Volume V of the UNESCO *General History of Africa* covers the history of Africa from the beginning of the sixteenth century to the close of the eighteenth century. Two major themes emerge: first, the continuing internal evolution of the states and cultures of Africa during this period; second, the increasing involvement of Africa in external trade - with major but then unforeseen consequences for the whole world.

In North Africa, we see the Ottomans conquer Egypt and establish Regencies in Tripoli, Tunis and Algiers. South of the Sahara, some of the larger, older states collapse (Songhay, Western Sudan, Christian Ethiopia), and new power bases emerge (Asante, Dahomey, Sakalava). Highly centralized political and administrative structures develop and societies with distinct social classes and, often, a strongly feudal character. Traditional religions continue to coexist with both Christianity (suffering setbacks) and Islam (in the ascendancy).

Along the coast, particularly of West Africa, Europeans establish a trading network which, with the development of New-World plantation agriculture, becomes the focus of the international slave trade. The immediate consequences of this trade for Africa are explored, and it is argued that the long-term global consequences include the foundation of the present world-economy with all its inbuilt inequalities.

Each chapter is illustrated with black and white photographs, maps and figures. The text is fully annotated and there is an extensive bibliography of works relating to the period, as well as a comprehensive glossary.

ENERAL HISTORY OF AFRICA · V

rica from the Sixteenth to the Eighteenth Century

Volume V of the *General History of Africa*
is accompanied by a corrigendum
reproducing some corrections which could
not have been made for technical reasons.
The publishers believe that this is necessary
to maintain the historical, political and
academic accuracy required of
such a *History*

UNESCO General History of Africa

ENERAL HISTORY
F AFRICA · V

frica from the Sixteenth
the Eighteenth Century

ITOR B.A. OGOT

NEMANN·CALIFORNIA·UNESCO

First published in 1992 by the
United Nations Educational, Scientific
and Cultural Organization,
7 Place de Fontenoy, 75700 Paris

and

Heinemann International Literature and Textbooks
a division of Heinemann Educational Books Ltd
Halley Court, Jordan Hill, Oxford OX2 8EJ
PMB 5205, Ibadan, PO Box 54314, Nairobi
PO Box 10103, Village Post Office, Gaborone

OXFORD   EDINBURGH   MADRID
PARIS   ATHENS   BOLOGNA   MELBOURNE
SYDNEY   AUCKLAND   SINGAPORE
TOKYO   PORTSMOUTH NH (USA)   HARARE

First published 1992
in the United States of America by the
University of California Press
2120 Berkeley Way, Berkeley
California 94720, United States of America

© UNESCO 1992

Maps drawn by John Gilkes

Heinemann International Literature
and Textbooks   ISBN 0435 948113

UNESCO   ISBN 92-3-101711-X

University of California Press   ISBN 0-520 039165

Filmset in 11pt Monophoto Ehrhardt by
Butler & Tanner Ltd, Frome and London

Printed in Great Britain by
Butler & Tanner Ltd, Frome and London

92 93 94 95 10 9 8 7 6 5 4 3 2 1

Contents

Note on chronology

It has been agreed to adopt the following method for writing dates. With regard to prehistory, dates may be written in two different ways.

One way is by reference to the present era, that is, dates BP (before present), the reference year being + 1950; all dates are negative in relation to + 1950.

The other way is by reference to the beginning of the Christian era. Dates are represented in relation to the Christian era by a simple + or − sign before the date. When referring to centuries, the terms BC and AD are replaced by 'before the Christian era' and 'of the Christian era'.

Some examples are as follows:

(i) 2300 BP = − 350
(ii) 2900 BC = − 2900
　　 AD 1800 = + 1800
(iii) 5th century BC = 5th century before the Christian era
　　 3rd century AD = 3rd century of the Christian era

Key for Maps

ASANTE	Ethnic groups
TAKRŪR	States
SAHARA	Regions
Agadir	Towns
Niger	Rivers, lakes
●	Site of town
⊙	Site of city

Additional information and keys are given on individual maps.

List of Figures

xiv

List of Plates

Acknowledgements for plates

Addo, M., 16.1
Aeschiman, M., Geneva, © and photo, 20.4
Bahimmi, Dr Al-Saghayar A., Tripoli, 9.11
Barth, H. *Travels and Discoveries in Northern and Central Africa*. Harper and Brothers, New York, 1857, © Royal Commonwealth Society Library, London, 2.1, 2.2, 11.1, 11.2, 11.4
Berjonneau, G., ART 135, Boulogne-Billancourt, © and photos, 12.1, 20.1, 20.2, 20.3, 20.7, 28.2
© Bertoni, M., Florence, front cover photo of ivory horn
© Bibliothèque nationale, Paris, 9.3, 9.4, 9.8
Binger, L. G., *Du Niger au golfe de Guinée par le pays de Kong et le Mossi, 1887–1889*, Hachette, Paris, 1892. © Royal Commonwealth Society Library, London, p. 295, 12.3, p. 47, 12.4
British Institute in Eastern Africa, Nairobi, 25.3, 25.4
British Museum, London, reproduced by courtesy of the Trustees, 18.2
© Collection Musée de l'Homme, Paris, photo D. Ponsard, 9.2, photo D. Destable, 18.3, photo M. Delaplanche, 18.4
© Chrétien, J. P., 26.1, 26.3, 26.4
Cultural Atlas, p. 57, © Spectrum Picture Library, 25.2
Dapper Foundation, Paris, 19.2
Dapper, O., *Description de l'Afrique*, Wolfgang, Waesberge, Boom and van Someren, Amsterdam, 1686, © and photos Dapper Foundation, Paris, 14.1, 19.4, 19.5, © and photo National Museum of Angola, Luanda, 19.6
Denham, D., *Narratives of Travels and Discoveries in Northern and Central Africa*, John Murray, London, 1826, © Royal Geographical Society, London, 17.3
Dubois, H., Brussels, 12.2, 15.3, 15.4, 15.5, 20.5, 20.6, 27.2
von Duisburg, A., *Im Lande des Chegbu von Bornu*, D. Reimer Verlag, Berlin, 1942, facing p. 81, 17.1
El Fasi, His Excellency M., 8.3
Etnografisch Museum, Antwerp, 18.5
French National Museums (Réunion des musées nationaux), Paris, 9.5
© Frobenius Institute, Frankfurt, 24.6, 24.7
Garrard, T., *Akan Weights and the Gold Trade*, Longman, London, 1980, p. 280, photos courtesy of T. Garrard, 14.3
© Holford, M., 4.2
© The Hulton-Deutsch Collection, London, 4.1, 4.5, 6.1, 23.3
The Illustrated London News, 1888, © The Mary Evans Picture Library, 7.1
Institut des musées nationaux du Zaïre, 18.6, 19.1
Institut fondamental d'Afrique noire (I.F.A.N. Cheikh Anta Diop), Dakar, photos G. Labitte, 10.5, 10.6
Institute of Egyptology, Charles University, Prague, 6.3, 6.4, 6.5, 6.9
Janzen, J., *Lemba, 1650–1930*, New York, 1982, courtesy of the Section of Ethnography, Royal Museum of Central Africa, 1980–Tervuren, Belgium, 19.13

Preface

AMADOU-MAHTAR M'BOW

Director-General of UNESCO (1974–1987)

For a long time, all kinds of myths and prejudices concealed the true history of Africa from the world at large. African societies were looked upon as societies that could have no history. In spite of important work done by such pioneers as Leo Frobenius, Maurice Delafosse and Arturo Labriola, as early as the first decades of this century, a great many non-African experts could not rid themselves of certain preconceptions and argued that the lack of written sources and documents made it impossible to engage in any scientific study of such societies.

Although the *Iliad* and *Odyssey* were rightly regarded as essential sources for the history of ancient Greece, African oral tradition, the collective memory of peoples which holds the thread of many events marking their lives, was rejected as worthless. In writing the history of a large part of Africa, the only sources used were from outside the continent, and the final product gave a picture not so much of the paths actually taken by the African peoples as of those that the authors thought they must have taken. Since the European Middle Ages were often used as a yardstick, modes of production, social relations and political institutions were visualized only by reference to the European past.

In fact, there was a refusal to see Africans as the creators of original cultures which flowered and survived over the centuries in patterns of their own making and which historians are unable to grasp unless they forgo their prejudices and rethink their approach.

Furthermore, the continent of Africa was hardly ever looked upon as a historical entity. On the contrary, emphasis was laid on everything likely to lend credence to the idea that a split had existed, from time immemorial, between a 'white Africa' and a 'black Africa', each unaware of the other's existence. The Sahara was often presented as an impenetrable space preventing any intermingling of ethnic groups and peoples or any exchange of goods, beliefs, customs and ideas between the societies that had grown up on either side of the desert. Hermetic frontiers were drawn between the civilizations of Ancient Egypt and Nubia and those of the peoples south of the Sahara.

It is true that the history of Africa north of the Sahara has been more closely linked with that of the Mediterranean basin than has the history of sub-Saharan Africa, but it is now widely recognized that the various civilizations of the African continent, for all their differing languages and cultures, represent, to a greater or lesser degree, the historical offshoots of a set of peoples and societies united by bonds centuries old.

Another phenomenon which did great disservice to the objective study of the African past was the appearance, with the slave trade and colonization, of racial stereotypes which bred contempt and lack of understanding and became so deep-rooted that they distorted even the basic concepts of historiography. From the time when the notions of 'white' and 'black' were used as generic labels by the colonialists, who were regarded as superior, the colonized Africans had to struggle against both economic and psychological enslavement. Africans were identifiable by the colour of their skin, they had become a kind of merchandise, they were earmarked for hard labour and eventually, in the minds of those dominating them, they came to symbolize an imaginary and allegedly inferior *Negro* race. This pattern of spurious identification relegated the history of the African peoples in many minds to the rank of ethno-history, in which appreciation of the historical and cultural facts was bound to be warped.

The situation has changed significantly since the end of the Second World War and in particular since the African countries became independent and began to take an active part in the life of the international community and in the mutual exchanges that are its *raison d'être*. An increasing number of historians has endeavoured to tackle the study of Africa with a more rigorous, objective and open-minded outlook by using – with all due precautions – actual African sources. In exercising their right to take the historical initiative, Africans themselves have felt a deep-seated need to re-establish the historical authenticity of their societies on solid foundations.

In this context, the importance of the eight-volume *General History of Africa*, which UNESCO is publishing, speaks for itself.

The experts from many countries working on this project began by laying down the theoretical and methodological basis for the *History*. They have been at pains to call in question the over-simplifications arising from a linear and restrictive conception of world history and to re-establish the true facts wherever necessary and possible. They have endeavoured to highlight the historical data that give a clearer picture of the evolution of the different peoples of Africa in their specific socio-cultural setting.

To tackle this huge task, made all the more complex and difficult by the vast range of sources and the fact that documents were widely scattered, UNESCO has had to proceed by stages. The first stage, from 1965 to 1969, was devoted to gathering documentation and planning the work. Operational assignments were conducted in the field and included campaigns to collect oral traditions, the creation of regional documentation centres for oral traditions, the collection of unpublished manuscripts in Arabic and Ajami (African languages written in Arabic script), the compilation of archival inventories and the preparation of a *Guide to the Sources of the History of Africa,* culled from the archives and libraries of the countries of Europe and later published in eleven volumes. In addition, meetings were organized to enable experts from Africa and other continents to discuss questions of methodology and lay down the broad lines for the project after careful examination of the available sources.

The second stage, which lasted from 1969 to 1971, was devoted to shaping the *History* and linking its different parts. The purpose of the international meetings of experts held in Paris in 1969 and Addis Ababa in 1970 was to study and define the problems involved in drafting and publishing the *History*; presentation in eight volumes, the principal edition in English, French and Arabic, translation into African languages such as Kiswahili, Hausa, Fulfulde, Yoruba or Lingala, prospective versions in German, Russian, Portuguese, Spanish and Chinese, as well as abridged editions designed for a wide African and international public.[1]

The third stage has involved actual drafting and publication. This began with the appointment of the 39-member International Scientific Committee, two-thirds African and one-third non-African, which assumes intellectual responsibility for the *History*.

The method used is interdisciplinary and is based on a multi-faceted approach and a wide variety of sources. The first among these is archaeology, which holds many of the keys to the history of African cultures and civilizations. Thanks to archaeology, it is now acknowledged that Africa was very probably the cradle of mankind and the scene − in the neolithic period − of one of the first technological revolutions in history. Archaeology has also shown that Egypt was the setting for one of the most brilliant ancient civilizations of the world. But another very important source is oral tradition, which, after being long despised, has now emerged as an invaluable instrument for discovering the history of Africa, making it possible to follow the movements of its different peoples in both space and time, to understand the African vision of the world from the inside and to grasp the original features of the values on which the cultures and institutions of the continent are based.

We are indebted to the International Scientific Committee in charge of this *General History of Africa,* and to its Rapporteur and the editors and authors of the various volumes and chapters, for having shed a new light on the African past in its authentic and all-encompassing form and for having avoided any dogmatism in the study of essential issues. Among these issues we might cite; the slave trade, that 'endlessly bleeding wound',

1. Volumes I and II have been published in Arabic, Spanish, Korean, Portuguese, Chinese and Italian; Volume I has been published in Kiswahili and Hausa; Volume II in Hausa; Volume IV and Volume VII in Arabic, Spanish and Portuguese.

which was responsible for one of the cruellest mass deportations in the history of mankind, which sapped the African continent of its life-blood while contributing significantly to the economic and commercial expansion of Europe; colonization, with all the effects it had on population, economics, psychology and culture; relations between Africa south of the Sahara and the Arab world; and, finally, the process of decolonization and nation-building which mobilized the intelligence and passion of people still alive and sometimes still active today. All these issues have been broached with a concern for honesty and rigour which is not the least of the *History*'s merits. By taking stock of our knowledge of Africa, putting forward a variety of viewpoints on African cultures and offering a new reading of history, the *History* has the signal advantage of showing up the light and shade and of openly portraying the differences of opinion that may exist between scholars.

By demonstrating the inadequacy of the methodological approaches which have long been used in research on Africa, this *History* calls for a new and careful study of the twofold problem areas of historiography and cultural identity, which are united by links of reciprocity. Like any historical work of value, the *History* paves the way for a great deal of further research on a variety of topics.

It is for this reason that the International Scientific Committee, in close collaboration with UNESCO, decided to embark on additional studies in an attempt to go deeper into a number of issues which will permit a clearer understanding of certain aspects of the African past. The findings being published in the series 'UNESCO Studies and Documents – General History of Africa'[2] will prove a useful supplement to the *History*, as will the works planned on aspects of national or subregional history.

The *General History* sheds light both on the historical unity of Africa and also its relations with the other continents, particularly the Americas and the Caribbean. For a long time, the creative manifestations of the descendants of Africans in the Americas were lumped together by some historians as a heterogeneous collection of *Africanisms*. Needless to say, this is not the attitude of the authors of the *History*, in which the resistance of the slaves shipped to America, the constant and massive participation of the descendants of Africans in the struggles for the initial independence of America and in national liberation movements, are rightly perceived for what they were: vigorous assertions of identity, which helped forge the

---

2. The following eleven volumes have already been published in this series: *The peopling of ancient Egypt and the deciphering of Meroitic script; The African slave trade from the fifteenth to the nineteenth century; Historical relations across the Indian Ocean; The historiography of Southern Africa; The decolonization of Africa: Southern Africa and the Horn of Africa; African ethnonyms and toponyms; Historical and socio-cultural relations between black Africa and the Arab world from 1935 to the present; The methodology of contemporary African History; The Educational Process and Historiography in Africa; Africa and the Second World War; Libya Antiqua.*

universal concept of mankind. Although the phenomenon may vary in different places, it is now quite clear that ways of feeling, thinking, dreaming and acting in certain nations of the western hemisphere have been marked by their African heritage. The cultural inheritance of Africa is visible everywhere, from the southern United States to northern Brazil, across the Caribbean and on the Pacific seaboard. In certain places it even underpins the cultural identity of some of the most important elements of the population.

The *History* also clearly brings out Africa's relations with southern Asia across the Indian Ocean and the African contributions to other civilizations through mutual exchanges.

I am convinced that the efforts of the peoples of Africa to conquer or strengthen their independence, secure their development and assert their cultural characteristics, must be rooted in historical awareness renewed, keenly felt and taken up by each succeeding generation.

My own background, the experience I gained as a teacher and as chairman, from the early days of independence, of the first commission set up to reform history and geography curricula in some of the countries of West and Central Africa, taught me how necessary it was for the education of young people and for the information of the public at large to have a history book produced by scholars with inside knowledge of the problems and hopes of Africa and with the ability to apprehend the continent in its entirety.

For all these reasons, UNESCO's goal will be to ensure that this *General History of Africa* is widely disseminated in a large number of languages and is used as a basis for producing children's books, school textbooks and radio and television programmes. Young people, whether schoolchildren or students, and adults in Africa and elsewhere will thus be able to form a truer picture of the African continent's past and the factors that explain it, as well as a fairer understanding of its cultural heritage and its contribution to the general progress of mankind. The *History* should thus contribute to improved international co-operation and stronger solidarity among peoples in their aspirations to justice, progress and peace. This is, at least, my most cherished hope.

It remains for me to express my deep gratitude to the members of the International Scientific Committee, the Rapporteur, the different volume editors, the authors and all those who have collaborated in this tremendous undertaking. The work they have accomplished and the contribution they have made plainly go to show how people from different backgrounds but all imbued with the same spirit of goodwill and enthusiasm in the service of universal truth can, within the international framework provided by UNESCO, bring to fruition a project of considerable scientific and cultural import. My thanks also go to the organizations and governments whose generosity has made it possible for UNESCO to publish this *History* in different languages and thus ensure that it will have the worldwide impact it deserves and thereby serve the international community as a whole.

Description of the Project

B. A. OGOT*

President, International Scientific Committee
for the Drafting of a General History of Africa (1978–1983)

The General Conference of UNESCO at its 16th Session instructed the Director-General to undertake the drafting of a *General History of Africa*. The enormous task of implementing the project was entrusted to an International Scientific Committee which was established by the Executive Board in 1970. This Committee, under the Statutes adopted by the Executive Board of UNESCO in 1971, is composed of thirty-nine members (two-thirds of whom are African and one-third non-African) serving in their personal capacity and appointed by the Director-General of UNESCO for the duration of the Committee's mandate.

The first task of the Committee was to define the principal characteristics of the work. These were defined at the first session of the Committee as follows:

(a) Although aiming at the highest possible scientific level, the history does not seek to be exhaustive and is a work of synthesis avoiding dogmatism. In many respects, it is a statement of problems showing the present state of knowledge and the main trends in research, and it does not hesitate to show divergencies of views where these exist. In this way, it prepares the ground for future work.

(b) Africa is considered in this work as a totality. The aim is to show the historical relationships between the various parts of the continent, too frequently subdivided in works published to date. Africa's historical connections with the other continents receive due attention, these connections being analysed in terms of mutual exchanges and multilateral influences, bringing out, in its appropriate light, Africa's contribution to the history of mankind.

(c) *The General History of Africa* is, in particular, a history of ideas and civilizations, societies and institutions. It is based on a wide variety of sources, including oral tradition and art forms.

(d) The *History* is viewed essentially from the inside. Although a scholarly work, it is also, in large measure, a faithful reflection of the way in

---

*During the Sixth Plenary Session of the International Scientific Committee for the Drafting of a General History of Africa (Brazzaville, 1983), an election of the new Bureau was held and Professor Ogot was replaced by Professor Albert Adu Boahen.

which African authors view their own civilization. While prepared in an international framework and drawing to the full on the present stock of scientific knowledge, it should also be a vitally important element in the recognition of the African heritage and should bring out the factors making for unity in the continent. This effort to view things from within is the novel feature of the project and should, in addition to its scientific quality, give it great topical significance. By showing the true face of Africa, the *History* could, in an era absorbed in economic and technical struggles, offer a particular conception of human values.

The Committee has decided to present the work covering over three million years of African history in eight volumes, each containing about eight hundred pages of text with illustrations, photographs, maps and line drawings.

A chief editor, assisted if necessary by one or two assistant editors, is responsible for the preparation of each volume. The editors are elected by the Committee either from among its members or from outside by a two-thirds majority. They are responsible for preparing the volumes in accordance with the decisions and plans adopted by the Committee. On scientific matters, they are accountable to the Committee or, between two sessions of the Committee, to its Bureau for the contents of the volumes, the final version of the texts, the illustrations and, in general, for all scientific and technical aspects of the *History*. The Bureau ultimately approves the final manuscript. When it considers the manuscript ready for publication, it transmits it to the Director-General of UNESCO. Thus the Committee, or the Bureau between committee sessions, remains fully in charge of the project.

Each volume consists of some thirty chapters. Each chapter is the work of a principal author assisted, if necessary, by one or two collaborators. The authors are selected by the Committee on the basis of their *curricula vitae*. Preference is given to African authors, provided they have requisite qualifications. Special effort is also made to ensure, as far as possible, that all regions of the continent, as well as other regions having historical or cultural ties with Africa, are equitably represented among the authors.

When the editor of a volume has approved texts of chapters, they are then sent to all members of the Committee for criticism. In addition, the text of the volume editor is submitted for examination to a Reading Committee, set up within the International Scientific Committee on the basis of the members' fields of competence. The Reading Committee analyses the chapters from the standpoint of both substance and form. The Bureau then gives final approval to the manuscripts.

Such a seemingly long and involved procedure has proved necessary, since it provides the best possible guarantee of the scientific objectivity of the *General History of Africa*. There have, in fact, been instances when the

Bureau has rejected manuscripts or insisted on major revisions or even reassigned the drafting of a chapter to another author. Occasionally, specialists in a particular period of history or in a particular question are consulted to put the finishing touches to a volume.

The work will be published first in a hard-cover edition in English, French and Arabic, and later in paperback editions in the same languages. An abridged version in English and French will serve as a basis for translation into African languages. The Committee has chosen Kiswahili and Hausa as the first African languages into which the work will be translated.

Also, every effort will be made to ensure publication of the *General History of Africa* in other languages of wide international currency such as Chinese, Portuguese, Russian, German, Italian, Spanish, Japanese, etc.

It is thus evident that this is a gigantic task which constitutes an immense challenge to African historians and to the scholarly community at large, as well as to UNESCO under whose auspices the work is being done. For the writing of a continental history of Africa, covering the last three million years, using the highest canons of scholarship and involving, as it must do, scholars drawn from diverse countries, cultures, ideologies and historical traditions, is surely a complex undertaking. It constitutes a continental, international and interdisciplinary project of great proportions.

In conclusion, I would like to underline the significance of this work for Africa and for the world. At a time when the peoples of Africa are striving towards unity and greater co-operation in shaping their individual destinies, a proper understanding of Africa's past, with an awareness of common ties among Africans and between Africa and other continents, should not only be a major contribution towards mutual understanding among the people of the earth, but also a source of knowledge of a cultural heritage that belongs to all mankind.

The struggle for international trade and its implications for Africa

M. MALOWIST

Introduction

In 1500 the geo-political map of the world revealed the existence of a number of major, relatively autonomous regions which were to some degree interlinked either through trade or through conflict. First, there was the Far East represented by Japan and China which, together with the Pacific and Indian Ocean regions covering the Molucca Islands, Borneo, Sumatra and India itself, were the world's source of spices. Next, was the Middle East which covered a vast area including the Arabian peninsula, the Safawid empire and the Ottoman empire which was soon to include North Africa. Then there was Europe with its Slavs, Scandinavians, Germans, Anglo-Saxons and Latins, all of whom still remained confined within its borders. Finally, there was Africa with its Mediterranean seaboard in the north and its Red Sea and Indian Ocean coastlines which were becoming increasingly involved in the international trade with the Far East and the Orient.

The period from 1500 to 1800 was to witness the establishment of a new Atlantic-oriented geo-economic system, with its triangular trading pattern linking Europe, Africa and the Americas. With the opening up of Atlantic trade, Europe – particularly Western Europe – gained ascendancy over the Americas and African societies. Henceforth, Europe was to play a leading role in the accumulation of capital generated by trade and plunder on a worldwide scale. The emigration of Europeans to trading settlements in Africa and the territories of North and South America gave rise to the establishment of supporting overseas economies. These were to play a decisive long-term role through their contribution to Western Europe's rise to power over the rest of the world.

The period from 1450 to 1630 is recognized in the historical sciences as a phase of considerable economic, political and cultural expansion in most European countries, particularly in western and south-western Europe. As time went on, Europe became more markedly divided into the economically advanced north-west, the less developed countries of the Iberian peninsula, and the vast areas of central and eastern Europe which, although not without development, were becoming more and more dependent on western markets.

This was also a period of overseas expansion into the vast territories bordering the Atlantic and even into the Pacific. From the beginning of the sixteenth century, the African coast was one such area, although the situation in North Africa differed from that in the sub-Saharan region. Competition in the basin of the Mediterranean was strong between Spain, Portugal, France and Muslim North Africa. Also, the Ottoman empire was gaining more and more influence. In 1517, the Ottomans conquered Egypt and subsequently subjugated a large part of the Arab peninsula, gradually establishing their rule over Tripoli, Tunis and Algiers, where Ottoman Regencies developed under Turkish protectorates. These constituted a great danger to European navigation and to the southern coasts of Italy and Spain. In Morocco, however, the Portuguese managed to dominate a large part of the coast as far as Agadir (Santa Cruz du Cap d'Aguer) and Safi, while the Castilians established bases in Tlemcen and Oran.[1]

These conquests were of great importance as they gave the Portuguese control of the termini of some long-established and important gold- and slave-trade routes from Western Sudan through the Sahara and the Maghrib to the Mediterranean. The termini of other important routes, running both latitudinally and longitudinally, were under the control of the Turks and of the more or less autonomous representatives of the Ottoman Porte in Africa – Algiers, Tunis and Tripoli. Portugal's control of the trade termini came after almost a century of expansion in West Africa and ensured that part of the gold and slave cargoes – previously sent in their entirety to the Muslim world – were intercepted by the Europeans.[2] The decrease in the supply of gold to the Maghrib resulting from the European expansion in Africa is a matter which should be investigated further. It seems likely that the results of such investigations would make the conquest of the curve of the River Niger by the Moroccans in 1591 more comprehensible; this conquest enabled the latter to control certain gold- and slave-trade routes running from West Africa to the Maghrib and Egypt. The famous campaign of Djūdar Pasha is a typical example of the great conquests so characteristic of the sixteenth century. It is worth adding that Djūdar Pasha himself was a renegade of Iberian background, that his army was dominated by similar types. These renegades brought with them the tradition of the Spanish and Portuguese conquests.[3]

The opinion of the age – that the coasts of West and East Africa would long remain under the economic and political domination of Portugal – was to be confirmed. Portugal also exerted a certain cultural influence on its black trading partners. Throughout the fifteenth and the early sixteenth centuries the Portuguese established numerous trading posts on the West African coast and made the coastal population and its rulers permanently interested in trade with the Europeans. After 1481–2 the most important

1. See ch. 9 below.
2. V. de Magalhães Godinho, 1969, pp. 184, 217.
3. See ch. 2 below.

place on the Gold Coast was the fortress of El Mina. Other trading posts also grew up in that region, such as Axim, Shamma and Accra. When setting up trading posts the Portuguese sought the permission of the local African rulers and, through various payments, tried to win their goodwill.

In East Africa, methods were different with the Portuguese crushing the defences of Sofala, Mombasa and other coastal towns, leaving garrisons there and levying taxes for the King of Portugal. At the same time, the Portuguese tried to take over the gold, ivory and metals trade between the coast, its hinterland and India. The profitability of the different factories and Portuguese trading posts in Africa varied. In the early sixteenth century, trade in El Mina, at the mouth of the River Gambia in Sierra Leone and in Sofala, brought large profits mainly from the purchase of cheap gold and also from the trade in slaves supplied from the hinterland. Arguin – the oldest Portuguese factory – continued to lose importance, however.[4]

Trade with Africa brought Portugal great profit. According to J. Lúcio De Azevedo's calculations, the Crown gains, which had amounted to some 60 million Portuguese reals in the 1480s, reached 200 million reals during the rule of King Manuel (1491–1521) and at least 279.5 million reals by 1534.[5] This increase was undoubtedly achieved through profits from trade not only with India but also to a large extent with Africa. Moreover, the considerable inflow of African gold made it possible for John II and his successor, Manuel, to stabilize their silver coinage, to mint the *cruzados* – a high-value gold coin – and, more importantly, to expand the fleet and the state and colonial administration.[6] This fact was of great significance, not only politically but also socially, as it opened opportunities for the aristocracy and gentry to obtain numerous prestigious and profitable offices. Former opposition from the aristocracy to the centralistic policies of the monarchs was thus eliminated and the state became a more cohesive entity.

Trade with Africa, and subsequently with India, accelerated the development of the Portuguese trader class which had been relatively weak even in the fifteenth century. Thus, Portugal might have been thought – in the early sixteenth century – to have entered upon a path of lasting economic and political expansion. However, its backward and sluggish socio–economic structure eventually prevented this from happening. Overseas expansion necessitated large financial outlay and the purchase of gold and slaves depended on supplying Africa with large quantities of iron, brass and copper goods, cheap textiles and some silver, foodstuffs and salt. These goods were not produced in Portugal but had to be bought from foreign visitors or in Bruges and, later, from the major European trade centres at that time. The expansion of the fleet depended on the import of timber and other forest products, mainly from the Baltic countries which also

4. V. de Magalhães Godinho, 1969, pp. 185–8.
5. V. de Magalhães Godinho, 1978, Vol. II, pp. 51–72.
6. M. Malowist, 1969, p. 219.

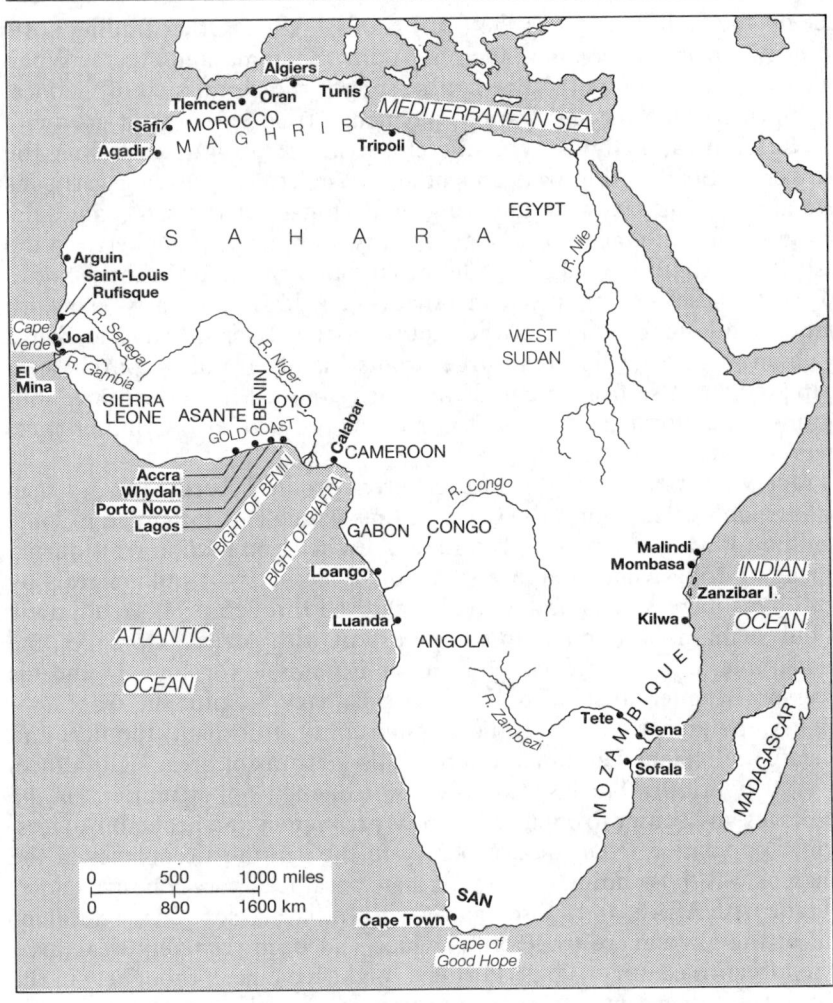

FIG. I.I *Africa: the main points of European trade contact during the sixteenth to eighteenth centuries*

supplied some grain – deficient in Portugal since the fourteenth century.[7] This matter has still not been fully investigated but obviously much of the profit from foreign trade would have been allotted to the purchase of the foreign goods needed for economic exchange in Africa. Portugal was unable to develop its own production because of its weak demographic potential (in 1550 it had only 1.4 million inhabitants)[8] and the severe competition from foreign, particularly industrial goods, long popular on the Portuguese market.

Europe's economic boom triggered a gradual rise in prices from the 1470s. During the second half of the sixteenth century this rise became enormous, affecting mainly agricultural products and industrial goods. The relationship between the rise in prices and the increase in Portugal's profits from overseas trade has not yet been investigated – although it seems that it was not to Portugal's benefit. Monopoly of trade with Africa or India helped but little. Besides, it had been instigated on quite different economic premises. The high expenditure associated with overseas expansion was profitable only when the Portuguese could impose on their black trading partners terms of trade profitable to themselves – that is, buying cheap and selling dear. This, however, made it necessary to limit or even exclude from the trading ports immigrants from Europe, particularly from countries other than Portugal. To this end, a strong fleet had to be maintained to deter European rivals heading for Africa. This was a costly enterprise which proved almost beyond Portugal's means to attain.[9]

By the 1470s, Portugal among others was already engaged in armed conflict with Castile. The outcome, thanks to the temporary supremacy of the Portuguese fleet and to diplomatic manoeuvres, was the elimination of Castile from West Africa by the treaties of Alcáçovas and Tordesillas in 1481 and 1493, and the granting to Portugal by Pope Alexander VI of exclusive rights for economic and political expansion in the south-eastern Atlantic. The discovery and conquest of America – and European politics in general – turned Castile's attention away from African affairs. Relations between Portugal and its other rivals on the West African coast and subsequently in East Africa developed differently, however, particularly as those rivals were countries more economically advanced than Portugal.

The Portuguese rulers, John II and Manuel, were compelled to seek support for their colonial activities among the big financiers of Italy and south Germany. The Italians, particularly those from Florence, who had settled in Lisbon and Antwerp or had commercial agents there, put large sums in cash or goods at the disposal of the Portuguese rulers. These loans were subsequently repaid by cash or goods imported from overseas. From the 1480s and possibly earlier, some of those bankers, such as Bartolomeo Mar-Chioni, Sernigi and others, became actively engaged in trade with

7. A. Da Silva Costa Lobo, 1904, p. 83.
8. V. de Magalhães Godinho, 1978, Vol. II, p. 25.
9. ibid., pp. 185–203.

Africa and rewarded the Portuguese kings adequately. The Portuguese king's accounts from Bruges and subsequently Antwerp reveal that there were strong financial links between the Crown and major firms such as those of Frescobaldi, Affaitati and Fuggers.[10] In the first stage of expansion, the Portuguese rulers managed to monopolize the importation of gold from Africa and, to a large extent, the slave trade – or at least its indirect profits. This was done by a system of costly trading licences granted mainly to Portuguese traders and to foreigners more rarely. During difficult periods, the Portuguese Crown often gave traders its rights in Africa, with the exception of El Mina. The geographical limits of the area in which trading was allowed were specified on the licences.

In the mid-1520s the Portuguese encountered their first difficulties in the purchase of gold, even in the region of El Mina.[11] It is probable that the Portuguese were by then already unable to supply the coast of Africa with enough goods to keep gold supplies steady. There is no doubt that vast resources of gold still existed in the hinterland of El Mina and Accra but the situation favoured Portugal's European rivals, namely the French, English and Dutch who had more capital at their disposal. Moreover, they traded in goods mostly produced in their own countries, not imported. Finally, neither France, England nor Holland was yet burdened by an overdeveloped administration controlling its overseas trade and colonies. The Portuguese apparatus was both costly and slow to adapt to the changes so characteristic of overseas trade. Traders arriving in Africa from France, England or Holland were able to supply more goods than the Portuguese and sell them more cheaply. Sources dating from the 1570s prove that although the Portuguese understood this situation they were unable to alter it.

The slave trade

Portugal was initially attracted to Black Africa by its gold, previously exported to the Islamic countries. The Portuguese, however, soon discovered a second African product attractive to Europeans, namely slaves. Though slavery in Africa differed from that known to Europeans, the tradition of exporting slaves to the Arab countries was an old one in large parts of the continent, particularly Sudan. This tradition seems to have facilitated somewhat the organization – during the 1400s and 1500s – of regular purchases of slaves by the Portuguese from a large part of West Africa, particularly Senegambia, a long-standing economic partner of the Maghrib. The Portuguese, who penetrated farther and farther inland in the south-eastern part of West Africa, successfully applied the trade methods used in Senegambia. Realizing success depended on the co-operation of local chiefs and traders, they worked to interest them in the slave trade. The Portuguese also realized that such trade would lead to

10. C. Verlinden, 1957, pp. 624–5; V. Rau, 1966.
11. M. Malowist, 1969, pp. 492, 500.

increased fighting between peoples and states, because prisoners of war soon became the main subject of the trade. The Portuguese soon abandoned their moral objections to the slave trade, believing, as did many in Europe, that it enabled blacks to reach salvation whereas had they remained in their own countries, they would as non-Christians have been damned to eternal perdition.

Soon another argument for the slave trade was propounded – that blacks were descended from Ham, who had been cursed, and for that reason were condemned to permanent slavery.[12] Such ideological motivations should not be underestimated. It should be added here that black slaves appeared in Europe at a time when trade in white slaves from the Black Sea zone was almost dead. From this time on slaves were identified as Negroes, other representatives of the black race being unknown.

Throughout the 1400s and early 1500s, the main market for 'the black merchandise' was Europe, particularly Portugal and the Spanish countries and, to a certain extent, islands in the Atlantic such as Madeira, the Canaries, the Cape Verde Islands and subsequently St Thomas Island – although the number of slaves transported to these islands was limited by the small size of the islands themselves. The main incentive for the slave trade in Madeira, the Cape Verde Islands and, in particular, St Thomas Island was the introduction of the cultivation of sugar cane and cotton. Slavery could not develop to any great extent on the European continent because there was no economic reason for it. The Africans who were brought into Portugal and the Spanish countries were mainly employed as domestic servants or semi-skilled artisans in the towns. There is no evidence that Africans played an important role in agriculture, the foundation of Europe's economy. V. de Magalhães Godinho estimated the number of slaves brought from Arguin between 1451 and 1505 as between 25 000 and 40 000.[13] The export of slaves from other parts of Africa was minimal then, except to Muslim countries. According to Curtin's estimates, the number of slaves taken from Africa by the Europeans between 1451 and 1600 amounted to about 274 900. Of these Europe and the Atlantic islands took about 149 000, Spanish America about 75 000 and Brazil about 50 000.[14] These figures are characteristic of the early period of the Atlantic slave trade – prior to the great development of the plantation system in the New World. They corroborate the thesis that it was the discovery of America and its economic development by the whites that gave impetus to the trade. The enormous shortage of labour in Spanish colonies where local populations were already too few to carry out the heavy production tasks demanded by the Spaniards is currently seen as the main reason.[15]

12. This was the opinion of many Portuguese writers. E. de Zurara, 1949, chs 7, 14, 25 and 38; J. De Barros and I. De Asia, 1937, p. 80.
13. V. de Magalhães Godinho, 1962, p. 193.
14. P. D. Curtin, 1973, p. 259, Table 7.1.
15. See ch. 4 below.

Certainly, in early modern times large numbers of blacks were concentrated in those areas of the American lowlands with a tropical climate. However, any attempts at large-scale black recruitment into the mining industry in the high Andes were unsuccessful, though great masses of Indian labourers managed to survive there. At the peak of Potosí's development in the late 1500s the number of Africans there was only about 5000 out of a total population of about 150 000.[16] Again, an attempt to recruit them to mining failed.

The first Africans in America were brought there from Europe by the Conquistadores. They were slaves mainly from Senegambia and either had been brought to Europe previously, or had been born there. They were called *ladinos* in America because they knew Spanish or Portuguese, and were at least partly influenced by the civilization of the Iberian countries. They were highly thought of, contrary to the *bozales*, who had been brought directly from Africa and had been influenced by quite a different culture.[17] The demand for black labour was already great in the Antilles in the early 1500s and grew rapidly with the territorial expansion following the Spanish conquests. Because of the high mortality rate of the Indians, and the largely unsuccessful defence of their interests by the Castilian clergy and the Crown, the demand for labour increased steadily and supplies of black slaves – from Europe and, above all, Africa – became a major concern for the new lords of America.

The Portuguese in Africa also had major problems. Throughout the fifteenth century they had been increasingly interested in buying slaves and, during the 1500s and later, those territories which could supply large numbers of slaves became more and more attractive to them. This was the basis for Portuguese expansion in Congo (which had no gold and silver) from the early sixteenth century, and their subsequent conquest of Angola, preceded by the rapid development of the slave trade in the island of Luanda. The need for large numbers of slaves also affected the settlers in St Thomas Island who wanted them for their own plantations and to sell to the Spanish American colonies and also, from the late sixteenth century, to Portuguese Brazil. The size of Brazil's black population was only several thousand by the late 1500s but the following century saw an increase in this number to 400 000/450 000, an increase associated with the development of the sugar-cane plantations.[18]

The conquest of America and the demand for black labour also created great problems for the Castilian Crown. While it was necessary to ensure supplies of slaves for the colonists it was also clear that this was a source of great profit to the Royal Treasury through the costly licencing system. (Licences were granted by the Castilian Crown and importers undertook to bring in a certain number of slaves for the colonists within a certain

16. J. Wolff, 1964, pp. 158–69, 172–4.
17. R. Mellafe, 1975, pp. 14, 15, 19, 21.
18. F. Mauro, 1960, pp. 179–80.

time, usually five years.) The price of the licence rose steadily as the demand for slaves grew. R. Mellafe correctly maintains that the Crown willingly granted import licences for huge numbers of slaves because the larger the number the higher the fee.[19] The first to obtain licences – often monopolistic – included aristocrats close to the throne, such as Charles V's Chancellor, Gouvenet, in 1518, and also great capitalists, such as the Welser family, Heinrich Ehinger and Jerome Seiler in 1528,[20] probably in connection with their settlement and mining plans in Venezuela. There were Africans in Venezuela from an early date brought there by financiers as well as Conquistadores and others who bought them as slaves from the Portuguese in Africa or Europe. It was, however, unavoidable that potential slave traders would try to eliminate the costly offices of the Portuguese and to intercept both the purchase and sales of 'the black merchandise'. In Africa those who wanted to break into the trade had to overcome obstacles set by the Portuguese, while in America they had to resort to contraband trade as the Castilian Crown permitted only those to whom it had granted licences to import slaves. This was not an insurmountable difficulty, however, as the Spanish colonists in America were permanently short of labour and were therefore willing to buy workers from smugglers. Slaves were brought in through illegal harbours – a procedure favoured by the Spanish colonial officers who derived an additional source of income from bribes. Foreigners found the system particularly attractive as they were often paid in gold or silver, the private export of which from Spanish America was officially allowed only as far as Seville and Cadiz, the centres of the strong Castilian colonial administration. Private people were in principle prohibited from exporting gold and silver from Spain.

Thus, all seemed to favour increased exports of blacks from Africa to America, except that the trade only really boomed when the great sugar-cane plantations began to be established. It transpired quite quickly that in both Spanish America and, subsequently, in Brazil that the Indian population could not stand the steady hard work on the plantations, whereas Africans made excellent plantation labourers. In mining their role seems to have been only small, with the possible exception of mines on the island of San Domingo, in Venezuela and in certain other tropical territories in Mexico.

Hence from the early 1500s, but more particularly from 1550, Africa played an extremely important though undesirable role as a supplier of labour and of some gold to the developing world economy.

It is worth mentioning, however, that the Portuguese position was becoming more precarious. In Morocco, they suffered severe blows from the Sa'ādī *sharīfs'* holy war against the infidels. In 1541 the Portuguese lost Agadir and soon after were compelled through financial difficulties to give up almost all their Moroccan ports. The year 1560 witnessed the first

19. R. Mellafe, 1975, p. 39.
20. G. Scelle, 1906, Vol. I, pp. 122–36.

9

bankruptcy of the Portuguese Crown. The maintenance of a colonial empire while bringing enormous profits to part of the aristocracy, the gentry and some traders, had ruined the Crown and its Treasury and had laid an increasing burden on many of the population.

Arrival of new European powers

From the 1520s, the French – and from the 1550s the English, too – became dangerous rivals of the Portuguese in Africa. From the late sixteenth century, however, the Dutch became even more dangerous. Initially, only individual French traders, such as the well-known Jean Ango of Dieppe, or individual trading companies, were active. In the trade with Africa neither the French King nor the English Crown were directly involved. In 1531, 1537 and 1539 Francis I even tried unsuccessfully to stop his subjects from making expeditions to Africa as he was wary of straining relations with Portugal at a time when France was in sharp conflict with the Spanish Habsburgs. Traders from Rouen, La Rochelle and Dieppe had sent ships to Africa even earlier. In 1525 the King of the Congo captured a small French ship and delivered it with its crew to the Portuguese.[21] French expansion was at its strongest in the region of Cape Verde and Senegal where the French often looted Portuguese ships returning with a cargo of African gold or goods from India. Many other French ports, such as Le Havre and Honfleur, participated in this French expansion during the sixteenth century. Nantes gradually came to dominate this trade. In the last quarter of the sixteenth century the position of the French in Senegambia became very strong, particularly in such centres as Gorée, Portudal, Joal and Rufisque (Rio Fresco) in Wolof country. The French brought with them textiles from Normandy and Brittany, spirits and metal goods, and possibly firearms. The latter seem to have made the situation favourable for the French, because the Portuguese Crown for a long time and very stubbornly prohibited imports of firearms to Africa, whereas the local rulers were very eager to get weapons. The French bought mostly gold and ivory, and also malaguetta pepper, hides and palm oil. Slaves were not yet important to them. They were dangerous rivals to the Portuguese on the Pepper and Gold Coasts in the mid-sixteenth century,[22] apparently importing many more goods than the Portuguese. This was particularly painful for the Portuguese in the region of El Mina where in 1556, for example, the French and English brought in so many goods and sold them at such low prices that the Portuguese agent in El Mina was unable to buy any gold.[23] This was exceptional, however, and the position of the Portuguese soon improved again. During the religious wars in Europe, French expansion may have weakened somewhat but this has not yet been

21. A. Brasio, 1952, Vol. I, pp. 138, 153.
22. C. A. Julien, 1948, p. 177; G. Martin, 1948, p. 4.
23. G. Martin, 1948; J. W. Blake, 1942.

corroborated. Some firearms were apparently sold to local rulers on the Cameroon coast but the position of the French was strongest in Senegal where they often co-operated with the *tangomãos*, emigrants from the Cape Verde Islands and predominantly mulatto. They pushed the Portuguese out of the estuaries of the Rivers Senegal and Gambia, only to be pushed out in turn by the English at the end of the sixteenth century.[24]

English expansion in Africa in the sixteenth century was similar to that of the French. Initially they had lively economic contacts with Morocco, following the expulsion of the Portuguese after 1541 from most of their Atlantic ports which were then left open to the ships of other European countries. In the 1550s and the early 1560s, English trading companies sent several expeditions, reports of which have survived. They visited the West African shores as far as the Gulf of Benin, buying mostly gold, hides and small numbers of slaves. Portuguese reports reveal that by the late 1500s the English were in contact with the population of the Gold Coast, though they do not seem to have been greatly interested in the slave trade.[25] Even as late as 1623, Richard Jobson refused to buy black slaves in the region of the Lower Gambia, though the Portuguese were quite active there and co-operating with African traders.[26] Little is yet known about English expansion in other regions of West Africa. However, by 1600 their position was very strong on the fringes of Senegambia, whence they had ousted both the Portuguese and the French. In 1588 the first English company for trading with Guinea was established mainly by merchants from London and Exeter already active in trading expeditions to the mouth of the River Gambia.[27] There is no evidence, however, that this company developed to any great size. Possibly the English found that looting Castilian ships on Atlantic waters was, at the end of the sixteenth century, more profitable than trading with Africa.

It was at exactly this time that the Dutch made their appearance on the shores of Africa. They were then in a state of war with Spain and repudiated the Pope's subdivision of the Atlantic. They treated Portugal, which was then ruled by Philip II, as an enemy state. The huge capital amassed by traders and their strong fleet made it possible for the Dutch to develop their expansion in India and Africa on a scale not yet achieved by the English or the French. A Dutch scholar, H. Terpestra, believed that the expeditions to the African countries had initially been organized by companies launched predominantly by medium-scale traders, interested in a quick return of capital. Expeditions to the East Indies were, however, organized by major capitalists, often rich emigrants from Antwerp, who could invest their capital for longer periods.[28]

24. L. Silveira, 1946, pp. 16, 17, 35–7, 44–6.
25. T. S. Willan, 1959, pp. 94–7, 139; J. W. Blake, 1942, pp. 129, 133, 138, 150–5.
26. R. Jobson, 1623, p. 112.
27. Cf. note 25 above.
28. H. Terpestra, 1960, pp. 341, 342.

From 1593 to 1607, about 200 ships sailed to Africa from Holland, and in 1610 and 1611 about twenty ships a year were apparently expedited. In 1594 and 1595 the Dutch came to Gorée. A few years later they reached the Cape of Benin where they bought cotton textiles and cowry shells which they took to the Gold Coast where they exchanged them for gold and silver. In 1611 the Dutch built the port of Nassau in Moree on the Gold Coast, their first fortified trading post on the West African coast. They also developed trade with the Accra region.[29] The Portuguese were no rivals for the Dutch who could supply large quantities of goods at low prices because of their wealth and their efficient trade networks. In this respect they had the edge over the English and the French. Dutch imports into West Africa consisted of iron, brass, copper and tin ware, cheap textiles of diverse origin, spirits, weapons, various adornments, goods of everyday use and even spectacles which enjoyed varying popularity. As a result of these imports (the large-scale character of which was such a surprise to Pieter de Marees in 1601–2)[30] supplies of gold from the interior to the Gold Coast increased again, predominantly to the benefit of the Dutch. The Dutch also imported to Africa sugar from St Thomas Island: they dominated this trade for some time, transporting the semi-finished product to the refineries of Amsterdam.[31]

Dutch expansion in West Africa developed more or less spontaneously. In 1617 the Dutch were so strong in Senegambia that they were a dominant force in the island of Gorée and had largely eliminated not only the Portuguese but also the English and the French from trade in Joal, Portudal and Rufisque. They held their strong position for over fifty years. At the same time their ships visited Loango, the Congo and Angola. Initially, like the English and the French, they were little interested in the slave trade. The turn of the sixteenth century, however, heralded a new phase of European expansion in Africa in which the slave trade grew in significance to become of the utmost importance to the Dutch as well. This phase began with the purchase of slaves in El Mina, Accra, Arda, Benin and the Nile delta and also Calabar, Gabon and Cameroon. The slaves were sold in return for sugar to the plantations on St Thomas Island (then occupied by the Dutch) or were transported to Brazil. From the area around the mouth of the River Senegal, the Dutch sent the Wolof, who – according to O. Dapper – were thought to possess great physical strength and be well-suited to work on the plantations.[32] The conquest of Angola in 1641 was closely associated with the labour needs of the Dutch in Brazil, thus following the Portuguese model.[33] Though the Dutch lost north-eastern Brazil and were also ousted from Angola in 1648, the close association of

29. K. Ratelband, 1953, pp. XXI–XXV, LXXV, LXXXIII; P. de Marees, 1912.
30. P. de Marees, 1912, pp. 45, 46, 51–4.
31. K. Ratelband, 1953, pp. XCV, CXV, 114, 118, etc.
32. ibid., pp. 8, 10, 27–35, 40–61; O. Dapper and A. F. C. Ryder, 1965.
33. M. Malowist, 1969, p. 569.

the two territories, based on slave-trading, continued until the nineteenth century.

Throughout this period, East Africa was of little interest to the Europeans. The Portuguese, who dominated Sofala and who politically subordinated other coastal towns, did not penetrate into the interior. They reached no farther than Tete and Sena on the River Zambezi, where they bought small quantities of gold on the local market.[34] Supplies of gold and possibly other goods from the hinterland to the coast had already diminished by the mid-sixteenth century, and there is nothing to indicate that they increased subsequently. The reduction in the supplies of gold to Sofala had a bad effect on the position of such towns as Kilwa, Mombasa and Malindi, which – prior to the arrival of the Portuguese – had been active in supplying gold and other goods to traders from India and Arabia. This decline may have been caused by the dislocation of Muslim trade on the East African coast, but it also seems likely that some political disturbances took place along the trade routes linking the ports with the hinterland.[35] This matter calls for further investigation. Attempts by the coastal inhabitants to secure the intervention of the Turks from the Arab Peninsula against the Portuguese miscarried. The expansion from the seventeenth century of the *Imāmate* of Oman to the East African coasts and islands brought about some changes in the late 1600s, confining Portuguese power to Mozambique alone.[36] However, it was not till the late eighteenth and the nineteenth centuries that these changes became very marked.

It should be added here that in the southern tip of Africa the first signs of European expansion appeared during the seventeenth century in the form of colonies of Dutch (and German) peasants, called the Boers, who were settlers sponsored by the Dutch East India Company. However, this phenomenon was insignificant during the seventeenth century and even long after. Nonetheless, the pressure of the Boers on the San which turned them into slaves, drove them off their lands and almost exterminated them, was a dangerous omen for the African population.[37]

Africa as a reservoir of labour

P. D. Curtin estimates that between 1451 and about 1600, 274 900 blacks were brought to America. Over the next few years this number increased to 1 341 100 to reach 6 million in the eighteenth century. Of these, according to estimates by F. Maura accepted by P.D. Curtin, some 400 000 to 450 000 slaves were imported to Brazil between 1575 and 1675. In the eighteenth

34. J. Lúcio De Azevedo, 1947, pp. 189–201; V. de Magalhães Godinho, 1969, pp. 253–75.
35. V. de Magalhães Godinho, 1962, pp. 272–3.
36. ibid., p. 273. R. Oliver and G. Mathew, 1963, Vol. I, pp. 141, 142.
37. See ch. 23 below.

century, the figure reached almost 2 million.[38] Throughout the 1700s, the importation of black labour to the English and French Antilles increased enormously and supplies to Cuba also grew. The above figures symbolize a radical, though gradual, change in European attitudes towards Africa which ceased to be a rich source of gold and became, first and foremost, a reservoir of labour without which many European estates in America could neither exist nor develop. This change – which was noticeable from the mid-seventeenth century – had, by the end of that century, become quite marked. The rapidly developing sugar-cane plantations were the main factor behind the enormous increase in demand for black labour. This process had started in Madeira, the Canaries and the Cape Verde Islands – particularly St Thomas Island – as early as the fifteenth century. It spread to Brazil in the second half of the sixteenth century, where it developed on a large scale in the north-eastern region. The Dutch occupation far from interrupting the process even stimulated it. The situation changed only when the Dutch were expelled from Brazil and transferred techniques used in the Brazilian sugar refineries to the islands in the Caribbean, which gradually became dominated mainly by the French and the English. Because of keen competition from the islands, the sugar-cane plantations were pushed into second place in the economic life of Brazil. With gold and diamond mining in Central Brazil (and from the 1800s, coffee production in South Brazil), the high demand almost trebled seventeenth-century slave imports.[39]

Supplies of slaves to English and French estates in the Caribbean also increased enormously. In the English colonies, slave imports rose from 263 700 in the seventeenth century to 1 401 300 in the eighteenth. The situation was similar in the islands occupied by France, with San Domingo importing the greatest number – almost 790 000 slaves, mostly direct from Africa, in the eighteenth century.[40] The cultivation of sugar cane was also started in Cuba, with similar consequences regarding labour requirements. Dutch Surinam and the English and French estates in Central America and the northern tip of South America also absorbed great numbers of black slaves. In North America, the tobacco plantations in Virginia and the rice plantations in Maryland laid the foundations for the further extension of the slave trade. A marked increase took place there in the eighteenth century when almost 400 000 slaves were brought into the English colonies.[41] Subsequent development of the cotton plantations in the nineteenth century changed the southern territories of the United States into a vast area based on a slave economy. In the northern part of the colonies, dominated by medium- and small-scale grain cultivation, there was little need to increase the import of slave labour.

38. P. D. Curtin, 1973, p. 259; F. Mauro, 1960, pp. 179, 180.
39. P. D. Curtin, ibid.
40. ibid.
41. Ibid.

PLATE 1.1   *Negro slaves washing for diamonds in Brazil*

Demand for black labour in the American colonies presented Western Europe with an unprecedented task. Moreover, it came at a time when radical political and economic changes were taking place in Europe. During the second half of the seventeenth century the decline of Spain and Portugal became increasingly evident. Holland, then at the peak of its power, started to be slowly ousted by England and France whose economies were developing rapidly. From the late 1600s England and France had had more and more influence regarding the character and pace of white expansion in Africa, while the Spaniards and even the Dutch came to play marginal roles. With the Portuguese, their progress in the conquest of Angola allowed them to retain an advantageous position in this important zone of the slave trade.

In the seventeenth century, Holland, England and subsequently France, as well as certain other countries, set up companies for trading with Africa and for transporting slaves to America. Thus resources began to be concentrated to this end. The companies obtained from their governments monopoly rights for trading with Africa and were therefore able to control prices. In return, they were obliged to build new forts and to maintain the old ones protecting the European trading posts on the coasts. The European position in Africa was therefore buttressed by the English, Dutch and French companies. The number of European forts increased greatly during the seventeenth and eighteenth centuries, particularly on the Gold Coast and nearby.

Meanwhile, whites in Africa were at loggerheads among themselves. Their rivalries did not merely echo the rivalry of the Great Powers in Europe. The traders and trading companies were striving to obtain the most convenient trading posts on the African coast. They did so in time of war, and there were frequent changes in possession among the diverse rival European groups, each of which was supported by its own government. The governments which backed the companies were interested specifically in the development of the American plantations based upon black labour and in increasing their profits from the slave trade. It was, therefore, unthinkable for the Great Powers, and also certain weaker European countries, to leave Africa to its own devices. Even Sweden, Denmark and Prussia tried to involve themselves in African affairs without, however much success and eventually withdrawing.

The activities of the companies, however, were not as fruitful as expected Of the English companies, the first two were not particularly active. The Royal African Company, founded in 1672 and in which the King of England himself had a share, met with constant difficulties despite controlling a large part of African external trade on the western coasts in the last quarter of the seventeenth century. Its policy met with strong disapproval from both the American planters in the English colonies and many merchants in England.[42] The planters protected the high slave prices imposed by the

42. D. P. Mannix, 1963, pp. 29–30.

PLATE 1.2   *Sale of estates, pictures and slaves in the Rotunda, New Orleans, America*

Company, while those English merchants who were not members of the Company also craved access to the African coasts and the highly profitable slave trade. After 1689, the Company's privileges were gradually curbed and access to the African trade was granted to others, too. In the mid-eighteenth century the Company ceased to exist.

In England an era of free trade with Africa had already begun a few years earlier. The merchants of Liverpool – which had been for almost half a century the main centre of what was known as the 'triangular trade' – were the most powerful. The trade operated as follows: the Liverpool merchants sent their ships with English goods to the African coast to be traded for slaves; these they transported to America to be sold to planters in the English, Spanish and Portuguese colonies; in turn, they brought back colonial goods to England.[43] In the eighteenth century the trade treaties which the English forced from both Spain and Portugal gave them easy access to Spanish and Portuguese possessions in America. The English West Indies, Barbados and Jamaica in particular were – during the seventeenth and eighteenth centuries – areas of large-scale, compulsory settlement for Africans brought there to work on the sugar-cane plantations and, subsequently, on cotton, coffee and other plantations, too.[44] Both Barbados and Jamaica sold slaves to the growing number of tobacco and rice planters in Virginia and Maryland in exchange for grain and other products from the North American colonies.

The great successes of the Liverpool merchants during the eighteenth century were made possible – as was realized long ago – through the rapid industrial development in the English Midlands, particularly of metals in Birmingham and of textiles in Manchester. The Liverpool merchants were able to supply Africa – more regularly and more cheaply than could other Europeans – with knives, weapons and other metal goods, which were in high demand, as well as with textiles. During the eighteenth century, England gradually became the power with the greatest economic involvement on the African coast. England's influence was felt from Senegal to the boundaries of Cameroon. Though England lost its outposts in Senegal to France in 1799, its position in the Gambia and Sierra Leone had become stronger. England also occupied a leading position in the Gold Coast's slave trade which had greatly increased since the mid-seventeenth century. Trade in the Bight of Biafra and the Benin Cape, including Calabar, was tremendously important: during the eighteenth century the number of slaves transported far exceeded 1.3 million. Slave exports from Whydah, Porto Novo, Lagos and other Gold Coast ports also increased enormously.[45] It was not only the English who were active there. Though France and Holland held weaker positions both, particularly France, developed a strong trade in the Slave Coast – in Senegal and in the region of Cameroon and

43. D. P. Mannix, 1963, pp. 69–74.
44. O. Patterson, 1967, pp. 16–29.
45. P. D. Curtin, 1973, pp. 259, 267.

Loango. The merchants of Nantes were in the forefront of this activity. Angola, in the late 1600s the most important source of black labour, was still under Portugal's influence during the second half of the eighteenth century and Portugal continued as a large-scale supplier of slaves to Brazil.

Attempts at settlement started on a modest scale with the whites in Angola. Along the coast, however, from Cape Verde to the Congo, European expansion retained its trading character. European factories and settlements such as Saint-Louis set up in 1626, were all scattered along the coast, near convenient bays and usually close to conglomerations inhabited by Africans. El Mina, Accra, Whydah, Porto Novo, Badagri and both old and new Calabar – all famous in the eighteenth century – and others were settlements where white incomers met the blacks who supplied the slaves and also took European goods. The African rulers mostly reserved for themselves priority in trading with Europeans, but the role of black traders was also important. Even in Angola the Portuguese caught few slaves themselves, using for that purpose local agents who bought or kidnapped slaves in the interior.

The territorial extent of the slave trade in Africa is difficult to assess. Herskovits and Harwitz are now thought to be wrong in believing that only the coastal zone was ravaged.[46] Undoubtedly the problem was most painful for the hinterlands of the ports, but information circulated as early as the sixteenth century concerning the long journeys made by slaves from their places of origin to the ports. During the large-scale export of Africans in the eighteenth century, slave-catchers had to penetrate the interior in order to reach their most important suppliers – the rulers of such powerful countries as Asante and Dahomey, and traders from Calabar. Their hunting zone must have been in the very heart of the continent, north of their own places of residence.[47] The old African states, such as Benin or Ọyọ, were much less involved. The Congo, which entered a period of complete disintegration in the eighteenth century, was never an important supplier of slaves.

The Europeans were not particularly interested at this time in territorial expansion in Africa (with the exception of Angola). They obtained slaves, through their factories and numerous bays where, moreover, they sold their own wares including rum and weapons. Europe was not yet ready to start the conquest of Africa mostly because of Africa's harsh climate and European helplessness in the face of tropical diseases. The early Europeans, the Brazilians and the North Americans who first made an appearance on the African continent therefore did everything to win the friendship of the African rulers by supplying them generously with whatever goods they wanted. In the seventeenth and eighteenth centuries, the community of interests between the European slave-traders and the slave-suppliers – the African rulers, dignitaries and traders – became even stronger. It is worth

46. M. J. Herskovits and M. Harwitz, 1964.
47. J. D. Fage, 1969a.

mentioning here that the movement for the abolition of slavery, started in the second half of the eighteenth century, was strongly resisted in England not only by the planters of the West Indies but also by merchants in the metropolis. It also became clear later that the kings of Asante and Dahomey, and no doubt certain other African rulers, were also definitely opposed to the abolition of the slave trade.

The main area of European interest in the seventeenth and eighteenth centuries was the west coast of Africa. There was little slave-trading on the eastern coast, and it was not until the eighteenth century that European slave-traders started to invade that area. The great distance from the east coast to the American markets made the transport of East Africans to the New World more difficult though not impossible. Numerous inhabitants of present-day Mozambique therefore had to face a tragic journey across the Atlantic to Brazil in particular. P. D. Curtin estimated the numbers brought to the Americas from central and south-east Africa between 1711 and 1810 at about 810 100, or 24 per cent of the total number of persons imported.[48] There is, however, no information as to the number of those who came from the eastern coast and its hinterland. Small numbers of black slaves were exported by the French after they occupied the islands of Réunion and Mauritius. And in East Africa, the export of slaves to Arabia, carried on by the subjects of the *Imām* of Oman, increased during the eighteenth century. When the centre of this activity shifted from Oman to Zanzibar, the effects were tragic for the population of East and Central Africa. It seems, however, that the ravaging raids of the Arab slave-catchers took place mainly in the nineteenth century.

In North Africa, the Europeans only put an end to the activities of the Barbary pirates in the eighteenth century, finally depriving them of their basic source of income. It would be interesting to find out whether this had any influence on the policies of the ruling élite in Algiers and Tunis – then deeply involved in the piratical expeditions – particularly concerning the local native populations.

The expedition to the River Niger in 1591 seems to have had no lasting effect on Morocco. The conquerors quickly made themselves independent of their metropolis, and their descendants – the Arma – set up their own small states which were, however, of short duration. There is no evidence of any important changes having taken place in the trade between Morocco and the curve of the Niger. Slaves and small amounts of gold continued to be exported from West Sudan. The slave trade, however, seems to have been considerable as, at the turn of the seventeenth century, the sultans of Morocco possessed an army composed of slaves which, for a certain period, also exerted a strong influence on the country's politics.

48. P. D. Curtin, 1973, p. 267, Table 7.2.

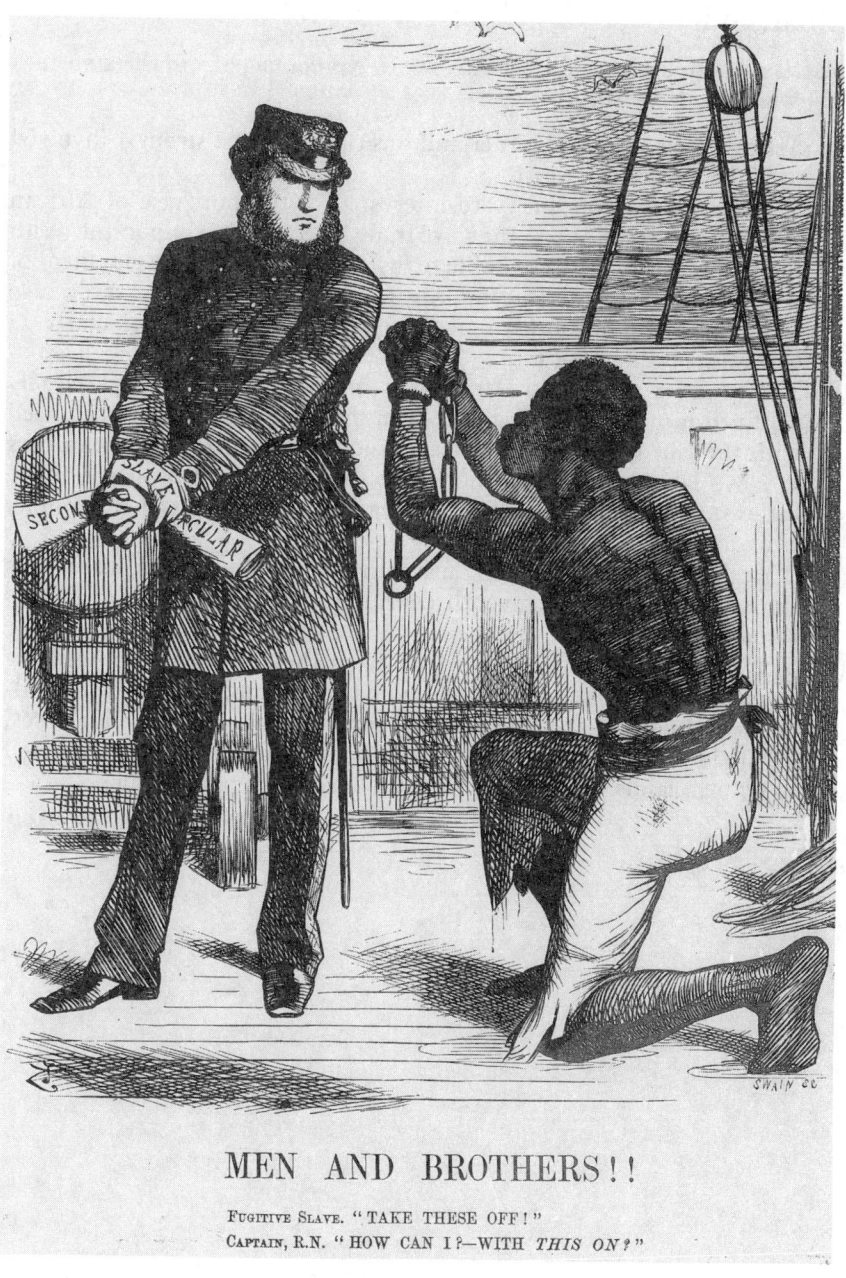

MEN AND BROTHERS!!

Fᴜɢɪᴛɪᴠᴇ Sʟᴀᴠᴇ. "TAKE THESE OFF!"
Cᴀᴘᴛᴀɪɴ, R.N. "HOW CAN I?—WITH *THIS ON?*"

PLATE 1.3   *The political cartoon, 'Men and Brothers!!'*

Conclusion

The following may be said of Africa's external contacts from the sixteenth to the eighteenth century:

(1) Africa's west coast and hinterland was the area most strongly involved with the rest of the world.

(2) Initially, the Europeans were interested in the purchase of African gold but, from the 1550s, the slave trade became more important. With slaves, the Europeans were able to foster the economic development of a large part of America and the Caribbean. The slave trade also accelerated the accumulation of capital in Europe, particularly in England, and in Africa.

(3) European expansion in Africa was proto-colonial and was largely confined to trade. Exchange between the two parties was unbalanced with the Europeans selling cheap goods in return for huge numbers of slave labourers. Thus, though at that time the Europeans made little attempt to conquer Africa, they greatly damaged its demographic situation.

(4) Africa's role as a market for European industrial products, as early as the sixteenth and seventeenth centuries, has probably been underestimated.

(5) The advantages accruing to Africa from these contacts included the introduction of new crops such as maize, manioc and cassava. This in no way could have compensated for the huge demographic losses, let alone the sufferings of large numbers of human beings abducted to strange lands overseas for hard labour on the plantations.

African political, economic and social structures during this period

P. DIAGNE

Largely as a result of internal factors such as demography and ecology or under the impact of external forces such as the slave trade, Christianity, Islam and capitalism, African social, economic and political structures were continuously transformed between 1500 and 1800. This chapter discusses these transformations and the new structures that emerged. It will be evident from this analysis that in most parts of the continent the idea of timeless African structures or institutions is a historical myth with no real substance.

New social structures

Islam and Christianity

The first noticeable changes and new structures were social. In the religious area, European and Middle Eastern philosophies and religions began to impinge, with Christianity and Islam becoming political forces in new areas. The religious problem became a crucial one for civilizations which, by virtue of their own visions of the world, had previously ignored conflicts of this kind.

Any ground gained by Christianity in the coastal areas of East Africa during this period was lost with the assassination of Father Conçalo da Silveira, a Portuguese priest who had been trying to bring the Mwene Mutapa Nogoma under Christian and Portuguese influence in 1560. Islam, on the other hand, made gains in Ethiopia with the conquests of Aḥmād Grañ (1531–5)[1] and those of the *Mai* of Borno (Bornu) and the *askiyas* of Songhay in the Sahara and Western Sudan.

---

1. See ch. 24 below.

The transition from captive to slave society

The second important change was the replacement in most of Africa of the black African *jonya* system by the European and Middle Eastern slave-owning system.

The *jonya* (from the Mande word *jon* meaning 'captive') was found mainly in Western Sudan and the Niger–Chad region. A *jon* (*jaam* in Waalo, *maccuba* in Fulfulde, *bayi* in Hausa) belonged to a certain lineage. He was not transferable, he owned the bulk of what he produced and, in societies in which the system flourished, he belonged to a socio-political category that was part of the ruling class and thus had a share in the sovereignty of the state and its political apparatus. Both as a system and a social class *jonya* played a considerable and novel role in the states and empires of Ghana, Takrūr, Mali, Kānem-Borno, Asante, Yoruba and Mutapa.[2] The élite of the royal slaves – the Mande *jon tigi*, the *farba* of the Takrūr *jaami buur* and the Hausa *sarkin bayi* – belonged to the dominant ruling class in the state and society. They exercised some power, made fortunes and could even themselves own slaves such as the Mande *jombiri jon* and the slaves-of-captives of Dahomey.[3]

Oriental and western slavery, on the other hand, in both its ancient and later its Western colonial form which gained a hold on eighteenth-century Africa, set out to base a mode of production on slaves as chattels or commodities with few rights, to be bought, sold and inherited. Sometimes they made up the bulk of a society's labour force, as in the Athenian system and the colonial plantation slavery of medieval Arabia and post-Columbian America. Its influence gave rise to a conflict that continued to afflict the African continent into the twentieth century.

Increasing instability and continual warring contributed, if only on demographic grounds, to the rise of *jonya* in the sixteenth century until it began to overlap geographically with the slave-owning system and the colonial form of slavery within the new overlying social structures. Where Islamic institutions were introduced, as in Songhay, Hausaland and the East African towns, the two systems were often confused.

With the setting up of Muslim states or emirates – which progressively took over Western Sudan through the *djihād*s and the revolutions of Karamokho Sambegu in Futa Jallon around 1725 and of Sulaymān Baal in Futa Toro in 1775 – Muslim law and tradition was established in the region. At the same time, the slave-owning system was replacing the *jonya*. The founding of the Sokoto caliphate by 'Uthmān dan Fodio at the

---

2. *Macamos* were gangs of slaves surrounding the Mwene Mutapa, i.e. they corresponded to the Sudanic royal captives (*furba jon*, *tonjon* or *jaami buur*).

3. The study of slavery within African societies has been undertaken in several major works, e.g. S. Miers and I. Kopytoff, 1977. This work reveals the wide range of related institutions to which the term 'slavery' could be applied and attempts to define 'slavery' in the indigenous African context. See also C. Meillassoux, 1975; P. E. Lovejoy, 1981; A. G. B. Fisher and H. G. Fisher, 1970.

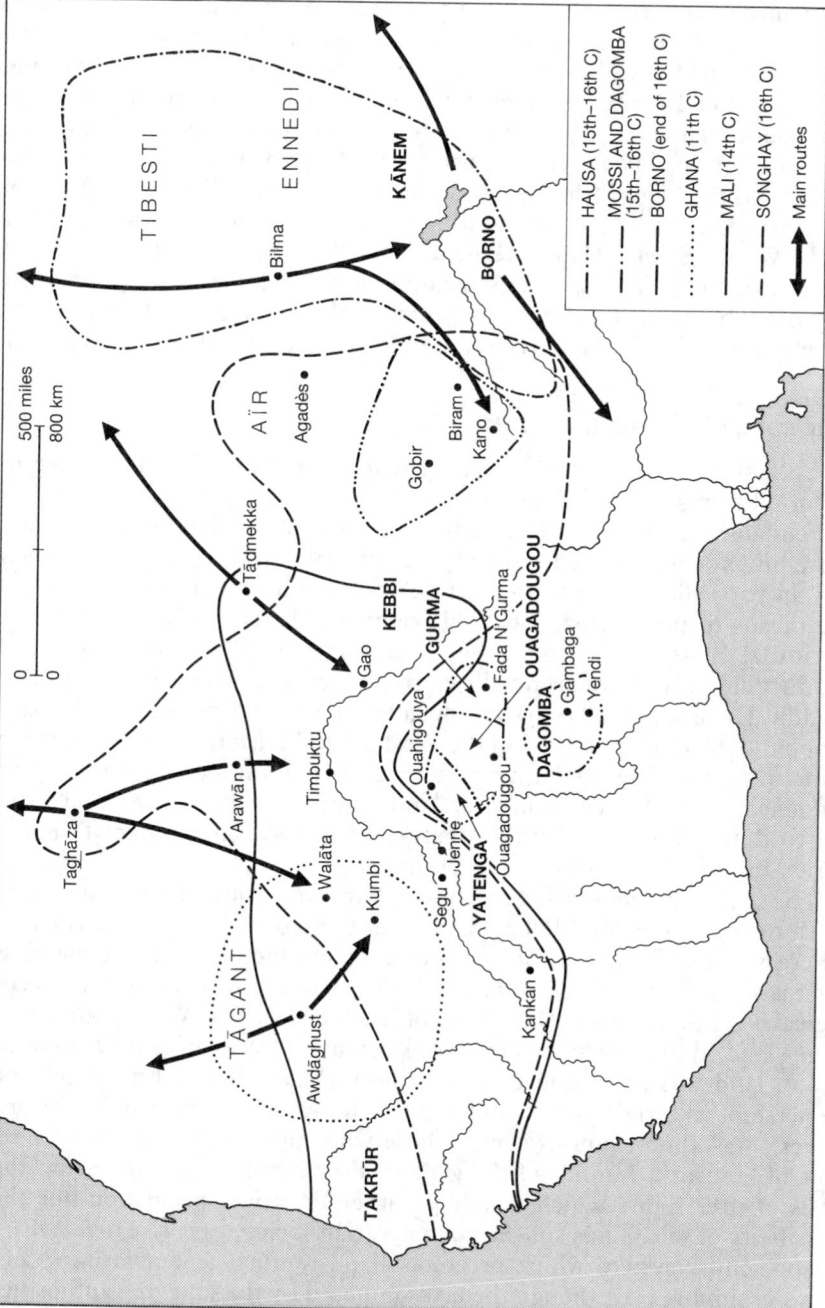

FIG. 2.1   *Political entities of the Sahel between the eleventh and sixteenth centuries*
Source: adapted from map drawn by P. Ndiaye, Department of Geography, University of Dakar

25

beginning of the nineteenth century further accelerated the process; and the Islamization of the Saharan Negro–Berbers and their conquest by the Saharan Arab Hassan *ḳabīla*s took it a step further, progressively converting the semi-feudal *ḥarāṭīn*[4] (which featured a warlike aristocracy combined with conquered sedentary peoples), into a more or less slave-owning system. *Jonya* did survive, however, amongst the traditional aristocracy of Western Sudan and the Niger–Chad region, which had suffered little or no Muslim influence. Until colonial conquest, *jonya* continued to wield some power in the Wolof, Sereer, Hausa, Kanēmbu and Yoruba states. The empire of Segu, with its *furba jon*, is reminiscent of that of the *mansa* with their *tonjon*. Until colonial conquest the states of Kayor, Siin and Yatenga were largely controlled by the warrior or administrative élite of the captive class.

The spread of feudal structures

The third change was the spread of feudal structures in either pure or distorted forms among the agrarian civilizations of Africa.

Feudalism as a political structure, a mode of production or a socio-economic system entailed not only ties of fealty, vassalage or suzerainty but, in particular, an opportunity to speculate and to make a profit out of the means of production. That this right was based on land ownership, territorial mastery, or control of a person, thing or some means of production, was unimportant. Property, which dominated European and Middle Eastern thought, system of government and political and socio-economic structure, featured in the Western and Eastern feudalisms which came to bear on the predominantly agrarian civilizations of Africa. Their influence was to be seen wherever land tenure or control over a territory led to duties, taxes, land rents, share-cropping systems, tenant farming, agricultural wage labour or land renting.

The socio-economic structures of sub-Saharan Africa differed from those of Europe and the Middle East and from the feudal system in particular. There was no speculation in the means of production, even in the class societies and states of sub-Saharan Africa, because of historical and eco-logical conditions. Before the advent of Islamic law or the Western-inspired *mailo* land system (which introduced a tenancy system into Uganda in 1900), land was not a source of income in black Africa. European-type ownership, as a right to use and transfer things and even people (that is, slaves), was almost non-existent. Those who appropriated or passed on a plot of land or a hunting, fishing or food-gathering area worked on the basis of user rights which entailed neither lucrative speculation nor the possibility of sale. Thus sub-Saharan agrarian society gave rise to *lamana* – a land tenure system which precluded land-renting, tenant farming and share-cropping, even though the taxes imposed by the state, the authorities and the chiefs were levied on agricultural and pastoral production. The

4. Originally serfs.

mode of production peculiar to black Africa entailed above all production for consumption. People produced for their own use, without the control of the means of production.

Interaction between the different social structures gave rise to hybrid, heterogeneous societies, generally rather poorly described by scholars blinkered by pre-conceived ideas of history. African society, from the sixteenth to the eighteenth century, thus contained marginal areas of debased feudalism mixed with *lamana*. Feudalism held sway where there was production for exchange and the *lamana* system of production for consumption had been broken down or modified.

In Egypt, the Turkish *beylik* (beylic) system helped to foster the feudal system and feudalization. The Ottoman regime took over in Egypt a landed nobility which had itself established cliental or seigniorial relationships. This rural aristocracy was protected, as in the Middle Ages in Europe, by *odjak*s (Turkish fortresses and garrisons). Great local chiefs ruled the *carsh* (ethnic area) and the *dwar*s (tented camps) according to a hierarchical system. They subordinated *khames* (vassals, serfs) and small communities to themselves, as in the case of the Makhzen. In the Sahel and the Mauritanian Sahara, religious families and *djuad* (warrior chiefs) took over and vassalized confederations of small communities under the cloak of religious brotherhood or by right of conquest. In southern Oran the Awlād Sīdī Shaykh imposed tribute on the Chaamba nomads, who undertook allegiance to them. The Hassan warriors established the same *worma*[5] (obligations of fealty) over the *harāṭīn* and the *marabout* families north of the Senegal river, and exacted the *muud al-hūrum* from the Haal-pularen.

The chief Turkish and native dignitaries in the Maghrib were often granted large estates by the *bey*s which they ran on a tenancy, rental or share-cropping basis. As in Egypt, the *beylik* controlled the up-to-date economic activities, and monopolized manufacturing industry, the mills, the arsenals, the mint, the building yards and the resources of piracy. It had a hold over the cereal, oil, salt and textile trades, and controlled the trade routes (caravan termini and sea-ports) and foreign trade. The guilds of craftsmen and merchants were under its supervision. The merchant middle class itself worked as an intermediary for the Ottoman regime.

In the rest of North Africa and northern Ethiopia the feudal system developed differently because of ecological conditions which in some areas made land ownership less concentrated. The great beylical estates of the Maghrib extended over a wide area, and gave rise to the widespread distribution of *azel* (fiefs) worked by the *khammāsat* (tenant farming) system on a one-fifth basis. At the regional level, the pattern was still one of *milk* (small family holdings) and *carsh* (community or group holdings) but always within the speculative feudal superstructure.

In Egypt and the rest of North Africa some centuries of Graeco–Roman

---

5. *Worma* introduced the idea of allegiance or fealty into Takrūr languages where such a bond did not exist.

rule had already prepared the ground for the transition to feudalism, the *iḳṭāʿ* system of the Mamluks. Under the Greek and Roman occupation these areas had become the granaries of the Imperial regime which had developed *ager publicus* and the Colonate there with the help of slave labour and thoroughly oppressed and exploited peasantry. In the sub-Saharan region the transition to feudalism took place under outside influence.

In northern Ethiopia, for instance, there emerged a landed gentry which created estates. This came about because the Ethiopian nobility subverted the principles of ambilineal descent and equal partible inheritance thereby creating among themselves trans-generational 'families'. They also claimed properties such as cattle and produce from such land. The economy of the region was based on plough agriculture, and a significant number of the emerging nobility were able to hand over their newly acquired estates intact to their heirs. Also, political office was gradually concentrated within this group and, hence, the holding of public office became critical to the accumulation of wealth. Consequently, northern Ethiopia exhibited marked tendencies towards greater class differentiation based on the accumulation of land property and political power.[6]

These semi-feudal situations were extended by Christian northern Ethiopia to the southern areas where the *ketema* (garrison towns) were established with a *neftenia* (landed élite) colonizing the *gasha* (occupied lands). The *gabar* (peasant) who worked the lands for the benefit of the landed élite was, like the *fallāh* (pl., *fallāḥīn*), similar to a serf, or at least a tributary or client obliged to pay the *gabir* or *siso*, depending on whether he was a share-cropper or a tenant farmer.

In the Great Lakes region, especially its southern area which comprises much of present-day western Tanzania, Burundi, Rwanda and Uvira in north-eastern Zaire, the institutions of clientship constituted a semi-feudal bond which developed to harmonize the relationship between pastoralists and agriculturalists. It was a contract between a pastoralist donor, who provided cattle, and an agriculturalist recipient who put his services and those of his family and future generations at the disposal of the donor and his heirs. These contracts differed from society to society and changed over the years.[7] In Takrūr a *surga* or *dag* would agree of his own free will to be maintained by a rich man or an influential political leader for his own benefit. Such manifestations of semi-feudal structures cannot apparently be attributed to external influence but have to be explained in terms of internal developments.

The main factors contributing to the adoption of the Ottoman feudal socio-economic system were the spread of the Muslim Emirate with the advent of the *askiya* in Western Sudan, the expansion of the empire of the Islamized *Mai* of Borno and the introduction of Ḳurʾānic law as a result of conversion and the *djihād*s. In Songhay the *askiya* kept part of the tra-

6. See ch. 24 below. See also A. Hoben, 1975.
7. E. Mworoha, 1977, chs 3 and 4. See also ch. 26 below.

ditional socio-economic structure. Like the Ethiopian aristocracy, who colonized southern Ethiopia, they introduced many innovations to the lands they conquered. *Askiya* Muḥammad and his successors distributed concessions after the Mamluk style: they set up *ikṭāʿ* (fiefs) on the *kharādj* lands seized from non-Muslims and gave to their favourites not the serfs, the non-transferable land or their property, but the usufruct of the duties, taxes and fees payable to the state. The *ta'rīkh*s (chronicles) are full of details of this kind.

In the emirates the Muslim law of the *djihād*s was adopted, thus implanting more firmly European and Middle-Eastern feudal, semi-feudal or tributary socio-economic structures. The *almamia* of Futa Toro and Futa Jallon and the Sokoto caliphate were simply copied from Ottoman land tenure and taxation systems. The *jom leydi* (master of the land), the *jom lewre, jom jambere* and *jom jayngol*[8] (who had the usufruct of the Futa lands) were progressively absorbed, not into feudal forms of allegiance but into a feudal-type socio-economic structure.

The new legal system established under the emirate introduced feudal-type land speculation. The *njoldi* (symbolic payments[9] attaching to the master of the land), *kawngal* (fishing grounds), *yial* (hunting grounds), *hore kosam* (grazing land) and *gobbi* (mines), were transformed into annual dues payable to those in power, and were collected under state supervision. Even the office of the tax-collector became negotiable for a fee, as did most of the official posts within the system. Share-cropping, tenant farming and land rental became the rule. In the Islamized areas the landless peasants, dispossessed by conquest or the new legal system, became an important factor. The Sereer *refo rekk* (serfs), the Takrūr, *samba remoru, baadolo* and *navetaan* and the Hausa *talakawa* emerged as counterparts of the Mediterranean and Saharan *khames, ḥarāṭīn, fallāḥīn* and *gaba*s. The *leydi hujja* (Fulfulde for land bond) introduced the Ottoman system of land tenure. The *njoldi* was the annual ground rent and the *cootigu* the fee payable by tenant farmers, share-croppers and sub-tenants. The eastern Muslim system of land control appeared in the *bayti maal* or *leydi maal* and the *leydi janandi* which were state-owned, and the *ḥabūs* which belonged to the religious community. The land was, however, only partly subjected to Maghribi forms of vassalage. In some cases Makhzen types of tax exemption were to be found.[10] Under the *leydi urum* allegiance was owed

8. *Jom lewre* – the first occupant and clearer of the land; *jom jambere* – a person entitled to clear the land with an axe; *jom jayngol* – a person entitled to clear the land by burning.

9. These dues, which were of various kinds (cereals, joints of game, honey beer, chicken, goat, etc) were originally primarily of ritual significance, i.e. meant as offerings to the 'spirit of the place' that was occupied. They were given on taking possession, sometimes at harvest time, and most commonly at funerals and ceremonies of succession to the *laman*, or first occupant.

10. The Makhzen *ḳabīla*s were exempted from tax and their lands were under the control of central authority. In return for this submission, the Makhzen chiefs levied taxes on the neighbouring *ḳabīla*s, the *raia*.

by means of the *worma* (bond of fealty), coupled with the *muud al-hūrum* or *muudul horma* tax.

From the sixteenth century onwards, socio-economic structures from different backgrounds were therefore combining. The result was the emergence of a new social order – an emiral or dominant form of government[11] in which feudal structures were superimposed on the African *lamana*. This development of socio-economic structures affected the form of the *mansaya* state: in Western Sudan and Nigeria, which were becoming Islamized, the eastern Muslim institution of the emirate replaced it or was superimposed on it. In the Gulf of Guinea and Central and East Africa, where Christian rulers appeared among the Mani Kongo and the Mwene Mutapa, the institutional influence of Christian feudal monarchy was increasingly apparent.

Architectural and artistic developments

Finally, there were also some important architectural and artistic developments. The men who built the towns in the Nile valley, the Maghrib, Sudan and the coast, and erected the Yoruba palaces, the edifice known today as the Zimbabwe ruins, the houses, palaces and mosques of the East African coast and the *tata* surrounding the Hausa cities were at once architects, masons, decorators and town planners. The round or pyramidal strong clay or stone huts and the tiered Jolla houses were in the same architectural traditions as the Koutoubia of Marrakesh, the tomb of the *askiya* at Gao and that of the caliphs at Cairo. In the earlier period great emphasis was placed on good architecture, as witness the ruins of Awdāghust, Kumbi, Kilwa, Jenne and Axum. After the sixteenth century new advances in architecture continued to be made, perhaps mainly in Western Sudan and Nigeria, but the towns of North Africa and the Nile valley declined with the collapse of their erstwhile prosperity. The *askiya*s, however, who carried on the tradition in West Africa, were great builders, like their Moroccan contemporary, Abū 'l-'Abbās al-Manṣūr.

Sonni 'Alī and *Askiya* Muḥammad resumed the construction of the great canal running along the River Niger. In Morocco, al-Manṣūr's accession to power coincided with a definite, if short-lived, vogue for large public works. The architectural traditions of the Sahel and the Islamic world nevertheless increasingly spread southwards. Sudanese architectural style, of which the mosques at Sankore and Jenne were the prototypes, spread from the sixteenth century. *Askiya* Muḥammad built Tendirma out of nothing and founded the Sīdī Yaḥya mosque. In this context, large bodies of masons, cabinet-makers and decorators grew up who, in Western Sudan and the Maghrib, gave rise to fraternities and castes.

In Ethiopia, the Gondar period (*c*.1632–*c*.1750) witnessed the development of new architectural styles promoted by the court. In Gondar itself

11. The term dominant or emiral regime is used here to denote the hybrid social forms that emerged in black Africa following contact with Islam; cf. P. Diagne, 1967.

and in other towns, the emperors' families erected huge and beautiful palaces, castles, churches and libraries with elaborate interior decorations.[12] In the Swahili-speaking coastal regions of East Africa major architectural changes occurred from about 1700 to 1850. New patterns and motifs were introduced, and the houses themselves were of original designs and great craftmanship with excellent plaster-carving. Architectural developments were accompanied by productivity in related fields such as wood-carving, especially door-carving and furniture-making.[13]

New economic structures

The main new economic structures that developed during this period were the caste system of production, which replaced the guild or corporation system; the predatory economy, mainly in North and East Africa; and the trading-post or entrepôt economy, mainly in Central and West Africa.

A craft economy and a caste-and-guild society

Medieval urban civilization had contributed to the division of labour through the development of crafts, manufacturing and industrial processes. But in the sixteenth century development was uneven – depending on the area and the type of society – with different tendencies showing themselves in the various social contexts.

The civilizations of Western Sudan, the Niger-Chad region and the Sahara, for instance, developed crafts, manufacturing and industrial activities on the basis of more or less closed, inbred castes. With the growing influence of Takrūr and the Saharan civilizations, the caste system crystallized, most noticeably in the civilizations of southern Senegal, Mande territory and Hausaland. The Takrūr caste system – and members of it – migrated to Kayor, Jolof, Siin and Salum. The Mande *nyamankala* (caste system) long raised the status of the blacksmith's trade until the *djihād*s brought the Takrūrians to the area. For example, Sumaguru Kante, who played a prominent role in the rise to power of the Mansa dynasty and the state of Mali, was originally a blacksmith. Metalworkers were held in high esteem among the Fon and Yoruba but there, too, the impact of immigration from Takrūr and the Sahara was to upset the prevailing order. In Songhay, the *askiya* already governed a society in which the caste system had developed, become stratified and taken ideological root.

The Torodo revolution at the end of the eighteenth century accentuated the caste system in Takrūr by deepening class divisions. The Sebbe peasants, the Subalbe fishermen and even the Buruure Fulbe nomadic herdsmen were progressively debased. They were not identified with the *enangatoobe* (*sakkeebe* or cobblers, *wayilbe* or blacksmiths or *gawlo*, griots,

12. See ch. 24 below.
13. J. de V. Allen, 1974. See also P. S. Garlake, 1966.

etc.), but were subject to segregation among the *nangatoobe* (upper caste). The Torodo *marabout* élite increasingly came to regard as low-caste the defeated *Ceddo* and Denyanke aristocracies and everyone except members of the *marabout* lineages eligible for high office. In the Negro–Berber societies of the Sahara, religious, ethnic and racial divisions gradually came into play in caste hierarchies.

One last striking aspect in the development of craft or industrial organization concerned state control. In Mediterranean civilizations, the trend was towards state monopolies in a number of activities, such as weaving, shipbuilding, arsenals, refining and foreign trade. The black African state seldom exercised such control, even with the expansion of the armaments and weapons industries.[14] One feature of this phase was the contrast between the versatility of country-dwellers and the marked specialization of townsmen. In agriculture and stock-breeding the division of labour and the proliferation of trades and crafts had developed little. Farmers, fishermen, stock-breeders and hunters remained versatile with each plying many trades such as blacksmith, basket-maker, mason, woodcutter, carpenter, weaver or shoemaker as needed. Sometimes women, or specific age-groups, specialized in a given type of work – mainly specific trades, such as metal-, wood- and leather-working, that were implicated in the development of castes.

State industries also developed, with arsenals for weapons and even for the building of river- and ocean-going fleets, both in Western Sudan and on the West Atlantic coast and also in Mediterranean and Indian-Ocean countries.

The multiplicity of wars sometimes lent fresh impetus to metal-working. In the sixteenth century Sonni 'Alī reorganized the Songhay arsenals, setting yearly production targets for the workshops. Egypt became skilled in metallurgy and produced Damascus steel. Large communities were engaged in iron-, copper-, gold- and silver-working. The precious-metal industry in Egypt and North Africa continued to be supplied with gold from Wādī Allaga in Nubia, Sofala and Western Sudan. The Mande blacksmiths, organized on a caste basis, exported their techniques to the new towns that had sprung up as a result of the Atlantic trade. The Sudanese *garassa*, *tëgg* and *maabo* – who made ploughs, axes, swords, spears, arrowheads and household tools – perfected their techniques and, by the end of the eighteenth century, were repairing firearms. It was in this sector that new technologies were most quickly absorbed. Craftsmen working in gold and silver stimulated trade in the *sūḳs* (markets) of towns in the Maghrib, Egypt and Western Sudan. Berber and Wolof jewellers were outstanding for their gold and jewellery filigree work. The minting of gold coinage – of long-standing in the north and on the Swahili coast, particularly at Zanzibar and Kilwa – moved southwards to Nikki. The

14. The large-scale development of state armaments industries in black Africa took place mainly in the nineteenth century.

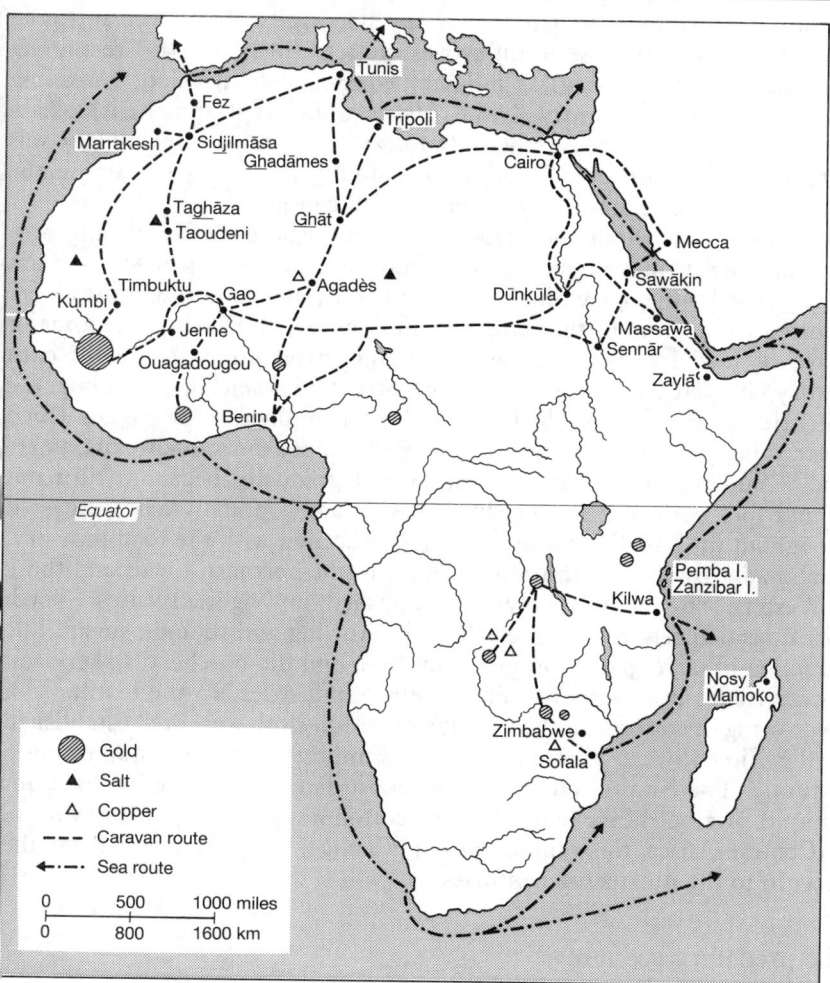

FIG. 2.2 *African trade routes in the sixteenth century*
Source: adapted from map drawn by P. Ndiaye, Department of Geography, University of Dakar

33

Swahili also manufactured beautiful jewellery and other silver and gold items. Ceramics gave rise to industries, pottery (like basketry) remaining a female preserve. The glass industry continued to develop, spreading throughout Yoruba country, Nupe, Hausaland, Egypt and the Maghrib. Among the Shona in the Southern Zambezi region, mining technology was quite advanced with gold- and copper-mining industries sustaining the economies of the region up to the eighteenth century.[15]

Leatherworking flourished most in Nigeria, where stock-breeding provided ample raw materials. Footwear from the new centres of Kano, Zaria and Abeche competed with the leather goods; and large quantities were exported from Siyu, in the Lamu archipelago which had become a major centre of leatherwork by 1700. From the sixteenth to the eighteenth century, basketry and carpet-weaving also took their place among the industries of the Niger–Chad region. The manufacture of paper, which replaced papyrus, developed chiefly in Egypt under the influence of Samarkand.[16] Sudan did not lag far behind and gradually began to turn out manuscripts with Kānem producing Ḳur'āns (Qorans) that were sold throughout the Muslim world.[17] Trades associated with the food industry, which had grown up in the Middle Ages in the northern towns and those of Western Sudan, also became established in Nigerian cities. North Africa, particularly Egypt, specialized in growing and refining sugar. The extraction of olive, palm and groundnut oil, and the butchery, bakery and grocery trades in general remained cottage industries. In the textile field, the growing of cotton and the weaving of cotton cloth were well established on the Zimbabwean Plateau and the Zambezi valley by the sixteenth century.[18] The Swahili city states were also famous for fabrics: Pate, for example, produced excellent silk,[19] and cotton was grown, spun and woven. In Central Africa the raphia cloth of Kongo was renowned from the fifteenth to the nineteenth centuries.

The predatory economy

Prior to the sixteenth century, long-distance trade had played a major role in the economy of Africa. This had encouraged high productivity and had led to the rise of urban civilizations and the forging of strong links between town and country which had slowly transformed the countryside. Between 1500 and 1800, however, the predatory economy – the outcome of Spanish and Portuguese expansionism, from 1600 both violent and destructive – was introduced with the decline of the ports and market towns that had been enriched by the medieval trans-Saharan trade apparent from 1592

15. D. N. Beach, 1980a, pp. 26–30.
16. G. Nachtigal, 1881.
17. G. Nachtigal, 1876.
18. D. N. Beach, 1980a, pp. 30–2.
19. G. S. P. Freeman-Grenville, 1962b, p. 142.

PLATE 2.1 (Left) *Sandal of Sudanese leather, made in the Kano area. Similar goods were exported in great quantities to North Africa*

PLATE 2.2 (Right) *Leather bag from the Timbuktu region*

onwards when the Christian kings of Spain and Portugal began expelling the large colonies of Jews and Muslims who had settled in the Maghrib and at Tunis and Algiers.

Spain had occupied Palma, in the Canary Islands, and had taken Tenerife in 1495, followed by Melilla in 1496. In 1505 it had established itself at Mars al-Kabīr and in the same year the Portuguese had occupied Agadir, followed by Sāfī in 1508. In 1509 Cardinal Ximenes had seized Oran and in the same year Algiers came under Spanish control followed, in 1510, by Bougie; Tunis Delys, Cherchel and Algiers all paid tribute to Spain. In 1513 Portugal had extended its sway to Azemmūr.

By this time the Arab–Berbers and the Ottoman Porte felt compelled to oppose European aggression and the corsairs, sailing under the Ottoman flag, helped to redress the balance of power. In 1514 one of the Barbarossa brothers, Abū Yūsuf, recaptured Djidjellī and Algiers with his brother, Khāyr al-Dīn, consolidating the reconquest. Tunisia and Algeria came under Ottoman sovereignty once again, and remained so, at least nominally, until the nineteenth century, despite Charles V of Spain's expeditions against them (he was defeated before Algiers in 1541). In 1551 Sinān Pasha occupied Tripoli in the name of the Ottoman Porte followed by Tunis in 1574. In the mid-1500s, Morocco asserted its independence having reconquered Agadir, Sāfī and Azemmūr from Portugal thanks to the *djihād* of the Banū Saʿād, founders of the Shārīfian dynasty. At al-Makhazen, Abū 'l-ʿAbbās al-Manṣūr, an ally of Queen Elizabeth I of England, routed an army of 20 000 Portuguese.

Despite their clashes with European powers, the North African states continued to preserve their freedom but their progress was impeded in the sixteenth century by the breakdown of the world economic order. Henceforth, the ports of the Maghrib and North Africa lived mainly by piracy and on tributes and duties, rather than by trade or new industries. The main activities of the states were dictated by the logic of the predatory economy. The Turkish corsairs took the place of the medieval merchant class in catering for the prosperity of the Ottoman ruling military élite. The ports of Salé (Morocco), Algiers, Tunis and Tripoli enjoyed the protection of the privateer fleet which, in the 1600s, enjoyed its golden age in the Mediterranean.

In 1558, thirty-five galleys and twenty-five brigantines were engaged in piracy from the port of Algiers, a city with a population of only 20 000. Nevertheless, economically it was in a sorry state. In 1580 it was stricken by famine and lost one-third of its population. It continued to attract people, however, and, by the eighteenth century, had a population of 100 000, including 25 000 Christian slaves. Sixteenth-century Tripoli had a population of 40 000 comprising 3500 Turks, 35 000 Arab–Berbers and 2000 Christians. Its corsairs ravaged the Mediterranean – the scene of the anti-European struggle – and throughout the eighteenth century, too, there was continual instability in the western Mediterranean. The Ottoman regencies of Algiers and Tunis were almost constantly at war with one or other European power with confrontations alternating with treaties. In this context mercantile capitalism and the merchant class stood to gain nothing.

It is against this background that the Moroccan expedition against Songhay in Western Sudan should be seen, likewise the *djihād*s which the Muslim communities of black Africa, influenced by the Maghrib, undertook against the entrepôt economy on the Atlantic coast. The Moroccan ruler, Abū 'l-ʿAbbās al-Manṣūr – who had defeated the Portuguese – endeavoured with the conquest of Songhay in 1591 to re-open the gold and slave routes. In 1593 the capture of Timbuktu made it possible to bring 1200 slaves across the Sahara. Djūdar Pasha's venture served only to hasten the downfall of this trade. It put an end to what was the largest if not the most powerful empire in Western Sudan in the sixteenth century.

Tripolitania and Egypt were more sheltered from the consequences of the decline of the Saharan trade and maintained their traditional trans-Saharan routes. The Ottoman Porte, which was established in Egypt and at Tripoli, bolstered Kānem–Borno by means of an alliance and deliveries of arms, and so maintained a flow of north–south trade – vital for its own supplies – until the nineteenth century.

The societies in this area did not, however, escape the overall decline. The oriental civilization of which they had become part was decaying. Its feudal structures did not facilitate the development of the areas it influenced in the Mediterranean, the Indian Ocean, or the interior – in the Niger–Chad region and Western Sudan.

The predatory economy, of which piracy in the Mediterranean was a component, certainly contributed to the halting of economic and technological growth in the southern Mediterranean. But socio-economic and political structures also played a part in the stagnation and under-development of the area and its hinterland. The decline of Mediterranean Africa meant the decline of a whole sub-system which played a prominent role in the economic and political geography of the medieval world.

All the countries of the Nile and East Africa, and those in the Niger–Chad region and Western Sudan, were affected in differing degrees. As Chapter 28 on Madagascar reveals, in the western Indian Ocean the years 1680 to 1720 became known as the 'the period of the pirates'. Countries in direct contact with the new European hegemonies were physically disrupted by the predatory economy, although their decline was also due to their inability to revivify a socio-economic structure increasingly influenced by the backward East. They were also handicapped by their inability to quickly establish power relationships that would have saved them from the unequal balance of trade characteristic of the period.

The decline of the countryside: poverty and insecurity among the peasantry

The predatory economy caused trade between town and country to stagnate and therefore affected the relationship between them. Their activities and produce had been complementary. Towns had broken the closed circle of subsistence farming, accentuated the division of labour and contained the seeds of the new society. They had provided the background for scientific and technological development and the growth of trade and specialized crafts and industries. They had created new economic, social and cultural values and represented the forefront of progress. They had given rise to new production technologies and more sophisticated consumption patterns. It was urban crafts and industries that had, until then, stimulated large-scale agriculture, stock-breeding, fishing and hunting and their auxiliary

37

industries. They had been responsible for the planting of sugarcane and cotton on an industrial scale and the growing of dye plants, such as madder, indigo, saffron and henna, and also perfume plants. Hydraulic installations, roads and stock-breeding for wool, milk and meat all owed their development to the towns.

The sixteenth century, however, brought disruption and crisis to that world. Urban depopulation brought decline to the rural economy, leading to widespread poverty among the peasants and the reversion to bush of large tracts of arable land. Increasingly insecure, the country-folk sought refuge in the depths of the forest where, cut off from the high-consumption culture of the towns, they withdrew more and more into family or village self-sufficiency subsistence farming and production for consumption. The Maghribi and Egyptian peasant produced olive oil and cereals for himself, and kept domestic animals. The West Atlantic peasant made palm oil, planted cassava and yams and learnt to grow bananas and maize. The farmer-stock-breeders of the savannah filled their barns with rice, millet and fonio, and made their own *karite-* (shea butter nut) groundnut- and palm-oil. Exchange of produce and barter were the main forms of trade.

This rustic life was further disrupted by the slave trade which drained the peasant population, for, when wars between rival aristocracies no longer furnished sufficient captives, the gap was bridged by slave-raiding and the devastation of the countryside, especially south of the Sahara. Depleted of able-bodied men, the village economy declined: people disappeared from traditionally inhabited areas and, in some regions, peoples continually on the run reverted to a migrant economy of hunting and food-gathering with many moving into the savannah region towards the forest.

Even methods of production regressed. The strong correlation between innovation, the need for sophisticated techniques and abundant means is well known; and the general unavailability of resources in the African countryside accentuated technological regression or stagnation.

The warrior aristocracy drained a great deal of manpower from the land which, in black Africa in particular, was demographically ruinous for the country areas. The ruling élites gave up farming and relied instead on raiding using the services of the freemen and slaves they had captured.

It became more and more burdensome for the peasantry to support these idle élites particularly in the troubled Western Sudan and Niger–Chad regions which, with their dry farming and extensive migrant agriculture, found it increasingly difficult to feed their people. The *baadolo*, the *samba remoru* (poor peasants of Takrūr) and the *talakawa* (poverty-stricken farmers and herdsmen of Hausaland and the Niger–Chad area), came to constitute the great mass of the peasantry in the savannah lands. They led as hard a life as the Egyptian *fallāḥīn*, the Ethiopian *gabar* and the Saharan and Maghribian *ḥarāṭīn*s and *khames*.

The oppression of the African peasantry by the rural and urban élites increased with the tightening of the fiscal screw on rural farmers. Under

Turkish Muslim law taxation was increased in the *daru khurudj* (non-Islamized) lands. Muslims were made to pay not only the *zakāt* (the only tax to which a Muslim was liable) but also the *kharādj*. There was also an increase in land speculation through share-cropping and tenancy.

As the black market in local taxation rights became widespread in Muslim countries, the weight of taxation imposed by the élites on the peasants and rural craftsmen increased. The plundering of wealth and the capture and enslavement of the peasant masses attained gigantic proportions. To the *galag* (tax) payable to the political chief of the Takrūr aristocracy was added the *moyal* (meaning literally spoliation) which entitled members of the élite to appropriate wealth wherever possible.

In such a situation the leaders of the *djihād*s and the Christian messianic movements found it easy to enlist the mass support of the peasantry. Men of religion promised equality and an end to all troubles. They designated the traditional aristocracies and the Europeans as the disruptive factors and the causes of social injustice.

From the seventeenth century, the peasantry's political role increased. Peasant revolts rooted in the decline of the countryside swept the continent like a religious revolution, thus paving the way for resistance to colonial conquest. It was a revolt not of captives or slaves but of the largest, most heavily exploited class, the small peasants. The Torodo revolution in the Senegal Futa, supported by the landless *samba remoru*, was a revolt against both the *muudul horma*, imposed by the Moorish *ḳabīla*s, and the oppressive eastern Muslim tax system introduced by the Islamized Denyanke aristocracy. The decline and breakdown of rural economies were not always similar in nature or extent, economic ossification being proportional to the under-development of the traditional commercial towns and their ruling classes.

The countries of the Nile and the Indian Ocean

The impact of the predatory economy on the countries of the Nile and the Indian Ocean was equally disastrous. The East African ports had been known for their trading activities since the eleventh century. Although not as important either in size or influence as the Western Sudanese and North African towns, they nevertheless formed the framework of a substantial urban commercial civilization in touch with Arabia, Persia, India, China and the Mediterranean.[20] The Portuguese invasion set off the progressive ruin of this urban commercial complex. By 1502 the destructive Portuguese occupation had begun and in the same year, Kilwa and Zanzibar were placed under tribute by Portugal. In 1505 Francesco d'Almeida sacked Kilwa and Mombasa, and then built Fort Santiago at Kilwa. He prohibited all trade between these towns, and the merchants left for Malindi and the

20. See UNESCO, *General History of Africa*, Vol. IV, ch. 18.

Comoros. Lamu and Pate were occupied. The process of disruption had begun.

With the exception of Luanda and Mozambique none of the stations set up by the Portuguese and later by the Dutch, English and French was as big as an average town in Western Sudan or as important even as the Swahili and East African ports of the tenth to sixteenth centuries.

The entrepôt or trading-post economy

While the predatory economy became widespread in the areas bordering the Mediterranean, the Nile and the Indian Ocean, the entrepôt or trading-post economy became the structure in the areas bordering the Atlantic Ocean. Trading entrepôts concerned themselves little with creative business. The new maritime entrepôt towns were fortresses before becoming centres of commercial civilization – scenes of violence and spoliation.

On the Guinea and equatorial coasts, the Portuguese – who established the entrepôt economy in the sixteenth century – looted more than they bought. They had little to offer economically: they even imposed tributes and the goods they exchanged rarely came from their own businesses. Apart from some wine and iron bars, the Portuguese goods were imported. It was local and regional produce that was exchanged for gold, slaves, leather, gum, ivory, amber, yellow civet, cowries, cotton and salt. In the Gulf of Guinea the Portuguese bought goods from the Akan and resold them on the Nigerian coast or in the Congo or Angola. In Senegambia, they took up residence in the ports and became successful local merchants. In the seventeenth century, when European industry began to produce textiles and hardware, deflation in the towns became still worse.

The depots contributed nothing to local prosperity. Before 1800, Albreda, Cacheu, Santiago de Cabo Verde, El Mina, Ketu, Calabar and San Salvador were the most important depots and none had as many as 5000 inhabitants. The principal feature of the entrepôt economy was the Atlantic slave trade. At the height of the trade none of these depots was also a centre for complex trading operations in local craft products or a market place for commercial or entrepreneurial activities of a large native population. The slave-trade depot was, above all, an instrument of depopulation. Statistics do not agree as to the number of slaves exported or the number of victims of the slave trade in Africa: figures range from 25 to 200 million.[21]

The direct and indirect contribution of the trading-post economy to world prosperity, however, was considerable. After the opening of the American mines, the trading posts supplied a substantial part of the world's gold and silver. Moreover, the bulk of the labour force which developed the American continent originated from them. In a word, they kept world trade going. They were the fountainhead of industry, finance and European

21. See ch. 4 below.

and international capitalism. France, a leading power in the eighteenth century, provides one example. Its trade, which in 1716 amounted to 100 million pounds, had grown by 1789 to 400 million pounds. In the same year it had a trade surplus of 36 million and 57 million pounds respectively. In 1774 the West Indies alone accounted for 126 million pounds' worth of exports to France and 185 million pounds' worth in 1788. In the same years, trading-post imports for all Senegambia did not exceed 5 million pounds.[22]

The predatory economy, moreover, operated on the basis of one-sided speculation. Contrary to general supposition, there was no genuine equal three-way trade until the middle of the eighteenth century. The European navigators who took up the entrepôt trade – particularly the Portuguese, as already noted – put nothing into it. European produce amounted to very little. The iron, copper, textiles and hardware that, in the eighteenth and nineteenth centuries, were to compete with local products were of little importance in the sixteenth and seventeenth centuries. The Portuguese were mainly middlemen. They bought salt, cowries, Senegambian loin-cloths and local or Indian fabrics on the coast of East Africa, and traded them for gold, gum, slaves and other goods to export to America or Europe. They took this trade away from the native merchants.

Thus, when European navigators gained a foothold in the economic network, they brought normal inter-African trade to a halt and set up their own monopoly of middlemen operating from the entrepôts. Africans no longer traded between Saint-Louis and Portendick, Grand Lahou and El Mina, Angola and Kongo or Sofala and Kilwa. *Pombeiros Lançados* and *tangomaos* (middlemen) made the role of the merchant class their exclusive preserve. The bulk of business was controlled by Portuguese, Spanish, Dutch, English and French monopoly concerns. The Portuguese middle-men, who lived either in the trading posts or in the interior, organized the network of trade on the basis of their markets and *feiras* (fairs) and defended them by force.

This Portuguese network was used by the other maritime powers from the sixteenth century onwards. The only impediment to monopolistic control was opposition by African governments when they were capable of it, and the difficulties and risks the Europeans faced in getting to the slave-trading points in the interior. It was a period of clashes between the Guinea coast *Lançados*, middlemen and slave-traders, on the one hand, and the companies on the other, with the former demanding a free hand in petitions to Santiago and Gorée. Detailed information is available on trade in the entrepôt fortresses and the seasonal trading stations from the time of the Portuguese until the arrival of the Dutch, French and English. It is a story of violence and continual conflict. The Atlantic and Indian Ocean trading posts were destroyed, rebuilt and changed hands in a struggle between the European, Ottoman and Omani maritime powers against the stubborn

22. P. D. Curtin, 1969.

resistance of local rulers, who levied dues and duties or *curva*[23] that were either paid or refused.

In addition to the risks of the business, the entrepôt economy had one main characteristic: it was not conducive to the rise of a merchant class such as might have created on the coast something comparable to the achievement of the long-distance trade which thrived on the integration of town and country and the growth of crafts, manufacturing and industry. In the trading posts, apart from the European merchants, most people were *laptos* (native interpreters). In 1582, out of the 15 000 inhabitants of Santiago and Fogo, 13 400 were slaves and 1600 were Europeans who controlled the economy. Before the nineteenth century,[24] the Atlantic trading posts, with the exception of the Loango coast, had no category of native slave-traders such as had operated in Kilwa, Mogadishu, Mombasa and the Mediterranean ports.

Finally, the technological innovations that revolutionized Europe had little impact. The African economy suffered most from competition from European industry and business. From the eighteenth century onwards, European traders ruined the native crafts and industries of the coast by wrecking the traditional networks. By cornering the ports they paralysed the links between the coast and the interior. Thus the European states which annexed the coastal areas demarcated Portuguese, Dutch, French and English spheres of influence even before the colonial conquest, and determined their development and political geography in the eighteenth century. From Moroccan expansion into Songhay to the shifting fortunes of the internecine wars in Western Sudan, most upheavals on the African political scene originated in the process of disruption set off by the European hegemonies in the sixteenth century.

New political structures

The African political scene had already reached a state of balance and stability in the period between the twelfth and sixteenth centuries. In the sixteenth century, Mediterranean Africa constituted a sub-system within Arab–Ottoman sovereignty, Morocco, Ifrīkiya and Tripolitania being one area of it. Egypt was an entity on its own. The Nile area, consisting of Nubia and Ethiopia, linked to the south with the Great Lakes state of Bunyoro–Kitara, the Swahili city states and Southern Zambezi which, in the late sixteenth century, was dominated by the state of Mutapa. Southern Africa as yet had few state structures. In Central Africa one system was dominated by the Kongo and Tio states, another by the Luba state. But the peoples in the forests had no state structures. Western Sudan and the Niger–Chad region adjoined each other, with ever-changing borders. Both were in contact with Nubia and Ethiopia.

23. *Curva* in areas under Portuguese control, and duty in English-speaking regions.
24. P. Diagne, 1976.

The development of the political map was to reflect external pressure and its repercussions. The internecine wars which played havoc with the political scene shattered the existing boundaries and balance of power. New states emerged: either those which were best-armed, such as Kānem–Borno, or those with most outlets to the sea, such as Kayor in Senegambia, Dahomey in the Gulf of Guinea, Angola in Central Africa and Changamire in Southern Zambezi.

The character of the African state itself altered. Huge areas without rulers or sovereigns and hitherto peopled by farmers, nomadic herdsmen and hunters, were conquered and turned into states with centralized structures. The village structures of Bantu Africa, and also of the Kabyle or Saharan Berbers, was replaced by the Maghribi *Makhzen*, the autocratic black African *mansaya* or *farinya*,[25] Ottoman *beylik* feudalism or the Muslim emirate. Political power increasingly passed out of the hands of the clan and ethnic community chiefs and *laman* (territorial chiefs) and into those of the political aristocracies of the *mansaya*, the landed nobility of the *neftenia*, the Maghribi *beylik* and sultanate, the Sudanese emirate or even the *mani* (Christianized Bantu kings) surrounded, European-fashion, by their princes, counts and chamberlains.

From the sixteenth century onwards, political life centred increasingly around the coastal areas, the privateering ports and the trading posts. The aristocracies collected tithes from them. African governments had revenue departments to tax foreign trade. The Mediterranean *alcaid*s had their counterparts in the *alkaati*, *alkaali* or simply *alcaid*s of Gorée, Portudal, San Salvador, Sofala and Kilwa. Many treaties were concluded in an attempt to codify this taxation system. Morocco, Tunisia, Algeria and Tripolitania signed many trade agreements and short-lived treaties of friendship with the Europeans and even the Americans. In 1780 a war between Morocco and Spain was ended by the Treaty of Aranjuez, which redefined their borders and codified their trade relations. About the same time, Algeria was at war with the United States of America and compelled it to pay ransom to the pirates: the United States of America also paid Morocco 10 000 dollars for the same reason. From 1796, they paid 83 000 dollars a year to Tripoli, and also paid 21 000 dollars to Algiers in 1797, in addition to 642 000 dollars for the freeing of some of their nationals.

At Saint-Louis in Senegambia at the end of the eighteenth century, the aristocracies shared between them 50 000 pounds – one-tenth of the budget of a colony that derived its revenue from foreign trade. In the sixteenth

25. *Farinya* comes from Fari and Pharaoh meaning ruler in Soninke, Mande, etc. The Mande *mansaya* was a socio-political system, whose dominant ruling class was a polyarchy composed of an élite of laymen or priests, freemen or slaves, caste or guild members, noblemen or commoners. It was financed by the taxes which those controlling the machinery of government levied on trade and produce. It was not a landed aristocracy or proprietor class whose appropriations of the means of production entitled them to a share of the surplus wealth generated.

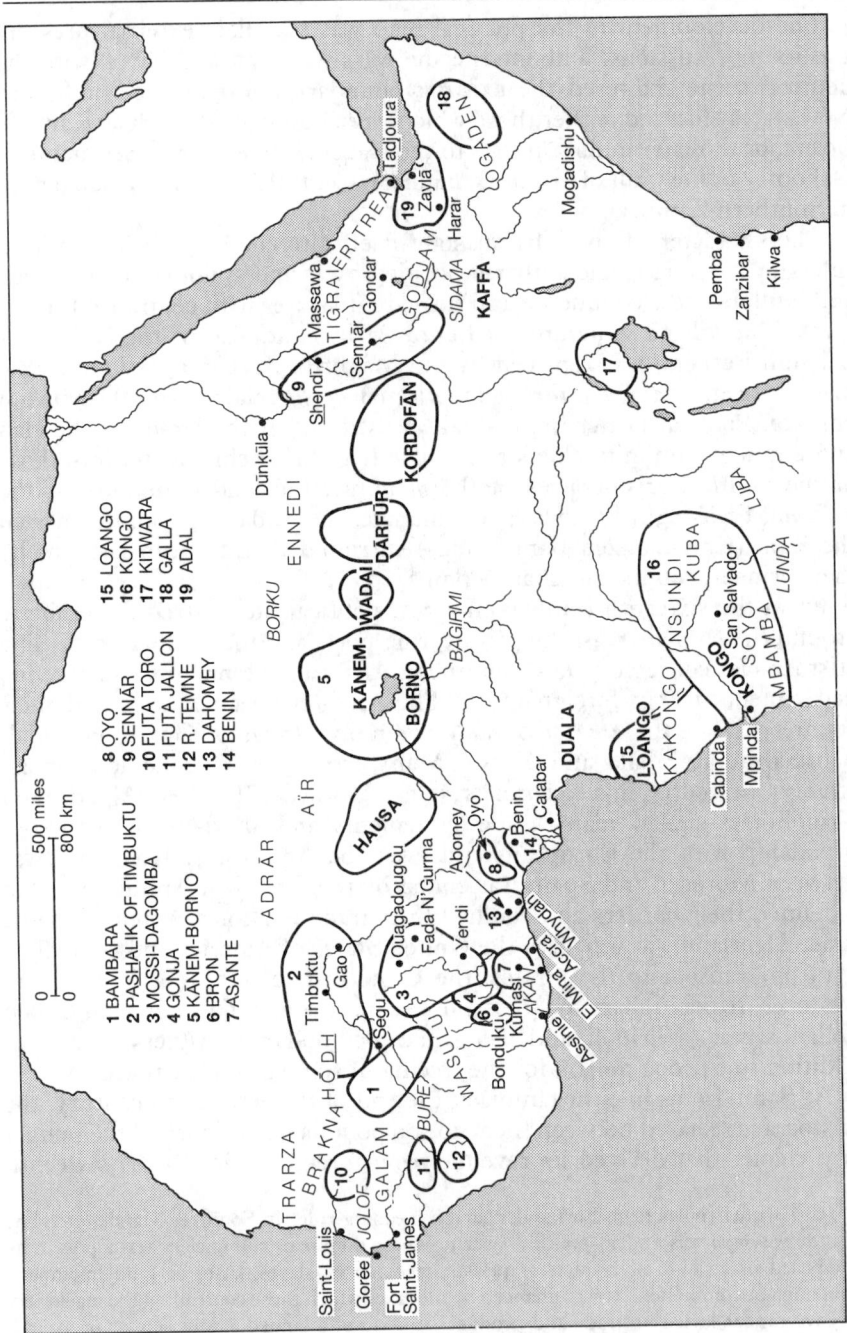

century, the Portuguese required tribute to be paid to them in the Swahili ports of Sofala, Kilwa and Mombasa.

It took wars, the destruction of trading posts (as the Zimba did in Mozambique in the sixteenth century) and prohibitions on trade (as often happened in Senegambia, Angola and the Kongo) to persuade the European powers and their merchants to resume paying taxes. But these more or less regular sources of income were the cause of wars among the aristocracies and ruling classes throughout the continent.

Political entities were predominantly areas in which a balance had been achieved and which had developed in relation to their domestic circumstances. They varied in size and in the stability of their frontiers and governments. Some were to remain unchanged until the colonial conquest. Some were confederations of states and others unitary states or chiefdoms with limited jurisdiction. Sometimes they were a clan, or an independent *lamana* in which the first occupants lived a completely autonomous existence.

The instability introduced by the predatory and entrepôt economies thus set the pattern, from the sixteenth to the eighteenth century, for states and economies which could no longer base their economic, social and political development on a foundation of order and cohesiveness.

Population movements and emergence of new socio-political forms in Africa

J. VANSINA

The nature of population mobility

One of the main ways in which the history of precolonial Africa differs from the history of Europe and most of Asia is in population mobility, especially the mobility of farmers. African farmers, working with tropical and subtropical soils, were much more mobile than farmers in Europe or Asia who practised intensive agriculture, renewing the fertility of the same plot of land year after year. This could not be done over most of Africa and agriculture had to be extensive, moving from field to field each year. This resulted in a population not tied to definite plots of land but more mobile than elsewhere. It was the same with the pastoralists, although their techniques of coping with the environment were more comparable with those used by Asians – especially central Asians – and with transhumance in Europe. Nevertheless, population mobility is a basic characteristic to be considered in any study or reconstruction of Africa's past, and its influence on both societies and cultures must be carefully assessed.[1]

This volume gives evidence of many migrations from the *trekboere* at the Cape to the Somali and Oromo in the Horn of Africa, to the Ngbandi of Ubangi,[2] the Jaga in Central Africa, the Tuareg in the Niger bend, the Mane in Sierra Leone, the Fulbe all over West Africa and all the populations of Madagascar. It may seem that between 1500 and 1800 nobody remained in the same place. By the late sixteenth century Portuguese reporters were already speculating that the Mane, Jaga, Zimba and Oromo migrations from West, Central and East Africa were all related.[3] They were caused, said the Portuguese, by a single mass of vagabonds. Migrants, they felt,

1. The bibliography of population mobility in Africa is congruent with the bibliography of African history itself. In this chapter, references will be made mostly to other chapters in this volume and their bibliographies should be consulted for further study.

2. H. Burssens, 1958, p. 43.

3. As late as 1883, A. Merensky still airs such views. He linked Oromo migrations to Jaga, Fulbe and Zimba movements – but not to those of the Mane – and claimed furthermore that the Zimba were responsible for the immigration of south-eastern Bantu speakers south of the Limpopo! As a Transvaal missionary his speculations reflect the Boer claims in South Africa. Sources such as these have left the impression that the sixteenth century saw a huge upheaval in sub-Saharan Africa. This impression is false, a product of the conflation

were the antithesis of a settled, well-regulated life: they were barbarians as opposed to civilized people. As late as 1963, a trace of this stereotyped attitude still exists in Trevor Roper's dismissal of African history as the 'meaningless gyrations of barbaric tribes'.[4] Although the stereotype coalesced in the sixteenth century, a discussion of population movement could be placed in any of the volumes of this history. We shall see that, continent-wide, it was no more characteristic of the period 1500 to 1800, than any other.

Much of the history of Africa was understood until recently as a 'saga of unrelenting migration',[5] comparable to the historiography of the great Germanic invasion that destroyed the Roman empire and left epithets such as 'Vandal' or 'Hun' in their wake. Apart from being derogatory, this conception also reduced all population movement to migration only, and mass migration at that – a view which has thoroughly confused the understanding of what happened in different cases.

'Migration' means the movement of a population from one country to settle in another. In zoology it means also the seasonal movement of populations but when speaking of people the correct term for this is 'transhumance'. So much for dictionary definitions. Migration is a concept expressing a relationship between people, space and time implying an alteration in this relationship. In this very general sense we speak of population movement and not of migration proper. Hence the causes have to do with the organization of space, either because the ratio of people to resources alters – through, for example, overpopulation or climatic catastrophe – or because people reorganize space and its resources on a relatively large scale. The prominent large-scale spatial organizations in Africa were states and trading networks.

Just as Europeans stressed migration, so did Africans in their oral traditions. Many speculated cosmological origins and told of founders or populations who came from elsewhere – a place of genesis. There was also a *countervailing* stereotype that people emerged from the soil and were thus owners of the land. But it was the first concept that fuelled the preconceived ideas already held by foreign scholars who envisaged constant invasions with peoples pushing each other around like billiard balls on a billiard table. With each conquest a new wave of refugees (*restvolker*) was sent out in search of a haven in some remote area, or perhaps themselves to disturb yet other populations. Ratzel incorporated in the very foundations of modern anthropology the notion that migration alone explained cultural and social similarities. Later the *Kulturkreise* school viewed cultures as mixes involving layers of pristine cultures: and resulting from countless

---

of data to suit subjective world views. For a general critique of this historiographical tradition cf. J. C. Miller, 1973, pp. 122–6.

4. T. Roper, 1963.
5. P. E. H. Hair, 1967.

migrations. Through Frobenius and Baumann these ideas found their way into African studies.

But the commonly held view that Africans were forever on the move does not hold, despite all the evidence of migrations. In a crucial article, Hair documented the remarkable 'stability' of all the coastal languages from Senegal to the Cameroons,[6] and this stability can be seen in most farming societies on the continent after 1500. The temptation now is to dismiss all migrations as figments of the imagination and to deny the very real mobility of both individuals and groups – for linguistic or cultural stability does not entail immobility.

Like the concept of 'migration', the notion of 'stability' in this context involves people, space and time and stresses the absence of change. But both concepts are generalizations – approximations of real occurrences in the past whose particulars are deleted. They are also relative concepts. Given a large enough area, such as the lands east and north of the White Nile, the migration of such people as the Jie[7] becomes a stability, a mere adaptation of people to the requirements of the land and its climate. At the other extreme, any displacement of a village ten kilometres away can become a migration. It is the same with time. When people drift over many centuries, and huge periods of time are taken as a unit, migrations appear where smaller temporal units would not show them. The Bantu migration, which extended over perhaps two millennia, is such an example. And the number of people required to move before the label migration can be applied varies from individuals to communities. In this essay the term migration will always apply to the movement of communities at least the size of villages.

Hence to understand the historical record we must first deal with normality: the usual movements of people in the making of their livelihood. With this background we can then better understand the unusual and the abnormal and discuss the different processes by which population movement actually occurs. Then we can turn to the kinds of evidence that survive about such unusual movements and conclude with an overview of major movements in Africa between 1500 and 1800 as they are discussed in the chapters to follow.

Mobility and land use

As there are four main ways to exploit the environment for food production – hunting and gathering, the herding of domestic animals, agriculture and fishing – so there are four main patterns of usual movement associated with these activities. Because they are normal, usual and do not lead to the displacement of communities over space, they cannot be called population movements, let alone migrations.

6. P. E. H. Hair, 1967.
7. J. E. Lamphear, 1976.

Hunters and gatherers roam a range which is fairly stable as long as the population density is adapted to the requirements of the way of life. Such people, organized in camps, need a range and must frequently move their camps within it, usually once every two weeks as is known from the Ituri pygmies[8] and the Kung San in Botswana.[9] This is necessary both to follow game and to find clusters of suitable vegetal food. With seasonal variation comes variation of movement. In the forest this is most obvious during the honey-gathering season; while in the near desert of the Kalahari, for instance, the movements of mammals towards or away from water-holes, as well as the fruiting of trees, dictate such annual movements. The mobility is high, yet such populations can sometimes remain stable for long periods, exploiting the range over and over again.

Herders are also mobile. The animals on which they depend need water, grass and salt and the availability of these commodities varies with the seasons. In the Sahara, for instance, nomads typically live near the edge of the desert or major oases during the dry part of the year and spread far and wide over the desert when the rains come.[10] Their movements are called transhumance and they often followed the same routes year after year. In regions with extremely low populations and particularly erratic rainfall, such as northern Fezzān, the same routes were not followed each year but the transhumance patterns were still regular when viewed over a decade or more.[11] Such movements could involve enormous distances for camel herders, such as the Rigeibat of the western Sahara, and often implied complex reciprocal movements between nomads herding different kinds of stock, according to the various requirements of camels, goats, cattle and sheep. Thus the ranges of the Tuareg and the Fulbe overlapped in the Sahel just as those of the cattle-keeping nomads (*Bakkāra*) in the Sudan overlapped with those of camel-herders, such as the Kabābīsh, further north. Moreover, nomads also cultivated a few crops and exchanged food with specialized hunters or gatherers where they existed – as did the eighteenth-century *trekboere* in South Africa. Otherwise they relied on vegetal food produced by farmers, so that at the edge of their ranges there had to be agricultural settlements. Thus space was exploited in various ways by different complementary groups, each with its own mobility over the same area. Herding, however, was more susceptible than hunting or gathering to climatic fluctuation, especially to short-term changes. In recent droughts, the hunter-gatherer San did not have to alter greatly their movements over the range, but the neighbouring Tswana farmers and stockbreeders suffered famine. There is evidence that some groups, such

8. C. M. Turnbull, 1961, 1966; P. Schebesta, 1952; R. B. Lee, 1968 and 1979. See also L. Demesse, 1978, 1980. M. Sahlins, 1972, demonstrated the relative security and affluence of this way of life, a fact with obvious historical consequences.

9. UNESCO, 1963, and E. E. Evans-Pritchard, 1940.

10. ibid.

11. A. Cauneille, 1957.

as the Khoi herders near the Kalahari, would become hunter-gatherers (San) during such times. But although herding was sensitive to variations in rainfall, the effects of drought were less dramatic than on farming, especially cereal farming.

Farmers were also mobile because they moved from field to field. Because soil fertility was restored by means of fallow regeneration, new fields had to be made each year to rest the exhausted soil. Villages had to move whenever the fields became too far from their homes. In recent times this has occurred every ten years on average, with some cycles as short as five years or as long as twenty. Favourite locales, with a combination of irrigation and the annual deposition of rich silt, were rare. Ancient Egypt was such an example and oasis agriculture developed from such practices. These farmers did not have to move from field to field and the population was quite stable. Apart from Egypt, and the belt of wet-rice cultivation on the western Guinea coast, permanent fields were extremely rare in Africa because methods of intensive fertilization could not usually be efficiently developed.

Most villages moved. But their movements were more or less circular over a stable territory, again given low densities of population. Mobility may have been greater before the introduction of cassava as a staple crop round about 1600. Moreover, mobility and direction of movement were not dependent on the state of the soils alone. In many cases – including for instance all the villages of the tropical rainforest in central Africa – farmers relied equally on trapping and hunting, with some gathering too. This meant that, as with the Nzabi of Gabon, the next siting of the village could be dictated as much by the needs of trappers as farmers.[12] Complex patterns of movement, but always in the same territory, could result. The greatest menace to this way of life was climatic variation: not enough rain, or too much, could destroy the year's crop. Moreover, the exact timing of the rains was crucial and even near the well-watered equator there could be famine. Thus at Loango near Pointe-Noire in Congo it was not the lack of rain that was feared but the timing. To have no rain after planting was a disaster and so was continuous rain which prevented planting. 'Normal' years were comparatively rare. Every five years or so the farmer in Zambia[13] had to expect drought, so he had to build up reserves each year in preparation. The frequency of drought was higher in regions close to the deserts but nowhere was it negligible. In most cases two successive years of drought brought a shortage of food and three could mean famine, despite other food-gathering activities which rapidly gave out where population densities were too high.

In short, for farmers as for herders or gatherers there were limits to population densities and there were optimal densities which varied with the environment – or the micro-environment. Soils, rainfall, topography

12. G. Dupré, 1982.
13. J. Allan, 1965.

and supplementary sources of food all had to be taken into account, as did existing technology and arrangements for the sharing or other distribution of food. The ratio of land to farmers could change without dramatic impact provided technology changed. Otherwise inward or outward movement was the mechanism used to adjust population density to land and vice versa. Outright population control was yet another mechanism.

Fishermen lived in fixed sites and their settlements rarely moved. Yet seasonal changes in the levels of the rivers forced them to undertake expeditions, sometimes of hundreds of kilometres as on the Zaire or Kasai rivers, to live in camps on sandbars while leaving their families at home. This pattern was most typical of the Zaire, Niger and Benue basins and provided the model for migratory movement. Stability was greatest on the shores of the oceans or the great lakes. Because they had boats fishermen had a cheap means of transport by water, and this turned many into traders, mediating between different land groups. Also, they could easily move themselves and their belongings to sites far away, if they felt so inclined. Thus fishermen, who needed to move least of all, were as well prepared to do so as hunter-gatherers or herders and could do so more easily.

So far, we have only considered the major factors involved in usual movement. Where symbiosis was more developed or economies were complex, the patterns and requirements for siting territory were also more complex. Imagine the farming village near the Congo bend that provided agricultural produce to both fishermen and hunter-gatherers while depending on them for meat, fish, pottery and perhaps other products. The movements of both hunters and farmers had to be co-ordinated and could not take them too far from the fixed points of the fishing villages. Moreover, as communal mobility was part of the way of life it obviously allowed people to move for other reasons than the requirements of land use. High mortality, quarrels or defensive needs easily led to a decision to move, especially among the farming population which, unlike herders, did not depend on fixed poles of transhumance during a few crucial weeks every year. This facility they shared with the hunter-gatherers even while paradoxically lacking the transport of the herders and fishermen.

Apart from collective movements, there was usually much individual mobility. Women often married into foreign villages; sons went to live with their mother's kin; slaves, pawnbrokers, traders and pilgrims, reputed medicine men, hunters and even other rare specialists were often on the road. The mobility of individuals in Africa was at least equal to that obtaining in most parts of the world and the stereotyped idea of untouched ethnic groups is as false as the one of perennial wandering.

Although the following sections deal only with movements by a community in an unusual fashion, it should be stressed that the boundary between usual and unusual movement for individuals was much more tenuous, even though the resulting population displacements could be spectacular. The sale of slaves after 1660 could be seen as a usual event with individuals moving. Yet the slave trade to the Americas was certainly the largest single demographic movement in Africa. Even the sale of slaves and their removal to North Africa and beyond, although possibly more than ten times smaller than the Atlantic slave trade, was still more important than any other movement of population within the continent, except perhaps the most massive migrations.

Urbanization also represents movement of population. By 1300, the population of Zimbabwe city[14] could have been 10 000. If so, it was the product of an internal migration that had absorbed a hundred villages. When Zimbabwe had to be abandoned, because its soils were exhausted and a permanent settlement could no longer be maintained,[15] the dispersal of its people to villages represents an equally important population movement.[16] But urbanization and the slave trade apart, there is very little evidence of such individual or even small family movements and more will only be known about them if and when it becomes possible to calculate population densities as they varied decade by decade and area by area. But such movements did exist and historians should never forget the possibility that individual mobility alone could build up or deplete population densities. Population increases have always been seen as an effect of natural increase but immigration is just as likely to have played a role, with the reverse holding for a decrease of population.

Processes of unusual movements of population

Unusual population movements by communities fall into two major groups – drift and migration. Drift is gradual, slow movement, an extension of the usual patterns of mobility and food production into new territory. Sudden movement, which departs sharply from the usual mobility and productive activities, is called migration. Drift does not ordinarily entail the desertion of the original settlements, although it may eventually. Migration, on the other hand, ordinarily means abandoning the territory of origin. Both drift and migration encompass several distinct processes. Drift is called expansion when it enlarges a territory held by a group and diaspora when it is discontinuous and new distinct settlement results.

14. D. N. Beach, 1980a.

15. P. S. Garlake, 1973; D. N. Beach, 1980. This is a cogent illustration of the constraints imposed on forms of settlement by shifting agriculture and herding on natural grazing grounds.

16. A clear case of considerable individual mobility leading to the re-ordering of the population over a landscape, is not only the growth of the early city of Jenne-Jeno, Mali, from about −200 onwards and especially after +250, but its decline after +1000 which was concurrent with the rise of Jenne city only some three kilometres away. Smaller satellite settlements grew along with Jenne-Jeno, with a certain time lag, and declined before the city itself was abandoned by +1400. The whole site-territory of Jenne-Jeno and of Jenne city, dramatically shows the effects of individual mobility over this small portion of space Cf. R. J. McIntosh and S. Keech-McIntosh, 1982.

Migration will be called mass migration when it occurs on a large scale involving a whole people; band migration when it concerns only a fraction of the population, usually warriors on the rampage; and élite migration when it involves minute groups, sometimes even individuals, whose immigration leads to changes of great significance in the host society. Elite migration is almost an individual movement but it must be included here because of its effects, its frequency and the claims made for it as a form of migration.

The number of people involved in such movements, their duration, the distance travelled, the motivations which triggered them – including push factors (factors which induce or force people to emigrate) and pull factors (factors which attract people to immigrate) – and their impact are the features which established the significance and the magnitude of a movement. These questions should be considered in each case studied. But such indicators cannot be used as a basis for classification because they are too variable in meaning. For instance, the distance travelled does not make sense by itself: several hundred kilometres in the Sahara, for example, may correlate to less than fifty in a densely settled area. Motivations are very varied. Natural catastrophes, such as drought, may or may not be involved. The mix of push/pull factors is so variable that each case risks becoming a type on its own. Numbers are often not available and usually too unreliable to be useful as criteria for a typology. Thus it is the characteristics of the movement itself – with its antecedents and consequences – which are now described for each of the five migration types.

Expansion

Expansion has occurred countless times because of the natural mobility of most African populations, and its character differs according to the way of life common in the parent society. Shifting cultivation becomes expansion when drift occurs primarily in one direction rather than in a haphazard or circular pattern. The unit of migration is the village, but the movement in the same direction of all the villages in a community or a large number of them, leads to expansion. The distances involved are usually small, often no more than ten to twenty kilometres. The frequency of movement is low, no more perhaps than once in every ten or more years. The time involved may therefore be very long and the population will always look stable even though expansion is in progress.

In the forest, Mongo expansion from the areas around the equator, in the great bend of the River Zaire to the south, began long before 1500 and was still in progress in 1900 in much of the area between the Zaire in the west and the Lomami in the east. The goal seems to have been the attractive environment of the river valleys of the lower Kasai and Sankuru and the richer fringes of the forest further east. The effect was to create a flow from nuclei of higher population density around the equator and the first degree

53

south, southwards to the river valleys and fringes.[17]

Such a movement could easily be accelerated either by increasing the distances travelled during each move or by moving more frequently, say every two or three years. The expansion then became conscious and in response to specific goals, often pull factors or attractions. The Nzabi people of Gabon/Congo, for example, in a mere half-century moved from their lands in the east of the great Ogowe bend to the south-west so as to be closer to the trade routes and derive wealth from them, and to exploit new mineral resources.[18] The rush of the Fang from the Upper Comoe to the Gabon estuary occurred in a mere twenty years and then continued for another forty towards the Ogowe delta at a slightly less feverish pace. Villages still moved only once every few years but long distances of up to, say, forty kilometres were not unusual. The Fang movements have been well studied with respect to the process of moving itself. At no point was it necessary to abandon the usual way of life. When a village moved, it by-passed other Fang villages on its way to the lands beyond. The whole expansion occurred by leap-frogging, all within a single environment, with scouting provided by hunters on their usual rounds.[19]

Expansion by pastoralists proceeds in different ways. The most common way is for members of a younger generation to leave the centre or pole of transhumance of their elders and move with stock into fresh pastures. Because such areas are only found where rainfall is too sparse or unreliable for farming, herders were usually constrained by environmental variables. Maasai expansion, for example, occurred first in this fashion until all suitable lands were occupied. The whole process lasted from about 1600 to about 1800.[20] A well-documented case is that of the *trekboere* in South Africa who had established their way of life near the Cape in the second generation of European settlement, from about 1680 onwards. From the start, the first pastoralists complained about overpopulation, even though the population was sparse. But the land was arid and great acreages were needed to pasture the flocks. By 1700 a family felt crowded if it could see the smoke from a neighbour's chimney. Then the younger sons would emigrate with part of the stock and an ox-wagon and venture further afield. Until about 1780 this expansion continued into lands occupied primarily by other stockbreeders (Khoi groups) who could be chased away. But then the *trekboere* came up against a frontier of much better-watered land held by Xhosa farmers and stockholders.[21]

In some cases, the transhumance routes were very long and involved more than one centre or pole. The Awlād Sulaymān of Libya had been

17. J. Vansina, 1981.
18. G. Dupré, 1982, pp. 25–39.
19. P. Alexandre, 1965, p. 532. His larger view of Fang migration is in error: cf. C. Chamberlin, 1977, pp. 23–80.
20. T. T. Spear, 1981, pp. 63–6.
21. L. Fouché, 1936, pp. 134–6.

moving back and forth between the Sirte area near the Mediterranean and the Fezzān oases in south Libya, according to the seasons. After a disastrous defeat in 1842 near Tripoli they were forced to abandon the Sirte pole. They established a new pole to the south of Fezzān along the caravan route to Borno. First their pole was in Borku, later in Kānem, despite the determined resistance of Tuareg groups into whose territories they were penetrating. By 1850 they had reached Lake Chad and after initial reverses came, by 1870, to dominate the whole area between Fezzān and Chad.[22] This movement involved armed bands and fighting so that it can be easily seen as a case of migration by bands. But the overall process is clearly similar to that of other pastoralists and consisted of the establishment of a new territory by shifting one of the two extreme poles of transhumance.

Even hunter-gatherers can show drift. This may be the explanation for the presence of Baka hunters in eastern Cameroon. These pygmies speak Ubangian languages but are to the west of any Ubangian settlement by farmers. The situation would be best explained not by a mass migration but by a gradual extension to the west of their hunting ranges from sites near the Upper Sanga river.[23]

Large expansion movements are diagnostic of population redistributions. Often they indicate the colonization of areas previously exploited in a more extensive fashion. One of the deepest and longest trends in the history of Africa has been the inexorable advance of people in larger and larger numbers, moulding the environment more and more to suit their ways of life, rather than being determined and limited by it. Thus the expansion of Bini-speaking peoples in the forest west of the Niger started around the onset of the Christian era and probably ceased only around 1200 when Benin City began to develop.[24] Although data are lacking for the Igbo expansion east of the lower Niger this was well under way by 1800 (Igbo–Ukwu) and resulted in a complete transformation of the landscape from a natural forest to a domesticated one, accompanied by the build-up of high population densities. In the case of the Bini speakers, there was more adaptation to an existing environment, exploited in a novel way by farmers. In the case of the Igbo, farmers destroyed the original environment. Hence it is natural that such expansions occurred from areas of relatively high densities to those of low densities. The overall effect was to raise densities everywhere as Africa's population expanded. To attribute such movements to over-population is only correct in a very limited sense, as the notion refers to how people such as the *trekboere* felt, while densities were in fact very low. Over-population is a relative measure of pressure put on the land by existing methods of exploitation. Shifts in technology could relieve this just as population control or emigration could.

Expansion movements must have occurred from early dates in Africa,

22. D. D. Cordell, 1972, and E. Rossi, 1968.
23. J. M. C. Thomas, 1979.
24. P. J. Darling, 1979.

first by hunters and gatherers and later by populations that had developed more land–intensive technologies. In some cases, long-term deterioration of resources due to climatic change was involved, the most spectacular one being the desiccation of the Sahara. The archaeology of Mauritania shows how farmers were gradually forced south by this phenomenon between perhaps -1500 and the rise of the kingdom of Ghana by +700.[25]

More rapid expansions, such as those of the Fang, Nzabi, or Awlād Sulaymān, are due to other causes. In the first two instances, the attraction of trading routes and centres provided a goal or pull factor. In the last, the defeat in Tripolitania was a push factor while the knowledge of the trade route to Chad provided a direction for travel.

In no case was a sudden catastrophe such as a famine or an epidemic a cause for the expansion of farmers. Under extreme crisis conditions their usual way of life could not be maintained. Economic and socio-political structures broke down and when movement occurred it was mass migration, rather than ordinary, orderly expansion. Moreover, such cases seem to have been extremely rare.

Expansion did not necessarily mean dispossession of the autochthones by the newcomers. Often a mixture of populations occurred and new societies emerged or, as in the Fang case, autochthones adopted the culture of the immigrants. New societies and cultures could be spawned by new mixes. Thus the Mongo drift southwards formed a variety of new societies, including what was to become the famous Kuba.[26] In other cases the autochthones were slowly displaced, as may have happened when south-eastern Bantu speakers met San hunters and perhaps also on meeting Khoi herders, although here there is also evidence of absorption. The billiard-ball effect – the expulsion of one population by another which then, in turn, dispossessed a third which itself then conquered or acquired new lands elsewhere – seems almost never to have happened. Expansions produced few refugees given the population densities usually involved.

Diaspora

When drift is discontinuous, and leads to new settlements separated from the parent settlements by foreign population, diaspora occurs. Nearly all diasporas are linked to trade or pilgrimage. Perhaps the only exception is the spread of Fulbe herders over suitable tracts of land all over West Africa. Such lands were ecological 'niches' not occupied by others who only found a very marginal use for their resources. Thus the autochthones did not oppose Fulbe occupation. It is best, in fact, to see this case as yet another example of ordinary expansion not much different from similar examples such as the Turkana, Nandi or Maasai in Northern Kenya and Tanzania.[27]

25. J. Devisse, 1982, pp. 171–3.
26. J. Vansina, 1978.
27. See ch. 27 below.

The most typical diasporas grew out of trade. The Phoenician, Greek and Arab settlements on the Horn coast, the European forts and the nucleus of the colony of Cape Town are all diasporas, having been founded by traders from overseas. Cases of carriers by water and fishermen were also numerous. In the period under review the Bobangi are an example. The inhabitants from a large village at the mouth of the Ubangi river began to found trading posts and daughter settlements all the way down the Zaire to the mouth of the River Kasai. They mixed with others, acquired large numbers of dependants, and formed a new ethnic group called the Bobangi, all this between about 1750 and 1850.[28] On the east coast Swahili society and culture developed in a similar way and spread from the coastal borderlands of Somalia and Kenya to as far south as Ibo island off Mozambique and the Comoros. Some medieval settlements on north-eastern Madagascar may be attributed to them.[29] But diasporas could also spring up along overland routes. Mande traders formed Jahanka diasporas from the Upper Niger to the coast of Senegal and Joola (Dyola) settlements from the Upper Niger to the Ajan coasts. Yarse traders, who were Mossi-speakers, organized a network of posts and trading centres in the Mossi countries.

Some diasporas were due to the yearly *hadjdj* to Mecca. Here individuals or small groups were in fact prominent. When for one reason or another they could not continue on their way, they settled. This is the origin of the nineteenth-century Takrūri settlements in Sudan. The Takrūri were people from West Africa who remained in the Sudan and congregated into settlements of their own, just as *djallāba* (traders), often from the Dongola reach, formed their own quarters or settlements along the trading routes. Most of the *marabtin bilbaraka* in Barḳa were the offspring of pilgrims, usually North Africans.

Diasporas also typically maintained contact with their centres of origin through trade or by being located on a pilgrim route. In some cases such contact was indirect or no longer maintained with the centre of origin. By the fifteenth century the inhabitants of Sofala, for example, communicated easily with Kilwa, less easily with cities further north, and no longer had special ties to the Lamu archipelago or the Bajun Islands in the Swahili heartland. This is merely a result of continual hiving off. It is no different from the case of Cerne, a colony of Carthage (and not of Tyr), on the Atlantic coast of Morocco. Even European diasporas had a tendency to become re-oriented by trade. Thus the culture of Cape Town was that of the East Indian Dutch empire, centred at Batavia, rather than that of Holland; Mozambique was for centuries directly dependent on Goa, while Angola, after 1648, almost became a Brazilian dependency.

Diasporas are highly visible movements of population. They are a sign of long-distance communication and they flourish when trade routes grow. Although some had begun long before 1500, most of the known cases

28. R. Harms, 1981.
29. UNESCO, *General History of Africa*, Vol. IV, ch. 18.

belong to the period after 1500 and attest to a further facet of man's control over space. They occur where populations are well settled and where their economies are beginning to be complementary to each other, or are beginning to exchange goods with the world outside Africa. Their presence is a sign of success in man's struggle to settle space.

Mass migration

When a whole people – men, women and children – leave their homeland with all their belongings to travel long distances for a year or more, this constitutes a true mass migration. Such spectacular upheavals of population are linked to spectacular catastrophes. The numbers involved may be very great. Some eighty thousand Vandals are said to have crossed into Africa in 429 at the invitation of an unhappy Byzantine governor and in the face of further defeats by the Visigoths of Spain at their rear. Their movement was, however, only part of the massive reshuffling of populations that was then occurring in Europe.[30] The greatest invasion of North Africa, by the Banū Hilāl and Banū Sulaym from 1052 onwards, has been linked tentatively to recurrent droughts in Arabia. Their numbers were large and the migration continued until about 1500 when it entered Mauritania. This migration, and the allied drift of Arabs in the Sudan and then Chad, changed the cultural map of all northern Africa which became fully Arabized.[31] True mass migrations are dramatic. They have immense consequences and it is not surprising, therefore, that they are rare. In the period between 1500 and 1800, the Oromo mass migration and expansion, with attendant movements by communities belonging to other cultures, was the only fully fledged mass migration in Africa. The famous Nguni migrations, that convulsed Africa from the Cape to Nyanza, are the only instance in the nineteenth century.

Mass migrations pose great problems. Scouts must have information as to where the migration can go. The migrants must be fed as they cannot sustain themselves by customary methods. The march usually required a different socio-political organization than had existed before. In many cases society was organized around military groupings. Subsequently migrants often had to create new economic and social forms as well as adapt to novel environments. This process often led to raiding and pillaging, even when pastoralists moved with their herds. Snowballing – the incorporation of numerous members of populations encountered on the way – was common, as such societies also became totally or partially disrupted. The process also usually occurred in spasmodic stages. It led to large-scale fighting, created refugees and set off ancillary migrations or rapid expansions. In short, such population movements are cataclysmic and lead to a dramatic new relationship and adaptation of people to space over huge areas. No

30. C. Courtois, 1955.
31. UNESCO, *General History of Africa*, Vol. III, chs 4, 5, 15 and 16.

wonder then that, although the primary movements might be fairly quick, the whole process, down to the settlement of the last refugee, could take more than a century. Thus the Oromo upheaval started perhaps in the 1530s but stable conditions returned only around 1700. However, compared to the great expansions by drift, such time scales are short.

Obviously, this picture applies best to the most extreme occurrences. Earlier, when documentation is scant, it is often difficult to distinguish between mass migration and fast but massive spread, especially by pastoralists. Thus the expansion of the Luo, over many centuries and over many varying environments, is often understood as a mass migration. It involved whole populations, it created many ancillary movements and it disturbed a large area, mainly east of the White Nile. For much of its duration, it was accompanied by similar large-scale movements of other groups in the southern Sudan and northern Uganda. But the time-scale is very deep, perhaps half a millennium, and what evidence there is[32] points to drift rather than mass migration as people usually moved with their flocks and stopped to raise crops. Parts of the Oromo movement also show such characteristics. These examples show that the distinction between mass migration and massive expansion is not always clear-cut and that drift will also occur during such times. In the end, however, there still remains a sharp distinction based on both the productive capacities and the militarized structure of a large body of people on the march. The processes are not identical.

Drift and mass migrations can be mixed. Thus the Luo movements were mostly expansion but the sudden explosion of the Kenya Luo during the eighteenth century can be regarded as a mass migration. They then overran populous areas and used force to gain control over new lands. Conversely, the Oromo movement began as a mass migration and in its later stages, before and especially after 1700, became an expansion.

Mass migrations are cataclysmic upheavals. Usually they are attributed to equally cataclysmic causes, often to a sudden change in climate, such as drought with ensuing famine and epidemics. Sometimes, however, they are not. The Vandal migration, for example, was not accompanied by natural disaster, although it is linked to other migrations and to the fall of the Roman empire. Relative over-population is advanced as a cause for the migration of the Banū Hilāl, the Oromo and the *mfecane* but so far there is little proof of this. Such proof as there is comes from attributing all mass migrations to over-population following a sudden unfavourable change in the ratio of population to resources. This may be a fallacy in so far as that while the *process* consists indeed of redistributing populations over land areas, the *cause* may vary. Pressure at the initial point of migration is only one possibility but whether or not there was population pressure in the Oromo heartland, it was the mutual destruction of Christian and Muslim kingdoms that triggered the direction of the Oromo flood, if not the flood

32. See ch. 26 below.

itself.[33] As to the *mfecane*, archaeologists are attempting to show a rise in population in the heartlands. By itself this is not a full cause. It needs to be linked convincingly to the rise of military leaders – of which there is evidence – and to what seem to be precursor movements in Zimbabwe.[34] Population pressure may well be involved in all cases – if only because there are so many migrants in mass migrations – but it is inadequate by itself as a complete explanation.

Band migration

Migration by bands, always armed, involves a relatively small number of people, mostly young males, constituting but a fraction of a population. Its consequences, while spectacular, are less severe than those of mass migration and less durable than large-scale drift. The usual process was for bands of warriors to strike out to conquer with or without a single leader. In the Zimba case, Santos speaks of the lord of a little kraal, most ambitious of human honour, who 'decided that for this purpose it would be expedient to sally out of his country with an armed force and destroy, rob and eat ... '[35] In the Jaga case, there may not have been a single leader. In the Tyokosi case, the band was composed of mercenaries.[36] In some instances – the Jaga and the Zimba, for example – the bands finally dissolved after defeat, in others – such as the Mane, the Tyokosi and the Imbangala – they succeeded in establishing chiefdoms or a kingdom.

Because the scale of band migration was small, even if the destruction wrought by it could be great, it created less turbulence than mass migrations, provoked fewer secondary migrations and less snowballing, and took less time than any of the other processes discussed so far. In most cases the pull factors were stronger than the push factors even though in some, such as the Korana and Gonaqua movement to the Orange and Caledon rivers,[37] the push factor, here the *trekboere* expansion, was at least equally strong. Such movements were sometimes the outgrowth of state formation – such as the Zimba from Maravi and the Tyokosi in relation to Asante – or a reaction to the expansion of trade from which the migrants wished to reap profits, as in the case of the Jaga. Again over-population, due to factors such as sudden drought or other calamities in the home area, may be involved – as with the Imbangala – but so far there is no hard proof in any of these cases. One of the major difficulties in discussing such band migrations is the question of whether or not they are part of a larger mass migration. Thus the Ndebele invasion of Zimbabwe and the Kololo

33. See ch. 24 below.
34. See UNESCO, *General History of Africa*, Vol. VI, chs 4, 5, 7 and 9; and Vol. V, ch. 22. See also, D. N. Beach, 1980a, p. 320.
35. M. D. D. Newitt, 1982, p. 156.
36. See chs 12 and 14 below.
37. See ch. 23 below.

invasion of Zambia[38] by themselves are band migrations, but they also form part of the mass migration of the *mfecane*. It is still not completely clear whether the Jaga and Imbangala bands were independent, as all authors now hold, or whether they formed part of a larger mass movement.

The Imbangala case is an instructive example. Bands formed near the Kwango river, perhaps produced by internal changes in the expanding Lunda state. They mixed with marginal autochthones of Ovimbundu and Mbundu polities. They went on the rampage for years as allies of the Portuguese, who were conquering and carving out a state in Angola, then settled by 1620, just out of reach of the Portuguese near the Kwango river. They drove out the original population, who migrated or drifted as far as the Kasai river. There had been no relative over-population in the area of origin of the first Imbangala bands and the movement did not alter the ratio of people to land between Cuanza and Kasai. But a state did result, namely the kingdom of Kasanje, which became the premier entrepôt for the processing of slaves from inner Africa on the route to Luanda. The Imbangala case, therefore, can only be called a re-organization of space in terms of socio-political structures and trade, nothing more.[39]

Elite migration

Elite migration is a favourite subject of oral traditions about the founding of states. The first king is a foreigner, often a hunter; he comes from elsewhere, alone or with a few companions; and while the population movement involved is insignificant the socio-cultural results are spectacular. In Malawi, for example, the foundation of the Maravi state was attributed to the Phiri clan whose ancestors were said to have come from Luba country far away in Shaba. In the north a series of related élites, the Ngulube, founded the kingdom and chiefdoms there.[40]

Some of these stories may well be fictitious and express no more than the stereotyped idea that a king had to be a foreigner, because kingship stood apart from the population, enveloped in an aura of sacredness and mystery. His place of origin had to be either the most prestigious place people could imagine or the one most removed from their own civilization. Some traditions, however, are better founded. Thus the Kuba tale of how Shyaam a Mbul a Ngoong, a Bushoong who had fled his country, came from the west and formed a kingdom out of antagonistic chiefdoms, at the very least reflects influences from the west on the Kuba. It has been shown that linguistic influences from the west entered the Kuba area and then radiated outwards, from the court, which supports the notion of cultural domination.[41] It is, however, unlikely that such an effect was obtained from

38. Cf. UNESCO, *General History of Africa*, Vol. VI, ch. 5.
39. J. C. Miller, 1976; J. Vansina, 1966a.
40. See ch. 21 below.
41. J. Vansina, 1978, pp. 59–65 and 187.

the immigration of one person and certainly not from an exiled person returning to his homeland.

In a study of population movements, such élite migrations of very few or indeed even one person are unimportant. But for a study of the development of socio-cultural formations, especially states, they can assume considerable importance. They do not change the ratio of people to resources over space in general, but they re-organize the space occupied by a population through a new distribution of resources according to a novel hierarchy. Hence an extended discussion of these episodes is found in Chapter 2.

Documenting population movements

The major sources documenting population movements in Africa are oral, linguistic, archaeological and written. But all present difficulties when used for this purpose. Unwise use of them has sometimes led in the past to the creation of spurious migrations. Hence a word about the documentation before an overview is given of the main movements between 1500 and 1800.

Oral literature cannot record long-term expansion because daily life is so little disturbed by it and the movement so slow that it is hardly noticeable. Therefore, if a tradition claims that a whole population came from a certain place by a process described as expansion it is suspect. No oral tradition can encompass a mass migration because the scale of events is too large. Traditions deal, therefore, with episodes of mass migrations and tend to confuse them with band migrations which, being more localized but equally spectacular, are well recorded. The expansion of a diaspora is often recorded in part because settlement A, for example, knows it was founded from settlement B and settlement B knows it was founded from settlement C and so on. The movements of élites can be very well recorded: the movements of the ruling family of the Mangbetu, for example, are told for almost two centuries before their kingdom was founded.[42]

But traditions are ideologies and they reflect cosmologies. If the researcher does not take this into account, erroneous conclusions can result. If a cosmology places all origins in one spot, then obviously it requires migrations from that spot to the territory where people live now. If it includes a paradise it has to record movement away from it. The Kuba, for example, claimed that they stemmed from downstream, from an ocean, and the Fang and the Komo claimed points of origin in relation to the most upstream or downstream points of the rivers they knew. All these people, moreover, orient themselves by upstream or downstream, so all movements can only be told in terms of such cardinal directions. Their traditions of origin are all spurious as history, except those dealing with

42. C. Keim, 1979; Col. Bertrand.

the last movements, of whole groups or élites, involving known and recognized sites nearby.[43]

Ideology is also responsible for such themes of origin as the foreign hunter becoming king, found from the Igala of lower Niger to the kingdoms of the southern savannah and those of the Great Lakes area, to the Shamba kingdom in Tanzania or the Fipa state between lakes Tanganyika and Rukwa. This is a stereotype, like the one in the African Sahel from the Nile to the Atlantic Ocean, in which foreign knights kill snakes and deliver people – itself a variant of the St George legend. This should not be taken literally as an élite movement, but as an expression of the ideology of the state.[44] Since, however, it is possible that a foreigner or a small group may have founded a state, each of these tales should be checked by other means. Certainly the precise symbolic value and the ideological worth of the statements must be studied. We reject, for example, the notion that the kings of Rwanda fell from heaven, but link them to the princes of Nkole on the basis of a linguistic clue. We must likewise reject the concept of the foreign origin of the first king of Burundi, the unkempt Ntare from the wilds. Ntare may have been foreign but the traditions cannot help us to determine whether he was.[45]

Another error often made in the interpretation of traditions is taking the part for the whole. The traditions of the origins of the Kamba, the Meru and the Gikuyu in Kenya may all have some truth in them. But they all seem to have elevated the story of one small portion of the population into that of the whole population.[46] This happened to such an extent with the Mangbetu that, after the kingdom had been established about 1800, a new genealogy was drawn up and imposed by the founder and the kingdom took the name of what may have been the name of an ancestor of this one man.

In general the stress on origins in traditions, and the abundant use of stereotypes even for clan, lineage, village or family histories, make it fairly easy to recognize doubtful portions of oral traditions and to establish whether and to what extent traditions can contribute as documentation to such questions.

The use of linguistics, which is quite common, can be more difficult because alternative historical explanations are often possible. The general rule is that when speakers of two languages mix, those in the majority end up by imposing their language on the minority. Hence massive expansion or mass migration leads to the spreading of the language of the expanding

---

43. J. Vansina, 1978, pp. 34–40; C. Chamberlin, 1977, pp. 26–34. Note the connection between still water and Fang orientation by streaming water.

44. J. S. Boston, 1969; S. Feierman, 1974, pp. 70–90; J. R. Willis, 1981, pp. 10–44; T. O. Reefe, 1981, pp. 23–40; E. Mworoha, 1977, pp. 96–105.

45. J. P. Chrétien, 1981a.

46. B. A. Ogot, 1976b, pp. 106–261; G. Muriuki, 1974; J. A. Fadiman, 1973; K. Jackson, 1978.

or migrating people. When, conversely, diaspora or band migration is involved, bringing small numbers of newcomers into contact with greater numbers of autochthones, it is the newcomers' languages that disappear. Most of the apparent exceptions are not exceptions. Thus, in diasporas, compact settlements of newcomers in contact with their homes of origin keep their languages, even though bilingualism is very common. Band migrants who maintain a closed community can also keep their language, as in the case of the Tyokosi or the Mende of Sierra Leone as opposed, say, to the Imbangala whose original kernel lost its language.

But there are genuine exceptions. In these cases the minority language can even take over the majority because of its special prestige. Ndebele and Kololo, for example, survived in Zimbabwe and Zambia after the conquests. Their prestige stemmed less from the conquest itself and more from the fact that soon afterwards their languages came to be committed to writing and were taught in school. Otherwise both Ndebele and Kololo would have been absorbed by the majority languages, Shona and Luyi, just as French at the English court finally gave way completely to English several centuries after the conquest.

A second basic rule for linguistic evidence is that in contact situations the ousted language always leaves traces. Such traces, in the form of loan words, expressions (calques), alternations in syntax, morphology and onomastics (personal and place names) can always be studied to document specific features of the contact. Examples include the impact of Khoi and San on the Bantu languages of south-eastern Africa; the position of the diaspora language called Bobangi as basically a northern language with very heavy Kongo influence (zone H); and the foreign inputs in Kiswahili.[47]

One can even distinguish between various processes of population movement. Diasporas are the easiest to detect because of the massive effects of prolonged plurilingualism and sometimes the creation of creoles. Afrikaans is a creole because of the massive changes in its morphology and even syntax, confirmed by the number of words it has of Malay, Portuguese, Bantu and Khoi or San origin. Bobangi is the equivalent of a creole between closely related Bantu languages, with typically simplified grammar and multiple-origin vocabulary. Expansion is characterized by much sparser loans unless the populations involved were fairly even in numbers. Signs of the absorbed languages are found in major toponyms and some loanwords. The situation is clearly differentiated from mass migration by the fact that the language distributions over an area larger than the region directly affected are fairly congruent with supposed genetic ties. One argument, for instance, against mass migration for the Fang and their related neighbours is that their language block (A 70) fits in well with other groups of A languages. At the same time, evidence for some disturbance stems from the fact that A 70 languages split A 80 languages into two unequal blocks. Mass migrations, such as the Oromo, impose their lan-

47. R. Anttila, 1972; T. Bynon, 1977; W. P. Lehmann, 1962; A. Meillet, 1925.

guages in very irregular-looking areas of distribution, but often still in a single block, or one with a few outliers. That block does not fit in well with genetic relationships. Considerable loans, due to the impact of snowballing, can be detected. Often more than two languages are involved in the mix. This situation allows us to state that a case such as the movements of the Langi, whose language is Luo with Karamo influences, is probably *not* due to mass migration, as there are only two sources for its composition.[48] The fact that it is basically a Luo language also indicates that the Luo were the majority, something not indicated by the oral traditions. Band migrations which form compact groups may leave their language behind them – or traces of it in several languages on their path – when they finally move on. If the numbers are small and the languages involved closely related, no distinct traces remain, which is the case of the Jaga and the Zimba, as opposed to the Mane, the Imbangala and others.

But the main difficulty is that loans, unless they are studied very extensively by the method of 'Words and Things' (*Worter und Sache*), can easily be attributed to other causes such as trade contacts, an official state language, a ruling family (as in the Kuba case), or a prestigious religious tongue. Detailed studies have very rarely been pursued in Africa, even though the results of admittedly arduous study can be very revealing. The organization of large-scale research in this field is urgently needed.

Archaeology has been a major source in the postulation of expansions or migration. Finding similar or identical elements of material culture (objects) or identical customs (such as burial in urns) in different places is usually interpreted as a sign of migration or other population movement. The rationale is that such elements, especially patterns of decoration and fabrication, are not likely to be invented independently, so that they must have been diffused. In such matters as burials or pottery, diffusion is thought to have been due to migration. However, in archaeological theory there has been a retreat from migrationism[49] with the recognition that independent invention occurs more often than was thought and that items could have been diffused by many other means.

Nevertheless, in many cases movement of population seems to have been involved. Given a sharp break in pottery style on a number of sites, for instance, and the introduction of a new uniform style, it is hard to avoid the inference. It is on such evidence that the assumption rests of an expansion or migration from south-east Africa to Zimbabwe around 1000. This supposed movement, called *kutama*, is as well-documented archaeologically as it could be.[50] Yet it is conceivable – although not probable – that a new style of pottery simply spread like a new fashion without any movement.

Unfortunately there are many more dubious cases. When pottery suc-

48. J. Tosh, 1978, pp. 17–34.
49. W. Y. Adams *et al.*, 1978.
50. T. N. Huffman, 1978.

cessions are divided into styles, with many transitions, not only is the number of styles unclear but the inference that immigrants brought new styles is unwarranted. Clearly this is a product of the analysis, not of the data themselves. Such mistakes have occurred on the Zimbabwe site and others.

Some authors still use ethnographic distributions as evidence for migration. This was fashionable once but the approach is now totally discredited. Thus to argue from the presence of crossbows among the Fang that they must stem from Ubangi where other populations used them, and that migration was involved, is clearly unreasonable. Similarly, to look for resemblances in hats, smelting furnaces or martial headgear as arguments for a northern origin of the Beti of Cameroon is unwarranted.[51] Such elements could spread without population movement, similarities could be accidental and in many cases independent invention is quite likely. Ethnographic similarities without linguistic evidence are useless and even if diffusion is shown, diffusion by movement of population remains to be proven.

The marshalling of valid data into an overall hypothesis can also lead to gross errors. One of the most famous cases is that of the so-called Fang migrations. The Fang, Bulu, Beti and Ntumu were all believed to have come from the north, crossing the Sanaga all together or with a separate crossing for the Bulu, and to have fled from attackers into an environment that was new to them: the rain-forest.[52] But this is a conflation of all sorts of traditions which are not identical and which are in large part an expression of cosmology. There is no evidence for any other early home of the Fang apart from the headwaters of the Comoe, Ntem and Ivindo. They moved after about 1840 not as a mass migration but as a rapid expansion.[53] And this movement has no relationship to those postulated for the Bulu, Beti or Ntumu.

A most difficult case is the Jaga migration, a band migration first reported in 1591 on the basis of the testimony of a Portuguese who arrived years after the event and left in 1583. The event occurred in 1568. Various authors have debated the question. Some are now convinced that there never were any Jaga. The most extreme opinion holds that the Portuguese invented the migration to intervene in the affairs of the kingdom of Kongo during a succession dispute.[54] Other authors do not agree and maintain that some immigrants definitely entered Kongo in 1568 even if most of the Jaga were Kongo peasants in revolt.[55] We may never know for certain.

---

51. P. Laburthe-Tolra, 1981, pp. 61–5.

52. P. Alexandre, 1965, is the latest author to attempt an overview. Cf. also H. Ngoa 1981.

53. C. Chamberlin, 1978.

54. F. Bontinck, 1980; J. C. Miller, 1973 and 1978.

55. J. K. Thornton, 1978; A. Wilson, 1979.

The major population movements 1500–1800

Only one part of the continent was subject during this period to major redistributions of population and the ensuing creation of new societies and cultures. This is the Horn area, south of the Abbay or Upper Blue Nile, including most of what is now Somalia and northern Kenya, as well as the lands east of the White Nile, north of Nyanza lake and south of the Sobat. Several movements were clearly involved. The most spectacular was the migration of the Oromo into Ethiopia about 1535. Other Oromo groups migrated or expanded to the south as far as the River Tana and even to the hinterlands of the coastal cities. From 1500 onwards, Somali movements of expansion occurred on a large scale. They are not well-known due to lack of study and, in part, because population movements have been obscured by the vagaries of the titanic struggle opposing Ethiopia of the Muslim emirate led by Aḥmad Grañ. By 1700 a large part of Ethiopia was under Oromo control, Christian and Muslim influences in the south-west had disappeared, the Somali and Oromo were locked in competition for good lands all the way to the Tana river and smaller stable populations had been driven out of Shungwaya, a territory just north of the Somali–Kenya border near the ocean. These groups, the future Miji-Kenda peoples, settled in *kaya*, which were large, well-defended sites behind the major port-cities of Kenya.[56]

Further west, population movements had begun much earlier, perhaps about 1000 when the movement labelled the 'Luo migration' started along the White Nile. East of the Nile there are no sound data for earlier periods. It is clear, however, that a large number of groups were involved, mostly the so-called Karamojong group and to their east, the Turkana, and southern Nilotes, such as the Nandi as well as the Maasai. All these people, like the Oromo and Somali, were primarily pastoralists, except for the Luo group. All were attempting to exploit 'empty' territories – lands with lower population densities – more intensively than the preceding hunters and gatherers or pastoralists.[57] The environments determined the arenas to a large extent. Luo groups needed well-watered lands, the Karamojong needed lands with a higher rainfall than the southern Nilotes or Maasai and they, in turn, needed wetter lands than the camel nomads – the Somali and some southern Oromo groups. The Oromo, who had been cattle keepers in their homeland, showed it was possible to acquire a new technology – in this case camels – and thus occupy new lands. But this was the exception. By and large, each group had its own strategy for exploiting resources in given environments, and its organization for defence (usually age-grades), and strove to occupy a maximum amount of land. In a few cases, however, during the later expansions, armed struggles occurred between populations which exploited their environments in similar ways.

56. See chs 24 and 25 below; also T. T. Spear, 1978.
57. See chs 26 and 27 below.

This occurred in the eighteenth century, when the Kenya Luo wrested land from their neighbours, and in Maasai country by the nineteenth century when different Maasai groups began to fight each other for land. Clearly population pressures were involved here.

These population movements were in effect the story of the colonization of marginal lands, at least until the eighteenth century. The wettest lands near the Nile were first occupied by farmers who also kept cattle and then defended the land against all comers. Groups arriving later sought to extend their ranges, often against competition as their numbers increased. The whole movement, compared to the state of affairs elsewhere in the continent, proves by contrast how stable Africa was as a whole. All other major areas had been occupied and settled by populations using technologies well suited to the land and to their levels of population at the time. Elsewhere in the continent man had mastered space: here the struggle was still going on.

It has been suggested that droughts played a major role in these movements.[58] One can imagine that they were a product of drier conditions associated with a supposed Little Ice Age, from 1450 to 1750, and point to drought conditions in the western Sahel too. There the collapse of Songhay and its rather ineffectual replacement by Moroccans[59] had led to sizeable Tuareg expansion south of the Niger bend and even to Tuareg–Fulbe clashes. But these movements were quite localized compared with the movements in north-eastern Africa. Even the advance of the Moors, or the evacuation of the lands near Aïr by Gobir Hausa who retreated south, although a possible consequence of desiccation, still remain mainly evidence for an orderly movement of cultural and ethnic boundaries along with shifting climatic borders. Space was still under control. The great movements occasioned by the Banū Hilāl, the Banū Sulaym and other Arabs in Sudan and Chad were over. The land was colonized and even the bad conditions from 1600 to 1750 did not disrupt the whole pattern of large-scale settlement. Therefore it is unlikely that, by themselves, droughts can explain the overall mobility of population in the north-east; nor is it likely that the collapse of a strong Ethiopian empire was the sole cause. We must think in terms of fundamental stresses between relatively high densities of population, in the Oromo heartland, for example, and on the Nilotic side of the south Ethiopian highlands perhaps, with the relatively low densities in northern Uganda and northern Kenya and in the dry rift valleys of both Kenya and Tanzania. By 1700 all of these lands had been occupied by new groups with societies and economies that permitted higher densities.

Elsewhere movements of this nature were occurring on a much more modest scale. In southernmost Africa the *trekboere* were colonizing the Karroo veld by ousting or killing its pastoral occupants, while in Namibia

58. See ch. 26 below.
59. See chs 11 and 16 below.

both Herero and Namib were expanding to the detriment of the original San and Dama. The fringes of the Kalahari were being settled as were the arid lands of northern Uganda and northern Kenya. Yet to the south-east a major area of disequilibrium was building up. In south-east Africa populations were becoming too numerous for their resource bases. The first signs, perhaps, were the movements of the Tonga north into south-eastern Zimbabwe, the band migrations of raiders in Zimbabwe itself, and the end of the 'filling up' of southern Zimbabwe by settlers from the better lands to the north.[60] The next big upheaval was to start there after 1800.

Massive but slow drift, a certain sign of adaptation of population densities to land, was occurring meanwhile in the rain-forest of Central Africa and in the savannahs of what is now the Central African Republic during the whole period. The drift of Mongo groups south from centres of higher density near the equator has been mentioned. Immigration led to the development of strong chiefdoms north of the lower Kasai and the Kuba kingdom. Further east, population densities were also low in some savannah areas and some Mongo language speakers settled there. Between the Rivers Zaire and Ubangi some higher densities built up – but in patches. It was still possible for a people such as the Ngbandi to drift south from the Ubangi river valley. But by the eighteenth century there were signs of relative over-population and after 1750 a new people, the Zande, were born. They expanded by rapid drift, creating successive chiefdoms east towards the Nile. On the grasslands of the Central African Republic and Cameroon there also occurred movements of slow drift by farmers, mainly Gbaya and Banda, but documentation for this area is still scant.[61] In the western part of the Central African rain-forest constant emigration by drift was taking place from the Mbam/Sanaga confluence to places of lower density further south and perhaps west, while a minor centre of density in Equatorial Guinea was sending immigrants northward.[62]

One can point to minor drifts almost everywhere, even in West or North Africa, as the mobile populations constantly adapted to relative differences of population density, as is evident by mentions of such movements in every regional chapter. But compared to mass migrations, the orderliness of the process is important. For that orderly and slow process was the sign of true stability.

Among the smaller movements, those that occurred around states being formed or collapsing are the most numerous. In West Africa, the breaking up of the Jolof state by 1520 may not have involved any of these, but the slow collapse of the Mali empire is said to have led to the Soso (Susu), Baga and Nalu drifts from Futa Jallon and to the Mane band migration which, after a rampage through parts of Liberia and Sierra Leone, led to the emergence of new chiefdoms and new cultures there. The Mande

60. See ch. 23 below.
61. See ch. 18 below.
62. D. Birmingham and P. Martin, 1983; P. Burnham, 1975, and 1980, pp. 10–39.

people are one of the main results. The development of the Mossi states may be connected to the northward movement of the Dogon who settled on the Bandiagara scarp, while further south Mande troops founded Gonja. The emerging state of Asante led to a small displacement of the Akwamu near the Volta river and, more importantly, to a larger expansion in the south-east by Baule and Agni groups.[63] The Tyokosi war band, which ultimately settled in northern Togo, comprised people from Asante but also Mande and was involved in mercenary operations for one of the Mossi kingdoms.

In Central Africa fewer such movements are known. The expansion of the Lunda empire first, then of the Yaka kingdom of the Kwango, led to movements of armed bands. The ones in southern Lunda and the one that founded the Kazembe kingdom are the best known. But a group of populations between Kwango and Kasai, near the fifth parallel south, may have begun to move before 1800 as a result of raids by both the Yaka and the Lunda, but perhaps also because of the inducement of more regular rainfall and better terrain.[64] In Malawi a spectacular rise of armed bands occurred as a byproduct of the creation of the Maravi and Lunda states about 1600.[65] The Zimba, who came from this area, first raided northern Mozambique and the hinterland of Kilwa. They are said – but are they the same band? – to have ravaged the coastal lands north to Malindi and further. At least one other band settled in the highlands of Zimbabwe but was later destroyed. In Zimbabwe itself small movements of expansion and raiding cannot be confidently associated with state expansion or contraction, except for a few cases such as the Manyika expanding to the barren Inyanga highlands and three smaller expeditions from the Changamire state. Other small movements here had more to do with the colonization of relatively empty land in the south. Madagascar is perhaps the prime example of population movements related to the emergence of kingdoms and chiefdoms. The story of the Maroserana movements, with the attraction of other groups and the flight from their path of yet others, is telling. By 1500 the population on the island was still very mobile and had not effectively settled and not all the land was yet under human control. By 1800 most of these lands had been organized into states of various sorts. Space had been tamed. A major difference from other parts of Africa, however, was the prominence of state formations during the taming process.[66]

Similar developments on the mainland were confined to portions of central Tanzania, all of southern Tanzania and northern Mozambique. Here the rise of the kingdoms and chiefdoms of the Bena, Sangu, Hehe, Makua, Lundu, Yao, and further consolidation of some Nyamwezi polities,

---

63. See chs 10, 11, 12, 13, 14 and 15 below; also C. H. Perrot, 1981.
64. See chs 19 and 20 below.
65. See chs 21 and 22 below; also D. N. Beach, 1980a.
66. See ch. 28 below.

similarly provided a framework for stabilization.[67]

The impressive further development of trading routes south of the Sahara led to the creation of new diasporas or the strengthening of older ones and also to some other population movements, usually over short distances. From west to east the Jahanka, Joola, Yarse, Hausa, Bobangi, Vili, Hungaan, Bisa, Yao and Swahili diasporas are the best known. To these must be added the European diasporas of which the French on the Senegalese coast, the Portuguese in Luanda and Mozambique, the Portuguese agents, *lançados*, *pombeiros* and *prazo* personnel, and the Dutch at the Cape influenced Africa most in this period. Many of both the European and the African diasporas were involved in the slave trade as the trading routes became busier, better organized and longer. Peoples living near such major routes sometimes moved closer to them and sometimes fled from them. Thus the Itsekiri expanded to the coast, not far from their former lands, in order to be on the sea route to Benin. The Efik moved from the vicinity of Arochuku to Old Calabar on the Cross river and founded a major port there.[68] The Duala descended the Wouri river for the same reason in the eighteenth century. In Gabon, a number of people drifted slowly towards the mouth of the Ogowe delta to participate more in the trade. Some, on the other hand, fled from these regions towards the Ngunie river.[69] The population between Kwongo and Kasai seems to have moved away from the trade route and the raiders in the vicinity, while Bemba groups in Zambia moved closer to the route developed in the nineteenth century. Many in Zimbabwe seem to have moved away from the turbulence created by the Portuguese *feiras* in colonizing the south. But all these movements at any given time were small-scale indeed. They too represent no more than dynamic readjustments to new larger-scale organizations of space for trade or for socio-political control. Movements similar to these also occurred in or near the trading routes and the new political centres in northern Africa.

Conclusion

Space had been tamed in most of Africa long before 1500 and no lands remained completely unused by that date. Over most of the continent, settlement was of sufficiently low density that processes of expansion solved problems of pressure on the land. The main exception was eastern Africa from the Horn to the Zambezi, excluding the Great Lakes area and including Madagascar. The northern half of this area saw mass migration, an uprooting of previous patterns of settlement and quite active drifts by expanding herders. In the southern half and on Madagascar, where farming was more prominent, social reorganizations with the emergence of a

67. See ch. 27 below.
68. See ch. 15 below.
69. See ch. 18 below.

network of kingdoms and chiefdoms provided the means for greater stabilization of settlement and more intensive use of the land.

Drought and famine are not sufficient explanations for the occurrence of mass migrations and active expansions in the northern part of this area because the fringes of the Sahara in both west and north Africa, also affected by droughts, were not similarly affected by migrations or rapid expansion. Slower drifts were the response here.

Population increase in Africa cannot have been dramatic during these centuries since it was mostly easily controlled by these mechanisms. Only here and there do we see the emergence of quite intensive technologies for land use which, in turn, allowed higher densities of population. The lower Casamance, Igbo country, the Cameroon grasslands with their 'domesticated' vegetation, the mountains in the Great Lakes area along the western rift with their systems of irrigation and/or intensive cultivation of bananas, small spots such as the Kukuya plateau with its novel forms of fertilization or the valley of the Upper Zambezi where floods were used, all are still exceptions in western and central Africa. In northern Africa, including Egypt, with the largest oasis in the world, intensive oasis agriculture was millennia old by this time. We cannot here go into the reasons why population increase was not greater but we must at least indicate that the large flow of emigrants from the continent, especially as a result of the trans-Atlantic slave trade, is part of this question. It is remarkable that the parts of the continent affected by this trade, West and Central Africa, were also quite stable compared to eastern Africa, and that the slave trade did not occasion massive turbulence (massive relocations of population) although minor movements are associated with it.

Outside eastern Africa, group mobility was affected most by the rise and fall of states and by the extension of trading networks. Despite the collapse of some larger states in the Sahel of West Africa, the percentage of areas controlled by states on the continent was higher by 1800 than it had been by 1500, and there was some turbulence around the fringes of each emerging state.

Long-distance trading routes and diasporas were old in West and North Africa by 1500 and even in Central Africa some elements existed. A network of such routes developed there in the seventeenth and eighteenth centuries, when routes reached from coast to coast. Diasporas developed everywhere as the need arose for the conduct of trade. Such trading networks enlarged the scale of resource exploitation just as states organized larger territories than chiefdoms or confederations of villages. Long-distance routes connected Africa to the world outside and were drawing the continent into the hierarchical organizations of space affecting most of the globe. From 1500 onwards this meant increasingly a world system in which Europe became dominant.

These three centuries must be seen as a portion of a much longer evolution. Compared to the previous half-millennium, the population was much more stable than before and the mastery of communities over space more evident. Yet, in the nineteenth century, one major upheaval was still to shake eastern and southern Africa when population build-up in southern Africa led to the *mfecane*, in the absence of a technological revolution that could have prevented it. But once again, the rest of the continent did not experience this instability and it is clear that most of Africa had achieved mastery over space long before 1500. The relationship of population to land resources and available technologies had produced a stable situation in which intricate cultural elaborations and such social complexities as urbanization flourished.

But, as this chapter also shows, we still know little about movements of population. Historical demography and technological history is just beginning in Africa. We need more data and we particularly need to replace the vague notion of 'migration' with more refined analyses. Then we shall be better able to chronicle a fundamental theme in African history. It is one that moves very slowly: the successive colonizations of Africa by its inhabitants.

Africa in world history: the export slave trade from Africa and the emergence of the Atlantic economic order

J. E. INIKORI

Introduction

While slaves from Africa south of the Sahara may have been sold in the area around the Mediterranean in ones and twos in ancient times, the export of slaves in significant quantities from black Africa to the outside world dates from about the ninth century.[1] This trade served mainly the area around the Mediterranean (including Southern Europe), the Middle East and parts of Asia. Though the export slave trade from Africa in this direction lasted several centuries, even into the early twentieth century, the numbers exported annually were never very great. However, with the opening up of the New World to European exploitation, following the voyage of Christopher Columbus in 1492, a much more extensive slave trade from Africa, in terms of annual volume, was added to the older trade. This is generally known as the trans-Atlantic slave trade which lasted from the sixteenth century to the mid-nineteenth. Both trades were conducted simultaneously for almost four centuries, removing millions of people from Africa. The place of this trade in world history has hitherto not been properly demonstrated.

It must be noted that trade in slaves has not been limited to Africa. In fact, the world has known chattel slavery and large-scale trade in slaves since the days of the Roman empire. An examination of the historical records will easily show that all races of the world have at one time or another sold their members into slavery in distant lands. The story is told that the mission to convert the English people to Christianity in the late sixth century was connected with the sale of English children in the market at Rome – victims of the frequent fights that the Anglo–Saxon tribes had among themselves during which they captured and sold one another as slaves.[2] The same is true of other European territories. For many centuries ethnic groups in East and Central Europe (particularly the Slavs from

1. R. A. Austen, 1979; R. Mauny, 1971.
2. The story is that a Roman monk once saw English children being sold in the market at Rome and felt sorry that the English people were not Christians. When later this monk became Pope Gregory the Great, he ordered in + 596 a party of monks to go and convert the English people to Christianity. See T. Cairns, 1971, p. 50.

whose ethnic name the word slave is derived) supplied slaves to the Middle East and North Africa.

Yet, from the point of view of world history, the export slave trade from Africa, particularly the trans-Atlantic trade, is unique in several respects. The sheer size of the trade, the geographical extent of the regions of the world involved, and the economics of the trade – at the level of slave supply, employment of slaves to produce commodities for an international market, and trade centred on the products of slave labour – all these put the slave trade from Africa apart from all other slave trades.

The difficulty of demonstrating the place of the export slave trade from Africa in world history is at once tied up with the problem of understanding and explaining the historical origins of the contemporary world economic order. The controversy surrounding the latter subject arises from a number of factors: first, the tyranny of differing paradigms conditioning the thought patterns of different scholars; second, the intrusion of political influences into scholarly explanations; and third, inadequate information at the disposal of many scholars. The views expressed on the subject by some well-known scholars may be quoted to illustrate.

In his analysis of the historical origins of the contemporary international economic order, the Nobel-Prize-winning black economist, W. Arthur Lewis, opined that: 'The Third World's contribution to the industrial revolution of the first half of the nineteenth century was negligible.'[3] Looking at the other side of the coin – the effects of the evolving international economy on Third-World economies – the late Bill Warren declared:

> There is no evidence that any process of underdevelopment has occurred in modern times, and particularly in the period since the West made its impact on other continents. The evidence rather supports a contrary thesis: that a process of *development* has been taking place at least since the English industrial revolution, much accelerated in comparison with any earlier period; and that this has been the direct result of the impact of the West ...[4]

Again, writing recently from the political angle, the development economist, P. T. Bauer, stated that

> Acceptance of emphatic routine allegations that the West is responsible for Third World poverty reflects and reinforces Western feelings of guilt. It has enfeebled Western diplomacy, both towards the ideologically much more aggressive Soviet bloc and also towards the Third World. And the West has come to abase itself before countries with negligible resources and no real power. Yet the allegations can be shown to be without foundation. They are readily accepted because

3. W. A. Lewis, 1978, p. 6.
4. R. Warren, 1980, p. 113.

the Western public has little first-hand knowledge of the Third World, and because of widespread feelings of guilt. The West has never had it so good, and has never felt so bad about it.[5]

While far from being the majority position, these are views for which support can be readily found in the literature on the subject. They all bear traces of the three factors stated earlier. However, one particularly striking feature of the three views quoted is the apparent non-consideration of the slave trade from Africa and New World slavery. This seems to be a fairly common feature of existing studies of the historical origins of the contemporary world economic order. The explanation is possibly that historians have not tried to show simultaneously the effects of the slave trade from Africa in global terms.

In this chapter, an attempt is made to analyse the consequences of the slave trade from Africa in the context of the evolution of a world economic order from the sixteenth century as a way of reaching a better understanding of the international economic issues of our time. For this purpose, an economic order may be defined as a single system of economic relations embracing several countries, simultaneously allocating functions and distributing rewards to the countries involved through the mechanism of a trading network. The development of such a system of international economic relations entails the evolution of economic, social and political structures in the individual member countries or sub-regions within the system which make it possible for the operation of the system to be maintained entirely by the forces of the market. Once so developed, any important modification of the system can only arise from a deliberate political action, occasioned possibly by a change of regime in one or more countries within the system.

It is held in this chapter that an economic order linking together a vast area comprising diverse regions of the world emerged in the Atlantic zone in the nineteenth century. The regions within the order were Western Europe, North America, Latin America, the Caribbean and Africa. This order was structured in such a way that Western Europe and later North America formed the core territories, while Latin America, the Caribbean and Africa formed the periphery, with economic, social and political structures to match. The extension of the Atlantic economic order to incorporate Asia and the rest of Europe in the nineteenth and twentieth centuries produced the world economic order of the twentieth century which has been undergoing more or less minor changes in its character to date. It is important to note that the core and peripheral areas of the nineteenth-century Atlantic economic order have continued to maintain their positions ever since, even within the wider order. The developments of the nineteenth and twentieth centuries only increased the core areas by one or two territories, while considerably expanding the periphery.

5. P. T. Bauer, 1981, p. 66.

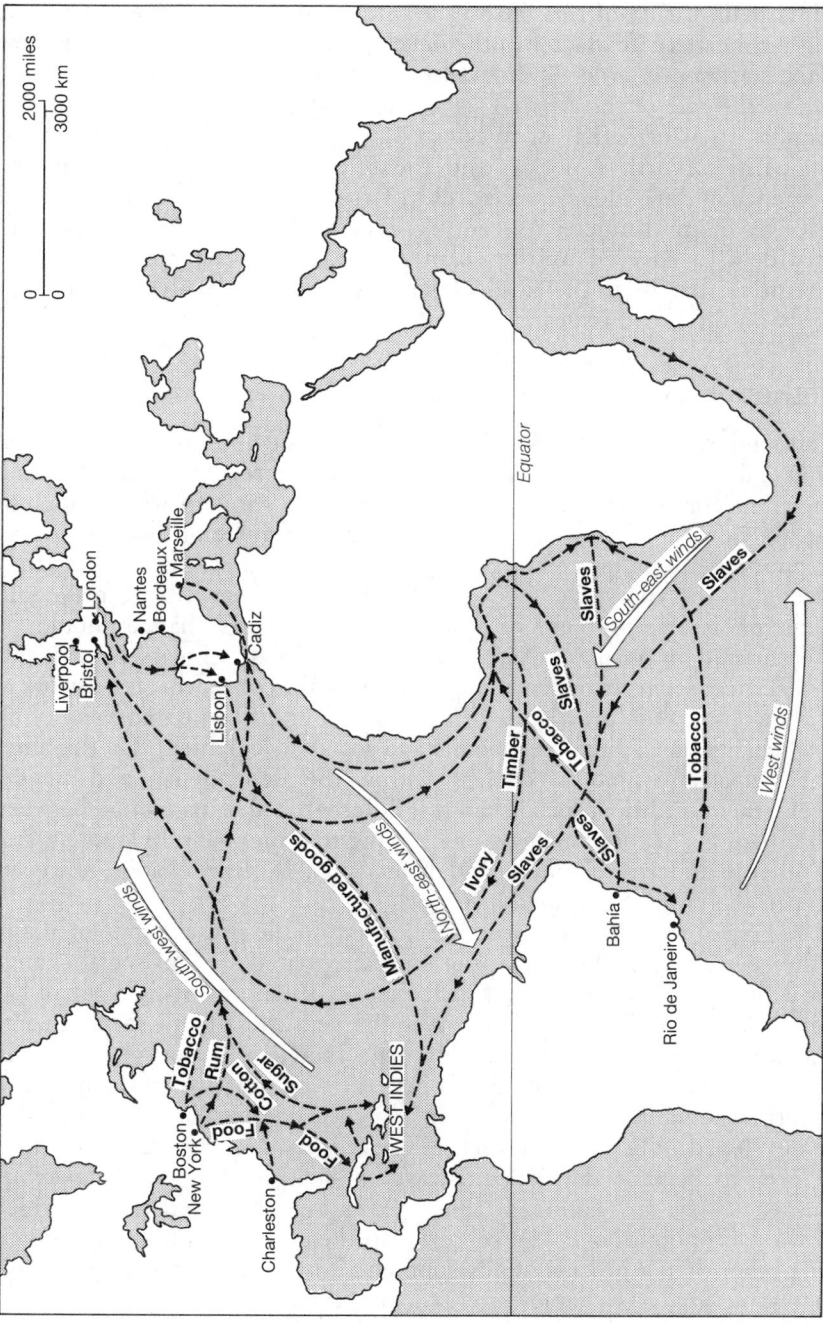

FIG. 4.1 *Atlantic commerce in the eighteenth and early nineteenth centuries*
Source: adapted from A. G. Hopkins, *An Economic History of West Africa*, London, Longman, 1973. Map reproduced by kind permission of Longman Group UK Ltd

The main thrust of this chapter is to demonstrate that the slave trade from Africa was a key factor in the development of the nineteenth-century Atlantic economic order. To develop this theme, efforts have been made to show the role of the African slave trade and New World slavery in the capitalist transformation of Western Europe (with special reference to Britain) and North America, and the role of the same factors in the emergence of dependency structures in Latin America, the Caribbean and Africa by the mid-nineteenth century. Due to the limitation of space and the wide area covered by the chapter, it has not been possible to give descriptive details at the level of sub-regions. The analysis is focused mainly on the broad issues.

Methodology

In all studies of society, a key factor that makes communication between scholars difficult and gives occasion to heated disagreement is the differing conceptual frameworks providing differing lenses through which different scholars view the same social facts. This explains much of the controversy surrounding discussions on underdevelopment and dependence, as is partly reflected in the views cited above. Central to the disagreement in the said discussion is the problem of whether or not social change should be differentiated for purposes of analysis. The practice by scholars, as far as this is concerned, seems to depend considerably on the conceptual framework at their disposal. One practice is centred on an undifferentiated view of all social change as leading to economic and social development. On the other hand, especially among scholars within the dependency and under-development tradition, social change is differentiated: a distinction between two directions of social change, one leading to economic development and the other to underdevelopment and dependence. Both are change, however, and can therefore, be studied historically.

Looking at the historical processes leading to the present state of affairs in the economies of the world, the undifferentiated view of social change proves incapable of offering a satisfactory explanation. Social change has been taking place in all societies over the centuries. If all social change leads ultimately to economic development, then surely most economies in the world should by now be developed. Yet, by any proper definition of the term 'economic development', only a few economies in the world today are developed. The vast majority still need very drastic measures if they are ever to become developed: measures such as those undertaken by Stalinist Russia and China. It thus follows that the social change which led these economies over the centuries to their present situation is something other than a process of development. The latter historical process is what some analysts characterize as a process of underdevelopment and dependence whose features are distinguishable analytically from those of the development process.

The approach of the underdevelopment and dependency tradition needs some further elaboration. Social change entails economic, social and political structuring. Some mixture of economic, social and political structures produces economic development, but others create a stumbling block for the attainment of economic development. Processes of social change that produce the structures for development should be seen as the development process, while social change giving rise to structures that ultimately create barriers to development which can only be eliminated through drastic political action, should be characterized as an underdevelopment and dependency process. Analytically, therefore, three types of economics are distinguishable: undeveloped, developed and underdeveloped economies.

For the purposes of understanding the analysis in this chapter, these three terms need to be defined. A developed economy should be taken to mean an economy with strong internal structural and sectoral linkages, supported by advanced technology and social and political structures that make it possible for self-sustained economic growth to be maintained.[6] An underdeveloped and dependent economy should be understood to mean an economy that is structurally and sectorally disarticulated by certain internal structures arising from the character of previous international relationships which make it extremely difficult, if not impossible, for advanced technology and strong structural and sectoral linkages to develop within the economy, giving rise to a situation where the economy's expansion or contraction depends entirely on the external sector.[7]

Finally, undeveloped economies are those that possess neither the structures of development nor those of underdevelopment and, hence, are still free to move easily in either of the two directions, depending on the kind of opportunities that are presented.[8]

6. By structural linkage we mean linkages between mining, capital-goods industry and consumer-goods industry. And by sectoral linkage we mean links between the sectors: mining and industry, agriculture, transport and commerce. For an economy to be described as developed, the sub-sectors within industry must be fully developed and linked, and all the sectors of the economy must be strongly integrated. Only in this way can self-sustained growth be maintained and dependency eliminated.

7. A situation of total dependence on the external sector must be distinguished from that of interdependence between the economies within the world trading system. As Dos Santos puts it: 'A relationship of interdependence between two or more economies or between such economies and the world trading system becomes a dependent relationship when some countries can expand through self-impulsion while others, being in a dependent position, can only expand as a reflection of the expansion of the dominant countries ...' T. Dos Santos, 1973, p. 76.

8. This type of economy must not be confused with underdeveloped economies. R. Warren (1980, p. 169) is certainly wrong in his statement that 'There is no reason to abandon the view that underdevelopment is non-development, measured in terms of poverty relative to the advanced capitalist countries.' Even if a literary meaning is sought, the term underdevelopment makes better sense if it means a process of capitalist transformation that is blocked and therefore incomplete. This situation cannot be the same as that of natural backwardness, which non-development or underdevelopment implies.

79

Thus, to understand the global effects of the process through which the international economy was created, we need to examine the kinds of economic, social and political structures to which that process gave rise in the different economies it embraced. Then, it will be possible to determine which of the structures conform with development or underdevelopment and dependence. Particularly useful for this purpose is an important hypothesis provided by the underdevelopment and dependency tradition: that during the mercantilist epoch,[9] the capitalist transformation of what became the core countries of the evolving world economy produced at the same time a consolidation and further extension of pre-capitalist social formations in what became the peripheral territories.[10]

If this is true, then the development of the core countries led to both underdevelopment and dependency structures in the periphery. This chapter is organized around this hypothesis for the purposes of testing it against the historical evidence.

The volume of the slave trade from Africa

To make a fair assessment of the role of the slave trade from Africa in world history, it is important to establish an estimate that is reasonably close to the real volume of the trade over the centuries. In this regard, considerable progress has been made with respect to the more important branch of the trade, the trans-Atlantic slave trade. This progress centres on the estimates published in 1969 by Philip Curtin.[11] Since then, other specialists have published the results of their detailed researchers centred on different portions of the estimates. A comparison of these recent estimates with those of Curtin for the relevant components is shown in Table 4.1.[12]

As can be seen from the table, the results of these researches since 1976 show unanimously that Curtin's figures are much too low. Much of the Atlantic slave trade still awaits detailed research. The kind of detailed work done by David Eltis for Brazilian slave imports, 1821–43, is yet to be extended to Brazilian imports in the eighteenth, seventeenth and sixteenth centuries. The volume of British slave exports in the sixteenth and seventeenth centuries, and many other subject areas, still await detailed research. When these researches are complete, it will be possible to have global figures based entirely on the detailed work of specialists. However,

9. The period 1500–1800 is usually referred to as the period of mercantilism whose central feature was the struggle among West-European countries to dominate the expanding world trade of the period to their exclusive advantage.

10. In Marxist terms, pre-capitalist social formations are constituted by the primitive communist, the ancient, the slave and the feudal modes of production. There are some other variants of the pre-capitalist modes of production. For a useful discussion of issues relating to pre-capitalist social formations, see J. G. Taylor, 1979.

11. P. D. Curtin, 1969.

12. J. E. Inikori, 1976; P. D. Curtin, R. Anstey and J. E. Inikori, 1976.

TABLE 4.1   *Estimates of the volume of the Atlantic slave trade made since*
1976

Author	*Component estimated*	*Estimated number of slaves*	*Curtin's estimate for the same component*	*Percentage difference*
J. E. Inikori	British slave exports from Africa 1701–1808	3 699 572	2 480 000[a]	49.2
C. A. Palmer	Spanish slave imports 1521–95	73 000	51 300[b]	42.3
E. Vila Vilar	Spanish slave imports 1595–1640	268 664	132 600[c]	102.6
L. B. Rout Jr.	Spanish slave imports 1500–1810	1 500 000	925 100[d]	62.1
D. Eltis 1977	Trans-Atlantic slave exports from Africa 1821–43	1 485 000	1 104 950[f]	34.4
D. Eltis 1979	Brazilian slave imports 1821–43	829 100	637 000[e]	30
D. Eltis 1981	Trans-Atlantic slave exports 1844–67	634 700	539 384[g]	17.7
R. Stein	French slave exports 1713–92/3	1 140 257	939 100[h]	21.4

[a] J. E. Inikori, 1976; P. D. Curtin, 1969, Table 41, p. 142.
[b] J. E. Inikori, 1976; P. D. Curtin, 1969, Table 5, p. 25.
[c] P. D. Curtin, 1969, Table 5, p. 25.
[d] P. D. Curtin, 1969, Table 77, p. 268.
[e] P. D. Curtin, 1969, Table 67, (p. 234) and Table 80 (p. 280).
[f] P. D. Curtin, 1969, Table 67 (p. 234) and Table 80 (p. 280).
[g] P. D. Curtin, 1969, Table 67 (p. 234) and Table 80 (p. 280).
[h] P. D. Curtin, 1969, Table 49, p. 170.

Sources J. E. Inikori, 1976; C. A. Palmer, 1976, pp. 2–28; E. Vila Vilar, 1977b, pp. 206–9;
L. B. Rout Jr, 1976; D. Eltis, 1977, 1979, 1981; R. Stein, 1978; P. D. Curtin, 1969.

the estimates resulting from the post-1976 research do show a clear pattern that can form the basis of a reasonable statistical inference relating to the whole trade. One major point about these estimates is that they cover all the important centuries of the trade. They suggest, in particular, that the most substantial upward revisions of Curtin's estimates are to be expected for the sixteenth and seventeenth centuries,[13] the period for which more detailed research is needed.

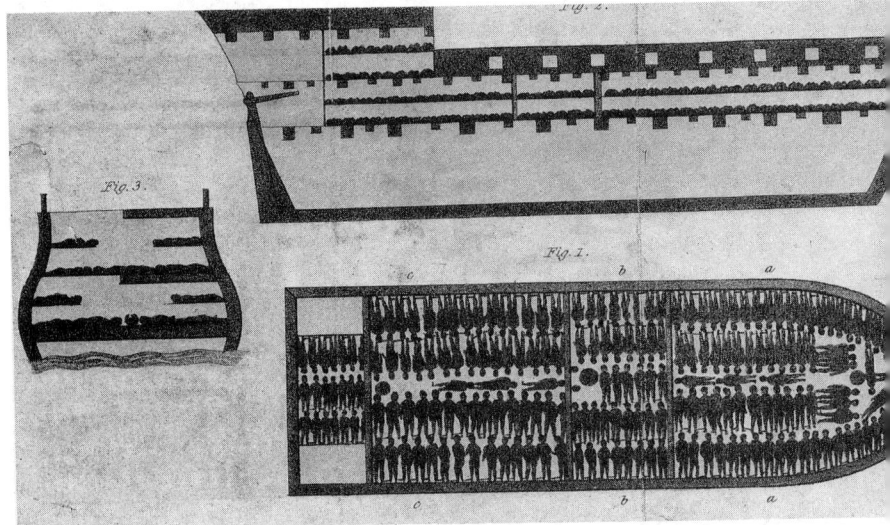

PLATE 4.1   *Plan and cross-section of a European slaving ship*

Both the pattern and the magnitude of the revisions shown by the post-1976 research suggest that a 40 per cent upward revision of Curtin's global figures would bring the estimate reasonably close to the real volume of the Atlantic trade. Applying this to Curtin's total figure of approximately 11 million worldwide, gives a figure of about 15.4 million.[14]

13. See the estimates given in Table 4.1.

14. Paul Lovejoy has given a rather amazing interpretation of the results of this recent research. Rather than studying the pattern of the revisions coming from the research and making a statistical inference, Lovejoy makes a questionable selection from them, mixes his selected figures with unrevised figures from Curtin (which form a large proportion of the total) and arrives at what he calls a 'new estimate'. This 'new estimate', Lovejoy claims, confirms the accuracy of Curtin's original estimate. See P. E. Lovejoy, 1982. Apart from the errors of judgement involved in Lovejoy's selection of figures, the most curious thing in his 'estimate' is the use of Curtin's own original figures to confirm the accuracy of Curtin's estimates. This is a misleading exercise, especially because the results of the researches since 1976 show clearly that Curtin's figures for the period before 1700 are the ones that require the largest upward revision. Yet these are the ones mostly used by Lovejoy. In my view, the method used by Lovejoy is unhelpful. If we must use global figures in our various works before the needed research is concluded, the best we can do is to make statistical inferences based on the results of recent research.

For the trade across the Sahara, the Red Sea and the Indian Ocean, the existing estimates are less firmly founded, due to the weaker database. However, there are two estimates of this branch of the trade which command a reasonable amount of confidence. These are the estimates by Raymond Mauny[15] and Ralph Austen.[16] Mauny computed 10 million for the period 1400–1900. Austen's figures, on the other hand, amount to roughly 6 856 000 for the period 1500–1890. The latter figure is made up of 3 956 000 for the trans-Saharan trade and 2 900 000 for the trade across the Red Sea and the Indian Ocean. In general Austen's estimates seem more securely based and are, therefore, to be preferred to Mauny's. Thus, taking both branches of the trade together, about 22 million people were exported from black Africa to the rest of the world between 1500 and 1890.

The capitalist transformation of Western Europe and North America in the era of slave trade and slavery

When Christopher Columbus arrived in the Caribbean in 1492, the West European economies were by definition undeveloped. Subsistence agriculture and self-employed handicraft manufacturing were still the dominant economic activities, in terms of the proportion of the working population employed. Manufacturing was still part and parcel of agriculture – a part-time occupation for a people whose main employment was agriculture in which the bulk of the output was consumed directly by the direct producer himself. Social and political structures were such that extra-economic coercion still dominated the distribution of the social product.

However, some important structural changes occurred in Western Europe during the three centuries or so preceding the arrival of Columbus in the New World. The growth of population and its regional redistribution during the Middle Ages stimulated considerable development of inter-regional and international trade within Western Europe and thus provoked important institutional changes in a number of countries.[17] Production for market exchange within and between the countries of Western Europe expanded while subsistence production began to weaken. There were important developments in the organization of land and labour intended to improve the efficient utilization of these factors, particularly the development of property rights in land. These were accompanied by some changes in social structure. All these developments which occurred between the

15. R. Mauny, 1971.

16. R. A. Austen, 1979.

17. For a stimulating discussion of these changes, see D. C. North and R. P. Thomas, 1970 and 1973; D. C. North, 1981; R. S. Lopez, 1976; D. B. Grigg, 1980. See also the debate provoked by R. Brenner, 1976; J. P. Cooper, 1978; M. M. Postan and J. Hatcher, 1978; P. Croot and D. Parker, 1978; H. Wunder, 1978; E. le R. Ladurie, 1978; G. Bois, 1978; R. Brenner, 1982.

late Middle Ages and 1492 were important in providing the conditions which made West European economies responsive to the opportunities offered by the emergence of the Atlantic system following the arrival of Columbus in the Americas.

While all the economies of Western Europe underwent changes in the late Middle Ages there were important differences from one country to another. In particular, the combined effects of the wool trade and population expansion in England made developments there most remarkable.[18]

In summary, in order to properly understand what happened between the sixteenth and nineteenth centuries, two points need to be stressed about developments in Western Europe during the centuries preceding the emergence of the Atlantic system. First, the commercialization of economic activities increased throughout Western Europe thereby enhancing the operation of market forces. This explains the ease with which the impact of the Atlantic system was communicated directly and indirectly to all the economies of the region. Second, significant differences in the level of institutional change in the different countries of Western Europe, coupled with further differences in access to opportunities emanating from the Atlantic system in the centuries that followed, explain the differing rates of capitalist transformation in the countries of Western Europe between the sixteenth and nineteenth centuries.

In analysing the impact of the evolving Atlantic system on the economies of Western Europe, two periods are distinguishable: 1500–1650 and 1650–1820.

Between 1500 and 1650 the economies and societies of the Atlantic region were not yet structured in a way that enabled market forces to fully maintain the operation in the area of a single economic system that could allocate functions and distribute rewards to the member units. In consequence, Western Europe used its military superiority to command resources from other economies and societies in the region. For this reason, the pre-Columbus transformation process in Western Europe continued in much the same pattern, with much of the international exchange of commodities occurring within Europe, as the resources from the rest of the Atlantic area were brought to Western Europe in exchange for little or nothing.

The most important resources that came to Western Europe from the rest of the Atlantic area during this period were silver and gold. These came mainly from Spanish America (the Spanish colonies in the New World), the gold trade from West Africa having declined as the economics of the slave trade and slavery took hold. From Spain, the silver and gold from the New World were distributed throughout Western Europe. Table 4.2 shows the quantities imported into Spain between 1503 and 1650.

As the imported bullion went into circulation as a medium of exchange, the process of commercialization of economic activities accelerated all over

18. J. E. Inikori, 1984.

TABLE 4.2 *Quantities of silver and gold imported into Spain from the Americas, 1503–1650*

Period	Silver (oz)	Gold (oz)
1503–10		175 133
1511–20		322 859
1521–30	5 256	172 453
1531–40	3 040 373	510 268
1541–50	6 263 639	880 323
1551–60	10 692 168	1 503 361
1561–70	33 258 031	406 740
1571–80	39 456 766	332 595
1581–90	74 181 368	426 881
1591–1600	95 507 751	686 107
1601–10	78 082 734	414 959
1611–20	77 328 761	312 383
1621–30	75 673 829	137 214
1631–40	49 268 753	43 739
1641–50	37 264 124	54 639

Source C. M. Cipolla, 1976, p. 210, based on E. J. Hamilton, 1934, p. 42.
Note The extent of smuggling was such that official figures can only provide an indication of the overall magnitude of the imports.

Western Europe. The interaction of the rapidly increasing quantity of money in circulation with population expansion produced what is known in European history as the price revolution of the sixteenth century. The conditions created by this phenomenon were particularly important for the early development of capitalist agriculture in Western Europe, particularly in England.[19]

The import of American bullion also gave a fillip to the growth of international trade within Europe. By law only Spanish nationals and Spanish-owned ships were allowed to take goods to and from Spanish America. The trade was restricted to only two ports in the whole of Europe, Cadiz and Seville. In addition, the Spanish American colonies were forbidden to produce their own manufactured goods. Yet, the mineral wealth of the colonies encouraged the dominant classes in Spain to depend on other European countries for all sorts of imports to meet the needs of Spaniards in Spain and in Spanish America. Even the trade of Cadiz and Seville with Spanish America was dominated by alien European merchants through various underground arrangements.[20]

In this way, Spain became the centre of a large-scale international trade within Western Europe in the sixteenth century. This trade, which was

19. E. J. Hamilton, 1929; J. D. Gould, 1964.
20. A. Christelow, 1948; J. O. McLachlan, 1940.

PLATE 4.2 *Spanish coin bearing the heads of Ferdinand and Isabella, 1474–1504. Such coins had a wide circulation*

dominated by Holland, France and England, provided the channel through which American bullion poured into the major economies of Western Europe and fuelled their transformation process. The silver and gold from Spanish America left Spain within months of arrival, so much so that it was said: 'Spain kept the cow and the rest of Europe drank the milk'.[21] This continued through the seventeenth and into the eighteenth century.

From 1650 to 1820, the structuring of the economies and societies of the Atlantic area reached its climax and the process of capitalist transformation in Western Europe came to depend on the Atlantic system. The role of the latter system in the economic development of Western Europe during the period can only be fully appreciated when viewed against the background of the general crisis of the seventeenth century in Western Europe.

The economic expansion of sixteenth-century Western Europe, associated with the growing imports of American bullion and population expansion, came to a halt as the effects of both factors weakened. The import of American bullion reached its peak in the 1590s and declined thereafter. Population growth also decelerated as European societies tailored their demographic behaviour to the level of economic opportunities. The situation was worsened by the policy of economic nationalism, bordering on

21. A. Christelow, 1948.

economic warfare, that was adopted by a number of West European countries particularly France, during the seventeenth century. The high tariff walls erected by France, England and others to protect home industries aggravated the economic situation in Western Europe, resulting in a general crisis. International trade within Western Europe collapsed.[22] The ongoing process of capitalist transformation was halted in some countries, while a reverse process occurred in others. The worst hit of all was Italy which was transformed 'from the most urbanised and industrialized country of Europe into a typical backward peasant area.'[23]

The nature and origin of the seventeenth-century crisis show clearly that for the capitalist transformation process in the region to be completed, Western Europe needed much greater economic opportunities than Europe alone could offer. As Professor Hobsbawm points out, 'The 17th century crisis cannot be explained by the inadequacies of the equipment for Industrial Revolution, in any narrowly technical and organizational sense.'[24] It cannot be explained by the shortage of capital either. '16th century Italians', says Hobsbawm, 'probably controlled the greatest agglomerations of capital, but misinvested them flagrantly. They immobilized them in buildings and squandered them in foreign lending ...' But the Italians were behaving rationally.

> If they spent vast amounts of capital non-productively, it may have been simply because there was no more room to invest it progressively on any scale within the limits of this 'capitalist sector.' (The 17th century Dutch palliated a similar glut of capital by multiplying household goods and works of art ...)[25]

Thus, what explains the crisis is inadequate economic opportunities in Western Europe. It follows from this, that for as long as Western Europe depended virtually on internal economic opportunities, the region had little or no chance for a full capitalist transformation.

The changes that occurred in the structuring of the economies and societies of the non-European areas of the Atlantic between 1650 and 1820, offered immense opportunities and challenges which completely altered the economic situation in Western Europe generally, but very much more so for those countries that had greater access to those opportunities. In the New World, a major element in the economic and social structuring of the period was the growth of plantation agriculture. The production of precious metals continued to be important, particularly as Brazil entered large-scale gold production in the eighteenth century. But the key element in the structuring of the economies and societies of the New World during the

22. R. Davis, 1969, chs 2 and 3.
23. E. J. Hobsbawm, 1954, p. 36.
24. ibid., p. 42.
25. ibid., pp. 42–3.

period was large-scale plantation agriculture. In mainland North America, the products were mainly tobacco and cotton, but in Latin America and the Caribbean, sugar was king. The scale of operation of the new economy necessitated a complete repopulation of the New World.

A great volume of trade was organized around the shipping of goods to Africa and the Americas, the shipping of slaves from Africa to the Americas, and the shipping of produce and precious metals from the Americas to Western Europe. As an example, sugar legally imported from the Americas into Western Europe reached at least 151 658 tons per annum in the 1740s and 193 005 tons in the 1760s.[26] Since the colony-owning West European countries restricted the movement of goods in and out of their American colonies, their control of the distribution of American commodities in Europe became a major factor in the growth of intra-European trade in the seventeenth and eighteenth centuries.[27] The main beneficiaries of these developments were England, France and Holland. As an illustration, the official value of England's foreign trade (imports plus exports) rose from an annual average of £8.5 million in 1663–9 to £28.4 million in 1772–4 and £55.7 million in 1797–8.[28] This growth was directly or indirectly due almost entirely to the expansion of the Atlantic system. France and Holland had similar experiences. For England, re-exports centred on New-World produce made up 37.1 per cent of all exports in 1772–4, while the comparable figure for France is 33.2 per cent in 1787.[29] It is not for nothing that a French economic historian declared:

> The eighteenth century can be truly called the Atlantic stage of European economic development. Foreign trade, and especially trade with the Americas, was the most dynamic sector of the whole economy (for instance, French colonial trade increased tenfold between 1716 and 1787), and furthermore the demand from overseas was stimulating the growth of a wide range of industries as well as increased specialization and division of labour. Owing to the superiority of sea transport over land transport, the eighteenth century European economy was organized around a number of big seaports, the most prosperous being those with the largest share in the growing colonial trade, such as Bordeaux or Nantes; each of these had, not only its own industries, but also its industrial hinterland in the river base of which it was the outlet.[30]

26. R. Sheridan, 1970, Table 1, p. 22.
27. R. Davis, 1969, chs 2 and 3; R. Davis, 1967.
28. For 1663–9 and 1772–4, see R. Davis, 1969, pp. 92, 119, 120. For 1797–8, see P. Deane and W. A. Cole, 1967, Table 13, p. 44. The 1797–8 figure is for Great Britain, while the others are for England and Wales. All the figures include all imports, domestic exports and re-exports. The eighteenth-century figures are at 1697–1700 constant prices.
29. P. Kriedte, 1983, Tables 39 and 40, pp. 124, 128.
30. F. Crouzet, 1964.

The growing economic opportunities associated with the expanding Atlantic system offered increased employment stimulating population growth all over Western Europe after the seventeenth-century decline.[31] This contributed considerably to the growth of domestic markets in England, France and Holland which combined with growing exports to provide the demand pressures that provoked the inventions and technological innovations of the eighteenth-century and nineteenth-century industrial revolutions in Western Europe. In this way, the phenomenal expansion of commodity production, trade, finance and shipping which occurred in the Atlantic area between 1650 and 1820 provided the needed opportunities for the economies of Western Europe to overcome the crisis of the seventeenth century, break the shackles of traditional economic and social structures, and complete the process of capitalist transformation. The first country to complete the process was England. The forces which this development unleashed, and the lessons that it offered, helped the rapid completion of the process in the other West European countries that had shared positively (directly or indirectly) in the opportunities emanating from the expanding Atlantic system.

The part of the New World that in 1783 became the United States of America, while operating under important political constraints as colonial territories between the seventeenth century and 1776, also shared positively in some important ways in the expanding Atlantic system during this early period. The economies of these territories were probably among the most undeveloped in the Atlantic area at the time Columbus arrived in the Americas. Population densities were among the lowest in the New World at the time, and there was nothing to compare with the ancient civilizations of South America in terms of economic and social organization. For many decades after their settlement by the European colonists, these territories were overwhelmingly dominated by subsistence activities. The growth of opportunities for market production which occurred in the eighteenth and nineteenth centuries was directly related to the expansion of the Atlantic system from the mid-seventeenth century to the nineteenth.[32]

Tables 4.3 and 4.4 show the magnitude of the involvement of these territories in the Atlantic system in the years immediately preceding the declaration of independence and the formation of the United States of America.

On average, the total annual value of the Atlantic trade of British North America during these years was £8.4 million (imports plus commodity and invisible exports). With a total population of 2.2 million in 1770,[33] the

31. It has now been firmly established that the growth of population in England in the eighteenth century was due to earlier and more universal marriage. This in turn was due to growing employment opportunities. See J. E. Inikori, 1984 for more details. The analysis is based on evidence produced by E. A. Wrigley, 1983 and D. N. Levine, 1977.

32. See J. F. Shepherd and G. M. Walton, 1972.

33. J. Potter, 1965, Table Ia, p. 638.

TABLE 4.3   *Total earnings (£) from commodity and invisible exports by British North America, 1768–1772*

Region	1768	1769	1770	1771	1772
Great Britain and Ireland	1 658 000	1 852 000	1 818 000	2 113 000	2 135 000
All the West Indies	979 000	1 131 000	1 272 000	1 287 000	1 498 000
Southern Europe and the Wine Islands	520 000	805 000	741 000	721 000	762 000
Africa	16 000	30 000	25 000	18 000	34 000
TOTAL	3 173 000	3 818 000	3 856 000	4 139 000	4 429 000

TABLE 4.4   *British North American imports (£), 1768–1772*

Region	1768	1769	1770	1771	1772
Great Britain and Ireland	2 908 000	2 151 000	3 112 000	5 382 000	4 135 000
All the West Indies	524 000	767 000	792 000	676 000	939 000
Southern Europe and the Wine Islands	81 000	85 000	80 000	69 000	88 000
Africa	56 000	189 000	85 000	104 000	265 000
TOTAL	3 569 000	3 192 000	4 069 000	6 231 000	5 427 000

Source J. F. Shepherd and G. M. Walton, 1972.
Note The invisible exports were made up largely of earnings from shipping.

Atlantic trade of these territories was £3.8 per head of population. This magnitude of involvement in the Atlantic system stimulated the growth of the domestic market and production for market exchange, as it encouraged specialization, raised per capita income and influenced the rate of migration into the area.

As the British North American colonies moved gradually from subsistence activities to market production under the impact of the Atlantic system, three economic regimes comprising the southern, middle and northern (mainly New England) colonies became distinguishable. The combination of natural resources and the availability of cheap African slave labour encouraged the southern colonies to expand plantation agriculture, first rice and tobacco, then cotton. The middle colonies, however, took to foodstuffs production on family-sized farms utilizing family labour. In the northern colonies, relatively poor natural resources for agriculture combined with the availability of deep natural harbours and forest resources for shipbuilding encouraged early specialization in trade and shipping.[34]

In this way, the south produced virtually all the plantation commodities

34. See D. C. North, 1961.

that were exported to Europe, while the north produced the bulk of the invisible exports – shipping, merchants' services, insurance, etc. The middle colonies, meanwhile, produced footstuffs for export as well as some invisible exports. Production in the south was dependent on African slave labour, while the market for the output was mainly in Europe. For the middle and northern colonies, the restructuring of the Caribbean economies that accompanied the growth of slave plantations produced a division of labour between the Caribbean (British and non-British) and North America which provided a large market in the Caribbean for the foodstuffs of the middle colonies and for the shipping and other services of the northern colonies. Thus, the economies of the three North American sub-regions were tied up with the slavery system of the Americas, either in the production process or in the market.[35]

British North America's large-scale involvement in the Atlantic system during the colonial period, produced differing economic and social structures in the southern, middle and northern colonies. In the middle and north, production was based on free white labour, property widely spread, and incomes more evenly distributed. In the south, the predominance of plantation agriculture dependent on African slave labour produced a population with a large proportion of slaves, a large concentration of property and an extremely uneven distribution of income. Of the 697 000 slaves in the United States in 1790, 642 000 were in the south, being 36 per cent of the total population of the southern states.[36] While the structures in the middle and northern territories encouraged the growth of the home

35. The economies of the southern colonies were tied to the slavery system at the level of production, while those of the middle and northern colonies were tied to New World slavery at the market level, since it was the structure of the slave plantations of the Caribbean that created the markets for foodstuffs and commercial services on which the middle and northern colonies largely depended at this time. The following figures of export earnings from the major commodities and services (annual averages for 1768–72) give an indication of the structure of North America's export trade during the colonial period:
£s sterling
Tobacco 766 000
Shipping earnings 610 000
Bread and flour 410 000
Rice 312 000
Fish 287 000
Indigo 117 000
These six items together made up 64.4 per cent of total export earnings for British North America during these years. Tobacco and rice were slave plantation products that came from the southern colonies. Bread and flour came from the family-sized farms of the middle colonies, while fish and shipping came largely from the northern colonies. (The figures here are from J. F. Shepherd and G. M. Walton, 1972, p. 258.) The imports were mainly manufactured goods, and came largely from England, while England retained only a small proportion of the colonies' exports. The tobacco went almost exclusively to England and Scotland, but over half of the quantity was yearly re-exported to continental Europe.

36. J. Potter, 1965, Table 2, p. 641.

market for mass consumer goods, the structures in the south restricted the growth of that kind of domestic market and encouraged the import of luxury goods from abroad. In this way, while the foundation for self-sustained economic growth was laid in the middle and northern colonies during the colonial period, dependency structures were built up in the south.

After the achievement of independence, the economy of the southern states continued to depend on African slave labour. The phenomenal expansion of cotton production in the southern states between 1790 and 1860, depended entirely on black slave labour.[37] In consequence, the economic and social structures of the colonial period were maintained in the south, even in the new territories into which cotton plantations expanded in the nineteenth century. In 1850, of the total population of 8 983 000 in the old and new south, 3 117 000 were slaves, being 34.7 per cent.[38] Property and income distribution remained skewed; the dependency structures were further strengthened.

However, with the attainment of independence, the politically independent US government adopted economic measures which gradually turned the south from dependence on Western Europe to dependence on the northern states. The ship-owners and merchants of the north-eastern states, aided by government protection, took over the shipping of southern cotton to Europe and the import of European manufactures for southern plantation owners and their slaves.[39] At the same time, the expansion of cotton production in the south provided a growing food market which stimulated the growth of commercial food production in the west and the flow of immigrants into the western territories. This regional specialization, centred on southern slave plantations, provided a large domestic market

---

37. Cotton production in the southern states increased from 4000 bales of 500 lb each in 1790, to 3 841 416 bales in 1860. In the 1850s, about 76.5 per cent of the total output was exported. H. U. Faulkner, 1924, pp. 201–2.

38. J. Potter, 1965, Table 11, p. 680.

39. An Act of 4 July 1789 allowed a discount of 10 per cent in the duties charged on imports into the United States carried by American-built and American-owned ships. Another Act of 20 July 1789 imposed a duty of 6 cents per ton on American-built and American-owned ships, and 30 cents per ton on foreign-built and foreign-owned ships, entering US ports. Both Acts encouraged the growth of ship-building and ship-owning in the north-eastern states of the USA. The tonnage registered in foreign trade grew from 123 893 in 1789 to 981 000 in 1810. During the same period, US imports carried by American-owned ships increased from 17.5 per cent to 93 per cent of the total, and US exports carried by American-owned ships from 30 per cent to 90 per cent. By 1862, US shipping tonnage registered in foreign trade was 2 496 894, and about 75 per cent of US exports by this time came from the south, cotton taking about 60 per cent and tobacco, rice and refined sugar taking the remaining 15 per cent. (For all these figures, see H. U. Faulkner, 1924, pp. 201, 202, 218, 219, 228 and 233.) The incomes generated directly and indirectly by southern exports, and the earnings made by north-eastern shipowners and merchants in foreign trade, formed the foundation of US industrialization from 1790 to 1860. See D. C. North, 1961.

which encouraged the growth of import-substitution industrialization in the north-east, nurtured by government import controls. In this way, the industrialization of the United States of America up to 1860 was based primarily on the southern slave plantations: the United States took advantage of its political independence at the right moment to manipulate the forces operating in the Atlantic area to the benefit of its economy, aided by the favourable structures that developed in the middle and northern colonies during the colonial period.[40] The dependency structures of the southern states thus acted as essential conditions for the capitalist transformation of the northern and western states.

The evolution of under-development structures in Latin America and the Caribbean

By our definition, the economies of Latin America and the Caribbean were undeveloped when Columbus arrived in the area. Three main factors were responsible for the general level of undevelopment: population, geography and isolation from the rest of the world.

The probable size of the population of all the Americas by 1492 has been a subject of much debate. There have been estimates as low as 8.5 million and as high as 112 million.[41] The more recent research of the Berkeley School, however, indicates that a range of 50 million to 100 million is more plausible.[42] Relative to the large geographical extent of the Americas, even the highest figure is small. Moreover, people were concentrated in about three areas – middle America, comprising the ancient kingdoms of the Aztecs and the Mayas; the Inca empire of ancient Peru; and the Caribbean island of Hispaniola, now made up of Haiti and the Dominican Republic.[43] The rest of the New World was characterized by extremely low population densities. It has been said that population densities of less than 10 persons per sq. km applied to over 90 per cent of the geographical area of pre-conquest Latin America.[44]

The low population densities in large areas of pre-Columbus America had adverse effects on the development of trade and the division of labour.

---

40. For further details relating to Western Europe and North America, see J. E. Inikori, 1979 and 1981.

41. B. Keen and M. Wasserman, 1980, pp. 30–1.

42. For the estimates of the Berkeley School see W. Borah and S. F. Cook, 1963; also S. F. Cook and W. Borah, 1971–4. For a recent synthesis see W. M. Denevan, 1976.

43. Based on a variety of Indian and Spanish records, and using sophisticated statistical methods, W. Borah and S. F. Cook have put the population of pre-conquest Central Mexico at between 18.8 million and 26.3 million. W. Borah and S. F. Cook, 1967, p. 205. Cook and Borah have also estimated the population of Hispaniola at between 7 million and 8 million by 1492. (B. Keen and M. Wasserman, 1980, p. 30.) Cook and Borah's estimates have been subject to considerable recent criticism as being on the high side.

44. A. Morris, 1981, p. 52.

Areas with high population densities, however, were separated from one another and from the sparsely populated areas by thick forest, mountains and deep valleys. These made communication difficult and restricted the development of intra-American trade. In this situation, sea-borne commerce would have been important in pushing the frontier of trade from the sea coast to the interior, as happened in North America in the eighteenth and nineteenth centuries. However, the isolation of the Americas from the rest of the world up to 1492 did not make this possible. Because of this isolation, the rich natural resources of the Americas had little commercial value and therefore made little or no contribution to the development of population and trade.

Consequently, while the ancient civilizations of Central and South America had reached a high level of cultural development by 1492, their economies were basically undeveloped. They needed external commodity trade with the rest of the world to give economic value to their resources, encourage the growth and spread of their populations, stimulate the development of intra-American trade, and set in motion the process of capitalist transformation.

Contrary to these requirements, the trading opportunities that followed the arrival of the Europeans in 1492, came under conditions which led to the evolution of structures of underdevelopment rather than development. First, the West European countries forcefully took control of the natural resources of Latin America and the Caribbean. The Indians were humiliated and demoralized. When the labour demands and the unfamiliar diseases brought by the Europeans were added, the Indian population collapsed everywhere in Latin America and the Caribbean. The demographic catastrophe of Central Mexico in the sixteenth century vividly demonstrates the point. The estimated population of 18.8 to 26.3 million in the area before the European conquest, fell to 6.3 million by 1548 and to 1.9 million in 1580. By 1605, it was down to approximately 1.1 million.[45]

The virtual elimination of the entire Indian population led to two important results. The first is that the phenomenal expansion of commodity production for sea-borne trade with Europe and North America – which occurred between the sixteenth and nineteenth centuries – was made possible only by a massive import of African slave labour. The second is that the agricultural land in Latin America and the Caribbean was taken over by European colonists and put into large estates that came to be known as *laciende* or *lazenda*. It will be shown subsequently that both developments provided trading opportunities that stimulated the capitalist transformation of Western Europe and North America, while at the same time producing underdevelopment and dependence in Latin America and the Caribbean.

The magnitude of contraband slave imports into Spanish America in

45. W. Borah and S. F. Cook, 1967, p. 204.

the sixteenth and seventeenth centuries makes it almost impossible to show the quantitative contribution of African slave labour to the production of precious metals in Spanish America during those centuries.[46] However, a census taken in Spanish America by the clergy in 1796 was reported to

PLATE 4.3   *Negro slaves working on a coffee plantation in Brazil, c. 1870*

46. The evidence produced by E. Vila Vilar indicates the magnitude of the contraband imports: 'D. Fernando de Sarria, the deputy governor of Cartagena, was able to verify that between 1516 and 1619 duty had been paid on only 4816 blacks, whereas in reality 6000 had entered in little more than a year – from May 1619 until December 1620. He contended that the boats that arrived with 15, 25, 37 and 45 'pieces' actually had on board 200, 300, and 400. The *visitador* Medina Rosales testified that it was common for merchants, when paying duty, to declare far fewer 'pieces' than they were actually transporting; he had proven that one vessel that declared 68 was carrying 440; another declaring 45 had 200 on board; and another that declared 65 introduced 260; and he contended that in one year, from 10 June 1620 to 18 July 1621, 6443 slave 'pieces' had entered the port of Cartagena. Juán de Orozco, treasurer of Santa Marta, wrote to the King in 1631 that every ship that arrived with blacks carried 400 'pieces', although duties were only paid on 100; and D. Martín de Saavedra, president of the *audiencia* of San Domingo, testified in 1637 that slaving vessels going to Cartagena with 150 registered, in reality carried 300.' E. Vila Vilar, 1977a, pp. 272–3; see also C. A. Palmer, 1976; L. B. Rout Jr., 1976, pp. 61–6.

95

have shown that people of African origin numbered 679 842 in Mexico and 539 628 in Peru.[47] While one cannot ascertain the accuracy of the census, these figures indicate that African slave labour was crucial to the economies of colonial Mexico and Peru. In Brazil, export production of sugar in the sixteenth and seventeenth centuries depended entirely on African slave labour. While the Brazilian gold boom of the eighteenth century brought many European traders and mining capitalists to the country, actual production still virtually depended on African slave labour. This is borne out by the ethnic composition of the Brazilian population in the eighteenth and nineteenth centuries. In 1798, of the total population of 3 250 000, people of African origin numbered 1 988 000, of whom 1 582 000 were slaves. In 1872, approximately 5.8 million out of the total population of 9.9 million were people of African origin, of whom 1.5 million were slaves.[48] Thus, people of African origin made up 61.2 per cent of the total Brazilian population in 1798, and 58 per cent in 1872. The slave populations were concentrated in those regions producing gold and agricultural products for export to Europe and North America. For example, of the 1 566 416 slaves in Brazil in 1873, 1 233 210 (79.2 per cent) were in six export-producing provinces: Bahia, Pernambuco, Rio de Janeiro, São Paulo, Minas Gerais and Rio Grande do Sul.[49] The largest concentration – 351 254 – was in Minas Gerais, the gold-producing province.

In the Caribbean Islands, the domination of export production by people of African origin is reflected by the transformation of the ethnic composition of their populations after 1650. Before the mid-seventeenth century, the production of subsistence crops had dominated the islands' economies and export production was marginal. From the second half of the seventeenth century, the large-scale import of African slave labour and the expansion of plantation agriculture made it possible for export production to grow rapidly, while the production of subsistence crops was drastically reduced. Thus, the combined populations of Barbados, Jamaica and the Leeward Islands in 1660 was made up of 33 000 whites and 22 500 African slaves, but in 1713 the whites numbered 32 000 and African slaves, 130 000.[50] This means that the slave population increased from 40.5 per cent of the total in 1660 to 80.2 per cent in 1713. Similarly, in the French West Indies, the combined population of Martinique and Saint-Domingue in 1678–81 was made up of 6786 whites and 7397 African slaves,[51] but by 1780 of the total population of 514 849 in all the French West Indies, only 63 682 were

47. J. E. Inikori, 1976, p. 204.
48. T. W. Merrick and D. H. Graham, 1979, Table III, 2, p. 29. The Indian population was 252 000 in 1798 and 386 955 in 1872. The European population in both years was 1 010 000 and 3 787 289, respectively.
49. R. B. Toplin, 1972, App., pp. 288–9.
50. Computed from R. S. Dunn, 1972, p. 312.
51. R. Sheridan, 1970, pp. 35 and 49.

whites, 437 738 were African slaves and 13 429 were free blacks.[52] So, the population of African origin in the French West Indies grew from about 52 per cent of the total in the late seventeenth century to about 88 per cent in 1780.

It was this massive transplantation of African labour into Latin America, the Caribbean Islands and the southern territories of North America that produced the phenomenal expansion of commodity production and trade in the Atlantic area between the sixteenth and nineteenth centuries. This, in turn, provided the stimulating opportunities and challenges under pressure of which the process of capitalist transformation was completed in the major West European countries and North America. This same historical process, however, produced structures of underdevelopment and dependence in Latin America and the Caribbean.

Because the total population was made up largely of slaves, the vast majority of the people in Latin America and the Caribbean earned incomes far too low to make them regular members of the market. In consequence, the growth of the domestic market for mass consumer goods was highly restricted. Lacking a growing mass domestic market to encourage the flow of resources into the development of industrial production for home consumption, the profits from mining and plantation agriculture went for the purchase of manufactures imported from Europe, or were repatriated to finance investment and consumption in Europe. The situation was aggravated by colonial laws which restricted the establishment of industries in Latin America and the Caribbean during the colonial period. In this way, Latin America and the Caribbean taken together, provided a stimulating market for manufacturers in Western Europe, particularly British manufacturers who supplied the British colonies as well as Spanish and Portuguese America, directly or via Spain and Portugal.[53] For example, the official value of British exports to the British West Indies between 1714 and 1773 amounted in total to £43.4 million (virtually all manufactured goods). During the same period, the official value of commodities exported to Britain by these British West Indian colonies amounted to £101.3 million.[54] This shows the importance of the New World markets to British manufacturers as well as the magnitude of resource repatriation from the slave plantation colonies.[55]

52. E. Williams, 1970, p. 153.
53. A. Christelow, 1948; J. O. McLachlan, 1940; H. E. S. Fisher, 1963.
54. E. Williams, 1970, p. 151.
55. A common feature of the slave plantation economies of the New World was the tendency for the level of production to exceed the level of consumption within the territory of production. This was also true of British North America. Between 1714 and 1773, the southern slave plantation colonies of Carolina, Virginia and Maryland exported to Britain commodities worth officially £46.6 million, while New England, New York and Pennsylvania (non-slave colonies) exported goods totalling only £7.2 million. However, the three slave plantation colonies imported from Britain during the same period goods worth only £26.8 million, while the three non-slave colonies imported goods worth £37.9 million.

PLATE 4.4   *Negro slaves cutting sugar cane on a plantation in the West Indies, c. 1833*

The non-development of any important industrial sector gave rise to disarticulated economies in Latin America and the Caribbean, with the mining and agricultural sectors linked strongly to economies in Western Europe and also, later, to the economy of the United States. Associated with this development was the emergence of vested economic interests tied strongly to imports and exports. The mining magnates and the agrarian oligarchies in Latin America and the Caribbean saw their interests only in imports and exports. The merchant class that grew out of the conditions that prevailed from the sixteenth to the eighteenth centuries also became enmeshed in imports and exports. The highly skewed distribution of property and incomes associated with the plantation and slave economies ensured that there were no other groups that could rival these three (the mine-owners, the agrarian oligarchy and the merchants) in economic and political power. Hence, even after the major countries of Latin America had become politically independent in the nineteenth century, state policies continued to favour the production of primary commodities for export and the import of manufactured goods. This was further encouraged by the outcome of the industrial revolutions in Western Europe and the United States in the nineteenth century. These industrial revolutions, nurtured by the Atlantic system, led to the explosion of demand for foodstuffs and raw materials of all types. At the same time, the tremendous reductions in manufacturing costs brought about by the industrial revolutions so cheapened manufactured goods traded in the Atlantic area that the opportunity cost of setting up the domestic production of manufactured goods for home consumption was raised considerably for the newly independent Latin American countries. Thus, by the mid-nineteenth century, the economies and societies of Latin America and the Caribbean had become so structured that underdevelopment and dependence had become entrenched.

The laying of the foundations of dependency structures in Africa

Christopher Wrigley wrote:

> ... there is one unexpected conclusion that does seem to be rather forcibly suggested by recent archaeological work, namely, that the intensive peopling of sub-Saharan Africa did not start with the first signs of agriculture, or of iron-working, but only about a thousand

---

(. Williams, 1970, p. 151.) Thus, commodity production occurred largely in the slave plantation territories, while consumption was concentrated mainly in the non-slave territories of the Atlantic. The non-slave territories of British North America derived their purchasing power largely from their sale of foodstuffs, shipping and merchants' services to the Caribbean slave plantations and also to the slave plantations of the southern colonies of British North America.

years ago or rather less, at the beginning of what in Bantu Africa is called the Later Iron Age. If this is really so, radically new perspectives are opened up. There is now room for demographic expansion to have been proceeding rapidly at the time of the first European contacts . . .[56]

The available indirect evidence lends much support to this conclusion. Local sources in Africa speak unanimously of general population migrations during the first half of the present millennium. While these sources often refer to political causes, these population movements certainly had something to do with increasing ratios of population to resources in the older places of settlement, forcing some groups to move into unsettled or sparsely settled territories.[57] Also, the fourteenth and fifteenth centuries are often referred to as a period in Africa history during which important changes occurred in the organization and technology of production, both in agriculture and manufacturing, and after the sixteenth century there followed a long period of stability and stagnation.[58] Again, rapidly growing population during the preceding centuries must have been an important factor in these changes.

The evidence thus shows that African societies were going through major processes of transformation when the Europeans arrived in the late fifteenth century. Recent archaeological findings indicate that a high level of social and economic transformation had already been attained in a number of

56. C. Wrigley, 1981, p. 18. According to Thurstan Shaw's calculation, the population of Africa in *c*. -10 000 was 2 million, and 5 million in *c*. -3000 (T. Shaw, 1981, p. 589). Further, Posnansky says that the total population of sub-Saharan Africa before + 1000 was 'well under 10 million'. (M. Posnansky, 1981, p. 727). For the year + 1500, Shaw has concluded that archaeological evidence supports the figure of 20 million as the population of West Africa (T. Shaw, 1977, p. 108). Taking these figures together, the indication is that the population of West Africa grew rapidly between 1000 and 1500. This is so because, if we assume that about one-third of the total population of sub-Saharan Africa in 1000 was located in West Africa, then the West African population increased from about 3 million in *c*.1000 to about 20 million in *c*.1500.

57. Jan Vansina says that most of the population migrations in the African rain-forest before 1600 involved movements from high to low densities (J. Vansina, 1981, p. 758). Again, Dike's account of migrations into the Niger delta in the fifteenth and sixteenth centuries also shows movement from high to low densities – from Benin to the Delta (K. O. Dike, 1956, pp. 22–5). See also ch. 3 above.

58. For Senegambia, Curtin says that the period from the seventeenth to the nineteenth century was one of comparative stability in agricultural technology, after the developments of the two previous centuries (P. D. Curtin, 1975, pp. 13–15). See also M. Malowist, 1966, and the debate which ensued between A. G. Hopkins, 1966 and Malowist. Neville Chittick also talks of the fourteenth and fifteenth centuries as the period of greatest prosperity on the East African coast (H. N. Chittick, 1977, p. 209). The process seems to have started somewhat later in the interior of East Africa. As Unomah and Webster say: 'The years from 1500 to 1800 were marked by considerable population movements throughout this region [the East African interior]. Sparsely populated areas were settled, larger societies were created and new states were founded.' (A. C. Unomah and J. B. Webster, 1976, p. 272).

places by that time.[59] However, the relatively short period of time the processes had covered by the late fifteenth century meant that economic and social structures in Africa still conformed basically to our definition of undevelopment. The total population relative to the available agricultural land was still very small. The relatively small population was scattered over the huge continent, with groups separated from one another by long distances and difficult terrain.[60] The emergence of massive desert between black Africa and the Mediterranean and the Middle East (the centres of international commerce for many centuries) reduced black Africa's trade with the rest of the world to commodities with very high value but relatively low transport costs – gold and slaves. Both conditions limited the development of the division of labour, the growth of internal trade, the evolution of market institutions, and the transformation of the pre-capitalist modes of production still overwhelmingly dominant. Thus, the ongoing population expansion needed to proceed for some centuries to raise the ratio of population to agricultural land sufficiently for social differentiation, economic and political organization to be further elaborated. More extensive external trade based on bulky commodities – agricultural, industrial, mineral, etc. – was also needed to interact with internal factors to speed up the process of structural transformation.

The establishment of a seaborne commerce between Africa and Western Europe from the second half of the fifteenth century seemed at first to offer the kind of opportunities that black Africa needed for rapid economic and social transformation. The gold trade expanded. Trade in agricultural commodities, such as pepper, was initiated. Some stimulus was even given to African cloth producers as the Portuguese and the Dutch participated in the distribution of African cloths to different parts of the African coast.[61]

These early developments, however, were short-lived. When the vast

59. See for example T. Shaw, 1970. Northrup says, 'Taken as a whole, the material remains of Igbo–Ukwu are evidence of a craft industry highly developed in skill and artistry. While both earlier and richer than other evidence, the Igbo–Ukwu finds do not diverge from the general trends of cultural development in southern Nigeria. Yet these craft industries were but the summit of an economy about whose base Igbo–Ukwu gives very little information. Despite this lack of direct evidence, it is clear that such specialists and their customers could only have existed in a society producing an agricultural surplus capable of supporting them.' (D. Northrup, 1978, p. 20).

60. In East Africa, the relatively prosperous coastal towns were not brought into regular trading contact with the East African interior until well into the eighteenth century. As Roland Oliver says: 'The reasons for this strange disjunction between coast and interior are certainly in large measure geographical. Behind the narrow coastal plain, the land rises towards the great central plateau, in shelf after shelf of dry thorn scrub, hard to inhabit and difficult to cross. ... During Iron Age times at least, then, the focal area of human development into dense populations and larger societies has lain in the centre of the sub-continent, 1300 kilometres or more from the sea.' R. Oliver, 1977b, pp. 621–2. See also A. C. Unomah and J. B. Webster, 1976, p. 272.

61. For these early developments see J. W. Blake, 1977, and A. F. C. Ryder, 1969.

PLATE 4.5 *Slaves being loaded onto a European slaving ship*

resources of the Americas became accessible to Western Europe after 1492
and with the virtual elimination of the Indian population as a consequence
of the conquest and the diseases introduced by the European conquerors,
the role of Africa in the evolving Atlantic economic system was altered.
The population which Africa needed to build up in order to provide the
internal conditions necessary for a complete structural transformation of
the continent's economies and societies was transferred massively to the
Americas where it was employed to develop large-scale commodity production and trade. The conditions created over a period of about three
centuries by this massive transfer of population discouraged the development of commodity production in Africa, both for internal trade and for
export, and laid the foundation for dependency structures in the continent.

The first crippling impact of this forced migration was the elimination
of the ongoing population growth and the outright depopulation of large
areas of the continent. Earlier in the chapter, it was estimated that about
22 million people were exported from black Africa to the rest of the world
between 1500 and 1890, 15.4 million across the Atlantic and 6.9 million
across the Sahara, the Red Sea and the Indian Ocean.[62] These figures of
actual exports have to be properly interpreted to relate them to demographic
processes in black Africa during the period.

The main issue to examine is the extent to which these exports reduced
the reproductive capacity of the populations of black Africa. This requires
an analysis of the age and sex composition of the exported population.

62. See above, pp. 80–83.

because it is the number of females of child-bearing age that will determine the magnitude of the reduction in reproduction capacity.

In the trade across the Sahara and the Red Sea, young and attractive females predominated because demand was largely for concubines. It is generally believed that the sex ratio in this branch of the trade was two females to one male. This view is not based on any hard data. However, it has been confirmed by census evidence relating to the population of black slaves in Egypt in the nineteenth century which shows that the ratio of female to male slaves was about three to one.[63]

For exports across the Atlantic, recent research now provides hard data with which to show sex ratios for the 404 705 Africans imported into different New World territories during the seventeenth, eighteenth and nineteenth centuries.[64] This represents about 3 per cent of the estimated total exports to the Americas. While the size and the spread of the sample over time and space are quite good, there is rather an over-representation of the Congo–Angola region, being over 50 per cent of the total. East Africa, however, is not represented at all in the sample, although it is reasonable to assume that the East African ratio must fall somewhere within the range for Western Africa. Overall, the sample shows that females made up 32.9 per cent of the 404 705 slaves in the sample.

An important element revealed by an examination of the data for the Atlantic trade is the consistent variation of the sex ratios according to regions of origin. A sample of 43 096 slaves analysed by the writer,[65] shows this clearly (see Table 4.5). The regional variation shown by this sample is further confirmed by a sample of 55 855 slaves landed in the West Indies in the years 1781–98 (see Table 4.6).[66]

From these two sets of data it is clear that the Nigerian area, from the Bight of Benin to the Bight of Biafra, exported the largest proportion of females, ranging from two-fifths to one-half of total exports. However, the other major exporting area, the Congo–Angola region, regularly exported a larger proportion of males than the general average. It is thus likely that the over-representation of the Congo–Angola region in the sample has had a depressing effect on the proportion of families calculated earlier from the 404 705 slaves. This regional variation of the sex composition of the population exported is very important in assessing the demographic impact of the exports at the micro-regional level.

63. G. Baer, 1967.

64. These figures come from: J. E. Inikori, 1982, p. 24 (129 570 slaves); H. S. Klein, 1978, Table 3, p. 30 (55 855 slaves); H. S. Klein, 1975, Table 9, p. 84 (181 909 slaves, mostly from Angola); J. Mettas, 1978, cited by P. Manning, 1981, (12 697 slaves); D. Northrup, 1978, App. D, pp. 335–9 (24 502 slaves); K. D. Patterson, 1975, p. 80 (172 slaves).

65. J. E. Inikori, 1982, Table 2, p. 23. The sample covers the years, 1764–88, and relates to slaves imported into Jamaica.

66. H. S. Klein, 1978, Table 3, p. 30.

TABLE 4.5   *Sex ratios of slaves from different regions of Africa, 1764–88*

African region	Percentage male	Percentage female
Gambia	72.1	27.9
Windward Coast	65.7	34.3
Gold Coast	66.8	33.2
Whydah	57.8	42.2
Benin	49.96	50.04
Bonny	56.5	43.5
Calabar	58.8	41.2
Gabon	68.8	31.2
Angola	68.2	31.8

Source J. E. Inikori, 1982, Table 2, p. 23.

TABLE 4.6   *Sex ratios of slaves landed in the West Indies, 1781–98, by region of origin*

African region	Slaves landed	Percentage male	Percentage female
Senegambia	190	67.5	32.5
Sierra Leone	5 544	64.9	35.1
Windward Coast	3 420	70.6	29.4
Gold Coast	2 721	64.4	35.6
Bight of Benin	315	54.5	45.5
Bight of Biafra	18 218	56.9	43.1
Congo–Angola	12 168	69.9	30.1
Unknown	13 279	65.3	34.7

Source H. S. Klein, 1978, Table 3, p. 30.

For the whole of black Africa, the evidence analysed above shows that the number of females annually exported was of a magnitude that must have drastically reduced the region's reproduction capacity. Considering the additional population losses caused by the exports to the Americas – losses due to mortality between the time of capture and the time of final export, and deaths arising from the wars and famines associated with the gathering of captives for export – along with the 6.9 million exported to the other parts of the world (mostly females), the evidence indicates strongly that the population of black Africa declined absolutely from at least 1650 to 1850.

This overall decline was not evenly shared among all the sub-regions. When the regional variations in the sex ratios shown earlier are related to the regional distribution of the total exports, a fair assessment of the

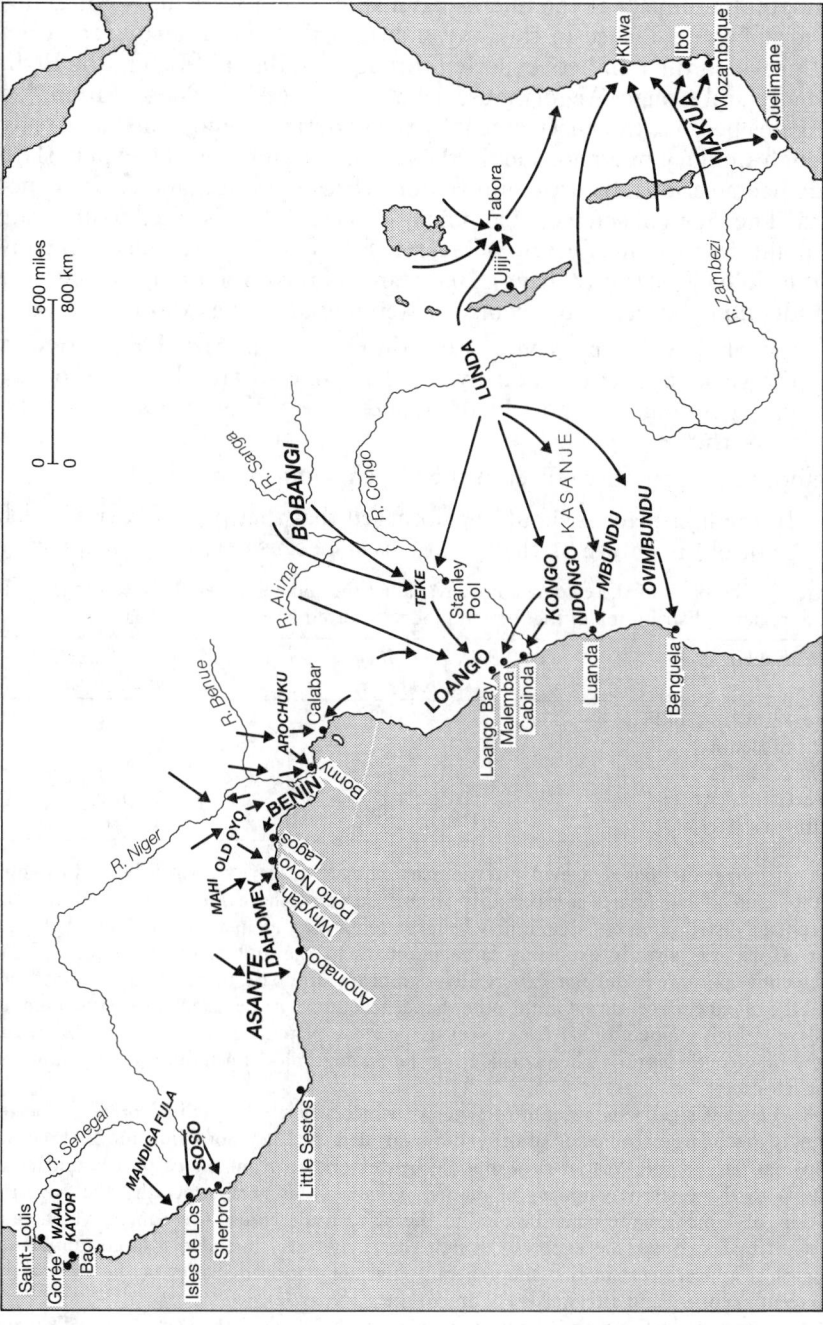

FIG. 4.2   *Sources of the Atlantic slave trade from Africa in the eighteenth and nineteenth centuries (after J. E. Inikori)*

105

demographic impact at the micro-regional level can be made.[67] An examination of the evidence in this way indicates that the ultimate territories that provided the numbers exported through the Bight of Benin, the Bight of Biafra and Congo–Angola must have suffered serious depopulation.[68]

Again, because the enslavement of the exported population was largely through military operations and other forms of violence, the export slave trade had a serious distorting impact on African political and social structures. The views of some contemporary observers may be cited to illustrate the point. In 1679, the Director-General of the Dutch West India Company on the Gold Coast (now Ghana), Heerman Abramsz, reported that since the introduction of firearms following the stepping up of the export slave trade,

> the whole Coast has come into a kind of state of war. This started in the year 1658, and gradually this has gone so far, that none of the passages could anymore be used, and none of the traders could come through.[69]

In about 1730, another officer of the Dutch company reported:

> In the first place it should be observed that that part of Africa which as of old is known as the 'Gold Coast' because of the great quantity

67. On the basis of the evidence now available, the following may be taken tentatively as the regional distribution of the total numbers exported by way of the Atlantic trade:

African sub-region	Percentage of eighteenth-century export	Percentage of nineteenth-century export
Senegambia to Gold Coast	24.8	10.3
Bight of Benin	23.2	17.5
Bight of Biafra	14.8	12.9
West Central Africa	37.5	48
South-east Africa		11.4

The percentages are based on evidence summarized by P. E. Lovejoy, 1982. While Lovejoy' method and global figures are certainly wrong, some of the evidence is useful and the percentage distribution based on it may be taken tentatively as an approximation. Although East Africa was already exporting large numbers to the Indian Ocean islands in the eighteenth century, it did not export any significant numbers to the Atlantic territories until the nineteenth century. On the other hand, account must be taken of the large number of slaves which mainland East Africa sent to the clove plantations of Pemba and Zanziba in the nineteenth century when considering the demographic impact of the slave trade on East Africa.

68. There is a growing amount of evidence which when properly interpreted indicate strongly that a large proportion of the exports through the Bights of Benin and Biafra came from that part of the West African middle belt extending from the eastern boundary of Nigeria to the eastern boundary of modern Ghana. This area, especially the Nigerian portion, also made large contributions to the slave trade across the Sahara which took mostly females. Since the exports through the Bights also included a large number of females, it appears certain that the generally low population densities of the area in the nineteenth century and afterwards are due to the slave trade.

69. Heerman Abramsz to Assembly of Ten, 23 November 1679, in A. van Dantzig 1978, p. 17. The Assembly of Ten was the governing body of the company in Holland.

of gold which was at one time purchased there by the Company as well as by Dutch private ships, has now virtually changed into a pure Slave Coast; the great quantity of guns and powder which the Europeans have from time to time brought there has given cause to terrible wars among the Kings, Princes and Caboceers of those lands, who made their prisoners of war slaves; these slaves were immediately bought up by the Europeans at steadily increasing prices, which in its turn animated again and again those people to renew their hostilities, and their hope for big and easy profits made them forget all labour, using all sorts of pretexts to attack each other, or reviving old disputes. Consequently, there is now very little trade among the coast Negroes except in slaves ...[70]

Later in the eighteenth century, an African observer, Olaudah Equiano, wrote in the same vein:

From what I can recollect of these battles, they appear to have been irruptions of one little state or district on the other, to obtain prisoners or booty. Perhaps they were incited to this by those traders who brought the European goods I mentioned amongst us. Such a mode of obtaining slaves in Africa is common; and I believe more are procured this way, and by kidnapping, than any other.[71]

These illustrative observations taken from a large body of similar evidence show the strong link that existed between the export slave trade and the frequency of wars in Africa during the period. The causal relationship was, of course, very complex. The illustrative observations have not adequately brought out the full complexity of the relationship. The fact is, however, that – directly and indirectly – the export slave trade stimulated frequent wars which distorted the political and social structures of African societies.[72]

One major distortion was the creation of military aristocracies that became so politically influential that they determined the direction of state policy in virtually all major African states of the period. The existence of a large export market for captives meant that the military aristocracies saw war more as a source of captives to be sold than as a means of acquiring more territories whose natural and human resources could be exploited for the benefit of the ruling class through an effective integration into a larger state. This had an adverse effect on the ultimate size of these states and on political stability within them. This is why many of the states that emerged during the period were very limited in size, never achieved real political

70. Enclosure in the Minutes of the meeting of the Directors of the Chamber of Zeeland, held 7 February 1730, in A. van Dantzig, 1978, p. 240.

71. P. D. Curtin, 1967, p. 77. The European goods mentioned earlier by Equiano to which reference is made here are fire-arms, gunpowder, hats and beads. The description by Equiano suggests that these goods were taken to his homeland by the Aro traders of south-eastern Nigeria.

72. For details of this see J. E. Inikori, 1982.

stability and collapsed rather quickly either from within or at the very first sign of trouble from a formidable enemy.

The existence of these military aristocracies, in interaction with the prevailing economic conditions, also stimulated the growth of the slave mode of production in several African societies. Under the structural impact of the export slave trade, first across the Sahara and the Red Sea, and more extensively later across the Atlantic, the various forms of personal dependence that had existed in Africa were transformed into institutions that more or less conformed to chattel slavery of the Western type. Large proportions of the populations of major African societies came to be held under these conditions by people who were connected directly or indirectly with the export slave trade, either as merchants or as government functionaries. With these structures already in place, and under conditions of extremely low population relative to the available cultivable land, the expansion of 'legitimate commerce' that followed the elimination of the export demand for slaves in the nineteenth century further provoked the expansion of the slave mode of production in Africa.[73]

The overall consequence of these historical processes covering a period of more than three centuries was to alter the direction of the economic process in Africa away from development and towards underdevelopment and dependence. The elimination of the population expansion that was in progress up to the sixteenth century, brought to a halt processes leading to the expansion of intra-African trade, the development of internal markets and market institutions, the commercialization of agriculture and a general development of the division of labour. The prevalence of generally low population densities throughout the continent, with vast areas such as the West African middle belt virtually empty of people, retarded the development of production for market exchange. The growth of the slave-trade mode of production in large areas of Africa during the period had the effect of further limiting the development of internal markets and market production. Moreover, the Atlantic slave trade in various ways obstructed the development of commodity trade with Europe that would have stimulated the growth of internal trade and market production.[74] Hence, subsistence production of foodstuffs remained overwhelmingly dominant in African economies by the middle decades of the nineteenth century. This virtually eliminated capital accumulation in agriculture and, therefore, the growth of productivity in food-crop farming for the domestic market. W. Arthur Lewis has demonstrated brilliantly that present-day prices received from the world market by African producers for their primary commodities, are determined by the low level of returns to African foodstuffs farmers producing for the domestic market, owing to the low

73. For more details see J. E. Inikori, 1982, and especially C. Meillassoux, 1982; also P. E. Lovejoy, 1983; S. Miers and I. Kopytoff, 1977; P. Manning, 1981.

74. For details of this point, see J. E. Inikori, 1983. See also J. E. Inikori, 1982, Introduction.

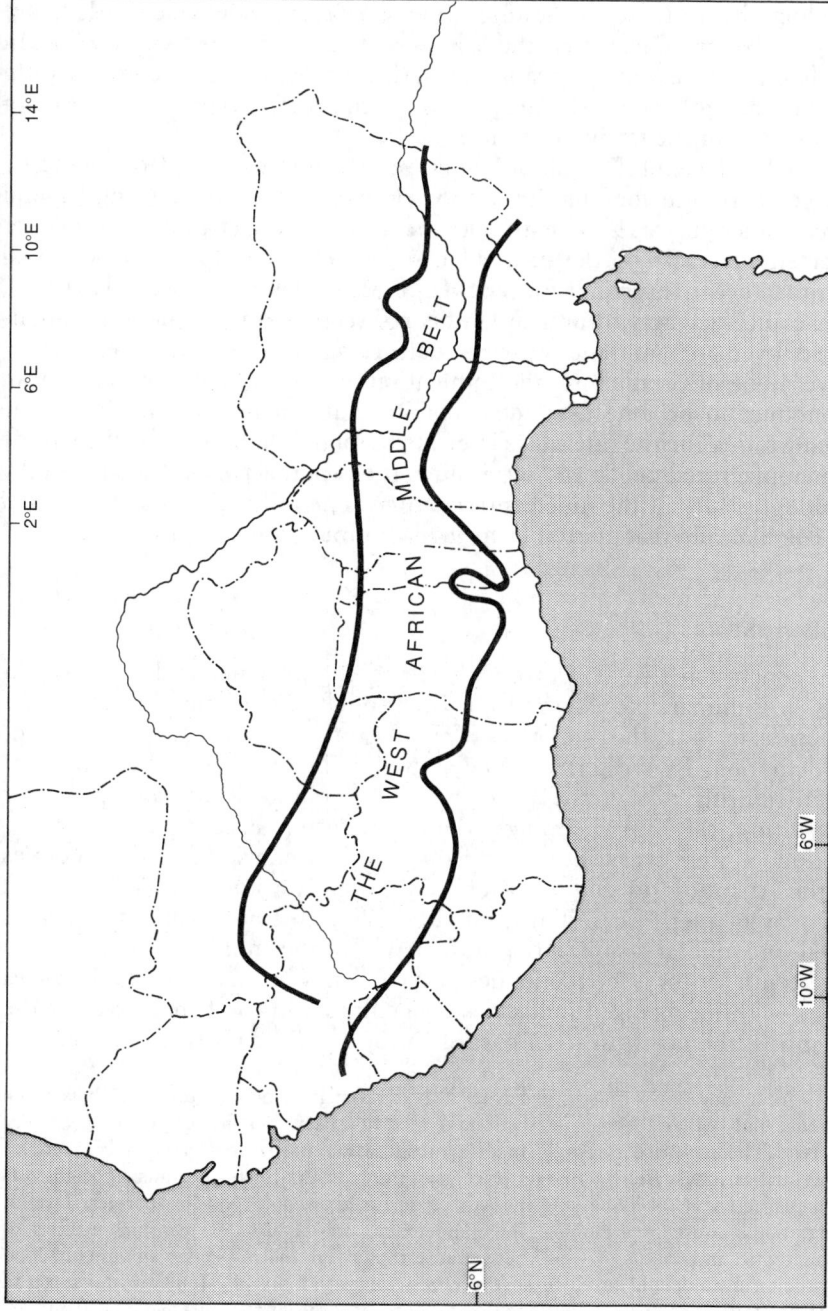

FIG. 4.3 *The West African middle belt*

Source: adapted from M. B. Gleave and H. P. White, 'The West African Middle Belt: Environmental fact or geographers' fiction?', *Geographical Review*, LIX, 1969, p. 124. Map published by kind permission of the American Geographical Society

productivity of these foodstuffs farmers.[75] What Arthur Lewis does not seem to be aware of is that the origins of the low productivity of African foodstuffs farmers are traceable through more than three centuries from the seventeenth century, further worsened by the economic impact of colonialism in the twentieth century.

The low level of division of labour and the limited size of the domestic market were unfavourable for the development of manufacturing beyond the handicraft stage. The development of manufacturing was further affected adversely by the uncontrolled import of European and Oriental manufactures in exchange for captives. Thus, with limited internal markets, non-capitalized agricultural and industrial sectors, small-scale states dominated by merchants and warriors depending for their subsistence on a slave mode of production, the foundation was firmly laid for the African economies to become dependent on the industrialized economies of the Atlantic area for the sale of their primary commodities and for the supply of manufactured goods and services, as the export slave trade ended in the middle decades of the nineteenth century. The full edifice was completed by colonial rule that started from the late nineteenth century.

Conclusion

The conclusion that flows from the foregoing evidence and analysis can now be summarized. At the time Christopher Columbus arrived in the Americas in 1492, the economies of the Atlantic area were all undeveloped, by definition. In Western Europe as well as in Africa and the Americas, manufacturing was at the handicraft stage and was part and parcel of agriculture, the overwhelmingly dominant sector. Precapitalist modes of production were everywhere dominant. In this circumstance, the economies of the Atlantic area could not effectively operate under a single system ruled by market forces. Thus, initially, Western Europe had to bring its naval and military superiority into play. By the middle decades of the nineteenth century, the economies of the Atlantic area had moved distances apart, with mechanized industries concentrated in the fringe areas of the Atlantic – the north-western part of Europe and the north-eastern part of

75. As Arthur Lewis puts it: 'A farmer in Nigeria might tend his peanuts with as much diligence and skill as a farmer in Australia tended his sheep, but the return would be very different. The just price, to use the medieval term, would have rewarded equal competence with equal earnings. But the market price gave the Nigerian for his peanuts a 700-lbs.-of-grain-per-acre level of living, and the Australian for his wool a 1600-lbs.-per-acre level of living, not because of differences in competence, nor because of marginal utilities of productivities in peanuts or wool, but because these were the respective amounts of food that their cousins could produce on the family farms. This is the fundamental sense in which the leaders of the less developed world denounce the current international economic order as unjust, namely that the factoral terms of trade are based on the market forces of opportunity cost and not on the just principle of equal pay for equal work.' 1978, p. 19.

the USA – while the greater part of the Atlantic region was dominated by the production of primary commodities: commercial foodstuffs production and plantation agriculture in the western and southern USA; plantation agriculture in the Caribbean; mining, large-scale livestock raising and plantation agriculture in Latin America; and subsistence food-crops farming and part-time gathering of wild products for export in Africa (the export of captives having been cut off). The economies and societies of the Atlantic area had become so structured that a single economic system ruled by market forces had emerged. Only determined political actions in one or more of the member countries could now radically alter the structures and the international (as well as inter-regional) division of labour that had become entrenched. Barring such actions, the situation was bound to be self-perpetuating, as the advantageously placed fringe areas of the Atlantic further exploited the situation to their economic and political advantage.

The evidence and analysis we have presented all show that these developments derived ultimately from the export slave trade from Africa. It is clear from the evidence that the industrial revolution in England in the eighteenth and early nineteenth centuries, and the one in the north-eastern USA in the nineteenth, could not have occurred at the time they did without the phenomenal expansion of commodity production and trade in the Atlantic area from the sixteenth to the nineteenth century. The same expansion of production and trade provided the basis for the industrial revolutions that occurred later in the nineteenth century in north-western Europe. There is no doubt whatsoever that it was African slave labour, provided through the export slave trade from Africa, that made possible this phenomenal expansion of commodity production and trade in the Atlantic area during the period.

While this expansion stimulated the growth of free wage labour to become the dominant form of labour in north-western Europe and the north-eastern USA, in the rest of the Atlantic area the slave mode of production expanded. Particularly in Latin America, the Caribbean and the southern states of the USA, the expansion of the slave mode of production provided the conditions for unequal development that facilitated the rapid development of capitalism in north-western Europe and the north-eastern USA. The concentration of mechanized industries in these fringe areas of the Atlantic by the nineteenth century was made possible by the large market which the conditions of unequal development made available to manufacturers in these areas. The evidence thus supports the hypothesis that the historical process that produced capitalism in north-western Europe and the north-eastern USA produced at the same time a consolidation and further extension of pre-capitalist modes of production in Africa, Latin America, the Caribbean and the southern states of the USA.

From the conditions created by the economic order that had emerged in the Atlantic area by the nineteenth century, the fringe areas of the Atlantic, equipped with their instruments of mechanized industry, launched an economic and political onslaught on Asia, the Pacific territories and the rest of Europe: an onslaught that finally produced the contemporary world economic order. It is important to note that at the time the Atlantic economic order was being constructed between the sixteenth and nineteenth centuries, Western Europe could not establish with Asia a firm trading link based on the exchange of European products with those of Asia. For several centuries Western Europe had to depend on American bullion to maintain its trade link with Asia for want of commodities the Asians considered a better bargain than their own products. This is borne out by the composition of exports to Asia by the English East India Company in the seventeenth and eighteenth centuries (see Table 4.7).[76] A large proportion of West European imports from Asia during the same period also went to Africa and the Americas as re-exports.

TABLE 4.7   *British East India Company exports to Asia*

Period	Total exports (Ten-year average in £s sterling)	Percentage precious metals
1661–70	133 464	67.0
1691–1700	332 613	71.4
1721–30	650 008	83.6
1751–60	988 588	65.7

Source P. Kriedte, 1980–3, Table 25, p. 84.

By the nineteenth century, however, Western Europe and North America were able to integrate the economies of Asia firmly into the Atlantic economic order, as the Asians found it difficult to resist the products of mechanized industry from Western Europe and North America. Machine-produced textiles from England and North America poured into Asia, forcing the region into the production of raw materials to meet the ever-growing demand of the new industries. In this way, assisted by colonial rule, the Atlantic economic order was extended to the rest of the world, resulting in the world economic order of the twentieth century. It can thus be validly said that the twentieth-century world economic order was constructed originally with the sweat and blood of Africans. Because the population of Africa was forcefully transferred to the Americas for this purpose at a time when Africa needed a growing population and external commodity trade in order to develop commodity production and transform its pre-capitalist social formations, all the latter developments were arrested. Hence, Africa entered the twentieth century as the most economically backward major region of the world. Between the late nineteenth and mid-twentieth century, colonial rule contributed immensely to the maintenance of this position of Africa among the major regions of the world. The latter subject, however, is beyond the scope of this chapter.

76. P. Kriedte, 1980–3, Table 25, p. 84.

The African diaspora in the Old and the New Worlds

J. E. HARRIS

Europe and the Americas

When Africans first arrived in Iberia or the rest of Europe is difficult to document. However, it is likely that some Africans north and south of the Sahara made their way into Iberia during the great trans-Saharan trade of ancient times.

Africans also accompanied Muslims on their Iberian campaign in 711 and the ensuing centuries of Muslim-Christian warfare saw Africans fighting as soldiers and serving as slaves. Indeed, as early as the thirteenth century Moorish merchants were selling sub-Saharan Africans at fairs at Guimarães, in northern Portugal.[1]

When Portugal captured Ceuta in 1415, a sustained European penetration of inner Africa was launched. By 1435 the Portuguese had reached Senegal and were in Congo by 1483. Africans were taken to Lisbon from 1441, a precedent which led to the forced immigration of Africans in the modern slave trade. Indeed, between 1450 and 1500 Portugal imported an estimated 700 to 900 African slaves annually. By the beginning of the seventeenth century there were an estimated 100 000 slaves in Portugal and its Madeira Islands. In 1468 the Portuguese crown initiated the famous *asiento* (monopoly) over the trade in slaves south of the Senegal river.

The growing number of African slaves had to be justified and the papal bulls of Nicholas V (1454) and Calixtus III (1456) provided the necessary justification by establishing Portugal's expansion into Africa as a crusade to Christianize. Consequently, enslavement of Africans by Christians came to be viewed as advantageous to the 'pagan' indigenes. This argument was further supported by the biblical myth of Ham whose descendants were said to be cursed and subjected to slave status. The strength of this biblical and church dimension provided an inestimable basis for earlier ideas on the 'savage' and 'inferior' nature of Africans.[2]

In Spain and Portugal black slaves worked in mines, on farms, in construction, as soldiers, guards, domestics, couriers, stevedores, factory labourers and concubines. Even those who were not slaves were invariably

1. A. Luttrall, 1964, p. 64.
2. J. Walvin, 1972, pp. 10–12, 32–47 and 115–52.

found doing the most menial and arduous tasks.

The sale and use of slaves were primarily urban phenomena, largely because the import of such labour occurred at port-cities and towns. The principal urban areas were Barcelona, Cadiz, Seville and Valencia in Spain, and Lisbon in Portugal. Urban life provided opportunities for slaves to escape and, in some cases, to purchase their freedom. It is not surprising, therefore, that 'free' blacks also congregated mainly in urban settings where they sought to cultivate a community spirit with institutions reflective of black concerns. Religious brotherhoods were organized in Barcelona about 1455, in Valencia in 1472 and in Seville in 1475. Those organizations sponsored recreational activities, festivals and social events; they raised money to purchase and free other slaves; and they bought burial plots which, for blacks, usually had to be in separate areas.[3]

Some free blacks achieved distinction in Spanish society. Cristóbal de Meneses became a prominent Dominican priest; Juán de Pareja and Sebastián Gómez were both painters; and Leonardo Ortez became a lawyer. In 1475 Juán de Valladolid was appointed supervisor over the blacks in Seville. More distinguished, however, was Juán Latino, a black scholar who received two degrees at the University of Granada in 1546 and 1556 respectively; he also taught there, although apparently without an official faculty appointment.[4]

Although African servants accompanied Nicholas Ovando when he assumed his post as the first Spanish governor of Hispaniola in 1502, and while appeals by Pierre Bartholome do Las Casas and others were made to increase the supply of African slaves, there was no official policy for the slave trade to the Americas until 1518 when Charles I of Portugal proclaimed the *Asiento do Negroes*, thereby accelerating competition for African slaves.

Portugal, although a part of Spain between 1580 and 1640, established a virtual monopoly of the slave trade in 1600 by securing from Spain a contract to supply the Spanish colonies with African slaves. The Dutch obtained the contract in 1640; the French in 1701; and in 1713 the monopoly went to England in the form of the *asiento*, following the War of the Spanish Succession. England thus became the greatest slave-trading power.

Although the English had a monopoly to supply slaves elsewhere, the number of Africans in England itself also increased. After William Hawkins sailed to West Africa in 1530, subsequent voyages brought African slaves to England. By 1556 Elizabeth I observed that there were too many 'blackmoores' in England and that they should be returned to Africa. From the eighteenth century in particular, West Indian planters on home visits brought with them Africans as domestic slaves and body-guards. Military and naval officers and captains of slave vessels did likewise. Indeed, to have such black servants became a mark of distinction. Gradually this status

3. L. B. Rout, 1976, pp. 15–16.
4. ibid., p. 18; V. B. Spratlin, 1938.

symbol achieved widespread acceptance, as did the recognition that such servants were cheap labour, and newspapers advertised widely for 'Negroes'.

Most of these Africans were brought to urban areas which facilitated escape into the crowd, the selling of their labour and the development of close relations with liberal persons who opposed slavery. Newspapers in London, Bristol, Liverpool and elsewhere not only advertised slaves but also appealed for the return of escaped slaves. As the demand for slaves increased, kidnapping increased. Slave-hunters in England gained a certain distinction as they specialized in tracking down Africans who did not have the protection of the society or its laws. Africans were frequently picked up and claimed by Europeans on the basis of colour, and in many cases identified by marks burnt into their skins by slave-owners. Colour made Africans targets for enslavement in Europe as in Africa; and the psychological effects of this control by whites over blacks cannot be overestimated. The process of dehumanising the African was thus well in practice by the eighteenth century.[5]

The presence of Africans in England increased demands to know their status. Some English people felt that conversion to Christianity should bring freedom and the rights of civilized men. Granville Sharp was one of the Englishmen who fought for the abolition of slavery. From 1767 and starting with the case of the African Jonathan Strong, Sharp championed the cause of the African slaves by rescuing Africans and fighting court cases for their freedom. The most important of these was that of James Summerset, in 1772, a slave who escaped and was recaptured. The African community in London followed the case closely as they knew the significance the outcome could have for them all. Lord Mansfield, who ruled on the case, did not in fact abolish slavery but he did rule that a slave-master could not legally compel a slave to accompany him abroad – a decision that signalled the beginning of the erosion of slavery in England. At that time it was estimated that some 15 000 Africans were resident in England, some of them living in poverty as pariahs.[6]

From the fifteenth century, the African presence in France received increasing attention. This was the period when French sailors frequented various parts of the West African Coast, particularly the Cape Verde Islands and the Senegal river. Many brought Africans to France, first as evidence of their voyages and later for sale. By 1595 the Portuguese captain, Álvarez d'Almeida, noted that many Africans in Africa spoke French and had visited France.

While enslavement of Africans did occur in France, it is clear that its development was not initially intended. Indeed, a royal court in 1571 proclaimed that: 'La France, mère de la liberté, ne permet aucun esclave'. However, practices varied and some Africans were enslaved while others

5. F. O. Shyllon, 1974, pp. 5–10.
6. ibid., pp. 17–23 and 141–64.

remained nominally free in hostile communities. Several observers noted the African presence in French cities such as Anjou, Lyon, Orléans, Nantes and Paris. They were active as servants, menial labourers and even as pages for the nobility; some were also used in parades and in other forms of entertainment. There were also those who distinguished themselves as soldiers, such as those in the Saxe-Volontaires Regiment which was formed with blacks from Guinea, Congo and Madagascar. In the eighteenth century they won acclaim in several European battles.[7]

The most distinguished black in the French military, however, was to be Alexandre Dumas who was born in the nineteenth century to a Frenchman and his African mistress. Subsequent generations of this Dumas family established their mark both in the military and the arts. But most Africans in France were domestics with lives less harsh than their brothers' in slavery.

From the end of the seventeenth century, Africans arrived in France in significant numbers and, during the eighteenth, royal policy permitted French slave-owners in the Americas to bring their slaves to France. Thus blacks became a more common sight in France.

Much less has been published about the African presence in other parts of Europe. However, a number of Africans, especially Ethiopian envoys and pilgrims, visited Europe during the late Middle Ages and by the fifteenth century Ethiopian monks and other Africans including some slaves, were living in Venice, the Vatican and neighbouring cities.[8]

Venetians were slave-traders and slave-owners too. Although most slaves seem to have been of European and Asian origin, some were Africans. Indeed, the trade in African slaves increased after the fall of Constantinople had restricted the Black Sea traffic. Most seem to have been obtained from Egyptian ports, a point which suggests that their origin included the Nile valley of the Sudan.[9]

Documentation is too scanty to generalize about the Africans' lives in Venice and neighbouring areas. Some reports assert that they became absorbed into local families, thereby accounting for their virtual disappearance by the late eighteenth century. Also relevant to their status is the fact that unfree persons were excluded from certain crafts, so African slaves and servants probably suffered this disadvantage. Some observers, however, have noted that slaves were granted the protection of the law. All slaves had to be baptised and this may have encouraged more lenient conditions.[10] However, slaves were unfree and unequal and the physical and psychological limitations suffered require more study before final conclusions are reached.

The most decisive and dramatic aspect of the African dispersion occurred

7. I. B. Kake, 1948, pp. 73–85.
8. T. Tamrat, 1977; W. L. Hansberry, 1965.
9. R. Smith, 1979.
10. ibid., pp. 53 and 57.

PLATE 5.1 *General Thomas Alexandre Dumas, 1762–1806*

across the Atlantic Ocean to the Americas.[11] For most of the fifteenth century that traffic in people was primarily a Caribbean, Central and South American phenomenon as the Portuguese developed plantations in Brazil and the Dutch in the Guyanas. The sixteenth-century phase of the traffic coincided with African participation in the exploration of the Americas. Thirty Africans accompanied Balboa during the exploration of Mexico and one reportedly planted and harvested the first wheat crop there; 200 accompanied Alvarado to Quito and some joined Pizarro's expedition in Peru. Perhaps the best known was Estevanico who played an important part in the Spanish exploration of New Mexico and Arizona territories. Africans also participated in the French expeditions in Canada, notably

11. Suggested sources include: J. E. Inikori, 1982 and P. D. Curtin, 1969.

with Jesuit missionaries, and in the conquest of the Mississippi valley.[12]

In 1619 a Dutch vessel brought twenty 'negars' to Jamestown as indentured servants. This initiated a demand for black labourers and led to various practices restricting the freedom of Africans and limiting their choice as workers. This culminated in the official establishment of slavery in the North American English colonies in 1660 and, by the end of the century, Africans were legally relegated to the position of chattel slaves – property to be disposed of as their masters saw fit, without regard to the African as a human being and with no likelihood of state restraint. This was a system of slavery designed for maximum economic gain and entrenched by the European belief in and argument for the inherent inferiority of Africans because of colour and physical type.[13]

Meanwhile, Britain and Spain were fighting for dominance in the Caribbean. In 1627 Britain took Barbados and in 1655, Jamaica. The sugar plantations there demanded a large labour force which, over the next forty years, increased almost ten-fold with large numbers of slaves being imported from the Gold Coast, Angola, Congo, Nigeria, Dahomey and, by the 1690s, Madagascar.

British and French dominance in the Caribbean was secured by the latter part of the seventeenth century. Chattel slavery in Jamaica and Barbados developed early and provided the model for North America. In addition, the Caribbean areas were utilized as 'seasoning' stations for the 'breaking in' of African slaves. But because a high proportion of seasoned Africans also knew about conditions in the Caribbean and, in some cases, were involved in plots and revolts, they also served as models for slave resistance in North America.

Slave revolts represented the highest stage of the struggle for freedom from slavery, and areas with high black-slave population densities generally had more frequent and severe conspiracies and revolts. In British Guyana, for example, the slave population at its peak constituted about ninety per cent of the total population; Jamaica, Brazil and San Domingo (Haiti) had similar large black concentrations; and Cuba was not far behind. In the United States, however, blacks were in the majority in only two states, Mississippi and South Carolina.

Excluding San Domingo, the greatest African slave revolts in the Americas occurred in Jamaica and Guyana. The first was the Maroon War in Jamaica in 1725, when bands of slaves fled into the mountains to establish their own community. In 1739, the British were forced to sign a treaty with Captain Cudjoe, from the Gold Coast, who agreed to send back any runaway slaves in return for rights of self-government and a tax-free existence.

Guyana, which included the areas of Essequibo, Berbice and Demarara,

12. R. W. Logan, 1940; J. W. Johnson, 1941.

13. The most authoritative single source on blacks in the United States is J. H. Franklin, 1967.

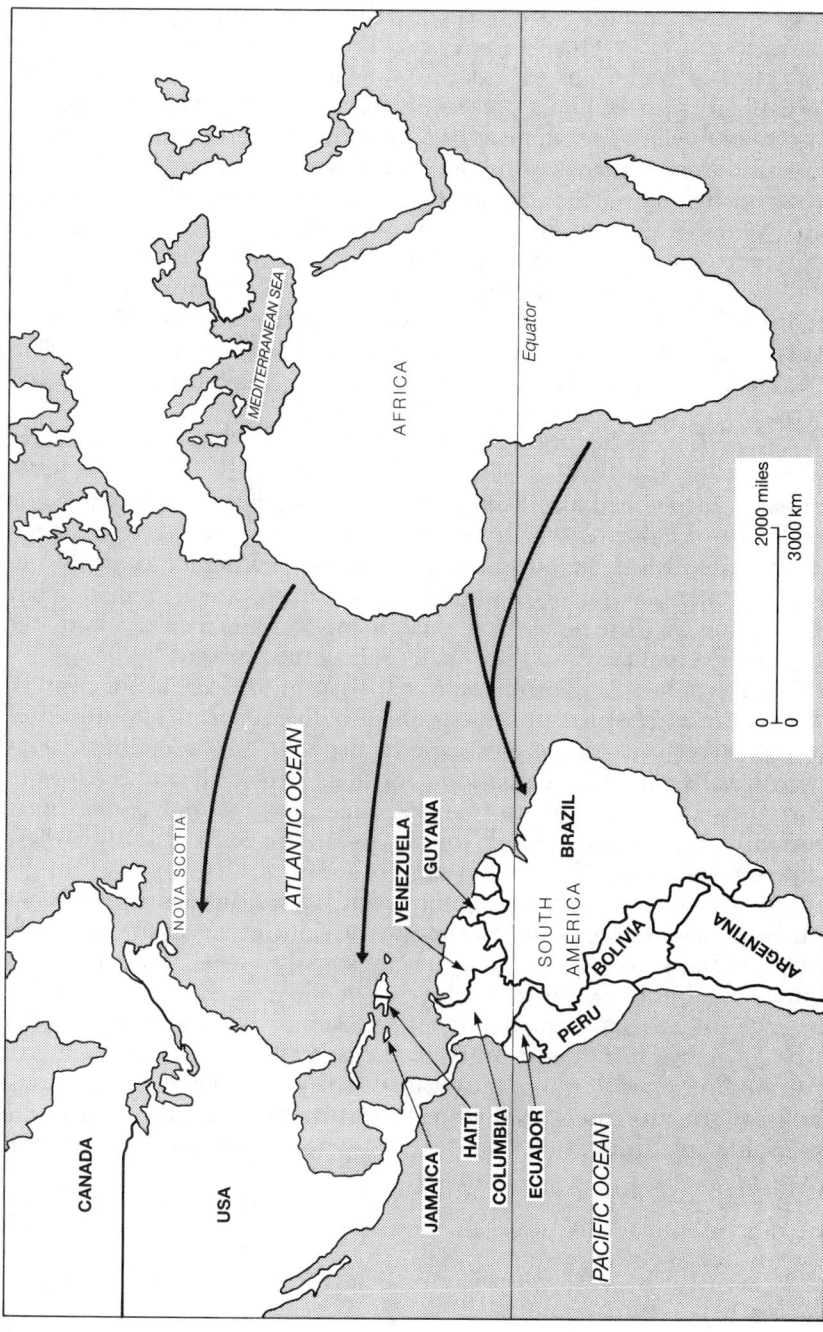

FIG. 5.1 *The Americas and Africa*
Source: adapted from map drawn by Dr Dulal C. Goswami, Geology and Geography Department, Howard University, Washington DC

suffered several serious revolts during the eighteenth century, culminating in the largest in 1823. During the 1740s black resistance led the Dutch to sign a treaty of friendship with the Coromante leader, Adoe. He and his followers had embarked on a programme of total European extermination but were confined to a small area. By mid-century another Coromante-led group made another unsuccessful bid to take over the colony. But the 1760s were especially noteworthy, marked by the Great Rebellion (1763–4) when Cuffy organized Africans and Creoles in what some observers have viewed as a prelude to the San Domingo revolt. In Mexico African slaves staged important revolts in the sixteenth and seventeenth centuries with the objective of organizing African communities, while similar efforts were pursued by Maroons in Panama, Colombia and Venezuela, by blacks in Peru and slaves in the Leeward and Windward Islands, Cuba and elsewhere.[14]

It was in Brazil that the African armed struggle reached impressive proportions for an extended period – prior to the San Domingo epoch. Small-scale revolts had long been part of Brazil's history of slavery but it was the state of Palmares which, for most of the seventeenth century, from 1605–95, established an autonomous African community estimated at 20 000 inhabitants originally Bantu from the Congo–Angola region. They sought to model their society on their homeland and resisted both the Dutch and Portuguese until they finally succumbed in 1695.[15]

These freedom struggles illustrate the nascent African nationalism in the Caribbean and Latin American segments of the diaspora. The objectives were not merely vengeance or escape to the hills but to establish areas where Africans would have political control and could defend themselves against their enemies. African religions such as *obeah* and *vodum*, were important as organizing tools. So too was Islam, especially in Bahia where it helped to solidify the Hausa and the Yoruba.[16]

Scores of major plots and conspiracies and several serious insurrections by Africans also occurred in North America during this same period.[17] Most plantations were far from any terrain suited to rebel activity, such as the mountains of Jamaica or the jungles of Guyana. But escape to live among the Indians or others was an option taken by a considerable number of slaves in some of the southern colonies, as in the flight to the Seminole Indians in Florida with whom the escaped slaves later raided neighbouring plantations. Insurrections also occurred in Virginia and Maryland in the early eighteenth century as soon as it became clear that a pattern of

14. R. Price, 1973; R. Bastide, 1971; A. D. Lara, 1978; R. Mellafe, 1964; C. F. Guillot, 1961; G. A. Beltran, 1958; M. A. Saignes, 1967; F. B. Figueroa, 1961; J. J. Uribe, 1963; F. Ortiz, 1916; E. V. Goveia, 1965; UNESCO, 1979.

15. C. Moura, 1959 and 1972; L. Luna, 1968; S. B. Schwartz, 1970 and 1977; R. K. Kent, 1965; E. D. Genovese, 1979; D. H. Porter, 1970, pp. 37–40.

16. E. Ignace, 1970.

17. H. Aptheker, 1943; E. D. Genovese, 1979.

enslaving Africans for life was replacing the indentured system, and as the Carolinas adopted extensive plantation production using slave codes developed in the Caribbean.

In 1730, conspiracies involving slaves were uncovered in the three colonies of Virginia, Carolina and Louisiana. They were led by Africans who had previously been involved in revolts in West Africa. The following year there was a mutiny aboard a slave ship lying off the shore of Rhode Island and, four years later, a group of slaves destroyed themselves and their captors aboard the slaver, *Dolphin*. The most serious revolt of this period took place in 1739 in South Carolina as Cudjoe was checkmating the British army in the mountains of Jamaica. It is recorded as Cato's Rebellion.[18]

In the northern American colonies, where there were fewer than 3000 Africans among approximately six times as many whites and where there were no plantations, there were similar troubles. In 1712 a group led by a Gold Coast African tried to burn down New York City. A similar attempt was made in Boston in 1723. In 1741, the most widely publicized episode occurred – another attempt at arson in New York City, the details of which are still in dispute. Two years before the Declaration of Independence was signed, there was another scare in Boston. It is significant that this first cycle of plots and revolts in North America tended to be led by Africans recently imported and still fighting against enslavement. By 1772 suggestions were being heard in several parts of the American colonies that all free blacks should be deported to Africa or the West Indies. Free blacks were regarded as instigators of resistance.[19] Hangings and similar brutal treatment were applied to those caught following revolutionary activities. There were certain safety valves in North America not present in the Caribbean. In the far north, for example, there was the possibility of escape. There were also European groups – particularly the Quakers – in both the north, and the south and in Canada, who spoke out against slavery and were prepared to assist escapees. Despite this, however, between 1700 and 1750, many North American Africans seem to have been influenced by the Maroon Rebellions in the Caribbean.

Between 1750 and 1775, events affecting Africans were moving towards a climax in both North America and the Caribbean. The establishment of British dominance was accompanied by the growth of the anti-slavery movement in Britain. This led, in 1772, to the famous Lord Mansfield Decision which made it illegal to hold a person a slave within the British Isles. In the American colonies a white movement developed whose objective was to sever English political power. It engendered a philosophical debate on whether or not blacks, too, should be free.

The North American colonies proclaimed their Declaration of Independence in 1776. Many of the Africans in the colonies, however, had long

18. ibid.
19. ibid.

been demanding their own freedom and it was therefore natural for the literate among them – both slaves and freemen – to join Europeans in expressions of the right to be free. Some Africans fought side by side with the whites against the British. Indeed, one, Crispus Attucks, was the first to die in the struggle against England in 1770, the prelude to the American War for Independence in which several took up arms and are recorded with their African names. Some deserted and were given their freedom by the British.[20]

In French San Domingo, where by now there was a sizeable mulatto population, a group of coloured volunteers helped the colonists fight the British at Savannah, Georgia. The struggle for freedom in North America had begun; but it was of a curious nature with Europeans in America seeking freedom from Britain while, at the same time, Africans were seeking freedom from both Britain and the American colonists and were fighting both groups.

The Africans of the American diaspora were an integral part of a world dominated by European powers where great economic and intellectual forces were reshaping political and social structures. Some had an understanding of those forces and by their very presence and actions in the midst of that European system had some influence on European decisions. They were divided, to be sure. Some were convinced that salvation lay in the assimilation of European values and goals; but others were committed to their African-ness and were prepared to risk their lives in protest and resistance against European suppression.

One means to salvation was the Sierra Leone experiment which followed Lord Mansfield's 1772 court decision that a master could not forcibly remove his slave from England. That decision, and the influx of Africans liberated because they had fought with England against the independence of the United States, resulted in a sizeable black community in London. Abolitionists thus pursued the idea of resettling liberated Africans in Africa where it was hoped that a society founded on free labour would spread Christianity, develop a western-style economy and contribute to the abolition of the slave trade. Thus, in 1787, over 400 liberated Africans were sent from England and settled in Sierra Leone. That was the first practical application of group repatriation of African ex-slaves.

Perhaps the first organized and self-financed effort by Africans to achieve that goal occurred under the leadership of Paul Cuffee in the United States. Cuffee was impressed by the potential of the Sierra Leone experiment and set himself a goal of reuniting blacks wanting to return to Africa; he also wanted to develop trade with Africa. Cuffee's ideas and efforts had little immediate effect other than the repatriation of thirty-eight Africans in 1814; however, his example was to inspire others of future generations.[21]

While Europeans in the United States were consolidating themselves

20. B. Quarles, 1961, is the best source for this subject.
21. H. N. Sherwood, 1923.

and establishing institutions as expressions of their culture and their independence, Africans, feeling disillusionment and frustration reinforced by racial pride, also established a number of institutions. They started calling themselves 'Africans' – a significant step as most had been kidnapped as children and had had little with which to cultivate and sustain as African ethnic identity. Black codes forbade them to speak African languages or practise their religions; and families were frequently divided by sale.

It is noteworthy, therefore, that in 1787 an African Methodist minister in the United States, Richard Allen, in protest against attempts to segregate him and others in a white church where they had been worshipping, broke away to form the Free African Society which had both religious and social objectives. Africans in other parts of the United States began to follow the same pattern, sometimes applying the same name to their own voluntary associations. At the same time, a Barbadian-born preacher and businessman in Boston, Prince Hall, who had been initiated as a Mason by some British soldiers during the American War of Independence, tried to secure a charter for a lodge of free black men. When the white Masons refused him, he made application to the Masons of the Scottish Right who granted the charter and authorized him to organize the African Lodge with himself as grand master. This was the first western-style fraternal organization among black men. In a sense it was a continuation of a practice enjoyed by Africans in Africa – the formation of secret societies. These activities laid the foundation for what became Afro-Americans' two strongest types of institution in the nineteenth century – lodges and religious organizations – which bound blacks together on a national scale.[22]

Another important institution came into being in 1787, founded not by blacks but whites wanting to assist blacks. It was called the Free African School of New York and was opened by the Manumission Society with forty students.

While the African label represented blacks' determination to identify themselves with the traditions and culture of their homeland, these organizations were also carriers of western values such as thrift, puritan theology, personal advancement through hard work and education, concern for the less fortunate and service to society. Such was the motivation of George Liele, for example, who founded Baptist churches in the United States and Jamaica in the late eighteenth century. Africans would later utilize those ideas in their concern for Africans elsewhere. Such pioneering innovations among American blacks would in future years help provide a basis for an evolving community identity in the United States, the Caribbean and Africa.

Most Afro-American leaders of these times were self-educated or had received only a few years of formal education. Some, however, made significant achievements: Phyllis Wheatley, who was born in Africa around 1753, became a renowned poet. Gustavus Vassa, who was born in Benin

22. See A. Hill and M. Kilson, 1969.

PLATE 5.2   *Phyllis Wheatley, an eighteenth-century servant who became a distinguished poet*

in 1745 and taken to America and later to England, was active in the anti-slavery movement and wrote the important book, *The Interesting Narrative of the Life of Oloudah Equiano, or Gustavus Vassa*, which condemned slavery. Benjamin Banneker, sometimes called 'the Ethiopian', became a noted mathematician and astronomer who prepared an almanac and served on the commission which defined and laid out Washington, DC.[23]

PLATE 5.3   *Benjamin Banneker, a free black who became a well-respected mathematician, an inventor and a planner of Washington D.C.*

Africans in Europe also contributed to the struggle for freedom and human dignity. Anton Armo studied at the Universities of Halle and Waltenberg and then returned to help his fellow Africans in the Gold

23. Banneker was referred to by contemporaries as 'fresh proof that the powers of the mind are disconnected with the colour of the skin'. See J. H. Franklin, 1967, p. 157.

Coast.[24] Likewise, Philip Quaque and Jacobis Capitein of the Gold Coast also studied in Europe and returned to work at home. Ottobah Cagoano, who was freed by the Mansfield Decision in 1772, later wrote *Thoughts and sentiments on the evil and wicked traffic of the slavery and commerce of the human species.* Ignatius Sancho's posthumously published letters confirm him too as an important spokesman for Africans abroad. In addition, a number of African emissaries were active in Europe, including representatives from Congo, Ethiopia, Guinea and the Gold Coast.[25] In Europe, as in the United States, African protestors found some white allies, such as the Paris-based Société des Amis des Noirs.

It was in the Americas, however, that the freedom struggle first reached dramatic international proportions. Throughout the Americas small groups of blacks had gained their freedom, a few had never been slaves, but they all developed their own way of life and although powerless to influence general public policy, followed with interest world developments affecting black people. As a group, both they and the black slaves were profoundly influenced by the events on the island of San Domingo (Haiti).

Just two years after the United States of America had adopted the constitution that gave moral and legal sanction to slavery, a revolution erupted in France with the slogan: Liberty! Equality! Fraternity! It shook the structure of the French settlement on San Domingo, a prosperous sugar colony where 500 000 slaves and 24 000 free persons of colour lived under the domination of some 32 000 French settlers known for their opulence and cruel treatment of their slaves. The free African population, which included several slave-owners, took the revolutionary French slogan seriously and demanded full equality with the whites. Then, in 1791, the great black masses moved under the leadership of an illiterate fieldhand, Boukman, who bound his followers with voodoo ritual and African-style secret oaths to rise against their masters. The revolutionary government in Paris dispatched an army to restore order. It was at this stage, that one of the most remarkable figures in history appeared on the scene – a literate, Christian, slave-coachman, diaspora-born with an African father – Toussaint who took the name L'Ouverture (The Opener).[26]

Toussaint called for guerrilla action to support his small army and, within five years, had defeated Napoleon's invading army – with assistance from yellow fever. He restored order and prosperity to Haiti and was proclaimed throughout the world for his military ability, administrative skills, humanity and statesmanship. His reputation spread rapidly, reaching blacks in the United States through black sailors who played an important role in disseminating information throughout the black world.

The success of the African liberation movement in Haiti created terror among whites in the United States who feared that American Africans

24. A. G. Armo, 1968.
25. W. Rodney, 1975; W. L. Hansberry, 1965.
26. C. L. R. James, 1963; P. M. Fontaine, 1970.

PLATE 5.4   *Toussaint L'Ouverture of Haiti*

might also seek their freedom through violence. More stringent legislation was passed, police security was tightened and steps were taken to restrict the movement of blacks in the country and prevent black immigration, especially from Haiti. On the other hand, Africans in the United States were inspired by the achievement of their brothers in Haiti. Haiti and Toussaint L'Ouverture thus became symbols inspiring blacks in other parts of the Americas and the Carribean to seek their freedom with the possibility that independence could be theirs.

The nineteenth century opened with a major conspiracy in the United States. Gabriel Prosser, a black preacher, organized and led over a thousand slaves in a march against Richmond, Virginia. The aim was to win freedom but word leaked out giving the governor time to call out the militia to re-establish order. Many Africans were arrested and executed including Prosser – but the link to the Haitian example and its legacy remained.

By the dawn of the nineteenth century, Africans in the Americas and Europe were on the brink of a new era. Despite the differences between the application of European and American laws pertaining to enslaved and free blacks, attitudes were basically the same. No European or American system accepted blacks as equal and really free, although there were several instances of greater flexibility in black roles. Blacks did learn to read and write, for example, even when laws forbade such; intermarriage occurred although repulsive to most; and travel – national and international – facilitated the development of networks. Africans of the diaspora knew they were pariahs abroad. Furthermore, they realized that their deprived status stemmed from their African identity and heritage. Consequently, their efforts to organize community institutions included aspirations to redeem black people and their heritage. This psychological unity prevailed and indeed became a source of strength among African peoples culminating in the Pan African movement of the nineteenth and twentieth centuries.

Africans in the diaspora, however, could not escape the influence of their physical and social environments. Their language and life-styles changed and their values and goals were modified. Their perspective of the world, themselves and others came to reflect the centuries of inculcation by Euro-American culture and the memory of their African heritage, though strong and determined, was nevertheless clouded by years of absence and miles in distance. Diaspora Africans in Europe and America thus became cultural intermediaries between indigenous Africans and Euro-Americans.

Asia

While the forced migration of Africans to Europe and the Americas is a relatively recent chapter in world history, the trade in black slaves to Asia constitutes a much older, continuous aspect of history. *The Periplus of the Erythraean Sea*, written $c. + 50$, refers to slaves taken from the Horn of Africa – and there is no reason to believe that this was the first instance of the trade.

The intermingling of peoples on both sides of the Red Sea seems to have roots in prehistoric times. But from the seventh century and the birth of Islam, a kind of cultural unity evolved throughout the Indian Ocean–Red Sea areas. Several coastal towns in East Africa became Islamized and Muslims increasingly dominated trade, including the slave trade. That it had become significant in parts of Asia is revealed by the Zandj revolts in Mesopotamia during the ninth century. Although the Zandj were exterminated, their revolts contributed to the collapse of the Abbasid Caliphate and what H. Deschamps called the 'first model of a great tropical construction project involving the labour of hundreds of Negro slaves' – constructing dams in southern Iraq. A little earlier, in the eighth century, two African slaves had been observed in the court of the Emperor of China; and in the twelfth century, some Cantonese were using African slave labour.[27] Sources also remind us of the continuity of the trade in East Africans: al-Mas'ūdī wrote about it in the eleventh century; al-Idrīsī in the twelfth century; and Ibn Baṭṭūṭa's fourteenth-century account of prosperity in Kilwa also related to the slave trade.

The northern coast of the Mediterranean Sea remains woefully under-investigated by researchers of African diaspora history. Serious research is particularly needed in Turkey and its neighbours on the major entrepôts for slaves from Tripoli and Benghazi over many centuries and the transit zone for the inland traffic. A notable example of that traffic was the purchase in Constantinople in 1696 of several African boys for Emperor Peter the Great of Russia. One was Abram Petrovich Gannibal, the great-grandfather of Aleksander Pushkin. Gannibal appears to have been born in Ethiopia where he was captured by Turks. How many other African slaves arrived in Russia and neighbouring areas via Turkey is not known but the numbers were probably small. That and the fact that in Russia slavery was abolished during the first quarter of the eighteenth century would probably explain why Africans there became servants instead of slaves.[28] Although more documentation is necessary, black slavery and its accompanying disabilities do not seem to have developed in Russia.

Most slaves imported into Asia were children, with girls constituting the largest numbers. From the East African ports, slaves were normally taken to the Arabian Red Sea port of al-Mukha (Mocha), from which many were either marched or reshipped to al-Hudaydeh (Hodeida), Djidda, Mecca and other entrepôts in Arabia. Others were reshipped to Persian Gulf ports such as al-Sharikah (Sharjah), Sur Muscar, Bandar 'Abbās, Bandar-e Lengeh, Bahrein, Būshahr (Bushire), Kuwait and Baṣra. Indian ports usually received shipments from al-Mukha or the Persian Gulf, although some allotments came directly from East Africa. The Indian ports included Bombay, Goa, Surat, Karikal, Pondicherry, Calcutta, and various places in Kutch, Gujarat, and the coast of south-east Asia and China, and on several islands in the Indian Ocean.[29]

In Arabia, Oman held the key position in the naval and commercial strategy of the Middle East and thus spearheaded Arab involvement in the slave trade. Its capital, Muscat, commanded the approach to the Persian Gulf, through which large numbers of African slaves were transported. Omani Arabs captured the East African ports of Kilwa and Zanzibar in 1784 and 1785 respectively, and from that time claimed sovereignty over several towns on that coast. After the Sultan of Oman had gained control

27. UNESCO, 1979 and 1980; C. M. Wilbur, 1967, p. 93; E. Bretschneider, 1871, pp. 13–22. For an up-to-date discussion of the African diaspora in Arabia and Asia before our period, see UNESCO, *General History of Africa*, Vol. III, ch. 26.

28. Pushkin memorialized his African heritage in one of his poems. See D. Magarshack, 1969, pp. 12–17; A. Perry, 1923; B. Modzalevskii, 1907; N. Malevanov, 1974; B. Kozlov, 1970; A. Blakeley, 1976.

29. J. E. Harris, 1977, pp. 264–8.

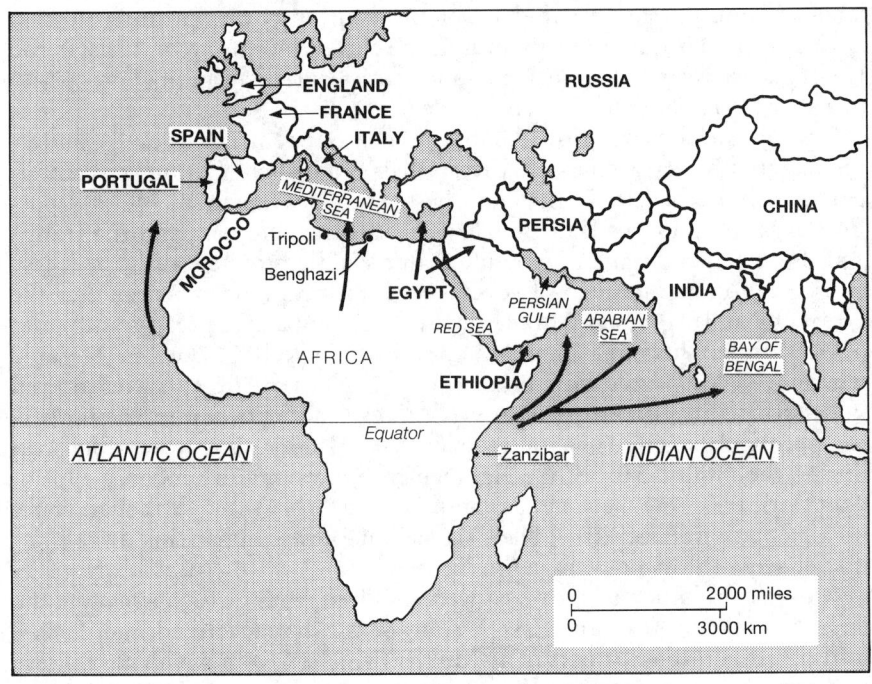

FIG. 5.2 *Africa, Europe and Asia*
Source: adapted from map drawn by Dr Dulal C. Goswami, Geology and Geography Department, Howard University, Washington DC

of Zanzibar and parts of the East African coast in the late eighteenth century, demand increased for slaves to harvest Arab-owned clove and coconut plantations in the region.[30]

There had been people of black African origin in Yemen and Ḥadramaut since ancient times. Most seem to have come from Ethiopia and in Aden they appear to have been seen as a caste of 'untouchables'. In several other areas of southern Arabia black slaves from Africa served in armies of local sultans, as concubines and domestic servants, eunuchs, crewmen and dock workers, administrators and agricultural labourers in salt marches and sugar and date plantations.[31]

Africans were settled on many Indian Ocean islands. The Dutch collected slaves in East Africa and Madagascar and took them to Indonesia; the French and the British settled East Africans as slaves on the Mascarene Islands of Bourbon (Réunion) and Mauritius. Indeed, one observer records that from 1670 to 1810 about 160 000 slaves were imported into the Mascarenes from Madagascar, the East African coast, West Africa and

30. See ch. 25 for details.
31. R. B. Serjeant, 1967, pp. 67 and 287; J. E. Harris, 1971, pp. 39–41.

India. Bourbon's slave population was estimated in 1808 at 53 726, mostly from Madagascar and Mozambique.[32] The African settlements of the Mascarene Islands were enlarged with the expansion of the slave trade in the nineteenth century. But even before then, there had emerged a community of Creoles whose influence would be exerted in the nineteenth and twentieth centuries. It has also been observed that some Africans reached the Malay states with merchants and with Muslim pilgrims returning from Mecca.[33]

There were far more African slaves in South Asia than other parts of Asia.[34] This may have resulted from its longer and more profitable trade with Africa due to strong Muslim control over the prosperous western coast of India and the settlement of Indians in East Africa. In any case, African slaves are prominent in India at least by the thirteenth century. Queen Raziya, sovereign of the Delhi Sultanate, for example, became attracted to a *Ḥabshī*[35] (African) slave named Djalalud-ud-dīn Yāḳūt whom she appointed as royal stable-master. Another African, Mālik Sarvar, was a slave of Sultan Muḥammad in Delhi and became deputy sultan in 1389.[36]

The second half of the fifteenth century witnessed the assertion of an African presence in another part of northern India, Bengal. Africans had migrated there from the coastal region of Calcutta, the area of Dacca, and several inland regions. The ruler of Bengal, Rukn-ud-dīn-Barbak (1459–74), used to promote loyal Africans to responsible military and administrative posts. There were thus several Africans of high rank among the king's estimated 8000 African slave-soldiers.

When Barbak died, a period of instability ensued. In 1486 Shāhzāda, eunuch commander of the palace guards, led a group of Africans in a successful coup and assumed the title of Barbak Shah. He was, however, subsequently murdered by another African, Amir-ul-Imona Malih Andil (Indīl Khān), loyal to the former Indian ruler. Indīl Khān became Saif-ud-dīn-Firuz and ruled for three years. When he died, he was succeeded by Nasr-ud-dīn Muḥammad, a minor whose identity remains unclear; but his regent, Ḥabesh Khān, was an African. Then in 1490 an African guardsman, Sīdī Badr, seized the throne as Hams-ud-dīn Abū Nasr Muzaffar Shah with an army of 30 000 including a reported 5000 Ethiopians. When he died in 1493, Africans were removed from their posts and

32. UNESCO, 1979.

33. R. Maxwell, 1932. This is another area demanding serious research.

34. The vast area of today's South Asia was not unified at this time and thus contained scores of different ethnic and political entities. The largest country to emerge, and which included most of the regions discussed in this section, was India, which is the term adopted here.

35. *Ḥabshī* and *Siddi* are terms used interchangeably to denote Africans in Asia. For a general history of this subject, see: J. E. Harris, 1971.

36. R. C. Majumdar, 1951, pp. 186–7, 188 and 698–702; and *The Cambridge History of India*, 1937, Vol. III, pp. 251–2.

expelled from the kingdom; but they left their mark during that short period of dominance.[37]

In Gujarat Africans served in armies from at least the thirteenth century, by which time they had become an important political and economic factor. In 1576 the government of Gujarat is reported to have paid a tribute of 400 slaves who were 'children of Hindu chiefs and Abyssinians'.[38] Some were descended from slaves captured during the Muslim Arab invasion of Ethiopia in 1527. Others were brought to Gujarat in 1531 by Mustafa bin Bahrām, a Turkish commander who helped Muslim Indians defend themselves against Portugal.[39] In 1537 Aḥmadābād is reported to have had as many as 5000 Africans in government service.[40] These early Africans seem to have formed a nucleus from which Africans migrated to other parts of the region.[41]

Several Africans distinguished themselves in Gujarat during the sixteenth century. Yākūt Sabit Khān Ḥabshī (Ulūgh Khān), Khayrāt Khān and Jhujhar Khān became important military commanders; while Ikhtiyar-ul-Mulk organized a force of some 20 000, including Afghans, Rajputs, Gujaratis and Africans, to challenge the troops of the Mughul Emperor Akbar. Although he was defeated, Ikhtiyar won the respect of Akbar and Gujaratis alike. One former African slave, Shaykh Sayyid al-Ḥabsh Sultani, served as a soldier in Jhujhar Khān's army. When he retired, he purchased some land, made the pilgrimage to Mecca and opened his lands to feed hundreds of poor people daily. He also established a library which attracted many scholars.[42]

In 1573 Sayyid (Saʿīd) constructed a mosque in Aḥmadābād and the chronogram for its construction reads: 'For the sake of Allāh he erected this mosque, and the builder Saʿīd.' The Sīdī Saʿīd mosque, as it is known is of simple design with a roof of arches and beautiful arched perforated windows with exquisite tracery and floral patterns. A renowned authority on Indian and Eastern architecture, James Fergusson, has observed of this mosque:

> It would be difficult to excel the skill with which the vegetable form are conventionalized just to the extent required for the purpose .. but perhaps the greatest skill is shown in the even manner in which the pattern is spread over the whole surface. There are some exquisite specimens of tracery in precious marbles at Agra and Delhi, but none quite equal to this.[43]

37. ibid., pp. 214 and 215.
38. K. K. Basu, 1932.
39. M. S. Commissariat, 1957, Vol. II, p. 470.
40. Ḥadjdjī al-Dabir, n.d., pp. 407 and 447.
41. For notes and paintings of Kutch personalities, including Africans, see B. N. Goswamy and A. L. Ballapeceola, 1978.
42. ibid., pp. 471, 508–24, 441–3 and 448; E. D. Ross, 1921, Vol. II, pp. 640–3.
43. J. Fergusson, 1876.

Fergusson and a colleague wrote:

> It is probably more like a work of nature than any other architectural detail that has been designed, even by the best architects of Greece of the Middle Ages.[44]

M.S. Commissariat wrote:

> This lovely and world-famous mosque is the last noble specimen of the great creative period of the Muslim architecture of Gujarat.[45]

Another African, Sīdī Bashīr, built a noted mosque in Aḥmadābād. It is unique in that it has two shaking minarets, each comprising three stories. When one minaret is shaken, the vibration is carried to the other. This style is reported to have been an innovation at the time.

Not far from Gujarat is Janjira Island which, in ancient times, was part of the prosperous commercial activity of northwestern India, including what are today Bombay and the Konkan coast. According to one tradition, the *Siddi*s of Janjira descended from Africans who arrived from Gujarat in 1489 when an Ethiopian in the service of the *niẓām* (king) of Aḥmadnagār disguised himself as a merchant and took 300 boxes of merchandise to the island. The merchandise included *Siddi* soldiers who, on command, took possession of the island, appointed one of their number king and thus laid the foundation for the dynasties of the *Siddi nawab*s (kings). Most of the Africans on Janjira, however, can probably be traced to the East African slave trade.[46]

From about the 1530s the Portuguese developed political and economic control over parts of the west coast of India, especially the Konkan coast where many African slaves were imported. The number of slaves imported at any one time was small – between six and ten – but their arrival was fairly continuous to about 1740, when Portuguese maritime dominance was seriously challenged by the French and the British. Most slaves were from Mozambique, although the Portuguese also seized African slaves when they defeated the Muscat Arabs in Diu in 1670. The slaves were generally used by the Portuguese in businesses, on farms, as domestics or in other menial jobs. Some were trained as priests and teachers for religious schools, especially in Goa which became Portugal's headquarters for its East African and Asian colonies.

During that time, Janjira retained its autonomy and, by the seventeenth century, the *Siddi*s had become the island's principal land-owners and comprised its largest Muslim group. A council of elders of the major *Siddi* leaders chose a *nawab* who acted as head of state and religion. With the advice of the council he could appoint and dismiss state and religious officials. From this political base the Janjira *Siddi*s expanded their power

44. J. Fergusson and T. Hope, 1866, pp. 86–7.
45. M. S. Commissariat, 1957, p. 505.
46. J. E. Harris, 1971, pp. 80–7, discusses Janjira's history.

over the island and along stretches of the Indian coast. They dominated the north-western coast as seamen and, in 1616, became an important ally of Mālik Ambar, a *Ḥabshī* king in the central part of India known as the Deccan. Both forces fought the Mughuls for many years. Some indication of the significance of the Janjira *Siddi*s' role is reflected in the assessment of the Indian scholar, K. M. Panikkar, who stated that their naval activities caused the Mughuls to develop an Indian fleet. The Indian military historian, Sir Jadunath Sarkar, has written that the 'Abyssinians of Janjira' were a mighty power.[47]

Because of the control the *Siddi*s wielded over the Konkan coast of India, the British East India Company made repeated efforts to enlist them as allies during the seventeenth century. The *Siddi*s continued to exercise independent power in the area, however, and later also negotiated with the Dutch. It was not until 1759 that the British were able to curb *Siddi* power, and Janjira did not become subject to direct British control until the nineteenth century.

The Janjira *Siddi*s exercised considerable influence on Indian history. How they were able to wield such power over the indigenous groups is not entirely clear, but without doubt their Muslim religion and their maritime and military skills were major factors. It is of great importance that this small group of African migrants had such an impact on the policies and actions of Great Britain, Portugal and the Netherlands, as well as on local Indian states.

Africans also settled along parts of the Malabar coast. Black Jews of Cochin and Kerala in southern India, who were descendants of African slaves, settled along the Malabar coast during the seventeenth and eighteenth centuries. Most became menial labourers and intermarried with local inhabitants and other Jews.[48] The Portuguese were responsible for settling African slaves along parts of the Malabar coast, especially around Goa which became one of its headquarters in the sixteenth century. Black slaves were used as soldiers in Goa and Ceylon and also in Macao in the sixteenth and seventeenth centuries.[49]

The Italian scholar and traveller, Pietro della Valle, reported that blacks from West and East Africa (Guineans and Mozambicans) were part of the shipments to the Portuguese territories.[50] In Portuguese India, black slaves performed several menial tasks throughout the territory, including the carrying of water in huge jugs. The slaves also served as bearers and escorts for the Portuguese and African women were frequently kept as mistresses.

Another part of India, the Deccan, witnessed the most dramatic assertion of power by a single African, Mālik Ambar, an Ethiopian who was sold as a slave in Ethiopia, the Hidjāz, al-Mukhā and Baghdad before finally

47. K. M. Panikkar, 1945, p. 8; J. Sarkar, 1919, Vol. IV, pp. 237–8.
48. A. M. Pescatello, 1972.
49. C. R. Boxer, 1969.
50. E. Grey, 1892, pp. 50–1.

PLATE 5.5   *Mālik Ambar, an African king in India in the seventeenth century*

reaching India. Ambar spent much of his life in Aḥmadnagār where there were thousands of Africans; Ambar himself recruited 1000 for his guard.

Ambar's greatness stems from the fact that he became a commander of a large army for the king of Aḥmadnagār and resisted several Mughul attacks, thereby preventing the Mughul emperors from conquering the Deccan during his lifetime. He ruled supreme in the area around Aḥmad-nagār for nearly a quarter of a century (1602–26). During that time he founded towns, constructed canals and irrigation schemes, stimulated trade with Asians and Europeans, attracted scholars and poets to his court and fostered the construction of some of the most impressive buildings in the Deccan.[51]

Mālik Ambar's activities confirm two significant points: first, that individual Africans played influential roles in Indian history; and second, that Africans managed to win support and respect from diverse Indians while retaining a sense of their own identity.

Conclusion

The history of African people has been so much influenced by perceptions stemming from the intercontinental slave trade that it is necessary to emphasize that Africans of their own volition migrated between continents as merchants, clerics, seamen, adventurers and so on. This early free black presence abroad is greatly in need of study to provide a more complete and realistic account of world civilization.

It was, however, the intercontinental slave trade which, more than anything else, established a world black presence.[52] It was the nature of this trade and its consequences which, especially in the Americas and the Caribbean, caused Africans to organize freedom struggles which over the years established the common concern for the redemption of Africa and the liberation of blacks throughout the world. This process began during the early modern era and by 1800 showed real signs of an international base when Haiti's Toussaint L'Ouverture emerged as an international symbol of black freedom. This process continued, despite colonial rule, and may indeed be the greatest historical consequence of the African diaspora.

51. J. E. Harris, 1971, pp. 91–8.
52. See ch. 4 above.

The Ottoman conquest of Egypt

R. VESELY

The history of much of sixteenth-century Africa and Arabia was dominated by the Ottoman empire, a new Islamic power that had formed in Asia Minor and the Balkan peninsula and which, during the 1500s, went on to subjugate a large part of the Arab countries in West Asia and North Africa.

It was in 1516 that the state of the Mamluk sultans in Syria and Egypt collapsed under the attack by the Ottoman army. Ottoman–Egyptian relations had been strained since the 1480s. But in 1514, when Sultan Selim I led his first successful campaign against Persia, the fast-expanding power on his eastern frontier, the Egyptian rulers finally decided to take a firm stand against the Ottoman threat. Selim responded with force. Two years later, during his second Persian campaign, he determined to break the Mamluk–Safawid (the Syrian dynasty) coalition once and for all.

On 24 August 1516, the Ottoman army routed the Mamluk troops at the battle of Mardj Dabiḳ plain north of Habab. The Ottoman victory was largely due to its army's technical superiority but it was also greatly helped by the defection to the Ottomans of the vice-regent of Habab, Amīr Khāyr Bey, and his troops at the critical moment. The victory behind him, Selim went on to occupy Damascus without encountering much resistance and then to take all Syria and Palestine south to the Sinai Desert making Syria a buffer state between the Ottoman empire's eastern frontier and Egypt.[1]

The new leaders in Egypt, however, seemed intent on regaining their lost Syrian territory and Selim was finally persuaded, both by his own advisors and the Mamluk amīrs who had defected to his side at Habab, to crown his campaign with the conquest of Egypt. He continued his march south meeting little resistance on the way to Cairo where he routed the Mamluk troops led by Tūmān Bey, the last of the Mamluk sultans, in a short battle at Raydāniyya on 23 January 1517 which brought the Mamluk sultanate to an end.

Military superiority was not the only reason for the Ottoman victory over the Mamluks, although the most obvious one. The main reason was the difference politically and economically between the two states. In Europe and Asia Minor the Ottomans dominated territories that were economically advanced. They had mines and raw materials, their pro-

1. Aḥmad b. al-Ḥādjdj Abū 'l-ʿAlī, 1962, pp. 143ff.

duction being concentrated in a number of centres connected by international trade which offered opportunities for the further growth of the empire. The Mamluk states, on the other hand, had almost no mineral resources and depended almost exclusively on agriculture and international transit trade, profits from which had rapidly declined particularly since its main branch – the trade in eastern spices – had been seized by the Portuguese. The importation of precious metals from other African countries was also declining. The Mamluks had been trying to solve these problems for many years by drawing on internal economic reserves, confiscating land and increasing taxes, all of which had intensified the local inhabitants' hatred of the foreign Mamluk exploiters and had fostered their hopes for the collapse of the regime.

Selim's victory at Mardj Dabiḳ in 1516 had far-reaching consequences for both West Asia and North Africa. It sealed the fate of the Egyptian Mamluk sultanate; it saved Persia from another Ottoman invasion; and it saved Syria from impending destruction by providing a period of stability during which to consolidate its strength – thus in time becoming, ironically, a permanent threat to the Ottomans. The conquest of Egypt also altered Ottoman policy which was now directed at controlling the Mediterranean Sea routes and led the empire to attempt the conquest of other North African Arab countries.

The newly conquered former Mamluk territory included regions of great economic, political and strategic importance. Egypt was particularly important because of its intensive agriculture, its large population and its Red Sea coastline which imposed upon its new rulers the task of continuing the fight for supremacy in the Indian Ocean against the Portuguese. In addition, the prestige of the Ottoman sultans was enhanced by the fact that – like the Mamluk sultans before them – they became guardians of the two sacred cities of Islam, Mecca and Medina, and also of the pilgrim routes from Asia and Africa.

Before leaving Egypt in September 1517, Selim placed Khāyr Bey, the Mamluk defector, at the head of the Egyptian province which was to be kept as one administrative unit. Khāyr Bey's rule saw the transition to full Ottoman control in the newly gained territory. He was entrusted with the management of all former Mamluk Egypt, although the extent to which he could enforce his power was limited. He governed more as a sultan's vassal than a provincial administrator, even though his commission was formally renewed so that he held office until his death in 1522. He retained his Mamluk title *Mālik al-umarā* (King of Commanders) and conducted his court according to Mamluk ceremonial. He surrounded himself with former Mamluk dignitaries willing to serve the new regime entrusting them not only with important tasks in the field of financial administration but also with political and military assignments. In addition, the old forms of administration were left untouched and the administrative personnel kept almost unchanged. The organization of justice continued to be based on

PLATE 6.1   *Sultan Selim I, conqueror of Egypt*

the system of four Supreme Judges, one for each School of Law.

Selim left Khāyr Bey to control the province's income at his own discretion. The regular presents sent by Khāyr Bey to Istanbul, the Ottoman seat of power, were not so much obligatory deliveries to the state treasury as gifts paid from his own resources and expressing his personal indebtedness to the sultan.

Khāyr Bey worked hard to control the resources of the new province. To do so – and also to curb the power of the Mamluk dignitaries – he abolished the *iḳṭāʿ* (extant feudatory tenures) and incorporated them into the state property, their former holders being alloted fixed salaries to be paid from the provincial treasury. He also revised endowment properties. These measures made it possible to draw up more accurate and detailed land registers and enabled him to fulfil his commitment to supply the two sacred cities, Mecca and Medina, with corn.

Khāyr Bey's powers, however, were not unlimited. Selim had left strong troops in Egypt to further consolidate Ottoman control and, if necessary, thwart any attempt by the Mamluks to re-seize power. They comprised infantry detachments (one of Janissaries and one of Azabs) and two cavalry detachments (the Tüfenkdjis and the Gönüllüs). To the Janissaries was allocated the most important task of guarding the Cairo Citadel, the administrative centre and seat of the provincial governor and the treasury. The Azabs were to guard all roads to Cairo, forming garrisons for the small fortresses built to protect agricultural areas from raiding nomads. The two cavalry detachments were used to slowly entrench Khāyr Bey's rule throughout the province. The units, however, were badly disciplined and in order to retain control of them Khāyr Bey formed cavalry detachments of his own, recruited from among former as well as new Mamluks.

When Khāyr Bey died in 1522 the process of incorporating Cairo – the centre of a state which had been independent for centuries before it became an Ottoman province – was well under way and everything augured well for the imminent completion of the exercise.

The Ottoman administration and conflicts within the ruling class

The beginning of the new period – which began with Khāyr Bey's death – was marked by revolts against Ottoman supremacy. The first revolt – a timid attempt at insurrection against the first vice-regent by two Mamluk regional administrators at the beginning of the period – was quickly suppressed. The second revolt in 1524, however, was far more serious being instigated by the new vice-regent himself, Aḥmad Pasha, who declared himself Sultan of Egypt and started minting his own coins. With the help of some Arab groups he succeeded in capturing Cairo but was ultimately ejected from the city after having been betrayed by the Beduin chiefs who had at first supported him.[2]

These events, however, made clear to the Istanbul government the need to define more precisely Egypt's position within the Ottoman empire. They did so by issuing a decree called the *Ḳānūn Nāme* which sought to regulate the political, military, civil and economic life of Egypt. The decree, in effect, introduced the Ottoman system of administration into Egypt. According to this system the ruler of Egypt, the *wālī* (vice-regent), who had always held the rank of *pasha*, was accorded certain privileges not enjoyed by the vice-regents of other provinces and reminiscent of the customs at the Istanbul court. As his seat he was given the Cairo Citadel, the seat of the former sultans. Four times a week he was to convene a meeting of the *Dīwān* (executive council) which consisted of military commanders, financial and court administrators, port commanders and other dignitaries. The vice-

---

2. The revolt of Aḥmad Pasha is usually connected with Safawid anti-Ottoman plans which also included subversive activities in Egypt.

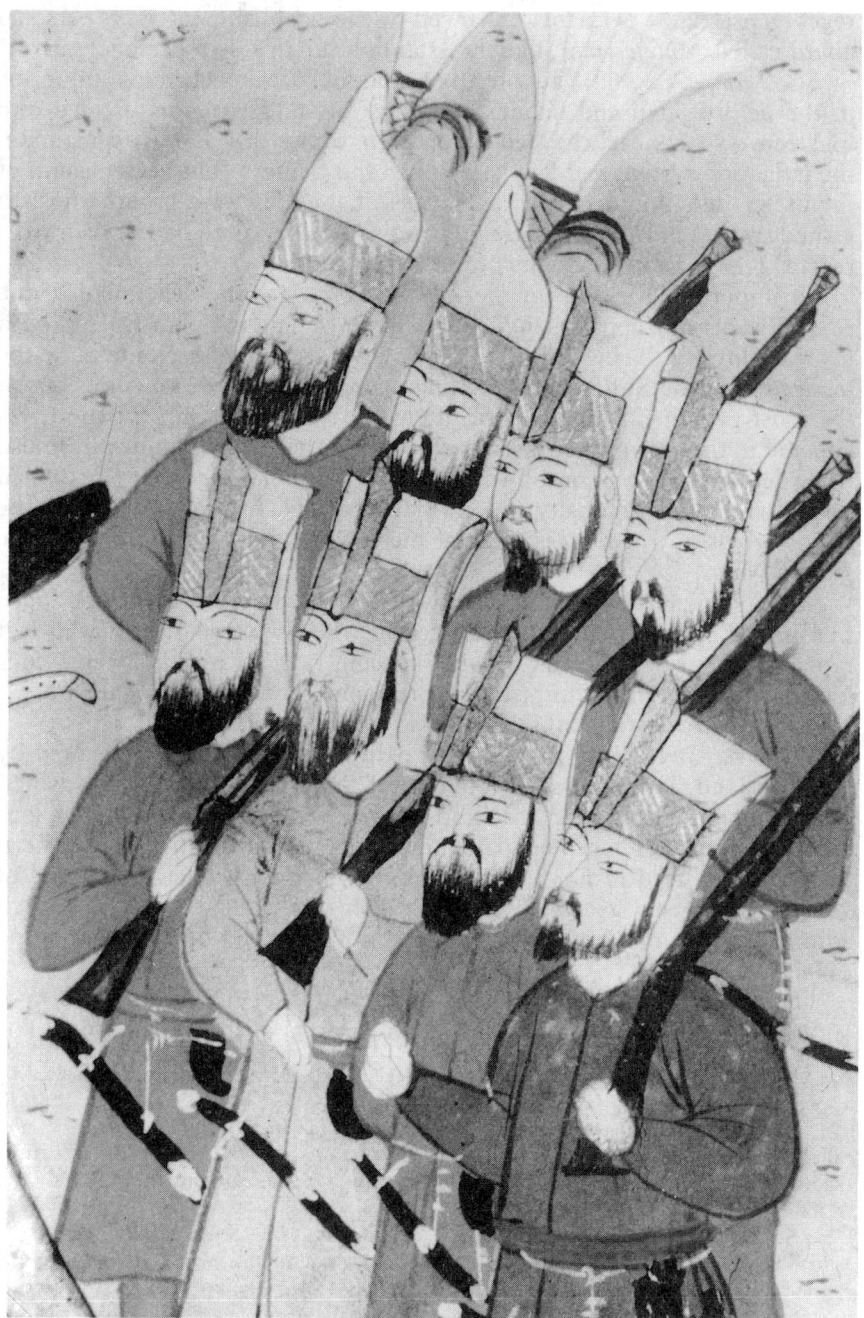

PLATE 6.2   *The Janissaries, as portrayed in a sixteenth-century Turkish miniature*

regent's prestige was further enhanced by the establishment of his personal guard called *Müteferriḳas*, like the Istanbul Sultan's own personal guard.[3]

The *Ḳānūn Nāme* also adopted a number of Mamluk customs and forms in the field of civil and financial administration. Egypt was divided into fourteen districts each headed by a *kāshif* whose task it was to maintain the irrigation system and levy taxes from the farmers. The region south of Asyūṭ was left under the Arab *shaykh*s of the Hawwāra group who had gained control of the area after 1517 and were recognized by the then vice-regent, Khāyr Bey, as regents of the Upper Nile.

An important function of the *Ḳānūn Nāme* was the enactment of the *odjaḳ*s (imperial troops) introduced to Egypt by Sultan Selim I.[4] In reward for their loyalty during Aḥmad Pasha's revolt, the Janissaries became the main prop of the Sultan's power. Their commander, the *Agha*, was one of the most prominent members of the executive council and the mint was situated in the area of their barracks in the citadel. The Mamluks were also rewarded by the creation of a new *odjaḳ* of *umerā-i-sherākise* (Circassian *amīr*s) which was gradually added to by Mamluks from Cairo as were the *Müteferriḳas* and *Ghaushe*s (central messengers), also established by the *Ḳānūn Nāme*.

All the soldiers based in Egypt drew regular payments from the provincial treasury. The top men – the vice-regent, the Supreme Judge (who had replaced the previous team of four Supreme Judges) and the twenty-four highest military and administrative personnel known as *Sandjaḳ Bey*s – were paid *sāliyāne* (annual salaries) also from the treasury.

These payments and salaries were paid from the income generated by taxes on land, industrial and commercial undertakings in the towns and cities, customs duties and the head tax paid by worshippers of religions other than Islam. These were paid under a new administrative and financial system introduced in Egypt according to which each village or group of villages comprised a *muḳataʿāt* and which was both a financial and an administrative unit. Each *muḳataʿāt* was administered by a civilian called *emīn*.[5]

The whole tax system was based on the feudal rent paid in the form of land tax[6] which was levied by the administrators of individual areas. The

3. In addition the reception of a new vice-regent by local dignitaries was regulated by a special ceremonial.

4. The Ottoman troops were composed of six *odjaḳ*s, to which Sulaymān added a seventh called the *Odjaḳ* of Çerkes (Circassian). The *odjaḳ*s were: the *Müteferriḳa*, the *Çavushān*, the *Gönüllüyān*, the *Tüfenkçiyān*, the *ʿAzabān*, the *Mustahfizān* and the *Çerākise*. See A. K. Rafiḳ, 1963, pp. 144–6.

5. S. J. Shaw, 1962a, p. 31.

6. The exact yield of the land tax was not known when the *Ḳānūn Nāme* was enacted as the cadastral survey was not completed until 1576. Due to the prevailing law and order in sixteenth-century Egypt, the countryside prospered and the amount of arable land was increased by cultivating new fields or recultivating old. It was not until the 1608 land register, that a complete inventory of agricultural land became available.

taxes on town-dwellers were levied by *kāshif*s, or *emīn* (tax collectors), who drew fixed annual salaries irrespective of the amounts collected. The Arab *shaykh*s in the region south of Asyūṭ were, in accordance with the *iltizam* system, assigned their respective areas from which, as *multazim*s,[7] they could levy taxes and retain them provided they guaranteed the agricultural work and paid a fixed part of their takings to the provincial treasury in return for their leased privileges.

From 1525 the income remaining after covering all expenses had been sent each year to Istanbul instead of Ḥidjāz. The regular dispatch of this *hazne* or *hazine* (treasury) was one of the vice-regent's most important tasks. During the sixteenth century it was sent regularly, its total several times exceeding the agreed sum of 400 000 guldens.[8] A separate sum was also set aside for the purchase of agricultural produce for the Sultan's kitchen. Egypt also fulfilled its obligations towards Mecca and Medina.[9]

The *Kānūn Nāme* also made it legal to take dues from individual holdings which were regarded as *iltizam*s. At first this new ruling applied to agricultural holdings, but it spread to other holdings during the sixteenth century as the *odjak*s and their officers grew more powerful and the power of the representatives of Ottoman rule decreased. Officers, and even regular soldiers, gradually took over all positions of control within the holdings while the tax collectors were slowly reduced to mere officials with no influence on taxation or any other aspect of fiscal policy.

This process reflected the changing political relations within the ruling class. Towards the end of the sixteenth century two levels of political power crystallized in the country. One consisted of official executors of political power appointed by Istanbul and headed by the vice-regent. The other consisted of the *odjak*s and their officers, and the *Sandjak Bey*s with their Mamluk retinues. Although unofficial, this group had at its disposal both military and economic power and, from the late 1500s onwards, its significance in Egypt's political life became more and more apparent.

---

7. According to the *iltizam* system, which superseded the *mukata'āt* system by about 1658, lands of every village or group of villages were offered for public auction and the highest bidders (the *multazim*s) were given the right to collect taxes from the peasants and such lands became their *iltizam*.

8. Corresponding to 16 million silver paras.

9. The endowments established for Mecca and Medina by the Mamluk sultans were broadly recognized and, in addition, the Ottoman sultans founded new ones. Egypt was sending not only considerable cash sums to Ḥidjāz but also natural produce and maize in particular. In addition, it was supplying a cover for the *Ka'ba* from the special endowments account.

PLATE 6.3 *Porcelain façade of the burial chamber of Ibrāhīm. Agha of the Janissaries c. 1062/1652, in the mosque of Akṣunḳur (747/1346–748/1347)*

Ottoman influence in North-east Africa

Throughout the sixteenth century Egypt played an important role in the expansionist foreign policy of the Ottoman empire. Because of its geographical position it formed a natural link between the Mediterranean Sea and the Indian Ocean, with the trade route bringing eastern goods to Europe passing through the Red Sea and Egypt itself.[10] At the time of Selim's conquest of Egypt, in 1517, Eastern trade was in Portuguese hands. After subjugating Egypt, therefore, the Ottomans faced the task of removing the Portuguese from the Indian Ocean or at least hindering their penetration of the Red Sea.

A welcome opportunity to intervene in the Indian Ocean was provided by the ruler of Gujarat in his entreaty to Sultan Sulaymān for help against the Portuguese who had occupied the port of Diu. Sulaymān Pasha, the Egyptian vice-regent, was entrusted with the campaign. On his way to Diu in 1538, he seized Aden, in Yemen, and established Ottoman administration there. Although his attempt at driving the Portuguese out of Diu failed, he disembarked on his return journey at the port of Ḳuṣayr in Upper Egypt and, after reaching Aswān, continued his march south along the River Nile to North Nubia, where he pushed the Arab groups out of the river valley area, finally reaching Wādī Halfa. On the island of Sāy he built a fortress which was to become the southernmost point of Ottoman Egypt.

It was difficult to secure Upper Egypt, dominated as it was by the Hawwāra *shaykh*s and, in the middle of the century, Ottoman supremacy there had to be re-established through an expedition, led by the former vice-regent of Yemen, Özdemir Pasha, who re-occupied Ibrīm, Aswān and Sāy, garrisoning them with Bosnian troops. A new province called Berberistan was established headed by a *kāshif* directly subordinate to the Cairo vice-regent.

In 1557, Özdemir Pasha took Massāwa on the Red Sea coast as well as Zaylaʾ (Zeila, Zalha), the town opposite Aden, and also conquered part of the interior ruled by the Ethiopian king. Massāwa became the centre of Ḥabesh, a new Ottoman province in Africa which played an important role in the Ottoman defence of the Red Sea against the Portuguese and also in securing trade with Yemen and the East African coast further south. As the Portuguese had succeeded in excluding both Arabs and Ottomans from the Indian Ocean trade, the creation of these Red Sea posts was of great importance to the continuation of the transit trade which, under the pressure of international developments, was changing from eastern spices to coffee beans. Because of the new popularity of coffee the Egyptian transit trade, far from declining, continued to bring considerable revenues to the country's coffers.

10. In the 1560s, the digging of a canal across the Isthmus of Suez was under consideration, having been suggested by the Grand Vizir Meḥmed Pasha Soḳollu. Later, however, this suggestion was forgotten.

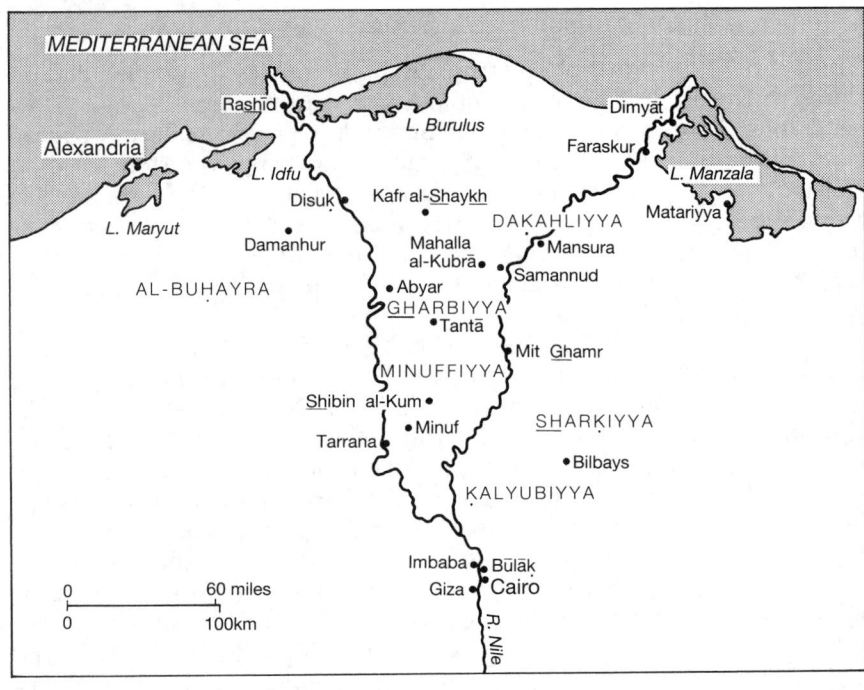

FIG. 6.1   *Lower Egypt (al-Delta)*
Source: adapted from 'Abd al-Rahim 'Abd al-Rahman and Wataru Miki, *Village in Ottoman Egypt and Tokugawa Japan – A Comparative Study*, Institute for the Study of Languages and Cultures of Asia and Africa, Tokyo, p. (ii) – (Maps published by kind permission of Professor Wataru Miki, Keio University, Tokyo)

The creation of the provinces of Egypt and Ḥabesh was the culmination of Ottoman influence in North-east Africa. From 1517 to the 1580s Ottoman power in Egypt was at its zenith. No symptoms of Istanbul's decline had yet appeared: on the contrary its power was even further consolidated. In 1575, for example, areas south of the southern town of Girgā were united into one administrative unit and in 1583 the Province of Upper Egypt was created, the Hawwāra chiefs being replaced as administrators by an official from Cairo.

Traditionally, Upper Egypt had occupied a distinctive place within the political organization of the Nile valley states. It was different from the rest of Egypt in its politics, its social systems, its peoples, its religions and its geography. Being so distinguished it had often been the refuge of movements directed against authority.[11] Its political importance had been enhanced by its economic importance which was based, among other things, on its control of the trade routes and the traffic on the Nile. The

11. The Upper Egypt sub-province was also very large and, during the 1600s, even increased in size. Arab *kabīlas* were ejected from the Bahnasā area in 1640, from the region of Asyūṭ and Aftīh in 1694, and from the vicinity of Aswān, Manfalūt and Minya in 1698.

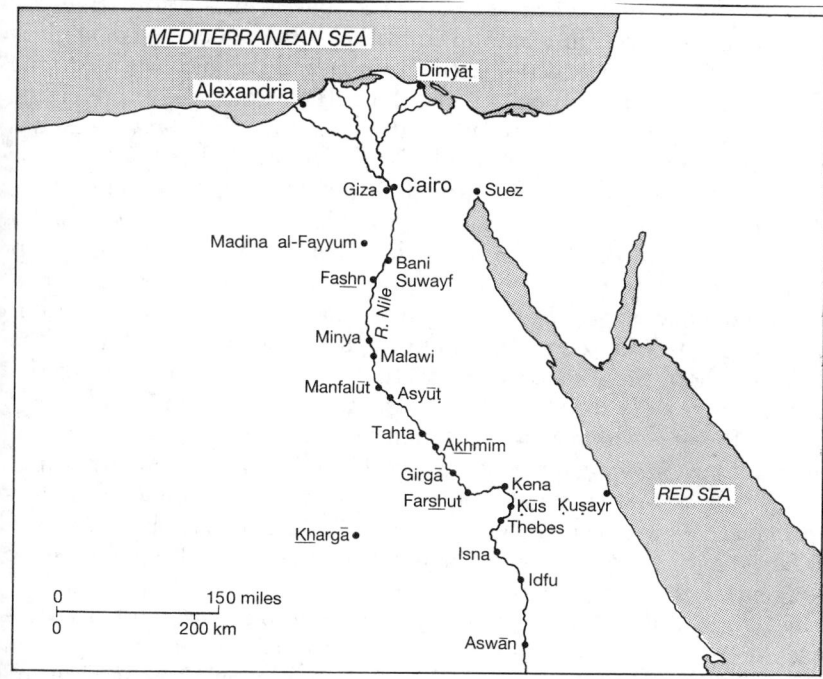

FIG. 6.2 *Middle and Upper Egypt (al-Saïd)*
Source: see Fig. 6.1

Ottomans showed their interest and respect for this vital territory by accrediting it a special position within the Egyptian province.

Like the administrator of all Egypt, the administrator of Upper Egypt bore the title of *walī* (vice-regent) and stood second in the administrative hierarchy to the provincial administrator himself. The office was held exclusively by an official with the rank of *Sandjak Bey* and the vast financial and administrative machinery under his control was organized according to the system used in Lower Egypt. His political importance and his loyalty were also emphasized by the considerable number of troops at his disposal.

Internal military conflicts

The period of internal peace started by the suppression of Aḥmad Pasha's revolt in 1524 lasted about sixty years. In the 1580s, as a result of its dependence on the general socio-economic well-being of the Ottoman empire, Egypt began to experience the first symptoms of economic difficulties. These soon sparked fierce conflicts between the various components of the ruling military stratum.

Between 1598 and 1609 a few revolts broke out, spearheaded by the economically weak *spahi* cavalry corps who had been most badly hit by the recent soaring inflation. Their revolts served to weaken the position of the vice-regents who were only able to fulfil their obligations to Istanbul by exploiting the rivalry between the *spahi* cavalry and the loyal *odjak*s, trying at the same time to balance one against the other for the sake of preserving peace in the province. As a result of these revolts, the *spahi* corps was henceforth excluded from the struggle for power among the *odjak*s.

The subsequent years saw the growth of the importance of the twenty-four *Sandjak Bey*s who came to form a group in some ways comparable to the highest *amir*s of the former sultanate. Their high rank entitled them to hold foremost political office and, until the 1620s, they were generally assigned the office of *Serdar*, commander of the military operating within or beyond Egypt's borders. In addition, they were entrusted with the command of both the *Amīr al-Khazna*, the units responsible for escorting the Egyptian treasury to Istanbul, and also with the command of the *Amīr al-Ḥadjdj*, the unit which gave protection to the pilgrim caravan travelling to Mecca. One *Sandjak Bey* was also appointed administrator of Upper Egypt. As *Defterdār*s they also controlled the financial administration of the province. The growth of their political influence was shown, at the beginning of the seventeenth century, when the *Ḳā'im Maḳam* (deputy vice-regent) was selected from among them.

Through skilful use of the military and economic powers of the vice-regent they reinforced the position they had gradually built up in political life by gaining control, as tax collectors, of a large section of the agricultural holdings.

Their first significant political coup was the removal in 1631 of vice-regent Mūsā Pasha, whom they replaced with the deputy vice-regent, Ridwān Bey al-Faḳārī, chosen from among their own ranks. Despite Mūsā Pasha's protests, the Sublime Porte complied with their wish, thus creating a precedent to be repeated several times in the years to come. Although Mūsā Pasha's removal seemed to have been prompted by the assassination of a certain Ḳaytās Bey, and the confiscation of his property, the real motives of the *bey*s and the *odjak*s went much deeper: Mūsā Pasha had started cutting back their salaries.

In 1517 the military had been allowed to introduce *himāye* (protection charges) – caution money protecting the conquered townsfolk from looting. Even the inhabitants of Cairo had paid it. Over the years, however, these charges had escalated until they had become a means by which the soldiers exploited urban populations for their own enrichment. Mūsā Pasha's attempt to eradicate what amounted to the illegal taxation of the townsfolk had caused his downfall. And the *odjak*s, newly reinforced by the admission of traders and craftsmen who now enjoyed the same extortionist privileges as they did, were too powerful for the Istanbul government to attempt to overrule them.

Mūsā Pasha was replaced by Ridwān Bey al-Faḳārī who ruled as vice-regent until his death in 1656. He was also the leader of the Faḳārīya, a political group made up of *bey*s and their Mamluk retinues. The Fakārīya was opposed by the Ḳāsimīya, which also consisted of *bey*s and their retinues and which also sought followers among the nomads and the townsfolk. The struggle between these two groups also involved the *odjak*s, the Janissaries supporting the Fakārīya and the Azabs the Ḳāsimīya, with the overall result that, by the end of the seventeenth century, Egyptian society was completely divided.

Riḍwān Bey secured his position by obtaining a Sultan's decree appointing him life commander of the pilgrim caravan while his ally in the south, 'Alī Bey, by another Sultan's decree, was appointed life vice-regent for Upper Egypt. The Fakārīya was thus well-placed politically, with its two top men firmly entrenched in the provincial hierarchy. By the mid-1600s Cairo was dominated by them. After Riḍwān Bey's death, however, the top positions in the Fakārīya were seized by younger men whose recklessness resulted in internal disagreements and the consequent collapse of the party.

In 1660, after driving the Fakārīya out of Cairo the Ḳāsimīya, with the vice-regent's support, succeeded in gaining, albeit briefly, the office of vice-regent of Upper Egypt and also that of deputy vice-regent of the province. But before the Ḳāsimīya could consolidate their position, their leader, Aḥmad Bey Boshnagī, was assassinated in 1662 on the orders of the vice-regent himself.

These events were testimony to the efforts of the Sublime Porte to reassert its authority in Egypt. Incontestable proof of its success had been provided in 1661 when it had managed to suspend all non-military personnel in the seven *odjak*s and also to increase by 20 per cent the *multazim*s' payments from their benefices in order to cover the treasury deficit caused by rapid inflation. Despite the unpopularity of these measures, the Istanbul court continued to introduce further steps. In 1670 the vice-regent, Ḳara Ibrāhīm Pasha, was instructed to carry out fiscal reform with the help of the army. After a radical rearrangement of the budget and four years of intensive negotiations with all interested parties, he doubled the sum of the treasury, bringing it to 30 million paras. (Some important benefices were still in the possession of the *odjak*s and these Ḳara Ibrāhīm had to confirm in 1672.)

The principles of this reform became the basis for solving fiscal problems from this time until 1798. But success was short-lived and soon the level of the treasury had fallen again. The decision to weaken the economic influence of the *odjak*s – whose financial resources included both legal holdings and illegal takings – had come too late. The legalization, in 1672, of the extant holding of benefices had significantly strengthened the position of the Janissaries and Azabs, who controlled the most lucrative holdings[12]

12. The Janissaries controlled profits from customs houses in all ports except Suez which was one of the vice-regent's benefices. The Azabs controlled profits from granaries, and landing places in Būlāḳ and Old Cairo, and entertainment tax.

to the detriment of the ghaushes and *müteferriḳas*. It also helped to turn the hitherto open system, which permitted easy changes in the holding of benefices, into a closed system dominated by acute controversy.

The weakening of the *pasha*'s position during the first half of the seventeenth century and the disposal of the *bey*s' parties in the 1660s had enabled the *odjaḳ*s to seize those benefices based on the exploitation of the townsfolk.[13] The *bey*s, with no means of access to urban exploitation, continued to exploit the rural people, drawing their income from the agricultural holdings.

Between about 1670 and 1750, political life became even more complicated. The *odjaḳ*s vied with one another but, in addition, they were also torn by internal conflict generated by party affiliation. Some factions supported the Faḳārīya and others the Ḳāsimīya, the rivalry between these two parties having become embedded in those *odjaḳ*s in which they were canvassing support with the aim of eventually dominating them completely. The most contentious issues were the main elements of political and economic power: the holding, and possible redistribution, of benefices, illegal takings from *odjaḳ*s' members' economic activities and illegal protection charges on traders and craftsmen attached to the *odjaḳ*s.[14]

The most strife-ridden *odjaḳ*s was the Janissaries' which controlled the most lucrative benefices. The protagonist of the internal struggle for almost twenty years was Bashodabashi Küchük Meḥmed. Meḥmed had been expelled from Egypt in 1680 because of his opposition to other top-ranking Janissary officials. Later he had returned and joined the Gönüllüyān *odjaḳ* where he won the support of the *Agha* who introduced him to the Faḳārīya. Ibrāhīm Bey, the Faḳārīya leader, helped Küchük Meḥmed rid the Janissary *odjaḳ* of its Ḳāsimī commanders and, from 1692, to dominate it himself. Before long he had forced the top officials of all seven *odjaḳ*s to approve his decision to abolish some of the protection charges and all the other illegal charges demanded by the Janissary and Azab tax-collectors from the customs houses in Alexandria, Rashīd and Būlāḳ. With the vice-regent's support, Küchük Meḥmed was able to put these new rulings into

---

13. The *odjaḳ*s' ambitions to possess holdings officially and also to create illegal sources of income were fuelled by their increasing contact with local inhabitants, resulting from their own economic activities and, in particular, from exposure to traders and craftsmen who were now admitted into their ranks. Their clients were, in particular, rich coffee dealers, and this rapprochement was the basis of the *odjaḳ*s' claim on protection charges as well as a 10 per cent cut of a deceased client's wealth. The new *odjaḳ*s' members, the traders and craftsmen, were not altogether losers, however, as membership guaranteed protection as well as exploitionist privileges, which turned them into an influential group closely connected to the *odjaḳ*s.

14. These practices also fell contrary to the *sharī'a* (Islamic law) and were criticized as *mazālim* (abuses). The Istanbul court wanted their removal to prevent possible political difficulties. The main burden of exploitation was borne by the people whose plight was worsened by bad harvests, inflation, famine and epidemics. In the late 1600s in 1678, 1687 and 1695 popular riots broke out which had some bearing on political leadership.

force. The main reason for this move – which, though favoured by the people, made enemies of many Janissaries, led by Mustafā Ḳazdoghlu – was fear of a repetition of the riots of 1678 which were caused by continuous inflation and rising maize prices.

In the summer of 1694, tension within the Janissaries' *odjaḳ* reached a critical level. At the same time a low flood of the River Nile caused a sudden rise in maize prices. True to form, Küchük Meḥmed moved against possible speculators, fixing grain prices and excluding middlemen from its distribution. He thus brought together the Janissaries and the Azabs who controlled the grain stores, a liaison which culminated in the assassination of Küchük Meḥmed. Once again the *odjaḳ*s had access to their lost benefices and the freedom to determine food prices. The subsequent escalation in the price of all basic commodities caused famine in 1695 followed by epidemics a year later. It was only the abundant floods of 1697 that brought an end to this series of crises.

Since 1688 conditions had been aggravated by the continuous decrease in the value of the currency and by 1692 the situation was critical. In an attempt to balance the deficit in the value of the treasury, the provincial administration increased by 4 per cent the deliveries from the *iltizam*s. Istanbul, however, demanded that the treasury be delivered in valuable coin, a move strongly opposed by the *odjaḳ*s who were deriving huge profits from the devaluation, as were their merchant-clients. It was this opposition that wrecked the attempt at financial reform and change in the tax system prepared by the financial expert, Yāsif al-Yahūdī, in 1697.[15]

A new wave of price increases, resulting from an influx of valueless currency from other parts of the Ottoman empire in the early 1700s, gave the Janissaries the opportunity to snatch the monopoly of the maize trade from the Azabs. The main problem, once again, proved to be the protection charges which neither *odjaḳ* would relinquish. The deadlock was finally solved by a compromise which avoided the main problem but which was acceptable to the *odjaḳ*s. It was decided that trimmed coins might be used only as weighed metal and that *fidda dīwānī* (fine silver coins) be minted instead. Price lists of basic commodities were issued and the export of coffee to Christian lands banned. But although the mint decree slowed down the decline of the para, the real problem of protection charges remained unsolved and tension between the *odjaḳ*s continued and yet another political crisis loomed.

It finally broke about 1710, its main cause being the export of coffee to Christian countries. The rapid increase in coffee exports, in response to rising demand in Europe, had caused prices to soar. The coffee wholesalers and their Janissary patrons had profited to such an extent that the other *odjaḳ*s felt quite overshadowed. The problem of protection charges once

15. Suggested reforms included the stamping of currency, the introduction of 10 per cent duty on coffee in stock, a state monopoly in coffee-roasting, the hall-marking of textiles and the taxation of houses and shops.

again came to the fore but discussions as to its solution were forestalled by the split of the Janissary *odjak* into a Fakārīya and a Ḳāsimīya party. The split resulted in an unprecedentedly fierce clash within the *odjak* in which the *beys* also participated.

The main instigator was Bashodabashi Ifrandj Aḥmad who was in favour of the Janissaries involving themselves in economic activities. Although he was backed by the Fakārīya, the Ḳāsimīya succeeded in expelling him from the *odjak* in 1707. By 1709 tension was again high with the Janissaries in isolation against the united front of the other *odjak*. At this point Ifrandj Aḥmad, still with the support of the Fakārīya, was taken back into the Janissary *odjak* and those Ḳāsimīya officers responsible for his expulsion in 1707 were themselves expelled. The Fakārīya position was now secure and the followers of Ifrandj Aḥmad's policy united. But a decree sent from Istanbul was to deal the Janissaries a serious blow. The decree, which stipulated official policy on the current problems, ordered that an immediate stop be put to all abuses as well as the patronising relations between military and non-military personnel. In addition, the mint was to be moved from the Janissary barracks into a new building.

At the end of 1710 the crisis was worsened still further by a rupture between the two leading Fakārīya *beys*, Ayyūb and Ḳaytās, with the latter going over to the Ḳāsimīya – a move which led to the return of the expelled officers. The delicate power balance thus disturbed, the crisis developed into an armed conflict in which the *beys* were also fully engaged. Ayyūb Bey, the Fakārīya leader, and the vice-regent of Upper Egypt, Maḥmūd Bey al-Kabīr, backed Ifrandj Aḥmad, while the rivals were joined by the Ḳāsimīya leader Aywaz Bey, Ibrāhīm Shanab, Meḥmed Bey Ḳutamish and the former Fakāritite, Ḳaytās Bey. After a two-month siege of the citadel, Janissary resistance collapsed in June 1711, the Fakārīya *beys* fled Egypt and Ifrandj Aḥmad was executed.

Following the events of 1711 and the preceding twenty years of struggle, the influence of the Janissary and other *odjak*s waned, leaving the field clear for the *beys* and their Mamluk retinues. Since the mid-1600s the *Sandjak Beys*, and also members of the Ottoman hierarchy, had been forming their own Mamluk retinues. By 1700 affranchized slaves and Mamluks of many houses, including the Ḳazdughlīya, Ḳutamishīya, Balfīya, and Djulfīya, were already holding most offices and many of the benefices. From 1711 there followed a period of about twenty years during which new political patterns took shape as the *beys* once again took the limelight on the Egyptian political stage.

Despite the economic and political crisis in its final years, the *odjak*s' rule in Egypt had witnessed great economic and social change. Agricultural production had increased as had trade in Egyptian goods, the profits from which were surpassed only by those from the transit trade. Profits from coffee in particular had contributed significantly to general prosperity.

The healthy state of the economy had been accompanied by a high rate of population growth which had resulted in the extensive cultivation of the land and the expansion of production and trade in the towns. The population of Cairo had soared to 300 000, surpassing its previous peak of 250 000 at the beginning of the fourteenth century.

An ongoing problem had been currency devaluation which had been noticeably aggravated by Ottoman defeats in Europe. Apart from this aspect, however, Egypt had not been affected by the events taking place on the battlefields of Europe: even trade was carried on as normal, while *odjak* participation in the wars was negligible. Under these conditions of peace, the social character of the *odjak*s had changed gradually. Permanently garrisoned in Egypt, the soldiers had begun to integrate with the local people, mostly through inter-marriages, until only their military status and some privileges and duties distinguished them from the Cairo townsfolk. Their discipline during these peaceful times, however, declined and they naturally deteriorated militarily.

The struggle for power, after 1711, continued at two levels both between and within the individual political groups. In 1714 the top man of the ruling Kāsimīya party, Kaytās Bey, was killed by his subordinates who thus seized *riyāsa* (leadership). However, one of them, Ibrāhīm Bey Abū Shanab, soon died, leaving Ismāʿīl Bey, son of Aywaz Bey, its only leader and their position of power soon collapsed. The Mamluks of Abū Shanab formed an opposition group, the Shanabīya, which, in co-operation with the Fakārīya *bey*s, ousted Ismāʿīl Bey together with the entire Aywazide faction of the Kāsimīya. The Shanabīya leader, soon formed a duumvirate together with the Fakārīya leader, Dhū ʾl-Fakār. This new liaison, which amounted to a political compromise, had been dictated by a new economic crisis precipitated by the fall of the previous Shanabīya leader, Mehmed Bey Cherkesī. Like others before him, Mehmed Bey Cherkesī had tried to alleviate the growing tension by forcing the *odjak*s to relieve taxation and relinquish their illegal takings. At first the *odjak*s seemed willing to compromise but upon hearing that traders and Hawwāra Arab members were to be expelled, tempers flared and Mehmed Bey Cherkesī was assassinated.

The relentless fight between the *bey*s gave the vice-regents an opportunity, after 1720, to strengthen their authority. It was for this end that they had taken part in the various infightings, even backing the assassinations of Ismāʿīl Bey and Mehmed Bey Cherkesī. After the collapse of the Kāsimīya party in 1729, the vice-regents continued their meddling with the Fakārīyas now headed by three men: Mehmed Bey Kutlumush, the Janissary Kāhya ʿUthmān (Osman) and the Azab Kāhya Yūsuf.

In 1736, the rivalry between these leaders offered vice-regent Bakir Pasha an opportunity to try to divert the *odjak*s' legal and illegal takings to the treasury. When he met resistance he had all three representatives assassinated. Although the Sublime Porte did not approve of this move it did, however, ban the alienation of the benefices of the *odjak*s – in the interests of the state. The new leadership of the Egyptian military stratum, represented by 'Uthmān Bey Dhu 'l-Faḳar and the Janissary Kāhya Ibrāhīm Ḳazdoghlu and supported by the *odjaḳs*, refused to submit. The opposition was reinforced by representatives of the *'ulamā'* (sing. *'ālim*) – the religious brotherhoods.

With Ibrāhīm Ḳazdoghlu at the head of the Janissary *odjaḳs*, the Ḳazdughlīya, a strong Faḳārīya faction which had hitherto remained in the background, came to the fore. Its leaders were not of the rank of *Sandjaḳ Bey* but the group had therefore not lost any of its leaders through assassination and had remained comparatively intact. From 1743, when Ibrāhīm Kāhya forced 'Uthmān Bey to emigrate, leaving himself as the only leader of the military stratum, the Ḳazdughlīya became the only ruling party and remained so until 1798.

After 'Uthmān Bey had left the country, Ibrāhīm Kāhya joined forces with Riḍwān, the Kāhya of the Azabs and the leader of the Djulfīya, a smaller Faḳārīya faction. This duumvirate, composed of the two most powerful military detachments in Egypt, ruled undisturbed for ten years from 1744. Neither took the rank of *Sandjaḳ Bey* but each nominated three of his own Mamluks to the *bey* corporation. While Riḍwān Kāhya indulged in building activities, his hobby, Ibrāhīm Kāhya, turned Egypt into his personal domain: he seized the richest material resources, built up a strong retinue of Mamluks and thoroughly enriched himself.

Despite the seeming stability of the duumvirate, however, symptoms were forming of the approaching doom of the socio-economic structures on which the power of the military rested.[16]

Under the duumvirs, the *odjaḳs*' collective authority was replaced by the personal power of what amounted to two despots. Only because of the sound economy – stable prices and a stable currency – was internal peace maintained. The underlying unrest became apparent as soon as Ibrāhīm Kāhya died in 1754. Riḍwān Kāhya was the first victim: he was killed during a Janissary revolt precipitated by his proposal to impose yet another tax on coffee. The *odjaḳs* were rebelling in defence of their much-eroded privileges but also as an expression of antagonism towards the increasing power of the Mamluks who, as *bey*s and *odjaḳ* officers, were now assuming substantial authority both politically and economically. The decline in the *odjaḳs*' political power was directly connected with their economic decline in the 1720s, 1730s and 1740s, caused by the loss of some profitable benefices and a decrease in the takings from other sources – in particular the trade in spices and coffee which was facing competition from the Antilles. The impoverishment of the merchants by the duumvirs had also

16. Within the traditional system of exploitation, the *odjaḳs* had offered their clients some of the privileges enjoyed by the ruling stratum. But the duumvirs' exploitation offered no such compensation. Exploitation was worsened by confiscations, forced loans and other drastic measures directed in particular at the traders. The booty, meanwhile, was divided quite openly between the two rulers.

impaired *odjaḳ*s profits. After 1760, *odjaḳs* power weakened still further as the *odjaḳ*s degenerated into mere reserves for Mamluk retinues whose members were allowed to hold the rank of officer.

Cultural development

The extinction of the sovereign Mamluk sultanate and the transformation of Egypt into a *wilāya* (province) of the Ottoman empire led to significant cultural changes that clearly reflected newly forming social, economic and national relations. Education was also affected, as was the role of Arabic as the medium of cultural expression.

After the fall of the Mamluk sultanate, Cairo ceased to be the spiritual centre of the Sunnite world, which it had been since 1261. Its exalted position was strengthened by the presence of the Abbasid Caliphs and the developed educational institutions headed by the ancient Azhar, to which seekers of knowledge came from all over the Islamic world. They came to Cairo to study, to teach at the numerous *madrasa*s there, or to work as officials in the state administration where political authority and economic prosperity were turning the capital into a city bursting with life. Although the Azhar remained a school of high prestige for students from Arab countries even after 1517, those who wanted to achieve success in public service were increasingly forced to attend Istanbul schools which prepared their graduates for service in any part of the vast Ottoman empire. No less attractive were teaching posts at these schools, from which a way was frequently found to high public office and rank. Istanbul and other cities of the Central Empire thus usurped the place which, until 1517, had incontestably belonged to Cairo, even in the eyes of Arab Ottoman subjects.

The incorporation of Egypt and other Arab countries into the Ottoman empire, in whose public and cultural life Ottoman–Turkish occupied a leading position, accentuated the decline of Arabic as mediator of Islamic-Arabic culture. At that time, New Persian literature and literature in Turkish languages was flourishing and the spiritual culture of Islam was being expressed through them. The loss of political independence by some Arab countries stopped the use of Arabic as a language of state administration, and also impaired its literary use. With the exception of religious and legal themes, literature – including scientific literature – was generated and consumed by the ruling stratum, which did not know Arabic but could appreciate works in Turkish or Persian. Unlike Arabic culture and literature, Persian culture experienced a period of great creativity between the fifteenth and eighteenth centuries.

As in all Arab provinces of the Ottoman empire, the culture of Egypt fell under strong Ottoman–Turkish political, social and cultural pressure resulting in its gradual integration into the new Ottoman–Turkish variation of Islamic civilization. It nevertheless retained a certain character of its own which was to become the starting-point and the regulator of the Arabic national revival in the nineteenth and twentieth centuries. This character was retained by the Arabic and Egyptian literature of the sixteenth, seventeenth and eighteenth centuries, although this literature fell into the background of official literary activities. This period, usually described as the time of deepest decline for Arabic literature, bore nothing new in the classical genres but did bring about a new orientation of literary production. Writings in the Arabic language were directed at readers from the middle strata of townsfolk, such as the *'ulamā'* of lower levels, the clerical intelligentsia, traders and craftsmen whose mother-tongue was Arabic. This reorientation resulted in literature with a strong popular character in genre and language.

This trend was particularly pronounced in poetry. As the Dervish orders became more widespread, mystic *ṣūfī* poetry gained much favour and popularity. It concentrated, under the influence of Ibn al-Fārid, on praising the Prophet Muḥammad, whose glory was also sung in the *mawlid*s (legendary prose narratives about Muḥammad).[17]

Satire was also introduced during this period, the most remarkable being *Hazz al-kuhūf* (Shaking the Peasants' Heads) by al-Shirbīnī (dated 1787) in which the author ridiculed the thick-headedness and rudeness of farmers as well as the narrow-mindedness and haughtiness of the *'ulamā'*, using the form of a commentary on a satirical poem by the fictitious village poet Abū Shaduf ibn Udjayl (Father of Weighbeam, son of Calf). The language of this work is the Arabic of Egyptian countryfolk. In one of his poems, Ḳaṣid Abū Shaduf, he deals with the exploitation of the peasants by the administration and relatives and the injustices meted out to them. Another poet was Ḥasan al-Badrī al-Ḥidjāzī (died 1719) who, in addition to a collection of poems on religious themes, wrote an independent collection of moralizing satires commenting upon remarkable events and criticizing contemporary society.

Apart from this poetry addressed to a wide public (one of the authors of which was also the Chancellor of the Azhar, 'Abdullāh al-Shubrawī (died 1758) who wrote a small collection of love poetry and seasonal poems and a panegyric on Muḥammad and other outstanding personalities) there appeared formalistic poetry with a tendency towards self-conceited eccentricities. Its representative in Egypt was Abdullāh al-Idkāwī (died 1770) who also, like his contemporary Yūsuf al-Hifnāwī (died 1764), wrote on art.

Narrative folk prose was enriched by another work, a novel on the conquest of Egypt by Selim I. It deals with the heroic resistance to foreign aggression by the last Mamluk Sultan, Tūmān Bey. The author of this novel was Aḥmad ibn Zunbul, the writer of a concise history of the same event which forms the thematic basis of the novel.

---

17. Muḥammad ibn Riḍwān al-Suyūti (died 1766) was the author of one such popular poem. Less popular (because of their rhetorical character) were the writings of Ā'isha al-Bā'ūniya and the physician 'Abd al-Raḥmān al-Humaydī (died 1587).

Scientific literature, however, did not develop during this period. On the contrary its decline continued, marked by a lack of originality in the processing of knowledge and fruitless comment on writings of reputable authorities from the past. The ideal of Islamic society, into which Ottoman ideologists tried to fit society, did not require or allow disturbance of critical analysis. Commentaries and glossaries – common enough during this period – although reacting to the demands of the times in detail, could not present an objective image of society.[18]

In this respect, historiography had better possibilities. However, in Egypt it suffered from a lack of patrons and persons interested in historical works. Apart from the works by Ibn Iyās which, although concluded in 1552, are considered to be part of Mamluk historiography, the historiographic works produced during this period were of poor quality, especially in their methodogy. Only a few books can be considered lengthy chronicles containing well-arranged materials.[19] Frequently, they are but dry chronological lists of sultans, vice-regents and supreme judges, or short summaries of Egyptian history until the author's time.[20] There are also a few detailed treatises on certain events, often based on personal experience.[21] A number of historical booklets were written in verse and others in the spoken language.[22] While the last Mamluk chronicle by Ibn Iyās covers the beginning of the Ottoman period, the last decades of the eighteenth century are described in the greatest work of this kind written in the nineteenth century, the chronicle by al-Djabarti, the last writing of its kind in the Arabic literature of the feudal period.

Mere commentary, although often sterile, produced a significant work by Muḥammad Murtadā al-Zabīdī (died 1791), the many-volume dictionary *Tādj al-arūs*, a commentary on al-Fīrūzabādī's *Al-Kāmūs*. Philology was also treated by al-Khafādji (died 1659), the author of a large collection of biographies of outstanding personalities.

A favourite genre was treatises on pilgrim routes to Mecca and Medina as well as writings on destinations of pilgrims and the tombs of outstanding personalities, in particular scholars and *shaykh* saints.

The veneration of Saints, an expression of the faithful, was connected with the rapid advancement of the Dervish orders and the interest in mystics, both of which spread widely in Egypt from the sixteenth century.

18. A number of small treatises were compiled on the problems of the times, particularly in the field of applied law, in addition to concise handbooks which were often of textbook character.

19. For example, the Chronicle of Aḥmad Chelebi covering the period from 1517 until 1737.

20. Typical of this kind of writing are the books by al'-'Shākī, Marʿī ibn Yūsuf and al-Sharkāwī.

21. The best of them is *Wak'at al-Sanādjik* (Clash of the *Sandjak Beys*) by as-Sālihi, dealing with the revolt of the Fakārīya *beys* in 1660.

22. There is a book by al-Ghamrī in verse and the Dermirdesh Chronicle in the spoken language.

Greatest popularity was enjoyed by the Aḥmadīya, an order founded by Aḥmad al-Badawī (died 1276), whose tomb in Tanṭā was the centre of a special cult. Its numerous branches were widespread, especially the Bayyūmīya, Shaʿrāwīya and Shinnāwīya. Among the influential orders, mention must be made of the Ḳādirīyya, Rifāʿīya and Nakshbandīya, whereas the Ibrāhimīya, Demirdāshīya, Bakrīya and many others were of less importance. The Dervish orders were headed by *naḳīb al-ashrāf* (a representative of the Prophet's descendants), a *shaykh* from the al-Bakrī family which derived its origins from the first Caliph Abū Bakr. The Dervish orders associated with certain social strata, including some social groups and had representatives of some professions within their ranks. The social structure of the orders and their firm organization gave their leaders significant political power through which to influence public life. The orders were also of cultural significance. They contributed to the education of the people through whom their members came in touch with spiritual culture mediated by written literature, mostly poetry. This contact also stimulated independent interest in the written word and independent creation. Mystic poetry was cultivated by a number of authors such as the pleiad of the members of the al-Bakrī family, ʿAbdullāh al-Shaʿrāwī, Aḥmad al-Dardīr and others who, in their poems, treatises and lectures to their colleagues, did not always conform to the dogma of Islam.

Throughout the eighteenth century, Egypt did not experience the advantage of the printing press, although from 1729 both Turkish and Arabic books were printed in Istanbul. Copying by hand continued to be the only way of multiplying literary works.

Cairo and other Egyptian cities are still adorned by numerous architectural monuments built during the Ottoman period. An outstanding place is occupied by buildings serving religious or educational aims and financed from endowments bequeathed by persons who had ordered them to be built – vice-regents, top *odjaḳ* officers, *bey*s and even Ottoman sultans and other members of the dynasty. Like the profane objects which often formed part of the material basis of the endowment, these buildings are marked by a number of local Egyptian elements represented, of course, in unequal proportion to the imported Ottoman elements. They can be found both in the general architectural conception and, more frequently, in the decor, such as the use of marble stucco or coloured windows,[23] the imported elements being mostly represented by the *manāra* (the large central dome), the faience wall panelling and the flowers painted on the ceiling and wall plates.[24] The extant relics also confirm that domestic architecture also

23. Local elements are represented, to the highest degree, in the al-Burdaynī Mosque (from 1611).

24. The best-known mosques are Sulaymān Pasha's, in the Cairo Citadel (1538), Sinān Pasha's in Būlāḳ (1571) and the Mālika Ṣafīya Mosque (1610). An important synthesis is represented by the Mosque of Muḥammad Bey Abū 'l-Dahab (1774).

PLATE 6.4   *The mosque of Maḥmūd Pasha, 975/1568*

PLATE 6.5   *The īwān of the mosque of Aḥmad al-Burdaynī, 1025/1616–1038/1629*

preserved the traditional arrangement in principle.[25] Although fashionable Ottoman elements found more place in interior decoration, especially in the use of faience panelling, the traditional use of wood and marble generally

25. For example, the houses of Zaynab Khatun (1713), Djamāluddīn al-Dahabī (1637) and al-Sihaymī (1648–1796).

prevailed here, too. The size and comfort of these dwellings testify to an advanced form of housing for the well-to-do townsfolk – a testimony to the progressive changes within Egyptian society and the increasing importance of traders, the nucleus of the future bourgeois class. These changes took place in Egypt analagously to development in the entire Ottoman empire, although somewhat delayed in comparison to its European counterparts and Syria.

Economic decline and attempts to achieve independence

After the deaths of Ibrāhīm Bey and Riḍwān Kāhya, fierce fighting broke out within the Kazdughlīya. For a while a number of *bey*s, all of them former Mamluks of Ibrāhīm Kāhya, took turns at its head. One of them, Ḥusayn Bey Sābundjī, had conferred upon him in 1756 the honorary title of *Shaykh al-Balad*, a title not previously in regular use.[26]

Shaykh al-Balad 'Alī Bey al-Ghazzāwī, who, in 1757, ousted Ḥusayn Bey, was opposed by a group led by 'Abd al-Raḥmān, an influential Janissary Kāhya. 'Abd al-Raḥmān, who was keen to preserve his influential position in the background of public events, decided to replace al-Ghazzāwī with a *bey* whom he considered to be his man, 'Alī Bey, also known as *al-Djinn* (the devil). In 1760, while al-Ghazzāwī was in Mecca, 'Abd al-Raḥmān forced the *bey*s to accept his man as the new *Shaykh al-Balad*.

'Alī Bey soon proved to be extraordinarily ambitious and energetic. He secured his position in Egypt[27] and then, through his contacts at the Sublime Porte, also succeeded in persuading Istanbul that he was the only person capable of putting Egypt to rights.

At the time of 'Alī Bey's ascent to power, relations between Egypt and the Sublime Porte were somewhat strained. The main reason was the ever-increasing treasury deficit, now tens of millions of paras. In 1761 the Istanbul government decided to intervene militarily in Egypt. However, in 1763, 'Alī Bey, exploiting the nervousness of the Egyptian party and the embitterment of the court, secured – in exchange for promising to eradicate the treasury deficit – financial assistance from Istanbul plus Sublime Porte approval of his retention of all the properties he had confiscated from his adversaries. He pledged to pay the treasury deficit for the past ten years

26. The first bearer of this unofficial title seems to have been Meḥmed Bey Cherkesī. It meant merely a senior grandee among the Egyptian *bey*s.

27. To neutralize the influence of the rest of the Kazdughlīya, 'Alī Bey promoted to the rank of *Sandjak Bey* Ibrāhīm Kāhya's Mamluk Ismā'īl and two Mamluks from his own retinue, Muḥammad Bey Abū 'l-Dahab and Aḥmad Boshnak who was later known as *al-Djazzār* (the butcher). He also disposed of a number of older leaders such as 'Abd al-Raḥmān', the Janissary Kāhya who was leader of the Kazdughlīya, and Ṣāliḥ Bey, the only remaining leader of the Kāsimīya.

PLATE 6.6   *The main room (ḳāʿa) in Ḏjamāluddīn al-Dahabī's house, 1047/1637*

PLATE 6.7   *The wooden screen (machrabia) in Ḏjamāluddīn al-Dahabī's house, 1047/1637*

a total of 91 million paras, and to deliver the sum of 50 million paras earned by the sale of the confiscated benefices.[28]

His repression of landowners and the politically influential triggered the

28. The confiscated benefices, or those whose holders had died, were re-allocated to beneficiaries against the payment of *hulwān*, a special tax usually eight times the annual income from the benefice.

formation of an opposition led by Ṣāliḥ Bey. In 1765 Ṣāliḥ left for Upper Egypt to join forces with Shaykh Humām who was, in practice, the independent leader of the Hawwāra Arabs who were already sheltering many of ʿAlī Bey's enemies.

Aware of the potential threat of this group, which had dominated Upper Egypt, ʿAlī Bey planned a campaign against it. But the leader of the expedition, Ḥusayn Bey Kashkash, a former Mamluk of Ibrāhīm, made use of the force entrusted to him and, in co-operation with opposition elements in Cairo, forced ʿAlī Bey to flee to Syria. A year later, however, he returned – with the support of the Sublime Porte – reconciled himself with Ṣāliḥ Bey of Upper Egypt and, in 1768, ejected Ḥusayn Bey Kashkash and Khalīl Bey who had ruled as duumvirs during his absence.

As soon as ʿAlī Bey had fulfilled his promise to the Sublime Porte to pay off the deficit, his policy underwent a radical change. Also in 1768 he deposed the vice-regent and appointed himself both vice-regent and deputy vice-regent. ʿAlī Bey's efforts to combine in himself both vice-regent – the titulary head of Egyptian administration – and *Shaykh al-Balad*, the foremost political power, were again demonstrated in 1769 when he deposed the new *walī* soon after he had been appointed. However, despite being ruler of Egypt, whose subjugation to the Sultan was entirely formal, ʿAlī Bey did not go so far as to declare himself an independent sovereign. Nevertheless, he usurped the right to mint coins of his own and his name was introduced into Friday prayers. He also tried to utilize all resources exclusively for strengthening his political and economic power by boosting the army and developing agriculture and trade. He also opened commercial negotiations with prominent European powers.

His ambition,[29] cleverly disguised as service to the Sultan, was further fuelled in 1770 when his office entitled him to take part in the dynastic strife of the Hāshimite *amīr*s in Mecca. The solution, through Egyptian intervention, and the replacement of the Ottoman vice-regent in Djidda by an Egyptian *bey*, was a definite gain for ʿAlī Bey against the Sultan's supremacy in Ḥidjāz. Stimulated by this success, ʿAlī Bey began cherishing the idea of unifying – under his reign but still within the framework of empire – the areas that had once formed the territory of the Mamluk sultanate: Egypt, Ḥidjāz (dominated by the vassal dynasty of the Hāshimī Katādites) and Syria.

That same year, 1770, ʿAlī Bey saw his chance to dominate Syria. The unsuccessful war currently being waged by the Ottomans against Russia, and the destruction of the Ottoman navy by the Russian fleet at Cheshme, practically excluded the possibility of a counter-measure against him, particularly as the vice-regent of Damascus was currently endangered by the rebellious administrator of Akka and Galilee, Shaykh Zāhir ʿUmar. Moreover, to harness support for his decentralizing activities – and assist-

---

29. His nickname was *Bulut Kapan* (Cloud-catcher).

ALI-BEY.
Bacha de la Crimes,
qui veut se faire reconnoitre Sultan d'Egipte

PLATE 6.8   *'Alī Bey, vice-regent of Egypt*

ance in time of need – 'Alī Bey had contacted the commanders of the Russian fleet in the Eastern Mediterranean.

Despite the initial reluctance of Ismā'īl Bey, the commander of the troops sent by 'Alī Bey to support Shaykh Zāhir 'Umar, the allied army, reinforced by further units led by Muḥammad Bey Abū 'l-Dahab, defeated the Istanbul troops and took Damascus. However, perhaps through fear of retaliation by the Porte, or because of the Porte's readiness to appoint Muḥammad Bey as the ruler of Egypt should he first dispose of 'Alī Bey, the two *beys* assured the sultan of their loyalty and returned to Cairo with their army. At the beginning of 1772, Muḥammad Bey was forced to take shelter in Upper Egypt where he joined the Hawwārī Arabs and the Ḳāsimīya supporters. And when a punitive expedition sent against the southern rebels had defected to the other side, together with their commander, Ismā'īl Bey, 'Alī Bey's power collapsed. In spring 1772 forces loyal to 'Alī Bey were defeated and 'Alī Bey had to commit his office to his rival, Muḥammad Bey. With the help of his allies in Syria and Palestine, 'Alī Bey made one more attempt to return to power but his scanty support was soon dispersed and he himself died soon after in captivity.

Although inspired by Egypt's past, some features of 'Alī Bey's career foreshadowed future developments. These included his ruthlessness in disposing of adversaries and, in particular, his activities in the Arab peninsula and Syria, his personal use of the country's economic resources and his increasing political independence of central government. That his success was shortlived no doubt resulted from the extent of his social and political ambition and its restraint by the Mamluk houses and the fickleness of their allegiance.

During 'Alī Bey's time, symptoms arose of the prolonged socio-economic crises which continued, with varying intensity, until the nineteenth century. 'Alī Bey's interest in agriculture was prompted by the need to increase the feudal rent. His harsh taxation, which first affected the rural areas, was undoubtedly a main cause of the impoverishment of the farmers. It drove them to the towns where they were also unable to make a living as more and more traders and craftsmen were also suffering from high taxes, to be paid in advance, and the high deliveries on inheritances. General impoverishment – the result of the drastic exploitation of every level of society – grew worse during subsequent years and was dramatically intensified by a series of epidemics.

The new *Shaykh al-Balad*'s fulfilment of obligations, characteristic of his loyalty, gave the Porte hope that at last they had a pro-Ottoman ruler in Egypt. In 1775 Muḥammad Bey dispatched more than 130 million paras as the annual payment. The same year he sent an expedition against Shaykh Zāhir 'Umar on the sultan's orders. But, during the siege of Akka, Muḥammad Bey died and Egypt's engagement in Syria came to an end. Egyptian troops vacated the occupied territory and henceforth the *beys* lost interest in Syria, confining their activities to Egypt alone.

PLATE 6.9   *The mosque of Muḥammad Bey Abū 'l-Dahab, 1188/1774*

The Porte took every opportunity to interfere in the struggles for power which broke out between members of the Mamluk élite after Muḥammad Bey's death. It supported whichever magnate promised, in exchange for the right to confiscate the estates of the defeated rivals, to send the Porte the largest portion of the tax levied from the new benefice holders. This attitude reflected an important change in the function and aims of the benefice system, and showed that the Porte had no intentions of intervening directly in Egyptian affairs, being content merely to utilize the Mamluk squabbles to drain as much money as possible from the province.

In the struggle for supreme power, which lasted almost ten years, the main protagonists were three Ḳazdughlīya *bey*s, Ismāʿīl, originally a Mamluk of Ibrāhīm Kāhya, and two former Mamluks of Muḥammad Bey Abū ʾl-Dahab, Murād Bey and Ibrāhīm Bey. The first phase of the struggle was concluded in 1778 when Murād Bey and Ibrāhīm Bey together succeeded in forcing Ismāʿīl and his followers to leave Egypt. The second phase consisted of fights between the two victors. Ibrāhīm, although officially recognized as *Shaykh al-Balad*, was prevented by Murād from entirely controlling the situation. This rivalry gave the Porte the chance to manoeuvre and manipulate the two adversaries with the aim of increasing to the maximum the sum of the annual payment. The Porte however was not able to make full use of this opportunity and the two leaders confiscated more and more resources, including the benefices explicitly reserved for certain offices which they were not able to hold.[30]

After 1778 they gradually gained control of the whole administration of the province, having seized all its resources which they utilized for their own ends, in particular to cover the costs of fighting one another. Ibrāhīm did not fulfil his obligations as *Shaykh al-Balad* sending, if anything, a small fraction of the stipulated amount to Istanbul. In 1784, at the beginning of an economic crisis that was to last until 1792 – when the two rivals were reconciled and agreed to rule the province together – the Sublime Porte considered its interests in Egypt endangered as it was unlikely that the duumvirs would pay the deficit of the last five years.

In view of this, central government decided to renew direct control over Egypt through military intervention. In July 1786 Ottoman expeditional troops, under the command of Ḥasan Pasha, disembarked at Alexandria and Rashīd. During their march they dispersed the Mamluk troops but Murād and Ibrāhīm retreated to Upper Egypt together with the remaining force. Ḥasan's first task in restoring the sultan's authority was to break the military power of the two usurpers and mould the loyal Mamluk element into an instrument obedient to the demands of the Porte. He accomplished this by creating a new set of *bey*s and garrison commanders appointed from among the various Mamluk houses. The Sultan's moral authority was

30. For example, the income from the customs house in Suez, seized in 1779 and formerly reserved as the *iltizam* for the vice-regent: it consisted mainly of duties on the import of coffee.

enhanced by a number of edicts emphasizing the Islamic character of his regime versus the tyranny of the two rebels. The sultan also promised tax relief and the return to the righteous principles of the *Ḳānūn Nāme*.

As the main aim of the punitive expedition was the enforcement of the regular delivery of the treasury, Ḥasan Pasha prepared a number of fiscal decrees to secure the fulfilment of the obligations of the province towards both the Porte and the sacred cities of Ḥidjāz. But before he could implement these instruments, he was sent elsewhere on a military mission.

The Porte's military intervention in Egypt did not have the expected results. Ḥasan Pasha had not succeeded in subduing the two rebel *beys*. Moreover, the division of Egypt into a lower part, ruled by the sultan's representative, and an upper part dominated by the two rebels, became accepted as a reality, particularly after the two rebels, following a brief expulsion to Nubia, had in 1787 restored control over all the points in Upper Egypt occupied by Ottoman or loyal troops. Although Ḥasan Pasha had made some changes in the holding of ranks and offices, Ismāʿīl Bey being appointed the new *Shaykh al-Balad*, the Mamluk regime remained intact and with it all the pre-conditions for the old problems to re-emerge.

The political crisis that followed the death of Muḥammad Bey Abū 'l-Dahab was seriously complicated from 1783 by economic and social difficulties such as poor harvests, starvation, price increases and currency devaluations. These problems were aggravated by the stormy political atmosphere, administrative disorganization and tax pressures. An unusually severe epidemic in 1791, however, simplified the political situation by claiming as its victims a large number of loyal *beys* including Ismāʿīl Bey. Murād and Ibrāhīm were thus able to enter Cairo again without resistance in the summer of the same year and take up rule over all Egypt.

The Porte consented to their rule on condition that the normal obligations be fulfilled. The two new leaders, in 1792, signed an agreement with the Porte stipulating the total sum to be paid and the method of payment. This agreement, however, was kept but reluctantly and the total sum sent was always insufficient. The return to power of the two *beys* meant the restoration of the harsh, extortionist regime that Egypt had experienced before Ḥasan Pasha's expedition, its consequences for the country being even more disastrous. Because Egypt had for ten years been disrupted by political anarchy, economic mismanagement and the relentless plundering of resources and reserves, all attempts to arrest the general decline were doomed to failure, despite the fact that almost all the money drained by the tax apparatus had remained in Egypt. The critical state of the economy was a reflection of the oppressive politics whereby the majority of the people was controlled by a small élite made up of Mamluk *beys* and their retinues. Central government lacked the strength to dispose of them and Egyptian society was not yet ready to do the deed itself. But the ousting of the Mamluks was not in fact so far away. In the summer of 1798 the first impulse was provided by a most unexpected source – the French military expedition to the Egyptian coast under the command of Napoleon Bonaparte.

Conclusion

The period from the fall of the Mamluk sultanate in 1517 to the French expedition of 1798 was one in which Egyptian development was largely determined by its own inner dynamics but also by the Ottoman empire of which it was a component. Unlike the European areas of the empire, however, Egypt was little affected by the political development of the centre, and its socio-economic development of the centre, and its socio-economic development did not reach the stage where the beginnings of a new social class, the bourgeoisie, was spawned. Socially, therefore, it did not cross the boundaries of the late stage of the social formation traditionally called feudalism.[31]

The incorporation of Egypt was, however, a significant gain for the Ottoman empire which undoubtedly enhanced its economic capacity and political strength. Relations between central government and the Egyptian province, however, fluctuated considerably throughout, leading to a permanent strained atmosphere between the two. First, as in other provinces, it was political and economic relations that were a source of conflict. But progressive Ottoman decline produced even more frequent and fierce social clashes which, combined with political and economic crises, led to continuous decentralizing efforts. The aim as yet was to dominate the economy of the country and its political institutions, not to create an independent state.

The growth of separatist forces in Egypt in the late 1700s was no isolated phenomenon in the Arab countries of the Ottoman empire. More or less independent states arose in Tripolitania, Iraq and Syria at this time, some of them being the hereditary holdings of their rulers.

In Egypt, however, some aspects of this first stage of the development of separatist forces were also characteristic of its development during the nineteenth and twentieth centuries. These included the activities of the Egyptian *beys* in the Arab peninsula and Syria (the first step of Meḥmed 'Alī's expansionist policy), and the reluctance of the *beys*, as well as Meḥmed 'Alī, to rid an almost independent ruler of the last vestiges of subjection to the Ottoman Sultan.

Ḥasan Pasha's expedition in 1787 foreshadowed that of Napoleon Bonaparte in its course and its effect on the subjected inhabitants. It also

---

31. The author is aware of the specific character of feudalism in the countries of West Asia and North Africa as treated by a number of scholars (cf. *Encyclopaedia of Islam*, s.v. *iḳṭāʿ*).

revealed the military inadequacy of the Mamluk regime – a vulnerability Napoleon's expedition showed up in full light. Moreover, as an attempt to destroy decentralizing forces and strengthen ties between the province and central government, the Ottoman expedition appears to have been the first significant example of the Ottoman's nineteenth-century attempts at centralization.

Egypt's increasing interest in territories beyond its borders, its contacts with the representatives of foreign powers and its efforts to enter into independent commercial relations with other regions, all showed that it had broken out of its centuries-long isolation and started to participate actively in the development of its region. The isolation from which it was slowly emerging was finally overcome when France embarked on its colonial expansion in the Eastern Mediterranean. In connection with the increasing problems of the Eastern question and the spread of European colonialism, Egypt became a country of major importance for world politics.

The Sudan, 1500–1800

7

Y.F. HASAN and B.A. OGOT

Introduction

The period under discussion has been characterized by population movements from within the Sudan[1] and from outside. In the north the slow penetration of the Muslim Arabs in large numbers over a long period of time – which was at an advanced stage at the beginning of our period,[2] – led to the gradual assimilation of the Christian Nubians and others in the larger pan-Islamic world. The process of cultural and ethnic assimilation was a two-way process: it led to the Arabization and Islamization of large numbers of Sudanese peoples on the one hand and the indigenization of the Arab immigrants on the other.

The impact of Islam and Arabic culture on the Southern Sudan was negligible. The expansionist energies of the Nilotes from the South had succeeded in arresting the southward march of the Arabs as well as the spread of Islam. Indeed the Nilotes, especially the Shilluk and the Jieng (Dinka), posed a serious threat to the northern Muslim states until the end of the period.

This chapter will therefore be dealing primarily with the establishment and expansion of the two Muslim savannah states (the Fundj and the Fūr sultanates), their relations with each other and their interaction with non-Muslim African societies which were also in the process of formation from diverse linguistic and cultural groups during this period.

The chapter will also attempt to show that the expansion of Islam constitutes an important factor in the history of the Sudan during this period.

In its southerly expansion, the process of the Arabization and Islamization was halted during this period in the water divide (consisting of the Sudd, Baḥr al-Ghazāl and Baḥr al-'Arab) thus creating a cultural

1. The Sudan refers to the eastern part of *Bilād al-Sūdān* which in Medieval times included the Christian Kingdom of Nubia, and then the Fundj and the Fūr Islamic sultanates, and in the present chapter is roughly equated with the modern Republic of the Sudan. The official usage of the term Sudan as a political or administrative entity is associated with the Turco–Egyptian regime 1821–85.

2. Cf. UNESCO, *General History of Africa*, Vol. IV, ch. 16.

frontier between what came to be known as the northern and southern Sudan. The existence of this cultural frontier has deeply coloured our interpretation of modern Sudanese history.

From the southern Sudanese perspective the relations between the two regions have been presented largely in terms of the aggression and economic exploitation of raiding parties from the Fundj in the Upper Nile, and later from the Fūr in the Baḥr al-Ghazāl region. From the northern perspective, on the other hand, political, economic and social changes have tended, until recently, to be explained in terms of Muslim and often Arab immigrants, 'The wise strangers' from the north or east. State formation in Northern Sudan is hence explained according to this perspective instead of historical analyses of the economic bases of these states and their social and cultural formation.

By the twentieth century the 'North' is presented as Arab and Muslim, and the 'South' as African (or negroid) and 'pagan' (or 'animist'). Thus the frontier becomes increasingly defined in religious and ethnic terms. Such a conception was largely propagated by the writings of anthropologists and colonial administrators. The elaborate racial terms and prejudices which evolved on both sides of the frontier tended to portray each region as a separate ethnic and religious entity with little or no contact between the two.

The historical reality was of course more complex than this. First, the 'frontier' between these two regions was frequently shifting – and not always southward or westward. For instance from about the middle of the seventeenth century to 1861, the Shilluk who occupied the Upper Nile, pushed the frontier northward to Ilays. From this area they raided the Fundj sultanate and the Nuba mountains.

Secondly, the frontier was not only constantly shifting; it was also a wide zone extending over a few hundred kilometres – for example, in the area of the Upper Nile. The same was true for the western area. What the Fūr sultanate raiders, the *djallāba* (traders) and the Baḳḳāra Arabs regarded as a frontier was, by 1800, a huge territory.[3] Furthermore, within the frontier itself, cultural, ethnic and social transformation was taking place all the time with people becoming Arabs, Fūr, Fundj, Shilluk, Naath (Nuer) or Jieng according to political and economic circumstances. Indeed, the process of social transformation and ethnic integration that was heralded by the coming of the Arabs and Islam in Nūba and Bēdja land was still at work along this huge frontier in the period under discussion.

Thirdly, within the northern Muslim sultanates themselves the process of ethnic change was a complex phenomenon. To begin with, the process of Arabization – which embraced Arabs and a host of indigenous Sudanese people – was more of a cultural connotation than an ethnic one. Regardless of a few exceptions, the term Arab was progressively being emptied of nearly all its ethnic significance. The Baḳḳāra Arabs who live along the

3. R. S. O'Fahey, 1980, pp. 137–9.

frontier between the two regions are a case in point. Another example is provided by the heterogeneous indigenous peoples such as the Bong–Bagirmi language group comprising the Kara, Binga and Gula,[4] the Nanda and Feroge. By the eighteenth century, each sultanate was divided into a number of chiefdoms most of which were plural societies. Moreover, the social formation of these sultanates was further complicated by the factor of slavery. Many of these slaves, who were brought from the southern regions, formed an important part of the armies of the sultans, others were completely assimilated in their new societies. Furthermore, trade in slaves as well as in other frontier commodities such as ivory and ostrich feathers, not only linked the two Sudanese regions but also linked Sudan in general and the frontier in particular to world markets.

Finally, largely as a result of migrations, political and economic factors, the population had crystalized during this period into the present population of the Sudan. With the exception of Westerners from central and Western *Bilād al-Sūdān* (such as the Takrūr and the Fulbe) and the Rashayida from Arabia, no new ethnic groups emerged in the Sudan in the nineteenth or twentieth centuries, and the major population movements were virtually completed by 1800.

The 'Abdallābi state

During the second half of the fifteenth century, a confederacy of Arab *ḳabīla*s led by their chief 'Abdallāh, nicknamed Djammā' (the Gatherer), succeeded in conquering the kingdom of "Alwa".[5] Contrary to what is commonly accepted, the conquest of Sōbā was not a joint undertaking of the Fundj and the Arabs, but was accomplished by the Arabs alone. The conquest of Sōbā was an indication of the preponderance of Arab influence and it marked the beginning of Arab ascendancy in eastern *Bilād al-Sūdān*.[6]

'Abdallāh Djammā' and his descendants, the 'Abdallābi, administered the new regime from Ḳerri, north of Sōbā, on the main Nile. Sōbā thus lost lost its importance and was indeed in ruins when Daudi Reubeni the Jewish traveller, passed by it in 1523.[7] The choice of Ḳerri was probably determined by its easy access to the Buṭāna Arabs whose support was essential to the 'Abdallābi. It also controlled movements, especially of trade, along the Nile valley and across it to the western bank.

The extent of the new state is not easy to determine. The 'Abdallābi hegemony seems to have extended over the Arabs in northern Djazīra, the Buṭāna, east of the Nile, and possibly over some of the Bēdja groups. The Arabized chieftainships which dotted the area between Shandī and the Egyptian border, and which seemed to have participated in the Arab assault

---

4. For this language group, see A. N. Tucker and M. A. Bryan, 1966, pp. 10–9.
5. For details see UNESCO, *General History of Africa*, Vol. IV, ch. 16, pp. 406–7.
6. P. M. Holt, 1960; Y. F. Hassan, 1972, pp. 23–6.
7. S. Hillelson, 1933, p. 60.

against Sōbā, remained loyal to the head of the Arab confederation. The exact relation between them is not clear; but later, the 'Abdallābi as overlords had the authority to confirm the appointment of new chiefs.

The independent existence of the 'Abdallābi state did not last long enough for it to evolve its own institutions. By the beginning of the sixteenth century it was confronted with a formidable enemy – the Fundj, who were cattle nomads migrating down the Blue Nile. The two migratory forces clashed, probably in competition over pasture in the northern part of the Djazīra. At Arbadjī, in 1504, the Fundj defeated the 'Abdallābi and their king was reduced to the position of vassal.[8] As junior partners, the 'Abdallābi continued to rule the northern part of the Fundj sultanate until the Turco–Egyptian conquest of 1820.

The Fundj sultanate

The Fundj were cattle nomads, whose remote origin gave rise to many contradictory hypotheses. Their kingdom is known in Sudanese traditions as *al-Sultana al-Zarḳa* (the Black Sultanate).[9] Daudi Reubeni, who visited them in 1522–3, described their monarch as a black Muslim who ruled over a nation of blacks and whites[10] – referring to the indigenous population and the Arabs respectively. While visiting Sennār in 1772, James Bruce, the Scottish traveller, recorded that the Fundj were by origin Shilluk raiders who descended from the White Nile.[11] Yet some Sudanese traditions, probably of Arab origin, attribute an Arab ancestry to them, through an Umayyad refugee who came via Ethiopia. He married an indigenous princess and hence inherited her authority. He is referred to in Sudanese traditions as the 'blessed man' who brought new customs.[12]

It is not clear at what date the Fundj dynasty began to claim Umayyad descent. In the light of Reubeni's remarks, at least king 'Umāra Dunḳus, who defeated the 'Abdallābi, was a Muslim. But it seems that, as a result of the impact of the new Muslim society over which they extended their hegemony and as a consequence of commercial and cultural relations with Egypt, the Fundj were rapidly Islamized.[13] Like other converts on the fringes of Islamic societies, the Fundj tended to associate themselves with the Arabs and thus adopted an Arab ancestry. By so doing they hoped to increase their prestige in the Muslim world and to enhance their moral authority over their Arab subjects. However, it is significant to note that Ibn (son of) Dayf Allāh, when referring to the ruling élite called them 'kings of the Fundj' and 'kings of the Arabs' (that is, kings of the 'Abdallābi

8. J. Bruce, 1805, Vol. III, pp. 370–2; Vol. 7, p. 96.
9. *Azraḳ* means black in Sudanese colloquial Arabic.
10. S. Hillelson, 1933, pp. 55–60.
11. J. Bruce, 1805, Vol. VII, p. 96.
12. Y. F. Hasan, 1965.
13. P. M. Holt, 1961, p. 20; J. L. Spaulding, 1972.

and the Dja'aliyyūn) implying that there was an ethnic difference between the two groups.[14]

Having asserted their suzerainty over the 'Abdallābi territories, the Fundj ruled their domains from Sennār which became their seat of government. The 'Abdallābi *shaykh* (chief), while retaining virtual autonomy in his former domains, became the Fundj vassal and bore the title of *Māndjil* or *Māndjuluk* which Fundj monarchs bestowed on their principal vassals. However, it appears that from the beginning, relations between the Fundj and their junior partners were antagonistic.

In an attempt to shake off Fundj dominance, Shaykh Adjīb I, who came to power just after the middle of the sixteenth century, challenged the Fundj, defeated them and drove them into Ethiopia. Under Dakīn (1568/9–1585/6) the Fundj were able to regain their former position but conceded to Adjīb I the right to appoint judges in his domains. Dakīn's policy of reorganizing the kingdom and introducing new regulations appears to have upset the delicate balance between the two sides and driven Adjīb into open rebellion. At Karkodj, a few miles north of Sōba, a Fundj army inflicted a crushing defeat on the 'Abdallābi and killed Adjīb I in 1611/12. His clan took refuge in Dūnkūla. A settlement between the Fundj and the 'Abdallābi was negotiated through the good office of Shaykh Idrīs wad al-Akbār, the influential religious dignitary.[15] Except for Arbadjī, which was transferred to Fundj, the *status quo* was restored: the descendants of Adjīb, bearing the title of *wad 'Adjīb*, continued to rule directly as far north as Hadjar al-'Asal, including over most of the nomadic groups and indirectly over the chieftaincies in the Nile valley to the border of Ottoman Nubia at the Third Cataract. The settlement gave the sultanate a fairly long period of stability. However, in about the middle of the seventeenth century, the Shaykīyya chieftaincy challenged the 'Abdallābi hegemony and asserted its independence from the Fundj sultanate.[16]

The extension of the Fundj sultanate

The extension of Fundj authority as far as lower Nubia, which was originally dependent on the 'Abdallābi, seems to have been viewed with suspicion by the Ottomans, who conquered Egypt in 1517. Although frontier clashes were reported, the Ottomans did not press the issue until the reign of Sultan Sulaymān the Magnificent (1520–66). To avert the Portuguese threat to the Red Sea, the Ottomans sent a naval expedition against them in the Indian Ocean; and decided to conquer Ethiopia, a Portuguese ally. On a return voyage from a naval expedition Özdemir was instructed to put an end to the 'rebellious' Fundj in Nubia, where two

14. Y. F. Hasan, 1965; Ibn Dayf Allāh Muḥammad 'Abd Nur, 1973, pp. 61, 90.

15. Aḥmad b. al-Ḥādjdj Abū 'l-'Alī, 1961, pp. 8–9; Ibn Dayf Allāh Muḥammad 'Abd Nur, 1973, pp. 63, 227, 296.

16. Y. F. Hasan, 1972, pp. 63–75.

factions were fighting one another. Özdemir captured the strategic frontier fortresses of Ibrīm and Dirr. At Sāy, between the Second and Third Cataracts, he built a fortress which constituted the southern limit of Ottoman Egypt. Effective administration of the new Ottoman province, hence known as Berberistan (the land of the Berberines or Nubians), appears to have been established when a garrison of Bosnian soldiers was installed at the fortresses of Aswān, Ibrīm and Sāy.[17]

After his retirement from the governorship of Yemen in November 1554, Özdemir Pasha had several interviews with the Sultan, during which they discussed the affairs of Egypt, Yemen and Habesistān.[18] He was later commissioned to conquer Habesistān. After detailed preparations in Egypt, the expedition started off up the Nile. At Aswān, Özdemir could not control his unruly troops and had to call off the campaign. There it was understood that the expedition was directed against Fundjistān (the land of the Fundj) and not Habesistān. Later, in 1577, a certain Sulaymān Pasha was instructed to undertake the conquest of Fundjistān. However, the campaign never materialized.[19] The Egyptian frontier was finally consolidated at Hannīk after some fighting between the 'Abdallābi and the Ottomans in about 1622. Hannīk lies half way between the Third Cataract and Mushu, the Fundj frontier post in the north.[20]

The administration of Ottoman Nubia was entrusted to an officer bearing the title of *Kashif*. The office then became hereditary in the family of the first *Kashif* who lived at al-Dirr. Likewise, the descendants of the original Bosnian troops, who intermarried locally, continued to garrison Ottoman fortresses in the district.

Özdemir is also credited with establishing an Ottoman base against the Portuguese and the Ethiopians: Sawākin, which was nominally dependent on Mamluk Egypt, passed to Ottoman suzerainty, and Massawa was annexed in 1557. Thenceforward the coastal strip between the two ports constituted the province of Habes. At Sawākin, an Ottoman garrison, headed by a governor with the rank of *sandjak* was stationed. When the Portuguese threat was over, Sawākin resumed its activites as the main commercial outlet of the Fundj sultanate. Relations between the Ottoman governor and the Fundj were at first unfriendly and at times deteriorated into armed confrontation. In 1571, according to Ottoman sources, the Fundj (or perhaps more accurately the Bēdja) attacked Sawākin and besieged it for three months. However, because of extensive commercial transactions between the two sides a more friendly atmosphere developed. Sawākin rose to a position of importance, which it retained unchallenged

17. G. Örhanlü, 1974, pp. 1–2, 21–2; P. M. Holt, 1961.
18. Ottoman sources use the term Habesistān or Abyssinia to include all territories south of Egypt as far as the island of Zanzibar or Mozambique in East Africa. See G. Örhanlü, 1974, p. 21.
19. ibid., pp. 34–5, 77.
20. P. M. Holt, 1961, p. 24.

PLATE 7.1   *The port of Sawākin, as portrayed in a nineteenth-century engraving*

until the beginning of the twentieth century. The Arabized Bēdja clan, the Ḥadāriba, who once dominated the region of ʿAydhāb, played a leading role in the trade. Later, it was from the Ḥadāriba that the Ottomans chose the local ruler known as the *Amīr*.[21]

By the beginning of the seventeenth century, the Fundj appeared to have consolidated their position at Sennār. Their direct rule extended from Arbadjī to the south of Fazūghlī, which probably constituted the northern limits of the Ethiopian border. The expansion of Fundj power in a westerly direction across the Djazīra into Kordofan was initiated by Sultan ʿAbd al-Kādir. In about 1554 he defeated the chiefs of the Sakadī and Moya Hills. Both chiefs were confirmed in their offices after embracing Islam and agreeing to pay an annual tribute.[22] The increasing pressure of the Nilotic peoples on the White Nile at the expense of Sennār apparently led to a direct confrontation between the Fundj and the Shilluk, who inhabited most of the region of the White Nile. Sultan Bādī II Abū Dikn (1644/5–1718), whose reign constituted the golden age of the Sultanate, established a Fundj garrison and a bridgehead at Alays on the White Nile. The administration of Alays was entrusted to a member of the Fundj dynasty whose rank was second to that of the ʿAbdallābi chief. From that strategic point the Fundj were able to check all movements across the river and also to check the Shilluk, who appear to have entered into an alliance with them.[23]

Then the Fundj penetrated the Nuba mountains, one of the principal slave-raiding regions. There the newly established Islamized kingdom of Takali was reduced to subordinate status.[24] Likewise the Fundj extended their suzerainty over the northern hills of al-Dāyr and Kordofan, which later became the scene of intensive competition with the Musabbaʿāt. The numerous prisoners captured from among the non-Muslim ʿhill-Nūbaʾ were accommodated in villages around Sennār. The prisoners formed a slave-bodyguard to protect the sultan. Their numbers were later increased by raids and purchase. The establishment of a slave-army dependent on the ruler is not unprecedented in Islamic annals: it was first adopted by the Abbasid Caliph al-Muʿtasim and also by the sultan of Dārfūr in the eighteenth century. The practice was viewed with grave concern by the traditional warriors, the Fundj aristocracy, who revolted against it during the reign of Bādī III (the Red, 1692–1716). Although the sultan succeeded in containing that outbreak, the Fundj aristocracy was able to assert its power and depose his son Unsa III who was accused of leading a dissolute private life. This marked the end of the direct line of ʿUmāra Dunkus.

21. G. Örhanlü, 1974, p. 76.
22. J. Bruce, 1805, Vol. IV, p. 368.
23. Aḥmad b. al-Ḥādjdj Abūʾl-ʿAlī, 1961, pp. 9–10; Y. F. Hasan, 1972, p. 68; R. S. OʾFahey and J. L. Spaulding, 1974, pp. 61–3.
24. There is disagreement regarding Fundj–Takali relations at this time. The earlier theory of a tributary relation has recently been challenged by J. Ewald, 1983, p. 10.

Unsa III was followed by Prince Nūl in 1720.

Despite the intervention of the Fundj aristocracy, the state continued to rely on the slave-army. A further crisis was precipitated during the reign of Bādī IV Abū Shullūkh (1721–62), the last effective Fundj monarch. During the first half of his reign, Bādī IV, described as 'just and prosperous', left the affairs of state to his minister Dōka. On Dōka's death, Bādī banished the *ahl al-usūl* (members of the old lineage and rank) and with the support of his Nūba slave-army and Fūr refugees, assumed arbitrary rule. To rid himself of the antagonized Fundj notables, Bādī sent them on a campaign against the Musabbaʿāt who had encroached on the Fundj domains in Kordofān. After initial setbacks, the Fundj army, under the command of Muḥammad Abū Likaylik, won a decisive victory in 1747. Thereafter, Abū Likaylik retained his command over the Fundj forces in Kordofān, where he ruled as viceroy for fourteen years.[25]

Meanwhile, the Fundj had fought two wars with Ethiopia, both largely triggered by border disputes but neither of which had led to any radical changes. The record of their relations includes many examples of positive co-operation and economic interdependence. To the Christians of Ethiopia, Sennār had long been their principal land outlet with the outside world. Through Sennār the Ethiopians obtained new bishops from Egypt and exchanged commercial commodities with the merchants. It was also along this route that European Christian missionaries found their way to Ethiopia – the land of Prester John.

The first Ethiopian war occurred at the beginning of the seventeenth century. When Sultan ʿAbd al-Ḳādir was deposed, he was granted political asylum by Emperor Susenyos of Ethiopia who appointed him governor of Chelega which controlled the movement of trade caravans on the border. The reigning Fundj sultan was anxious because, despite an exchange of gifts between Susenyos and Bādī I, relations had deteriorated into border skirmishes and slave-raiding. Frontier clashes escalated during 1618 and 1619, when large numbers of troops, using a limited number of muskets, were involved. The fact that the two monarchs conducted the war from their capitals, indicates that the war did not constitute a formidable threat to either side. The war ended in favour of Ethiopia.[26]

The second Ethiopian war began in the form of border raids against the Ḳalābāt–Dindera region to impose tributes. In March 1744, Iyasu II marched at the head of a large Ethiopian army against Sennār. The two armies met on the banks of the Dindera, in a pitched battle, during which the Ethiopians were routed and the emperor barely escaped death. The resounding Fundj victory was attributed to Prince Khamīs Djunḳul of the Mussabbaʿāt and his followers who had taken refuge in Sennār. Although relations between Sennār and Gondar remained strained for many years,

25. Aḥmad b. al-Ḥādjdj Abū' l-ʿAlī, 1961, pp. 9–10; P. M. Holt, 1961, pp. 20–2; Y. F. Hasan, 1972, pp. 71–7.

26. W. Aregay and S. H. Sellassie, 1971, Vol. VI, pp. 65–6.

trade routes were kept open. The Fundj victory was celebrated with religious fervour by Bādī IV and his subjects. It was also echoed in Istanbul where the Ottoman Caliph was said to have been 'pleased with the victory of Islam'.[27]

The progress of Islam

The establishment of the Fundj–'Abdallābi sultanate gave the country a measure of unity and stability that facilitated the spread of Islam by individual Muslim scholars who brought Islamic learning and introduced *ṣūfī* mysticism. They were welcomed by the rulers and encouraged to settle in the country. Before this the spread of Islamic doctrine had been accomplished by two groups – traders and, primarily, nomadic Arabs. The first group, whose contacts continued for more than nine centuries, acted as propagators of Islam: the combination of commercial activity with proselytization had always been a visible phenomenon on the margin of Islamic societies. The second group, although not well versed in Islamic doctrine and not moved by religious zeal, was largely responsible for the spread of Islam primarily through intermarriage with the indigenous Sudanese people. The process of Arabization was normally followed by Islamization.[28] The efforts of these two groups were, at times, augmented by those of individual teachers.

The early Fundj period witnessed a rise in the number of Muslim teachers, some of whom came from Egypt, the Ḥidjāz, Yemen and the Maghrib. The majority were, however, Sudanese some of whom had studied in Cairo and other holy places. On his return from Cairo in the middle of the sixteenth century Maḥmūd al-'Arakī, the first Sudanese Muslim scholar, established seventeen schools on the White Nile. In about 1570, Ibrāhīm al-Būlād ibn Djābir, a descendant of Ghalām Allāh ibn 'Ayd, introduced the teaching of the two Māliki textbooks: the *Risāla* by Abū Zayd al-Kayrawānī, and the *Mukhtasar* by Khalīl ibn Isḥāk. These books helped in establishing the predominance of the Māliki rite. Its ascendancy was further sustained by cultural impact from the Maghrib and western *Bilād al-Sūdān*, where the Māliki school predominated.

The first trained Muslim scholars were primarily concerned with the teaching of the *sharīʿa* (Muslim law), and with its administration. To transmit orthodox teaching and to raise the level of religious sophistication were not easy tasks in a vast, isolated and backward country. Before orthodox Islam had struck root, a more popular and less exacting type of Islam was introduced.

Most of the *ṣūfī tarīḳas* (religious orders) were introduced from the Ḥidjāz. The first of these and probably the most popular was the Ḳādiriyya, after 'Abd al-Ḳādir al-Djīlānī (1077–1166) of Baghdad. It was introduced

27. ibid., pp. 67–8; Aḥmad b. al-Hadjdj Abū 'l-'Alī, 1961, pp. 22–2.
28. J. S. Trimingham, 1949, p. 82.

by Tādj al-Dīn al-Baḥārī, of Baghdad, who came from Mecca in 1577 at the invitation of a Sudanese merchant pilgrim. He stayed for seven years in the Djazīra, during which he initiated many prominent Sudanese (including Shaykh ʿAdjīb I) into the Ḳādirīyya order.

Another order, the the Shādhiliyya, was introduced by Hammād ibn Muḥammad al-Madjdhūb (1693–1776), a member of the Djaʿaliyyūn Ḳabīla, who studied in the Ḥidjāz. The Madjdhūbiyya, as the order came to be known locally, and the Madjādhīb clan developed into an ethnic theocracy in the region south of the Atbara confluence. There, they played an important role in temporal and spiritual matters.

When *Ṣūfism* reached the Fundj kingdom, it had already reached a low ebb throughout the Islamic world, being no longer merely a means of deepening religious conviction, as it had become tainted by some unorthodox practices. In the absence of proper religious instruction, people had come to believe that *baraka* (blessings or goodness) emanated from a holy man who acted as an intermediary between man and God. They also believed that such mystical powers or functions could be inherited by such a man's descendants or could be exhibited by him after his death. This attitude led to a significant emphasis on the cult of saints. *Ṣūfi* teachers were generally endowed with grants of land, or tax exemption and some acquired considerable political influence such as that attained by Idrīs wad al-Akbār and the Madjādhīb. They became more revered by the rulers and their subjects than the jurists.

However, by the seventeenth century, the two functions could no longer be distinguished. The jurists, realizing the gratifying position attained by their rivals, tended to combine the teaching of law with *ṣūfi* leadership. This development was clearly reflected in local usage, where the title *fakī* (a corruption of the Arabic *fakīh*, a jurist; pl. *fukahāʾ*) was indiscriminately applied to the jurist and the mystic.

Through the many centres of religion they established, and through the great influence they wielded, the *fakī*s offered elements of continuity and stability to the heterogeneous and fluid Fundj society. Through their teaching of Islamic doctrine they provided a unifying factor and through the loyalty they enjoyed they superimposed a wider loyalty to Islam. Their missionary zeal was not confined to the Fundj kingdom, but radiated as far as Kordofān, Dārfūr and Borno. Indeed, celebrated Sudanese jurists attracted students from the region between the Djazīra and Borno.[29]

Islam progressed in a similar manner in Kordofān and the newly established Fūr sultanate. Dārfūr was affected by Islamic currents initially from the Maghrib and central *Bilād al-Sūdān* and then increasingly from the Fundj kingdom. Islamic influences were felt in Kānem, which wielded great influence all over the region, well before the eleventh century.[30]

29. For example, al-Ḳaddāl had 1500 students from the Takrūr and Arbāb al-Khashin had 1000 students from the region between the Djazīra and Bornu.

30. Y. F. Hasan, 1971; Ibn Dayf Allāh Muḥammad ʿAbd Nur, 1973, pp. 3–23.

Trade and the state

The territories of the Fundj and the Fūr sultanates were traversed by a number of long-distance trade routes that connected them with Egypt and the Red Sea. These routes played an important role in strengthening economic and cultural links with the outside world. The Fundj and the Fūr sultans, like most kings of the Sudanic belt, had a vested interest in long-distance trade which enjoyed their patronage and protection. The exchange of slaves, gold, ostrich feathers and other African products for fine cotton textiles, jewellery, weapons and other luxury items complemented one another. Besides the revenue they levied at the customs posts, the sultans needed luxury goods to maintain their prestige and to reward their loyal supporters.

External trade ran along two main axes which took a west–east and a south–north direction. The first connected Borno–Wadai with Sennār, through Kobbie – the principal commercial centre in Dārfūr – and Kordofān. From Sennār it proceeded directly to Ḳoz Radjab and Sawākin, or by way of Shandī. Beside commercial transactions, it also carried Muslim pilgrims across what came to be called the Sudan Road.

Through the Sudan Road, the Eastern Sudan was laid open to cultural influences from the Western Sudan and North Africa. African Muslim scholars – who developed strong relations with the Nile valley and the Ḥidjāz – followed this route whose starting-point seems to have been Dārfūr, which also attracted pilgrims from the countries west of Lake Chad. By the beginning of the nineteenth century the route was known throughout the Sudan belt as far as Futa Toro in the west. Being shorter and less expensive it was traversed by pilgrims who could not afford the cost of a desert journey through Egypt in the company of commercial caravans. Pilgrims travelled mostly on foot, and benefited from the charity and the protection of the Muslim peoples. Although some of these pilgrims, including scholars, settled in the Eastern Sudan, they should not be confused with the migratory trends of some West Africans such as the Fulbe who had established sizeable communities in Dārfūr (and elsewhere) by the beginning of the nineteenth century. These pilgrims seem to have carried on considerable trading activities en route, in asses, books, and other merchandise. The writing of amulets was also one of their major activities.

The second route commenced at Sennār from which a regular trade caravan set out twice a year to Egypt. It went through Ḳerrī (and later Halfāyat al-Mulay) directly across the Bayūda Desert (or from another point down the Nile) through Dūnḳula and Salima to Asyūṭ in Upper Egypt. However, owing to the chaos caused by the rise of the Shayḳīyya in the eighteenth century, this standard route was abandoned in favour of another that followed the eastern bank. This one went from Sennār via Shandī, al-Damār, across the Atbara to Berber and then across the Nubian

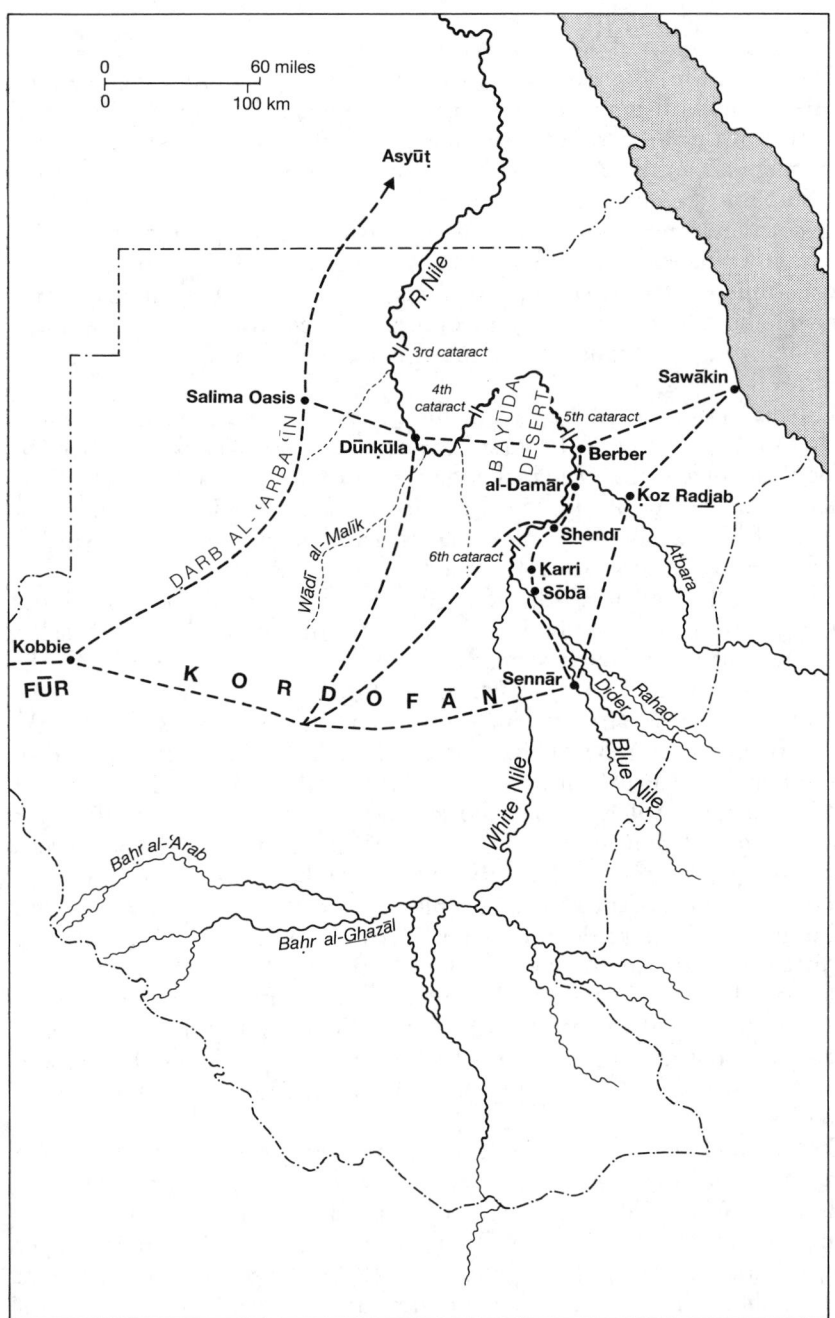

FIG. 7.1   *Trade routes of the Sudan (after Y. F. Hasan)*

Desert under the protection of the 'Abābda Arabs, to Isna in Upper Egypt.

At the Salima Oasis, the Nile route was joined by the *Darb al-'Arbaʿīn* (Forty-Days Road), the main artery of Fūr trade to Egypt. It started at Kobbie then went to Suwaynī, the last Fūr border point, across the desert via the Salima and the Khārdja oases into Asyūṭ. Another trade route took a north-westerly direction to Tripoli and Tunisia via Fezzān.[31]

Through its wide hinterland and strategic position Sennār developed into an important commercial centre. Describing Sennār in 1701, Father Krump wrote:

> In all Africa, as far as the Moorish lands are concerned, Sennār is close to being the greatest trading city. Caravans are continually arriving from Cairo, Dūnḳūla, Nubia, from across the Red Sea, from Nubia, Ethiopia, Dārfūr, Borno, the Fezzān and other kingdoms. This is a free city and men of any nationality or faith may live in it without a single hindrance.[32]

Most of the foreigners who came to Sennār were merchants and a few were craftsmen. The bulk of the trade was probably in the hands of the Sudanese *Djallāba* (traders). As middlemen in the trade between Sennār and Egypt, the Danāḳla and the Djaʿaliyyūn of Shandī acquired commercial experience and adequate capital to venture into new territories. The enterprising *Djallāba* also played an important role in the Fūr trade and were instrumental in the development of commercial centres in Dārfūr. Although the Sudanese *Djallāba* and others from Upper Egypt were the chief financiers of the long-distance trade, the ultimate control of that trade, its organization and safety seemed to rest with the sultans of the respective kingdoms. At times the sultans dispatched their own caravans to Cairo.[33] In Dārfūr, the long-distance trade was more or less under state control. Through these trading caravans, the Fūr sultanate became better known to the outside world.

The commercial ascendancy of Sennār was affected by the Fundj–Fūr rivalry over Kordofān and by the Shilluk raids which rendered the Kobbie-(al-ʿObeyd)-Sennār route unsafe. Hence that trade took a northerly direction into Shandī.[34] When Bruce visited Shandī in 1773 it was a large commercial centre, under the autonomous rule of the Saʿdāb Djaʿaliyyūn.[35] By the beginning of the nineteenth century Shandī had attained such great commercial importance that Burckhardt described it as having succeeded Sennār as the grand rendezvous for Nubian caravans and the market for Ethiopian and Fūr commerce.[36]

31. R. S. O'Fahey and J. L. Spaulding, 1970, pp. 6, 9; P. M. Holt, 1961, pp. 12–14; Y. F. Hasan, unpublished and also 1977; U. al-Naqar, 1972, pp. 92–113.

32. T. Krump, 1710.

33. R. S. O'Fahey and J. L. Spaulding, 1974, p. 68.

34. J. L. Burckhardt, 1819, pp. 321–2.

35. J. Bruce, 1805.

36. J. L. Burckhardt, 1819, pp. 321–2.

In the East the Ḥadāriba of Sawākin were also active in the long-distance trade between the Red Sea and the Nile. They procured African products and slaves from Shandī and exchanged them for Indian goods at Sawākin – the most important slave centre after Cairo and Massawa.[37]

The movement of slaves down the Nile was an ancient phenomenon. The practice was continued by the Arabs when they concluded the *baḳt* treaty with the Nubians, after which through the dispatch of four hundred Nubian slaves annually, the Arab world came to favour them as domestic employees. Their fighting qualities as bowmen also recommended them to serve as slave troops. Black slaves had been eagerly sought by the Tulunids (868–935), the Ikhshidids (935–69) and the Fāṭimids (969–1171) of Egypt to fill the ranks of their armies.

As a result of this long practice, demand for black slaves increased. However, because of its sparse population, Nubia could not meet the needs of the Islamic world and Arab traders had to tap other sources south-west of Nubia. It was through this Arab (the term is used vaguely to include Arabs and their subjects) intervention that the slave trade received further stimulus acquiring great importance which continued until the last decades of the nineteenth century. At first the slaves included Nubians and Bēdja, then with the increase in demand, they were procured from Kordofān, Dārfūr and, eventually, from the Baḥr al-Ghazāl, Borno–Wadai and other adjacent lands in central *Bilād al-Sūdān*. Slaves offered for sale at Shandī by the end of the eighteenth century included Ethiopians and Nūba from Kordofān, Dārfūr, Borno and Dār Silla.

Slaves were acquired through conquest, kidnapping or purchase and the role of Arab dealers varied from time to time and from one region to another. It seems, however, that most Arab traders were not engaged in the primary acquisition of slaves (except during the nineteenth century) but relied mostly on African suppliers or middlemen. Both Arab traders and African suppliers utilized fully ancient customs and institutions that lent themselves to such practices. The Arab merchants were mostly content to obtain slaves in return for the commodities they peddled.

The external demand for black slaves for military purposes shrank during the time of the Ayyubids (1172–1251) who disbanded black troops in favour of white slaves. This policy was continued by the Mamluks (1251–1517) during whose regime the army was almost exclusively recruited from white slaves.

However, demand for black soldiers continued to be felt in other places, particularly in the newly established Fundj and Fūr sultanates where they constituted the core of the army. In the nineteenth century Muḥammad 'Alī Pasha, Viceroy of Egypt, began to recruit black slaves for his modern army, most of whom were purchased from the Sudan. Although Muḥammad 'Alī abandoned his original idea of a black army, Sudanese soldiers

37. For a more detailed discussion of this point, see Y. F. Hasan, unpublished and 1977; R. S. O'Fahey, 1970; J. L. Spaulding, 1971, p. 150 and T. Walz, 1975.

continued to constitute a sizeable section of the Egyptian army throughout the nineteenth century.

The decline of the Fundj sultanate

The visible decay of Sennār as the leading commercial centre was matched by political decline. At Sennār, with the increase of Bādī IV's repressive measures, members of the Fundj aristocracy who had accompanied Abū Likaylik to Kordofān and whose families had suffered most, induced the general to depose the sultan. Abū Likaylik marched with his army into Sennār, deposed Bādī and replaced him with his son Nāṣir in 1762. The success of the revolt of Abū Likaylik was an important landmark in the history of the sultanate. Henceforward Shaykh Muḥammad Abū Likaylik and his successors, who were called *wazirs*, became effective hereditary rulers or regents of the kingdom until its downfall. The Fundj sultans were indeed no more than puppets in the hands of the Hamadj regents. The shift in power is aptly summarized by the Fundj chronicler in the following words: Bādī ' ... was the last of the kings with power and with him ended the real monarchy. After him the power of binding and loosing passed to the Hamadj.'[38]

The term 'Hamadj' was applied by Sudanese Arabs to some of the ancient peoples of the Djazīra. Although accredited with a Djaʿali pedigree they were neither Fundj nor Arabs. The emergence of the Hamadj hegemony, under the leadership of Abū Likaylik probably represented the resurgence of an ancient people who became Arabized and Islamized.[39]

On the death of Abū Likaylik in 1776/7, the Fundj kings began to conspire with the provincial governors, particularly the ʿAbdallāb, to oust their regents. The descendants of Abū Likaylik were themselves handicapped by their own internal struggle for power. Indeed, the last fifty years of the Fundj sultanate were punctuated by intrigues, revolts and civil wars among the competing factions.

In the north, the control of the 'Abdallāb chiefs over the Nile valley also declined: the Saʿdāb of Shandī, and the Madjādhīb of al-Damar became virtually autonomous. The Shayḳīyya warriors who became a major force in the region of Dūnḳula were harassed by the Mamluks of Egypt. In 1811, they fled from Muḥammad ʿAlī's massacre, established a camp at Dūnḳula al-ʿUrdī and fought the Shayḳīyya. In the west, the Fundj, harassed by the Fūr sultanate, were ultimately driven out of Kordofān. When the Turco-Egyptian forces approached Sennār in 1821, the sultanate was too feeble to muster any resistance.

---

38. J. L. Burckhardt, 1819, p. 310.
39. Aḥmad b. al-Ḥādjdj Abū 'l-ʿAlī, 1961, p. 21; R. S. O'Fahey and J. L. Spaulding, 1974, p. 94.

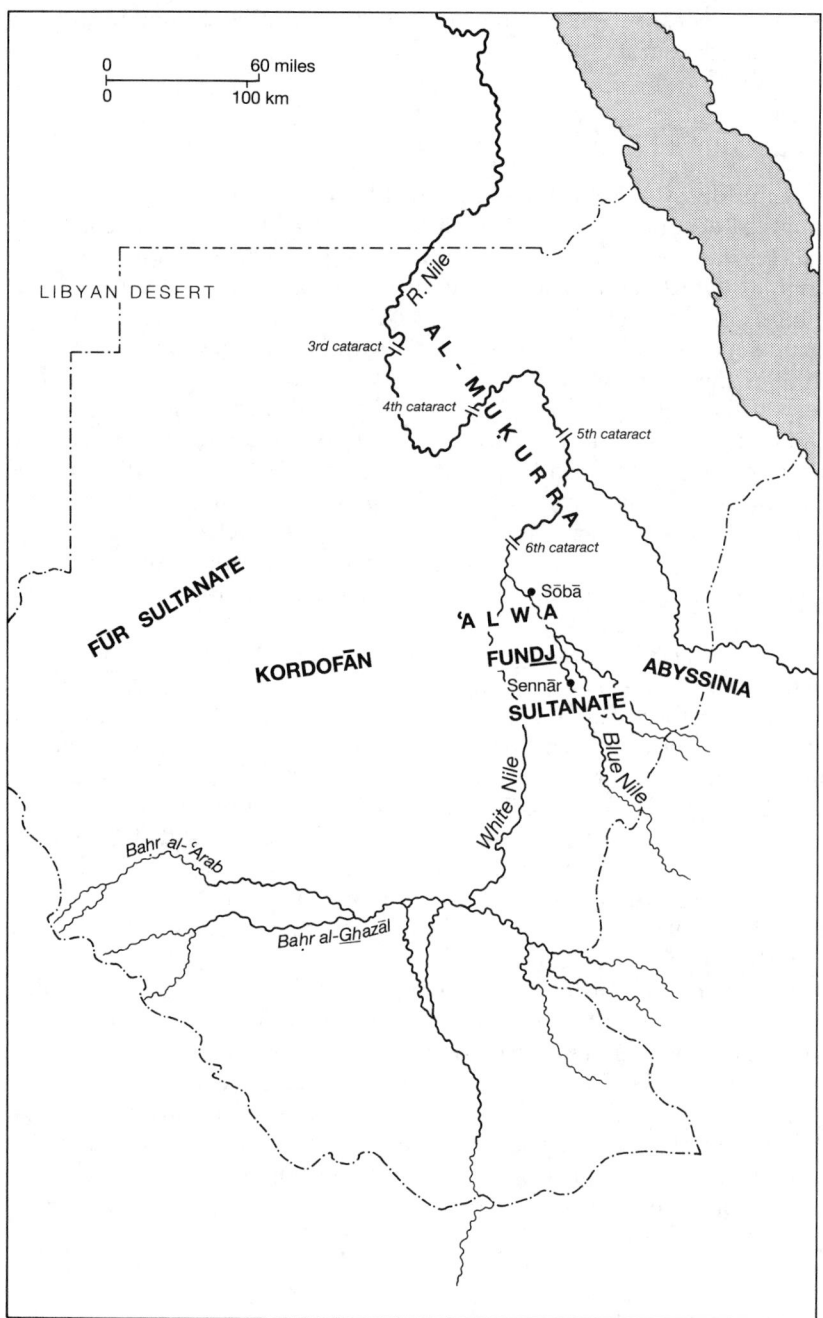

FIG. 7.2   *Kingdoms and sultanates of the Sudan (after Y. F. Hasan)*

The Fūr sultanate

The Fūr sultanate was one of the Islamic kingdoms that flourished in the savannah belt of *Bilād al-Sūdān*. It occupied the western fringe of the eastern *Bilād al-Sūdān*. To the west lay the Sultanate of Wadai, and between the two states there existed a number of small semi-independent kingdoms whose allegiance was divided between the two sultanates. To the east, the plains of Kordofān, which separated the Fūr sultanate from the Fundj kingdom, were a cause of dispute between the two states, primarily for economic reasons. There, the Musabbaʿāt, cousins of the Fūr sultans, were also at loggerheads with the rival states, while attempting to consolidate their hold over Kordofān. The Libyan Desert in the north and Bahr al-ʿArab in the south formed natural borders to the state. The central region, dominated by Djabal Marra, the cradle of the Fūr sultanate, was the meeting place for a number of trade routes. These caravan routes brought economic prosperity, cultural influences and human immigration.

The early history of the Fūr sultanate is obscure because of the scarcity of written sources. According to oral tradition the Fūr state was preceded by two indigenous dynasties: Dādjū and Tundjūr. The Dādjū kingdom flourished during the thirteenth and fourteenth centuries. On losing control over the trade they were succeeded by the Tundjūr at the beginning of the fifteenth century. They first established their authority over the central region and gradually over Dārfūr and parts of Wadai.[40] It was probably during the reign of the Tundjūr (*c.*1400–1600) that Islamic influences were first felt. They resulted from wide commercial contact with the Muslim world, and the gradual penetration of the region by Arab immigrants.[41] However, the proper Islamization of the region began with the establishment of the Fūr sultanate in the early seventeenth century.

The Fūr sultanate owed its name to the Fūr, an indigenous Sudanese people who lived around Djabal Marra, and who originally might have been connected with the peoples of western Bahr al-Ghazāl. It is not clear why they moved down to the savannah from their mountain base.

R. S. O'Fahey has suggested that the rise of the Fūr sultanate, like that of other Islamic kingdoms of the Sudanic belt, was a product of the long-distance trade. He links its establishment with expansion of trade across the Forty-Days Road.[42] The association between trade and the spread of Islam has been noted by many scholars; in the case of the Fūr sultanate, trade was an important factor in developing the state itself and strengthening its contacts with its neighbours.

The Kayra sultanate flourished from about 1640 to 1874. It was restored in 1898 and was finally annexed to the Anglo–Egyptian Sudan in 1916. Sulaymān Solongdungu was probably the founder of the dynasty (*c.*1640–

40. Y. F. Hasan, 1972, pp. 72–82.
41. ibid., pp. 82–5; P. M. Holt, 1961; R. S. O'Fahey and J. L. Spaulding, 1974, p. 121.
42. R. S. O'Fahey, 1971, p. 87.

60). He is remembered as a conqueror who drove out the Tundjūr and annexed the area around Djabal Marra. He was assisted in these campaigns by Arab groups comprising camel and cattle nomads such as the Ḥabāniyya, the Maʿāliyya, the Rizayḳāt, and the Misayriyya.

The policy of expansion and consolidation started by Sulaymān Solong-dungu was pursued by his successor Aḥmad Bukr b. Mūsā (*c*.1682–1722), who pushed on to the north and north-west annexing the strategic state of Dār Ḳimr. This expansion brought the Kayra dynasty into contact with the Zaghāwa whose territories became a source of conflict between the Sultanates of Wadai and Dārfūr. The Kayra consolidated their position in Dār Zaghāwa by marriage alliances and by supporting one section against the other. Competition for control of the borderlands was resolved in favour of the Kayra sultanate, and Wadai continued to pay the tribute which it had formerly paid to the Tundjūr kings. However, Sultan Yaʿḳūb renounced the tribute, invaded Dārfūr and penetrated as far as the import-ant commercial centre of Kabkābiyya. After two years of military prep-aration, during which he obtained weapons and firearms from Cairo, Bukr drove the invaders out of the country.[43]

Until the end of the eighteenth century the political history of Dārfūr was dominated by the struggle of two factions of the Kayra dynasty: the sultans who sought to centralize their own power and other princes who wanted to strengthen the powers of the dynasty as a whole. The struggle was triggered by Sultan Bukr's desire that the sultanate should pass to each of his sons in turn. Bukr had no less than a hundred children, five of whom ascended the Fūr throne. His first successor, Muḥammad Dawra, started by eliminating his brothers or proscribing them in Djabal Marra, and naming his son Mūsā as successor. However, he soon changed his mind and replaced Mūsā by his younger brother ʿUmar Lel. Mūsā retaliated by revolting against his own father. When ʿUmar Lel came to power hostility between him and his uncles, the sons of Bukr, increased. Sulaymān ibn Aḥmad Bukr took refuge with the Musabbaʿāt who, after an unsuccessful bid for the Kayra throne had to migrate to Kordofān. Sulaymān's attempt to enlist the support of the Musabbaʿāt and that of the Sultan of Wadai failed. However, his action provoked ʿUmar Lel to invade Wadai in about the middle of the eighteenth century. After heavy fighting, the Sultan of Wadai, Muḥammad Djawda, defeated the Fūr army and captured the sultan.

The conflict continued into the reign of the sixth sultan, Abu ʾl-Ḳāsim b. Aḥmad Bukr. To consolidate his position, Abū ʾl-Ḳāsim turned against his brothers and recruited slave troops rather than the traditional ethnic levies. By this action the sultan 'completely alienated himself from the free men of his country preferring slaves and heaping upon them riches and places of honour'.[44]

43. R. S. O'Fahey and J. L. Spaulding, 1974, pp. 126–8; Y. F. Hasan, 1972, pp. 86–8.
44. G. Nachtigal, 1971, Vol. IV, p. 285.

Abū 'l-Ḳāsim's dependence on slave troops was opposed by large numbers of the traditional title-holders. Indeed, it produced tensions similar to those that developed in the Fundj kingdom during the reign of Bādī IV.

During the battle against the Wadaians, Abū 'l-Ḳāsim was deserted by the traditional war chiefs and ethnic levies and was left with his slave troops. There he was wounded after he had lost the day. The old Fūr nobility and traditional soldiers hailed Muḥammad Tayrāb ibn Aḥmad Bukr as the new sultan. Muḥammad Tayrāb followed his predecessor's practice and created a standing slave-army called the *Kurkwā* (spearmen in Fūr). Slaves from the Turundj of the Nuba mountains, the Dading from Dār Tama and others were incorporated into it. One of the *Kurkwā* corps, Muḥammad Ḳurra, a eunuch, became one of Tayrāb's masters of the royal grooms. Later he attained great distinction and became *Āb Shaykh*, a post that commanded great authority.[45]

Having failed to expand westward against his formidable foe, the Sultan of Wadai, Tayrāb, concluded a treaty which remained effective for a hundred years. He then turned his efforts eastward against the Musabbaʿāt, who must have regained power in Kordofan after the withdrawal of Abū Likaylik in 1761–2. The change in the direction of expansion was probably dictated by other factors such as Tayrāb's desire to curb the Musabbaʿāt's attempt to establish a strong state in Kordofan and to control the trade routes, the sources of slaves and gold in southern Kordofan. The arrival of large numbers of enterprising *djallāba* and religious teachers from the Fundj kingdom and the increasing commercial links with Egypt might have influenced the sultan in that direction. His immediate objective was probably to remove his brothers and other members of the old Fūr nobility out of Dārfūr to pave the way for the succession of his son, Isḥāḳ: Tayrāb, at the head of a large army moved against Hāshim, Sultan of Kordofan. The latter, deserted by his army, took refuge in the Fundj kingdom; while Kordofan remained in the hands of the Fūr until the Turco–Egyptian conquest. Tayrāb himself died at Bara.

A struggle over succession ensued between the supporters of Isḥāḳ and his uncles, the sons of Aḥmad Bukr. Muḥammad Ḳurra succeeded in rallying the support of the second faction for ʿAbd al-Raḥmān, the youngest son of Aḥmad Bukr. ʿAbd al-Raḥmān was a pious and scholarly young man with neither ethnic connections nor support from among the new forces in the state. In the civil war, ʿAbd al-Raḥmān emerged victorious. The new sultan rewarded Muḥammad Ḳurra with the position of *Āb Shaykh* – a rank that was second only to that of the sultan. As the chief, Muḥammad Ḳurra was from about 1790 to 1804 the strongest man in the state.[46]

45. R. S. O'Fahey and J. L. Spaulding, 1974, pp. 129–37, 171–5; Y. F. Hasan, 1972, pp. 87–8.

46. P. M. Holt, 1961, pp. 26–8; R. S. O'Fahey and J. L. Spaulding, 1974, pp. 134–40; Y. F. Hasan, 1972, p. 91.

'Abd al-Raḥmān marked his victory by establishing a new *fāshir* (royal residence) at Khor Tandalti, east of Djabal Marra, in 1741–2. Until then the Fūr sultans had had no fixed capital. The growth of a permanent capital at al-Fāshir, and the consolidation of the centralizing forces and Islamizing influences in the reign of 'Abd al-Raḥmān marked the apogee of the Kayra sultanate. His reign was marked by increasing contacts with the outside world through trade and the arrival of religious teachers. The state prospered from trade along the Forty-Days Road. G. W. Browne, who visited Dārfūr in 1793–6, describes the role of the king as follows:

> The king is the chief merchant in the country, and not only despatches with every caravan to Egypt a great quantity of his own merchandise, but also employs his slaves and dependants to trade with the goods of Egypt, on his own account, in the countries adjacent to the Sudan.[47]

The sultans utilized the trade to strengthen their political position by purchasing arms, armour and luxury goods with which to reward their loyal subordinates and allies.

Both trade and religion were stimulated by the infiltration of the Dja'aliyyūn and the Danākia. 'Abd al-Raḥmān exchanged presents with the Ottoman sultan, who bestowed on him the honorific title of *al-Rashīd* (the just). He also corresponded with Bonaparte in 1799 during the French occupation of Egypt.

The adoption of Islam in Dārfūr was probably a much slower process than in the Fundj kingdom. Earlier trends of Islamization were speeded up in the eighteenth century. Sulaymān Solongdungu was credited with the introduction of Islam as a court religion and the promotion of Islamic practices. Some of Dārfūr's religious families claim that their ancestors had settled in the sultanate during the reign of Sulaymān. However, African religious practices and rituals co-existed with Islam at the Kayra court for some time.[48] Islam received further encouragement from Aḥmad Bukr who built mosques and schools; while Muḥammad Tayrāb obtained religious books from Egypt and Tunisia. 'Abd al-Raḥmān al-Rashīd, himself a Muslim scholar, encouraged jurists and mystics from other countries to settle in his land. Among these was 'Umar al-Tunisi, a Tunisian Arab, who was later followed by his own son, Muḥammad, whose account of Dārfūr is one of the main sources for its history.[49] Other scholars came from Egypt, the Ḥidjāz, the Nilotic Sudan and western *Bilād al-Sūdān*. From the last region came Mālik al-Futāwī, a member of a religious family, who taught 'Abd al-Raḥmān before he became sultan. Later, he became minister to Sultan Muḥammad al-Faḍl. Since the execution of justice rested in the hands of the sultan and the traditional title-holders according to customary law, the appointment of 'Izz al-Dīn al-Djāmī as the Grand Ḳāḍī (Chief

47. G. W. Browne, 1799, p. 301.
48. Y. F. Hasan, 1972, pp. 90–1.
49. al-Tunisi, 1965.

Judge of the *Sharīʿa* Court) was probably in an advisory capacity.

As an inducement to settle, the sultan offered religious teachers lands through the *hakura* (tax exemption) system, as enjoyed by their counterparts in the Fundj kingdom; some holy men adopted a mediatory role.[50]

By the end of the eighteenth century, it is clear that the sultan and his immediate associates who had no ethnic affiliations had gone a long way in developing external trade and adopting Islamic institutions to govern the affairs of the state. This approach helped in changing the ethnic structure of the state and weakening the ancient religious practices that had existed for some time. The emergence of a new class of merchants, jurists and mystics was instrumental in bringing this change about. However, the Kayra dynasty, despite its connection with an Arab ancestry, had its roots among the Fūr. Although Arabic was used in diplomacy and trade, Fūr remained the language of the court.

On the death of ʿAbd al-Raḥmān in 1801–2 his son Muḥammad al-Faḍl succeeded him with the help of Muḥammad Ḳurra. The new sultan soon fell out with his chief minister, Muḥammad Ḳurra, and killed him. Muḥammad al-Faḍl ruled for forty years, during which the state began to decline.[51]

The Southern Sudan

Despite the existence of major anthropological works by eminent scholars such as W. Hofmay, D. Westermann, C. G. Seligman, E. Evans-Pritchard and his many students and F. M. Deng on the Jieng, Naath, Anywa, Shilluk and Azande, historical research on Southern Sudan is still in its infancy. The same applies to archaeological investigations, which have been concentrated on Northern Sudan, and to historical linguistic research.[52]

From the meagre evidence, however, certain broad outlines are beginning to emerge. From linguistic evidence, for example, it is becoming increasingly clear that the homelands of both Nilotic and probably Central Sudanic cultures lie within Southern Sudan.[53] According to available data it is also evident that most of the language groups involved in the history of Southern Sudan belong to Greenberg's Nilo–Saharan family, as shown overleaf.

Much of Southern Sudan and Northern Uganda was probably occupied by speakers of Central Sudanic languages until the last decades of the last millennium when the area began to be colonized by Eastern and Western Nilotic speakers. Indeed, one of the major historical themes during our period is the progressive Niloticization of the former Central Sudanic

50. Y. F. Hasan, 1971, pp. 83–5; R. S. O'Fahey, 1971, pp. 87–95.

51. R. S. O'Fahey and J. L. Spaulding, 1974, pp. 162–4, 167; Y. F. Hasan, 1972, pp. 95–6; R. S. O'Fahey, 1970, pp. 3, 9.

52. For an assessment of the extent of our ignorance, see J. Mack and P. Robertshaw, 1982.

53. C. Ehret, 1982.

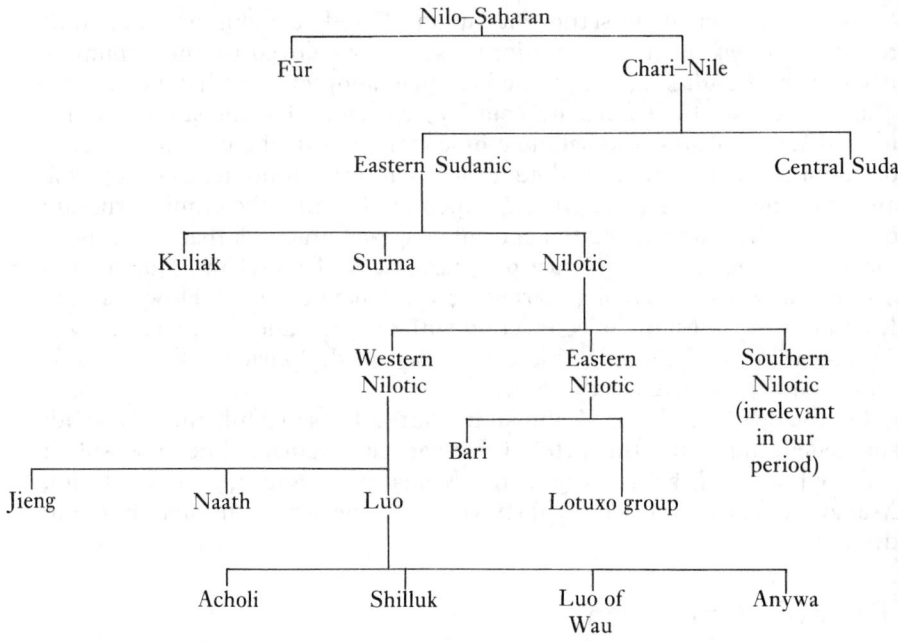

speakers in Southern Sudan. Today the region is mostly occupied by the Nilotes, with only the Moru and Madi living to the west of the White Nile to remind us of the former presence of the Central Sudanic speakers.

Roland Oliver has attempted a synthesis of Iron Age archaeological evidence on the early history of this region which tends to confirm the linguistic picture.[54] He envisages two centres of Iron Age cultures, one to the east of the Nile swamps in the Sudan–Ethiopian borderlands and the other on the ironstone plateau of the Nile–Congo watershed. These two cultures – the former Nilotic and the latter Bantu – were separated by Central Sudanic cultures. As the Nilotes moved southwards into the Bantu areas, there occurred a meeting of two Iron Age cultures which had hitherto developed separately. The result was an intensive Iron Age pastoralism among the Bantu-speakers, which he argues, could only have come from the Nilotes.

Regarding the Sudan, Oliver identifies two Iron Age periods among the Nilotes. First, there was the Early Iron Age, which coincided with the Later Iron Age of the Bantu. In Western Equatorial and Baḥr al-Ghazāl

54. R. Oliver, 1982. See also his chapter in J. Mack and P. Robertshaw, 1982.

provinces, this period is identified with Iron Age pastoralists, the Luel, who kept humpless cattle and who built artificial mounds in order to raise their wet-season settlements above flood level. It has been suggested by J. M. Stubbs, C. C. T. Morison, S. Santandrea and G. Lienhardt that the Luel were probably an advance party of Northern Luo-speakers. Their pottery was mostly plain or decorated with twisted fibre roulettes.

Then there was the Later or Recent Iron Age of the Nilotes, and it is this that concerns us in this chapter. The transition from the earlier to the later cultural complex seems to have coincided with the appearance of the humped cattle on the Baḥr al-Ghazāl and the full development of transhumance, especially among the Jieng. The humped cattle probably spread southwards with the Baḳḳāra Arabs following the fall of the kingdom of Dūnḳūla. It is also worth noting that this Arab penetration of the Northern and Central Sudan which occurred in the thirteenth and fourteenth centuries not only coincided with, but might have triggered, the Western Nilotic migrations.[55]

The rapid expansion of the Western and Eastern Nilotes southwards and eastwards may therefore be linked with the spread of intensive cattle-keeping made possible by the introduction of humped cattle and combined with cereal agriculture. This combination provided a means of food production suited to drier areas which enabled the Nilotes to occupy many areas which had hitherto been avoided by Bantu-speakers.

The Shilluk kingdom

In Southern Sudan, the Shilluk constitute the largest component of the Northern Luo group, the others being the Luo of Baḥr al-Ghazāl and the Anywa who straddle the Sudan–Ethiopia border. Their first settlement was near Malakal, under their leader, Nyikang (*c.*1490–1517) after defeating and driving out the Fundj – the previous inhabitants of what was soon to be the heartland of the Shilluk, the area between Tonga in the south and Muomo in the north. This area which lies at the confluence of the Nile and the Sobat and controls Lake No, must have been of the highest strategic importance. This small group of Luo-speakers incorporated Fundj and Nūba elements among others. It was these diverse elements, reflecting different cultures and economic traditions, that combined in the crucible of history to form what became known as the Shilluk nation from the second half of the seventeenth century.

During this formative century, the Shilluk established a mixed economy of cattle-herding and cereal agriculture. The population was essentially sedentary: transhumance, which characterized the life of the Jieng and Naath, was lacking. The Shilluk lived in a string of villages on the west bank stretching from Muomo to Tonga, a distance of one hundred miles.

55. D. W. Cohen, 1973; I. Hrbek, 1977, pp. 78–80.

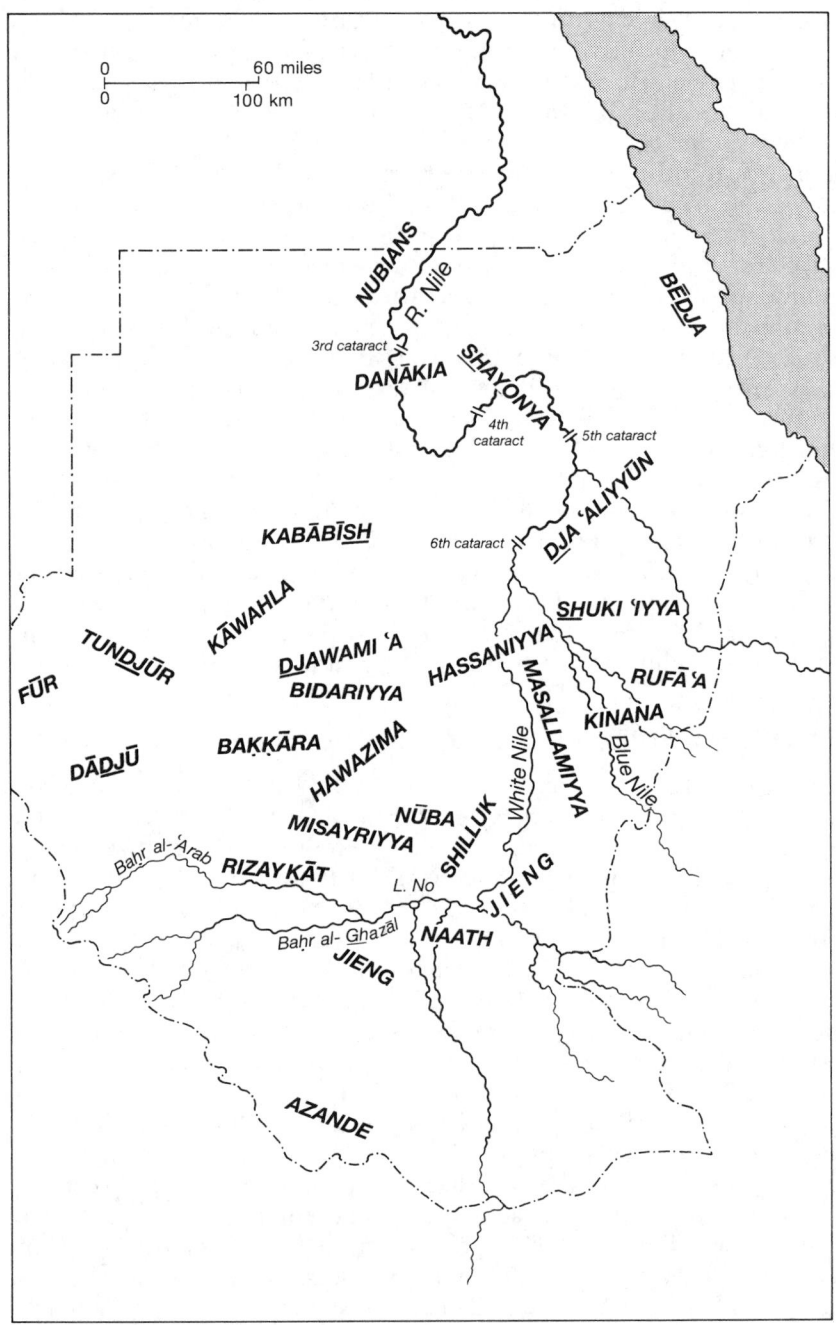

FIG. 7.3 *Peoples of the Sudan (after Y. F. Hasan)*

Frontiers and socio-economic interdependence

By the beginning of the seventeenth century, this area already had a bigger population than it could support. The intensive pressure on the land had not changed even by the nineteenth century, according to G. Schweinfurth who claims it was the most densely populated region of those parts of Africa then known to the outside world, including the Nile valley in Egypt.[56] The Shilluk began to expand into two frontier areas. Northwards, they attempted to control the White Nile from Muomo to Alays, a distance of about three hundred miles, studded with islands and thick mimosa forests. Although unsuitable for agriculture the region provided abundant game, fish and honey to the Shilluk frontiersmen. From the reign of Odak Ocollo (c.1600–35) to 1861, the Shilluk dominated this region which was named by the Muslim peoples 'Baḥr Scheluk', and the inhabitants as the 'River Shilluk'.

The second frontier area was the region between the Nile and the Nuba Hills. The numerous references in tradition to Shilluk–Nūba activities in this area imply that it was an important frontier zone for both the Nūba and the Shilluk before it was occupied by the Baḳḳāra Arabs in the second half of the nineteenth century.

In their book, *The Kingdoms of the Sudan*, R. S. O'Fahey and J. L. Spaulding have written:

> The fourteenth and fifteenth centuries were a period of change in the riverain Sudan, of adjustment to cultural and economic development impinging from the surrounding countries, and of accommodation to two intrusive groups – the Arabs and the Nilotic-speakers, particularly the Shilluk. The unification of Nubia early in the sixteenth century may be seen as both a Nubian reaction against the invaders and a positive response to the new economic and social circumstances that the intrusive forces had created.[57]

The history of the Shilluk during this period must be viewed against this broader canvas. They looked to the northern and western frontiers as areas of economic opportunities which provided what P. Mercer has termed 'an alternative source of supply.'[58] These zones also absorbed excess population.

We learn from Shilluk traditions, for example, that during the reign of *Reth* (King) Odak Ocollo, they supported Dārfūr in its struggle with the Fundj sultanate for the control of the White Nile trade. With the capitulation of Taḳali, the Fundj and the Shilluk were left confronting each other along the White Nile, both apparently exhausted after three decades of warfare.

56. G. Schweinfurth, 1873, p. 85.
57. R. S. O'Fahey and J. L. Spaulding, 1974, p. 15.
58. P. Mercer, 1971, p. 414.

But this temporary peace was soon disturbed by the arrival of another Jii-speaking people[59] – the Jieng – who invaded the southern region of the Fundj from about 1630 onwards.[60] Throughout the seventeenth and eighteenth centuries, the Jieng expanded into southern Djazīra, and gradually altered the balance of power in the region. Their presence there was a threat to both the Shilluk and the Fundj, and the two combined forces against the Jieng, whom they regarded as a common enemy. They succeeded in preventing the Jieng from expanding northwards or westwards, and instead forced them eastwards towards the Ethiopian border.

This alliance between the Fundj and the Shilluk against the Jieng marked the beginning of a socio-economic interdependence that the Shilluk established with different groups at different times – the Fundj, the *djallāba*, the Baḳḳarā Arabs, the Arab freebooters, the European traders and the Mahdists – usually to exploit the Jieng. It shows that such socio-economic alliances had not yet adopted a racial or ethnic ideology, for we see the Shilluk again and again combining with the above groups to exploit a related Jii-speaking group. Racial ideology in the Southern Sudan was to be a post-Mahdiyya-period phenomenon. Historians concerned with the development of patterns of socio-economic dependence should study the relationships between the different groups in the Upper Nile – the Shilluk, Fūr, Fundj, Nūba, Arabs, Jieng and Naath – to appreciate how often frontiers changed and how various groups became incorporated into different socio-economic systems.

The development of political and social institutions

During the second half of the seventeenth century, political developments occurred which were to affect significantly the socio-economic processes in Shillukland. A sense of national unity was forged among the diverse peoples who had settled in the country, and a more centralized form of administration was established under the *Reth*. One of the main consequences of this development was the gradual introduction of the royal monopoly of economic resources as well as of local and long-distance trade.

The three names associated in Shilluk history with this development are Abudhok, a queen and daughter of *Reth* Bwoc, and one of the many powerful women in Shilluk history; her half-brother Dhokoth; and Tugo, Dhokoth's son *Reth* Dhokoth (*c*.1670–*c*.1690) is remembered for having organized successful raids down the Nile and westwards into the Nuba mountains. The Great Famine of 1684 (*Umm Laham* in Arabic) was probably responsible for sending many Shilluk fleeing northwards, to raid or settle in Baḥr Scheluk. The Great Famine and the Shilluk have been

59. The Jii-speaking peoples are the Western Nilotic-speaking peoples comprising the Luo-speakers as well as the Jieng and Naath. They all use the term '*jii*' meaning 'people', hence the name.
60. R. S. O'Fahey and J. L. Spaulding, 1974, pp. 61–3.

held responsible for the destruction of seventeen religious schools located between Alays and the confluence of the Blue and White Niles.[61] The raiding parties of Dhokoth returned with much booty. They also brought back many captives, largely from the region to the east of Kākā, who were settled at Athakong where they formed part of the bodyguard for *Reth* Dhokoth.

The military and economic successes of *Reth* Dhokoth were largely responsible for the centralization of the powers of the *Reth*. The process of consolidation was completed by his son and successor Tugo (*c*.1690–*c*.1710), who founded the village of Fashoda and made it the permanent residence of the *Reth*. Formerly, each Shilluk *Reth* reigned from, and was buried in, his native village. The elaborate installation ceremony for a Shilluk *Reth* was also instituted by Tugo. His fame spread rapidly both within and outside the kingdom. There seems also to have been a correlation between the rate of political centralization and the development of a social hierarchy in Shilluk society.

By the beginning of the eighteenth century, the Fundj empire was disintegrating as discussed above. As the power of the Fundj along the White Nile declined, that of the Shilluk increased correspondingly. By 1772, when James Bruce was at Sennār, he had no doubt that the Shilluk were in control at Alays.[62] He further suggested that the Shilluk raided as far down the river as the confluence of the two Niles. This suggestion was later confirmed by Brun-Rollet who contended that the site of the present Khartoum had been a settlement of importance until 1780 when the Shilluk raided the town, destroyed it and massacred all its inhabitants.[63]

The last two decades of the eighteenth century witnessed the final collapse of the Fundj sultanate. This further helped to consolidate Shilluk control of the White Nile region. The English traveller, George William Browne, who stayed in Dārfūr for four years (1793–6) and who wrote a book on commercial activities in the region, recorded that the Shilluk were in complete control of the river at Alays, where they provided an important ferry service for the caravan traders travelling between Sennār and al-ʿObeyd.[64]

The decline of Shilluk power

During the reign of *Reth* Nyakwaa (*c*.1780–1820) there occurred a mass migration of the Jieng, probably the Rueng and Ngok sections, across the River Sobat. This meant that the White Nile area from Lake No in the south to Alays in the north, which for one-and-a-half centuries had been completely dominated by the Shilluk, was henceforth to be shared with

61. Ibn Dayf Allāh Muḥammad ʿAbd Nur, 1973, pp. 95, 344; P. Mercer, 1971, p. 410.
62. J. Bruce, 1805, Vol. VI, p. 390.
63. C. E. J. Walkley, 1935, p. 227.
64. W. G. Browne, 1799, pp. 452–3.

other Jii-speakers. But that was not all. A year after the death of Nyakwaa, the armies of Muḥammad 'Alī Pasha, Viceroy of Egypt, invaded Sudan, ended the Fundj administration and installed Turco–Egyptian rule, whose aim was to exploit the Sudan for the benefit of Egypt. A clash with the Shilluk, the dominant power along the White Nile, was inevitable. Despite sustained Shilluk resistance, from 1821 the Shilluk frontier steadily retreated southwards before the encroaching Arab intrusion and the Turco–Egyptian regime.

In order to dominate the White Nile the Shilluk had to control the waterways. This control, in turn, depended on their canoe or water power. They possessed a large number of vessels and were fine oarsmen. During a raid or a military expedition, groups of thirty or forty canoes travelled together. They therefore constituted a formidable military force in the region. To quote Mercer again, ' . . . before the foundation of the Turkish White Nile shipyards, the Shilluk canoes had no superiors or even rivals in the region.'[65] But a Turco–Egyptian government shipyard had been established in 1826 at Mandjara and, thenceforth, the naval supremacy of the Shilluk on the White Nile was successfully challenged.

The peoples of the Baḥr al-Ghazāl

The country south of the Baḥr al-Ghazāl and west of a line from Meshra al-Rek, Rumbek, and the point where the boundaries of modern Sudan, Zaire and Uganda meet, was occupied by peoples belonging to two major language families: the Ubangian (Niger–Congo) and the Central Sudanic (Sahara–Nile). Speakers of these languages had been settled there since remote times. Indeed, Central Sudanic seems to have developed in the Nuba area many millenia before the Christian era, either close to the Baḥr al-'Arab or in the area of Wau.[66] These people there were farmers with cereal crops, who also kept cattle and hunted a good deal, the area only being settled along the water-courses. The site of Djabal Tūkyī (lat. 5°19 N, long. 30°27 E), dating to *c.*180–220, can be attributed to them.[67] Speakers of these languages were found before 1800 from the vicinity of Hofrat-en-Nahas to the borders of the rainforest in the south and on both banks of the Upper Nile downstream from Lake Albert.

Ubangian speakers arrived from the west (Central African Republic) and settled mostly to the west of the Central Sudanic speakers or in between Central Sudanic speaking communities, which is understandable given the very light settlement of peoples in the area. Ubangians were farmers who had first based their economy on yams but later shifted in part to cereal crops, in part to bananas, according to the local environment. They did not keep cattle, which implies substantially different attitudes towards

65. P. Mercer, 1971, p. 412.
66. C. Ehret, 1974, p. 86; N. David, 1982, pp. 80–1.
67. N. David, 1982, pp. 81–2.

wealth, including bride-wealth, from those of the Central Sudanic people.[68]

We know very little about the past of these people before 1800 because nineteenth-century developments led to the breaking up of their communities. By 1800 slave-raiders from Dārfūr were already active in Dār Fertīt and Dār Banda, south of Hofrat-en-Nahas, while the Zande conquest of the peoples further south was beginning. The Zande absorbed the people they overran and elsewhere, especially in the north, large-scale emigration into the Central African Republic occurred as Banda speakers and others fled from the slave-raiders. The inquiries of F. Santandrea[69] show yet another reason why oral traditions have remembered so little of the earlier history: there were no large political units in the area. This alone explains the relative ease of the Zande conquest. It also means that clan traditions – the traditions of the leading families of small units living in dispersed settlements, hamlets or sometimes villages – simply did not go back very far. No narrative tradition could be found about any event before 1800. The only genealogies that went back further were three lists of Bongo clans[70] where the founding generations of the chiefly line started between 1650 and 1705. This merely indicates that the people were there then, in the Wau–Tonj area during the eighteenth century, and also that the social organization of these Bongo groups was of a slightly larger scale than that of other groups, although less than neighbouring Nilotic groups. A Bongo tradition also shows, however, how much centralization was resisted. Several Bongo political units followed Ngoli, a hero who organized resistance against the Azande. But 'rival chieftains' murdered him as soon as he had successfully repulsed the Azande![71]

All that can be said, therefore, for the period covered by this chapter is that Dārfūr began to exercise informal control over Dār Fertīt well before 1800 and required tribute in copper from the inhabitants near Hofrat-en-Nahas, while some Arab or Fūr families established themselves as leaders over small groups in the area of Raga. More research is obviously needed throughout the area. Data on ways of life, exchange and trade, eventual population movements before 1880 could perhaps still be gathered.

68. D. E. Saxon, 1982; N. David, 1982, pp. 88–91; L. Bouquiaux and L. Hyman, 1980, pp. 807–22.
69. F. Santandrea, 1964 and 1981.
70. F. Santandrea, 1964, pp. 136–8.
71. ibid., p. 132.

Morocco

M. EL FASI

In Volume IV it was shown that during the fifteenth century Spain and Portugal had launched their offensive against North Africa, particularly against Morocco. Since 1415 – the year in which the Portuguese conquered Ceuta – they gradually occupied many important coastal places on the Atlantic littoral, making them into bases for their raids into the Moroccan hinterland.

All these events had lively repercussions; they aroused firm resistance and a keen desire to liberate the towns conquered by the Portuguese. The various *zāwiya Shaykhs*[1] and religious brotherhoods actively encouraged this spirit, using it to consolidate their power and prepare the population to fight the invaders, who were regarded as the protagonists of a new crusade.

Some of the *sharīfs* of Dar'a, led by Abū 'Abd Allāh, known as al-Ḳā'im bi-'Amr Allāh (he who rises at the command of God), accordingly appointed themselves to fight the infidels and drive them from the forts they were occupying. The proclamation of al-Ḳā'im bi-'Amr Allāh, made in 1511, marks the beginning of the Sa'ādī dynasty. The struggle lasted some forty years, and was directed partly against the Portuguese and partly against the Waṭṭāsid kings.

In southern Morocco, the Portuguese were threatened to such a degree that they remained within their fortified places. Subsequently, Portuguese colonization declined at an increasing pace. The *sharīfs* and the religious leaders (called *marabouts* by European historians) stepped up their attacks on the Portuguese forts, and the assaults were often bloody.

The Portuguese were also threatened from the north by the fighters of Salé, who continually harried Arzila (Asīla) and the other *presidios* occupied by the Portuguese, who were thus driven out of Ma'mura (now called al-Mahdiyya), at the mouth of the Sebū river.

During this period, the struggle between the new dynasty of the Sa'ādī settled in the south and the old Waṭṭāsid–Marinid dynasty had a disastrous effect on Morocco, since it weakened both sides and prevented them from freeing all the posts occupied by the Portuguese. Fortunately, after an

---

1. The *zāwiya* is a cultural and religious centre; when fortified and manned by defenders of the faith, it is called a *ribāṭ*.

indecisive battle between the Waṭṭāsid Sultan Aḥmad and the *Sharīf* Aḥmad al-Aʿradj at Tadla in 1527, a treaty was concluded which gave the Saʿādī the Sūs and Marrakesh and left the rest of the country in the hands of the Sultan, with Fez remaining the capital.

These provisions gave Morocco twelve years of peace, of which the Saʿādī took advantage to strengthen and organize their forces and concentrate on the struggle against the Portuguese.

At this juncture an important event took place. The Governor of Sūs, the *Sharīf* Muḥammad al-Mahdī, had extended the sugar plantations on his land[2] and developed the sugar trade. But the Portuguese held the export monopoly from the port of Agadir, which they still occupied. The Saʿādī Sultan therefore decided to liberate Agadir, which the Portuguese called Santa-Cruz du Cap d'Aguer. Muḥammad al-Shaykh had already built up an army strong enough to tackle the Portuguese and drive them out of Agadir. With the help of artillery he began to besiege the Portuguese port. After six months, the sultan at last managed to breech the defences.

The capture of Agadir created a considerable stir in Portugal. The Portuguese immediately evacuated the towns of Sāfī and Azemmūr (1542), though they held on to Mazagān (al-Djadīda) because it was easier to defend.

With these victories the *sharīf*s appeared as champions of the *djihād* and Muḥammad al-Shaykh as the hero of national liberation, which brought him great prestige throughout the country. He could now renew his struggle against the Waṭṭāsids and attempt to reconquer the north of Morocco, which the latter were still governing under the Treaty of Tadla.

Muḥammad al-Shaykh, after expelling his rival brother, Aḥmad al-Aʿradj to Tafilālet, became the sole leader of the Saʿādī and was free to finish with the Waṭṭāsids. He set out to capture Fez, possession of which would give him supreme power in Morocco.

The struggle between the old and new dynasties swayed to and fro for some ten years, until Muḥammad al-Shaykh finally entered Fez on 13 September 1554. But the Sultan's main concern was the threat from the Turks in Algiers. In his view, the only real danger for Morocco came from the Ottoman Empire, which had subjugated all the eastern and western Arab countries, a fate which the Moroccans, with their traditional sense of independence, could never accept. To safeguard his country from a Turkish invasion, he therefore decided to force the Ottomans out of Africa. The two elder sons of the Saʿādī Sultan, ʿAbdallāh and ʿAbd al-Raḥmān, had taken Tlemcen in 1550, but the Turks had reacted immediately. The Pasha of Algiers formed a large army commanded by the convert Ḥasan Corsa (historians call the European converts who served the Maghreb states

2. It is known that the production of sugar dates back to the early Middle Ages, and that Morocco was the chief exporter. See D. de Torres, 1667, ch. XXXV; and recently, P. Berthier, 1966. Mr Berthier's research was encouraged by the author's ministry during the 1950s and is the best work on the subject.

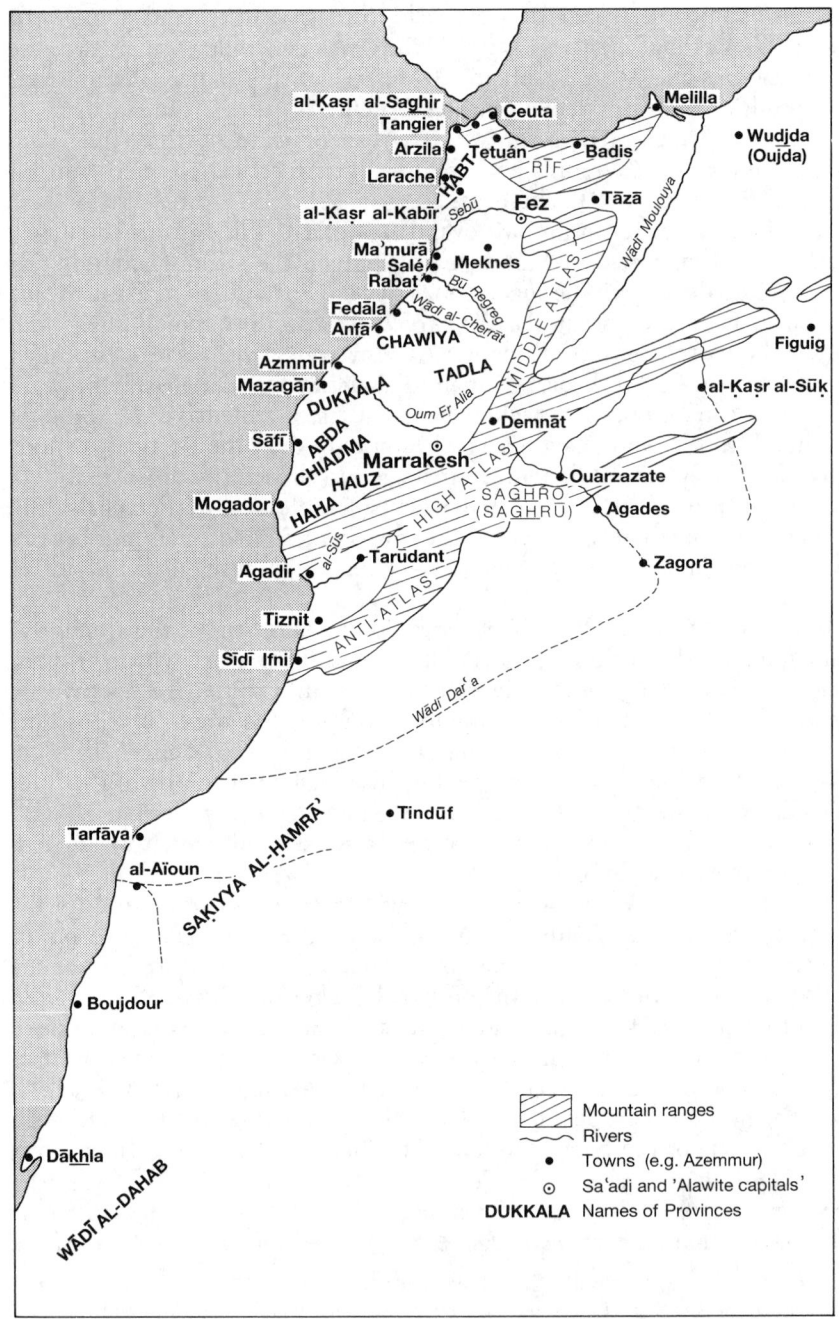

FIG. 8.1   *Morocco in the sixteenth and seventeenth centuries (after M. El Fasi)*

'renegades') and sent it against the Moroccan troops, who were defeated. Tlemcen was then reoccupied by the Turks (1552).

To carry through his grand design of conquering Algeria, Muḥmmad al-Shaykh sought an alliance with Spain. Talks were arranged with the Count of Alcaudete, the Spanish Governor of Oran, and the two sides agreed to mount an expedition against Algiers. Two thousand Spanish cavalry in the pay of the Sultan were to join this Moroccan-led operation. The Turks got wind of the preparations and Ṣalāḥ Ra'īs therefore asked the Sublime Porte for money and reinforcements to attack Oran, then occupied by Spain. At this point, Ṣalāḥ Ra'īs died, and it was Ḥasan Corsa who led the attack on Oran. However, the Turkish fleet, which was to have blockaded the Spanish fort by sea, was recalled to fight the Christian fleet of Andrea Doria, then threatening the Bosphorus. The Sultan, now rid of a dangerous rival, could turn to the conquest of Algeria. He began by laying siege to Tlemcen and succeeded in capturing it.

In 964/1557 the Sultan Muḥammad al-Shaykh was assassinated by an officer of his own guard who was in the pay of the Ottoman government.

This dramatic end, however, made no difference to the determination of the Saʿādī to press on with clearing Morocco of all foreign occupants and defending it against all fresh incursions by foreign powers, even a Muslim one such as the Ottoman empire which, as already noted, had extended its domination over all the Arab countries. In other words, the new Caliph, Abū Muḥammad ʿAbdallāh, who had been proclaimed uncontested Sultan after the murder of his father, followed the policy laid down by his predecessor. He was given the name of al-Ghālib Billāh (victor through the strength of God).

Although unavenged for his father's murder, the new Sultan felt in a position to turn against the Portuguese in an attempt to dislodge them from Mazagān. He set out to rebuild his army, obtain the most modern weapons and organize a vast psychological campaign with the help of the *zāwiya* and the chiefs of the brotherhoods. In particular, Sīdī Aḥmad u Mūssā, who had great influence in the Sūs and a reputation for holiness not only in his own region but throughout Morocco, roused all the *kabīla*s against both the Turks and the Portuguese. When, therefore, al-Ghālib Billāh felt himself strong enough to besiege Mazagān (then called al-Briza, and later al-Djadīda), he made preparations and assembled a large force of infantry and cavalry armed with highly efficient weapons, including twenty-four pieces of artillery, ten of which were heavy guns and comprised the famous Maymūn ('lucky charm').

Although this attempt to deliver Mazagān was unsuccessful, it showed the Portuguese that they had to reckon with a genuine new power. As for the Sultan, he considered that the Portuguese threat to the interior of Morocco was averted, and he turned to developing his kingdom's prosperity. He encouraged trade with the European states, especially France. A document reveals, for example, that in 1570 the merchants of

Rouen signed an act of association with Morocco whereby they were allowed to trade with that country, chiefly with the towns of Sāfī, Tarūdant and Marrakesh.[3]

In architecture, al-Ghālib Billāh is known as one of the greatest builders of the Sa'ādī dynasty. He constructed a great mosque in Marrakesh, and he also restored the Almohad Mosque in the present-day Casbah of Agadir. In general, Moroccan art, handed down from the previous dynasties, became more ornamental and splendid.

The reign of Mawlāy 'Abdallāh al-Ghālib Billāh was on the whole calm and prosperous. He died peacefully in 1574 after seventeen years as Sultan.

His succession proved more difficult. Transgressing the long-established rule whereby the family's eldest male had a prior right to succeed over the eldest son of the late ruler, it was Muḥammad, the son of al-Ghālib Billāh, who was proclaimed Sultan. This ushered in a period of turbulence for Morocco, fortunately very short, which ended with the victorious Battle of the Three Kings.

The new Sultan took the title of al-Mutawakkil, but is still known mainly by the descriptive name of al-Maslukha.

Mawlāy 'Abd al-Mālik, the eldest of the Sa'ādī princes and uncles of al-Maslukha, considered that the throne should have been his. When al-Ghālib Billāh's son was proclaimed Sultan of Fez, he took refuge first at Sīdjilmāsa, later in Algiers and eventually in Constantinople. He entered the Ottoman army and took part in the Turkish reconquest of Tunis, where he displayed great courage.

On his return to Constantinople, Mawlāy 'Abd al-Mālik therefore found the Caliph very well disposed to help him regain the throne of his ancestors. Murād ordered the *Walī* of Algiers el-Hadj 'Alī to provide the Sa'ādī prince with a small armed force. When this force reached Morocco it met with no opposition, since the people were all on his side. Al-Mutawakkil was abandoned by his army and forced to flee, leaving Mawlāy 'Abd al-Mālik to enter Fez on 31 March 1576, where he was welcomed by the population with wild enthusiasm.

Al-Mutawakkil escaped towards the south. Pursued and defeated by the Sultan at the Wādī al-Cherrāt between Rabat and Fedāla, he succeeded in fleeing once again and managed to retake Marrakesh. The Vice-Sultan of Fez, the Sultan's brother Mawlāy Aḥmad, was given the task of driving him out of Marrakesh and taking him prisoner. The first part of this task was duly performed, but al-Mutawakkil managed to escape, for the last time. He made towards the north and asked the Governor of Vélez de la Gomera for refuge in his town. The request was passed on to King Phillip II, who authorized the Governor to take in the fugitive, on condition that he be accompanied by no more than ten members of his family.

Mawlāy 'Abd al-Mālik, once freed – at least for the time being – from the encumbrance of al-Mutawakkil, began to reorganize the state, replenish

3. H. de Castries, 1905–36, Vol. I, p. 303.

its coffers and rebuild the army, and he made his brother Mawlāy Aḥmad Caliph in Fez.

He found the treasury empty, and could have levied fresh taxes to redress the situation, but he felt that this would ruin rather than enrich the country. He therefore thought of more effective methods which would not involve his subjects financially. He expanded the navy, had new ships built and repaired or modernized the older ones. This stimulated many different crafts and increased trade with the rest of the world, especially Europe. His policy was a success and had beneficial effects in all fields.

Success was however also due to the personality of Mawlāy 'Abd al-Mālik, who was highly esteemed by the Europeans. There are many eulogies of him by foreign authors. The French writer and poet Agrippa d'Aubigné in particular gave a flattering portrait of this king, telling us among other things that the Saʿādī Sultan 'knew Spanish, Italian, Armenian and Slav. He was also an excellent poet in Arabic'.

The Battle of the Three Kings

In the sixteenth century, as noted above, Portugal built up a powerful empire which controlled vast territories in America, Asia and Africa. At the time when the dethroned Saʿādī Sultan al-Mutawakkil took refuge at Vélez de la Gomera, this empire was ruled by the young King Don Sebastián, who since his earliest childhood had dreamed of conquering Morocco, using it as a base for conquering the entire Maghrib, and finally pushing on towards the East to deliver Christ's tomb from Muslim hands. In his search for help to regain his throne, al-Mutawakkil turned to the King of Spain, who refused to receive him or to grant him the least support in his desperate venture. He then contacted Don Sebastián. The King of Portugal seized the opportunity for, having decided – against the advice of his counsellors – to mount the expedition of which he had always dreamed, he regarded the dissident Moroccan's arrival as a key factor in bringing round all his opponents. Public opinion in Portugal, worked up by extremist propaganda – especially among the clergy – was enthusistic, and greatly encouraged the reckless expedition being prepared by the young king.

For his part, Mawlāy 'Abd al-Mālik, informed of all these preparations, tried to dissuade the young King of Portugal from his rash venture; it was not that he doubted his own possibilities or courage – indeed, he was supported by his people and especially by the Djazūlite religious movement and its leader Abū 'l-Maḥāsin Yūsuf al-Fāsī;[4] but since he was anxious to preserve his people and country from the evils of war, and to work for the maintenance of peace, he decided to try to persuade King Don Sebastián to give up his expedition. He therefore wrote the king a letter which is unique in the history of diplomacy, not only for its substance but for its

4. The chief of the Shadilite Djazūlism was the forebear – eleven generations ago – of the author of this chapter.

moving tone of sincerity, wisdom and desire for peace. The French archives possess the Italian translation of this document, which has been published in Count Henry de Castries' *Sources inédites de l'histoire du Maroc*. Substantially it reads as follows:

> That which you are preparing to do, that is, to wage war against me in my country, is an injustice and an act of aggression without reason, for I wish you no ill, think no evil of you and have taken no evil action against you. Why then do you venture to deprive me of my rights and to give them to another in exchange for vain promises which he will be unable to keep so long as I am alive? You come to drive me from my kingdom, even though, with all that you possess and all that your states contain, you will be unable to gain your desire. Do not believe that my words spring from cowardice. On the contrary, know that if you do not heed these recommendations you will expose yourself to certain destruction.
>
> I am ready to come to an agreement with you in person, at whatever place you choose. I do all this in order to save you from destruction. I add that I am willing to come with you before your court of law, which never takes things away from one person to give them illegally and unjustly to another. And I accept in advance the judgement of that court . . .
>
> God is my witness for everything I say! Know further that I am informed that certain of your attendant lords proffer advice which will lead you to disaster.[5]

This letter, which displays the lofty sense of responsibility and deep love of peace of Sultan Mawlāy 'Abd al-Mālik, also shows his diplomatic skill: in facing Don Sebastián squarely with his responsibility, he made it clear at the same time by his warning that the real aggressor and fomenter of trouble in the Mediterranean region was in fact the young King of Portugal.

However, Don Sebastián continued to prepare for war.

Another example of Mawlāy 'Abd al-Mālik's understanding of Don Sebastián's psychology and character emerges from the accounts of Moroccan historians. They relate how, knowing that the King of Portugal saw himself as the paragon of chivalry and fearless courage, and that he was imbued with the noblest sentiments, Mawlāy 'Abd al-Mālik wrote to him as follows on learning that he had landed at Arzila (Asīla):

> It is no mark of chivalry or of a noble soul to attack defenceless people living peacefully in their townships, and not to wait for one's opponents to come and match one's strength. If therefore you are a true Christian, wait where you are until I arrive in your vicinity.

5. H. de Castries, 1905–36, Vol. I, pp. 383–7.

When Don Sebastián received this letter, his attendants, especially Muḥam-mad al-Maslukh, advised him not to comply because, they said, it was a trick; on the contrary, he should make haste to attack and occupy first Larache (al-Arīsh) and then al-Ḳaṣr al-Kabīr. But Don Sebastián's lofty concept of honour prevented him from exposing his reputation to ignominious dishonour. He therefore decided not to move from Arzila, where he remained nineteen days until the eve of the battle.

There is no trace of this correspondence in the European documents.[6] On the other hand, it is noted that Don Sebastián hesitated between following the coast by sea, or going overland, to besiege Larache. A council of war was held at Arzila to consider the two alternatives. Most members of the council, led by al-Maslukh, were for going by sea, but the King favoured going by land so as to be able to display his valour and martial accomplishments – and so it was decided.

The Sa'ādī forces set out from Marrakesh northwards and were continually joined by large numbers of volunteers. In addition the Sultan had ordered his brother, the Caliph at Fez, to get to al-Ḳaṣr al-Kabīr before him with the contingents from Fez and its region and in particular with the élite corps of young archers (the Rima) from the capital, together with the disciples of the Djazūlī *zāwiya* of al-Ḳaṣr al-Kabīr.

Mawlāy 'Abd al-Mālik had decided to establish his command post at al-Ḳaṣr al-Kabīr because this city was near the Portuguese possessions from which the King of Portugal was expected to attack. It was, moreover, the centre of the Djazūlite movement led by Abū 'l-Maḥāsin Yūsuf al-Fāsī, who lived there and had his *zāwiya* there.[7]

When the Sa'ādī army arrived at al-Ḳaṣr al-Kabīr, Mawlāy Aḥmad was already there with the élite corps of young archers from Fez. Mawlāy 'Abd al-Mālik charged them – once Don Sebastián had crossed the Wādī al-Makhāzin (which gave its name to this decisive battle) – to destroy the bridge across the river so as to prevent the defeated Portuguese from finding their way towards the sea; the order was carried out during the night of 3–4 August 1578.

The next day the 'Battle of the Three Kings' took place, which should be regarded as one of the most important battles in the history of mankind, and especially in the history of Morocco and Islam. Among Arab historians it is known as the Battle of Wādī al-Makhāzin, and among Spanish and Portuguese historians as the Battle of Alcazarquivir.

6. Only Moroccan historians have commented on it.

7. For full information about this great man see *Al-Istiḳsa*, by Narciri, in H. de Castries, 1905–36, Vol. V, pp. 131, 134, 135, 138 and in E. Lévi-Provençal, 1922, pp. 240–7 and J. Berque, 1982, pp. 137–45.

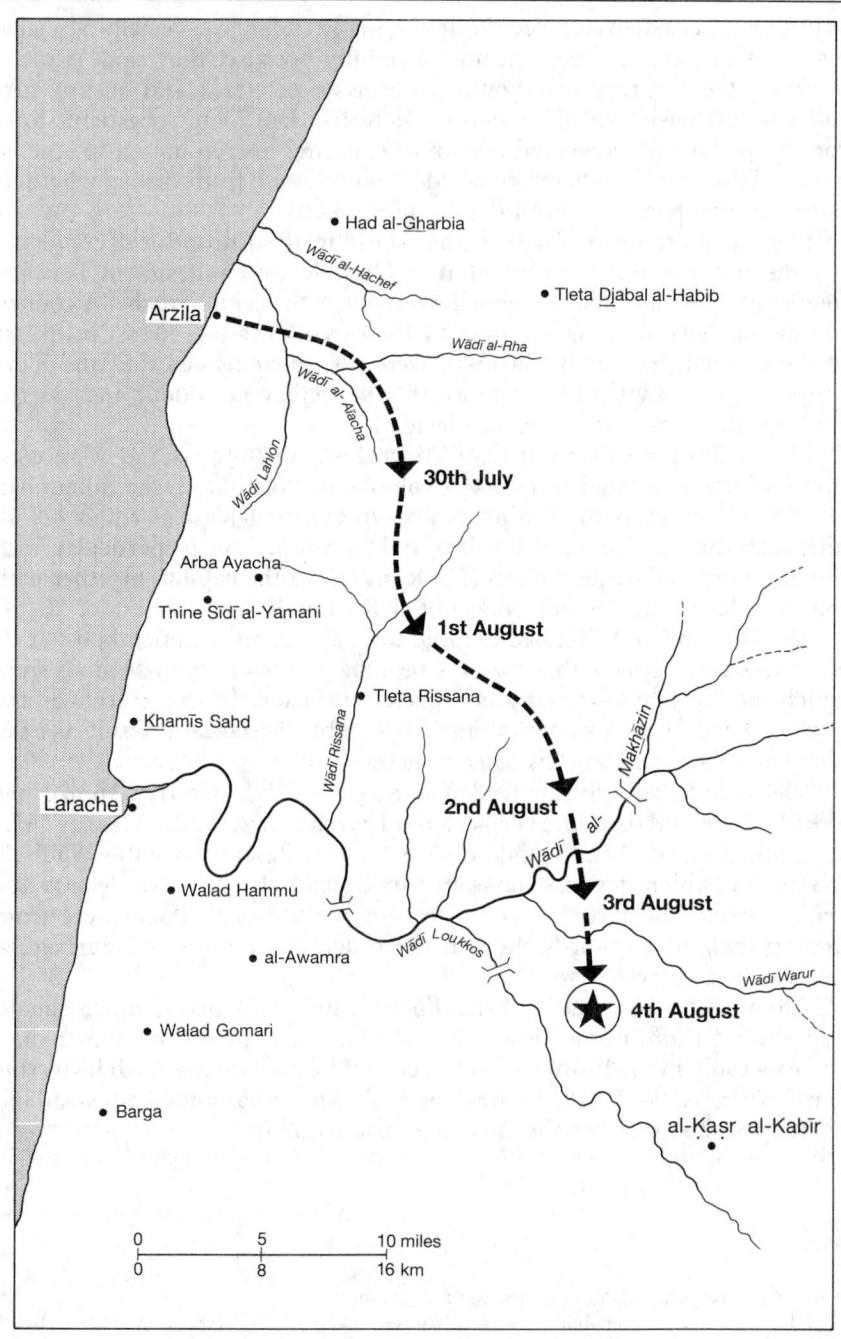

FIG. 8.2 *The stages of Don Sebastián's progress towards the site of the 'Battle of the Three Kings' at Wādī al-Makhāzin, 30 July to 4 August 1578 (after M. El Fasi)*

The day of the battle

After meticulous preparations to raise one of the largest armies of that time, which he based at Tangier, Don Sebastián made for al-Ḳaṣr al-Kabīr, the headquarters of Mawlāy ʿAbd al-Mālik.

On the Monday morning at the end of the month of Djumādāʾ 11 in the year of 986 of the Hegira (4 August 1578) the opposing camps prepared for battle. It was an historic day; the culmination of centuries of conflicts between Muslims and Christians, which had begun in Spain and then spread to Morocco. It was also the day for which Don Sebastián had been preparing since his childhood, and which would in his eyes be the first step in his conquest of the world. For the Muslims, on the other hand, it was a day on which thousands of martyrs would fall in the defence of their just cause.

The opposing forces prepared to attack, each employing its own tactics. The Christian army was drawn up on the field of battle in a square, with a body of legionaries in front. German troops held the right flank and Spanish and Italian ones the left. The cavalry, less numerous than the infantry, advanced on each wing. There was also a small body of supporters of Muhammad 'the Flayed' (from three hundred to six hundred men, depending on the source).

The Moroccan army was deployed in the form of a crescent, from within which the Sultan Mawlāy ʿAbd al-Mālik directed the battle from a litter. He had been taken ill on the way from Marrakesh but, though his state had worsened so that he could not move, his mind remained clear and active. The tips of the crescent were manned by the cavalry, with the infantry and artillery in the centre.

After the dawn prayer, the mercenaries flung themselves on the left flank of the Muslims, taking them completely by surprise. Sultan ʿAbd al-Mālik, seeing his troops beginning to crack, rose from his litter and drawing his sword, he managed to push his way forward. The Sultan's action gave new courage to his soldiers; unfortunately he succumbed from his efforts but, before passing away, he instructed his servants to conceal his death, since the battle had only just begun.

As the battle raged, with many men killed on both sides, the Muslims continued to advance while the Christians fell back, until they eventually turned and fled across the fields towards the bridge. Finding it destroyed, they threw themselves into the river in an effort to cross, but were carried away by the current and drowned.

Don Sebastián however stood firm, displaying the greatest courage. But his courage could not save him: he was struck down on the field of battle along with thousands of his soldiers and devoted servants. Muhammad the Flayed tried to flee and threw himself into the river, where he drowned. His body was recovered and brought to Aḥmad al-Manṣūr, who was proclaimed king after the victory (which gave him his name, al-Manṣūr, the Victorious).

It is not known exactly how many were killed on each side, but the slain Muslims numbered several thousands. Of the Portuguese and their allies almost none escaped, since nearly all those who avoided drowning or who survived the battle, were taken prisoner. Tradition has it that there were nearly fourteen thousand Christian prisoners.

While negotiations were proceeding on the ransom to be paid for Don Sebastián's body, it was taken first of all to Fez; but al-Manṣūr was too proud to accept any offer, especially as the ransoms for the prisoners, in particular for those of noble blood, had yielded him sums which certain historians see as the origin of his nickname *al-Dhahabī* (the Golden). More gold was received from the Portuguese than had been brought back after the conquest of the Sudan. Al-Manṣūr refused a ransom for the body of the unfortunate King. He therefore decided during the negotiations to inform the King of Spain, Philip II (the successor to his nephew, who had died unmarried) that he was willing to return the King's body without any payment of any kind.

The consequences of the Battle of the Three Kings

This decisive battle had major consequences which for many centuries set their mark not only on Islam and Morocco, but also on Europe and Portugal. The victory imparted fresh vitality to the Saʿādī dynasty and gave Morocco peace and prosperity in all fields of economic and cultural life. The ransoms paid for the thousands of Portuguese prisoners also greatly enriched the Saʿādī dynasty, and its fame spread throughout the world.

In regard to economic development, one particular case deserves note: the sugar industry, temporarily in decline (although Morocco was the world's principal exporter of sugar), again became flourishing.

The same was true for industry of all kinds and the arts. Encouraged by the Saʿādī and the newly-rich middle class, architecture in particular[8] developed and achieved outstanding refinement, as attested by the masterpieces which are still to be seen, especially in Marrakesh. The Moroccans' newly recovered stability and their lofty feelings of pride also produced a wealth of art, poetry and literature during this period, such as for example, the works of ʿAbd al-ʿAzīz al-Fishtālī and al-Makkarī ibn al-Ḳāḍī.

The repercussions of the Battle of the Three Kings on international politics were equally impressive. The result was a substantial decline in Portuguese influence in the Muslim world, particularly in the Gulf countries. The battle finally put an end to the threat from crusaders to the countries of the East. It was in fact the last of its kind, and scotched any intention of those harbouring the idea of a crusade. The Saʿādī victory also strengthened the power of the Ottoman empire, and Europeans are right

8. Architecture had stagnated for some time after the weakening of the Waṭṭāsid dynasty.

PLATE 8.1   *A sugar-loaf mould from the 1960 excavations of the Chichāwa sugar mill*

to consider this Moroccan victory as a victory of all the Muslims, precisely because it epitomized Muslim solidarity.

On the other hand, the victory resulted in the Ottomans abandoning any idea of conquering Morocco, which remained the only Arab territory outside Turkish influence. The Arabic language thus retained its purity and authenticity in Morocco, and continued to be used for many centuries. The style of Moroccan epistolary literature and of the decrees issued by the king's ministries remained untainted by any foreign influence. This explains why the texts written during the time of the Saʿādī and ʿAlawites (and up to the reign of Mawlāy Ḥassan I) give the impression of having been written during the glorious age of the Umayyads in Spain and of the Almoravids, Almohads and Marinids in Morocco.

We have dwelt at length on the Battle of the Three Kings because of its intrinsic importance, particularly for Morocco. As Professor Lévi-Provençal rightly says:

> One must not criticize Moroccan historians for dwelling on this famous battle and according it the importance which it truly merits ... We can now prove that the ransom of the Portuguese nobles taken prisoner during this battle contributed even more than the conquest of Sudan to the immense wealth of Sultan 'Abū l-'Abbās al-Manṣūr (winning him his nickname of *al-Dhahabī*, 'the Golden'). All the European powers in financial straits tried to negotiate loans from Morocco. The Chorfa Empire even practised a policy of alliances, and, especially if 'Abd al-Mālik had not died, might very well have joined the European concert of nations in the same way as the Ottoman Empire'.[9]

Saʿādī expansion in the sixteenth century

Al-Manṣūr reigned for a quarter of a century and devoted himself to consolidating the power of the Saʿādī, developing his kingdom in every possible way and establishing economic relations with the main states of the time.

After the victory of Wādī al-Makhāzin, he set out to liberate the cities still in the hands of Europeans: Arzila (Asīla), Tangier, Ceuta and Mazagān. He succeeded in driving the foreign occupants from Arzila (1589), but Tangier was not liberated until the following century, by the 'Alawite Sultan Mawlāy Ismāʿīl, and Mazagān (al-Djadīda) by his grandson Muḥammad III: Ceuta passed into the hands of Phillip II, King of Spain, who inherited the kingdom of Portugal. Along with Melilla and three other *presidios* it remains a Spanish dependency to this day.

Al-Manṣūr's consummate success encouraged him to look beyond Morocco's traditional boundaries with a view to restoring the situation as it was at the time of the Almoravids and thus unifying Islam. But this was in fact only a pretext, the real motive for his campaign being expansionism, an age-old desire of all great powers. This is why one should avoid judging historical events according to present-day concepts and ideas, bearing in mind that, from Alexander the Great to Napoleon, and before and after them, history has produced many conquerors.

Moroccan opinion was, however, against al-Manṣūr's Sudanese expedition, a most unusual attitude for that time and much to Morocco's credit. Al-Manṣūr called a council of war before undertaking the campaign, and explained his plans. In his history of Morocco, H. Terrasse writes that 'Almost everyone was against the venture, because it was too risky and *above all* because it would mean waging war against other Muslims'.[10] The

9. E. Lévi-Provençal, 1922, p. 107, note 1.
10. H. Terrasse, 1949–50, Vol. II, p. 203.

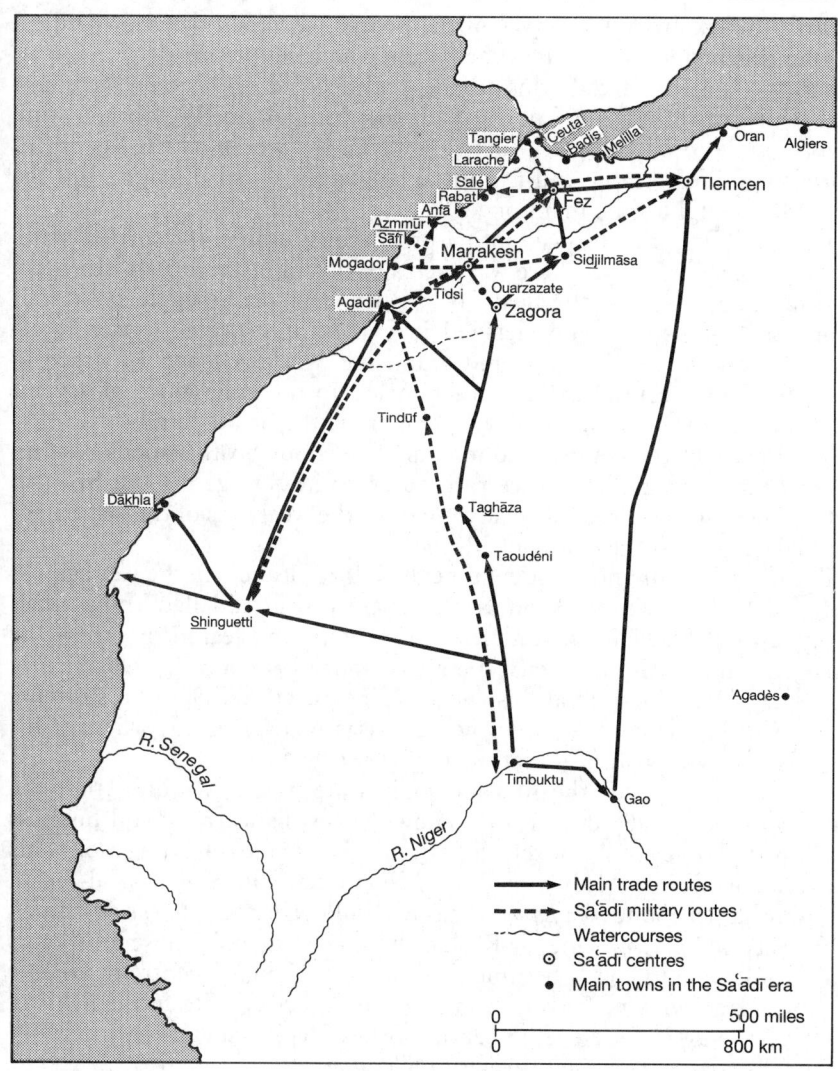

FIG. 8.3 *The empire of Aḥmad al-Manṣūr, 'the Golden' (1578–1603) (after M. El Fasi)*

'*ulamā*', the true representatives of the people, also took this view and, in judging this historic event, it is their view which counts.

But al-Manṣūr overrode this advice, and decided on his own to mount what Moroccan historians call the Sudanese Expedition. We do not think it worthwhile to describe it in detail since all the works on the history of Morocco, in both Arabic and European languages, do so at length, but the salient facts ought to be mentioned.[11]

After building up Morocco into a prosperous, united and envied state, al-Manṣūr died in 1603. There was then a period of instability in Morocco. As often happens after the death of a ruler, a power struggle broke out among his successors, who engaged in endless internecine strife. In al-Manṣūr's case it was his sons and grandsons who drenched Morocco in blood for half a century. This situation led to the emergence of several claimants to power over and above members of the Saʿādī family.

In all parts of the country, adherents of religious brotherhoods rose up in the name of patriotism to restore peace and fight against the Spanish and Portuguese, who had taken advantage of the weakness of the last Saʿādī and had blockaded the coasts of Morocco.

The most famous and most genuine of all these leaders in the war against the first colonizers of modern times was certainly Abū ʿAbdallāh Muḥammad al-ʿAyyāshī of Salé. A war leader loved by some and feared by others, he managed temporarily to pacify the areas under his control, in particular the town of Fez. Despite all his successes he never laid claim to supreme power, since he was a true saint; he was assassinated, on the orders of his enemies, the Moriscos of Rabat, in 1051/1641.

In 1046/1636–7, for the first and only time in the Middle Atlas, the grandson of a *Shaykh* universally renowned for his learning and holiness rose up and declared himself Sultan of the whole of Morocco. This claimant's name was Muḥammad ibn M'Ḥammad ibn Abū Bakr al-Dalāl. His grandfather founded a *zāwiya* in the Middle Atlas which was destroyed by the second ʿAlawite king, al-Rashīd ibn al-Sharīf, and whose location is almost unknown today. It became almost as prestigious a centre of Islamic studies as Ḳarāwiyyīn University at Fez. Several celebrities in the fields of Islamic learning in the eleventh century of the Hegira (seventeenth century of the Christian era) passed through Dila *zāwiya*.

Abū Bakr Muḥammad's son followed in his father's footsteps and went on running the spiritual and intellectual affairs of the *zāwiya*, which developed still further. On his death, he was succeeded by his son.

Since al-Manṣūr's death in 1012/1603, ten of his descendants competed for power for a little over half a century. During this long period two kings managed to reign for more than twenty years, with interruptions for the success of their brothers and cousins, who took power and later lost it – to

11. H. Terrasse, 1949–50, Vol. II, pp. 202–5; see also al-Nāṣirī, 1954–6, in H. de Castries, 1905–36, Vol. V, pp. 195–8 and 209–18; and Cossac de Chavrebière, 1931, pp. 330–4. See ch. 11 below.

say nothing of the claimants from among heads of *zāwiya*s and other adventurers. Other rebel claimants to the throne made life difficult for the last Saʿādī in the north and the south. In the Tangier area of al-Khaḍr Ghaylān, a disciple of Muḥammad al-Ayyāshī claimed to continue the wars against the Portuguese undertaken by the great warrior of Islam. What is remarkable about these events is that all these claimants to the throne of Morocco made themselves out to be saviours of the unity of the country and champions of stable government.

The Ghanāte were a faction of the Aʿrāb (Arab nomads) who were driven out of Cairo by the Fāṭimids and invaded the Maghreb in successive waves, destroying everything in their path including houses, forests and all kinds of installations. In the sixth century of the Hegira (twelfth century of the Christian era) they had been brought into Morocco by the Almohad Yaʿḳūb al-Manṣūr. The Almohads, Marinids and Saʿādīs used them as mercenaries in their wars inside and outside Morocco. In the end they settled – where they remain to this day – on the fertile plains of the Atlantic coast, driving its inhabitants into the mountains of the Middle Atlas; it was they who were responsible for the real Arabization of Morocco.

In 1069/1658–9, in the reign of Abū al-ʿAbbās Aḥmad ibn Muḥammad al-Shaykh ibn Zaydān, a caid of the Shbanāte by the name of ʿAbd al-Karīm ibn Abū Bakr al-Shbāni and known as Ḳarrūm al-Ḥādjdj rose up in Marrakesh against Sultan Aḥmad, known as Mawlāy al-ʿAbbās (though the sultan's mother was a Shbanāte). She advised him to approach his maternal uncles and try to win them over. Once Ḳarrūm al-Ḥādjdj had Sultan Aḥmad in his hands, he put him to death, declared himself Sultan and occupied the Royal Palace at Marrakesh. His reign lasted some ten years, marked by extortion, injustice and cruelty. Poverty became the rule, particularly in the south. Even his followers and supporters, exasperated by these ills raining on the country, wanted to get rid of this tyrant. One of those close to him surprised him in his palace and threw a spear at him which killed him on the spot. His son Abū Bakr ibn ʿAbd al-Karīm was proclaimed sultan in his place, and reigned for a time until he died forty days before the ʿAlawite sultan Mawlāy al-Rashīd reached Marrakesh.

The early sultans of the ʿAlawite dynasty

All these pretenders to the throne and would-be unifiers of Morocco who stained the country with blood after al-Manṣūr's death failed in their attempts. The honour of setting up a strong, lasting and beneficent government was to fall to the Shārīfian dynasty of the ʿAlawites, who reigned over Morocco for three and a half centuries. This longevity was due to the principles enshrined in the policy always followed by the ʿAlawite sultans: their firm attachment to the integrity of the country; fidelity to all the noble ideals of Muslim civilization; and the importance attached to the development of education at all levels.

This means that unlike the motives underlying all the preceding dynasties, except the Marinids, the 'Alawites were not out to champion a religious cause. Their aim was solely political, namely to unify the country, set up a strong, stable government and propagate learning.

The first question, however, is who these 'Alawites were. They were a family whose descent from the Prophet has been scientifically established by the great scholars of Morocco: al-Arabī al-Fāsī, his nephew, the Shaykh al-Islam 'Abd al-Ḳādir, al-Imām al-Yūsī and others quoted by the author of the *Kitāb al-Istiḳsā*.[12]

The descendants of the family formed a religious aristocracy which acquired great prestige among all the peoples of the Tafilālet. Al-Ḥasan's great-grandson Mawlāy 'Alī al-Sharīf became very famous. He had nine sons, one of them being Mawlāy al-Sharīf, who went on living in the Tafilālet and whose fame spread throughout southern Morocco. The instability that prevailed in Morocco led the Filālī to proclaim him Sultan. At the time, as we have seen, Morocco was divided between the Dilāwīyya of the Middle Atlas, who occupied Fez; Ibn Ḥassūn, who reigned over the Sūs and the High Atlas; al-Khaḍr Ghaylān, who was ravaging the northwest; and other adventurer-bandits who took advantage of this instability to pillage towns and villages.

In the Tafilālet itself, a family was occupying a fortress, Tabousamt, in opposition to the 'Alawite *sharīf*s. One side was supported by the Dilāwīyya and the other by Abū Ḥassūn, and there was fighting between them. Mawlāy al-Sharīf was captured and imprisoned by Abū Ḥassūn, but was rescued by his son, Mawlāy M'ḥammad. His father abdicated in his favour and he was enthroned as king of Morocco in 1050/1640. This was the beginning of the 'Alawite dynasty. The word "Alawite"[13] comes from the name of their ancestor Mawlāy 'Alī al-Sharīf of Marrakesh. This dynasty is also called Ḥasanī or Filālī, from Tafilālet, the old Sidjilmāsa.

Mawlāy Muḥammad was not acknowledged by his brother Mawlāy al-Rashīd, and left the Tafilālet. He began by roaming about in the towns and among the *ḳabīla*s of the south and the north: he went to the Todgha valley, to Demnāt, to the Dila *zāwiya* and to Fez.

His brother for his part raised an army and marched on the Dar'a, which was occupied by Abū Ḥassūn. He fought several battles against the latter, and drove him out of this area. He then marched on the *zāwiya* of Dila and gave battle against the Dilāwīyya, but was defeated. He decided to lay siege to Fez. This time he succeeded in occupying it in 1060/1650. But he had to abandon it forty days later in order not to expose his soldiers to certain defeat. Having failed to establish himself in Fez, he made for eastern Morocco. He occupied the town of Udjda and advanced on Tlemcen. The

12. al-Nāṣirī, 1954–6, Vol. VII, pp. 3–4.
13. Generally speaking the word "Alawī" is used to denote all the descendants of 'Alī, cousin and son-in-law of the Prophet. But the 'Alawite of Syria have nothing to do with the Caliph 'Alī.

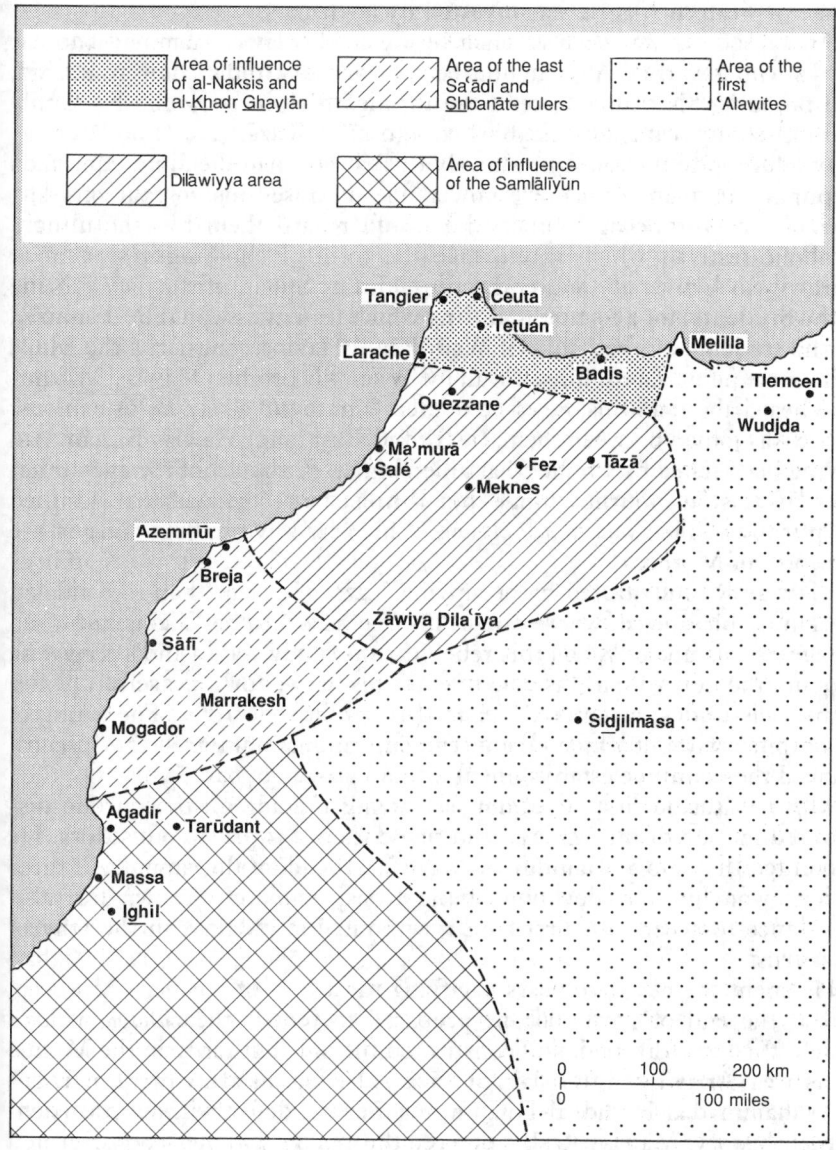

FIG. 8.4 *The principalities of northern Morocco in the early seventeenth century (after M. El Fasi)*

whole of western Algeria was invested by his troops.

An agreement was then reached between Mawlāy M'hammad and the Turks who governed Algeria, and he returned to Udjda. Mawlāy Rashīd, still pursuing his plan to ascend the throne of Morocco which his family had just set up, came and established himself at Tāzā.

In addition to the renown, Mawlāy Rashīd now had the money and men to pursue his plans to achieve power. He promised his companions that once on the throne of Morocco he would regard them by instituting a symbolic festival, which would take the form of choosing a student at Ḳarāwiyyīn University and enthroning him as Sultan of the *Tolba* (King of the Students) for a fortnight, during which festivities would be organized by the students on the banks of Wādī Fāz.[14] Having conquered the whole Tāzā area, he declared himself Sultan. When his brother Mawlāy M'hammad heard about all this, he came to meet him to put a stop to his exploits. Battle was joined between them, but did not last long, Mawlāy M'hammad having been felled by a bullet that killed him at the outset of the encounter. Mawlāy Rashīd mourned him – but it must be recognized that it suited his purposes. This was in 1075/1664. This year saw the beginning of the conquest of Morocco.

Mawlāy Rashīd started by occupying Tāzā. He went then to Tafilālet, the family birthplace, where one of his deceased brother's sons had risen up against his uncle. When this rebel learnt of Mawlāy Rashīd's arrival he fled and the new sultan was able to enter his native town peacefully. After many vicissitudes, he entered Fez in triumph in 1076/1666. The taking of this capital, without which no government can maintain itself in Morocco, marked the definitive establishment of the 'Alawite dynasty.

Mawlāy Rashīd first set about organizing the administration. He distributed money to the *'ulamā'*, and made them his privy counsellors. He appointed the scholar Ḥamdūn al-Mazwār al-Ḳāḍī of the capital. All these actions won him the devotion of the Fāsīs, who were known for their reluctance to accept the first comer without first judging him worthy of their trust.

He spent the next two years pacifying the whole of northern Morocco, and at the end of 1078/1668 he prepared to reduce the *zāwiya* of Dila which, though weakened, still constituted the only authority in the Middle Atlas area. Arriving in the plain of Fāzāz, al-Rashīd's army met the troops of Muḥammad al-Hadjdj al-Dilāʿī who suffered a defeat without precedent in their history. Mawlāy Rashīd entered the *zāwiya* with his troops, treated its occupants humanely and did not shed one drop of blood. He ordered the aged Dilāʿī to be moved to Fez, to live there with all the members of his family. This happened in the first month of 1079/1668.

14. This student tradition lasted from the days of Mawlāy Rashīd to the present. As it had been discontinued, I reintroduced it in the early days of independence, when I was Minister of Education and Rector of Moroccan universities. It has since fallen into disuse again.

After this victory, it only remained for Mawlāy Rashīd to crush the last pockets of resistance in southern Morocco. In the month of Safar 1079/July 1668 he decided to liberate Marrakesh from the Shbanāte. He succeeded in occupying it, captured Abū Bakr ibn Ḳarrūm al-Ḥādjdj al-Shabānī and some members of his family and had them put to death.

The last local power still to survive in the Sūs was that of the Samlālīyūn. The founder of this principality had died in 1070/1659 and been replaced by his son Muḥammad. In 1081/1670 Mawlāy Rashīd besieged the town of Tarūdant, occupied it and marched on the fortress of Ighīl, capital of the Samlālīyūn. He took it and killed the members of this maraboutic family and their leading supporters. With this victory the whole of Morocco was pacified and ʿAlawite power finally established.

A year and a half later, in 1082/1671, Mawlāy Rashīd met his death in a riding accident.

This account of the last Saʿādī and the beginning of the ʿAlawite dynasty has been largely a history of events, because the strife that then prevailed, the insecurity and the instability of the government did not permit developments in letters and arts. It was only under Mawlāy Rashīd that Morocco resumed its cultural traditions and its social and economic achievements. Mawlāy Rashīd held scholars and men of letters in great esteem. He had himself studied at the Ḳarāwiyyīn University.

Mawlāy Rashīd built the biggest *madrasa* (college) in Fez. This is the *madrasa* modestly called Madrasa Cherraṭīn,[15] from the name of the street in which it was built. He built another *madrasa* in Marrakesh. Among his monumental works he was responsible for the construction of the bridge over the Wādī Sebū, fifteen kilometres east of Fez.

On the economic side, he lent traders considerable sums to develop their businesses and thus create prosperity for all the people. He ordered a reform of the coinage which took the form of devaluing the mouzouna from 48 fals to 24 fals. The bronze coins which were shaped, were struck in order to make them round. As regards his work for the community, he took a great interest in the water problem, especially in the desert areas: thus he had many wells dug in the deserts of eastern Morocco, particularly in the Darʿa, which was on the route taken by caravans of traders and pilgrim caravans on their way to Mecca.

By and large, historians all agree that Mawlāy al-Rashīd's reign was marked by remarkable progress in all realms, unbroken peace and beneficent prosperity after the long years of strife and poverty.

---

15. When I was Rector of Ḳarāwiyyīn University, I officially renamed it al-Madrasa al-Rāshidīyya.

The reign of Mawlāy Ismāʿīl

The history of Mawlāy Ismāʿīl is full of outstanding achievements. This ruler completed the task begun by his two brothers – that of unifying Morocco by putting it under a single throne as it had been in the days of its might and greatness. It was he also who strengthened the basis of the state founded by his two brothers and laid the foundations of the State of Morocco that has safeguarded Morocco's heritage up to the present. Lastly, it was he who saw to it that Muslim law was extended to all parts of Morocco, in order to give the country religious as well as political unity.

He concerned himself greatly with matters relating to the Muslim religion and proselytization on its behalf, even with European kings such as Louis XIV of France and James II of England, to whom he wrote inviting them to embrace Islam. He strictly observed the precepts of Muslim law and led an austere life, having never in his entire life drunk any intoxicating drink. Christian historians have described him as cruel, violent, despotic and prone to anger for no reason except for the pleasure of seeing bloodshed. All these allegations are false. What led them to paint this picture of him was that they believed the stories of European prisoners, who had naturally been treated in accordance with the fashion of the time – that is, with retaliatory violence. Every one of these prisoners, once released and back in their own countries, started to give exaggerated descriptions of the ordeals they had endured – so much so that the idea of Mawlāy Ismāʿīl's violence and cruelty came to be believed by Europeans.

Moreover, the Sultan's ambassadors were sent to European capitals: Ibn Ḥaddū to London, and al-Ḥadjdj Muḥammad Tamīm in turn to Paris and Versailles. Conversely, delegations from the European states came to seek his friendship. He maintained personal relations with the Kings of England and France, and intervened in the affairs of these two states: he had intelligence agents there, who enabled him to be thoroughly conversant with what was going on. He showed perspicacity in politics, saying, for instance: 'The King of Spain is a child, who leaves it to Heaven to govern his country; the King of England has no freedom of action; the King of Austria is obliged to satisfy the great electors. The King of France is the only one who really governs'. Here he was referring to Louis XIV, who at that time was one of the greatest monarchs in Europe.

Such was the ruler who came to the throne of Morocco after the death of his brother Mawlāy Rashīd. His proclamation took place on Wednesday 16 Dhū 'l-Ḥidjdj 1082 (16 April 1672).

The notables of the towns and *ḳabīla*s came to swear allegiance to him, except for those from Marrakesh. This was because his nephew Aḥmad ibn Muḥriz, having learnt of the death of his uncle Mawlāy Rashīd, had gone in haste to that city and asked its inhabitants to proclaim him Sultan. He had the support of many followers, especially among the people of the Sūs. Mawlāy Ismāʿīl thus had no choice but to nip this threat in the bud.

PLATE 8.2   *Sultan Mawlay Ismāʿil*

Only a few days after his proclamation he marched against his nephew and did battle with him and with the Hauz *ḳabīla*s who had joined cause with him. He defeated them, entered Marrakesh and forgave the people their lack of haste in swearing allegiance to him, excusing them because of his nephew's rebellion. The latter had fled after his defeat, but started scheming again, urging the people of Fez to revolt and proclaim him Sultan, in which he succeeded.

When he heard about all this unrest, Mawlāy Ismāʿīl decided to deal first of all with his nephew. He marched against him and forced him to flee a second time, into the Sahara. Then he advanced on Fez and laid siege to it until it surrendered, but later decided to make Meknes his capital. On his return to that town he gave orders for the building of palaces, houses, walls, stables, warehouses and other large buildings. He had gardens and ponds laid out, to such good effect that this town came to rival Versailles (which King Louis XIV, abandoning Paris, had taken as his capital). At Meknes, the building work went on for several years.

Aḥmad ibn Muḥriz, having twice tried in vain to seize power in the capitals of both the north and the south, tried a third time to revolt against his uncle. He entered Marrakesh for a second time, occupied it in 1085/ 1674–5 and fortified himself there, where his uncle pursued and besieged him. The siege lasted nearly two years, at the end of which time Ibn Muḥriz fled for the third time, to the Sūs. Mawlāy Ismāʿīl then made his entry into Marrakesh and this time he gave his army orders to castigate those of the townspeople who had supported Ibn Muḥriz.

One of the domestic political events of Mawlāy Ismāʿīl's reign was the revolt by three of his brothers, Mawlāy al-Ḥarrān, Mawlāy Hāshim and Mawlāy Aḥmad, which broke out at the end of Ramaḍān of 1089/ 1678–9. The rebels were recognized and supported in their campaign by the Aït ʿAttā *ḳabīla*. The Sultan marched against them at the head of an impressive army, and the opposing forces met at Djabal Saghrū. Victory went to Mawlāy Ismāʿīl, whose soldiers showed great courage. Following this victory the three brothers fled into the Sahara.

After taking refuge in the Sūs, Ibn Muḥriz suffered various ups and downs, while his uncle, taken up with the important domestic and foreign affairs of state could not give him his full attention. In 1096/1684–5, when in Meknes, Mawlāy Ismāʿīl learnt that his brother al-Ḥarrān and his nephew Ibn Muḥriz had joined forces and occupied the town of Tarūdant. The Sultan marched against them at the head of a huge army and besieged Tarūdant. During the siege Ibn Muḥriz was killed. Thus ended the adventures of this rebel, who had caused Mawlāy Ismāʿīl much anxiety for over fourteen years. As for Mawlāy al-Ḥarrān, he remained besieged in Tarūdant. When the royal army took Tarūdant by storm, al-Ḥarrān fled into the Sahara.

Mawlāy Ismāʿīl's campaigns to recover the Moroccan towns occupied by the Europeans

Before the advent of the ʿAlawite dynasty, Morocco was split between agitators and Christians, and was coveted by all other nations: this state of affairs having been brought about, as we have seen, by the betrayals and civil strife for which the last Saʿādī rulers were responsible. Mawlāy Mʿhammad and then his brother Mawlāy Rashīd after him of course endeavoured to put an end to this situation and unify Morocco under a single throne and a single king; and they were followed in this by their brother, the great Mawlāy Ismāʿīl. It was to the latter that the role fell, after consolidating the achievements of his two predecessors, of completing the unification of Morocco by liquidating Christian colonization.

The re-taking of al-Mahdiyya

The port of al-Mahdiyya which was then called al-Ma'mūra, was one of the biggest ports in Morocco. Pirates of various nations attempted to occupy it. It was from this port, which came under Salé, a town then settled by Andalusians, that Moroccan ships sailed to fight the Spaniards and other enemies. Taking advantage of the Moroccans' weakness as a result of the quarrels between al-Manṣūr's sons, the Spaniards in 1023/1614 occupied al-Mahdiyya and held it until Mawlāy Ismāʿīl decided to re-take it from them. He marched against the town, besieged it and cut off its water supply, and in 1092/1681 occupied it and took prisoner all the Spaniards who were there.

The re-taking of Tangier

Tangier had fallen under the sway of the British after one of their kings married a Portuguese princess. Already Mawlāy Rashīd had sought to make this town part of Morocco again, but he died before he could liberate it. Given its importance, Mawlāy Ismāʿīl did his utmost to rescue it, and to this end he deputed one of his greatest generals, by name ʿAlī ibn ʿAbdallāh al-Rīfī, to besiege it. Here there is a discrepancy between the Moroccan and European versions of the reason why the English evacuated this town. Though both versions agree that the English evacuated Tangier without striking a blow and after demolishing the towers and fortifications, Moroccan historians say that the English did this because of the severity of the siege to which General ʿAlī al-Rīfī subjected them. European historians claim that this evacuation took place for reasons of domestic politics: the English government and Parliament were afraid that the Duke of York, who had converted to Catholicism, would take Tangier as an operational base in order to attack King Charles II and seize power. This is why the English sovereign supposedly ordered Lord Dartmouth to evacuate Tangier.

Nevertheless, it is acknowledged that another reason for this evacuation was the difficulty the English had found in repelling the Moroccans' attacks. Experience has sufficiently taught us that Europeans did not as a rule give up an inch of occupied Muslim land without being beaten and compelled to do so.

Be that as it may, Moroccan troops led by General 'Alī ibn 'Abdallāh al-Rīfī, entered Tangier in Rabi'I of 1095/February 1684. Wasting no time, the General set about rebuilding what the English had demolished and restoring the mosques, walls, towers and everything else that they had destroyed during their stay and in their flight.

The re-taking of Larache

The loss of Larache was one of the greatest disasters for the Muslims of Morocco; for this town had not been forcibly occupied by the Spanish enemy, but had been ceded to them by one of the kings of Morocco in exchange for their support in regaining power. While the sons and grand-sons of al-Manṣūr the Sa'ādī fought for the throne, the Europeans tried to exploit this situation: they all wanted to occupy Larache, which was then an important strategic centre. Muḥammad Shaykh had fled to Europe to ask the foreign kings for military assistance against his two brothers. King Philip III of Spain heard of this and negotiations took place, at the end of which the pretender to the Moroccan throne agreed to cede Larache to the King of Spain in return for help in regaining his throne. The bargain having been struck, Muḥammad Shaykh returned to Fez and the Spaniards occupied Larache in 1019/1610. Larache remained under Spanish rule for over eighty years, until the advent of Mawlāy Ismā'īl. This great king threw a large army against the town, besieged it and hemmed in the Spaniards for over five months. Fierce fighting took place between besiegers and besieged, and the Moroccans won a brilliant victory. The re-taking of Larache, which took place on Wednesday 18 Moharram of 1101/1 November 1689, gave the Moroccans enormous joy, equalled in intensity only by the grief they had felt at its loss.

The re-taking of Arzila

The port of Arzila had fallen into the hands of the Portuguese at the beginning of the reign of the Banū Waṭṭās. After being recovered by the early Sa'ādī kings, it was re-taken a second time by the Portuguese. Changing hands in this way, it eventually fell to the Spaniards. When General Ibn Ḥaddū had finished with Larache he received orders from the Sultan to advance on Arzila and besiege it. Worn out, the besieged inhabitants sued for their lives; and this was granted subject to the Sultan's approval. But fearing the worst, they fled by night in their ships. The Moroccans then entered Arzila in 1102/1691.

The Armies of Mawlāy Ismāʿīl

The Wadāya militia

The Moroccan kings raised their armies either from *kabīla*s of their own clan or from allied *kabīla*s. The Almoravids, for example, relied on the Ṣanhādja *kabīla*s (Lamtūna, Lamṭa and others), while the Almohads were supported by the Maṣmūda *kabīla*s. This was so until the advent of the Saʿādī: they recruited their soldiers from the *kabīla*s of Beduin Arabs introduced into Morocco in the time of al-Manṣūr the Almohad, who had settled in the south of the country. From these *kabīla*s the Saʿādī raised a body of troops known as the 'Wadāya militia'. The Wadāya had dispersed following the decline of the Saʿādī. During his stay in Marrakesh, Mawlāy Ismāʿīl had the idea of reassembling them and making them into soldiers in order to buttress his regime. These new recruits were given uniforms and taken to Meknes, the capital. They were merged with the men of the Shbanāte and the Zirāra.

Their numbers having grown, Mawlāy Ismāʿīl divided them into two groups: the first was sent to Fez, and the second stayed at Riyād in Meknes.

The Bawākhir militia

Mawlāy Ismāʿīl pondered a great deal about what makes nations strong, stable and feared. Eventually he realized that this depends on their military might. But he also realized that a nation's decadence results from the acquisition of excessive authority by the army and its chiefs. He therefore decided to establish a militia composed of slaves. Such people are naturally inclined to obedience, which is an essential prerequisite for discipline; and since they are at their masters' mercy, they are naturally inclined to obey them.

Mawlāy Ismāʿīl bethought himself of this solution when he was organizing the Wadāya militia, as mentioned above. One of the secretaries of the Makhzen was Muḥammad ibn al-Kāsim ʿAlīlīsh;[16] whose father was also secretary to al-Manṣūr the Saʿādī. 'The king had a militia of slaves' he said to Mawlāy Ismāʿīl, 'and I possess the book in which my father recorded their names'. He showed him this register, and told him that there were still a great many of these slaves in the Marrakesh area and that he would be able to collect them together and enter their names again in a special register in order to make them do military service. Mawlāy Ismāʿīl entrusted this task to him, and gave orders in writing to the chiefs of the *kabīla*s in the area to give him help and assistance. ʿAlīlīsh accordingly set about tracking down these slaves and eventually enrolled them all. He carried

16. Contrary to what is stated in al-Nāṣirī, 1954–6, Vol. IV, p. 26, where his name is given as ʿUmar ibn Kāsim, I actually possess a letter in his handwriting written on behalf of the Vizir al-Yaḥmadi and signed Muḥammad Ibn Kāsim. The same name is given for this person in a letter from Mawlāy Ismāʿīl to our ancestor Shaykh al-Islām Sīdī Muḥammad ibn ʿAbd al Kādir al-Fāsī. Al-Duʿa ysjif-Ribāti also refers to him by this name.

out a full recruitment – to such good purpose that not a Negro remained in all these *kabīla*s, whether slave, half-caste or freeman. Public opinion was shocked by this measure, especially the *'ulamā'*, repositories of Islamic law, which forbids the exploitation of free men. This question gave rise to a long controversy between the king and the *'ulamā'* of Fez, and to a voluminous correspondence part of which still exists. These are the famous letters from Mawlāy Ismāʿīl to the Shaykh al-Islām Abū 'l-Suʿūd al-Fāsī.[17]

To revert to Mawlāy Ismāʿīl, I must make the following general comment about him. If, as Europeans claim, he was really savage, cruel and despotic, then a mere scholar, strong only in faith and law, could not have stood up to him. But Mawlāy Ismāʿīl was convinced that he was acting in accordance with Muslim law in this matter which he regarded as the best thing he could do for Morocco and Islam. What encouraged him further to maintain his position was the diminution of his responsibility in the matter by virtue of the part played by Muḥammad ibn Ḳāsim ʿAlīlīsh in reducing free men to slavery: ʿAlīlīsh claimed that they, or at any rate their fathers, had already been slaves in the days of the Saʿādī. Furthermore, Mawlāy Ismāʿīl had the concurrence of certain more accommodating *'ulamā'*, such as the scholar who wrote an undated and unsigned letter to Shaykh al-Islām al-Fāsī, saying *inter alia*:

> Why did you not say in your letter [the one to Mawlāy Ismāʿīl]: Lord, victorious by God's grace and rightly guided in all his actions, particularly the recruitment of these slaves before their reduction to slavery and the precautions taken as regards Muslim law: this question having been thoroughly considered, nothing remains to be done after all the justifications that have been put forward. Everything is in the hands of our Lord – God send him victorious! – who acts in accordance with the directives of ourselves and the other *'ulamā'* of the day; all that in order to have a clear conscience, may God keep him forever for ourselves and all Muslims! Moreover he has an ample sufficiency of papers on this subject, such as to convince any sceptic or critic. To speak thus is to speak the truth. This is what you ought to have done, without fear of contravening divine or human laws in any way. I hope you will show yourself more conciliatory in your correspondence to our Lord – may God support him! So that he may be satisfied with it. It is because I hold you in esteem that I have given you this advice.

The correspondence on this subject between the Sultan and the *'ulamā'* went on until the death of Sīdī M'ḥammad ibn ʿAbd al-Ḳādir al-Fāsī in 1116/1704–5, and had certainly begun in the last decade of the eleventh century. But the earliest letter from this correspondence that has survived is the one dated 28 Dhū 'l-Kaʿda 1104/July 1693. In it, the Ruler asked the aforesaid Sīdī M'ḥammad to study ʿAlīlīsh's arguments about the reduction of free men to slavery, to state whether this operation was in accordance

17. al-Nāṣirī, 1954–6 Vol. IV, p. 42, Cairo edition.

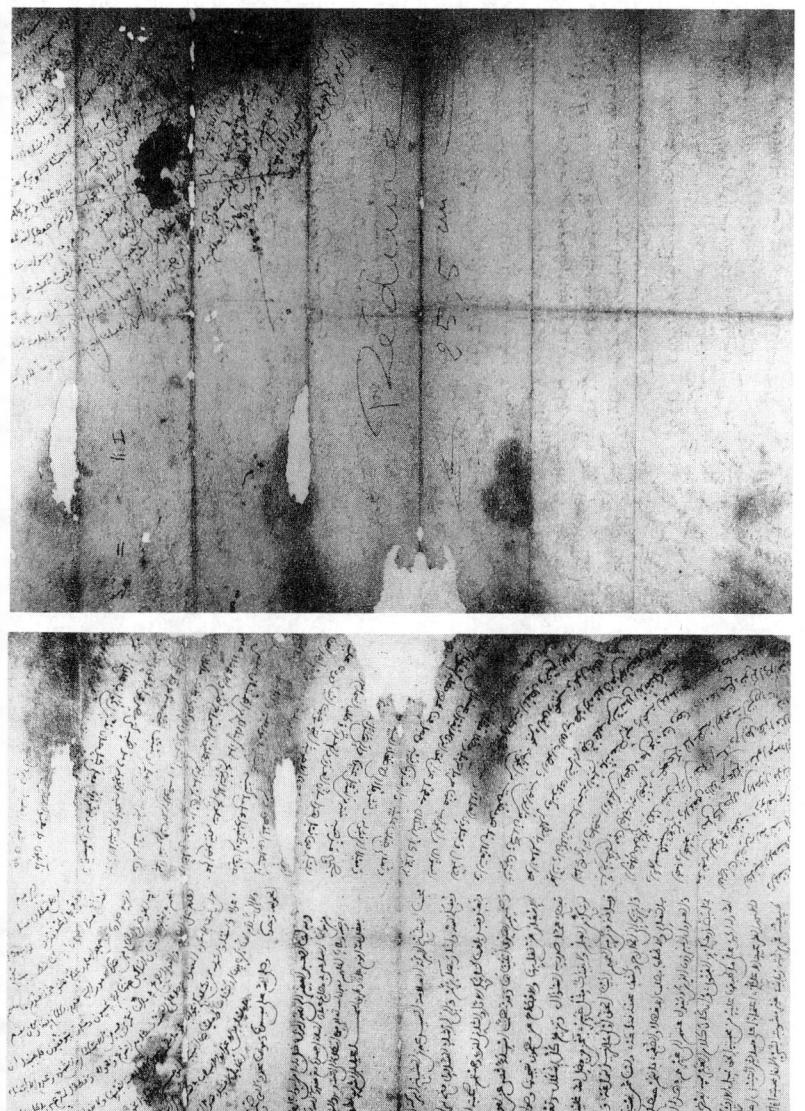

PLATE 8.3 *Letter No. 12, part of the correspondence between Sultan Mawlāy Ismāʿy Ismāʿīl and Shaykh al-Islām Sīdī Muḥammad al-Fāsī*

with the law, and to say whether he approved of it or not. This scholar no doubt answered this question frankly, or else insinuated that the law did not allow free men to be reduced to slavery. The disagreement got worse, until the Sultan, vexed, wrote a letter about which the author of *al-Istiḳsā* said[18]

> In the same month of Dhū 'l-Ḳaʿda of the same year, that is 1108/ 1696–7, the *ḳāḍī* and the *ʿulamāʾ* of Fez received a letter from the Sultan upbraiding them for not giving their agreement to the reduction to slavery of the men entered on the register. A second letter arrived in which the monarch praised the people of Fez, severely criticized the *ʿulamāʾ*, and ordered the dismissal of the *ḳāḍī* and the notaries public of this city.

The first letter to which this passage from *al-Istiḳsā* refers is part of my family collection. It deals with many repeated questions which may be summarized as follows: the Sultan had thought it necessary and essential to organize an army to defend the territory of Islam. In this long letter he developed his point of view about the institution of this army of slaves, and asked the recipient to distribute it to the *ʿulamāʾ* and ask them for their replies. We possess only one letter of reply, from Sīdī M'ḥammad, in which he says his last word: 'As to the man who cannot be proven to be a slave, scholars are unanimous that he is free and that it is by no means lawful to own him or to dispose of his person either by selling it or in any other way, for men are born free'.

It was at this juncture that the Ruler, in order to convince the Shaykh al-Islām of the need to organize the army of the Bawākhir, resorted to the following method: by a letter dated Djumādā' I of 1110/December 1698, he called him to witness that he had freed all the slaves he had made into a militia and that he held them in mortmain to defend the territory of Islam.

We do not know what Sīdī M'ḥammad's reply was, but in some correspondence on this subject dated not far from the scholar's death (Radjab 1115/Autumn of 1703) we find a clue which is not directly related to the matter but refers to the enrolment of the people of Fez in the corps of archers. It seems that the Sultan had also consulted the scholar about this latter question, and had probably received an unsatisfactory reply. So he took the opportunity to write him a long letter, the full text of which will be found in the collection of Mawlāy Ismāʿīl's letters referred to above.

In the following year Sīdī M'ḥammad died, and Mawlāy Ismāʿīl continued to ask the *ʿulamāʾ* of Fez for their agreement. The affair had all sorts of ups and downs until 1120/1708–9, when the King finally forced them to

18. This correspondence, which is of fundamental importance from the historical, social, legal and religious points of view, was published by the author of this chapter, with photocopies of the documents, in a special number of the journal *Hesperis-Tamuda* published in 1962 for the third centenary of Mawlāy Ismāʿīl's accession to power.

approve the *Dīwān al- 'Abīd* (Register of Slaves).

Such is the history of the formation of the Bawākhir militia – in concise form, admittedly, but based on unique and important documents. This militia initially helped a great deal to maintain peace and security in the unified country. Mawlāy Ismāʿīl had established forts and citadels (*kaṣaba*s) in all parts of Morocco, from the frontier with Algeria to the southernmost limits of the Sahara. These forts were garrisoned by soldiers who lived with their families and whose sons received special training, an account of which is called for here.

PLATE 8.4 *Walad Dāwūd Aït Hamū or Manṣūr Ḳaṣaba at Skoura in the province of Ouarzazate probably built in the eighteenth century*

Thanks to this powerful militia, Mawlāy Ismāʿīl managed to restore Morocco's strength and prestige in the eyes of the great nations of the day, which then began to fear it. This militia also enabled him, as we have said above, to maintain security in Morocco and give people confidence and peace of mind.

Mawlāy Ismāʿīl appoints his sons viceroys in the various parts of Morocco

This selection was one of the things that caused Mawlāy Ismāʿīl the greatest difficulty. The point was that the sovereign had a very large number of children: at the time of his death, there were 500 boys and as many girls. Hence he could not satisfy them all. In these circumstances, he would have done better to have adopted from the outset the solution he finally arrived at after bitter experience.

In 1111/1699–1700, he divided the provinces between his sons as follows: Mawlāy Aḥmad (nicknamed *al-Dhahabī*) was sent to Tadla with 3000 Negro soldiers; Mawlāy 'Abd al-Mālik was sent to the Dar'a at the head of 1000 horsemen; Muḥammad al-'Alem to the Sūs with 3000; and Mawlāy al-Ma'mūn al-Kabīr to Sidjilmāsa. The latter set up his base at Tizīmī with 500 horsemen, but he died two years later and was replaced by Mawlāy Yūsuf in 1113/1701–2. Mawlāy Zaydān was sent to eastern Morocco, and launched expeditions against the Turks, once even entering the town of Mascara where he sacked *Amīr* 'Uthmān Bey's palace. His father removed him from office, in view of the pact between himself and the Ottoman Caliph, and replaced him with Mawlāy Ḥāfiḍ.

Those of Mawlāy Ismā'īl's elder sons who did not receive viceroyships felt injured. Indeed, some of them even tried to occupy provinces by force, such as Mawlāy Abū Naṣr, who attacked his brother Mawlāy 'Abd al-Mālik, defeated him and took possession of the Dar'a. The defeated prince fled. The Sultan sent his son Mawlāy Sharīf to recover the Dar'a province from Abū Naṣr, and it was then assigned to him instead of to 'Abd al-Mālik, who had shown himself incapable of defending himself. In the midst of all this, Mawlāy Muḥammad al-'Alem rose up in the Sūs, had himself proclaimed Sultan and marched on Marrakesh, which he besieged and occupied. Mawlāy Ismā'īl sent his son Mawlāy Zaydān against him, and fought against the rebel for two years. Having seen the untoward consequences of this experiment in the shape of squabbles between his sons during his lifetime, some of them even going so far as to claim the throne, Mawlāy Ismā'īl began to send to Tafilālet all his sons who had reached the age of puberty. He set each of them up in a house, mostly with their mothers; he gave them a certain number of palm-trees and a plot to cultivate, and also a certain number of slaves to help them in their work. The sovereign was wise to do this, for he had too many sons, who could not all lead a princely life in Meknes or the other towns of Morocco. Thus by sending them to Sidjilmāsa he solved this problem. In 1130/1717–18 he removed all his sons from office except Mawlāy Aḥmad al-Dhahabī, Governor of Tadla, who had succeeded in his task given that in his twenty unbroken years of operation there had been not one uprising in his province either directed against him or fomented by him against his father.

Following this measure the country had peace and quiet, and Mawlāy Ismā'īl's constructive work during the last ten years of his life was apparent. The Moroccans took up trade and agriculture and helped to develop the country's wealth, encouraged as they were by complete security. Thus historians agree that during this period there were no robbers or highwaymen any more, thanks to the severe measures taken both against people guilty of crimes and also against their accomplices. The result of this situation was great well-being and easy circumstances, as a result of the means possessed by the overwhelming majority of the population.

Mawlāy Ismāʿīl had stayed on the throne for fifty-seven years. No king of Morocco or of anywhere in Islam before or after him had reigned for so long except al-Mustanṣir al-ʿUbaydī, who was proclaimed at the age of seven and reigned until he was sixty-seven. He died on Saturday 28 Radjab 1139/21 March 1727.

Mawlāy Ismāʿīl's successors

After Mawlāy Ismāʿīl's death the inevitable occurred, that is to say that his many sons, who already during his lifetime had fought over the regional government their father had granted them, started to rise up with the object of acceding to supreme government. For decades none of the claimants managed to establish a strong and lasting government. The first of them, Mawlāy ʿAbdallāh, was enthroned and deposed several times.

The part played by the Bawākhir militia, set up to maintain order and ensure peace, was a pernicious one. Similar institutions in the Muslim dynasties from the Abbasids of Baghdad to the Ottomans with their Janissaries were a disaster for the dynasties and for the people who suffered under them.

Towards the end of the eighteenth century a great king, Sīdī Muḥammad ibn ʿAbdallāh or Muḥammad III, came to the throne of Morocco. He restored order, strengthened the power of the monarchy and made Morocco a country respected by all nations.

His primary interest lay in the development of trade and to that end he set about modernizing the ports, in particular the port of Mogador, which has since been given the name of Essaouira (meaning 'little wall' or, according to another etymology, 'little plan', after a construction plan of the port which was circulated among the workers). He signed trade agreements with a number of European states, including an agreement in 1757 with Denmark concerning the port of Sāfī.

Muḥammad III's reforms extended to other domains.[19] He took an active interest in the Ḳarāwiyyīn of Fez and drew up reforms concerning syllabuses, texts to be studied, subjects to be taught, and so on.

As far as religion is concerned, he believed in the original purity of Islam, which rejects what is known as maraboutism, or the veneration of saints and the act of requesting them to intercede with God for the good of humankind. Such fundamentalist tendencies remained in check, however, because in the late eighteenth century the Wahhābī movement in Arabia was demanding much more radical reforms than any of those which Muḥammad III wished to see. During this period he was on excellent terms with the *Sharīf* of Mecca, Sourour, to whom he had given one of

19. al-Nāṣirī, 1954–6, Vol. IV, ch. on the reign of Muḥammad III.

his daughters in marriage. As the Wahhābīs were enemies of the *Sharīf*s of Mecca, Muḥammad III wished to avoid any reform which coincided too closely with Wahhābī ideology. Nevertheless, the power of the brotherhoods declined considerably during his reign and during the reign of his son, Mawlāy Sulaymān.

As regards foreign relations, Muḥammad III continued throughout his reign to conclude agreements with foreign countries. He recognized the independence of the United States of America; suggested to Louis XIV that he abolish slavery; and supported the Ottoman empire in its conflict with the Russian empire. In 1767 he expelled the Portuguese from Mazagān,[20] but died suddenly while preparing to besiege Ceuta.

In conclusion, the reign of Muḥammad III can be said to have had a major stabilizing effect on the State and on the authority of the ʿAlawite dynasty. So peace-loving was he that he went to war only once, to liberate Mazagān, and he resolved all domestic and foreign issues through negotiation and dialogue. Overall, such prudent and realistic policies were beneficial to the Moroccan people, who, during the second half of the eighteenth century, enjoyed general prosperity and complete security.

20. Contrary to common belief, the name of this coastal town on the Atlantic, to the south of Casablanca is not of foreign origin. It is the name of a Berber *ḳabīla*, the Banū Mazghawa, who lived in the vicinity of Mazagān. For the same reasons, the town of Algiers also bore this name, known to geographers and Arab historians as ʿJazu un Bani Mazghawaʾ.

Algeria, Tunisia and Libya: the Ottomans and their heirs

M. H. CHERIF

The early sixteenth century was marked by a profound crisis which put an end to the old state structures in the Maghrib and the former balances implicit in them. Thanks to the intervention of the Ottomans in Algiers, Tunis and Tripoli – and of the _shārīfs_ of the Saharan provinces in Morocco – this troubled time gave way to a new order which took longer to emerge in some countries than others but which finally brought some stability to the Maghreb until the structural crisis of the early nineteenth century which heralded colonial domination.

What was the underlying significance of this crisis? How did the Ottomans help to establish stability in the sixteenth century? To what extent did they remain alien to the societies they dominated, and to what extent did they become integrated into the conquered countries? It is clear that the situation of Algiers was different from that of Tunis, and that of Tunis from that of Tripoli – although how different is hard to determine. It is also clear that the eighteenth century, a period of relative stability, exhibits new characteristics in addition to those of the seventeenth century, which was marked by experiment and fluctuation.

The sixteenth-century crisis and the Ottoman solution in the Maghreb

This crisis affected the entire Arab world. It was an economic crisis, evidenced by the decline of the monetary economy in favour of the subsistence economy, and was due in part to the re-routing of the main trade traffic. It was also a social and political crisis consequent upon the weakening of the unifying factors of society – political and military forces, groups formed by large-scale traders, and the class of the _'ulamā'_ (Islamic scholars). It was also a cultural crisis involving great change and with it a pathological attachment to things of the past – ideas, behaviour, customs and tastes. This multi-faceted crisis occurred at a particularly dangerous time since a rival world, Europe, was awakening economically (through major discoveries and the rise of capitalist trade), politically (through increasing centralization and the increase in absolute monarchies) and culturally (through the Renaissance which was changing ways of thinking, habits and techniques).

Only the Osmanli Turks, on the fringe of the Muslim world, adapted to the times to some extent by using certain modern techniques or ideas including firearms and efficient military and administrative organization. Although limited (it did not involve significant internal changes in Muslim society), the Ottoman response to the challenges of the period was nonetheless a way out for societies and states in full decline and exposed to outside threats such as the Maghreb states at the beginning of the sixteenth century.

The crisis in the Maghreb

The Maghreb was in a state of crisis at the end of the 'Middle Ages',[1] plagued by a dwindling population, the dislocation of the economy and of society, and incurable political weakness.

The numerous underlying reasons were inherently structural. First, there was the alarming proximity of the desert and its rapid encroachment on substantial areas of the Maghreb whenever there was a prolonged drought or land was left untended for long periods as at the end of the 'Middle Ages'. Second, there was the juxtaposition of different modes of production and societies: Arab *gaba'il* (groups); groups assimilated with the Arabs; Berber mountain communities, sedentary rural populations and town-dwellers. Third, there was the very flexibility of society's unifying elements, whether social, economic or spiritual and, fourth, the lack of technological and cultural progress.

The Hilālian nomads[2] have often been blamed for the decadence of the Maghreb during the late 'Middle Ages' but this accusation has been ruled out – at least in its unqualified and partisan form.[3] However, through their activities and organization, their division into opposed or allied (but always separate) segments, their way of life and their warrior ethic (their 'noble irregularity', to quote Jacques Berque), the Arab *gaba'il* (or groups assimilated with the Arabs) represented an element of weakness for the central government – the Maghreb's soft underbelly. When drought or political crisis weakened central authority, these groups would promptly seize the opportunity to take up arms to restore the means of their livelihood or to participate in the general struggle for power.

1. The term 'Middle Ages' is inadequate when applied to Muslim history, but we have borrowed it from European historiography as a universally accepted convention. We might also add that the end of the fifteenth century was a real turning-point not only for Europe but also for the other civilizations. With firearms, the development of world trade and the beginnings of capitalism, modern times really began.

2. Arab groups from Upper Egypt, who invaded the Maghreb from the mid-eleventh century onwards and swarmed over the plains in the interior, subjugating the former populations of these regions or converting them to their mode of life and their culture.

3. J. P. Poncet, 1967.

During the 1300s and 1400s epidemics and famine, as in Europe, had the peoples of the Maghreb reduced in total population to between 3 and 6 million. As a result production had decreased, cultivation in lands perpetually under threat from encroaching desert had been compromised and security in sparsely occupied territories had deteriorated. At the same time the treasures of America, which poured into Seville from 1503 to 1505, were to devalue considerably the Old World's money reserves and help establish the power first of their original owners, the Iberians, and later of those who had seized them in the service of the New World economy, particularly the Dutch, English and French.[4]

The gradual decline which affected the cities of the Maghreb from the eleventh and twelfth centuries onwards (except for certain towns on the great trade routes or on the coast and with a few interruptions in the thirteenth century) became a rapid deterioration by the late 1400s and early 1500s. Commercial life was paralysed, trade delayed and food shortages and poverty were rife. Leo Africanus invariably attributed this poverty, which he saw everywhere, both in the cities and in the regions cultivated by sedentary populations, to oppressive taxation – which sometimes weighed absurdly on the populations still liable to it – and to the consequent depredations of the nomads.

The nomads were indeed freeing themselves from the yoke of the state and extending their control and pastoral way of life to the greater part of the country. They took advantage of the vacuum created by depopulation and the low level of farming and used violence in order to subsist – or to obtain food in excess from weaker populations. The areas cultivated by sedentary populations began to shrink as a result of the nomad offensive. It even happened that tiny fields in which cereals were grown were protected by great walls. Leo Africanus, who noted this around Tunis, concluded: 'Think of the amount of grain obtainable from a small walled enclosure, tended with such care and toil! The harvest is not enough for even half the year!'[5]

Such were the circumstances in which the multi-secular states of the Zayyānids (or Banū 'Abd al-Wadids) in Tlemcen and the Ḥafṣids in Tunis began to founder. The disorganization of trade and the decrease in taxable commodities led to a dwindling of their resources. Troops and the bureaucracy, already badly maintained, became far less efficient. Added to this were the effects of the *iḳṭā'* (concessions) of land or taxes granted by impecunious sovereigns to the powerful warrior groups. Soon the cities which were far from the centre of power were to become autonomous (Tripoli, Bougie, Constantine in the Ḥafṣid kingdom) and the great confederations were to reign supreme in the areas over which they ranged. The *Bilād al-Makhzen* (country under state authority) was gradually reduced to a limited area around the sultan's residence with the exception of a few

4. I. Wallerstein, 1974.
5. Leo Africanus, 1956, Vol. II, p. 383.

pockets of allegiance farther afield. Insecurity was still rife and the Ḥafṣid sultan himself had to take up arms in the early 1540s to defend his herds from nomad raiders almost under the walls of his residence.[6]

The domination of the Zayyānids in Tlemcen and the Ḥafṣids in Tunis and the eastern Maghreb had already been severely shaken – from the late 1400s and from 1530 respectively when the Spaniards and the Ottomans gained a foothold in these possessions.

Foreign intervention in the central and eastern Maghreb

The political vacuum or the lesser resistance put up by the Maghreb could account for this intervention but it was motivated, above all, by the needs or the designs of the conquerors. Their initiatives must be seen in the light of the religious passions of the time: the crusading spirit of the Spaniards, who had barely completed the *reconquista* of their land; and the defence of *Dār al-Islām* combined with the ideal of *ghāzī* (conquest)[7] on the part of the Ottomans. Moreover, the coastal strongholds of the Maghreb were of undeniable strategic interest to the two protagonists, either to protect their own possessions from the assaults of the other (who might be aided by religious minorities such as the Muslims from Andalusia or the Christians from the Balkans), or as bases for a possible offensive.[8] Significantly the Spanish offensive in the Maghreb, from 1505 onwards, came shortly after the first arrivals (1503–4) of precious metals from America,[9] which afforded them the means of pursuing a vigorous expansionist policy.

The Spaniards in the central and eastern Maghreb

From 1505 to 1574, the kings of Spain repeatedly tried to secure footholds on the coasts of the Maghreb. One has only to recall the great expeditions of Pedro Navarro in 1505–11 (against Oran, Bougie and Tripoli), of the Holy Roman Emperor in 1535–41 (against Tunis and Algiers), and those of Don John of Austria, who recaptured Tunis from the Turks in 1573 (two years after his great victory over the Turkish fleet at Lepanto). The gains were limited, however, as the conquest of the interior of the Maghreb and the conversion of the indigenous inhabitants rapidly proved impossible. The Spaniards contented themselves with occupying a few *presidios* (towns) (Oran in 1509–1708 and 1732–92; Tripoli in 1510–51) and building a number of powerful fortresses on African soil, such as Peñon at the entrance to Algiers (1511–29) or Goulette in the outer harbour of Tunis (1535–74). With Goulette, the aim was to hold the town in check and, above all, to guard the southern coastline of the Strait of Sicily.

This policy of limited occupation had to be supported by a constant

6. Ibn Abī Dīnār, 1967, p. 169.
7. A. Temini, 1978; K. R. Sahli, 1977.
8. F. Braudel, 1928 and 1935.
9. H. Chaunu and P. Chaunu, 1955, Vol. VIII(2), pp. 14 *et seq.*

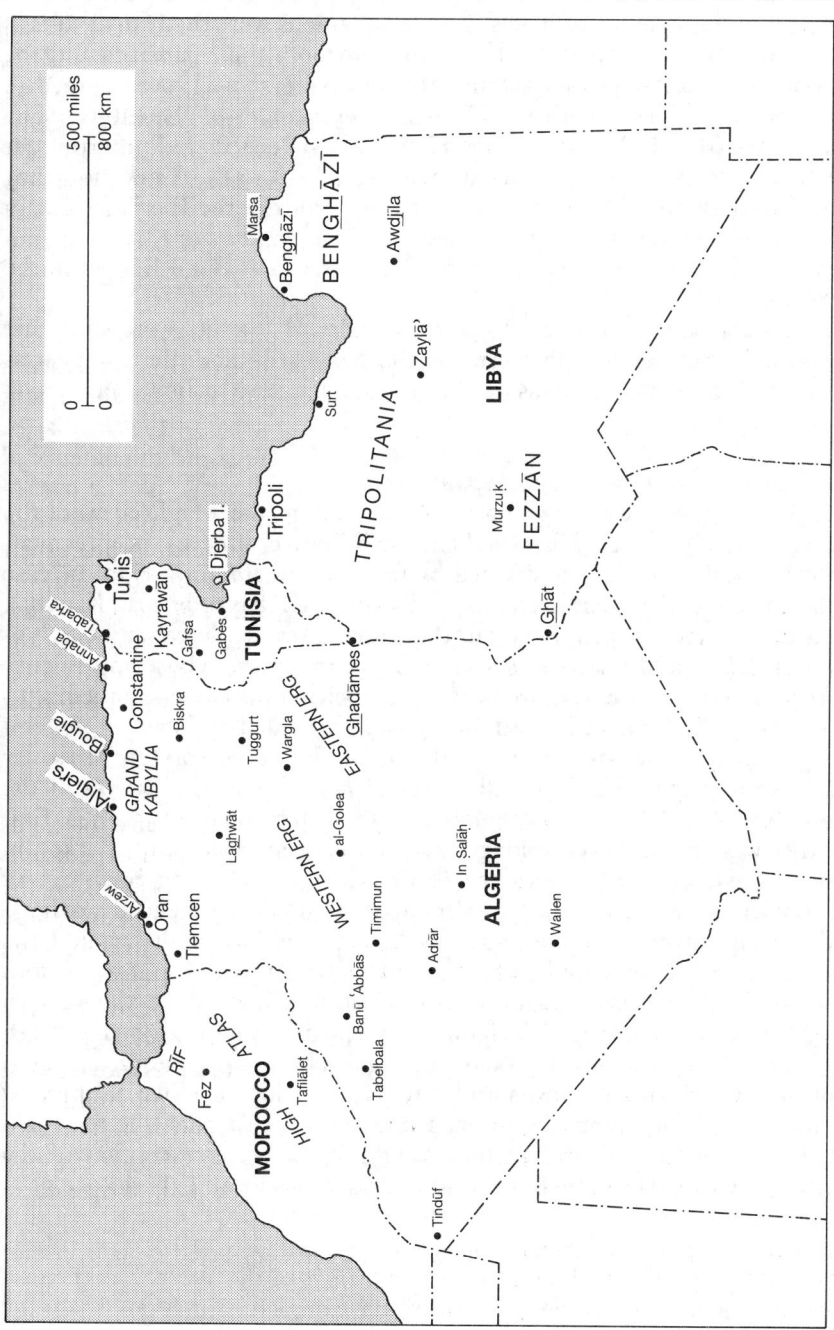

FIG. 9.1 *Algeria, Tunisia and Libya in the sixteenth to eighteenth centuries*

search for local allies or protégés. The most famous were the Ḥafṣid sultans who, from 1535, subtly played see-saw with both the Spaniards and the Ottomans. The last Ḥafṣid sultan, Muḥammad (1573–4), even agreed to share power in Tunis with the Christian commander of the capital. The last Zayyānids of Tlemcen, like Ḥafṣids, also contracted intermittent alliances with the Spaniards, until their capital fell to the Turks and they were finally removed from power in 1551–4. Nor did the Iberians disdain alliances with lesser chiefs, such as the Shābbiya, masters of Ḳayrawān and central Tunisia in about 1550, or the Banū Amīr and Banū Rāshid in the Oran area.

In general, however, the religious and cultural barriers were such that no durable rapprochement between the Spaniards and the indigenous chiefs was possible. As was to be expected, the Muslim Turks took advantage of this.

The Ottomans' fight against the Spaniards

The first Turks to wage war on the Christians in the Maghreb were the *Raʿīs* corsairs. They acted first on their own initiative, although in agreement with the local sovereigns and aided by the local inhabitants, as in the case of the Barbarossa brothers, ʿArrūdj (or ʿUrūdj) and Khayruddīn (or Khidhr), from about 1500 to 1519. At about that time, after the defeat and death of ʿArrūdj, Khayruddīn appealed to the Ottoman sultan, whose sovereignty he recognized and the Maghreb *iyāla* (regencies) thus came into being.

Thanks to the Janissaries and the weapons provided by Istanbul, Algeria was gradually subjugated by Khayruddīn and his successors, in particular Ṣalaḥ Raʾīs (1552–6) and the all-powerful *beylerbey* of the *'odjak*s of the West', Killidj or ʿIldj ʿAlī (1568–87). For about forty years (1534–74), East Ifrīḳiya was the scene of a long struggle between Spain and Turkey in which Ḥafṣid sovereigns and the local chiefs, such as the Shābbiya of Ḳayrawān, intervened actively – although not always to their advantage – and corsairs of great repute, such as Torgut (or Dragut) – around the middle of the century and until his death just off Malta in 1565 – won renown. The principal stages in the Turkish conquest of the eastern Maghreb were the taking of Tripoli in 1551, Ḳayrawān in 1557, Djerba in 1558 and, lastly, Tunis in 1569 and again in 1574. Thereafter, both protagonists, Spaniards and Ottomans, were called to other theatres of operations and the situation stabilized in favour of the Turks who remained masters of the central and eastern Maghreb, with the exception of the enclave of Oran, Marsa el-Kabīr and the small island of Tabarka.

The organization of the Ottoman Regencies

These outlying military borderlands, the *'odjak*s of the West' – as the new African provinces were called – were never completely integrated into the Ottoman political and military system. No regular tribute was paid, nor was there any direct administration by Istanbul, nor were the institutions characteristic of Europe, such as the *tīmār* (fiefs) introduced into North Africa. Initially under the authority of a single warlord, the *beylerbey* of Algiers, the three Maghreb Regencies were separated after the death of the omnipotent Killidj in 1587.

Each province was entrusted to a *pasha* appointed by Istanbul and assisted by the *dīwān* (council of high-ranking Turkish officers). The militia of the Janissaries, several thousand in number, was responsible for territorial defence, maintained a minimum of order and played an active part in the raising of taxes and the running of the 'administration'. As such, it was from the start the mainstay of the new regime and its members settled down as lords and masters of the lands they had conquered. Allied to the Janissaries were the corsairs from the Greek archipelago, Albania or nearby European countries such as Italy, Provence and Spain. They had all been converted to Islam, although some were less sincere than others, and like their counterparts in the militia, they were uniformly considered Turks and included in the caste of conquerors whose privileged status they enjoyed.

The Makhzen (administration) fulfilled various simple functions. It collected taxes to meet the cost of waging war and maintaining the corps of conquerors in the country; it kept order and dispensed justice, at least in the towns inhabited by the subject sedentary populations; and it managed the postal service. A small staff of *khudja* (scribes) and accountants, a few high-ranking political figures (including the *pasha*), or religious ones (including the *ḳāḍī* or magistrate) and, above all, soldiers of all ranks carried out the many tasks. In time, the Makhzen had to recruit auxiliaries from among the local inhabitants: soldiers such as the Kabyles, or the local horsemen who were taken into the service of the Turks; and civilians such as the Arabic scribes, advisers of all kinds and administrators and *lazzām* (tax-farmers).

In other respects, society was still managed by local indigenous institutions with the new masters intervening now and then. There were, for instance, local communities which continued to obey their own *shaykh*s (elected chiefs) and to observe their own *'urf* (customs). There were also religious institutions which continued to dispense justice (except when peace was seriously disturbed or the Turks were involved) and to be responsible for public worship, education and charitable works.

Although slight and rudimentary, the new Ottoman organization gave the Maghreb what it needed most – the means of adapting to the modern world. It introduced a disciplined army using firearms, a relatively centralized administration and the acquisition by privateering of some of the money being circulated in the Mediterranean. The new regime was generally well received in the cities which were directly exposed to Christian assault and threatened with asphyxiation since the countryside had regained autonomy. It was also well received by the clergy, particularly the *'ulamā'* who favoured a strong central power. Lastly, some people, including leading urbanites, prominent rural figures and entire *makhzen* (groups), entered its service out of self-interest, choice or tradition. Opposed to the Turks were all those who had benefited from the freedom of the early eleventh century, the rural populations which had had their own social and war-making organizations and to which the new masters signified only harsh rule and burdensome exploitation. The Turks had to wage long wars to subjugate the useful areas of hinterland and to establish *mah'alla* (armed camps) there, through which to raise taxes and impose a minimum of order. They also became skilled at playing off *saff*, (pl. *sufuf*, confederations), one against the other. Without the power to control the area by force of arms alone, diplomacy was as important as coercion.

The seventeenth century in the Maghreb: in search of equilibrium

In the seventeenth century Maghreb society, mostly little changed by the Ottoman episode, gradually recovered from the crisis of the 1500s. Its coastal cities, and perhaps its sedentary population, had even developed to some extent. It was nonetheless still susceptible to the grave crises of epidemics, famines and civil wars which continued to shake it from time to time. The Turkish ruling class had undergone some internal changes, being joined by new elements and becoming to some extent rooted in the Maghreb. The interests, horizons and characteristics of rulers and ruled diverged and throughout the seventeenth century the long and complex hostilities between opposing factions increased. Certain foreign problems arose concerning relations with the mother-city, Istanbul, and Barbary privateering, which enjoyed its golden age between 1600 and 1650. The Regencies grew further apart with their political development following different lines.

Seventeenth-century Ottoman Maghreb society

Ottoman North Africa comprised the following socio-economic groups: the city, suburban farmers, semi-sedentary farmers who practised transhumance from one to three months a year, nomadic shepherds who travelled far from their *watan* (homeland), nomadic camel-herders of the deep desert and sedentary oasis dwellers. The main urban strata included notable clerics and merchants, workers, the *kulughli* (prosperous descendants of locally married Ottoman immigrants), the Ottoman military establishment and civilian imperial officers.

The rural people belonged to various *kabīlas*[10] which were communities

10. *kabīla* (pl. *kabā'il*): 'A large agnatic group, the members of which claim to be "descended from one common ancestor" and who may "jointly own an area of grazing land"' (*Encyclopaedia of Islam*, new edn., Vol. IV, pp. 334–5). In the *General History of Africa* the plural is given as *kabīlas*.

thought to share a common patrilineal descent. Genealogies justified why and how various smaller groups were entrusted to an elected *shaykh* assisted by an informal council composed of the heads of the smaller *kabīlas*. Above the *kabīla* there existed *saff* (pl. *sufuf*) – confederations formed by alliances between *kabīlas*. These were stable alignments occurring either within a single ecological zone or uniting groups from different ecological and economic spheres, such as camel-herders, shepherds, semi-sedentary farmers and urban factions. Some territorial groups developed long-term centralized leadership such as the great Tuareg principalities (*amenokal*-led groups). Some *kabīlas* allied through attendance at a common shrine, or allegiance to a common *turuk* (brotherhood).

Historians, therefore, should not view the rural people as a medley of groups and factions capriciously rebelling against or submitting to the Ottomans. Conversely, it was the dynamics of ecological change and the shifts in *saff* alignments which dictated whether groups should rebel or co-operate. The existence of the *saff*s also meant that a single system of political relations operated over large portions of the Maghreb. City politics were only a small part of this wider context. Great blocks, allied to or dominated by the Makhzen, stood in opposition to the *sība* (dissident blocks).

This increase in territorial stability and consequent reduction in turbulence – at least in the Maghreb's well-watered regions, the newly-strengthened Makhzen and the *saff* system – distinguished the 1600s from earlier centuries.

While most of the countryside was Arabic-speaking there still remained substantial Berber-speaking communities, often still Ibāḍites. They occupied refuge areas such as the mountains of the Tripolitanian Djabal Nafūsa, the Awrās (Aurès), the Grand Kabylia in the central Maghreb and the mountainous areas of the Atlas and the Rīf on the west. Berber communities were distinguished from Arab communities by the continued success of their resistance to the Ottomans. They owed this to their location in refuge zones and to their elaborate defence systems. Their successful resistance allowed them to preserve a strong attachment to the different forms of Berber culture. The Berber communities remained distrustful towards the new Ottoman authorities. They remained Berber and mostly preserved their autonomy, refusing, for example, to pay taxes. When they could not maintain their autonomy they became Arabized. Certain over-populated Berber areas, such as Kabylia, however, became zones for the recruiting of regular soldiers for service in Algiers or Tunis (the famous Zwāwa) and perhaps also centres providing seasonal workers and rural pedlars (the emigration of labour witnessed in the nineteenth century doubtless existed before that time).

The village areas (the Tunisian Sahel, for example), the southern oases, the wheat-producing regions under urban control (the Tunisian *hanshīr* and Algerian *h'aoush* regions), and the flat country of the towns (such as the Algiers Sahel and the Tripoli Manshiya) were occupied by a society very different from that of the mountain areas. Its members led a sedentary existence. They had some trading links with the outside, well-established or better-defined *milk* (land ownership) and were influenced by urban economy and culture. All this suggests complex social structures and relationships, attitudes and behaviour more akin to those of town-dwellers than those of the Beduins. The omnipresent patrilineal kinship went hand-in-hand with hierarchical relationships, such as those linking the owner of the means of production to the *khammā* (one-fifth share-cropper) in the large cereal-producing areas. Certain specialized occupations emerged, including crafts and religious or administrative functions, urban values such as submission to authority spread more easily than in the mountain areas, and the influence of written law – essentially canonical in nature – was stronger. These traits, which were clearly structural, must have been accentuated in the seventeenth century (and even more so in the following century) with the modest but genuine progress in security, the consolidation of urban society and the extension of its influence and, lastly, the establishment of relations with the mercantile European states. These relations must have stimulated the extension of export crops and the economic and social system on which they were based, in particular, the large estates on which cereals were grown with the help of the one-fifth share-croppers.

The oases, far from the sea and the central authorities and maintainers of the caravan trade with Black Africa or the East, were inhabited by better-integrated societies and gave rise to well-entrenched oligarchies or local dynasties, such as that of the Fāsīs in the Fezzān.

Although the cities were less prestigious than those of the Arab or Muslim East, they nonetheless made their presence and influence felt throughout the Maghreb. They included the coastal capitals of Algiers, Tunis and Tripoli and also former colonizing cities such as Ḳayrawān, Constantine and Tlemcen. Trade and handicrafts stemming from time-hallowed traditions or stimulated by new discoveries took on renewed vigour from the first half of the seventeenth century onwards. Examples are the *chechia* (red woollen bonnet) industry in Tunis, whose development was encouraged by the Muslims or Moors driven out of Spain after 1609, and the luxury textile industry which grew up in Maghreb towns. Trade was encouraged, particularly in the coastal towns, initially by privateering and the products and money derived from it, then, from the late 1600s, by the links established with European capitalist trade. *'Ilm* (religious knowledge) slowly revived after the crisis of the sixteenth century, stimulated by the comparative material prosperity of the towns and the consequent increase in the number of *wakfs* (religious foundations). The revival was also encouraged by the new Turkish authorities who granted their protection above all to the Hanafite scholars of their rite but also to the indigenous Mālikites, for reasons perhaps more secular than spiritual (the desire to legitimize their power, which was alien and largely military).

PLATE 9.1 *Seventeenth-century earthenware vase for storing oil and other liquids, from the Ķallaline district of Tunis. Height: 45 cm*

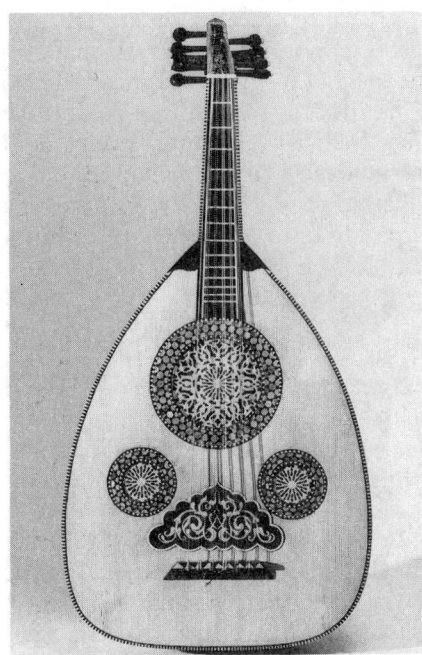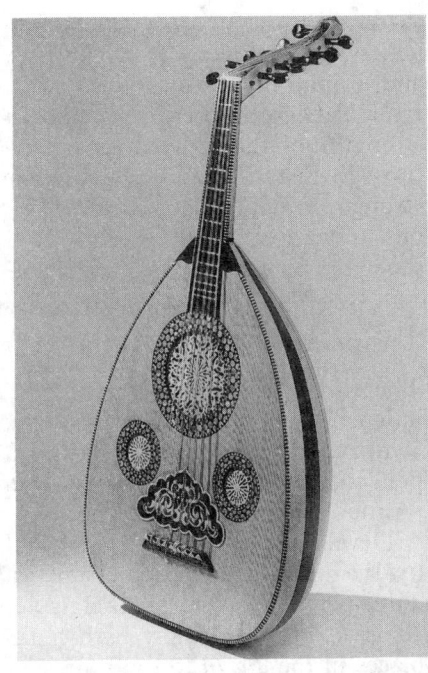

PLATE 9.2 *A Tunisian-made, eleven-stringed, melon-ribbed lute ('ūd) of Egyptian type, with ovoid belly in glued wood and mother-of-pearl inlay. Length: 81 cm*

At the top of the political and social hierarchy was the ruling class. Although, in theory, made up solely of members of the Turkish army, it was also open to other categories. It was open first to Christians who had converted to Islam, invariably called Turks despite names such as Francīs, Inglīz, Kūrsū (Corsican), Sardū (Sardinian) or others hardly Turanian in origin. Their golden age was perhaps in the first half of the seventeenth century, for it was they who introduced modern European technology, especially with regard to military matters and seafaring. They (the corsair captains in particular) played an active role not only in those fields but also in various political and administrative posts (some even attaining to the supreme function of *dey* (chief of the Turkish militia) in Tunisia and Tripolitania). In these two Regencies, the Turks quickly gave their children by indigenous women (the *kulughli* whom they regarded as Turks) the functions and privileges previously reserved for themselves. The Turks in Algiers were more exclusivist and refused to do likewise, thus provoking a serious *kulughli* insurrection which ended in the defeat of the latter and their total exclusion between about 1630 and 1680.

Whereas in Tunis and Tripoli some indigenous people were gradually appointed advisers, secretaries, *ḳā'īds-lazzām* (tax-farmers) and even com-

244

manders of the auxiliary military forces recruited locally, in Algiers indigenes were excluded. In short the seventeenth-century ruling class in Tunis and Tripoli began to associate with the local élites, whilst that of Algiers remained fiercely alien. This difference may have stemmed from the relative strengths of the indigenous élites. The Tunisian élite was strong both through historic traditions and their activities. The Tripolitan élite was strong through the large-scale trans-Saharan trade. However, in Algiers, a new town created almost entirely by the Turks in the sixteenth century, the élite was but poorly established.

The political regimes in the Regencies of the seventeenth century

The three Regencies, in principle Ottoman provinces, became largely independent of the mother-city from the beginning of the seventeenth century, more because of Istanbul's impotence than a desire for independence. Each Regency developed differently depending on the composition of its ruling class and society.

Development was most rapid in Tunis. Soon stripped of any real power by the high-ranking officers of the territorial forces in the *dīwān*, the Tunisian *pasha* was nonetheless kept as a symbol of Ottoman allegiance. In 1591, however, these high-ranking officers had, in turn, to cede their places in the *dīwān* to the representatives of the Janissaries. The military democracy thus installed did not last long. In 1598, a single Turkish leader – the *dey* – set up an autocratic regime which tried to balance the interests of the Turkish caste and those of the indigenous notables. Around 1630, a new authority emerged in the country, the *bey* or commander of the territorial forces. This office, held by a *mamlūk* (freed man) of Genoese origin, Murād, enabled its holder to conquer the hinterland at the expense of the large confederations, until then independent. With the country's inland resources and military forces – part Turkish, part local – at his disposal and through alliances with local notables, the *bey* gradually consolidated his position, concentrated power within his family (the Muradite dynasty) and adopted a veritable monarchical policy in keeping with the country's traditions and the interests of the indigenous notables. In the end, he prevailed over his rival, the *dey*, particularly during the armed conflict of 1673. But the Muradite triumph was shortlived. The crisis of the late 1600s, the weakening of the Turkish militia, which had been the most effective instrument of unification, internecine strife between rival *bey*s, Algiers' intrigues and interventions and lastly, the pro-Turkish reaction of a high-ranking officer in the militia, brought this first experiment in semi-national monarchy to an end in 1702.

A similar development was to take place in Tripoli, although with some delay. A *dey* was appointed there in 1603–4 and a policy analogous to that of the Tunisian Muradites was adopted between about 1630 and 1672. The *bey* was pre-eminent, particularly during the time of Murād al-Maltī (1679–

86) and climaxing in the ultimate triumph of the *kulughli bey*, Aḥmad Ḳaramānlī, in 1711. This progress towards a monarchical regime better integrated into the country was, however, counteracted or delayed in Tripoli by many factors. These included the ill-timed interventions of Istanbul which was trying to regain real power in the country (*c*.1610 and 1689); the omnipotence of the Beduin confederations (the Maḥāmid, Tarhūna and others) which, unable to destroy them, the Turkish power in Tripoli treated with care; the repeatedly lost and regained autonomy of the eastern province, Benghāzī, and the southern province, Fezzān; and, lastly, the meagreness of the country's own resources. Real power rested on the balance struck between the Turks and the civic authorities (which had grown rich through their control of the great caravan trade and through handicrafts), between maritime and land interests, between the towns and the great *kabīla*s, and between the centre and the provinces. In this delicate balance lay the instability of power.

The Algiers régime preserved for longest its original characteristics as a Turkish military province. There the *pasha* kept some privileges until 1659, after which the *dīwān* of the *āghas* (high-ranking officers of the militia) seized power. This was not for long, however, as a *dey*, representing first the corsair captains then the Janissaries, succeeded in seizing power in 1671. His power, however, remained precarious, exposed to the moods of the soldiery, clan conflicts and the hazards of circumstance. From 1671 to 1710, no less than eleven *dey*s were to hold that supreme office. Most were overthrown and killed during revolts by the Janissaries. The Algiers regime was therefore a military regime which became more democratic during the seventeenth century but only for the benefit of the Turkish caste, in the absence of a strong group of indigenous civic authorities capable of exercising their influence over the political regime, as in Tunis and even in Tripoli. However, even the Algiers regime concentrated its power in the *dey*s, although they did not really manage to prevail over the egalitarian or aristocratic tendencies of the Turkish caste until the late 1700s.

The Regency regimes, whether or not exclusive of local leaders, remained close to Istanbul. Their policy towards local communities was of the utmost severity. It was largely based on the use of armed force and aimed at pressurizing their subject peoples to the limits of their capacity to contribute or to resist. From the seventeenth century, however, the ruling class began to use certain local forces – group alliances or rural chiefs – to impose their domination, at least in Tunis. In general, however, antagonistic relationships prevailed. Hence the tendency of the Beduins to revolt, their apparently spontaneous support for any pretender and, finally, the instability of the Maghreb regimes.

That they should survive, let alone achieve a certain degree of success, was dependent on external resources.

External revenue: privateering and trade

Some colonial historiography has improperly reduced modern Maghreb history to privateering equated with piracy. But privateering, as different from piracy as war on land from banditry, only concerned a tiny minority of the Maghreb population and, during the latter part of the seventeenth century, had to contend with the mercantile interests of the powerful European states and their local allies. What was the true position with regard to this privateering and this trade?

Maghreb privateering in the seventeenth century

A legacy of the great struggles of the Ottomans against their Christian enemies in the sixteenth century, privateering became the prerogative of the Turkish Regencies in the Maghreb once the Ottomans had made peace with the Spaniards in the Mediterranean and the Ottoman provinces in the West had acquired freedom of action. Privateering continued to be organized or strictly controlled by the various Maghreb states and their principal dignitaries. It observed certain rules, even if these were often transgressed in the course of an activity by definition hazardous and violent. Practised by Turks, Albanians or converted Christians, for personal gain, it remained a monopoly of a faction of the Ottoman ruling class. Much of the material and most of the techniques used in boat-building were borrowed from outside. As a result, privateering never ceased to be a marginal, if not alien, activity in Maghreb life despite bringing in big profits and having considerable political and military significance. Its aims and purposes were many: as a holy war *par excellence*, it helped to justify Turkish conquest and power in the Regencies, bringing in huge profits from slave ransoms and the capture of Christian boats; it was an extremely lucrative activity for the privateers and corsairs taking part in it, the states which took a considerable share of the profits and, indirectly, the entire population of the corsair ports involved in this rather special traffic; and, finally, it helped to make the states practising it feared because of the damage they could do to the trade of even the powerful European states.

The importance of privateering obviously varied from period to period. Its history as an independent force in the Regencies began in about the 1580s. It thus benefited from the prosperity of the Mediterranean in the late 1500s and early 1600s. It then unquestionably reached its zenith as a result of the European wars of the first half of the seventeenth century. Improving their armaments by the adoption of round vessels and Berthon boats (through the self-interested help of the Dutch, the English and others), Regencies were able to build up considerable fleets. Around 1610–30, Algiers is supposed to have maintained some eighty vessels and Tunis some thirty to forty vessels of all sizes.[11] The second half of the century saw the irreversible decline of Maghreb privateering with the growth of

11. P. Grandchamp, 1937.

PLATE 9.3 *View of the city and port of Algiers, by the eighteenth-century French engraver F. A. Aveline*

PLATE 9.4 *View of the city and port of Tripoli, by the eighteenth-century French engraver F. A. Aveline*

the fire power of European fleets and the mercantile progress made by the big Christian powers. From the 1680s onwards, France and England forced the Regencies to respect their ships and their trade and privateering was practised only against the nationals of the small Christian powers, with the tacit agreement or secret encouragement of the big powers, who saw this as a means of eliminating competition from their less fortunate rivals such as the Italians and Spaniards. From then on it was only in exceptional circumstances, such as the European wars (particularly those of the late 1700s and early 1800s) that Maghreb privateering could regain its freedom of action – and then only temporarily.

Progress in trade between Europe and the Maghreb in the seventeenth century
It may seem paradoxical to discuss progress in trade during this century of privateering. But in fact privateering never completely obstructed peaceful transactions and, moreover, it began to die out in the second half of the seventeenth century. This change would seem to be due, in the first place, to the influence of the big European states won over to mercantilism and able, at a certain stage, to impose their views on the Maghreb authorities. These powers were, for their part, divided into a military faction (preponderant in Algiers) and a civilian faction, favourable to trade and prevailing over its rival mainly in Tunis (in the last third of the seventeenth century). These were the circumstances in which trade links with Europe were strengthened, but on new bases and to the advantage of new partners.

The traditional transit trade declined greatly, with the exception of trans-Saharan links through Tripoli (where European goods such as metals and salt were traded for gold dust, slaves, ostrich feathers and senna) and the time-honoured and imposing pilgrim caravans between the Moroccan south and Mecca, through the Algerian and Tunisian oases, Tripoli and Egypt. With these exceptions, it was the maritime trade imposed by the European states for their advantage which prevailed in quantity and value.

As for exports, the products of the Maghreb countryside were being directed in ever greater quantities to Europe. Cereals, in particular, were increasingly in demand in the southern provinces of western Europe. In response to this demand and to strained finances, the Maghreb states weighed heavily on trade in rural products – either through the collection of some, such as cereals, or through the granting of contracts for some of them to tax farmers (a typical case being the purchase and export of leather, for which the Leghorn Jews had secured a monopoly in Tunis by the end of the seventeenth century), or by the charging of heavy taxes on exported rural products. (The *teskere* (export permit) was the most usual form of taxation.) Of secondary importance was the export, mainly to other Muslim countries, of handicraft products such as red woollen bonnets from Tunis, luxury textile products and worked leathers.

As for imports, besides the inevitable luxury products for the use of a small élite, they included the means of controlling the hinterland, such as weapons (notwithstanding official prohibitions), money, writing paper and, lastly, some products for the use of local craftsmen (wool and dye-stuffs

PLATE 9.5 *Late seventeenth- or
eighteenth-century Algerian embroidered
scarf in muslin, natural silk,
and gold and silver thread.
Length: 302 cm*

for red blankets accounting in the main for the imports of value in Tunis
at the end of the seventeenth century).

Without doubt the main beneficiaries of these trade relationships were
the European states and their merchants and carriers on whose initiative
the ties were established. The great naval expeditions of the 1670s and
1680s aimed to lessen privateering and put European trade on a more
convenient basis, with the safety of Christian subjects guaranteed, import
duties reduced (to 3 per cent for the English and later for the French) and
permission to extract a country's products on payment of certain duties
and on certain conditions. This was the beginning of the policy of unequal
treaties.

Paradoxically, these treaties were mostly accepted by the Maghreb authorities not only out of fear of European fire power but also out of self-interest for they derived substantial profits from the sea trade in addition to acquiring European products and weapons with which to control the hinterland. Moreover, a few social groups also stood to gain. These included the tax-farmers connected with European trade (such as the leather-dealing Leghorn Jews), the retail traders, the red-blanket makers who depended on Christians for raw materials and to sell the finished product (Europeans were responsible for transporting it to the Levant) and possibly certain categories of producers (such as the Tunisian Sahel olive-growers and the owners of the large estates on which cereals were grown).

These different trends which emerged in the late 1600s were to continue and be consolidated during the eighteenth century.

The eighteenth century: achievement or respite?

Historians traditionally see the Ottoman eighteenth century as a period of crisis or increasing decadence. How far is this true of the Regencies or Sandjak of the west?

Maghreb societies in the eighteenth century

The Maghreb did not undergo any fundamental changes during the eighteenth century – unlike during the seventeenth. The means of production, social structures, institutions, attitudes and habits all remained unchanged. Some progress, however, can be seen, even if limited to certain regions or groups, such as the extension of cereal-growing on large estates and of the valuable prickly pear which spread well beyond the Andalusian settlements where it was first introduced. There were many favourable signs but not enough to revolutionize the means of production or the structures of society.

These retained the distinctive traits inherited from a distant past (such as patrilinearity and separate communities) or from a recent past (such as an imported ruling class and the ethnic hierarchy in the towns). The only noteworthy changes were those introduced through public service or the growth of trade with Europe. These included the consolidation of certain notable local families at the head of rural communities, in certain religious functions (such as the *zāwiya* and fraternities distinguished and honoured by those in power), in administrative offices such as provincial government or purchasable offices which included various types of leasing. There are well-known incidences of the rise of *kulughli* families in the Algerian *beyliks*, such as al-Gullī in Constantine and Bū-Shlaghīm in Oran. Equally well-known are the Algerian Jewish families in Bacri and Bushnāk, who played a leading role in relations between Algiers and Europe in the late 1700s and early 1800s. In Tunis, large-scale *lizma* (farming-out of the provinces,

PLATE 9.6 *Eighteenth-century wedding chest from Kabylia, Algeria (ḳabīla of the Aghil-ʿAlī), made of cedar wood, brass and iron. Length: 198 cm*

customs, etc.) enabled certain families to acquire wealth and power. Families such as the Banū ʿAyyād and the Djallūlī eventually provided the state with its most valued servants. They and their less illustrious counterparts were to give the Tunisian state remarkable stability, greater than elsewhere.

The Tunisian state in the eighteenth century

In the eighteenth century, Tunisia was the best-consolidated Maghreb state and the best-integrated, both for geographical reasons (its plains opening onto the sea) and for historical reasons (its influential urban notables and its long monarchical traditions).

Yet Tunisia remained a province of the Ottoman empire ruled by a *veli* (governor) appointed by Istanbul. The Turkish caste continued to dominate, both politically and socially, and the regime continued to depend on the militia of the Janissaries and to rule the mass of the population with an iron hand. Turkish sovereignty, however, became increasingly national inasmuch as the *bey* of Tunis enjoyed complete autonomy. The Ottoman ruling class included the *kulughli* (the cross-bred offspring of the Turks and the indigenous people) who were entirely integrated into local society, and became more and more accessible to local notables. The militia of the

252

Janissaries was restricted to a strictly military role, totally divorced from political life, while at the same time, its military influence was counter-balanced by other armed units recruited in the country such as the *awāwa*, 'Arab' *spahi*s, and the mountain horsemen. Lastly, the effects of the policy of force were attenuated by the *bey*s' practice of contracting alliances with indigenous notables, especially religious leaders, won over to the dynasty by various means and advantages. The eighteenth-century Tunisian regime was therefore of a dual nature, which can be explained both by its origins (foreign military conquest) and by its gradual adaptation to the society of local notables. This dual nature could easily account both for the regime's difficulties and then, later – in the eighteenth century – its success.

Taking advantage of the 1705 invasion of the Tunisian countryside by the Turkish troops of Algiers, Ḥusayn b. ʿAlī, a *kulughli*, had himself proclaimed *bey* and led the resistance against the invader. He then used his victory to eliminate his rivals and found a lasting semi-monarchical regime. Restricting the Turks to purely military tasks, and their rep-resentatives – *pasha* and *dey* – to a mere honorary role (albeit a necessary one which gave Ottoman sovereignty concrete form), he secured the support of the *kulughli*, the Andalusians and the local notables and managed to achieve relatively advanced centralization. Economically, this meant that *mushtarā* (rural products) were bought cheaply, some being sold to Euro-pean merchants. 'The bey has such a hold over trade that he can be said to be the only trader in the State', wrote, not without exaggeration, the French consul in Tunis, Saint-Gervais, in about 1730.[12]

Nonetheless, contradictions were accumulating between the attempts at centralization and the mostly segmentary nature of rural society, between the removal of the Turks from political life and the Regency's status as an Ottoman province, and between the subsistence economy and the extensive trade in which the *beylik* was involved. In 1728, ʿAlī Bāshā, the *bey*'s nephew revolted. The country split immediately into the *bāshiya* or pashists, followers of the *bey*'s nephew, and the *ḥusayniya* or husseinists, subjects loyal to the reigning *bey*. The crisis lasted until 1762. ʿAlī Bāshā's side triumphed first (1735–56), then the sons of Ḥusayn b. ʿAlī. The Algiers troops invaded in support of one or the other, in 1735 and 1756 in particular, with sporadic revolts by various people until 1762.

From that time until just after 1815, peace reigned once again in the Regency of ʿAlī Bey (1759–82) and Ḥammādī Pasha (1782–1814). It was a relatively good period despite the terrible plague from 1784–5 and the famines of 1777–8 and 1804 which indeed seem only to have re-established the precarious balance between the country's resources and the size of the population. Revenue from external sources increased appreciably owing to the strengthening of trade links with Europe up to about 1790, high European demand for food products during the Napoleonic Wars (1792–1814) and, finally, because the corsairs took advantage of those wars,

12. de Saint-Gervais, 1736.

PLATE 9.7 *Eighteenth-century ceramic panel from the Ḳallaline district, Tunis, used as an interior wall decoration. Height: 151 cm*

vigorously resuming their activities. This enabled the state to lighten the tax burden or, at least, not to increase it, thus lessening political tensions. In addition, the *bey*s followed a policy of alliance with notables of every opinion. As proof of success there was an absence of serious revolt from 1762 until shortly after 1815 and the *bey*'s foreign triumphs at Venice (1784–92), Tripoli (1793–4) and, above all, Algiers (1807). The domination of Algiers over Tunis, established in 1756, was brought to an end by this military victory.

This period of equilibrium and success, which Tunis enjoyed for over half a century, came to an end just after 1815 with the resumption of European expansion in new circumstances, unfavourable to all countries outside Europe. Thus began a new era heralding colonial imperalism.

The Algiers Regency in the eighteenth century

As already shown, the Algiers Regency kept an alien and military ruling class longer than the other two Maghreb regencies. Yet it still underwent some changes.

Although privateering had greatly declined it was still practised selectively against certain Christian countries such as Spain. The Scandinavian countries and some Italian states, such as Venice, agreed to pay tribute to Algiers in order to safeguard their merchant ships. Despite privateering, trade with the great mercantile states of France and England also developed. These states were particularly interested in buying cereals, first from the east, through 'Le Bastion de France', near 'Annāba, in La Calle, then from the west, through Arzew and later Oran after its recapture by the Regency in 1792.

Another external source of revenue, war against neighbouring states, brought in huge profits for the ruling class in Algiers. In particular, interventions in Tunis in favour of pretenders, in 1735 and 1756, yielded considerable spoils picked up in passing and a disguised tribute paid by Tunis from 1756 until about 1807.

In the interior, taxes continued to be exacted in the most traditional fashion through the *mah'alla* (armed expedition). These taxes were for the benefit of the Turkish exclusivist caste. The *kulughli*s, the offspring of Turks and indigenous women, were excluded from the militia and higher state offices, a policy which continually gave rise to opposition. There were countless Kabyle insurrections, including that of 1767–71, which resulted in a considerable reduction in taxes. Even more serious were the popular uprisings in Oran, led by religious fraternities, and the revolts in Constantine in the early 1800s led by local feudal lords who had detected a certain mobilization of opinion against the Turks. The Constantine revolts marked the revival of the local chiefs' powers at a time when the militia of the Janissaries was showing signs of weakness.

The deterioration of the Janissary militia was not in itself a tragedy as

PLATE 9.8 *The city of Constantine, as portrayed in a nineteenth-century French lithograph*

the same thing had happened in Tunis and Tripoli and had long been anticipated in Algiers. Since the late 1600s power had largely been monopolized by a single chief, the *dey*. In the eighteenth century, the *dey* increasingly gained the support of the small body of Turkish dignitaries from amongst whom he had been chosen. Thus the military democracy dear to the Janissaries and the Ottoman *rāʿīs* was gradually eroded. As a result the Algerian regime became more stable and effective. Only one of the eleven *dey*s who took power from 1671 to 1710 remained in office until he died a natural death, whereas seven of the nine *dey*s who acceded to this supreme office from 1710 to 1798 died naturally. Muḥammad b. ʿUthmān's exceptionally long reign (1766–91) afforded the Algerian state undeniable stability.

In the provinces, the change was even more marked, for the *bey*s of Constantine, Titteri and the west, with only a small number of Janissaries at their disposal, were forced to rely more on local dignitaries and chiefs. There were even *kulughli bey*s who were blood relations of the great indigenous families (the Quilī in Constantine and the Bū-Shlaghīm or the family of Muḥammad b. ʿUthmān al-Kabīr in the west). In short, better-integrated into the country, more civilian than in Algiers, the *bey*s in the provinces showed more clearly that the Algerian regime was changing along the same lines as Tunis and even Tripoli.

PLATE 9.9 *Eighteenth-century silver conical headdress from Algeria. Height: 15 cm*

These changes were to occur belatedly in the capital itself. At the end of 1817, with the support of the *kulughli* and the Zwāwa, *dey* ʿAlī Khōdja decimated the militia of Janissaries, or what remained of it, thus permanently eliminating Turkish military influence as had the *bey*s of Tunis and Tripoli a century earlier. A more rapid nationalization of the Algerian regime could then have been expected, but the French conquest of 1830 put a stop to a trend which had possibly begun too late or in unfavourable conditions when the divorce between the population and its leaders had already become an accomplished fact.

The Regency of Tripoli in the eighteenth century

As in Tunis at the beginning of the century, in 1711 a *kulughli* officer, Aḥmad Ḳāramānlī, took power in Tripoli and founded a dynasty of *bey*s which was to rule until 1835. The success of this family is explained by many factors. First, there was the length of the reigns of Aḥmad (1711–45), 'Alī (1754–93) and Yūsuf (1794–1832). Second, there was the existence of multiple alliances between the *kulughli* and the great urban families of Tripolitania. Third, and perhaps most important, there was the size of the *beylik*'s revenue from external sources. These included privateering which was revived after 1711 and again from 1794–1805; the resulting direct revenue from captures and prisoners' ransoms and indirect revenue from the tribute paid by many European states to ensure the security of their merchant ships; the great trans-Saharan traffic across the Fezzān of which Tripoli gained control by repeated expeditions; and the Mediterranean trade with Leghorn and the Levant. This trade was probably responsible for the power of the trading groups in the Tripolitan towns and the prosperity of the Jewish colony in the late 1700s and early 1800s.

The Tripoli Regency experienced grave difficulties during this period. First, there were the many natural disasters, including the 1767–8 famine and the terrible plague of 1785. The country's resources were limited – hence the serious tensions between the state with its high demands (for it lived in the modern world) and the populations with their modest capacity to contribute.

Second, there was the organization of most of the populations into two great confederations whose memberships fluctuated. Without the support of one or the other the Ottomans could not rule. The struggle between them was perennial and the adversaries of the rulers of Tripoli were always branded as rebels. When rivals to the throne found support in the competing confederations, civil wars erupted such as that in 1791–3 which pitted different members of the Ḳāramānlī family against each other.

In the third place, Istanbul did not give up its attempts to regain real power in Tripoli, the soft underbelly of the Ottoman Maghrib. In 1793, for example, a Turkish officer, 'Alī Burghūl, entered Tripoli during a civil war and drove out the Ḳāramānlīs. Extending this action to Djerba in Tunisian territory, he was counter-attacked by the *bey* of Tunis, who dislodged him from Tripoli and re-established one of the contending Ḳāramānlī as *bey* there in 1794. With the reign of Yūsuf Ḳāramānlī there followed at first a period of prosperity. He successfully resisted an early attempt by the United States of America to unseat him. Later, however, he was forced to accept treaties with Britain and France that virtually suppressed privateering and protection monies. Thus a major source of revenue was lost for which the trans-Saharan trade could not compensate.

Higher taxation led to strong rural opposition, and declining standards of living fuelled discontent in Tripoli. The dynasty eventually lost credit.

PLATE 9.10 *Part of a street in the Saharan city of Ghadāmes, Libya*

PLATE 9.11 *Interior of a living room in a house in the old city, Ghadāmes, Libya*

In addition Yūsuf also made major miscalculations in his relations with the Djabal Nafūsa people and the *saff*, led by the Awlād Sulaymān of the Surt and Fezzān, so that he lost his rural power-base. There was also discontent over the increased power of the French and British consulates in Tripoli, from where these powers intervened on occasion in the relationships between Libyans.

So when an Ottoman force landed in Tripoli in May 1835, it was well received and the Porte resumed direct control over Libya.

The final source of difficulties for the Regency lay in the Christian endeavours to reduce privateering and impose favourable trading conditions on Tripoli. The most famous war declared on privateering was that waged from 1801–5 by the United States of America when it was first appearing on the international scene. The war ended, however, with a compromise peace. Such was not the case after 1815, however, when the Europeans succeeded in imposing their conditions unilaterally. They eliminated privateering and opened the country to their trade on their own terms. They then began to demand compensation from the Tripolitan regime on every occasion and even without occasion: France demanded payment of 800 000 francs in 1830 because its consul had been insulted, and England demanded no less than 200 000 piastres because the son of its consul had been insulted. With its financial resources exhausted, the Tripolitan state found itself completely paralysed. Undermined in addition by revolts, which it was unable to put down, it was easy prey for the Ottoman empire which re-established itself there in May 1835 to rule for a long time.

Conclusion

In the sixteenth century the Maghreb experienced a grave crisis, the fundamental cause of which was its failure to adapt to the period of fire-arms, centralizing monarchies and American treasures. The Ottomans provided the countries of the central and eastern Maghreb with a solution to this crisis, by setting up modern systems – military and administrative – capable of ensuring external defence and the minimum of internal order required for collective survival. While fulfilling these functions, however, the Ottomans imposed on their subjects an iron rule and whenever possible, the severe exploitation of their resources – thus contributing to the stagnation of indigenous societies. The Ottoman Maghreb thus superimposed states and ruling classes that were modern, dominating and exploitative, although the situation differed to some extent between Algiers, Tunis and Tripoli at various times.

Rapidly gaining independence from Istanbul (without ever renouncing official allegiance to the mother-city) the '*odjaḳ*s of the West' gradually separated into independent states which were inclined to be antagonistic. Ten wars took place between the regimes of Tunis and Algiers between 1600 and 1800. During the seventeenth and eighteenth centuries the states developed along different lines (or at a different pace). While the Ottoman ruling class gradually became accessible to the *kulughli*s and local dignitaries in Tunis and Tripoli, in Algiers it was uncompromisingly exclusivist.

Semi-national monarchies thus emerged in Tunisia and Tripolitania in the eighteenth century while Algiers long remained under a regime greatly influenced by its conquering and alien origins. Nonetheless the general trend towards greater integration of the ruling élite with the local population and greater centralization of a monarchical type was also experienced in the Algerian Regency. But it occurred initially in the provinces and only belatedly from 1817, in the capital. Moreover, this separate and different development of the three Regencies (later accentuated by the diversity of their colonial situations) was to determine the partition of the Maghreb into separate states until today.

The history of Ottoman Maghreb was also determined by its relations with Christian Europe. The latter was the source of many of the instruments of modernity which afforded the states and ruling classes of the Maghreb the means of exercising their hegemony over the local populations: firearms and modern armies, writing paper, currency tokens, precious metals and, finally, men who brought new techniques and ideas with them. Relations with Europe were thus vital to the ruling classes of the Maghreb. First came relations of war (privateering), established by the Ottoman military from their own initiative and mainly for their own benefit. Then came relations of peace – mainly commercial – which were imposed by the great mercantile states and willingly accepted by the civilian faction of the ruling classes and its local allies. These relations first benefited the European capitalism which had established them and, second, the Maghreb states and their local partners – but only while they could defend their interests and attitudes against their European protagonists, until about 1815. This year clearly marked the end of one period and the opening of another – that of exclusive domination by Europe.

Senegambia from the sixteenth to the eighteenth century: evolution of the Wolof, Sereer and 'Tukuloor'

B. BARRY

Introduction

Senegambia, which comprises the basins of the Senegal and Gambia rivers, lies some distance from the Niger Bend, midway between the Sahara and the forest. Until the fifteenth century it remained a dependency of the states of the Sudan and the Sahara. But its opening up on its Atlantic side with the arrival of the Portuguese gave Senegambia its full geopolitical importance as an avenue for the penetration of expanding Europe's economic and political domination and as an outlet for the products of Western Sudan.

Despite regional geographical variations and the diversity of its population – which comprised Wolof, Fulbe, Mande (Mandinka), Sereer, Tukuloor, Joola (Dyola, Jola), Nalu, Baga and Tenda – all Senegambia shared a common destiny linked to the meeting in this tip of West Africa of influences from the Sudan, the Sahara and the forest. This unity was enhanced from the fifteenth century onwards by the impact of the Atlantic trade which from then on played a decisive role in the economic, political and social evolution of all the states of Senegambia.

From the fifteenth century, Portuguese trade in gold, ivory, leather and slaves diverted the trade routes from the interior towards the coast and, in the sixteenth century, precipitated the break-up of the Jolof confederacy and the rise of the Denyanke kingdom in the Senegal river valley and of the Kingdom of Kaabu (Gabu) in the Southern Rivers.

During the seventeenth century the division of the coast into Dutch, French, English and Portuguese spheres of influence coincided with the development of the Atlantic slave trade which remained, throughout the eighteenth century, the cornerstone of the Atlantic trade. The Atlantic slave trade led to an era of violence and the warlike and arbitrary *ceddo* (warlord) regimes exemplified by the reigns of the *Damel-Teen* of Kayor and Bawol, Lat Sukaabe Fall, and of the *Satigi* of Futa Toro, Samba Gelaajo Jeegi. Faced with *ceddo* violence, Islam formed the sole bulwark against the arbitrary rule of the aristocracy. At the end of the seventeenth century the adherents of Islam took up arms in the *Marabout* War and, although defeated, went on to cause three revolutions in Bundu, Futa

Jallon and Futa Toro during the eighteenth century. The opposition of the Muslim theocracies against the *ceddo* regimes forms the background to the history of Senegambia suffering the consequences of the Atlantic trade.

The Portuguese monopoly and the re-drawing of the political map in the sixteenth century

At the western tip of Africa, Senegambia is the sector of the African coast most clearly open to the west. Long a dependency of the Sudan and the Sahara, in the fifteenth century it was subjected to the influence of the Atlantic with the arrival of the Portuguese who invested in the area. Portuguese trade in gold, ivory, spices and, before long, slaves, led to the diversion of trade routes towards the Atlantic. This first victory of the caravel over the caravan gave rise, from the middle of the sixteenth century, to profound political, economic and social changes and, in particular, to the re-drawing of the political map of Senegambia.

The Portuguese trade

Senegambia, a dependency of Mali, was soon dominated along the River Gambia by the Mande Juula (Dyula) who, through stages in Wuli, Niani, Niumi and Kantora, linked the Niger Bend to the kola, iron and indigo trade from the forest areas. The Mande conquerors thus founded the Kingdom of Kaabu to the south of the River Gambia which, in the name of Mali, came to dominate all southern and part of northern Senegambia, given that the Gelowar dynasty of Siin and Salum was of Kaabu origin.[1]

But in the fourteenth century, the succession crisis that followed Mansa Sulaymān's death in 1360 facilitated the creation of the Jolof confederacy whose ruler, Njajaan Njaay, extended his rule over all northern Senegambia between the River Gambia and the River Senegal. Jolof's hegemony was soon undermined, however, and finally broke up in the sixteenth century under the impact of the invasion led by Koly Tengella who, in the fifteenth century, left the Malian Sahel with many Fulbe and settled in the high plateaux of Futa Jallon. In the 1490s the many companions of Koly or his son turned northwards and founded the Denyanke dynasty of Futa Toro in the Senegal valley. During their travels, they undermined the Mande principalities of the Gambia and, despite the resistance of the Beafada, completely transformed the political equilibrium in Senegambia.[2]

The appearance of the Denyanke kingdom thus coincided with the arrival of the Portuguese, the first Europeans to explore the African coast. They established themselves at Arguin in about 1445 with the aim of diverting towards the Atlantic the trade of the Sudan and Senegambia which, traditionally, had been directed northwards across the Sahara. However, although they tried to penetrate inland, their failure to build a

1. Y. Person, 1974a, p. 7.
2. J. Boulègue, 1968, p. 177.

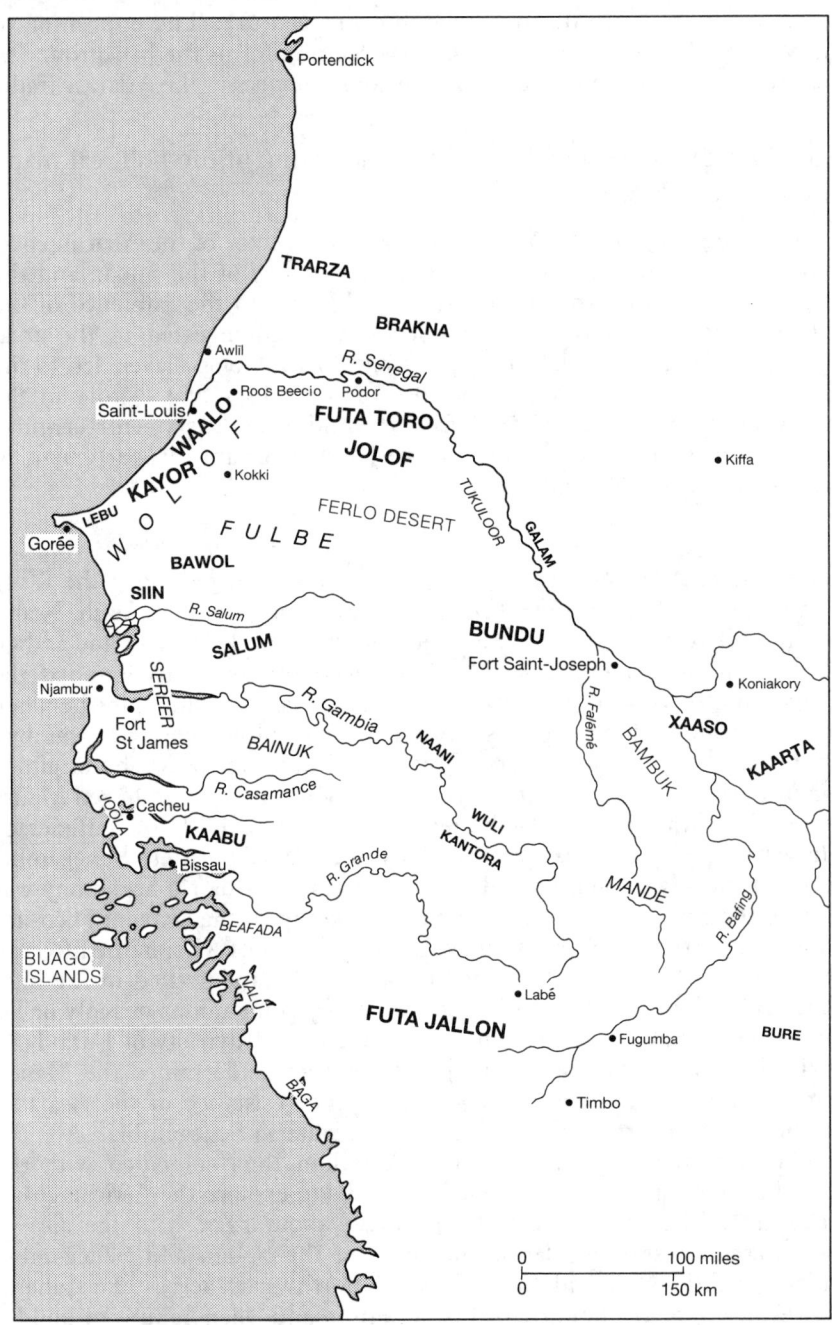

FIG 10.1   *Senegambia in the sixteenth to eighteenth centuries*

fort, in 1488, on the banks of the River Senegal, navigation of which is impeded by the Felu Falls, together with the effective presence of Mali in the Gambia, meant that they had to confine themselves to the coast.

The Portuguese, working out of the Cape Verde Islands, participated in the trade along the coast and at the mouths of the Senegal and Gambia rivers, in the form of cabotage. They established themselves firmly in the Southern Rivers and in the Gambia which was important in the inter-regional trade of Senegambia. Portuguese trade in gold, ivory, hides, spices and slaves was grafted onto the old inter-regional trade in kola nuts, salt, cotton goods, iron and indigo. Even more advantageously, the Portuguese were soon heavily engaged in the major trading centre of Wuli at the starting-point of the caravans that linked the Gambia northwards to the upper Senegal and eastwards towards the Niger Bend. Mali, which was by now in decline, thus had to turn increasingly towards the Atlantic to market its gold.

The Sudanese gold trade, which now ended in the fairs of Wuli and Kantora, occupied a special place in Portuguese trade and contributed much to splitting off the Bambuk and Bure area from its links with the Niger Bend and the Sahara and making it part of Senegambia. The leather trade which at its peak in 1660 involved 150 000 hides as a result of strong European demand, was Senegambia's second export item after gold. In addition there was the trade in ivory, wax and above all slaves, for which Senegambia – half way between Europe and America – was the first and main source of exports by sea to Europe in the sixteenth century. Trade in slaves was particularly important with the Canary Islands, the Cape Verde Islands and Madeira being opened up and, later, the plantation economy in the New World being developed. Walter Rodney estimates that at least 5000 slaves a year were exported from the Southern Rivers between 1562 and 1640. Moreover, from the start, the Portuguese who traded horses for slaves developed a plantation economy in the Cape Verde Islands which enabled them to produce sugar, cotton and indigo and to take over the inter-regional trade of Senegambia.[3] The *Lançados* or *tangomãos* (the Afro-Portuguese) gradually asserted themselves as the indispensable middlemen between the European trade and Senegambia which, by the second half of the sixteenth century, was undergoing profound political, economic and social changes and, notably, the re-drawing of the political map.

The re-drawing of the political map of the states of Senegambia in the second half of the sixteenth century

Despite its relatively minor scale, sixteenth-century Portuguese trade was already giving rise to an economic and political crisis in the Southern Rivers and accelerating the break-up of the Jolof confederacy in northern Senegambia.

3. W. Rodney, 1970b, pp. 153–61.

The crisis occurred first in the Southern Rivers – the key to the inter-regional trade of Senegambia – because of its early take-over by the Portuguese.

The crisis thus came early to the area between the Casamance river and the Rio Cacheu where numerous Cape-Verdian traders were operating. Here the Bainuk and Kasanga, who were highly skilled at weaving and dyeing, rapidly became the main customers for cotton from the Cape Verde Islands. The Bainuk also became prosperous through their agricultural produce which was needed both by the European residents and for the provisioning of the slave cargoes. The favourable position occupied by the Bainuk provoked conflict with the *Lançados* who, in 1570, sought help from Mansa Tamba of the Kasanga. The rivalry between the Bainuk of Buguendo and Bishangor, on the one hand, and the Kasanga states stirred up by Portuguese interests on the other, only ended in about 1590 with the death of Mansa Tamba of Kasa.[4]

From the beginning, however, the slave trade – the hub of Portuguese trading activities – upset the economic, political and social situation in the Southern Rivers in a more enduring way. The Mande, who were specialists in large-scale slave-hunting, consolidated the power of Kaabu which controlled all the land between the River Gambia and Futa Jallon. Kaabu profited from the ruin caused by the passage of Koly Tengella's forces through the Bainuk, Papel, Kasanga and Beafada, and imposed its rule over most of the Southern Rivers to take advantage of the sea-borne trade.

Similarly, the inhabitants of the Bijago Islands organized themselves systematically so as to participate actively in the hunt for slaves on the mainland. While the women devoted themselves to farming, fishing and house-building, the men made *almadies*, the famous boats that made up a veritable war fleet and enabled them to spread terror in the Southern Rivers. Thus the mosaic of peoples in the Southern Rivers – the Bainuk, Joola, Papel, Balante, Nalu, Landuma and Baga – were the first victims of the overseas slave trade. The tendency to isolation, especially among the Joola, was therefore intensified in this mangrove region designed by nature as a refuge. However, it was the minority groups in the Tenda area, the Bassari, the Koniagui and the Badyaranke, between the highlands of Futa Jallon and the Southern Rivers, who were the main victims of the slave trade.[5]

The economic, political and social crisis thus came early to the Southern Rivers where it encouraged the isolation of certain coastal peoples to the benefit of the mainland power of Kaabu. The political evolution of the Southern Rivers lineage states towards developed monarchical forms was blocked by the pressure of neighbouring peoples and by the violence engendered by the hunt for slaves which induced defensive and isolationist

4. G. E. Brooks, 1980, p. 19.
5. W. Rodney, 1970b, p. 110.

266

reactions. This blockage continued almost until the nineteenth century and the period of colonial rule.

Kaabu, however, became the dominant power in the region after the final decline of the Mali empire. Kaabu, a military power, controlled to its own advantage the Bainuk and Beafada trading network and also seized the Mande principalities along the River Gambia. The Farim of Kaabu continued to be the most active slave-hunters in the area. The Maane and the Saana, who formed the ruling Naanco dynasty in Kansala, strengthened their warlike character and from the beginning symbolized the rule of the *ceddo*, who dominated political life in Senegambia during the era of the overseas slave trade. The conquest of Siin and Salum by the Gelowar dynasty, which came from Kaabu, bears ample testimony to the power of this kingdom.

The sixteenth and seventeenth centuries marked the apogee of the Kingdom of Kaabu which replaced Mali throughout the Southern Rivers until the triumph of the theocratic revolution in Futa Jallon at the beginning of the eighteenth century, which brought expansion inland to an abrupt halt. But the expansion of Kaabu coincided with the development of the overseas slave trade and above all with the take-over by Europeans of the Southern Rivers trade. The initiative in inter-regional trade in the Southern Rivers, so vital for Senegambia, passed from the indigenous peoples to the Portuguese who inserted themselves into the old north-south trading network along the coast and reduced the Beafada, the Bainuk, and especially the Mande and the Bijago, to mere slave-hunters or brokers in the Atlantic trade towards the interior.

Similarly, northern Senegambia between the River Gambia and Senegal in turn saw a profound and lasting re-drawing of the political map in the second half of the seventeenth century.

The Jolof confederacy, already shaken by the massive invasion led by Koly Tengella, broke up completely under the impact of the Portuguese trade which, by favouring the coastal provinces, accelerated the political disintegration of Senegambia. Thus Amari Ngoone, after his victory at Danki over the Buurba Jolof, declared the independence of the maritime province of Waalo, at the mouth of the Senegal river, and Bawol, in the south-west, thus restricting Jolof, strictly defined, to the hinterland. In this way Jolof was much reduced in size, deprived of direct relations with the dominant Atlantic trade and cut off from the trans-Saharan trade to the north by the power of the Denyanke kingdom of Futa Toro.[6]

The break-up of Jolof followed numerous battles that inaugurated the era of warlord violence. The *ceddo* monarchies introduced violence into not only relations between the states of Senegambia but also political and social relations within each state. The same process also gave birth to the kingdoms of Siin and Salum, both of which finally freed themselves from the Jolof empire during the sixteenth century.

6. J. Boulègue, 1968, p. 212.

After the break-up of the Jolof confederacy, the *Damel* of Kayor, Amari Ngoone, at first tried to impose his rule by annexing Bawol and part of Waalo – the mouth of the Senegal river which was in touch with the Atlantic trade. He took the title of *Damel-Teen* thus initiating a long series of short-lived unions between the Kingdom of Kayor and the Kingdom of Bawol. The dream of every *Damel* of Kayor was to become *Teen* of Bawol and vice-versa. But the duel between Kayor and Bawol soon prevented the *Damel* from achieving his ambition of unifying the former provinces of the Jolof confederacy under his rule. This failure, however, also facilitated the rise to power of the Denyanke kingdom of Futa Toro.

The *Satigi*, whom European sources describe as the 'Great Ful', took advantage of the break-up of the Jolof confederacy to extend his domination over most of northern Senegambia. The Denyanke dynasty thus reached its apogee at the beginning of the seventeenth century during the reign of Samba Lamu. Futa Toro, through its occupation of the mouth of the Senegal river and part of the Malian and Mauritanian Sahel, now had a dual vocation to control both the trade of the Sudan towards the Sahara and the European sea-borne trade.[7]

The partition of the Senegambia coast and Muslim reaction in the seventeenth century

At the beginning of the seventeenth century, the Portuguese monopoly of the coasts of Africa was successfully challenged by the arrival one after the other of the Dutch, the English and the French. These new European powers settled on the African coast and embarked on what was to become the encirclement of Africa.

The European powers engaged in sharp competition, imposing themselves on Senegambia through the creation of spheres of influence jealously protected by fortified trading posts along the coast at Arguin, Saint-Louis, Gorée, Fort St James, Cacheu and Bissau.

These trading posts served above all as entrepôts for slaves, the trade in which, from the mid-seventeenth century, became the main activity of the European powers on the African coast. The intense slave trade with its corollary, the hunt for slaves, was the source of profound economic, political and social crises. It brought about violence in relations between states, the militarization of power and the advance of militant Islam. Thus, by the end of the seventeenth century, Senegambia was the scene of a widespread *marabout*-led movement which sought to unify the states of the Senegal river valley against the noxious effects of the overseas slave trade.

7. J. Boulègue, 1968, p. 244.

The trading posts and the partition of the coast

The re-drawing of the political map was accompanied by the recrudescence of violence between states and the development of the overseas slave trade which accelerated the political disintegration of Senegambia. It also coincided with the arrival of the Dutch, the French and the English, whose presence on the Senegambian coast was consolidated during the second half of the seventeenth century at the expense of the Portuguese monopoly. The Atlantic slave trade, which had become the cornerstone of colonial mercantilism following the development of the sugar-cane industry in the New World, led to the partition of Senegambia into spheres of influence through the building of fortified trading posts along the coast.

In 1621 the Dutch established themselves on Gorée Island, to be followed in 1659 by the French at Saint-Louis, opposite the Senegal river mouth, while the English built Fort St James in 1651 at the mouth of the River Gambia. The Portuguese were thus progressively eliminated from northern Senegambia and were restricted, apart from their permanent base in the Cape Verde Islands, to Cacheu and Bissau. But they were already being forced to share the rich market of the Southern Rivers with the new European powers. At any event, the building of a string of fortified trading posts, stretching along the coast, completed the redirection of Senegambian trade towards the sea.

The fort of Saint-Louis, at the Senegal river mouth, enabled the French to control all trade along the river between February and May at the various *escales* (factories) of Desert in Waalo, and Coq and Terrier Rouge in Futa Toro. The building of Fort Joseph in Gajaaga at the end of the seventeenth century ensured a French monopoly throughout the Senegal valley from the river-mouth to the upper river at the gateway to Sudan. France thus sought to make the Senegal river the main highway of the trade of northern Senegambia by attracting to the *escales* the trade of Arguin and Portendick on the Mauritanian coast and that of the Sudan centred on the Niger Bend.[8]

Gorée Island, which held the monopoly of trade along the *petite côte*, was first occupied by the Dutch and later taken by the Portuguese in 1629 and 1645, then by the English in 1667, and finally by the French in 1677. Thus, from Gorée, the French traded with Kayor at the *escale* at Rufisque, with Bawol at the *escale* at Portudal and finally with Siin at the *escale* at Joal. Gorée also tried to extend its sphere of influence southwards into the Gambia through the factory at Albreda and to the Southern Rivers through Bissau and Cacheu. Here the French encountered competition from the Portuguese and above all from the English who were solidly established in the Gambia. Fort St James, originally built by the English, controlled all the trade along the River Gambia, with factories at Jufure and Bintang, as far as the Barakunda Falls, with factories at Sutuku and Fatatenda in Wuli.

8. B. Barry, 1972, pp. 111–26.

PLATE 10.1 *Saint-Louis, at the mouth of the River Senegal, drawn by E. de Bérard, after Nouveaux*

Each Mande principality along the River Gambia, which had the enormous advantage of being navigable all year round, was a potential *escale* for the dominant English trade. The English were thus well placed to conquer the *escales* of the *petite côte* in the north and the rivers in the south and, above all, to offer dangerous competition to French trade on the upper river.[9] The Gambia had more facilities to attract the Sudan trade into its orbit, which explains the early colonization of this area by the Mali empire. The Portuguese, driven out of the north, fell back on the Southern Rivers where they established the trading posts at Bissau and Cacheu. But it was already the *Lançados* from the Cape Verde Islands who kept up the presence here of a Portugal whose economic power in Europe could no longer compete with that of the English, French and Dutch.

Senegambia thus bore along its sea frontage a series of forts, built preferably on islands, whose main function was to divert Senegambian trade towards the coast. These permanent buildings had two purposes: to protect each sphere of influence against competition from other European powers and prevent the states of Senegambia from uniting against the monopoly of European trade.

The massive presence of the Dutch, French and English – following the Portuguese presence in Senegambia (the like of which was at the time only to be found on the Gold Coast) – was closely linked with the emergence of colonial mercantilism. The fever to accumulate money-wealth seized, after Portugal and Spain, the other Atlantic powers who threw themselves into the conquest of the markets of Africa, Asia and the New World.

Each of the European powers, in addition to their fortified trading posts

9. P. D. Curtin, 1975, pp. 105–9.

on the African coast, also set up chartered trading companies whose aim was the monopoly of sea-borne trade. The companies, whose area of activities often extended beyond Senegambia, comprised the Dutch West India Company set up in 1625, the French West India Company set up in 1665 and, finally, the Royal African Company established by the English in 1672. Established with the blessing of the monarchies, these companies symbolized the rise of nation-states in Europe and reflected the new spirit of competition between these powers for the conquest of markets.

The chartered companies to some extent enabled the nobility, which was losing economic ground to the bourgeoisie, to devote itself to overseas trade without risking social disgrace. Hence rivalries in Europe were echoed in Senegambia where the trading posts changed hands among the powers depending on the local or metropolitan balance of power.

The Dutch, who had been the first to upset the Portuguese monopoly, were eliminated from the Senegambian coast in 1677 by the English and the French, except for Arguin and Portendick on the Mauritanian coast where their presence continued until the first half of the eighteenth century in the growing gum trade. Senegambia then remained divided between the French sphere of influence from Saint-Louis to Gorée and the English sphere of influence in the Gambia, while the French and the English contested for the Southern Rivers with the Portuguese. Because of its proximity to Europe and America, possession of Senegambia was vital at a time when the development of the plantations was accelerating, tripling demand for slaves bound for the French or English West Indies between 1651 and 1700.[10]

Saint-Louis, Gorée, Fort St James, Cacheu or Bissau were transformed into entrepôts for slaves from the interior markets to the slave ships destined for the New World. But until the hunt for slaves and their consignment to the coast from the Niger Bend became systematically organized, it was the coastal peoples and particularly those in Senegambia who formed the main source of supply.

Senegambia's proximity to both Europe and America, combined with the fact that the great slave markets of the Gulf of Guinea and Angola were not opened up until later, explains Senegambia's importance during the early days of the slave trade in the sixteenth and seventeenth centuries. It seems clear that Philip Curtin underestimates this region's share in the trade which, despite the lack of reliable statistics, he puts at less than 10 per cent after 1640.[11] The large size of the Senegambian trade however is no myth, as is shown clearly by Lemaire's account in 1682:

> These Negroes are exchanged for cotton pieces, copper, tin, iron, brandy and a few glass trinkets. The profit from this trade is 800%. The hides, ivory and gum are taken to France while the slaves are

10. P. D. Curtin, 1975, p. 102.
11. ibid.

PLATE 10.2 *Trophy of weapons and other objects of the peoples of Senegal, drawn by J. Pelcoq at the French colonial exhibition*

sent to the French islands in the Americas to work in the sugar plantations. Better ones can be had at ten francs each and they can be re-sold for upwards of 100 écus. For four or five jars of brandy one can often get quite a good slave, and in this way the expense is less in the purchase than in the transport because of the heavy expenses of the ships.[12]

It is of course impossible to estimate exports from Senegambia quantitatively, but the unequal exchange relations that existed between Europeans and Senegambians must be emphasized as must the consequences of the Atlantic trade on the historical development of this region. Moreover, the scale of the trade is evidenced by the existence of a profound political and social crisis which was the source of a widespread movement led by *marabouts* in the Senegal river valley a few years after the building of the fort at Saint-Louis.

The *Marabout* Wars

After the reorganization of the states during the sixteenth century under impact of Portuguese trade, Senegambia underwent, in the first half of the seventeenth century, an acute economic, political and social crisis. This crisis was manifest particularly in northern Senegambia and was linked both to the intensification of the overseas slave trade and to the Atlantic trade as a whole.

The *marabout* movement, led in the name of Islam by the Moorish *marabout* Nāṣir al-Dīn, was aware of the crisis brought about by the European presence in Senegambia.[13] Under cover of puritanical Islam, the *marabout* movement began in southern present-day Mauritania where Berber society was suffering an acute economic crisis following the decline of the trans-Saharan trade which had accelerated since the establishment of the French at Saint-Louis in 1659.

The island of Saint-Louis, by virtue of its strategic position at the mouth of the Senegal river, was drawing the valley's trade towards the Atlantic, thus breaking up the age-old complementary relationship between the nomadic Berbers of Chamama and the sedentary agriculturalists along the river. The trading monopoly of Saint-Louis thus not only deprived the Moors of the slave labour that had been used for centuries in production and trade with North Africa, but also of the grains from the valley which supplied all the countries of the Sahel north of the Senegal river. The development of slave entrepôts on the coast had redirected the grain trade to the trading posts to meet the growing needs of the slave cargoes during the long wait before departure and the crossing to the New World. This economic crisis exacerbated the political and social antagonism between the

12. P. Lemaire, 1695, p. 68.
13. B. Barry, 1972, pp. 135–59. I have studied this *marabout* movement in detail.

Hasaniyya warriors, of Arab origin, the Banū Maghfar, and the Ṣanhādja *marabouts* of Berber origin.

Berber society was caught in a vice between the southward movement of the Hasaniyya Arab warriors and the monopoly of Saint-Louis which was diverting for its own benefit the trade of the Senegal valley. Nāṣir al-Dīn raised a religious movement based on puritanical Islam to save Berber society from disintegration by conquering the Senegal valley – so vital to the economy of the Sahel. The struggle between the Hasaniyya warriors and the Berber *marabouts* was thus extended by the proclamation of a *djihād* in the kingdoms along the Senegal valley. In its original home, Nāṣir al-Dīn's movement was an attempt to regulate political and social life according to the teachings of the *sharīʿa* (Islamic law) in its purest orthodox form, by putting an end to the arbitrary power of the Hasaniyya warriors and establishing a Muslim theocracy.

The proclamation of a *djihād* in the kingdoms of the river valley was motivated by both economic and religious considerations, to conquer the trade in grains and slaves and to convert the peoples and purify the practice of Islam. In 1677, the success of the holy war in Waalo, Futa Toro, Kayor and Jolof was greatly assisted by the situation in northern Senegambia, then suffering the noxious consequences of the intensification of the Atlantic slave trade during the second half of the seventeenth century. The consequences of the large-scale hunt for slaves formed the main themes of the creed of Nāṣir al-Dīn's movement.

This puritanical, even reformist, movement was initially opposed to the continuance of the overseas slave trade and strongly condemned the tyranny of the kings participating in the hunt for slaves.[14] The lack of figures is not sufficient argument to deny the disastrous consequences – economical, political and social – of the Atlantic slave trade.[15]

From the beginning, however, the *marabout* movement was above all a

14. Chambonneau, the main eye-witness to these events, clearly shows the causes of the movement led by Nāṣir al-Dīn who, as the Great Servant of God, had the mission 'to admonish all the kings to change their life style by performing their prayers better and more often, contenting themselves with three or four wives, getting rid of all their griots, minstrels and *gens de plaisir*, and finally that God did not want them ever to pillage their subjects, much less to kill and enslave them'. He went on, 'God does not ever allow kings to pillage, kill or enslave their people; rather they must keep and protect them from their enemies, the people not being made for the kings, but the kings for the people'. Until recently, the Mauritanian aspect of this *marabout* movement was known through the *Taʾrīkhs* of Berber origin published by Ismāʿīl Hamet. Chambonneau's description, contemporary with the movement, published by C. I. A. Ritchie, throws more light on the true scale of this Muslim revolution in the states along the River Senegal. See C. I. A. Ritchie, 1968, pp. 338 and 339.

15. All the travellers who visited the area after Chambonneau were at one in considering that the success of the Tubenan or *marabout* movement was due to the effects of the overseas slave trade. Lemaire in 1682 speaks of the *Brak* who made slaves in his country for the least crime and shows clearly that the success of the *marabout* was due to the promise made to the inhabitants of Waalo to 'avenge them for the tyranny of their kings'. Gaby in

defensive reaction by the trans-Saharan trade against the increasingly powerful monopoly of the trading post at Saint-Louis. It opposed not only the trading monopoly of Saint-Louis in the Senegal valley, but also and above all the continuation of the overseas slave trade.

Opposition to the overseas slave trade in no way signified a desire to suppress domestic slavery or the small-scale sale of slaves, an age-old practice whose development within the framework of the trans-Saharan trade had never precipitated such crisis as had the Atlantic trade. Islam, which served as an excuse for the *marabout* movement, was changing its character. From the religion of a minority caste of merchants and courtiers in the royal courts, it became a popular resistance movement against the arbitrary power of the ruling aristocracies and against the noxious effects of the Atlantic trade.

With the connivance of indigenous Muslims and popular support, the *marabout* movement swept away one after the other the ruling aristocracies in Futa Toro, Waalo, Kayor and Jolof without any great resistance. After the defeat of the four kingdoms, Nāṣir al-Dīn replaced the fallen aristocracies with religious leaders who espoused his cause. Chambonneau calls them *Burr Jullit* (Great Prayer Masters). This marked the triumph in northern Senegambia of Muslim theocracies under the political and spiritual authority of Nāṣir al-Dīn, with specific features in each of the kingdoms taken over by the *marabout* movement.

In Futa Toro, although details are lacking, the victory of the *marabout*s was swift and marked by massive and violent participation in the overthrow of the rule of the *Satigi*. In Waalo the *Brak*, Fara Kumba Mbodji, put up strong resistance but was overcome by new *marabout* recruits from the Futa Toro countryside. The death of *Brak* Fara Kumba in battle, finally enabled the *marabout*s to establish themselves and appoint a puppet *Brak*, Yerim Kode, a member of the royal family, who accepted the conditions of the theocratic system set up by Nāṣir al-Dīn.[16]

In Kayor, oral tradition is more detailed on the success of the *marabout* movement which was greatly assisted by the political crisis within the aristocracy. Here the *marabout* movement, led by the *Xaadi*, espoused the cause of the *Linger*, Yaasin Bubu, who had been removed from office by the new *Damel*, Decce Maram Ngalgu, who replaced her with his mother. Yaasin Bubu converted to Islam, bringing with her part of the *garmi* (ruling

1689 after Lacourbe in 1689 said the same: 'The kings have no right to impose tributes on their peoples. Their whole income consists of slaves and cattle. They often go and pillage their subjects on the excuse that there has been evil talk about them or that there has been stealing or killing, so that no one is secure in his goods and his liberty since he enslaves them and this is what has caused the revolution in their kingdom.' All these eye-witness reports do not prevent Philip Curtin from shutting his eyes to our interpretation of the economic, political and social context of the *marabout* movement: see P. D. Curtin, 1975, p. 50.

16. B. Barry, 1972, pp. 137–42. Our interpretation of the movement in Waalo was here distorted by an unfortunate confusion with events in Kayor.

class) and its clients. She married the *marabout* Njaay Sall who killed the *Damel*, Decce Maram Ngalgu, and installed another ruler, Mafaali Gey, also a convert to Islam because of his political ambition. But Mafaali was soon killed for not respecting the Ḳur'ānic laws, by the *marabout* Njaay Sall who proclaimed himself viceroy within the framework of the 'Tubenan' movement led by Nāṣir al-Dīn. Mafaali's assassination led to a split between the *marabout* movement and the *garmi* who, when they lost their claim to the throne of Kayor, appealed to the *Buur* Salum, Maxureja Joojo Juuf, to intervene.[17]

But in 1674, the death of Nāṣir al-Dīn, in battle against the Hasaniyya warriors in Mauritania, precipitated the decline of the *marabout* movement, as did also contradictions in the vice-royalties of the states along the Senegal river. The decline enabled the French at Saint-Louis to intervene directly to give their support to the fallen aristocracies in Futa Toro, Waalo, Kayor and Jolof. This reaction by those at Saint-Louis, whose trading activities were almost suspended until the complete defeat of the *marabout* movement in 1677, had several justifications. They wanted first to prevent the consolidation in the Senegal valley of a large political grouping which, under cover of Islam, might be able to dicatate to them their terms of trade. Moreover, they wanted to resume the trade in slaves which was so vital for the prosperity of the plantations in the New World and hence, to the maintenance of the triangular trade. The French at Saint-Louis therefore gave military and financial aid to the various fallen aristocracies to help them regain power.[18]

Despite Chambonneau's clear evidence, Philip D. Curtin, on the pretext of 'decolonizing African history', tries to deny any relationship between the European presence and the evolution of the societies of Senegambia which he studies in isolation.[19] But it was only with their own interests at heart that the French put their support behind the *Brak* of Waalo, Yerim

17. L. G. Colvin, 1974, pp. 587–9; M. Diouf, 1980, pp. 122–3.

18. Chambonneau, an eye-witness to events, is again quite explicit on the participation of those at the trading post of Saint-Louis in the annihilation of the *marabout* movement. In a first campaign between May and 20 June 1674 De Muchin won the support of the Waalo chiefs and he again went 60 leagues up the river in early July 1674 with 'the same ships and other small boats so that with the fleet being larger than on the first voyage, it would have struck fear in all those of the Negroes when they were all assembled. ... This Naval Army came back down river after a month and a half where on their arrival in the month of August there were nothing but fireworks and entertainments and a straw Negro was burned'. C. I. A. Ritchie, 1968, pp. 345, 346.

19. This is the major shortcoming of the otherwise very well-documented work by Philip Curtin on Senegambia. I have never intended to deny African societies their own internal dynamism, but to assert that from the fifteenth century onwards their evolution was more and more determined by the European presence. This presence incorporated Africa into the capitalist system whose formation was underway, thus inaugurating the process of its dependence which continues down to the present day through the alliance between foreign capital and the African ruling classes. This evidence cannot be denied on the pretext of 'decolonizing African history' unless the intention is to perpetuate the

Kode, who immediately deserted the *marabout* movement in Futa Toro, Jolof and Kayor. Thus, by 1677, the movement had been almost wiped out and the old aristocracies had recovered their former prerogatives. The failure of this first popular resistance against the overseas slave trade and the arbitrary power of the establishment had lasting consequences for the development of the kingdoms of Senegambia.

In Mauritania, the movement's original home, the defeat of the Berber *marabout*s ensured the survival of the political power of Hasaniyya warriors who founded the emirates of Trarza and Brakna. In the eighteenth century, enabled through the development of the gum trade to participate profitably in the Atlantic trade, these emirates kept up constant military pressure on the states on the left bank of the Senegal. The *Marabout* War – known as the Tubenan movement in the European sources and Shurbuba in the Berber chronicles – had more lasting consequences than the Almoravid movement which had started in the same area in the eleventh century.

The Almoravid movement had embarked upon the conquest of the north whereas Nāṣir al-Dīn's movement had turned southward. Despite its failure, the Almoravid movement had left a permanent mark on the inexorable orientation of the Chamama Berbers who were attracted by the Atlantic trade towards the Senegal valley. They participated increasingly in the political, economic and religious history of Senegambia. While the emirates of Trarza and Brakna participated in the widespread violence between states in the Senegal valley, the *zwāwiya marabout*s continued to forge close links with the established *marabout* parties in the kingdoms of Senegambia, thus participating in the Islamic opposition to the military powers. By the end of the seventeenth century, Chamama had become an integral part of Senegambia.

The long *Marabout* War gave rise to a series of famines throughout the region and above all to the repression of the Muslims. They thus increased considerably the volume of the slave trade to the advantage of the trading post at Saint-Louis and the victorious aristocracy. The defeat of the *marabout*s, with the complicity of the aristocrats who were the only Africans to benefit from the Atlantic trade, ensured the continued commercial expansion of Saint-Louis. The French at Saint-Louis had finally succeeded in preventing the formation of a large political grouping which might have dictated their terms of trade along the Senegal river.

Political disintegration proceeded ever more rapidly as a result of civil wars and wars between the various kingdoms over who should supply the slave trade. The use of fire-arms became widespread, and autocratic and military governments came to power in all the kingdoms with the *ceddo* or captives of the crown used as an instrument of the arbitrary rule of the governing aristocracies. But the victory of those at Saint-Louis accentuated the contradiction between the aristocracy and the rest of the population

dependence of Africa. On this theme, see P. D. Curtin's review of B. Barry, 1972 (P. D. Curtin, 1973b).

which turned more and more towards Islam, the chief centre of opposition to the ruling regimes throughout Senegambia.

From this time many *marabout* families began to leave the coastal areas and the Senegal valley and take refuge inland, notably in Bundu and Futa Jallon, where they tried to consolidate the autonomy of the Muslim communities. The Muslim revolutions in Bundu and Futa Jallon at the beginning of the eighteenth century thus marked the triumph of militant Islam as a reaction against the consequences of the overseas slave trade. Opposition between Muslim theocracies and *ceddo* rulers thus dominated the history of Senegambia throughout the eighteenth century, the apogee of the era of the overseas slave-traders.

The impact of the overseas slave trade: *ceddo* rule and Muslim revolutions in the eighteenth century

The Atlantic trade, particularly the slave trade, accentuated the political, economic and social crises in the states of Senegambia throughout the eighteenth century.

In an atmosphere of widespread violence, the *ceddo* aristocracies strengthened their warlike character and imposed centralized monarchical rule through the support of the crown slaves. In reaction against the arbitrary rule of the aristocracies, Muslim communities formed enclaves within the states or organized revolutions as in Bundu, Futa Jallon and Futa Toro.

The strengthening of *ceddo* rule and political crises

The Wolof kingdoms of Kayor, Bawol and Waalo, and the Sereer kingdoms of Siin and Salum, underwent the same evolution towards the strengthening and centralization of monarchical power.

Kayor, during the reign of Lat Sukaabe Fall, was the supreme example of the evolution of the *ceddo* regime towards an autocratic regime and the advent of the warlords in Senegambia. Lat Sukaabe Fall (1695–1720) is seen by tradition as a usurper who took advantage of the unrest in Kayor to bring together the two crowns of Bawol and Kayor under the title of *Damel-Teen*. He enforced royal monopoly over the sale of slaves and the purchase of fire-arms and thus strengthened monarchical rule by eliminating the Dorobe and Gelowar royal branches to the benefit of his *meen* (maternal family), the Geej. He also favoured his supporters within the lineages holding hereditary offices and made many marriage alliances to create a vast clientage network which henceforth formed a permanent feature of political life.

Lat Sukaabe instituted sweeping institutional reform to ensure integration of the *marabout*s into the political system. He appointed *Serin Lamb* (holders of new titles) to attract the junior branches of the *marabout* party. The *Serin Lamb*, of *garmi* or *doomi Buur* origin, became agents of central government responsible for the defence of the frontiers and soon adopted the military ways of the ruling *ceddo* party. Conversely, the *Serin Jakk* rejected any compromise with the *ceddo* rulers and, while devoting themselves to religious activities and teaching, continued to focus the discontent of the peasant masses who were subject to pillaging by the *ceddo* aristocracy.[20]

But the strengthening of central authority and especially of the Geej matrilineage, considerably harmed the interests of French trade as Lat Sukaabe Fall, as the head of Kayor and Bawol, could now impose his prices on the posts at Gorée and the factories at Rufisque and Portudal. Furthermore, Lat Sukaabe was a supporter of free trade for all European nations. In 1701, he had André Brué, Director-General of the Compagnie du Sénégal, arrested while attempting to impose a French trading monopoly in this area at the expense of the English in the Gambia.[21]

Lat Sukaabe's reign is particularly interesting because it marks the eventual advent of the warlords in the Wolof and Sereer kingdoms. He imposed himself through his skill at settling internal political disputes to his own advantage and also because of the royal monopoly on arms import. However, on his death, the French took advantage of the succession crisis to prevent the reunification of Kayor and Bawol under the authority of a single ruler – as was the case in 1736 during the reign of Maysa Ten Wejj. Furthermore, succession disputes between the rulers of Kayor and the rulers of Bawol formed the major source of supply for the slave trade and consequently for the supply of arms to these new warlords who reigned over the Wolof kingdoms on the coast.[22]

Waalo is another striking example of political and social crisis caused by regular interference by the French at Saint-Louis in the succession crises between the three royal families – the Tejek (Teedyekk), the Loggar and the Joos. This interventionism came at a time when the economic situation was changing due to the growing importance of the gum trade. From the beginning of the eighteenth century, stimulated by the European textile industry, the gum trade – which was monopolized by the Moors in the emirates of Trarza and Brakna – not only helped solve the economic crisis of the late 1600s but also to exert pressure on the kingdoms of the Senegal valley. Waalo, Kayor, Jolof and Futa Toro were all ultimate victims of the contradiction brought about by the French desire to attract the gum trade towards the posts on the Senegal river, to their own exclusive advantage. Their reason was vigorous competition from the Dutch and English in the factories at Arguin and Portendick on the Mauritanian coast. This

---

20. The particularly interesting reforms of Lat Sukaabe Fall have been revealed by Lucy Colvin and dealt with at length by Mamadou Diouf and Abdoulaye Bara Diop: L. G. Colvin, 1974, pp. 587–97; M. Diouf, 1980, pp. 124–30; and A. B. Diop, 1981, pp. 167 and 226.

21. J. Boulègue, 1968, pp. 171–93.

22. C. Becker and V. Martin, 1975.

PLATE 10.3   *A Wolof chief in his residence, drawn by E. de Bérard, from life*

competition gave rise to the first gum war between 1717 and 1727 which had lasting consequences, particularly on the development of the Kingdom of Waalo.[23]

After the failure of Rigaudière's 1723 expedition to recapture the Mauritanian factories from the Dutch, Brué, the officer in charge at Saint-Louis, sought an alliance with the *Beccio*, Malixuri, the *kangam* (provincial chief) of Roos Beecio. The aim of this alliance was to induce Alichandora, the *Amīr* of Trarza, to give back the Arguin fort to the French and also to act as a counterweight to the enmity shown by the *Brak* of Waalo and the *Damel* of Kayor against the trading post at Saint-Louis. In 1724, supported by Saint-Louis, Malixuri rebelled against Yerim Mbanik, *Brak* of Waalo. This attempt at secession is a significant reflection of the policy adopted by the French at Saint-Louis who now aimed at defending their interests by promoting political disintegration within the states of Senegambia.[24]

Furthermore, with the failure of the attempt at mediation between Saint-Louis and Alichandora, Malixuri lost the company's support. This was followed by his defeat at the hands of Yerim Mbanik. By 1734, Yerim Mbanik, with an army of 200 to 300 horsemen and 3000 infantry, half of them carrying fire-arms, had naturally become one of the most powerful kings in the region. This enabled his successors, his two brothers, Njaag

23. A. Delcourt, 1952, p. 240.
24. B. Barry, 1972, pp. 186–9.

Aram Bakar (1733–57) and in particular, Naatago (1756–66) to exercise hegemony over the neighbouring kingdoms, particularly Kayor which had been undermined by famine and seven years of civil war. The two brothers then claimed possession of all the territory near the estuary and tried to confiscate all the dues paid by Saint-Louis to the *Damel*.

This policy of open hegemony pursued by Waalo was overthrown by the English, who occupied Saint-Louis from 1758 onwards, following numerous harassments by the *Brak*, Naatago Aram, now sufficiently powerful to impose his will on Saint-Louis whose access to trade on the Senegal river he controlled. In his role as gate-keeper of the river, Naatago Aram repeatedly demanded an increase in the dues and the price of slaves. In 1764, Naatago Aram twice blocked Saint-Louis' trade and forbade access to the upper river through Waalo. The English reacted by giving assistance to the *Damel* of Kayor, Makoddu Kumba Jaaring, who, by August 1765, had succeeded in recovering most of the territory annexed from him by Waalo.

The English governor, O'Hara, who at first thought of building a fort on the mainland to protect the Saint-Louis trade, took advantage of Naatago Aram's death finally to break the power of Waalo. O'Hara, whose chief concern was clearly to get as many slaves as possible out of the region for his own plantations in the West Indies, supplied arms to the Moors who overran all the Senegal river area. In 1775, in the Kingdom of Waalo alone, the English took more than 8000 slaves in less than six months. The over-supply of slaves was such that in the streets of Saint-Louis a slave was being sold for one piece of cloth.[25]

This tremendous drain of manpower coincided with the beginning of a long civil war lasting almost twenty-nine years, during which two royal families, the Loggar and the Joos, tried to recover the power which the Tejek family had monopolized since the early 1700s. (The succession to the Waalo throne of the two brothers, Aram Bakar and Naatago Aram Bakar, had marked the victory of the Tejek matrilineage over the Joos and Loggar matrilineages following a process identical to the one that had given rise to the Geej monopoly in Kayor.)

But Waalo soon felt the pressure of the Trarza Moors who were becoming increasingly powerful because of the importance of gum. The Moors intervened regularly in the succession disputes which completely ruined the power of the kingdom, which was henceforth incapable of pursuing an independent policy and generating an internal dynamism sufficient to promote the emergence of warlords of the stature of Lat Sukaabe Fall.

The Sereer kingdoms of Siin and Salum underwent a development similar to that of the Wolof kingdoms. But the history of Siin was marked by its small size while the prevailing climate of violence forced it to close itself off from external influences and to practise extensive agriculture to maintain its cohesion. The *Buur* Siin nevertheless developed a high degree

25. B. Barry, 1972, pp. 208–10.

PLATE 10.4   *Warriors from Waalo.*

of administrative centralization to control the *Sax-Sax* appointed in each village by the central government. Conversely, Salum's development differed because of its larger size, the cosmopolitan character of its population and, above all, its advantageous commercial position on the River Salum. The rich salt pans provided the *Buur* with significant income and enabled him to participate in the slave trade and ensure the expansion of Salum towards the Gambia.[26]

Futa Toro, under Denyanke rule since Koly Tengella, underwent an evolution identical to that of the Wolof kingdoms through the permanent disputes between pretenders to the throne, and through the use of violence and the massive use of fire-arms. This endemic political crisis opened the way to frequent intervention by the Moors and the post at Saint-Louis which was above all concerned to satisfy its needs for slaves and gum.

From the beginning, the *Satigi*'s lack of fixed rules of succession encouraged war among the various claimants, not to mention the numerous usurpations made possible by the power of the *sebbe*, (sing. *ceddo*) – the war chiefs. In this climate of violence Bubakar Sire called on the Moroccans for help in 1716 thus giving them the opportunity to interfere in the affairs of Futa Toro which from then on was forced to pay the *muudul horma* (grain tax).[27] In addition, Futa Toro took a direct part in the struggle between Alichandora, the *Amīr* of Trarza, and Brakna. This was the source of the increasing interference by Morocco which used its troops, known as Ormans, in the affairs of the Senegal valley from Waalo to Gajaaga.

In 1720, Alichandora deposed and driven out by his powerful northern neighbours, the Ulad Dellim, sought the help of the Sultan of Morocco. While Alichandora wanted to end Brakna hegemony in southern present-day Mauritania, the *Shārīf* wanted to secure recognition of his suzerainty over the Moorish emirates to the south of Morocco. But the Ormans, numbering 5000 according to Saint-Robert, subsequently acted quite independently and put all the countries along the Senegal river to fire and sword. They ended by splitting into two factions, one of which allied with Trarza and the other with Brakna. Alichandora was defeated in 1722 by the Brakna faction and took refuge with the *Beecio*, Malixuri, in Waalo. From this time onwards the Ormans intervened actively in the numerous succession crises in Futa Toro during the first half of the eighteenth century. Thus, between May 1721 and December 1724, there was total confusion as Bubakar Sire and Babu Musa replaced one another on the *Satigi*'s throne at dizzying speed until the legendary Samba Gelaajo Jeegi seized power in 1725 with the help of the Ormans of Gaidy and the commander of Fort Saint Joseph.[28]

Samba Gelaajo Jeegi (1725–31) is the prototype of the warlord whose exploits, love of danger, boldness and courage still fuel the legendary tales

26. M. A. Klein, 1968, pp. 26–9.
27. O. Kane, 1974, p. 245.
28. ibid., p. 246.

of the griots in Futa Toro. *Sambayel mo Lamotako* (little Samba who does not reign) – for having usurped power by force without being enthroned – with his famous mare, *Umulatum*, and his famous gun, *Bubu Lowake* (*Bubu* meaning that which does not need charging), illustrates the violence in Futa Toro's political life. Samba Gelaajo Jeegi was the *ceddo* leader par excellence, who, with his army of *Sebbe* equipped with fire-arms, waged forty-five battles during his reign, to the sound of *bawdi peyya yiyan* (blood drums) and *dadde yiyan* (war songs/blood songs).[29]

The saga of Samba Gelaajo Jeegi, still marvellously sung in Futa Toro, is magnificently evoked in the two versions published by Amadou Ly and Amadou Abel Sy.[30] This poetical evocation of the *ceddo* epic through the saga of Samba Gelaajo Jeegi is still sung by the *Sebbe* in their war songs: *Gumbala*, a hymn to dash and courage, is above all the epic song of death in which the *ceddo* assumes his destiny as a warrior, his faithfulness to his ancestors and to the ethic of his caste. Thus, what is most striking in the *Gumbala* is the poetry of violence and death and fantastic and excessive horse-rides. The poetry of the *Gumbala* is a poetry of the macabre, a hymn to the warrior, to his horse, his gun and his lance:

> That one is the man who said . . .
> Through the prayers of my mother,
> Through the prayers of my father,
> God, do not make me die a shameful death,
> Do not let me die in my bed,
> In the midst of my children's tears,
> And the wailing of the old people.[31]

Similarly, the *Lenngi*, sung solely by *Sebbe* women at marriages or circumcisions, are heroic songs summoning up contempt for death and the protection of honour. The singing of them is thus a great communing both to reaffirm that the future spouses belong to the *Sebbe* caste and to remind them of the values they have to perpetuate.[32] But the saga of Samba Gelaajo Jeegi is unfortunately evoked out of its true historical context which was dominated by the violence born of the overseas slave trade and which ultimately explains the emergence of this type of warlord shaped by the *ceddo* ethic. Futa Toro's permanently violent state could be accredited to two factors. Morocco, through its army of Ormans, intended to control the Moorish emirates tied into the Atlantic trade circuit through the trade in gum and slaves. Meanwhile, the French at Saint-Louis, whose presence was felt in the Senegal valley from the estuary to the upper river, had one main aim: to extract as many slaves from the area as possible. These external factors created a situation of chronic instability in Futa Toro

29. O. Kane, 1970b.
30. A. Ly, 1977; A. A. Sy, 1979.
31. A. A. Sy, 1979, pp. 365–7.
32. ibid., pp. 438–9.

where the Denyanke military aristocracy was constantly challenging the power of the *Satigi* by calling on either the Moors and their Orman allies, or the French. Thus, Samba Gelaajo Jeegi, who had first allied with the Moors, later sought help from the French at Saint-Louis to shake off the Moroccan yoke. In 1725, he asked for fire-arms, gunpowder and cannon in exchange for a hundred slaves and for a port to be built in his capital at Jowol. In July 1725, he tried to protect French interests against pillaging by the Moors. It was perhaps this alliance that enabled him to reign without interruption from 1725 to 1731 despite the claims of his two rivals, Bubu Mūsā and Konko Bubu Mūsā.[33]

But the French, far from their Saint-Louis base, were unable to put a final stop to the pressure of the Moors who 'held all Nigritia crawling under them'.[34] The French ended, however, by using some factions to bring to his knees Konko Bubu Mūsā (an ally of the *Tunka* of Gajaaga) to the advantage of Samba Gelaajo Jeegi, their ally once again in exile in Bundu. Samba, whose army was made up of an Orman faction, conscripted by Saint Adon in exchange for 2000 bars of merchandise reconquered power from Konko Bubu Mūsā between 1738 and 1741. Samba, however, remained a prisoner of his Orman and Moorish allies and attempted in vain to persuade the French to build a fort at Jowol to counteract Orman–Moorish control over him. Samba died shortly afterwards in obscure circumstances. According to tradition, he died according to the *ceddo* warrior's ideal of courage – at the treacherous hand of his wife suborned by his enemies during his second exile in Bundu:

> 'You have put *Lalo* in my meal and that follows our conversation the other day. I know that I shall die from eating this meal, but I shall eat it all the same. No one will ever say that I am afraid of death. I never recoil from death, though I recoil from dishonour'.[35]

However, the circumstances of the death of Samba Gelaajo Jeegi, legendary hero of sacred violence in a Futa Toro sapped by war, matter little, as, in 1752, the new *Satigi*, Sube Njaay, holding his *fergo* in Galam, was in turn driven out by Yaye Hoola and his warriors who ravaged Bundu with the help of Xaaso and the Ormans. Futa Toro seemed to be at its nadir, as the *Satigi* followed one another in bewildering succession to the sole profit of the Moors who dominated a country having all the necessary conditions for the success of the Muslim revolution in 1776.[36]

33. O. Kane, 1974, pp. 246–7.
34. ibid., p. 248.
35. O. Kane, 1970b, p. 924.
36. 'The land of the Foulah as usual provides the same thing to say. It is still the prey of the Moors and no one takes any notice any more of the revolutions that happen there because they have no effect at all on the situation of the country. We pay the dues to the one who happens to be there. That happens quickly today.' Col. C6–16. Letter from the Conseil Supérieur du Sénégal, 25 July 1752.

Gajaaga, on the upper river, had also been integrated into the Atlantic trade circuit since the end of the seventeenth century, to the considerable advantage of Soninke traders at the meeting-point of the three ecological regions of Senegambia – the coast, the savannah and the Sahel. But despite the dynamism of Soninke trade which was the main supplier of the countries of the Niger Bend in salt and European goods and of western Senegambia in cotton goods, Gajaaga suffered the same political and economic crises linked to the overseas slave trade and the invasion by the Ormans. The political crisis, which began in about 1700 with the struggle between *Tunka* Naame of Maxanna, and his cousin, Maxan of Tamboukane, in the province of Kammera, was extended in 1730 by the war between Gwey and Kammera. This conflict broke out after the removal of *Tunka* Mussa Jaabe of Ciaabu, who was replaced by Bukari Sette of Maxanna, who was then proclaimed head of the Gajaaga confederacy.

These tensions multiplied and led to a series of civil wars between 1744 and 1745 which finally destroyed the unity of the Soninke confederacy, thus paving the way for the invasion of the country in 1750 by Xaaso in alliance with the Bambara of Kaarta. Although the Xaasonke invader was driven back, Gwey and Kammera had been weakened by the endless disputes that had permanently compromised the future of the Gajaaga confederacy.[37]

Little is known about the development of the Kingdom of Kaabu which dominated southern Senegambia until the victory of the Muslim revolution in Futa Jallon. But the power of Kaabu, which lasted beyond the eighteenth century, was based on trade in slaves which considerably strengthened the warlike character of the Nanco kingdom. Thus, in about 1738, the *Mansa* of Kaabu was in a position to deliver some 600 slaves a year to the Portuguese alone, while the Southern Rivers, also under Kaabunke control, exported thousands of slaves annually. Kaabu thus strengthened its hold over the coastal provinces while also raiding its inland neighbours, the Bajaranke, Fulakunda, Koniagui and Bassari. With Baram Mansa, who died in about 1705, Kaabu seemed to be at the height of its power under the leadership of the Nanco aristocracy. But the state of permanent war, by its very existence, strengthened the position of the *Khorin* (provincial war chiefs) and the Soninke warriors famous for their excessive consumption of *dolo* (alcohol). Here, too, as evidenced by the political crisis of the nineteenth century, dissension among the three royal lineages, Sama, Pacana and Jimara, was the source of numerous civil wars aimed at imposing a single central authority over the kingdom. This situation, more amply documented in the nineteenth century, explains the success of the holy wars

'The land of the Foulah has again changed kings. That is virtually all we have to say about it, as it really makes no difference at all on whose head this crown falls since all power is really in the hands of the Moors.' Col. C6–14. Letter from the Conseil Supérieur du Sénégal, 20 June 1753.

37. A. Bathily, 1975.

later led from Futa Jallon and Bunda and of the internal Muslim revolutions against the Soninke state of Kaabu.[38]

Muslim revolutions in the eighteenth century

The military defeat of the *marabout* movement led by Nāṣir al-Dīn in the second half of the seventeenth century was followed by the spread of underground action by Islam against *ceddo* rule and the disastrous consequences of the overseas slave trade throughout Senegambia.

Within the states controlled by the powerful military aristocracies, the Muslim communities gradually strengthened themselves to win political and social autonomy under the leadership of influential *marabout* families. But, increasingly, these Muslim communities, linked to one another throughout Senegambia by a long chain of religious, political and economic ties which transcended national frontiers, embarked on creating new states or seizing power where they were through violence and the proclamation of a holy war.

Thus, at the end of the seventeenth century, Maalik Sy founded the Muslim theocracy of Bundu which was followed at the beginning of the eighteenth century by the Muslim revolution in Futa Jallon under the leadership of Karamokho Alfa. After this victory on the borders of Senegambia, there was an interval until the second half of the eighteenth century before the triumph of the Torodo *marabout* party led by Sulaymān Baal in Futa Toro, the stronghold of the Denyanke regime. These three successes proved the continuity and the solidarity of the *marabout* movement throughout Senegambia, whose history henceforth was to be dominated by the struggle between the Muslim theocracies and the *ceddo* rulers.

The Muslim revolution in Bundu

The repression directed against the *marabout*s after the defeat of Nāṣir al-Dīn led to the mass departure of Muslims from Futa Toro to Bundu where Maalik Sy founded the first Muslim theocracy on the borders of Senegambia in about 1690. Maalik Sy doubtless continued the *marabout* movement being one of the group of Muslim leaders who had received their religious education in Pir or Kokki in Kayor, which had close connections with the Berber *zāwiya*.

Maalik Sy was born at Suyuma, near Podor. After completing his religious education he travelled through Senegambia and finally settled on the borders of Gajaaga with the permission of the *Tunka* of Ciaabu. But the alliance sealed between Maalik Sy and the *Tunka*, who had granted him a piece of land according to the custom of the Jonnu, was soon broken because of the strategic position of Bundu at the terminus of the trade routes from the Gambia.[39] Maalik Sy, settled in a cosmopolitan area

38. M. Mane, 1978, p. 128.
39. A. Bathily, 1975, pp. 57–9.

inhabited by Bajaranke, Koniagui, Bassari, Jaxanke, Soninke and many Fulbe from Futa Toro, took advantage of the weakness of Gajaaga to declare a holy war. His religious prestige, and the military organization he set up with the help of Muslims, most of whom had come from Futa Toro after the defeat of the *marabout* movement, enabled him to found the theocratic state of Bundu.[40]

Maalik Sy supported the Jaxanke *marabout*s whose commercial interests were constantly threatened by the pillaging of the Gajaaga military aristocracy. The Muslim party thus ensured for itself the control of Falémé whose commercial importance and agricultural wealth were to make it, over the following centuries, the basis of the power of the Sisibe dynasty.[41] Maalik Sy then took the title of *Almamy*, a Fulfulde version of the title *al-Imām* which had earlier been adopted by Nāṣir al-Dīn.

Philip Curtin has clearly demonstrated the religious and family connections between Nāṣir al-Dīn's movement and the revolution in Bundu. Although he did not take a direct part in the *marabout* war, Maalik Sy was nevertheless a keen follower who achieved some of the political and religious aims of the *marabout* party.[42]

There is no documentation to explain why the first Muslim revolution was successful. But a clear trend can be seen for Muslim communities to consolidate themselves far from the coast, on the borders of Senegambia, to escape the oppressive policy of the *ceddo* establishment. In this way the fate of Bundu was linked to that of the Muslim communities in Futa Toro and Futa Jallon which lay one on either side of Bundu. Bundu was well situated on the trade routes linking the Niger Bend to the trading posts in the Gambia and it gradually consolidated its position under the Sisibe dynasty at the expense of Gajaaga.[43]

The Muslim revolution in Futa Jallon

The success of the Muslim revolution in Bundu was followed a few years later by a revolution in Futa Jallon, which took place in much the same circumstances. The fate of the mountainous massif of Futa Jallon – a natural obstacle which over the centuries had become a place of refuge for the Jallonke, the Soso and the Fulbe – underwent a complete upheaval during the sixteenth and seventeenth centuries. Koly Tengella's invasion and, above all, the development of the Atlantic trade soon had powerful cultural consequences while also accelerating the movement of the people of the Sudan towards the forest or the coast with many choosing to pass through the highlands of Futa Jallon. Moreover, this major crossing-point was economically revitalized by the existence of large herds of cattle belonging to Fulbe herdsmen who had flooded into the area from the

40. P. D. Curtin, 1971, pp. 20–2.
41. A. Bathily, 1975, p. 58.
42. P. D. Curtin, 1971, p. 22.
43. S. Diagne, 1975, p. 1.

fifteenth century onwards, drawn by the abundant grazing areas in the Futa Jallon highlands.

Futa Jallon, now incorporated into the Atlantic trade, was the scene of a profound economic and social transformation which was to give rise to the Muslim revolution at the beginning of the eighteenth century. Walter Rodney gives an excellent account of the economic, political and social context of the 1725 revolution which ended in the setting up of the theocratic state of Futa Jallon by the *marabout* party. He shows that to present the revolution merely as a struggle between the unfortunate Fulbe and their Jallonke masters and exploiters is simplistic.

During the seventeenth century, the Fulbe had probably become the richest and most powerful social group in the country. This was a result of the combination of three factors. First, the quest for new grazing grounds had considerably increased the numbers of Fulbe from Bundu, Futa Toro, Macina and the Sahel. Second, expansion of the Atlantic trade had led to large-scale development of the trade in cattle and hides and had thus strengthened the economic position of the cattle-owning Fulbe. Third, militant Islam had emerged to serve as an ideology for the construction of a new economic, political and social order.[44]

The Muslim revolution in Futa Jallon was, clearly, as in Bundu, a reaction to the violence and upheavals precipitated by the overseas slave trade. In fact, the leaders of the Muslim revolution in Futa Jallon were not all from Macina but also from the Senegal valley where they had had direct links with Nāṣir al-Dīn's *marabout* movement.

Philip Curtin and Levtzion have both clearly shown the religious, political and matrimonial links between the various *marabout* families of Futa Toro, Bundu and Futa Jallon.[45] The route linking the Senegal valley to the Futa Jallon highlands through Falémé was a permanent feature of the history of the peopling of Senegambia, as is well illustrated by the travels of Shaykh 'Umar in the nineteenth century. Bundu was the link in this *marabout* movement, whose defeat at the end of the seventeenth century in Futa Toro was followed by its triumph in Futa Jallon at the beginning of the eighteenth, with the participation of the various Fulbe, Mande and Jaxanke peoples of the area. In the context of the large-scale slave-hunts organized by the powerful state of Kaabu, the Muslim revolution in Futa Jallon appears as the victory of the *marabout* party whose prime aim was to ensure the security of the Muslim community.

This essentially Muslim revolution was not at all an ethnic war between Fulbe herdsmen and Jallonke settled farmers. Tradition clearly demonstrates the multi-ethnic character of the revolution initially led by twelve Fulbe *marabout*s and ten Mande *marabout*s, who were certainly of Jaxanke origin. Conversely, the movement was confronted with opposition from the leaders of Kafu, who were Jallonke, and also from the non-Muslim

44. W. Rodney, 1968, pp. 274-6.
45. P. D. Curtin, 1971, pp. 21-2; N. Levtzion, 1971a.

PLATE 10.5 *Fulbe woman of the Futa Jallon*

Fulbe, who lived in the bush with their cattle. The Muslim Fulbe, who wanted to abolish cattle taxes, and the Mande Juula or Jaxanke, whose trading way of life had always been associated with the practice of Islam, certainly allied to create a vast political grouping in place of the tiny Jallonke chiefdoms which had become incapable of ensuring the security of the populations in the context of the overseas slave trade.

The Muslim revolution was certainly not the work of rootless itinerant pastors, but of Muslims of every background, firmly settled in the refuge area in the Futa Jallon highlands. The *marabout* party, most of whose members had been schooled in the famous Jaxanke educational centre of Jaxaba, on the River Bafing, was in fact consolidated by the participation of numerous Fulbe who could put their cattle wealth to profitable use in the framework of a gradual sedentarization. The trade in cattle and hides towards the coast gave them economic power while Islam gave them the ideology necessary for the construction of a new political and social order.

Thus, after the victory of the *marabout* party following the holy war against the various ruling Jallonke aristocracies, the Muslim leaders created the Confederation of Futa Jallon under the leadership of Ibrahima Sambegu. Sambegu, known as Karamokho Alfa, was the head of the Sediyanke lineage of the Barry family of Timbo, and carried the title *Almamy*. The Confederation was divided into nine *Diwe*, sing. *Diwal* (provinces) whose chiefs bore the title of *Alfa* and were appointed from among the leaders of the *djihād*. The territorial division thus corresponded, initially, to the territory liberated by each of the leaders of the Muslim revolution. Thus Karamokho Alfa, the *Almamy* and head of the Confederation of Futa Jallon, was above all the *Alfa* of the *Diwal* of Timbo, the capital. From the beginning, the power of the *Almamy*, with his seat at Timbo, was limited by the wide autonomy granted to the chiefs of the

PLATE 10.6 *The old mosque at Labé, Futa Jallon*

provinces of Labé, Buriya, Timbi, Kebaali, Kollade, Koyin, Fugumba and Fode Haaji and also by the existence of a Council of Ancients acting as a parliament at Fugumba, the religious capital.[46]

The Muslim theocracy in Futa Jallon was thus the outcome of a series

46. T. Diallo, 1972, p. 28.

of military campaigns between the *marabout* party and the leaders of Jallonke Kafu who were fighting to defend their political sovereignty. But the holy war that sealed the victory of the *marabout* party, at the famous battle of Talansan, was continued by the attempt to convert to Islam the non-Muslim populations of the massif of Futa Jallon. At this level, the Muslims met more opposition from the Fulbe pastoralists who had been leading a nomadic way of life in the area for centuries and were hostile to Islam, which they saw as synonymous with decentralization and political and economic control. This opposition sprang from those Fulbe who subsequently came to form the lowest class of bush Fulbe, exploited by the ruling *marabout*s. Its very existence belies any superficial racial interpretation of the Muslim revolution as the outcome of an invasion by Fulbe to enslave the indigenous Jallonke. Its existence also explains why hostilities lasted so long and why the theocratic regime was so slow to consolidate itself, obliged as it was to create throughout the first half of the eighteenth century a new political structure to replace Jallonke Kafu.[47]

On the death of Karamokho Alfa in about 1751, the *Almamy*ship devolved onto Ibrahima Sory, known as Sory Mawdo (Sory the Great). The religious leader of the *djihād* was thus followed by the commander of the army who involved Futa Jallon in an aggressive policy against neighbouring countries, on the excuse of waging the *djihād*. This policy became the main method of slave-hunting for the domestic needs of the ruling aristocracy and also and above all for meeting the growing demand of the overseas slavers on the coast.

As with the Kingdom of Dahomey or the Asante confederacy, the evolution of Futa Jallon is incomprehensible outside the global context of the dominating overseas slave trade. These kingdoms, originally formed in reaction against the noxious consequences of the hunt for slaves, eventually came to participate in this trade, either to defend themselves against neighbouring kingdoms or purely for financial gain. Islam then became just one ideology among many to maintain and consolidate the power of the ruling aristocracy.

Sory Mawdo, assisted by the leader of the Jallonke kingdom of Solimana, thus engaged in a series of wars against his neighbours to procure slaves and booty. But the alliance was defeated in 1762 by Konde Burama, king of Sankaran, who, in 1762, was able to occupy Timbo following the defection of Solimana. It took an outburst of national energy to stop Konde Burama's army at the gates of Fugumba and it was only in 1776 that Sory Mawdo finally eliminated the threat. The defeat of Sankaran inaugurated a long period of domination of Futa Jallon of Solimana to the east of Timbo. This victory went a long way towards consolidating the power of Sory Mawdo who, until his death in 1791, asserted the authority of the military faction over the religious faction.

Sory Mawdo's death gave rise to much political confusion as his son

47. N. Levtzion, 1975, p. 208.

Sadu was assassinated in 1797/8 by supporters of 'Abdulay Bademba, son of the first *Almamy*, Karamokho Alfa. It is certainly from this time that the system of alternating rule dates between the two families of Alfaya, descendants of Karamokho Alfa, and Soriya, descendants of Ibrahima Sory Mawdo. This duality, which was a throwback to the political structures of the *ceddo* kingdoms where there were two or three royal lineages, considerably weakened the central government: it enabled the Council of Ancients, responsible for ensuring respect for the *sharī'a*, to control the power of the *Almamy* and also enabled the provincial chiefs to consolidate their autonomy.

Despite this weakness inherent from the beginning in the political system, the Kingdom of Futa Jallon was able to preserve its independence up to the period of colonial rule and even to extend its frontiers. But the new regime gradually lost its revolutionary character as the *marabout* party, once it had made itself safe within the Futa Jallon highlands, changed into a religious and military aristocracy actively participating in the overseas slave trade. As elsewhere, trade in slaves became the monopoly of the state which supervised the trade routes and organized the caravans to the coast. The predominance of the overseas slave trade was a permanent feature of the eighteenth century as the Europeans abandoned products such as gold, ivory and hides in favour of slaves. Thomas Winterbottom, who visited Timbo in 1794, gives a good explanation of the dynamic of the overseas slave trade that forced the *Almamies* to wage war to obtain slaves as the sole article to be traded for European goods.[48]

Under these circumstances, the holy war lost its religious character and Islam became a mere pretext for a hunt for slaves amongst the infidels on Futa Jallon's frontiers. The fact that only slaves could be exchanged for European goods explains the oppressiveness of the new regime towards the non-Muslims who, captured in vast numbers, were either sold on the coast or kept in *runde* (slave villages). The *runde* was the most typical institution of the new regime in Futa Jallon throughout the eighteenth century[49] – for the development of domestic slavery served not only to meet the food requirements of the political and religious aristocracy but also to meet the grain needs of the slave ships. Situated between the Bambara states and the coast, Futa Jallon both participated in raids and bought slaves for its domestic production while also selling the surplus at the coast to buy European goods and the salt needed for its pastoral economy. This trade introduced into Futa Jallon, during the eighteenth and nineteenth centuries, a larger number of slaves from many different areas including Bambara, Kisi, Jallonke, Fulbe, Bassari and Koniagui.

This massive presence of slaves, explicable only in the context of the overseas slave trade, has led to a misunderstanding of the internal development of Futa Jallon. For numerous historians, the history of Futa Jallon

48. T. M. Winterbottom, 1803.
49. W. Rodney, 1968, pp. 280–2.

is nothing more than the result of the massive invasion of Fulbe who enslaved the Jallonke inhabitants thus triggering a bitter conflict between two ethnic groups. It is, however, quite clear that Futa Jallon's internal development was in fact dominated by the formation of a hierarchical and essentially inegalitarian society based on Islam as the ideology of power. Non-Muslims were discriminated against, having a servile status within the new society governed by the *shari'a*, while Muslims had all the rights of free men. The predominance of the Fulfulde language and culture should not obscure the true dynamism of internal development which was marked by the existence of distinct social classes based on Muslim ideology.

Beyond the basic distinction between *rimbe* (sing., *dimo*) or free men and *maccube* or slaves, within the dominant society of free men there was a hierarchical ranking reflecting relations of inequality and exploitation. Among the *rimbe* there were at the top the *las li* (the aristocracy of the sword and the lance and the book and the pen). These were the descendants of the great *marabout* families who had launched the holy war and who monopolized power completely. They formed the political and religious class with its large clientele of vassals and dependants who exploited the vast number of slaves concentrated in the *runde*.

Next there was the great mass of free men whose condition derived from their position in relation to the ruling political *marabout* class of learned men. Classed lowest amongst free men were the bush Fulbe, mostly descendants of Fulbe slow to convert to Islam after the *djihād*. Owning almost no slaves, they worked the land themselves, a task considered unclean by the aristocracy. With cattle as their sole wealth, they were subject to endless taxes and labour dues payable to the ruling political *marabout* class. However, it was the development of domestic slavery, closely correlated with the Atlantic slave trade, that was the major feature of the evolution of the societies of Senegambia during the eighteenth century. The concentration of slaves into *runde* in Futa Jallon and in the Southern Rivers was on such a scale that at the end of the eighteenth century there was a series of slave revolts.

The practice of domestic slavery doubtless lay behind the cultural revolution in Futa Jallon where the *marabout* and political class, freed from agricultural work, came to devote itself to teaching. According to the account of Winterbottom, who visited Timbo in 1794, the new regime set up many Ḳurʿānic (Qoranic) schools throughout the country. A strong political and social organization, based on the *shari'a* and the prohibition of the sale of Muslims, enabled Futa Jallon to avoid anarchy and depopulation.[50] It also explains why Futa Jallon should be over-populated despite its relative poverty in natural resources. The theocratic state thus enjoyed a degree of stability guaranteed to its own benefit by the Muslim ruling class which ensured the security and unity of the Muslim community. Despite its limitations the Muslim revolution was followed by a genuine

50. T. M. Winterbottom, 1803, p. 8.

cultural revolution for the *marabouts* soon translated the Ḳur'ān (Qoran) into Fulfulde to facilitate the religious instruction of the masses. This cultural revolution was doubtless speeded up by Cerno Samba Mombeya who, in his well-known work *Le filon du bonheur éternel*, launched the manifesto for the use of Fulfulde as the instrument for the religious education of the people.

> I shall quote the Authorities in Fulfulde to make
>   it easier for you to understand.
> When you hear them, accept them.
> For each man, only his own language enables him
>   to grasp what the Authorities are saying.
> Many Fulani do not really understand what they
>   are taught in Arabic and remain uncertain.
> Remaining uncertain, in the works of Duty,
>   is not enough in words, is not enough in acts.
> He who seeks the Light, free from uncertainty,
>   let him read in Fulfulde these lines by an
>   ordinary man.[51]

The outcome was not only a plentiful and rich literature in Fulfulde but also the deeper Islamization of the masses. Thus, the Islam of the cities of the Middle Ages, such as Timbuktu and Jenne, became, through the Muslim revolution in Futa Jallon, a popular Islam which subsequently inspired the formation of a string of theocratic states throughout West Africa. In this connection, Futa Toro constitutes the third link in the long chain of victorious Muslim revolutions in Senegambia during the eighteenth century.

The Muslim revolution in Futa Toro

After its successes in Bundu and Futa Jallon, Islam triumphed in Futa Toro during the second half of the eighteenth century through the Torodo *marabout* party. Here more so than in Bundu and Futa Jallon, there is a clear link between the Torodo movement and Nāṣir al-Dīn's movement in the late seventeenth century, for the trade movement was a direct continuation of al-Dīn's both in the forms it took and in its basic aims. At the same time, however, through working closely with the Moorish *zāwiya*, the Torodo movement did take much of its inspiration from the success of the *Djihād* in Bundu and Futa Jallon at the beginning of the eighteenth century. Thus the leaders of the Torodo *marabout* party, Sulaymān Baal and 'Abd al-Ḳādir were former students at the schools at Pir and Kokki in Kayor, which were in close relations with the Daimani *zāwiya*s in Mauri-

51. A. I. Sow, 1971, p. 43.

tania. These spiritual heirs of Nāṣir al-Dīn's movement later moved to Futa Jallon or Bundu to consolidate their faith in the hope of eventually establishing a theocratic regime in Futa Toro where the latent crisis of the Denyanke regime was to facilitate the victory of the Torodo revolution.

As Saint-Louis is so close to Futa Toro, there are European sources to shed light on the political, economic and social conditions of the success of Islam there, which is not the case in Bundu and Futa Jallon. It seems clear that the same crisis observed in Waalo in the Delta during the eighteenth century also existed in Futa Toro in the middle of the Senegal river valley because of the scale of the Atlantic slave trade and the proximity of the emirates of Brakna and Trarza.

The succession crisis, opened in about 1716 by Bubakar Sire, continued throughout the eighteenth century plunging Futa Toro into insecurity and civil war. The situation worsened during the second half of the eighteenth century with the recrudescence of the overseas slave trade organized by the new English Governor, O'Hara, who facilitated the occupation of Futa Toro by the Brakna and Trarza Moors. In these circumstances the Torodo revolution was directed not only against the Denyanke régime, now incapable of ensuring security in the country, but also against domination by Brakna and the sale of Muslims as slaves. The Torodo party, led by Sulaymān Baal, was therefore able at once to win a military victory against the Ulad ʿAbdallāh at Mboya and thus put an end to the *muudul horma* (the annual tribute payable in grain to the Moors). After establishing its authority in central Futa Toro, the Torodo party put an end to several centuries of Denyanke domination and, in July 1776, forbade all English trade with Galam in reaction to the ravages perpetrated by O'Hara in 1775 to procure slaves.[52]

The Torodo victory coincided with the death of its famous leader, Sulaymān Baal, who was succeeded by ʿAbd al-Ḳādir Kan, chosen for his religious learning to consolidate the new theocratic regime. Once elected *Almamy*, ʿAbd al-Ḳādir borrowed many ceremonial practices from Futa Jallon while also maintaining some of the traditions of the Denyanke kingdom – some of whose chiefs retained their domains by going over to the Torodo party. He also redistributed *bayti* (vacant lands), while confirming the rights of the powerful Torodo families over most of central Futa Toro through the three 'Abe' families – the Bosseyabe, the Yirlabe, and the Hebbyabe. From the beginning, ʿAbd al-Ḳādir's power was limited by 'Abe' families who provided most of the great *Jaggorde* (the Council of Electors), the most well-known of whom were the Ac of Rindiaw, ʿAlī Dundu's family, which dominated Bosea, ʿAlī Sīdī Yirlabe's and ʿAlī Mamadu's. Nevertheless, ʿAbd al-Ḳādir consolidated the new regime and extended its religious influence beyond the frontiers of Futa Toro where its success gave rise to high hopes of change among the Muslim communities which already formed powerful enclaves within the Wolof and

52. O. Kane, 1973, p. 622.

Sereer states. The example of Futa Toro thus increased the tension between the Muslim reformers and the *ceddo* ruling classes of Waalo, Jolof, Kayor and Bawol. Many peasants emigrated to Futa Toro in search of security, now reassured by the new regime which had forbidden any trade in Muslim slaves. In addition, 'Abd al-Ḳādir promoted religious education in every village and the construction of mosques each in the charge of an *Imām* responsible for ensuring respect for Ḳur'ānic law in the new theocratic state.

The Torodo regime, which was consolidating its position in Futa Toro, embarked in 1786 on the conquest of Trarza where 'Abd al-Ḳādir wanted to impose, as he had on Brakna, his authority and the payment of tribute. With the Brakna's help, he defeated Trarza, whose *amīr*, Ely Kowri, was killed in battle. 'Abd al-Ḳādir's victory, celebrated in a *ḳaṣīda* by Mukhtar Wuld Buna, a disciple of the Moorish *zāwiya* of the Daimani, symbolized the triumph of Islam, as conceived a century earlier by Nāṣir al-Dīn, against the Hasaniyya warriors who blocked the trade routes. 'Abd al-Ḳādir rightly considered himself the Commander of the Faithful, the legitimate heir of Nāṣir al-Dīn. His ambition was thus to impose Islamic law on the rulers of Waalo, Jolof and Kayor and extend his rule over the upper river.

But in 1790, the new *Damel* of Kayor, Amari Ngoone Ndeela, renounced the submission made by his predecessors to Futa Toro and harshly suppressed all attempts at independence on the part of the reformers in the Muslim enclaves in the province of Njambur. He killed 'Abd al-Ḳādir's envoy, Tapsir Ḥammādī Ibra, and the survivors of the defeat – including the *marabout* of Kokki's son – appealed to the *Almamy* to save the cause of Islam. This prompted 'Abd al-Ḳādir to organize a great military expedition with nearly 30 000 people, including women and children, to colonize Kayor.

But the expedition ended in the disaster of Bungoy where the great army was beaten through the scorched-earth tactic brilliantly organized by Amari Ngoone. Numerous Futanke were sold to the slavers and 'Abd al-Ḳādir was held prisoner in Kayor although later sent back to Futa Toro. Amari Ngoone was assured that henceforth there would be no more invasions. Oral tradition still retains the memory of the magnanimity of Amari Ngoone who defended with conviction the secular nature of the *ceddo* state against the religious proselytization of the theocratic state that 'Abd al-Ḳādir sought to impose through the holy war.[53] But Baron Roger suggests that the victory of the *ceddo* party was due to the help given by the slavers in Saint-Louis and Gorée to Amari Ngoone against 'Abd al-Ḳādir.[54] This support is to be explained by 'Abd al-Ḳādir's opposition to the sale of Muslims and to the numerous conflicts between Futa Toro and Saint-Louis between 1787 and 1790 which prevented boats from moving to the upper river and

53. D. Robinson, 1975, pp. 201–8.
54. L. G. Colvin, 1974, p. 601; Baron R. Keledor, 1829, p. 129.

interrupted the supply of millet to the island.[55]

With the defeat at Bungoy, 'Abd al-Ḳādir's authority began to wane. Opposition to him in Futa Toro came from 'Alī Sīdī of Yirlabe and 'Alī Dundu of Bosea, both influential members of the *Jaggorde*. The powerful Torodo family of Thierno Molle, hostile to the religious strictness of 'Abd al-Ḳādir, obliged the *Almamy* to leave his capital for Kobbilo, on his own lands, while the new unlettered princes, 'Alī Sīdī and 'Alī Dundu, imposed themselves as sole intermediaries between central government and the western and eastern provinces of Futa Toro.

This internal power struggle coincided with the development of hostilities between Futa Toro and the post at Saint-Louis, whose trade on the river was interrupted between 1801 and 1803. Saint-Louis not only refused to pay the usual dues but also embarked on a punitive expedition of twelve ships to burn a dozen villages in western Futa Toro and capture 600 prisoners, most of whom belonged to the Torodo ruling class. In 1805 Futa Toro took its revenge and in 1806, as the stoppage of commercial activities was already hurting both parties, accepted a new agreement confirming that of 1785.

'Abd al-Ḳādir, who had not for some years had access to the fire-arms and goods needed to reinforce his increasingly disputed authority, then embarked on an expedition to the upper river to put down the ravages of *Almamy* Sega, at the expense of the *marabouts* of Bundu. He had Sega executed and appointed his own candidate, Ḥammādī Pate, thus precipitating an alliance between Ḥammādī Aissata, the unsuccessful but popular claimant and leader of Bundu, and the king of Kaarta.

The growing hostility of Saint-Louis and the increasing internal opposition by the *Jaggorde* prevented 'Abd al-Ḳādir from breaking the Kaarta-Bundu alliance. In fact, al-Ḳādir was soon deposed by the *Jaggorde* after which he allied with Gajaaga and Xaaso. In 1807, however, he was killed by the combined forces of Bundu and Kaarta with the connivance of the second generation Torodo party. His death opened the way for the triumph of the *Jaggorde* who could now impose an *Almamy* devoted to their cause and retain a wide degree of autonomy in their respective chiefdoms.[56]

As in Bundu and Futa Jallon, the *marabout* party, initially made up of learned men, gave way to a political system in the hands of a warrior aristocracy with no pretence to religious learning, as in the *ceddo* kingdoms. Power became the monopoly of hereditary lineages now involved in sharp competition and a new Torodo oligarchy came into being, bearing no relation to the ideal of the revolution of 1776. Nevertheless, the Muslim revolution did consolidate for ever the Islamic character of both state and society in Futa Toro in contrast to the *ceddo* regimes which were still controlling the Wolof and Sereer kingdoms in northern Senegambia.

'Abd al-Ḳādir's failure to impose Islam as the state ideology in the Wolof

55. D. Robinson, 1975, p. 202.
56. ibid., pp. 209–14.

kingdoms was largely compensated by the considerable progress made by the indigenous *marabout* parties. Growing numbers of Muslims tried to challenge *ceddo* violence from within. In Kayor in particular, 'Abd al-Ḳādir's defeat at Bungoy led to the departure of large numbers of Muslims from the province of Njambur for the Cape Verde peninsula where they helped to found a theocracy under the leadership of Jal Joop. From Cape Verde the exiles encouraged Lebu opposition to the exactions of the *Alkaati* of the *Damel* and Kayor separatist movements. After several years of resistance the *marabout* party won independence which sealed the first territorial breach and the victory of Islam in the kingdom of Kayor.[57]

Conclusion

The evolution of Senegambia from the sixteenth to the eighteenth century was profoundly influenced by the impact of the Atlantic trade at the beginning of the process whereby Black Africa became dependent on the dominating power of Europe. Barter (for gold, ivory, gum, hides and slaves) without territorial occupation gave rise, from the second half of the sixteenth century, to the diversion of the trade routes from the interior towards the coast. During this period the Jolof confederacy disintegrated – giving way to the kingdoms of Waalo, Kayor, Bawol, Siin and Salum – while the Denyanke kingdom became dominant in the Senegal valley. In Southern Rivers, Portuguese trade ruined the inter-regional trade of the Bainuk, Beafada, Nalu and Baga and facilitated the rise of the military power of Kaabu which took over from the declining empire of Mali.

The dominance of the slave trade in overseas exchanges during the seventeenth century rapidly led to the partition of the coast into spheres of influence and the building of fortified trading posts. It also led to the strengthening of the violent nature of the *ceddo* regimes which, in turn, gave rise to a widespread *marabout* movement hostile to the military aristocracies. After the failure of Nāṣir al-Dīn's movement (1673–7), the adherents of militant Islam organized themselves in Bundu, Futa Jallon and Futa Toro.

At the end of the eighteenth century, however, the theocratic states themselves gradually lost their revolutionary character just when Europe was thinking of abolishing the slave trade whose role in the accumulation of finance capital was diminishing. Europe then tried to integrate Senegambia into the developed capitalist system as a direct periphery of the European centre for the supply of raw materials for industry. Senegambia, already ravaged by the profound political economic and social crises of the slavery era, stood no chance of resisting the military conquest embarked upon by Europe during the second half of the nineteenth century.

---

57. M. Diouf, 1980, pp. 134–9.

The end of the Songhay empire

M. ABITBOL

The collapse of the Songhay empire

Reasons for the Moroccan invasion

Mawlāy Aḥmad al-Manṣūr, who was installed in power after the battle of
Wādī al-Makhāzin in 1578, could not have come to the Saʿādī throne in
more propitious circumstances. The victory over Portugal had placed him
among the great defenders of Islam, and the money paid to ransom his
Christian captives had made him one of the most influential figures on the
world scene.

As Caliph, *Imām* and Prince of the Faithful his ambition was to bring
all Muslims together in a 'single same way of thought' and to revive the
tradition of the *djihād*. Thus the profits he planned to derive from the
Saharan salt deposits at Taghāza would be devoted to replenishing the
Bayt al-Māl (Treasury) and slaves won in the conquest of Songhay would
be set to work in the navy that would eventually fall on the infidel.

But al-Manṣūr's more lofty motives far from excluded others less intangible – gold and slaves from the Sudan.[1]

The slaves were to be used especially in the sugar industry in the south
of Morocco, where installations had suffered greatly in the fighting of the
previous decades.[2] As for gold, supplies had dwindled rapidly since the
rise of the Songhay empire in the Niger Bend. Al-Manṣūr's predecessors
had twice tried to change this situation: once, between 1537 and 1547, by
raiding Wazzān, and again, in 1556–7, by seizing Taghāza. But, clearly not
wanting to jeopardize the supply of salt to Black Africa, al-Mahdī, al-
Manṣūr's grandfather, had made an agreement with *Askiya* Dāwūd of

---

1. The main sources of this well-documented phase of the history of relations between
Morocco and Sudan are: Sudanese: al-Saʿdi, 1964; M. Kaʿti, 1913–14; and O. Houdas, 1966;
Moroccan: al-Fishtali, 1964; al-Slawi, 1936; al-Wafrani, 1888–9; European: see H. de
Castries, 1923, for a full account of the Moroccan invasion by an anonymous Spaniard.

2. P. Berthier, 1966.

Songhay over the immediate sharing-out of dues collected.[3]

But there were still threats to Morocco's trade with the Sudan: the Portuguese, who in 1565 tried to reach Timbuktu via Senegal,[4] and above all the Turks, some of whose moves suggested that they aimed at extending their supply lines to the southern Maghrib. Examples of the latter include Ṣālaḥ Ra'īs's expedition to Wargla in 1552, Djaʿfar Pasha's conquest of the Fezzān in 1557 and Ḥasān Veneziano's expedition to Tūwāt in 1578–9.[5]

The Saʿādīs' hopes of benefiting from Taghāza faded as the Songhays developed the new salt desposits at Taghāza al-Ghizlān (Taoudéni).[6]

In 1582 al-Manṣūr seized the oases of Tūwāt and Gurāra. Their occupation was officially presented as a measure to restore order in an area where 'the royal yoke had been thrown off'. But the real objective was to conquer the Sudan and build up a huge empire on the southern flanks of the Ottomans' African possessions.[7]

In 1583 the King of Borno, May Idrīs Alaōma, gave al-Manṣūr an unhoped-for opportunity to realize his ambitions. Fearing a Turkish advance into his territories from the Fezzān, May Idrīs asked al-Manṣūr for fire-arms with which to fight the non-Muslim groups 'on the borders of the Sudan'. Al-Manṣūr agreed after extracting from the King of Borno a *bayʿa* (an act of allegiance) which was duly drawn up and signed.[8]

The following year a Moroccan expeditionary force entered the Atlantic Sahel in the direction of Senegal, but was obliged to turn back in circumstances which are not clear.[9]

The order to attack the Songhay empire was almost given in 1586, but in view of the difficulties presented by the operation, al-Manṣūr put it off for five years. He used the interval to train and equip his army, to obtain all possible intelligence about the *Askiya* empire, and to persuade his own leading citizens – merchants, *ʿulamāʾ* and army officers – of the soundness of his plan.

Tondibi and the causes of Songhay's collapse

On 30 October 1590 a Moroccan column of between three and four thousand soldiers, together with several hundred auxiliaries, set out from Marrakesh under the command of Djūdar Pasha. The force crossed the High Atlas and went down the Darʿa valley to Ktawa, where it entered the Sahara. On 1 March 1591, after a forced march of sixty days, it reached the banks of the Niger and eleven days later arrived at Tondibi, only some

3. al-Saʿdi, 1964, pp. 163–4; al-Fishtali, 1964, p. 55.
4. A. Teixeira da Mota, 1969.
5. E. Rossi, 1936, pp. 74–5; A. G. P. Martin, 1908, pp. 119–23.
6. al-Fishtali, 1964, p. 55.
7. ibid., pp. 36–40.
8. ibid., pp. 61–3; A. al-Nāṣirī, 1954–6.
9. al-Fishtali, 1964, pp. 60–1; E. Fagnan, 1924, pp. 415–16; al-Saʿdi, 1964, p. 194.

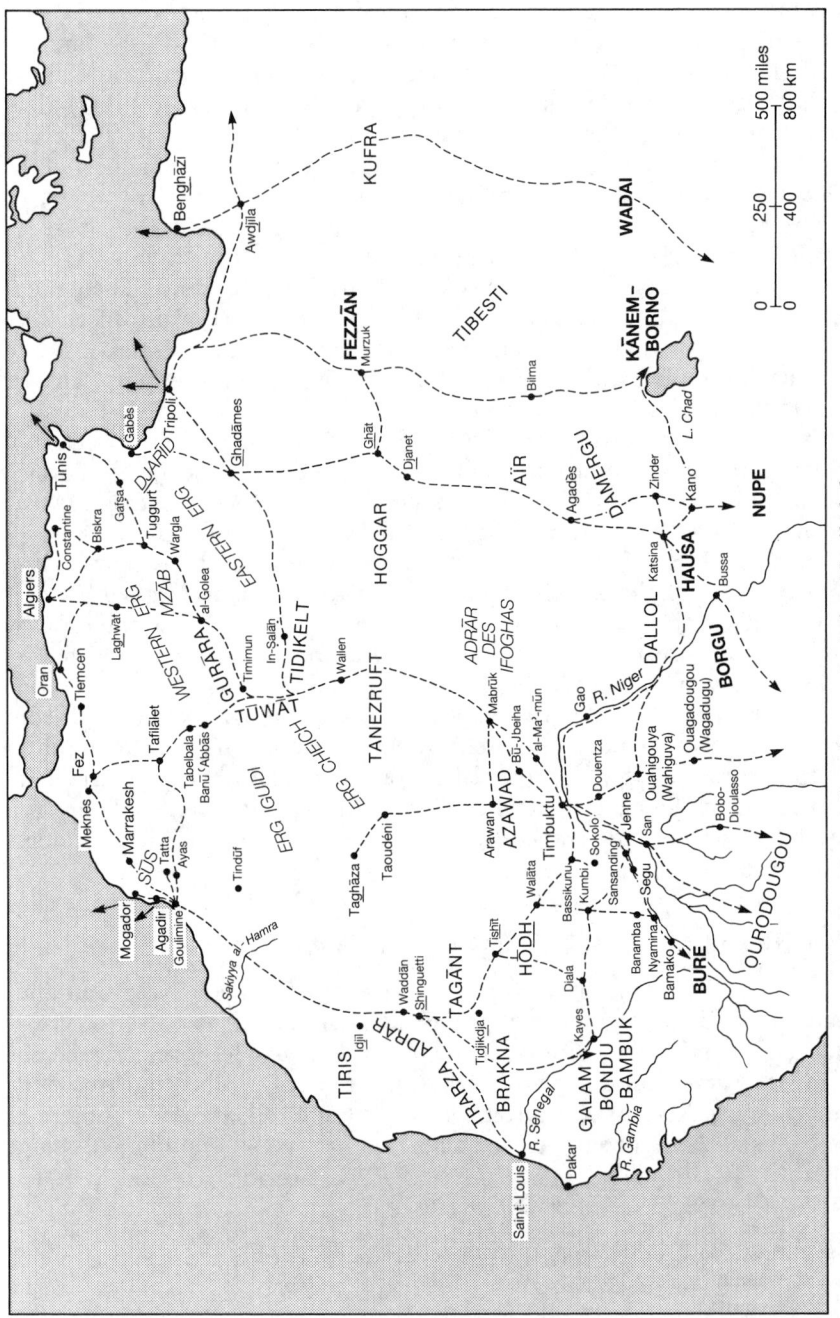

FIG. 11.1   *Trans-Saharan routes in the sixteenth to eighteenth centuries (after M. Abitbol)*

fifty kilometres from Gao, the Songhay capital.

Although *Askiya* Isḥāḳ II waited until the last moment before mobilizing his troops, he faced the invader with a considerable force. Confronted, however, with the Moroccans' guns, the Songhay army was crushed on 12 March 1591, after a day of heroic resistance.[10] And so collapsed the last great Sahel empire whose rulers, absorbed in their domestic quarrels, had failed to recognize the extent of the Moroccan threat.

Since the fall of the great *Askiya* Muḥammad al-Ḥādjdj in 1529, the court at Gao had been the scene of relentless struggles between different pretenders to the throne which soon turned into revolts threatening the empire itself with destruction. Barely five years before the Moroccan invasion the Songhay empire was almost divided into two as a result of the rebellion of *Balama* al-Ṣaḍḍuḳ, whose headquarters were in Timbuktu. Isḥāḳ II put down the revolt, but was left with little time to reunite the country before the Moroccan invasion.[11]

Economically Songhay had for several decades been suffering from the adverse effects of the Portuguese coastal trade. Military reverses in Dendi, Borgu and Mossi (Mosi) country – all traditional sources of slaves for the empire – together with the loss of Taghāza in 1585, exacerbated the social consequences of the economic setbacks. In addition the empire was afflicted with a series of natural disasters including epidemics, drought and food shortages.[12]

In its last days, the empire built up by Sonni ʿAlī and *Askiya* Muḥammad stretched over a vast area but it lacked the ethnic and socio-cultural framework which had lent a larger measure of unity to Ghana and Mali, its great predecessors in the region. Songhay had not succeeded in binding together its various peoples. Unity was particularly lacking under the Great *Askiya* Muḥammad who was closer to the Arab–Berber values of Timbuktu than the traditional values of Gao and Kūkya, to which he was a stranger by birth. Although Gao was the political capital, neither it nor Songhay itself was the driving force of the empire whose centre of gravity lay, paradoxically, in conquered territory, in Timbuktu and Jenne.

The setting up of the Moroccan Pashalik

In pursuit of the remains of the Songhay army, Djūdar Pasha marched on to Gao, which had already been deserted by its inhabitants. Isḥāḳ II, although still in control of the Niger river, did not attempt any counter-offensive. Instead he began to negotiate with Djūdar the conditions of his return to Morocco. Djūdar, disappointed at Gao's lamentable state and realizing that his own men were in poor physical shape, was prepared to

10. al-Fishtali, 1964, pp. 64–71; al-Wafrani, 1888–9, pp. 160–2; M. Kaʿti, 1913–14, pp. 263–75; al-Saʿdi, 1964, p. 194.

11. M. Kaʿti, 1913–14, pp. 230–9 and 246–54; al-Saʿdi, 1964, pp. 197–206.

12. M. Kaʿti, 1913–14, pp. 164, and 174 and 230; al-Saʿdi, 1964, pp. 151–82 and 195.

accept Ishāk's suggestions. But al-Manṣūr was not: he recalled Djūdar immediately and replaced him with the second-highest-ranking officer in the Moroccan army, Maḥmūd b. Zarkūn. Zarkūn's orders were quite simply to conquer the whole of the Sudan and destroy the various Sudanese forces which had taken advantage of the general disorder to try to fill the vacuum left by the rout of the Songhay army.[13]

Maḥmūd Pasha immediately set about destroying Songhay political power. He seized the traditional capital of Kūkya, drove Ishāk II from the country to his death among the Gurmanche, laid a fatal trap for Ishāk's appointed successor, Muḥammad-Gao, and endeavoured to wipe out the last pockets of Songhay resistance in Dendi (1592–4).[14]

Having thus done away with the Songhay menace, Zarkūn returned to Timbuktu to destroy the educated classes there as a political force. Dozens of *'ulamā'* were slain or sent into exile in Morocco. Among the latter was the celebrated Aḥmad Baba whose fame was to spread 'from the region of Sūs to the towns of Bougie and Algiers'.[15]

Zarkūn was killed in 1594 in an ambush laid by the Songhay resistance in Bandiagra,[16] before he had completed the occupation of the area around Jenne. This task was now given to Djūdar, but soon proved impossible in the face of fierce opposition from Fulbe (Fulani), Bambara and Mande (Malinke), temporarily grouped around Mansa Maḥmūd. After a series of inconclusive skirmishes a *modus vivendi* was established between the Moroccans installed in Jenne and the people of the area who came to accept, although 'only in words', the Moroccan occupation.[17]

Al-Manṣūr's army was forced to limit itself to the occupation of certain river ports, where they installed *kaṣabas* (permanent garrisons). These included Jenne, Wandiaka, Kubi, Konna, Sebi, Tendirma, Issafay, Kabara, Timbuktu, Bamba, Bourem, Gao and Kūkya.[18] For obvious economic reasons most were on the river line from Jenne to Timbuktu. On both sides of the Niger, the spine of the Pashalik, lay vast areas scarcely touched by Moroccan influence.

The *pashas* did not try to change the systems of local administration left behind by the Songhay. Whenever a native chief was appointed he had to receive the endorsement of the *pasha*, who backed the investitures of *kāḍīs* and *imāms* in the big towns as well as those of their Fulbe and Tuareg equivalents, *ardos* and *amenokals*. In this, the representatives of Morocco were only doing what the *Askiyas* had done before them and, like them, they rarely interfered in the choice of candidates.

13. al-Sa'di, 1964, pp. 220–1; al-Fishtali, 1964, pp. 170–1; H. de Castries, 1923, p. 473.
14. al-Sa'di, 1964, pp. 230–4; M. Ka'ti, 1913–14, pp. 275–6 and 287–95; al-Fishtali, 1964, pp. 83–7.
15. M. Ka'ti, 1913–14, pp. 300–8; al-Sa'di, 1964, pp. 258–66; al-Wafrani, 1888–9, p. 170.
16. al-Sa'di, 1964, p. 268.
17. al-Fishtali, 1964, p. 94; al-Sa'di, 1964, pp. 273–9.
18. The Moroccans later built two more *kaṣabas* at Gundam and Arawān.

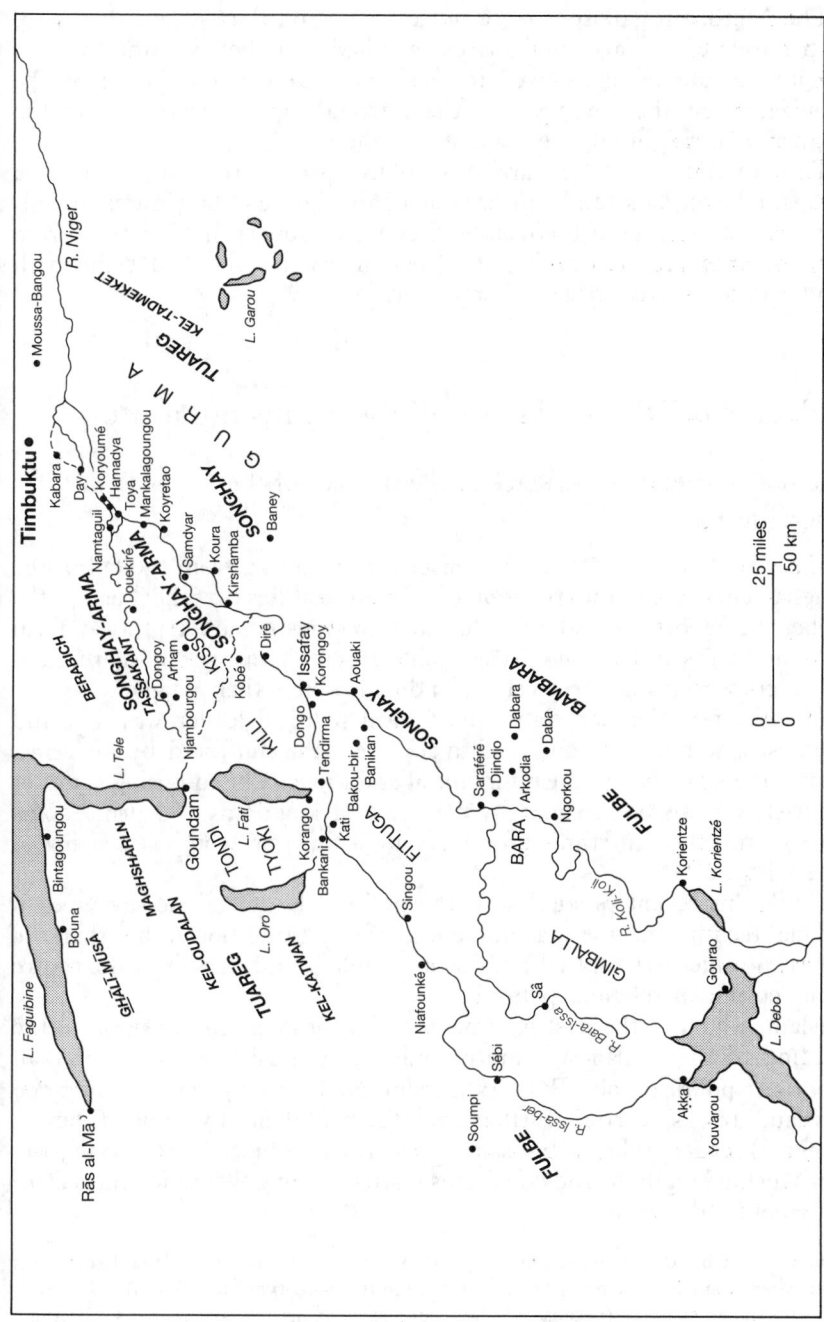

FIG. 11.2 *The Timbuktu region (after M. Abitbol)*

The Moroccan garrisons were not closed in on themselves: they were neither isolated enclaves nor fortresses. Al-Manṣūr believed the fruits of conquest would be short-lived if pacification were not followed by the colonization of the country and the introduction of peoples from the Maghrib who might take permanent root there.

Thus the Sudan saw the arrival of Guish people from Sūs, and Haha groups and also Maʿḳil and Djusham elements whom al-Manṣūr was anxious to get rid of because of the trouble they were causing in Morocco. From 1599 onwards the legionaries of Christian origin, who had come with Djūdar Pasha, were sent back home to Morocco.[19]

Sudanese politics to the end of the eighteenth century

The post-imperial experience of the peoples of the Niger Bend: general features

In the climate of uncertainty and insecurity resulting from the fall of the Songhay empire and the irruption of ethno-social forces – the Tuareg, the Fulbe, the Moors, and so on – that had previously been kept away from cultivated areas and urban centres, political power was within the reach of any rulers who could effectively defend and protect their peoples.

All over the Nigerian Sahel the typical political leader was first and foremost a warrior, his only legitimacy the right conferred by his arms. Such leaders rarely had great territorial ambitions. The imposing states of the past were to be replaced by a mosaic of kingdoms and princedoms usually limited to an ethnic group, a clan, a town or even just a string of large villages.[20]

Unlike his recent predecessors, the political leader of the seventeenth and eighteenth centuries was influenced by local tradition rather than the universal values transmitted by Muslim scholars, and was rarely the centre of any cosmic or religious pattern.

Islam, which in the past had made such a brilliant contribution to the building of the Sudanese empires, now temporarily ceased to play an important political rôle. But it still continued its long march along the grassland tracks, carried further and further afield by Juula (Dioula, Wangara) traders who at the same time had no objection to serving the non-Muslim kingdoms and chiefdoms scattered along the trade routes from the Sahel to the forest.

19. al-Fishtali, 1964, p. 93 and pp. 113–15. As a result of these moves the descendants of the Moroccan soldiers bore little resemblance to the stereotyped image of them as some kind of Muslim convert (because of their supposedly Christian or 'renegade' origins), speaking Spanish rather than Arabic.

20. M. Abitbol, 1979.

Timbuktu, Jenne and the Arma

From 1618 onwards, Morocco stopped appointing the chief officials of the Pashalik or sending military reinforcements, and the last survivors of al-Manṣūr's army and their descendants, the Arma, were left to their own fate. They made themselves the lawful masters of the Timbuktu area and remained so until the beginning of the nineteenth century.

Although its military power had dwindled, the *Pasha* state proved remarkably durable and lasted with its structures almost intact until the time of Shaykhū Aḥmadu. And yet, before the foundation of the Fulbe empire of Macina, there were forces in the Niger Bend capable of wiping out the remains of the old Moroccan colony. First there were the Bambara of Segu, who not only refrained from extending their domination as far as Timbuktu but avoided even entering Jenne. There were also the powerful Tuareg confederations of the Kel-Awllimiden and above all the Kel-Tadmekket who, despite their overwhelming victory over the Arma in 1737, never thought of seizing political power in Timbuktu. Similarly, the influential clerical group, the Kunta, did no more than offer to mediate, through its Azawad *zāwiya*, between the Arma and their nomad enemies. The Kunta only entered Timbuktu on the eve of its conquest by the Fulbe in 1825–6.

At first there seem to have been no special rules governing appointment to the various offices within the Pashalik, including that of the *Pasha* himself. But from the middle of the seventeenth century, when the first generation of locally-born Arma came to power, rules for the transmission of authority began to emerge, based on the rotation of the chief offices between the three great Divisions to which all the Arma belonged. The Division whose turn it was to provide a *Pasha* chose its candidate who then had to be endorsed by the rest of the military. If this endorsement was not forthcoming it became the turn of another Division to choose a candidate and so on until a choice was made that was acceptable to all.[21]

Such a system was bound to produce two results. First, there were frequent interregnums and often several months would go by before all the Divisions could agree on a candidate. Secondly, 'reigns' themselves tended to be short, since the *Pasha* was obliged to resign as soon as a single 'army leader' withdrew his support.[22] In these circumstances the same individuals were inevitably called to power more than once. This led to the emergence of a number of great families or lineages distinguished from the rest of society by their political power and economic influence built up as the result of repeated periods in office. There thus came into being a 'ruling class', described in local chronicles as a 'class of chiefs'.[23]

21. O. Houdas, 1966, pp. 21, 50–1 and 136–7.
22. It was not unusual for a *pasha* to be forced to resign on the very day of his appointment.
23. O. Houdas, 1966.

Between 1646 and 1825, 145 *pasha*s were appointed in Timbuktu, most of them belonging to the three lineages of the Tazarkini, Mubarak al-Dar'i and al-Za'ri. It was the last of these three which produced Manṣūr b. Mas'ūd al-Za'ri Pasha who seized power by force in 1716, exiled all who opposed him and plunged Timbuktu into a reign of terror unparalleled in all its history. In 1719 the people, losing patience with al-Za'ri's excesses, rose in rebellion, drove the *Pasha* and his *legha* (henchmen) from the city and restored the old Arma political system with its chronic instability, its domestic conflicts between the Divisions, and its long interregnums.[24]

In 1766 the Arma elected as *Pasha* Bā-Haddū b. Abū Bakr al-Dar'i, who performed the unusual feat of remaining in office for more than eight years. After his death in 1775, Timbuktu remained without a *pasha* for eighteen years. But even this long interregnum did not entail the final disappearance of Arma institutions: in 1794, when the great Divisions, which had meanwhile become ethnic clans, agreed on a *pasha*, their choice, al-Muṣṭafā al-Tazarkini, restored all the former offices of the Pashalik.[25]

Under his successor, Abū Bakr b. Aḥmad al-Dar'i, the office of *pasha* became hereditary and on his death in 1815 his two sons, Muḥammad and 'Uthmān, succeeded him. Ḳā'īd 'Uthmān was the last *pasha* of Timbuktu.[26]

By the end of the seventeenth century, as a result of its military decline and the chronic instability of its central government, the Pashalik began to break down into a number of more or less autonomous units grouped around each of the great *ḳaṣaba*s of Gao, Bamba, Timbuktu and Jenne. While continuing to recognize the official but distant authority of Timbuktu, each garrison elected its own leaders quite independently. The *pasha*s themselves seldom interfered in the garrisons' affairs, calling on them only when there was some serious external threat.

The garrison at Jenne was as independent as the rest, and was not disturbed by the Bambara of Segu throughout the eighteenth century. In 1754, shortly before the presumed death of Mamari Kulibali, the *Biton* (Commander), a Bambara army got as far as Gomitigo, some ten kilometres from Jenne, but did not attack Jenne itself.[27]

The Arma administration remained intact throughout the period we are concerned with: the *ḳā'īd* (commander, army chief) of Jenne continued to be chosen by his Arma peers unless there was a particularly enterprising *pasha* in Timbuktu. Thus in March 1767, Bā-Haddū Pasha himself appointed a new governor of Jenne, Ḳā'īd Alfa b. Masik, who was succeeded by Ḳā'īd Aḥmad b. Sharīf. The latter remained in office until his death in 1772.[28]

24. O. Houdas, 1966, pp. 70–85.

25. See *Timbuktu Chronicle*, Bibliothèque nationale, Paris, Fonds arabe, Ms 5259, ff. 25–6 and 32r.

26. ibid., f.34. B. de Mézières, 1912, pp. 36–7; R. Caillié, 1828, Vol. II, pp. 306–8.

27. Institut de France, Fonds Gironcourt, Ms 2405, pièce 5, ff. 7 and 13.

28. Bibliothèque nationale, Paris, Fonds arabe, Ms 5259, f. 26v.

PLATE 11.1 *General view of Timbuktu from the terrace of the travellers' house*

The commercial links and political relations between Timbuktu and Jenne were never interrupted: in 1773 two messengers were sent to Jenne to announce the death of Bā-Haddū Pasha.[29] In 1785–6 two *ḳāʿid*s of Timbuktu took their armies to Jenne to punish a band of robbers who had taken refuge in the town.[30] In 1794 Timbuktu was notified of the death of the governor of Jenne, Ḳāʿid Abū Bakr b. Saʿīd, and the following year the *pasha* of Timbuktu appealed to the late *ḳāʿid*'s successor and the merchants of Jenne to replenish Timbuktu's supplies of cowries.[31]

But in 1796 Mungo Park, the Scottish explorer, was told in Segu that Jenne officially belonged to the Bambara kingdom though in fact it was governed by the 'Moors'.[32]

Should this be taken to indicate that the Bambara exercised a 'protectorate' over Jenne? Such local sources as are available hardly support this hypothesis. They tend rather to confirm René Caillié's view that Jenne lived 'alone and independent' until it was conquered by the Fulbe of Macina in 1818–19.[33]

The Songhay of Dendi

After being driven out of Gao and having lost two kings and dozens of members of the imperial family within a few months, the Songhay, led by Askiya Nuh, managed to hold back the Moroccan advance in Dendi. As pitched battles had resulted in a series of defeats, they began to rely instead upon ambush and, with help from Kebbi[34], succeeded in holding back Zarḳūn's troops. But after the latter's death in Bandiagara, his successor, Manṣūr b. ʿAbd al-Raḥmān Pasha (1595–6), made them pay dearly for their victory: Nuh, defeated and forced to leave some of his people in the hands of the Moroccans, withdrew to Dendi where he was deposed by his brothers in 1599; the Moroccans then appointed an *askiya* for the Songhay who remained under their control.[35]

The Songhay of Dendi gradually reverted to 'paganism' and broke down into several kingdoms, although they did succeed in maintaining their unity until the middle of the seventeenth century.

In 1630 they signed a peace treaty with the Moroccans who subsequently began to interfere in their internal affairs and arbitrate in their quarrels over succession. In 1639, for example, Masʿūd al-Zaʿri Pasha entered Lulami, the capital of Dendi, with his army, in order to establish a new king.[36]

29. Bibliothèque nationale, Paris, Fonds arabe, Ms 5259, f. 26v.
30. ibid., f. 30r and v.
31. ibid., f. 32r and v.
32. M. Park, 1808, p. 301.
33. R. Caillié, 1828, Vol. II, p. 206.
34. See A. Ganun, 1964, pp. 127–32, for the threatening letter from the Moroccan sultan to the Kanta of Kebbi.
35. al-Saʿdi, 1964, p. 270.
36. ibid., pp. 394–5, 399–400 and 423.

PLATE 11.2   *A Songhay village*

The new king was deposed almost as soon as the Moroccan troops had departed but the Songhay of Dendi did not follow up this attempt at reasserting themselves. Broken up into a number of small and insignificant political units they ceased to be a major political factor in the region. They did, however, retain their freedom until the beginning of the nineteenth century, despite strong pressure from Fulbe and Tuareg nomads from Liptako and Aïr.

The Bambara kingdoms of Segu and Kaarta

After the break-down of Songhay's westward advance and the defeat of the *Mansa* of Mali at Jenne in 1599, the Bambara peasants of Niger were dangerously exposed to Fulbe and Arma incursions.

The Bambara, who practised their own religion, were divided into several *kafu* whose Marka and Muslim chiefs maintained reasonably amicable relations with Jenne and Timbuktu. They appealed for protection to the traditional hunter confraternities or to clans specializing in warfare, such as the Samake, who rapidly assimilated Moroccan fighting methods.[37]

In the middle of the seventeenth century, in a movement much like a peasant revolt, the Bambara rebelled against their Marka chiefs. It is probably from this background that the Kulibali clan emerged, which was to found the kingdoms of Segu and Kaarta.[38]

In Segu, Biton Kulibali (*c.*1710–*c.*1755) imposed his authority with the help of his *ton-dyon*, mostly captives or former captives taken in war. But no sooner had he established his position than, in or around 1739, his kingdom was attacked by the Joola of Kong led by Famagha Wattara. The Joola remained in Segu until 1745 when they received news of the death of the Faama of Kong, Sekou Wattara.[39]

Biton Kulibali, now enfeebled, spent the rest of his life consolidating his kingdom and getting rid of competition from his Masa-si cousins who were installed to the north-west of Segu in the region of Murdia. In 1753–4 he carried the war into their own territory, destroyed their capital Sunsanna and captured their chief, Fulakoro, who was put to death in Segu. After this the Masa-si, led by Sebamana (1754–*c.*1758), moved away and imposed their rule on Kaarta.[40]

After Biton Kulibali's death, the Kingdom of Segu went through a long period of anarchy until about 1766 when a new dynasty rose to power, founded by Ngolo Diarra. After restoring the kingdom to unity, Ngolo Diarra engaged in large-scale military operations in Macina and Fuladugu, and even against the Mossi and Yatenga countries. His excellent relations with the Azawad Kunta and their chief, Shaykh al-Mukhtār (1729–1811),

37. al-Saʻdi, 1964, p. 276.
38. ibid., pp. 406–20. See also C. Monteil, 1924; L. Tauxier, 1942.
39. O. Houdas, 1966, pp. 112–13.
40. See P. Marty, 1927, pp. 367–9.

seem to have made Ngolo Diarra treat Timbuktu with circumspection.

He was succeeded by his son, Monzon (*c.*1789–1808), who was the real organizer of the Kingdom of Segu. Like Biton Kulibali before him he had to deal with rivalry from the Masa-si who, since 1754, had extended their power over a large area between the Kingui and the Beledugu. In 1792 they even seized Nyamina on the River Niger, thus cutting one of Segu's main supply routes. Monzon's reply to this was terrible: after liberating Nyamina he turned to Kaarta where he sacked Guemu, the capital, and forced the Masa-si king, Desekoro, to flee to Guidimakha. He then attacked the Awlād M'Bark Moors in the Nioro region for having refused to help him in his war against Kaarta. Back in Segu he followed his father's example by giving his sons chiefdoms in the territories he had conquered and supplying each of them with a considerable army.[41]

Monzon died in 1808. Three years later Shaykh al-Mukhtār died not far from Timbuktu. The almost simultaneous disappearance of these two leaders was an important factor in the unrest which prevailed in the Niger Bend until Shaykhū Aḥmadu's time, and for which the Fulbe and Tuareg forces, which the two leaders had held in check, were largely responsible.

Fulbe and Tuareg

One of the chief consequences of the collapse of the Songhay empire was social disorganization. From the early 1600s one of the main features was the irresistible advance of the Saharan nomads towards the Niger valley and the lake area south of Timbuktu.

The Fulbe achieved complete preponderance in Macina. While preserving their independence by offering fierce resistance to Moroccan attacks from Timbuktu and Jenne, they speeded up their migration towards Futa Jallon in the west and Liptako and Hausa country in the east. But they were subject to raids by the Bambara armies of Ngolo and Monzon and, during the second half of the eighteenth century, were forced to accept Segu sovereignty. Meanwhile, among the pastoral Kunari, a slow process of sedentarization and Islamization began.

Also contemporary with the Moroccan occupation was the expansion of the Tuareg of Adrār – the Kel-Tadmekket and the Kel-Awllimiden. While the first remained in the background until the end of the seventeenth century, the Kel-Awllimiden soon brought all their weight to bear on the eastern part of the Niger valley, especially between Gao and Dendi.

They became the scourge of Timbuktu, intercepting communications between it and its outport, Kabara, interfering in the conflicts between the Arma chiefs and pillaging the agricultural villages along the river. The eighteenth century was full of confrontations and clashes between the Tuareg, who were usually victorious, and the weakened Arma who suffered defeat after defeat.

41. C. Monteil, 1924, pp. 66–90 and 110–16.

In May 1737, about twenty kilometres south-east of Timbuktu, Ameno-kal Oghmor ag Alad overwhelmed the Arma forces at Toya, inflicting considerable losses. Three hundred to three hundred and fifty were killed, among them the ruling *pasha*.[42] Despite this, the chiefs of other Tuareg groups, including the Kel-Āwllimiden, continued to come to Timbuktu to receive their investiture at the hands of the *pasha*s.[43]

In 1770 the Tadmekket laid siege to Timbuktu, reducing the population to starvation after a group of Arma had murdered their Amenokal Habatīt.[44] The city was only saved by the intervention of the *Shaykh* of the Kunta, al-Mukhtār al-Kabīr, who managed to reconcile Bā-Haddū Pasha and Habatīt's successor, Amenokal Hammiyuk. The terms of the agreement concluded between the two parties in August 1771 provided that the Arma should pay the Tuareg a surety in horses and gold-dust.[45]

But the Tuareg broke the pact, and the *Shaykh* withdrew his moral support from Hammiyuk and set up another as his rival, thus causing the Tadmekket to break up into two rival branches, the Tingirigif and the Irriganaten. At the same time he won the confidence of the Awllimiden and their chief, Amma ag Ag Shaykh, who took advantage of the disunity among the Tadmekket to try to extend his rule over the Saharan nomads of the Timbuktu region. The Awllimiden thus became the chief support of the Kunta who, as the Arma grew weaker, succeeded in filling the political vacuum they left and in limiting the effects of the resulting anarchy. But until the founding of the Fulbe empire of Macina they took care not to annex any political rights in Timbuktu nor to drive out the last vestiges of Arma power. Thus Kawa ag Amma, the powerful *amenokal* of the Kel-Awllimiden, followed the old custom and, in July 1796, went to Timbuktu to receive investiture at the hands of Abū Bakr Pasha.[46]

Western Sudan and the outside world

Despite Morocco's gradual withdrawal from Sudan after al-Manṣūr's death, the *pasha*s of Timbuktu were steadfastly loyal to the last sultans of the Saʿādī dynasty. The Friday *khuṭba* (sermon in a mosque) was recited every week in the name of the rulers in Marrakesh, who took the trouble to announce their accession to the throne to the *pasha*s in Timbuktu and the heads of the garrisons in Gao and Jenne.

When the last Saʿādī monarch was assassinated in 1659 the *bayʿa* (oath of allegiance) binding the *pasha*s to the dynasty immediately lapsed. In 1660,

42. O. Houdas, 1966, pp. 168–78.
43. ibid., p. 253.
44. Bibliothèque nationale, Paris, Fonds arabe, Ms 5259, ff. 26v–27v.
45. ibid., f.28v; see also Bibliothèque nationale, Paris, Ms 5334, the *Kitab al-Taraʿif*, by Shaykh al-Mukhtār's son.
46. Bibliothèque nationale, Fonds arabe, Ms 5259, f. 32r; Institut de France, Fonds Gironcourt, Ms 2406, pièce 75 (Taʿrikh Fittuga).

understandably enough, the *khutba* ceased to be recited in the name of Mawlāy Aḥmad al-Manṣūr's descendants 'in all Takrūr, from Kūkya to Bina'.[47] But ten years later, after the 'Alawite dynasty had seized power in Morocco, the Arma renewed their allegiance to the Moroccan throne, first to Mawlāy al-Rashīd and then to Mawlāy Ismā'īl.[48]

Unlike the Saʿādīs, the 'Alawites paid little attention to the Nigerian Sahel. Their policy was oriented towards Mauritania rather than Sudan. While the Europeans fought over Arguin and the trade in gum arabic, Mawlāy Ismā'īl firmly established his power in Mauritania by supporting the *Amīr* (Prince) of the Trarza, and even by occasionally sending more or less regular troops to the Senegal valley. These were the Ormans, who terrorized all the riverside regions of Senegal until the 1720s.[49] They gained control of Futa Toro where they made and unmade the *satigi* (rulers) to suit themselves and brought strong pressure to bear on the inhabitants of Upper Senegal. The captives they took there went to swell the ranks of the famous black army of the *'Abid* formed by the Sultan of Morocco. The excursions of the *'Abid* wrought havoc in Bondu and Bambuk and above all in Galam where, on several occasions, they threatened the French trading-post of Fort Saint-Joseph.

Despite all this the Arma continued to show a certain respect to the 'Alawite kings and according to the English writer, J. G. Jackson, the Timbuktu Pashalik went on paying allegiance to Mawlāy Ismā'īl's successors.[50]

With the coming to power of Sultan Sīdī Muḥammad (1757–90), Morocco's policy in the Sudan made a fresh start, based on the revival of trade across the Sahara. Like the last of the Saʿādī kings, the 'Alawite Sultan referred to himself as 'sovereign of Gao and Guinea' in his correspondence with European governments. This might seem boastful without the evidence of the highly trustworthy English counsul, J. Matra, who served in Morocco between 1786 and 1806.[51]

Moreover his claim seems to correspond to the attitude taken in the Sudan towards the status of Timbuktu on the eve of the Fulbe *djihād*. Such at least is the suggestion arising from the writings of Nuh b. al-Tahir, a scholar of Macina who was one of Shaykhū Aḥmadu's closest collaborators. One of these texts proclaims the advent of the last Caliph of Islam, Shaykhū Aḥmadu. It was addressed to the 'Sultan of Gharb and Marrakesh and his dependencies of Timbuktu, Arawān, Bū-Jbeīha, Taoudéni, as of Sūs Near and Far, and of Touat'.[52]

47. O. Houdas, 1966, p. 145.
48. ibid., p. 185; Bibliothèque nationale, Fonds arabe, Ms 6399, ff. 214–18.
49. See A. Delcourt, 1952; B. Barry, 1972.
50. J. G. Jackson, 1811, p. 296.
51. Archives nationales, Paris, Fonds des affaires étrangères. B1, 831; R. Hallet, 1964, p. 81.
52. Bibliothèque nationale, Fonds arabe, Ms 5259, ff. 74–8.

This classification may have no basis in fact. But the political evolution of Timbuktu, while reflecting the internal autonomy of the former Moroccan territory on the banks of the Niger, is also comparable in many respects to the evolution of the Berber Regencies of the seventeenth and eighteenth centuries, when Constantinople's sovereignty, though now nominal, continued to be significant.

Economic and social development

Natural calamities and human environment

By the end of the 1700s, western Sudan was no longer the dazzling and prosperous country of which al-Manṣūr spoke in 1591.

The turn of the seventeenth century brought a series of disasters: drought, food shortages, epidemics and famines destroyed harvests and decimated populations, exacerbating tensions between nomads and sedentary people. From 1639, respites became shorter and crises longer and more acute. That same year there was a famine in the Jenne region, the granary of the Niger Bend. From the central Delta it spread for four consecutive years over all the Bend. The resulting distress was probably the origin of the social movement that preceded the rise of the Bambara kingdom of Segu.[53]

There were few years without crises in the eighteenth century. There was an early seven-year food shortage from 1711 to 1718. Then, from 1738, western Sudan underwent one of its worst famines ever, which affected all the Sahel and a large part of the Maghrib.[54]

In 1741 famine combined with a plague epidemic to bring about a disaster of catastrophic proportions during which 'People ate the corpses of animals and human beings'. This period was full of wars and minor conflicts which set the peoples of the Sudan one against the other.[55] After 1744 the effects of the famine began to fade but plague remained endemic erupting every few years, in 1748–9, 1762–6 and, above all, 1786–96.[56]

Thus the Niger Bend suffered as much if not more from natural disasters as from the misdeeds of man, and both its people and its landscape bore the scars.

The land between Timbuktu, the Great Lakes and the River Niger, was the confluence of various ethnic groups. For a large part of each year it became a mosaic of peoples and a zone of contact between two ways of life – pastoral and rural sedentary. But because the good grazing land was also the best arable land, this contact often produced conflicts, all the more serious because there was no political force in the area strong enough to

53. Al-Saʿdi, 1964, p. 339.
54. O. Houdas, 1966, pp. 14, 63, 102, 105 and 191–2; P. Marty, 1927, pp. 562 and 565.
55. O. Houdas, 1966, pp. 116–19.
56. Bibliothèque nationale, Paris, Fonds arabe, Ms 5259, ff. 24r–v; 26r–v, 31 v–32v.

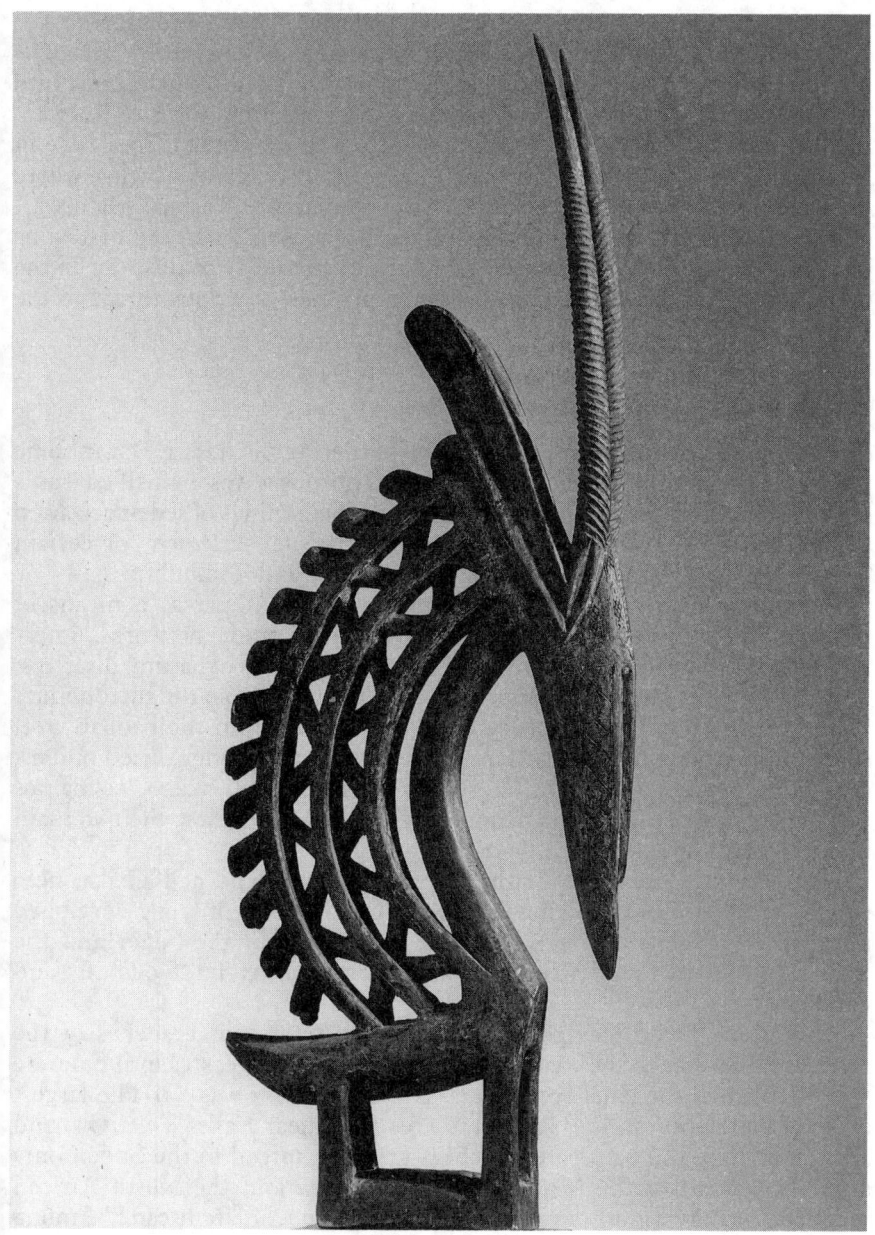

PLATE 11.3   *Tyi-wara antelope headdress, used by the Bambara in rites re-enacting the mythical birth of the bringer of agriculture*

limit the incursions of herders' tracks onto farmers' fields and vice-versa.

Thus the hot season became a period of trouble and insecurity through-out the region. The Kel-Tadmekket east and south of Timbuktu came into close proximity with the Berabich, the Kel-Maghsharen, the Kel-Katwan, the Ghālī-Mūsā and other *baydan* (nomads) who descended from Aklé in Mauritania towards Rās al-Mā' and the northern edge of Macina where they and the Fulbe fought each other over the meagre seasonal pastures.

Pressure was greatest at the end of the hot season when the first rains brought the peasants out into the fields again: any delay or disorder in the withdrawal of the nomads was enough to produce a serious threat to the harvest.

Local production and regional trade

Agriculture tended to recede in the areas bordering the desert. But in some places the occupation of land for agricultural purposes was intensified – as is shown by the Bambara migrations in Bara, the beginnings of sedentarization among the Fulbe of Macina, and the permanent settlement of certain Tuareg or Tuareg-ized (Kel-Antasar) groups around Timbuktu.

Furthermore, because of the advantages of the Niger as a means of communication and the extension of traditional trade networks, inter-regional commerce helped to mitigate the consequences of natural disasters.

Local food production at Jenne was supplemented from the surrounding region of San which produced ground-nuts, flour from the baobab tree, shea (a tree from whose kernels a butter is obtained), honey, dried onions, pimentos, beans and fonio. There were also cotton, indigo, senna for making soap, wool, wax, iron from Bendugu and, of course, the two main imports from the forest area, kola nuts and gold.[57]

After leaving Jenne for Timbuktu, boats would land at Kubaka, near which – at Sofara in the eighteenth century – the Joola of Kong developed a centre for fattening horses.[58] At the confluence of the Niger and the Bani stood Isaqa (later Mopti) with its large market for foodstuffs and handicrafts.[59]

After Lake Debo, navigation followed the two main branches of the river, the Issa-bar to the west and the Bara-Issa to the east. Until Sarafére was established the chief settlement on the Bara-Issa was Sâ. The largest areas of cultivation in the Timbuktu area were near Lakes Tele, Oro and Fati, and along the backwaters. Wheat-growing spread in the Sudan only after the advent of the Moroccans as the Arma and the North African merchants in the big towns were the only people who ate bread.[60] Among the industrial plants produced were tobacco and gum arabic which were

57. R. Callié, 1828, Vol. II, pp. 210–17; C. Monteil, 1977 edn. pp. 11–14.
58. ibid., p. 236; al-Sa'di, 1964, pp. 303 and 488–9.
59. ibid., pp. 239–40; al-Sa'di, 1964, p. 303.
60. O. Houdas, 1966, p. 117.

collected in large quantities around Gundam and Lake Faguibin.[61]

Underlying the commercial life of Timbuktu were numerous artisans: salt-processors, weavers, tailors, tanners, shoe-makers, goldsmiths, potters and manufacturers of agricultural implements and weapons. Each craft was the monopoly of an ethno-professional corporation: all dyers, for example, came from Sansanding while the Arma had the exclusive privilege of making shoes.[62]

The eastern part of the Niger valley was the area which had suffered most since the days of the Songhay: following the decline of Gao, it had been isolated from trade networks and as a result of persistent drought and soil erosion most of its people had become nomadic.

Trans-Saharan trade and the Atlantic trade

Despite the political upheavals from the end of the sixteenth century, trade in the Niger Bend was established on firm geographical, economic and social foundations which survived both the Moroccan conquest and the intensification of European trade on the coast. Trans-Saharan trade overcame all political and military difficulties resulting from the weakening of the central powers bordering the Sahara Desert and remained the main economic activity of vast regions of the Maghreb and the Sahel. What suffered inexorable change from the sixteenth century was not the volume of trade but its economic significance in relation to the development possibilities of the countries and regions involved.

Routes

After 1591 the route from Dar'a to Taghāza to Timbuktu became the royal road for trade between Sa'ādī Morocco and Western Sudan. It was used both by army convoys and by merchant caravans organized and supervised by the Sultan's men. This route was the first to be affected by the disturbances which followed the death of al-Manṣūr. The merchants gradually neglected Dar'a and Taghāza for Sūs and Tafilālet, where local religious leaders wielded a beneficial influence. Thus, less than fifty years after the Moroccan conquest the road network had almost reverted to what it had been in the Middle Ages. The most lasting changes were those affecting the Sahelo–Sudanese part of the network.

The Atlantic route   The Saharan part of the Atlantic route corresponded to the old Trīk Lamtūnī, and its revival in the 1620s was reinforced by the 'Alawites.

Under Mawlāy Ismā'īl, caravans from Tegdaoust and Gulimin crossed the territories of the Ma'kil people who, for various reasons, had thrown in their lot with the Sharīfian dynasty. Special mention should be made of

61. R. Caillié, 1828, pp. 314–21.
62. A. Dupuis-Yacouba, 1921, pp. 25–8, 38–9, 61–3 and 79–80.

PLATE 11.4   *Travellers approaching Timbuktu*

the Tadjukant who were masters of all caravan traffic between south Morocco and Mauritanian Adrār.[63]

Furthermore, the dissemination in the Western Sahara of religious doctrines, such as those of the Ḳādirīyya and Tīdjānīyya brotherhoods, caused considerable circulation of men and ideas between the religious centres of south Morocco and those of the southern Sahara. Aḳḳa, Tindūf, Smāra, Shinguetti and Boutlimit were well-known centres of the Ḳādirīyya as well as important trading posts. Caravans from Shinguetti or Waddān travelled to Fort Saint-Louis in Senegal via Trarza country, Galam via Brakna country, and Hōdh by the Dhār track leading to Tishīt and Walāta. In Galam, Moorish trade enjoyed complete predominance, despite the existence of the French fort of Saint-Joseph.[64] From Hōdh, several tracks led south towards the Bambara kingdoms of Kaarta and Segu via posts at Diara in Kingui, Gumbu, Bassikunu and Sokolo.[65]

Moorish caravans travelled as far as Segu, Banamba and even Nyamina, but most Bambara trade was transacted at Sansanding. Sansanding was a trans-shipment point for canoes going up the Niger from the Sotuba rapids, and the port of trade for the Kingdom of Segu. It gradually became less dependent on Jenne for its supplies from the Sahara and by the 1790s its commercial network was as busy as that of the capital of Bani.[66]

Caravans from Walāta also maintained direct links with Jenne via Rās al-Mā' and Timbuktu.[67]

The eastern route   This group of roads started in Tafilālet in Morocco and crossed Tūwāt, providing also a passage for the great caravans of Moroccan pilgrims. At Timimun the road from Tūwāt to the Sudan connected with the tracks from central Maghrib: one from al-Golea to Mzāb to Laghwāt and another from al-Golea to Wargla to Tuggurt to Tozeur to Gafṣa – both controlled by the Shaamba and Ughramma nomads whose only occupation was to guide and protect the caravans.[68]

Further south, at In-Ṣalāḥ, was the junction with the track from Ghadāmes, quarelled over throughout the eighteenth century by Tripoli and Tunis, and the channel by which Sudanese goods flowed to both capitals. The merchants there, who were among Timbuktu's wealthiest clients, maintained permanent relations with Hausa country via Ghāt and Agades, and with Borno via Murzuk and Bilma.[69]

63. P. Marty, 1910–11, Vol. III, pp. 97–8 and 132–4.

64. See the correspondence of the Fort's commanders, Archives nationales, sous-collection Colonies, C6.

65. M. Park, 1799, pp. 233–4; A. Golberry, 1802, pp. 287–8.

66. M. Park, pp. 303–4; R. Caillié, 1828, Vol. II, p. 380.

67. O. Houdas, 1966, pp. 21–5 and 102–4; H. Barth, 1857–8, Vol. V, pp. 481–2.

68. E. Carrette, 1844, p. 91; A. Daumas-Chancel, 1848, pp. 111–16; H. Duveyrier, 1859, pp. 6–7, 16–17 and 19–24.

69. L. de Tassy, 1757, Vol. II, pp. 180–2; R. Hallet, 1964, pp. 82–4; E. Carrette, 1844, p. 143.

After Tidikelt the caravans skirted the western border of Ahnet and on, after the arduous crossing of Tanezruft, to Azawad and the Kunda encampments. The Kunda, who provided services, knowledge and *baraka* (blessings) and who acted as arbiters in most of the conflicts arising among the nomads or between the nomads and the sedentary peoples played an important role in the region. Their presence alone was enough to make them the best guarantees and the most effective protectors of the road to Timbuktu.[70]

From Arawān and Bū-Jbeiha some caravans went directly to Bamba or Gao, but it was Timbuktu which attracted most of the traffic along this route.[71]

After presenting gifts to the Arma chiefs of the town, the Maghrib merchants were taken over by *diatigui*, who supplied them with hospitality, means of transport and, if necessary, an armed guard.[72] For many travellers the journey did not end at Timbuktu as goods from North Africa were carried on to Jenne by the same men. It was only upstream from Jenne that a different trade infrastructure emerged, of which the most important element was the Joola network.

The Juula network Jenne was linked by two main routes to the forest regions and the countries that produced kola nuts and gold. The first route, to the south-west, ran in the direction of Bure or Wurodugu, the outskirts of kola country. The second, to the south-east, went towards Kong and Asante.[73]

Kong supplied Jenne with kola nuts and gold from Lobi and the Gold Coast. Both were carried by the same Juula traders who sold slabs of salt from Taoudéni to Buna. The rest of their load would be made up of cotton goods and European products which were marketed around Kumasi.[74]

Parallel to this route the Yarse, a Mossi group, had established direct links between Timbuktu and Asante country, skirting Jenne and the inner Delta and proceeding via Douentza, Korientze, Aouaki and Diré or via Wahiguya (Ouahigouya), Bandiagara, Konna and Korientze.

Apart from these Mossi side-roads, there seems to have been a small amount of traffic between Timbuktu and Hausa country along the river to Ansongo, Dallol and Mauri. This was the route followed by the pilgrims, who, after reaching Kano, went north to the Fezzān and then on to Egypt via Awdjīla and Sīwa.[75]

Moroccan exports to the western Sudan were extremely varied. They

70. Bibliothèque nationale, Paris, Fonds arabe, Ms 5334, f. 79*r*; P. Marty, 1920–1, Vol. I, pp. 27 and 49–51.

71. H. Barth, 1857–8, pp. 457–8.

72. O. Houdas, 1966, pp. 138 and 203.

73. R. Caillié, 1828, Vol. II, pp. 99–103; L. G. Binger, 1892, Vol. II, pp. 141–2.

74. L. G. Binger, 1892, Vol. I, pp. 316–17 and 373–4. Red fabrics said to be from Kumasi were known in Timbuktu in the mid-1900s: O. Houdas, 1966, p. 96.

75. Bibliothèque nationale, Paris, Fonds arabe, Ms 5713, ff. 30–1.

consisted of local products, ranging from cereals and religious books to silk garments and tobacco from Meknes, and goods from the eastern Mediterranean (spices and silk) and from Europe (textiles, sugar, coffee, tea, glassware and fire-arms).

In the central Maghreb, Sudanese trade was the chief source of activity for the provinces of Tūwāt, Mzāb, Sūf and Djarīd. It covered a wide variety of goods, from indigo cloth and *turkedī* from Kano to kola nuts from Asante; the latter were eaten throughout the southern Maghreb where there were large black populations.[76]

This trade, both varied and continuous, was very lucrative.[77] Its economic significance may seem small in comparison with trade as a whole at that time, but the trans-Saharan trade was transporting not only merchandise, but also the ideas and values of a whole civilization.

Trade goods

Salt played a very small part in trade between the people of the Maghrib and those of the Sahel and the Sudan. Since the beginning of the seventeenth century, and despite the presence of Moroccan ḳāʾids both in Taghāza and in Taoudéni,[78] the towns along the River Niger has had access to Saharan salt deposits by means of separate and independent routes: the Moorish and Tuareg *azalai*. It was therefore essential for caravans from the north to diversify the goods exported to the Sudan. In addition, Sudan itself, apart from its traditional exports of gold, slaves and ivory, also needed to dispose of certain manufactured goods, such as cloth and jewellery, the proportion of which grew as the export of gold and slaves declined or stagnated.[79]

Although the amount of gold exported never again equalled the huge amounts taken out of the Sudan after the Moroccan conquest, gold formed part of the freight of all caravans returning from the Sudan. At the end of the seventeenth century there was an appreciable increase in the export of slaves after Mawlāy Ismāʿīl had formed his ʿAbīd army and, in the second half of the eighteenth century, gum arabic played an important role in Sudanese exports to Morocco. The opening of the port at Mogador provided Sudanese caravans with a new maritime outlet where, in addition to the goods already mentioned, they also sold large quantities of ostrich feathers and ivory.

76. R. Leselle, 1957; L. Valensi, 1967.

77. See among others: G. Lemprière, 1891, p. 290; J. Gräberg, 1834, p. 146; L. Godard, 1859, pp. 117–20; Prax, 1845.

78. Moroccan ḳāʾids are said to have been in Taoudéni until just before the French conquest. See the Pichon report on the Arawān region, Archives nationales du Sénégal, Dakar, IG 254.

79. R. Caillié, 1828, Vol. II, pp. 383–4; Prax, 1845, p. 344.

Cultural and religious development

Islam in the Sudan just before the *djihād*s of the nineteenth century

The period we have been examining is often said to be one of decadence and cultural stagnation. But if by this is meant a decline or regression of Islamic culture, the description needs to be revised. Through the continuous commerce across the Sahara, through the *zāwiya* (sanctuaries), the fraternities and the *marabout* groups, and through the highly organized networks of the Juula traders, the influence of Islam continued to spread in varying degrees through all the peoples of the Niger valley.

As René Caillié observed at the beginning of the nineteenth century, all the inhabitants of Timbuktu and Jenne were able to read and write Arabic. The best proof of how widely this powerful means of communication was spread is the abundance of written sources available to the historian of the region. The *ta'rīkh*s, the famous chronicles of Timbuktu, were all written between the seventeenth and nineteenth centuries.

Islam was no longer a purely urban phenomenon as it had been in the Middle Ages. It was no longer transmitted exclusively by the city-dwelling *'ulamā'*, nor organically linked to just one social group, the merchants, nor connected with one economic activity.

Islam spread into the country and affected both the Bambara peasants and the Fulbe herdsmen. Its new propagators were the Berber or Sudanese *marabout* groups who had adopted as their main business the study and dissemination of the Word of the Prophet.

The emergence of the *marabout* groups (*zuwaya* or *insilime*) is one of the most spectacular aspects of the ethno-social stratification which occurred on the southern edge of the Sahara during the second half of the seventeenth century. After demographic upheavals or armed struggles about which we still know very little, nomad society, from Senegal to Aïr, split into two distinct strata: the 'warrior' and the clerical groups, who enjoyed great religious prestige and devoted themselves entirely to the study and practice of Islamic law and mystical theology.

Their *zāwiya* attracted students as well as travelling merchants seeking protection. Many of these sanctuaries, carefully placed along the trading routes, later became important caravan posts. Examples of this were Arawān and Bū-Jbeiha (north of Timbuktu), which were founded by the *marabout* group of the Kel al-Sūk, later to be supplanted in its own territory by the Kunta. Others were Mabrūk and al-Ma'mūn, also former Kel al-Sūk encampments which, in the eighteenth century, under Shaykh al-Mukhtār, were to become two of the most important centres of Kunta influence.

The *shaykh*s of the desert were to eclipse the *'ulamā'* of the towns and become the spiritual masters of most of the instigators of the *djihād*s of the eighteenth and nineteenth centuries. It was with the Ait Dayman of Shinguetti that *Amīr* 'Abd al-Kādir of Futa Toro began his studies, before

PLATE 11.5 *A mosque in Timbuktu*

the *djihād* of 1775. It was among the *insilimen* sector of the Ait Awari of
Aïr that 'Uthmān dan Fodio met his teacher Djibrīl ibn 'Umar. The influ-
ence of the Kunta on Shaykhū Aḥmadu is well-known, as is that of the
Ida-u-'Alī of Shinguettī on Ḥādjdj 'Umar Tall.

The Islam of the *marabouts* was to a certain extent a continuation of
the Almoravid tradition, and its militancy contrasted with the tolerant
syncretism which characterized the 'Black Islam' of the Sudanese towns
and the Juula centres. Also, by quickly associating itself with brotherhoods
and religious orders as universal as the Ḳādirīyya (of which the chief
representatives in the Sudan were the Kunta), the Islam of the *marabout*
offered its followers not only a religion but also a framework which went
beyond the traditional categories of identification, such as ethnic groups
or clans.

Whereas traditional Islam in the Sudan was closely linked to the ruling power and the chiefs, the Islam of the *marabouts* before the *djihāds* exercised its influence from below, through the combined action of the brotherhoods and the herdsmen who in the nineteenth century were to set out to attempt the religious conquest of the whole of the Sahel. It was a rallying point, a force for social and political emancipation, and as such it attracted all the Tukuloor of Futa Toro who were struggling against the established power of the Denyanke dynasty. It also attracted the Fulbe of Macina, who were shaking off the yoke of the Bambara and the *ardo*, as well as the Fulbe and the farmers of Hausa country who were struggling against the hegemony of the royal powers established at Gobir, Kano, Katsina and other places.

From the Niger to the Volta

12

M. IZARD AND J. KI-ZERBO

After the fall of the Gao empire in 1591 – following the Moroccan invasion – the basic edifice of political power at the top of the Niger Bend disintegrated, thus creating a major political vacuum which other powers gradually began to fill. Over the following centuries, power became localized under the impact of centrifugal forces emanating from the heart of the fallen empire and integrative forces at work on its periphery. In the Niger Bend and the upper reaches of the Voltas, four poles emerged during the seventeenth and eighteenth centuries: the Bambara kingdoms of Segu and Kaarta, the Mossi kingdoms, the Kingdoms of Kong and Gwiriko, and the Gulmanceba kingdoms. This took place against a back-cloth of numerous ethnic groups with non-centralized authority. It has been said that power was 'tribalized' during this period, especially under the impact of the slave trade which, even for countries as far inland as the Niger Bend and the River Volta, formed the economic backdrop.[1] But this is inaccurate, as shown later, because the African kingdoms were established in geographical areas that were, inevitably, ethnically diverse. In other words, the traditions of Mali and Gao continued but on a smaller scale, by other means and in a context increasingly dominated by external factors and internal conflicts that shaped new political structures. In addition, certain socio-economic and religious factors, that were in no way 'tribal', influenced the reorganization processes and, at the end of the eighteenth century, precipitated the first cracks that heralded the upheavals of the nineteenth.

---

1. The Bambara appeared in the lists of names of the slave-traders and it is quite possible that their sudden rise to prominence in the seventeenth century was also linked to the slave-raiding of the time.

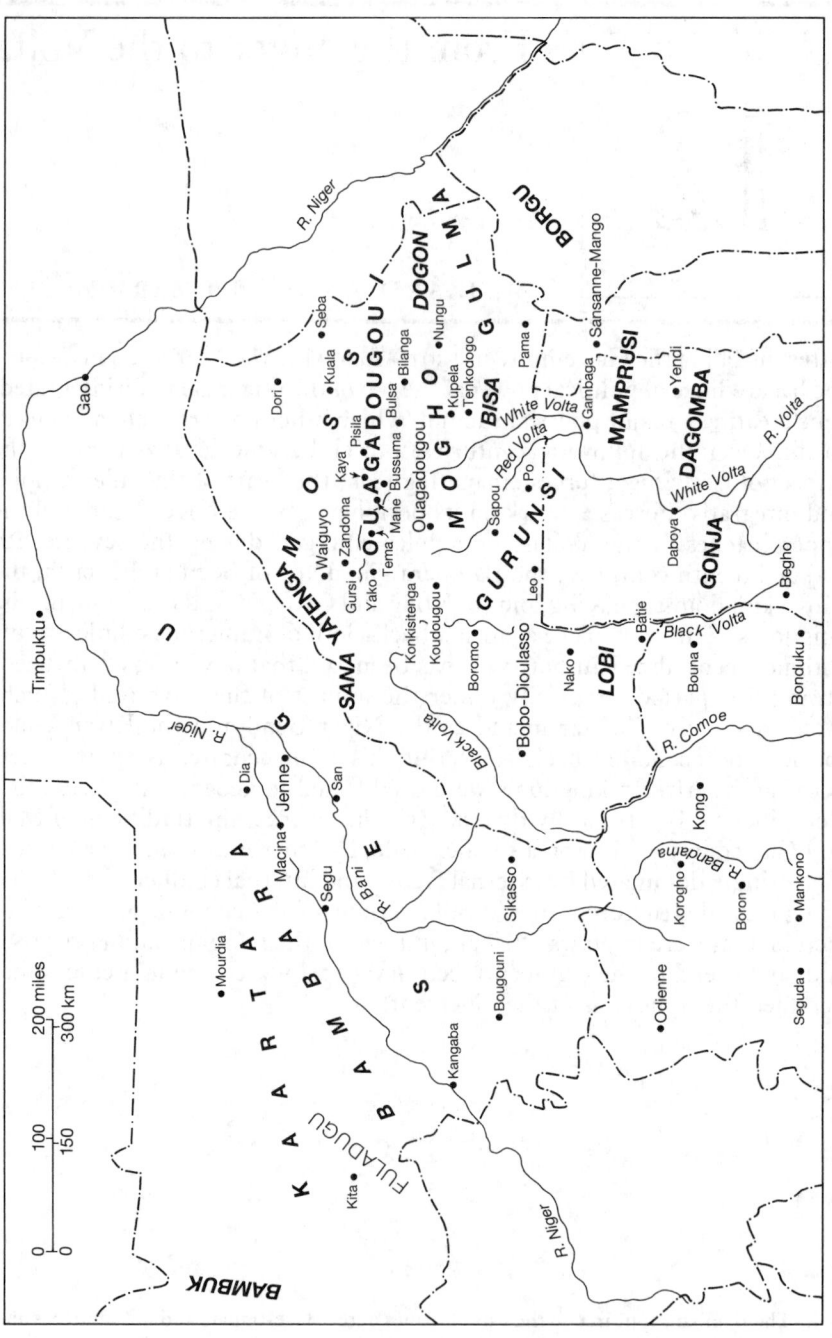

FIG. 12.1 *The Niger–Volta region in the sixteenth to eighteenth centuries*

Peoples, chieftaincies and kingdoms

The Bambara kingdoms of Segu and Kaarta from the sixteenth to the nineteenth century

Political evolution

The origins of the Bambara[2] kingdoms, while not ancient, are obscured by the diversity of the oral traditions and the chronicles. The former, collected or compiled by European travellers, officers and administrators just before and after Gao's fall, as well as by African traditionalists have now become crystallized in writings that contain a variety of viewpoints. The order of succession of rulers is not always the same, nor is the length of reigns.[3]

This study, however, is more concerned with the development of the societies that gave birth to and formed great men than with their actions. And here, after a brief discussion of events, we shall deal mainly with the organization and relations of the forces that moved these peoples from the sixteenth to the nineteenth century.

Another disputed issue relates to the peoples responsible for taking the historical initiative in the Bambara kingdoms. Tauxier is categorical on this point: 'In the final analysis', he writes, 'the Bambara were never capable by themselves of founding kingdoms: the kings of Segu and Kaarta were of Fulbe origin, those of Sikasso and Kong of Mande–Juula origin. As for the ordinary Bambara, he is a true Negro, rather inferior, but a reasonably good worker and farmer'.[4] As Bambara is a Mande language and as peoples have been mixing together since the earliest times, our main interest today obviously lies elsewhere[5] even despite the many biological and political alliances (and wars) between the Bambara and the Fulbe, for example, to repel the last emperor of Mali, Mansa Magan (1645), or the attack on Kong. Although Bambara's origins are certainly lost, contemporary movements are reflected in traditions that make it possible to assert that they have long been indigenous to the Niger Bend. The Bozo were almost certainly there before them and they also mixed with the Soninke, Soso, Malinke, Fulbe and others. Raffenel mentions a myth of origin that talks of the land of Toron, at a moon's march from Segu, which clearly cannot

2. The Bambara call themselves Bamanaw, but we shall retain here the official present-day spelling of their name.

3. From this viewpoint, the works that are most often in agreement are: on the one hand, A. Raffenel, 1846 and L. Tauxier, 1942; and, on the other hand, M. Delafosse, 1912 and 1913, and C. Monteil, 1924. In matters of chronology we prefer the first two.

4. L. Tauxier, 1942, p 8.

5. Further on, L. Tauxier, talking of physical anthropology writes: 'Quatrefages and Hamy conclude p 359 that the Mandingo [Mande] and Bambara Negroes who live in the upper Niger valley seem to belong to both the Hausa and Sudanic races, the latter representing the inferior negroes, the true negroes, the Hausa race representing a superior negro race or one mixed with Ethiopian or Hamitic elements' (1942, p 16).

be a reference to Toron in Wasulu quite nearby to the south-west. In fact, the existence of a *sanankunya* (joking relationship) between the Kulibali (Kurubari) and the Keita or Ture is evidence of long-standing relations between the Bambara and the Malinke[6] who, moreover, speak two dialects of the same language.

Whatever the case, the story of the migration of the eponymous ancestors of the Bambara dynasties contains the theme of the river crossing that is to be found in so many legends of origin in Africa. Two brothers, Bara-mangolo and Niangolo, pursued by an enemy and having no canoe, crossed the river (possibly the Baule or the Niger) thanks to an enormous *m'polie* (catfish) which saved them at the last minute.[7]

The striking aspect of this story of origin is the rapid association that came about, sometimes from choice, often by force, with the Soninke (also called the Marka). The Soninke were traders who had been settled for centuries, sometimes as slave-dealers, and had little interest in soldiering although the Bambara newcomers made it almost a profession. One of the brothers, Baramangolo, sought asylum on the right bank of the Niger with the Buare of Segu. The Segu Buare, who were Soninke, gave him a district which, although separate, allowed the newly arrived Bambara to defend the entire Segu kingdom. Meanwhile, the other brother, Niangolo, crossed the river and built a *tata* (fort) at Baïko. After failing to take the fort by storm, the Marka eventually settled down to peaceful and complementary relations with the Bambara newcomers – until the time when captives brought from Toron by the Juula seized their freedom and provided considerable reinforcement to Niangolo's forces. Hence the Bambara's (no doubt gradual) movement from the status of refugees to that of protector of their hosts and then to that of masters. This process stands out clearly in most accounts of the origins of Bambara power.

Another key aspect of this history was the strategic importance of the middle Niger where the bend of the river reaches farthest into the desert and towards the routes to North Africa. By unifying the two banks, the middle Niger had polarized political power for four centuries. It was difficult for power to be shared, which is why the two sister kingdoms, Segu and Kaarta, were to attack one another continually, mobilizing for this purpose peoples from as far apart as the river Senegal and northern Upper Volta.

It is difficult to relate the two earliest legendary ancestors of the Bambara dynasties to the first leaders known historically. Regarding Segu, we are told that one of Baramangolo's descendants was Kaladian Kulibali who is

6. See R. Pageard, 1957. Some writers explain the marginalization of these people during the time of the *Mansa* of Mali by their refusal to accept Malian power and the Muslim religion, whence their name *Ban mâ na*, 'Refusal of the Master'.

7. The fact that they crossed the river without a canoe is said to be the origin of the patronym Kulibali (Kurubari) (from *kulu*, canoe, and *bali*, privative); but there are other etymologies.

PLATE 12.1 *Soninke statuette of a kneeling hermaphrodite made of wood with a patina derived from sacrifices. Height: 29 cm*

said by several authors to have been the great-grandfather of Mamari
Kulibali through Danfassari and Soma.[8] Kaladian, who does not appear in
the oral traditions, is represented as having almost restored the greatness
of Mali in the seventeenth century, notably by reconquering Timbuktu
from the Moroccans.[9]

Meanwhile in Kaarta, on the left bank of the Niger, according to Niono
legend, Sunsan (*c*.1635), the son of Niangolo, is said to have founded
Sunsana near Mourdia. His son, Massa (*c*.1666), was a famous farmer and
also a prolific father who systematically married off his dozens of daughters
not to princes he could not win over but to poor men on condition that
they come and live with him and also espouse his cause. The periodic raids
he launched also attracted many adventurers who were only admitted on
condition that they first proved their worth at farming.[10] Massa's son
Benefali (*c*.1710–45), continued the same policy and considerably extended
the power of the Massasi using methods that skilfully combined the
patriarchal farming life with the brutality of military raids.

Fulakoro, who succeeded his brother Benefali, was unable to avoid the
first serious clash between the Massasi and the kings of Segu. The latter
were more powerful because their territory comprised the valleys of the
river and its main tributaries, and had a larger, more varied population of
producers including Bambara peasants and warriors, Soninke and Juula
traders, Fulbe and Moorish cattle-herders, and Somono and Bozo fishermen and transporters. Segu's power was counterbalanced by the superiority
complex of the Massasi who claimed a more authentic nobility, especially
after the change of dynasty in Segu.

Fulakoro, however, had to confront an able ruler in Segu's Mamari
Kulibali (1712–55), great grandson of Baramangolo the true founder of the
kingdom. Mamari who was endowed with extraordinary strength and
whose mother brewed *dolo* (millet beer) and hydromel rapidly became
leader of a *ton* (an association of boys circumcised at the same time) whence
his name, Biton or Tiguiton. Hunting, farming, and drinking and larking
with his age-mates produced in Mamari a social – and later a political
leader outside the gerontocratic and religious institutions of the country.
Conflict ensued both within the *ton* and without: internal conflict arose
from Mamari's decision to monopolize the weekly Monday meetings – and
the contributions of his guests – instead of sharing the privilege as formerly.
But the main clash was between Mamari and the Soninke traders whose
youthful champion, Kassum was eventually killed after a series of

---

8. C. Monteil, 1924, p 21; L.G. Binger, 1892, Vol. II, p 386.

9. L. Tauxier, 1942, p 63.

10. It is Massa who gave his name to the dynasty. Massasi means: 'son of Massa', but
also 'descendants of the king'.

11. The process by which the Bambara state was formed from the social institution of
the *ton* will be shown in detail below.

disputes.[12] As the elders showed some concern over his increasing power, Mamari broke with the gerontocracy and eliminated the elders of Donkouna and Banankoro so as to win over their young men.

When the adults in these villages asked for help, Mamari seized the chance to consolidate his domestic achievements with external successes – first against Kong, which offered the Wattara gold to secure their services, and also against the Massasi.

Mamari was only able to repel the first intervention by Kong (*c*.1725) through his coalition with the Macina Fulbe who were in the process of settling Fuladugu (the land of the Upper Bakoy around Kita). Sekou Wattara is even said to have attacked Malinke territory and to have thus been caught between the Segu Bambara and the Fuladugu Fulbe. The second attack, by Kong, was driven off with the aid of the Tyero Somono using swarms of bees against the Kong cavalry.[13] After relieving San and driving back the Senufo, the master of Segu nevertheless reduced the heavy taxes afflicting the people of Kong.

Fulakoro was reigning in Kaarta at this time.[14] He was besieging the city of Mourdia which sent an appeal for help to Mamari. Mamari, who was only waiting for such a signal to intervene, defeated Fulakoro and took him prisoner and Fulakoro later died in captivity. Once again the Massasi had to move westward. Mamari Kulibali, called Biton, also conquered the whole of Bambara territory including Beledugu. Macina and Jenne were placed under his authority and he had palaces built there by a Jenne architect. Finally, in 1751, Mamari easily conquered Niani, the capital of declining Mali whose ruler, Massa Maghan Keita, paid him tribute. The *pasha*s of Timbuktu had to do likewise after Biton's fleet and cavalry had cleared the Niger Bend of Tuareg exactions. Biton's successors, however, were rulers of no great stature.

The first was his son Denkoro (1755–7), an arrogant bloodthirsty man, who had seized the golden axe – the symbol of royal power – and was soon executed by the war chiefs. The average length of reign was less than three years. Only Ngolo Diarra (1766–90) reigned long enough to develop a policy: but he had first to get rid of Nankoroba Nzangue and then persuade the military chiefs to swear on magical objects that Mamari himself had appointed him ruler. Ngolo thus put an end to the agitation by the *ton-dyon* chiefs who had become mercenaries, and restored a true monarchy to which he gave concrete form by abandoning Segu-Koro to settle up-river

12. Thus, for example, Kassum suggested settling fines in cattle, with the aim of drawing the association into the area of movable property where the Soninke were certain to come out on top.

13. L. Tauxier, 1942, p. 74. It should be noted that the Juula also often raised bees which might provide useful help in time of war.

14. This episode is absent from the tradition recorded by Tammoura and Monteil, but is mentioned by Robert Arnaud and Adam. Fulakoro is further said to have seduced Bassana, one of Mamari's daughters. See L. Tauxier, 1942, p. 75.

at Segu-Si-Koro. Like Biton, he also had palaces built for him at Jenne and Timbuktu and it was he who strengthened the Bambara hold on both Timbuktu and Macina where civilian officials descended from the 'Moroccans' (Arma) were now to be watched over by Bambara war-chiefs. His campaign against the Fulbe chief Sila Makan Yero took him even into Dogon country. Many Fulbe then emigrated towards Wassalu and Ganadugu.[1] Even when very old he went on an expedition against Yatenga which failed and he died on the return journey, having created a new dynasty at Segu.

After Ngolo internal conflict erupted again and only Monson Diarra (1792–1808) made the power of Segu felt from San to Timbuktu and from the land of the Dogon to Kaarta.[16]

But Kaarta was not yet finished. After Fulakoro (who died in captivity during Mamari's reign), it had recovered through raids and at the expense of Beledugu, Bambuk and Khassonke country. Then, after Deniba Bo (1758–61), a great warrior – Sira Bo Kulibali (1761–80) – had established the royal residence at Guemu. He had seized half of Bakhunu while Ngolo Diarra was occupied in the north and east. He pillaged Kita, a large Malinke town in Fuladugu and, taking advantage of a dispute between two Diawara clans, the Sagone and the Dabora, he drove the latter out. The Dabora took refuge in Bundu or Segu while the Sagone, who were considered as free, were exempted from paying tribute but were obliged to provide a contingent of warriors in the event of war.

The socio-political organization of the Bambara kingdoms

The most striking feature of the Bambara's move towards a state form and the development of institutions suitable for the rule of far-flung communities, is the novel formula they evolved for reconciling Bambara practices with the imperatives inherent in the life of large-scale multi-ethnic kingdoms. Nothing seems to have been borrowed from outside. The most inspired aspect is that, starting from the working of an ordinary *ton* they gradually forged the machinery of a state. While this procedure is not exceptional in African history it has the advantage here of showing, in striking miniature, in the space of a few decades, the passage from 'clans' to empires'.[17]

In the kingdom of Segu   The starting-point was the *fla-n-ton* (peer association) led by Mamari Kulibali. A *fla-n-ton* (or *ton*) was an association of young men who had undergone the initiation rite of circumcision together.[18] In theory, successive promotions were organized into three groups: youths, adults and elders.

15. L. Tauxier, 1942, p. 96, citing L. G. Binger, 1892.
16. C. Monteil, 1924, p. 89.
17. ibid., pp. 290 *et seq*.
18. In fact the *fla-n-ton* brought together the members of three successive promotions of those circumcised.

The *ton-den* (association members) elected a *ton-tigui* (chief) who might equally well be a house captive as a son of a notable. The prime characteristic of the *fla-n-ton* was the absolute egalitarianism among people of all social backgrounds, which contrasts with the prevailing clan or gerontocratic hierarchy.

The other office-holders of the association comprised someone responsible for settling disputes and ensuring respect for the rules; the convenor, who called meetings and, because he declared the decisions, was nicknamed the *ton-djeli* (*ton*'s *griot*); and the *ton-masa* (leader) who acted as spokesman for the chief. The *ton*'s aims were mutual assistance and the sharing of resources for participation in social life.

As shown above Mamari Kulibali strengthened his group both against the take-over bids by Kassum's rival group of young Soninke, and against the elders who opposed his *ton* plan, using first their role as *faaya* (fathers) and then the demands of farm work. By killing the elders of Donkouna and Banankoro, Mamari at once broke with gerontocratic authority and replaced it as *faa* (father) of the *ton-den*. But, as leaders' successes mounted many other association members had joined the original group – insolvent debtors, pardoned condemned men, prisoners who had broken parole and young adventurers. Such new recruits were admitted with the status of *ton-dyon* (captives of the *ton*). But after the massacre of the elders, Mamari convened the *ton-den* (association members) and brutally had their hair cut to resemble the *ton-dyon*.[19] Tradition puts significant words into Mamari's mouth at this moment: 'We shall no longer eat together the *ton*'s groundnuts, we shall no longer drink together the *ton*'s beer; I am the son of God!' Then some are said to have called out: 'How cruel today's *ton* (*bi-ton*) is!', whence the nickname Biton given to Mamari.

When the members of the association – which basically coincided with the Bambara state's army – poured in, it was no longer a matter of *fla-n-ton* (peers) but of *foroba-dyon* (captives on the big common field) or *furuba-dyon* (captives of the Great Union), the first *ton-dyon* of which formed the aristocracy. This structure was further strengthened by the involvement of the *ton-dyon* in cults of which Mamari was the grand-master; by the assignment of contingents of *ton-dyon* to the control of his own relatives; by the selection of the *ton-masa* not from the *ton-dyon* but from among his personal slaves; and finally by the rule that a *foroba-dyon* remain so for life and that his children be born *foroba-dyon* and remain so.

This process – which represented the abstraction and also the personalization and accumulation of power and, more precisely, arms around the leader of this politio-military machine – resulted in the attribution of the title *faama* (lord holding supreme power).[20] The confusion of this status

19. Three tufts of hair spaced from the forehead to the nape.
20. Mamari Kulibali was thus both *faa* (father of a biological community) and *faama* (man of power and authority). See C. Monteil, 1924, p 303. This typically Mande title later passed to the Juula dynasts, including Samori.

with that of patriarch of a family community was one of the system's serious contradictions. Originally property – accumulated through contributions, raids and war-takings – had remained in the *foroba* (public treasury) and profited the whole community. However, the community fiction did not long mask the privatization of state property. Eventually the collective oath (a bilateral oath binding the *ton-tigui* himself at a given point in his election) was replaced by a unilateral oath imposed by Ngolo Diarra on his electors. From then on the *faama* had discretionary control of state property which he used in particular to reward the bravest military leaders, by giving them the wherewithal 'to repair the tears in their clothes'. The ruler was indeed assisted by a consultative senate of forty members including warriors and holy men but these notables had sworn fidelity to him at secret rituals on an island in the River Niger and had sworn allegiance after the investiture.

Another serious contradiction was the attempt by Mamari's successors to settle the *foroba-dyon* as state serfs tied to farming, a move which precipitated a serious resistance crisis among the warriors. Eventually, however, some military leaders attempted to withdraw to their lands, which brought down terrible reprisals by the central government.

Except during the reigns of strong figures such as Mamari Kulibali and Ngolo Diarra, however, the egalitarian and almost anarchical spirit of the *fla-n-ton* never completely disappeared. It was this spirit that impelled the assembly of *ton-dyon* to eliminate Denkoro, Mamari's son and successor, 'to change the seed'. Initially, the *ton-dyon* sometimes had the *faama* at their mercy – by refusing mobilization and marching orders, for example. However, although the *ton-dyon*'s Monday and Thursday general meetings continued to be held for a long time, eventually they 'no longer had a deliberative, or even a consultative, role, except in serious circumstances'.[21] The council of military leaders gradually supplanted the general meeting, itself becoming weakened, however, as some of its members moved away from Segu as the kingdom expanded – thus accelerating the slide towards autocracy of the *faama*, now influenced above all by his immediate entourage. Nevertheless, to rekindle his troops' devotion to him the *faama* still convened a general meeting at least once a year for the re-swearing of loyalty oaths, the performance of religious rites and the incorporation of young recruits.

Segu's army

At the time of the election, the royal insignia comprised the bow, the quiver and the golden axe – unequivocal symbols of the main activity of the state. Oral tradition records the feats of the *faama* of Segu's army, notably in the siege of towns through the use of battering rams to undermine walls or stockades, ladders to scale them and burning arrows to spread fire. The basic army unit was the *sẽn* (foot) and several *sẽn* formed a *bolo* (arm). When the army was arrayed in battle order, the main mass – the *sofa*

21. C. Monteil, 1924, p. 309.

(grooms) corps[22] was in the centre, called *disi* (chest). This main body of troops was flanked right and left by the *kini-n-bolo* (right arm) and the *numa-n-bolo* (left arm) which were made up of *foroba-dyon* officered by *ton-dyon*. Behind the *disi* was a reserve corps of experienced *ton-dyon* called *ton-koro-bolo*. The *faama* alone appointed the *keletigui* (war-leader or leader of an expedition).

In addition to this regular army, there were allied volunteer contingents also outfitted by the *faama* or by suppliers bound by contracts to the ruler.

Arms consisted of axes (the chiefs' were made of precious metals), arrows, lances and guns, the first of which, of blunderbuss type, seem to have come from Kong. The drums played an important role either the great *tabala* drum associated with each ruler who announced war, or the *dunuba* drum which, skilfully played, transmitted messages over considerable distances. There were also trumpets and xylophones.

The man responsible for inspiring this whole body was the *griot* who had to ensure the men had heart for the battle on the eve of expeditions, for example, when war-chiefs would bind themselves on oath to perform acts of valour.

The army was the main arena for people of different nationalities to rub shoulders. It contained men of every social, ethnic and geographical background: a former captive could command nobles and a Fulbe might march at the head of a contingent made up of Bambara. Young people were thus attracted, being assured – if they survived – of rapidly making their fortunes. While one-quarter of the booty went to the king, one-quarter to the religious chiefs and one-quarter to the Somono who supplied the river transport, the remaining quarter went to the troops. There was also the booty from raids by individuals for soldiers attached to 'proconsular' command.

The overall organization of the territory, as in most African kingdoms, was concentric – from the original core along the River Niger from the capital, Segu-Koro, to Kirango, to the territories annexed over the years, along the stretch of river from Kangaba to Timbuktu. This main area of state activity by the kings of Segu was given the evocative name *too-daga* (*too* pot).[23] The eldest son played a special role in the running of this area's affairs, a role which increased as his father grew older so as to prepare him for his future responsibilities. As a result of the increasing confusion of state property and personal wealth, the eldest sons of kings were generously provided for and their residences dotted the course of the River Niger. In the outlying areas, it was almost a matter of delegated power, either to the indigenous chiefs or to governors appointed by Segu.

22. The *sofa* were in theory grooms, but did not necessarily practise this occupation; they were part of the *faama*'s household. Sometimes, to secure the undying devotion of the 'young men', the *faama* presided at their 'birth' to manhood through circumcision, making sure that some of his own sons were also involved.

23. *Too*: millet paste that forms the staple diet among the Bambara.

Particular use was made in the organization of the army and the kingdom of two communities – the Somono and the Fulbe. The River Niger was the kingdom's main artery, vital for the supply of fish, for civil transport and military logistics. The Somono fishermen, backed by *foroba-dyon*, were thus enrolled in the service of the state, to provide transport and supply fish in the form of dues. It was understood that this group benefitted from the special protection of the king and that they were free to organize their professional work technically and ritually.

It was the same for the Fulbe through the institution of the *foroba-fulaw* (Fulbe public officials), only a minority of whom were ethnic Fulbe. They were freemen, also backed by *foroba-dyon*, and expected to raise the public herds. Their sons, like those of the Somono, retained the status of their fathers. To these two groups must be added the numerous *foroba-dyon* established as peasants on agricultural lands for the needs of the rulers of Segu.

In the Kingdom of Kaarta   The socio-political organization of the Massasi kingdom of Kaarta was similar to that of the kingdom of Segu, but more autocratic. When the king was enthroned, certain rituals were particularly meaningful. The head of the *ton-dyon* took over the running of the king's house, confiscated the dead king's wives' jewellery and put it in the royal treasury. It was a member of the allied family of the Kassi Konare who had the duty of seating the newly elected ruler on the sheepskin, putting the red cap on his head and putting on the gold rings and silver amulets. He then made a speech to him recalling the political programmes of his predecessor and what the royal clan was expecting of him. The head of the *ton-dyon* then prostrated himself before him to swear allegiance and submission in the name of the troops. The royal succession did not pose problems among the Massasi as they had firm control over the country through provincial governors and heads of army corps. Moreover, the *sofa* corps directly bound to the king was highly organized and could be used to discourage the heads of the *ton-dyon* from any idea of rebellion. The supreme leader of the *ton-dyon* was a creature of the ruler, and all men in authority, all the corps of troops and the allies of the clan were members of the brotherhood that venerated the guardian spirit of the clan.

In short, the Massasi clan seems to have been more homogenous than that of Segu because it was not initially locked into a pre-existing indigenous institution. It was formed and developed freely under the initiative of the Massasi family which always jealously kept its leadership for itself.[24]

24. C. Monteil, 1924, p. 330. The author likens this structure to that of Khasso.

On the Central Volta Plateau: Mossi[25] kingdoms from the sixteenth to the nineteenth century

Origins[26]

The most important development on the Volta plateau during this period is undeniably the formation of the Mossi kingdoms, the earliest of which dates from the twelfth century. Assuming, as most authors do, that the Na Gbewa and Na Nedega of Mossi traditions are the same person, through Naaba Rawa and Naaba Zungrana, the sons of Naaba Wedraogo (himself the son of Yennenga who was the daughter of Na Nedega), the Mossi dynasties are linked to the Mamprusi, Nanumba and Dagomba kingdoms. With Naaba Wubri – whose advent at the head of the future kingdom of Ouagadougou dates to about 1495[27] – and Naaba Yadega – Naaba Wubri's agnatic grandson who founded the Kingdom of Yatenga in about 1540 – there began a process of organizing the political structures of the Mossi kingdoms which was to develop over the following two centuries.

Of the three kingdoms (Mamprusi, Nanumba, Dagomba) founded by Na Gbewa's descendants, only Dagomba was to play a major role, from the time of Na Nyaghse (1460–1500).[28] Little is known about succeeding reigns from the early sixteenth[29] to the mid-seventeenth century: internal domestic strife seems to have been the main feature. But in the second half of the sixteenth century a Mande chief (*Naaba*), established the kingdom of Gonja.[30]

In the second half of the seventeenth century, the Gonja kings launched expeditions from their capital, Yagbum. One of these wars, led by Lata-Jakpa (1622/3–1666/7) against Dagomba, was successful. Na Dariziegu of Dagomba was killed, and the Gonja took Daboya, the centre of a salt-producing area. But in 1713 during the reign of Na Zangina, a convert to Islam, the Dagomba held off a new invasion by the Gonja who were crushed at the battle of Tunuma (Tuma). The peace that followed put an end to acts of aggression by Gonja which, under Lata-Jakpa, also harried the Nanumba kingdom.

In about 1740, however, a serious war of succession broke out in Dagomba itself between the newly designated Na Garba and a prince who had been an unsuccessful candidate for the throne. Taking advantage of Dagomba's state of turmoil, in 1744 the Asante ruler, Opoku Ware,

---

25. On the Moose or Mossi, it should be recalled that the singular is Moaga, the country is Mogho, the language is More and the proper name of Ouagadougou in More is Wogodogo. But, in accordance with current spelling, we use Ouagadougou.

26. On origins see UNESCO, *General History of Africa*, Vol. IV, ch. 9.

27. ibid.

28. On the Mamprusi–Nanumba–Dagomba group of kingdoms, see H. A. Blair and A. Duncan-Johnstone, 1932; S. J. Eyre-Smith, 1933; and E. F. Tamakloe, 1931, p. 193.

29. See N. Levtzion, 1964c.

30. Cf. J. Goody, 1967a.

mounted an expedition against Yendi in support of the faction opposed to the new king. Na Garba was taken prisoner and only freed after undertaking to send to Kumasi an annual tribute of 2000 prisoners – an enormous number, even with eastern Gonja contributing its share.[31] Dagomba's future was dogged by the aftermath of this treaty which compelled it to continually find new sources of prisoners. The main role of Dagomba warriors became one of man-hunting among ethnic groups less organized politically and militarily for which purpose mercenaries were recruited. By the end of the eighteenth century, Dagomba was no more than a channel for Asante influence which reached as far as the borders of Mogho.

The Kingdom of Ouagadougou

Twenty-three successors to Naaba Wubri are known in central and southern Mogho between 1500 and 1800. The *nanamse* (princes) had until then consolidated their territorial hold as far as the Yako and Gursi area, thus laying claim to the legacy of Naaba Rawa whose sway had extended over a large part of the White Volta river basin.[32] Naaba Kumdumye,[33] the son of Naaba Nyingnemdo who had established Mossi government over the old settlement of Ouagadougou (Wogodogo), began his reign with a dynastic dispute which was to have serious consequences. Naaba Kumdumye had competed for the kingship with another candidate, Naaba Yadega, who even after being rejected still had the support of his eldest sister, Pabre,[34] who had stolen Naaba Wubri's regalia for him. With these insignia of royal legitimacy, Naaba Yadega made for Gursi and, after brutally killing his former tutor, Naaba Swida, conquered the region which subsequently bore his name, Yatenga (from *Yadega-tenga*: the land of Yadega).[35]

Naaba Kumdumye put his sons to rule in Yako and Tema which were both later to become independent chiefdoms. Mossi organization in the territories it occupied or claimed was still loose and finding a place for princes whose loyalty was not always above suspicion, the king was killing two birds with one stone: he was occupying the ground politically and also keeping happy the potential candidates for the throne. Ironically, however, it was through this process that several peripheral chiefdoms were, in fact, transformed into kingdoms or independent principalities: initially loyal dynasties became less so as they became genealogically and territorially more distant from the royal line.

31. See below, ch. 14, p. 420.
32. See UNESCO, *General History of Africa*, Vol. IV, ch. 9.
33. See M. Izard, 1970, Vol. I, pp. 150–70.
34. The interregnum between the announcement of the king's death and the appointment of his successor was bridged by the deceased king's eldest daughter, who bore the title *napoko*. Pabre was a *napoko*.
35. It was perhaps from Naaba Kumdumye's reign that the rulers descended from Naaba Wubri began to take the title *Mogho-Naaba* (*Naaba* of the Mossi country), as if to assert their sovereignty over the whole of the territory, despite Yadega's secession.

Other sons of the king were placed at Mane, at Konkistenga (a name derived from Naaba Konkise) and at Bussuma. His successors continued this policy, the aim of which seems to have been to create between them and Yatenga a protective screen made up of these northern marches.

At the end of the sixteenth century, Naaba Kuda moved the royal residence to Sapone, which shows that the state apparatus was still poorly developed. He also placed his sons in areas such as Laale, Zorgo and Riziam.

Almost nothing is known of Ouagadougou until the reign of a Fulbe usurper, Naaba Moatiba (1729–37)[36] in the eighteenth century. He is said to have been warlike, an essential requirement to have defended himself against the united Mossi princes. He is also said to have died by poisoning and his name, and those of his descendants, was erased from the official genealogy of the court.

The reign of Naaba Warga (1737–44) was short but full of new moves to strengthen the monarchy.[37] Wars followed one another, perhaps to bring back under Ouagadougou's control regional chiefdoms such as Yako and Mane and Tatenga (Riziam) – Tatenga had almost acquired its independence and its chief Naaba Manzi was even expansionist. But Naaba Warga was a great legislator. According to Yamba Tiendrebeogo, he established the ritual announcement of *zabyuya* at the ceremonial investiture of chiefs. On this occasion three mottoes were proclaimed: the first was an expression of thanks to the great electors; the second indicated the new chief's programme, often with a discreet warning to his adversaries; and the third illustrated the chief's character. Naaba Warga also organized the royal court, establishing two corps of servants, one Mossi and the other of prisoners, each comprising *sorondamba* (young servants) and *bilbalse* (adult servants). In addition, some duties were assigned to eunuchs. Naaba Warga also institutionalized the royal *pogsyure* (*napogsyure*) system – a system of capitalizing and distributing women – to enable royal servants to have children. The girls received or collected were married to servants, and the firstborn children of these marriages were earmarked either for royal service, in the case of boys, or for capitalization for the *napogsyure*, in the case of girls.

With regards to criminal law, Naaba Warga may have instituted the punishment of castration. Regarding customary law, he is said to have codified it to the state in which it existed in the precolonial period, although the details of these moves are obscure. In short, the end of the seventeenth century and the first half of the eighteenth saw the final establishment of

36. This name may be a corruption of the Muslim first name Modibo. This usurpation no doubt throws some light on the darkness of the seventeenth century, suggesting that it must have been very troubled.

37. See Y. Tiendrebeogo, 1964, pp. 25–32. It may be that this king was not the instigator of all the initiatives attributed to him by this author, as he is a more controversial figure than it appears from his book.

the Mossi political system both in Yatenga and in central and southern Mogho. After Naaba Zombre's long and peaceful reign (1744–*c*.84) and that of Naaba Kom (1784–*c*.91) who was the first to spread Muslim influence, the reign of Naaba Saaga (1791–6) was marked by internal conflicts which heralded the upheaval of the nineteenth century.[38]

The small kingdoms of central Mogho

The small kingdoms and chiefdoms of southern Mogho are little known despite the considerable contribution of information by Jonzo Kawada. Such is the case of the problematical Kingdom of Tankudgo (Tenkodogo).[39]

In the east and north-east, however, three kingdoms stand out: Bulsa, Busuma[40] and Tatenga, the last of which dominated the region in the seventeenth century and the second, Busuma, in the eighteenth. The principality of Bulsa probably dates back to the beginning of the sixteenth century with the installation of Naaba Namende, son and *kurita*[41] of Naaba Wubri.

The Kingdom of Busuma absorbed one by one the chiefdoms that were still scattered in this area at the beginning of the seventeenth century, namely Naamtenga (in the Luda region) at the beginning of the eighteenth century, then the chiefdom of Pisila, and finally Salmatenga (in the Kaya region). But Busuma's future was decided in the second half of the eighteenth century when the neighbouring state of Tatenga, founded by one of Naaba Kuda's sons, saw a formidable and ambitious warrior, Naaba Manzi, accede to the throne. Nonetheless, at the end of the seventeenth century, Busuma's Naaba Ruubo, with the help of Mégé and Salogo, succeeded in eliminating the terrible Manzi in battle. His son Wema had no choice but to take refuge in the farthest parts of the Riziam massif, which was later to lose more land to Yatenga during the nineteenth century.

Yatenga[42]

We have already described how Naaba Yadega went into exile from Ouagadougou. His successors held sway over a limited area gradually moving their royal residences northwards from Gursi and Lago, throughout the sixteenth century. The north, however, was occupied by the kingdom of Zandoma under the sway of Naaba Rawa's descendants. Naaba

---

38. L. Frobenius, 1911–13 and 1924.

39. See J. Kawada, 1979. Tankudgo means 'the old mountain', and so the current official spelling Tenkodogo does not come from *teng kudgo*, 'the old land', as has often been stated.

40. On Busuma and Bulsa and also Mane and Tema see G. Chéron, 1924; and M. Izard, 1970, Vol. II, pp. 230–52.

41. The king's *kurita* is his representative on earth after death; *kurita* means 'reigning death'. He is chosen from among the deceased king's sons unlikely to accede to the throne; once chosen, he is excluded from the throne; he is exiled far away from the court since it is forbidden for him to meet his father's successor.

42. See L. Tauxier, 1917; M. Izard, 1970, 1980, and 1981, Vol. II, pp. 275–381.

Lambwega's political and military activity consisted precisely in dismantling Naaba Rawa's inheritance, while in the east he incorporated the former Kurumba chieftaincies of Lurum.[43]

In the late seventeenth and early eighteenth centuries, Naaba Lambwega's descendants tried to saturate the considerably enlarged area of the kingdom, by establishing Mossi chieftaincies there reserved for princes, by settling Lurum, and by containing the Macina and Jelgoji Fulbe, but also by maintaining the internal territorial *status quo* in Mogho.[44] Thus about the middle of the eighteenth century, a series of clashes with Yako[45] began which were to last until the beginning of the nineteenth century over control of the small chiefdoms of Busu-Darigma and Nyesga. Naaba Nabasere died engaged in this task.

Naaba Kango

On the death of his son Naaba Piiyo (1754), who was probably responsible for the introduction of the first guns into Yatenga, his younger brother Naaba Kango came to the throne. No sooner had he been appointed than he was faced with violent opposition from princes led by Naaba Wobgo and he was obliged to abdicate and go into exile with a handful of trusty followers. He reached Kong and then moved on to Segu where he won the support of the Kulibali to regain his throne. In 1757, he returned to Yatenga at the head of an army of mercenaries comprising Bambara riflemen and Bwaba and Samo archers. But after his stay in places famous for their economic importance and their political pluralism, it was no longer the same prince who was returning to his country. His policy strikingly testified to this. After beating Naaba Wobogo, who went into exile, Naaba Kango began his reign with a spectacular gesture: he refused to make the *ringu* (enthronement) journey, which alone gave the ruler of Yatenga – who on appointment was only a *naaba* (chief) – the rank of *rima* (king).[46] This refusal to have his power legitimized marked a decisive break with the past.

He also founded the capital at Waiguyo (Ouahigouya), in about 1780, not far from the former royal seat at Biisigi. It was a new town around a vast palace built in the Mali style and bringing together his old comrades in exile. Until then, royal seats had been ordinary villages. This was the first time the inhabitants of a capital had consisted exclusively of

43. The Kurumba (Fulse in More) occupied a vast area from northern Gulma to Yatenga; they are said to have established the 'kingdom' of Lurum which covered part of present-day Jelgoji (Jibo region). The king living at Mengao, bore the title of *Ayo* or *Lurum'ayo* or *Lurun'yo*.

44. Thus the *Naaba* of Zitenga (capital: Tikare) in the south-east of Yatenga was considered a *kombere* of Yatenga; a *kombere* (pl. *kombemba*) was a regional chief with broad autonomy marked notably by the right to appoint local chiefs; practically, Zitenga was independent of Yatenga.

45. D. Nacanabo, 1982.

46. *Rima* and *ringu* have as shared radical the verb *ri*, meaning 'to absorb or eat food that is not chewed'.

representatives of the state apparatus, the world of politics, people of the royal household, either prisoners or free. Here again, he was demonstrating a clear determination to break with custom and organize sovereignly a power that he owed to no one but himself, making it more centralized by strengthening the corps of royal servants.[47] The name of the new capital, Waiguyo, is itself indicative of a whole programme: 'come and bow down and make your submission'. This demand was addressed first and foremost to all members of the royal lineage, royal *nakombse* (princes of the blood) who had until then been dominant, who had supported the usurper Wobogo and who now had to be brought down through the action of the royal staff. This marked a sharp turning-point in the political relations of force within the Mossi monarchy. But, up to the time of colonization, the princes refused to acknowledge defeat and the balance of power oscillated dangerously between them and the authority of the palace. The latter was reorganized. The war-chief of Ula was made the first army commander and his office was brought into the *cursus honorum* of the court, so that it stopped being hereditary and became available as a reward for the personal merits of valorous warriors.

To restore order, which had been seriously disturbed during the years of instability, Naaba Kango put down banditry mercilessly. Thieves and murderers were burnt alive; the same fate befell the Bambara mercenaries from Segu who had been used against Yako and then been accused of having become turbulent. The indiscipline of chiefs was severely punished, as also sometimes was their munificence – this being interpreted in high places as a presumptuous way of competing with the king's lifestyle.

Did the massacre of the Bambara mercenaries precipitate an expedition by Segu against Yatenga? There is no reference to such an expedition in Mossi tradition, whereas there is in Bambara traditions.[48] In any event, Naaba Kango, who intended to give royal prisoners a special place in the system of government, needed many more of them. Some were taken from among prisoners-of-war; but most were captured during raids against Dogon villages in the Gondo plain and the Kurumba villages in the east and north-east.

Naaba Kango's war against Yako was a politico-military success but it had no follow-up; hostilities resumed at the beginning of the nineteenth century.

When Naaba Kango died in 1787, he was buried in his capital and not in the royal cemetery. His death must have come as a relief to many, for he ruled without pity. The princes' resentment was so great that they had the only daughter of the dead king stifled to death. But the court aristocracy which had remained loyal were able to have one of his life-long companions, Naaba Saagha (1797–1803), nominated to succeed him.

47. See M. Izard, 1975.
48. See M. Izard, 1970, Vol. II, pp. 320–8.

The socio-political structures of Mogho

By the Mossi kingdoms is meant not states comprising a homogenous society – the Mossi ethnic group – but composite socio-political formations resulting from the conquest, by warriors called Mossi, of the White Volta basin. And this conquest must not be seen crudely and romantically as wave after wave of horsemen sweeping down. The process of intermarriage[49] and infiltration by slow settlement carried out by Mossi peasants, which continues down to the present day, was certainly much more decisive. But each time that an area was taken over, it was organized on the Mossi socio-political model. Strictly speaking, the Mossi were the holders of political power in the Mossi kingdoms; they recognized each other as being all agnatic descendants of a common ancestor, Naaba Wedraogo. In the case of Yatenga, at the end of the nineteenth century the population comprised three distinct societies: Mossi society, Silmiga (Fulbe) society, and Silmi–Mossi society. The first alone was made up the population of the kingdom, in that it was subject to the authority of the king, the *Yatenga-Naaba*. The Fulbe or Silmiise had, as it were, the status of guests, on the basis of settlement contracts under which a broad strip of territory in the northern part of the country was reserved for them. The Fulbe had been settled in Yatenga since the seventeenth century and had established permanent villages there from which the seasonal transhumance of cattle was organized. In these permanent settlements lived the *rimaibe* (prisoners tied to working the land). It is perhaps misleading to speak of Silmi–Mossi society, but these sedentary small stockbreeders, quite numerous in the south-east of Yatenga, certainly fall into a separate category. Their compound name, Silmi–Mossi, is a reminder that they were the offspring of mixed marriages (which anyway were forbidden) between Fulbe (Silmiise) men and Mossi women. Arriving in the eighteenth century from Tema, and settling in hamlets on the fringes of Mossi village lands, they did not come under Mossi authority, and passed under the somewhat distant protection of the Fulbe politico-religious centre at Todiam in the east of the kingdom.

But what of Mossi society itself? Its internal cleavages were linked to the distinction made by the Mossi between the *naaba* (chief), *naabiise*, sing. *nabiiga* (chiefs' sons) and the *nakombse*, sing. *nakombga* (sons or descendants of sons of princes who had not become chiefs). This distinction rested on one of the rules of eligibility for a chieftaincy – that only chiefs' sons could become chiefs. Because of this, a *nakombga* had no hope of holding *naam* (power). Thus, strictly speaking, except for the tiny minority of chiefs and sons of chiefs, all other Mossi who claimed to be descendants of Wedraogo could be regarded as *nakombse*. This led to a narrow definition of the status of *nakombga* which distinguished between this class and that of the *talse* (commoners). Thus in Yatenga, only the agnatic descendants of the twelfth

49. It might be recalled that the first king of Ouagadougou, Wubri, was himself the fruit of a marriage between a Mossi prince and an indigenous girl.

PLATE 12.2 *Mossi statuette commemorating a female ancestor, made of wood with a natural patina. Height: 47 cm*

Yatenga-Naaba are *nakombse*, all other Mossi – except for the chiefs and sons of chiefs – being regarded as *talse*. The royal *nakombse* (the royal lineage) were themselves divided into five branches, each normally consisting of one generation of princes. The royal lineage was apparently very early seen as having to be of constant generational depth (five generations), the appearance of a new generation entailing the exclusion of the oldest generation from the royal lineage and its transfer to the *talse* group. This system was linked to the need for every new king to provide his sons with village chieftaincies, when there was only a limited number of villages; thus old local dynasties in the villages were regularly replaced by new ones.

To the extent that they held village chieftaincies, the *nakombse* constituted a category of power-holders below the chiefs. There were two others: the *tasobnamba* (war-chiefs) and the king's household staff. The war-chiefs were appointed from the oldest genealogical stocks of *nakombse*, the dynastic descent groups founded before the formation of Yatenga, and from the first two dynastic generations of Yatenga. The war-chiefs, who did not necessarily have any military duties, were thus local notables of ancient stock, whereas the local power of the *nakombse* was always of recent origin. During the reign of Naaba Kango, royal servants, of free or prisoner origin, were appointed to posts as local chiefs on an *ad hominem* basis. This represented a departure from the traditional idea of incompatibility between authority and service posts and stemmed from the central government's intention to create a Mossi colonization front towards Fulbe country to the east. In the case of court offices, the structure that prevailed on top of the political hierarchy around the king was the same as that around each local chief. Three dignitaries assisted the chief: the *Togo-Naaba*, the chief's spokesman who was responsible for ritual ceremonies; the *Balum-Naaba*, who looked after supply problems and domestic affairs; and the *Weranga-Naaba*, who looked after the horses. These were the chief's *nesomba* (honest men). These posts were closed to non-Mossi as well as the *nakombse* and to members of castes such as blacksmiths.

The royal court had the same core of dignitaries, but with a fourth as well – the *Bin-Naaba* or *Rasam-Naaba*, chief of the royal prisoners. Each headed a large group of servants.[50] Thus members of the royal lineage too deeply involved in the struggle for the throne could not serve the king. Lastly, the institutional holders of power were actually effectively divided into two sub-groups with opposing interests: those – the war-chiefs and royal servants – on whom the king relied to govern; and those – the *nakombse* – against whom he governed. This division went deep among the Mossi as these men of lowly origin who held the great offices of state were

50. At the court of the king of Ouagadougou, around the *Mogho-Naaba*, were the *Widi-Naaba*, the political spokesman, the *Gounga-Naaba*, with military responsibilities, the *Larhle-Naaba*, who combined military and ritual functions, the *Balum-Naaba*, and the *Kamsaogo-Naaba*, an eunuch responsible for the harem. There was also the *Tasoba*, the war-chief.

at the same time the great electors who chose a new *Mogho-Naaba* and sometimes held territorial commands. Internal conflicts have always punctuated the history of all the Mossi kingdoms. They were almost always about the transmission of power over which the rival interests of the nobles and the political experience of the king's ministers – men of lowly extraction but with the power to select the best among those eligible – clashed. Generally, the main rivalry was between the ruling monarch's younger brothers and his sons.

In contrast to the world of government, to which the royal prisoners belonged, lay the world of the land. The people or sons of the land were, in theory, the descendants of the indigenous peoples, blacksmiths excepted. Deprived of all political power, they were responsible for the earth rituals which concerned both the fertility of the soil and the harvests, law and order and the perpetuation of the local group. Thus the figure of the *naaba* (chief) was contrasted with that of the *tengsoba* (earth-priest), the holder of sacred power. This dualism was reflected cosmogenically in the divine world through Naaba Wende, the King-God, and Napaga Tenga, the Queen-Land, although the King-God Wende had no altar and no ritual cult.

But the definition of the category of people of the land changed substantially down the centuries because the true Mossi became absorbed into the category of indigenes and used this status to become earth-priests. About one-third of Yatenga's earth-priests are of Mossi origin although some Mossi became blacksmiths and Yarse.

Alongside the earth-priest there was also the *bugo* (fertility priest), pl. *buguba*, with his own *tiido* (altar). This office, which was even open to *nakombse* and also to blacksmiths, seems to have been of Dogon origin.

The political world and the world of the land were integrated into a unitary system with the king as its hub through the medium of great yearly rituals involving the monarch and the power-holders, the earth-priests and the fertility priests. The Yatenga Mossi (like the Kurumba) had an annual solar calendar divided into lunar months, the discrepancy between the lunar year and the solar year being compensated for by an intercalary month every three years. After the new year *filiiga* (thanksgiving festival) came the ceremonies of *napusum* (greeting the king) at which, in three separate ceremonies, the royal servants, the war-chiefs and the *nakombse* paid homage to the king and gave him presents. As the new year fell approximately at the winter solstice, the period from the second to the sixth month was taken up with a great ceremonial cycle called *bega* which involved the king and all the dignitaries of the land in sacrifices intended to ask for a good harvest. The feasts of the *bega* ended at the beginning of the rainy season. Ceremonial activity was resumed during the harvest season, with two festivals of first fruits, one for the war-chiefs and the other for the fertility priests.

This highly complex political-cum-religious system gave cohesion to state society which was made up of groups of varied origin, the biggest of which had usually retained several cultural features from their pre-state past, starting with their own socio-political stratification. Thus the division of society as a whole into four large functional groups – power-holders, people of the land, blacksmiths and craftsmen, and traders – turns up with certain differences among the Kurumba or Fulse. Indeed, it was probably from the Kurumba that the Mossi of Yatenga borrowed their ideas about blacksmiths who, here, unlike in the rest of Mogho, form an endogamous group.

Considering society as a whole, all the ethnic groups were divided in two ways: into descent groups and local groups.

In this composite society, patrilineal and patrilocal, the Mossi term *budu* denotes any descent group, from the broadest and the oldest to the narrowest, that operates as the exogamous reference unit. It is this latter sense that is generally understood. Society was thus made up of a certain number of *budu* – such as the group of royal *nakombse*. With a history of its own, distinguished by the name of a founder and a place of foundation, a *budu* defined its individuality by the existence of a *bud-kasma* (head), a *kiims'rogo* (ancestral shrine) and a heartland where the *bud-kasma* lived and the *kiims'rogo* was, and also by having (usually not in exclusivity) one or more *sonda* (collective names or mottoes), sing. *sondre*, a key word which was used as a patronymic.

The patrilineage only existed territorially at its first level of segmentation, the *saka* (section). The section was divided in turn into *yiiya* (households), sing. *yiiri*; production and consumption units themselves being divided into *zakse* (smaller units), sing. *zaka*. *Zakse* have nowadays become the economically meaningful family units. Work on the common fields of the household was favoured to the benefit of the *yiir-kasma* (head the *yiiri*). The reserves of the head of the family were redistributed as a last resort when the stores of heads of compounds had been exhausted.

The sections belonging to one lineage were generally scattered, and hence came under several village units. In other words, a Mossi village[51] contained parts of several lineages, whilst a lineage was likewise dispersed over several villages, the largest local lineage unit being the section.

The Gulma and the Borgu

For a long time the Gulma (or Gurma) bank of the Niger – the right bank downstream from the Bend – was little known from the historical viewpoint. This, however, has changed recently thanks to research carried out in the

51. There has been much discussion recently about the appositeness of the term 'village' to denote the biggest unit of habitat among the Mossi. Even though the pairing of sections does not form village 'communities' as in West Volta, nevertheless they still constitute meaningful entities in terms of the logic of economic and social relationships, if only because of the intersection of administrative units incorporated in a local chief, and units of land control represented by an earth-priest.

north of Gulma territory by the Voltaic historian, Georges Madiega, so that it is now possible to give on the Gulma information still incomplete but scientifically sound at least.

The Dogon (Kumbetieba in the Gulma language) constitute one of the oldest populations of North Gulma. After them came the group today called the Tindamba (people of the earth)[52] who were originally from the region known today as Moaga but would belong to a pre-Moaga population group, and the Woba from the south. North Gulma was also peopled by the Kurumba and it is possible that the group name, Koarima – as the Gulmanceba from the south called those from the north – is a modification of the term Kurumba. In south Gulma, for which our information is still very limited, one finds, amongst the former inhabitants, some Tindamba and Woba. The latter certainly occupied a huge area before being over-whelmed and partially assimilated by the Gulmanceba and other peoples who set up states there. Thus, Woba from Gulma and Waba from Borgu (north Benin today) would form one and the same group.

On this substructure of early populations a foreign power superimposed itself, namely the Bemba or Buricimba, sing. Buricima, who later gave rise to the Gulmanceba states. We do not yet possess a satisfactory chronological framework for early Gulmance history, but Georges Madiega's two major hypotheses are first that the ancestors of the Mamprusi passed through Gulma before the arrival of the Buricimba, and second that the first Gulmance dynasties were contemporary with the first Mossi dynasties. This would suggest that the beginning of Gulma's history as a state was probably during the fifteenth century or the end of the fourteenth at the earliest. The figure of a historical-mythical ancestor called Jaba is associated with the birth of the Gulmance states. That he was a guerrilla leader like Naaba Wedraogo in Mossi history, seems unlikely; and the powers attributed to him have more to do with magic than with generalship. What seems certain is that the links suggested by the Mossi between Na Bawa's descendants and Jaba's (known by the Mossi as Jaba Lompo, though Jaba and Lompo were probably two separate individuals, Lompo being Jaba's son) are nothing but late reconstructions thought up at the court of the *Mogho-Naaba* to justify the virtual amalgamation of Gulmance power and Mossi power during the colonial period. Alternatively the converse may be the case – that the colonial administrative organization of the old chieftaincies or states, which gave the *Mogho-Naaba* a kind of absolute pre-eminence, may have led some people to give it a historical basis. All the evidence suggests that, from the point of view of dynasty origins, the Mossi and Gulmanceba hegemonies must be treated separately.

Where the Buricimba came from is questionable. As in many other areas that were organized as states in central West Africa, we find references in Gulma to the effect that the conquerors came from Borno; but in fact there

52. Cf. Y. G. Madiega, 1982.

is at present no way of knowing which warlike migrations gave rise to the Gulmance empire. At least we know that the earliest Gulmance political centre was Lompotangu or Sangbantangu, south-east of Nungu (Fada N'Gourma). From Lompotangu the Buricimba moved to Kujuabongu, south of Pama. The ruins that mark this second stage of Buricima penetration suggest the remains of an old capital, that of the earliest Gulmance political structure; and this must have been the focal point from which the conquerors set out and gave rise to the present-day dynasties. It is noteworthy that the Buricima were not at the time the only founders of kingdoms in this area. The Jakpangu dynasty is of Berba origin, and the Gobnangu dynasty of Hausa origin. There are also dynasties whose founders came from Yanga, an interface between the Mossi and the Gulmance, whose present-day chiefs can be connected with the descendants of Naaba Wedraogo. The Gulmance dynasties of Yanga comprise the Boarigu, Komin–Yanga, Sudugo, Kamseongo, Dogtenga and Yutenga.

Buricimba expansion continued throughout the sixteenth and seventeenth centuries, and the apogee of Gulmance power can be put at about the middle of the eighteenth century. At that time the Gulmanceba held sway over an enormous (though no doubt sparsely populated) territory, bounded to the south by the Mamprusi kingdom and Borgu, to the east by Torodi and the last vestiges of the Songhay empire, to the north by the Sahel areas inhabited by Kurumba, Songhay and Fulbe, and to the west by the Mossi chiefdoms of Tuguri, Bulsa, Kupela and Tankudgo. What were to become the Fulbe emirates of Liptako (the Dori area) and Yaga (the Seba area) were then under Gulmance rule, and it was not until the early 1800s that the Fulbe drove the Gulmanceba southwards.

In the middle of the eighteenth century two large kingdoms, Bilanga and Kuala, shared most of the territory of north Gulma between them, plus three fairly new minor states, Piala, Bongandini and Con. From the village of We, north-east of Nungu, which the Buricimba reached in about the mid-1500s, the Gulmance empire expanded northwards at a great rate. The result was a sparse scattering of regional and local chiefdoms, which shrewd chiefs were later to set about federating into kingdoms.

While, thanks to Georges Madiega, we now understand the history of north Gulma, that of central and southern Gulma remains obscure. It is, therefore, all the harder to take an overall view of the history of Gulma because in the south we have eleven kingdoms, one of which, Nungu, is especially important because of the status of its king, the Nunbado (chief of Nungu).[53] Nungu was founded by Yendabri, a descendant of Jaba's, in the mid-1700s. That was the time when southern Gulma was over-run by the Tyokosi, Mande mercenaries belonging to the Wattara group (who turn up at Kong and Bobo-Dioulasso). Originally in the service of the Mamprusi kings, the Tyokosi were headed by a chief from Gonja. They

53. *Bado* is the equivalent of the More *naaba*.

351

first settled in what is now northern Togo, then launched expeditions against the Gulmanceba kingdoms while continuing to hire themselves out as mercenaries. Thus the chief of Pama sought the support of the Tyokosi against the chief of Kujuabongu. Yendabri, ruler of Nungu, soon took on the leadership of a coalition of kingdoms and set about driving the Tyokosi out of Gulma. The kings of Pama, Macakoali, Boarigu and Botu rallied around Yendabri, as did the Mossi rulers of Bulsa, Kupela and Tankudgo. Hard-pressed by their enemies, the Tyokosi withdrew to their capital, Sansane-Mango, to which the allies laid siege.[54] It is questionable whether the victorious Yendabri then took advantage of his success to strengthen his authority over the league he had formed. What is certain is that, in the eighteenth century, the Nunbado became a sort of overlord of part of Gulma, his authority outside the borders of his own kingdom also being more spiritual than political. 'The Nunbado', writes Georges Madiega, 'exerted direct authority over Nungo ... He also exerted a more remote control over the *diema* (regional kingdoms or chiefdoms) of the *batieba* (regional rulers or chiefs) who were not of Lompo descent. The dynasties that were of Lompo descent regarded him simply as the *nikpelo* (eldest member) of the lineage'. In the document quoted, Lompo is seen as Jaba's son.[55] Thus the Nunbado gradually developed into the chief sovereign of Gulma and, in the meantime, his royal seat became the main town of the land, largely because of the economic role of the Hausa traders there. (Their name for Nungu was Rojo or Fada N'Gourma.) It is still difficult today to interpret the relationship the Nunbado had with the Gulmanceba rulers. There does not seem to have been a Gulmance confederation, and the Nunbado's real authority was no doubt just as territorially limited as that of the other kinds, several of whom indeed were more powerful than he. But the Nunbado acquired exceptional moral and ritual prestige in that he became – belatedly – regarded as the direct heir of Lompo and hence of his 'father' Jaba. Hausa trade did the rest: Nungu became an important centre for east–west caravan traffic.

Borgu[56] extends to the south-east of Gulma. Its history, somewhat confused, comprises several state-type entities, the earliest having apparently been Busa, from which the Wasangari warriors spread. Here again, the chiefs claim that the royal dynasties originated in Borno. The Wasangari military aristocracy imposed its rule over long-established peoples, some of them pre-Gulmance, who in the sixteenth and seventeenth centuries absorbed Mande groups (Busa is a south-Mande language) trading between what is northern Ghana and Hausaland. Busa reached its apogee in the sixteenth century, then declined. The other kingdoms, such as Nikki, are

54. Cf. R. Cornevin, 1964 and D. Rey-Hulman, 1975. We also follow Y. G. Madiega's account (1978).

55. See above, p. 350: Jaba Lompo, the single figure of (no doubt late) Mossi traditions, is replaced in Gulmance traditions by two persons, Jaba and his son Lompo.

56. Cf. M. Izard, 1975.

more or less direct offshoots from Busa. In the eighteenth century Nikki was at war with the Kingdom of Nupe. Nikki gave rise to the little states of Kaiama, Paraku, Kuande and Kandi. The Borgu states, incidentally, are known as the Bariba kingdoms, after one of the main indigenous peoples of the area.

The peoples with non-centralized authority

These peoples are described in this way for lack of a better term.[57] They were settled in the upper Volta basins and had existed from a very early date, either there or elsewhere.[58] Although, unlike the centralized societies, these peoples did not dominate the political stage or the flow of events, their contribution must not be overlooked – particularly as they form the underlying human population onto which external contributions were biologically grafted. The conquering peoples rarely arrived in all-engulfing waves, annihilating all before them. The Mossi, for example, are the product of a mixing of various ethnic groups brought together by a group of chieftaincies, under the authority of an apparently absolute king but governed by strict custom. In this process of expansion, the steady advance of Mossi peasants was unquestionably more important than the establishment of contingents of horsemen. The slow penetration of the pre-existing human fabric was a phenomenon with a double meaning, thanks to intermarriage and cultural and economic exchanges.

The biological contributions are so important that Dim Delobsom noted that the very term Moaga (pl. Mossi) means mixed.[59] We cannot insist too strongly in this connection on the role of the Nioniosse mentioned by several authors[60] as existing at a very early date. There has been so much biological mixing that the people of Yatenga treat the Mossi of central Mogho as Gurunsi; while in Ouagadougou this term is used solely for the Mossi of Koudougou who are neighbours of the Gurunsi. Nor have the people of Yatenga themselves been untouched by contributions from the Mande peoples of the Niger Bend, who had a decisive military impact on the history of Yatenga with Naaba Kango's recourse to troops from Segu. These same Mande peoples, however, had long been mixed with the population through cohabitation by their traders, the professional and even biological ancestors of the important Yarse group.[61] It is this biological

57. The expressions 'stateless societies' or 'acephalous societies' must be rejected. But even the term 'people with non-centralized authority' can be criticized because it is negative, and because it refers only to political power. Moreover, a people of this type can in turn become centralized (the Bambara) and then cease to be so.

58. UNESCO, *General History of Africa*, Vol. IV, ch. 9.

59. See A. D. Delobsom, 1929. It is true that the author adds that this rather unfavourable judgement emanated from nobles describing commoners; but tradition (see Yamba Tien-drebeogo) reports that the mother of Wubri, the first king of Ouagadougou, was herself an indigenous woman.

60. ibid.; R. Pageard, 1969.

61. See below in this chapter: p. 361.

mixing that probably lies behind the *rakire* (joking relationship) between the Mossi and the Samo (Sana). On the cultural and economic levels, here as elsewhere – such as in the Great Lakes region – the contribution of the indigenous peoples has often been played down or even concealed. We have seen how, in the area of political and religious organization, the Dogon (particularly the earth-priest) and the Kurumba contributed to the system of dynastic rule in Yatenga. If only through the management of farming rituals and through the ministry of earth-priests, who were usually from the indigenous peoples, they continued to have a strong influence on the daily life of every single peasant. But at the highest political level, the descendant of the chief of the indigenes, who had become the Ouagadougou Naaba,[62] had an important role to play in the enthronement of the *Mogho-Naaba*.

While slavery developed during this period – usually at the expense of the indigenous peoples, particularly the Gurunsi and the Fulse[63] – it escalated above all with the rise of the slave trade on the Guinea coast and its repercussions as far as the Asante empire and its tributary countries to the north.

Moreover, the indigenous peoples, whether of Mande or Voltaic culture, were open to exchanges but refused to accept domination – a strategy that was highly successful until the colonial period. Naaba Kumdumye died on an early expedition to Boromo when he was probably trying to bring under Mossi control the area between the Red and Black Voltas. This great design failed and the Red Volta, except in a few restricted areas, became the natural western border of Mogho.

Despite the absence of a centralized state, the Gurunsi[64] and the Bwaba who inhabit this region developed a marked individual personality. The Gurunsi, whose main centres were Po, Leo, Sapouy and Rep, spread into present-day Ghana. They lived withdrawn into family groups in remarkably designed huts and were fiercely opposed to any form of complex political hierarchy. Often the earth-priest or masquerade societies constituted a link between families. In the east, however, there did exist a more organized structure under a canton chief with a court, and a religious adviser responsible for the cult of his *kwara* (magical symbol).

The Bwaba[65] appear to have emerged as a specific entity between the tenth and fifteenth centuries. They do not recognize any political authority above the village level. The religion of *Do* also forms a bond between the initiated in one village and those in neighbouring villages.

---

62. Ouagadougou (Wogodogo) is, in the narrow sense, the district where the indigenous chief lives.

63. Fulse or Kurumba; see above, p. 343.

64. In fact there is no people calling itself Gurunsi (sing. *gurunga* in More); but Nunuma, Lela, Sisala, Kô, Kasena, etc.

65. See J. Capron, 1973. The Bwaba are related culturally but not linguistically to the Bobo. See A. Le Moal, 1976.

Near Yatenga were the northern Samo[66] whose concentrated settlements are marked by enormous grain stores. Political organization consisted of reasonably stable confederations of dozens of villages around a few political centres corresponding to the *kafu* (Mande canton). The San system rested on both clan alliances – between the Zerbo chiefs and the blacksmiths, for example – and territorial coalitions. Before coming to the throne, Naaba Kumdumye and other princes, including Naaba Yadega, had made war against the Sana. Later, Naaba Kango attempted to draw north-eastern San country into the bosom of Yatenga but failed. The Sana, hardened warriors and peasants fiercely attached to their freedom, again resisted Yatenga pressures as they had earlier – in the time of Naaba Yadega and during the reign of Naaba Lambwega, in particular – and as they were to do again throughout the nineteenth century. During this last period, moreover, their country was to act as a fallback zone for the Yatenga princes who gathered mercenaries there to make or unmake the kings in Waiguyo. As for the Bisa, who were related to the Sana and separated from them after a clan dispute, they were based in south-eastern Mogho. They, too, would put up remarkable resistance despite mutual cultural exchanges and a tribute in captives at the end of the 1700s. But they seem to have been expanding until the colonial period.

The south-west of present-day Burkina Faso was almost uninhabited although the Bwaba went hunting as far as the River Buguriba. In about 1730, the Kulango expanded into the same area where, a decade later, the Pwa (Puguli) settled with the permission of the Bwaba. Then, within fifty years, followed the Dorobe and Gan, who settled initially at Nako, the first Dyan, Lobi and Wiile and, finally, the Birifor who occupied the area of Batie abandoned by the Lobi.

Kong and Gwiriko
Since the time of the Sudanese empires from the tenth to the fifteenth centuries, Juula traders, called Wangara, had been travelling the routes to the forest where gold and kola (whence the name Worodugu) were to be found. But, from the sixteenth century, a new factor arose along the Gulf of Guinea: the trade in slaves and fire-arms. This single event is enough to explain why groups of Juula – now traders, now soldiers, now Muslim missionaries – went further and further south into the savannah areas where the goods most demanded by the new dispensation were increasingly traded. It was Juula who helped to establish the great trading centre of Begho. The Begho route was soon linked to the one crossing present-day Côte d'Ivoire from Assinie to Bobo and Bamako through Yakasso. While the Diomande settled in the centre-west, the Wattara turned Boron and Mankono into great trading centres. At the end of the sixteenth century,

66. The term Samo comes from the Mande name Samogo. But this people calls itself Sanã (sing. San).

the Gonja kingdom came into being and, at the end of the seventeenth century, after the destruction of Begho, Juula refugees fell back into the Bron (Abron) kingdom and founded Bonduku.

A number of important circumstances gave a sharp push to the activities of the Juula from the seventeenth century onwards. First there was the fall of the Empire of Gao and, second, the creation of the Asante empire which constituted a major centre for the supply of gold, arms, salt and manufactured goods. Third, there were the Voltaic savannah societies, which were quite densely populated compared to neighbouring societies, most of which had no centralized political authority, and which therefore could supply slaves, and also the cattle and gold that the coastal areas wanted. It is thus easy to understand why the Dagomba should have organized the Kulango[67] kingdom of Buna in Lorhon country on the same model as their own. It was a highly centralized kingdom based on military districts administered by princes. They exploited the gold deposits of Lobi – possibly in competition with the Bron kingdom – which gave rise to bloody clashes during the seventeenth and eighteenth centuries.

After subduing the southern Kulango, the Bron of the Akan group disputed with Buna control of the northern route along the River Comoe. It was the consolidation of their power by two great rulers, Tan Date (in the seventeenth century) and Kousounou (in the early eighteenth century) that attracted the Juula to Bonduku. But the Baule soon decided to close the Bandama river to trade with the north. The Juula, who had been driven westwards, wanted to open up the Comoe river route down to Bassam so as to use this round-about way to reach the forts in Nzima and Fanteland.

It was in this overall context that a new diaspora of settlements that were at once commercial, political, military and religious came into being on the initiative of the Juula. In the middle of the eighteenth century, armed bands that had come down from Segu – the Diarrasouba – brushed the Senufo aside and set up a Mande (Nafana) kingdom at Odienne.

The Senufo belong to the Voltaic group of language-speakers. They were settled in clans around Korogho, Seguela, Odienne and Kong, and the fall of Mali seems to have opened up to them possibilities of territorial expansion northwards as far as Sikasso and Bougouni where, however, they adopted the Bambara language and southwards into the region of Bouaké where they would be absorbed into the Baule block. In the east they gave rise to isolated groups, such as the Nafana who became gold-diggers at Begho, before falling under Bron control. As for the Pallaka, they would fall under the domination of Kong. The Senufo were, above all, excellent peasants who worked the land around their compact villages with great efficiency. They were egalitarian and independent-minded and the fact that they only had one large-scale social institution – the Poron, which had a religious character – also helped to regulate the social hierarchy. They also

67. Kulango: 'Those who do not fear death'.

PLATE 12.3   *General view of Kong*

had consummate artists who, since an early date, had been producing some of the masterpieces of the Negro-African symbolist style. It was only in about the nineteenth century that the Senufo set themselves to building up a few centralized kingdoms – with the Traore dynasty of Kenedugu (Sikasso) for example – perhaps imitating the Mande in this respect.

At the beginning of the eighteenth century the Mande added the famous centre of Kong to the chain of Juula settlements. This region appears to have been occupied, if not organized, at an early date by the Tiefo, as is suggested by the string of Tiefo villages that still run from Noumoudara to Kong. It was there that Keita and Kulibali Mande, who had later become Wattara, subdued the indigenes. One of them, Sekou Wattara, eliminated the other Juula groups at the beginning of the eighteenth century, and reigned at Nafana and Kong thanks to a powerful army in which Senufo served under Juula officers. This military force enabled it to conquer western Upper Volta as far as Dafina (the Black Volta bend). Subsequently, the Kong forces subdued Turka country and Folona, laid waste the Sikasso region and part of Minianka and Macina, and even got as far as Sofara, opposite Jenne on the River Bani. We have seen how this expedition was finally driven back by Biton Kulibali. After Sekou Wattara's death in 1740 the empire was profoundly disrupted – because of its enormous size, the diversity of its peoples and its lack of a firmly established system of government. Finally, there was a split: the caste of non-Muslim Joola and Senufo warriors, the Sohondji, seceded from the Salama Juula, who were traders and Muslims. Kong had indeed become a great centre of Islamic learning. But its attempt to control Jenne clearly shows that the Wattara's grand design was above all economic: to control the trade routes linking the forest to the Niger Bend over the greatest possible distance. After the failure of this ambitious project, the Juula groups fell back on more limited undertakings. One of the boldest was the creation of the Kingdom of Gwiriko.[68] There, around Sya (Bobo-Dioulasso),[69] Famaghan Wattara founded a replica of the Kingdom of Kong in an area around the watershed of the River Banifin (a tributary of the Niger), the Comoe and the Black Volta. As the Comoe and the Black Volta cross gold places along their middle and lower reaches and the Comoe flows through Beni towards the Jenne region, the strategic character of Famaghan Wattara's decision, and his refusal to pay allegiance to his young nephews, Sekou Wattara's sons, in Kong, is clear. He seized more or less completely, and more or less permanently, Tiefo, Dafin and Bwamu (the country of the Bwaba). In Bobo, he subdued and allied with the Bobo-Juula who had arrived from Jenne after the Bobo-Fing in about the eleventh century. His successors, Kere Massa Wattara (1742–9) and Magan Oule Wattara (1749–1809), only

68. Gwiriko means 'at the end of the long stage' in Juula.

69. See N. Levtzion, 1971; E. Bernus, 1960; and D. Traoré, 1937. On the *Gonja Chronicle*, which forms the basis of a reliable chronology for the events reported in this paragraph, see J. Goody, 1967a; and N. Levtzion, 1971b.

managed to contain the revolts by peoples reduced to Juula domination by repeated repression (as in 1754 against the large Bwa town of San). This domination was above all economic, even when it was made to appear as proselytism.

Economic life from the Niger to the basin of the Voltas

It is also to the middle of the eighteenth century, with the arrival of the Bobo-Juula, that J. B. Kietegha dates the period of high gold production from the Black Volta. The newcomers practically monopolized the exploitation of the gold of Pura and introduced technological improvements in its extraction. Kietegha hypothesizes, however, that the exploiters of the earlier period (from the fifteenth to the mid-eighteenth century) were already Mande-Juula, perceived by the Gurunsi of Pura as Mossi.[70]

Traders and trade routes were the busiest in the western and northern half of the area between the River Niger and the basin of the Voltas. But during the seventeenth and eighteenth centuries – even in the Mossi kingdoms and among the people with non-centralized authority, such as the Gurunsi, above the subsistence-economy base – there gradually came into being a trading network in exotic goods, which came to involve more and more professional traders.

Mossi country is an area of near monoculture in millet on exhausted soils with irregular rainfall. In each decade there were on average two bad and two very bad years. Shortages, even famines, occurred not uncommonly in Yatenga – during the reign of Naaba Zana at the end of the seventeenth and beginning of the eighteenth century and in the 1830s for example.[71] In addition to millet, the staple food, crops included maize (an off-season crop), groundnuts, cowpeas, beans, sesame and some potherbs. Cotton, the main plant used in crafts, seems to have been grown for a long time. The Muslim Yarse have been associated with weaving since the beginning of Mossi history, and strips of cotton cloth formed their cargo goods in the north-south caravan trade, of which they were the main operators. The Marase (Songhay), who specialized in dyeing, used indigo. Many wild plants were gathered, both potherbs and substitute foods used in times of shortage, the main ones being *nere*, whose fruit had many uses, and the shea nut, from which cooking oil was made.

In Lurum's pre-Mossi era (up to the fifteenth and sixteenth centuries) the Kurumba had among them Marase who engaged in the Saharan salt trade. The formation of the northern Mossi states, including Yatenga, had a twofold effect on the caravan trade: first, the Marase were supplanted by the Yarse and, second, the Yarse, in addition to the Saharan salt trade, took up trade in kola nuts, which they bought on the northern fringe of

70. See J. B. Kietegha, 1983, p. 158.
71. A proper listing of the famines in Mogho has still to be compiled.

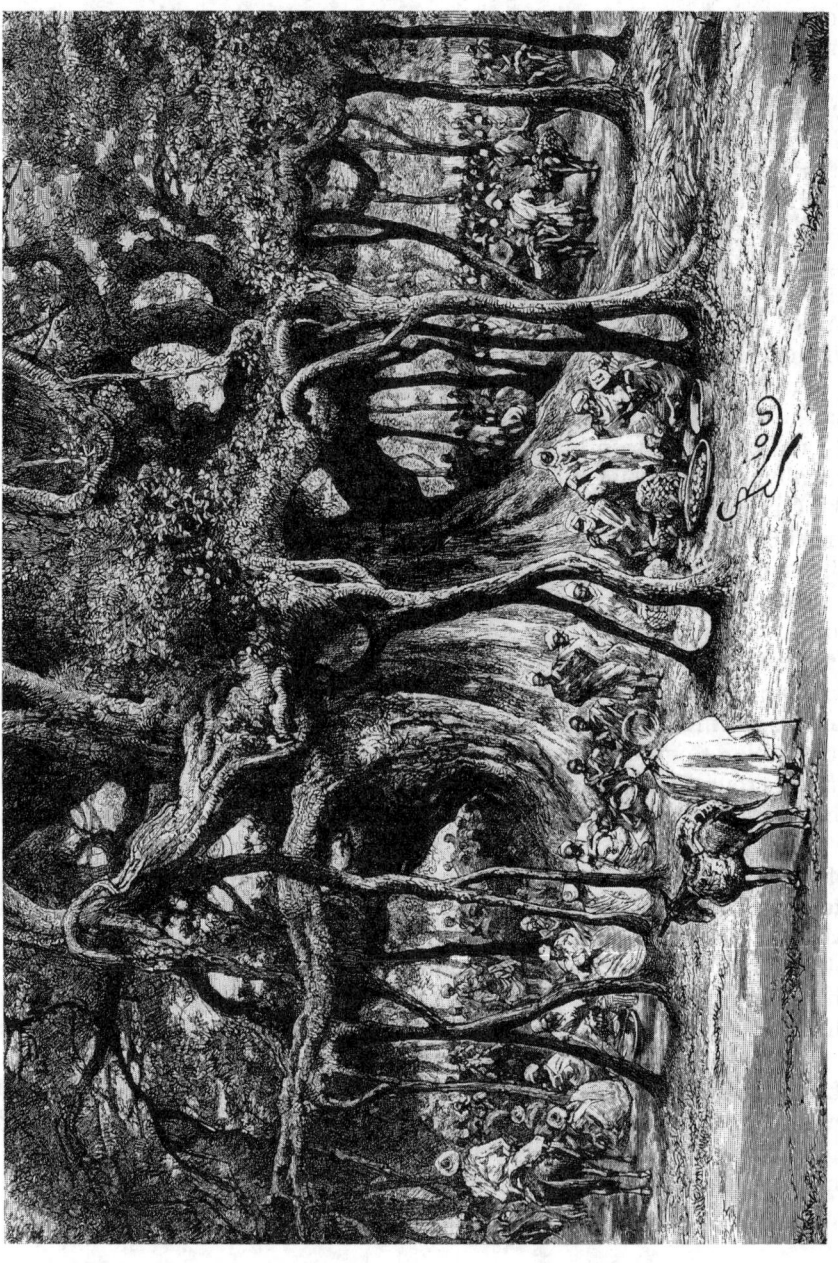

PLATE 12.4   *Market traders gathering under the shade of a banyan tree*

the Asante world. Naaba Kango's reign gave trade a fillip; the prosperity of the village of Yuba, near Waiguyo, for example, dates from this time.

The eighteenth century saw the formation of large settlements of traders in which the Yarse were joined by the Marase. The latter could no longer maintain an independent trading system because the Kurumba lost their independence and even their identity after their country gradually came under the sway of the Mossi (Yatenga) and the Fulbe (Jelgoji). The large markets of the kingdom, such as Yuba and Gursi, were the termini of the salt and kola caravans. The Yarse of Yatenga were a dynamic group of traders found not only at Timbuktu, the starting-point for the salt caravans, but also in the valley of the Bani and throughout Macina. Naaba Kango's policy towards Segu may perhaps have been aimed at getting these Yarse settled in countries bordering Yatenga. For in Mossi country these judicious traders lived in symbiosis and compromise with the leaders. In return for certain privileges (the right to pardon, exemption from services and armed escorts), they undertook not to encourage any subversion, to sell to the *Naaba* as a matter of priority, to give him their blessing and support through appropriate rituals and even on occasion to act as intelligence agents.[72]

While the accounting unit for the traders was the cowrie, other units, in particular the cubit of cotton strip, were used both in the caravan trade and in everyday business. There were various systems of equivalence between the cowrie, the cubit, the block of salt, slaves and horses.

Alongside the Yarse, who combined cotton crafts with long-distance trade, the blacksmiths engaged in heavy metal-working, metal-refining, pottery (made by women) and the export trade to central Mogho, which was poor in iron ore. Yatenga was, after all, one of the great metal-working areas of central West Africa; and the trade in manufactured goods (iron parts for weapons and farm implements) brought the blacksmiths substantial incomes.

The Waiguyo site had certainly not been chosen without economic ulterior motives. Frobenius[73] reports a tradition to the effect that Naaba Kango meant to make his capital a salt depot. It may also have been Naaba Kango's reign that saw the formation of a corps of chiefs of the market, drawn from captives, with the task of levying a royal tax on imported goods. Naaba Zombre had earlier created a corps of chiefs of the market in the Kingdom of Ouagadougou; they were drawn from the royal captives and were responsible for the collection of taxes on goods displayed. The aim was, of course, to provide the court with extra revenue; but it also sought to reduce the taxing rights of local chiefs, who were often very harsh on traders.

During this period, which corresponds to the height of the slave trade on almost every part of the coast of Black Africa, the terrible logic it introduced into the mechanism of trade flows and the content of socio-political relations must always be present in the mind, from the moment

72. A. Kouanda, 1984, p. 248.
73. L. Frobenius, 1924, p. 281.

fire-arms, slaves and political power were made part of the same question. We have noted it in the greatest kings of the time: the Massasi, the rulers of Segu, Naaba Kango of Yatenga, the Wattara of Kong and Bobo, not to mention the Dagomba and Asante rulers. But the slaving activities of kings were augmented and fuelled by the host of local chiefs who, willy-nilly embarked on this business to enter the political game.

We have seen how, in the Bambara system, the status of captive had been ingeniously institutionalized by turning to account the already existing institution of the *ton-den* (association member) to create the *ton-dyon* (captives of the *ton*). But while it was Mamadou Kulibali who had this idea, it was because it was 'in the air' and had been established in social praxis for centuries.

A further step was taken with the *foroba-dyon* (crown slaves). These were prisoners-of-war grouped into contingents each of which was defined by the *faama* who had formed it. Usually their fate was to be sold as trade goods produced by war, in Bambara, *san'dyon* (trade slaves). Purchased by a community, the woman, as soon as she produced a child, acquired the status of *woloso* (born in the house) and the man could acquire the same status as soon as his master had sufficient confidence in him. Later, the *woloso* might become a *dyon goron* when his children took his place and paid an annual indemnity to his master. After reaching the status of *woloso* the slave became a caste member. He could no longer be put on sale, and had a right to property and to transmit his estate to his children, such that his living conditions, if not his status, were preferable to those of a free but poor man who might suddenly find himself in captivity. Many people in the turbulent world of the eighteenth century, obviously finished up accepting the powers of a protector and a master just as they did in the European High Middle Ages. It is true that the condition of a *woloso* was transferred to his descendants in perpetuity, even if, as happened at royal courts, a few caste men might rise to the highest positions. Although their lofty positions made it impossible for any ordinary person to refer to their caste status, the thought persisted ineradicably in the collective mind.[74]

Thus, the great king Ngolo Diarra's family was unable to eradicate the memory of the servile status of their ancestor, which provoked taunts from the Massasi of Kaarta. Ngolo's case nevertheless shows that doors were not closed to the cleverest captives. In theory, they were subject to the discretion of their master but in practice, by making use of the good offices of people in favour, they could influence top-level decisions.[75] Even in the rigid Mossi system – where everyone was born and died in his status, with no transfer or break possible[76] – a eunuch, the *Kamsaogo-Naaba* had heavy

74. Cf. A. Raffenel, 1846, Vol. I, p. 371.

75. See C. Monteil, 1924, p. 301.

76. The king could not dismiss or demote a noble. The chief who the king wanted to remove received a poisoned arrow from him with which he was supposed to commit suicide; if he did not, war would follow.

responsibities. It is true that other eunuchs destined for this purpose, were traded towards the Fezzān, North Africa and the Near East.[77]

Islam and traditional African religions

It was common, both before and after the colonial conquest,[78] to say that the Bambara and the Mossi had constituted strong barriers to the advance of Islam in West Africa. This is a simplistic assertion that needs revision. Islam, at work since the eighth century if not before, increased its influence in the great empires from the Empire of Ghana to the Empire of Gao. But even in these areas there were obstacles and resistance. Even as late as the eighteenth century, the Jelgoobe and Feroobe Fulbe, who had left Macina for the north-east of the Volta region, were often followers of traditional religions.[79]

For a millennium, however, from the eighth to the nineteenth century, Islam continued to penetrate the whole of this region diffused through numerous channels including traders, prayer-leaders, even violence, all the while getting round obstacles and adapting to the specific circumstances presented by the multiplicity of peoples, particularly when they seemed resistant. The peoples of the interior of West Africa, however, did not look upon Islam or, later, Christianity, in the same way as the followers of these religions did when they judged the continent's traditional religions. The Bambara initially looked upon Islam syncretistically: its presence impelled them to stress once again the Supreme God, Maa Ngala, the sovereign above the spirits honoured by particular cults. Having assimilated Islam in this way, the kings of Segu and Kaarta saw no obstacle to consulting the ministers of this great God through the persons of the *marabout*s while remaining faithful to their own cults – of which they were practically *ex officio* the high priests – and to the magician. The latter is deemed to have invoked the universal and invisible Energy, provoking in this way a sort of materialization of his desire. The magician 'names' and thus creates what he calls upon with his prayers.[80]

Although they practised such traditional rites, the Kulibali, including the highest chiefs, took part in Muslim religious festivals, at least by their presence and by offering lavish gifts to the Sarakolle *marabout*s. The festival of the *tabaski* (sacrifice) coincided, moreover, according to Raffenel, with the general meeting of the Massasi clan which involved secret rites such as those of Komo and Makongoba and oaths of allegiance. But these same Bambara repeated as well as they could the gestures of the officiants at Muslim prayers and some even sacrificed a sheep. These syncretisms – which in time developed with Christianity in Afro-American worship in Brazil, Haiti and Cuba – were one of the characteristics of the Negro-

77. See Y. Tiendrebeogo, 1964.
78. C. Monteil, 1924 p. 23 *et seq.*
79. See I. P. Diallo, 1981.
80. See UNESCO, *General History of Africa*, Vol. I, ch. 8.

African religious spirit. Thus, if the appeals to the spirits failed to provide a clear and satisfactory response, the intervention of the *marabout* was then sought and welcomed piously by Mamari Kulibali as well as by Tonmasa Ngolo and others. Biton moreover paid the *zakāt* to the *marabouts* of Jenne and maintained a group of forty divines, including the Kamite who although Muslims, were also priests of a *faro* (spirit of the River Niger). When Denkoro the Bloodthirsty was intercepted and killed by the Tonmasa, he was at the time getting ready to perform his ablutions followed by his faithful blacksmith who was carrying a *satala* (kettle).

The magician-blacksmith also had no difficulty in adopting the geomantic divination introduced by the Muslims.[81] It is true, however, that the 'Alī Bakary's Islamized successor at Timbuktu, who had learned Arabic from a *shaykh* of the Bekkai family, was soon murdered with all his family. This murder has been attributed to the fact that he was intending to ban the consumption of *dolo* (millet beer) and the cult of the spirits or ancestors. In fact, this is far from certain as the ambitious Tonmasa, who carried out all these massacres, was soon to kill Dion Kolo, Mamari's last son.

What is certain is that Islam presented itself to the Bambara with institutions such as polygamy, divorce, repudiation and slavery that did not systematically challenge their own. Moreover, the *marabouts* themselves did nothing that might put off Bambara neophytes. Thus at Dia,[82] probably one of the oldest centres of Islam in the Western Sudan, teaching generally adapted itself to indigenous customs and gave plenty of attention to magic.[8] The most numerous *marabouts* among the Bambara were the Marka, the Bozo and the Somono who claimed to be in the line of the great master of Moorish or Fulbe Islam and, through them, to belong to this or that brotherhood. The fact was that some ethnic groups, such as the Soninke, the Marka, the Fulbe and the Torodbe, Islamized long before and enjoying religious toleration, acted as models and catalysts. The same was true of the Bozo and Somono fishermen whom tradition associates with the earliest days of the Kulibali clan of Segu.

In short, this mutual tolerance was of great benefit to both parties: it associated the Muslim leaders with government and it used endogenous channels to win these peoples to the faith of the Ḳur'ān (Qoran). But it also contributed to the strengthening of the power of monarchs who, faced with the ethnic and social heterogeneity of their states, could not afford the luxury of religious discord. Thus,

> the pagan, by taking advantage of Islam according to his own concepts Sudanized it; such that between these two poles, the Islamic and pagan, there exists an infinity of intermediate states linking them to

81. One of the terms to describe the divine, the consultant is *turndala* (through the sand), derived from the Arabic *al-tareb* (the land) whereas the others are strictly Sudanese words – *buguridala* and *kyekyedala* from *buguri* (dust) and *kyekye* (sand).

82. Dia is situated on the left bank of the Niger in Macina.

83. P. Marty, 1920–1, Vol. IV.

one another, and which, depending on the angle from which they are observed, appear now as the Islamization of the Sudanese and now as the Sudanization of Islam.[84]

Such was the state of affairs in the Niger Bend before the dissimilar *djihād*s of Sekou Ahmadu Barry and Al-Ḥādjdj 'Umar. In Mossi country the beginning of Muslim influence at the court of Ouagadougou probably dates from the reign of Naaba Kom, son of Naaba Zombre (*c*.1744–*c*.1784).

Contrary to what the historic process of the expansion of Islam across the Sahara might suggest, Islam in the Volta basin was not the result of penetration from the north. On the contrary, Yatenga remained practically closed to Islam until the colonial period, despite (or because of) the existence there of two large Muslim minorities, the Fulbe and the Yarse traders. Recent research has shown that Islam spread into the Volta basin in the wake of Juula traders and warriors along a north-south line in the west of the Volta area, along the Black Volta valley; and that the town of Bobo-Dioulasso was one of the main centres of Muslim proselytism, and that the Marka *dafing* (clan) of the Sanogho was one of its most active carriers through its intellectuals and *marabout*s.

The founders of Gonja were Muslim Mande. From Gonja, Islam moved into Dagomba country. Levtzion puts Muslim penetration among the Dagomba at the time when, in the mid-1600s, for reasons of security, the capital of their kingdom was moved eastwards from Yendi Dabari to the site of present-day Yendi.[85] Trading centres in these areas soon became religious centres, distinguished by the presence of *malam*s (Muslim scholars). The evangelists of the faith were to enter the White Volta basin behind the kola caravans. The first Dagomba king to be converted was Na Zangina, who reigned at the very beginning of the eighteenth century. It is possible that the conversion of the king of the Dagomba facilitated the conclusion of a lasting peace with Gonja.

Islam penetrated Mamprusi country at roughly the same time. Gambaga, the main market, quickly became a Muslim centre. Thus it was from the south that Islam came to Mogho at the end of the eighteenth century, during the reign of Mogho-Naaba Zombre. The ruler of Ouagadougou whose mother was Muslim and to whom Islam was therefore familiar, although he did not convert, used to say the daily prayers and showed himself generally sympathetic to Muslims, including proselytes. It was during the reign of Naaba Dulugu (*c*.1796–*c*.1825) that the decisive step was taken. The *Mogho-Naaba* formally converted; he built the first mosque in Ouagadougou and made the town *imām* one of the top dignitaries at court. This early Mossi Islam, like that which then prevailed in the Mamprusi and Dagomba kingdoms, was an aristocratic Islam; and for the *Mogho-Naaba* and the other chiefs and dignitaries, its practice was in no

84. C. Monteil, 1924, p. 332.
85. See N. Levtzion, 1968, pp. 194–203.

365

way inconsistent with observance of the traditional religion. They were, however, far from trying to impose the new religion on their subjects Although a convinced Muslim, Naaba Dulugu seems to have been afraid that Islam might make too rapid progress in his kingdom. He moved away his eldest son, the future Naaba Sawadogo, and dismissed the chief of Kombisiri – both of whom were fervent Muslims, possibly rather too prone to engage in proselytizing among their entourages. It can thus be seen that, in the Bambara kingdom as in Mogho, although there was a decided tolerance towards Islam, the traditional religion remained, despite everything, on its guard and meanwhile sought compromise formulae. For the other two political centres of this period, the Empire of Kong and Gwiriko, on the one hand, and the Gulmance kingdoms on the other, the general attitude was decidedly different. At Kong, as among the Bobo-Juula, the Islamic religion was both a reason to live and a way of life, such that their policy, imbued with a militant faith, foreshadowed the *djihād*s and the conquests of the nineteenth century, particularly by Samori. Conversely, the Gulmanceba were resolute upholders of the traditional religion.

Conclusion

For the countries of the Niger Bend and the Upper Volta basin, the period from the sixteenth to the eighteenth century was unquestionably a state-building phase.

In accordance with an ancient tradition in the region, the Juula, Mossi, Gulmanceba and Bambara states were all units made up of several ethnic groups. Even if the dominant ethnic group claimed certain privileges, it was itself the outcome and source of an intermixing of such groups. Hence they were not ethnic states. The sometimes highly sophisticated political machinery devised here was nevertheless vulnerable, mainly because of the almost total lack of a written form of administration.

Moreover, the states in question were undermined with internal contradictions. In the first place, the devolution of power often gave rise to serious difficulties. When Naaba Kumdumye of Ouagadougou found positions for the unsuccessful candidates for the chieftaincy – to appease them and keep them out of the way, but also to scatter dynastic power geographically – little did he suspect that his successor, Naaba Warga, would have to wage war on the descendants of those chiefs. Likewise, some of the 'companions' of Biton Kulibali whom he appointed, became unruly governors. This political difficulty was compounded by a social problem, for the princes excluded from the power system turned their animosity against the peasants, who were thus exploited mercilessly.

These initial contradictions obscure another equally dangerous inconsistency, namely the opposition between the royal entourage, made up of commoners, and the king's relatives, who were held in check by a series of measures the most striking instance of which was the policy of Naaba

Kango of Waiguyo. In the case of the Bambara, the swift transition to statehood makes more conspicuous the confrontation between the three competing forces represented by the clan, the political association (*ton*) and the territorial state. This conflict of interests abated only under sovereigns of exceptional stature.

The question of religion must not be played down. It is true, however, that, before the 1800s the Mossi and Bambara states succeeded in maintaining a *modus vivendi* with the Muslim groups (Soninke, Juula, Yarse) in a compromise based on tolerance, syncretism and an exchange of service that cemented co-operation among their ruling classes. As the case of the Yarse demonstrates in particular, the Muslims in the region were often traders indispensable to the state. But there was a noteworthy difference between the Mossi and Bambara states, on the one hand, and the Kong empire and the Gulmanceba kingdoms, on the other. In Kong, Bobo and the Kenedugu, the model of militant Islam prevailed. Among the Yarse of Mogho and the Soninke of Segu and Kaarta, however, the chosen course was to refrain from politics and even initially, in the case of the Yarse, to avoid proselytism, as the traditional religion enjoyed official status. But this may merely have been a question of a time-lag, explained because the balance of power was still far from being upset. The extreme case here is that of the Gulmanceba, who were to switch abruptly from a position of power based upon the traditional religion to submission to the Muslim Fulbe after the Liptako *djihād*, in the early nineteenth century.

State-building in the region, however, fitted into an overall economic context which spelt ultimate doom for such political experiments. All those countries lay between the southern edge of the Sahara and the Atlantic coast which was increasingly controlled by the Europeans. European bargaining policies reshaped commercial circuits and the structure and terms of trade to their advantage, so that established patterns of supply and demand were gradually disrupted. In the economic chain that each ruler attempted to control in his region, the relative importance of the commodities used to win and maintain power (horses, arms and captives) constantly increased. It was thus that the shadow of the slave trade began to loom behind these processes in which the peoples living under non-centralized political power systems were anything but passive onlookers.

By comparison with the African rulers along the coast – who were directly confronted with the Europeans and had no other choice but submission or war – these countries of the interior certainly enjoyed a respite and seemed to be freely going their own ways. But their destiny was, in fact, pre-ordained in a process that was increasingly dependent on the outside world. For this reason the hegemonies of the region often did not have enough time to establish a *de jure* state providing the stability and order mentioned by chroniclers in reference to the previous empires. The all-important fact here, however, is that in difficult circumstances people proved capable of building a state with their own African means.

13

The states and cultures of the Upper Guinean coast

C. WONDJI

Introduction

From the Casamance to the Republic of Côte d'Ivoire inclusive, there stretches an enormous area of coasts and forests, inhabited by many and various peoples. This area is far bigger than the one historians normally call Upper Guinea.[1] This chapter aims at sketching the outline of its development between 1500 and 1800.

The societies

By comparison with the big ethnic masses of the Sudan, where state-type societies predominate, the area under consideration here is characterized by many small socio-cultural units organized on the basis of lineages, clans and villages.

The people of the Guinea countries are remarkable for being fragmented into many ethnic groups. From the River Casamance to the River Tanoe, between the northern savannah and the southern coastline and the mountain ranges of Futa Jallon and the Guinea Spine and the western and southeastern coastline, there are more than a hundred ethnic groups and subgroups.

This multiplicity of human groups explains the many linguistic differences that characterize the cultural landscape. Each ethnic group, speaking a language distinct from those of its neighbours, is aware of its individuality. There are sometimes many dialectal variants within a single language, which oddly restricts linguistic intercomprehension within a single ethnic group. Thus each ethnic group contains striking distinctions: for example the Joola are differentiated into Flup (Felup), Bayotte, Blis-Kianara, Kassa and Fooni. In the Côte d'Ivoire, We in the north (the Facobli) and the

1. The West Atlantic coastal area (Guinea) was divided into Upper Guinea, from the Senegal to Cape Palmas, and Lower Guinea, from Cape Palmas to the Niger delta in the Bight of Biafra. W. Rodney uses the term 'Upper Guinea Coast' for the coast between the Gambia and Cape Mount. Thus the Côte d'Ivoire was not part of Upper Guinea as defined by historians, although from a strictly anthropological point of view, the western part belongs to this region.

centre (the Duekoue) have difficulty in understanding their Nidru relatives in the south (the Toulepleu); and the Baga are divided into the Baga-Sitemou, Baga-Fore and Baga-Kakissa.[2]

Despite the diversity of ethnic groups and languages due to the continual overlapping of migratory flows, there are wider linguistic entitles. Three big language families, themselves subdivided into groups and sub-groups, share the area between the Casamance and Tanoe rivers. Within the family of Mande languages, the Southern Mande sub-group is predominant – Northern Mande only appearing in the form of the Mande spoken in the Gambia, Casamance, Guinea–Bissau, Sierra Leone and Liberia. South of the Mande languages, along the coastline from the Casamance river to Liberia, the so-called West Atlantic languages are also divided into northern and southern groups: they are less homogeneous than the previous family and show internal variety reflecting the ethnic complexity described above. Lastly, to the east and south-east the so-called Kwa languages comprise the Kru-Bete and Akan languages, which show the same heterogeneity as the West Atlantic languages.[3]

The difficulty of producing an historical synthesis

Tracing the development of the countries of the coast of West Africa from the Casamance river to the Côte d'Ivoire between the fifteenth and nineteenth centuries is one of the most difficult tasks of African historians. It deals not only with peoples and societies, most of which have recently become states whose national history is being reconstructed, but also with territories that did not all belong to the big political entities of pre-colonial Africa and whose histories pose many difficult methodological problems for the historian.

These difficulties relate first to the sources themselves. After the fifteenth century, European written sources, which grew in number and accuracy as trade intensified, provide material about the Atlantic coast of Africa. Like the mercantile interests of the European nations, they are unevenly distributed by periods and regions: they are plentiful for Senegambia, the Rivers Coast and the sector from the Gold Coast to the Niger delta, but less so for Liberia and the Côte d'Ivoire; before the fifteenth and even into the sixteenth century they are virtually non-existent for certain sectors. Although they reflect the prejudices of Europeans, in line with their nationalities and the ideas then current, they nevertheless give a good picture of the coastal area, including the geographical setting and the economic activities, systems of government and habits and customs of the peoples visited. But the coast is better depicted than the hinterland, for

---

2. For the Joola see C. Roche, 1976, pp. 28–46; for the We and Baga see D. T. Niane and C. Wondji.

3. See J. H. Greenberg, 1980.

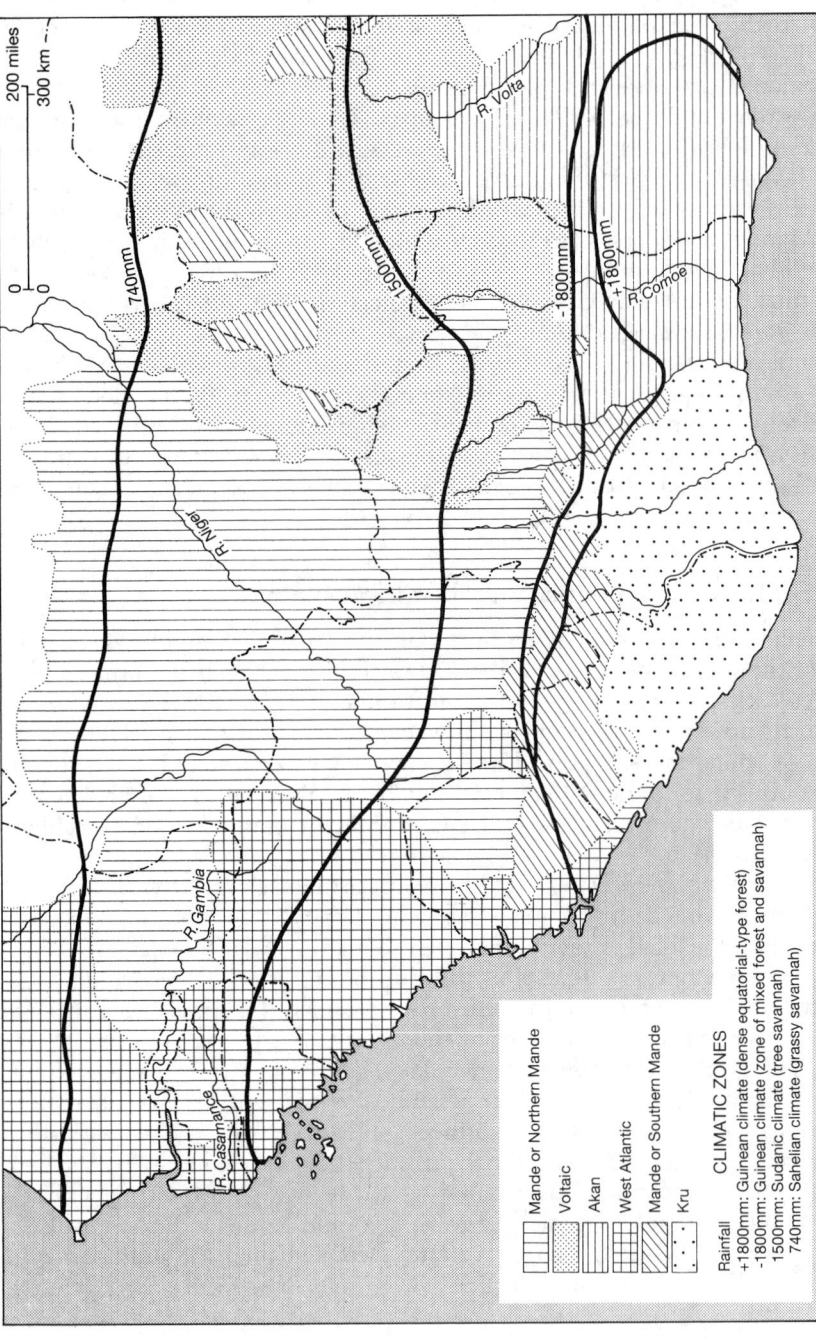

FIG. 13.1 *Major population groups of West Africa (after C. Wondji)*

which no records exist before the nineteenth-century missions into the interior.

These inadequate or non-existent written sources need to be supplemented or amplified by archaeology, oral tradition and other sources. The scope, however, is unevenly distributed, although the archaeology of the dry Sudan–Sahel area is developing, that of the humid Guinea area is still in its infancy despite excavations – in Casamance, Guinea–Conakry, Sierra Leone and the Côte d'Ivoire – which show traces of human occupation going back to the third millennium. Research on oral tradition has made crucial progress in the Mande and Fulbe sectors but has not yet given full measure elsewhere because the necessary knowledge of the languages and their many dialects and the prerequisite analysis of the societies and cultures call for many painstaking surveys whose findings will appear only after lengthy efforts. Moreover, in the light of the few results already recorded it seems that oral tradition rarely goes back beyond the seventeenth century. Lastly, apart from the Mande-speaking groups (where the homogeneity of the Mande languages allows significant and fruitful cross-checking), historical linguistics in this area of amazing linguistic complexity and discontinuity is still at the planning stage.

There are also difficulties relating to the socio-political fragmentation typical of this region. Historians of the states that came into being as a result of the sharing out of colonies often give more space to the peoples of the Sudanic parts than to those of the coast, who are only mentioned in connection with developments concerning the former. Moreover, no overall historical study of these peoples of the coasts and forests is possible at present without precise knowledge of each of their histories. Thus the Soso of Guinea, a Mande group, are better known than their Baga compatriots; and the Anyi of south-eastern Côte d'Ivoire, an Akan group, are more comprehensible than their lagoon-dwelling and Kru compatriots to the west.

Whether references by European travellers of the mercantilist period, observations by modern ethnologists and recent studies by historians can enable us to overcome the difficulties of fragmentation and build up a chronologically structured historical summary is questionable. Here we come up against the problems of the general line of development and the starting-point for historical movements; and the keys to these are not to be found in accounts furnished by a fragmented and disparate oral tradition.

Our study will keep to historical reality as experienced by the peoples themselves and reconstruct the time of West Africa in its most dynamic part (the Sudan) without losing sight of the flow of world history. The West African coast acted as the link between the historical pressures of the Sudan and those of European trade; and down the centuries different parts of it became active, came to life again and settled down.

Population movements

The Mande movements

In the area between the Gambia and the rivers of Guinea and Sierra Leone signs of the first Mande (Malinke) advance towards the Atlantic stem from the twelfth century. Oral traditions collected in Gambia, Casamance and Guinea–Bissau mention Mande agricultural settlement between the end of the twelfth and the beginning of the thirteenth centuries. Peasant villages are reported among the Bainuk, Balante and other indigenous peoples; within these scattered groups the Muslim Fati and the ancestor-venerating Sane clans predominated, these being the original nucleus of the reigning families of what was to be the Empire of Kaabu (Gabu).

This peaceful peasant migration was followed at the end of the fifteenth century by the conquering migration of the soldiers of Tiramaghan Traore, one of Sundiata's retired generals. The conquest of the Atlantic Joola, Balante and Bainuk territories – facilitated by the complicity of the early settlers – gave Mali wide access to the sea and control of the area between the Gambia and Sierra Leone.[4]

A deeper analysis of the traditions of this western expansion suggests social and economic factors inherent in Mande society as its possible causes. The practice of collateral succession – brother succeeding brother until the last male of the eldest generation died – made it difficult for sons of rulers to succeed their fathers. Many gathered willing family members, warriors and slaves and moved westward to establish their own states. Many of these migrating groups were also attracted by the desire to participate in the increasing trade in, and the growing affluence of, the western frontier region. It is therefore misleading to describe these movements purely as military conquests involving the warriors only: other members of Mande society, such as traders, hunters and farmers – intent on exploiting the western commerce and on finding areas for settlement – as well as artisans and slaves, were actively involved in the expansion. The movements also involved considerable interaction among the various ethnic and language groups which resulted in new amalgams.

The peoples of the coastal belt and the hinterland in 1500

The peopling of the coasts and forests before the European voyages of the fifteenth and sixteenth centuries is one of the most obscure areas in West African history. No doubt some written sources dealing with the Sudanese empires and the gold trade exist that can give us some information about the peoples of Senegambia, the Southern Rivers and the Gold Coast – that is, the north-western and south-eastern sectors of this region. For the areas

4. See S. M. Cissoko, 1972, pp. 1–3; B. K. Sidibé, 1972, pp. 5–13; and W. F. Galloway, 1974.

in between we can only guess the history on the strength of hasty notes by Portuguese travellers and the sometimes baffling oral traditions of some peoples of the interior who claim 'to have always been there'.

The Southern Rivers between the Gambia and Cape Mount

Southern Senegambia – Casamance and Guinea–Bissau   Most of the peoples living in this sector were already there when the Portuguese arrived, as witnessed by Cà da Mosto and V. Fernandes.[5] Three main groups occupied the estuaries and lower river valleys, namely the Bainuk or Banhun, a people of Mande origin who had come from the east in the fourteenth century; the Joola, who had come from the south (Rio Cacheu) before the fifteenth century; and the Balante from the east, who had imposed themselves on the Bainuk before the fifteenth century. These big groups had attached to themselves the little related peoples of the coast and the immediate hinterland: the Kasanga, Papel, Beafada and Bijago. Behind these coastal groups, in the middle and upper basins of the rivers between the Gambia and the Rio Grande, were the Mande who arrived from the east in the twelfth and thirteenth centuries driving the other peoples westward towards the sea; after the Mande in the fifteenth century, came the Fulbe from Macina.[6]

Guinea–Conakry and Sierra Leone   Fyfe and Rodney have given accounts of the peopling of this area. Archaeological discoveries at Yengema in Kono country (Sierra Leone), confirmed by linguistic research, have prompted C. Fyfe to suggest that, contrary to widely-held opinion, the Windward Coast has long been inhabited – since the third millennium before the Christian era. The earliest inhabitants were probably the Limba of Sierra Leone, who speak a different language from others in the neighbourhood: they occupied the Scarcies. Next came the Temne and Baga, with their related languages. The Temne came from the north, moving from Senegal to Futa Jallon. Lastly came the Kisi and Bullom, two related groups, who had followed the River Niger to its source. The Kisi and the Bullom merged then later split up, the former remaining in the interior and the latter going on to the sea.[7]

At the end of the twelfth century, movements following the fall of Ghana and Sosso brought the Soso to Futa Jallon, where the Dyallonke, Baga, Nalu, Landuma and Tyapi were already. There followed a mingling of peoples which ended in some migratory movements to the west. Small groups of these peoples headed towards the coast and its immediate neighbourhood: the Nalu settled in the sector between the Rio Tomboli

---

5. See, for example, A. da Cà da Mosto, 1937.
6. C. Roche, 1976, pp. 21–66; W. Rodney, 1970b, pp. 6–8; J. Richard-Molard, 1949, p. 108.
7. C. Fyfe, 1964, pp. 149–65.

and the Rio Nuñez, the Baga between the Rio Nuñez and the Rio Componi, and the Landuma–Tyapi in the immediate hinterland of the Nalu and the Baga. The Temne remained in the interior until the beginning of the sixteenth century, reaching the sea only at the end of that century. The Bassari and Koniagui of the Tenda group, having come from middle Gambia to Futa Jallon, were to stay there until the arrival of the Fulbe in the fifteenth century.[8] At the end of that century the pressure of the Fulbe on the Soso–Dyallonke–Baga and Temne set off new migratory movements which enabled the Baga to spread southwards along the coast, thus coming into contact with the Bullom. Behind the Baga and Nalu some isolated Soso–Dyallonke groups were already trying to reach the sea. Most of these earliest peoples belong to what is known as the West Atlantic group.

Cape Mount to the River Bandama – Liberia and western Côte d'Ivoire
This area was the home of the Kru, part of the Kwa-speaking peoples. Its coastal sub-sector was the area of the malaguetta ('grains of paradise', Guinea or 'fool's' pepper) trade. Its hinterland was the realm of high forest in the eastern heights of the Guinea Spine, which allowed only limited links with the world of the Sudanic savannahs.

The European navigators of the late fifteenth century encountered peoples along this coast from Cape Mesurado to Cape Lahou. The descriptions given by D. Pacheco Pereira and Eustache de la Fosse suggest the Kru, Bassa and Grebo.[9] Should we conclude from this that an early Kru population already existed on this coast in the fifteenth century? C. Fyfe observes that the sickle-cell trait is significant among the Kru, and infers from this evidence that they must have lived for a long time in isolation. Y. Person concludes from the same evidence that the Kru must have settled early in the coastal forest belt.[10] As some authors report the presence of Kru groups on the high mountains northeast of Liberia,[11] we must therefore suppose that the movement of these peoples from the interior to the coast began before the European voyages of the fifteenth century. Archaeology and recent research in oral tradition also show that this region has been populated for a long time. West of the Bandama river prehistoric tools have been found in the alluvial valleys of the Sassandra basin, and there are ancient caves in the area between the Bandama and the Sassandra rivers testifying to human occupation going back to the Mesolithic period. A historian of oral tradition, the Ivorian A. L. T. Gauze, has revealed the existence of an ancient people, the Magwe, who came from the north and followed the River Bandama to its mouth. These people, the ancestors of the Bete-Dida, fanned out into the western forest between the rivers

8. W. Rodney, 1970b, pp. 1–15.
9. D. Pacheco Pereira, 1937, pp. 99–115; E. de la Fosse, 1897, pp. 180–90.
10. C. Fyfe, 1964, pp. 152–3; Y. Person, 1970.
11. C. Behrens, 1974, pp. 19–38.

Sassandra and Bandama during the first millenium of the Christian era.[12]

We must therefore suppose that the savannah north of the forest in the Côte d'Ivoire, Liberia and Guinea–Conakry, the home of the Kru, was occupied at the same time by the Southern Mande groups, the Guerze, Manon, Toma, Dan, Guro, Toura and Gagu. In the fifteenth century they had, no doubt, already begun to thrust south into the forest regions under pressure from the Northern Mande ('Mandingo') from the Upper Niger. The momentum of this north–south drive must have brought many little groups of Kru to the seaward fringe of the forest.

Population movements from Sierra Leone to the Côte d'Ivoire
In the sixteenth century new peoples came from the interior to join those found by the Portuguese in the second half of the fifteenth century. They were mainly Mande, compelled by Mali's political and economic difficulties to move southwards on the routes to the forests and the coast. This expansion to the forest fringes was the work not only of warriors but also of merchants:

> Hemmed in to the north, the warriors from the savannah drove southward in the middle of the forest galleries as far as their horses survived. They followed in the hasty footsteps of the peddlers in search of kola, who brought Mandingo language and civilization to the fringes of the great forest all the way from the borders of Sierra Leone and the sources of the Niger in the west to the banks of the Bandama.[13]

The first of the Mande to move were the Kongo–Vai who came from the Upper Niger at the turn of the fifteenth and sixteenth centuries under the leadership of the Mande Camara clan. They came to Bopolou, in the northwest of what is now Liberia, and reached the coast along the rivers Mano and Moa which flow through Sierra Leone and Liberia. According to Holsoe *et al.*, the Vai migrated to the coast between 1500 and 1550 in search of salt and to establish trade routes into the interior. At the beginning of the seventeenth century the Vai occupied the mouths of these rivers and their Kono relatives the immediate hinterland.[14]

In the mid-sixteenth century, the Mane–Sumba, a group of Mande invaders from the Upper Niger also arrived on the coasts of Sierra Leone and Liberia. The origin of this migration is still unclear but Y. Person sees it as a major part of the Mande's movement southward, and says that the Mane followed the River Niger to Kouroussa then on to Konyan and Liberia. In 1545 they finally reached the coast at Cape Mount having followed the rivers Mano and Moa. From Cape Mount they moved north-

12. A. L. T. Gauze, 1969 and 1982.
13. Y. Person, 1981, p. 624.
14. C. Fyfe, 1964, p. 159; S. E. Holsoe, 1967; and S. E. Holsoe, W. L. d'Azevedo and Gay, 1974.

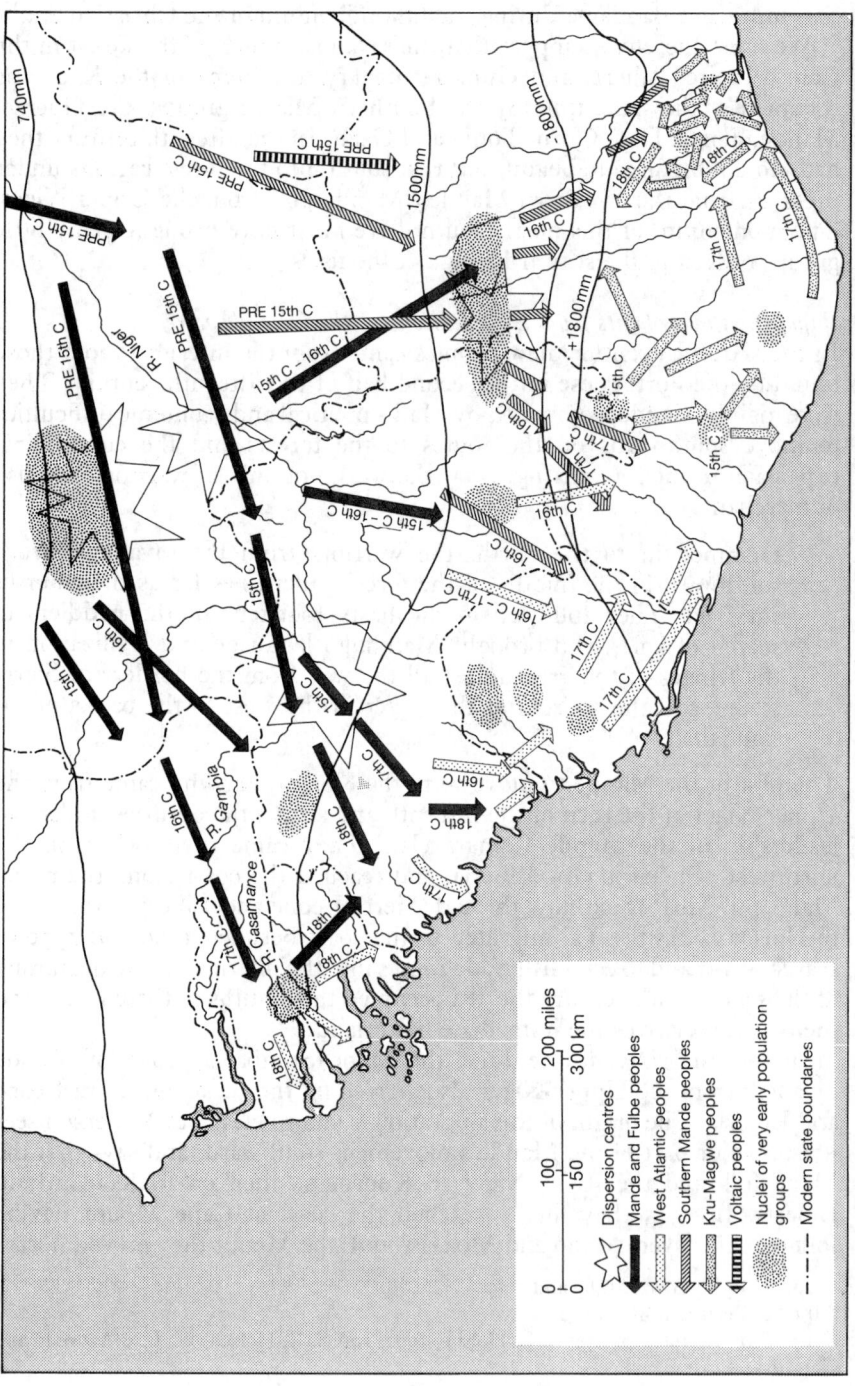

ward along the coast, crushed the indigenous peoples of Sierra Leone and made an incursion into the Futa Jallon mountains via the Scarcies. They were driven back by the Soso, the allies of the Fulbe, and had to return to the coast, which they occupied from Liberia to the islands of Los, merging with the original inhabitants.

The exact composition of the groups that brought about this migratory flow is not yet clear. Who were the Mane? Who were the Sumba? J. D. Fage thinks that the Mane were Mande warriors who may have recruited auxiliaries or Sumba from the Kru and West Atlantic peoples. But Y. Person thinks that the Mane were a Northern Mande aristocracy who led the invasion using Southern Mande warriors, in particular the Toma who may have been the Sumba. Whatever the case, this invasion had important social and cultural consequences for all the peoples in this area – Southern Mande, Kru and West Atlantic – starting with the destruction of the famous kingdom of the Sapes and continuing with the building up of a new political society under Mande direction. The peoples of this coast were reorganized into four kingdoms, themselves sub-divided into chief-taincies or principalities: Bullom (from the islands of Los to Cape Tagrin); Loko (around Port Loko); Bure (from the Sierra Leone channel to Sherbro Island); and Sherbro. These peoples were then integrated socio-culturally. Having during their conquest used the Bullom and Temme against the Limba and the Soso, and the Fulbe and the Kru peoples of the Grain Coast against the Kisi and Bullom, the Mane embarked on a process of miscegenation which led to the implantation of Mande influence in this region. The Loko, a small Temne group, adopted the Mande language; the Temne kept their West Atlantic culture, but introduced Mande chiefs; and the Kru, who kept their Kwa language, were influenced politically. The Mane also introduced military innovations – new weapons, tactics, sieges and fortifications which developed the warlike prowess of the peoples of the coast through practice in the art of attack and defence. By the end of the sixteenth century the invaders seem to have become naturalized, and by the beginning of the seventeenth the original Mane had been completely absorbed.[15]

In the sixteenth century a Southern Mande group, the Mande (Malinke) of the Upper Niger Camara clan, moved into Liberia and western Côte d'Ivoire causing not only the movement of the Kono and Vai towards the coasts of Sierra Leone and Liberia but also that of the Toma, Guerze and kindred groups (the Galla and the Manon) towards the forests of what are now the republics of Guinea and Liberia. At the same time the Diomande, brothers of the Camara, were moving eastward, settling at Touba (in Côte d'Ivoire) and driving out the Dan–Toura who moved south to occupy the Man (also in Côte d'Ivoire). Advancing still further east, the Mande entered Worodugu (the Seguela–Mankono sector of Côte d'Ivoire) and displaced

15. See J. D. Fage, 1969b, pp. 37–9; Y. Person, 1964; and C. Fyfe, 1964, pp. 158–9.

the Guro who moved south and southeast as far as the forest.[16]

This north–south and northwest–southeast thrust by the southern Mande brought pressure to bear on the Kru, who moved deeper into the forest in the direction of the coast. Studying the Kru peopling of Liberia, C. Behrens thinks that by the middle of the sixteenth century, the north–south movement was already completed, the Kru having left northeastern Liberia and settled on the coast. In the Côte d'Ivoire sector the movements seem to have taken place later. For example, the Nidru of Toulepleu, a We group who originally lived in the savannah, were driven into the forest in the middle of the sixteenth century.[17] At the same time the Zehiri Dida had had to leave Divo for the mouth of the Bandama in what is now Avikam country (Grand Lahou).[18]

Population movements in the seventeenth and eighteenth centuries

Unlike those before them, the population movements of the seventeenth and eighteenth centuries affected the whole coastal and sub-coastal area, and took the form of multidirectional migratory flows. These flows ran not only from north to south or from the interior to the coast but also from south to north, east to west and west to east. The sector most affected by them was that from Liberia to the River Tanoe. Warren L. d'Azevedo has suggested that these population movements were largely stimulated by the desire to control the slave trade which in turn led to conflicts and the consequent formation of inter- and intra-ethnic military and commercial alliances. These developments led to the establishment of strong cultural relations among the various ethnic groups in the region.[19]

From Gambia to Sierra Leone

Casamance and Guinea–Bissau In the seventeenth and eighteenth centuries no new peoples appeared in this sector; but with the boom in the slave trade there was a mingling of peoples due in particular to the devastating raids of the Mande backed by the expansion of Kaabu, then at its peak. The appeal of European goods stimulated slave raids which in turn aroused resistance from the groups under attack. Hence the interminable wars from which no people was immune; in the Rio Cacheu in the seventeenth century they set the Bainuk, Kasanga, Papel, Joola and Balante against one another. Some groups showed themselves to be particularly aggressive, such as the Bijago and Beafada of the islands who attacked the mainland Nalu and Balante peoples. But the Mande and their Kasanga vassals, the prime-movers in the slave raids, continually harassed the Bijago, Joola, Balante

16. Y. Person, 1964, pp. 325–8.
17. A. Swartz, 1971.
18. M. Sékou-Bamba, 1978, pp. 167–8.
19. W. L. d'Azevedo, 1959 and 1962.

and Bainuk. To escape the pressure of the slave-traders many peoples sought refuge in the coastal swamps, abandoning to Mande control the rivers leading into the interior.[20]

Guinea–Conakry and Sierra Leone   The growing influence of the Atlantic trade on the peoples of the Sudanic zone and the expansion of Islam which the Fulbe revolution in Futa Jallon brought about in the eighteenth century, were the phenomena that formed the background to the population movements in this sector in the seventeenth and eighteenth centuries.

In the first third of the eighteenth century, the Fulbe of the Muslim holy war set off the movement of the peoples of the Tyapi group towards the coasts of what is now the Republic of Guinea. This continued an old trend, for as early as the fifteenth and sixteenth centuries, as indicated above, under pressure from the Mande and Fulbe, small Baga, Nalu and Landuma groups from Futa Jallon had occupied the coastal area where the Portuguese had met them at the mouths of the rivers Nuñez and Pongo. But the Fulbe Muslim revolution that started between 1720 and 1730 drove the Tyapi peoples out of their old habitat for ever. Rejecting the authority of the masters of the new religion, and having lost several hard-fought battles, such as that of Talansam (1725–30) fought by the Baga, the last groups left the Futa Jallon hills for the coast; the Landuma left Mali for the upper Nuñez basin; and the Baga came from Labé to occupy the coast between the Rio Pongo and the Scarcies.[21]

Another major movement was the one that brought powerful waves of Soso–Dyallonke to the coast. Driven from Futa Jallon, the Soso moved slowly towards the coast which was already occupied by the Nalu and Baga. But the big wave started in 1760 when the Soso, under the leadership of Soumba Toumane, invaded the Baga and set up the chieftaincy of Toumania in the immediate hinterland of the Kaloum peninsula. They welcomed their Dyallonke relatives, who had also been driven from the Futa mountains by the Fulbe, and by the end of the eighteenth century dominated the coast between the Rio Pongo and Sierra Leone.[22]

Not all the inhabitants of Futa Jallon were driven out. The peoples of the Tenda group, for example, on the north-western spurs of the mountains, resisted the Muslim Fulbe. So did the Koniagui and the Bassari who, since the fifteenth century, had escaped domination by the invaders although some of them had taken part in Koly Tengella's bands in the sixteenth century. Nevertheless, symbiosis did occur in some cases: the Badyaranke were a mixture of Tenda and Mande–Sarakolle and the Fulbe managed to Islamize some groups who became the Tenda–Boeni.[23]

Other prime movers of this population movement into Guinea and Sierra

20. See W. Rodney, 1970b, pp. 1–15; J. Suret-Canale, 1976 edn, pp. 456–511.
21. See Dr Méo, 1919.
22. J. Suret-Canale, 1976 edn, pp. 504–10.
23. A. Delacour, 1912; F. de Coutouly, 1912.

Leone were the Northern Mande ('Mandingo'), who caused the Toma, Guerze and Manon migrations into the forest zone of Guinea, those of the Mende into Sierra Leone and those of the Quoja into Sierra Leone and Liberia. We must distinguish here between movements connected with the already long-established Mande migration south to the sea, and those which stemmed from the expansion of Islam for which the Mande were as responsible as the Fulbe.

In addition, during the seventeenth century the continuous movement of the Mande from Konyan drove the Toma (Loma), Guerze (Kpelle) and Manon (Mani) from the savannahs on the forest fringe north of Beyla (in the Kerouane and Bissandougou sectors) to the forests of Guinea and Liberia which they continued to penetrate throughout that century. Other Mande from the east followed the same route as the Mane and entered Sierra Leone where they intermingled with the Kisi, Bullom, Loko and Temne to give rise in the late 1600s and early 1700s to the Mende people.[2] The Mende long remained in the interior, only reaching the sea in the nineteenth century. In the 1620s other Mande from the interior, intermingled with Liberian Kru, were to give rise to the Quoja and Karou hegemony which dominated the coast from Cape Verga to Cape Mesurado.[25]

The Mande acted as religious proselytizers. Leaders in both trade and Islam, they set up Ḳur'ānic schools (in particular among the Bena-Sose and the Kuranko), and until the 1700s lived as groups of scholars and traders among the coastal agricultural peoples. But with the advent of the Muslim revolution in Futa Jallon they joined with the Fulbe to convert or subjugate the Soso, Baga, Bullom and Temne. Thus they occupied the Mellacorie in the eighteenth century, organized Muslim Mande chieftaincies, and were represented all along the coast from the Island of Matacong to the Saint Paul river. At the end of the eighteenth century however, resistance to Islamization broke out among the Soso and the West Atlantic peoples when the *Almamy* of Futa Jallon sought to impose his authority over the whole area through the Fulbe–Mande religious alliance. The Baga, Bullom and Temne, however, refused to recognize his authority as did the kingdom of Falaba, northeast of Port Loko, which was led by a Soso group fiercely opposed to Islam. Nevertheless, the society of the Guinea and Sierra Leone rivers was not to escape the influence of Futa Jallon, nor the more specific political and cultural influence of the Mande trader-*marabouts*.[26]

24. K. Little, 1951; A. P. Kup, 1961b, suggests that the Mende are descendants of the Sumba and Mane warriors who entered the hinterland of Sierra Leone in the sixteenth century, sometime after the Vai migration.

25. For the Toma, Guerze and Manon see J. Suret-Canale, 1970, p. 169 *et seq.* and S. S. Bouet and L. T. Bouet, 1911. For the Mende, Quoja and Karou see C. Fyfe, 1965, p. 159 and O. Dapper, 1686 edn, pp. 256–4.

26. On Islam and the West Atlantic peoples see W. Rodney, 1970b, pp. 229–39; C. Fyfe, 1964, pp. 162–4; and J. Suret-Canale, 1976, pp. 509–10.

Liberia to the River Bandama

The migrations that helped establish the peoples of this sector in the seventeenth and eighteenth centuries were primarily a continuation of the north–south movements – from the savannah to the forest and the coast – that took place during the fifteenth and sixteenth centuries. They were also due to the upheavals in the Akan world during the seventeenth and eighteenth centuries, and to the various attractions and disadvantages of life at the coast at that time. The results were migratory flows in various directions: north–south, east–west, south–north, west–east and, in the forest, sometimes even in circles.

The Mande and the We   The Quoja–Karou invasion that fell upon the coasts of Sierra Leone and Liberia shows that the Mande thrust was still pressurizing the forest and coastal peoples in the eighteenth century. The Northern Mande (Malinke) had continued their advance to the south and south-east across the Sassandra river as far as the River Bandama. Their movement intensified that of the Southern Mande: the Dan continued to move south-south-eastward through Côte d'Ivoire (to Touba-Man) and south-south-westward (to Danané in Côte d'Ivoire and the Liberia forest); and the Guro and Gagu were heading south-south-east towards the Bandama river and beyond (the Guro to Bouake and the Gagu to Tiassalé and Dabou).[27]

This southern Mande thrust affected the movement of the We who were continuing towards the forest, in particular the We from Toulepleu in Côte d'Ivoire (to Nidru and Bewa). They reached the Guiglo in the forest in the middle of the seventeenth century and the Cavally river in the late 1600s and early 1700s. Associated with the Akan thrust and the rearrangement of the Kru world in Liberia, there were to be other migrations in the eighteenth century from the south-west (Zibiao), the north-east (Zarabaon) and the north (Semien).[28]

The Magwe–Kru   C. Behrens thinks that the Kru moved into Liberia along the coast from east to west during the sixteenth century. There they split up into the Bassa, the Krahn and the Grebo, etc. and, after fighting the Berkoma and the Quoja in the Cape Mount area in the mid-seventeenth century, occupied what is now Grand-Bassa County. According to Behrens the Karou hegemony reflected the Kru's determination to control the whole of the Grain Coast from Liberia to Sierra Leone. Thus the Kru of Grand-Cess, west of Cape Palmas, came from Grebo country in the late 1600s and early 1700s and an east–west movement followed the original north–south movement.[29]

27. A. Clérici, 1963, p. 24.
28. A. Swartz, 1971.
29. C. Behrens, 1974, pp. 19–38.

As regards the Kru settlement of Côte d'Ivoire, it seems that a west–east movement followed the north–south one. Thus the Kru of Grand-Béréby came to Côte d'Ivoire from Liberia following the fragmentation of Guerre groups (the We) from the north. Most of the Bakwe and Neyo, who probably belong to the same migratory flow, also came from the west, from the Tai–Grabo forest and the valley of the Cavally.

This great migratory wave led large groups of the Magwe (the Bete, the Godie and the Dida) from the Cavally basin in the west to the Sassandra basin and beyond to the River Bandama. It supplied population for the settlement of the area between the Sassandra and the Bandama rivers until the end of the eighteenth century.

Political mutations and socio-economic changes

The establishment of sea routes: late fifteenth to early seventeenth centuries

Once open to traffic and trade, the sea shore became a magnet to the coastal and sub-coastal peoples and the Sudanese traders from the interior. The establishment of sea routes had begun before the arrival in the fifteenth century of the Portuguese caravels when Mande expansion linked the Central Sudan to the Atlantic coast from Senegambia to the Gold Coast. When the Portuguese arrived they found the coastal fringe of the Guinea area open in two directions, towards the hinterland and towards the outside of the African continent.

Internal factors leading to the establishment of sea routes
In the fourteenth and fifteenth centuries, Mali, with its spontaneous agricultural settlement and military and political expansion westward, created the conditions for the commercial expansion of the Mande into the coastal area. From 1312 onwards, Joola corporations linked the coastal countries to the line of the River Niger between the River Casamance and Sierra Leone. The Gambia and Casamance, having become western provinces of Mali, exchanged their agricultural produce (rice and millet) and their craft products (cotton cloth) for iron and other metals from the interior. The trading cities of Kantora ran this trade which used the waterways, particularly the Gambia and Casamance rivers whose mouths were linked by a busy coasting trade. A different trade flowed south from the River Niger to the forest area where the Joola exchanged salt, copper, cotton goods and fish for kola nuts and sometimes palm oil. In the fifteenth century the economy of this north-west area was thus oriented towards the interior, and Kisi and Temne country was already affected by Mande (Malinke) influence from the Upper Niger (at Doma and Hamana).[30]

30. D. T. Niane, 1975a, pp. 67–88.

Beyond Sierra Leone, between Liberia and the Gold Coast, it is hard to specify the outlets of Joola trade at this time, although the names of Monrovia and Grand Lahou are sometimes mentioned. But it is certain that the Joola brought goods from the Niger Bend to El Mina, as they are reported at Begho in the first half of the fifteenth century.

The trading sphere of the Mande thus relied on a network of routes and market staging-posts with which the forest fringes were amply supplied and which the alluvial valleys and big river outlets extended coastwards. As a Portuguese observer, V. Fernandes, remarked:

> They (the Malinke) trade their goods very far into the interior, further than any other people in this region, and they even go to Mina Castle by way of the interior.[31]

External circumstances: the Portuguese explorations

The Portuguese were the first Europeans to explore the West African coasts in the fifteenth century, once the development of the caravel had enabled them to round Cape Bojador in 1434. They were at Arguin Island in 1443, in Senegal and Gambia between 1445 and 1456, and in Sierra Leone and Liberia in 1460–2. Between 1462 and 1480 they explored the whole of the Gulf of Guinea, touching what is now the Côte d'Ivoire in 1469–70 and the Gold Coast in 1470–1.[32]

From 1481 to 1560 the coasts of West Africa thus came under the influence of the Portuguese. In search of gold and spices, they joined their emergent maritime empire to the Mande trading sphere, developed by Mali expansion since the fourteenth century. They must surely have wanted to obtain the gold of Galam, Bambuk, Bure, Lobi and Asante, the legend of which had long haunted Europe and which was now needed to buy the spices and other oriental produce so valued by European markets.

Portuguese documents of the time, such as the meticulous registrations by the treasurer of the Casa de Guiné, provide us with the instructive list of goods which, apart from gold, formed the cargo of caravels returning to Lisbon from the newly discovered sites of the West African coast, and on which custom duties were levied. They include rice, copal, civet, palm mats and sacks, and carved ivory objects – mainly spoons, pedestal bowls, and oliphants. The latter group is particularly important because its surviving specimens, preserved today as precious rarities in the museums of three continents, and the finest of which are safely attributed to the Bullom of Sherbro Island, bear witness to the high level of technical skill and aesthetic taste reached by the coastal peoples before their contacts with Europeans. At the same time, they represent the very earliest class of African sculptures known to have been introduced into Europe and

31. Quoted by D. T. Niane, 1975a, p. 83.
32. R. Mauny, 1970; A. F. C. Ryder, 1964; A. Teixeira da Mota, 1975.

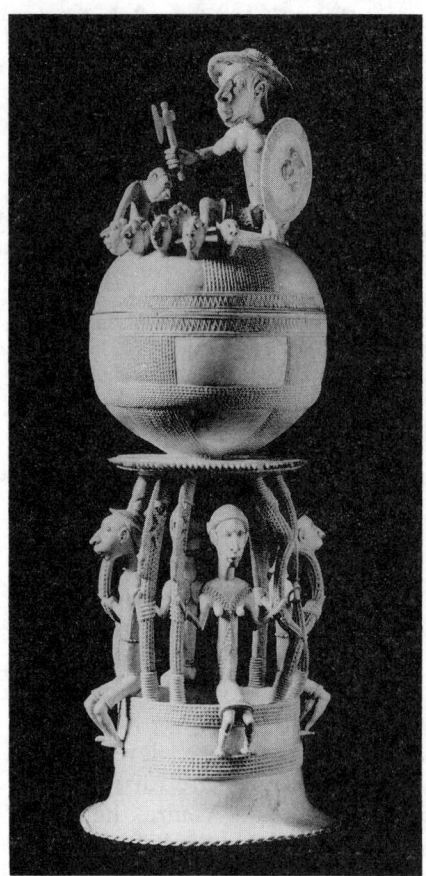

PLATE 13.1 *Sixteenth-century carved ivory salt-cellar from Sherbro Island (Bullom), Sierra Leone. Height: 43 cm*

admiringly appreciated and collected in Western societies.[33]

Throughout the sixteenth century the Portuguese maintained maritime and commercial supremacy on the West African coast from Arguin to Angola. In Upper Guinea they travelled by river in search of Sudanese gold, particularly along the Gambia, the Casamance and the rivers of Guinea-Bissau. They traded without aiming at territorial occupation. In what was then Mali's ocean gateway, they helped to improve the links between the Rivers Coast on the one hand and the Upper Gambia, Upper Senegal and Upper Niger on the other. The gold-bearing basins of the Rivers Bambuk and Bure were thus gradually separated from the Niger

33. A. F. C. Ryder, 1964; A. Teixeira da Mota, 1975.

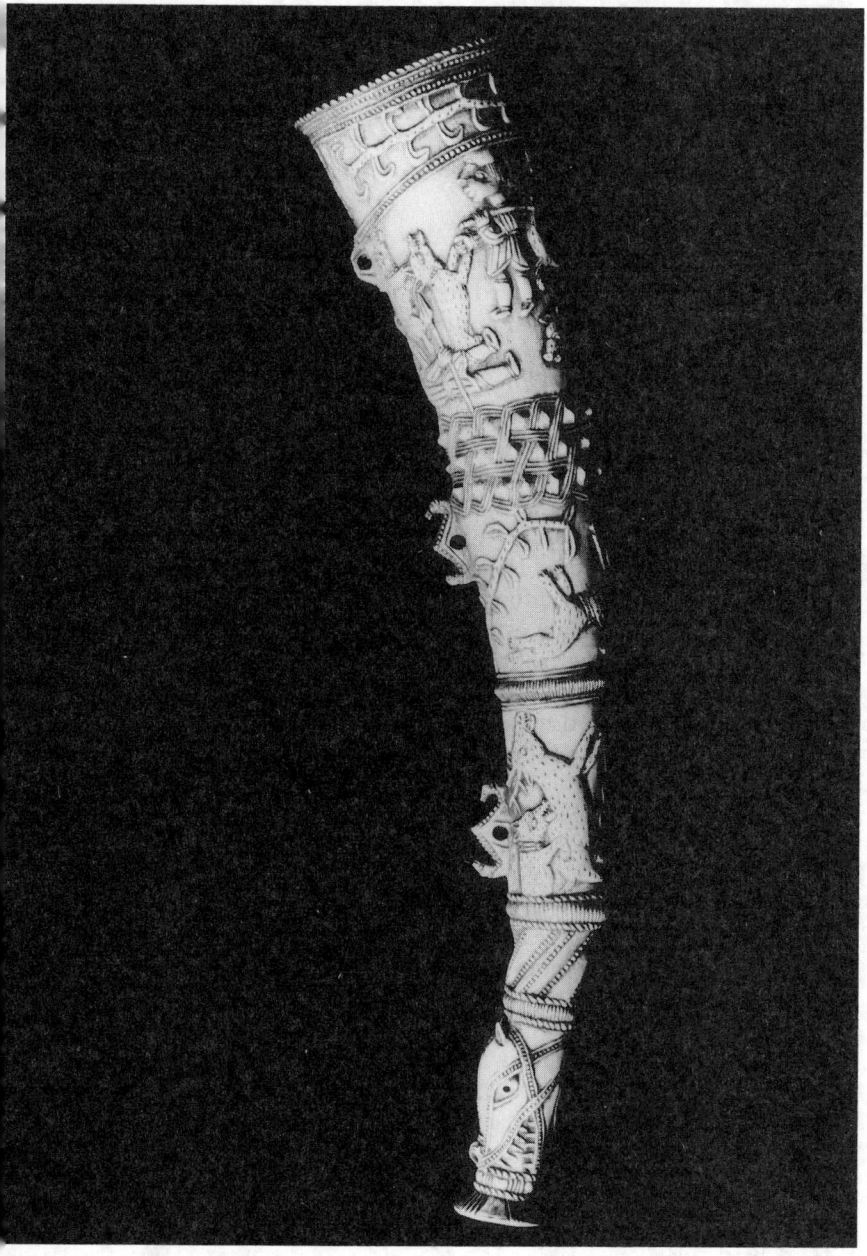

PLATE 13.2 *Sixteenth-century carved ivory hunting-horn from Sherbro Island (Bullom), Sierra Leone. Height: 43 cm*

basin and the Sahara, to the advantage of the Atlantic coastal fringe.[34]

Thus in the sixteenth century Joola inland trade routes in the Guinea coast, from the north-west to the south-east, led to coastal positions occupied by the Portuguese. Sudanese gold therefore reached Lisbon together with malaguetta which was sold cheap on the markets of Antwerp in competition with real pepper from the islands.[35] Thus the Mande and European trading spheres were linked and Saharan traffic began to be taken over for commercial purposes.

European voyages and early trading

The Portuguese, however, had to contend with French and English pirates operating on the Guinea coast from 1530 onwards. Their supremacy was also threatened by Dutch competition. Already masters of Gorée (1621), El Mina (1637) and Arguin (1638), the Dutch took the monopoly of Guinea from a Portugal already weakened by its annexation by Spain in 1580. Dutch ships began to ply to West Africa in the 1590s and a decade later the Netherlands were doing more West African trade than most European nations put together. With a total of 200 voyages between 1593 and 1607, they were later making twenty voyages a year. In 1614, for example, there were thirty-six Dutch ships lying off the El Mina coast at one time[36] and Portuguese supremacy was doomed.

Before Dutch supremacy established itself, however, the Atlantic coast had turned into a trading front of a new type, destined – in the eighteenth century – to become the scene of a busy maritime trade. But the Portuguese, by the 1700s, had opened up the area to trade and set up the strategy that was to prevail during the following centuries.

Early social formations and the 'Kingdom of the Sapes'

The West Atlantic civilization, which stretched from the Joola of Casamance to the Temne of Sierra Leone, was characterized by its adaptation to the ecological environment of the lowlands and stagnant waters. It consisted of swamp agriculture, the extraction of salt, paddy rice-growing, and the use of waterways for transport and communications in boats called *almadies*. Organized into village societies without slaves or castes but with age groups and work associations, the Joola had already reached iron age development when they came into contact with the Mande. Rejecting the epithet 'primitive' assigned to the 'West Atlantic' peoples, W. Rodney[37] stresses their ingenious adaptation to the natural environment, shows the commercial relationships that existed between them, and deduces their social and cultural homogeneity from their languages, dress and customs. They had no primordial state structure but did have a unified civilization and culture.

34. B. Barry, 1981.
35. F. Braudel, 1946.
36. A. F. C. Ryder, 1965b, pp. 217–36.
37. See W. Rodney, 1970b.

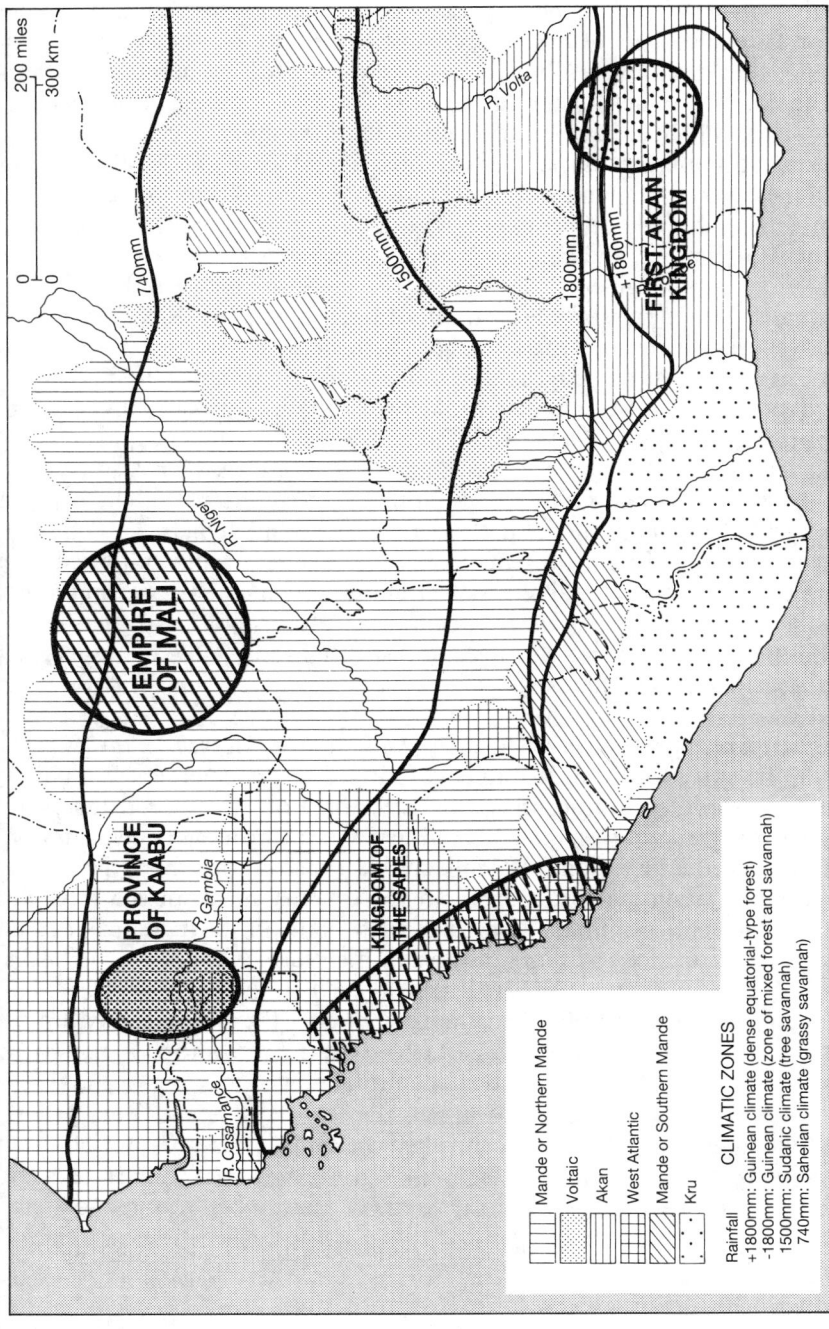

FIG. 13.3 *The main states of West Africa, pre-sixteenth century (after C. Wondji)*

Paddy rice-growing and the Kingdom of the Sapes were conceivably the historical expressions of this unity. Whether paddy rice-growing was an independent invention or a borrowing from the Mande has become a subject of controversy among historians such as P. Pélissier and B. Davidson.[38]

Social and political organization raises fewer problems than paddy rice-growing, for all the authors apparently accept that the caste system, patrilinear succession and state structure are institutions of foreign origin. Thus, under Mande influence brought about by the westward expansion of the Mali empire, the various peoples of the coast were organized into chieftaincies and principalities subject to the suzerainty of the *Mandi-Mansa*, the Emperor of Mali. In the fifteenth century the Portuguese observed the existence of these 'western provinces' (the kingdoms of Fogni and Casa, etc.) but reported the presence to the south of the 'Kingdom of the Sapes'. This raises another problem. Was Sapes a big confederation comprising the Baga, Nalu, Landuma, Limba and Temne peoples, as D. T. Niane thinks? Or, was it a kingdom formed between Cape Verga and Cape Saint-Anne following the infiltration southward of the Tyapi-Landuma-Baga-Nalu under the leadership of Mande chiefs, as J. Suret-Canale supposes? In our present state of knowledge it is difficult to choose between these two hypotheses.[39] Even more fundamentally, we should be cautious about accepting what appears to be a diffusionist explanation for all the social and political systems and institutions in the region, especially patrilinear succession and state structures.

Kaabu: from emancipation to hegemony (sixteenth–eighteenth centuries)
While the spread of Mande influence had led to the emergence of chieftaincies and proto-royalties in southern Senegambia, the establishment of the Atlantic trade in the sixteenth century was to encourage new states on the ruins of the hegemony of Mali. Mali's expansion to the Atlantic via the Gambia basin had brought about the establishment, in the fifteenth century, of politico-military structures such as the little kingdoms of (the) Gambia, Casamance and Guinea-Bissau which formed the western fringes of the Mande empire. Their rulers paid tribute to the *Mansa* of Mali through his *fariba/farin* (intermediaries). But by the sixteenth century it was the *farin* of Kaabu province, east of the Geba river, who were receiving tribute from the Mande chiefs throughout Gambia.

Lying between the middle Gambia, the Rio Grande and Futa Jallon, the Malian province of Kaabu controlled the trade of Kantora, which dealt in gold from the Falémé and Bambuk. In the sixteenth century Kaabu annexed the province of Sankola, south of the Upper Casamance, and

38. For this discussion, see P. Pélissier, 1966, pp. 42–44; B. Davidson, 1965, pp. 132–5. *Oryza glaberrima* is the indigenous African rice, as opposed to *Oryza sativa* or white rice, of Asian origin.

39. For this other discussion see F. Mahoney and H. O. Idowu, 1965, p. 141; D. T. Niane, 1975b, p. 51; J. Suret-Canale, 1976 edn, p. 507.

became a powerful province, although still a dependency of Mali. But as the old Mali empire weakened under attack from Songhay most of its western provinces freed themselves from its sway with the *farin* setting themselves up as independent kings, and Kaabu did likewise in 1537.

After its emancipation Kaabu unified all Mande countries between the Gambia, the Upper Casamance and the Upper Geba and supplanted the *Mansa* of Mali in this region. It then extended its sway to the Kasanga, Balante, Joola (Flup) and Beafada peoples. Its *farin* 'was like an emperor among them', wielding authority over all southern Senegambia and controlling trade as far as the borders of Guinea and Sierra Leone.[40]

Atlantic trade and the peoples of the Southern Rivers

While the Portuguese traders were facing competition and opposition from the Mande they were also attracting 'West Atlantic peoples' into their stations on the coast and were in direct contact there with the Joola, Balante, Papel and Kasanga.

In Sierra Leone the Bullom, Temne and neighbouring groups played an active part in trade with the Portuguese. The Bullom, who traded sea salt for gold from Mali to the north, now sold this gold to the Portuguese on the coast for cotton goods, copper bells and various metal utensils. At the end of the sixteenth century the Temne, themselves keen to profit from the maritime trade, reached the estuary of the Sierra Leone, thus splitting the Bullom into two.

By the sixteenth century the Rivers Coast of Upper Guinea had been transformed. Not only had the Portuguese set up many trading settlements there, but they had also established numerous points of contact with the Mande in the middle and upper reaches of the rivers. Links with the hinterland were thus intensified and north–south links considerably strengthened: the Cape-Verdians traded directly with the region of the Sierra Leone rivers, selling their cotton on the way to the Bainuk and Kasanga weavers; printed cloth travelled between Cacheu and Nuñez; and handicraft articles from the coast reached the Scarcies travelling back along the old kola trade route.[41]

The coastal area as a new West African trading front in the seventeenth and eighteenth centuries

By opening the West African coast to world trade, the great European explorations committed the countries of Guinea to an unprecedented process of historical development. The main changes in the seventeenth and eighteenth centuries were the expansion of trade, population movements from the interior to the coast and the emergence of new societies. These changes brought about the gradual marginalization of the Sudanic

40. S. M. Cissoko, 1972, pp. 3–8; D. T. Niane, 1975b, pp. 49–51.
41. W. Rodney, 1970b, pp. 71–94.

zone which, to survive, had to join the Atlantic trade by re-activating the routes leading to the forest and the sea.

The implantation and consolidation of European trade

The development of European trade on the West African coast was characterized by three features: its definitive implantation, not to say consolidation, by the systematic organization of trade; the increasing importance of the slave trade which, in the eighteenth century, accounted for an unprecedented proportion of total transactions; and the bitter competition between European nations for the possession of bases in West Africa.

In the seventeenth century European trade implanted itself for ever with the development of the sea-power of the Dutch who perfected the organization of the world mercantilist system by creating chartered companies. Moving from small commercial ventures to an organization on a grand scale, the Dutch, in 1621, set up the West India Company. With a charter giving it a twenty-four-year monopoly over trade with America and Africa from the Tropic of Cancer to the Cape of Good Hope, it had a military and naval warranty from the state and could pursue its commercial and colonial expansion in complete security. Basing itself on its forts and factories, the former to protect supply lines and the latter to exchange produce, the company contributed to Holland's trade boom in the first half of the seventeenth century. As maritime transporters the Dutch redistributed in Europe the produce they imported from Asia, Africa and America, in particular a great quantity of gold and ivory, and thus made huge profits. As masters of the seas they purveyed slaves to the American colonies of the other European nations (Spain, Portugal, France and England) which, in 1641, acknowledged their trading monopoly over the whole of the Guinea coast.

Between 1650 and 1672 Dutch predominance was reduced. The expansion of the American plantations had given a fillip to the sugar-based economy and called for increased supplies of slave labour. This had intensified the slave trade, which gained by the concomitant boom of manufacturing industry in Western Europe (fire-arms in particular), and had increased the desire of European nations to break away from dependence on Holland. Thus France and England embarked on a merciless struggle against the Dutch monopoly, equipping themselves with the same tools of power as their great rival. There followed the golden age of their chartered companies: the English Company of Royal Adventurers (1660) and later the Royal African Company (1672); the French *Compagnie française des Indes occidentales* (1664) and later the *Compagnie de Guinée* (1685); and also Swedish, Danish, Portuguese and Brandenburger companies.

All the European nations imitated the system of organization perfected by the Dutch because isolated merchants could not engage in West African trade unless they were members of or had support from a national company.

Only powerful companies were able to meet the expenses of building and maintaining forts. Between 1640 and 1750 many forts and trading stations were built on the coasts of Africa but changed ownership continually according to the vicissitudes of war between the slave-trading nations. There were some in Senegambia and many in the Gold Coast but none in between. War with Holland ended in 1713 with the Treaty of Utrecht which gave England the privilege of *asiento*.

From the shelter of these forts, and from around the trading stations, the Europeans pursued the commercial exploitation of the Atlantic coast. From Gorée to Sherbro Island, in Sierra Leone, trade flourished; but no French or English company could monopolize trade because of the many coastal islets and offshore islands that gave anchorage to any ship wanting to trade with the *mulatto* merchants. This part of the coast was thus a happy hunting-ground for slavers of all nations who were not associated with the big companies. In the eighteenth century there was no system of forts in this sector; it was claimed by Portugal, although her writ only ran effectively in the neighbourhood of the trading station at Cacheu. The chartered companies did not bother with the Grain Coast or Côte d'Ivoire, because malaguetta pepper was no longer prized on world markets; ivory was in decline, and anchoring difficulties kept ships away from the coast. A French fort built at Assinie, in south-east Côte d'Ivoire at the end of the seventeenth century was abandoned a few years later. But by 1700 the growing demand for slaves in America was encouraging individual traders to take an interest in this sector.[42]

Changes in the Sudan

Parallel with the establishment of European trade, the Sudanic hinterland underwent important changes which had a decisive effect on the development of the coastal area between the Casamance and the Bandama rivers.

In the Sudan, and particularly in the Mande world, effects of the Atlantic trade, dominated by the slave as merchandise, were various. At the socio-economic level, relations with the coast became more important and the spread of the trade was accompanied by the spread of fire-arms by Joola merchants. At the socio-cultural level, Islam having lost its sway with the fall of the great empires, the ruling class split into two rival factions, one traditional and political and the other made up of *marabouts* and merchants. The former, relying on cavalry and trade guns, set itself up as a military aristocracy; the latter, supporting the advance of Islam to the countries of the south, inspired politico-religious revolutions. The former led to the Bambara military monarchies and the latter to the Muslim Fulbe revolutions, both of which sought to solve the social crisis born of the break-up of the empires and the spread of the slave trade.

After the political fragmentation that followed the decline of the great empires, surrogate hegemonies tried (especially in the eighteenth century)

42. See J. D. Fage, 1969b, pp. 65–73.

to reconstruct the various parts of the hinterland. In the north and north-west, the Grand Foul empire arose in the seventeenth century on the ruins of Songhay but later, in the second half of the eighteenth century, gave way to the Empire of Kaarta. Along the Atlantic, the countries that had resulted from the dismemberment of Mali were unified by Kaabu in the seventeenth and eighteenth centuries, and then by Futa Jallon in the eighteenth and nineteenth centuries. Along the River Niger the recovery took place at the beginning of the eighteenth century under the aegis of the Bambara of Segu, under Biton Kulibali. But in the south, from the Upper Niger to the Bandama river and eastward into the Volta-Senufo area, the Joola increased their influence thanks to their numbers and wealth. In the eighteenth century they organized the Empire of Kong to keep traffic going on the trade routes from the middle Niger to the forest and the Gold Coast; and west of the Bandama river they founded market towns to control the tracks to the sea and the kola-growing areas of the forest.[43]

Just as trans-Saharan trade had helped bring the Sudanic political hegemonies into being along the Sahel strip between the seventh and sixteenth centuries, so the intensification of European trade encouraged the emergence of political hegemonies on the coast and in the hinterland in the seventeenth and eighteenth centuries. In line with these political mutations, socio-economic changes (which have been variously interpreted) affected the coastal peoples living at the terminus of the best trade routes into the interior.

The sub-coastal hegemonies of the north-west: from Kaabu to Futa Jallon

In the seventeenth century Kaabu established itself as the big power in the Southern Rivers sector from the Gambia to Sierra Leone. Organized into twelve confederated Mande provinces, including Fulbe enclaves and Bainuk, Balante and Joola groupings, Kaabu was led by a supreme *mansa* (with his seat at Kansala) supported by an aristocracy of soldier-officials and a standing cavalry corps. This kingdom, which had become an empire, controlled the trade of the Gambia valley and the Guinea rivers (the Casamance, the Rio Cacheu and the Rio Geba) on which were the European trading stations of Cacheu, Farim, Ziguinchor, Bissau, Geba, Albreda and Fort James. At the end of the seventeenth century Mansa Biram was selling 600 slaves a year, buying all kinds of merchandize and levying customs through his licensed *alcali* (collectors).[44]

In the second half of the eighteenth century the Fulbe Muslim confederation of Futa Jallon established itself. It emerged from the Muslim revolution that shook the Guinea–Sudan massif in about 1725–30, and gradually became the hub of relations between the Rivers Coast and the countries of the hinterland. Situated at the confluence of the rivers that run down to the sea from the Upper Niger area, Futa Jallon was to set

43. Y. Person, 1981, pp. 47–55.
44. S. M. Cissoko, 1972, p. 10.

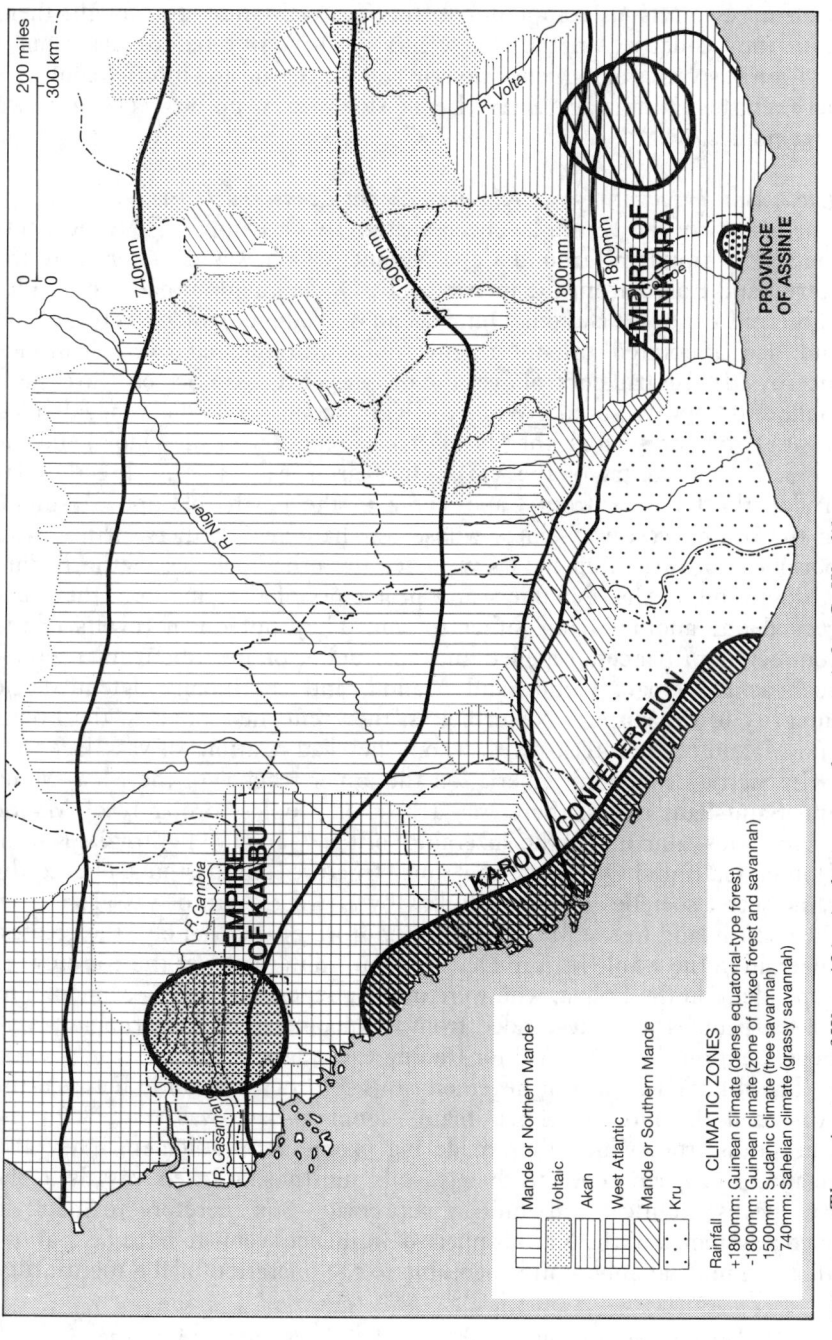

FIG. 13.4 *The main states of West Africa in the seventeenth century (after C. Wondji)*

Mande or Northern Mande

Voltaic

Akan

West Atlantic

Mande or Southern Mande

Kru

CLIMATIC ZONES

Rainfall
+1800mm: Guinean climate (dense equatorial-type forest)
–1800mm: Guinean climate (zone of mixed forest and savannah)
1500mm: Sudanic climate (tree savannah)
740mm: Sahelian climate (grassy savannah)

EMPIRE OF KAABU

KAROU CONFEDERATION

EMPIRE OF DENKYRA

PROVINCE OF ASSINIE

R. Casamance

R. Gambia

R. Niger

R. Volta

200 miles

300 km

740mm

1500mm

1800mm

+1800mm

itself up as a serious competitor to the Kaabu Mande, and fought them until they collapsed in the nineteenth century. But before that time a division of spheres of influence covering all the coastal and interior countries between the Gambia and Sierra Leone slowly grew up between these two hegemonies.[45]

The coastal hegemony of the Karou in Sierra Leone and Liberia

The history of the Karou has been written by O. Dapper. First there was the Quoja kingdom, around Cape Mount, which was conquered by the Karou and Folgia from the interior. The Quoja kingdom had the peoples of Sierra Leone (the Bullom, Quilliga and Carrodoboe) under its protection and had appointed provincial governors who reigned over them like viceroys. It also had control over the peoples of the Rio Sestos, the eastern Galla and Cape Mesurado. When the Karou conquered Quoja they divided it into two main sectors: the *Quojabercoma* (country of the Quoja) and the *Veybercoma* (country of the Vai). The Karou leaders, who directly controlled the territory from Cape Verga in the north to Cape Mesurado in the south, were war-chiefs whose war-hardened soldiers, armed with poisoned arrows, often held sway over the other peoples of the region. Absolute monarchs, defenders and protectors of the kingdom, they succeeded one another from father to son. They put down revolts in the conquered provinces, repelled the onslaughts of neighbouring peoples, such as the Dogo, Gebbe and Manou, and continually defended the integrity of the empire. Nevertheless, they remained allied to the Folgia and Manou of the interior with whom they had relations of vassalage.

In Sierra Leone and Liberia, on the upper reaches of the Moa, Mano and Saint-Paul rivers, there was a host of peoples, probably of Mande origin, who came under the suzerainty of the Manou. The Folgia, Karou, Hondo, Galla and Quoja had the same structures and customs, obeyed the same secret societies and were linked by a rising chain of vassalage from the coast inland to the *Mandi-Mani* (the Lord of the Manou), the greatest suzerain in the whole region. Despite their military power the Karou were dependent on the Folgia, who were in turn dependent on the Manou. The coastal peoples were descended from the peoples of the interior but were dependent on their goodwill for trading exchanges.[46]

The function of Karou hegemony was to order this trade between the coast and the interior. Their main economic base was trade with the Europeans from which they made big profits as middlemen. They also retailed European goods to their vassals and those of their vassals to the Europeans. Political and military supremacy was therefore to maintain such a system, and the Karou sphere of influence seems to have been above all a commercial sphere indispensable to the operation of the mercantilist

---

45. J. Suret-Canale, 1976 edn, pp. 486–504; W. Rodney, 1970b, pp. 223–39.
46. O. Dapper, 1686 edn, pp. 252–74.

slave-trading system in this region in the seventeenth and eighteenth centuries.

European trade and the comprador *peoples of the coast*

The development of trade in the seventeenth and eighteenth centuries brought about the formation among the coastal peoples of merchant groups acting as intermediaries between the European ships and the African societies of the interior. Such were the *Mestizos* (half-castes) and *Creoles* (people born in a locality but with origins elsewhere) of the rivers in Casamance, Guinea and Sierra Leone.

From the Portuguese Lançados *to the* Mestizos *and* Creoles *of the rivers in Guinea and Sierra Leone*

Whether Afro-Portuguese, descended from the Portuguese settlers of the fifteenth and sixteenth centuries, or Anglo-Africans descended from the British merchants of the seventeenth and eighteenth centuries, the *mulatto* groups made up a very special people. Their influence on the historical development of the coast between the Gambia and Sierra Leone was decisive.

Lançados *and Afro-Portuguese*   Portuguese influence in West Africa was due to deliberate immigration but particularly to the many expatriates who populated the Southern Rivers and the Atlantic islands (especially Cape Verde) from the fifteenth century onwards. They included merchant adventurers and agents of the trading companies and were called the *lançados*. W. Rodney defines the latter as people who were thrown (*lançar*, to throw) among the blacks to do business. Most of them were Portuguese, with a sprinkling of Greeks, Spaniards and even Indians. They recruited African *grumetes* (auxiliaries) and plied the valleys of the Senegal, the Gambia, the Casamance and the little rivers of Guinea. Many settled in the Cacheu and Geba sectors (partly Guinea-Bissau now), and some in Sierra Leone at Port Loko. By the late 1500s and early 1600s they had penetrated Soso country and encountered the Mande traders from the interior.

The *lançados* soon laid the foundations of an Afro-Portuguese community: settled in villages and living close to blacks, they took African wives or mistresses. Portuguese soon became a local *lingua franca* second to Mande. The Portuguese presence was thus secured during the following centuries despite the decline of the mother country.

The *lançados* and their descendants controlled local trade in Upper Guinea in the seventeenth and eighteenth centuries. But the racial composition of the group changed conspicuously. In the seventeenth century the flow of migrants decreased until the number of pure Portuguese fell below that of the *mulattos*, and the *lançados* came to include more and more halfbreed children, the *filhos da terra* (children of the land), who dominated the Beafada and Port Loko areas in the mid-1600s. The *Mestizos* became blacker and blacker until they could hardly be distinguished from Africans. By the end of the eighteenth century the Afro-Portuguese community thus comprised few whites and many blacks; but it was run by the *Mestizos*, who had imparted to it its main socio-cultural features.

The *lançados* had produced a socio-cultural group new to the coasts of Africa. Speaking Portuguese, dressing in European style and living in oblong houses with whitewashed walls and sleeping verandahs, they nevertheless adopted even such African customs as tattooing and making ethnic markings. They practised a distorted Catholicism in which the wearing of the cross went hand-in-hand with a strong belief in charms, and the celebration of the Christian saints did not inhibit ancestor veneration.

The *lançados* were first bound to the peoples of the coast by bonds of friendship – Bibiana Vaz of Cacheu, for example, co-operated closely with the Papel and Bainuk and owned property at Farim among the Mande. Later some were integrated into the social, political and cultural life of the African peoples by kinship ties – José Lopez de Moura, for example, grandson of a Mane king of Sierra Leone, often took part in the political life of this sector where he became the greatest kingmaker of the second half of the eighteenth century. Others were quite simply Europeanized Africans, such as Francisco Correia, a Mande from Geba who spoke fluent Portuguese, was highly educated and dressed elegantly in the European style.[47]

This Afro-Portuguese group drew its strength from its function as a *comprador* class. Its members did no productive work but purveyed goods to the European ships and carried on a seasonal trade related to the agricultural activities of the indigenous Africans. They thus made big profits and so came under attack from the European trading companies which tried to by-pass them.

While most were dependent on the European ships some became rich enough to do without them. These included the great *mulatto* families of the time: the Vaz of the Rio Cacheu and Rio Nuñez; the Tomba Mendez and Antonio Vaz in the Gambia; Sittel Fernando of the Rio Pongo and Rio Nuñez; and José Lopez de Moura in Sierra Leone. The Bibiana Vaz family became prominent in the Cacheu sector in the seventeenth century. Bibiana lived in Cacheu in Papel country but had a house among the Bainuk and another at Farim among the Mande. She had a two-masted ferry-boat and her brother, Ambrosio, at Cacheu, and her nephew, Francisco, ran a substantial business on the Rio Nuñez. Senhora Bibiana Vaz's counterpart in Sierra Leone was Senhor José Lopez de Moura, the richest man in this area in the first half of the eighteenth century.

There were many disagreements between the wealthy *mulatto* traders and the trading companies, particularly between supporters of free and unrestricted trade and supporters of regulation and monopolies. The middlemen had to resist the trading companies' attempts to by-pass them.

47. For full details about the Afro-Portuguese see W. Rodney, 1970b, pp. 200–22.

From 1684 to 1685, for example, Bibiana Vaz quarrelled with Captain José Gonçalves Doliveira of the Cacheu Company for refusing non-Portuguese ships permission to trade in the area even if they had paid their anchorage dues. The Afro-Portuguese merchants, led by Bibiana Vaz, petitioned against the measure and won over the local Papel who finally compelled Doliveira to permit trade with the English.

The determination of the middlemen groups to control the economic and political destinies of the coast by advocating free trade as against the monopoly of the big European companies, expressed itself in Sierra Leone in the form of José Lopez de Moura's struggle with the Royal African Company. The British company aimed in particular at breaking the alliance between the African rulers and the *mulattos* and put an end to the latter's role as middlemen. Led by Lopez de Moura, the *mulattos* reacted against this threat to their existence and, at the height of the struggle, destroyed the company's factory which was never able to resume its activities in Sierra Leone.

From the English merchant adventurers to the Anglo-Africans of Sierra Leone
Another *mulatto* group was the Anglo-Africans of Sierra Leone who came into being in the eighteenth century. By 1800 they formed a group of nearly 12 000 people among whom the Tuckers, Rogers, Corkers and Clevelands were the leading families.

The Tuckers, Rogers and Caulkers (later Corkers) came from England in the seventeenth century and were initially involved in the trade of the English companies. They took African wives and thus penetrated indigenous society within which they were associated with the ruling class. The Rogers and the Corkers, for example, married into the royal family of Sherbro Island. As with the Afro-Portuguese, a culturally hybrid social group came into being here in which a man such as James Cleveland, whose mother was a Kisi woman, could occupy a prominent position in the secret society of the Poro.

As servants of the trading company the ancestors of the Anglo-Africans initially did menial factory jobs such as store-keepers, carpenters and locksmiths. But they soon became important commercial middlemen and enriched themselves considerably. In about 1690 the Tuckers dominated Sherbro Island; and in the mid-eighteenth century Henry Tucker was its leading representative. In the second half of the eighteenth century, James Cleveland came to prominence in Sierra Leone.[48]

Thus in the seventeenth and eighteenth centuries the Afro-Portuguese and Anglo-Africans constituted a social group with specific economic functions, and provided a cultural milieu in which Europeans and Africans, whites and blacks, came together. Conscious of this role, they managed to make their mark with whites and blacks alike. But conscious of their interests they exploited the Africans from whom they extracted maximum

48. ibid.

profits; and although they rebelled against the rigid monopoly of the trading companies, they were none the less agents in the service of European mercantile capitalism.

Trade and peoples from the Grain Coast to the Tooth Coast
From Cape Mesurado to Cape Lahou, the development of European trade in the seventeenth and eighteenth centuries did not give rise to any dynamic merchant groups among the Kru peoples. Although poorly linked to the Sudanic hinterland, this coastal sector nevertheless boasted many villages built at the mouths of the rivers, and abounded in a great variety of produce. The English and Dutch ships took on supplies of malaguetta pepper at the River Sestos, Cape Palmas and Cavally and slaves at Bassa, Drewin and Saint Andrew: ivory they bought everywhere.

This sector's lack of economic dynamism, despite its wealth of ivory, was no doubt due to the malaguetta crisis and the mentality of the people who were poor and more concerned with receiving presents than organizing trading relations with the Europeans. The one exception was the Saint Andrew river area which offered the ships its gold and slaves and its 'elephants' teeth' weighing over 100 kilograms. Its 'amiable and dignified' chiefs were draped in loincloths as on the Quaqua Coast.

Conclusion

Despite the difficulties inherent in drawing up a historical synthesis of this region, it can be seen that between 1500 and 1800 these peoples and countries experienced a unified development. From relative isolation they were gradually integrated into the circuits of the world market built up by the Europeans' Atlantic voyages since the great explorations. This integration was accompanied by population movements from the interior to the coast and by sharp social and political changes wherever the people tried to take advantage of the opportunities European trade offered them.

The states and cultures of the Lower Guinean coast

A. A. BOAHEN

For the peoples of the Lower Guinea coast, from modern southern Côte d'Ivoire to modern Benin, or from the Bandama to the Mono rivers in general and the Akan, the Ga and the Ewe rivers in particular, 1500–1800 was – possibly – one of the most revolutionary periods in their history. It witnessed, first and foremost, the completion of the migrations of these peoples from their various cradles into their present areas of abode and the evolution of most of the ethno-linguistic groups into which they are divided today. Secondly, it saw the intensification of the trading and cultural links between these peoples and those of western Sudan, the Sahara and the Maghreb, and the opening of a completely new channel of communication and trade across the Atlantic – first with Europe and then with the Americas. Thirdly, it saw the gradual centralization of states and the evolution of larger political entities or kingdoms and empires. Indeed, by 1800 nearly the whole area was organized into a single empire under the rule of one dynasty. Finally, the period was one of radical social and cultural transformation and the evolution of new classes and new religions. These four themes form the subject of this chapter.

The migrations and the evolution of new ethno–linguistic groups

Both oral and documentary evidence confirms that, in 1500, although some of these peoples had penetrated and occupied the areas in which they live today, most were still concentrated in their various cradles. Some of the Akan, for example, had penetrated southwards to the coast, to modern south-eastern Côte d'Ivoire and south-western Ghana.[1] But most were still living in their cradle, in the area of modern Adansi and Amanse in the Ofin-Pra basin where they were divided into eight matrilineal Adangbe (clans) – the Ada, Osudoku, Shai, La, Ningo, Kpone, Gbugbla and Krobo clans.

The Ga–Mashi, the Nungua and the Tema had long broken away from their Adangbe kinsmen in the lower Volta basin around the Lolorvor hills

1. A. A. Boahen, 1977.

and had founded a host of settlements in the Accra plains north of the coastal region where they now live.[2] According to the archaeologist Ozanne, Ayawaso, regarded as the last such settlement, was founded towards the end of the sixteenth century.[3]

The Ewe of modern Togo and Ghana had not yet begun their migrations but were all concentrated in their third ancestral home, Nuatsie or Notsie in modern Togo, the first two being Tado and Ketu.[4]

Between 1500 and 1800, particularly in the 1600s and early 1700s, the final phase occurred of the dispersions of these peoples into the areas in which they live today. Partly for economic reasons – to tap the new discovered gold- and kola-producing regions, partly for social reasons – population pressure, but mainly for political reasons, the Akan, the Ga–Adangbe and the Ewe began to move out in all directions, usually in small clan and lineage groups. The Akan, for instance, in the sixteenth century moved first north and east into the present Kumasi, Mampong and Akyem areas, and south and south-west into the present Wassa, Igwira, Sanwi and Assini areas. In the seventeenth century, more Akan moved in different matrilineal clan groups north into the present Asante, Asante–Akyem and Kwahu areas, northwest into the Kulango areas and southwest into the Wassa-Sehwi and the Lagoon areas of Côte d'Ivoire. Mainly for political reasons, 1680–1730 saw a particularly large and persistent migration of the Akan from the Kumasi, Anwianwia and Denkyira areas into the present Nzima, Aowin, Sehwi, Ahafo and northern Bono areas and the Anyi and Baule areas of Côte d'Ivoire. By the mid-1750s the Akan flow seems to have dried up.

During the Akan migration, the Ga also continued their dispersion from inland to the coast largely in response to the European presence there and the consequent greater economic opportunities. The Ga–Mashi, the Nungua and the Tema were the first to move in the sixteenth century and they were followed in the seventeenth by the Osu and Teshi peoples. Their kinsmen, the Adangbe, also began to spread out southwards and northwards into the Accra plains during the sixteenth and seventeenth centuries, some who moved north-eastwards into the mountainous regions becoming the Manya Krobo of today. Others, in the seventeenth century, moved to the coast to found such settlements as Ningo, Prampram and Ada.

The most dramatic migrations, however, were those involving the Ewe. In the late 1500s or early 1600s, mainly for political reasons and especially to escape the tyrannical rule of their king, Agokoli, the Ewe left Notsie in two main groups, the southern Ewe (Dagboawo or Dzieheawo) and the northern or interior Ewe (Demeawo or Numeawo).[5] The southern group

2. C. C. Reindorf, 1898, pp. 6–12.

3. P. Ozanne, 1962, p. 69.

4. N. L. Gayibor, 1977, pp. 11–15; H. W. Debrunner, 1965, pp. 3–10; C. M. K. Mamattah, 1979.

5. C. M. K. Mamattah, 1979, pp. 121–2.

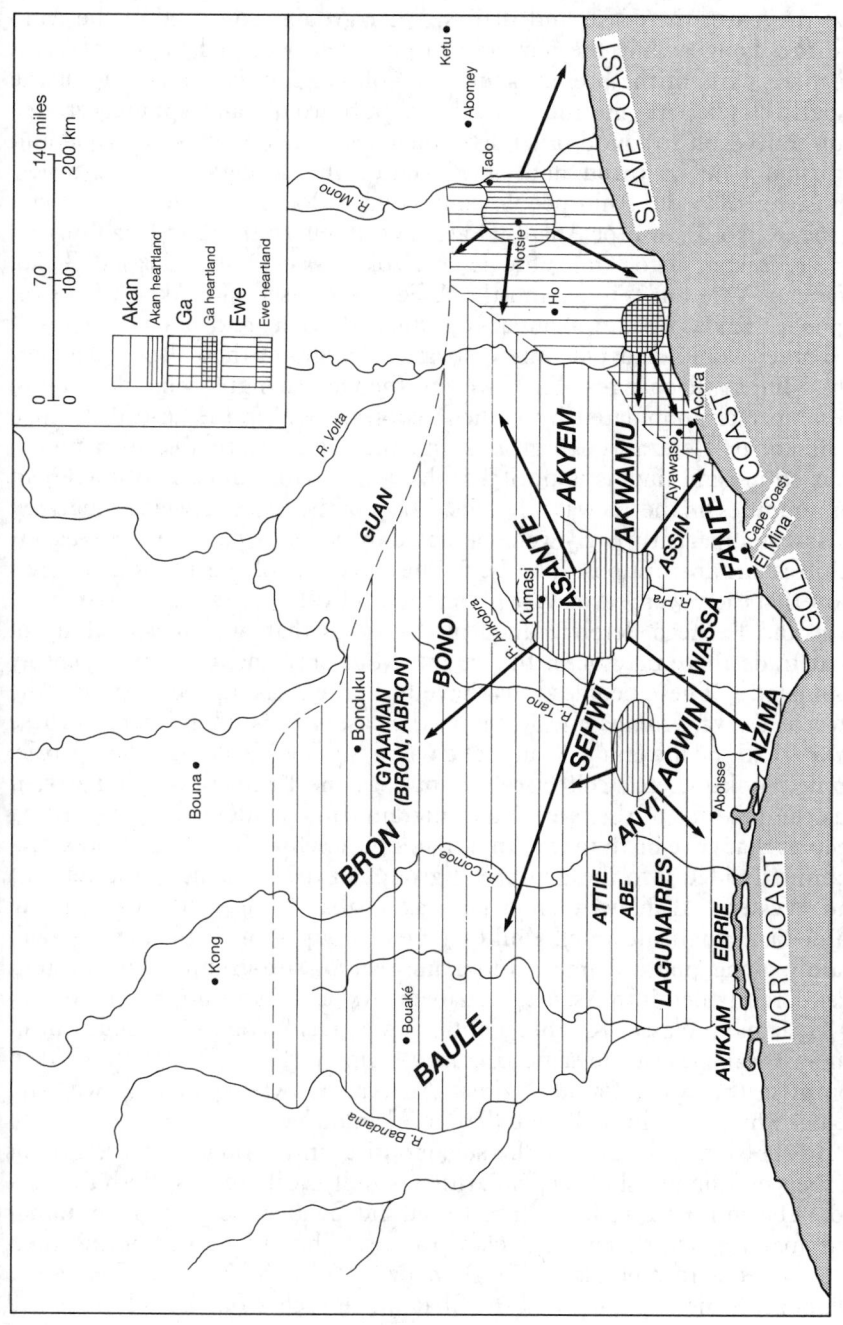

FIG 14.1   *The Akan, Ga and Ewe peoples (after A. A. Boahen)*

that moved to the coast, and their splinter groups, consisted of the Anlo and the Tongu while the northern groups that occupied the central and northern parts of the present southern Volta region were made up of the Asogli, Hopke, Akpini and Awudome. Sub-groups and splinter groups soon moved off to found other settlements and this process of fission and diffusion went on throughout the seventeenth and eighteenth centuries. Thus, by 1800 the Anlo people comprised Anlo, Afife, Ave, Xevi, Veta, Some, Kliko, Flawu (or Aflao), Dodze and Avenori; the Tongu comprised Agave, Bakpa, Bato, Dofo, Fievie, Fodzoku, Mofi, Mefa, Sokpoe, Tefle, Togome, Volo and Vume; and the Asogli comprised Ho, Akoefe, Hodzo, Kpenoe, Takla, Adaklu, Abutia, Agotime, Akoviefe, and so on.[6]

These peoples did not only disperse or migrate: they also underwent ethno-linguistic changes. The Ewe and the Ga–Adangbe, who moved into areas sparsely populated by earlier peoples, such as the so-called Togo Remnant or Central Togo groups and the Guan, were able to maintain their ethnic and linguistic purity. Indeed, the main influence of the Guan communities on the Ga was religious. Many of the Akan, however, migrated into areas apparently fairly well populated by peoples of different languages, cultures and institutions. The Portuguese records of the 1480s and 1490s show that there were seven villages on the Côte d'Ivoire east of the Bandama river and Pacheco Pereira added in the 1550s that 'we know nothing of what trade there may be in this country but only know that it is densely populated'.[7] These peoples must have been the Adisi in the west, and the Ewotre, Agwa, Kompa and Mono in the east. It was the mixture of these groups and the incoming Akan that gave rise to the Mbalo, Alladian, Ebrie, Eotile, Avikam, etc., collectively known as the Lagunaires. Similarly, it was the mixture of the later Akan migrants and some of the pre-existing peoples that gave birth to the Anyi, Baule and Sehwi. The Akan, therefore, became divided into the two broad groups of today, namely, the Eastern and Western Akan between whom, as Diabate insists, 'there is not an immediate linguistic intelligibility'. Each group is now further divided, mainly along political lines, into a number of sub-groups. The Eastern Akan are divided into Asante, Akuapem, Akyem, Akwamu, Bron (Abron) or Gyaaman, Wassa, Kwahu, Fante, Assin, Denkyira and Gomua, all of whom speak almost the same language, namely, Twi. The Western Akan comprise the Anyi, Baule, Nzima, Ahanta, Sanwi (Afema), Aowin and Sehwi who speak mutually intelligible Akan dialects.

By the sixteenth century the sociopolitical institutions of these groups in their new homes showed similarities as well as differences. Both the Ga–Adangbe and the Ewe lived in scattered independent settlements in minor and major patrilineages and clan groups. The Adangbe, for instance, are divided into nine clans: the Asinodze, Blaka, Kpoku, La, Lekpodze, Lenodze, Nangla, Sepote and the Shalom. In each group each lineage had

6. C. M. K. Mamattah, 1979, pp. 147 and 155–8.
7. Quoted by T. F. Garrard, 1980, p. 48.

its own senior god whose priests were its leaders. However, by 1600 the Ga-Mashi had developed the office of king, based at Ayawaso.

The Akan, conversely lived in towns ruled by kings and queens and villages ruled by chiefs. Each town or village was made up of families belonging to the eight matrilineal clans into which they are all divided. These matrilineal clans are Ekoona (Asanwule among the Nzima), Oyoko (Anona among the Fante, or Alonroba or Nvavile among the Nzima and Anyi and Dwum or Dwimina among the Fante), Asenee, Agona, Bretuo (Twidan among the Fante), Asakyiri, Aduana or Atwea (Aberadze among the Fante and Asamangama or Ahwea among the Nzima).[8] Each family had an *abusuapanin* (head, leader) and so did each clan. It appears that each family or clan had its own god or gods and so did each village or settlement whose priests wielded considerable power. Among the Ga and Ewe these priests acted not only as religious but also as political leaders. In other words, society had already become stratified, with a ruling aristocracy consisting of priests and kings, ordinary subjects and relatively small number of domestic slaves. However, this social set-up was greatly altered by the political and economic developments of the 1500–1700s.

Economic changes in Lower Guinea

Equally far-reaching economic developments, both internal and external, took place in Lower Guinea from 1500–1800. Internally, already-established economic activities were continued and greatly expanded. These included collecting, farming, livestock-raising, hunting, fishing, salt-making and gold-mining.[9] Collecting was quite widespread, its most important feature being the collection of kola nuts from trees which grew wild in the forest areas of the Gold Coast, especially near modern Asante, Ahafo and Akyem, the home of the eastern Akan. These nuts formed the mainstay of trade between the Akan and the Gur, Mande and Hausa speakers of the savannah and western Sudan.

Farming also grew in importance, the main crops being plantain, bananas, yams and rice. To these were added, in the sixteenth and seventeenth centuries, a host of new crops, introduced into the Guinea coast by the Europeans from Asia and the Americas and including corn (maize), cassava (manioc), various types of yam, tomatoes, onions, eggplants, avocado pears, sweet potatoes, citrus fruits and groundnuts.[10] The rapid adoption of these crops by small farmers diversified the agricultural economy of the Guinea coast and must have thereby accelerated population growth.

Livestock-raising involving poultry, sheep, goats and pigs was practised, as were fishing and hunting. Fishing was the main economic activity of the

8. A. A. Boahen, 1966, p. 4.
9. K. B. Dickson, 1969, pp. 72–89.
10. J. P. Murdock, 1959, pp. 21–4; D. G. Coursey, 1966.

Ewe, and Ga and other coastal peoples such as the Fante, the Ahanta, the Nzima and the Lagunaires. Hunting was done by all, first with spears, bows and arrows and sticks and later with guns.

Two of these primary activities, salt-making and gold-mining, became increasingly important between 1500 and 1800. Nearly all salt was produced by the coastal inhabitants,[11] while gold-mining was the exclusive preserve of the inland forest people, especially the Akan in the Wassa region and the areas referred to in sixteenth- and seventeenth-century European records as Arcany or Akanny or Arcania – that is, modern Asante, Kwahu and Akyem[12] as well as Brong Ahafo, Bron or Gyaaman and Baule. These were the areas which also produced kola nuts, the mainstay of trade with northern and western Sudan. Gold was obtained in two ways, by panning the alluvial soils from riverbeds and dry valleys and *nkoron* (deep-mining). While panning had been in use since ancient times, deep-mining was probably introduced into Akan territory by the Mande in the thirteenth or fourteenth century.[13]

Gold-mining, which in many areas was rigidly controlled by the state and formed the main source of income of the rulers, reached its peak in the late 1600s when about 2 000 000 oz of gold was produced.[14] Throughout this period gold-mining remained the exclusive monopoly of the Akan themselves and all European efforts – particularly Dutch – to participate directly in its production were resisted.[15]

At the same time there developed another increasingly important economic activity, namely trade, in which slaves played a prominent role as porters. Trade fell into two sectors: internal and external. The Ewe, the Ga and the Akan had long been trading among themselves: fish and salt, produced by the Ewe, the Ga and the Fante, and Adangbe pottery being exchanged for the gold, *tweapea* (chewing sticks), ivory and iron or metalwear produced by the Akan of the interior. Oral traditions and European records clearly show that this internal trade, conducted in local and regional markets or fairs, increased in volume and importance. Of the salt trade between the coast and the interior Bosman says:

> It is not to be imagined what vast riches the Negroes get by boiling of salt and if they (i.e., the Fante) were always, or for the most part in Peace, those who follow that Employment would in a short time amass unwieldly sums; for all the Inland Negroes are obliged to fetch their salt from the Sore, from whence it is easy to infer that it must cost them very dear . . .[16]

11. For a vivid description of the different ways in which salt was produced on the Guinea Coast, see W. Bosman, 1967, pp. 308–9.

12. A. A. Boahen, 1973.

13. T. F. Garrard, 1980, pp. 24–5; I. G. Wilks, 1962c, p. 166.

14. T. F. Garrard, 1980, p. 166.

15. W. Bosman, 1967, p. 80.

16. ibid., p. 308.

But even more important was the development of external trade. Two branches developed, the older with the savannah and western Sudan and the other across the Atlantic with Europe and later, the Americas. Arabic sources such as the *Kano Chronicle*, Portuguese records from 1470–1500 and oral traditions clearly show that by 1500 the Ga, the Ewe and the Akan had established trading links with the Guan and Gur to their north, with the Hausa of northern Nigeria to the north-east and the Mande of the Niger Bend to the north-west in gold, kola nuts, textiles, slaves and salt. Between 1500 and 1800 these links were strengthened, the Akan in particular building up trade with the Mande and Hausa during the sixteenth and seventeenth centuries.[17] With the rise and expansion of Songhay in the fifteenth and sixteenth centuries and consequent order and peace, trade between Akan and Mande boomed. It was to control this trade that the Joola established a number of trading posts or refreshment centres, such as Bobo-Dioulasso, Kong, Bonduku, Buna (Bouna) and Begho, between the Niger Bend and the gold-producing countries to the south. Jenne and Begho, the main entrepôts of the north-west trade became extremely wealthy during the sixteenth century, as is evident from both written and archaeological sources. In these north-western markets, the Akan exchanged mainly gold, kola nuts and, later, European imports for cloths, blankets, Turkish carpets, striped and blue silks, leather goods, iron-ware, brassware and salt.[18]

The overthrow of Songhay in the late 1500s and the subsequent insecurity was thought to have destroyed trade along the north-west routes. Now, however, it has been convincingly shown that trade did not decline during the eighteenth century but increased in volume instead.[19] It was with a view to tapping that trade that Asante expanded, conquering Bron or Gyaaman, Banda and Bono during the early 1700s. In fact this trade continued even into the nineteenth century in the new market centres that emerged, such as Atebubu and Kintampo.

Trade between the Akan and Hausaland and Borno also continued. It was already in progress and of some importance by the beginning of the sixteenth century, as substantiated by the eye-witness accounts of Leo Africanus who visited Songhay and Hausaland.[20] And it grew in intensity and volume, particularly during the seventeenth and eighteenth centuries following the growth of the Mole-Dagbane states of Mamprusi, Dagomba, Nanumba and Mossi and also the Hausa state. Nothing illustrates this better than the wealthy state in which the eighteenth- and early nineteenth-century European explorers and travellers found such towns as Kano and Katsina in Hausaland and, above all, Salaga in northern Gold Coast which

17. For evidence, see A. A. Boahen, 1977.
18. V. Lamb, 1975, pp. 86–92.
19. E. W. Bovill, 1968, p. 195; J. R. Willis, 1971; E. A. McDougall, 1980; C. C. Stewart, 1976.
20. Leo Africanus, 1956; N. Levtzion, 1968, pp. 14–22.

was then the main southern entrepôt for the north-east trade.

Gold may have been exported by the Akan to Hausaland in the sixteenth century, but it seems that gold exports had ceased during the eighteenth century, probably because of strong European competition. Akan kola, however, continued as the mainstay of the north-east trade from 1500–1800. Kola nuts were re-exported from Hausaland and Borno into the Sahara and Barbary states: in the 1780s Lucas met a Shereef in Tripoli who told him of the trade between Tripoli and Asante.[21] The nuts were conveyed in caravans of bullocks, asses, horses and slaves. In exchange, the Akan imported cotton cloths, blankets, Turkish carpets, smocks, sandals and other leather goods, natron, brassware and red glass beads. A far more important and voluminous trade, however, was also developing – the trans-Atlantic trade between the Lower Guinea coast and Europe and the Americas. It started when the Portuguese dropped anchor off the coast of modern Ghana in 1471. Then followed, in the sixteenth century, the French, English and Dutch and, in the seventeenth, the Danes, the Swedes and the Brandenburgers. The last two, however, abandoned the Guinea coast in 1661 and 1732 respectively. Direct trade with the West Indies began in 1518 when the first cargo of slaves was sent there in a Spanish ship. Trade with the North American mainland commenced in 1619 when a Dutch frigate discharged the first load of West African slaves at Jamestown in the state of Virginia.[22] Thus, by the mid-1600s, the triangular trade linking the Guinea coast, Europe and the Americas was fully established.

The commodities the Lower Guinea coast sold to Europeans varied from region to region and from century to century. Until the 1690s the Akan between the Bandama and the Ankobra rivers sold mainly ivory, while the Akan and the Ga between the Ankobra and the Volta rivers sold mostly gold. Throughout the sixteenth century, there seems to have been very little trade between the Ewe and the Europeans between the Volta and the Mono rivers. Most Portuguese avoided that stretch, sailing straight from the Accra region to Whydah in Dahomey and Benin in Nigeria.[23] Only from 1650 did the Dutch and the Danes operate there, slaves being the main commodity.

As a result of this specialization, European traders divided the coast of Lower Guinea into the Côte d'Ivoire, the Gold Coast and the Slave Coast. Until the end of the seventeenth century, however, gold was by far the most important commodity and of prime concern to both Europeans and Africans. Every European nation tried to gain a footing on the Gold Coast, and a huge number of forts and castles was built there between the Ankobra and the Volta rivers. According to Lawrence, as many as forty-two forts and castles were built in West Africa from Senegal to Cameroon, with

21. J. Beecham, 1841, pp. 149–55.
22. A. A. Boahen, 1971, p. 315. See also UNESCO, 1979, Document 12.
23. H. W. Debrunner, 1965, pp. 21–3.

PLATE 14.1 *Fort St George at El Mina, as it was in the time of the Portuguese*

thirty-two on the Gold Coast alone. None were built on the Nigerian coast.[24]

From 1650 to 1800, however, the export trade between the Ga and the Eastern Akan and Europe underwent a revolutionary change. The records clearly show that, in the fifteenth and sixteenth centuries, slaves were imported into the Gold Coast from Benin, São Tomé and Whydah – obviously to be used in the gold mines. In April 1529, for example, 2060 slaves were imported into the Gold Coast from Benin, and 80 from São Tomé to El Mina in 1535.[25] But from the mid-1600s the Ga and Akan of the Gold Coast began to export slaves and did so in such increasing numbers that by 1710 trade in slaves had exceeded that in gold. In 1704, the Dutch representative at El Mina, William de la Palma, reported that 'the Negroes ... now pay more attention to the slave trade than the gold trade as they do better by it'.[26] William Smith, an Englishman who visited the Fante Coast in 1726, remarked in disgust: 'Why this is called the Gold Coast, I do not know'.[27] The trade continued to grow throughout the first half of the eighteenth century: according to Daaku, 5–6000 slaves were being exported annually by 1700, rising to 6–7000 in the eighteenth century when, according to Curtin, a total of 474 000 slaves[28] was exported. The

24. A. W. Lawrence, 1969, pp. 12–13.
25. W. Rodney, 1969a.
26. Furley Collections (F.C.), W. de la Palma to the X, 31 Aug. 1704. See also K. Y. Daaku, 1970, pp. 46–7.
27. W. Smith, in T. Astley, 1745, Vol. II, p. 138.
28. P. D. Curtin, 1969, p. 221.

accuracy of Curtin's figures has been heatedly debated and there is now a general concensus that he underestimated the number exported from West Africa, especially during the eighteenth century, by as much as between 7.3 and 18.4 per cent.[29] The Ewe areas also exported large numbers, especially after 1730 when the Akwamu invaded the region.

Why, then, did the slave trade supersede that of gold on the Gold Coast in the eighteenth century? There are three main answers to this question. The first is the great increase in the demand for slaves following the introduction from the 1640s of the plantation system of sugar cultivation into the Caribbean Islands and the mainland of America. This demand was almost insatiable throughout the seventeenth and the eighteenth centuries.[30] The second answer is the enormous rise in the number of war-captives owing to a great increase in the incidence of wars and also from 1650, the growing use of fire-arms. The war-captives could not be contained locally and had to be exported. The period from 1670 to 1750, when the slave trade was at its peak, coincided with the rise and expansion first of the Denkyira and Akwamu and then of the Asante empires. Most slaves were war- or raid-captives.[31] The third answer, which follows from the second, is the increase in the number of slaves collected as tribute from vassal states especially following the rise of the three new empires. Most of their vassal states – especially Asante's – paid tribute in the form of slaves. Like gold, the supply of slaves to Europeans on the Gold Coast remained the exclusive preserve of the Africans themselves.

Although the Ewe, Ga and Eastern Akan exported more slaves than gold from the end of the seventeenth century, the western Akan of Côte d'Ivoire continued to export primarily ivory and gold throughout the seventeenth and eighteenth centuries.

Imports into Lower Guinea also underwent revolutionary changes both in volume and quality. In the late 1400s and the 1500s the principal imports were clothes mostly manufactured not in Europe but in the Barbary states, Benin and Côte d'Ivoire.[32] Clothes from the Barbary states, referred to in early Portuguese sources as *lanbens, hallabens* and *aljaravais*, the cloths of Benin and the Quaqua cloth of the Ivory Coast were popular on the Gold Coast before the arrival of the Portuguese who immediately took advantage of the demand and started trading in cloth. The export of Benin and Quaqua cloths to the Gold Coast certainly continued into the seventeenth century. Other imports, according to the list provided by Pacheco Pereira in the 1500s, were brass bracelets, handkerchiefs, corals and certain 'red

29. J. E. Inikori, 1976; P. D. Curtin, R. Anstey and J. E. Inikori, 1976; R. Stein, 1978. See also ch. 3 above.
30. J. E. Inikori, 1976, pp. 4–5.
31. P. E. H. Hair, 1965; P. D. Curtin, 1969.
32. V. Lamb, 1975, pp. 84–5.

shells which they prize as we prize precious stones, white wine and blue beads which they call coris'.[33]

By the seventeenth century the list of imports had increased considerably. Pieter de Marees, writing in the early 1600s, has left the following account of goods brought in by the Dutch alone:

> Great store of light linen cloth whereof there is very much spent in those for they apparell themselves therewith besides great store of basons of all sizes, for drinking, washing in, burials, kettles to fetch water in, red copper pots, castle pots; iron used to make assagaie, cutting knives; great store of red, blue, yellow and green Rupish cloth, used for girdles about their middles to hang their knives, purses etc. Spanish serges, Dutch knives, great store of Venice beads of all kinds, and colours which they break and grind and put them on strings made of bark of trees and sold, pins used to make fish hooks, looking glasses and small copper milk cans. But the chiefest wares that are wanted there and most used among them is Linen cloth, brass and copper things, basons, kettles, knives and corals.[34]

This list shows that these imports, including both textiles and beads, now came mainly from Europe. There is no mention of fire-arms, probably because the import of guns and gunpowder only began in earnest in the 1640s when the English and the interlopers started selling arms on the coast.[35] So popular did fire-arms become that in 1658 the Dutch could report that 'only musquets sell well' and that 'the natives take the field with thousands of them'.[36] In 1660 the Dutch lifted their fire-arms export ban and started exporting in quantity. Between 1673 and 1704 the Royal African Company alone shipped almost 66 000 fire-arms and more than 9000 barrels of gunpowder to West Africa, mostly to the Gold Coast. Fire-arms exports increased throughout the eighteenth century and remained the item most in demand on the Gold Coast. According to Inikori, from 1750 to 1807 a total of 49 130 368 pounds of gunpowder was exported to West Africa from Britain alone giving an annual average of 847 075 pounds.[37]

The value of non-slave exports from West Africa to England between 1750 and 1807 was £5 443 682 (£900 000-worth of gold) while that of slaves exported by English merchants alone totalled £53 669 184. If the English share of the trade in slaves was 45 per cent, the total value of exports from West Africa during the second half of the eighteenth century would have been £131 361 920 or £2 264 861 annually.[38]

33. D. P. Pereira, 1937.
34. P. de Marees, in S. Purchas, 1905, Vol. VI, pp. 281–2.
35. R. A. Kea, 1971; K. Y. Daaku, 1970a, pp. 148–52.
36. F. C. Valkenburgh's Report to the XIV, June 1658.
37. J. E. Inikori, 1977.
38. J. D. Fage, 1969a; W. Rodney, 1969a.

The effects of the economic developments

Economically the Lower Guinea coast changed dramatically from 1500 to 1800 and the effects of this change were several. One was the evolution of a complicated network of major and minor trade routes. These first linked the peoples of the area to one another, then linked them to the Mole–Dagbane and Hausa to the north-east, the Mande to the north-west and to the Barbary states across the Sahara and the Muslim world. Finally the network spread across the Atlantic, first to Europe and, from the sixteenth century, to the Americas. At the centre of this network lay the town of Kumasi.

Another effect was the emergence mainly along these routes of a number of urban centres which served as entrepôts, market centres or termini. These included Kong, Bobo–Dioulasso, Buna, Begho and Bonduku to the north-west; Salaga, Yendi and Sansanne-Mango to the north-east and Tiassalé, Sakasso, Yakasso, Krinjabo, Kumasi, Kete–Krachi and Akwa-mufie in the south.

The European presence on the coast accelerated the growth of the towns there at the expense of the former capital towns immediately inland. By 1800 these towns had broken away from those inland and developed into independent city-states. Thus Mouri had broken away from Asebu, Cape Coast from Fetu, El Mina from Aguafo and Anomabo from Mankesim.

Another effect of the new network was the integration of the economy of the Lower Guinea coast into that of western Europe and America and also that of the Mande–Hausa–Muslim world. In time the latter link weakened, however, while that with Europe and the Americas grew stronger.

As a result of this integration economic and industrial developments in Lower Guinea were destroyed or stunted. Trade in slaves – the most destructive, hideous and inhuman of all trades – steadily replaced trade in natural products. Moreover, it denuded the area of its labour force and - some of its skilled artisans, craftsmen and artists. Instead of exporting goods which would have stimulated existing industries and the creativity of the Ewe, the Akan and the Ga, Europe exported only cheap mass consumer goods thereby killing existing industries or seriously retarding their growth. In short, from 1500 to 1800 there was economic growth in Lower Guinea but without economic development. Moreover, since Europe controlled both importation and exportation, she kept most of the profits. Herein lie the roots of the process of underdevelopment, aggravated in the 1900s by the abolition of the slave trade and the establishment of colonialism in Africa.

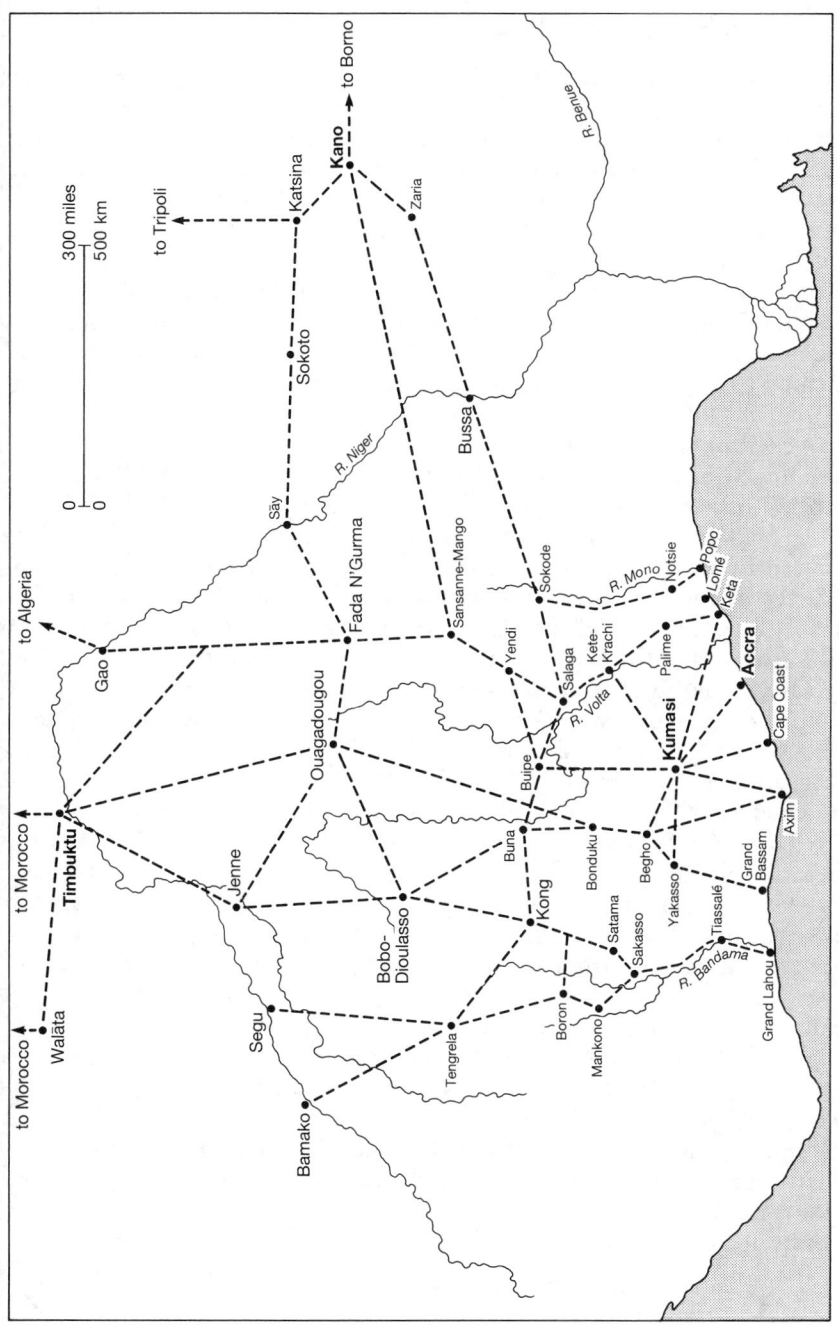

FIG 14.2 *Principal trade routes of the Bandama–Volta–Mono basins (after A. A. Boahen)*

Political changes on the Lower Guinea coast

Political change between 1500 and 1800 was even more radical than economic.

By 1500 the process of state formation had already begun and a number of states had emerged on the coast and in the northern savannah regions. The Portuguese arrived to find the coastal states of Ahanta, Shama Aguafo, Fetu, Asebu, Agona and Accra already in existence in addition to the Mole–Dagbane cluster of Mamprusi, Dagomba, Nanumba and Ouagadougou (Wagadugu) and the Akan state of Bono in the savannah belt.[39] The process of state-building continued to gather momentum with the first Akan kingdom, Bono, emerging in the second half of the fifteenth century and reaching its peak through the lucrative trade with the Mande and the Akan centred around Begho.[40]

During the sixteenth century, the Ga-Mashi, the Nungua and the Tema were joined in the Accra plains by the Labadi and the Osu, all of whom founded numerous settlements. Before 1300 the Ga had had no kings, being ruled by priests. But by 1600 secular kingship had evolved, probably inspired by their Akan or Adangbe neighbours. During the early 1600s, attracted by the European presence, some Ga moved to the coast. The Ga-Mashi, the Nungua and the Osudoku were the first to move followed by the La who founded Labadi on lands conquered from the Nungua while the Osu seized land from the Osudoku. The last Ga principality to be founded on the coast was Teshi built on land presented by the Nungua to a group that had migrated from Labadi. All these coastal towns, however, recognized the suzerainty of the Ga *Mantse* (king) at Ayawaso which remained the kingdom's capital until 1680 when it was moved to the coast.

What seems to have happened among the Akan in the 1500s was the formation in the Pra-Ofin basin of a number of small communities and city-states or chiefdoms bound together not by allegiance to a common sovereign but by kinship, agnatic and clan ties and linked by trade routes. However, it appears from the oral traditions of Adansi that, from about 1550, some move towards centralization was made by the clan and city-states around Fomena and Akrokyere led by Awurade Basa, king of Fomena.[41] This led to the formation of the Adansi confederation of states but also precipitated the migrations of some Akan northwards and southwards to found their own chiefdoms, city-states and principalities, such as Kwahu, Akyem Abuakwa, Akyem Kotoku and Akwamu; Wassa Twifo, Igwira and Adom further south; and Tafo, Suntreso, Kaasa and Amakom all now part of the municipality of Kumasi.[42]

State formation seems to have accelerated between 1580 and 1630 as

39. A. A. Boahen, 1966b and 1977.
40. C. K. Effah-Gyamfi, 1978.
41. K. Y. Daaku, 1969, p. iii.
42. K. Y. Daaku, 1966a, pp. 10–13.

demonstrated by a most revealing map of the states of southern Gold Coast between the Tano and Volta rivers drawn by a Dutch cartographer on 25 December 1629. The map depicts about thirty-eight states and kingdoms. All except two, Great Incassa and Incassa Igwira,[43] have been identified and still exist in the same areas.

These states were founded by the migratory Ga and Akan mentioned above. With so many states in so limited an area, they must have been small, many being mere city-states or small chiefdoms. However, though different in size, all appear to have been similarly structured, with a single ruler or chief, or a king and queen. The Adansi confederation, for example, rotated the headship among the royal families of its various states. In the single states, the king was selected (in accordance with the matrilineal principle in the case of the Akan) from its royal family – usually the first family or clan to arrive in the area. He was advised by a council of family – or clan – leaders and was more the first among equals than a dictator. Each state had its own gods – river, lake or rock gods, for example – and their priests wielded considerable influence in society.

Between 1630 and about 1670 two main political developments took place in the Ga and Akan areas. The first was the steady consolidation and growth of the states shown on the 1629 map and the second was the emergence of new states. Oral sources show that kingdoms like Akwamu, Denkyira, Accra or Ga, Fante, Wassa and Adom greatly expanded their frontiers largely through peaceful means. The Ga, for instance, extended northwards from the coastal plains to include the Guan principalities below the Akuapem Hills where they established their important market centre of Abonse – A.B.C. of the 1629 map – and westwards to include the Guan principalities of Awutu and Senya. Ga was at its biggest and most powerful peak under King Okai Akwei (*c*.1640–77).

At the same time the Aduana state of Akwamu also became a strong kingdom occupying present-day Asamankese, Kade, Nsawan and Akuapem. Meanwhile Denkyira broke away from the Adansi Confederation, after a series of wars in the 1650s and 1660s and firmly established itself at the confluence of the Ofin-Pra rivers.[44] On the coast the Fante extended their territory inland and European records frequently refer to wars between Fante and Etsi peoples to the north.[45] Wassa and Adom in the south and west also expanded.

The Denkyira–Adansi wars (1650–70) and the Bono wars had greatly accelerated migration southwards and westwards into the forest where older peoples, such as the Adisi, Ewotre, Agwa, Kompa and the Lagunaires,

---

43. Great Incassa and Incassa Igwira have been identified by some scholars such as Fynn and Porter with the Sehwi states whose rise will be discussed below. This, however, is doubtful since their oral traditions do not mention the former nor claim any relationship with them. See R. Porter, 1974, p. 37; J. K. Fynn, 1971, p. 43.

44. I. G. Wilks, 1957; K. Y. Daaku, 1970b, pp. 144–61.

45. A. A. Boahen, 1965, pp. 175–80.

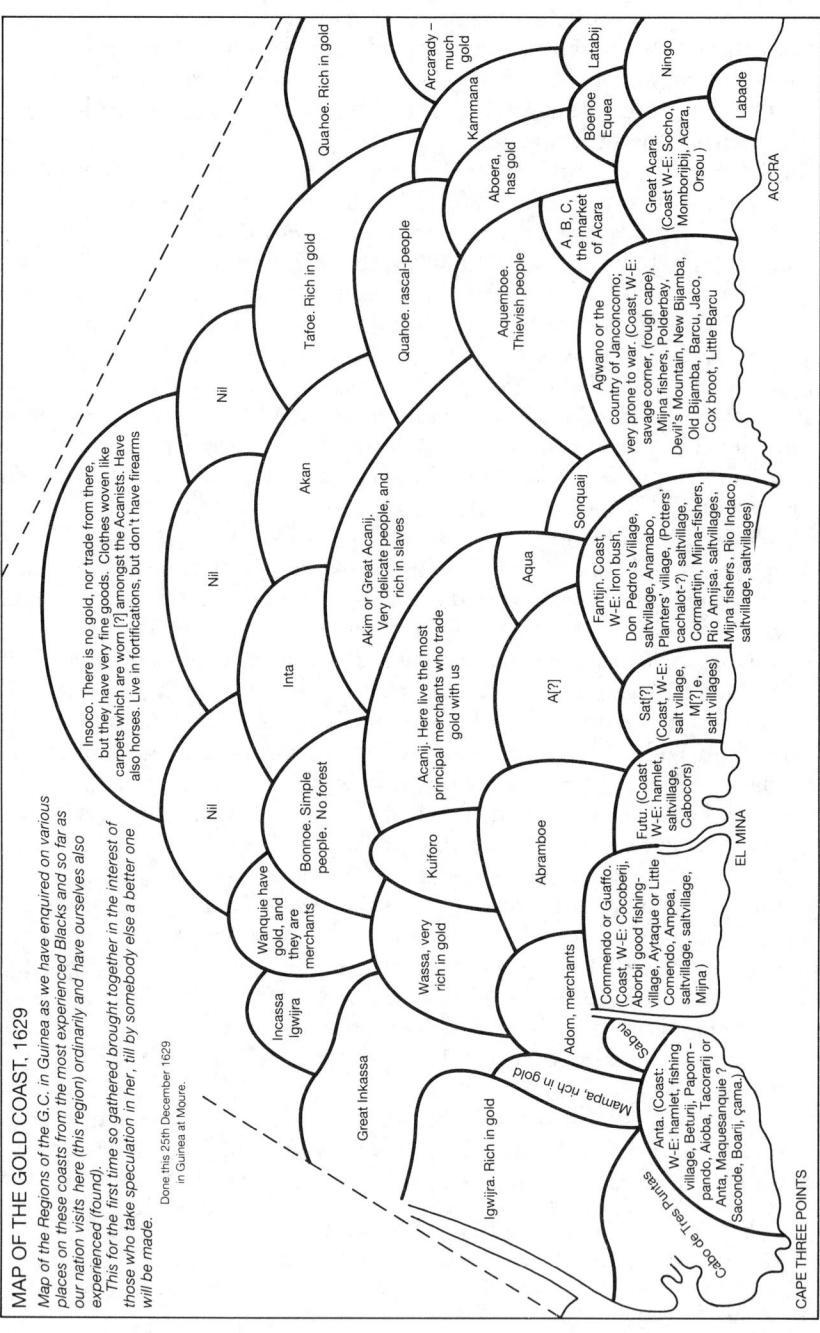

FIG 14.3 *Re-drawing of a 1629 map of the Gold Coast*

lived. These new groups founded not only Aowin, near present-day Wassa Amanfi, with its capital Enyini Nsu near the village of Anwianwia,[46] but also the three Sehwi states – Anwhiaso, Bekwai and Wiawso – in the south, states such as Assini, Abripiquem and Ankobra and a host of coastal towns. In one of the richest gold areas and on the main trade route linking the northern markets of Begho and Bonduku with the coast, by the 1670s Aowin had grown into a strong and rich kingdom.[47]

The Denkyira–Adansi migrants who moved northwards founded the Oyoko states of Kumasi, Kokofu, Dwaben, Nsuta and later Bekwai and the Bretuo states of Mampong and Afigyaase all within a fifty-kilometre radius of Kumasi. Further north others founded the Aduana state of Gyaaman or Abron among the resident Gbin, Nkoran, Nafana, Fantara and Kulango.[48]

The new states seem to have been organized like the old. The Sehwi and Aowin states, for instance, superimposed the sophisticated Akan clan system and the institution of matrilineally elected kingship on the existing socio-political structure based on *asago* (warrior) companies grouped around living-quarters.

However, between 1570 and 1600, a political revolution took place marked not by the emergence of new states but by the centralization of existing ones, apparently pioneered by Aowin and Denkyira (Fig. 14.4). In the 1670s and 1680s Aowin conquered the Sehwi states to the north and west and expanded far west to embrace such Côte d'Ivoire towns as Keteso, Yawu, Brako and Sikasso.[49]

While Aowin was expanding so was Denkyira, from her capital of Abankieso, at the Pra-Ofin confluence, in almost every direction. In the 1670s and 1680s, in a series of brilliant campaigns, the Agona rulers of Denkyira conquered all the Adansi and the pre-Asante states near Kumasi to the north and Assin and Twifo to the south. Between 1686 and 1690, they also defeated Aowin, the Sehwi states and Wassa to the south-west and the coastal kingdoms Adom and Fetu.[50] By 1690, Denkyira dominated the south-western Gold Coast and parts of the Côte d'Ivoire.[51]

In the south-eastern regions, meanwhile, Akwamu was also consolidating its power, expanding outwards from the newly established capital, Nyanoase, near modern Nsawan. The Akwamu rulers first attacked the Ga kingdom which was finally conquered in 1681. Then they turned westwards to subdue the coastal kingdom, Agona, in 1689. In their final campaigns (1702–10) they conquered the Adangbe states to the east and Kwahu to

46. Personal communication from H. Diabaté (1977).
47. K. Y. Daaku, n.d.
48. E. A. Agyeman, 1965, pp. 36–9; M. A. Clerici, 1962, pp. 27–8.
49. K. Y. Daaku, n.d.
50. ibid., pp. 156–60.
51. W. Bosman, 1967, pp. 72–3.

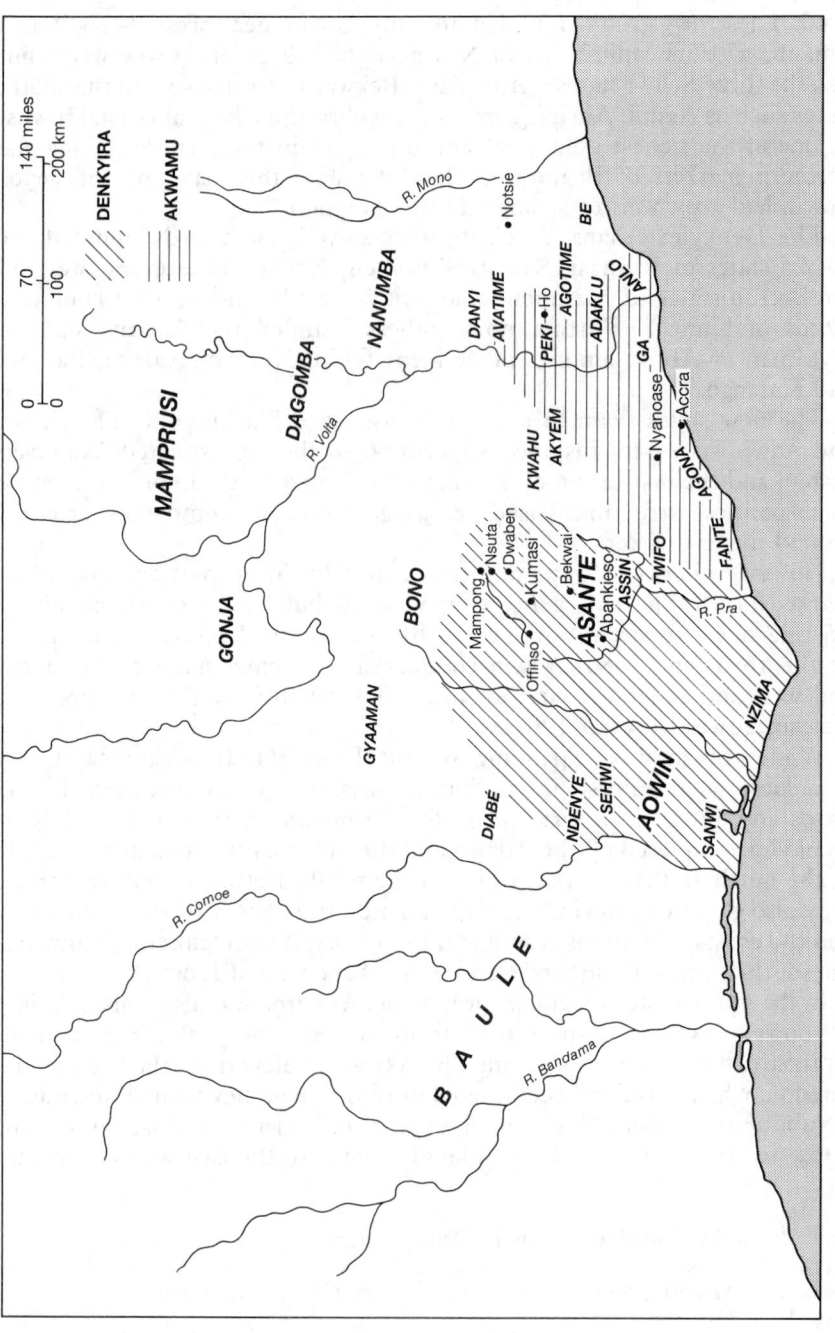

FIG 14.4 *States of the Lower Guinea coast, 1700 (after A. A. Boahen)*

the north, even crossing the River Volta and subduing the Ewe states of Peki, Ho and Kpandu.[52]

The Denkyira and Akwamu evolved similar machinery to administer their empires. Each was divided into two areas, metropolitan and provincial. The metropolitan centred around the capital headed by the *Omanhene* (king) who was also king of the whole empire. Under him was a series of officials or kings who performed certain functions at court, such as the *Batahene* (Minister of Trade), the *Sanaahene* (Finance), the *Gyaasehene* (Home Affairs), the *Akyeamehene* (Foreign Affairs and Head Linguist) and the *Sumankwaahene* (Religious Affairs). For politico-military purposes, each state was divided into wings, three in Denkyira and five in Akwamu. The Denkyira divisions were *Akumatire* (Right wing), *Kyeremfem* (Left wing) and *Agona Adontendom* (Advance Guard).[53] The Akwamu wings were *Benkum* (Left wing), *Nifa* (Right wing), *Adonten* or *Krontire* (Advance guard), *Kyidom* (Rear guard) and *Gyaase*. Each wing was headed by a king of a town or state within the metropolitan area or in the capital town itself. He exercised political control over his wing during peace time and became its *Osafohene* (war-leader) during wars. All the wing chiefs were members of the council that advised the *Omanhene*. The provincial area consisted of all the conquered states now part of the empire. Each continued to be ruled by its own king but was placed directly under the control of the *Omanhene* or a wing chief. Each state was expected to pay annual tribute and to fight in the wing of its head during battles.

Since Denkyira was the first state to develop into an empire, and since it had three wings while Akwamu had five, three of which were the same as those of Denkyira, Akwamu obviously borrowed the new imperial politico-military system from Denkyira, merely improving upon it by adding two more wings, namely *Kyidom* and *Gyaase*.

Many historians have seen the political history of the Gold Coast in the 1700s almost exclusively in terms of the rise of the Asante empire. But it was much more complex. First, there was the rise of other new states besides Asante. Secondly, there was the revival albeit brief, of Aowin and the overthrow of Denkyira and Akwamu by Akyem and Asante respectively. Thirdly, there was the expansion of the Fante kingdom to its widest territorial extent. Then, finally, there was the rise of the Asante empire, admittedly the most brilliant event of the century.

The other new eighteenth-century states included Nzima, the Aowin or Anyi states of Sanwi, Ndenye, Diabe, Moronou and Bettie, and many Baule principalities. After being defeated by the Denkyira in the 1680s, Amo Aseman led the Aowin or Anyi from Anwianwia across the River Tano to conquer the Agwa (Sohie and Anabula) and recreate their kingdom around Enchi. They were still consolidating when, in 1715, the Asante attacked forcing some Aowin westwards to found the kingdom of Sanwi

52. I. G. Wilks, 1957; K. Y. Daaku, 1970b, pp. 153–6.
53. J. K. Kumah, 1966, pp. 33–5; K. Y. Daaku, 1970b, p. viii.

after conquering the Aqua, Aboisse, Abakulo and Ekuebo and then the Eotile.[54] After establishing their capital, at Krinjabo, they soon conquered Assin thereby gaining control over trade between the interior and the Aby Lagoon.

North of Sanwi emerged the other Anyi states, Ndenye and Diabe, founded at the same time as Sanwi by the branch of Anwianwia refugees that moved north-westwards[55] into the area formerly occupied by the Agwa, Abure and other Lagunaires. The Anyi of Ndenye owed allegiance to Aowin until about 1715 but a section that refused to accept this moved away to found the kingdom of Bettie. Some Anyi, the Monfwe, crossed the River Comoe to establish the kingdom of Moronou.[56] The relations that existed between these latter states are not known but Ndenye was definitely brought under the control of Asante. Both Perrot and Gross thought that Ndenye served the *Asantehene* through the Sehwi state of Wiawso but recent research has confirmed Daaku's view that they did so through the *Bantamahene* of Kumasi.[57]

Northwest of the Anyi, between the Comoe and Bandama rivers, there also arose, during the first half of the eighteenth century, a host of Baule principalities or chiefdoms. The oral traditions of the founders clearly show that they arrived in two waves from the Gold Coast.[58] The first, the Alanguira Baule, arrived in 1700 about the same time as the Anyi. They came from Denkyira after its defeat by Asante in 1700–1. They settled in the area of the modern Canton of Agba whence some moved west to live among the Guro and Koro.

The second much larger wave, the Assabu, came from Kumasi following the disputed succession that broke out after the death of Osei Tutu in 1717. According to their oral traditions, they were led by their Queen Abla Poku who sacrificed her son to the spirit of the River Comoe before they could cross, hence their name *Baule* (the infant is dead). Some moved north to form the Ando and others south to Grand-Morie among the Attie and the Abe. The rest, still under Queen Abla Poku, moved south across the Bandama river and then north again to the Bouaké region. This group was divided into eight large families or clans: the Faafuwe, Nzipri, Aitu, Nanafowe, Warebo, Saafowe, Agba and Ngan.[59] Akwa Boni, who succeeded Queen Abla Poku, was apparently able to establish his authority over the Baule, the Malinke and the Mande who occupied the Warebo region. After his death, however, the kingdom broke up into independent chiefdoms.

54. Personal communication from H. Diabaté, 1977. See also R. A. Horowitz, 1974, pp. 330–79; H. Diabaté, 1977; M. A. Clerici, 1962, pp. 27–31.

55. C. H. Perrot, 1970 and 1974.

56. M. A. Clerici, 1962, pp. 27–31.

57. C. H. Perrot, 1970 and 1974, K. Y. Daaku, 1971.

58. J. P. Chaureau, 1979, pp. 24–5; M. A. Clerici, 1962, pp. 28–9; T. C. Weiskel, 1980, pp. 5–8.

59. M. A. Clerici, 1962, pp. 28–9; J. P. Chaureau, 1974.

Both waves of invaders soon mixed with the Guro, the Malinke, the Senufo and the Goli to form the modern Baule people.

The Nzima kingdom which also emerged at this time was the creation of three brothers, Annor Blay Ackah, Bua Kpanyili and Amihere II who amalgamated under their rule the three states of Jomoro, Abripiquem and Ankobra through their wealth gained from European trade. The most famous brother, Amihere II, was to become extremely rich in the 1760s. He extended the frontiers of the new kingdom, increasing its population by deliberately encouraging outsiders to settle there. Known in European records as Apollonia, this new state dominated the south-western corner of the Gold Coast throughout the eighteenth century.

Meanwhile some of the older states, such as Bron, Sehwi Wiawso, Aowin and Fante were extending their power and influence. Aowin, for example, appeared to have regained its independence from Denkyira in the 1690s. Greatly strengthened by refugees, who poured in from the Asante–Denkyira wars, it came to dominate the Sehwi states and from 1700–10 began the conquest of the gold- and ivory-producing regions to the north. So powerful and intrepid did it grow that, in 1718–19, under its commander Ebri Moro, it invaded the Asante, sacking the capital, Kumasi, and returning home with loot and captives including some members of the Asante royal family.[60]

Also in the early 1700s, the state of Bron conquered the Kulango to the south and part of the Nafana to the north and extended its power as far west as the Comoe river thereby dominating the trade routes from Bonduku to Kumasi and Krinjabo. The new Bron state was unique, being made up of Akan, Kulango, Nafana and Mande elements. At the top politically were the Akan invaders who maintained their clans, their matrilineal system of inheritance, their judicial system and aspects of their traditional religion. But they adopted Kulango and Nafana folklore, songs and dances and left untouched Nafana social structures and political orders at village and rural levels. In addition some of these three groups accepted Islam, introduced by the Mande–Joola who also greatly influenced the economic system of the kingdom.[61]

It was also between 1700 and 1710 that the Akwamu extended their empire across the River Volta to its widest territorial limits.[62] By 1730, in response partly to Akwamu expansion and later to Asante and Akyem expansion the Fante had conquered their neighbouring coastal states, Aguafo and Fetu to the west and the Agona to the east,[63] giving them control of the coast from the Pra river to the Ga kingdom.

The political changes that occurred in the central forest regions between the Comoe and Volta rivers between 1500 and 1800 were even more

60. K. Y. Daaku, n.d.; J. K. Fynn, 1971, p. 43.
61. M. Toure, 1974, pp. 463–78.
62. I. G. Wilks, 1957.
63. A. A. Boahen, 1965, pp. 180–2.

dramatic. First was the defeat and overthrow of the Denkyira empire in a series of wars (1699–1701) by the young Asante confederation of states. This was followed by the conquest of all Denkyira's former vassal states, such as the Sehwi states (1701–2), Twifo (1712–13) and Wassa (1713 and 1726). The Asante then conquered Aowin (1715–21), Nzima (1715) and the Anyi state of Ndenye (1715) to the south-west, and Wenchi (1711–14), Bono (1723–4), the Bron state (1731–40) and Gonja (1732) to the north-west.[64] Thus, by 1730, from the Comoe to the Volta rivers was under Asante control.

Second was the defeat in 1731 of Akwamu by Akyem Abuakwa and her allies the Ga, Kotoku and Agona.[65] The Akwamu rulers were driven from their traditional homelands across the Volta river where they founded their present capital town, Akwamufie, and the Birim–Densu basin was annexed by Akyem Abuakwa. Thus by 1733, from the Comoe to the Volta rivers was partitioned among the Asante, the Akyem and the Fante.

Centralization was completed between 1731 and 1750 when the Asante conquered Akyem Kotoku and Akyem Abuakwa (1742) and the Ga state (1744–5) to the south, Eastern Gonja and the Dagomba state (1744) to the north of the Volta river, and the Krakye and Bassa states (1744–5) to the north-east.[66] By the mid-1700s the Asante empire stretched from the middle reaches of the Comoe river in the west to the River Volta in the east and from beyond the Volta in the north, south to the sea except for the Fante state directly south of Kumasi. The Fante maintained their sovereign existence throughout the eighteenth century through their own diplomatic skills and strong support from the British who wanted to stop the Asante gaining control over the whole coast.[67]

Asante's structure and government was similar to Akwamu's and Denkyira's. It was divided into metropolitan Asante and provincial Asante (Greater Asante, as Arhin calls it). Metropolitan Asante – unlike Metropolitan Denkyira or Akwamu – consisted not of just one town or state but, significantly, of all the former states within a fifty-kilometre radius of Kumasi. These included Dwaben, Kokofu, Bekwai, Nsuta, Mampong, Offinso, Asumenya, Denyasi, Adansi and Kumawu all of which recognized the *Ohene* (king) of the Kumasi state as their *Asantehene* (paramount king) and Kumasi as their capital. They accepted the Golden Stool as the soul and sacred symbol of the unity and survival of the Asante nation and were represented by their own *Omanhene* on the Asanteman Council, the governing body of the confederation and the entire empire. For politico-military reasons, metropolitan Asante was divided, like Akwamu, into five wings with the same names as their Akwamu counterparts: *Benkum, Nifa,*

64. For details of these campaigns and conquests, see J. K. Fynn, 1971, pp. 40–83; K. Y. Daaku, 1970, pp. 173–81; I. G. Wilks, 1975, pp. 18–29.

65. F. Addo-Fening, 1980.

66. I. G. Wilks, 1975, pp. 18–29; J. K. Fynn, 1971, pp. 57–80.

67. For further details, see A. A. Boahen, 1965, pp. 182–5; and 1974.

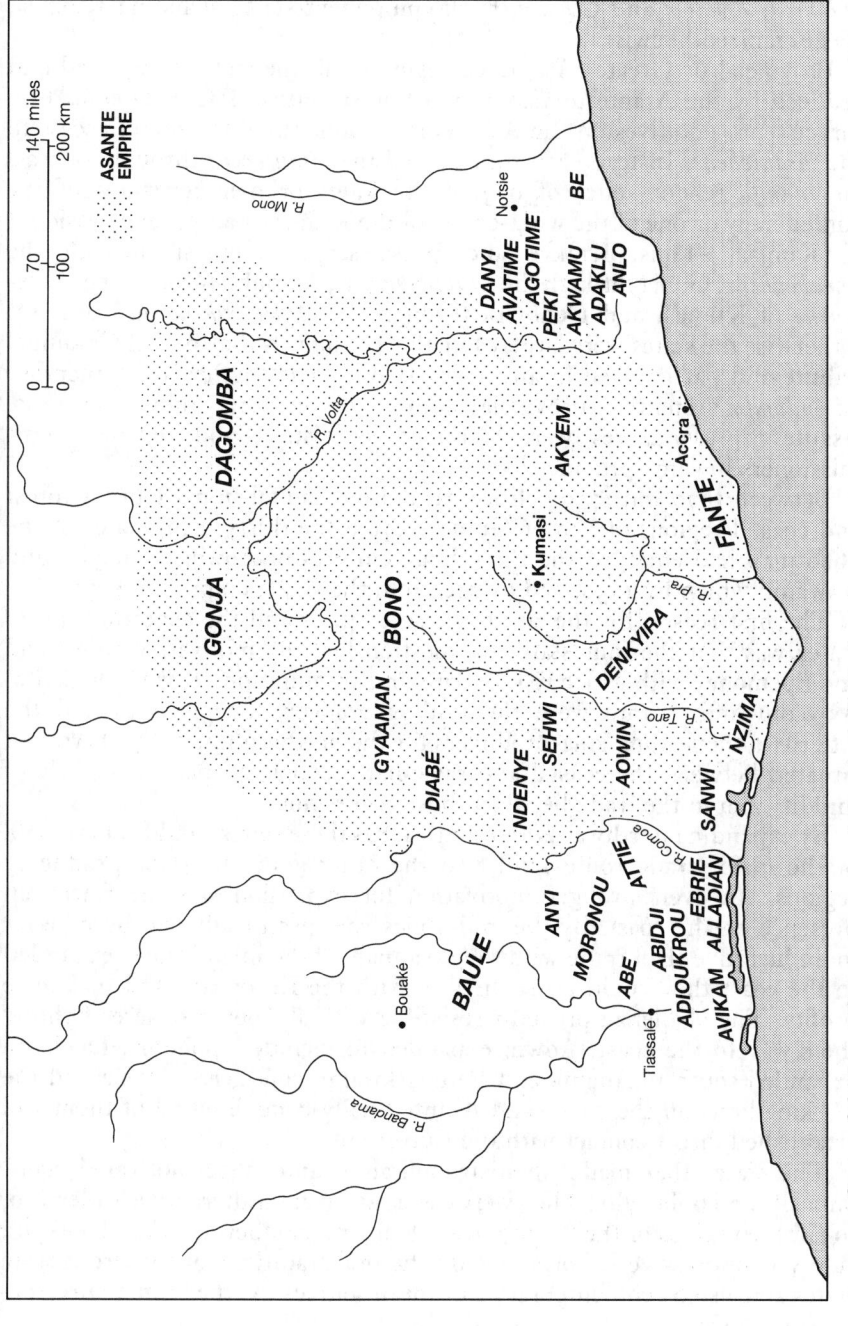

FIG 14.5 *States of the Lower Guinea coast, 1750 (after A. A. Boahen)*

Adonten, Kyidom and *Gyaase*. Each component state, including Kumasi, was organized likewise.

Provincial or Greater Asante consisted of all the states conquered and reduced by the Asante to vassal or tributary status. These states had no direct representatives on the Asanteman Council nor any direct access to the *Asantehene*. Instead each state served the *Asantehene* through, or was, an *adamfo* (client state) of one of the kings or member-states of the confederacy or one of the wing-chiefs of the Kumasi state, usually resident in Kumasi. Thus, Krakye and Bassa served Kumasi through the *Dwabenhene*, Gonja through the *Mamponghene*, Atebubu through the *Adontehene* of Kumasi and Denkyira through the *Akwamuhene* of Kumasi.[68] Otherwise the states were largely left alone as long as they paid their annual tribute and participated in any wars. It was to strengthen this otherwise lax *adamfo* system of provincial administration that, from 1760–1800, Asante representatives were stationed as district and regional commissioners in some provincial states.[69]

Between 1670 and 1750 political revolution had taken place in the forest and coastal regions of Lower Guinea. From the thirty-eight states of the 1629 map had emerged the three large empires of Aowin, Denkyira and Akwamu which by 1750, had merged into the single empire of Asante.

The first reason for the rise of these empires and the centralization of states was that the four states in question had the motivation to expand and the money with which to buy arms and ammunition. Aowin, Denkyira, Akwamu and Asante were the leading gold-producing states and the latter two the leading kola-producers for the northern trade. Furthermore, situated between the coastal and savannah regions, all played the role of middle-men in the trade between those two regions.

By expanding northwards and southwards these states would gain control of the major trade routes and also the other gold- and kola-producing regions. An even stronger motivation for expansion was the European presence on the coast. By the mid-1600s European trade had become far more lucrative than trade with the savannah. If the inland states expanded to the coast they could trade directly with the Europeans and maximize profits. The challenge proved irresistible with all sooner or later fighting their way to the coast. Aowin expanded to include Apollonia, Denkyira expanded south to Ahanta and Fetu, Akwamu conquered Agona and the Ga kingdoms on the coast, and Asante finally conquered all of them and established direct contact with the Europeans.

The states that made up metropolitan Asante were motivated economically and politically. They were eager, given good alternative leadership, to rid themselves of their tyrannical Denkyira conquerors. That Denkyira rule was oppressive is borne out by the oral traditions of the pre-Asante states and also by contemporary European sources. As the Dutch Director-

68. I. G. Wilks, 1975, pp. 39 and 151.
69. A. A. Boahen, 1965, pp. 342–4.

General at El Mina, J. Van Sevenhuysen, remarked in 1701: 'The Denkyiras, for a long time past have been very bellicose and proud over their victories and have been intolerable to their neighbours.' Bosman, a contemporary observer, also notes that: 'Denkyira elevated by its great Richness and Power, became so arrogant, that it looked on all other Negroes with a contemptible Eye, esteeming them no more than its slaves; which rendered it the object of their common hatred, each impatiently wishing its downfall.'[70] What they needed was leadership and this was provided by Osei Tutu and Opoku Ware, the founders of the Asante empire.

The other reason behind the rise of the three great empires was that the four expansionist states were free from interference in their internal affairs. The Akyem and the coastal states, although not without money or motivation, failed to develop into empires because they were denied such freedom. Sandwiched between expanding Denkyira and, later, Asante to the west and Akwamu to the east, the Akyem states were on the defensive throughout the seventeenth and eighteenth centuries. Similarly, the coastal states' internal affairs were subjected to all sorts of interference by rival European nations on the coast, at times resulting in armed conflict, such as the Komenda–Dutch wars of the 1690s. Indeed, throughout the seventeenth and eighteenth centuries, cardinal European policy was to prevent any coastal state from gaining ascendancy. The inland states of Aowin, Denkyira, Akwamu and Asante, however, were initially free from direct European interference and could sufficiently consolidate their power before encountering them.

Two other factors should also be taken into account in explaining the rise of the three empires: the adoption of a new technology and the high quality of leadership. Guns and gunpowder had become the most prized European import from 1650 onwards and, with their gold and other resources, the rulers of these states, could purchase what ammunition they needed. With guns their expansionist activities were obviously greatly accelerated. In traditional warfare two enemies faced each other in dense columns using spears, swords, axes, knives, bows and arrows and even hand combat in battle. The use of guns introduced fighting in different wings. This led to the evolution of the three wings by Denkyira followed by the five wings of Akwamu and Asante. This new military formation was superimposed on the traditional political structure of king plus advisory council of clan and lineage heads. Without able rulers these states could not have adapted their traditional warfare and old political structure to the new technology.

At this stage little is known about the Aowin kings but both oral and European documentary sources acclaim the courage, tact and prowess of the rulers of Denkyira, Akwamu and Asante. The Denkyira kings included Werempe Ampem, Boadu Akafu Brempon and the most illustrious, Boa Amponsem; Akwamu's included Ansa Saskraku, Basua and Akwono and

70. W. Bosman, 1979, pp. 74–5.

Asante's Osei Tutu and Opoku Ware.[71] These kings converted their small kingdoms into huge empires in a series of brilliant, carefully-timed and well co-ordinated campaigns.

Many historians believe that these empires were products of the slave trade. Fage, for instance, has contended that

> on the whole it is probably true to say that the operation of the slave trade may have tended to integrate, strengthen and develop military, territorial authority but to weaken more segmentary societies. Whether this was good or evil may be a nice point; historically, it may be seen as purposive and perhaps as more or less inevitable.[72]

Clerici and others also maintain that 'On peut même dire que ces royaumes (i.e. Dahomey et Achanti), qui n'existaient pas auparavant, sont nés de la traite.'[73] This may be true of other parts of West Africa but not for this area. On the Gold Coast the slave trade only became significant economically from 1700–10 while expansionist activities had begun in the 1670s and 1680s. In the Gold Coast the slave trade was the consequence not the cause of the state-building process.

In the Akan areas west of the River Tano and the Ewe areas east of the Volta river, home of the Lagunaires, the Anyi and the Baule, no such dramatic political change took place at this time. Political conditions in 1800 were much as they had been fifty or a hundred years earlier with small kingdoms or chiefdoms, each made up of loosely united family groups from clans of common ancestry.

In 1800 Ewe territory was still split into many independent *dukowo* (territorial divisions or what Amenumey calls chiefdoms and paramountcies) of varying sizes ranging from the single town of Wodze to Anlo of thirty-six independent towns and villages scattered far and wide.[74] By 1900 the number of Eweland *dukowo* had grown to 120, each ruled by a *fia* (king) elected patrilineally from one or two lineages of the founding families. He was assisted by a Council of Elders, consulted on every issue. Under him were the chiefs of the villages of the *dukowo* and, in turn, each village was made up of lineages under the lineage head. At village or town level, all able-bodied male adults participated in open discussions on all matters before a decision could be taken by the chief and his elders. There are several reasons why the Western Akan of the Tano–Bandama basin and the Ewe of the Volta–Mono basin did not consolidate themselves. First, the migrations into their lands continued throughout the seventeenth and eighteenth centuries and the breakaway movements into smaller and smaller settlements even into the nineteenth. By 1800 therefore, the Ewe

71. For details of the roles played by these rulers, see J. K. Fynn, 1975; A. A. Boahen, 1965; K. Y. Daaku, 1970b; J. K. Kumah, 1966; I. G. Wilks, 1957.

72. J. D. Fage, 1969a.

73. M. A. Clerici, 1962, p. 67.

74. D. E. K. Amenumey, 1969; C. K. Nukunya, 1969.

and Western Akan were not sufficiently settled to embark on wars of expansion. Secondly, as these migrants were themselves escaping the centralization and tyrannical behaviour of their former rulers, they were not likely to recreate the same socio-political structures in their new homes. Thirdly, in the case of the Ewe, economic motivation for state-building was lacking. As Amenumey puts it:

> Eweland lacked the economic incentive, a necessary prerequisite to the evolution of centralized political entities. It is the production of economic surpluses that provides the first incentive for centralization.[75]

Without gold, ivory or kola nuts, the Ewe could not participate in the long-established and lucrative north-south Atlantic trade. During the seventeenth and eighteenth centuries, their main export was slaves, an activity which jeopardized peace, stability and orderly government – the requirements for political expansion or centralization.

The Western Akan did have gold, ivory and kola but because the trade routes to the north were controlled by the Mande, the Senufo, the Kulango and the Eastern Akan, especially the Asante, they profited little from that trade. Nor did they take part in the lucrative trade with Hausaland and Borno to the north-east. They therefore had no money for large-scale expansionist activities.

The third reason for the Ewe and Western Akan's failure to consolidate was ecological.[76] Because they were cut off from inland areas by numerous lagoons no Europeans would settle there, thus depriving them of any real economic incentive to expand southwards to the coast.

The fourth and probably most important reason was their neighbours' constant interference in their political affairs which kept the Ewe and Western Akan on the defensive. The Western Akan faced the threat of the Sehwi and especially the Asante throughout the eighteenth century. Likewise, from the 1680s, the Ewe faced active interference first by the kings of Grand and Little Popo, then by the Akwamu and, in the eighteenth century, by Dahomey to the east and all-conquering Asante to the west.

Social and cultural changes in Lower Guinea

The most obvious socio-cultural change in Lower Guinea between 1500 and 1800 was demographic. With so many new food crops from the Americas and Asia, especially maize and some species of yams, the populations of the Lower Guinea coast greatly increased during the sixteenth and seventeenth centuries – as is borne out by contemporary European documents. During the eighteenth century, however, largely as a result of the slave trade, the population remained stagnant or even decreased. As

75. D. E. K. Amenumey, 1969.
76. Personal communication by C. Wondji.

Inikori has shown,[77] the population of Lower Guinea would be much higher today had it not been for the Atlantic slave trade.

Secondly, society had become more sophisticated. In 1500 it had been composed of a ruling aristocracy consisting of a religious élite of priests (who wielded most power) and a political élite of kings and queens, ordinary subjects and domestic slaves. By 1800, however, the political élite had superseded the religious, except among the Ga–Adangbe and the Ewe. Furthermore, the tremendous increase in economic activities, especially in gold-mining and long-distance trade, and the numerous wars of expansion and domination, had led to an increase in domestic slaves. Slaves in Lower Guinea at this time were allowed to own property and marry free citizens. Some held responsible jobs and could even inherit the property of their owners by whom they were regarded as part of the family. By 1800 most had become integrated into society and it had become a sacred law, especially among the Akan, not to divulge the origins of such people.

Moreover, as a result of trading activities and the European presence, three new classes emerged unknown to traditional society. They were most prominent in the coastal areas between the Tano and the Volta rivers, and included a wage-earning class, an independent class of wealthy traders and middlemen merchant princes, and a *mulatto* group.[78] The first class consisted of people employed by Europeans as masons, carpenters, bricklayers, interpreters, writers or secretaries, goldbrokers, civil-servants, ambassadors and public-relations officers. European records abound in references to such people. Some were literate and acted as intermediaries between Europeans and traditional rulers and their subjects.

The second class consisted of Africans, individuals or groups, who, through their own efforts in farming or trade, became exceedingly wealthy and more powerful even than the traditional rulers. This class included, on the Gold Coast, people such as John Ahenakwa and John Claessen of Fetu, Asomani of Akwamu, John Kabes of Komenda, John Konny of Ahanta and John Currantee of Anomabo (also known in oral tradition as Eno Baisie Kurentsi). On eastern Ivory Coast there also emerged the Kosehirange and the Essouma who acted as brokers or middlemen between the Europeans and the Avikam, Eotile, Abure, Sanwi, Aowin and Sehwi of the interior. By 1800 the Kosehirange in particular had become extremely wealthy and powerful and were playing a key role in the choice of lineage heads.[79] Trade between the coast and inland was brisk. Ordinary people as well as traditional rulers could participate in it and the forest peoples played the lucrative role of middlemen–cum–producers. If a wage-earning group did not emerge, at least a group of wealthy traditional rulers and independent merchant princes must have arisen. Unfortunately, European sources and oral traditions are both silent on this subject.

77. J. E. Inikori, 1979, pp. 68–71.
78. K. Y. Daaku, 1970b, pp. 96–143.
79. Based on a contribution by C. Wondji.

The *mulatto* group was the product of miscegenation between European traders and African women. Such people could be found all along the Lower Guinea coast. Although contemporaries such as Bosman have spoken of them disparagingly as a 'bastard strain ... made up of a parcel of profligate villains neither true to the Negroes nor us',[80] some, such as Geenlendonck, Bosman, Barter, Gordon and, above all, the descendants of Richard Brew, played important roles in commercial and political life.[81]

Another important social change was the introduction of Christianity and western education by the Europeans, and of Islam by the Mande and Hausa traders. Both Dutch and English established elementary schools in their castles at Cape Coast, El Mina and Accra and, in the 1750s, the Society for the Propagation of the Gospel sent missionaries to Cape Coast. Moreover, some *mulattos'* and some traditional rulers' children were sent abroad to be educated with several, including Christian Pedersen, Svane, Capitein and Philip Quacoe, returning home as teachers and missionaries. Thus, by 1800 a small educated élite and a few Christian converts could be found in such coastal towns as Accra and Cape Coast.

Even earlier than Christianity was the spread of Islam and Muslim culture along the northern trade routes, into northern Ghana by the fourteenth century and Asante and Baule by the 1750s. By 1800 Kumasi had a thriving Muslim quarter with a Kur'ānic school and, according to Wilks, the last eighteenth-century *Asantehene*, Osei Kwame (1777–1801), was deposed because of his attachment to the Muslim religion.[82]

By 1800, however, both Christianity and Islam had made little impact on most peoples of the Lower Guinea coast, although the art of reading and writing in both Arabic and European languages had been firmly established.

As substantiated by fast-growing archaeological evidence,[83] the Guinea-coast societies had, by 1800, developed the arts and crafts of potting, sculpture (in wood, ivory and clay), weaving, smithing and casting (in brass, copper and gold) with some groups specializing in a particular craft. Equally developed were their music, drumming and dancing.

Potting, one of the world's oldest crafts, dating in Ghana, for example, from the Later Stone Age (after − 3000),[84] was highly developed by 1700 particularly among the Adangbe whose pots were exported as far as Bonduku in Côte d'Ivoire. According to Anquandah, pottery was raised to a fine art by the Asante who produced 'some of the best-quality polymorphic pottery with complex motifs such as the *abusua kuruwa*, clan pot and the

80. W. Bosman, 1967, pp. 141–2.
81. M. Priestley, 1969.
82. I. G. Wilks, 1961 and 1966a.
83. J. Anquandah, 1982.
84. ibid., p. 53

mogyemogye ceremonial jaw-bone pot, a wine jar used for pouring libation on the Golden Stool'.[85]

Carving and sculpting in wood, ivory and clay was also developed during this period – particularly among the Akan. Wooden stools, drums, umbrella tops and linguist staffs were made. Wood-carving reached its zenith during the sixteenth century when the Denkyira kings, to quote Anquandah, 'developed the political and cultural ideology connected with the Adanse stool'.[86] Seventeenth- and eighteenth-century European visitors to the Ghana coast, such as Bosman, were impressed by the beauty of the ivory-side-blown trumpets that they found. Particularly well-known are the *akuaba* (fertility dolls) in wood and clay and the sculptured clay portraits of deceased kings and queens.

Weaving also developed during this period. According to a recent study, weaving on narrow horizontal looms was introduced to the Akan, Ewe and the Ga from western Sudan probably via the Nile valley rather than the western Maghreb.[87] We do not know exactly when this knowledge reached the forest and coastal regions but it must have been before the arrival of the Portuguese, becoming widespread in the sixteenth and seventeenth centuries. Both Brun and Barbot reported that cloth of six stripes from Côte d'Ivoire was being exported to the Gold Coast. According to the 1629 map, Nsoko (now identified as Begho) was an important centre 'where cloths are woven like carpets which are worn among the Acanists'.[88] Those weavers also produced blankets, known among the Akan as *kassa*, *bomo* and *nsaa*, which are still highly valued by them. But it was in the eighteenth century, as Lamb has clearly shown, that weaving among the Akan and the Ewe attained its maturity and highest sophistication. This is amply demonstrated by the now famous colourful *kente* cloths of the Akan and the rich *adanudo* cloths of the Ewe who originated them (Plate 14.2).[89] The making of *adinkra* cloth, a broad cloth with Akan traditional motifs and symbols stamped on it, also became famous in the Brong region and was later copied by the Asante.

However, it was in smithing and casting, especially in gold and brass, that the greatest development occurred among the Akan in particular. Using mainly the *cire-perdue* (lost-wax) process, these smiths produced exquisite gold and silver regalia including sword ornaments, rings, bangles, chains and headgear. Goldsmithing was well established before the advent of the Europeans but drawing on the expertise of their Muslim craftsmen, the Brong, then the Denkyira and particularly the Asante developed the art during the 1600s and 1700s, to a degree of excellence not since superseded. The Akan smiths also produced thousands of geometric and figur-

85. J. Anquandah, 1982, p. 40.
86. ibid.
87. J. Lamb, 1975, p. 219.
88. S. Brun, 1624 and J. Barbot, 1732.
89. ibid., pp. 91–9.

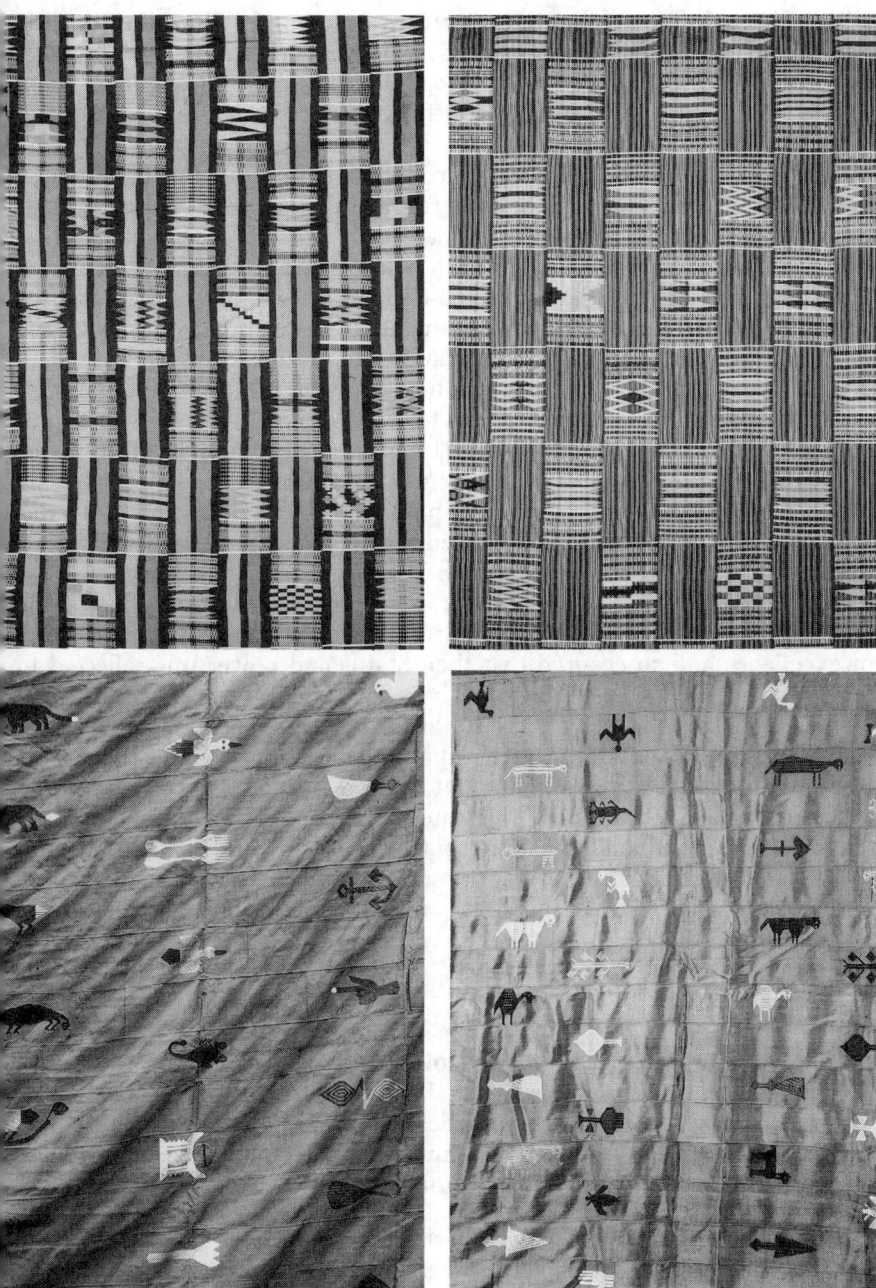

PLATE 14.2   *West African weaving; (above) Kente cloths, Asante silks (below) Adanudo cloths, Ewe silks*

ative gold or brass weights, now a great attraction for European tourists and found in famous art museums worldwide (Plate 14.3).[90] Casting, especially in brass, was also developed at this time and exquisite brass caskets for keeping gold dust in and brass vessels for storing shea butter were also made.

With the rise of the Asante empire in the eighteenth century the arts and crafts of the Lower Guinea coast reached their peak. The Asante kings expanded not only territorially and politically but did everything in their power to promote arts and crafts. Following the defeat of Denkyira, Tekyiman and Akyem, they collected their best craftsmen and goldsmiths and sent them to Kumasi,[91] as Anquandah has pointed out: 'with the establishment of the Asante confederation, the Asante kings centralised all Asante arts and crafts in the neighbourhood of the capital, Kumasi'.[92] Ahwiaa was established as the centre for stool-making, Bonwire for kente-weaving, Tafo for pottery, Fumesua for iron work and Krofofrom for brass-casting. Moreover, the *Asantehene* established the Apagyafie – a group of goldsmiths and other craftsmen from Denkyira whose duty was to make his regalia. He also introduced the golden *Asomfo* stool whose first occupant, Nana Tabiri, was the son of a Denkyira chief.[93]

By blending expertise and artistic traditions, the Asante kings of the eighteenth century brought Akan cultural development to its highest peak of excellence and so ensured that their status and power was reflected in art forms of the highest quality. They developed a golden culture and civilization symbolized by their sophisticated golden regalia, their rich, multi-coloured kente cloth, their elaborate court protocol and their complicated and artistic gold weights that amazed Europeans visiting Kumasi in the 1700s and early 1800s.[94] Despite the impact of colonialism, and the iconoclasm of and condemnation by Christian missionaries in the nine-teenth and twentieth centuries, the goldsmiths' art never died out and fascinating regalia in gold and silver are still being produced, particularly by the Asante.

Conclusion

1500 to 1800 was indeed a period of radical change for the states and peoples of the Lower Guinea coast. Politically the process towards cen-tralization was completed. Economically, trade in gold and ivory was eclipsed by the slave trade; the commercial and economic centres moved from inland to the coast; strong commercial links were forged with the

90. For a fascinating study of Akan gold weights, see T. F. Garrard, 1980, pp. 171–363.
91. ibid., p. 198.
92. J. Anquandah, 1982, p. 40.
93. T. F. Garrard, 1980, p. 299.
94. T. F. Garrard, 1980, pp. 47–8; M. D. McLeod, 1981, pp. 72–6; J. Anquandah, 1982, pp. 39–44 and 100–12.

PLATE 14.3 *Akan brass weights for weighing gold-dust. Geometric forms (left) were used from the fifteenth century onwards: figurative forms (right), in use from the seventeenth century, also served to illustrate popular proverbs and maxims*

PLATE 14.4 *Nana Otuo Siriboe II*, Omanhene *of Dwaben state, in a rich Kente cloth and wearing some of the gold state regalia*

Americas and Europe, thereby integrating the local economy with the global. Above all, this was a period of social change: the evolution of new classes, although on a limited scale and confined mainly to the coast; the introduction of literacy, western education and Christianity; the spread of Islam; and the flowering of indigenous cultures, especially in weaving and metal-work. These were indeed dynamic centuries for the peoples of the Lower Guinea coast, all the more so because at the end they were in full control of their own destiny and sovereignty.

Fon and Yoruba: the Niger Delta and the Cameroon

E. J. ALAGOA

Introduction

This chapter covers the region extending from the valley of the River Volta in the west to the River Cameroon in the east. Most of the area is tropical forest bordered by savannah with shrub forest to the north. The western part, from the border of Nigeria to the River Volta, is also savannah. The region can also be defined as the territory contained between the coastline of the Bights of Benin and Bonny (formerly Biafra) in the Gulf of Guinea. The peoples living within this part of the Guinea forest and the surrounding savannah comprise the Fon or Aja of the modern Republic of Benin, the Yoruba, the Ijo of the Niger Delta in the centre of the area, the Igbo to the north-east of the Delta in the centre of the area, the Igbo to the north-east of the Delta, the Ibibio, and various peoples of southern Cameroon.

All the languages of the area belong to the Niger–Congo family, the vast majority of them being within the Kwa sub-family. The Efik/Ibibio and other languages of the Nigeria–Cameroon border area of Nigeria, and the languages of the Cameroon itself are, however, closely related t ɔ the Bantu languages of Central, Eastern and Southern Africa. The eastern section of the region is, therefore, in many ways, an extension of the great Bantu complex of languages and cultures into West Africa. The peoples and cultures in this border region form a unifying link between West Africa and Bantu Africa. Among the Kwa language group, the Yoruba and Igbo are the largest in terms of the numbers of speakers (8–12 million) and geographical spread. The Edo group is also large with a spread of related peoples from deep within its hinterland to the Delta and its western peripheries, including such groups as the Isoko and the Urhobo and, to the north, the Ishan (Esan) and others. Among the Kwa languages, Ijo in the Niger Delta is the most divergent from its neighbours, Igbo, Edo, and Yoruba.[1]

The comparatively high degree of differentiation of Ijo from Igbo, Edo and Yoruba is, in part, the result of the long period in which it has been a separate language. Glotto-chronological estimates give the period of

1. K. Williamson, 1971.

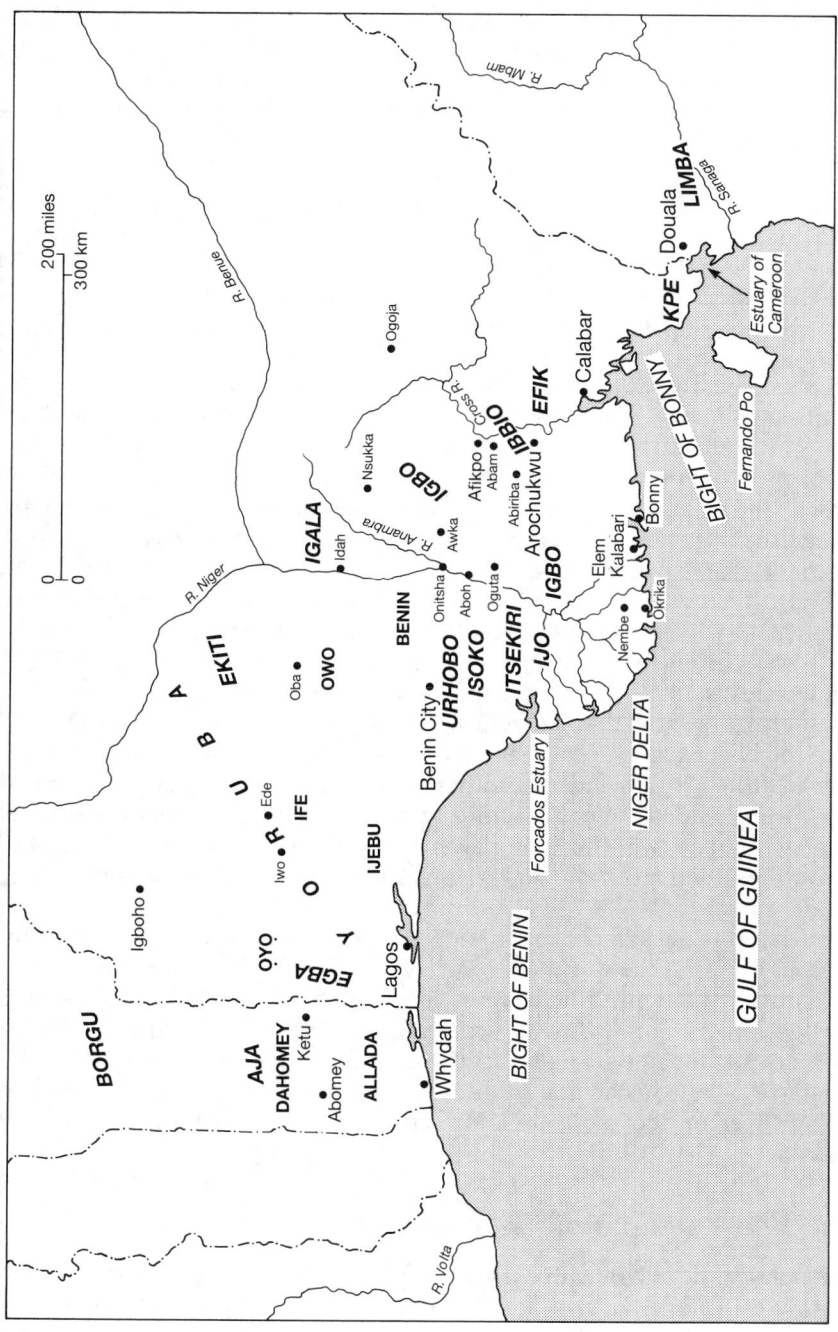

FIG. 15.1 *The Niger Delta area and Cameroon in the sixteenth to eighteenth centuries*

separation as more than 5000 years, which indicates the stability of the language communities in the region. Separation times for dialect clusters within the Ijo group itself, between the Central and Eastern Delta, for example, have been estimated at 1–2000 years. A similar estimate of 2000 years is made for Yoruba and the related language, Igala.

The long continuities in this region's history should be borne in mind when evaluating the changes supposedly induced by the arrival of Europeans on the Atlantic coast from the end of the fifteenth century. It may be noted that the predominant influence of developments in the savannah and the hinterland on this region was only equalled over a long period and only recently superseded by the influences of the European impact from the coast.

The sixteenth century was the beginning of European activity of any significance in the Bights of Benin and Bonny. The Portuguese reached Benin in 1486 and established relations with the *Oba* of Benin. They also established commercial relations at various points all along the coast. During the following centuries European activity on the coast began to change the direction of trade from north to south, and the coast gradually became the major origin of stimuli to change.

The overseas slave trade was the obvious focus of European activity from the sixteenth to the eighteenth century. The region covered in this study was one of the main markets for slaves on the West African coast. Some states, such as the Kingdom of Dahomey, derived great impetus for their formation and growth from the trade. The development of others, from the Niger Delta to the Cameroon, was influenced by the profits to be derived from it. Other communities, especially those organized in non-state forms, tended to be the victims of slave-raids and to constitute supply sources. In one way or other, every community was affected by the disruptions, depopulation and changes induced by the overseas slave trade.

During this period, the main impact of the slave trade was to draw the communities into the world economy as suppliers of slaves for work in the American plantations. The increase in the local slave supply led to social and political changes within the communities. The arrival of forced African migrants in the Americas also created additional forces for change in the New World. But in the oral traditions of the communities, what emerges is the effect of the trade on the fortunes of local lineages, groups or dynasties.

The Fon kingdom of Dahomey

The political development of the Kingdom of Dahomey and of the neighbouring states of Allada, Whydah, Popo, and Jakin was largely related to the activities of the European slave-traders on the coast, and to the influence of the Yoruba kingdom of Oyọ to the north-east. According to a study of

PLATE 15.1 *Fifteenth- or sixteenth-century commemorative head from Benin, Nigeria, cast in bronze and inlaid with iron. Height: 22 cm*

this area by Akinjogbin,[2] developments before the early nineteenth century relate closely to the effects of the slave trade and the attempts by Ọyọ to impose its authority.

The traditional institutions of the small communities and states of the area were weakened by the introduction of the slave trade and, by the end of the seventeenth century, a political vacuum had been created. It was at this point that the founders of the Kingdom of Dahomey re-established order by fashioning a new form of political organization out of various groups of Aja peoples comprising Egun (Gun), Fon, Arada and others from the southern part of the modern Republic of Benin. By 1700 Dahomey had become a major power in the area. Between 1724 and 1727 its ruler, Agaja, embarked on a conquest of the small but older states surrounding

2. I. A. Akinjogbin, 1967, p. ix and 1976.

437

Abomey. This provoked intervention by Ọyọ, but not to establish a system of its own. After 1730 Dahomey accepted the political authority of Ọyọ and agreed to live within the economy of the slave trade in co-operation with the European traders on the coast. But the study concludes that it was the very 'inadequacies of the slave trade economy' that ended the brief period of prosperity. The depression that began about 1767 culminated in the fall of the Agaja dynasty in 1818, and the rise of the new dynasty of Gezo.

The new dynasty adapted fully to the slave-trade economy and made it the basis of its strength. It thereby benefitted from the breakdown of the Ọyọ kingdom and the wars in Yoruba country in the nineteenth century.

These, then, were the two predominant influences on Aja country: the Yoruba (specifically, the Ọyọ) and the slave-trade from the coast.

The inter-relationship between the Aja communities and the Yoruba to the east and north-east was deep and long-standing. Traditions of origin relate to earlier homelands in Yoruba country even among those communities with traditions of recent migration from the west. Others have traditions of direct migration from Yoruba homelands. Such traditions need not derive from the experiences of Ọyọ–Yoruba political and military activity from the seventeenth to the nineteenth century. There are, indeed, states of Yoruba origin and culture within the area, and the incidence of cultural affinity is high. The Aja kingdoms tend to derive their affinities from Ketu, a migrant community of Yoruba from Ile–Ife.

The states, then, were largely organized in systems similar to the Yoruba pattern. The 'father' kingdom in the area was Allada, which had been founded about 1575 and played the same role as Ile–Ife played in Yorubaland. The rise of Dahomey as a centralized state swallowing all others and organized on new lines offended against tradition and invited the intervention of Ọyọ. Ọyọ intervention at several points, then, was disruptive in the tradition of all military interventions. Such interventions served to weaken Dahomey as a military power but were not negative in every way. The peace enforced by Ọyọ prevented the young Dahomey state from dissipating all its energies on military adventure and enabled it instead to strengthen its internal administration. Some aspects of Ọyọ organization were taken over, such as the *ilari* system introduced by Tegbesu, the last of the founding dynasty. It was the stability of its internal system that enabled Dahomey to finally break away from Ọyọ in the nineteenth century.

The important factor in the effect of the European slave trade on Aja country was that at the beginning of the sixteenth century when the trade started, the states in the area were still weak. The kidnapping and seizure of the weak by the strong was disruptive in the extreme and would have removed people from productive agricultural and industrial pursuits. Normal economic activities were undermined and the rules of society destroyed. Insecurity and brutal force prevailed over respect for authority, elders and the family.

The pattern of rivalries and competition for European trading posts also destroyed the precedencies and traditional relationships between the states. Early in the seventeenth century, the Dutch established agents at Assim, the capital of Allada, the senior state. After the French had failed to establish Christian missions in Allada, they set up a rival trading station at Whydah in 1671. Economic rivalry between the two kingdoms set in, finally destroying the already weakened traditional ties. It was in this atmosphere of cynicism concerning the normal values of society, of insecurity and political and commercial rivalries, that the Kingdom of Dahomey was created by migrants who travelled from Allada.

The dissident migrants from Allada settled in Abomey, out of reach of the Europeans, in about 1625, and tried to set up a new political system that would endure despite the disturbed times. They repudiated the traditional view of the state as a larger version of the family, likening it instead to a perforated pot, symbolized by the king. For the perforated pot to hold water, each citizen had to place a finger over a hole thus sinking his identity in an absolute state. It was the dogged development of this idea of a strong centralized state with an absolute king demanding unreserved loyalty that marked Dahomey out from other states. It was thus that it was able to survive the slave trade and the attacks from Ọyọ and gradually bring all other states in the neighbourhood under its control.

The predominant role attributed to the Atlantic slave trade assumed in the above account of the history of Dahomey is currently being revised by recent research. Peukert[3] directly challenges the two central concepts, first, that the history of Dahomey was determined by the processes of the slave trade and, second, that its economy was archaic, its external trade being monopolized by the monarchy and domestic exchange being redistributive rather than through the open market-place. In place of these old hypotheses, it is suggested:

(1) that the Dahomean state did not account for more than 20 per cent of the kingdom's foreign trade and that small traders did most of the external trade;
(2) that the Atlantic trade accounted for little more than 2.5 per cent of the Dahomean economy; and
(3) that even in the external trade, slaves and guns did not form the major items – Brazilian tobacco, for example, being more important an import than guns.

These are significant points for a revision of the old ideas and form bases for future research.

---

3. W. Peukert, 1978. See reviews by P. Manning, R. A. Austen and A. Van Dantzig, 1980.

The Yoruba kingdoms

The history of the Yoruba communities of south-western Nigeria may be briefly summarized.

First, there are the problems of reconciling the oral traditions of origin and the archaeological evidence. The problems here mainly concern the traditions which make Ile–Ife the centre of creation and the origin of all Yoruba kingdoms from where their rulers obtained their beaded crowns. Ife, of course, also merits attention because of the unique naturalistic art in bronzes and terracotta which have been known to the world since Frobenius proclaimed them the proof of a Greek settlement in the heart of Africa. Second, there was the rise of the military and political power of Ọyọ, thought by some to have co-existed with the spiritual authority of the *Oni* of Ife over the whole of Yoruba country. Ọyọ became the flag-bearer of Yoruba power in the northern and western areas of the region. Ọyọ's imperial role in the affairs of the Fon and their neighbours is well known. It also came into close direct contacts with the Nupe and Borgu, known to the Yoruba as the Tapa and the Ibariba respectively. Ọyọ also seems to have had relations with the Hausa and through them contact with the trans-Saharan trade. Third, there is the nature of the political, cultural and social development in other Yoruba communities and kingdoms.

The primacy of Ife in Yoruba history is based on many factors. Its founder, Oduduwa, was supposed to have come from heaven or Mecca, and his sons or grandsons to have founded all the other Yoruba states. Recent interpretations of these traditions suggest that Oduduwa, or a group of migrants, came to the area about 1000 years ago but that the land was already occupied, possibly by the Igbo of Ife traditions.[4] Some of the place-names in the traditions also suggest the existence of a number of mini-states and the names of some of the 400 deities may represent the names of rulers of such states before their unification. In addition, the movement outwards from Ife did not take place at one time and not all the crowns were obtained directly from Ife.

The famous Ife bronzes have played a part in confirming the traditions of the relationship between Ife or Yorubaland and the Edo kingdom of Benin to the east. But the bronzes also relate Ife to Nupe and regions around the Niger. Clear similarities have been found between the large bronzes found in Nupe country and those of Ife. Accordingly, it has become clear that the 'Mecca' of the traditions did not refer to any place in the Middle East, to Egypt or to Meroe but to regions just across the River Niger to the north of present-day Yoruba territory. In addition, the art of Ife has been compared to the Nok terracotta art in central Nigeria, despite the time gap between the two cultures ($-900-+c.200$ for Nok, and $c.+900-1300$ for the height of Ife art).

Ọyọ not only became pre-eminent among the Yoruba kingdoms, but

4. A. Obayemi, 1976.

PLATE 15.2 *Brass commemorative head of an* oba *from Benin, Nigeria. According to popular stories, the last king of the mythical dynasty of the Ogiso reigning in Benin before the arrival of the Yoruba, was dethroned following a revolt. He was replaced by a prince of Ife, named Oranmiyan, the son of the* oni *of Oduduwa. From that time, custom required that the* oba *of Benin be decapitated after his death, that his skull be sent to Ife for burial in the sacred enclosure* (orun oba ado) *and that, in return, a brass commemorative head be sent to Benin, to be placed on the altar of the royal ancestors. At the end of the fourteenth century, the sixth* oba. *Oguola, is said to have suggested that a metal-caster from Ife come to Benin to teach his art. The* oni *is said to have sent Ighehae. This master, who may be mythical, is venerated today as the founding patron of the* igun eromwon *guild of casters, and has a shrine. The masculine sex of this commemorative head is indicated by the three vertical stripes above each eye (a woman would have four). The* oba *comes from the so-called middle period, from the mid-sixteenth to the end of the seventeenth century. The vertical inlays of iron, characteristic of the early period have disappeared; the neck and chin are hidden beneath twenty coral necklaces; and the face no longer has any realism. The greater thickness of the metal may be due to the casting technique which had become less rigorous, but it did serve a useful purpose since the increased weight made them more suitable for use as pedestals for the carved ivory needles which were customarily inserted in the circular opening in the headdress. Height: 23 cm*

also developed special features. Some of these derived from its location close to the Nupe and Borgu. For example, Ọyọ relied more heavily on officials of slave origin in the military and social organizations than did other Yoruba states. In the armed forces, Ọyọ's supremacy was probably the result of its use of cavalry and archers, derived from its early contact

with the trans-Saharan trade and the northern states, from about the period'
of Songhay ascendancy in the fourteenth century. Ọyọ may have obtained
horses, *kanun* (potash) and *obuotoyo* (rock salt) among other products from
the north, while exporting kola nuts, shea butter and palm products.[5]
These external contacts as well as its location in the savannah enabled Ọyọ
to make innovations in the Yoruba concepts it shared with the other
kingdoms. One peculiar innovation made by Ọyọ was the supremacy of
the *Sango* (thunder cult) in its religious system.

The foundation of Ọyọ is related to Ife and Benin through its legendary
founder, Oranyan (*Oranmiyan*), who is stated to have reigned at both Ife
and Benin before moving to Ọyọ. But other states already existed in the
locality, such as Iwo, Owu and Oba in the Igbomina area; Ira in the Ibolo
area; and Oyokoro, Ikoyi and others. Ọyọ eventually made several of them
into vassal states including Owu in the south and Ede in the south-east.
Ọyọ expansion was finally stopped by the forest-dwelling Ijesha, as the
Ọyọ cavalry could not operate in wooded regions. The Ijebu and the hill
country of the Ekiti also escaped direct Ọyọ control. The Benin kingdom
to the east proved another barrier to Ọyọ expansion and one tradition says
that the two powers established a tree boundary at the town of Otun. Ọyọ
ran a trade route to the coast through the territory of the Egba and Egbado
and it was through this route in south-western Yoruba country that Ọyọ
power expanded to Dahomey.

Ọyọ power developed out of adversity. In the fifteenth century its rulers
had been driven out of Old Ọyọ (Ọyọ Ile or Katunga) and had taken refuge
in Kusu among the Borgu and later at Igboho. Undaunted, Ọyọ had
reorganized its army and adopted a new policy of militarism. The town of
Ikoyi became the home of the *eso* warriors devoted to 'training in warfare'.
By the beginning of the sixteenth century Ọyọ had reconquered her former
territory and pushed the Nupe back. The friendship between the Ọyọ and
the Borgu also broke down and Ọyọ tried to expand in their direction too.

Ọyọ remained outside the area of direct European influence before
the nineteenth century, developing its major institutions and starting its
expansion independently. The adventure into Dahomey may have been
connected with participation in the coastal trade. But other traditions say
that Ọyọ kept out of the slave trade and contact with Europeans because
of an early experience of European duplicity when 800 messengers sent to
greet a professed friend on the coast never returned. Whatever the case,
Ọyọ did not use such conspicuous elements of the European trade as guns
until the nineteenth century.

The areas of Yoruba country beyond Ọyọ expansion, to the east and
north, consisted of smaller state forms in the Ekiti area anu others, such
as the Igala, which tended to relate developments in Yoruba country to
those in the Niger–Benue valley. Other states, such as the Owo and Ijebu,
also appear to have had much more to do with the Edo kingdom of Benin

5. I. A. Akinjogbin, 1976, p. 380.

PLATE 15.3   *Yoruba female statuette, dedicated to the worship of the* orisha *of creativity, Obatala. She is usually clothed with a white cloth like the priests and devotees of that god, an iron bracelet and, here, a necklace of white pearls with a pendant. The bowl that she is holding is intended to receive an offering of the white blood of the snail, a symbol of peace and calm. It is the female element of the* orisha, *the male element being represented by a statuette holding a fan and a fly-whisk. This bowl-bearer should not be confused with the* olumeye, *or vessel for kola nuts, represented by a much larger kneeling maternal figure holding a bowl which often has a lid. Height: 49 cm*

than with Ǫyǫ. Works of art recovered from excavations at Owo suggest that, by the fifteenth century, Owo sculptural forms were already related to both Ife and Benin styles and that there was a third independent style, which could possibly indicate a single prototype for the two better-known styles.

PLATE 15.4 *Seventeenth-century bronze mask which was worn at the waist, from Benin, Nigeria. Height: 9.3 cm*

The Niger Delta

The history of the Niger Delta is linked with the history of parts of the coastal region east to the Cameroon and west to the lagoons of Lagos and beyond. Until the nineteenth century – and until the disruption by European imports at different points of the coast – trade routes crossed the region from east to west and north to south. Cloth made in the Ijebu area of Yorubaland was sold in the Western Delta and appears to have been resold as far east as Nembe in the Eastern Delta. The Itsekiri kingdom of the Western Delta, for example, was related to the Ijebu, as shown by the similarity of language, although the Itsekiri also say that their rulers came from the Benin kingdom, and its political system is similar to that of the Edo kingdom of Benin. The Itsekiri also derived some of their cultural values from the Ijo of the Western Delta among whom they lived, and traded in pottery, salt and cloth with the states of the Eastern Delta, especially Nembe.

In the western Niger delta, Ode Itsekiri, the capital of the Itsekiri kingdom, was the focus of political power. When the Portuguese came to this area, the Itsekiri became their major delta contacts and attempts were made to establish Christianity there as well as trade. There was another trading post at the estuary of the Forcados river, but the Portuguese moved through the Western Delta to the mainland at Ughoton which they used as a base for contact with the capital of the Edo kingdom at Benin. The Itsekiri also moved out in some numbers from Ode Itsekiri in the eighteenth century to establish settlements at the estuary of the Benin river at points of vantage for the trans-Atlantic trade.[6] It was mainly from these new centres, such as Bobi, that the Itsekiri served as the agents of the Benin kingdom and as middlemen in their own right for the export of the produce of the hinterland peoples, namely, the Urhobo, the Isoko and the western Igbo.

The Ijo of the western Niger Delta were mostly organized in loose stateless communities and tended to participate in the overseas trade by preying on it as pirates. The Gbaramatu of the Escravos estuary and the Ogulagha and Iduwini of the Forcados estuary appear to have benefited to some extent from the trade system. The bronzes found among these Ijo groups, and also among the Mein and Kabowei, may be indications of affluence derived from participation in internal and external trade, as well as contact with Benin and other hinterland centres.

The Ijo of the Central Delta formed the heartland of the group. Oral traditions suggest migrations from this area to the Eastern Delta and Western Delta, and on to the Delta peripheries. From the lexicostatistical estimates of the distance between Ijo and the mainland languages of Yoruba, Edo and Igbo, the first settlements in the Delta may have been established up to 5000 years ago. Palaeontological studies of a core taken

6. P. C. Lloyd, 1963.

PLATE 15.5 *Seventeenth-century bronze plaque from Benin, Nigeria, showing a warrior wearing a padded coral costume, and holding a lance and sword. At each side is an escort with a shield. All three are wearing necklaces of leopards' teeth, and have bells on their chests. Between them are two small musicians. Height: 39 cm*

near Nembe in the Eastern Delta suggest that human life was possible there 3000 years ago.[7] But according to linguistic and oral traditional estimates, the present communities in the Eastern Delta were settled in the area only 1000 years ago. And radio-carbon dating of finds from sites at Ke and Saikiripogu (Ewoama) only confirms that people were living there before +800.

The excavations in the eastern Niger delta carried out by Drs. Anozie and Nzewunwa, following Professor Alagoa's survey of oral traditions, have opened up new vistas for Niger Delta history.[8] The excavations show that

7. M. A. Sowunmi, 1978.
8. E. J. Alagoa, 1972 and 1976; F. N. Anozie, 1976.

the earliest settlers knew how to exploit the shell-fish of the salt-water delta and also kept some animals. The abundance of pottery at such sites as Onyoma suggests a complex economy which included some farming, although most agricultural products were obtained through trade with the hinterland. In the oral traditions palm fruits, peppers and bananas are indicated as local products. The excavations also revealed some iron-working on a small scale. This again suggests contacts with the hinterland for raw materials and for finished goods. Numerous brass or bronze objects have been found on the surface at various locations in the Niger Delta, but a single coiled object alone has been recovered *in situ* as a grave-good at Onyoma.

Current art in the Niger Delta consists almost solely of sculpture in wood depicting water spirits or ancestors as shrine furniture or masks for dancing. The excavations have recovered a small but significant number of masks in terracotta from Ke and human figures from Onyoma. These finds are unique among Nigerian terracotta but one of the human heads from Onyoma has features reminiscent of Nok and Ife terracotta in the treatment of the eyes.

The Atlantic slave trade and, prior to it, internal long-distance trade, played a large part in the formation of the states of the eastern Niger delta – namely Bonny, Elem Kalabari (New Calabar), Okrika and Nembe. From the oral traditions it would appear that their founders came from earlier homes in the fresh-water Central Delta and adapted to life in the salt-water Eastern Delta. The adaptations included changing from an economy based on fishing and farming to one based on fishing, salt-boiling and trading. Social and political adaptations were made and kingship institutions were set up from about the thirteenth century. The Atlantic slave trade tended to accelerate the pace of change and the form of state established by the eighteenth century has been named the city-state or trading state.[9] The slave trade provided wealth as a base of power for the *amanyamabo* (king) and ruling élite, a system for recruiting labour and increasing the population and men for the fighting forces.

Igboland

A number of stone-age sites in the Igbo heartland suggest a longer history of human habitation than had been credited to the culture. A rock shelter at Afikpo produced stone tools and pottery 5000 years old and sites with similar evidence have been found in the Nsukka area. A stone factory has been discovered also at Nsukka and is now under study by Dr Anozie of the University of Nigeria. It seems clear that people farmed there at least 3000 years ago, with yams as their main crop. Other crops which appear to be of local origin include oil palms, *okro*, *egusi* and some varieties of kola nut. Cassava, rice, coco-yams, banana, plantain and other important crops

9. K. O. Dike, 1956; G. L. Jones, 1963.

from the Americas were introduced through the Atlantic slave trade. Cassava was established in the Niger Delta (from the Western Delta eastwards) by the seventeenth century but only penetrated parts of Igboland two to three hundred years later.

Oral traditions in places like Nri relate the origin of agriculture to their founding fathers. Iron-working, too, was established early and the bronze art of this area has become world-famous through the excavations at Igbo-Ukwu.[10] The bronzes are thought to derive from a different tradition from those of Ife and Benin and to equal them in beauty and high quality. They are associated with the Nri divine kingship and ritual centre. The Nri priests exercised authority over wide areas of Igboland with power to install *ozo* and *eze* title-holders and wash away abomination. The *eze Nri* also controlled *ifejioku* (the yam force). It could have been the income brought back by travelling Nri priests which provided the wealth that sustained the bronze art.

The Nri priesthood performed a vital role in Igboland because of the small-scale organization of the communities based on the title system. But some Igbo groups west of the River Niger and on its east bank adopted kingship institutions through contact with communities that had similar institutions. Thus the Aboh, Onitsha and Oguta kingdoms apparently derived their *obi* from the *oba* kingship of Benin. These states developed from migrants from areas under Benin influence in the sixteenth and seventeenth centuries. From the oral traditions it would seem that the movements occurred during the *oba*ship of Esigie (*c.* 1517–*c.*1550) in Benin. The presumption is that wars or other disturbances in eastern Benin prompted groups to migrate eastwards to establish new polities modelled on their homeland.

Other states on the River Niger, such as the Osomari, claim ancestors from the Igala kingdom of Idah to the north. But Igala influence on Igboland was probably more pronounced among northern Igbo in the Anambra valley and in the Nsukka region. There is evidence of Igala raids into the area, while the Nri claim that they and the Igala shared a distant ancestor. The Igbo states along the Niger river became the first participants in the overseas slave trade and later in the palm-oil trade of the nineteenth century in collaboration with the Niger Delta states. The northern Igbo groups traded with the Igala and other groups to the north.

The Igbo political and social systems had mechanisms for wider control than the village or town. One was religious sanction by an oracle. Various oracles have operated in Igboland at different times and places, including Kamalu of the Etche, Igwe Kala of Umunoha, Agbala of Awka and Ibini Okpube (Long Juju) of Arochukwu. The last two achieved the widest influence because other sectors of the community actively demonstrated their faith in them. Thus, the Awka blacksmiths, who worked at markets and settled all over Igboland and the Niger Delta, spread the influence of

10. T. Shaw, 1970.

PLATE 15.6 *Ornamental sixteenth-century bronze plaque from Benin, Nigeria, showing a chief wearing his regalia: coiffure with a high collar of coral beads, leopards'-teeth necklace, bracelets and anklets. He is not an oba, since he is wearing a protective war bell on his chest, an item not worn by the king. The leopard's head decorating the war dress is believed to frighten enemies. He is accompanied by two warriors playing a trumpet and a double bell, and a naked servant carrying his ceremonial sword. These three figures, although close, are smaller – indicating their lesser importance. The representation of the Portuguese, with their plumed helmets, long hair, beards and buttoned jeckets, makes it possible to date this plaque to the time of Oba Esegie. In 1515, he received military assistance from the Portuguese in a war with the Ata of the Igala. The four-leaved motif engraved in the background is known as owen iba ede ku ('the sun does not forget a day'); it is associated with Olokun, the god of water. Hundreds of these plaques decorated the great rectangular pillars that supported the canopies of the various courtyards of the palace of the oba of Benin. Their arrangement reflected complex themes. Height: 45.7 cm*

the Agbala oracle. But the Arochukwu oracle was the most successful thanks to the Aro traders, the major slave-dealers, who spread word of him far and wide. The Aro trade network probably developed in relation to the trade in slaves through the Cross river estuary at the port of Calabar but also came to deal with the Delta states, developing rapidly from about the seventeenth century. Aro traders established settlements and markets throughout Igboland and used the utterances of the oracle to procure slaves. Unlike the Nri priesthood, the Aro were willing to use violence and enlisted the help of the warriors of Abam, Edda, Ohafia, Abiriba and others with whom they shared the loot.

The areas of Igboland without strong centralized political government probably suffered most from the effects of slave-raiding and kidnapping. In the eighteenth and early nineteenth centuries, the eastern Niger delta ports were prominent in the export of slaves from West Africa most of whom came from the Igbo hinterland. Internally, too, insecurity and the disruption of communities and institutions was considerable.

The Cross river valley and the Cameroons

The peoples in this region show affinities of language and also of historical origins. Most of the languages are related to Bantu languages, forming a north-western extension of the great Bantu languages of Central, Eastern and Southern Africa into West Africa.

The largest ethnic group in the Cross river valley, the Ibibio, have been so long established there that they no longer remember any traditions of migration from outside. In the northern parts of the valley, the Ogoja area is occupied by a wide variety of peoples with traditions of migration from the Benue valley further north, or from the Cameroon. Some communities in the Ibibio group or closely related to them, such as the Andoni of the eastern Niger delta fringe and the Ibeno (Ibuno), also claim ancestral homelands in the Cameroon. Likewise, some communities in the Cameroon, such as the Isangele, are of Ibibio origin.

Communities in this region were largely organized in non-centralized political systems of great complexity. Age organizations as well as secret societies provided effective social and political control. Among the Ibibio, the *Ekpo* secret society among others was widespread. But the *Mgbe* (leopard society) of the northern Cross river valley and the Cameroons which became the *Ekpe* of the Efik state of the Cross river estuary, was the best-known and most formally organized.

The Efik are closely related to the Ibibio, their proximate home having been Uruan Ibibio on the west bank of the River Cross. Some traditions state that they had previously lived at Ibom, near Arochukwu in Igboland. They had left Ibom because of wars involving groups characterized as Akpa who could have been related to the communities known by that name in the Benue valley, such as the Jukun. These early contacts of the Efik are important as their final settlement at Ikot Etunko (Creek Town), Obutong (Old Town) and Atakpa (Duke Town) by the beginning of the seventeenth century made them the major centres for the overseas slave trade in the region.

The state the Efik founded on the lower Cross river – now known as Calabar – exported Igbo-hinterland slaves from the collecting centre at Arochukwu which obtained slaves through its oracle and mercenaries. But most slaves sold in Calabar were Ibibio or members of groups in the Cross river valley and the neighbouring areas of the Cameroons.

The slave trade was partly responsible for the reshaping of the Ibibio *Ekpo* secret society and the Ekoi *Mgbe* into the *Ekpe* at Calabar. The *Ekpe* became a class-structured society uniting the free aristocratic elements and keeping in control the slave classes and the poor. It also enforced political and social rules, collected debts and imposed order. Because of the common influences of the slave trade and trans-Atlantic contacts, Calabar developed lineage-based organizations similar to the Houses of the Eastern Delta states. Calabar, however, was different in that it had mainland farms where it kept most of its slaves in isolation rather than integrate them like the open masquerade society, *Ekine* or *Sekiapu* in the Delta states.

The most important groups on the Cameroon coast were the north-west Bantu groups of the Kpe–Mboko, the Duala, the Limba and the Tanga–Yasa. There were numerous groups of fishermen, farmers and hunters. Most were organized in small village units but by the eighteenth century the Bubi, the Duala and the Isuwu had organized larger political units. These groups were either connected with the slave trade or took advantage of it. The Cameroons river thus became a minor centre of the slave trade beyond the Cross river estuary with which it retained close contact.

The secret society was also an important focus of social and political control and, among the Duala, the Isuwu and other neighbouring groups, the *Jengu*, based on the veneration of water spirits, became the most prestigious.

Conclusion

The major external influence in the history of this region of coastal swamp and rainforest from the fifteenth to the eighteenth century was without doubt the overseas slave trade. It is, however, hard to assess its exact role in relation to internal factors for change long present in the region.

In many oral traditions the slave trade features as an enriching activity that brought both wealth and people. This was the case for the coastal communities which took part as middlemen, not themselves engaging in hunting or fighting for slaves but buying from others to sell to the slave ships and adding some of the local population. The Niger Delta states and the Efik state of Calabar would fall into this category. For them the slave trade was mainly a factor of economic change, social change in the integration and control of slaves, and political change in the shifts in the power base through differentials in wealth and manpower.

The Fon kingdom of Dahomey exemplifies a second type of participation in the slave trade – that of active procurement of slaves. In Igboland the

Aro and their mercenary allies played a similar role hunting for slaves. These communities gained from the trade but only at the expense of the normal development of their social, political and moral systems which were disrupted by the violence involved in procuring slaves.

The third category of community affected by the trade may be seen as victims. They were those from whom most slaves were taken for sale on the coast, and included parts of Yorubaland, Igboland and Ibibioland. The economic and social systems of communities were probably disrupted mostly by raids, kidnapping, wars and the general cheapening of human life. Villages were destroyed or dispersed, farms were abandoned and people lived in terror.

Against this gloomy picture, however, it is sometimes argued that the slave trade brought these tropical regions of Africa out of isolation. Formerly remote from European centres of civilization they became the vanguard of enlightenment and contact with the rest of the world. It was the slave trade which brought these communities into the international economy. In addition, the introduction of food crops such as maize, cassava and rice could be seen as redressing the demographic balance by enabling an increase in population. These are speculative hypotheses. For the African peoples of the region, the slave-trade era is seen as a bad dream best cast into the dark recesses of memory.

The Hausa states

D. LAYA

Introduction

The region discussed in this chapter is today readily associated with the idea of wealth. One author considers that two other factors should be added to the economic potential referred to in Volume IV: first, Hausaland's interaction with nearby regions as a producer of grain, leather and iron and a consumer of gold and kola nuts; and second, the integrated aspect of the West African economy, with the Wangara, Hausa and Kanuri in the savannah, and the Fante, Bini, Ijaw and Arochukwu in the forest.[1]

The documentation available on the region's development between 1500 and 1800 is of very uneven quality. Source materials on the Hausa states are extremely varied. One category comprises eye-witness reports, surveys and reference works, although both reports and surveys are open to dispute.[2] In addition to these easily obtainable publications of a general nature, there are a number of theses which, while of uneven academic level, are mainly written by researchers from the region.[3] A third category comprises the proceedings of regular seminars attended by specialists from various countries and covering such fields as history and archaeology. These proceedings are almost always published.[4] Lastly, the point of view of the people directly concerned[5] is set out in a number of documents published in English or Hausa. With the *Kano Chronicle*, for instance, the

1. UNESCO, *General History of Africa*, Vol. IV, pp. 295–6; M. Adamu, forthcoming.
2. Tilho, 1911; Y. F. Urvoy, 1936; Leo Africanus, 1956; al-Sa'di, 1964; E. Séré de Rivières, 1965; B. Hama, 1966; H. J. Fisher, 1975, 1977; J. F. A. Ajayi and M. Crowder, 1976; J. Ki-Zerbo, 1978; T. H. Hodgkin, 1979; O. Ikime, 1980; M. Ka'ti, 1913–14; M. Hiskett, 1984.
3. B. Hama, 1966, 1967(a), 1967(b), 1968, 1969; M. Adamu, 1968; M. Alkali, 1969; M. H. Piault, 1970; A. Salifou, 1971; G. Nicolas, 1975; D. M. Hamani, 1975; N. Echard, 1975, pp. 34–97; M. Karimou, 1977; G. Na-Dama, 1977; M. Adamu, 1978; Y. B. Usman, 1981; M. Saley, 1982.
4. Y. B. Usman, 1979b; Y. B. Usman and N. Alkali, 1983; B. M. Barkindo, 1983; M. Adamu, forthcoming; and H. W. El-Hasanwi, 1982.
5. H. R. Palmer, 1967; M. A. al-Hajj, 1968; A. A. Dokaji, 1978; Y. F. Urvoy, 1978; R. M. East, 1979; for the discussions, see M. Last, 1983 and forthcoming; M. G. Smith, 1983.

errors in the English version, which was published long ago, were corrected in the Hausa version, but this still contains errors of interpretation of the original text, as well as printing errors, and new editions of all these sources are urgently needed. However, the discussions to which they give rise underscore their exceptional quality. They are proof of the vitality and seriousness of current research and the queries that are continually being raised guarantee that the present shortcomings will gradually be made good.

Indirect references to the Nupe and Kwararafa may be found in some of the above-mentioned publications. For the moment, until the thesis by the late Mūsa Idrīs[6] has been published, it is difficult to provide new information on Borgu.

The nature of the documentation is such that the various political entities cannot all be treated with the same degree of thoroughness: this is a consequence of the uneven pattern of research and perhaps also of the relatively peripheral role played by Borgu, the Kwararafa and the Nupe during the period under consideration.

The Hausa states

Political development

Whenever post-1500 Central Sudan is being considered, it has become customary to point to the specific influence of Western Sudan – Mali and Songhay and the Kānem–Borno empire. This is understandable as a number of doubts still exist, particularly in connection with fourteenth-century history.[7] The sixteenth century opened with Askiya Muḥammad's campaign in Azbin – research in progress[8] is expected to explain why Azbin was so coveted at various times in its history. There was also a feeling of nostalgia for the *sarakunan noma* (masters of the crops) emperors,[9] the *Mai* (King) of Kānem, who experimented with sugar cane crops, and the *Mansa* (Emperor) of Mali, who had the robber of *kafi* beheaded. Indeed, the war was to take on another dimension and to become an enterprise whose fundamental aim was to consume the stocks that had been built up through

6. See J. Lombard, 1965; O. Bagodo, 1978; D. M. Debourou, 1979. We have high hopes of M. Idris' thesis, particularly as it has been entrusted to specialists of the highest repute; cf. M. Adamu, 1979, note 89.

7. The extension of Mali's power to include Tādmekka or Takedda: this assertion was made by Ibn Khaldūn, but has been rejected by H. J. Fisher, 1977, p. 265. This was the place where the *Mansa* Sakura died on returning from a pilgrimage, cf. D. Lange, 1977, p. 73, note 19(4). Likewise, according to one of Ibn Khaldūn's informants, the name Zaghai designates the Takrūr. If it is the name of the country to which the copper from Tādmekka was exported, as Ibn Baṭṭūṭa suggested, it may be identified with Songhay, Zaghāwa or more simply Zaghai, Birnin Katsina's original name; cf. J. M. Cuoq, 1975, pp. 319 and 343; M. Last, 1983, p. 73.

8. D. Hamani, 1975.

9. J. M. Cuoq, 1975, p. 209 (Kānem), pp. 266–7 (Mali).

the producers' labours. One final reason was that, since Western and Eastern Sudan were better known, little attention had been paid until that time to the changes taking place in Central Sudan. However, it was soon to be integrated into the commercial and ideological system uniting the societies of Western Sudan with the Muslim world. Its political development came to be viewed in terms of its relationships with the neighbouring states, the conflicts between Kano and Katsina, and interludes involving Kebbi, Zamfara and Gobir.

The chronological framework adopted here is based on research which provides an extremely evocative view of the overall situation, despite some difficulties and occasional differences of opinion.[10] A distinction can be made between the following three periods:

(1) 1500 to 1620, when the states gained in strength but there were bitter conflicts between Kano and Katsina, and Kebbi remained the dominant power in the western part of Hausaland. As far as relations with their neighbours were concerned, Songhay was eliminated once and for all, and the *Mai* of Borno could do little more than vent his annoyance at the hardly aristocratic behaviour of *Sarkin* Kano Muḥammad Kisoki (1509–65).
(2) 1620 to 1730, when Kano was on its way to becoming a caliphate,[11] at a time when Zamfara and Gobir were consolidating their positions following the decline of Kebbi and Kwararafa was further increasing its capacity for attack.
(3) 1730 to 1808, a period marked by the collapse of Zamfara and Gobir's rise to the peak of its power.

Relations with the neighbouring regions

Although Hausaland's relations with its neighbours are being studied in increasing depth, there still remains some controversy over interpretation.

With Songhay,[12] undue importance has been attached to the authority of Askiya Muḥammad. The economic and political issues can be gauged from the Kano sources, according to which 'Abdullāh Burja (1438–52) opened up the Gwanja–Kano–Borno route when the Sunnis were organizing the western part of their empire. Kubbel's point of view may, therefore, be readily accepted – that the *Askiya* 'only knew of one way' of opposing the growth in trade along the eastern route, and that was to control it by conquering the region with his army. The main outcome of his campaign in Azbin was the emergence of Kebbi as an independent state

10. H. R. Palmer, 1967; M. Alkali, 1969; G. Na-Dama, 1977; D. Lange, 1977; Y. B. Usman, 1978 and 1981; I. Maïkassoua, 1982.
11. M. Last, 1983, pp. 67–91.
12. See UNESCO, *General History of Africa*, Vol. IV, ch. 2, pp. 280–9; L. E. Kubbel, 1974, p. 97.

in 1516. Songhay was subsequently to attempt to regain control over Kebbi.[13] Askiya Muḥammad II Benkan Kiriai (1531–7) led an expedition in about 1533: 'The Kanta inflicted a shameful defeat on his adversary, who fled with his entire army. ... The prince arrived in Kagho and since that time, none of the Askiya has led an expedition against the Kanta.' In fact, another expedition was organized under the reign of Askiya Dāwūd (1549–83), the conflict being brought to an end by the conclusion of a peace treaty in 1553. Kanta Dāwūd (c.1589–1613) was to provide shelter and assistance to the Songhay resistance movement: despite the Sultan of Morocco's threats, he did not yield, confident as he was of his military strength, and perhaps also wishing to handle the Songhay with tact, as they had supported the first Kanta and were represented at his court by a high-ranking dignitary, the *Gulma*.[14]

Azbin[15] was to provide the pretext for the clash between Kebbi and Borno. The latter had extended its influence through the conquest of Agades in about 1532, the conclusion of treaties with various Tuareg groups, and the appointment of a delegate. As Kebbi continued its repeated forays, Borno was in 1561 called to Azbin's aid. After initially winning the day at Surame, the 100 000-man Borno army was compelled to withdraw: the Kanta defeated it at Nguru but died on the return journey in a village in Katsina.[16] Then, at the end of the century, a dynastic crisis flared up in Azbin. Yūsuf, after being deposed by Muḥammad ben al-Mubārak (c.1601) appealed to Kanta Dāwūd for support. The latter, who wished to maintain his influence, was forced to come to his assistance on two occasions to help him defeat his rival, who was backed by Borno. This success checked the *Mai*'s designs on the Azbin,[17] which was at its peak under the reign of Muḥammad al-Mubārak (c.1653–87). In 1674, taking advantage of the continual conflicts between Gobir and the eastern part of Hausaland (Kano and Katsina), and between Zamfara and Kebbi, Muḥammad dispatched an expedition led by his son Agabba, who conquered Adar and thereby hastened Kebbi's decline.[18] From then onwards, it was left to Zamfara and Gobir to temper the influence of Azbin in the Kwanni regions. In 1675, Zamfara's army set an ambush and massacred some 700 Kel-Ewey Tuareg. In the same year, Azbin took its revenge, and Zamfara left a thousand dead on the battlefield. Gobir, which was pillaging the same area, was attacked and defeated by Azbin in about 1689. Finally Agabba, who had become

13. Al-Saʿdi, 1964, pp. 146–7, 168; J. O. Hunwick, 1976, p. 285. For the political context to 1590, see Z. Dramani-Issifou, 1982, pp. 186, 207, 218–19. There are reservations as to what the Kebbi Chronology has to say; M. Alkali sets the date of Kanta I's death at 1554, and al-Saʿdi at 1561; the author has chosen the first date.

14. M. Alkali, 1969, pp. 62–3.

15. J. O. Hunwick, 1976, pp. 283–4; H. J. Fisher, 1977, p. 266; see ch. 17 below.

16. Y. B. Usman, 1981, pp. 31–2; see ch. 17 below.

17. M. Alkali, 1969, p. 76; J. O. Hunwick, 1976, p. 283.

18. M. Alkali, 1969, pp. 78–84; R. A. Adeleye, 1976, pp. 585–6; D. M. Hamani, 1975, p. 91; G. Na-Dama, 1977, pp. 217–25.

Sultan, marched on Surame in 1721, and killed Kanta Aḥmadu. In 1722, the Kebbi court withdrew towards the western areas. However, Azbin was entering a period of dynastic crises and disasters, and this left Zamfara and Gobir to occupy the leading role.

Before 1561, Borno was in a position of strength; Sarkin Kano 'Abdullāhī (1499–1509) was attacked by the *Mai* and adopted a subservient attitude which prompted the aggressor to depart. It is difficult to describe the political climate in Kano at the time except to say that the Queen Mother Auwa managed to contain a rebellion fomented by the *Dagacih*, an important figure who appears to have been a court dignitary. The reasons for that move are unclear. However the *Sarkin*'s successor, Muḥammad Kisoki (1509–65) made for the city of Nguru in Borno where he gave orders that only horses and clothing were to be seized. Caught by surprise, the *Mai* took the initiative the following year and attacked Kano but was again made to withdraw.[19] Two historians have recently commented on these events.[20] When the domestic situation in the two states is examined more closely, it can be seen that Kano had just emerged victorious from a long struggle with Katsina, while Idrīs Katakarmabi (c.1497–1519) was having to consolidate the fruits of his victory. The humiliation inflicted by Kisoki was a sign of the might of Kano at a time when Borno was suffering from internal strife and several years of famine: the second attack against Kano, however, seems to have taken place before the time of Idrīs Alowoma (1564–96).

It was not long before Kano was subjected to repeated attacks from Kwararafa: between 1582 and 1618, its population was forced to seek refuge at Daura. The sovereign of Kano was again driven out in 1653, and its inhabitants once more sought refuge in Daura in 1671. According to Palmer, the peace treaty signed between Kano and Katsina (c.1649–51) was inspired by fear of the Kwararafa, who were eventually to be defeated by Borno in 1680.[21]

To be objective, due allowance has to be made for the political situation in each of the states who were involved at the different stages in their political development. Apart from the profits they generated from plunder, these conflicts point to the unstable equilibrium between powerful neighbours.

19. H. R. Palmer, 1967, pp. 112–13. There is a discrepancy between the English text and the Hausa version which suggests, provided there is no printing error, that the *Dagaci* was about to go to Kagara (a village).

20. Y. B. Usman, 1983, pp. 181–4; M. Last, 1983, pp. 68–74. For the situation in Borno, see D. Lange, 1977, pp. 79–81; ch. 17 below.

21. H. R. Palmer, 1967, pp. 83, 116, 121–2.

The struggle for hegemony

Leo Africanus describes Kano as a city whose 'inhabitants consist of civilized craftsmen and rich merchants'. By contrast, Katsina was regarded as a kingdom both rural and poor. It should be recalled that the Gwanja–Kano–Borno route had been opened up between 1438 and 1452. Moreover, in the fifteenth century, Agades had replaced Takedda as a caravan centre, thereby making Katsina a terminus of the trans-Saharan caravan route, and a trading centre for all Hausaland.[22]

According to a recent article, the explanation that the military conflicts between the two states were due to the struggle for control of the trans-Saharan terminus, has to be reconsidered – nothing is known of the nature and scale of these wars, their political background or general context. It is therefore necessary to re-examine these conflicts indicating, if possible, their causes, the name of the aggressor and the location, as well as the internal and external political situation.

The first conflict[23] broke out during the reign of Rumfa (c.1463–99). Rumfa had amassed so much wealth that he was the first to be escorted by eunuchs – in full trappings in the war against Katsina – and to entrust them with official duties. The causes of the conflicts are not known, but it is known that Korau, Ibrāhīm Sura and Aliyu Murābit reigned in succession in Katsina. With sovereigns such as these to be reckoned with, it was not surprising that the war lasted for eleven years, with no decisive outcome.

The second conflict took place at the time of Abū Bakr Kado (c.1565–73), when Ibrāhīm Badankarī (c.1565–73) was reigning in Katsina. The Katsinawa advanced to the very gates of Kano and camped at Salanta, defeated Kano and then returned home.

To avenge this defeat Muḥammad Shāshīrī (c.1573–82) organized an expedition against Katsina, where Muḥammad Wari (c.1575–87) was ruler. The battle took place at Kankiya, not far from Katsina. It was said that: 'The Katsinawa were victorious because they outnumbered the enemy'. Civil war then broke out in Kano, and although the sovereign escaped death, he was deposed.

These first three conflicts seem to have had well-founded political causes. For some reason unknown to us, the attack on Kano was unsuccessful; the Katsinawa advanced to the gates of Kano in a bid for victory, after which Kano, in its turn, advanced to a point not far from Katsina, where it was defeated. At least one Katsina source[24] states that it was under the control of Kano at one time.

22. Leo Africanus, 1956, pp. 2, 476–7; H. R. Palmer, 1967, p. 109; J. O. Hunwick, 1976, pp. 275–6; R. A. Adeleye, 1976, pp. 562–3.

23. H. R. Palmer, 1967, pp. 111–12, 115–16. It was not possible to consult 'Abdullāhi Mahadi's recent thesis on Kano.

24. I. Dankoussou, 1970, p. 28.

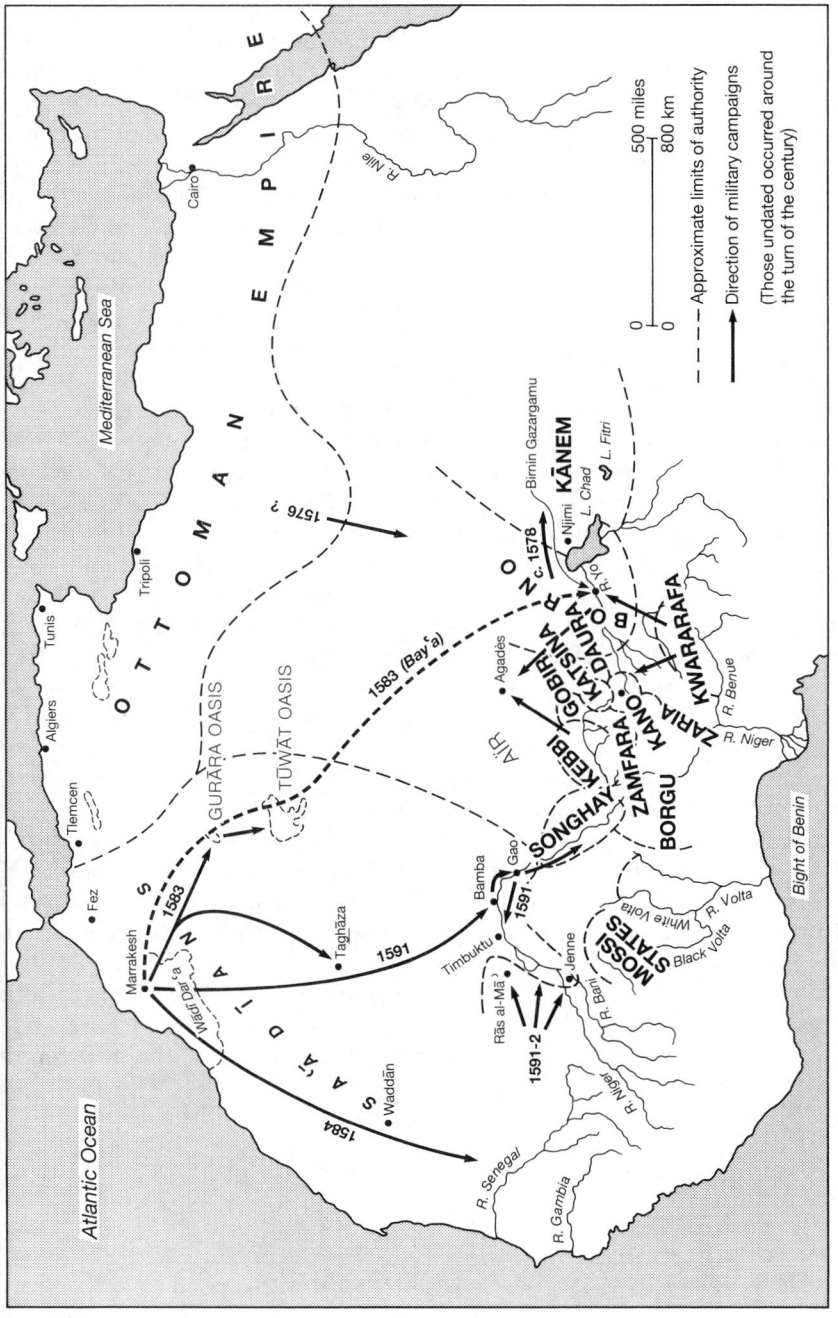

FIG. 16.1 *North Africa and the Central Sudan in 1600*
Source: adapted from J. F. A. Ajayi and M. Crowder, *History of West Africa*, 1976, Vol. 1, London, Longman, *p. 286*. Map adapted by kind permission of Longman Group
UK Ltd

The next conflict broke out[25] during the reign of Muḥammad Zakī (*c*.1582–1618) of Kano. In Katsina, Muḥammad Wari (*c*.1575–87) was succeeded by Sulaymān (*c*.1587–1600) and 'Uthmān Nayinawa (*c*.1600–18). There is some confusion as to what happened next. There may have been a change of dynasty, as the chronology is not precise. Katsina, however, was so powerful that Kano was afraid it might be attacked and one author stresses that one precaution, taken on the advice of the dignitaries, was to adopt *Cokana* and *Dirki* as talismans before launching an attack. Despite even this precaution, however, the Kwararafa invaded Kano, defeating it and sapping its strength. Shortly afterwards, Kano's Muḥammad Zakī consulted the '*ulamā*' and obtained a talisman at a very high price. Suitably protected, Kano then attacked Katsina's military encampments and finally emerged victorious.

As soon as he assumed power in Kano, Muḥammad Nazaki (*c*.1618–23) made peace proposals to Katsina which, however, rebuffed them and instead attacked. The encounter took place at Karaye, not far from Kano, and Katsina was defeated. The *Wambai* of Kano was posted to Karaye, from where he launched constant attacks against Katsina.[26]

Under Kutumbi (*c*.1623–48), Kano's Prince Bako dan Kutumbi kept up the pressure on Katsina. He pillaged a town with his ninety mail-clad horsemen and their six hundred horses. Another conflict then broke out, the pretext being the assassination in Katsina of a slave belonging to a representative of Kano on a mission there. Kutumbi set up camp at Dugazawa and subjected Katsina to a long siege. He then organized a second expedition but his army was taken by surprise and put to flight and he himself was killed at Rumarawa, on the Katsina–Kano border. Kutumbi's successor, al-Hādjdjī, was deposed after eight months and his successor, Shekarau (*c*.1649–51), managed to sue for peace after negotiations conducted by the '*ulamā*'. Katsina's power was further consolidated by Muḥammad Wari (*c*.1631–41), Muḥammad Uban Yara (*c*.1641–71) and Muḥammad Jan Hazo (*c*.1671–84), without the peace treaty with Kano being broken.[27]

There was accordingly a long political struggle for control of eastern Hausaland. As shown, the neighbouring states of Borno and Kwararafa had to be reckoned with, but the other factor involved was the situation in western Hausaland.

25. H. R. Palmer, 1967, pp. 81, 116–17; I. Dankoussou, 1970, p. 30; R. A. Adeleye, 1976, p. 580; Y. B. Usman, 1978, and 1981, p. 63.

26. R. A. Adeleye, 1976, p. 581; Y. B. Usman, 1981, p. 33.

27. H. R. Palmer, 1967, pp. 118–19; R. A. Adeleye, 1976, p. 581.

Interludes

Until the end of the sixteenth century, Kebbi feared none of its enemies, not even Morocco. Among the specific factors instrumental in consolidating Kebbi's position, one author has suggested the mixed origins of the population, the polarization of the protests against Songhay domination, and the importance its military leaders attached to maintaining independence. However, there is no proof that Kebbi invaded the region or laid claim to Songhay.[28]

Indeed, it was Kebbi's independence that altered the political map in the Rima basin: north-east Zarma was integrated into it, thus depriving Zamfara of a region to pillage.[29] This was to give rise to a series of clashes under Zartai, who ruled after Taritu (*c*.1531) and led a number of indecisive attacks in the middle of the century, after which a peace treaty was concluded. The pressure was thus taken off Kebbi which, by defeating Borno in 1561, rose to occupy the leading place in the political life of Hausaland: 'It rapidly became the most fearsome military power in the Hausa world'.[30] The exact nature of its political relations with the states is not known. Some writers feel that most paid tribute to the Kanta, but others disagree. Zamfara, for example, was attacked by Kebbi on only one occasion and there is no evidence to show that Zamfara was ever a vassal of Kebbi. Both, however, had reason to fear Gobir.[31]

The capital of Gobir had been transferred from Azbin to Hausaland to Birnin Lalle, in the centre of the densely populated and well-watered region of Gulbin Tarka, probably founded in about 1450. The rulers remained there until about 1600 when the Tuareg launched an attack which degenerated into a massacre. The Gobirawa were forced to take up their wanderings again and set out in the direction of Kufan Kuturu and Hisatau in the Gulbi Maradi, further south. (The last of Hisatau's sovereigns,[32] Muḥammad Mai Gici, was killed there by the ruler of Katsina, who was

28. M. Alkali, 1969, pp. 58–67.

29. The most recent information regarding Zamfara is taken from G. Na-Dama, 1977; for Zamfara's relations with Kebbi, cf. pp. 220–8.

30. D. M. Hamani, 1975, p. 83.

31. Information regarding the *sarauta* system in Gobir is provided by Ibn Baṭṭūṭa, in J. M. Cuoq, 1975, p. 323. Quoting an eyewitness, the author says that the sovereign was buried with several of his entourage, together with slaves and thirty sons and daughters of persons of note. The striking fact was the religious aspect of such a tradition, although its political significance is quite clear. Archaeological research will no doubt eventually identify a site for the capital of Gobir. The new facts and the chronology prior to 1700 are taken from Maikassoua's research. His findings are awaited with interest, particularly as Gobir is a subject that intrigues researchers, for instance J. E. G. Sutton, 1979, pp. 192–5 and G. Nicolas, forthcoming.

32. I. Maikassoua, 1982, pp. 39–45. The findings of J. Tilho, 1911, and Y. B. Usman, 1978 and 1981, suggest that these events must have taken place between the beginning of Sulaymān's reign (*c*.1587–1600) and the end of that of the sovereign of Katsina, 'Uthmān Tsagarana (*c*.1600–18).

concerned at the encroachments onto his territory and anxious not to lose control of the Katsina–Tessawa–Azbin route.) The Gobirawa then struck out towards the north-west and founded the 'new' Gwaran Rama (*c*.1685–90). Uban Doro launched attacks from Gwaran Rama against Kebbi, and even against Yorubaland and Gurma and his successor, Soba, attacked Adar, Kebbi and Maradi. However, he also, established friendly relations with Zamfara, which opened up Alkalawa to the farmers and traders of Gobir.

This gradual expansion of Gobir southwards brought about another change in the political context. Kebbi maintained its position and prospered until 'The old military aristocracy ... was eclipsed by a new aristocracy based on money'.[33] It started to decline as Zamfara was clearly gaining strength. In the mid-seventeenth century, Zamfara was governed by a series of strong sovereigns who drew their support from Islam; the position it occupied can be gauged from its relations with Katsina,[34] which were excellent until the day when a Zamfaran prince was killed by Muḥammad Uban Yara (*c*.1641–71). Sarkin Zamfara Zaudai planned to retaliate but encountered opposition from the dignitaries of the court, who argued that the two states were on good terms. His death, however, put an end to the plan and the electors appointed as his successor his brother, Aliyu, who became Zamfara's first Islamic sovereign. There can be no doubt that he helped to spread Islam through Katsina, as he built mosques in the towns. Zamfara then stopped making its sporadic raids and instead concentrated its forces on Kebbi's major towns. In 1674 Sulaymān organized a full-scale attack and the army of Kebbi, with its 6000 troops and the support of a contingent from Adar, was put to flight and many of its troops captured. In the same year, Kebbi lost Adar, which was wrested from it by Prince Agabba, as seen above. It was a series of separate defeats rather than a concerted action by Azbin, Gobir and Zamfara.[35] Zamfara became the leading power in the area: its might is revealed by the victory won by the commander of its cavalry, Yakubu dan Mazuru, at Yargana against Kano's army, during the reign of Muḥammad Sharīf (*c*.1703–31). It was after this defeat that Muḥammad Sharīf constructed ramparts around many towns.[36]

Zamfara had thus recovered from the defeat it suffered at the hands of Azbin, but the military strength of Gobir was also growing: 'Under his reign (Kumbari *c*.1731–43), there was a fierce war between Kano and Gobir. The *Sarkin* of Gobir's name was Soba. Whenever the Gobirawa inflicted a defeat on the Kanawa, the latter took their revenge the following

33. D. M. Hamani, 1975, p. 85.
34. G. Na-Dama, 1977, pp. 231–4; Y. B. Usman, 1981, pp. 30–1.
35. M. Alkali, 1969, pp. 78–9; D. M. Hamani, 1975, p. 91; G. Na-Dama, 1977, pp. 224–5.
36. H. R. Palmer, 1967, p. 123; G. Na-Dama, 1977, pp. 240–5.

year, and this alternating pattern went on for a long time.'[37] Ibrāhīm Babārī
(*c*.1741–70), Soba's successor, sent a delegation to al-Hādjdjī Kabi (*c*.1743–
53) to make peace, but al-Hādjdjī Kabi refused. A year later, Babārī took
the initiative and attacked, and the encounter at Dumi turned into a
complete rout for Kano, 'because of Babārī's magical power'. The massacres
perpetrated on both sides only came to an end at Kabi's death. Gobir was
soon to feel the weight of various restrictions imposed upon it by Sarkin
Zamfara, who was worried by his restive neighbour. At the outset, Gobir
was content with harassing its enemy from time to time, but then, taking
advantage of a dynastic crisis, it destroyed Birnin Zamfara in about 1762.[38]

This development had significant repercussions on the political situation
in the peripheral areas. In the east,[39] the Sultanate of Damagaram was
founded towards the beginning of the eighteenth century, while the Tsotsebaki states were consolidating their position before subsequently splitting
up. This area, which marked the transition between Borno and Hausaland,
was extremely sensitive to political and cultural movements.

In the north-west, the history of Adar is better known.[40] However, it is
not clear what its links were with Kurfay – which is associated with Adar
in some accounts and with Borno in others – although the proximity of
Arewa suggests the latter. The date of the foundation of political authority
in the area is highly controversial, but the various dynasties were identified
with Borno at times and with Daura at others.

According to the traditions of the Zarma and the Gobirawa,[41] Zarma –
the easternmost part of the Songhay empire – first established links with
Hausaland when Gobir was part of Azbin. At this time Kebbi, Zamfara
and Gobir all fought over the area. Kebbi is thought to have been eliminated
in 1722. Before that, however, its political role was decisive in Zarmatarey,
where its name was associated with cavalry protected by *lifidi* (quilted
armour) which spread terror and desolation.

Finally, in the west, on the *gurma* (right) bank of the River Niger, certain
Gulmanceba dynasties claimed to originate from Central Sudan, Borno or
Hausaland – a claim seemingly substantiated by archaeological excavations
at least for the areas along the *Hausa* or left bank.[42]

In the south, occupied by Kebbi, Yawuri, Nupe and Borgu, the growth

37. H. R. Palmer, 1967, pp. 124–5.

38. G. Na-Dama, 1977, pp. 378–86.

39. For Damagaram, see A. Salifou, 1971, pp. 31–42; for the Tsotsebaki states, see
M. Saley, 1982, pp. 24–58.

40. For Adar, see D. M. Hamani, 1975, pp. 25–125 and N. Echard, 1975, pp. 34–97;
for Arewa, see M. H. Piault, 1970, pp. 49–124 and M. Karimou, 1977.

41. For the relations between Gobirawa and Zarma, see B. Hama, 1967(a), 1967(b) and
1968; B. Gado, 1980; and I. Maikassoua, 1982; on the influence of Kebbi in Zarmatarey,
see M. Alkali, 1969, pp. 90–6.

42. See G. Y. Madiega, 1982, pp. 30–41 (Borno origins of the Bemba) and pp. 50–4
(dynasties of Gobnangu and Jabo); for the archaeological data, see B. Gado, 1980, pp. 35–
119.

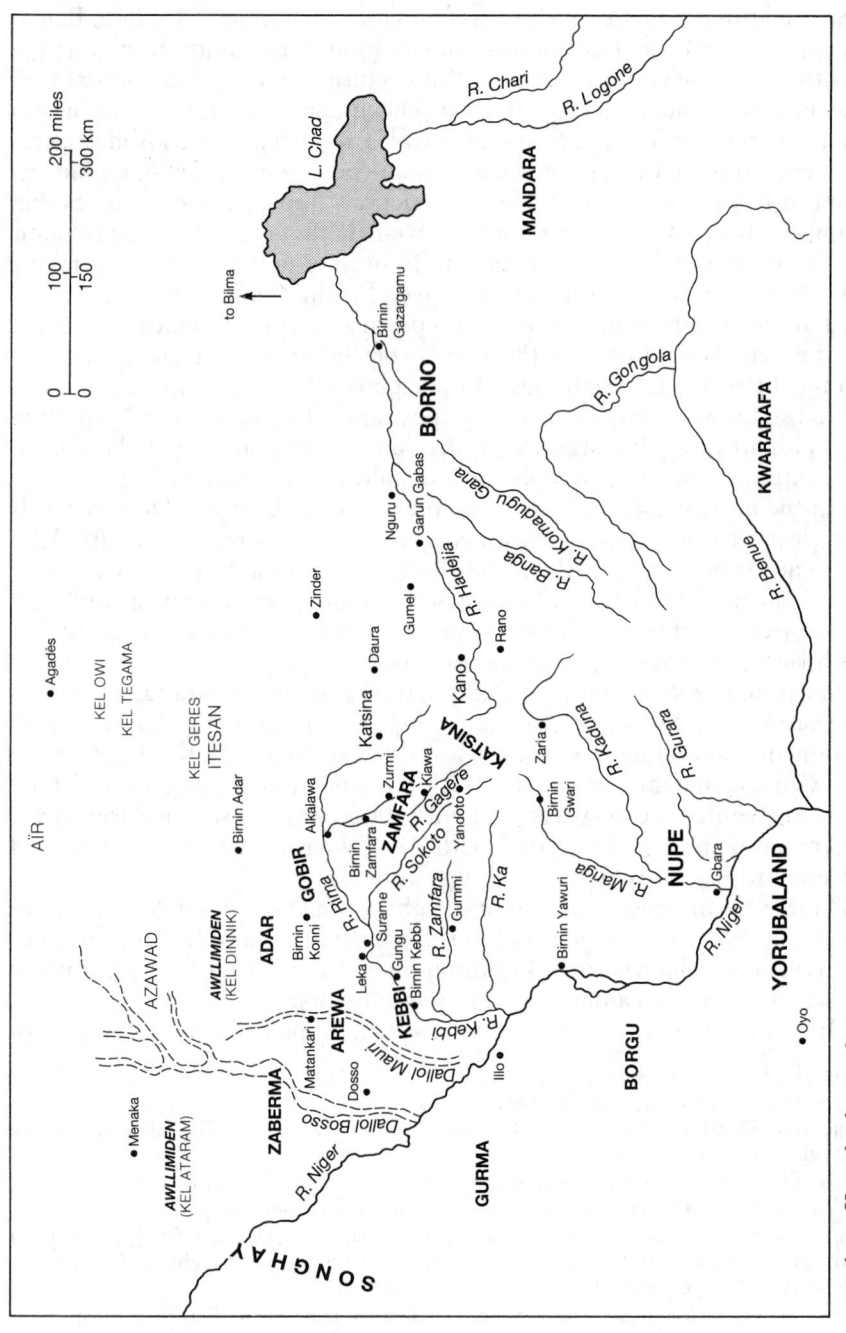

FIG. 16.2   *Hausaland, pre-1800*

and consolidation of the Zarma–Songhay people has not been clearly determined. In this area's mythology the most powerful divinities include *Manda Hausakoy*, the fisherman-blacksmith from Yawuri, and *Dongo*, a Borgu hunter whose powers were identical to those of *Shango* in the Yoruba culture.[43]

The situation, however, stabilized considerably after Zamfara's defeat in 1762. Katsina, despite a domestic crisis, was to defeat Gobir, while in Kano,[44] Babba Zaki (*c.*1768–76) felt compelled to terrorize his collaborators.

Political and administrative organization

Thus, despite the military conflicts, which assumed alarming proportions, this host of states remained in existence. After their severe defeats, the sovereigns of Kebbi and Zamfara retrenched to an even smaller territory to safeguard their power. Explanations for this development are being sought in the process whereby the *sarauta* system as it evolved in Central Sudan was introduced and transformed.[45]

The Sarki

At the head of the state, which was first and foremost a *kasa* (territory), there was the *Sarki*,[46] whose ancestor had seized political power: in Kano, Katsina and Zamfara, it has been wrested from the hands of a high priest, while in Kebbi it was a *magaji* (warrior) who rose to the rank of *Sarki*.

The appointment of the successor to the throne from among the princes was the responsibility of an electoral college. In Katsina, this consisted of four members.[47] It is difficult to say whether such a college existed in Kebbi at this time, but it certainly appeared there at a later stage. In Zamfara, Gobir and Kano, it bore the name *Tara* (the Nine),[48] followed

43. See Fondation SCOA Seminar, 1981, pp. 45–109.

44. H. R. Palmer, 1967, p. 126; R. A. Adeleye, 1976, pp. 588–93; Y. B. Usman, 1981, pp. 92–3.

45. A general survey has been produced by A. Mahadi (forthcoming); see also M. Alkali, 1969, pp. 43–62; G. Na-Dama, 1977, pp. 80–9; Y. B. Usman, 1981, pp. 5–19; the sociological viewpoint is expounded by N. Perchonock (forthcoming). The outline is reminiscent of the information provided by written sources on the subject of Western Sudan; see J. M. Cuoq, 1975, p. 99 (sacred forest of Ghana), p. 108 (meal of the *Kanda* in Kāw-Kāw), p. 122 (magic stone of the Amima), etc.

46. There continue to be discussions as to the significance of the term; it should be noted that the sovereign's sister in Zamfara bore the title *Asarki*, cf. G. Na-Dama, 1977, p. 345.

47. Galadima, Kaura, Durbi and Yandaka, cf. Y. B. Usman, 1981, p. 78.

48. In Zamfara: Danau, Basace, Sarkin Rafi, Sarkin Tudu, Sarkin Bazai, Sarkin Kaya, Magajin Gari, Ubandawaki and Galadima; see G. Na-Dama, 1977, pp. 86–7. In Gobir: Ubandawaki, Ubandoma, Sarkin Rafi Babba and Karama, Sarkin Tudu Babba and Karama,

by the name of the state. The titles and functions of the various electoral colleges differ, but some of the incumbents can be identified as follows: an elder holding an ancient, long-forgotten office, the *Basace*, in Zamfara; governors of cities and important regions, five in Zamfara and seven in Gobir which added two deputies to Zamfara's list, and high-ranking public servants, three in Zamfara, two in Gobir and nine in Kano. They also included representatives of ousted dynasties, such as the Durbi in Katsina, and reigning dynasties, such as the Ubandoma in Gobir.

The successor had to be chosen unanimously by the electors. Once he had been appointed, the enthronement and installation ritual took place. The electoral college also formed the council of the *Sarki*, and it was not uncommon, for one reason or another, for the Council to clash with the *Sarki*, or for the latter to debar one of the Council members.[49]

The government

The *Sarki* exercised his authority through three groups of officials: members of the dynasty, public servants, governors of the towns and regions. The members of the dynasty were assigned important duties. As different generations were involved, the brothers and children of the sovereign usually bore titles showing that they held administrative positions. The wide range of titles and the duties they entailed does not make it easy to draw up a single list.[50]

The sovereign's sister played a leading political role, although she did so through the traditional form of worship. In Zamfara she was called the *Asarki* or *Inna*[51] – a name which Gobir also used. The history of Kano is signposted by the names of celebrated princesses: for example, if the *Madaki* (the Queen Mother) Auwa had not energetically intervened, 'Abdul-lāhī (1499–1509) would most certainly have been driven out by a rebellion. His son, Kisoki governed the city with the support of the same Madaki Auwa, his grandmother, Iya Lamis, his mother and Gulli, Auwa's brother. During the reign of S͟h͟arīf (*c*.1703–31), a dignitary of Kano had musical

---

Magajin Kukuta, Sarkin Bazai and Sarkin Kaya; see I. Maikassoua, 1982, pp. 47–8. For Kano, the Gazetteers give the following list: Galadima, Madaiki (Madawaki?) Wambai, Makama, Sarkin Dawaki Maituta, Sarkin D. Tsakanin Gida, Sarkin Bai, Giroma and Dan Iya; although they all belonged to the nobility, they held administrative and/or military offices, but such a structure appears to have been very recent, since figures as important as the *Dagaci*, the *Barde* and the *Santuraki* were not included.

49. See below regarding the events that took place at Zaudai in Zamfara. In Kano, Kisoki appointed his brother Dabkare dan Iya to replace the *Barde* on the Council of Nine, cf. H. R. Palmer, 1967, pp. 112–13.

50. For Maradi, see P. H. David, 1969, pp. 657, 665–6; for Damagaram in the nineteenth century, see A. Salifou, 1971, pp. 117–33; for Zamfara, see G. Na-Dama, 1977, p. 348.

51. See G. Na-Dama, 1977, pp. 345–8.

instruments from Yawuri brought to him which he kept for three months and then gave them to Madaki Maryama 'because she had attained the limits of power and she had no equal in the seven Hausa States'.[52]

In what might be called the central government, there were several categories of officials:

(1) The court dignitaries managed the affairs of the palace and the city. The composition of the list and the duties varied from one state to another, but their role was above all administrative. In Katsina, the most important officials included the *Galadima* (who deputized for the Sarki), the *Ajiya* (treasurer), the *Turaki* and *Shantali* (protocol officers) and the *Madawaki* (officer-in-charge of the royal stables).[53] They were in a position to act as middlemen between the *Sarki* and the regional governments. In Kebbi, internal security was the responsibility of the *Magajin Gari, Galadiman Gari* and the *Doka*; the *Magajin Baberi* seems to have been in charge of external affairs, and the *Maishanu* collected the livestock that was the state's due.[54]

(2) The representatives of the guilds were appointed from among the skilled craftsmen, such as blacksmiths, weavers, dyers, tanners, masons, butchers and hunters. They were responsible for relations with the different trades and occupations and, in particular, for collecting the state dues. When necessary, the blacksmiths and hunters, for instance, provided contingents for the army.

(3) The autochthonous groups had their own representatives. The village of Sarkin Naya and the region of Sarkin Mazum, for example, kept their titles even after Gobir established its capital at Hisatau.[55] The Maguzawa of Kano were disbanded by order of Bugaya (*c.*1385–90), but they were to be summoned by Kukuna (*c.*1652–60) who allowed them to indulge in their favourite sport for three weeks, showered them with riches, and confirmed their patriarch Zanko in his office, expecting from him a tribute in kind each year consisting of a certain number of days work.[56] It has to be asked whether some of the states did not relegate certain autochthonous peoples to the status of bondsmen or tributaries.

(4) The numerous immigrants were also allowed to have their own representatives. In Gobir, Sarkin Azbin handled relations with the Tuareg living in the territory, and Sarkin Fullani did likewise for the Fulbe (in Gobir, Zamfara, Katsina and Kano), as did Sarkin Sillubawa for the Sillube (in Kano and Katsina). From this point of view, the

52. H. R. Palmer, 1967, pp. 112–13, 123; R. M. East, 1979, p. 38.
53. Y. B. Usman, 1981, p. 80.
54. M. Alkali, 1969, pp. 73–107.
55. I. Maikassoua, 1982, p. 48.
56. H. R. Palmer, 1967, pp. 107, 120–1.

situation regarding the Fulbe in Kebbi is most instructive.[57] The titles *Galoji* and *Magajin Sangeldu*, which were created under the Kanta, could only be conferred upon Fulbe in contact with the herdsmen. The title of *Dikko*, however, which was created in the eighteenth century, was borne for the first time by a Pullo whose mother was the sovereign's daughter.

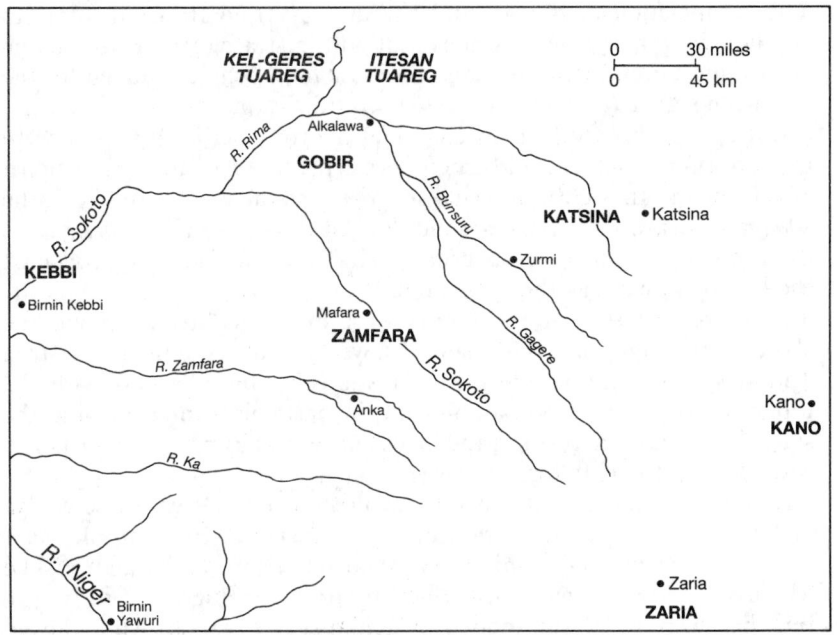

FIG. 16.3   *Hausa states in the eighteenth century*
Source: adapted from P. Lovejoy, *Caravans of Kola The Hausa Kola Trade, 1700–1900*, 1980, *p. 55*, Zaria, Ahmadu Bello University Press

(5) The Islamic community was present everywhere with its *mallamai* (scholars). In terms of regional government or, more specifically, territorial control, a distinction also has to be made between several categories:

(a) The authority of the governors of certain cities was independent of the dynasty; this was true of Rano, Gaya, Dutse, Karaye (in Kano), Maska, Samri, Dugui (in Katsina); and Zurmi, Kiawa, Tunfafi and Bakura (in Zamfara). On occasions, their relations with the sovereign could be difficult as they were eventually reduced to the status of vassals. The vassals of Kano were quick to rebel, and the Kano ruler Dadi (*c.*1670–1703) was forced to execute Farin Dutse, the governor of Gaya.[58]

57. M. Alkali, 1969, pp. 34–5, 113.
58. H. R. Palmer, 1967, p. 122.

(b) The governors of other cities and regions were nobles whose ancestors had become allies of the dynasty while preserving their own authority, or they were public servants. Zamfara provides an illustration of the first case with the *Danau* who owed his title to the name of the town in which he resided, an important trading centre from where he kept watch over the roads leading south and west of Kebbi;[59] the governor of Bazai resided in the north, while the governor of Kaya moved from Kavatau in the north to Maradun in the centre of the territory. In Kebbi, the *Innamme* kept watch over the western frontier.[60] In Katsina, the *Marisa* (Destroyer) resided in Gwiwa from where he supervised the eastern border, while the *Gatari* (Axe) of Ruma kept an eye on the north-western frontier.[61] Two rather curious titles were to be found in Zamfara: *Sarkin Tudu* (Governor of the Hills) controlled the east of the territory, and *Sarkin Rafi* (Governor of the Valleys) the villages at the confluence of the Bunsuru and Gagare rivers. These titles may well have been inspired by the natural relief of the regions concerned.

(c) The other governors became mere cogs in the governmental machinery. The immigrants retained a local hierarchy – known by the Fulbe as *ardo*, or *rugga*.

(d) Finally, certain titles were the outcome of historical developments. In Kebbi, for example, the *Kokani* was responsible for relations with the population, after the conquest of Kwanni; the office of *Saburu* was created in about 1650 to provide security on the roads that led to Kwanni and the Azbin which were regularly pillaged by Zamfara and Gobir.[62]

All these dignitaries, nobles, commoners or slaves performed duties of a non-military nature except that, when the occasion demanded, they became valiant warriors and formed their own armed groups.

Military organization

The foundation of Kebbi signified the increasingly important role played by military leaders in the affairs of the state.[63] The Kanta's first companions were from the country's leading families but, subsequently, the elements that had participated in the struggle for independence were granted two representatives, one of whom, the *Kunduda*, was to be Kebbi's military

59. G. Na-Dama, 1977, pp. 86–7.
60. M. Alkali, 1969, p. 108; initially the title was conferred upon a dignitary who was a slave by origin.
61. Y. B. Usman, 1981, p. 80.
62. M. Alkali, 1969, pp. 73–4, 108–9; it is not known where the *Kokani* resided.
63. See J. P. Smaldone, 1977, for a general survey. M. Alkali, 1969; G. Na-Dama, 1977; Y. B. Usman, 1981 and A. Salifou, 1971 provide information on Kebbi, Zamfara, Katsina and Damagaram in the nineteenth century.

leader.[64] In south-western Katsina, the proximity of Zamfara, Kebbi and Katsina inhibited the formation of a large state centred around Kwianbani, Birnin Gwari, Koriga, etc. The large number of Katsinawa immigrants meant that the area towards Katsina was included but as it was constantly coveted by its neighbours, it had to be content with being dependent on Katsina.[65]

As we have seen, this subservient role was further emphasized by the need to seek protection against its neighbours, even distant ones such as Azbin, Borno and Kwararafa, and to provide for security on the borders and the roads. The number of military leaders increased, a ranking order was instituted and efficiency increased. The highest-ranking title varied from state to state: it was *Kunduda* in Kebbi, *Kaura* in Katsina, *Ubandawaki* in Zamfara and Gobir, while in Kano it appears to have been the *Galadima*.

As weapons improved, so strategies and tactics changed. In the event of mobilization, the services of the different trades and occupations, such as hunters and blacksmiths, were called upon. The weapons used included swords, lances, knives and arrows; shields (made of oryx skin in Zamfara) were used for protection prior to the appearance of the Nupe shields. The army consisted of two main corps – the infantry, subdivided into archers and lancers, and the cavalry. Kebbi also had river flotilla.[66]

The horses mainly originated from Azbin and Borno and were treated with special care. The sovereign imported them and set up stables: the kanta of Kebbi, for example, had stables in three places. The role played by the horse in military affairs can also be seen from the number and rank of the titles pertaining to them, such as *Ubandawaki*[67] *Madaki/Madawaki* (leader of the cavalry and/or commander-in-chief of the army) and *Sarkin Dawaki* (general in the cavalry division). The enhanced status of horses was also due to the innovations introduced by the acquisition of *sulke* (coats

---

64. See UNESCO, *General History of Africa*, Vol. IV, pp. 277–8. The Kanta was surrounded by the Magajin Kulalo, Magajin Leka, Galandu, Mayalo, Lelaba and Tak-wamba (names of persons); they were joined by the *Gulma* (for the Songhay element) and the *Kunduda* (for the Kwararafa element), cf. M. Alkali, 1969, pp. 59, 61, 72, 114.

65. Y. B. Usman, 1981, pp. 83–4.

66. M. Alkali, 1969, p. 11. It may be asked what the relationship is between the 'small canoe made of a single hollowed-out tree trunk' that Ibn Baṭṭūṭa took in Timbuktu, and the 'small and extremely narrow boats, made of half a hollowed-out tree trunk' observed by Leo Africanus in Jenne; there are grounds for doubting whether Sonni 'Alī Ber's flotilla was effective with such craft, and the Sultan of Morocco certainly did not ask the Kanta of Kebbi to send them to him. L. E. Kubbel, 1974, p. 87, rightly asks whether the *abara*, the dugout canoes of Hausa (and Kebbi and Nupe), did not spread as far as the Timbuktu–Jenne area.

67. The meaning of the title must not be confused with the duties pertaining to it, cf. A. Salifou, 1971, p. 124; a glossary of military titles is supplied by J. P. Smaldone, 1977, pp. 216–19. A. Salifou mentions, in order of their qualifies, nine breeds of horses known in Damagaram in the nineteenth century, pp. 153–4.

of mail) and the manufacture of *lifidi* (horse-trappings), whence the titles *Sarkin Lifidi* (general in the heavy cavalry division) and *Lifidi* (commander-in-chief of the heavy cavalry division) which were among the highest-ranking military officers.

Rifles had been introduced to Kano[68] by a Borno prince under Dauda's reign (1421–38), but it was not until three centuries later – at the time of Kumbari (*c*.1731–43) – that they were imported from Nupe: Babba Zaki (*c*.1768–76) was the first sovereign to set up a corps of fusiliers to serve as his personal bodyguard. Borno took to rifles but Songhay, which had been able to gauge their deadly effectiveness at its own cost, did not bother to retrieve those abandoned by the Moroccan soldiers half a century later (1591 to 1640).[69] Hausaland seems to have deliberately neglected a weapon that it could have procured for itself with its wealth, despite, as has been suggested, Borno's attempts to prevent it from doing so. Songhay and Hausaland could boast neither of venerating horsemanship more devoutly than Borno, nor of having used slave labour and participated in the slave trade to a greater extent than Borno and the Mande.

The war tactics used consisted of surprise attacks, ambushes, direct clashes and sieges. The stepped-up construction of fortifications around the cities was also justified by the frequent sieges and conflagrations. Campaigns were meticulously prepared and often the scholar-priests prayed for the army's victory.

In this region, in which the pace of economic development had increased, improvements in the art of war were to lead to the growth of pillaging. It is not easy to distinguish between wars waged for purposes of conquest or consolidation, the repression of rebellions, wars of intimidation, and simple raids. As a state, Gobir was continually obliged to fight for its survival. Because it lasted so long after acquiring a relatively rich and well-populated territory, it is worth continuing to investigate the meaning of its existence. The political, administrative and military aristocracy indulged in pillaging, as the *Kano Chronicle* clearly shows: it grew rich and presented gifts to the sovereigns and scholars. In Kano, in the space of two centuries – between 1573 and 1768 – the aristocracy became so powerful that it urged the state to wage war, participated in plots, flaunted its wealth and its generosity and gave the sovereign cause for concern. Kukuna obliged Madawaki Kuma to tour the city on a donkey led by young servant girls, and Babba Zaki had the idea of continually terrorizing his collaborators, and did not hesitate to humiliate them.[70]

The total number of dignitaries varied from one state to another: Gobir

68. H. R. Palmer, 1967, pp. 109, 124, 126.

69. During an ambush, Ibnou Bentsi massacred 400 Moroccan fusiliers, but he apparently had their rifles thrown into the rivers; M. Ka'ti, 1981, pp. 294–5. Up to 1640, the Songhay people of Dendi were in a position to retrieve the rifles, but no trace of this has been found in the traditions collected so far.

70. H. R. Palmer, 1967, pp. 120, 126.

had twenty-two (thirteen noblemen and nine commoners) and Katsina forty-six (sixteen nobles and thirty commoners).[71]

Resources

The Hausa state developed an ingenious system for controlling the territory and levying taxes to provide the treasury with the resources needed to run it. Four major sources may be singled out:

Taxes and duties

Taxes and duties were the most regular sources. They included the following:

kudin kasa (land tax) was paid by the farmers. The unit taken into account seems to have been the *gandum gida* (the family field). In Kano, Naguji (*c*.1197–1247) was the first to set the tax to be paid by each farmer at one-eighth of his harvest. There were taxes both on lowland crops and on others, such as indigo and groundnuts.[72]

kudin sana'a (professional tax) and paid by craftsmen and traders. In Kebbi, every producer of salt gave the Kanta one gourd a year.[73] With the development of crafts and trade, and as a result of the establishment of guilds, these taxes could represent a substantial source of earnings.

kudin hito (customs duty) was payable on certain products entering the territory. In Kebbi, in addition to this entry duty, the caravans journeying from Dallol Fogha towards Hausaland and Nupe–Gwanja, as well as those travelling from Hausaland to Gwanja, had to pay another duty. In addition, salt shipped to Zarmatarey and Arewa was subject to tax.

jangali[74] (the livestock tax) was paid by the stock-breeders, particularly the Fulbe. In Kano, it was levied for the first time by Kutumbi (*c*.1623–48): 280 head of cattle were supplied by four groups, no doubt depending on the size of their herds. It was on this occasion that the office of *Sarkin Shanu* (livestock tax-collector) was created.

In Kebbi, the nomadic Fulbe paid *kudin haki* (grazing duty) while a dignitary, called the *Nono*, collected the milk and butter intended for the sovereign.

71. J. Tilho, 1911, pp. 519–21. For Damagaram in the nineteenth century, an extremely detailed and impressively long list (of over 50 incumbents), is supplied by A. Salifou, 1971, pp. 117–36.

72. Y. B. Usman, 1981, p. 83; H. R. Palmer, 1967, p. 101.

73. M. Alkali, 1969, pp. 103–6.

74. The author believes that this noun was formed from *jaɓa* (to take, snatch) and that it implies the idea of extortion; however, the correct form is *jaɓ(u) ngal, janngal*. For Kano, cf. H. R. Palmer, 1967, pp. 118–20, 123–4; the first time *Sarkin Fullani* is mentioned is under Shārīf, a century later, but there is nothing to suggest that the title did not exist before.

Gifts

Governors, dignitaries and other figures sent the sovereign a *gaisuwa* (gift made to a superior). This was a political act whereby the interested party paid tribute to the *Sarki*, hoping in return to enjoy his favours. The value of the gift was in proportion to the rank of the giver and, in exchange, the sovereign[75] did not fail, when the occasion arose, either to manifest his satisfaction or displeasure. One common method of obtaining the where-withal to send a *gaisuwa* was precisely by pillaging. Those who were appointed to high office also presented gifts to the *Sarki*.

Spoils

Pillaging brought in slaves, horses, cattle and a variety of goods. The latter were all rapidly consumed, while the horses and their trappings increased combat capacity. The *Kano Chronicle* stresses the value attached to horses between 1582 and 1623.[76] Having conquered the Katsinawa at Garaya: 'the Kanawa took 400 horses and 60 sets of horse trappings; nobody knew how many had been killed and made prisoner'. Shortly afterwards, the *Wambai* formed a team of 100 mail-clad horsemen, with a reserve of 1000 horses, and this was certainly to the detriment of Katsina. The slaves were sold or divided among the great royal properties of which Kano is still the most outstanding example. Kutumbi, for instance, was jealous of Sarkin Dawaki Magari and ventured out on a raid. On his return, he left 500 slaves at Indabo, a property that had been set aside for him.

Other resources

There were countless measures whereby the *Sarki* could fill the coffers of the state. In almost every instance, when the sovereign pardoned an offender the latter had to pay *kudin laifi* (forgiveness tax). Thanks to the *Kano Chronicle*, it is possible to follow the process whereby the taxes and other duties were created for the benefit of the state. Shārīf (*c*.1703–31) instituted seven taxes that were regarded as oppressive, including duty payable when girls were married. His successor, Kumbari (*c*.1731–43), increased the tax payable in the Kasuwa Kurmi market so much that the market collapsed. The following year, he made the scholars pay a duty, as a result of which the Arabs left and went to Katsina and the *talakawa* were scattered throughout the country.

75. Nazaki was very pleased with the gift that Wambai Giwa made him, while Kutumbi, his successor, did not appreciate Sarkin Dwa Dawaki Magari's gesture, cf. H. R. Palmer, 1967, pp. 117–18.

76. H. R. Palmer, 1967, pp. 117, 123; R. M. East, 1979, p. 28.

Overview

In catering for the development and management needs of the state, the *sarauta* system evolved in such a way that commoners and slaves could occupy the highest offices if they were considered highly trustworthy. Thus it was that royal slaves, particularly eunuchs, came to constitute an essential cog in the state machinery throughout the region.

This resulted in opposition between the *mai sarauta* (the ruler) and the *talaka* (the ruled) which was to become so pronounced that Sarkin Kano Kumbari (*c*.1731–43) was said to have 'loved his advisers, and hated the people'.

To a lesser degree, the governors of the cities and regions were potential opponents. The frequent uprisings fomented by the governors of Gaya and Dutse illustrate the recurring friction between sovereign and vassals in Kano's history.

The political, administrative and military aristocracy represented a uniform group which grew rich by various methods of exploitation, ranging from levies on the income derived from pillaging to almost mandatory political gifts. This aristocracy adopted a way of life commensurate with its resources and decked itself out splendidly to show its prestige, while at the same time becoming increasingly difficult to keep under control because of the bribery and corruption in which it indulged. This combination of circumstances fathered an ideology designed to deny its aristocratic origins yet unable to conceal the system's capacity for oppression, admirably conveyed by the various meanings of the word *iko* (power).

Diagne has described this system as an oligarchical monarchy characterized by the close interdependence between the monarch and the oligarchs.[77] Usman, however, criticizes the notion of the city-state and considers that the main feature of Hausaland was 'the existence of numerous urban centres, which formed the nuclei of a political community into which the immigrants of differing origins were integrated and became Katsinawa, Kebbawa, and Kanawa, with each centre maintaining its legal status and some degree of autonomy with respect to the capital and the other centres.'[78]

Economic relations

A brief review of a number of areas of production and distribution is necessary to understand the main features of social relations.

77. P. Diagne, 1967, pp. 244–52.
78. Y. B. Usman, 1981, p. 53.

Agriculture and stock-raising

From 1500 to 1800 Hausaland remained primarily a region of *manoma* (farmers) who made judicious use of the agricultural potential through a variety of techniques, including fertilizers and crop rotation and association. Their tools were as numerous as elsewhere in Africa, with a wide range of hoes adapted to the nature of the soil and the function required of them. The bulk of the labour force came from the *gida* (extended family) and the *gayya* (mutual-aid system). Mention must also be made of the tradition of the *bukin duku* (Feast of Thousands) whereby it had to be proved that a yield of 1000 sheaves of millet or sorghum could be obtained. Careful technical, material and psychological preparations were made for the attempt and successful candidates were awarded the title of *Sarkin poma* (master of the crops).[79]

The farmers grew millet, sorghum, rice, maize, peanuts and beans as well as cotton, indigo, henna, tobacco and onions. Shea, tamarind and *nere* were also cultivated, and honey was collected. They also engaged in fishing and hunting. *Jibda* (musk) was removed from the civet-cat and used for making perfume.

There was a substantial amount of stock-raising for domestic purposes. Goats were sacrificed – by having their throats slit – for certain ceremonies, while donkeys were used as a means of transport, particularly by traders. However, Hausaland attracted many Fulbe,[80] Azbinawa and Shuwa Arabs, who had been pastoralists for several centuries. Kel-Geres, Itesan and Kel-Tegama Tuareg moved southwards to northern and central Zamfara to graze their herds of camels, goats and sheep during the dry season, and some took up residence there. The Fulbe, with their sheep and cattle, settled in several areas of Katsina (at the confluence of the Rivers Karaduwa and Bunsuru), Kebbi (at Gulbin Kebbi, Dallol Boso, Fogha and Mauri) and Zamfara (in the area watered by the Bunsuru, Gagare and Sokoto rivers). Agriculture and stock-raising became closely associated and pockets of economic life developed based on a combination of the two, such as in the region of Ingawa in Katsina.[81]

79. For this tradition, see G. Nicolas, 1975, pp. 114–17, 297–9 and G. Na-Dama, 1977, pp. 91–101.

80. For the migration of some of the Fulbe to Borno and Hausaland, see M. Idrissou, 1979. However, B. Hama (1968, pp. 92–6) asserts that some of the Fulbe came direct from the Sahara to Central Sudan and the middle reaches of the Niger, passing through Azawad. Archaeological research carried out in the region of In Gall–Tegiddan Tesemt, has brought to light skeletons of buried cattle; the only date available is 1435 (see F. Paris, 1984, pp. 1–75). The question thus remains open.

81. M. Alkali, 1969, pp. 34–5, 73, 113–14; G. Na-Dama, 1977, pp. 110–20, 169–84, 197–9; Y. B. Usman, 1981, pp. 64–7, 73–5.

Crafts

The diversity and high technical standards attained by craftsmen were already remarkable at the time of Leo Africanus.[82] People worked with iron, wood and leather, and also engaged in basket-making and pottery, while there was spectacular growth in weaving and dyeing. The raw materials iron and cotton were abundant and high demand stimulated high-quality crafts. Craftsmen became highly specialized: leatherwork seems to have become distinct from shoemaking, while spinning, weaving, dyeing, sewing and embroidery became quite separate trades. A system of guilds was set up, each with a representative responsible for its interests and for its relations with the state.[83]

A trend towards group specialization can also be observed. In Kebbi, weaving and dyeing were in the hands of the Kebbawa, while Zamfara attracted weavers and dyers from Kano. In both Kebbi and Zamfara, the Zoromawa,[84] who arrived from Macina (Massina) in the sixteenth century, specialized in silver jewellery and pottery; in Kano, pottery was made by the Bambadawa.

There was also a wide variety of manufactured articles. Leather, sandals, harnesses and saddles were exported; jewellery, which was regarded as a luxury, was purchased by the wealthy, while clothing, such as tunics, and textile cloth were famed for their quality. Hausaland was also among the areas producing the highest quality woven and dyed goods.

Trade

The stereotype of the *bahaushe* (trader)[85] became widely recognized and it is impossible to overstress his integration into the trading networks of Western Africa and the international trader class in the savannah which comprised the Wangara, Juula (Dyula), Mossi (Mosi) and Kanuri. However, the starting-point was the availability of considerable agricultural surpluses, plus a flourishing crafts sector geared to the market and offering a wide range of goods.

The area of influence of the markets differed considerably. Some were important locally and retained their social and economic character: goods were traded, but social life on market day was considerably enlivened by the exchange of information, games and so on. At a higher level, the regional market was a centre to which local products were brought and where imported articles in daily use were distributed. In some cases, such

82. Y. B. Usman, 1981, pp. 472–9.

83. The most frequently mentioned guilds are those of the stonemasons, blacksmiths, weavers, dyers, coopers, tanners and shoemakers. It is not easy to classify the barbers and butchers. The representative of the coopers in Kebbi, who was appointed by the sovereign, was called the *sakke*, a well-known name throughout the savannah in Western Sudan.

84. These were the Jawambe (a group of the Fulbe), whom the Mande named the Jogorame; see P. J. Shea, 1983, p. 111.

85. See H. J. Fisher, 1975, pp. 84–92 and 1977, pp. 269–87 and, in particular, M. Adamu, 1978, and 1979, pp. 60–104.

PLATE 16.1   *Hausa loin-cloth called* Goranka da nono, *literally 'there is milk in your gourd'*

PLATE 16.2   *Hausa robe worn by men, and showing a strong Islamic influence. Made of cotton dyed blue with indigo and embroidered with silk*

markets were situated on a trade route and were thereby in privileged positions: Kebbi, for example, took care of Kwanni as Katsina did of Tessawa. In Zamfara itself, the northern and north-eastern markets of Baje, Fahai, Birnin, Zamfara and so on, supplied cotton, indigo, tobacco, onions and cattle, while their southern counterparts – Kiawa, Jata, Tsohu-

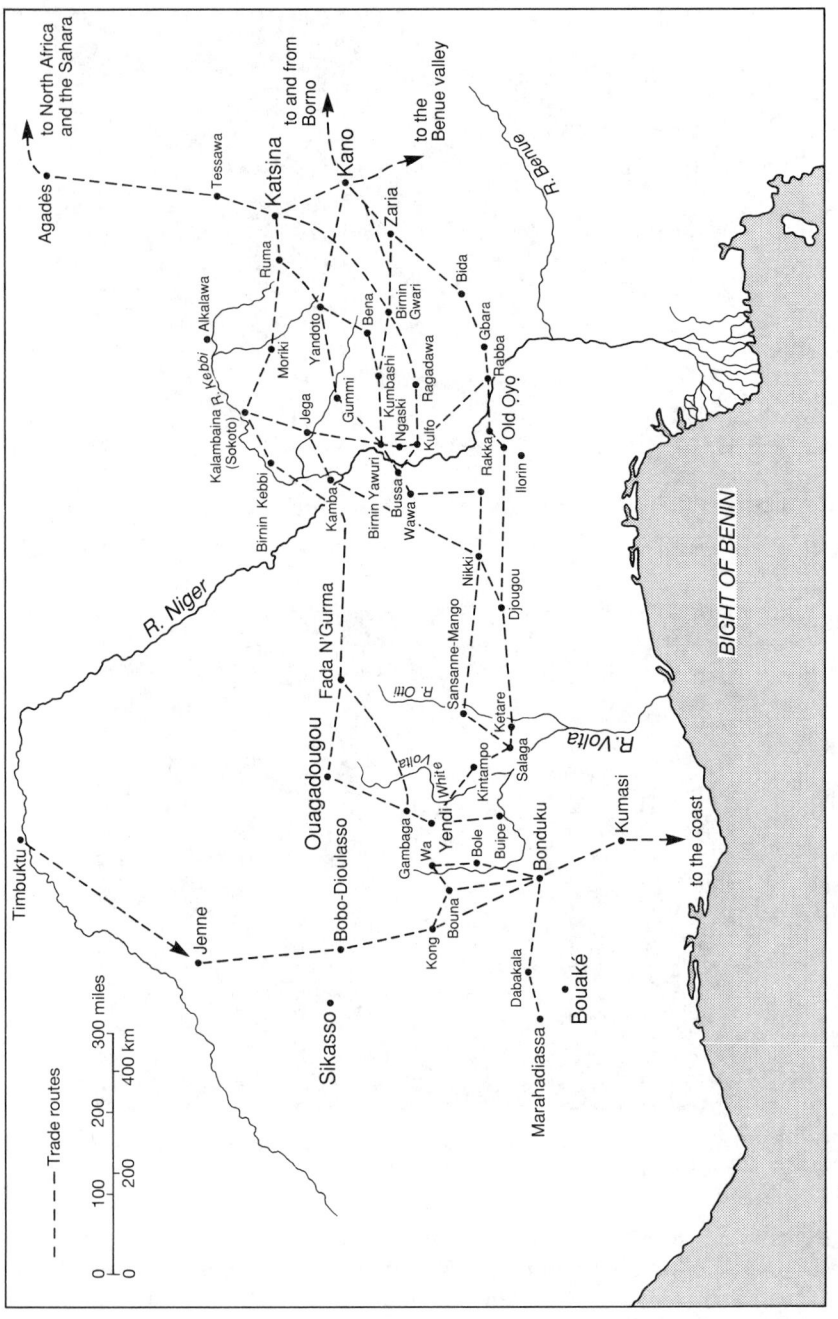

FIG. 16.4 *Trade routes between Hausaland and the Volta basin*

war, Barrago and others – received abundant supplies of cereals. Upper Kebbi sent yarn, fabrics and slaves to Lower Kebbi, which supplied nets, harpoons, hides and *abara* (large dugout canoes).[86]

The growth in domestic trade, a consequence of Hausaland's development and also a contributory factor, has received little attention. However, because trade prospered revenues increased – in the form of various taxes and the *gaisuwa* which the traders often had to provide. External trade remained in the hands of the Hausa, although some Azbinawa, Arabs, Kanuri and Wangara also took part.

External trade immediately suggests the caravans. Regardless of whether these were the *azalai* travelling from Kawār to Gao, the *ayari* linking Azbin and Hausaland, or the *fatake* plying the Kano–Gwanja route, their first concern was to ensure that their assignment could be successfully carried out.[87] As already mentioned, each sovereign took security precautions to protect the caravans in his own territory as they paid taxes to the states through which they travelled.

Before presenting the overall situation, several regional variants[88] should be mentioned. In Zamfara, the *Karfi* assembled everything the *sarakunan rafi* (grazing-tax collectors) had levied. Here, salt and natron from Nguru, gathered on the shores of Lake Chad, were marketed at an earlier date than salt from Bilma or Dallol Fogha. Similarly, the *dan Bahar* breed of horse, from Baḥr al-Ghazāl and highly prized throughout Hausaland, was used in the cavalry and for cross-breeding with local stock. Kebbi sent salt to Nupe, Ilọrin and Gwanja, from which it received tunics and kola nuts.

There were several international markets within the region and on its periphery. In the north, Agades and Bilma continued to serve as links with northern Africa; in the centre, Katsina and Kano were staging-points in north–south and east–west relations; and in the south, Zaria, Birnin Gwari and Birnin Yawuri enabled the networks to be extended towards Yoruba, Nupe, Borgu, Gwanja (and Timbuktu for Yawuri). A considerable volume of merchandise circulated in Hausaland.

The Sahara and Azbin sent Arab and European goods to these markets, including mirrors and paper, but particularly horses (the *dan Azbin* breed, also called *bagazam*, from Azbin), camels, dates, henna, salt (*balma* after the city of Bilma), swords and other articles. Part of the salt and sword consignments were in transit and bound ultimately for the south. In return, Hausaland supplied them with slaves, clothes, fabrics, millet, hides, iron, gold dust and kola nuts from Gwanja.

Borno had horses (*dan Bahar* or *Bahargazal*), natron and salt to offer, and in exchange received metal articles, gold dust and kola nuts, again from Gwanja.

Hausaland exported salt, swords, condiments, hides, clothes and fabrics,

86. G. Na-Dama, 1977, pp. 137–42; M. Alkali, 1969, pp. 41–2.
87. For details see H. J. Fisher, 1977, pp. 267–9; G. Na-Dama, 1977, pp. 149–51.
88. G. Na-Dama, 1977, pp. 253–4; M. Alkali, 1969, p. 42.

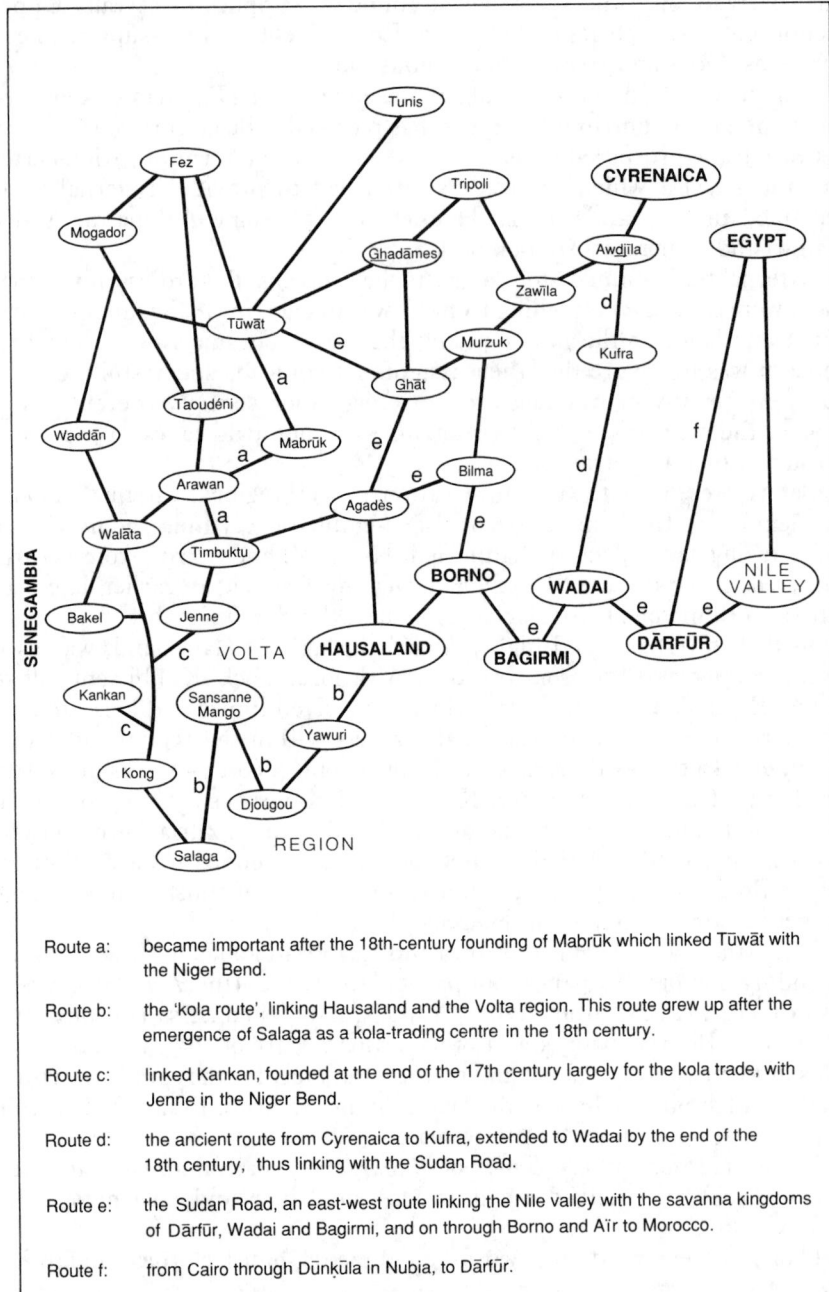

Route a: became important after the 18th-century founding of Mabrūk which linked Tūwāt with the Niger Bend.

Route b: the 'kola route', linking Hausaland and the Volta region. This route grew up after the emergence of Salaga as a kola-trading centre in the 18th century.

Route c: linked Kankan, founded at the end of the 17th century largely for the kola trade, with Jenne in the Niger Bend.

Route d: the ancient route from Cyrenaica to Kufra, extended to Wadai by the end of the 18th century, thus linking with the Sudan Road.

Route e: the Sudan Road, an east-west route linking the Nile valley with the savanna kingdoms of Dārfūr, Wadai and Bagirmi, and on through Borno and Aïr to Morocco.

Route f: from Cairo through Dūnḳūla in Nubia, to Dārfūr.

FIG. 16.5 *Diagram showing the main trade and caravan links in the Sahara and west and central Sudan, c.1215*
Source: adapted from M. Hiskett, *The Development of Islam in West Africa*, 1984, *p. 321*, London, Longman. Adapted by kind permission of Longman Group UK Ltd

slaves and horses to Gwanja, Borgu, Nupe and Yoruba and received in return various European goods, local iron, antimony, slaves and eunuchs, rifles from Nupe (for Kano), and kola nuts from Gwanja for general consumption.

Social relations

Despite the large number of immigrants into Hausaland, an individual's ethnic origin had little social significance, while religious affiliation itself was so unreliable that Muḥammad Alwālī's defeat was attributed to the profanation of the *Dirki*.[89] It is for this reason that we shall distinguish between three basic groups.

Producers of material goods

Farmers formed the largest category. The more intensive exploitation of the land and the improvements in farming practices – overshadowed by the importance of agrarian rites, but highlighted in the Feast of Thousands – were to bring about far-reaching changes. Until that time, the main source of labour had been the extended family. It is clear that some population groups had been reduced to a state of bondage: the Mazumawa, for example, lost their independence as soon as Gobir reached the Birnin Lalle area. Furthermore, the dispersal of the Maguzawa on the orders of Bugaya and the fact that they were summoned by Kukuna[90] seem to imply that they had a different status, since Zanku, their patriarch, was not an elector, whereas Sarkin Mazum had to be consulted, at least for the sake of appearances. The Maguzawa of Fankui were subordinate as a group and thus tributaries, but their relations with the state differed from those existing between the sovereign Sarkin Kano and his vassal Sarkin Gaya. The last source of labour was slave labour.

Alongside the farmers was a wide variety of craftsmen. Intense specialization had produced the high standards already described. Moreover, many slaves engaged in craft activities at their master's behest and for his benefit – at least to begin with.

A large number of herdsmen came to adopt a sedentary life-style and to employ slaves both for cereals production and to guard their herds. This process increased the pace of their integration into the political community.

Whether the producers were free men, tributaries or slaves, they were all members of the political community and their relations with the state were codified. Distinctions based on wealth and on proximity to the machinery of the state were gradually introduced.

89. H. R. Palmer, 1967, p. 127.
90. ibid., pp. 107, 121.

Traders

In the fifteenth century, Gwanja was linked to Borno through Kano. In the early 1500s the Azbinawa brought salt to Gobir, while the traders in Gwanja made trips to Katsina where Kanuri and Arabs were beginning to settle. Subsequently, the Kambarin Barebari, who originated from Borno, were to make a name for themselves in long-distance trade, but the documentation currently available does not suggest that there was specialization by ethnic groups. Despite this, traders were divided into several categories, ranging from wholesalers engaging in *fatauci* (trade over medium and long distances), to retailers who organized the *kasuwanci* (retail trade).[91]

A group of *attajirai* (rich traders) was formed which probably included merchants dealing in slaves, horses, kola nuts and clothing. In Zamfara,[92] aristocrats and traders used their slaves to enhance the value of the *gandaye*. There is little information on the production of cereals or industrial crops, such as cotton. However, traders and scholars always seem to have been closely linked.

The main unifying factor among the traders lay in their common interests; even specialization along ethnic lines could become established only if it brought in increased profits. The traders offered the aristocracy luxury goods, and did not hesitate to emigrate when they felt they were being taxed excessively: some Arabs left Kano and settled in Katsina because Kumbari was increasing the tax burden.[93]

Between 1500 and 1800, the different Wangara and Hausa subgroups succeeded in uniting the trade networks throughout Western Africa and, according to Ki-Zerbo,[94] constituted the middle class in the main towns. The traders continued to consolidate their position as a class, while improving their techniques and spreading the Islamic faith to their advantage.

The aristocracy

The ruling class included the *masu sarauta* (all those with any political authority). It was subdivided into several levels.

The *Sarki* was at the head of the nobility which was composed of the princely families, families governing the semi-autonomous cities and vassal provinces, and representatives of the various nationalities, particularly the Azbinawa, the Shuwa Arabs and the Fulbe. The nobility performed various duties within the machinery of the state, and tended to become a homogeneous group whose cohesion was strengthened by marriage ties: ʿAbdullāh Burja (1438–52) was the first sovereign of Kano to marry one daughter of

91. H. R. Palmer, 1967, pp. 109–111; M. Adamu (forthcoming); and UNESCO, *General History of Africa*, Vol. IV, p. 294.
92. G. Na-Dama, 1977, pp. 147–8.
93. H. R. Palmer, 1967, p. 124.
94. J. Ki-Zerbo, 1978, p. 175.

Sarkin Dutse, one of Sarkin Shira, one of Sarkin Kano and one of the *Galadima*.[95]

All the dignitaries appointed by the *Sarki* to run the state formed the second level. They were of commoner or serf origin, but their position gave them access to wealth and esteem through the gifts they received, but particularly through pillaging. In some instances, they held key military offices.[96] Wambai Giwa decided to enlarge the city of Kano to please Nazaki (*c*.1618–25) and 'went to the site each day with a thousand dishes of food and fifty oxen up until the time the building work was finished', but he was stripped of his office by the subsequent *Sarki*. This section of the ruling class ultimately controlled the state. For example, it urged Muḥammad Nazaki to counter Katsina's authority, and it opposed the attack against Katsina planned by Zaudai. Kebbi's decline began when the dignitaries holding the military offices had grown so rich that they lost interest in the affairs of the state.

The aristocracy, primarily the princes and the royal slaves, confiscated the property of the *talakawa* (ruled), particularly when the sovereign showed signs of weakness.

The question of social relations appears to have been dominated by two factors. The sale of Africans by certain sovereigns and the participation of Kawār and Zawīla in the slave trade had already been stressed by al-Ya'ḳūbī as early as 891. Moreover, it was said of the *Mai* of Kānem, Arku (*c*.1023–67) that: 'Reflecting one day on the large number of slaves he possessed, he installed 300 of them in Dirkou, 300 in the Saguedine mosque and a further 300 in Zaylan'. These appear to be the first indicators[97] of both the export of slaves from the region and their use within it. In Kano,[98] Tsamia (*c*.1307–43) refused 200 slaves brought to him by the followers of traditional religion, but the Kwararafa were compelled to send some to Yaji (*c*.1349–85) and to his son Kanajeji (*c*.1390–1410). As 'Abdullāh Burja (1438–52) was about to make a return Galadima Dawuda asked him to rest and began to wage war in his stead: 'every two months he sent Sarkin Kano a thousand slaves. Each day Sarkin Kano sent him horses, clothing and horse trappings'. By the end of the campaign, he had accumulated 21 000 slaves, distributed among twenty-one villages and all named Indabo. Contrary to the recent view of one specialist[99] who regarded this development as a population movement, it was in fact a genuine slaving expedition, well organized and profitable. Proof of this can be seen from the emergence of the category of the Indabawa (Rumfa was to seize their daughters), who were distinct from the Maguzawa: it should be added that the term *indabo*

95. H. R. Palmer, 1967, p. 110.
96. H. R. Palmer, 1967, p. 117 (Kano); D. M. Hamani, 1975, p. 85 (Kebbi); G. Na-Dama, 1977, p. 351 (embezzlement).
97. J. M. Cuoq, 1975, p. 49; D. Lange, 1977, p. 67.
98. H. R. Palmer, 1967, pp. 103–12.
99. M. Hiskett, 1984, pp. 101–2.

is reminiscent of the Soninke *debe*, the Fulfulde *debeere* and the Songhay *dabey* (a village of slaves). The Indabo engaged in production activities and crafts, and particularly in agriculture. In Katsina, the city of Tsagero was a royal property where large numbers of slaves were kept, and where even princes were sent.[100] The towns in the Gozaki area, in the south, stepped up their relations with Kano and Zazzau (Zaria): the cotton-growing on the estates in that area eventually came to depend on slaves imported from Zazzau, and part of the crop was exported to Kano.

Whether the slave was a commodity, a servant, a high-ranking public official or a producer in a subordinate position, he had a role to play in the development of the economy and the state. However, the export of slaves has to be examined regarding the sources of supply in Europe and in the Orient, even before the Atlantic trade began to claim its share. The contribution of slavery to the prosperity of the region will become clearer when it has been singled out from all other forms of subordination. From this point of view, the transition from the status of *bawa* (captive) to that of *bacucane* (house-born slave) is found in other areas of the savannah, the terms *woloso* (Mande), *forso* (Songhay), *dimaajo* (Fulfulde) being the equivalents of *bacucane*. Research should be focused on the growth of slavery during this period, in which the development of mercantile relationships simplified the social stratification. We already have enough evidence to show that the lot of the slaves was not preferable to that of the *talaka*.[101]

The *masu sarauta* (aristocrats) can be regarded as opposing the *talakawa*, who were free producers but had no political power. As the aristocracy, the cultivated members of society, and the traders grew rich, the distinction shifted to an economic level, with the *masu arziki* or *attajirai* being the wealthy, and the *talakawa* the poor. The *bawan Sarki* (royal slave) ceased to be a *talaka*, from both the political and economic standpoints. The situation was thereby clarified, because the ethnic and religious differences had been relegated to the background, and this left those in power and the second-class citizens confronting one another.

Culture and religion

Political and economic developments gave rise to many cultural changes. On a material level, for instance, the architecture was improved and, even today, the cities still compete with each other in their building styles. In music, some instruments became widespread (such as the *kakaki* and the

100. Y. B. Usman, 1981, pp. 43, 49; P. E. Lovejoy, 1983, p. 113.

101. See F. Cooper, 1979. See also the bibliography in P. E. Lovejoy, 1983. Particular attention is given to the Songhay empire by L. E. Kubbel, 1974; his ideas are of great interest for the savannah as a whole. The presence of the term *talaka* in many of the African languages (Tamajaq, Kanuri, Hausa, Fulfulde, Songhay, Gulmancema, Moore. etc.) should be noted. It more or less corresponds to *badolo* in Takrūr. However, in Takrūr and in Kebbi, two expressions emphasize the position of agriculture in the savannah's economy; *samba remooru* and *Bakabban kumbu* are farmers who have turned back to the land.

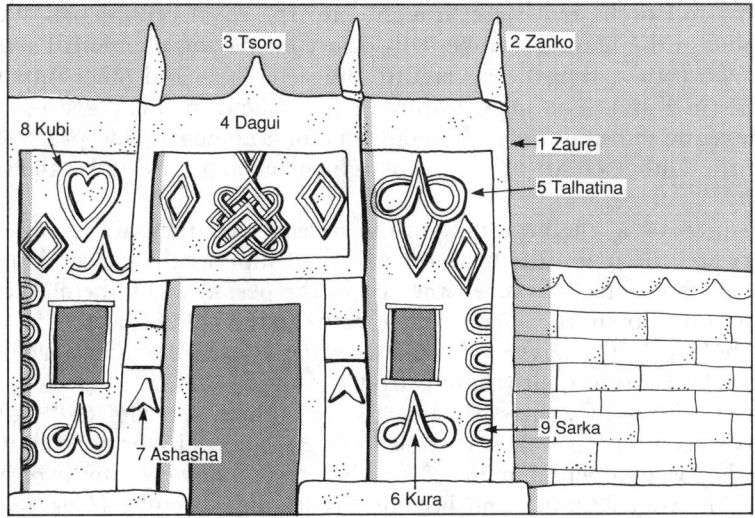

PLATE 16.3   *The decorated façade of a Birni house in Zinder*

Key to the 'speaking' decoration, as explained by the Zinder master craftsman, Dandibi, and recorded by his nephew, Cheffou Malam:

1 *The vestibule*: Zaure

2 *Corner horns*: Zanko, *the cock's crest, is the name of a type of plait made from women's hair.*

3 *The peak of the pediment*: Tsoro, *the wrestler's plait* (*to which his talisman is attached*) *which frightens the enemy.*

4 *The main strapwork decoration on the pediment*: Dagui *is the term used to describe the embroidery on Hausa men's robes, the lion's print, the sign indicating hopes of greatness.*

5 *The Agades Cross, this jewel of Hausa blacksmiths in the service of Tuareg masters, was to be interpreted as a fertility symbol by Jean Gabus.*

6 *The sign under every window*, Kura, *the hyena, equals a hook for pulling up a water-scoop.*

7 *The sword blade*, Ashasha, *on each side of the entrance, is located on the pillars called* Dogari, *the Prince's guards.*

8 Kubi: *symbols from playing cards, a personal contribution by Dandibi.*

9 *Embroidery design known as* Sarka, *which is one of the principal themes of traditional decoration* (*as used in the Sultan's palace at Daura, the cradle of the Hausa people*). *It is also known as* Durgusum taguwa, *or Strapwork of threads.*

algaita) and orchestras were brought into the royal ceremonial. We are indebted to the literate members of society for having mentioned some of the *kirari* (praise-songs) dedicated to the sovereigns and other important persons in Kano. The main feature of Hausaland in this respect was its richness and cultural unity – the outcome of a homogenizing process that made the Guber of Africa's greatest vehicular languages under the name *Hausa*.[102]

Islamization at the beginning of the sixteenth century, was confined to traders and the political élite, who used it to support the consolidation of power at the centre. However, the end of the period was to be marked by an intensification of the open struggle between the political aristocracy and the scholars.[103] The *Kano Chronicle* and the *Wangarawa Chronicle* show the development of their relations from the inside.

Kano witnessed a massive and regular influx of scholars.[104] Under Kisoki's reign (1509–65), several scholars arrived. The first, Shaihu Ba-Tunashe, brought with him the *Ashafa* book; the following year he received a student from Zazzau, who became his leading disciple. He asked the sovereign to build a mosque for the Friday sermons for the Rumawa, and this was granted. The second scholar, Dan Gwarandume, took up residence at the place where Abū Bakr Kado, Kisoki's successor, was to read the *Ashafa* book. The third, Shaihu Abdussalami, introduced three books. Abū Bakr, who made the princes learn the Ḳur'ān, was to be the first to read one of them. There was also a group of three brothers from Borno: one, Shaihu Kursiki turned down the post of *ḳāḍī* which his brother Magume accepted, while Kabi, the third remained a simple scholar. Three others, Watasanu, Buduru and Kudu arrived later. Under the reign of Abū Bakr Kado (*c*.1565–73), a second group immigrated to Kano, including Tama, Malam Sharīf, Getso and Wuri; they came from Bagirmi (or Lagumi according to other sources) and had first spent some time in Katsina before settling in Godiya where Tama, their leader, married. Muḥammad Zakī (*c*.1582–1618) married one of Tama's daughters, and instituted the *Cokana* and the *Dirki* talismans before attacking Katsina. It was on account of the scholars that the Katsinawa did not sack Kano. However, Kano attacked in its turn one morning when the feast of *Ramāḍān* was being celebrated, and was victorious. In the end, the scholars negotiated peace between Kano and Katsina in the period between 1648 and 1651. Kano thus occupied a privileged position at this time and attracted many scholars, at least a third of whom came from Borno. They brought books with them and were often much travelled. One of them, Kursiki, remained remote from the centre of power but another, Tama, became the sovereign's father-in-law.

102. Leo Africanus, 1956, Vol. I, p. 16.

103. H. J. Fisher, 1975, pp. 92–7; R. A. Adeleye, 1976, pp. 596–601; S. A. Balogun, 1980; M. Hiskett, 1984, pp. 68–109.

104. H. R. Palmer, 1967, pp. 112–16, 120–2.

In Birnin Katsina,[105] a distinction could be made between several groups descending from Wālī Abū 'Abdullāhī b. Masānī, Malam Buhārī (who had declined an invitation to settle in the capital) and from Malam 'Uthmān (who had come from Borno) and so on. Many cultivated people from differing backgrounds, ethnic groups and places of origin lived in other cities. This intelligentsia, which was scattered over a territory whose population and leaders considered themselves Islamized, did not occupy any important offices in government. They were conscious that they were a separate group and kept their distance from the ruling class.

Zamfara[106] differed in that Islam did not take root there until a late stage probably because most of its towns were far from the major cities and the caravan routes of Central Sudan. Nevertheless, Kanuri scholars may have participated in converting the sovereign to Islam. Unlike in the other states, the *Imām* of Anka had a real fief; the *Imām*'s residence was a sanctuary and a place of refuge for all those who incurred the wrath of the rulers. Three other offices were reserved for the scholars: the *Limanin Ciki* was responsible for the education of the royal family, while the *Dan Kodo* and *Dan Dubal* were advisers on religious affairs, the custodians of Zamfara's history and responsible for praying for the army's victory. The first Muslim sovereign reigned in about 1670, and Babba (*c.*1715) had 100 educated members of the community pray for Zamfara's success against Kebbi.

For their income the scholars relied on the generosity of the aristocracy who contributed to their physical welfare and most probably made them gifts of money. However, it is difficult to fault the objectivity of the educated members of the community even when their own situation is involved. For example, Shaykh 'Abd al-Raḥmān Zagaiti[107] prayed for his descendants to be founts of wisdom so that they could become advisers to the king; Rumfa gave two properties to each of the Shaykh's two sons; while the *Wambai*, who resided in Karaye, presented Ḥabībullāhi, the third son, with a fief as a reward for his blessing. It could be concluded from this that, in Kano at least, the scholars were in a position to enjoy the benefits of large estates.

Their critical attitude was also reflected in the *Kano Chronicle*.[108] Muḥammad Shārīf (*c.*1703–31) introduced seven measures that were regarded as *zālunci* (injustice) and included the constant increase in the rate of taxation, the tax on the marriage of young girls and so on. His successor Kumbari (*c.*1731–43) was to make the scholars pay a tax; the Arabs accordingly left and went to Katsina, where peace and prosperity reigned, and the *talakawa* deserted the city.

105. Y. B. Usman, 1981, pp. 71–6.
106. G. Na-Dama, 1977, pp. 185–7, 320–6.
107. M. A. al-Hajj, 1968, pp. 11, 14. Only Professor Hunwick has attempted to trace the Wangara (Diakhite?) whose name the chronicler wished to transcribe; cf. J. O. Hunwick, 1976, p. 278.
108. H. R. Palmer, 1967, pp. 123–5. The Hausa version contains significant corrections.

PLATE 16.4 *Decorated pages of a miniature Hausa Qoran, late seventeenth- to early eighteenth-century. Height: c. 7.5 cm*

The regular travelling of the scholars and the introduction of books are the reasons already put forward to explain the area's intellectual awakening. However, there can be no doubt that this must be ascribed to the existence of centres of learning and, in particular, to the use of the *ajami* script in Kano and Katsina in the sixteenth century. A *madrasa* had grown up in Katsina after al-Balbali[109] had passed through it, and it is likely that the use of *ajami* had not been introduced by the beginning of the sixteenth century even though, according to some sources, it had been developed during Rumfa's reign. The scholars wrote in Arabic, Fulfulde and Hausa. Between 1500 and 1800, the fact of being part of the same political community, the same movement towards urbanization and economic development, the same population movements and spread of education and literature, all made for increasingly simple social relations. The examples of Kano, Katsina and Zamfara show that the scholars' place of origin is easier to identify than their ethnic origin: in Kano and Zamfara the majority came from the east (Borno), whereas scholars from the west (Malle in the broadest sense) predominated in Katsina. They prayed for victory in war, they were consulted on legal matters, they rejected appeals, and their advice was prized, so that they came to have a decisive influence on social life, particularly through the *wa'azi* (sermons). Several names deserve mention. In Zamfara[110] among the most celebrated, mention has been made of

109. M. Hiskett, 1984, pp. 80–3.
110. G. Na-Dama, 1977, pp. 252, 325.

488

Ramaḍān b. Aḥmadu (from Fezzān), Hashimu Bazanfane (a master of Shehu 'Uthmān), Maman Tukur dan Binta and al-Mustafa Gwani, a Kanuri who confronted 'Uthmān – while he was touring Zamfara – on the issue of the simultaneous presence of men and women during the sermons.

Two outstanding names are associated with Katsina.[111] One, Abū 'Abdullāhī b. Masānī b. Muḥammad al-Barnāwī al-Kashinawī (c.1595–1667), was born in Katsina of Borno parents. The other was Muḥammad al-Sabbāgh al-Kashinawī – better known as Dan Marina – who was extremely active in about 1650 and was considered by local traditions to be Muḥammad al-Kashinawī. These two were at the root of an authentic intellectual renaissance which was to be given expression in the poem composed by Dan Marina in praise of Mai 'Alī, who defeated the Kwararafa in about 1680. The name of Muḥammad al-Kashinawī, who died about 1741 and many of whose works have survived, should also be mentioned, as well as that of Muḥammad b. 'Abd al-Mahman al-Barnāwī, who died about 1755 and whose works served as sources for 'Uthmān.

However, there can be no doubt that it was Malam Djibrīl dan 'Umaru who stood out most strikingly from the group.[112] This scholar, with his encyclopaedic knowledge, was born in Adar and died there, after having been on several pilgrimages. His main subject of preoccupation lay in the Islamic reforms in Sudan. After his failure among the Tuareg in Adar, he approached the Hausa princes, whose hostility he aroused. 'Uthmān ('Usmān) and 'Abdullāhī dan Fodio were his disciples. Despite his criticism of some of Djibrīl's attitudes 'Uthmān regarded himself as his disciple and successor. The second half of the eighteenth century was to be marked by a wealth of intellectual activity and heated debate among scholars, by way of a simple form of opposition to the established order represented by the *masu sarauta*.

Conclusion

Just before the *djihād*, there was a marked decline in the turbulent character of the relations between the states. Kebbi and Zamfara had been defeated, but the others were faced with difficult problems. In Kano, peace and stability were punctuated by two serious disagreements between the *Sarki* and the dignitaries: the latter prohibited Babba Zaki (c.1768–76) from residing in Takai, and Muḥammadu Alwālī (c.1781–1807) refused to give them the forty head of cattle intended for the *Dirki*, and had them slaughtered with an axe instead. In Gobir, Bawa (c.1777–89) for the first time introduced a tax on a certain variety of maize, and several stock-raisers in that state had to pay the *jangali* on several occasions during the same year. Two dynastic crises shook Katsina in 1767 and 1796. The risk

111. I. Dankoussou, 1970, pp. 38–52; Y. B. Usman, 1981, pp. 71–2 and 1983, pp. 199–200; M. Hiskett, 1984, pp. 81–2; A. M. Kani, forthcoming.

112. D. M. Hamani, 1975, pp. 136–41; A. M. Kani, forthcoming.

of instability was noted almost throughout the region, due to resistance on the part of the dignitaries, the increased weight of tyranny, and the latent opposition of the *talakawa*. The political authorities had attained a threshold of oppression which no longer spared the scholars, but they were the only ones who ventured to combat the established orders openly.[113]

The historiography of Central Sudan is gradually emerging from the stage when it was devoted almost exclusively to an apologia of the *djihād*, and is now beginning to look at the changes that took place in the course of the preceding periods.

Economically the apparent opposition to progress that seemed to characterize the years between 1600 and 1790 has been overstressed. It is true that neither the wheel nor the windmill was used, and even the rifle was scorned. However, as far back as about 1582–6 the 'Takrūr people' of Gao were having fierce discussions with the 'Sudanese', who claimed that Kano was more important and greater than Gao.[114] Despite a host of natural calamities,[115] the area developed in a remarkable manner that has been too readily ascribed to trade although trade did indeed increase thanks to state intervention in various forms. However, the progress achieved in respect of production and processing should not be underestimated. It earned the region sufficient renown as to soon attract many European expeditions – although the reasons they gave for going there may have been of a scientific nature, such as to investigate the courses of the Nile and Niger rivers.

Politically, despite the armed conflicts, none of the states in the area disappeared during the period under consideration. Elsewhere, Ghana, Mali and Songhay disintegrated, perhaps because they were empires, yet Kānem–Borno whose longevity was remarkable was also an empire. In between the two, Hausaland and its economic successes relegated the great stability of the state as an institution to a position of secondary importance. Its bureaucratic and oppressive nature was highlighted by the measures introduced by Sharīf in Kano. One of them was called *kwaro*. Several authors do not know what this word means. If it has been correctly spelt and read, it is an obsolete term signifying 'to exchange a coin for cowries'. Since cowries were introduced into Hausaland under Sharīf in Kano's reign, he must have ordered them to be brought into circulation. One author misinterpreted *kwaro* – possibly because of a printing error – as meaning harvest tax, which was payable in Damagaram, for instance. However *kwaro* is interpreted, the meticulous detail with which the state was managed is evident. The foresight of Muḥammadu Alwali (*c.*1781–1807), who stock-piled food in his palace in anticipation of disturbances

113. H. R. Palmer, 1967, pp. 126–7; R. M. East, 1979, pp. 42–3; G. Na-Dama, 1977, pp. 396–402; M. A. al-Hajj, 1979; Y. B. Usman, 1981, pp. 84–99.

114. For the opposition to change, see H. J. Fisher, 1975, pp. 66–7; for the discussion regarding Kano and Gao, see M. Kaʿti, 1981, p. 262.

115. Between 1539 and 1564, 1639 and 1688, 1697 and 1715, 1729 and 1750, for instance; see S. Maley, 1981, pp. 57–81; P. E. Lovejoy, 1983, pp. 69–70.

and famine, vouch for that fact – although, ultimately, even he was unable to prevent the famine.[116] The machinery of the state, however, was very obviously efficient and few alterations were made to it by the regimes that followed.

116. H. R. Palmer, 1967, p. 125; R. M. East, 1979, pp. 37–8.

Kānem–Borno: its relations with the Mediterranean Sea, Bagirmi and other states in the Chad basin

B. M. BARKINDO*

In the thirteenth century the Muslim state of Kānem was one of the most extensive in the *Bilād al-Sūdān*. The Sēfuwa *mai*s (kings) controlled the vast area from the eastern shores of Lake Chad in the south to the Fezzān oasis in the north. Their expansion, however, had not been accompanied by appropriate political and economic development. The emergence of various groups as semi-autonomous units distinct from the main Sēfuwa ruling dynasty had prevented the development of a centralized political system. In addition, Kānem, mostly desert and semi-desert, lacked the primary resources needed to support such a large system.

There followed a serious crisis which finally led to the collapse of the Kānem state in the latter part of the fourteenth century. Mai 'Umar b. Idrīs (1382–87), leading the Magumi group (of which the royal Sēfuwa was a lineage) and its supporters, migrated to Borno to the west of Lake Chad where the necessary resources existed and where the Sēfuwa had already planted their vassals. The Sēfuwa had been preceded by a large number of individual Kānem immigrants who had already settled there, particularly in the south and west.[1]

The Sēfuwa's main objective on arrival in Borno appears to have been the building of a strong regional economy to support a well-organized Sēfuwa-dominated political structure. However, during their first century there, they faced many problems which at times posed threats to their very survival. There was constant civil strife, regular dynastic crises, periodical attacks from the Bulala and the problems of overmighty title-holders.[2]

Mai 'Alī Gaji and the foundation of the Borno califate c.1465–97

Civil conflict terminated with the accession of 'Alī ibn Dunāma, commonly known as 'Alī Gaji, who was able to consolidate power in his own branch of the ruling dynasty. When in about 1471 the Bulala made one of their

---

*I am grateful to Dr Philip Shea and John Lavers, who read the draft of this chapter, for their useful comments and suggestions.

1. For discussions see B. M. Barkindo, 1971.
2. ibid.

predatory incursions into Borno, 'Alī Gaji met and defeated them although he did not pursue them further.

In about 1472, 'Alī Gaji built the fortress of Birnin Gazargamu in the fork of the Rivers Yobe and Gana.[3] This eventually developed into the capital of the Sēfuwa and remained so throughout their rule in Borno. Several other fortified settlements were probably founded at about the same time.[4]

'Alī Gaji is remembered as a reviver of Islam as he attempted to eliminate, at least in the ruling group, the syncretism which had become rife amongst the Sēfuwa. He also tried to found a proper Islamic government. Following the traditions of his predecessors and in response to the Islamic fervour of the period, 'Alī surrounded himself with *'ulamā'* (Muslim scholars) whose advice he sought on any major decision. Two of these were Aḥmad b. 'Abd al-Ḳuwwata his *Ḳāḍī al-Kabīr* (chief judge), and Masbarma 'Umar b. 'Uthmān, his *Wazir* and chief *Imām*.[5]

Many of the overmighty title-holders had their powers reduced, especially the *kaigama* and *yerima* (governor of the northern provinces) who, during the period of crisis, made and unmade kings at will.[6] It may have been during 'Alī Gaji's reign that the division of the royal harem with its four titled wives and a number of titled concubines was created.[7] The office of the *chiroma* (heir-apparent) may also have had its origins in this period.

During his pilgrimage in about 1484, 'Alī Gaji was said to have been invested as the *Khalīfa* of Takrūr by the Abbasid claimant 'Abd al-'Azīs b. Ya'ḳūb.[8] From this time onwards Borno rulers regarded themselves as *Khalīfas*, a claim that came to be accepted by many scholars and rulers in the *Bilād al-Sūdān*.[9]

Problems and opportunities in expanding the Borno califate: 1497–1564

'Alī Gaji's policies were continued by his son and successor Idrīs b. 'Alī surnamed Katakarmabe (*c.*1497–1519) who consolidated his gains and tried to expand the state. But for the next fifty years or more Katakarmabe and his successors faced many challenges which diverted their attention from their expansionist goals.

The Sēfuwa's first problem was the resumption of the Bulala attacks after 'Alī Gaji's death. The Bulala appear to have been determined to

3. *Brief Dīwān.*
4. 'Alī's praise song was 'He of the tall towns and long spears'.
5. H. R. Palmer, 1936, pp. 21–2 and 23–8.
6. H. Barth, 1965, Vol. II, p. 589.
7. H. R. Palmer, 1967, p. 158.
8. *Brief Dīwān*, pp. 5–9.
9. J. E. Lavers, 1971, p. 32.

frustrate economic and political development in Borno[10] and Katakarmabe had to face a Bulala attack as soon as he became *Mai*. Not only did he defeat them but he victoriously re-entered Ndjīmī, the former Sēfuwa capital which, however, was never re-occupied. After concluding a treaty with the Bulala, Idrīs returned to Borno. It was, however, a short-lived peace and intermittent conflict continued well into the reign of Idrīs Alawoma (1564–96).

Another problem for the Sēfuwa kings was the emergence of many states both in the Chad basin and elsewhere in the Sudan. This forced the Sēfuwa to change or modify their programmes in order to deal with individual states.

By the early 1500s numerous petty kingdoms had emerged in the Chad basin along the southern border of Borno. These included Bagirmi, Mandara, the Kotoko states, Northern Bolewa of Daniski, the Yamta and the Margi.[11] Such a potentially dangerous development attracted the king's attention. Some states were attacked and forced to recognize some form of Sēfuwa hegemony. But more often the Sēfuwa tried to enter into some form of peaceful relations with the nascent states. Those mentioned above had records of early co-operation with the Sēfuwa and the king's intention must have been to use the emerging states in the building of a regional economic system. Most were encouraged to develop their own economies and to establish regular trade with Borno. Through this association the emerging states absorbed much of the Borno culture, which may have contributed to their rapid development.[12]

In the same period many states also emerged in Hausaland. Katsina and Kano soon developed as the termini of the trans-Saharan route as well as the entrepôts of the west–east route by which the Akan gold and kola were taken to Borno.[13] In the Sahara, there was a slight shift of the trans-Saharan route when Agades developed and supplanted Takedda as the main entrepôt.

Borno must have reacted to these developments. The new trade route between Hausaland and Borno was soon rendered unsafe to travellers by the raids of the Ngizim and the Bedde as well as the Bulala. Much energy must have been spent in trying to safeguard the route, although it was only during the rule of Idrīs Alawoma that the problem was alleviated. The trade-route problem and the question of the control of the new settlements which soon developed along the route may have contributed to the conflicts between Mai Idrīs Katakarmabe and the two kings of Kano, 'Abdullāhī (*c*.1499–1509) and Muḥammad Kisoki (*c*.1509–65).[14]

10. B. M. Barkindo, 1971.

11. For details see B. M. Barkindo, 1980, pp. 204–41.

12. ibid.

13. H. R. Palmer, 1967, p. 109; P. E. Lovejoy, 1978, pp. 185–6; Y. B. Usman, 1981, p. 16.

14. H. R. Palmer, 1967, p. 113.

Borno must have also had to adjust to the shift of the trans-Saharan route. Borno had long-standing relations with Takedda but must have now wanted to control Agades, particularly in the face of increasing Songhay power. In 1501 and 1515 Songhay's Askiya Muḥammad (*c.*1493–1528) sent military expeditions against Agades with the intention of bringing the area under Songhay's influence.[15] The result is not clear but in about 1532 Borno is said to have sent its own military expedition which succeeded in subjugating the town.[16] However, the emergence of Kebbi under Muḥammadu Kanta (*c.*1516–54) frustrated the efforts of both Songhay and Borno. The problems of Agades continued to bedevil the Sēfuwa kings almost throughout their rule.

The period from about 1480 to 1520 was a time of active Islamization in the *Bilād al-Sūdān*. In the east, the Fundj sultanate, which was founded in about 1504, soon adopted Islam. In Ḥausaland many scholars from Mali, North Africa, Egypt and the Saharan oases visited the area during this period, all contributing to the proper Islamization of the area. In the far west, Songhay rose to prominence under Askiya Muḥammad whose rule coincided with Islamic fervour in the area. It is of interest to note that Askiya Muḥammad during his pilgrimage to Mecca (*c.*1496–8) asked to be – and was – invested as *Khalīfa* of Takrūr[17] as Mai 'Alī Gaji had been ten years earlier.

Islamic fervour in this period presented an opportunity to the kings of Borno. The facts that the Sēfuwa *mai*s had been Muslims since the eleventh century; that 'Alī Gaji had been invested *Khalīfa* some ten years before the *Askiya*, who alone seems to have openly contested the title; and that Borno rulers traditionally surrounded themselves with reputable scholars tended to give the *mai*s an edge on the other rulers. The chronicle which Masbarma 'Umar b. 'Uthmān wrote for Idrīs Katakarmabe and the later chronicle written by Imām Aḥmad b. Farṭūwa for Idrīs Alawoma appear to have been attempts to justify the caliphal claims of the *mai*s. The decline and collapse of Songhay later in the century, finally established the primacy of the Borno claim.

Borno was also becoming a great centre of learning visited by scholars from the *Bilād al-Sūdān* and other parts of the Muslim world.[18] That the claim of the Borno kings was accepted by many scholars contributed greatly towards laying the foundation of the cultural influence of Borno in many states. In Hausaland, these developments must have been largely responsible for the introduction of the payment of regular gifts (*gaisuwa* or *tsare* in Hausa) to the Borno *Khalīfa* by the Muslim rulers in Hausaland.[19]

15. J. O. Hunwick, 1971, p. 221.
16. ibid.
17. J. O. Hunwick, 1962. It must have been an attempt by the *Askiya* to strengthen his position at home and to offer challenge to Borno, the only other great power in the region.
18. J. E. Lavers, 1971.
19. H. R. Palmer, 1967, pp. 9–10 and 83; A. Hassan and A. S. Naibi, 1952.

From the reign of Idrīs Katakarmabe, some records exist of diplomatic and commercial relations between the Sēfuwa and the authorities controlling the North African littoral. In about 1512 Katakarmabe sent a diplomatic and trade mission to the Spaniards – who had recently occupied Tripoli – to renew commercial ties. Trade relations with whoever controlled the area continued under succeeding kings.[20] When the Ottomans were established in the Maghrib, Dunāma b. Muḥammad in about 1555 sent an embassy which established with Tighūrt Pasha a treaty of 'friendship and commerce' which was continually renewed by succeeding rulers.[21] Strong ties must have also been established with Egypt which lay on the Borno pilgrim route. There is evidence of trade relations,[22] although information is still fragmentary.

Katakarmabe's sons and grandsons inherited the Bulala incursion problem and that of the emerging states. There was also the Kebbi-Borno war (*c.*1561) over control of Agades, which Borno appears to have lost.

Establishment of a strong regional economy and a centralized political system and the emergence of the Kanuri, *c.*1564–77

Most scholars agree that Borno reached its apogee during the rule of Idrīs b. 'Alī, posthumously surnamed Alawoma (1564–96). The first twelve years of his reign were described in a panegyric by his *Imām*, Aḥmad ibn Furṭūwa.[23] At home he was seen as a military and administrative innovator and an Islamizer, and in foreign affairs as a skilled diplomat who was comparable to the major Muslim leaders of his day.

His main objective as king appears to have been the realization of the objectives of his ancestors, namely the building of a strong economic and political system. Attempts were made for the first time to bring the whole metropolitan province firmly under the control of the *mais*. The cavalry, which was the mainstay of the army, was reorganized. There was also a corps of Turkish gunmen which had been developing under his predecessors. Larger boats were said to have been built for easier crossing of rivers. It was with such a force that Alawoma launched his conquests.

Most of the hostile groups which refused to be persuaded or coerced into submission were continually attacked until they surrendered. These included the Ngafata, the Talata, the Dugurti, the Maya, the Ngizim and

20. D. Girard, *L'histoire chronologique du royaume de Tripoli*, Bibliothèque nationale, Paris, MSS. français (ancien fonds) 12219, 12220.

21. ibid.

22. See J. E. Lavers, 1982.

23. A. ibn Furṭūwa, 1862.

the Bedde. Some, such as the Mukhulum who submitted after a defeat, were allowed to retain their homes upon a promise of tribute in corn.[24] Others, such as the Ngafata, the Talata and the Dugurti, who were considered unmalleable were ejected from the metropolitan province.[25]

In place of the ejected, other groups – mostly from Kānem – were brought in and settled. One of Alawoma's most significant contributions to Borno history was the large-scale demographic changes which he effected in the metropolitan province. This, and extensive intermarriage with female slaves caught during the conflicts or exchanged with satellite states such as Mandara and Bagirmi, contributed to the development and spread of the Kanuri group within the metropolitan province.

In southern Borno dissident groups such as the Gamergu were contained by a series of *ribāṭ*s (frontier fortresses) and formal agreements were entered into with satellite-state rulers for joint military expeditions against the dissidents.[26]

The final solution to the problems of Kānem

After the pacification and integration of most of the metropolitan province, Idrīs Alawoma turned his attention to Kānem to finally solve the menace it posed for Borno. He had three lines of action: to destroy completely the military strength and power base of the Bulala; to try to destroy the economic base of the Kānem state; and to transfer as many groups as possible to Borno.

Alawoma undertook several expeditions to Kānem in which the Bulala were defeated and continually harassed.[27] Other groups, such as the Kananiya who supported the Bulala, were also ruthlessly attacked until they were weakened.[28] During one of the expeditions, three of the most productive valleys of Kānem were ravaged, some of the most important towns situated there, such as Ikima, Aghafi and Ago, were destroyed and the population removed and settled in Borno.[29]

The Kānem groups taken to and settled in Borno included the Tubu, the Koyam, the Kulu and the Shuwa Arabs. The Kulu and the Shuwa Arabs, who were both cattle-owners, were settled along the southern shores of Lake Chad and to the west of the metropolitan province.[30] The Tubu and the Koyam were encouraged to engage in commerce both within Borno and with neighbouring Hausaland and Fombina.[31] Some of the Koyam,

24. A. ibn Furṭūwa, 1862, p. 238.
25. ibid., p. 219; the Dugurti migrated to Kānem.
26. B. M. Barkindo, 1980, ch. 5.
27. H. R. Palmer, 1967, p. 14 suggests the expeditions took place in *c*.1571–5.
28. ibid., pp. 64–6.
29. ibid., p. 49.
30. For the Kulu, ibid., p. 49; for the Shuwa, J. C. Zeltner, 1979, p. 22.
31. H. Barth, 1965, Vol. II, p. 31; G. Nachtigal, 1881, Vol. II, p. 148; B. M. Barkindo, 1980, pp. 164 and 286–90.

who were camel-drivers, were employed in the camelry which had been established as a transportation unit of the army.[32] Many groups were also settled north of the lake in an area through which the Bulala used to pass to attack Borno. Others, in particular the Tubu, were settled on the desert margin, both for strategic reasons and to participate in the production and marketing of the Bilma and Muniyo salt. Other groups must also have been utilized for economic or military reasons but as yet no evidence has been found.

By the 1580s, Alawoma had achieved most of his objectives and the Kānem state, by common agreement, was partitioned between Borno and the Bulala, the latter accepting some form of loose control by Borno.[33]

Internal reforms

Alawoma seems to have made a pilgrimage to Mecca in about 1571.[34] On his return he tried to introduce a number of reforms to bring the country into line with other Islamic states. In government he tried to separate the functions of the judiciary from the administration – but was not, it seems, successful.[35] He does, however, seem to have succeeded in establishing a court of appeal where 'The learned men and Imams held disputations before the Amīr 'Alī concerning doubtful points of law and dogma.'[36]

Mai Alawoma was said to have replaced the old mosques made of reeds with those built of mud-bricks. Numerous North African and other scholars were attracted to his court which thereby gained a cosmopolitan character.

The rise of a strong regional economy

The conquests of and demographic changes under Idrīs Alawoma, as well as his other reforms, led to the emergence of a strong regional economy based on the metropolitan province, an area of some 20 000 sq. km. Three important commercial centres seem to have arisen in the eastern and western extremities of the area as well as around Birnin Gazargamu which lay between the two.[37]

In the eastern part there was large-scale fishing along the banks of Lake Chad by the Buduma and Kānembu,[38] while the good grazing lands

32. H. R. Palmer, 1967, p. 55.

33. J. E. Lavers, 1980, p. 199.

34. H. Barth, 1965, p. 596, suggests that Idrīs performed the pilgrimage in the ninth year of his rule, i.e. in 1571. This also fits in with the date suggested for the start of the Kānem wars by H. R. Palmer (see footnote 27 on p. 497). These dates support the chronologies of D. Lange, 1977, which are being used in this study.

35. J. E. Lavers, 1971, p. 37.

36. H. R. Palmer, 1936, pp. 33–6. Elsami some 170 years later called this *burguram*; see S. W. Koelle, 1968, p. 276.

37. M. N. Alkali, 1983, pp. 64–9.

38. P. M. Redmond (at press).

attracted a large number of Kānembu, Shuwa and Fulbe cattle nomads.[39] *Kilbu* (natron) and *manda* (salt) were also produced by the sedentary Kānembu and Buduma.[40] Important urban centres grew up rapidly in this area due to population increase and economic development. These included Munguno, Kauwa, Burwa and Ngurno.

In the west of the metropolitan province large natron deposits were also found. These were worked by the Manga and the Tubu.[41] In the south was a large concentration of farming peoples including the Ngizim and the Bedde. This area, following the activities of Alawoma and his immediate successors, received more varied immigrants than the east. Many of the urban centres which developed there were therefore more cosmopolitan than their eastern counterparts. They included Nguru Ngilewa, Mashina Kabshari and Maja Kawuri.

Birnin Gazargamu and its environs formed the third economic centre. It had direct and easy access to both areas through the east–west trade route which passed through the city. The Rivers Yobe and Gana also served as waterways, particularly for the transport of fish, and along their banks cattle were transported from east to west. Birnin Gazargamu was also the terminus for the Borno–Kawār–Tripoli trade route as well as for the main route connecting the area with Hausaland. It therefore served as the nerve-centre of the economy of the state, with a large market and a nucleus of foreign merchants.[42] In the fertile irrigated Yobe valley there was a heavy concentration of the emerging Kanuri group settled in many urban centres in addition to Birnin Gazargamu. After the rule of Idrīs Alawoma, the Kanuri started to spread both southwards to the banks of the River Gana and beyond, and northwards towards Garu Kime and beyond.

Attempts were also made towards tighter control over the satellite states. For example, a regular supply of iron and slaves was obtained from Mandara, and skins, ivory and slaves from the Kotoko and Bagirmi.

The development of basic industries led to the establishment of supporting ones such as pottery, weaving, leather work, dyeing and transportation.[43]

Natron and salt were traded to the Atlantic coast, Hausaland, the Volta region and northwards to Azbin and Adrār. Dried fish was traded within the metropolitan province, with Mandara and Hausaland and with the Saharan oases. Slaves, eunuchs, animal skins, ivory, perfumes, leather goods and gold were sent across the Sahara to North Africa and Egypt. In exchange horses, horse-trappings, armoury, copper, bronze and other

39. M. N. Alkali, 1978, p. 158.
40. P. E. Lovejoy (at press).
41. ibid.
42. M. S. ibn Isḥāḳu, 1929, pp. 544–7.
43. M. N. Alkali, 1978, p. 152.

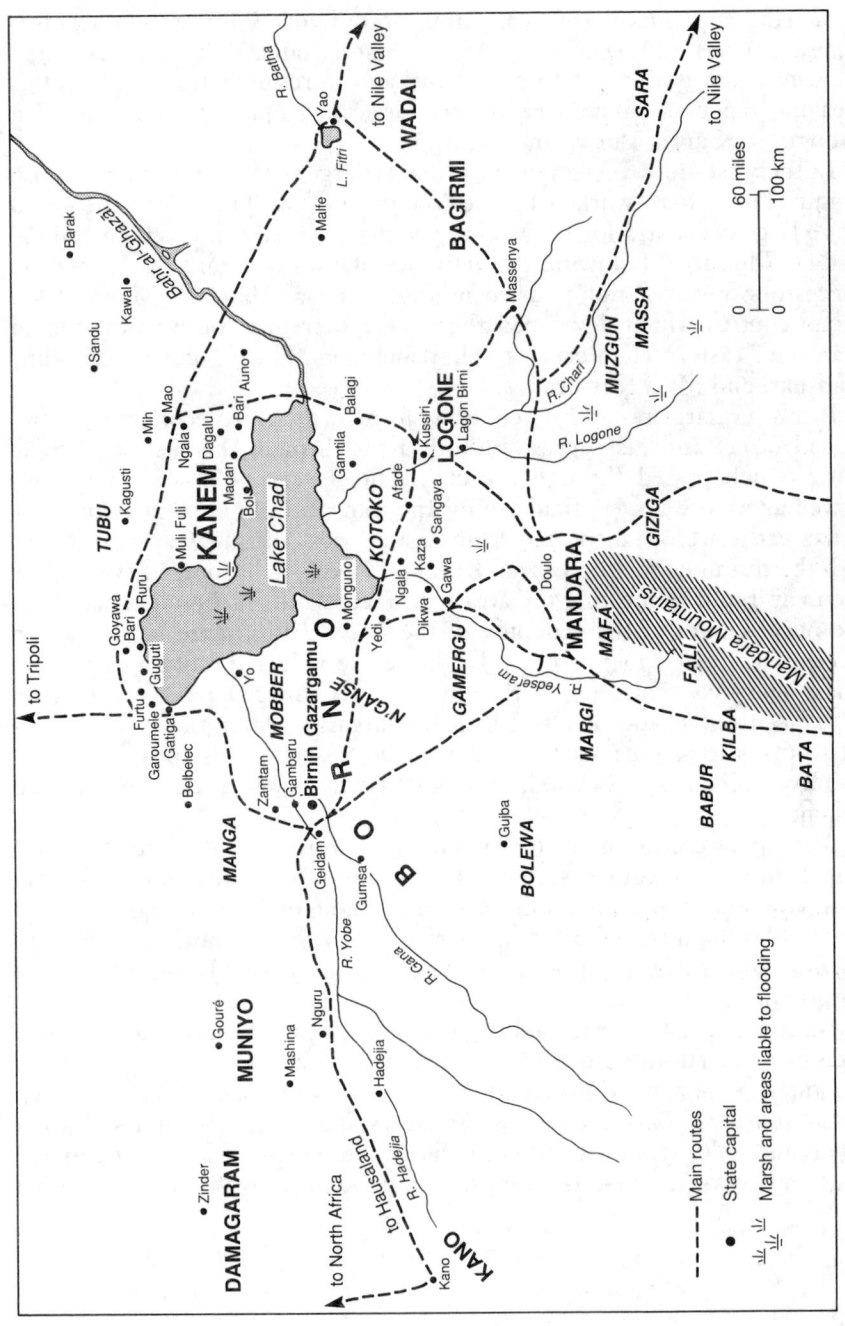

FIG. 17.1   *Borno, Kānem and their immediate neighbours in the eighteenth century*

PLATE 17.1 *A Bornoan weaver making cotton strips* (gabaga) *from which clothes were made*

European and North African products were received for distribution within Borno and other parts of the *Bilād al-Sūdān*.

From the reign of Alawoma various peoples around the Chad basin were apparently encouraged by the Sēfuwa to engage in commercial activities. We have already mentioned the Tubu and the Koyam. The Kotoko and Mandara appear to have come to Kano;[44] Komboli traders from Bagirmi settled in the Zamfara valley;[45] while the Tubu under the Kadella settled in Zaria.[46] Significantly, were all referred to as Bornoans[47] and must have helped to spread the emerging Bornoan culture in Hausaland and other areas. It was through its regional economy, its control of trade and its primacy in Islam that Borno came to dominate the affairs of the *Bilād al-Sūdān* during this period.

The *mai*s interfered little with the trade itself, limiting their role to the provision of security by making the routes safe from marauders, such as the Ngizim and the Tuareg, and by entering into agreements with Saharan and North African governments to ensure the flow of trade both on state

44. Anonymous, 1967, pp. 112–14.
45. P. E. Lovejoy, 1973b *Komboli* is the Kanurized Bagirmi term *umboli* meaning 'trader'.
46. A. Smith, 1970, pp. 88–9. On the *Kadella* title and its spread in Borno and neighbouring areas see B. M. Barkindo, 1980, p. 179.
47. Anon., 1967, pp. 112–14.

and individual levels.[48] It was in the organization of the market that the Sēfuwa government was more involved – to encourage traders and to obtain revenue. In the capital and the other major centres, the *Wasili* (North African traders) were recognized as guests of the government. A *wasiliram* (special quarter) was assigned to them and a *Zanna Arjinama* (titled official) looked after their affairs.[49] In the markets, the *Mala Kasuube* supervised sales and attempted to ensure justice and fair play during major commercial transactions. Each profession or craft had its own head nominated by its members and recognized by the government. These helped the *Mala Kasuube* in the administration of the market and in the collection of revenue.

The diplomatic relations of Idrīs Alawoma with the sultans of Turkey and Morocco

Alawoma's diplomatic relations with the Ottomans and the Saʿādī thanks to the discovery of some documents, have received the attention of several scholars.[50] However, due to the one-sidedness of the documents – they deal mainly with replies to letters sent by Alawoma – understanding of these relations is still not complete. However, the evidence shows as incorrect the general assumption that Alawoma's main objective was to obtain arms.

Ottoman–Borno relations started with the arrival of the former in the Maghrib. From about 1549 – when the Ottomans took control of Fezzān – to about 1570, these relations appear to have been cordial. However, in about 1571 the annual tribute of Fezzān to the Ottomans was suddenly raised to 3000 from the normal 1140 *mithḳal*s of gold.[51] This high-handed Ottoman action unfortunately coincided with a period of famine, and these two events forced many people to migrate to Hausaland and Borno. Ottoman officials in Fezzān forced those who remained, many of them old people, to pay the additional sum between them. Several marauding expeditions were sent against many fortresses in the Sahara oases ostensibly to catch those avoiding taxation. Even the pilgrims from Hausaland and Borno were stopped and forced to pay taxes and the properties of those who died during the pilgrimage were confiscated.[52]

It must have been in 1571 that Alawoma went to Mecca, thereby obtaining first-hand information of the situation. Certainly, this was when he travelled to Kawār to receive the submission and complaints of the

48. J. E. Lavers, 1980, p. 206.
49. M. N. Alkali, 1983, p. 72.
50. For example, see B. G. Martin, 1972 and M. A. al-Hajj, 1983.
51. C. Orhanlu, 1969. I am grateful to John Lavers for the English translation of this document.
52. ibid.

people of Jado who were probably among the Ottoman victims.[53]

Borno's interest in the Fezzān,[54] and the interests of the *mai*s in the security of the route both for pilgrimage and for commerce, must have forced Alawoma, in about 1574 to dispatch a six-man embassy to Istanbul with three specific demands: a guarantee of security of life and property to all Borno travellers in Ottoman territory; proper management or failing that the ceding to Borno of all the recently acquired fortresses south of Fezzān, including Guran; and co-operation between the two powers in dealing with the troublesome Tuareg and any other power disturbing peace in the area. There appears to have been no mention or solicitation of arms.[55]

Sultan Murād III's reply, dated 5 May 1577, agreed with all the requests except the ceding of the Guran fortress – which, however, he promised would henceforth be properly managed.[56] Letters were sent to the governors-general of Tripolitania and Egypt and to the district officer of Fezzān telling them of Alawoma's requests and ordering them to comply.[57] From then on, cordial and beneficial commercial and diplomatic relations continued between the two powers.

Moreover, the claim that the sole purpose of the embassy sent by Alawoma to Sultan al-Manṣūr of Morocco in about 1583 was to solicit arms may not be true either.

The Moroccan victory at Ḳaṣr al-Kabīr in 1578 was generally hailed as an ideological victory for Islam over Christendom.[58] There were congratulatory delegations from Borno and all the leading Muslim powers: Algiers, the Ottomans and Songhay.[59] In addition, Alawoma must have also feared a proposed Ottoman-Saʿādī joint expedition which might have had the Saharan oases or even the Sudan as its target.[60] It appears that Alawoma, a skilful diplomat, aimed at frustrating that proposed venture by suggesting instead a joint Borno-Moroccan expedition to the Saharan oases, once again in some state of insecurity. The outcome of this embassy, according to Moroccan sources, was that Alawoma accepted al-Manṣūr's claim to be *Khalif* of the age as the price for his demands.[61]

Contrary to the views of some authors, the negotiations must have greatly satisfied both parties. Morocco would have gained ideologically to have one of the leading powers in the Sudan recognize al-Manṣūr's Caliphate,

53. A. ibn Furṭūwa, 1862, p. 203.
54. On Borno's interest in Fezzān see B. G. Martin, 1969; J. E. Lavers (at press).
55. See reproduction of the draft letter of Murād's reply to Idrīs in C. Orhanlu, 1969 and M. A. al-Hajj, 1983.
56. C. Orhanlu, 1969.
57. ibid.
58. D. Yahya, 1981, p. 105.
59. ibid.
60. ibid., p. 112. In 1581 the Ottomans suggested a joint Ottoman-Moroccan enterprise 'to improve their positions'.
61. ibid., pp. 150–1. Yaḥyā cautions the acceptance that Idrīs paid the *bayʿa* to al-Manṣūr.

thus strengthening his demands on Songhay.[62] For Alawoma, the price was worth paying if it forestalled joint Moroccan-Ottoman action – whether real or assumed – against Borno or any area where its interests lay.

As yet little is known about the remaining fifteen years of Idrīs Alawoma's reign. He was probably occupied with consolidating his reforms and innovations in Borno. Towards the end of his reign a major problem must have been the fast development of the Mandara and Bagirmi states. Mandara not only abandoned its earlier agreements with Alawoma regarding joint expeditions against the Gamergu but also started to encourage buffer zones between it and Borno. Alawoma was forced to lead several expeditions against Mandara, most of them unsuccessful.[63] In Bagirmi, 'Abdullāh b. Lubetko (*c.*1561–1602), despite having probably gained the throne with Bornoan assistance, started making trouble. It was on a campaign against 'Abdullāh that Alawoma was said to have been assassinated by a Gamergu.

The death of Idrīs Alawoma, contrary to the views of some writers, did not lead to the collapse of the Borno empire. It was in fact, during the rules of his four immediate successors (*c.*1596–1677) that the earlier conquests were consolidated and the administrative machinery finally took shape. It was also at this time that the Kanuri finally emerged as an ethnic group with a distinct culture.

The social and material culture of the Kanuri

The term Kanuri probably came into use in the early seventeenth century.[64] It refers to the dominant ethnic group of Borno upon whom the power of the Sēfuwa kings was based. It was produced by the inter-marriage of the peoples and cultures of the immigrant Magumi from Kānem and the Chadic speakers of Borno – a development, as noted above, accelerated by the activities of Idrīs Alawoma. Within the Kanuri group itself there were many sub-ethnic distinctions but it is not our aim here to go into such details. It was the Kanuri culture that formed the base of the Bornoan culture which spread beyond the metropolitan province as the Kanuri travelled out or as other groups adopted the Kanuri culture through political or economic domination or association or through Islamization.

Most Kanuri lived in villages in compounds containing several round huts either of wooden frameworks or of mud walls with conical grass roofs. Many compounds were surrounded by *sugedi* (grass matting). In the larger towns most huts and mosques were made of mud walls and houses of men with means were usually surrounded by high mud walls.[65]

---

62. Al-Manṣūr was then thinking of invading the Songhay which he finally did in 1591.
63. B. M. Barkindo, 1980, ch. 5.
64. The earliest mention of the term is in a satirical poem by Muḥammad al-Tahir b. Ibrāhīm al-Fallati (d. 1776) quoted in M. Bello, n.d.
65. A. von Duisburg, 1942, pp. 92–5.

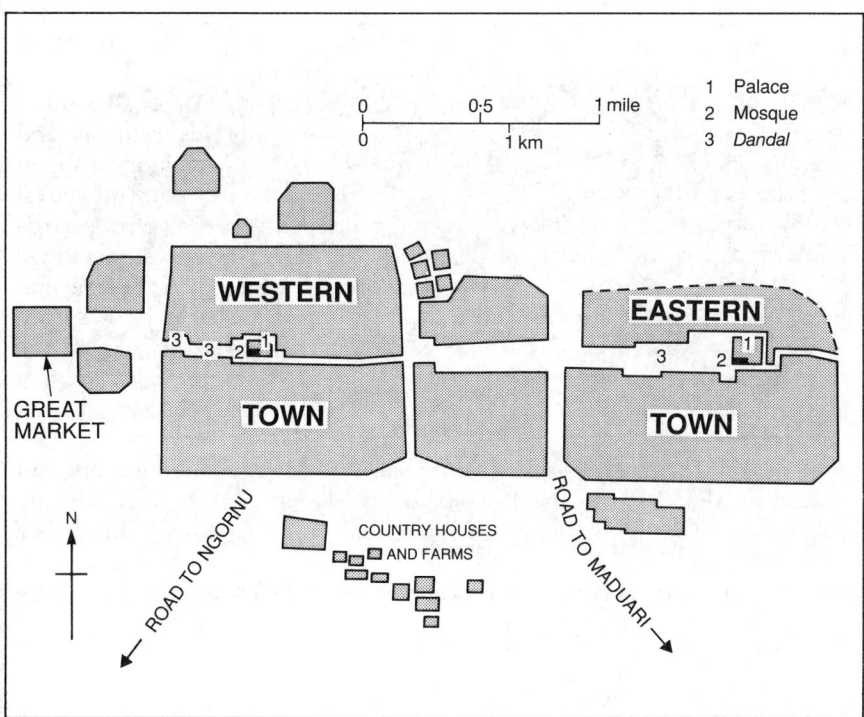

FIG. 17.2 *Plan of Kukawa, the nineteenth-century capital of Borno, built in a double form of the traditional Kanuri design*
Source: adapted from H. Barth, 1857, II, pp. 50–1. Adapted by kind permission of Longman Group UK Ltd

Most Kanuri towns and villages were U-shaped. The *dandal* (the opening of the U) was the settlement's main street. It faced westwards and led to the palace of the governor of the town, beside which was situated the settlement's main mosque.

At Birnin Gazargamu and in some of the most important towns, such as Nguru, Mashina and Gambaru, the houses were usually rectangular with thick mud walls and flat roofs. Royal palaces at Birnin and Gambaru, their main mosques, and the palaces of important dignitaries, such as the *Galadima* at Nguru and the *Mashinama* of Mashina were surrounded by impressive walls of fired bricks,[66] one of the distinguishing traits of Kanuri culture which seems to have flourished from the mid-sixteenth to the early eighteenth century.[67] Such walls must have been introduced to give additional protection during the period of conquests and insecurity. Birnin Gazargamu and other important towns were surrounded by a *garu* (mud

66. A. D. H. Bivar and P. C. Shinnie, 1962.

67. H. R. Palmer, 1936, p. 253 has a reference to a brick palace built by Muḥammad b. Hamdūn (c.1729–44).

PLATE 17.2   *A wall of the* Mai's *summer palace at Gambaru, built* c. *1570–80*

wall) and *belaga* (ditch) for additional defence.

A typical Kanuri could have been distinguished by his language and physical appearance. Both men and women had distinguishing vertical marks on each cheek. An unmarried girl usually wore her hair in a *kela yasku* (a special style) while a married woman wore her hair in a *jurungul* (crown).[68] All women ate kola nuts and stained their teeth with *gorongo* or *fure* (tobacco flower)[69] dyed their hands and feet with *nalle* (henna) and put a coral bead or metal stud into one nostril. They usually wore *gimaje* (long dyed cotton dresses) and women of distinction wore a *kalaram* (turban).

Men wore *tobe* (large open cotton gowns either plain or dyed blue) while those of the upper class wore a multiplicity of gowns of expensive imported cloth. In the late-eighteenth century they wore outsize unwieldly turbans which appear to have been borrowed from seventeenth-century Ottoman practice.[70]

68. D. Denham, 1826, Vol. II, p. 144, footnote; G. Rohlfs, 1875, Vol. 2, p. 7; R. E. Ellison, 1936, p. 529; I. Imam, 1969, p. 514. The hair-styles in Borno changed several times so that the earlier styles are difficult to ascertain. Usman Geidam, Amina and Jakingi Mala, personal communication.

69. Tobacco was introduced into Borno in the 17th century. The practice therefore may date from that time.

Marriage was one of the distinguishing traits of Kanuri culture which, if properly studied, would reveal the many elements which went into its formation: Islamic rite and both Magumi and Bornoan practices.[71] The *nyia* (marriage contract) itself was made under Islamic rites but ceremonies both before and after the marriage contract betray other cultural traits. One such example is the *kalimbo barata* when the bride's friends went into the bush to collect branches from the *kalimbo* thorn-tree with which the bridegroom and his best friend were supposed to be beaten. Another was the *kalaba*, the final ceremony of the marriage, which comprised the reading of the Ḳur'ān together with what appears to have been some pre-Islamic initiation ceremony.[72]

Kanuri society was highly stratified. It was broadly divided into two classes, the *Kontuowa* (ruling class or nobility) and the *tala'a* (commoners) and both these had several divisions. Differences of speech, dress, household furniture, architecture and residence distinguished the classes and their sub-divisions. Status was based on ethnic membership, occupation, birth, age and residence. Upward mobility was achieved through obtaining more wealth, association with the ruling class or obtaining a highly ranked profession.[73]

The emphasis on inferior–superior relations was an important aspect of Kanuri socio-political culture. A social inferior was always required to show his superior respect in public. In addition, a social inferior had to render *nona* (respectful visits) to the house of his social father for whom he was supposed to run any errand required of him.[74] The superior reciprocated by providing his inferior with his basic needs and protecting and advancing his interests in society. A Kanuri's most valuable socio-economic and political asset, according to Cohen, was probably to have a large number of people dependent on and subordinate to him.[75]

As already indicated, Islam was one of the bases of Kanuri culture. Islam was deeply rooted in ordinary everyday life and had even penetrated the fabric of Kanuri folklore. Much of the technical vocabulary of Islam had been so 'Kanurized' that its original meaning had been modified. For example, the word *kasalla* (meaning washing of any sort even of animals) had been adopted from the Arabic word *sallah* (prayers).[76]

Borno by this time was a centre of learning which attracted large numbers

70. D. Denham, 1826, Vol. I, illustration opp. p. 230.

71. R. E. Ellison, 1936, pp. 531–2; I. Imam, 1969, p. 515.

72. Both the *kalimbo barate* and part of *kalaba* ceremonies are said to have been adopted by the Magumi from the so-called Sao peoples whom they first met and intermixed with upon their arrival.

73. R. Cohen, 1970.

74. R. Cohen, 1965, p. 363.

75. ibid., p. 364.

76. S. W. Koelle, 1968, p. 114. For more information see J. E. Lavers, 1971.

of students and visiting scholars from the *Bilād al-Sūdān*, North Africa and the Middle East. Borno specialized in *tafsīr* (commentary on the Ḳurʾān) in the Kānembu language[77] and the art of writing the Borno language in Arabic letters must have been developed by the seventeenth century.[78]

There were two types of scholars. The first were the bearers of Islamic offices of state – the *imām*s, the *ḳāḍī*s, the *mainin kinendi* (Islamic and legal adviser to the *mai*), the *Talba* (head of police and magistrate), *khazin* (treasurer) and the *wazir*. These were the great *ʿulamāʾ* who helped the *mai* in running the Islamic government and their positions were hereditary and restricted to a few leading scholarly families. The great scholars were supposedly learned and pious but as they held institutionalized offices and were thus associated with worldly power they became increasingly alienated from the non-court scholars who criticised them for supporting *bidʿa* (religious innovation) and *ada* (traditions of the country) for reasons of political expediency.[79]

The more austere scholars lived away from the court and the city in *malamti* (scholarly families) in the rural areas where they taught and spread the religion. During the time of the Sēfuwa most of these scholars were supported and patronized by the kings who also gave many of them *mahrams*.[80] It was they who helped spread Islam in the rural areas of the metropolitan province and beyond into the neighbouring states. However, it was also they who produced the first intensive criticism of Sēfuwa rule.

Most of the Sēfuwa kings tried to enhance their powers not only through patronizing the *ʿulamāʾ* but also through an outward show of piety and in becoming learned in their own rights. This attitude – which appears to have been partly an attempt to reinforce the pre-Islamic supernatural powers of rulers,[81] since knowledge provided its holder with a reputation for having access to supernatural powers – was adopted by many neighbouring rulers who adopted their religion and political structure from Borno.[82]

Political organization

The *mai* was the head of the institutionalized royal family, the supreme head of state and the *larde kangema* (nominal owner of the land). He was the symbol of the unity and continuity of the state. As the *Amīr al-muʿminīn*

77. A. D. H. Bivar and P. L. Shinnie, 1960, pp. 199–205.

78. ibid.

79. M. Bello, n.d.

80. *Mahram*s are documents of privileges and exemptions from taxation and military services granted by the *mai*s to some scholarly families and a few trading groups. See the various *mahram*s in H. R. Palmer, 1936 and 1967.

81. For example, ʿAlī b. ʿUmar was considered to have been learned and pious and to have possessed miraculous powers. He performed the *ḥadjdj* five times, dying near Cairo while returning from the fifth.

82. For a Mandara example, see B. M. Barkindo, 1979, p. 44.

(commander of the faithful) he was head Muslim and a final court of appeal in both public and private matters of justice.[83]

Many of the sacred attributes of the pre-Islamic kings, vividly described by al-Muhallabī in the tenth century,[84] seem to have survived into the Islamic period. The king was still largely secluded, appearing in public in a *fanadir* (cage), and people spoke to him only through intermediaries.[85] Muslim scholars appear to have enhanced the sacred attributes of the king in several ways. The scholar in the *Idara*, for example, claims that God 'has made certain peoples kings and has perfected the characters of those chosen to be kings ... '[86]

Ibn Furṭūwa, in the sixteenth century, echoed the belief of many Muslims in other parts of the world when he said: 'A place where there is an evil Sultan is better than a place where there is none.'[87]

The *mai* was selected from amongst the *maina* (eligible princes) whose fathers had been kings. Succession, however, was not always smooth. There was both internal opposition from other segments of the royal dynasty and external opposition from rebellious tributary states. To avoid rebellion during an interregnum it was essential to select a new king with minimum delay. However, the office of the heir-apparent does not appear to have functioned well.[88] From the time of Mai Idrīs b. 'Alī (c.1677–96) or earlier, the kings seem to have resorted to eliminating rival candidates, a habit they probably learnt from the Ottomans.[89]

Subordinate to the king were the other members of the institutionalized royal family. This consisted of the king's four titled wives, headed by the *gumsu* (headwife), the concubines, the princes and the *mairam* (princesses). It also included the *magira* (queen-mother) and the *magram* (the king's official sister). The *gumsu* was responsible for administering the palace, and the *magira*, in addition to being the holder of the largest number of fiefs in the state, had the right to grant sanctuary. The official sister usually supervised the cooking of the king's food.

The royal wives were generally drawn from the families of the leading officials of state,[90] while the princessess were given in marriage to leading religious dignitaries and *torwe* (specially designated title-holders).[91] Most princes resided outside the palace and were strictly controlled although some were given fiefs. The most important of these were the *chiroma* (heir-apparent) and the *yerima* (governor of the northern provinces) who was

83. M. N. Alkali, 1985.

84. J. F. P. Hopkins and N. Levtzion, 1981, p. 171.

85. R. Cohen, 1970.

86. Muḥammadu Yanbu in J. F. A. Ajayi and B. Ikara, 1985.

87. A. ibn Furṭūwa, 1862.

88. For example, even Idrīs Alawoma was not immediately succeeded by his *Chiroma* (Biri).

89. See B. M. Barkindo, 1979, pp. 41–2.

90. G. C. Lethem, 1919.

91. J. C. Petterson, 1920.

PLATE 17.3 *Reception of the Denham-Clapperton mission by the* Mai *of Borno in the 1820s*

always a *maidugu* (grandson of a previous king) which meant he would never become king.

The highest council of state was the *majlis* which was normally presided over by the king and composed of military and religious notables who were said to have been twelve although the accounts vary from source to source. It normally included most of the Islamic advisers already mentioned as well as military commanders: *yerima*, *kaigama* and *galadima*. Other sources include powerful slaves of the king some of whom were eunuchs. The *noguna* (*mai*'s court), which consisted of all the notables in the capital, met daily.

All towns, villages and ethnic units were grouped into *chidi* (fiefs) and all major officials of state were *chima*s (fief-holders). These were responsible for the maintenance of order in their fiefs, for the collection of taxes and for the raising of troops for the army. All fief-holders, except the *galadima*, resided in the capital and were represented by their *chima gana* (junior fief-holders). All fiefs were held at the pleasure of the king who had the right to confiscate, reduce or re-arrange their holdings. Rural people were ruled by *mbarma* or *bulala* (local or ethnic leaders).

The Sēfuwa's income included the *zakāt* (alms), *dibalram* (road tolls), *kultingo* (tribute) and war booty. All those who participated in tax collection reserved some portion for themselves while the major title-holders reserved large portions, paying the rest as tribute to the king. Both the *mai* and fief-holders, however, were expected to redistribute the major portions of their income as gifts to their subordinates who, in turn, were required to do the same to their followers.

The golden age in Borno

The seventeenth century – not the sixteenth as popularly claimed – should be regarded as Borno's golden age. Idrīs Alawoma's conquests were completed and consolidated and administrative reforms were made to facilitate the management of the growing empire. It was during the rule of 'Umar b. Idrīs (*c.*1619–39) that the offices of the *galadima* at Nguru and the *alifa* of Mao at Kānem were established as semi-autonomous vassals to take care of the western and eastern extremities of the state respectively.[92] Buffer states were established along the desert fringe at Muniyo and Mashina (and at Gaskeru, Tunbi and Damagaram in the eighteenth century) as barriers to Tuareg attacks on the metropolitan province.[93]

This was the period when 'Abd al-Karīm b. Jame (*c.*1611–55), who studied in Borno, founded Wadai – no doubt with Borno's blessing, since the emergence of Wadai checked for some time the expansionist attitude of Bagirmi, into what was considered Borno territory. As with the other

92. A. Benisheikh, 1983, p. 41; J. E. Lavers, 1980.
93. J. E. Lavers, 1980, p. 203.

neighbouring states, Wadai also fell within the political, cultural and commercial orbit of Borno.[94]

Diplomatic and commercial relations with the Mediterranean littoral entered one of its briskest periods. Trade became so active that in about 1636 Muḥammad Saḳizli (c.1633–49) of Tripoli wrote to Mai ʿUmar that the two of them, together with the Sultan of Fezzān, should monopolize it completely[95] – a venture which after some years was found to be impossible. Relations with Egypt must also have been good, through trade and because Egypt lay on the pilgrimage route. It probably was during this period that new crops such as maize, tomatoes and paw-paw were introduced into Borno from the Mediterranean littoral, particularly Egypt.[96]

By the seventeenth century, particularly by the rule of ʿAlī b. ʿUmar (c.1639–77), Borno had become the dominant power in the *Bilād al-Sūdān*. Not only was it a centre of learning and culture but also the controller of all the easily accessible sources of mineral salts – at Muniyo, Bilma and around Lake Chad. Its close trade connections with the Mediterranean coast led to its domination of the redistribution of Mediterranean imports to the central Sudanic states.[97] It was also in possession of a strong regional economy at home. The *mai*s were recognized as the undisputed leaders of the Islamic states of the region and Borno was acknowledged throughout the area as the fourth sultanate of the Islamic world.[98] Most of the states appear to have placed themselves voluntarily under the protection of the *Khalif* (caliph), to benefit from his *baraka* (blessing) and to obtain the goods they needed. It was the general erosion of this system that led to the decline and final collapse of the Sēfuwa.

The kings of the late seventeenth and the first half of the eighteenth centuries tried to maintain the system they had inherited and appear to have done their job well. Most of what the oral traditions regard as classical Borno is based on the Sēfuwa system as it existed in the eighteenth century.

Crises of the late-eighteenth century

With the reign of ʿAlī ibn Dunāma (c.1742–92) Borno entered a period of crisis which climaxed in the *djihād* of the nineteenth century.

In western Borno, the Bedde were intensifying their raids on the trade routes to Hausaland while in the north the increasing raids of the Tuareg of Agades finally led to the loss, in about 1759, of the important Bilma salt

94. G. Nachtigal, 1874, p. 50.

95. D. Girard, Ms. 12219.

96. The words for maize (*Masara*, i.e. 'Egyptian') and paw-paw (*Bambus Massarabe*, i.e. 'Melon from Egypt') in Kanuri and many other languages of people around Lake Chad and Hausaland further support the claim of Egyptian origin for these crops.

97. P. E. Lovejoy, 1978.

98. M. Kaʿti, 1913–14, p. 65. The *Taʾrīkh* has been edited several times, this passage could have been written any time between 1591 and 1655.

mines and later the abandonment of many towns on the desert fringe.[99] This precipitated the southward shift of the Manga groups into Hausaland, the Sosebalki states and the Ngazir province.

In Bagirmi, Muḥammad al-Amīn (*c*.1715–85) threw off Borno's over-lordship and launched a series of attacks on Borno's eastern frontiers while Wadai under Jawda (*c*.1747–95) continued its expansionist policies towards Baḥr al-Ghazāl.[100] These attacks set in motion the migrations of the Tubu, Kānembu and Shuwa Arabs into Kānem and the metropolitan province[101] thereby causing conflicts over grazing lands among the pastoralists which were exacerbated by the long and severe famines.

In about 1781, Mandara revolted and after several engagements severely defeated the forces of Borno.[102] This was followed by the revolt of the Sosebalki states[103] and, in about 1785, of Gobir.[104]

Faced with insecurity, famines and impoverished grazing lands, many of the Fulbe nomads abandoned metropolitan Borno and drifted into Hausaland, Mandara and Fombina. Nowhere, however, did they find the peace and security they were looking for[105] and this may partly explain their dominant participation in the *djihād*.

The non-court scholars and the ordinary Muslims blamed the crisis on the increasing corruption of the Sēfuwa rulers and the inability of the *mai*s to prevent the growing syncretism among the people. The court scholars were equally blamed for their acquiescence to the increasing syncretism of the rulers. Other scholars, such as the *karabiwa mallam*s attempted to withdraw completely from the society which they considered corrupt. When the *djihād* broke out, the client-rulers in Hausaland called upon the *mai* to fulfil his obligation as *Khalif* and patron and come to their aid. That he could not and that he could not even prevent his own expulsion from his capital by the same djihādists meant that the *khalif* had lost his primacy.

However, although the *djihād* did contribute to the loss of the vassal states and to the end of the Sēfuwa rule, the system that the *mai*s had built, particularly in metropolitan Borno, did survive albeit with modification well into the twentieth century.

---

99. J. E. Lavers, 1980, p. 208.

100. G. Nachtigal, 1874, pp. 100–1; J. E. Lavers, 1980, p. 208.

101. Anon., n.d.

102. B. M. Barkindo, 1980, pp. 390–1.

103. I. Landorein, 1910–11, pp. 427 and 429.

104. A. ibn Mustafā, particularly MS. 49, ff. 46 and 76.

105. For Hausaland see Y. B. Usman, 1981; for Mandara see B. M. Barkindo, 1980; for Fombina, see A. Sa'ad, 1977.

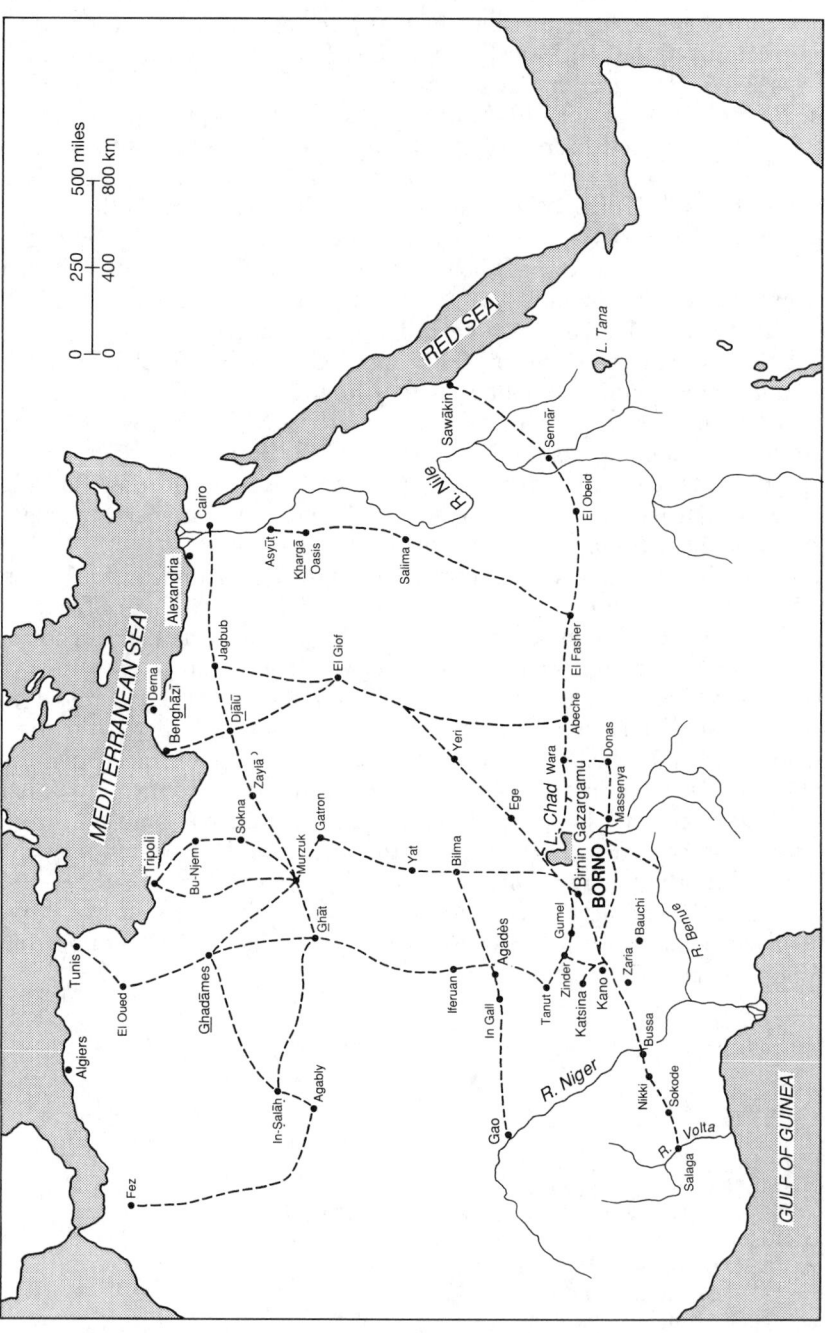

FIG. 17.3   *Borno's links with North Africa and the Nile valley in the eighteenth century*

From the Cameroon grasslands to the Upper Nile

E. M'BOKOLO

In this part of Africa, historical information for the period 1500–1800 is less plentiful, coherent and reliable than for other regions. This is not only because research has been unsystematic and, in general, recent, but also because, for the period prior to the nineteenth century, the possibilities for research seem extremely limited. In areas where political organizations took the form of states, these were mostly formed very late, in the eighteenth and nineteenth centuries. Oral traditions among their peoples, who had only a limited degree of hierarchy, appear uninformative and rarely go back more than a few generations, five or six at best. Those which do exist often record the individual history of a particular lineage and raise, in addition to the usual problems of interpretation, the problem of how to relate them to one another and integrate them into an overall view. Any synthesis based on this type of source is therefore provisional – but other sources are very sparse. A few travellers' accounts, from the sixteenth century onwards, exist for the areas in closest contact with foreigners: the Atlantic coast, for example, is relatively well covered whereas the northern borders close to Muslim areas were only really visited by Muslim travellers in the nineteenth century. Finally, archaeological research, historical linguistics and ethnolinguistics are only just beginning in the area.

There is, moreover, no single factor uniting the different parts of this region. The forest is certainly its dominant physical feature – particularly as it must have covered a larger area in the sixteenth, seventeenth and eighteenth centuries than it does today – but many parts of the region have long been savannah. The low population density appears to be another common characteristic but then, as now, there were areas of relatively high density, notably in the savannah and along the waterways. As for the peoples, their languages, ways of life and forms of organization were extremely diverse. This diversity and the inevitable uneven distribution of information necessitate a regional approach to the area.

The northern border area

The northern part of this region, from the central Cameroon highlands in the west to the River Nile in the east, is the area for which historical information is most lacking. It is significant, for example, that the best chronologies currently available contain few facts from before 1800.[1] Before the beginning of the nineteenth century the historian, to use E. M. Chilver's words, is in the domain of 'reasonable conjecture', and these conjectures can only be made within narrow geographical limits. The tendency of ethnological and historical works to restrict themselves first to the limits of ethnic groups and then, more recently, to the limits of contemporary states, makes any regional synthesis difficult and hazardous. It seems wiser, therefore, to try to define micro-regions which have some degree of cultural homogeneity or, at least, some degree of common destiny at this time.

The central Cameroon highlands

These relatively fertile grasslands were probably settled very early, certainly before the population movements whose consequences are still visible and which probably took place in the sixteenth and seventeenth centuries.[2] There are at least two indications of this early settlement. The first is the vegetation which is today wooded savannah but was once dense forest. The savannah-ization (the chronology of which is not yet established and the mechanisms of which appear to be highly complex) might be attributed to the slow and progressive action of compact human communities, to the sudden and brutal action of a small number of immigrants, or even to climatic influences. The second indication is the presence of numerous stone tools that testify to settled human occupation prior to the diffusion of iron-working which probably occurred in this area in the second half of the first millennium. But it remains impossible to identify these ancient inhabitants. They might have been Pygmy hunters, a few of whose descendants still survive on the banks of the Mbam; or proto-Bantu language-speakers who had not discovered metal-working; or a fluid mixture of several distinct peoples.

It is only from the sixteenth century that facts begin to crystallize. The population movements recorded in the traditions involved many different sorts of people: family or kinship groups; compact, thrusting bodies of people; and also isolated individuals. All the evidence suggests that the number of migrants was small for, while they dominated the peoples they found already settled (which indicates some technological superiority), everywhere they abandoned their own language and adopted that of the country where they settled. The same process may also have applied to political institutions. The traditions also reveal the countless reasons for

1. See for example P. Kalck, 1980 and E. M. Chilver, 1981.
2. C. Tardits, 1981, pp. 14 and 459–84; T. Eyongetah and R. Brain, 1974, p. 34.

these movements, which included internal disputes, the search for iron ore and wood to work it, the quest for new land, perhaps precipitated by the introduction of maize or the development of the oil palm, the salt trade, and the pressure of invaders from the north. The northern factor, particularly the Fulbe raids, which is well known for the nineteenth century, was relevant much earlier, from the mid-eighteenth century or even before. The famous book, *History and Customs of the Bamum*, prepared at the request of and under the supervision of Njoya, king of the Bamum, refers to mounted invaders at a time which corresponds to the eighteenth century. In addition the vocabulary and syntax of the Mbum language, spoken in the central Cameroon highlands, include many borrowings from Fulfulde (Adamawa variant). It thus seems that the Fulbe drove the Mbum southwards and that they in turn forced the Voute to move southwards, and that this migration led to the migration of the Fang and Beti.

This constant jostling of populations, spread over several centuries, accompanied by mixing and borrowing in every direction, is a main factor in the striking cultural homogeneity of the peoples of Central Cameroon.[3] The peoples there all speak Bantoid or Semi–Bantu languages. There are numerous similarities in political and social institutions. Human communities, for example, are organized into chiefships, or even kingdoms, in which the chief has sacred attributes and heads a body of titleholders with the help of a princess of high status (the queen-mother or queen-sister), and males belong to countless associations – secret societies and/or military groups – with ritual or police functions. Technologies were often comparable too, especially in the working of iron and copper. The smith was believed to have magical powers and is prominent in myths and historical traditions. This homogeneity, well established by about 1800, had been formed gradually during the previous centuries.

Three of these numerous peoples deserve special attention. The first are the Tikar who are important because many other peoples in the Cameroon highlands either claim to derive from them or have been strongly influenced by them.[4] They are said to descend from a trader from Borno who settled and left offspring among the Mbum. Their various traditions put their origin in north-east Cameroon (Tibati, Banyo, Kimi, Ndobo). *Tikar* was initially the nickname of the first group of Mbum to leave their homeland for the highlands but in time it came to be applied to all Mbum emigrants and the peoples they had conquered. The major part of this great migration probably took place in the seventeenth century under pressure from the Fulbe, internal troubles and the quest for new lands. When they reached the Bamenda region, the Tikar met the Tumu whom they first allied with and then dominated. But the price of victory was their adoption of the language of the conquered and their institutions, particularly the political titles and secret societies. Several groups among the conquered chose to

3. T. Eyongetah and R. Brain, 1974, pp. 36–8; M. McCulloch *et al.*, 1954, p. 11 *et seq.*
4. C. Tardits, 1980, pp. 80–9; T. Eyongetah and R. Brain, 1974, pp. 38–41.

migrate to the west and north-west where they founded several states, notably the Kingdom of Nsaw. Some of its features were later transmitted to the other kingdoms in the region, such as divine kingship, the cult of dead kings, the rigid socio-political hierarchy, the reservation of certain titles or functions for princes and princesses, the existence of a large palace nobility, and male secret societies in every village.

The foundation of the Bamum kingdom was the work of a group of emigrants related to the royal dynasty of the Tikar of Nsaw.[5] The exact chronology of these events is difficult to establish: we may simply observe that in the *History and Customs of the Bamum* ten kings are listed between the founder, Nchare, and Kuotu, the ruler immediately before Mbuembue, whose reign is dated to the first half of the nineteenth century. According to some traditions Nchare was driven out of Rifum, while others say he emigrated freely with several companions to the present location of the Bamum. He was a conqueror who crushed some eighteen rulers, some of whose peoples fled while others were absorbed and he also founded the capital of the Bamum, Foumban, then called Mfomben (from *fom* (ruins) and Mben (the conquered former inhabitants). Nchare also endowed the kingdom with political institutions mostly taken from those of the Tikar. He set up a body of numerous title-holders, including the *kom ngu* (counsellors of the kingdom), with whom he divided up the available lands; he formed two secret societies one of which, *ngiri*, was for princes only, while the other, *mitngu*, was open to the rest of the population irrespective of social status (descendants of conquered peoples, great state retainers, counsellors of the kingdom, and so on). However, the Bamum gave up Tikar and adopted Mben, the language of the conquered. The nine kings who followed Nchare get short shrift from the codified traditions of the Bamum which say that each 'lived long without doing anything, living on what the hands of Nchare had done'. These rulers were not conquerors, for territorial expansion only began at the beginning of the nineteenth century during the reign of Mbuembue. Apart from internal dissension the kingdom also faced the serious threat of Chamba and Fulbe invaders from the north, particularly during the eighteenth century. However, some significant developments can be detected during this period. The growth in large-scale royal polygamy led to a vast increase in the number of princely lineages (sixty-one by the end of the eighteenth century). The palace nobility also grew substantially (twenty-seven lineages of great retainers were formed) with the king recruiting most of his retainers from twins and the sons of princesses. Material and social developments remain little known. At the end of the eighteenth century the kingdom had perhaps ten to twelve thousand inhabitants, among whom there was a small number of slaves, reduced to this state as a result of offences or debts. The economy, heavily agricultural, was open to external trade and from a very early date

5. This history has been completely revised by Claude Tardits, 1980, pp. 83–126.

the Bamum were importing salt, iron, beads, cotton goods and copper objects.

As for the Bamileke, their ancient history is closely linked to that of the two previous groups.[6] The word itself, whose origin and meaning are still the subject of debate, has been incorrectly applied to many groups (about a hundred chiefdoms) which did indeed share a common culture but did not describe themselves as Bamileke. All came from the north, from the region today occupied by the Tikar. Their migration southwards probably began in the seventeenth century, and was related to the Tikar population movements and Fulbe pressures. It took place over a long period, in successive waves led by distinct elements of the population. These migrants occupied present Bamum country where they founded several villages before being driven out of most by the Bamum: those who remained were assimilated. Among the various Bamileke groups, the Baleng were the first to cross the River Nun, almost certainly at the beginning of the eighteenth century, soon to be followed by the Bandeng, Bapi and Bafoussam. The settlement of these groups in their present location continued into the nineteenth century. The various chiefdoms had features common to the political societies of the Cameroon highlands (the existence of a chief, the importance of councils, and the role of associations, for example). One of their distinctive traits was the high mobility of people which appears to date from early times and be linked to their fairly high population growth and the inheritance system that transferred an estate to a single heir, thus obliging the other sons to secure land from the chief or settle elsewhere.

The areas around the Uele and the Ubangi rivers

A close look at the hypotheses and conclusions currently available suggests that knowledge of the areas around the Uele and the Ubangi rivers, at least before the nineteenth century, has hardly advanced since the works of the first anthropologists, in particular those of Hutereau, Calonne-Beaufaict and Lagae.[7] Contemporary researchers constantly use the same expressions (probabilities, conjectural knowledge, provisional conclusions) which reveal the tentative state of existing knowledge as well as the extreme complexity (confusion, patchwork of races, puzzle) of the phenomena being studied.

The most vexed question is undeniably that of the settlement of these lands. Despite minor divergences, relating to the most suitable qualifiers to describe the human groups involved, all research agrees in recognizing three types of populations: neolithic, Bantu and Sudanic. The main difficulties appear in detailing the vagaries and modalities of settlement and the content and successive forms of the relations between these various peoples.

Traditionally, more as a matter of convenience than of choice, two sub-

6. T. Eyongetah and R. Brain, 1974, pp. 43–6; and C. Tardits, 1981.
7. A. de Calonne-Beaufaict, 1921; Hutereau, 1922; Lagae, 1926.

regions were distinguished, the Ubangi and the Uele.[8] The Ubangi area, today inhabited mostly by Sudanic peoples – Banda, Ngbaka and Ngbandi, speaking languages belonging to the eastern Adamawa family – was probably occupied until the seventeenth century by Bantu, themselves supposed to have taken possession of the region from little-known populations whose neolithic implements have survived. These Bantu are scarcely better known, since most became acculturated to the Sudanic peoples. The Sudanic peoples probably began to move into the region from Dārfūr and Kordofān in the seventeenth or early eighteenth century. Those who were to form the Ngbandi group probably arrived first, then the Banda and the Ngbaka. The succession of human groups in the Uele area, today dominated by Zande, Zande-ized peoples and Mangbetu, seems to have been different. Until the sixteenth or early seventeenth century, the Uele, Mbomu and Aruwimi basins were probably occupied by neolithic populations, the present-day survivors of whom are said to be the Momvu, the Logo and the Makere. These short-statured peoples used implements of wood, bone and especially polished stone (axes, grind-stones and sling-stones). Two population groups, traditionally portrayed as invaders, grafted themselves onto this underlying population. These original migrations took place from 1500–1800. The first movement of the Sudanic peoples, from whom came the Mangbetu, Ngbandi and Zande peoples, took them in a north–south direction as far as the Ubangi and the Mbomu rivers and west–east from there. The seventeenth century also saw the arrival of the Bantu following the rivers northwards. It was during this period – the seventeenth to early eighteenth centuries – that the ethno-political groups were formed.

Other researchers have proposed a synthesis covering all Ubangi and Uele areas (see Fig. 18.1).[9] Their argument rests on linguistic and ethno-linguistic data and distinguishes three broad stages of settlement. First, in the first millennium before the Christian era, there was a large-scale west-east movement bringing the proto-Ubangians to the River Nile, with the Gbaya-Manga settling in the west, the Band in the centre, the Ngbaka–Sere–Ngbandi in the triangle formed by the river Baḥr al-Ghazāl and the White Nile, and the Zande–Nzakara in the south between the Uele river and the Nile. The populations were still settled there in about 1000 when a Nilotic drive from the north occurred. The first effect of this was to break up the Ngbaka–Sere–Ngbandi group and drive southwards the Ngbandi in the region between the Rivers Ubangi and Zaire. Here they met the Pygmies and the Bantu. This Nilotic drive also drove the Zande–Nzakara populations westward into the lands watered by the Uele and Mbomu rivers. The third stage, which began in the eighteenth century, corresponds to the drive by the Bantu from the south and fleeing the effects of the slave trade.

8. J. Vansina, 1966b, pp. 27–52; A. de Calonne-Beaufaict, 1921, pp. 135–49; E. de Dampierre, 1968, p. 156.
9. L. Bouquiaux and L. Hyman, 1980.

PLATE 18.1 *Head in volcanic tuff, Uele, of unknown date*

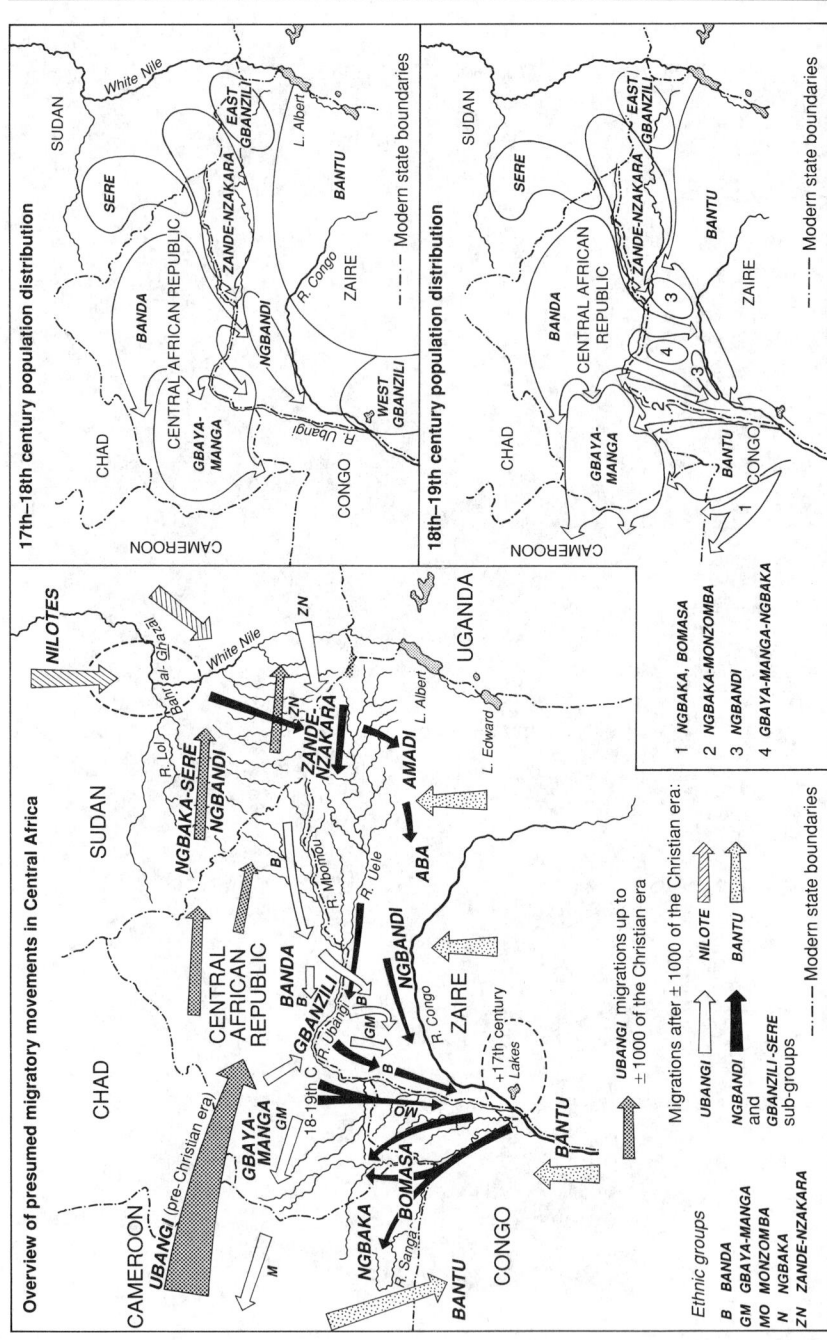

FIG 18.1 *Population migrations in the Uele–Ubangi regions*

This synthesis is attractive, although it calls for two basic reservations. First, it seems difficult to speak of migrations as this word means movements by large numbers of people. In the best-known cases, those of the Zande and the Mangbetu, the processes at work had more to do with politics than with demography since the invaders were élites, remarkably well-organized technologically and politically, and content to regroup the local populations into chiefdoms and kingdoms. However, it would be false to suggest that the states and ethnic groups, whose history in the nineteenth century is known, had always existed. But all the traditions, particularly the genealogies of the major clans, show that it was only during the seventeenth century that 'conglomerations of peoples' (E. de Dampierre) came into being as a result of the various waves of migration: the Nzakara, speaking a Zande-related language, the Ngbandi-speaking Baza and the Zande-speaking Mbomu. At the same time, a few clans began to stand out: the Vou–Kpata among the Nzakara, the Bandia among the Bangbandi (sing. Mongbandi), the Bakunde and the Vungara among the Mbomu. Later developments, probably dating to the eighteenth century, enabled two clans, the Vungara and the Bandia, to assert their dominance at the expense of the others. The Vungara, initially settled on the River Shinko, one of the tributaries of the River Mbomu, obtained recognition as the sole chiefs of the Mbomu by eliminating the Bakunde. They then embarked on a long migration eastward and southward which was to last until the late 1800s and during which they were to conquer, reduce, assimilate or make allies of the most diverse populations. It was above all their skill in politically organizing these populations that cemented Zande society which then appeared, more so than today, 'an extraordinary puzzle of uprooted clans and lineages' (E. de Dampierre) linked by their common allegiance to the ruling Vungara aristocracy. As for the Bandia, their starting-point was the upper Ubangi above the confluence of the Mbomu and the Uele rivers. The high point of their expansion came during the eighteenth century thanks to Ngubenge who carried through the conquest of Nzakara country and helped to drive the Vungara eastward.[10]

Little is known of the material civilization of these peoples; the quite considerable information available for the nineteenth century can only be projected back to earlier centuries with the greatest caution.[11] It seems likely, however, that the conquering aristocracies had long and effectively engaged in hunting. Among the Zande, hunting remained a highly valued activity: they learned their farming skills from the conquered populations and, whatever interest Zande princes may have had in agriculture, work in the fields remained the preserve of women, clients and slaves. Iron-working was held in high esteem and among some groups, such as the Ngbandi, smiths were grouped in strictly closed professional associations. The major

10. E. de Dampierre, 1968, pp. 156–73; E. E. Evans-Pritchard, 1971, pp. 267–78 and 414–35.

11. In addition to the authors cited above, see also P. Denis, 1961, pp. 7–20.

river network formed by the Ubangi, the Uele, the Mbomu, the Aruwimi and their numerous tributaries was the basis for a busy trade. Regular markets were held every five to seven days with craft products (iron knives and spears), foodstuffs and animals (fish, goats and dogs) together with slaves, being the main items traded. This trade grew rapidly as the trade carried on by Europeans on the Atlantic coast penetrated inland.

The coastal societies and the Atlantic trade

The period from 1500 to 1800 also saw the establishment and large-scale development of the coastal trade, soon to be reduced to the slave trade. The coastal fringe, which experienced all sorts of upheavals precipitated by this new trade, was only the last link of a long trading chain into the interior. By 1800 this chain reached the upper Mungo, the grasslands of Cameroon and the upper Ogoze and, through the River Congo (Zaire), the River Ubangi.

Peoples

The state in 1500 of the populations and societies in the coastal zone remains obscure and continues to fuel controversies among specialists. Just south of the original home of the Bantu-speaking peoples and half way between the two centres of Guinean Coast and Kongo where state systems flourished, this region probably underwent a complex evolution in its settlement and its political, social and cultural organization, whose major stages remain obscure. The traditions concerning origins and migrations tell little: the precise migration routes of the Duala populations and their kin can only be traced from the Sanga valley; and for the Mpongwe of Gabon, the Mitsogo and the Okande, the only identified starting-point is the upper Ivindo. The writings of European navigators and traders add little more. Written by men whose main concerns were the usefulness and profitability of the countries they were visiting, these texts name places, describe resources and indicate modes of settlement but say nothing of the identity of the human groups. But they do show that the whole region was occupied, even if they do not tell by whom. Thus, according to *Esmeraldo de Situ Orbis*, written by Pacheco Pereira in about 1505, 'all the sea coast, from (the) Serra de Fernam do Poo to Cabo de Lopo Goncalves, is densely populated. ... This country is very near the Equator, which the Ancients declared to be uninhabitable, but experience has shown that it is not so'.[12] The *Report of the Kingdom of Congo and the surrounding countries*, published in Rome in 1591, confirms this ancient settlement: 'The island of St. Thomas trades with the people of the mainland, who frequent the mouths of the rivers'.[13]

12. D. P. Pereira, 1937.
13. F. de Pigafetta, 1591.

Who were these people? For the coast itself, two additional types of source are available. Travellers' reports and, particularly, O. Dapper's *Description de l'Afrique* ..., which contains a list of the numbers used by the peoples on the coast, make it possible to assert that in about 1660 they were definitely Bantu-speaking.[14] These same written sources make it possible to date the reigns of several rulers named in oral traditions. Thus the height of the reign of Mulobe, the third historical king of the Duala, can be put at about 1650. This precise dating makes it possible to date to the sixteenth century the exploits of his grandfather Mbedi, and to beyond the sixteenth century those of the legendary Mbongo, to whom the Duala and related peoples refer.[15]

While it is thus possible to accept a Bantu peopling of the coast by the beginning of the sixteenth century, one is still reduced to conjecture for the neighbouring regions of the interior. Thus, for the Minlaaba region and Beti country, six levels of populations have been established with no chronological data, the oldest of which was the Pygmies, followed by hunter-gatherers, such as the Ola, then various Bantu groups such as the Maka, Muumbo, Beti and Basa, whose migrations continued into the nineteenth century.[16] Further south, in modern Gabon, the picture is clearer. At the end of the fifteenth century, the Portuguese found Mpongwe populations in the estuary region. These had reached the coast at an unknown date and had found Pygmies there. Around the Mpongwe, the Akele and Seke were possibly already living. The lands along the lower Ogowe (Cape López and Fernán-Vaz) did not yet have any Bantu populations, whose establishment in the region occurred after the development of trade with the Europeans. The peoples there were probably predominantly Negrillo. The only organized state was in the Gabon estuary. According to the later description by Dapper in the seventeenth century, the king bore the title of *Mani Pongo*: the word *mani*, of Kongo origin, may indicate the direct or indirect influence of the political model of the kingdom of Kongo, unless European traders, familiar with Kongo, used it to refer to this monarchy simply as a matter of convenience.[17] In the far south, the Kingdom of Loango was well established by about 1500, since all the voyagers' accounts of the early sixteenth century refer to the Mani Loango and Mbanza Loango by name. The only uncertainties, which are difficult to resolve, concern its foundation and extent. Some traditions make Loango a state derived from the Kingdom of Kongo – whose founder is said to have been related to the first king of Loango – but according to other traditions, the foundation of the Kingdom of Loango resulted from processes internal to Vili society. It is possible that Loango may have main-

14. O. Dapper, 1668.
15. E. Ardener, 1956 and 1968; M. Mdoumbe-Moulongo, 1968; H. Ngoa, 1969.
16. P. Laburthe-Tolra, 1977, pp. 77–413.
17. J. A. Avaro, 1981, pp. 23–30 and 39–59; E. M'Bokolo, 1981, pp. 11–28; K. D. Patterson, 1975, pp. 1–25.

PLATE 18.2   *Front and side views of a Kuba royal statuette, seated in front of a mascara board*

tained close, perhaps vassalage, relations with Kongo until the late fifteenth century. Loango made its influence felt intermittently as far as Cape Sainte-Catherine and, perhaps, Cape López. As in many states in Central Africa, the king's main functions were ritual ones. The institution of royalty, founded by a family of smiths, was linked to the fire cult. During the coronation ceremony, each *Maloango* lit the *ntufia* (sacred fire) which was to burn until his death and torches lit from this fire were ceremoniously transported to the provincial capitals and thence to the lineage homes. Another important ritual concerned rain, for which the king was responsible. Each year, at the beginning of the rainy season, a great festival was held in the capital. The people, after thanking the king for his protection, would implore him to make rain and at the end of the festivities, the king, standing on this throne, would shoot an arrow into the sky and, reports a witness, 'there is great rejoicing on that day, because sometimes they would have rain'. The most striking feature of this society was certainly its complex economy. A dynamic food-crop agriculture blended with diversified craft production which included the making of palmcloth for clothing and use as currency; the working of ivory, copper and redwood; and salt-making. These products were sold on the local markets, notably the one in Buali, the capital, and also reached markets outside the kingdom. A trading network, based on the alliance between the Vili chiefs of Loango and those of the neighbouring peoples, made it possible to reach the Gabon estuary, Kunyi country and Malebo Pool, dominated by the Teke.[18] The Atlantic trade thus did not create trade in this region: it merely gave a new intensity and a new dimension to an already well-established trading system.

The Atlantic trade

The local history of the Atlantic trade in this part of Africa is still little known. The account books of European traders, many of which have not survived, are often fragmentary. In the seventeenth and eighteenth centuries many descriptions of Central Africa give as original and certain information which was second- or even third-hand. But some facts have been established.

At first Portugal had a monopoly of the trade and the navigators Fernão do Po and Lope Gonçalves reached respectively the island of Formosa and the Gabon in 1472 and 1473. Trade only began to increase after 1500 when the Portuguese settled on the island of São Tomé which needed slaves for its own sugar-cane plantations while also serving as an entrepôt for cargoes destined for the Americas. The islands of Príncipe and Annobón, uninhabited when the Portuguese settled there, were also peopled by slaves drawn from the neighbouring coasts. The trade seems to have been small-scale. At the end of the sixteenth century, slave revolts, the most important of which took place on São Tomé in 1574 and 1586, ruined Portuguese trade in the region. The Dutch arrived after 1598 and developed the new trading centres of Douala, at the mouth of the Wouri in the Gabon estuary, and Cape López, and also eliminated the Portuguese from Loango. A new stage was reached in about 1660 when the slave trade underwent a massive expansion which continued until about 1850. France and Great Britain became the main trading powers in the region, but the activity of the Portuguese, Dutch and Danes succeeded in maintaining a competitive situation, which caused regular increases in the price of slaves and the number of points of sale on the coast.

The exact size of this trade which varied from point to point along the coast, is hard to quantify. The position of these lands, at the bottom of the

18. P. M. Martin, 1972, pp. 1–32; R. Gray and D. Birmingham, 1970, pp. 141–6.

Gulf of Guinea, constituted some hindrance to the development of the trade there. The slaving vessels often followed the 'small route', which obliged them to stop at the various slaving stations along the Atlantic coast, from Senegambia to Calabar, before reaching Cameroon, the Gabon and Loango which were thus visited at the end of the journey when the boats had already placed much of their cargo. The other route, the 'great route', allowed boats to avoid these intermediate stops and, taking the best advantage of winds and sea currents, to arrive directly south of Cape López and begin trading at Loango or in the neighbouring ports. Slaving captains also preferred slaves from Loango and farther south, 'the flower of the slave trade, soft and quiet, used to servitude ... always satisfied with their lot', unlike those from the Gabon or Cameroon who reputedly had a low tolerance for the physical effects and constraints of slavery.[19]

There were thus the following variations. On the Cameroon coast trade entered its busiest phase in about 1750[20] with the Wouri estuary and, more precisely, Douala, its main centres. It was mostly Dutch ships that came there, although between 1732 and 1759, of the 153 trading expeditions organized by the Middelburgsche Commercie Company to Africa, only 10 percent were destined for the Cameroon.[21] The number of Dutch ships belonging to other companies and the number of English ships remain unknown, however, and there is every indication that many came to the region. Douala was supplied from the north and north-east; there is no evidence of any trading relations at this period with the south. To the north, the River Mungo gave access to the grasslands where, from about 1750, the Chamba wars supplied numerous slaves, and to the north-east, the River Wouri led to Nun–Mbam country. As yet any estimate of the numbers involved in this trade would be risky.

This uncertainty has led some historians to play down the export of slaves in favour of other products, particularly ivory, of which the Dutch took large quantities in the eighteenth century. On the River Gabon, the main trading centre was the estuary region: Cape López only began to take an active part in the Atlantic trade in the reign of Reombi-Mpolo (*c.* 1790–1810). Here again, despite the sparsity of figures, the slave trade was quite extensive, to judge from the seriousness of the conflict between the Portuguese and the Dutch over possession of the Gabon at the beginning of the eighteenth century and from the number of ships sent to this region by the French port of Honfleur. In addition to slaves, there were large quantities of ivory, wax and sandalwood supplied by the Kele and Fang hunters and gatherers of the neighbouring region. The slaves came from the middle Ogowe which also supplied Cape López. The Loango trade is the best known. Its trade in slaves lasted a short time compared to that of the Slave Coast or Angola. It began on a large scale about 1670 but by

19. L. Degrandpré, 1801, cited by E. M'Bokolo, 1981, p. 17.
20. E. Ardener, 1968; J. Bouchard, 1952, pp. 79–104.
21. R. A. Austen and K. Jacobs, 1974, p. 7.

1780 was almost over. Until the mid-1600s Loango supplied mainly ivory, dyewoods and palm-cloth. The latter was widely sought after in Central Africa as a currency and two or three Portuguese ships from Luanda would come each year to take on board 6–7000 pieces of cloth which the Portuguese used to pay their soldiers. The number of slaves exported by the Loango coast (Loango, Malemba, Cabinda) – a hundred a year in about 1639 – rose to 12 500 a year in the period 1762–78 and to 13–14 000 annually between 1780 and 1790.[22] Slaving captains' account books have left valuable indications of the ethnic origins of slaves bought by Europeans at Loango. The Vili of Loango are hardly mentioned among those destined for external markets. Three groups predominated: the Mayombe, the immediate neighbours of the Vili; the Monteques (Teke from Malebo Pool); and the Quibangues (Bubangi and 'river people' from the Congo and Ubangi rivers). This last name shows that, at its peak, the Atlantic trade had reached the heart of the continent. About 1780, Loango lost its importance to Apomande on Cape López and Malemba and Cabinda, the respective ports of two small states, Kakongo and Ngoyo, formerly vassals of the Maloango.

Complex dynamics

Over such a small region, an analysis of the effects of this system of intense and prolonged trade must be conducted with rigour and care. One long-established trend in research stresses the destructive effects of the Atlantic trade.[23] The demographic losses resulting from the exports of slaves but also from the wars to capture them and the diseases imported from Europe and the Americas, take on a crucial importance in this perspective. Walter Rodney, using the example of Loango, highlighted the technological stagnation brought about by the massive imports of European and American goods and the ruin of local metal-working and textile industries.[24] Another more recent trend in research tends to play down the measurable losses suffered by African societies. Thus, for Philip Curtin, the effects of the 'three transatlantic migrations' (the export of slaves from Africa to the Americas and, in the opposite direction, the spread of previously unknown diseases and new food plants) may perhaps have balanced each other out.[25] The debate remains open. We shall limit ourselves here to stressing, in relation to these exchanges, the dynamisms of all sorts, the long-term changes affecting social organization, political structures, peopling and mentalities.

One of the most important changes was the introduction of food crops from the Americas: maize, cassava, groundnuts, beans and tobacco.[26] From

22. R. Gray and D. Birmingham, 1970, p. 149.
23. R. F. D. Rinchon, 1929; W. Rodney, 1972.
24. W. Rodney, 1972, pp. 103–23.
25. P. D. Curtin, 1969, pp. 270–1.
26. J. Vansina, 1979.

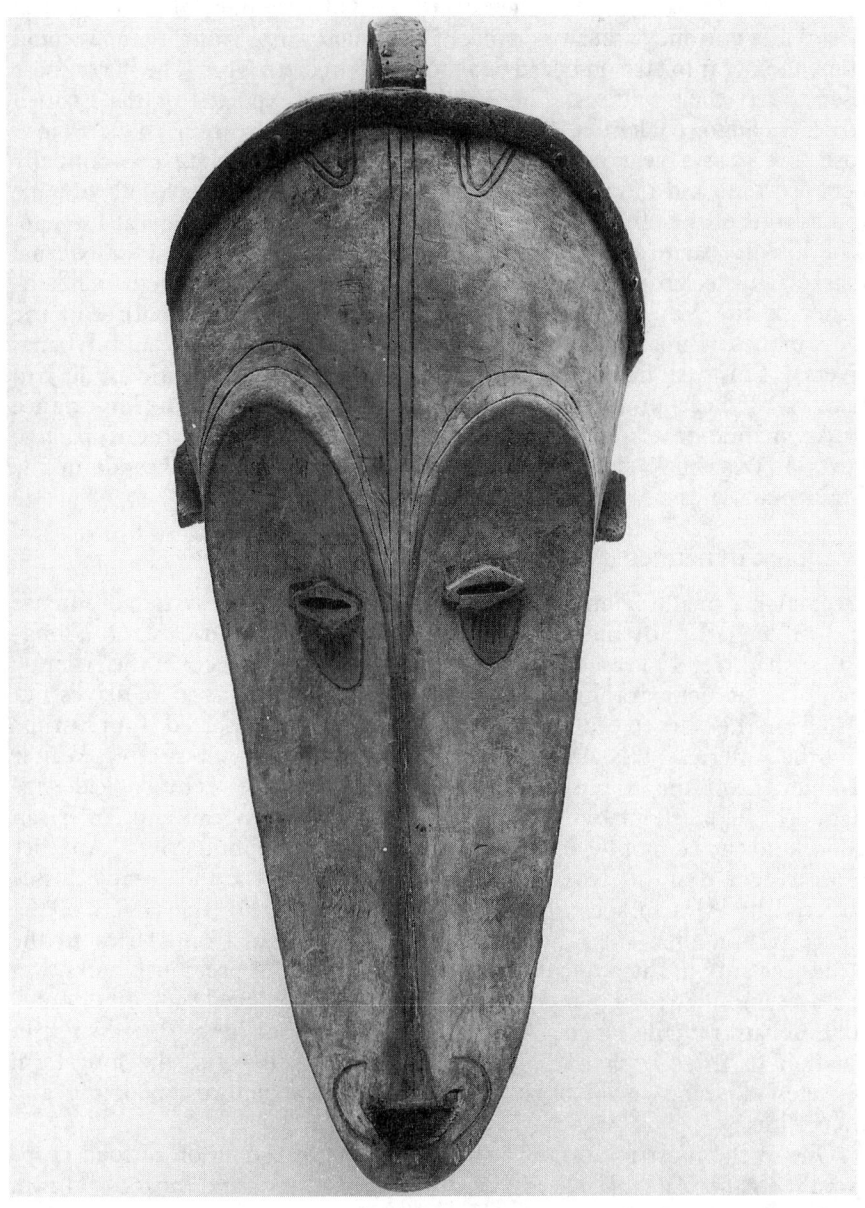

PLATE 18.3 *Fang mask worn by a member of the Ngil society, an association of men organized on the basis of specific initiations, whose members maintain order in the community and protect it from evil spells. Height: 70 cm*

530

about 1600, it took two and a half centuries for these crops to replace, and sometimes eliminate, the old plants, bananas, sorghum, millet and yams. The diffusion of these crops did not take place only in the coastal region: they moved rapidly inland, sometimes along trade routes, sometimes independently of them. Cassava had the most success. Mentioned on the coast of Loango in 1608, it was already being cultivated in Teke country at the end of the seventeenth century. This success was due to several factors. Its yield was distinctly higher than that of yams. It also offered great protection against the vagaries of the climate and social disorders since its root could remain in the soil unspoiled for up to two years. It was a plant with many uses: its leaves could be eaten, while the root lent itself to several techniques of processing and conserving, one of which gave a well-known bread (*chikwange* among the Kongo) which would keep for up to six months. During the eighteenth century, cassava spread throughout the Congo basin following the course of the River Congo (Zaire) and its many tributaries. Doubtless more slowly and less spectacularly, maize, whose presence on the coast is recorded before 1600, replaced sorghum. The other crops were gradually incorporated into the various systems of crop rotation. The scale and speed of these changes were such that it has been described by J. Vansina as a veritable 'agricultural revolution'. They testify to a great capacity for technological innovation among the peasant communities of Central Africa. But it remains difficult to interpret their effects. Did they, as has often been stressed, contribute through a more secure and more diversified food supply, to a greater physical resistance among the populations and a higher rate of population growth? Nothing could be less certain. The nutritional value of cassava is limited and, at least in the nineteenth century, serious signs of malnutrition were reported among the peoples who used it most, the Tio and the Mbosi. More generally, the extensive clearing of land required by these crops may perhaps have facilitated the spread of mosquitoes, malaria and yellow fever. Socially, this agricultural revolution contributed, along with the trade itself, to the establishment of a new division of labour. Numerous agricultural tasks, such as land clearing, cultivation and preparation of crops were gradually abandoned by men – who preferred to devote themselves to trade, which was more lucrative – and entrusted to women and slaves. The development of domestic slavery and other forms of dependence was a direct consequence of these agricultural changes.

In the regions nearest the coast, in direct touch with overseas trade, the transformations were highly complex. In the seventeenth and eighteenth centuries the peopling stabilized and a process of redistribution began which was to be completed in the nineteenth century. These population movements were particularly complex in Cameroon and Gabon. The seventeenth century saw the occupation of the Gabon estuary by new Mpongwe clans; and the eighteenth century saw the arrival of the Orungu

531

at Cape López and the Nkomi at Fernán-Vaz.[27] The slow spread of the Fang began in the eighteenth century from somewhere on the right bank of the Sanga near the sea.[28] As regards political structures, the coastal trade had contradictory effects.[29] In only one case, among the Orungu of Cape López, did it lead to the formation of a strong, centralized state, whose royal clan – Abolia or Alombe – held the exclusive monopoly over trade with the Europeans. The formation or strengthening of this state occurred quite late, when the slave trade was at its height, in the reign of Reombi-Mpolo (c.1790–1810). Elsewhere on the coast the opposite mechanism was at work – a breakdown of centres of authority and a splintering of political power. In this case, organization of trade, on the African side, was not a state monopoly: competition benefited a few individuals, princes, commoners and even some ex-slaves who formed a new aristocracy jealous of its privileges and keen to secure political power. In Douala, rivalry crystallized between the Bela family ('King Bell') and the Ngando family ('King Akwa') and ended in a final break in the nineteenth century. On the River Gabon, the right bank was controlled by the two branches of the Aguekaza clan and the left bank by the Assiga and Agoulamba clans. At Loango it was the new men – brokers, traders, caravan leaders and other middlemen – who came out best as they had the means to purchase land from the king and build up an entourage of many free or servile dependants. At the end of the eighteenth century there is mention of commoners with 700 dependants who were making war or cultivating land on their own account. The Maloango was reduced to selling high state offices to these *nouveaux riches*. It is quite certain that in Douala, on the River Gabon or at Loango the condition of the ordinary people was deteriorating. Significantly, the old vocabulary of these societies is rich in terms describing countless forms of dependence and different degrees of servitude. Collective mentalities also underwent major modifications although, in this area still neglected by research, one must not jump to conclusions. Thus the eighteenth century saw the appearance or the development of new magical practices and new conceptions of sickness centred on the individual instead of on the family group, with the main aim being to ensure protection against attacks from all sides.[30] This development is no doubt related to a greater degree of insecurity, as the case of Loango shows very clearly. In the traditional kingdom anybody could appeal to royal justice; he had merely to go to the capital along special roads, *Nzila zi Nzambi* (God's paths) or *Nzila Ivanga Nzambi* (God-created paths), which ensured him total immunity. In the eighteenth century, however, numerous traditions testify to examples of flagrant violation of this immunity.

27. H. Bucher, 1977, pp. 149–70; J.A. Avaro, 1981, pp. 97–146 and 175–93.

28. P. Alexandre and J. Bynet, 1958, pp. 13–17; P. Laburthe-Tolra, 1977, pp. 410–11.

29. J. A. Avaro, 1981, pp. 143–6; J. R. Brutsch, 1950, pp. 213–16; P. M. Martin, 1972, pp. 158–74; E. M'Bokolo, 1981, pp. 19–28.

30. J. M. Janzen, 1979 and E. M'Bokolo, 1983.

PLATE 18.4   *Ngunie-style mask from Gabon. Worn by a dancer on stilts, it represents the spirit of a pretty young woman who has returned to earth to take part in funeral celebrations as a member of the community of the living even after her death. Height: 26 cm*

The Congo river axis and large-scale Congolese trade

Describing the River Congo (Zaire) as a 'starting-line', the geographer Gilles Sautter has strikingly emphasized the role of the majestic Central African river:

> The Congo is not only, by virtue of its channels and its widely scattered islands, a world unto itself that juxtaposes the (neighbouring) areas. It also represents for these latter a factor of co-ordination and regional integration. Its influence is at once direct, as a regulating waterway, and indirect, as a great navigable highway open to human initiatives.[31]

Until colonization the river acted as a powerful factor bringing together the various peoples of the vast Congo basin. This role did not only involve the river itself, along its navigable portion above Malebo Pool: it also involved its many tributaries, particularly the Alima, the Likwala, the Sanga, and the Ubangi on the right bank and the Kwa, the Ruka, the Ikelemba and the Lulonga on the left bank. Since early times, a remarkable trading network had been organized, ever-growing in size and complexity and moulding most of the riverine human societies along the river and its tributaries.

An ancient exchange economy

There is much evidence of this antiquity. Given that traditions rarely go back more than fifteen generations, it obviously remains difficult to reconstruct the chronological stages and the precise lines of the settlement of this region. It is, however, possible – with the help of linguistics, archaeology and traditions – to distinguish two main movements. The first and oldest is a large-scale movement that brought these Bantu-speaking peoples into this region from their original home. This movement seems to have been in a north-west to south-east direction. Most of these peoples belong, in Guthrie's classification, to Zone C. Today, some languages still show very strong similarities to certain Nigero–Cameroonian languages: as, for example, does Bobangi to Tunen and Jawara.[32] This fact suggests a direct migration from the Nigero–Cameroonian homeland towards their present location following the waterways, particularly the Sanga, which form the most convenient routes in this marshy and heavily forested area. At the end of the fifteenth century and the beginning of the sixteenth, Portuguese writings mention several peoples, notably the Bolia, the Boma

31. G. Sautter, 1966, p. 231.
32. J. H. Greenberg, 1963, pp. 35–8; J. D. Fage and R. A. Oliver, 1970, pp. 131–40.

and the Tio, in their present locations.[33] Besides this first movement, there were also smaller-scale movements which probably occurred later and were in an east–west direction and which gradually led to the stabilization and separating-out of some groups. Thus, in the 'land of the rivers', drained by the Likwala-Massaka and its tributaries, all the peoples place their origin to the east, on the other side of the river.[34]

These latter movements no doubt helped to create the conditions for or to broaden the bases for an exchange economy by distributing the population over complementary ecological zones including waterfronts, floodlands, and even dry lands. Agricultural activities and fishing went on simultaneously during the dry season, which was also the period of low water in the rivers and their tributaries. People thus had to make a choice, the river people opting for fishing, whose harvest was traditionally highly valued and which they could easily trade for foodstuffs or goods produced by local industries.

Archaeology fortunately bears out these assertions. In the first place it is striking that all the known layers of Zairean–Congolese archaeology are to be found around Malebo Pool, thus bearing witness to a highly unusual degree of continuity in both the density of settlement and the variety of human activities. Two sites are particularly revealing on the subject of trade. In the first, at Kingabwa near Kinshasa, on the right bank of Malebo Pool, several types of pottery have been uncovered, one of which, with very fine decoration, has been found at other minor sites in the Kinshasa region and along the river, as far as Lake Mai-Ndombe. This pottery, dated 1450 to 1650, is the best evidence of very old commercial relations along the Congo (Zaire) and its tributaries. At the other site, at Mafamba, near the confluence of the Kwa and the Congo, many clay pipes of various styles have been discovered. Most have not been used, which suggests that Mafamba was a production centre or an entrepôt redistributing the pipes in the region.

Pottery and pipes were not the only goods traded. Two products seem to have dominated the long-distance trade: camwood, for cosmetic purposes, and copper mined from the deposits on the lower Congo. The low trade value and the high transport costs limited to local trade, within a certain radius, products whose raw materials were easy to find and whose technology was relatively simple, such as salt, cloth, mats and baskets.[35] This trade was already flourishing before the fifteenth century and was to be given a great boost by the development of trade on the Atlantic coast.

33. J. Vansina, 1965, pp. 78, 80, 81 and 1973b, pp. 439–46; G. Sautter, 1966, p. 363.
34. G. Sautter, 1966, pp. 212, 243–7.
35. P. de Maret, F. van Noten and D. Cahen, 1977; pp. 495, 497–8; R. Harms, 1981, pp. 20–3.

The grafting of the Atlantic trade and its consequences

This took place in several stages.[36] In the first, from the late fifteenth century to about 1560, the Kingdom of Kongo played the leading role. Documents of Portuguese origin dating from 1529 indicate that the Malebo-Pool region was one of the main suppliers of slaves, through the routes linking it to Mbanza Kongo (San Salvador) and Mpinda. In the mid-sixteenth century, the Anzikos (Tio, Pool Teke) made up large contingents of the slave population of Peru, Colombia and Brazil. At this time these slaves were traded along with quantities of ivory, palm-cloth and redwood: in the opposite direction, the Pool began to receive *nzimbu* (shells used as currency in the Kingdom of Kongo), beads and European cloth and alcohol. The second stage, 1560–1750, witnessed a decline in Kongo's trade, although it did not lead to a consequential decline in the externally-oriented trade of the Pool and its offshoots. The reason was that while Kongo was suffering from the growing competition of Angola and internal problems caused particularly by the Jaga, these same Jaga established themselves in the areas between the Pool and the coast, controlling the Kingdom of Bungu, the Kongo province of Nsundi and the copper mines at Mindouli. Consequently, the decline of the routes linking the Pool to the coast through Kongo was largely compensated for by the new dynamism of the Pool–Loango axis. During the third stage, from 1750 to about 1850, the basin of the Congo and its tributaries became the principal supplier of slaves for the Americas with a dense network of caravan routes linking it to a long chain of ports on both sides of its mouth, Loango, Cabinda, Boma, Ambrizette, Ambriz and Luanda.

Throughout these three stages, Malebo Pool – the point where loads were divided up between the land paths and tracks round the unnavigable Congo rapids and the waterways higher up – was also the meeting-point between long-distance Congolese trade and the Atlantic trade. The latter's galvanizing effect on the regional economy was based on mechanisms that are easy to understand. The export trade involved high-value goods and this made long-distance transport on the Congo and its tributaries profitable. Trade in locally used goods, therefore, even if transported over long distances, also became profitable, and this in turn stimulated regional specialization. Large-scale trade was thus not a simple superimposition, but involved the complex articulation of one trade system oriented towards the outside world and another towards the satisfaction of regional needs. Each, however, was based on specific products, rules and structures.

The geographical area encompassed by these various levels of trade grew continuously from about 1500. By about 1690, Malebo Pool was in permanent trading relations with the lower Kasai and the lands around the River Alima. A century later, the River Ubangi was fully integrated into this commercial space as were all the rivers in between, together with their

36. R. Harms, 1981, pp. 24–8.

PLATE 18.5   *Kuba statuette in wrought iron, c. 1515. Height: 18.7 cm*

tributaries, the Alima, Likwala and Sanga on the right bank and the Lulonga, Ruka, Mfimi, Lake Mai-Ndombe, Kasai and Kwango on the left bank. The only uncertainty relates to the depth of commercial penetration along these various waterways. Only in the nineteenth century does the trade frontier appear to reach the confluence of the Ubangi and the Uele rivers.

PLATE 18.6   *Kuba anvil. Height: 28 cm*

Numerous markets existed along these waterways, particularly at the confluences, and archaeology should be able to provide a complete count of them. The largest were naturally at the biggest junction, Malebo Pool, where there were four markets by the eighteenth century and perhaps earlier: Ntamo and Kinshasa on the left bank and Mpila and Mfwa on the right bank. Nineteenth-century observers estimated that each of these four markets had 3000 to 5000 permanent inhabitants to whom must be added people passing through, who were especially numerous during the trading season. This was during the dry season, from April or May to September, with business heavily concentrated in August. During the rainy season, business slowed but merchandise destined for the overseas market continued to be exported and the small markets above the Pool remained open.

In the absence of statistics, it is difficult to estimate the exact volume of trade but a few indications are available. In the nineteenth century, the typical canoe – whose dimensions seem not to have changed since the middle of the previous century – was fifteen metres long by eighty to ninety centimetres wide, and could carry one-and-a-half to three tonnes of merchandise. The average capacity of a paddler was about sixty-five to ninety kilograms transported over about eighty kilometres a day downstream or fifty kilometres upstream. In the nineteenth century, when the slave trade had disappeared, it was estimated that at least a tonne of merchandise passed through the Pool daily, and up to forty tonnes during the height of the trading season.[37]

The trading system directed towards the outside world rested essentially on two items – slaves and ivory. Slaves, trade in whom really boomed after 1750, came mainly from four regions: the Lulonga basin; the lands around the River Alima; Boma country between the confluence of the Congo and the Kwa and Lake Mai-Ndombe; and the Ubangi basin. The slave trade in the Lulonga valley, for example, shows the extreme complexity of this trade. Around the main market, Basankusu, there were numerous villages where the slaves cultivated the fields until they could be sold. Some of the slaves sold followed the course of the river to be exported; others went up the River Ubangi to be sold to the Loi in exchange for ivory destined for the markets at the Pool and on the Atlantic coast.[38] The slaves, therefore – the main export item – also had their local uses. This had come about through the changes in agriculture already discussed, but also through trade requirements and the changes in social and political structures. Thus the riverine peoples along the Kwa would buy from the Boma the slaves who were used to carry their goods to the Pool and *vice versa*.

Among the Tio, domestic slavery was so developed that the word *mboma* (man of the Boma ethnic group) came to mean a stupid person or anyone in a lowly occupation. With the development of the slave trade, the number of mechanisms of enslavement grew. Among the Bobangi, the main trading people in the Congo basin, a distinction was made between a *montonge* (captured slave) and a *montamba* (slave sold by his kin) which indicates how far social values had been overturned by the slave trade. Throughout

37. J. Vansina, 1977, pp. 255–8.
38. R. Harms, 1981, pp. 30–1.

the region this trade was seen as luxurious because it benefited only a tiny minority of lineage and village heads and Bobangi middlemen, and shameful because during trade negotiations not the word 'slave' but the euphemism 'dog' was used.

The second export item, ivory, appears in sixteenth-century Portuguese texts as one of the most profitable lines. Ivory had long been used locally for bracelets and hair-pins but compared to copper, also used for jewellery and decoration, its trade value in the region seems to have remained low.

There were numerous herds of elephants in the forest zone, especially in the Sanga basin and in the valleys of the Lulonga and its two tributaries, the Lopori and the Maringa. The Pygmies almost monopolized elephant-hunting but the network of rights over slaughtered animals was so complex that the hunters themselves made little profit. Among the Likuba the chiefs had to be given both tusks, leaving the hunter with only the meat; among the Tio and Mbosi the chiefs claimed the ground tusk; in addition, among the Tio, the remainder of the ivory was divided into three parts, one each for the hunter, land chief and political chief. Until the late 1700s ivory took the same routes and went through the same hands as the slaves who, by value, provided the bulk of the trade. The relationship between the two items of trade was only reversed after 1830. The range of goods received in exchange from the coast, at first limited to salt, *nzimbu* (shells) from Luanda, cloth and beads, was widened in the mid-1600s by the introduction of metal objects, particularly knives, and mirrors. The eighteenth century saw a dramatic increase in muskets and gunpowder, copper and tin products, and alcoholic beverages.

How these items circulated in the Congo basin is poorly understood. It seems that the very organization of trade – the variation in the value of goods from place to place and according to different tastes – prevented an equal distribution. Until about 1750 there was a segmented trade with each ethnic group controlling a portion of the river or its tributaries. This system facilitated the monopolization of certain highly valued goods, such as mirrors and porcelain. The speed of circulation of these goods has also been the subject of speculation since Stanley estimated, in about 1880, that it took an average of five years for a European article to move from the coast to the Ubangi.

The trade in locally used goods covered the same area, perhaps slightly larger, as that in export goods. Thus the lands around the upper Ogoze produced iron objects that reached the river region through Kukuya and Tio middlemen. Individuals or groups often engaged in both trades at once. Among the Kasai and its tributaries, from the eighteenth century onwards, the Nunu and the Ntomba were producing pottery, salt and sugar-cane alcohol for the Congo river market, and also ivory and gum destined for the coast. Similarly, the Bobangi, the principal middlemen in the region, also produced various goods mainly handicrafts for the local markets.

This local trade involved two main sorts of goods. Foodstuffs had the advantage of an enormous market because, from the eighteenth century, the high and ever-rising level of external demand led many villages to specialize in trade. This was the case particularly round the Pool, in the Alima, Likwala-Massaka and Sanga valleys and in the trading centres in the forest zone that no longer managed to feed themselves. Cassava, cultivated and processed by women, was one of the most sought-after items. The oil-palm provided various useful commodities: oil for domestic use, profits from the sale of which were divided among the owner of the tree, the man who had climbed it to cut the stem and the woman who had extracted the oil from it; and palm wine, produced exclusively by men. Salt was another vitally important item, whether rock salt from Mbosi country or vegetable salt produced mostly by riverine peoples along the waterways. These peoples supplied many species of fish according to well-developed techniques. Finally, there were tobacco and local alcohols.

Handicrafts also contributed to trade. This was the work of specialists: amongst agriculturalists, the women farmed leaving handicrafts a male preserve; among fishing communities, however, catching fish was the men's job, which left women free to make handicrafts. The most sought-after products were: mats, a speciality of the land people not the river people; red camwood powder, produced by women; palm-cloth, for which the Tio were famous; iron implements; pottery, made in most villages but using different techniques and decorations, which stimulated trade; and finally, canoes of all sizes, the larger ones for trade measuring up to twenty metres long or more, while the small three-metre ones were used for short-distance journeys between fishing villages.[39]

There were thus considerable differences between the two types of trade. The export trade was based on an economy of destruction – the extraction of men and hunting – and was little concerned with the replacement of the riches on which it depended: it profited only a tiny minority. The trade in local goods was based on an economy of production, which grew uninterruptedly over the centuries and which contributed either to the maintenance or to the improvement of village technologies: its beneficiaries were the ordinary people, men and women, each according to how much he or she produced.

Diverse societies

This internal trade, which lasted for a very long time, promoted the progressive unification of the various peoples of the Congo basin, despite the obstacles that encouraged variety. Among these was the way trade was organized. It was a segmented trade and remained so until the mid-nineteenth century. The river and its tributaries were divided into spheres

39. G. Sautter, 1966, pp. 272–8; J. Vansina, 1977, pp. 276–81; R. Harms, 1981, pp. 51–69.

of influence each of which was controlled by one ethnic group – for
example, the Sakata and the Nunu on the Rivers Kwa and Mfimi, the

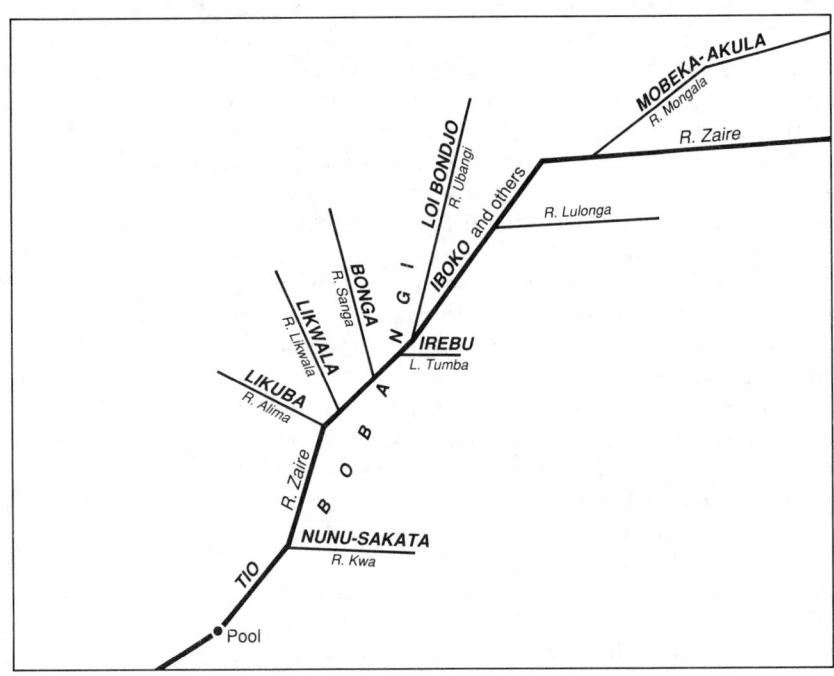

FIG 18.2   *Peoples and spheres of influence along the Congo–Zaire axis*
Source: adapted from R. Harms, *River of Wealth, River of Sorrow. The Central Zaire Basin in the Era of the Slave
and Ivory Trade, 1500–1891*, 1981, New Haven and London: YUP, p. 76 © Yale University Press

Likuba on the River Alima, and the Loi on the lower Ubangi. It was only
during the eighteenth century that the Bobangi began to control all the
Congo–Ubangi axis. Mistrust had long ruled relations among the various
partners and pillaging was not uncommon. To protect themselves from it,
trading expeditions were large involving ten big canoes or more each with
between thirty and sixty paddlers. Conflicts of interest often led to full-
scale wars such as that between the two groups most involved in the trade,
the Bobangi and the Tio, who only reached a lasting agreement in the early
1800s. Among the many factors making for unification, most important
were the trading techniques themselves. Thus, from the eighteenth century,
the whole region began to adopt the same currencies for transactions –
palm-cloth, *nzimbu*, cowries and copper rods – which seem to have been
in competition locally with currencies of more limited usage. In the same
way, the widespread practice of credit created long chains of solidarity
throughout the trading area. The profitable conduct of trade also led to
strategies of extended alliances through marriage and, above all, blood
brotherhoods that created numerous obligations between partners (pro-

542

tection and lodging, financial help in case of debt, military assistance, moral and financial help at bereavements). The river trade thus brought different peoples into contact, spread the same customs and beliefs and facilitated the rise of hegemony of Bobangi, an excellent trade language. This shared civilization, the formation of which speeded up in the eighteenth century, reached its apogee between 1850 and 1880.

This growing unity went hand in hand with a degree of diversity, linked partly to the variety of ways in which peoples became involved in and adapted themselves to large-scale Congolese trade.

For not all engaged in trade. Where water was plentiful, fishing, one of the oldest activities of the Bantu peoples of the Congo basin, remained the basic activity of many groups. Fishing societies were characterized first by their high geographical mobility, which was determined by variations in the water level and the regular movements of fishing banks. Depending on the season, men would live in fixed villages or in fishing camps built during low water and abandoned as the level of the river rose. Socially and politically there was a distinct lack of congruence between political and economic units. The basic political unit was still the village: the chief's authority, essentially ritual and religious, operated solely within this limited framework. Many aspects of village life, however, escaped his control, particularly the endless comings and goings of fishermen between village and fishing camps and the activities of short-lived fishing teams. The basic economic unit was a loosely structured fishing team based on the initiative of a renowned fisherman and including some of his kin and other volunteers. In this way, the family cells on which the villages were based were dislocated to meet the requirements of fishing. While this system encouraged some individualism, it also guaranteed that each family received foodstuffs regularly as one fishing kinsman or another would always have fish to send home.[40]

Many societies in the Congo basin which were integrated into the exchange economy also profited from the new economic situation to develop their productive activities. This economic particularism no doubt partly explains the survival of the original political structures of the numerous Mongo groups whose history remains little understood.[41]

Those who specialized in trading activities evolved differently as shown by the contrasting evolution of the Bobangi and the Tio. The details of the Bobangi's long migration from the middle or lower Ubangi to Malebo Pool are hard to reconstruct. According to the earliest colonial administrators, writing in about 1885, the Bobangi had been settled on the River Congo for only three or four generations, that is, since the beginning of the nineteenth century. But other European sources mention numerous Quibangue slaves on the coast in the eighteenth century and Fra Luca da Caltanisetta's *Diaire Congolais 1690–1701* notes the arrival of unidentified

40. R. Harms, 1981, pp. 111–25.
41. G. Van der Kerken, 1944; G. Hulstaert, 1972.

immigrants at the Pool during the seventeenth century.[42] What is certain is that what was originally a society of fishermen rapidly switched to trade, which became the sole foundation of all social life. Henceforth, there was complete convergence between the political and the economic unit. Bobangi society was based on trading firms belonging to wealthy traders. These were not built on kinship ties as each trader preferred to acquire dependants – women and slaves – over whom his authority would be greater than over kin, and exclusive. It was an open society, with much social mobility: anyone active and successful in trade could acquire wealth which was the means to increase dependants, to power and to lay claim to political titles, the highest of which, *mokondzi* (chief), strengthened its holder's position at the head of his firm, facilitated the making of alliances throughout the region and brought him into the councils responsible for settling the various problems arising from trade.

The Tio had the unique good fortune of living at the biggest crossroads and main break-of-bulk point in the Congolese trading network. Trade had not apparently upset the political structures of the kingdom. Despite a feeling of common origin and cultural identity, it was widely decentralized. The underlying structure consisted of relatively autonomous chiefdoms. The chief had major ritual prerogatives but limited political powers; he could not forbid the settlement of newcomers on his territory or oppose the final departure of his discontented subjects in the event of serious dissent. The same situation occurred at the next level. The *ôkoo* (deformed by the Europeans into *makoko* but meaning king) had above all a spiritual role. Temporal power belonged to a few high notables such as the *ngaailiino*, responsible for collecting tribute and heading the administration, and the *muidzu*, the country's chief justice. Unlike the chiefship, the dignity of *ôkoo* was not hereditary: the king was elected from among the leading chiefs in the kingdom by his peers, meeting in a college of eleven electors chaired by the *ngaailiino*. This old structure retained its essential features until the advent of colonization. It was at the social level that the most lasting changes occurred. There was first an increasing dissociation between the riverine peoples, who monopolized trading activities, and the Tio in the interior, who specialized in agricultural production (cassava and tobacco) for the river market. This intensive agricultural work required ever more manpower and led to the increasing accumulation of women and slaves. Among the riverine peoples, those who profited most from trade were the chiefs, especially those at the Pool who exploited to the maximum their exclusive right to sell men and ivory. Conversely, the chiefs and titleholders established away from the Pool, such as the king who resided at Mbe more than one hundred kilometres to the north, participated only fitfully in trade by sending their dependants there. They held political power but their economic power was less than that of the riverine peoples.

These Bobangi and Tio trading economies did not become capitalist.

42. G. Sautter, 1966, pp. 243–5; P. M. Martin, 1972, p. 124.

Large profits were made but these could not be invested in the productive sector. It was impossible to buy land or a labour force, except in the form of slaves. Money, accepted in some dealings, was not a universal equivalent which could purchase all goods. It was accumulated in various forms and lent out, but generally without interest. Some goods and some social and religious services, such as fines and dowry payments, never came within the money economy.

The picture thus drawn of the peoples and societies of Central Africa clearly demonstrates their diversity as well as their aptitude for innovation, even in constraining situations. It also shows, through the gaps in knowledge, the directions in which researchers should urgently move, both in large-scale research with large means, directed principally towards collecting new materials through archaeology and oral traditions, and in detailed theoretical modelling in the study of social structures, cultural evolution and the history of mentalities.

The Kongo kingdom and its neighbours

J. VANSINA

based on a contribution by
T. OBENGA

The western part of Central Africa, to the south of the equatorial forests, is inhabited by peoples who speak dialects of the Kongo language and of other closely related languages.[1] This unity is strengthened by a profound cultural unity. This enthnolinguistic group occupies a territory stretching from southern Gabon to the Benguela plateau and from the Atlantic Ocean to well beyond the River Kwango. To the north-east this complex has always bordered upon a Teke area centred on the Bateke plateaux and, to the south, on the Ovimbundu area of the Benguela plateau.

The history of this region is well documented from 1500 onwards. The number of contemporary pages written on the period 1500–1800 is estimated at over half a million: more than for any other area of comparable size on the continent.

Over the past hundred years, texts and guidebooks have been published in many editions,[2] and a historiographical school has been developing since the seventeenth century.[3] Naturally this chapter can be no more than an introduction in which even recent bibliography must be kept selective.

The movement of history in these areas in the sixteenth and seventeenth centuries was very different from that of later times. Territories of great size were organized by man, using political structures, to form states. After about 1665, however, these territories were reorganized on an even greater scale, the states becoming far less important. The organizing principle now derived from the imperatives of an economic structure which was the product of an intensive slave trade. In our approach to the early centuries, therefore, we shall give priority to the history of the kingdoms; and then,

---

1. M. A. Bryan, 1959, pp. 56–62; T. Obenga, 1969 and 1970.
2. Summary of sources: A. Brasio, 1952–71; T. Filesi and E. de Villapadierna, 1978; L. Jadin, 1961 and 1975; and the works of A. de A. Felner, L. M. Jordão, J. Cuvelier and F. Bontinck. Bibliographies in W. G. L. Randles, 1968; J. K. Thornton, 1983b. Among the authors of the past: G. Cavazzi, 1687; O. de Cadornega, 1681 (1940); O. Dapper, 1668; L. Degranpré, 1801; F. de Pigafetta, 1591; A. Proyart, 1776; and E. Da Silva Correa, 1782? (1937) are the most important.
3. J. K. Thornton, 1983b, pp. xvii–xx, for recent historiography.

when the dynamics of trade have brought the kingdoms low, trade shall be the focus of attention.

The potential of these regions is determined by the relief and the rainfall. Where the dry season is short, the fertile ground is in the valleys. The dry season however varies in duration from two to six months depending on the latitude and the distance from the coast, which is drier. The generally mountainous nature of the terrain explains why a population in search of better habitats was unevenly distributed, with inhabited areas the size of small districts or provincial centres alternating with deserts. The region best favoured by this diversity of habitats lay to the north of the Zaire/Congo river, from the coast to the area called Mayombe. Here, too, there were worthwhile mineral deposits (copper, lead and iron ore). This was where the two largest states of the coast, the Kingdoms of Kongo and Loango, came into being.

Since − 400 at least farmers speaking western Bantu languages had been settled to the north and south of the lower Zaire, where they produced yams, vegetables and palm kernels. From the second to the fifth century, this population was augmented by the arrival from the east of people speaking eastern Bantu languages. These people grew grain and, where the tsetse fly allowed – especially in Angola – kept herds of cattle. Before they arrived, by + 100 or earlier, iron-working had reached the region. Lastly, perhaps during the sixth century, banana-growing was introduced to round out the production pattern.[4]

Thereafter the socio-political organizations became more complex, and chiefdoms formed between the ocean and the Zaire river upstream from Pool. It was in the well-endowed area north of the lower river, in the region called Mayombe, that the regional division of labour developed furthest. By about 1500 the coastal dwellers were supplying salt and fish and had transformed the coastal plain of Loango, towards the estuary of the Zaire, into a vast palm-grove producing palm-oil. The estuary-dwellers were potters. Inland, copper and lead were produced from Mboko Songho to Mindouli, and iron in the Manyanga (Nsundi) area. Further north, near the edges of the great forest, raffia palm was cultivated and large quantities of fabric produced. Lastly, in the same area and further into the forest, forest products such as red dyewood were exchanged for products of the savannah. This was the birthplace of the Kongo civilization. The Teke civilization developed on the plateaux, but on the basis of contributions from groups living on the forest fringe and in the neighbourhood of the Kongo groups, and of contributions – at least of political ideas – from the Middle Zaire/Congo. The Teke kingdom, mentioned in literature from 1507 onwards, was perhaps the oldest of all: at least during the seventeenth century it was reputed to be so.[5]

The Kongo kingdom began in the Vungu chiefdom north of the Zaire

4. J. Vansina, 1984b.
5. O. Dapper, 1668, p. 219 (German translation, 1670).

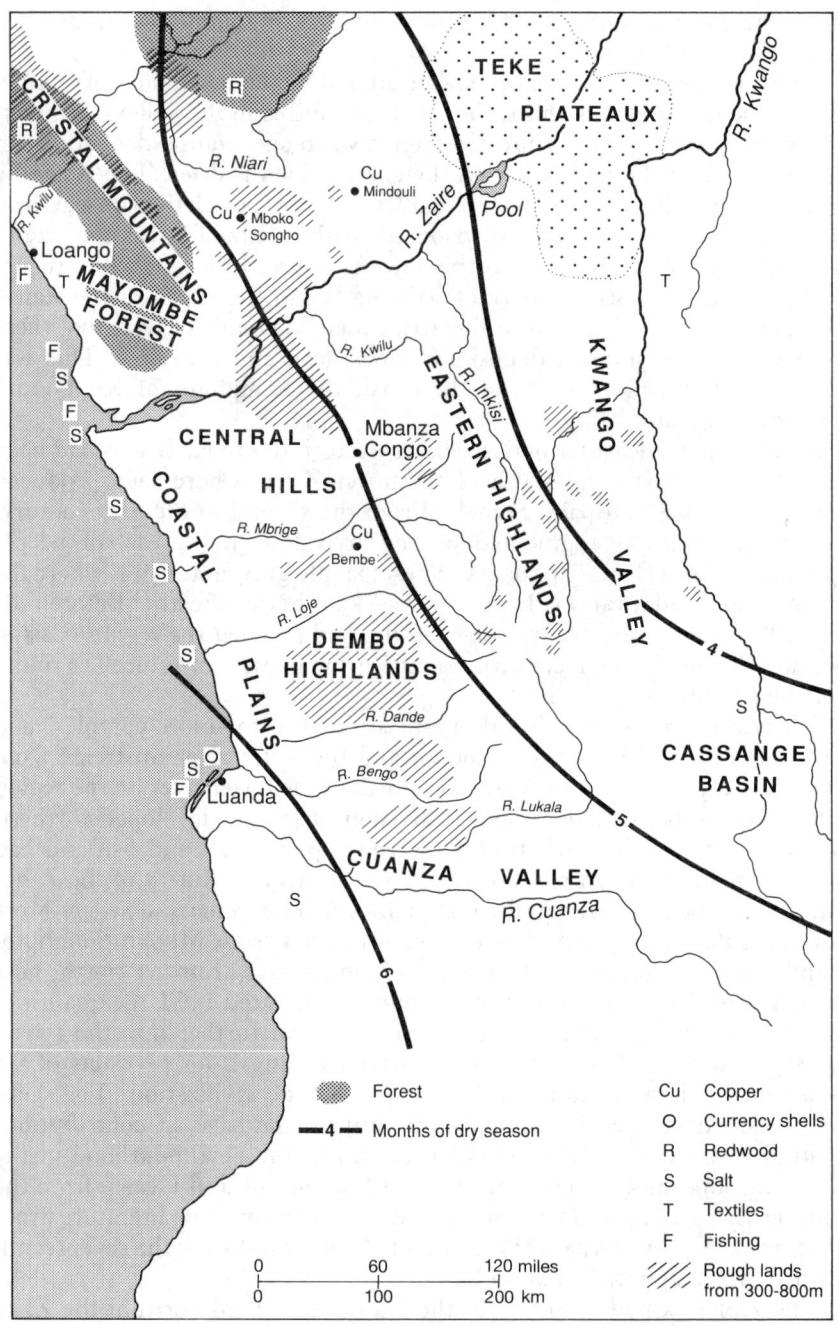

FIG. 19.1 *Topography and natural resources of Kongo (after J. Vansina)*

PLATE 19.1 *Yombe pottery. Height: 37.5 cm*

river.[6] At the time, chiefdoms and even small kingdoms and clusters of chiefdoms, covered the lands of the lower river to both north and south. Nimi Lukeni, the founder of the Kingdom of Kongo, founded the town of Mbanza Kongo where San Salvador now stands. His kingdom was constituted partly by alliance with the local chief, the *Kabunga*, and with a king further east who ruled the Mbata in the Inkisi valley, and partly by the conquest of other lands towards the sea and the lower Inkisi valley. The date of the kingdom's creation is unknown. Some writers emphasize the length of a process whose beginning, reasoning by analogy, they place in the ninth century.[7] Others limit themselves to dating the founding of this kingdom, placing it around 1400 at the latest, and at least a century before that at the earliest.[8]

Scholars generally agree, despite the absence of any evidence in firm

6. J. Vansina, 1963.
7. For the reasoning, see M. M. Dufeil, 1980, 1981.
8. W. G. L. Randles, 1968, p. 18.

549

support, that the Tio kingdom was probably founded earlier. The Kingdom of Loango, which developed not far from Vungu to the north of the river, is thought by some scholars to have reached its zenith in the sixteenth century, whereas others, arguing from the fact that it did not attract the attention of metropolitan Portugal before 1576, contend that it was not by then highly developed or very old. To the south of Kongo, the State of Ndongo, whose king bore the title *ngola* – a title deformed to Angola – was taking shape about 1500. In contrast with Kongo and Loango, which were coalitions of large provinces, Ndongo represented a merger of many small chiefdoms and thus marked the culmination of a trend towards a form of state organization far less deep-rooted than that in Kongo or Loango. Moreover around 1520 it was still partly dependent on Kongo, as were the Dembo chiefdoms which separated it from Kongo proper.

A hegemony: Kongo

In the fifteenth and sixteenth centuries a single state, Kongo, held sway over the entire region between the Benguela plateau and the Bateke plateaux and from the sea to beyond the River Kwango. Around 1500 the borders of the state proper followed the bank of the River Zaire from its mouth upstream to above the confluence with the Inkisi, in places – at Manyanga for example – extending northward beyond the river. It included the Inkisi basin and all the lands to the south as far as the Loje. It was expanding southwards and perhaps towards the River Kwango. It influenced, and sometimes levied tribute on, all political entities except the Tio kingdom. The kingdom proper had a large population, although we have only very rough estimates to guide us. Most authors accept the figure of two million, although one speaks of four or even eight million, whereas another scouts the idea of more than half a million.[9] The areas in Kongo's sphere of influence at least equalled the kingdom in population. The population of the Tio kingdom must have been very sparse except around Pool.

In view of the crucial role played by Kongo in the historical evolution of the region, we here propose a table of organization for it. Its structural base was divided between a large town, the capital Mbanza Kongo, and the countryside. Three well-defined social strata co-existed: the nobility, the villagers and the slaves, who differed in legal status, occupation and life-style. The language expressed this difference by a terminology which opposed the concepts of 'civilization' and 'politeness', associated with urban life, to that of 'rusticity', associated with the countryside. The same word meant both 'slave' and 'war captive', thus indicating the source of slaves.[10]

9. J. K. Thornton, 1977a; W. G. L. Randles, 1968, pp. 146–8.

10. J. K. Thornton, 1983b, pp. 17, 21–2; J. Van Wing and C. Penders, 1928: *kifuka* (urbanity); *kifuka kia ntinu* (court of the king); *uvata* (rusticity); *vata* (to cultivate); *evata* (village). This dictionary, which dates from 1650–2, was probably compiled by Roboredo, a canon and cousin of the king. It remains one of the main sources for the studying of mentalities.

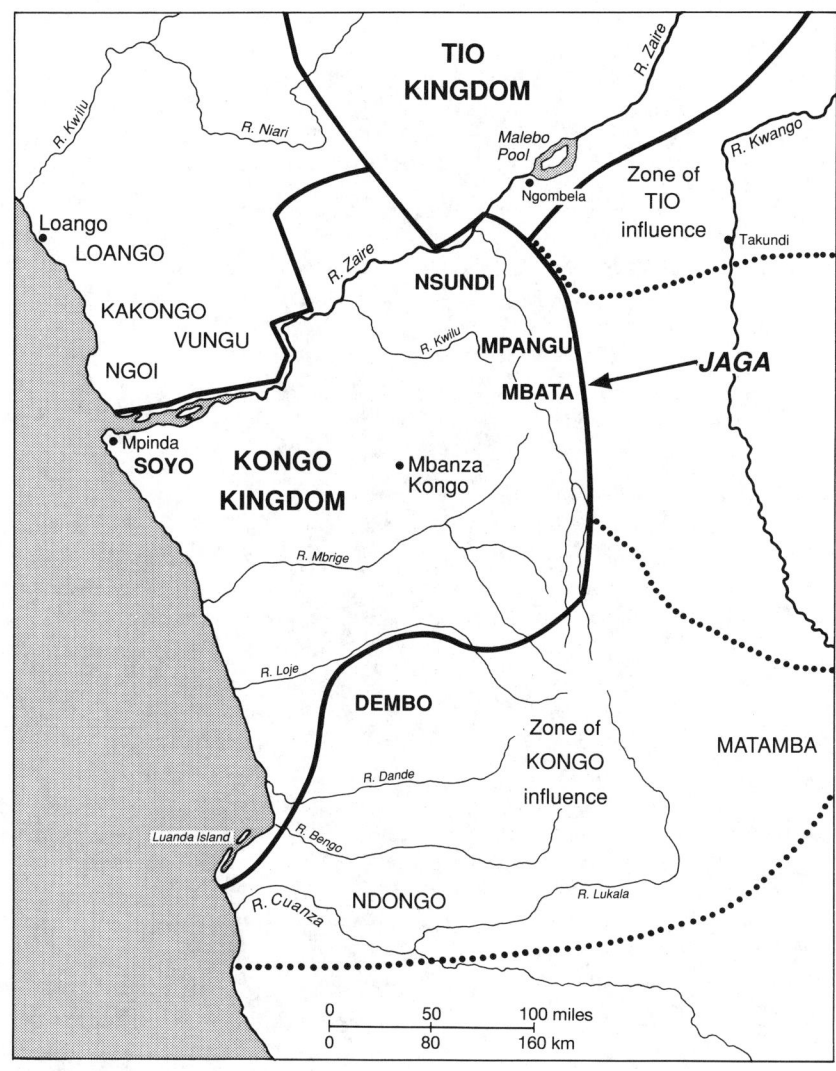

FIG. 19.2 *Kongo and its neighbours in the sixteenth century (after J. Vansina)*

The nobility formed the structural framework of the kingdom, and the town its hub. The nobles lived in town except when required to serve as provincial governors. The upper nobility was composed of relatives of the king or one of his predecessors. It was made up of bilateral houses interconnected by marriage and by the fact that individuals belonged to more than one house simultaneously. In relation to the villages, the nobility formed a bloc. Matrilineality determined access to the land, residence and

BANSA ofte te Stadt SALVADOR
Hooft-flat van het Rijk
CONGO.
BANSA ou S.SALVADOR Capitale de CONGO.

A. *Palcis des Kominge.*
B. *Slaven, en Slavrani, die uit de*
Stadt brengen.
C. *Kerken.*
D. *Kerggre-rolling of Stecklie.*
E. *Spring-bron, met zeer*
zoet water.

A. *Palais du Roy*
B. *Esclaves qui vont puiser de l'eau*
dans la rivieres
C. *Eglises*
D. *Conduite*
E. *Source d'eau douce*

The River Lelunda

DE RIEVIERE LELUNDA.

PLATE 10.2 *San Salvador, the capital of Kongo, on the site of Mbanza Kongo*

succession to the headship of the village.[11] Social cohesion was much weaker between villages than in the noble bloc. Here the king appointed his close relatives to key posts in, for example, provincial government, high public office and/or the central tax system. Royalty was elective; the royal council was made up of twelve members including four women who, according to A. Hilton, represented the clans of the king's grandparents.[12] This institution notwithstanding, struggles for succession were commonplace. After a struggle between the lords of the north and those of the capital and south, Nzinga Mbemba, otherwise known as Afonso I, succeeded his father Nzinga Nkuwu in 1506.[13]

The kings, much given to polygamy, had many children, and their houses quickly reached huge proportions. After a reign of twenty-five years Afonso had 300 grandsons and great-grandsons,[14] and no doubt as many nephews and great-nephews. The king's principal wife had to be a daughter or sister of the governor of Mbata, a province where government was hereditary in the female line of the Nsaku Lau. The reigning prince of Mbata, in his turn, married a close relative of the king. A branch of his kin, the Nsaku Vunda, provided the kingdom's supreme religious dignitary, the *Mani* (lord) Kabunga of Mbanza Kongo, who was in charge of the cult of the territorial spirit of the capital area. The two Nsaku lords enthroned the king. There is a clear trace here of how the kingdom came to be constituted.

Kongo, governed by a network of the king's relatives, was nonetheless highly centralized. The king appointed the territorial governors except the governor of Mbata and, after 1491, the governor of Soyo where the port of the Kingdom of Mpinda was situated. He dismissed governors and other officials as he saw fit. The nobility had no hereditary functions and lived forgotten at Mbanza Kongo. At every generation its hierarchy was redefined in relation to the new kings. Another factor favouring centralization was the existence of a currency issued under the king's control. It consisted of shells of *Olivancilaria nana*, called *nzimbu*, which came from the fishing-grounds of the Island of Luanda, part of the kingdom. There was also military centralization. In the late sixteenth century the royal guard, composed of slaves, was 16 000 to 20 000 strong[15] and was the sole standing armed force of the kingdom. In time of war abroad, the peasants were called up in territorial units. Every noble house, centred around a great

---

11. A. Hilton, 1985, gives a number of indications; proof is given by J. Van Wing and C. Penders, 1928: *unguri* (relationship); *unguri ankama* (seigniory) – a title still in use among the southern Suku about 1900 – and *nguri* (mother). The prefix *u*- denotes an abstraction, and the expression translated 'seigniory' signifies that a territory was perceived as relationship on a large scale, *unguri* meaning 'the mother principle'.
12. A. Hilton, 1985, p. 194.
13. L. Jadin and M. Dicorato, 1974, pp. 54–64.
14. ibid., p. 181.
15. F. de Pigafetta, 1591, p. 120; A. Hilton, 1985, p. 196 (1595).

man, also had its people (dependants and slaves), and the royal house had in addition slaves sent by all the nobility.

PLATE 19.3   Nzimbu *vessel*

The ideology of royalty, called *nkisi*, derived from religious conceptions in general, in which three important cults played a role. These were ancestor worship, for which the holy place was the royal cemetery grove; the worship of territory spirits, the spirit of Mbanza Kongo being served by the *Mani Kabunga* (the name given to the clergy assigned to the spirits, from the village level to that of the kingdom); and the worship of royal charms. The *nkisi* concept was fundamental, and the Christians were to adopt the term, using it to mean 'that which is sacred'. The church was 'the house of the *nkisi*', the Bible 'the book of the *nkisi*', the priest the *nganga* of the *nkisi*,[16] *nganga* being the recognized term for a religious expert, especially in *nkisi*. Diseases and misfortunes were attributed to *ndaki* (sorcerers) whom *nganga ngombo* (diviners) were able to identify, sometimes by ordeal. The use of oracles, including the oracle of poison in the administration of justice, stemmed from this notion; so did the perpetual suspicion that the king was a sorcerer. Royalty was sacred. The king was addressed as *Nzambi mpungu* (Supreme Creator) and court etiquette and ceremonies expressed this sacredness, which was confirmed by the ceremony of investiture. By his *tumba* (blessing) the king expressed his protection of the royal officials and, in general, guaranteed fertility, principally through his control over the rainfall.[17] The king himself was, in a real and profound sense, the *nkisi* of the country.

Structures in the neighbouring kingdoms were different but the ideology was almost identical. These kingdoms were less centralized. In Loango the noble houses had not supplanted matrilineal groupings, and this class was much less cohesive than in Kongo.[18] Ndongo had no territorial structure above the petty chiefdom level, and the military system was intended to make good the deficiency.[19]

Afonso I's victory ushered in the longest reign in Kongo's history, from 1506 to 1543. The role played by this king was crucial. He opened up the country to Portugal, thus setting in train a vast economic and political reorganization and a deliberate assimilation of features of Christianity that was to prove permanent. On becoming king, this factional chief – a Christian since 1491 and protector of the rare missionaries before 1506 – rapidly made the Catholic Church the state religion under the direction, from 1518 to 1536, of his son Henrique, who was consecrated bishop in Rome. The bishopric was later to fall under the control of Portugal. The slave trade developed from 1514 onwards. The king first tried to control it, just as the sovereign of Portugal had tried to do, by establishing royal monopolies, and then, in 1526, to abolish it. This attempt failed, and even the royal monopolies were constantly breached by the Afro-Portuguese of São Tomé, by the kingdom's neighbours – both on the Loango coast and in Ndongo – and even in Luanda, which was an integral part of the kingdom. The king used his revenue from the slave trade, the ivory trade and the trade in raffia fabric to attract Portuguese technicians and, above all, missionaries. Before he died, social and political life had been transformed. The gulf between the nobility and the ordinary people had

16. F. Bontinck and D. Ndembe Nsasi, 1978: *nzo amuquissi* (269), *nganga* (269), *muquissi mucanda ua ucua* (268), *unganga* (271), *uquissi* ('holiness') (271); J. Van Wing and C. Penders, 1928: *mukisi* (evil-spell, witchcraft, crime of poisoning), but *ukisi* (holiness, divinity, divine will) and *kia nkisi* (holy, sacred).

17. O. Dapper, 1668, p. 583. For *tumba*, see personal communication from Mr. Obenga.

18. In general, see P. M. Martin, 1972, and O. Dapper, 1668, who give very long descriptions of Loango.

19. Its structure is described by B. Heintze, 1970 and 1977 (for the Kisama).

PLATE 19.4   *Kongo noblemen of the Kingdom of Loango wearing cat-hair aprons*

widened: the former had become literate, espoused Christianity and took part in the slave trade, while the ordinary people were harshly exploited.[20] The royal house had been strengthened by the importation of slaves from Pool and beyond for the royal guard, and by the proliferation of Afonso's descendants, to the point where the succession was affected. All the subsequent kings were descendants of Afonso through one or other of his three principal daughters. The ever-increasing number of claimants led to a scission of the royal house into enemy factions and, after 1665, to a civil war which destroyed the kingdom as it had been to that date. The presence of Portuguese in the town introduced a new political dimension. Connected by marriage to various noble houses, they were split up into Afro-Portuguese and people from the mother country, who led the opposing parties at court until 1665 and took part in all the struggles for succession.

Intercontinental trade, which had been very slight before 1506, developed after it started dealing in slaves. From 1515 until 1526, when it was placed on a regular footing, slavery was a disorderly business. From

20. L. Jadin and M. Dicorato, 1974, p. 179: 'Be careful also lest the great ones of your kingdom subject the common people to ill-treatment' (late 1529).

then onwards only foreigners – mainly from Pool and possibly from the Kwango valley – and criminals became slaves. The *mulatto* community in the capital was sending *pombeiros* (agents from *pombo*, the Kikongo name for Pool people) to Pool even before 1529. The previous origins of these slaves are still unknown. Many were Bateke, but some certainly came from other areas, whence they were shipped along the rivers to Pool. Exports totalled some 4000 to 5000 slaves yearly until about 1540, and 6000 to 7000 thereafter.[21] Imports from Pool must have been larger, for many slaves were recruited at Mbanza Kongo for service in the royal guard or for work in the food plantations which fed the capital, and other slaves were assigned to the port of Mpinda or to the retinue of provincial nobles. In addition to this supervised trade, a clandestine slave trade carried on by the inhabitants of São Tomé developed on the northern and southern borders of the kingdom, especially after 1526 when exports from the Kingdom of Benin came to an end. This trade remained on a small scale except in Luanda, where Ndongo's wars of expansion yielded many slaves.

Portugal took a keen interest in the mineral products of the country and wanted to control them. Throughout the sixteenth century the Portuguese believed that Kongo possessed hidden gold-mines, which they wanted to take over and work. The king of Kongo, however, was determined to keep the mining of Bembe copper and the working of Mbanza Kongo iron under tight control. Successive kings never allowed mineral prospecting and even restrained the exports of copper which, before 1506, had kindled the covetousness of the Portuguese. The Portuguese sovereign permitted no sale of ships to Kongo and opposed its attempts to lay on its own transport to São Tomé or Europe. The Portuguese kept control of trade and made it an unequal exchange. The Kongo court used the resulting revenues to pay Portuguese technicians and missionaries, and also to bear its share of the expenses of Kongolese nobles studying in Portugal. From the outset, however, a substantial part of the revenue was also absorbed by imports of fabrics, wine and luxury items which the king redistributed to his nobility. Such imports quickly became an ostentatious necessity for the nobility, and by the end of Afonso I's reign they absorbed the entire revenue.

Under Afonso I's successors the trends continued, despite the attempts made by Diogo I to limit the effects of the European incursion. Kongo's relative power diminished, especially in relation to Ndongo, which was gaining strength mainly through the clandestine traffic with São Tomé. In 1561 Kongo cut itself off from Portugal almost completely, but the successive deaths of two kings during a war with the Tio of Pool in 1566 and 1567 led to a disarray which, with the invasion of warriors called Jaga from the east, turned to catastrophe.

21. L. Jadin and M. Dicorato, 1974, p. 203 (1536); P. E. Lovejoy, 1983, pp. 37–8.

Three states: 1575–1640

The Jaga routed the royal forces, and the court had to take refuge on an island in the lower Zaire. Numerous refugees were sold as slaves by the Jaga to the people of São Tomé. The king had to appeal to Portugal, which sent expeditionary forces that reconquered the country between 1571 and 1573, although the troops were not withdrawn before 1575 or 1576. The hegemony of Kongo over the region was destroyed for the colony of Angola was founded in 1575 and the Portuguese, in large numbers, came to Loango to trade from that year onwards.

The identity of those who invaded Kongo has never been established.[22] The name Jaga (*Yaka* in Kikongo) is used in the sources as a synonym for barbarian and applied to a whole range of more or less nomadic warrior groups. The first Jaga appeared to the east of Mbata, or to the south of Pool, and from there to the River Kwango. The invasion must be associated with the Kongo–Tio wars, and probably with the complete cessation of the slave trade in 1561. It is thought that the ranks of the invaders were swollen by a great many villagers who were weary of being exploited by the nobility. Their aim was no doubt to secure a bigger share of the wealth generated by the slave trade and, once victorious, they were to be found selling slaves on the coast. There is no evidence, direct or indirect, to support the suggestion that a drought and subsequent famine drove the Jaga to invade Kongo.

Paulo Dias de Novaes, after a stay at the court of Ndongo, worked to such purpose that he obtained a contract for conquest and colonization from the Portuguese court. The colony was to be named Angola, from the title of the king of Ndongo. Dias arrived in 1575, founded Luanda in 1576 and began trading in slaves, endeavouring to supplant a community of Afro-Portuguese from São Tomé who were plying the trade in Luanda. The community yielded the market to him and moved to the *ngola*'s court. In 1579, however, pressure from the mother country forced Dias to perform his contract. When the king of Ndongo was told of this, he had all the Portuguese at his court massacred as a preventive measure, thus furnishing the pretext for a war which was to last for almost a century, until 1671. At first, the fortunes of war fluctuated, with local alliances divided between the adversaries. Nevertheless, the Portuguese did manage – with great difficulty – to erect a few fortifications inland. In 1612, however, the Portuguese entered into an alliance with some Mbangala (called Jaga). These were communities of nomadic warriors who had been in the region since before 1600 and who lived by pillage. With their aid, and especially that of the Jaga Kasanje, the Portuguese occupied a large part of the kingdom from 1617 to 1621; its king fled to the east of the country. The

22. The last article in a debate which brought together D. Birmingham, J. Vansina, J. C. Miller, J. K. Thornton, F. Bontinck and A. Hilton (1963–81!) was by A. Hilton, *The Jaga Reconsidered*, suggesting that they were the ancestors of the Yaka of the Kwango.

allies sacked the region and the country was laid waste. Even the slave trade had come to a standstill, and famine was rife.[23] A peace treaty was therefore drawn up in 1622 and 1623, the *ngola* being represented by his sister Nzinga Mbande, who was baptized and named Anna at Luanda. But Nzinga became the leader of an anti-Portuguese party; at the beginning of 1624 the king died (he may have been murdered or have committed suicide) and Nzinga became regent, then queen in 1626. Meanwhile the Jaga Kasanje was still occupying the best part of Ndongo. War accordingly broke out again in 1626 against Nzinga, but also against Kasanje, and the Portuguese tried to install a puppet king. In the course of operations, Kasanje found a base in the Kwango valley in 1626 and built the Imbangala state ther during the 1630s, while Nzinga conquered the Kingdom of Matamba, where she established a formidable base of opposition to the Portuguese regime.[24] When the Dutch occupied Luanda she was still campaigning, and she formed an alliance with them.

The colony of Angola, ruled by a governor appointed by Lisbon every three years, was divided into the town of Luanda and a few *presidios*. Luanda was governed by a city council in conjunction with the governor, while military captains administered the territories around their *presidios*. The administrative structure was feudal in the strict sense of the term, its legal basis being contracts of vassalage which linked the *soba* (petty chiefs) to the Portuguese court through their ties with the *amos* (Portuguese overlords) and later through the contract of vassalage with the governor and captains. The revenues of the state and of its representatives were derived from feudal tributes all of which, whether due in goods or in labour, were payable in slaves. This system was not replaced until the eighteenth century, with the introduction of a poll-tax and the reduction of the ties of vassalage to a legal instrument justifying the sovereign rights of Portugal.[25]

Meanwhile Kongo had recovered. Despite its loss of hegemony and the gradual changes taking place in the structure of the nobility, the kingdom remained sound and even spread eastwards. But territory was lost in the south, especially in 1622, with the loss of the fishing-grounds of the Island of Luanda and lands in Luanda town. A large Kongo army of provincial origin was defeated by the Angolans, allied to the Jaga, at Bumbe. But the war then came to a stop, halted mainly by general mobilization in Kongo. In addition Kongo successfully resisted other Portuguese attempts at control by forming a diplomatic alliance with the Vatican, by pitting Portugal against Spain, and even pitting both countries against the Netherlands. The most serious loss suffered was that of the maritime province of Soyo with the port of Mpinda. After 1636 this province became independent, although its prince retained the right to take part in the election

23. D. Birmingham, 1966, pp. 30–89.
24. B. Heintze, 1977; J. C. Miller, 1975a and 1976, pp. 151–264.
25. B. Heintze.

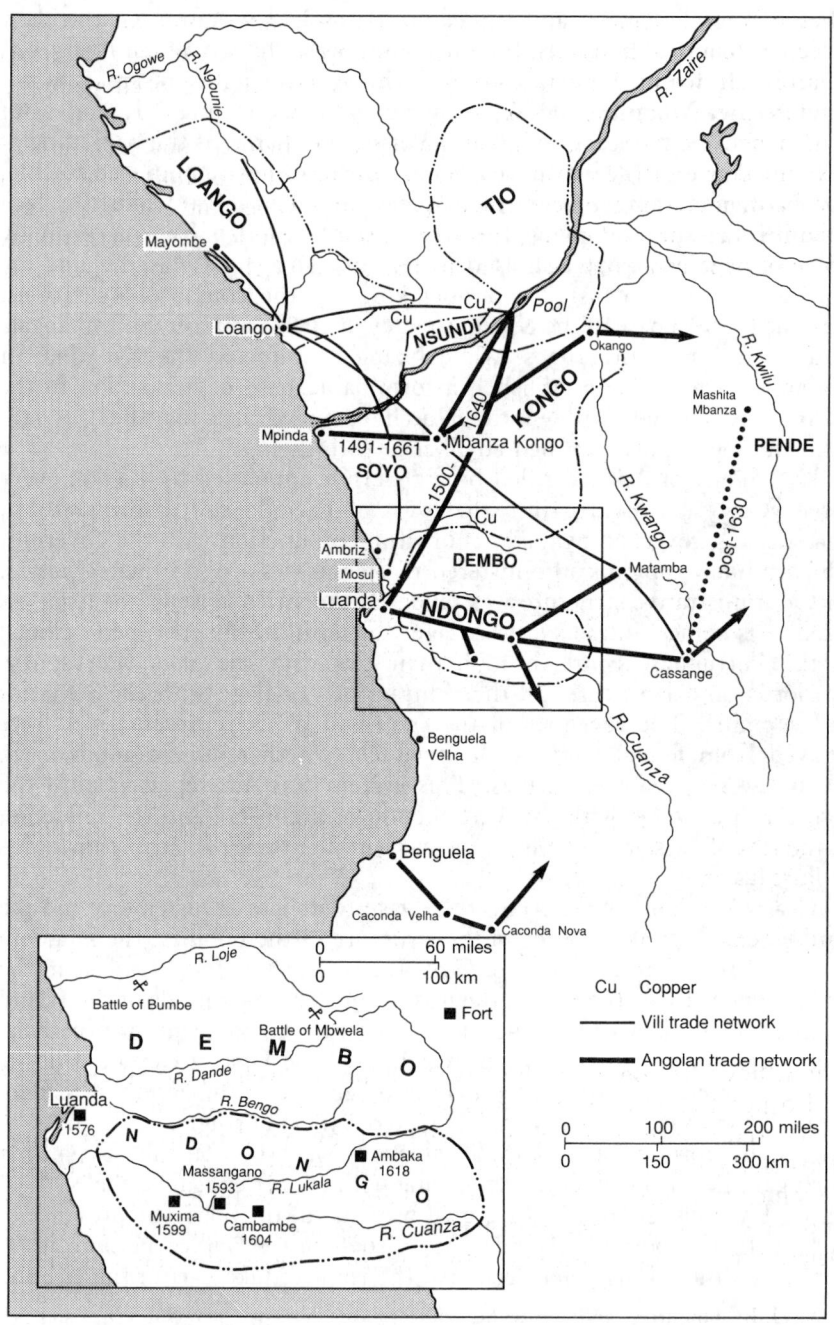

FIG. 19.3 *Kingdoms and trade of the Kongo region in the seventeenth century, with inset map of Ndongo (after J. Vansina)*

of the king of Kongo. The same year, the dominant noble house lost the election to a rival house; and the electors were so far weakened that in 1641 Garcia II, fortified by the support of his house, dispensed with their endorsement and took power.[26]

Loango had become a great power even before 1600. Its territory extended from the Fernán Vaz lagoon to the south of Pointe-Noire, and probably included the best part of the Ngunie valley and part of the Niari plain. Its cultural influence, spread by trade, extended even further afield. Traces of it can even be found to the north of the Gabon estuary. We

PLATE 19.5   *Court of the King of Loango, 1668*

know, however, almost nothing of its political development before 1700.[27]

Loango traded in ivory – produced by pygmies among others – and in hides, red dyewood and raffia fabrics, but exported relatively few slaves. This traffic was conducted with some Afro-Portuguese who carried on a very lucrative coasting trade between the coast of Benin, São Tomé, Loango and Luanda. Raffia fabrics from Loango became the currency in Angola, where they began competing with those from the east of the Kingdom of

26. J. K. Thornton, 1983b., p. xiii; J. Vansina, 1965, pp. 101–4, 107–9, 130–4 and 138–42.

27. P. M. Martin, 1972, pp. 1–32; D. Ngoie Ngalla, 1978 and 1982.

Kongo in 1600.[28] Moreover, from 1600 onwards the Dutch frequented Loango and Soyo. Loango, not being Catholic like Mpinda, afforded them a better trading base, and the king co-operated with them from the start.[29] Dutch ships had better goods to offer at lower prices. They bought copper and, above all, they had guns and gunpowder for sale. The upshot was that the traders on the Loango coast, the Vili, who organized the caravan traffic to the interior, extended their networks at an astonishing rate. By 1626 they were south of Dande,[30] and by about 1650 they were trading at Mbanza Kongo and even in Matamba and Kasanje. Their principal route led to Pool via the mineral deposits of Nsundi, where the Vili mined iron ore and possibly copper. Along the coast they advanced far into Gabon, as far as the confluence of the Ngunie and the Ogowe.

At this period the Vili network was in competition with the existing networks not only for the sale of ivory or fabrics but also for the slave trade. The Kongo and Angola network was disrupted by the founding of Luanda which, from the start, exported more slaves than Mpinda; the first exports varied between 12 000 and 13 000 slaves a year, mainly prisoners

PLATE 19.6 *The port of Luanda in the seventeenth century*

of war.[31] In 1625 the total number legally exported was 11 000. This figure decreased between 1618 and 1640 but never fell far below 10 000 a year. After the first few years, more and more slaves came from purchases made inland, either in Pool (without passing through Mbanza Kongo) or in the market of Ocanga on the River Kwango. From there a caravan route

28. P. M. Martin, 1972, pp. 33–52.
29. ibid., pp. 42–5.
30. B. Heintze; P. M. Martin, 1972, pp. 69–70.
31. B. Heintze.

crossed the Kwango, advancing in the direction of the Kwilu.[32] In the 1630s slaves from beyond the Kwango began arriving in Luanda from Matamba and Cassange, the capital of Kasanje.

These developments affected Kongo adversely, for its capital was no longer the mandatory repository for goods and slaves, although its slave trade continued, probably on a diminishing scale. Furthermore, its currency greatly depreciated, the Portuguese having imported other shells. By 1619, the *nzimbu* had lost two-thirds of its value – and the king two-thirds of his revenue.[33] The king, however, managed to redress the situation and the currency gradually regained its former value. The revenues of the king and the nobility must have, in fact, suffered far more from the diversion of trade to Luanda and Loango.

This period saw the introduction first of maize cultivation (between 1548 and 1583) and, soon after 1600, that of manioc, tobacco[34] and probably beans, groundnuts and other New World plants, apart from citrus fruits which were found on the coast before 1600. Pigs are mentioned from 1583 onwards,[35] and these were probably imported livestock. They were to spread mainly in Kongo and central Angola.

The crops from the New World transformed agriculture in the seventeenth century, especially after 1650, increasing yields and providing, through manioc, a diet better suited to occasional drought and war conditions. Manioc came to be associated with all the trade routes, for it was also used to feed slaves. Nutritional standards generally improved as a result of this. As early as 1560, however, reference is made to smallpox, an epidemic introduced from Europe which was to become a recurrent scourge.

The first half of the seventeenth century thus witnessed changes in nutrition and health conditions – and the introduction of the slave trade. All this inevitably set up new population trends of which the details are unknown. In Angola in particular, however, the population must have declined.[36]

---

32. With regard to Ocanga, L. Jadin and M. Dicorato, 1974, p. 175, note 9, believe that as early as 1529 the plural of *pumbo* referred to this market. Mentioned as a kingdom from 1584 onwards and then as the starting-point of a caravan route, Ocanga is mentioned regularly until about 1640. It is known that towards 1680 the market and the route to the Kwilu were abandoned by the traders. Kongo and various European influences probably followed this route as far as the Kuba country (J. Vansina, 1978, pp. 187–91). The well-known site of Mashita Mbanza was perhaps located on this route, not far from the Kwilu (Kodi Muzong, 1976, pp. 179–83).

33. J. Cuvelier and L. Jadin, 1954, pp. 306–12.

34. J. Vansina, 1978, pp. 11–13.

35. B. Heintze, 1977, p. 773; A. Brasio, 1952–71, Vol. 2, p. 510.

36. Even J. K. Thornton, 1981b, whose model seems to us over-optimistic (p. 685, one-quarter rather than one-third women among the slaves, and omission of young children), concludes on p. 713 that there was a decline in the eighteenth century.

Towards a new order: 1641–1700

In 1641 the Dutch captured Luanda and occupied a vast part of the colony of Angola before a fleet fitted out in Brazil drove them out in 1648.[37] From then on the Brazilians dominated Angola's trade, totally until 1730 and

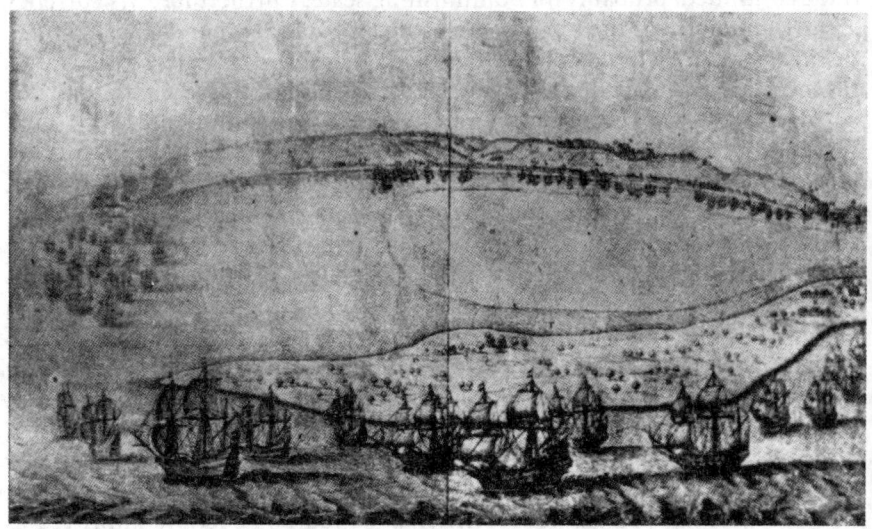

PLATE 19.7   *The bay and city of San Paulo of Luanda during the Dutch occupation in the 1640s*

partly thereafter. Also in 1641, Garcia II became king of Kongo and, like Nzinga, formed an alliance with the Dutch. The Restoration left them face-to-face with a great Portuguese army with which they had to come to terms. Kasanje, which had stayed out of the wars, signed a treaty of friendship and became an ally of Portugal for more than a century. Meanwhile, from 1645 onwards, large numbers of Italian Capuchin missionaries arrived in Kongo, and this helped Garcia II to come to terms with the Portuguese. The new missionary effort in Kongo and later in Angola was to bring in four hundred missionaries – almost all in the seventeenth century – and hasten the conversion to Christianity of many rural areas of Kongo even after the kingdom collapsed – for the disagreements over the treaty ultimately led the Angolans to invade Kongo. Antonio I of Kongo declared war, assembled all his nobles and was defeated in 1665 at the battle of Mbwila – indisputably the greatest battle of the century.[38] António perished in the battle together with many nobles. But a second Portuguese army was so disastrously beaten at Soyo in 1670 that Angola gave up its

37. C. R. Boxer, 1952; A. Da Silva Rego, 1948.
38. C. R. Boxer, 1960a; J. K. Thornton, 1983b, pp. 73–83.

PLATE 19.8 *Decorative tiled panel from the principal façade of the Church of Our Lady of Nazareth, Luanda, 1665*

PLATE 19.9 *Detail from the above, showing the head of King António I, who is buried in the church*

attempts to conquer Kongo. In 1671 the last vestige of Ndongo was conquered and by about 1680 peace had been imposed on Matamba (Nzinga), Kasanje and the chiefs to the south of central Cuanza. The conquest was complete.

The Kingdom of Kongo did not recover from Mbwila. The disputed royal succession rapidly led to a civil war between noble houses, which worsened and resulted in Mbanza Kongo being destroyed in 1666 and totally abandoned in 1678. Since the town was the pivot of the political system, everything collapsed. When a single king at last returned to Mbanza Kongo in 1709, his kingdom was no longer a centralized entity but a collection of principalities often still rent by internal struggles between claimants. Everything had fallen apart except Soyo, and even Soyo had the greatest difficulty in remaining united and had to give up a few districts. The nobility, having deserted Mbanza Kongo between 1666 and 1678, had to adapt itself to life in the countryside and contended there for the posts of command. During and after this period a sizeable number of nobles crossed the river northward to found small principalities in Mayombe and between the rivers Zaire and Niari.

The upheaval was total and traumatic. It demolished the very foundations of society, calling its world outlook into question: so much so that prophetesses began to appear. In 1704 Dona Beatrice Kimpa Vita, a Joan of Arc, began preaching a refurbished Christianity called Antonianism. She rejected the missionaries and the whites, but above all she exhorted rival claimants to the throne to give up the struggle, restore a king and repopulate Mbanza Kongo. She had a large popular following (she herself belonged to the petty nobility) and persuaded a claimant to the throne to settle in Mbanza Kongo, where she crowned him with the black Antonian crown. But in 1706 she was captured by the pretender Pedro II and burnt as a heretic, despite which the movement survived for another few years.[39] Pedro II restored the kingdom and repopulated Mbanza Kongo, but a forty-year tide of political evolution could not be turned back.

With the Kongo, the organization of a vast area disappeared. The structural framework of this area, like that of Angola, was henceforth to be economic, with a framework of trade routes articulated by places of trans-shipment. Angola, which had expanded towards 1680, was also weakened. Neither the governors nor the *Camara* of Luanda could maintain their ascendancy over the *quimbares* and *ovimbali* (the Afro-Portuguese) who begin to be mentioned in the sources, or over the Brazilian traders. The control of the colony was slipping away from them. In Loango the state still appeared to be strong. But when the king died in 1701, a twenty-five-year-old 'sister' became regent, and her council governed. It took more than a year to elect a new king.[40] In a kingdom which was so trade-oriented,

39. A. C. Gonçalves, 1980.
40. P. M. Martin, 1972, pp. 162–3.

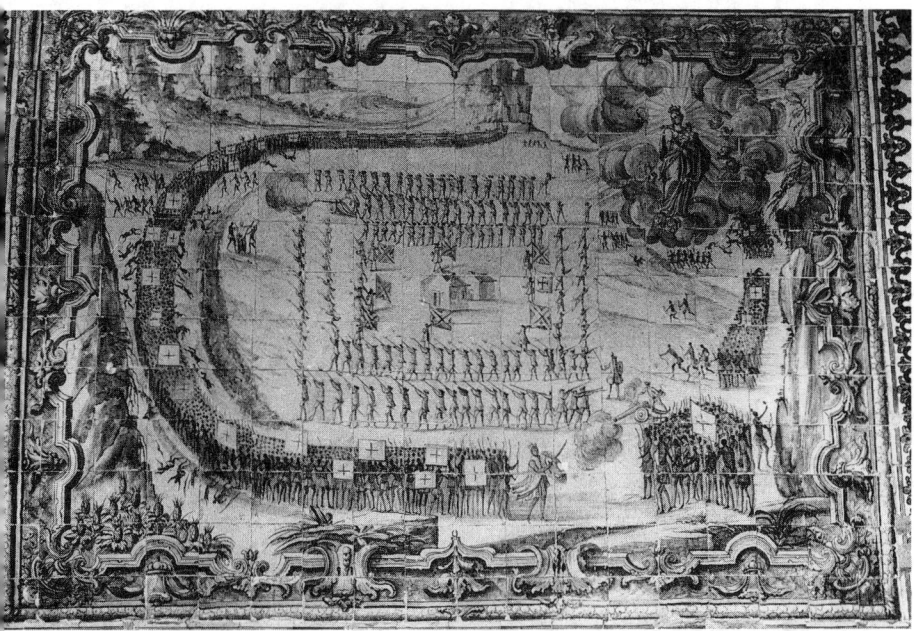

PLATE 19.10 *Decorative tiled panel from the Church of Our Lady of Nazareth, Luanda, showing the battle of Mbwila*

it was to be expected that the members of the regency council would also be the heads of trading firms and that royalty, for all its religious prestige, would begin to be redefined with regard to its authority over trade.

On the periphery of the slave-trading areas, states strengthened themselves through a growing trade which they controlled, or at least remained sound for such time as they controlled it. Kasanje had become a great power on the Kwango river because it controlled an increasing flow of slaves after 1648; by about 1680 part of this flow was coming from far-away Lunda. Building its kingdom from widely varied components from 1630 onwards, Kasanje displaced a part of the original population, the Pende, who had to emigrate beyond the Kwango.[41] For fear of being raided, the Pende departed north-eastwards towards Mashita Mbanza, a population centre near the Kwilu, and then eastwards as far as central Kasai, where they established chiefdoms.[42] In the north the Tio kingdom held its ground, apparently without great changes, but mention is made of other kingdoms in this area, some of which were probably founded in the seventeenth century.[43]

The Dutch conquest and the Restoration had substantial economic consequences. Currencies – fabrics and *nzimbu* – depreciated. A square of

41. Kodi Muzong, 1976, pp. 91–169.
42. ibid., pp. 170–267.
43. They include the Boma kingdom of 'Giriboma'; cf. E. Sulzmann, 1983.

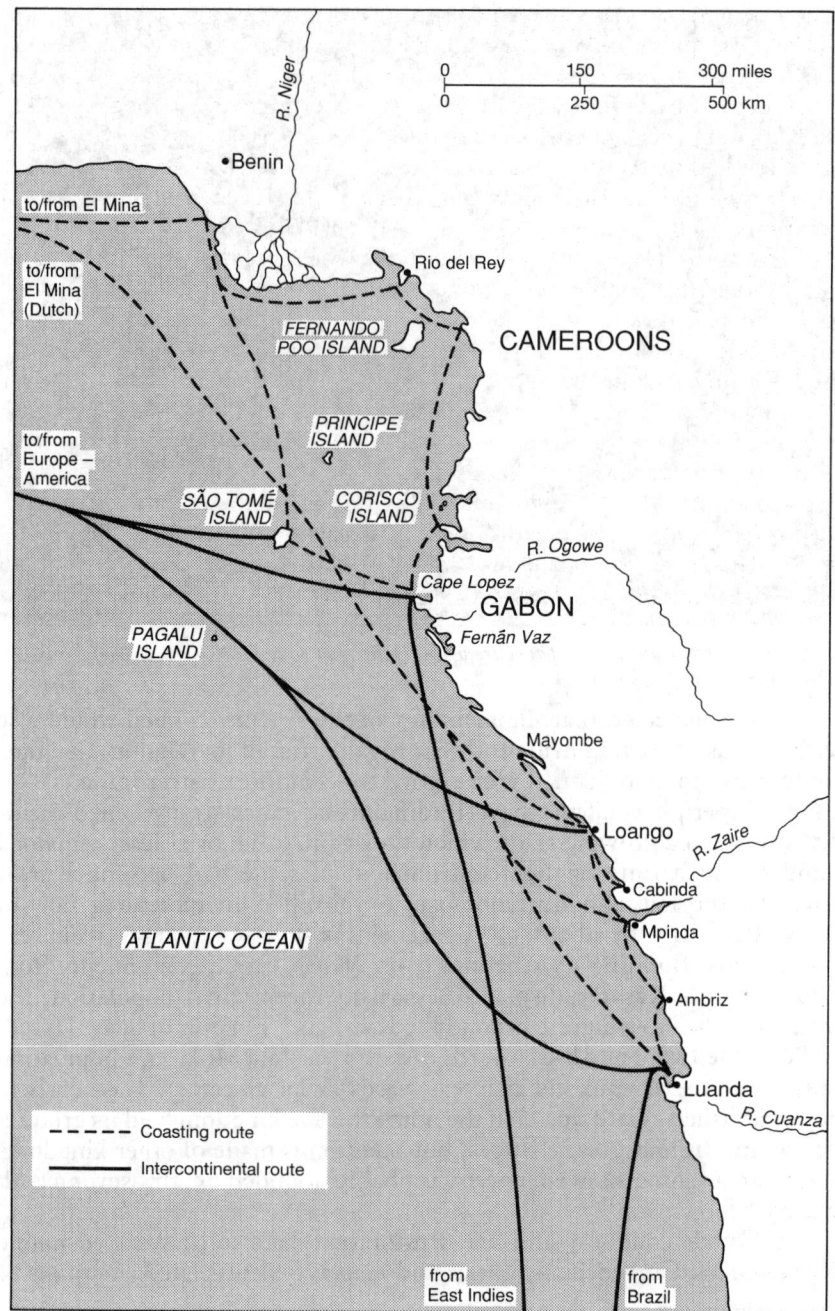

FIG. 19.4 *Shipping routes to Central Africa, seventeenth and eighteenth centuries (after J. Vansina)*

raffia which was worth 12 reis in 1640 fell to 5 reis in 1649. Despite this fall, the government did not succeed in introducing a copper currency, and the fabric rose in value once more. In Soyo it stood at 10 reis in 1813. The *nzimbu* depreciated from 2000 reis a *cofo* (unit) in 1640 to 1600 in 1649. The civil wars accelerated its fall – to 800 reis in 1698 – after which the unit value stabilized at about 1000 reis.[44] These changes were not due solely to political developments but began to reflect an economic transformation which was to be profound.

In Angola this transformation consisted in the reorganization of the slave trade by the Brazilians, who supplied capital, ships and European goods and who acted, through their factors in Luanda and Benguela, in concert with the organizers of caravans – the Afro-Portuguese slavers. Portuguese capital was invested in Brazil not directly in Angola and this remained true until about 1730. Since capital was lacking, the traders pressed for war as a source of captives for merchants. The big Lisbon companies calculated that their profit was made on goods and not on slaves, and tried, therefore, to possess as few slaves as possible. They imported goods for the captains and the Afro-Portuguese against bills of exchange which were converted into Brazilian sugar or local ivory.[45] The principal market was Brazil.

The situation on the Loango coast was entirely different. With an insatiable demand for slaves making itself felt in the West Indian colonies, English and French ships began to appear in 1660–5 and entered into hard-driving competition with the Dutch, who were also beginning to buy slaves in large numbers. Here companies financed in Europe carried on the triangular trade. The slave trade, initially favoured by the troubles in Kongo, developed essentially through purchase rather than capture. The contribution made regularly by Vili caravans buying in markets as distant as Pool or Cassange was far greater than the supply of prisoners of war. These were the conditions that saw the start of the large-scale slave trade which was to reach its full development in the eighteenth century.

Social and cultural transformations: the sixteenth and seventeenth centuries

We shall deal here mainly with Kongo, about which we are best informed. The division into three social strata, those of the *mwisikongo* (nobles), the *babuta* (sing. *mubata*) (rustics) and the *babika* (sing. *mubika*) (slaves), was to persist until sometime between 1666 and 1678, each stratum having different social structures. The general change was set in train first among the nobility and then in the countryside. The stratum of nobles and the terms used to designate it disappeared round about 1700.

44. J. Cuvelier, 1946, pp. 309–12.
45. J. C. Miller, 1979; 1984; and 1983, pp. 134–5.

The term *ekanda* (root: *kanda*), which is attested from this period onwards, today means 'matriclan' or 'matrilineage'. At that time it meant 'family' – matrilineal, to be sure – but also 'ethnic group, family, republic': in short, any community.[46] The people of a village made up an *ekanda* just as did a matrilineal group within that village, or the Christian community. The village was thought of as belonging to a group of people related through the female line and descended from the founder of the village, who was represented by the village leader, the *nkuluntu* (old one). In fact, since women followed their husbands and their sons did not always go to live in their uncle's village, the village group – always small in the old Kongo – was bound together by a territorial tie, although the *nkuluntu*, in running his community, took account of the various sections of clans other than his own: in other words he took counsel. The village held the rights to the land, and the spirit that dwelt in that land was perpetuated by the village *kitomi*. Ideologically these rights belonged to the matrilineage of the founder, but in practice the village acted as a body. This can be seen in particular in the existence of associations such as *khimba*, *nzo longo* or *kimpasi*, all of which were initiation cults for boys or healing cults which differed from one area to the next. Marriage defined lineage and kinship in general. Marriages between crossed cousins were preferred, and no marriage portions were paid apart from a few gifts to the wife herself.[47] The great unknown is whether the local matrilineal sections were linked together from village to village to form big clans comprising noble and peasant sections. We do not believe they were. The villages were in reality sharply cut-off from one another despite the web of marriage connections.

In the course of time, the power of matrilineage and of the village diminished. The villagers were already being harshly exploited by 1525. They may have revolted with the Jaga in 1568, and rebellions took place during the reign of Garcia II. At that time the *kimpasi*, a cult whose aim was to banish *mpasi* (suffering, poverty, need, calamity or affliction) was very active coincidentally with acts of oppression or natural disasters. The villagers' lot became more and more precarious as the nobles increasingly intervened, even at this level, to demand concubines and set the sons they bore them to keep the villages under surveillance. The status of rural women suffered most, and the distinction between wives and slaves (persons without lineage) grew more and more blurred as the wife became a person without local family connections to defend her. In the seventeenth century, even for men, matters reached a point where some took refuge as *fuku*

46. Most authors tend to take the known social institutions of the nineteenth and twentieth centuries and date them back to this period. There is no justification for this. Even A. Hilton is not entirely free from this shortcoming.

47. A. Hilton, 1985. The reconstruction ventured here is pieced together from a series of minor indications and arrived at by analogy with what is known of recent village organizations. It is simply a model that is not contradicted by the sources.

(clients) in noble houses, while some villagers branded their children (not their nephews) to save them from being taken into slavery.[48]

The bilateral noble houses, taking the royal house as their model, grew in size and importance. They absorbed a great many slaves. Their heads had large harems of wives from other noble or rural families. They paid high bride-prices for their principal wives, thus securing for themselves the ownership of the future children; the bride-price went to the wife. In this way the noble ladies grew in economic and political importance. Such growth was also favoured by the persistence of a residual matrilineal ideology when divisions occurred in the houses of highest rank. As we have seen, the great schism in the house founded by Afonso I had to do with the issue of three of his daughters. The senior woman of a house by bilateral descent was its standard.

In practice the position of patrilineal descendants – sons – grew in importance. Movable property acquired by trade belonged to the sons who, after about 1550, no longer took their father's name but a Portuguese surname symbolizing their house. The inheritances, however, were less substantial than might be thought. Everything acquired through the performance of public functions – tributes, fines or gifts – reverted to the king after the death or dismissal of the incumbent, and it is thought that the same custom prevailed at lower levels for functions in the gift of the great lords.

After 1666 the houses underwent two different series of changes. In Soyo the reigning house became increasingly patrilineal, continuing the tendency to neglect nephews in favour of sons, including even sons by female slaves. Eventually, in the nineteenth century, the whole of Soyo, rural and otherwise, adopted the patrilineal ideology. In Kongo, on the other hand, the nobles, having lost their town, had to make a new place for themselves in the countryside. The great houses melted away like the snow in summer, to be replaced around 1700 by the formation of large matrilineal groups, the *mvila* (clans). Government had been decentralized and ruralized.[49]

When the slaves – initially war captives – were once put to work in the fields of the capital or in the household, they did not remain a single stratum for long. A new distinction became vital: that between saleable slaves and domestic slaves who could no longer be sold. The latter were attached to noble houses, and some groups – such as the royal slaves (serving in the guard or elsewhere) and mission-station slaves – became independent locally powerful groups and so remained up to the nineteenth century. Since the saleable slaves were exported, these unfortunates never formed cohesive groups. In the seventeenth century social mobility was

48. A. Hilton, 1985, p. 203 (children). *Fuku*, from *fuka* (to cover, to shelter); *mfuka* (debt); *mfuku* (usefulness, benefit); *kifuka* (urbanity, politeness – i.e. the behaviour of a client).

49. The word *mvila* is not mentioned before the nineteenth century.

greater for domestic slaves than for villagers. They were members of a noble house – manumission was common practice – and the children of female slaves and noble fathers were equal or almost equal in rank to their father. In the villages, only the son of a minor noble's concubine could hope to rise in the social scale. In time, Kongo's three strata thus became compressed into two stable ones – the nobility who benefited from labour relationships, and their exploited subjects. Nevertheless, as Thornton[50] has proved, the difference in life-style of these two stable strata should also be emphasized. The urban nobility, literate and wont to parade its Catholicism, housed, clothed, fed and amused itself in an entirely different way from rural folk.

In Angola the indigenous social structure – which comprised the same strata as in Kongo although the nobles were less united as a group – was headed by a Portuguese stratum. But here, and indeed all over Central Africa, the situation was complicated by the emergence of an Afro-Portuguese stratum: *mulatto* traders who, in culture and language, were as much Angolan or Kongolese as they were Portuguese. This group first formed in São Tomé through miscegenation with Kongo nobles, then hived off to the Kongo capital and to Luanda. After 1575 a group formed in the Ndongo capital, but some remained in Luanda and from there emigrated in 1615 to Benguela and inland, near the chief towns of *presidios*. By about 1680 there were two large groups in existence, one around the fortress of Ambaka, the other founding Cacunda Velha in 1680. About this time the term *quimbares* or *ovimbali* made its appearance and was to be used to designate this stratum for the next two centuries. In the eighteenth century they were to spread most widely on the Benguela plateau. These groups were neither chiefs nor vassals but represented a floating population of caravaneers and traders who worked in concert with African chiefs and married into the local nobility.[51]

The history of religions and ideologies is marked on the surface by conversion to Catholicism which, in Kongo, spread first among the urban nobility and in the chief towns of the provinces. The ecclesiastical structure remained chiefly Portuguese until 1645, when the Italian Capuchin missionaries began an intense campaign of conversion to Christianity which continued in Kongo until about 1700. A very large proportion of the population was baptized, and the Christian religion was implanted even in remote villages. In Angola the Catholicism imposed by the conquerors did not progress beyond the colony except in Matamba. This religion did not spread in Loango, despite the conversion of a king in 1663.[52]

The evolution of religious ideas and practices in Kongo shows that the Christian doctrine influenced the old religion and coexisted with it. A. Hilton has documented the existence of belief in a group of celestial

50. With respect to the Kingdom of Kongo.
51. J. L. Vellut, 1972, pp. 94–9; J. C. Miller, 1983, pp. 132–5.
52. J. K. Thornton, 1983a.

spirits other than those associated with the sun and moon. These conceptions are completely foreign to the rest of Central Africa. On the other hand, the ways of thinking of the old religion reappear in Catholic texts, as witness the catechism of 1624.[53] An older example is the notion of *nkadi ampemba* (demon).[54] *Nkadi* is a dangerous ancestral spirit and *mpemba* (kaolin) reinforces the notion of ancestor. The Christian terminology stems from the domain of the *nkisi*, the *ndoki* and the *nganga*, the *nkisi* being 'that which is sacred' or 'grace'. The missionaries fought against the rites of the *kitomi* and of witchcraft, ancestors worship and healing associations (such as *kimpasi* or *marinda*), but tolerated the medicine practised by the *nganga*. The Capuchins used processions and the accompanying prayers to replace fertility rites, and could practise exorcism. The beliefs and practices of the old religion varied in matters of detail from region to region, and these local features, with the exception of those of Mbanza Kongo, were not reflected in Catholicism.

From the sixteenth century onwards there can be said to have been a single religion in which, at least among the nobles, features of Christianity and features of the old religion had merged. The main spread of this religion took place in the seventeenth century. This explains how Garcia II came to be the defender both of Catholicism and of the *kitomi*. He was even nicknamed 'the sorcerer'.[55] This new religion was the source of Haitian voodoo.

Various religious movements have been recorded since the 1630s when a first attempt was made to establish an indigenous church.[56] The first brotherhoods of Mbanza Kongo and the coming of the Capuchins led to a resurgence of *kimpasi* rites and of the influence wielded by the *kitomi* at court. Among the nobility, ancestor worship had been on the decline since Afonso I's time and was replaced by a ritual of burial in church which was associated with the brotherhoods. It is possible that worship of the saints, especially St Francis and St Anthony, took over part of the role formerly played by the worship of great ancestors. Lastly, the Reformation, introduced by the Dutch and opposed by the Kongo kings, nevertheless had a degree of influence which has not yet been documented.

In 1704 Dona Beatrice preached a far-reaching reform which cannot be explained solely in terms of the political situation. She called for thorough Africanization. As she claimed to be in direct contact with heaven she was regarded as a *munaki* (prophetess). The Holy Family was black and hailed from Mbanza Kongo, and the symbols she used were evocative local symbols associated with water, the soil and local vegetation and were similar to those used, in particular, in the healing cults led by women. Perhaps

53. F. Bontinck and D. Ndembe Nasasi, 1978.
54. Mentioned by E. Lopes in 1583 (*ncariampemba*) – see F. de Pigafetta, 1591 – and in 1624; F. Bontinck and D. Ndembe Nasasi, 1978, p. 269; A. Wilson, 1978.
55. W. G. L. Randles, 1968, p. 110.
56. J. Jadin, 1967.

the ideas of the Reformation also played a part. But Dona Beatrice recognized the Pope, despite her desire to drive out the white missionaries who falsified revelation. In short, her views were even more syncretic than the religion practised in her time.[57]

It has been said that after 1700 Kongo lost its Catholicism. This is false. The simple fact is that the Christian missionaries of the late nineteenth century, steeped in the atmosphere of colonialism, failed to recognize the indigenous Catholicism which was henceforth inherent in Kongo religion. If we examine modern Kikongo vocabulary, however, we find the same religious terminology, and the continuity is striking.

The arts express culture. While nothing survives in Kongo of the performing arts, such as music, dance and oral art,[58] visual art objects have survived together with many texts on the subject. These objects, created to symbolize class differences (vestiary art objects, for example),[59] political concepts (emblems and ceremonial objects) and religious concepts (Christian art, objects used in divination, statues of ancestors and spirits and masks) were commissioned by the court, the Catholic Church, the leaders of villagers and of village cults and even heads of families.

Although the study of Kongo art in historical perspective is still in its infancy, what is striking is the continuity of stylistic elements, allied to a dynamism of form that assimilates the many European influences. Examples include geometrical decorations criss-crossing at acute angles on a royal emblem (an ivory horn) from before 1553; fabrics from about 1650 to 1800; and basketwork, tattoos and mats from the nineteenth and even the twentieth century. Again, a motif characteristic of nineteenth-century sculpture is already represented on the Kongo coat-of-arms of the early sixteenth century. European influence was strong and was reflected in the importation of European stone architecture (churches and palaces), symbols of authority (swords, crowns, flags and vestments) and, above all, religious objects (medals, *agnus dei*, statues, crucifixes and paintings – there was a Spanish painter working in Kongo before 1650). Almost all characteristics of Kongo art, especially statuary and the graphic arts, have been attributed to Christian influence. In both sculpture and graphic art, however, these assertions are baseless: the facts go to prove the opposite.

Thus the manifestations of ancient graphic art – rock drawings surviving from different periods – have hitherto been ignored. In the seventeenth century we find alongside stylized drawings a series of pictograms which are clearly derived from writing and clearly an expression of popular culture. Letters were used as symbols and transformed. This use of pictograms was to continue and merge with the production of geometrical

57. A. C. Gonçalves, 1980; L. Jadin, 1961; and J. Cuvelier, 1953, have published the known sources.

58. T. Obenga, 1981.

59. Narrative bas-reliefs and pictograms merge, for example, on ceremonial swords and on pottery lids from the country north of the river.

PLATE 19.11 *Ruins of the former bishop's palace. Mbanza Kongo (San Salvador), 1548, photographed in 1955*

decoration. This is plainly an achievement inspired by the introduction of writing. Alongside these drawings, however, a more varied figurative tradition was still practised, as witness the narrative bas-reliefs and wall paintings of the eighteenth and nineteenth centuries.

Sculpture is represented first by many Christian objects, mainly crucifixes and walking-stick handles but also statues of saints; and it does exhibit elements of the European canon of proportions. But the stylization allied to Kongo realism was there from the beginning. In the course of time the European canon was gradually modified to one that is found in ordinary sculpture, the oldest known example of which dates from before 1694.

Artists used the most varied materials – copper, ivory, wood, stone, ceramics, fibres and fabrics – and worked on the most diverse objects, including even cooking utensils. The very first chronicles extol the merits of Kongo raffia fabrics, embroidered or worked in velvet. Even the clergy used them to make priestly robes to supplement those which they imported from Italy in particular and which gave the Kongo artists certain ideas. The sculpting of cult objects used in the old religion was forbidden and opposed and work was destroyed at various times, especially under Afonso I and Garcia II and by Kimpa Vita. However, the demand for these objects was constantly renewed – for the *kimpasi*, for example, during Garcia II's time. Most of the Christian sculpture was produced before 1700 and many objects of this kind have survived. Other creative activities inspired by

Europe were the casting of dress-swords and the making of standards embroidered with coats-of-arms and symbols.

The influence of Kongo art extended north and east during the centuries under review. The spread of the so-called 'white' masks from Gabon derives from northern Kongo masks and probably accompanied the expansion of Loango, especially in the seventeenth century. The technique of making raffia velvet spread along the Okango route to the east and was the forerunner of the 'velvets of Kasai', and especially of Kuba. It also appears that some features of Kongo art were passed on to the Americas.[60]

The eighteenth century: the northern areas

In the eighteenth century the whole of West Central Africa was re-organized. The trading networks – not the states – became the dominant factor. As the states declined so did the old ruling classes, while a merchant class arose to replace or complement them. As we have seen, there were two slaving networks: one Portuguese, trafficking from Angola to Brazil and the other in the north, where the other European powers trafficked but where the overland trade remained firmly in African hands.

This trade in the northern areas, that of the Loango coast, was fuelled by companies which financed the entire triangular trade. The Dutch, for example, were represented by the Dutch West India Company whose capital came from all the states of the Netherlands, northern Germany and the Baltic countries. At every stage of this intercontinental trade there was fierce competition between the different nationalities and European firms and this was an even greater factor in driving up prices than the increased demand for slaves in the West Indies and North America. It caused the trade to expand and the trade routes to lengthen as slaves were exported to ever more distant countries. Demand increased steadily from about 1665 to 1755, when it grew even more sharply, attaining its peak between 1755 and about 1797 when the great European wars brought it to a temporary halt.[61]

The ports used were first Loango and then Malemba, Cabinda and Boma in the estuary. After 1750 Malemba replaced Loango as the main trading centre. Towards 1780 Cabinda became the busiest port, to be supplanted in its turn by Boma after 1800. The European traders rented warehouse buildings in the ports, where they exchanged their merchandise for slaves through the agency of brokers, the *mercadores* of 1700 who later took local titles such as *Mafouk*.[62] Brokers were indispensable, for the monetary systems were not identical and it was necessary to agree on exchange values. To that end, a unit of goods – the parcel – was established,

60. R. F. Thompson and J. Cornet, 1982, pp. 141–210.
61. P. D. Curtin, 1969; J. C. Miller, 1983, pp. 146–51; P. E. Lovejoy, 1983, pp. 46–54.
62. R. F. D. Rinchon, 1964, for specific cases; N. Uring, 1928, pp. 26–8 (*mercadores*, p. 28); R. F. D. Rinchon, 1929.

PLATE 19.12   *Ndongo mask from Loango*

corresponding to a unit value of slaves, the standard slave being the adult male. The value and composition of the parcel were discussed first. Components were of three kinds: guns and gunpowder, fabrics and miscellaneous goods especially metal goods such as cutlery and copper basins. Once agreement had been reached on the parcel, negotiations began on the exchange of people, valued by reference to the standard slave, for actual goods, valued by reference to the standard parcel. By common consent, one type of merchandise could be replaced by another: for example, some of the fabrics could be replaced by beads or mirrors, or a fabric of a given quality by one of another. Europeans calculated in terms of the purchase price of the goods in European money; the broker calculated on the basis of the currencies in use on the coast and inland. Raffia money, which was still in use around 1700, was replaced by money made of a fabric imported during the eighteenth century, but this was not accepted everywhere inland for all types of merchandise. Beads, for example, were objects of adornment in Loango but a medium of exchange in Manyanga and a supplementary currency in Pool. In addition to the purchase prices, the European merchant had to pay trade duties and make gifts to the local king and the notable in charge of European trade. The broker, for his part, earned a large commission on the selling price of the slaves, the proceeds of which went to the slave-owner, through the leader of the caravan.

About one million slaves and small quantities of ivory, copper and wax were exported during the eighteenth century.[63] Imports consisted mainly of fabrics and weapons. It is estimated that 50 000 guns a year were imported during the second half of the century, with gunpowder to match, and the number of spans of fabric imported must have been even greater.[64]

The caravans were led by guides who maintained institutionalized relations (as 'mates') with the leaders of trade centres along the routes: they were skilled in negotiating rights of passage and had an expert knowledge of the big inland markets such as that of Pool. The caravans were composed of these guides, numerous armed guards, and porters. They sometimes travelled very long distances, possibly taking many months and sometimes spending the entire rainy season cultivating food crops during the outward journey. They took with them not only European products but also salt, salted and dried fish and locally manufactured items such as jewels from Loango. On the way they were able to buy other local products which they sold elsewhere, thus carrying on a kind of land-borne coasting trade.

The principal route linked the ports to Pool, where the slaves shipped along the river and its tributaries arrived in large numbers. Specialized carriers coalesced into ethnic groups, the best known being the Bobangi

63. According to the figures given by P. D. Curtin, 1969, and P. E. Lovejoy, 1983, 982 000 slaves were put aboard ship between 1660 and 1797.

64. P. M. Martin, 1970, p. 153. Compared with Van Alstein's calculations this estimate seems rather high, but the figures were of the order of tens of thousands per annum (see D. Rinchon, 1964).

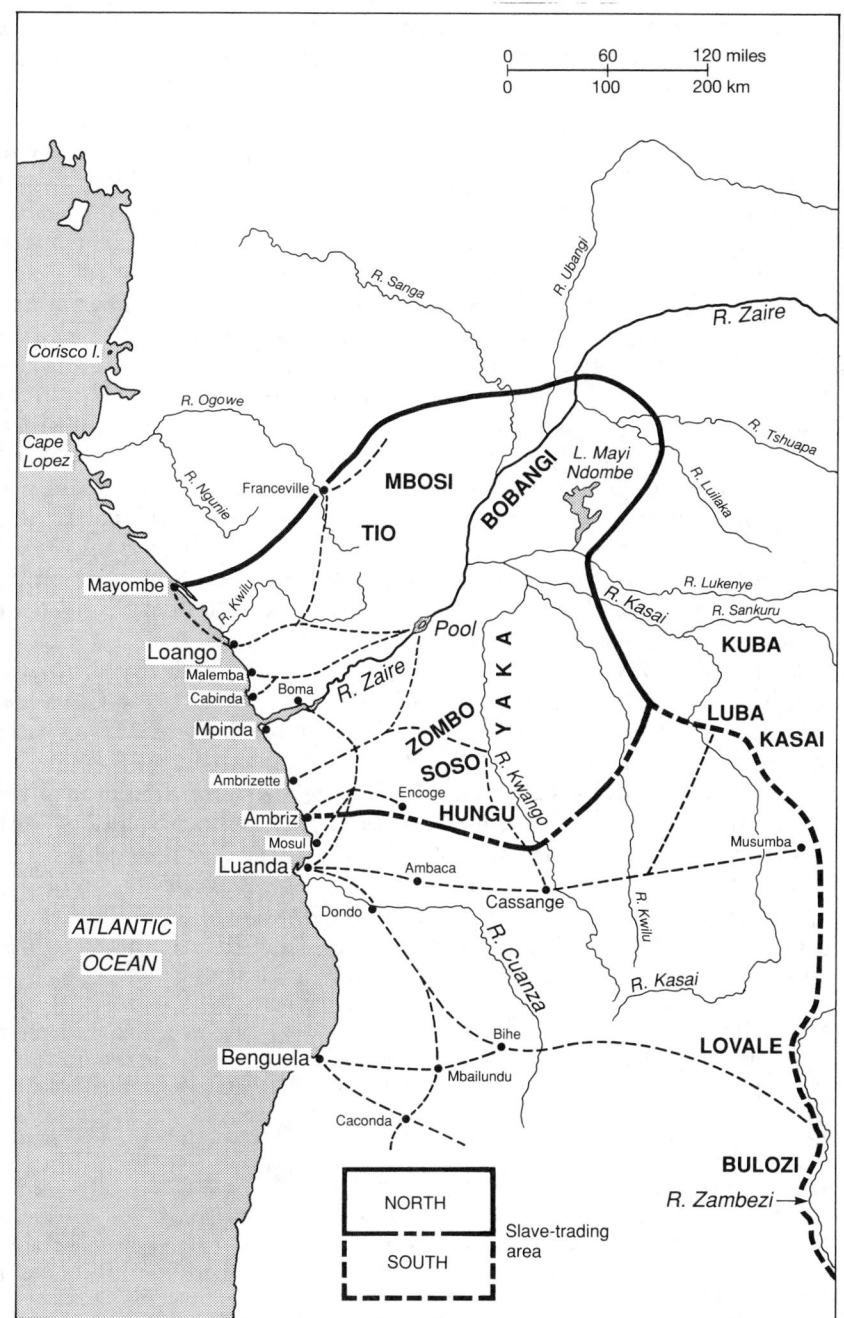

FIG. 19.5 *The slave trade in Central Africa in the eighteenth century (after J. Vansina)*

579

who gave up fishing for commerce and whose trade network, from the 1750s onwards, stretched from the Ubangi river to the Kwa. These water-borne carriers also conducted an extensive trade in other products, for heavy merchandise of low unit value could be carried by water at a profit. The river and its tributaries were accordingly the scene of a lively trade in pottery, fish, mats, food, beer, red dyewood and other commodities bought in one place and sold in another; this encouraged different areas to specialize in different goods. This slave-trading zone had reached the Ubangi, the lower Tshuapa and the areas around Lake Mayi Ndombe well before 1800[65] and continued to expand as the demand for slaves grew. We know nothing of its progress along the Lukenye, lower Kasai and Kwilu, but these rivers do not seem to have been much affected by the slave trade. We do not, however, know why. A branch of the route from Pool ran to the north of the Congo, passing through what is now Franceville, until it reached Mbeti and Mbosi country, competing with the slave trade up the Ogowe river. Other caravan routes traversed Kongo, reaching Matamba and Cassange on the upper Kwango, where the Vili had to compete with regional carriers of whom the Zombo and Soso were the best known. About 1750 the capital of the new Yaka state of the Kwango river became a slave-trading centre into which thronged the slaves taken in the constant military campaigns waged by the Yaka beyond the Kwango.[66]

The northern slave trade was so lucrative compared with that of Angola that it pushed the latter's field of operations towards Luanda and Cassange. This led to Portuguese military action against the port of Mosul (later Ambriz) and to the occupation of Encoge (1759) in central Kongo and subsequently in 1783 of Cabinda. The Portuguese were driven out by a French squadron supported by local forces. Briefly, military solutions were of no avail in halting the progress of the trade on the Loango coast.

We are only beginning to learn the effects of the slave trade. Its demographic effects in particular are still largely unknown. A million slaves means perhaps almost two million people torn from their homes,[67] a third of them women.[68] They came however from a vast area. Even so, it is

65. R. Harms, 1981; E. Sulzmann, 1983. Traces of it have come to light in the form of mugs originating from Westerwald (in what is now the Federal Republic of Germany) and manufactured in the eighteenth century, which were found between Ruki, Mayi Ndombe and Momboyo.

66. On the Yaka, see M. Plancquaert, 1971; J. K. Thornton, 1981a, pp. 5 and 8; D. Birmingham, 1966, pp. 148–52.

67. Taking into account deaths on the routes and in the barracoons. Figures given for Angola by J. C. Miller, 1979, p. 103, note 90, indicate that two-thirds of the slaves died before embarkation. These figures are exaggerated, and the slave trade was more lethal in Angola than on the northern coast, especially on the routes. Doubling the export figures is certainly not an exaggeration, and the result is probably still short of the truth.

68. See H. S. Klein, 1972, p. 914. This applies to the slave trade in general, but is also valid for Angola in the nineteenth century and the Dutch slave trade in general. The figures for children, pp. 903–5, were in the area of 5 per cent.

probable that the population actually fell in old Kongo and Mayombe, although we cannot estimate by how much. Elsewhere the main result was to slow down population growth.

We know more about the economic effects. To the north of the Zaire river a vast area organized itself into a well-knit aggregate of specialized areas. In one, raffia was produced, in another tobacco, in another cane-sugar wine, in another ivory, in another foodstuffs, ironware, pottery, boats and so on. This led to technological impoverishment in each individual area. The Tio, for example, gave up iron-smelting, boat-building and, to some extent, even weaving and pottery, finding it cheaper to import the products from neighbouring areas. The economic vitality of the aggregate, however, increased steadily, due mainly to the development of waterborne transport.

The social and political effects were far-reaching. The brokers and notables in charge of the slave trade steadily gained in importance at the courts of Loango, Ngoyo and Kakongo. They used their acquired wealth to surround themselves with large retinues and thus displaced the old nobility linked to the royal house. Royal authority suffered accordingly. In Loango the royal council witnessed the replacement of territorial nobles of the royal house by these nobles, the titles being sold by the king to the highest bidder. The system of succession deteriorated,[69] and it was the councillors who elected a king and favoured long-lived regency councils. Then, in or before 1750, the royal line became extinct. Six factions contended for the throne, but the royal *kitomi* eventually succeeded in imposing a neutral king at the cost of gravely weakening his power. A little later the new royal line suffered a schism, and royalty grew so weak that after 1787 no more kings were appointed for almost two centuries. Moreover, distant provinces such as Mayumba began seceding from 1750 on.

The Tio kingdom was also in difficulties. The regional great lords trading on their own account had grown rich and adopted a new ideology legitimizing their secession. This power was spiritual, centred upon a talisman, the *nkobi*, and could dispense with the support of terrestrial spirits. From about 1780 onwards the Tio state was in the grip of civil war and did not recover until about 1830. The *nkobi* ideology served to justify an impressive series of new chiefs who took power in, or incorporated into their own jurisdiction, an area extending from the region of Makua, via the west of the Teke (Kukuya) plateaux, as far as Tsayi country near the route from Loango to Pool.

In the middle Zaire basin the expansion of the slave trade led to renewed population movements on a small scale and to hostilities both in the Mayi Ndombe area and further north, while large centres of population began

69. P. M. Martin, 1970. F. Hagenbucher Sacripanti, 1973, although confused, confirms and gives details.

to take shape beside the river at points where it had to be crossed. These centres became market towns in the nineteenth century.[70] Between Loango and Pool, especially in the copper-mining area of Mindouli, an immigration of Kongore nobles displaced the Teke villages. Alongside small chiefdoms, however, a greater number of independent villages sprang up along the Loango–Pool axis. These villages agreed among themselves to maintain common markets by establishing a market tribunal composed of judges from the different villages. The *lemba* association cemented alliances between them.

In Kongo itself Christian ideology, and especially the use of the Order of Christ to which the rulers belonged, remained the basis of the ruling ideology. Its centres were the king, who was now no more than a supreme *nkisi*, and the former mission stations run by former mission slaves. Territorial units broke up again and again (the Kongo syndrome),[71] sometimes down to village level. To the east of Mbanza Kongo the Zombo carriers adopted the institution of market judges or agreed to rotate between leading families the government of small chiefdoms composed of only a few villages. At the same time, however, large *mvila* (clans) appeared, structured in lineages that had become anchored to the land. This network of clans became the cement that bound the independent villages together, establishing a setting in which they co-operated and competed with one another.

These transformations were accompanied by significant cultural changes. The role of the great ancestors – linked with the clans – increased. Cemeteries and churches, particularly those of Mbanza Kongo, grew bigger. The notion of *zombi*, a kind of corpse-slave,[72] took hold, as did the confusion of saints with great ancestors. Until about 1700[73] the burial of prominent people was still a fairly simple event, but soon they were being buried with ever greater ostentation. The fabric wrapping around the corpse was now replaced by a funerary bundle so enormous that routes had to be mapped out and wagons used to take the body to the cemetery, at least in places near the coast. In the nineteenth century the bundle became a giant doll, or a small shrine came into being. The wooden heads or busts which were positioned on the bundles in the eighteenth century became wooden or stone statues or ceramic monuments to adorn the tombs on which an increasing number of broken imported objects were also laid.[74] The Boma area and Mayombe were at the centre of these developments. South of the river, the funerary stelae of Ambriz[75] were their counterparts.

The group-healing cults prospered everywhere. The *lemba*, an already old example of these *nkisi* in Loango, changed in character. It became a

70. J. Vansina, 1983b, pp. 112–13.
71. S. Broadhead, 1971, 1979 and 1983.
72. Already mentioned in 1701 by N. Uring, 1928, p. 47.
73. N. Uring, 1928, pp. 35–6.
74. R. F. Thompson and J. Cornet, 1982.
75. Museu de Angola, Luanda, 1955, Nos 137–146 (Ambrizette), pp. 86–7.

PLATE 19.13   *Lemba medicine-chest* (nkobi) *made of bark, with characteristic petal motif on lid, from Ngoyo. Height: 24 cm*

nkisi of protection for members of the élites who could pay the high enrolment fees. When an important man fell ill, the *lemba* priest came to treat him. To be cured he had to become an initiate member of the association, together with his first wife. The cult ideology sanctified alliances between élite families (marriage, members of the *lemba* cell), legitimized initiate judges and heads of families and, indirectly, legitimized the market tribunals. Different forms of the *lemba* developed after 1700, including one in Haiti, where the *lemba* Petro was the fourth voodoo.[76]

Christianity held its ground and evolved. The scarcity of foreign or local priests left the initiative to the missionaries' former helpers, their slaves and, at court, the king's entourage. The reliefs of Ambriz show crucifixion scenes in which the spear has become a python, reminiscent of Mbumba or Bomba, associated with the slave trade and wealth, while the scene is accompanied by drummers. Christian statuary was still preserved and statues were possibly manufactured in Soyo and at Mbanza Kongo, as were the crucifixes which were emblems of authority and, in what was essentially a judicial role, the emblem of *nkangi* (the saviour). Other crosses developed, such as *santu*, or charms associated with divination by hunting and used to discover the cause of collective misfortunes. These were the two sides of the same official religion.

Angola in the eighteenth century

As already stated, the Angolan slave trade was on a significant scale long before that of the north developed. The system, which was aimed mainly at Brazil, was highly fragmented by comparison with that of the north.[77] Before 1730 it had the following components: the export merchant in Portugal; brokers in Brazil; shippers; slave-dealers in Luanda or Benguela; Afro-Portuguese caravaneers; and African lords and traders offering slaves for sale at the markets. A single firm could supply several components but rarely all of them together, not even those in Brazil and Portugal. Everyone tried to avoid risks and to maximize profits. The greatest risk was *o risco dos escravos*: the risk that slaves would die of malnutrition, untreated diseases and ill-treatment. All these causes of death resulted from attempts to avoid spending what was necessary on food, medical care and competent custodians. Each segment tried to shift responsibility for the slaves, and hence the ownership thereof, to the weaker segments. The firms in Portugal and Brazil were in a strong position; the shippers, the dealers in Luanda and Benguela and the caravaneers were in the weakest. It was they who tried to cut costs at the expense of the slaves, with consequent high mortality. J. C. Miller quotes[78] an estimate to the effect that half the slaves

76. J. M. Janzen, 1982.
77. See in particular H. S. Klein, 1972; J. C. Miller, 1975b, 1979, and 1984.
78. J. C. Miller, 1979, p. 103, note 90.

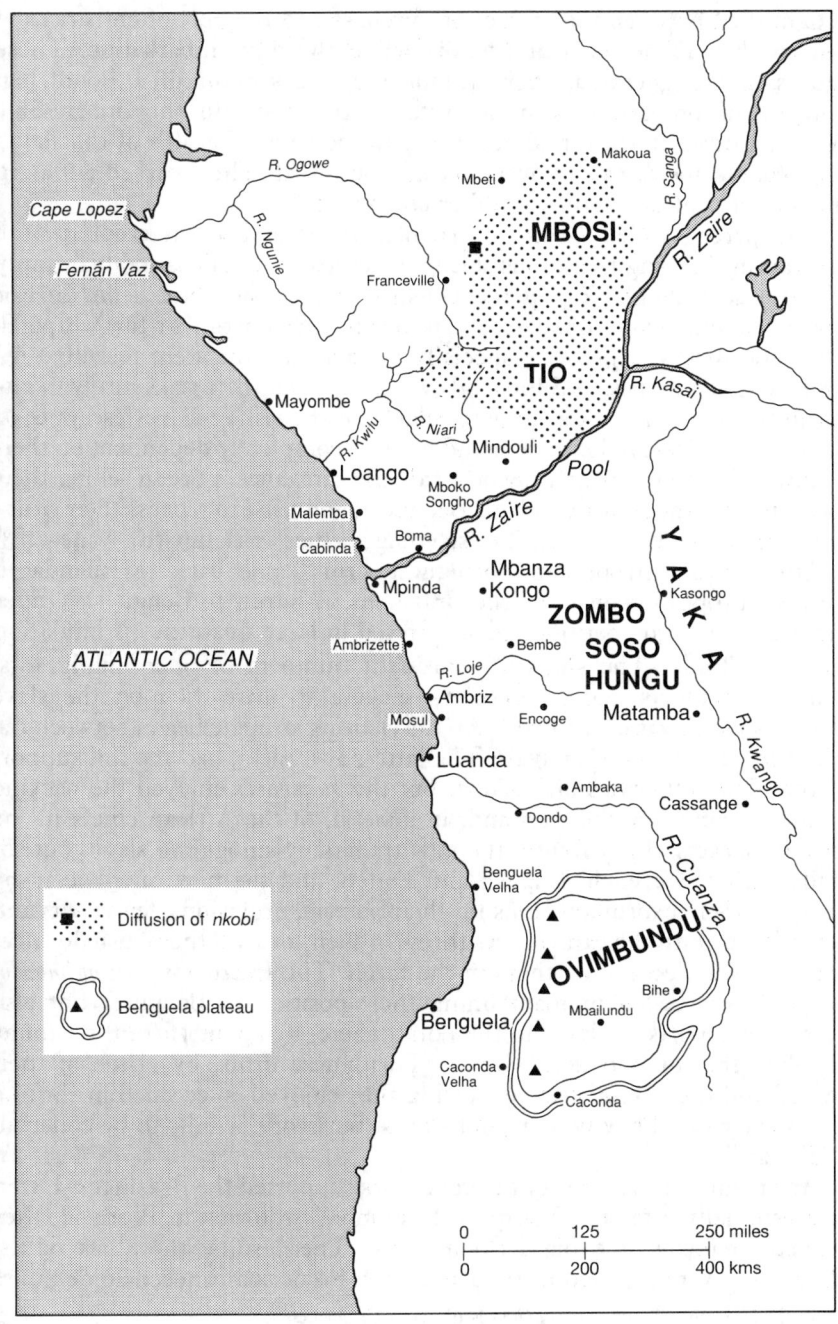

FIG. 19.6   *West Central Africa in the eighteenth century (after J. Vansina)*

bought died between the market of purchase and the port of embarkation and another 40 per cent at Luanda while awaiting embarkation. These figures are exaggerated; their author was the servant of a Pombalian company in competition with this system in the 1770s. But they are credible figures. Losses at sea varied according to the state of health of the slaves shipped and the degree of overcrowding on board. They worked out at 10 and 15 per cent of the total number embarked.[79]

The parcel, called *hanzo* in Angola, was supplied on credit to the caravaneer, binding him to his sleeping partner, who calculated his supply of slaves accordingly. The parcel consisted mainly of fabrics from Goa or Europe, brandy from Brazil, local salt, beads and sometimes a few weapons. The caravaneers' expenses (especially for porters, who were recruited inland by state officials, and for food) were high and their risks heavy (waiting in the African market, in particular, and the risk of slaves escaping or dying). They soon fell into debt and became completely dependent on their creditor. But from about 1760 onwards the caravaneers began selling their slaves to any trader in Luanda or Benguela, and tried to redress their situation with the goods obtained. The sleeping partner was left with a write-off.[80]

After 1730 metropolitan Portuguese firms came back to Luanda to supply European goods, and the Brazilians withdrew to Benguela. Under the pressure of competition, goods arrived in large quantities, stimulating the slave trade. The ships also brought numbers of poor immigrants, common convicts and adventurers seeking to grow rich on the slave trade, especially as caravaneers. An unrelenting struggle began between the *quimbares* and the new arrivals. The latter, as traders, had the full support of the high authorities of Luanda, but the *quimbares* enjoyed the backing of the provincial authorities and, in general, of the African chiefs in the inland markets. They fought the new traders by smuggling slaves out for trade with the French, English and Dutch, and the new caravaneers by charging them exorbitant sums for their porters, provisions, ferryboats and other items until the caravaneers threw in their lot with them, usually after leaving their sleeping partners in the lurch. The Brazilians and *quimbares* not only succeeded in maintaining their position in Benguela but also increased exports of slaves to the point where, by about 1690, the volume equalled that of Benguela. But the Portuguese firms, by virtue of their capital and the administrative backing they enjoyed, succeeded in shifting the 'slave risk'. They bought, not slaves, but ivory or bills to be collected in Brazil.[81]

At the turn of the century the governors supported the Brazilians. Later, and especially after the Márques de Pombal's reforms in Portugal, they tended to favour the big Lisbon firms. The Jesuits, the allies of the Brazilians, were expelled in 1660, and with Francisco Innocencio de Sousa

79. P. E. Lovejoy, 1983, p. 47 (losses of 10 to 15 per cent).
80. E. Da Silva Correa, 1937; J. C. Miller, 1979, pp. 90–1.
81. J. C. Miller, 1983, pp. 146–51.

Coutinho (1664–72)[82] a vigorous effort was made to re-establish the mother country's control in Angola. De Sousa tried to regain control of the administrative posts in the interior, to lay down regulations for the slave trade in the inland markets and to diversify the country's economy. Neither he nor his successors achieved this. The Afro-Portuguese emigrated once again, moving mainly to the Benguela plateau where massive military campaigns from 1772 onwards succeeded merely in hastening the emergence of two large kingdoms, Mbailundu and Bihe, of which the latter in particular became a haven for the *quimbares*. A new bridgehead for trade with the interior developed here, and before 1794 the caravans reached the Upper Zambezi in Lozi country. The slaves were taken to Benguela, avoiding Luanda. Luanda continued to attract the slave trade through the Kingdom of Kasanje. The Imbangala travelled by caravan to the northeast, reaching central Kasai and the Luba who lived there before 1755. But their main axis was the route from Cassange to Mussumba, the capital of the Lunda empire.

The Lunda empire took shape during the eighteenth century. Constant military campaigns yielded large numbers of slaves, while tributes in slaves flowed into the capital from the subject regions. After 1750 the empire succeeded in founding the Kingdom of Kazembe on the Luapula river and in establishing communications with Tete and Zumbo in Mozambique. Before then, westward expansion had reached the River Kwango, where a captain founded the Yaka kingdom between 1740 and 1760, causing thousands of people to flee from Hungu to Kongo between 1761 and 1765.[83] This great Yaka state occupied a large part of the Kwango valley downstream of Kasanje and extended its conquests eastward in the direction of the Kwilu. Large numbers of captives were brought back from there to be sold to the Zombo, Soso and Vili, but also to the Imbangala and to caravans passing through Nkoje. During the late eighteenth century and more so during the nineteenth, these conquests and raids caused large population movements from the Kwango river towards the Kwilu as people fled from the Yaka.

In Angola the slave trade had such an ascendancy that, despite the efforts of de Sousa Coutinho and others, the country failed to develop a diversified economy for lack of capital not tied to the slave trade. The colony remained economically dependent on Brazil; around 1800, 88 per cent of its revenues still came from the slave trade with Brazil and a little less than 5 per cent from the ivory sent to Portugal.

82. R. Delgado, 1948–55.
83. Making 1 032 000 slaves, according to the figures given by D. Birmingham, 1966; P. D. Curtin, 1969; H. S. Klein, 1972; P.E. Lovejoy, 1983. See also J. C. Miller, 1975b and 1979. In this case 2 million is certainly an underestimate. The real figure might be nearer 3 million. As to demography, see J. K. Thornton, 1980; 1977a, 1977b and 1981b; he concedes, 1981b, p. 713, that there was a loss of population, but his model underestimates the number of women (according to him, one-quarter and not one-third) and children (according to him, none were put aboard ship). These figures are crucial to the population picture.

The political system of the Luba and Lunda: its emergence and expansion

20

NDAYWEL è NZIEM

The history of the Luba is the story of the development of a political system which first emerged in Shaba, in the present-day Republic of Zaire, and subsequently spread into a large part of the southern grasslands, over an area stretching almost from the River Kwango to the River Zambezi.[1] Although a whole series of societies evolved along individual lines in this area, they were all closely intertwined, springing as they did from the same basic impulses. This pattern clearly demonstrates the capacity for unification which already existed among African peoples in the precolonial period.

The connection and the differences between the Luba and Lunda states are implicit in their two names which reflect not so much ethnic distinction as two political and cultural systems within which a whole range of separate ethnic referents sprang up. The history of the Luba covers matters affecting the present-day Luba of both Shaba (the Luba Shankadi) and Kasai (the Luba Lubilanji) as well as matters relating to the Songye, Kanyok, Kete, Sala Mpasu, Bindji and Lulua. The history of the Lunda deals both with the Rund groups (the Lunda in the narrow sense) and the Lozi, Ndembo, Lwena, Imbangala and other groups (the Lunda in the broad sense).[2] The linguistic classification given to the Luba and Lunda languages are indicative of this intertwined relationship. While Guthrie classifies them all in his Zone L, the Lunda languages are put into Group 50 and the Luba languages into Group 30. This bears eloquent testimony to both the

1. This political system affected the three Central African countries of Zaire, Angola and Zambia.
2. There is an extensive literature on these people. This includes the old ethnographical works: H. A. Dias de Carvalho, 1890; C. Van Overbergh, 1908; R. Colle, 1913; E. Verhulpen, 1936; L. Van den Byvang, 1937; P. Denolf, 1954; E. D'Orjo de Marchovelette, 1950–1; L. Duysters, 1958; W. F. Burton, 1956. Recent works are mostly unpublished doctoral theses. Whether the history of the region is looked at from Bemba materials (A. D. Roberts, 1973), Luba materials (T. Q. Reefe, 1977; J. C. Yoder, 1977) or Lunda materials (J. C. Miller, 1972b; J. L. Vellut, 1972; W. F. Pruitt, 1974; R. E. Schechter, 1976; J. J. Hoover, 1979), one comes back to the problematic of those who deal with these cultures as a whole (S. A. Lucas, 1968; L. De Heusch, 1972; B. Crine-Mavar, 1973; S. K. Ndua, 1978); R. J. Papstein, 1978.

similarities and differences between the two languages.[3]

There is general agreement that the archaeological finds of the Upemba Depression at Sanga and elsewhere are to be attributed to the ancestors of the Luba.[4] Emblems of rule, later common among the Luba, appear by the thirteenth century at the latest, along with evidence at Katota and Sanga of the formation of two chiefdoms. Yet Katota and Sanga were not the direct forerunners of the Luba kingdom. Oral chronology cannot be pushed back reliably much beyond 1700 in this case. All we know is that the main Luba kingdom came into being as one among many and began to expand before the Rund state, fountainhead of the Lunda empire, was developed. The formation of the Rund state cannot be dated by oral tradition[5] but at least the state is mentioned in the traditions by 1680. How long before that date it took shape, we do not know.

The emergence of the Luba and Lunda states

Shaba and the adjoining parts of Zambia and Angola are covered by woodlands, its soils are poor and the dry season is very long. The best lands lie mostly in the river valleys and their quality decreases from north to south and east to west, being worst in eastern Angola. The further north the less the risk of drought. But the southern, half-barren country contains mineral treasure – copper, iron and salt – all in its south-eastern quadrant.

It is not surprising, therefore, that the population lived in pockets of fertile land, whether near major mineral sites or not, with vast expanses of almost uninhabited areas in between, used mainly for hunting. This population distribution was reflected in the location of the early territorial organizations: which comprised small chiefdoms each governing one settlement. Thus the Sanga charter of settlements becomes the later chiefdom of Kikondja while Katota upstream, at the other end of the Lualaba lake system, formed another chiefdom. In both these areas people were fishermen and farmers. There were many other chiefdoms, all located in major river valleys, where the inhabitants were mostly farmers: namely the Kalundwe, Kanyok, Kanincin, Nsanga, Mpimin, the early Rund and various Hemba chiefdoms.

None of these population clusters lived in isolation. They were linked by trade and, presumably, intermarriage. From the north came raffia and palm oil, from the Lualaba river fish, from the south copper and salt, from the central southern area *mbafu* oil. There is no evidence for extended east-

3. M. Guthrie, 1948, p. 54. The linguists at Tervuren consider that the two groups of speakers settled in neighbouring areas at a fairly late date (A. Coupez, E. Evrard and J. Vansina, 1976).

4. See UNESCO, *General History of Africa*, Vol. IV, ch. 22; J. Vansina, 1984a, pp. 564–70.

5. Such attempts all rested on the supposed emigration of Kinguri from the Rund capital to Angola. We now know that this is a later elaboration of tradition dating at the earliest from *c*.1700; cf. J. K. Thornton, 1981a.

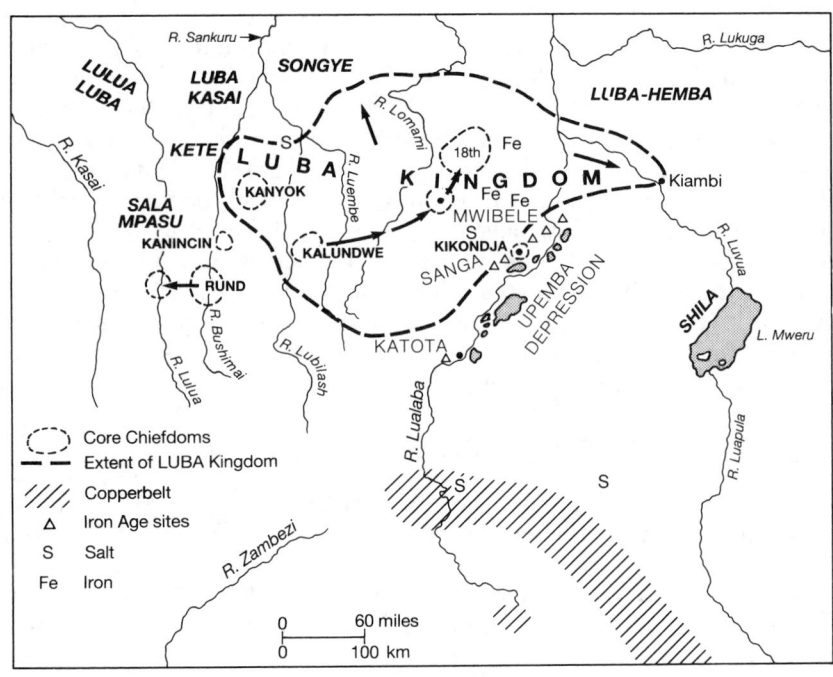

FIG. 20.1   *The states in Shaba before 1700 (after J. Vansina)*

west trade at an early date and apart from copper the usual movement of products was on a north–south axis from the limits of the equatorial forest in the far north, southwards to central Zambia. The trade was important enough for currencies to develop from at least 1000. In the Upemba Depression around 1300 the copper cross became the currency. By 1500 such crosses were standardized as to weight and by 1600 they had become quite small, so that they could be used for minor as well as major purchases. But the decline in size may also have been an index of devaluation. After 1700 crosses disappeared and, by the nineteenth century, imported beads were becoming the new currency.[6]

In this context developed the political ideology that later would be central to the main Luba kingdom. This consisted of two interlocked *bulopwe* (principles), that of the sacred character of kingship and that of rule through a closed association. In the kingdom's northernmost area, in Songye country, and in some eastern areas, rule by association became dominant, but in the kingdom's heartland balance between the two came into being, although the sacred character of kingship clearly predominated.

According to some traditions the forerunner of the Luba kingdom was

6. P. de Maret, 1981, pp. 139–43.

PLATE 20.1 *Hemba, Zaire: monoxyloid caryatid seat, the bottom of which is worn away. Note the prominent scarifications and the quality of the bracelets. Height: 35 cm*

the small Kalundwe kingdom founded between the Luembe and Lubilash rivers by a coalition of three clans.[7] Its capital was at Cifinda. One of its kings, Kongolo (Rainbow), moved to found a capital on the plains at Mwibele, not far from Lake Boya, in what would be the heartland of the future Luba state. Other accounts, however, have Kongolo coming from elsewhere. The epic narrative of foundations, for example, tells in vivid detail how Kongolo was defeated and slain by Kalala Ilunga – Ilunga the hunter, a foreigner from the east – who moved his capital to Munza, closer to a district rich in iron ore and not far from salt pans. As *Mwine Munza* (master of Munza), Kalala represents a founding-father figure that depicts what an ideal Luba king should be. Kongolo may well not be an authentic figure but at least the traditions can be accepted as to the situations of the former capitals. Unlike almost all the other chiefdoms, the Luba kingdom did not have its centre in a river valley but in the heart of the great plains north of the Upemba Depression. It dominated, perhaps from the onset, the Kalundwe to the west, Kikondja to the south and controlled the major north–south trading routes. Nonetheless, until the eve of the eighteenth century it would remain a fairly small kingdom.

Meanwhile, further west other political units were being formed. The foremost among them, Nkalany, developed in the Mbuji Mayi valley from the fusion of several small areas headed by *tubung* (masters of the land). Their Kete neighbours to the north had a similar organization but, to the north-west, their closest relatives in speech and material culture, the Sala Mpasu, organized themselves very differently, by age organizations and by allowing powerful men to monopolize authority. Political succession to existing positions, and hence aristocracy, was rejected by them.

Nothing really predestined the Rund lands to become an empire. The areas further north with better soil were more densely settled. Their agriculture was much more advanced and they were better placed on the north–south trading routes. Yet at one point the northern *tubung* were united under one of the Rund lands, although they only formed a chiefdom centred along a stretch of river. The northern *tubung* traditions begin with an explanation as to why a chief Nkond left his office to his daughter, Rweej or Rueji, who married Cibinda Ilunga (Ilunga the Hunter) from the Luba court and then abandoned office in his favour. The episode of the hunter is an obvious cliché also found elsewhere in the region.[8] According to the story, Cibinda Ilunga organized his court on the Luba model. But even in this, tradition may only be partially correct as scholars have found as many Rund influences on the Luba as the other way round.[9]

Another element of the tales must still be mentioned. According to

7. For a critical examination of traditions, see T. Q. Reefe, 1977 and 1981; for notations of historical traditions, see H. Womersley, 1984.

8. H. A. Dias de Carvalho, 1890; P. Pogge, 1880. The Curse by Nkond of his sons recalls the episode of Noah under the tree and is probably of late invention.

9. T. Q. Reefe, 1981, pp. 75–8.

Carvalho, after the conquest stage, power went to Rweej's first son, Yav, who became the *Mwant Yav* (Lord Yav). It was his name which was to become a political title designating the aristocracy of the new court. On his death, power is thought to have been assumed by his brother Naweej, who was to become the real organizer of the empire. However, the versions that have been collected more recently claim that Rweej was sterile. In order not to jeopardize the succession, she gave her husband a second wife, Kamonga, who was first in succession. This situation accounts for the institutionalized existence of two female dignitaries at the court of the Mwant Yav: the *Swan Murund* or *Swana Mulunda*, the symbolic mother of the society, who symbolized the perpetuation of the role played by Rweej who, although sterile, founded the empire; and the *Rukonkesh* or *Lukonkeshia*, the queen-mother, who occupied the role played by Kamonga and all other women in the same situation.

More commonly, reference is made to the existence of the right-hand mother (*Swan Murund*), who has to be differentiated from the left-hand mother (*Rukonkesh*). It was the latter who gave birth to the successor.

This testimony explains the different institutions that evolved after the appearance of the Luba hunter: first, the two female aristocracies, one symbolizing social fertility and the other biological fertility; and second, the royal title based on the chiefly title *Mwant*, to which the name of the first king was added.

The Luba: internal organization and development to 1800

As with Mwine Munza, a state appeared on the plains as a result of influences from the east across the Lualaba river. It incorporated the Kikondja kingdom in the Upemba Depression south of the plains and the Kalundwe kingdom to the west. It further expanded, then or somewhat later, to the south-east to control the lower reaches of the Lovua river.

The foundation and first consolidation of the kingdom led to some disturbances in the region and a number of emigrants left the lower Lovua to found the Shila state on the western shore of Lake Mweru and along the lower Luapula.[10] It is likely that this account deals only with the group that ruled the Shila before about 1750 and not with most of the inhabitants. These rulers may not even have come from the Luba kingdom but may have been given this area as a prestigious place of origin, although they really stemmed from Kiambi on the lower Lovua. The Kanyok to the north-west were also subjected to the kingdom by Luba immigrants who organized (or founded) a kingdom there, although in the early 1800s, they threw off their allegiance to the Luba.[11]

The most important emigration is reported towards the north. Following the troubles when the kingdom was founded, later wars of succession and

10. M. Musambachime, 1976, pp. 15–32.
11. J. C. Yoder, 1977; 1980, pp. 88 and 90.

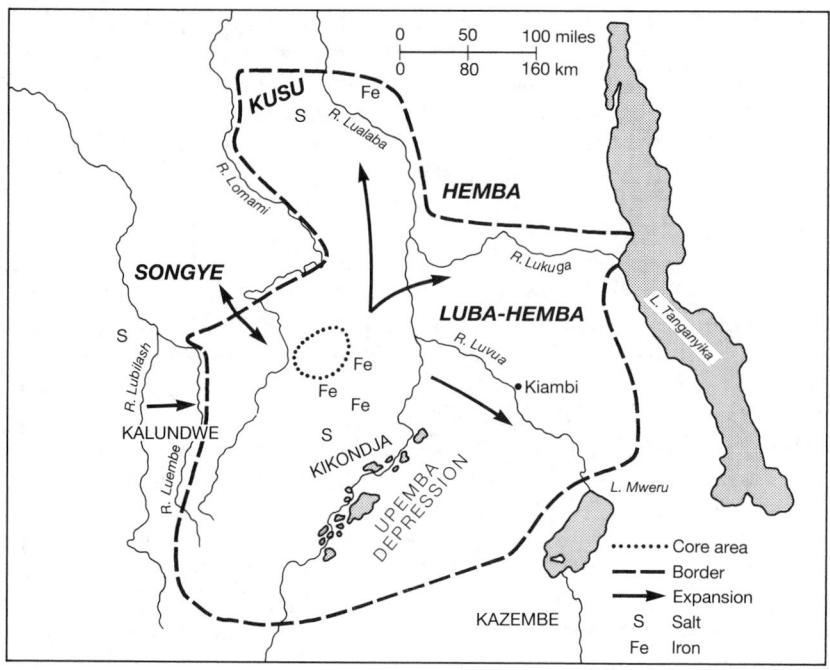

FIG. 20.2 *The Luba kingdom in the eighteenth and nineteenth centuries (after J. Vansina)*

famines, groups of Luba Kasai left Shaba to spread northwards along the Lubilash river fanning out into the better-watered lands.[12] Famine is given as a major motive for movement in many traditions of kinship groups in Kasai, not only for leaving Shaba but also when explaining why they left the Lubilash in Kasai to move west towards the Lulua river. They point to a real dynamic of population shift. But all the Luba Kasai could not have left Shaba in one or two waves. Probably, whenever famine hit, some southerners moved north and continued to do so until at least the early 1800s.[13] In this area Ciluba and related languages and dialects are spoken, all markedly different from Kiluba, spoken in Shaba. Central Kasai, therefore, must have been occupied by such speakers for many hundreds of years, just as the northern country between Lubilash and Lualaba was occupied by Songye whose speech forms another branch in the Luba family of speech.

Although to the south, in Shila and Kanyok country, a variant of the

12. P. Denolf, 1954; Mabika Kalanda, 1959, p. 83; Kabongo Mukendi, 1973, pp. 48–50; L. M. Mpoyi, 1966, pp. 34–6.

13. Luba came into contact with Kuba c.1750 and immigrated (the Bena Coofa) just after 1800.

Shaban Luba political system was set up, in Kasai this did not occur. Here the political organization was either limited to the village and its land or higher office was given for life – or even for a limited period – to the highest bidder, a system also found among some Songye. The Luba Kasai also adopted some emblems and some political practices from the Kanyok. Most Songye were, however, ruled differently. By the 1880s, and probably some centuries earlier, the Songye lived in huge farming settlements or towns, ruled by the Bukishi association – membership of which required high fees and was dominated by chiefs with a few titled notables.[14] This, too, differed from the model of the main Luba kingdom.

The organization of the Luba state was imagined as a pyramid of pyramids. At village level, households were linked by patrilineage. Relations between villages were also thought of as relations between lineages, although each district had a titled chief of a given family whose authority was held to stem from his connection with a local *vidye* (spirit). Above this the kingdom itself was ruled from the capital (imagined as a summit in expressions referring to it), the very lay-out of which reflected this structure with royal quarters and quarters for titled officials of both sexes, separated by military or civilian function. At its centre stood the *bulopwe* (royal office). A less careful scrutiny of the layout showed the presence of *Bambudye*, the closed association which helped the king to rule. The king was not supposed to have a lineage or clan although the office was normally handed down from father to brother to son. But the Luba saw this as a rotation in office of different lineages, namely those of the mother's kings. Hence the king was at the same time above the political fray and yet linked by kinship to many of the district heads. He stood at the apex of the pyramid of pyramids of kinship. This is the meaning of the title *mulopwe* which signifies the indivisibility of power that could not be shared.[15] The rituals of investiture (royal incest, for instance) and the emblems underscored the uniqueness and the supremacy of the ruler as well as his position as a mere incumbent of the office for he was but one in a line of kings. Those who came before him were now powerful ancestors with their shrines and gave voice through the medium of the women attached to their shrines.

The *mulopwe* was surrounded by a household and titled officials. First was his harem reflecting the real political alliances that bound the kingdom together. His officials saw to it that tribute was paid in *mingilu* (unpaid labour), in *milambu* (taxes payable in food and local produce such as salt, iron, raffia and baskets) and in gifts paid at the investiture of *Kugala* (dignitaries). The territorial administration was in the hands of the *bilolo* (singular *kilolo*), each responsible for a *kibwindji* (region), and normally chosen by the local people from amongst the ruling family of the district and confirmed by the court. Sometimes the choice of *kilolo* was imposed

14. N. Fairley, 1978, pp. 118–60.
15. J. Van Avermaet and B. Mbuya, 1954; S. K. Ndua, 1978, p. 337; T. Q. Reefe, 1975, p. 11.

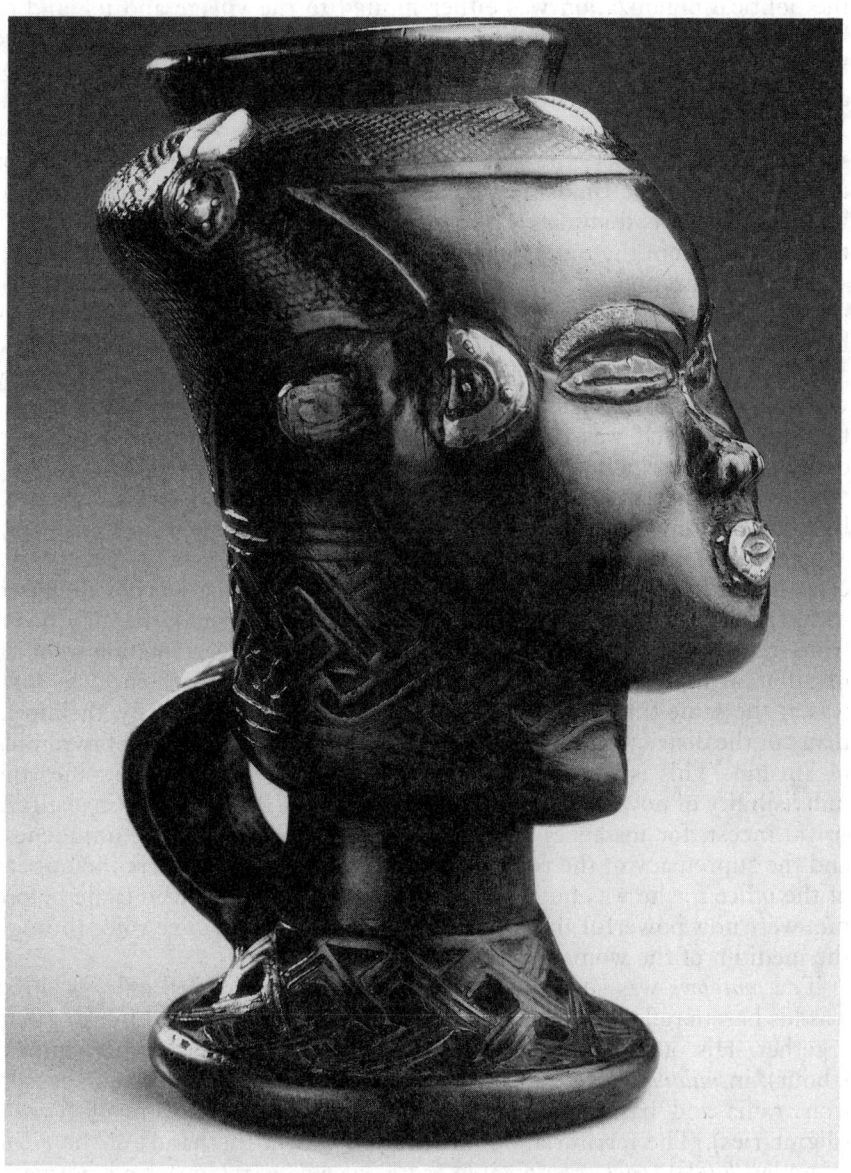

PLATE 20.2 *Kuba, central Zaire: cephalomorphic ritual cup for drinking palm wine. It is inlaid with cowries on the neck and handle, and with brass on the mouth, temple and back of the head. Height: 18 cm*

PLATE 20.3   *Luba, southern Zaire: the knob of a ceremonial cane, in the form of a human head decorated with a very tall headdress surmounted by two figures holding each other by the waist. Overall length: 164 cm*

597

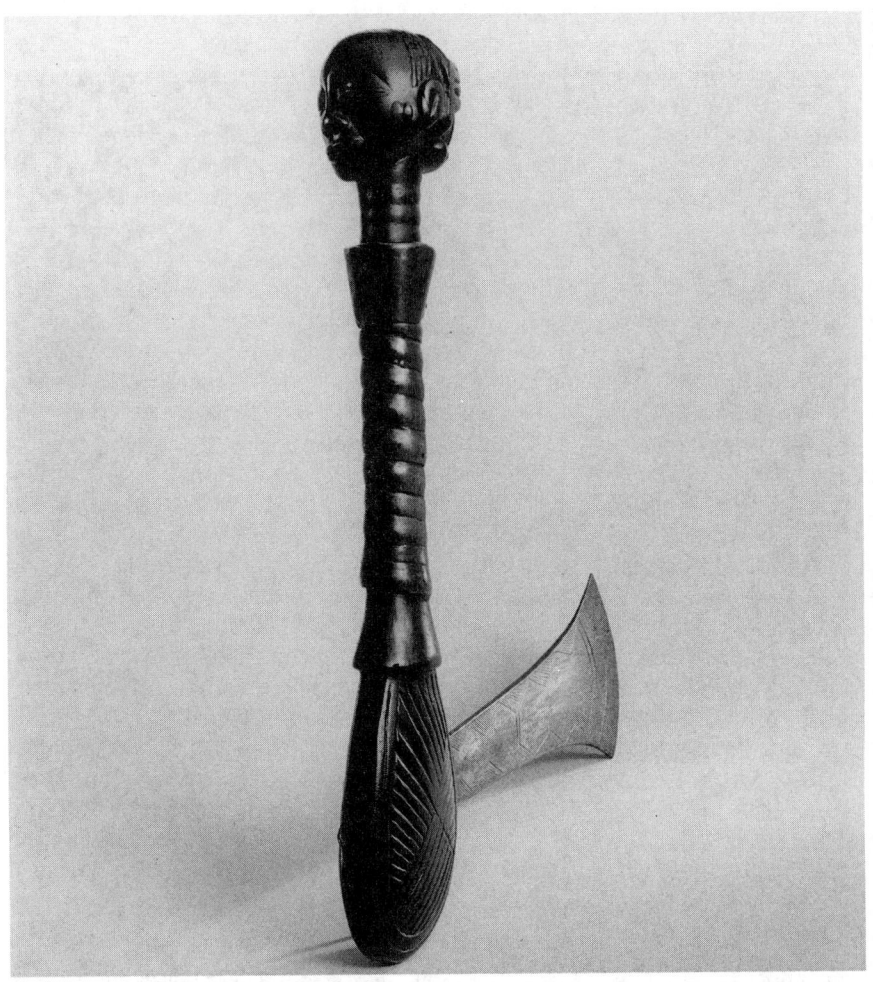

PLATE 20.4 *Luba, Zaire: ceremonial weapon whose handle, covered with twisted brass, ends in a carved head. Incised iron blade. Length: 37 cm*

by the court, in which case he was usually a close relative of the king. The central administration supervised the collection of tribute, organized the military when it was necessary to coerce tribute and advised the king through the *tshidie* (general council) and the *tshihangu* (court). The main officers were the *twite* (who represented the king in secular contexts), the *nabanza* (keeper of the regalia and supervisor of rituals), the *lukanga* (senior judge), the *mwana Mwilamba* (head of the army), the *mwine Lundu* (keeper of tradition and particularly of the unwritten constitution), the *fumwa pamba diyumbi* (the keeper and maker of charms and royal diviner) and the *ndalamba* (queen-mother with ritual role).[16]

Beyond this the same officials and probably others also acted at sessions of the *Bambudye* association which had numerous lodges. We do not know exactly how this functioned as the *Bambudye* secrets have not been revealed. But the effects of *Bambudye* were to exert both ritual and secular control over the country and even its king, while continually promoting the ideology of Lubahood and of the state.[17]

In practice, local courts were patterned after the organization of the capital and local chiefs had some sacred paraphernalia and links to local territorial spirit cults, often for their own ancestors, so that the centrifugal forces in the kingdom were always strong. The coercive power of the king's warriors was the practical force that kept the country together. But there was no standing army, so that the ideological force constituted by the *Bambudye* was of great importance. This meant also that heavy tribute (and many traditions speak of this) could only be enforced when central districts were willing to back the king against internal or external forces.

It is not surprising, therefore, that the kingdom did not expand rapidly. There is little information about territorial history until about 1700[18] and the reign of King Kadilo. At that time there were campaigns to the north against the adjacent Songye towns, 'but, in the end, Kadilo met with defeat. Alliance with some Songye towns followed and by the end of the century Songye influence was being felt in the affairs of the state during a succession crisis.'[19] The real expansion of the kingdom occurred in the valley of the Lualaba, along the Lovua (Kiambi) and south of the Upemba depression'. Such expansion faltered as a major succession crisis developed from about 1780 to 1810. During this crisis the Kanyok freed themselves from Luba overrule, and Songye political and cultural influence reached a high point as shown by the introduction of the Bukasandji society. After 1800 however, expansion continued towards the east, with the conquest of the lands between the River Lualaba and Lake Tanganyika and a push by military leaders invested with the sacred fire towards the north along the Lualaba river as far as Buli.[20] Explanations given for this expansion[21] are not entirely convincing. It is better to acknowledge that the inner rationale of this dynamic is still not understood than to try and force explanations in terms of access to trade routes or raw materials about which almost nothing is known so far.

16. J. Vansina, 1965, pp. 57–8; K. Y. Tundu, 1981, pp. 83–99.
17. T. Q. Reefe, 1981, pp. 46–8.
18. ibid., pp. 107–24, and pp. 58–9 for dates.
19. N. Fairley, 1978.
20. T. Q. Reefe, 1981, pp. 124–8.
21. A. Wilson, 1972.

PLATE 20.5 (Left) *Luba, Zaire: the knob of a cane, in the form of a scarified woman with a pearl necklace. Overall length: 160 cm*

PLATE 20.6 (Right) *Luba, Zaire: the knob of a cane, in the form of a scarified woman with her hands on her shoulders. Overall length: 80 cm*

The Lunda: internal organization and development to 1800

The Rund kingdom became a Lunda empire in the eighteenth century. Its earlier organization is not fully known, except for some titles at court and that its military character was much more developed than in the Luba kingdom. A little is known, however, about the principles of social and political organization.

The succession of the *tubung* had been matrilineal but succession for the royal title and at court was bilateral. The imaginary representation of society was based on positional succession and perpetual kinship. This meant that every incumbent to a position or title was supposed to almost become his predecessor. The incumbent took on the name of his predecessor, his wives, children and other relatives. Indeed the personality of his predecessor almost became his personality and as a consequence kinship was perpetual. The incumbent of a title might have been in the king's case, a grandson, for another title-holder his nephew or, for the *mwant a ngaand* (district headman), his uncle. Five generations later this system would still stand and so the ravages of time were negated.

It was possible, therefore, to imagine the state as an organization run by a single family, headed by the *Mwant Yav* (emperor). New chiefs could be incorporated by giving them a kinship link (as son-in-law, for instance, after a marriage alliance) and providing them with a stable position in the empire. Historians have rightly pointed out that positional succession and perpetual kinship provided the mechanism by which the incorporation of far-flung territories became possible. Moreover, the provision of a family model for the empire automatically regulated relationships between officials. Division by notional generation was strict.[22] Thus all 'sons' and 'nephews' owed obedience to all 'fathers' and 'uncles'; all 'grandsons' were allies of their 'grandfathers'. Division by direct descent or affinal station complemented this. 'Sons-in-law' were clients of their fathers-in-law, and 'sister sons' were in ambiguous relationship to 'mother's brothers' as a result.

So, to the Rund the state was a family writ large – very large indeed as the empire came to stretch from the River Kwango to beyond the River Luapula. But it was a family of warriors and a family that would thrive on slavery. By about 1700, Lunda war expeditions had subdued the populations around the empire's core, incorporated them and then moved further afield. By 1750 to 1760 strong subsidiary kingdoms were taking shape from the Yaka on the Kwango river to Kazembe on the River Luapula, along an east–west axis that encompassed the mineral resources

22. The model is clearly akin to that of the Sala Mpasu who were not even organized into a chiefdom. But their age organization and 'big men' correspond to Rund categories of age and titled positions. Cf. W. F. Pruitt, 1973.

of Shaba and access to the Portuguese emporia on the River Zambezi as well as the trading routes from the Rund to the Imbangala on the River Kwango.

The imperial administration was loose. The empire consisted of a core plus peripheral kingdoms whose rulers merely paid occasional tribute to the court.[23] At the core the lowest level of territorial organization was the canton ruled by the district headman who still succeeded to this office by matrilineal succession. Above him was the *Cilol* (district ruler) appointed from the capital. At the centre the *tubung* and titled officials assisted the king.

To control the *bilolo* the king had created the *tukwata*, sing. *kakwata*, (special officials), who roamed the countryside with a military detachment to force the *bilolo* to surrender tribute. Apart from these forces there still existed a major military organization headed by a *kazembe* (general). Even before 1700 generals were appointed to head expeditionary forces to distant areas. The title itself was given to any sanguinary warrior who had killed a dangerous enemy.[24] Such a general wielded all power in his operational terrain but once the area was incorporated, he either lost his status or became a ruler in his own right, a *kilolo* of the emperor.

The *mussumba* (capital) was laid out like an army camping overnight, with front and vanguards, wings and centre. Its hub was the royal palace with the *Mwant Yav* (emperor), the *Swan Murund* (symbolic queen-mother named Rweej), the *rukonkesh* (queen-mother and head of the logistics for the court) and the officials foremost among whom were military officers such as the *Kalala* (head of the vanguard) and the *Swan Mulopwe* (heir-presumptive and commander of the army). Power was vested in the emperor; his title *Mwant Yav* (Lord of the Viper) referred to the distance between king and mortals but also to his ambiguity as he stood for both peace and war, prosperity and destruction.

By comparison, the role of the Lunda emperor was much less ritualized and his power was more despotic. Until recently the expansion of the Lunda empire was thought to have begun with an emigration of warriors to the River Kwango. But recent research has shown that the traditions about the so-called first wave of emigration are later interpolations, resulting from trading contacts between the Imbangala and the Rund.[25] In fact, the expansion started before 1700. The first expedition went south-east towards the salt pans of the Lualaba river, near present-day Kolwezi. Then around 1700, a breakaway group, under the leadership of Musokantanda and Kanongesha, went south into present-day Zambia and set up a state in the Ndembu area after partly assimilating the Mbwela autochtons and pushing some of them southwards.[26] Some Lunda may have been involved earlier

23. J. L. Vellut, 1972, p. 70.
24. Again the parallel to the Sala Mpasu (head hunter); W. F. Pruitt, 1973.
25. J. K. Thornton, 1981a.
26. R. E. Schechter, 1980, pp. 113–24 and 1976.

in the formation of the Lozi kingdom. Historians accept some early influence of the Lunda on Bulozi but hard proof of such contacts is still lacking. As Lunda expansion southwards started after 1700 it is likely that the Lozi kingdom had already taken shape by the time Lunda influence reached it.[27]

From the salt pans of the Lualaba river a further expedition took the Lunda generals eastwards towards the copper mines and beyond to the rich Luapula valley. The Lunda army beat off a Luba attack against them and subjugated the chiefs of Shaba (one of them called Katanga) and the Shila state of Luapula. They extended this state and, by the second half of the eighteenth century, Kazembe of the Luapula was lord of a large tightly knit kingdom.[28] Soon after their settlement the Lunda of Kazembe took up contacts with the Portuguese of Sena and Tete. A mission led by de Lacerda visited the new kingdom from 1798 to 1799.[29] It was impressed by the military power of the Kazembe and with the severity of coercive measures still being used by the court against the local inhabitants. The Portuguese visit inaugurated a period of intense trade relationships between Kazembe and the lower Zambezi. This was to strengthen the autonomy of Kazembe towards Mussumba, so that the regular tribute payments of the 1790s had become more an equal exchange of gifts by the 1830s.[30]

Towards the north and west other Lunda expansion was closely linked to the development of the slave trade in Angola. Contacts with the Angolan slave-trading system date from the 1670s at the latest[31] and developed after 1630.[32] The Imbangala developed a system of trading by caravans which brought European goods, such as cloth, beads and crockery, to the Lunda capital where they served as luxury goods for the aristocracy and new emblems of status and power. The Lunda rejected the offer of guns and retained their faith in the *mpok* (broadsword).[33] In return, they exported slaves captured first in the areas north and east of the Rund core in the lands of the Sala Mpasu, Kete, Kanincin and even Kanyok. Later, Mbwela captives from northern Zambia and eastern Angola were also added to those exports. At the same time, demand for slaves grew in Lunda proper. They were settled around the capital to cultivate large fields and along the major roads of the country in deserted sites to provide cassava from plantations, as well as ferry services and, eventually, porterage assistance to caravans crossing the wastes between the Rivers Kwango and Nkalany as well as from the Nkalany to the River Lualaba.[34]

Also shortly after 1700 the Lunda sent expeditions westwards, so that

27. Mutumba Mainga, 1973, pp. 213–14.
28. E. Labrecque, 1949, p. 27; M. W. Kolungwe, 1974, p. 50.
29. J. Vansina, 1965, p. 133.
30. J. Vansina, 1966, pp. 165–74; F. de Lacerda e Almeida, 1944, pp. 175–261; A. C. P. Gamitto, 1960, Vol. II, pp. 9–130.
31. O. de Cadornega, 1940, Vol. III, p. 219.
32. Probably after 1965; cf. J. K. Thornton, 1981a, p. 6.
33. M. C. Correia Leitão, 1938, p. 25.
34. J. L. Vellut, 1972.

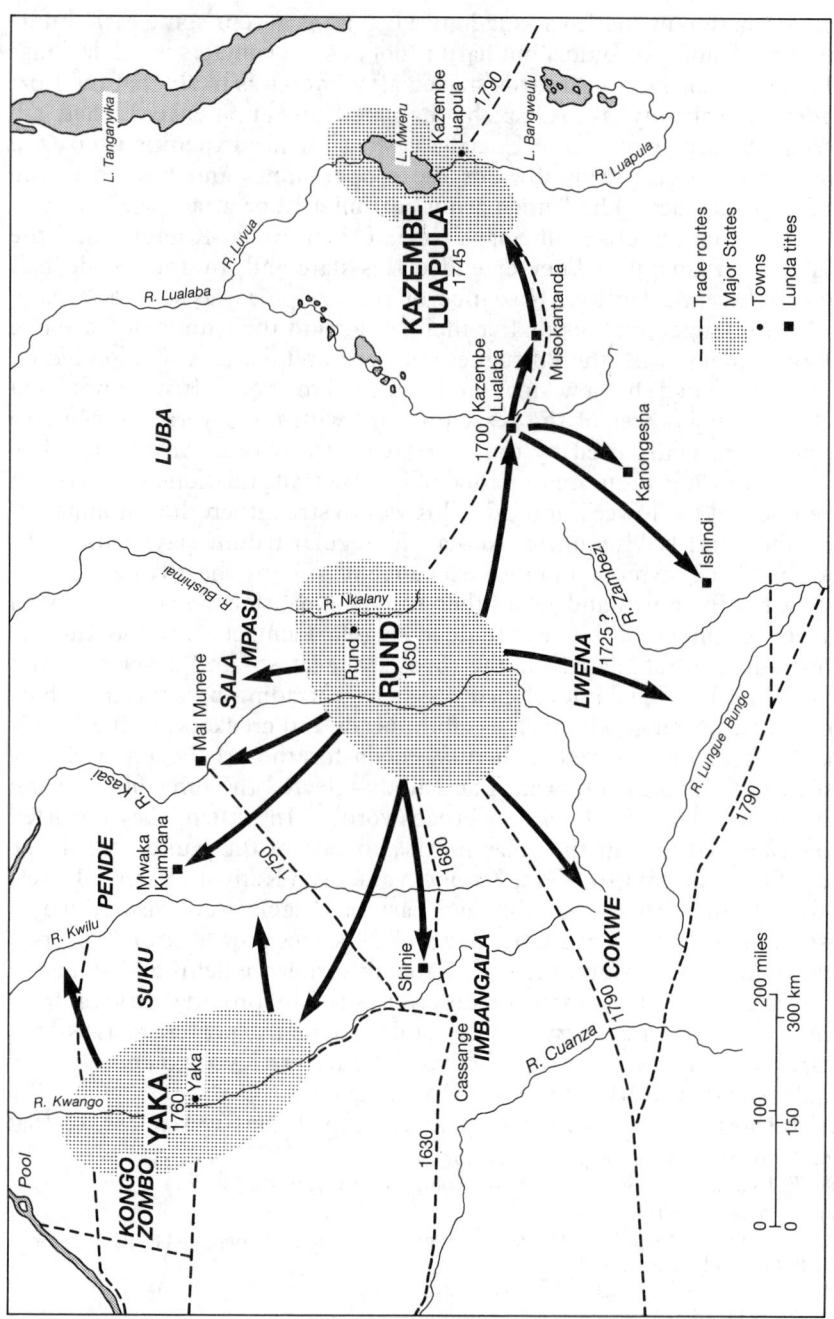

FIG. 20.3   *The Lunda empire in the eighteenth century (after J. Vansina)*

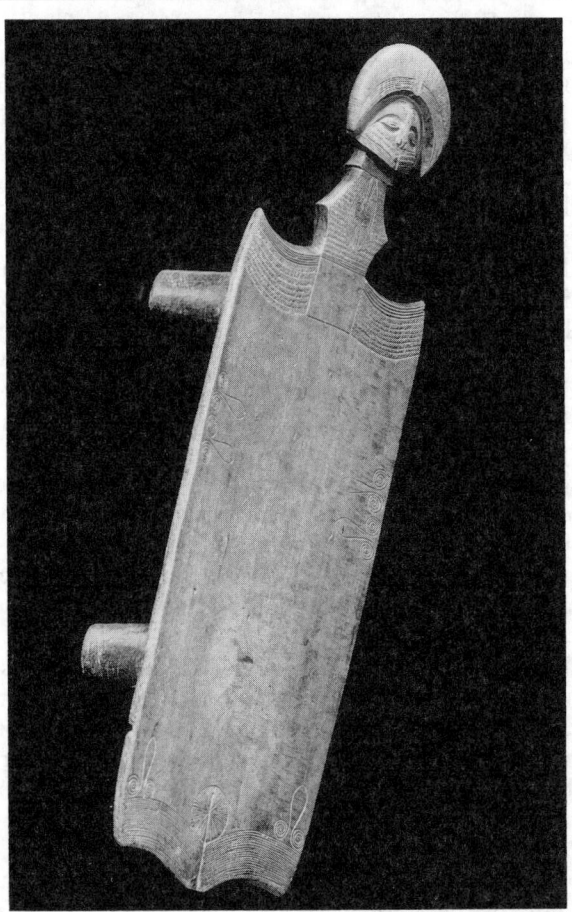

PLATE 20.7 *Chokwe, Angola and Zaire: a wooden ritual bed (?) with four feet, extended by a head with a typical Chokwe headdress. It is decorated by carvings reminiscent of the earrings known as* ukulungu. *Length: 131 cm*

by about 1750 Lunda chiefs were found on the River Kwango. Eastern Angola, the land of the Lwena, was their first goal. Several small states were created, the main one under the leadership of Ciniama. The Lunda leaders superimposed themselves on fairly large-scale societies organized around matrilineal genealogies of great depth. The Lunda *mwangana* (chief) obtained his position first as arbitrator to settle feuds, but the local people also accepted the belief that strong supernatural powers were vested in him. By genealogical reckoning the first Lunda chiefs here date from about 1750 but the process certainly started a good generation earlier, if only because by 1750 Lunda chiefs were installed on the eastern banks of the

River Kwango.[35] West of the River Lwena various Chokwe, Minungo and Songo chiefdoms were also created by the Lunda by superimposing themselves on existing societies. With the Shinje, however, they overran a pre-existing kingdom.[36] Among the former the Chokwe were later to prove the most important. Even in the eighteenth century as metallurgists, skilled carvers and hunters, they were valuable to the empire. The central Lunda, who had little metallurgical or carving skills,[37] derived both weapons and carvings from this area.

The Lunda invaders hunted slaves as they conquered. They built great fortified military camps, with ditches and extensive palissades.[38] In the Kwango valley they found Yaka, Suku and perhaps at Okango yet other chiefdoms structured after the Kongo pattern. These they overran, while many inhabitants fled. But the structures were not destroyed. Instead the Lunda established superior or parallel *kilolo* (chiefs). As a result a complex, three-tiered political structure came into being in which even the ideology of the state was split between 'autochthons' and Lunda invaders. But the leader of the Yaka, the *kiamfu* (a term derived from *Yav*, the imperial title), could not control all his own men. In the north a semi-independent state arose, that of the Pelende, whilst a group called the Sonde–Luwa emigrated east of the Middle Kwango and founded chiefdoms of their own.[39]

Once established, the Yaka kings started raiding the lands towards the Kwilu to gather slaves for sale to Angolan, Kongo and Vili traders. This provoked major upheavals in the region. The Suku kingdom arose as a result of successful resistance, but elsewhere people fled north-eastwards provoking, by the nineteenth century, the high densities of population observed around the fifth degree of latitude south.[40]

The final expedition went from the west of the Kasai river northwards, probably along the valley of the Tshikapa. It founded two small states: one at the main falls of the Kasai with a capital at Mai Munene which soon became a major market for caravans from the River Kwango; and the other, called Mwaka Kumbana, on the River Loange. In both areas the Lunda

35. C. M. N. White, 1962, pp. 15–8; J. K. Thornton, 1981a, p. 5 and footnote 29 (Shinje; Malonda).

36. Evidence from Lunda tradition and from the stylistic study of art used at the Lunda court related to a later period (19th century) but may well be (certainly with regard to metal) valid for the second half of the 18th century as well. The carving activities of the Chokwe at that time are attested by stylistic borrowing from late Portuguese Renaissance and indeed from Portuguese Rococo objects.

37. M. C. Correia Leitão, 1938, p. 25. Similar fortifications were known in the heartland, among the Kanyok and in the Luba heartland. Military technology diffused throughout the region.

38. ibid.

39. M. Plancquaert, 1971; J. K. Thornton, 1981a.

40. The ethnic groups now called Mbala and Ngongo all moved north as a result of Yaka raids.

mixed with the other recent immigrants – the Pende – as well as with autochthons. The resulting political systems were much less like the organization of the central Rund than other Lunda states. This was due to the political influence of the Pende in the area and the continuing existence of almost independent Pende chiefdoms.[41]

Conclusion

By 1800 Luba and Lunda expansion had structured all the savannah area of Central Africa east of the River Kwango. They had spread a common general culture over the whole area giving its various peoples common world views, common rituals and common emblems and symbols. Some objects, such as the Lunda horned caps, are found from the River Kwango to the Lualaba. Some institutions, such as the boys' *mukanda*, known from west of the Kwango valley since the 1650s, spread at first with the Pende then with the Lunda and, in the north, from the Pende to the Kuba.[42] Such widespread movement was facilitated by the existence of the trading routes and even by raids. Population mobility especially through marriage alliances, was astonishing, as evidenced by the diffusion of names for although women went to live with their husbands, clan-names were inherited through the mother. Common names are found from the River Kwango to the Kasai and from the Kasai to the Luapula.

Lunda expansion, however, also led to devastation over huge areas. The militaristic nature of the Lunda states should not be underestimated, nor their large-scale slave-raiding. The low population densities in southern Kwango and eastern Angola were probably partly due to these raids. Certainly the bunching of populations along the fifth parallel between Kwango and Kwilu was a result of these activities. This, and the presence of a common political culture from Kwango to the Luapula river, still constitutes the contemporary heritage throughout this huge area.

41. Kodi Muzong, 1976, pp. 268–342.
42. J. Vansina, 1983a, pp. 332–3, and 1978, pp. 204–5; Kodi Muzong, 1976, pp. 136 and 163.

The Northern Zambezia – Lake Malawi region

21

K. M. PHIRI, O. J. M. KALINGA AND H. H. K. BHILA

The region discussed in this chapter is bounded on the south by the Zambezi, on the north by the Songwe and Ruvuma rivers, on the west by the Luangwa, and on the east by the Indian Ocean. The southern zone of this region was dominated by the Chewa speakers with their sub-groups: the Manganja of the lower Shire valley and Nyanja around the southern end of Lake Malawi. To the west of the Chewa were the Nsenga and to the east the Lolo–Makua–Lomwe speakers and the Yao. The northern zone stretched on the western side of Lake Malawi from the Chewa–Tumbuka marginal zone in the south to the Songwe river in the north. Three language families occupy this zone: the Tumbuka, the Ngonde–Nyakyusa, and the Sukwa–Lambya–Nyiha. In 1500, all the people of the southern zone and the Tumbuka of the north belonged to the 'matrilineal cluster of Central Bantu speakers' which stretched from southern Zaire in the west to the Indian Ocean in the east. In the centuries after 1500, however, the Tumbuka changed to patrilineal descent. The Ngonde–Nyakyusa and Sukwa–Lambya–Nyiha had always been patrilineal since the dawn of their historical tradition. The region today comprises eastern Zambia, all of Malawi, and northern Mozambique.

In the period under discussion, the southern zone was dominated in the fifteenth century by the arrival of the Maravi and the rise of their state system, and in the sixteenth and seventeenth by its expansion over the Nsenga to the west and the Lolo–Makua–Lomwe to the east. In the north, in the sixteenth century the people were organized in clusters of autonomous clans except for the Simbowe and Mbale chiefdoms in the Karonga plain and Phoka highlands respectively. Late in the same century, however, an immigrant group – the Ngulube – founded the states of Lambya, Ngonde, Chifungwe, Sukwa and a number of Nyakyusa chiefdoms. In the same period, the expansion of the Maravi into the Tumbuka–Chewa marginal zone led to the establishment of new Chewa chiefdoms such as Kanyenda, Kabunduli, Kaluluma and Chulu over Tumbuka peoples, creating in the main the Tonga people and language. In both zones the trade in ivory was a major factor in the eighteenth century. The southern zone was then characterized by the decline of the Maravi state system, the rise of successor states, and the outward spread of the Yao

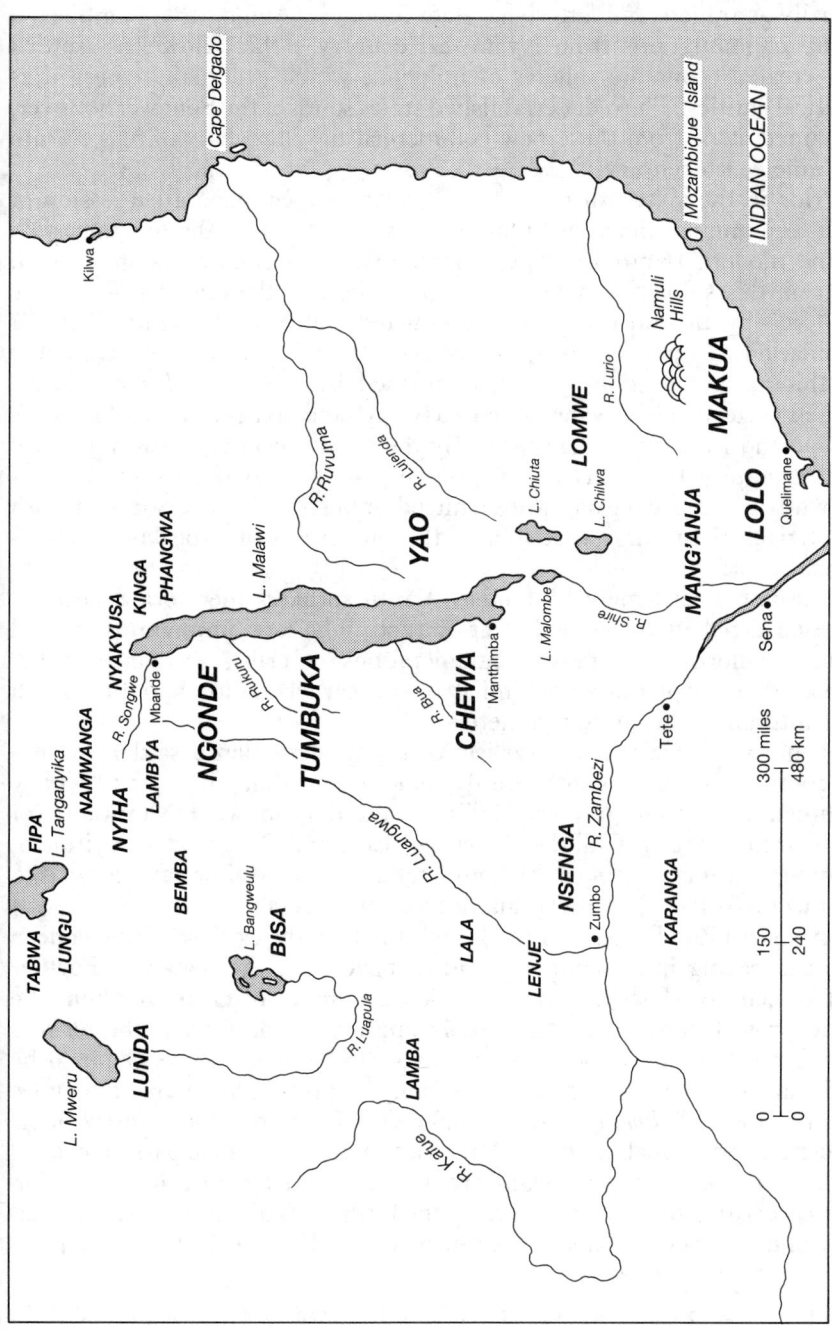

FIG. 21.1 *Peoples of the Northern Zambezia region in the eighteenth century*
Source: adapted from A. D. Roberts, *A History of the Bemba Before 1900*, London, Longman, 1973, p. xxv. Map adapted by kind permission of Longman Group UK Ltd

initially as traders and latterly as state founders. Among the Tumbuka, a group of immigrants from Nyamwezi country – the Balowoka – settled and created economic spheres of influence which eventually emerged as political entities. The older established states south of the Songwe, however, remained aloof from these new commercial developments until well into the nineteenth century.

Prior to the sixteenth century, the region experienced a succession of Iron Age immigrations, including those which brought the first ancestors of the modern Bantu-speaking inhabitants. Archaeology has shed much light on this subject. It tells us, for example, that the region began to be occupied by an iron-using, food-producing and possibly Bantu-speaking population as early as $+300$. Until the eleventh century, the Iron Age inhabitants in question were distinguished by their use of such closely related pottery as Mwavarambo and Mwamasapa in the north, and Kapeni, Nkope and Longwe in the south.[1] By the twelfth century, however, these earlier pottery traditions had begun to give way to fresh ones such as Mawudzu and Luangwa, whose introduction has been associated with the arrival of the first ancestors of the modern Bantu-speaking populations.[2]

The initial settlement by modern Bantu-speakers therefore appears to have occurred in the period after $+1200$. The new immigrants arrived from the north in clans or agglomerations of clans, and once in the region they displaced or assimilated the earlier Bantu and pre-Bantu agriculturalists and hunter-gatherers.

In northern Malawi, the earliest of the modern Bantu settlers were a predominantly stateless or pre-dynastic population (Fig. 21.2). They included the clans of Sikwese, Chilima, Silumbu, Simwayi, Namwenes (of the Karonga plain), Chiluba, Mzembe, Luhanga, Nyanjagha, Nyirongo, Kanyinji, Mtonga and so on, whom later and stronger immigrants tried to organize into states, with varying degrees of success.

In eastern Zambia, east of the Luangwa river, the earliest of the modern Bantu-speaking inhabitants are said to have been the Katanga. Further east in central Malawi, they comprised a number of clans to whom the term 'proto-Chewa' has been loosely applied. In particular, the term is associated with the Banda, Mbewe and Zimba clans which claim to be indigenous to the area. In oral tradition, the proto-Chewa are sometimes referred to as *Kalimanjira* (Path-makers) who cleared the country of its earlier nomadic inhabitants, the Batwa and Kafula. In some parts of central Malawi, the proto-Chewa clans are also associated with a local creation myth according to which man and all the birds and animals of his Malawian environment were created at Kapirintiwa Hill which is located on the

1. G. Y. Mgomezulu, 1981, pp. 450–1; K. R. Robinson, 1966, pp. 183–8; and K. R. Robinson and B. Sandelowsky, 1968.
2. G. Y. Mgomezulu, 1981, pp. 450–1.

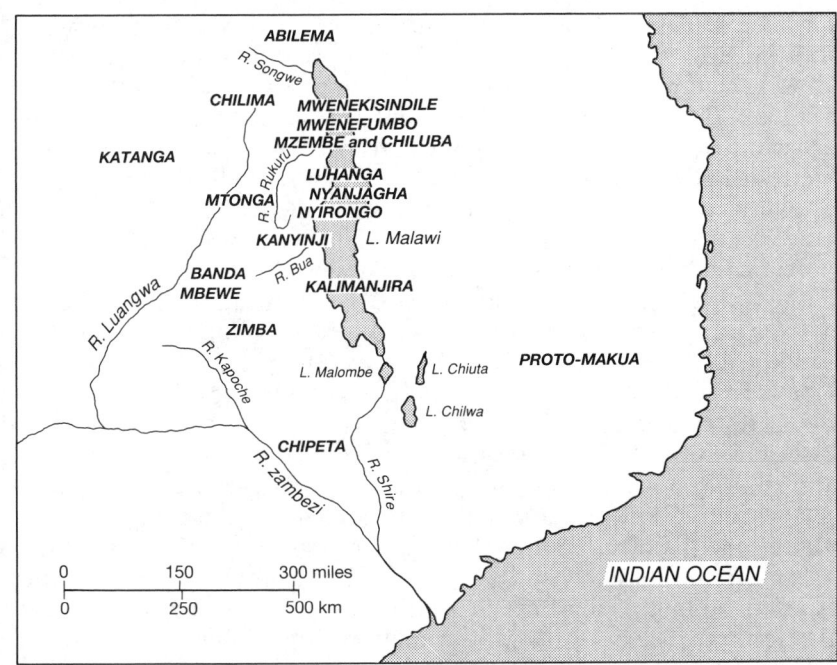

FIG. 21.2 *Pre-dynastic groups in Northern Zimbabwe (after K. M. Phiri and O. J. M. Kalinga)*

boundary between Central Malawi and Western Mozambique.[3]

It is not possible, on the other hand, to be definite about the origins and early composition of the Lolo–Makua–Lomwe and Yao of northern Mozambique. None of them has clear traditions of how they occupied their present homelands. This is probably because they occupied their country many centuries ago and have therefore long since lost memory of their exact origins. At the beginning of the sixteenth century, the Lolo already occupied the south-western part of northern Mozambique, while the Makua and other Lomwe-speaking groups inhabited the coast opposite Mozambique Island and its hinterland as far as the highlands in the central part of the country. The Yao had their homeland to the north-west of the Makua, between the Ruvuma river in the north and the Lujenda in the south.[4]

In the northern zone, the earliest modern Bantu-speaking inhabitants

3. The following are among the main sources on the interaction between the modern Bantu-speakers and the earlier inhabitants of this region: H. L. Vail; H. W. Langworthy, 1969b; K. M. Phiri, 1975b; and A. J. William-Myers, 1978b.

4. Field research on the oral history of northern Mozambique was not possible before 1975 because of the national liberation struggle there. The situation has probably changed now as the Centro de Estudos Africanos in Maputo is currently committed to rectifying

for whom there are records settled in the area between the Songwe and South Rukuru rivers. They included the Sikwese, Chilima, Mwenekisindile and Mwenefumbo clans of the Chitipa and Karonga plains, and the Mzembe and Chiluba clans of the mountainous Phoka area south-west of Karonga. Their traditions of origin claim that they came from the north-eastern side of Lake Malawi and may have been related to the *abilema* who are believed to have lived in Unyakyusa before the Lwembe lineage settled there.[5] Not long afterwards, however, fresh and in most cases more powerful groups also began to infiltrate the area. These included the Simbowe who occupied the Karonga plain and the Mbale who invaded the Phoka area. They too came from the north, with the Mbale claiming to have migrated into the Lake Malawi region from the area south of Lake Victoria.

The Mbale migration into the Phoka highlands probably occurred in the fourteenth century. The new immigrants were noted iron-smelters and they easily established good relations with the autochthons, the Mzembe and Chiluba, on whom they came to depend for agricultural produce and some of the coal deposits which they needed for their furnaces. The Mzembe and Chiluba, on the other hand, began to depend on the Mbale for iron agricultural tools and weapons.[6] Thus it would appear that there was a general migration of people southwards using the corridor between Lakes Tanganyika and Malawi as a main passage. Some of these people probably moved further south into central Malawi or the Chewa-speaking zone.

Between the Phoka and Chewa areas in the north and south respectively, there lived various Tumbuka-speaking clans. The Nkamanga plain, Henga and Kasitu valleys were inhabited mainly by the Luhanga, Kachali, Nyirongo, Mtika and Nyanjagha clans. Some of these groups seem to have spread as far east as the lakeshore and as far west as the Luangwa valley in modern Lundazi district of eastern Zambia.[7] The Nsenga, the present-day inhabitants of the latter region, seem to have evolved into a 'tribe' as a result of interaction between Tumbuka groups moving in from the east and Luba/Lunda-related immigrants from the west. They speak a language that is akin to Tumbuka and share the same clan-names with the inhabitants of Tumbukaland. In the eighteenth and nineteenth centuries,

the situation. The historical traditions of the Yao in Malawi, on the other hand, have been collected systematically of late, see K. Lapukeni, P. Rashid, N. Kumwembe and J. B. Webster, 1978; K. M. Phiri, M. Vaughan and D. Makuluni, 1978; and R. B. Misomali, G. Mkondiwa and H. K. Bhila, 1978; Y. B. Abdallah, 1919a; L. D. Soka, 1953; and E. A. Alpers, 1975a. The Yao, according to their traditions, originated around 'Yao Hill' in the area between the Rovuma and Luambala rivers. According to Alpers, the Makua spread to other parts of north Mozambique from the Namuli Hills in the central part of northern Mozambique.

5. See M. Wilson (1958). For a summary of the migration traditions of modern Bantu-speakers onto the Chitipa and Karonga plains, see O. J. M. Kalinga, 1985.

6. H. K. Msiska, 1978a and 1978b.

7. H. L. Vail, 1972b.

they tended to act as a bridge between the Tumbuka in the east and the Bisa in the west.

Thus prior to about 1500, the political structure of the entire region from the Songwe river in the north to the Zambezi in the south, with the exception of a few pockets, was characterized by the prevalence of stateless or small-scale polities. The different ethnic groups were each comprised of local chieftaincies with a two-tier hierarchy of authority. This form of political organization revolved around a local chieftain as the uppermost authority. The chief presided over a group of closely related lineage-based villages of which his own was the most senior genealogically. To the community of villages surrounding him, he rendered religious, judicial and military services, and was in turn entitled to the allegiance of all his followers.

Though politically and sometimes physically divided into ethnic and clan spheres of influence, the Lake Malawi region enjoyed a certain degree of social and religious cohesion. Religious affiliation in particular provided a basis of cohesion within and across the different socio-linguistic groups. Indeed over the greater part of this region, religious action was expressed at a local as well as territorial level. At a local level, religion played the function of ensuring the moral and material well-being of the population, while at a territorial level it also fostered cultural and ecological cooperation.[8]

Religious practice for most people in this part of Africa involved ancestor veneration, spirit possession, rain-making, and control of witchcraft. Among the Chewa-speaking peoples, for example, the Nyau Secret Society (Plate 21.1) was an important vehicle for expressing and dramatizing ethnic creation myths, the moral code, and so on. Among other things, a Nyau performance dramatized the interdependence of the natural and spirit worlds, and the Chewa creation myth according to which man, animals and spirits once lived together in harmony. The chief manifestation of a territorial religious experience, on the other hand, was the rain cults. A number of these spanned large areas were dedicated to a territorially acknowledged god or spirit, and controlled by an élite of priests and functionaries. The Chikha-ng'ombe and Chisumphe cults of the Tumbuka and Chewa respectively belonged to this category.

It has been shown that at least within the matrilineal belt extending from the Tumbuka–Chewa marginal zone in the north to the Zambezi valley in the south, there was a considerable degree of interaction and overlap between the various territorial religious cults. The deity was represented in the same way throughout. Among the Tumbuka and Chewa, for example, he took the physical form of a snake, was thought to be a male force, and had several spirit wives devoted to his service. The functionaries dedicated to the services of this deity were possessed and set apart for their

8. This view is strongly supported by T. O. Ranger, 1973, and J. M. Schoffeleers, 1979a, pp. 6–23.

PLATE 21.1 *Mask used by the Nyau Secret Society, the most revered institution among the Chokwe/Maravi peoples.*

special role in society. Noting these structural similarities between the different rain cults north of the Zambezi, Schoffeleers has postulated that the different cults in Malawi, Mozambique and Zimbabwe may have belonged to the same cult-complex.[9] Be that as it may, religion provided an important means of communication and interaction between peoples who were otherwise divided politically.

Among the Chewa and related peoples of the southern zone, the loose political structure which prevailed before 1500 was greatly transformed by the emergence of the Maravi state system at the beginning of the sixteenth century and its expansion later in the same century and in the seventeenth.[10] The Maravi thus dominate the sixteenth- and seventeenth-century political history of the lower northern Zambezia region just as the builders of the Mutapa state dominate that of Southern Zambezia in the fifteenth and sixteenth centuries.

It is now generally agreed that the Maravi arrived in the Lake Malawi region as immigrants who originated in the Luba area of south-eastern Zaire, and that they entered central Malawi from the west after migrating through the great plateau of north-eastern Zambia. On reaching the southern end of Lake Malawi, they rapidly established themselves as rulers over the earlier proto-Chewa inhabitants, consolidated their rule, and then embarked on a campaign of territorial expansion which took them beyond central and southern Malawi into adjacent parts of Zambia and Mozambique (Fig. 21.3). By the early seventeenth century, therefore, their confederation of states encompassed the greater part of eastern Zambia, central and southern Malawi and northern Mozambique. In this way, the Maravi state system came to have a political, military and economic impact over a vast area.

However, the process which led to this political configuration is not yet clearly understood by historians. No one is yet clear how the Maravi state was created or the factors which were conducive to state growth in the region.

One view holds that the Maravi arrived in the country as a group of invaders who were fully equipped with the symbols of chiefly power with the help of which they established themselves as a ruling class over what must have been a stateless indigenous population.[11] This theory emphasizes the external origins of Maravi kingship and political institutions and

9. M. J. Schoffeleers, 1979a, pp. 22–3. See also H. L. Vail, 1979, and M. J. Schoffeleers, 1979b. On the religious aspects of Nyau, see M. J. Schoffeleers, 1976, and N. E. Lindgren and M. J. Schoffeleers, 1978.

10. The only evidence to date the arrival of the Maravi in the Lake Malawi area is archaeological. C-14 dates from Maravi occupation sites that have been excavated range from 1420–80, thus suggesting that the Maravi arrived in the fifteenth century. See K. R. Robinson, 1972, pp. 61–3, and M. J. Schoffeleers, 1973, pp. 48–53. Dr Newitt, however, is of the opinion that the Maravi did not occupy the northern banks of the Lower Zambezi until the early sixteenth century: see M. D. D. Newitt, 1982, pp. 47–8.

11. This theory was first advanced by R. A. Hamilton. After a close reading of Chewa

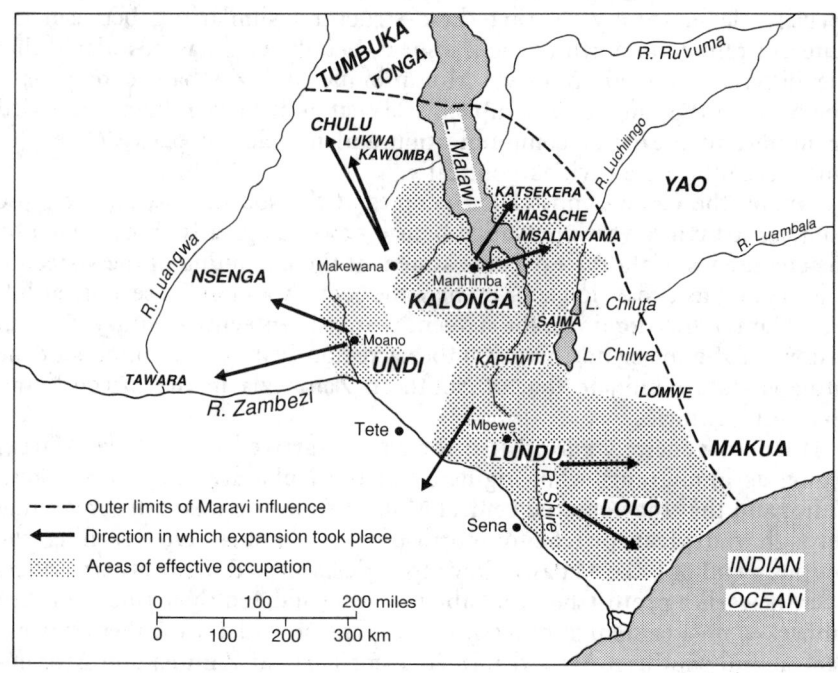

FIG. 21.3   *The Maravi expansion, c.1650 (after K. M. Phiri)*

therefore possibly underplays the intricate interweaving of indigenous and immigrant ideologies in the formation of the state. Andrew Roberts, for example, has argued that although invasion and conquest may have been crucial steps in the creation of states in some parts of tropical Africa, historians should also think in terms of how newcomers acquired authority by virtue of importing useful techniques and ideas.[12] He has a vision of what would have happened in a socially and economically differentiated society where a group possessing ideas and techniques – which could be used to exploit the natural environment or to resolve long-standing conflicts or feuds, for example – was also likely to dominate the others.

Other hypotheses have also been popular with different writers. One of these would have us take into account the role of demographic factors. Agnew, for instance, speaks of geographical momentum – soil fertility,

oral traditions, he concluded that a major political change occurred in the fourteenth or fifteenth century. A group of incoming chiefly invaders known by the clan name Phiri then superimposed themselves over a long established and loosely organized indigenous population. See R. A. Hamilton, 1955a, p. 21. Since then, this view has been echoed by several writers, including M. G. Marwick, 1963, pp. 377–8; and M. J. Schoffeleers, 1972a, pp. 96–9.

12. A. D. Roberts, 1976, p. 84.

adequate rainfall and reliable food supply – which from early times has been conducive to the greater concentration of population on the western side of Lake Malawi than in the neighbouring areas to the east and west. A growing population engaged in surplus production, albeit modest, would have served as a suitable basis for the accumulation of dynastic power.[13]

Another hypothesis takes into account the trade factor, maintaining that the formation of a state at the southern end of Lake Malawi in the fifteenth or sixteenth century arose from the need for an authority to control the development of the trade in ivory between the southern shores of the lake and the east coast of Africa via the Shire–Zambezi water system. The argument, in other words, is that it was by exercising control over the growth of this trade that the early Kalongas (as Maravi paramounts were called) were able to accumulate power.[14]

Lastly, there is the conflict hypothesis which maintains that the Maravi state evolved out of the dialectics of interaction between the incoming Maravi–Phiri group and the indigenous proto-Chewa inhabitants. On this, Chewa oral traditions specifically point to how – after an initial period of conflict – an acceptable relationship was worked out, according to which the Maravi–Phiri invaders would act as rulers of the country while the indigenous proto-Chewa–Banda acted as 'owners of the soil'.[15] As to what might have prompted the indigenes to accept the leadership of the immigrants, a possible answer is to be found in the strength of the Maravi kinship organization. In later periods, it was this which served as a unifying link between the various Maravi sub-divisions as they dispersed.

Oral tradition, the main source of information on the early history of the area, on the other hand, is rather reticent on exactly how the Maravi state was founded. It simply maintains that under the leadership of Kalonga Chidzonzi, who headed the most senior Phiri royal lineage, the Maravi established their first kingdom around Mankhamba and Manthimba on the south-western side of Lake Malawi. Here, the Kalonga set up his headquarters at Manthimba or Maravi and designated the village of Mankhamba (which probably predated the Maravi advent) as the religious centre of the kingdom. It is furthermore maintained that the Kalonga surrounded himself with a bureaucracy of administrators. They included the commander of the army, *khombe*, the public executioner, *mkomba*, and a land divider, *mgawi*. From Portuguese written sources of the seventeenth century, on the other hand, we learn that Manthimba developed into an important commercial and political centre. According to one observer in 1624, it was a densely populated place, within three kilometres of the lake

13. S. Agnew, 1972, pp. 32–3.
14. E. A. Alpers, 1975a, pp. 46–9.
15. M. J. Schoffeleers, 1973, pp. 47–60; K. M. Phiri, 1975a, pp. 47–51; and M. J. Schoffeleers, 1979a, pp. 147–61.

with whose inhabitants Portuguese traders from Tete on the Zambezi conducted a prosperous trade.[16]

Oral tradition, however, provides the only indication of the institutional mechanisms through which the Kalonga's state was held together. One of these was the *mlira* cult. Once every year, about the month of September, heads of the different Phiri royal lineages were invited to Manthimba for the ritual veneration of Mlira, the spirit of the great Kalonga Chinkhole who led their ancestors into the country at the time of the migration from the north. The ritual culminated in the burning of the Marimba bush which stretched for a considerable distance along the lake, from Mankhamba in the south to the Chilua river in the north. This ritual, we believe, was a surface manifestation of a royal cult which had a significant integrative function within the Maravi state. Equally important to the integration of the kingdom was the manner in which appointive offices of state were allocated. The Kalonga is said to have appointed some heads of proto-Chewa clans to important leadership positions in his state. The Banda, an important proto-Chewa clan, were caretakers (*amatsano*) of the Kalonga's shrine at Mankhamba while the Mwale under Khombe led the Kalonga's warriors in battle. Traditions to this effect clearly underscore the extent to which non-Phiri or non-Maravi clan leaders were involved in the making of decisions pertaining to land tenure, the distribution of wealth, and the making of war.[17]

The extent to which the Kalonga was able personally to direct the affairs of his kingdom may have begun to decline towards the last quarter of the sixteenth century when the state began to expand. This expansion was affected through heads of the junior Phiri lineages. Such heads were sent out from the Manthimba–Mankhamba area into adjacent territories. Mpinganjila was sent eastwards into the land adjoining the eastern bank of the Upper Shire. Nyangu went south and occupied the country on the western bank of the Upper Shire; Changamire occupied the present Kirk Range area to the west of Manthimba; Chauma went to settle to the north-west of Mankhamba; while Chinsamba went to occupy the country north of the Manthimba–Mankhamba area. Taken together, the territories controlled by the Kalonga and these subordinate chiefs formed the heartland of the Maravi state system as it evolved in the seventeenth century.

Another dimension of the Maravi expansion involved the migration of the Kalonga's senior kinsmen into distant lands to the south and south-west of the heartland. This may have been a calculated move on the part of the early Kalongas as they sought to distance those who would have contested for the throne at Manthimba. Kaphwiti and Lundu migrated into and colonized the Lower Shire valley. Of the two, Kaphwiti was senior

16. Luiz Marianno, a Portuguese resident of Sena in 1924. His observations on the state of the 'Maravi empire' are summarized in J. Batalha-Reis, 1889.

17. I. Linden, 1979, pp. 188–93; K. M. Phiri, 1975a, pp. 52–5, and S. J. Nthara, 1948, pp. 17–24.

and controlled the whole valley before he lost much of his authority to Lundu. The paramountcy of Kaphwiti, however, did not last for long. It had suffered an enigmatic blow by 1572 when it was reported that Lundu ruled the greater part of the valley from the Mamvera or Murchison rapids in the north to the confluence of the Zambezi with the Shire in the south. The desire to control the Sena ivory trade with the Portuguese probably accounted for the Lundu's expansion of his sphere of influence, just as it might have led to the decline of the Kaphwitis who later found themselves cut off from this trade.[18]

It was the Lundu who, after his ascendancy in the Lower Shire valley, spearheaded Maravi expansion eastwards into Lolo and Makua country. The process of Maravi expansion in this part of Northern Zambezia started in the mid-sixteenth century. According to Nurse's historical linguistic analysis, the Maravi or Chewa in this part of northern Mozambique must have begun to interact with the Lolo and Makua not later than *c.* 1560.[19]

Maravi invasion and conquest of Lolo–Makua country first owed much to the fanaticism of the Lundu's warriors, whom some historians of Eastern Africa have identified with the notorious Zimba marauders of the late sixteenth century.[20] If they are correct, then the Lundu must have employed a mercenary army drawn from the truculent inhabitants of the area west of the Lower Shire valley.[21] According to dos Santos, the Zimba originated in that area before they moved toward Sena where they routed the Portuguese and their African allies in 1592. Thereafter, they swept through northern Mozambique and sacked the towns of Kilwa and Mombasa. It was not until they reached Malindi on the northern coast of Kenya that they were defeated by an alliance between the Swahili inhabitants of the town and the Segeju, a hinterland ethnic group with which the Sultan of Malindi was on friendly terms.[22]

Secondly, the success of the Lundu's warriors in the east was due to the statelessness of the Lolo and Makua societies. It has been said of the Lolo in particular that 'they had never been and seem never to have wanted to be notable or important'. Their political system was segmentary. The functions of government were performed by village headmen assisted by councils of elders. Together, these took decisions on all the military, judicial and religious affairs of their communities. Like the Lolo, the Makua also had a segmentary political system, but among them lineages belonging to

18. For a summary of the relative positions held by the Kaphwiti and Lundu in the pre-colonial politics of the Lower Shire valley, see H. H. K. Bhila, 1977. The expansion of the Lundu's kingdom is in J. dos Santos, 1901. See also E. A. Alpers, 1968, pp. 20–2, and M. J. Schoffeleers, 1968, pp. 143–59.

19. G. T. Nurse, 1977, p. 126.

20. N. J. Hafkin, 1973, pp. 10–14.

21. Schoffeleers, however, has proposed that the Zimba originated on the southern bank of the Zambezi where they were displaced by the wars of Portuguese colonial expansion between Sena and Tete: see M. J. Schoffeleers, 1980, pp. 15–19.

22. J. dos Santos, 1901, pp. 290–304.

the same clan sometimes combined under the leadership of the one who headed the most powerful lineage. Under this kind of impetus and as a result of pressure from the Portuguese, strong chieftaincies emerged among the coastal Makua in the late sixteenth century.[23]

The Lundu's warriors conquered both the Lolo and Makua and had them incorporated into a tributary state which the Portuguese residents of the Lower Zambezi termed 'Bororo'. In this conquest state, about which more is known than any aspect of Makua–Lolo history up to 1800, the Maravi established several chieftainships to govern their subjects some of whom did become auxilliary vassals. Politically, it was expedient then for many Makua to claim a Maravi origin. Culturally, however, there was considerable synthesis of Maravi and Makua customs and traditions, particularly in the Quelimane area.[24]

As a result, by the beginning of the seventeenth century, the Lundu controlled a vast territory north of the Zambezi, from the Lower Shire in the west almost to the Indian Ocean in the east. Not only was he recognized as 'the second most powerful person in the empire of Maravi (the first being Kalonga)', but his warriors periodically descended on the Makua part of the coast to raid Portuguese settlements.[25]

The Lundu held his vast kingdom together with the help of loyal military generals and vassals drawn from junior lineages within his clan. Furthermore, his state had an economic underpinning in that the different peoples whom it encompassed depended on the salt, iron and *machila* cotton cloths that were produced by the Lundu's Manganja subjects in the Lower Shire valley. Manganja religion was another unifying factor in the state. Centred on the Mbona cult whose central shrine was at Khulubvi in the Lower Shire valley, the theology of Manganja religion encompassed many elements of commoner protest against the misuse of royal power and pregogative. Consequently, the official cult of the Lundu paramountcy found many adherents over a large territory stretching from the seat of the Lundus in the Lower Shire valley to the Zambezi delta on the east coast.[26]

The immense prestige enjoyed by the Lundu in the eastern part of the Maravi confederation did not go unchallenged. The Kalonga who himself controlled a vast territory on the western and eastern sides of Lake Malawi as well as along the Upper Shire became extremely anxious about the Lundu's growing power. In the 1620s and 1630s, therefore, Maravi expansion eastward was stalled by the vicious internal rivalry which developed

23. The best description of the Lolo and Makua political system in the sixteenth century is that given by J. dos Santos, 1901, p. 308. Examples of emergent and powerful Makua chiefs of the time are Maviamuno and Mauruka whose relations with the Portuguese are treated at considerable length by E. A. Alpers, 1975a, pp. 14–85.

24. N. J. Hafkin, 1973, pp. 15–22.

25. M. Barreto, 1899, p. 475, and E. Axelson, 1960, pp. 132–3.

26. E. A. Alpers, 1975a, pp. 25–6; E. C. Mandala, 1977, pp. 39–41; and M. J. Schoffeleers, 1972b, p. 76.

between the Kalonga and Lundu.[27] Thereafter, the scene of dramatic events as far as Maravi expansion was concerned shifted from the east to the south-west. In this latter direction, Undi then established his own kingdom which he later expanded as the Lundu had done in the Lower Shire and further east.

According to one version of the traditions relating to the establishment of Undi's kingdom, the founder was sent out by the Kalonga to occupy the sandy plains near Nsengaland. Another version, however, suggests that Undi's departure for the south-west was occasioned by a major conflict within the ruling Phiri clan at Manthimba.[28] The second version seems more reliable because most traditions have it that Undi left Manthimba with many followers after quarrelling with the Kalonga over such issues as political succession and the distribution of tribute.

In the west, Undi and his followers successfully colonized the Kapoche river area, a tributary of the Zambezi. Thereafter, they extended the boundaries of their nascent kingdom from the banks of the Kapoche river westward toward the confluence of the Zambezi with the Luangwa. In that direction, Undi's warriors came into conflict with the Tawara along the Zambezi and the Nsenga along the eastern bank of the lower Luangwa. But the extent to which the Maravi then came to dominate the Nsenga has been the subject of some debate.

Historians approaching the subject from the Malawian side maintain that the first notable event in the history of the Nsenga was this invasion of their country by Undi and his warriors in the mid-seventeenth century. This invasion, it is claimed, was directed by Chimwala, the Undi's classificatory nephew, and initially aimed at the subjugation of Mundikula who then headed the largest and most important Nsenga clan, that of the Mwanza. According to William-Myers, one of the few researchers who have approached the debate from the Zambian side, however, about three-quarters of the Nsenga on the eastern side of the Luangwa were at one time or another in a tributary relationship with Undi. The conclusion to draw from this is that during its expansive phases, Undi's state encompassed a number of Nsenga chieftaincies, but that this did not apply to all the Nsenga as such. The south-western Nsenga near Feira in Zambia, for example, have no traditions of having been a part of Undi's 'empire'.[29]

Despite the debate, there is still the question of how Undi may have established a certain degree of political control over the Nsenga. The traditional argument is that Undi and his subordinates used force and the creation of perpetual kinship relationships according to which the conquered Nsenga chiefs were recognized as 'sons' or 'nephews' of the

27. R. A. Hamilton, 1954; E. A. Alpers, 1975b, p. 517.
28. H. W. Langworthy, 1969a, pp. 148–63; and K. M. Phiri, 1977, p. 9.
29. Among the sources which reflect a Maravi bias are: E. H. Lane-Poole, 1934, pp. 39–41, and H. W. Langworthy, 1969a, pp. 215–16. A more recent work is that by A. J. William-Myers, 1978a.

Maravi chiefs. Of late, however, a stronger argument has been presented. This is that trade and famine may have played a crucial role in the expansion of Undi's influence over neighbouring peoples. Undi, it has been shown, enjoyed immense influence with Portuguese traders at Tete, and this fact enabled him to exercise indirect control over participants from neighbouring polities. Secondly, Nsenga chiefdoms along the Luangwa valley suffered from endemic famine and their inhabitants often sought relief in Undi's territory which was more fertile than their own. The combined control and regulation of trade and famine relief placed Undi in an extremely strong position *vis-à-vis* the neighbouring peoples and polities.[30]

There is every indication, on the other hand, that Undi and his kinsmen allowed the Nsenga chieftains who came under their influence to continue to administer the affairs of their clans and areas, as long as they sent tribute in ivory and slaves to Undi's headquarters on the Kapoche river. Nevertheless, from the time of the conquest, the Nsenga adopted the Maravi system of chieftainship which they also adapted to suit their own customs. This explains why the Mundikula (or Kalindawalo), Chimfombo and Chifuka chiefly lines maintain that Undi installed them as chiefs in the olden days.

The Maravi and their Chewa surrogates also expanded northwards into Tumbuka country. Among the princely leaders who migrated in that direction were Chulu, Kaluluma, Kanyenda and Kabunduli. Their presence there resulted in the creation of mixed socio-linguistic groups of whom the Tonga of northern Khota Khota and Nkhata–Bay districts are the most obvious.

Chulu and Kaluluma, for example, moved into the southern Tumbuka area known as Chimaliro and the surrounding plains. Here, they encountered a Tumbuka people who were self-sufficient economically but loosely organized politically. There was little political or military co-operation among the different Tumbuka clans: Zimba, Kanyinji, Nyirongo, Mtonga, and so on. The manner in which Chulu or Kaluluma established himself as ruler over a predominantly Tumbuka-speaking population, however, is subject to conflicting interpretations in Chewa and Tumbuka oral traditions. In the case of Kaluluma, Chewa oral traditions have it that the Tumbuka initially welcomed him and his entourage. Later, however, they decided to rebel but were crushed in the fighting which ensued. The Tumbuka version, on the other hand, is more elaborate. It maintains that Kaluluma was given permission by the Tumbuka headmen to settle in the area as a commoner. Not long afterwards, however, he began to tour the countryside to compel everyone to recognize him as chief, and to force the Tumbuka headmen to help him carry the grinding stone (*mphelo*) on which his favourite snuff was ground. In protest, therefore, the Tumbuka tried to expel him, but he defeated them instead.[31]

30. G. M. Theal, 1899–1902, Vol. III, pp. 480–1; and J. D. Clark, 1965, pp. 276–80.
31. H. L. Vail, 1971; T. C. Young, 1932, p. 186; and S. S. Murray, 1922, p 224.

These traditions suggest that lacking the institution of territorial chief-tainship, the Tumbuka tried to resist early Maravi attempts to impose it on them. It is also possible that the conflict had an economic origin since as immigrants who still lacked a solid economic foundation of their own, the Maravi/Chewa immigrants may have become a burden on the surplus production of their Tumbuka hosts.

PLATE 21.2 *The royal stool, made of iron, of Chief Kanyenda of Khota Khota central Malawi, probably seventeenth-century*

Kanyenda and Kabunduli migrated into what later became Tongaland. Both originally came from the heartland of the Maravi empire near the Linthipe river in the south. Their migration northward brought them to Khota Khota mid-way along the western side of the lake where Kabunduli split from Kanyenda. Kabunduli then migrated further north into Tonga-land via Chimaliro in the west. In Tongaland, Kabunduli soon earned a reputation for re-organizing the once scattered Tonga groups whom he apparently defeated and brought under his own control. As his reputation increased, he was followed by a number of Chewa commoner families from the Chewa heartland, such as the Kapunda Banda who claim to have come from Chauwa's area in what is now eastern Lilongwe.[32]

This intermingling of the Maravi with the original inhabitants of Ton-

32. F. Kwaule and E. J. Chakwera, 1978; J. Van Velsen, 1959; C. Z. Mphande, 1969; F. R. Mkandawire, 1978.

galand accounts for the peculiarities of Tonga society as we know it today. Chitonga, the language of the area, is a bridge between the Tumbuka and Chewa languages. The Tonga are also the only group in northern Malawi to have remained matrilineal in descent and inheritance customs to this day. This shows that Tonga society has acted as a bridge historically between the matrilineal Chewa complex in the south and the patrilineal Tumbuka–Phoka complex in the north.

For the Chewa–Maravi peoples, the seventeenth century was a 'golden age' when as a result of their territorial expansion they emerged as the most renowned power-brokers north of the Zambezi. Even the Portuguese, ensconced as they were in their settlements along the Zambezi, were forced to co-operate with them. This was because the Maravi did not confine their interest to the area north of the Zambezi. From the 1590s through to the 1630s, they actively interfered in what was the Portuguese sphere-of-influence south of the Zambezi. They were interested in the lucrative gold and silver mines of the Munhumutapa's domains, and in exercising a certain amount of control over traffic along the Zambezi.[33]

For two generations at the beginning of the seventeenth century, therefore, the Portuguese, from Angoche on the east coast to Tete up the Zambezi, sought to contain the Maravi, by collaborating with them. They recruited large numbers of Maravi warriors to help them in their campaigns against the Karanga or Shona south of the Zambezi as well as against local enemies in the immediate vicinity of their Zambezi settlements. For example, in 1608 the Portuguese at Tete received 4000 warriors from the Kalonga Muzula for their campaign against rebellious subjects of their ally, Munhumutapa Gatsi Rusere. Six years later in 1614 the Portuguese at Sena sought the assistance of the Lundu in mounting an armed expedition to Chicoa north-west of Tete, to search for silver. The Kalonga was again called upon to assist the Portuguese in 1623. This time he dispatched thousands of warriors across the Zambezi to help the Portuguese suppress some Karanga chiefs who took to arms following the death of Gatsi Rusere. The campaign was a success for these Maravi warriors, for they are reported to have retreated to their side of the Zambezi laden with loot in the form of gold and cattle. Again in 1635, the Lundu aided the Portuguese in crushing an uprising of Swahili chieftains in the Angoche (Quelimane) district north of the Zambezi delta.[34]

There is also evidence, on the other hand, to indicate that the Portuguese co-operated with the Maravi out of necessity rather than choice. Up to the end of the seventeenth century, the Portuguese residents of Sena and Tete dreaded the Maravi whom they regarded as 'very bad neighbours', unlike the Lolo and Makua who gave them no trouble.[35]

33. D. W. Beach, 1980a, pp. 125–8; and M. D. D. Newitt, 1982, pp. 158–60.

34. A. Gomes, 1959, p. 183; G. M. Theal, 1899–1902, Vol. III, p. 395; and E. A. Alpers, 1975a, pp. 54–6.

35. G. M. Theal, 1899–1902, Vol. III, p. 480; and M. D. D. Newitt, 1973, p. 80.

The Maravi expansion had several effects. For example, the creation of the Lundu state east of the Lower Shire valley made it possible for the Mbona cult among the Manganja to spread its influence more widely than would otherwise have been possible. The economic and cultural effects were perhaps as significant. Within territory encompassed by the Maravi confederation in the seventeenth century, trade in ivory flourished. As a result, Northern Zambezia had considerable interaction with the world's mercantile capitalist economy. The 'Maravi empire' may also have fostered cultural uniformity between the different matrilineal peoples of the Northern Zambezia region, as can be attested by the fact that they share the same clan-names and have a common descent-system.[36]

While the Maravi were expanding over the southern zone in the sixteenth and seventeenth centuries, the north was being penetrated by the Ngulube immigrants from the north-east. Like the Maravi advent in the south, the coming of the Ngulube is a major event in the history of the northern zone.[37] Their coming also enables more precise dating, since regnal lists for the major chieftaincies can be reconstructed back to the time of their founding. The only problem is that although the regnal lists seem fairly reliable, the number of reigns per dynastic generation is not always easy to determine, since informants are not always clear on the way the system of succession operated. The regnal list of the Kyungus who ruled Ungonde, for example, contains fifteen names prior to about 1940. One suggestion is that this represents a minimum of nine dynastic generations. The list of the Mwaulambyas, the rulers of Ulambya, contains sixteen names prior to 1940, representing a maximum of twelve dynastic generations.[38] It is also worth noting that the founding rulers of Ungonde, Ulambya and Unyiha were near contemporaries, with those of Ulambya having preceded the others by perhaps a few generations.

In the vanguard of the Ngulube migration, the Mwaulambya crossed the Songwe river south of the Misuku hills into what came to be called Ulambya. There he found the Sikwese and Chilima clans. The Mwaulambya assumed political control through more peaceful means than the Kyungu who was shortly to invade the Karonga plain. This was partly because the former's migration party was probably smaller than the latter's. Consequently, the Mwaulambya was more accommodating than the Kyungu whose close advisers were chosen exclusively from those who had accompanied him for all, or part of, the migration. The major officials of the Mwaulambya on the other hand were drawn from the families found in the region, the latter sharing prestige and political power with the new

---

36. E. A. Alpers, 1975a, pp. 56–8. Alpers also holds the view that as time passed, participation in this trade was unremunerative for most peoples of East-Central Africa. The similarity between social institutions has been noted by J. B. Webster, 1977, pp. 4–5.

37. O. J. M. Kalinga, 1985, pp. 41–63.

38. O. J. M. Kalinga, 1975, and 1978, pp. 57–61.

rulers.[39] Similarly, the Msukwa assumed political power over the Simwayi and Silumbu clans without the use of excessive force. Both Ulambya and Misuku were founded on compromise.

The modern language situation reflects something about the numerical strength of the various immigrant parties who founded chieftaincies as well as the means by which they assumed power and later governed the people. Cilambya and the language of Kameme are dialects of the indigenous Nyiha while Kyangonde and Kinyakyusa are dialects of the Ngulube peoples' language. In other words, the Mwaulambya and Kameme and their followers were assimilated linguistically while in Ungonde and Unyakyusa the indigenous people were assimilated by the immigrants. Modern Cisukwa is a dialect of Ndali (a linguistic group north of the Songwe) understood by the Nyiha-speakers and relatively easier to learn by the Ngonde than Nyiha proper. Cisukwa thus forms a bridge between the Nyiha and Ngonde languages.

The Kyungu, Kameme and party migrated to the Karonga plain via Unyiha, Uiwa, Unamwanga and then Ulambya and Misuku in the west. Although Ngonde court traditions claim that their ancestors established political authority in Unamwanga and Uiwa, those of the latter area dispute this and point to Ubisa and ultimately the Luba country as the original home of their present line of rulers. At any rate, within a short time of their arrival in Karonga, Kameme returned and settled in the area immediately west of Ulambya. Here he established political authority over a people who were mainly of Nyiha stock although in later years many Mambwe and Namwanga migrated into the Kameme chiefdom. How the Kameme established his state is not clear. It was clearly a smaller polity than that of his brother, the Kyungu, who founded his kingdom on an already established state ruled by the Simbowe.

Simbowe is a clan name and evidence suggests that it was a title used by a long list of rulers. The Simbowe clan came from Unyiha in modern Tanzania and had established itself at Mbande hill in the west-central section of the Karonga lakeshore. The basis of Simbowe's power is not clear but it would appear that he was a trader, and part of a trading network which might have extended to the east coast. Archaeological excavations carried out by Robinson at Mbande and the surrounding area have yielded artifacts which include glass beads, porcelain and conus shells. Indeed, Robinson himself concluded that the fifteenth- to sixteenth-century artifacts probably belonged to the pre-Portuguese period on the east coast, that is, during the height of Arab power and commercial influence.[40]

Simbowe's relations with the indigenous people do not appear to have been easy; after his arrival, the Kyungu formed an alliance with the Mwenekisindile who were the custodians of an important religious shrine associated with a snake cult. Indeed, it seems that the Mwenekisindile

39. O. J. M. Kalinga, 1978, pp. 55–66 and 1977.
40. The section that follows is based on O. J. M. Kalinga, 1979a.

assisted the Kyungu in planning and executing the attack upon Simbowe. The Kyungu assumed power at Mbande by force and gradually was able to establish a new order. Once settled, the Kyungus maintained their supremacy over their new subjects by establishing a ritual centre devoted to the cult of their royal ancestors. The Kyungu did not attend the ritual centre, but gave his blessings to Mulwa, a senior official who had accompanied him to the area and who became the centre's head. In addition, adults in the kingdom attended an annual ceremony in which all fires were extinguished and new ones lit from the central fire at the royal court, a ceremony during which the people renewed allegiance to the Kyungu.[41] On a more frequent basis the people were expected to pay tribute to the Kyungu and work in the royal gardens. The Kyungu and his officials further established themselves in the area by marrying into the original local families.

Before the arrival of the Kyungu clan the people seem to have worshipped the high god through intermediary spirits such as the divine snake. The Kyungus employed the ancestors as mediums for the worship of their own high god, Ngulube, thus introducing and promoting royal ancestor worship. As the people slowly accepted the growth of ancestral worship they also accepted the divinity of the Kyungu. He became priest-king and communicator with the royal ancestors. To the Ngonde, the Kyungu became the living representative of god. His health determined their welfare and prosperity and to safeguard this he was restricted to his residence. Should the Kyungu show even minor signs of illness he was immediately smothered by his councillors, the *makambala*. As ancestral veneration gained popularity in the area, the snake cult – and with it the Kisindile clan – became much less influential.

These developments occurred during the reigns of the first four Kyungus, roughly between 1600 and 1720. Soon after the death of the third Kyungu, Mwakalosi, his son and successor renounced the throne because he feared that should he fall ill, the *makambala* would kill him. He also refused to have all but one of his children killed. The two practices were designed to avoid competition for the throne. The *makambala* were also protecting their own position by ensuring that a ruler was of their own choice. The crisis caused by the refusal of Mwakalosi to accede to the throne was averted when the *makambala* installed his brother Magemo as Kyungu.

The Kameme, Mwaulambya and Msukwa chiefdoms also promoted royal ancestral veneration. However, they became more Nyiha in their philosophy as in their language, and smothering the monarch, restricting his movements and killing royal children never featured in their history. However, all these chiefdoms represent the introduction into the area of a

41. More details are to be found in R. J. Mwaipape, 'History and social customs of the Ngonde of Northern Malawi' (unpublished manuscript completed in 1982 and in author's possession).

new form of political organization which brought together religion and politics under more elevated and prestigious leaders and where relations among the citizenry were based more upon political than upon kinship ties.[42]

An even greater crisis occurred in the Ngonde kingdom upon the death of Kyungu Magemo whose only successor, Mwangonde, was too young to succeed him. His sister's son, Kasyombe, became Kyungu. Kasyombe's father, a Ndali, was the ruler of a small area on the north-western corner of the Karonga plain. With Kasyombe's accession to power in about 1750, therefore, this new region was incorporated into an enlarged Ngonde kingdom.

Another important change resulting from the accession of Kasyombe was that the *makambala* began to lose some of their powers to the Kyungu. Kasyombe had been brought up at Ngana in the northern part of the kingdom. He insisted on personally touring the kingdom and ended the practice of killing the male children of the Kyungus. The number of princes proliferated leading in turn to a further increase in the powers of the monarch, especially after some of his successors such as Mwangonde (*c*.1785–1839) assigned portions of land to some princes thereby ensuring that the Kyungus' influence was felt throughout the domain.[43] There can be no doubt, however, that by 1800, the Ngonde kingdom was confident enough to begin asserting itself in the international politics of the wider region south of the Songwe.

Thus between the mid-thirteenth and mid-eighteenth centuries the area south of the Songwe river had developed through a number of stages. From an early network of religious shrines associated with a snake cult, to a system of dominant clans and, finally, in the northern and southern sections to the foundation of a number of states; in the north Ulambya, Kameme, Misuku, Ungonde and Mwaphoka Mwambale, and in the south Kanyenda and Kabunduli, Kaluluma and Chulu. In the north Kyangonde had been introduced as a new language by the Ngonde and Nyakyusa founders while in the south Chitonga was evolving out of a fusion of the Tumbuka and Chewa peoples and languages. The central part of the region was dominated by the Tumbuka. Their original clans, the Luhanga and various branches of the Mkandawire were joined by the Munthali from the Ndali hills north of the Songwe river. Further west in the Luangwa region the Tumbuka clans included the Zolokere, Mwavintiza, Goma and others. These Tumbuka groups had no centralized government and their early history is an extremely difficult one to chart. Their genealogies are shallow and so is their conception of how they were organized prior to the eighteenth century. However, in the eighteenth century the most significant

42. O. J. M. Kalinga, forthcoming.

43. O. J. M. Kalinga, 'A History of the Ngonde Kingdom,' pp. 180–250; and R. J. Mwaipape, 1982, pp. 34–41.

events of the region occurred in Tumbuka country. These will be discussed later.

The kinds of religious change which occurred in the Karonga lakeshore following the establishment of the Ngonde state were also discernible in the Maravi zone of influence. The Maravi state system encompassed a network of pre-Maravi or proto-Chewa rain-shrines centred on Msinja in what is western Lilongwe today. Each of the Maravi state-builders tried to exercise control over the shrines that fell within his jurisdiction. He was anxious to play a role in the appointment of officials and to offer assistance and protection, and he usually made annual pilgrimages to the shrines. Both the Kalonga and Undi tried to gain control of the Msinja shrine in this way, while in the Lower Shire valley the Lundu managed to establish a considerable degree of control over the Mbona shrine at Nsanje. With this level of dynastic participation in the affairs of the rain-cults, their theology gradually became syncretic. It began to accommodate the veneration of the royal ancestral spirits, while purely Chewa creation myths like those which obtained in Nyau were suppressed.[44]

However, the most notable religious change of the period occurred where the dynasts failed to gain control over the pre-existing rain-cults. They then tended to establish their own cults which tried to rival the pre-existing ones. These were royal cults and one of their functions was to deify the royal family. For this reason, it has been suggested that their link with commoners was rather tenuous. The king or his nominee presided over the rain-making ceremonies and other rituals.

Towards the middle of the eighteenth century, while the Ngonde in the north were preoccupied with the balance of power among internal factions and between religious institutions, the Maravi state system began to decline. The most articulate expression of this decline took the form of secessions from or revolts against the Kalonga, Lundu and Undi paramountcies. There were revolts against the Kalonga by a number of chiefs in the Lilongwe area of present-day central Malawi. During the same period, Undi was also confronted with the revolts led by Biwi and his other subordinates, while out in the east the Lolo and Makua also revolted against the Lundu's overlordship.[45]

However, the factors accounting for the decline of what had been a powerful confederation of Maravi states in the seventeenth century are not clear. In the case of Undi, the Portuguese who invaded his kingdom during the gold rush of the 1740s and 1750s did play a minor role in undermining his authority. It has also been argued that both Undi and the Kalonga were weakened by the growing reluctance of Makewana, who controlled the central Chewa religious shrine at Msinja in Lilongwe, to use her ritual power in their interest. This is because – unlike the *svikiro* mediums who faithfully served the interest of the Mutapa state south of the Zambezi –

44. M. J. Schoffeleers, 1979b, pp. 152–60; I. Linden, 1979, pp. 188–93.
45. K. M. Phiri, 1975a, pp. 78–9; A. F. Isaacman, 1972b, pp. 14–15.

Makewana and her subordinate rain-callers did not always exercise their authority in a manner that would have bolstered the institution of Maravi kingship.[46] The early Makewanas, it should be noted, had been key links in the religious unity of the Kalonga and Undi kingdoms. They were entrusted with the performance of the religious rituals upon which the Kalonga and Undi depended for the well-being of their followers. The Makewanas of the eighteenth century, on the other hand, developed secular ambitions as well. They carved out their own sphere of influence between the kingdoms of Kalonga and Undi, and on one occasion even sent warriors to raid into the domains of the Kalonga. Since Makewana and her acolytes belonged to the proto-Chewa clans of the Banda and Mbewe, their resistance to the Kalonga and Undi was probably indicative of an attempt by the proto-Chewa to reassert their autonomy. In any case, the defection of Makewana meant that both the Kalonga and Undi were deprived of the mystical sanctions which they had hitherto exercised over their followers through the agency of Makewana.

Finally, a factor which proved crucial to the decline of the Lundu's influence east of the Shire river was the emergence of Makua–Lolo ethnic consciousness or nationalism in the eighteenth century. According to Hafkin, the Makua became extremely power-conscious then, much to the surprise of contemporary observers who had previously under-rated their military capacity.[47] Their nationalism was primarily directed against the Portuguese. The coastal Makua in particular objected to the 'divide and rule' policies of the Portuguese as well as to the capricious trade policies of individual Portuguese. However, it was not until they began to acquire firearms from the French and Brazilian slave-dealers that the Makua began to challenge the Portuguese with impunity. Led by powerful chiefs like Mauruka and Murimuno, they waged a bitter war of attrition against the Portuguese and their African allies from 1749 to the end of the century. The challenge which the coastal Makua posed for Portuguese imperialism on the Mozambique coast must have inspired the Makua and Lolo further inland from the coast into similar campaigns against foreign domination. In the inland areas, however, it was the Maravi rather than the Portuguese who became the object of Makua–Lolo hostility. Maravi supremacy then began to be shaken from Quelimane in the east to Mount Murambala on the Shire in the west.[48]

The people of Northern Zambezia in the period under consideration were also greatly affected by their growing economic contacts with the outside world.[49] Such contacts are usually traced back to the period of Arab–Swahili commercial dominance on the east coast and along the

46. A. F. Isaacman, 1972b, p. 15.

47. N. J. Hafkin, 1973, pp. 23–6.

48. A. Rita-Ferreira, 1966, p. 34; E. C. Mandala, 1977, pp. 43–4; and E. A. Alpers, 1975a, pp. 104–13.

49. This subject is ably reviewed by E. A. Alpers, 1975a, Introduction.

Zambezi before 1500. Their frequency, however, was rather limited until the advent of the Portuguese and particularly after their settlement along the Zambezi in the mid-sixteenth century. Thereafter, Portuguese traders regularly sailed up the Shire river from Sena to purchase iron-ware, *machila* cloth, salt and ivory from the Manganja, with imported cloth, beads and brass-ware. With some of these Manganja products – including iron-ware and *machila* cloths – the Portuguese conducted further business in the lands of the Munhumutapa south of the Zambezi river.[50] Further up the Zambezi, the Portuguese who settled at Tete established trading connections with Undi's kingdom and the heartland of the Maravi state system as far as the Upper Shire and the southern littoral of Lake Malawi. With the founding of a *feira* at Zumbo in 1716, the Portuguese gained access to the ivory market in several societies as far west as southern and central Zambia.[51] But it was the rise and spread of the Zambezia *prazos* which played a decisive role in the expansion of Portuguese commercial influence north of the Zambezia.

Prazos came into existence when a number of Portuguese or Goanese colonists assumed the status of political chiefs over land that initially belonged to the indigenous African peoples. The process began around Sena at the close of the sixteenth century and gradually spread to other parts of the Lower Zambezi valley in the seventeenth.[52] According to Axelson, the grant of *prazos* to prominent Portuguese settlers was seen by the Crown in Lisbon as a way of encouraging private initiative in the colonization of the Zambezi valley. In addition, it was hoped that with the prospect of acquiring land, immigrants would be attracted to the Zambezia where their presence was required in order to increase the Portuguese population.

In the eighteenth century, *prazos* dominated the whole Lower Zambezia region from the Luabo or Zambezi delta in the east to Chicoa midway between the towns of Tete and Zumbo in the west. They were acquired in different ways. One way was by conquest, usually after the white conqueror had exploited the divisions which existed among the original African occupants: the other was by demanding land as compensation for some special service that had been rendered to a local ruler.

The big *prazos* were more than private estates. They amounted to areas of jurisdiction in which the estate-owners commonly known as *prazeros* 'had absolute power of justice, waged war, imposed tribute, and were often guilty of great barbarities'. Of the many issues about these *prazos* which are of interest to the historian, two stand out. One is that of the complex

50. G. M. Theal, 1899–1902, Vol. III, pp. 480–1; E. A. Alpers, 1975a, pp. 25–7; E. C. Mandala, 1977, p. 41.

51. N. Sutherland-Harris, 1970; M. D. D. Newitt, 1973, pp. 75–9; and T. I. Mathews, 1981, pp. 23–31.

52. For a full discussion of the process, see A. F. Isaacman, 1972b; M. D. D. Newitt, 1973; and E. Axelson, 1960.

relationships which they maintained with neighbouring African polities. The other is that of the economic impact which they had on the rest of the Northern Zambezia region.

The *prazeros* were notorious for their harsh treatment of the African peoples who surrounded them as voluntary retainers or conquered subjects. In addition, most of them entered into diplomatic and military relations with the surrounding African polities with the explicit aim of exploiting their human resources. For example, the Chikunda, who served the *prazeros* as retainers, were recruited from different African societies both north and south of the Zambezi. In this way, the *prazeros* had access to labour from among the Makua, Manganja, Sena, Kalanga, Tonga, Tawara, Nsenga, Tumbuka and others.[53]

Through their interest in the gold and ivory trades, the *prazeros* played an important role in the development of commerce north of the Zambezia. Using some of their Chikunda retainers (*vashambadzi*) as middle-men, they established a network of trade links with different African peoples in the region: Manganja, Chewa, Nsenga, Lenje and Southern Lunda. From these inland peoples, their trade caravans obtained copper, ivory, wax and slaves in exchange for imported cloth, beads, brass-ware, alcoholic beverages and salt. From about 1740, the *prazeros* were also involved in the mining and exchange of gold north of the Zambezia, particularly in Undi's kingdom. Here *bares* or mines were opened at Michonga, Maano (the Undi's capital), Java and Muchinga. The Portuguese or Goanese miners from Tete insisted upon absolute ownership of the diggings and all essential means of production. In return for this privilege, they made token offers of gifts and royalties to the Undi and his subordinates. Under this system of production, approximately 100 kilograms (3500 ounces) of gold were extracted annually before the supply began to dwindle in the 1780s.[54]

Unfortunately for the *prazeros* and the Portuguese community on the Zambezi generally, this gold rush led to their loss of the ivory trade. The diggings attracted an interest that was out of proportion to their actual worth. Meanwhile, the ivory trade increasingly fell into the hands of other competitors for the northern ivory market. These were the Yao, a people who have been singularly associated with the development of long-distance trade throughout East-Central Africa.

The Yao emerged as a dominant trading nation in the late seventeenth and early eighteenth centuries; and there are two related interpretations of how they rose to this position and status. Abdul Sheriff maintains that the Yao orientation to coast-bound trade was the result of a chain-reaction. The Yao, in other words, may have simply responded to commercial influences which first affected their Ngindo and Makua–Lomwe neighbours who were nearer to the coast than themselves. Of late, Webster has proposed that what made the Yao response to trade with the coast so spectacular,

53. A. F. Isaacman, 1972a.
54. A. F. Isaacman, 1972b, pp. 70–1; and M. D. D. Newitt, 1973, pp. 79–84.

was their occupation of hilly and marginal agricultural country in which it was not possible for them to make a success of farming or hunting. Their Nyanja or Chewa neighbours to the west and Lomwe to the east were better agriculturalists and hunters, respectively.[55]

According to Yao oral tradition as recorded by Yohanna B. 'Abdallāh, it was the Chisi ironsmiths who pioneered trade to the coast. The Chisi are said to have depended on their iron-working skills and local trade in iron-ware for their livelihood. It is thus possible that once Yaoland was adequately supplied with iron goods, the Chisi took their merchandise further afield until they established contact with the coast. Once this had been achieved, the further development of Yao commercial enterprise was facilitated by the creation of a stable market for ivory at Kilwa between 1635 and 1698. This was a period when having conquered the East African coast as far north as Malindi, the Portuguese entered a phase of peaceful commercial interaction with the various coastal cities. Kilwa therefore attracted much trade from the interior. When the Kilwa market for ivory fell after 1698 as a result of Omani–Portuguese conflicts the Yao found an alternative market at Mossuril opposite Mozambique Island. Trade, it would seem, had by that point become indispensable to the Yao way-of-life. The Yao would carry their ivory to either Mozambique or Kilwa, as dictated by circumstances.[56]

In the interior to the west of their own homeland, the Yao had a rich source of ivory in Maravi country. Furthermore, from about 1750, they began to receive more ivory from the Bisa of north-eastern Zambia for onward transmission to Kilwa. The Bisa who dealt with the Yao in this way began their commercial career as entrepreneurs in the service of Kazembe, the Lunda king, whose capital on the Luapula was a regular terminus of a route used by traders from both the east and the west coasts. By 1775 at the latest, the Bisa had acquired a reputation for being one of the most commercially minded nations in the region.[57]

For the Bisa, trade probably offered compensation for their political impotence at home. Agriculturally, they occupied a country that was marginally productive, between the Luapula river and the Muchinga range. Politically, they were trapped between the expansionist forces of the Lunda and Bemba kingdoms. Thus trade and travel were important avenues to opportunities further afield. In the course of pursuing them, the Bisa opened many new routes between the Luapula region in north-eastern Zambia and the east coast. Between 1790 and 1830, they also tried to develop commerce between the Lunda kingdom and the Portuguese on the Zambezi. In both cases, they played a middle-man's role. They procured ivory, copper and slaves from different places in the interior of Central Africa and bore them to the coast or Zambezia settlements to be exchanged

55. A. M. H. Sheriff, 1971, pp. 208–17; and J. B. Webster, 1977, pp. 3–6.
56. E. A. Alpers, 1975a, pp. 58–62, 70–81; J. B. Webster, 1977, pp. 7–10.
57. F. M. Thomas, 1958, p. 26; R. F. Burton, 1873, p. 95; J. Vansina, 1966a, pp. 171–2.

for goods such as cloth, beads, guns and gun-powder.

One consequence of their trade with the east coast was that their own settlements began to drift eastward into the Luangwa valley and beyond. The initial impetus of this migration was famine and the desire to tap the ivory trade between the Luangwa valley and Lake Malawi. In this way, several Bisa villages were established in the Luangwa valley by the 1760s and by the end of the eighteenth century there were Bisa villages in the western part of central Malawi. This eastward drift of Bisa communities was intensified in the 1820s and 1830s when the Bemba intermittently raided their settlements in the Muchinga area.[58]

Thus for at least four decades before the close of the eighteenth century, the Bisa had close dealings with the peoples to their east. Their presence among the Chewa in particular was a factor in the growth of the power of several chieftainships including Mwase Kasungu and Mkanda. The Bisa immigrants were enterprising and often more loyal to the ruling families than the local subjects.

For the Portuguese, the failure of the gold-diggings and the loss of the ivory trade to the Yao and Bisa were factors in their active participation in the slave trade. In turn this led to a remarkable change in the nature of long-distance trade north of the Zambezi in the late eighteenth century. Ivory began to be superseded by slaves as the main trade commodity that could be exported from the region. This change, though by no means complete, was pronounced enough to warrant the identification of the eighteenth century with the ivory trade and the nineteenth with the slave trade. Portuguese participation in the slave trade was remarkable enough in the 1780s when slaves from Northern Zambezia were exported to the French island colonies of Réunion and Bourbon in the Indian Ocean.[59]

As the slave trade became more lucrative than the trade in ivory, the Portuguese already in it were joined by the Yao and Bisa. According to 'Abdallāh, the Yao turned to slave-trading because of the coastal demand for slaves rather than ivory. Indeed, the Kilwa market to which the Yao took their wares from the interior began to be dominated by the slave trade from the 1770s onwards.[60] The market-conscious Yao probably then began to displace ivory with slaves in their caravans from the interior.

The entire northern zone was also drawn into the long-distance trading network. Until the early eighteenth century, no part of the region had been involved in the long-distance trade although a vigorous local trade had existed all round the shores of Lake Malawi and from Tumbuka country into Nsengaland and the northern Chewa area. During the first four decades of the eighteenth century the Tumbuka region was linked to a trading network which stretched from Katanga in the north-west to Kilwa in the

58. A. C. P. Gamitto, 1960, pp. 55–6, 161–92; and A. D. Roberts, 1973, pp. 104–67.

59. R. F. Burton, 1873, pp. 81–7; E. A. Alpers, 1975a, pp. 201–19; A. F. Isaacman, 1972b, pp. 85–94.

60. Y. B. 'Abdallāh, 1973, pp. 29–37; G. S. P. Freeman-Grenville, 1965, pp. 43–8.

east. The people responsible for this change were heads of families known as *balowoka* – those who crossed the lake – who arrived in the area over a period of three to four decades.

The most famous of these new men was Kakalala Musawila Gondwe,

PLATE 21.3 *The remains of a Tumbuka iron-smelting kiln* (ng'anjo). *The fame of the Tumbuka as iron-smelters was rivalled only by that of the Phangwa on the east side of Lake Malawi*

PLATE 21.4 *A Tumbuka-made iron hoe. This particular example was made in the Vipya, Mzimba district, northern Malawi, in the 1940s*

probably a Yao-influenced Nyamwezi who for sometime had been involved in the trade to the east coast. Searching for ivory, Gondwe crossed the lake at Chilumba and settled in the Nkamanga plain near the Luangwa valley which at that time was heavily populated with elephants. He established contact with the head of the Luhanga clan, Chilundanya Luhanga, who was pleased with the goods – beads, *mphande* shells and cloth – which the newcomer had brought. Later Gondwe married into the Luhanga and their other influential families thereby firmly establishing himself in Tumbuka society. To fully tap the resources of the region, he gave turbans – the type which he himself wore – to various local leaders as a symbol of authority derived from himself.[61]

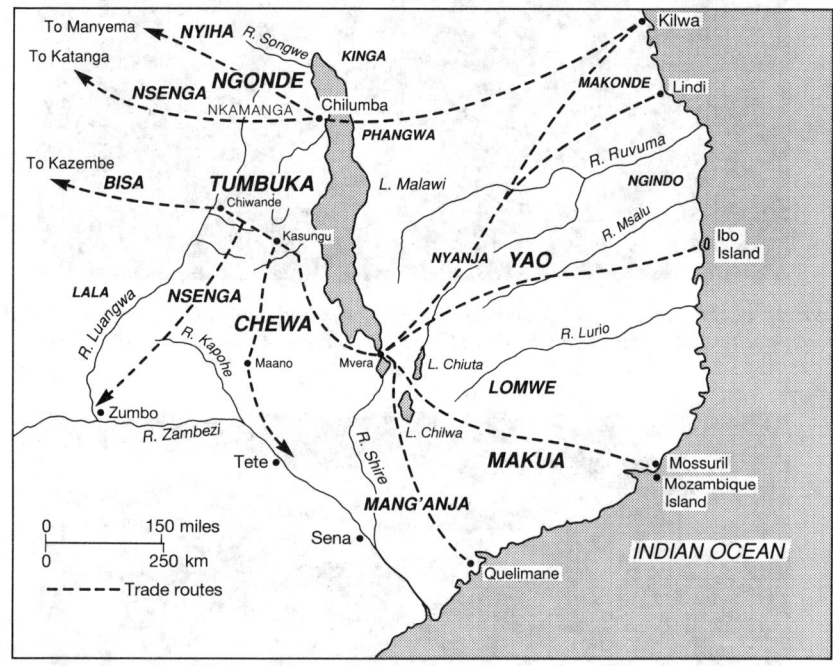

FIG. 21.4 *Ivory trade routes in East-Central Africa in the eighteenth century (after E. A. Alpers, UCLA)*

Other immigrant families from east of the lake established themselves in the areas adjacent to Nkamanga. In the district that is today known as Hewe, Katumbi Mulindafwa Chabinga had begun to organize a smaller yet more viable state than that of Gondwe. He too came from Nyamwezi territory and also crossed the lake at Chilumba, but unlike Gondwe, he went into the mountainous area which adjoins the Misuku hills and the

61. This section has benefited from H. L. Vail, 1972b, 1974; and H. K. Msiska, 1978a.

Nyika plateau and settled at Chigoma in Nthalire.[62] Again like Gondwe he distributed turbans to local leaders as a symbol of his recognition of their authority. From Chigoma, Katumbi extended his trading contact westwards to Malambo in the ivory-rich Luangwa valley. Later, his descendants moved some miles south-westwards to modern Hewe – the centre of the state when the Europeans arrived.

Another trader, Katong'ongo Mhenga whose original home was in the Ubena–Uhehe region crossed the lake shortly after Gondwe and Katumbi had settled. Katong'ongo was not a trader in the same sense as Katumbi and Gondwe. He was looking for land where he and his family could settle, and this he found in the Henga valley. Katong'ongo had many skills; he was a hunter, an artisan who made ornamental bracelets and, most important of all, he knew how to produce salt. The latter skill proved very useful in that he soon came to control the high-quality salt-pans at Kamembe. Katong'ongo also married into local families such as the Munthali, Mzumara and Mkandawire some of which were well established in the Henga valley. He gradually became influential and came to be known as Mwahenga, owner of the Henga area. He traded with Mwaphoka Mbale's people and with Gondwe's Nkamanga.[63]

Although the three immigrant families, Musawila Gondwe, Katumbi Mulindafwa Chabinga and Katong'ongo Mhenga, began to dominate the trade of most of the area south of the Songwe and east to the Luangwa valley, it was difficult for them to carry on for long without clashing with each other. Gondwe felt particularly threatened because Katumbi controlled access to the region that was rich in ivory; furthermore, it was important for him to have free use of – if not control of – the Chilumba ferry in order to transport his ivory to the east coast. Thus he became involved in the succession crisis following the death of Katumbi. He succeeded in promoting a weak candidate for the chieftaincy. He then worked out an arrangement with Mwahenga whereby the latter agreed not to impede his trade and was given cloth and other valuable goods in return. Gondwe made similar arrangements with the rulers east of the Henga valley. These included Mwafulirwa, Mwamlowe, Mwankunikila and Kachulu. Thus by 1800 Gondwe was able to claim a trade monopoly of the area between the Luangwa and the western shores of Lake Malawi. In the Nkamanga plain he had achieved political authority and was thus able to extend his trading empire in which the Chikulamayembe was assisted by the fact that families – mainly the Msiska and Nyirenda probably also from Unyamwezi and also traders – took over political control of the area ruled by the Mwaphoka, ending a long period of Mbale supremacy in the

62. The Nthalire state was established sometime in the eighteenth century, by the Kawonga who were from southern Tanzania. They were hunters who married into the Kyungus of Karonga and it was they who suggested that they should settle in what later came to be called Nthalire.

63. O. J. M. Kalinga, 1979b.

area. The Phoka country – between Nkamanga and the Henga valley on the one hand and the Chilumba ferry on the other – had long been the nexus of local trading.

There were smaller polities established in the eighteenth century by families from the eastern side of the lake and many of their founders were, like Gondwe and Katumbi, ivory-traders. Just south of Ungonde, the Mwafulirwa family founded the Fulirwa state in the area that had been dominated by the Mkandawire clan. A relation of the Mwafulirwa, Mwendamunjila Mushani Kaira later went west and finally settled at Zibang'ombe some miles west of the Mwafulirwa mountains. They overcame the indigenous Simwaka who were Nyiha and they began to forge the Wenya state which by the end of the eighteenth century had extended northward to the southern borders of Ulambya. At about the same time the area south-west of Wenya fell under the rule of a Mlowoka family, the Mughogho. This area, Uyombe, which today forms part of the Isoka district of Zambia, was rich in elephants and in later decades became popular with many hunters. The Mughogho established good relations with the older polities of Chifungwe and Utambo near the source of the Luangwa, an area also rich in elephants.

There were other families which crossed the lake further south and settled not far from the present Nkhata-Bay *boma*. Amongst them were the forebears of modern Mankambira. They were hunters and left their homes sometime in the 1720s probably because they were attracted by the possibility of finding abundant ivory along the western shores of Lake Malawi. They displaced the Phiri rulers and after a generation became the dominant family in the area.[64]

In the eighteenth century, therefore, the Tumbuka area was dominated first by ivory-hunters, then traders whose control of wealth led to the assumption of political authority. Political decentralization gave way to the power of trader-chiefs. The hunters and traders had chosen the area because successful trade normally requires political influence of some kind. Such political influence was not possible in the northern states which remained outside the network of long-distance trade for almost a century after the Tumbuka had been drawn into it. In the eighteenth century the Maravi empire was disintegrating and the states of the Tumbuka–Chewa marginal zone in the south were being left in total control of their own affairs. However even within chiefdoms such as Kanyenda, the fissiparous tendencies which frequently accompanied the ivory trade were beginning to make themselves felt and the stage was thus set for the events which led to the creation of Mankhambira's hegemony in the area. After 1800 all states and people would become deeply involved in the commercial age of ivory and later of slaves, with unsettling to disastrous results.

The beginning date for this volume does not coincide with historical periodization in this region. An historical age opens in the southern zone

64. This paragraph is based partly on O. Y. Kaira, 1970–1; and J. B. C. Nkhoma, 1978.

c.1400 with the coming of the Maravi, and in the northern zone *c*.1600 with the migration of the Ngulube. However, the closing date is apt because new themes dominate the historiography of the entire region in the nineteenth century. They include the change-over in trade from ivory to slaves and the involvement of all parts of the region in externally manipulated commerce, the development of a whole series of Yao chiefdoms in areas formerly under the Maravi, and the arrival of a conglomerate of new peoples – the Nguni, Swahili, Kololo and Europeans – who would ultimately seek to wield political authority, regardless of their disparate motives for coming.

Southern Zambezia

22

H. H. K. BHILA

The period 1500 to 1800 is characterized in Southern Zambezia by a scarcity of records. We have to rely largely on the accounts of the Portuguese travellers and traders who penetrated the region during the first decade of the sixteenth century. This chapter will therefore concentrate on three selected polities, notably the Mutapa, Rozvi and eastern Shona states. The Mutapa and Rozvi polities evolved from the Great Zimbabwe culture (1200–1450) whose origins and development are dealt with elsewhere.[1]

Great Zimbabwe gradually declined from the mid-fifteenth century[2] onwards and its decline has been closely associated with the decrease in gold production in the Zimbabwe plateau at this time. Great Zimbabwe's decline gave rise first to an obscure state known as Torwa or 'Butwa', according to Portuguese sources.[3] Its first capital was situated at Khami and the second at Danangombe.[4] The first capital, which was probably founded in the mid-1400s, was destroyed by fire during the second half of the seventeenth century.[5] From what is known of its architecture and pottery, the Torwa state was a replica of Great Zimbabwe. The second capital was much smaller than the first. The available archaeological evidence suggests two things, first that almost all the prestige stone buildings in the Torwa state were constructed before 1650; and secondly that the Rozvi Changamire dynasty, which annexed the Torwa state in the 1690s, undertook no prestige stone construction at all.[6]

The second important political development after the fall of Great Zimbabwe was the emergence of the Mutapa empire which, by the beginning of the sixteenth century, had brought under its control the fertile and agricultural lands of the plateau region and 'a section of the Zambezi valley dry lands which also commanded parts of the trade routes'.[7] The empire comprised heterogeneous Karanga-speaking populations. In theory it

1. UNESCO, *General History of Africa*, Vol. IV, ch. 21.
2. P. S. Garlake, 1973; I. R. Phimister, 1974 and 1976; T. N. Huffman, 1972.
3. P. S. Garlake, 1982, pp. 30–1.
4. ibid.
5. D. N. Beach, 1984, pp. 26, 82, notes 60, 61.
6. ibid., p. 27.
7. ibid.

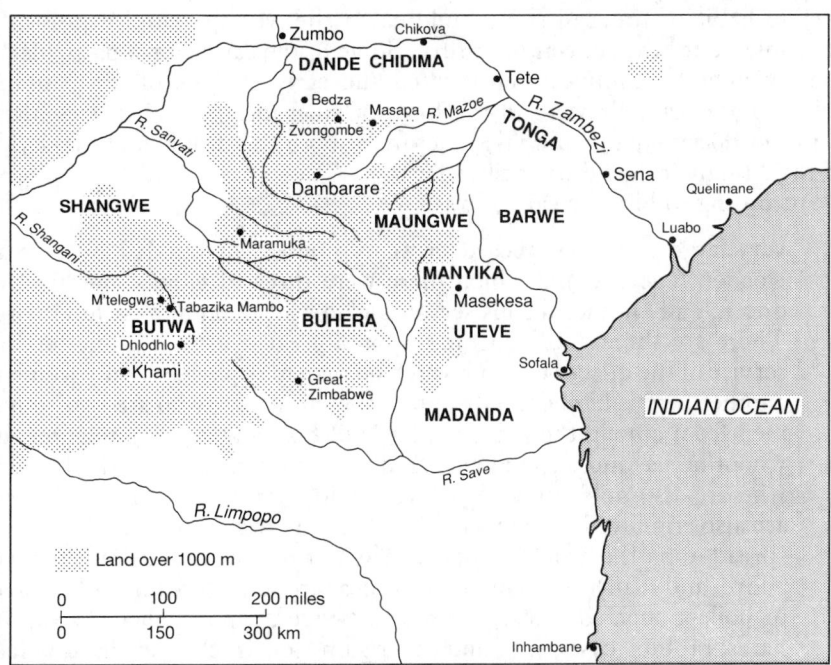

FIG. 22.1 *Central and south-eastern Africa during the period of the Mutapa and Torwa states*
Source: adapted from S. I. Mudenge, *A Political History of Munhumutapa c. 1400–1902*, Zimbabwe Publishing
House, Harare, 1988; and *Zimbabwe Epic*, published by the National Archives of Zimbabwe, Harare, p. 47

extended from the southern margins of the Zambezi to the Indian Ocean
but in practice the Mutapa rulers exercised a much more limited authority
outside the plateau country. There is evidence that the Kingdoms of
Manyika, Uteve, Barwe and Danda hived away from the parent empire
during the sixteenth century. However, they continued to perform their
ritual and tributary obligations until the rise of Dombo Changamire in the
late seventeenth century.[8] The evidence is slender but it would seem that
the 'rebel' kingdoms continued to pay tribute to the Mutapa rulers long
after the rise of Dombo Changamire. There is a suggestion that even the
Changamires occasionally paid tribute to the Mutapa emperors during the
eighteenth century.[9] The Rozvi tribute-bearers however, were 'received
with honours accorded the ambassadors of the kings'.[10] Similar developments occurred in the Lower Zambezi where the Tonga and Sena rulers
successfully resisted all efforts by the Mutapa rulers to impose their political
hegemony over them. These developments reduced the empire to its core,
the region spanned by the Dande and Chidima territories.

8. Vasco Fernandes Homen to Luys da Sylva in E. Axelson, 1940, p. 269.
9. L. F. de Carvalho Dias, 1954.
10. ibid.

The habit of prestige stone-building in the Mutapa empire probably continued until the sixteenth century. Some of the early ruins, particularly the Zvongombe complex, represented the early capitals of the Mutapa rulers. Later capitals were in the form of stockades several metres high. Antonio Bocarro painted a vivid picture of both the capital and life-styles of the Mutapa rulers during the 1620s.

According to him the capital was:

> very large and is composed of many houses surrounded by a great wooden fence, within which there were three dwellings, one for the queen, and another for his servants who wait upon him within doors. There are three doors opening upon a great court-yard, one for the service of the queen, beyond which no man may pass, but only women, another for his kitchen, only entered by his cooks, who are two young men from among the principal lords of his kingdom, his relations in whom he has most confidence, and the lads who serve in the kitchen who are also nobles between fifteen and twenty years of age. These are also employed to lay food when the king wishes to eat, which they spread upon the ground, upon a carpet or mat, with muslin extended above, and many different kinds of meat are set before him, all roasted or boiled, such as hens, pigeons, partridges, capons, sheep, venison, hares, rabbits, cows, rats, and other game, of which after the king has eaten a portion is given to some of his servants who are always provided from his table.[11]

However, in the first half of the eighteenth century the Mutapas lost direct control of the plateau and the core of the empire shifted to the southern lowlands of the Zambezi bounded by Zumbo and Tete. This loss of political control was the culmination of a long process of fragmentation which began in 1629, when the Portuguese defeated Mamvura Mutapa,[12] and ended in 1917, when the Mutapa polity finally disappeared. The weakening of the Mutapa state invited distant as well as neighbouring Shona groups to take lands for themselves. The Budya who fanned out from the Lower Zambezi are a notable example. Consequently the Mutapa rulers invited other groups to settle in the core of the empire.[13]

Administratively the empire was controlled at three levels – the capital, the province and the village. The Mutapas delegated authority to chiefs at village and provincial levels. It would seem, however, that the nature of those appointed to these positions varied according to the Mutapas' political circumstances. In the empire's early days, only relatives of the Mutapas were entrusted with the government of the villages and provinces. It was customary for a prince and heir-apparent to govern the Dande lands. He was known as senior *nevanje*. Next to him was another prince with the title

11. A. Bocarro, in G. M. Theal, 1899–1902, Vol. III, pp. 356–7.
12. G. M. Theal, 1892–1902, Vol. V, pp. 290–2.
13. D. N. Beach, 1980a, pp. 164–5.

PLATE 22.1 *Ruins in the Matendere area*

PLATE 22.2 *Mutoko-type ruins*

of junior *nevanje* who was ranked second in succession to the throne.[14] Besides members of the royal lineage, those who though not related to the Mutapas had aided in the process of conquest, were appointed to authority.

14. W. G. L. Randles, 1979, p. 58; A. P. de Miranda in A. A. Andrade, 1955, pp. 307–8.

As the Mutapas came to feel more secure and confident in the seventeenth century, they allowed the villages and provinces to elect their own leaders. In the capital the Mutapas were assisted by high-ranking officials who, in exchange for their services, were granted land. Each of the emperor's wives was also assigned specific duties.[15]

Beliefs and methods of administrative control

The Mutapas manipulated several mechanisms to control the empire. A typical example was the practice whereby the territorial chiefs had to rekindle their royal fires annually from the Mutapa original royal fire.[16] This was an act of renewal of loyalty to the central authority. Once a year the Mutapa rulers sent out orders to the territorial chiefs to extinguish their royal fires and proceed immediately to the Mutapa court to rekindle their royal fires. This ritual of fidelity was also repeated at the enthronement of a new Mutapa ruler. Following the death of a ruling Mutapa an order was sent out to the territorial chiefs to extinguish their royal fires until a successor from whom they would rekindle their fires had been selected.

Failure to perform this ritual was regarded as an act of rebellion which was accordingly severely punished. This was done through an efficient army which has been estimated variously at '100 000 men into the fighting line',[17] 30 000 regulars during the sixteenth century and 3000 men during the eighteenth century.[18] These figures suggest that, before the decline of the empire, the Mutapa rulers were in a position to mobilize many peasants *ad hoc* to join the army but were much less able to do so when the empire fell into decay and disorder during the eighteenth century. The statistics provided by contemporary Portuguese observers are extremely unreliable.

The Mutapa also manipulated religion to control their subjects through the close relationship between the monarchy and the spirit mediums. It was either the spirits of the ancestors of the emperors themselves or 'past representatives of the original owners of the soil',[19] who possessed a medium. In addition to his other duties, the emperor was expected to maintain a close contact with the powerful dead on behalf of the nation. It was the emperor who propitiated the national spirit and interceded on behalf of his subjects. The system of observing the cult of royal graves also enhanced the emperor's image, prestige and, ultimately, his control over his people. He was expected to visit his ancestors' graves before any major military expedition was undertaken.

15. ibid.; A. Bocarro, in G. M. Theal, 1892–1902, Vol. III, pp. 356–7.
16. G. M. Theal, 1899–1902, Vol. I, p. 96; Vol. III, p. 130; Vol. VI, p. 170.
17. Vasco Fernandes Homen to Luup de Sylivia in E. Axelson, 1940, p. 274.
18. W. G. L. Randles, 1979, p. 60.
19. T. O. Ranger, 1979, p. 19.

PLATE 22.3 *An eighteenth-century engraving of Mutapa, reflecting the richness, glory and power of the emperor*

PLATE 22.4   *Musimbira-type ruins*

The owners of the soil, like Dzivaguru, were rain-makers and ritual officers at the Mutapa royal court. This religious system was duplicated at the various levels of administration. Religion was an important mechanism of social control, particularly in an economy dominated by agriculture. The participation of the emperor in rain-making rituals was seen as crucial to the economic prosperity of the empire. Indeed, the Mutapa emperors held 'monthly new moon' dances for their ancestors[20] – great annual feasts to appease their ancestral spirits. There are also references to musicians 'who awakened the spirits to the people's need for rain'.[21]

Religion, therefore, played a crucial role as a social mechanism for political control. Indeed, the spirit mediums enjoyed a higher status than the emperors. It was for this reason that they were and still are called *mhondoro* (lion), and it was their function to advise the emperor in all matters of state.[22]

The most common method of political control was tribute. The Mutapa emperors levied tribute in the form of agricultural produce, lion and leopard skins, ostrich feathers, small and large stock, the brisket of every

20. R. Gray and S. Marks, 1975, p. 388.
21. ibid.
22. Anon., 1890, p. 223; D. P. Abraham, 1969; G. K. Garbett, 1965; see also E. G. Parrinder, 1967, p. 61.

646

animal killed and, for an elephant, the tusk on which it fell when it died.[23] Tribute also took the form of labour rent. According to João de Barros:

> All the officers and servants of his court and the captains of the soldiers, each with his men, must serve him in the cultivation of his fields or other work seven days in every thirty. And the lords to whom he gives any land which contains vassals receive the same from them. Sometimes, when he wishes for a particular service he sends to the mines where they dig gold, one or two cows, according to the number of people there to be divided among them as a sign of love, and in return for this service each of them gives a little gold, to the value of five hundred reis. In the markets also the merchants give a certain amount instead of service, not that any penalty is inflicted on those who do not pay, but they are not allowed to appear before Benomotapa which is considered a great disgrace.[24]

The practice of labour rent was also adopted by vassal rulers who seem to have varied its application. Instead of sending people to cultivate the emperor's fields, the villages and hamlets in Uteve cultivated 'a large field of Sorghum for the king; all the inhabitants of the place were obliged to work in it certain days of the year; fixed in advance ...'. The harvest, however, was done by 'stewards maintained all over for this purpose'.[25]

When opening a new mine the Mutapa rulers usually sent their trusted agents to collect the tribute. The gold-miners erected a shelter to house the tribute-collectors as well as the tribute itself. The tribute was assessed as 'the product of one of the trips from the mine to the water that each miner accomplished daily'.[26] As will be shown later, the extraction of minerals, particularly gold, involved washing it in a river or pond. The nature of the tribute system does not seem to have changed until the demise of the Mutapa polity in the early twentieth century.

It could be argued that the various mechanisms of control partially succeeded in maintaining a centralized empire at a time when vast distances rendered the close supervision of the territorial chiefs impossible. The army's inability to deal effectively with rebellions in the far-flung parts of the empire, internal political intrigue which was exploited by Portuguese traders, and civil wars, all account for the gradual decline and fall of the Mutapa empire.

23. J. de Barros in G. M. Theal, 1899–1902, Vol. I, Book 10, ch. 1; J. dos Santos, in G. M. Theal, 1899–1902, book 2, ch. 15; A. P. de Miranda in L. F. de Carvahlo Dias, 1954, Vol. VII, p. 135.
24. G. M. Theal, 1899–1902, Vol. VI, p. 271.
25. J. dos Santos, in G. M. Theal, 1899–1902, Vol. VII, Book 2, ch. 15, p. 222.
26. W. G. L. Randles, 1979, p. 66.

The Portuguese factor

Although the Portuguese arrived at Sofala in 1506 it was only from 1550 to 1630 that they made serious attempts to gain control of the Mutapa empire. Until 1540 trade between the Portuguese and the Shona was conducted on a non-official basis. However, in 1540 commercial relations between the Portuguese traders and the Mutapa rulers and their subjects were regularized.[27] This was done through the establishment of a Portuguese diplomatic-cum-trade mission at the Mutapa royal court headed by an officer called the Captain of the Gates. He was elected for life by the Portuguese traders but his appointment had to be confirmed by the Mutapa emperors. His main duties were to transmit presents, requests or complaints from the Portuguese traders to the Mutapa emperors and *vice-versa*.[28] Relations between the Portuguese community and the Mutapa rulers were essentially tributary with the Portuguese paying a tribute called *curva*. At the assumption of his office, each new captain of the Portuguese fortress of Mozambique was:

> under obligation to pay to Monomotapa the value of three thousand cruzados in cloth and beads for the three years of his office, that he may during this term open his lands to all merchants, both Christians and Moors, as all of them trade with cloth obtained from the said Captain; and the greater part of the gold exported from these rivers goes into the hands of the captain of Mozambique.[29]

In exchange for this tribute the Mutapa emperors granted freedom of passage to the traders to sell their cloth and beads throughout the empire. According to the experience of a Jesuit missionary, João dos Santos, it was an:

> unheard of thing for Kaffier thieves to attack the Portuguese on the road or to rob them, unless by order of Monomutapa himself, as he has sometimes given such orders to avenge some injury he received or pretended to have received from the Portuguese especially when the captain who has newly entered office at Mozambique has not paid him or delayed until the second year the cloth which it is usual to pay him during the first.[30]

27. J. dos Santos, in G. M. Theal, 1899–1902, Vol. II, ch. 9; Fr. Monclaro in G. M. Theal, 1899–1902, Vol. III, p. 186.
28. J. dos Santos, in G. M. Theal, 1899–1902, Vol. II, p. 271.
29. ibid., p. 272.
30. P. B. de Rezende in G. M. Theal, 1899–1902, Vol. II, pp. 414, 427 and 429. The value of the *curva* is given as fifteen or sixteen thousand *cruzados* every three years. This sounds a little exaggerated.

In situations of this kind the emperor order the seizure without compensation of all the merchandise in his empire. This actually happened in 1610 when Gatsi Rusere declared a *mupeto* (forcible confiscation) of traders' merchandise which resulted in the raiding and killing of Portuguese traders.[31] In addition to the tribute the Portuguese Captain paid to the Mutapa emperors, both the Portuguese emperor and the Swahili–Arab traders had to pay a tribute of one piece of cloth out of every twenty pieces brought into the empire.[32] Besides cloth and beads, which were widely circulated, the Mutapa emperors acquired as presents from the Portuguese imported luxury items such as silks, carpets, ceramics and glassware which they used to enhance their prestige through a system of patronage.

This system of tributary relations persisted with little change until the second half of the sixteenth century when the Portuguese began to win control over the Mutapa rulers. This came about as a result of Portugal's aggressive wars in Southern Zambezia between 1569 and 1575[33] – when it succeeded in entrenching itself in the eastern Kingdoms of Uteve and Manyika. After several battles, in 1575 the Portuguese concluded a treaty with the King of Uteve whereby the captain of Sofala and his successors were obliged to pay an annual tribute of 200 pieces of cloth to the Teve rulers.[34] In exchange for this tribute the Portuguese traders secured freedom of passage to the Kingdom of Manyika where, as later events proved, they erroneously believed there was an abundance of gold. In addition, the inhabitants of the Portuguese fortress at Sofala were allowed freedom of passage into the interior along the Sofala river to buy provisions. As with the Mutapa emperors, each Portuguese trader who wanted to pass through Uteve to Manyika had to pay a duty to the Teve ruler of one cloth out of every twenty pieces brought into the kingdom. However, African merchants, who traded 'cloth, beads and other merchandise with the Portuguese', paid 'three in every twenty pieces to the King'.[35] It is not clear why the African merchants were required to pay more than their Portuguese counterparts but it was probably to prevent the rise of a powerful merchant class which would ultimately challenge the king's political authority. A similar treaty was concluded with the King of Manyika in 1573.[36]

This limited success tempted the Portuguese to2 make further encroachments into the Mutapa empire. The rebellions which broke out there between 1590 and 1607 provided the Portuguese with an opportunity to delve into the complexity of Mutapa politics. One Mutapa ruler, Gatsi Rusere, turned for help to the Portuguese and concluded a treaty with

31. J. dos Santos in G. M. Theal, 1899–1902, Vol. II, p. 272.
32. Fr. Monclaros in G. M. Theal, 1899–1902, Vol. III, pp. 202–53.
33. R. Gray and S. Marks, 1975, p. 390.
34. J. dos Santos in G. M. Theal, 1899–1902, Vol. II, p. 219.
35. G. M. Theal, 1899–1902, Vol. VII, p. 222.
36. ibid., p. 218.

PLATE 22.5 *Father Conçalo da Silveira, who introduced Christianity into the Mutapa empire in 1560. He was killed on the orders of the emperor when rumours circulated that he had led an advance party of Portuguese invaders*

them for military assistance in exchange for which he promised to cede all his gold, copper, iron, lead and tin mines.[37] The treaty bestowed upon the Portuguese the prestige of ownership although they lacked the expertise and the manpower to exploit the metals. In fact the treaty turned out to be of limited value because the Portuguese left Gatsi Rusere to his own devices while the civil wars continued to rage until he died in 1624. Gatsi Rusere was succeeded by his son Nyambu Kapararidze, the legitimacy of whose claim to the Mutapa royal throne was challenged by his uncle

37. G. M. Theal, 1899–1902, Vol. III, pp. 367–70.

Mamvura. In the war that ensued between these two pretenders Mamvura sought and, in 1629, obtained Portuguese military assistance. The Portuguese extorted promises from Mamvura, after which they made a common cause with him against Kapararidze. These promises involved a treaty of vassalage and the cession of the silver and gold mines. As with Gatsi Rusere in 1607, Mamvura succeeded to the Mutapa throne with Portuguese military assistance. The treaty which he subsequently concluded with the Portuguese required Mamvura to allow the Portuguese traders freedom of passage throughout the empire, to expel the Swahili–Arab traders from the empire, and to allow the Dominican missionaries to preach their religion. It also required Mamvura to stop the *curva*, which the Portuguese had been paying to the Mutapa rulers as tribute almost since the mid-1500s, and instead to pay tribute to the Portuguese thenceforth. After this treaty the number of Portuguese traders and adventurers within the Mutapa empire increased. Both Mamvura and his wife were baptized and changed their names to Domingos and Luiza respectively.[38] The treaty of 1629 encouraged Portuguese adventurers to seize land subsequently recognized by the Portuguese crown as *prazos* (crown land). From being the guests of the African rulers, the Portuguese traders now almost became the controllers of land but their individualism and lawlessness led to what may be viewed as a period of chaos and anarchy. Portuguese penetration of the Mutapa empire therefore, could be said to have led to its disintegration and to have given rise to a phenomenon called the *prazo* system as well as the birth of a new polity, the Rozvi empire.

The *prazo* system

The acquisition of land by individual Portuguese adventurers proceeded almost unchecked with the result that many *prazos da coroa* (crown-land estates) were created.[39] They were owned by Portuguese officials, traders, religious orders and frontiers-men.

The *prazo* system was a synthesis of two socio-economic systems. The first was that of the Shona which consisted of a ruling oligarchy and peasant producers; the second, which was superimposed on the Shona system, consisted of the *prazeros*, as a dominant class, and the *achikunda* (armies of slaves). In other words the *prazeros* maintained the socio-political system they found in existence in Zambezia. An African chief continued to perform his traditional duties but he 'no longer had absolute authority'[40] as the *prazero* assumed the status of overlord so that the relationship resembled that of chief and sub-chief in the Mutapa empire.

The relations of production on the *prazos* were esentially feudal. The

38. For the full text of the treaty, see J. Coelho in G. M. Theal, 1899–1902, Vol. V, pp. 290–2.

39. A. F. Isaacman, 1972b, ch. 2; M. D. D. Newitt, 1973, ch. 4.

40. A. F. Isaacman, 1969.

African chief paid tribute to the *prazero* in the form of agricultural produce; butter, locally woven cloth, honey, tobacco, sugar, large and small stock, ivory and gold dust.[41] In his position as a *de facto* chief, the *prazero* adopted African social practices in matters of religion and married into chiefly families to disguise his usurpation of African traditional authority, to enhance his image among Africans, and to overcome his major weakness – his lack of legitimacy in African traditional politics. These considerations led Professor Isaacman to postulate an Africanization theory which claims that the *prazo* as a Portuguese land-tenure system was so transformed and adapted to the African situation that it became completely African.[42] This indigenization process began at the turn of the seventeenth century.

However, Isaacman's total Africanization theory is difficult to maintain when it is realized that, throughout the *prazo* system was always more or less linked to mercantile capitalism. As Isaacman points out, the *prazeros* served as middle-men in the long-distance trade between Mozambique and India and, ultimately, Europe with the *prazeros* during the eighteenth century exporting mainly ivory and slaves to Brazil and the French islands of the Mauritius group. In this way, the *prazo* system maintained its economic connections with Europe and it can therefore be argued that the *prazero* society retained, even in its decadent stage, a non-African feature. In addition the internal organization of the *prazos* had features which could hardly be called African, a notable example being the co-existence of the *colono* and the *chikunda* (slave army). Even at the acme of its supposed mutation into an African institution, an opposite process, that of the de-Africanization of the traditional African societies of the *prazos*, was taking place. As the *prazo* system responded to the internal demand for slaves, the *prazeros* enslaved and sold their African neighbours and victimized their *colonos* and slaves alike. Consequently, a system of *aringas* came into existence in which the life of the *colonos* was so disturbed that the previous distinction between *colono* and slave became blurred.

It has been argued that 'in terms of the day to day governing of the *colonos* the *mambo*'s position remained virtually unaltered'.[43] It is true that the *mambo* enjoyed prestige and obedience from his people by virtue of his connection with the founding lineages. As Isaacman points out, 'when a *mambo* entered a village all work ceased; he was welcomed by a chorus of hand clapping – the traditional signal of respect and royality'.[44] But these were the empty trappings of royalty. Ultimately the *prazero* had the last word in deciding judicial cases, disputes or the appointment of an African chief himself. The tusk on which an elephant fell no longer went to the *mambo* nor did 'the choicest parts of the other animals which had died on

41. W. F. Rea, 1976, p. 102.
42. A. F. Isaacman, 1972b, pp. 56–63.
43. A. F. Isaacman, 1969, p. 158.
44. ibid.

his lands'.[45] Even the right to distribute land had been usurped by the *prazero*. It cannot, therefore, be argued that the 'arrival of the *prazero* did not lead to the destruction or modification of the traditional political system'.[46] It may not have been destroyed but it was certainly greatly modified. The *prazos* represented the first phase of the Portuguese colonization of Mozambique: they were pockets of political and economic exploitation by the Portuguese merchants achieved only through a modification of African political and social institutions.

The geographical spread of the *prazos*

The *prazos* were dotted on both sides of the Zambezi river. There were, however, significant differences between the *prazos* to the north and those to the south of the river.[47] Those to the south were *terras da coroa* (Portuguese crown property), while those to the north were not. The *prazeros* who held the crown lands did so under clearly specified obligations. In theory the grant of a *terra da coroa* was restricted to three generations, the land could only be inherited through a female, it could not be more than three leagues in size, and the holder was subject to an annual quit rent. The *prazo*-holders in the north were free from all these conditions and acquired land as a result of a direct arrangement with the indigenous African chief. These differences led to great disparities of value between *prazos* of the same size. Besides, the *prazo*-holders placed greater value on the northern *prazos* as they were near the market, the *Feira* of Zumbo, and also the eighteenth-century gold-workings of the *bares*.

The *prazo* system was sustained by a variety of categorized slaves. The top slave was the *chuanga*[48] – the 'eyes and ears' of the *prazero*, appointed because of his loyalty. Every *prazo* village had its *chuanga* whose primary function was to spy on the traditional leaders and to collect taxes and ivory. The *prazero* relied on him for information about the local Africans and for the recruitment of disaffected African chiefs in the neighbourhood. The size of the African community on a *prazo* was of crucial importance to the *prazero* as he depended on it for gold production, trade, tribute which was paid in kind, defence and, often, to wage wars for territorial aggrandisement. For the enforcement of his authority the *prazero* depended on a *chikunda* whose main function was to police the local population, ensure that the laws of the *prazero* were obeyed and deal also with acts of rebellion. A *chikunda* army usually ranged from twenty to thirty men on small *prazos* while on large *prazos*, it could comprise thousands. A *chikunda* was divided into *nsaka* (groups of ten men) under the control of a *sachikunda*. A *sachikunda* and his *nsaka* received orders from a *mukazambo* (slave chief).

45. ibid.
46. ibid.
47. W. F. Rea, 1976, pp. 88–9.
48. A. P. de Miranda in A. A. Andrade, 1955, pp. 266–70.

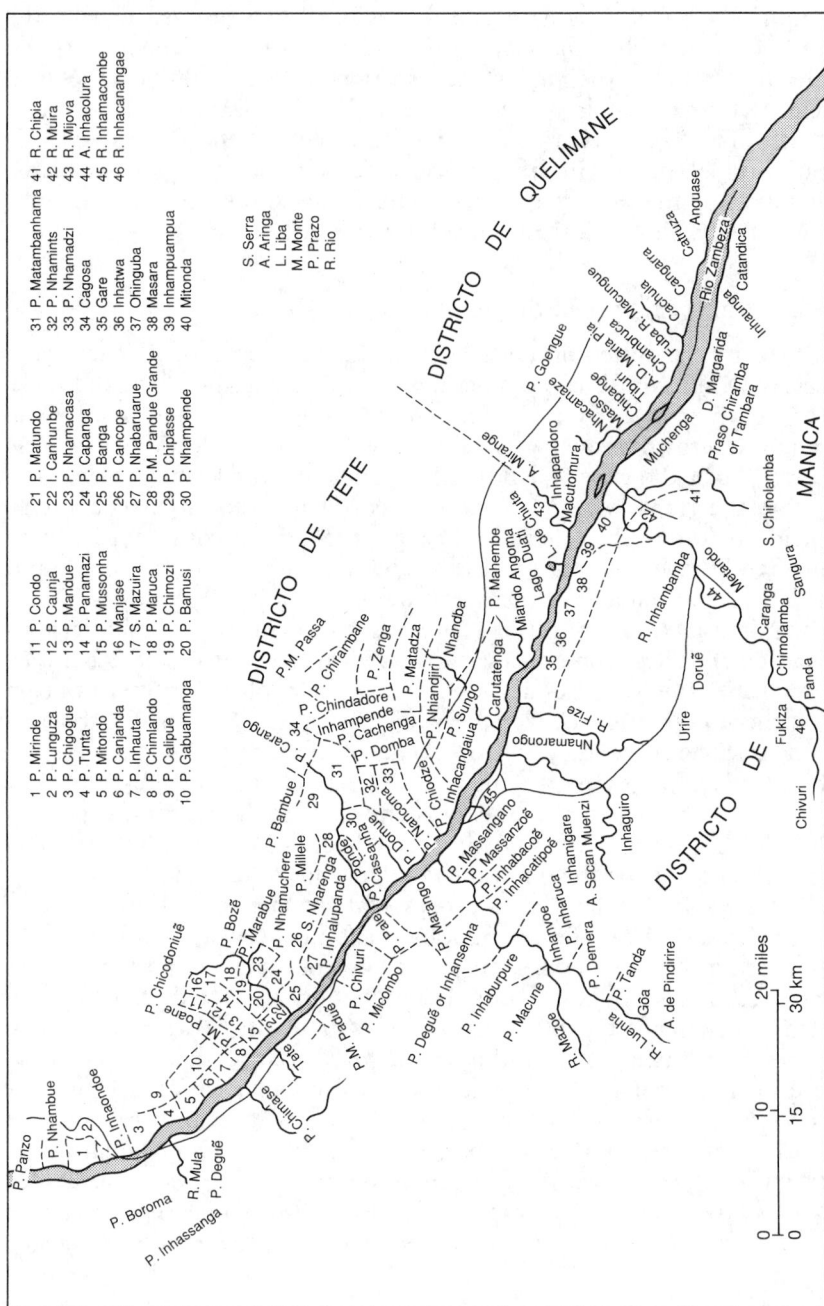

FIG. 22.2 *The prazos of the lower Zambezi valley*

1 P. Mrinde	11 P. Condo	21 P. Matundo	31 P. Matambanhama
2 P. Lunguza	12 P. Caunja	22 I. Canhunbe	32 P. Nhamints
3 P. Chigogue	13 P. Mandue	23 P. Nhamacasa	33 P. Nhamadzi
4 P. Tunta	14 P. Panamazi	24 P. Capanga	34 P. Cagosa
5 P. Mitondo	15 P. Mussonha	25 P. Banga	35 P. Gare
6 P. Canjanda	16 Manjase	26 P. Cancope	36 P. Inhatwa
7 P. Inhauta	17 S. Mazuira	27 P. Nhabaruarue	37 P. Ohinguba
8 P. Chimlando	18 P. Maruca	28 P.M. Pandue Grande	38 P. Masara
9 P. Calipue	19 P. Chimozi	29 P. Chipasse	39 P. Inhampuampua
10 P. Gabuamanga	20 P. Bamusi	30 P. Nhampende	40 P. Mitonda

41 R. Chipia	S. Serra
42 R. Muira	A. Aringa
43 R. Mijova	L. Liba
44 A. Inhacolura	M. Monte
45 R. Inhamacombe	P. Prazo
46 R. Inhacanangae	R. Rio

There could be as many as twenty or thirty slave chiefs on one *prazo* whose main functions were to resolve cases and administer *muavi* (a poison ordeal) to establish the guilt or innocence of a person accused of witchcraft.

In his report of 1766 concerning the coast of Africa, Antonio Pinto de Miranda discussed the main methods by which slaves were obtained. According to him slave-hunters stole children and sold them to Portuguese traders, Arab–Swahili traders and African agents; some people were sold or pawned as slaves in times of famine; and, convicted criminals, prisoners-of-war and credit defaulters sold as slaves.[49] The picture which emerges from other Portuguese sources is one of voluntary enslavement.

There is sufficient evidence, however, that some who were sold believed that 'they were not really slaves, but were serving in the same way as a European servant who agrees on a payment with his master but does not become his slave'.[50] Children were occasionally sold to meet tributary demands on the *prazo*, in which case a man could only redeem his child by exchanging him for a slave. Clearly some chiefs and *colonos* found themselves with no choice but to sell their dependents.

The decline of the *prazo* system

The *prazo* system declined during the second half of the eighteenth century for several reasons. The first was that the *prazero*'s authority was ill-defined compared with that of the traditional African ruler.[51] Often this tempted the *prazero* to abuse his authority by compelling the African peasants to sell their agricultural produce to him exclusively and at artificially low prices. He also imposed heavy taxes on the peasants, tortured them and committed 'hundreds of bloody, ferocious atrocities and cruel killings without these ever coming to the attention of the government'.[52] The *colonos* reacted sharply by revolting against the *prazeros* and even migrating. Miranda has drawn our attention to the abortive slave rebellions and *mussitos* (fugitive slave strongholds) in the late 1700s. These revolts and migrations led to a decline in agricultural production, drought and famine.[53] The *prazero* and his slave armies relied for their food on what the peasants produced; the *chikunda* used force to get food-stuffs from the peasants and the *colonos*, again, reacted by migrating from the *prazos* to look for food and security elsewhere.

The slave trade was another factor that led to the decline of the *prazo* system. The overseas slave trade increased in the 1640s as a result of the Dutch occupation of Angola.[54] The supply of Angolan slaves to Brazil was

---

49. A. P. de Miranda in A. A. Andrade, 1955, pp. 266–70.
50. ibid.
51. ibid.
52. A. F. Isaacman, 1969, p. 170.
53. A. P. de Miranda in A. A. Andrade, 1955, pp. 266–70.
54. ibid.

stopped and Lisbon had to turn to south-east Africa as a source. The establishment of a plantation economy in the French Mascarene Islands in the 1730s created additional demand for slaves. But despite all these new demands, the numbers of slaves exported from Southern Zambezia by 1752 were relatively small; 300 had been obtained from the Zambezi and 200 from Sofala. A German missionary who lived in the region from 1758–9 also observed that 'few slaves were sent overseas, and it was considered so terrible a fact that those condemned to it would commit suicide in order to avoid it'.[55] Towards the end of the eighteenth century, however, the slave trade gathered such momentum that the *prazeros* in the Zambezi valley saw it as an opportunity for wealth. Slave-raiding parties brought caravan loads of slaves from the Chewa, Nsenga and Manganja territories. The *prazeros* also began to sell the slaves on their estates, thus undermining the very foundation of the *prazo* system. However, beyond the Zambezi valley the rest of Southern Zambezia was little affected by the trade. The decline of the *prazo* system south of the Zambezi was accelerated instead by the rise of a new polity in the second half of the seventeenth century – the Rozvi Changamire dynasty.

The Rozvi empire

The origins of the Rozvi empire are a matter of speculation. The issue has been further complicated by the name Changamire, which is associated with the founder of the Rozvi empire in the second half of the seventeenth century but first mentioned in the fifteenth century.[56] There are occasional references to a Changamire dynasty in the sixteenth century and 'the last that had been heard of these earlier Changamires was their defeat in 1547–8'.[57] However, there seems some consensus on four points:[58] first, that the Rozvi were an integral part of the historic Karanga of the Mutapa empire until they broke away in the seventeenth century and acquired a separate identity; secondly, 'that the designation Rozvi was first applied to a section of those historic Karanga who were associated with the rise to power between 1684 and 1695 of Changamire Dombo I';[59] thirdly, that the creation of the Rozvi empire was the work of Changamire Dombo I; and fourthly, that the appellation Rozvi, which was derived from the Shona verb *kurozva* (to destroy), was either assumed by the 'followers of Dombo ... out of vanity'[60] because of the destruction they had committed during their wars of conquest or was given to them as a nickname by their victims.

55. Cited in W. F. Rea, 1976, pp. 117–18.
56. D. de Alcacova to the king, Cochin, 20 Nov. 1506 in *Documentos Sobre os Portuguezes em Moçambique*, Vol. I, p. 393.
57. D. N. Beach, 1980a, p. 228.
58. S. I. Mudenge, 1974a.
59. ibid.
60. ibid.

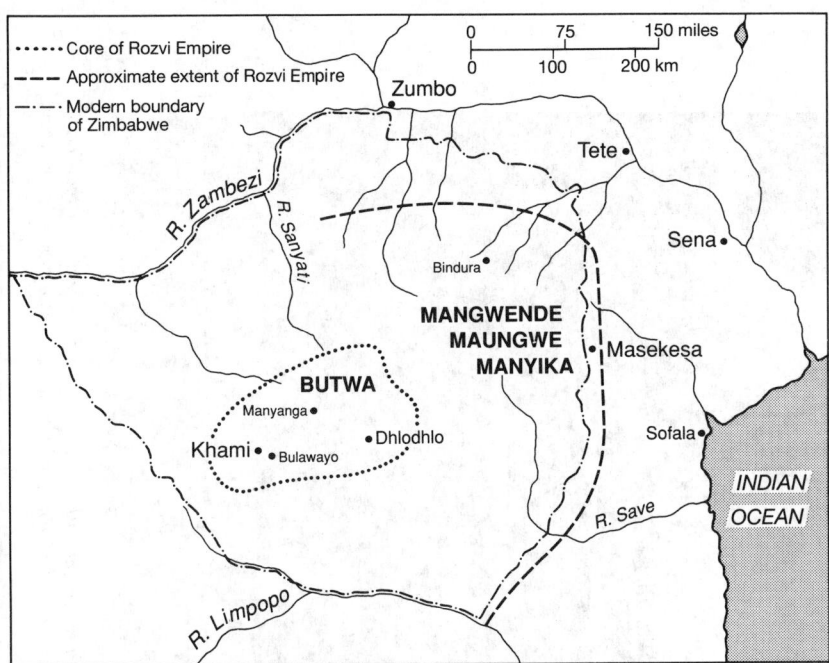

FIG. 22.3 *The Rozvi empire*
Source: adapted from D. N. Beach, *Zimbabwe before 1900*, 1984, p. 38, Harare, Mambo Press

Between 1684 and 1695 Dombo Changamire gradually rose to power in the north-east.[61] How he did so is still unclear. He was a herdsman of the Mutapa emperors who rebelled taking himself and his followers first to the Torwa state in the south-west, then to the Kingdoms of Manyika and Uteve in the east.[62] The Portuguese traders, while conquering these areas, were expelled in 1684 from the Kingdom of Maungwe, from the plateau country in 1693 and from the Kingdom of Manyika in 1695. They fled to Zumbo, where they established a new settlement in 1710, then returned to their former settlement of Masekasa in Manyika. In every case, however, there was a tacit understanding that they were under the authority of the Rozvi Changamire overlords. In this way the Rozvi rulers were able to create an empire that stretched as far as Buhera, Bocha, Duma and the south-eastern highlands in the south; to the sandveld in the north-west, to the sodic soils in the north and to the lowveld in the south-west.[63] The core of the empire probably spanned the same area as that of the Ndebele which succeeded it in the 1840s. The early capital was situated at Danangombe but later the Rozvi emperors seem to have lived at Khami and Natetale from time to time.

61. D. N. Beach, 1980a, pp. 228–31.
62. ibid.
63. ibid., p. 236.

PLATE 22.6 *Decorative walling at Danangombe. Possibly built in the seventeenth century as one of the centres of the Torwa state, it appears to have become its capital in the 1630s or 1640s, after the burning of Khami. Its population was probably c. 2,000*

Our idea of a Rozvi capital comes from a nineteenth-century description,[64] although it had probably changed little since the 1600s and 1700s. The royal court, according to our account, consisted of three large stone houses, each with many rooms, in which the Rozvi emperor used to store his belongings. The houses were surrounded by walls of ivory tusks. The Rozvi Changamire had many rifles which he obtained from Portuguese traders at Sena. He bred 'pigs and fine dogs' and:

> does not eat any fresh food, only old and he drinks his *pombe* by himself. On certain days he goes hunting with his courtiers, other times he sends his hunters; when he dies he is buried in his house and there is no wailing or mourning because the very next day his wives present to elders a new Changamire selected by them and the first wife crowns him with two caps ...[65]

The Rozvi maintained their identity as a foreign élite amidst people who shared the same *moyo* (heart) totem, their allies during the wars of conquest of the Kalanga-speaking people as well as those of the Torwa state.

Provincial administration

The Rozvi rulers used methods similar to those of the Mutapas to maintain their empire. The mechanisms involved the allocation of land, the payment of tribute, religion and the training of an efficient army.

The Rozvi rulers distributed land to newly installed chiefs and levied tribute from them. They also manipulated the priestly class in the installation of chiefs, libation practices and various spirit cults. They introduced innovations in religion and the collection of tribute. Under the Mutapa emperors, as already noted, the tributary chiefs used to send their tribute with bearers directly to the royal court. The Rozvi emperors, however, organized their tribute in a hierarchical pyramid with the village as the base and the Rozvi court, the apex. The principal officer and commander of the *tumbare* army supervised the collection of tribute throughout the empire, sending out teams of special tribute-collectors to the various provinces and villages. The collection of tribute was therefore a specialized function within the overall administration of the empire. Some tribute-collectors were backed by the army.

The Rozvi developed a religious system altogether different from that of the *mhondoro* (spirit mediums) prevalent among the northern and eastern Shona. The Rozvi 'cult of the oracular deity', Mwari, was based on a belief in a High God who expressed himself through natural phenomena such as lightning or earthquakes. The principal officers of the Mwari oracle were

64. A. H. U. Lisbon Moc. Caixa 2, João Julião da Silva, Sofala 8th August 1844. 'Memoria Respectiva a Villa de Sofala' (1836–47).

65. Anon., A. H. U. Moc. Caixa 7, 'Descripção Corografica do Reino de Manhica, seus custumes e leis' (1794).

the Mouth, the Ear and the Eye whose main purpose was to collect information. The Mwari cult was manipulated by the Rozvi rulers for a political end.

The proverbial efficiency of the Rozvi army calls for some clarification. Portuguese observers, during the eighteenth century, never ceased to marvel at both the discipline and efficiency of the Rozvi armies which were generally well equipped with bows and arrows, daggers, assegais, battle axes and cudgels. Its organization very much resembled that of Shaka, a nineteenth-century[66] Zulu king. Like the Zulu, the Rozvi organized their armies into regiments and also adopted the crescent formation in battle. Under certain circumstances, however, this method could be abandoned. A typical example was the battle of Maungwe in 1684 when the 'wily and cunning' Dombo Changamire vanquished the Portuguese 'with his strategems'.[67] Like most armies in pre-colonial African societies, the Rozvi armies performed certain rituals which instilled military prowess and self-confidence before they went into battle. The Portuguese came to believe that the Rozvi emperor 'had magic oil with which he could kill any one simply by touching the person with it'[68] and there is no doubt that this and other beliefs played an important role in Rozvi military victories.

The prowess of the Rozvi armies in battle can also be explained by the thorough training the soldiers underwent which involved military exercises as well as archery. The elements of training and hierarchy in the Rozvi army have tempted some historians to make comparisons with the organization and terminology of a Roman army.[69] It is more more likely, however, that the Rozvi armies were organized and trained much after the fashion of the early nineteenth-century Zulu, Ndebele and Sotho armies, as already indicated.

Another aspect of the Rozvi army that has been mystified is its invincibility – the defeat of the Portuguese at the end of the seventeenth century is often cited as an example – but these military victories are seen in isolation from the totality of the Portuguese presence in East and Central Africa during this period. The Portuguese were fighting for their survival along the East African coast from the 1650s to 1729 when their fortress at Mombasa was destroyed by the Sultans of Oman.[70] The Sultan of Oman established himself at Pate and mounted unsuccessful military attacks against Mombasa in 1661 and Mozambique in 1670. In March 1696, a fleet from Muscat, which was reinforced at Pate, laid seige to Fort Jesus at Mombasa. Fort Jesus collapsed and with it Portuguese control of the East African coast north of Cape Delgado.[71] In other words, what the Rozvi

66. S. I. Mudenge, 1974b, p. 378.
67. Cited in S. I. Mudenge, 1974, p. 379.
68. ibid.
69. ibid., p. 377.
70. C. R. Boxer and C. de Azevedo, 1960.
71. ibid. See also G. S. P. Freeman-Grenville, 1963, pp. 141–2.

Changamires encountered in Southern Zambezia was not the totality of organized Portuguese military effort as the Portuguese were concentrating on re-establishing their control of the East African coast. The Rozvi defeat of the Portuguese during this period can, therefore, hardly be used as an index for the efficiency of the Rozvi army.

The Portuguese military effort in Southern Zambezia was based on the *prazeros*, themselves badly disunited by rather conflicting economic interests. The *prazeros* had also engendered disunity in most African societies, notably in the lands of Mutapa and the Kingdom of Uteve. If these factors are not taken into account when assessing the glory and power of the Rozvi empire, it is easy to exaggerate the efficiency of the Rozvi military machine.

The Economy

Agriculture

The dominant branches of production among the Shona societies were agriculture, animal husbandry, hunting, gathering, fishing and metal-work. Long-distance and inter-regional trade complemented the economy. The Shona cultivated three main cereals, finger-millet, drought-resistant bulrush millet and various sorghums.[72] The unit of production was the household, and there is no solid evidence that the division of labour was rigidly based on sex as has been suggested by some writers.[73] What evidence there is, suggests that the situation differed from society to society. In some, as Barber observed, 'adult males in the community were responsible for the construction of shelters and for the clearing and preparation of new lands',[74] while the women sowed and cultivated the fields. The harvesting was done by both men and women. In other words, the men performed the heavier tasks within the agricultural cycle and the women the lighter, more in the spirit of co-operation than strict division of labour. In some societies, however, such as the Hlengwe of the lowveld, there was some division of labour with the adult males devoting most time to trapping and hunting game while the juveniles herded cattle and the women cultivated the fields.

The ploughing season stretched from September to November with the hoe the basic technology. The limited nature of this technology necessitated shifting agriculture whereby the old land was abandoned whenever it became exhausted and new land opened up. The opening of new land involved the 'clearing of the bush, burning it and allowing the ash to fertilize it'.[75] The destructive nature of the slash-and-burn techniques of

72. D. N. Beach, 1977, p. 41.
73. W. J. Barber, 1964, p. 46.
74. ibid.
75. ibid., p. 45.

agriculture has been criticized as wasteful of land. But as Lord Hailey observed in his *African Survey*, it was 'less a device of barbarism than a concession to the character of the soil'.[76] Shona agriculture, like most pre-colonial agrarian economies, was adapted to local conditions so that there were many practices of shifting agriculture.

The period 1500 to 1800 witnessed the piecemeal introduction into Southern Zambezia of new crops from Europe and Asia. The new crops were introduced mainly along the coast and in regions where the Portuguese had built their settlements. In Sofala and the Lower Zambezi, the region between the Tendaculo and the Luabo rivers, the African peasants cultivated rice and yams although these never became their staple diet.[77] They also cultivated sugar-cane to eat rather than to make sugar as they lacked both the expertise and the appliances. The African peasants also planted many fruit trees from India and Portugal, such as figs, pineapples, guavas, pawpaws and oranges; they also grew melons, cucumbers, sweet potatoes and lemons. Some of these fruits grew on their own in the bush, as noted by João dos Santos in 1596:

> In two places along the Sofala river there are two unowned thickets full of orange and lemon trees of which all who choose may freely gather the fruit, and the lemons are so abundant that the Kaffirs [Africans] load vessels with them and go down the river to Sofala where they are sold almost for nothing. The inhabitants of the fortress salt and fill barrels and jars with them, which they send to India where they are greatly esteemed and are eaten with rice.[78]

It would seem, therefore, that the cultivation of these exotic fruits was stimulated mainly by demand from foreign traders. There is also evidence that wheat was being cultivated in the Kingdom of Manyika during April and May. According to Father Gaspar Macedo, the yield was quite good with one grain of wheat producing 'fifty ears'.[79] There is also evidence that by 1778 peanuts were being cultivated in Manyika.[80]

In addition to the cereals and fruits, 'two grain legumes were grown everywhere, notably groundnuts, *voandzeia subterranea* and cowpeas, *vigna unquiculata*'.[81] As already noted, none of the crops introduced from Euro–Asia ever constituted the main diet of the Shona. The case was different with maize which was introduced into Southern Zambezia during the eighteenth century. This gradually caught up with millet and sorghum to constitute one of the staple diets of the Shona in the twentieth century, particularly among urban populations.

76. Cited in W. J. Barber, 1964, p. 45.
77. J. dos Santos in G. M. Theal, 1899–1902, Vol. II, p. 269.
78. ibid., p. 190.
79. G. Macedo, 1890, p. 150.
80. J. Baptista Moutaury in A. A. Andrade, 1955, p. 362.
81. W. G. L. Randles, 1979, p. 49.

The Nyanga and lowveld

The agrarian economy of the Nyanga and lowveld areas was in many ways different from that of the plateau. The Nyanga highlands were characterized by poor soils and steep slopes. The greater part of the landscape in northern Nyanga was terraced with dry stone walls about a metre high. These terraces were made on the hillsides and their purpose was 'simply to conserve the soil and dispose neatly of the stones'.[82] In other words, terrace-building was a method of controlling a precarious environment that was used for three or more centuries until 1800. It is possible that the numerous terraces 'represent the accumulated evidence of small-scale cultivation in many different years'.[83] There is also evidence that a limited amount of irrigation was practised but only in a supplementary role as the Nyanga area usually enjoys a fair amount of annual rainfall. It is more likely that the irrigation of dry-season gardens of vegetables, maize and bananas, which is still being practised in this region, is an agricultural tradition of eighteenth-century origin. Equally, evidence of this agricultural tradition can be observed in the terracing of lower slopes and contouring of valley lands in the Nyanga area. According to Roger Summers, the Tonga/Sena practised this kind of agriculture before they were absorbed into Manyika society during the eighteenth century.[84]

The lowveld economy

The lowveld economy was different. Here a riverine people, the Hlengwe, practised mainly hunting, gathering and fishing and agriculture only to a limited extent.[85] The lowveld has very low annual rainfall so that gathering plays an important role in the economy even at present. The fruits gathered were mainly those from which beverages were made including *nkanyi* (marula – *Sclerocarya caffra*), *mahanga* (ilala palm – *Hyphaene natalenis*) the sap of which was used to make an intoxicating wine called *njemani* or *chemwa*; the *kwaka* tree (monkey orange – *Strychnos madagascariensis*) and the baobab fruit. These fruits were gathered by women and children while the men hunted big game. The women and children killed mice, gathered the large silvery caterpillars from trees and collected locusts.

The Hlengwe were, as they still are today, proficient hunters. The abundance of many species of game in the lowveld, it has been said, rendered it 'a hunters' paradise'.[86] Fishing was also an important occupation. The lowveld rivers, then as now, were rich in fish. Like hunting, fishing was essentially done by the men year-round. The most

82. J. E. G. Sutton, 1983, p. 12.
83. ibid.
84. ibid.
85. J. H. Bannerman, 1981.
86. ibid.

effective method of catching fish in large quantities was to use nets made of reeds. These nets were skilfully laid at the confluence of streams or, alternatively, young men and sometimes women were sent to walk downstream so as to drive the fish like a flock into the nets. It should be noted, however, that the difference between the hunting and fishing activities of the Hlengwe and the rest of the people in Southern Zambezia during this period was only one of degree as both hunting and fishing were practised by people in the plateau country and the coastal kingdoms. Commenting on the subject of fishing at the end of the sixteenth century, João dos Santos noted that 'In Winter when the river Sofala rises it frequently overflows its banks and inundates the fields, the ponds in them which become full of fish from the river.'[87] He then went on to describe the various kinds of fish. The Nyanga region was and still is famous for its trout. Fishing then, as now, was practised in both the large and small rivers in Southern Zambezia.

As with fishing, hunting as a way of earning a living was not the exclusive monopoly of the Hlengwe of the lowveld. In various parts of the Mutapa empire men hunted countless species of animals including lions, tigers, leopards, rhinocerous, elephant, buffalo, wild cows, eland and wildebeste to cite only a few. There was no limit as to what could be killed for food. Guineafowl were found in their hundreds in the bush close to the fields. The traditional professional hunters used traps, spears, clubs and bows and arrows to kill animals. However, with the introduction of fire-arms by the Portuguese in the early sixteenth century, the hunters' efficiency improved.

It would be incorrect to create the impression or rather, perpetuate the 'myth about the Hlengwe being solely hunters'.[88] That they were able to differentiate between various kinds of soil demonstrates that they paid as much attention to agriculture as their Shona counterparts elsewhere in Southern Zambezia. The Hlengwe differentiated soils mainly on their relative ability to retain moisture.[89] They called the sandy soils where they built their homesteads *nthlava*. This type of soil was good for the cultivation of cucumbers, gourds, cowpeas, groundnuts and peanuts. They also grew millet and sorghum on *nthlava*. soil but in the valleys or their neighbourhoods. Since rainfall was erratic, the dew that fell in these valleys played an important role in the growth of sorghum. The Hlengwe called the basalt soils *tsovolo*. This was a fertile type of soil on which they grew maize and a variety of vegetables. Its advantage over other types of soil was that it retained moisture for a long period after the heavy rains. This was important for the cultivation of maize which requires a lot of rain, in a region where the rainfalls were erratic. It would seem that there was no

87. J. dos Santos, in G. M. Theal, 1899–1902, Vol. II, p. 264.
88. J. H. Bannerman, 1981, p. 19.
89. ibid.; interview with my mother, Pertenia Kwatini Bhila (aged *c*. 67–8 years), 19/5/85, Borrowdale.

shortage of land and the only restriction was the erratic rainfall. In a good year, the Hlengwe peasants produced surplus grain which 'may not have always carried them through all the lean years but did ameliorate the situation'.[90]

Various views have been expressed concerning the efficiency of the agrarian economies of the Shona societies between 1500 and 1800. In 1569 Father Monclaro castigated African peasants 'because they are not provident, but quickly waste and consume the new crops in feasts and drinking'.[91] In 1648, however, Antonio Gomes observed that the African peasants produced a surplus that lasted until the following year; further 'they never see the bottom of their grain bins'.[92] Conversely, in 1667 Manuel Barreto maintained that the Africans 'have not, and cannot possibly have, any provision from one year to another'.[93] In 1696 Antonio da Conceicao observed that in the Mutapa empire people 'do their own farms and the king has one cultivated by his *cafres* which stretches where the eyes cannot see and sometimes sees personally but in a grave manner. He eventually collects so much food that he lives in plenty and even luxury, not only he but also his women'.[94] We also learn from Jesuit Father Julio Cesar, who visited the Mutapa court in 1620, that this reigning Mutapa paid much attention to agriculture. Julio Cesar reported that the Mutapa did not despise the title of farmer; on the contrary, this priest says that he was quickly dispatched because the Emperor wanted 'to go and see to his farming activities because it was time to sow the fields'.[95]

These contradictory statements by Portuguese observers clearly underscore the need to heed date and location when discussing the efficiency of pre-colonial agriculture in Southern Zambezia. The evidence cited above referred to situations which prevailed in certain years in specific places in Southern Zambezia and should not be used as a justification for generalization. The problem of famine and drought should be discussed in the context of time and space. As will be shown later, Portugal's aggressive wars during the seventeenth century led to famines which caused the peasants to abandon their lands. It is possible that Barreto's report referred to some place in the Kingdom of Maungwe where in 1667, the Portuguese and the Swahili–Arabs were fighting for commercial supremacy. Likewise, the anonymous eighteenth-century writer was concerned largely with the situation in the Kingdom of Manyika – or, probably with famine in a certain part of Manyika. It has been necessary to dwell on this theme of frequent famine and the improvidence of African peasants because the Portuguese accounts on this subject from 1500 to 1800 and later have led

90. J. H. Bannerman, 1981, p. 19.
91. Father Monclaro, in G. M. Theal, 1899–1902, Vol. III, p. 231.
92. A. Gomes, 1959, p. 220.
93. M. Barreto, in G. M. Theal, 1899–1902, Vol. III, p. 478.
94. F. de Souza, 1710, Vol. I, p. 837.
95. A. da Conceicao, p. 66.

some historians, such as David Beach to over-generalize about famines both in pre-colonial and colonial Southern Zambezia.

Beach has characterized Shona pre-colonial agriculture as 'useful but dangerously static'.[96] This, according to him, was because 'no selection of crops and soil and no expertise in predicting *shangwa* (famine) could ward off these disasters, whether caused by climate, locusts and other blights'.[97] He further argues that the grain stores could not 'keep grain in store to feed the people throughout the really bad shangwa'.[98] First it should be noted that the Shona societies themselves were not 'static'. The various Shona societies had contacts among themselves as well as with other neighbouring African societies – the Swahili–Arabs from the tenth century or earlier and the Portuguese from the beginning of the sixteenth century. These contacts represented efforts to modify their material conditions through barter and exchange. The Shona peasants, as already noted, had been adopting new crops throughout the period from 1500 to 1800. These developments could hardly have been features of a static pre-colonial agrarian economy. The myths about the static nature of African agrarian economies have already been dispelled, in the case of West Africa, by A. G. Hopkins. As he aptly remarks:

> the agricultural history in the pre-colonial period is a story of inno-
> vation rather than stagnation. The assumption that the economy was
> static, having been frozen at the very dawn of African history, is
> untenable, and the timeless concept of the 'traditional' society to be
> used with care or better still, not used at all. Although contact with
> other continents led to introduction of some weeds, such as spear
> grass, there is no doubt that on balance the import of seeds and plants
> was of great benefit to West Africa. The new crops offered the means
> of improving nutrition, they reduced the risk of famine and made
> possible the support of a larger population.[99]

The idea that the Shona peasants were helpless victims of droughts and famines has been shown to be dated. Dr Richard Mutetwa showed that, in the case of the Duma people in the south-east, for example, 'they had several ways of predicting droughts'.[100] They also had several methods of fighting famine such as bartering salt, meat, fish, tusks, mats, pots, baskets, spears, arrows and jewels for grain and, sometimes, begging. The Shona also obtained grain during famine through a system called *mukomondera*[101] whereby one borrowed grain on the understanding that it would be refunded without interest in the following good season. In difficult situations a man pawned his daughter. It should be remembered that the other

96. D. N. Beach, 1984, p. 40.
97. ibid.
98. ibid.
99. A. G. Hopkins, 1983, p. 31.
100. R. M. G. Mutetwa, 1976 unpublished, pp. 238–9.
101. ibid.

branches of production, notably hunting, fishing and gathering, did not disappear after the introduction of new crops; they were adapted to the new agrarian economy and consequently constituted an important means of combating drought and famine.

In his study, Mutetwa has also convincingly argued that the problem of storage was not serious because the three Shona staple crops, millet, bulrush millet and sorghum, could store very well for more than three to four years.[102] Beach's observation that humidity increased the moisture in the grain bin during the rainy season – which caused the grain either to rot or made it easier for stock-borers to eat into the grain bins – has not sufficiently taken into account the precautions the Shona peasants took to preserve their grain. The grain bins were carefully plastered 'on the inside and sealed off'.[103] This rendered them airtight. The grain bins were also situated on bare rock to prevent termites reaching them. In the absence of such a rock, the grain bins were placed on reasonably high poles so that termite activity could easily be spotted before any damage was done. There has been a danger, as Mutetwa keenly observed, of 'stressing the drought years at the expense of the normal or above average years, and, it may be added, without regard to date and location'.[104] Parallels elsewhere in Africa concerning the efficiency of pre-colonial agriculture suggest that the 'darker picture' of the efficiency of Shona agriculture to satisfy the needs of the peasants can hardly be justified. As Walter Rodney argues, most African societies actually increased the cultivation of their lands notwithstanding the periodic famines.[105] In a different historical context, Miracle observed that:

> We have much to learn about the tribal economies of tropical Africa, but it is increasingly clear that a number of current stereotypes about them are in need of revision.[106]

This observation was no more true about pre-colonial peasant agriculture elsewhere than it was of the Shona.

Stock-raising

Stock-raising was an important branch of production in both the Mutapa and Rozvi empires. Stock-raising included the rearing of sheep, goats and cattle. The economic significance of cattle in African societies has attracted much interest among economic historians. Cattle provided meat, milk and manure which farming communities either consumed or sold.[107] Possession

102. ibid., pp. 236–7.
103. ibid.
104. ibid.
105. Cited in R. M. G. Mutetwa, 1976, pp. 240–1.
106. Cited in R. M. G. Mutetwa, 1976, p. 241.
107. W. J. Barber, 1964, p. 47.

of cattle also performed a social function in that it bestowed a social status upon an individual. The more cattle a man owned in society, the more he was respected 'not for his unthinking devotion to ascribed values, but for his skill in controlling a major resource'.[108] In a region which sometimes experienced severe droughts, cattle had the advantage of lasting longer 'than stored grain'.[109] This may explain why the Shona societies expressed their exchange values in terms of cattle. Portuguese documents stress the central role of cattle in the economy of both the Mutapa and Rozvi empires. Large herds of cattle flourished particularly in the highveld where they were not threatened with the tsetse fly.[110] There is every likelihood that the Mutapa and Rozvi Changamire rulers practised transhumance or the seasonal movement of cattle. In general the practice of transhumance was determined by three factors.[111] First, the size of the herd was important: the larger the herd the more land the cattle-owning community needed. The threat of disaster explains why, from the days of Great Zimbabwe, from the thirteenth to the fifteenth century, to the end of the eighteenth century, there was an annual trek of cattle from the highveld to the lowveld during the dry season in search of better grazing land.[112] The herdsmen moved their cattle to the highveld at the onset of the rainy season which would spread fly-borne disease. Secondly, transhumance was determined by the degree of concentration on animal husbandry. Water and salt were scarce and pasture tended to be poor on the highveld during the dry season. Again cattle were taken to the lowveld. In other words, the natural distribution of essential foodstuffs was an important factor in the practice of transhumance. Thirdly, transhumance was undertaken for purposes of trade. The cultivators and pastoralists needed one another's products and one of the reasons behind transhumance was to exchange animal products for grain. As a result, conflicts occasionally erupted between the pastoralists and the cultivators whenever cattle destroyed the cultivators' crops. This in turn led to a shift in the orbit of transhumance and/or migrations to entirely new areas – which is how pastoralists became colonists. Beach has carefully documented most of these population movements from the late seventeenth century onward and the resultant new settlements in the north, east and south of the Shona plateau.[113]

However, he has explained these phenomena in terms of the demographic factor. It is possible that the human population pressures he has identified were also linked to the bovine population and scarcity of grazing land. Jeffy Guy has drawn our attention to a similar situation in Zululand during the

108. A. G. Hopkins, 1983, p. 42.
109. D. N. Beach, 1984, p. 42.
110. W. G. L. Randles, 1979, p. 51.
111. For the general theory of transhumance, see A. G. Hopkins, 1983, p. 41.
112. For the practice of transhumance in Southern Zambezia see P. S. Garlake, 1978.
113. D. N. Beach, 1980a, ch. 8; J. M. Gray, 1979, ch. 1.

last decade of the eighteenth century and the importance of ecology, climate and vegetation in history.[114]

The practice of transhumance, it may be argued, enabled the Mutapa and Rozvi populations to maintain large herds. Essentially there were two types of cattle breed: the small type which was reared in the north-east and the mountainous region of Nyanga, and the large type which was reared in the north-west.[115] However, both archaeology and the Portuguese documents tell us little about cattle management and their distribution from the sixteenth century to the end of the eighteenth century. Portuguese sources continually point to the fact that Southern Zambezia was 'rich in cattle and other animals' and that the Africans 'cook their meat in milk instead of water'.[116] The latter was an overstatement but nevertheless underscores the abundance of cattle in the region. Some of these cattle were exchanged for cloth or other exotic articles. The Torwa at Khami, for example, used to export cattle to the Zambezi valley during the sixteenth century.[117]

There are several testimonies concerning the central role of cattle in the Rozvi economy from the sixteenth to the eighteenth centuries. In the early 1500s, Diogo de Alcacova recorded that 4000 hornless cows were paid as tribute to a reigning Mutapa by a ruler of Butwa in the south-west.[118] In 1569, Father Monclaro likened the large size of cattle in Butwa to the large oxen of France.[119] In the sixteenth century, Father João dos Santos attributed the small-scale production of gold to the fact that the African peasants were pre-occupied with herding cattle 'which were in great numbers in these lands'.[120] In 1648, Antonio Gomes exaggeratedly reported that the cows in Butwa were so big that one had to stand up to milk them.[121]

Besides cattle the African peasants reared goats and sheep and chickens for food and exchange. As João dos Santos observed in 1595 in Uteve:

> Their meat is generally hens which are innumerable. The Kaffirs breed them to sell to the Portuguese and in Sofala they give twelve for a black cotton cloth, which is there worth two testoons at most; and if the purchaser goes up the river to their dwellings to buy them, they will give sixteen or eighteen for the same piece of cloth which makes eleven or thereabouts for each hen. There are also many

---

114. D. N. Beach, 1980, ch. 8.
115. W. G. L. Randles, 1979, p. 51.
116. A. Gomes, 1959, p. 189.
117. D. N. Beach, 1984, p. 42.
118. Diogo de Alcacova to King, Cochin, 20 Nov. 1506, in G. M. Theal, 1899–1902, Vol. I, p. 64.
119. Father Monclaro, in G. M. Theal, 1899–1902, Vol. III, p. 237.
120. J. dos Santos, in G. M. Theal, 1899–1902, Vol. II, p. 274.
121. A. Gomes, 1959, p. 197.

domesticated pigs which are bred among the houses, many goats and cows and an abundance of venison, wild pigs . . .[122]

Mining of metals: iron and copper

A large amount of iron, copper and lead was mined throughout the Mutapa and Rozvi empires although the available literature leads one to believe that African peasants were only interested in mining gold. This, however, is a reflection of the interests of the Portuguese and Arab–Swahili traders. The African peasants extracted iron from which they made objects such as hoes, assegais and axes.[123] The Njanja of Wedza acquired a reputation as hoe manufacturers,[124] selling their hoes as far afield as Manyika, Bocha, Buhera and Ndau country. They also mined copper from which they made bangles which both men and women wore round their arms and legs. Eighteenth-century evidence suggests that copper came from Duma where it was plentiful. Admittedly the Duma people did not produce copper in large quantities but they probably exported the little they mined: a geological survey carried out in 1952 showed that four-fifths of total copper production in Zimbabwe came from Duma.[125] A considerable quantity, however, also came from Urungwe in the north-west.[126]

Salt

The salt industry was very important for the Shona economy between 1500 and 1800. It was largely the preoccupation of regions that did not enjoy sufficient rainfall to grow crops and raise cattle, such as the Middle Save where the salt-workers exchanged their product for grain.[127] The Middle Save was also rich in clay and the local inhabitants took advantage of this resource to specialize in pottery manufacture. Like salt, the pots were exchanged for grain, particularly during famine years.

Cloth

Textile production was also an important economic activity among the Shona peasants of Southern Zambezia. Cotton-growing and weaving flourished mainly on the eastern bank of the Zambezi river.[128] Some cotton was also grown in the north-east of the highveld. The Shona wove a cloth from this cotton and also from the bark of the baobab tree. The cotton-growing lowveld area was complemented by the highveld region which abounded in cattle and this largely determined the pattern of inter-regional trade.

122. J. dos Santos, in G. M. Theal, 1899–1902, Vol. II, p. 190.
123. A. Gomes, 1959, pp. 186–8.
124. See J. M. Mackenzie, 1975.
125. H. H. K. Bhila, 1982, p. 40.
126. P. S. Garlake, 1983, p. 27.
127. H. H. K. Bhila, 1982, p. 39.
128. A. Gomes, 1959, pp. 203, 222.

Gold and silver

The existence and extraction of silver from the sixteenth to the eighteenth century was a matter of great speculation among the Portuguese authorities both in Lisbon and Southern Zambezia, but throughout the period under review and even later no silver mines were located. Silver was instead obtained as a by-product of gold-mining and there was plenty of gold on the highveld, in Butwa, in the south-west and in Manyika and Uteve in the east.

The amount of gold present in Southern Zambezia was greatly exaggerated by the Portuguese during the sixteenth century. In 1633 Gaspar Macedo was told by African peasants that until that time nobody had had to dig for gold in Torwa state but had simply collected it from the rivers and creeks and exchanged it for cloth at the *feira* of Masekesa in Manyika. The king's treasure, he was told, consisted of 'gold bars each of them weighing seven or eight *arratels*'.[129] It was also claimed that 'the whole "Mucaranga" is a gold mine wherever you dig you find gold'.[130] Although these were exaggerations, there was still plenty of gold in the Mutapa empire and Portuguese expectations were largely fulfilled from the early sixteenth century to the second half of the seventeenth century, despite their protestations to the contrary.

Historical references to Shona mining practices strongly suggest that mining was not a year-round activity. However, in the Kingdom of Manyika in the east the extraction of gold was carried out year-round mainly because most of the rivers were, and still are, perennial.[131] It is possible that mining was carried out by peasants either to assuage the aristocracy's demands for exchangeable commodities or to trade themselves.[132]

Shona mining activities were concentrated within the months of August, September and October in order to combine them with general land clearance.[133] Agriculture was 'the matrix in which all other indigenous economic activity' was set: a peasant could combine farming with other economic enterprises, such as trade or gold-mining, which remained subsidiary occupations. Often it was the sale of surplus agricultural produce that financed other projects. Another reason for mining during the dry months of August, September and October was that miners could sink shafts fairly deep as a result of a seasonal fall in the water-table. Moreover, the alluvial deposits of the previous summer could easily be found before being carried away by the floods of the next season.

Mining operations followed a pattern prevalent in much of Southern Africa. The basic tools used to break out the ore were hammerstones and

129. G. Macedo, 1890, p. 151.
130. A. Gomes, 1959, p. 186.
131. H. H. K. Bhila, 1982, p. 46.
132. P. Sinclair, 1977.
133. I. R. Phimister, 1976, p. 5.

iron gads.[134] A gad was used to hammer into cracks and crevices, as a wedge for prizing the rock apart. The miners also used a type of crowbar consisting of a piece of iron inserted into the end of a heavy stick, probably hafted like a hoe and used as a pick.[135] Shovels were also used to gather together the broken rock and ensure no valuable pieces were left behind. The method for gold-reef mining was fire-setting – as can be deduced from the large quantities of charcoal which Roger Summers found in many of the ancient mines.[136] In one he also came across troughs containing charcoal standing against the face of the reef. According to him, they formed a hearth concentrating the heat against the hard rock face. By cooling the heated rock rapidly the Shona were able to crack the rock face. They controlled the amount of cold water applied by using a specially shaped clay vessel to obtain the maximum splitting of the rock. Using a wooden container, the miners took the ore to the surface where they sorted it with small axes removing the gold-bearing quartz. The pieces thus sorted were stacked amongst piles of firewood and roasted, after which the burnt quartz was crushed and the gold washed out of it.

With alluvial gold the recovery process was village-based.[137] During the mining season groups of 400 or more miners, including women and children, assembled in one place under the command of their respective village heads. They washed the alluvium in wooden bowls and the gold that was recovered was packed into hollow reeds or quills ready for exchange. The peasants preferred gold panning to reef mining as the workings were shallow and gold-rich levels could be easily reached; gold washing was not expensive as the miner did not need picks to crack the rock nor did he have to buy or look for firewood. Moreover, panning did not involve the crushing or roasting of rocks, nor expose miners to the hazards of tunnels through soft soils that regularly caved in.

The Mutapa and Rozvi rulers exercised great control over the production of gold within their empires.[138] It has been estimated that almost 50 per cent of gold production within the Mutapa empire was appropriated directly by the ruling élite. If a person stumbled upon a gold deposit he was required to cover it up and report it immediately to the local chief. Commenting on this in 1648, Antonio Gomes said 'no matter what a Portuguese promises them, they will not reveal that place and very often that they have tried, up to now no one has known of any'.[139] Failure to comply with this law was punishable by death.[140] The Mutapa and Rozvi

134. I. R. Phimister, 1976, p. 5.
135. ibid.
136. ibid.
137. M. Barreto, 1899, p. 491.
138. A. Gomes, 1959, p. 186; G. Macedo, 1890, pp. 148–9; J. dos Santos in G. M. Theal, 1899–1902, Vol. II, pp. 280–1.
139. A. Gomes, 1959, p. 185.
140. A. Gomes, 1959.

rulers did not want the Portuguese who traded with their empires to know the location of the gold mines as this would tempt them to conquest; moreover, control of the mines enabled them to dictate better terms of trade for their subjects.

The decline of gold production during the seventeenth century.

The dangerous nature of gold mining led not only to low production but ultimately to its decline during the seventeenth century.[141] Sometimes water burst into the shafts, flooded them and killed the miners. Moreover, by the seventeenth century the Shona miners, it has been argued, had mined deep enough to reach the water-table, and it was not possible to mine below this without the aid of a new technology capable of pumping out both the water and mud.[142] The third reason for the decline was that the price the Portuguese traders paid for gold was too low to induce the peasants to risk their lives.

One aspect that has not been examined in detail was the impact of war on gold production. The first half of the seventeenth century witnessed the height of Portuguese aggression towards the Mutapa empire. Its intervention into internal Shona politics resulted in wars among the Mutapa rulers themselves and also between the Mutapa rulers and their tributaries. These wars resulted in temporary and permanent migrations, and famine through the disruption of agricultural production even in areas rich in resources and with favourable weather patterns. In 1683, for example, there was anarchy in Makaranga where the country was 'depopulated ... and consequently without mines',[143] as a result of which 'the Portuguese live from what they can scratch by the banks of the rivers or from the gold that appears at the surface of the earth'.[144] The second half of the seventeenth century was characterized by the even more devastating Changamire wars which resulted in the reorganization of populations into several states.

Warfare, therefore, could be blamed for the disruption of gold production in Shonaland during the seventeenth century in the same way that a natural calamity disrupts agriculture by reducing the amount of land available for production. The impact of war on the decline of gold production has so far been ignored by historians in favour of 'the fundamental constraints imposed by a hostile and capricious geological environment which severely limited the gold available to Shona mining operations'.[145]

In addition, the methods adopted by the Portuguese traders alienated

141. J. dos Santos in G. M. Theal, 1899–1902, Vol. II, p. 219.
142. I. R. Phimister, 1976, pp. 22–3.
143. Anon., 'Descipcao dos Rios de Cuama', Biblioteca da Ajuda, Lisbon, 51–VII–43 and 51–7–44.
144. ibid.
145. I. R. Phimister, 1976, pp. 22–3.

them from the peasants largely responsible for producing gold. African rulers protested against Portuguese insistence that peasants – and their rulers – trade their products exclusively with the Portuguese. According to captain Francisco Figuira de Almeida of Sena, relations started to sour when the Portuguese changed their original method of trade. In the early 1500s African peasants used to take their produce directly to the Portuguese *feiras* in the interior. Later in the century, however, the Portuguese sent middlemen into the interior who took merchandise 'in small bundles wrapped in wild palm-tree mats as big a load as a man can carry on his back' to the peasants' doors.[146] De Almeida further reported that usually a Portuguese trader travelled with anything between three and five hundred local peasants who 'steal anything they come across and the natives from the villages move to other places so as not to be subjected to such humiliation'.[147] Another Portuguese mistake was to sell merchandise on credit to the African peasants who often defaulted with the result that a Portuguese trader would have to send twenty to thirty of the peasants in his employ to recover the debt. If the defaulter failed to pay the debt he became 'the traders' slave and with the same ease he goes with his wife and children and started doing the same as the other do'.[148] In this way a Portuguese trader could end up with several hundred enslaved middlemen. As one African ruler pointed out:

> the Portuguese were causing great damage and if they wanted to sell cloth to the Africans they should bring it to him and he himself would sell it to those who could pay for it, otherwise some run away, the others are taken by the Portuguese and thus the population of the villages was dwindling.[149]

By the mid-1600s the king of Uteve had ordered his people not to extract any gold but 'to till the land and grow food in order to become rich and have more peace and quiet'.[150] Social factors, therefore, were probably more important than climate or geological factors in the decline of gold production during the seventeenth century.

Trade

Trade records also provide historical evidence of the diversity of Shona peasant economies. The peasants' main aim, however, was to produce use-values rather than exchange values. But the production of commodities inevitably resulted in the exchange of products among the peasants them-

146. A. Gomes, 1959, p. 192.
147. ibid.
148. ibid.
149. ibid.
150. ibid., p. 193.

selves and between peasants and craftsmen and this led to the emergence of regional trade. The important regional trade networks will be identified in the subsequent discussion.

The Swahili traders established several bazaars in the Mutapa empire. It is difficult to say exactly when they did so but one Portuguese adventurer found them in existence when he travelled inland from Sofala in 1514–15.[151] We can, however, safely assume that the first bazaars in Sofala and its immediate neighbourhood were established during the tenth century when the Arab–Swahili traders, who depended on African peasants for their food supplies, started trading with African peasants in the Mutapa empire.[152] The bazaars were operated on Mondays,[153] with the African peasants exchanging their agricultural produce and gold dust for beads, cloth and other exotic items. Little is known about the volume and organization of this trade but it is reasonable to assume that the demand for food by the Swahili–Arabs must have stimulated the production of surplus grain, large and small stock for meat, and a variety of vegetables. The demand for food supplies must have increased when the Portuguese established a fortress at Sofala in 1506 which became an entrepôt between the Portuguese traders and the African peasants who went there to sell their produce.

The establishment of this fortress must be seen in the context of Portuguese commercial activities from 1498 when Vasco da Gama made his famous voyage to India. It was at this time that the Portuguese learnt about the gold mines in Sofala and its hinterland and that King Emmanuel consequently ordered the setting up of a factory at Sofala. Portugal's main aim at this time was to occupy all strategic points along the Indian Ocean. The fortresses of Sofala and Kilwa were built in 1506 to protect the gold trade while three others – in Quilon, Angediva and the Red Sea – were built to control the pepper trade. Sofala was therefore integrated into Portugal's trade network and the stage was set for further exchange between African and Portuguese traders. On arrival at Sofala in 1506, the Portuguese as already mentioned, found the Arab–Swahili traders well established and a rivalry, characterized by several military encounters, consequently developed.[154] The Portuguese emerged victorious, however, and the Arab–Swahili fled north to various strategic points on the Zambezi river from where they continued to undermine Portuguese commercial activities along the Zambezi trade route as well as trade routes into the interior. The Portuguese reacted swiftly by ousting them from most of these places and, in 1531, establishing Sena and Tete as their main trade centres. Portuguese

151. H. Tracey and A. Fernandes, 1940, pp. 20–30; see also Gaspar Velosco's report in *Documentos Sobre*, Vol. III, pp. 181–9; A. H. Quiring, 1949; W. A. Godlouton, 1945.

152. *Archaelogia e contecimento de passado*, 1980, pp. 4–6.

153. Notes made by Gaspar Velosco, Clerk of the Factory of Mozambique and sent to the king (1572), *Documentos Sobre*, Vol. III, p. 183.

154. For details of this rivalry, see A. Lobato, 1954a.

trading activities accordingly shifted northwards thus decreasing the commercial importance of the Sofala region.[155]

The defeat of the Swahili in 1512 and the effective occupation of Sena and Tete in the 1530s – which gave the Portuguese a monopoly over the supply of goods – brought to an end the independent trade of the Swahili–Arabs. But as they had neither the skill nor the manpower, and as the Swahili–Arabs were anxious to continue as traders in the region, a natural though uneasy trading alliance developed between them. For the next century Swahili–Arabs were the main agents of Portuguese trade in the interior. African *vashambadzi* (traders) had been acting as middlemen for the Swahili–Arab traders long before the advent of the Portuguese, and their role was formally institutionalized within the Swahili–Arab/Portuguese alliance. The Swahili–Arabs continued to trade, albeit clandestinely, in the Torwa interior until the late 1600s. By the early 1700s they had lost much of their Islamic culture and had adopted Lemba and Venda culture.[156]

The defeat of the Swahili–Arabs left the Portuguese traders without major competition along the Zambezi trade route and in the interior. Initially the aim of the Portuguese crown was to monopolize the entire trade in Sofala and the interior. But this proved impossible as greed drove individual traders inland to make independent trade agreements with African rulers. As already noted, by 1541 there were so many Portuguese traders in the interior that it became necessary to formalize and regulate their trading activities within the Mutapa empire.

As with the Swahili–Arab traders, the African peasants exchanged their produce for a variety of exotic items. Peter Garlake's archaeological excavations of the *feiras* of Luanze, Dambarare and Rimuka indicate that beads were the most popular commodity of trade during the early sixteenth century.[157] The popularity of the most common black, yellow, green and blue beads varied from region to region but red and black beads – known as Cambay beads – were preferred in all kingdoms. The Portuguese found beads in circulation when they arrived and tried in vain to control their market. The popularity of beads was determined by a set of beliefs prevalent among the Shona[158] that the Portuguese plucked them from trees. The black beads, it was thought, had acquired their colour through being left on the tree long enough to petrify and turn black. The green beads had been plucked before they were ripe while the yellow ones had been plucked when ripe and before the sun burnt them black. There was also a variety of imported beads, including those 'of coral, crystal, pewter, jet, amber and blue Venetia glass',[159] but these were unpopular. Consequently, a

155. *Documentos Sobre os Portuguezes em Moçambique*, Vol. III, pp. 237–48; A. Lobato, 1954a, pp. 19 and 103.
156. D. N. Beach, 1984, p. 32.
157. P. S. Garlake, 1954.
158. A. Gomes, 1959, p. 196.
159. P. S. Garlake, 1954, p. 43.

locally-made variety known as *caracoes* (small stone beads), which were also exempt from royal bead-trade monopoly, captured the market between 1516 and 1518. The *caracoes* were rated seven times as popular as the European imported beads. Cloth was another important trade item, particularly the brightly coloured cloth which was measured by arm-lengths.

In exchange for these articles, the Shona brought to the fortress's daily market sorghum, maize, groundnuts, cowpeas, baskets, mats, pots, chickens, eggs, honey, trapped animals and birds, and a wide range of vegetables and wild fruits. This type of trade was also carried on in the *feiras* and presumably continued when the *feiras* themselves were destroyed at the end of the seventeenth century. There was, possibly, as in the markets of West Africa,[160] some segregation of merchants according to products sold and also to sex; that is, women traders probably sold different articles from those sold by men. Most smiths, other craftsmen and miners exchanged their goods either among themselves or with the Portuguese traders. The farmers found ready market for their cattle, goats, sheep or pigs. The Sofala fortress and the *feiras* in the interior struck deep roots into Shona society and became an essential part of its economic and social framework.

Feiras in Shona country

The period 1575–1684 witnessed a change in the pattern of trade between African peasants and Portuguese traders. The Portuguese traders consolidated their commercial and military victory over the Swahili–Arabs by adapting and transforming the bazaars into Portuguese *feiras*. The land on which the *feiras* were established was granted by local African chiefs. In time the *feiras* became the main focal points of Afro–Portuguese commercial intercourse. They were large areas enclosed by low timber-palisade walls, with a few residential pole-and-mud huts near the gold-mining areas.[161] Each *feira* had a fortress, a garrison of ten to fifteen soldiers, in theory a church with a priest, and a *capitão-mor*. Some *feiras* were administered by the government of the Rivers of Sena while others were privately owned. The *capitães-mores*, whose role and position in Portuguese commerce in the Rivers of Sena were clearly defined during the eighteenth century, bore some resemblance to the guards of the medieval Portuguese *feiras*. The position of *capitães-mores* in Manyika, Butwa and Karanga country was comparable to that of the *capitão-mor dos Banianes* on the island of Mozambique, and other similar representatives of merchants who were sometimes organized into guilds. Their *soldo* (payment) was regarded only as a subsidy – and it was the policy of the Portuguese administrators to appoint only wealthy individuals from the Portuguese settlement of Sena to such posts. On the island of Mozambique, the *capitão-mor dos Banianes* was

160. E. P. Skinner, 1964, p. 86.
161. P. S. Garlake, 1954, p. 49.

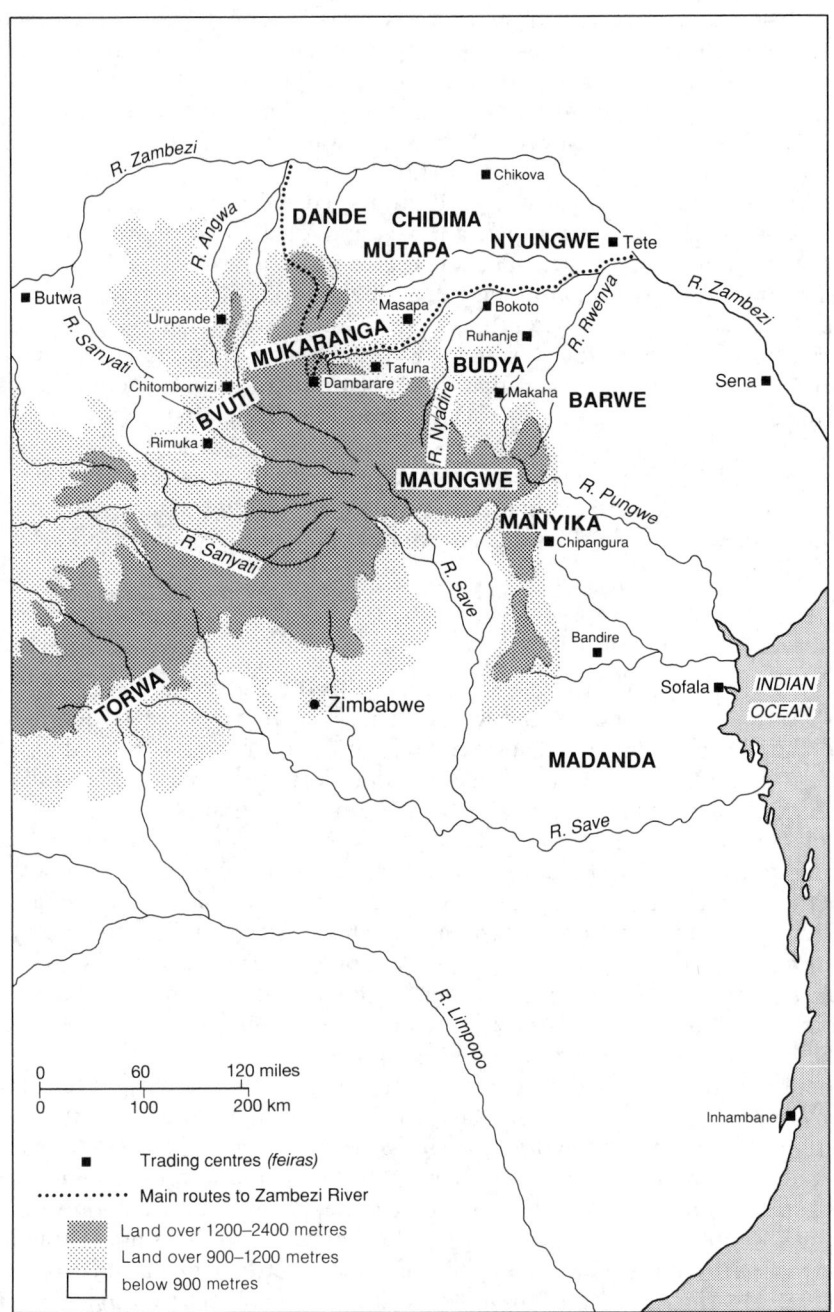

FIG. 22.4 *The main feiras in the sixteenth and seventeenth centuries*
Source: adapted from map 3 of H. H. K. Bhila, *Trade and Politics in a Shona Kingdom. The Manyika and their African and Portuguese Neighbours, 1575–1902*, London, Longman. Adapted by kind permission of Longman Group UK Ltd

usually the wealthiest of the Indian merchants from Diu. This was also true of Mozambique's less well-known *capitão-mor dos muros*, who was often a wealthy ship-owner.

The duties of the *capitães-mores* involved taxation, price control, arbitrating between Portuguese and African traders, granting of licences, protecting caravans, raising soldiers, and the enforcement of laws relating to weights and measures.[162] These powers and duties were greatly modified as *capitães-mores* interacted with various African rulers. The *feira* as an institution was formalized and regulated by a series of instructions which the Portuguese Crown sent to Vincente Regado, *capitão-mor* of Sofala and Mozambique in 1531.[163] These instructions provided for the circulation of merchandise, the determination of titles and excise duty, the establishment of shops and the drawing up of licences to sell merchandise and the holding of law suits.

The main *feiras*

The *feira* of Dambarare was acclaimed the best of all the *feiras* in the Rivers of Sena, where almost all the rich influential merchants of Sena traded and thence scattered to other places such as Chitomborwizi, Rimuka, Luanze and Matafuna. Dambarare was the headquarters, second only to the administrative headquarters of the Captain of the Gates at Masapa. The Dambarare *feira* was three days' journey from that of Angwa, where there was much gold but few residents as it was so far from both Sena and Tete.[164]

A similar situation obtained in Uteve where the Portuguese held an annual *feira* in Bandire to purchase articles from the interior.[165] This custom lasted from the sixteenth century to the early eighteenth century when the Teve authorities stopped it. The Portuguese claimed that the right to hold the Bandire *feira* was accorded them by the Munhumutapa in 1580. This may be so in theory, but the Mutapas' control over their feudatories, Uteve not excluded, had almost disappeared by 1580. The annual *feira*, as its subsequent history shows, was sustained and controlled by the Teve rulers. Teve methods of controlling Portuguese trade were somewhat different from those of other Shona societies. In Manyika, for example, *feira* trade was controlled personally by both the kings who with their councillors occasionally visited the *capitão-mor* and the prince or princess of the *feira* area. But in Uteve the *feira* was operated largely by an *inyamasango* (village head) under whose jurisdiction the administration

161. P. S. Garlake, 1954, p. 49.
162. M. D. D. Newitt, 1973, p. 43.
163. J. J. T. Botelho, 1936, p. 146.
164. For a discussion of individual *feiras*, see 'Extracts from the Decade written by Antonio Bocarro of the performances of the Portuguese in the East', in G. M. Theal, 1899–1902, Vol. III, p. 354; Biblioteca da Ajuda, Lisbon, 51-VII-40: 'Brief Account on the Rivers of Cuama' by Father Philipe de Tssumao.
165. J. dos Santos, in G. M. Theal, 1899–1902, Vol. II, pp. 380–1.

of Bandire fell.[166] He was required to pay an annual tribute to the *Sachiteve* in the form of a Turkish tunic, one piece of cloth, a barret, some linen, one *rola* (turtle-dove) and some Bengal muslin. Apparently these articles were supposed to be yellow in colour to symbolize the abundance of gold at Bandire. A survey of the area in 1890 by Renato Baptista testified to the abundance of gold. The Portuguese do not seem to have created any *feiras* north of the Zambezi until the early eighteenth century when Zumbo and Michonga were established.[167] Two reasons may account for the late development of the *feiras* of both Michonga and Zumbo: the discovery of *bares* north of the Zambezi during the eighteenth century, and the need for the Portuguese to look elsewhere for trade after their expulsion from Shona country by the Rozvi emperor, Dombo Changamire, between 1693 and 1695.

The expulsion of the Portuguese from their *feiras* by Changamire forced the Portuguese to adopt the trading methods they had used during the sixteenth century. When they abandoned their *feiras* in Makaranga they established a new one, Zumbo, at the Luangwa–Zambezi confluence between 1710 and 1788 and came to depend on the *vashambadzi* for their trade with the Rozvi empire.[168] They were, however, able to revive the *feira* of Masekesa in Manyika in 1719 but none in Uteve. The system of having one officer to co-ordinate Portuguese relations with African rulers was no longer possible in the case of the Mutapa emperors as there was no effective central political authority among the African rulers. It is therefore necessary to briefly examine relations between the Portuguese and some important African rulers during the eighteenth century.

In the east, the King of Uteve did not allow the Portuguese to mine gold in the *bares* in his kingdom. His subjects, however, could buy cloth and beads from the Portuguese settlers at Sena. Even in this trade, the king and his princes were accused by Portuguese traders of causing 'infinite damage', 'robbery' and violence to Portuguese merchandise, much of whose profit was spent trying to buy safety. Teve policy during the eighteenth century was decidedly anti-Portuguese.[169] In the Kingdom of Manyika, Portuguese traders were allowed freedom of passage throughout the land but their trading activities were strictly controlled by Manyika rulers. The *capitão-mor* and the Portuguese merchants paid a regular tribute.

Similarly, to keep the *feira* of Zumbo and the trade route to Butwa safe,

166. R. Baptista, 1892, p. 14.

167. A. Lobato, 1954b, p. 43 ff.; H. Capello and R. Ivens, 1886, Vol. II, p. 306.

168. The term Zumbo refers to three settlements which the Portuguese established and abandoned in succession on the Zambezi–Luangwa confluence during the eighteenth century. The first and earliest settlement was founded probably in 1710 on the island of Chitacativa on the River Zambezi; the second settlement, founded in 1715, is on the Mozambique angle of the Zambezi–Luangwa confluence; the third settlement known as Mucariva, now marked on Zambian maps merely as 'Feira', was founded in October 1788. For full discussion see S. I. Mudenge, 1977.

169. X. Caetano in A. A. Andrade, 1955, p. 155.

the Portuguese traders paid a regular tribute to Changamire. This involved great expense and he used to send his envoys to the *feira* of Zumbo asking for additional gifts – usually to the value of six *pastas* – over and above the usual tribute.[170] The precarious nature of the trade route between Zumbo and Butwa via Dande country was illustrated by an incident in 1757 when prince Chirimba of Dande seized merchandise intended for Butwa. For the next seven years, Changamire, his soldiers and the gold producers of Butwa carried on continual raids so that the once prosperous Butwa trade was destroyed. Changamire's famous raid of 1756–7, which confiscated property worth 1000 *pastas* (800 000 *cruzados*) was a case in point.[171] The Zumbo trade was also compromised by recurring civil war and famine during the 1760s. Despite the Portuguese raids, however, the Changamires valued their trade with them. The Rozvi rulers sent expeditionary forces on three occasions – in 1743, 1772 and 1781 – to protect the *feira* of Zumbo from attacks by the neighbouring African rulers. In addition to beads, the articles of special interest to the Rozvi rulers included umbrellas, seashells, rosaries of fake coral, chinaware, brass bells, scissors and *aguadente* (fire-water), a kind of brandy.[172]

The nature of relations between the Mutapa and the Portuguese appears to have changed little during the eighteenth century. The Portuguese continued to maintain a garrison of twenty soldiers, a *capitão-mor*, a lieutenant, a captain-general and a Dominican friar at the Mutapa royal court. It would also seem that the 'old custom of baptizing the Mutapa rulers was maintained' even though there is nothing Christian about those kings as they generally have as they all do, a thousand or more concubines'.[173] Another sixteenth-century practice which survived into the eighteenth century was that:

> Every three years, this King sends a emissary to the General of Sena, who meets him at Tete always on the first year of his term of office, and they discuss the continuation of the old state alliance with the said King and some matters concerning the traders of Zumbo who necessarily have to travel across his territory and if any other business comes up outside the scope of that triennial visit, there will be more respective emissaries sent from one and the other side.[174]

Despite these arrangements, trade between the Portuguese and the Mutapa rulers continued to decline during the eighteenth century. This decline has been explained in the context of three developments in Southern Zambezia during the eighteenth century. First, there was the gold rush north of the

170. H. H. K. Bhila, 1982, p. 119.
171. ibid., pp. 119–20.
172. ibid.
173. Anon., 'Descipcao dos Rios de Cuama', 1683, Biblioteca da Ajuda, Lisbon, 51-VII-43.
174. ibid.

Zambezi with individual Portuguese adventurers discovering *bares* and starting to mine gold themselves. Secondly, gold production had almost completely declined by the eighteenth century; and thirdly, both the African and Portuguese traders on either side of the Zambezi river took to elephant hunting for ivory.

Ivory trade played an important role in the Mutapa empire. A sixteenth-century Portuguese account tells us that elephants used to 'go about in droves almost like a herd of cows'[175] in the Mutapa empire and that 'four or five thousand elephants die every year which is confirmed by the large quantity of ivory sent thence to India'.[176] The advantage of elephant hunting was that it was not as amenable as gold to control by African rulers as the hunting usually took place in remote areas. However, little is known about its organization and there are suggestions that much eighteenth-century elephant hunting took place in Buhera and Rimuka.[177]

Conclusion

Portuguese penetration of Southern Zambezia eroded the power of the indigenous ruling class and facilitated direct forms of peasant exploitation by Portuguese mercantile capital and, later, British industrial capital in Southern Zambezia. The convergence of regional trade networks with long-distance trade gave rise to an African merchant class called *vashambadzi*. With the arrival of the Swahili-Arab traders in the tenth century and the Portuguese at the beginning of the sixteenth century, some Africans were hired to act as middle-men between the foreign traders and the African peasant producers.

The Portuguese merchants were largely concerned with trade in gold and ivory and, consequently, the main commodities of regional trade – iron, salt and copper – were relegated to second position in terms of commercial importance. By the 1530s the Portuguese merchants had already penetrated the interior of the Mutapa empire and trade in salt, copper and iron and in gold and ivory converged. Trade in one commodity stimulated trade in another, hence the emergence of an African merchant class. For long-distance trade to flourish there had to be gold and ivory and porters, food to feed the carriers, hoes to cultivate the crops and iron to make the hoes. The *vashambadzi* transported not only ivory and gold but salt and iron hoes which they exchanged for food on the way. The African cultivators who lived near the trade routes were gradually transformed as they grew more and more surplus agricultural produce for sale to the traders and their porters. Needless to say the peasants, who were mostly ignorant of the international value of the commodities they sold, were ruthlessly exploited by the Portuguese merchants.

175. G. M. Theal, 1899–1902, Vol. VI, p. 266.
176. ibid.
177. D. N. Beach, 1984, p. 35.

Dependence and interdependence: southern Africa from 1500 to 1800

23

D. DENOON

Between 1500 and 1800 much of southern Africa was transformed. New communities established themselves in the region; many pre-existing communities changed their means of living, their location or both; and the relationships which grew up within and between communities were radically different from any before. Many of these drastic changes were because of changes in southern Africa's external linkages. When the first European, Vasco da Gama, rounded the Cape in 1497, southern Africa had only the most tenuous links with the rest of the world, but by 1800 the region was firmly enmeshed in world-wide patterns of trade and strategy. It is worth considering the changing international context itself before trying to evaluate its effect on southern Africa.

In 1500 the great population concentrations of the world were around the Mediterranean and in Asia. Neither sub-Saharan Africa nor the Americas had been drawn into regular relationships with the rest of the world. International trade was particularly concerned with Europe and Asia, and it was conducted almost entirely over land, at very great expense.[1] The objective of da Gama's mission was to pioneer a sea route which would reduce the costs of international trade and curb the rapacity of the many middle-men who battened upon the land route. To the Portuguese, who first developed this trade route, and to the Dutch, English and French, who followed them round the Cape, southern Africa was merely a dangerous navigational hazard. The mapping of its coast-line, however, gradually ended its isolation but the consistent lack of interest from Arab and European traders is worth looking at.

During the late Iron Age, the temperate climates of the southern hemisphere were not very attractive. With only rudimentary tools it was difficult to produce a regular surplus of food, even in regions which permitted cultivation, and what surplus there was was difficult to store or invest in further production. Population densities in the temperate regions of the southern hemisphere – including Australasia and the southern cone of South America – were much lower than in the neighbouring tropical regions. The tropical regions nurtured relatively dense human populations, permitting surplus production and a high degree of specialization. Not

1. F. Braudel, 1981, ch. 1.

surprisingly, therefore, the temperate regions were unattractive to international traders. They did not regularly produce commodities for export, and they would not do so until very recent times when large volumes of capital, advanced technology and improved transport became available.[2] The Arabs, who conducted a flourishing trade along the east coast of Africa, were not tempted further south because the gold, ivory and slaves, which bulked large in their cargoes, were much more readily available on the tropical coasts than in the temperate extremity of the continent. Similarly, Europeans travelled round the Cape for 150 years before taking much interest in the region for its own sake. The names the Portuguese gave their anchorages – Algoa and Delagoa – speak of their determination to travel to and from Goa, and their lack of interest in the trading potential of southern Africa itself.

Sea-borne influences were negligible, and land contacts not much more important. Many communities in the south had historic and linguistic ties to the north, but these had little significance in daily life. The Khoi Khoi who herded animals, caught fish and gathered food from the field along the southern coastal belt, were effectively isolated from most northern contacts and so were the San hunters and gatherers in the southern interior. The speakers of the Nguni languages, mainly east of the dividing range, had little regular contact with their northern neighbours in 1500. In the far west (in today's Namibia) the Herero and Ovambo had close linguistic ties with each other and with their northern neighbours. The central Tswana and Sotho traded to the north from time to time, but even when trade took place, the quantity of goods was small, and the commodities traded (including copper, iron and *dagga*) were not essential to anyone's survival.[3] As late as 1500 these societies were effectively independent of the rest of the world: their external links were sporadic, *ad hoc* and marginal. The European fleets, which sometimes anchored off the coast and took fresh water and supplies on board, did little to dent this self-sufficiency for another century or more.

Although European interest in the region was slow to develop, when it did finally express itself it was powerful. In the mid-1600s a new community was planted at the Cape by the Dutch East India Company which continued to see southern Africa simply as a way-station to the East. As late as 1800 'Cape Town was a seaward-looking community, a caravanserai on the periphery of the global spice trade',[4] with the character of 'a residency city, closer in spirit to Asia than to the African continent on which it stood'.[5] The regional consequences of establishing the Cape Town settlement were, however, much more profound than the Company planners intended. The region as a whole was securely linked to Europe and Asia, although it was

2. D. J. N. Denoon, 1983.
3. M. Wilson, 1969a.
4. R. Elphick and R. Shell, 1979, p. 161.
5. ibid., p. 126.

not yet resolved whether the Dutch (who held the Cape from 1652 to 1795) or the British (who seized the Cape in 1795) would be the agents. The new settlement at the Cape was, and would remain, a dependency, responding swiftly to new external pressures and incentives. As that dependency expanded into its hinterland, it would draw the whole region into durable new relationships tinged with dominance and dependence. Through the little settlement entered capitalist relations of production, together with colonialism and imperialism which would transform southern Africa more abruptly and more thoroughly than any other part of sub-Saharan Africa. These developments are the focus of this chapter.

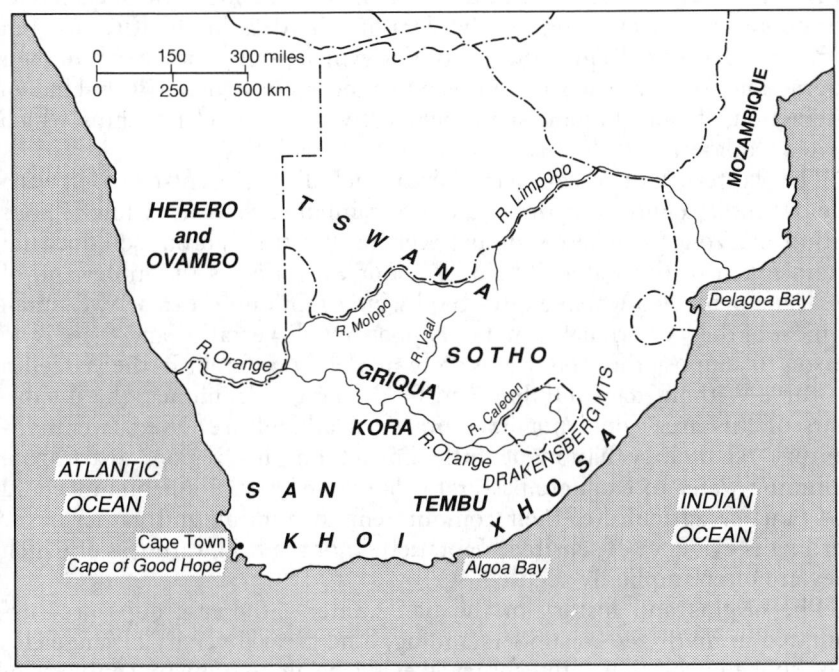

FIG. 23.1 *Southern Africa in the sixteenth to eighteenth centuries*

It is possible to reconstruct the conditions and events of the sixteenth century but it is difficult to strike any kind of scholarly balance in reviewing these conditions. Wherever hunting and gathering communities have come into conflict with cultivators during the past two centuries, they have been destroyed as viable societies. Cultivators have survived in sufficient numbers to force themselves upon the attention of historians: nomads have been less fortunate. The general destruction of Aboriginal, Red Indian, gaucho, Siberian and southern African nomadic societies has reinforced the set theories in which we customarily view past and present, so that some scholars can scarcely conceal their impatience in anticipating the evolution of nomads into cultivators and, ultimately, into industrial pro-letarians.[6] The American Indians at least left behind them sufficient evidence to form the basis of imaginative and sometimes romantic reconstructions:[7] southern African nomads were destroyed or transformed too early, and too comprehensively, to permit such literary creation.[8]

Some very interesting relationships prevailed in southern Africa in the sixteenth century that defy all notions of historical inevitability. Environmental differences permitted a degree of specialization between communities; these specialist societies interacted upon each other; and this interaction was compatible with the durability of the life-style of each one. Hunters were not evolving into herders, nor herders into cultivators, but rather co-existing despite the hostilities which sometimes marked their interaction. It is worth spending some time reconstructing this kind of interaction, if only to gain some perspective on the relationships which developed later.

The western half of southern Africa, including present-day Botswana and Namibia, enjoys less than 40 cm of rainfall each year. A few regions within this zone have better annual averages but their porous soil does not retain much of the water. The only major exception is the hinterland of the Cape peninsula which enjoys good winter rain quite regularly. Rainfall in most of the western half is not only poor but also erratic,[9] and there is no reason to suppose that conditions were markedly different in the sixteenth century. Without dam-building and food-storage techniques, the inhabitants of this area could not have practised agriculture. Even twentieth-century technology has made little impact on this region, apart from damming water to facilitate pastoral production. As the inhabitants could not practise agriculture, their commitment to hunting and gathering or herding is evidence of sensible adaptation – not the backwardness of which they are often implicitly accused.

The origins and history of the San hunter-gatherer groups are surrounded in myth and misunderstanding. The great diversity of languages they spoke in the sixteenth century is evidence alone of many centuries of adaptation within the western half of southern Africa.[10] Hunting and gathering were not nearly as risky then as they would be now. Travelling light, knowing their territory and the flora and fauna intimately, and rarely venturing beyond familiar terrain, a hunting band was probably quite secure as long as human population density did not outgrow environmental resources.[11] Fifty to seventy was reported as the average size of a hunting

6. R. L. Meek, 1976.
7. P. Farb, 1969, chs 7, 8 and 14.
8. J. Wright, 1977.
9. N. C. Pollock and S. Agnew, 1963.
10. R. Elphick, 1977, chs 1 and 2.
11. M. Sahlins, 1974.

band and while there were substantial areas free of agriculture and intensive pastoralism, there would have been ample wild game. Hunting and gathering provided a reliable livelihood independent of other societies, but the San also interacted with other people. Sometimes a group of hunters would attach themselves as clients to herding patrons, obtaining dairy products in exchange for game or advice on animal movements. Although the hunters were clients, the relationship cannot have been oppressive because the San always retained the option of returning to specialist hunting on their own. Some hunting groups also lived outside the western-central interior region and indeed, a few survived in the foothills of the Drakensberg range until well into the nineteenth century, supplementing their diet by occasional raids upon the herds of the mixed farmers of that area.[12] This form of livelihood relied absolutely on mobility. Mobility would have been impaired by the presence of many old, young or otherwise immobile people; and, therefore, a hunting life-style itself would have imposed restraints on population growth so that the balance between population and resources was not jeopardized. The need for mobility imposed yet another constraint: the accumulation of property could only depress living standards by hampering the band's speed.

In his masterly review of the evidence for Khoi Khoi origins, Elphick proposes that the most likely explanation is that San groups acquired cattle and sheep long before 1500 and expanded with them through the riverine regions of the interior into the southern coastal belt where they were observed by European travellers in the sixteenth century.[13] Possession of stock meant that the Khoi had to cling to well-watered areas rather than roam the arid regions; but it also permitted the gradual growth of a population and the size of individual bands. Since oxen could carry baggage, the Khoi could build tents and transport them instead of making fresh shelters whenever they moved. Similarly, the presence of immobile old and young people was no longer the handicap it had been. Private property could be accumulated on a small scale (and even on a large scale in the form of stock), and within these pastoral societies, a measure of stratification developed differentiating them from the more egalitarian and property-less San. The need for social control did not require the Khoi to develop a formal structure of political authority; but individuals did exercise some authority among their clans and, in the early days of sporadic trading with European ships, some accumulated considerable power and livestock wealth.

Herding may have offered a higher level of consumption than hunting during good times, but herds were vulnerable to drought and animal disease, as well as theft and confiscation in war. When such disasters occurred the Khoi often had to hunt for a living, at least until they could build up fresh herds of stock. The knowledge and techniques of herding

12. J. Wright, 1971.
13. R. Elphick, 1977, ch. 1.

were not much different from those required in hunting, so Khoi could easily revert to San whenever necessary.[14] Near the Cape peninsula, where hunting opportunities were limited, dispossessed herders took to the sea-shore living off fish and shellfish until they gained access to stock or attached themselves as clients to more fortunate stock-owners. These transitions were not difficult: neither language nor culture distinguished one group sharply from another. Life might have been unstable but it was not miserable. The rare Khoi who was taken overseas on one of the ships which watered at the Cape found nothing to induce dissatisfaction with conditions at home.[15]

Interaction between Khoi and Nguni, on the eastern flank of Khoi territory, took place across quite sharp cultural and technical boundaries. The region in which Khoi and Xhosa interacted was good grazing country but marginal for the purposes of agriculture because the rainfall was little more than 40 cm a year. There could be no clear ecological boundary between Khoi and Xhosa, as both modes of livelihood were possible. Instead inter-penetration seems to have been common.[16] Individual Xhosa abandoned settled farming for herding and sometimes hunting. Whenever a crisis struck the Khoi, they could become clients of established Xhosa nearby because agricultural production recovers more rapidly from famine conditions than stock-farming. There must have been two-way traffic between mixed farming and specialist herding – usually small-scale but occasionally massive. Robert Ross demonstrates this relationship with reference to the Gonaqua, Gqunukhwebe and Ntinde societies which were all – in his view – former Khoi who became mixed farmers and were incorporated *en masse* into Xhosa society, language and tradition. However, we are not dealing with a single transition from herding to cultivation. Physically, the Gonaqua resembled the Xhosa more than the Khoi, so they may have made more than one transition (from agriculture to herding and back again) before the eighteenth century. Most of the evidence comes from the eighteenth century when the Khoi were under enormous pressure: but we cannot assume that, in earlier centuries, the Xhosa were generally expanding, nor that Khoi territory was consistently contracting, as earlier historical orthodoxy maintains.[17] It is only in the light of hindsight that Khoi pastoralism seems a transitional and obsolete means of livelihood. For most of the period under review, the Khoi interacted intensively with other specialists but without sacrificing the viability of their own life-style.

For years the study of the mixed-farming communities in south-eastern Africa has been confounded by historians' obsession with one question: when was the mass migration from the tropical north?[18] It is now clear that

14. R. Elphick, 1977.
15. ibid., ch. 4.
16. R. Ross, 1978.
17. G. M. Theal, 1910.
18. ibid.

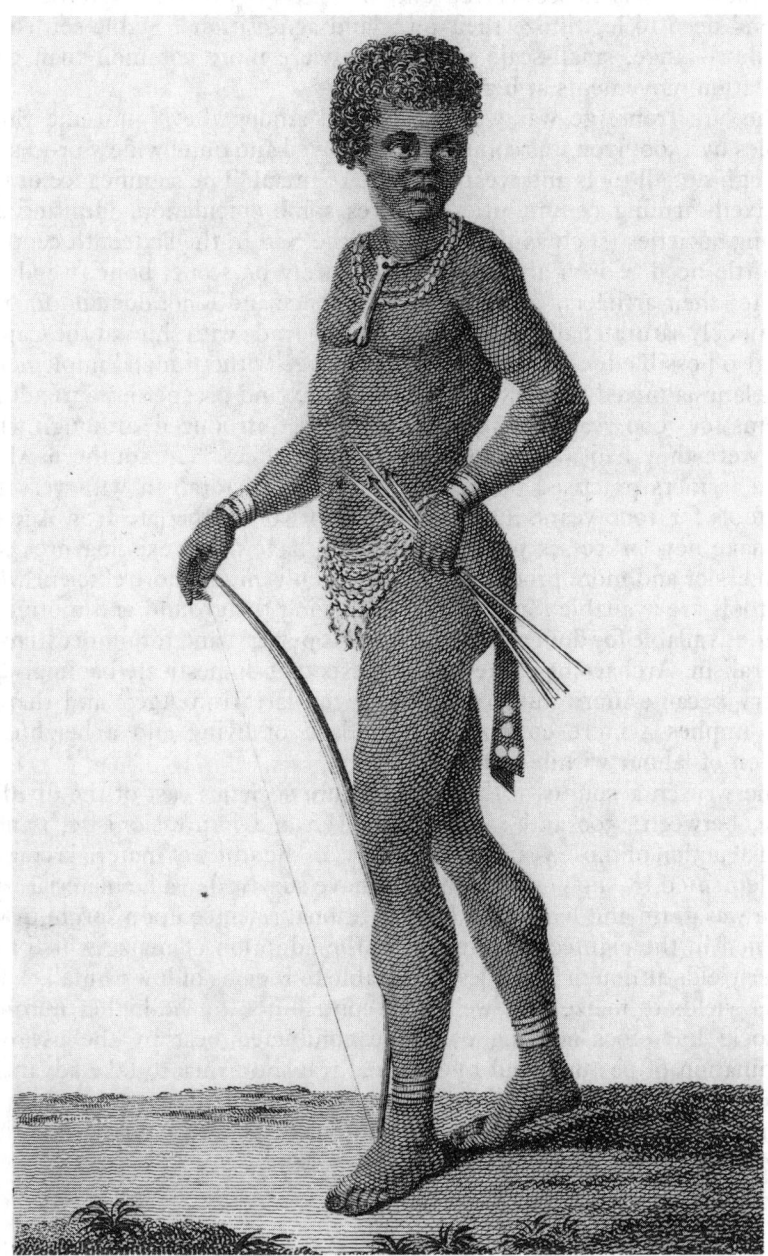

PLATE 23.1   *A Gonaqua (Griqua) huntsman*

this question was misconceived and that it was provoked by the white settlers' need to legitimize their own land acquisitions. Stable settlement and short-range, small-scale movements were more common than great population movements at high speed.

The late Iron Age was well established among the Nguni and Sotho peoples by 1500. Iron was commonly employed and quite widely processed, although not all tools and weapons were of metal. The significance of iron in mixed-farming communities requires some elucidation. Hunting and herding societies (such as the Khoi and the San in the sixteenth century) had little need of iron and could rely entirely on stone, bone, wood and fibre for their artifacts. Iron was a convenience and Khoi demand for iron was quickly saturated during the early, casual trade with ships at the Cape.[19] It is also possible for mixed farmers to manage without metal implements: in Melanesia mixed farmers operated complex and prosperous agricultural systems for 5000 years before steel tools were introduced, although when they were they had a marked labour-saving effect.[20] In southern Africa mixed farmers practised both agriculture and pastoralism with very few iron tools for 1000 years. The abundance of iron in the late Iron Age did not make new processes possible but must have made existing processes much easier and more productive. Cultivation is much more efficient when iron tools are available for clearing and hoeing the ground and more time is made available for domestic crafts, such as pottery, and for more extensive pastoralism. Archaeological record suggests that domesticated animals and pottery became more numerous during the late Iron Age[21] and that, in turn, implies a more comfortable standard of living and a heightened division of labour within each community.

The written accounts of the life of Nguni societies east of the dividing range, between 1500 and 1800, are uneven and impressionistic;[22] and a reconstruction of those years relies heavily on the study of material remains, supplemented by such oral accounts as have survived.[23] The material basis of life was grain and livestock. The traditional reliance upon sorghum was modified in the eighteenth century by the adoption of maize which gave higher yields although it was less adaptable to regions of low rainfall.[24] The higher yields of maize may well have contributed to the higher numbers of stock; but stock-farming could be conducted best by the use of a combination of pastures and by seasonal transhumance to take advantage of the differing qualities of sweet and sour grazing. The pressures on mixed farming of this kind were, presumably, intensified by the climatic variations

19. R. Elphick, 1977, ch. 4.
20. R. F. Salisbury, 1962; D. J. N. Denoon and C. Snowden, 1981.
21. G. M. Hall, 1976.
22. M. Wilson, 1969b.
23. J. B. Peires, 1981.
24. G. M. Hall, 1976.

which Hall proposes for the eastern coastal belt as a whole.[25] In particular, a general decline in rainfall in the first half of the eighteenth century, and a serious drought at the end of the 1700s, would have intensified competition for those pastures which were usable even in dry years.

Human population densities appear to have been much lower than we are now accustomed to. Peires estimates that there were no more than 100 000 Xhosa-speaking people by 1800, despite the accumulation of ex-Khoi during the preceding century or longer.[26] If those figures are typical of the eastern coastal belt, then there cannot have been serious population pressure on land at any time between 1500 and 1800, despite the extensive agricultural and pastoral methods then used. This is important in considering the political systems recorded for the Nguni in this era. Their essential constituent, and the irreducible unit of viability, was a household of stock-owning and land-using people. For most day-to-day purposes, the household could behave as an independent unit, trading and exchanging commodities and wives with other households, almost at will. In practice, each household was linked through patrilineal kinship to a lineage, and hence to a clan; and from the time of Tshawe the Xhosa, for instance, had been loosely bound together by allegiance to the royal clan of Tshawe's descendants. The leader of the royal clan, however, had few sanctions with which to enforce his authority over other Xhosa-speakers, except the manipulation of marriage links and gifts whereby other clans (including non-Xhosa clans such as the neighbouring Khoi) became indebted to him. The ability to bestow wives, gifts and land depended ultimately on the royal household's ability to out-produce other households and clans. The chief usually had more wives – hence more units of production – than others, but there was no particular barrier to a commoner becoming wealthy in stock and wives[27] so that the margin favouring the chief was not always wide. And against the centralizing ambitions of the chiefs commoners also had ambitions, including the desire to live as free of chiefly demands as possible. The incessant wrangles within dominant Xhosa clans and, presumably, among other Nguni societies were undoubtedly encouraged by thoughtful commoners who sought to paralyse the central authority by turning it against itself. These constraints on the evolution of a despotic style of administration were not broken until the end of the 1700s. Until then, daily life seems to have been relaxed and usually comfortable. Certainly the occasional white castaways who found their way into Nguni households during this period, and who have left some records, evinced no great anxiety to return to their own strictly ranked, tightly controlled societies.[28]

Even less is known about the Sotho and Tswana peoples west of the

25. ibid.
26. J. B. Peires, 1981.
27. ibid.
28. ibid.; and M. Wilson, 1969a.

PLATE 23.2   *Khoi Khoi farmers threshing grain*

Drakensberg where lighter rainfall encouraged a greater emphasis on stock (within a mixed-farming regime) than east of the dividing range. In the 1500s there was some risk of attack from north of the Limpopo river;[29] towards the end of the 1700s there was a more immediate threat from new communities moving northwards into the valleys of the Orange and Caledon rivers. In between, Sotho and Tswana must have interacted with Khoi and San and Nguni and Shona as there was small-scale trade in all those directions,[30] but in the present state of knowledge little more can be said.

Like the San and the Khoi, therefore, the southern Bantu communities interacted with other specialists but were not transformed by that interaction. Nor did they transform the societies with which they interacted. Peires cites evidence of alliances between Xhosa chiefs and Khoi groups, such as the Chainouqua in the seventeenth century, and interprets this evidence as subordination of some Khoi to leading Xhosa.[31] In view of the difficulty with which Xhosa chiefs dominated even settled Xhosa, however, these claims should perhaps be treated with some scepticism, especially as Khoi groups seem to have looked to such alliances as long-term insurance rather than daily subordination. In any event, even if these Xhosa claims were conceded, the picture of interaction suggests the durability of each of the specialist occupations. The different African groups were, it seems, capable of long-term co-existence without entrenching the hegemony of one mode of production over another.

The historiography of southern Africa is dominated by accounts of the Dutch settlement at Cape Town, its expansion and its influence on the lives of everyone within the region. In fact, the Portuguese were not only the first navigators to round the Cape but also the first Europeans to establish a permanent settlement in the region. Something of the revolutionary quality of the Dutch settlement can be grasped if it is contrasted briefly with the earlier, longer-lasting, though less influential Portuguese settlement.

Portugal in the sixteenth century was feudal, small and poor. Its overseas expansion was organized by the monarchy as a trading monopoly to India buttressed by the Church which, in the absence of any other source of skilled manpower, had a pervasive influence on the style and substance of administration. By 1510 the centre of overseas rule was Goa and the sea route was protected by forts commanding the Mozambique channel from Delagoa Bay to present-day Tanzania.[32] With superior ships and fire-arms, it was not difficult to conquer the Arab and Swahili ports: but military superiority offered no mechanism for day-to-day government. The security of the Portuguese along the African coast, and particularly at Mozambique which became the regional headquarters, was expressed in fortresses com-

29. M. Wilson, 1969a.
30. R. Elphick, 1977; and J. B. Peires, 1981; and M. Wilson, 1969a.
31. J. B. Peires, 1981, pp. 22–4.
32. M. V. Jackson-Haight, 1967; and R. Elphick, 1977.

manding the mainland but not always connected to it. This was a sea-borne empire, tentative in its territorial control. It was also an essentially feudal empire in which important and lucrative offices were sold by the Crown for an annual fee. It was populated by Portuguese criminals, non-Portuguese traders and adventurers with short-term ambitions. Profit was to be had through the gold and ivory trades, and later the slave trade, recognizing the authority of existing African rulers and provoking in them the most anti-social behaviour. By the end of the sixteenth century the Portuguese empire in the Indian Ocean had been disrupted by competition from other trading powers: the Arabs had recovered their East African possessions while the Dutch, English and French had firmly established themselves in the Indies. The Mozambique channel had been reduced in strategic significance by the development of more direct routes from Europe to Asia via Cape Town or Mauritius or even without any pause for refreshment.

The exploitation of Mozambique was inefficient. Instead of introducing new forms of production, the Portuguese and Indian traders strove to become middle-men. The land was parcelled up into *prazos* and leased to *prazeros*, which had the quality of feudal and subsistence-based manors rather than commodity-producing farms. The supply of the export staples – ivory, gold and slaves – depended on indigenous collectors. Such exploitation could only take place with the co-operation of indigenous societies. For this reason the Cape itself, with its sparse population and scant commodities, offered no opportunity to the Portuguese. Even in Mozambique the absence of an effective government to attend to the long-term interests of traders permitted the degeneration from trade to short-term raiding. Merchant capitalism without capital, and colonization without colonists, could certainly disrupt south-eastern Africa: what it could not encompass was a durable transformation of existing societies.

During the long struggle against the Portuguese trading monopoly, the Dutch East India Company was formed in 1602 by associating all the smaller Dutch trading companies interested in the Asian trade. Like the contemporary English trading companies, it was founded by merchants with royal support whose aim was a national (and, if possible, an international) monopoly of trade between specified regions. The Company was innocent of any religious enthusiasm and independent of the reformed churches as the religious organizations no longer enjoyed a monopoly of education in a reformed Europe. The Heren XVII, the governing body in the Netherlands, could afford to be single-minded in the pursuit of trading profits. Equally important, the Company could afford considerable outlays which would be recouped only over a long term. The garrison settlement at the Cape was precisely such an outlay – of a kind which only an affluent clear-thinking and long-sighted trading company could envisage.[33] Like the French in Mauritius and the Portuguese in Mozambique, the Heren

33. G. Schutte, 1979.

XVII considered the Cape Town garrison a strategic point premised upon continuing Asian trade. They also envisaged a therapeutic purpose, whereby the garrison would buy fresh meat from the Khoi and grow vegetables to provision the Dutch fleets sailing to and from Batavia. For this reason it was appropriate that the first commander of the settlement was Jan van Riebeeck, a surgeon: and when neither the Khoi nor company employees could produce victuals on a sufficient scale, the Company took refuge in a modified form of capitalist production whereby company employees were released as free burghers to engage in production, the Company itself retaining control over marketing. The Company's rationale and its tactics were as thoroughly capitalist as the Portuguese were feudal; and, accordingly, it reaped the profits of careful planning.

Like other European powers which expanded into temperate grasslands with scant populations, the Dutch found that the dynamics of their new settlement were quite different from those of their tropical dependencies. For over a century, until the encounter with settled mixed farmers, their experience was similar to that of the Spaniards in the grasslands of the South American pampa, and of the British in the prairies of North America and south-eastern Australia.[34]

Perhaps the fundamental determinant of the Cape settlement was the painfully slow evolution of agriculture. For the first forty years of its history, the settlement imported much of its staple food despite the enormous stock of agricultural knowledge they brought with them from western Europe.[35] The most lucrative use of land was pastoralism, of an extensive and expansive nature. The second great determinant of the settlement was the absence of a coercible, indigenous labour force. Whereas Indonesians could be directed into commodity production in large numbers by the manipulation of existing social structures, it was impossible to turn Khoi into commodity-producers without the total destruction of Khoi society. The few Khoi who survived and remained within the boundaries of the settlement merged with other elements of a new community – the Khoi Khoi, later the nucleus of the Cape Coloured. The Company could not, and did not, rely upon the Khoi for labour. Instead, labour was introduced from other parts of Africa and from the East Indies in the form of slavery. These relations of production left no room for Khoi or San except as individual units of labour fully separated from the means of production. In the language of development studies, pastoral capitalism did not articulate with other modes of production: it obliterated them.

This characteristic of the new society might not have mattered much had it not been combined with a persistent expansionism. Neumark thought that pastoral expansion was fuelled mainly by the growth of external markets for fresh meat.[36] Guelke and Ross prefer to see the mainspring of

34. D. J. N. Denoon, 1983.
35. A. J. Boeseken, 1969.
36. S. D. Neumark, 1957.

expansion as integral to the society itself.[37] A capitalist organization has to expand to survive, so the question of external *versus* internal impulses can perhaps be ignored. At the Cape, labour was expensive and scarce while land was cheap and plentiful, so the obvious manner of achieving the expansion of capitalism was not through the more intensive use of land but through territorial expansion. The geographical extension of the settlement had the curious consequence of replicating the sparse population levels which had characterized Khoi land usage; and, indeed, commercial pastoralism meant little more than grazing much the same cattle and sheep on the same land as before, sometimes with Khoi employed as herdsmen. It was not land usage so much as social relations which were changed by the new regime. On the frontier of commercial expansion it was particularly difficult for the Dutch settlers to control their Dutch labourers as it was easy for disgruntled workers to flee eastwards or northwards to escape an irksome working situation. In addition, only settlers (and occasionally Khoi converts) could have land registered in their own names. In these circumstances it was almost impossible to discipline a Dutch labour force, and frontier pastoralists had to rely instead on costly slaves or Khoi both of whom had considerable opportunities for escape although a series of *ad hoc* treaties between the company and Khoi leaders officially provided for runaway slaves to be returned to the settlement.

During the eighteenth century the imperatives of extensive commercial pastoralism expressed themselves in a series of social relationships which have more in common with those of the South American pampa and nineteenth-century Australia than with the rest of Africa. Cape Town was the entrepôt, the focus of all trading relationships and meeting point of international cultures and ideas. Company officials not only administered the settlement but also often traded on their own account – a crime which was likely to go unpublished unless it caused the Company itself to lose money.[38] They consorted with the more prosperous local land owners, traders and inn-keepers of the town, and lorded it over the large and strictly disciplined slave population. They felt superior, too, to the pastoralists who came to town occasionally to sell meat, hides and tallow. Speaking a crude form of Dutch, barely literate and wearing unfashionable but functional clothes, the pastoralists obviously lacked urban sophistication and could easily be cheated by the urban meat-merchants. They were rough, too, in their management of labour as they often lived far from the disciplining officers of the town. But while they were gauche, they were also the mainstay of the colonial economy. The slave population was constantly being increased by importation but the pastoral population increased just as fast, both by immigration and natural increase.[39] One hundred and fifty years after foundation, the settlement comprised more

37. L. Guelke, 1979; and R. Ross, 1975.
38. G. Schutte, 1979.
39. R. Ross, 1975.

than 20 000 free burghers and more than 25 000 slaves.[40]

The territorial expansion of the settlement tended to disperse the Khoi and San from the western interior. At the same time the strict hierarchy and discipline within the new society tended to extrude the more vigorous and independent-minded of the slaves and the ex-Khoi. An occasional white settler also fled to the frontier, either to escape the law, or in search of quick wealth, or for a combination of these reasons. Some of the refugees were armed, and many were accomplished horsemen so – like the gauchos generated by similar social forces on the South American pampa – they were a hardy community, specialists in violence.[41] Their options were three. First, they could seek and obtain employement with the state, as frontier law-enforcers, a choice which was regularized in 1795 with the formation of the Hottentot Corps.[42] Secondly, they could try to live a settled life among the white frontiersmen, either as wage-labourers (as the whites wanted them to be) or as independent pastoralists (as they themselves wished). Although this was an attractive prospect, it was difficult to realize because the consolidation of the Cape settlement and the protection of private property in land made the coloured frontiersmen vulnerable to expropriation. Only rarely could Khoi register title to land in their own names, and the extension of colonial authority made the white pastoralists bold enough to challenge Khoi *de facto* landowners. It was, therefore, the third option which was the most promising: to stay one step ahead of the frontier of white pastoral expansion.

The wide, dry region to the north of the Company settlement, particularly along the Orange river and its tributaries, was a typical region for the evolution of new societies. Here evolved the Kora, Griqua and Nama societies and from 1730 to about 1780 they were seldom troubled by Company authority.[43] Their title to land was not explicitly recognized by the whites, but neither was it challenged. To make a living, the new little societies captured, bred and sold cattle, relying on fire-arms and gun-powder acquired through the settlement. Accordingly, leadership fell on those of the frontier who were able to converse with and understand the whites and the Company authorities – white outlaws, such as Bloem, or descendants of slaves, such as the Kok family. Many knew, and remembered, their descent from Khoi bands. The Griqua chose their name because they derived from the Chariguriqua community. However, the Griqua were not merely refugees from the Company settlement but also its cutting edge. They aspired to the status of independent commercial pastoralists which whites already enjoyed, not to the culture and condition of subsistence pastoralism whose time was clearly past. Yet their personal aspirations were largely irrelevant. Dependent upon fire-power from the

40. R. Ross, 1975; W. M. Freund, 1979.
41. S. R. Duncan-Baretta and J. Markoff, 1978.
42. W. M. Freund, 1979.
43. M. Legassick, 1979; R. Ross, 1976.

PLATE 23.4   *A seventeenth-century impression of a Namaqua family*

settlement, and obliged to stay ahead of their white rivals, they could not in the long term become a settled community. Such precarious security as they built for themselves had to be purchased by the dispossession of others. Their lands constituted the penumbra of violence which was an essential component of the new, commercial pastoralist economy and society. When that frontier was at length 'closed' in the nineteenth century, by a combination of environmental conditions and reinforced colonial administration, the day of the Griqua would end. That end was implicit in the inter-group relations of the eighteenth century, and while it could be postponed, it could not be averted.

The northern frontier of the settlement was the classic environment for new racially-mixed societies and similar developments also occurred on the eastern frontier. There, however, the course of events was swifter, and the climax in the 1790s more dramatic, as it involved not only the white pastoralists, the Cape Town authorities and the refugee communities but also the southernmost Bantu. There was a penumbra of insecurity on the fringe of Xhosa territory as on the white pastoral frontier and when these two zones of insecurity overlapped life became dangerous.

A degree of control over most Xhosa-speakers may have been exercised by the ruler Phalo, but his death in 1775 unleashed the rivalry of his two most important sons, Rharhabe and Gealeka.[44] Gealeka's death three years later released further sub-dividing forces among his followers; and the

44. J. B. Peires, 1981.

death of Rharhabe in 1782 (in a war against the Tembu) similarly split his followers between the regent Ndlamba and the young heir Ngqika. Each of these factions aspired to dominance over the entire Xhosa-speaking community and the neighbouring Khoi who were enlisted as allies. From the perspectives of both factions, the white pastoralists seemed much like the brown pastoralists – potential allies and eventual clients of wealthy Xhosa. The practice of transhumance, whereby herds of cattle were driven considerable distances for seasonal grazing, meant that white, Khoi and Xhosa were intermingled from the start, meeting each other in small numbers. It took a generation for the Xhosa to grasp the unique quality of *commercial* pastoralism, with its limitless and constantly-increasing appetite for grazing land. Meanwhile they behaved as if the pastoralist threat was marginal.

The Company's reluctance to spend shareholders' money, and the difficulty of administering a remote and sparsely populated region propelled the white pastoralists into providing for their own protection and expansion. The Company paid for a resident magistrate – a *landdrost* – at major centres, but the *landdrost* alone could not maintain control. In his judicial functions he was assisted by burghers – *heemraden* – who, in military affairs, took matters more and more into their own hands. Every adult male of fighting age was potentially a landowner and they all recognized a rough equality among themselves despite the growing inequalities of wealth. Each adult male was, at least potentially, the patriarch of a small community comprising his family, his slaves and his employees; and each patriarchy conducted its affairs largely outside the formal judicial framework. When fighting was imminent, therefore, the patriarchs would elect an *ad hoc* leader and form a commando unit which would be disbanded once the spoils had been divided. It was as difficult for this loosely structured society to commit itself to a long-term strategy as it was for the Xhosa in their divided state. As white numbers increased late in the eighteenth century, so the burghers became impatient with the Company. In 1795, during the last days of Company rule, the burghers on the frontier formally denounced the Company, and declared themselves for two independent republics of white patriarchs, the short-lived republics of Swellendam and Graaf Reinet.[45]

Meanwhile, a much more serious rebellion was brewing. A necessary consequence of white pastoral expansion had been the dispossession of Khoi communities and of individual Khoi commercial pastoralists such as Klaas Stuurman.[46] To the whites it seemed appropriate that the Khoi should be content to be farm labourers rather than independent farmers. To the Xhosa faction-leaders it seemed appropriate that the Khoi should be content to become clients of wealthy Xhosa. The Khoi themselves were, of course, disgruntled with the status of 'Hottentot' which the Company

45. H. Giliomee, 1979.
46. ibid.

allowed and with the status of client which the Xhosa offered. In 1799 many of them rebelled, drawing in reinforcements from the armed Khoi in the service of the new British administration. Unlike the burgher republicans, who wished to preserve the *status quo* but throw off the Company yoke, the Khoi farm servants, soldiers and farmers sought to overthrow the *status quo* on the frontier. The former was a revolt, the latter an incipient revolution.

During the French revolutionary wars, the British navy seized a number of garrisons around the world to consolidate their naval supremacy on a global scale. One of these was the garrison at Cape Town, captured after a short tussle in 1795. There is no reason to suppose that the British naval and military officers who took charge at Cape Town had much interest in the hinterland, except to maintain order. As usual in such a conquest, the simplest method of maintaining order was to acknowledge the local hierarchy of power-holders; and accordingly the burgher republics were quickly suppressed but the burghers' control over their land was confirmed. The Khoi revolt, however, could not be put down so easily. With insufficient troops for a protracted frontier campaign, General Dundas was content to calm matters. Some land was granted to individual Khoi, including Stuurman and his brothers; others were encouraged (but not forced) to return to their employment or to the Hottentot Corps; and the troubles were left to simmer for a few years until they broke out again early in the nineteenth century.[47]

The Cape which the British acquired at the end of the 1700s already had many of the characteristics which would distinguish it in the nineteenth century. Cape Town, with a mere 15 000 inhabitants, was still mainly a garrison and an entrepôt for Asian and European trade; but it had also acquired its role as outlet for an export economy based on the hinterland, and the abandonment of old monopoly trading arrangements would provoke a massive increase in export production in the new century. In the colony as a whole there were some 22 000 'Christians', most of whom were white with a few liberated blacks. The Khoi and San were enumerated at about 14 000 and slaves at 25 000.[48] As the terms of the census imply, the Cape had a strictly defined series of castes, each distinguished by different access to the means of production. Only 'Christians' could hold land, although the Khoi had not been entirely squeezed out; and only slaves were entirely without civil rights although, again, the Khoi were in an ambiguous position which varied with local conditions and numbers.

Increasingly, the Khoi were cast in an intermediate situation between the settlement on one side and the Xhosa, Sotho and Tswana on the other. By the end of the 1700s that intermediary role had been exhausted on the eastern frontier – hence the explosion of revolt – but it had another two or three generations to run on the more open northern frontier. Because it

47. W. M. Freund, 1979.
48. ibid.; R. Ross, 1975.

was Khoi – as Khoi Khoi, Griquas, Nama and Kora – who bore the brunt of the pastoral expansion from the western Cape, most of the mixed-farming communities of the whole region were at this point only marginally affected. We have seen that the Xhosa could treat the white pastoralists as if they were merely pale Khoi: further north, among the northern Nguni, the emergence of the strong confederacies, which led ultimately to the formation of the Zulu state, was entirely independent of events at the Cape. Nevertheless, in the long run it was the transforming force of commercial pastoralism, itself provoked by the capitalist transformation of Europe and Asia, which would prove the most durable social force of the nineteenth century.

The Horn of Africa

24

E. HABERLAND

Introduction

The sixteenth and seventeenth centuries are the most dramatic in the history of north-east Africa. The mighty political and military power and the outstanding cultural development of the Christian Ethiopian empire disintegrated and collapsed. Enemy invasions not only decimated large sections of the Christian population, but also tore whole provinces away from the empire for long periods. For a time the *mangest egzi 'abḥērāwit* (Holy Empire), hardpressed on all sides, was but a shadow of its former self. Only where the emperor actually faced the enemy at the head of his troops could the authority of the state, otherwise non-existent, be said to have any reality; and these external, political tribulations were aggravated by equally destructive spiritual disorders which constantly marred the unity of empire, the Christians and the Orthodox Church. The remarkable influence of a handful of Portuguese missionaries won an increasing number of converts to the Catholic faith, including even Emperor Susenyos who, in 1630, embraced the new faith and raised it to the status of the official religion of the state. Civil wars of unprecedented violence swept over the enfeebled empire until eventually the foreign faith and its supporters were driven out by force.

Until the end of the seventeenth century there now followed a period of consolidation of empire and restoration of the Christian Ethiopian faith and culture that once again bore fruit, though less exuberantly than in former times. Then, from 1700, a period of fragmentation of empire began which, by analogy with Old Testament precedents, has been called the 'Age of Princes/Judges'. The steadily increasing anarchy during this period only came to an end in 1855, when Theodore II ushered in the age of the great emperors whom the Ethiopian empire had to thank for its restoration and its survival through the colonial era.

North-east Africa, however, does not only comprise the Christian Ethiopian empire. Around 1500, Islamic culture, too, reached its peak in the east and centre of the subcontinent, and warlike Islam was soon to achieve its greatest triumphs. Fired by the concept of *djihād* (Holy War), Aḥmad ibn Ibrāhīm al-Ghazi, a brilliant military leader and champion of the faith, recorded in the Christian Ethiopian chronicles under the nickname *Grañ* (the lefthander), won victory after victory. Year after year, in the dry season, his hosts overran the land of the Amhara and the Tigrai, destroying and subjugating and forcing whole provinces to embrace Islam, even if only temporarily. But eventually the forces supporting these political and civilizing activities proved too weak. They exhausted themselves and, after the death of their leader, collapsed. The Christian empire started to counter-attack. Finally the migrations of the great Oromo (Galla) people, with inexhaustible forces at their disposal, destroyed the once flourishing communities and cultures of the Islamic peoples in central Ethiopia, leaving hardly a vestige.

Two important peoples now came on the scene, the Oromo and the Somali, who were to play a decisive role in the history of north-eastern Africa. Their evolution followed completely different paths. The Oromo spread out in all directions, in a series of individual migrations, completely separate from one another, in western, central, eastern and even northern Ethiopia. They advanced into areas depopulated through the religious wars; they subjugated and assimilated other peoples; yet, at the same time, the conquerors adapted themselves voluntarily to the superior cultures of other peoples. As a result, they failed to develop a true national culture of their own.

Not so the Somali. The participation of large groups in Grañ's Holy War, and the steadily increasing influence of Islam which set them apart from most other peoples of north-east Africa, were powerful factors in the development of a strong national consciousness. Regardless of their division into many genealogically determined ethnic groups, at least from this time on, the Somali considered themselves one people with one culture and one religion. Their expansion between 1500 and 1700 in a south-westerly direction at least as far as the River Juba was due not only to their military strength and growing numbers but also to their ability to assimilate.

The political and cultural events in northern, central and eastern north-east Africa are historically fairly well substantiated; but the history of the west and south-west was little known until recently. We know today that this period saw the beginnings of a cultural development which, in its creativity and dynamism, is one of the most significant events in African history. Direct influence from the Christian empire to the north which, since 1300 or before, had been trying to influence southern Ethiopia, led to the growth of large states and sophisticated cultures extending south to the natural highland boundary. Of particular importance were the foundations of the states of Inariya: Boša, Kaffa and Sekko, as well as Wolayta, Dauro and the small states of the Gamo highlands.

The Christian Ethiopian empire around 1500

By about 1500 the Christian Ethiopian empire had politically, culturally and, indeed, in every respect reached heights that it was not to approach again for centuries.[1]

In respect of foreign policy and military power, it enjoyed undisputed hegemony in north-east Africa. Sudan was not yet Islamic. Christian groups – all that was left of the state of Sōba – still subsisted around the confluence of the White Nile and the Blue Nile, soon to be overrun by the Fundj. The Islamic towns on the shores of the Red Sea – in what is now Eritrea – were politically insignificant. Even the coast around Massawa – the island and the city itself was Islamic-Arabic – was indisputably part of he Ethiopian empire, under the control of the governor of the provinces to the north of the Bahr Nagaš (River Mareb), inhabited by the Tigrai.[2]

The power of the many small Islamic dominions and states in eastern and central Ethiopia had been cut back by the crushing blows of the Ethiopian emperors of the preceding century, in particular Emperor Zera-Yakob (1434–68). Most of these states paid tribute, however unwillingly, to the Christian empire. Christian military colonists had settled there. Relationship by marriage between the ruling classes of the Christian empire and the Islamic border areas strengthened these contacts. (Empress Helena, for example, daughter of an Islamic Hadiyya chief, was one of the most influential figures at the Ethiopian court for two generations.)[3]

The influence and the military and cultural expansion of the Christian state were even stronger towards the south and south-west. New states with a Christian ruling class emerged; formerly independent peoples and states were made to recognize the political and cultural supremacy of the Northern Empire by force, diplomacy and purposive missionary work.[4] The moral justification of this imperial expansion and power drive was provided by the *magna carta* of the Ethiopian empire, the *Kebra Nagast* (Glory of the Kings).[5]

This work was probably compiled about 1300, shortly after the so-called restoration of the dynasty that from then until 1974 was called the Solomonid dynasty. Folk legends, biblical, talmudic and Kur'ānic traditions were brought together here and harmonized with a divine mission of salvation. The *Kebra Nagast* thus took on a significance for the development of Ethiopia comparable only to that of the *Aeneid* where, in similar pro-

---

1. This is a generally accepted historical fact which can be duduced too, from all known evidence. Cf. T. Tamrat, 1972, pp. 206 *et passim*; F. Alvares, 1961, *passim*. For the paintings, see J. Leroy, 1967 and J. Leroy, St. Wright and O. A. Jäger, 1961. For the literature, see E. Cerulli, 1968, pp. 81f.
2. F. Alvares, 1961, Vol. I, p. 54.
3. J. Perruchon, 1893, pp. 125 and 176; T. Tamrat, 1972, p. 289.
4. Cf. U. Braukamper, 1980, pp. 91f.
5. Cf. C. Bezold, 1905; E. Haberland, 1965, pp. 25f.

phetic fashion, the Roman mission was established. It explains how the Queen of Sheba – here equated with Ethiopia – undertook a journey to Jerusalem to learn the wisdom of Solomon. By him she had a son, Menelik, who was born after her return to Ethiopia and was later to become the first Ethiopian king. Later, on a visit to his father in Jerusalem, Menelik carried off the Ark of the Covenant, the most important sacred symbol in the world, and brought it back to Ethiopia. It was preserved thereafter in the famous cathedral of Axum where the Ethiopian emperors were enthroned. The book ends with the announcement of the spiritual division of the world between the two great Holy Empires of Rome and Ethiopia which are to establish the Kingdom of Christ. Everything that could serve to elevate the Christian Ethiopian people and its dynasty is woven together here in most artistic fashion: the lineage of the emperors, descended from Solomon and David, the Prophet and Psalmist and the relationship with Jesus Christ thus implied and, finally, the transfer to Ethiopia of the Ark of the Covenant, the symbol of the True Presence of God among mankind. The story makes Christian Ethiopians the chosen people of both the Old and New Testaments for, unlike the Jews, they have accepted the Gospel:

> The chosen of the Lord are the people of Ethiopia. For that is the abode of God, the heavenly Zion. ... I have made a covenant with my chosen people; I have sworn to my servant David: I will preserve thy seed for all eternity and maintain thy throne for ever and ever.

The fact that Ethiopia – the 'Christian island in a heathen sea' – was able to withstand so many storms, not least those of the sixteenth century, is due above all to the geographical position of this mountainous land. But the feeling of being the new chosen people must have given spiritual conviction to the empire's determination to extend dominion over most of north-east Africa.

Internally, the empire enjoyed the utmost tranquillity at that time. This is evident in particular from the reports of Francesco Alvares who, from 1520 to 1526, accompanied the Portuguese mission from Massawa to Shoa as chaplain and travelled extensively throughout the country.[6] Order and security reigned; the Governor's instructions were obeyed and the emperor's word carried absolute authority throughout an empire that measured at least a thousand kilometres from north to south. Although the individual provinces and districts possessed some regional autonomy, and although communication within the Ethiopian Highlands was severely limited especially during the rainy season, the unity of this state was strongly established. The concept of the Holy Christian Empire, the undisputed claim to power of the House of Solomon and, finally, the Christian faith and common culture of the two peoples who formed the state, the Amhara and the Tigrai, constituted strong and effective bonds. The culture and language of these two peoples exerted a powerful assimilating effect on

6. F. Alvares, 1961, Vol. I, *passim*.

other ethnic groups which came into contact with them. The history of this period is, therefore, also the history of the rise of other ethnic groups in association with the two largest populations. This is particularly true of the different groups of the Agaw, the indigenous inhabitants of central and northern Ethiopia, who were almost completely assimilated by the Amhara and Tigrai. The assimilation process gathered strength during the sixteenth century and reached its zenith in the extirpation of the groups in northern Ethiopia who linguistically and culturally belonged to the Agaw but practised the Jewish faith, especially in the provinces of Samen, Dambiya and Waggara. Their survivors have been living ever since as a sort of pariah caste called the Falasha scattered over all northern and central Ethiopia.[7] In the south, too, in the parts of Shoa province now inhabited mainly by Oromo, not only Christianity but also the Amharic language and culture must have spread at the expense of other ethnic groups living there, in particular members of the Hadiyya.

The attempt by Emperor Zera-Yakob (1434–68) to centralize the empire's political organization and replace the constantly changing provincial and district chiefs (recruited from among the influential families of the regions by people of his own choosing, with unlimited tenure of office) failed,[8] but the word of the emperor still carried absolute authority, even after 1500. From the chronicles, which are not always forthcoming on this point, we can infer that, as regards the autonomy of individual provinces and the question of land law closely bound up with it, conditions were very similar to those still obtaining in the nineteenth and twentieth centuries.[9] Most land was the residual property of ethnic and family groups who decided how it should be divided among their members. The Church was also an important landowner, although its share is usually overestimated. It served to provide the livelihood of a caste made up of peasant secular priests who, in return, had to conduct divine service. Finally there were the imperial lands, granted by the emperor on a short- or long-term basis to deserving people or for specific purposes. This feudal land – to adapt the European expression to African conditions – was known as *gult*. The same word is also used to denote the right conferred by the emperor – in connection with the grant of an office – to levy tribute and services. The ownership of the land by the inhabitants was not affected by this dependency status.

The extraordinary dynamism of Ethiopian society, with its ideal of the *tellek saw* (great man) who had constantly to prove himself anew and in whom qualities and achievements alone counted, was not conducive to the rise of a nobility. In theory, the way to office was open to any free man belonging to a respectable family. In his district peoples' assembly he could

7. Cf. W. Leslau, 1951, pp. ix–xliii, which despite its brevity, is still the best introduction to the Falasha problem.

8. Cf. J. Perruchon, 1893, pp. 95f., 102 and 112.

9. Cf. E. Haberland, 1965, pp. 200f; B. Abbebe, 1971; A. Hoben, 1973.

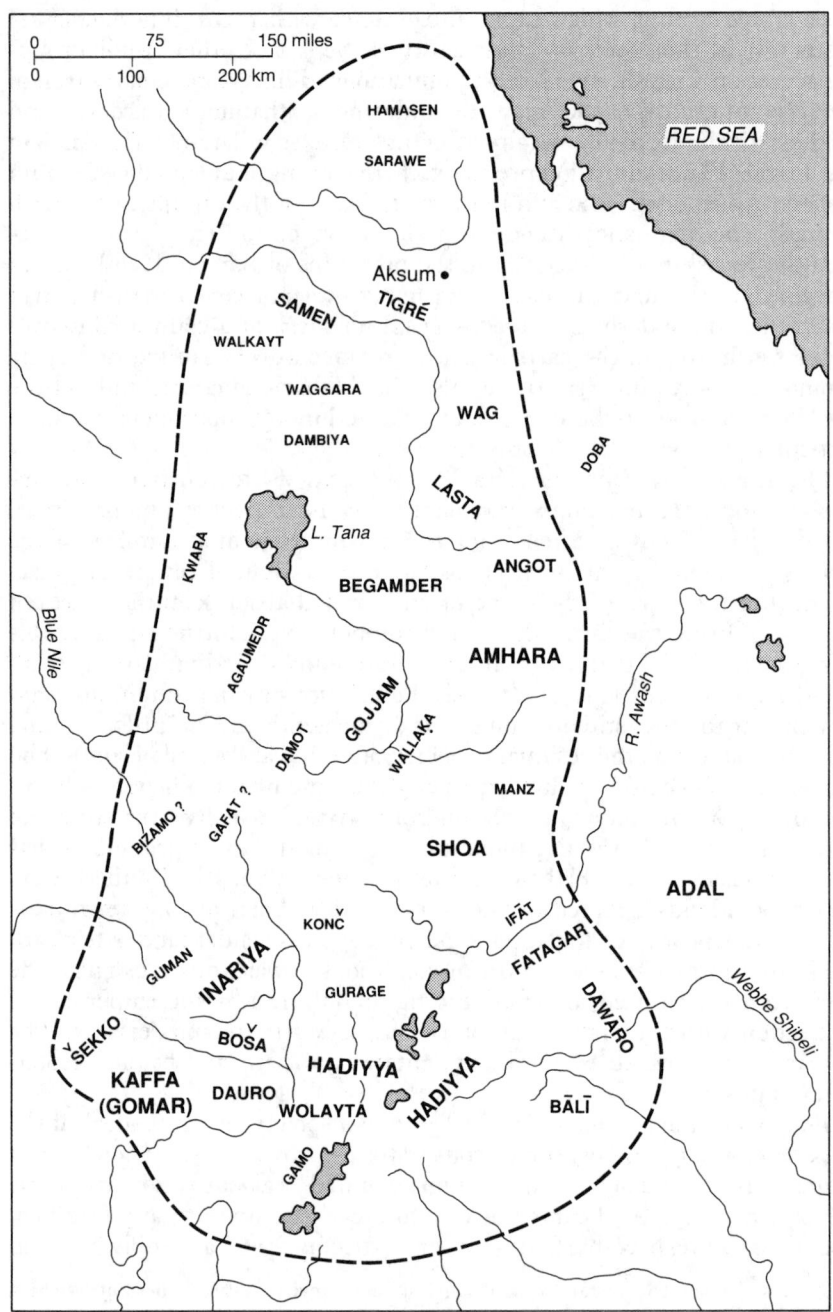

FIG. 24.1   *The Ethiopian empire and its dependencies,* c. *1550 (after E. Haberland)*

be elected to office or demoted. The emperor participated in this democratic process in as much as confirmation of election or dismissal fell to him as supreme authority. Thus monarchical power and democratic election complemented one another, preventing the formation of a hereditary nobility with political privileges which could have disturbed the unity of the empire. This only happened with the increasing enfeeblement of imperial power after 1700 and later led people to talk of feudalism, a term originally characteristic of Ethiopia.[10]

Roads were safe and travellers faced no problems. Imperial rest-houses abounded and also great weekly markets.[11] General well-being – not just of a ruling class – surpassed anything later known. Taxes in kind flowed from the provinces and the tributary states to the emperor's court where they were distributed. (Until 1636, when Gondar became the court's permanent residence, the emperors knew only mobile courts consisting of large tent encampments.) Although neither minted coins nor commercial correspondence were known, there was nevertheless extensive trade over long distances in which important consumer goods were imported from India and the Near East. (Salt was carried from one end of Ethiopia to the other, and luxury goods such as jewellery and costly fabrics).

Ethiopia was closely linked with distant lands as far away as Europe, not only economically but also culturally, in contrast with its later isolation. Edward Gibbon's famous and often quoted words: 'Encompassed on all sides by the enemies of their religion, the Ethiopians slept near a thousand years, forgetful of the world, by whom they were forgotten,'[12] do not hold true for this period. Ethiopian monasteries in Jerusalem and Cyprus had active contacts with Europe.[13] Ethiopian monks – the main purveyors of education, art and science – received their training in Egypt and took part in both Coptic and Islamic cultural life.[14] Although literary production was limited to two fields – religious and historical – it flourished until at least 1650. In addition the graphic arts – of which, above all, book illuminations have survived – were also stimulated by contact with the Christian east and with Europe. Important themes depicted in religious painting were taken over and further developed. Evidence of these contacts are the casual mentions in the chronicles of the presence of Italian and Spanish artisans and artists. The existence of hitherto little-known ruins of churches and palaces is further proof of the richness and artistic creativity of this period.[15]

---

10. M. Perham, 1948, pp. 267f. and 273.
11. The description by Alvares of his journey from Massawa to Shoa is very instructive.
12. E. Gibbon, 1956, Vol. V, p. 69.
13. Cf. E. Cerulli, 1943–7, 1947; T. Lefèbre, 1845–54.
14. The chronicles of Galawdewos and Sartsa Dengel and also the *History of the Galla* were apparently written by monks who got part of their instruction in Egypt or elsewhere in the Orient. See J. Perruchon, 1894 and 1896; C. Conti Rossini, 1907; A. W. Schleicher, 1893.
15. Cf. S. Chojnacki, 1969.

Islamic states and cultures: the *djihād*, the Somali and the Hadiyya

By 1300, if not before, Christianity had developed a vigorous missionary activity carried on by monks and secular priests in central and southern Ethiopia. As the official religion of the Ethiopian empire, Christianity could always rely on state support – if necessary backed by fire and sword. The spread of Islam in north-east Africa, however, was not the result of missionary purpose and state help but depended on the spread of Arab culture and – at least in this area – on trade and communications. Arab and Islamic influences on the north-east African coast are age-old. Trade between the Arabian peninsula, the Ethiopian coast opposite and the Somali coast dates to pre-Islamic, even pre-Christian times. These trading relationships led to the foundation of a number of towns with mixed populations but with the Arab element predominating. The most important centres, starting from the north, were: Massawa, the off-shore Dahlak Islands, Assab, Oboek, Tadjūra, Djibouti, Zaylāʿ, Berberā, Obbia, Mogadishu, Merka and Brava (here the East African coast proper begins, with strong Swahili influence). The strength and direction of the spread of Arab–Islamic culture from these centres shows clearly just how dependent it was upon trading relationships with the hinterland and, likewise, on the fertility of the hinterland, the goods it produced and its population density. The map of the spread of Islam during the fifteenth and sixteenth centuries clearly shows that it was concentrated on both sides of the Rift Valley – along the great trade route into central Ethiopia. On the southern edge of the highlands lay a number of Islamic cities of which imposing ruins remain, and states that stretched south towards Lake Zway as far as the Shebele river.[16] Harar is the only city remaining. From the coast inland, there were a number of states: Adal, the largest, extending from Zaylāʿ on the Indian Ocean west to Harar and north to the Aussa Oasis in Afar territory, Dara, Dawāro, Bālī, Arababnī (or Arʾen), Šarha and Hadiyya.[17] Islamic influence probably extended westwards across the Rift Valley. This is suggested by traditions that explain the name of the former Kingdom of Yamgor (commonly called Ǧangero) on the middle Gibe as meaning Yemen Land, as well as by records that tell of the Arab origin of the *nagado* (merchant) caste in Kaffa.[18] To the north of the Rift Valley on the southern slopes of the Shoa highlands lay the twin Islamic states of Ifāt and Fatagar (Fatadjar) with a population still known today as Argobba. Many people in these states must have spoken Semitic languages which spread alongside and overlay the Kushitic languages originally spoken there, particularly the dialects of the Hadiyya–Sidama linguistic family. The only ones remain-

16. F. Azais and R. Chambard, 1931, pp. 129f. and 203, plates LXIII and LXIV; C. Conti Rossini, 1942; E. Cerulli, 1941; and R. and H. Joussaume, 1972.

17. G. W. B. Huntingford, 1965, pp. 53f.; al-Makrīzī, 1790.

18. F. J. Bieber, 1920–3; H. Straube, 1963, pp. 274f.

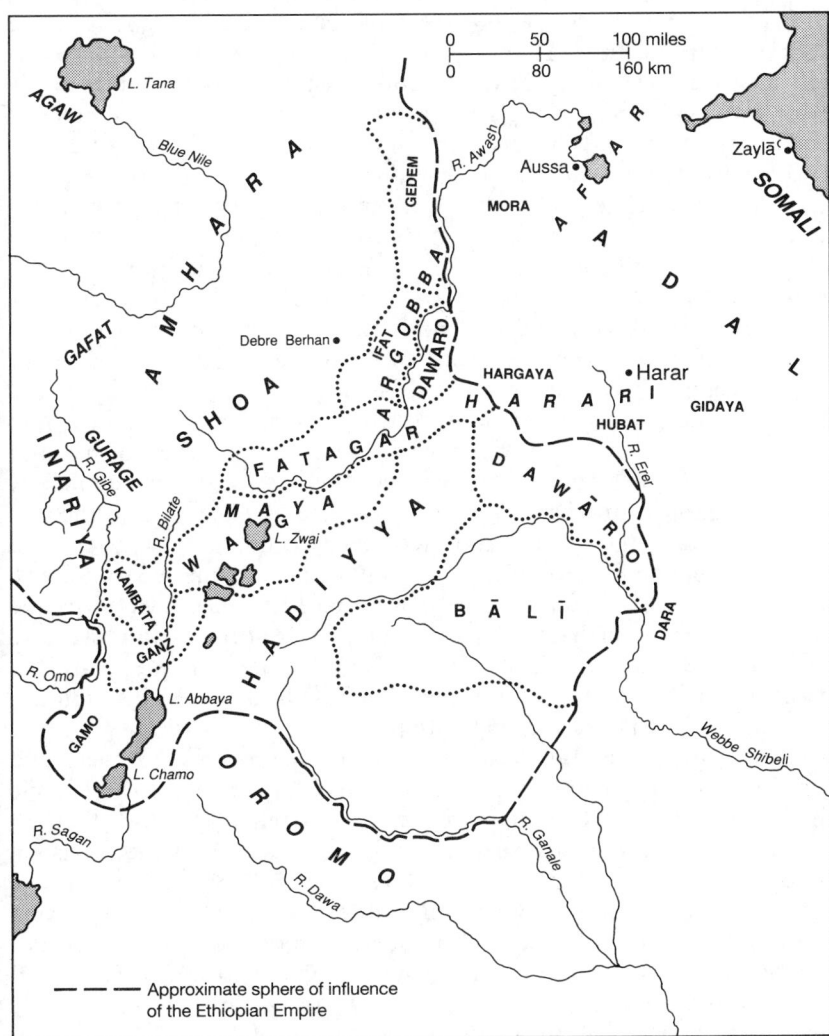

FIG. 24.2   *South-eastern Ethiopia, c. 1500 (after E. Haberland)*

ing are the languages of the Harari, East Gurage and Argobba.[19]

These states were all marked by the influence of Arab–Islamic culture from the coast. The cultural elements that still persist today – long after the destruction of the states – are also Arab–Islamic. The most striking example of the town settlements that once dominated the area is Harar, the only genuinely ancient city on Ethiopian soil. The city-like fortified

19.   Cf. P. V. Paulitschke, 1888; V. Stitz, 1974; W. Leslau, 1963 and 1979.

villages of the Argobba to the south-east of Harar and the Argobba on the eastern edge of Shoa must also be mentioned here, as must the stone-built single-storey or two-storey town dwellings with flat roofs and beautiful interior furnishings, betraying Arab influences, and the large number of walled holy sepulchres. Whenever Arab influence was felt, it left its traces in intensive horticulture (with terracing and irrigation systems), still practised today, and a multitude of food crops not normally cultivated in Ethiopia such as oranges, lemons, peaches, vines, bananas and sugar-cane.[20] Also traceable to Arab influence is cotton-growing and the consumption of coffee and *khat* or *čat* (celastrus) which were not used until recently in non-Islamic Ethiopia. Widespread in central Ethiopia are numerous religious concepts, rites and words that stem from the Arabic, even though the original Muslims there later renounced Islam.[21]

The spread of Islam and its culture from east to west brought it into conflict with the Christian Empire wherever it crossed the north–south course of the empire's political and religious drive. This happened mainly in central Ethiopia, in what is now the province of Shoa, and to the east of it. This was also the scene of repeated bloody conflicts between the two powers that went on for several centuries and remained indecisive until well into the fifteenth. Although the Christian Empire remained the undisputed dominant power in north-east Africa, forcing most of the Islamic states to pay tribute, it was nevertheless unable – mainly for geographical reasons – to eliminate or destroy the Islamic states although they were insignificant in relation to its own size and population.[22]

We are still not certain what brought an end to this stalemate and changed the hitherto mainly politically motivated war between the Islamic trading states and the Christian Empire into a religious 'Holy War' or *djihād*, and why the political leadership of the Sultans of Adal, the Walasma, was transferred to the religious leaders (*imām*). Nor do we know what gave the Islamic armies – a motley collection of ethnic groups – the cohesion and fanaticism to bring the mighty Christian Empire to the brink of defeat. One explanation no doubt lies in the brilliant Aḥmad ibn Ibrāhīm al-Ghazi (Aḥmad Grañ) who emerged from obscurity to become the charismatic leader of the *djihād*.[23] With his death in 1543 the Islamic impetus soon collapsed, although his talented and bold successor, Amīr Nūr, tried with some initial success to continue the fight. There is also no doubt that the rest of the Islamic world, which at that time held the northern Somali tightly in its grip, provided its armies in Ethiopia with a recruiting potential

20. H. Straube, 1963, pp 292f. and 301f.
21. I would like to mention words like *šayh* (religious chief), *djinn* (spirit), *al-hayr* (welfare, form of greeting), *iblis* (devil), *awliya* (saint), *ṣaum* (fasting) and *halika* (creation) which are found, often in corrupted forms, in many languages in Southern Central Ethiopia.
22. Cf. G. W. B. Huntingford, 1965; U. Braukamper, 1980, pp. 91f.
23. The best source is the history of the wars of Aḥmad ibn Ibrāhīm by his lieutenant Sihāb al-Dīn; see R. Basset, 1897.

several times the size of the comparatively small populations of the Islamic states.

A war with the state of Adal, provoked by the Christians, and initially successful wars in the Chercher area during the reign of the weak Emperor Lebna Dengel (1508–40), who appears to have lacked all leadership qualities, seemed to herald no more than another indecisive conflict between the two adversaries. But the fortunes of war suddenly changed. In the decisive battle of Šembera Kure (1529) on the western edge of the Chercher Mountains, the Ethiopian empire lost not only a whole army but also a considerable part of its ruling élite. 'Until this time the (Christian) country had never been laid waste or overrun by the enemy', writes the Ethiopian chronicler, in great pride and great distress in the imperial annals.[24] The consequences were to be fearful. Until 1543, Islamic armies swept over the Ethiopian Highlands, in the south and the north, each dry season, systematically defeating and subjugating one province after another. In southern and eastern Ethiopia, in Hadiyya and Bālī, the population went over to the Muslims, for they often shared their religion and greeted them as liberators from the yoke of Christian rule. In the old Christian provinces, especially the regions inhabited by the Amhara and Tigrai, the population was given the choice of accepting Islam or being put to the sword so that often whole districts converted – if only nominally – to Islam. Churches and monasteries were ruthlessly plundered and sacked and their treasures destroyed or given to the Islamic army if they consisted of sacred gold or silver objects or costly fabrics. Many of the treasures of Ethiopian literature and painting, miniatures in books or murals on church walls, were destroyed and such relics which by chance escaped destruction can today give only a rough idea of the achievements of those creative and productive centuries. Each dry season another province was conquered and destroyed. In 1531 Dawāro and Shoa, two large, densely populated provinces in the southeast and in the heart of the Ethiopian Highlands, were subjugated. Amhara and Lasta, two of the empire's central provinces, followed in 1533. The same year Ethiopia's most important holy place, Axum, with the Maria Zion cathedral where the emperors were enthroned and the Tablets of the Law from Mount Sinai preserved, was razed to the ground. (The Tablets were saved and later brought back to Axum where they are still to be found today.)

But even in the most desperate times, the steadfastness of the Christian people and the strength of the concept of the Holy Ethiopian Empire were apparent. Those forcibly converted to Islam abandoned their new faith the moment the Islamic armies withdrew. (The Ethiopian Church later organized a penitential and reinstatement ceremony for these temporary apostates.) Similarly, the conquered provinces soon rose against their new masters. Even the weak Emperor Lebna Dengel, continually on the run,

24. R. Basset, 1882, pp. 103f.

did not submit when forced by the victorious Islamic general to take a grave decision:

> Maḥammad Grañ sent a messenger to the Emperor to say to him: Give me your daughter to wife and let us make a pledge of friendship. If you do not follow me, there will soon be nobody to whom you can flee. The Emperor answered him: I will not give you my daughter, for you are an unbeliever. It is better to trust in the might of the Lord than in you, for His power is as great as His mercy. He gives the weak strength and the strong He makes weak. Thereupon the Emperor was hunted and pursued by hunger and sword. He was plagued by misfortunes such as cannot be imagined.

Lebna Dengel died a hounded fugitive, in 1540, in the impregnable monastery-citadel of Dabra Damo in Tigré. But within a few years an unforeseeable change had occurred in the political situation. The accession to the throne of the young Emperor Galawdewos (Claudius), one of the most outstanding figures in Ethiopian history, was followed in quick succession by the extraordinarily rapid restoration of the Ethiopian empire, the arrival of the Portuguese expeditionary corps (and with it the Portuguese mission) and, finally, the decisive defeat of the Muslims.

By the sixteenth century, Portugal had reached the peak of its imperialist expansion. The Indian Ocean and its inlets had become a Portuguese sea. Portuguese fortresses, which were never completely subjugated, sprang up on the coasts at Hormuz, Oman, Socotra, Mombasa, and so on. Like Spain, its rival for world conquest, Portugal was enjoying its golden age, albeit brief, and the zenith of its cultural development. Certainly the riches of three continents were flowing into Portugal, but they were bought at the cost of the enslavement of countless people, the destruction of whole cultures and appalling bloodshed from which it took the Portuguese people generations to recover. They had overestimated their own strength.[25]

It was an historical accident, but one that was to have far-reaching and long-lasting effects, that, in 1541, brought a Portuguese fleet into Massawa which, at that time, still belonged to the Ethiopian empire, and that Portuguese soldiers joined battle on the Ethiopian side. Ethiopia was no unknown quantity for Europe. Since the fourteenth century it had been identified with the empire of the legendary Prester John, a Christian ruler in the 'third India', whose existence remains a myth to this day. For centuries attempts were made to find him and win him as an ally against the oriental enemies of Christendom, whether Mongols, Arabs or Turks.[26] Official Portuguese missions had already twice visited Ethiopia to form an alliance between the emperor, whom they quite gratuitously called Prester John, and the Portuguese crown. The first mission (1487) was not allowed to return to its homeland, but Francesco Alvares, chaplain to the second

25. C. Verlinden, 1971, pp. 86f. and 114f.; H. Kellenbenz, 1971, pp. 123f.
26. F. Zarncke, 1876–9.

(1520–6), left a remarkable account soon afterwards translated into many European languages so that Europe was well-informed about the Christian Empire.[27]

In 1540 a Portuguese fleet was sent from Goa in India to the Red Sea to combat the growing expansion of the Turks who, after the conquest of Egypt, were gaining ground in Arabia and even in Sudan. Part of the fleet anchored at Massawa in the spring of 1541. Soon after, the *Baḥar nagāš* (sea-king), governor of the northernmost province of the Ethiopian empire, appeared bearing letters and requesting support for the Christian state in its fight for survival. By July 1541 a volunteer corps of 400 Portuguese, under the leadership of Cristóvão da Gama, one of the younger sons of the famous Vasco da Gama, had marched into the Ethiopian Highlands. Their modern combat tactics and, above all, their superior fire-arms, made them formidable opponents for the Muslim occupation troops in northern Ethiopia. A growing number of Ethiopian volunteers accompanied the Portuguese who inflicted severe defeats on the hitherto invincible army of Imām Aḥmad Grañ in two battles. By invoking the *djihād* and the common cause of Islam, the *imām* nevertheless succeeded in obtaining decisive assistance in the form of new types of artillery and sharpshooters from the Turkish commanders in the Yemen. Before the Portuguese could link up with the emperor's army they were forced to engage in a third battle and were defeated. The Portuguese commander was captured and, when he refused to adopt Islam, executed. Fortune nonetheless favoured the Christians. The imperial army and the remaining Portuguese joined forces and, in February 1543, the Muslim army was destroyed on the plateau to the east of Lake Tana. The *imām* was killed by a Portuguese bullet and his troops went to pieces. Whether it was Portuguese assistance that tipped the balance in this long-drawn-out war is uncertain. From a purely military point of view this may well have been the case in the final battles as their tactics and their guns had restored a certain strategic equilibrium. What was to be of greater consequence for Ethiopia, however, was the Catholic mission that followed the Portuguese soldiers (see below). The Muslim forces were no doubt strong enough to conquer Ethiopia militarily but too weak to keep the two great peoples, the Tigrai and the Amhara, under control permanently – particularly as they did not succeed in forcing Islam on the Christians. After 1543 the Christians emerged victorious from the struggle and, during the next few decades, the empire succeeded in winning back lost territory. The might of Islam had been broken for centuries to come.[28]

27. The best edition is that of C. F. Beckingham and G. W. B. Huntingford (F. Alvares, 1961).

28. After the terrible last wars between Christians and Muslims during the reign of Galawdewos (1550–9) the Muslim states are not mentioned again in the imperial chronicles.

The Oromo (Galla)

'But', as the Ethiopian chronicler laments, like the prophet Joel, 'that which the palmerworm hath left hath the locust eaten, and that which the Muslim has spared have the Galla laid waste'. Since the middle of the sixteenth century, members of the great Oromo people – hitherto usually known as the Galla, the name bestowed on them by their neighbours – had been penetrating central, eastern and western Ethiopia in ever increasing numbers amounting to a migration. Their arrival, their settlement and their quarrels with other groups already there had far-reaching effects, both political and cultural, and brought about fundamental changes for all north-east Africa. The Ethiopian empire suffered more and longer through the Oromo than the Muslims, and lost many provinces for ever. It was not until about 1700 that some imperial consolidation again took place, and even this did not halt the momentum of the Oromo culture. The Oromo became the largest ethnic group in north-east Africa but, unlike the Amhara or the Somali, they only recently developed a unifying national consciousness. Furthermore, individual Oromo groups were exposed to a variety of cultural and political influences.

There are few ethnic groups in Africa about whose origins and culture so much that is untrue has been written.[29] Although it is still not possible to specify the reasons for the great Oromo migrations, they were not undertaken – as is sometimes stated – to escape the pressure of other peoples. Their own traditions say nothing about the matter except that they started out to seek new grazing-lands for a growing population. The Somali, who are said to have exerted pressure on them, had little contact with them at the time. It is also unlikely that the Somali – split into numerous autonomous groups – would have been a military threat to the Oromo who, at that time, were still united, and drove the well-organized armies and conscripts of the Amhara before them and completely wiped out the Islamic states of south-east Ethiopia.

Notwithstanding the fanciful accounts of Amharic and European authors, who pinpoint their original home as Madagascar, Mombasa or northern Somalia, the Oromo are a true Ethiopian people. This is proven by their whole culture and their traditions. The cool highlands surrounding what is today the province of Bālī were their home, whence they set out on their great migrations into the heart of the Ethiopian Highlands and south, to present-day Kenya and the Indian Ocean.

Equally erroneous are the descriptions of the Oromo as *barbariores barbari* (savages) or primitive cattle-raisers. These originated from proud Amharic historians, and the Amhara generally, who described the Oromo as barbarians, non-Christians (and also non-Muslims), with no sophisticated social strata, no script and no monarchy. The false estimation of the Oromo as primitive cattle-raisers with no farming skills derives from their cattle-

29. Cf. E. Haberland, 1963; A Legesse, 1973; E. Cerulli, 1922.

complex: they had a close emotional relationship with their cattle unknown elsewhere in Ethiopia, that went far beyond economic interest. On their great migrations they were obviously unable to practise any agriculture but wherever they settled they unfolded the full splendour of their culture. They also readily adopted many local cultural elements entering into a close symbiosis with the populations they conquered.

The Oromo were and are a people with a highly developed, sophisticated culture admired by their neighbours. It would be impossible otherwise to explain their political successes, their massive expansion and their capacity to assimilate. How strongly developed this capacity was is evident from the fact that today most Oromo do not stem from true Oromo stock but belong to Oromo-assimilated groups. Their spread was partly the result of a chain reaction in the face of their military superiority, and because of their much-admired social organization other ethnic groups voluntarily joined them. It was particularly true of members of the great ethnic group between Harar and Gurage, the Hadiyya, almost all of whom went over to the Oromo. Only the names of their ethnic groups and a few traditions bear witness to their identity. Many of the Hadiyya who became Oromo are settled in the province of Wallaga.[30]

Oromo culture is marked by several distinctive features. There is the close relationship with their cattle already mentioned. Cattle were not only the basis of their livelihood but the object of emotional and ritual concern. This cattle-complex, with its moral overtones, permeated the whole culture, and the emotional significance of agriculture was by comparison quite secondary. Its roots lay in the Oromo myth of creation which maintains that when God created man, he cried, '*Eh, Kota, abba loni!*' ('Hey, come forth, ye owners of cattle!').[31]

Like the Somali, the Oromo consisted of numerous genealogically connected groups and clans which, as the population increased, tended to break away and form new, politically independent groups. Borana and Barentu (or Baraytu) were the mythical ancestors and founders of the two halves of the original stock that bore their names. After the migrations began, these became large genealogically kindred units embracing many sub-groups. The Barentu made their home mainly in the east, while the Borana (not to be confused with the Boran on the Kenya border) settled in the south, centre and west. Towards the end of the last century, when the Oromo were defeated by Emperor Menelik and incorporated into the Ethiopian empire, they split into more than eighty politically independent groups of various sizes.[32]

Of still greater importance for the social and political organization of the Oromo was the *gada* system, classification by age groups based on an abstract numerical principle. The *gada* was a central institution that ruled

30. U. Braukamper, 1980, p. 152.
31. J. L. Krapf, 1858, Vol. I, p. 267.
32. Cf. the map at the end of E. Haberland, 1963.

the life of the Oromo with an exclusivity unknown among any other people. Nothing was not subject to its rules: birth, baptism, marriage, circumcision, emancipation from paternal authority, permission to beget and bring up children, conscription for war and for hunting, obligation to kill and to sacrifice, civil death by exclusion from the system, burial, the style of adornments, hairstyles, clothing, furniture and ceremonial trappings, the installation of house and kraal and more. It represented the sum total of the laws by which life was governed. Forty years after his father had done so, each Oromo, regardless of his actual age, had to enter the children's class. Ideally he had to pass through ten classes, each of eight years, during his lifetime. All those entering a class together formed a *gada* group, which remained an insoluble warrior fraternity for life. Specific rights and duties were associated with membership of a certain class, and the activities of each class – apart from social and religious regulations – were in keeping with the corresponding age-group. The fifth and sixth classes constituted the leadership and warrior class. As it was a community of free men with equal rights, there was no hereditary hierarchy. The leader of the ethnic group, who usually took the name of *abba gada*, was elected from among the members of the fifth class (*gada* or *luba*). He was supported by the *hayu* (judges), also elected from his class, and by other dignitaries. Of decisive significance for the military aggressiveness of the Oromo was the *gada* rule that at least once during the eight years of the ruling *gada* class a fighting and killing expedition had to be undertaken. The ideal of the hero as successful killer and hunter was common to all the peoples of north-east Africa. Only one who had distinguished himself as a brave warrior and hunter and had killed enemy warriors or dangerous big game, such as lion, elephant, buffalo or rhinoceros, could occupy a position of eminence in the community. To achieve this, the Oromo was prepared to make sacrifices and risk his life in the wild to win the coveted trophies. The warrior had the right to wear the killer's adornments which included ear-rings, feathers and butter for his hair and phallic forehead ornaments. Nowhere in north-east Africa was the killer-complex so integrated into the system of society as among the Oromo. As the rules demanded of each ruling *gada* class a fighting and killing expedition, every eight years the Oromo warriors burst upon their neighbours who, until they came to understand the *gada* system, remained perplexed and helpless in the face of these cyclical episodes. Many of the Oromo's neighbours – the Sidama, Darasse, Burgi, and all members of the Konso group[33] – saw the *gada* system as a strengthening of military might and adopted it in somewhat modified form.

The Oromo religion was one of remarkable solemnity. Belief in a god who was creator and heavenly father took Old Testament forms. The Oromo possessed a rich treasure of oral literature, both sacred and profane,

33. For the *gada* system see: Ad. E. Jensen, 1936, pp. 315–82; E. Haberland, 1963, pp. 167–223, 308–21, 380–97, 451–75; A. Legesse, 1973; S. Stanley and D. Karsten, 1968; and C. R. Hallpike, 1972, pp. 180–221.

including prayers and invocations to the deity but also lyrical love poetry.

In their early migrations at least, the Oromo had one advantage other than their military prowess: they were advancing into regions virtually depopulated or only thinly settled after fifteen or so years of fierce warfare between Muslims and Christians. This was particularly true of central Ethiopia, today the province of Shoa, through which the Islamic armies had marched every year on their way north. Once densely populated, central Shoa had become an uninhabited wilderness, which as late as 1800 was still scarcely settled. After 1530 the warriors of the Mudana *gada* group crossed the Wabi river; after 1538 the Kilole group devastated the adjacent area to the north, the predominantly Muslim-populated country of Dawāro and, still further north, the lowlands of the Hawaš river; after 1546 the Bifole invaded the province of Fatagar; and after 1554 the Mesale destroyed the greater part of the Islamic state of Adal. At this time the Oromo became acquainted with the horse and soon became renowned horsemen.[34]

Meanwhile the wars between Christians and Muslims continued. Amīr Nūr, the brave and gifted successor of Imām Aḥmad Grañ, made a last heroic but fruitless attempt to revive the *djihād* against the Christians; and even though Emperor Galawdewos fell in a battle for which the Christians were ill-prepared, Muslim might rapidly declined.

Catastrophic for Christian and Muslim alike were the attacks of the Harmufa group of Oromo (1560–70). They invaded the provinces at the heart of the Ethiopian empire which were just beginning to recover from the devastation of the *djihād*: Angot, Amhara and Bagemder, where the armies of the new Emperor, Minas, confronted them. At the same time other Oromo groups again attacked Adal, where there was famine and plague, Amīr Nūr himself falling victim to it. Except for a few small groups who fled to the Awsa Oasis in the Afar desert, and the inhabitants of the city of Harar, which was protected by its high walls, the Muslims disappeared from this part of Africa for several centuries. When Emperor Minas died, a third of the Ethiopian empire was already permanently settled by the Oromo.[35]

But this was not the end of Oromo expansion. Even before 1500, other groups had already moved out from the highlands around Bālī into the endless savannahs to the south and, in their constant search for new and more extensive grazing-lands for their cattle, had finally reached the Indian Ocean at the mouth of the River Tana. These were the Guği, Boran and Orma. In the centre the Arusi established themselves in the vicinity of the former state of Bālī; and pushed their borders westwards until they reached the Bilate river in 1880. The Barentu spread over the area of the earliest Islamic states of Fatagar, Dawāro and Adal. The fortified city of Harar and – thanks to the Oromo's religious tolerance – the famous pilgrimage centre of Šek Hussen survived as Islamic islands. Numerous small groups

34. A. W. Schleicher, 1893, p. 20.
35. See Fig. 24.3; cf. V. Stitz, 1974, p. 80.

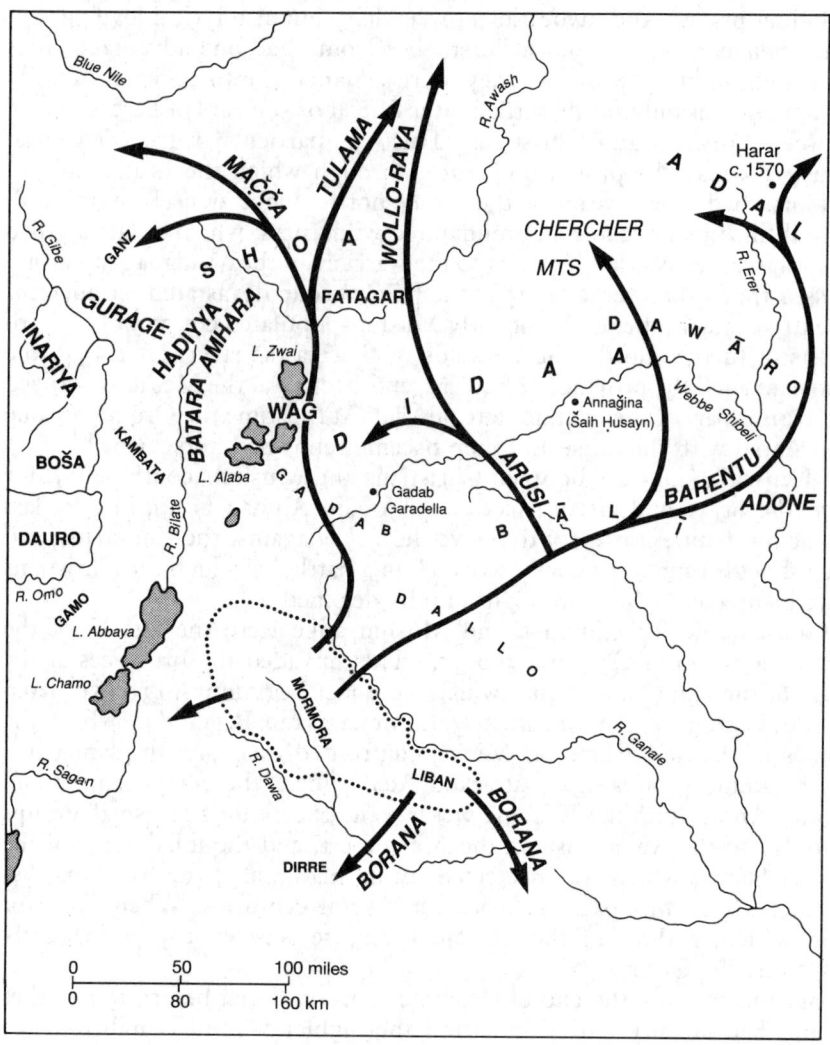

FIG. 24.3 *Oromo migrations in the sixteenth century (after E. Haberland)*

of the so-called Tulama Oromo settled in Shoa. Only in the hot, easily defended lowlands, in the gorges of the great rivers and on a few tablelands did pockets of Amhara hold out: in Moret, Marhabete, Tagulat, Wagda, Manz, Geše, Efrata and Gedem. From these places they gradually climbed onto the tablelands again, and it was from here, around 1700, that the reconquest of the former Christian areas began under Nagasi, a descendant of a collateral branch of the Solomonid dynasty. The Wollo and Yeǧǧu

Oromo spread over the fertile provinces of Angot and Amhara, once inhabited by Christians now confined to Amhara Saynt. Although they soon adopted the local Amharic language, because of their conversion to Islam the Oromo remained sworn enemies of the Christians. Other Oromo occupied the fertile lowlands to the east of the Ethiopian Highlands as cattle-raisers. These were the Karayu, Ğile, Artuma, Rike, Raya and Azebo.[36]

At the beginning of the seventeenth century, a last wave of Oromo, consisting of several groups mainly belonging to the large Mačča family, pushed westwards into what are today the provinces of Wallaga and Ilubabor, stopping only when they reached the western slopes of the Ethiopian Highlands. We know little about the early history of the western part of this region. It was probably only sparsely settled, by small groups of Sudanese farmers whose survivors are the Gunza–Gumuz still living there today, and by members of the Gonga group (see below) of whom the Mao–Afillo and the Šinaša have survived. The situation was quite different in the east and south of this region. Here the Oromo came upon well-organized, densely populated kingdoms in close contact with the Ethiopian empire to the north and whose populations were partly Christianized. Supported to some extent by the Ethiopian empire, they put up a stubborn resistance. But because of the vigorous Oromo expansion, communications between the empire to the north and its dependencies in the south-west weakened parallel with the decline in the strength of the empire. Thus Boša and Guman disappeared from the political map and became the Oromo dominions of Gimma and Gumma. The indigenous substratum remained so strong here that the Oromo took over much of their culture, in particular the state constitution and the monarchy, while the *gada* system gradually disappeared. Inariya, famous for its gold treasures, was the last of these states to fall, defeated by the Limmu Oromo. After 1700 its king fled to the south, where the other Gonga kingdoms of Kaffa and Šekko and the many Ometo kingdoms held their ground against the Oromo, thanks to the natural strongholds provided by their terrain, and even expanded to some extent[37] (see below).

The Somali

The penetration and expansion of the Oromo in central, eastern and western Ethiopia was reflected in both Christian Ethiopian and European writings. During the same period, if not earlier, another great people – the Somali – began an expansion which had comparable significance for large sectors of the eastern part of the Horn of Africa. Written sources say little about the rise of the Somali who, stimulated by the *djihād* of Imām Aḥmad

36. See the map at the end of E. Haberland, 1963.
37. F. J. Bieber, 1920–3; H. Straube, 1963, pp. 274f.; W. Lange, 1980, *passim*.

Gran, now began to play an active role in the history of north-east Africa.[38]

The Somali country of origin is generally taken as the area north of where they live today. From there they spread – probably from the eleventh century onwards – south and west. As early as the thirteenth century, Arab geographers tell of Somali settlements in the area of Merka, to the south of the city known today as Mogadishu. As cattle-rearing nomads, the Somali were driven by the pressure of increasing population to seek new grazing-lands in the direction of the Ethiopian Highlands, and they probably reached the eastern edge of the Harar plateau about 1500, coming into contact with the Islamic states there. Names and genealogical data left by the chronicler Šihāb al-Dīn suggest that they played an important role as supporters of Imām Aḥmad Gran's *djihād*.

To date, the stimulating and unifying effect of the Arab–Islamic influence exerted by the towns on the northern and eastern coasts of Somali country and the Islamic states in south-east Ethiopia (Adal, Dawāro, and so on) has been greater on the Somali than any other north-east African people. Islam became an integrating element in Somali culture, in sharp contrast with its effect on other culturally related Kushitic peoples, such as the Oromo and the Hadiyya. The intensity of the Somali's faith was constantly strengthened by the missionaries who drifted in from Arabia. These became the holy men and founding fathers of the Somali people, such as the famous Ismā'īl Gabarti from whom many Somali are descended.

This Arab–Islamic cultural influence also gave the Somali a sense of cultural superiority and strengthened their assimilation capacity in relation to the other mainly kindred groups in the huge area between Ogaden and Lake Turkana. Here a whole series of different ethnic groups, mainly of Kushitic language and culture and all dependent on cattle-rearing activities, had formed before the advent of Islam. As the existence of the Rendille proves, the Somali had taken part in this process before their great north-east–south-west migrations. Whether this area had once been populated by a negroid, possibly Bantu people is doubtful. It is more likely that groups racially different from the Somali, such as the Adone on the upper Shebele river, the Shebeli and Makanna on the middle Shebele and the Gobawoin on the upper Juba, owe their existence to isolated historical processes. We know for certain, for example, that the Gosa on the lower Juba are the descendants of former slaves from East Africa who banded together there to form free communities.[39]

It is extraordinarily difficult to pinpoint individual stages in the expansion of the Somali and their assimilation of other groups because many

38. Unfortunately we still know very little about the history of this important people at that time, especially in the interior of the Horn of Africa. Certainly a better knowledge of the oral traditions and the historical events connected with the genealogies is needed. Historical research should be an urgent matter for Somalia. Still the best works are E. Cerulli, 1957–64 and I. M. Lewis, 1955, pp. 11–55; 1961, pp. 1–30.

39. V. Grottanelli, 1953.

groups which attached themselves to the Somali nation deliberately suppressed all reference to their former ethnic differences and assumed a
Somali genealogy. The most important groups that merged into the Somali
in this way were the Sab (Digil, Rahanwein, and so on) and possibly some
of the Hawiyya. There is still a whole series of ethnic groups in the Somali–
Oromo border area who now describe themselves as Somali but were
formerly considered to belong to the Oromo (the Gurra, Garri, Gabra and
Sakuya) and who provide an instructive example of cultural transfer and
assimilation. Today a single family tree unites all Somali with each group
having its place within the common genealogy.[40]

Under the influence of Islam the Somali culture changed, especially in
the south. (The northern Somali, the Issa for example, still preserve
many elements of the common East Kushitic culture.) The Somali thus
differentiated themselves more than any other group from the large family
of north-east African peoples, linked by many common historical, cultural
and – not least – geographical factors. The influence exerted by the
geographical environment is by no means to be underestimated. Apart
from the Afar who, in the desolate wastes of their homeland, had little
opportunity for cultural development, the Somali are the only inhabitants
of north-east Africa whose territory consists exclusively of dry savannah
and semi-desert. This ecological environment caused them to develop a
completely different type of culture from that of other north-east African
peoples, who are mostly highland-dwellers. Thus the *gada* system, so
important to most East Kushites, either never gained a foothold with the
Somali or was given up under the influence of Islam.

The Ethiopian empire's struggle for survival, 1529–1632: the Portuguese episode and the restoration of Empire after 1632

Between 1529 (the start of the *djihād*) and 1632 (the beginning of the
Restoration) the Ethiopian empire was struggling for survival. It was a
dramatic period not only in political and military events. It was also a time
of intense intellectual and cultural conflict, an age in which ideas from
another continent stirred up revolt and civil war but also stimulated both
the culture and the Ethiopian Church. Compared with the 100 years of
intellectual and political stagnation between 1755 and 1855, this period
appears extraordinarily active and lively.

The Christian Empire – or its two great peoples, the Amhara and the
Tigrai – showed astonishing strength and capacity for survival in the face
of pressure from external and internal enemies. It was during the time of
Emperor Sartsa Dengel (1563–97) when – as in the last years of the reign
of Lebna Dengel – the empire was more a fiction than a political reality,

40. I. M. Lewis, 1961, pp. 127–95.

that the spiritual strength of the concept of the Holy Empire was forcefully demonstrated. The Turks were consolidating their power on the shores of the Red Sea, seizing all Ethiopian ports and penetrating deep into the Highlands to Tigré; in the central provinces of Bagemder and Samen a bitter civil war was being waged against the Ethiopians of Jewish faith; and the Oromo had not only overrun and destroyed the south-eastern tributary states and cut the empire off from its western and south-western dependencies, but also periodically invaded Bagemder and Gojjam (Godjam, Gojam) and settled permanently in originally Christian heartlands such as Angot, Wallaka, Amhara and Shoa. Real state power may have been reduced to the area the emperor occupied with his troops, but the immortality of the 'evangelical Empire' was apparently never in doubt. This at least is how it appears in the imperial chronicles, our main source of information. It was also this ideology that prevented the empire from disintegrating altogether towards the end of the 100 years' anarchy between 1755 and 1855.

Moreover, the importance for the empire's political survival of the disappearance of the Islamic states and culture from eastern and central Ethiopia as a result of the fearful upheavals of the *djihād* and, above all, through the Oromo migration, can scarcely be overestimated. In the centuries to come Islam was to pose no serious threat.

The empire did, of course, suffer considerable territorial and ethnic losses in this struggle for survival. Finally, at least as from the Restoration of 1632, the great southward thrust of the empire – indeed the whole imperial policy of the preceding centuries – while not officially renounced, was scarcely pursued. As the imperial power steadily declined, efforts were concentrated on maintaining stability at the centre, and no particularly noteworthy or successful political or military action was undertaken. The transfer of the emperor's residence to Gondar in 1636 is a sign of this withdrawal. Before this the emperors – in a country where towns were unknown – had moved their encampments of tents to a different place every year or half year. This had been a hard-and-fast rule, followed even when there was no political or military necessity for undertaking a journey or change of residence. Although the Ethiopian chronicler says that 'the Emperors moved from province to province until the hour of their last sleep'[41] they were not permanently on the move from one end of the empire to the other. Often the residence remained in one region, at the hub of the empire, for long periods apart from short moves. Thus the rulers of the Zagwe dynasty (twelfth and thirteenth centuries), who followed the Aksumite kings, established their residences in Waǧ and Lasta. The first Emperor of the Solomonid dynasty, Yekuno Amlāk (1270–85), resided mainly in the province of Amhara; Emperor Zera-Yakob (1434–40) preferred north-eastern Shoa (Dabra Birhan); Emperor Lebna Dengel (1508–40) had pitched his camp in south-eastern Shoa when the Portuguese

41. J. Perruchon, 1893, p. 149.

mission arrived; and Emperor Galawdewos (1540–59) finally had an important residence in Munesa in the Wağ district of what is known today as Arusi. It was therefore not just a break with this tradition but also a symbolic renunciation of former dynamic imperial policy, when Fasiladas built a fixed residence in Gondar in 1636 after the last great civil wars of

PLATE 24.1   *The castle at Gondar, the Ethiopian capital built by Emperor Fasiladas*

religion had ended. Gondar was to remain the centre of what was left of Christian Ethiopia until 1855.[42]

Thus between 1529, the start of the *djihād*, and 1597, the death of Emperor Sartsa Dengel and the beginning of the civil wars, Imperial policy was concentrated on defence against external and internal enemies. Emperor Galawdewos carried on the struggle against the Muslims, in particular those in the state of Adal–Harar, with great success. Broad areas of the south, Dawāro and Wağ, were reunited with the empire, although they were shortly to fall into Oromo hands. Former contacts with the south-west were renewed, the influence of Christian–Amharic culture was restored there and the Oromo driven back, at least temporarily. Under the leadership of Amīr Nūr ibn Muğahid, the brave and politically gifted successor to Ibrāhīm Grañ, the Adal–Harar Muslims, despite fearful famine

42. Monti della Corte, 1945.

and epidemics which ravaged large sections of an already decimated population, once more attempted to confront the Christian Empire. Although the poorly prepared Ethiopian army was beaten back in an attack on Adal in 1559 and Emperor Galawdewos fell on the field of battle, this marked the end of Islamic power. Within a few decades the Islamic states and Islamic culture had disappeared from this region. There remained only the fortified town of Harar and the small sultanate of Awsa, in the Hawaš river-delta oasis, protected by the surrounding wastelands.[43] Galawdewos' successor, Emperor Minas (1559–63), had mostly to fight the Turks who, from their bases in the Red Sea ports at Massawa and Suākin, tried repeatedly to establish a foothold in the Ethiopian Highlands. Sartsa Dengel (1563–97), Minas's son who acceded to the throne while still a child, spent his short life and his relatively long reign in uninterrupted campaigns heading in all directions. Although the Oromo, constantly growing in numbers and strength, never presented so serious a threat as the armies of the *djihād*, they allowed the empire no peace.[44]

Wars of frightful violence were waged to annihilate the Ethiopians of Jewish faith in the northern Highlands, mainly in Samen, Waggara, Dambiya, Belasa, Sallamt and Sagade, where formerly they had had their own chiefs and enjoyed a certain autonomy. Their forefathers had probably been converted to Judaism by Jewish missionaries as early as pre-Christian times. Unlike Jews in other parts of the world, they were completely integrated into the culture in which they lived, so much so that their holy books (the Old Testament, for example) were not written in Hebrew but in Ge'ez, the Ethiopian literary and liturgical language.

It is not known why this religious war broke out at the very time when the empire was already hard-pressed by external enemies. The Jews were faced with the choice of embracing Christianity or being exterminated. The description of these wars, like that of the extirpation of the Christians by the Muslim armies of the *djihād* a generation earlier, is one of the darkest chapters in Ethiopian history. Despite their heroic courage, which went as far as self-destruction, the Jewish population was practically wiped out as the majority refused to be converted. The few survivors were stripped of their civic rights and their land expropriated. They were therefore forced to become artisans and the word Falasha came to be synonymous with smith, potter, carpenter or weaver, indeed with any type of skilled labourer. Despite the importance of these occupations, a stigma was attached to them in a society whose ideal was the free and independent man who never worked for a wage. Thus social degradation went hand-in-hand with religious persecution.[45]

43. P. V. Paulitschke, 1888; E. Cerulli, 1931, 1936, 1942; E. Wagner, 1979.

44. The chronicle of the Emperor Sartsa Dengel relates only wars. C. Conti Rossini, 1907.

45. W. Leslau, 1951, gives an exhaustive bibliography on the Falasha. Cf. J. M. A. Flad, 1869.

It is astonishing how the Ethiopian empire found the strength, despite three generations of furious and unrelenting struggle, to confront not only the Turks in the north, the Adal Muslims in the east and the Oromo in the south and centre but also, in massive campaigns in the south-west, to force the large states of Inariya, Boša and Kaffa (Gomar) to become once more closely linked to the Ethiopian Church and northern Ethiopian culture. The compiler of the *History of the Galla* (probably the Court Chaplain to Emperor Sartsa Dengel) when chronicling this important campaign merely reports laconically that, during a campaign in the south-west, the Emperor was unable to bring the Dawe Oromo to battle because they had withdrawn.

> As he was unable to fight against flesh and blood, he decided to fight against the Devil and captured the souls of the peoples that men call Inariya, Boša and Gomar. They were told: 'Become Christians!' and they did so, and were baptized with the Christians' baptism.[46]

The writer of the imperial chronicle, however, devotes many pages to the mass baptism. His eye-witness account vividly shows the Amhara's conviction of their mission and their superiority as purveyors of the Christian faith and the imperial concept. Sartsa Dengel offered to halve the Inariya tribute on condition that all became Christians. Under the pressure of the Most-Christian Emperor, but also mindful of the support to be expected against the Oromo, whose strength was constantly increasing, King Badančo of Inariya decided to be baptized. The ceremony was performed with great solemnity for the king and all his people together. The Emperor of Ethiopia himself, 'the new Apostle, the new Constantine, who closes the temples of the idolaters and opens churches', became the King of Inariya's godfather and his elders the godfathers of the Inariya nobles. The baptism ceremony was performed by the highest church dignitaries of the Ethiopian court. It is no mere panegyrizing when the chronicler, himself a monk, cries,

> Oh, how great was the joy of the Christian Emperor this day for the souls of the believers who received baptism on the same day. Come, let us gladly take our Emperor Sartsa Dengel and praise him: Teacher of peoples, you who obey the Christian Law, not through fear of the sword, but in the hope of attaining the Kingdom in Heaven.[47]

Following the ceremony and the presentation of robes of honour and finery to the Inariya, the Emperor proclaimed the Church rules and gave the country 'orthodox teachers', priests and deacons who entered the Church founded by King Badančo, now christened *Zamaryam* (belonging to Mary).

46. C. Conti Rossini, 1907, pp. 140f.; A. W. Schleicher, 1893, p. 31.
47. C. Conti Rossini, 1907, p. 144.

Shortly thereafter the king of the neighbouring Boša was christened George. These events, which took place shortly before 1600, represent the swan-song of imperial expansion, never to be repeated in this form. (Despite brave resistance, Inariya was conquered by the Oromo in 1710, the king fleeing with some of his people to Kaffa in the south). We can conclude from oral traditions still surviving among south-west Ethiopian peoples that the contacts thus made during the time of Sartsa Dengel had a particularly lasting and stimulating effect on southern Ethiopia and its cultural development.

Of far greater consequence for the existence of empire, however, was the almost century-long ideological conflict with the Catholic Church from 1542 to 1632.

With the creation of the Society of Jesus (the Jesuits) in 1540 the Catholic Church acquired an extremely effective instrument not only for carrying on the fight against the Reformation in Europe, but also for converting the 'heathen' and recovering the 'heretical' Christian churches not subject to the dogma and authority of Rome. Apart from the mission to India, China and Japan, led by no less a figure than Saint Francis Xavier, the recovery of the Church of Prester John was also considered important. Even before 1540 letters had been exchanged between the Portuguese kings and the Ethiopian emperors and these contacts were now seized upon. The decisive factor was, of course, the presence in Ethiopia of members of the Portuguese expeditionary force who had remained behind, and their families. Following the extraordinary episode of one João Bermudez (who had accompanied the second Portuguese mission (1520–6), some say as a barber, and later returned to Ethiopia claiming to be the Roman Patriarch for Ethiopia, ordained by the Pope), in 1557 Andrea da Oviedo was consecrated bishop and sent to Ethiopia with some other Portuguese Jesuits to prepare the work of reinstatement – that is, the union of the Orthodox Church with Rome. His discussions with Ethiopian clerics and, more particularly, with Emperor Galawdewos, brought no advantage to the Catholic faith in Ethiopia but did provoke a brilliant exposé of the Ethiopian Christian faith through the mouth of the Emperor, which has gone down in history as *haymanota* Galawdewos (Galawdewos' profession of faith).

Here a voice is raised for the first time in Africa pointing out that Christianity is a religion without limitations of time or place, about which no people and no continent can claim that its own interpretation is the only true path. At once self-assured and tolerant, the African Christian here confronts the European. He puts him in his place when, for example, he shows that certain customs and practices of the Ethiopian Church are neither 'heathen' nor 'Jewish', but have their origins in Ethiopian folk culture, just as European culture has found expression in European Christendom. He says

With regard to circumcision we Ethiopians do not have ourselves circumcised like the Jews, for we know what Paul, the fountain-head of wisdom, said of it ... Circumcision is practised among us simply as a custom of our country, just as the Nubian people score their faces or the Indians pierce their ears. Thus we do it, not in order to follow the law of Moses, but out of human habit. ... And as regards eating [i.e. the ban on eating] pork, this occurs so that we can observe the law of Moses like the Jews. We do not abominate anyone who eats pork; we do not consider him unclean, but if someone does not eat it, we do not force him to do so. ... Some prefer to eat fish, others fowl, and others eat no mutton. Let each follow where his heart is inclined, even as men's inclinations and wishes are different. ... To the pure all things are pure, and as Paul says: he who really believes may truly eat all things.

This document also discusses the Ethiopian Christians' practice of keeping Saturday holy by celebrating Holy Communion and *mahabbar* (*agape* – a 'love-feast' connected with the Lord's supper) on that day.[48]

Under Emperor Sartsa Dengel the Jesuits were given Fremona, near Adwa in Tigré, as their centre. There they were allowed to live in complete freedom and – not without success – to engage in missionary work. Oviedo died in 1577 and it was many years before there was a successor to lead the mission, for the Turks controlled the Red Sea ports and seized all Portuguese who came there. It was not until 1603 that Pedro Paez, a Spaniard, took over the mission after a dangerous journey lasting several years. Of all the European missionaries of the time he was undoubtedly the most important and also an outstanding and tolerant human being. Hence during his time the Ethiopians carried on the most stimulating theological discussions. The challenge forced the Ethiopian Church out of its customary lethargy into a period of debate and active struggle among the most lively in Ethiopian Church history. To reach the people, the Church carried on and recorded the religious discussions in Amharic. This ceased after the Restoration of 1632 with the reintroduction of the official Church language, Ge'ez, which was as little understood by the mass of the population as was Latin by the European peasants of the time. The fruitful effect of this contact, however, was short-lived and the constructive debate soon turned into open enmity between Orthodox and Catholic factions.[49]

Literary production experienced a remarkable upsurge and the works written at this time, mainly theological and historical, are among the most important in Ethiopian literature. Theological works that may be mentioned are the *Fekkare Malakot* (Explanation of the Divinity) which

48. H. Ludolf, 1681, Vol. III, ch. 1.

49. The abbreviated chronicle remarks laconically that during the reign of Susenyos: 'he had revolted for the sake of the Francs' (i.e. the Catholic faith); 'the people perished in Wag by reason of the Francs'; 'he perished by reason of the Francs', etc. See R. Basset, 1882, pp. 129f.

discusses the problem of the knowledge of God; the *Mazgaba Haymanots* (Treasury of Faith) which, like the *Sawana Nafs* (Refuge of the Soul), summarizes the arguments of the Orthodox clergy in favour of the Monophysite belief, or the all-embracing *Haymanota Abaw* (Faith of the Fathers), translated from Coptic Arabic and serving the same purpose. Walatta Petros was a nun who died in 1644 after spending most of her life struggling against Catholic dogma. The vivid story of her life and suffering is an important record of this turbulent period. For the reinstatement of those Christians who had temporarily embraced Islam, the *Mashafa Keder* (Book of Impurity) was written in connection with the atonement rites and the *Mashafa Nesseha* (Book of Penance) was translated from the Arabic.[50]

An author who occupied a special position was Enbakom (Habakuk), an Arab Muslim converted to Christianity who rose in the Ethiopian Church hierarchy to the rank of *abbot* of the famous Dabra Libanos monastery and became *eččage*, leader of the Ethiopian clergy. The remarkable book *Ankasa Amin* (Gates of the Faith), a defence of Christianity against Islam, in which quotations from the Ḳurʾān are constantly used as evidence for the truth of the Christian faith, is from his pen. Furthermore, with the translation of *Barlaʾam and Josaphat*, Enbakom made an important work of Eastern literature accessible to the Ethiopian people. It was also perhaps he who translated and adapted the *Song of Alexander* (*Zena Eskender*) the effect of which on the whole of Ethiopia was much more important than is generally supposed.[51]

The three works or Annals concerning the reigns of the Emperors Galawdewos, Sartsa Dengel and Susenyos and the short *History of the Galla* by the monk Bahrey are also to be numbered among the important literary productions of this period. (Bahrey may also be the compiler of the Chronicle of Sartsa Dengel.) These works are characterized by their lively presentation, individual style and strong personal involvement, and also by their authors' awareness that they are writing as representatives of the empire.[52]

Emperor Sartsa Dengel had appointed his brother's grown-up son, Za Dengel, as his successor, as his own son, Yaʿekob, was still a child; but his widow together with some influential dignitaries, managed to set Yaʿekob on the throne. Revolt and civil war followed. Za Dengel finally won but he was rash enough to make an over-hasty alliance with the Catholic mission and the Portuguese in the country, who were still to be reckoned with, and to announce his devotion to the Pope. Thereupon the *abuna* (the metropolitan of the Ethiopian Church) released the subjects from their oath of allegiance and excommunicated the emperor. Civil war broke out again, Za Dengel fell in the battle, and Yaʿekob was reinstated until finally a great-grand-nephew of Sartsa Dengel, Susenyos, succeeded in becoming

50. E. Cerulli, 1968, pp. 145f.
51. E. Cerulli, 1968, pp. 125f.; L. Ricci, 1969–71 and 1971.
52. J. Perruchon, 1893; C. Conti Rossini, 1907; A. W. Schleicher, 1893.

emperor, thanks to his superior political and military abilities, and in re-establishing peace and order.

The accession of Susenyos (1607) marks the beginning of the final decisive phase of the confrontation between the Ethiopian Orthodox Church and the Catholic Missionary Church. In the first five years of his reign Susenyos overthrew the most dangerous enemies, both outside the empire and within, in a series of successful campaigns: the few remaining Falasha were extirpated, the Agaw (the indigenous population of central and western Ethiopia, who had hitherto enjoyed a certain autonomy) were definitively subjugated and, finally, the Oromo were dealt such blows that they remained quiet for a considerable time. The exceptional talents of the head of the Jesuit Mission, Pedro Paez, as theologian, preacher, teacher and architect, had gained him access to the imperial court and, under the influence of his strong personality, the emperor began to incline increasingly towards Catholicism. This inclination was strengthened when the emperor's influential brother, Ras Se'ela Krestos, officially turned Catholic in 1612 and set up a Catholic mission in his province of Gojjam. Despite the remonstrances of the *abuna*, who threatened him with excommunication, in 1622 the emperor himself also embraced the Catholic faith. Pedro Paez died shortly afterwards.[53]

The confrontation between the two doctrines and civilizations, hitherto carried on with intellectual weapons and mutual respect, now turned into open war. Alphonso Mendez, the new Spanish bishop sent by the Pope, was the opposite of his tolerant and understanding predecessor. His bigotry and arrogant manner inevitably led to a hostile reaction in a freedom-loving nation which had had close links with its own national Church for centuries. Under the emperor's protection, and with all the relentless logic and intolerance of a Jesuit of his time, Mendez began to set the Ethiopian Church on what he saw as the right path. All Ethiopian priests had to be re-ordained, all churches re-consecrated and their interior decorations altered to fit the European pattern. The calendar was Europeanized; circumcision was forbidden; and all Ethiopians even had to be re-baptized. 'Everything was done in fact that could antagonize not only the clergy but the simple worshipper.'[54]

Two incidents aroused particular hostility: the remains of a highly respected *abbot* were removed from his grave in the monastery church of Dabra Libanos because Mendez felt the body of a schismatic meant desecration; and a woman was indicted for witchcraft after the European pattern. (Until then Ethiopia had remained free of witch trials, the scourge of the early modern age in Europe.)

Revolt after revolt broke out, uprising against the hated new church being particularly fierce in the central provinces of Bagemder, Lasta and Waǧ. The emperor, once so loved, who had brought peace to the land,

53. P. Pais, 1945–6; J. Lobo, 1728; B. Tellez, 1710.
54. A. H. M. Jones and E. Monroe, 1978, p. 97.

now had to subdue his subjects in bloody wars during which the fanatical zealotry of the Jesuits increased tension still further. In 1632 there was another great battle from which the emperor emerged victorious despite fearful losses on both sides. As Crown Prince Fasiladas was riding across the field of battle at his father's side, he pointed at the bodies of the rebels, saying: 'These were once your loyal subjects!' At this the emperor, whose doubts had been increasing, broke down and abdicated. As he did so he issued the following proclamation:

> Hear ye, hear ye! We first gave you this faith believing it was good. But innumerable people have been slain ... and now these peasants. For which reason we restore to you the faith of your forefathers. Let the former clergy return to the churches, let them put in their altars, let them say their own liturgy. And do ye rejoice.[55]

Susenyos died shortly afterwards, a broken man and the Catholic mission came to an end. The people, insofar as they had adopted the new religion, returned in a body to the traditional faith. The new emperor, Fasiladas, had the Jesuits deported and any who remained in defiance of the imperial decree were put to death. The gradually dwindling number of Ethiopians who persisted in the Catholic faith were persecuted and their most prominent leaders, amongst them Ras Se'ela Krestos, were executed. In his endeavour to reconsolidate the empire and eliminate all foreign influence, Fasiladas went so far as to conclude an agreement with the Turkish governor of Massawa in which the governor undertook to kill any European missionaries landing at Massawa in exchange for head money. Thus ended, through the fault of the Europeans, a contact between Africa and Europe that had lasted almost a hundred years, at first enriching and significant, later only negative. The Christian brothers from overseas, originally greeted as friends and helpers, now lived on in Ethiopian memories as 'the wolves from the west'.[56]

The Ethiopian empire now began a period of deliberate isolation from the rest of the world and deliberate stabilization that, by the end of century, turned into stagnation. The establishment of a permanent imperial residence at Gondar, in the militarily secure centre of the empire, was part of this process. Although the great campaigns and migrations of the Oromo gradually died down and many Oromo were assimilated into the Christian Ethiopian civilization, it was no longer possible to pursue an aggressive and dynamic policy from Gondar. There is therefore little political activity to report in Christian Ethiopia during the second half of the seventeenth century. Under Emperor Yohannes (1667–82) the few remaining Catholic Ethiopians were given the choice of accepting the Orthodox faith or leaving the country. There was a certain accommodation with the Muslims still in Christian Ethiopia – mainly *gabarti* (merchants) – who were allowed to

55. R. Basset, 1882, p. 132; A. H. M. Jones and E. Monroe, 1978, p. 98.
56. H. Ludolf, 1681, Vol. III, ch. 13.

practise their religion freely but made to live in separate settlements.

Iyasu I (1682–1706) was the last of the great emperors who fully exercised their power. He undertook the last and unsuccessful attempt to re-establish contact with south-western Ethiopia and even visited Inariya. During his reign there were no internal or external enemies to endanger the empire. The important port of Massawa, although nominally belonging to the Turkish empire and under the control of a Bēdja governor (*nā'ib* of Arkiko), remained open for trade with Ethiopia. Shortly after Iyasu's death, however, internal weaknesses began a disintegration of the empire that degenerated into complete anarchy after about 1755.[57]

During this period intellectual and cultural life flourished for the last time. It was mainly the patronage of the imperial court at Gondar that stimulated the arts and sciences (so that we now speak of the Gondar Period in Ethiopian art). To a greater extent than ever, art and science proved to be the sphere of a small élite, a superstructure rising above the peasant folk culture. It is not possible here to give a complete account of the different aspects of the intellectual life of the period – particularly as the extraordinary richness of cultural achievements has not yet been sufficiently recognized. We shall therefore restrict our remarks to literature, architecture and painting.

In contrast to the previous great century, literature took on a stereotyped, edifying and courtly character, with translations from Coptic Arabic predominating. Worthy of mention are *Faws Manfasawi* (Spiritual Medicine), a devotional book of penance, and the *Fetha Nagast* (Jurisdiction of the Monarchs), a collection of laws and instructions taken from ecclesiastical, civil and constitutional law intended for the use of Coptic communities in Egypt. Despite often being cited by later European writers, this work never achieved any practical significance in Ethiopia. Not only was the translation unusually full of errors and misleading, but the instructions contained in this codex had little relevance to the Ethiopian situation. Finally, this period saw the creation of a great many sacred hymns in praise of the Holy Trinity, Jesus Christ, the Virgin Mary, saints or angels. They had different names according to their metre or the tradition of their origin: *deggwa, kene, malke'e* or *salam*.[58]

The graphic arts, too, are marked by this relationship with court life. The famous rock churches, which are among the most important and original creations of Christian Ethiopian civilization, were still being hewn in the rock at the end of the fifteenth century, not only in the main centres of Wağ, Lasta and Geralta but also in many of the provinces further south. Their exact number is still not known – nor have they been accurately described. This type of construction ceased completely after 1500, pre-

57. The following period until 1855, when Tewodros was crowned is therefore called, in allusion to the Biblical Book of the Judges, (the era of the princes/judges) *Zamana Masāfent*.

58. E. Cerulli, 1968, pp. 162f.

PLATE 24.2 *Eighteenth-century Coptic painting on cloth of the Virgin and Child, Gondar*

sumably because of the religious wars, and was never taken up again.[59] What appeared later, after 1632 in Gondar and a few other places, was something completely different – huge castles, libraries, court chapels and annexes to the palaces of the emperors and members of the imperial family. The forms of these structures often indicate foreign models. Most were probably erected by Indo–Portuguese master-builders who came to Ethiopia in connection with the Portuguese mission from the areas under Portuguese influence around Goa. This also happened in the wake of the expulsion of the Portuguese missionaries after 1632. The gradual decline of the empire, the destruction of the city of Gondar by Tewodros and the dervishes, and centuries of neglect have since completely robbed these buildings of their architectonic finery and their costly interior decoration.

59. R. Sauter, 1963.

PLATE 24.3 *Eighteenth-century Coptic painting on cloth of St George and the dragon, Gondar*

All that remains today is bare walls or ruins which give little idea of the level of civilization at the time.[60] In this Restoration period there must also have been active cultural contacts with India although little is known about them. Thus, for example, the Ethiopian emperor appears in religious pictures in the court dress of the Great Moguls of Delhi.[61]

Ethiopian painting expressed itself mainly in two media: church wall paintings and book illuminations in religious works. (In comparison with these, the relatively few folding wooden altars, despite their high quality, play only a subsidiary role in quantitative terms.) While only little remains

60. Monti della Corte, 1945.
61. For example, on several icons of the Institute of Ethiopian Studies, University of Addis Ababa.

PLATE 24.4   *Eighteenth-century wall painting in the church of Dabra Birhan, Gondar*

of the church murals (paintings on stone or on cotton fabrics stuck onto the walls) before the seventeenth century, many manuscripts date back to the fourteenth and clearly show the development of this type of painting. Ethiopian painting has always been distinguished by two characteristics: its readiness to take up foreign models and stimuli, and its ability to rework these forms into typically Ethiopian creations. Each of the great epochs of Ethiopian history gave rise to quite specific developments in style.[62]

About 1500, book illumination reached a peak that corresponded to the peak of Christian Ethiopian civilization at that time and also to the imperial greatness of the Ethiopian empire. The highly stylized figures show a majestic dignity but also a remarkable depth of feeling. Independently of the text they illustrated, the paintings were intended to move the onlooker

62. Cf. J. Leroy, S. Wright and O. A. Jäger, 1961; J. Leroy, 1967; O. A. Jäger, 1957.

PLATE 24.5 *Eighteenth-century Coptic fresco of hell and the devil, in the church of Dabra Birhan, Gondar*

through the force of their representation and strengthen him in his beliefs. Despite a canon binding on all, these painters nevertheless had great artistic freedom in their execution, so that their individuality is easily perceived.[63] The paintings of the second half of the sixteenth century and the early seventeenth are quite different in character. They reflect the multiplicity of foreign influences now penetrating Ethiopia and are witnesses to the intense intellectual conflict. An illuminating example is provided by the form of the crucifixion adopted by several Ethiopian painters – a copy of the famous woodcut, from the *Small Passion*, by the German painter and illustrator Albrecht Dürer. In 1591 Propaganda Fide in Rome had printed

63. I would like to refer to the unpublished miniatures in the manuscripts of Birbir Maryam (Gamu), or to the paintings reproduced in J. Leroy, 1967, pl. VI–XV.

an *Evangelium Arabicum* to support Catholic missionary work in the East and had illustrated it with many copper engravings, in which they also had recourse to older models, including Dürer. Copies of this work reached Ethiopia in the wake of the Portuguese mission and became favourite models for miniatures.[64] All these pictures bear witness to the remarkable capacity of the Ethiopians for integrating foreign models into their own culture. They are also a lively expression of a turbulent age, characterized by conflict with foreign forms that did not easily fit the style of traditional Ethiopian art.

The pictures of the Restoration, the Gondar Period, finally stand out above all for their courtly elegance and graceful form. (Many of these too are inspired by European models.) They reflect the slowly vanishing splendour of the empire and are painted for a society of courtiers who found delight in their elegant and increasingly conventional forms. They are painted by artists who were integrated into court society. Pictures such as *Christ on the Mount of Olives* represent a peak in the painting of this period with its artistic arrangement of the figures, carefully balanced colours and love of detail. In the so-called Second Gondar Period of paintings, from about 1700, the force of the artistic creation steadily diminishes and finally degenerates into a canon of repetitive forms.[65]

South-western Ethiopia: the emergence of a new culture and new states

We are reasonably well informed about contacts between south-east Ethiopia and the Christian Empire to the north between 1500 and 1700 (and even earlier) from Christian–Ethiopian and Islamic written sources (see above). As early as the first half of the fourteenth century, the Hadiyya, who at that time still inhabited the Chercher Mountains and the area to the south thereof, were named in the Ethiopian imperial legend, the *Kebra Nagast*. The Chronicles of the Emperors Amda Seyon (1314–44) and Zera-Yakob (1434–68) are full of accounts of conflicts with the Islamic states in the east and south-east.[66] The situation is quite different, as regards written sources, with the west and south-west – the area now occupied by the provinces of Wallaga, Ilubabor, Kaffa, Gamo–Gofa and the western and south-western parts of Shoa and Sidamo–Borana. It is true that the famous songs in praise of particular fifteenth-century emperors mention the names of peoples and states that then paid tribute to the Ethiopian empire. But we cannot be certain that they are identical with the peoples and states of the same name in the nineteenth century as names changed and migrations brought names to very distant regions. The most important names men-

64. H. Buchthal, 1960.

65. Cf. O. A. Jäger, 1957, pl. 17 and 18; J. Leroy, 1967, pl. LIX and LX; E. Hammerschmidt, 1977, pp. 121–7, 138–50 and 151–5.

66. Cf. G. W. B. Huntingford, 1965, *passim*; J. Perruchon, 1893, *passim*.

tioned were: Inariya, Boš(a) Zenğaro, Kambat(a) Ennamor, Ḳuččạ, Zergo, Walamo, Gamo, Halaba, Gudela, Wağ and finally Damot and its king Motolomi (or Motilami).[67]

How much influence Christian Ethiopia actually had beyond political domination and exaction of tribute cannot be determined from these texts. More significant is the semi-mythical life story of St Takla Haymanot (early fourteenth century) in which it is described in detail how she went to Damot to baptize 'King Motolomi'. It is possible that the 'King' element was not actually a title. Also, it has not yet been established where Damot was – it might have been Wolamo (Wolayta), as oral tradition has it. As a name given to districts and mountains, Damot occurs frequently in southern Ethiopia.[68] Although Emperor Zera-Yakob (1434–68) led or sent military and missionary expeditions to southern Ethiopia, the surviving texts of his Annals say almost nothing about them. His name, however, lives on today in the oral traditions of the Ethiopian south and, sometimes in the garbled form '*Zerako*', has become a synonym for 'Emperor'. The Chronicle of Emperor Galawdewos only briefly mentions activities in the south. The final note is sounded by the remarkable description of Sartsa Dengel's expedition to Inariya (see p. 727).

But what were the real consequences of these military, religious and cultural contacts between north and south? The oral traditions surviving in the Ethiopian south today provide a wealth of historical information which has unfortunately still not been fully recorded. Family trees, analyses of cultures as a whole and archaeological findings also give valuable clues to these events and their consequences. They prove that northern influence on the south was so far-reaching as to cause the emergence of a new culture.

The cultural situation in southern Ethiopia before the fifteenth century, when influence began to be exerted by the north, can only be deduced today, for want of other possibilities, from the picture of cultural conditions of ethnic groups in the outer fringes of the Ethiopian oecumene, who remained untouched by this influence until recently. Among these are the different groups of the Gimirra, Ari or Dizi peoples. States and sophisticated political institutions are still lacking here today. Only the steadily growing stimulus provided by the Christian Empire to the north was able to bring about decisive changes. Before this a great number of small and very small clan groups must have lived side-by-side in the south, held together by nothing more than the sharing of a common language and culture, recognition of a common lineage and, finally, perhaps veneration of a high priest or elder, who embodied the sum total of the religious affinities of the group. He was surrounded by a certain religious aura by virtue of his descent from the first man and founder of the group whose birth was surrounded by propitious omens. He was credited with supernatural powers, mainly expressed in those functions that were most important to

67. E. Littmann, 1914.
68. West of Gojjam in Wolayta, in Ğanğero, in Basketto, in Koyša (Kaffa).

the peasant community, namely power over rain and food-plant growth, successful crops and rich harvests. Compared with their overriding religious significance, the political functions of these dignitaries seem to have been unimportant and often almost non-existent. Many would have had difficulty in enforcing their will and imposing sanctions. (Significantly, words for 'command', 'punish' and 'decree' are still lacking in the linguistic usage of many groups in southern Ethiopia.) These dignitaries were, of course, the undisputed symbol of their community but the real holders of political power were the clans and their leaders as autonomous, originally self-contained units. It was here that the real decisions over war and peace, right and wrong, were made.[69]

The conquerors from the north with their rigid concepts of state and kingship swooped down upon this unsophisticated world of simple peasants. Conquest and assimilation often proceeded comparatively peacefully, the people of the south recognizing the cultural superiority of the north. Thus the conquest of what was later to become the important state of Wolayta is supposed to have happened as follows: in the year 1600, a Tigrai noble, Mika'el, came south in the wake of one of the last great campaigns of the Ethiopian Emperor Sartsa Dengel. He was accompanied by armed horsemen and Christian priests. According to the legend he crossed a raging torrent by dividing the waters with his staff, like Moses, and arrived in the as yet small land of Wolayta, where he married the daughter of the chief. Upon the death of the chief, which followed shortly and of which his descendants have unpleasant tales to tell, Mika'el usurped the throne. The Wolayta rose against him and he would soon have been defeated, despite his bravery and his use of cavalry hitherto unknown to the Wolayta, had he not resorted to a ruse. This ruse is a perfect illustration of the intellectual superiority and political shrewdness of the invaders. In the battles, which took the form of individual actions involving small groups, instead of throwing spears at their opponents the northerners threw fabrics (weaving was then unknown to the Wolayta), strings of beads or pieces of meat. 'If you are so rich and powerful that you can throw away such treasures', the Wolayta cried, 'then shall you also rule over us!' Thus the invaders took possession of Wolayta which under their influence, soon changed its character completely and from a land of insignificant peasant folk became a dynamic, aggressive state.[70]

It was often accepted without question that monarchically-led states, whose warriors were better armed and possessed cavalry, originally unknown in the south, were superior to the democratically organized communities. There are therefore reports of groups voluntarily surrendering to the northern invaders and accepting the leaders as their new rulers. There are even reports of people expressly praying for a prince who

69. H. Straube, 1957.
70. E. Haberland, 1965, pp. 260f.

would establish a new dynasty and found a new state.[71]

In this way a whole series of new states of various sizes came into being, states that were never to forget their links with the north, whose ruling classes faithfully preserved and developed the traditions and institutions of the north, and whose kingdoms and general structure have reflected the great model of the north to the present day.

In addition to the purely external, formal structure of state organization and court life, the state myth of the Ethiopian empire also made its mark. This involved the claim that they were the chosen people and theirs the true kingdom, and the associated claim that they were able to subjugate and assimilate all neighbouring peoples. The history of southern Ethiopia, as it is known from 400 years of oral tradition, is the story of the great expansion of these newly created states which widened their spheres of domination at the expense of independent democratically organized smaller groups and often contributed to the founding of new dynasties among their neighbours. This process worked in a chain reaction. Thus, according to oral tradition the first Gonga state, Inariya (or Hinnaro), was founded before 1500 by an immigrant from Tigré (Kaba Seyon). The conversion to Christianity of Inariya by the Ethiopian Emperor Sartsa Dengel has already been mentioned (see pp. 727–8), but the founders of Inariya had presumably already been Christians and their followers had only temporarily accepted the faith of their rulers. Inariya maintained its contacts with the Christian Empire as long as possible, remaining Christian until it collapsed under constantly growing Oromo pressure. In the sixteenth and seventeenth centuries, members of the Busaso dynasty of Inariya founded further dominions: Boša, which was absorbed into the Oromo kingdom of Gimma in the nineteenth century; Kaffa, which is reputed to have been the most important and powerful state in all south-eastern Ethiopia for generations, and finally Šekko (Močča) in the virgin forest on the western edge of the Ethiopian Highlands. Further groups of Gonga, or their ruling élite, pushed northwards where they probably founded Bizamo now vanished in Wallaga. Traces of them remain in the Afillo–Busase to the north of Dembidollo and the Šinaša settled along the Abbay.[72]

Oral tradition has it that the Kingdom of Gangero was originally founded by Islamic migrants from Arabia, hence its name *Yam gor* (Yemen land). Later an originally Christian dynasty from Gondar assumed rule. Similar accounts survive concerning the area occupied by the Ometo peoples: in Dawāro another group of migrants priding themselves on their Gondar origin succeeded, after years of struggle, in uniting many small groups of indigenous inhabitants into a powerful state.

About 1600 Wolayta was conquered by the descendants of one šum Tamben from Tigré. Other states, both large and small, such as Kučča, Uba, Zala, Dorze, Amarro and Eli, have similar traditions. Members of

71. E. Haberland, 1959, p. 197.
72. W. Lange, 1980; V. L. Grottanelli, 1940 and 1941.

the Gošanaa dynasty, probably also of northern Ethiopian origin, founded a total of ten dominions (Gofa, Doko, Balta, Basketto, Oyda, Gozza, Gayla, Abba Malo, Konto and Koyša). As late as 1800 or so, a member of this dynamic family, Gobe, succeeded in founding the Kingdom of Konta in the no-man's-land between Kaffa and Dawāro. Some of the former ruling families of the Dizi (Maği) in the far south-west can also trace their origins back to immigrants from Tigré.[73]

In southern Ethiopia the social structure was originally characterized by the coexistence and mutual acceptance of free and equal people. Only religious leaders, such as clan elders or rain priests and warrior heroes, occupied a certain but not unduly privileged position. But in the newly-created states under the influence of the hierarchical concepts of the Christian north things were quite different. Equality was replaced by a complicated hierarchical system of ranks. At the summit stood the revered king, inaccessible and often invisible to his subjects and surrounded by special ceremonial laws. His hallowed family enjoyed special privileges, as in High Ethiopia, often occupying the most important state offices, such as district governor or chief justice. The exaggerated pomp and ceremony of the royal households, often in flagrant disproportion to the small size of the country and population, is reminiscent of the megalomania of the European baroque princes who tried to reproduce Versailles in miniature. In Amarro (Amhara), one of the southernmost of these kingdoms whose total population never exceeded a few thousands, there were hundreds of different state and court offices representing nothing more than honorary titles. These titles, such as *abeto* (highness), *mikirečˇo* (royal counsellor), *gabirečˇo* (page), are without exception borrowings from the Amharic. As the kingdoms expanded, so did the royal households, developing into independent, powerful institutions with hundreds of members. They were in sharp contrast to the former high priests or clan leaders who had lived by their own labour and that of their families and voluntary gifts from others.

The dimensions a royal court could attain is illustrated by Wolayta to the north of Lake Abbaya. Here the royal court was not only the centre of political life but also a sacral district, protected by a multitude of ritual and ceremonial laws. If the king appeared in public, it was only at a proper distance from the crowd or surrounded by his followers. The protection of the royal court with its three ramparts and three gates, each one triply secured (this too was the classical High Ethiopian pattern), was entrusted to the members of specific castes (hunters, potters, tanners and smiths) who watched the entrances, fetched water and firewood, guarded prisons and treasuries, and each morning and evening played the large instruments (drums and trumpets) reserved for the king, to announce that sun and ruler had risen or retired. While entry was more or less unrestricted by day, by evening all except the king, his wives and his pages had to leave the

73. E. Haberland, 1980.

PLATE 24.6 *Fourteenth-century (?) former church bell from Tigré (?) used as a sacral ox-bell by a Dizi chief in south-western Ethiopia*

743

PLATE 24.7   *The walls of Wolayta, southern Ethiopia*

hallowed district. The dignitaries and court servants withdrew to their houses against the ramparts of the royal enclosure. Only the king could slaughter animals on the soil of his hallowed residence or indeed exercise the second most important right for all Ethiopians: any kind of sexual activity. Therefore the pages who took direct care of the king's person, washed his clothes, cooked his food and served him, were sexually innocent, forbidden just as strictly as the pages of the Christian Ethiopian emperor to leave the royal court and come into contact with other people. They were pseudo-children, from respectable families, who were replaced when they reached age at which their sexual purity became questionable. The ground covered by the royal court was so hallowed that sexual intercourse between a man – other than the king as master of the house – and a woman would have resulted in the death of the offenders and the transfer of the palace to a new site.

It was not only the palace precincts, the officers, ranks and ceremonial that were given a completely new content and dimension under northern influence: even the most revered royal insignia with whose possession royal dignity was associated, were transformed. These had formerly been symbolic objects, simple in material and form, such as sacred spears, two-pronged forks, grass rope, and so on. Their place was now taken by rings, mostly finger or arm rings, fashioned in the two precious metals, gold and silver, which were the mark of royalty in High Ethiopia. They were known

744

everywhere by the Amharic words *wark* (gold) and *birr* (silver).

This High Ethiopian influence was not confined to the introduction of new offices and institutions but had far-reaching effects on the whole social structure. Although most southern Ethiopians were members of a single homogeneous class, which we might call freemen, a sophisticated system of ranks developed after the High Ethiopian pattern which found its most marked expression in the worth-complex that extended over all Ethiopia. Worth was not inheritable like riches or a respected name (although this was not without significance), but had to be earned anew by every man, so that he could find his publicly recognized place in society. The central concepts were success in war and big-game hunting, and the warrior's obligation to kill. Political ability as judge or leader, or self-made riches were only secondary considerations. Only a person who earned worth could aspire to one of the innumerable elected offices, the holding of which was the decisive criterion for a man's status. Name and rank were often designated by the same word, and to lack a name was synonymous with social failure. It must have been the endeavour of every man to hold office at least once, even for a short period (office-bearers were elected yearly). The official kept the name – or title – of his rank even after the office had changed hands.[74] Here again the influence of the north is obvious, for the names of the ranks are borrowings from the Amharic or Tigrai languages, such as *dana* or *dayna* (judge from the Amharic *danya*); *guda* or *goda* (master from the Amharic *geta* or the Tigrai *goyta*); and *rasa* or *erasa* (head or chief from the Amharic *ras*). The further from the north, the weaker the recognizable forms of the worth-complex until, among the southernmost of the vestigial groups still living in the Ethiopian Highlands, they disappear altogether.[75]

The free peasants were followed in the hierarchy by the artisans, who were members of specific castes and who occupied a comparatively low position. Despite their great economic importance – they wove garments, produced ceramics, forged tools, weapons and ornaments and tanned hides – they were nevertheless looked down upon. They could own no land, and were subjected to defamatory regulations, and physical contact with them was considered to be defiling for people of higher birth.[76]

In the lowest position came the slaves who, in many countries, made up more than a third of the total population. Most lived as serf-like peasantry on their masters' fields, with farms and property of their own. It was their labour and their productivity that made possible the formation of a rich dominant class which, in Wolayta for example, was the driving force in the great wars of conquest.

All these states had well educated administrators, elected by the people and confirmed in their positions by the king. The states were divided into

74. E. Haberland, 1965, pp. 187; H. Straube, 1957.
75. Ad. E. Jensen, 1959.
76. E. Haberland, 1964b.

communities, districts and provinces. They had public markets, supervised by the state, and were criss-crossed by a network of well-built roads. They were protected against external enemies by great ramparts and walls with carefully guarded gates.

The material advances brought from the north to the south since the fourteenth century are many. Curiously enough the plough, the most important agricultural implement in the north, has for some reason never gained acceptance in the south. Although its principle was known to many peoples, it was not used. Agriculture is, however, indebted to the north for a considerable number of crops. It was probably not until after the four-teenth of fifteenth century that peas (*Pisum sativum*), broad beans (*Vicia faba*), chickpeas (*Cicer arietinum*), onions (*Allium cepa*) and garlic (*Allium sativum*) reached the south. Later came lentils (*Ervum lens*) and various oilseeds including linseed (*Linum humile*), sesame (*Sesamum indicum*), safflower (*Carthamus tinctorius*) and nogo (*Guizotia abyssinica*) all from the Near East. These, however, played as unimportant a role in the diet of the population in general as the fruits from the East, brought into the country from Arabia *via* Harar and limited to specifically Islamic centres: lemon (*Citrus limonium*), banana (*Musa paradisiaca*) and peach (*Prunus persica vulgaris*). Of great importance later were the plants of the New World brought from America to Africa in post-Columbian times, probably by the Portuguese. Of these, red pepper (*Capsicum conicum*), maize (*Zea mays*) and tobacco (*Nicotiana tabacum*) are of such significance today that it is hard to imagine life in southern Ethiopia without them. The pumpkin (*Cucurbita maxima*), sweet potato (*Ipomoea batatas*), potato (*Solanum tuberosum*) and tomato (*Solanum lycopersicum*) spread to a lesser extent.[77]

Even today the techniques used by the descendants of the artisans from the north still bear witness to the impetus they gave this sector: treadle-loom weaving (associated with the cultivation of cotton), goldsmithing and silversmithing with sophisticated tools (blacksmithing was and still is practised using stones), leather-work with needles and fine woodwork for the production of door panels, wooden platters and large bowls. (Wood-turning or indeed, the use of rotary operations of any kind in handicrafts, including the potter's wheel, was unknown in both north and south Ethiopia until recently.) Finally, the introduction to the south of the horse should be mentioned, although it was without economic significance, being used only in battle and as a prestige symbol.

Let us now turn to the influence of Christianity: was it strong enough to have a permanent effect on the south and provide a long-term, lasting drive, or did it disappear after emperor and troops, bishop and missionaries had withdrawn? Even today it is clear that the cultural influence was very strong, its vestiges still being visible as far as the borders of Kenya and Sudan and perhaps even beyond. Apart from external tangible mani-festations, Christianity had a great impact on the moral system of the

77. W. Kuls, 1958, pp. 32f.; H. Straube, 1963, pp. 26f. and 288f.

individual folk cultures, on customs and usage and spiritual life in general. This type of transformation can often only be recognized with great difficulty.

The most striking Christian monuments in this area, by no means rich in durable man-made works, are the many sacred groves, mainly on hills and mountain tops, marking the sites of former Christian churches as their names indicate: *Kitosa* (Christ), *Mairamo* (Mary), or *Gergisa* (George). A survey carried out by the author proves that south-west Ethiopia was once dotted with a multitude of Christian churches. The materials used to build them were perishable and all have disappeared. However, their sites are still regarded as sacred and the descendants of the former Christian priests, who have become members of non-Christian clans, still perform sacrifices to the god in heaven and the god of creation and other ceremonies that are variants on the sacrifice of the Mass. In the turbulent centuries that followed the Christian mission to southern Ethiopia, the new generations of priests could not go to northern Ethiopia to be ordained by the *abuna* – the only Ethiopian bishop. The expansion of the Oromo set up a broad barrier between the empire to the north and the colonial territories in the south-west, so that the south was gradually cut off.

How strongly Christianity as a religious entity, not just as a collection of rites, influenced the essence of the southern Ethiopian religious ethics has not yet been thoroughly investigated. Neither has there been a satisfactory analysis of Ethiopian Christianity's understanding of itself. Enough has been written about official dogma but little on the views of peasants and peasant priests on their faith. Such an investigation should also consider the problem of the exceptionally important role of Mary in Ethiopian Christianity, a role that relegates Jesus Christ to the background. The function of Mary as a helpful and forgiving deity, particularly well-disposed towards women, can be seen in both north and south Ethiopia.

As regards external forms, an astonishing number of vestiges of Christian laws and ceremonies survived in the south until recently, when the Ethiopian Orthodox Church began another mission. Fasting on specific days (even if not every Wednesday and Friday as in northern Ethiopia) survived, with people abstaining from food until midday and then from animal food, including milk, butter and eggs, until midnight. The Sabbath was also observed with all work in the fields prohibited at least for the successors of former Christian priests. The seven-day Christian week, regulating the frequency of markets, continued to be observed instead of southern Ethiopia's original four-day week. Christian Sundays have now become public holidays on which the *kesiga* (successors of the Christian priests) gather their congregations together and in mutilated ritual invoke God, Christ and Mary, make the sign of the cross, burn grain instead of incense and use any other available vestiges of Christian paraphernalia. Neither were the great Christian holidays forgotten, especially the Feast of the Holy Cross (27 September) which became the New Year feast, with the exorcising

747

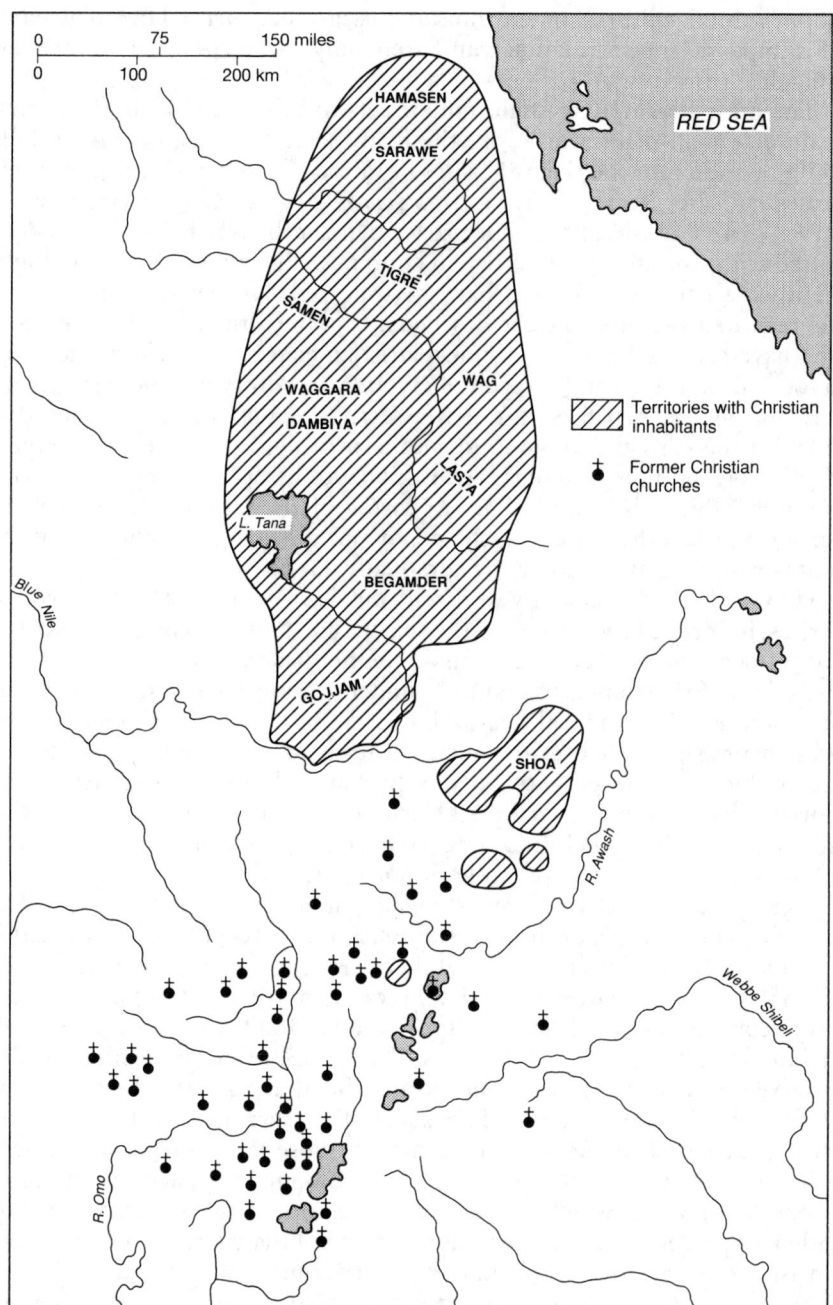

FIG. 24.4   *Christianity in north-eastern Africa, c. 1700 (after E. Haberland)*

of devils and a great, exuberant folk festival where everyone received gifts of meat and new clothes. Christmas and Epiphany, of such importance in the north, were celebrated only by a few groups in the south, while Easter, remarkably, became the day of the great ritual hunt.

East Africa: the coast

A. I. SALIM

The sixteenth, seventeenth and eighteenth centuries opened with the advent of the Portuguese[1] to East African waters and closed with the attempts by the Omani Arabs to establish some kind of overlordship on the littoral. In between these two prominent milestones, the coastal towns and peoples experienced important – at times revolutionary – economic, social and political changes. Some towns fell from great heights; others rose from obscurity to prominence; many disappeared for ever; and only a few maintained significance throughout the three centuries. The ebb and flow in their fortunes can be attributed to many factors, of which Portuguese intervention is but one, albeit important.

The coast at the beginning of the sixteenth century

In 1500, the coast was still enjoying its 'Golden Age' as shown by the surviving ruins and material culture of the fifteenth and sixteenth centuries. Prosperity was reflected in the stone buildings and increased population in the thriving 'stone-cities', 'with their elaborate sanitation and their narrow courts . . . the taste for many beads, the common use of porcelain'.[2]

This is the overall picture: a closer look reveals differing degrees of economic and material well-being. The prosperity of the island state of Kilwa, which was growing in the fifteenth century, was levelling off if not declining, on the eve of Portuguese intervention.[3] Kilwa had owed much of its efflorescence to the control of the Sofalan gold trade which it had wrested from Mogadishu in the late 1200s or early 1300s. Its trade, until the advent of the Portuguese, had been sea- rather than land-oriented. There is no documentary or archaeological evidence for any overland trade routes linking Kilwa Kisiwani and the gold-producing region of southern Zambezia.[4] The only trade the island state seems to have had with the mainland, prior

---

1. For Portuguese primary sources, which are numerous, consult C. R. Boxer and C. de Azevedo, 1960; R. Oliver and G. Mathew, 1963; E. B. Martin, 1973 and E. A. Alpers, 1975a.
2. G. Mathew, 1963, pp. 121–2.
3. ibid., p. 124.
4. E. A. Alpers, 1975a, p. 41.

to the arrival of the Portuguese, was in foodstuffs. By the end of the fifteenth century, however, Kilwa had lost control over Sofala. Politically too, its influence was declining on the coast to the north, an area important for it commercially. Internally, the rapid succession of rulers – thirteen in the fifty-six years between 1442 and 1498 – was symptomatic of a malaise that sapped its strength and vitality, whilst its hostile relations with Zanzibar reflected a recurrent weakness of Swahili towns – internal factionalism and dissension encouraging intervention by outside forces. This phenomenon was often found in later years in other coastal towns and facilitated Portuguese and, later, Omani Arab intervention and overlordship.

By 1454, Zanzibar was attempting to impose its nominee on Kilwa. At this time, Zanzibar was not, however, a leading coastal town politically or economically. It was itself divided into at least five settlements each with its own ruler. Mombasa, however, ranked with Kilwa and Malindi as a leading city state. By 1500 it had grown enormously. Ibn Baṭṭūṭa had described it in 1331 as having no mainland extension and no native-grown grain, even if it had banana and citrus trees. But by the time Vasco da Gama visited it in 1498, it had become a 'great city of trade with many shops'.[5] Its merchants played an important rôle in the commerce of the southern coast as far south as Angoche. By then, the island town had also established trade links with its hinterland in honey, wax and ivory which may have explained its remarkable and sudden rise until, by the time the Portuguese came, it had become 'the most powerful city-state on the coast'.[6]

Malindi, Mombasa's arch-rival, was also prosperous by 1500. Its trade was based largely on the export of ivory and, secondarily, on the sale of such goods as gold from Sofala, beeswax, ambergris and gum copal. Unlike most other settlements, Malindi, even in the sixteenth century, had large plantations of millet and rice worked by slaves.[7] The earliest Portuguese visitors were impressed by the great variety and quality of its fruits, vegetables and meats and by its attractive lay-out. The fact that Portuguese ships would have been assured of a regular supply of water and provisions may have been behind the establishment of cordial relations with the town.

Further north, petty sultanates were to be found in the Lamu archipelago with three on one island alone, namely Pate, Siyu and Faza. These quarrelled so much among themselves that they found it impossible to present a united front against the Portuguese intruders. By 1500 Lamu had not yet seen its most prosperous times. These came long after neighbouring Manda's days of efflorescence at the end of the ninth century. Lamu town existed on its present site by the mid-1300s, but it was to flourish only

5. Quoted by E. B. Martin, 1973, p. 31.

6. E. A. Alpers, 1975a, p. 45.

7. E. B. Martin, 1973, p. 30. Portuguese sources do not mention the existence of any appreciable slave trade south of the Somali coast during their presence. Vespucci, on whom Martin relies as a source for the presence of slaves in Malindi, states that they were from Guinea.

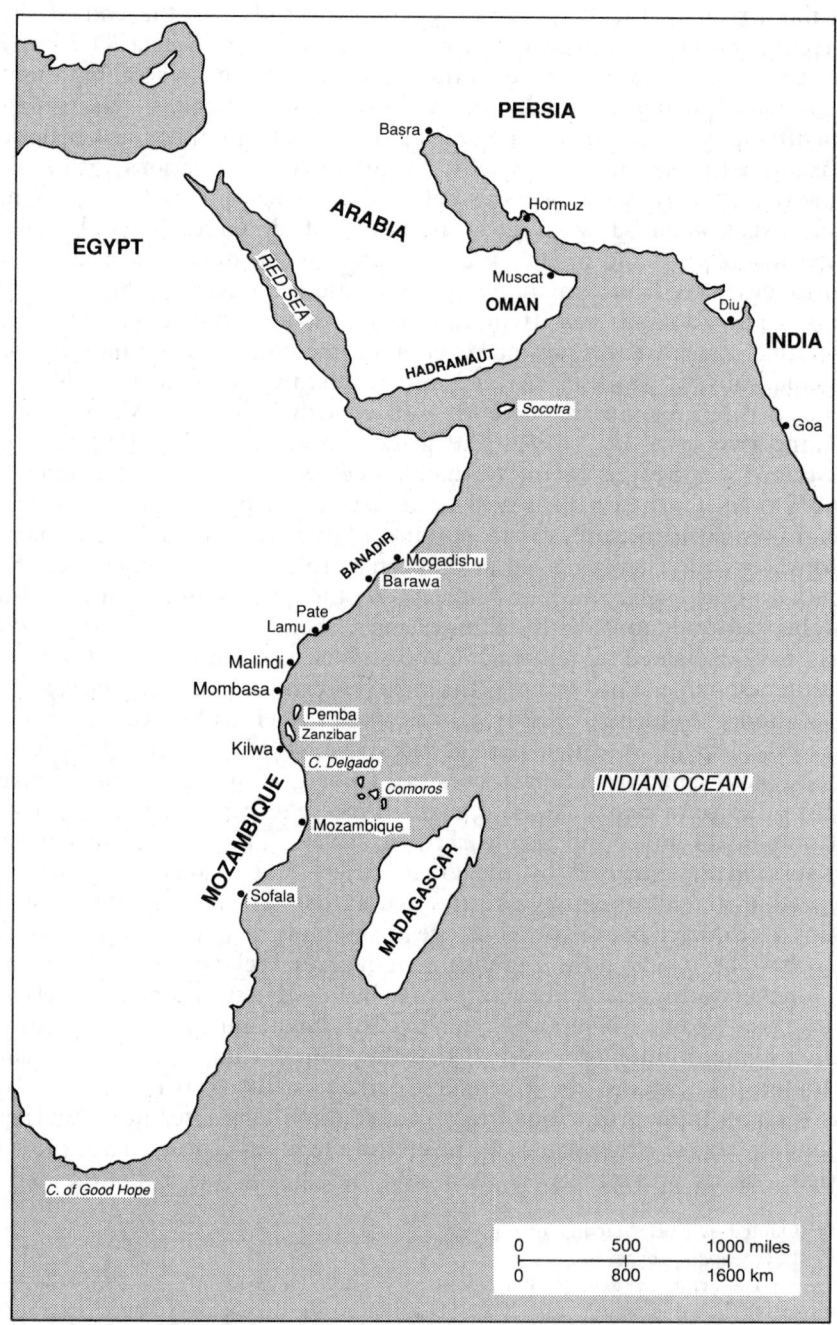

FIG. 25.1   *The western Indian Ocean basin (after A. I. Salim)*

after 1650. Like Kilwa, it was probably founded by immigrants from the Middle Eastern region of the Muslim empire.[8]

In between these largest, most commercially prominent settlements were numerous smaller ones, interspersed among them and often falling within their spheres of influence. Thus Kilwa had some control over the Mafia islands and Mombasa enjoyed a similar rôle regarding Mtangata and Vumba. The larger towns looked more towards international maritime trade than the smaller which depended on agriculture and fishing. The number of East African coastal settlements between the Benadir coast and the mouth of the Zambezi river from the ninth to the twentieth centuries has been estimated at 173.[9] While this estimate is not definite or exact it gives a picture of general trends and development, confirming that the greatest proliferation of settlements (over 100) was between 1200 and 1500, the coast's Golden Age.

It is harder to estimate the size of these settlements in terms of area and population, although, some data are available with which to estimate figures for a few towns. Malindi, for example, is said to have covered a smaller area than it does today and the walled town could not have extended more than 600 metres north–south along the sea front and 240 metres inland.[10] The walled town is dated to 1498, with a population of approximately 3500 based on the occupation of some 1000 stone houses.[11] This obviously does not include the plantation labourers or the poor who probably lived in mud-and-thatch huts. Thus figures can only be rough estimates if not speculative. Mombasa and Lamu enjoyed longer continuous 'stone-town' existences than the other settlements which all suffered temporary or permanent eclipse.[12]

The political fragmentation of the coast was much compensated for by religious and cultural homogeneity well-established since 1500. Ethnically the population was mixed – African, Arab and so-called Shīrāzī blood, intermingled in various degrees to form a new cultural group known later as the Swahili (people of the coast). Swahili is a generic term the coastal people did not apply to themselves until recently. In the 1500s, they merely formed urban groups whose élite and ruling families, for prestigious purposes, often claimed dubious, Arabian or Shīrāzī origins even if they were ethnically mixed. Others chose names that reflected their areas of origin on the coast itself, such as Wachangamwe, Wafaza, Wapate, etc.[13]

While the coast was politically fragmented and its people came from different groups with loyalty to individual settlements, certain factors in its development helped to forge a fairly homogenous culture. The most

8. J. de V. Allen, 1981, p. 1; E. A. Alpers, 1975a, p. 40.
9. ibid., pp. 320–1.
10. E. B. Martin, 1973, pp. 19–20.
11. ibid., p. 28. Kilwa's population was estimated by Vasco da Gama in 1502 at 12 000.
12. J. de V. Allen, 1974.
13. See, for example, F. J. Berg, 1971 and 1968, pp. 35–6.

important was the common African denominator and the Kiswahili language that was soon to evolve into a *lingua franca* for the entire coast. Other important influences were the Islamic and, to a lesser degree, the Arab factors, although the latter only became dominant in the nineteenth century. The infusion of Arab and Shīrāzī blood into a predominantly African, probably Bantu society must have contributed to ethnic and, with the rise of Islam, cultural differentiation on the littoral.

There is no denying the profound impact Islamic culture had on the coast. In J. de V. Allen's words:

> The advent of Islam had a profound and long-lasting effect upon Swahili culture. It must have introduced a whole new set of cultural and religious dimensions to the concept of urbanisation: henceforth townsmen, or at least some of them, were to be marked off by religion as well as other factors. ... Nor was it only in religious learning that Islam would have an impact. The Muslim World between the tenth and fifteenth or early sixteenth centuries, enjoyed a more advanced knowledge of science and philosophy, a more sophisticated technology and better building techniques, and a higher standard of civilisation generally than any other part of the world. The Swahili coast was now, so to speak, plugged into this source of boundless intellectual creativity – albeit by wires that were somewhat tenuous and occasionally faulty – and received periodic visits from scholars like Ibn Baṭṭūṭa, craftsmen, artists and many others who had contributions to make to the development of Swahili culture.[14]

In fact, Swahili culture and civilization is a regional example of Islamic culture. It is regional because it was influenced by the indigenous East African culture which, to a significant degree, was incorporated into and became an integral part of it. The Swahili language which developed into the *lingua franca* of the coastal people, although it adopted a large number of Arabic words over the years, is the most important single manifestation of that African contribution to Swahili culture. Others include rituals related to birth and marriage, funerary and investiture ceremonies, a belief in spirits and traditional dances. Swahili culture represented 'a fusion, in an urban "melting pot" context, of the values and customs of many people, both from the African continent and from other lands bordering the Indian Ocean'.[15]

The material prosperity of some coastal towns in 1500 was very impressive. The rulers lived in palaces and the élite in stone dwellings, many of which were multi-storied and built around central courtyards. 'The rich houses were embellished with those elaborately carved wooden doors which

14. J. de V. Allen, 1976c, pp. 17–18.
15. ibid.

754

PLATE 25.1   *Carved door, Zanzibar*

were such a striking feature of the old Swahili culture'.[16] The townsmen's high standard of living is reflected in the importation and use of such luxury items as damasks, silks, satins, copper objects, Chinese porcelain, Middle Eastern glass vessels and glass beads. Men from Kilwa, Malindi and Mombasa were seen as far east as Malacca selling East African goods such as gold, ivory, copal and ambergris, and bringing back the cottons, silks and satins which found their way into the various coastal towns through the commercial traffic that linked them. Not all could have lived in luxury, however. The life of the tiny but wealthy minority in the multi-storied stone houses contrasted with that of the poor and servile majority in the mud-and-thatch quarters which were probably in and outside every settlement.

The populations of these settlements were predominantly African, with

16. C. R. Boxer and C. de Azevedo, 1960, p. 16.

initially a tiny minority of Arabs whose numbers increased substantially in the eighteenth and nineteenth centuries. There was also a steadily growing number of people of mixed origin. Rulers may have carried legitimate Arab dynastic names, such as al-Nabhānī, al-Mahdalī, al-Bā-ʿAlawī, but they were invariably of mixed descent and often black.[17] Colour was of no social or political consequence: it was the *ukoo* (lineage, descent) that distinguished someone and indicated his place in society and his degree of belonging.

The Portuguese intrusion

The Portuguese, like their Spanish neighbours in the Iberian peninsula, embarked upon their voyages of exploration with the din of battle against the Muslims still ringing in their ears. The Spaniards did not oust the last Muslims from their land until 1492, only five years before Vasco da Gama reached the East African coast. The motives behind the Portuguese expeditions were to outflank Islam commercially, politically, militarily and religiously – to break Mamluk (later Ottoman) monopoly of the trade routes to Asia and China, to link up with other Christians to eradicate Muslim rule wherever it was found, and, indeed, in the belief that non-Christians possessed no rights to property, to take over all Muslim territories. Pope Martin (1417–31) and Pope Nicholas (1452) had issued their papal bulls to Spanish and Portuguese rulers on the assumption that their expeditions would also serve Christendom.

The man behind Portuguese plans to outflank the Muslims, Prince Henry, was also the Grand Master of the Order of Christ under whose banner he had fought the Muslims in Morocco in the early fifteenth century. Also, in the Maghrib the Portuguese had learnt that Arab Muslims had travelled by sea to Eastern Africa and that Africa could therefore be circumvented, the Muslims there checkmated and their commerce taken over.[18]

A series of expeditions was embarked upon to put into effect this grand plan. In January 1498, Vasco da Gama's fleet reached the southernmost fringes of the Swahili coast at the mouth of the Quelimane river where they found an Afro-Arab settlement that was in touch with the sought-after lands of the East, namely, the island and town of Mozambique which, the Portuguese learnt, fell under the influence of Kilwa. The richly clad *shaykh* there welcomed his visitors until he discovered they were not Muslims after which mutual suspicion led to the first skirmishes between coastal Muslims and Portuguese. Da Gama did not visit Kilwa on this trip because of unfavourable winds. His reception in Mombasa was hostile because news of the Mozambique skirmishes had preceded him. In contrast, the *Shaykh* of Malindi greeted them warmly, either because of a shrewd

17. G. S. P. Freeman-Grenville, 1963, p. 143.
18. J. Strandes, 1968 ed., p. 2.

and far-sighted design to acquire a powerful ally against Mombasa or by an equally shrewd sense of *real-politik* or self-preservation. In any event, both sides remained faithful to the alliance they set up until after Malindi's *shaykh* had acquired Mombasa with Portuguese assistance at the close of the sixteenth century. On da Gama's return journey from India, the *Shaykh* of Malindi sent one of his subjects on board one of the Portuguese vessels as ambassador to Portugal.[19]

Da Gama's first voyage was successful in its objective to reach India. It had also yielded valuable intelligence concerning Muslim trade on the Swahili coast and towns like Mozambique, Mombasa and Malindi had impressed the Portuguese with their material culture. This largely exploratory voyage was followed by others. One, in 1501, gave the Portuguese a glimpse of Kilwa's size and trade but its *shaykh*, Ibrāhīm, would not be persuaded to co-operate with them in establishing a trading agency in Sofala. Only force, the Portuguese realized, could make him change his mind.

The following year, 'to the accompaniment of incessant salvoes, which were intended to spread alarm and despondency,'[20] Vasco da Gama's vessels sailed into Kilwa harbour and, under the threat of the destruction of his town, Ibrāhīm agreed to the payment of an annual tribute and to become a vassal of the Portuguese king.[21] In 1503, Ruy Lourenço Ravasco indulged in plunder and piracy in and around Zanzibar, capturing considerable booty in the form of grain, ivory and silver from ships before landing in Zanzibar and using force to impose tribute. In 1505, on the pretext that it was behind in the payment of tribute and that the ruler had not hoisted the Portuguese flag as a sign of subservience, Kilwa was attacked by Dom Francesco de Almeida, later viceroy of India. Exploiting the factional rivalries and intrigues in Kilwa, de Almeida installed a pro-Portuguese elder, Muḥammad Ankoni, as ruler and, at Kilwa's expense, work was started to build Portugal's first fort on the Swahili coast.

Mombasa had shown hostility towards da Gama in 1498 so it was not surprising that, when de Almeida's fleet sailed into Mombasa harbour on 13 August 1505, it was met by fire from a canon recovered earlier from a sunken Portuguese ship. This canon was destroyed by a lucky hit from one of de Almeida's ships but the King of Mombasa and his people continued their determined resistance. Using rocks and arrows against the Portuguese muskets and cross-bows, the Mombasans, supported by hundreds of mainland African allies, fought the Portuguese in the narrow alleys of the town all the way to the king's palace. Eventually, the two-pronged Portuguese assault on the palace forced the king to surrender. The town was looted and burnt before de Almeida's fleet departed and no garrison was left behind to occupy it. It seems, as Strandes notes,[22] that the Portuguese aim

19. ibid., p. 28.
20. J. Strandes, 1968, p. 40.
21. ibid., p. 43.
22. ibid., p. 64.

was to break the power and prosperity of Mombasa in order to enhance that of Kilwa which was to be their stronghold.

The following year Hoja (or Oja, and thought to be Ungwana), then enjoying relations with Mamluk Egypt, decided to submit to the Portuguese rather than meet a similar fate. But Brava (Barāwa) put up resistance before being overpowered and completely looted by a force some 1000-strong. The casualties of both sides were estimated to be higher than those of any other battle then fought by the Portuguese on the Swahili coast.

Portuguese actions on the East African coast were blatantly punitive and destructive. In 1528 Mombasa was attacked again and occupied for some four months. With no long-term policy or plans for the island (the King of Malindi was not keen to take it over), the Portuguese razed the town once again before withdrawing. During that short occupation the Portuguese had destroyed Mombasa and lost many lives through fighting and disease.[23]

Sixteen years earlier, in 1512, the Portuguese had been compelled to vacate their fort in Kilwa after becoming embroiled in the internal struggle for succession following the death of Ankoni. By then the Portuguese had been made to realize that the town could not produce the tribute they had so rapaciously demanded. The sum that could be extracted barely covered the cost of maintaining a garrison. They had hoped to monopolize the Sofalan gold trade, on which the town and other parts of the coast had thrived, but had only succeeded in disrupting it with their ill-considered behaviour and commercial controls. By 1506, the garrison in Sofala, stricken by disease and death, was no longer functioning and in 1512, the Kilwa garrison was withdrawn and transferred to India.

With the departure of the Portuguese, Kilwa's trade improved significantly although the ruler remained nominally a vassal of the Portuguese crown. The town's commercial pattern underwent an interesting change. Its traders avoided Portuguese-controlled Sofala and, together with traders from Mombasa and Malindi, sought greater contacts with the Angoche coast south of Mozambique which had long-established commercial ties with the Zambezi hinterland. Their aim was to undermine Portuguese control of Sofala; and it was to forestall this that the Portuguese ventured inland to establish themselves at Sena and Tete.

Kilwa had been heavily dependent on the carrying trade of gold and ivory from Zimbabwe as it had little to export itself. Much of the ivory, as well as the gold, had come from Sofala[24] and once Sofala was lost, Kilwa had to develop new trade links with the interior. Ivory became its most important export: 'Effectively cut off by the Portuguese from the gold of Zimbabwe after 1530, it was the Muslim traders of Kilwa who sought to develop the previously insignificant ivory trade with the hinterland of their own town.[25] This re-orientation of Kilwa trade coincided with the

23. J. Strandes, 1968, p. 110.
24. E. A. Alpers, 1975a, p. 46.
25. ibid.

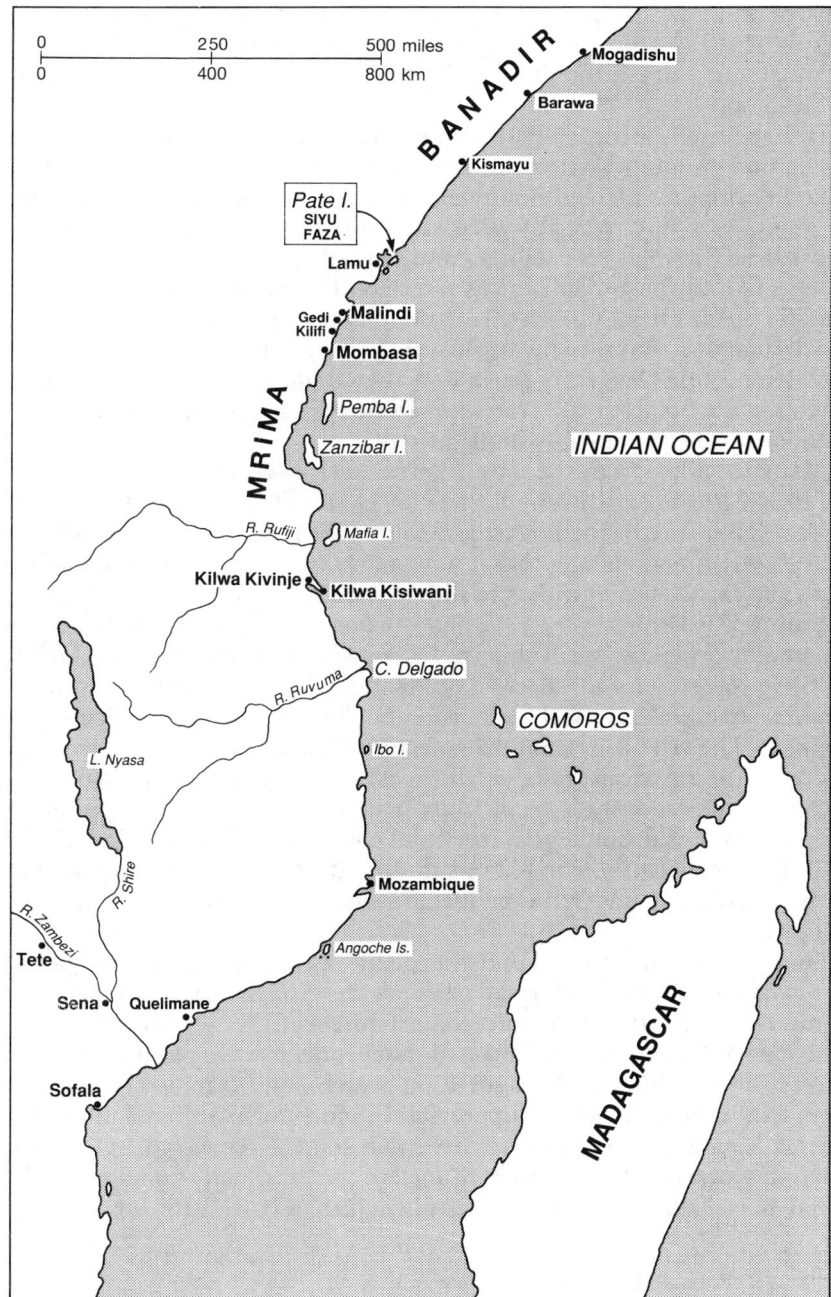

FIG. 25.2 *The East African coast (after A. I. Salim)*

expansion of the Maravi and the Yao. It was the struggle between two Maravi chiefs, Kalonga and his nominal subordinate, Lundu, which was eventually to unleash the Zimba who were to deal Kilwa a crippling blow in the 1590s.

In conclusion, then, the Portuguese failed to devise a clear-cut policy of occupation or administration on the Swahili coast. They had only a mercenary desire to control, if not monopolize, all commercial traffic. Even in this they were only partially successful. Because Portuguese occupation was so brief (they left Mozambique and Malindi only twenty-five years after leaving Kilwa) the Swahili towns managed to continue their commercial activities. Ships from Cambay, for example, brought goods such as cotton and beads, and ships from nearby Mogadishu, Brava, Pate, Lamu and Mombasa would then carry on an exchange trade with the southern coast, including the Sofala area.[26] Measures to stamp out this trade were neither assiduously nor successfully implemented.

Many say that, from the onset, Portuguese interests really lay beyond the East African coast in the East. This contention is sometimes used to explain the failure of the Portuguese to establish themselves effectively on the east coast, maintaining that it was only considered a minor part of the *Estado da India* (state of India), headquartered at Goa where the Portuguese viceroy resided. However, a 'Captain-major of the Sea of Malindi' was appointed with a few small ships at his disposal to patrol the East African coast, in the absence of effective occupation. It was also his job to issue *carataze* (passes) to vessels and run the Portuguese trading factory at Malindi. The establishment of this factory is proof enough of Portuguese interest in the African trade on the coast and inland. It imported goods such as cotton and beads from India which it exchanged for local goods such as gum-copal, ambergris, ivory and coir. The Captain at Malindi also played an important role in Kilwa's trade and a factor of his was placed on Mafia island, still under the political influence of Kilwa, to acquire coir and pitch.

Until the advent of the Turkish expeditions in the later 1500s, sources give only the scantiest information about the Swahili coast. In general it seems that a politico-economic compromise had been enforced by circumstances: Swahili towns remained independent so long as no conflict of interest arose with the Portuguese, in which case, commerce would be curtailed but not altogether suppressed.[27] Some towns suffered more than others. Mombasa despite destructive punishment recovered well and in 1569 was described by Father Monclaro as 'large and populous'.[28] He found Kilwa almost deserted but still trading in ivory with the Comoros

26. J. Strandes, 1968, p. 100.
27. C. R. Boxer and C. de Azevedo, 1960, pp. 18–19.
28. R. Oliver and G. Mathew, 1963, p. 136. It has been suggested that its trade with the hinterland helps to explain Mombasa's recovery and resilience: E. A. Alpers, 1975a, p. 45.

and the interior. By this time a factor whose impact is even harder to gauge than that of the Portuguese, had entered the picture: population movements on the mainland and their effect on the Swahili towns. Zanzibar was said to be in conflict with invaders from the mainland; Malindi was partly in ruins as a result of pressure from the Segeju;[29] and, according to J. Kirkman,[30] Gedi was declining prior to the advent of the Turkish commander, Mir 'Alī Bey, and his threat to the Portuguese presence.

From the moment they had entered the Indian Ocean, the Portuguese had aroused the hostility of not only the local Muslim rulers but also the rulers of the Muslim superpower, the Mamluks of Egypt. With the defeat of the Mamluks by the Ottomans in 1517 leadership in the struggle against the Portuguese intruder passed to the Turkish sultan in Constantinople. Several naval battles took place between Portuguese and Turks on the west coast of India and in the Persian Gulf. Then, in 1570–1, an insurrection broke out in the Portuguese stronghold of Hormuz, whose inhabitants had called for Ottoman help.

The uprising was suppressed, but its example was followed as the Turkish fleets periodically harassed the Portuguese. The first Turkish raids had occurred in the neighbourhood of Malindi even before the appearance of Mir 'Alī Bey. Although they had little impact, the Portuguese had been concerned and the Crown had advised the Viceroy at Goa to put an end to the misconduct of Portuguese officials on the Swahili coast about which the Swahili *shaykh*s had sent complaints. The Portuguese king had feared that these leaders would be encouraged or forced to seek Turkish help to free themselves from the Portuguese yoke.

Lisbon's fears were well-founded. When Mir 'Alī Bey appeared in 1585, his single galley and his message of liberation were warmly welcomed by all Swahili towns between Mogadishu and Kilwa except Malindi. He left with a promise to return with a stronger force, after collecting booty and taking prisoner some fifty Portuguese soldiers in Lamu. The Portuguese responded with a punitive expedition directed particularly at Faza and Mombasa. The former put up stiff resistance, its inhabitants inflicting heavy casualties on the Portuguese before being overpowered, having their town razed and their *shaykh*'s head taken to Goa for display. Mombasa's inhabitants made a tactical withdrawal until the Portuguese left, but the town was sacked.

True to his promise, in 1588 Mir 'Alī Bey returned with five ships and, once again, won the support of most towns, except Malindi which only put up token resistance. When the Turkish commander began to implement his plan to make Mombasa a Turkish base, the Portuguese responded by setting sail for East Africa with a bigger fleet in January 1589.

The threat of Portuguese retribution coincided with the arrival of the

29. ibid. The presence of the Segeju in the area, however, proved fortuitous because they helped Malindi survive the Zimba attack.
30. Quoted by Freeman-Grenville in R. Oliver and G. Mathew, 1963, p. 137.

cannibalistic Zimba who threatened Mombasa from the mainland as they had Kilwa before.[31] Thus the townspeople and their Turkish deliverers found themselves caught between two unrelated enemies. The destruction of the Turkish fleet by the Portuguese allowed the Zimba access to the island where they went on a rampage of destruction. Some 200 inhabitants and Turks sought safety aboard Portuguese ships. The Zimba menace proceeded northwards and it was only the Segeju who stemmed their trail of destruction and saved Malindi from a similar fate. Meanwhile, the Portuguese expedition sailed north and wreaked vengeance on Lamu for supporting the Turks. The _shaykh_ and several other notables were taken to Pate and beheaded in the presence of the Sultans of Pate, Faza and Siyu, as an object lesson to them. Neighbouring Manda island was attacked and its capital, Takwa, sacked.

To what extent the Zimba menace, like that of the Oromo later, contributed to the depopulation and decline of some Swahili towns is difficult to gauge. Kilwa was at first eclipsed but it slowly recovered thanks to the will of its people, the presence of the commercial agent of the Portuguese Captain of Mombasa and the emergence of Yao trade towards the end of the sixteenth century.[32] Mombasa was sufficiently weakened for her erstwhile enemy, Malindi, to take the town with the help of the Segeju. Thus ended the reign of the Mombasa Shīrāzī dynasty that had put up continued resistance to Portuguese overlordship. It was replaced by the dynasty of her arch-rival, Malindi whose ruler, Sultan Aḥmad, was thus rewarded for his consistent loyalty to the Portuguese. But the long-term effect of the transfer to Mombasa of the Portuguese Captain and his garrison, together with Malindi's royal house, was the gradual decline of Malindi itself from which it was not to recover until the second half of the nineteenth century.[33]

The role played at this time by Kilifi between Mombasa and Malindi is an interesting one, although sources tend to disregard its rivalry with Malindi. The rulers of Mombasa and Kilifi are said to have been related. Soon after the Zimba onslaught, Kilifi seems to have fought Malindi for the seat of Mombasa. She did so possibly on the basis of her dynastic relations or through mere ambition. Whatever the case, relations between Kilifi and Malindi on the eve of the latter's take-over of Mombasa were hostile, with Malindi complaining of Kilifi's encroachments and raids. The battles between the two gave Malindi an opportunity to kill two birds with one stone: to end Kilifi's provocations and also her claims to Mombasa. After this defeat Kilifi seems to have suffered an irreversible decline. Ruins

31. As noted above, the Zimba were originally the warriors of the Lundu. In the 1580s, one of their chiefs led his men on a rampage against the people to their east. About 1588 his growing army reached Kilwa, slaughtered most of its inhabitants and left it a ghost-town before marching north to Mombasa. See also J. dos Santos, 1609, Vol. I, pp. 65–71 and R. Avelot, 1912.

32. E. A. Alpers, 1975a, pp. 58–62.

33. E. B. Martin, 1973, pp. 40–1.

testify today to the existence of a town which once had a palace and houses on top of a hill and a mosque, with beautifully carved verses of the Ḳur'ān around the recess of the *mihrab*, and the rest of the town laid out below.

The two Turkish expeditions had revealed the fragility of the Portuguese hold on the Swahili coast. To strengthen it and thereby cope with future challenges, the Portuguese decided to erect a fortress in Mombasa and place a garrison there. Fort Jesus was built in 1593–4 by masons from India and labourers from Malindi working under the direction of an Italian architect.[34] A garrison of 100 men was placed there under a captain whose jurisdiction stretched from Brava in the north to Cape Delgado in the south.

PLATE 25.2   *Fort Jesus, Mombasa, built by the Portuguese in 1593–4*

But despite their relatively strong presence in Mombasa, Portuguese administration of the rest of the Swahili coast did not undergo any significant change. Elsewhere, their presence remained minimal and payment of tribute was all they expected from the town rulers. The Mombasa garrison made it easier for the Portuguese to react quickly to resistance and revolts which might break out. But their proximity did not intimidate all.

34. For details of the building, see C. R. Boxer and C. de Azevedo, 1960, pp. 87–117.

In 1603, for example, the ruler of Pate rose up in arms thereby inviting condemnation and execution. But this ruthless punishment did not prevent subsequent defiance and uprisings by Pate and other towns.

Human dispersal and resettlement along the coast

Several important developments took place during the seventeenth century. One was the entry of the Dutch and British into the Indian Ocean to challenge the Portuguese. Another was the deterioration of relations between the Portuguese and the new rulers of Mombasa, their traditional allies. A third was the human dispersal and resettlement along the coast which led to the emergence of new populations and groups.

Increased insecurity, arising largely from the pressure of the Oromo and to some extent, probably, from environmental changes, led to the movement of Swahili groups from the more northerly to the southern towns. Pemba island and Mombasa both acquired immigrants from northern centres and it was during this period that most of the ancestors of the nine nations (Miji–Kenda) of Mombasa settled on the island. While some northern settlements declined or were abandoned others, to the south, were strengthened and further north – on the Tanzanian coast known as Mrima,[35] for example – new ones appeared. Vumba Kuu developed further during the seventeenth century to acquire a distinctive identity.

Equally important was the dispersal south from Shungwaya (or Singwaya) of groups which later developed into the Miji–Kenda peoples and the Pokomo. Shungwaya cannot be discussed as a mythical state.[36] Evidence is weighted more in favour of its existence – whether settlement or state. The Miji–Kenda oral traditions and those of Swahili-speaking groups such as the Bajuni, for example, furnish substantial evidence for its existence.[37] The evolution of the Miji–Kenda has only been studied recently, filling thereby an important gap in coastal history.[38] Briefly, the story is one of movement southwards from Shungwaya and settlement by different groups in fortified villages (*makaya*; sing.: *kaya*) on the hills overlooking the Swahili towns between Malindi and just south of Mombasa. Fortification probably contributed towards the development of group identity and solidarity. In time, the *makaya* became more than mere havens of security from Oromo and later, Maasai threats. They came to occupy a central place in the socio-religious life of the Miji–Kenda which outlasted the days when people lived within the fortified villagers. The Miji–Kenda groups developed commercial and cultural relations with the neighbouring Swahili

35. G. S. P. Freeman-Grenville, 1963, pp. 146–9.

36. R. F. Morton, 1973.

37. J. de V. Allen, 1977b. Also, see V. L. Grottanelli, 1955 and 1975, who identified the archaeological site near modern Bur Kavo (Port Durnford) with historical Shungwaya.

38. T. T. Spear, 1974. The Nine Nations (Miji Kenda) are the Digo, Giriama, Rabai, Ribe, Kombe, Kauma, Duruma, Chonyi and Jibana.

towns. The Digo and Segeju, for example, entered into socio-cultural and economic relations with Vumba Kuu.[39] Each Miji-Kenda *kaya* established a special economic and political association with one of the Twelve Nations of Mombasa whose settlement in the town had been completed by the eighteenth century.

The Portuguese–Mombasans' Conflict

The amicable relations between the Portuguese and Sultan Aḥmad lasted only three or so years after the transfer of the sultan's seat of government to Mombasa. It soon became clear that the Captain of Mombasa was ignoring orders from Goa to keep on good terms with their ageing ally and was not honouring the administrative and fiscal agreements made with him. The sultan complained of obstacles placed on Mombasa's commerce and shipping and, significantly, appealed to Lisbon to relieve other towns of the tribute imposed after the Turkish expeditions. He also asked for recognition as ruler of Pemba which he seems to have conquered with his own forces but which the Portuguese wished to be controlled by a puppet of their own choosing. Finally, Sultan Aḥmad was given Pemba but only on lease, his annual payment being 300–500 sacks of rice.

After Sultan Aḥmad died in 1609, his son, al-Ḥasan, found himself at loggerheads with the new Portuguese Captain, Manuel de Mello Pereira, over his rights and privileges in Mombasa and over Pemba. The poisoned atmosphere between the two, worsened by the intrigues of al-Ḥasan's uncle, drove the sultan to seek refuge in Arabaja (probably Rabai), rather than submit to a decision from Goa to be tried there. At first the Musungulos[40] gave him refuge but later betrayed him killing him in return for a Portuguese bribe of pieces of cloth.

Lisbon was not party to this treachery and, to make amends, insisted that al-Ḥasan's son Yūsuf be made ruler after a period of education in Goa. On arrival in Goa, Yūsuf was converted to Christianity and given a Portuguese-Asian wife. He also served in the Portuguese armed forces in the Persian Gulf and acquired distinction as a soldier and gunner. But in 1630, when he was sent back to Mombasa as ruler (under the Christian name Dom Jerónimo Chingulia) he faced severe problems for neither Mombasans nor Portuguese would accept him. His relatives resented his change of faith and he found himself socially ostracized by the whole community. At the same time, the Portuguese officials did not treat him with the respect he deserved or show appreciation of his services to the Portuguese crown.

39. See A. I. Salim, 1973, ch. 1 and W. F. Mckay, 1975.

40. This group is mentioned by the Portuguese sources but they appear not to have outlasted the Portuguese period. They were probably absorbed by subsequent groups of settlers from Shungwaya, perhaps those whose descendants became the Rabai, one of the Miji–Kenda groups.

765

In August 1631, the Portuguese Captain, Pedro Leitão de Gamboa, decided that Yūsuf's habit of praying at his murdered father's tomb in the Muslim fashion amounted to renunciation of the Christian faith verging on treason and planned to ship him back to Goa for trial. Like his father, Yūsuf decided not to submit to trial but, unlike al-Ḥasan, he decided instead to fight.

The story of Yūsuf's surprise entry into Fort Jesus on 15 August 1631 during the Portuguese celebration of the Feast of Our Lady of the Assumption and the massacre of all but a handful has often been told.[41] Yūsuf saw his dramatic return to Islam as the beginning of a *djihād* to oust the Portuguese from the whole coast. But his call was not heeded so well as Amīr 'Alī Bey's had been some decades earlier and no other town would support his revolt. Nevertheless, when the first punitive expedition was sent against them in January 1632, he and his several hundred Swahili and African followers forced it to withdraw after suffering heavy casualties. But he would not wait for another expedition. Disheartened by the lack of military support from other towns, he left for Arabia – probably to enlist Turkish help.

When this was not forthcoming, Yūsuf returned to East Africa where he provoked minor coastal uprisings until his death in 1637. The most rebellious was the Lamu archipelago and a lengthy punitive expedition had to be undertaken in 1636–7 to subdue Faza, Lamu, Manda and Pate. A 1635 inscription over the gate of Fort Jesus boasts of the victory which reduced the coast to subjection to the Portuguese crown.

Anglo–Dutch intruders

By then, however, the tide had already turned against the Portuguese in the Indian Ocean. The appearance of the Dutch and English in the area had already contributed to the decline of Portuguese supremacy by the time of Yūsuf's revolt. The Dutch had long been involved in the Eastern trade as agents, shipping to other parts of Europe colonial goods brought to Lisbon. But when Spain and Portugal were united in 1580, the Spanish king sought to cut out the Dutch who had been fighting since 1566 to liberate themselves from Spanish overlordship. This determined the Dutch to reach the East independently of Spain and Portugal and, by the end of the sixteenth century, Dutch ships were challenging Portuguese in the Indian Ocean. In 1607, Dutch ships blockaded Mozambique town for several months before sickness forced them to withdraw. But they had entered the Indian Ocean determined to stay.

The English, meanwhile, had embarked upon piratical raids on Spanish ships since 1580 when unity between the two Iberian powers made Portuguese interests in the Indian Ocean legitimate targets. Before the turn of the century, English ships had rounded the Cape of Good Hope. In 1591

41. For a study of this event, see G. S. P. Freeman-Grenville, 1980.

one landed in Zanzibar before proceeding to India, and in 1608 another landed at Pemba. Thenceforth, the Portuguese fought a futile battle to keep out these European intruders. The area of conflict was largely the Persian Gulf, along the Malabar coast of India, Sri Lanka and the Malay archipelago. Neither the Dutch nor the English sought to replace the Portuguese by permanently occupying any East African town. Stop-overs in Zanzibar and Pemba were for provisions and water supplies only.

Nevertheless, Anglo–Dutch raids and harassment stretched Portuguese resources. English involvement in fighting between local inhabitants and their Portuguese overlords turned the tide decidedly against the latter. Eventually, the shockwaves of setbacks in the Persian Gulf began to reach the East African coast.

Although officially at peace with Spain and Portugal, in 1622 England helped the Shah of Persia drive the Portuguese from their strategic entrepôt of Hormuz[42] thus depriving the Portuguese Indian state of its main source of revenue. To compensate for this loss, the Portuguese fell back on Muscat, one of the Omani coastal towns they had dominated since the early sixteenth century, plundering it as they had many Swahili towns. Muscat was the Omani equivalent of Mombasa. In 1588, soon after the Turkish raids, the Portuguese had built a fort there as a base from which to reconquer Hormuz and also as an entrepôt for the Indian–Persian Gulf trade.

The end of Portuguese rule in East Africa

Soon after the fall of Hormuz to the Persians, a new dynamic dynasty came to power in the Omani interior, determined to liberate the country from the Portuguese yoke. This was the Ya'rubi dynasty whose founder and first *Imām* was Nāṣir bin Murshid. Between 1640 and 1650, the Portuguese were forced by military defeats to demolish their fortresses and evacuate Muscat. With control over their own coastline, the rulers of Oman used their seasoned seafaring inhabitants to build a strong naval force that started challenging the Portuguese beyond the Gulf. It was inevitable that historical, social, cultural and commercial ties should turn the attention of the Ya'rubi rulers to East Africa.

With the recapture of Mombasa after Yūsuf's revolt, the Portuguese decided to rule the town directly. As noted above, revolts broke out periodically, especially in Pate which seems to have assumed leadership in the struggle for liberation. The town seems to have entered a period of prosperity during this time which led the Portuguese to establish a custom-house there in 1633. But Portuguese interference with the town's trade, which, in their estimation, was making Pate too wealthy and powerful, led to the deterioration of relations between the two. Meanwhile, complaints of ill-treatment from other towns, such as Siyu, Pemba, and Otondo,

42. S. B. Miles, 1919.

reached not only Lisbon but also the new rulers of Oman of whom help against the Portuguese was requested.

What followed was a prolonged period of struggle during the second half of the seventeenth century between the Portuguese and the Omani Arabs in East African waters. In 1652, an Omani expedition encouraged by the local rulers, attacked the Portuguese position in Zanzibar, killing a number of Portuguese. The Portuguese retaliated by raiding the island and driving away the queen and her son, the ruler of Otondo, for refusing to pay tribute and encouraging the Omani Arabs. In 1660 a combined fleet from Oman and Pate landed in Mombasa and sacked the Portuguese quarter seemingly without any serious opposition. Other Omani raids were made as far south as Mozambique in 1669. In August 1678, the Portuguese viceroy himself led a major expedition against 'Pate the swaggering'. He was joined by the ruler of neighbouring Faza which at the time was involved in its perennial squabbles with Pate. The expedition was of limited success as it was forced to withdraw on the appearance of Omani ships in January 1679 – but not before having seized the rulers of Pate, Siyu, Lamu and Manda who were then beheaded together with several other notables. But the loss of her ruler did not quell Pate and in 1687 yet another move was made against it. It was invaded and looted and its new ruler seized and sent to Goa together with twelve councillors.

An attempt was made to reach a compromise agreement whereby the *Shaykh* of Pate would retain his throne – instead of being replaced by his enemy, the ruler of Faza – in return for accepting Portuguese overlordship. But this provisional agreement reached in Goa was repudiated by Lisbon as the Portuguese king wished to end Pate's independence and reward Faza for its 'conspicuous loyalty'.[43] But by then, Pate had been lost to an Omani force and, on Christmas Day 1688, the captive ruler and his councillors were killed in an attempt to escape from captivity in Panjim.

For some years, civil strife at home interrupted the Omani raids on Portuguese positions in East Africa. When they were resumed, their target was Pemba upon whom Mombasa depended for food and where a revolt had broken out against the Portuguese. In 1694, however, the Portuguese managed to suppress the revolt and expel the Omani Arabs.

But the following year came the greatest challenge from Oman. In March 1696, seven Omani ships, carrying 3000 men and the ruler of Lamu, landed in Mombasa. They easily occupied the town and the island before laying siege to Fort Jesus. The siege lasted for more than two and half years, until December 1698 when the fortress finally surrendered. It demonstrated not only the heroism of the defenders, who were supported by allies from Malindi and Faza, but also the remarkable ineptitude and cowardice of the Portuguese commanders sent from time to time to relieve those in the fort. Invariably they limited themselves to sending supplies to the beleaguered fortress without attempting to attack the besiegers. When the Omanis

43. C. R. Boxer and C. de Azevedo, 1960, p. 51.

persuaded the neighbouring Miji–Kenda to cut off supplies to the defenders, disease and malnutrition took their toll. When the expedition from Goa arrived in November 1698, with orders to engage the enemy, the red flag of Oman was already flying over the fort.

From 1728–9 the Portuguese managed a brief return to Mombasa, taking advantage of the scanty Omani presence after the fall of Mombasa and Swahili disillusionment in some towns with the Arabs who were reportedly ill-treating the wealthy and interfering with local trade. Such reports may well have been exaggerated in Goa by dispossessed Swahili notables such as the Prince of Faza. But there is no doubt that the ruler of Pate was at odds with the Arab garrison in his town. When a faction rose against him, supported by the Omanis, he finally sought support from Goa late in 1727. From Pate the Portuguese expedition moved against Mombasa where the Omani garrison in the fort had rebelled during the absence of its commander, calling for help from the King of Pate against other Arab garrisons guarding smaller forts on the island. The fort and town surrendered to the joint Portuguese–Patean forces and rulers from Wasini(?) Vumba, Pangani, Mtangata, Tanga, Zanzibar and Pemba were summoned to Mombasa to renew pledges of loyalty.

But the return of the Portuguese and the Portuguese–Patean alliance was shortlived. The ruler of Pate had been so anxious for help against the local rival faction and its Arab supporters that he had made reckless promises to Portugal, such as the payment of tribute and the monopoly of the ivory trade. Within six months the King of Pate was accusing the Portuguese of oppression with regard to the ivory monopoly and complaining about other trade restrictions. In June 1729 an armed clash finally convinced the Portuguese that they should withdraw.

By then, trouble was brewing for them in Mombasa. A combined force of Mombasans and Musungulos (mainland Africans), under the leadership of a Mombasa notable who had earlier gone to Goa to urge the Portuguese return, attacked Portuguese positions in the town before besieging the small garrison in the fort. In November 1729, the half-starved garrison surrendered and was allowed to sail to Mozambique. Other towns, including Zanzibar, Pemba and Mafia, had followed Mombasa's lead, murdering or driving out the Portuguese.

The Swahili towns, therefore, were responsible for the final expulsion of the Portuguese. But soon Pate and Mombasa were once again occupied by the Omanis, and the Swahili coast entered a new era in its history.

The Portuguese defeat has been credited to a variety of factors: their weak, incompetent and confused colonial system; the personal irresolution, caprice, ineptitude and greed of officials interested primarily in lining their own pockets, who often alienated the local Swahili population; the harsh vagaries of climate and disease that took many lives among an already small Portuguese population; and the local factional struggles, often a double-edged sword, now working for the Portuguese now against them. Towards the end, Portuguese resources were overstretched and an expeditionary force hard to muster. Goa itself, for example, was denuded of defence forces in a last, desperate and abortive effort to regain an East African foothold in January 1730.

These military activities took place amidst significant political, economic and cultural development on the littoral. In the southern part of the coast there developed an important trade between the Yao and Kilwa, initially in hides, iron-ware and agricultural products but, by the end of the seventeenth century, including 'a thriving, well-organized trade in ivory'.[44] This trade suffered a temporary setback in the early 1700s when the Portuguese lost Mombasa whose captain had purchased a large part of Kilwa's exports. Their Omani successors failed to provide sufficient demand for these goods or for the exchange goods of cloth and beads with which Kilwa obtained ivory and other goods from the interior. As a result, Yao ivory was diverted from Kilwa to Mozambique. But the advent of the Būsaʻidi dynasty in Oman, in the mid-1700s, ushered in another period of revival for Kilwa.

Further north, Vumba Kuu had undergone consolidation and its Sharī-fite ruling family, the Bā-ʻAlawī, had become indigenized. Each $\overline{diwān}$ (ruler) adopted a Bantu nickname and his investiture ceremonies combined both Bantu and Islamic rites. The Segeju had settled around the Diwanate, as had the Digo, one of the Miji-Kenda groups. Both had entered into an intimate relationship with Vumba Kuu, providing the foundation of its economy and participating in the installation of its rulers and succession disputes during the eighteenth century and later. The influence of the Sharīfite families' religions proved decisive in the conversion to Islam of the coastal Digo and Segeju who, however, retained certain aspects of their religious beliefs including rain-making ceremonies.

In the Lamu archipelago, Pate witnessed its most glorious decades during the seventeenth century and into the eighteenth, enjoying great wealth and influence over parts of the coast to the south and playing a leading rôle in the liberation of the coast. Its prosperity was based on maritime trade which it exploited at a time when other towns such as Malindi, Mombasa and Kilwa were recovering from attacks by inland peoples such as the Zimba. Pate even established profitable relations with the marauding Oromo, who provided the town with hides for export, and traded in ivory from the mainland.[45] Material culture collected and preserved reflects the great heights of prosperity and civilized living enjoyed by Pate during this period. Sources do not adequately explain its seemingly rapid decline sometime during the second half of the eighteenth century.

44. E. A. Alpers, 1975a, p. 63.
45. A. Nāṣir, 1977, pp. 17–18; J. de V. Allen, 1974.

PLATE 25.3 *Roundel from a mosque at Vumba Kuu*

The Omani factor in East Africa

It is this fall from great heights that forms the subject of one of the greatest *tenzi* (epic poems) in Kiswahili, *Al-Inkishafi*. Its author, Sayyid ʿAbdallāh bin ʿAlī bin Nāzir, was a member of the Sharīfite élite of Pate. His ancestor, Shaykh Abū Bakr bin Sālim was the celebrated Saint of Ināt in the Hadramaut and had been asked by a sixteenth-century ruler of Pate to pray for the town to be freed from her enemies – whether Portuguese or Oromo it is not clear. The *sharīfs* settled and multiplied, became indigenized and with the *sharīfs* of Lamu, came to play a leading role in the development of Swahili literary and religious traditions. It was Sharīfian immigrants from South Arabia who, even before the arrival of the Portuguese, came to determine the Shāfiʿī madhhab (school of thought) of the vast majority of the coast's Muslim population.

The methods of teaching Islam, the manuals used, the cult of the saints, the veneration of *sharīfs* and the form and content of poetic verse constitute the cultural legacy of these descendants of the Prophet Muḥammad who settled not only in the Lamu archipelago but also elsewhere on the coast and formed the main part of its religious intelligentsia. By the nineteenth century a

> cultural traffic linked South Arabia to the Banadir, to the coast southwards to Mozambique and to the offshore islands: the Lamu archipelago, Zanzibar, Pemba, Mafia and the Comoro islands. Hadrami towns like ʿInāt and Tarīm, Mecca and Medina, sometimes

771

Cairo, and occasionally Istanbul helped to mould the scholastic minds of the East African Muslim scholars. Students from the East African towns travelled to the Hidjaz, Hadramaut, and sometimes Egypt to study under renowned scholars. The acquisition of an *Idjāza* (certificate) from one of these scholars established its recipient as a teacher in a mosque or in his own home of the Arabic language, Kuranic exegesis, *hadith*, Sharia, etc. From this educational system there developed a strong body of *ulama* from among whom the Busaidi rulers appointed their Kadis.[46]

The Omani factor contributed significantly towards the economic resurgence of Kilwa as did the slave trade. Together with the ivory trade, the slave trade was to dominate the economic history of the east coast for much of the nineteenth century. The first major catalyst for the trade was France whose acquisition of the Mascarene Islands – Ile-de-France (Mauritius) and Ile Bourbon (Réunion) – and their development after 1735 as plantation colonies, acted as strong incentives to both Kilwa and Zanzibar to provide slaves. Initially, the French turned to Portuguese Mozambique and the Kerimba Islands for their slaves as the Portuguese were anxious to prevent the French trading directly in slaves or ivory with the Makua, Yao and the Swahili merchants on the mainland.

But Mozambique's domination began to decline in the mid-1700s, partly because of Portuguese conflicts inland with the Makua, which disturbed the Mozambique route, and partly because of the challenge from Swahili and also Arab merchants who had increased their activities along the coast after the Būsaʿidi dynasty had strengthened its dynastic grip on Oman. Parallel to this was the growth of Indian merchant capital at Zanzibar, deliberately encouraged by the new Omani rulers, who had made Zanzibar their major stronghold on the coast. Kilwa once again became a major trading centre to which mainland African slave and ivory traders were drawn, to the consternation of the Portuguese. All measures, military and otherwise, to stamp out Arab and Swahili commercial rivalry, which was seen as a deadly threat to the economic backbone of Mozambique, failed to stem the tide of Arab and Swahili competition.

By 1785, Mozambique's domination of the ivory trade in East and Central Africa had almost ended although it continued to thrive on the slave trade, owing to the increased demand of the French Indian Ocean colonies.[47] In this it faced competition from Swahili mainland coastal settlements, such as Ibo, to which the French turned more and more for slaves. Yao slave-traders turned increasingly to Kilwa as a destination for their ivory and slaves, as Kilwa became a greater emporium for desired Indian–Omani imported goods, such as Surat cloth. It is this growing resurgence of Kilwa that led the French trader-adventurer, Jean-Vincent

46. A. I. Salim, 1980, pp. 885–91.
47. E. A. Alpers, 1975a, p. 127, fn 8.

PLATE 25.4 *The Great Siwa of Mwinyi Mkuu, Zanzibar*

Morice, to sign a treaty with the town in 1776 for 1000 slaves a year to be sold to the French colonists on the Mascarene Islands.[48] By the 1780s there is already evidence of the pioneering trading ventures of the Swahili and Swahilized traders into the interior and across Lake Malawi. Two of the three newly established routes reached Kilwa and the Swahili coast around Bagomoyo, testifying to the 'revitalization of the trading economy of the Swahili coast during the second half of the eighteenth century'.[49] New trade routes were opened to link with the coast peoples such as the Bolowoka, the Bisa and the Ngonde.

48. For the French trade at Kilwa, see G. S. P. Freeman-Grenville, 1965.
49. E. A. Alpers, 1975a, p. 161.

Proof that trade and profit were often divorced from politics is provided by the Omani Arabs who traded with Kilwa although its sultan jealously guarded his independence from Oman. From 1784, however, the newly installed *Imām* of Oman, Saʿīd bin Aḥmad, embarked upon a military campaign to impose his will on a number of coastal towns, including Kilwa which had been used as a base by a rebel uncle of his, Saif bin Saʿīd. Kilwa's ageing Sultan, Ḥasan Ibrāhīm, could only put up token resistance. He was forced to relinquish his sovereignty and over half of his custom dues to the Omani overlord and accept the presence of an Omani governor and garrison. But these political developments only helped to increase commerce on the Kilwa coast since they created greater stability and introduced more Indian capital investment.[50] No doubt Muscat gained from this arrangement. By 1804, the Omani Governor of Kilwa was sending to his *Imām* 6000 piastres a year which sum was at least doubled by 1811.[51] Zanzibar, already the Būsaʿidi's most stable, loyal and lucrative base in East Africa added no less than 40 000 piastres to the Omani coffers in 1796 and nearly 60 000 piastres in 1811.

By the turn of the century the economic value of the few points at which they were represented was becoming evident to the Omani Būsaʿidi. This and other political and strategic considerations, contributed to the policy adopted by Sayyid Saʿīd bin Sultan (1804–56) of extending his dynastic authority on the coast and, eventually, establishing his capital in Zanzibar.[52]

Conclusion

Between 1500 and 1800 there were important changes on the coast. Hitherto independent Swahili towns endured Portuguese intrusion. Their internal rivalries and intrigues sometimes facilitated Portuguese intervention, although the Portuguese occasionally found involvement more a liability than an asset.

The Portuguese occupation was violent and ruthless, determined to strike at Muslims everywhere, to take over their lands and trade and even convert them and the so-called heathens of the area to Christianity. In effect, the religious impact was negligible. Barring a few exceptions, such as Yūsuf bin Ḥasan, or some female companions, most Muslims were impervious to Christianity. Certainly, by the end of the Portuguese occupation no trace of Christianity remained.

As for the control of trade and commercial traffic in the Indian Ocean, Portuguese efforts were to prove of limited success. The Swahili towns were able to continue with a significant degree of commercial activity although Portuguese controls, such as monopolies and *carataze* licences depressed trade to some extent. Greed and incompetence amongst local

50. E. A. Alpers, 1975a, p. 166.
51. R. Oliver and G. Mathew, 1963, p. 156; E. A. Alpers, 1975a, p. 177.
52. See UNESCO, *General History of Africa*, Vol. VI, ch. 8.

officials were responsible for such developments as the decline of the Sofalan gold trade. While the coast was initially regarded as of secondary importance to the Asian trade, it enriched Portuguese officials, if not the Portuguese crown.

Swahili towns during this period experienced vacillating fortunes. Mombasa's resilience enabled it to recover several times from serious Portuguese punishment. Kilwa took the blows less well. Towards the end of the eighteenth century it recovered, thanks to the slave trade with the Ile-de-France. But recovery was short-lived since it was to be overshadowed by mainland Kilwa Kivinje early in the nineteenth century. Other coastal towns disappeared for ever or reverted to villages. To ascribe this decline to Portuguese action is erroneous. Human pressures, such as those of the Oromo and the Zimba, plus environmental changes, are probably more plausible explanations. A notable exception to this general decline is Pate, which enjoyed its greatest prosperity during the seventeenth and eighteenth centuries – a fact which probably explains the Portuguese obsession with the island. But by the end of the eighteenth century, Pate was on the decline again, as her great poet, Sayyid 'Abdallāh, author of *Al-Inkishafi*, records. More research, however, is needed to answer many questions concerning these Swahili towns, their sizes, the factors leading to their growth and development and their eventual decline.

The Great Lakes region, 1500–1800

J. B. WEBSTER, B. A. OGOT

and J. P. CHRETIEN

This period can be divided into three: 1500 to about 1580, the droughts and famines of 1580 to 1680, and the era of state formation and expansion from about 1680 to 1800. Before 1580 the major concern of the southern and central sections of the region was the consolidation of the successor states to the Bachwezi empire while, in the north, it was the interaction among the linguistic families consequent upon the first intrusion into the Great Lakes region of Eastern Nilotic-speaking peoples.

The second period (c.1580–1680) was dominated by droughts and famines. It also witnessed the region's most massive movement of peoples for the last thousand years. There were large-scale migrations out of Baar, the scattering of the Luo associated with Pubungu, and massive Banyoro invasions to the south with ramifications as far as Rwanda and Usukuma. In the east the drought was associated with the appearance of the Central Eastern Nilotes, their interaction with earlier peoples including Luo and a substantial southern drift of population.

The third period (c.1680–1800) was primarily concerned with the pro-liferation and expansion of state structures. It began with a dynastic crisis in Bunyoro which signalled the decline of that empire and, through the Paluo, was responsible for the creation of states from the Alur Highlands to the mountains on the Acholi–Karamoja border and, through the Banyoro princes, for a string of states along the southern borderlands. Nyanza Luo, Basoga, Bakonzo, Kakwa, Banyangoma and Babinza states were all multiplying. The Mpororo state was founded and fragmented. The period ends with the rise and expansion of Buganda in the central area and Rwanda in the south as the 'super-powers' of the Great Lakes region and, in the north, with the broad outlines of the modern configurations of Central Eastern Nilotic ethnic entities such as the Iteso, the Jie, the Eastern Luo, the Lango Omiro and the Kumam.

The Northern and Central areas

The formation of new groups and societies

Before + 1000 the Central Sudanic were probably the predominant peoples over the entire Great Lakes region. They were divided into many groups, including the ancestors of such ethnic groups as the Lendu, Kebu and Moro. 'Muru' was the Luo term for all these indigenous peoples and will be used when the ethnic identity of a Central Sudanic people is not known and especially to distinguish the early peoples of the region from the later Madi immigrants who were also Central Sudanic and probably the earliest-known inhabitants of Baar. Most of the Central Sudanic peoples were organized on segmentary and gerontocratic lines. They were agricultural, revered an earth god and used rain stones or mixed oil and water to call rain. They had a complex totemic system and buried their dead in recessed graves. Mostly they were known by later migrants as expert iron-miners, smelters and blacksmiths. By 1500 they had been assimilated into Bantu culture south of the Nile–Kyoga divide but still dominated the north from the Alur Highlands to the mountains of Karamoja.

About + 1000 the Nilotic Luo cradleland of Dog Nam broke up.[1] One group moved to Tekidi and a secessionist group from Tekidi migrated to and settled in Pakwac-Pawir. Out of this section came the major linguistic element of the Alur, Abwor, Padhola, Nyanza Luo and possibly the Babito of Bunyoro. From Dog Nam another section settled in Wipac (Rumbek) out of which emerged the Shilluk, Western Acholi and possibly the Paluo dialects. By 1500 there must have been a substantial dialectical difference between the two groups. In all three Luo enclaves a form of hereditary leadership associated with the bushbuck totem had been established well before 1400.[2]

The period from about 1400 to 1580 was given over to the internal consolidation of the successor states[3] and the diplomatic manoeuvring of the great power blocs, the Bahinda and Babito. The new rulers rewarded collaborators with offices and recognized certain indigenous rulers, notably those of Bwera and Buyaga. There were few succession disputes. A cult developed among the Babito to revere the fallen Cwezi which was a potential threat to the new rulers.

1. See the contributions of J. M. Onyango-ka-Odongo *et al.*, 1976; A. M. Garry, 1976; and R. S. Herring, 1976. See also R. S. Anywar, 1954 (1969); L. Okech, 1953 and 1968; J. P. Crazzolara, 1950–4; V. Pellegrini, 1963/1972; A. Malandra, 1947/1971.
2. See UNESCO, *General History of Africa*, Vol. IV, ch. 20.
3. Published works on the successor states include J. W. Nyakatura, 1947 and G. N. Uzoigwe, 1973; P. Bikunya, 1927; H. K. Karubanga, 1949; J. W. Nyakatura, 1971; A. G. Katate and L. Kamugungunu, 1953; K. N. Nganwa, 1948; F. X. Lwamgira, 1949 and E. R. Kamuhangire, 1968; F. X. Lwamgira (manuscript); H. Rehse, 1910 and Mrs. Denne, n.d.

The Babito and Bahinda were the major contenders for overall hegemonic power. Tradition claims that Kitara came to the military support of the indigenous ruler of Kiziba when a Muhima from the court in Buganda sought to overthrow him. The Banyoro armies invaded Buganda, killed the Muhima king, Nakabinge and may have been instrumental in replacing him with a ruler from the Sesse Islands, a man of the lion-leopard totem of the earlier Kintu dynasty. A disaffected section of the new dynasty in Buganda crossed Nyanza to the south-west where the Batundu population, fearful of Bahinda expansion, accepted them as rulers. This was the foundation of the Babinza clan, also of the lion-leopard totem.[4] The Banyoro killed the Muhima aspirant to the Kiziba throne and dispatched Kibi who seized power in Kiziba. In addition, according to traditions, the Banyoro encouraged the Balisa clan to found Buhweju and Buzimba (*c.*1523–50) as buffer states on their southern border against threats from the Bahima states. The Banyoro also roundly defeated Nkore but their further plans were cut short when their army fled in disarray during an eclipse of the sun in 1520.

North of the Nile–Kyoga divide, the year 1500 is important because it possibly coincides with the first major appearance of the Northern section of Eastern Nilotes or Bari cluster of the Eastern Nilotes. It has been argued that this northern section of Eastern Nilotes moved out of their homeland in the Ethiopian borderlands[5] in three waves, the first of which (*c.*1490–1517) possibly contained some ancestors of the Pajulu, the second (*c.*1517–44) of the Bari–Kakwa–Kuku and the third (*c.*1544–71) of the Lotuho. These migrations were certainly not distinct and people from the second and third waves did find their homes among the Pajulu. The waves have been tentatively dated by the generations in which Eastern Nilotes from the north-east attacked Tekidi. There are, of course, widespread doubts about the accuracy of the Tekidi regnal list from which the dates are calculated and, except for the third, the Lotuho invasion, no firm identification of the migrants in the Tekidi tradition. This division, however, finds some support in the published genealogies of the northern group of Eastern Nilotes. Each group in turn attacked Tekidi until this Luo settlement was broken up by the Lotuho.

Given the undeveloped state of the Northern group of Eastern Nilotic historiography the following outline must be considered tentative in the extreme. Between the Turkana escarpment and the Agoro mountains the

---

4. For Buganda, see M. S. M. Kiwanuka, 1971; A. Kaggwa, 1908, 1949 and 1971; M. B. Nsimbi, 1956 and C. E. S. Kabuga, 1963. For the Sukuma, see B. Itandala, 1979.

5. No major research has been done in this northern group of Eastern Nilotes, but see M. Loro, 1971 and J. B. Baba, 1972. L. F. Nalder, 1937, is a useful source; J. P. Crazzolara, 1950–4, pp. 337 and 342–3 and J. M. Onyango-ka-Odongo and J. B. Webster, 1976, are helpful, the latter especially for dating. There are, however, several works on the Central groups of the Eastern Nilotes: J. E. Lamphear, 1976 and unpublished; R. S. Herring, unpublished.

group seems to have split in two directions, one westward through Central Sudanic country (Muru and Lukoya) to the Nile in Baar, the homeland of Madi, and the other south through Karamoja where they were responsible for the withdrawal of the Kalenjin-type peoples from the northern part of that region.[6] The evidence seems to suggest that they introduced to the Central Sudanic peoples their age organization, the fire-making ceremony, a sky god, the spear and shield, the sacred spear for inducing rain, the long straight hoe and elaborate head-dresses. In many areas their interaction with the Central Sudanic peoples probably promoted chieftaincy and their language spread as a new *lingua franca*.

The second Eastern Nilotic invasions may have been affected by the Oromo who spread out from their cradleland north of Lake Turkana about 1517–44 and attacked Tekidi about the same time as they began their invasions of Southern Ethopia.[7] Ancestors of the modern Kakwa were possibly moving within this migration. Kakwa tradition goes back to Meme living at Kapoeta (now in Toposa country). The same tradition provides a genealogy to Jaki who lived at Korobe Hill far to the west, a dispersal point for many ruling clans among the Pajulu and Kakwa. Jaki became a hero-ancestor to the Kakwa. The Kakwa also recognize their connection with a sub-stratum of the Iteso, and an early northern group of the Eastern Nilotic presence in eastern Uganda may be indicated by, along with other evidence, variations of the word 'Kakwa' from Eastern Acholi to Western Kenya among the Luo.

The land of Baar became an area of extensive mixing of Eastern Nilotes and Madi. A variety of types of hereditary leadership probably developed but for those who went to the west of the Nile – the Pajulu, Kakwa and Kuku – it was usually Eastern Nilotic leaders and Madi followers; those who went south-east towards Agoro were possibly Eastern Nilotes under either Madi or Luo leadership; those who remained in Baar created a hereditary rain-maker leadership of supposedly Madi origin but speaking an Eastern Nilotic dialect. Among the Pajulu, Kakwa and Kuku the new societies seemingly adopted an Eastern Nilotic language and combined the Eastern Nilotic sky god and spear with the Sudanic earth god and bow and arrow. They apparently abandoned the Eastern Nilotic age organization and adopted Madi dress, burial practices and rain stones. The secular leadership was usually Eastern Nilotic, while the ritual experts were Madi. The Pajulu, Kakwa and Kuku were culturally Sudanic and linguistically Eastern Nilotic.

The Bari fusion was similar with somewhat stronger Eastern Nilotic influence. A prominent feature of Bari and Kuku society was that the *dupi*

6. J. E. Lamphear (unpublished) gives the Jie traditions about the Kalenjin. C. Ehret, 1971, also discusses their withdrawal.

7. H. S. Lewis, 1966, fixes the beginning of the Oromo movement to 1530–8 by documentary evidence. The 1517–44 date is calculated from the genealogy in J. M. Onyango-ka-Odongo et al., 1976.

(servile class) were occasionally physically distinct from the freeborn. In Kakwa and Pajulu society the *dupi* were clients rather than serfs. Since the *dupi* were often assistants in the rain-making ritual and notable miners and smiths, they could have been of Muru rather than Madi origin on the assumption that modern Madi, who first appear later in Luo traditions, were themselves mixtures of at least different Sudanic peoples, including Moro and possibly Muru. To the Luo, all Sudanic peoples came to be called Madi and were renowned iron-workers. The Madi, however, deny this, saying that the iron-workers were the indigenous people among whom they settled, here assumed to be Muru, Moro, Lendu or Okebu. The latter three peoples still exist and claim to have been iron-workers who were accorded special status in Madi society.[8]

The final invasion of the northern group of Eastern Nilotes was associated in Luo Tekidi tradition with the Lotuho. The Lotuho overran the Luo settlement of Tekidi and the king, Owiny Rac Koma (*c.*1544–71), fled with the majority of his subjects to the sister Luo settlement in Pakwac-Pawir. It would seem that the Didinga and Dongotono-Murle survived the invasions by defending their highland strongholds. Probably a Central Sudanic group, the Okarowok, became Eastern Nilotic-speakers through the influence of the Lotuho. One section of the Okarowok, the Koriuk, was brought under Lotuho linguistic, cultural and finally political influence; a second, the Ilogir, came under linguistic and cultural but not political influence; while a third, the Lokoya or Oxoriuk, remained separate while adopting Eastern Nilotic speech. Slim as the evidence is that the Oxoriuk became the Okarowok (a major Eastern Nilotic clan in Uganda), this is the direction in which the evidence points.

Apparently the Lotuho assimilated the small Okarowok clans into the four large Lotuho clans and introduced Okarowok totemic prohibitions. They also introduced the fire-making ceremony and age organization and – probably because of the insecure situation – built populous closely packed villages in an area formerly characterized by a dispersed settlement pattern. This was the furthest eastward spread of totemic clans and rain stones – possibly indicating the eastward limit of Central Sudanic settlement.

While a group of the proto-Luo was forced by the incursions of the Eastern Nilotes to move to the Tekidi area, another group moved northward to Wipaco Dwong' in Rumbek. This settlement later broke up, between 1382 and 1418, and the group moved west to the Nile to found a riverain settlement. This cluster later divided, with one group – the proto-Shilluk and its allies – going north and establishing their settlement (*c.*1490 and 1517) after defeating the Fung, while the Patiko and Padibe moved southwards from Baar into Pakwac-Pawir. The Luo intrusions into Baar

---

8. No Madi traditions have been collected in their homeland in Baar. The only Madi traditions we have come from the Uganda region. Everywhere in the Eastern and Western Nilotic areas of Northern Uganda, hoes which were associated with Central Sudanic speakers are called Madi hoes.

apparently induced the Madi-led Panyimur, Atyak and Koc-Pagak to migrate south to the Mount Kilak area. A Madi–Luo struggle for power ensued in Pakwac-Pawir. In the chiefdom of Atyak it was prophesied that a child of the princess, Nyilak (*c*.1517–62), would assassinate her father the king and seize the throne. Consequently the king locked up his daughter but a wandering Luo (said in one tradition to have been Keeno, King of Patiko) impregnated Nyilak and her son, as predicted, killed the Madi king. Possibly out of this two states emerged: Attyak (later Okoro), Luo-led and from whose royal line Nyipir was born, and Atyak (Acholi), Madi-led. The plot of the Nyilak story is a stereotype, the characters varying in each incident, to explain the overthrow of Sudanic leadership by either Luo in the north or Bantu in the south.[9]

The Madi–Luo struggle for hegemony in Pakwac-Pawir intensified when the large Luo migration entered Owiny of Tekidi's kingdom. Under Owiny's predecessor, Owiny Rac Koma, the Payera ruling house had been founded by Ayera, a Luo-speaking common girl whose mother was East Nilotic and whose father was a Muru trader, an apt origin for the ethnic mixture which later characterized the Payera state. The children of Ayera, who moved west to the Nile, were raised primarily as Muru and attached many Madi to themselves. In about 1560 the Lotuho overwhelmed Tekidi most of whose citizens fled with their king to Pakwac-Pawir. Others fled into the hills, returning temporarily after the Lotuho had withdrawn. The main chiefdom to emerge from the Lotuho was Puranga.[10] This Luo group, infiltrated over the centuries by new migrants from Anywa and elsewhere and much influenced by Eastern Nilotes, may be called the Eastern Luo. They formed a predominant element of the population in East Acholi, Labwor, Nyakwai and Lango and they and the Eastern Nilotes had a significant impact on the dialects spoken in these areas.

The period of droughts and famines

No major area of the Great Lakes region, nor indeed of east-central Africa, was unaffected by the climatic disaster of droughts and the resulting famines which occurred in the late sixteenth and early seventeenth centuries. During this period, rainfall in the northern and central areas was only normal in two years. The four worst periods of drought were probably: 1588–90, 1601–2, 1613 and 1617–21. In 1621 the summer Nile reached its lowest level since 622 when records were first kept. The records suggest that

---

9. J. P. Crazzolara, 1950–4, pp. 180–3; R. J. Ocamali, 1970; A. W. Southall, 1954; R. S. Anywar, 1954; A. Malandra, 1947/71. A similar Bantu tradition is that of Bukuku in Nyakatura's *Abakama*.

10. We here follow the Luo tradition as given by J. M. Onyango-ka-Odongo *et al.*, 1976. This important tradition, which deals largely with the early history of the Luo, deserves much more critical attention than it has received so far. It provides a useful corrective to Luo oral traditions, most of which have up to recently, dealt largely with the Western Luo.

during the whole period crops could have been normal only twice, failed totally in eleven years, and were marginal or failures in twenty-four. What was the toll in human lives, in civilized norms of behaviour and human dignity during these periods of drought?

In Northern Uganda, the entire period is called *Nyarubanga* (Luo word for 'sent by god') because it was the worst natural disaster in their remembered history. It ended with the Great Famine of 1617–21, accompanied by a disease which wiped out the cattle herds.

The stark spectre of mass starvation leaps from the traditions. The stories from Egypt are horrendous. Cannibalism became commonplace and an estimated half of the population died of starvation. What was true of Egypt was probably also true of most parts of the Great Lakes region, especially the northern section.

If half the people died, most others were forced to migrate or flee towards regions of refuge, clustering around rivers and lakes, along the Nile, Lake Victoria and the chain of lakes stretching southward into central Africa. Twelve major traditions of migration have been collected from this period, most recalling swift movements towards large rivers and lakes. Some migrations were organized on military lines, such as the Nkanda invasion of Sukuma country, the 'Lomukudit' movement through Baar, or the Banyoro invasion southward at least as far as Buzinga. Traditions also report the drying up of the Albert and Victoria Niles and also of Smith Sound which must have represented a massive shrinkage of Nyanza.

The *Nyarubanga* re-structured the ethno and political geography of much of the Great Lakes region and possibly a much wider area. It probably dealt a massive and destructive blow to leadership built on the principles of control over supernatural forces, particularly to those who claimed rain-making powers. It led to the rise of a new leadership based often on migration leaders whose skills as commanders, warriors and hunters had been responsible for a sizeable group of survivors. When the trauma was over, the leaders of the survivors set up new political entities in new regions – probably uninhabited or sparsely populated, or at best with no political leadership of their own. It is not just because the newcomers' descendants wanted to claim ownership of the soil that traditions argue that the land was empty. In some areas it probably was or was nearly so.

Nor is it surprising that when the immigrants found people they are recalled as hunters, nor that the leader of the newcomers was himself a hunter. The animals also migrated to the regions of refuge and were clustered around the permanent water holes. Finally, it is not surprising that traditions give the impression that around 1600 there was a new beginning. Most groups experienced a new ethnic mix, a new location and new leadership. Just because pre-1600 traditions are skeletal and vague, historians should not assume that they are an accurate reflection of conditions, because the *Nyarubanga* wiped out traditions and destroyed their mechanisms of transmission and probably most of the older people who were their carriers. As the worst climatic disaster in the remembered history of the Great Lakes region, it set rapidly moving waves of migration in motion, broke up states, overthrew dynasties and even shook the foundation of pastoralist societies normally adapted to cope with prolonged dry weather.[11]

The migration out of Baar greatly accelerated during the *Nyarubanga*. Madi Opei, Palabek and Padibe moved to Agoro; Attyak, Koc-Pagak, Aliba, Laropi, Parabongo, Alero and Palaru were among those Madi who poured into Pakwac-Pawir. Eastern Nilotic-speakers moved south to Korobe Hill and Mount Liru where a number of ruling families claim to descend from Jaki, his sons and following. These include the chiefly families of Nyangilia, Obule and Midia (all Kakwa-speaking), Yemele and Paranga (Madi-speaking). One group moved east to the Nile creating a belt of Eastern Nilotic speakers which divided the Madi Moyo and Meta from the southern Madi later known as Lugbara.

It was also in this period that Pakwac-Pawir gained its renown as a major Luo dispersal centre. Because Luo-speakers had lived in this area since before the Babito takeover in Bunyoro–Kitara, and because they remained firm Babito supporters, the Babito naturally took an interest in what happened there. This was important, since the area also attracted non-Luo migrants from the north, whom the Babito wished to control. Their interest in this area is perhaps best epitomized by the story of Omukama Cwa Nyabongo and Daca.

At some point near the beginning of the *Nyarubanga*, Cwa gathered his army, crossed the Victoria Nile (probably using a sudd bridge, a possible sign of low water) and fought and killed the Madi King of Koc-Pagak, an important non-Luo polity in the area. It then seems that he appointed another Madi, Abok, who had lived in Kitara, to rule Koc-Pagak under the supervision of one of his Paluo queens named Daca. In so doing he was apparently trying to more than merely subdue a troublesome neighbour, for using royal females as agents in a form of indirect administration was apparently typical of the first Babito dynasty's administration of outlying territories. While this policy was normally successful, in this instance he failed, to the extent at least that three sons of the original Madi leader successfully broke away to form the Pagak, Paboo and Pawoor polities. Its impact was still important, however, because it ensured that Cwa and his agents would play a rôle in the history of this area during the *Nyarubanga*.

It seems clear that the drought turned Pakwac-Pawir into a region of refuge for a mixture of starving and desperate people of various languages and cultures – including the Owiny Luo from Tekidi, the Omolo and Paluo indigenes, and Luo–Madi, Madi–Eastern Nilotic, and Luo–Eastern Nilotic mixtures from Baar. The influx of these people apparently destroyed the position of the Paluo north of the Nile, and made the question of who would control the Luo and other groups there even more pressing. This,

11. For evidence of this drought, see J. B. Webster, 1979b.

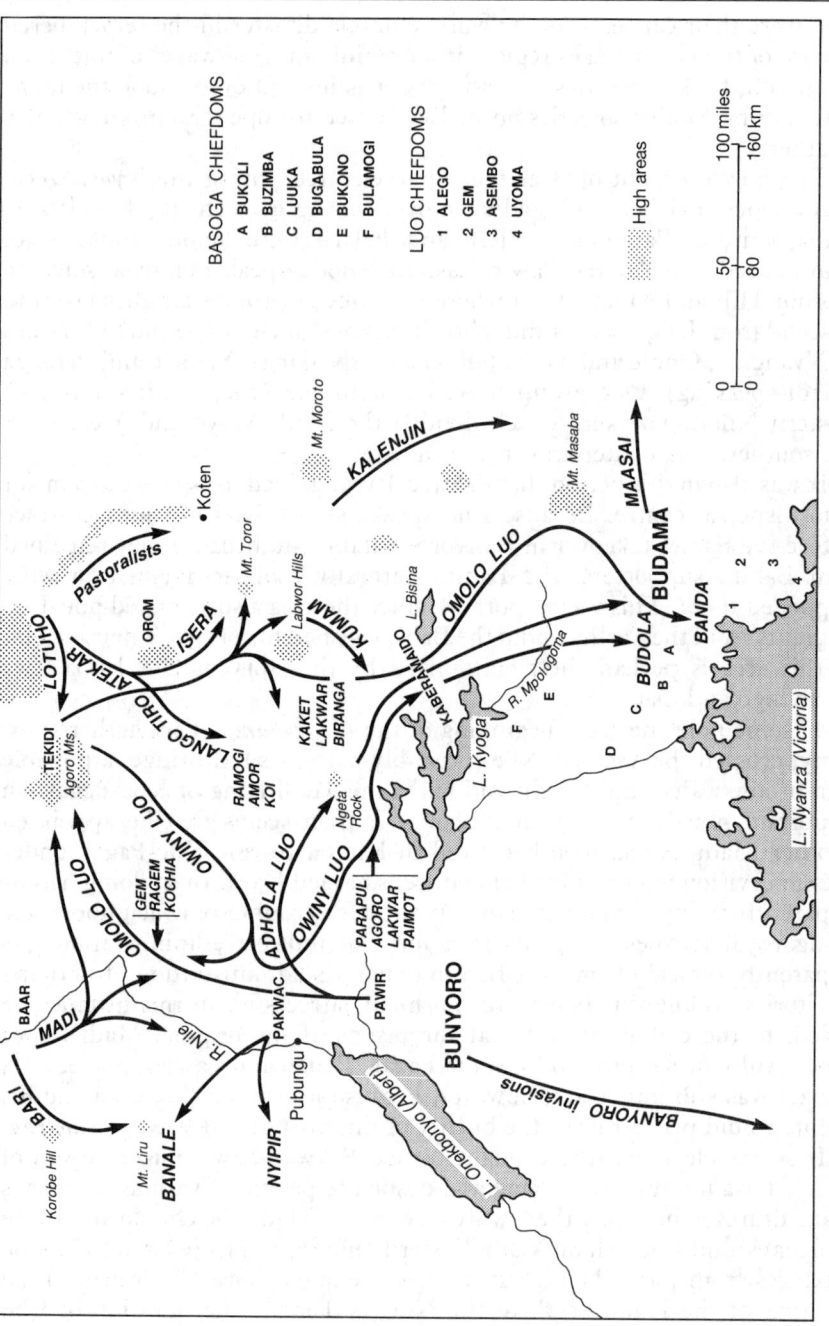

FIG. 26.1   *The Nyarubanga and the fragmentation of the Luo, c. 1570–1720 (after J. B. Webster)*

in turn, eventually led to a quarrel between Cwa Nyabongo (and his agents) and Nyipir. This dispute is recounted within the spear-and-bead tradition. If the elephants are seen as Madi (Abok being of the elephant totem) and the *Min Lyec*[12] as Daca, then this tradition demonstrates how the latter facilitated the ambitions of Nyipir. Nyipir and Tifool (of possible Baar Luo origin), whose followers were largely Owiny and Omolo Luo, moved west of the Nile away from the jurisdiction of Cwa, Nyipir according to tradition driving an axe into the dry bed of the Nile as a symbol of eternal separation. Nyipir, leader of Attyak, founded the Alur kingdom of Okoro Tifool, a state which fragmented into Nyiganda and Angal. The main body of the Owiny apparently moved south-east passing north of Lake Kyoga into the Budola camps in eastern Busoga. The Omolo, whose movements are more debatable, may have left for Agoro and thence via Karamoja to the same area.

According to Jonam traditions, the remaining Luo, led by Daca, deposed Abok and the Koc state split into three. The first, Koc Ragem under Cua, son of Daca by Cwa Nyabongo, became the largest of the Jonam states west of the Nile. The second, Koc Labongo, east of the Nile, was founded by Kaladua, son of Daca by Abok. The third was Koc Paluo under Madi leadership in the sphere of influence of Pawir and under a Munyoro royal female supervisor.[13] It may have been out of this fragmentation of Koc that Kakaire emerged to lead the Pakoyo migration south of Lake Kyoga into northern Busoga in the latter part of the seventeenth century.

The Luo founder of the Terego chiefdom of the Lugbara may have also emerged out of the dispersal from Pakwac-Pawir. Banale and his nephew Raoule arrived east of the Nile in Madi country completely destitute. Banale had been expelled from his home because the famine had driven him, like so many others of this period, to cannibalism. He had been assisted by a leprous Madi woman and when their secret relationship was discovered, a council of Madi elders decided surprisingly to accept him as leader and thereby founded Terego, the largest chiefdom among the Lugbara or southern Madi. Jaki and his ambitious sons were at this time extending their rule over neighbouring Madi, and it is possible that the Madi elders preferred Banale to absorption into the Eastern-Nilotic-speaking Jaki group.[14] By their decision they preserved their language and remained essentially Madi in culture.

The *Nyarubanga* and the spear-and-bead dispersal at Pubungu set three migrations of Luo in motion towards the south-eastern littoral of Nyanza,

12. *Min Lyec* means 'queen of the elephants'. This section follows R. A. Sargent, 1979. Also see A. Apecu, 1972. Since the details of the spear-and-bead tradition have been published so often and are widely known, they have been omitted here.

13. Sargent's interpretation is adopted here. It is stimulating, though controversial, and relates a number of events which hitherto have been treated separately and distinctly in the traditions of the Madi, Banyoro and Luo.

14. See O. J. E. Shiroya, unpublished (a) and (b).

an area that had already been pioneered by such Luo-speaking groups as the Joka Jok of Western Kenya. Many of the Adhola clans left Pakwac-Pawir and caught up with the Owiny in Kaberamaido. One of their leaders was Amor and the Amor clan later emerged in Padhola with a royal drum, sacred spear and bushbuck totem. Other well-known clans within the Adhola complex were the Ramogi (probably part of the early Joka Jok complex), the Bwobo and their relations, the Koi. The latter was related to Olum Panya, the second king of Bwobo (of Acholi), who led them to Ngeta rock where the Koi separated from the main Bwobo group and joined the Adhola on their march to the south-east. The Adhola and Owiny groups rapidly moved south to settle in camps at Budola in eastern Busoga. Another group of clans – the Gem, Ragem and Kochia, who were part of the Omolo cluster and ultimately of Luo–Sudanic origin – were led out of Pakwac-Pawir north along the Nile east to Tekidi and south through Otuke towards Mount Elgon. Possibly the Kaket, Lakwar and Biranga joined the Omolo complex in the east. The Biranga may have been an off-shoot of the royal clan of Puranga since both included important ritual experts ministering the oracles of an earth goddess.[15] There was thus a gradual build-up of Luo settlers in eastern Uganda who then coalesced, probably with the arrival of *Nyarubanga* refugees, to form two separate clusters.

By 1600, the early settling and migrant clans had joined together to form at least four clusters: the Omolo cluster in the Banda camps; an Owiny–Adhola cluster in the Budola camps; a couple of future Adhola clans (the Ramogi and Lakwar) in the forests of West Budama; and a group of future Basoga clans on the northern Mpologoma river. Between about 1598 and 1650 both the Budola and Banda camps broke up, presumably under the severe drought of the 1620s near the end of the *Nyarubanga*. The Owiny moved through Samia-Bugwe and into the Alego region in Siaya District in Western Kenya. One section of the Omolo followed and the two groups came into conflict. The Adhola clans were the last to leave the Budola camps and join their brothers in West Budama.

Among those who retained their Luo speech in Western Kenya, some established chiefdoms (for example, Alego, Gem and Kadimo). They did this, it seems, partly because of their earlier political development, partly because they required some kind of political structure to mediate the process of absorption of the earlier settling Bantu, and partly because they often fought both one another and their neighbours. The majority, however, were like the Padhola, who settled in an unoccupied area and were content with an acephalous political system which preserved peace among the thirty-one clans. Ethnic unity was fostered by the myth that all the clans were descended from the sons and descendants of Adhola, their great migration leader from Kaberamaido to West Budama.[16] Thus, although

15. See J. M. Onyango-ka-Odongo *et al.*, 1976; R. S. Anywar, 1959 (1969); B. A. Ogot, 1967.
16. See B. A. Ogot, 1967.

they included such groups as the Amor, who owned royal regalia and could claim royal ancestry, the Padhola could choose to do without chiefly leadership.

The Padhola gradually pioneered land to the south and east of their original settlements. They clashed with the Bagisu and thereafter concluded a lasting peace with them. After about 1650 they also fought the Maasai in the Tororo area. The Maasai withdrew to the east and Tororo remained a no-man's-land until the Iteso began to settle there in the late eighteenth century.

Eight clans of the Owiny and Omolo complexes moved out of the Budola camps into Busoga.[17] All were of the bushbuck totem and all had pastoral and hunting traditions, although the Owiny cluster also had a farming tradition. Those of Owiny origin were the Mudola, Ngobi, Naminha and Kibiga. The Omolo were the Bandha, Wakoli, Kiruji and Kiranda. All the Owiny, and the Wakoli of the Omolo, became ruling clans in Busoga. The Mudola clan first achieved power in Bukoli. Out of the Mudola came the Mukama figure who moved westward across northern Busoga attracting a large clientage, his sons and grandsons of the Ngobi clan founding the Chiefdoms of Luuka, Buzimba, Buzaaya and Bugabula. A second stream of migrants from the northern Mpologoma settlements of the Luo founded the Chiefdoms of Busiki, Bukono and Bulamogi. The Omolo were more pastoral, reluctant settlers, and only one of their clans became dominant.

Thereafter followed the Pakoyo migrations from Pawir south of Lake Kyoga and their founding of the Chiefdoms of Bagweri and Bugaya. In seeking a sense of ethnic unity the Basoga have tried to make Mukama the leader of all these migrations, to do for him what Padhola traditions have done for Adhola. The Luo migrations gathered numerous clients through inter-marriage and by using or seizing the principal shrines which became centres of ritual and royal pilgrimage. Wherever the Luo went they readily fitted themselves into the existing ritual and religious establishments: spiritual adaptability was one of their greatest political assets.

By 1750 the nine major states noted above had been founded. By the late nineteenth century the initial nine had fragmented into nearly thirty states, the Ngobi or bushbuck clan being dominant in almost twenty. Those states which remained father-to-son in succession and made extensive use of commoner administrators such as Luuka and Bugabula experienced no secessions and few civil wars. On the other hand those which practised fraternal succession and used royal princes as office-holders suffered repeated disputes over the throne and numerous civil wars. Buzimba split into eight independent polities, Busiki and Bugweri each into four, and Bukoli into two. Both Bunyoro and Buganda had experienced both types of administration with similar consequences. Those dynasties which held to their original Luo principles were more stable than those which gave in to the principles of heredity espoused by their Bantu subjects.

17. See D. W. Cohen, 1972.

The *Nyarubanga* and the associated spear-and-bead dispersal was a momentous and historic occasion for the Luo because it determined their modern geographical distribution. The *Nyarubanga* also promoted a massive Banyoro invasion of the Bahima–Batutsi-dominated south and the greatest effort of the agricultural classes to throw off pastoralist overlordship. The first phase of the invasion consisted of unorganized and ravenous hordes, eating banana leaves and sorghum stems. They were clearly not promoting an imperial policy formulated in the royal court of Kitara. Driven by starvation, the hordes swept over the whole of the southern region, some ultimately settling in Buzinza, Burundi and beyond. They in turn set in motion migrations which followed the chain of lakes into Central Africa.

As the drought persisted, a cattle disease wiped out the royal herds of Kitara. This bestirred Cwa II (not Cwa Nyabongo) to lead his armies south to replenish the royal herds and reinforce imperial authority. The pastoralists were the obvious target of the Banyoro, and the agriculturalists Cwa's natural allies. The struggle which ensued is discussed below in the section dealing with the agro-pastoral kingdoms of the south.

The *Nyarubanga* also introduced the Central group of Eastern Nilotes to the scene of the Great Lakes history.[18] Historically this group, whose core population was the Karimojong-Teso cluster, was divided into Isera (agriculturalists with some cattle) and Koten pastoralists (cattle-keepers who engaged in some agriculture). While Isera and pastoralist elements are contained in all peoples of the Central group of the Eastern Nilotes, the ethnic groups to emerge primarily from the former, and whose dialects are similar, are the Iteso, Toposa and Dodos and, out of the latter, the Karimojong, Jie and Turkana.

Furthermore all the modern Central group of Eastern Nilotes have Luo elements among them. One problem for the historian is to explain why, when clan names, age and ritual organizations, homelands and migration traditions are much the same for the Lango Omiro, Eastern Acholi, Kumam and Iteso, the first three had become Luo-speaking and the last Eastern-Nilotic-speaking by 1830. A second problem surrounds three small Luo-speaking groups – the JoAbwor, JoAkwa and Kumam – who resemble the Central group of Eastern Nilotes culturally and who have received more than their share of attention because their history was expected to throw some light on the enigma of the Lango Omiro and Iteso. A third complication is the Nyangiya group – the Nyangiya, Tepes (Sor), Teuso and Didinga – who inhabit mountainous areas in north-eastern Uganda. In clan origins they are almost 90 per cent Central Eastern Nilotic or Luo in origin, yet these people maintain a very distinct language and culture.

The Okarowok (Ikarebwok) is a major clan among the Central group of

18. J. E. Lamphear, unpublished; R. S. Herring, 1979; J. B. Webster *et al.*, 1973; J. P. Crazzolara, 1960; R. Ogwal, 1969; J. A. Otima, unpublished; D. H. Okalany, unpublished; P. Odyomo, unpublished; J. Weatherby, 1979 and unpublished (a) and (b).

Eastern Nilotes. As noted earlier it seems to have emerged in the Agoro region when the Lotuho imposed their language and customs over a Muru population, the Lukoya. Agoro was a major centre of Isera-Omiro dispersal. The migrants carried place-name memorials of their Agoro homeland wherever they went: Magoro, Mukongoro, Itengor, Ngora, Bokora, Igoria.

The major migrations to the south-east of the Luo associated with the Owiny and Omolo were very much mixed with the Isera, especially the Omolo who traversed the Agoro–Karamoja corridor to the south. The Owiny left behind pockets of Luo-speakers in what later became Lango Omiro country, at Amac on the northern littoral of Lake Kyoga and near Karuma Falls. Many of the people who eventually identified with the Omolo may have been Eastern Nilotic in background. Those who reached Western Kenya were known to the Luo as Omia, the Lomia being one of the four great clans of the Lotuho, and Omiya Anyiima and Omia Pacua being memorials to them in East Acholi. The last wave of settlers to arrive in Siaya also included some migrants from eastern Uganda, the most notable of whom were the Owila (the dominant clan of Uyoma), the Matar (the dominant clan of Sakwa) and the Bayuma (the dominant clan of Wanga), all probably Isera-Omiro from the Bako of Ethiopian origins.

In addition to the Central Sudanic peoples and the Northern group of Eastern Nilotes the Isera contained clans of Luo and Ethiopian origin. Other than Luo left behind by the Owiny and Omolo, there were the Puranga survivors of Tekidi. These groups were reinforced by migrants who can be traced back to Anywa or Pari, to Baar, and to Pakwac-Pawir. The most important Pakwac-Pawir groups were the Patiko, Payera, and Paluo (discussed below). Moreover, some 'Ethiopian' emigrants may have entered this region as a result of the Oromo invasion.[19]

During the seventeenth and eighteenth centuries, these migrant groups settled together and formed clusters which were defined by their territory of residence and, in some instances, some degree of self-identification. The largest of these were the Bako cluster in Central Jie, the Okii (or Miro) cluster in the Mount Moroto–Omanimani River area of Central Karamoja, the Abwor cluster in the Labwor Hills, the Kuman cluster in Western Teso, and (what we can call) the Iworopom–Iteso cluster in Central and Southern Karamoja. All of these clusters included both Luo and the Central group of Eastern Nilotes, though in quite different proportions, and bilinguality was common by the eighteenth century. The Iworopom–Iteso cluster was unique in that it seems to have had the least coherence: its people spoke a Central Eastern Nilotic and/or Kalenjin-type language, and its Iworopom elements had large herds of cattle.

19. We believe that these 'Ethiopian' emigrants possibly included the Bako groups in Lango (cf. Bako people in Ethiopia), the Ober people in Lango (cf. the Uober clan among the Bako people), and the Oromo, which is the proper name for the so-called Galla. There are no traditions that explicitly link these groups to Ethiopia, so our association must be seen as a very tentative hypothesis.

Pastoralists and farmers

In the Great Lakes region, it has been the practice among historians and anthropologists to divide societies into two water-tight compartments of pastoralists and agriculturalists. These were supposed to be distinct economic categories into which all societies in the region fell. Attempts have therefore been made to identify certain ethnic groups with particular economic pursuits. This is an over-simplification of what was a very complex, dynamic and fluid situation. In northern and eastern Uganda, for example, the relationship between farmers and cattlemen was evolving throughout our period. Numerous attempts were made by all groups – farmers, pastoralists, mixed farmers, fishermen, hunters and gatherers – to improve their economies, form stable communities and, when they chose or were compelled to migrate, plan their movements rationally. Such movements of population and other social dislocations threw together groups whose socio-political, religious and economic ideas and practices often varied considerably. Consequently, people were compelled to mix and compromise their cultural heritages if they wished to form stable communities. Throughout our period, different linguistic groups of farmers and pastoralists were fusing together to form new and reasonably well integrated societies. Most of these cultural syntheses formed the bases of the new ethnic groups that emerged in the area during the eighteenth and nineteenth centuries. We give below a few examples to illustrate the nature of this social transformation.

Although a few of the pastoralist Central–Eastern Nilotic groups may have joined the Isera at an early date,[20] and others (the Lokorikitak) stayed in Dodoth during their emigration from the Sudan, the majority settled in the Mount Koten–Magos Hills area of north-eastern Karamoja. These Koten–Magos people (as they have been called) apparently already had a pastoralist orientation before they came south. Hence, while they entered Karamoja as cattle-poor refugees, they quickly developed a mixed pastoral, farming, and hunting and gathering economy that was better adapted to the climate of this region than the economies of the more agricultural groups. The results of this became evident between 1680 and 1830, when the Koten–Magos groups moved into their modern homelands and the agricultural groups either joined them and adopted their economy or retreated to the west.

This process started in about 1680–1750 with the expansion of the pastoralists in four directions: one group, the Ngimonia, spread along the River Tarash and formed the core of the Turkana; another, the Korwakol, moved west to the Longiro river, forced many of the Bako groups to leave Jie, and became the most important moiety of the Jie; a third, consisting of some future Karimojong and Dodos, moved south to the Apule river; and a fourth, the Ngikora, migrated north into Dodoth (where they formed

20. See R. S. Herring, 1974.

the core of the Toposa). The last stages of this process may have been influenced by a drought in the 1720s which resulted in the 'Nyamdere' famine, for the traditions of the agriculturalists indicate that many of them left Jie and Labwor because of famine and moved to eastern Acholi and the Ngeta Rock area of Lango. Some of the groups in eastern Acholi then retraced their steps and resettled north-central Jie where they eventually joined the Korwakol and formed the Rengen moiety of the Jie.

The situation then stabilized for a time, but a combination of land pressure in some of the pastoralist-dominated areas and droughts in the 1780s and 1830s started the movements again. Most of the Abwor and Bako groups in Labwor pushed west into Lango and, in a few cases, south into Teso (where some joined the Kuman cluster). Likewise, many of the Okii-cluster people left central Karamoja for Nyakwai, Labwor, Lango and northern Teso, while many of the agricultural groups in southern Karamoja moved through the Magoro area into central and southern Teso.[21] Others from both areas joined the Sor. Most of the groups that moved into Nyakwai, Labwor, eastern Acholi, and Lango were at least bilingual in a Luo dialect and, since all of them joined or were joined by Luo-speakers from further west, these societies became Luo-speaking. The same was true of those who joined the Kumam.[22] Those who went into Teso, however, included fewer Luo-speakers, and the Iteso thus became an Eastern-Nilotic-speaking people.

This western flow of agriculturalist refugees, especially in its later stages, was accelerated by the renewed expansion of the pastoralists. In the 1780s, the proto-Dodos groups on the Apule river moved north into Dodoth, where they and the Lokorikituk combined to force the Toposa community there to move north into their present homelands. Both the Dodos and Toposa pastoralists assimilated a number of Isera groups and thus adopted a somewhat more agriculturally oriented economy than their southern brethren. Then, in the 1820s, the Korwakol and Rengen Jie combined to destroy a large community of agriculturalists, the Poet, who lived on the Kapoeta river. And, finally, in the same period, the proto-Karimojong groups on the Apule river pushed south into the homelands of the remnants of the Okii and Iteso-Iworopom clusters, and either absorbed them into their society or forced them to leave. In the case of the Iworopom people, this involved a great deal of violence, probably because they had large herds of cattle and were thus the direct competitors of the Koten-Magos groups. In either case, these developments and the 1830s drought precipitated the last large-scale migrations from this area to the west.

21. According to tradition, 'Karimojong' means the 'old men left behind' who, fearing their youths were dead, said to the messengers, 'look for their *atesin* (graves)', thus originating the word 'Teso'. While most age-sets are named after animals, 'Kangarak' means 'Those who go ahead'.

22. J. E. Ekadu, 1961 and 1971. For analysis see A. B. Eilu, 1976; D. H. Okalany, unpublished; J. B. Webster, unpublished (a).

The case of Bunyoro-Kitara illustrates the interrelationship between the pastoralists and the farmers even better. Edward I. Steinhart's study emphasizes the close 'correlation between drought/famine and pastoral expansion, agricultural dislocation, and state formation in Kitara and her southern marches'.[23] Bunyoro lost valued grazing lands in Kooki, Bwera and the southern marches of Kitara to Buganda between about 1760 and 1783. Also, the increasing autonomy of the pastoral societies of Nkore, Buhweju and Buzimba further restricted the Bunyoro state to largely agricultural lands. Consequently, the Kitara pastoralists infiltrated both into the Bito dynasty as well as into the agricultural lands. Pastoralists settled among agriculturalists and fused with them to form new compound communities. A new class system emerged and a new state structure based on it gradually developed. Land and not cattle became the basis of political authority, and the new chiefly élite was recruited from the settled Bahuma, members of the Bito clan and the Bairu farmers. These three groups intermarried extensively and they provided both the chiefs and the land-lords, who collected tribute from the subjects for the *omukama* (king). Thus, in the words of Steinhart, a new Nyoro state, 'based on the development of a subordinate tribute-paying peasantry', gradually came into being in the eighteenth century.[24]

Social and political institutions

It was not only language and economy which distinguished the pastoralists from the Isera groups and both from the Luo-speakers. The pastoralists perfected their age organizations as instruments of gerontocratic control, and these became the key social and political institutions in their societies. Age organizations also existed among the Isera and Isera-influenced societies, but in a truncated form. The main social and political institutions in these latter societies were multi-clan ritual groupings – called *etogo* in Lango, *otheme* (sing. *othen*) in Labwor and *itemwan* (sing. *etem*) in Teso and Kumam – which were used for settling disputes and performing religious ceremonies. The more mixed in origins the group of clans, the stronger these institutions were.[25]

In the ethno-cultural mix north of the Nile–Kyoga–Bisina divide, hereditary chieftaincy was a Luo idea. Since the majority of the Eastern Luo either were Eastern Nilotic in origin or had been strongly influenced by Eastern Nilotic ideas, this type of hereditary leadership was rejected by many and opposed by the elders. Nevertheless, it had an impact on the political institutions of not only many of the Luo-speaking groups, but also on some of the Isera groups and, through their influence, on such

23. E. I. Steinhart, 1981, p. 132.
24. ibid., p. 135.
25. For the Jie age organization see J. E. Lamphear, 1979. For the *etem*, see D. H. Okalany, unpublished.

groups as the Jie and Dodos. Among the Luo-speakers, those that followed chiefs tended to move into eastern Acholi, where their ideas were reinforced when some Paluo groups arrived there between 1680 and 1760. Even then, however, the Eastern Acholi remained so distinct that the western Luo peoples viewed them as Lango rather than Luo until the last half of the nineteenth century. In Labwor, Lango, Nyakwai and Kumam, the people generally rejected the idea of hereditary chieftaincy in favour of gerontocratic ritual leadership.

This is not to say that these groups did not sometimes entrust individual leaders with a good deal of secular authority. Oral traditions give the impression that the eighteenth and nineteenth centuries witnessed a significant increase in warfare among the Eastern Luo and Central-Eastern Nilotes. This in turn tended to increase the influence of war leaders and their councils and also of the younger generation at the expense of the gerontocracy, youth and eldership being a potential line of division in these age-organized societies. Thus, in Lango, powerful war leaders formed extensive military confederacies which they used to conquer their homeland, attack their neighbours, and raise large mercenary armies which fought in Bunyoro, Toro and Buganda. Similar confederacies were formed in northern Teso, Sebei (Mount Elgon), Kumam and Padhola, but in these areas the leaders were *emuron* (seers) whose roles seem to have been adopted from the Kalenjin peoples, probably by way of the Iworopom. Because of their crucial military roles, these men also gained considerable political influence, but none was able to secure a chiefly status for his family. Thus the institution of *emuron* created yet another power centre and challenge to both the war council and the gerontocracy, but did not combine readily with chieftaincy.

The Iteso who settled in the 'thigh of the cow', an unusually fertile area in Ngora and Kumi and those areas – Serere and southern Soroti – colonized from it, most closely resembled the original Isera. They had no age organization, no ritual *etem* and no *emuron*. They depended upon three great assimilating clans – Atekok, Ikarebwok and Irarak – as the vehicles of social cohesion. The northern Iteso plus those in Bukedea possessed all the institutions noted above, being much more mixed in origin. Among them migrations were often organized by *etem*, western Teso having been occupied by three, with one, the Isolata, giving its name to Soroti. Many Iteso filtered into the Bantu and Luo areas to the south as seekers after land or as mercenaries being especially welcome in some Busoga states as a counterbalance to military and political pressure from Buganda. In Bugwere, for example, the first Iteso settlers led by Laki of the Irarak clan settled from 1706 to 1733, became wealthy and drew clients, Laki's son split the kingdom and became chief of one part after the Laparanat famine.[26] In Bulamogi, an Etesot ruled temporarily. Probably the greatest of the mercenaries was the Etesot, Oguti among the Padhola.

26. R. R. Atkinson, at press. For the Iteso in Padhola, see B. A. Ogot, 1967.

In the Central area, Buganda stood in distinct contrast to Bunyoro. Without a royal clan or cattle and with a king who could and often did appoint officials without regard to custom, tradition or heredity, Buganda had developed, by the beginning of the nineteenth century, little class institutionalization, unusual vertical mobility and a greater degree of social inequality than Bunyoro but less than Rwanda. Everyone in Buganda was involved in a dyadic relationship of super-ordination and subordination. Social and economic ties were vertical rather than horizontal.

Politically and socially, Bunyoro-Kitara sat in the middle. From a northern Nilotic perspective it was despotic and class-ridden and from Buganda it appeared loosely organized and class-conscious. The royal Babito clan had originated as mixed farmers but the dynasty increasingly acquired a pastoral orientation. However, the non-royal branches of the Bito clan who became, during our period, the largest and most dispersed clan group in Kitara, were found at all economic levels. Many possessed no wealth or power but maintained the myth of belonging to a ruling clan. These commoner Bito clans intermarried extensively with other social and kinship groups, thus helping to create a homogenous national image for the dynasty.

Furthermore, the creation of this national image was enhanced by the appointment of representatives of other social strata and kinship groups to various court and state offices. Gradually, these offices were made hereditary and, in this way, a permanent class of privileged persons, whose fortunes and aspirations were interlocked with those of the Bito dynasty, was created.

The Mukama of Bunyoro had much less power and wealth than the Kabaka of Buganda. The Kabaka retained more of the wealth he received than the Mukama who emphasized the redistribution of wealth and surplus by the royal court. In Bunyoro power was more dispersed: most positions remained hereditary with the Mukama merely confirming the chosen candidate and in consequence few peasants ever attained high office. The clans in Bunyoro did not achieve the cohesion, nor their heads the status, of those in Buganda. While in Buganda the thirty clans were theoretically equal – in practice their status rose and fell according to their political fortunes – in Bunyoro there was a clear distinction between high- and low-status clans.

Among the Nilotic Luo there were those organized in states and those who were non-centralized. State structures were less elaborate than in Bunyoro or Buganda and Luo kings exercised influence but little real power. Office-holders were almost exclusively hereditary with the king unable to interfere with the chosen candidate of the family or clan. These differences were the result of geography and economics, historical developments and cultural biases. Although some royal lines stretch back many centuries and are as old as those in the south and west, most of the Luo states came into existence late. Furthermore, repeated droughts had forced so many migrations, re-locations and re-formations of societies that many Luo states in their present location and their present populations date to about 1680 or even later. It is true that the same droughts substantially affected the south-west but they never caused the physical removal of a state such as in northern Uganda where Padibe, one of the oldest and by the nineteenth century most sophisticated of the Luo states, ultimately came to be located over 500 miles from where it was originally founded.

Also, none of the Luo states enjoyed the fertile agricultural base of Buganda, Rwanda or the Bahima states. Neither did they possess the rich iron and salt deposits of Bunyoro or the Busongora area. Prior to the *Nyarubanga* it seems likely that the Luo owned substantial hards of cattle. However, by about 1800 these had been destroyed and it seems possible that the Acholi at least probably had the lowest incidence of cattle of any of the cattle-rearing peoples of the Great Lakes region. Without cattle and without rich agricultural lands or trade items it was difficult to amass and maintain surplus wealth. Consequently the Luo states did not exhibit the disparities in wealth nor the class consciousness which distinguished the states of the south-west. In all the Luo states the Eastern Nilotic population was influential and became more pronounced from west to east, until it formed a majority in the states of Eastern Acholi. The Eastern Nilotes were extremely egalitarian in their political and social philosophy. It must have been difficult to convert them to ideas of chieftaincy, superordination and subordination, class and heredity. As one moves eastwards, Luo kings appear more and more like chairmen of, and spokesmen for, Eastern Nilotic councils of elders.

In the Luo states the theory and the nineteenth-century practice regarding class differ. The theory may represent an older pre-*Nyarubanga* practice when the Luo were distinguished by their ownership of cattle. The theory is that Luo societies are divided into royal and commoner classes. What had become more important by about 1800 were distinctions based on origins, those of Luo and those of non-Luo ancestry. Often royal has come to be identified with Luo and non-Luo with commoner. The royal clan is normally the largest. Membership of it gives only a modicum of prestige unless one belongs to the royal lineage. In popular thought non-Luo commoners are often graded according to how long ago their ancestors entered the society and became Luo. However, a royal separated by ten generations from the chiefly line will be treated little differently and have no greater control over wealth than an alien who joined the society ten generations ago. In the Acholi states the royal clan is exogamous and aliens are rapidly assimilated.

There is a more realistic way to look at class in the Luo states. In the political compromises over the centuries, many non-Luo clans came to hold positions or perform ritual functions which gave the lineages of the office-holders more prestige (and sometimes tribute) than the royal clan. If there was an upper class it consisted of the nuclear families of the king,

795

his councillors, the owner of the soil, the ritual experts including the rain-caller and the *jagos* (territorial sub-heads).

The acephalous Luo and the Central–Eastern Nilotes had no class institutionalization. There were no chiefs and no hereditary offices. Individuals were seldom memorialized either in clan or place names as was customary among the Nilotes. People rarely recalled ancestors prior to their grandfather. Clans were huge but families almost of the nuclear variety. The gerontocracies were governed by the oldest age-set sitting in *etem* or *etogo* where their decisions were believed to be sanctioned by the ancestors. The gerontocracies were often linked in large military confederacies in which one prominent warrior leader and his subordinates were recognized and supported by an *emuron* (seer) and his sub-agents, who consulted the spirits about the advisability of war, presided over ritual preparations and advised on strategy. The *emuron* was often a rain-caller as well. The war leaders and ritual experts were usually fairly prosperous. In the gerontocracies the lines of tension and potential cleavage were between the governing elders and the younger warriors. The elders maintained tight, even oppressive, control over the younger men, monopolizing both women and cattle and delaying marriage and economic independence for the young. Younger age-sets occasionally migrated to escape their frustrations.[27]

Acephalous Luo and Eastern Nilotic societies often exhibited great disparities in wealth and economic inequality. In Teso, for example, the average family might possess three to five head of cattle, 10 per cent owning 500 to 1000. Prosperous elders might be heard more often and more attentively in *etem* but while they had more influence they had no greater power than others. Wealth brought respect and aroused expectations of lavish hospitality but it did not result in social inequality. Vertical mobility upward was achieved by raising a large family of girls for whom cattle bridewealth was secured and few boys for whom bridewealth had to be paid, achieving fame and cattle as a great warrior, or by being a skilled animal husbandman. Cattle were widely distributed through the bride-wealth system. In the south-west the same bridewealth custom was so hedged about with rules and prejudice that it made inter-marriage difficult and prevented Bairu and Bahutu from becoming cattle-owners.

The change in the balance of power: the decline of Bunyoro and the rise and expansion of Buganda

After the *Nyarubanga* the most significant themes in the northern and central sections of the Great Lakes history were the crisis in Bunyoro which led to its decline and the internal developments in Buganda which caused its dynamic rise and expansion. These two developments led to a dramatic

27. For the discussion of social stratification, we have followed the schema of M. L. Perlman, 1970; A. W. Southall, 1970.

change in the balance of power. The Bunyoro crisis began with the death of Cwa in the *Nyarubanga* invasion of the south. Cwa's only son, Winyi II, was captured and lived in Ihangiro.[28] Kitara was ruled by a regent, Cwa's sister, Mashamba. Cwa had no sons by a Luo wife (those eligible to succeed him under the rules of the royal house) and the boy later found in Ihangiro may not have been a son at all, but he was of the Babito clan. Winyi II murdered Mashamba and seized the throne. Thereafter the old tradition of the heir being of a Luo or Paluo mother became the exception rather than the rule. Candidacy for the throne was opened to all sons of the king and succession disputes became more frequent, more bitter and more prolonged.

Under the first dynasty, the chiefdom of Pawir had held a prestigious position within the imperial structure. The new turn of events at the imperial capital caused general unrest in Pawir. A succession of what the Paluo called 'Bantu kings' sought to deal with the unrest by encouraging separatist tendencies so that the unified sub-chiefdom of Pawir in 1650 had become six petty chieflets by 1750.[29] Under Isansa all six chieflets were placed under a country chief by which Paluoland lost its semi-autonomous status and was integrated into metropolitan Bunyoro. The Paluo regularly opposed Bantu candidates to the throne while other Paluo migrated away to the north and east because of the closing of political opportunities, the loss of status and outright persecution. The frequency of succession disputes combined with Paluo dissidence undermined the central power of Kitara. King Isansa (*c.*1733–60) came to power against strong Paluo opposition. Once in power he carried out a severe persecution of the Paluo which in turn accelerated their outward migration.

The most immediate result of the crisis in Bunyoro was the exodus of Paluo-Pakoyo.[30] into Acholi, northern Busoga, Alur and even into Padhola and Western Kenya east of the lake. The first exodus was led by Labongo, Kakaire and Atiko, the first two claiming a relationship to the royal house of the first Babito dynasty. They were not agents of Banyoro imperialism but they did carry drums and the political ideology of Babito rule. Both were influenced in founding chieftaincies where they had not existed and in enlargement of political scale where they had. While the Paluo helped to spread their language in the north, the Pakoyo linguistically assimilated into Basoga society.

In the north the major form of political organization was gerontocracies or tiny chiefdoms. The Paluo popularized royal drums, enhanced the dignity of the chief and incorporated small units into larger states, allowing them to retain their hereditary leadership. They founded new states such as Lira Paluo and Paimol or enlarged and restructed old ones such as

28. J. B. Webster, unpublished (b).

29. A. Adefuye, 1973, 1979 and unpublished.

30. On the exodus, see J. B. Webster, unpublished (a); R. R. Atkinson, 1976; A. M. Garry, 1976 and J. B. Webster, 1976c.

Padibe, Patongo, Alero and Koc. Both Puranga (taken over by the Paluo) and Payera under its traditional leadership were inspired by Paluo theories and incorporated a number of subordinate units in the process of expansion. Atiko was very much influenced by Paluo political philosophy and enlarged his insignificant polity in a move to the east until it was a chiefdom of size and significance. Although he was twelfth in line from the founder, so pronounced was his contribution that his name was given to his state. Those who imitated Paluo methods were often more successful than the Paluo themselves. Of the twenty chiefdoms west of the Aswa river in 1800 only three had Paluo monarchies and of the nine major Acholi chiefdoms in 1900 only Lira Paluo and Puranga were governed by Paluo.

Luo-ization proceeded both by incorporation and political fragmentation and proliferation. Lira Paluo was an example of the former, the Alur of the latter. The Paluo entered the Lapono area and persuaded one non-Luo gerontocracy, two small Luo chieflets and the large Lira chiefdom to join them. After a later expansion they created two royal governorships. Since further expansion was blocked, Lira Paluo formed a confederacy with small neighbouring chieflets which were gradually brought into clientship. With this political expansion went a popularization of the Luo language and culture.

The Alur developments were different. Prior to 1680 there was only one Alur chiefdom, Okoro, among the Central Sudanic peoples of the highlands. Luo settlers moved out of Okoro, inter-marrying and popularizing the Luo language and culture and ultimately inviting an Okoro prince to rule over them. This was usually done with the support of the indigenous people and it brought many Kebu, Lendu and Madi under Alur Luo rule. Alur states proliferated; Panduru was founded about 1670–1700; Paidha, Padiya, Padel and Acer Paluo between 1700 and 1790; and Ucego about 1820–50. This became the Alur family of states.[31]

Omukama Isansa was as crucial to the decline of Bunyoro as Kabaka Mawanda was to the rise of Buganda. Isansa's rule was a peculiar mixture of military success and political disaster. We have noted the mistakes in his northern policy: his southern policy was even more disastrous. He swept south once again demonstrating Bunyoro's military might. During the military campaign he encouraged royal princes to head governorships in Kooki, Kitagwenda and the Busongora states of Kisaka and Bugaya and a favourite of the Bamooli clan in Kiyanja. Predictably, all except Kitagwenda had thrown off allegiance to the empire within a generation of his death.[32] Isansa was overturning a policy of administering outlying territories which had worked tolerably well for three centuries presumably in the interest of getting rid of the multiplicity of contenders to the throne created by the new succession policies of his dynasty.

31. J. B. Webster, unpublished (a).

32. A. Wheeler, unpublished; E. R. Kamuhangire, unpublished; S. Lwango-Lunyiigo, 1972–3.

Isansa's greatest political blunder was his attack upon the palace of Wamara, head of the Cwezi cult in Bwera. The first Babito dynasty had carefully cultivated relations with the cult, being more successful in this policy than the Bahinda states. While the Babito worshipped Wamara, the Bahinda had nothing to do with the cult even though their subjects did. Presumably Wamara opposed the second Babito dynasty because it violated the traditional rules of succession. The kings in turn withheld their normal tribute to Wamara's court. Isansa decided upon a military confrontation. It was the most momentous blunder in Kitara's history.

So great was the sacrilege that the trees 'bled' and Wamara cursed Isansa, prophesying that Buganda would swallow Bunyoro. The working out of this curse became a major historical theme well into the twentieth century. Isansa's blunder not only related to Buganda but to the whole southern borderlands where Banyoro authority partly at least rested upon the support of the Cwezi cult. A new cult headquarters was created within the imperial palace but the cult and, Banyoro authority with it, disappeared in the southern borderlands. Consequently the new princely states threw off allegiance with ease as did the ancient tributary states of Buhweju and Buzimba. The nadir of the empire's fortunes came about 1830 with the secession of Toro and Paluoland.[33] Not only did Wamara's curse prove accurate, in that Buganda seized much territory of Bunyoro proper, but the string of small southern states could not stand in isolation. They became ideal targets for the imperial ambitions of Buganda, Nkore and Mpororo.

The rise of Buganda

While the Banyoro kings were busy dismantling a political system which had assured their pre-eminence for three centuries, the Baganda monarchs were correcting many of the political evils which had crippled Buganda from its foundation.[34] Buganda was bedevilled by three inter-related problems. The first arose from the growing strength of the monarchy and its appointed bureaucracy pitted against the clan heads or Bataka chiefs where ties or supposed ties of kinship were utilized to strengthen clan loyalties and mould clans into cohesive political factions. The second surrounded the multiplicity of ambitious royal princes in or out of office looking for an opportunity to manipulate clan political factions in order to seize the throne. Where the bureaucracy was largely hereditary and therefore protected when the monarch changed, throne disputes might be less bitter and kingmakers more disinterested and amenable to compromise. But in Buganda the new monarch's control of bureaucratic patronage meant that behind each princely candidate stood clientages of potential office-holders for whom the outcome of the succession struggle would mean either position and prestige or oblivion and even exile. Compromise was difficult

33. J. F. M. Wilson, unpublished (a) and (b).
34. M. S. M. Kiwanuka, 1971a, whose interpretation is adopted here.

because potential office-holders sought not only personal advancement but patronage for the clan they felt they represented. The third problem was the bloody succession disputes and wars which followed the death of most kings and the numerous royal assassinations. Succession disputes were more damaging in Buganda than they ever had been in Kitara. In the latter the struggle for the throne could be fierce but once a king had been chosen and crowned he was rarely assassinated or overthrown. Not so in Buganda where a monarch might be killed or overthrown at any time during his reign. A number of Buganda kings never did appear to secure control of the kingdom, their reigns being a bloody series of civil wars among brothers and sons. Furthermore, in Kitara brothers did not succeed except in unusual circumstances. In Buganda three brothers might reign in succession with all their sons struggling to succeed.

Buganda was more favourably situated climatically and geographically than the other major Great Lakes states. There is no reference to drought in its lengthy and detailed traditions. It was rather a region of refuge. Its economy had not been shaken at least twice every century nor occasionally destroyed as during the *Nyarubanga*. Buganda had a diverse and secure agricultural base which, unlike in the other major states, freed its male population for war and politics. Because it was located along the littoral of Nyanza it conducted a water-borne trade – probably long before the mid-to-late eighteenth century – and this factor is normally advanced to explain its expansion. It produced bark cloth, a commodity much prized by neighbouring peoples and, in its expansion, it secured control of iron-ore deposits, a resource it originally lacked. With the possible exception of the southern Basoga states, no other state in the Great Lakes region possessed such a favourable geographical and economic environment.

Unlike other Great Lakes states, Buganda had no royal clan, each prince belonging to the clan of his mother contrary to the general population which followed the rules of patriliny. Any clan therefore had a chance to provide the monarch. This system gave all the people a feeling of being part of the monarchy but also encouraged each clan to give a wife to the new *kabaka* with the consequent rapid proliferation of potential royal heirs. The kings of Buganda were therefore forced to be more extravagantly polygamous than most other rulers. Contrast the Acholi system where upon coronation the king was given a wife by the elders, the heir to come from the sons of this queen only. In addition the Baganda king was merely the first among equals of the Bataka chiefs. Outlying districts were governed by an indirect-rule system where indigenous chiefs became new Bataka and were employed as local agents of the kings; they were hereditary and not removable by the monarch.

In the sixteenth and seventeenth centuries Buganda was merely a tiny state like many in Busoga which tolerated fraternal succession and relied upon royal administrators. It was unstable and wracked by interminable civil wars. However, Baganda nationalism (having developed in the shadow of Banyoro imperialism) was strong enough to prevent secession and fragmentation of the state – in contrast, for example, with the Basoga state of Buzimba which disintegrated into eight independent chieflets. However, the reluctance to secede meant that the struggle for the throne was even more fierce than where secession was an option.

Kabaka Tebandeke (c.1644–74) strengthened royal power by a successful attack upon the ritual religious officers whose extortionate practices lay heavy upon the monarchy and the populace. Tebandeke greatly reduced the power of these religious officers leaving Buganda unique among Bantu peoples in its indifference to supernatural forces. That Tebandeke was successful while Isansa failed in a similar policy relates to the different organization of religion in the two kingdoms. In Kitara the Cwezi cult was a centralized institution, while in Buganda each ritual officer was apparently independent of the next.

Buganda's territorial expansion was associated with three outstanding kings of the eighteenth century. Mawanda (c.1674–1704) seized Singo, overran Kyaggwe and took over Bulamogi from Bunyoro. Bunyoro, pre-occupied with its domestic problems related to the change in the dynasty, did not rally wholeheartedly to the protection of its territory. Given this immense territorial expansion Mawanda wisely abandoned the old indirect-rule system and the king's favourites – many of commoner origin and called the king's men – were appointed to the expanded bureaucracy. These royal appointees became more influential than the Bataka chiefs: Mawanda even appointed and dismissed Bataka chiefs. In theory all positions became appointive. This outstanding monarch was not only a military genius but also an imaginative statesman and is rightly credited with being the father of the modern Kiganda system of government. Both Junju and Kamanya, between about 1734 and 1794, further expanded the kingdom. Junju annexed Buddu, brought Kooki into tributary relationship and demonstrated Buganda's military might by marching into Kiziba and as far as Karagwe. Junju was reaping the fruits of Isansa's 'southern charter' of the generation before. Kamanya seized Buwekula from Bunyoro. By 1800 Buganda had conclusively established her pre-eminence over Bunyoro.

Semakokiro, in the mid-eighteenth century, turned his attention to the problem of the royal princes. He began the practice of executing unsuccessful rivals, even royal sons if necessary. He purged princes from the administration to prevent them from using their positions to plot against the throne. This gave immense power to the king and paved the way for the absolute monarchy which emerged in the nineteenth century. Ironically, while Semakokiro was seeking to reduce the destructiveness of succession disputes by controlling the number of candidates and removing them from offices of authority, Isansa was opening up the contest to all sons of the king. Not surprisingly, succession disputes became something less of a problem in Buganda and far more of a problem in Bunyoro, reversing the conditions of earlier centuries. Given the turbulence of the early politics of Buganda, it is easy to overrate the great centralizers and imperial *kabaka*s of the eighteenth century as heralding a golden age. It is well to recall that despotism was achieved at the expense of lengthy rebellions, severe opposition to the *kabaka*s, considerable political violence and growing numbers of exiles to neighbouring states. It might be argued that the eighteenth century was even more violent than the centuries before it.

For centuries Buganda had existed under the shadow of Banyoro imperialism, first as a pawn of that empire but by the end of the eighteenth century ready to challenge the imperial structure itself. Buganda developed an intense nationalism which permitted the kings to gather power around the throne and develop an efficient administrative and military machine where the energies of the citizenry were devoted to their personal advancement by finding favour with the *kabaka*. Every man became a politician and many became addicted to jealousy, spying and blackmail in pursuit of royal favour. Great kings directed this energy to the service of the state and nation. Despite a vague 'establishment' of the Manis, Lungfish and Monkey clans, by 1800 Buganda had a highly competitive society, a society more upwardly mobile and secular than any other in the Great Lakes region.

The agro-pastoral kingdoms of the South

The term 'interlacustrine culture' employed for almost a century by Africanist ethnologists, is usually based on observations carried out in the southern half of the region, in particular in the Rwandan monarchy which has been singled out by several authors as an ideal example thereof.[35] The formation of this cultural complex has been dated to a relatively recent period, from the sixteenth to the eighteenth centuries, the period discussed here. The work done by historians over the last twenty years or so has helped to expose the fallacies of this image presented by European ethnologists, and to set in their true historical dimension, one which is broader, better-balanced and more rigorously defined, peoples with a past known to be rooted in an ancient iron age going back to the beginning of the Christian era, if not earlier. The sixteenth century is a turning point, an age of legends and the socio-cultural bases of its history.

A geocultural area

The region's natural features and cultural heritage give it a physical and human landscape full of contrasts. In the west a gigantic fault scarp over 2000 metres high, the Kibira range, extended north by the Virunga volcanoes, dominates the Lake Tanganyika depression (less than 800 metres above sea level) and the Lake Kivu basin.

To the east the high hills of Burundi and Rwanda gradually slope

35. J. J. Maquet, 1954; L. de Heusch, 1966.

towards the terraced plateaux reaching down to the shores of Lake Victoria (some 1200 metres above sea level). At over 1000 kilometres from the Indian Ocean, which gives the region its climate, this varied relief gives rise to very marked differences in rainfall between the highlands of the west and the shores of Lake Victoria, which have a yearly rainfall exceeding 1500 mm, while the narrow valley of the Kagera receives less than 1000 mm. The actual figures and, above all, the period of the rainy season (roughly September–October) vary considerably from one year to the next. Climatic variations which – as we shall see – seem to have particularly influenced the period under study, have had widely varying repercussions in the different areas, all leading to changes in the region's ecology and to movements among its populations.[36]

The pattern of language distribution was similarly somewhat heterogeneous. The regions concerned were divided into two zones in which Bantu languages were spoken. In the west, according to Guthrie's classification, zone D encompassed the Kinyarwanda–Kirundi–Giha group and the languages of the present-day Zairean province of Kivu. In the east, zone E, represented by Kizinza, Ruhaya and Runyambo, corresponded to the Bantu-speaking area of Uganda. People were able to understand each other without much difficulty from the Virunga volcanoes south to lower Malagarazi, and from Lake Lutanzige (or Onekbonyo, formerly Lake Albert) to the south of Lake Victoria: in the former area kings were called *mwami*, and in the latter *mukama* or *mugabe*. These long established geographical and cultural divides were, however, to become less clear-cut from the sixteenth century onwards, as the kingdoms took shape.

Written and oral traditions

In addition to archaeological datings and linguistic hypotheses, oral sources also provide information concerning the history of the last five centuries. Unfortunately, the wealth of this original cultural heritage was wasted on the Europeans from the time of their first contacts at the end of the nineteenth century, due to their obsession with the 'Hamitic theory'. A written colonial tradition was established which set traps on all sides for those seeking to interpret history. In the interests of methodology we recall this tradition's main characteristics. The new mid-nineteenth century definition of *Hamite* – to denote Africans of a superior race – as opposed to *negroes as such* (a terminology popularized by Seligman), was applied from the earliest 'explorations' onwards to the Hima and Tutsi groups on the basis of stereotyped aesthetic impressions and political considerations. The entire civilization of the Great Lakes was attributed to a 'Hamito–Semitic' migration from the East which is assumed to have introduced the

36. P. Gourou, 1953; W. T. W. Morgan, 1969; J. P. Chrétien, 1983; J. B. Webster, 1979a.

cow, the system of royalty and even some aspects of monotheism.[37]

The hypothesis put forward by Speke in 1863 of an Oromo invasion between the sixteenth and eighteenth centuries, which supposedly made the region a second Ethiopia, permeated the accounts of German travellers and officers from 1890 to 1914 (Emin Pasha, Franz Stuhlmann, Count Von Goetzen, Hans Meyer) and the many publications of the White Fathers combining the fruits of their local investigations with the general anthropological conclusions of British or German authors (H. H. Johnston on Uganda, Friedrich Ratzel, Jan Czekanowski, Hermann Rehse).[38] The traditional sources of the history of the southern kingdoms were until recently deeply marked by this hypothesis. These include the *District Books* of the Territory of Tanganyika, written by Hans Cory, articles by Father Edmond Césard and Father H. Van Thiel on the Bahaya and the Bazinza respectively, works by Father Albert Pagès and Father Louis de Lacger on Rwanda, and by Father Julien Gorju on the entire region and on Burundi.[39]

The oral traditions themselves were retrieved from modern mythologies in the light of the culture of their possessors and the contacts established with them. Examples are the material gathered by the first educated inhabitants of the region, catechizers, minor civil servants and local chiefs, who were long considered the only worthy repositories of tradition. Apollo Kaggwa and John Nyakatura had their emulators. For instance, the 'Haya traditions' quoted by historians are usually traced to the work of one man, Francisco Rwamugira (or Lwamgira). An aristocrat, close to King Mutahangarwa of Kiziba, interpreter to the German Resident, Von Stuemer, and later secretary to the council of 'chiefs' at Bukoba under the British, Lwamgira wrote at the beginning of the twentieth century a *History of the Kiziba* (*Amakuru ga Kiziba*) which served as a source for Rehse's book, an article by Césard, the *District Book* of Bukoba, and the general *History of the Bahayas* by Father Otto Mors.[40] We might also mention the influence of Chief Pierre Baranyanka and of Counsellor Joseph Rugomana in the historiography of Burundi, also the exceptional role of intermediary played by Alexis Kagame in the history of Rwanda. Kagame was at one

---

37. E. Sanders, 1969; J. P. Chrétien, 1977; J. L. Amselle and E. M'Bokolo, at press.

38. Emin Pasha, 1891; F. Stuhlmann, 1894; G. A. von Goetzen, 1895; H. H. Johnston, 1902; H. Rehse, 1910; H. Meyer, 1916; J. Czekanowski, 1917; F. Ratzel, 1885, pp. 451–78. For the White Fathers see the review *Missions d'Afrique des Pères Blancs* and J. M. Van der Burgt, 1903.

39. *District Books* of Bukoba, Biharamulo, Mwanza, Kasulu, Kibondo, Kigoma, H. Cory, *c*.1960 (copies available at SOAS, London). The Cory Papers, Dar es Salaam University library, also contain a great deal of information. E. Césard, 1927, 1935–7; P. Césard, 1931; H. Van Thiel, 1911; A. Pagès, 1933; L. de Lacger, 1939/1959; J. Gorju, 1920 and 1938. On the same lines of thought concerning the Banyamwezi, see F. Boesch, 1930; with regard to East Zaire, see A. Moeller, 1936.

40. On the role of F. Lwamgira, see H. Rehse, 1910, p. 237; O. Mors, 1957; R. A. Austen, 1968, pp. 89–90; J. P. Chrétien, 1986 and at press. Lwamgira's text is reproduced unchanged in E. Césard, 1937, pp. 32–57.

and the same time a dignitary close to King Mutara Rudahigwa, a priest trained for the purpose by Canon de Lacger and a genuine investigator seeking information.[41]

These chronicles, summarizing traditions refined and interpreted according to the criteria of western ethnohistory, were then made available to schoolchildren, readers of newspapers written in African languages (such as *Munno* in Uganda, *Mambo Leo* in Tanganyika, *Rusizira Amarembe* in Burundi and *Kinyamateka* in Rwanda) and all those who attended missionary and administrative centres.[42] Many leading personalities began to locate their clan origins in Egypt (*Misri*) or Ethiopia (*Bisinya*).[43] More extensive and rigorous oral surveys were conducted from the end of the 1950s onwards. The traditions of the court were thus put into perspective, with due emphasis being given to those of more lowly families and, above all, to the diversity of regional variations and the wealth of information compiled from sources other than the small group of educated people. Knowledge of the region's history grew with the collecting of recordings, the accurate transcription of oral texts and the establishment of reliable linguistic bases.[44]

The traces left by Ruhinda and the Bachwezi

The states of the south may have grown out of the disintegration of an ancient monarchy founded between the sixteenth and eighteenth centuries by a conqueror called Ruhinda: this, at least, was the prevailing belief until the 1950s. The 'Empire of Ruhinda', comprising all the Haya and Zinza territory, except Kiziba, and at times including Burundi and even Rwanda, was considered the southern extension of the 'Empire of the Bachwezi', brought about by a new wave of expansion by Bahima herdsmen. The event, if it actually took place, is now believed to have occurred at an earlier period, about the fifteenth century; more importantly, different traditions have handed down widely varying versions of the 'Ruhinda legend'. In

---

41. A. Kagame, 1943–7/1959; J. Rugomana, 1957; P. Schumacher, 1949, uses P. Baranyanka, as also J. Gorju, 1938 and J. P. Chrétien, 1981a and 1981b.

42. On the transmission channels of these traditions at the start of the twentieth century, see *District Book* of Bukoba [copies available from the School of Oriental and African Studies (SOAS), London], Vol. VII, pp. 5–6, which contains translated extracts from J. Gorju, 1920 and H. Rehse, 1910 and references to F. Lwamgira; also the *District Book* of Biharamulo, *History of Migrations*, 1931. It is worth noting that the pupils of the Kome mission are better acquainted with this history than the people in the locality.

43. See H. Cory and M. M. Hartnoll, 1945/1971.

44. J. Vansina, 1961, 1971, 1972; A. Kagame, 1972; C. W. Newbury, 1976; E. Mworoha, 1977; L. Ndoricimpa, 1984; *Culture et société* (Bujumbura); *Études rwandaises* (Butare); I. K. Katoke, 1975; P. Schmidt, 1978. The study by S. R. Karugire, 1971, is also of use for the kingdoms of the south. An important international symposium was held in Bujumbura in 1979: see Centre de civilisation burundaise, 1981. It was followed by a similar meeting in Bukavu in December 1982.

Bunyoro and Nkore the hero Ruhinda is described as the illegitimate son of Wamara, the last Cwezi 'king' and a woman servant, Njunaki, while in Haya and Zinza country his father is generally said to have been Igaba or Bugaba, one of the local names for the supreme deity. The Hinda dynasties of Nkore, Karagwe, Kyamutwara, Ihangiro and Buzinza took as their respective founders either a brother, a son or a grandson of Ruhinda, who is said to have given each of them a country and a drum. These traditions relate primarily to two locations between which the hero's remains are said to have been divided when he died: towards the north, the Nkore–Karagwe complex, where his memory is associated in particular with the Isingiro and Bugara regions on both sides of the Kagera, and towards the south, the Buzinza–Ihangiro complex in which he is depicted as the assistant or even the son of the blacksmith Kayango. The traditions of the different kingdoms were built up in relation to these two locations and were not always compatible; Kyamutwara, Nyarubamba, the son or grandson of Ruhinda, came from Karagwe; in Ihangiro, the founder was himself described as a son of Nyarubamba, but bore the name of Ruhinda Kayanga in keeping with Zinza tradition. As for Ruhinda's legendary odyssey from Bunyoro to the extreme south of the region, it follows two different itineraries depending on the traditions. In one version it is overland, passing through Karagwe, in another the hero sailed the lakes north to Buzinza, from which he is said to have returned north-westwards by land.[45]

All the evidence suggests that the reference to Ruhinda reflected the meeting of two waves of traditions, connected with two major clan groups, Bahinda and Bayango, which had adopted the same taboo, that of the monkey *nkende* (a grey *cercopithecus*).[46] With regard to the founding of the Hinda dynasties, the traditions relate that this happened only one or more generations after that of the legendary conqueror. Probably the most interesting historical fact is the continued existence of the Ruhinda tradition, a source of political legitimacy, well after the sixteenth century. Ruhinda was invoked in the eighteenth century in Kyamutwara against usurpers from the Hima clan of the Bankangos; his name was associated in the nineteenth century with the remembrance of past greatness (in Karagwe), and of shattered unity (in Buzinza); it was also used in the

45. Apart from the titles already quoted, see material in the Cory Papers, for example No. 69 (*Chronology of the Bahinda*) and Nos 413 and 416 (notes by A. M. D. Turnbull in 1925 and 1926 on the history of Buzinza). See also the *District Books* of Bukoba and Biharamulo and, in the Archives of the Maison genéralice des Pères Blancs, several manuscripts including J. B. Lapioche, *Le Buhava et son histoire*, 1938; A. D. Kakaira, *Histoire d'Uzinza*, 1930.

46. L. de Heusch (1966, pp. 50–1) interpreted this as an old rivalry between the two clans, basing himself on the erroneous deduction he drew between the *nkende* and *tumbili* monkeys (quoted in H. Cory and M. Hartnoll, 1945/1971), whereas in fact these are the same animal, named in Ruhaya and Kiswahili respectively.

nineteenth century to rally the Bunyoro and Haya peoples against the petty imperialism of the Baganda.[47]

The differences between the court and the popular versions reflect[48] the tenacious persistence of a cycle of traditions in the form of legends. In most cases they probably represent the spread of a particular type of ruling power rather than an expedition by a single conqueror. In Gisaka the Bagesera Bazirankende dynasty (the reader is referred to the *nkende* (taboo)) attributed its origins to Nyakacende (or Nyiragakende), the daughter of Ruhinda or of one of his successors in Karagwe. In Kiziba the Bito dynasty identified Kibi, its founder, with Nyakiru, the brother of Ruhinda, and held that the two brothers had fought for control over their mother; the Bahinda clan was responsible for demarcating administrative boundaries. The Bukerebe Silanga dynasty, which came from Ihangiro towards the end of the seventeenth century, claimed that it originally descended from Ruhinda. Hinda influence is manifest as far as Buha in the south, as evidenced in the royal titles (in Heru and Bushingo) and in the reference to *nkende* (the taboo of the kings of Bujiji).[49] In the west, on the other hand, oral accounts brought forward other heroes. In Rwanda, Gihanga, a hero with a genuinely civilizing role was raised to the rank of father of all the neighbouring kingdoms. In Burundi, Ntare Rushatsi, a name which seems to apply to the founders of two dynasties in the sixteenth and seventeenth centuries, is associated with Ruhinda in European writings only.[50]

The traditions concerning Ruhinda drew their strength from the links between this legendary figure and the heroic exploits of the Bachwezis. Whatever may have been the reality or the extent and duration of the 'Empire of Kitara', as a political and religious model it most obviously had its origins in the plateaux of western Uganda. In the south, however, Isimbwa, Ndahura and Mulindwa hardly exist outside accounts circulating relatively recently. Here the foremost roles are played by Wamara, Mugasha and Ryangombe. The south developed its own mythology – for example, the manner in which Wamara, accompanied by Mugasha and Irungu, brought back from the domain of the terrible Kintu not only cattle and

---

47. This ideological use appears in: Emin Pasha, 1891, pp. 353–5 (in Bunyoro); F. Stuhlmann, 1894, pp. 713–15 (in Lyamutwara); the *District Book* of Bukoba, copy available from SOAS, pp. 42–3 (in Karagwe); A. Brard, *Rapport sur les tribus insulaires du Nyanza méridional*, Archives of the White Fathers, Jan. 1897; and A. E. Kitching, 'Tribal history and legends of the Wazinza', 1925, in the *District Book* of Biharamulo (in Buzinza).

48. See the traditions compiled in Maruku by P. Césard, 1931.

49. Cory Papers, No. 413 (Turnbull, 1925). G. W. Hartwig, 1972; *The District Book* of Kigoma (copy available from SOAS), Vol. VII, p. 203; J. P. Chrétien, 1975.

50. Hinda traditions appear in Rwanda in the accounts of Ruganzu Ndori's 'return' from Karagwe in the company of Muyango. In Burundi, Ntare Rushatsi opposed a king of Bushingo called Ruhinda, and J. M. Van der Burgt, 1903, attributed the founding of this kingdom to Ruhinda 'the great', a theory somewhat unthinkingly accepted in the general studies by Roland Oliver.

seeds but death as well; Wamara's conflicts with Mugasha to whom he refused his daughter and who unleashed a storm (in a Rwandan version it is Ryangombe who is involved), and with Kagoro who in the end burned down the enclosure sheltering his beautiful cow Kitare.[51] These deities are only the most important in a pantheon of thirty or more gods, continually increased by circumstances. Each is associated with a field of activities: Wamara with the dead; Mugasha with water, rain and lakes, hence with fishing and agriculture (in particular, the banana tree); Irungu with the bush, hence with hunting and travel; Kagoro with lightning; and Ryangombe with cattle and hunting.

While Wamara, whose great sanctuary was in Masaka in Bwera (Uganda), is a recurrent name in the traditions of Kitara, Nkore and Karagwe, the influence of Mugasha seems to have spread out from the Sese Islands, on Lake Victoria.[52] Accounts of Ryangombe are to be found mostly in the west, from Rwanda to Lake Tanganyika, his origin being located by some traditions in Ndorwa and by others, by identification with Kiranga, in Burundi (it is actually related that he died in an area which was then under Bugesera), or even east of present-day Zaire. Kiranga, a hunting hero, is also associated with agriculture through the spirits Nyabashi and Serutwa.[53] Far from being merely monarchical institutions, these religions appear to have had very ancient origins, pre-dating the founding of the modern dynasties. Popular traditions see in Wamara the protector of the old ruling clans, such as the Basita or the Bayango, and by contrast relate the conflicts between him and his 'servant' Ruhinda. Mugasha is said to have enacted with Kabambo, the scene mentioned above; and when the waters of Lake Victoria rose, this King of Buzinza is said to have been forced to give up his daughter to him. And Ryangombe ridiculed the King of Rwanda, Ruganzu Ndori.[54]

This *Cwezi* religion (or religion of the *Imandwa*) was independent in matters of both worship and mythology. In the east (in Haya and Zinza country), the same families maintained hereditary functions as mediums and were responsible for temples. In the west (Rwanda, Burundi, Buha), initiation to the *kubandwa* was widespread. Symbolism and vocabulary seemed to associate the religion with royalty in Haya country and Nkore, while the acts of worship performed in the shade of the *erythrina*, the sacred tree of Ryangombe/Kiranga, seemed to be of a more popular nature. But in all cases, these were practices of initiatory divination and healing, offering protection against threats coming from near ancestors or abuses of

51. E. Césard, 1927; Manuscript by J. B. Lapioche, 1938; A. Arnoux, 1912–13.

52. For the question as a whole, see I. Berger, 1973; F. Richter, 1899; Cory Papers, No. 79; D. W. Cohen, 1968; C. Wrigley, 1958.

53. F. Geraud, 1972; P. Smith, 1981.

54. See F. Boesch, 1930, for a version originating from Karagwe; O. Mors, 1957; H. Van Thiel, 1911; A. Coupez and T. Kamanzi, 1962, narrative No. 13. These accounts led L. de Heusch, 1966, to put forward the theory of a primarily anti-Hinda movement.

PLATE 26.1   *The sacred wood of Bunywankoko in Nkoma*

power.[55] Mechanistic and ethnic explanations of this cultural phenomenon[56] have, with a kind of naive euhemerism, thrown an almost total veil of obscurity over the deep divide between the specific history of this religion (of which fresh developments will be studied below) and the end of an ancient reign in Kitara.[57]

A choice between 'clans' and 'castes'

Faced with a written tradition which laid emphasis on the theory of 'caste' and indeed 'racial' opposition between 'Hima and Tutsi lords' and 'Iru and Hutu serfs', recent historiography has devoted more attention to the 'clan' structure.[58] The clan (*umuryango* in Kirundi and Giha, *ubwoko* in Kinyarwanda, *uruganda* in Runyambo and Ruhaya), despite its universal presence in oral culture (elderly people identify themselves primarily as belonging to a clan), has not the organic simplicity of a group of kinsfolk, even if it is sometimes experienced as such. Lineages, in the strict sense of the term, are classified in units characterized by collective name, by their

55. In addition to the titles quoted above see: B. Struck, 1911; A. Vix, 1911; H. Rehse, 1910; H. Meyer, 1916; B. Zuure, 1929.
56. An example of a moot point: L. de Heusch, 1964 and C. Vidal, 1967, for the reply.
57. J. P. Chrétien, 1981a and 1981b.
58. D. W. Cohen, 1972; M. D'Hertefelt, 1971; G. W. Hartwig, 1976; C. Buchanan, 1974.

respect for one or two taboos (*imiziro*) and sometimes by traditions relating to their origins or by the protection of a god belonging to the Cwezi pantheon (particularly in Haya country); but they have no territorial unity.[59] Clans are sometimes sub-divided into sub-clans (*amashanga* in Rwanda, *amahiga* in Haya country), but the system is not segmentary. Some clans appear in the long history of several of the kingdoms of the Great Lakes region, examples being the Bayangos of Nkore in Buzinza, the Bakimbiri of Nkore in South Buha, and the Basita of Bunyoro in Bukerebe. Taboos sometimes concern even larger groups: the toad is respected in Rwanda by the Bega, the Bakono and the Baha (three large clans which provided the queen mothers); there are instances of the spread of the *nkende* taboo, the most surprising example being the Kiziba, which is respected both by the dynastic clan of the Babito and by the Bahinda, while the *ngabi* bushbuck taboo, usually associated with the Babito, has been taken over by the old royal clan of the Bakuma. Some clans also see themselves as being related to different clans at different times. In Rwanda, the Banyiginya have been connected at times with the Basindi and at others with the Bahondogo.

The historical background of the clans is clear in Rwanda. As in Nkore (four units), the structure in Rwanda is exceptionally limited to eighteen large clans which all comprise Bahutu, Batutsi and Batwa members.[60] But studies carried out recently on the people living on the banks of Lake Kivu in the west[61] show that these 'clan corporations' were still in the making two centuries ago. Elsewhere, in Burundi, Buha, Karagwe and the lands bordering on Lake Victoria, there were hundreds of clans but each had different forms of association, either exogamic units (among the Bahaya) or associations based on a joking relationship or the taking of an oath (the *endahiro* of the Bakiga, in the north of present-day Rwanda). Identity was often closely linked with the exercise of political or religious duties of relatively long standing. The fact of belonging to a given clan defined the individual's social status. The oldest traditions bear witness to the large number of local functions for which one or the other of these clans was responsible, without this necessarily implying that each of these principalities comprised a homogeneous group. For example the Basita, associated with the old Cwezi rulers in Bunyoro and Nkore, are said to have reigned in Karagwe (King Nono) and chosen the heir to the Bukerebe throne. The Batundu are said to have reigned over what was Kyamutwara, themselves following on the Bahunga dynasty, that of King Kashare, and they are sometimes associated with the Baheta, who formed the clan of King Nsansama in Buzinza.

59. H. Cory and M. Hartnoll, 1945/1971.

60. The Batwa represent a small minority group in Rwanda, Burundi, and Buha (where they are called Bakiko). They specialize in hunting, fishing and pottery, and are outcasts on account of numerous taboos. They have been defined as 'pygmoid' but this term is debatable.

61. C. W. Newbury, 1976; D. S. Newbury, 1981.

Ihangiro is thought to owe its name to a former king of the Bayango clan (belonging to the larger group of Barongo blacksmiths). Here the Bahutu (a very powerful Hima clan) are said to have fought first the Bayango and then the Bahinda, under the leadership of Nkumbya, or Mukumbya. The fate of the latter, sometimes presented as a king and sometimes as a rain-maker, differs with different traditions: killed by Ruhinda, exiled at the court of Kashare, fleeing with Katobaha to Bukerebe or, alternatively, the ancestor of Ntumwa, the king of the Bukuma dynasty done to death by Kibi in Kiziba.[62] In Rwanda there are also many pre-Nyiginya political entities: the Bazigaba in Mubari and Cyingogo; the Bagesera in Gisaka, Bushiru and Busozo; the Badanda in Nduga, Bwana-mwali, Buhoma and Bukonya; the Basindi in Busigi and Ruhengeri; the Bacyaba in Bugara; the Basinga in Burwi and elsewhere (old Renge dynasties); the Bongera in Bumbogo, Buriza and Bwanacyambwe; the Batsobe in Rukoma, and so on. A number of these lineages have retained ritual *biru* functions in modern Rwanda.[63] In Burundi, the custody of the drums and the religious duties devolving on clans such as those of the Bajiji, the Bashubi and the Bahanza probably reflect ancient ruling powers. All of these clan principalities were gradually absorbed between the fifteenth and the seventeenth centuries (sometimes later) by the new dynasties, as will be seen below. Notwithstanding these regional changes and influences (resulting from lineage migrations or the flow of ideas and oral accounts), small subregional entities retained a living individuality until the twentieth century. Studies have yet to be carried out on the *ibihugu* (countries) of Rwanda and Burundi, on the Bayoza of Kyamutwara and the Bahamba of Kyanja (groups existing before the great state of Kyamu-twara or Bumbwiga, split up at the end of the eighteenth century).[64]

The distinction between pastoralists and farmers is not so clearly obvious in this context as to lend credence to the generally prevailing hypothesis of invasions and conflicts (ascribed to the grave political crises of the mid-twentieth century). It is not only in Rwanda that clans are of mixed composition: this is also the case for 20 per cent of the clans in Haya country,[65] over 10 per cent of Bahutu, over 50 per cent of Batutsi and 90

---

62. See the sources already quoted, in particular O. Mors, 1957. On Bukerebe see E. Hurel, n.d. The Bahutu or Baitira (H. Cory and M. Hartnoll, 1945/1971, p. 282) are confused in J. B. Webster, 1979b, p. 14, with the Hutu category of Rwanda or Burundi. In Haya country there is also a Hima clan among the Batwa, which bears no relationship with the Batwa potters. The narrative published by H. Rehse, 1910, p. 286, on the massacre which followed the death of Kashare, the ancient sovereign of Kyamutwara, also related the savagery of the Hinda King Karemera, especially towards the members of his own family; it in no way signifies a 'pogrom of reprisals against farmers'.

63. M. D'Hertefelt, 1971; A. Kagame, 1954; F. Nahimana, 1981.

64. The term Bahaya, before being applied in the colonial period to all the populations of the district of Bukoba, designated only the people living on the shores of Lake Victoria in the region of Maruku.

65. Including Karagwe.

per cent of Batwa clans in Burundi.[66] Other clans are in an intermediate or indeterminate situation, described as *bairu* (ennobled) (the Bayango) or *bahutu* (from a good family background) (the Bajiji). The Basita are described in some cases as pastoralists (in Rwanda for example), in others as farming-blacksmiths, having relinquished their dynastic drum in exchange for cereal farming.[67] In general the Bajiji are classified as Bahutu in Burundi and Batutsi in Bujiji (Buha). While the hypotheses concerning a meeting in the ancient past between Bantu-speaking groups and groups speaking south Kushitic or central Sudanese languages[68] are interesting, they bear on too remote a period (the first millennium) to throw light on the situation obtaining in the sixteenth century, given the cultural fusion of these populations. As we saw above, ethnic differentiation occurred along regional, clan or political lines which reflected the Hima/Tutsi and Iru/Hutu categories, although it would be risky to attempt a precise definition of what these categories represented four centuries ago. One single fact seems to stand out – the extent of pastoral activities on the middle plateaux from Nkore to Buha, through Karagwe, Gisaka and Bugesera. The Hamitic conquest which is so often mentioned in connection with this period appears to be no more than another way of presenting the regional and politico-economic pattern of the relations between predominantly pastoral and predominantly agricultural sectors between the sixteenth and eighteenth centuries.

The formation of the modern kingdoms: a geopolitical study

Problems posed by dates in general

The wealth of oral sources contributes to the complex problem of reconstructing the chronology of the region. Dynastic lists and the genealogies of princes have many variants especially before the seventeenth century. A number of chroniclers tried to substantiate the age of their kingdoms by compiling data from external sources. The average span of a generation, fixed at thirty-three years by Alexis Kagame, would seem in fact to be about twenty-seven to twenty-eight years. Two solar eclipses provide absolute references, but they cannot be identified beyond doubt.

The first was probably that of 1520, during the battle of Biharwe, between Ntare Nyabygaro (Nkore) and Olimi Rwitamahanga (Bunyoro) – an eclipse which has implications for datings in Buganda and Rwanda. The second was probably that of 1792, which coincided with the enthronement

66. F. M. Rodegem, 1964.

67. Oral traditions, even when they go back as far as fifteen or more generations, do not throw light on the earlier origins of population formation as such: or else they are 'traditions' permeated, through the channels described above, by the ideas of Speke, Emin or Gorju, for example, the Ethiopian hypotheses on the origin of the Basita put forward in the study by C. Buchanan, 1974, pp. 98–9.

68. See C. Ehret, 1973.

of Mibambwe Sentabyo (Rwanda). The *mwami* of Rwanda whose body was exhumed in 1968–9 by the team of F. Van Noten and ascribed to the first half of the seventeenth century, could, given the imprecision of the oral studies in this respect, have been either Mutara Semugeshi or Cyirima

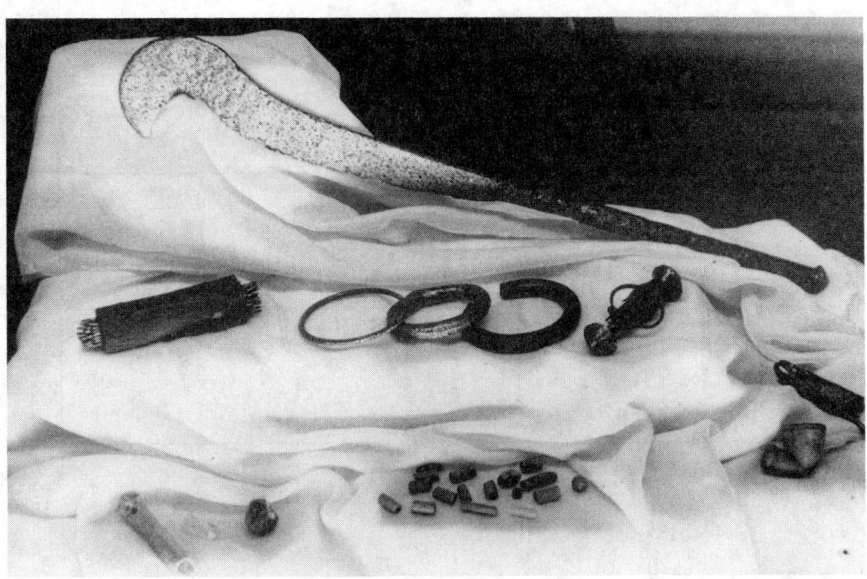

PLATE 26.2 *Objects found in the tomb of Cyirima Rujugira,* Mwami *of Rwanda*

Rujugira. In spite of the scepticism of authors such as David Henige, we can thus arrive at acceptable probabilities. Using all the concordances found in the sources and adopting the syntheses suggested by David Cohen and J. B. Webster, we suggest the chronology shown in Table 26.1.[69]

The 'invasions' organized towards the south by the Bito sovereigns of Bunyoro also appear as a binding influence between the different kingdoms. But the traditions compiled in each of the kingdoms ascribe the event to different periods. In fact, the Banyoro must have mounted numerous cattle raids. Moreover, the repetition in the dynastic lists of names such as Cwa (Bunyoro), Ntare (Nkore), Ntare and Karemera (Karagwe), Magembe (Kiziba) and Nyarubamba (Ihangiro) has led to chronological confusion.[70] None the less, three large expeditionary waves can be distinguished:

(1) In the first half of the sixteenth century, after their victory in 1520

69. The first attempt to bring together the dynastic lists is in J. Czekanowski, 1917. See also A. Kagame, 1959; J. Vansina, 1962a, 1962b and 1967; S. R. Karugire, 1971; D. Henige, 1974; D. W. Cohen, 1970; J. B. Webster, 1979a; F. Van Noten, 1972.

70. For example in O. Mors, 1957, Ntare Ktabanyoro of Karagwe is said to have been at odds with Magembe Kitonkire and Magembe Kagaruki, two kings of Kiziba who reigned a century apart.

TABLE 26.1 *Synchronological table of dynasties, fifteenth–nineteenth century*

	BUHA (SOUTH)	BURUNDI	RWANDA	GISAKA	KARAGWE	KIZIBA	KYAMUTWARA	IHANGIRO	BUZINZA
1500			RUGANZU Bwimba	KIMENYI	RUHINDA	KIBI ?	RUHINDA	NYARUBAMBA	KAYANGO ?
	KIMENYI	NTARE Karemera	CYIRIMA Rugwe	KABUNDA	NTARE Mihingoeta-yomba	ISHAMURA	?	RUHINDA Kayango	
1600	NTARE ?	?	KIGERI Mukobanya /MIBAMBWE Mutabazi	KIMENYI Shumbusho	RUHINDA	WANNUMI	NYARUBAMBA	NTARE	RUHINDA NTARE C Mugangazara
	RUHINDA	NTARE Kibogota	YUHI Gahima	MUTUMINKA	NTARE	MATWI	KAREMERA BWOGI		KABURA
		MUTAGA Nyamubi	NDAHIRO Cyamatare C	NTAHO	KAREMERA Ndagara	MAGEMBE Kitonkire	KAREMERA	NTARE	KABAMBO
			RUGANZU Ndori C	?	RUHINDA	MUZINGA Nyakashoke	"RUKAMBYA Gihume C	?	KATOBAHA /KINWA
			MUTARA Semugeshi C	KIMENYI Rwahashya	NTARE	MWIGARA	RUGOMORA Mahe	MURAMIRA Kikongera	KYENDANZIGU /NYAMURASA C
			KIGERI Nyamuheshera	KWEZI	RUSATIRA	BURUNGU	KAHIGI Kasita	BUTO	
1700	MAZIGA	NTARE Rushatsi	MIBAMBWE Gisanura	RUREGEYA	MEHINGA	MAGEMBE Kagaruki	SKWENGE /KARUMUNA Rugomora	NYARUBAMBA Kicumbu	KABURA Nyabureza
	MASIMBA	MWEZI	YUHI Mazimpaka		KAREMERA Bwirangenda	MBONEKO C Hangi		MUGUNDA /KAHIGI	KYENDANZIGU Kisamba
	KIVUNANGOMA	MUTAGA Senyamwiza	KAREMERA Rwaka	BAZIMYA	RUZENGA /NTARE C Kitabanyoro	NYARWANGU /RUHANGARAZI C	MBOGI Mpangukando C	NYARUBAMBA	KAKARAZA
	NTARE	MWAMBUTSA Mbariza C	/CYIRIMA Rujugira C	KIMENYI Getura					
	KANYONI		KIGERI Ndabarasa		RUHINDA	RUTAJWAHA	KAREMERA Mwiru	RUHINDA	MHIHAHABI
1800	RWASA	NTARE Rugamba	MIBAMBWE Sentabyo	?		BURUNGU /KIBI C Kakindi	KINYONI — KAJURUNGA	NTARE	NTARE RUHINDA Muhire Muhan-gakyaro
	NTARE		YUHI Gahindiro		NDAGARA	RUHANGARAZI	RUGOMORA	NYARUBAMBA +1906	RUSIMBYA
	KANYONI — NTARE RWASA +1906/07	MWEZI Gisabo +1908	MUTARA Rwogera	(anneri)	RUMANYIKA	MUTATEMBWA +1903	KAHIGI +1916		ISEKANYERE MANKORONGO +1885/90
		KIGERI Rwabugiri +1895			KAYENJE				
					NDAGARA +1892/93				

Heru / Bushingo

Maruku / Kyarja

Buzinza / Rusubi

N.B. Sources indicated in notes. Maximum use has been made of the most fully documented sources and has not been confined to standardized lists. The most accurate are those of Rwanda and Kiziba. Considerable uncertainty exists as regards the period before the seventeenth century.

in Nkore, the Banyoro are said to have invaded Rwanda twice, under the leadership of Prince Cwa, the son of Nyabongo, Olimi's successor. The *bami*, Kigeri Mukohanya and Mibambwe Mutabazi were forced to flee, one to the west of Nyabarongo and the other as far as Bushi. The King of Bugesera, Nsoro Sangano, is also said to have been killed during this invasion. Only with the death of Cwa was the tide to turn.

(2) During the first half of the seventeenth century, the small Bito Kingdom of Kiziba seems to have been subject to raids by its protector, Bunyoro, which occurred thoughout the century, for example during the reign of Magembe Kitonkire. Karagwe (under kings called Ntare and Ruhinda) was also affected during this same period.

(3) During the first half of the eighteenth century the most famous raid occurred which is attributed to a *mukama* called in some accounts Cwa (Cwamali) and in others Kyebambe. After having for years laid waste all the Haya lands, this sovereign is said to have been defeated and killed by King Nyarubamba Kicumbu in Ihangiro. His retreating warriors are then said to have been crushed by the *mukama* Ntare Kitabanyoro of Karagwe, who had returned from Buha where his mother had taken him into exile. At the same time another Banyoro group was defeated by a *mugabe* from Nkore, also known as Kitabanyoro ('Banyoro killer'). The kingdoms of the south were thus finally rid of the activities of the Babito. The memory left behind by the Babito was both terrible and confused but their influence was probably substantial especially with regard to the military organization of the kingdoms.[71]

The Kagera plateau states

This region of grassy plateau has always represented an important geo-political axis offering an easy route from the valley of the Katonga to that of the Malagarazi. Unfortunately its political history is the worst recorded in the region, because of the difficulties besetting its different kingdoms since the nineteenth century, resulting in some cases in their dismemberment or destruction, and bringing about the rapid erosion of their traditions. There is not a single study on either Bushubi or Bugesera, and what has been written about old Gisaka or Buha is either sketchy or superficial. Only the northern part, comprising Mpororo, Nkore and Karagwe, is relatively well known.

Despite its prestigious origins (the Sita dynasty, the principal starting-point of the Ruhinda complex), Karagwe began to assert itself chiefly from the seventeenth century onwards, taking advantage of the first ebb of Nyoro

71. D. Henige, 1974; A. R. Dunbar, 1965; S. R. Karugire, 1971; E. Césard, 1927; I. K. Katoke, 1975; O. Mors, 1957; H. Rehse, 1910; A. Kagame, 1972. These expeditions are to be distinguished from the more remote establishment of a Bito dynasty in Kiziba and in no way lend support to the hypothesis that the Hinda movement was Luo in origin, as suggested by L. de Heusch, 1966.

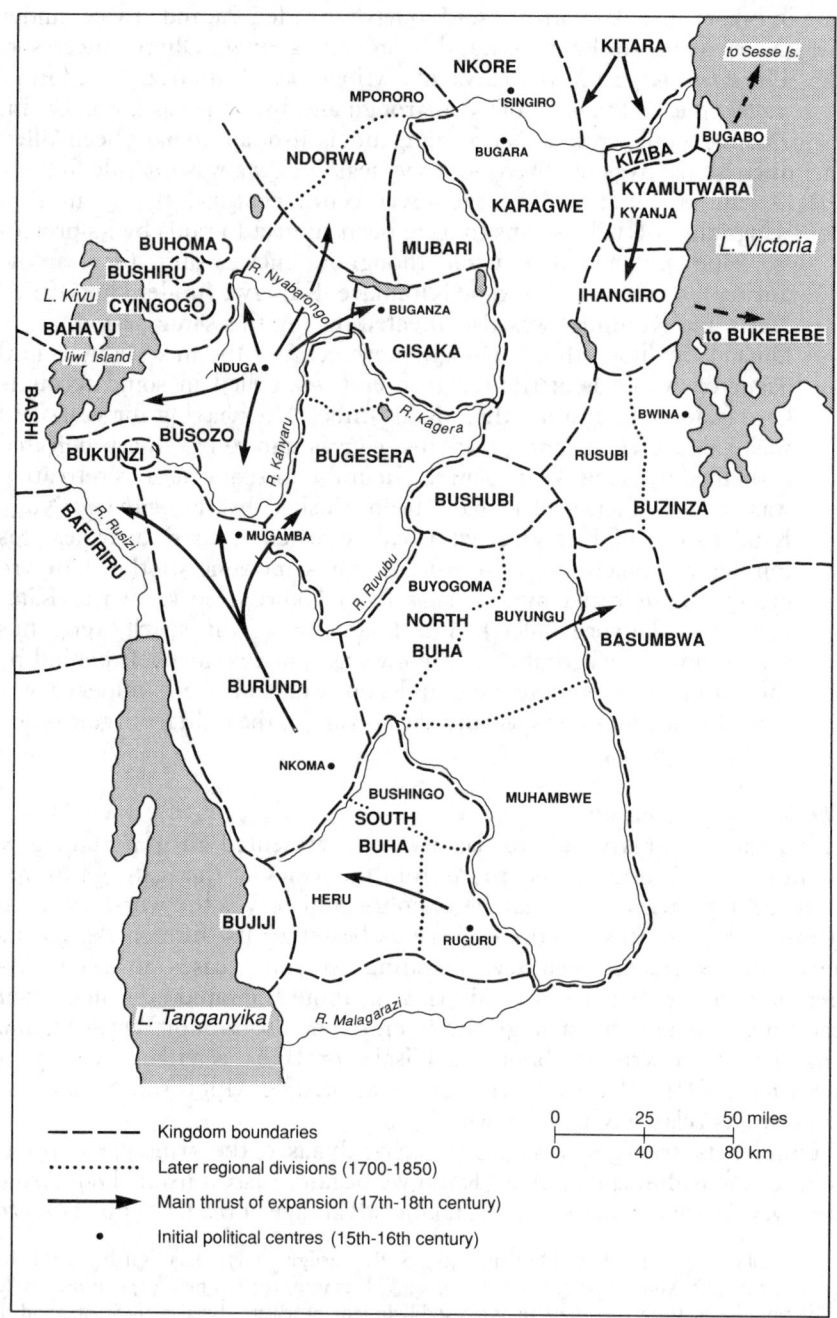

FIG. 26.2   *The southern Great Lakes region at the end of the seventeenth century (after J. P. Chrétien)*

influence (the crisis of the succession leading to the accession of Winyi, the successor of Nyabongo). Little is known about the Ntare and Ruhinda who came after, save that they were more powerful than their neighbours to the east: the attack on Kiziba ended in the death of a son of King Magembe Kitonkire. They maintained better relationships with Gisaka and Rwanda, including marriage alliances. The crisis precipitated in the eighteenth century by the Nyoro invasion led to a fresh upsurge, embodied in the person of Ntare Kitabanyoro, and later consolidated by the establishment of trade relations with Buganda and the people of Nyamwezi.

Mpororo, or Ndorma, inherited a rich tradition of government by clans. The Bakimbiri are said to have been governed by Ryangombe himself, and the Baishekatwa by Queen Kitami, the first incarnation of the spirit Nyabingi, who was held to be very active until well into the twentieth century. Overall government was taken over by a Hima dynasty from the Bashambo clan who took advantage of the vacuum created by the Banyoro defeat in Rwanda. The Bashambo contracted marriage alliances with the Bahinda of Nkore, who at that time were less powerful than the Bashambo: in the mid-seventeenth century, King Gahaya, the son of Ishemurari, attacked Gisaka and alarmed Rwanda. The culminating point was reached at the beginning of the eighteenth century; but fifty years later, when Gahaya Rutindangyezi died, Prince Ndabarasa, the son of the Rwandan *mwami* Cyirima Rujugira, occupied the entire south of the country; the kingdom split up into rival principalities; and the Murorwa drum was hidden near Lake Bwinyoni in the western mountains.

The Gisaka dynasty claimed to have two different clan origins, namely the Bagesera and the *nkende* totemic group (the Bazirankende). At the end of the fifteenth century King Kimenyi threatened to annex the tiny territory of the Rwandan *mwami*, Ruganzu Bwimba. In the mid-sixteenth century Kimenyi Shumbusho took advantage of the Nyoro attack to occupy the heart of old Rwanda, Buganza and Bwanacyambwe: Rwanda was only to regain this lost territory a century later. With Ndorwa and many Rwandan rebels as allies, Gisaka tried to take its revenge under Kimenyi Getura in the mid-eighteenth century, but Cyirima Rujugira's warriors defeated him also. The latter's son, Kigeri Ndabarasa, also occupied Mubari, an old kingdom ruled by the Bazigaba, with its centre in the islands of the Kagera.

Bugesera could also be seen as a precursor of the political powers which were later to establish themselves in the western mountains. The Bahondogo dynasty seems to be so closely linked with that of the Banyiginya of early Rwanda that Jan Vansina suggested that the latter descended from it. Marriages and military alliances marked the history of the two countries from the sixteenth to the eighteenth centuries. Ruganzu Ndori took action against Burundi, and Yuhi Mazimpaka gave hospitality to King Nsoro Nyabarega who was in difficulties. Until the end of the seventeenth century Bugesera covered a very large territory extending from the Kanyaru to the Ruvubu (the entire northern third of present-day Burundi) and, with its watering-places and rituals, was a typical pastoral habitat. Trouble came with the growth of the Baganwa dynasty in Burundi, which tended to side with Gisaka. The nineteenth century began with the country being divided up.

Farther to the south, several kingdoms were established in the Malagarazi basin. From the sixteenth century a 'north Buha' is said to have consisted of Buyungu, Muhambwe, Ruguru, Buyogoma (east of present-day Burundi), and even Bushubi. The Rwandan *mwami* Mibambwe Mutabazi is said to have found a wife there. The Bahumbi dynasty (of the kings known as Ruhaga, Nkanza and Gihumbi) remained very powerful until the eighteenth century: it gave hospitality to King Ntare of Karagwe fleeing from the Banyoro; it defeated Kakaraza, the *mugabe* of Buzinza; and it expanded into Sumbwa territory. Early on, however, to the south of the river, Ruguru became the centre of another state, comprising Heru and Bushingo and ruled by the Bakimbiri dynasty (that of Kings Ntare, Ruhinda, Rwasa and Kanyoni) which, with the principality of the Bajiji in Nkarinzi, took a greater interest in the mountains overlooking the eastern shore of Lake Tanganyika. It was only towards the mid-nineteenth century that Buha declined and began to break up.[72]

The states on the shores of Lake Victoria

These countries, which were more thickly populated, extended over grassy highlands and fertile, humid plains and valleys with waters teeming with fish. These differing geographical features affected the characteristics of communities and states and accounted in part for the splitting up of Kyamutwara and Buzinza in the nineteenth century.

Kiziba, wedged in between Lake Victoria and the River Kagera, was torn between its traditional links with Kitara–Bunyoro (its kings were buried there until the end of the seventeenth century, and its princes brought up in this foreign court) and with the Sese Islands (the origin of a ritual fire used at enthronement). Moreover, it was constantly warring with its neighbours in the south-west, Kyamutwara and Karagwe, which turned a succession of conflicts to their advantage. The Nyoro menace was followed at the end of the eighteenth century by attacks by the Baganda. King Burungu Kakindi appealed to Kabaka Semakokiro, for help against the rebel princes who, for their part, gained the support of the pretender, Kamanya.

In Kyamutwara, permanent Hinda supremacy seems to have been established in the seventeenth century by King Karenera. His insane cruelty is said to have led him to have his son Mukanbya blinded. It is possible that, after a long regency under Kayango, it was the latter's successor, who in fact founded a new dynasty. This was Rugomora Mahe who, following his

72. I. K. Katoke, 1975; J. Freedman, 1979; F. Geraud, 1972; S. R. Karugire, 1971; J. P. Chrétien, 1975 and 1984; A. D'Arianoff, 1952; A. Kagame, 1972; J. Vansina, 1962a and 1962b.

long and roundabout voyage from Ihangiro to the Sese Islands and Kitara, was regarded as a civilizing hero. He and his descendants exploited the weaknesses of Kiziba and Ihangiro, until at least the end of the eighteenth century when Kyamutwara was in its turn weakened by internal dissension. The *mukama*, Karemera Mwiru, eliminated his predecessor, Bwogi Mpangukano, with the support of the Baziba and the Baganda. His sons, Kajurunga and Kinyoni, were to share Hinda power, thus leading to the formation of the principalities of Maruku and Kyanja in the nineteenth century. During the eighteenth century two Hima lineages of the Bankango clan, originating from Buzinza in the reign of Kahigi Kasita (who is thought to have married the sister of the two founders, Karamagi and Mutashaba), gained increasing military and political influence. At the beginning of the nineteenth century they established an independent government in Bugabo and a small-scale 'Kyamutwara', implanted on the shores of Lake Victoria where the Germans were to found Bukoba in 1890.

In Ihangiro there was a sharp division between a flat lake region called Ihaya and an inland plateau called Mugongo. Succession conflicts, especially under Muramira, gave the kings of Kyamutwara, Rugomora and Kahigi, the opportunity for intervention in the plateau region at the end of the seventeenth century. Justification could be provided by the dynastic relationship. Here again, with Buto, we find the theme of a king blinded by his father; the question also arises of a break with the reign of Nyarubamba, the conqueror of the Banyoro. At the close of the eighteenth century Nyarubamba II appealed to the Baganda to help him recover the plateau region from a rebel prince. From then on there developed along the whole western shore of Lake Victoria in the nineteenth century what could be termed Ganda imperialism.[73]

Buzinza introduces us to another cultural and ethnic region where the influences of the Baha, the Basukuma and even the Tatoga Nilotes intermingled. It was also the main home of the Barongo blacksmiths whose links with the Yango clan have been mentioned. The three main sources of the political history of this kingdom[74] provide dynastic lists which contradict one another with regard to length and order; the most accurate is that of Van Thiel. After the reigns surrounded by the legend of Ntare Muganzara and the first Kabambo, there was, as it were, a second founding under Kabambo Kinwa, who was also born of the incest committed by a blind prince. In the eighteenth century the *mugabe* Kakaraza had to fight off attacks from the Baha in the west and the Tatoga in the east. His son Mwihahabi was the last sovereign of a unified Buzinza. The war of succession led to the separation of Rusubi under Ntare Muhire, and of all the coastal regions under Ruhinda Muhangakyaro, at the start of the nineteenth century.

73. H. Rehse, 1910; E. Césard, 1927; O. Mors, 1957; P. Schmidt, 1978. *District Book of Bukoba, passim.*
74. H. Van Thiel, 1911; O. Mors, 1957; P. Betbeder, 1971.

The history of Bukerebe is one of complex regional influences. From the cultural standpoint, this country, made up of an island and a peninsula, forms part of the Zinza group. In the nineteenth century, however, the Silanga dynasty claimed to be of Ruhindan (even Bunyoro) origin, whereas its founder, Katobaha, is said to have come from Ihangiro in the seventeenth century, and its taboo was the *enfunzi* (a kind of goldcrest) which was also that of the Bahutu or the Baitira, a clan which, as we saw above, fought with the Bayango and the Bahinda (under King Nkumbya at the end of the sixteenth century). The kings (*bakama*) gradually gained the upper hand in the eighteenth century over the Sita and Kula clans, but the Tatoga menace forced them to establish their capital in the island. The important trade in ivory was considerably developed by this principality at the start of the nineteenth century.[75]

The states in the western mountains

Whereas in the east the developing pattern of kingdoms led to fragmentation, in the west, the trend favoured concentration to the advantage of two powers – Rwanda and Burundi – each of which had over one million inhabitants at the end of the nineteenth century.

The tiny Rwandese principality which came into being in the fourteenth century south of Lake Mohazi (in Buganza), in the shadow of Bugesera and Gisaka, succeeded in firmly establishing itself along the River Nyabarongo, thanks to the long reign of Cyirima Rugwe who annexed the lands of the Bongera. But the serious crises of the sixteenth century were to affect this kingdom's stability. The two Nyoro invasions, which led King Kigeri Mukobanya and King Mibambwe Mutabazi to flee westwards, culminated in the shifting of the centre of political power to Nduga, while the original territory (Buganza and Bwanacyambwe) was captured by Gisaka. After the warlike reign of Yuhi Gahima, who launched expeditions in every direction, the succession conflict between his sons, Juru and the *mwami* Ndahiro Cyamatara, was exploited by the Bashi, the Bahavu and the people of Bugara in the west. The king was killed and the drum of the Rwoga dynasty captured. Notwithstanding the pious tradition recounting that the rightful prince had been hidden in the home of his aunt in Karagwe and despite the claims by the Banyiginya to an unbroken line from the country's origins (from the time of the mythical Kigwa and the legendary Gihanga), Ruganzu Ndori probably founded a new dynasty of the Kalinga drum at the beginning of the seventeenth century. He re-occupied Nduga and from there he and his successors extended the kingdom as far as Lake Kivu and the River Kanyaru, recapturing Bwanacyambwe (in the region of Kigali) in the east at the same time. The growth of a new dynasty in Burundi put a stop to expansion at the end of the century, but it recommenced in the eighteenth century as a result of the exceptional military organization set up by Cyirima

75. G. W. Hartwig, 1972 and 1976; E. Hurel, n.d.

Rujugira and Kigeri Ndabarasa. Burundi and Gisaka were compelled to retreat; Ndorwa broke up; Mubari was occupied and settlements on the shores of Lake Kivu were extended up to Kinyaga. At the end of the eighteenth century, Bugesera, an old ally, was divided up between Rwanda and Burundi under Mibambwe Sentabyo. This expansion continued in the nineteenth century, especially in the north-west and south-east, but the old Hutu and Tutsi powers preserved their independence for a long time under a kind of protectorate of the Banyiginya.[76]

There is much less information concerning the history of Burundi during this period. At the start of the sixteenth century an initial dynasty created by Ntare Karemera seems to have become established in the mountains of the north-west, on the borders of the powerful Bugesera. Among the Bami, Mutara Semugeshi, who was the son of Ruganzu Ndori, and Mutaga Nyamubi are said to have established a kind of alliance which was consolidated by exchanges of pastoral rituals. Then at the end of the seventeenth century Ntare Rushatsi or Rufuku founded the Baganwa dynasty in Nkoma which maintained relations with South Buha. This dynasty unified the south (where the so-called Nyaburunga Burundi was weakened by the conflict with Nsoro and Jabwe), the centre and the north – the fusion of the clan powers of the old kingdom (Bahanza, to which Ntare, Bajiji, Babibe and Bashubi would seem to have belonged) – and rose up against Bugesera whose king, Nsoro Nyabarega, had to take refuge in Rwanda. Burundi then extended to the south of present-day Rwanda; it was the defeat of Mutaga Senyamwiza by Cyirima Rujugira in the mid-eighteenth century that fixed its borders along the River Kanyaru. It was only at the time of the long reign of Ntare Rugamba, during the first half of the nineteenth century, that the kingdom expanded west to reach the River Rusizi, and east as far as the Malagarazi basin (at North Buha's expense).[77]

Further west, around Lake Kivu, the Bashi on the one hand, and on the other, the Bafuriru of the Rusizi plain and the Bahavu dwelling on Ijwi island and the west coast, were all ascribed a common origin in the Nyindu region (in Lwindi). The political structure of the *mwami* could be connected with the socio-religious institution of *Bwami* which would seem to have formed the basis for Bembe and Rega societies. Traditions also testify to the very long history of relations between these small kingdoms and Burundi and Rwanda. They have been masked only by the spread of the Hamitic theory of the 'Ethiopian invasions' and by the carving out of colonial frontiers at the end of the nineteenth century.[78]

---

76. A. Kagame, 1972; J. Vansina, 1962a and 1962b; J. K. Rennie, 1972.
77. J. Vansina, 1961 and 1972; E. Mworoha, 1977; J. P. Chrétien, 1981 (a) and (b), and 1984.
78. C. Bishikwabo, 1982; D. S. Newbury, 1978 and 1979.

States, economies and societies

This history of politics and warfare should not overlook the question of population movements, the evolving pattern of landscapes and crop production, and institutional and even ideological changes.

Development of the relationship between herding and farming

At the outset, geographical factors determined the two areas which served for these activities – pastoralism on the Kagera plateaux and agriculture on the shores of Lake Victoria and in the western mountains. During the period considered here, however, the two activities were to a greater and greater extent carried out in conjunction throughout the region and in a variety of ways. In reality, they had never been in strict opposition to one another: the association of the earliest cereals, eleusine and sorghum, with cattle-raising would seem to be a very old practice, as regards both production and consumption (meal and milk).[79] Ancient Karagwe is famous, according to tradition, not only for its cattle but also for its farming and its beer made from sorghum.[80] Cattle were not limited to a single variety, the long-horned Sanga, and their preserve in the region goes back much further than was thought. Early accounts mention the use of manure whose importance in intensive farming with two harvests a year in the wettest regions has been sadly overlooked. This complementarity was especially evident in countries such as Kiziba and Kyamutwara – the banana tree gradually assuming the same importance there as in Buganda, where the Bahima settled only in small numbers and where social hierarchies were based on land relationships and not on contracts concerning cattle. The renown of Rugomora Mahe in the seventeenth century (or that of Katobaha in Bukerebe) rested essentially on the introduction of the banana tree and the raphia palm (with which he is credited) and on his relations with Mugasha, god of water and cultivation.[81]

But towards the west in particular, factors other than those of an agricultural kind led to the increasing influence of the herders at that time. These were droughts and famines. Close analysis of the oral sources available concerning the countries in question reveals a vast number of such calamities during the first half of the seventeenth century (Rwanda, Kyamutwara, Buzinza) and the second half of the eighteenth century (Burundi, Rwanda, Kiziba, Karagwe), and this is in line with several of the hypotheses put forward by R. S. Herring and J. B. Webster based on data on the old Nile regime and the traditions of the Nilotes of Uganda already discussed above. As was very well demonstrated by E. I. Steinhart

79. J. P. Chrétien, 1982.
80. O. Mors, 1957; J. B. Lapioche, MS, *op. cit.*, fn 51.
81. A. O. Anacletti and D. K. Ndagala, 1981. For the socio-political role of the banana tree, see C. P. Kottak, 1972; concerning Rugomora Mahe, see a very fine account published by P. Schmidt, 1978.

in the case of Nkore and the principalities which emerged from Ndorwa, these ecological and subsistence crises were particularly detrimental to farmers; they were forced to seek the help of the herders who, through the practice of transhumance, were able to ensure the survival of their cattle. The shifting of the centres of political gravity from the area of the Rivers Kagera and Malagarasi towards the wooded heights of Kiriba overlooking Lakes Kivu and Tanganyika which occurred in the seventeenth century was not simply the result of expeditions or dynastic changes but was also due to the growth of a system of tribute which was favourable to pastoral groups and their values. The 'civilization of watering-places' which obtained in Bugesera is also reflected in the oldest historical traditions concerning Rwanda and Burundi. Worship by the *mwami* Yuhi Mazimpaka at the end of the seventeenth century, of the most beautiful cows in his herd, is an illustration of this.[82]

In the case of Rwanda or Burundi (and of Nkore), however, it can be said that those who benefited from the regimes established 300 years ago represented only a part of the herd-owners, the rich Batutsi and the ruling circles that had links with royalty (for example, the princes of Baganwa in Burundi). In short, they were those who had succeeded, through the actual introduction of the cow or its use as a symbol, in acquiring political control over agricultural production which provided an additional means of redistribution and statute labour. Agriculture was of little interest to ethnological accounts, and yet its importance is evident in the rituals and even the ideology of royalty. In Burundi, for example, the annual *muhanuro* festival – during which royal authority and the drums symbolizing it were renewed – celebrated the sowing of sorghum, and determined the most favourable date for this in a country with a long rainy season. Moreover, with regard to food crops, the introduction of plants of American origin (sweet potatoes, maize, *Phaseolus vulgaris* bean) which, to judge by the references to tobacco in oral traditions, could have occurred in the region in the seventeenth century, presented farmers with new ways of intensifying their activities, providing them with the possibility of two harvests a year and ensuring the supply of plant protein (present in beans).[83]

The relationship between herders and tillers, then, does not have the immutable and universal character that the socio-biological stereotypes would lead us to believe. Even assuming that the Barundi, Banyarwanda or Bahaya farmers were termed Bahutu or Bairu at the start of our period,

82. See 'C' indicated in Table 26.1. J. B. Webster, 1979a, chs 1, 2 and 7; E. I. Steinhart, 1981, pp. 115–56; J. P. Chrétien, 1984; P. Schumacher, 1958. Concerning the same development in Buha, see J. F. Mbwiliza, 1981.

83. J. P. Chrétien, 1979 and at press; M. Bahenduzi, 1977; L. Ndoricimpa, 1984; E. Mworoha, 1977; C. Vidal, 1974. In spite of her misuse of feudal terminology and a tendency to underestimate the impact of colonization, Claudine Vidal deserves credit for underlining the importance of the land in old Rwanda. It will also be seen that *mwami* refers to fructification (*kwama* in Kirundi) whereas *mukama* means 'the milker', a revealing contrast.

PLATE 26.3   *The sanctuary of Banga in Mugamba, north-east Burundi*

PLATE 26.4   *The ancient royal drums preserved in the sanctuary of Banga in Mugamba, north-east Burundi*

the economic, political and territorial changes which took place between the seventeenth and nineteenth centuries brought about the development of Hima–Iru or Tutsi–Hutu relations from one of local trade to a more comprehensive hierarchical relationship, its flexibility depending on the

824

states involved or the particular moment in time.[84]

Consolidation: monarchical rulers in the seventeenth and eighteenth centuries
Before colonization each state had a system of tribute which varied according to the ecological situation, the relationship between the different forces of production, the clan pattern and the institutional forms that existed. Everywhere, the sovereign exercised direct control over areas close to his residences and assigned chiefs (*bakungu, batware*) elsewhere. They were often princes of royal blood (*Balangira* in Haya country, *Baganwa* in Burundi), and were assisted by delegates who were usually from the most influential local lineages (farmers or herders). Tribute was paid to these courts in the form of labour or in kind (cattle, baskets of provisions, special products such as salt, honey or weapons). The ruling aristocracy could thus extend its influence by redistribution, for there was little luxury (clothing was of skins or bark; local vegetation was used for the construction of residences).[85] Nevertheless, royal power was consolidated, particularly from the eighteenth century onwards, in four ways:

Exploitation of clientship (the relationships which were known as *ubugabire* or *ubuhake*) were increasingly removed from their private context and used for political purposes – protection guaranteed to a family in exchange for increased obligations. In Rwanda the *buhake* was used more especially to subjugate influential Hutu lineages in the peripheral regions conquered by the Banyiginya, particularly in the reign of Yuhi Gahindiro at the very end of the eighteenth century. It was at this same time that the *gikingi* land system became established, granting exclusive grazing rights to the most important herd-owners with administrative authority over families residing in these areas. This network of privileges which has prompted a number of authors to refer to feudalism, was accompanied in Rwanda by a remarkable increase in the size of herds resulting from the conquests of the eighteenth century.[86]

Military organization: Employing the same model as the *emitwes* of Nkore, Rwanda developed – especially from the time of the reign of Cyirima Rujugira – a system of hereditary standing armies, consisting of young men of certain lineages who were stationed in camps located on borders which were under threat. This militia also looked after the herds belonging to or protected by the king. It included Bahutu as well as Batutsi, and even foreigners, some of whom were refugees from the kingdoms defeated by Rwanda (Ndorwa, Gisaka, Burundi). In the nineteenth century, the role

84. Colonization then gave this opposition an ethnic aspect, making the two categories castes in a racial substratum.
85. E. Mworoha, 1977 and 1981; O. Mors, 1957; A. Nsanze, 1980.
86. J. P. Chrétien, 1974; A. Ndikuriyo, 1975; C. W. Newbury, 1976; J. Rwabukumba and V. Mudandagizi, 1974; L. Meschi, 1974.

of this institution was reduced to a mainly tax-gathering function, termed *umuheto* ('of the bow') in the service of important chiefs who were ranked above land chiefs and grass chiefs. The importance of the military factor was also marked in the other kingdoms at the end of the period.[87]

Trade possibilities: Until a recent date, institutionalized exchanges and local barter played a more important commercial role than specialized trading. None the less, regional products such as salt from Katwe in Busongora, or from Uvinza, articles made of iron (hoes made by the Bazinza and the Bashi) or raphia bracelets (*amatega*) formed the basis of the earliest pedlars' wares. Judging from the objects found in the tomb of the Rwandese *mwami* who died in about 1635, or the traditions concerning Yuhi Mazimpaka, articles from the Indian Ocean coast, including glass beads and ornamental shells, would appear to have spread through the region from one centre to another, in the seventeenth century. Trade in copper (from present-day Shaba?) is also thought to have existed from the eighteenth century onwards in Burundi, Karagwe and Buganda. But it was only in the nineteenth century that rulers in Rusubi, Karagwe, and Rwanda made attempts, as had been done in Buganda, to control this trade in luxury articles.[88]

Ideological control: The break-up of lineages, which had become an ill-assorted mixture of clan groups of a political character, was fostered by the changes brought about in society as a result of the agrarian crises, the wars of conquest of the seventeenth and eighteenth centuries, and the movement of the population in search of food, better irrigated lands, or richer pastures. The success of Cwezi religion in the seventeenth century (for example, the emergence of Ryangombe or of Kiranga in Rwanda and Burundi) is understandable for it offered a kind of refuge in the face of this instability. To a great extent the new monarchies derived their legitimacy from this religious movement, as testified by myth and ritual. Initiates were, however, also capable of sparking off subversive movements among the people or blocking royal action. The *mukama* Wannumi of Kiziba, was, for example, driven mad by the medium of Wamara whose cows he had seized!

Ultimately the monarchies, supported by the ruling system and encouraged by their war conquests, set about controlling this double-edged religion and turning it to their advantage. In Kiziba the cult of dead kings counterbalanced the power of Cwezi spirits. In Kyamutwara, the monarchy, from the time of Rugomora Mahe onwards, was based on the cult of Mugasha. In Rwanda a 'King of the Imandwa' was installed at the court from the reign of Cyirima Rujugira. During the same period the Rwandese monarchy had an official body of panegyric poetry and historical

87. D. S. Newbury, 1979; A. Kagame, 1963.

88. R. Gray and D. Birmingham, 1970; J. E. G. Sutton and A. Roberts, 1968; D. S. Newbury, 1980; F. Van Noten, 1972.

narratives compiled. This oral literature was disseminated by the army. The sacred code of *ubwiru* established royal rituals and the dynastic genealogy incorporated allied Tutsi lineages (those of the queen-mothers).

The remarkable character of Rwandese oral literature reflects the exceptional nature of the country's political centralization. In the other states, the different strata of society retained a greater degree of independence right up to the eve of colonization.[89]

Conclusion

By the end of the eighteenth century the modern ethnographic and linguistic configurations in the Great Lakes region had emerged. The major population movements in the region had mostly come to an end, and the outlines of the last ethnic groups to be formed in the region – the Bakiga, Iteso and Lango Omiro – were being defined, the process being completed by about 1830. Most people already occupied the homelands in which their modern descendants live. Also, with very few exceptions, the era of state formation had come to an end with Rwanda having emerged as the dominant state of the southern section. In the central area, Bunyoro continued to decline until the secession of Toro and Paluoland in 1830 which brought to a close a lengthy theme of Great Lakes history with ramifications from Mounts Otuke and Elgon in the east to the Alur and Kigezi highlands in the west, and from Agoro in the north to the undulating plains of Usukuma in the south. By the beginning of the nineteenth century, Buganda had emerged as the pre-eminent state in the central area. Henceforth, the main concern of the historian shifts from the growth of central authority to the efforts of the chiefs to control and limit the power of the monarch. During the nineteenth century, a multiplicity of new themes was to dominate the Great Lakes history.[90]

89. J. P. Chrétien, 1981(b); A. Kagame, 1981; J. Vansina, 1962a and 1962b; P. Schmidt, 1978; J. N. Nkurikiyimfura, 1983.
90. See UNESCO, *General History of Africa*, Vol. VI, ch. 10.

The interior of East Africa: the peoples of Kenya and Tanzania, 1500–1800

27

W. R. OCHIENG'

In East Africa, the year 1500 is generally considered the high watershed between archaeology and historical linguistics, on the one hand, and oral traditions, on the other, as rewarding sources for historical studies. Before 1500 historians have to rely heavily on archaeology and historical linguistics but thereafter oral traditions are the major source and, from the nineteenth century, oral traditions join hands with written sources.[1]

This does not mean, however, that there are adequate sources, oral or written, on which to rely for the perception or reconstruction of the period under study. As in the period before 1500, unevenness and even the lack of documentation remain fundamental problems. For example, little historical research, if any, has been done on interior societies such as the Gorowa, Zigua, Gogo, Turkana, Maasai and most of the Kalenjin groups, to mention only a few. The gap is slowly being filled but there remains a crippling imbalance in the sources for the history of this region for this period. It follows that what can legitimately be asserted must be tempered by the knowledge that much was taking place that remains unknown. As Professors Alpers and Ehret have correctly observed, the themes yet to be recovered through research might well be of equal or greater weight than the dominant social and economic interpretations that have emerged from existing materials.[2]

The period 1500 to 1800 saw the emergence of societies and social and economic systems that are still characteristic of the interiors of Kenya and Tanzania. Variety of experience is perhaps the key feature of the history of this region at this time. The centre of the stage was occupied by the Maasai, Chagga, Pare, Shambaa, Gogo and Hehe. On the eastern periphery lived the Kikuyu, Kamba, Miji-Kenda, Zigua and Zaramo. To the north-west lived the Abaluyia, Kalenjin, Luo, Abagusii and Abakuria, and to the south-west the Tanzanian communities such as the Sukuma, Iramba, Nyamwezi, Zinza and Kimbu.

All these peoples – with the exception of the coastal societies – were still

---

1. Most history books in East Africa on the pre-colonial period which are based largely on oral traditions open around 1500. See G. Muriuki, 1974; H. A. Mwanzi, 1977; W. R. Ochieng', 1974a.

2. E. A. Alpers and C. Ehret, 1975, p. 470.

isolated from the ocean and could still resolve their problems without confronting the economic and allied challenges that would emanate from the coast during the nineteenth century. There is no record of any penetration of the interior by Arabs or Swahili before 1700, and 'no significant collection of imported objects has yet been found at any interior site north of the Zambezi dating to the period before 1600'.[3] From the mid-1600s, however, it is possible to begin to see clearly the rise of chieftaincies and articulate – though often decentralized – political organizations, and changes towards a general tributary mode of production. Sustained attempts were being made to effect social and political integration into larger economic and political communities in which rulers extracted tribute from their subjects by which to maintain themselves, their families and their followers. Oral traditions portray this development as one of conquest and assimilation by the stronger migrating communities. Alternatively, the process can be viewed as a gradual neutralization and stabilization by the local populations of the disruptive activities of hitherto unsettled or migrating communities.

All history is transition from one stage to another. In the centuries following 1500 the interior societies of Kenya and Tanzania were evolving into the distinct ethnic groups that exist today with their own peculiar linguistic and cultural characteristics. The overwhelmingly dominant economic activity was agriculture. In all the settled agricultural communities people observed the distinctive features of their own local environment and tried to find techniques for dealing with them in a rational manner. As John Iliffe has put it: 'The men followed the dictates of the land.'[4] Advanced methods were used in some areas – such as terracing, crop rotation, green manuring, mixed farming and regulated swamp farming.

While most East Africans were agriculturalists, the Maasai, Pokot and Turkana were largely cattlemen who drove their livestock for pasture and water all over the plains of central Kenya and Tanzania. As is discussed later, both the agriculturalists and cattlemen at no time attempted to pursue exclusive, or specialized, economic activities. Each economic pursuit shaded imperceptibly into the next and all were subject to fluctuation and change.[5] Often the agriculturalists such as the Luo and Abagusii, also kept large herds of livestock, while cattlemen such as the Samburu and Arusha Maasai also practised some agriculture. The Baraguyu, the Kalenjin and the Akamba (Kamba) were semi-pastoralists.

The Sanye, Okiek, Sandawe and Hadzapi remained gatherers of berries, vegetables and fruits, and hunters of wild animals and birds – but even among these hunters and gatherers, growing variety of subsistence patterns

3. R. Oliver, 1977, p. 621.
4. J. Iliffe, 1979, p. 6.
5. See E. A. Alpers and C. Ehret, 1975, pp. 469–511; A. M. H. Sheriff, 1980; and R. M. A. van Zwanenberg and A. King, 1975, pp. 79–109.

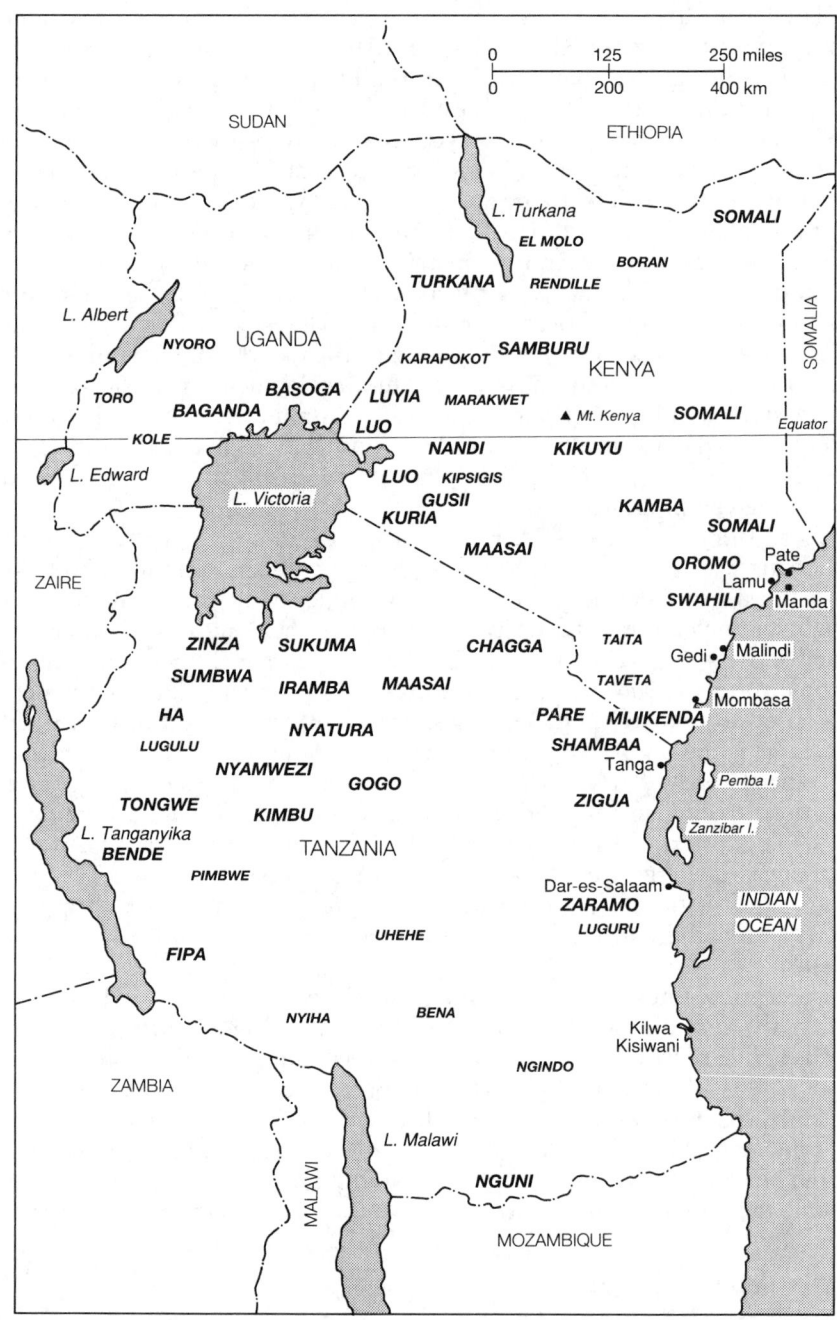

FIG. 27.1   *Ethnic groups of Kenya and Tanzania*
Source: adapted from map drawn by M. Kivuva, Moi University, Kenya, after W. R. Ochieng'

were to be observed.[6] For example, the Okiek traded honey for agricultural products, while the Dorobo and Athi hunters were involved in the long-distance ivory trade and, by the nineteenth century, were beginning to acquire stock. Henry Mwanzi informs us that when the nineteenth-century Swahili caravan-traders came to Kipsigis country it was those of Okiek extraction who were first to secure what was required – namely ivory. They excelled in hunting techniques and in elephant tracking, and 'they thus acted as middlemen who hunted for ivory, which they sold to the caravan traders'.[7] During most of the seventeenth and eighteenth centuries both agriculturalists and cattlemen were locked in competition over the higher, richer and better-watered grasslands and plateaux. At the same time, however, they invaded the domains of the hunters and gatherers which led to the systematic absorption, decimation or isolation of the latter.

Economic evolution

By 1500 the two major economic pursuits in the Kenya-Tanzania interior were agriculture and cattle-keeping. Famine, John Iliffe has argued, was man's biggest challenge during this period.[8] It resulted from East Africa's poor soils and its unreliable rainfall which affected both crops and pasture.

Not even the most favoured regions were spared the pangs of famine. Bananas might have thrived in Usambara, but the traditions of the Shambaa record a famine at least once every fifteen years. 'Deliver us from death by starvation', men prayed in the fertile Unyakyusa on the shores of Lake Malawi.[9] Many Haya, Miji-Kenda, Hehe and Kamba traditions also tell of frequent periods of starvation, and famine is the chief explanation of migration and social change in most Kenyan and Tanzanian traditions. Most of the ancient clans of southern Usambara claim to have come up into the fertile hills during famines in Zigua 'and having moved to the mountains, they had the advantages of increased rainfall and hardy banana trees'.[10] In 1899 a terrible famine hit Usambara: 'people ate tree roots and banana peels, and hundreds became Christians to fill their stomachs'.[11] When rains failed, men had two alternatives:

> Some sought food in the bush. Here hunting and gathering skills were crucial, and such experts as the Sandawe were less often decimated than their neighbours. Others fell back on the reserves embodied in their cattle, not eating them but exchanging them for grain with

6. R. H. Blackburn, 1982 and 1976.
7. H. A. Mwanzi, 1977, pp. 155–66.
8. J. Iliffe, 1979, pp. 6–9.
9. ibid., p. 13.
10. S. Feierman, 1968, p. 12.
11. ibid., p. 14.

more fortunate groups, or exploiting the social ties created by prior exchanges of cattle.[12]

The first line of defence against famine was the cultivator's skill. From 1500 there was continued experimentation with the crops introduced much earlier by the Bantu and Nilotes. In forested regions with heavy rainfall, sorghum, eleusine and millet were less important than bananas and tubers. After 1500 a number of European and American crops were introduced by the Portuguese in East Africa. These included maize, groundnuts, sweet potatoes and cassava, all now well-established. Although only recently introduced to East Africa, little is known of their routes of dispersion. They seem, however, to have varied with the habitat requirements of each crop. Cassava, for example, is thought to have reached the Great Lakes area of East Africa from both Zaire and Zanzibar,[13] while maize may have arrived in the same area from the east, through Ethiopia.[14] Other foods, including numerous varieties of peas, beans and nuts, were also cultivated and are still grown today.

The East African cultivator experimented with all available crops and sought to produce as many as possible.

> Since communications and markets were relatively poorly developed, the farmer had to sow a great variety of crops with a great variety of characteristics, in order to survive no matter what the climatic variations, so that he would not be, in effect, wiped out. By taking a single ecological zone, understanding its complexity with a thoroughness incomprehensible to even a Westerner, developing a rich and subtle language with a profusion of terms for the understanding of local ecology, planting dozens of crops to which the environment was peculiarly suited, the farmer sought to defeat famine, to cheat death.[15]

In Western Kenya the Abagusii, on penetrating the Southern Kenya Highlands in the mid-1700s from the plains around Winam Gulf, were faced with instant crop failure which led to famine and many deaths. They were forced to reduce their dependence on several varieties of sorghum and other lowland crops and expand production of finger-millet and root crops that flourished in their new environment.[16] Only long experience could give such skill, on which rested the authority of age.[17] By the 1700s the Kenya–Tanzania interior supported many different agricultural systems.

As already noted, all communities observed the peculiarities of their own environment and tried to find techniques for dealing with it in a rational

12. J. Iliffe, 1979, p. 13.
13. M. D. Gwynne, 1975, pp. 268–70; and B. W. Langlands, 1966, p. 12.
14. A. C. A. Wright, 1949, p. 80. See also M. D. Gwynne, 1975, p. 253.
15. S. Feierman, 1974, p. 19.
16. M. H. Y. Kaniki, 1979, p. 14.
17. R. W. July, 1974, p. 180.

manner. One common practice was the cutting and burning of the bush to make room for cultivation. After a few seasons, when the soil was exhausted the farmer would move elsewhere to allow the soil to recover. The little available evidence suggests that all agricultural systems in the Kenya and Tanzania interiors rested on the labour of the homesteads with the same simple technology – axes, hoes, *pangas* and digging sticks.

Livestock-raising involving poultry, sheep and goats continued to be a vital economic and cultural activity, particularly in the drier and less-densely settled areas of the Kenyan Rift Valley and the open grasslands of central Tanzania. As Abdul Sheriff has observed, it was more convenient to store wealth in the form of cattle than vegetable foodstuffs.[18] Cattle manure was also important for agricultural intensification. Livestock provided clothing and food, weapons and utensils. Among the pastoralists, such as the Maasai and Turkana, livestock governed the daily routine and kinship relations, its ownership being a measure of family prosperity and individual security.[19] Even among settled agricultural peoples and in mixed agricultural and pastoral societies, ownership and control of cattle and other livestock had high economic and social value. In many predominantly agricultural societies, the Kikuyu and Abagusii for example, the acquisition and ownership of cattle was an important indication of wealth and prestige, 'and relationships with neighbouring peoples, the Maasai and Akamba, were made in this context.'[20] Among the Turkana, Luo, Kalenjin and Maasai, stock changed hands through loans freely begged and granted and through bridewealth. In this way each family herd came to be widely dispersed among friends and relatives often in distant parts, and the benefit rebounded on both the individual and on society as a whole. 'Through the broad dispersal of his cattle, each man reduced the dangers of catastrophe – the destruction of his herds through disease, enemy raid and drought.'[21] By freely loaning his stock a man increased the number of his friends, relatives and acquaintances on whose assistance he could rely in time of need.

Apart from cattle, the predominantly pastoral people were also wealthy in land. Groups such as the Somali, Maasai and Oromo expanded their pastoral activity over wide areas of East Africa. 'With their ease of mobility, their political cohesion and their general health and strength, based on high protein diet of milk, blood and meat, the nomadic pastoralists were militarily dominant over much of East Africa.'[22] The economic geography of the Kenyan and Tanzanian interiors by the mid-1700s can rightly be described as a 'sea' of pastoralism surrounding a few 'islands' of agricultural production. In its social value, wealth, control of territory and political and

18. M. H. Y. Kaniki, 1979, p. 14.
19. R. W. July, 1974, p. 180.
20. R. M. A. van Zwanenberg and A. King, 1975, p. 80.
21. R. W. July, 1974, p. 180.
22. R. M. A. van Zwanenberg and A. King, 1975, p. 80.

military power, pastoral production and the pastoral way of life was predominant, and envied.

Supplementary to agriculture and livestock-keeping was hunting, both as a food source and for protecting cultivated crops. Many East African traditions refer to the importance of hunting, particularly among those who were poor in livestock and, therefore, in domestic sources of protein. Oral accounts, especially those of the Luo, Shambaa, Pare and Abakuria, frequently explain the movement of people by stating that they were hunting an animal that led them to a desirable location where they decided to settle. The myth of the origin of the Shambaa kingdom tells of the appearance of Mbegha, a Ngulu hunter, who killed the wild pigs that were uprooting their crops and gave meat freely to the people. 'The Shambaa, in admiration and gratitude, gave him wives and made him king of all Usambara.'[23] The founder of the ruling Muyinga dynasty of the Hehe is said to have come from Ikombagulu in Usagara on a hunting expedition.[24] The founders of chiefdoms among the Sumbwa, Vinza, Tongwe and Bende are also said to have been 'hunters from Buha, Burundi, Rusuubi or Rwanda'.[25] Hunting, thus, was an important and respectable economic activity.

Men hunted animals for their flesh to supplement their vegetable diet. Cultivated crops and domesticated animals had to be protected from wild animals and birds, and men had to prevent burrowing and grazing animals from destroying crops by using trenches, pit-traps, nooses, spears, arrows and dogs.

In contrast to early importance assigned by tradition to farming, live-stock-raising and hunting, fishing activities are not accorded much significance, except among the groups who lived along Lakes Turkana, Victoria, Baringo, Eyasi and the Indian Ocean. Various types of fish were caught by hook and line, basket-nets and fence traps. Dried fish were, and are, traded to those far from fishing areas.

The traditions of most of the East African peoples indicate an ancient knowledge of iron-working, both smelting and forging. Archaeologists and linguists have also established that iron technology had been introduced into East Africa by the Bantu, probably six centuries before the Christian era. The earliest Iron Age sites in East Africa are around Lake Victoria – at Buhaya, Rwanda, Nyanza and Chobi – and date from the fifth or sixth century before the Christian era in Buhaya and to the third or fourth century of the Christian era in the Winam Gulf and northern Uganda.[26] 'These sites are characterized by tall cylindrical smelting furnaces, a distinctive style of pottery termed Urewe-ware, dense village settlements, and

23. A. D. Roberts, 1968a, p. 5.
24. ibid., p. 39.
25. ibid., p. 120.
26. H. N. Chittick, 1975, p. 18; T. T. Spear, 1981, p. 12.

agriculture.'[27] Another series of early Iron Age sites is found at Kwale, Pare, Kilimanjaro and Usambare, dating from the second or third century. 'These have their own distinctive pottery style, termed Kwale-ware; and also show evidence for permanent settlements and agriculture.'[28] Smithing was usually the guarded occupation of a few groups and carried much prestige and, occasionally, wealth. Among the Nyiha, the iron-smelting was accompanied by great ritual, including the absolute prohibition of the presence of women near the kiln.[29] Several Ugweno traditions indicate that by about 1500, it had lineages specializing in iron-smelting and iron-forging. The major iron-working lineage, the Washana, controlled political power in the country. They were later overthrown by the Wasuya who transformed what were hitherto clan initiation rites into an elaborate state institution with unlimited coercive powers.[30] In western Kenya, the Abagusii claim that they had worked iron since the sixteenth century. Their smiths are said to have become rich from the sale of their manufactures.[31] Among the Luo to the north of the Winam Gulf, the Walowa of Yimbo were the major smiths.[32] They manufactured hoes, arrowheads, ornaments, needles, axes, spears, knives and razors. Also important were salt-mining and crafts such as drum-making, pottery and canoe-building. Traditionally, these were the guarded specialities of particular clans. Such crafts as basketry and housebuilding were not specialist activities, but were undertaken by anyone who had time for them.

It must be re-emphasized that, between 1500 and 1800, food production was a crucial factor in the survival and expansion of society, stimulating a steady increase in population. As most of East Africa was put under extensive cultivation, and grazing, and as production rose above the bare necessity, man could start to look ahead – accumulating and preserving food for future consumption, and utilizing the time thus freed for purposes other than subsistence. He could now afford to specialize, to exempt certain individuals from the task of food production to follow other pursuits such as commodity distribution, war-making, statecraft, art, religion, medicine or philosophy and the improvement of technology.

Trade

Until the late 1700s most societies in the Kenyan and Tanzanian interiors developed independently of external global forces. They were independent politically, economically and socially. As Sheriff puts it, 'their economy

27. T. T. Spear, 1981, p. 12.
28. ibid., pp. 12–13; D. W. Phillipson, 1977. For further discussion, see UNESCO, *General History of Africa*, Vol. II, ch. 23.
29. B. Brock, 1968, p. 75.
30. I. N. Kimambo, 1969, pp. 45–64.
31. W. R. Ochieng', 1974a, p. 213.
32. W. R. Ochieng', 1970, p. 8.

PLATE 27.1   *Forging hoes*

was symmetrical and internally integrated, by which we mean that they produced what they consumed and the surplus was retained within the community to support the development of non-agricultural crafts and social differentiation'.[33] The exchange of various forms of surplus is termed trading.

Trading, the exchange of goods for mutual benefit, is a universal human habit found even among the most simple societies. Although simple communities are commonly thought to have self-sufficient subsistence economies, trade in the sense of a regular series of acts of exchange is frequently reported even among those who live by hunting and collecting. The need to trade arises from the simple fact that at no time have all groups and

33. A. M. H. Sheriff, 1980, p. 36.

areas been endowed with similar facilities and resources. People traded because their neighbours had vital commodities which they themselves lacked but needed either for their livelihood or their pleasure.

Take, for example, the relationship between pastoralism and agriculture. There is, of course, the misconception that regards pastoralism as historically separate from, and essentially opposed to, agriculture. Indeed colonial literature has built a picture of continuous feud between pastoralists and farmers. While one can talk about contrasts between the two, there was also much that encouraged co-operation and pastoralists exchanged their products with farmers.

Much has been written about the trade connections that for centuries existed between East Africa and the Orient. Indeed even before the establishment of the long-distance trade which, in the nineteenth century, was to become the lifeline of this commercial exchange between East Africa and overseas countries, there existed trade relations between East Africa and Asiatic states.[34] But it must be emphasized that significant trade relations in East Africa also included important internal economic ties between cultural and ecological regions.

African trade has long been stimulated by contact between distinct ecological regions and different and complementary cultures. Indeed, this trade may have been more significant to the African peoples, as it dealt in basic necessities often determined by climatic and ecological factors. Internal African trade had a different purpose and dynamic to that of Arab or European trade. In some areas, for instance, one of its dominating concerns was to overcome famine. It was therefore irregular and sporadic. It was also a means of accumulating wealth in the form of cattle and foodstuffs.

Let us look at several instances of this trade. Traditions from Kikuyuland talk of ancient trading connections between the Kikuyu and the neighbouring Akamba and Maasai. The Kikuyu economy was diverse. While they were predominantly farmers, certain sections, such as the Kikuyu of Tetu and Mathira in Nyeri, were so influenced by their Maasai neighbours as to have evolved a semi-pastoral economy, almost a Maasai way of life. Conversely, the Athi Kikuyu specialized in hunting and extracting forest products, such as beeswax and honey. To the Maasai, the Kikuyu offered a variety of manufactured, as well as agricultural products – including pots, calabash containers, spears and swords, as well as honey, tobacco, elephant-mat and ochre. For these the Maasai paid in livestock, magic, milk, skins and leather cloaks.

Kikuyuland also constituted the best markets for the Akamba after 1760. From the Kikuyu communities of Muranga and Nyeri, the Akamba traders sought the staple crops that they could not grow themselves in sufficient abundance: *nzavi* (a preservable bean), *ikwa* (a tuber yam), *nduma* (the arrowroot plant of the inland water-holes), *njaki* (a common Kikuyu bean), *mwembe* (traditional maize) and, sometimes *ndulu* (a green of which the

34. See ch. 25 above.

Akamba were particularly fond). The Akamba paid in *mbua* (animal skins) and *uki* (a type of beer, longer fermented than that of neighbouring communities). Sometimes, the Akamba traded their labour in harvesting for an equivalent share of the food crops.[35]

Further west, on the eastern lip of Lake Victoria, there was a widespread trading network linking the various communities. The Abagusii and the Luo were the major trading partners. The Abagusii sold to the Luo agricultural products and iron items such as axes, spears, razors and arrowheads, and also soapstone and leopard and baboon skins. These were exchanged for a variety of Luo goods – chiefly livestock but also including cattle-salt, hides, ghee, milk, fish, pots and poison. Trade between the Maasai and their Nyanzan neighbours was negligible, although the broad-bladed Maasai spears and their magic were widely sought after by the Abagusii and Luo. In return the Maasai were paid in foodstuffs.[36]

Further south, in Tanzania, traditions from Western Unyamwezi and Uvinza speak of pre-1800 immigrant groups from the north exchanging grain crops for pots with the earlier inhabitants, 'fishermen who had lived along river banks and only cultivated crops'.[37] Among the Nyamwezi, forest products – bark-cloth, bark-boxes, spearshafts, honey and beeswax – were also traded between villages and were in special demand in the northern countries of the Iramba, Sumbwa and Sukuma. In Unyakyusa most women made pottery, but volcanic areas lacked suitable clay and so depended on specialists such as the Kisii women of the Nyasa lakeshore, who bartered their pots from house to house in Nyakyusa villages, or the people of Ngaseni who traded their huge beer pots along the road which ran around the upper slopes of Kilimanjaro.[38]

The two most important items in early trade in central Tanzania were probably iron and salt. The main area of iron-working was in the north, among the Ha and the Zinza. The scarcity of iron in general was a major stimulant to trade. Throughout central, western and northern Tanzania iron was needed in a variety of forms as hoe-blades for cultivation, as knife-blades and axe-heads for building and other crafts, and as spear-blades and arrowheads for hunting, fishing and fighting. Many traders from the north and the south travelled to the land of the Ha and the Zinza to buy these iron items which they sold back home at a profit. The northern Nyamwezi introduced iron hoes to the Nyatura. Andrew Roberts explains that iron hoes from the north-west were reworked to make spears, not only among the Sukuma and Wakiko fishermen of the lower Malagarasi, but also among the Western Maasai and the Baraguyu.[39] In the north-east, the Chagga and Maasai obtained iron products from Pare smelters while, in the late 1700s,

35. K. Jackson, 1976.
36. W. R. Ochieng', 1974, pp. 68–9.
37. A. D. Roberts, 1970c, p. 43.
38. J. Iliffe, 1979, p. 18.
39. A. D. Roberts, 1970c, pp. 45–6.

the Mamba chiefdom became the iron-working centre for much of Kilimanjaro. In the south, Fipa smiths exchanged their produce for cloth woven in the Rukwa valley while the Nyakyusa climbed the Livingstone mountains to barter food for the products of Kinga furnaces. Iron was a scarce and precious commodity: only the wealthy possessed iron hoes. Those used on Kilimanjaro towards the end of the eighteenth century were only a few centimetres broad. The Sandawe used them until they were worn down to the tang.[40]

The other staple of regional exchange was salt, a necessity of life to men who lived chiefly on vegetable foods. Most people produced small quantities by burning grass or collecting surface deposits but high-quality sources were rare. The major saltpans were located in Ugogo and at Ivuna, Kanyenye, Lake Balangida, Singida and Lake Eyasi, and at Bukune and Bulungwa south of Kahama. The most important brine springs were in Buha and Uvinza. Salt was traded widely, 'especially to the north and south'.[41] The Uvinza springs, in particular, seem to have been exploited since + 1000.[42] This Vinza salt industry was later stimulated by the foundation of the original Vinza chiefdom in 1800, 'which would have extended the range of social contacts and created a social group that would profit directly, through taxation, from increased salt production'.[43]

Trade among the Miji-Kenda of south-east Kenya and north-eastern Tanzania had only begun to develop appreciably by the beginning of the eighteenth century. At this time most Miji-Kenda, who had previously isolated themselves in fenced-in hill-top settlements behind the coastal plains, began to expand outwards. Later, with their population greatly expanded, they embarked on secondary migrations settling in the less fertile lower parts of their hilly country, where they frequently clashed with the Oromo and Maasai.[44]

The Miji-Kenda were largely cultivators of millet, rice and fruits. Throughout the eighteenth century they were staunch allies of the Mazrui, supplying the many coastal settlements with ivory, gum copal, honey, beeswax, tobacco, grain, foodstuffs and timber for building dhows. In return the Miji-Kenda traders obtained salt, beads, cloth, iron hoes and other goods. John Lamphear has suggested that by 1750 at least, the Miji-Kenda were the middlemen of Swahili–Arab trade.[45]

In the trade between the coast and the interior, the Miji-Kenda sent their trading caravans both north and north-west. Northwards, they travelled to the countries of the Oromo and Borana from whom they obtained mainly livestock in exchange for cloth and beads. In the north-west, they

40. J. Iliffe, 1979, p. 19.
41. A. D. Roberts, 1970c, p. 47.
42. J. Iliffe, 1979, p. 19.
43. A. D. Roberts, 1970c, p. 47.
44. T. T. Spear, 1976 and 1978.
45. See J. E. Lamphear, 1970 and W. R. Ochieng', 1975b.

penetrated Akamba and Chagga countries, obtaining ivory, honey and beeswax.[46] But Miji-Kenda control of the interior trade was shortlived and by the mid-1700s, they had been replaced by the Akamba.

From the foregoing survey, we may conjecture that the trade of the interior of Kenya and Tanzania may well, by 1700 or before, have involved exchanges over considerable distances. It is, however, clear that it was only in about 1800 that the interior of East Africa began to participate in long-distance trade and thus to be linked to economies beyond it.

Social and political activity

Social and political institutions and organizations were important for the cohesion of society and the protection of property and trade. Society in the East African interior, between 1500 and 1800, was far from settled. Although the linguistic map of modern East Africa was taking final shape, there were still significant internal migrations into sparsely-settled or empty areas. These internal movements sometimes brought together peoples of different languages or dialects and with different political and economic practices. Internal conflicts multiplied as clans and clan membership expanded, necessitating more sophisticated methods of conflict resolution. When disputes arose between different clans, the parties involved sought arbitration from individuals respected for their wisdom. In some areas, such as Shambaa,[47] Yimbo,[48] Nandi,[49] and Unyiha, the immigrant groups or families assumed political leadership over those whom they found already settled. In other areas the immigrants were absorbed into the local social set-ups. In both cases internal migrations set into motion processes of cultural and political integration which continued into the colonial period.

The period 1500–1800 therefore saw a movement towards political centralization and the evolution of larger and larger linguistic and social groups. A number of factors dictated in favour of the expansion of political scale. There was, for example, the need for more effective means of defence than those offered by the clan or the village and to expand areas of economic activity. But while a variety of societies emerged in the East African interior the two that contrasted most conspicuously were the pastoralists and farmers.[50]

Pastoralists, like hunters, were parasites upon herbivores. Like hunters, too, they pursued a wandering life, travelling comparatively large distances in search of grass for their animals. They often followed a regular migrational pattern designed to discover the richest feeding and watering grounds for their herds at each season of the year. Above all, the pastoralists

46. W. R. Ochieng', 1974a and 1974b.
47. S. Feierman, 1968, pp. 1–8.
48. W. R. Ochieng', 1975c and 1976.
49. See W. R. Ochieng', 1977, pp. 58–76 and B. J. Walter, 1970.
50. B. Brock, 1968.

had to protect their herds from rival carnivores, whether animals or men. Such a life required articulate leadership and clearly defined lines of authority to determine routes of march and take command in emergencies whenever rivals attempted to intrude upon the community's traditional pastureland or steal their flocks and herds.[51]

The political history of the Kenya–Tanzania interior partly depended on population growth which was made possible by a farming existence and the disciplined politico-military organization required by pastoralism. The balance tipped in favour of one or other protagonist, depending on the fluctuations in social organization and cohesion, and on the development of technology. By 1800 the pastoralists were beginning to lose both economic and military power to the farmers who were rapidly perfecting their political institutions through social integration and the expansion of their farming capability. The pastoral Maasai, in particular, declined militarily and economically throughout the nineteenth century due to cattle diseases, epidemics and civil wars.[52] It could thus be said that the pace of socio-political evolution throughout the Kenya–Tanzania interior was accelerated by the increased variety of societies and stimulated by migrations.

By 1700 two main types of socio-political organization existed in the Kenya–Tanzania interior. Societies such as the Kikuyu, Miji-Kenda, Kamba and Maasai lived in scattered independent settlements in minor or major patrilineages and clan groups with no form of centralized, traditional bureaucracy. Decentralization, however, as shown later, did not mean disorganization or lack of political or social cohesion. Decentralized societies had family, village and neighbourhood councils. At the highest level they had clan or district councils made up of elders, and from these elders was chosen the ruling council. Group relationships were maintained among family, clan and neighbourhood members, and these relationships defined and governed the actions of individuals and established mutual obligations and rights. Indeed, among the Kikuyu the idea of individual initiative was sharply discouraged as self-seeking, 'whereas concepts of corporate effort and group responsibility were regarded as the cardinal virtues'.[53]

Conversely, the centralized (or centralizing) societies, such as the Shambaa, Pare, Sukuma, Nyamwezi and Wanga, entertained rudimentary chiefly bureaucracies that provided socio-political control. By the end of the eighteenth century some of these groups, such as the Shambaa and Pare, had strong despotic kings and paramount chiefs, assisted by various councils, ministers and district chiefs.

Let us look at specific cases of these developments. Before 1300 central Tanzania was occupied by scattered populations of settled agricultural Bantu, the cattle-herding and Kushitic-influenced Mbugu, Gorowa, Burungi, Alagwa and Aramanik, and the hunting and gathering Sandawe

51. R. M. A. van Zwanenberg and A. King, 1975, pp. 79–87.
52. G. S. Were and D. A. Wilson, 1972 edn, pp. 89–96.
53. R. W. July, 1974, pp. 177–8.

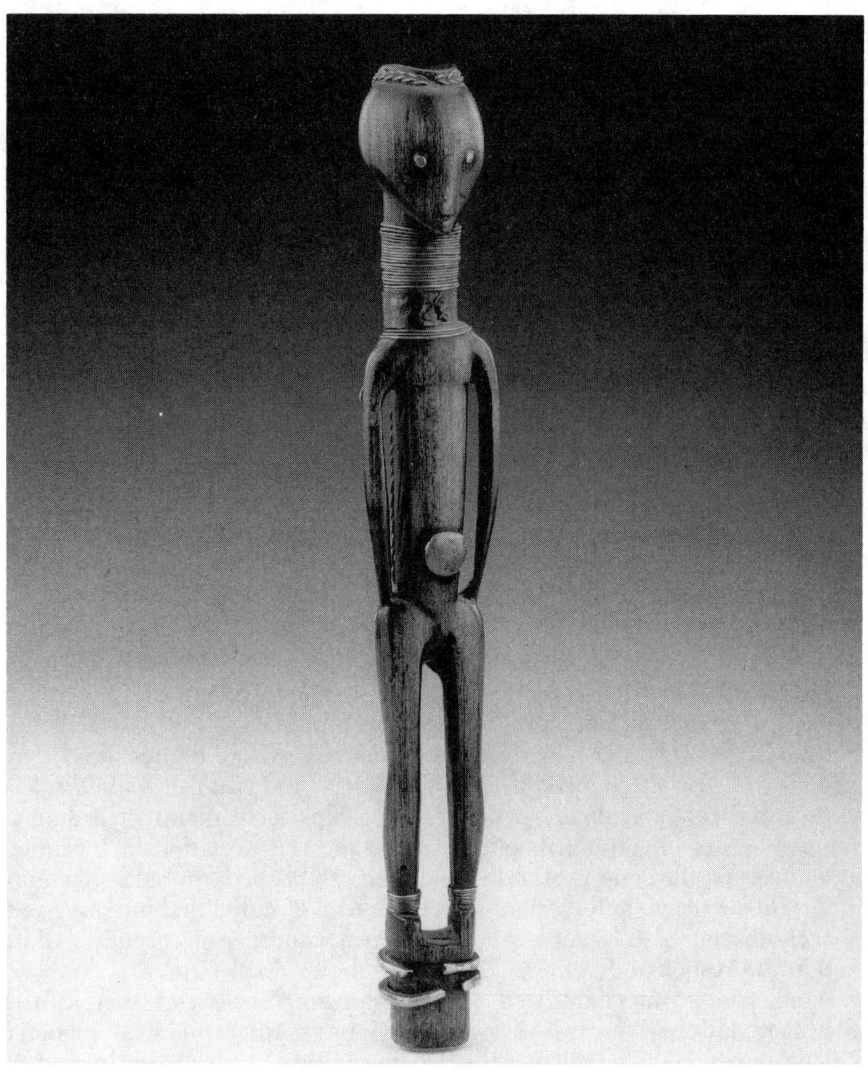

PLATE 27.2 *Kamba statuette of a female figure, made of wood having a clear natural patina. There are numerous brass rings round the neck and ankles, and the eyes, navel and hair are inlaid with metal. Height: 26.5 cm*

and Hadzapi. They lived in villages, the ruins of some of which – particularly those of the Bantu farmers – are still scattered all over Tanzania. These early villages governed themselves on family lines, authority being vested in the hands of two or three influential families. Indeed, most Tanzanian communities seem to have recognized the importance of some kind of organization from the time they migrated and settled in their respective areas. But because the migrations were individual or small-group migrations, the organization also emphasized kinship ties. Within each kinship group there were seeds of political leadership.

Among the Pare, the first stage of articulate political leadership was accomplished when each clan established itself in its territory and accepted one ritual leader whose descendants would succeed him. Thus the religious needs of the community were at the heart of Pare political evolution.[54] After settling in an area, each Pare group gradually established its *mpungi* (sacred shrine) which linked it with the ancestors who had founded the group and, periodically, all members gathered to worship. As the population increased it became necessary for people of different clans to come together. The formative period, when clans first came together, is enshrouded in myth, but Isaria Kimambo says that about 'sixteen generations ago' a leader from the Washana iron-smiths emerged who was recognized by many Ugweno clans as their chief. The Washana were later overthrown by the Wasuya who took over the loose political organization that had existed and established a centralized state. Angovi was the coup-maker but it was his son, Mranga, who consolidated the Ugweno state. Kimambo considers Mranga 'one of the great' political reformers of Tanzania:

> He transformed what were hitherto clan initiation rites into an elaborate state institution with unlimited coercive powers. He organized a hierarchy of councils, he maintained a large group of officials wholly dependent on him and, finally, he sent his sons to rule districts and thus expanded the kingdom over the whole plateau of North Pare.[55]

At the apogee of its power the Ugweno state had at its head a *Mangi Mrwe* (paramount chief) who was assisted by a council of ministers and the *wamagi* (district chiefs).

As already explained, population expansion aided by the emergence of ritual leaders and iron-smith experts, led to the coalescence of clans for mutual political and economic benefits in Ugweno (and later the entire Pare Highlands). North Pare, for example, formed a single geographical unit which allowed a greater concentration of population. In addition, were the resolute leaders whose wealth and claim to supernatural powers attracted followers beyond their lineages.

Bukoba was another area of Tanzania where chiefly institutions were strong by 1600. Several ruling lineages had evolved among the agricultural communities, including Karagwe, the Buhaya states, Buzinza and the Ha states. Their political system, which was more centralized than in other Tanzanian states, involved control of land and cattle in such a way that the tribute system was more exploitative. These states belonged to the

54. I. N. Kimambo, 1969, p. 4.
55. I. N. Kimambo, 1968, p. 19.

great Lakes region.[56] Further south, by 1600 many chiefships had sprouted all over Tanzania resembling one another in many ways. For example, each consisted of a small group of villages and neighbourhoods ruled by a single chief whom the villagers appointed from the ruling lineage. Such chiefs were known as *ntemi* or *mtemi*. The chief presided over the chiefdom's councils and supreme court. He was the holder of special regalia or rulership symbols, such as sacred spears. He also maintained a royal fire from which all fires of his chiefdom were supposed to be kindled.

The striking similarity in the organization and regalia of these chiefdoms at one time led scholars such as Roland Oliver and J. D. Fage to propound the theory of common origin, ultimately from the Nile valley and immediately from local Ugandan, Rwandese and Burundi examples.[57] But scholars of Tanzanian political history have repudiated such diffusionist (at times racist)[58] theories. Kimambo, in particular, has argued that the problem of explaining similarities between African political units, at regional or continental level, has to be sought in agricultural peoples, and the differences in the scale of organization have to be understood in terms of adjustment both to local environment and to special external factors.

Andrew Roberts tells us that the origins of numerous Nyamwezi chiefdoms are probably not to be sought in any single process of migration or diffusion: they sprang from the Nyamwezi environment. 'From an early stage – just how early, we cannot say – certain men were respected as rainmakers and magicians, as pioneers in opening up woodland and as arbitrators in dispute.'[59] It was from these roots that the Nyamwezi chiefships emerged. 'A Nyamwezi (ntemi) exercised both ritual and administrative power in a manner broadly similar to that of other chiefs in eastern and central Africa.'[60] But unlike in Upare where development was towards centralization, in Unyamwezi the small chiefdoms tended to increase in number, 'not only through migrations, but also as a result of chiefdoms splitting up'. Only in the nineteenth century was there rapid centralization in Unyamwezi 'due to expansion of trade' and the emergence of ruthless traders and organizers such as Mirambo.

Among the Fipa of south-western Tanzania, the earliest traditions of origin are tied up with the origin of the (Mlansi) Fipa kingdom. According to one version, recorded by Roy Willis, 'the first man in the world, who was called Ntatakwa, fell from the sky when the world began and founded the Milansi line of chiefs'.[61] The early settlers of Ufipa were farmers who lived in compact villages. This encouraged a collective defence arrangement which culminated in the building of fortifications. The ruling lineage,

56. See ch. 26 above.
57. R. Oliver and J. D. Fage, 1963, pp. 44–52; I. N. Kimambo, 1969, pp. 1–10.
58. C. G. Seligman, 1957, p. 85.
59. I. N. Kimambo, 1968, p. 18.
60. A. D. Roberts, 1968b, p. 119.
61. R. G. Willis, 1968, pp. 82–3.

which most probably came from around Lake Mweru, seems to have derived its power from its iron-smithing skills. 'The fact that the present chief of Mlansi is an ironsmith, a hereditary occupation,' Willis has argued, 'supports the theory that the founders of the Milansi chiefdom were themselves smiths.'[62] Milansi traditions indicate that the first ruler, Ntatakwa, sent out his sons to found villages and govern other parts of the country. The Fipa kingdom seems to have been a confederation of chiefdoms ruled by related chiefs.

Later in the eighteenth century, the Fipa political style was changed due to an invasion by some pastoralists from the north who introduced political ideas resembling those of Buganda, Bunyoro and Ankole. They introduced a principle of government not based on relationships between 'father chiefs' and 'son chiefs', as formerly practised in Ufipa, but on a personal bond of loyalty between a ruler and a number of followers chosen by him. These rulers at the periphery had no kinship relation with the king. There was probably a coup which overthrew the traditional ruling Milansi lineage and ushered in the Twa dynasty. Some of the lesser chiefs, still loyal to the Milansi dynasty, apparently had to be overcome by force. The Twa, however, did not rule in peace, as Ufipa was again invaded towards the end of the eighteenth century, by the Nyiha who burnt down Milansi villages. By 1800 civil war between the two rivals for the Twa kingship was still raging.

Clearly, between 1500 and 1800 a number of *ntemi* chiefships, of varying sizes and centralization, sprang up in Tanzania in response to human, political and economic needs. They were shaped by the physical and human environment and, while centralization and economic expansion was the objective of most Tanzania states, the process of nation-building was often painful. Sometimes, as with the Nyamwezi, these states faced fission or secession. Sometimes, as with the Fipa, they faced coups and civil wars. In many ways they faced similar nation-building problems to those faced by modern African states.

In western Kenya, the Luo seem to have emphasized their kinship system, ancestral cults and hereditary leadership, with the result that they tended to form jural communities organized around ritually important *megpiny* (land-owning clans) and their nominally hereditary leaders. When they arrived in Nyanza they tended to create polities that were more centralized and stratified than the earlier communities. And, while the Luo clans and lineages were equal in most respects, the presence of chiefly, priestly and commoner groups indicated a degree of clan inequality rarely found in Kenyan societies.

Probably the best elaboration on the Luo socio-political system in precolonial times is that by Peter C. Oloo Aringo in his study of the Alego Luo.[63] He agrees with B. A. Ogot that, at the highest level of political

62. R. G. Willis, 1968, p. 84.
63. P. C. Oloo, 1969 and B. A. Ogot, 1963.

organization, the Luo were divided into twelve or thirteen *ogendini* (sub-ethnic groups) of varying sizes. Membership of the sub-ethnic group was through *gweng'* (pl. *gwenge*), a semi-autonomous political and territorial unit. Ideally *gweng'* was occupied by clansmen but parts were often leased to *jodak* (stranger lineages and clans), 'either because of the latter's part in assisting in the conquest of the new territory, or on terms laid down by the dominant clan who claimed to possess all land in the territorial unit. *Gweng'* society, thus, tended to be a plural society.'[64]

The highest political council in any *gweng'* was the *buch jodong gweng'* (council of the elders). In Alego, membership of this council was open to all heads of lineages of the dominant clan, with only select and talented representation by the elders of *jodak* communities. (In Yimbo, another Luo chiefdom, there was no such discrimination.)[65] The *gweng'* council was the custodian of clan land. It accepted or rejected new strangers and acted as the final court of appeal in cases affecting the *gweng'*. It also carried out ritual ceremonies and declared war or negotiated peace with other *gwenge*. A decision of the *jodong gweng'* was binding on all subjects: those who defied its regulations and decisions could be cursed. An effective curse of *jodongo* was believed to inflict *chira* (an incurable disease supposedly imposed by the ancestors on the wrong-doers and his descendants). The *gweng'* council could also expel persistent criminals and their families from the territorial unit and inflict corporal punishment and fines on wrong-doers for various crimes.

Above the *gweng'* council was the *buch piny* (council of the sub-ethnic group). Members of this council were the heads of the various *gweng'* councils, together with prominent diviners, healers, rainmakers and outstanding warriors. The *buch piny* was usually chaired by the *ruoth* or *wuon piny* (chief). The council dealt with major political, judicial and economic matters affecting the *piny* (territory of a sub-ethnic group) – such as murder, cattle-theft, boundary disputes, famine, pestilence, invasion, defence, trade and inter-clan and inter-*gweng'* conflicts. In a few centralized *pinje*, such as Yimbo, the *buch piny* was an effective instrument of control and coercion. In places such as Sakwa or Asembo, where centralization was yet to be achieved, the *buch piny* tended to have limited powers and confined its role to arbitration in internal disputes.

The Kalenjin, who have lived for centuries in the western highlands of Kenya, formed a typically decentralized society. B. E. Kipkorir says that until the 1800s the political system was egalitarian and decentralized.[66] The elders and influential specialists monopolized authority. Eloquence, the ability to voice acceptable views at councils, and a command of precedence and custom were considered important for political leadership. Above all, a man had first to distinguish himself as a happily married and socially

64. P. C. Oloo, 1969.
65. W. R. Ochieng', 1975c.
66. B. E. Kipkorir, 1974.

established member of a clan or neighbourhood community to be accorded the accolade of leadership. Among the Nandi, a section of the Kalenjin, there is evidence to indicate that between the eighteenth and nineteenth centuries a new dimension of governance of society entered the scene in the adoption of a spiritual leader called the *orkoiyot* (pl. *orkoik*). H. A. Mwanzi asserts that while the socio-political structure of Nandi society remained largely unchanged, with the clan and neighbourhood councils as the basis of social and political life, by the end of the nineteenth century the *orkoiyot* had transformed the Nandi polity into a theocracy with himself as the sovereign.[67]

In time the *orkoiyot* was able to demand a share of the war booty and to impose his authority over sectional and neighbourhood councils through having his personal representatives as consultants to each council. This intervention in the political field created strong ties between the sectional warriors and the *orkoik*, but in many other matters the *orkoik* had little direct power or influence. There is evidence to suggest, however, that by 1890 the Nandi *orkoik*, like the Maasai *laibons* (ritual leaders), were beginning to pretend to a greater degree of political authority than their predecessors had envisaged. These pretensions were encouraged by the regional councils which had profited from the *orkoik*'s ministrations, and had consequently developed an unreasoning belief in his supernatural attributes.

Thus, a special class of officials was created among the Nandi to maintain communication between these councils and the *orkoiyot*. These officials accompanied the warrior leaders when the *orkoiyot*'s permission was sought for a projected raid. They also acted as secret-service agents for the *orkoiyot*, so that he could be kept informed of events and public opinion in their areas. These arrangements progressively centralized Nandi society in the second half of the nineteenth century.[68]

Conclusion

Scattered all over Kenya and Tanzania by 1800 was a bewildering number of differing Nilotic, Kushitic, and Bantu-speaking communities. Only in the Great Lakes areas of East Africa had there developed large states and kingdoms.[69] In the Kenya–Tanzania interior, the typical polity was small and clan-oriented. Most Bantu-speakers were farmers, though wherever possible they kept and prized their livestock. Pastoralists, such as the Turkana, Oromo and Maasai, with their more aggressive societies, controlled substantial portions of territory between the agricultural Bantu.[70] Along the coast were the Swahili city-states, dominated by local Arab

67. H. A. Mwanzi, 1973.
68. W. R. Ochieng', 1977, pp. 58–76.
69. See ch. 26 above.
70. R. M. A. van Zwanenberg and A. King, 1975, pp. 79–109.

oligarchies. The city populations were mixed, the dominant language being Swahili, and the tempo of life considerably different from that of the interior.

The end of the eighteenth century marked the end of independent East African growth – centuries of Iron Age growth during which most inland people were isolated from outside influences. Soon after 1800 the independent people of Kenya and Tanzania were faced with events of new and often terrible meaning as great waves of Arab and European invasion intruded upon their lands. Much of their traditional civilization was seriously damaged or submerged in a rising flood of violence. Many long-established customs and beliefs were undermined and many ancient ways of keeping law and order set aside.

East Africa was badly placed to meet this harsh and sudden challenge from outside. Africa as a whole had fallen far behind the strong powers of the rest of the world in its ability to produce goods, whether for war or peace. After 1500 Europe had entered a period of far-reaching mechanical and scientific discovery and development. Inland Africa, by contrast, had not: it had continued instead with the steady but slow development of its own civilization.[71] This Iron Age civilization had many achievements. There was much advancement and invention in the arts of community life, the adoption of new crops, the spread of metal-working skills, the growth of trade and, more important, the methods of self-rule and ways of keeping the peace. These were definitely important gains but they could not compete with the growing power of the strong industrialized nations of Europe. By 1800 the technical power of the Europeans was far greater than that of the Africans.[72] By 1900 the power gap had become enormous. It underlay much of post-1800 African history and was part of the background to imperialism in Africa. It went far to explain the crisis which began after 1800, and although it did not make itself directly felt until after 1850, it had an indirect effect on the inland peoples long before that.

71. W. Rodney, 1970a and 1972. Also W. R. Ochieng', 1975d.
72. See E. A. Alpers, 1973 and A. M. H. Sheriff, 1980.

28

Madagascar and the islands of the Indian Ocean

R. K. KENT

Madagascar

The mould of modern Madagascar was cast in the course of the nineteenth century when the Merina of its heartland attained political supremacy, imposed a blend of their own and imported European features on many other populations, and became virtually the only Malagasy to be perceived by outsiders. The colonial period, which began with a military defeat of the Merina, made them even more omnipresent in the current century. Yet, beyond the impact of relatively recent events, there is a different and more inclusive past in which the three hundred years before 1800 stand as a monument in the history of Madagascar as a whole. It is almost certain that most of the inhabitants of Madagascar coalesced during these three centuries into the wider social, economic, religious, cultural and political aggregates that make up the Malagasy people today – the Antankara, Antandroy, Antambahoaka, Antanosy, Antemoro, Antesaka, Antefasy, Bara, Betsimisaraka, Betsileo, Bezanozano, Merina, Mahafaly, Sakalava, Sihanaka, Tanala and Tsimihety.[1]

By the mid-sixteenth century there was an end to settlers from overseas who merged into new populations; some of the inhabitants of Madagascar had come into contact with Europeans, mostly Portuguese; and at least one of the more lasting and influential royal families, the *Maroserana*, had started to form. In the early 1600s Madagascar was a political honeycomb of mostly small and self-contained chiefdoms. Before the end of the century much of western Madagascar went under a Sakalava empire and several kingdoms emerged among the highlanders like the Betsileo and Merina, among the south-eastern Antemoro, Antesaka, Antefasy and Antanosy, among the southernmost Antandroy, the south-western Mahafaly, and the

---

1. As the ethnic names have never been standardized other spellings also exist. In general the prefix *an-* (or *ant-*) denotes 'people of' but is swallowed in everyday speech (viz. Antanosy = 'Tanus' as the Malagasy 'o' comes out as 'oo' or 'ou' in French); *be-* and *-be* reflect 'many' or 'numerous' and also 'great' to denote importance; and *tsi-* or *-tsi* is a negative. Excluded from the above list are some 70 000 Makua, descendants of Africans imported via Mozambique in the first half of the nineteenth century. Recent suggestions that a number of the main ethnic names were formed under Merina hegemony are incorrect.

Bara of the southern interior. In the same century contacts with Europeans became less confined and more intense at times as the Dutch, English and French East India Companies turned to the great African island; the slave trade shifted from exports mainly to Eastern Africa and Arabia via three outlets bunched up in the north-west to exports at several points of Madagascar's vast coastal belt and toward the Cape, the Mascarenes and the New World; and fire-arms began to spread in relatively small quantities but not without instances of political impact. In the eighteenth century, the Sakalava empire and especially Iboina,[2] its northern component, reached its apogee while a good part of the eastern littoral became politically united for the first time into the Betsimisaraka Confederation. Before 1800 the northern Sakalava and the Betsimisaraka were in a state of decline which could not be reversed because of events within and outside Madagascar. In contrast, a weak and disunited Imerina augmented its food production, increased its population, and underwent a political rebirth which gave the Merina a solid base for their future expansion.

Newcomers and coalitions

In time the Antemoro became famous in Madagascar as the only group to have a scribal tradition in Malagasy (using the Arabic script) before the 1800s and the people with special abilities in the domains of magic and religion. Full agreement is still lacking on the questions of when and where the ancestral Antemoro first landed in Madagascar, where they came from, the degree of their own Islamization, and their impact within the island. Earlier writers tended to place them in north-eastern Madagascar around the 1400s and to regard them as Arabs from Arabia.[3] Even more recently, the extent to which Islam has been and is a real force in the past and present of the Antemoro has been questioned.[4] Gustave Julien was the first scholar to propose an Eastern African origin,[5] supported in the past decade on several grounds, along with the suggestion that the early Antemoro had Islamic religious training and organization but could not maintain either in the face of total isolation from the Islamic world.[6] One aspect should remain beyond dispute: the Antemoro did not develop a society and state in Madagascar prior to the arrival of their ancestors at the Matitana river in the south-east. This is where both emerged after the ancestors intermixed

2. The prefix *I-* stands for 'place of' in toponyms; it is also found as a personal article in individual and group names; and it represents an African survival.

3. A. Grandidier, 1908–28, Vol. IV, part I, p. 156. He suspected an Eastern African sojourn for some of the Antemoro ancestors but found no African cultural influences to modify the ultimate Arab origin.

4. J. Faublée, 1958, p. 71. He was following A. Van Gennep, 1904, pp. 4–11, who demanded proof of Islamic origins. E. de Flacourt, 1661, p. 171, outlined the Muslim hierarchy in the south-eastern part of the island.

5. G. Julien, 1929, p. 75.

6. R. K. Kent, 1970, pp. 108–14.

with the *tompon-tany* (master of the soil; original inhabitants). It is however possible to date rather closely the Matitana settlement because three Portuguese sea captains happened to visit the area at the right time, between 1507 and 1514. At a year apart, the first two neither found nor reported any 'Moors' there but did note that local residents were no strangers to trade with them.[7] The third was sent directly to Matitana to establish a factory in 1514. By then Matitana had a 'town densely inhabited by Moors'. After some six months of their opposition to a Portuguese commercial presence the *tompon-tany* forced him to abandon Matitana for good.[8] As the ancestral Antemoro are the only serious candidates for the 'Moors' in this particular instance, the Matitana settlement must have developed between 1509 and 1513.

Written Antemoro traditions regarding both the formative period ('when Matitana did not yet have seven villages') and the ensuing centuries are not only documents which record events of the past but are also aspects of a self-reflective process. They tell us in general about encounters with those who inhabited the south-eastern littoral before the first Antemoro arrived; about newcomers steeped in patrilineal concepts meeting the *tompon-tany* who defined themselves in matrilineal terms; about not one but several arrivals of the 'proto-Antemoro' at Matitana and about the many conflicts among the newcomers themselves.[9] Only the ultimate ancestor, Ramakararube, remains above all strife as he returned to 'Maka' (Mecca).[10] In a more precise way, it was in the first three-quarters of the sixteenth century that the Antemoro prevented their own incorporation into one or more of the *tompon-tany* groups and formed a society dominated by and centred around four aristocratic and four sacerdotal clans. Indeed, most of what is known of Antemoro internal history well into the 1800s is but a reflection of conflict among the aristocratic Anteoni, Antemahazo, Anteisambo and Zafikasinambo, each clan having its own territory within the kingdom.[11] The *Andrianoni*, or ruler of all the Antemoro, could come from any of the four (sometimes collectively called Anteoni). At the same time, the sacerdotal clans vied for primacy in religious and cultural functions. The Tsimeto, Zafimbolazi, Anakara and Anterotri sought, for example, to be the guardians of sacred Antemoro manuscripts, (*sorabe*), to become the high priests of the realm, or to have the closest proximity to an *Andrianoni*

7. A. Grandidier *et al.*, 1903–20, Vol. I, pp. 18–19 and 48–9 for the visits of Ruy Pereira and Diego Lopes de Sequeira (who was much more than a sea captain) in 1507 and 1508.

8. A. Grandidier *et al.*, 1903–20, Vol. I, p. 53; *Documentos Sobre ...*, 1962–75, Vol. III, p. 508, for the voyage of Luis Figueira.

9. G. Julien, 1929, pp. 1–23 and 1933, pp. 57–83; G. Mondain, 1910, pp. 50–191 (Arabico–Malagasy texts and French translations).

10. Cf. G. Mondain, 1910, p. 51 and G. Ferrand, 1891–1902, Vol. II, p. 57.

11. These were reduced to three in the 1600s. The Anteoni and Antemahazo occupied the lower and middle Matitana. The Andrianoni's capital was Ivato. The sacerdotal clans, collectively called Antalaotra, centred around Vohipeno. Cf. H. Deschamps, 1961, p. 93 and map on p. 110.

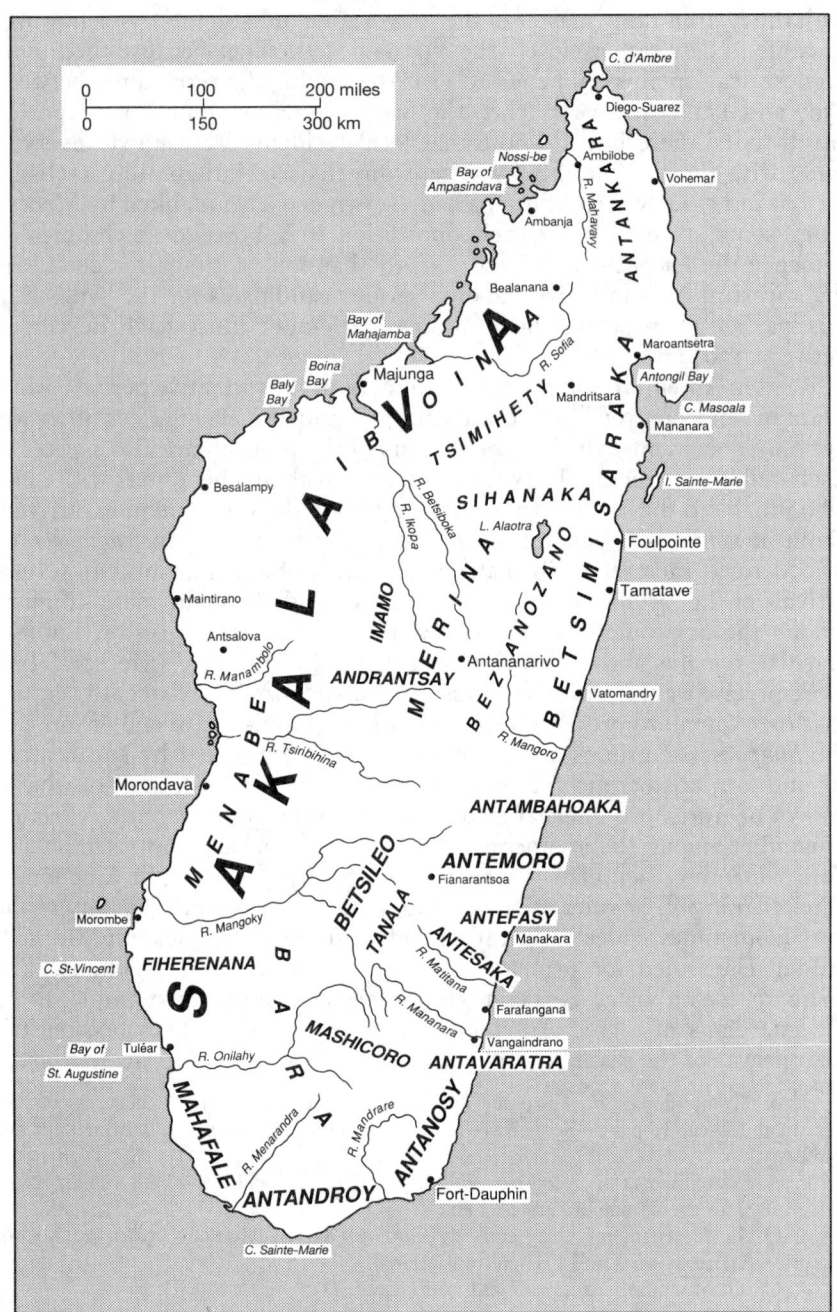

FIG. 28.1 *Ethnic groups of Madagascar*
Source: adapted from map of Madagascar from *Early Kingdoms in Madagascar, 1500–1700* by Raymond K. Kent,
© 1970 by Holt, Rinehart and Winston, Inc. Map adapted by kind permission of the publisher.

852

and his clan.[12] As could be expected, the aristocrats were not free of ambition to control the religious aspects of Antemoro society, while the Antalaotra sought temporal power as well. The divisions would blur in the 1800s as the sacerdotal Anakara gained a monopoly over both political and religious power, unchallenged until revolts by commoners began to erode it despite their suppression by foreign troops from Imerina.[13]

When the Antemoro established themselves on the eastern littoral of Madagascar they found that it contained, besides several *tompon-tany* groups, other relative newcomers who had been there since earlier times.[14] Concentrated among the Antambahoaka, the northern neighbours of the Antemoro, but also scattered along the central and southern sections of the eastern coast, were the descendants of Raminia, the Zafindraminia, whose great ancestors were also reputed to have been from 'Maka'. Various origins have been proposed for Raminia and his companions[15] but there is agreement that their advent in Madagascar should antedate at least the fifteenth century. One of the few Zafindraminia traditions to survive without being incorporated into Antemoro texts suggests that – wherever Raminia ultimately came from – Eastern Africa provided an important point of transition en route to Madagascar.[16] By the time of the Antemoro arrivals, the Zafindraminia enjoyed, on the whole, privileged positions among the *tompon-tany*, the ongoing custom (*sombili*) being that only a descendant of Raminia should slaughter domestic animals. As could be expected and as their own texts confirm the Antemoro ancestors sought to intermarry with the Zafindraminia females. There were rivalries over them but the unions were 'barren'.[17] In the end the conflict became one between the more recent and the older newcomers creating considerable insecurity which was echoed in some oral traditions of the *tompon-tany* as a fight of two 'giants' (Darafify and Fatrapaitanana).[18] The peak of this general conflict coincides with the emergence of the aristocratic Zafikasimambo as the new and powerful rulers at Matitana around 1550. Not without some difficulties, the Antemoro texts derive the Zafikasimambo founder (Zafika-zimambobe) from Ramarohala, the immediate ancestor of the aristocratic Anteoni who represents the third indigenous generation and two of whose seventeen sons were founders of the aristocratic Antemahazo and Ante-

---

12. Cf. G. Ferrand, 1891–1902, Vol. II, pp. 69–72 and Vol. I, pp. 1–41; H. Deschamps and S. Vianès, 1959, pp. 41–5.

13. G. Huet, 1901.

14. Some thirteen *tompon-tany* are mentioned as group-names in Antemoro texts, with the Antemanampatra and Manankarunga as the more important ones. A small number of earlier newcomers called *Onjatsy* (phon. *Undzatse*) retained some privileges under the Antemoro rulers, some of whom married Onjatsy females.

15. *Inter alia*, Javanese, Shīrāzī and Indian.

16. See G. Ferrand, 1902, pp. 219–22.

17. G. Mondain, 1910, pp. 52–5. The 'lack of progeny' is a symbolic claim.

18. The tradition is outlined in A. Grandidier, 1908–28, Vol. IV, part I, p. 135 and note 1.

isambo.[19] While such genealogical texts show that it took several generations to become assimilated into the language and culture of the area, they also point to their own cohesive function. They require that the Zafikasimambo issue forth from the Anteoni and that they be given a proper aristocratic and local origin. Nonetheless, it is known from an independent source of the mid-1600s, well-acquainted with south-eastern Madagascar, that the Zafikasimambo were the last of overseas newcomers at Matitana and that their name came through a *tompon-tany* female spouse.[20] They were uniformly regarded as sacerdotal persons (*ombiasa*) and scribes sent from Mecca fifteen decades from the date of writing (1658) to instruct the local inhabitants.[21] The Zafikasimambo influenced the course of Antemoro society in some decisive ways after the 1550s. They took over the Zafindraminia ritualistic prerogative of *sombili* and applied it with rigidity, as an economic and political tool; they reduced the freedoms of commoners; and they pushed religion into the centre of political life. They also settled the Antemoro–Zafindraminia conflicts by putting to death as many male descendants of Raminia as possible and by placing their women and children in confined areas.[22] It could be said that the Zafikasimambo created the first strong Antemoro kingdom at Matitana and gave it two capable Andrianoni, namely Rabesirana (*c*.1580–1615) and Andriapanolaha (*c*.1630–60).[23]

The ferment at Matitana had an impact beyond this homeland of the Antemoro. It produced, for example, expatriation which became a permanent feature of their society.[24] As the sacerdotal clans sired more of the specialists than could be absorbed into the subdivisions of the Antemoro kingdom, it became a common practice to fan out among other populations and offer the special skills to those in need.[25] This could be done either by itinerant *ombiasa*[26] or by those who took up residence, usually to serve a ruler. There are no satisfactory chronological steps through which to measure the impact of the Antemoro expatriates on other populations from the mid-1500s to the end of the eighteenth century. Yet, in a cumulative sense, there is little doubt that they came to assist (as perhaps the earliest pan-Malagasy) a major and ongoing political change – the transition from self-contained and inward-looking chiefdoms, uninterested in territorial expansion and frequently unaware of others at some distance apart, to

19. G. Mondain, 1910, pp. 56–9. The other sons were deme-founders.

20. E. de Flacourt, 1661, p. 17. It should be noted that *mambo* and *kazi* are titles found in south-east-central Africa.

21. E. de Flacourt, 1661, p. 17.

22. ibid., de Flacourt placed the pogrom in the 1630s.

23. R. K. Kent, 1970, pp. 98–9.

24. See B. F. Leguével de Lacombe, 1823–30, Vol. II, p. 187.

25. See G. A. Shaw, 1893, p. 109, for one instance of Antemoro expatriation.

26. Phonetically *umbias* (pl. and sing.) and often translated as 'priest', 'medicine man', 'doctor'. *Ombiasa* encompass a number of functions and have a number of categories into which they are subdivided among the Malagasy.

wider and more ambitious political unions. As is known from de Flacourt, the *ombiasa* from Matitana (the name Antemoro was not known to him) were not only the 'masters' of the *ombiasa* in other sections of the south-east; they also trained foreign religious specialists, some of whom may have been nothing less than pivotal in their own societies. Constant ferment at Matitana also led to occasional aristocratic exiles and the pogrom carried out by the Zafikasimambo against Zafindraminia adult males must have sent not a few involuntary migrants towards the interior of Madagascar. From such exiles may have come the Zafirambo, rulers among the Tanala or Ikongo,[27] some ancestors of nobility in future Imerina,[28] or even the Zafindraminia among the Antanosy.

According to de Flacourt, the Zafindraminia came to Antanosy at the turn of the sixteenth century.[29] Others have argued for a much later arrival there, around 1625.[30] The earlier date appears to be the better one but, again, it is not improbable that the Zafindraminia newcomers among the Antanosy received an infusion of their co-descendants fleeing from Matitana. A Zafindraminia–Antanosy genealogy, which is far from being a reliable chronological document, suggests that there was a 'royal line' extending back for seventeen generations.[31] In effect, written accounts by resident Europeans falling between 1614–80 as well as a study soon to be completed,[32] show in clear terms that the Zafindraminia were not able to create a centre of authority among the Antanosy. They introduced the *sombili* into the area; they excelled in the construction of wooden huts; they amassed cattle which was the main source of wealth even in a predominantly agricultural society; they had an idea of kinship and a 'will-to-power'; and they attained a position of privilege in the lands of Antanosy. Yet their acquisitive impulse, internal rivalries, and inability to find symbols that would transcend the needs of individual *Rohandrian* (as the highest Zafind-raminia estate was called) and unite all of the Antanosy, all went against the formation of a single state ruled by the Zafindraminia kings. Instead, two parallel societies developed with the Zafindraminia copying the *tompon-tany* hierarchy. When the French established Fort Dauphin in Antanosy during 1643 the two societies were in a state of interpenetration not only as a result of exogamy but also because the upper estates on both sides

27. H. Deschamps, 1965 (third edn.), p. 55, (from Ms. 13, Bibliothèque nationale, Paris).

28. A somewhat suspect Antemoro text (or rather Antemoro-influenced) suggests that late in the 1800s (when the Merina were victorious in most of Madagascar) some of the early Zafindraminia had gone to Imerina.

29. E. de Flacourt, 1661, p. 5. In his preface de Flacourt placed the advent of Zafind-raminia in Madagascar some 500 years before his time.

30. A. Grandidier oscillated between the two dates, for example.

31. Bibliothèque nationale, Paris, Fonds Français, Ms. 20181, ff. 146v-147; H. de Flacourt, 1661, pp. 48–53; and L. Mariano, *Relation*, 1613–14, in A. Grandidier *et al.*, 1903–20, Vol. II, p. 49.

32. R. K. Kent, n.d.

were shifting toward political centralization. During its three decades on local soil, from 1643 to 1674, Fort Dauphin deflected this process completely and political unity would continue to be elusive.[33]

The Zafindraminia were not kingdom-builders, the Antemoro represent a rare instance of newcomers who created their own society and state, but the Maroserana stand out as a pan-dynastic family, the most important one in the political history of Madagascar. Ultimately, the Maroserana would give rulers to the Mahafaly, the Sakalava of Menabe and Boina, to a part of the Antandroy and of the Bara. Once formed, like the Zafindraminia and the Antemoro, the Maroserana were no longer outsiders to Madagascar, unassimilated foreigners who maintained their own language and culture. The origin of the Maroserana and their formative period have been (as in the cases of other newcomers) matters of controversy. To begin with, the Mahafaly and Sakalava oral traditions are not in accord about the ultimate Maroserana ancestor or about where the 'proto-Maroserana' arrived from. Oral texts collected when most of the Sakalava were still independent advance two very different origins at the same time. One is assigned to Andrianalimbe from the interior of Madagascar and the other to Andriamandazoala from overseas.[34] To compound the problem, a number of traditions claim that the Maroserana founder was Rabaratavokoka.[35] The Mahafaly of south-western Madagascar, among whom the Maroserana were born sometime in the 1500s, have given Olembetsitoto as the founder of their royal family.[36]

These contradictions are in part responsible for the claims of some authors that the Maroserana originated, for example, in south-eastern Madagascar; that they were stranded Indians from India who had landed near present-day Fort Dauphin around 1300 and gone north and founded the Zarabehava, the royal family of the Antesaka; and that, from there, they had moved westward giving royal families to the southernmost Antandroy (the Zafy Manara), to the Bara of the southern interior (the Zafy Manely) and still later to the Mahafaly and the Sakalava.[37] The term Maroserana has been interpreted to mean 'those who had many ports' – 'nom donné surtout aux princes du sang que Radama I envoya comme gouverneurs aux divers ports de mer ou il établit des douanes'[38] – suggesting

33. ibid., see also below.

34. Cf. C. Guillain, 1845, pp. 10–11.

35. *Inter alia*, L. Thomassin, 1900, p. 397, where it is spelled Rabavavatavokoka. Still other traditions give him a father.

36. C. Poirier, 1953, pp. 34–5. In fact 'Andriamaroserana' is the generic name of the first Maroserana ruler whose skull, called Andriamaro, became the protector of all Mahafaly (see text below). The difficulty with Mahafaly genealogies stems from the political fact that there developed four states among this south-western group, complicating versions of the early royal tree.

37. A. Grandidier, 1908–28, Vol. IV, part I, pp. 127–8 (note 1), pp. 168, 212, 214, 278–80 (note 4).

38. A. Abinal and V. Malzac, 1888, p. 557.

an ancient strategy of coastal control. Several corrections have been made to all these claims in recent years, especially by reference to the primary sources.[39] As the Antesaka royal traditions have stated, the ruling Zarabehava were a branch of the west-coast Sakalava who crossed Madagascar sometime before 1650 but not earlier than 1620.[40] This passage is also attested by other evidence.[41] Thus there was no dynastic Maroserana movement from east to west and there is no longer any real doubt that this family formed in south-western Madagascar. The Zafy Manely, royal family of Ibara, came from the south-west into the southern interior, not the other way around, while the would-be Indian origin is not supported by evidence, including linguistic items, as nothing Indian has ever been found in the Maroserana royal vocabularies. No less damaging to an Indian political influence is the span of some 250 years between the supposed arrival in 1300 and the birth of the Maroserana at about 1550. Finally, some 135 years ago, Charles Guillain showed *in situ* that a title instituted early in the 1800s by the Merina King Radama I (1810–28), with the intent of securing control over ports, did not have the same meaning at all in south-western Madagascar around 1840.[42]

The two divergent Sakalava traditions are by no means antagonistic. Andriamandazoala and Rabaratavokoka mean respectively 'Lord-who-withered-the-forest' and 'Noble-bent-reed'. As both the Mahafaly and the Sakalava renamed their departed monarchs (this linguistic taboo is called *anaratahina* in Mahafaly and *fitahina* by the Sakalava), and since their idioms did not tolerate the use of the word 'dead' in respect to monarchs no longer living, it is likely that the idea of a 'bent' reed (reed being a concept analogous to the Zulu *uthlanga*)[43] points to Rabaratavokoka as a *fitahina* for Andriamandazoala. Another argument in favour of this *fitahina* is the absence of any tomb for Rabaratavokoka and the claim that Andriamandazoala always had one (although it was found empty when opened).[44] The tomb of Olombetsitoto is in Mahafaly.[45] At the same time, newcomers from the interior (possibly exiled by other newcomers) – represented by

39. R. K. Kent, 1969.

40. Cf. Marchand, 1901, pp. 485–6; H. Deschamps, 1936, pp. 162–4, *passim*, and 1965, p. 94.

41. See J. Boto, 1923, pp. 252–3. In addition a number of wars were fought by the Sakalava while crossing the interior, leaving memories behind.

42. C. Guillain, 1845, p. 11, note 1. He was told near Tuléar that the term *maroserana* meant 'many paths' reflecting the custom of the first Maroserana kings in Mahafaly to place their residences in the middle of habitations with paths radiating in all directions to villages around them; but Guillain did not find the explanation satisfactory. He was also aware what meaning had been assigned to the term in Imerina.

43. Cf. C. Callaway, 1870, pp. 2–3 and note.

44. Reported by E. Birkeli, 1926, p. 32.

45. M. A. Marion, 1971.

Great-Lord-ʿAlī (Andrianalimbé)[46] – and those from overseas – reflected in the person of Andriamandazoala – gravitated toward each other through both coalition and conflict, a pattern for newcomers in Madagascar. It is highly probable that some of the Maroserana ancestors arrived in south-western Madagascar by a sea route. The ruling Maroserana branch among the Sakalava was known as the Zafivolamena (Sons-of-gold) while the tombs of Maroserana rulers in Mahafaly are still called *volamena* (red silver, i.e. gold). There certainly are traditions which claim that a large amount of gold was unloaded near present-day Tuléar by the Sakalava-Maroserana ancestors.[47] Given that gold was neither found nor mined in the entire southern half of Madagascar (Portuguese sailors showing gold encountered indifference among the coastal inhabitants in the 1500s), traditions which record that it was imported cannot be wrong in substance. Equally, the fact that *volamena* became a sacred (*fady, faly*) metal is a reflection of its pan-dynastic agents. With the proximity of vast Rhodesian gold mines, with men capable of bringing it to Madagascar in a single crossing (the Afro–Arab traders or even self-exiled Portuguese holding on to large quantities of gold with nowhere to go) and with the presence of several words and customs in Madagascar with parallels in Rhodesia, one can hardly avoid the strong possibility of Maroserana–Mwene Mutapa connections.[48]

Some extremely interesting traditions, collected and published by a Sakalava at the turn of the 1900s, throw light on the Maroserana beginnings. They point to initial failures of newcomers to the south-west to become politically established, with many starts which led nowhere in particular. They reveal that political successes were not forthcoming until kinship evolved with local chiefly families, grouped under the name of a nearby forest, the Analamahavelona.[49] They also reveal that innovation was an important asset to the early Maroserana. They had a sense of territorial expansion; they began to introduce fortifications and build on elevated sites; they used irregular soldiers; they arbitrated disputes; they knew how to attract followers by redistributing food and cattle (their first capital was known as Itsororobola, a name suggesting a constant flow of abundance); and they began using pre-existing diviners for the purposes of state.[50] An

46. Andrianalimbé may have a better translation as simply 'nobles by the tens of thousands' (*andriana* = lords, nobles + *ali*, from *alina* = ten thousand, and *mbe/be* meaning numerous, many). Andriana should not be understood as a functional title that applied to those in office.

47. Tovonkery, 1915, p. 7.

48. R. K. Kent, 1970, *passim*. Nonetheless, the nature of the connections may not be direct in terms of customs and until parallels can be increased beyond the most disputable levels, by additional research on both sides of the Mozambique Channel, a Zimbabwean origin of some Maroserana ancestors will remain controversial.

49. Analavelona is a ridge in the Fiherenana valley, partly parallelling the western coast between the rivers Fiherenana and Mangoky.

50. Sgt. Firinga, 1901, pp. 664–9.

analogous situation obtained among the Mahafaly where alliances with the chiefly families – the Andriantsileliky – interrupted by several years of conflict, ended in the Maroserana political supremacy. Yet the chiefly families retained many important privileges and were not dispossessed.[51] It would appear that a combination of the high birth rate among the Maroserana and attempts to adhere to primogeniture in royal succession began to issue forth endless collaterals and princes without the right to rule. The Sakalava texts (sometimes by 'extending' the Maroserana genealogy back in time) refer to this bifurcation into the legitimate rulers and collaterals as the *volamena* and *volafotsy* (white silver) phase. It was probably as a response to this problem that new lands (*orin-tany*) came to be actively sought, assisting nonetheless an expansion of Maroserana influence, as non-ruling kin were given villages to rule over. But this problem would not go away, even as late as the 1800s, and it led from time to time to self-exile of the collaterals (*longon'mpanilo* or *vohitsy mananila*), alliances with opponents of the Maroserana and even to the formation of rival dynastic families, like the Andrevola, rulers of the Fiherenana valley who would give the Maroserana a great deal of trouble.

Outsiders and their impact

The accounts of outsiders from Europe who visited Madagascar prior to the colonial period have had one cumulative and lasting effect. They are and will continue to be of inestimable value to the study of the island's past.[52] Such a unilineal view cannot be advanced in respect to what the local impact of Europe had been by about 1800.[53] In a general way, the sixteenth-century Portuguese affected negatively the Muslim-dominated trade and its outlets in the western Indian Ocean.[54] At the turn of the 1500s Madagascar had four such outlets, one near the north-eastern town of Vohemar and three in the north-west, not far from present-day Majunga. The north-western trading posts were located on small islets in the Bays of Mahajamba, Boina and Bombetock. They were controlled and inhabited by communities of Swahili-speakers who exported mainly rice and slaves to Eastern Africa and Arabia. Their north-eastern counterpart, called Iharana, was different in several respects. The Iharanians lived on the mainland, they did not rival the north-west in exports of grains and humans, and they were in essence an original local culture of long-standing,

51. E. Mamelomana, n.d., pp. 1–3.

52. Many of the sources will be found in the *COACM*, Vols. I–IX (1903–20), started and inspired by Alfred and Guillaume Grandidier, the main editors. The volumes do not go beyond 1800 and there is no comparable collection for the nineteenth century as yet.

53. The most stinging and sweeping condemnation of all Europeans in and around Madagascar before 1800 came from the pens of the Grandidiers, undoubtedly the most important students of Madagascar. Cf. A. Grandidier, 1908–28, Vol. IV, part II pp. 106–8.

54. Cf. J. Strandes, 1961 edn, pp. 12–155.

centred around the polished stone and building crafts.[55] Moors from Malindi were reported as the founders of Iharana by the Portuguese in the early 1500s and there is little doubt that it began to decline only after Europe interfered with Muslim commerce in the Indian Ocean. By the eighteenth century Iharana was a ghost and its material culture died out without reappearing in any solid fashion elsewhere in the Great Island. In 1506 the Portuguese attacked the main Swahili trading post in the north-west, called Lulangane (on the islet of Nosy Manja in the Mahajamba Bay). They planned to destroy Boina without a clear result and they spared Bombetock altogether as its *shaykh/shaykh*s proved to be friendly.[56] The Portuguese also discovered a dense colony of Africans further north, in the Bay of Anorontsanga. Some two thousand strong, they massed on the beach armed with bows and arrows (weapons which have since disappeared from Madagascar) as well as spears and shields, but changed their mind before a battle could take place and disappeared inland. Their huts were burned as the 'whole mountain seemed ablaze'. Yet this particular colony was not a part of the Muslim trade network: the Africans in question were escaped slaves from Malindi, Mombasa and Mogadishu.[57]

After a bellicose beginning, however, the Portuguese in Mozambique changed their tune and began to send a ship annually to north-western Madagascar for cattle, ambergris, raffia cloth and slaves.[58] According to Do Couto, his compatriots even became the most active buyers of slaves from the north-western middlemen by the mid-1500s.[59] In adding to the demands for exports, the Portuguese were a factor in the emergence of several minor political unions on the north-western mainland, not very far from the Swahili trading posts. There were no less than five such new groupings along the littoral and partly inland between latitudes 14°S and 16°S.[60] One of the five was growing rapidly in importance under a ruler whose title was *Tingimaro*, called with exaggeration the 'most powerful *rei* in the island', who was 'continuously at war with his neighbours'.[61] Tingimaro was visited half a century later, in June 1614, by Father Luis Mariano of the Order of Jesus in Mozambique. He travelled three times some twenty-four kilometres inland to Tingimaro's capital of Cuala and back in the hope of securing a religious (and Portuguese secular) foothold in a state which the coastal middlemen were beginning to fear.[62] After one of Tingimaro's subjects underwent a poison ordeal to ascertain the

55. For an outline of previous work on Iharana, see P. Vérin, 1971, pp. 225–9. P. Gaudebout and E. Vernier, 1941, remain the starting point of description.

56. Albuquerque and de Barros, in A. Grandidier *et al.*, 1903–20, Vol. I, pp. 15, 20–1 and 24–31.

57. Albuquerque, in A. Grandidier *et al.*, 1903–20, Vol. I, p. 22.

58. J. dos Santos, 1609/1891, Vol. II, ch. 19, pp. 332–3; and 1901, p. 332.

59. Do Couto, in A. Grandidier *et al.*, 1903–20, Vol. I, p. 100.

60. ibid.

61. ibid., war prisoners were sold to the coastal middlemen.

62. Samamo, the Swahili ruler of New Mazalagem told Paulo Rodrigues da Costa in

intentions of Father Mariano he was well-received but Tingimaro refused a treaty with the Portuguese and would not allow any missionary activity inland.[63] He was a Buque (from the Swahili *wa-Buque*), the name the Portuguese adopted to distinguish speakers of Malagasy from the Cafres on the mainland of Madagascar who spoke Bantu idioms, but one by which the Swahili-speakers designated all the inhabitants of the island.[64] As Tingimaro eventually came to control also the Bay of Anorontsanga, it would appear that the colony of escaped slaves from the Swahili coast of Africa had been absorbed by the Buques in close to five generations.

In the late 1580s, the Moors of Mazalagem (the names 'Old' and 'New' Mazalagem were given to the trading posts in the Bays of Mahajamba and Boina by Europeans, in a variety of spellings) refused to trade with the Portuguese and a Dominican priest seeking local converts lost his life.[65] Only royal orders from Lisbon prevented a war[66] but not before a show of force and some reprisals against Moors outside Madagascar.[67] In 1590 north-western Madagascar was placed in the trading zone of the Mozambique Island.[68] Several attempts were made between 1614 and 1620, especially by the ubiquitous Father Mariano, to establish a church in north-western Madagascar. As a recently published diary makes clear, this did not serve the Christian cause. Relatively lax local practitioners of Islam, who seldom went to the mosque, were driven to more rigorous observances and tighter ties with the Sunnite Muslims from Eastern Africa and Arabia.[69] About half a century later, in 1667, Father Manuel Barreto was able to write that he had:

> Often heard Bartholomew Lopes, a man of great judgement ... and well experienced in voyages to Madagascar, say that if the king (of Portugal) would give him six armed vessels with oars, carrying Portuguese soldiers, he would go there with his launch and several boats manned (by) Kaffirs of another race and would prevent any ships of the Moors from Mecca, Brava and Magadoxo, putting into the island to carry on the trade in Buques, of whem they make Moors, at the rate of more than three thousand and a half every year, there being sheiks in various ports for this purpose, who in the course of

---

1613 that his uncle and himself had been forced to abandon Old Mazalagem by Tingimaro and that he feared attempts by Tingimaro to capture New Mazalagem too.

63. A. Grandidier *et al.*, 1903–20, Vol. II, pp. 66–70.

64. Madagascar was only called Ubuque in the north-west and the distinction between Buques and Cafres in Da Costa's *Diário* and Mariano's accounts was deliberate.

65. J. dos Santos, 1609/1891, Vol. I, p. 286.

66. *King to de Meneses*, 6/2/1589, *BFUP*, I, 302.

67. J. dos Santos, 1609/1891, Vol. I, pp. 286–7.

68. Placed, that is, from Goa.

69. P. R. da Costa, 1613/1970, pp. 61–72, to be compared with Mariano to de Medeiros, 24 August 1619, in A. Grandidier *et al.*, 1903–20, Vol. II, pp. 303–11.

the year buy and catechise them, to the great opprobrium of the Christian name.[70]

The Portuguese also signed several treaties with rulers along the western littoral of Madagascar in 1613 and a Jesuit mission was sent to the Kingdom of Sadia, on the Manambovo river in 1616 and 1617. The mission triggered a civil war which had been in the making for some time[71] and which would have important consequences in the foundation of the Sakalava kingdom of Menabe. In 1641 the Portuguese formally annexed western Madagascar in a Luso–Dutch treaty.[72] But, in practical terms, this meant little more than the wishful thinking of Mozambique's main trader with Madagascar. Indeed, by 1700, north-western Madagascar was under Sakalava–Maroserana control and, just a century later, the Malagasy would come to raid not only Portuguese vessels in the Mozambique Channel but also their bases at the Querimba and Ibo islands.[73] It is certain that some stranded Portuguese had been in southern Madagascar sometime between 1510 and 1550 and stories linking them with a large quantity of gold were recorded by de Flacourt.[74] One such group settled in Antanosy, where a small stone fort (*trano-vato*) was found bearing inscriptions, and some of the Zafindraminia claimed inter-marriage with the Portuguese who were absorbed without leaving much of an impact behind in this part of the island.[75]

It would appear that early in the 1600s the Portuguese took fewer slaves from Madagascar than their competitors from Africa and Arabia. Moreover, the Portuguese were paying considerably more. At the same time, the Comoro Islands became the point at which slaves and material items from Madagascar were collected for trans-shipment to Malindi, Mombasa, Mogadishu and Arabia (particularly the Gulf of Aden). Traders from Domoni, for example, obtained 'abundant numbers' of slaves from north-western Madagascar 'because of everlasting civil wars' among its rulers. In 1614, slaves were bought in Madagascar for nine or ten piasters and resold to the Portuguese for 100 piasters each.[76] As not a few of Domoni's merchants spoke Portuguese 'rather well' at the time, it would seem that the Portuguese were shifting their commerce toward the Comoros. Also in 1614, Anjouan was reported teeming with male and female slaves from Madagascar about to be taken to Arabia and exchanged for Indian cotton

70. See supplement to M. Barreto, 1899, pp. 503–4.

71. L. Mariano, *Letter*, 24 May 1617, in A. Grandidier *et al.*, 1903–20, Vol. II, p. 236.

72. G. M. Theal, 1898–1903, Vol. I, p. 407. It was ratified in Portugal and Holland in 1641 and 1642.

73. See E. de Froberville, 1845.

74. E. de Flacourt, 1661/1920, pp. 32–3.

75. L. Mariano, *Relation*, in A. Grandidier *et al.*, 1903–20, Vol. II, pp. 41–8; E. de Flacourt, 1661/1920, pp. 32–4.

76. Walter Peyton's visit to Moheli, in A. Grandidier *et al.*, 1903–20, Vol. II, p. 84.

and opium.[77] Some three decades later, a dhow from Boina Bay (New Mazalagem) was seen at Anjouan with 500 slaves, mostly children and youths purchased for 'two to four pieces of 8th real'. At Anjouan they had already quadrupled in price, at Malindi they went for ten times more than at Boina and even this price doubled by the time they reached the Red Sea area.[78] Dhows from S̲h̲ihir, in the Gulf of Aden, also made direct voyages to Madagascar to buy rice, millet, young men and women.[79] Clearly, the Portuguese were losing out to traditional buyers in Madagascar and – after about 1620 – they seem to have lost interest in the island altogether.

As the seventeenth century edged toward its second half, new buyers still began to visit Madagascar and they would hardly be confined to its north-western outlets. At least eight ships are known to have supplied the Dutch at Mauritius with rice and slaves from Madagascar, especially from the Bay of Antongil, between 1639 and 1647.[80] A treaty was signed with Antongil's ruler in March 1642 which bound him to supply slaves only to the Dutch East India Company and, in 1646, Mauritius' third governor planned to built and arm a fort in that bay – but orders from Batavia halted further efforts from Mauritius.[81] Until they began to make journeys to Madagascar from the Cape in 1655, the Dutch had frequent (and at times quite brutal) conflicts with the eastern Malagasy. They also took part in local conflicts. Yet the eastern littoral was disunited and neither a Dutch commercial presence nor occasional participation in local wars can be said to have produced any long-lasting effects. In the 1700s, however, the Dutch would combine with other Europeans to exert considerable commercial influence in several parts of Madagascar, more strongly along its western coast than elsewhere.

English vessels came to Madagascar hundreds of times between 1600 and 1800, mostly to its western shores and especially to the Bay of Saint Augustine. Sometimes eight or more ships would be moored there at the same time. Pidgin English became the local language of trade and some of the local residents took English names and titles.[82] Puritans from England were sent to Saint Augustine Bay in 1645 to establish a colony. Five years later, another colonial venture was started at the north-western islet of Nosy Be. Both attempts failed, with considerable loss of life, the potential

77. Pieter van den Broecke's visit to the Comoros, in A. Grandidier *et al.*, 1903–20, Vol. II, p. 93.

78. Smart to Kynnaston, 23 June 1646, in A. Grandidier *et al.*, 1903–20, Vol. V, pp. 515 and 518.

79. P. v. d. Broecke (1614).

80. See tentative table in G. Grandidier and R. Decary, 1958, Vol. V, part III, section 1, p. 208.

81. For the treaty's text see *Corpus Diplomaticum Neerlando-Indicum*, erste deel (1596–1650), The Hague, 1907, pp. 360–2; French transl. in A. Grandidier *et al.*, 1903–20, Vol. VI, pp. 19–21.

82. See A. Grandidier *et al.*, 1903–20, Vol. V, p. 255 as an example.

settlers having been misled about Madagascar as an earthly paradise.[83] Unlike the Portuguese and the Dutch, the English did not develop any bases around Madagascar but they nonetheless became the most active exporters of slaves from the island to the New World, especially to Barbados and Jamaica. A census taken at Barbados at the end of the 1600s showed 32 473 slaves, half of whom were from Madagascar.[84] Not a few participants in the slave trade between 1688 and 1724 were English and American pirates. They visited all the trading sections of Madagascar but also had colonies at Diego Suárez, Bay of Antongil, and the eastern islet of Sainte-Marie. Pirates took part in local wars and contributed to a state of insecurity and the constant supply of humans for export.[85] It was sometime in this period of the pirates that two marked changes could be noted in terms of trade and in items of exchange. First, as a variety of Europeans started to compete for the same suppliers, the coastal rulers converted this advantage into prices which mostly fluctuated upward. The second change may have been the consequence of the first as it became more and more expedient to trade discarded and faulty fire-arms for the much-sought-after slaves. As an English medical doctor put it in 1754: the fire-arms sold to the residents of Saint Augustine were of such poor quality that they often exploded maiming and killing those who used them.[86]

France was the only one of Europe's nations seeking a long-term foothold in Madagascar to register a modest success in the form of Fort Dauphin, a fortified settlement in south-eastern Madagascar which lasted just over three decades, from 1643 to 1674. At times, the French can even be perceived as occupying an intermediate position between 'outsiders' and 'newcomers'. Many of the men at Fort Dauphin married local women. Among the better-known instances were those of Pronis, Fort Dauphin's first governor, who married into the Zafindraminia *Rohandrian*, and of the French soldier nicknamed 'La Case' who came to Fort Dauphin in 1656, married an heiress-apparent in the northern reaches of Antanosy-land, and became a local military hero.[87] Frenchmen also fought on loan to various rulers, using their fire-arms to great advantage at a time when few were as yet in local hands. The best-educated and the most durable of Fort Dauphin's governors, Etienne de Flacourt (1648–58), author of two fundamental works about Madagascar,[88] became in effect a local potentate, forced to fend for himself without much support from France. Indeed, not a single ship came to Fort Dauphin during half of his tenure as governor.

The impact of Fort Dauphin has been generally underestimated. It has

---

83. See A. Grandidier *et al.*, 1903–20, Vol. III, pp. 44–64, 69–183, 184–7 and 221–58. A number of essays exist on the subject as well.

84. G. Grandidier and R. Decary, 1958, Vol. V, part III, section 1, p. 213.

85. H. Deschamps, 1972, remains the basic work on the subject.

86. Account of Dr. Edward Yves, in A. Grandidier *et al.*, 1903–20, Vol. V, p. 256.

87. See E. F. Gautier and H. Froidevaux, 1907, *passim*.

88. E. de Flacourt, 1658/1913 and 1661/1920. See also A. Malotet, 1898.

PLATE 28.1   *Etienne de Flacourt, governor of Fort Dauphin, Madagascar, 1648–58*

two dimensions: one local; one wider. The Antanosy were, for example, about to attain their elusive political union with the Zafindraminia under the leadership of Dian Ramack, a former prince of the Matikassi sub-division who had been to Goa. Fort Dauphin became an obstacle. When ships no longer came to it (1650–4), a period of intense struggle for supremacy came into the foreground, with the *Rohandrian* newcomers on one side and the French outsiders on the other, and with most hut-dwellers and tillers of the land fleeing into the forests from the mounting violence. By 1653 Dian Ramack and many *Rohandrian* were dead and a number of chiefs made their submissions (*mifaly*) to de Flacourt who had no interest in becoming a builder of a local state. Matters grew worse after his departure but the Second French East India Company nonetheless made another colonial effort in Madagascar. Outposts were set up in 1665 at Antongil, Matitana and Sainte-Marie. In 1667, ten ships disembarked some 2000 *colons* and soldiers from France at Fort Dauphin. This prompted a series of *mifaly* as rulers in Antanosy gave up the struggle for good. Outside Antanosy, the French presence at Fort Dauphin accelerated the founding of Menabe by the Maroserana ruler, Andriandahifotsy, who sought an alliance with Fort Dauphin.[89] Another case in point outside the Antanosy lands consists of the campaigns of La Case at Matitana where he ended the political supremacy of the Zafikasimambo. Fort Dauphin was abandoned in 1674 and its last residents were evacuated to Mozambique, India and Bourbon (now Réunion) but its thirty-year presence came to be felt in Ibara, among the southern Betsileo, in Antandroy and Mahafaly lands, as well as throughout south-eastern Madagascar.

As nearby plantation economies, the Mascarene Islands of Bourbon and Ile-de-France (Mauritius, abandoned by the Dutch in 1710 and occupied from Bourbon from 1715–21) were destined to have a disruptive impact on Madagascar, especially on its eastern side during the 1700s. In 1744 Bourbon exported 1.14 million kilograms of coffee and its population comprised 10 338 slaves and 2358 whites. In 1797 over 80 per cent of its total population of 56 800 were slaves. In Mauritius – whose total population in 1978 was less than 43 000 – close to 36 000 slaves were counted and in 1797 over 83 per cent were counted as slaves among a total of 59 000 residents.[90] It is generally agreed that most of the slaves imported into the two Mascarenes between 1664 and 1766 came from Madagascar but that the royal French administration which bought both Mascarenes from the French East India Company for over 7.5 million pounds sterling gradually supplanted the Malagasy with slaves from Africa.[91] It should not be overlooked, however, that imports of slaves doubled between 1766 and

89. See R. K. Kent, 1970, p. 199.
90. Cf. A. Toussaint, 1972, pp. 335–6.
91. The formal decision was made in 1740 but slaves were sought even earlier in Mozambique and the reason for the change came from the Malagasy Maroon colonies which could not be dismantled: cf. C. Grant, 1801, pp. 75–8.

1788, the first generation of royal government, and that Madagascar was hardly left alone by the Mascarenes after 1766. By 1784, there was a royal agent at Foulpointe, the main outlet for the Mascarenes in Madagascar. Two years later, when a Polish-Hungarian nobleman and libertine named Benyowsky tried to interfere with Mascarene commercial interests in eastern Madagascar, he was shot by soldiers from Ile-de-France. In fact, north-eastern Madagascar, between Tamatave and Foulpointe, was becoming a satellite plantation for Mascarene enterpreneurs.

The western and northern states: Mahafaly, Sakalava, Antankara, Tsimihety

After the political success of the early Maroserana in the south-west, a new society emerged between the Menarandra and the Onilahy rivers. Its name, Mahafaly (to make sacred), is connected with social differentiation and with rituals of royalty. Traditions recall that the first Maroserana went into total seclusion, advised and protected by the ruler's *ombiasa*. He became sacred (*faly*) when no longer seen and, by extension, he made the land and the people on it *maha-faly*.[92] The principal Maroserana deity, cranium Andriamaro, could not be seen either as it inhabited a misty peak and spoke only through a medium (*vaha*) to express its will. In a society with long-established pastoral habits and little love of authority, Andriamaro seems to have been able to impose a moral code based on fear.[93] After the Maroserana came to power, Mahafaly society consisted of the privileged (*renilemy*), the commoners (*valohazomanga*), and those who came to Mahafaly from elsewhere (*folahazomanga*). The descendants of the most powerful chief at the time of Marosenara's formation, Tsileliki (who-could-not-be-vanquished); his former subjects with special status; all those who came with the proto-Maroserana; and occasionally rewarded individuals or families: these became the new élite.[94] Some of the numerous Mahafaly clans had special functions which brought them into proximity with the *mpanjaka* (king, chief, ruler), as royal smiths, for example, or collectors of honey for the court. The clans elected their own heads, who were confirmed as royal friends (*rainitsy ny mpanjaka*) and were assisted by their own high councillors (*ondaty-bé*). The Mahafaly kings had a chief priest, *mpisoro*, who presided over the group-altar, *hazomanga-lava*, where animals were sacrificed.[95]

Mahafaly history before 1800 is marked by conflicts with its neighbours, by the division into four separate and independent kingdoms (Sakatovo,

92. As told to A. Grandidier, 1908–28, Vol. IV, part I, section 1, p. 213, note 1.
93. D. Jakobsen, 1902.
94. E. Mamelomana, n.d., *passim*; and Centre for the Study of Customs, University of Madagascar, n.d., pp. 1–3. Both were probably written in the early 1960s.
95. G. Grandidier and R. Decary, 1958, Vol. IV, part III, section 1, Appendix 31, pp. 235–6.

Menarandra, Linta and Onilahy), and by the annexation of lands belonging to the westernmost Antandroy (Karimbola). De Flacourt throws some light on the conflicts. He mentions an embassy of twelve Mahafales (Mahafaly) who came to Fort Dauphin in June 1649 from Dian Manhelle (not the *anaratahina*). They asked for French mercenaries to fight against a ruler of the Machicores (the generic name of the peoples of the southern interior, now spelt Mashicoro) who had taken many cattle from their king. De Flacourt agreed for the usual fee of half the cattle taken with the help of these men.[96] By mid-1653, on the eve of Dian Manhelle's own death, the people of the southern interior were in complete disarray, having lost two successive rulers in wars against him.[97] It would appear that the Mahafaly were also parting in the 1650s – the given approximate date of the first two breakaway kingdoms, the Menarandra and the Sakatovo. Somewhat later, Menarandra would spawn two more kingdoms, the Linta (*c.*1670) and the Onilahy (*c.*1750), the northernmost of the Mahafaly states ruled by the Maroserana.[98] It was one of the Menarandra kings who conquered the western Karimbola–Antandroy in the first half of the 1700s.[99] An Antemoro influence can be detected in the Onilahy kingdom since its first ruler carried the Antemoro title of *Andrianoni* as his own name. There were six rulers in Sakatovo before 1800, seven in Linta, three in Menarandra (after the breakaway about 1750) and two in the Onilahy kingdom. The divisions reflect much strife among the Maroserana, but the internal history of the Mahafaly prior to the late 1800s is not well known as yet.

While the earliest political successes of the Maroserana took place among the *tompon-tany* living south of the Onilahy, the largest waterway of the south-west, this dynastic family did not grow in political importance until some of its members crossed the river and went north into the valley of the Fiherenana, the area between the Onilahy and the Mangoky. This is where the Maroserana–Volamena were born and from where they crossed the Mangoky to become the dynasty of the Sakalava states, the Menabe and Iboina. There is no doubt that Andriandahifotsy was the founder of Menabe and most likely of the Volamena branch as well. As his *fitahina* states, he was the lord-who-humbled-thousands (Andrianihananinariyo).

De Flacourt's map indicates southern Menabe as the land of Lahe Fonti (*lahe/dahe*, man; *fonti/fouti/foutchy/fotsy*, white) before 1660. The foundings of the Volamena and of Menabe have their religious and secular aspects. A royal *moasy* (priest), associated with crocodiles, Ndriamboay (noble crocodile), is credited with introducing the cult of the ancestors

96. E. de Flacourt, 1661/1920, p. 263. It took fifteen Frenchmen and 2000 Mahafaly some twelve days to reach the Machicores and take 10 000 head of cattle and 500 slaves.

97. E. de Flacourt, 1661, pp. 74–5.

98. The Mahafaly–Maroserana genealogies and dates were worked out by Speyer, an Austrian, who spent thirty years among the Mahafaly and advised their last king, Tsiampondy (1890–1911). The dates are tentative.

99. E. Defoort, 1913, pp. 168 and 172, places the event close to 1750.

(*dady*) to the Maroserana so that the rulers became the *Ampagnito-be* (great royal ancestors; fathers of the people). In reward Ndriamboay was included in the Maroserana *dady*, either as the father (the idea of submission) of Andriandahifotsy or as his uncle, and given the posthumous name of Andriamisara ('*ishara* means to divine in Arabic).[100] Other traditions hold that it was Ndriamboay who carried out the sacrifice of Andriandahifotsy's wife from whose blood came both the Volamena (silver which became red) and the name Menabe (Great Red).[101] Human sacrifices are known to have taken place in some Maroserana funerals but a more reliable tradition reveals that Andriandahifotsy's spouse (a member of the numerous Sakoambe whose tombs are still near Morondava) managed to bring the first fire-arms to him during a crucial battle.[102] The ten weapons became part of the royal regalia[103] and her sons became the Volamena.

When the Maroserana came into contact with peoples of Menabe they were no longer in the lands of south-western pastoralists, and the *tompontany* of Menabe were quite different as well. The coastal belt roughly between Majunga and Morondava some 640 kilometres long, was inhabited by fishermen and farmers with few cattle. Excepting the densely inhabited Sadia (with a capital of 10 000 in 1614), most of its residents lived in small communities, had no weapons and constantly surprised Da Costa in this particular respect.[104] The 640-kilometre belt was known as Bambala. Its residents spoke not Malagasy but Bantu idioms: they were Cafres not Buques; and their language had been 'made richer' by the intrusion of Malagasy loan-words, without any linguistic flooding.[105] The origin of the Sakalava has been made into a greater problem than it should have been, particularly through linguistic arguments. They were from the Bambala coast, from Sadia, and they connected with the Maroserana somewhere near the Mangoky river, probably at one of its smaller affluents called the Sakalava. All traditions agree that the Sakalava were the outstanding warriors of their time and Mariano's testimony confirms this function among the Suculamba of Sadia who had broken off in 1616 and were reported raiding far and wide by 1620.[106] Moreover, the *dady* cult, described by Mariano during his stay in Sadia,[107] was the model adopted by the Maroserana–Volamena. The Sakalava were the spearhead of political auth-

---

100. Académie malgache, Antananarivo, anon. mss. 2238/2, *c*.1908, *Niandohan'ny Fivavahan'ny* (Origins of the Sakalava Religion), ff. 1–7.

101. C. Betoto, 1950b, p. 3.

102. E. Birkeli, 1926, p. 33.

103. See R. K. Kent, 1970, p. 200 and note 163.

104. P. R. Da Costa, 1613/1970, pp. 72–126.

105. L. Mariano in his *Relation* and *Letters*; cf. A. Grandidier *et al.*, 1903–20, 21–3, Vol. II, pp. 315, 241, 225 and 256 (in small print, on 'richer' aspect).

106. This was made clear by Mariano in his *Letter* of 24 August 1619; see A. Grandidier *et al.*, 1903–20, Vol. II.

107. L. Mariano, *Letter*, 22 October 1616, in A. Grandidier *et al.*, 1903–20, Vol. II, pp. 226–9 and 232–3.

ority for the Volamena kings but the *dady* cult gave this authority a religious base which survived the formidable warriors and their direct descendants. A feature which came into Menabe from outside, probably not directly with the Maroserana,[108] was the formula for making royal posthumous names with the prefix *andria* (lord, noble) and suffix *arivo* (thousand, thousands). While the variable infix usually depicted what a ruler had represented in local memory, the formula contained the political idea that a true king must have many subjects.

Southern Menabe (an area roughly between the Mangoky and Manambovo rivers) was under Andriandahifotsy by the early 1670s when this ruler was visited by a French cattle-trader from Fort Dauphin, who saw a disciplined army of some 12 000 men and received fifty prime bulls as a gift for the Fort's governor.[109] By best estimates, Andriandahifotsy died around 1685. Conflicts over the succession left one of his sons, Trimonongarivo (died *c.*1718/19 as Andriamanetriarivo), at the helm of Menabe which he expanded[110] and populated with many new subjects attracted from the south-western pastoralists.[111] His younger brother, Tsimanatona (by *fitahina* Andriamandisoarivo), crossed the Tsiribihina river and went north with less than 1000 Sakalava warriors to found Iboina in the 1690s. As some of the royal names do not accord in oral texts and contemporary European accounts, it is difficult to tell whether Menabe had four or six rulers between 1720 and 1800.[112] Nonetheless, it remained stable during this period apart from one case of regicide reported in the 1730s. In the ensuing decade an important alliance with the Andrevola rulers of the Fiherenana valley was concluded through the royal blood-covenant (the *fatidra*) which made the southern boundaries of Menabe safer. There was also a marriage alliance with a powerful ruler in western Imerina – an alliance which impelled his rival in central Imerina to seek the submission of Menabe toward the end of the 1700s but without success.[113] In Iboina, protected from the south by its sister-state, Menabe, the Muslim trading posts and traders were brought forcibly under the royal Volamena protection. Analalava and Anorontsangana (once under Tingimaro) were added to the kingdom along with some new subjects. Majunga grew into the commercial capital of Iboina and its kings and their court at Marovoay attained a splendour unknown elsewhere in Madagascar. At the time of Andrianinevenarivo (known as Andrianbaga, died 1752), Iboina was at its height. Just as the influx of south-western pastoralists had

108. The formula may have been Antemoro as some of their *sorabe* reflect it.

109. Du Bois, 1674, pp. 105–8.

110. At its peak, Menabe encompassed the area between the Fiherenana and Manambao rivers, reaching unevenly inland to the massifs of Isalo, Midongy, Lava, Tsara and Bongo: cf. L. Thomassin, 1900, p. 397.

111. R. Drury, 1729/1890, pp. 274–5.

112. E. Fagering, 1971, pp. 22–4, attempts to resolve this problem.

113. C. Guillain, 1845, p. 16 *et seq.*; F. Callet, 1878–1902, pp. 659–61; E. Fagering, 1971, pp. 23–4.

virtually replaced the land cultivators in Menabe during the Maroserana ascent, now migrants from the north, moving south with their cattle herds, gradually absorbed most of the remaining Bambala populations.[114] This meant not only the linguistic flooding-out of the Bantu-speaking *tompontany* but also an adverse economic change which came at a time when the Sakalava states needed more, not fewer, inhabitants who could plant and harvest. Eventually, as it became harder to obtain agricultural labour from other parts of Madagascar, the Sakalava began to raid the Comoro Island and even south-eastern Africa.[115]

The last three decades of Iboina, in the 1700s, evolved under a single monarch, Queen Ravahiny (*c.*1767–1808), who is usually credited with the stable government and economic prosperity of her lands.[116] Nonetheless, Iboina began to decline during her rule. The Volamena had run out of dynamic kings by the 1750s while the Iboina Muslims, who had gone the Sakalava way constituted Iboina's most dynamic element. As the Iboina–Sakalava followed the proper line of royal succession and accepted, not without periodic turbulence, three successive queens (Ravahiny was the third), the Muslims aimed at capturing the throne. Ravahiny's son and heir-apparent was, for example, a Muslim convert and frictions between the *silamos* (from *Islam/Islamos*) and traditionalist Sakalava élites were not an asset for Iboina. Another weakness came out indirectly, by way of the eastern littoral where Count Benyowsky had persuaded a number of Betsimisaraka rulers to cease paying tribute to Iboina. Warriors sent in 1776 to punish the former tributaries and eliminate Benyowsky failed in their mission and some Sakalava even came over to his side,[117] revealing thus to the peoples of the interior that Iboina was no longer omnipotent. Finally, Ravahiny handed Iboina a major long-range foreign policy error by deciding to support the ruler of central Imerina, Andrianampoinimerina, against other local rivals.

The Sakalava kingdoms were both despotic and regal.[118] The rulers' daily lives were regulated by the royal *moasy* (priests) and nothing would be undertaken without sacerdotal advice. There was a Royal Council composed of six elders who resided at the court. The first minister, *Manantany*, dealt directly with the many royal collaborators and his power usually expanded or shrank in inverse proportion to the king's direct involvement in the affairs of state. An aide to the first minister, the *Fahatelo*, was usually selected for his knowledge of clans and lineages as well as of Sakalava custom. Each village of any size had its own royal official (often

---

114. Cf. E. Birkeli, 1926, pp. 9–48; R. K. Kent, 1968.

115. Cf. E. de Froberville, 1845, pp. 194–208; R. K. Kent, 1970, pp. 203–4, 296–8.

116. H. Deschamps, 1965 edn, pp. 101 and 104; M. A. de Benyowsky, 1790, Vol. II.

117. For the terms, see J. Vansina, 1962a.

118. This also shielded the Maroserana kings who could always blame their *moasy* for errors of judgement when something went wrong. Several royal *moasy* are known to have been put to death in Menabe under royal disgrace.

also called the *Fahatelo*) who saw that the royal rice fields were worked four days a week and that the royal cattle-pens were constantly renovated through various gifts since a regular tax did not exist and quotas were fixed according to position and ability to contribute. Officials called *Talempihitry* and *Hanimboay* acted as overseers of the *dady* cult to which all the Sakalava adhered. No monarch could rule without being in possession of the royal *dady* (ancestral Volamena relics), especially since a new king automatically became the sole intermediary with the sacred royal ancestors (*Ampagnito-be*). As custom ruled the Sakalava even more than the royal *dady*, its interpreters were highly regarded and the Royal Council of elders had its counterpart in the *sojabe* (village elders) concerned with the minutiae of social life.[119] Royal relatives were often made into minor rulers (*mpanjaka*) through the *fehitra* (village fiefs, for lack of a better term) which assured their economic well-being but which gave them little political influence. This organization is a model which mutated in both Iboina and Menabe during the period from 1700 to 1800. Provincial governors often had considerable powers and sometimes declared their independence. Some of the monarchs had little regard or use for the channels of authority and royal power was often used differently at the ports which were the source of external wealth going directly to the throne.

The Tsimihety grew out of acephalous refugee groups from the eastern littoral, men and women who had fled the slave wars and settled with their cattle in the great Mandritsara plain that could be reached without scaling the high escarpment that divides much of eastern Madagascar from the interior.[120] In contrast, the Antankara were the *tompon-tany* of Madagascar's far north, people of the rocks (*ant-ankara*) which are such a visible mark of this part of the island. Neither had developed states[121] on their own and both came to accept Maroserana collaterals (the *Volafotsy*, descendants of white silver, sons of non-Maroserana women and Maroserana royals) who could not rule among the Sakalava and who migrated into the northern interior in search of their own kingdoms. The Tsimihety, nonetheless, did not accept rule by the Volafotsy (or the Volamena) and deliberately adopted their collective name (*tsi-mihety*) to indicate, by refusing to cut their hair, non-submission to Maroserana authority. Because a centralized kingdom failed to emerge among the Tsimihety their eighteenth-century history remains virtually unknown. They intermarried with the Iboina–Sakalava and the Antankara and although their numbers increased greatly before 1800 there were no serious external attempts to

119. C. Betoto, 1950a, and R. K. Kent, field notes, 1966.

120. The exact origin of the 'proto-Tsimihety' is a matter of some dispute: cf. B. Magnes, 1953, pp. 13–14 and A. Grandidier, 1908–28, Vol. IV, part I; p. 227.

121. It would appear that a section of the Antankara coast was once controlled from the islet of Nosy Be by a powerful chief who had opposed Muslims and who was in the process of political expansion but perished in a gunpowder explosion along with his family: N. Mayeur, 1912, p. 128 and pp. 148–9.

place them under political control. This is all the more surprising as the Tsimihety had no warriors, paid no tribute and often crammed, with their herds of cattle, the high Sofia river valley, an artery of Iboina's political supremacy among the east-coast Betsimisaraka until the 1780s.

The Antankara reactions were quite different. Some came to place themselves under Iboina's founder and part of the Antankara would be under Sakalava control at one time or another well into the 1800s.[122] Nonetheless, a royal line took among them, going back to a Volafotsy named Kazobe. A fully centralized kingdom did not evolve, however, until the time of his grand-nephew, Andriantsirotso, who ruled either from *c*.1697 to 1710 or between 1710 and *c*.1750, depending on the texts.[123] Alternately in exile among the Betsimisaraka of Maroantsetra and a ruler forced to pay tribute to Iboina, it was Andriantsirotso who established the royal necropolis at Ambatosahana (where he had once fled from Iboina's King Andrianbaba). In the absence of a royal *dady* cult he introduced the unifying symbol of Antankara royalty, the *saina*, the flag with crescent[124] and star brought back from Maroantsetra. He associated his power with a formidable female *moasy* who fashioned the royal amulets, *mandresirafy* (purveyors of invincibility, sacred objects passed on from ruler to ruler), advised two of his successors and lived to be over a hundred years old.[125]

Andriantsirotso's son and successor, Lamboina (despite probable 'telescoping'), had one of the longest rules in Madagascar (the texts differ with 1710–1790 and *c*.1750–1802). He sired over thirty sons, according to tradition, and his rule had one outstanding feature in that it was without wars. With one attempted exception, he paid regular tribute to Iboina, some fifty outrigger-loads of tortoise-shell each year, and concluded a treaty with Benyowsky's envoy and interpreter, Nicolas Mayeur, in 1775. A decade later Lamboina was persuaded by Benyowsky to shift his allegiance to France and cease paying tribute to Iboina's kings, advice followed with brevity since the Count was himself killed in 1786.[126] The Antankara political organization was borrowed from the Iboina–Sakalava without the *dady* cult. Officials analogous to the *Fahatelo* in Iboina were called *Rangahy* at Ambilobe (the later-day Antankara capital); the Royal Council, called *Famoriana*, was probably more powerful among the Antankara; and they, too, did not have a system of regular taxation and used the method of periodic collection (*tatibato*) to finance the state.

---

122. G. Grandidier and R. Decary, 1958, pp. 153–6.
123. M. Vial, 1954, p. 5; G. Grandidier and R. Decary, 1958, pp. 154–6 and 232–3 (Appendix 25).
124. Although the royal Antankara family converted to Islam in the 1840s (in exile) the flag itself and its crescent had no connections with this religion other than visual (copy of the crescent).
125. M. Vial, 1954, pp. 19–22.
126. N. Mayeur, 1912, pp. 119–24; C. Guillain, 1845, pp. 369–70.

States of the Interior: Betsileo, Merina, Sihanaka, Bezanozano, Tanala and Bara

The Betsileo derive their name from a ruler named Besilau who is known to have opposed the Menabe Sakalava expansion into the interior highlands during the 1670s, apparently with success (-*silau/tsileo*, the invincible).[127] Yet the populations that became known as the Betsileo in more recent years did not, on the whole, support internal attempts at political unity and came under one government only through external force in the 1800s.[128] A mixture of diverse *tompon-tany* and newcomers, sometimes migrating in groups or as individuals in search of their own political fortunes, subdivided the Betsileo into four main states: Arindrano in the south, merging into Ibara; Isandra in the centre, facing west and the Sakalava; Lalangina in east-central Betsileo with the Tanala as neighbours; and Manandriana, the northernmost Betsileo state, closest to Imerina, the last to form and the first to accept Merina over-rule in the late 1700s. Although complex genealogical trees could be extended into the 1500s it is doubtful that kingdoms developed among the Betsileo before the 1650s. Isandra and Arindrano (a name also applied to the southern Betsileo who had sought French mercenaries at Fort Dauphin) were under a host of minor and independent chiefs as late as 1648, while Lalangina had little strength as a state even in 1667, when La Case took from it many cattle with only a small force of men.[129] Oral traditions confirm that Lalangina had internal difficulties at the time. Its founder, Rasahamanarivo, was forced to abdicate (because of leprosy, a disease which seems to have been connected with royal persons more than once) in favour of his brother but went to Arindrano around 1680 and was accepted in turn, by the southern Betsileo as their ruler.[130] Struggles for succession and wars with neighbours arrested the growth of Lalangina and, after a case of regicide, it broke up into four provinces, each with its own ruler.[131] Nonetheless, the usurping branch of Lalangina's royal family produced at least three strong rulers in the 1700s: Raonimanalina, who re-unified the kingdom with the aid of fire-arms obtained from the Sakalava ('3,000 flintlocks for 3,000 slaves') and introduced an internal militia to reduce dissentions; Andrianonindranarivo, who carried out a number of important economic and social reforms which resulted in much greater rice production, the growth of the population and a period of domestic tranquillity; and his son and successor, Ramaharo,

127. F. Martin, *Memoire*, in A. Grandidier *et al.*, 1903–20, Vol. IX, pp. 480 and 620.

128. See G. Grandidier and R. Decary, 1958, Vol. V, part III, section 1, pp. 12–13 and 16–19.

129. E. de Flacourt, *Histoire*, in A. Grandidier *et al.*, 1903–20, Vol. VIII, p. 23; E. de Flacourt, *Relation*, in A. Grandidier *et al.*, 1903–20, Vol. IX, pp. 41–2, 85 and 376.

130. G. Grandidier and R. Decary, 1958, Vol. V, part III, section 1, p. 11; H. M. Dubois, 1938, sections on Lalangina, and on Arindrano early history, pp. 169–206 and 218–19.

131. G. Grandidier and R. Decary, Vol. V, part III, section 1, p. 11 and note 8.

who transformed the militia into an economic adjunct of state meant to ensure a still greater harvest of rice (indeed, during the 1700s the Betsileo became the foremost rice-growers of Madagascar). The eighteenth-century rulers of Lalangina were not fortunate in external relations but Ramaharo would not submit to Merina rule toward the end of the 1700s.[132]

Conflicting traditions hold that the ancestor of Isandra's royal family, the Zafimanarivo, was either an Antemoro female or a Maroserana prince in exile.[133] Geography certainly favours a Maroserana antecedent. An early Zafimanarivo is associated with the term *volamena* (gold). Finally, like the Maroserana of Menabe, Isandra's departed rulers were drained of their humours prior to final rest. Unlike the Menabe Sakalava, however, the western Betsileo came to believe that the royal humours transformed themselves into large snakes (*fanane*), the objects of a pre-existing but less elevated cult.[134] It is also very possible that a sacerdotal person coming from south-eastern Madagascar entered the royal genealogy for services rendered, as had earlier been the case with the celebrated priest of the Maroserana in Menabe. One could not call Isandra a notable Betsileo state until the 1750s, when it came under an outstanding monarch, Andriamanalina I. Sometimes called the 'jester king' because of his ability to win political arguments through humour, Andriamanalina I was the first Betsileo to conceive of a unified, single state, and to attain this end as well. When diplomacy failed, as with parts of Lalangina and Arindrano (long eclipsed by the former in the 1700s), Andriamanalina became a military conqueror. He also expanded westward, placing his Betsileo on the Midongy massif, and south into Ibara where he obtained an important vassal, the Bara ruler Andriamanely II. Retaining the traditional structure in each area, Andriamanalina I placed his sons at the head of four new provinces which contained most of the Betsileo. Indeed, at his death in 1790, the Betsileo were at their political apex.[135] As for Manandriana, it had a very short span as an independent state having formed after about 1750 and with its second ruler placing himself under the Merina, quite willingly,[136] *c.*1800.

In a strict sense, the Merina history begins with Ralambo, the ruler to whom an important body of oral traditions assigns not only the first use of this collective name[137] but also the introduction of new institutions and hierarchy. Before his time, variously estimated between 1610 and 1640,[138] Imerina did not contain a state organization. It had numerous village

132. G. Grandidier and R. Decary, 1958, p. 10.

133. H. M. Dubois, 1938, pp. 112–39, sections on early Isandra; G. Grandidier and R. Decary, 1958, pp. 4 and 5 and note 3.

134. F. Callet, 1958 edn, Vol. III, pp. 234–7; R. K. Kent, 1970, pp. 294–5 (Appendix).

135. G. Grandidier and R. Decary, 1958, pp. 5–6.

136. G. Grandidier and R. Decary, 1958, p. 3; H. M. Dubois, 1938, pp. 102–4.

137. F. Callet, 1953 edn, Vol. I, pp. 284–5.

138. M. Cheffaud, 1936, pp. 46–7; A. Jully, 1898, pp. 890–8; and A. Grandidier 1908–28, Vol. IV, part I, pp. 83–5. Also, R. K. Kent, 1970, p. 229 and note.

chiefdoms peopled either by the Vazimba, its *tompon-tany*, or by the Hova[139] whose clans attained Imerina in two major migratory movements probably not later than about 1500.[140] Intermittent conflicts appear to have been the rule in the 1500s but their resolution did not necessarily depend on warfare. Disputes were also arbitrated by local sages and astrologers, the elders of Ampandrana, who had settled among the Vazimba prior to the Hova arrivals.[141] As neither the Hova nor the Vazimba of that time were ethnic groups or peoples with a centre of political authority, the Ampandrana gradually assumed a position of leadership from which came the future dynasty of Andriana, starting with Andriamanelo, Ralambo's father. It was Andriamanelo who created the first fortifications at Alosara and who started using iron for weapons as well as limited domestic use. Although his iron-tipped spears gave him absolute superiority over the clay-heads, to consolidate his power he also married into the family of the powerful Vazimba chieftain at Ambohitrabiby.[142]

With Ralambo come the first of the twelve *sampy*, amulet-guardians of Imerina; royal circumcision and incest; the *fandroana* or annual royal-bath ceremony;[143] divinization of departed monarchs; the noble (*andriana*) classes and smithing units (silversmiths and ironsmiths) to serve the state; the head tax; consumption of beef; and a small but standing army.[144] His son and successor, Andrianjaka, turned decisively against the Vazima using fire-arms obtained from west-coast traders under royal protection.[145] Under Andrianjaka, the Merina monarchy became more elevated and more distant from its subjects, and some of its internal measures inspired fear. Nevertheless, he founded Antananarivo and secured the marshes for considerable harvests of rice which, as Hubert Deschamps has observed, gave the Merina an economic base early enough to become the most numerous among the Malagasy.[146]

The growth of population in Imerina also increased the risk of famine (*tsimiompy*) and compelled its rulers to continuously expand the irrigated areas, a practice followed without exception by Andrianjaka's three successors well into the eighteenth century. While his son and grandson distinguished themselves mainly by adding letters to their royal names (lord-above-lords and lord-above-greatest-of-lords, with thirty-three

---

139. Although still used for the early period of local history, the term Hova did not reflect ethnicity and, after Ralambo and to the end of Merina state, Hova (with whom the Merina were often interchanged) designated *commoners*.

140. C. Savaron, 1928, p. 63; R. K. Kent, 1970, p. 220.

141. F. Callet, 1953 edn, Vol. I, pp. 28–9, 18, 540; C. Savaron, 1928, pp. 65–6; and R. K. Kent, 1970, pp. 227–8 (note 112) and 233–5.

142. R. K. Kent, 1970, pp. 308–9, Appendix; F. Callet, 1953 edn, Vol. I, pp. 27 and 126.

143. The best work on this subject is G. Razafimino, 1924.

144. R. K. Kent, 1970, p. 235; H. Deschamps, 1965 edn, p. 116.

145. F. Callet, 1953 edn, Vol. I, p. 461; R. K. Kent, 1970, pp. 241–2.

146. H. Deschamps, 1965 edn, p. 117.

letters in Malagasy), Andrianjaka's great-grandson, Andriamasinavalona, was another pivotal ruler. Largely with the help of his astute adviser, Andriamampiandry, he deposed an older brother who fled among the Sakalava and even sought their military help.[147] Andriamasinavalona pursued a policy of aggressive expansion and allowed little independence to the many chiefs who came under his authority. He increased the number of the noble clans from four to six and rewarded the more deserving nobility with village fiefs and the title of *tompon-menakely* (masters-of-the fief).[148] His advanced age also led him to consider the problem of succession while still in office. Against the advice of Andriamampiandry, he divided Imerina into four provinces and placed a son at the head of each. In effect, he soon found himself amid four independent kingdoms: two in the north, centred around Ambohitrabiby and the necropolis of Ambohimanga (where 'no boar, dog or stranger could set foot', as tradition has it); one in the south, ruled from Antananarivo; and one in the west with its capital at Ambohidratrimo. He also suffered the humiliation of being imprisoned (for 'seven years') by Andriantomponimerina, his son and ruler of the western area (Marovatana).[149] The old king died about 1750,[150] and Imerina became a site of internal wars in which even outsiders took part. By the 1770s, Ambohimanga had conquered Ambohitrabiby and seemed quite strong under its ruler Andrianbelomasina. Although his son Andrianjafy inherited the throne it was his nephew Ramboasalama who became the ruler at Ambohimanga *c.*1777/8 and who came to be regarded as the most important of Imerina's kings.

Assuming the name of Andrianampoinimerina, he first managed to secure peace with his royal brothers and rivals. He then fortified his borderlands by peopling them with those pledged to defend them, and secured a considerable quantity of fire-arms through western Madagascar. Antananarivo fell in 1797,[151] Ambohidratrimo shortly thereafter, and several less defined sections of Imerina also came into his hands before about 1800. He went beyond the obvious drive for unification in Imerina and began sending especially selected envoys to rulers in other parts of Madagascar with the offer to become his vassals and retain autonomy or face eventual conquest by the Merina. This form of diplomacy worked at times, as among the Manandriana Betsileo, the Andrantsay of Betafo (a mixture of Antandrano who had fled western Madagascar during the Sakalava expansion, of Betsileo and some assimilated Merina), and in western Imamo. It also failed in places as in Menabe or parts of Lalangina

147. C. Guillain, 1845, p. 42; V. Malzac, 1912, pp. 54–65.

148. This institution went back to the times of Andrianjaka and his brother Andriantompokoindrindra when twelve Menakely were created: cf. J. Rasamimanana and L. Razafindrazaka, 1909, 1957 edn., p. 37.

149. G. Grandidier, 1942, Vol. V, part I, pp. 62 and 64.

150. A. Tacchi, 1892, p. 474.

151. G. Grandidier, 1942, p. 91, note 2 and p. 92; H. Deschamps, 1965, pp. 121–2.

and Isandra, but there is slight doubt that Imerina under Andrianampoinimerina no longer paid tribute to the Sakalava and that it was becoming a power to be reckoned with, despite its small territorial size.[152] Andrianampoinimerina was a tough monarch and it is said that he did away with not only theft in Imerina but also the consumption of intoxicating beverages and the smoking of tobacco. In essence, Andrianampoinimerina made himself the centre of all authority, high and low, building on the earlier ideas of Andriamasinavalona, but tempered by constant advice from reputable elders, the flow of information through the public assemblies (*kabary*) and the Council of Seventy which represented every collective within the kingdom.[153] Through unification and the restructuring of Imerina, he paved the ground for its nineteenth-century empire.

Although neither the Sihanaka nor the Bezanozano developed into powerful state-structures their histories remain of considerable interest. The Sihanaka evolved around Lake Alaotra (the largest lake in Madagascar), while the Bezanozano came to inhabit an area between the tropical rain forest of the eastern littoral and its escarpment. Both were thus ideally situated – the Bezanozano on the main commercial route linking Imerina with the eastern coast and the Sihanaka on its counterpart in the direction of the north-western entrepôts. It is almost certain that the first 'Ova' (Hova) sold into slavery in 1614, as reported by Father Mariano, reached the entrepôts through Sihanaka intermediaries.[154] Conversely, the Bezanozano were the main suppliers from Imerina to the Mascarene traders in eastern Madagascar.[155] Indeed, both the Sihanaka and the Bezanozano were in possession of so many slaves that, in 1768, they even sought help from Europeans to suppress their own internal slave rebellions.[156] In 1667, when François Martin penetrated into Sihanaka territory from the eastern side (after an eighteen-day journey), he found them inhabiting fortified hill-top villages, surrounded by high stone walls (held together by reddish mortar) and wide, deep trenches. They were excellent potters; they had the only bridge seen in Madagascar until that time by Europeans; and they were extremely well armed, using bows and arrows to rout Martin's party of forty-four compatriots and some 3000 Betsimisaraka.[157] Martin also confirmed the Sihanaka as one of the most important trading groups in the island, all of which would presuppose considerable political organization. Yet there is no evidence that the Sihanaka ever had central authority. There was an attempt to establish a dynasty among the *tompon-tany* of the Lake

152. About twenty miles in diameter: see the map based on detailed work of Savaron in H. Deschamps, 1965 edn, p. 118.

153. For an outline of changes see H. Deschamps, 1965 edn, pp. 121–7; otherwise the French texts of F. Callet, 1953 edn, Vols. II and III.

154. L. Mariano, *Relation*, in A. Grandidier *et al.*, 1903–20, Vol. II, pp. 12–13.

155. N. Mayeur, 1806, p. 123.

156. G. Grandidier and R. Decary, 1958, pp. 120, 121 and note 1, and p. 132.

157. F. Martin, *Mémoire*, December 1667, in A. Grandidier *et al.*, 1903–20, Vol. IX, pp. 552–9.

Alaotra area by Rabenifananina who probably came from Betsileo and left behind the collective name of Antsihanaka but no political successors.[158] In fact, the Sihanaka paid tribute to Iboina in the eighteenth century but not without at least one serious attempt to repudiate it through a major attack which ended in failure.[159] The Bezanozano, whose group name even indicated a lack of central authority according to William Ellis,[160] and whose land was called originally Ankay, were also ruled by village chiefs (*mpifehy*) and lived in fortified villages. Unlike the Sihanaka, however, they had at least one unifying institution in the form of amulets representing eleven protector-deities said to have arrived from Sakalava land. As several bear Sakalava names,[161] their west-coast origin seems beyond dispute, although it is also likely that the Bezanozano *ombiasa* fashioned some of them. Toward the end of the 1700s, in contrast to the Sihanaka, the Benzanozano seem to have accepted the pre-eminence of Randrianjomoina, their first king, but this was an evolution cut short by the Merina who demanded and secured the Bezanozano ruler's submission.[162]

Wedged between the Betsileo highlanders and the coastal Antemoro, the Tanala took as their own a purely environmental name, 'people of the forest' (Antanala) which was used in other parts of Madagascar as well but not in such a lasting, ethnic sense. Indeed, the Tanala developed into a highly mixed population. As many as twenty-three of their clans have claimed Betsileo descent; and none of the Tanala ever had a state. Some of them, however, do stand out in local history, the so-called Tanala of Ikongo, a huge rock accessible only by artificial passages.[163] While completely isolated from the Betsileo highlands, the Tanala–Ikongo area has been the natural hinterland of the coastal region (only about forty-five kilometres away), accessible (apart from the rock itself) by such waterways as the Sandrananta and the Faraony, and the Matitana river of the Antemoro.[164] It is therefore not surprising that the Ikongo–Tanala accepted migrants from the eastern littoral and that one of them, Rambo, said to have been an Anteony–Antemoro, sired the local dynasty of the Zafirambo, first mentioned by outsiders in 1668.[165] According to Tanala traditions, collected by Ardant Du Picq around 1900, Rambo became the king of Ikongo through his knowledge of the curative amulets (*fanafody*) and of the *sorabe*. Rambo was also remembered as the 'law-giver' and several of his successors also fashioned amulets to protect the Ikongo–Tanala and

158. G. Grandidier and R. Decary, 1958, p. 117, note 3.

159. C. Guillain, 1845, p. 24; N. Mayeur, 1912, p. 70.

160. W. Ellis, 1838, Vol. I, p. 131. Mayeur called the Bezanozano a 'republic'.

161. Vallier, 1898, pp. 80–1.

162. F. Callet, 1908 edn, Vol. I, pp. 77–84, and 1909 edn, Vol. II, p. 527; V. Malzac, 1912, p. 92; and G. Grandidier and R. Decary, 1958, pp. 133–4.

163. A. du Picq, 1905, pp. 541–2.

164. ibid., p. 543.

165. See R. K. Kent, 1970, p. 92 and note 14. Deschamps places the exile of Rambo in the 1500s.

were reputed to predict natural phenomena. Pre-dynastic chiefs, the Anak-andriana and Andriambaventy, retained a number of privileges and although the Zafirambo practised the *sombili* (prerogative to slaughter domesticated animals) they applied it only to themselves. The Zafirambo were also known as Zanaka Isandrananta (children of the Sandrananta) because, after Rambo, the humours of departed rulers were thrown into this river, creating the belief that crocodiles hatched from them.[166] Most of the 1700s were marked by conflicts between the Ikongo-Tanala and the Antemoro, leading to a devastating Tanala invasion of the lowlands late in the century. At the turn of the 1800s, one of the Zafirambo, Andri-amamohotra, allied himself with Andrianampoinimerina.[167]

The Bara, major pastoralists of Madagascar who have often been given an African origin,[168] seem to have emerged somewhere in the southern reaches of Arindranoland, along the River Ihosy. De Flacourt mentions a site in this approximate area, called Varabei,[169] a name duplicated in Bara-be (*Varabei* and *Bei/be* meaning great, or numerous) one of the three great Bara clans. The Bara-be settled on the Horombe Plateau with the Bara Ianstsantsa to their east and the Bara Imamono on the western side, toward the Sakalava. Two important but smaller Bara clans, the Vinda of south-western Ibara and the Antivondro who inhabit the eastern side of the River Ionaivo, are of more recent origin, the Vinda having formed only in the early 1800s.[170] The Bara seem to have expanded until the more or less natural boundaries were attained with the Sakalava, Mahafaly, Antandroy, Antanosy, Antesaka and Antefasy. There were two distinct dynastic periods in the southern interior (of which Ibara is by far the largest), one which coincides with the proto-Maroserana and which is likely to remain inad-equately known,[171] and the more recent one, the period of the Zafimanely, after about 1650. A total absence of succession rules and the ease with which dissenters could migrate with their cattle to even better grazing grounds undoubtedly facilitated the disintegration of political authority by the 1640s, when the Mahafaly ruler, Dian Manhelle, invaded the southern interior and began to instal his kinsmen as local rulers. After his death in 1653, Dian Manhelle's descendants, the Zafimanely, gradually assumed positions of authority in Ibara but not necessarily to its benefit. Ibara's history between about 1650 and 1800 is dominated by competition among the Zafimanely kinglets (*mpanjaka-kely* in distinction from *mpanjaka-be*, the title of a king given only to rulers of the great Bara clans) and their proliferation which added countless subgroups (*tariki*) to the Bara family. Their internal competition was not political so much as economic in nature.

166. A. du Picq, 1933, pp. 27–39.
167. ibid., p. 39.
168. R. K. Kent, 1970, pp. 116–20 and notes on this subject.
169. E. de Flacourt, 1661/1913, p. 33.
170. R. K. Kent, 1970, p. 124.
171. ibid., pp. 123–37.

PLATE 28.2 *Bara ethnic group of Ambusitra, south-eastern Madagascar: memorial statue called* alualu, *erected when a person dies without male issue or when the corpse does not rest in the family grave. The statue was surrounded by an enclosure of posts bearing the horns of zebu cows sacrificed at the funeral ceremonies. The rule was that it was a female figure that becomes the replacement for the dead male and symbolizes the element destined to ensure issue. Made from the hard wood of the camphor tree. Height: 107 cm*

Without a system of regular tribute the Zafimanely maintained themselves as local lords by securing a part of their wealth through legal decisions[172] and a much larger one through raids for cattle, the main source of wealth.

172. This may be the reason why Bara justice involved a great variety of trials-by-ordeal.

As they could not afford to raid their own subjects or embark easily upon foreign wars, the Zafimanely raided each other's cattle-pens, more or less constantly and without any political vision. This cycle of artificial tension was broken only after 1800 by Raikitroka, an extremely interesting ruler who deserves to be studied in greater depth.[173] The Bara kings did not, in practice, govern their clans as absolute rulers, and they could not declare war without the approval of their councils of ministers (called *Tandonaka* among the Imamono) and their provincial governors (*Mamandranomay*), appointed by the *mpanjaka-be* in office but also controlled by local councils of elders (the *Ionaka* in Imamono).[174]

The Eastern and Southern states: Betsimisaraka, Antemoro, Antambahoaka, Antefasy, Antesaka, Antanosy and Antandroy

The Betsimisaraka, often divided into 'Northerners' (*Antavaratra*) and 'Southerners' (*Antatsimo*), and the Betanimena who separated the two, evolved along the eastern littoral of Madagascar roughly between the Bay of Antongil and Vatomandry. As is attested by a large number of sources, the *tompon-tany* of this area were strangers to larger political unions prior to the 1700s and remained under chiefs (*filohany*) seldom in control of more than one or two villages. Nevertheless, chiefs around the huge Antongil Bay seem to have been better organized and to have had office regalia, at least since the late 1500s.[175] The Antavaratri were also favoured by nature. They had all the ports (in Antongil, at Titingue, Foulpointe, Fenerive and Tamatave) while the Betanimena coast had none. As the Mascarenes came to depend increasingly on eastern Madagascar for its rice, cattle and slave labour, the control of these ports assured not only wealth for their *filohany* but also firepower for protection and attack. This was also the section of Madagascar most heavily settled by European, especially English and American, pirates from the 1680s until the 1720s. Many intermarried among the Antavaratra and sired *métis* who became the Zana Malata, often allied to the *filohany* as sons of their daughters. Out of one such union, around 1694, came a Zana Malata named Ratsimilahoe[176] whose father took him to England and India for brief periods.[177] A political change among the Betanimena (then known as Sicoua or Tsikoa in modern

173. See J. Rabemanana, 'Le pays des Kimoso et son histoire depuis les origines jusqu'à l'an 1820', 1911–12, MS in the Archives of the Académie malgache, Antananarivo, p. 98; and R. K. Kent, 1970, p. 124, note 44, and p. 129, note 65.

174. L. Michel, 1957, pp. 34–51; C. Le Barbier, 1916–17, pp. 97–100.

175. In the 1590s, the Dutch saw a ruler who monopolized the colour red and wore a sort of crown with two horns.

176. N. Mayeur, *Ratsimilahoe*, 1806, typescript copy, p. 132.

177. ibid., p. 11; G. Grandidier and R. Decary, 1958, p. 28, note 1.

Malagasy) gave Ratsimilahoe his political start. Around 1700 the Sicoua began to unite around strong chiefs. By about 1710 they elected the chief of Vatomandry as their supreme ruler, one who would lead them into the northern ports. It was in response to an invasion of these ports that Ratsimilahoe managed to unite most of the Antavaratra despite his youth.

Ratsimilahoe recaptured Fenerive in 1712 and the hasty retreat of the Sicoua, across fields of soggy red clay which stuck to their feet, led to their name *Be-tani-mena* (the many-of-red-earth).[178] Ratsimilahoe coined the name Betsimisaraka (the indivisible-many) to stress the lasting nature of the political union and in distinction to the Betanimena. He also secured peace with them by leaving the port of Tamatave to their king and was elected as king (*mpanjaka-be*) of all the Betsimisaraka and renamed Ramaroumanompou (modern Ramaromanompo, Lord-served-by-many) at his capital of Foulpointe.[179] The Betsimisaraka–Betanimena peace broke down within six months, however, and Ratsimilahoe took Tamatave, forcing the Betanimena king into an inaccessible area further south.[180] He also contracted alliances with the Antatismo (Southerners) and the Bezanozano.[181] By the 1730s Ratsimilahoe was one of the most powerful kings in Madagascar, holding together a confederation of clans and families with rather independent habits. He did this by allowing the traditional chiefs to keep their autonomy and pay as much tribute as each saw fit, in slaves, cattle and rice. He also compensated the relatives of various *filohany* who had fallen in battles against the Betanimena with royal gifts (*vilipate*) and allowed the Betanimena to buy back relatives taken during the hostilities. He took the sons of high and low *filohany* as hostages at his court but used them productively as the *ompanghalalan*, royal messengers, who took his orders to the Betsimisaraka. He also administered high justice, permitting any Betsimisaraka to by-pass his own ruler.[182] Keenly aware of the strong centrifugal tendencies within his kingdom, Ratsimilahoe married Matave, the sole daughter of Iboina's king Andrian Baba to be linked with the Volamena and the Sakalava empire.[183] Ratsimilahoe died in 1754, after about forty years as the leader and unifier of the Betsimisaraka. He had three successors between 1755 and 1803. The first lost his life in slave raids. The second was speared to death by his own subjects. The middle one, Iavy, became illustrious only as the biggest slaver in Madagascar. Indeed, in the second half of the 1700s, Betsimisaraka-land came to resemble Angola in the height of its slaving tragedies early in the 1600s.

There is no longer any real doubt that both the Antesaka and the Antefasy of south-eastern Madagascar were founded by migrants from

---

178. N. Mayeur, *Ratsimilahoe*, 1806, typescript copy, pp. 28–36.
179. ibid., pp. 36–48.
180. ibid., pp. 64–77.
181. ibid., pp. 83–90.
182. ibid., pp. 116–24.
183. ibid., pp. 124–30.

the west. Differences between the ruler of Sakalava–Menabe, Andri-andahifotsy, and his brother (or uncle), Andriamandresi, impelled the later to leave Menabe and go into the southern interior with his own followers. Andriamandresi crossed the Horombe Plateau and may even have reached the Bara–Tanala gap (providing passage to the eastern littoral). It was not until his grandson Behava, however, that Nosipandra (later Vangaindrano) was attained and became the Antesaka capital, seat of the Zarabehava rulers and rice-basket of their kingdom.[184] According to Antesaka informants, the collective name is meant to reflect Sakalava origins.[185] De Flacourt's map suggests that the Antesaka migration was over by the 1650s. As for the Antefasy, their traditions hold that the ultimate ancestor, Ndretsileo, came from the African mainland to the River Menarandra at a time when the Maroserana were already established among the Mahafaly, in Menabe and in parts of Ibara. With a companion named Isoro (who would later separate to found the Zafisoro) Ndretsileo settled in Ibara. Difficulties with the Zafimanely nonetheless became acute by the time of his grandson Ndrem-bolanony. He went further east and sided in a local war with the ruler of Antevatobe whose daughter became, in turn, the spouse of Ndrem-bolanony. One of his three sons, Marofela, coined the name Antefasy (sand-people) to suggest that his kingdom would be densely populated by the analogy with sand.[186]

The most important Antefasy ruler prior to the 1800s was undoubtedly Ifara who resided at Ambaky (the old name of Farafangana). Ifara gained a monopoly of trade with the first European vessels to visit his coast and became so powerful at one point that he was widely regarded as the sole owner of the Manampatra river.[187] Another Zarabehava ruler particularly recalled is Maseba who detached the Antefasy from a brief Antemoro dominance. Ifara was Maseba's successor, but dates are hard to come by. The Antefasy (who sometimes claim kinship with the Zarabehava) undoubtedly formed after the Antesaka – possibly in the 1670s – and Maseba might have been the last seventeenth-century ruler. From Antemoro sources, conflicts between the Antemoro and the Antefasy can be dated to the 1680s.[188] They also continued during the 1700s but the wars were never conclusive. The Antesaka were more inward-looking and they had considerable difficulties over successions. Tradition recalls that one of their Zarabehava kings, Ratongalaza, 'either killed or expelled all of his brothers'. His grandson, Lengoabo, was the last eighteenth-century king and he extended the Antesaka boundaries to their greatest limit.[189] The history of Antambahoaka and the Antemoro during the 1700s remains

184. H. Deschamps, 1936, p. 166.
185. H. Deschamps, 1936, pp. 162–4; Marchand, 1901, pp. 485–6.
186. M. Fontoynont and E. Raomandahy, 1939, pp. 1–5.
187. ibid., pp. 6–7.
188. G. Mondain, 1910, p. 73; R. K. Kent, 1970, pp. 98 and 157.
189. H. Deschamps, 1936, pp. 166–7.

unknown despite the fact that Matitana is cited by European accounts as one of the main exporters of rice and slaves, especially after 1724.[190] Another aspect of considerable interest for the 1700s, particularly after about 1750, is the general restlessness of commoners under Zafindraminia and Anteony rulers, a restlessness which would explode in the 1800s and force at least the Anteony to seek Merina support against their own subjects.

Of some 4000 settlers and soldiers sent from France to Fort Dauphin by 1674, two-thirds perished from malaria, famine and violent death.[191] Twenty-four years later, amid the ruins of this Fort in Antanosy-land, a Dutch sea-captain found that the local 'king' was a pirate from Martinique named Samuel. He commanded some twenty Europeans and about 300 Antanosy, had a fleet of fifteen large outriggers, and was at constant war with the traditional ruler Diamarang Diamera.[192] The European connection within Antanosy was not only sustained by earlier links through Fort Dauphin but also because, after the 1720s, the Mascarenes became plantation economies with an insatiable demand for slaves, rice and cattle. The Count of Modave, sent as the governor of the second French establishment at Fort Dauphin (1767–70), discovered no less than thirty-five rulers between the valley of Ambolo and the River Mandrare. They were at war with each other over slaves and cattle, causing frequent external migrations of their own subjects (especially among the Antandroy), and the most powerful of the local rulers controlled fewer than 3000 villagers.[193] Modave, who opposed the slave trade and came to replace it with a legitimate counterpart, was abandoned by France (much like de Flacourt before him) and ended by becoming a slaver to pay for his debts and resupply his own plantations on Ile-de-France (Mauritius).[194] It should be recalled that Fort Dauphin was built at a time when Antanosy-land had been among the most densely populated in Madagascar, when its agriculture produced considerable surpluses, and even when it had a good possibility of becoming unified into an important state. Shortly after the collapse of the Modave mission another French visitor saw Antanosy-land as the 'poorest' and 'saddest' in the island, barely populated and virtually without 'resources'. Even slaves and cattle were few in number and had to be brought from far away.[195]

There have been two very different sections of Antandroy, the southern-

190. C. Grant, 1801, pp. 167–71, from a 1763 report.
191. G. Grandidier and R. Decary, 1958, p. 103, note 2.
192. Jan Coin, *Voyage*, 1698, in A. Grandidier *et al.*, 1903–20, Vol. VI, pp. 41–7.
193. Modave, *Journal*, 1768, quoted in G. Grandidier and R. Decary, 1958, p. 10. There was a revolt in Antanosy in the 1730s against the Zafindraminia who were dispossessed of their cattle according to Le Gentil, 1779–81, Vol. II, pp. 511–22, but it may also have taken place in the 1770s according to A. Grandidier, *Notes*, MS, folios 316, 410 and 551; G. Grandidier and R. Decary, 1958, p. 104, note 5.
194. H. Deschamps, 1965 edn, pp. 80–1.
195. M. de la Haye, 1774, quoted in G. Grandidier and R. Decary, 1958, p. 10, note 1(a).

most state of Malagasy. The Karimbola have been the *tompon-tany* of western Antandroy, the area between the Menarandra and the Manambovo rivers, and they have no memory of a migration. The eastern Antandroy (called by de Flacourt the land of Ampatres), extending from the Manambovo to the Mandrare, was once occupied mainly by the Mahandrovato who were submerged by an influx of migrants from Ibara and Antanosy seeking refuge in the arid south from political uncertainties at home.[196] It would appear that the ruling dynasty of Zafimanara emerged among the Mahandrovato (who welcomed the earliest migrating groups) and that their rule was gradually accepted by the Karimbola as well. The collective name, Antandroy, was given by the Zafimanara to all the peoples between the Menarandra and the Mandrare and it reflected a sense of political unity, a 'Zafimanara Confederation'. The Karimbola, who retained their autonomy under chiefs residing at Ambahy, accepted the Zafimanara kings through marriage alliances and because of their constant need for self-defence against Maroserana-Mahafaly expansion eastward.[197] In the long run, the Karimbola saw little help from the Zafimanara, having stopped the Mahafaly at the Menarandra until about 1750 but not thereafter.[198] At about the same period, repeated migrations from the interior and from Antanosy diluted the Zafimanara authority in eastern Antandroy. By the 1790s, the Zafimanara were confined to the Manombo plateau having been flooded out and unable to cope with the changing nature of their former domain. As for many other populations in Madagascar, the end of the eighteenth century did not augur well for the Antandroy.

The Comoro Islands: Grande Comore, Anjouan, Moheli and Mayotte

The Comoro Islands are roughly half-way between Madagascar and Africa. The Grande Comore is nearest to the African mainland, Mayotte faces Madagascar, while Anjouan and Moheli are in between. Their past is, among other things, a mirror of their geographical situation. There is general agreement that the Comoros were settled by Bantu-speaking mainlanders who had no discernible ties to Islam, that this great religion was imported by the Afro-Shīrāzī, and that the lasting supremacy of Sunnite Islam among the Comoreans must also be attributed to some political successes of more recent Muslim arrivals from Africa. In the traditional

196. E. Defoort, 1913, pp. 161–72, outlines the various migrations.

197. ibid., pp. 162 and 166.

198. ibid., p. 168.

199. The names of the four Comoros vary infinitely in older sources but their local ones were Ngazija, Anzuani, Muali (at times M'heli), and M'samburu (after Mayotte's largest group of Bantu-speakers, M'Chambara), sometimes also M'Ayata; cf. J. Repiquet, 1902, p. 110, and A. Gevrey, 1972, p. 74. The names in this short essay are the current ones.

accounts collected by Ṣaʿīd Ahmad ʿAlī,[200] the pre-Islamic and Shīrāzī periods are associated with the ancient chiefs (*bēdja*) and their *fani* successors whose own daughters (*jumbe*) would come to marry the Sunnite newcomers.[201] Almost nothing is known of the *bēdja* and the two periods cannot be sharply defined,[202] but the *fani* are connected with construction in stone and the erection of the earliest mosque in the Comoros.[203] Although the three segments tend to duplicate those often expressed for the history of East Africa,[204] a chronology of the *bēdja* and *fani* cannot as yet be worked out in the absence of detailed archaeological, linguistic and historical studies. Such studies are not merely overdue. They could go a long way towards new understanding of three monumental events – the migrations of the Bantu-speakers, Indonesian migrations to Africa and Madagascar, and the advent of Swahili culture itself.[205]

The clearest innovation of the latest Muslim arrivals was political in

200. *Essai sur l'Histoire d'Anjouan*, 29 December 1927, typescript, pp. 1–45, Bibliothèque Grandidier, Tsimbazaza-Tananarive (Antananarivo now), Malagasy Republic; pagination of typescript is followed. Parts of the S. A. ʿAlī *Essai* have appeared in a local ephemeral publication, *Promo Al-Camar*, May 1971, most inadequately. Despite many confusing passages, the 1927 *Essai* must continue to be regarded as the most interesting and still quite valuable attempt to deal with local history. The *Essai* is dedicated to the Governor-General of Madagascar and Dependencies. The Comoros were attached to Madagascar from 1914 to 1946. Mayotte became a French Protectorate in 1843. The other Comoros were taken over by France in 1886.

201. S. A. ʿAlī, 1927, pp. 3–7.

202. The Bēdja appear sometimes as the earliest Shīrāzī chiefs. For example, M. Fontoynont and E. Raomandahy, 1937, picked up the following oral tradition: 'Grâce à leurs connaissances botaniques, pharmaceutiques et médicales, ces Chiraziens échappèrent aux maladies et ils se multiplièrent rapidement puis se dispersèrent, se choisissant des chefs auxquels ils donnèrent le nom *Bedja* que l'on retrouve *ensuite* chez *plusieurs Sultans*, tel *Fabedja*', p. 12, (italics added). The same reservation, expressed for East Africa quite well by James Kirkman in his note on 'Persian' for Justus Strandes (pp. 309–10 of the English translation, edn. of 1971), applies to would-be sharp distinctions between the Shīrāzī and Arabs as well as *fani* and Sunnite periods used as a matter of simple convenience.

203. The earliest mosque reported is on Mayotte at Chingoni but A. Gevrey, 1972, p. 207, reads the carved *hidjra*-calendar date of 944 while S. A. ʿAlī, 1927, p. 4, gives it as 844, providing the corresponding Christian dates of 1566 and 1441.

204. See, *inter alia*, H. N. Chittick, 1971, pp. 100–17.

205. An early date for the presence of mainlanders on the Comoro Islands could produce considerable revisions of virtually all the many theories and hypotheses regarding the Bantu-speaking migratory impulses and stages; it is equally possible that settlers from the mainland were of intermixed Afro-Indonesian origins, especially since the Wamatsaha who represent the first Comorean settlers offer a number of physical, ethnographic and even linguistic features which point to such a conclusion. Cf. J. Repiquet, 1902, p. 51 and photo.; S. A. ʿAlī, 1927, p. 1; also James Hornell's comparative studies of the outrigger in Madagascar, Comoros and Eastern Africa (e.g., J. Hornell, 1934). The earliest available Comorean vocabularies are already Swahili: for example, the fourteen words reported by Walter Peyton in 1613, see S. Purchas, 1613; *His Pilgrims*, British Library, London, Add. Mss, no. 6115, Vol. I, fos. 488–90; and A. Grandidier *et al.*, 1903–20, Vol. I, p. 491 and note; see also L. Aujas, 1920, pp. 51–9.

concept. For the first time, the four Comoros were perceived as a single entity and attempts were made to place them under one monarch (*Sultan*) residing in the the centrally located Anjouan. The sultanic period may have started as late as 1506 or even before about 1400, depending upon how one reads the slender evidence.[206] One or more of the Comoros might well have been under the control of traders from Mozambique and Kilwa[207] before 'Muslim Arabs of the same tribe that founded Malindi' arrived at Grande Comore,[208] which could be seen from the African mainland whenever Mount Kartala erupted.

Telescoped as well as functional traditions hold that the first Comorean dynasty was born on Anjouan despite the initial migration of the ultimate ancestor into Grande Comore.[209] This may not be far-fetched. Grande Comore is the largest island but it has no sweet water and its soil is generally unproductive. As late as 1727, Alexander Hamilton described it as an island endowed with the bare necessities of life and a handful of inhabitants.[210] The penultimate ancestor, Ḥasan/Ḥasanī, the real founder of the dynasty, is also depicted as a prolific builder of mosques on Anjouan, first at Sima and later at Domoni. He is also seen as the main carrier of the Shāfiʿīte rite and, indeed, his ascent seems hardly separable from the general adoption of Sunnite Islam by the Anjouanaise. His sons had dual names, Bantu and Arabic, and they extended the Hassanite dynasty to the other Comoros, probably along with the new religious influence.[211] Thereafter, Comorean history is dominated by internal rivalries, even to the level of tiny sultanates within each island. Thus, while Sunnite Islam took hold across the Comoros and brought about a new system of justice with its *ḳāḍī*s, *nā'ib*s (village judges), and the *Madjelisse* (body of jurists), political rivalry among kinsmen and between some of the old *fani* and the new *sultan*s became both an unchanging and dynamic feature of the Comorean society.

Europeans who visited the Comoros left accounts which can seldom be matched with local traditions or at least those set on paper so far. Yet both

206. Cf. A. Gevrey, 1972, pp. 78–9, 148, 184, 206–7; S. A. 'Alī, 1927, pp. 2–5; J. Repiquet, 1902, pp. 111–12. Gevrey gives a list of Mayotte's eighteen Sultans (the last of whom was from Madagascar) on p. 227, spanning the period 1530 to 1843. He states that some dates are accurate while others represent approximations. Unfortunately, his base date of Lancaster's visit to the Comoros, given as 1561, is inaccurate by thirty years (1591 and it is *not* a simple inversion of the 9/6).

207. J. Strandes, 1971 reprint, p. 85; J. de Barros, 1552–1613, Vol. I, pp. 214–5; A. Gevrey, 1972, p. 123.

208. Do Couto, *Da Asia*, Dec. VII, Bk. IV, ch. 5, pp. 310–18; A. Grandidier *et al.*, 1903–20, Vol. I, p. 103.

209. The fact that the earliest mosque is on Mayotte and not on Anjouan (and all the more so since its building is attributed to Haissa, the son of Ḥasanī) seems to confirm the functionalist aspect but judgement cannot be firm as, properly speaking, there is no real work of professional history for the Comoros before the nineteenth century.

210. A. Hamilton, 1727, Vol. I, pp. 16–22; *Antananarivo Annual*, Vol. IV (1892), p. 498 (from the second edn of 1744).

211. S. A. 'Alī, 1927, p. 3. Their Bantu names were Machinda and Chivampe.

types of sources, external and internal, do reveal the constant rivalry and the fact that local history is dominated not by the larger Grande Comore and Mayotte but by Anjouan and Moheli, the pace-setters. At the turn of the 1600s, independent visitors from different parts of Europe confirmed that Anjouan did have a monarch – a queen – regarded as the supreme head of all four Comoros.[212] One can equally deduce from the same sources that each island had a *de facto* ruler of its own, a ruler who held the Anjouanaise queen in esteem as a dynastic matriarch,[213] not necessarily as a military or administrative power to fear. In 1602 Moheli was ruled, for example, by an independent and imposing Muslim monarch who stunned visitors from Europe with a dazzling knowledge of navigation and charts from the Red Sea to the East Indies, with his first-hand acquaintance with Africa and Arabia, and – not least – with his command of the Portuguese language.[214] This extremely interesting Comorean died in 1613, just one day before the arrival of Christopher Newport who noted that only the royal death could have brought a temporary halt to the Mohelian, outrigger-riding war parties which often sailed to Anjouan and 'other' Comoro Islands.[215] Other English visitors found, a year later, that Grande Comore was divided among ten 'Lords'; that the Anjouanaise queen (the 'old Sultaness') had 'delegated' power on Moheli to her two sons, Amar-Adel, the *sultan*, and his brother, the vice-*sultan* and *sharīf* (the main sacerdotal figure), both of whom lived in the interior, near Fombony; and that Moheli's principal port was under Fombony's governor, a man of very considerable influence.[216] Also in 1614, the old *fani* of M'samudu proclaimed himself an independent *sultan* and also master of northern Anjouan as the venerable queen no longer controlled her island.[217] Martin Pring also came across a powerful *fani* in 1616 at Moheli.[218] By 1626 there were

212. Notably the Dutch in 1599 and 1601–2, and François–Martin de Vitré also in 1602, see A. Grandidier *et al.*, 1903–20, Vol. I, pp. 256, 272 and 317.

213. Several accounts refer to the *sultan*'s 'queens' who are at times spouses and at other times mothers. The queen-mother (of a *sultan*) seems to have been held in great esteem, see the account of John Saris for Moheli in 1611, A. Grandidier *et al.*, 1903–20, Vol. I, p. 497.

214. Reports from Admiral G. Spilberg's visit in 1602, translated from the Dutch in De Constantin, 1725, Vol. IV, pp. 29–30 and 42–60; A. Grandidier *et al.*, Vol. I, pp. 312–13.

215. A. Grandidier *et al.*, 1903–20, Vol. I, p. 490.

216. Accounts of Walter Peyton and Thomas Roe, 1614, in S. Purchas, 1613, *His Pilgrims*, British Library, London, Add. Mss, no. 6115, Vol. I, fos. 529 and 536ff; A. Grandidier *et al.*, 1903–20, Vol. II, pp. 83–9.

217. A. Gevrey, 1870, p. 185; A. Grandidier *et al.*, 1903–20, Vol. II, pp. 90ff. Both Gevrey and Grandidier state that *Magné-Fané* (*fani*) was the name of the rebel *sultan* of M'samudu, and both cite Pieter van den Broecke, an astute observer and officer in the Dutch fleet under General Reynst, who visited the Comoros in 1614. However, P. van den Broecke does not mention this name.

218. A. Grandidier *et al.*, 1903–20, Vol. II, p. 100. The name cited by M. Pring in *Fanno Mary O Fannadill*.

two contenders for the Mohelian Sultanate, a descendant of the *fani* (probably deceased by then) and an 'Arab'. Both owed their 'fortunes' and, apparently, most of their rivalry to their spouses, daughters of the 'last sultan'.[219]

With exceptions,[220] Comorean rulers sought good relations with the Europeans who came to their islands. It became customary for captains of European vessels to send more or less imposing swords and pistols to local rulers upon arrival.[221] In turn, the *sultan*s and their 'port' governors secured letters of recommendation from the captains upon departure. These documents were subsequently shown to incoming captains as proof of international friendship.[222] Nearly all of the 'English Shipping bound to Mocha, Persia and Surat', wrote Hamilton, paused at 'Johanna' (Anjouan) for 'Refreshments', leading to long-lasting Anglo-Anjouanaise amity on which the local *sultan*s would call from time to time. The Comorean traders had been for a long time, middlemen between Madagascar, Africa and Arabia but it does not follow (as can be read on occasion) that the four islands had nothing to export themselves. Wars within an island, such as the one reported on Grande Comore in 1620,[223] and frequent sea-raids from one island to another went beyond purely political tensions. Many were simply glorified *razzias* for slaves to be exported at considerable profit. This duality of purpose became more pronounced by the time M'samudu had built its great mosque in 1670 and, yet was still less acute than during the pirate times in the Western Indian Ocean (1680–1720), when Comorean *sultan*s used and were, in turn, abused by such major pirates as Mission and Caraccioli, when the sackings and destruction of Comorean towns became commonplace.[224] It was precisely between 1700 and 1720 that British naval squadrons, under Captain Cornwall and Commodore Littleton, abandoned the neutrality of their flag and gave

219. Thomas Herbert's account, A. Grandidier *et al.*, 1903–20, Vol. II, pp. 394–9.

220. For example, thirty-five sailors under the command of J. Lancaster were killed in an ambush on Grande Comore in 1591, an act which gave this island a bad reputation decades and even a century later; cf. A. Grandidier *et al.*, 1903–20, Vol. I, p. 161.

221. In 1608, when Alexander Sharpy sent some trinkets and two knives to the ruler at the landing site of Grande Comore, the gifts were 'rejected with disdain'; A. Grandidier *et al.*, 1903–20, Vol. I, p. 419.

222. For example, in 1620 General de Beaulieu was shown letters in English and Dutch dated respectively 16 August 1616 and 8 August 1618 as 'attestations'; cf. A. Grandidier *et al.*, 1903–20, Vol. II, p. 358. The practice of international letters of recommendation undoubtedly grew out of the local Swahili scribal culture since it is known that the heads of at least Mayotte communicated with the *sultan* at Anjouan via state letters. In 1599, for example, the Dutch were given a letter of recommendation for the queen at Anjouan by Mayotte's ruler; cf. A. Grandidier *et al.*, 1903–20, Vol. I, p. 256; in 1646, John Smart took 'letters' from the 'King of Mayotte' to Anjouan: Smart to Kynnaston, 26 June 1646, cf. A. Grandidier *et al.*, 1903–20, Vol. V, pp. 514–17.

223. A. Grandidier *et al.*, 1903–20, Vol. II, p. 365.

224. ibid., Vol. III, pp. 480–514.

active help to Anjouan and its *sultan* of the year.[225] This naval and military assistance reflected a desire to extend Anjouan's effective control over the other Comoros and pre-empt any local shelter for the pirates in return. The pirate supremacy had ended by 1720 but not the interventions of British arms on behalf of Anjouan.

In 1736, according to Saʿīd Aḥmad ʿAlī, Anjouan obtained a new monarch, Sultan Aḥmad, who believed – as did the early Hassanites – that all the Comoros should be under a supreme ruler. He lasted a long time, 'over 40 years', but his tenure was marked by a nearly successful dynastic coup in 1743, a full-scale political war with Mayotte some years later (ending in Anjouan's humiliating defeat) and, above all, by an internal revolt of major proportions. The original inhabitants of Anjouan (the Wamatsaha), led by a charismatic commoner named Tumpa (who claimed descent from a *fani*), rose in 1775 against the ruling Arab element demanding full equality and the 'right to marry Arab women'. Domoni fell with ease providing the rebels with enough fire-arms to lay siege to M'samudu itself. Fortunately for the Hassanites, they had on loan a platoon of British marines who found Tumpa with their first shots as he was riding on an elevated platform under a large red umbrella.[226] Tumpa's death ended a movement that could have had far-reaching consequences for Anjouan as well as for the other Comoros. Yet, as the eighteenth century drew to an end, the real problems were just beginning for the Comoro group. Outrigger fleets from Madagascar, manned by the Sakalava and Betsimisaraka, began to raid the four islands for slaves and caused lasting terror among the local inhabitants. The sea raids ended by about 1825, largely because of British interventions.[227] Moreover, upheavals caused by the Merina expansion in Madagascar resulted in at least one unexpected event. Mayotte became Malagasy-speaking, following the massive Sakalava flights from Iboina, and the island acquired Malagasy *sultans* (Ramanetaka, a kinsman of Radama I, and Andriantsoli, the last Sakalava–Iboina ruler).[228] Indeed, for the Comoros, being half-way between Africa and Madagascar was not at all easy.

225. ibid., Vol. V, pp. 53, 156 and 159. (The French Captain, Péron, gave aid in 1790 to Anjouan against Mayotte which would be turned over to France as a protectorate fifty-three years later.)

226. S. A. ʿAlī, 1927, pp. 12–4.

227. For the Malagasy sea raids see note 109 above; and the account of Austin Bissel, November 1798, in A. Grandidier *et al.*, 1903–20, Vol. V, pp. 415–16. (English text in A. Dalrymple, 1806, Vol. I, pp. 5–12); also M. Fontoynont and E. Raomandahy, 1937, pp. 15–21.

228. A brief account of Ramanetaka and Andriantsoli appears in A. Gevrey, 1870, pp. 217–25.

The Mascarene Islands: Réunion, Mauritius and Rodrigues[229]

In contrast to Madagascar and the Comoros, the three Mascarene Islands remained uninhabited until the arrival of Europeans in the Indian Ocean.[230] Their location east of Madagascar was instrumental in transforming Réunion (Bourbon) and Mauritius (Ile-de-France) into strategic maritime stations controlled by the large overseas trading companies. The two larger islands in the Mascarene group also grew into plantation economies which came to affect, at different times and with different intensity, not only eastern Madagascar but also eastern and south-eastern Africa and even coastal India. After 1638, the Dutch concentrated on Mauritius, exploiting its timber and developing a slave trade with Madagascar, but in 1710 they abandoned the island.[231] Réunion obtained its earliest settlers in 1646 and 1654 from Fort Dauphin, roughly an equal number of French and Malagasy rebels against the initial French East India Company which, nonetheless, made Bourbon into its preserve from 1664 until 1719.[232] The French had colonized Mauritius from Réunion by 1721 and both islands were under their second East India Company until 1767, when the Mascarenes were turned over to the royal administration.[233] Having learned of the French Revolution in 1790, the planters of Réunion and Mauritius began to assert a form of local nationalism which stood against such metropolitan measures as the abolition of slavery in 1794 and the Convention's attempt to send its agents, two of whom were expelled in 1796. The Napoleonic Wars proved adverse to the French Mascarenes. Mauritius passed to British control for good and there was a temporary halt in the supply of slaves. Beyond the changing political aspects, however, Réunion and Mauritius were about to enter the period of their most pronounced economic successes.

Around 1710, Réunion and Mauritius together had some 2000 inhabitants. A third were slaves. By mid-century the population had increased by 300 per cent but more than two-thirds of it now consisted of servile

229. Rodrigues, a volcanic rock of some sixty square miles located several hundred nautical miles from both Réunion and Mauritius, is not included here. For this island see J. F. Dupon, 1969, and A. J. Bertuchi, 1923. The three islands obtained their present collective name in the 1820s and A. Toussaint, 1972, is the standard work on the subject. Réunion was formerly named Bourbon, and the French re-named Mauritius as Ile-de-France. Current names are retained.

230. This central fact also argues against direct population movements from Indonesia to Madagascar across the Pacific, movements which should otherwise have given the Mascarenes their *tompon-tany* as well.

231. For the Dutch at Mauritius see A. Pitot, 1905.

232. See Father J. Barassin, 1953.

233. For an excellent summary of the post-1719 periods see A. Toussaint, 1972, pp. 38–106 (Company and royal administrations). Among the longer accounts, see A. Pitot, 1899; C. Grant, 1801; and A. Lougnon, 1956 and 1958.

labour. By the end of the 1700s the two islands had 120 000 inhabitants including some 94 000 slaves.[234] Already, early in the eighteenth century, there were five visible groupings in the local society – whites of the first-settler families; white creoles; *mulatto* creoles; resident white foreigners (including many English ex-pirates and some Dutch refugees from their own East India Company); and slaves who were further sub-divided into black creoles and those not born in the islands.[235] There were few emancipated slaves before 1797 – for example, in 1788, there were only 950 on Réunion out of 45 800 inhabitants and on Mauritius only 2456 out of a total of 42 828 inhabitants in the same year.[236] An important change nonetheless occurred within the local slave population as the Mascarene buyers turned gradually away from Madagascar and toward Africa and India in search of new labourers. At least one cause of this shift was the belief that the Malagasy were especially prone to form fugitive-slave colonies. 'Slaves from Madagascar', according to a 1758 report, 'have the greatest propensity to escape. Many among them, out of love for liberty, fled into the mountains, amid inaccessible forests, and came in groups to attack the plantations on which they had been slaves'.[237] In fact, *marronnage* in Réunion and Mauritius was, like everywhere else, a response to slavery made possible by the environment and it lasted as a chronic problem until far more recent times, when almost no Malagasy were involved.

Although sugar cane had been grown on Mauritius since 1639 its first sugar-mill only came into being during the administration of Mahé de Labourdonnais (1735–46), who also re-organized the Mascarenes into a base against the British in India.[238] But, Mauritius did not really export sugar before the advent of royal French government which discarded the restricted-trade policies of the French East India Company and opened the islands to all French nationals at the end of the 1760s.[239] Coffee, introduced to Réunion in 1715 to become its main crop, attained its last bumper harvests in the early 1740s. It was in such a state of decline by 1767 (as a result of Antilles competition) that Réunion's planters had to diversify into spices.[240] During the next three decades, the Mascarene

234. A. Toussaint, 1972, statistical tables, pp. 335–8.
235. Based on the 1714 report: cf. Father J. Barassin, 1953, p. 309, and A. Toussaint, 1972, p. 32. Citing a 1763 report by a British naval officer, Grant held that early settlers had children almost exclusively with Malagasy women; that there was not one creole in fifty who did not reflect this union; and that local creoles had, roughly, the same privileges as petty nobility in France: cf. C. Grant, 1801, pp. 163–71, and A. Grandidier *et al.*, 1903–20, Vol. V, p. 303.
236. A. Toussaint, 1972, statistical tables, pp. 335–8.
237. C. Grant, 1801, pp. 75–8, and A. Grandidier *et al.*, 1903–20, Vol. V, pp. 316–17.
238. On Mahé de Labourdonnais, undoubtedly the most innovative figure, see his own *Mémoire des Iles de France et de Bourbon*, edited and annotated in 1937 by A. Lougnon and A. Toussaint. On the sugar industry, see A. North-Coombes, 1937.
239. A. Toussaint, 1967, p. 94.
240. A. Toussaint, 1971, pp. 35–6.

Islands became 'the focal point of a real *"route des Iles"*' as 'commercial interest shifted from the Atlantic to the Indian Ocean'.[241] Mauritius, which used to be visited by some thirty ships a year during the Company days, saw a tenfold increase in incoming vessels by 1803, many of them belonging to foreign merchants, especially from the United States after the North American War of Independence. It could be said that, around 1800, the privileged minorities in the Mascarene Islands had a standard of living equal to or superior to those of all other colonial outposts.

241. A. Toussaint, 1967, p. 94.

The historical development of African societies, 1500–1800: conclusion

B. A. OGOT

Various historical labels have been applied to the period 1500 to 1800 in African history. In many history books the period is referred to as 'the era of the slave trade'. Such works tend to over-emphasize the importance of the slave trade as a factor in African history; they overlook the fact that, in West and Central Africa, 'the slave-trade era' extended to about 1850 and, in East Africa, the nineteenth century was the period of the slave trade, if we exclude the earlier slave trade to the Muslim world. The label also ignores the fact that some parts of Africa, for instance South Africa, were hardly affected by the trade at any time. Other historians, especially the neo-marxists, identify the gradual integration of Africa into the world capitalist economy dominated by Europe as the main feature of the period. More emphasis is therefore placed by such historians on Africa's external relations than on internal developments. The African peoples are portrayed as hapless victims of world forces which they can neither comprehend nor control. Africa begins to be marginalized and racist ideas about the continent and its peoples become intensified and consolidated. Yet other historians single out population mobility and the final settlement of the continent as the distinguishing characteristic of the period. They fail to see that, with the exception of a few cases, there were hardly any mass migrations in Africa after 1500. Still other writers would wish to discuss the history of the three centuries in terms of a series of ecological catastrophes. They regard droughts and famines as the chief determining factors during this period.

Each of these labels has some element of truth, but none of them can adequately describe the complexity and dynamism of these three centuries of African history. In this final chapter, we shall attempt to characterize the historical development of African societies during this period, basing our discussion largely on the various chapters in this volume.

Perhaps it might be appropriate to begin with the fundamental question of population mobility. It was important for this period of African history but, as Vansina warns in Chapter 3, 'no more characteristic of the period 1500 to 1800 than any other'.[1] Most of Africa was already colonized by 1500 and what oral traditions refer to as migrations in such areas were, in

1. Ch. 3, p. 46.

effect, population expansion and drift. Only north-east Africa, covering modern Somalia, southern Ethiopia, southern Sudan, northern Kenya and northern Uganda, experienced mass movements of population during this period. The peoples involved were the Oromo, the Somali, the Luo, the Karamojong, the Kalenjin, the Turkana and the Maasai. These movements, according to Vansina, were 'in effect the story of the colonization of marginal lands ... All other major areas had been occupied and settled'.[2]

What is of greater significance than the usual concern with migration is the fact that the period 1500 to 1800 is crucial for social formations on the continent. Most of the inhabitants of the different regions of Africa coalesced during these three centuries into the wider social, economic, religious, cultural and political aggregates that make up the African peoples today.

As African societies evolved into distinct ethnic groups with their own peculiar linguistic and cultural characteristics, much of Africa was being transformed because of changes in Africa's external relations. In 1500 most African societies were relatively independent of the rest of the world, their external links being tenuous. But by 1800 much of Africa had become integrated into the circuits of the world market which securely linked it to Europe, America and Asia. The process of integration was facilitated by the establishment of new communities on the continent such as the Dutch settlers in southern Africa, the Portuguese in Angola and on the east coast and the Ottomans in Egypt and the Maghrib. Many African societies gradually changed their means of living, their location or both. Soon relationships radically different from any before grew up within and between societies. These new relations were characterized by dominance and dependence both internally and in a world system in which Europe became dominant.

Pathe Diagne has identified the main new economic structures that developed during this period as the caste system of production which developed in Western Sudan, the Niger–Chad region and the Sahara; the predatory economy which became widespread in the areas bordering the Mediterranean, the Nile, and the Indian Ocean; and the entrepôt or trading-post economy which characterized the area bordering the Atlantic Ocean.[3]

The predatory economy, for example, was the outcome of Spanish and Portuguese expansionism and depended mainly on piracy and tributes and duties rather than on trade and industry, as was the case before 1500. The Mediterranean and Indian Ocean sub-systems, for example, were completely disrupted by the predatory economy. It pauperized the country-side which was later further disrupted by the slave trade. A military aristocracy that relied on piracy and raiding using the services of freemen and slaves emerged. This exploitative and oppressive system provoked

2. Ch. 3, pp. 68–9.
3. See ch. 2.

several peasant revolts, especially in Western Sudan, the Niger–Chad region, Egypt, the Sahara, the Maghrib, Ethiopia and Lower Zambezia.

Like the predatory economy, the entrepôt economy concerned itself little with creative business. The new maritime entrepôt towns were fortresses and scenes of violence and spoliation, rather than commercial or industrial centres. On the Guinea and equatorial coasts, in the Kongo, Angola and Senegambia, the Portuguese looted more than they bought. From 1650 to 1800, the principal feature of the entrepôt economy was the Atlantic slave trade.

The societies affected by the entrepôt economy were gradually transformed in the seventeenth and eighteenth centuries. This was a complex process which involved major reorganizations. The main feature of the reorganizations, particularly in West-Central Africa, was that the trading networks, not the states, became the dominant factor. In most places on the coast, there was a general breakdown of centres of authority and a splintering of political power. As M'Bokolo has shown,

> Organization of trade, on the African side, was not a state monopoly: competition benefited a few individuals, princes, commoners and even some ex-slaves who formed a new aristocracy jealous of its privileges and keen to secure political power ... At Loango it was the new men – brokers, traders, caravan leaders and other middlemen – who came out best as they had the means to purchase land from the king and build up an entourage of many free or servile dependants. At the end of the eighteenth century there is mention of commoners with 700 dependants who were making war or cultivating land on their own account.[4]

In other words, as the states declined so did the old ruling classes, which a merchant class arose to replace or complement. The Portuguese penetration of Southern Zambezia, for instance, eroded the power of the indigenous ruling class and facilitated direct forms of peasant exploitation by Portuguese mercantile capital. 'The convergence of regional trade networks with long-distance trade', writes Bhila, 'gave rise to an African merchant class called *vashambadzi* ... [They acted] as middle-men between the foreign traders and the African peasant producers.'[5]

Similar developments produced the 'Mestizos and Creoles' of the Rivers Casamance, Guinea and Sierra Leone. The Afro-Portuguese and the Anglo-Africans of Sierra Leone were merchant groups which acted as middle-men between European ships and the African societies of the interior. They were mostly agents in the service of European mercantile capitalism and they enriched themselves considerably.

Even in the case of the Fundj and Fūr sultanates, where the *sultan*s appeared to patronize and protect the long-distance trade linking them

4. See ch. 18, p. 532.
5. See ch. 22, p. 682.

with Egypt and the Red Sea, the bulk of the trade was in the hands of the Sudanese *djallāba* (traders) who acted as the middle-men and financiers of the long-distance trade.

Thus from relative isolation in 1500, the various peoples of Africa gradually became integrated into the world economy. In most cases, this integration was accompanied by sharp social and political changes.

Despite the collapse of large states in Western Sudan and north-east Africa at the beginning of our period, 'the percentage of areas controlled by states on the continent', writes Vansina, 'was higher by 1800 than it had been by 1500'.[6] But it was not only the area covered by states that had increased during the three centuries: the period also witnessed many examples of political consolidation through the expansion and centralization of political institutions. Thus the two processes of state-building and centralization of political authority characterize this period.

In north-east Africa, for example, although the sixteenth and seventeenth centuries witnessed the collapse of the Christian Ethiopian empire and anarchy continued intermittently until 1855, when Theodore II inaugurated the age of the great emperors, there was expansion of the Christian Ethiopian empire southwards which stimulated the growth of new states such as Boša, Kaffa, Šekko, Wolayta and Dauro.

In the case of Madagascar, we have the opposite process of centralization. By the beginning of the seventeenth century, Madagascar still consisted mainly of small and self-contained chiefdoms. But by the end of that century, western Madagascar under a Sakalava empire, and several kingdoms, emerged among the highlanders and among the south-eastern, south-western and southern peoples. In the eighteenth century, the Sakalava empire reached its apogee and the eastern littoral became politically united for the first time into the Betsimisaraka confederation. By 1800, these two states were in decline and the state of Imerina, formerly weak and disunited, was on the ascendancy.

A similar process of consolidation and centralization occurred in the Lower Guinea coast. According to a 1629 map, there were thirty-eight states and kingdoms in the region, founded by the Ga and Akan peoples. Between 1670 and 1750, a major political revolution took place in the forest and coastal regions of Lower Guinea. From the thirty-eight states of the 1629 map had emerged the three large empires of Aowin, Denkyira and Akwamu which by 1750 had merged into the single empire of Asante.

Other examples of states that expanded and evolved centralized political systems during this period are Buganda, Rwanda and Maravi.

A more common political phenomenon during the three centuries was for a declining or collapsed state to be succeeded by several localized states or by economic systems. In Central Africa, for example, larger and larger states were formed and by the sixteenth century the Kongo, the Tio, Loango and Ndongo (future Angola) kingdoms were in existence, with the

6. Ch. 3, p. 72.

Kongo kingdom being the most dominant and centralized. But from 1665 the states began to decline and territories were reorganized on a larger scale on the basis of economic imperatives dictated by the slave trade.

In the Upper Guinea coast, successor states to the empires of Songhay and Mali arose in the seventeenth and eighteenth centuries. The Grand Foul empire arose in the seventeenth century on the ruins of Songhay, but gave way to the empire of Kaarta during the second half of the eighteenth century. Along the Atlantic, the countries that had resulted from the dismemberment of Mali were unified by Kaabu (Gabu) in the seventeenth and eighteenth centuries and then by Futa Jallon in the eighteenth and nineteenth centuries. In the centre, the recovery took place at the beginning of the eighteenth century under the aegis of the Bambara of Segu and in the south, the Dyula (Juula) organized the empire of Kong in the eighteenth century.

A similar process can be witnessed in Southern Zambezia. The decline of the Great Zimbabwe gave rise first to the Torwa state and later and more importantly to the Mutapa empire at the beginning of the sixteenth century. Fragmentation and decline of the Mutapa state began in 1629. The empire fell into decay and disorder during the eighteenth century, although the Mutapa polity did not finally disappear until 1917.

In most of the new states that emerged, original systems of government and administration were developed. Dahomey, for instance, represented a new idea of the state. It had been created by migrants from Allada in about 1625 who established their rule over diverse groups. The traditional view had regarded the state as a larger version of the family. The new idea developed in Dahomey was that of a strong centralized state ruled by an absolute king demanding unreserved loyalty from all citizens. The novel ideas of the state and systems of government developed in different regions of Africa, especially in the seventeenth and eighteenth centuries, call for further study.

There also emerged in most of these states various social classes: aristocrats, military groups, commoners and slaves. For example, the Kanuri society in Borno was highly stratified. It was broadly divided into two classes, the *kontuowa* (ruling class or nobility) and the *talia* (commoners) and both these had several divisions. Differences of speech, dress, household furniture, architecture and residence distinguished the classes and their divisions. In Hausaland, as the aristocrats and traders grew rich, the distinction shifted to an economic level with the *attajirai* (the wealthy) and the *talakawa* (the poor).

The aristocracy – administrative and military – grew rich by various methods of exploitation. It soon developed an ideology of oppression. In Egypt, for instance, as the Ottoman empire declined, internal struggles between different social strata developed: not for political independence, but for the control of the economy and the country and its political institutions. The critical state of the economy was a reflection of the oppressive politics whereby the majority of the people was controlled and exploited by a small élite made up of Mamluk *beys* and their retinues. This oppressive situation led to the rise of popular literature in Arabic, especially poetry and satire, dealing with the exploitation of the peasants.

As we have already emphasized when discussing the results of a predatory economy, there were several peasant revolts against these oppressive regimes in west, north, east, central and southern Africa. There is an urgent need for a thorough study of these peasant uprisings in the seventeenth and eighteenth centuries. To begin with, we need a typology of these peasant resistance movements. Secondly, the lower classes in many areas were not a homogenous group: some were not even peasants. But generally speaking, it can be stated that the lower classes, whoever they were, fought against a deterioration of their position, at least in order to maintain the *status quo*.

The slave trade

The usual questions raised in connection with this subject, such as slave censuses or the effects of the slave trade on African societies, have been discussed in Chapter 4 and in the relevant sections of most chapters in this volume. It is therefore unnecessary to repeat such discussions in this concluding chapter. Rather I wish to draw attention to a few basic questions regarding the slave trade which, I feel, African historians should be raising.

First, to what extent should the slave trade be emphasized in African history? In other words, as African historians, what is our interest in the slave trade? All races have been enslaved in the past: even the word itself is derived from 'slavs', who are East Europeans. But all other groups have found a way of removing it from their consciousness. The Jews, for example, were once slaves, but they now interpret their slavery as a special and unique condition assigned to them by God. The Africans are keen to over-emphasize the importance of slavery in their history to such an extent that the term 'slave' is almost being equated with 'African'. As D. B. Davis has brought out clearly in his *The Problem of Slavery in Western Culture* and *Slavery and Human Progress*, slavery is a major phenomenon in the ideology of the modern Western world which we must attempt to understand.[7] It inspires much of the negative attitude towards Africa and the Africans.

In Chapter 4, Inikori attempts to assign quantitative weight to the rôle of black slavery in the economic progress of the Western world. This is another fundamental question which must be faced and dealt with exhaustively. Marx and Engels argued that though slavery is and always was immoral, it has nevertheless been essential for economic and therefore social progress. Without slavery, they argued, there would have been no Greek or Roman civilization. Inikori argues that African slavery was crucial

7. D. B. Davis, 1966 and 1975; 1984.

for the development of the Atlantic-oriented geo-political and economic system and the industrialization of Western Europe. On the other hand, Fernand Braudel has presented in his three-volume *Civilization and Capitalism* a different picture of the rise of European capitalism to world power, starting with the unchanging subsistence economy of the peasantry, through the market place and, finally, the story of how a few bankers and merchants, by monopolizing trade and maximizing profit, helped create a series of world economies centred in Europe and so extended the growing power of European capitalism. He attributes the growth of European capitalism to the multi-national combines such as the House of Fugger of sixteenth-century Augsburg and the East India Company of the seventeenth and eighteenth centuries.[8] The role of the African slavery in this debate needs a radical reassessment.

J. E. Harris has raised in Chapter 5 one other important question related to chattel slavery. From all the available evidence, it is clear that the process of dehumanizing the African intensified during 1500 to 1800, as a result of the increase in chattel slavery from 1619.

The intercontinental slave trade, more than anything else, established a world black presence. It led to a major African diaspora, especially in the Americas and the Caribbean. According to Harris

> It was the nature of this trade and its consequences which, especially in the Americas and the Caribbean, caused Africans to organize freedom struggles which over the years established the common concern for the redemption of Africa and the liberation of blacks throughout the world ... This process continued, despite colonial rule, and may indeed be the greatest historical consequence of the African diaspora.[9]

Indeed, this was the foundation of the Pan-African Movement of the nineteenth and twentieth centuries.

Introduction of new food crops

The introduction of new crops from the Americas has been seen by many writers as a positive aspect of the Atlantic trade system. Some have argued that the introduction of the new crops – which inevitably led to changes in diet – improved the health of the Africans and, consequently, led to population increase. As a standard textbook on African history has put it:

> New crops from the Americas made it possible for tropical Africa, and especially the forest regions, to sustain populations several times larger than those of the past. Maize, peanuts, and manioc – to name

8. F. Braudel, 1984. Also, see I. Wallerstein, 1976.
9. Ch. 5, p. 136.

only three – permanently altered the relations of Africans to their environment.[10]

But as M'Bokolo has cautioned, the effects of these agricultural changes on the African population are difficult to interpret. 'Did they, as has often been stressed, contribute through a more secure and more diversified food supply, to a greater physical resistance among the populations and a higher rate of population growth?' He finds no evidence for these claims. On the contrary, he points out, cassava has limited nutritional value and the people who relied on it most, such as the Tio and the Mbosi, suffered from serious malnutrition.[11]

Population trends during the seventeenth and eighteenth centuries are difficult to discern because new diseases such as smallpox that were to become recurrent scourges were introduced into Africa at the same time. It was also during this period that the Atlantic slave trade reached its peak.

What is certain, however, is that the new crops from the Americas and Asia introduced by Europeans to various African regions between 1500 and 1800 diversified the agricultural economy of the continent. These included maize, cassava (manioc), groundnuts, various types of yam, sweet potatoes, citrus fruits, tomatoes, onions and tobacco. Many African food crops, such as bananas, sorghum, millet and yams, were gradually superseded during this period by cassava and maize. Thus the present-day heavy reliance by Africans on maize and cassava as the main staple diet date back to this period.

Socially, according to M'Bokolo, this agricultural revolution contributed, along with trade, to the establishment of a new division of labour. He contends that men gradually abandoned agricultural tasks such as land clearing, cultivation and preparation of crops to the women and slaves, preferring instead to devote themselves to trade which was more lucrative. The development of domestic slavery and other forms of dependence was therefore a direct consequence of these agricultural changes.[12]

Ecological catastrophies

Attempts have been made to provide a periodization of African history primarily based upon climatic conditions and to argue that there is a meaningful correlation between severe periods of aridity and major historical events. Our period in particular is seen as drought-prone.[13]

Such analyses tend to give the physical environment such importance that Africans are reduced to hopeless victims of nature. There is also the danger of stressing the drought years at the expense of the normal and

10. P. D. Curtin, S. Feierman, L. Thompson and J. Vansina, 1978, p. 214.
11. Ch. 18, p. 531.
12. See ch. 18.
13. J. B. Webster, 1979a, 1980; S. E. Nicholson, 1978, 1979; J. C. Miller, 1982; D. J. Schove, 1973; J. Thornton, 1981a. Also, see ch. 26.

above-average years. This has led some historians to over-generalize about famines in pre-colonial Africa.[14] Nowhere do such historians discuss how Africans creatively responded to the droughts. How, for example, did droughts affect and contribute to changes in systems of production and distribution, the ennoblement of food crops and methods of food preservation?

The question of droughts and famines also relates to the larger issue of the efficiency of African agriculture in the pre-colonial period. As Vansina has pointed out, the 1500–1800 period, for example, witnessed the emergence of intensive technologies for land use which, in turn, allowed higher densities of population.

> The lower Casamance, Igbo country, the Cameroon grasslands with their 'domesticated' vegetation, the mountains in the Great Lakes area along the western rift with their systems of irrigation and/or intensive cultivation of bananas, small spots such as the Kukuya plateau with its novel forms of fertilization or the valley of the Upper Zambezi where floods were used, all are still exceptions in western and central Africa. In northern Africa, including Egypt, with the largest oasis in the world, intensive oasis agriculture was millennia old by this time.[15]

In short, although the practice of intensive agriculture in most parts of Africa was not as old as it was in Northern Africa, small pockets of intensive farming emerged, especially in Western and Central Africa. In such areas, advanced agricultural methods, such as terracing, crop rotation, green manuring, mixed farming and regulated swamp farming, were used. These topics deserve more attention from historians than the usual generalizations about famine and drought in Africa.

Christianity and Islam

Christianity declined in Africa during the period 1500 to 1800, especially in Ethiopia, on the east coast and, to a lesser degree, in the Kongo. Islam, on the other hand, gained momentum in West Africa, Sudan, Ethiopia and on the east coast.

On the Lower Guinea coast, for example, Christianity was introduced into the region by the Dutch and the British. Initially, they established elementary schools in their castles at Cape Coast, El Mina and Accra. Later, in the 1750s, missionaries were sent to Cape Coast by the Society for the Propagation of the Gospel. Also, some of the new converts, especially the children of *mulattos* and traditional rulers, were sent abroad for further education, and many returned home as teachers and missionaries. Thus the foundation of the Christian revolution that was to take place in West Africa in the nineteenth century was being laid during this period.

14. See ch. 22.
15. Ch. 3, pp. 71–2.

In the Kongo, Christianity was introduced during Afonso I's reign (1506–43). Under the direction of his son Henrique, who was consecrated bishop in Rome, he made the Catholic Church the state religion. But Christian fervour declined in the Kongo until 1645 when a large number of Italian Capuchin missionaries arrived. About 400 missionaries came to the Kongo and later Angola during the seventeenth century, to spread the gospel, especially in the rural areas. As Vansina has explained, Christianity was first introduced into the Kongo by the Portuguese and was confined largely to the urban nobility, with the ecclesiastical structure remaining chiefly Portuguese. But from 1645 to 1700, the Italian missionaries were engaged in an intense campaign to convert as many people as possible, particularly in the rural areas.[16]

Both Christianity and Islam, during this period, were syncretic. Christianity in the Kongo, for example, co-existed with traditional religion. Indeed, they had so much influence on one another that, as Vansina concludes,

> From the sixteenth century onwards there can be said to have been a single religion in which, at least among the nobles, features of Christianity and features of the old religion had merged. The main spread of this religion took place in the seventeenth century ... This new religion was the source of Haitian voodoo.[17]

Attempts to organize independent churches also date back to this period. In the Kongo, attempts to establish an indigenous church started in the 1630s and reached a peak in 1704 when Dona Beatrice Kimpa Vita began to preach a reformed Christianity called *Antonianism* which rejected the missionaries and the whites. Henceforth, indigenous Catholicism prevailed in the Kongo.

Turning now to Islam, it is evident that the expansion of the Islamic frontier in Africa constitutes one of the important themes of the period 1500 to 1800. In the Lower Guinea coast, for example, the Mande and Hausa traders introduced Islam. It spread along the northern trade routes reaching Asante and Baule in the 1750s. By 1800 Kumasi had a thriving Muslim quarter with a Ḳur'ānic school. In the Upper Guinea coast, the Fulbe and the Mande were responsible for the expansion of Islam. They formed a Fulbe–Malinke religious alliance, not only to convert the peoples of the region but also to subjugate them. Thus the spread of Islam was associated with political domination in many regions of Africa. This comes out clearly in the Senegambia where the opposition between the Muslim theocracies against the *ceddo* (warlord) regimes forms the background to the history of the region. In the Sudan, Islamization of northern Sudan created an ideological frontier between northern and southern Sudan which is still strong. The period saw the establishment and expansion of two

16. See ch. 19.
17. Ch. 19, p. 573.

Muslim savannah states – the Fundj and Fūr sultanates. In the seventeenth and eighteenth centuries Islam continued to spread in the Bambara, Mossi, Kong and Gwirika kingdoms, through traders, prayer-leaders and even violence. The same process of Islamic expansion was witnessed in Hausaland and in Borno.

Apart from the simple geographical spread of Islam in Africa at this time, Muslim fundamentalism was an important factor in many areas. There was the Nāṣir al-Dīn movement, for example, which started in Mauritania and was directed southwards. Its motives were partly economic (to control the trade in grains and slaves) and partly religious (to purify and reform Islam by replacing arbitrary rule with Muslim theocracy). The same reformist tendency is discernible among the Muslims in Hausaland, especially during the eighteenth century. A community of Muslim scholars, with similar political, economic and religious backgrounds developed in various centres and became critical of the established order represented by the aristocrats. The most outstanding of these scholars was Malam Djibrīl dan 'Umaru who advocated Islamic reforms. Both 'Uthmān and 'Abdullāhī dan Fodio were his disciples. As the rule of the aristocrats became more oppressive, the scholars openly attacked the established order. This is the background to the *djihād* of the nineteenth century.

As a result of the oppression of the African peasantry by the rural and urban élites, especially in Western Sudan, the Niger–Chad region, Egypt, the Sahara, the Maghrib, Ethiopia and Kongo, the Muslim leaders and the Christian messianic movements found it easy to enlist the mass support of the peasantry. Men of religion promised equality and an end to injustice. They condemned the traditional aristocracies and the Europeans as the disruptive factors and causes of social injustice.

Finally, it should be noted that the Africans looked at Islam, as they viewed Christianity, syncretistically. They accepted Islam while at the same time remaining faithful to their traditional religion. As Izard and Ki-Zerbo point out, these syncretisms later developed with Christianity in Africa and in Afro-American worship in Brazil, Haiti and Cuba. Thus they conclude, for example, that 'Islam presented itself to the Bambara with institutions such as polygamy, divorce, repudiation and slavery that did not systematically challenge their own.'[18]

18. Ch. 12, p. 364.

Members of the International Scientific Committee for the Drafting of a General History of Africa

The dates cited below refer to dates of membership.

Professor J. F. A. Ajayi
(Nigeria), from 1971
Editor Volume VI

Professor F. A. Albuquerque Mourao
(Brazil), from 1975

Professor D. Birmingham
(UK), from 1985

Professor A. A. Boahen
(Ghana), from 1971
Editor Volume VII

The late H. E. Boubou Hama
(Niger), 1971–8 (resigned in 1978;
deceased 1982)

Dr (Mrs) Mutumba M. Bull
(Zambia), from 1971

Professor D. Chanaiwa
(Zimbabwe), from 1975

Professor P. D. Curtin
(USA), from 1975

Professor J. Devisse
(France), from 1971

Professor M. Difuila
(Angola), from 1978

The late Professor Cheikh Anta Diop
(Senegal), 1971–86; deceased 1986

Professor H. Djait
(Tunisia), from 1975

Professor J. D. Fage
(UK), 1971–81 (resigned)

H. E. M. El Fasi
(Morocco), from 1971
Editor Volume III

The late Professor J. L. Franco
(Cuba), from 1971; deceased 1989

The late Mr M. H. I. Galaal
(Somalia), 1971–81; deceased 1981

Professor Dr V. I. Grottanelli
(Italy), from 1971

Professor E. Haberland
(Germany), from 1971

Dr Aklilu Habte
(Ethiopia), from 1971

H. E. A. Hampaté Bâ
(Mali), 1971–8 (resigned in 1978; deceased
1991)

Dr I. S. El-Hareir
(Libya), from 1978

Dr I. Hrbek
(Czechoslovakia), from 1971
Assistant Editor Volume III

Dr (Mrs) A. Jones
(Liberia), from 1971

The late Abbé Alexis Kagame
(Rwanda), 1971–81; deceased 1981

Professor I. N. Kimambo
(Tanzania), from 1971

Professor J. Ki-Zerbo
(Burkina Faso), from 1971
Editor Volume I

Mr D. Laya
(Niger), from 1979

Dr A. Letnev
(USSR), from 1971

Dr G. Mokhtar
(Egypt), from 1971
Editor Volume II

Professor P. Mutibwa
(Uganda), from 1975

Professor D. T. Niane
(Senegal), from 1971
Editor Volume IV

Professor L. D. Ngcongco
(Botswana), from 1971

Professor T. Obenga
(People's Republic of the Congo),
from 1975

Professor B. A. Ogot
(Kenya), from 1971
Editor Volume V

Professor C. Ravoajanahary
(Madagascar), from 1971

The late Professor W. Rodney
(Guyana), 1979–80; deceased 1980

The late Professor M. Shibeika
(Sudan), 1971–80; deceased 1980

Professor Y. A. Talib
(Singapore), from 1975

The late Professor A. Teixeira da Mota
(Portugal), 1978–82; deceased 1982

Mgr T. Tshibangu
(Zaïre), from 1971

Professor J. Vansina
(Belgium), from 1971

The late Rt Hon. Dr E. Williams
(Trinidad and Tobago), 1976–8;
resigned 1978; deceased 1980

Professor A. A. Mazrui
(Kenya)
Editor Volume VIII, not a
member of the Committee

Professor C. Wondji
(Ivory Coast)
Assistant Editor Volume VIII, not
a member of the Committee

*Secretariat of the International
Scientific Committee*
A. Gatera, Division of Cultural Identities
and Intercultural Relations
1, rue Miollis, 75015 Paris

Biographies of authors

CHAPTER 9   M. H. Chérif (Tunisia): specialist in North-African social and political history; author of several articles on North-African history; University Professor and Dean, Faculté des sciences humaines et sociales, Tunis.

CHAPTER 10   B. Barry (Senegal): Doctor in History; author of numerous works on Waalo, Senegambia and Futa Jallon; former Secretary-General of the Association des historiens africains; now teacher at the Faculty of Arts, Université Cheikh Anta Diop, Dakar.

CHAPTER 11   M. Abitbol (Israel): specialist in Nigerian Sudan; author of works on the history of the Sudan; Senior researcher at the Hebrew University of Jerusalem.

CHAPTER 12   M. Izard (France): specialist in the pre-colonial history of the Mossi kingdoms (Burkina Faso); anthropologist and historian; author of numerous publications and articles, especially on the ancient kingdom of Yatenga; Senior Researcher at the Centre national de la recherche scientifique (Laboratory of Social Anthropology), Paris.

J. Ki-Zerbo (Burkina Faso): specialist in the methodology of African history; author of a number of works dealing with Black Africa and its history; Professor of History, University of Dakar.

CHAPTER 13   C. Wondji (Côte d'Ivoire): specialist in the modern and contemporary history of Africa; author of numerous works on African cultures and the history of Côte d'Ivoire; formerly Head of the Department of History, Faculté des lettres de l'Université nationale de Côte d'Ivoire (Abidjan) and Deputy Director of the Institut d'art et d'archéologie, University of Abidjan; at present Counsellor at the Permanent Delegation of Côte d'Ivoire at UNESCO, Paris.

CHAPTER 14   A. A. Boahen (Ghana): specialist in West African history; author of numerous publications and articles on African history; former Professor and Head of the Department of History, and now Emeritus Professor, University of Ghana.

CHAPTER 15   E. J. Alagoa (Nigeria): specialist in African history and historiography; author of various studies of the Ijo, the techniques and methodology of oral tradition and archaeology; Professor of History, University of Port Harcourt.

CHAPTER 16   D. Laya (Niger): specialist in West African cultures; sociologist; author of works on the subject; Director of the Centre d'études linguistiques et historiques par tradition orale (CELHTO), Niamey.

CHAPTER 17   B. Barkindo (Nigeria): specialist in State formation and inter-state relations in the Chad basin; author of numerous works on the subject; Reader in History, Bayero University, Kano.

CHAPTER 18   E. M'Bokolo (Zaire): specialist in the history of Black Africa; author of numerous works on the subject; Senior Researcher at the Ecole des hautes études en Sciences sociales (EHESS); lecturer at the Institut d'études politiques (IEP), Paris; producer at Radio France Internationale.

CHAPTER 19   J. Vansina.

T. Obenga (People's Republic of Congo): specialist in African languages; author of a number of articles on African history and of works on Africa in the ancient world; formerly Professor at the Faculty of Letters of Marien N'Gouabi University, Brazzaville; at present Director-General of the Centre international des civilisations bantu (CICIBA), Libreville.

CHAPTER 20   Ndaywel è Nziem (Zaire): specialist in the history of Central Africa; author of works on the subject; teaches History at the University of Kinshasa and at the Institut pédagogique national; Director of the Bibliothèque nationale du Zaire.

CHAPTER 21   K. M. Phiri (Malawi): specialist in the history of Malawi, and of Central and Southern Africa; formerly lecturer and senior lecturer in History, University of Malawi; at present Associate Professor in History, University of Malawi.

O. J. M. Kalinga (Malawi): specialist in the history of the Lake Malawi region; author of works on the subject; Professor of History, National University of Lesotho.

H. H. K. Bhila (Zimbabwe): specialist in the history of South-Eastern Africa; author of works on Southern Africa; former Chairman of the Department of History, University of Zimbabwe; at present Deputy Secretary to Parliament of Zimbabwe.

CHAPTER 22   H. H. K. Bhila.

CHAPTER 23   D. Denoon (UK): specialist in Southern and East Africa; author of works on the subject; formerly visiting lecturer at the University of Ibadan; currently Professor at the Australian National University, Canberra.

CHAPTER 24   E. Haberland (Germany): specialist in pre-colonial Ethiopia and West Africa; author of works on Ethiopia; Director of the Frobenius Institute, Frankfurt; Professor of the Chair of Ethnology and African history, University of Frankfurt; Director, Centre of African Studies in Frankfurt.

CHAPTER 25   A. I. Salim (Kenya): specialist in East African history; author of many articles on the Swahili-speaking peoples; Professor and currently Chairman, Department of History, University of Nairobi.

CHAPTER 26   J. B. Webster (Canada): specialist in pre-colonial history, with special attention to climate; author of works on Acholi and Iteso history as well as *Chronology, Migration and Drought in Interlacustrine Africa*; formerly Professor and Head of History at Makerere and the University of Malawi; now Professor of African history, Dalhousie University.

B. A. Ogot.

J. P. Chrétien (France): specialist in the history of Burundi; author of numerous works on the Great Lakes kingdoms and German East Africa; Senior Researcher at the Centre de recherches africaines (C.R.A.), University of Paris I.

CHAPTER 27   W. R. Ochieng' (Kenya): specialist in the history of Kenya; author of numerous works on the subject; formerly Senior Lecturer in Kenyan history, Kenyatta University College, Nairobi; currently at MOI University, Eldoret, Kenya.

CHAPTER 28   R. K. Kent (USA): specialist in the history of Madagascar; author of numerous works on the subject; Professor of African History, University of California, Berkeley.

CHAPTER 29   B. A. Ogot.

Bibliography

The publishers wish to point out that while every effort has been made to ensure that the details in this Bibliography are correct, some errors may occur as a result of the complexity and the international nature of the work.

Abbreviations and list of periodicals
AA   Antananarivo Annual, Antananarivo
Abbia   Abbia, revue culturelle camerounaise, Yaoundé.
ABUP   Ahmadu Bello University Press, Zaria
AE   Annales d'Ethiopie, Rome
AEH   African Economic History, Madison, Wisconsin
AESC   Annales: Economies, sociétés, civilisations, Paris
Africa   Africa, Rome
AHS   African Historical Studies (now *IJAHS*), African Studies Center, Boston University
AL   Africana Linguistica, Tervuren: Musée royal de l'Afrique centrale
ALR   African Language Review (now *African Languages*) London: International African Institute
Anais   Anais da Junta de Investigações do Ultramar
Annual Review of Anthropology   Annual Review of Anthropology, Palo Alto, CA
Anthropos   Anthropos: Revue internationale d'ethnologie et de linguistique, Fribourg
Arabia   Arabia: the Islamic World Review, Slough, UK: Islamic Press Agency
Arnoldia   Arnoldia, Salisbury: National Museums of Rhodesia
ARSOM   Académie royale des sciences d'Outre-mer (formerly 'Institut royal colonial belge' and 'Académie royale des sciences coloniales'), Brussels
AS   African Studies (continues as *Bantu Studies*), Johannesburg: WUP
ASR   African Social Research, Lusaka: University of Zambia
ASR   African Studies Review, Camden, NJ
AVG   Annuaire des voyages et de la géographie
Azania   Azania: Journal of the British Institute of History and Archaeology in Eastern Africa, London

BAM   Bulletin de l'Académie malgache, Antananarivo
BARSOM   Bulletin de l'Académie royale des sciences d'Outre-mer, Brussels
BCAF   Bulletin du Comité de l'Afrique française – Renseignements coloniaux, Paris
BCEHSAOF   *Bulletin du Comité d'études historiques et scientifiques de l'Afrique Occidentale française*, Dakar
BCGP   Boletino cultural da Guiné portuguesa, Bissau
BEM   Bulletin économique de Madagascar, Antananarivo
BGHD   Bulletin de géographie historique et descriptive, Paris
BIEA   British Institute in Eastern Africa, Nairobi
BIFAN   Bulletin de l'Institut français (later *fondamental*) *d'Afrique noire*, Dakar
BIHBR   Bulletin de l'Institut historique belge de Rome
BJIDCC   Bulletin des juridictions indigènes et du droit coutumier congolais (now *Bulletin des tribunaux coutumiers*), Elisabethville: Societé des Etudes Juridiques du Katanga
BLLE   Bulletin de liaison – Linguistique-ethnosociologie, Abidjan: Centre universitaire de recherches de développement, University of Abidjan
BLS   Bulletin de liaison saharienne, Algiers
BM   Bulletin de Madagascar, Antananarivo
BODE   Bulletin officiel de la Direction de l'enseignement, Madagascar
BS   Bantu Studies, Johannesburg
BSGL   Boletim da Sociedade de Géografia de Lisboa, Lisbon
BSOAS   Bulletin of the School of Oriental and African Studies, London

CA   Codices Aethiopici
CCAH   Cahiers congolais d'anthropologie et d'histoire, Brazzaville
CCB   Centre de civilisation burundaise, Bujumbura
CEA   Cahiers d'études africaines, Paris: Mouton
CEDA   Centre d'études et de diffusion africaine, Paris/Abidjan

CHM   *Cahiers d'histoire mondiale*, Paris: Librairie des Méridiens
CIS   *Cahiers Internationaux de Sociologie*, Paris: PUF
CJAS   *Canadian Journal of African Studies*, Ottawa: Canadian Association of African Studies, Department of Geography, Carleton University, Ottawa
CNRS   Centre national de la recherche scientifique, Paris
CNRSS   Centre nigérien de recherches en sciences sociales, Niamey
Congo   *Congo*, Brazzaville: Centre National de la Statistique et des Études Economiques
CRA   Centre de recherches africaines, Paris
CRDTO   Centre de recherche et de documentation pour la tradition orale [Research and Documentation Centre for Oral Tradition] Niamey
CSCO   *Corpus Scriptorum Christianorum Orientalium*, Paris
CUP   Cambridge University Press
CUP   Caribbean University Press
CVRS   Centre voltaïque des recherches scientifiques, Ouagadougou
CZA   *Cultures au Zaïre et en Afrique*

EALB   East African Literature Bureau, Nairobi, Kampala and Dar es Salaam
EAPH   East African Publishing House, Nairobi
EHA   *Etudes d'histoire africaine*, Kinshasa
EHR   *Economic History Review*, Cambridge: Economic History Society
EN   *Etudes nigériennes*, Niamey: IRSH
EUP   Edinburgh University Press, Edinburgh

GASS Accra
GNQ   *Ghana Notes and Queries*, Legon
GSSJ   *Ghana Social Science Journal*, Legon
GUP   Ghana Universities Press

HAJM   *History in Africa: A Journal of Method*, Waltham, Massachusetts
HAHR   *Hispanic American Historical Review*, Durham, NC: Duke University Press
Hespéris   *Hespéris*, Rabat: Institut des hautes études marocaines
HUP   Harvard University Press
HUP   Howard University Press, Washington, DC

IAI   International African Institute, London
IAS   Institute of African Studies, University of Nairobi
ICS   Institute of Commonwealth Studies, London
IFAN   Institut français d'Afrique noire, Dakar
IJAHS   *International Journal of African Historical Studies*, Boston: African Studies Center, Boston University
IJMS   *International Journal of Middle-Eastern Studies*, Cambridge: CUP
IRES   Institut de recherches économiques et sociales, Léopoldville
IRSH   Institut de recherches en sciences humaines, Niamey
IUP   Ibadan University Press

JA   *Journal asiatique*, Paris
JAAS   *Journal of Asian and African Studies*, Tokyo
JAE   *Journal of Arid Environments*, London: Academic Press
JAH   *Journal of African History*, Cambridge: CUP
JAS   *Journal of the African Society* (later *African Affairs*), London
JEH   *Journal of Economic History*, Wilmington, DE: Economic History Association
JES   *Journal of Ethiopian Studies*, Addis Ababa: Institute of Ethiopian Studies, Haile Salassie I University
JHSN   *Journal of the Historical Society of Nigeria*, Ibadan
JHUP   Johns Hopkins University Press, Baltimore
JIMM   *J. Inst. Mining Met.*
JMBRAS   *Journal of the Malayan Branch of the Royal Asiatic Society*, Singapore
JNH   *The Journal of Negro History*, Washington, DC
JRAI   *Journal of the Royal Anthropological Institute of Great Britain and Ireland*, London
JRAS   *Journal of the Royal Asiatic Society of Great Britain and Ireland*, London
JSA   *Journal de la Société des Africanistes*, Paris

913

JSH *Journal of Social History*, Pittsburgh, PA: Carnegie – Mellon University Press
JSS *Journal of Semitic Studies*, Manchester: Department of Near Eastern Studies, Manchester University

KASP *The Kroeber Anthropological Society Papers*
KHR *Kenya Historical Review, The Journal of the Historical Association of Kenya*, Nairobi
KHS Kenya Historical Society, Nairobi
KLB Kenya Literature Bureau
KS *Kano Studies*, Kano, Nigeria
KUP Khartoum University Press

LA *L'éducation africaine*
LSJ *Liberian Studies Journal*, Newark, Delaware: University of Delaware

MAM *Mémoires de l'Académie malgache*, Antananarivo
Man *Man*, London
MJSS *Malawi Journal of Social Science*
MRAC *Musée royal de l'Afrique centrale – Annales Sciences humaines, Tervuren*
MRAL *Memorie in Italian della Reale Accademia nazionale dei Lincei*, Rome
MUP Manchester University Press, Manchester

NA *Notes africaines: Bulletin d'information de l'IFAN*, Dakar
NADA *The Rhodesian Native Affairs Department Annual*, Salisbury
NEA *Nouvelles éditions africaines*, Dakar
NJ *Nyasaland Journal*
NNPC Northern Nigerian Publishing Company, Zaria
NRE *Notes, reconnaissances et explorations*, Madagascar
NRJ *Northern Rhodesian Journal*
NUP Northwestern University Press, Evanston, Illinois
Nyame Akuma *Nyame Akuma*, Calgary: Department of Archaeology, University of Calgary

Odu *Odu: Journal of West African Studies* (previously *Journal of African Studies*, Ife; preceded by *Journal of Yoruba and Related Studies*, Ibadan), Ife: University of Ife
Oduma *Oduma*, Port Harcourt, Nigeria
OHCIS Ohio University Centre for International Studies
ORSTOM Office de la recherche scientifique et technique d'Outre-mer, Paris
OUP Oxford University Press

PA Présence africaine, Paris
Paideuma *Paideuma: Mitteilungen zur Kulturkunde*, Frankfurt-am-Main
Phylon *Phylon*, Atlanta, GA: University of Atlanta
PP *Past and Present*, Oxford
PS *Population Studies*, London
PTRSA *Proceedings and Transactions of the Rhodesian Scientific Association*, Bulawayo
PUF Presses universitaires de France, Paris
PUP Princeton University Press

RA *Revue africaine, Journal des travaux de la Société historique algérienne*, Algiers
REI *Revue des études islamiques*, Paris
RFHOM *Revue française d'histoire d'Outre-mer*, Paris
RH *Revue historique*, Paris: PUF
RHM *Revue d'histoire maghrébine*, Zaghovan, Tunisia
RLJ *Rhodes-Livingstone Journal* (now *African Social Research*), Lusaka
RM *Revue de Madagascar*, Antananarivo
RR *Research Review*, University of Ghana
RS *Revue sémitique*, Paris
RSE *Rassegna di studi etiopici*, Rome
RT *Revue tunisienne*, Algiers/Tunis: Jean-Baptiste Salvago
RTC *Revue des troupes coloniales*
RV *Recherches voltaïques*, Ouagadougou: Centre Voltaïque de la Recherche Scientifique

Saeculum *Saeculum*, Freiburg

SAJS   *South African Journal of Science*, Johannesburg
SELAF   Société d'études linguistiques et anthropologiques de France, Paris
SEVPEN   Service d'édition et de vente des publications de l'Education nationale, Paris
SFHOM   Société française d'histoire d'Outre-mer, Paris
SGM   Scottish Geographical Magazine, Edinburgh: Royal Scottish Geographical Society
SM   Sudanese Memoirs
SMJ   Society of Malawi Journal, Blantyre, Malawi: Society of Malawi
SNP   Kaduna, Nigeria: National Archives
SNR   Sudan Notes and Records, Khartoum
SOAS   School of Oriental and African Studies, University of London
SSL   Studi storici e Linguist
SSM   Social Science and Medicine, New York: Pergamon Press
Studia   Studia, Lisbon
SUP   Stanford University Press, Stanford, CA

Target   Target, Dar es Salaam
TD   Travaux et documents
THSG   Transactions of the Historical Society of Ghana (previously *Transactions of the Gold Coast and Togoland Historical Society*), Legon
TJH   Transafrican Journal of History, Nairobi: EALB
TNR   Tanganyika Notes and Records (now *Tanzania Notes and Records*), Dar es Salaam
TPH   Tanzania Publishing House
Trav. IRS   Travaux de l'Institut de recherches sahariennes, Algiers: University of Algiers

UCLA   University of California, Los Angeles
UCP   University of California Press, Berkeley, CA
Ufahamu   Ufahamu, Los Angeles, CA: UCLA
UJ   Uganda Journal, Kampala: Uganda Society
ULP   University of London Press, London
UNCP   University of North Carolina Press, Chapel Hill
UTP   University of Tennessee Press
UWP   University of Wisconsin Press, Madison

WAJA   West African Journal of Archaeology, Ibadan
WMQ   William and Mary Quarterly, Williamsburg, VA
WUP   Witwatersrand University Press, Johannesburg

YUP   Yale University Press

Zaïre   Zaïre, Kinshasa
Zamani   Zamani, Nairobi: History Association of Kenya
ZFE   Zeitschrift für Ethnologie, Berlin
ZH   Zimbabwean History
ZJH   Zambia Journal of History, Lusaka: University of Zambia

Bibliography

Abbebe, B. (1971) *Evolution de la propriété foncière au Choa (Ethiopie)* (Paris: Imprimerie Nationale et Librarie Orientaliste, P. Geuthner).
'Abd al-Azīz b. Muḥammad b. Ibrahīm al-Ṣinhādjī al-Fishtālī (16th cent.) *Manāhil al-Safā' fi akhbār al-Nulūk al-Shurafā*; 1964 ed. 'Abd Allāh Gannun (Tetuan).
Abdallah, Y. B. (1919a) *Chiikala cha wa yao* (Zomba: Government Printer).
Abdallah, Y. B. (1919b) *The Yaos* (arranged, ed. and tr. by M. Sanderson, Zomba; 2nd edn, London: Frank Cass, 1973).
Abinal, A. and Malzac, V. (1888) *Dictionnaire malgache–français* (Antananarivo: Imprimerie de la Mission Catholique; 2nd edn 1889).
Abitbol, M. (1979) *Tombouctou et les Arma de la conquête marocaine du Soudan nigérien en 1591 à l'hégémonie de l'Empire du Maçina en 1833* (Paris: Maisonneuve & Larose), 297 pp.
Abraham, D. P. (1969) 'The roles of Chaminuka and the Mhondoro cults in Shona political history', in E. Stokes and R. Brown (eds), pp. 28–46.

Abubakar, S. (1978) *The Lamibe of Fombina: A Political History of Adamawa, 1809–1901* (Zaria: ABUP), 190 pp.

Abun-Nasr, J. M. (1975) *A History of the Maghrib* (2nd edn, Cambridge: CUP), 422 pp.

Achi, B. and Bitiyong, J. I. (1983) *Warfare and Urban Growth in Hausaland: The Case of Birnin Zaria c.1400–1808 A.D.* (Zaria: ABUP).

Adams, W. Y. (1977) *Nubia – Corridor to Africa* (London: Allen Lane), 797 pp.

Adams, W. Y., Van Gerven, D. P. and Levy, R. S. (1978) 'The retreat from migrationism', *Annual Review of Anthropology* 7, pp. 483–532.

Adamu, M. (1968) 'A Hausa government in decline: Yawuri in nineteenth-century Zaria' (MA thesis, Ahmadu Bello University, Zaria).

Adamu, M. (1978) *The Hausa Factor in West African History* (Zaria: ABUP) 224 pp.

Adamu, M. (1979) 'Distribution of trading centres in the central Sudan in the eighteenth and nineteenth centuries', in Y. B. Usman (ed.), pp. 59–104.

Adamu, M. (forthcoming) 'Some essential features of the economy of Hausaland, 1500–1804', in M. Adamu (ed.).

Adamu, M. (ed.) (at press(a)) *Economic History of Central Savannah of West Africa* (Zaria: ABUP).

Adamu, M. (ed.) (at press(b)) *Central Sudan before 1804*.

Addo-Fening, F. (1980) 'Akyem Abuakwa, c.1874–1943: A study of the impact of missionary activities and colonial rule on a traditional state' (PhD thesis, University of Ghana, Legon).

Adefuye, A. (1973) 'A political history of the Palwo c.1400–1911' (PhD thesis, University of Ibadan).

Adefuye, A. (1976) 'Palwo Jogi: impact on political history', in Onyango-ka-Odongo and J. B. Webster (eds), 1976a, pp. 215–30.

Adefuye, A. (unpublished) 'The Palwo: from prestigious to persecuted minority', in J. B. Webster (ed.), *Uganda before 1900*, Vol. I.

Adeleye, R. A. (1971) 'Hausaland and Bornu, 1600–1800', in J.F.A. Ajayi and M. Crowder (eds), pp. 485–530.

Agnew, S. (1972) 'Environment and history: the Malawian setting', in B. Pachai (ed.), pp. 28–48.

Agyeman, E. A. (1965) 'Gyaman – Its relations with Ashanti, 1720–1820' (MA thesis, University of Ghana, Accra).

Aḥmad b. al-Ḥādj dj Abū 'l-'Alī (1962) *Makhtūtat Katib al-Shūna fi ta'rīkh al-Saltana al-Sinnariyya* (ed. al-Shātir Busaylī 'Abd al-Jalil, Cairo).

Ajayi, J. F. A. (ed.) (1989) *General History of Africa*, Vol. VI, (Paris/Oxford/Berkeley: UNESCO/ Heinemann/University of California Press) 861 pp.

Ajayi, J. F. A. and Alagoa, E.J. (1980) 'Nigeria before 1800: aspects of economic developments and inter-group relations', in O. Ikime (ed.), pp. 224–35.

Ajayi, J. F. A. and Crowder, M. (eds) (1971) *History of West Africa* (London: Longman; 2nd edn 1976).

Ajayi, J. F. A. and Espie, J. (eds) (1965) *A Thousand Years of West African History* (Ibadan/London: IUP/Nelson), 543 pp.

Ajayi, J. F. A. and Ikara, B. (eds) (1985) *Evolution of Political Culture. in Nigeria* (Lagos: Lagos University Press and Kaduna State Council for Arts and History), 227 pp.

Akinjogbin, I. A. (1967) *Dahomey and its Neighbours, 1708–1818* (Cambridge: CUP), 234 pp.

Akinjogbin, I. A. (1976) 'The expansion of Oyo and the rise of Dahomey, 1600–1800', in J.F.A. Ajayi and M. Crowder (eds), 1976 edn, pp. 373–412).

Alagoa, E. J. (1972) *A History of the Niger Delta: an Historical Interpretation of Ijo Oral Tradition* (Ibadan: IUP) 231 pp.

Alagoa, E. J. (1976) 'Dating Ijo oral tradition', *Oduma* (Port Harcourt), 3, 1, pp. 19–22.

Alexandre, P. (1965) 'Proto-histoire du groupe beti-bulu-fang: essai de synthèse provisoire', *CEA*, 20, pp. 503–60.

Alexandre, P. and Binet, J. (1958) *Le groupe dit pahouin (Fang-Boulou-Beti)*, (London/Paris: IAI/PUF), 152 pp.

Alkali, M. B. (1969) 'A Hausa community in crisis: Kebbi in the nineteenth century' (MA thesis, Ahmadu Bello University, Zaria).

Alkali, M. N. (1978) 'Kanem-Borno under the Sayfawa', (PhD thesis, Ahmadu Bello University, Zaria).

Alkali, M. N. (1983) 'Economic factors in the history of Borno under the Saifawa', in M. N. Alkali and B. Usman (eds), pp. 57–77.

Alkali, M. N. (1985) 'Political and administrative structure of Kanem-Borno under the Saifawa Mais', in J. F. A. Ajayi and B. Ikara (eds), pp. 33–49.

Allan, J. (1965) *The African Husbandsman* (London: Oliver and Boyd).

Alldridge, T. J. (1901) *The Sherbro and its Hinterland* (London: Macmillan), 356 pp.

Allen, J. de V. (1974) 'Swahili culture reconsidered', *Azania*, 9, pp. 105–138.

Allen, J. de V. (1976) 'Swahili culture and identity', (Seminar paper, Department of History, University of Nairobi).

Allen, J. V. (1981) *Lamu Town: A Guide* (Lamu: Rodwell Press).

Allen, J. de V. and Wilson, T. (1979) *Swahili Houses and Tombs of the Coast of Kenya* (London).

Alpers, E. A. (1968) 'The Mutapa and Maravi political systems to the time of the Ngoni invasions', in T. O. Ranger (ed.), pp. 1–28.

Alpers, E. A. (1973) 'Rethinking African economic history', *KHR*, 1, 2, pp. 163–88.

Alpers, E. A. (1975a) *Ivory and Slaves in East-Central Africa to the Later 19th Century* (London: Heinemann), 296 pp.

Alpers, E. A. (1975b) 'Eastern Africa', in R. Gray (ed.).

Alpers, E. A. and Ehret, C. (1975) 'Eastern Africa, 1600–1790', in R. Gray (ed.), pp. 469–536.

Alvares, F. (1961) *The Prester John of the Indies* (trans. by Lord Stanley of Alderley, rev. and ed. by C. F. Beckingham and G. W. B. Huntingford; Cambridge: CUP, for the Hakluyt Society, 2 vols).

Amenumey, D. E. K. (1969) 'The pre-1947 background to the Ewe unification question', *THSG*, 10, pp. 65–84.

Ameyaw, K. (1966) 'Kwahu, an early Akan forest state', *GNQ*, 9, pp. 39–45.

Amselle, J. L. and M'Bokolo, E. (eds) (at press) *Une ethnicité forgée à l'ombre du colonialisme: Hutu et Tutsi au Rwanda et au Burundi.*

Anacletti, A. O. and Ndagala, D. K. (1981) 'The cattle complex in the ancient west lake kingdoms', *CCB.*

Andrade, A. A. (1955) *Relações de Moçambique Setecentista* (Lisbon: Agencia General do Ultramar).

Anjan, L. (1911–12) 'Notes historiques et ethnographiques sur les Comores', *BAM*, 9, pp. 125–41 and 10, pp. 183–200.

Anonymous (nd) 'Entry of Kanembu into Bornu', *Kanembu District Notebook*, Maiprof File No. 38 (Kaduna, Nigeria: National Archives).

Anonymous (1890) 'Descripção do Imperio de Moanamotapa', in *Memoria e Documentos acerca dos direitos de Portugal aos territorios de Machona e Nyassa* (Lisbon: Imprensa nacional).

Anonymous (1967) 'Tarikh erbab hadha 'l-belad al-Mussama Kanu', trans. by H. R. Palmer as 'Kano Chronicle', *SM*, 3, pp 92–132.

Anozie, F. N. (1976) 'Onyoma and Ke: a preliminary report on archaeological excavations in the Niger Delta', *WAJA*, 6, pp. 89–99.

Anquandah, J. (1982) *Rediscovering Ghana's Past* (London: Longman), 161 pp.

Anttila, R. (1972) *An Introduction to Historical and Comparative Linguistics* (New York: Macmillan), 438 pp.

Anywar, R. S. (1954) *Acoli Ki Ker Megi* (Kampala: Eagle Press). Trans. by N. E. Odyomo as *The Acholi and their Chiefdoms* (1969), Department of History, Makerere University.

Apecu, A. (1972) *The Pre-colonial History of the Jonam Chiefdoms* (graduating essay, Makerere).

Aptheker, H. (1944) *American Negro Slave Revolts* (2nd printing, New York: Columbia University Press), 409 pp.

Ardener, E. (1956) *Coastal Bantu of the Cameroons* (London: IAI, Ethnographic Survey of Africa, Western Africa, Part. 11), 116 pp.

Ardener, E. (1968) 'Documentary and linguistic evidence for the rise of trading politics between Rio del Rey and Cameroons, 1600–1650)', in I. M. Lewis (ed.), pp. 81–126.

Aregay, W. and Sellassie, S. H. (1971) 'Sudanese-Ethiopian relations before the nineteenth century', in Y. F. Hasan (ed.), pp. 62–72.

Arhin, K. (1967) 'The structure of Greater Ashanti (1700–1824)', *JAH*, 8, 1, pp. 65–85.

Arhin, K. (1979) *West African Traders in Ghana in the Nineteenth and Twentieth Centuries* (London: Longman), 146 pp.

Arhin, K. and Goody, J. (1965) *Ashanti and the Northwest* (Legon: Institute of African Studies, University of Ghana).

Armo, A. G. (1968) *Anton Gulielmus Armo Afer of Axim in Ghana: Translation of his works* (Halle: Martin Luther University).

Astley, T. (1745) *A New Collection of Voyages and Travels* (4 vols, London: Thomas Astley).

Atherton, J. H. (1972) 'Excavations at Kamabai and Yagala rock shelters, Sierra Leone', *WAJA*, 2, pp. 39–74.

Atkins, G. (ed.) (1972) *Manding: Focus on an African Civilization* (London: SOAS).

Atkinson, R. R. (1976) 'State formation and development in Western Acholi', in Onyango-ka-Odongo and J. B. Webster (eds), 1976, pp. 262–90.

Atkinson, R. R. (at press) 'Bugware before 1900: a survey', in D. Denoon (ed.).

Aubigné, T. A. d' (1616–20) *L'histoire universelle du sieur d'Aubigné . . .*, 3 vols; 2nd edn, 1626, 3 vols; another edn published by the Baron A. de Ruble, 1886–1909, 10 vols (Paris).

Aujas, L. (1920) 'Remarques sur quelques étymologies des noms de lieux géographiques à Mayotte', *Revue d'Ethnographie et des Traditions populaires*, 1, pp. 51–9.

Austen, R. A. (1968) *Northwest Tanzania under German and British rule, 1889–1939* (New Haven: YUP).

Austen, R. A. (1979) 'The trans-Saharan slave trade: a tentative census', in H. A. Gemery and J. S. Hogendorn (eds), pp. 23–76.

Austen, R. A. and Jacobs, K. (1974) 'Dutch trading voyages to Cameroon, 1721–1759: European documents and African history', *Annales de la Faculté des lettres et sciences humaines* (University of Dakar), 6, pp. 1–27.

Avaro, J. A. (1981) *Un peuple gabonais à l'aube de la colonisation: Le Bas Ogowe au XIXe siècle* (Paris: Karthala/CRA), 290 pp.

Avelot, R. (1912) 'Les grands mouvements de peuples en Afrique: Jaqa et Zimba', *BGHD*, pp. 76–216.

Axelson, E. (1940) *South-East Africa, 1488–1530* (London: Longman), 306 pp.

Axelson, E. (1960) *The Portuguese in South-East Africa, 1600–1700* (Johannesburg: WUP), 226 pp.

Axelson, E. (1973) *The Portuguese in South-East Africa, 1488–1600* (Johannesburg: WUP), 276 pp.

Azaïs, Rév. père F. and Chambard, R. (1931) *Cinq années de recherches archéologiques en Ethiopie, province du Harar et Ethiopie méridionale*, 2 vols (Paris: Librairie Orientaliste Paul Geuthner).

Azevedo, L. J. de (1947) *Epocas de Portugal Economica* (2nd edn, Lisbon).

Azevedo, W. L. de (1959) 'The setting of Gola society and culture: some theoretical implications of variations in time and space', *KASP*, 21, pp. 43–125.

Azevedo, W. L. de (1962) 'Some historical problems in the delineation of a Central West Atlantic region', *Annals of the New York Academy of Sciences*, 96, pp. 512–38.

Baba, J. B. (1972) 'Adiyo: the coming of the Kakwa and the development of their institutions', (student essay, University of Makerere).

Baer, G. (1967) 'Slavery in nineteenth-century Egypt', *JAH*, 8, 3, pp. 417–441.

Bagodo, O. (1978) 'Le royaume Borgou Wasangari de Nikki dans la première moitié du XIXe siècle' (MA thesis, Université nationale, Cotonou).

Bahenduzi, M. (1977) 'Le munganuro et l'umwaka: deux fêtes rituelles du Burundi ancien' (thesis ENS, Bujumbura).

Balogun, S. A. (1980) 'History of Islam up to 1800', in O. Ikime (ed.), pp. 210–23.

Balogun, S. A. (1983) 'A reconsideration of the Hausa folklore: the Bayajida legend' (Sokoto, mimeograph).

Bannerman, J. H. (1981) 'Hlengweni: the history of the Hlengweni of Lower Save and Lundi rivers from the late eighteenth to mid-twentieth century', *ZH*, 12, pp. 1–45.

Baptista, R. (1892) *Africa Oriental, Caminho de ferro da Beira a Manica* (Lisbon: Empresa Nacional), 121 pp.

Barassin, Father J. (1953) *Bourbon des origines jusqu'en 1714*.

Barber, W. J. (1964) *The Economy of British Central Africa: a Case Study of Economic Development in a Dualistic Society* (London: OUP), 271 pp.

Barbot, J. (1732) *A Description of the Coasts of North and South Guinea* (London).

Barkindo, B. M. (1979) 'Islam in Mandara: its introduction and impact upon the state and people', *KS*, 1 and 4.

Barkindo, B. M. (1980) 'Origins and history of the sultanate of Mandara' (PhD thesis, Ahmadu Bello University, Zaria).

Barkindo, B. M. (ed.) (1983) *Studies in the History of Kano* (Ibadan: Heinemann Educational Books, Nigeria), 214 pp.

Barreto, Father M. (1899) 'Informaçao do Estado e conquista dos Rios de Cuama, December 1667' [Report upon the state and conquest of the rivers of Cuama], in G. M. Theal (ed.), 1898–1903, vol. 3, Eng. trans. pp. 463–495.

Barros, J. de (1552–1613) *Da Asia: Dos Feitos que os Portuguezes fizeram na Conquista e Descubrimento das Terras e Mares do Oriente* (vol. 1: 1552; vol. 2: 1553; vol. 3: 1563; vol. 4: 1613; Lisbon).

Barry, B. (1972) *Le royaume du Waalo: Le Sénégal avant la conquête* (Paris: Maspéro), 393 pp.

Barth, H. (1857–8) *Reisen und Entdeckungen in Nord und Central Afrika in den Jahren 1849 bis 1855* (Gotha: J. Perthes), 5 vols. Engl. edn, *Travels and Discoveries in North and Central Africa: Being a Journal of an Exploration undertaken under the Auspices of HBM's Government in the Years 1849–55*, 1857 (London: Longman, Brown, Green, Longmans & Roberts), 5 vols; reprint, 1965 (London:

Ward, Lock, Centenary Ed.), 3 vols. French edn, *Voyages et découvertes dans l'Afrique septentrionale et centrale pendant les années 1849 à 1855*, 1860–1 (Paris: A. Bohné), 4 vols.

Basset, R. (1882) *Etudes sur l'histoire d'Ethiopie* (Paris).

Basset, R. (1897) *Histoire de la conquête de l'Abyssinie (XVIe siècle) par Chihab Eddin Ahmed ben 'Abd El Qāder surnommé Arab-Faqih* (2 vols, Paris: Publications de l'École supérieure de lettres d'Alger).

Bastide, R. (1971) *Les Amériques noires: les civilisations africaines dans le Nouveau Monde* (Paris: Payot), trans. as *African Civilizations in the New World* (London: Hurst), 232 pp.

Basu, K. K. (1932) *The Tarikh-i-Mubarak Shadi by Yahya bin Ahmad bin 'Abdullah as-Sihrindi* (Baroda: Gackwad's Oriental Series, No. 63).

Batalha-Reis, J. (1889) 'The Portuguese in Nyasaland', *SGM*, 5, 5, pp. 252–60.

Bathily, A. (1975) 'Imperialism and colonial expansion in Senegal in the nineteenth century with particular reference to the economic, social and political developments in the Kingdom of Gajaaga' (PhD thesis, University of Birmingham).

Bauer, P. T. (1981) *Equality, the Third World and Economic Delusion* (London: George Weidenfeld and Nicolson Ltd.).

Beach, D. N. (1976) 'Second thoughts on the Shona economy: suggestions for further research', *RH*, 7, pp. 1–11.

Beach, D. N. (1977) 'The Shona economy: branches of production', in R. Palmer and N. Parsons (eds), pp. 37–65.

Beach, D. N. (1980a) *The Shona of Zimbabwe from 900 to 1850: an outline of Shona history* (Gweru: Mambo Press).

Beach, D. N. (1980b) 'The Zimbabwean plateau and its peoples, 1400–1900' (Paper presented to the Conference on the Social, Political and Economic History of Central Africa, University of Kent, Canterbury, 7–11 July).

Beach, D. N. (1984) *Zimbabwe before 1900* (Gweru: Mambo Press).

Becker, C. and Martin, V. (1975) 'Kajor et Bawol: royaumes sénégalais et traite des esclaves au XVIIIe siècle', *RFHOM*, 226–7, pp. 286–99.

Beckingham, C. F. and Huntingford, G. B. W. see F. Alvares, 1961.

Beecham, J. (1841) *Ashantee and the Gold Coast: Being a Sketch of the History, Social State and Superstitions of the Inhabitants of those Countries . . .* (London: John Mason), 376 pp.

Behrens, C. (1974) *Les Kroumen de la côte occidentale d'Afrique* (Talence: CNRS, Centre d'études de géographie tropicale), 243 pp.

Bello, M. (nd) 'Infāq al-Maysūr fī ta'rīkh bilād al-Tukrūr', trans. and ed. in 1932 by E. J. Arnett as *Rise of the Sokoto Fulani* (Kano: Emirate Printing Department); and by C. E. J. Whitting in 1951 (London: Luzac and Co.).

Beltran, G. A. (1958) *Cuijla: esbozo etnografico de un pueblo Negro* (Mexico).

Benisheikh, A. (1983) 'The 19th-century Galadimas of Bornu', in Y. B. Usman and M. N. Alkali (eds).

Benyowsky, M. A. de (1790) *Memoirs and Travels* (2 vols, London: G. G. J. and R. Robinson).

Berg, F. J. (1968) 'The Swahili community of Mombasa, 1500–1900', *JAH*, 9, 1, pp. 35–56.

Berg, F. J. (1971) 'Mombasa under the Busaidi sultanate: the city and its hinterland in the nineteenth century' (PhD thesis, University of Wisconsin).

Berger, I. (1967) 'Migration of the Central Kenya Bantu: a reconsideration of the Shungwaya hypothesis' (MA thesis, University of Wisconsin).

Berger, I. (1973) 'The Kubandwa religious complex of interlacustrine East Africa: an historical study c.1500–1900' (PhD thesis, University of Wisconsin).

Bernstein, H. (ed.) (1973) *Underdevelopment and Development: The Third World Today* (New York: Penguin Books).

Bernus, E. (1960) 'Kong et sa région', *Etudes éburnéennes*, 8, pp. 239–324.

Berque, J. (1982) *Ulemas, fondateurs, insurgés du Maghreb* (Paris: La bibliothèque arabe, Sindbad).

Berthier, P. (1966) *Les anciennes sucreries du Maroc et leurs réseaux hydrauliques* (2 vols, Rabat: Imprimeries française et marocaine).

Bertrand, Col. *Notes d'histoire mangbetu*, manuscript (in possession of J. Vansina).

Bertuchi, A. J. (1923) *The Island Rodriguez: A British Colony in the Mascarenhas Group* (London: John Murray).

Betbeder, P. (1971) 'The kingdom of Buzinza', *CHM*, 13, 4, pp. 736–62.

Betoto, C. (1950a) 'The social organization of the Sakalava royalty', in C. Betoto (ed.), 1950 (b).

Betoto, C. (ed.) (1950b) *Histoire de la royauté sakalava* (Paris: Ecole nationale de la France d'Outre-mer, typescript), pp. 1–32.

Bezold, C. (1905) *Kebra Nagast: Die Herrlichkeit der Könige* (München: Verlag de K. B.).

Bhila, H. H. K. (1975) 'Some aspects of pre-colonial African trade south of the Zambezi', *MJSS*, 4, pp. 101–16.

Bhila, H. H. K. (1977) 'The Kaphwiti-Lundu complex in the Lower Shire valley, Malawi, to 1800 AD: myth and reality' (paper presented to the International Conference on Southern African History, National University of Lesotho, Roma, 1–7 August).

Bhila, H. H. K. (1982) *Trade and Politics in a Shona Kingdom. The Manyika and their Portuguese and African Neighbours, 1575–1902* (London: Longman).

Bieber, F. J. (1920–3) *Kaffa: ein altkuschilisches Volkstum in Inner Afrika*, vol. 1 (Münster: W. Aschendorffsche Verlagsbuchhandlung); vol. 2 (Wien).

Bikunya, P. (1927) *Ky'Abakama ba Bunyoro-Kitara* (London: Sheldon Press).

Binger, L. G. (1892) *Du Niger au golfe de Guinée par le pays de Kong et le Mossi, 1887–1889* (2 vols, Paris: Hachette).

Biobaku, S. O. (ed.) (1973) *Sources of Yoruba History* (Oxford: Clarendon Press).

Birkeli, E. (1926) *Marques de boeufs et traditions de race: documents sur l'ethnographie de la côte occidentale de Madagascar* (Oslo, Bulletin No. 2 of the Oslo Ethnografiske Museum).

Birmingham, D. (1966) *Trade and Conflict in Angola: The Mbundu and their Neighbours under the Influence of the Portuguese, 1483–1790* (Oxford: Clarendon Press).

Birmingham, D. (1975) 'Central Africa from Cameroun to Zambezi', in R. Gray (ed.) pp. 325–83.

Birmingham, D. (1981) *Central Africa to 1870: Zambezia, Zaïre and the South Atlantic* (Cambridge: CUP).

Birmingham, D. and Gray, R. (eds) (1970) *Pre-colonial African trade: Essays on Trade in Central and Eastern Africa before 1900* (London: OUP), 308 pp.

Birmingham, D. and Martin, P. (eds) (1983) *History of Central Africa*, vol. 1, (London: Institute of Commonwealth Studies), 314 pp.

Bishikwabo, C. (1982) 'Histoire d'un état shi en Afrique des Grands Lacs (c.1850–1940)' (PhD thesis, Louvain-la-Neuve).

Bishop, W. W. and Clark, J. D. (eds) (1967) *Background to Evolution in Africa* (Chicago: University of Chicago Press).

Bivar A. D. H. and Shinnie, P. L. (1960) 'A dated Kuran from Bornu', *Nigerian Magazine*, 65, (Lagos).

Blackburn, R. H. (1976) 'Okiek history', in B. A. Ogot (ed.), 1976b, pp. 53–83.

Blackburn, R. H. (1982) *Kenya's Peoples: Okiek* (London: Evans).

Blair, H. A. and Duncan-Johnstone, A. (1932) *Enquiry into the Constitution and Organization of the Dagbon Kingdom* (Accra: Government Printer).

Blake, J. W. (1937/1977) *West Africa, Quest for God and Gold, 1454–1578: A Survey of the First Century of White Enterprise in West Africa, with particular reference to the Achievement of the Portuguese and their Rivalries with other European Powers* (London: Curzon Press), 1st edn, 1937.

Blake, J. W. (1942) *Europeans in West Africa, 1450–1560* (tr. and ed. by J. W. Blake, London: for the Hakluyt Society, 2nd edn, 2 vols).

Blakeley, A. (1976) 'Gannibal, Abram Petrovich', in *Modern Encyclopaedia of Russian and Soviet History*, vol. 12, ed. by J. L. Wieczynski (Gulf Breeze: Academic International Press).

Boahen, A. A. (1964) *Britain, the Sahara and the Western Sudan, 1788–1861* (Oxford: Clarendon Press, Oxford Studies in African Affairs), 268 pp.

Boahen, A. A. (1965) 'Asante and Fante, A. D. 1000–1800', in J. F. A. Ajayi and I. Espie (eds), pp. 160–85.

Boahen, A. A. (1966a) *Topics in West African History* (London: Longman).

Boahen, A. A. (1966b) 'Origins of the Akan', *GNQ*, 9, pp. 3–10.

Boahen, A. A. (1971) 'The coming of the Europeans', in A. M. Josephy, Jr. (ed.).

Boahen, A. A. (1973) 'Arcany or Accany or Arcania and the Accanists of the 16th and 17th centuries' European Records', *THSG*, XIV, I, 6, pp. 105–12.

Boahen, A. A. (1974) 'Fante diplomacy in the eighteenth century', in K. Ingham (ed.), pp. 25–49.

Boahen, A. A. (1977) 'Ghana before the coming of the Europeans', *GSSJ*, 4, 2.

Boesch, F. (1930) *Les Banyamwezi: peuple de l'Afrique orientale* (Münster: Anthropos Bibliothek).

Boeseken, A. J. (1969) 'The settlement under the van der Stels', in C. F. J. Muller (ed.), pp. 26–38.

Bois, G. (1978) 'Against the neo-Malthusian orthodoxy', *PP*, 79, pp. 60–9.

Bonnel de Mézières, A. (1912) *Le Major A. Gordon Laing* (Paris: Larose) (2nd edn, 1927).

Bontinck, F. (1980) 'Un mausolée pour les Jaga', *CEA*, 79, pp. 387–9.

Bontinck, F. and Ndembe Nsasi, D. (1978)) *Le catéchisme kikongo de 1624: Réédition critique* (Brussels: ARSOM, Classe des Sciences morales et politiques, NS, XLIV-5).

Borah, W. and Cook, S. F. (1967) 'The Aboriginal population of Central Mexico on the eve of Spanish conquest', in L. Hanke (ed.), vol. I.

Bosman, W. (1967) *A New and Accurate Description of the Coast of Guinea* (London: Frank Cass, reprint of 1705 1st edn, with Introduction by J. R. Willis).

Boston, J. S. (1969) 'Oral tradition and the history of the Igala', *JAH*, 10, 1, pp. 29–43.

Botelho, J. J. T. (1936) *Historia militar e politica dos Portugeses em Moçambique da Descoberta a 1833* (Lisbon: Governo Geral de Moçambique).

Boto, J. (1923) 'Tradition relative à l'origine des Betsimisaraka–Betanimena', *BODE*, 25, pp. 252–3.

Bouchaud, J. (1952) *La côte du Cameroun dans l'histoire et la cartographie, des origines à la conquête allemande* (Yaoundé: Mémoires de l'IFAN, Centre du Cameroun, No. 5), 217 pp.

Bouet, S. S. and Bouet, L. T. (1911) 'Les Toma', *BCAF*, 8, pp. 185–246.

Boulègue, J. (1968) 'La Sénégambie du milieu du XVe siècle au début du XVIIe siècle' (PhD thesis, 3rd cycle, University of Paris).

Boulègue, J. (1972) 'Aux confins du monde malinke: le royaume du Kasa (Casamance)' (paper presented to the Conference on Manding Studies, London University).

Bouquiaux, L. and Hyman, L. (eds) (1980) *L'expansion bantoue* (3 vols, Paris: SELAF).

Boutillier, J. L. (1971) 'La cité marchande de Bouna dans l'ensemble économique ouest-africain précolonial', in C. Meillassoux (ed.), pp. 240–52.

Boutillier, J. L. (1975) 'Les trois esclaves de Bouna', in C. Meillassoux (ed.), pp. 253–80.

Bovill, E. W. (1958) *The Golden Trade of the Moors* (London: OUP), 281 pp; 2nd rev. ed. 1968, 293 pp; London: OUP).

Boxer, C. R. (1952) *Salvador de Sa and the struggle for Brazil and Angola, 1602–1686* (London: Athlone Press), 444 pp.

Boxer, C. R. (1960a) 'Uma relação inedita et contemporanea da batalha de Ambuila em 1665', *Museu de Angola*, 2, pp. 66–73.

Boxer, C. R. (1960b) 'The Portuguese on the Swahili coast, 1593–1729', in C. R. Boxer and C. de Azevedo (eds), pp. 11–86.

Boxer, C. R. (1961) *Four Centuries of Portuguese Expansion, 1415–1825: A Succinct Survey* (Johannesburg: WUP).

Boxer, C. R. (1963) *Race Relations in the Portuguese Colonial Empire, 1415–1825* (Oxford: Clarendon Press), 136 pp.

Boxer, C. R. (1969) *The Portuguese Seaborne Empire* (London: Hutchinson).

Boxer, C. R. and Azevedo, C. de (eds) (1960) *Fort Jesus and the Portuguese in Mombasa, 1593–1729* (London: Hollis & Carter), 144 pp.

Boyer, G. (1953) *Un peuple de l'ouest soudanais, les Diawara: Contribution à l'histoire des Songhay par J. Rouch* (Dakar: Mémoires de l'IFAN, 29), 259 pp.

Brasio, A. (ed.) (1952–71) *Monumenta Missionaria Africana – Africa Occidental* (11 vols, Lisbon: Agencia Geral do Ultramar).

Braudel, F. (1928) 'Les Espagnols et l'Afrique du Nord de 1492 à 1577', *RA*, pp. 184 *et seq.* and pp. 315 *et seq.*

Braudel, F. (1935) 'Philippe II et la Goulette', *RA*, pp. 386–91.

Braudel, F. (1946) 'De l'or du Soudan à l'argent d'Amérique', *AESC*, 1, pp. 9–22.

Braudel, F. (1981) *The Structure of Everyday Life: the Limits of the Possible* (trans. and rev. by S. Reynolds, London).

Braudel, F. (1984) *Civilization and Capitalism* (3 vols, New York: Harper & Row).

Braukämper, U. (1978) 'The ethnogenesis of the Sidama', *Abbay*, 9, pp. 123–30.

Braukämper, U. (1980) *Geschichte der Hadiya Süd-Äthiopiens* (Wiesbaden).

Brenner, R. (1976) 'Agrarian class structural and economic development in pre-industrial Europe', *PP*, 70, pp. 31–75.

Brenner, R. (1982) 'The agrarian roots of European capitalism', *PP*, 97, pp. 16–113.

Bretschneider, E. (1871) *On the Knowledge Possessed by the Ancient Chinese of the Arabs and Arabian Colonies* (London).

Brief Diwan, compiled 1165 A.H. (1751–2), reproduced in *Kitab fi Sha'n Sultan Idris*, 1932 (Kano), with a trans. by H. R. Palmer in the introduction.

Broadhead, S. (1971) 'Trade and politics on the Congo coast: 1770–1870' (PhD thesis, Boston University).

Broadhead, S. (1979) 'Beyond decline: the kingdom of the Kongo in the eighteenth and nineteenth centuries', *IJAHS*, 12, 4, pp. 615–50.

Broadhead, S. (1983) 'Slave wives, free sisters, Bakongo women and slavery c.1700–1850', in C. C. Robertson and M. Klein (eds), *Women and Slavery in Africa*, pp. 160–81.

Brock, B. (1968) 'The Nyika', in A. D. Roberts (ed.), 1968a, pp. 59–81.

Brooks, G. E. (1980) *Kola Trade and State-building in Upper Guinea Coast and Senegambia, 15th-*

17th centuries (African Studies Centre Working Papers, No. 38, Boston University).

Browne, W. G. (1799) *Travels in Africa, Egypt and Syria, from the year 1792 to 1798* (London: Longman & Rees, 496 pp.; (2nd edn, 1806, London: Longman & Co, 632 pp.).

Bruce, J. (1805) *Travels to Discover the Source of the Nile in the Years 1768, 1769, 1770, 1771, 1772 and 1773* (2nd edn, 8 vols, Edinburgh: A. Constable & Co., Manners and Miller); (1st edn, 5 vols, 1790, Edinburgh: J. Ruthren).

Brutsch, J. R. (1950) 'Les relations de parenté chez les Duala', *Etudes camerounaises*, **3**, 31–32 (September–December), pp. 211–30.

Bryan, M. A. (1959) *The Bantu Languages of Africa* (London: OUP, Handbook of African languages, Part 4, published for the IAI), 170 pp.

Buchanan, C. (1974) 'The Kitara complex: the historical tradition of Western Uganda to the 16th century' (PhD thesis, Indiana University, Bloomington), 273 pp.

Buchthal, H. (1960) 'An Ethiopian miniature of Christ being nailed to the Cross', in *Atti del Convegno Internazionale di Studi Ethiopici* (Rome), pp. 331–4.

Burckhardt, J. L. (1819) *Travels in Nubia* (London: John Murray), 543 pp.

Burnham, P. (1975) 'Regroupement' and mobile societies: two Cameroon cases', *JAH*, **16**, 4, pp. 577–94.

Burnham, P. (1980) *Opportunity and Constraint in a Savanna Society* (London: Academic Press), 324 pp.

Burssens, H. (1958) *Les peuplades de l'entre-Congo-Ubangi* (London: IAI).

Burton, R. F. (ed. and trans.) (1873) *The Lands of Kazembe: Lacerda's Journey to Kazembe in 1798* (London: John Murray).

Burton, W. F. (1956) 'L'organisation sociale des Balumba', *BJIDCC*, **4**, pp. 150–3.

Bynon, T. (1977) *Historical Linguistics* (Cambridge: CUP), 301 pp.

Cà da Mosto, A. da (1937) *The Voyages of Cadamosto and Other Documents on Western Africa in the Second Half of the Fifteenth Century*, (trans. and ed. by G. R. Crone, London: Hakluyt Society), 159 pp.

Cadornega, A. de Oliveira de (1940–2) *História geral das Guerras Angolanas* ... (3 vols, ed. by J. M. Delgado and M. A. da Cunha, Lisbon: Imprensa Nacional).

Caetano, X. (1954) 'Relação do estado presente de Moçambique, Sena, Sofala, Inhambane e todo o Continente da Africa Oriental', in L. F. de Carvalho Dias (ed.), pp. 171–215.

Caillié, R. (1828) *Journal d'un voyage à Tombouctou et à Jenne* (Paris: Imprimerie royale).

Cairns, T. (1971) *Barbarians, Christians and Muslims* (Cambridge: CUP).

Callaway, C. (1870) *The Religious Systems of the Amazulu* (London: Trübner & Co.).

Callet, F. (1878–1902) *Tantaran'ny Andriana* (2nd edn, Antananarivo; 3rd edn, 1908–9; trans. by G. S. Chapus and E. Ratsimba as *Histoire des rois*, 1953–8, Antananarivo. Popularly referred to as *Tantara*, general word for 'history'.

Calonne-Beaufaict, A. de (1921) *Azande; introduction à une ethnographie générale des bassins de l'Ubangi–Uele et de l'Aruwimi* (Brussels: M. Lamertin).

Capello, H. and Ivens, R. (1886) *De Angola a Contra-Costa: Descripção de Uma Viagem atravez do Continente Africano* (2 vols, Lisbon: Imprensa Nacional).

Capron, J. (1973) *Communautés villageoises bwa (Mali, Haute-Volta)* (Paris: Institut d'ethnologie, Mémoire No. 9), 379 pp.

Carreira, A. (1947) *Mandingas da Guiné Portuguesa* (Bissau: Centro de Estudos da Guiné Portuguesa).

Carrette, E. (1844) *Recherches sur la géographie et le commerce de l'Algérie méridionale* (Paris: Sciences historiques et géographiques).

Carvalho Dias, H. A. de (1890) *Expedição ao Muatiamvo: Ethnographia e história tradicional dos povos da Lunda* (8 vols, Lisbon: Imprensa Nacional).

Carvalho Dias, L. F. de (ed.) (1954) 'Fontes para a historia, geografia e comercio de Moçambique, sec. XVIII', *Anais*, **9**, 1.

Castries, H. de (1905–36) *Les sources inédites de l'histoire du Maroc de 1530 à 1845* (18 vols, Paris: Paul Geuthner).

Castries, H. de (1923) 'La conquête du Soudan par el-Mansour', *Hespéris*, **3**, 4, pp. 433–88.

Cauneille, A. (1957) 'Le nomadisme des Zentan (Tripolitaine et Fezzan)', *Trav. IRS*, **16**, 2, pp. 73–99.

Cavazzi, G. A. (1965) *Descripção histórica dos três reinos do Congo, Matamba e Angola ... 1687* (Portuguese trans. and annotated by G. M. de Leguzzano, 2 vols, Lisbon: Junta de Investigações do Ultramar).

Centre de Civilisation burundaise (ed.) (1981) *La civilisation ancienne des peuples des Grands Lacs* (Paris: Karthala), 495 pp.

Centre for the Study of Customs (ed.) (nd) *Enquête sur . . . les Mahafaly* (University of Madagascar).

Cerulli, E. (1922) *The folk-literature of the Galla of Southern Abyssinia* (Harvard African Studies No. 3, Cambridge, Mass.).

Cerulli, E. (1931) 'Documenti arabi per la storia dell'Ethiopia', *MRAL*, 4, Ser. 6, pp. 39–101.

Cerulli, E. (1936) *La lingua e la storia di Harar* (Rome).

Cerulli, E. (1941) 'Il sultanato dello Scioa nel secolo XII secondo un nuovo documento storico', *RSE*, 1, pp. 5–42.

Cerulli, E. (1942) 'Gli emiri di Harar dal secolo XVI alle conquista egiziana (1875)', *RSE*, 2, pp. 3–20.

Cerulli, E. (1943–7) *Etiopi in Palestina* (2 vols, Rome: Libreria dello Stato).

Cerulli, E. (1947) 'Il "Gesù percosso" nell'arte etiopica e le sue origini nell'Europa del XV secolo', *RSE*, 6, pp. 109–29.

Cerulli, E. (1957–64) *Somalia – Scritti vari editi ed inediti* (3 vols, Rome: Amministrazione Fiducitaria Italiana di Somalia).

Cerulli, E. (1968) *La letteratura etiopica* (Firenze/Milano: Sansoni/Accademia Sancasciano vul di Pesa, Stianti).

Césard, E. (1927) 'Comment les Bahaya interprètent leurs origines', *Anthropos*, 22, pp. 440–65.

Césard, E. (1935, 1936, 1937) 'Le Muhaya', *Anthropos*, 30, pp. 75–106 and pp. 451–62; 31, pp. 97–114, pp. 489–508 and pp. 821–49; 32, pp. 15–60.

Césard, P. (1931) 'Histoires des rois du Kyamtwara d'après l'ensemble des traditions des familles régnantes', *Anthropos*, 26, pp. 533–43.

Chamberlin, C. (1977) 'Competition and conflict: the development of the bulk export trade in Central Gabon during the nineteenth century' (PhD thesis, University of California).

Chamberlin, C. (1978) 'The migration of the Fang into Central Gabon during the nineteenth century: a new interpretation', *IJAHS*, 11, pp. 429–56.

Chaunu, H. and Chaunu, P. (1955) *Séville et l'Atlantique, 1504–1650* (11 vols, Paris: Ecole des Hautes études).

Chauveau, J. P. (1974) 'Note sur les échanges dans le Baule précolonial', in *Bondouku Colloque*, pp. 262–305.

Chauveau, J. P. (1979) '*Notes sur l'histoire économique et sociale de la région de Kokumbo*, (Paris: Office de la Recherche Scientifique et Technique d'Outre-Mer, Travaux et Documents, No. 104), 277 pp.

Cheffaud, M. (1936) 'Note sur la chronologie des rois d'Imerina', *BAM*, 19 (NS), pp. 37–47.

Chéron, G. (1924) 'Contribution à l'histoire du Mossi: Traditions relatives au cercle de Kaya', *BCEHSAOF*, 7, 4, pp. 635–91.

Chilver, E. M. (1981) 'Chronological synthesis: the western region', in C. Tardits (ed.), pp. 453–73.

Chittick, H. N. (1962) *A Guide to the Ruins of Kilwa, with Some Notes on Other Antiquities in the Region* (Dar es Salaam: National Culture and Antiquities Division, Ministry of Community Development and National Culture), 20 pp.

Chittick, H. N. (1963) 'Kilwa and the Arab settlement on the East African coast', *JAH*, 4, 2, pp. 179–90.

Chittick, H. N. (1969) 'A new look at the history of Pate' *JAH*, 10, 3, pp. 375–91.

Chittick, H. N. (1971) 'The coast before the arrival of the Portuguese', in B. A. Ogot and J. A. Kieran (eds), 1974 reprint, pp. 100–18.

Chittick, H. N. (1974) *Kilwa: An Islamic Trading City on the East African Coast* (2 vols, Nairobi: BIEA, Memoir).

Chittick, H. N. (1975) 'The peopling of the East African coast', in H. N. Chittick and R. I. Rotberg (eds), pp. 16–43.

Chittick, H. N. (1977) 'The East coast, Madagascar and the Indian Ocean', in R. Oliver (ed.), pp. 183–231.

Chittick, H. N. and Rotberg, R. I. (eds) (1975) *East Africa and the Orient: Cultural Synthesis in the Pre-Colonial Times* (New York: Africana Publishing Company), 343 pp.

Chojnacki, S. (1969) 'Däj Giyorgis', *JES*, 7, 2, pp. 43–52.

Chrétien, J. P. (1974) 'Echanges et hiérarchies dans les royaumes des Grands Lacs de l'est africain', *AESC*, pp. 1327–37.

Chrétien, J. P. (1975) 'Le Buha à la fin du XIXe siècle: un peuple, six royaumes', *EHA*, 7, pp. 9–38.

Chrétien, J. P. (1977) 'Les deux visages de Cham: points de vue français du XIXe siècle sur les races africaines d'après l'exemple de l'Afrique orientale', in P. Guiral and E. Temime (eds), *L'idée de race dans la pensée politique française contemporaine* (Paris: Editions du CNRS), pp. 171–99.

Chrétien, J. P. (1979) *Histoire rurale de l'Afrique des Grands Lacs* (Paris: Université de Paris).

Chrétien, J. P. (1981a) 'Du Hirsute au Hamite: les variations du cycle de Ntare Ruhatsi, fondateur du royaume du Burundi', *HA*, 8, pp. 3–41.

Chrétien, J. P. (1981b) 'Pouvoir d'Etat et autorité mystique: l'infrastructure religieuse des monarchies des Grands Lacs', *RFHOM*, pp. 112–30.

Chrétien, J. P. (ed.) (1983) *Histoire rurale de l'Afrique des Grands Lacs* (Paris: AFERA-Karthala), 285 pp.

Chrétien, J. P. (1984) 'Nouvelles hypothèses sur les origines du Burundi', in L. Ndoricimpa (ed.), pp. 11–52.

Chrétien, J. P. (1986) 'Confronting the unequal exchange of the oral and the written', in B. Jewsiewicki and D. Newbury (eds), pp. 75–90.

Christelow, A. (1948) 'Great Britain and the trades from Cadiz and Lisbon to Spanish America and Brazil, 1759–1783', *HAHR*, 28, 1, February, Part II.

Cipolla, C. M. (1976) *Before the Industrial Revolution: European Society and Economy, 1000–1700* (London: Methuen).

Cissoko, S. M. (1968a) *Histoire de l'Afrique occidentale* (Paris: PA), 233 pp.

Cissoko, S. M. (1968b) 'Famines et épidémies à Tombouctou et dans la Boucle du Niger du XVIe au XVIIIe siècle', *BIFAN*, Ser. B, 30, 3, pp. 806–21.

Cissoko, S. M. (1969) 'La royauté (mansaya) chez les Mandingues occidentaux, d'après leurs traditions orales', *BIFAN*, Ser. B, 31, pp. 325–38.

Cissoko, S. M. (1972) 'Introduction à l'histoire des Mandingues de l'ouest: l'empire de Kabou (XVIe–XIXe siècle)' (paper presented to the Conference on Manding Studies, London).

Cissoko, S. M. and Sambou Kaoussa (1969) *Recueils des traditions orales des Mandingues de Gambie et de Casamance* (Niamey: UNESCO), 269 pp.

Clark, J. D. (1965) 'The Portuguese settlement at Feira', *NRJ*, 6, pp. 275–92.

Clérici, M. A. (1962) *Histoire de la Côte d'Ivoire* (Abidjan: CEDA).

Cohen, D. W. (1968) 'Review of L. de Heusch, *Le Rwanda et la civilisation interlacustre*, 1966', *JAH*, 9, 4, pp. 651–7.

Cohen, D. W. (1968/73) 'The River-Lake Nilotes from the fifteenth to the nineteenth century', in B. A. Ogot (ed.), pp. 142–57 in 2nd edn.

Cohen, D. W. (1970) 'A survey of interlacustrine chronology', *JAH*, 11, 2, pp. 177–201.

Cohen, D. W. (1972) *The Historical Tradition of Busoga, Mukama and Kintu* (Oxford: Clarendon Press), 218 pp.

Cohen, D. W. (1989) 'Peoples and states of the Great Lakes region', in J. F. A. Ajayi (ed.), pp. 270–93.

Cohen, D. W. (at press (a)) 'Retracing the footsteps of Mukama', in J. B. Webster (ed.), *Uganda Before 1900*, (at press).

Cohen, D. W. (at press (b)) 'Emergence and crisis: the states of Busoga', in D. Denoon (ed.), (forthcoming).

Cohen, R. (1965) 'Some aspects of institutionalized exchange: a Kanuri example', *CEA*, 5.

Cohen, R. (1970) 'Incorporation in Bornu', in R. Cohen and J. Middleton (eds), *From Tribe To Nation In Africa*, (Scranton: Chandler Int. Co.), pp. 150–74.

Colle, R. (1913) *Les Baluba* (Brussels: Van Overbergh, Collection de monographies ethnographiques, Vols 10 & 11).

Colvin, L. G. (1974) 'Islam and the State of Kajoor: A case of successful resistance to Jihad', *JAH*, 15, 4, pp. 587–606.

Commissariat, M. S. (1957) *A History of Gujarat* (Calcutta).

Conti Rossini, C. (1907) 'Historia Regis Sarṣa Dengel – Malak Sagad', *CSCO*, Scr. Aeth., Ser. alt., Vol. 3.

Conti Rossini, C. (1942) 'Sulla communità abissina di Cipro', *RSE*, 1, pp. 98–9.

Cook, S. F. and Borah, W. (1971–4) *Essays in population history, Mexico and the Caribbean* (2 vols, Berkeley: UCP).

Cooper, F. (1979) 'The problem of slavery in African studies', *JAH*, 20, 1, pp. 103–25.

Cooper, J. P. (1978) 'In search of agrarian capitalism', *PP*, 80 (August), pp. 20–65.

Cordell, D. D. (1972) *History of the Awlad Sulayman* (MA thesis, University of Wisconsin).

Cornevin, R. (1964) *Note sur l'histoire de Sansanné Mango* (London, Survey on African Chronology).

Cory, H. and Hartnoll, M. M. (1945/1971) *Customary Law of the Haya Tribe* (London: Frank Cass, Cass Library of African Studies, Library of African Law, No. 7).

Cossac de Chavrebière (1931) *Histoire du Maroc* (Paris: Payot).

da Costa, Capt. P. R. (1613/1970) 'Diário', 1613, in H. Listao, *Os Dois Descobrimentos da Ilha de*

Sao Lourenco mandalos fazer pelo vice-rei D. Jeronimo de Azevedo nos anos de 1613 a 1616 (Lisbon), pp. 47–192.

Coupez, A., Evrard, E. and Vansina, J. (1976) 'Classification d'un échantillon de langues bantoues d'après la lexicostatistique', *AL*, 6, 81, pp. 131–58.

Coupez, A. and Kamanzi, T. (1962) *Récits historiques du Rwanda* (Tervuren: MRAC), 327 pp.

Coursey, D. G. (1966) 'The cultivation and use of yams in West Africa', *GNQ*, 9, pp. 45–54.

Courtois, C. (1955) *Les Vandales et l'Afrique* (Algiers: Arts et Métiers Graphiques), 441 pp.

Crazzolara, J. P. (1950–4) *The Lwoo* (3 vols, Verona: Missioni Africana).

Crazzolara, J. P. (1960) 'Notes on the Lango Omiru and the Labwor and Nyakwai', *Anthropos*, 55, pp. 174–214.

Crine-Mavar, B. (1973) 'Histoire traditionnelle du Shaba', *CZA*, 1, pp. 5–103.

Crooks, J. J. (1923) *Records Relating to the Gold Coast Settlements, 1750–1874* (Dublin: Browne and Nolan), 557 pp.

Crosby, C. A. (1980) *Historical Dictionary of Malawi* (New York: Scarecrow Press), 169 pp.

Cruickshank, B. (1853) *Eighteen Years on the Gold Coast of Africa* (2 vols, London: Hurst and Blackett).

Cullen-Young, T. (1970) *Notes on the History of the Tumbuka–Kamanga Peoples in the Northern Province of Nyasaland* (London: Frank Cass), 192 pp.

Cuoq, J. M. (1975) *Recueil des sources arabes concernant l'Afrique occidentale du VIIIe au XVIe siècle (Bilād al-Sūdān)* (Paris: Editions du CNRS), 490 pp.

Curtin, P. D. (ed.) (1967) *Africa Remembered: Narratives by West Africans From the Era of the Slave Trade* (Madison: UWP), 363 pp.

Curtin, P. D. (1969) *The Atlantic Slave Trade: A Census* (Madison: UWP), 338 pp.

Curtin, P. D. (1971) 'Jihad in West Africa: early phases and interrelations in Mauritania and Senegal', *JAH*, 12, 1, pp. 11–24.

Curtin, P. D. (1973a) 'The Atlantic slave trade 1600–1800', in J. F. A. Ajayi and M. Crowder (eds), vol. 1, pp 240–68.

Curtin, P. D. (1973b) 'Review of B. Barry, *Le royaume du Waalo: Le Sénégal avant la conquête* (Paris: Maspéro), *IJAHS*, 6, 4, pp. 679–81.

Curtin, P. D. (1975) *Economic Change in Pre-Colonial Africa, Vol. I: Senegambia in the Era of the Slave Trade; Vol. II: Supplementary Evidence* (Madison: UWP).

Curtin, P. D., Anstey, R. and Inikori, J. E. (1976) 'Discussion: Measuring the Atlantic slave trade', *JAH*, 17, 4, pp. 595–627.

Curtin, P. D., Feierman, S., Thompson, L. and Vansina, J. (1978) *African History* (Boston/Toronto: Little Brown Company), 612 pp.

Cuvelier, J. (1953) *Relations sur le Congo du père Laurent de Lucques, 1700–1717* (Brussels: Institut royal colonial belge, Section des sciences morales et politiques. Mémoires in 8° 32 (C)).

Cuvelier, J. (1957) *Koningin Nzinga van Matamba* (Brugge).

Cuvelier, J. and Jadin, L. (1954) *L'ancien royaume du Congo d'après les archives romaines, 1518–1640* (Brussels: ARSOM).

Czekanowski, J. (1917) *Forschungen im Nil-Kongo Zwischengebiet. Ethnographie: Zwishenseengebiet* (Leipzig: Klinkhardt & Biermann), 412 pp.

Daaku, K. Y. (1966) 'Pre-Ashanti states', *GNQ*, 9, pp. 10–13.

Daaku, K. Y. (1968) 'A note on the fall of Ahwene Koko and its significance in Asante history', *GNQ*, 10, pp. 40–4.

Daaku, K. Y. (1969) *Oral Traditions of Adansi* (Accra-Legon: Institute of African Studies).

Daaku, K. Y. (1970a) *Trade and Politics in the Gold Coast, 1600–1720* (Oxford: Clarendon Press, Oxford Studies in African Affairs), 219 pp.

Daaku, K. Y. (1970b) *Oral Traditions of Denkyira* (University of Ghana).

Daaku, K. Y. (1971) 'A history of Sehwi: a survey of oral evidence', *RR*, 7, 3.

Daaku, K. Y. (nd) *Unknown Aowin, Its People and Their Traditional History* (University of Ghana, unpublished).

Dalrymple, A. (1806) *Collection of Nautical Memoirs and Journals*.

Dampierre, E. de (1968) *Un ancien royaume Bandia du Haut-Oubangui* (Paris: Plon, Recherches en sciences humaines, 24), 601 pp.

Dankoussou, I. (1970) *Traditions historiques des Katsinaawa après le Jihad* (Niamey: CRDTO).

Dantzig, A. van (1978) *The Dutch and the Guinea Coast, 1674–1742: A Collection of Documents from the General State Archives at The Hague* (Accra: GASS), 375 pp.

Dapper, O. (1668) *Naukeurige Beschrijvinge der Afrikaensche gewesten van Egypten, Barbaryen, Libyen,*

925

Biledulgerid ... (Amsterdam: Van Meurs); 1670 Engl. trans. and adaptation, J. Ogilby, *Africa: Being an Accurate Description of the Regions of Aegypt, Barbary, Libya, etc.* (London); 1670 German trans., *Beschreibung von Afrika* ... (Amsterdam: Van Meurs); 1686 French trans., *Description de l'Afrique* ... (Amsterdam: Wolfgang, Waesberge *et al.*).

Dapper, O. (1676) *Umstaendliche und Eigentliche Beschreibung von Africa* (Amsterdam: Jacob von Meurs).

Dapper, O. and Ryder, A. F. C. (1965) 'Dutch trade on the Nigerian coast during the 17th century', *JHSN*, 3, 2, pp. 196–210.

D'Arianoff, A. (1952) *Histoire des Bagesera, souverains du Gisaka* (Brussels: Institut royal colonial belge), 138 pp.

Darling, P. J. (1979) 'Fieldwork surveys in the Benin and Ishan kingdoms', *Nyame Akuma*, **15**, pp. 35–9.

Darling, P. J. (1983) *Iron Smelting in and around Hausaland, Northern Nigeria* (University of Jos).

Da Silva Correa, E. (1937) *Historia de Angola (1782?)*, (2 vols, Lisbon: Editorial Atica, Coleção dos classicos da expansao portuguesa no mondo).

Da Silva Costa Lobo, A. (1904) *História da Sociedade em Portugal no seculo XV* (Lisbon).

Da Silva Rego, A. (1948) *A Dupla Restauração de Angola (1641–1648)* (Lisbon: Agencia Geral das Colonias).

Daumas-Chancel, A. (1848) *Le grand désert* (Paris).

David, N. (1982) 'Prehistory and historical linguistics in Central Africa: Points of contact', in C. Ehret and M. Posnansky (eds), pp. 78–95.

David, P. H. (1969) 'Maradi precolonial', *BIFAN*, 31, 3, pp. 638–88.

Davidson, B. (1965) *The Growth of African Civilisation: A History of West Africa, 1000–1800* (London: Longmans), 320 pp.

Davis, D. B. (1966/1975) *The Problem of Slavery in Western Culture* (2 vols, New York: OUP).

Davis, D. B. (1984) *Slavery and Human Progress* (New York: OUP), 374 pp.

Davis, R. (1967) *A Commercial Revolution: English Overseas Trade in the Seventeenth and Eighteenth Centuries* (London: Historical Association).

Davis, R. (1969) 'English foreign trade, 1660–1774', in W. E. Minchinton (ed.), pp. 78–120.

Deane, P. and Cole, W. A. (1967) *British Economic Growth, 1688–1959* (2nd edn, Cambridge: CUP).

Debourou, D. M. (1979) *Commerçants et chefs de l'ancien Borgou, des origines à 1936* (Paris: Université de Paris 1, CRA).

Debrunner, H. W. (1965) *The Church in Togo: A Church Between Colonial Powers* (London: Lutterworth), 368 pp.

Debrunner, H. W. (1967) *A History of Christianity in Ghana* (Accra: Waterville Publishing House), 375 pp.

De Constantin (1725) *Recueil des Voyages ... de la Compagnie des Indes Orientales.*

Defoort, E. (1913) 'L'Androy', *BEM*, 13, 2, pp. 127–246.

Degrandpré, L. (1801) *Voyage à la côte occidentale d'Afrique, fait dans les années 1786 et 1787* (2 vols, Paris: Dentu).

Delafosse, M. (1912) *Le Haut-Sénégal–Niger (Soudan français)* (3 vols, Paris: Larose).

Delafosse, M. (1913) 'Traditions historiques et légendaires du Soudan occidental', *Publications du Comité de l'Afrique française.*

Delcourt, A. (1952) *La France et les établissements français du Sénégal entre 1713 et 1763* (Dakar: Mémoires de l'IFAN No. 17), 432 pp.

Delgado, R. (1948–55) *História de Angola* (4 vols, Benguela: Edição da Tip. do Jornal de Benguela).

Delobsom, A. D. (1929) *'Les "Nionissés" de Goupana,'* *Cahiers d'Outre-Mer*, 1, 4, pp. 419–46.

Demesse, L. (1978) *Changements techno-économiques et sociaux chez les pygmées Babinga* (2 vols, Paris).

Demesse, L. (1980) *Techniques et économies des pygmées Babinga* (Paris: Institut d'Ethnologie), 301 pp.

Denham, D. (1826) *Narratives of Travels and Discoveries in Northern and Central Africa* (London: John Murray).

Denis, P. (1961) *Histoire des Mangbetu et des Matshaga jusqu'à l'arrivée des Belges* (Tervuren: MRAC, archives d'ethnographie, No. 2), 167 pp.

Denne, Mrs (nd) (tr.) *Kiziba: Land and People (Kiziba: Land und Leute).*

Denolf, P. (1954) *Aan den rand van der Dihese* (Brussels: ARSOM, Coll. in 8°, Vol. 34, No. 1).

Denoon, D. (ed.) (1972) *A History of Kigezi in South-West Uganda* (Kampala: The National Trust).

Denoon, D. (1983) *Settler Capitalism: The Dynamics of Dependent Development in the Southern Hemisphere* (Oxford).

Denoon, D. (ed.) (forthcoming) *Uganda Before 1900*, vol. 2.

Denoon, D. and Snowden, C. (eds) (1981) *A History of Agriculture in Papua New Guinea* (Port Moresby).

Deschamps, H. (1936) *Les Antaisaka* (Antananarivo).

Deschamps, H. (1949/1972) *Les pirates à Madagascar aux XVIIe et XVIIIe siècles* (2nd edn, 1972, Paris: Berger-Levrault), 1st edn, 244 pp.

Deschamps, H. (1961/1965) *Histoire de Madagascar* (2nd and 3rd edns, Paris: Berger-Levrault, Monde d'Outre-mer, Série Histoire), 348 pp.

Deschamps, H. (1962) *Traditions orales et archives au Gabon: contribution à l'ethno-histoire* (Paris: Berger-Levrault), 172 pp.

Deschamps, H. and Vianès, S. (1959) *Les Malgaches du sud-est* (Paris: PUF), 118 pp.

Devisse, T. (1982) 'L'apport de l'archéologie à l'histoire de l'Afrique occidentale entre le Ve et le XIIe siècle', *Comptes rendus de l'Académie des inscriptions et belles lettres* (Paris, January–March), pp. 156–77.

Diabaté, H. (1977) 'Mlan Alua, Blahima du Sanwi', *BIFAN*, **39**, 2, Ser. B, pp. 304–340.

Diabaté, H. (1984) 'La formation du royaume Sanvi, 1700–1843' (MA thesis, University of Paris I).

Diagne, P. (1967) *Pouvoir politique traditionnel en Afrique occidentale: essai sur les institutions politiques précoloniales* (Paris: PA), 249 pp.

Diagne, P. (1976) *Formations sociales africaines* (Manuscript, UCLA).

Diagne, S. (1975) 'Le Bundu des origines au protectorat français de 1858' (MA thesis, Dakar).

Diallo, I. P. (1981) *Liptako Speaks – History From Oral Tradition In Africa* (Irwin Paul, PUP).

Diallo, T. (1972) *Les institutions politiques du Fouta Djalon au XIXe siècle* (Dakar: IFAN, Initiations et études africaines), 276 pp.

Dickson, K. B. (1969) *A Historical Geography of Ghana* (Cambridge: CUP), 379 pp.

Dike, K. O. (1956) *Trade and Politics in the Niger Delta, 1830–1885: An Introduction to the Economic and Political History of Nigeria* (Oxford: Clarendon Press, Oxford Studies in African Affairs), 250 pp.

Diop, A. B. (1981) *La société wolof, tradition et changement: les systèmes d'inégalité et de domination* (Paris: Karthala), 355 pp.

Diouf, M. (1980) 'Le Kajoor au XIXe siècle et la conquête coloniale' (PhD thesis, Paris, University of Paris I).

Documentos Sobre os Portuguezes em Moçambique e na Africa Central, 1497–1840 [*Documents on the Portuguese in Mozambique and Central Africa, 1497–1840*] (Lisbon: National Archives of Rhodesia and Centro de Estudos Historicos Ultramarinos; (1962–1975 in progress); 8 vols, covering the period 1497–1588.

Dokaji, A. A. (1978) *Kano Ta Dabo Cigari* (Zaria: NNPC).

D'Orjo de Marchovelette, E. (1950–1) 'Notes sur les funérailles des chefs Ilunga Kabala et Kabongo Kumwimba. Historique de la chefferie Kongolo, *BJIDCC*, 18, pp. 350–68 and 19, pp. 1–12.

Dramani-Issifou, Z. (1982) *L'Afrique noire dans les relations internationales au XVIe siècle: analyse de la crise entre le Maroc et le Sonrhai* (Paris: Karthala), 257 pp.

Drury, R. (1729/1890) *Madagascar or Robert Drury's Journal During Fifteen Years of Captivity on That Island (ca. 1701–1717)* (London), 464 pp.

Dubins, B. (1969a) 'The Comoro Islands: A bibliographical essay', *African Studies Bulletin*, **12**, 2, pp. 131–7.

Dubins, B. (1969b) 'Nineteenth-century travel literature on the Comoro Islands: A bibliographical essay', *African Studies Bulletin*, **12**, 2, pp. 138–46.

Dubois, H. M. (1938) *Monographie des Betsileo (Madagascar)* (Paris: Institut ethnologique).

Du Bois, W.E.B. (1974) *Les voyages faits par le Sieur D.B. aux Iles Dauphine ou Madagascar, et Bourbon ou Mascarene, es années 1669–1672* (Paris).

Dufeil, M. M. (1980–81) 'Afrique, taxinomie, historie', *CCAH*, **5**, pp. 7–30 and 6, pp. 7–37.

Dugast, I., McCulloch, M. and Littlewood, M. (1954) *Peoples of the Central Cameroons* (London: IAI, Ethnographic survey of Africa: Western Africa, Part 9), 174 pp.

Duisburg, A. von (1942) *In Lande des Chegbu von Bornu* (Berlin: D. Reimer), 162 pp.

Dumestre, G. (1974/1980) *La geste de Ségou* (Paris: A Colin) (2nd edn, 1980), 1st edn, 579 pp.

Dunbar, A. R. (1965) *A History of Bunyoro-Kitara* (Nairobi: EALB), 265 pp.

Dunn, R. S. (1972) *Sugar and Slaves: The Rise of the Planter Class in the English West Indies, 1624–1713* (New York: Chapel Hill, UNCP).

Dupire, M. (1962) *Peuls nomades* (Paris: Institut d'ethnologie), 336 pp.

Dupon, J. F. (1969) *Recueil de documents pour servir à l'histoire de Rodrigues* (Port Louis, Mauritius: Mauritius Archives Publications No. 10).

Dupré, G. (1982) *Un ordre et sa destruction* (Paris: ORSTOM), 446 pp.

Dupuis, J. (1824/1966) *Journal of a residence in Ashantee* (London: Colburn); 2nd edn, 1966, London:

Frank Cass, Part I: 264 pp., Part II: 135 pp.

Dupuis-Yacouba, A. (1921) *Industries et principales professions des habitants de la région de Tombouctou* (Paris: Publications du Comité d'études historiques et scientifiques), 193 pp.

Duveyrier, H. (1859) *Coup d'oeil sur le pays des Beni-Mzab* (Paris: Imprimerie L. Martinet).

Duysters, L. (1958) 'Histoire de Aluunda', *Problèmes de l'Afrique centrale*, **12**, pp. 75–98.

East, R. M. (1979) *Labarun Hausawa Da Makwabtansu* (2 vols, Zaria: NNPC).

Echard, N. (1975) 'L'expérience du passé – Histoire de la société paysanne hausa de l'Ader', *EN*, **36** (Niamey: CNRSS).

Effah-Gyamfi, C. K. (1978) 'Bono-Manso: Archaeological investigation into an early Akan urbanism' (PhD thesis, University of Ghana: Accra).

Ehret, C. (1971) *Southern Nilotic History: Linguistic Approaches to the Study of the Past* (Evanston: NUP), 200 pp.

Ehret, C. (1973) 'Patterns of Bantu and Central Sudanic settlement in central and southern Africa (1000 BC–500 AD)', *TJH*, **3**, 1, pp. 1–71.

Ehret, C. (1974) 'Some thoughts on the early history of the Nile–Congo watershed', *Ufahamu*, **5**, 2, pp. 85–112.

Ehret, C. (1982) 'Population movement and culture content in the Southern Sudan, *c.* 3000 B.C. to A.D. 1000 – a preliminary linguistic overview', in J. Mack and P. Robertshaw (eds), pp. 19–48.

Ehret, C. and Posnansky, M. (eds) (1982) *The Archaeological and Linguistic Reconstruction of African History* (Berkeley: UCP), 299 pp.

Eilu, A. B. (1976) 'Migration and settlement of the Kumam', in Onyango-ka-Odongo and J. B. Webster (eds), pp. 398–413.

Ekadu, J. E. (1961) *Kumam Ikare One Asonya* (London: Longmans). (Trans. into English by A. B. Eilu as 'The Kumam during the Asonya', unpublished, History Department, Makerere University, 1971).

El-Ḥasnāwī, H. W. (ed.) (1982) *A History of Trans-Saharan Trade Routes* (Tripoli).

Ellis, W. (1838) *History of Madagascar* (2 vols, London: Fisher).

Ellison, R. E. (1936) 'Marriage and childbirth among the Kanuri', *Africa*, **9**, 4, pp. 524–35.

Elphick, R. (1977) *Kraal and Castle: Khoikhoi and the Founding of White South Africa* (New Haven: YUP, Yale Historical Publications, Miscellany, 116), 266 pp.

Elphick, R. and Giliomee, H. (eds) (1979) *The Shaping of South African Society, 1652–1820* (Cape Town/London: Longman), 415 pp.

Elphick, R. and Shell, R. (1979) 'Intergroup relations: Khoikhoi, settlers, slaves and free blacks, 1652–1795', in R. Elphick and H. Giliomee (eds), pp. 116–69.

Eltis, D. (1977) 'The export of slaves from Africa, 1821–1843', *JEH*, **37**, 2.

Eltis, D. (1979) 'The direction and fluctuation of the transatlantic slave trade, 1821–1843: a revision of the 1845 Parliamentary Paper', in H. A. Gemery and J. S. Hogendorn (eds), pp 273–330.

Eltis, D. (1981) 'The direction and fluctuation of the Transatlantic trade, 1844–67' (paper presented at the African Studies Association annual meeting, Bloomington).

Emerit, M. (1954) 'Les liaisons terrestres entre le Soudan et l'Afrique du Nord au XVIIIe siècle et au début du XIXe siècle', *Trav. IRS*, **11**, pp. 29–47.

Emin Pasha (1891) 'Zur Ethnologie de Gebiete um dem Albert-See', *Das Ausland*, **18**, pp. 351–55.

Evans-Pritchard, E. E. (1940) *The Nuer* (Oxford: OUP), 271 pp.

Evans-Pritchard, E. E. (1971) *The Azande: History and Political Institutions* (Oxford: Clarendon Press), 444 pp.

Ewald, J. (1983) 'Kingdom of Taqali' (PhD thesis, University of Wisconsin).

Exelson, E. (1969) *Portuguese in Southeast Africa, 1600–1700* (Johannesburg: WUP), 179 pp.

Eyongetah, T. and Brain, R. (1974) *A History of the Cameroon* (London: Longman) 192 pp.

Eyre-Smith, S. J. (1933) *A Brief Review of the History and Social Organization of the Peoples of the Northern Territories of the Gold Coast* (Accra), 45 pp.

Fadiman, J. A. (1973) 'Early history of the Meru of Mount Kenya', *JAH*, **14**, 1, pp. 9–27.

Fage, J. D. (1969a) 'Slavery and the slave trade in the context of West African history', *JAH*, **10**, pp. 393–404.

Fage, J. D. (1969b) *A History of West Africa: An Introductory Survey* (4th edn, Cambridge: CUP), 239 pp. (Earlier edn publ. as *An Introduction to the History of West Africa*).

Fage, J. D. and Oliver, R. A. (eds) (1970) *Papers in African Prehistory* (Cambridge: CUP), 331 pp.

Fage, J. D. and Oliver, R. A. (eds) (1977) *The Cambridge History of Africa*, vol. 3, (Cambridge: CUP), 803 pp.

928

Fagering, E. (1971) *Une famille de dynasties malgaches: Zafindravola, Maroserana, Zafimbolamena, Andrevola, Zafimanely* (Oslo: Universitets forlaget).

Fagnan, E. (ed.) (1924) *Chronique anonyme saadienne* (Rabat: F. Moncho).

Fairley, N. (1978) 'Mianda ya Ben 'Ekie' (A History of the Ben 'Ekie) (PhD thesis, State University of New York).

Farb, P. (1969) *Man's Rise to Civilisation* (New York: Datton), 332 pp.

Faublée, J. (1958) 'L'Islam chez les Antemuru', *REI*, 1, pp. 65–72.

Faulkner, H. U. (1924/60) *American Economic History* (New York: Harper and Row); 1st edn 1924, 201 pp.; 8th edn 1960, 202 pp.

Feierman, S. (1968) 'The Shambaa', in A. Roberts (ed.), 1968a, pp. 1–15.

Feierman, S. (1974) *The Shambaa Kingdom: A History* (Madison: UWP), 235 pp.

Felner, A. de A. (1933) *Angola: Apontamentos sobre a ocupação é início do estabelecimento dos Portugueses no Congo, Angola e Benguela* (Coimbra: Imprensa da Universidade).

Fergusson, J. (1876) *History of Indian and Eastern Architecture* (London: Murray), 756 pp.; rev. edn J. Burgess, 2 vols, 1910 (London: Murray); reprinted 1967, Delhi).

Fergusson, J. and Hope, T. (1866) *Architecture at Ahmadabad* (London).

Fernandes, V. (1951) Descripção de Cepta por sua costa de Mauritania e Ethiopia [Description de la côte occidentale d'Afrique] ed & French trans. by T. Monod, A. Teixeira da Moka and R. Mauny. Bissau: Centro des Estudos da Guiné Portuguesa, Publicações No. 11.

Ferrand, G. (1891–1902) *Les musulmans à Madagascar et aux Iles Comores* (3 vols, Paris: Leroux).

Ferrand, G. (1902) 'La légende de Raminia', *JA*, 19, 2, 9th series, pp. 185–230.

Figueroa, F. B. (1961) *Los insurrecciones de los esclavos negros en la sociedad colonial venezolara* (Caracas).

File, N. and Power, C. (1981) *Black Settlers in Britain, 1555–1958* (London: Heinemann Educational Books).

Filesi, T. and Villapadierna, E. de (1978) *La 'Missio Antiqua' dei Cappuccini nel Congo (1645–1835): Studio Preliminare et Guida delle Fonti* (Rome: Istituto Storico Cappuccini), 269 pp.

Firinga, Sgt. (1901) 'La dynastie des Maroserana', *RM*, 3, 9, pp. 658–72.

Fisher, A. G. B. and Fisher, H. G. (1970) *Slavery and Muslim Society in Africa* (London: C. Hurst), 182 pp.

Fisher, H. E. S. (1963) 'Anglo-Portuguese trade, 1700–1770', *EHR*, 16, 2nd Series, reprinted in W. E. Minchinton (ed.), pp. 144–64.

al-Fishtālī, 'Abd al-Azīz (1964) *Manahil al-Safa fi Akhbar al-Muluk al-Shurafa* (Rabat: Gunum Allan).

Flacourt, E. de (1658/1661/1913) *Histoire de la Grande Ile de Madagascar* (1st edn 1658; 2nd edn 1661, Paris: Clougier). (Also reprinted in modern French in A. Grandidier *et al.* (eds), vol. 8 (1913).

Flacourt, E. de (1661) *Relation de ce qui s'est passé en Ile de Madagascar depuis l'année 1642 jusqu'en 1660* (also reprinted in modern French in A. Grandidier *et al.* (eds), vol. 9 (1920).

Flad, J. M. A. (1869) *A Short Description of the Falashas and Kamants in Abyssinia* (London: MacIntosh).

Flint, J. E. (ed.) (1976) *The Cambridge History of Africa*, vol. 5 (Cambridge: CUP).

Fontaine, P. M. (1970) 'West Indian contribution to nationalism', in *The Black Prism* (New York).

Fontoynont, M. and Raomandahy, E. (1937) *La Grande Comore* (Mémoires de l'Académie malgache, vol. 23).

Fontoynont, M. and Raomandahy, E. (1939) 'Les Antaifasy', *BAM*, n.s., 22, pp. 1–7.

Forde, C. D. and Jones, G. I. (1950/1962) *The Ibo and Ibibio-speaking Peoples of South-Eastern Nigeria* (London: IAI, Ethnographic Survey of Africa, Part III), 94 pp.

Forde, C. D. and Kaberry, P.M. (eds) (1967) *West African Kingdoms in the Nineteenth Century* (London: IAI/OUP), 289 pp.

Forde, D. (1951) *The Yoruba-speaking Peoples of South-West Africa* (London: IAI, Ethnographic Survey of Africa, Part IV), 101 pp.

Forde, D. (ed.) (1956) *Efik Traders of Old Calabar* (London: OUP).

Fortes, M. (1940) 'The political system of the Tallensi of the Northern Territories of the Gold Coast', in M. Fortes and E. E. Evans-Pritchard (eds), *African Political Systems* (London: OUP), pp. 239–71.

Fortes, M. (1945) *The Dynamics of Clanship among the Tallensi* (London: OUP), 270 pp.

Fosse, E. de la (1897) 'Voyage à la côte occidentale d'Afrique en Portugal et en Espagne (1479–1480)', *Revue Hispanique* (Paris), 4, pp. 174–201.

Fouché, L. (1963) 'Foundation of the Cape Colony, 1652–1708', in E. A. Benians, J. Butler, P.N.S. Mansergh & E. A. Walker (eds), *The Cambridge History of the British Empire*, vol. 8, pp. 113–45 (CUP).

Franklin, J. H. (1967) *From Slavery to Freedom: A History of American Negroes* (first published 1956) (New York: Knopf), 686 pp.

Freedman, J. (1979) 'Three Muraris, three Gahayas and the four phases of Nyabingi', in J. B. Webster, (ed.), 1979a, pp. 175–88.

Freeman-Grenville, G. S. P. (1960) 'East African coin finds and their historical significance', *JAH*, I, pp. 31–43.

Freeman-Grenville, G. S. P. (1962a) *The Medieval History of the Tanganyika Coast* (Oxford: Clarendon Press), 238 pp. (2nd edn 1966, 314 pp).

Freeman-Grenville, G. S. P. (ed.) (1962b) *The East African Coast: Select Documents from the First to Earlier Nineteenth Century* (Oxford: Clarendon Press), 314 pp.

Freeman-Grenville, G. S. P. (1963) 'The coast, 1498–1840', in R. Oliver and G. Mathew (eds), pp. 129–68.

Freeman-Grenville, G. S. P. (1965) *The French at Kilwa Island: An Episode in Eighteenth-Century East African History* (Oxford, Clarendon Press), 243 pp.

Freeman-Grenville, G. S. P. (ed.) (1980) *The Mombasa Rising against the Portuguese, 1631, from Sworn Evidence* (London: OUP), 166 pp.

Freund, W. M. (1979) 'The Cape under the transitional governments, 1795–1814', in R. Elphick and H. Giliomee (eds), pp. 211–40.

Frobenius, L. (1911–13) *Und Africa Sprach* (3 vols, Berlin, Charlottenburg: Vita, Deutsches Verlagshaus, S. D.).

Frobenius, L. (1924) *Dichten und Denken im Sudan*, vol. 5 (Jena: Atlantis).

Froberville, E. de (1845) 'Historique des invasions Madécasses aux Iles Comores et à la côte orientale d'Afrique', *AVG*, 2, pp. 194–208.

Fyfe, C. (1964) *Sierra Leone Inheritance* (London: OUP), 352 pp.

Fyfe, C. (1965) 'Peoples of the Windward Coast, A.D. 1000–1800', in J. F. A. Ajayi and I. Espie (eds), pp. 149–65.

Fyfe, C. and McMaster, D. (eds) (1977 and 1981) *African Historical Demography*, vol. 1, 1977, 473 pp; vol. 2, 1981 (Edinburgh: EUP).

Fynn, J. K. (1971) 'Ghana-Asante (Ashanti)', in M. Crowder (ed.), *West African Resistance*, pp. 19–52.

Fynn, J. K. (1975) *A Junior History of Ghana* (London: Longman).

Gado, B. (1972) *Gazetters of the Northern Province of Nigeria*, vol. 1 (London: Frank Cass).

Gado, B. (ed.) (1980), ' "*Le Zarmatarey*": *Contribution à l'histoire des populations d'entre Niger et Dallol Mawri*', *EN*, vol. 45, (Niamey: IRSH), 356 pp.

Galloway, W. F. (1974) 'A History of Wuli from the thirteenth to the nineteenth century', (PhD thesis, Indiana University).

Gamitto, A. C. P. (1960) *King Kazembe and the Maravi, Chewa, Bisa, Bemba, Lunda and Other Peoples of Southern Africa*, trans. by I. Cunnison (2 vols, Lisbon: Junta de Investigações do Ultramar, Centro de estudos politicos e sociais, Estudos de ciencias politicas e sociais No. 43).

Gannun, A. (ed.) (1964) *Al-Rasa'il al-Sa'diyya* (Tetuan/Rabat: 'Abd Allāli Gannun).

Garbett, G. K. (1966) 'Religious aspects of political succession among the valley Korekore', in E. Stokes and R. Brown (eds), pp. 137–71.

Garlake, P. S. (1954) 'Excavations at the seventeenth-century Portuguese site of Dambarare, Rhodesia', *PTRSA*, **54**, 1, pp. 23–61.

Garlake, P. S. (1966) *The Early Islamic Architecture of the East African Coast* (Nairobi, London: BIEA, Memoir No. 1, published for the Institute of History and Archaeology in East Africa by OUP), 207 pp.

Garlake, P. S. (1973) *Great Zimbabwe* (London: Thames and Hudson), 224 pp.

Garlake, P. S. (1978) 'Pastoralism and Great Zimbabwe', *JAH*, 19, 4, pp. 479–93.

Garlake, P. S. (1982) *Life at Great Zimbabwe* (Gweru: Mambo Press).

Garlake, P. S. (1983) *Early Zimbabwe: From the Matopos to Inyanga* (Gweru: Mambo Press).

Garrard, T. F. (1980) *Akan Weights and the Gold Trade* (London: Longman), 393 pp.

Garry, A. M. (1976) 'Pajule: the failure of Palwo centralization', in Onyango-ka-Odongo and J. B. Webster (eds), pp. 320–34.

Gaudebout, P. and Vernier, E. (1941) 'Notes sur une campagne de fouilles à Vohémar', *BAM*, new series, **24**, pp. 91–114.

Gautier, E. F. and Froidevaux, H. (1907) 'Un manuscrit arabico-malgache sur les campagnes de La Case dans l'Imoro, 1656–1663', *Académie des Inscriptions et Belles Lettres, Notices et extraits* (Paris), **39**, 1, pp. 31–177.

Gauze, A. L. Téty (1969) 'Contribution à l'histoire du peuplement de la Côte d'Ivoire', *Annales de l'Université d'Abidjan*, Series F.

Gauze, A. L. Téty (1982) 'Histoire des Magwe', in *Godo-Godo* (University of Abidjan) Special Number, pp. 13–43.

Gayibor, N. L. (1977) *Recueil des sources orales du pays Aja-Ewe* (Lomé).

Gemery, H. A. and Hogendorn, J. S. (eds) (1979) *The Uncommon Market: Essays in the Economic History of the Atlantic Slave Trade* (New York: Academic Press), 442 pp.

Genovese, E. D. (1979) *From Rebellion to Revolution* (Baton Rouge: Louisiana State University Press), 173 pp.

Geraud, F. (1972) 'The settlement of the Bakiga', in D. Denoon (ed.), pp. 23–55.

Gevrey, A. (1870/1972) *Essai sur les Comores* (1st edn 1870; 1972 edn, Antananarivo: Travaux et documents du musée d'art et d'archéologie de l'Université, No. 10).

Gibbon, E. (1956) *The Decline and Fall of the Roman Empire* (6 vols, London: J. M. Dent and Sons; New York: E. P. Dutton and Co.).

Giliomee, H. (1979a) 'The Eastern Frontier, 1770–1812', in R. Elphick and H. Giliomee (eds), pp. 291–337.

Giliomee, H. (1979b) 'The burgher rebellions on the Eastern Frontier, 1795–1815', in R. Elphick and H. Giliomee (eds), pp. 338–356.

Glass, D. V. and Eversley, D. E. C. (eds) (1965) *Population in History: Essays in Historical Demography* (London: Edward Arnold), 692 pp.

Gleave, M. B. and White, H. P. (1969) 'The West African Middle belt: environmental fact or geographers' fiction?', *Geographical Review*, **59**, pp. 123–39.

Godard L. (1859) *Le Maroc, notes d'un voyageur* (Algiers).

Godinho de Magalhães, V. (1962) *A economia dos descobrimentos henriquinos* (Lisbon: Sá da Costa).

Godinho de Magalhães, V. (1969) *L'économie de l'empire portugais aux XVe et XVIe siècles* (Paris: SEVPEN).

Godinho de Magalhães, V. (1978) *Ensaios Sobre Historia de Portugal* (2 vols, Lisbon: Sá da Costa).

Godlouton, W. A. (1945) 'The journeys of Antonio Fernandes: the first known European to find the Monomatapa and to enter Southern Rhodesia', *PTRSA*, **2**, pp. 71–103.

Goertzen, G. A. von (1895) *Dutch Afrika von Ost nach West* (Berlin: D. Reimer), 417 pp.

Golberry, A. (1802) *Fragments d'un voyage en Afrique* (Paris: Treuttel et Würtz), 522 pp.

Gomes, A. (1959) 'Viagem que Fez O Padre Antonio Gomes da Companhia de Jesus, ao Imperio de (sic) Manomotapa e Assistencia que Fez nas Ditas Terras de Algunos Annos', with notes by E. Axelson, *Studia*, **3**, pp. 155–242.

Gonçalves, A. C. (1980) *La symbolisation politique: le 'prophétisme' Kongo au XVIIIe siècle* (Cologne: Neltforum Verlag).

Goody, J. (1956) *Social Organization of the Lowili* (London: IAI/OUP), 119 pp.

Goody, J. (1964) 'The Mande in the Akan hinterland', in R. Mauny, L. V. Thomas and J. Vansina (eds), pp. 193–218.

Goody, J. (1967) 'The over-kingdom of Gonja', in D. Forde and P. M. Kaberry (eds), pp. 179–205.

Gorju, J. (1920) *Entre le Victoria, l'Albert et l'Edouard* (Marseilles: Procure des Pères Blancs), 372 pp.

Gorju, J. (1938) *Face au royaume hamite du Ruanda, le royaume frère de l'Urundi* (Brussels: Vromant), 118 pp.

Goswamy, B. N. and Ballapeceola, A. L. (1978) 'Paintings in Kutch: Preliminary notes on a group of miniatures', *Artibus Asiae*, **40**, 1, pp. 62–74.

Gould, J. D. ((1964) 'The price revolution reconsidered', *EHR*, **17**, 2nd series, December, pp. 249–66.

Gourou, P. (1953) *La densité de la population du Ruanda-Urundi: Esquisse d'une étude géographique* (Brussels: Institut royal colonial belge), 239 pp.

Goveia, E. V. (1965) *Slave Society in the British Leeward Islands at the End of the Eighteenth Century* (New Haven: YUP), 370 pp.

Grandchamp, P. (1937) 'Une mission délicate en Barbarie au XVIIe siècle', *RT*, **31–32**, 3rd-4th quarters, pp. 471–3.

Grandidier, A. (1908–28) *Ethnographie de Madagascar* (Paris).

Grandidier, G. (1942) *Histoire politique et coloniale (de Madagascar)*, vol. 5 (Paris).

Grandidier, A., Charles-Roux, J., Delherbe, C. Froidevaux, H. and Grandidier, G. (eds) (1903–20) *Collections des ouvrages anciens concernant Madagascar* (9 vols, Paris: Comité de Madagascar).

Grandidier, G. and Decary, R. (1958) *Histoire politique et coloniale (de Madagascar)* vol. 5, part 3 (Antananarivo).

Grant, C. (Baron) (1801) *The History of Mauritius or the Isle of France and the Neighbouring Islands* (London: W. Bulmer and Co.), 571 pp.

Gray, J. M. (1948) 'A journey by land from Tete to Kilwa in 1616', *TNR*, 25, pp. 37–45.

Gray, J. M. (1958) *Early Portuguese Missionaries in East Africa* (London: MacMillan, in association with the EALB), 53 pp.

Gray, J. M. (1962) *History of Zanzibar from the Middle Ages to 1856* (London: OUP), 314 pp.

Gray, R. (1961) *A History of the Southern Sudan* (London: OUP), 219 pp.

Gray, R. (ed.) (1975) *The Cambridge History of Africa*, vol. 4 (Cambridge: CUP), 738 pp.

Gray, R. and Birmingham, D. (eds) (1970) *Precolonial African Trade: Essays on Trade in Central and Eastern Africa Before 1900* (London: OUP), 308 pp.

Gray, R. and Ehret C. (1975) 'Eastern Africa', in R. Gray (ed.), pp. 469–536.

Gray, R. and Marks, S. (1975) 'Southern Africa and Madagascar', in R. Gray (ed.), pp. 385–408.

Greenberg, J. H. (1963) *The Languages of Africa* (The Hague: Mouton, for Indiana University), 177 pp.

Greenberg, J. H. (1980) 'Classification of African Languages', *General History of Africa*, Vol. I, ch. 12 (Paris: UNESCO; London: Heinemann; Berkeley: University of California Press), pp. 292–308.

Grey, E. (ed.) (1892) *The Travels of Pietro della Valle in India* (London).

Grigg, D. B. (1980) *Population Growth and Agrarian Change: An Historical Perspective* (Cambridge: CUP).

Grottanelli, V. L. (1940) *I Mao* (Rome).

Grottanelli, V. L. (1941) 'Gli Scinascia del Nilo Azurro', *RSE*, I, 3, pp. 234–70.

Grottanelli, V. L. (1953) 'I Bantu del Giuba nelle tradizioni dei Wazegua', *Geographia Helvetica*, 8 (Bern: Geographische gesellschaft).

Grottanelli, V. L. (1955) 'A lost African metropolis', in *Afrikanistische Studien D. Westermann Zum 80. Geburtstag gewidmet* (Berlin: Deutsche Akademie der Wissenschaften za Berlin), pp. 231–42.

Grottanelli, V. L. (1975) 'The peopling of the Horn of Africa', in H. N. Chittick and R. I. Rotberg (eds), pp. 44–75.

Guelke, L. (1979) 'The white settlers, 1652–1789', in R. Elphick and H. Giliomee (eds), pp. 41–74.

Guillain, C. (1845) *Documents sur l'histoire, la géographie et le commerce de la partie occidentale de Madagascar* (Paris).

Guillot, B. (1973) *La terre Enkou* (Paris: Mouton), 126 pp.

Guillot, C. F. (1961) *Negros rebeldes y negros cimarrones: perfil afro-americano en la historia del Nuevo Mundo durante el siglo XVI* (Montevideo: Farina).

Guthrie, M. (1948) *The Classification of the Bantu Languages* (London: OUP, for the IAI), 91 pp.

Gutman, H. G. (1976) *The Black Family in Slavery and Freedom* (New York: Pantheon Books), 664 pp.

Guy, J. (1979) *The Destruction of the Zulu Kingdom: The Civil War in Zululand, 1879–1884* (London: Longman), 273 pp.

Gwynne, M. D. (1975) 'The origin and spread of some domestic food plants of Eastern Africa', in H. N. Chittick and R. I. Rotberg (eds), pp. 248–71.

Haberland, E. (1959) 'Die Basketto', in Ad. E. Jensen (ed.), pp. 189–226.

Haberland, E. (1963) *Galla Süd-Äthiopiens*, with a contribution of K. Reinhardt (Stuttgart: W. Kohlhammer), 815 pp.

Haberland, E. (1964a) 'The influence of the Christian Ethiopian Empire on Southern Ethiopia', *JSS*, 9, pp. 235–8.

Haberland, E. (1964b) *König und Paria in Afrika* (München: K. Renner).

Haberland, E. (1965) *Untersuchungen zum äthiopischen Königtum* (Wiesbaden: Franz Steiner Verlag), 353 pp.

Haberland, E. (1976) *Atles Christentum in Süd-Äthiopien: Eine vergessene Missionsepoche*, Frankfurter Historische Vorträge 2 (Wiesbaden: Steiner) 23 pp.

Haberland, E. (forthcoming) *Caste and Hierarchy – The Case of the Dizi (Southern Ethiopia)*.

Hacquard, A. (1900) *Monographie de Tombouctou* (Paris: Société des éditions coloniales et maritimes), 119 pp.

Hafkin, N. J. (1973) 'Trade, society and politics in Northern Mozambique, *c.* 1753–1913' (PhD thesis, Boston University).

Hagan, G. P. (1971) 'Ashanti bureaucracy', *THSG*, 12, pp. 43–62.

Hagenbucher Sacripanti, F. (1973) *Les fondements spirituels du pouvoir au royaume de Loango, R. P. du Congo* (Paris: ORSTOM), 214 pp.

Haig, Sir W. (ed.) (1937) *The Cambridge History of India*, vol. 3 (London: CUP).

Hair, P. E. H. (1965) 'The enslavement of Koelle's informants', *JAH*, 6, 2, pp. 193–203.

Hair, P. E. H. (1967) 'Ethnolinguistic continuity on the Guinea coast', *JAH*, 8, 2, pp. 247–68.

932

Hair, P. E. H. (1968) 'An ethnolinguistic inventory of the Lower Guinea coast before 1700: Part I', *ALR*, 7, pp. 47–73.

Hair, P. E. H. (1974) 'From language to culture: some problems in the systematic analysis of the ethnohistorical records of the Sierra Leone region', in R. P. Moss and R. J. A. R. Rathlone, *The Population Factor in African Studies* (London: ULP), pp. 71–83.

Hair, P. E. H. (1976) 'Some minor sources for Guinea, 1519–1559: Enciso and Alfonce Fonteneau', *HA*, 3, pp. 30–1.

al-Hajj, M. A. (1968) 'A seventeenth-century chronicle on the origins and missionary activities of the Wangarawa', *KS*, 1, 4, pp. 7–42.

al-Hajj, M. A. (1979) 'The meaning of the Sokoto jihad', in Y. B. Usman (ed.), 1979b, pp. 3–19.

al-Hajj, M. A. (1983) 'Some diplomatic correspondence of the Sefuwa Mais of Borno with Egypt, Turkey and Morocco', in Y. B. Usman and M. N. Alkali (eds).

Hall, G. M. (1976) 'Dendroclimatology, rainfall and human adaptation in the Later Iron Age in Natal and Zululand', *Annals of the Natal Museum* (Durban), 22, 3, pp. 693–703.

Hallet, R. (ed.) (1964) *Records of the African Association, 1788–1831* (London: Nelson, for the Royal Geographical Society), 318 pp.

Hama, B. (1966) *Enquête sur les fondements et la genèse de l'unité africaine* (Paris: PA).

Hama, B. (1967a) *Histoire du Gobir de Sokoto* (Paris: PA), 167 pp.

Hama, B. (1967b) *Histoire traditionnelle d'un peuple: les Zarma-Songhay* (Paris: PA), 273 pp.

Hama, B. (1968) *Contribution à la connaissance de l'histoire des Peuls* (Paris: PA), 362 pp.

Hama, B. (1969) *Histoire traditionnelle des Peuls du Dallol Boboye* (Niamey: CRDTO), 160 pp.

Hamani, D. M. (1975) *Contribution à l'étude de l'histoire des états Hausa: l'Adar précolonial (République du Niger)* (Niamey: IRSH), 277 pp.

Hamani, D. M. (1989) *Au carrefour du Soudan et de la Berbérie: le sultanat touareg de l'Ayar* (2 vols, Paris: Université de Paris I Panthéon-Sorbonne), 521 pp.

Hamilton, A. (1727) *A New Account of the East Indies, Being the Observations and Remarks of Capt. A. Hamilton who spent his time there from 1688 to 1723* (2 vols., Edinburgh).

Hamilton, E. J. (1929) 'American treasure and the rise of capitalism', *Economica*, 9 (November), pp. 338–57.

Hamilton, E. J. (1934) *American Treasure and the Price Revolution in Spain, 1501–1650* (Cambridge, Mass.: Harvard Economic Studies, vol. 43), 428 pp.

Hamilton, R. A. (1954) 'The route of Gaspar Bocarro from Tete to Kilwa in 1616', *NJ*, 7, 2, pp. 7–14.

Hamilton, R. A. (1957a) 'Oral tradition: Central Africa', in R. A. Hamilton (ed.), pp. 19–23.

Hamilton, R. A. (ed.) (1957b) *History and Archaeology in Africa, Second Conference held in 1957 at SOAS*. (London: SOAS), 99 pp.

Hammerschmidt, E. (1977) 'Illuminierte Handschriften der Staatsbibliothek Preubischer Kulturbesitz und Handschriften vom Tānāsee', *CA*, 1.

Hanke, L. (ed.) (1969) *History of Latin American Civilization: Sources and Interpretation* (2 vols, London: Methuen).

Hansberry, W. L. (1965) 'Ethiopian ambassadors to Latin courts and Latin emissaries to Prester John', *Ethiopia Observer* (Addis Ababa), 9, 2, pp. 90–9.

Harms, R. (1981) *River of Wealth, River of Sorrow: The Central Zaire Basin in the Era of the Slave and Ivory Trade, 1500–1891* (New Haven and London: YUP), 277 pp.

Harris, J. E. (1971) *The African Presence in Asia: Consequences of the East African Slave Trade* (Evanston, Ill.: NUP), 156 pp.

Harris, J. E. (1977) 'The Black peoples of Asia', in *World Encyclopaedia of Black Peoples* (St. Clair Shores, Michigan: Scholarly Press Inc.).

Harris, J. E. (1982) *Global Dimensions of the African Diaspora* (Washington DC: HUP).

Harris, M. (1964) *Patterns of Race in the Americas* (New York: Walker and Co.).

Hartwig, G. W. (1972) 'Les Bakerebe', *CHM*, 19, 3, pp. 353–76.

Hartwig, G. W. (1976) *The Art of Survival in East Africa: The Kerebe and Long-distance Trade, 1800–1895* (New York/London: Africana Publishing), 253 pp.

Hasan, Y. F. (1965) 'The Umayyad genealogy of the Funj', *SNR*, 46, pp. 27–32.

Hasan, Y. F. (1967) *The Arabs and the Sudan* (Edinburgh: EUP), 298 pp.

Hasan, Y. F. (1971) 'External Islamic influences and the progress of Islamization in the Eastern Sudan between the fifteenth and the nineteenth centuries', in Y. F. Hasan (ed.) *Sudan in Africa* (Khartoum), pp. 73–86.

Hasan, Y. F. (1972) *Muqaddima fi Tarīkh al-Mamālik al-Islamiyya fi al-Sūdān al-Sharqi* (Khartoum: KUP).

933

Hasan, Y. F. (1975) *Dirāsāt fi Tarīkh al-Sūdān* (Khartoum: KUP).

Hasan, Y. F. (1977) 'Some aspects of the Arab slave trade from the Sudan', *SNR*, 57, pp. 85–106.

Hasan, Y. F. (unpublished) *The Fur Sultanate and the Long-distance Trade, 1650–1850* (Khartoum: KUP).

Hassan, A. and Naibi, A.S. (1952) *A Chronicle of Abuja* (Ibadan: IUP), 92 pp.

Heintze, B. (1970) 'Beitrage zur Geschichte und Kultur der Kisama, Angola', *Paideuma*, 16, pp. 159–86.

Heintze, B. (1977) 'Unbekanntes Angola: der Staat Ndongo im 16 Jahrhundert', *Anthropos*, 72, pp. 749–805.

Henige, D. (1974) 'Reflections on early interlacustrine chronology: an essay in source criticism', *JAH*, 15, 1, pp. 27–46.

Herring, R. S. (1974) 'A history of Labwor hills' (PhD thesis, University of California, Santa Barbara).

Herring, R. S. (1976) 'The Nyakwai: on the borders of the "Lwo" world', in Onyango-ka-Odongo and J. B. Webster (eds).

Herring, R. S. (1979) 'The view from Mount Otuke: migrations of the Lango Omiro', in J. B. Webster (ed.), 1979a, pp. 283–316.

Herring, R. S. (unpublished) 'The Nyakwai: on the borders of two worlds; the political history of Labwor', in D. Denoon (ed.) (forthcoming).

Herskovits, M. J. and Harwitz, M. (eds) (1964) *Economic Transactions in Africa* (London: Routledge and Kegan Paul), 444 pp.

D'Hertefelt, M. (1971) *Les clans du Rwanda ancien: éléments d'ethnosociologie et d'ethnohistoire* (Tervuren: MRAC), 85 pp.

Heusch, L. de (1964) 'Mythe et société féodale: le culte du Kubandwa dans le Rwanda traditionnel', *Archives de sociologie des religions*, juillet-décembre, pp. 133–46.

Heusch, L. de (1966) *Le Rwanda et la civilisation interlacustre* (Brussels: Université libre de Bruxelles), 417 pp. (See also D. W. Cohen, review of same in *JAH*, 1968, 4, 9, pp. 651–57).

Heusch, L. de (1972) *Le roi ivre ou l'origine de l'Etat* (Paris: Gallimard), 331 pp.

Hichens, W. (ed.) (1972) 'Sayyid Abdallah bin Ali bin Nasir bin Sheikh Abubaker bin Salim', *Al-lukishafi* (The Soul's Awakening) (London: Sheldon Press); reprinted, Nairobi: OUP, 190 pp.

Hill, A. and Kilson, M. (eds) (1969) *Apropos of Africa* (London: Frank Cass), 390 pp.

Hillelson, S. (1933) 'David Reubeni: an early visitor to Sennar', *SNR*, 16, pp. 55–66.

Hilton, A. (1985) *Family and Kingship* (Oxford: OUP).

Hiskett, M. (1962) 'An Islamic tradition of reform in the Western Sudan from the sixteenth to the eighteenth century', *BSOAS*, 25, 3, pp. 577–96.

Hiskett, M. (1984) *The Development of Islam in West Africa* (London: Longman), 353 pp.

Historia de Portugal, (1931) Vol. III (Barcelona).

Hoben, A. (1973) *Land Tenure among the Amhara of Ethiopia: The Dynamics of Cognatic Descent* (Chicago and London: University of Chicago Press).

Hoben, A. (1975) 'Family, land and class in Northwest Europe and Northern Highland Ethiopia', in H. G. Marcus (ed.), *Proceedings of the First United States Conference on Ethiopian Studies, 1973* (Michigan: African Studies Center, Michigan State University).

Hobsbawm, E. J. (1954) 'The general crisis of the European economy in the seventeenth century, Part I', *PP*, 5, pp. 33–53.

Hodgkin, T. H. (1975/1979) *Nigerian Perspectives: An Historical Anthology* (London: OUP). (1st edn 1975; 2nd edn 1979).

Holsoe, S. E. (1967) 'The cassava-leaf people: an ethno-historical study of the Vai people with particular emphasis on the Tewo chiefdom' (PhD thesis, Boston University).

Holsoe, S. E., d'Azevedo, W. L. and Gay (1969) 'Chiefdom and clan maps of Western Liberia', *LSJ*, 2, pp. 23–39.

Holsoe, S. E., d'Azevedo, W. L. and Gay (1974) 'The first "Vai" migration', Paper presented at the 6th Annual Liberian Studies Conference, University of Wisconsin, Madison).

Holt, P. M. (1960) 'A Sudanese historical legend: the Funj conquest of Sūba', *BSOAS*, 23, pp. 1–12.

Holt, P. M. (1961/1963) *A Modern History of the Sudan, from the Funj Sultanate to the present day* (London: Weidenfeld and Nicolson), 241 pp. (2nd edn 1963, 248 pp.).

Holt, P. M. (1966) *Egypt and the Fertile Crescent, 1516–1922* (London: Longman), 337 pp.

Holt, P. M. (1967) 'Sultan Selim I and the Sudan', *JAH*, 8, 1, pp. 19–22.

Holt, P. M. (ed.) (1968) *Political and Social Change in Modern Egypt: Historical Studies from the Ottoman Conquest to the United Arab Republic* (London: OUP).

Hoover, J. J. (1979) 'The seduction of Ruwej' (PhD thesis, Yale University).

Hopkins, A. G. (1966) 'Underdevelopment in the empires of the Western Sudan: a contribution to a debate started by Malowist', *PP*, **33**, pp. 149–56 (with a rejoinder by M. Malowist, pp. 157–62).

Hopkins, A. G. (1973/1975/1983) *An Economic History of West Africa* (London: Longman). (1st edn 1973, 337 pp.).

Hopkins, J. F. P. and Levtzion, N. (1981) *Corpus of Early Arabic Sources for West African History* (Cambridge: CUP), 492 pp.

Hopkins, N. S. (1971) 'Mandinka social organisation', in C. T. Hodge (ed.), *Papers on the Manding* (Bloomington: Indiana University Press), pp. 99–128.

Hornell, J. (1934) 'Indonesian influence on East African culture', *JRAI*, **64**, pp. 305–33.

Houdas, O. (tr.) (1966) *Tadhkirat al-Nisyan* (anon.), Arabic text and French trans. (Paris: Maisonneuve).

Hrbek, I. (1977) 'Egypt, Nubia and the Eastern deserts', in J. D. Fage and R. Oliver (eds), pp. 10–97.

Huet, G. (1901) 'Histoire de l'occupation du territoire des Antaimorona par les Hova', *RM*, **3**, 2, pp. 761–7.

Huffman, T. N. (1972) 'The rise and fall of Zimbabwe', *JAH*, **13**, 3, pp. 353–66.

Huffman, T. N. (1978) 'The origins of Leopard's Kopje: an 11th-century Difaqane', *Arnoldia*, **7**, 33, pp. 1–23.

Hulstaert, G. (1972) 'Une lecture critique de l'ethnie mogo de G. van der Kerken', *EHA*, **3**, pp. 27–60.

Huntingford, G. W. B. (trans. and ed.) (1965) *The Glorious Victories of Amda Seyon, King of Ethiopia* (Oxford: Clarendon Press, the Oxford Library of African Literature), 142 pp.

Hunwick, J. O. (1962) 'Note on the appointment of Askia al-Hajj Muhammad Ture as Khalifa of Western Sudan', *JHSN*.

Hunwick, J. O. (1964) 'A new source for the biography of Ahmad Baba al-Timbukti', *BSOAS*, **27**, 3, pp. 568–93.

Hunwick, J. O. (1971) 'Songhay, Bornu and Hausaland in the 16th century', in J. F. A. Ajayi and M. Crowder (eds), pp. 202–39.

Hutereau, A. (1922) *Histoire des peuplades de l'Uele et de l'Ubangi* (Brussels: Goemaere, Bibliothèque Congo, No. 1), 334 pp.

Ibn 'Abd al-Zāhir, Muhyī al-Dīn (1961) *Tashrīf al-ayyām wa 'l-uṣūr fī sīrat al-Malik al-Manṣūr* (Cairo: M. Kamil).

Ibn Abī Dīnār, al-Ḳayrāwān (1967) *Kitāb al-Mu'nis fī akhbār Ifrīḳiya wa Tūnis* (Tunis), 169 pp.

Ibn Dayf Allāh Muḥammad 'Abd Nur (1973) *Kitāb al-Ṭabaqak fī Khusus al-awliya wa 'l-Salahin fī al-Sūdān*, 2nd edn, Y. F. Hasan (ed.), (Khartoum).

Ibn Furṭūwa, Aḥmad (16th cent.) *Ta'rikh mai Idrīs wa ghazawātihi lil Imām Aḥmad Burnuwī*, 1932 ed. H. R. Palmer (Kano: Amir's Press), 1926 Engl. transl. H. R. Palmer, *History of the first twelve years of the reign of mai Idris Alooma of Bornu (1571–83), by his Imam* ('together with the 'Diwān of the sultans of Bornu') (Lagos: Government Printer): 1932 edn (Kano: Amir's Press), reprinted London, 1970.

Ibn Isḥāḳu, M. S. (1929) 'An account of Birni Gazergamu (written in Arabic in *c.*1658–9)', trans. and published in *BSOAS*.

Ibn Khaldūn Walī al-Dīn 'Abd al-Raḥmān b. Muḥammad (14th cent.) *Kitāb al-'Ibār wa-diwan al-mubtada wa 'l-Khabar* ('Universal History'), 1967 edn, vol. 2 (Beirut): Commission libanaise pour la traduction des chefs-d'oeuvre.

Idrissou, M. (1979) 'Kalfu, or the Fulbe emirate of Bagirmi and the Toorobbe of Sokoto', in Y. B. Usman (ed.), 1979b, pp. 336–75.

Ignace, E. (1970) 'A revolta dos Males', *Afro-Asia*, **10–11**, pp. 121–36.

Ikime, O. (1972) *The Isoko People* (Ibadan: IUP), 166 pp.

Ikime, O. (ed.) (1980) *Groundwork of Nigerian History* (Ibadan: Heinemann Educational Books).

Iliffe, J. (1979) *A Modern History of Tanzania* (Cambridge: CUP), 616 pp.

Imam, I. (1969) 'Kanuri marriage', *Nigerian Magazine*, **102**.

Ingham, K. (ed.) (1974) *Foreign Relations of African States* (London: Butterworth, Colston Paper, No. 75), 344 pp.

Inikori, J. E. (1976) 'Measuring the Atlantic slave trade: an assessment of Curtin and Anstey', *JAH*, **17**, 2. pp. 197–223.

Inikori, J. E. (1977) 'The import of firearms into West Africa, 1750–1807: a quantitative analysis', *JAH*, **18**, 3, pp. 339–68.

Inikori, J. E. (1979) 'The slave trade and the Atlantic economies, 1451–1870', in *The African Slave Trade from the 15th to the 19th Century: Reports and Papers of the Meeting of Experts Organised by UNESCO at Port-au-Prince, Haiti, 31 January–4 February 1978*, The General History of Africa – Studies and Documents, 2 (Paris: UNESCO), pp. 56–87.

Inikori, J. E. (1981) 'Market structure and the profits of the British African trade in the late eighteenth century', *JEH*, **41**, 4 (December), pp. 745–76.

Inikori, J. E. (ed.) (1982) *Forced Migration: The Impact of the Export Slave Trade on African Societies* (London: Hutchinson University Library for Africa; New York: Africana Publishing Company), 349 pp.

Inikori, J. E. (1983) 'West Africa's seaborne trade, 1750–1850: Volume, structure and implications' (Paper presented at the Symposium on the quantification and structure of the import and export trade of Africa in the nineteenth century, held at St. Augustin (near Bonn), Germany, 3–6 January).

Inikori, J. E. (1984) 'Slave trade, slavery and the development of industrial capitalism in England in the eighteenth century: a reassessment' (Paper presented at the Conference on capitalism and slavery in the British West Indies: the contribution of Eric Williams, Bellagio, Italy, 21–25 May).

Isaacman, A. F. (1969) 'The prazos da Coroa, 1752–1832: A functional analysis of the Portuguese political system', *Studia*, **26**, pp. 149–78.

Isaacman, A. F. (1972a) 'The origin, formation and early history of the Chikunda of South-Central Africa', *JAH*, **13**, 3, pp. 443–62.

Isaacman, A. F. (1972b) *Mozambique: the Africanization of a European Institution: the Zambezi Prazos, 1750–1902* (Madison: WUP), 260 pp.

Isichei, E. A. (1973) *The Ibo People and the Europeans: the Genesis of a relationship – to 1902* (London: Faber and Faber).

Isichei, E. A. (1976) *A History of the Igbo People* (London: Macmillan), 303 pp.

Itandala, B. (1979) 'Ilembo, Nkanda and the girls', in J. B. Webster (ed.), 1979a, pp. 145–73.

Izard, M. (1970) 'Introduction à l'histoire des royaumes mossi', *RV*, **12–13** (2 vols, Paris and Ouagadougou CNRS/CVRS).

Izard, M. (1971) 'La formation de Ouahigouya', *JSA*, **41**, 2, pp. 151–87.

Izard, M. (1975) 'Les captifs royaux dans l'ancien Yatenga', in C. Meillassoux (ed.), pp. 281–96.

Izard, M. (1980) 'Les archives orales d'un royaume africain: Recherches sur la formation du Yatenga', (MA thesis, Université de Paris V-Descartes).

Izard, M. (1981) *Histoire du Yatenga des origines à 1895* (Ouagadougou).

Jackson, J. G. (1811) *An Account of the Empire of Morocco* (London), 328 pp.

Jackson, K. (1976) 'The dimensions of Kamba pre-colonial history', in B. A. Ogot (ed.), 1976b, pp. 174–261.

Jackson, K. (1978) *The Works of the Past: A History of the Precolonial Kamba* (Stanford).

Jackson-Haight, M. V. (1967) *European Powers and South-East Africa, 1796–1856* (London: Routledge and Kegan Paul).

Jadin, L. (1961) 'Le Congo et la secte des Antoniens: restauration du royaume sous Pedro IV et la "Sainte-Antoine" congolaise (1695–1718)', *BIHBR*, **33**, pp. 411–615.

Jadin L. (1967) 'Pero Tavares, missionaire jésuite, ses travaux apostoliques au Congo et en Angola, 1629–1635', *BIHBR*, **38**, pp. 271–402.

Jadin, L. (1975) 'L'ancien Congo et l'Angola (1639–1655), d'après les archives romaines, portugaises, néerlandaises et espagnoles', *BIHBR*, **20–22** (3 vols).

Jadin, L. and Dicorato, M. (1974) *Correspondance de Dom Afonso, roi du Congo, 1506–1543* (Brussels: ARSOM **41–3**), 245 pp.

Jäger, O. A. (1957) *Aethiopische Miniaturen* (Berlin: Mann).

Jakobsen, D. (1902) 'Note sur Andriamaro, idole célèbre chez les Mahafaly', *BAM*, **1**, 1, pp. 50–2.

James, C. L. R. (1963) *The Black Jacobins: Toussaint L'Ouverture and the San Domingo Revolution* (New York: Vintage).

Janzen, J. M. (1979) 'Ideologies and institutions in the precolonial history of Equatorial African therapeutic systems', *SSM*, **13**, 4, Part B.

Janzen, J. M. (1982) *Lemba, 1650–1930: The Regional History of an African Drum of Affliction* (Lawrence, Kansas).

Jensen, Ad. E. (1936) *Im Landes des Gada* (Stuttgart: Frobenius Institute), 608 pp.

Jensen, Ad. E. (1959) *Altvölker Süd-Äthiopiens*, with a contribution by E. Haberland (Stuttgart: Kohlhammer).

Jobson, R. (1623) *The Golden Trade or a Discovery of the River Gambia and the Golden Trade of the Aethiopians* (Teignmouth, Devonshire), 218 pp.

Johnson, J. W. (1941) 'Negro companions of the Spanish explorers', *Phylon* (Atlanta University, GA), 2 (Fourth Quarter).

Johnson, J. W. (1954) *Traditional History, Customary Laws, Mores, Folkways and Legends of the Vai Tribe* (Monrovia: Department of the Interior, Republic of Liberia).

936

Johnson, J. W. (1961) *Traditional History and Folklore of the Gola Tribe in Liberia* (Monrovia: Department of the Interior, Republic of Liberia).
Johnston, H. H. (1902) *The Uganda Protectorate* (2 vols, London: Hutchinson).
Johnston, M. (1966) 'The ounce in 18th-century West African trade', *JAH*, 7, pp. 197–214.
Jones, A. (1981) 'Who were the Vai?', *JAH*, 22, pp. 159–78.
Jones, A. H. M. and Monroe, E. (1978) *A History of Ethiopia* (Oxford: OUP), 196 pp.
Jones, D. H. (1964) *The Borgu Dynasties* (London: SOAS).
Jones, D. H. (1967) 'Jakpa and the foundation of Gonja', *THSG*, 6, pp. 1–29.
Jones, G. I. (1963) *The Trading States of the Oil Rivers* (London: OUP), 262 pp.
Jordão (Levy Maria), Viscount of Paiva Manso (1877) *História do Congo* (Lisbon: Academia das Scencias de Lisboa).
Josephy, A. M., Jr. (ed.) (1971) *The Horizon History of Africa* (New York: American Heritage Publications Co.), 528 pp.
Joussaume, R. and Joussaume, H. (1972) 'Anciennes villes dans le Tchertcher (Harar)', *AE*, 8, pp. 21–30.
Julien, C. A. (1948) *Les voyages de découverte et les premiers établissements (XVe-XVIe siècles)* (Paris), 177 pp.
Julien, C. A. (1951–6) *Histoire de l'Afrique du Nord: Tunisie, Algérie, Maroc. De la conquête arabe à 1830*, 2nd edn (2 vols, Paris: Payot).
Julien, G. (1929) 'Pages arabico-madécasses', *Annales de l'Académie des sciences coloniales* (Paris), pp. 1–123.
Jully, A. (1898) 'Origine des Andriana' *NRE*, 4, pp. 890–8.
July, R. W. (1974) *A History of the African People* (London: Faber), 650 pp.

Kabongo Mukendi (1973) 'Les migrations luba vers le Kasai et leurs conséquences' (first degree dissertation, Northwestern University, Evanston, Ill.).
Kabuga, C. E. S. (1963) *Eby'Obwakabaka bwa Buganda* (Kampala).
Kagame, A. (1943–7) *Inganji Kalinga*, reprint Kabgayi, 1959.
Kagame, A. (1954) *Les organisations socio-familiales de l'ancien Rwanda* (Brussels: Académie royale des sciences coloniales), 355 pp.
Kagame, A. (1959) *La notion de génération appliquée à la généalogie dynastique et à l'histoire du Rwanda du Xe-XIe siècle à nos jours* (Brussels: Académie royale des sciences coloniales), 117 pp.
Kagame, A. (1963) *Les milices du Rwanda précolonial* (Brussels: Académie royale des sciences coloniales), 196 pp.
Kagame, A. (1972) *Un abrégé de l'ethno-histoire du Rwanda* (Butare: Editions universitaires du Rwanda), 286 pp.
Kagame, A. (1981) 'La documentation du Rwanda sur l'Afrique interlacustre des temps anciens', *CCB*, pp. 300–30.
Kaggwa, A. (1908/1949) *Mpisa Za Baganda* (Kampala), 1908; 2nd edn, *Ekitabu Kye Bika bya Baganda* (Kampala), 1949.
Kaggwa, A. (1971) *Basekabaka be Buganda*, tr. and ed. by M. S. M. Kiwanuka as *The Kings of Buganda* (Nairobi: EAPH, Historical texts of Eastern and Central Africa, No. 1), 256 pp.
Kaira, O. Y. (1970–1) 'A survey of the history of the Kaira Clan of Northern Malawi' (Student seminar paper, Chancellor College, University of Malawi).
Kake, I. B. (1948) *Les Noirs de la Diaspora* (Libreville, Gabon), 190 pp.
Kalanda, M. (1959) *Baluba et Lulua, une ethnie à la recherche d'un nouvel équilibre* (Brussels: Editions de Remarques congolaises, Etudes congolaises, No. 2), 106 pp.
Kalck, P. (1980) *Historical Dictionary of the Central African Republic* (Metuchen, N. J. and London: The Scarecrow Press), 152 pp. (African Historical Dictionaries, No. 27).
Kalinga, O. J. M. (1974) 'The Ngonde Kingdom of Northern Malawi c.1600–1895' (PhD thesis, University of London).
Kalinga, O. J. M. (1975) 'The problem of chronology in the study of Ngonde history', *MJSS*, 4, pp. 26–35.
Kalinga, O. J. M. (1977) 'The Ngonde and Lambya kingdoms: a comparison of relations between indigenous and dominant immigrant groups', (paper presented to the Conference on Southern African History, National University of Lesotho, Roma, 7–9 August).
Kalinga, O. J. M. (1978) 'The establishment and expansion of the Lambya Kingdom, 1600–1750', *ASR*, 21, 2, pp. 52–66.
Kalinga, O. J. M. (1979a) 'Trade, the Kyungus and the expansion of the Ngonde Kingdom', *IJAHS*, 12, 1, pp. 17–39.

Kalinga, O. J. M. (1979b) 'The Balowoka traders and state builders', (paper presented to the Goethe-Institut sponsored Conference on state-formation in Eastern Africa, Nakuru, Kenya, 12–14 September).

Kalinga, O. J. M. (1985) *A History of the Ngonde Kingdom* (Berlin/New York: Mouton).

Kalinga, O. J. M. (forthcoming) 'Ngonde and Lambya historical texts'.

Kamuhangire, E. R. (forthcoming) 'State formation in the salt lakes region, 1500–1850', in D. Denoon (ed.).

Kane, O. (1970a) 'Chronologie des Satigi du XVIIIe siècle', *BIFAN*, 33, Series B, No. 3, pp. 755–65.

Kane, O. (1970b) 'Samba Gelajo Jegi', *BIFAN*, 32, Series B, No. 4, pp. 911–26.

Kane, O. (1973) 'Les unités territoriales du Futa Toro', *BIFAN*, 35, Series B, No. 3, pp. 614–31.

Kane, O. (1974) 'Les Maures et le Futa Toro au XVIIIe siècle', *CEA*, 14, 2, pp. 237–52.

Kani, A. M. (forthcoming) 'The rise and influence of scholars in Hausaland before 1804', in M. Adamu (ed.), (at press (a)).

Kaniki, M. H. Y. (ed.) (1979) *Tanzania Under Colonial Rule* (London: Longman), 391 pp.

Karimou, M. (1977) *Les Mawri Zarmaphones*, *EN*, 39 (Niamey: IRSH).

Karubanga, H. K. (1949) *Bukya Nibwira* (As the sun rises and sets) (Kampala: Eagle Press).

Karugire, S. R. (1971) *A History of the Kingdom of Nkore in Western Uganda to 1896* (Oxford: Clarendon Press), 291 pp.

Katate, A. G., Nyankore, Y. and Kamagungunu, L. (1955/1967) *Abagabe b'Ankole* (History of the Kings of Ankole) (2 vols, Kampala: Eagle Press); 1967 edn, Nairobi: EALB.

Ka'ti, Maḥmūd b. al-Ḥadjdj al-Mutawakkil (1913–14) *Ta'rīkh al-fattāsh fi Akhbar al-Buldān*; Arabic text and French trans. by O. Houdas and M. Delafosse (Paris: Publications de l'Ecole des langues orientales vivantes, 5e série, No. 10), (revised 1964); 1981 UNESCO reprint of 1913–14 edn & trans. (Paris: Maisonneuve).

Katoke, I. K. (1971) 'The kingdom of Ihangiro', *CHM*, pp. 700–13.

Katoke, I. K. (1975) *The Karagwe Kingdom: A History of the Abanyambo of North Western Tanzania c.1400–1915* (Nairobi: EAPH), 182 pp.

Kawada, J. (1979) *Genèse et évolution du système politique des Mosi méridionaux* (Tokyo: A study of languages and cultures of Asia and Africa, Monograph series, 12).

Kea, R. A. (1971) 'Firearms and warfare on the Gold and Slave Coasts, from the 16th to the 19th centuries', *JAH*, 12, 2, pp. 185–213.

Keen, B. and Wasserman, M. (1980) *A Short History of Latin America* (Boston: Houghton Mifflin), 574 pp.

Keim, C. (1979) 'Precolonial Mangbetu rule: political and economic factors in nineteenth-century Mangbetu history' (PhD dissertation, Indiana University, Bloomington).

Kélédor, Baron R. (1829) *Histoire africaine* (Paris).

Kellenbenz, H. (1971) 'Die Rückwirkungen der Kolonien auf die Muttedänder', *Saeculum Weltgeschichte*, 6, pp. 123–40.

Kent, R. K. (n.d.) *Southern Madagascar and the French, 1642–74* (typescript).

Kent, R. K. (1965) 'Palmares: an African State in Brazil', *JAH*, 6, 2, pp. 161–75.

Kent, R. K. (1968) 'The Sakalava', *JAH*, 9, 4, pp. 517–46.

Kent, R. K. (1969) 'Alfred Grandidier et le mythe des fondateurs d'états malgaches d'origine asiatique', *BM*, 277–8, pp. 603–20.

Kent, R. K. (1970) *Early Kingdoms in Madagascar, 1500–1700* (New York: Holt, Rinehart and Winston).

Kesteloot, L. (1972) *Da Monzon de Ségou, épopée bambara* (4 vols, Paris: F. Nathan).

Kesteloot, L. (1983) *Biton Koulibaly, fondateur de l'empire de Ségou* (Dakar: NEA), 96 pp.

Kietegha, J. B. (1983) *L'or de la Volta Noire* (Paris: Karthala, CREA), 247 pp.

Kimambo, I. N. (1968) 'The Pare', in A. D. Roberts (ed.), 1968a, pp. 16–36.

Kimambo, I. N. (1969) *A Political History of the Pare of Tanzania* (Nairobi: EAPH), 253 pp.

Kimambo, I. N. and Temu, A. (eds) (1969) *A History of Tanzania* (Nairobi: EAPH), 276 pp.

Kimble, D (1963) *A Political History of Ghana: The Rise of Gold Coast Nationalism, 1850–1928* (Oxford: Clarendon Press), 587 pp.

Kipkorir, B. E. (1974) 'The inheritors and successors', *KHR*, 2, 2, pp.. 143–73.

Kipkorir, B. E. and Welbourn, F. B. (1973) *The Marakwet of Kenya* (Nairobi: EALB), 97 pp.

Kirkman, J. S. (1954) *The Arab City of Gedi, Excavations at the Great Mosque, Architecture and Finds* (Oxford: OUP), 197 pp.

Kirkman, J. S. (1964) *Men and Monuments on the East African Coast* (London: Lutterworth Press), 224 pp.

938

Kirkman, J. S. (1970) *Fort Jesus, Mombasa* (Nairobi).
Kiwanuka, M. S. M. (1971a) *A History of Buganda* (London: Longman), 322 pp.
Kiwanuka, M. S. M. (1971b) *The Kings of Buganda* (Nairobi: EAPH, Historical Texts of Eastern and Central Africa, No. 1), 256 pp.
Ki-Zerbo, J. (1978) *Histoire de l'Afrique noire* (Paris: Hatier), 702 pp.
Klein, H. S. (1967) *Slavery in the Americas: A Comparative Study of Virginia and Cuba* (Chicago: University of Chicago Press), 270 pp.
Klein, H. S. (1972) 'The Portuguese slave trade from Angola in the eighteenth century', *JEH*, **32**, 4, pp. 894–918.
Klein, H. S. (1975) 'The Cuban slave trade in the period of transition, 1790–1843', *RFHOM*, **62**, 226–7, pp. 67–89.
Klein, H. S. (1978) 'The English slave trade to Jamaica, 1782–1802', *EHR*, 31.
Klein, M. A. (1968) *Islam and Imperialism in Senegal Sine-Saloum, 1847–1914* (Edinburgh: EUP), 285 pp.
Kodi Muzong (1976) 'A pre-colonial history of the Pende people (Republic of Zaire)' (PhD thesis, Northwestern University, Evanston, Ill.).
Koelle, S. W. (1854) *African Native Literature Or Proverbs, Tales, Fables, and Historical Fragments in the Kanuri or Bornu Language* (London: Church Missionary House), 434 pp. (reprinted 1968).
Kolungwe, M. W. (1974) 'Les Bambuile du lac Moero' (MA thesis, Lubumbashi).
Kopytoff, B. K. (1978) 'The early development of Jamaican Maroon societies', *WMQ*, **35**, 2 (April).
Kottak, C. P. (1972) 'Ecological variables in the origin and evolution of African states: the Buganda example', in *Comparative Studies in Society and History*, pp. 351–80.
Kouanda, A. (1984) 'Les Yarse: fonction commerciale, religieuse et légitimité culturelle dans le pays moaga (Evolution historique)' (PhD thesis, University of Paris I).
Kozlov, B. (1970) 'Kogda rodilsia praded pushkina Gannibal?' (When was Pushkin's great-grandfather born?), *Novoe Yusskoe Slovo*, 11, (January).
Krapf, J. L. (1858) *Reisen in Ost-Africa ausgefuhrt in den Jahren 1837–1855* (2 vols, Stuttgart: Kornthal); English edn: *Travels, Researches and Missionary Labors During An Eighteen Years' Residence in Eastern Africa* (Boston: Ticknor & Fields), 1860.
Kriedte, P. (1980/1983) *Peasants, Landlords and Merchant Capitalists: Europe and the World Economy, 1500–1800* English trans. S. Leamington, Berg Publishers Ltd., 1983; (original edn, Gottingen: Vandenhoeck and Ruprecht, 1980).
Krump, T. (1710) *Hoher und Frucht-barer Palm Baum de Heiligen Evangelij*, Augsburg, relevant parts translated by J. L. Spaulding: *Sudanese Travels of Theodro Krump, 1710–1712* (New York: Hambata Publications, No. 39).
Kubbel, L. E. (1974) *Songaiskaia derzhava* (Moscow: Hayka), 430 pp.
Kuls, W. (1958) *Beitrage zur Kulturgeographie der südäthiopischen seen-Region* (Frankfurt-am-Main: Kramer).
Kumah, J. K. (1966) 'The rise and fall of the kingdom of Denkyira', *GNQ*, **9**, pp. 33–5.
Kup, A. P. (1961a) *A History of Sierra Leone, 1400–1787* (London: CUP), 212 pp.
Kup, A. P. (1961b) 'An account of the tribal distribution of Sierra Leone', *Man*, **60**, pp. 116–19.
Kwaule, F. and Chakwera, E. J. (1978) 'Successors to the Kolonga's state: Kanyenda and Dzoole' (Student research paper, Chancellor College, University of Malawi).

Labarthe, P. (1803) *Voyage à la Côte de Guinée* (Paris: Bossange, Masson & Besson), 310 pp.
Labourdonnais, M. de (1937) *Mémoire des Iles de France et de Bourbon*, ed. by A. Lougnon and A. Toussaint (Paris: Ernest Leroux), 203 pp.
Labrecque, E. (1949–51) 'Histoire des Mwata Kazembe, chefs Lunda du Luapala, 1700–1945', *Lovania*, 16, pp. 9–33; 17, pp. 21–48; 18, pp. 18–67.
Laburthe-Tolra, P. (1911/1977) 'Minlaaba: histoire et société traditionnelle chez les Beti du Sud-Cameroun' (3 vols, printed 1977, Lille: Reproduction of theses, University of Lille III).
Laburthe-Tolra, P. (1981) *Les seigneurs de la forêt* (Paris: Publications de la Sorbonne), 490 pp.
Lacerda e Almeida, F. J. M. de (n.d.) *Travessia da Africa* (Lisbon: Agencia Geral das Colonais), 171 pp.
Lacerda e Almeida, F. J. M. de (1944) *Diarios de Viagem* (Rio de Janeiro: Biblioteca popular Brasileira, vol. 18).
Lacger, L. de (1939) *Ruanda* (Kabgayi); reprinted 1959 (Namur: Grands Lacs), 729 pp.
Lagae, Mgr. C. R. (1926) *Les Azande ou Miam-Miam: l'organisation zande: croyances religieuses et magiques: coutumes familiales* (Brussels: Vromant et Cie, Bibliothèque du Congo vol. 18), 224 pp.
Lamb, V. (1975) *West African Weaving* (London: Duckworth).

Lamphear, J. E. (1970) 'The Kamba and the Northern Mrima coast', in R. Gray and D. Birmingham (eds), pp. 75–101.

Lamphear, J. E. (1976) *The Traditional History of the Jie of Uganda* (Oxford: Clarendon Press, Oxford Studies in African Affairs), 281 pp.

Lamphear, J. E. (1979) 'When the Ngitome speared their oxen: problems in reconstructing the chronology of the Jie', in J. B. Webster (ed.), 1979a, pp. 263–282.

Lamphear, J. E. (at press) 'The origins and dispersal of the central Paranilotes', in J. B. Webster (ed.), at press (a).

Landorein, I. (1910–11) 'Du Tchad au Niger: notice historique', in *Documents scientifiques de la mission Tilho, 1906–1909*, vol 2 (Paris).

Lane-Poole, E. H. (1934) *The Native Tribes of the East Luangwa Province of Northern Rhodesia* (Lusaka: Government Printer).

Lange, D. (1977) *Chronologie et histoire d'un royaume africain* (Wiesbaden: Franz Steiner).

Lange, W. (at press) *History and Sociopolitical Structure of the Gonga Peoples* (Wiesbaden: Franz Steiner).

Langlands, B. W. (1966) 'The banana in Uganda, 1860–1920', *UJ*, 30, pp. 39–62.

Langworthy, H. W. (1969a) 'A history of Undi's kingdom to 1890: aspects of Chewa history in East-Central Africa' (PhD thesis, Boston University).

Langworthy, H. W. (1969b) 'Sources for Chewa history in East-Central Africa: a collection of interviews', (Unpublished copies in University of Boston Library and University of Malawi Library).

Langworthy, H. W. (1969c) 'Understanding Malawi's pre-colonial history', *SMJ*, 23, 1, pp. 28–45.

Langworthy, H. W. (1971) 'Conflicts among rulers in the history of Undi's Chewa kingdom', *TJH*, 1, pp. 1–23.

Langworthy, H. W. (1972) 'Chewa or Maravi political organization in the pre-colonial era', in B. Pachai (ed.), pp. 104–22.

Lapukeni, K., Rashid, P., Kumwembe, N. and Webster, J. B. (1978) 'Amachinga Yao traditions, Vol. I' (History Department, University of Malawi).

Lara, O. D. (1979) 'Negro resistance to slavery and the Atlantic slave trade from Africa to Black Americas', (working paper, Meeting of Experts organized by UNESCO on *The African Slave Trade from the 15th to the 19th century*, Port-au-Prince, Haiti, 31 January–4 February 1978, *The General History of Africa – Studies and Documents*, 2 (Paris: UNESCO) pp. 101–14.

Laroui, A. (1970) *L'histoire du Maghreb: un essai de synthèse* (Paris: Maspéro), 390 pp.

Last, M. (1983) 'From sultanate to caliphate: Kano c.1450–1800', in B. M. Barkindo (ed.), pp. 67–91.

Last, M. (forthcoming) 'Historical metaphors in the intellectual history of Kano before 1800', in M. Adamu (ed.), at press (a).

Lavers, J. E. (1971) 'Islam in the Bornu caliphate: a survey', *Odu*, 5, pp. 27–53.

Lavers, J. E. (1980) 'Kanem and Borno to 1808', in O. Ikime (ed.), pp. 187–209.

Lavers, J. E. (1982) 'The trans-Saharan trade before 1800: towards quantification', in H. W. El-Ḥasnāwī (ed.).

Lavers, J. E. (1983) *Some Observations on the Remains of Hausa Iron Smelting* (Jos: Jos University Press).

Lavers, J. E. (forthcoming) 'Fezzan, a Sudanic or Saharan state?', in M. Adamu (ed.), *Central Sudan Before 1804* (Zaria: ABUP).

Lavers, J. E. (at press) 'Fezzan, a Sudanic or Saharan state?', in M. Adamu (ed.), at press (b).

Lawrence, A. W. (1969) *Fortified Trade-Posts: The English in West Africa, 1645–1822* (London: Jonathan Cape), 237 pp.

Le Barbier, C. (1916–17) 'Notes sur le pays des Bara-Imamono, région d'Ankazoabo', *BAM*, new series, 2, pp. 63–162.

Lee, R. B. (1968) 'What hunters do for a living or how to make out on scarce resources', in R. B. Lee and I. De Vore (eds), *Man the Hunter* (Chicago: Aldine), pp. 30–43.

Lee, R. B. and De Vore, I. (eds) (1976) *Kalahari Hunter-Gatherers: Studies of the Kung San and Their Neighbours* (Cambridge, Mass: HUP), 408 pp.

Lee, R. B. (1979) *The Kung San: Men, Women and Work in a Foraging Society* (Cambridge: CUP), 526 pp.

Lefèbvre, T. (1845–54) *Voyage en Abyssinie* (6 vols, Paris: A. Bertrand).

Legassick, M. (1979) 'The northern frontier to 1820: the emergence of the Griqua people', in R. Elphick and H. Giliomee (eds).

Le Gentil (1779–81) *Voyage dans les mers de l'Inde, 1760–1771* (2 vols, Paris).

Legesse, A. (1973) *Gada: Three Approaches to the Study of African Society* (New York/London: The Free Press), 340 pp.

Leguével de Lacombe, B. F. (1840) *Voyage à Madagascar et aux Iles Comores* (2 vols, Paris).

940

Lehmann, W. P. (1962) *Historical Linguistics* (New York: Holt, Rinehart and Winston), 297 pp.

Leitão, H. (1970) *Os Dois Descobrimentos da Ilha de São Lourenço* edited and annotated by H. Leitão (Lisbon).

Leitão, M. C. Correia (1938) 'Relação breve sumário da viagem que eo, o sargentomor das moradoresdo Dande fiz as remotas partes de Cassange e Olos ... 15 Agosto 1756' in G. Sousa Dias (ed.), 'Uma viagem a Cassange nos meados do Século XVIII, *BSGL*, **56**, pp. 19–25.

Lemaire, P. (1695) *Les voyages du Sieur Lemaire aux Iles Canaries, Cap Vert, Sénégal et Gambie* (Paris).

Le Moal, A. (1976) 'Le peuplement du pays bobo; bilan d'une enquête', *Cahiers ORSTOM*, Sciences humaines, **13**, 2, pp. 137–42.

Lemprière, G. (1891) *Voyages dans l'Empire du Maroc* (Paris: Tavernier, Legras et Cordier).

Leo Africanus [Jean Léon l'Africain] (1956) *Description de l'Afrique*, tr. by A. Epaulard, with notes by E. Epaulard, T. Monod, H. Lhote and R. Mauny (2 vols, Paris: Maisonneuve).

Le Roy Ladurie, E. (1978) 'A reply to Professor Brenner', *PP*, **79**, pp. 55–9.

Leroy, J. (1967) *Ethiopian Paintings in the Middles Ages*, in G. Gerster (ed.), (London: Phaidon Press Ltd).

Leroy, J., Wright, St. and Jäger, O. A. (1961) *Aethiopien-Budmalereien* (New York).

Leselle, R. (1957) 'Les noirs du Souf', *BLS*, Supplement to Vol. 8, pp. 1–76.

Leslau, W. (1951) *Falasha Anthology: The Black Jews of Ethiopia*, trans. from Ethiopian sources with an introduction by W. Leslau (New York: Schocken Books), 222 pp.

Leslau, W. (1963) *Etymological Dictionary of Harari* (Berkeley and Los Angeles: UCP Near Eastern Studies, vol. 1), 240 pp.

Leslau, W. (1979) *Etymological Dictionary of Gurage (Ethiopic)* (3 vols, Wiesbaden: Harrasowitz, Otto-Verlag).

Lethem, G. C. (1919) 'Special Report on Nguru district, Bornu Emirate', *SNP*, **10**, 258 pp.

Levine, D. N. (1977) *Family Formation in an Age of Nascent Capitalism* (New York: Academic Press).

Lévi-Provençal, E. (1922) *Les historiens des Chorfa* (Paris: Larose).

Levtzion, N. (1964a) *Chronology from Genealogical Evidence: The Volta Basin* (London: SOAS, Survey on African Chronology).

Levtzion, N. (1964b) *Notes on the Expansion of Islam in Northern Ghana* (London: SOAS, Survey on African Chronology).

Levtzion, N. (1964c) 'Outlines of the development of Islam in Mossi (Wagadugu)', (London: SOAS, Survey on African Chronology).

Levtzion, N. (1968) *Muslims and Chiefs in the West Africa: A Study of Islam in the Middle Volta Basin in the Precolonial Period* (Oxford: Clarendon Press, Oxford Studies in African Affairs), 228 pp.

Levtzion, N. (1971a) 'Notes sur les origines de l'Islam militant au Fouta Djalon', *Notes africaines*, October, No. 132, pp. 94–6.

Levtzion, N. (1971b) 'Notes sur les Etats dyula de Kong et de Bobo', *BLLE*, **1**, pp. 61–2.

Levtzion, N. (1975) 'North-West Africa: from the Maghrib to the fringes of the forest', in R. Gray (ed.), pp. 192–272.

Lewis, H. S. (1966) 'The origins of the Galla and Somali', *JAH*, **7**, 1, pp. 27–47.

Lewis, I. M. (1955) *Peoples of the Horn of Africa: Somalia, Afar and Saho* (London: IAI, Ethnographic survey of Africa: North-Eastern Africa, Part I), 204 pp.

Lewis, I. M. (1961) *A Pastoral Democracy: A Study of Pastoralism and Politics Among the Northern Somali of the Horn of Africa* (London/New York/Toronto: OUP, for the IAI), 320 pp.

Lewis, I. M. (ed.) (1966) *Islam in Tropical Africa* (London: OUP, for the IAI), 470 pp.

Lewis, I. M. (ed.) (1968) *History and Social Anthropology* (London: Tavistock Publications, A.S. Monographs, No. 7), 307 pp.

Lewis, W. A. (1978) *The Evolution of the International Economic Order* (Princeton: PUP).

Linden, I. (1979) 'Chisumphi theology in the religion of Central Malawi', in M. J. Schoffeleers (ed.), 1979(a), pp. 189–207.

Lindgren, N. E. and Schoffeleers, M. J. (1978) *Rock Art and Nyau Symbolism* (Lilongwe: Department of Antiquities).

Little, K. (1951) *The Mende of Sierra Leone* (London: Routledge & Kegan Paul), 307 pp.

Littmann, E. (1914) *Die altamharischen Kaiserlieder* (Strasburg).

Lloyd, P. C. (1963) 'The Itsekiri in the nineteenth century: an outline social history', *JAH*, **4**, 2, pp. 207–31.

Lobato, A. (1954a) *A expansão Portuguesa em Moçambique de 1498 a 1530: Politica da Capitania de Sofala e Moçambique de 1530* (Lisbon: Agencia Geral do Ultramar).

Lobato, A. (1954b) *Evolução administrativa e economica da Moçambique 1753–63. Fundamentos da criacão do Governo Geral em 1752*, vol. 1 (Lisbon: Agencia Geral do Ultramar), 412 pp.

Lobato, A. (1962) *Colonização Senhorial da Zambezia e Outros Estudos* (Lisbon: Junta de Investigaçoes do Ultramar), 228 pp.

Lobo, J. (1728/1928) *Voyage historique d'Abyssinie du R. P. Jérôme Lobo*, ed. & trans. by J. Le Grand, 1928 (Paris).

Logan, R. W. (1940) 'Estevanico: Negro discoverer of the Southwest', *Phylon*, 1, 4th quarter.

Lombard, J. (1965) *Structures de type 'féodal' en Afrique noire: étude des dynamismes internes et des relations sociales chez les Bariba du Dahomey* (Paris/The Hague: Mouton), 544 pp.

Lopes, E., see F. de Pigafetta.

Lopez, R. S. (1976) *The Commercial Revolution of the Middle Ages, 950–1350* (Cambridge: CUP).

Loro, M. (1971) 'The pre-colonial history of the Kakwa' (Student essay, University of Makerere).

Lougnon, A. (1956) *L'Ile de Bourbon pendant la Régence*.

Lougnon, A. (1958) *Le mouvement maritime aux Iles de Bourbon et de France (1727–35)*.

Lougnon, A. and **Toussaint, A.** (eds) (1937) *Mémoire des Iles de France et de Bourbon* (Paris: Librairie Ernest Leroux), 203 pp.

Lovejoy, P. E. (1973a) 'The Hausa kola trade: a commercial system in the continental exchange of West Africa' (PhD thesis, University of Wisconsin).

Lovejoy, P. E. (1973b) 'The Kambari Beriberi: the formation of a specialized group of Hausa kola traders in the nineteenth century', *JAH*, 14, 4, pp. 633–51.

Lovejoy, P. E. (1978) 'The role of the Wangara in the economic transformation of the Central Sudan in the fifteenth and sixteenth centuries', *JAH*, 19, 2, pp. 173–93.

Lovejoy, P. E. (ed.) (1981) *The Ideology of Slavery in Africa* (Beverly Hills, Ca: Sage).

Lovejoy, P. E. (1982) 'The volume of the Atlantic slave trade: a synthesis', *JAH*, 23, 3, pp. 473–501.

Lovejoy, P. E. (1983) *Transformations in Slavery: A History of Slavery in Africa* (Cambridge: CUP), 349 pp.

Lovejoy, P. E. (1985) *Salt of the Desert Sun: A History of Salt Production and Trade in Central Sudan* (Cambridge: CUP), 351 pp.

Lovejoy, P. E. (at press) 'Salt industry of the Central Sudan', in M. Adamu (ed.), at press (a).

Lucas, S. A. (1968) 'Baluba et Aruund: étude comparative des structures socio-politiques' (PhD thesis, Ecole pratique des hautes études).

Ludolf, H. (1681) *Historia Aethiopica* (Franco Furti-ad-Moenum).

Luna, L. (1968) *O negro na luta contra a escravidao* (Rio de Janeiro: Leitura).

Luttrall, A. (1964) 'Slavery and slaving in the Portuguese Atlantic', in *The Transatlantic Slave Trade from West Africa* (Edinburgh).

Lwamgira, F. X. (1949/1968) *Amakuru ga Kiziba Bukoba* (trans. by E. A. Kamuhangire as *A History of Kiziba*, History Department, Makerere, 1968).

Lwamgira, F. X. (n.d.) *The History of Karagwe, Ihangiro and Kyamatwalo* (unpublished).

Lwanga-Lunyiigo, S. (1972–3) 'The foundation of the Babito kingdom of Khooki' (Makerere Seminar Paper, No. 6).

Ly, A. (1958) *La compagnie du Sénégal de 1673 à 1686* (Paris: PA), 316 pp.

Ly, A. (1977) 'L'épopée de Samba Guela Diegui' (PhD thesis, Dakar).

Macedo, G. (1890) 'Informação do Padre Frei Gaspar Macedo', in *Memoria e Documentoa Acerca dos Direitos de Portugal Aos Territorios de Machona e Nyassa 1890* (Lisbon: Imprensa Nacional), pp. 147–51.

MacGaffey, W. (1975) 'Oral tradition in Central Africa', *IJAHS*, 7, 3, pp. 421–36.

Mack, J. and **Robertshaw, P.** (eds) (1982) *Culture History in the Southern Sudan: Archaeology, Linguistics and Ethnohistory* (Nairobi: BIEA, Memoir No. 8), 179 pp.

McKay, W. F. (1975) 'A pre-colonial history of the Southern Kenya coast' (PhD thesis, Boston University), 303 pp.

Mackenzie, J. M. (1975) 'Pre-colonial industry: the Nyanja and iron trade', *NADA*, 2, 2, pp. 200–220.

MacMichael, H. A. (1922) *A History of the Arabs in the Sudan* (2 vols, Cambridge: CUP).

Madiega, G. Y. (1978) 'Le Nord-Gulma précolonial (Haute-Volta): origine des dynasties, approche de la société' (PhD thesis, University of Paris I).

Madiega, G. Y. (1982) *Contribution à l'histoire précoloniale du Gurma (Haute-Volta)* (Wiesbaden: Franz Steiner).

Magarshack, D. (1969) *Pushkin* (New York: Grove Press).

Mage, E. (1868) *Voyage dans le Soudan occidental (1863–1866)* (Paris: Hachette). (New edn by Karthala, 1980, Frobenius Institute).

Magnes, B. (1953) 'Essai sur les institutions et la coutume des Taimihety', *BM*, **89**, (October), pp. 1–95.

Mahadi, A. (forthcoming) 'Some observations on the emergence and development of the sarauta (kinship) system in the Central Sudan before 1804', in M. Adamu (ed.), at press (a).

Mahoney, F. and Idowu, H. O. (1965) 'The peoples of Senegambia', in J. F. A. Ajayi and I. Espie (eds), pp. 131–43.

Maïkassoua, I. (1982) 'Some considerations relating to the contribution of Gobir migrants to the transformation of neighbouring communities' (Department of History, Ahmadu Bello University, Zaria, mimeograph).

Majumdar, R. C. (1951) *The History and Culture of the Indian People* (Bombay: Bhasatiya Vidya Bhavan).

al-Maḳrīzī, Abu 'l-ʿAbbās Aḥmad b.ʿAli (before 1442) *Macrizi historia regum islamiticorum in Abyssinia una cum Abulfeda descriptione regionum nigritarum*, 1790 ed. and Latin transl. F. T. Rinck (Leiden: Luchtmans).

Malandra, A. (1947/1971) *Tekwaro Acholi* (Nairobi: Longman), trans. 1971 by C. A. R. Oywa as *Acholi Traditions* (Makerere: Department of History).

Malevanov, N. (1974) 'Praded Poets' (The Poet's Great-Grandfather), *Zuezda*, pp. 156–65.

Maley, J. (1981) 'Etudes palynologiques dans le bassin du Tchad et paléoclimatologie de l'Afrique nord-tropicale de 30 000 ans à l'époque actuelle', *TD*, vol **129** (Paris: ORSTOM).

Malotet, A. (1898) *Etienne de Flacourt ou les origines de la colonisation française à Madagascar, 1648–1661* (Paris).

Malowist, M. (1966) 'The social and economic stability of the western Sudan in the Middle Ages', *PP*, **33**, (April), pp. 3–15.

Malowist, M. (1969) *Western Europe and West Africa at the Beginning of the Colonial Expansion* (Warsaw).

Malzac, V. (1912/1930) *Histoire du royaume Hova depuis ses origines jusqu'à sa fin* (Antananarivo: Imprimerie catholique). (Reprinted 1930).

Mamattah, C. M. K. (1976) *The Ewes of West Africa; Oral Traditions*, vol. 1 (Accra: Volta Research Publications), 768 pp.

Mamelomana, E. (n.d.) *Les Mahafaly*, (typescript, probably written in the 1940s, in the Bibliothèque Charles Poirier, University of Madagascar).

Mandala, E. C.. (1977) 'The Kololo interlude in Southern Malawi, 1861–1895', MA thesis, University of Malawi.

Mané, M. (1978) 'Contribution à l'histoire du Kaabu, des origines au XIXe siècle', *BIFAN*, **40**, 1, pp. 87–159.

Manning, P. (1981) 'The enslavement of Africans: a demographic model', *CJAS*, **15**, 3, pp. 499–526.

Manning, P., Austen, R. A. and van Dantzig, A. (1980) Reviews of *Der atlantische Sklavenhandel von Dahomey (1740–1797)*, *AEH*, **9**, pp. 131–9.

Manning, P., Caldwell, J. C. and Inikori, J. E. (1982) 'Discussion', *CJAS*, **16**, 1, pp. 127–39.

Mannix, D. P. (1963) *Black Cargoes: A History of the Atlantic Slave Trade, 1518–1865* (London: Longman), 306 pp.

Maquet, J. J. (1954) *Le système des relations sociales dans le Ruanda ancien* (Tervuren: MRAC), 221 pp.

Marchand (1901) 'Les habitants de la province de Farafangana', *RM*, 3, pp. 481–91.

Marees, P. de (1602/1605/1905) *A Description and Historical Declaration of the Golden Kingdom of Guinea*, abridged English trans. of 1602 Dutch original, published in S. Purchas (1613/1905), vol. 6, pp. 247–396; French trans. 1605, *Description et récit historique du riche royaume d'or de Guinée* (Amsterdam: Claessen).

Maret, P. de (1981) 'L'évolution monétaire du Shaba central entre le VIIe et le XVIIIe siècle', *AEH*, 10, pp. 117–49.

Maret, P. de, Van Noten, F. and Cahen, D. (1977) 'Radiocarbon dates from West Central Africa: a synthesis', *JAH*, 18, 4, pp. 481–505.

Marion M. A. (1971) 'Notes sur l'art funéraire Mahafaly et Antandroy', *BM*, **21**, pp. 463–76.

Martin, A. G. P. (1908) *A la frontière du Maroc: les oasis sahariennes (Gourada-Touat-Tidikelt)* (Algiers: Imprimerie algérienne), vol. 1, 406 pp.

Martin, B. G. (1969) 'Kanem, Bornu and the Fezzan: notes on the political history of a trade route', *JAH*, 10, 1, pp. 15–27.

Martin, B. G. (1971) 'Notes on some members of the learned classes of Zanzibar and East Africa in the nineteenth century', *AHS*, **4**, 3, pp. 525–45.

943

Martin, B. G. (1972) 'Mai Idris of Bornu and the Ottoman Turks, 1576–78', *IJMS*, **3**, 1, pp. 470–90.

Martin, E. B. (1973) *The History of Malindi: A Geographical Analysis of an East African Coastal Town from the Portuguese Period to the Present* (Nairobi: EALB), 301 pp.

Martin, G. (1948) *Histoire de l'esclavage dans les colonies françaises* (Paris: PUF), 318 pp.

Martin, P. (1970) 'The trade of Loango in the seventeenth and eighteenth centuries', in R. Gray and D. Birmingham (eds), pp. 139–61.

Martin, P. M. (1972) *The External Trade of the Loango Coast, 1576–1870: The Effects of Changing Commercial Relations on the Vili Kingdom of Loango* (Oxford: Clarendon Press, Oxford Studies in African Affairs), 193 pp.

Marty, P. (1927) *Les Chroniques de Oualata et de Nema* (Paris: Geuthner).

Marty, P. (1920–1) *Etudes sur l'Islam et les tribus du Soudan* (4 vols, Paris: E. Leroux, Collection de la Revue du monde musulman, No.4).

Marwick, M. G. (1963) 'History and tradition in East-Central Africa through the eyes of the Northern Rhodesian Cewa', *JAH*, **4**, 3, pp. 375–90.

Mathew, G. (1963) 'The East African coast until the coming of the Portuguese', in R. Oliver and G. Mathew (eds), pp. 94–128.

Mathews, T. I. (1981) 'Portuguese, Chikunda and peoples of the Gwembe valley', *JAH*, **22**, 1, pp. 23–42.

Maugham, R. C. F. (1910) *Zambezia: A General Description of the Zambezi River From its Delta to the River Aruangwa, with its History, Agriculture, Flora, Fauna and Ethnography* (London: John Murray), 408 pp.

Mauny, R. (1970) 'Les navigations anciennes et les grandes découvertes', in H. Deschamps (ed.), *Histoire générale de l'Afrique noire* (Paris: PUF), vol. 1, Part II, pp. 203–18.

Mauny, R. (1971) *Les siècles obscurs de l'Afrique noire* (Paris: Fayard), 314 pp.

Mauny, R., Thomas, L. V and Vansina, J. (eds) (1974) *The Historian in Tropical Africa* (London: OUP, for the IAI), 428 pp.

Mauro, F. (1960) *Le Portugal et l'Atlantique au XVIIe siècle, 1570–1670* (Paris: SEVPEN).

Maxwell, R. (1932) 'The law relating to slavery among the Malays', *JMBRAS*, **10**, 1, pp. 247–97.

Mayeur, N. (1912) 'Voyage à la côte de l'ouest de Madagascar (pays des Sadaves), 1774', *BAM*, **10**, pp. 49–91.

M'Bokolo, E. (1983) 'Histoire des maladies, histoire et maladie: l'Afrique', in M. Augé and S. Herzlich (eds), *Le sens du mal* (Paris: Editions des Archives contemporaines).

M'Bokolo, E. (1981) *Noirs et blancs en Afrique équatoriale: les sociétés côtières et la pénétration française* (Paris/The Hague: Mouton, Civilisations et Sociétés, No. 69), 302 pp.

Mbwiliza, J. F. (1981) 'The hoe and the stick: a political economy of the Heru kingdom', *CCB*, pp. 100–16.

McCulloch, M., Littlewood, M. and Dugast, I. (1954) *Peoples of the Central Cameroons* (London: IAI, Ethnographic Survey of Africa, Western Africa, Part IX), 172 pp.

McDougall, E. A. (1980) 'The Ijil salt industry: its roles in the pre-colonial economy of the Western Sudan' (PhD thesis, University of Birmingham).

McIntosh, B. G. (ed.) (1969) *Ngano: Studies in Traditional and Modern East African History* (Nairobi: EAPH), 181 pp.

McIntosh, R. J. and Keech-McIntosh, S. (1982) 'The field season at Jenne-Jeno: preliminary results', *Nyame Akuma*, **20**, pp. 28–32.

McLachlan, J. O. (1940) *Trade and Peace with Old Spain, 1667–1750: A Study of the Influence of Commerce on Anglo-Spanish Diplomacy in the First Half of the Eighteenth Century* (Cambridge: CUP).

McLeod, M. D. (1981) *The Asante* (London: British Museum Publications).

Mdoumbe-Moulongo, M. (1968) 'Origines et migrations des Duala', *Abbia*, **20**, (June), pp. 79–150.

Meek, R. L. (1976) *Social Science and the Ignoble Savage* (Cambridge: CUP, Cambridge Studies in the History and Theory of Politics), 249 pp.

Meillassoux, C. (ed.) (1971) *The Development of Indigenous Trade and Markets in West Africa* (London: OUP, for the IAI), 444 pp.

Meillassoux, C. (ed.) (1975) *L'esclavage en Afrique précoloniale* (Paris: F. Maspéro), 582 pp.

Meillassoux, C. (1982) 'The role of slavery in the economic and social history of Sahelo-Sudanic Africa', in J. E. Inikori (ed.), pp. 74–99.

Meillet, A. (1925) *La méthode comparative en linguistique historique* (Oslo).

Mellafe, R. (1964) *La esclavitud en Hispanoamerica* (Buenos Aires: Editorial Universitaria).

Mellafe, R. (1975) *Negro Slavery in Latin America* (Berkeley, CA: UCP), 172 pp.

Méo, Dr (1919) 'Etudes sur le Rio Nuñez', *BCAF*, pp. 282–381.

Mercer, P. (1971) 'The Shilluk trade and politics from mid-seventeenth century to 1861', *JAH*, 12, 3, pp. 407–26.

Merensky, A. (1883) 'Ueber die Afrikanische Volkerwanderung des 16 Jahrhunderts', *Zeitschrift der Gesellschaft für Erdkunde zu Berlin*, pp. 67–75.

Merrick, T. W. and Graham, D. H. (1979) *Population and Economic Development in Brazil, 1800 to the present* (Baltimore: The Johns Hopkins University Press).

Meschi, L. (1974) 'Evolution des structures foncières au Rwanda: le cas d'un lignage hutu', *CEA*, 53, pp. 39–51.

Metcalfe, G. E. (1964) *Great Britain and Ghana: Documents of Ghana History, 1807–1957* (London: Thomas Nelson and Sons), 779 pp.

Mettas, J. (1978) *Répertoire des expéditions négrières françaises au XVIIIe siècle*, ed. by S. Daget (Nantes).

Meyer, H. (1916) *Die Barundi* (Leipzig: O. Spamer), 206 pp.

Mézières, B. de (1912) *Le Major A. Gordon Laing, Tombouctou, 1826* (Paris: Larose).

Mgomezulu, G. Y. (1981) 'Recent archaeological research and radio-carbon dates from Eastern Africa', *JAH*, 22, 4, pp. 435–56.

Michel, L. (1957) 'Moeurs et coutumes des Bara', *MAM*, 40.

Miers, S. and Kopytoff, I. (eds) (1977) *Slavery in Africa: Historical and Anthropological Perspectives* (Madison: UWP), 474 pp.

Miles, S. B. (1919) *The Countries and Tribes of the Persian Gulf* (2 vols, London: Frank Cass).

Miller, J. C. (1972a) 'A note on Casanze and the Portuguese', *CJAS*, 6, pp. 45–56.

Miller, J. C. (1972b) 'The Imbangala and the chronology of early central African history', *JAH*, 13, 4, pp. 549–74.

Miller, J. C. (1973) 'Requiem for the Jaga', *CEA*, 49, pp. 121–49. (See also *CEA*, 69 and 70).

Miller, J. C. (1975a) 'Nzinga of Matamba in a New Perspective', *JAH*, 13, pp. 201–16.

Miller, J. C. (1975b) 'Legal Portuguese slaving from Angola: Some preliminary indications of volume and direction, 1760–1830', *RFHOM*, 62, pp. 135–76.

Miller, J. C. (1976) *Kings and Kinsmen: Early Mbundu States in Angola* (Oxford: Clarendon Press, Oxford Studies in African Affairs), 312 pp.

Miller, J. C. (1979) 'Some aspects of the commercial organization of slaving at Luanda, Angola, 1760–1830', in H. A. Gemery and J. S. Hogendorn (eds), pp. 77–106.

Miller, J. C. (ed.) (1980) *The African Past Speaks: Essays on Oral Tradition and History* (London: Hamden, Dawson & Archon), 284 pp.

Miller, J. C. (1982) 'The significance of drought, disease and famine in the agriculturally marginal zones of West Central Africa', *JAH*, 23, pp. 17–61.

Miller, J. C. (1983) 'The paradoxes of impoverishment in the Atlantic zone', in D. Birmingham and D. Martin (eds), pp. 118–59.

Miller, J. C. (1984) 'The accounts of Antonio Coelho Guerreiro (1684–1692)', *IJAHS*, 17, pp 1–56.

Miller, J. C., 'Thanatopsis', *CEA*, pp. 229–31.

Minchinton, W. E. (ed.) (1969) *The Growth of English Overseas Trade in the 17th and 18th Centuries* (London: Methuen).

Misomali, R. B., Mkondiwa, G. and Bhila, H. K. (1978) 'Yao traditions, Vol. III', (History Department, University of Malawi).

Mkandawire, F. R. (1978) 'The corridor in Tumbuka and Chewa history: the migration and settlement of Kabunduli, 1650–1860', (student research paper, Chancellor College, University of Malawi).

Modzalevskii, B. (1907) *Rodoslavnia Gannibalov* (Genealogy of the Hannibals) (Moscow: Yakovlev Press).

Moeller, A. (1936) *Les grandes lignes des migrations des Bantous de la province orientale du Congo belge* (Brussels: Institut royal belge, Section des sciences morales et politiques, Mémoires, vol. 6), 578 pp.

Mokhtar, G. (ed.) (1981) *General History of Africa. Vol. II: Ancient Civilizations of Africa* (Paris/London/Berkeley: UNESCO/Heinemann/University of California Press).

Mondain, G. (1910) *L'histoire des tribus de l'Imoro au XVIIe siècle d'après un manuscrit arabico-malgache* (Paris: Ernest Leroux).

Monteil, C. (1903) *Monographie de Djenné* (Tulle: Imprimerie J. Mazeyrie).

Monteil, C. (1915) *Les Khassonké* (Paris: Leroux), 528 pp. (reprinted, 1974).

Monteil, C. (1924) *Les Bambara de Ségou et du Kaarta* (Paris: Larose), 404 pp; 2nd edn, 1977 (Paris: Maisonneuve), 441 pp.

Monteil, C. (1932) *Une cité soudanaise, Djenné, métropole du delta central du Niger* (Paris: Société d'études géographiques, maritimes et coloniales); 2nd edn, 1971 (Paris: Anthropos).

Monti della Corte (1945) *I Castelli di Gondar* (Rome).

Morgan, W. T. W. (ed.) (1969) *East Africa: Its People and Resources* (Nairobi: OUP, in association with D. A. Hawkins), 312 pp.

Morris, A. (1981) *Latin America: Economic Development and Regional Differentiation* (London: Hutchinson), 256 pp.

Mors, O. (1957) *Geschichte der Bahaya* (Fribourg: Anthropos), 207 pp.

Mortimore, M. J. (ed.) (1970) *Zaria And Its Region* (Zaria: Ahmadu Bello University, Occasional Paper No. 4), 192 pp.

Morton, R. F. (1972) 'The Shungwaya myth of Miji Kenda origins: a problem of late nineteenth-century coastal history', *IJAHS*, 5, pp. 397–423.

Moura, C. (1959) *Rebelioes da Senzala: quilombos, insurreicoes, guerrilhas* (São Paulo: Editora Zombi). 1972 edn (Rio de Janeiro: Conquista).

Mphande, C. Z. (1969) 'Some aspects of the history of the Tonga to 1934' (student research paper, Chancellor College, University of Malawi).

Mpoyi, L. M. (1966) *Histoire wa Baluba* (Mbuyi-Mayi).

Msiska, H. K. (1978a) 'Established on iron and undermined by ivory: the creation and fragmentation of the Mwaphoka kingdom, *c*.1380–*c*.1810' (student research paper, Chancellor College, University of Malawi).

Msika, H. K. (1978b) 'Phoka historical texts' (Chancellor College, University of Malawi, unpublished).

Mudenge, S. I. (1972) 'The Rozvi empire and the feira of Zumbo' (PhD thesis, University of London).

Mudenge, S. I. (1974a) 'An identification of the Rozvi and its implications for the history of the Karanga', *RH*, 5, pp. 19–31.

Mudenge, S. I. (1974b) 'The role of foreign trade in the Rozvi empire: a reappraisal', *JAH*, 15, 3, pp. 373–91.

Mudenge, S. I. (1976) 'The Dominicans at Zumbo: an aspect of missionary history in the Zambezi valley, *c*. 1726–1836', *Mohlomi*, 1, pp. 32–63.

Mudenge, S. I. (1977) 'Eighteenth-century Portuguese settlements on the Zambezi and the dating of the Rhodesian ruins: some reflections on the problems of reference dating', *IJAHS*, 10, 3, pp. 1–13.

Murdock, J. P. (1959) *Africa: Its Peoples and their Culture History* (New York: McGraw-Hill), 456 pp.

Muriuki, G. (1974) *A History of the Kikuyu, 1500–1900* (Nairobi: OUP), 190 pp.

Murray, S. S. (comp.) (1922) *A Handbook of Nyasaland* (London: published for the Government of Nyasaland by the Crown Agents for the Colonies).

Musambachime, M. (1976) 'Changing roles: the history and development disintegration of Nkuba's Shila State to 1740' (MA thesis, University of Wisconsin, Madison).

Mutetwa, R. G. (1976) 'The political and economic history of the Duma people of south-eastern Rhodesia from the early eighteenth century to 1945' (PhD thesis, University of Rhodesia).

Mutumba, M. (1973) *Bulozi under the Luyana Kings. Political Evolution and State-Formation in Pre-Colonial Zambia* (London: Longman), 278 pp.

Mwaipape, R. J. (1982) 'History and social customs of the Ngonde of northern Malawi' (Unpublished manuscript).

Mwanzi, H. A. (1973) 'Politics and religion among the Nandi in the nineteenth and early twentieth century' (Seminar paper, Department of History, Nairobi University).

Mwanzi, H. A. (1977) *A History of the Kipsigis* (Nairobi: EALB), 171 pp.

Mworoha, E. (1977) *Peuples et rois de l'Afrique des lacs* (Dakar: NEA), 352 pp.

Mworoha, E. (1981) 'Redevances et prestations dans les domaines royaux du Burundi précolonial', *Mélanges R. Mauny. Le sol, la parole et l'écrit: 2000 ans d'histoire africaine* (Paris: SFHOM), pp. 751–68.

Nacanabo, D. (1982) 'Le Royaume maagha de Yoko' (PhD thesis, University of Paris I).

Nachtigal, G. (1874) 'Zur Geschichte Bagirmis', *Zeitschrift der Gesellschaft für Erdkunde zu Berlin* (Berlin: D. Reimer).

Nachtigal, G. (1876) *Le voyage de Nachtigal au Ouadai: Traduction de Van Vollenhoven* (Paris).

Nachtigal, G. (1879/1881/1971–4) *Sahara und Sudan: Ergebnisse Sechsjähriger Reisen in Afrika*, Vol. 1 (Berlin: Weidmann), 749 pp.; Vol. 2 (Berlin: Weidmann), 790 pp.; Vol. 3 (Leipzig: F. A. Brockhaus), 548 pp.; 1881, French trans., *Sahara et Soudan*, by J. Gourdault (Paris: Hachette); 1967 complete reprint (Graz: Akademie Drüker); 1971, 1974, Engl. trans., *Sahara and Sudan*, by A. G. B. Fisher and H. J. Fisher of Vol. 1, Fezzan and Tibesti, and Vol. 3, Wadai and Darfur (London: C. Hurst).

Na-Dama, G. (1977) 'The rise and collapse of a Hausa state: a social and political history of Zamfara' (PhD thesis, Ahmadu Bello University, Zaria).

Nahimana, F. (1981) 'Les principautés hutu du Rwanda septentrional', *CCB*, pp. 115–37.

Nalder, L. F. (ed.) (1937) *A Tribal Survey of Mongala Province* (London: OUP), 232 pp.

al-Naqar, U. (1972) *The Pilgrimage Tradition in West Africa* (Khartoum: KUP).

Nāṣir, A. (1977) *Al-Inkishafi: Catechism of a Soul*, trans. and annotated by J. de Vere Allen (Nairobi: EALB).

al-Nāṣirī, A. (1954–6) *Kitāb al-Istiḳṣā' li-akhbār al-Maghrib al-Aḳṣā* (9 vols, Casablanca); also (Cairo) 1894; see also French trans. 'Part 1: Les Ŝaadiens', *Archives marocaines*, 34.

Ndikuriyo, A. (1975) 'Contrats de bétail, contrats de clientèle et pouvoir politique dans le Bututsi du 19e siècle', *EHA*, 7, pp. 59–76.

Ndoricimpa, L. (ed.) (1984) *L'arbre mémoire. Traditions orales du Burundi* (Paris/Bujumbura: Editions Karthala/Centre de Civilisation Burundaise).

N'dua, S. K. (1973) 'Mwant Yaav Mushid (1856–1907)', *EHA*, 5, pp. 25–50.

N'dua, S. K. (1978) 'Histoire ancienne des populations Luba et Lunda du Plateau du Haut Lubilashi' (PhD thesis, Lubumbashi Campus).

Neumark, S. D. (1957) *Economic Influences on the South African Frontier, 1652–1836* (Stanford: SUP), 96 pp.

Newbury, C. W. (1976) 'The cohesion of oppression: a century of clientship in Kinyaga, Rwanda' (PhD thesis, University of Wisconsin, Madison).

Newbury, D. S. (1978) 'Bushi and the historians: historiographical themes in Eastern Kivu', *HA*, 5, pp. 131–51.

Newbury, D. S. (1979) 'Kings and clans: state formation in Ijwi island (Zaire), c.1780–1840' (PhD thesis, University of Wisconsin, Madison).

Newbury, D. S. (1980) 'Lake Kivu regional trade in the XIXth century', *JA*, 50, 2, 2, pp. 6–30.

Newbury, D. S. (1981) 'The clans of Rwanda: a historical hypothesis', *CCB*, pp. 186–97.

Newitt, M. D. D. (1973) *Portuguese Settlement on the Zambezi: Exploration, Land Tenure and Colonial Rule in East Africa* (London: Longman), 434 pp.

Newitt, M. D. D. (1982) 'The early history of the Maravi', *JAH*, 23, 2, pp. 145–62.

Nganwa, K. N. (1948) *Abakozire Eby'Okutangaaza Omuri Ankole* (Nairobi: EALB).

Ngoa, H. (1969) 'Situation historico-généalogique des Ewondo: étude critique', *Abbia*, 22, May-August, pp. 65–88.

Ngoa, H. (1981) *Tentative de reconstitution de l'histoire récente des Ewondo*.

Ngoie Ngalla D. (1978) 'Réflexions sur le peuplement de la vallée du Niari par les Kongo', *CCAH*, 2, pp. 13–25.

Ngoie Ngalla, D. (1982) 'Les rapports politiques du royaume de Loango et de la vallée du Niari, d'après les textes et la tradition orale (XVIe-XIXe siècles)', *CCAH*, 7, pp. 25–32.

Niane, D. T. (1975a) *Recherches sur l'empire du Mali au Moyen-Age* (Paris: PA).

Niane, D. T. (1975b) *Le Soudan occidental au temps des grands empires, XIe-XVIe siècles* (Paris: PA).

Niane, D. T. (ed.) (1984) *General History of Africa. Vol. IV: Africa from the Twelfth to the Sixteenth century* (Paris/London/Berkeley: UNESCO/Heinemann/University of California Press).

Niane, D. T. and Wondji, C. *Enquêtes orales faites en Côte d'Ivoire (1973–1980) et en Guinée (1966–1970)*.

Nicholson, S. E. (1978) 'Climatic variations in the Sahel and other African regions during the past five centuries', *JAE*, 1.

Nicholson, S. E. (1979) 'The methodology of historical climate reconstruction and its application to Africa', *JAH*, 20, 1, pp. 31–49.

Nicolas, G. (1975) *Dynamique sociale et appréhension du monde au sein d'une société hausa* (Paris: Institut d'ethnologie, Travaux et mémoires de l'Institut d'ethnologie, No. 78), 661 pp.

Nicolas, G. (forthcoming) 'The question of Gobir', in M. Adamu (ed.), at press(a).

Nkhoma, J. B. C. (1978) 'Immigrant politics and the Mankhambira paramountcy, c.1720–1820' (student research paper, Chancellor College, University of Malawi).

Nkurikiyimfura, J. N. (1983) 'Généalogies, chronologie et sources orales au Rwanda' (PhD thesis, Paris).

North, D. C. (1961) *The Economic Growth of the United States, 1790–1860* (Englewood Cliffs, N.J.: Prentice Hall), 304 pp.

North, D. C. (1981) *Structure and Change in Economic History* (New York: Norton).

North, D. C. and Thomas, R. P. (1970) 'An economic theory of the growth of the Western world', *EHR*, 2nd series, 22, 1, pp. 1–17.

North, D. C. and Thomas, R. P. (1973) *The Rise of the Western World: A New Economic History* (Cambridge: CUP).

North-Coombes, A. (1937) *The Evolution of Sugarcane Culture in Mauritius* (Port Louis, Mauritius: General Printing).

Northrup, D. (1978) *Trade Without Rulers: Precolonial Economic Development in South-Eastern Nigeria* (Oxford: Clarendon Press), 269 pp.

Nsanze, A. (1980) *Un domaine royal au Burundi: Mbuye (env. 1850–1945)* (Paris: SFHOM), 93 pp.

Nsimbi, M. B. (1956) *Amannya Amaganda N'Emnono Zaago* (Kiganda names and their origins) (Nairobi: EALB).

Nthara, S. J. (1968) *Mbiri ya Achewa* (Blantyre: Hetherwick Press); (earlier edn, 1948).

Nukunya, C. K. (1969) *Kinship and Marriage among the Ewe* (London: Athlone Press).

Nurse, G. T. (1977) 'The people of Bororo: a lexicostatistical enquiry', in B. Pachai (ed.), pp. 123–35.

Nyakatura, J. W. (1947/1973) *Abakama ba Bunyoro-Kitara*; 1974 trans. by T. Muganwa and ed. by G. N. Uzoigwe as *Anatomy of an African Kingdom* (New York: Nok Publishers Ltd.), 282 pp.

Nyakatura, J. W. (1971) *Aspects of Bunyoro Customs and Traditions* (Nairobi: EALB), 117 pp.

Nziziwe, I. (1972) *Studies in Ibo Political Systems: Chieftaincy and Politics in Four Niger States* (London: Frank Cass), 287 pp.

Obayemi, A. (1976) 'The Yoruba and Ebo-speaking peoples and their neighbours before 1600', in J. F. A. Ajayi and M. Crowder (eds), 2nd edn, pp. 196–263.

Obenga, T. (1969) 'Le royaume de Kongo', *Africa*, 24, pp. 323–48.

Obenga, T. (1970) 'Le Kikongo, fondement de l'unité culturelle', *Africa*, 25, pp. 131–55.

Obenga, T. (1976) *La cuvette congolaise: Les hommes et les structures* (Paris: PA).

Obenga, T. (1979) 'Habillement, cosmétique et parure au royaume de Kongo, (XVe–XVIIIe siècles)', *CCAH*, 4, pp. 21–38.

Obenga, T. (1981) 'Instruments de musique au royaume de Kongo, (XVIe–XVIIIe siècles)', *CCAH*, 6, pp. 39–56.

Ocamali, T. J. (1970) 'A pre-colonial history of the highland Alur' (graduating essay, Makerere).

Ochieng', W. R. (1970) 'Walowa – The ironworkers of East Africa', *Target*, March.

Ochieng', W. R. (1974a) *A Pre-Colonial History of the Gusii of Western Kenya, 1500–1914* (Nairobi: EALB), 257 pp.

Ochieng', W. R. (1975b) *An Outline History of Nyanza up to 1914* (Nairobi: EALB), 104 pp.

Ochieng', W. R. (1975a) *The First Word* (Nairobi: EALB), 195 pp.

Ochieng', W. R. (1975b) *Eastern Kenya and its Invaders* (Nairobi: EALB), 104 pp.

Ochieng', W. R. (1975c) *A History of the Kadimo Chiefdom of Yimbo in Western Kenya* (Nairobi: EALB), 78 pp.

Ochieng', W. R. (1975d) 'Undercivilization in Black Africa', in W. R. Ochieng' (ed.), 1975a, pp. 1–20.

Ochieng', W. R. (1976) 'The transformation of a Bantu settlement into a Luo Ruothdom', in B.A. Ogot (ed.), 1976a, pp. 44–64.

Ochieng', W. R. (1977) *The Second Word: More Essays on Kenya History* (Nairobi: KLB).

Odyomo, P. (at press) 'Consensus and leadership in the Alido confederacy in nineteenth-century Lango', in D. Denoon (ed.).

O'Fahey, R. S. (1970) 'The growth and development of Keeraa Sultanate of Dār Fūr' (PhD thesis, University of London).

O'Fahey, R. S. (1970) *States and State Formation in the Eastern Sudan* (Khartoum: Sudan Research Unit, University of Khartoum, African Studies Seminar Paper, No. 9).

O'Fahey, R. S. (1971) 'Religion and trade in the Kayra Sultanate of Dār Fūr', in Y. F. Hasan (ed.), *Sudan in Africa* (Khartoum: KUP), pp. 87–97.

O'Fahey, R. S. (1980) *State and Society in Dār Fūr* (London: Hurst).

O'Fahey, R. S. and Spaulding, J. L. (1974) *The Kingdoms of the Sudan* (London: Methuen), 235 pp.

Ogot, B. A. (1963) 'British administration in the central Nyanza district of Kenya', *JAH*, 4, 2, pp. 249–73.

Ogot, B. A. (1967) *A History of the Southern Luo, Vol. 1: Migration and Settlement, 1500–1900* (Nairobi: EAPH), 250 pp.

Ogot, B. A. (ed.) (1974) *Zamani* (Nairobi: EAPH and Longman), 407 pp.

Ogot, B. A. (ed.) (1976a) *History and Social Change in East Africa* (Nairobi: EALB), 235 pp.

Ogot, B. A. (ed.) (1976b) *Kenya Before 1900* (Nairobi: EAPH), 291 pp.

Ogot, B. A. and Kieran, J. A. (1971) *Zamani: A Survey of East African History* (Nairobi: EAPH); a new edition of B. A. Ogot (ed.), 1974, 407 pp.

Ogwal, R. (1969) *History of Lango Clans*, trans. by J. A. Otima and W. Okot-Chono (Makerere: History Department).

Okalany, D. H. (at press) 'The Iteso: migration and developing institutions', in J. B. Webster (ed.), *Uganda Before 1900*, vol. 1.

Okech, L. (1953) *Tekwaro ki ker Lobo Acholi* (Kampala: EALB); 1968 trans. by J. Nyeko, *History and Chieftaincy Records of the Land of the Acholi People* (Makerere: History Department).

Oliver, R. (ed.) (1977a) *The Cambridge History of Africa, Vol. 3: From c.1050 to c.1600* (Cambridge: CUP), 803 pp.

Oliver, R. (1977b) 'The East African interior', in R. Oliver (ed.), pp. 621–69.

Oliver, R. (1982) 'The Nilotic contribution to Bantu Africa', *JAH*, 23, pp. 433–42.

Oliver, R. and Fage, J. D. (1962) *A Short History of Africa*, 2nd edn 1970 (Harmondsworth: Penguin).

Oliver, R. and Mathew, G. (eds) (1963) *A History of East Africa*, vol. 1 (Oxford: Clarendon Press), 500 pp.

Oloo, P. C. (1969) 'History of settlement: the example of Luo clans of Alego: 1500–1918' (undergraduate dissertation, Nairobi University).

Onyango-ka-Odongo and Webster, J. B. (eds) (1976) *The Central Luo during the Aconya* (Nairobi: EALB).

Orhanlu, C. (1969) 'Osmani-Bornu Munasebetine al belger', *Tarikh Dergisi*, 23, trans. by S. E. Brown as 'Documents relating to Ottoman-Borno relations'.

Orhanlu, C. (1974) *Osmanli Imparatorlugu'num güney si yaseti Habes eyalati* (Istanbul: University of Istanbul).

Ortiz, F. (1916) *Hampa afro-cubana: los negros esclavos* (Havana: Revista Bimestre Cubana).

Otima, J. A. (at press) 'The Atek of Oumolao in Aputi', in J. B. Webster (ed.), *Uganda Before 1900*, 1.

Ott, T. O. (1973) *The Haitian Revolution* (Knoxville: UTP), 232 pp.

Ozanne, P. (1962) 'Notes on the early historic archaeology of Accra', *THSG*, 6, pp. 51–70.

Pachai, B. (ed.) (1972) *The Early History of Malawi* (London: Longman), 454 pp.

Pachai, B. (1973) *Malawi: A History of the Nation* (London: Longman), 324 pp.

Pacheco Pereira, D. (1937) *Esmeraldo de Situ Orbis, 1506–1508*, trans. and ed. by G. H. T. Kimble (London: Hakluyt Society, 2nd series, vol. 79), 193 pp.

Pageard, R. (1957) *Notes sur l'histoire des Bambara de Ségou* (Paris).

Pageard, R. (1963) *Civilisation mossi et Egypte ancienne* (Geneva: Institut africain).

Pageard, R. (1969) *Le Droit privé des Mossi – Traditions et révolution*, vols 1 and 2 (Paris/Ouagadougou: CNRS/CVRS).

Pagès, A. (1933) *Au Rwanda, sur les bords du lac Kivu: Un royaume hamite au centre de l'Afrique* (Brussels: Institut royal colonial belge), 703 pp.

Pais, P. (1945–6) *Historia da Etiopia* (Porto: Libraria Civilização), 3 vols.

Palmer, C. A. (1976) *Slaves of the White God: Blacks in Mexico, 1570–1650* (Cambridge, Mass: HUP), 234 pp.

Palmer, H. R. (1936) *The Bornu, Sahara and Sudan* (New York: Negro University Press), 296 pp.

Palmer, H. R. (1967) *Sudanese Memoirs* (London: Frank Cass), 373 pp.

Palmer, R. and Parsons, N. (eds) (1977) *The Roots of Rural Poverty in Central and Southern Africa* (London: Heinemann).

Panikkar, K. M. (1945) *India and the Indian Ocean* (London: Allen & Unwin), 109 pp.

Papstein, R. J. (1978) 'The Upper Zambezi: a history of the Luvale people, 1000–1900' (PhD thesis, University of California, Los Angeles).

Paris, F. (ed.) (1984) 'La région d'In Gall-Tegi-en-Tesemt (Niger) III: Les sépultures du néolithique final à l'Islam', *EN*, vol 50, 233 pp.

Park, M. (1799) *Travels in the Interior Districts of Africa. .... in the years 1795, 1796 and 1797* (London: G & W. Nicol).

Parrinder, E. G. (1967) *The Story of Ketu* (Ibadan: IUP).

Patterson, K. D. (1975) *The Northern Gabon Coast to 1875* (Oxford: Clarendon Press), 167 pp.

Paulitschke, P. V. (1888) *Harar* (Leipzig: Brockhaus).

Peires, J. B. (1981) *The House of Phalo: A History of the Xhosa People in the Days of their Independence* (Johannesburg: Raven Press).

Pélissier, P. (1966) *Les paysans du Sénégal: les civilisations agraires du Cayor à la Casamance* (Saint-Yrieix, Haute-Vienne: Imprimerie Fabrègue), 941 pp.

Pellegrini, V. (1963/1972) *Acoli Macon* (Gulu); trans. by C. Okeng as *A History of the Acholi* (History Department, Makerere University).

Perchonock, N. (forthcoming) 'The territorial principle and the evolution of social organization in Kasar Hausa before 1500', in M. Adamu (ed.), at press (a).

Perlman, M. L. (1970) 'The traditional systems of stratification among the Ganda and the Nyoro of Uganda', in A. Tuden and Plotnicov (eds), *Social Stratification in Africa* (London: Macmillan), pp. 125–62.

949

Perrot, C. H. (1970) 'L'histoire dans les royaumes Agni de l'est de la Côte d'Ivoire', *AESC*, **25**, 6, pp. 1659–77.

Perrot, C. H. (1974) 'Ano Asemã: mythe et histoire', *JAH*, **15**, 2, pp. 199–222.

Perrot, C. H. (1982) *Les Anyi-Ndenye et le pouvoir politique aux XVIIIe et XIXe siècles* (Abidjan/Paris: CEDA).

Perruchon, J. (1893) *Les Chroniques de Zar'a yâ'eqôb et Ba'eda Mâryâm, rois d'Ethiopie de 1434 à 1478* (Paris: Bouillon).

Perruchon, J. (1894) 'Règne de Galâdêwos ou Aṣnaf Sagad', *RS*, **2**, pp 154–166 and 263–270.

Perruchon, J. (1896) 'Règne de Minas ou Admas Sagad. Règne de Sarṣa Dengel ou Malak Sagad. Règnes de Ya'qob et Za Dengel', *RS*, **4**, pp. 87–90.

Perruchon, J. (1897) 'Règne de Susenyos ou Seḷṭan Sagad', *RS*, **5**, pp. 173–89.

Perruchon, J. (1897–8) 'Règne de Fasiladas ou Alam Sagad', *RS*, **5**, pp. 360–72; and **6**, pp. 84–92.

Perruchon, J. (1901) 'Règne de Iyassu Ier', *RS*, **9**, pp. 71–8, 161–7 and 258–62.

Perry, A. (1923) 'Abram Hannibal, the favourite of Peter the Great', *JNH*, **8**, 4, pp. 359–66.

Person, Y. (1961) 'Les Kissi et leurs statuettes de pierre', *BIFAN*, **23**, Series B, vol 1, pp. 1–59.

Person, Y. (1964) 'En quête d'une chronologie ivoirienne', in J. Vansina, R. Mauny and L. V. Thomas (eds), *The Historian in Tropical Africa* (Oxford: OUP), pp. 322–38.

Person, Y. (1970) 'Le Soudan nigérien et la Guinée occidentale', in H. Deschamps (ed.), *Histoire générale de l'Afrique noire*, vol 1, (Paris: PUF), pp. 271–304.

Person, Y. (1971) 'Ethnic movements and acculturation in Upper Guinea since the fifteenth century', *AHS*, **4**, 3, pp. 669–89.

Person, Y. (1972) *The Dyula and the Manding World* (London: SOAS, Conference on Manding Studies, duplicated).

Person, Y. (1974a) 'La Sénégambie dans l'histoire', in R. C. Bridges (ed.), *'Senegambia: Proceedings of a Colloquium at the University of Aberdeen, African Studies Group'*, pp. 1–32.

Person, Y. (1974b) 'The Atlantic coast and the southern savannahs, 1800–1880', in J. F. A. Ajayi and M. Crowder (eds), *The History of West Africa*, vol 2, pp. 262–307.

Person, Y. (1981) 'Nyaani Mansa Mamadu et la fin de l'empire du Mali', in *Mélanges en hommage à R. Mauny*.

Pescatello, A. M. (1972) 'The African presence in Portuguese India', *JAH*, **2**, 1, pp. 26–48.

Petterson, J. C. (1920) *Special Report on Uje District, Bornu Province* (Kaduna, Nigeria: National Archives, SNP), 69 pp.

Peukert, W. (1978) *Der atlantische sklaventandel von Dahomey (1740–1797)* (Wiesbaden: Steiner), 412 pp.

Phillipson, D. W. (1974) 'Iron Age history and archaeology in Zambia', *JAH*, **15**, 1, pp. 1–25.

Phillipson, D. W. (1977) *The Later Prehistory of Eastern and Southern Africa* (London: Heinemann), 323 pp.

Phimister, I. R. (1974) 'Ancient mining near Great Zimbabwe', *JIMM*, **74**, pp. 233–7.

Phimister, I. R. (1976) 'Pre-colonial gold mining in Southern Zambezia: a reassessment', *ASR*, **21**, June, pp. 1–30.

Phiri, K. M. (1975a) 'Chewa history in Central Malawi and the use of oral tradition, 1600–1920' (PhD thesis, University of Wisconsin).

Phiri, K. M. (1975b) 'Chewa history fieldnotes' (unpublished, copies available in University of Wisconsin Library and National Archives of Malawi).

Phiri, K. M. (1976) 'Pre-colonial economic change in Central Malawi, 1750–1875', *MJSS*, **5**, pp. 15–27.

Phiri, K. M. (1977) 'The Maravi state system and Chewa political development about 1850' (History Teachers' Conference, Chancellor College, August), p. 9.

Phiri, K. M. (1980) 'The pre-colonial history of Southern Malawi: an interpretative essay', *MJSS*, **8**, pp. 28–46.

Phiri, K. M., Vaughan, M. and Makuluni, D. (1978) 'Yao and Nyanja historical texts, Vol. II' (History Department, University of Malawi).

Piault, M. H. (1970) *Histoire Mawri: introduction à l'étude des processus constitutifs de l'Etat* (Paris: Editions du CNRS), 206 pp.

Picq, Col. A. du (1905) 'Les Tanala de L'Ikongo', *Le Tour du Monde* (Paris), 18–25 November, pp. 541–64.

Picq, Col. A. du (1932) 'L'influence islamique sur une population malayo-polynésienne de Madagascar: Tanala', extract from *RTC*, **26**, pp. 191–208, 266–79 and 370–401.

Pigafetta, F. de (1591/1881/1970) *Relatione del Reame di Congo et delle circonvicine contrade tratta dalli scritti e ragionamenti di Odoardo Lopez Portoghese* (Rome: B. Grassi), 82 pp; Eng. trans. in 1881 by M. Hutchinson, *A Report of the Kingdom of Congo and the Surrounding Countries* (London: John Murray), 175 pp; 1970 reprint (London: Frank Cass).

Pike, J. G. (1965) 'Pre-colonial history of Malawi', *SMJ*, 18, 1, pp. 22–54.

Pike, J. G. (1968) *Malawi: A Political and Economic History* (New York: Praeger).

Pitot, A. (1899) *Ile de France: Esquisses Historiques (1715–1810)* (Port-Louis, Mauritius: E. Pezzani), 447 pp.

Pitot, A. (1905) *T'Eylandt Mauritius: Esquisses Historiques (1598–1710)*.

Plancquaert, M. (1971) *Les Yaka: essai d'histoire* (Tervuren: MRAC, Annales sciences humaines, vol. 71).

Pogge, P. (1880) *Im Reich des Muata Jamwo* (Berlin: D. Reimer).

Poirier, C. (1953) 'Généalogie des rois Maroserana du sud de l'Onilahy', *BAM*, new series, 31, pp. 29–35.

Pollock, N. C. and Agnew, S. (1963) *A Historical Geography of South Africa* (London: Longman), 242 pp.

Poncet, J. P. (1967) 'Le mythe de la "catastrophe" hilalienne', *AESC*, 22, pp. 1099–1120.

Porter, D. H. (1970) *The Abolition of the Slave Trade in England, 1784–1807* (New York: Archon).

Porter, R. (1974) 'European activity on the Gold Coast, 1620–1667' (PhD thesis, University of South Africa).

Posnansky, M. (1974) 'Archaeological aspects of the Brong Ahafo region' (Legon: Brong Studies Seminar).

Posnansky, M. (1981) 'The societies of Africa south of the Sahara in the early iron age', in G. Mokhtar (ed.), pp. 718–31.

Postan, M. M. and Hatcher, J. (1975 and 1978) 'Population and class relations in feudal society', *PP*, 75, pp. 37–47 and 78, pp. 24–37.

Potter, J. (1965) 'The growth of population in America, 1700–1800', in D. V. Glass and D. E. C. Eversley (eds), pp. 631–88.

Prax (1849) *Commerce de l'Algérie avec La Mecque et le Soudan* (Paris: J. Rouvier), 32 pp.

Price, R. (ed.) (1973) *Maroon Societies* (Garden City: Anchor).

Price, R. (1976) *The Guiana Maroons: A Historical and Bibliographical Introduction* (Baltimore: JHUP), 184 pp.

Priestley, M. A. (1961a) 'English gifts to the King of Ashanti in the 18th century', *GNQ*, 2, pp. 4–7.

Priestley, M. A. (1961b) 'The Ashanti question and the British', *JAH*, 2, 1, pp. 35–59.

Priestley, M. A. (1969) *West African Trade and Coast Society* (London: OUP), 207 pp.

Pring, M. *Fanno Mary O Fannadill*.

Proyart, A. (1776) *Histoire de Loango, Kakongo et autres royaumes d'Afrique* (Paris); 1968 reprint (Gregg International), 393 pp.

Pruitt, W. F. (1973) 'An independent people: the history of the Sala Mpasu of Zaire and their neighbors' (PhD thesis, Northwestern University, Evanston, III.).

Purchas, S. (1613/1905–7) *Purchas: His Pilgrims* (London: W. Stansby), 752 pp.; numerous later edns including that for the Hakluyt Society in 1905–7 (20 vols, Glasgow: J. MacLehose and Sons).

Quarles, B. (1961) *The Negro in the American Revolution* (Chapel Hill: UNCP), 231 pp.

Quiring, H. (1949) *Trade Routes, Trade and Currency in East Africa* (Livingstone: Rhodes-Livingstone Museum Occasional Paper).

Raffenel, A. (1846) *Voyage dans l'Afrique occidentale (1843–1844)* (Paris: Bertrand), 512 pp.

Rafik, A. K. (1963) *Misr wa-Bilād al-Shām* (Damascus).

Rahmān, A. R. A. and Miki, W. (1977) *The Village in Ottoman Egypt and Tokuga Japan – A Comparative Study* (Tokyo, Studia Culturae Islamicae No. 7, published by the Institute for the Study of Languages and Cultures of Asia and Africa), 106 pp.

Randles, W. G. L. (1958) 'South-East Africa and the Empire of Monomotapa as shown on selected and printed maps of the 16th century', *Studia*, 2, pp. 103–63.

Randles, W. G. L. (1968) *L'ancien royaume du Congo, des origines à la fin du XIXe siècle* (Paris/The Hague: Mouton), 275 pp.

Randles, W. G. L. (1979) *The Empire of Monomotapa: From the Fifteenth to the Nineteenth Century* trans. into English by R. S. Roberts (Gweru: Mambo Press), pp. 38–55.

Ranger, T. O. (ed.) (1968a) *Aspects of Central African History* (London/Nairobi: Heinemann/EAPH), 291 pp.

Ranger, T. O. (ed.) (1968b) *Emerging Themes of African History* (Nairobi: EAPH), 230 pp.

Ranger, T. O. (1973) 'Territorial cults in the history of Central Africa', *JAH*, 14, 4, pp. 581–97.

951

Ranger, T. O. (1979) *Revolt in Southern Rhodesia, 1896–1897: A Study in African Resistance*, 1st paperback edn (London: Heinemann), 403 pp.

Ranger, T. O. and Kimambo, I. N. (eds) (1972) *The Historical Study of African Religion* (London: Heinemann), 307 pp.

Rasamimanana, J. and Razafindrazaka, L. (1909) *Contribution à l'histoire des Malgaches – Fanasoavana ny Tantaran'ny Malagasy* (Ambohimalaza and Antananarivo); 1957 reprint, a-b, i-iii, pp. 1–45.

Ratelband, K. (1953) *Vijf Dagregisters van het Kasteel Sao Jorge Da Mina (Elmina) aan de Goudkust (1645–1647)* Uitgegeven door ... – Linschoten Vereeniging, V. LV (The Hague).

Ratzel, F. (1885) *Völkerkunde* (Leipzig), pp. 451–78.

Rau, V. (1966) 'Les marchands – banquiers étrangers au Portugal sous le règne de Joao III (1521–1557)', in *Les aspects internationaux de la découverte océanique aux XVe et XVIe siècles* (Paris).

Razafimino, G. (1924) *La signification religieuse du Fandroana ou de la fête du nouvel an en Imerina* (Antananarivo).

Rea, W. F. (1976) *The Economics of the Zambezi Missions, 1580–1759* (Rome: Institutum Historicum).

Redmond, P. M. (at press) 'Notes on the trade in dried fish in the Central Sudan', in M. Adamu (ed.), at press (a).

Reefe, T. Q. (1975) 'A History of the Luba Empire to 1895' (PhD thesis, University of California, Berkeley).

Reefe, T. Q. (1977) 'Traditions of genesis and the Luba Diaspora', *HAJM*, 4, pp. 183–206.

Reefe, T. Q. (1980) 'The eastern savanna of Central Africa and Northern Zambezia to the 1890s' (Paper presented to the Conference on the Social, Political and Economic History of Central Africa, University of Kent, Canterbury, 7–11 July).

Reefe, T. Q. (1981) *The Rainbow and the Kings: A History of the Luba Empire to 1891* (Berkeley: UCP), 286 pp.

Rehse, H. (1910) *Kiziba: Land und Leute* (Stuttgart), trans. by Mrs Denne as *Kiziba: land and people* (n.d.), 394 pp.

Reindorf, C. C. (1898/1966) *The History of the Gold Coast and Asanti* (Basle: Kegan Paul, Trench, Trübner & Co); 1966 reprint (Accra: GUP), 349 pp.

Rennie, J. K. (1972) 'The precolonial kingdom of Rwanda: a reinterpretation', *TJH*, 2, 2, pp. 11–53.

Repiquet, J. (1902) *Le Sultanat d'Anjouan, îles Comores* (Paris).

Rey-Hulman, D. (1975) 'Les dépendants des maîtres tyokossi pendant la période pré-coloniale', in C. Meillassoux (ed.), pp. 297–320.

Ricci, L. (1969–71) 'La "Vita" di 'enbāqom e di Yoḥannes abbati di Dabra Libānos di Scioa', *RSE*, 23, pp. 79–220 and 24, pp. 134–232.

Richard-Molard, J. (1949) *Afrique occidentale française* (2nd edn, Paris: Editions Berger-Levrault).

Richter, F. (1899) 'Der Bezirk Bukoba', *Mitteilungen von Forschungsreisenden und Gelehrten aus den deutschen Schutzgebieten*, 12, pp. 67–105.

Rinchon, R. F. D. (1929) *La traite et l'esclavage des Congolais par les Européens: Histoire de la déportation de 13 millions 250.000 Noirs en Amérique* (Brussels: Wetteren), 306 pp.

Rinchon, R. F. D. (1964) *Pierre Ignace Liévin van Alstein, capitaine négrier: Gand, 1733 – Nantes, 1793* (Dakar: IFAN, Mémoire No. 71), 452 pp.

Rita-Ferreira, A. (1966) *Os Chevas da Macanga* (Lourenço Marques).

Ritchie, C. I. A. (1968) 'Deux textes sur le Sénégal, 1673–1677', *BIFAN*, 30, Series B, No. 1, pp. 289–353.

Roberts, A. D. (ed.) (1968a) *Tanzania Before 1900* (Nairobi: EAPH), 162pp.

Roberts, A. D. (1968b) 'The Nyamwezi', in A. D. Roberts (ed.), 1968(a), pp. 117–50.

Roberts, A. D. (1970a) 'Chronology of the Bemba', *JAH*, 2, 2, pp. 221–40.

Roberts, A. D. (1970b) 'Pre-colonial trade in Zambia', *ASR*, 10, pp. 715–37.

Roberts, A. D. (1970c) 'Nyamwezi trade', in R. Gray and D. Birmingham (eds), pp. 39–74.

Roberts, A. D. (1973) *A History of the Bemba: Political Growth and Change in North-Eastern Zambia Before 1900* (London: Longman), 420 pp.

Roberts, A. D. (1976) *A History of Zambia* (London: Heinemann), 288 pp.

Robinson, D. (1975) 'The Islamic revolution of Futa Toro', *IJAHS*, 8, 2, pp. 185–221.

Robinson, K. R. (1966) 'A preliminary report on the recent archaeology of Ngonde, Northern Malawi', *JAH*, 7, 2, pp. 178–92.

Robinson, K. R. (1972) 'The Iron Age in Malawi: a brief account of recent work', in B. Pachai (ed.), pp. 54–72.

Robinson, K. R. and Sandelowsky, B. (1968) 'The Iron Age of Northern Malawi: recent work', *Azania*, 3, pp. 107–46.

Roche, C. (1976) *Conquête et résistance en Casamance* (Dakar: NEA).

Rodegem, F. M. (1964) *Onomastique rundi* (Bujumbura, mimeograph).

Rodney, W. (1967a) *West Africa and the Atlantic Slave Trade* (Nairobi: EAPH, Paper No. 2), 28 pp.

Rodney, W. (1967b) 'A reconsideration of the Mane invasions of Sierra Leone', *JAH*, 8, 2, pp. 219–46.

Rodney, W. (1968) 'Jihad and social revolution in Futa Djalon in the eighteenth century', *JHSN*, 4, 2, pp. 269–84.

Rodney, W. (1969a) 'Gold and slaves on the Gold Coast', *THSG*, 10, pp. 13–28.

Rodney, W. (1969b) 'Upper Guinea and the significance of the origins of Africans enslaved in the New World', *JNH*, 54, 4, pp. 327–45.

Rodney, W. (1970a) 'The historical roots of economic underdevelopment' (paper delivered at the 1970 (December) Universities of East Africa Social Science Conference, Dar es Salaam).

Rodney, W. (1970b) *A History of the Upper Guinea Coast, 1545–1800* (Oxford: Clarendon Press), 283 pp.

Rodney, W. (1972) *How Europe Underdeveloped Africa* (Dar es Salaam/London: TPH and Bogle L'Ouverture), 316 pp.

Rodney, W. (1975) 'Africa in Europe and the Americas', in J. D. Fage and R. Oliver (eds), *The Cambridge History of Africa*, vol 4 (Cambridge: CUP), pp. 578–651.

Rohlfs, C. (1875) *Quer durch Afrika* (2 vols, Leipzig: Brockhaus).

Roper, T. (1963) 'The rise of Christian Europe', *The Listener*, 28 November, p. 871.

Ross, R. (1975) 'The "White" population of the Cape colony in the eighteenth century', *PS*, 29.

Ross, R. (1976) *Adam Kok's Griquas: A Study in the Development of Stratification in South Africa* (Cambridge: CUP, African Studies Series No. 21), 194 pp.

Ross, R. (1978) 'Patterns of relationships between agriculturalists and pastoralists in Southern Africa' (Paper presented at the Conference on the Iron-using Bantu-speaking Population of Southern Africa before 1800, Leiden, September).

Rossi, E. (1936) 'La Cronaca Araba Tripolitana di Ibn Galboun', *SSL*, 3.

Rossi, E. (1968) *Storia di Tripoli e della Tripolitania* (Rome: Istituto per l'Oriente).

Rotberg, R. and Mazrui, A. (eds) *Protest and Power in Black Africa* (New York: OUP), 1274 pp.

Rout, L. B. Jr. (1976) *The African Experience in Spanish America, from 1502 to the Present Day* (Cambridge: CUP), 404 pp.

Rubin, V. and Tuden, A. (eds) (1977) *Comparative Perspectives on Slavery in New World Plantation Societies* (Annals of the New York Academy of Science, Vol. 292).

Rugomana, J. (1957) 'Le roi du pays rundi et les hommes qui y sont venus les premiers', *Zaire*, 11, 6, pp. 625–36.

Rwabukumba, J. and Mudandagizi, V. (1974) 'Les formes historiques de la dépendance personnelle dans l'état rwandais', *CEA*, 53, pp. 6–25.

Ryan, V. M. (1864) *Mauritius and Madagascar* (London: Seeley, Jackson and Halliday), 340 pp.

Ryder, A. F. C. (1964) 'A note on Afro-Portuguese ivories', *JAH*, 5, pp. 363–5.

Ryder, A. F. C. (1965a) *Materials for West African History in Portuguese Archives* (London: Athlone Press), 92 pp.

Ryder, A. F. C. (1965b) 'Portuguese and Dutch in West Africa before 1800', in J. F. A. Ajayi and I. Espie (eds), pp. 212–32.

Ryder, A. F. C. (1969) *Benin and the Europeans, 1485–1897* (London: Longmans), 372 pp.

Saʻad, A. (1977) *Lamibe of Fombina* (Oxford: Asian Broadcasting Union).

al-Saʻdī, ʻAbd al-Raḥmān b. ʻAbd Allāh (1656) *Taʼrīkh al-Sūdān*; 1898 ed. O. Houdas and E. Benoist, with 1900 French transl. O. Houdas, 2 vols (Paris: Leroux); 1964 rev. transl. (Paris: Maisonneuve et Larose), 540 pp..

Sahli, K. R. (1977) 'Kathaiqʻan al-Maghrab al-ʻUthmānī' (Documents concerning the Ottoman's Maghrib), *RHM*, 7–8, January, Arab section, pp. 40–60.

Sahlins, M. (1972) *Stone-Age Economics* (Chicago: Aldine-Atherton), 348 pp; 2nd edn 1974 (London: Tavistock).

Saignes, M. A. (1967) *Vida de los esclavos en Venezuela* (Caracas: Hesperides).

Saint-Gerrais de (1736) *Mémoires historiques qui concernent le gouvernement de l'ancien et du nouveau Royaume de Tunis, avec des réflexions sur la conduite d'un Consul, et un détail du commerce ...* (Paris: Ganeau Fils).

Saley, M. (1982) 'Les états tsotsebaki des origines au XIXe siècle' (MA thesis, University of Niamey).

Salifou, A. (1971) *Le Damagaram ou Sultanat de Zinder au XIXe siècle*, (Niamey: IRSH, *EN*, vol. 27), 320pp.

Salim, A. I. (1973) *The Swahili-speaking Peoples of Kenya's Coast, 1895–1965* (Nairobi: EAPH), 272 pp.

Salim, A. I. (1980) 'Kenya, Muslims' in *Encyclopedia of Islam*, new edn (Leiden/Paris: Brill/Maisonneuve et Larose).

Salisbury, R. F. (1962) *From Stone to Steel* (Melbourne: Melbourne University Press/CUP).

Sanders, E. (1969) 'The hamitic hypothesis: its origin and functions in time perspective', *JAH*, 10, 4, pp. 521–32.

Santandrea, F. (1964) *A Tribal History of the Western Bahr el-Ghazal* (Bologna: Editrice Nigrizia), 345 pp.

Santandrea, F. (1981) *Ethno-Geography of the Bahr el-Ghazal (Sudan): An Attempt at a Historical Reconstruction* (Bologna: Editrice Nigrizia).

Santos, J. dos (1609/1895) *Ethiopia Oriental*, 1895 edn (2 vols, Lisbon).

Santos, J. dos (1901) 'Ethiopia Oriental', in G. M. Theal (ed.), 1898–1903, vol. 7, pp. 1–182 (in Portuguese); pp. 183–370 (English trans.).

Santos, T. dos (1969) 'The crisis of development theory and the problem of dependence in Latin America', in H. Bernstein (ed.), pp. 57–80.

Sargent, R. A. (1979) 'The generations of turmoil and stress: a proliferation of states in the northern interlacustrine region *c*.1544–1625', in J. B. Webster (ed.), 1979 (a), pp. 231–61.

Sarkar, J. (1919) *History of Aurangzib* (Calcutta/London: Longmans, Green & Co.).

Sauter, R. (1963) 'Où en est notre connaissance des églises rupestres d'Ethiopie?', *AE*, 5, pp. 235–92.

Sautter, G. (1966) *De l'Alantique au fleuve Congo, une géographie du sous-peuplement* (Paris: Imprimerie nationale), 1102 pp.

Savaron, C. (1928 and 1931) 'Contribution à l'histoire de l'Imerina', *BAM*, new series, 11, pp. 61–81 and 14, pp. 57–73.

Saxon, D. E. (1982) 'Linguistic evidence for the eastward spread of Ubanguian peoples', in C. Ehret and M. Posnansky (eds), pp. 66–77.

Scelle, G. (1906) *La traite négrière aux Indes de Castille* (2 vols, Paris: L. Larose and L. Tenin).

Schebesta, P. (1952) *Les pygmées du Congo belge* (Brussels: Verhandelingen), 432 pp.

Schechter, R. E. (1976) 'History and historiography on a frontier of Lunda expansion: the origins and early development of the Kanongesha' (PhD thesis, University of Wisconsin, Madison).

Schechter, R. E. (1980) 'Apropos the drunken king: cosmology and history', in J. C. Miller (ed.), pp. 108–25.

Schleicher, A. W. (1893) *Geschichte der Galla* (Berlin: T. Fröhlich).

Schmidt, P. (1978) *Historical Archaeology: A Structural Approach to an African Culture* (Westport Connect.: Greenwood Press), 365 pp.

Schoffeleers, M. J. (1968) 'Symbolic and social aspects of spirit worship among the Mang'anja' (PhD thesis, Oxford University).

Schoffeleers, M. J. (1972a) 'The meaning and use of the name "Malawi" in oral traditions and precolonial documents', in B. Pachai (ed.), pp. 93–106.

Schoffeleers, M. J. (1972b) 'The historical and political role of the M'bona cult among the Mang'anja', in T. O. Ranger and I. N. Kimambo (eds), pp. 73–94.

Schoffeleers, M. J. (1973) 'Towards the identification of a proto-Chewa culture: a preliminary contribution', *MJSS*, 2, pp. 47–60.

Schoffeleers, M. J. (1976) 'The Nyau societies: our present understanding', *SMJ*, 29, 1, pp. 59–68.

Schoffeleers, M. J. (ed.) (1979a) *Guardians of the Land: Essays on Central African Territorial Cults* (Gweru: Mambo Press).

Schoffeleers, M. J. (1979b) 'The Chisumphe and M'bona cults in Malawi: a comparative history', in M. J. Schoffeleers (ed.), 1979 (a), pp. 147–86.

Schoffeleers, M. J. (1980) 'Trade, warfare and social inequality: the case of the lower Shire Valley of Malawi, 1590–1622 A. D.', *SMJ*, 33, 2, pp. 1–24.

Schove, D. J. (1973) 'African droughts and the spectrum of time', in D. Dalby and R. J. H. Church (eds), *Droughts in Africa* (London: IAI), pp. 38–53; 2nd edn, 1977.

Schumacher, P. (1949) 'Urundi', *Aequatoria*, 12, pp. 129–32.

Schumacher, P. (1958) *Ruanda* (Fribourg: Anthropos), 1300 pp.

Schutte, G. (1979) 'Company and colonists at the Cape', in R. Elphick and H. Giliomee (eds), pp. 173–210.

Schwartz, S. B. (1970) 'The "Macambo": slave resistance in colonial Bahia', *JSH*, 3, 4.

Schwartz, S. B. (1977) 'Resistance and accommodation in eighteenth-century Brazil: the slaves' view of slavery', *HAHR*, 57, February.

Schweinfurth, G. (1873) *The Heart of Africa: Three Years' Travels and Adventures in the Unexplored Regions of Central Africa, 1886–71* (2 vols, London: Low, Marston, Low & Searle).

Sékou-Bamba, M. (1978) 'Bas-Bandama precolonial' (PhD thesis, University of Paris).

Seligman, C. G. (1957) *Races of Africa*, 3rd edn (London: Butterworth), 236 pp.

Séré de Rivières, E. (1965) *Histoire du Niger* (Paris: Berger-Levrault), 311 pp.

Serjeant, R. B. (1963) *The Portuguese off the South Arabian Coast: Hadrami Chronicles with Yemeni and European accounts of Dutch Pirates off Mocha in the Seventeenth Century* (Oxford: Clarendon Press).

Serjeant, R. B. (1966) 'South Arabia and Ethiopia – African elements in the south Arabian population', in *Proceedings of the Third International Conference of Ethiopian Studies* (Rome).

Serjeant, R. B. (1967) 'Société et gouvernments en Arabie du Sud', *Arabia*, 14 October.

al-Sharqāwī, M. (1957) *Misr fi 'l-qarn al-thāmin 'ashar* (Egypt in the 18th century) (3 vols, Cairo).

Shaw, Rev. G. A. (1893 and 1894) 'The Arab element in South-East Madagascar', *AA*, 5, pp. 99–109 and 6, pp. 205–10.

Shaw, S. J. (1962a) *The Financial and Administrative Organization and Development of Ottoman Egypt, 1517–1798* (Princeton: NJ: PUP, Princeton Oriental Studies No. 19), 451 pp.

Shaw, S. J. (1962b) *Ottoman Egypt in the Eighteenth Century: The Nizamname i Misir of Cezzar Ahmed Pasha*, ed. and tr. by S. J. Shaw (Cambridge, Mass.: HUP, Harvard Middle Eastern Monograph 7).

Shaw, S. J. (1969) *The Budget of Ottoman Egypt, 1005–1006/1596–1597* (The Hague: Mouton), 210 pp.

Shaw, T. (1970) *Igbo-Ukwu: An Account of Archaeological Discoveries in Eastern Nigeria* (2 vols, London: Faber & Faber for the IAS, University of Ibadan).

Shaw, T. (1977) 'Questions in the holocene demography of West Africa', in *African Historical Demography I: Proceedings of a Seminar held in the Centre of African Studies, University of Edinburgh (29th and 30th April* (Edinburgh: EUP), pp. 105–21.

Shaw, T. (1978) *Nigeria: Its Archaeology and Early History* (London: Thames & Hudson).

Shaw, T. (1981) 'Towards a pre-historic demography of Africa', *African Historical Demography* (Edinburgh), 2.

Shea, P. J. (1983) 'Approaching the study of production in rural Kano', in B. M. Barkindo (ed.), pp. 93–115.

Shepherd, J. F. (1969) 'Estimates of "invisible" earnings in the balance of payments of the British North American colonies, 1769–1772', *JEH*, 29, 2.

Shepherd, J. F. and Walton, G. M. (1972) *Shipping, Maritime Trade, and the Economic Development of Colonial North America* (Cambridge: CUP).

Sheridan, R. (1970) *The Development of the Plantations to 1750: An Era of West Indian Prosperity, 1750–1775* (Bridgetown, Jamaica: CUP), 120 pp.

Sheriff, A. M. H. (1971) 'The rise of a commercial empire: an aspect of the economic history of Zanzibar, 1770–1873' (PhD thesis, University of London).

Sheriff, A. M. H. (1980) 'Tanzanian societies at the time of partition', in M. H. Y. Kaniki (ed.), *Tanzania Under Colonial Rule* (London: Longman), pp. 11–50.

Sherwood, H. N. (1923) 'Paul Cuffee', *JNH*, 8, 2, pp. 153–229.

Shiroya, O. J. E. (unpublished (a)) 'The Lugbara: at the nexus of three worlds', in J. B. Webster (ed.), *Uganda Before 1900*, vol 1.

Shiroya, O. J. E. (unpublished (b)) 'Ethnic assimilation and political integration: the Lugbara, Alur and their neighbours', in D. Denoon (ed.), forthcoming.

Sidibé, B. K. (1972) 'The story of Kaabu: its extent and people' (unpublished paper, Conference on Manding Studies, London).

Sidibé, B. K. (1974) 'The Nyanchos of Kaabu' (unpublished paper, Indiana University African Studies Programme).

Silveira, L. (1946) *Ediçāo Nova do Tratado Breve dos Rios de Guiné pelo Capitāo André Alvares D'Almada* (Lisbon).

Sinclair, P. (1977) 'First steps towards the reconstruction of the rural economy of the Zimbabwe state' (Paper presented at the International Conference on Southern African History, National University of Lesotho, Roma).

Skinner, E. P. (1964) *The Mossi of Upper Volta: The Political Development of a Sudanese People* (Stanford: SUP), 236 pp.

Smaldone, J. P. (1977) *Warfare in the Sokoto Caliphate* (Cambridge: CUP), 228 pp.

Smith, A. (1970) 'Some notes on the history of Zazzau under the Hausa kings', in M. J. Mortimore (ed.), pp. 82–101.

Smith, A. (1976) 'The early states of the Central Sudan', in J. F. A. Ajayi and M. Crowder (eds), 2nd edn, pp. 158–201.

Smith, M. G. (1967) 'A Hausa kingdom: Maradi under Dan Baskore, 1845–75', in C. D. Forde and P. M. Kaberry (eds), pp. 93–122.

Smith, M. G. (1983) 'The Kano chronicle as history', in B. M. Barkindo (ed.), pp. 31–56.

Smith, P. (1981) 'Personnages de légende', *CCB*, pp. 244–53.

Smith, R. (1979) 'Carpaccio's African gondolier', *ISAR*, 34, pp. 47–52.

Soka, L. D. (1953) *Mbiri ya Alomwe* (London: Macmillan).

Southhall, A. W. (1953) *Alur Society* (Nairobi: OUP), 397 pp.

Southhall, A. W. (1954) 'Alur tradition and its historical significance', *UJ*, 18, 2, pp. 137–65.

Southhall, A. W. (1970) 'Rank and stratification among the Alur and other Nilotic peoples', in A. Tuden and Plotnicov (eds), *Social Stratification in Africa* (London: Macmillan), pp. 31–46.

Sow, A. I. (1971) *Le filon du bonheur éternel par Mouhammadou Samba Mambeya* (Paris: Colin).

Sowunmi, M. A. (1978) *Palynological Studies in the Rivers State* (University of Port Harcourt, School of Humanities Seminars).

Spaulding, J. L. (1971) 'Kings of sun and shadow: a history of the Abdallab provinces of the Northern Sinnar Sultanate, 1500–1800 A.D.' (PhD thesis, Columbia University).

Spaulding, J. L. (1972) 'The Funj: a reconsideration', *JAH*, 13, 1, pp. 39–53.

Spear, T. T. (1974) 'Tradition myths and historian's myths: variations on the Singwaya theme of Miji Kenda origins', *HA*, 1, pp. 67–84.

Spear, T. T. (1976) 'The Miji Kenda, 1550–1900', in B. A. Ogot (ed.), 1976 (b), pp. 262–85.

Spear, T. T. (1978) *The Kaya Complex: A History of the Miji Kenda Peoples of the Kenya Coast to 1900* (Nairobi: KLB & EALB).

Spear, T. T. (1981) *Kenya's Past* (Nairobi: Longman), 155 pp.

Spratlin, V. B. (1938) *Juan Latino: Slave and Humanist* (New York: Spinner Press Inc.).

Stanley, S. and Karsten, D. (1968) 'The Luwa system of the Garbiččo', *Paideuma*, 14, pp. 93–102.

Stein, R. (1978) 'Measuring the French slave trade, 1723–1792', *JAH*, 19, 4, pp. 515–21.

Steinhart, E. I. (1981) 'Herders and farmers', in C. C. Steward and D. Crummey (eds), *Modes of Production in Africa* (London: Sage Publications), pp. 115–56.

Stewart, C. C. (1976) 'Southern Saharan scholarship and the *Bilād al-Sūdān*', *JAH*, 17, pp. 73–93.

Stitz, V. (1974) *Studien zur Kulturgeographie Zentraläthiopiens* (Bonn: Dümmler).

Stokes, E. and Brown, R. (eds) (1966) *The Zambezian Past: Studies in Central African History* (Manchester: MUP), 427 pp.

Strandes, J. (1899/1961) *Die Portugiesenzeit von Deutsch – und Englisch-Ost Afrika* (Berlin: D. Reimer); English trans. J. F. Wallwork, *The Portuguese Period in East Africa* (Nairobi: EALB), 378 pp.

Straube, H. (1957) 'Das Dualasystem und die Halaka-Verfassung der Dorse', *Paideuma*, 6, pp. 342–53.

Straube, H. (1963) *Westkuschitische Völker Süd-Äthiopiens*, with a contribution by Schutz-Weider (Stuttgart: Kohlhammer), 411 pp.

Struck, B. (1911) 'Bemerkungen uber die "Mbandwa" des Zwischenseengebiets', *ZFE*, 43, 3/4, pp. 516–21.

Stuhlmann, F. (1894) *Mit Emin Pascha ins Herz von Afrika* (Berlin: D. Reimer), 902 pp.

Sulzmann, E. (1983) 'Orale Tradition und Chronologie: Der Fall Baboma-Bolia', in Feik Nzuji *et al.* (eds), *Mélanges de culture et linguistique africaine publiés à la mémoire de Leo Stappers* (Berlin: Mainzer Afrika Studien Bd. 3), pp. 525–86.

Suret-Canale, J. (1970) *La République de Guinée* (Paris: Editions sociales), 431 pp.

Suret-Canale, J. (1971) 'The Western Atlantic coast, 1600–1800', in J. F. A. Ajayi and M. Crowder (eds), pp. 387–440; 1976 edn, pp. 456–511.

Sutherland-Harris, N. (1970) 'Zambian trade with Zumbo in the 18th century', in R. Gray and D. Birmingham (eds), pp. 231–42.

Sutton, J. E. G. (1979) 'Towards a less orthodox history of Hausaland', *JAH*, 20, 2, pp. 179–201.

Sutton, J. E. G. (1983) 'A New look at the Inyanga terraces', *ZH*, 19, pp. 12–19.

Sutton, J. E. G. and Roberts A. (1968) 'Uvinza and its salt industry', *Azania*, 3, pp. 45–86.

Swartz, A. (1971) *Tradition et changements dans la societé guéré* (Paris: ORSTOM, Mémoires No. 52), 259 pp.

Sy, A. A. (1979) 'La geste tiedo' (PhD thesis, Dakar).

Tacchi, A. (1892) 'King Andrianampoinimerina and the early history of Antananarivo and Ambohimanga', *AA*, pp. 474–96.

Tamakloe, E. F. (1931) *A Brief History of the Dagbamba People* (Accra: Government Printer), 76 pp.

Tamrat, T. (1970) 'The Abbots of Däbrä Hayq, 1248–1535', *JES*, 7, pp. 87–117.

Tamrat, T. (1972) *Church and State in Ethiopia, 1270–1527* (Oxford: Clarendon Press), 327 pp.

Tamrat, T. (1977) 'Ethiopia, the Red Sea and the Horn', *Cambridge History of Africa*, vol. 3 (Cambridge: CUP), pp. 98–182.

Tardits, C. (1980) *Le royaume bamoum* (Paris: Armand Colin), 1078 pp.

Tardits, C. (ed.) (1981) *Contribution de la recherche ethnologique à l'histoire des civilisations du Cameroun* (2 vols, Paris: Editions du CNRS), 597 pp.

Tassy, L. de (1757) *Histoire des états barbaresques qui exercent la piraterie* (Paris: Chaubert).

Tauxier, L. (1912) *Le Noir du Soudan* (Paris: Larose).

Tauxier, L. (1917) *Le Noir du Yatenga* (Paris: Larose), 790 pp.

Tauxier, L. (1921) *Le Noir de Bondoukou* (Paris: Leroux).

Tauxier, L. (1924) *Nouvelles notes sur le Mossi et le Gourounsi* (Paris: Larose).

Tauxier, L. (1942) *Histoire des Bambara* (Paris: Librairie orientaliste P. Geuthner), 226 pp.

Taylor, J. G. (1979) *From Modernization to Modes of Production: A Critique of the Sociologies of Development and Underdevelopment* (London: Macmillan).

Teixeira da Mota, A. (1954) *Guiné Portuguesa* (2 vols, Lisbon: Agencia Geral do Ultramar).

Teixeira da Mota, A. (1969) 'Un document nouveau pour l'histoire des Peul au Sénégal pendant les 15ᵉ et 16ᵉ siècles', *BCGP*, **96**, pp. 781–860.

Teixeira da Mota, A. (1975) 'Gli avori africani nella documentazione portoghese dei secoli XV-XVII', *Africa*, **30**, 4, pp. 580–9.

Tellez, B. (1710) *Travels of the Jesuits in Ethiopia* (London).

Temini, A. (1978) 'Al-Khalfiya al-dīniya lis-sirā al-isbani al-'uthmani' (The religious background to the duel between Spain and the Ottoman), *RHM*, **10–11**, January, Arab section, pp. 5–44.

Temini, A. (1983) *Mujaz al-dafātir al-arabiya wa'l-turkiya bil-Jazā'ir* (Sommaire des registres turcs et arabes d'Alger) (Tunis: Publications de l'ISD), 169 pp. in Arabic + 26 pp. in French.

Terpestra, H. (1960) 'Nederlands gouden tijd an de Goudkust', *Tijdschrift voor Geschiedenis*, **73**, 3.

Terrasse, H. (1949–50) *Histoire du Maroc* (2 vols, Casablanca: Atlantides).

Theal, G. M. (ed.) (1898–1903) *Records of South-Eastern Africa* (9 vols, London/Cape Town: Government of Cape Town).

Theal, G. M. (1910) *Ethnography and Condition of South Africa before A.D. 1505* (London: George Allen & Unwin).

Thomas, F. M. (1958) *Historical Notes on the Bisa Tribe of Northern Rhodesia* (Lusaka: Rhodes-Livingstone Institute), 52 pp.

Thomas, J. M. C. (1979) 'Emprunt ou parentés', in S. Bahuchet, *Pygmées de Centrafrique* (Paris), pp. 141–69.

Thomassin, L. (1900) 'Notes sur le royaume de Mahabo', *NRE*, **6**, pp. 395–413.

Thompson, R. F. and Cornet, J. (1982) *The Four Moments of the Sun: Kongo Art in Two Worlds* (Washington: National Art Gallery).

Thornton, J. K. (1977a) 'Demography and history in the kingdom of Kongo, 1550–1750', *JAH*, **18**, 4, pp. 507–30.

Thornton, J. K. (1977b) 'Eighteenth-century baptismal register and the demographic history of Manguezo', in C. Fyfe and D. McMaster (eds), pp. 405–15.

Thornton, J. K. (1978) 'A resurrection for the Jaga', *CEA*, **69–70**, pp. 223–7.

Thornton, J. K. (1980) 'The slave trade in eighteenth-century Angola: Effects on demographic structures', *CJAS*, **14**, 3, pp. 417–28.

Thornton, J. K. (1981a) 'The chronology and causes of the Lunda expansion to the west c.1700–1852', *ZJH*, **1**, pp. 1–13.

Thornton, J. K. (1981b) 'The demographic effect of the slave trade on Western Africa, 1500–1800, in C. Fyfe and D. McMaster (eds), vol 2, pp. 691–720.

Thornton, J. K. (1983a) 'Catholicism in Kongo, 1491–1750', *JAH*, **25**, pp. 147–67.

Thornton, J. K. (1983b) *The Kingdom of Kongo in the Era of the Civil Wars, 1641–1718* (Madison: UWP), 193 pp.

Tiendrebeogo, Y. (1964) *Histoire et coutumes royales des Mossi de Ouagadougou*, new edn with annotations by R. Pageard (Ouagadougou: Naba).

Tilho, J. (1911) *Documents scientifiques*, vol 2 (Paris: Imprimerie du NLE).

Timowski, M. (1974) *Le développement et la régression chez les peuples de la Boucle du Niger à l'époque précoloniale* (Warsaw: Warsaw University).

Toplin, R. B. (1972) *The Abolition of Slavery in Brazil* (New York: Atheneum).

Torres, D. de (1667) *Histoire des chérifs …* trans. Duc d'Angoulême (3 vols, Paris: T. Jolly).

Tosh, J. (1978) *Clan Leaders and Colonial Chiefs in Lango, the Political History of an East African Stateless Society, 1800–1939* (Oxford: Clarendon Press, Oxford Studies in African Affairs), 293 pp.

Toure, M. (1974) *Mande Influences in the Gyaman Kingdom*, Colloquium, Bonduku, January.

Toussaint, A. (1967) *La Route des Iles: Contribution à l'histoire maritime des Mascareignes.*

Toussaint, A. (1971) *Histoire de l'Ile Maurice* (Paris: PUF), 128 pp.

Toussaint, A. (1972) *Histoire des Iles Mascareignes* (Paris: Berger-Levrault), 351 pp.

Tovonkery (1915) *Lovantsofina Milaza ny Tantara Nihavian'ny Mpanjaka Sakalava Samy Hofa Eto Amin'ny Faritany Maromandia,* Document 620, Bibliothèque Poirier, University of Madagascar.

Tracey, H. (1940) *António Fernandes, Descobridor do Monomotapa, 1514–1515* (Lisbon/Lourenço Marques: Imprensa nacional), 92 pp.

Traoré, D. (1937) 'Notes sur le royaume mandingue de Bobo', *L'éducation africaine*, **26**, pp. 58–9.

Trimingham, J. S. (1949) *Islam in the Sudan* (Oxford: Clarendon Press), 280 pp.

Trimingham, J. S. (1964) *Islam in East Africa* (Oxford: Clarendon Press), 198 pp.

Trimingham, J. S. (1970) *A History of Islam in West Africa* (Oxford: OUP), 262 pp.

Tucker, A. N. and Bryan, M. A. (1966) *The Non-Bantu Languages of North-Eastern Africa* (London: OUP).

Tundu, K. Y. (1981) 'Le royaume de Bene Kalundwe: des origines à 1902' (First degree dissertation, Lubumbashi).

al-Tunisi, Muḥammad ibn 'Umar (1951) *Voyage au Oaday* trans. by Perron (Paris).

al-Tunisi, Muḥammad ibn 'Umar (1965) *Tashid al-adhhan bi-sirat Bilad al-'Arab wa l'Sudan* (Cairo: Egyptian General Organization for Authorship, Information and Publishing).

Turnbull, C. M. (1961) *The Forest People* (London: Chatto and Windus), 249 pp.

Turnbull, C. M. (1966) *Wayward Servants: The Two Worlds of the African Pygmies* (London: Eyre and Spottiswoode), 390 pp.

UNESCO (1963) *Nomades et nomadisme au Sahara* (Paris), 195 pp.

UNESCO (1979) *The African Slave Trade from the Fifteenth to the Nineteenth Century,* General History of Africa, Studies and Documents No. 2 (Paris: UNESCO), 330 pp.

UNESCO (1980) *Historical Relations across the Indian Ocean,* General History of Africa, Studies and Documents No. 3 (Paris: UNESCO), 198 pp.

Unomah, A. C. and Webster, J. B. (1976) 'East Africa: the expansion of commerce', in J. E. Flint (ed.), pp. 270–318.

Uribe, J. J. (1963) 'Esclavos y señores en la sociedad colombiana del siglo XVIII', *Anuario colombiano de historia social y de la cultura*, vol. 1.

Uring, N. (1928) *The Voyages and Travels of Captain Nathaniel Uring, 1701,* ed. by A. Dewar (London: Cassel and Co.).

Urvoy, Y. F. (1936) *Histoire des populations du Soudan central* (Paris: Larose), 350 pp.

Urvoy, Y. F. (1949) *Histoire de l'empire du Bornu* (Paris: Larose, Mémoires de l'IFAN No. 7), 562 pp.

Urvoy, Y. F. (1978) *Wakar Bagauda Ta Kano* (Zaria: NNPC).

Usman, Y. B. (1978) 'The dynastic chronologies of three polities of Katsina', *BIFAN* (B), **40**, 2, pp. 396–414.

Usman, Y. B. (1979a) 'The transformation of political communities', in Y. B. Usman (ed.), 1979 (b), pp. 34–55.

Usman, Y. B. (ed.) (1979b) *Studies in the History of the Sokoto Caliphate – The Sokoto Seminar Papers* (Lagos: Third Press International), 504 pp.

Usman, Y. B. (1981) *The Transformation of Katsina (1400–1883) – The Overthrow of the Sarauta System and the Establishment of the Emirate* (Zaria: ABUP).

Usman, Y. B. (1983) 'A reconsideration of the history of relations between Borno and Hausaland before 1804 A. D.', in Y. B. Usman and N. Alkali (eds), pp. 175–204.

Usman, Y. B. and Alkali, M. N. (eds) (1983) *Studies in the History of Precolonial Borno* (Zaria: NNPC).

Vail, H. L. (1971) 'Tumbuka historical interviews: oral sources compiled in 1969–71.' (Unpublished, copies deposited in Department of History, Chancellor College, University of Malawi).

Vail, H. L. (1972a) 'Religion, language and tribal myth: the Tumbuka and Chewa of Malawi', in M. J. Schoffeleers (ed.), 1979 (a), pp. 209–33.

Vail, H. L. (1972b) 'Suggestions towards a reinterpreted Tumbuka history', in B. Pachai (ed.), pp. 148–67.

Vail, H. L. (1974) 'Trade and politics in pre-colonial northern Malawi: the strange relationship' (Department of History, University of Zambia, Seminar No. 7).

Valensi, L. (1967) 'Esclaves chrétiens et esclaves noirs à Tunis au XVIIIe siècle', *AESC*, **22**, pp. 1267–88.

Valensi, L. (1969) *Le Maghreb avant la prise d'Alger, 1790–1830* (Paris: Flammarion), 141 pp.

Valensi, L. (1977) *Fellahs tunisiens: l'économie rurale et la vie des campagnes aux 18e et 19e siècles* (Paris/The Hague: Mouton), 421 pp.

Vallier (1898) 'Etudes ethnologiques sur les Bezanozano', *NRE*, 3, pp. 65–84.

Van Avermaet, J. and Mbuya, B. (1954) *Dictionnaire kiluba-français* (Tervuren: MRAC, ser. in 8°, No. 12).

Van den Byvang, L. (1937) 'Notice historique sur les Balunda', *Congo*, 1, 4, pp. 426–38; 1, 5, pp. 548–62; 2, 2, pp. 193–208.

Van der Burgt, J. M. (1903) *Dictionnaire français-kirundi* (Bois-le-Duc: Société de l'illustration catholique), 648 pp.

Van der Kerken, G. (1944) *L'ethnie mongo* (Brussels: Institut royal colonial belge).

Van Gennep, A. (1904) *Tabou et totémisme à Madagascar* (Paris: E. Leroux, Mondes d'Outre-mer, série Histoire).

Van Noten, F. (1972) *Les tombes du roi Cyirima Rujugira et de la reine Nyirayuhi Kanjogera: description archéologique* (Tervuren: MRAC), 82 pp.

Van Overbergh, C. (1908) *Les Basonge* (Brussels: A. de Witt), 564 pp.

Vansina, J. (1961) *De la tradition orale; essai de méthode historique* (Tervuren: MRAC, Mémoire No. 36).

Vansina, J. (1962a) 'A comparison of African kingdoms', *Africa*, 32, 4, pp. 218–39.

Vansina, J. (1962b) *L'évolution du royaume Rwanda des origines à 1900* (Brussels: ARSOM), 100 pp.

Vansina, J. (1962c) 'Long-distance trade routes in Central Africa', *JAH*, 3, 3, pp. 375–90.

Vansina, J. (1963) 'Note sur l'origine du royaume du Congo', *JAH*, 4, pp. 33–8.

Vansina, J. (1965) *Les anciens royaumes de la savane* (Léopoldville: IRES), 250 pp.

Vansina, J. (1966a) *Kingdoms of the Savanna: A History of Central African States until the European Occupation*, trans. of *Les anciens royaumes de la savane* (Madison: UWP), 364 pp.

Vansina, J. (1966b) *Introduction à l'ethnographie du Congo* (Kinshasa: Université Lovanium, Editions universitaires du Congo, No. 1), 227 pp.

Vansina, J. (1967) 'Note sur la chronologie du Burundi ancien', *BARSOM*, 3, pp. 429–44.

Vansina, J. (1971) 'Once upon a time: oral traditions as history in Africa', *Daedalus*, 100, 2, pp. 442–68.

Vansina, J. (1972) *La légende du passé: Traditions orales du Burundi* (Tervuren: MRAC), 257 pp.

Vansina, J. (1973a) 'L'influence du mode de compréhension historique d'une civilisation sur ses traditions d'origine', *BARSOM*, pp. 220–40.

Vansina, J. (1973b) *The Tio Kingdom of the Middle Congo, 1880–1892* (London: OUP), 586 pp.

Vansina, J. (1974) 'Les langues bantoues et l'histoire', in *Mélanges H. Deschamps* (Paris), pp. 171–84.

Vansina, J. (1978) *The Children of Woot: A History of the Kuba Peoples* (Madison: UWP), 394 pp.

Vansina, J. (1978) 'Finding food and the history of pre-colonial Equatorial Africa: a plea', *AEH*, 7, pp. 9–19.

Vansina, J. (1981) 'Tentative hypothesis: Long-term population history in the African rain forests', in C. Fyfe and D. McMaster (eds), vol. 2, pp. 757–60.

Vansina, J. (1983a) 'Is elegance proof? Structuralism and African history', *HA*, 10, pp. 307–48.

Vansina, J. (1983b) 'The peoples of the forest', in D. Birmingham and P. Martin (eds), pp. 75–117.

Vansina, J. (1984a) 'Equatorial Africa and Angola: migrations and the first states', in D. T. Niane (ed.), pp. 551–77.

Vansina, J. (1984b) 'Western Bantu expansion', *JAH*, pp. 131–49.

Van Thiel, H. (1911) 'Buzinza unter der Dynastie der Bahinda', *Anthropos*, pp. 497–520.

Van Velsen, J. (1959) 'Notes on the history of the lakeside Tonga of Nyasaland', *AS*, 18, 3, pp. 105–17.

Van Wing, J. and Penders, C. (1928) *Le plus ancien dictionnaire bantu* (Leuven: Bibl. CXXVII).

Vellut, J. L. (1972) 'Notes sur le Lunda et la frontière luso-africaine 1700–1900', *EHA*, 3, pp. 61–166.

Verhulpen, E. (1936) 'Baluba et Balubaises du Katanga' (Anvers: Les éditions de l'avenir belge).

Vérin, P. (1971) 'Notes sur les collections de Vohémar', *Taloha*, 4, pp. 225–9.

Vérin, P. (1975) *Les échelles anciennes du commerce sur les côtes nord de Madagascar* (2 vols, Lille: University of Lille).

Verlinden, C. (1957) 'La colonie italienne de Lisbonne et le développement de l'économie métropolitaine et coloniale portugaise', in *Studi in Onore di A. Sapori*, Vol. I (Milan).

Verlinden, C. (1971) 'Die überseeischen Kolonialreiche', in *Saeculum Weltgeschichte*, 6, pp. 73–122.

Vial, M. (1954) 'La royauté Antankarana', *BAM*, 92, pp. 3–26.

Vidal, C. (1967) 'Anthropologie et histoire: le cas du Ruanda', *CIS*, pp. 143–57.

Vidal, C. (ed.) (1974) 'Le problème de la domination étatique au Rwanda: histoire et économie', *CEA*, 53, pp. 1–191.

Vienne, E. (1900) *Notice sur Mayotte et les Comores* (Exposition universelle).

Vila Vilar, E. (1977a) 'The large-scale introduction of Africans into Vera Cruz and Cartagena', in V. Rubin and A. Tuden (eds), pp. 267–80.

Vila Vilar, E. (1977b) *Hispano-America y el comercio de esclavos: los asientos portuguesos* (Seville: Escuela de Estudios hispanoamericanos).

Vix, A. (1911) 'Beitrag zur Ethnologie des Zwischenseengebiets von Deutsch-Ostafrika', *ZFE*, 43, 3/4, pp. 502–15.

al-Wafrani, Muḥammad al-Saghir (1888–9) *Muzhat al-Hadi*, trans. by O. Houdas (Paris: E. Leroux).

Wagner, E. (1975) 'Imamat und Sultanat in Harar', *Saeculum*, 26, pp. 283–92.

Wagner, E. (1976) 'Die Chronologien de frühen muslimischen Herrscher in Äthiopien nach den Harariner Emirislisten', in *Festschrift Eugen Ludwig Rapp* (Meisenheim-an-der-Glan), pp. 186–204.

Wagner, E. (1979) 'Neues Material zur "Ausa-Chronik", in *Festschrift Hans Robert Roemer* (Beirut: Fritzsteiner-Austria), pp. 657–73.

Walkley, C. E. J. (1935) 'The story of Khartoum', *SNR*, 18, Part 2, pp. 221–41.

Wallerstein, I. (1974) *Capitalist Agriculture and Organ of the European World Economy in the Sixteenth Century* (London: Academic Press).

Wallerstein, I. (1976) 'The three stages of African involvement in the world economy', in P. C. W. Gutkind and I. Wallerstein (eds), *The Political Economy of Contemporary Africa* (London: Sage Publications), pp. 30–57.

Walter, B. J. (1970) 'Territorial expansion of the Nandi of Kenya, 1500–1905' (PhD thesis, OHCIS).

Walvin, J. (1972) *The Black Presence: A Documentary History of the Negro in England* (New York: Schocken Books).

Walvin, J. (1973) *Black and White: the Negro and English Society, 1555–1945* (London: Allen Lane and Penguin Press), 273 pp.

Walz, T. (1975) 'The trade between Egypt and Bilād al-Sūdān, 1700–1820' (PhD thesis, Boston University).

Warren, R. (1980) *Imperialism: Pioneer of Capitalism* (London: NLB and Verso).

Weatherby, J. (1979) 'The rain drums of the Sor', in J. B. Webster (ed.), pp. 313–31.

Webster, J. B. (1976a), 'Lira Palwo: an expanding Acholi state', in Onyango-ka-Odongo and J. B. Webster (eds), pp. 291–319.

Webster, J. B. (1976b) 'Noi! Noi! Famine as an aid to interlacustrine chronology', in Onyango-ka-Odongo and J. B. Webster (eds), pp. 1–37.

Webster, J. B. (1977) 'Ivory and slaves and the southwestern expansion of the Yao', (History research paper, Chancellor College, University of Malawi).

Webster, J. B. (ed.) (1979a) *Chronology, Migration and Drought in Interlacustrine Africa* (London: Longman and Dalhousie University Press), 345 pp.

Webster, J. B. (1980) 'Drought, migration and chronology in the Lake Malawi littoral', *TJH*, 9, 1–2, pp. 70–90.

Webster, J. B. (at press (a)) 'Otuke and Mugoro: the age of Asonya', in J. B. Webster (ed.), *Uganda Before 1900*, vol. 1.

Webster, J. B. (at press (b)) *The Palwo-Pakoyo Exodus, 1680–1760*.

Webster, J. B. (at press (c)) 'The second Babito dynasty in Bunyoro-Kitara and the formation of the new states, c.1650–1780', in D. Denoon (ed.), *Uganda Before 1900*, vol. 2.

Webster, J. B. (at press (d)) *Nyilak and Nyipir: Hero Ancestors of the Alur*.

Webster, J. B. *et al.* (1973) *The Iteso During the Asonya* (Nairobi: EAPH), 189 pp.

Weiskel, T. C. (1980) *French Colonial Rule and the Baule Peoples, 1889–1911* (Oxford: Clarendon Press), 323 pp.

Were, G. S. (1967) *A History of the Abaluyia of Western Kenya c. 1500–1930* (Nairobi: EAPH), 206 pp.

Were, G. S. and Wilson, D. A. (1968 and 1972) *East Africa through a Thousand Years* (Nairobi: Evans Bros.), 344 pp; 2nd edn 1972.

Wheeler, A. (at press) 'Mwenge and Kitagwenda', in D. Denoon (ed.), forthcoming.

White, C. M. N. (1962) 'The ethno-history of the Upper Zambezi', *AS*, 21, pp. 10–27.

Wilbur, C. M. (1967) *Slavery in China during the Former Han Dynasty* (New York: Russell and Russell).

Wilks, I. G. (1957) 'The rise of the Akwamu Empire, 1650–1710' *THSG*, 3, 2, pp. 99–136.

Wilks, I. G. (1960) 'The Ashanti kings in the eighteenth century', *JAH*, 1, 1, pp. 83–96.

Wilks, I. G. (1961) *The Northern Factor in Ashanti History* (Legon-Accra: IAS, University College of Ghana), 46 pp.

Wilks, I. G. (1962a) *The Tradition of Islamic Learning in Ghana* (Legon).

Wilks, I. G. (1962b) 'A Medieval trade-route from the Niger to the Gulf of Guinea', *JAH*, 3, 2, pp. 337–41.

Wilks, I. G. (1962c) 'The Mande loan element in Twi', *GNQ*, 4, pp. 26–8.

Wilks, I. G. (1965) 'A note on the early spread of Islam in Dagomba', *THSG*, 8, pp. 87–98.

Wilks, I. G. (1966a) 'Aspects of bureaucratization in Ashanti in the 19th century', *JAH*, 7, pp. 215–32.

Wilks, I. G. (1966b) 'The position of Muslims in Metropolitan Ashanti in the early nineteenth century', in I. M. Lewis (ed.), pp. 318–23.

Wilks, I. G. (1971a) 'The Mossi and Akan states, 1500–1800', in J. F. A. Ajayi and M. Crowder (eds), pp. 344–86.

Wilks, I. G. (1971b) 'Asante policy towards the Hausa trade in the 19th century', in C. Meillassoux (ed.), pp. 124–141.

Wilks, I. G. (1975) *Asante in the Nineteenth Century: The Structure and Evolution of a Political Order* (Cambridge: CUP), 800 pp.

Willan, T. S. (1959) *Studies in Elizabethan Foreign Trade* (Manchester: MUP), 349 pp.

William-Myers, A. J. (1978a) 'The Nsenga of Central Africa: political and economic aspects of clan history, 1700–1900' (PhD thesis, UCLA, Los Angeles).

William-Myers, A. J. (1978b) 'Nsenga historical texts: interviews from Petauke and Feira districts of Zambia' (Unpublished, copies in University of California at Los Angeles and Department of History, University of Malawi).

Williams, E. (1970) *From Columbus to Castro: The History of the Caribbean, 1492–1969* (London: Andre Deutsch), 576 pp.

Williamson, K. (1971) 'The Benue-Congo languages and Ijo', in J. Berry and J. H. Greenberg (eds), *Linguistics in Sub-Saharan Africa* (Mouton), pp. 245–306.

Willis, J. R. (1971) 'The Western Sudan from the Moroccan invasion to the death of al-Mukhtar al-Kunti' in J. F. A. Ajayi and M. Crowder (eds), pp. 441–83.

Willis, J. R. (1981) *A State in the Making* (Bloomington, Ind.).

Willis, R. G. (1968) 'The Fipa', in A. D. Roberts (ed.), 1968 (a), pp. 82–95.

Wilson, A. (1972) 'Long-distance trade and the Luba Lomani empire', *JAH*, 13, 4, pp. 575–89.

Wilson, A. (1978) 'The kingdom of Kongo to the mid-seventeenth century' (PhD thesis, London University).

Wilson, A. (1979) 'The kingdom of Kongo in the 16th and 17th centuries' (approximate title) (dissertation, SOAS, London).

Wilson, J. F. M. (at press (a) 'Guineafowl and bushbuck in Toro', in J. B. Webster (ed.), *Uganda Before 1900*, vol. 1.

Wilson, J. F. M. (at press (b) 'The foundations of Toro kingdom, 1830–1860', in D. Denoon (ed.), forthcoming.

Wilson, M. (1958) *Peoples of the Nyasa-Tanganyika Corridor* (Cape Town: AS), 75 pp.

Wilson, M. (1969a) 'The Sotho, Venda and Tsonga', in M. Wilson and L. Thompson (eds), vol. 1, pp. 131–86.

Wilson, M. (1969b) 'The Nguni people', in M. Wilson and L. Thompson (eds), vol. 1.

Wilson, M. and Thompson, L. M. (eds) (1969, 1971) *The Oxford History of South Africa* (Oxford: Clarendon Press), 2 vols.

Wolff, J. (1964) *Negersklaveri und Negerhandel in Hochperu 1545–1640 in Lateinamerika* (Köln: Böhlan-Verlag).

Womersley, H. (1984) 'Legends and the history of the Luba', in T.Q. Reefe (ed.), *Legends and History of the Luba* (Los Angeles: Cross Roads Press).

Wondji, C. (1973–80) *Enquêtes orales en pays neyo, bété, godie et dida*, (unpublished).

Wright, A. C. A. (1989) 'Maize names as indicators of economic contacts', *UJ*, 13, pp. 61–81.

Wright, J. (1971) *Bushman Raiders of the Drakensberg, 1840–1870* (Pietermaritzburg: University of Natal Press), 235 pp.

Wright, J. (1977) 'San history and non-San historians', in *The Societies of Southern Africa in the 19th and 20th Centuries*, vol. 8 (London).

Wrigley, C. C. (1958) 'Some thoughts on the Bachwezi', *UJ*, 22, 1, pp. 11–21.

Wrigley, C. C. (1981) 'Population and history: some innumerate reflexions', in *African Historical Demography – Vol. II: Proceedings of a seminar held in the Centre of African Studies, University of Edinburgh, 24th and 25th April 1981* (Edinburgh: University of Edinburgh), pp. 17–31.

Wrigley, E. A. (1983) 'The growth of population in eighteenth-century England: A conundrum resolved', *PP*, **98** (February).
Wunder, H. (1978) 'Peasant organization and class conflict in East and West Germany', *PP*, **78**, pp. 47–55.

Yahya, D. (1981) *Morocco in the 16th century* (Ibadan: Humanities Press).
Yoder, J. C. (1977) 'A people on the edge of empires: a history of the Kanyok of Central Zaire (PhD thesis, Northwestern University).
Yoder, J. C. (1980) 'The historical study of a Kanyok genesis myth: the tale of Citend a Mfumu', in J. C. Miller (ed.), pp. 82–107.
Young, T. C. (1932/1971) *Notes on the History of the Tumbuka-Kamanga Peoples in the Northern Province of Nyasaland* (London: The Religious Tract Society); 1971 edn (London: Frank Cass).

Zahan, D. (1958) 'La notion d'écliptique chez les Bambara et les Dogon du Soudan français', *NA*, **80**, October, pp. 108–11.
Zahan, D. (1960) *Sociétés d'initiation bambara: le N'domo; le Kore* (Paris/The Hague: Mouton), 438 pp.
Zahan, D. (1967) 'The Mossi kingdoms', in C. D. Forde and P. M. Kaberry (eds), pp. 152–78.
Zarncke, F. (1876–9) *Der Priester Johannes* Abhdl.d.philhist.Cl.d.kgl. sachs.Ges.d.Wiss., vols 7 and 8 (Leipzig: Hirzel S. Verlag).
Zeltner, J. C. (1979) *Les Arabes dans la région du lac Tchad* (Sarh, Chad: Centre d'études linguistiques, Collège Charles Lwanga).
Zurara, G. E. de (1896, 1899) *Cronica dos feitos de Guiné* (*The Chronicle of the Discovery and Conquest of Guinea*), ed. and Eng. trans. by C. R. Beazley and E. Prestage (2 vols, London: Hakluyt Society, Nos 95 and 100).
Zuure, B. (1929) *Croyances et pratiques religieuses des Barundi* (Brussels: Essorial), 208 pp.
Zwanenberg, van R. M. A. and King, A. (1975) *An Economic History of Kenya and Uganda – 1800–1970* (Nairobi: Macmillan), 326 pp.
Zwanenberg, van R. M. A. and King, A. (at press) (a) 'Retracing the footsteps of Mukama', in J. B. Webster (ed.), *Uganda Before 1900*, vol. 1.
Zwanenberg, van R. M. A. and King, A. (at press) (b) 'Emergence and crisis: the state of Busoga', in D. Denoon (ed.), forthcoming.

GLOSSARY

abara: the (large) dugout canoes of Hausa, Kebbi and Nupe.

abba gada: in Oromo Society (Ethiopia), the leader of an ethnic group, elected from among the members of the *gada*.

Abbot (title) (from the Aramaean *abbā*, father): the head or superior of an abbey; also a title of respect given to monks.

abeto: an Ethiopian honorary title: highness.

'abīd (sing. *'abd*: is the ordinary word for 'slaves' in Arabic, more particularly for 'male slaves', 'female slaves' being *imā'* (sing. *ama*).

abilema: the earliest inhabitants of Unyakyusa (Lake Malawi region).

Āb Shaykh (title) (Arabic): a rank that was second only to that of the Sultan; a post that commanded great authority.

abuna (title): the Patriarch of the Abyssinian Church; the metropolitan of the Ethiopian Church.

abusua kuruwa: Asante clan pot.

abusuapanin: head, leader (of a (Akan) family, etc.).

achikunda: in the *prazo* system, armies of slaves, i.e. the lower class, as opposed to the dominant class or *prazeros*.

ada ('traditions of the country'): sword, emblem of authority (in Borno).

adamfo ('client state'): in Greater Asante, a system of provincial administration in which each of the states composing the confederacy served the *Asantehene* through one of the kings or member-states of the confederacy or one of the wing-chiefs of the Kumasi state, usually resident in Kumasi.

adanudo: a rich Ewe cloth (in Ghana).

adinkra: broad cloth with Akan traditional motifs and symbols stamped on it.

Adontehene (title): one of the wing-chiefs of the Kumasi state, vassals of the *Asantehene*.

Adonten or *Krontire*: the Advance Guard division of the Akwamu state and metropolitan Asante.

agape: a 'love-feast' connected with the Lord's Supper.

āghas (Arabic): high-ranking officers of the militia.

Āgha (title): Commander of the Janissaries (in Egypt).

Agona Adontendom: the Advance Guard division of the Denkyira state.

aguadente (Portuguese): fire-water, a kind of brandy.

ahl al-usūl (Arabic): members of the old lineage and rank.

ajami: transcription in Arabic of African languages (e.g. the Hausa *ajami* manuscript).

Ajiya (title of an official in Katsina, Hausaland): treasurer.

akuaba: small wooden or terracotta maternity dolls. Still to be found in Ghana.

Akumatire: the Right wing of the Denkyira state.

Akwamuhene (title): 'the King of Akwamu'; one of the wing-chiefs of the Kumasi state, vassals of the *Asantehene*.

Akyeamehene (title): Minister of Foreign Affairs and Head Linguist, in the Akwamu and Denkyira empires.

alcaid (from the Spanish *alcaide*, formerly *alcayde*, captain); the governor or commander of a castle or fortress (as among Spaniards, Portuguese or Moors) – see *ḳaʿīd*.

alcali: collectors (in Maninka).

Alfa: title borne by the chiefs of the provinces (*diwe*) in the Confederation of Futa Jallon.

algaita: a musical instrument (in Hausaland).

Alifa: title of an officer (in Kānem).

aljaravais (Portuguese): clothes from the Barbary states.

alkaali or *alkaati*: the African counterpart of the Mediterranean *alcaid*.

Almamia: land tenure and taxation systems (in Futa Jallon, Futa Toro and the Sokoto caliphate).

almadies: boats (in Senegambia).

Almamy (title in Bundu, Futa Jallon and Futa Toro): a Fulfulde version of the title *Imām*.

amahiga: sub-clans, in Haya country.

amanyamabo ('owner of the town'): king (in the Niger delta).

amashanga: sub-clans (in Rwanda).

amatega: raphia bracelets.

amatsano: in the Maravi state, the caretakers of the Kalonga's shrine at Mankhamba.

amenokal (title): The Tuareg equivalent of the Muslim *imām* and *ķāḍī*.

amīr (Arabic): title given to generals, commanders, provincial rulers and sometimes to the sovereigns of small countries (splet '*emir*' in the West).

Amī al-Ḥadjdj (Arabic): the unit which gave protection to the pilgrim caravans travelling to Mecca.

Amīr al-Khazna (Arabic): the units responsible for escorting the Egyptian treasury to Istanbul.

Amīr al-mu'minīn (Arabic): caliphal title meaning 'prince, Commander of the Faithful'.

amos: Portuguese overlords.

Ampagnito-bé (Malagasy royal title): great, sacred royal ancestor; father of the people.

anaratahina: linguistic taboo (in Mahafaly, Madagascar).

andria: lord, noble (in Malagasy).

andriana: the noble classes (in Merina, Madagascar).

Andrianoni: Antemoro title carried by the first ruler of the Onilahy kingdom in Madagascar.

ant-ankara: 'people of the rocks', i.e. the Antankara of Madagascar far north.

Apagyafie: a group of goldsmiths and craftsmen from Denkyira.

ardo or *rugga*: the Fulbe equivalent of the Muslim *imām* and *ķāḍī*.

aringas: in the *prazos*, a system in which the previous distinction between *colono* and slave had become blurred.

arivo: thousand, thousands (in Malagasy).

arratels: in Portuguese, a weight measure equivalent to a pound.

'arsh (Arabic): ethnic area; community or group holdings; communal land.

asago: an Akan warrior.

Asantehene: title of the paramount king of Asante.

Asarki or *Inna*: title of the sovereign's sister in Zamfara (Hausaland).

asiento or *assiento* (Spanish *asiento*, seat, meeting place of a tribunal, treaty, contract, from *asentar*, to seat, make an agreement): a contract or convention between Spain and another power or company or individual for furnishing African slaves for the Spanish dominions in America.

Askiya: royal title adopted by the Songhay sovereigns to distinguish themselves from the preceding Sonni dynasty.

asomfo: a golden stool of the Asante.

atesin: graves, in Teso (Great Lakes region).

attajirai (or *masu arziki*): rich traders; the wealthy (in Hausa society).

audiencia: 1) a tribunal in which the sovereign of Spain gave his personal attention to matters of justice; an ecclesiastical or secular court representing the king of Spain; 2) a high court of justice in a Spanish colony frequently exercising military power as well as judicial and political functions; 3) a provincial or territorial high court in modern Spain; 4) the jurisdiction of an *audiencia*.

awāwa (Arabic): armed unit.

awliya (Arabic): saint.

ayari (Hausa): caravans linking Azbin and Hausaland.

Ayilol: see *Cilol*.

Ayo (or *Lurum'ayo* or *Lurun'yo* (a Mossi title): king of Lurum.

'Azabān (sing. *'azab*): an Arabic word meaning 'an unmarried man or woman', 'a virgin', applied to several types of fighting men under the Ottoman and other Turkish regimes between the thirteenth and the nineteenth centuries. They were a component of the imperial Ottoman troops or *odjaķ*s.

azalai or *azalay*: a term for the great caravans made up of several thousand camels (or to be more precise, dromedaries), which in the spring and autumn carry salt from the salt deposits of the Southern Sahara to the tropical regions of the Sahel and the Sudan. The salt deposits of Taoudéni have replaced those of Taghāza, a source of wealth of the kings of Mali and of Gao (fourteenth–fifteenth centuries).

azel: fiefs.

baadolo: serfs (in Takrūr).

babika or *bampika* (sing. *mubika*): the slaves, one of the strata in Kongo society.

babuta (sing. *mubata*, from *vata* or *evata*, 'village'): the rustics, one of the strata in Kongo society.

bacucane: a house-born slave (in Hausaland).

bado: the Mossi equivalent of the Moorish *naaba*

badolo: serfs, in Takrūr.

Baganwa: title of the princes of royal blood (in Burundi).

bagazam: see *dan Azbin*.

Bahargazal: see *dan Bahar*.

Bāḥar nagāš ('sea-king'): the governor of the northernmost province of the Ethiopian empire.

bahaushe: trader (in Hausaland)

bahutu: see *muhutu*.

bairu: ennobled (clans).

Bakabban kumbu: in Takrūr, farmers who have turned back to the land.

bakama: see *mukama*.

bakungu: chiefs (in Burundi and Rwanda).

balama or *kanfari*: in the Songhay empire, a kind of viceroy or inspector-general of the empire; commander of the army.

Balangira: in Haya country, princes of royal blood.

balma: salt, so called after the city of Bilma (in Hausaland).

balowoka ('those who crossed the lake'): in the Tumbuka region (northern Zambezia), heads of families.

Baum-Naaba (Mossi title): a dignitary who looked after supply problems and domestic affairs.

(the) *Bambudye*: the closed association which helped the Luba king to rule.

Bambus Massarabe ('Melon from Egypt'): paw-paw (in Kanuri).

bami: see *mwami*.

Bantamahene (title): one of the wing-chiefs of the Kumasi state, vassals of the *Asantehene*.

baraka (Arabic): 'divine favour', 'gift of working miracles', 'charisma'; a blessing dispensed by *marabouts* and especially by descendants of the Prophet Muḥammad (*shurafāʿ*).

barbariores barbari: savages (Ethiopia).

Barde (title in Kano): captain.

bares: mines, in Northern Zambezia region.

Basace (title in Zamfara, Hausaland): an elder holding an ancient, long-forgotten office, member of a *Tara*.

(the) *bāshiya* (Arabic) or pashists: the followers of ʿAlī Pasha.

Batahene (title): Minister of Trade, in the Akwamu and Denkyira empires.

batieba: Mossi region rulers or chiefs.

batware: chiefs (in Burundi and Rwanda).

bawa: captive (in Hausaland).

bawan Sarki: royal slave (in Hausaland).

bawdi peyya yiyan: blood drums (in Futa Toro).

bayʾa (Arabic): oath of allegiance to a sovereign; investiture oath; oath of fidelity.

baydan (Arabic): nomads.

baye (pl. *bayii*): captive (in Zarma).

bayi: captive in Hausa; slave who had been captured or bought and who had few rights.

Bayt al-māl: the (public) Treasury, in Arabic.

bayti: vacant lands (in Futa Toro).

bayti maal or *leydi maal*: state-owned land.

Beecio: a title (in Waalo).

bega (Mossi): a great ceremonial cycle which involved the king and all the dignitaries of the land in sacrifices intended to ensure a good harvest.

belaga: ditch (in Kanuri).

benangatoobe: in the caste system in Takrūr, the class involving the *sakkeebe*, *wayilbe* and *gawlo*.

Benkum: the Left wing of the Akwamu state and metropolitan Asante.

bey (gentleman, chief, prince in Turkish): 1) the governor of a district or minor province in the Ottoman Empire; 2) the sovereign vassal of the sultan (e.g. the *bey* of Tunis); 3) a high-ranking official, senior officer, in the Ottoman empire; 4) the bearer of a courtesy title, formerly used in Turkey and Egypt.

beylerbey (pl. *beylerbeyi*): the governor-general of a province, head of a *sandjak-beylik*.

beylik: the term *beylik* denotes both the title and post (or function) of a *bey* and the territory (domain, jurisdiction) under the rule of a *bey*. Later, by extension, it came to mean also 'state, government' and, at the same time, a political and administrative entity sometimes possessing a certain autonomy.

bidʿa (Arabic): innovations, i.e. traditional religious practices grafted onto islam.

bilād al-Makhzen: in the Maghreb, a country under state authority.

Bilād al-Sūdān: literally 'the country of the Blacks' in Arabic; this expression is nearly always used by Arab authors in reference to the Blacks of West Africa, a very extensive zone comprising not only the Senegal, Niger and Chad basins but also the more southern countries of savanna and forest. The term 'Sudan' now attaches to a state in the Nile valley never so designated in ancient writings.

bilbalse (Mossi): adult servants.

bilolo: see *kilolo*.

Bin-Naaba or *Rasam-Naaba* (Mossi title): chief of the royal prisoners.

birr: silver, in Amharic (Ethiopia).

Biton: Bambara title meaning 'the Commander'.

bolo ('arm', in Bambara): a division of the infantry in Samori Ture's army, formed of several *sēn*.

boma (Swahili): an enclosure or stockade used for herding beasts and for defensive purposes.

bomo: blanket (among the Akan).

bozales (Spanish): unlike the *ladinos*, the *bozales* were slaves brought directly from Africa and who had had no previous contact with Europe.

Brak: title in Waalo.

buch jodong gweng': council of the elders (among the Luo).

buch piny: council of Luo sub-ethnic groups.

bud-kasma: (Mossi) head of a *budu*.

budu: in the patrilineal and patrilocal Mossi society, this term denotes any descent group, from the broadest and the oldest to the narrowest, that operates as the exogamous reference unit.

bugo (pl. *buguba*): (Mossi) fertility priest.

buguba: see *bugo*

buguridala (from *buguri*, dust): Sudanese word to designate the divine, the consultant.

buhake: a type of clientele link (in Rwanda).

bukin duku ('Feast of Thousands'): a tradition in Hausaland whereby it had to be proved that a yield of 1000 sheaves of millet or sorghum could be obtained.

bulala: see *mbarma*.

bulopwe: the Luba concept of power (Luba royalty was founded on the principle of *bulopwe* or 'sacredness').

Bulut Kapan: 'Alī Bey's nickname meaning 'Cloud-catcher'.

burguram: a court of appeal (in Kānam-Borno).

Burr Jullit ('Great Prayer Masters'): religious leaders, in Senegambia.

Buur: a title (in Kayor).

Bwami: socio-political-religious institution in Bemba and Rega societies.

cafre (from Arabic *kāfir*, infidel): an inhabitant of the *Cafrerie*, i.e. the non-Muslim territories of Africa south of the Equator (see Kaffirs).

capitão-mor (pl. *capitãos-mores* (Portuguese): in Shona country, a representative of merchants in a *feira*, appointed by the Portuguese administration.

caracoes (shells, shellfish, cowries in Portuguese): small stone beads found in the Zambezia region.

carataze: passes for vessels.

Cavushān: one of the components of the imperial Ottoman troops (*odjaks*).

ceddo (pl. *sebbe*): warlord, war chief (in Senegambia).

Çerākise: Cerkes is a general designation applied to a group of people who form the northwest branch of the Ibero-Caucasian peoples. They were one of the components of the imperial Ottoman troops or *odjaks*.

chāt: see *kāt*.

chechia: red woollen bonnet.

chemwa: see *njemani*.

chidi: fiefs (in Borno).

chikunda: in the *prazo* system, a slave army under the authority of a *sachikunda*.

chikwange: a well-known bread among the Kongo, obtained from the cassava root.

chimas: fief-holders (in Borno).

chima gana: junior fief-holders (in Borno).

chira: in Luoland, an incurable disease supposedly imposed by the ancestors on wrong-doers and their descendants.

chiroma (a Borno title): heir apparent.

chuanga: in the *prazo* system, top slave.

Cilol (pl. *Ayilol*): district ruler (in Lunda).

cire perdue: lost wax.

cofo: a unit of the *nzimbu* (Kongo).

Cokana: a talisman (in Hausaland).

colono (Portuguese): colonist, settler (in *prazos*).

comprador (from Portuguese *comprar*, to purchase, buy): 1) Formerly, the name of a native servant employed by Europeans, in India and the Far East, to purchase necessaries and keep the household accounts; a house-steward. 2) Now, in China, the name of the principal native servant, employed in European establishments, and especially in houses of business, both as head of the staff of native employees, and as intermediary between the house and its native customers. 3) One held to be an agent of foreign domination or exploitation.

cootigu: fee payable by tenant farmers.

Creole (from Spanish *criollo*, 'native to the locality, country'): a person of European ancestry born in the former colonies (West Indies, Guyana, Reunion); Creole: a language, born of the black slave trade (sixteenth-nineteenth centuries), that has become the mother tongue of those slaves' descendants (in the West Indies, Guyanas, Indian Ocean Islands, etc.). There exist Creoles based on French, English, Portuguese, etc.: the Creole of Guadeloupe, the English Creoles of the Caribbean, etc.

cruzado (or *crusado*) (pl. *cruzados* or *cruzadoes*) (from Portuguese *cruzado*, literally 'marked with a cross'): an old gold coin of Portugal, originally issued by Alfonso V (1438–81) about the year 1457, having a cross on the reverse in commemoration of the king's crusading struggle against the Muslims of North Africa; also: a similar Portuguese coin in silver first issued by John IV (1640–56).

curva: known as 'customs' in lands under Portuguese influence, 'duty' in English; a tribute paid by the Portuguese to the Mutapa rulers.

dabey: in Songhay, a village of slaves.

dadde yiyan: war songs; blood songs (in Futa Toro).

dady: in Sakalava country (Madagascar), the cult of the ancestors; ancestral Volamena relics.

dafing: clan (among the Marka).

Dagaci (title): a court dignitary (in Kano).

dagga (from Zulu and Xhosa *daka*, mud, clay, mortar): a mortar used in Southern Africa that consists chiefly of kneaded mud (mixture of mud and dung).

Damel: title of a ruler (in Kayor).

Damel-Teen: title of a ruler (in Kayor).

dana or *dayna* (from the Amharic *danya*): judge.

Danau (title in Zamfara, Hausaland): a governor who owed his title to the name of the town in which he resided, an important trading centre from where he kept watch over the roads leading south and west of Kebbi.

dan Azbin or *bagazam*: a breed of horses from Azbin.

dan Bahar or *Bahargazal*: a breed of horses from Baḥr al-Ghazāl.

dandal ('the opening of the "U"'): the settlement's main street of most Kanuri U-shaped towns and villages.

Dan Dubal (a title in Hausaland): in Zamfara, an adviser on religious affairs, the custodian of Zamfara's history and responsible for praying for the army's victory.

Dan Kodo (a title in Hausaland): see *Dan Dubal*.

Dār al-Islām: 'the world, the house, the sphere of Islam' in Arabic; privileged territory (as opposed to the *Dār al-ḥarb/Dār al-kufr* inhabited by 'infidels' and 'pagans') under the sovereignty of the Muslims, where the Muslim community lives and where: (1) canon law or *sharīʿa* is observed; (2) the social and political order of Islam reigns and public worship is Muslim (even if not all the inhabitants are Muslim).

(the) *Darb al-ʾArbaʿīn* ('Forty-Days' Road' in Arabic): the great trans-Saharan route that linked the Darfur region to Egypt in about forty days.

daru khurudj (non-Islamized lands) (Arabic): This refers to the non-Muslim territories (as opposed to the *Dār al-Islām*), the rest of the world that is not yet under the rule of Islam but, in theory, is destined to disappear one day and merge into the Islamic world, as stated in the Ḳurʾān (IX, 33). (See the *Dār al-kufr/Dar al-ḥarb*, 'the world, the sphere of war', in Vol. III).

debe: a village of slaves (in Soninke).

debeere: a village of slaves (in Fulfulde).

Defterdār (Arabic): comptroller of the financial administration of the province (in Egypt).

deggwa: in Ethiopia, sacred hymns in praise of the Holy Trinity, Jesus Christ, the Virgin Mary, saints or angels. They had different names according to their metre or the tradition of their origin (see *kene*, *malke'e* and *salam*).

dey (from Turkish *dāyī*, 'maternal uncle') (honorific title): 1) a ruling official of the Ottoman empire in northern Africa, especially the head of the Algiers Regency from 1671 to 1830, i.e. before the French conquest in 1830; 2) also designated a lower rank in the Janissary militia; towards the end of the tenth/sixteenth century in Tunis, the name was born by the heads of the 40 sections of the militia.

al-Dhahabī (from *dhahab*, pure gold in Arabic): 'the Golden': nickname of Aḥmad al-Manṣur, the sixth sovereign of the Moroccan dynasty of the Saʿādī.

diatigui: a title (in Timbuktu).

dibalram: road tolls (in Borno).

diema: Mossi regional kingdoms or chiefdoms.

Dikko: title created in the eighteenth century in Kebbi (Hausaland), and which was borne for the first time by a Pullo whose mother was the sovereign's daughter.

dimaajo: house-born slave (in Fulfulde).

dimo (pl. *rimbe*): free man (in Futa Jallon).

Dirki: a talisman (in Hausaland).

disi ('chest', in Bambara): the centre of Segu's army when arrayed in battle order.

diwal (pl. *diwe*): a province (in Futa Jallon).

dīwān (Arabic): central state coffers or treasury; Council of State; military pension roll; collection of poetry; large hall or chamber; ministerial departments; ruler.

diwe: see *diwal*.

djallāb (Arabic): slave merchants, slave traffickers, called 'importers'. They acted as the middlemen and the financiers of the long-distance trade.

djamā'a (Arabic): meeting, assembly. In the religious language of Islam, it denotes 'the whole company of believers', *djamā'at al-mu'minīn*, and hence its most usual meaning of 'Muslim community', *djamā'a islāmiyya*.

Djammā' ('the gatherer' in Arabic): the nickname of 'Abdallāh, leader of the 'Abdallābi state.

al-Djazzār ('butcher' in Arabic): the nickname of Aḥmad Boshnak, a *mamlūk* from the Egyptian *bey* 'Alī Bey's retinue.

djihād: literally 'effort' in Arabic; *djihād akbar*: 'supreme effort'; 1) the struggle against one's passions; the greatest effort of which one is capable; an effort to attain a specific goal; 2) personal effort of the believer to serve the Islamic faith, particularly the struggle to defend Islam, its land and the Muslims against the impious enemy, or to enlarge Islamic territory (*Dār al-Islām*); by extension, 'holy war'.

djinn (Arabic): spirit.

al-Djinn ('the devil' in Arabic): the nickname of the Egyptian *bey* 'Alī Bey.

djuad (Arabic): warrior chiefs.

Doka (title in Kebbi, Hausaland): official responsible for internal security.

dolo: millet beer; wine; alcohol (in Soninke).

Dongo (divinity): in Hausaland, a Borgu hunter whose powers were identical to those of *Shango* in the Yoruba culture.

doomi Buur: see *garmi*.

dukowo: territorial divisions (in Eweland).

dunuba (Bambara): in Segu, a drum which, skilfully played, transmitted messages over considerable distances.

dupi: the servile class (in Western Nilotic societies).

Dwabenhene ('the king of Dwaben'): the leader of two of the vassal states (Krakye and Bassa) that formed the Confederacy of Greater Asante.

dwar: tented camp.

dyon goron (Bambara): status acquired by a *woloso* when his children took his place and paid an annual indemnity to his master.

eččage: the leader of the Ethiopian clergy.

egusi: a local crop (in Igboland).

ekanda: in Kongo society, matriclan, matrilineage, but also ethnic group, republic: in short, any community.

Ekine or *Sekiapu*: a mask-dancing secret society; a masquerade society of the Delta states.

Ekpe: the *Ekpe* society of Calabar was an adaptation of a cult of the leopard (*Mgbe*) present among many forest groups in the Cross river valley and in parts of the Cameroon.

Ekpo: a secret society (among the Ibibio).

emīn (from Arabic *amīn*, faithful, trustworthy): an Ottoman administrative title usually translated 'intendant' or 'commissioner'; tax collector. His function or office was called *emānet*.

emitwe: in Ankore (present-day Uganda), a system of military organization.

emuron: a seer (in Teso).

endahiro: taking of an oath (in Ankore).

enfunzi: a kind of goldcrest, the taboo of the Bahutu, Bahinda and Silanga dynasties (of the Great Lakes region).

erasa: see *rasa*.

erythrina: the sacred tree of Ryangombe/Kiranga (in Haya country).

escales: factories.

eso (Yoruba): in Ọyọ, warriors devoted to 'training in warfare'.

etem (pl. *itemwan*): in Teso and Kumam, multi-clan ritual grouping.

etogo: in Lango (present-day Uganda), multi-clan ritual groupings.

evata (Kikongo): village (Kongon kingdom).
eze (Igbo title): king.
eze Nri (title meaning 'ruler', 'the king of Nri', among the Igbo): priest-king with ritual and mystic, but not military power.

faa (Bambara): father of a biological community.
faama (Bambara title): lord holding supreme power; man of power and authority.
faaya: fathers (in Bambara).
fady/faly: sacred (in Malagasy).
Fahatelo: in Iboina (Madagascar), first minister; royal official.
fakī: a corruption of *fakīh*.
fakīh (Arabic pl. *fukahā'*): 'doctor of the law'; 1) scholar versed in *fikh*; jurist; 2) literate person; 3) theologian.
fallāh (pl. *fallāhīn*) (Arabic): a peasant (in North Africa).
Famoriana: the Antankara Royal Council (Madagascar).
fanadir: cage (in Borno).
fanafody: curative amulets (Madagascar).
fanane: snakes (in Malagasy).
fandroana: annual royal-bath ceremony (in Merina, Madagascar).
fani: in the Comoro Islands, the first Islamic chiefs who had originally succeeded the Bēdja of pre-Islamic times.
farba: government officials.
fari or *farma*: title of the Mande sovereigns.
farin or *faren*: rulers of provinces; governor.
Farinya (comes from *Fari* and pharaoh): 'ruler' in Soninke, Mande, etc. *Farinya* denotes a monocracy as opposed to the controlled monarchical oligarchy of the original *mansaya*.
faro ('spirit of the River Niger'): a religious cult among the Bambara.
fāshir (Arabic): royal residence.
fatāke (sing. *farke* or *falke*): professional merchants engaged in *fatauci*.
fatauci: in Hausaland, trade over medium and long distances; wholesale trade.
fatidra: royal blood-covenant (in Madagascar).
fehitra: village fiefs (in Madagascar).
feiras: fairs (in Portuguese).
fia: the king of a *dukowo* (in Eweland).
fidda dīwānī (Arabic): fine silver coins.
fikh (Arabic): the science that codifies and explains the prescriptions of the *sharī'a*; canon law; jurisprudence; Islamic law.
filiiga: a Mossi thanksgiving festival.
filohany: chief (in Malagasy).
fitahina: a linguistic taboo (among the Sakalava of Madagascar).
fla-n-ton (or *ton*): peer association; the *fla-n-ton* brought together the members of three successive promotions of those circumcised.
folahazomanga (in Malagasy, 'those who came to Mahafaly from elsewhere'): a component of Mahafaly society, Madagascar.
fom: ruins (in Bamum, Cameroon).
fonio: a crabgrass (*Digitaria exilis*) of northern Africa with seeds that are used as a cereal.
Foroba: public treasury (in Bambara).
foroba-dyon ('captives of the big common field') or *furuba-dyon* ('captives of the Great Union'): crown slaves.
Foroba Fulaw: Fulbe public officials.
forso: in Songhay, house-born slave.
fuku (from *fuka*, to cover, to shelter): clients (in Kongo).
fumwa pamba diyumbi (in Kikongo): the keeper and maker of charms and royal diviner at the court of the Luba king.
furba jon: Sudanic royal captives; Mande royal slaves.
fure: see *gorongo*.
furuba-dyon: see *foroba dyon*.

gaba'il (Arabic): in the Maghreb, groups assimilated with the Arabs.
gabar: in Ethiopia, a peasant who worked the lands for the benefit of the landed élite and was, like the

fallāh, similar to a serf, or at least a tributary or client obliged to pay the *gabir*, depending on whether he was a share-cropper or a tenant farmer.

gabarti: merchant (in Ethiopia).

*gaba*s: serfs.

gabir or *siso*: a tax paid by the *gabar*.

gabirecco (an honorary title in Ethiopia): page.

gada or *luba*: a classification of the Oromo society of Ethiopia by age groups based on an abstract numerical principle. It is an egalitarian system which involves rule by rotation age-groups.

gaisuwa or *tsare*: payment of regular gifts to superiors (in Hausaland).

Galadima (a Borno title): a kind of prime minister or grand vizier in whom the conduct of all affairs of state was vested. The title was borrowed from Borno, but there it designated the governor of the western provinces, that is, those nearest to Hausaland; in Katsina, an important official who deputized for the *Sarki*; in Kano, a military leader; in Sokoto, the caliph's adviser, acting as the caliph's link with the emirates.

Galadiman Gari (a title in Kebbi, Hausaland): an official responsible for internal security.

galag: a tax payable to the political chief of the Takrūr aristocracy.

Galoji: in Kebbi (Hausaland), title conferred upon Fulbe in contact with the herdsmen.

gan: guest, foreigner, in Wolof.

gandu (pl. *gandaye*): collective household farm (in Zamfara, Hausaland).

gandun gida (Hausa): the family field, generally known as *gona*, the generic name for any field.

garassa: Sudanese blacksmiths.

garmi or *doomi Buur*: the ruling class (in Kayor).

garu: mud wall (in Kanuri).

gasha (Arabic): occupied lands.

Gatari ('Axe'): in Katsina (Hausaland), title of a governor who watched over the north-western frontier.

gawlo: a griot (in Takrūr).

gayya: in Hausaland, mutual aid system; communal work.

ghaushes: central messengers (in Egypt).

ghāzī (Arabic): conquest.

gida (pl. *gidaje*): extended family; groups of families (in Hausaland).

gikingi: a land system granting exclusive grazing rights to the owner (in Rwanda).

gimaje: long dyed cotton dresses (in Kanuri).

gobbi: an annual tax on mines.

gonüllüyān (sing. *gönüllü*): a Turkish word meaning 'volunteer'; in the Ottoman empire it was used as a term for three related institutions: 1) from the earliest times of the Ottoman state, volunteers coming to take part in the fighting were known as *gönüllüyan*; 2) in the tenth/sixteenth century we find an organized body known as *gönüllüyān* in most of the fortresses of the Empire; they might be called out to serve on a campaign or take part in frontier-fighting; 3) in the eleventh/seventeenth century a body known as *gönüllüyān* is mentioned also among the paid auxiliaries who, under various names, were recruited in the provinces to serve on a campaign.

gorongo or *fure*: tobacco flower (in Kanuri).

Gounga-Naaba (Mossi title): a dignitary with military responsibilities.

Grand Ḳāḍī (title): Chief Judge of the *sharī'a* Court.

grumetes: African auxiliaries recruited by the *lançados*.

guda or *goda* (from the Amharic *geta* or the Tigrai *goyta*): master.

Gulma: title of a high-ranking dignitary among the Songhay.

gult: in Ethiopia, feudal land; certain rights possessed by the lord (e.g. the right to collect tribute in kind from each household in the district and to appropriate labour for work on his farms or on other projects he might designate).

gumbala: in Futa Toro, the war song of the *sebbe*, which consist of hymns to courage. It is the epic song of death in which the *ceddo* assumes his destiny as a warrior, his faithfulness to his ancestors and to the ethic of his caste.

gumsu: the king's headwife (in Borno).

gurma (Hausa): right (e.g. the *gurma* bank of the river, as opposed to *hausa*, the left bank).

gweng' (pl. *gwenge*): a Luo semi-autonomous political and territorial unit.

Gyaase: one of the divisions of the Akwamu state and metropolitan Asante.

Gyaasehene (title): Minister of Home Affairs (in the Akwamu and Denkyira empires).

Ḥabshī: one of the terms used in India to denote those African communities whose ancestors originally came to the country as slaves, in most cases from the Horn of Africa, although some doubtless sprang from the slave troops of the neighbouring countries. The majority, at least in earlier times, may well have been Ethiopian, but the name was applied indiscriminately to all Africans, and in the days of the Portuguese slave trade with India many such *Ḥabshī* were in fact of the Nilotic and Bantu peoples.

ḥabūs (Arabic): lands belonging to religious communities.

ḥadīth (Arabic): account of an act or word of the Prophet Muḥammad, reported and transmitted by his companions; the collection of the *ḥadīth*, called *sunna*, is regarded by the Muslims as the second source – after the holy scripture – of the dogma and law of Islam (the *ḥadīth* in Islam is the nearest equivalent of the Christians' New Testament reporting the acts and words of Jesus).

ḥakura: tax exemption.

ḥalika (Arabic): creation.

ḥallabens (Portuguese): clothes from the Barbary states.

Hanimboay: in the Sakalava kingdoms (Madagascar), officials acting as overseers of the *dady* cult.

hanshīr (Arabic): wheat-producing regions under urban control (in Tunisia).

hanzo (from *nso*, 'house' in Kikongo): parcel (in Angola).

h'aoush (Arabic): wheat-producing regions under urban control (in Algeria).

Ḥarāṭīn (sing. *Ḥarṭānī*) (Arabic): originally, serfs (*haratin*) in Maghreb. The term denotes black peoples throughout the Sahara, but particularly in the west – e.g. the oases of southern Morocco and Mauritania. Their origin is uncertain: they have been called black Berbers.

al-hayr (Arabic): welfare, form of greeting.

hayu: judges (among the Oromo of Ethiopia).

hazne or *hazine*: treasury.

hazomanga-lava (Malagasy): group-altar.

heemraden: burghers (in Southern Africa).

hidjra: the usual translation 'the flight' is incorrect as the true meaning of the Arabic word is 'severing previous ethnic ties and entering into new ones': the term denotes the emigration of Prophet Muḥammad and his followers from Mecca to Medina (the former oasis town of Yathrib) on 16 July 622, a date that has become the first year of the Muslim calendar (*hegira*).

himāye (Arabic): protection charges; caution money protecting the conquered townsfolk from looting.

hore kosan: grazing land.

hulwān (Arabic): special tax usually eight times the annual income from the benefice.

(the) *ḥusayniya* (Arabic) or husseinists: the followers of Ḥusayn b. ʿAlī.

ibihuya: country.

iblis (Arabic): devil.

Idara: the common name in modern Arabic, Persian, Turkish, etc., for administration. The term appears to have acquired its technical significance during the period of European influence.

idjāza (Arabic): certificate.

ifejioku ('the yam force'): one of the *eze Nri*'s powers (in Igboland).

igihugu: countries (in Rwanda and Burundi).

iharana: trading-post in north-eastern Madagascar.

iko: power (in Hausaland).

ikṭāʿ (Arabic): 1) the fiscal allocation of an emir, always strictly monitored and updated, of the revenue of one or more localities, according to status and the number of men in his service; 2) delegation of tax-collecting powers granted by the prince to a military or civilian officer in regard to a fiscal district, as remuneration for a service rendered to the state; this concession was revocable; 3) distribution of fiscal concessions for maintenance of the military class; 4) military fief system.

ikwa (Kikuyu): a yam.

ilari (system): an aspect of Ọyọ state organization introduced in the Dahomey state by Tegbesu, the last of the Dahomey founding dynasty.

ʿilm (Arabic): religious knowledge.

iltizam (Arabic): according to the *iltizam* system which superseded the *muḳataʿat* system by about 1658, lands of every village or group of villages were offered for public auction and the highest bidders (the *multazim*s) were given the right to collect taxes from the peasants and such lands became their *iltizam*.

imām (Arabic): honorary title awarded to the eminent legal experts who, between the second/eighth and the third/ninth centuries, codified the whole body of Muslim law in various intellectual centres of the Muslim world, particularly Medina and Baghdad; a title given to the founders of law schools and to major theologians; chiefs, supreme leader of the Muslim community; among the Shīʿites, equivalent of a caliph (must be a descendant of ʿAlī).

imāmate: the leadership of the Muslim community; caliphate or inherited power; office or rank of an *imām*; function of the *imām* as head of the Muslim community; the region or country ruled over by an *imām* (e.g. the *imāmate* of Yemen).
imiziro: a taboo (in Burundi and Rwanda).
indabo: a village of slaves (in Hausaland).
Inna: see *Asarki*.
Innamme: in Kebbi (Hausaland), title of a governor who kept watch over the western frontier.
Ionaka: the Imamono councils of elders (Madagascar).
insilimen: see *zuwaya*.
inyamasango: a village head in Shona country.
itemwan: see *etem*.
iyāla (*eyālet*, in Turkish) ('management, administration, exercise of power'): in the Ottoman empire the largest administrative division under a *beylerbey* or governor-general. In this sense it was officially used after 1000/1591.

jaam: captive (in Waalo).
jaami buur: Sudanic royal captives.
jadak: guest, foreigner, tenant (in Luo).
Jaggorde: the Council of electors (in Futa Toro).
jagos: territorial sub-heads (among the Luo).
jamana: see *kafu*.
jangali: the livestock tax paid by stockbreeders (in Hausaland).
Jengu: the most prestigious secret society among the Duala, Isuwu and other neighbouring groups, based on the veneration of water spirits.
jibda: musk (in Hausaland).
jodak: stranger lineages and clans to whom parts of the Luo *gwenge* were leased.
jodong gweng': see *buch jodong gweng'*.
jodongo: elders (see *buch jodong gweng'*).
jombiri jon (in Mande): slaves owned by the *jon tigi*, the *farba*, the *jaami buur* or the *sarkin bayi* who, although slaves themselves, belonged to the dominant ruling class in the state and society.
jom jambere: in the Futa land tenure system, a person entitled to clear the land with an axe.
jom jayngol: in the Futa land tenure system, a person entitled to clear the land by burning.
jom lewre: in the Futa land tenure system, the first occupant and clearer of land.
jom leydi: in the Futa land tenure system, the master of the land.
jon: captive (in Mande).
jon tigi: royal captive, royal slave (in Mande).
jonya (from the Mande word *jon* meaning 'captive'): Black African captive.
jumbe: in the Comoro Islands, this term denoted the daughters of the *fani*, who came to marry the Sunnite newcomers.
jurungul ('crown'): a special coiffure worn by a Kanuri married woman.

(the) Ka'ba: the vast cube-shaped edifice (*ka'ba* comes from the Greek *kubos*, a die) of grey stone in the centre of the Great Mosque at Mecca, towards which Muslims face when praying. Sealed in its wall is the Black Stone, which, according to the Ķur'ān, was brought to Abraham by the Angel Gabriel, and which every Muslim should, if possible, go and venerate at least once in his or her life.
kabaka: ruler, king (in Buganda).
kabary: public assemblies (in Madagascar).
ķabīla (Arabic pl. *ķabā'il*): a large agnatic Arab or Berber group the members of which claim to be descended from one common ancestor and who may 'jointly own an area of grazing land'.
kabunga: chief (in Kongo).
ķāḍī (Arabic): among Muslims, a magistrate concurrently discharging civil, judicial and religious functions in accordance with Muslim law (*sharī'a*).
ķāḍī al-kabīr (Arabic): chief judge.
Kaffir (from Arabic *kāfir*, pl. *kuffār*): a word meaning infidel, ungodly person, unbeliever; someone with no revealed religion; someone who does not adhere to monotheism in accordance with Muslim law. It is applied by the Arabs to all non-Muslims, and hence to particular peoples or nations.
kafi: a plant that may be related to yam.
kafu or *jamana* (in Mande): provinces; small state-like territorial units (among the Malinke and the Bambara).
ķā'īd (Arabic): commander, army chief; provincial governor; *ķabīla* chieftain.
ķā'īds-lazzām (Arabic): tax farmers (in the Maghreb).

kaigama (Borno title): governor of the northern provinces (in Kano).

ḳāʿim maḵām (Arabic): deputy vice-regent.

kakaki: a long trumpet (in Hausaland).

kakwata (pl. *tukwata*): a special Lunda official.

kalaba: the final ceremony of the marriage (in Kanuri).

Kalala: head of the vanguard (among the Lunda).

kalaram: turban (in Kanuri).

kalimbo barata: marriage ceremony (in Kanuri).

Kamsaogo-Naaba (Mossi title): a eunuch responsible for the harem.

kangam: a provincial chief in Senegambia.

kanun: potash.

ḳānūn or *lḳanūn* (from the Greek *kanôn*, rule): the corpus of legal regulations (canon law).

Ḳānūn Nāme: a decree which sought to regulate political, military, civil and economic life in Egypt under the Ottoman administration.

karabiwa mallam: a scholar (in Borno).

Karfi (title): in Zamfara (Hausaland), the official entrusted with assembling everything the *sarakunan rafi* had levied.

karite: shea butter nut.

kasa: territory (in Hausaland).

ḳaṣaba or *gaṣba* (Arabic) (casbah/kasbah in English): capital; (small) town; citadel, castle or fortress (in North Africa).

kasalla (from the Arabic word *sallah*, prayers): washing of any sort, even of animals (in Kanuri).

Kāshif (Arabic): head of district (in Egypt) whose task it was to maintain the irrigation system and levy taxes from the farmers; tax collector.

ḳaṣida: an Arabic or Persian panegyric, elegiac or satirical poem or ode, usually having a tripartite structure. The term is derived from the root *ḳaṣada*, 'to aim at', for the primitive *ḳaṣida* was intended to eulogize the *ḳabīla* of the poet and denigrate the opposing *ḳabīla*s. Later it was concerned with the eulogy of patrons.

kassa: blanket (among the Akan).

kasuwanci: retail trade (in Hausaland).

ḳāt (in Arabic) and *chāt* (in Amharic): a shrub (*Catha edulis* F.) native to Arabia, with mildly stimulating properties, grown in Ethiopia and Yemen and exported under the name of *ḳāt* or *chāt*; also the narcotic drug obtained from the leaves of this plant.

Kaura (title): a military leader (in Katsina, Hausaland).

kawngal: fishing ground.

kaya (pl. *makaya*): a fortified village; an enclosed or fortified settlement (among the Miji-Kenda people of East Africa).

kazembe: a general (among the Lunda).

kazi: a title found in south-east central Africa; it is a variant of the Muslim *ḳāḍī*.

kela yasku: a special coiffure usually worn by a Kanuri unmarried girl.

keletigui (Bambara): in Segu's army, a war-leader or leader of an expedition.

kene: sacred hymns, in Ethiopia (see *deggwa*).

kente (also Kente): colourful *kente* clothes (of the Akan); in Ghana, a banded material; also, a long garment made from this material, loosely draped on or worn around the shoulders and waist.

kesiga: the successors of the Christian priests (in Ethiopia).

ketema: garrison towns.

khalif or *khalīfa* (a title) (Arabic): caliph, successor of the Prophet, sovereign responsible for ensuring observance of Islamic law on earth.

khames (Arabic): vassals, serfs (in the Maghreb).

khammā (Arabic): one-fifth share-cropper.

khammāsat (Arabic): fifth share-cropping of the land; tenant farming.

kharādj (Arabic): a land tax, sometimes paid in kind (and in addition to the cash poll tax or *djizya*) on land belonging to the *dhimmī* (non-Muslims living in Muslim territory under the status of 'protégés of Islam'); by extension designates all land taxes (see also *raia*).

khazin (Arabic): treasurer.

khimba (an association in Kongo): an initiation cult for boys.

khombe: the commander of the army, in the Maravi administration.

khorin: provincial war chiefs (in Senegambia).

khūdja (Arabic): scribes.

khuṭba (Arabic): address delivered by the *khaṭīb* (preacher), from the top of the *minbar* (mosque chair) of the Great Mosque, during the noontime Friday prayer, in which God's favour was invoked on the recognized caliph in the city and, where applicable, the prince from whom the governor of the town held his delegated power.

kiamfu (derived from *Yav*, the imperial title): the leader of the Yaka.

kia ukisi: holy, sacred.

kibwindji: region under the responsibility of the *kilolo* (Luba).

kifuka (Kikongo): 'urbanity', 'politeness', i.e. the behaviour of a client.

kifuka kia utinu: court of the king (in Kikongo).

kiims'rogo: a Mossi ancestral shrine.

kilbu: natron (in Kānembu).

kilolo (pl. *bilolo*): territorial administrators; chiefs (among the Luba/Lunda).

kimpasi (a healing association in Kongo): a cult whose aim was to banish *mpasi*.

kini-n-bolo (Bambara): the right arm of Segu's army.

kirari: praise-songs dedicated to sovereigns and other important persons in Kano (Hausaland).

kitomi: in Kongo, former lords of the land.

Kokani (a title in Kebbi, Hausaland): the official responsible for relations with the population.

kombere (pl. *kombemba*) (Mossi): a regional chief with broad autonomy marked notably by the right to appoint local chiefs.

kom ngu: the counsellors of the kingdom (in Bamum).

korin: provincial war chiefs.

kontuowa: the ruling class or nobility (in the Kanuri society in Borno).

kraal (from Portuguese *curral*, pen for cattle, enclosure): 1) a village of Khoi Khoi or Kaffirs, or other South or Central African natives, consisting of a collection of huts surrounded by a fence or stockade, and often having a central space for cattle, etc.; also designates the community of such a village; 2) an enclosure for cattle or sheep, especially in South or Central Africa; a stockade, pen, fold.

Krontire: see *Adonten*.

kubandwa: a practice of initiatory rites in Rwanda, Burundi and Buha.

kudin haki: grazing duty paid by the nomadic Fulbe (in Kebbi, Hausaland).

kudin hito: customs duty (in Hausaland).

kudin kasa: a land tax paid by the farmers (in Hausaland).

kudin laifi: forgiveness tax paid by an offender when pardoned by the sovereign (in Hausaland).

kudin sana'a: a professional tax (in Hausaland).

kugala: dignitaries at the court of the Luba *mulopwe*.

kultingo: a tribute (in Borno).

Kulturkreis (pl. *Kulturkreise*) (German) (the *Kulturkreise* school): a culture complex developing in successive epochs from its centre of origin and becoming diffused over large areas of the world; the concept of the *Kulturkreise* was developed by the Vienna school of ethnology (the term is associated especially with the German anthropologists F. Graebner and W. Schmidt).

Kulughli (from Turkish *ḳuloghlu*, 'son of slave'): in the period of Turkish domination in Algeria and Tunisia, this word denoted those elements of the population resulting from marriages of Turks with local women.

Kunduda (title in Hausaland): a Kebbi's military leader.

kurita: a Mossi word which means 'reigning dead man', is constructed by analogy with *narita*, 'reigning chief'. The *kurita* is the representative among the living of a dead chief, and is generally chosen from among the sons of the dead chief; he has no power by virtue of his title and is debarred from the succession, but he can become a chief in an area outside his family's command; if a *kurita* becomes a chief, he retains the *nom-de-guerre* (*zab yure*) of *naaba kurita*.

(the) *Kurkwā* corps (spearmen in Fūr): a standing slave-army created by Muḥammad Tayrāb ibn Aḥmad Bukr.

kutama: migration movement (from south-east Africa to Zimbabwe around 1000).

kwaka tree or monkey orange: 1) either of two deciduous African shrubs or small trees (*Strychnos inocua* and *Strychnos spinosa*) having a hard globose fruit with edible pulp; 2) the fruit of a monkey orange.

kwama: fructification (in Kirundi).

kwara: a magical symbol (in Mossi).

kwaro (an obsolete term meaning 'to exchange a coin for cowries'): possibly a harvest tax, which was payable in Damagaram, for instance.

kyekyedala (from *kyekye*, sand): a Sudanese word to designate the divine, the consultant.

Kyeremfem: the Left wing of the Denkyira state.

Kyidom: the Rear guard division of the Akwamu state and metropolitan Asante.

laciende or *lazenda*: large estates; large plantations in Latin America.

Ladinos (Spanish): the first Africans in America brought there from Europe by the Conquistadores. They were mainly from Senegambia and had either been previously brought to Europe, or were born there. They were called *ladinos* in America because they knew Spanish or Portuguese, and were at least partly influenced by the civilization of the Iberian countries.

laibon: a Maasai ritual leader.

laman (first occupant): a territorial chief.

lamana (from the Sereer 'master of the land'): denotes a system of land tenure and a political system in which the masters of the land also exercised power. The *lamana* of the masters of the land developed into the *Mansaya* of purely political chiefs.

lanbens (Portuguese): clothes from the Barbary states.

lançados (from Portuguese *lançar*, to launch out an adventure) or *tangomãos* ('people who had adopted local customs'): emigrants who had settled on the (African) continent with the agreement of the African sovereigns, intermarried and set themselves up as commercial middlemen. They formed part of the many expatriates who populated the southern rivers and the Atlantic islands (especially Cape Verde). Most of them were Portuguese, with a sprinkling of Greeks, Spaniards and even Indians. They also came to include more and more halfbreed children, the *filhos da terra* (children of the land).

landdrost: a resident magistrate (in southern Africa).

lapto (literally, 'translator'): a native interpreter.

larde kangema: the nominal owner of the land (in Borno).

Larhle-Naaba (a Mossi title): a dignitary who combined military and ritual functions.

las li: the descendants of the great *marabout* families who constituted 'the aristocracy of the sword and the lance and the book and the pen' at the top of the *rimbe* (in Futa Jallon).

lazenda: see *laciende*.

lazzām (Arabic): tax farmers.

legha (Arabic): henchmen.

lemba ('to appease, to divert the anger of a *nkisi*'): in Kongo, the *lemba* association was an association of *bitomi* or high priests consecrated to a *nkisi* called *Lemba*. The activities of these priests were all related to the *lemba*: to appease the anger of a *nkisi* or to invoke a *nkisi* (*lemba nkisi*); to remove a danger (*lemba sunga*); to restore peace in the country (*lemba nsi*), etc.; also: judges.

Lenngi: in Futa Toro, the *Lenngi*, sung solely by *Sebbe* women at marriages or circumcisions, are heroic songs summoning up contempt for death and the protection of honour.

leydi hujja: land bond (in Fulfulde).

leydi janandi: state-owned lands.

leydi maal: see *bayti maal*.

leydi urum: a system of land control under which allegiance was owed by means of the *worma*, coupled with the *muud al-hūrum* tax.

lifidi (Hausa): a quilted armour; horse trappings; the quilted protection for war-horses.

Lifidi (title in Hausaland): Commander-in-chief of the heavy cavalry division.

Limanin Ciki (title in Hausaland): a Kanuri scholar responsible for the education of the royal family.

Linger: a title (in Kayor).

lizma (Arabic): in the Maghreb, farming-out of the provinces, customs, etc.; tax-farming.

longon'mpanilo or *vohitsy mananila*: collaterals, in Madagascar.

luba: see *gada*.

lukanga: a senior Luba judge.

Lukonkeshia: see *Rukonkesh*.

Lurum'ayo or *Lurun'yo*: see *Ayo*.

Lurun'yo: see *Lurum'ayo*.

maabo: Mande blacksmiths.

macamos: the *macamos* were gangs of slaves surrounding the *Mwene Mutapa*, i.e. they corresponded to the Sudanic royal captives (*furba jon*, *tonjon* or *jaami buur*).

maccube: slaves, captives (in Fulfulde).

machila: cotton clothes produced by the Lundu's Mang'anja subjects in the Lower Shire valley.

Madaki: the title of the queen-mother (in Kano).

Madawaki: in Katsina (Hausaland), officer-in-charge of the royal stables; leader of the cavalry and/or commander-in-chief of the army.

madhhab (pl. *madhāhib*) (Arabic): legal schools named after their founders who bear also the honorific title of *Imām*. There are four of these schools: Mālikism, Shāfi'ism, Hanafism and Hanbalism.

(the) *Madjelisse* (Arabic): a body of jurists.

madrasa (Arabic): a primary and secondary Ḳur'ānic school: *madrasa* designates more particularly an establishment of higher religious education (as a rule attached to a mosque) for the training of the Sunnite clergy, the *'ulamā'*.

Mafouk: in Central Africa, a title borne by the *mercadores*.

magaji: a warrior; a successor (in Hausaland).

Magajin Baberi (a title in Kebbi, Hausaland): an official in charge of external affairs.

Magajin Gari or *Sarkin Gari* (a title in Kebbi, Hausaland): a village chief; an official responsible for internal security; in Sokoto, the caliph's adviser, acting as the caliph's link with the emirates.

Magajin Sangeldu: in Kebbi (Hausaland), a title conferred upon Fulbe in contact with the herdsmen.

magira: the queen-mother (in Kānem-Borno).

magram: the king's official sister (in Kānem-Borno).

(the) Maguzawa: there are non-Muslim groups in both Nigeria and Niger who speak only Hausa and who share the Hausa culture, but who refuse to be called Hausa people. In Nigeria these people call themselves, and are called by other Hausa, Maguzawa (or Bamaguje), whereas in Niger they are known by the name Azna (or Arna) – the Hausa word for 'pagan'. Since the name Maguzawa is probably derived from the Arabic *madjūs* (originally 'fire-worshippers', then 'pagans' generally) it is possible that the polarization between Hausa and Maguzawa/Azna began only with the spread of Islam among the common people in Hausaland, after the seventeenth and eighteen centuries.

mahabbar: in Ethiopia, an agape, i.e. a 'love-feast' connected with the Lord's Supper.

mah'alla (Arabic): in the Maghrib, an armed expedition; armed camps.

mahanga (ilala palm – *Hyphaene natalenis*): a tree found in the lowveld areas of Southern Zambezia, the sap of which was used to make an intoxicating wine called *njemani* or *chemwa* (in Hlengwe).

mahram (Arabic): the granting – by chiefs – of privileges to families or religious notables.

mai: king, ruler (in Kānembu).

maidugu: grandson of a previous king (in Borno).

(the) *mailo* system: the system of land tenure introduced into East Africa under British colonization; it combines chiefdom with ownership and the right to speculate in land.

maina: eligible princes (in Borno).

Mainin Kinendi (title in Borno): the Islamic and legal adviser to the *mai*.

mairam: princess (in Borno).

mai sarauta: ruler (in Hausaland).

Maishanu (title in Kebbi, Hausaland): the official who collected the livestock that was the state's due.

Majlis: in Kānem, the highest council of state normally presided over by the *mai* and composed of military and religious notables.

makambala: the councillors of the Kyungu (a priest-king worshipped by the Ngonde).

makaya: see *kaya*.

makhzen (Arabic): privileged peoples from whom Moroccan state officials are recruited.

(the) Makhzen: originally meant 'treasury', but came to be used for the official system of government in Morocco, and more broadly the political and religious élite of the country.

makoko: king, among the Tio of Kongo.

Mala Kasuube (a title in Borno): the official who supervised sales in the markets and attempted to ensure justice and fair play during major commercial transactions.

malams: Muslim clerics and scholars.

malamti: in Borno, scholarly families.

malke'e: Ethiopian sacred hymns (see *deggwa*).

mallamai: scholars (in Hausaland).

Maloango: king (in Central Africa: Angola, etc.).

Mamandranomay: Bara provincial governors (Madagascar).

mambo: a title found in south-east/central Africa.

mamlūk: a freed man, a former slave of Christian origin who has been converted and suitably trained to serve at court or in the army.

(the) Mamluks: a dynasty that reigned over Egypt and Syria (1250–1517), whose sultans were chosen from among the militias of slave soldiers (*mamlūks*).

Mamponghene ('the king of Mampong'): the leader of Gonja, one of the vassal states that formed the Confederacy of Greater Asante.

Manantany: the first minister, in Sakalava kingdoms (Madagascar).

manāra: the large central dome (in architecture).

manda: salt, in Kānembu.

Manda Hausakoy (a divinity): the fisherman-blacksmith from Yawuri.

Mandi-Mani ('the Lord of the Manou'): the title of the greatest suzerain in the Sierra Leone-Liberia region.

Mandi-Mansa: the title of the Emperor of Mali.

Māndjil or *Māndjuluk*: the title which Fundj monarchs bestowed on their principal vassals.

mandresirafy: among the Antankara of Madagascar, the purveyors of invincibility, sacred objects passed on from ruler to ruler.

mangeśt egzi ʿabḥērāwit: the 'Holy Empire', i.e. Ethiopia.

Mangi Mrwe: the paramount chief of the Ugweno clans of Tanzania.

mani: in the Kongo kingdom, a high-ranking noble; a landlord; a governor.

Mani Kabunga: in Kongo, name given to the clergy assigned to the spirits, from the village level to that of the kingdom.

Mani Kongo: the ruler of the Kongo.

manoma: farmers in (Hausaland).

mansa (in Maninka): the king, the holder of the most important political power (in Mali).

mansaya (in Maninka): 1) royalty; political territorial groups headed by a *mansa*; 2) a socio-political system, whose dominant ruling class was a polyarchy of an élite of laymen or priests, freemen or slaves, caste or guild members, or noblemen or commoners. It was financed by the taxes which those controlling the machinery of government levied on trade and produce. It was not a landed aristocracy or proprietor class.

mantse: king, among the Ga.

marabout: the word does not have the same meaning in the Maghreb as in Black Africa. In the former it applies both to a holy person who has founded a brotherhood and to his tomb; in sub-Saharan Africa it designates any person with some knowledge of the Ḳurʾān and other sacred writings who uses that knowledge to act as interceder between the believer and God, while drawing upon traditional divinatory sources and the use of talismans. In the eyes of the public he is a scholar in the religious sense of the word, a magician, a soothsayer and a healer.

marabtin bilbaraka: in Barḳa, the offspring of pilgrims, usually North Africans.

marinda: a healing association (in Kongo).

Marisa (title meaning 'the Destroyer'): in Katsina (Hausaland), the title of a governor who kept watch over the eastern border.

maroserana ('many paths' in Malagasy): reflects the custom of the first Maroserana kings in Mahafaly to place their residences in the middle of habitations with paths radiating in all directions to villages around them.

marula or *nkanyi*: the *marulu* (*Sclerocarya caffra*) is a tree of the family Anacardiaceae, found in central and southern Africa, and bearing an oval yellow fruit about two inches long that is used locally for making an intoxicating beverage; also *marula plum*: the fruit of this tree.

Masara ('Egyptian'): maize (in Kanuri).

Mashinama: the title of an important Kanuri dignitary.

masu arziki: see *attajirai*.

masu sarauta: in Hausaland, all those with any political authority; aristocrats.

*mawlid*s (Arabic): legendary prose narratives about Muḥammad.

mazālim (abuses) (Arabic): a word whose singular *mazlima* denotes an unjust or oppressive action. At an early stage in the development of Islamic institutions of government, *mazālim* came to denote the structure through which the temporal authorities took direct responsibility for dispensing justice.

mbafu: red dyewood, in Luba (Zaire).

mbarma or *bulala*: local or ethnic leaders (in Kānem).

mboma (a man of the Boma ethnic group): among the Tio, the word designates a stupid person or anyone in a lowly occupation.

mbua: animal skin (in Kikuyuland).

meen: maternal family (in Kayor).

mercadores (Portuguese): brokers; merchants, tradesmen.

mestizo: a Spanish or Portuguese half-caste (Afro-Portuguese ...); also applied to other persons of mixed blood, such as Afro-Asians.

(the) *Mfecane* (crushing), in Nguni languages and *Lifaqane*/*Difaqane* (hammering) in Sotho-Tswana: a social and political revolution that took place in Bantu-speaking Southern Africa and beyond, during the first decades of the nineteenth century.

mfuka (Kikongo): debt.

mfuku (Kikongo): usefulness, benefit.

mgawi: the land divider (in the Maravi administration).

Mgbe: leopard secret society (of the northern Cross river valley and the Cameroon).

mhondoro ('lion'): in the Mutapa empire, spirit mediums whose function was to advise the emperor in all matters of state; national ancestor spirits.

mifaly: submission (in Malagasy).

mihrab (Arabic): 1) a niche, chamber, or slab in a mosque, indicating the direction of Mecca; 2) a niche motif of an Oriental prayer rug, resembling the shape of a *mihrab* in a mosque.

mikireččo (a honorary title in Ethiopia): a royal counsellor.

milambu: taxes payable (to the Luba *mulopwe*) in food and local produce.

milk: small family holdings; property; possession, ownership.

mingilu: unpaid labour (a tribute paid to the Luba *mulopwe* by his officials).

mithḳal (of gold, etc.) (Arabic): the Sudanese *mithḳal* weighs approximately 4.25 g.

mitngu: a secret society opened to the rest of the population irrespective of social status (in Bamum).

mkomba: the public executioner (in the Maravi administration).

mlira (the *mlira* cult): the ritual veneration of Mlira, the spirit of the Great Kalonga Chinkhole, an ancestor of the Phiri royal lineages (see Chapter 21).

moasy: a priest (in Madagascar).

Mogho-Naaba (a title): the *Naaba* of the Mossi country.

mogyemogye ('ceremonial jaw-bone'): an Asante wine jar used for pouring libations on the Golden Stool.

mokondzi: chief (in Lingala).

Monomotapa: see *Mwene Mutapa*.

montamba: among the Bobangi of the Congo basin, a slave sold by his kin.

montonge: a captured slave (among the Bobangi).

moyal (literally 'spoliation'): in Takrūr, a tax which entitled members of the élite to appropriate wealth wherever possible.

moyo: heart, in the Rozvi empire; soul, spirit in Kikongo.

mpanjaka: king, chief, ruler (in Madagascar).

mpanjaka-bé: title of a king given only to rulers of the great Bara clan (Madagascar).

mpanjaka-kely: the Zafimanely kinglets (in Madagascar).

mpasi (Kikongo): suffering, poverty, need, calamity or affliction.

mphande: shells, among the Tumbuka of northern Zambezia.

mphelo: a Tumbuka grinding stone.

mpifehy: village chiefs (in Madagascar).

mpisoro: the chief priest of the Mahafaly kings (Madagascar).

mpok: a Lunda broadsword.

m'polio: a catfish (in Bambara).

mpungi: the sacred shrine of the Pare of Tanzania.

mtemi: see *ntemi*.

muavi: in the *prazos*, a poison ordeal done to establish the guilt or innocence of a person accused of witchcraft.

mubata: see *babuta*.

mubika: see *babika*.

mugabe ('the milker') or *mukama* (pl. *bakama*): king (in Bunyoro and Buganda).

muhanuro: an annual festival in Burundi, during which royal authority and the drums symbolizing it were renewed, and which celebrated the sowing of sorghum, and determined the most favourable date for this in a country with a long rainy season.

muhutu (pl. *bahutu*): ethnic group in Burundi, Rwanda and several other states in eastern and central Africa.

muidzu: the country's chief justice (in Kongo).

mukama: see *mugabe*.

mukanda: institution.

muḳata'āt (Arabic): financial and administrative unit (in Egypt).

mukazambo: in the *prazo* system, a slave chief having under him a *sachikunda* and his *nsaka*.

mukisi (Kikongo): evil-spell; witchcraft; crime of poisoning; the poison itself.

mukomondera: a cultivation system through which the Shona used to obtain grain during famine.

mulatto (Spanish *mulato*, from *mulo*, mule): one who is the offspring of a European and a Black; also used loosely for anyone of mixed race resembling a *mulatto*.

mulopwe: the title of the Luba king which signified the indivisibility of power that could not be shared.

multazims (Arabic): the bidders who collected taxes from the peasants.

munaki: a prophetess (in Kongo).

Munhumutapa (a title): see *Mwene Mutapa*.

mupeto: in the Mutapa empire, forcible confiscation.
mushtarā (Arabic): rural products.
mussitos: in the *prazo* system, fugitive slave strongholds.
mussumba: a capital (town) (among the Lunda).
Mustahfizān: one of the components of the Ottoman imperial troops or *odjak̲*s.
Müteferrik̲as: the personal guard of the vice-regent of Egypt; the personal guard of a sultan.
muud al-hūrum or *muudul horma*: in the Senegal Futa, an annual tribute payable in grain (grain tax) to the Moors.
mvila: clans (in Kikongo).
mwami (pl. *bami*): the royal title of the former kings of Rwanda and Burundi.
mwangana: chief (in Lunda).
mwana Mwilamba: the head of the (Luba) army.
Mwant or *Mwaant*: the chiefly title to which the name of the first Luba king (Yav or Yaav) was added to become the imperial title *Mwant Yav*.
mwant a ngaand: a Lunda district headman.
Mwant Yav: the highest Luba/Lunda title meaning 'Lord Yav', 'Lord of the Viper', referring to the distance between king and mortals: emperor.
mwembe: traditional maize (in Kikuyuland).
Mwene Mutapa or *Monomotapa* ('lord of metals', 'master of pillage'): a title borne by a line of kings who ruled over a country rich in gold, copper and iron, whence the title 'lord of metals'. This country lay between the Zambezi and Limpopo rivers, in what is now Zimbabwe and Mozambique, from the fourteenth to the seventeenth century. It was often called the empire of the *Mwene Mutapa*, and is associated with the site known as Great Zimbabwe in south-western Zimbabwe.
mwine Lundu: the keeper of the Luba tradition and particularly of the unwritten constitution.
Mwine Munza: a Luba title meaning 'master of Munza'.
mwisikongo: the nobles, one of the strata in Kongo society.

naaba (a Mossi title): chief.
naabiiga (pl. *naabiise*): Mossi chief's son.
naabiise: see *naabiiga*.
naam (Mossi): power; those who held the power.
nabanza: the keeper of the regalia and supervisor of rituals at the court of the Luba king.
nagado: the merchant caste (in Ethiopia).
nā'ib (literally 'substitute, delegate, deputy'): the term applied generally to any person appointed as deputy of another in an official position, and more especially, in the Mamluk and Dihlī sultanates, to designate: a) the deputy or lieutenant of the sultan and b) the governors of the chief provinces. In its most common form, in Persian and Turkish as well as later Arabic, *nā'ib* signified a judge-substitute, or delegate of the *k̲ād̲ī* in the administration of law.
nak̲īb al-ashrāf (Arabic): a representative of the Prophet's descendants.
nakombga: see *nakombse*.
nakombse (sing. *nakombga*) (Mossi): princes of the blood; sons or descendants of sons of princes who had not become chiefs; the royal *nakombse* = the royal lineage.
nalle: henna (in Kanuri).
nanamse: Mossi princes.
nangatoobe: the upper caste (in Takrūr).
napogsyure: see *pogsyure*.
napoko (literally, 'chief woman'): the eldest daughter of a Mossi chief or king. On the death of a Mossi chief or king, between the official announcement of his death (not to be confused with the actual time of his death) and the appointment of his successor, his position is temporarily assumed by his eldest daughter, who is given the title of *napoko*; the *napoko* is a substitute for her father, whose clothes she wears.
napusum: Mossi ceremonies of greeting the king.
navetaan: serfs (in Takrūr).
nawab: king.
ncariampemba (Kikongo): see *nkadi ampemba*.
ndalamba: queen mother with ritual role (among the Luba).
ndoki (pl. *bandoki*): worker of spells, sorcerer (in Kongo).
ndulu: a Kikuyu green vegetable.
nduma: the arrowroot plant of the inland water holes (in Kikuyuland).
neftenia: landed élite, landed nobility.

nere: an African tree whose roots and seeds are used in traditional medicine.

nesomba: see *nesomde*.

nesomde (pl. *nesomba*) (Mossi): honest man; high-ranking dignitary at the head of groups of royal servants.

nevanje: a prince and heir-apparent in the Mutapa empire of Southern Zambia.

ngaailiino (Tio): in Kongo, the official responsible for collecting tribute and heading the administration.

ngabi: bush-buck taboo, usually associated with the dynastic clan of the Babito.

nganga: in Bantu languages, healer; sorcerer; medicine man; in Kongo, the recognized term for a religious expert, especially in *nkisi*.

nganga ngombo: diviners (in Kongo).

ng'anjo: iron-smelting kiln.

ngiri: a secret society for princes only (in Bamum).

Ngola: a title born by the king of Ndongo, a state to the south of Kongo.

nguri: mother (in Kikongo).

Nifa: the Right wing of the Akwamu state and metropolitan Asante.

nikpelo (Mossi): the eldest member (e.g. of a lineage).

nizām (from Turkish *nizām*, order, disposition, arrangement): the hereditary title of the rulers of Hyderabad, India, belonging to the dynasty founded by Asaf Jāf, Subahdar of the Deccan from 1713 to 1748.

njaki: a common Kikuyu bean.

njemani or *chemwa*: in Southern Zambia, an intoxicating wine made from the *mahanga* or ilala palm.

njoldi: symbolic payments attaching to the master of the land; annual ground rent.

nkadi ampemba or *ncariampemba* (from *nkadi*, a dangerous ancestral spirit, and *mpemba*, the hereafter): the demon (in Kikongo).

nkangi ('the saviour'): in Kongo, a crucifix which was the emblem of the judicial power.

nkanyi: see *marula*.

nkende: a grey cercopithecus (a genus of long-tailed African monkeys comprising the guenons and related forms) used as a taboo by the kings of Bujiji.

nkisi: the term, which means 'initiation; magic power; mystic powers; spirit; ancestral force; sacred medicine; idol; fetish', designates, in Kongo, the ideology of royalty derived from religious conceptions in general, in which three important cults played a role: ancestor worship; the worship of territory spirits and the worship of royal charms.

nkobi: a talisman (in Kikongo).

nkoron: deep-mining (in Akan).

nkuluntu ('old one'): the elder; hereditary village chiefs (in Kongo).

noguna: the *mai*'s court (in Borno).

nona: in Kanuri, respectful visits rendered by a social inferior to the house of his social father for whom he was supposed to run any errand required of him.

Nono (a title): in Kebbi (Hausaland), the dignitary who collected the milk and butter intended for the sovereign.

nsaa: blanket (among the Akan).

nsaka: in *prazos*, a unity of the *chikunda* army, comprising ten men, under a *sachikunda*.

ntemi or *mtemi*: a chiefship consisting of a small group of villages and neighbourhoods ruled by a single chief whom the villagers appointed from the ruling lineage (in Tanzania).

nthlava: the sandy soils where the Hlengwe used to build their homesteads.

ntufia: the sacred fire lit at his coronation by each king (*maloango*) of Loango, and which was to burn until his death.

numa-n-bolo (Bambara): the left arm of Segu's army.

nyamankala: the caste system (in Mande).

Nyarubanga (the Luo word for 'sent by God'): in Northern Uganda, the period of droughts and famines that ended with the Great Famine of 1617–21, accompanied by a disease which wiped out the cattle herds.

nyia: the Kanuri marriage contract.

Nzambi mpungu ('Supreme Creator', 'superior spirit'): the way the King of Kongo was addressed.

nzavi: a Kikuyu preservable bean.

nzimbu (shells of *Olivancilaria nana*): shells used as currency in the Kingdom of Kongo.

nzo longo (association in Kongo): an initiation cult for boys.

oba (in Edo): the title of the founder of the ancient Kingdom of Benin, holder of religious and political powers.

obeah (or *obi*): an African religion, probably of Asante origin, characterized by the use of sorcery and magic ritual; also: a charm or fetish used in *obeah* and: the influence of *obeah* (e.g. put *obeah* on a person).

obi: an Igbo term, of probable Yoruba origin, for king or chief. The *obi* was appointed by the *oba* of Benin.

obuotoyo: rock salt (in Yoruba).

odjaḳ: a corps of imperial troops introduced in Egypt by Sultan Selim I; also Turkish fortresses and garrisons.

ogendini: sub-ethnic groups (among the Luo).

ohene: the king of the Kumasi state.

ôkoo (makoko): king (among the Tio).

okro or *okra*: a tall annual plant (*Hibiscus* or *Abelmoschus esculentus*) indigenous to Africa, and its green seed-pods, used for soup, salad and pickles (also called *gumbo*).

omanhene: the king of the Akwamu and Denkyira empires.

ombiasa: often translated as 'sacerdotal person'; priest; medicine man; doctor, etc.; *ombiasa* encompass a number of functions and have a number of categories into which they are subdivided among the Malagasy.

ompanghalalan: royal messengers (in Malagasy).

omukama: king.

oni: king (e.g. the *oni* of Ife).

ondaty-bé: high councillors of the Mahafaly clans (in Madagascar).

onjatsy: earlier newcomers (on a land) (in Madagascar).

orin-tany: new lands (in Madagascar).

Oranmiyan: title of Oranyan, a son of Oduduwa (the founder and first *oni* of Ife) and the legendary founder of the Yoruba kingdom of Oyọ, who is stated to have reigned at both Ife and Benin before moving to Oyọ; now the title of a god.

orkoiyot (pl. *orkoik*): a spiritual leader (among the Nandi); also, a traditional leader (in Kenya).

osafohene: war leader in the Akwamu and Denkyira states.

othen (pl. *otheme*): in Labwor (Great Lakes region), multi-clan ritual grouping.

ovimbali or *quimbares*: the Afro-Portuguese (in Kongo).

ozo: a high-ranking person (in the Igbo hierarchy).

panga (Swahili): a large broad-bladed knife used in Africa for heavy cutting (as of brush or bananas) and also as a weapon (machete).

pasha (Turkish): honorary title attaching to senior office, particularly of military commander and provincial governor, in the Ottoman empire.

pastas (Portuguese): 1000 *pastas* = 800 000 *cruzados* (*c.* 1756–7) – see *cruzado*.

pinje: see *piny*.

piny (pl. *pinje*): the territory of a Luo sub-ethnic group.

(the royal) *pogsyure* (*napogsyure*) system: a system of capitalizing and distributing women (among the Mossi).

pombe (Swahili): in Central and East Africa, a (possibly intoxicating) drink made by fermenting many kinds of grain and some fruits.

pombeiros (in Portuguese): agents from *pombo*; barefoot *mulatto* merchants.

pombo: the Kikongo name for Pool people.

prazeros: in the *prazo* system, a dominant class, holder of the crown lands (*prazos*); estate-owners.

prazos (Portuguese): crown lands; agricultural estates; the *prazo* was also a Portuguese land-tenure system.

prazos da coroa (Portuguese): crown land estates.

presidios (Portuguese): towns.

pumbo ('market'): slave market in Pumbo, in Stanley Pool region.

quimbares: see *ovimbali*.

Quojabercoma: the country of the Quoja (Sierra Leone and Liberia).

raia (from Arabic *ra'iyah*, flock, herd, subjects, peasants): a non-Muslim subject of the Sultan of Turkey, subject to payment of such taxes as the *djizya* (poll tax) and the *kharādj* (land tax). (See the *dhimmī* of Vol. III).

rainitsy ny mpanjaka ('royal friends'): the heads of the Mahafaly clans (in Madagascar).

ra'is (or *reis*): a Muslim chief or ruler; a Muslim ship's captain.

rakire: joking relationship (in Mossi).

Ramādạn the ninth month of the Muslim lunar calendar, during which Muslims observe a fast (*ṣaum*).

Rangahy (Malagasy): a royal official (at Ambilobe, Antankara capital, Madagascar).
ras (Amharic *rās*, head, chief, from Arabic *raʿīs*) (a title): an Ethiopian king, prince, or feudal lord; also, the ruler of an Ethiopian province.
rasa or *erasa* (from the Amharic *ras*): head or chief.
Rasam-Naaba (a Mossi title): see *Bin-Naaba*.
al-Rashīd (Arabic): an honorific title meaning 'the Just'.
real-politik: a German word used to denote the notion of realism in politics.
(the) *Reconquista*: the process of Christian resistance to Muslim domination and the wars to eliminate Islam from the peninsula, covering the period between 722 (the battle of Covadonga) and 1492 (the fall of Granada).
refo rekk: serfs, in Sereer.
Regimento (Portuguese): instructions from the King of Portugal, granting privileges, especially to missionaries.
reis: see *rāʿīs*.
remoru: serfs, in Samba.
renilemy: the privileged, in Mahafaly society (Madagascar).
restvölker (German): refugees.
reth: king, in Shillukland.
ribāt (or *rābiṭa*): (from the Arabic *rabaṭa*, to link, to tie): a link, a tie, a connection; an outpost that is fortified (against external threat); a fortress, a hermitage; a fortified centre devoted to religious and ascetic practices and/or to propagating the faith; also a body of Islamic precepts (*daʿwat al-ḥakk*).
rima (a Mossi title – from *ri*, 'to absorb or eat food that is not chewed'): king.
rimaybe or *bellah* (Mossi): prisoners tied to working the land; captives and serfs.
rimbe: see *dimo*.
ringu (from *ri* – see above, under *rima*): enthronement.
riyāsa (Arabic): leadership.
Rohandrian: the name of the highest Zafindraminia estate in Madagascar.
rola: turtle-dove (in Shona country).
rugga: see *ardo*.
Rukonkesh or *Lukonkeshia* (Luba/Lunda title): the queen-mother and head of the logistics for the court.
runde: slave villages (in Futa Jallon).
ruoth or *wuon piny*: the chief of the Luo *buch piny*.

Saburu (a title in Hausaland): the official responsible for security on the roads.
sachikunda: in *prazos*, the head of a *chikunda* army.
Sachiteve: a title (in Uteve).
saff (pl. *sufuf*) (Arabic): a confederation formed by alliances between *ḳabilas*.
saka: the section, the first level in the Mossi patrilineal and patrilocal society.
sakke: in Kebbi (Hausaland), the representative of the coopers, appointed by the sovereign.
sakkeebe: cobblers (in Takrūr).
salam: Ethiopian sacred hymns (see *deggwa*).
sāliyāne (Arabic): annual salaries.
samba remoru: in Kebbi, farmers who have turned back to the land; poor peasants of Takrūr.
sampy: the royal divinity guaranteeing the well-being of the Imerina state (Madagascar).
Sanaahene: the Minister of Finance in the Akwamu and Denkyira empires.
sanankunya: joking relationship.
sandjaḳ (from Turkish *sanjāḳ*, literally, flag, standard): in the former Turkish empire, one of the administrative districts into which an *eyalet* or *vilayet* (province) was divided.
Sandjaḳ Bey (a title, in Egypt): the governor of a *sandjaḳ*; the highest military and administrative personnel of a district.
sandjaḳ-beylik: the most important and fundamental military and administrative unit of the Ottoman empire grouped, regionally, under the authority of a *beylerbey*.
san'dyon: trade slaves (in Bambara).
Sango: the thunder cult (in the Ọyọ religious system).
sanjag: see *sandjaḳ*.
santu (Kikongo): a type of cross; a crucifix, but also a saint.
Santuraki (a title in Kano): a court dignitary.
sarakunan noma: a title meaning 'master of the crops' (in Hausaland).
sarakunan rafi: in Zamfara (Hausaland), grazing-tax collectors.
sarauta: kingship (in Hausaland).

sarki (pl. *sarakuna*) (a title): head of state; chief; king (in Hausaland).
Sarkin (a title): chief; king (in Hausaland).
Sarkin bayi (a title in Hausaland): the king of slaves.
Sarkin dawaki (a title in Hausaland): a general in the cavalry division.
Sarkin fullani: a title in Hausaland.
Sarkin lifidi (a title in Hausaland): a general in the heavy cavalry division.
Sarkin poma (a title in Hausaland): chief, master of the crops.
Sarkin rafi (a title in Hausaland): Governor of the Valleys.
Sarkin shanu (a title in Hausaland): livestock tax-collector.
Sarkin tudu (a title in Hausaland): Governor of the Hills.
satala (Bambara): a kettle; prayer beads.
Satigi (a title in Futa Toro, meaning 'the Great Ful'): ruler.
ṣaum (Arabic): compulsory dawn-to-dusk fast during the month of *Ramaḍān*, with abstinence from all physical pleasures (food, drink, sexual relations, etc).
Sax-sax: in Kayor, administrative officers appointed in villages by the central government.
šayh: an Ethiopian religious chief.
sebbe: see *ceddo*.
Sekiapu: see *Ekine*.
señ (literally 'foot' in Bambara): the basic unit of the *faama* of Segu's army.
Serdar: the commander of the military operating within or beyond Egypt's borders.
Serin Jakk (a title in Kayor): the *Serin Jakk* devoted themselves to religious activities and teaching.
Serin Lamb: agents of central government (in Kayor) responsible for the defence of the frontiers.
Shango: a Yoruba divinity.
shangwa: famine (in Shona).
Shantali: a protocol officer in Katsina (Hausaland).
sharī'a (literally 'way', 'good road' in Arabic): detailed code of conduct; the *sharī'a* comprises the precepts governing the ritual of worship, standards of behaviour and rules of living. It consists of laws that prescribe, permit and distinguish between true and false. The Ḳur'ānic prescriptions it covers are complemented by prohibitions and explanations contained in the law (*fikh*). The sources of the Islamic *sharī'a* are the Ḳur'ān and the *ḥadīth*.
sharīf (Arabic pl. *shurafā'*): literally 'noble'; an honorary title given to all the descendants of 'Alī and of Fāṭima.
shaykh (Arabic pl. *mashāyikh*): old man; chief of an Arab *ḳabīla*; spiritual master; title given to the founders of mystical brotherhoods, to great scholars and to teachers.
Shaykh al-Balad (Arabic): an unofficial honorary title, only indicating a senior among the Egyptian *beys* (senior grandee).
sība (Arabic): dissident blocks.
Siddi: one of the terms used to denote blacks or African slaves in Asia.
silamos (from *Islam/Islamos*): Muslim converts (in Malagasy).
siso: see *gabir*.
soba: petty chief; leaders (in Angola).
sofa (Bambara): the infantry corps (in the *faama*'s army). The *sofa* were in theory grooms, but did not necessarily practise this occupation; they were part of the *faama*'s household. Sometimes, to secure the undying devotion of the 'young men' the *faama* presided at their 'birth' to manhood through circumcision, making sure some of his own sons were involved in it too.
sojabe: among the Sakalava of Madagascar, the village elders, concerned with the minutiae of social life.
soldo (Portuguese): the payment of the *capitãos-mores*.
sombili: (ongoing) custom; prerogative (practised by the Zafirambo in Madagascar) to slaughter domesticated animals.
sonda (sing. *sondre*) (Mossi): collective names or mottoes.
sondre: see *sonda*.
sorabe (or *volan'Onjatsy*) (in Malagasy): Arabic script used to transcribe the Malagasy language; Arabic-Malagasy characters; manuscript in the Antemoro language written in Arabic characters. These are *katibo*'s (scribes specializing in the writing and interpretation of the *sorabe*) traditions.
sorondamba (Mossi): young servants.
spahi (from Turkish *sipāhī*, horseman, mounted soldier): a horseman forming one of a body of cavalry which formerly constituted an important part of the Turkish army and was to some extent organized on a feudal basis.
ṣūfi (literally 'dressed in wool', from the Arabic root, *ṣūf*, meaning 'wool' to denote 'the practice of

wearing the woollen robe' (*labs al-ṣūf*), hence the act of devoting oneself to the mystic life on becoming what is called in Islam a *ṣūfī*: an adept of Muslim mysticism (*Ṣūfism* or *taṣawwuf*).

*ṣūfī tarīḳa*s: see *tarīḳa*.

Ṣūfism (*taṣawwuf* in Arabic): ascetic Islamic mysticism originating in the eighth century and developing especially in Persia into a system of elaborate symbolism of which the goal is communion with the deity through contemplation and ecstasy.

sugedi: grass matting (in Kanuri).

sūḳ: an Arab market or market-place, a souk, a bazaar; shops grouped by corporations.

sulke: coats of mail (in Hausaland).

sultan: the sovereign or chief ruler of a Muslim country; especially (formerly) the sovereign of Turkey; also formerly, a prince or king's son, a high officer.

Sunankwaahene: the Minister of Religious Affairs in the Akwamu and Denkyira empires.

surga or *dag*: in Takrūr, in the context of clientship, the relationship between the pastoralists (the donors) and the agriculturalists (the recipients) of one who agreed of his own free will to be maintained by a rich man or an influential political leader for his own benefit.

svikiro: the word *svikiro* is derived from the verb *kusvika* meaning 'to arrive at or reach a place'. *Svikiro* literally means the person, vehicle or instrument through which gods and spirits communicate with the people. Thus a priest, rabbi and prophet in western culture and a caliph and *mallam* in Muslim culture could be a *sviriko* in the Shona society. The *sviriko* should not be confused with a medical practitioner, *nganga*, or with a fortune-teller. The *sviriko* was a priest, an intellectual, an educator, and a leader, wrapped into one person.

Swana Mulunda: see *Swan Murund*.

Swan Mulopwe: heir-presumptive and commander of the Lunda army.

Swan Murund or *Swana Mulunda* (a Luba/Lunda title): the symbolic mother of the society; symbolic queen-mother named Rweej.

tabala (Bambara): in Segu, a drum associated with each ruler and which announced war.

tabaski ('sacrifice'): a Muslim religious festival in which the Bambara kings used to take part.

tafsīr (Arabic): commentary of the Ḳur'ān; exegesis.

tala'a: the commoners, one of the classes in Kanuri society.

talakawa (sing. *talaka*): the ruled; in Hausa society, serfs; free commoners; the poor; poverty-stricken farmers and herdsmen of Hausaland and the Niger-Chad area.

Talba: head of police and magistrate (in Borno).

Talempihitry: in the Sakalava kingdoms of Madagascar, officials acting as overseers of the *dady* cult.

talia: commoners in the Kanuri society (in Borno).

talse: Mossi commoners.

Tandonaka: councils of ministers (among the Imamono of Madagascar).

tangomãos: see *lançados*.

Tara (a Hausa title meaning 'The Council of Nine'): in Zamfara, Gobir and Kano, designated an electoral college responsible for the appointment of the successor to the throne from among the princes.

tarīḳa (Arabic pl. *turuḳ*): literally 'way'; association or brotherhood (each *tarīḳa* bears the name of its founder); congregation, *Ṣūfī* religious brotherhood; local centre of a religious brotherhood; lodge of brotherhoods.

ta'rīkh (Arabic): history in general, annals, chronicles; usually synonymous with 'historical account'. It is the title of a great many historical works, like *Ta'rīkh al-Sūdān* (the history of the Sūdān, or Negroes of West Africa – see *Bilād al-Sūdān*); *Ta'rīkh al-Andalus* (the history of Andalusia), etc.

tariki: subgroups (in Malagasy).

Tasoba (a title): war chief; general-in-chief.

tasobnamba ('masters of war' in Mossi): war chiefs.

tata: a fort (in Bambara).

tatibato: method of periodic tax collection used by the Antakara of Madagascar to finance the state.

Teen: a title (in Kayor).

tëgg: Mande blacksmiths.

tellek saw ('great man'): designates the ideal of greatness in Ethiopian society.

tengsoba ('the master of the land' in Mossi): earth priest.

tenzi: epic poems (in Kiswahili).

terras da coroa: in the *prazo* system, a Portuguese crown property.

teskere: an export permit.

tiido: an altar (in Mossi).

timār (Arabic): fiefs.

Tingimaro: title of a ruler (in Madagascar).

tobe (Kanuri): large open cotton gowns either plain or dyed blue.

Togo-Naaba (a Mossi title): the chief's spokesman who was responsible for ritual ceremonies.

tompon-menakely (a Malagasy title meaning 'masters-of-the-fief'): chiefs of village fiefs.

tompon-tany ('masters of the land'): original inhabitants (in Madagascar).

ton (Bambara): an association of boys circumcised at the same time; political association.

ton-den (Bambara): association members.

ton-djeli (Bambara): the *ton*'s griot.

ton-dyon ('captives of the *ton*', in Bambara) mostly captives or former captives taken in war.

tonjon: crown slaves (at the *mansa*'s court).

ton-koro-bolo (Bambara): in Segu's army, a reserve corps of experienced *ton-dyon* behind the *disi*.

ton-masa: leader (in Bambara).

ton-tigui (Bambara): chief; in the cavalry, quiver-bearers.

too: millet paste that forms the staple diet among the Bambara.

too-daga: *too* pot (in Bambara).

Torodo: the Torodo revolution of 1776 in Futa Toro was begun by the Torodo *marabout* movement which took much of its inspiration from the success of the *djihād* in Bandu and Futa Jallon at the beginning of the eighteenth century. It was a revolt of the small peasants against both the *muudul horma*, imposed by the Moorish *ḳabīla*s, and the oppressive eastern Muslim tax system introduced by the Islamized Denyanke aristocracy.

torwe: in Borno, specially designated title-holders.

trano-vato: a fort (in Madagascar).

Trek (the Great Trek – 1834–9): an emigration movement of the Cape Boers towards the Vaal and the Orange following the British thrust in South Africa.

trekboer: the *trekboers* were the Boer immigrant farmers who went across the Orange river in search of land before the Great Trek. They settled mostly in the south of what later became the Orange Free State.

tsare: see *gaisuwa*.

tshidie: a general council (at the court of the Luba king).

tshihangu: the court of the Luba king.

tsi-mihety: the collective name adopted by the Tsimihety (Madagascar) to indicate, by refusing to cut their hair, non-submission to Maroserana authority.

tsimiompy: famine (in Malagasy).

tsovolo: name given by the Hlengwe to the basalt soils.

tubung ('masters of the land'): heads of small political units (among the Luba/Lunda).

Tüfenkçiyān: one of the components of the Ottoman imperial troops or *odjaḳ*s.

tukwata: see *kakwata*.

tumba: blessing (in Kongo).

tumbili: monkey (in Kiswahili).

tunka (a Soninke title): king.

Turaki: a protocol officer in Katsina (Hausaland).

turndala ('through the sand', in Bambara): derived from the arabic *al-tareb*, the land, and designates the divine, the consultant.

turuḳ: see *tarīḳa*.

tweapea: (Akan) chewing-sticks.

twite: the officer who represented the Luba king in secular contexts; military chief.

Ubandawaki (a title): a military leader (in Zamfara and Gobir, Hausaland).

ubuhake: in Rwanda, a type of clientele link (see *buhake*).

ubugabire: a type of clientele link (in Burundi).

ubwiru: in Rwanda, the sacred code establishing royal rituals and the dynastic genealogy.

ubwoko: see *umuryango*.

uki: a type of beer made by the Akamba; it is fermented for longer than that of neighbouring communities.

ukisi: in Kongo, holiness; divinity; divine will.

ukoo: lineage, descent.

'ulamā' (sing. 'ālim) (Arabic): Muslim scholars, erudite persons, doctors of law or theologians.

umboli: trader (in Kānem-Borno).

umerā-i-sherākise: Circassian *amīr*s.

Umm Laḥam: the Great Famine of 1684 in Shillukland.

umuheto ('of the bow'): tax-gathering (in Rwanda).

umuryango, in Kirundi and Giha; *ubwoko*, in Kinyarwanda; *uruganda*, in Runyambo and Ruhaya: clan.

unguri ('the mother principle' in Kikongo): maternal, matrilineal relationship; matriarchy.

unguri ankama: seigniory (a Kikongo title still in use among the southern Suku about 1900).

'urf: customs.

uruganda: see *umuryango*.

uthlanga: reed (in Zulu).

uvata: rusticity (in Kikongo).

vaha: a medium.

valohazomanga: the commoners in Mahafaly society (Madagascar).

vashambadzi: traders; African merchant class, in the Zambezi region.

vata: to cultivate (in Kikongo).

veli: governor of a province (see *wālī*).

Veybercoma: the country of the Vai (Sierra Leone and Liberia).

vidye: spirit (in Luba).

vilipate: royal gifts (in Malagasy).

visitador (Portuguese): inspector.

voandzeia subterranea (from Malagasy *voandzou*): a genus of tropical creeping herbs (family Leguminosae) with trifoliolate leaves and small axillary flowers, commonly called 'ground nut'.

vodun: an African religion.

vohitsy mananila (Malagasy): see *longon'mpanilo*.

(the) *Volafotsy* ('white silver'): in Madagascar, the collaterals of the ruling Maroserana, descendants of white silver, sons of non-Maroserana women and Maroserana royals.

volamena ('red silver', i.e. gold): in Mahafaly (Madagascar), the tombs of the Zafivolamena (sons-of-gold), the ruling Maroserana branch among the Sakalava.

wa'azi: sermons (in Hausaland).

Waḳ'at al-sanādjik ('Clash of the *Sandjaḳ Bey*s'): an Egyptian treaty dealing with the revolt of the Faḳariya *bey*s in 1660.

wakf (Arabic pl. *awḳāf*): 1) an Islamic endowment of property to be held in trust and used for a charitable or religious purpose; 2) a Muslim religious or charitable foundation created by an endowed trust fund; 3) a juridical-religious measure taken by the owner of land or other real estate to vest its ownership in a religious institution (a mosque) or some public or social facility (a *madrasa*, hospital, etc.), and/or his or her descendants.

wālī (pl. *wulāt*) (from Turkish *vālī*): governor or vice-governor of a province (*wilāya*).

wamagi: district chiefs, in the Ugweno state (Tanzania).

Wambai: a Kano title.

wark: gold (in Amharic).

washambadzi: see *vashambadzi*.

wasili: North African traders (in Borno).

wasiliram: in Borno, a special quarter assigned to *wasili*.

watan: fatherland; homeland; ancestral land.

wayilbe: blacksmiths (in Takrūr).

wazir (Arabic) (title of the successors of S͟haykh Muḥammad Abū Likaylik): in the Ottoman empire, title of high-ranking state officials or ministers and of the highest dignitaries; holders of positions analogous to that of Muslim viziers; vice-regents, viceroys.

weg-piny: land-owning clans (among the Luo of Kenya).

Weranga-Naaba (a Mossi title): a dignitary who looked after the horses.

Widi-Naaba (a Mossi title): the political spokesman.

wilāya (pl. *wilāyāt*) (Arabic): one of the chief administrative divisions (provinces) of the Ottoman empire having as its head a *wālī* who represents the government and is assisted by an elective council, and being subdivided into *caza*s (districts).

woloso ('born in the house', in Mande): the status acquired by a woman purchased by a community, as soon as she produced a child. A man could also acquire the same status as soon as his master had sufficient confidence in him; house-born slave.

worma: obligations of fealty. *Worma* introduced the idea of allegiance or fealty into Takrūr languages where such a bond did not exist; bond of fealty.

wuon piny: see *ruoth*.

Xaadi: a title (in Kayor).

Yav: see *Mwant Yav*.

Yadega-tenga: the land of Yadega (Yatenga), in Mossi country.

Yatenga-Naaba (a Mossi title): the king of Yatenga.

yerima: the governor of the northern provinces (in Borno).

yial: hunting grounds.

yiiri (pl. *yiiya*): the household, the second level in the Mossi patrilineal and patrilocal society.

yiir kasma (Mossi): the head of the *yiiri*.

yiiya: see *yiiri*.

zabyuya: a ritual announcement at the ceremonial investiture of Mossi chiefs.

zaka (pl. *zakse*): the smaller unit in the Mossi patrilineal and patrilocal society.

zakāt (Arabic): compulsory alms-giving that, for any Muslim enjoying a certain income, consists of distributing a proportion – ranging from 2.5 per cent to 10 per cent – to the poor and to a specific category of the needy. The *zakāt* is the fourth pillar of Islam.

zakse: see *zaka*.

zalunci: injustice (in Hausaland).

Zanna Arjinama: a titled official (in Borno).

zāwiya (pl. *zawāyā*) (Arabic): religious brotherhood; brotherhood seat (and funerary sanctuary of the founding saint); cultural centre; when fortified and manned by defenders of the faith, it is called *ribāṭ*.

zombi or zombie (of Niger-Congo origin; akin to Kongo and Kimbundu and Tshiluba *nzambi*, god, Kongo *zumbi*, good-luck fetish, image): 1) the deity of the python in West African voodoo cults; the snake-deity of the voodoo rite in Haiti and the southern USA; the supernatural power or essence that according to voodoo belief may enter into and reanimate a dead body; a will-less and speechless human in the West Indies capable only of automatic movement held to have died and been reanimated but often believed to have been drugged into a catalepsy for the hours of interment; 2) a person thought to resemble the so-called walking dead; a person markedly strange or abnormal in mentality, appearance, or behaviour.

zuwaya or *insilimen*: Berber or Sudanese *marabout* groups.

Zwayiya (the *Zwayiya marabout*s): a branch of the *marabout* movement.

Index

MAP PAGES

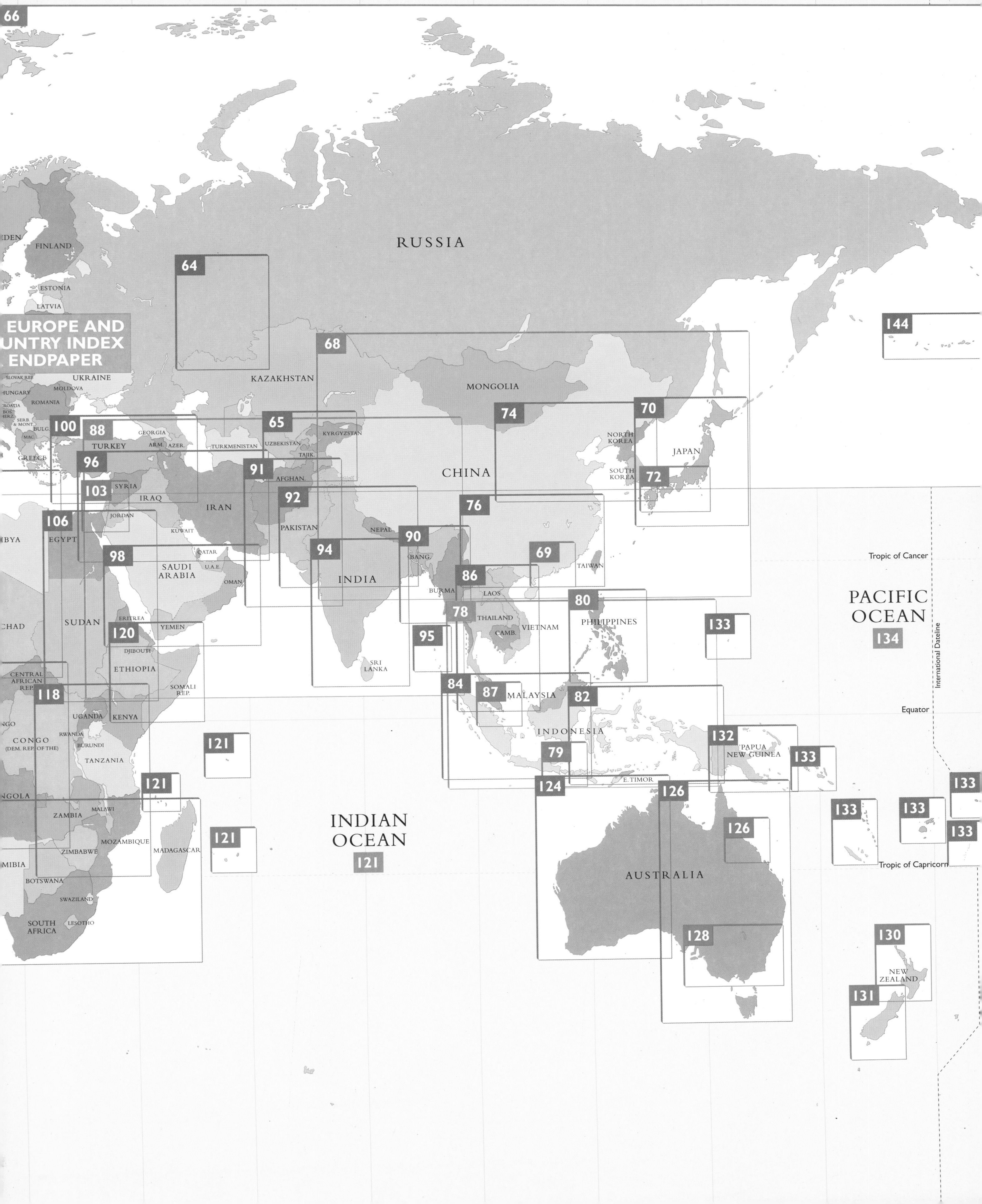

Rachel-
Congrats! Many years of exploration, fun, learning and laughter to you. Enjoy! Joreya &
Eric

Rachel,
Congratulations! Good luck in all your life journey's
Love
Shaun

Rachel As This book shows, No Matter Where You Are! There you Are! Love Dad & Bobbi

Rachel,
We'll miss you at
N 45° 51' 07" W 92° 45' 48"
this year. Good luck in everything!
Love
Lee Guthrie

RACHEL
Happy wanderings on this next adventure But remember page 154!
LOVE
Dale
&
GORDON

Rachel -
I have no doubt that where-ever you go, you will leave a mark. There will always be one on my heart - where you will be no matter where you go... Love, Cathy Mother

OXFORD

ATLAS
OF THE
WORLD

ELEVENTH EDITION

ACKNOWLEDGEMENTS

IMAGES OF EARTH (PAGES IX–XXIV)
All satellite images in this section courtesy
of NPA Group Limited, Edenbridge, Kent
(www.satmaps.com)

THE GAZETTEER OF NATIONS
TEXT Keith Lye

INTRODUCTION TO WORLD GEOGRAPHY
PICTURE ACKNOWLEDGEMENTS
Courtesy of NPA Group, Edenbridge,
  UK 9, 48
Science Photo Library/Earth Satellite
  Corporation 20
NASA/GSFC 22 bottom left and right

ILLUSTRATIONS
Stefan Chabluk, William Donohoe,
Bernard Thornton Artists /Steve Seymour

STAR CHARTS
John Cox and Richard Monkhouse

CARTOGRAPHY BY PHILIP'S

CITY MAPS
PAGE 11, DUBLIN: The town plan of Dublin
is based on Ordnance Survey Ireland by
permission of the Government Permit
Number 7617. © Ordnance Survey Ireland
and Government of Ireland.

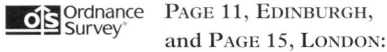 PAGE 11, EDINBURGH,
and PAGE 15, LONDON:
This product includes mapping data licensed
from Ordnance Survey® with the permission
of the Controller of Her Majesty's Stationery
Office. © Crown copyright 2003. All rights
reserved. Licence number 100011710.

VECTOR DATA: Courtesy of Gräfe and Unser
Verlag GmbH, München, Germany (city
center maps of Bangkok, Beijing, Cape Town,
Jerusalem, Mexico City, Moscow, Singapore,
Sydney, Tokyo and Washington D.C.)

Copyright © 2003 Philip's

Philip's, a division of
Octopus Publishing Group Limited,
2–4 Heron Quays, London E14 4JP

Published in North America by
Oxford University Press, Inc.,
198 Madison Avenue,
New York, N.Y. 10016

www.oup-usa.org/atlas

Oxford is a registered trademark of
Oxford University Press

*Library of Congress Cataloging-in-Publication
Data available*

ISBN 0–19–521986–4

Printing (last digit): 9 8 7 6 5 4 3 2 1

Printed in Spain

FOREWORD

AN AUTHORITATIVE AND SERIOUS REFERENCE WORK, the Oxford *Atlas of the World* is one of the finest atlases available anywhere in the world. The atlas incorporates computer-derived maps which have been produced using the very latest in digital cartographic techniques.

The Oxford *Atlas of the World* has been revised and updated with the help of a panel of specialist geography consultants from the United Kingdom and the United States, whose specialties range from the history of cartography, urban and social geography, epidemiology, and the European Union to biogeography and applied geomorphology. The result of their valuable input can be seen in the wealth of up-to-date maps and data contained in the "*Introduction to World Geography*" section of this atlas.

Country names are shown in conventional English form and are those that are in common usage. They are the forms used by publications such as *Newsweek* and *The Washington Post,* and by the BBC and the British Foreign Office. Alternative country names appear in brackets on the maps where space permits – for example, Burma (Myanmar) – and are cross-referenced in the index, for example, Côte d'Ivoire = Ivory Coast.

HOW TO USE THE ATLAS
The atlas is divided into a number of sections which are explained below.

WORLD STATISTICS AND IMAGES OF EARTH
World statistics on topics such as area and population for every country in the world, and physical dimensions – including the largest islands, lakes and seas, the highest mountains and the longest rivers, by continent. Also included in this section is a selection of detailed, up-to-date maps highlighting regions around the world that are currently in the news, such as Iraq, Afghanistan, the Near East, Kashmir, and Colombia. This section is followed by a beautifully illustrated satellite section showing 16 of the world's major regions and cities in the Americas, Europe, Africa, Asia, and Australasia.

THE GAZETTEER OF NATIONS
A comprehensive A–Z reference providing concise profiles of every country's geography, climate, history, politics, and economy, together with ready-reference tables, and illustrated with flags and locator maps.

INTRODUCTION TO WORLD GEOGRAPHY
A richly informative section comprising 48 pages of maps, charts, graphs, and diagrams which explain key themes about the world in which we live. The topics covered include the Solar System, oceans, climate, the environment, energy, and trade. Explanatory text on each spread describes the patterns shown by the data.

CITY MAPS
A detailed selection of maps for 67 urban areas around the world. These are useful for planning trips abroad as well as for comparative studies of cities worldwide. Also included is a 7-page index to the city maps.

WORLD MAPS
An outstanding collection of 176 pages of distinctive Philip's cartography. The highly acclaimed physical world maps combine relief shading with layer-colored contours to give a striking visual picture of the Earth's surface. Roads, railroads, canals, and airports are accurately depicted on the maps, and towns and cities are clearly marked. More information on the key features employed in the construction and presentation of the maps is given on the facing page.

GEOGRAPHICAL GLOSSARY AND INDEX
The 75,000-name index to the world maps includes geographical features as well as towns and cities, with both latitude/longitude and letter/figure grid references. Preceding the index is a list of geographical terms from various foreign languages that may be found in the place names on the maps and also in the index, together with their meanings.

SPECIALIST GEOGRAPHY CONSULTANTS

THE EDITORS are grateful to the following people for acting as specialist geography consultants on the "*Introduction to World Geography*" front section:
Professor D. Brunsden Kings College, University of London, UK
Dr C. Clarke Oxford University, UK
Professor P. Haggett University of Bristol, UK
Professor M-L. Hsu University of Minnesota, Minnesota, USA
Professor K. McLachlan Geopolitical and International Boundaries Research Centre, School of Oriental and African Studies, University of London, UK

Professor M. Monmonier Syracuse University, New York, USA
Professor M. J. Tooley University of St Andrews, UK
Dr T. Unwin Royal Holloway, University of London, UK

THE EDITORS would also like to thank:
Keith Lye
Robin Scagell
Dr I. S. Evans Durham University, UK
Dr Andrew Tatham The Royal Geographical Society

WORLD MAPS

The reference maps which form the main body of this atlas have been prepared in accordance with the highest standards of international cartography to provide an accurate and detailed representation of the Earth. The scales and projections used have been carefully chosen to give balanced coverage of the world, while emphasizing the most densely populated and economically significant regions. A hallmark of Philip's mapping is the use of hill shading and relief coloring to create a graphic impression of landforms: this makes the maps exceptionally easy to read. However, knowledge of the key features employed in the construction and presentation of the maps will enable the reader to derive the fullest benefit from the atlas.

MAP SEQUENCE

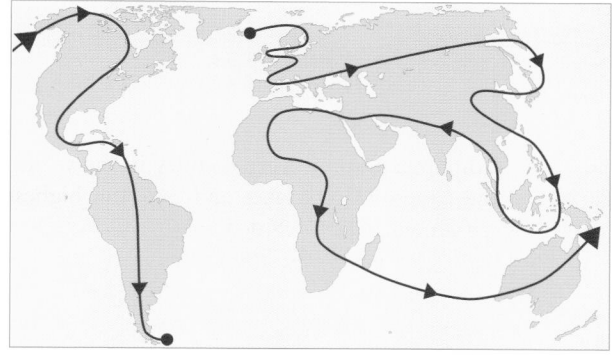

The atlas covers the Earth continent by continent: first Europe; then its land neighbor Asia (mapped north before south, in a clockwise sequence), then Africa, Australia and Oceania, North America, and South America. This is the classic arrangement adopted by most cartographers since the 16th century. For each continent, there are maps at a variety of scales. First, physical relief and political maps of the whole continent; then a series of larger-scale maps of the regions within the continent, each followed, where required, by still larger-scale maps of the most important or densely populated areas. The governing principle is that by turning the pages of the atlas, the reader moves steadily from north to south through each continent, with each map overlapping its neighbors.

MAP PRESENTATION

With very few exceptions (for example, for the Arctic and Antarctic), the maps are drawn with north at the top, regardless of whether they are presented upright or sideways on the page. In the borders will be found the map title; a locator diagram showing the area covered; continuation arrows showing the page numbers for maps of adjacent areas; the scale; the projection used; the degrees of latitude and longitude; and the letters and figures used in the index for locating place names and geographical features. Physical relief maps also have a height reference panel identifying the colors used for each layer of contouring.

MAP SYMBOLS

Each map contains a vast amount of detail which can only be conveyed clearly and accurately by the use of symbols. Points and circles of varying sizes locate and identify the relative importance of towns and cities; different styles of type are employed for administrative, geographical, and regional place names to aid identification. A variety of pictorial symbols denote landforms such as glaciers, marshes and coral reefs, and man-made structures including roads, railroads, airports, and canals. International borders are shown by red lines. Where neighboring countries are in dispute, for example in parts of the Middle East, the maps show the *de facto* boundary between nations, regardless of the legal or historical situation. The

symbols are explained on the first page of the World Maps section of the atlas.

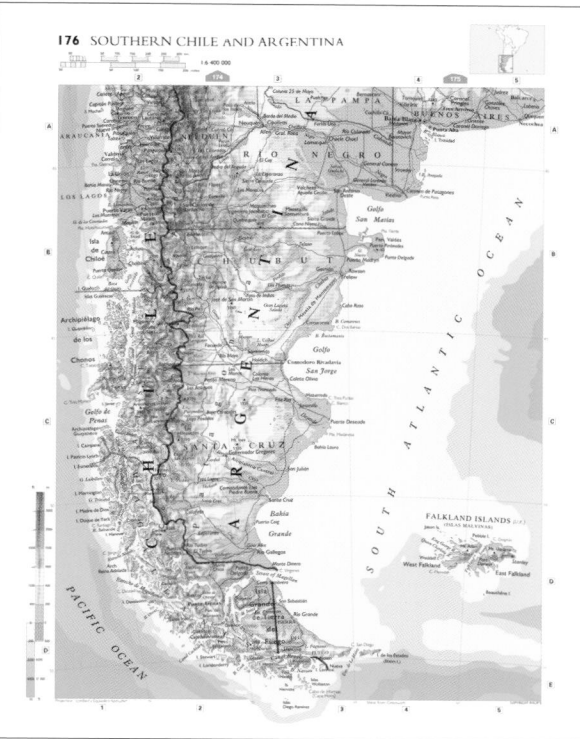

MAP SCALES

1:16 000 000
1 inch = 252 statute miles

The scale of each map is given in the numerical form known as the "representative fraction." The first figure is always one, signifying one unit of distance on the map; the second figure, usually in millions, is the number by which the map unit must be multiplied to give the equivalent distance on the Earth's surface. Calculations can easily be made in centimeters and kilometers, by dividing the Earth units figure by 100 000 (i.e. deleting the last five 0s). Thus 1:1 000 000 means 1 cm = 10 km. The calculation for inches and miles is more laborious, but 1 000 000 divided by 63 360 (the number of inches in a mile) shows that 1:1 000 000 means approximately 1 inch = 16 miles. The table below provides distance equivalents for scales down to 1:50 000 000.

LARGE SCALE		
1:1 000 000	1 cm = 10 km	1 inch = 16 miles
1:2 500 000	1 cm = 25 km	1 inch = 39.5 miles
1:5 000 000	1 cm = 50 km	1 inch = 79 miles
1:6 000 000	1 cm = 60 km	1 inch = 95 miles
1:8 000 000	1 cm = 80 km	1 inch = 126 miles
1:10 000 000	1 cm = 100 km	1 inch = 158 miles
1:15 000 000	1 cm = 150 km	1 inch = 237 miles
1:20 000 000	1 cm = 200 km	1 inch = 316 miles
1:50 000 000	1 cm = 500 km	1 inch = 790 miles
SMALL SCALE		

MEASURING DISTANCES

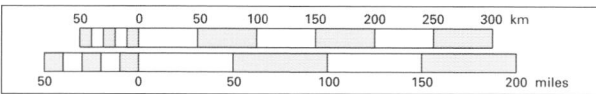

Although each map is accompanied by a scale bar, distances cannot always be measured with confidence because of the distortions involved in portraying the curved surface of the Earth on a flat page. As a general rule, the larger the map scale, the more accurate and reliable will be the distance measured. On small-scale maps such as those of the world and of entire continents, measurement may only be accurate along the "standard parallels," or central axes, and should not be attempted without considering the map projection.

MAP PROJECTIONS

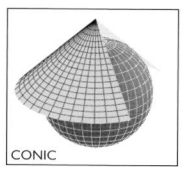 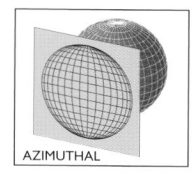 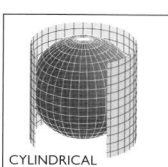

Unlike a globe, no flat map can give a true scale representation of the world in terms of area, shape, and position of every region. Each of the numerous systems that have been devised for projecting the curved surface of the Earth on to a flat page involves the sacrifice of accuracy in one or more of these elements. The variations in shape and position of land masses such as Alaska, Greenland and Australia, for example, can be quite dramatic when different projections are compared.

For this atlas, the guiding principle has been to select projections that involve the least distortion of size and distance. The projection used for each map is noted in the border. Most fall into one of three categories – conic, azimuthal, or cylindrical – whose basic concepts are shown above. Each involves plotting the forms of the Earth's surface on a grid of latitude and longitude lines, which may be shown as parallels, curves, or radiating spokes.

LATITUDE AND LONGITUDE

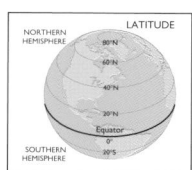 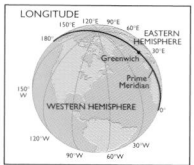 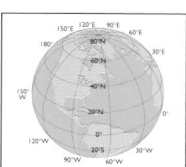

Accurate positioning of individual points on the Earth's surface is made possible by reference to the geometrical system of latitude and longitude. Latitude parallels are drawn west–east around the Earth and numbered by degrees north and south of the Equator, which is designated 0° of latitude. Longitude meridians are drawn north–south and numbered by degrees east and west of the prime meridian, 0° of longitude, which passes through Greenwich in England. By referring to these co-ordinates and their subdivisions of minutes (1/60th of a degree) and seconds (1/60th of a minute), any place on Earth can be located to within a few hundred yards. Latitude and longitude are indicated by blue lines on the maps; they are straight or curved according to the projection employed. Reference to these lines is the easiest way of determining the relative positions of places on different maps, and for plotting compass directions.

NAME FORMS

For ease of reference, both English and local name forms appear in the atlas. Oceans, seas, and countries are shown in English throughout the atlas; country names may be abbreviated to their commonly accepted form (e.g. Germany, not The Federal Republic of Germany). Conventional English forms are also used for place names on the smaller-scale maps of the continents. However, local name forms are used on all large-scale and regional maps, with the English form given in brackets only for important cities – the large-scale map of Russia and Central Asia thus shows Moskva (Moscow). For countries which do not use a Roman script, place names have been transcribed according to the systems adopted by the British and US Geographic Names Authorities. For China, the Pin Yin system has been used, with some more widely known forms appearing in brackets, as with Beijing (Peking). Both English and local names appear in the index, the English form being cross-referenced to the local form.

CONTENTS

WORLD STATISTICS: COUNTRIES

This alphabetical list includes all the countries and territories of the world. If a territory is not completely independent, the country it is associated with is named. The area figures give the total area of land, inland water and ice. The population figures are 2002 estimates. The annual income is the Gross Domestic Product per capita[†] in US dollars. The figures are the latest available, usually 2001 estimates.

Country/Territory	Area km² Thousands	Area miles² Thousands	Population Thousands	Capital	Annual Income US $
Afghanistan	652	252	27,756	Kabul	800
Albania	28.8	11.1	3,545	Tirana	3,800
Algeria	2,382	920	32,278	Algiers	5,600
American Samoa (US)	0.2	0.08	69	Pago Pago	8,000
Andorra	0.45	0.17	68	Andorra La Vella	19,000
Angola	1,247	481	10,593	Luanda	1,330
Anguilla (UK)	0.1	0.04	12	The Valley	8,600
Antigua & Barbuda	0.44	0.17	67	St John's	10,000
Argentina	2,767	1,068	37,813	Buenos Aires	12,000
Armenia	29.8	11.5	3,330	Yerevan	3,350
Aruba (Netherlands)	0.19	0.07	70	Oranjestad	28,000
Australia	7,687	2,968	19,547	Canberra	24,000
Austria	83.9	32.4	8,170	Vienna	27,000
Azerbaijan	86.6	33.4	7,798	Baku	3,100
Azores (Portugal)	2.2	0.87	234	Ponta Delgada	12,600
Bahamas	13.9	5.4	301	Nassau	16,800
Bahrain	0.68	0.26	656	Manama	13,000
Bangladesh	144	56	133,377	Dhaka	1,750
Barbados	0.43	0.17	277	Bridgetown	14,500
Belarus	207.6	80.1	10,335	Minsk	8,200
Belgium	30.5	11.8	10,275	Brussels	26,100
Belize	23	8.9	263	Belmopan	3,250
Benin	113	43	6,788	Porto-Novo	1,040
Bermuda (UK)	0.05	0.02	64	Hamilton	34,800
Bhutan	47	18.1	2,094	Thimphu	1,200
Bolivia	1,099	424	8,445	La Paz/Sucre	2,600
Bosnia-Herzegovina	51	20	3,964	Sarajevo	1,800
Botswana	582	225	1,591	Gaborone	7,800
Brazil	8,512	3,286	176,030	Brasília	7,400
Brunei	5.8	2.2	351	Bandar Seri Begawan	18,000
Bulgaria	111	43	7,621	Sofia	6,200
Burkina Faso	274	106	12,603	Ouagadougou	1,040
Burma (= Myanmar)	677	261	42,238	Rangoon	1,500
Burundi	27.8	10.7	6,373	Bujumbura	600
Cambodia	181	70	12,775	Phnom Penh	1,500
Cameroon	475	184	16,185	Yaoundé	1,700
Canada	9,976	3,852	31,902	Ottawa	27,700
Canary Is. (Spain)	7.3	2.8	1,694	Las Palmas/Santa Cruz	18,200
Cape Verde Is.	4	1.6	409	Praia	1,500
Cayman Is. (UK)	0.26	0.1	36	George Town	30,000
Central African Republic	623	241	3,643	Bangui	1,300
Chad	1,284	496	8,997	Ndjaména	1,030
Chile	757	292	15,499	Santiago	10,000
China	9,597	3,705	1,284,304	Beijing	4,300
Colombia	1,139	440	41,008	Bogotá	6,300
Comoros	2.2	0.86	614	Moroni	710
Congo	342	132	2,958	Brazzaville	900
Congo (Dem. Rep. of the)	2,345	905	55,225	Kinshasa	590
Cook Is. (NZ)	0.24	0.09	21	Avarua	5,000
Costa Rica	51.1	19.7	3,835	San José	8,500
Croatia	56.5	21.8	4,391	Zagreb	8,300
Cuba	111	43	11,224	Havana	2,300
Cyprus	9.3	3.6	767	Nicosia	11,500
Czech Republic	78.9	30.4	10,257	Prague	14,400
Denmark	43.1	16.6	5,369	Copenhagen	28,000
Djibouti	23.2	9	473	Djibouti	1,400
Dominica	0.75	0.29	70	Roseau	3,700
Dominican Republic	48.7	18.8	8,722	Santo Domingo	5,800
East Timor	14.9	5.7	953	Dili	500
Ecuador	284	109	13,447	Quito	3,000
Egypt	1,001	387	70,712	Cairo	3,700
El Salvador	21	8.1	6,354	San Salvador	4,600
Equatorial Guinea	28.1	10.8	498	Malabo	2,100
Eritrea	94	36	4,466	Asmara	740
Estonia	44.7	17.3	1,416	Tallinn	10,000
Ethiopia	1,128	436	67,673	Addis Ababa	700
Faroe Is. (Denmark)	1.4	0.54	46	Tórshavn	20,000
Fiji	18.3	7.1	856	Suva	5,200
Finland	338	131	5,184	Helsinki	25,800
France	552	213	59,766	Paris	25,400
French Guiana (France)	90	34.7	182	Cayenne	6,000
French Polynesia (France)	4	1.5	258	Papeete	5,000
Gabon	268	103	1,233	Libreville	5,500
Gambia, The	11.3	4.4	1,456	Banjul	1,770
Gaza Strip (OPT)*	0.36	0.14	1,226	–	630
Georgia	69.7	26.9	4,961	Tbilisi	3,100
Germany	357	138	83,252	Berlin	26,200
Ghana	239	92	20,244	Accra	1,980
Gibraltar (UK)	0.007	0.003	28	Gibraltar Town	17,500
Greece	132	51	10,645	Athens	17,900
Greenland (Denmark)	2,176	840	56	Nuuk (Godthåb)	20,000
Grenada	0.34	0.13	89	St George's	4,750
Guadeloupe (France)	1.7	0.66	436	Basse-Terre	9,000
Guam (US)	0.55	0.21	161	Agana	21,000
Guatemala	109	42	13,314	Guatemala City	3,700
Guinea	246	95	7,775	Conakry	1,970
Guinea-Bissau	36.1	13.9	1,345	Bissau	900
Guyana	215	83	698	Georgetown	3,600
Haiti	27.8	10.7	7,064	Port-au-Prince	1,700
Honduras	112	43	6,561	Tegucigalpa	2,600
Hong Kong (China)	1.1	0.4	7,303	–	25,000
Hungary	93	35.9	10,075	Budapest	12,000
Iceland	103	40	279	Reykjavik	24,800
India	3,288	1,269	1,045,845	New Delhi	2,500
Indonesia	1,890	730	231,328	Jakarta	3,000
Iran	1,648	636	66,623	Tehran	6,400
Iraq	438	169	24,002	Baghdad	2,500
Ireland	70.3	27.1	3,883	Dublin	27,300
Israel	20.6	7.96	6,030	Jerusalem	20,000
Italy	301	116	57,716	Rome	24,300
Ivory Coast (= Côte d'Ivoire)	322	125	16,805	Yamoussoukro	1,550
Jamaica	11	4.2	2,680	Kingston	3,700
Japan	378	146	126,975	Tokyo	27,200
Jordan	89.2	34.4	5,307	Amman	4,200
Kazakhstan	2,717	1,049	16,742	Astana	5,900
Kenya	580	224	31,139	Nairobi	1,000
Kiribati	0.72	0.28	96	Tarawa	840
Korea, North	121	47	22,224	Pyŏngyang	1,000
Korea, South	99	38.2	48,324	Seoul	18,000
Kuwait	17.8	6.9	2,112	Kuwait City	15,100
Kyrgyzstan	198.5	76.6	4,822	Bishkek	2,800
Laos	237	91	5,777	Vientiane	1,630
Latvia	65	25	2,367	Riga	7,800

*OPT = Occupied Palestinian Territory N/A = Not Available

Country/Territory	Area km² Thousands	Area miles² Thousands	Population Thousands	Capital	Annual Income US $
Lebanon	10.4	4	3,678	Beirut	5,200
Lesotho	30.4	11.7	2,208	Maseru	2,450
Liberia	111	43	3,288	Monrovia	1,100
Libya	1,760	679	5,369	Tripoli	7,600
Liechtenstein	0.16	0.06	33	Vaduz	23,000
Lithuania	65.2	25.2	3,601	Vilnius	7,600
Luxembourg	2.6	1	449	Luxembourg	43,400
Macau (China)	0.02	0.006	462	–	17,600
Macedonia (FYROM)	25.7	9.9	2,055	Skopje	4,400
Madagascar	587	227	16,473	Antananarivo	870
Madeira (Portugal)	0.81	0.31	241	Funchal	16,800
Malawi	118	46	10,702	Lilongwe	660
Malaysia	330	127	22,662	Kuala Lumpur/Putrajaya	9,000
Maldives	0.3	0.12	320	Malé	3,870
Mali	1,240	479	11,340	Bamako	840
Malta	0.32	0.12	397	Valletta	15,000
Marshall Is.	0.18	0.07	74	Dalap-Uliga-Darrit	1,600
Martinique (France)	1.1	0.42	422	Fort-de-France	11,000
Mauritania	1,030	398	2,829	Nouakchott	1,800
Mauritius	2	0.72	1,200	Port Louis	10,800
Mayotte (France)	0.37	0.14	171	Mamoundzou	600
Mexico	1,958	756	103,400	Mexico City	9,000
Micronesia, Fed. States of	0.7	0.27	136	Palikir	2,000
Moldova	33.7	13	4,435	Chişinău	2,550
Monaco	0.002	0.001	32	Monaco	27,000
Mongolia	1,567	605	2,694	Ulan Bator	1,770
Montserrat (UK)	0.1	0.04	8	Plymouth	2,400
Morocco	447	172	31,168	Rabat	3,700
Mozambique	802	309	19,608	Maputo	900
Namibia	825	318	1,821	Windhoek	4,500
Nauru	0.02	0.008	12	Yaren District	5,000
Nepal	141	54	25,874	Katmandu	1,400
Netherlands	41.5	16	16,068	Amsterdam/The Hague	25,800
Netherlands Antilles (Neths)	0.99	0.38	214	Willemstad	11,400
New Caledonia (France)	18.6	7.2	208	Nouméa	15,000
New Zealand	269	104	3,908	Wellington	19,500
Nicaragua	130	50	5,024	Managua	2,500
Niger	1,267	489	10,640	Niamey	820
Nigeria	924	357	129,935	Abuja	840
Northern Mariana Is. (US)	0.48	0.18	77	Saipan	12,500
Norway	324	125	4,525	Oslo	30,800
Oman	212	82	2,713	Muscat	8,200
Pakistan	796	307	147,663	Islamabad	2,100
Palau	0.46	0.18	19	Koror	9,000
Panama	77.1	29.8	2,882	Panamá	5,900
Papua New Guinea	463	179	5,172	Port Moresby	2,400
Paraguay	407	157	5,884	Asunción	4,600
Peru	1,285	496	27,950	Lima	4,800
Philippines	300	116	84,526	Manila	4,000
Poland	313	121	38,625	Warsaw	8,800
Portugal	92.4	35.7	9,609	Lisbon	17,300
Puerto Rico (US)	9	3.5	3,958	San Juan	11,200
Qatar	11	4.2	793	Doha	21,200
Réunion (France)	2.5	0.97	744	St-Denis	4,800
Romania	238	92	22,318	Bucharest	6,800
Russia	17,075	6,592	144,979	Moscow	8,300
Rwanda	26.3	10.2	7,398	Kigali	1,000
St Kitts & Nevis	0.36	0.14	39	Basseterre	8,700
St Lucia	0.62	0.24	160	Castries	4,400
St Vincent & Grenadines	0.39	0.15	116	Kingstown	2,900
Samoa	2.8	1.1	179	Apia	3,500
San Marino	0.06	0.02	28	San Marino	34,600
São Tomé & Príncipe	0.96	0.37	170	São Tomé	1,200
Saudi Arabia	2,150	830	23,513	Riyadh	10,600
Senegal	197	76	10,590	Dakar	1,580
Serbia & Montenegro	102.3	39.5	10,657	Belgrade	2,250
Seychelles	0.46	0.18	80	Victoria	7,600
Sierra Leone	71.7	27.7	5,615	Freetown	500
Singapore	0.62	0.24	4,453	Singapore	24,700
Slovak Republic	49	18.9	5,422	Bratislava	11,500
Slovenia	20.3	7.8	1,933	Ljubljana	16,000
Solomon Is.	28.9	11.2	495	Honiara	1,700
Somalia	638	246	7,753	Mogadishu	550
South Africa	1,220	471	43,648	C. Town/Pretoria/Bloem.	9,400
Spain	505	195	38,383	Madrid	18,900
Sri Lanka	65.6	25.3	19,577	Colombo	3,250
Sudan	2,506	967	37,090	Khartoum	1,360
Suriname	163	63	436	Paramaribo	3,500
Swaziland	17.4	6.7	1,124	Mbabane	4,200
Sweden	450	174	8,877	Stockholm	24,700
Switzerland	41.3	15.9	7,302	Bern	31,100
Syria	185	71	17,156	Damascus	3,200
Taiwan	36	13.9	22,548	Taipei	17,200
Tajikistan	143.1	55.2	6,720	Dushanbe	1,140
Tanzania	945	365	37,188	Dodoma	610
Thailand	513	198	62,354	Bangkok	6,600
Togo	56.8	21.9	5,286	Lomé	1,500
Tonga	0.75	0.29	106	Nuku'alofa	2,200
Trinidad & Tobago	5.1	2	1,164	Port of Spain	9,000
Tunisia	164	63	9,816	Tunis	6,600
Turkey	779	301	67,309	Ankara	6,700
Turkmenistan	488.1	188.5	4,689	Ashkhabad	4,700
Turks & Caicos Is. (UK)	0.43	0.17	19	Cockburn Town	7,300
Tuvalu	0.03	0.01	11	Fongafale	1,100
Uganda	236	91	24,699	Kampala	1,200
Ukraine	603.7	233.1	48,396	Kiev	4,200
United Arab Emirates	83.6	32.3	2,446	Abu Dhabi	21,100
United Kingdom	243.3	94	59,778	London	24,700
United States of America	9,373	3,619	280,562	Washington, DC	36,300
Uruguay	177	68	3,387	Montevideo	9,200
Uzbekistan	447.4	172.7	25,563	Tashkent	2,500
Vanuatu	12.2	4.7	196	Port-Vila	1,300
Vatican City	0.0004	0.0002	1	Vatican City	N/A
Venezuela	912	352	24,288	Caracas	6,100
Vietnam	332	127	81,098	Hanoi	2,100
Virgin Is. (UK)	0.15	0.06	21	Road Town	16,000
Virgin Is. (US)	0.34	0.13	123	Charlotte Amalie	15,000
Wallis & Futuna Is. (France)	0.2	0.08	16	Mata-Utu	2,000
West Bank (OPT)*	5.86	2.26	2,164	–	1,000
Western Sahara	266	103	256	El Aaiún	N/A
Yemen	528	204	18,701	Sana	820
Zambia	753	291	9,959	Lusaka	870
Zimbabwe	391	151	11,377	Harare	2,450

† Gross Domestic Product per capita has been measured using the purchasing power parity method. This enables comparisons to be made between countries through their purchasing power (in US dollars), showing real price levels of goods and services rather than using currency exchange rates.

WORLD STATISTICS: PHYSICAL DIMENSIONS

Each topic list is divided into continents and within a continent the items are listed in order of size. The bottom part of many of the lists is selective in order to give examples from as many different countries as possible. The order of the continents is the same as in the atlas, beginning with Europe and ending with South America. The figures are rounded as appropriate.

World, Continents, Oceans

	km²	miles²	%
The World	509,450,000	196,672,000	–
Land	149,450,000	57,688,000	29.3
Water	360,000,000	138,984,000	70.7
Asia	44,500,000	17,177,000	29.8
Africa	30,302,000	11,697,000	20.3
North America	24,241,000	9,357,000	16.2
South America	17,793,000	6,868,000	11.9
Antarctica	14,100,000	5,443,000	9.4
Europe	9,957,000	3,843,000	6.7
Australia & Oceania	8,557,000	3,303,000	5.7
Pacific Ocean	179,679,000	69,356,000	49.9
Atlantic Ocean	92,373,000	35,657,000	25.7
Indian Ocean	73,917,000	28,532,000	20.5
Arctic Ocean	14,090,000	5,439,000	3.9

Ocean Depths

Atlantic Ocean

	m	ft
Puerto Rico (Milwaukee) Deep	9,220	30,249
Cayman Trench	7,680	25,197
Gulf of Mexico	5,203	17,070
Mediterranean Sea	5,121	16,801
Black Sea	2,211	7,254
North Sea	660	2,165

Indian Ocean

	m	ft
Java Trench	7,450	24,442
Red Sea	2,635	8,454

Pacific Ocean

	m	ft
Mariana Trench	11,022	36,161
Tonga Trench	10,882	35,702
Japan Trench	10,554	34,626
Kuril Trench	10,542	34,587

Arctic Ocean

	m	ft
Molloy Deep	5,608	18,399

Mountains

Europe

		m	ft
Elbrus	Russia	5,642	18,510
Mont Blanc	France/Italy	4,807	15,771
Monte Rosa	Italy/Switzerland	4,634	15,203
Dom	Switzerland	4,545	14,911
Liskamm	Switzerland	4,527	14,852
Weisshorn	Switzerland	4,505	14,780
Taschorn	Switzerland	4,490	14,730
Matterhorn/Cervino	Italy/Switzerland	4,478	14,691
Mont Maudit	France/Italy	4,465	14,649
Dent Blanche	Switzerland	4,356	14,291
Nadelhorn	Switzerland	4,327	14,196
Grandes Jorasses	France/Italy	4,208	13,806
Jungfrau	Switzerland	4,158	13,642
Grossglockner	Austria	3,797	12,457
Mulhacén	Spain	3,478	11,411
Zugspitze	Germany	2,962	9,718
Olympus	Greece	2,917	9,570
Triglav	Slovenia	2,863	9,393
Gerlachovka	Slovak Republic	2,655	8,711
Galdhöpiggen	Norway	2,468	8,100
Kebnekaise	Sweden	2,117	6,946
Ben Nevis	UK	1,343	4,406

Asia

		m	ft
Everest	China/Nepal	8,850	29,035
K2 (Godwin Austen)	China/Kashmir	8,611	28,251
Kanchenjunga	India/Nepal	8,598	28,208
Lhotse	China/Nepal	8,516	27,939
Makalu	China/Nepal	8,481	27,824
Cho Oyu	China/Nepal	8,201	26,906
Dhaulagiri	Nepal	8,172	26,811
Manaslu	Nepal	8,156	26,758
Nanga Parbat	Kashmir	8,126	26,660
Annapurna	Nepal	8,078	26,502
Gasherbrum	China/Kashmir	8,068	26,469
Broad Peak	China/Kashmir	8,051	26,414
Xixabangma	China	8,012	26,286
Kangbachen	India/Nepal	7,902	25,925
Trivor	Pakistan	7,720	25,328
Pik Kommunizma	Tajikistan	7,495	24,590
Demavend	Iran	5,604	18,386
Ararat	Turkey	5,165	16,945
Gunong Kinabalu	Malaysia (Borneo)	4,101	13,455
Fuji-San	Japan	3,776	12,388

Africa

		m	ft
Kilimanjaro	Tanzania	5,895	19,340
Mt Kenya	Kenya	5,199	17,057
Ruwenzori (Margherita)	Ug./Congo (D.R.)	5,109	16,762
Ras Dashan	Ethiopia	4,620	15,157
Meru	Tanzania	4,565	14,977
Karisimbi	Rwanda/Congo (D.R.)	4,507	14,787
Mt Elgon	Kenya/Uganda	4,321	14,176
Batu	Ethiopia	4,307	14,130
Toubkal	Morocco	4,165	13,665
Mt Cameroon	Cameroon	4,070	13,353

Oceania

		m	ft
Puncak Jaya	Indonesia	5,030	16,503

		m	ft
Puncak Trikora	Indonesia	4,750	15,584
Puncak Mandala	Indonesia	4,702	15,427
Mt Wilhelm	Papua New Guinea	4,508	14,790
Mauna Kea	USA (Hawaii)	4,205	13,796
Mauna Loa	USA (Hawaii)	4,169	13,681
Mt Cook (Aoraki)	New Zealand	3,753	12,313
Mt Kosciuszko	Australia	2,237	7,339

North America

		m	ft
Mt McKinley (Denali)	USA (Alaska)	6,194	20,321
Mt Logan	Canada	5,959	19,551
Pico de Orizaba	Mexico	5,610	18,405
Mt St Elias	USA/Canada	5,489	18,008
Popocatepetl	Mexico	5,452	17,887
Mt Foraker	USA (Alaska)	5,304	17,401
Ixtaccihuatl	Mexico	5,286	17,342
Lucania	Canada	5,227	17,149
Mt Steele	Canada	5,073	16,644
Mt Bona	USA (Alaska)	5,005	16,420
Mt Whitney	USA	4,418	14,495
Tajumulco	Guatemala	4,220	13,845
Chirripó Grande	Costa Rica	3,837	12,589
Pico Duarte	Dominican Rep.	3,175	10,417

South America

		m	ft
Aconcagua	Argentina	6,962	22,841
Bonete	Argentina	6,872	22,546
Ojos del Salado	Argentina/Chile	6,863	22,516
Pissis	Argentina	6,779	22,241
Mercedario	Argentina/Chile	6,770	22,211
Huascaran	Peru	6,768	22,204
Llullaillaco	Argentina/Chile	6,723	22,057
Nudo de Cachi	Argentina	6,720	22,047
Yerupaja	Peru	6,632	21,758
Sajama	Bolivia	6,542	21,463
Chimborazo	Ecuador	6,267	20,561
Pico Colon	Colombia	5,800	19,029
Pico Bolivar	Venezuela	5,007	16,427

Antarctica

	m	ft
Vinson Massif	4,897	16,066
Mt Kirkpatrick	4,528	14,855

Rivers

Europe

		km	miles
Volga	Caspian Sea	3,700	2,300
Danube	Black Sea	2,850	1,770
Ural	Caspian Sea	2,535	1,575
Dnepr (Dnipro)	Black Sea	2,285	1,420
Kama	Volga	2,030	1,260
Don	Black Sea	1,990	1,240
Petchora	Arctic Ocean	1,790	1,110
Oka	Volga	1,480	920
Dnister (Dniester)	Black Sea	1,400	870
Vyatka	Kama	1,370	850
Rhine	North Sea	1,320	820
N. Dvina	Arctic Ocean	1,290	800
Elbe	North Sea	1,145	710

Asia

		km	miles
Yangtze	Pacific Ocean	6,380	3,960
Yenisey–Angara	Arctic Ocean	5,550	3,445
Huang He	Pacific Ocean	5,464	3,395
Ob–Irtysh	Arctic Ocean	5,410	3,360
Mekong	Pacific Ocean	4,500	2,795
Amur	Pacific Ocean	4,400	2,730
Lena	Arctic Ocean	4,400	2,730
Irtysh	Ob	4,250	2,640
Yenisey	Arctic Ocean	4,090	2,540
Ob	Arctic Ocean	3,680	2,285
Indus	Indian Ocean	3,100	1,925
Brahmaputra	Indian Ocean	2,900	1,800
Syrdarya	Aral Sea	2,860	1,775
Salween	Indian Ocean	2,800	1,740
Euphrates	Indian Ocean	2,700	1,675
Amudarya	Aral Sea	2,540	1,575

Africa

		km	miles
Nile	Mediterranean	6,670	4,140
Congo	Atlantic Ocean	4,670	2,900
Niger	Atlantic Ocean	4,180	2,595
Zambezi	Indian Ocean	3,540	2,200
Oubangi/Uele	Congo (D.R.)	2,250	1,400
Kasai	Congo (D.R.)	1,950	1,210
Shaballe	Indian Ocean	1,930	1,200
Orange	Atlantic Ocean	1,860	1,155
Cubango	Okavango Delta	1,800	1,120
Limpopo	Indian Ocean	1,600	995
Senegal	Atlantic Ocean	1,600	995

Australia

		km	miles
Murray–Darling	Indian Ocean	3,750	2,330
Darling	Murray	3,070	1,905
Murray	Indian Ocean	2,575	1,600
Murrumbidgee	Murray	1,690	1,050

North America

		km	miles
Mississippi–Missouri	Gulf of Mexico	6,020	3,740
Mackenzie	Arctic Ocean	4,240	2,630
Mississippi	Gulf of Mexico	3,780	2,350
Missouri	Mississippi	3,780	2,350
Yukon	Pacific Ocean	3,185	1,980
Rio Grande	Gulf of Mexico	3,030	1,880
Arkansas	Mississippi	2,340	1,450

		m	ft
Colorado	Pacific Ocean	2,330	1,445
Red	Mississippi	2,040	1,270
Columbia	Pacific Ocean	1,950	1,210
Saskatchewan	Lake Winnipeg	1,940	1,205

South America

		km	miles
Amazon	Atlantic Ocean	6,450	4,010
Paraná–Plate	Atlantic Ocean	4,500	2,800
Purus	Amazon	3,350	2,080
Madeira	Amazon	3,200	1,990
São Francisco	Atlantic Ocean	2,900	1,800
Paraná	Plate	2,800	1,740
Tocantins	Atlantic Ocean	2,750	1,710
Paraguay	Paraná	2,550	1,580
Orinoco	Atlantic Ocean	2,500	1,550
Pilcomayo	Paraná	2,500	1,550
Araguaia	Tocantins	2,250	1,400

Lakes

Europe

		km²	miles²
Lake Ladoga	Russia	17,700	6,800
Lake Onega	Russia	9,700	3,700
Saimaa system	Finland	8,000	3,100
Vänern	Sweden	5,500	2,100

Asia

		km²	miles²
Caspian Sea	Asia	371,800	143,550
Lake Baykal	Russia	30,500	11,780
Aral Sea	Kazakhstan/Uzbekistan	28,687	11,086
Tonlé Sap	Cambodia	20,000	7,700
Lake Balqash	Kazakhstan	18,500	7,100

Africa

		km²	miles²
Lake Victoria	East Africa	68,000	26,000
Lake Tanganyika	Central Africa	33,000	13,000
Lake Malawi/Nyasa	East Africa	29,600	11,430
Lake Chad	Central Africa	25,000	9,700
Lake Turkana	Ethiopia/Kenya	8,500	3,300
Lake Volta	Ghana	8,500	3,300

Australia

		km²	miles²
Lake Eyre	Australia	8,900	3,400
Lake Torrens	Australia	5,800	2,200
Lake Gairdner	Australia	4,800	1,900

North America

		km²	miles²
Lake Superior	Canada/USA	82,350	31,800
Lake Huron	Canada/USA	59,600	23,010
Lake Michigan	USA	58,000	22,400
Great Bear Lake	Canada	31,800	12,280
Great Slave Lake	Canada	28,500	11,000
Lake Erie	Canada/USA	25,700	9,900
Lake Winnipeg	Canada	24,400	9,400
Lake Ontario	Canada/USA	19,500	7,500
Lake Nicaragua	Nicaragua	8,200	3,200

South America

		km²	miles²
Lake Titicaca	Bolivia/Peru	8,300	3,200
Lake Poopo	Bolivia	2,800	1,100

Islands

Europe

		km²	miles²
Great Britain	UK	229,880	88,700
Iceland	Atlantic Ocean	103,000	39,800
Ireland	Ireland/UK	84,400	32,600
Novaya Zemlya (N.)	Russia	48,200	18,600
Sicily	Italy	25,500	9,800
Corsica	France	8,700	3,400

Asia

		km²	miles²
Borneo	Southeast Asia	744,360	287,400
Sumatra	Indonesia	473,600	182,860
Honshu	Japan	230,500	88,980
Sulawesi (Celebes)	Indonesia	189,000	73,000
Java	Indonesia	126,700	48,900
Luzon	Philippines	104,700	40,400
Hokkaido	Japan	78,400	30,300

Africa

		km²	miles²
Madagascar	Indian Ocean	587,040	226,660
Socotra	Indian Ocean	3,600	1,400
Réunion	Indian Ocean	2,500	965

Oceania

		km²	miles²
New Guinea	Indonesia/Papua NG	821,030	317,000
New Zealand (S.)	Pacific Ocean	150,500	58,100
New Zealand (N.)	Pacific Ocean	114,700	44,300
Tasmania	Australia	67,800	26,200
Hawaii	Pacific Ocean	10,450	4,000

North America

		km²	miles²
Greenland	Atlantic Ocean	2,175,600	839,800
Baffin Is.	Canada	508,000	196,100
Victoria Is.	Canada	212,200	81,900
Ellesmere Is.	Canada	212,000	81,800
Cuba	Caribbean Sea	110,860	42,800
Hispaniola	Dominican Rep./Haiti	76,200	29,400
Jamaica	Caribbean Sea	11,400	4,400
Puerto Rico	Atlantic Ocean	8,900	3,400

South America

		km²	miles²
Tierra del Fuego	Argentina/Chile	47,000	18,100
Falkland Is. (E.)	Atlantic Ocean	6,800	2,600

WORLD: REGIONS IN THE NEWS

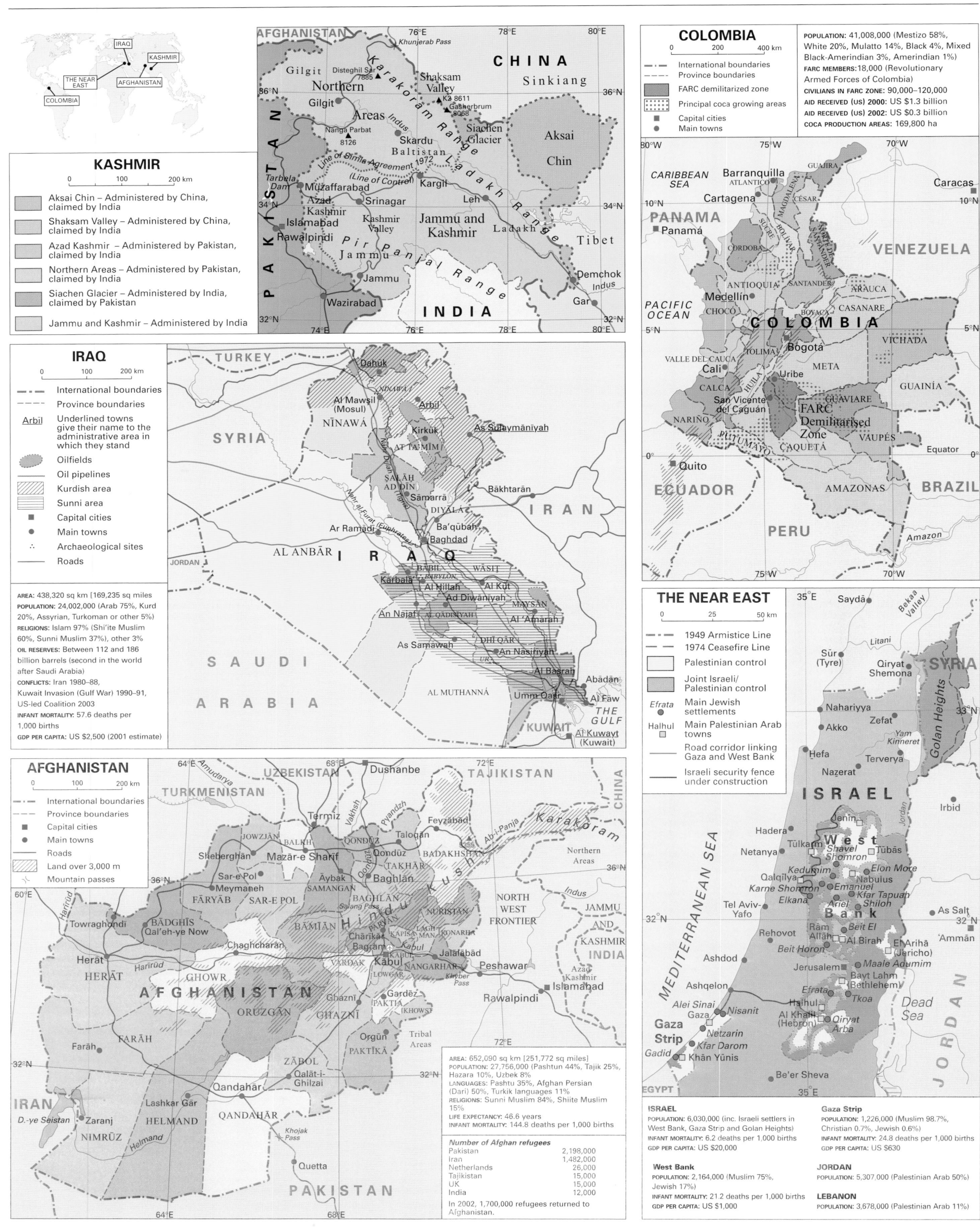

KASHMIR

0   100   200 km

Aksai Chin – Administered by China, claimed by India

Shaksam Valley – Administered by China, claimed by India

Azad Kashmir – Administered by Pakistan, claimed by India

Northern Areas – Administered by Pakistan, claimed by India

Siachen Glacier – Administered by India, claimed by Pakistan

Jammu and Kashmir – Administered by India

IRAQ

0   100   200 km

— · — International boundaries

— — — Province boundaries

Arbil Underlined towns give their name to the administrative area in which they stand

Oilfields

Oil pipelines

Kurdish area

Sunni area

■ Capital cities

● Main towns

∴ Archaeological sites

— Roads

AREA: 438,320 sq km (169,235 sq miles)
POPULATION: 24,002,000 (Arab 75%, Kurd 20%, Assyrian, Turkoman or other 5%)
RELIGIONS: Islam 97% (Shi'ite Muslim 60%, Sunni Muslim 37%), other 3%
OIL RESERVES: Between 112 and 186 billion barrels (second in the world after Saudi Arabia)
CONFLICTS: Iran 1980–88, Kuwait Invasion (Gulf War) 1990–91, US-led Coalition 2003
INFANT MORTALITY: 57.6 deaths per 1,000 births
GDP PER CAPITA: US $2,500 (2001 estimate)

AFGHANISTAN

0   100   200 km

— · — International boundaries

— — — Province boundaries

■ Capital cities

● Main towns

— Roads

Land over 3,000 m

↗ Mountain passes

AREA: 652,090 sq km (251,772 sq miles)
POPULATION: 27,756,000 (Pashtun 44%, Tajik 25%, Hazara 10%, Uzbek 8%)
LANGUAGES: Pashtu 35%, Afghan Persian (Dari) 50%, Turkik languages 11%
RELIGIONS: Sunni Muslim 84%, Shiite Muslim 15%
LIFE EXPECTANCY: 46.6 years
INFANT MORTALITY: 144.8 deaths per 1,000 births

Number of Afghan refugees

Pakistan	2,198,000
Iran	1,482,000
Netherlands	26,000
Tajikistan	15,000
UK	15,000
India	12,000

In 2002, 1,700,000 refugees returned to Afghanistan.

COLOMBIA

0   200   400 km

POPULATION: 41,008,000 (Mestizo 58%, White 20%, Mulatto 14%, Black 4%, Mixed Black-Amerindian 3%, Amerindian 1%)
FARC MEMBERS: 18,000 (Revolutionary Armed Forces of Colombia)
CIVILIANS IN FARC ZONE: 90,000–120,000
AID RECEIVED (US) 2000: US $1.3 billion
AID RECEIVED (US) 2002: US $0.3 billion
COCA PRODUCTION AREAS: 169,800 ha

— — — International boundaries

— · — Province boundaries

FARC demilitarized zone

Principal coca growing areas

■ Capital cities

● Main towns

THE NEAR EAST

0   25   50 km

— · — 1949 Armistice Line

— — — 1974 Ceasefire Line

Palestinian control

Joint Israeli/ Palestinian control

Efrata ● Main Jewish settlements

Halhul ☐ Main Palestinian Arab towns

Road corridor linking Gaza and West Bank

Israeli security fence under construction

ISRAEL
POPULATION: 6,030,000 (inc. Israeli settlers in West Bank, Gaza Strip and Golan Heights)
INFANT MORTALITY: 6.2 deaths per 1,000 births
GDP PER CAPITA: US $20,000

West Bank
POPULATION: 2,164,000 (Muslim 75%, Jewish 17%)
INFANT MORTALITY: 21.2 deaths per 1,000 births
GDP PER CAPITA: US $1,000

Gaza Strip
POPULATION: 1,226,000 (Muslim 98.7%, Christian 0.7%, Jewish 0.6%)
INFANT MORTALITY: 24.8 deaths per 1,000 births
GDP PER CAPITA: US $630

JORDAN
POPULATION: 5,307,000 (Palestinian Arab 50%)

LEBANON
POPULATION: 3,678,000 (Palestinian Arab 11%)

IMAGES OF EARTH

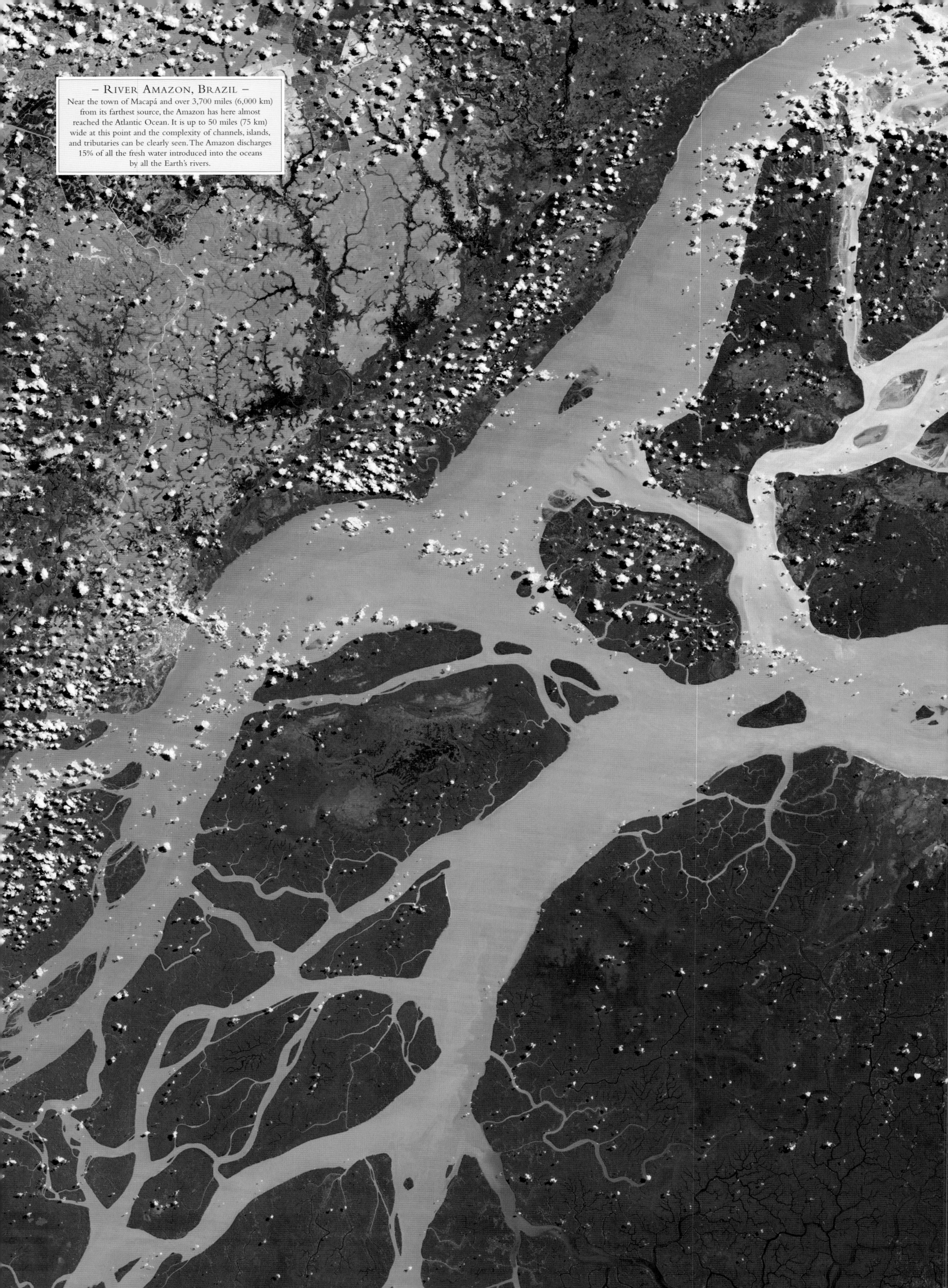

– RIVER AMAZON, BRAZIL –
Near the town of Macapá and over 3,700 miles (6,000 km)
from its farthest source, the Amazon has here almost
reached the Atlantic Ocean. It is up to 50 miles (75 km)
wide at this point and the complexity of channels, islands,
and tributaries can be clearly seen. The Amazon discharges
15% of all the fresh water introduced into the oceans
by all the Earth's rivers.

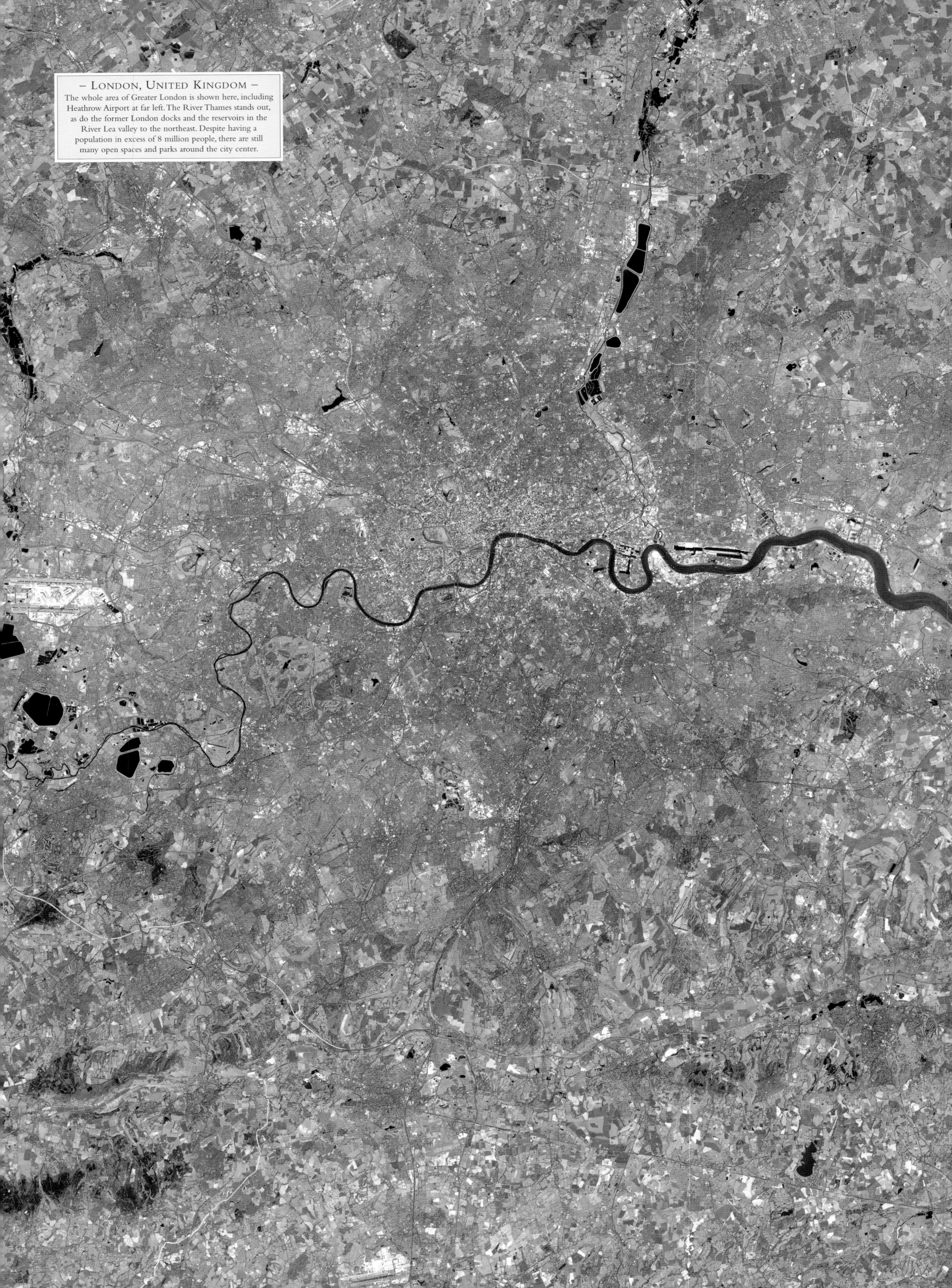

— NAPLES, ITALY —

The city, situated in the northeastern corner of the
Bay of Naples, has a population in excess of 1 million
inhabitants. The cone of the active volcano Vesuvius,
4,200 ft (1,281 m) high, dominates the bay. Evidence of
other volcanic activity can also be seen to the west of the
town in the area known as the Phlegraean Fields. Pompei,
once buried by its lava, lies near the mountains to the
southeast. On the southern peninsular is the town
of Sorrento, and beyond, the island of Capri.

— CAIRO, EGYPT —

The largest city in Africa with almost 10 million inhabitants,
Cairo evolved on the eastern bank of the River Nile, near
its delta. This image clearly shows the differences between the
arid desert areas to the southeast and southwest, the fertile
lands of the Nile flood plain, and the urban area itself.
The shadows of the Pyramids on the Giza Plateau can
be seen on the left-hand edge of the cultivated area,
below where the road crosses it.

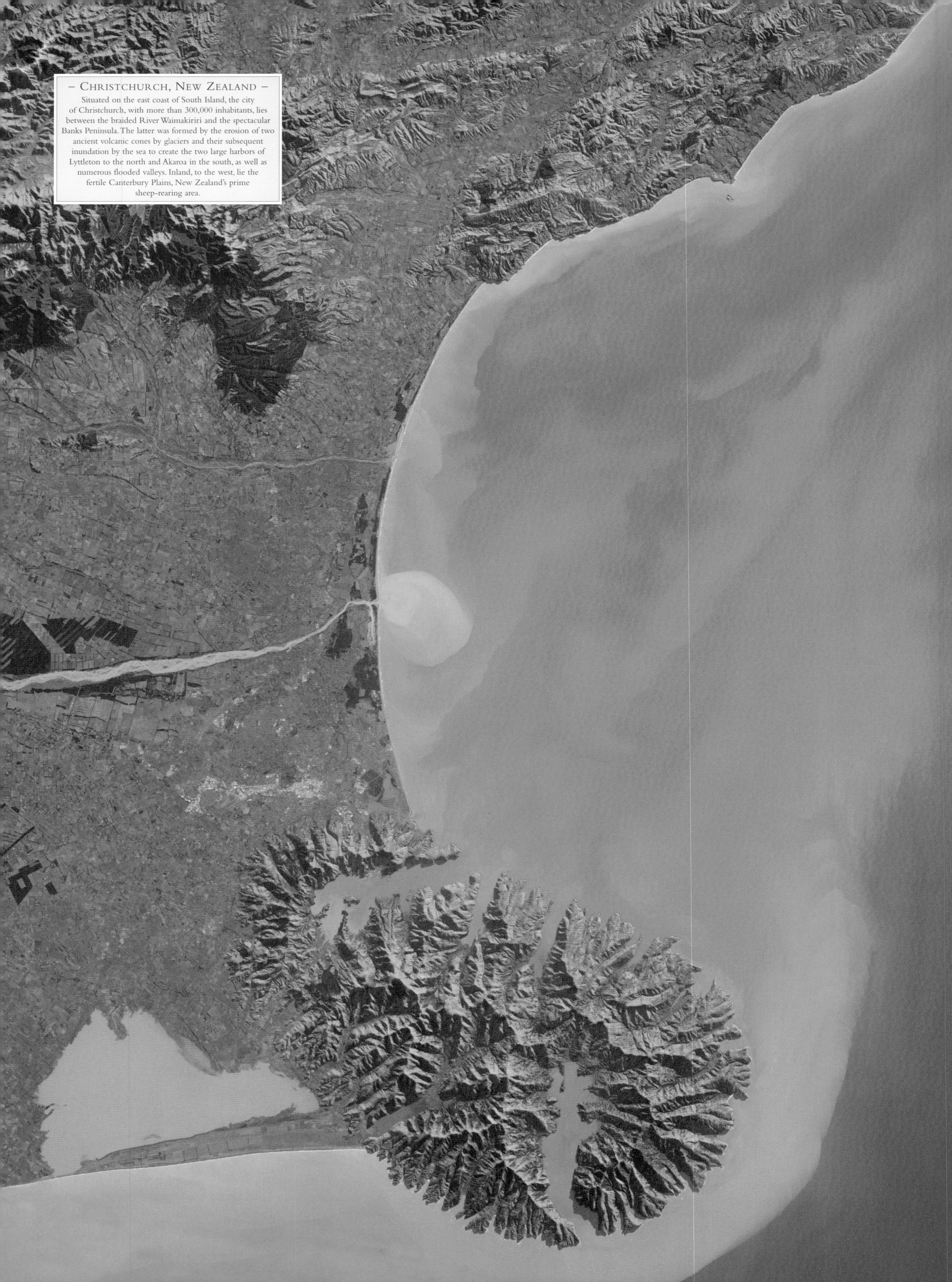

THE GAZETTEER OF NATIONS

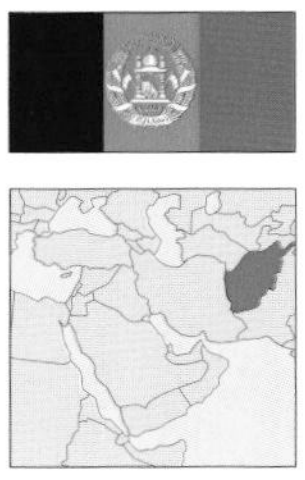

AFGHANISTAN

GEOGRAPHY The Republic of Afghanistan is a landlocked, mountainous country in southern Asia. The central highlands reach a height of more than 22,966 ft [7,000 m] in the east and make up nearly three-quarters of Afghanistan. The main range is the Hindu Kush, which is cut by deep, fertile valleys.

In winter, northerly winds bring cold, snowy weather to the mountains, but summers are hot and dry.

POLITICS & ECONOMY The modern history of Afghanistan began in 1747, when the various tribes in the area united for the first time. In the 19th century, Russia and Britain struggled for control of the country. Following Britain's withdrawal in 1919, Afghanistan became fully independent. Soviet troops invaded Afghanistan in 1979 to support a socialist regime in Kabul, but they withdrew in 1989. By the early 21st century, a group called the Taliban ("Islamic students") controlled 90% of the country. In 2001, following the refusal of the Taliban government to hand over the terrorist leader Osama bin Laden, an international force overthrew the Taliban regime and a coalition government was set up.

Afghanistan is one of the world's poorest countries. About 60% of the people live by farming. Many people are seminomadic herders. Natural gas is produced, together with some coal, copper, gold, precious stones and salt.

AREA 251,772 sq mi [652,090 sq km] **POPULATION** 27,756,000
CAPITAL (POPULATION) Kabul (1,565,000)
GOVERNMENT Islamic state **ETHNIC GROUPS** Pashtun ("Pathan") 38%, Tajik 25%, Hazara 19%, Uzbek 6%, others 12%
LANGUAGES Pashtu, Dari/Persian (both official), Uzbek
RELIGIONS Islam (Sunni Muslim 84%, Shiite Muslim 15%)
CURRENCY Afghani = 100 puls

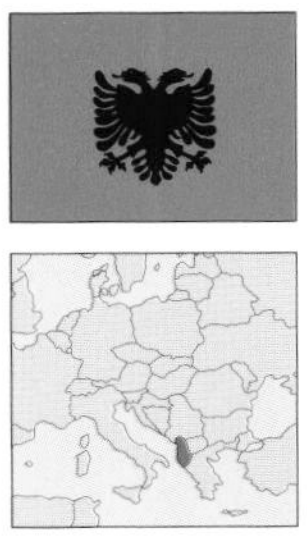

ALBANIA

GEOGRAPHY The Republic of Albania lies in the Balkan peninsula, facing the Adriatic Sea. About 70% of the land is mountainous, but most Albanians live in the west on the coastal lowlands.

The coastal areas of Albania experience a typical Mediterranean climate, with fairly dry, sunny summers and cool, moist winters. The mountains have a severe climate, with heavy winter snowfalls.

POLITICS & ECONOMY Albania is one of Europe's poorest nations. A former Communist country, Albania adopted a multiparty system in the early 1990s. The change proved difficult. But after elections in 1997, a socialist government committed to a market system took office. In 2001, the stability of the region was threatened when Albanian-speaking Kosovars and Macedonians, many of whom favored the creation of a Greater Macedonia, fought with government forces in northwestern Macedonia.

In the early 1990s, agriculture employed 56% of the people. The land was divided into large collective and state farms, but private ownership has been encouraged since 1991. Albania has some minerals and chromite, copper and nickel are exported.

AREA 11,100 sq mi [28,750 sq km] **POPULATION** 3,545,000
CAPITAL (POPULATION) Tirana (251,000) **GOVERNMENT** Multiparty republic **ETHNIC GROUPS** Albanian 95%, Greek 3%, Macedonian, Vlachs, Gypsy **LANGUAGES** Albanian (official) **RELIGIONS** Many people say they are non-believers; of the believers, 65% follow Islam and 33% follow Christianity (Orthodox 20%, Roman Catholic 13%)
CURRENCY Lek = 100 qindars

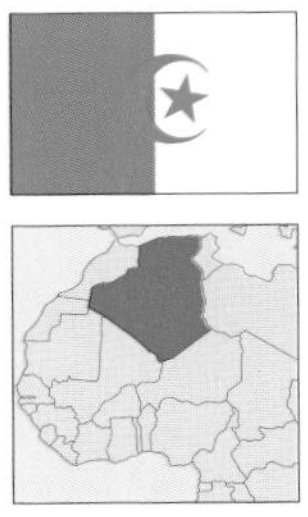

ALGERIA

GEOGRAPHY The People's Democratic Republic of Algeria is Africa's second largest country after Sudan. Most Algerians live in the north, on the fertile coastal plains and hill country bordering the Mediterranean Sea. Four-fifths of Algeria is in the Sahara. The coast has a Mediterranean climate, but the arid Sahara is hot by day and cool at night.

POLITICS & ECONOMY France ruled Algeria from 1830 until 1962, when the socialist FLN (National Liberation Front) formed a one-party government. Following the recognition of opposition parties in 1989, a Muslim group, the FIS (Islamic Salvation Front), won an election in 1991. The FLN canceled the elections and civil conflict broke out. About 100,000 people were killed in the 1990s. In 1999, following the withdrawal of the other candidates who alleged fraud, Abdelaziz Bouteflika, who was assumed to be favored by the army, was elected president. Bouteflika's peace offensive reduced the violence, but sporadic conflict continued into 2003.

Algeria is a developing country, whose chief resources are oil and natural gas, which were discovered in the Sahara in 1956. The natural gas reserves are among the world's largest, and gas and oil account for 90% of Algeria's exports. Cement, iron and steel, textiles and vehicles are manufactured. Barley, citrus fruits, dates, potatoes and wheat are the major crops.

AREA 919,590 sq mi [2,381,740 sq km] **POPULATION** 32,278,000
CAPITAL (POPULATION) Algiers (1,722,000)
GOVERNMENT Socialist republic **ETHNIC GROUPS** Arab-Berber 99%
LANGUAGES Arabic and Berber (both official), French **RELIGIONS** Sunni Muslim 99% **CURRENCY** Algerian dinar = 100 centimes

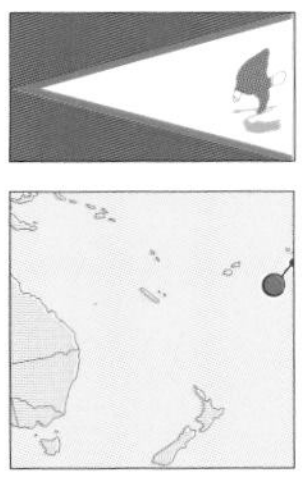

AMERICAN SAMOA

An "unincorporated territory" of the United States, American Samoa lies in the south-central Pacific Ocean.

AREA 77 sq mi [200 sq km]
POPULATION 69,000 **CAPITAL** Pago Pago

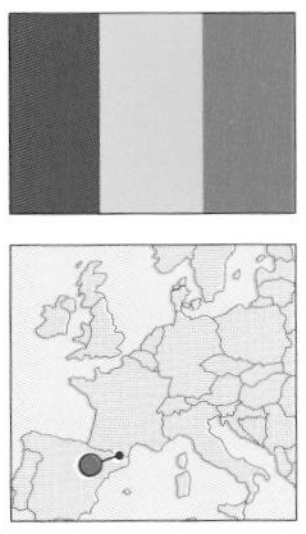

ANDORRA

A mini-state situated in the Pyrenees Mountains, Andorra is a co-principality whose main activity is tourism. Most Andorrans live in the six valleys (the Valls) that drain into the River Valira.

AREA 175 sq mi [453 sq km]
POPULATION 68,000 **CAPITAL** Andorra La Vella

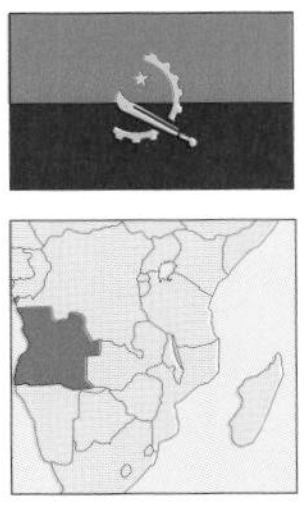

ANGOLA

GEOGRAPHY The Republic of Angola is a large country in southwestern Africa. Much of the country is part of the plateau that forms most of southern Africa, with a narrow coastal plain in the west.

Angola has a tropical climate, with temperatures of over 68°F [20°C] throughout the year, though the highest areas are cooler. The coastal regions are dry, but the rainfall increases to the north and east.

POLITICS & ECONOMY A former Portuguese colony, Angola gained its independence in 1975, after which rival nationalist forces began a struggle for power. A long-running civil war developed which, despite a ceasefire in the mid-1990s, continued until 2002, when the rebel leader, Jonas Savimbi, was killed in action and his successors negotiated peace.

Angola is a developing country, where 70% of the people are poor farmers. The main food crops are cassava and maize. Coffee is exported. Angola has much economic potential. It has oil reserves near Luanda and in the Cabinda enclave, which is separated from Angola by a strip of land belonging to Congo (Dem. Rep.). Oil is the leading export. Angola also produces diamonds and has reserves of copper, manganese and phosphates.

AREA 481,351 sq mi [1,246,700 sq km] **POPULATION** 10,593,000
CAPITAL (POPULATION) Luanda (2,250,000)
GOVERNMENT Multiparty republic
ETHNIC GROUPS Ovimbundu 37%, Kimbundu 25%, Bakongo 13%, others 25% **LANGUAGES** Portuguese (official), many others
RELIGIONS Traditional beliefs 47%, Roman Catholic 38%, Protestant 15%
CURRENCY Kwanza = 100 lwei

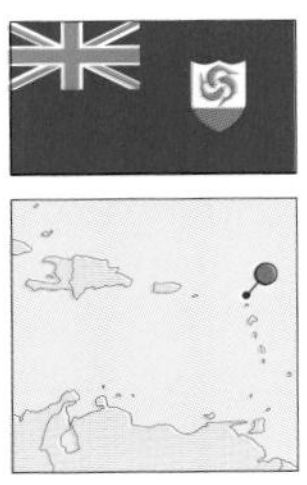

ANGUILLA

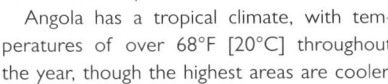

Formerly part of St Kitts and Nevis, Anguilla, the most northerly of the Leeward Islands, became a British dependency (now a British overseas territory) in 1980. The main source of revenue is now tourism, although lobster still accounts for half the island's exports.

AREA 37 sq mi [96 sq km] **POPULATION** 12,000
CAPITAL The Valley

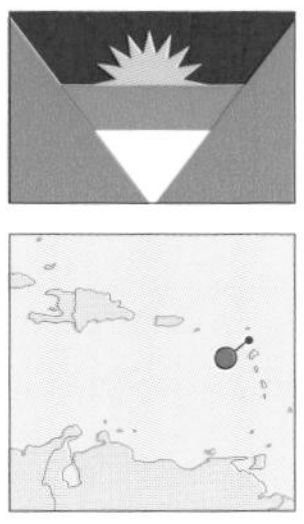

ANTIGUA & BARBUDA

A former British dependency in the Caribbean, Antigua and Barbuda became independent in 1981. Tourism is the main industry, though sugar is an important product.

AREA 170 sq mi [442 sq km]
POPULATION 67,000 **CAPITAL** St John's

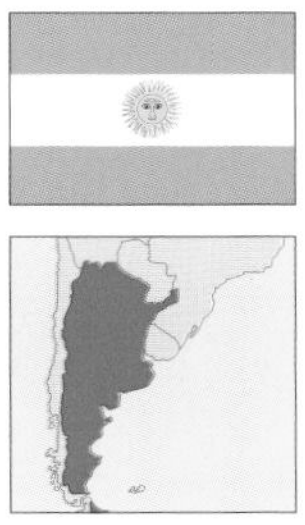

ARGENTINA

GEOGRAPHY The Argentine Republic is South America's second largest and the world's eighth largest country. The high Andes range in the west contains Mount Aconcagua, the highest peak in the Americas. In southern Argentina, the Andes Mountains overlook Patagonia, a plateau region. In east-central Argentina lies a fertile plain called the pampas.

The climate varies from subtropical in the north to temperate in the south. Rainfall is abundant in the northeast, but is lower to the west and south. Patagonia is a dry region, crossed by rivers that rise in the Andes.

POLITICS & ECONOMY Argentina became independent from Spain in the early 19th century, but it later suffered from instability and periods of military rule. In 1982, Argentina invaded the Falkland (Malvinas) Islands, but Britain regained the islands later in the year. Elections were held in 1983 and a new constitution was adopted in 1994.

According to the World Bank, Argentina is an "upper-middle-income" developing country. Large areas are fertile and the main agricultural products are beef, maize and wheat. But about 87% of the people live in cities and towns. Industries include food processing and the manufacture of cars, electrical equipment and textiles. Oil is the chief natural resource. Major exports include meat, wheat, maize, vegetable oils, hides and skins, and wool. In 1991, Argentina, Brazil, Paraguay and Uruguay set up Mercosur, an alliance aimed to create a common market. However, in late 2001, a severe economic crisis threatened anarchy, but the government struggled to restore confidence in 2002 and 2003.

AREA 1,068,296 sq mi [2,766,890 sq km] **POPULATION** 37,813,000
CAPITAL (POPULATION) Buenos Aires (10,990,000)
GOVERNMENT Federal republic **ETHNIC GROUPS** European 97%, Mestizo, Amerindian **LANGUAGES** Spanish (official)
RELIGIONS Roman Catholic 92%, Protestant 2%, Jewish 2%
CURRENCY Peso = 10,000 australs

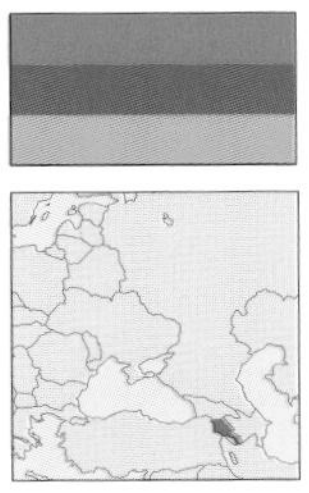

ARMENIA

GEOGRAPHY The Republic of Armenia is a landlocked country in southwestern Asia. Most of Armenia consists of a rugged plateau, criss-crossed by long faults (cracks). Movements along the faults cause earthquakes. The highest point is Mount Aragats, at 13,419 ft [4,090 m] above sea level.

The height of the land, which averages 4,920 ft [1,500 m] above sea level gives rise to severe winters and cool summers. The highest peaks are snow-capped, but the total yearly rainfall is generally low.

POLITICS & ECONOMY In 1920, Armenia became a Communist republic and, in 1922, it became, with Azerbaijan and Georgia, part of the Transcaucasian Republic within the Soviet Union. But the three territories became separate Soviet Socialist Republics in 1936. After the breakup of the Soviet Union in 1991, Armenia became an independent republic. Fighting broke out over Nagorno-Karabakh, an area enclosed by Azerbaijan where the majority of the people are Armenians. In 1992, Armenia occupied the territory between it and Nagorno-Karabakh. A ceasefire agreed in 1994 left Armenia in control of about 20% of Azerbaijan's land area. Talks aimed at settling the dispute failed in 2001.

The World Bank classifies Armenia as a "lower-middle-income" economy. The conflict has badly damaged the economy, but the government has encouraged free enterprise, selling farmland and government-owned businesses.

AREA 11,506 sq mi [29,800 sq km] **POPULATION** 3,330,000
CAPITAL (POPULATION) Yerevan (1,256,000)
GOVERNMENT Multiparty republic
ETHNIC GROUPS Armenian 93%, Azerbaijani 3%, Russian, Kurd
LANGUAGES Armenian (official) **RELIGIONS** Armenian Orthodox
CURRENCY Dram = 100 couma

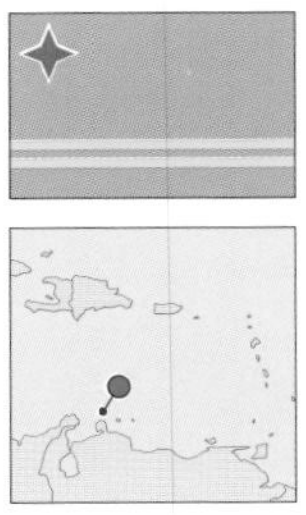

ARUBA

Formerly part of the Netherlands Antilles, Aruba (the most western of the Lesser Antilles) became a separate self-governing Dutch territory in 1986.

AREA 75 sq mi [193 sq km]
POPULATION 70,000 **CAPITAL** Oranjestad

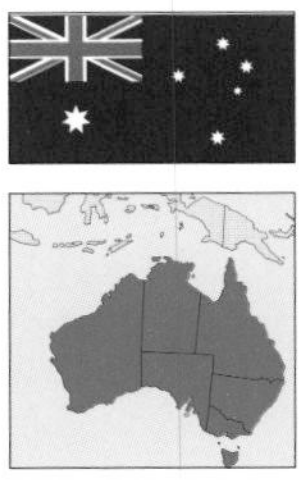

AUSTRALIA

GEOGRAPHY The Commonwealth of Australia, the world's sixth largest country, is also a continent. Australia is the flattest of the continents and the main highland area is in the east. Here the Great Dividing Range separates the eastern coastal plains from the Central Plains. This range extends from the Cape York Peninsula to Victoria in the far south. The longest rivers, the Murray and Darling, drain the south-eastern part of the Central Plains. The Western Plateau makes up two-thirds of Australia. A few mountain ranges break the monotony of the generally flat landscape.

Only 10% of Australia has an average yearly rainfall of more than 39 inches [1,000 mm]. These areas include the tropical north, where Darwin is situated, the northeast coast, and the southeast, where Sydney is located. The interior is dry, and water is quickly evaporated in the heat.

POLITICS & ECONOMY The Aboriginal people of Australia entered the continent from Southeast Asia more than 50,000 years ago. The first European explorers were Dutch in the 17th century, but they did not settle. In 1770, the British Captain Cook explored the east coast and, in 1788, the first British settlement was established for convicts on the site of what is now Sydney. Australia has strong ties with the British Isles. But in the last 50 years, people from other parts of Europe and, most recently, from Asia have settled in Australia. Ties with Britain were also weakened by Britain's membership of the European Union. Many Australians believe that they should become more involved with the nations of eastern Asia and the Americas rather than with Europe. In 1999, Australia held a referendum on whether the country should become a republic or remain a constitutional monarchy. By a majority of about 55 to 45, the country retained its status as a monarchy.

Australia is a prosperous country. Crops can be grown on only 6% of the land, but dry pasture covers another 58%. Yet the country remains a major producer and exporter of farm products, particularly cattle, wheat and wool. Grapes grown for winemaking are also important. The country is a major producer of minerals, including bauxite, coal, copper, diamonds, gold, iron ore, manganese, nickel, silver, tin, tungsten and zinc. Australia also produces oil and natural gas. Metals, minerals and farm products account for the bulk of exports. Australia's imports are mostly manufactured products, although the country makes many factory products, especially consumer goods, such as foods and household articles. Major imports include machinery.

AREA 2,967,893 sq mi [7,686,850 sq km] **POPULATION** 19,547,000
CAPITAL (POPULATION) Canberra (325,000) **GOVERNMENT** Federal constitutional monarchy **ETHNIC GROUPS** Caucasian 92%, Asian 7.5%, Aboriginal 1.5% **LANGUAGES** English (official)
RELIGIONS Roman Catholic 26%, Anglican 26%, other Christian 24%, non-Christian 24% **CURRENCY** Australian dollar = 100 cents

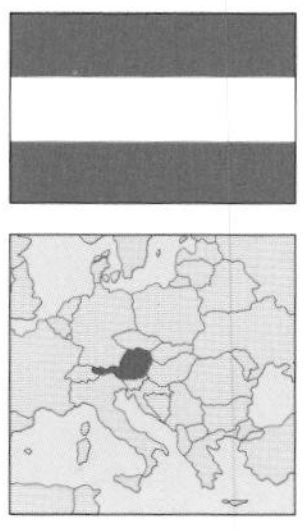

AUSTRIA

GEOGRAPHY Austria is a landlocked country in Europe. Northern Austria contains the valley of the River Danube, which flows from Germany to the Black Sea, and the Vienna basin. Southern Austria contains ranges of the Alps, their highest point at Grossglockner, 12,457 ft [3,797 m] above sea level.

The climate is influenced by westerly and easterly winds. Moist westerly winds bring rain and snow, and moderate temperatures. Dry easterly winds bring cold weather in winter and hot weather in summer.

POLITICS & ECONOMY Formerly part of the monarchy of Austria-Hungary, which collapsed in 1918, Austria was annexed by Germany in 1938. After World War II, the Allies partitioned and occupied the country. In 1955, Austria became a neutral federal republic. It joined the European Union on January 1, 1995, but was a focus of controversy when, in 2000, a coalition government was formed by the right-wing People's Party and the extreme right-wing Freedom Party. The Freedom Party lost much of its support in 2002, but it remained part of the ruling coalition.

Austria has a highly developed economy, with plenty of hydroelectric power and some oil, gas and coal reserves. The country's leading economic activity is manufacturing metals and metal products. Crops are grown on 18% of the land, and another 24% is pasture. Dairy and livestock farming are the leading activities. Major crops include barley, potatoes, rye, sugar beet and wheat. Tourism is a major activity in this scenic country.

AREA 32,374 sq mi [83,850 sq km] **POPULATION** 8,170,000
CAPITAL (POPULATION) Vienna (1,560,000) **GOVERNMENT** Federal republic **ETHNIC GROUPS** Austrian 93%, Croatian, Slovene, other
LANGUAGES German (official) **RELIGIONS** Roman Catholic 78%, Protestant 5%, Islam and other **CURRENCY** Euro = 100 cents

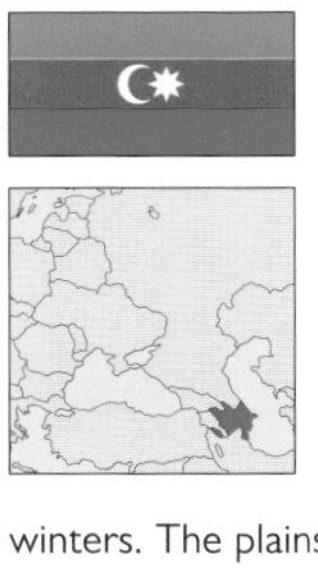

AZERBAIJAN

GEOGRAPHY The Azerbaijani Republic is a country in the southwest of Asia, facing the Caspian Sea to the east. It includes an area called the Naxçivan Autonomous Republic, which is completely cut off from the rest of Azerbaijan by Armenian territory. The Caucasus Mountains border Russia in the north.

Azerbaijan has hot summers and cool winters. The plains are fairly dry, but the mountains are rainy.

POLITICS & ECONOMY After the Russian Revolution of 1917, attempts were made to form a Transcaucasian Federation made up of Armenia, Azerbaijan and Georgia. When this failed, Azerbaijanis set up an independent state. But Russian forces occupied the area in 1920. In 1922, the Communists set up a Transcaucasian Republic consisting of Armenia, Azerbaijan and Georgia under Russian control. In 1936, the three areas became separate Soviet Socialist Republics within the Soviet Union. In 1991, following the breakup of the Soviet Union, Azerbaijan became an independent nation. After independence, the country's economic progress was slow, partly because of the conflict with Armenia over the enclave of Nagorno-Karabakh, a region in Azerbaijan where the majority of people are Armenians. A ceasefire in 1994 left Armenia in control of about 20% of Azerbaijan's area, including Nagorno-Karabakh. Attempts to resolve the problem failed in 2001.

In the mid-1990s, the World Bank classified Azerbaijan as a "lower-middle-income" economy. Yet by the late 1990s, the enormous oil reserves in the Baku area, on the Caspian Sea and in the sea itself, held out great promise for the future. Oil extraction and manufacturing, including oil refining and the production of chemicals, machinery and textiles, are now the most valuable activities.

AREA 33,436 sq mi [86,600 sq km] **POPULATION** 7,798,000
CAPITAL (POPULATION) Baku (1,713,000) **GOVERNMENT** Federal multiparty republic **ETHNIC GROUPS** Azeri 90%, Dagestani 3%, Russian, Armenian, other **LANGUAGES** Azerbaijani (official)
RELIGIONS Islam 93%, Russian Orthodox 2%, Armenian Orthodox 2% **CURRENCY** Manat = 100 gopik

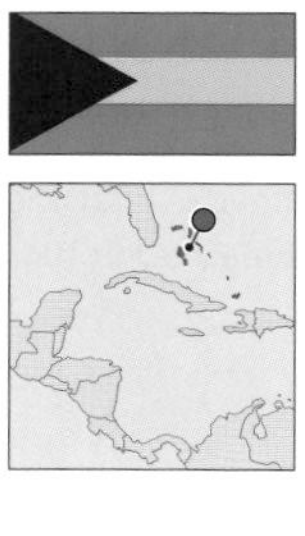

BAHAMAS

A coral-limestone archipelago off the coast of Florida, the Bahamas became independent from Britain in 1973, and has since developed strong ties with the United States. Tourism and banking are major activities.

AREA 5,380 sq mi [13,940 sq km]
POPULATION 301,000 **CAPITAL** Nassau

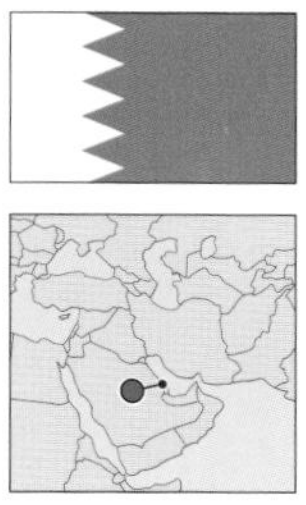

BAHRAIN

The Kingdom of Bahrain, an island nation in the Gulf, became independent from the UK in 1971. Oil accounts for 80% of the country's exports.

AREA 262 sq mi [678 sq km]
POPULATION 656,000 **CAPITAL** Manama

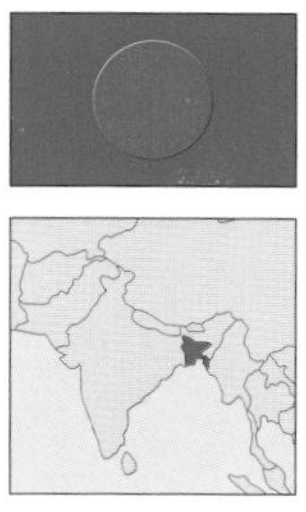

BANGLADESH

GEOGRAPHY The People's Republic of Bangladesh is one of the world's most densely populated countries. Apart from hilly regions in the far northeast and southeast, most of the land is flat and covered by fertile alluvium spread over the land by the Ganges, Brahmaputra and Meghna rivers. These rivers overflow when they are swollen by the annual monsoon rains. Floods also occur along the coast, 357 mi [575 km] long, when cyclones (hurricanes) drive seawater inland. Bangladesh has a tropical monsoon climate. Dry northerly winds blow in winter, but, in summer, moist winds from the south bring monsoon rains. Heavy monsoon rains cause floods. In 1998, about two-thirds of the entire country was submerged, causing great suffering.

POLITICS & ECONOMY In 1947, British India was partitioned between the mainly Hindu India and the Muslim Pakistan. Pakistan consisted of two parts, West and East Pakistan, which were separated by about 1,000 mi [1,600 km] of Indian territory. Differences developed between West and East Pakistan. In 1971, the East Pakistanis rebelled. After a nine-month civil war, they declared East Pakistan to be a separate nation named Bangladesh.

Bangladesh is one of the world's poorest countries. Its economy depends mainly on agriculture, which employs over half the population. Bangladesh is the world's fourth largest producer of rice.

AREA 55,598 sq mi [144,000 sq km] **POPULATION** 133,377,000
CAPITAL (POPULATION) Dhaka (7,832,000)
GOVERNMENT Multiparty republic **ETHNIC GROUPS** Bengali 98%, tribal groups **LANGUAGES** Bengali, English (both official)
RELIGIONS Islam 83%, Hinduism 16% **CURRENCY** Taka = 100 paisas

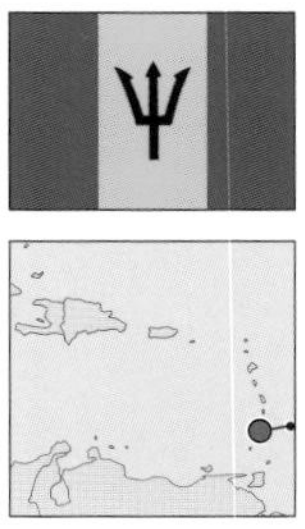

BARBADOS

The most easterly Caribbean country, Barbados became independent from the UK in 1960. A densely populated island, Barbados is prosperous by comparison with most Caribbean countries.

AREA 166 sq mi [430 sq km]
POPULATION 277,000 **CAPITAL** Bridgetown

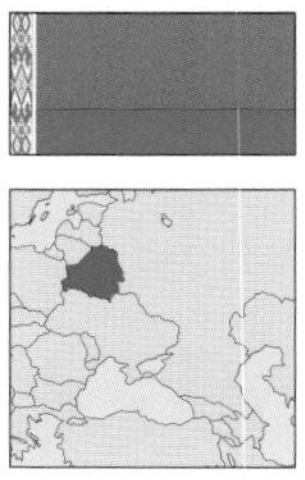

BELARUS

GEOGRAPHY The Republic of Belarus is a landlocked country in Eastern Europe. The land is low-lying and mostly flat. In the south, much of the land is marshy and this area contains Europe's largest marsh and peat bog, the Pripet Marshes. The climate is affected by both the moderating influence of the Baltic Sea and continental conditions to the east. The winters are cold and the summers warm.

POLITICS & ECONOMY In 1918, Belarus (White Russia) became an independent republic, but Russia invaded the country and, in 1919, a Communist state was set up. In 1922, Belarus became a founder republic of the Soviet Union. In 1991, Belarus again became an independent republic, though Belarus continued to support re-unification with Russia. In 1998, Belarus and Russia set up a "union state," with plans to have a common currency, a customs union, and common foreign and defense policies. But any surrender of sovereignty was not expected. In 2003, the Russian President Vladimir Putin agreed to deepen ties with Belarus, but also stated that he did not wish to create anything like the Soviet Union.

The World Bank classifies Belarus as an "upper-middle-income" economy. Like other former republics of the Soviet Union, it faces many problems in turning from Communism to a free-market economy.

AREA 80,154 sq mi [207,600 sq km] **POPULATION** 10,335,000
CAPITAL (POPULATION) Minsk (1,717,000)
GOVERNMENT Multiparty republic **ETHNIC GROUPS** Belarussian 81%, Russian 11%, Polish, Ukrainian **LANGUAGES** Belarussian, Russian (both official) **RELIGIONS** Eastern Orthodox 80%, other 20%
CURRENCY Belarussian rouble = 100 kopecks

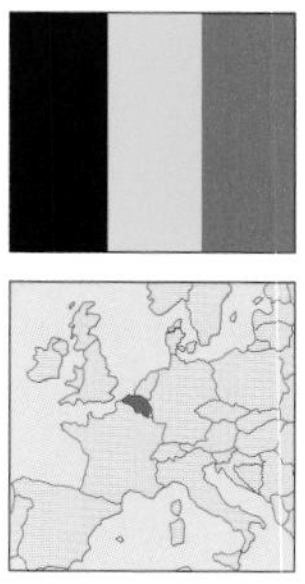

BELGIUM

GEOGRAPHY The Kingdom of Belgium is a densely populated country in western Europe. Behind the coastline on the North Sea, which is 39 mi [63 km] long, lie its coastal plains. Central Belgium consists of low plateaux and the only highland region is the Ardennes in the southeast.

Belgium has a cool, temperate climate. Moist winds from the Atlantic Ocean bring fairly heavy rain, especially in the Ardennes. In January and February much snow falls on the Ardennes.

POLITICS & ECONOMY In 1815, Belgium and the Netherlands united as the "low countries," but Belgium became independent in 1830. Belgium's economy was weakened by the two World

Wars, but, from 1945, the country recovered quickly, first through collaboration with the Netherlands and Luxembourg, which formed a customs union called Benelux, and later through its membership of the European Union.

A central political problem in Belgium has been the tension between the Dutch-speaking Flemings and the French-speaking Walloons. In the 1970s, the government divided the country into three economic regions: Dutch-speaking Flanders, French-speaking Wallonia and bilingual Brussels. In 1993, Belgium adopted a federal constitution, with each region having its own parliament. Elections under this system were held in 1995 and 1999.

Belgium is a major trading nation, with a highly developed economy. Most of the materials needed for manufacturing are imported. Its main products include chemicals, processed food and steel. The textile industry is important. It has existed since medieval times in the Belgian province of Flanders. In 2002, the parliament voted to phase out the use of nuclear energy by 2025.

Agriculture employs only 3% of the people, but Belgian farmers produce most of the food needed by the people. Barley and wheat are the chief crops, followed by flax, hops, potatoes and sugar beet, but the most valuable activities are dairy farming and livestock rearing.

AREA 11,780 sq mi [30,510 sq km]
POPULATION 10,275,000
CAPITAL (POPULATION) Brussels (948,000)
GOVERNMENT Federal constitutional monarchy
ETHNIC GROUPS Belgian 91% (Fleming 58%, Walloon 31%), other 11% **LANGUAGES** Dutch, French, German (all official)
RELIGIONS Roman Catholic 75%, other 25%
CURRENCY Euro = 100 cents

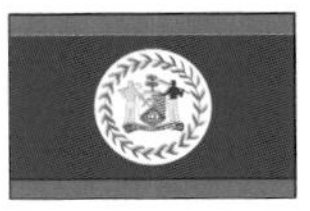
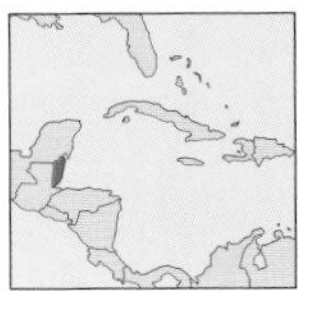

BELIZE

GEOGRAPHY Behind the southern coastal plain, the land rises to the Maya Mountains, which reach 3,674 ft [1,120 m] at Victoria Peak. The north is mostly low-lying and swampy. Temperatures are high all year round, while the average annual rainfall ranges from 51 inches [1,300 mm] in the north to over 150 inches [3,800 mm] in the south. Hurricanes sometimes occur. One in 2001 killed 22 people and left 12,000 homeless.

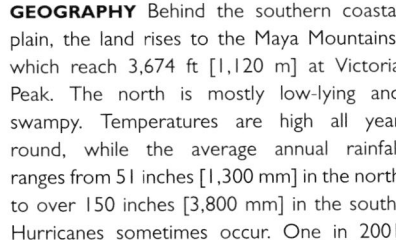

POLITICS & ECONOMY From 1862, Belize (then called British Honduras) was a British colony. Full independence was achieved in 1981, but Guatemala, which had claimed the area since the early 19th century, opposed Belize's independence and British troops remained to prevent a possible invasion. In 1983, Guatemala reduced its claim to the southern fifth of Belize. Improved relations in the early 1990s led Guatemala to recognize Belize's independence and, in 1992, Britain agreed to withdraw its troops from the country.

The World Bank classifies Belize as a "lower-middle-income" developing country. Its economy is based on agriculture and sugarcane is the chief commercial crop and export. Other crops include bananas, beans, citrus fruits, maize and rice. Forestry, fishing and tourism are other important activities.

AREA 8,865 sq mi [22,960 sq km] **POPULATION** 263,000
CAPITAL (POPULATION) Belmopan (4,000)
GOVERNMENT Constitutional monarchy **ETHNIC GROUPS** Mestizo (Spanish-Indian) 44%, Creole (mainly African American) 30%, Mayan Indian 11%, Garifuna (Black-Carib Indian) 7%, other 8%
LANGUAGES English (official), Creole, Spanish **RELIGIONS** Roman Catholic 62%, Protestant 30% **CURRENCY** Belize dollar = 100 cents

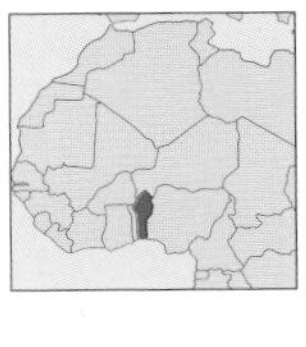

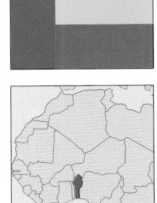

BENIN

GEOGRAPHY The Republic of Benin is one of Africa's smallest countries. It extends north–south for about 390 mi [620 km]. Lagoons line the short coastline, and the country has no natural harbors.

Benin has a hot, wet climate. The average annual temperature on the coast is about 77°F [25°C], and the average rainfall is about 52 inches [1,330 mm]. The inland plains are wetter than the coast.

POLITICS & ECONOMY After slavery was ended in the 19th century, the French began to gain influence in the area. Benin became self-governing in 1958 and fully independent in 1960. After much instability and many changes of government, a military group took over in 1972. The country, renamed Benin in 1975, became a one-party socialist state. Socialism was abandoned in 1989, and multiparty elections were held in 1991, 1996, 1999 and 2001.

Benin is a poor developing country. About 70% of the people earn their living by farming, though many remain at subsistence level. The chief exports include cotton, petroleum and palm products. Cocoa, coffee, groundnuts (peanuts), tobacco and shea nuts are also grown for export.

AREA 43,483 sq mi [112,620 sq km] **POPULATION** 6,788,000
CAPITAL (POPULATION) Porto-Novo (179,000)
GOVERNMENT Multiparty republic **ETHNIC GROUPS** Fon, Adja, Bariba, Yoruba, Fulani **LANGUAGES** French (official), Fon, Adja, Yoruba
RELIGIONS Traditional beliefs 50%, Christianity 30%, Islam 20%
CURRENCY CFA franc = 100 centimes

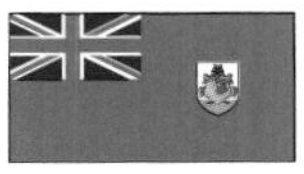
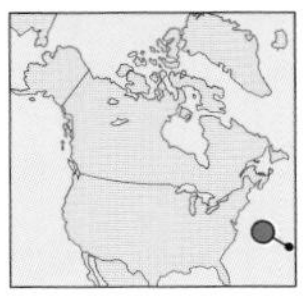

BERMUDA

A group of about 150 small islands situated 570 mi [920 km] east of the USA. Bermuda remains Britain's oldest overseas territory, but it has a long tradition of self-government.

AREA 20 sq mi [53 sq km] **POPULATION** 64,000
CAPITAL Hamilton

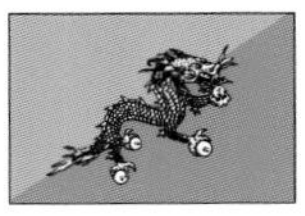
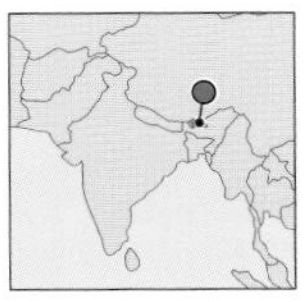

BHUTAN

GEOGRAPHY A mountainous, isolated Himalayan country located between India and Tibet. The climate is similar to that of Nepal, being dependent on altitude and affected by monsoonal winds.

POLITICS & ECONOMY The monarch of Bhutan is head of both state and government and this predominantly Buddhist country remains, even in the Asian context, both conservative and poor. Bhutan is the world's most "rural" country, with about 87% of the population dependent on agriculture and only 7% living in towns.

AREA 18,147 sq mi [47,000 sq km] **POPULATION** 2,094,000
CAPITAL (POPULATION) Thimphu (30,000)
GOVERNMENT Constitutional monarchy **ETHNIC GROUPS** Bhutanese 50%, Nepali 35% **LANGUAGES** Dzongkha (official) **RELIGIONS** Buddhism 75%, Hinduism 25% **CURRENCY** Ngultrum = 100 chetrum

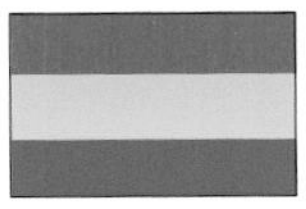
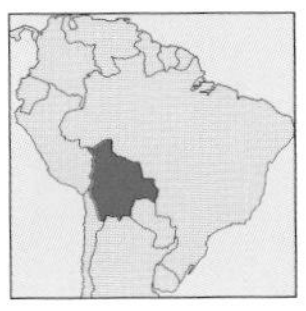

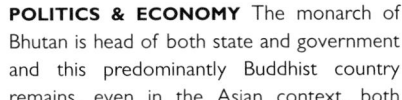

BOLIVIA

GEOGRAPHY The Republic of Bolivia is a landlocked country which straddles the Andes Mountains in central South America. The Andes rise to a height of 21,464 ft [6,542 m] at Nevado Sajama in the west.

About 40% of Bolivians live on a high plateau called the Altiplano in the Andean region, while the sparsely populated east is essentially a vast lowland plain.

The Bolivian climate is greatly affected by altitude, with the Andean peaks permanently snow-covered, and the eastern plains remaining hot and humid.

POLITICS & ECONOMY American Indians have lived in Bolivia for at least 10,000 years. The main groups today are the Aymara and Quechua people.

In the last 50 years, Bolivia, an independent country since 1825, has been ruled by a succession of civilian and military governments, which violated human rights. Constitutional government was restored in 1982. From the 1980s, Bolivia has pursued economic reforms and free-market policies.

Bolivia is one of the poorest countries in South America. It has several natural resources, including tin, silver and natural gas, but the chief activity is agriculture, which employs 47% of the people. Coca, which is used to make cocaine, is exported illegally. In 2002–3, the production of coca plummeted, causing much social unrest and ethnic tensions. The government hoped that oil and gas would soon replace coca as the chief export.

AREA 424,162 sq mi [1,098,580 sq km] **POPULATION** 8,445,000
CAPITAL (POPULATION) La Paz (1,126,000)
GOVERNMENT Multiparty republic **ETHNIC GROUPS** Mestizo 30%, Quechua 30%, Aymara 25%, White 15%
LANGUAGES Spanish, Aymara, Quechua (all official)
RELIGIONS Roman Catholic 95%
CURRENCY Boliviano = 100 centavos

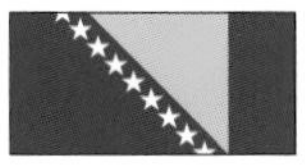
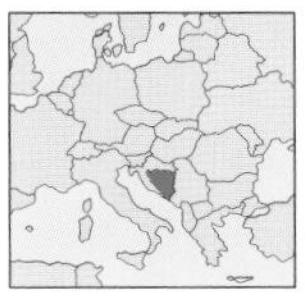

BOSNIA-HERZEGOVINA

GEOGRAPHY The Republic of Bosnia-Herzegovina is one of the five republics to emerge from the former Federal People's Republic of Yugoslavia. Much of the country is mountainous or hilly, with an arid limestone plateau in the southwest. The River Sava, which forms most of the northern border with Croatia, is a tributary of the River Danube. Because of the country's odd shape, the coastline is limited to a short stretch of 13 mi [20 km] on the Adriatic coast.

A Mediterranean climate, with dry, sunny summers and moist, mild winters, prevails only near the coast. Inland, the weather is more severe, with hot, dry summers and bitterly cold, snowy winters.

POLITICS & ECONOMY In 1918, Bosnia-Herzegovina became part of the Kingdom of the Serbs, Croats and Slovenes, which was renamed Yugoslavia in 1929. Germany occupied the area during World War II (1939–45). From 1945, Communist governments ruled Yugoslavia as a federation containing six republics, one of which was Bosnia-Herzegovina. In the 1980s, the country faced problems as Communist policies proved unsuccessful and differences arose between ethnic groups.

In 1990, free elections were held in Bosnia-Herzegovina and the non-Communists won a majority. A Muslim, Alija Izetbegovic, was elected president. In 1991, Croatia and Slovenia, other parts of the former Yugoslavia, declared themselves independent. In 1992, Bosnia-Herzegovina held a vote on independence. Most Bosnian Serbs boycotted the vote, while the Muslims and Bosnian Croats voted in favor. Many Bosnian Serbs, opposed to independence, started a war against the non-Serbs. They soon occupied more than two-thirds of the land. The Bosnian Serbs were accused of "ethnic cleansing" – that is, the killing or expulsion of other ethnic groups from Serb-occupied areas. The war was later extended when Croat forces seized other parts of the country.

In 1995, the warring parties agreed to a solution to the conflict. This involved keeping the present boundaries of Bosnia-Herzegovina, but dividing it into two self-governing provinces, one Bosnian Serb and the other Muslim-Croat, under a central unified government. Elections were held in 1996, 1998 and 2000, and, in the early 21st century, hopes of future stability were high.

The economy of Bosnia-Herzegovina, the least developed of the six republics of the former Yugoslavia apart from Macedonia, was shattered by the war in the early 1990s. Before the war, manufactures were the main exports, including electrical, machinery and transport equipment, and textiles. Farm products include fruits, maize, tobacco, vegetables and wheat, but food has to be imported.

AREA 19,745 sq mi [51,129 sq km] **POPULATION** 3,964,000
CAPITAL (POPULATION) Sarajevo (526,000)
GOVERNMENT Federal republic **ETHNIC GROUPS** Bosnian 49%, Serb 31%, Croat 17% **LANGUAGES** Serbo-Croatian **RELIGIONS** Islam 40%, Serbian Orthodox 31%, Roman Catholic 15%, Protestant 4%
CURRENCY Convertible mark = 100 paras

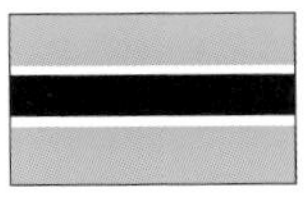
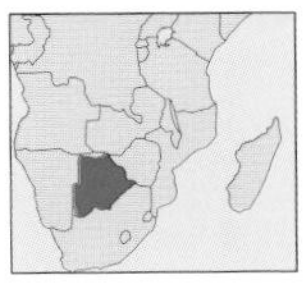

BOTSWANA

GEOGRAPHY The Republic of Botswana is a landlocked country in southern Africa. The Kalahari, a semidesert area covered mostly by grasses and thorn scrub, covers much of the country. Most of the south has no permanent streams. But large depressions in the north are inland drainage basins. In one of them, the Okavango River, which rises in Angola, forms a large, swampy delta.

Temperatures are high in the summer months (October to April), but the winter months are much cooler. In winter, night-time temperatures sometimes drop below freezing point. The average annual rainfall ranges from over 16 inches [400 mm] in the east to less than 8 inches [200 mm] in the southwest.

POLITICS & ECONOMY The earliest inhabitants of the region were the San, who are also called Bushmen. They had a nomadic way of life, hunting wild animals and collecting wild plant foods.

Britain ruled the area as the Bechuanaland Protectorate between 1885 and 1966. When the country became independent, it was renamed Botswana. Since then, the country has been a stable, multiparty democracy. However, a major setback occurred in the early 21st century, when health officials announced that around 25% of the people were infected with HIV/AIDS. In 1966, Botswana was extremely poor, depending on meat and live cattle for its exports. But the discovery of minerals, including coal, cobalt, copper, diamonds and nickel, has boosted the economy. About 22% of the people now depend on agriculture, raising cattle and growing crops. Industries include the processing of farm products.

AREA 224,606 sq mi [581,730 sq km] **POPULATION** 1,591,000
CAPITAL (POPULATION) Gaborone (133,000)
GOVERNMENT Multiparty republic **ETHNIC GROUPS** Tswana 75%, Shona 12%, San (Bushmen) 3% **LANGUAGES** English (official), Setswana **RELIGIONS** Traditional beliefs 50%, Christianity 50%
CURRENCY Pula = 100 thebe

BRAZIL

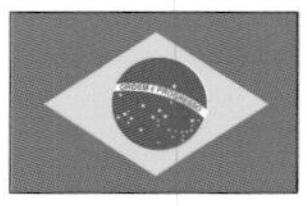

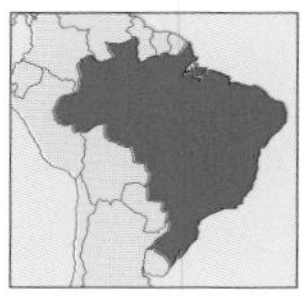

GEOGRAPHY The Federative Republic of Brazil is the world's fifth largest country. It contains three main regions. The Amazon basin in the north covers more than half of Brazil. The Amazon, the world's second longest river, has a far greater volume than any other river. The second region, the northeast, consists of a coastal plain and the *sertão*, which is the name for the inland plateaux and hill country. The main river in this region is the São Francisco.

The third region is made up of the plateaux in the southeast. This region, which covers about a quarter of the country, is the most developed and densely populated part of Brazil. Its main river is the Paraná, which flows south through Argentina.

Manaus has high temperatures all through the year. The rainfall is heavy, though the period from June to September is drier than the rest of the year. The capital, Brasília, and the city Rio de Janeiro also have tropical climates, with much more marked dry seasons than Manaus. The far south has a temperate climate. The northeastern interior is the driest region, with an average annual rainfall of only 10 inches [250 mm] in places. The rainfall is also unreliable and severe droughts are common in this region.

POLITICS & ECONOMY The Portuguese explorer Pedro Alvarez Cabral claimed Brazil for Portugal in 1500. With Spain occupied in western South America, the Portuguese began to develop their colony, which was more than 90 times as big as Portugal. To do this, they enslaved many local Amerindian people and introduced about 4 million African slaves. Brazil declared itself an independent empire in 1822 and a republic in 1889. From the 1930s, Brazil faced periods of military rule and widespread corruption. Civilian rule was restored in 1985. Brazil adopted a new constitution in 1988.

The United Nations has described Brazil as a "Rapidly Industrializing Country," or RIC. Its total volume of production is one of the largest in the world. But many people, including poor farmers and residents of the *favelas* (city slums), do not share in the country's fast economic growth. Widespread poverty, together with high inflation and unemployment led to the election as president of left-winger Luiz Inácio Lula da Silva (popularly known as "Lula") in 2002.

By the early 1990s, industry was the most valuable activity, employing 25% of the people. Brazil is among the world's top producers of bauxite, chrome, diamonds, gold, iron ore, manganese and tin. It is also a major manufacturing country. Its products include aircraft, cars, chemicals, processed food, including raw sugar, iron and steel, paper and textiles.

Brazil is one of the world's leading farming countries and agriculture employs 22% of the people. Coffee is a major export. Other leading products include bananas, citrus fruits, cocoa, maize, rice, soybeans and sugarcane. Brazil is also the top producer of eggs, meat and milk in South America.

Forestry is a major industry, though many people fear that the exploitation of the rain forests, with 1.5% to 4% of Brazil's forest being destroyed every year, is a disaster for the entire world.

AREA 3,286,472 sq mi [8,511,970 sq km] **POPULATION** 176,030,000
CAPITAL (POPULATION) Brasília (2,051,000)
GOVERNMENT Federal republic **ETHNIC GROUPS** White 55%, Mulatto 38%, African American 6%, other 1%
LANGUAGES Portuguese (official)
RELIGIONS Roman Catholic 80%
CURRENCY Real = 100 centavos

BRUNEI

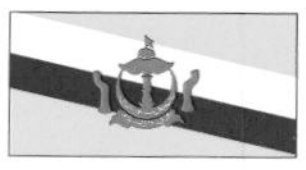

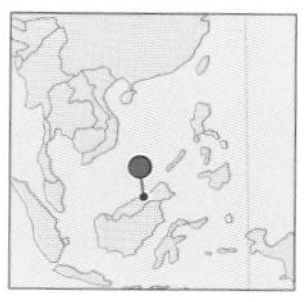

The Islamic Sultanate of Brunei, a British protectorate until 1984, lies on the north coast of Borneo. The climate is tropical and rain forests cover large areas. Brunei is a prosperous country because of its oil and natural gas production, and the Sultan is said to be among the world's richest men.

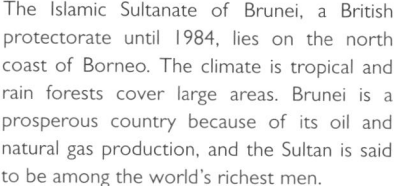

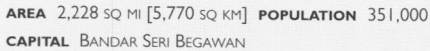

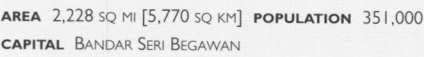

AREA 2,228 sq mi [5,770 sq km] **POPULATION** 351,000
CAPITAL Bandar Seri Begawan

BULGARIA

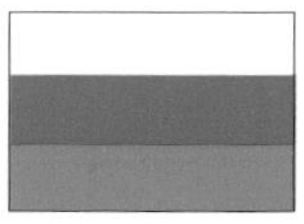

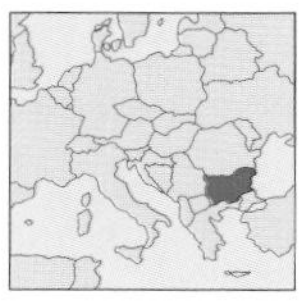

GEOGRAPHY The Republic of Bulgaria is a country in the Balkan peninsula, facing the Black Sea in the east. The heart of Bulgaria is mountainous. The main ranges are the Balkan Mountains in the center and the Rhodope (or Rhodopi) Mountains in the south.

Summers are hot and winters are cold, though seldom severe. The rainfall is moderate.

POLITICS & ECONOMY Ottoman Turks ruled Bulgaria from 1396 and ethnic Turks still form a sizable minority in the country. In 1879, Bulgaria became a monarchy, and in 1908 it became fully independent. Bulgaria was an ally of Germany in World War I (1914–18) and again in World War II (1939–45). In 1944, Soviet troops invaded Bulgaria and, after the war, the monarchy was abolished and the country became a Communist ally of the Soviet Union. In the late 1980s, reforms in the Soviet Union led Bulgaria's government to introduce a multiparty system in 1990. A non-Communist government was elected in 1991, the first free elections in 44 years. Throughout the 1990s, Bulgaria faced many problems. In 2001, a coalition led by the former King Siméon, who had left Bulgaria in 1948, won the elections. Siméon became prime minister.

According to the World Bank, Bulgaria in the 1990s was a "lower-middle-income" developing country. Bulgaria has some deposits of minerals, including brown coal, manganese and iron ore. But manufacturing is the leading economic activity, though problems arose in the early 1990s, because much industrial technology is outdated. The main products are chemicals, processed foods, metal products, machinery and textiles. Manufactures are the leading exports. Bulgaria trades mainly with countries in Eastern Europe.

AREA 42,822 sq mi [110,910 sq km] **POPULATION** 7,621,000
CAPITAL (POPULATION) Sofia (1,139,000) **GOVERNMENT** Multiparty republic **ETHNIC GROUPS** Bulgarian 83%, Turkish 8%, Gypsy 3%, Macedonian, Armenian, other **LANGUAGES** Bulgarian (official), Turkish **RELIGIONS** Christianity (Eastern Orthodox 87%), Islam 13%
CURRENCY Lev = 100 stotinki

BURKINA FASO

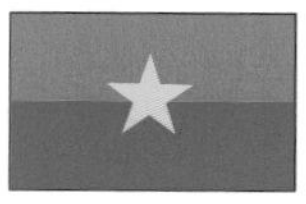

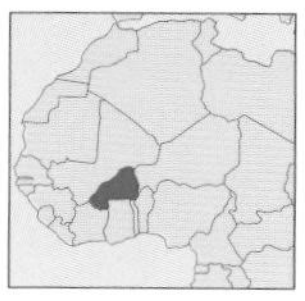

GEOGRAPHY The Democratic People's Republic of Burkina Faso is a landlocked country, a little larger than the United Kingdom, in West Africa. But Burkina Faso has only one-sixth of the population of the UK. The country consists of a plateau, between about 650 ft and 2,300 ft [300 m to 700 m] above sea level. The plateau is cut by several rivers.

The capital city, Ouagadougou, in central Burkina Faso, has high temperatures throughout the year. Most of the rain falls between May and September, but the rainfall is erratic and droughts are common.

POLITICS & ECONOMY The people of Burkina Faso are divided into two main groups. The Voltaic group includes the Mossi, who form the largest single group, and the Bobo. The French conquered the Mossi capital of Ouagadougou in 1897 and they made the area a protectorate. In 1919, the area became a French colony called Upper Volta. After independence in 1960, Upper Volta became a one-party state. But it was unstable – military groups seized power several times and political killings took place. In 1984, the country's name was changed to Burkina Faso. In 1991 and 1998, the former military leader, Captain Blaise Compaoré, was elected president, but the military continued to play an important part in the government.

Burkina Faso is one of the world's 20 poorest countries and has become very dependent on foreign aid. Most of Burkina Faso is dry with thin soils. The country's main food crops are beans, maize, millet, rice and sorghum. Cotton, groundnuts and shea nuts, whose seeds produce a fat used to make cooking oil and soap, are grown for sale abroad. Livestock are also an important export.

The country has few resources and manufacturing is on a small scale. There are some deposits of manganese, zinc, lead and nickel in the north of the country, but there is not yet a good enough transport system there. Many young men seek jobs abroad in Ghana and Ivory Coast. The money they send home to their families is important to the country's economy.

AREA 105,869 sq mi [274,200 sq km] **POPULATION** 12,603,000
CAPITAL (POPULATION) Ouagadougou (690,000)
GOVERNMENT Multiparty republic **ETHNIC GROUPS** Mossi 48%, Gurunsi, Senufo, Lobi, Bobo, Mande, Fulani **LANGUAGES** French (official), Mossi, Fulani **RELIGIONS** Islam 50%, traditional beliefs 40%, Christianity 10% **CURRENCY** CFA franc = 100 centimes

BURMA (MYANMAR)

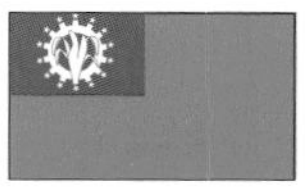

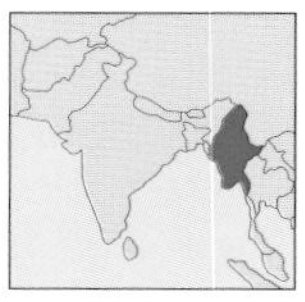

GEOGRAPHY The Union of Burma is now officially known as the Union of Myanmar; its name was changed in 1989. Mountains border the country in the east and west, with the highest mountains in the north. Burma's highest mountain is Hkakabo Razi, which is 19,294 ft [5,881 m] high. Between these ranges is central Burma, which contains the fertile valleys of the Irrawaddy and Sittang rivers. The Irrawaddy delta on the Bay of Bengal is one of the world's leading rice-growing areas. Burma also includes the long Tenasserim coast in the southeast.

Burma has a tropical monsoon climate. There are three seasons. The rainy season runs from late May to mid-October. A cool, dry season follows, between late October and the middle part of February. The hot season lasts from late February to mid-May, though temperatures remain high during the humid rainy season.

POLITICS & ECONOMY Many groups settled in Burma in ancient times. Some, called the hill peoples, live in remote mountain areas where they have retained their own cultures. The ancestors of the country's main ethnic group today, the Burmese, arrived in the 9th century AD.

Britain conquered Burma in the 19th century and made it a province of British India. But, in 1937, the British granted Burma limited self-government. Japan conquered Burma in 1942, but the Japanese were driven out in 1945. Burma became a fully independent country in 1948.

Revolts by Communists and various hill people led to instability in the 1950s. In 1962, Burma became a military dictatorship and, in 1974, a one-party state. Attempts to control minority liberation movements and the opium trade led to repressive rule. The National League for Democracy led by Aung San Suu Kyi won the elections in 1990, but the military continued their repressive rule throughout the 1990s, earning Burma the reputation for having one of the world's worst human rights records. Its admission to ASEAN (Association of Southeast Asian Nations) in 1997 may have implied regional recognition of the regime. However, the European Union continued to voice its concerns over human rights abuses, even after the release of the opposition leader Aung San Suu Kyi in 2002.

Agriculture is the main activity, employing 64% of the people. The chief crop is rice. Maize, pulses, oilseeds and sugarcane are other major products. Forestry is important. Teak and rice together make up about two-thirds of the total value of the exports. Burma has many mineral resources, though they are mostly undeveloped, but the country is famous for its precious stones, especially rubies. Manufacturing is mostly on a small scale.

AREA 261,228 sq mi [676,577 sq km] **POPULATION** 42,238,000
CAPITAL (POPULATION) Rangoon (2,513,000) **GOVERNMENT** Military regime **ETHNIC GROUPS** Burman 69%, Shan 9%, Karen 6%, Rakhine 5%, Mon 2%, Kachin 1% **LANGUAGES** Burmese (official), Shan, Karen, Rakhine, Mon, Kachin, English, Chin **RELIGIONS** Buddhism 89%, Christianity, Islam **CURRENCY** Kyat = 100 pyas

BURUNDI

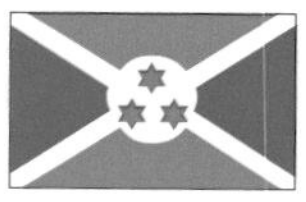

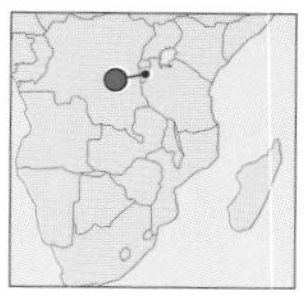

GEOGRAPHY The Republic of Burundi is the fifth smallest country in mainland Africa. It is also the second most densely populated after its northern neighbor, Rwanda. Part of the Great African Rift Valley, which runs throughout eastern Africa into southwestern Asia, lies in western Burundi. It includes part of Lake Tanganyika.

Bujumbura, the capital city, lies on the shore of Lake Tanganyika. It has a warm climate. A dry season occurs from June to September, but the other months are fairly rainy. The mountains and plateaux to the east are cooler and wetter, but the rainfall generally decreases to the east.

POLITICS & ECONOMY The Twa, a pygmy people, were the first known inhabitants of Burundi. About 1,000 years ago, the Hutu, a people who speak a Bantu language, gradually began to settle the area, pushing the Twa into remote areas.

From the 15th century, the Tutsi, a cattle-owning people from the northeast, gradually took over the country. The Hutu, though greatly outnumbering the Tutsi, were forced to serve the Tutsi overlords.

Germany conquered the area that is now Burundi and Rwanda in the late 1890s. The area, called Ruanda-Urundi, was taken by Belgium during World War I (1914–18). In 1961, the people of Urundi voted to become a monarchy, while the people of Ruanda voted to become a republic. The two territories became fully independent as Burundi and Rwanda in 1962. After 1962, the rivalries between the Hutu and Tutsi led to periodic outbreaks of fighting. The Tutsi monarchy was ended in 1966 and Burundi became a republic. Instability continued with frequent coups and massacres of thousands of people as Tutsis and Hutus fought for power. In 2001, leaders signed a power-sharing agreement, but conflict continued despite efforts to implement it.

Burundi is one of the world's ten poorest countries. About 93% of the people are farmers who live mostly at subsistence level. The main food crops are beans, cassava, maize and sweet potatoes. Cattle, goats and sheep are raised and fishing is also important. However, Burundi has to import food.

AREA 10,745 SQ MI [27,830 SQ KM] **POPULATION** 6,373,000
CAPITAL (POPULATION) BUJUMBURA (300,000) **GOVERNMENT** REPUBLIC
ETHNIC GROUPS HUTU 85%, TUTSI 14%, TWA (PYGMY) 1%
LANGUAGES FRENCH AND KIRUNDI (BOTH OFFICIAL)
RELIGIONS ROMAN CATHOLIC 62%, TRADITIONAL BELIEFS 23%, ISLAM 10%, PROTESTANT 5% **CURRENCY** BURUNDI FRANC = 100 CENTIMES

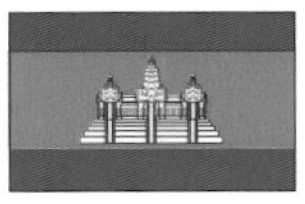

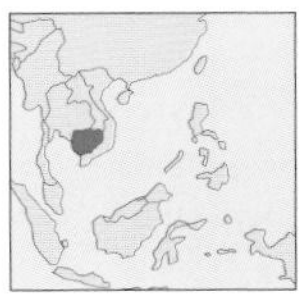

CAMBODIA

GEOGRAPHY The Kingdom of Cambodia is a country in Southeast Asia. Low mountains border the country except in the southeast. But most of Cambodia consists of plains drained by the River Mekong, which enters Cambodia from Laos in the north and exits through Vietnam in the southeast. The northwest contains Tonlé Sap (or Great Lake). In the dry season, this lake drains into the River Mekong. But in the wet season, the level of the Mekong rises and water flows in the opposite direction from the river into Tonlé Sap – the lake then becomes the largest freshwater lake in Asia.

Cambodia has a tropical monsoon climate, with high temperatures throughout the year. The dry season, when winds blow from the north or northeast, runs from November to April. During the rainy season (May to October), moist winds blow from the south or southeast. The high humidity and heat often make conditions unpleasant. Rainfall is heaviest near the coast, and rather lower inland.

POLITICS & ECONOMY From 802 to 1432, the Khmer people ruled a great empire, which reached its peak in the 12th century. The Khmer capital was at Angkor. The Hindu stone temples built there and at nearby Angkor Wat form the world's largest group of religious buildings. France ruled the country between 1863 and 1954, when the country became an independent monarchy. But the monarchy was abolished in 1970 and Cambodia became a republic.

In 1970, US and South Vietnamese troops entered Cambodia but left after destroying North Vietnamese Communist camps in the east. The country became involved in the Vietnamese War, and then in a civil war as Cambodian Communists of the Khmer Rouge organization fought for power. The Khmer Rouge took over Cambodia in 1975 and launched a reign of terror in which between 1 million and 2.5 million people were killed. In 1979, Vietnamese and Cambodian troops overthrew the Khmer Rouge government. But fighting continued between factions. Vietnam withdrew in 1989, and in 1991 Prince Sihanouk was recognized as head of state. Elections were held in May 1993, and in September 1993 the monarchy was restored. Sihanouk again became king. In 1997, the prime minister, Prince Norodom Ranariddh, was deposed, so ending four years of democratic rule. Further elections were held in 1998 and, in 2001, the government set up courts to try leaders of the Khmer Rouge.

Cambodia is a poor country whose economy has been wrecked by war. Until the 1970s, the country's farmers produced most of the food needed by the people. But by 1986, it was only able to supply 80% of its needs. Farming is the main activity and rice, rubber and maize are major products. Manufacturing is almost non-existent, apart from rubber processing and a few factories producing items for sale in Cambodia.

AREA 69,900 SQ MI [181,040 SQ KM] **POPULATION** 12,775,000
CAPITAL (POPULATION) PHNOM PENH (570,000)
GOVERNMENT CONSTITUTIONAL MONARCHY **ETHNIC GROUPS** KHMER 90%, VIETNAMESE 5%, CHINESE 1%, OTHER 5% **LANGUAGES** KHMER (OFFICIAL)
RELIGIONS BUDDHISM 95%, OTHER 5% **CURRENCY** RIEL = 100 SEN

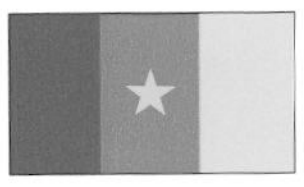

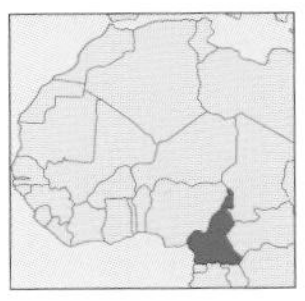

CAMEROON

GEOGRAPHY The Republic of Cameroon in West Africa got its name from the Portuguese word *camarões*, or prawns. This name was used by Portuguese explorers who fished for prawns along the coast. Behind the narrow coastal plains on the Gulf of Guinea, the land rises to a series of plateaux, with a mountainous region in the southwest where the volcano Mount Cameroon is situated. In the north, the land slopes down toward the Lake Chad basin.

The rainfall is heavy, especially in the highlands. The rainiest months near the coast are June to September. The rainfall decreases to the north and the far north has a hot, dry climate. Temperatures are high on the coast, whereas the inland plateaux are cooler.

POLITICS & ECONOMY Germany lost Cameroon during World War I (1914–18). The country was then divided into two parts, one ruled by Britain and the other by France. In 1960, French Cameroon became the independent Cameroon Republic. In 1961, after a vote in British Cameroon, part of the territory joined the Cameroon Republic to become the Federal Republic of Cameroon. The other part joined Nigeria. In 1972, Cameroon became a unitary state called the United Republic of Cameroon. It adopted the name Republic of Cameroon in 1984, but the country had two official languages. In 1995, partly to placate English-speaking people, Cameroon became the 52nd member of the Commonwealth.

Like most countries in tropical Africa, Cameroon's economy is based on agriculture, which employs 73% of the people. The chief food crops include cassava, maize, millet, sweet potatoes and yams. The country also has plantations to produce such crops as cocoa and coffee for export.

Cameroon is fortunate in having some oil, the country's chief export, and bauxite. Although Cameroon has few manufacturing and processing industries, its mineral exports and its self-sufficiency in food production make it one of the better-off countries in tropical Africa.

AREA 183,567 SQ MI [475,440 SQ KM] **POPULATION** 16,185,000
CAPITAL (POPULATION) YAOUNDÉ (800,000) **GOVERNMENT** MULTIPARTY REPUBLIC **ETHNIC GROUPS** FANG 20%, BAMILEKE AND BAMUM 19%, DUALA, LUANDA AND BASA 15%, FULANI 10% **LANGUAGES** FRENCH AND ENGLISH (BOTH OFFICIAL), MANY OTHERS **RELIGIONS** CHRISTIANITY 40%, TRADITIONAL BELIEFS 40%, ISLAM 20% **CURRENCY** CFA FRANC = 100 CENTIMES

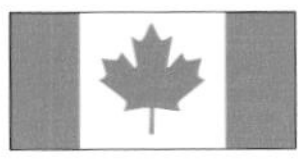

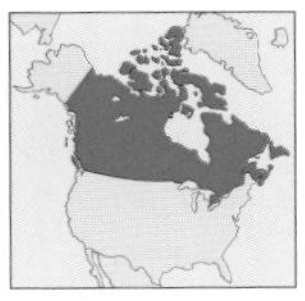

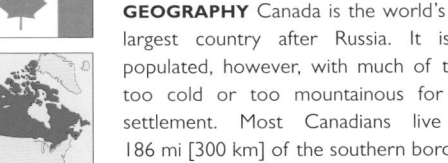

CANADA

GEOGRAPHY Canada is the world's second largest country after Russia. It is thinly populated, however, with much of the land too cold or too mountainous for human settlement. Most Canadians live within 186 mi [300 km] of the southern border.

Western Canada is rugged. It includes the Pacific ranges and the mighty Rocky Mountains. East of the Rockies are the interior plains. In the north lie the bleak Arctic islands, while to the south lie the densely populated lowlands around lakes Erie and Ontario and in the St Lawrence River valley.

Canada has a cold climate. In winter, temperatures fall below freezing point throughout most of Canada. But the southwestern coast has a relatively mild climate. Along the Arctic Circle, mean temperatures are below freezing for seven months a year.

Western and southeastern Canada experience high rainfall, but the prairies are dry with 10 inches to 20 inches [250 mm to 500 mm] of rain every year.

POLITICS & ECONOMY Canada's first people, the ancestors of the Native Americans, or Indians, arrived in North America from Asia around 40,000 years ago. Later arrivals were the Inuit (Eskimos), who also came from Asia. Europeans reached the Canadian coast in 1497 and a race began between Britain and France for control of the territory.

France gained an initial advantage, and the French founded Québec in 1608. But the British later occupied eastern Canada. In 1867, Britain passed the British North America Act, which set up the Dominion of Canada, which was made up of Québec, Ontario, Nova Scotia and New Brunswick. Other areas were added, the last being Newfoundland in 1949. Canada fought alongside Britain in both World Wars and many Canadians feel close ties with Britain. Canada is a constitutional monarchy, and the British monarch is Canada's head of state.

Rivalries between French- and English-speaking Canadians continue. In 1995, Québeckers voted against a move to make Québec a sovereign state. The majority was less than 1% and this issue seems unlikely to disappear. Another problem concerns the rights of the Aboriginal minorities, who would like to have more say in the running of their own affairs. To this end, in 1999, Canada created a new territory called Nunavut for the Inuit population in the north. Nunavut covers approximately 64% of what was formerly the eastern part of Northwest Territories.

Canada is a highly developed and prosperous country. Although farmland covers only 8% of the country, Canadian farms are highly productive. Canada is one of the world's leading producers of barley, wheat, meat and milk. Forestry and fishing are other important industries. It is rich in natural resources, especially oil and natural gas, and is a major exporter of minerals. The country also produces copper, gold, iron ore, uranium and zinc. Manufacturing is highly developed, especially in the cities where 78% of the people live. Canada has many factories that process farm and mineral products. It also produces cars, chemicals, electronic goods, machinery, paper and timber products.

AREA 3,851,788 SQ MI [9,976,140 SQ KM] **POPULATION** 31,902,000
CAPITAL (POPULATION) OTTAWA (1,107,000)
GOVERNMENT FEDERAL MULTIPARTY CONSTITUTIONAL MONARCHY
ETHNIC GROUPS BRITISH 28%, FRENCH 23%, OTHER EUROPEAN 15%, NATIVE AMERICAN (AMERINDIAN/INUIT) 2%, OTHER 32%
LANGUAGES ENGLISH AND FRENCH (BOTH OFFICIAL)
RELIGIONS ROMAN CATHOLIC 42%, PROTESTANT 40%, JUDAISM, ISLAM, HINDUISM **CURRENCY** CANADIAN DOLLAR = 100 CENTS

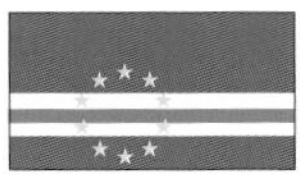

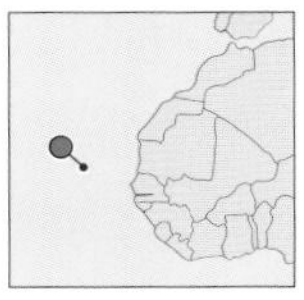

CAPE VERDE

Cape Verde consists of ten large and five small islands, and is situated 350 mi [560 km] west of Dakar in Senegal. The islands have a tropical climate, with high temperatures all year round. Cape Verde became independent from Portugal in 1975 and is rated as a "low-income" developing country by the World Bank.

AREA 1,556 SQ MI [4,030 SQ KM]
POPULATION 409,000 **CAPITAL** PRAIA

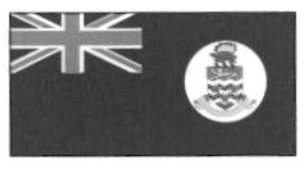

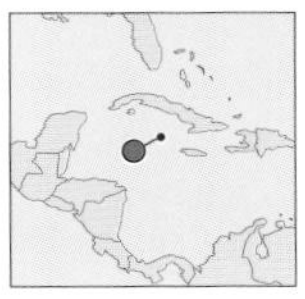

CAYMAN ISLANDS

The Cayman Islands are an overseas territory of the UK, consisting of three low-lying islands. Financial services are the main economic activity and the islands offer a secret tax haven to many companies and banks.

AREA 100 SQ MI [259 SQ KM]
POPULATION 36,000 **CAPITAL** GEORGE TOWN

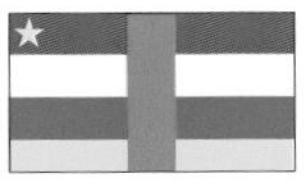

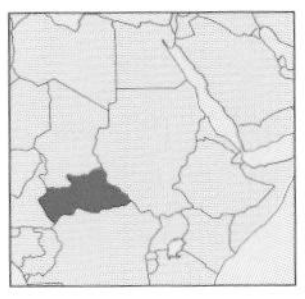

CENTRAL AFRICAN REPUBLIC

GEOGRAPHY The Central African Republic is a remote, landlocked country in the heart of Africa. It consists mostly of a plateau lying between 1,970 ft and 2,620 ft [600 m to 800 m] above sea level. The Ubangi drains the south, while the Chari (or Shari) River flows from the north to the Lake Chad basin. The climate is warm throughout the year, while the annual average rainfall in the capital Bangui totals 62 inches [1,574 mm]. The north is drier, with an average annual rainfall of about 31 inches [800 mm].

POLITICS & ECONOMY France set up an outpost at Bangui in 1899 and ruled the country as a colony from 1894. Known as Ubangi-Shari, the country was ruled by France as part of French Equatorial Africa until it gained independence in 1960.

Central African Republic became a one-party state in 1962, but army officers seized power in 1966. The head of the army, Jean-Bedel Bokassa, made himself emperor in 1976. The country was renamed the Central African Empire, but after a brutal reign, the tyrannical Bokassa was overthrown in a military coup in 1979. The country again became a republic.

The country adopted a new, multiparty constitution in 1991. Multiparty elections were held in 1993 and 1998. However, an army uprising began in 2002, culminating in the overthrow by a military coup of the elected President Patassé in 2003. He was succeeded by General François Bezize.

The World Bank classifies Central African Republic as a "low-income" developing country. Over 80% of the people are farmers, and most of them produce little more than they need to feed their families. The main crops are bananas, maize, manioc, millet and yams. Coffee, cotton, timber and tobacco are produced for export, mainly on commercial plantations. The country's development has been impeded by its remote position, its poor transport system and its untrained work force. The country depends heavily on aid, especially from France.

AREA 240,533 SQ MI [622,980 SQ KM] **POPULATION** 3,643,000
CAPITAL (POPULATION) BANGUI (553,000) **GOVERNMENT** MULTIPARTY REPUBLIC **ETHNIC GROUPS** BAYA 34%, BANDA 27%, MANDJIA 21%, SARA 10%, MBAKA 4%, MBOUM 4% **LANGUAGES** FRENCH (OFFICIAL), SANGHO
RELIGIONS TRADITIONAL BELIEFS 57%, CHRISTIANITY 35%, ISLAM 8%
CURRENCY CFA FRANC = 100 CENTIMES

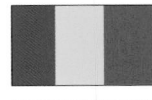

CHAD

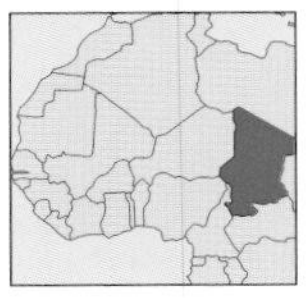

GEOGRAPHY The Republic of Chad is a landlocked country in north-central Africa. It is Africa's fifth largest country and is over twice the size of France, the country which once ruled it as a colony.

Ndjamena in central Chad has a hot, tropical climate, with a marked dry season from November to April. The south of the country is wetter, with an average yearly rainfall of around 39 inches [1,000 mm]. The burning-hot desert in the north has an average yearly rainfall of less than 5 inches [130 mm].

POLITICS & ECONOMY Chad straddles two worlds. The north is populated by Muslim Arab and Berber peoples, while black Africans, who follow traditional beliefs or who have converted to Christianity, live in the south.

French explorers were active in the area in the late 19th century. France finally made Chad a colony in 1902. After becoming independent in 1960, Chad has been hit by ethnic conflict. The 1970s were marked by civil war and coups. Chad and Libya agreed a truce in 1987 and, in 1994, the International Court of Justice ruled against Libya's claim on the Aozou Strip. Chad enjoyed more stability in the 1990s. A new constitution was adopted in 1997.

Hit by drought and civil war, Chad is one of the world's poorest countries. Farming, fishing and livestock raising employ 83% of the people. Groundnuts, millet, rice and sorghum are major food crops in the south, but the chief export crop is cotton. Chad has few manufacturing industries, but its oil reserves hold out hope for development in the 21st century.

AREA 495,752 SQ MI [1,284,000 SQ KM] **POPULATION** 8,997,000
CAPITAL (POPULATION) NDJAMENA (530,000)
GOVERNMENT MULTIPARTY REPUBLIC **ETHNIC GROUPS** BAGIRMI, KREISH AND SARA 31%, SUDANIC ARAB 26%, TEDA 7%, MBUM 6%
LANGUAGES FRENCH AND ARABIC (BOTH OFFICIAL), MANY OTHERS
RELIGIONS ISLAM 50%, CHRISTIANITY 25%, TRADITIONAL BELIEFS 25%
CURRENCY CFA FRANC = 100 CENTIMES

CHILE

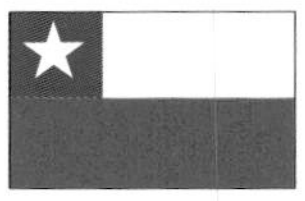

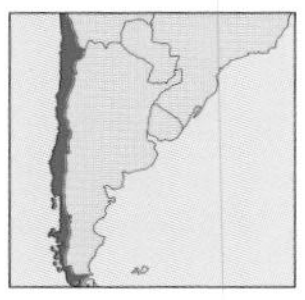

GEOGRAPHY The Republic of Chile stretches about 2,650 mi [4,260 km] from north to south, although the maximum east–west distance is only about 267 mi [430 km]. The high Andes Mountains form Chile's eastern borders with Argentina and Bolivia. To the west are basins and valleys, with coastal uplands overlooking the shore. Most people live in the central valley, where Santiago is situated.

Santiago has a Mediterranean climate, with hot, dry summers from November to March and mild, moist winters from April to October. The Atacama Desert in the north is one of the world's driest places, while southern Chile is cold and stormy.

POLITICS & ECONOMY Amerindian people reached the southern tip of South America 8,000 years ago. In 1520, Portuguese navigator Ferdinand Magellan was the first European to sight Chile. The country became a Spanish colony in the 1540s. Chile became independent in 1818. During a war (1879–83), it gained mineral-rich areas from Peru and Bolivia.

In 1970, Salvador Allende became the first Communist leader to be elected democratically. He was overthrown in 1973 by army officers, who were supported by the CIA. General Augusto Pinochet then ruled as a dictator. A new constitution was introduced in 1981 and elections were held in 1989. In 2000, a socialist, Ricardo Lagos, was elected president. Pinochet, who had been charged with presiding over acts of torture, was found to be too ill to stand trial in 2001.

The World Bank classifies Chile as a "lower-middle-income" developing country. Mining is important, especially copper production. Minerals dominate exports. The most valuable activity is manufacturing; products include processed foods, metals, iron and steel, transport equipment and textiles. The chief crop is wheat, while beans, fruits, maize and livestock products are also important. Chile's fishing industry is one of the world's largest.

AREA 292,258 SQ MI [756,950 SQ KM] **POPULATION** 15,499,000
CAPITAL (POPULATION) SANTIAGO (4,691,000)
GOVERNMENT MULTIPARTY REPUBLIC **ETHNIC GROUPS** MESTIZO 95%, AMERINDIAN 3% **LANGUAGES** SPANISH (OFFICIAL)
RELIGIONS ROMAN CATHOLIC 89%, PROTESTANT 11%
CURRENCY PESO = 100 CENTAVOS

CHINA

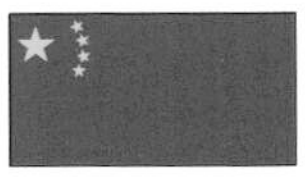

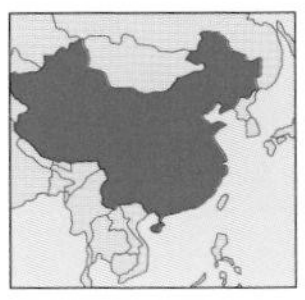

GEOGRAPHY The People's Republic of China is the world's third largest country. Most people live in the east – on the coastal plains or in the fertile valleys of the Huang He (Hwang Ho or Yellow River), the Chang Jiang (Yangtze Kiang), which is Asia's longest river at 3,960 mi [6,380 km], and the Xi Jiang (Si Kiang). Western China is thinly populated. It includes the bleak Tibetan plateau which is bounded by the Himalaya, the world's highest mountain range. Other ranges include the Kunlun Shan, the Altun Shan and the Tian Shan. Deserts include the Gobi Desert along the Mongolian border and the Taklimakan Desert in the far west.

Beijing in northeastern China has cold winters and warm summers, with a moderate rainfall. Shanghai, in the east-central region of China, has milder winters and more rain. The southeast has a wet, subtropical climate. In the west, the climate is severe. Lhasa has very cold winters and a low rainfall.

POLITICS & ECONOMY China is one of the world's oldest civilizations, going back 3,500 years. Under the Han dynasty (202 BC to AD 220), the Chinese empire was as large as the Roman empire. Mongols conquered China in the 13th century, but Chinese rule was restored in 1368. The Manchu people of Mongolia ruled the country from 1644 to 1912, when the country became a republic.

War with Japan (1937–45) was followed by civil war between the nationalists and the Communists. The Communists triumphed in 1949, setting up the People's Republic of China. In the 1980s, following the death of the revolutionary leader Mao Zedong (Mao Tse-tung) in 1976, China encouraged formerly forbidden policies, namely private enterprise and foreign investment. But the Communist leaders have not permitted political freedom. Opponents are still harshly treated, while attempts to negotiate some degree of autonomy for Tibet have been rejected.

China's economy has expanded greatly since the 1970s, with many Communist policies being abandoned. Foreign investors have help to set up many new industries in the east. Between 1989 and 2002, the economy grew by an average of 9.3% per year. With its cheap labor, trained managers and engineers, China has overtaken Japan to become the fourth largest exporter to the United States. It has benefited from the return of Hong Kong in 1997 and its admission to the World Trade Organization (WTO) in 2001. China would also like to regain the prosperous island of Taiwan, also a member of the WTO, but this seems unlikely in the near future.

Despite its recent success, China remains a poor country. In the late 1990s, agriculture still employed nearly half of the people, although only 10% of the land is farmed. Products include rice, sweet potatoes, tea and wheat, and many fruits and vegetables. Livestock farming is important. Pork is popular – China has more than a third of the world's pigs. Resources include coal, iron ore and other metals. Leading manufactures include cement, chemicals, fertilizers, machinery, telecommunications and recording equipment, and textiles. In recent years, China has also become one of the world's leading producers of consumer goods. It now produces more than half of the world's cameras, 30% of its air conditioners and TV sets, 23% of its washing machines, 20% of its refrigerators, 37% of its hard disk drives and 10% of its computer monitors.

AREA 3,705,386 SQ MI [9,596,960 SQ KM]
POPULATION 1,284,304,000 **CAPITAL (POPULATION)** BEIJING (12,362,000) **GOVERNMENT** SINGLE-PARTY COMMUNIST REPUBLIC
ETHNIC GROUPS HAN CHINESE 92%, 55 MINORITY GROUPS
LANGUAGES MANDARIN CHINESE (OFFICIAL) **RELIGIONS** ATHEIST (OFFICIAL)
CURRENCY RENMINBI YUAN = 10 JIAO = 100 FEN

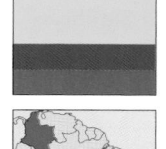

COLOMBIA

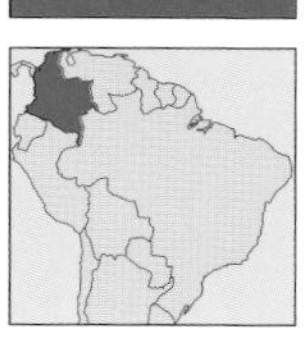

GEOGRAPHY The Republic of Colombia, in northeastern South America, is the only country in the continent to have coastlines on both the Pacific and the Caribbean Sea. Colombia also contains the northernmost ranges of the Andes Mountains.

There is a tropical climate in the lowlands, but the altitude greatly affects the climate of the Andes. The capital, Bogotá, which stands on a plateau in the eastern Andes at about 9,200 ft [2,800 m] above sea level, has mild temperatures throughout the year. The rainfall is heavy, especially on the Pacific coast.

POLITICS & ECONOMY Amerindian people have lived in Colombia for thousands of years. But today, only a small proportion of the people are of unmixed Amerindian ancestry. Mestizos (people of mixed white and Amerindian ancestry) form the largest group, followed by whites and mulattos (people of mixed European and African ancestry).

Spaniards opened up the area in the early 16th century. They set up a territory known as the Vice-royalty of the New Kingdom of Granada, including Colombia, Ecuador, Panama and Venezuela. In 1819, the area became independent, but Ecuador and Venezuela soon split away, followed by Panama in 1903. Instability has marked its recent history. Political rivalries led to civil wars in 1899–1902 and 1949–57, when a coalition government was formed. The coalition ended in 1986 when the Liberal Party was elected. Colombia faces economic and security problems, notably combating left-wing guerrillas and right-wing paramilitaries, while controlling a large illicit drug industry. In the early 2000s, the US provided aid to help Colombia fight drug-trafficking. Colombia exports oil, coffee and chemicals.

AREA 439,733 SQ MI [1,138,910 SQ KM] **POPULATION** 41,008,000
CAPITAL (POPULATION) BOGOTÁ (6,005,000)
GOVERNMENT MULTIPARTY REPUBLIC **ETHNIC GROUPS** MESTIZO 58%, WHITE 20%, MULATTO 14%, BLACK 4% **LANGUAGES** SPANISH (OFFICIAL)
RELIGIONS ROMAN CATHOLIC 90% **CURRENCY** PESO = 100 CENTAVOS

COMOROS

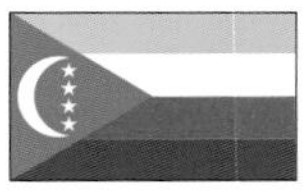

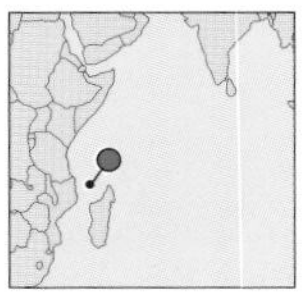

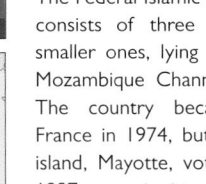

The Federal Islamic Republic of the Comoros consists of three large islands and some smaller ones, lying at the north end of the Mozambique Channel in the Indian Ocean. The country became independent from France in 1974, but the people on a fourth island, Mayotte, voted to remain French. In 1997, secessionists on the island of Anjouan, who favored a return to French rule, defeated forces from Grand Comore and, in 1998, they voted overwhelmingly to break away from the Comoros. Most people are subsistence farmers, although cash crops such as coconuts, coffee, cocoa and spices are also produced. The main exports are cloves, perfume oils and vanilla.

AREA 861 SQ MI [2,230 SQ KM] **POPULATION** 614,000 **CAPITAL** MORONI

CONGO

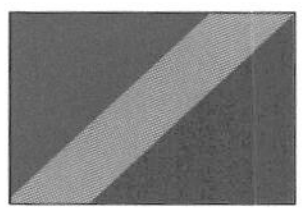

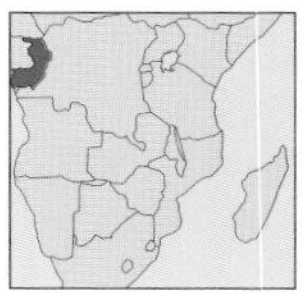

GEOGRAPHY The Republic of Congo is a country on the River Congo in west-central Africa. The Equator runs through the center of the country. Congo has a narrow coastal plain on which its main port, Pointe Noire, stands. Behind the plain are uplands through which the River Niari has carved a fertile valley. Central Congo consists of high plains. The north contains large swampy areas in the valleys of the tributaries of the River Congo.

Congo has a hot, wet equatorial climate. Brazzaville has a dry season between June and September. The coast is drier and cooler than the rest of Congo, because of the cold offshore Benguela ocean current.

POLITICS & ECONOMY Part of the huge Kongo kingdom between the 15th and 18th centuries, the coast of the Congo later became a center of the European slave trade. The area came under French protection in 1880. It was later governed as part of a larger region called French Equatorial Africa. The country remained under French control until 1960.

Congo became a one-party state in 1964 and a military group took over the government in 1968. In 1970, Congo declared itself a Communist country, though it continued to seek aid from Western countries. The government officially abandoned its Communist policies in 1990. Multiparty elections were held in 1992, but the elected president, Pascal Lissouba, was overthrown in 1997 by former president Denis Sassou-Nguesso. Civil war again occurred in January 1999, but peace was restored. In 2002, Sassou-Nguesso was elected president.

The World Bank classifies Congo as a "lower-middle-income" developing country. Agriculture is the most important activity, employing more than 60% of the people. But many farmers produce little more than they need to feed their families. Major food crops include bananas, cassava, maize and rice, while the leading cash crops are coffee and cocoa. Congo's main exports are oil (which makes up 70% of the total) and timber. Manufacturing is relatively unimportant at the moment, still hampered by poor transport links, but it is gradually being developed.

AREA 132,046 SQ MI [342,000 SQ KM] **POPULATION** 2,958,000
CAPITAL (POPULATION) BRAZZAVILLE (938,000)
GOVERNMENT MILITARY REGIME **ETHNIC GROUPS** KONGO 48%, SANGHA 20%, TEKE 17%, M'BOCHI 12% **LANGUAGES** FRENCH (OFFICIAL), MANY OTHERS **RELIGIONS** CHRISTIANITY 50%, ANIMIST 48%, ISLAM 2%
CURRENCY CFA FRANC = 100 CENTIMES

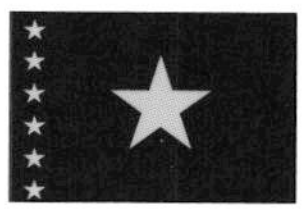
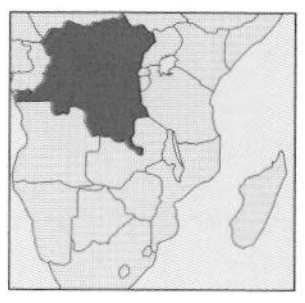

CONGO (DEM. REP. OF THE)

GEOGRAPHY The Democratic Republic of the Congo, formerly known as Zaïre, is the world's 12th largest country. Much of the country lies within the drainage basin of the huge River Congo. The river reaches the sea along the country's coastline, which is 25 mi [40 km] long. Mountains rise in the east, where the country's borders run through lakes Tanganyika, Kivu, Edward and Albert.

The equatorial region has high temperatures and heavy rainfall throughout the year.

POLITICS & ECONOMY Pygmies were the first inhabitants of the region, with Portuguese navigators not reaching the coast until 1482, but the interior was not explored until the late 19th century. In 1885, the country, called Congo Free State, became the personal property of King Léopold II of Belgium. In 1908, the country became a Belgian colony.

The Belgian Congo became independent in 1960 and was renamed Zaïre in 1971. Ethnic rivalries caused instability until 1965, when the country became a one-party state, ruled by President Mobutu. The government allowed the formation of political parties in 1990, but elections were repeatedly postponed. In 1996, fighting broke out in eastern Zaïre, as the Tutsi–Hutu conflict in Burundi and Rwanda spilled over. The rebel leader Laurent Kabila took power in 1997, ousting Mobutu and renaming the country. A rebellion against Kabila broke out in 1998. Rwanda and Uganda supported the rebels, while Angola, Chad, Namibia and Zimbabwe assisted Kabila. A peace treaty was signed in 1999, but fighting continued. Kabila was assassinated in 2001. His son, Major-General Joseph Kabila, who became president, worked to end a war which, by early 2003, had claimed over 2 million lives.

The World Bank classifies the Democratic Republic of the Congo as a "low-income" developing country, despite its reserves of copper, the main export, and other minerals. Agriculture, mainly at subsistence level, employs 65% of the people.

AREA 905,365 SQ MI [2,344,885 SQ KM] **POPULATION** 55,225,000
CAPITAL (POPULATION) KINSHASA (2,664,000)
GOVERNMENT SINGLE-PARTY REPUBLIC
ETHNIC GROUPS OVER 200; THE LARGEST ARE MONGO, LUBA, KONGO, MANGBETU-AZANDE
LANGUAGES FRENCH (OFFICIAL), TRIBAL LANGUAGES
RELIGIONS ROMAN CATHOLIC 50%, PROTESTANT 20%, ISLAM 10%, OTHERS 20%
CURRENCY CONGOLESE FRANC = 100 CENTIMES

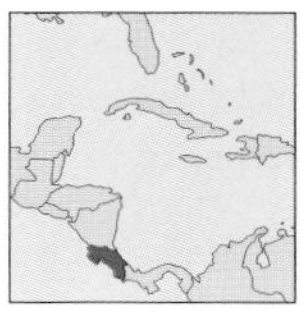

COSTA RICA

GEOGRAPHY The Republic of Costa Rica in Central America has coastlines on both the Pacific Ocean and also on the Caribbean Sea. Central Costa Rica consists of mountain ranges and plateaux with many volcanoes.

The coolest months are December and January. The northeast trade winds bring heavy rain to the Caribbean coast. There is less rainfall in the highlands and on the Pacific coastlands.

POLITICS & ECONOMY Christopher Columbus reached the Caribbean coast in 1502 and rumors of treasure soon attracted many Spaniards to settle in the country. Spain ruled the country until 1821, when Spain's Central American colonies broke away to join Mexico in 1822. In 1823, the Central American states broke with Mexico and set up the Central American Federation. Later, this large union broke up and Costa Rica became fully independent in 1838.

From the late 19th century, Costa Rica experienced a number of revolutions, with periods of dictatorship and periods of democracy. In 1948, following a revolt, the armed forces were abolished. Since 1948, Costa Rica has enjoyed a long period of stable democracy, which many in Latin America admire and envy.

Costa Rica is classified by the World Bank as a "lower-middle-income" developing country and one of the most prosperous countries in Central America. There are high educational standards and a high life expectancy (to an average of 73.5 years). Agriculture employs 20% of the people.

The country's resources include its forests, but it lacks minerals apart from some bauxite and manganese. Manufacturing is increasing. The United States is Costa Rica's chief trading partner. Tourism is a fast-growing industry.

AREA 19,730 SQ MI [51,100 SQ KM] **POPULATION** 3,835,000
CAPITAL (POPULATION) SAN JOSÉ (1,220,000)
GOVERNMENT MULTIPARTY REPUBLIC **ETHNIC GROUPS** WHITE 85%, MESTIZO 8%, BLACK AND MULATTO 3%, EAST ASIAN (MOSTLY CHINESE) 1%
LANGUAGES SPANISH (OFFICIAL) **RELIGIONS** ROMAN CATHOLIC 76%, EVANGELICAL 14% **CURRENCY** COLÓN = 100 CÉNTIMOS

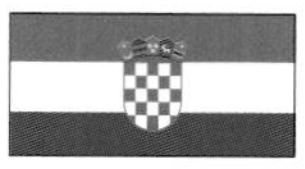
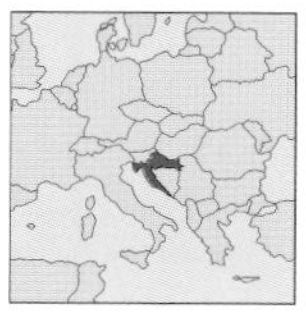

CROATIA

GEOGRAPHY The Republic of Croatia was one of the six republics that made up the former Communist country of Yugoslavia until it became independent in 1991. The region bordering the Adriatic Sea is called Dalmatia. It includes the coastal ranges, which contain large areas of bare limestone. Most of the rest of the country consists of the fertile Pannonian plains.

The coastal area has a typical Mediterranean climate, with hot, dry summers and mild, moist winters. Inland, the climate becomes more continental. Winters are cold, while temperatures often soar to 100°F [38°C] in the summer months.

POLITICS & ECONOMY Slav people settled in the area around 1,400 years ago. In 803, Croatia became part of the Holy Roman empire and the Croats soon adopted Christianity. Croatia was an independent kingdom in the 10th and 11th centuries. In 1102, the king of Hungary also became king of Croatia, creating a union that lasted 800 years. In 1526, part of Croatia came under the Turkish Ottoman empire, while the rest came under the Austrian Habsburgs.

After Austria–Hungary was defeated in World War I (1914–18), Croatia became part of the new Kingdom of the Serbs, Croats and Slovenes. This kingdom was renamed Yugoslavia in 1929. Germany occupied Yugoslavia during World War II (1939–45). Croatia was proclaimed independent, but it was really ruled by the invaders.

After the war, Communists took power with Josip Broz Tito as the country's leader. Despite ethnic differences between the people, Tito held Yugoslavia together until his death in 1980. In the 1980s, economic and ethnic problems, including a deterioration in relations with Serbia, threatened stability. In the 1990s, Yugoslavia split into five nations, one of which was Croatia, which declared itself independent in 1991.

After Serbia supplied arms to Serbs living in Croatia, war broke out between the two republics, causing great damage. Croatia lost more than 30% of its territory. But in 1992, the United Nations sent a peacekeeping force to Croatia, which effectively ended the war with Serbia.

In 1992, when war broke out in Bosnia-Herzegovina, Bosnian Croats occupied parts of the country. But in 1994, Croatia helped to end Croat–Muslim conflict in Bosnia-Herzegovina and, in 1995, after retaking some areas occupied by Serbs, it helped to draw up the Dayton Peace Accord which ended the civil war there.

The wars of the early 1990s disrupted Croatia's economy, but following the election of a pro-democratic coalition government in 2000, stability, which is so vital for the valuable tourist industry, appeared to be increasing. Croatia has many manufacturing industries. Manufactures are the chief exports.

AREA 21,824 SQ MI [56,538 SQ KM] **POPULATION** 4,391,000
CAPITAL (POPULATION) ZAGREB (868,000)
GOVERNMENT MULTIPARTY REPUBLIC **ETHNIC GROUPS** CROAT 78%, SERB 12% **LANGUAGES** SERBO-CROATIAN **RELIGIONS** ROMAN CATHOLIC 77%, EASTERN ORTHODOX 11%, ISLAM 1% **CURRENCY** KUNA = 100 LIPAS

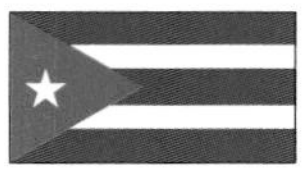
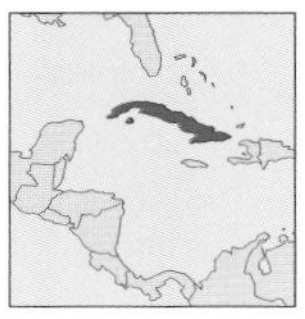

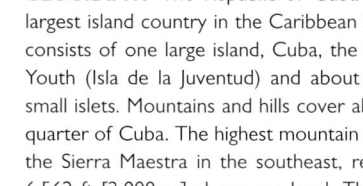

CUBA

GEOGRAPHY The Republic of Cuba is the largest island country in the Caribbean Sea. It consists of one large island, Cuba, the Isle of Youth (Isla de la Juventud) and about 1,600 small islets. Mountains and hills cover about a quarter of Cuba. The highest mountain range, the Sierra Maestra in the southeast, reaches 6,562 ft [2,000 m] above sea level. The rest of the land consists of gently rolling country or coastal plains, crossed by fertile valleys carved by the short, mostly shallow and narrow rivers.

Cuba lies in the tropics. But sea breezes moderate the temperature, warming the land in winter and cooling it in summer.

POLITICS & ECONOMY Christopher Columbus discovered the island in 1492 and Spaniards began to settle there from 1511. Spanish rule ended in 1898, when the United States defeated Spain in the Spanish–American War. American influence in Cuba remained strong until 1959, when revolutionary forces under Fidel Castro overthrew the dictatorial government of Fulgencio Batista.

The United States opposed Castro's policies, when he turned to the Soviet Union for assistance. In 1961, Cuban exiles attempting an invasion were defeated. In 1962, the US learned that nuclear missile bases armed by the Soviet Union had been established in Cuba. The US ordered the Soviet Union to remove the missiles and bases and, after a few days, when many people feared that a world war might break out, the Soviet Union agreed to the American demands.

Cuba's relations with the Soviet Union remained strong until 1991, when the Soviet Union was broken up. The loss of Soviet aid greatly damaged Cuba's economy, but Castro maintained his left-wing policies. In 2000, the United States lifted its food embargo on Cuba, but Cuba again came under fire in 2003 following the arrests of 78 opponents of the regime.

The government runs Cuba's economy and owns 70% of the farmland. Agriculture is important and sugar is the chief export, followed by refined nickel ore. Other exports include cigars, citrus fruits, fish, medical products and rum.

Before 1959, US companies owned most of Cuba's manufacturing industries. But under Fidel Castro, they became government property. After the collapse of Communist governments in the Soviet Union and its allies, Cuba worked to increase its trade with Latin America and China.

AREA 42,803 SQ MI [110,860 SQ KM] **POPULATION** 11,224,000
CAPITAL (POPULATION) HAVANA (2,204,000)
GOVERNMENT SOCIALIST REPUBLIC **ETHNIC GROUPS** MULATTO 51%, WHITE 37%, BLACK 11% **LANGUAGES** SPANISH (OFFICIAL)
RELIGIONS ROMAN CATHOLIC 40%, PROTESTANT 3%
CURRENCY CUBAN PESO = 100 CENTAVOS

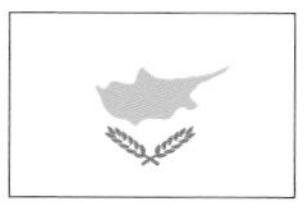
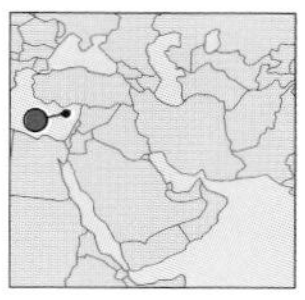

CYPRUS

GEOGRAPHY The Republic of Cyprus is an island nation in the northeastern Mediterranean Sea. Geographers regard it as part of Asia, but it resembles southern Europe in many ways.

Cyprus has scenic mountain ranges, including the Kyrenia range in the north and the Troodos Mountains in the south, which rise to 6,401 ft [1,951 m] at Mount Olympus. The island also contains several fertile lowlands, including the broad Mesaoria plain between the Kyrenia and Troodos mountains.

Cyprus has a Mediterranean climate, with hot, dry summers and mild, moist winters. But the summers are hotter than in the western Mediterranean lands; this is because Cyprus lies close to the hot mainland of southwestern Asia.

POLITICS & ECONOMY Greeks settled on Cyprus around 3,200 years ago. From AD 330, the island was part of the Byzantine empire. In the 1570s, Cyprus became part of the Turkish Ottoman empire. Turkish rule continued until 1878 when Cyprus was leased to Britain. Britain annexed the island in 1914 and proclaimed it a colony in 1925.

In the 1950s, Greek Cypriots, who made up four-fifths of the population, began a campaign for *enosis* (union) with Greece. Their leader was the Greek Orthodox Archbishop Makarios. A secret guerrilla force called EOKA attacked the British, who exiled Makarios. Cyprus became an independent country in 1960, although Britain retained two military bases. Independent Cyprus had a constitution which provided for power-sharing between the Greek and Turkish Cypriots. But the constitution proved unworkable and fighting broke out between the two communities. In 1964, the United Nations sent in a peacekeeping force, but communal clashes recurred in 1967.

In 1974, Cypriot forces led by Greek officers overthrew Makarios. This led Turkey to invade northern Cyprus, a territory occupying about 40% of the island. Many Greek Cypriots fled from the north which, in 1979, was proclaimed an independent state called the Turkish Republic of Northern Cyprus. But the United Nations still regarded Cyprus as a single nation under the Greek-Cypriot government in the south. In 2002, the European Union invited Cyprus to become a member in 2004. However, attempts to reunify the island in 2003 ended in failure.

Cyprus got its name from the Greek word *kypros*, meaning copper. But little copper remains and the chief minerals today are asbestos and chromium. However, the most valuable activity in Cyprus is tourism. Manufactures include cement, clothes, footwear, tiles and wine.

In the early 1990s, the United Nations reclassified Cyprus as a developed rather than a developing country. But the economy of the Turkish-Cypriot north lags behind that of the more prosperous Greek-Cypriot south.

AREA 3,571 sq mi [9,250 sq km] **POPULATION** 767,000 **CAPITAL (POPULATION)** Nicosia (189,000) **GOVERNMENT** Multiparty republic **ETHNIC GROUPS** Greek Cypriot 78%, Turkish Cypriot 18% **LANGUAGES** Greek and Turkish (both official), English **RELIGIONS** Greek Orthodox 78%, Islam 18% **CURRENCY** Cyprus pound = 100 cents

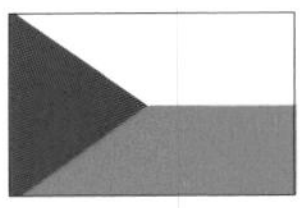
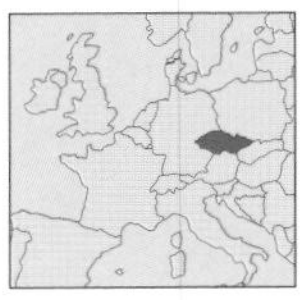

CZECH REPUBLIC

GEOGRAPHY The Czech Republic is the western three-fifths of the former country of Czechoslovakia. It contains two regions: Bohemia in the west and Moravia in the east. Mountains border much of the country in the west. The Bohemian basin in the north-center is a fertile lowland region, with Prague, the capital city, as its main center. Highlands cover much of the center of the country, with lowlands in the southeast.

The climate is influenced by its landlocked position in east-central Europe. Prague has warm, sunny summers and cold winters. The average rainfall is moderate, with 20 inches to 30 inches [500 mm to 750 mm] every year in lowland areas.

POLITICS & ECONOMY After World War I (1914–18), Czechoslovakia was created. Germany seized the country in World War II (1939–45). In 1948, Communist leaders took power and Czechoslovakia was allied to the Soviet Union. When democratic reforms were introduced in the Soviet Union in the late 1980s, the Czechs also demanded reforms. Free elections were held in 1990, but differences between the Czechs and Slovaks led to the partitioning of the country on January 1, 1993. The Czech Republic became a member of NATO in 1999 and, in 2002, the European Union invited the country to become a member in May 2004.

Under Communist rule the Czech Republic became one of the most industrialized parts of Eastern Europe. The country has deposits of coal, uranium, iron ore, magnesite, tin and zinc. Manufacturing employs about 40% of the Czech Republic's entire work force. Farming is also important. Under Communism, the government owned the land, but private ownership is now being restored. The country was admitted into the OECD in 1995.

AREA 30,449 sq mi [78,864 sq km] **POPULATION** 10,257,000 **CAPITAL (POPULATION)** Prague (1,203,000) **GOVERNMENT** Multiparty republic **ETHNIC GROUPS** Czech 81%, Moravian 13%, Slovak 3%, Polish, German, Silesian, Gypsy, Hungarian, Ukrainian **LANGUAGES** Czech (official) **RELIGIONS** Atheist 40%, Roman Catholic 39%, Protestant 4% **CURRENCY** Czech koruna = 100 haler

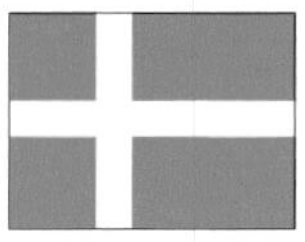
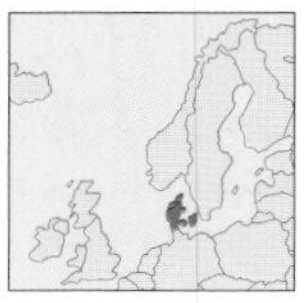

DENMARK

GEOGRAPHY The Kingdom of Denmark is the smallest country in Scandinavia. It consists of a peninsula, called Jutland (or Jylland), which is joined to Germany, and more than 400 islands, 89 of which are inhabited.

The land is flat and mostly covered by rocks dropped there by huge ice sheets during the last Ice Age. The highest point in Denmark is on Jutland. It is only 568 ft [173 m] above sea level.

Denmark has a cool but pleasant climate, except during cold spells in the winter when The Sound between Sjælland and Sweden may freeze over. Summers are warm. Rainfall occurs all through the year.

POLITICS & ECONOMY Danish Vikings terrorized much of Western Europe for about 300 years after AD 800. Danish kings ruled England in the 11th century. In the late 14th century, Denmark formed a union with Norway and Sweden (which included Finland). Sweden broke away in 1523, while Denmark lost Norway to Sweden in 1814.

After 1945, Denmark played an important part in European affairs, becoming a member of the North Atlantic Treaty Organization (NATO). In 1973, Denmark joined the European Union, although it rejected the adoption of the euro in 2000. The Danes now enjoy some of the world's highest living standards, although the extensive social welfare provisions exert a considerable cost.

Denmark has few natural resources apart from some oil and gas from wells deep under the North Sea. But the economy is highly developed. Manufacturing industries, which employ about 17% of all workers, produce a wide variety of products, including furniture, processed food, machinery, television sets and textiles. Farms cover about three-quarters of the land. Farming employs only 4% of the workers, but it is highly scientific and productive. Meat and dairy farming are the chief activities.

AREA 16,629 sq mi [43,070 sq km] **POPULATION** 5,369,000 **CAPITAL (POPULATION)** Copenhagen (1,362,000) **GOVERNMENT** Parliamentary monarchy **ETHNIC GROUPS** Danish 97% **LANGUAGES** Danish (official) **RELIGIONS** Lutheran 95%, Roman Catholic 1% **CURRENCY** Krone = 100 øre

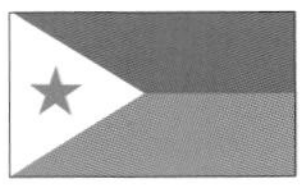
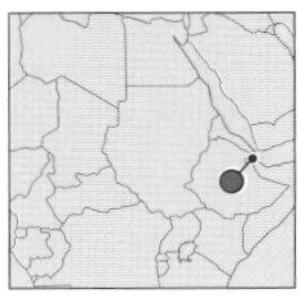

DJIBOUTI

GEOGRAPHY The Republic of Djibouti in eastern Africa occupies a strategic position where the Red Sea meets the Gulf of Aden. Djibouti has one of the world's hottest and driest climates.

POLITICS & ECONOMY France set up a territory called French Somaliland in 1888. Its capital, Djibouti, became important when a railroad was built to Addis Ababa and Djibouti became the main outlet for Ethiopian trade. In 1967, France renamed the dependency the French Territory of the Afars and Issas, but it was renamed Djibouti on independence in 1977. It became a one-party state in 1981, but a new constitution (1992) permitted four parties which had to maintain a balance between the country's ethnic groups. Conflict between the Afars and Issas flared up in 1992 and 1993, but a peace agreement was signed in 1994. Djibouti is a poor country. Its economy is based largely on the revenue it gets from its port and the railroad to Addis Ababa.

AREA 8,958 sq mi [23,200 sq km] **POPULATION** 473,000 **CAPITAL (POPULATION)** Djibouti (383,000) **GOVERNMENT** Multiparty republic **ETHNIC GROUPS** Somali 60%, Afar 35% **LANGUAGES** Arabic and French (both official) **RELIGIONS** Islam 94%, Christianity 6% **CURRENCY** Djibouti franc = 100 centimes

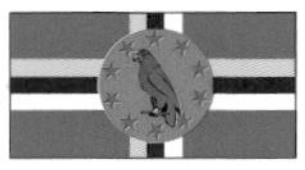
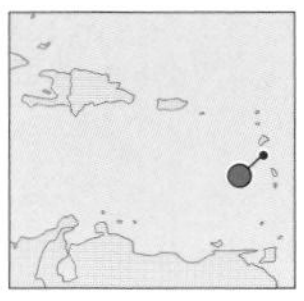

DOMINICA

The Commonwealth of Dominica, a former British colony, became independent in 1978. The island has a mountainous spine and less than 10% of the land is cultivated. Yet agriculture employs more than 60% of the people. The manufacturing of coconut-based soap is important, while mining and tourism are other minor activities.

AREA 290 sq mi [751 sq km] **POPULATION** 70,000 **CAPITAL** Roseau

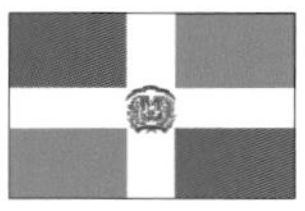
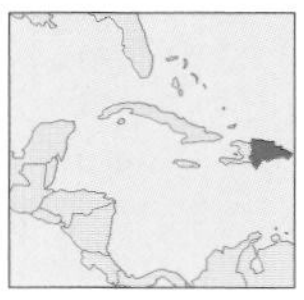

DOMINICAN REPUBLIC

GEOGRAPHY Second largest of the Caribbean nations in both area and population, the Dominican Republic shares the island of Hispaniola with Haiti, with the Dominican Republic occupying the eastern two-thirds. The country is mountainous, and the generally hot and humid climate eases with altitude.

POLITICS & ECONOMY The Dominican Republic has chaotic origins, having been held by Spain, France, Haiti and the United States at various times. Civil war broke out in 1966 but the conflict soon ended after US intervention. Since 1966, a young democracy has survived violent elections under the watchful eye of the USA.

AREA 18,815 sq mi [48,730 sq km] **POPULATION** 8,722,000 **CAPITAL (POPULATION)** Santo Domingo (2,135,000) **GOVERNMENT** Multiparty republic **ETHNIC GROUPS** Mulatto 73%, White 16%, Black 11% **LANGUAGES** Spanish (official) **RELIGIONS** Roman Catholic 95% **CURRENCY** Peso = 100 centavos

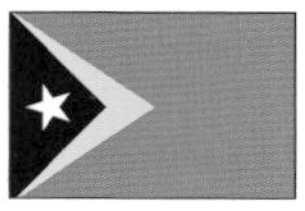
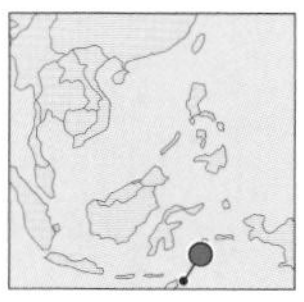

EAST TIMOR

The Republic of East Timor became fully independent and the world's newest country on May 20, 2002. The land is mainly rugged. Temperatures are generally high and the rainfall is moderate. Portugal ruled the area from the late 19th century, when it was called Portuguese Timor. Portugal withdrew in 1975 and Indonesia seized the area. Guerrilla activity mounted under Indonesian rule and, in 1999, the people voted for independence. Agriculture is the main activity. East Timor is heavily dependent on foreign aid, but its offshore deposits of oil and natural gas are due to come on line in 2004.

AREA 5,731 sq mi [14,870 sq km] **POPULATION** 953,000 **CAPITAL** Dili

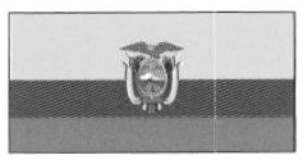
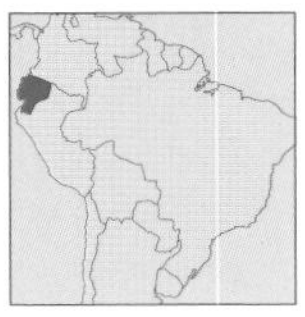

ECUADOR

GEOGRAPHY The Republic of Ecuador straddles the Equator on the west coast of South America. Three ranges of the high Andes Mountains form the backbone of the country. Between the towering, snow-capped peaks of the mountains, some of which are volcanoes, lie a series of high plateaux, or basins. Nearly half of Ecuador's population lives on these plateaux.

The climate in Ecuador depends on the height above sea level. Though the coastline is cooled by the cold Peruvian Current, temperatures are between 73°F and 77°F [23°C to 25°C] all through the year. In Quito, at 8,200 ft [2,500 m] above sea level, temperatures are 57°F to 59°F [14°C to 15°C], though the city is just south of the Equator.

POLITICS & ECONOMY The Inca people of Peru conquered much of what is now Ecuador in the late 15th century. They introduced their language, Quechua, which is widely spoken today. Spanish forces defeated the Incas in 1533 and took control of Ecuador. The country became independent in 1822, following the defeat of a Spanish force in a battle near Quito.

In the 19th and 20th centuries, Ecuador suffered from political instability, while successive governments failed to tackle the country's social and economic problems. A war with Peru in 1941 led to a loss of territory. Disputes continued until 1995, but a border agreement was signed in January 1998. Economic crises in the early 21st century led the government to abolish the sucre, its official currency, and replace it with the US dollar.

The World Bank classifies Ecuador as a "lower-middle-income" developing country. Agriculture employs 30% of the people and bananas, cocoa and coffee are all important crops. Fishing, forestry, mining and manufacturing are other activities.

AREA 109,483 sq mi [283,560 sq km] **POPULATION** 13,447,000 **CAPITAL (POPULATION)** Quito (1,574,000) **GOVERNMENT** Multiparty republic **ETHNIC GROUPS** Mestizo (mixed White and Amerindian) 40%, Amerindian 40%, White 15%, Black 5% **LANGUAGES** Spanish (official), Quechua **RELIGIONS** Roman Catholic 92% **CURRENCY** US dollar = 100 cents

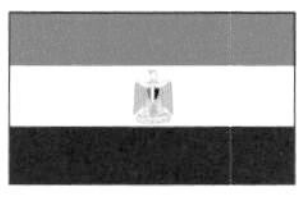
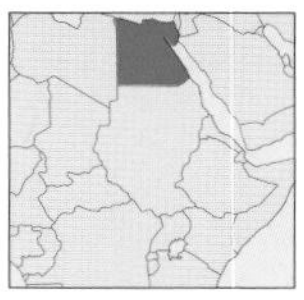

EGYPT

GEOGRAPHY The Arab Republic of Egypt is Africa's second largest country by population after Nigeria, though it ranks 13th in area. Most of Egypt is desert. Almost all the people live either in the Nile Valley and its fertile delta or along the Suez Canal, the artificial waterway between the Mediterranean and Red seas. This canal shortens the sea journey between the United Kingdom and India by 6,027 mi [9,700 km]. Recent attempts have been made to irrigate parts of the western desert and thus redistribute the rapidly growing Egyptian population into previously uninhabited regions.

Apart from the Nile Valley, Egypt has three other main regions. The Western and Eastern deserts are parts of the Sahara. The Sinai peninsula (Es Sina), to the east of the Suez Canal, is a mountainous desert region, geographically within Asia. It contains Egypt's highest peak, Gebel Katherina (8,650 ft [2,637 m]); few people live in this area.

Egypt is a dry country. The low rainfall occurs, if at all, in winter and the country is one of the sunniest places on Earth.

POLITICS & ECONOMY Ancient Egypt, which was founded about 5,000 years ago, was one of the great early civilizations. Throughout the country, pyramids, temples and richly decorated tombs are memorials to its great achievements.

After Ancient Egypt declined, the country came under successive foreign rulers. Arabs occupied Egypt in AD 639–42. They introduced the Arabic language and Islam. Their influence was so great that most Egyptians now regard themselves as Arabs.

Egypt came under British rule in 1882, but it gained partial independence in 1922, becoming a monarchy. The monarchy was abolished in 1952, when Egypt became a republic. The creation of Israel in 1948 led Egypt into a series of wars in 1948–9, 1956, 1967 and 1973. Since the late 1970s, Egypt has sought for peace. In 1979, Egypt signed a peace treaty with Israel and regained the Sinai region which it had lost in a war in 1967. Extremists opposed contacts with Israel and, in 1981, President Sadat, who had signed the treaty, was assassinated.

While Egypt plays a major part in Arab affairs, most of its people are poor. Some Islamic fundamentalists, who dislike Western influences on their way of life, have resorted to violence. In the 1990s, attacks on foreign visitors caused a decline in the valuable tourist industry. In 1999, Hosni Mubarak, president since 1981, was himself attacked by extremists, but he was re-elected to a fourth term in office.

Egypt is Africa's second most industrialized country after South Africa, but it remains a developing country and income levels remain low for the vast majority of Egyptian people. Oil and textiles are the chief exports.

AREA 386,660 SQ MI [1,001,450 SQ KM] **POPULATION** 70,712,000
CAPITAL (POPULATION) CAIRO (6,800,000)
GOVERNMENT REPUBLIC
ETHNIC GROUPS EGYPTIAN 99%
LANGUAGES ARABIC (OFFICIAL), FRENCH, ENGLISH
RELIGIONS ISLAM (SUNNI MUSLIM 94%), CHRISTIANITY (MAINLY COPTIC CHRISTIAN 6%)
CURRENCY POUND = 100 PIASTRES

EL SALVADOR

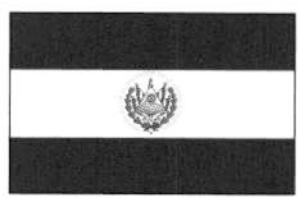

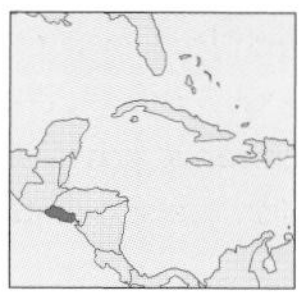

GEOGRAPHY The Republic of El Salvador is the only country in Central America which does not have a coast on the Caribbean Sea. El Salvador has a narrow coastal plain along the Pacific Ocean. Behind the coastal plain, the coastal range is a zone of rugged mountains, including volcanoes, which overlooks a densely populated inland plateau. Beyond the plateau, the land rises to the sparsely populated interior highlands.

The coast has a hot, tropical climate. Inland, the climate is moderated by the altitude. Rain falls on practically every afternoon between May and October.

POLITICS & ECONOMY Amerindians have lived in El Salvador for thousands of years. The ruins of Mayan pyramids built between AD 100 and 1000 are still found in the western part of the country. Spanish soldiers conquered the area in 1524 and 1525, and Spain ruled until 1821. In 1823, all the Central American countries, except for Panama, set up a Central American Federation. But El Salvador withdrew in 1840 and declared its independence in 1841. El Salvador suffered from instability throughout the 19th century. The 20th century saw a more stable government, but from 1931 military dictatorships alternated with elected governments and the country remained poor.

In the 1970s, El Salvador was plagued by conflict as protesters demanded that the government introduce reforms to help the poor. Kidnappings and murders committed by left- and right-wing groups caused instability. A civil war broke out in 1979 between the US-backed, right-wing government forces and left-wing guerrillas in the FMLN (Farabundo Marti National Liberation Front). In 12 years, more than 750,000 people died and hundreds of thousands were made homeless. A ceasefire was agreed on February 1, 1992, and elections were held in 1993 and 1999. By 2003, the economy had shown signs of recovery, but the World Bank still classifies El Salvador as a "lower-middle-income" economy.

About three-quarters of the country is farmed. Coffee, grown in the highlands, is the main export, followed by sugar and cotton, which grow on the coastal lowlands. Fishing for lobsters and shrimps is important, but manufacturing is on a small scale.

AREA 8,124 SQ MI [21,040 SQ KM] **POPULATION** 6,354,000
CAPITAL (POPULATION) SAN SALVADOR (1,522,000)
GOVERNMENT REPUBLIC **ETHNIC GROUPS** MESTIZO (MIXED WHITE AND AMERINDIAN) 89%, WHITE 10%, AMERINDIAN 1%
LANGUAGES SPANISH (OFFICIAL) **RELIGIONS** ROMAN CATHOLIC 86%
CURRENCY US DOLLAR; COLÓN = 100 CENTAVOS

EQUATORIAL GUINEA

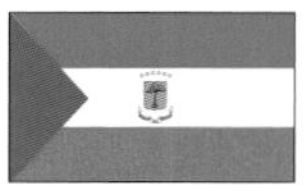

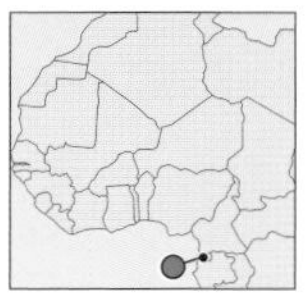

GEOGRAPHY The Republic of Equatorial Guinea is a small republic in west-central Africa. It consists of a mainland territory which makes up 90% of the land area, called Rio Muni, between Cameroon and Gabon, and five offshore islands in the Bight of Bonny, the largest of which is Bioko. The island of Annobon lies 350 mi [560 km] southwest of Rio Muni. Rio Muni consists mainly of hills and plateaux behind the coastal plains.

The climate is hot and humid. Bioko is mountainous, with the land rising to 9,869 ft [3,008 m], and hence it is particularly rainy. However, there is a marked dry season between the months of December and February. Mainland Rio Muni has a similar climate, though the rainfall diminishes inland.

POLITICS & ECONOMY Portuguese navigators reached the area in 1471. In 1778, Portugal granted Bioko, together with rights over Rio Muni, to Spain.

In 1959, Spain made Bioko and Rio Muni provinces of overseas Spain and, in 1963, it gave the provinces a degree of self-government. Equatorial Guinea became independent in 1968.

The first president of Equatorial Guinea, Francisco Macias Nguema, proved to be a tyrant. He was overthrown in 1979 and a group of officers, led by Lt-Col. Teodoro Obiang Nguema Mbasogo, set up a Supreme Military Council to rule the country. In 1991, the people voted to set up a multiparty democracy. Elections were held in the 1990s, but accusations of human rights abuses continued.

Equatorial Guinea is a poor country. Agriculture employs over half of the people. The most valuable crop is coffee. Oil has been produced since 1966, but oil revenue has done little to ease poverty.

AREA 10,830 SQ MI [28,050 SQ KM] **POPULATION** 498,000
CAPITAL (POPULATION) MALABO (35,000) **GOVERNMENT** MULTIPARTY REPUBLIC (TRANSITIONAL) **ETHNIC GROUPS** FANG 83%, BUBI 10%, NDOWE 4% **LANGUAGES** SPANISH AND FRENCH (BOTH OFFICIAL) **RELIGIONS** ROMAN CATHOLIC 89% **CURRENCY** CFA FRANC = 100 CENTIMES

ERITREA

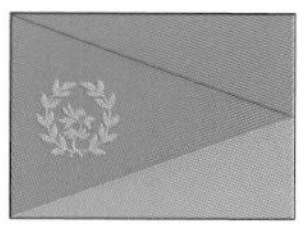

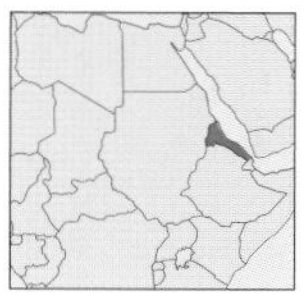

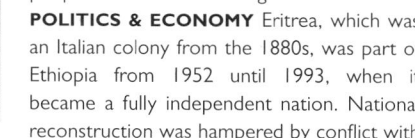

GEOGRAPHY The State of Eritrea consists of a hot, dry coastal plain facing the Red Sea, with a fairly mountainous area in the center. Most people live in the cooler highland area.

POLITICS & ECONOMY Eritrea, which was an Italian colony from the 1880s, was part of Ethiopia from 1952 until 1993, when it became a fully independent nation. National reconstruction was hampered by conflict with Yemen over three islands in the Red Sea, while in 1998–9, border clashes with Ethiopia caused loss of life. However, a peace agreement was signed in 2000. Farming and livestock rearing are the main activities in this war-ravaged territory. Eritrea has few manufacturing industries, based mainly in Asmara.

AREA 36,293 SQ MI [94,000 SQ KM] **POPULATION** 4,466,000
CAPITAL (POPULATION) ASMARA (367,500)
GOVERNMENT TRANSITIONAL GOVERNMENT **ETHNIC GROUPS** TIGRINYA 49%, TIGRE 32%, AFAR 4%, BEJA 3%, SAHO 3%, KUNAMA 3%, NARA 2%
LANGUAGES AFAR, AMHARIC, ARABIC, TIGRINYA **RELIGIONS** COPTIC CHRISTIAN 50%, ISLAM 50% **CURRENCY** NAKFA

ESTONIA

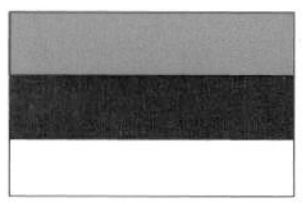

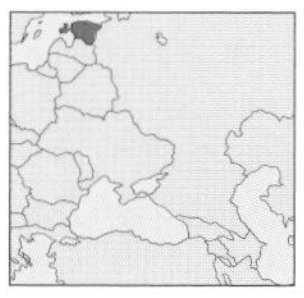

GEOGRAPHY The Republic of Estonia is the smallest of the three states on the Baltic Sea, which were formerly part of the Soviet Union, but which became independent in the early 1990s. Estonia consists of a generally flat plain which was covered by ice sheets during the Ice Age. The land is strewn with moraine (rocks deposited by the ice).

The country is dotted with more than 1,500 small lakes, and water, including the large Lake Peipus (Chudskoye Ozero) and the River Narva makes up much of Estonia's eastern border with Russia. Estonia has more than 800 islands, which together make up about a tenth of the country. The largest island is Saaremaa (Sarema).

Despite its northerly position, Estonia has a fairly mild climate because of its nearness to the sea. This is because sea winds tend to warm the land in winter and cool it in summer.

POLITICS & ECONOMY The ancestors of the Estonians, who are related to the Finns, settled in the area several thousand years ago. German crusaders, known as the Teutonic Knights, introduced Christianity in the early 13th century. By the 16th century, German noblemen owned much of the land in Estonia. In 1561, Sweden took the northern part of the country and Poland the south. From 1625, Sweden controlled the entire country until Sweden handed it over to Russia in 1721.

Estonian nationalists campaigned for their independence from around the mid-19th century. Finally, Estonia was proclaimed independent in 1918. In 1919, the government began to break up the large estates and distribute land among the peasants.

In 1939, Germany and the Soviet Union agreed to take over parts of Eastern Europe. In 1940, Soviet forces occupied Estonia, but they were driven out by the Germans in 1941. Soviet troops returned in 1944 and Estonia became one of the 15 Soviet Socialist Republics of the Soviet Union. The Estonians strongly opposed Soviet rule. Many of them were deported to Siberia.

Political changes in the Soviet Union in the late 1980s led to renewed demands for freedom. In 1990, the Estonian government declared the country independent and, finally, the Soviet Union recognized this act in September 1991, shortly before the Soviet Union was dissolved. Estonia adopted a new constitution in 1992, when multiparty elections were held for a new national assembly. In 1993, Estonia negotiated an agreement with Russia to withdraw its troops.

Under Soviet rule, Estonia was the most prosperous of the three Baltic states. Since 1988, Estonia has begun to change its government-dominated economy to one based on private enterprise and, in 2002, the European Union invited Estonia to become a member in May 2004. Estonia's resources include oil shale and its forests. Industries produce fertilizers, machinery, petrochemical products, processed food, wood products and textiles. Agriculture and fishing are other important activities.

AREA 17,300 SQ MI [44,700 SQ KM] **POPULATION** 1,416,000
CAPITAL (POPULATION) TALLINN (435,000) **GOVERNMENT** MULTIPARTY REPUBLIC **ETHNIC GROUPS** ESTONIAN 65%, RUSSIAN 28%, UKRAINIAN 3%, BELARUSSIAN 2%, FINNISH 1% **LANGUAGES** ESTONIAN (OFFICIAL), RUSSIAN **RELIGIONS** LUTHERAN, RUSSIAN AND ESTONIAN ORTHODOX, METHODIST, BAPTIST, ROMAN CATHOLIC **CURRENCY** KROON = 100 SENTS

ETHIOPIA

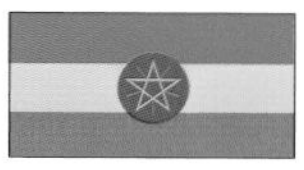

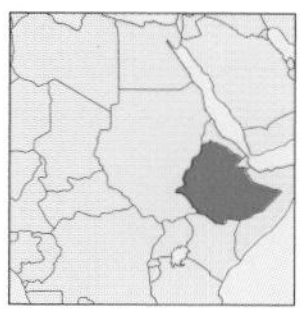

GEOGRAPHY Ethiopia is a landlocked country in northeastern Africa. The land is mainly mountainous, though there are extensive plains in the east, bordering southern Eritrea, and in the south, bordering Somalia. The highlands are divided into two blocks by an arm of the Great Rift Valley which runs throughout eastern Africa. North of the Rift Valley, the land is especially rugged, rising to 15,157 ft [4,620 m] at Ras Dashen. Southeast of Ras Dashen is Lake Tana, source of the River Abay (Blue Nile).

The climate in Ethiopia is greatly affected by the altitude. Addis Ababa, at 8,000 ft [2,450 m], has an average yearly temperature of 68°F [20°C]. The rainfall is generally more than 39 inches [1,000 mm]. But the lowlands bordering the Eritrean coast are hot.

POLITICS & ECONOMY Ethiopia was the home of an ancient monarchy, which became Christian in the 4th century. In the 7th century, Muslims gained control of the lowlands, but Christianity survived in the highlands. Ethiopia resisted attempts to colonize it, but Italy invaded the country in 1935. The Italians were driven out in 1941 during World War II.

In 1952, Eritrea, on the Red Sea coast, was federated with Ethiopia. But in 1961, Eritrean nationalists demanded their freedom and began a struggle that ended in their independence in 1993. Clashes along the border with Eritrea occurred in 1998 and 1999, but a peace agreement was signed in 2000, though a disagreement arose in 2003 about the status of Badme, the village where the conflict began. Some Ethiopian minorities would like self-government and, in 1995, the country was divided into nine provinces, each with its own regional assembly.

Ethiopia is one of the world's poorest countries, particularly in the 1970s and 1980s when it was plagued by civil war and famine caused partly by long droughts. Many richer countries have sent aid (money and food) to help the Ethiopian people. Agriculture remains the leading activity.

AREA 435,521 SQ MI [1,128,000 SQ KM] **POPULATION** 67,673,000
CAPITAL (POPULATION) ADDIS ABABA (2,316,000)
GOVERNMENT FEDERATION OF NINE PROVINCES
ETHNIC GROUPS OROMO 40%, AMHARIC 32%, SIDAMO 9%, SHANKELLA 6%, SOMALI 6% **LANGUAGES** AMHARIC (OFFICIAL), 280 OTHERS
RELIGIONS ISLAM 47%, ETHIOPIAN ORTHODOX 40%, TRADITIONAL BELIEFS 11% **CURRENCY** BIRR = 100 CENTS

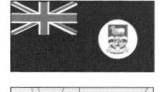

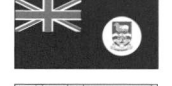

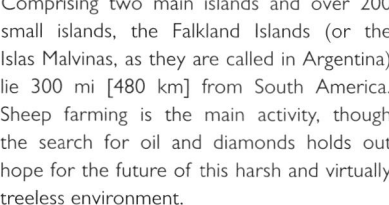

FALKLAND ISLANDS

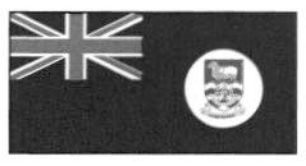

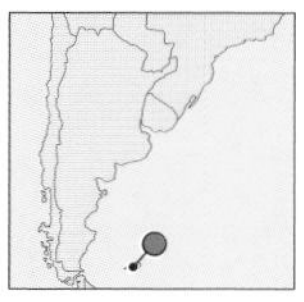

Comprising two main islands and over 200 small islands, the Falkland Islands (or the Islas Malvinas, as they are called in Argentina) lie 300 mi [480 km] from South America. Sheep farming is the main activity, though the search for oil and diamonds holds out hope for the future of this harsh and virtually treeless environment.

AREA 4,699 SQ MI [12,170 SQ KM] **POPULATION** 3,000
CAPITAL STANLEY

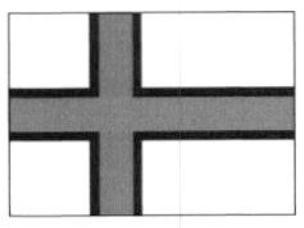

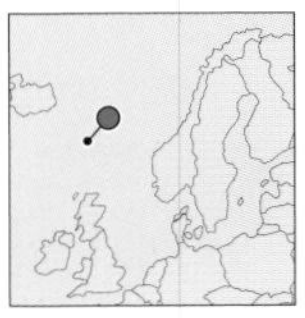

FAROE ISLANDS

The Faroe Islands are a group of 18 volcanic islands and some reefs in the North Atlantic Ocean. The islands have been Danish since the 1380s, but they became largely self-governing in 1948. In 1998, the government of the Faroes announced its intention to become independent of Denmark.

AREA 541 sq mi [1,400 sq km]
POPULATION 46,000 **CAPITAL** Torshávn

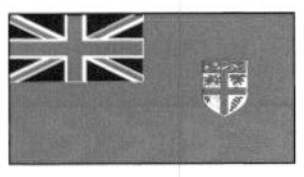

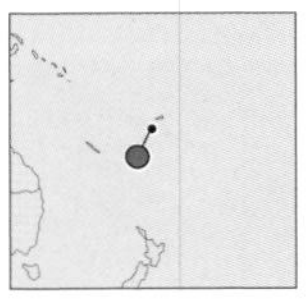

FIJI

The Republic of Fiji comprises more than 800 Melanesian islands, the biggest being Viti Levu and Vanua Levu. The climate is tropical, with southeast trade winds blowing throughout the year. A former British colony, Fiji became independent in 1970. Its recent history has been marred by efforts by ethnic Fijians to impose their rule, stopping members of the ethnic Indian community from holding senior cabinet posts. Their actions have provoked international criticism.

AREA 7,054 sq mi [18,270 sq km] **POPULATION** 856,000 **CAPITAL** Suva

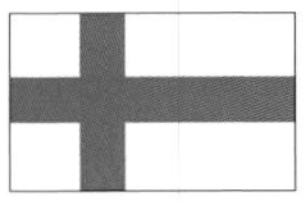

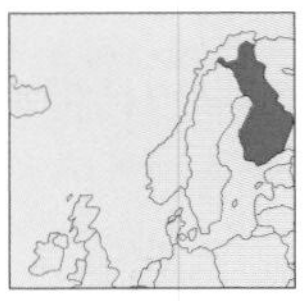

FINLAND

GEOGRAPHY The Republic of Finland is a beautiful country in northern Europe. In the south, behind the coastal lowlands where most Finns live, lies a region of sparkling lakes worn out by ice sheets in the Ice Age. The thinly populated northern uplands cover about two-fifths of the country.

Helsinki, the capital city, has warm summers, but the average temperatures between the months of December and March are below freezing point. Snow covers the land in winter. The north has less precipitation than the south, but it is much colder.

POLITICS & ECONOMY Between 1150 and 1809, Finland was under Swedish rule. The close links between the countries continue today. Swedish remains an official language in Finland and many towns have Swedish as well as Finnish names.

In 1809, Finland became a grand duchy of the Russian empire. It finally declared itself independent in 1917, after the Russian Revolution and the collapse of the Russian empire. But during World War II (1939–45), the Soviet Union declared war on Finland and took part of Finland's territory. Finland allied itself with Germany, but it lost more land to the Soviet Union at the end of the war.

After World War II, Finland became a neutral country and negotiated peace treaties with the Soviet Union. Finland also strengthened its relations with other northern European countries and became an associate member of the European Free Trade Association (EFTA) in 1961. Finland became a full member of EFTA in 1986, but in 1992, along with most of its fellow EFTA members, it applied for membership of the European Union, which it finally achieved on January 1, 1995. On January 1, 2002, the euro became Finland's sole official unit of currency.

Forests are Finland's most valuable resource, and forestry accounts for about 35% of the country's exports. The chief manufactures are wood products, pulp and paper. Since World War II, Finland has set up many other industries, producing such things as machinery and transport equipment. Its economy has expanded rapidly, but there has been a large increase in the number of unemployed people.

AREA 130,552 sq mi [338,130 sq km] **POPULATION** 5,184,000
CAPITAL (POPULATION) Helsinki (532,000)
GOVERNMENT Multiparty republic **ETHNIC GROUPS** Finnish 93%, Swedish 6% **LANGUAGES** Finnish and Swedish (both official)
RELIGIONS Evangelical Lutheran 88% **CURRENCY** Euro = 100 cents

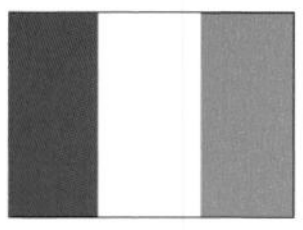

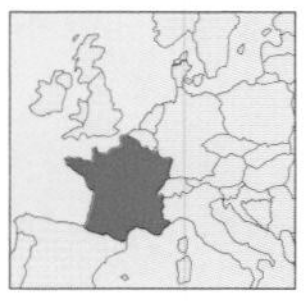

FRANCE

GEOGRAPHY The Republic of France is the largest country in Western Europe. The scenery is extremely varied. The Vosges Mountains overlook the Rhine valley in the northeast, the Jura Mountains and the Alps form the borders with Switzerland and Italy in the southeast, while the Pyrenees straddle France's border with Spain. The only large highland area entirely within France is the Massif Central between the Rhône-Saône valley and the basin of Aquitaine in southern France.

Brittany (Bretagne) and Normandy (Normande) form a scenic hill region. Fertile lowlands cover most of northern France, including the densely populated Paris basin. Another major lowland area, the Aquitanian basin, is in the southwest, while the Rhône-Saône valley and the Mediterranean lowlands are in the southeast.

The climate of France varies from west to east and from north to south. The west comes under the moderating influence of the Atlantic Ocean, giving generally mild weather. To the east, summers are warmer and winters colder. The climate also becomes warmer as one travels from north to south. The Mediterranean Sea coast has hot, dry summers and mild, moist winters. The Alps, Jura and Pyrenees mountains have snowy winters. Winter sports centers are found in all three areas. Large glaciers occupy high valleys in the Alps.

POLITICS & ECONOMY The Romans conquered France (then called Gaul) in the 50s BC. Roman rule began to decline in the fifth century AD and, in 486, the Frankish realm (as France was called) became independent under a Christian king, Clovis. In 800, Charlemagne, who had been king since 768, became emperor of the Romans. He extended France's boundaries, but, in 843, his empire was divided into three parts and the area of France contracted. After the Norman invasion of England in 1066, large areas of France came under English rule, but this was finally ended in 1453.

France later became a powerful monarchy. But the French Revolution (1789–99) ended absolute rule by French kings. In 1799, Napoleon Bonaparte took power and fought a series of brilliant military campaigns before his final defeat in 1815. The monarchy was restored until 1848, when the Second Republic was founded. In 1852, Napoleon's nephew became Napoleon III, but the Third Republic was established in 1875. France was the scene of much fighting during World War I (1914–18) and World War II (1939–45), causing great loss of life and much damage to the economy.

In 1946, France adopted a new constitution, establishing the Fourth Republic. But political instability and costly colonial wars slowed France's post-war recovery. In 1958, Charles de Gaulle was elected president and he introduced a new constitution, giving the president extra powers and inaugurating the Fifth Republic.

Since the 1960s, France has made rapid economic progress, becoming one of the most prosperous nations in the European Union. But France's government faced a number of problems, including unemployment, pollution and the growing number of elderly people, who find it difficult to live when inflation rates are high. One social problem concerns the presence in France of large numbers of immigrants from Africa and southern Europe, many of whom live in poor areas.

A socialist government under Lionel Jospin was elected in 1997. Under Jospin, France adopted the euro, the single European currency, and shortened the working week. The French system of high social security seems likely to continue. France has a long record of independence in foreign affairs and, in 2003, it angered the United States and some of its EU allies by opposing the invasion of Iraq.

France is one of the world's most developed countries. Its natural resources include its fertile soil, together with deposits of bauxite, coal, iron ore, oil and natural gas, and potash. France is also one of the world's top manufacturing nations, and it has often innovated in bold and imaginative ways. The TGV and hypermarkets are typical examples. Paris is a world center of fashion industries, but France has many other industrial towns and cities. Major manufactures include aircraft, cars, chemicals, electronic and metal products, machinery, processed food, steel and textiles.

Agriculture employs about 4% of the people, but France is the largest producer of farm products in Western Europe, producing most of the food it needs. Wheat is the leading crop and livestock farming is of major importance. Fishing and forestry are leading industries, while tourism is a major activity.

AREA 212,934 sq mi [551,500 sq km] **POPULATION** 59,766,000
CAPITAL (POPULATION) Paris (11,175,000) **GOVERNMENT** Multiparty republic **ETHNIC GROUPS** Celtic, Latin, Arab, Teutonic, Slavic
LANGUAGES French (official), Breton, Occitan **RELIGIONS** Roman Catholic 90%, Islam 3% **CURRENCY** Euro = 100 cents

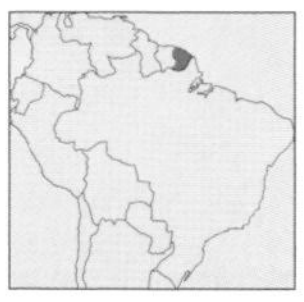

FRENCH GUIANA

GEOGRAPHY French Guiana is the smallest country in mainland South America. The coastal plain is swampy in places, but some dry areas are cultivated. Inland lies a plateau, with the low Tumachumac Mountains in the south. Most of the rivers run north toward the Atlantic Ocean.

French Guiana has a hot, equatorial climate, with high temperatures throughout the year. The rainfall is heavy, especially between December and June, but it is dry between August and October. The northeast trade winds blow constantly across the country.

POLITICS & ECONOMY The first people to live in what is now French Guiana were Amerindians. Today, only a few of them survive in the interior. The first Europeans to explore the coast arrived in 1500, and they were followed by adventurers seeking El Dorado, the mythical city of gold. Cayenne was founded in 1637 by a group of French merchants. The area became a French colony in the late 17th century.

France used the colony as a penal settlement for political prisoners from the times of the French Revolution in the 1790s. From the 1850s to 1945, the country became notorious as a place where prisoners were harshly treated. Many of them died, unable to survive in the tropical conditions.

In 1946, French Guiana became an overseas department of France, and in 1974 it also became an administrative region. An independence movement developed in the 1980s, but most people want to retain their links with France and continue to obtain financial aid to develop their territory.

Although it has rich forest and mineral resources, such as bauxite (aluminum ore), French Guiana is a developing country. It depends greatly on France for money to run its services and the government is the country's biggest employer. Since 1968, Kourou in French Guiana, the European Space Agency's rocket-launching site, has earned money for France by sending communications satellites into space.

AREA 34,749 sq mi [90,000 sq km] **POPULATION** 182,000
CAPITAL (POPULATION) Cayenne (42,000) **GOVERNMENT** Overseas department of France **ETHNIC GROUPS** Mulatto 66%, Chinese and Amerindian 12%, White 10% **LANGUAGES** French (official)
RELIGIONS Christianity (Roman Catholic 80%, Protestant 4%)
CURRENCY Euro = 100 cents

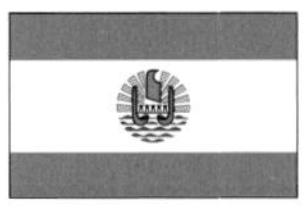

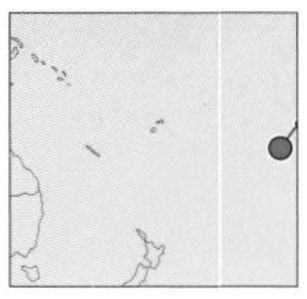

FRENCH POLYNESIA

French Polynesia consists of 130 islands, scattered over 1.5 million sq mi [4 million sq km] of the Pacific Ocean. Tribal chiefs in the area agreed to a French protectorate in 1843. They gained increased autonomy in 1984, but the links with France ensure a high standard of living.

AREA 1,520 sq mi [3,941 sq km]
POPULATION 258,000 **CAPITAL** Papeete

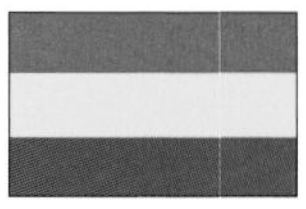

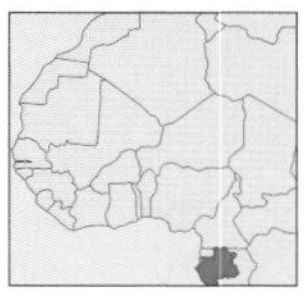

GABON

GEOGRAPHY The Gabonese Republic lies on the Equator in west-central Africa. In area, it is a little larger than the United Kingdom, with a coastline 500 mi [800 km] long. Behind the narrow, partly lagoon-lined coastal plain, the land rises to hills, plateaux and mountains divided by deep valleys carved by the River Ogooué and its tributaries.

Most of Gabon has an equatorial climate, with high temperatures and humidity throughout the year. The rainfall is heavy and the skies are often cloudy.

POLITICS & ECONOMY Gabon became a French colony in the 1880s, but it achieved full independence in 1960. In 1964, an attempted coup was put down when French troops intervened and crushed the revolt. In 1967, Bernard-Albert Bongo, who later renamed himself El Hadj Omar Bongo, became president. He declared Gabon a one-party state in 1968. Opposition parties were legalized in 1991, but Bongo was re-elected president in 1993 and 1998.

Gabon's abundant natural resources include its forests, oil and gas deposits near Port Gentil, together with manganese and uranium. These mineral deposits make Gabon one of Africa's better-off countries. But agriculture still employs about 41% of the population and many farmers produce little more than they need to support their families.

AREA 103,347 sq mi [267,670 sq km] **POPULATION** 1,233,000
CAPITAL (POPULATION) Libreville (418,000)
GOVERNMENT Multiparty republic
ETHNIC GROUPS Four major Bantu tribes: Fang, Eshira, Bapounou and Bateke **LANGUAGES** French (official), Bantu languages **RELIGIONS** Roman Catholic 65%, Protestant 19%, African churches 12%, traditional beliefs 3%, Islam 2%
CURRENCY CFA franc = 100 centimes

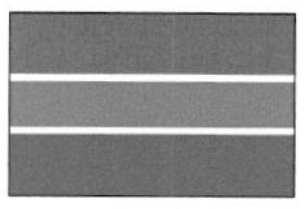
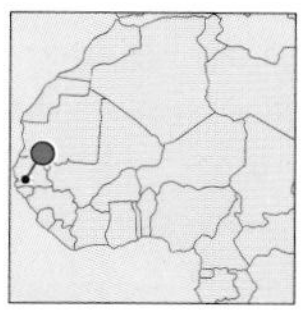

GAMBIA, THE

GEOGRAPHY The Republic of The Gambia is the smallest country in mainland Africa. It consists of a narrow strip of land bordering the River Gambia. The Gambia is almost entirely enclosed by Senegal, except along the short Atlantic coastline.

The Gambia has hot and humid summers, but the winter temperatures (November to May) drop to around 61°F [16°C]. In the summer, moist southwesterlies bring rain, which is heaviest on the coast.

POLITICS & ECONOMY English traders bought rights to trade on the River Gambia in 1588, and in 1664 the English established a settlement on an island in the river estuary. In 1765, the British founded a colony called Senegambia, which included parts of The Gambia and Senegal. In 1783, Britain handed this colony over to France.

In the 1860s and 1870s, Britain and France discussed the exchange of The Gambia for some other French territory. But no agreement was reached and Britain made The Gambia a British colony in 1888. It remained under British rule until it achieved full independence in 1965. In 1970, The Gambia became a republic. Relations between the English-speaking Gambians and the French-speaking Senegalese form a major political issue. In 1981, an attempted coup in The Gambia was put down with the help of Senegalese troops. In 1982, The Gambia and Senegal set up a defense alliance, called the Confederation of Senegambia. But this alliance was dissolved in 1989. In July 1994, a military group overthrew the president, Sir Dawda Jawara, who fled into exile. Captain Yahya Jammeh, who took power, was elected president in 1996 and re-elected in 2001.

Agriculture employs more than 80% of the people. The main food crops include cassava, millet and sorghum, but groundnuts and groundnut products are the chief exports. Tourism is a growing industry.

AREA 4,363 SQ MI [11,300 SQ KM] **POPULATION** 1,456,000
CAPITAL (POPULATION) BANJUL (171,000)
GOVERNMENT MILITARY REGIME
ETHNIC GROUPS MANDINKA 42%, FULA 18%, WOLOF 16%, JOLA 10%, SERAHULI 9%
LANGUAGES ENGLISH (OFFICIAL), MANDINKA, WOLOF, FULA
RELIGIONS ISLAM 90%, CHRISTIANITY 9%, TRADITIONAL BELIEFS 1%
CURRENCY DALASI = 100 BUTUT

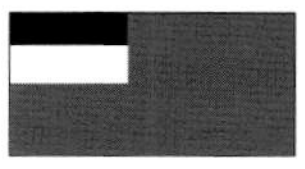
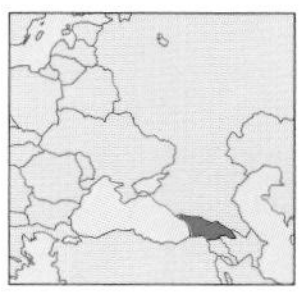

GEORGIA

GEOGRAPHY Georgia is a country on the borders of Europe and Asia, facing the Black Sea. The land is rugged with the Caucasus Mountains forming its northern border. The highest mountain in this range, Mount Elbrus (18,481 ft [5,633 m]), lies over the border with Russia.border in Russia.

The Black Sea plains have hot summers and mild winters, when the temperatures seldom drop below freezing point. The rainfall is heavy, but inland Tbilisi has moderate rainfall, with the heaviest rains in the spring and early summer.

POLITICS & ECONOMY The first Georgian state was set up nearly 2,500 years ago. But for much of its history, the area was ruled by various conquerors. Christianity was introduced in AD 330. Georgia freed itself of foreign rule in the 11th and 12th centuries, but Mongol armies attacked in the 13th century. From the 16th to the 18th centuries, Iran and the Turkish Ottoman empire struggled for control of the area, and in the late 18th century Georgia sought the protection of Russia and, by the early 19th century, Georgia was part of the Russian empire. After the Russian Revolution of 1917, Georgia declared its independence, but Russia invaded, making the country part of the Soviet regime. Georgia declared itself independent in 1991. It became a separate country when the Soviet Union was dissolved in December 1991.

Georgia contains three regions containing minority peoples: Abkhazia in the northwest, South Ossetia in north-central Georgia, and Adjaria (also spelled Adzharia) in the southwest. Civil war broke out in South Ossetia in the early 1990s, while fierce fighting continued in Abkhazia until the late 1990s. In 2000, Georgia agreed to recognize Adjaria's autonomy in the country's constitution. In 2002, Russian and Georgian troops attacked Chechen rebels in Pankisi Gorge in northeastern Georgia. The USA also alleged that terrorists from Afghanistan and elsewhere were hiding in the area.

Georgia is a developing country. Agriculture is important. Major products include barley, citrus fruits, grapes for winemaking, maize, tea, tobacco and vegetables. Food processing and silk and perfume-making are other important activities. Sheep and cattle are reared.

AREA 26,910 SQ MI [69,700 SQ KM] **POPULATION** 4,961,000
CAPITAL (POPULATION) TBILISI (1,253,000)
GOVERNMENT MULTIPARTY REPUBLIC **ETHNIC GROUPS** GEORGIAN 70%, ARMENIAN 8%, RUSSIAN 6%, AZERI 6%, OSSETIAN 3%, GREEK 2%, ABKHAZ 2%, OTHERS 3% **LANGUAGES** GEORGIAN (OFFICIAL), RUSSIAN
RELIGIONS GEORGIAN ORTHODOX 65%, ISLAM 11%, RUSSIAN ORTHODOX 10%, ARMENIAN APOSTOLIC 8%
CURRENCY LARI = 100 TETRI

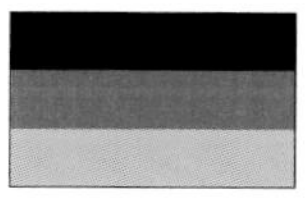
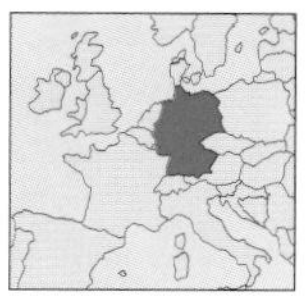

GERMANY

GEOGRAPHY The Federal Republic of Germany is the fourth largest country in Western Europe, after France, Spain and Sweden. The North German plain borders the North Sea in the northwest and the Baltic Sea in the northeast. Major rivers draining the plain include the Weser, Elbe and Oder.

The central highlands contain plateaux and highlands, including the Harz Mountains, the Thuringian Forest (Thüringer Wald), the Ore Mountains (Erzgebirge), and the Bohemian Forest (Böhmerwald) on the Czech border. South Germany is largely hilly, but the land rises in the south to the Bavarian Alps, which contain Germany's highest peak, Zugspitze, at 9,721 ft [2,963 m] above sea level. The scenic Black Forest (Scharzwald) overlooks the River Rhine, which flows through a rift valley in the southwest. The Black Forest contains the source of the River Danube.

Northwestern Germany has a mild climate, but the Baltic coastlands are cooler. To the south, the climate becomes more continental, especially in the highlands. The precipitation is greatest on the uplands, many of which are snow-capped in winter.

POLITICS & ECONOMY Germany and its allies were defeated in World War I (1914–18) and the country became a republic. Adolf Hitler came to power in 1933 and ruled as a dictator. His order to invade Poland led to the start of World War II (1939–45), which ended with Germany in ruins.

In 1945, Germany was divided into four military zones. In 1949, the American, British and French zones were amalgamated to form the Federal Republic of Germany (West Germany), while the Soviet zone became the German Democratic Republic (East Germany), a Communist state. Berlin, which had also been partitioned, became a divided city. West Berlin was part of West Germany, while East Berlin became the capital of East Germany. Bonn was the capital of West Germany.

Tension between East and West mounted during the Cold War, but West Germany rebuilt its economy quickly. In East Germany, the recovery was less rapid. In the late 1980s, reforms in the Soviet Union led to unrest in East Germany. Free elections were held in East Germany in 1990 and, on October 3, 1990, Germany was reunited.

The united Germany adopted West Germany's official name, the Federal Republic of Germany. Elections in December 1990 returned Helmut Kohl, West Germany's Chancellor (head of government) since 1982, to power. His government faced many problems, especially the restructuring of the economy of the former East Germany. Kohl was defeated in elections in 1998 and was succeeded as Chancellor by Social Democrat Gerhard Schröder. In 1999, Germany's parliament moved from Bonn to the reconstructed Reichstag building in Berlin.

West Germany's "economic miracle" after the destruction of World War II was greatly helped by foreign aid. Today, despite all the problems caused by reunification, Germany is one of the world's greatest economic and trading nations.

Manufacturing is the most valuable part of Germany's economy and manufactured goods make up the bulk of the country's exports. Cars and other vehicles, cement, chemicals, computers, electrical equipment, processed food, machinery, scientific instruments, ships, steel, textiles and tools are among the leading manufactures. Germany has some coal, lignite, potash and rock salt deposits. But it imports many of the raw materials needed by its industries.

Germany also imports food. Major agricultural products include fruits, grapes for winemaking, potatoes, sugar beet and vegetables. Beef and dairy cattle are raised, together with many other livestock.

AREA 137,803 SQ MI [356,910 SQ KM] **POPULATION** 83,252,000
CAPITAL (POPULATION) BERLIN (3,426,000)
GOVERNMENT FEDERAL MULTIPARTY REPUBLIC **ETHNIC GROUPS** GERMAN 93%, TURKISH 2%, SERBO-CROAT 1%, ITALIAN 1%, GREEK, POLISH, SPANISH
LANGUAGES GERMAN (OFFICIAL) **RELIGIONS** PROTESTANT (MAINLY LUTHERAN) 38%, ROMAN CATHOLIC 34%, ISLAM 2%
CURRENCY EURO = 100 CENTS

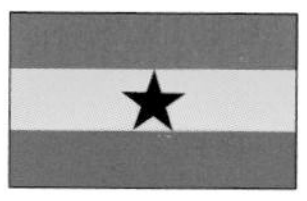
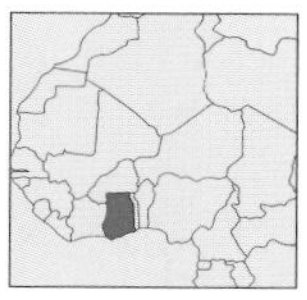

GHANA

GEOGRAPHY The Republic of Ghana faces the Gulf of Guinea in West Africa. This hot country, just north of the Equator, was formerly called the Gold Coast. Behind the thickly populated southern coastal plains, which are lined with lagoons, lies a plateau region in the southwest.

Accra has a hot, tropical climate. Rain occurs all through the year, though Accra is drier than areas inland.

POLITICS & ECONOMY Portuguese explorers reached the area in 1471 and named it the Gold Coast. The area became a center of the slave trade in the 17th century. The slave trade was ended in the 1860s and, gradually, the British took control of the area. After independence in 1957, attempts were made to develop the economy by creating large state-owned manufacturing industries. But debt and corruption, together with falls in the price of cocoa, the chief export, caused economic problems. This led to instability and frequent coups. In 1981, power was invested in a Provisional National Defense Council, led by Flight-Lieutenant Jerry Rawlings.

The government steadied the economy and introduced several new policies, including the relaxation of government controls. In 1992, the government introduced a new constitution, which allowed for multiparty elections. Rawlings was elected president in 1992 and 1996, but he retired in 2002.

The World Bank classifies Ghana as a "low-income" developing country. Most people are poor and farming employs 59% of the population.

AREA 92,100 SQ MI [238,540 SQ KM] **POPULATION** 20,244,000
CAPITAL (POPULATION) ACCRA (1,781,000) **GOVERNMENT** REPUBLIC
ETHNIC GROUPS AKAN 44%, MOSHI-DAGOMBA 16%, EWE 13%, GA 8%
LANGUAGES ENGLISH (OFFICIAL), AKAN, MOSHI-DAGOMBA, EWE, GA
RELIGIONS CHRISTIANITY 63%, TRADITIONAL BELIEFS 21%, ISLAM 16%
CURRENCY CEDI = 100 PESEWAS

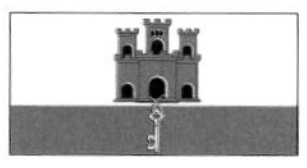
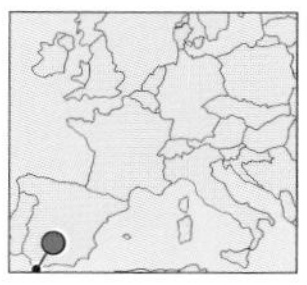

GIBRALTAR

Gibraltar occupies a strategic position on the south coast of Spain where the Mediterranean meets the Atlantic. It was recognized as a British possession in 1713 and, despite Spanish claims, its population has consistently voted to retain its contacts with Britain.

AREA 2.5 SQ MI [6.5 SQ KM] **POPULATION** 28,000
CAPITAL GIBRALTAR TOWN

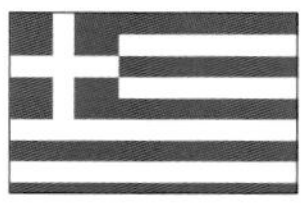
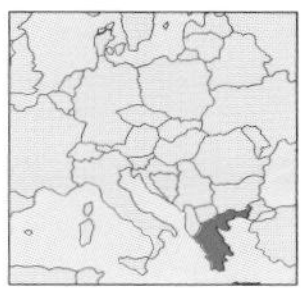

GREECE

GEOGRAPHY The Hellenic Republic, as Greece is officially called, is a rugged country situated at the southern end of the Balkan peninsula. Olympus, at 9,570 ft [2,917 m] is the highest peak. Islands make up about a fifth of the land.

Low-lying areas in Greece have mild, moist winters and hot, dry summers. The east coast has more than 2,700 hours of sunshine a year and only about half of the rainfall of the west. The mountains have a much more severe climate, with snow on the higher slopes in winter.

POLITICS & ECONOMY After World War II (1939–45), when Germany had occupied Greece, a civil war broke out between Communist and nationalist forces. This war ended in 1949. A military dictatorship took power in 1967. The monarchy was abolished in 1973 and democratic government was restored in 1974. Greece joined the European Community (now the EU) in 1981. Despite efforts to develop the economy, Greece remains one of the EU's poorest nations. On January 1, 2002, the euro became Greece's sole official unit of currency.

Manufacturing is important. Products include processed food, cement, chemicals, metal products, textiles and tobacco. Greece also mines lignite (brown coal), bauxite and chromite.

Farmland covers about a third of the country, and grazing land another 40%. Major crops include barley, grapes for winemaking, dried fruits, olives, potatoes, sugar beet and wheat. Poultry, sheep, goats, pigs and cattle are raised. Greece's beaches and ancient ruins make it a major tourist destination.

AREA 50,961 SQ MI [131,990 SQ KM] **POPULATION** 10,645,000
CAPITAL (POPULATION) ATHENS (3,097,000)
GOVERNMENT MULTIPARTY REPUBLIC **ETHNIC GROUPS** GREEK 98%
LANGUAGES GREEK (OFFICIAL) **RELIGIONS** GREEK ORTHODOX 98%
CURRENCY EURO = 100 CENTS

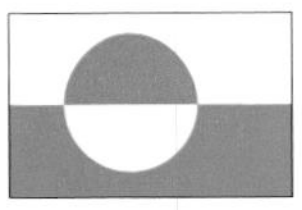
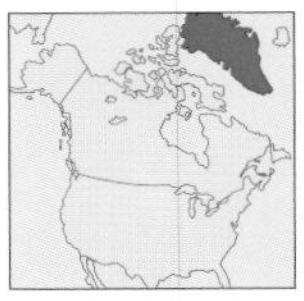

GREENLAND

Greenland is the world's largest island. Settlements are confined to the coast, because an ice sheet covers four-fifths of the land. Greenland became a Danish possession in 1380. Full internal self-government was granted in 1981 and, in 1997, Danish place names were superseded by Inuit forms. However, Greenland remains heavily dependent on Danish subsidies.

AREA 838,999 sq mi [2,175,600 sq km] **POPULATION** 56,000
CAPITAL Nuuk (Godthaab)

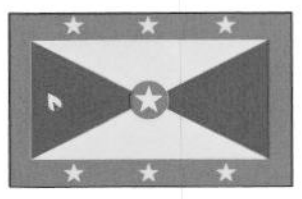
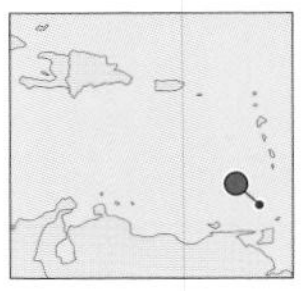

GRENADA

The most southerly of the Windward Islands in the Caribbean Sea, Grenada became independent from the UK in 1974. A military group seized power in 1983, when the prime minister was killed. US troops intervened and restored order and constitutional government.

AREA 131 sq mi [340 sq km]
POPULATION 89,000 **CAPITAL** St George's

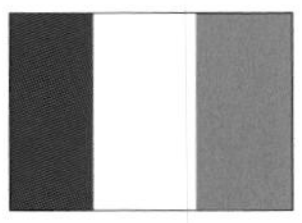
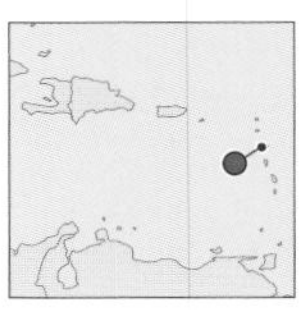

GUADELOUPE

Guadeloupe is a French overseas department which includes seven Caribbean islands, the largest of which is Basse-Terre. French aid has helped to mantain a reasonable standard of living for the people.

AREA 658 sq mi [1,706 sq km]
POPULATION 436,000 **CAPITAL** Basse-Terre

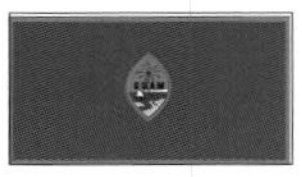
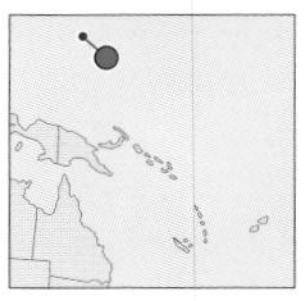

GUAM

Guam, a strategically important "unincorporated territory" of the USA, is the largest of the Mariana Islands in the Pacific Ocean. It is composed of a coralline limestone plateau.

AREA 212 sq mi [549 sq km]
POPULATION 161,000 **CAPITAL** Agana

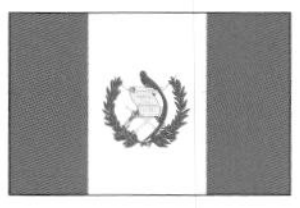
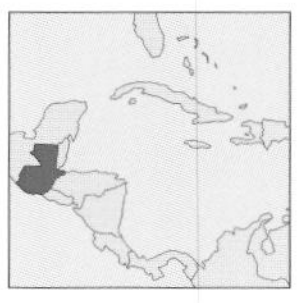

GUATEMALA

GEOGRAPHY The Republic of Guatemala in Central America contains a thickly populated mountain region, with fertile soils. The mountains, which run in an east–west direction, contain many volcanoes, some of which are active. Volcanic eruptions and earthquakes are common in the highlands. South of the mountains lie the thinly populated Pacific coastlands, while a large inland plain occupies the north.

Guatemala lies in the tropics. The lowlands are hot and rainy, but the central mountain region is cooler and drier. Guatemala City, at about 5,000 ft [1,500 m] above sea level, has a pleasant, warm climate, with a marked dry season between November and April.

POLITICS & ECONOMY In 1823, Guatemala joined the Central American Federation. But it became fully independent in 1839. Since independence, Guatemala has been plagued by instability and periodic violence.

Guatemala has a long-standing claim over Belize, but this was reduced in 1983 to the southern fifth of the country. Violence became widespread in Guatemala from the early 1960s, because of the conflict between left-wing groups, including many Amerindians, and government forces. A peace accord was signed in 1996, ending a war that had lasted 36 years and claimed perhaps 200,000 lives.

The World Bank classifies Guatemala as a "lower-middle-income" developing country. Agriculture employs nearly half of the population and coffee, sugar, bananas and beef are the leading exports. Other important crops include the spice cardamom and cotton, while maize is the chief food crop.

AREA 42,042 sq mi [108,890 sq km] **POPULATION** 13,314,000
CAPITAL (POPULATION) Guatemala City (1,167,000)
GOVERNMENT Republic **ETHNIC GROUPS** Ladino (mixed Hispanic and Amerindian) 55%, Amerindian 43%, other 2%
LANGUAGES Spanish (official), Amerindian languages
RELIGIONS Roman Catholic 75%, Protestant 25%
CURRENCY US dollar; Quetzal = 100 centavos

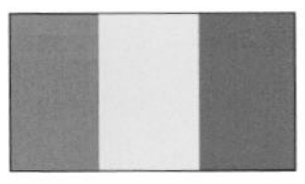
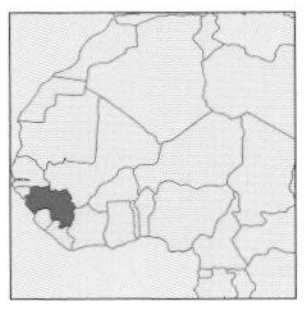

GUINEA

GEOGRAPHY The Republic of Guinea faces the Atlantic Ocean in West Africa. A flat, swampy plain borders the coast. Behind this plain, the land rises to a plateau region called Fouta Djalon. The Upper Niger plains, named after one of Africa's longest rivers, the Niger, which rises there, are in the northeast.

Guinea has a tropical climate and Conakry, on the coast, has heavy rains between May and November. This is also the coolest period in the year. During the dry season, hot, dry harmattan winds blow southwestward from the Sahara Desert.

POLITICS & ECONOMY Guinea became independent in 1958. Its president, Sékou Touré, pursued socialist policies, though he had to resort to repressive policies to hold on to power. After his death in 1984, a military government, under President Lansana Conté, introduced free enterprise policies. In the late 1990s and early 2000s, Guinea was drawn into the civil conflicts which were taking place in neighboring Liberia and Sierra Leone.

The World Bank classifies Guinea as a "low-income" developing country. It has several natural resources, including bauxite (aluminum ore), diamonds, gold, iron ore and uranium. Bauxite and alumina (processed bauxite) account for 90% of the value of the exports. Agriculture, however, employs 78% of the people, many of whom produce little more than they need for their own families. Guinea has some manufacturing industries. Products include alumina, processed food and textiles.

AREA 94,927 sq mi [245,860 sq km] **POPULATION** 7,775,000
CAPITAL (POPULATION) Conakry (1,508,000)
GOVERNMENT Multiparty republic
ETHNIC GROUPS Peuml 40%, Malinke 30%, Soussou 20%, other 10%
LANGUAGES French (official)
RELIGIONS Islam 85%, Christianity 8%, traditional beliefs 7%
CURRENCY Guinean franc = 100 cauris

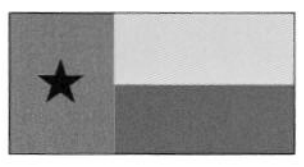
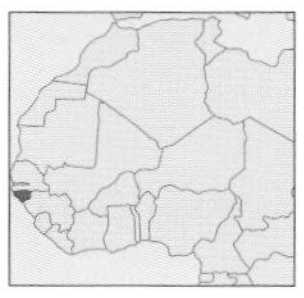

GUINEA-BISSAU

GEOGRAPHY The Republic of Guinea-Bissau, formerly known as Portuguese Guinea, is a small country in West Africa. The land is mostly low-lying, with a broad, swampy coastal plain and many flat offshore islands, including the Bijagós Archipelago.

The country has a tropical climate, with one dry season (December to May) and a rainy season from June to November.

POLITICS & ECONOMY Portugal appointed a governor to administer Guinea-Bissau and the Cape Verde Islands in 1836, but in 1879 the two territories were separated and Guinea-Bissau became a colony, then called Portuguese Guinea. But development was slow, partly because the territory did not attract settlers on the same scale as Portugal's much healthier African colonies of Angola and Mozambique.

In 1956, African nationalists in Portuguese Guinea and Cape Verde founded the African Party for the Independence of Guinea and Cape Verde (PAIGC). Because Portugal seemed determined to hang on to its overseas territories, the PAIGC began a guerrilla war in 1963. By 1968, it held two-thirds of the country. In 1972, a rebel National Assembly, elected by the people in the PAIGC-controlled area, voted to make the country independent as Guinea-Bissau.

In 1974, newly independent Guinea-Bissau faced many problems arising from its under-developed economy and its lack of trained people to work in the administration. One objective of the leaders of Guinea-Bissau was to unite their country with Cape Verde. But, in 1980, army leaders overthrew Guinea-Bissau's government. The Revolutionary Council, which took over, opposed unification with Cape Verde. Guinea-Bissau ceased to be a one-party state in 1991 and multiparty elections were held in 1994. Civil war broke out in 1998 and a military coup occurred in May 1999. In elections in 1999 and 2000, Kumba Ialá was elected president.

Guinea-Bissau is a poor country. Agriculture employs more than 80% of the people, but most farming is at subsistence level. Major crops include beans, coconuts, groundnuts, maize and rice.

AREA 13,946 sq mi [36,120 sq km] **POPULATION** 1,345,000
CAPITAL (POPULATION) Bissau (145,000)
GOVERNMENT "Interim" government
ETHNIC GROUPS Balanta 30%, Fula 20%, Manjaca 14%, Mandinga 13%, Papel 7% **LANGUAGES** Portuguese (official), Crioulo
RELIGIONS Traditional beliefs 50%, Islam 45%, Christianity 5%
CURRENCY CFA franc = 100 centimes

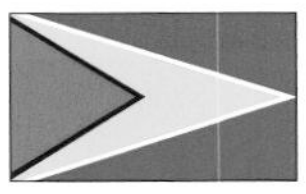
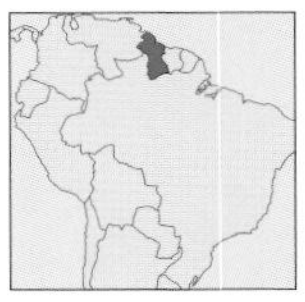

GUYANA

GEOGRAPHY The Cooperative Republic of Guyana is a country facing the Atlantic Ocean in northeastern South America. The coastal plain is flat and much of it is below sea level.

The climate is hot and humid, though the interior highlands are cooler than the coast. The rainfall is heavy, occurring on more than 200 days a year.

POLITICS & ECONOMY British Guiana became independent in 1966. A black lawyer, Forbes Burnham, became the first prime minister. Under a new constitution adopted in 1980, the president's powers were increased. Burnham became president until his death in 1985. He was succeeded by Hugh Desmond Hoyte. Hoyte was defeated in elections in 1993 by an ethnic Indian, Cheddi Jagan. Jagan died in 1997 and was succeeded by his wife, Janet. In 1999, Bharrat Jagdeo was elected president.

Guyana is a poor country. Its resources include gold, bauxite (aluminum ore) and other minerals, forests and fertile soils. sugarcane and rice are leading crops. Electric power is in short supply, although the country has great potential for producing hydroelectricity from its many rivers.

AREA 83,000 sq mi [214,970 sq km] **POPULATION** 698,000
CAPITAL (POPULATION) Georgetown (200,000)
GOVERNMENT Multiparty republic **ETHNIC GROUPS** East Indian 49%, Black 32%, Mixed 12%, Amerindian 6%, Portuguese, Chinese
LANGUAGES English (official), Creole, Hindi, Urdu
RELIGIONS Protestant 34%, Roman Catholic 18%, Hinduism 34%, Islam 9% **CURRENCY** Guyana dollar = 100 cents

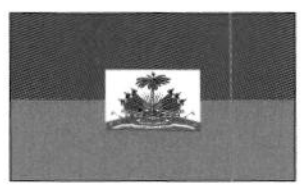
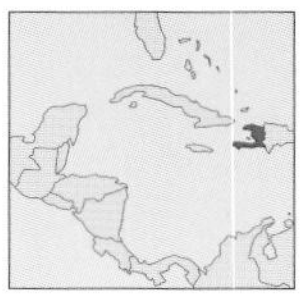

HAITI

GEOGRAPHY The Republic of Haiti occupies the western third of Hispaniola in the Caribbean. The land is mainly mountainous. The climate is hot and humid, though the northern highlands, with about 79 inches [200 mm], have more than twice as much rainfall as the southern coast.

POLITICS & ECONOMY Visited by Christopher Columbus in 1492, Haiti was later developed by the French. The African slaves revolted in 1791 and the country became independent in 1804.

Since independence, Haiti has suffered from instability, violence and dictatorial rule. Elections in 1990 returned Jean-Bertrand Aristide as president, but he was overthrown in 1991. Following US intervention, he returned in 1994. In 1995, René Préval was elected president, but Aristide was again elected president in 2000 amid accusations of vote-rigging.

AREA 10,714 sq mi [27,750 sq km] **POPULATION** 7,064,000
CAPITAL (POPULATION) Port-au-Prince (885,000)
GOVERNMENT Multiparty republic **ETHNIC GROUPS** Black 95%, Mulatto 5% **LANGUAGES** French and Creole (both official)
RELIGIONS Roman Catholic 80%, Voodoo
CURRENCY Gourde = 100 centimes

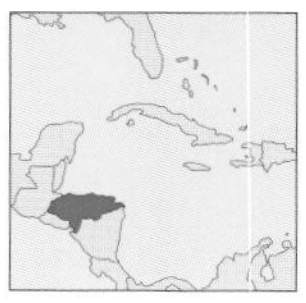

HONDURAS

GEOGRAPHY The Republic of Honduras is the second largest country in Central America. The northern coast on the Caribbean Sea extends more than 373 mi [600 km], but the Pacific coast in the southeast is only about 50 mi [80 km] long.

Honduras has a tropical climate, but the highlands, where the capital Tegucigalpa is situated, have a cooler climate than the hot coastal plains. The months between May and November are the rainiest. The north coast is often hit by hurricanes. In 1998, Hurricane Mitch caused the worst destruction in the area in modern times.

POLITICS & ECONOMY In the 1890s, American companies developed plantations in Honduras to grow bananas, which soon became the country's chief source of income. The companies exerted great political influence in Honduras and the country became known as a "banana republic," a name that was later applied to several other Latin American nations. Instability has continued to mar the country's progress. In 1969, Honduras fought the short "Soccer War" with El Salvador. The war was sparked off by the treatment of fans during a World Cup soccer series. The real reason was that Honduras had forced Salvadoreans in Honduras to give up land. Since 1980, civilian governments have ruled Honduras, though the military remain influential.

Honduras is a developing country – one of the poorest in the Americas. It has few resources besides some silver, lead and zinc, and agriculture dominates the economy. Bananas and coffee are the leading exports, and maize is the main food crop.

Honduras is the least industrialized country in Central America. Manufactures include processed food, textiles, and a wide variety of wood products.

AREA 43,278 sq mi [112,090 sq km] **POPULATION** 6,561,000
CAPITAL (POPULATION) Tegucigalpa (813,000)
GOVERNMENT Republic **ETHNIC GROUPS** Mestizo 90%, Amerindian 7%, Black (including Black Carib) 2%, White 1%
LANGUAGES Spanish (official) **RELIGIONS** Roman Catholic 85%
CURRENCY Honduran lempira = 100 centavos

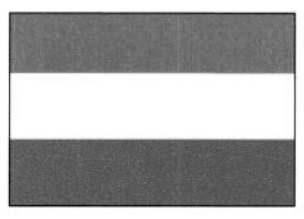

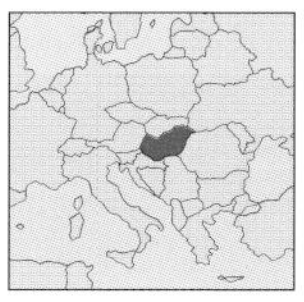

HUNGARY

GEOGRAPHY The Hungarian Republic is a landlocked country in central Europe. The land is mostly low-lying and drained by the Danube (Duna) and its tributary, the Tisza. Most of the land east of the Danube belongs to a region called the Great Plain (Nagyalföld), which covers about half of Hungary.

Hungary lies far from the moderating influence of the sea. As a result, summers are warmer and sunnier, and the winters colder than in Western Europe.

POLITICS & ECONOMY Hungary entered World War II (1939–45) in 1941, as an ally of Germany, but the Germans occupied the country in 1944. The Soviet Union invaded Hungary in 1944 and, in 1946, the country became a republic. The Communists gradually took over the government, taking complete control in 1949. From 1949, Hungary was an ally of the Soviet Union. In 1956, Soviet troops crushed an anti-Communist revolt. But in the 1980s, reforms in the Soviet Union led to the growth of anti-Communist groups in Hungary. In 1989, Hungary adopted a new constitution making it a multiparty state. Elections held in 1990 led to a victory for the non-Communist Democratic Forum. In 2002, the Hungarian Socialist Party, in alliance with the liberal Free Democrats, won a majority in parliament. In 2003, a majority of Hungarians voted in favor of joining the European Union in May 2004.

Before World War II, Hungary's economy was based mainly on agriculture. But the Communists set up many manufacturing industries. The new factories were owned by the government, as also was most of the land. However, from the late 1980s, the government has worked to increase private ownership. This change of policy caused many problems, including inflation and high rates of unemployment. Manufacturing is the chief activity. Major products include aluminum, chemicals, and electrical and electronic goods.

AREA 35,919 sq mi [93,030 sq km] **POPULATION** 10,075,000
CAPITAL (POPULATION) Budapest (1,885,000)
GOVERNMENT Multiparty republic **ETHNIC GROUPS** Magyar 90%, Gypsy, German, Croat, Romanian, Slovak **LANGUAGES** Hungarian (official) **RELIGIONS** Roman Catholic 64%, Protestant 23%, Orthodox 1%, Judaism 1%
CURRENCY Forint = 100 fillér

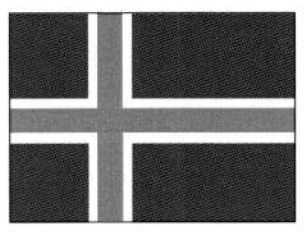

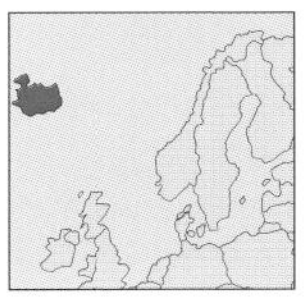

ICELAND

GEOGRAPHY The Republic of Iceland, in the North Atlantic Ocean, is closer to Greenland than Scotland. Iceland sits astride the Mid-Atlantic Ridge. It is slowly getting wider as the ocean is being stretched apart by continental drift.

Iceland has around 200 volcanoes, and eruptions are frequent. An eruption under the Vatnajökull ice cap in 1996 created a subglacial lake which subsequently burst, causing severe flooding. Geysers and hot springs are other common volcanic features. Ice caps and glaciers cover about an eighth of the land. The only habitable regions are the coastal lowlands.

Although it lies far to the north, Iceland's climate is moderated by the warm waters of the Gulf Stream. The port of Reykjavik is ice-free all the year round.

POLITICS & ECONOMY Norwegian Vikings colonized Iceland in AD 874, and in 930 the settlers founded the world's oldest parliament, the Althing.

Iceland united with Norway in 1262. But when Norway united with Denmark in 1380, Iceland came under Danish rule. Iceland became a self-governing kingdom, united with Denmark, in 1918. It became a fully independent republic in 1944, following a referendum in which 97% of the people voted to break their country's ties with Denmark.

Iceland has played an important part in European affairs and is a member of the North Atlantic Treaty Organization. Conflict with Britain over fishing rights have occurred since Iceland extended its territorial waters in the 1970s. Other fishing disputes with Norway, Russia and others continued in the 1990s.

Iceland has few resources besides the fishing grounds which surround it. Fishing and fish processing are major industries which dominate Iceland's overseas trade. Barely 1% of the land is used to grow crops, mainly root vegetables and fodder for livestock, but 23% of the country is used for grazing sheep and cattle. Vegetables and fruits are grown in greenhouses heated by water from hot springs.

AREA 39,768 sq mi [103,000 sq km] **POPULATION** 279,000
CAPITAL (POPULATION) Reykjavik (103,000)
GOVERNMENT Multiparty republic **ETHNIC GROUPS** Icelandic 97%, Danish 1% **LANGUAGES** Icelandic (official)
RELIGIONS Evangelical Lutheran 92%, other Lutheran 3%, Roman Catholic 1%
CURRENCY Króna = 100 aurar

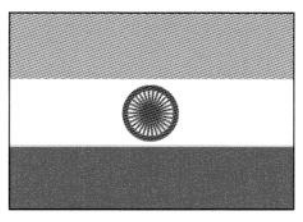

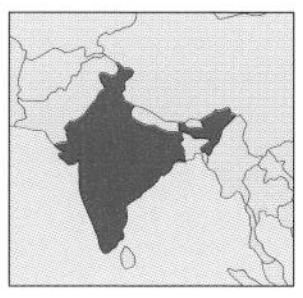

INDIA

GEOGRAPHY The Republic of India is the world's seventh largest country. In population, it ranks second only to China. The north is mountainous, with mountains and foothills of the Himalayan range. Rivers, such as the Brahmaputra and Ganges (Ganga), rise in the Himalaya and flow across the fertile northern plains. Southern India consists of a large plateau, called the Deccan. The Deccan is bordered by two mountain ranges, the Western Ghats and the Eastern Ghats.

India has three main seasons. The cool season runs from October to February. The hot season runs from March to June. The rainy monsoon season starts in the middle of June and continues into September. Delhi has a moderate rainfall, with about 25 inches [640 mm] a year. The southwestern coast and the northeast have far more rain. Darjeeling in the northeast has an average annual rainfall of 120 inches [3,040 mm]. But parts of the Thar Desert in the northwest have only 2 inches [50 mm] of rain per year.

POLITICS & ECONOMY In southern India, most of the people are descendants of the dark-skinned Dravidians, who were among India's earliest people. Most northerners are descendants of lighter-skinned Aryans who arrived around 3,500 years ago.

India was the birthplace of several major religions, including Hinduism, Buddhism and Sikhism. Islam was introduced from about AD 1000. The Muslim Mughal empire was founded in 1526. From the 17th century, Britain began to gain influence. From 1858 to 1947, India was ruled as part of the British empire. An independence movement began after the Sepoy Rebellion (1857–9) and, in 1885, the Indian National Congress was formed. In 1920, Mohandas K. Gandhi became its leader and it soon became a mass movement. When independence was finally achieved in 1947, British India was divided into modern India and Muslim Pakistan. Partition was marred by mass slaughter as Hindus and Sikhs fled from Pakistan, and Indian Muslims poured into Pakistan. In the ensuing disputes, some 1 million people were killed.

Although India has 15 major languages and hundreds of minor ones, together with many religions, the country remains the world's largest democracy. It has faced many problems, especially with Pakistan, over the disputed territory of Jammu and Kashmir. Two wars in 1965 and 1972 failed to alter greatly the 1948 ceasefire lines. In the late 1980s, Kashmiri nationalists in the Indian-controlled area waged a campaign, demanding either integration into Pakistan or independence. India sent in troops and accused Pakistan of intervention. In the 1990s, Pakistani-backed guerrillas fought to break India's hold on the Srinigar valley, Kashmir's most populous region. The tense situation was further aggravated by the testing of nuclear devices by both India and Pakistan in 1998. Between 2000 and 2002, attempts were made to achieve a lasting ceasefire in the region, but the negotiations were unsuccessful.

Economic development has been a major problem and, according to the World Bank, India is a "low-income" developing country. After socialist policies failed to raise the living standards of the poor, the government introduced private enterprise. Farming employs 64% of the people. The main crops are rice, wheat, millet, sorghum, peas and beans. India has more cattle than any other country. Milk is produced but Hindus do not eat beef. India has reserves of coal, iron ore and oil, and manufacturing has expanded greatly since 1947. Iron and steel, machinery, refined petroleum, textiles and transport equipment are major products. India also imports rough diamonds and exports jewelry.

AREA 1,269,338 sq mi [3,287,590 sq km] **POPULATION** 1,045,845,000
CAPITAL (POPULATION) New Delhi (7,207,000)
GOVERNMENT Multiparty federal republic
ETHNIC GROUPS Indo-Aryan (Caucasoid) 72%, Dravidian (Aboriginal) 25%, other (mainly Mongoloid) 3%
LANGUAGES Hindi, English, Telugu, Bengali, Marati, Urdu, Gujarati, Malayalam, Kannada, Oriya, Punjabi, Assamese, Kashmiri, Sindhi and Sanskrit are all official languages **RELIGIONS** Hinduism 83%, Islam (Sunni Muslim) 11%, Christianity 2%, Sikhism 2%, Buddhism 1%
CURRENCY Rupee = 100 paisa

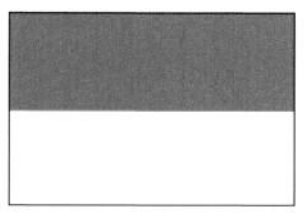

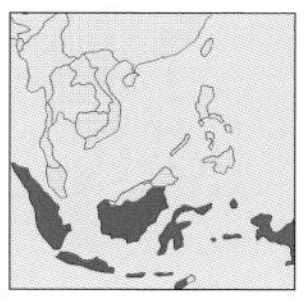

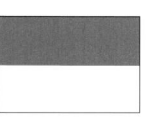

INDONESIA

GEOGRAPHY The Republic of Indonesia is an island nation in Southeast Asia. In all, Indonesia contains about 13,600 islands, less than 6,000 of which are inhabited. Three-quarters of the country is made up of five main areas: the islands of Sumatra, Java and Sulawesi (Celebes), together with Kalimantan (southern Borneo) and Irian Jaya (western New Guinea). The islands are generally mountainous and volcanic. The larger islands have extensive coastal lowlands. The climate is hot and humid, with a high rainfall. Only Java and the Sunda Islands have relatively dry seasons.

POLITICS & ECONOMY Indonesia is the world's most populous Muslim nation, though Islam was introduced as recently as the 15th century. The Dutch became active in the area in the early 17th century and Indonesia became a Dutch colony in 1799. After a long struggle, the Netherlands recognized Indonesia's independence in 1949. The economy has expanded, but ethnic and religious conflict have slowed down economic progress. In the early 21st century, Indonesia was facing many problems, arising from widespread corruption in the government and the army. Separatists were operating in Aceh province in northern Sumatra and in West Papua (formerly Irian Jaya), Christian-Muslim clashes led to loss of life in the Moluccas, and East (formerly Portuguese) Timor became an independent country in May 2002. In October 2002, terrorists bombed a night club in Bali, killing more than 180 people, most of them tourists.

Indonesia is a developing country. Its resources include oil, natural gas, tin and other minerals, its fertile volcanic soils and its forests. Oil and gas are major exports. Timber, textiles, rubber, coffee and tea are also exported. The principal food crop is rice. Manufacturing is increasing, particularly on Java.

AREA 729,613 sq mi [1,889,700 sq km] **POPULATION** 231,328,000
CAPITAL (POPULATION) Jakarta (11,500,000)
GOVERNMENT Multiparty republic
ETHNIC GROUPS Javanese 45%, Sundanese 14%, Madurese 7%, Coastal Malays 7%, more than 300 others
LANGUAGES Bahasa Indonesian (official), others
RELIGIONS Islam 88%, Roman Catholic 3%, Hinduism 2%, Buddhism 1%
CURRENCY Indonesian rupiah = 100 sen

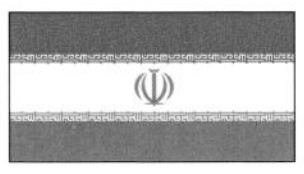

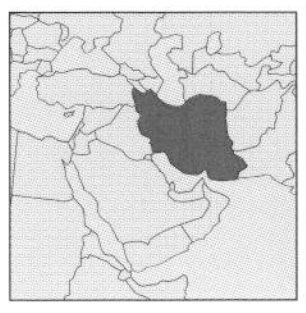

IRAN

GEOGRAPHY The Republic of Iran contains a barren central plateau which covers about half of the country. It includes the Dasht-e-Kavir (Great Salt Desert) and the Dasht-e-Lut (Great Sand Desert). The Elburz Mountains north of the plateau contain Iran's highest peak, Damavand, while narrow lowlands lie between the mountains and the Caspian Sea. West of the plateau are the Zagros Mountains, beyond which the land descends to the plains bordering the Gulf.

Much of Iran has a severe, dry climate, with hot summers and cold winters. In Tehran, rain falls on only about 30 days in the year and the annual temperature range is more than 45°F [25°C]. The climate in the lowlands, however, is generally milder.

POLITICS & ECONOMY Iran was called Persia until 1935. The empire of Ancient Persia flourished between 550 and 350 BC, when it fell to Alexander the Great. Islam was introduced in AD 641.

Britain and Russia competed for influence in the area in the 19th century, and in the early 20th century the British began to develop the country's oil resources. In 1925, the Pahlavi family took power.

Reza Khan became shah (king) and worked to modernize the country. The Pahlavi dynasty was ended in 1979 when a religious leader, Ayatollah Ruhollah Khomeini, made Iran an Islamic republic. In 1980–8, Iran and Iraq fought a war over disputed borders. Khomeini died in 1989, but his fundamentalist views and anti-Western attitudes continued to dominate politics. In 1997, Mohammad Khatami, a liberal, was elected president. His reform policies won support in elections in 2000, but the conservative clerics made actual reform difficult.

Iran's prosperity is based on its oil production and oil accounts for 95% of the country's exports. However, the economy was severely damaged by the Iran–Iraq war in the 1980s. Oil revenues have been used to develop a growing manufacturing sector. Agriculture is important even though farms cover only a tenth of the land. The main crops are wheat and barley. Livestock farming and fishing are other important activities, although Iran has to import much of the food it needs.

AREA 636,293 SQ MI [1,648,000 SQ KM] **POPULATION** 66,623,000
CAPITAL (POPULATION) TEHRAN (6,759,000)
GOVERNMENT ISLAMIC REPUBLIC
ETHNIC GROUPS PERSIAN 51%, AZERI 24%, GILAKI AND MAZANDARANI 8%, KURD 7%, ARAB 3%, LUR 2%, BALUCHI 2%, TURKMEN 2% **LANGUAGES** PERSIAN 58%, TURKIC 26%, KURDISH
RELIGIONS ISLAM 99% **CURRENCY** RIAL = 100 DINARS

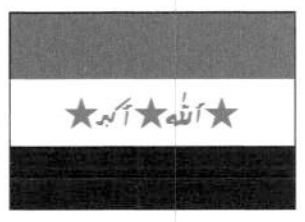

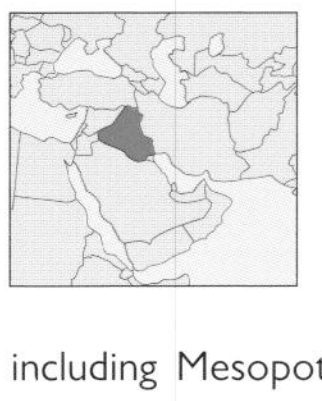

IRAQ

GEOGRAPHY The Republic of Iraq is a southwest Asian country at the head of the Gulf. Rolling deserts cover western and southwestern Iraq, with part of the Zagros Mountains in the northeast, where farming can be practised without irrigation. The northern plains, across which flow the rivers Euphrates (Nahr al Furat) and Tigris (Nahr Dijlah), are dry. But the southern plains, including Mesopotamia, and the delta of the Shatt al Arab, the river formed south of Al Qurnah by the combined Euphrates and Tigris, contain irrigated farmland, together with marshes.

The climate of Iraq ranges from temperate in the north to subtropical in the south. Baghdad, in central Iraq, has cool winters, with occasional frosts, and hot summers. The rainfall is generally low.

POLITICS & ECONOMY Mesopotamia was the home of several great civilizations, including Sumer, Babylon and Assyria. It later became part of the Persian empire. Islam was introduced in AD 637 and Baghdad became the brilliant capital of the powerful Arab empire. But Mesopotamia declined after the Mongols invaded it in 1258. From 1534, Mesopotamia became part of the Turkish Ottoman empire. Britain invaded the area in 1916. In 1921, Britain renamed the country Iraq and set up an Arab monarchy. Iraq finally became independent in 1932.

By the 1950s, oil dominated Iraq's economy. In 1952, Iraq agreed to take 50% of the profits of the foreign oil companies. This revenue enabled the government to pay for welfare services and development projects. But many Iraqis felt that they should benefit more from their oil.

Since 1958, when army officers killed the king and made Iraq a republic, the country has undergone turbulent times. In the 1960s, the Kurds, who live in northern Iraq and also in Iran, Turkey, Syria and Armenia, asked for self-rule. The government rejected their demands and war broke out. A peace treaty was signed in 1975, but conflict has continued.

In 1979, Saddam Hussein became Iraq's president. Under his leadership, Iraq invaded Iran in 1980, starting an eight-year war. Iraqi Kurds supported Iran and the Iraqi government attacked Kurdish villages with poison gas. In 1990, Iraqi troops occupied Kuwait, but an international force drove them out in 1991. Since 1991, Iraqi troops have attacked Shiite Marsh Arabs and Kurds. In 1998, Iraq's failure to permit UN inspectors, charged with disposing of Iraq's deadliest weapons, access to suspect sites led to the Western bombardment of Iraqi military sites. Another major offensive occurred in February 2001. In 2002 and 2003, pressure mounted on Iraq to dispose of its alleged weapons of mass destruction. Its failure to do so led to a coalition force, headed by the United States and the UK, to invade Iraq and overthrow the Saddam regime in March–April 2003.

Civil war, war damage in 1991 and 2003, UN sanctions and mismanagement have all contributed to economic chaos. Oil remains Iraq's main resource, but a UN trade embargo in 1990 halted oil exports. Farmland, including pasture, covers about a fifth of the land. Products include barley, cotton, dates, fruit, livestock, wheat and wool, but Iraq still has to import food. Industries include oil refining and the manufacture of petrochemicals and consumer goods.

AREA 169,235 SQ MI [438,320 SQ KM] **POPULATION** 24,002,000
CAPITAL (POPULATION) BAGHDAD (3,841,000)
GOVERNMENT REPUBLIC **ETHNIC GROUPS** ARAB 77%, KURDISH 19%, TURKMEN, PERSIAN, ASSYRIAN **LANGUAGES** ARABIC (OFFICIAL), KURDISH (OFFICIAL IN KURDISH AREAS) **RELIGIONS** ISLAM 96%, CHRISTIANITY 4%
CURRENCY IRAQI DINAR = 20 DIRHAMS = 1,000 FILS

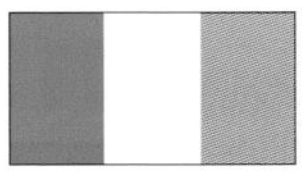

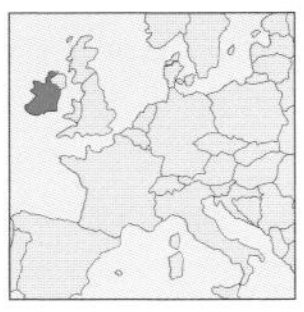

IRELAND

GEOGRAPHY The Republic of Ireland occupies five-sixths of the island of Ireland. The country consists of a large lowland region surrounded by a broken rim of low mountains. The uplands include the Mountains of Kerry where Carrauntoohill, Ireland's highest peak at 3,415 ft [1,041 m], is situated. The River Shannon is the longest in the British Isles. It flows through three large lakes, loughs Allen, Ree and Derg.

Ireland has a mild, damp climate greatly influenced by the warm Gulf Stream current that washes its shores. The effects of the Gulf Stream are greatest in the west. Dublin in the east is cooler than places on the west coast. Rain occurs throughout the year.

POLITICS & ECONOMY In 1801, the Act of Union created the United Kingdom of Great Britain and Ireland. But Irish discontent intensified in the 1840s when a potato blight caused a famine in which a million people died and nearly a million emigrated. Britain was blamed for not having done enough to help. In 1916, an uprising in Dublin was crushed, but between 1919 and 1922 civil war occurred. In 1922, the Irish Free State was created as a Dominion in the British Commonwealth. But Northern Ireland remained part of the UK.

Ireland became a republic in 1949. Since then, Irish governments have sought to develop the economy, and it was for this reason that Ireland joined the European Community in 1973. In 1998, Ireland took part in the negotiations to produce a constitutional settlement in Northern Ireland. As part of the agreement, Ireland agreed to give up its constitutional claim on Northern Ireland.

Major farm products in Ireland include barley, cattle and dairy products, pigs, potatoes, poultry, sheep, sugar beet and wheat, while fishing provides another valuable source of food. Farming is now profitable, aided by European Union grants, but manufacturing is the leading economic sector. Many factories produce food and beverages. Chemicals and pharmaceuticals, electronic equipment, machinery, paper and textiles are also important.

AREA 27,135 SQ MI [70,280 SQ KM] **POPULATION** 3,883,000
CAPITAL (POPULATION) DUBLIN (1,024,000)
GOVERNMENT MULTIPARTY REPUBLIC **ETHNIC GROUPS** IRISH 94%
LANGUAGES IRISH AND ENGLISH (BOTH OFFICIAL)
RELIGIONS ROMAN CATHOLIC 93%, PROTESTANT 3%
CURRENCY EURO = 100 CENTS

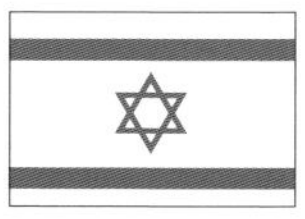

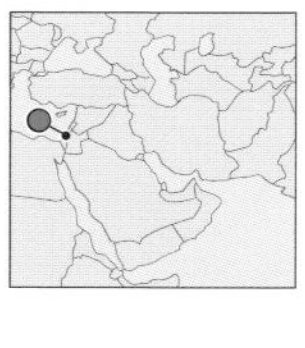

ISRAEL

GEOGRAPHY The State of Israel is a small country in the eastern Mediterranean. It includes a fertile coastal plain, where Israel's main industrial cities, Haifa (Hefa) and Tel Aviv-Jaffa are situated. Inland lie the Judaeo-Galilean highlands, which run from northern Israel to the northern tip of the Negev Desert. To the east lies part of the Great Rift Valley which contains the River Jordan, the Sea of Galilee and the Dead Sea. Summers are hot and dry. Winters on the coast are mild and moist, but the rainfall decreases from west to east and from north to south.

POLITICS & ECONOMY Israel is part of a region called Palestine. Some Jews have always lived in the area, though most modern Israelis are descendants of immigrants who began to settle there from the 1880s. Britain ruled Palestine from 1917. Large numbers of Jews escaping Nazi persecution arrived in the 1930s, provoking an Arab uprising against British rule. In 1947, the UN agreed to partition Palestine into an Arab and a Jewish state. Fighting broke out after Arabs rejected the plan. The State of Israel came into being in May 1948, but fighting continued into 1949. Other Arab-Israeli wars in 1956, 1967 and 1973 led to land gains for Israel.

In 1978, Israel signed a treaty with Egypt which led to the return of the occupied Sinai peninsula to Egypt in 1979. But conflict continued between Israel and the PLO (Palestine Liberation Organization). In 1993, the PLO and Israel agreed to establish Palestinian self-rule in two areas: the occupied Gaza Strip, and in the town of Jericho in the occupied West Bank. The agreement was extended in 1995 to include more than 30% of the West Bank. Israel's prime minister, Yitzhak Rabin, was assassinated in 1995. In 1996, his successor, Simon Peres, was defeated by the right-wing Benjamin Netanyahu, under whom the peace process stalled. In 1999, the left-wing Ehud Barak defeated Netanyahu and revived the peace process. But, following violence between the Palestinians and Israeli forces, Barak resigned. In 2001, Barak was defeated by the right-wing Ariel Sharon, who adopted a hardline policy against the Palestinians. In 2003, after Sharon won re-election, the United States exerted pressure on him to agree to the setting up of a Palestinian state.

Israel's most valuable activity is manufacturing and the country's products include chemicals, electronic equipment, fertilizers, military equipment, plastics, processed food, scientific instruments and textiles. Fruits and vegetables are leading exports.

AREA 7,960 SQ MI [20,600 SQ KM] **POPULATION** 6,030,000
CAPITAL (POPULATION) JERUSALEM (591,000)
GOVERNMENT MULTIPARTY REPUBLIC **ETHNIC GROUPS** JEWISH 82%, ARAB AND OTHERS 18% **LANGUAGES** HEBREW AND ARABIC (BOTH OFFICIAL)
RELIGIONS JUDAISM 80%, ISLAM (MOSTLY SUNNI) 14%, CHRISTIANITY 2%, DRUZE AND OTHERS 2% **CURRENCY** NEW ISRAELI SHEQEL = 100 AGORAT

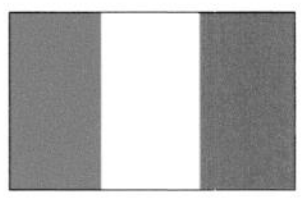

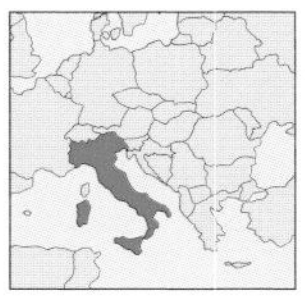

ITALY

GEOGRAPHY The Republic of Italy is famous for its history and traditions, its art and culture, and its beautiful scenery. Northern Italy is bordered in the north by the high Alps, with their many climbing and skiing resorts. The Alps overlook the northern plains – Italy's most fertile and densely populated region – drained by the River Po. The rugged Apennines form the backbone of southern Italy. Bordering the range are scenic hilly areas and coastal plains. Southern Italy contains a string of volcanoes, stretching from Vesuvius, through the Lipari Islands, to Etna on Sicily, the largest Mediterranean island. Northern Italy has cold, often snowy, winters, but the summer months are warm and sunny, with brief summer thunderstorms. Rainfall is abundant. The south has mild, moist winters and warm, dry summers.

POLITICS & ECONOMY Magnificent ruins throughout Italy testify to the glories of the ancient Roman Empire, which was founded, according to legend, in 753 BC. It reached its peak in the AD 100s. It finally collapsed in the 400s, although the Eastern Roman empire, also called the Byzantine empire, survived for another 1,000 years.

In the Middle Ages, Italy was split into many tiny states. These states made a great contribution to the revival of art and learning, called the Renaissance, in the 14th to 16th centuries. Beautiful cities, such as Florence (Firenze) and Venice (Venézia), testify to the artistic achievements of this period.

Italy finally became a united kingdom in 1861, although the Papal Territories (a large area ruled by the Roman Catholic Church) was not added until 1870. The Pope and his successors disputed the takeover of the Papal Territories. The dispute was finally resolved in 1929, when the Vatican City was set up in Rome as a fully independent state.

Italy fought in World War I (1914–18) alongside the Allies – Britain, France and Russia. In 1922, the dictator Benito Mussolini, leader of the Fascist party, took power. Under Mussolini, Italy conquered Ethiopia. During World War II (1939–45), Italy at first fought on Germany's side against the Allies. But in late 1943, Italy declared war on Germany. Italy became a republic in 1946. It has played an important part in European affairs. It was a founder member of the North Atlantic Treaty Organization (NATO) in 1949 and also of what has now become the European Union in 1958.

After the setting up of the European Union, Italy's economy developed quickly. But the country faced many problems. For example, much of the economic development was in the north. This forced many people to leave the poor south to find jobs in the north or abroad. Social problems, corruption at high levels of society, and a succession of weak coalition governments all contributed to instability. Elections in 1996 were won by the left-wing Olive Tree alliance led by Romano Prodi, who was replaced in 1998 by an ex-Communist, Massimo d'Alema, who tried but failed to introduce a two-party system. In 2001, a center-right coalition won a substantial majority in parliament and its leader, media tycoon Silvio Berlusconi, became prime minister.

Only 50 years ago, Italy was a mainly agricultural society. But today it is a leading industrial power. It lacks mineral resources, and imports most of the raw materials used in industry. Manufactures include textiles and clothing, processed food, machinery, cars and chemicals. The chief industrial region is in the northwest.

Farmland covers around 42% of the land, pasture 17%, and forest and woodland 22%. Major crops include citrus fruits, grapes which are used to make wine, olive oil, sugar beet and vegetables. Livestock farming is important, though meat is imported.

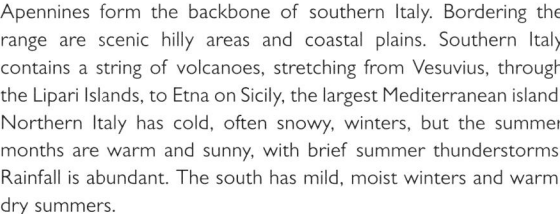

AREA 116,320 sq mi [301,270 sq km] **POPULATION** 57,716,000
CAPITAL (POPULATION) Rome (2,654,000) **GOVERNMENT** Multiparty republic **ETHNIC GROUPS** Italian 94%, German, French, Albanian, Ladino, Slovene, Greek **LANGUAGES** Italian 94% (official), German, French, Slovene **RELIGIONS** Roman Catholic 83%
CURRENCY Euro = 100 cents

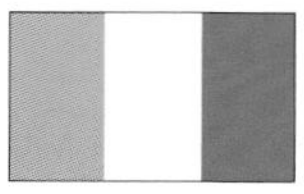

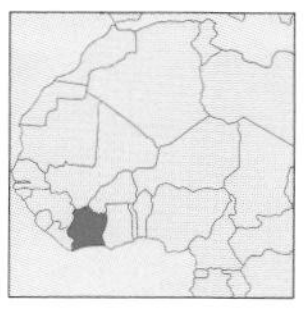

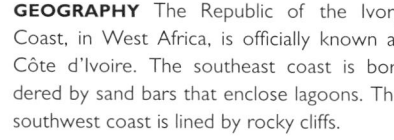

IVORY COAST

GEOGRAPHY The Republic of the Ivory Coast, in West Africa, is officially known as Côte d'Ivoire. The southeast coast is bordered by sand bars that enclose lagoons. The southwest coast is lined by rocky cliffs.

Ivory Coast has a hot and humid tropical climate, with high temperatures all year. The south has two rainy seasons: between May and July, and from October to November. Inland, the rainfall decreases and the north has one dry and one rainy season.

POLITICS & ECONOMY From 1895, Ivory Coast was governed as part of French West Africa, a massive union which also included what are now Benin, Burkina Faso, Guinea, Mali, Mauritania, Niger and Senegal. In 1946, Ivory Coast became a territory in the French Union.

Ivory Coast became fully independent in 1960. Its first president, Félix Houphouët-Boigny, became the longest serving head of state in Africa with an uninterrupted period in office which ended with his death in 1993. Houphouët-Boigny, a pro-Western leader, made Ivory Coast a one-party state. In 1983, the National Assembly voted to make Yamoussoukro, the president's birthplace, the new capital. In 1999, a military coup occurred, but civilian rule was restored in 2000, when Laurent Gbagbo was elected president. An army rebellion began in September 2002. It continued into 2003 when a power-sharing coalition was set up, including members from rebel groups.

Agriculture employs about two-thirds of the people, and farm products make up nearly half the value of the exports. Manufacturing has grown in importance since 1960; products include fertilizers, processed food, refined oil, textiles and timber.

AREA 124,502 sq mi [322,460 sq km] **POPULATION** 16,805,000
CAPITAL (POPULATION) Yamoussoukro (120,000)
GOVERNMENT Multiparty republic **ETHNIC GROUPS** Akan 42%, Voltaic 18%, Northern Mande 16%, Kru 11%, Southern Mande 10%
LANGUAGES French (official), Akan, Voltaic
RELIGIONS Christianity 34%, Islam 27%, traditional beliefs 17%
CURRENCY CFA franc = 100 centimes

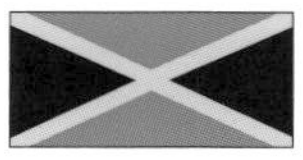

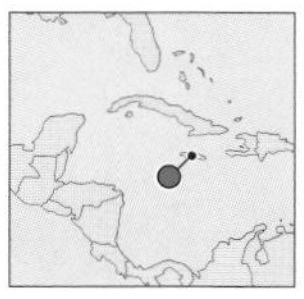

JAMAICA

GEOGRAPHY Third largest of the Caribbean islands, half of Jamaica lies above 1,000 ft [300 m] and moist southeast trade winds bring rain to the central mountain range.

The "cockpit country" in the northwest of the island is an inaccessible limestone area of steep broken ridges and isolated basins.

POLITICS & ECONOMY Britain took Jamaica from Spain in the 17th century, and the island did not gain its independence until 1962. Some economic progress was made by the socialist government in the 1980s, but migration and unemployment remain high. Farming is the leading activity and sugarcane is the main crop, though bauxite production provides much of the country's income. Jamaica has some industries and tourism is a major industry.

AREA 4,243 sq mi [10,990 sq km] **POPULATION** 2,680,000
CAPITAL (POPULATION) Kingston (644,000)
GOVERNMENT Constitutional monarchy
ETHNIC GROUPS Black 91%, Mixed 7%, East Indian 1%
LANGUAGES English (official), Creole
RELIGIONS Protestant 61%, Roman Catholic 4%
CURRENCY Dollar = 100 cents

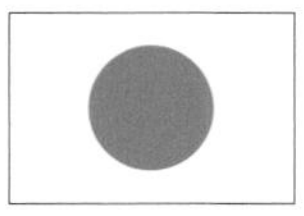

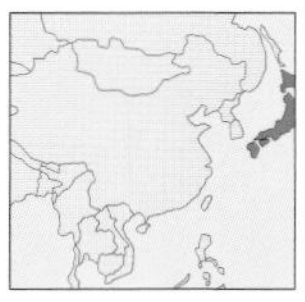

JAPAN

GEOGRAPHY Japan's four largest islands – Honshu, Hokkaido, Kyushu and Shikoku – make up 98% of the country. But Japan contains thousands of small islands. The four largest islands are mainly mountainous, while many of the small islands are the tips of volcanoes. Japan has more than 150 volcanoes, about 60 of which are active. Volcanic eruptions, earthquakes and tsunamis (destructive sea waves triggered by underwater earthquakes and eruptions) are common because the islands lie in an unstable part of our planet, where continental plates are always on the move. One powerful recent earthquake killed more than 5,000 people in Kobe in 1995.

The climate of Japan varies greatly from north to south. Hokkaido in the north has cold, snowy winters. At Sapporo, temperatures below 4°F [–20°C] have been recorded between December and March. But summers are warm, with temperatures sometimes exceeding 86°F [30°C]. Rain falls throughout the year, though Hokkaido is one of the driest parts of Japan. Tokyo has higher rainfall and temperatures, while the southern islands of Shikoku and Kyushu have warm temperate climates. Summers are long and hot. Winters are cold.

POLITICS & ECONOMY In the late 19th century, Japan began a program of modernization. Under its new imperial leaders, it began to look for lands to conquer. In 1894–5, it fought a war with China and, in 1904–5, it defeated Russia. Soon its overseas empire included Korea and Taiwan. In 1930, Japan invaded Manchuria (northeast China) and, in 1937, it began a war against China. In 1941, Japan launched an attack on the US base at Pearl Harbor in Hawaii. This drew both Japan and the United States into World War II.

Japan surrendered in 1945 when the Americans dropped atomic bombs on two cities, Hiroshima and Nagasaki. The United States occupied Japan until 1952. During this period, Japan adopted a democratic constitution. The emperor, who had previously been regarded as a god, became a constitutional monarch. Power was vested in the prime minister and cabinet, who are chosen from the Diet (elected parliament).

From the 1960s, Japan experienced many changes as the country rapidly built up new industries. By the early 1990s, Japan had become the world's second richest economic power after the US. But economic success has brought problems. For example, the rapid growth of cities has led to housing shortages and pollution. Another problem is that the proportion of people over 65 years of age is steadily increasing.

Japan has the world's second highest gross domestic product (GDP) after the United States. [The GDP is the total value of all goods and services produced in a country in one year.] The most important sector of the economy is industry. Yet Japan has to import most of the raw materials and fuels it needs for its industries. Its success is based on its use of the latest technology, its skilled and hard-working labor force, its vigorous export policies and its comparatively small government spending on defense. Manufactures dominate its exports, which include machinery, electrical and electronic equipment, vehicles and transport equipment, iron and steel, chemicals, textiles and ships. However, from the late 1990s, Japan experienced an economic slowdown, which merged in a recession in the early 21st century.

Japan is one of the world's top fishing nations and fish is an important source of protein. Because the land is so rugged, only 15% of the country can be farmed. Yet Japan produces about 70% of the food it needs. Rice is the chief crop, taking up about half of the total farmland. Other major products include fruits, sugar beet, tea and vegetables. Livestock farming has increased since the 1950s.

AREA 145,869 sq mi [377,800 sq km] **POPULATION** 126,975,000
CAPITAL (POPULATION) Tokyo (17,950,000)
GOVERNMENT Constitutional monarchy
ETHNIC GROUPS Japanese 99%, Chinese, Korean, Ainu
LANGUAGES Japanese (official) **RELIGIONS** Shintoism and Buddhism 84% (most Japanese consider themselves to be both Shinto and Buddhist) **CURRENCY** Yen = 100 sen

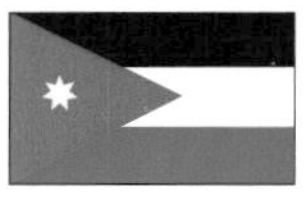

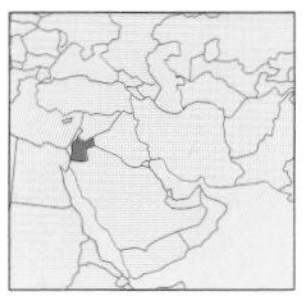

JORDAN

GEOGRAPHY The Hashemite Kingdom of Jordan is an Arab country in southwestern Asia. The Great Rift Valley in the west contains the River Jordan and the Dead Sea, which Jordan shares with Israel. East of the Rift Valley is the Transjordan plateau, where most Jordanians live. To the east and south lie vast areas of desert.

Amman has a much lower rainfall and longer dry season than the Mediterranean lands to the west. The Transjordan plateau, on which Amman stands, is a transition zone between the Mediterranean climate zone to the west and the desert climate to the east.

POLITICS & ECONOMY In 1921, Britain created a territory called Transjordan east of the River Jordan. In 1923, Transjordan became self-governing, but Britain retained control of its defenses, finances and foreign affairs. This territory became fully independent as Jordan in 1946.

Jordan has suffered from instability arising from the Arab–Israeli conflict since the creation of the State of Israel in 1948. After the first Arab–Israeli War in 1948–9, Jordan acquired East Jerusalem and a fertile area called the West Bank. In 1967, Israel occupied this area. In Jordan, the presence of Palestinian refugees led to civil war in 1970–1.

In 1974, Arab leaders declared that the PLO (Palestine Liberation Organization) was the sole representative of the Palestinian people. In 1988, King Hussein of Jordan renounced Jordan's claims to the West Bank and passed responsibility for it to the PLO. Opposition parties were legalized in 1991 and elections were held in 1993. In October 1994, Jordan and Israel signed a peace treaty, ending a state of war that had lasted more than 40 years. Jordan's King Hussein commanded respect for his role in Middle Eastern affairs until his death in 1999. He was succeeded by his eldest son who became Abdullah II.

Jordan lacks natural resources, apart from phosphates and potash, and the economy depends substantially on aid. The World Bank classifies Jordan as a "lower-middle-income" developing country. Because of the dry climate, less than 6% of the land is farmed or used as pasture. Jordan has an oil refinery and manufactures include cement, pharmaceuticals, processed food, fertilizers and textiles.

AREA 34,444 sq mi [89,210 sq km] **POPULATION** 5,307,000
CAPITAL (POPULATION) Amman (1,752,000)
GOVERNMENT Constitutional monarchy **ETHNIC GROUPS** Arab 99%, of which Palestinians make up roughly half **LANGUAGES** Arabic (official) **RELIGIONS** Islam (mostly Sunni) 93%, Christianity (mostly Greek Orthodox) 5% **CURRENCY** Jordan dinar = 1,000 fils

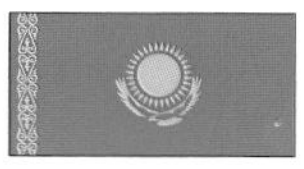

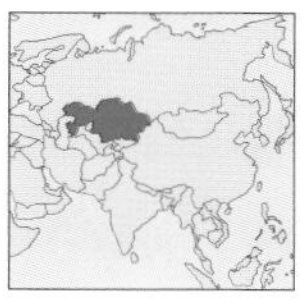

KAZAKHSTAN

GEOGRAPHY Kazakhstan is a large country in west-central Asia. In the west, the Caspian Sea lowlands include the Karagiye depression, which reaches 433 ft [132 m] below sea level. The lowlands extend eastward through the Aral Sea area. The north contains high plains, but the highest land is along the eastern and southern borders. These areas include parts of the Altai and Tian Shan mountain ranges. Eastern Kazakhstan contains several freshwater lakes, the largest of which is Lake Balkhash. The water in the rivers has been used for irrigation, causing ecological problems. For example, the Aral Sea, deprived of water, shrank from 25,830 sq mi [66,900 sq km] in 1960 to 12,989 sq mi [33,642 sq km] in 1993. Large areas are now barren desert.

Kazakhstan lies far from the moderating influence of the oceans and it has an extreme climate. Winters are cold and snow covers the land for about 100 days at Almaty. The rainfall is generally low.

POLITICS & ECONOMY After the Russian Revolution of 1917, many Kazakhs wanted to make their country independent. But the Communists prevailed and in 1936 Kazakhstan became a republic of the Soviet Union, called the Kazakh Soviet Socialist Republic. During World War II and also after the war, the Soviet government moved many people from the west into Kazakhstan. From the 1950s, people were encouraged to work on a "Virgin Lands" project, which involved bringing large areas of grassland under cultivation.

Reforms in the Soviet Union in the 1980s led to its breakup in December 1991. Kazakhstan maintained contacts with Russia through the Commonwealth of Independent States (CIS). In 1997, the government moved its capital from Almaty to Aqmola (later renamed Astana), a town in the Russian-dominated north. It hoped that this would bring some Kazakh identity to the area. In the early 21st century, Kazakhstan's economy was in better shape than any other of the Central Asian ex-Soviet republics. However, its President Nursultan Nazarbaev was criticized for cracking down on political dissent and independent newspapers.

The World Bank classifies Kazakhstan as a "lower-middle-income" developing country. Livestock farming, especially sheep and cattle, is an important activity, and major crops include barley, cotton, rice and wheat. The country is rich in mineral resources, including coal and oil reserves, together with bauxite, copper, lead, tungsten and zinc. Manufactures include chemicals, food products, machinery and textiles. Oil is exported via a pipeline through Russia; however, to reduce dependence on Russia, Kazakhstan signed an agreement in 1997 to build a new pipeline to China. Other exports include metals, chemicals, grain, wool and meat.

AREA 1,049,150 sq mi [2,717,300 sq km] **POPULATION** 16,742,000
CAPITAL (POPULATION) Astana (280,000) **GOVERNMENT** Multiparty republic **ETHNIC GROUPS** Kazakh 53%, Russian 30%, Ukrainian 4%, German 2%, Uzbek 2% **LANGUAGES** Kazakh (official); Russian, the former official language, is widely spoken **RELIGIONS** Islam 47%, Russian Orthodox 44% **CURRENCY** Tenge = 100 tiyn

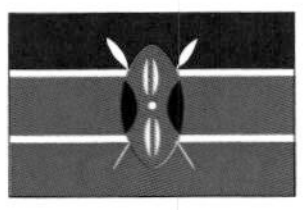

KENYA

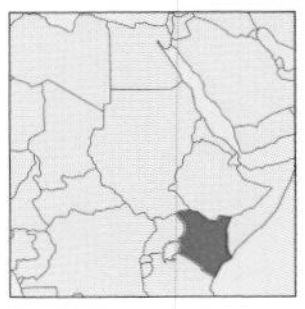

GEOGRAPHY The Republic of Kenya is a country in East Africa which straddles the Equator. Behind the narrow coastal plain on the Indian Ocean, the land rises to high plains and highlands, broken by volcanic mountains, including Mount Kenya, the country's highest peak at 17,057 ft [5,199 m]. Crossing the country is an arm of the Great Rift Valley, on the floor of which are several lakes, including Baringo, Magadi, Naivasha, Nakuru and, on the northern frontier, Lake Turkana (formerly Lake Rudolf).

Mombasa on the coast is hot and humid. But inland, the climate is moderated by the height of the land. As a result, Nairobi, in the thickly populated southwestern highlands, has summer temperatures which are 18°F [10°C] lower than Mombasa. Nights can be cool, but temperatures do not fall below freezing. Nairobi's main rainy season is from April to May, with "little rains" in November and December. However, only about 15% of the country has a reliable rainfall of 31 inches [800 mm].

POLITICS & ECONOMY The Kenyan coast has been a trading center for more than 2,000 years. Britain took over the coast in 1895 and soon extended its influence inland. In the 1950s, a secret movement, called Mau Mau, launched an armed struggle against British rule. Although Mau Mau was eventually defeated, Kenya became independent in 1963.

Many Kenyans felt that Kenya should have a strong central government, and Kenya was a one-party state for much of the time since 1963. But democracy was restored in the early 1990s and elections were held in 1992, 1997 and 2002. In 1999, Kenya, with Tanzania and Uganda, set up an East African Community, which aimed to create a customs union, a common market, a monetary union, and, ultimately, a political union.

According to the United Nations, Kenya is a "low-income" developing country. Agriculture employs about 80% of the people, but many Kenyans are subsistence farmers, growing little more than they need to support their families. The chief food crop is maize. The main cash crops and leading exports are coffee and tea. Manufactures include chemicals, leather and footwear, processed food, petroleum products and textiles.

AREA 224,081 SQ MI [580,370 SQ KM] **POPULATION** 31,139,000
CAPITAL (POPULATION) NAIROBI (2,000,000)
GOVERNMENT MULTIPARTY REPUBLIC
ETHNIC GROUPS KIKUYU 21%, LUHYA 14%, LUO 13%, KALENJIN 12%, KAMBA 11% **LANGUAGES** KISWAHILI AND ENGLISH (BOTH OFFICIAL)
RELIGIONS PROTESTANT 45%, ROMAN CATHOLIC 33%, TRADITIONAL BELIEFS 10%, ISLAM 10% **CURRENCY** KENYA SHILLING = 100 CENTS

KIRIBATI

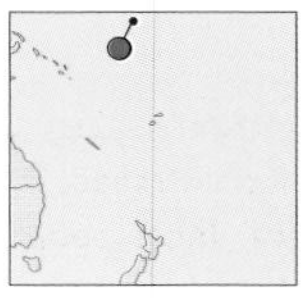

The Republic of Kiribati comprises three groups of corall atolls scattered over about 2 million sq mi [5 million sq km]. Kiribati straddles the equator and temperatures are high and the rainfall is abundant.

Formerly part of the British Gilbert and Ellice Islands, Kiribati became independent in 1979. The main export is copra and the country depends heavily on foreign aid.

AREA 281 SQ MI [728 SQ KM] **POPULATION** 96,000 **CAPITAL** TARAWA

KOREA, NORTH

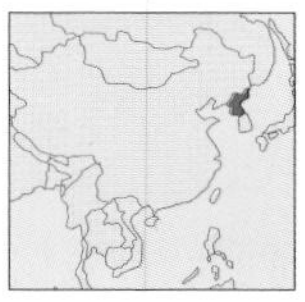

GEOGRAPHY The Democratic People's Republic of Korea occupies the northern part of the Korean peninsula which extends south from northeastern China. Mountains form the heart of the country, with the highest peak, Paektu-san, reaching 9,003 ft [2,744 m] on the northern border.

North Korea has a fairly severe climate, with bitterly cold winters when winds blow from across central Asia, bringing snow and freezing conditions. In summer, moist winds from the oceans bring rain.

POLITICS & ECONOMY North Korea was created in 1945, when the peninsula, which had been a Japanese colony since 1910, was divided into two parts. Soviet forces occupied the north, with US forces in the south. Soviet occupation led to a Communist government being established in 1948 under the leadership of Kim Il Sung. He initiated a Stalinist regime in which he assumed the role of dictator, and a personality cult developed around him. He was to become the world's most durable Communist leader.

The Korean War began in June 1950 when North Korean troops invaded the south. North Korea, aided by China and the Soviet Union, fought with South Korea, which was supported by troops from the United States and other UN members. The war ended in July 1953. An armistice was signed but no permanent peace treaty was agreed. After the war, North Korea adopted a hostile policy toward South Korea in pursuit of its policy of reunification.

The ending of the Cold War in the late 1980s eased the situation and both North and South Korea joined the United Nations in 1991. The two countries made several agreements, including one in which they agreed not to use force against each other. However, North Korea remained as isolated as ever.

In 1993, North Korea began a new international crisis by announcing that it was withdrawing from the Nuclear Non-Proliferation Treaty. This led to suspicions that North Korea, which had signed the Treaty in 1985, was developing its own nuclear weapons. Kim Il Sung, who had ruled as a virtual dictator from 1948 until his death in 1994, was succeeded by his son, Kim Jong Il. In the early 2000s, attempts were made to reconcile the two Koreas, though the prospect of reunification seemed remote. In 2003, North Korea's relations with the United States deteriorated sharply when the US accused North Korea of developing nuclear weapons.

North Korea has considerable resources, including coal, copper, iron ore, lead, tin, tungsten and zinc. Under Communism, North Korea has concentrated on developing heavy, state-owned industries. Manufactures include chemicals, iron and steel, machinery, processed food and textiles. Agriculture employs about a third of the people of North Korea and rice is the leading crop. Economic decline and mismanagement, aggravated by three successive crop failures caused by floods in 1995 and 1996 and a drought in 1997, led to famine on a large scale.

AREA 46,540 SQ MI [120,540 SQ KM] **POPULATION** 22,224,000
CAPITAL (POPULATION) PYŎNGYANG (2,741,000)
GOVERNMENT SINGLE-PARTY PEOPLE'S REPUBLIC
ETHNIC GROUPS KOREAN 99%
LANGUAGES KOREAN (OFFICIAL)
RELIGIONS BUDDHISM AND CONFUCIANISM
CURRENCY NORTH KOREAN WON = 100 CHON

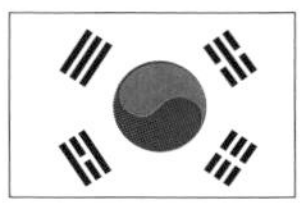

KOREA, SOUTH

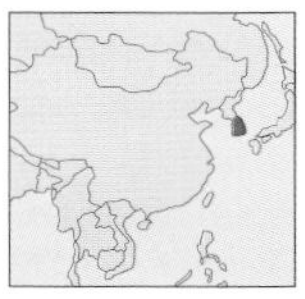

GEOGRAPHY The Republic of Korea, as South Korea is officially known, occupies the southern part of the Korean peninsula. Mountains cover much of the country. The southern and western coasts are major farming regions. Many islands are found along the west and south coasts. The largest of these is Cheju-do, which contains South Korea's highest peak, Halla-San, which rises to 6,398 ft [1,950 m].

Like North Korea, South Korea is chilled in winter by cold, dry winds blowing from central Asia. Snow often covers the mountains in the east. The summers are hot and wet, especially in July and August.

POLITICS & ECONOMY After Japan's defeat in World War II (1939–45), North Korea was occupied by troops from the Soviet Union, while South Korea was occupied by United States forces. Attempts to reunify Korea failed and, in 1948, a National Assembly was elected in South Korea. This Assembly created the Republic of Korea, while North Korea became a Communist state. North Korean troops invaded the South in June 1950, sparking off the Korean War (1950–3).

In the 1950s, South Korea had a weak economy, which had been further damaged by the destruction caused by the Korean War. From the 1960s to the 1980s, South Korean governments worked to industrialize the economy. The governments were dominated by military leaders, who often used authoritarian methods and flouted human rights. In 1987, a new constitution was approved, enabling presidential elections to be held every five years. In 1991, South and North Korea became members of the United Nations and they signed agreements, including one in which they agreed not to use force against each other. Tensions continued, though hopes were raised when negotiations between the two countries took place in the early 21st century.

The World Bank classifies South Korea as an "upper-middle-income" developing country. It is also one of the world's fastest growing industrial economies. The country's resources include coal and tungsten, and its main manufactures are processed food and textiles. Since partition, heavy industries have been built up, making chemicals, fertilizers, iron and steel, and ships. South Korea has also developed the production of such things as computers, cars and television sets. In late 1997, however, the dramatic expansion of the economy was halted by a market crash which affected many of the booming economies of Asia. However, South Korea recovered faster than any other country in the region, and huge inflows of foreign investment and strict financial measures, including the restructuring of its short-term debt, led to the restoration of confidence and economic growth.

Farming remains important in South Korea. Rice is the chief crop, together with fruits, grains and vegetables, while fishing provides a major source of protein.

AREA 38,232 SQ MI [99,020 SQ KM] **POPULATION** 48,324,000
CAPITAL (POPULATION) SEOUL (10,231,000)
GOVERNMENT MULTIPARTY REPUBLIC
ETHNIC GROUPS KOREAN 99% **LANGUAGES** KOREAN (OFFICIAL)
RELIGIONS CHRISTIANITY 49%, BUDDHISM 47%, CONFUCIANISM 3%
CURRENCY SOUTH KOREAN WON = 100 CHON

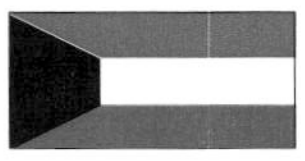

KUWAIT

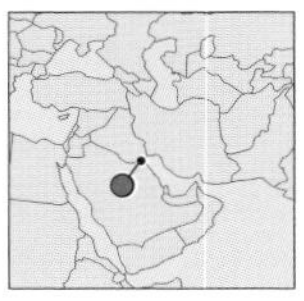

The State of Kuwait at the north end of the Gulf is largely made up of desert. Temperatures are high and the rainfall low. Kuwait became independent from Britain in 1961 and revenues from its oil wells have made it highly prosperous. Iraq invaded Kuwait in 1990 and much damage was inflicted in the ensuing conflict in 1991 when Kuwait was liberated.

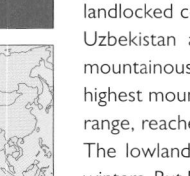

AREA 6,880 SQ MI [17,820 SQ KM] **POPULATION** 2,112,000
CAPITAL KUWAIT CITY

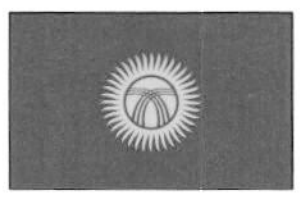

KYRGYZSTAN

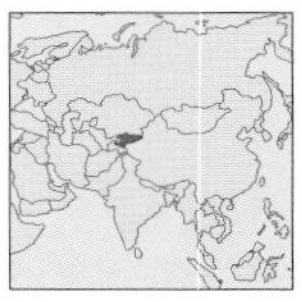

GEOGRAPHY The Republic of Kyrgyzstan is a landlocked country between China, Tajikistan, Uzbekistan and Kazakhstan. The country is mountainous, with spectacular scenery. The highest mountain, Pik Pobedy in the Tian Shan range, reaches 24,406 ft [7,439 m] in the east. The lowlands have warm summers and cold winters. But January temperatures in the mountains plummet to –18°F [–28°C]. Kyrgyzstan has a low annual rainfall.

POLITICS & ECONOMY In 1876, Kyrgyzstan became a province of Russia and Russian settlement in the area began. In 1916, Russia crushed a rebellion among the Kyrgyz, and many subsequently fled to China. In 1922, the area became an autonomous oblast (self-governing region) of the newly formed Soviet Union but, in 1936, it became one of the Soviet Socialist Republics. Under Communist rule, local customs and religious worship were suppressed, but education and health services were greatly improved.

In 1991, Kyrgyzstan became an independent country following the breakup of the Soviet Union. The Communist party was dissolved, but the country maintained ties with Russia through an organization called the Commonwealth of Independent States. Kyrgyzstan adopted a new constitution in 1994 and parliamentary elections were held in 1995. In the early 21st century, many people were alarmed when Islamic guerrillas sought to set up an Islamic state in the Fergana valley, where Kyrgyzstan borders Tajikistan and Uzbekistan.

In the early 1990s, when Kyrgyzstan was working to reform its economy, the World Bank classified it as a "lower-middle-income" developing country. Agriculture, especially livestock rearing, is the chief activity. The chief products include cotton, eggs, fruits, grain, tobacco, vegetables and wool. But food must be imported. Industries are mainly concentrated around the capital Bishkek.

AREA 76,640 SQ MI [198,500 SQ KM] **POPULATION** 4,822,000
CAPITAL (POPULATION) BISHKEK (589,000) **GOVERNMENT** MULTIPARTY REPUBLIC **ETHNIC GROUPS** KYRGYZ 52%, RUSSIAN 18%, UZBEK 13%, UKRAINIAN 3%, GERMAN, TATAR **LANGUAGES** KYRGYZ AND RUSSIAN (BOTH OFFICIAL), UZBEK **RELIGIONS** ISLAM **CURRENCY** SOM = 100 TYIYN

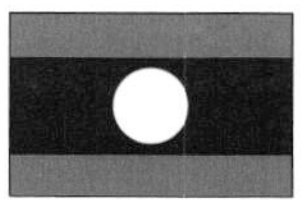

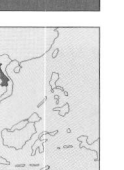

LAOS

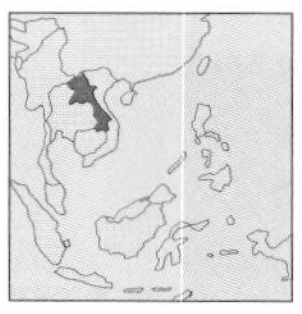

GEOGRAPHY The Lao People's Democratic Republic is a landlocked country in Southeast Asia. Mountains and plateaux cover much of the country. Most people live on the plains bordering the River Mekong and its tributaries. This river, one of Asia's longest, forms much of the country's northwestern and southwestern borders.

Laos has a tropical monsoon climate.

Winters are dry and sunny, with winds blowing in from the northeast. The temperatures rise until April, when the wind directions are reversed and moist southwesterly winds reach Laos, heralding the start of the wet monsoon season.

POLITICS & ECONOMY France made Laos a protectorate in the late 19th century and ruled it as part of French Indochina, a region which also included Cambodia and Vietnam. Laos became a member of the French Union in 1948 and an independent kingdom in 1954.

After independence, Laos suffered from instability caused by a long power struggle between royalist government forces and a pro-Communist group called the Pathet Lao. A civil war broke out in 1960 and continued into the 1970s. The Pathet Lao took control in 1975 and the king abdicated. Laos then came under the influence of Communist Vietnam, which had used Laos as a supply base during the Vietnam War (1957–75). From the early 1980s, the economy deteriorated and opposition appeared when bombings occurred in Vientiane in 2000. They were attributed to rebels in the minority Hmong tribe or to politicians who wanted faster economic reforms.

Laos is one of the world's poorest countries. Agriculture employs about 76% of the people, compared with 7% in industry and 17% in services. Rice is the main crop, and timber and coffee are both exported. But the most valuable export is electricity, which is produced at hydroelectric power stations on the River Mekong and is exported to Thailand. Laos also produces opium.

AREA 91,428 sq mi [236,800 sq km] **POPULATION** 5,777,000
CAPITAL (POPULATION) Vientiane (532,000)
GOVERNMENT Single-party republic **ETHNIC GROUPS** Lao Loum 68%, Lao Theung 22%, Lao Soung 9% **LANGUAGES** Lao (official), Khmer, Tai, Miao **RELIGIONS** Buddhism 58%, traditional beliefs 34%, Christianity 2%, Islam 1% **CURRENCY** Kip = 100 at

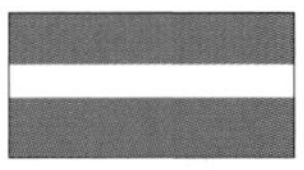
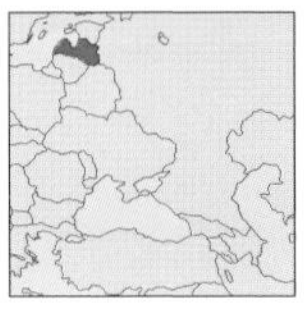

LATVIA

GEOGRAPHY The Republic of Latvia is one of three states on the southeastern corner of the Baltic Sea which were ruled as parts of the Soviet Union between 1940 and 1991. Latvia consists mainly of flat plains separated by low hills, composed of moraine (ice-worn rocks).

Riga has warm summers, but the winter months (from December to March) are subzero. In the winter, the sea often freezes over. The rainfall is moderate and it occurs throughout the year, with light snow in winter.

POLITICS & ECONOMY In 1800, Russia was in control of Latvia, but Latvians declared their independence after World War I. In 1940, under a German-Soviet pact, Soviet troops occupied Latvia, but they were driven out by the Germans in 1941. Soviet troops returned in 1944 and Latvia became part of the Soviet Union. Under Soviet rule, many Russian immigrants settled in Latvia and many Latvians feared that the Russians would become the dominant ethnic group.

In the late 1980s, when reforms were being introduced in the Soviet Union, Latvia's government ended absolute Communist rule and made Latvian the official language. In 1990, it declared the country to be independent, an act which was finally recognized by the Soviet Union in September 1991.

Latvia held its first free elections to its parliament (the Saeima) in 1993. Voting was limited only to citizens of Latvia on June 17, 1940, and their descendants. This meant that about 34% of Latvian residents were unable to vote. In 1994, Latvia restricted the naturalization of non-Latvians, including many Russian settlers, who were not allowed to vote or own land. However, in 1998, the government agreed that all children born since independence should have automatic citizenship. Since 1990, Latvia has cultivated closer ties with the West and, in 2002, it was invited to become a member of the European Union in May 2004.

The World Bank classifies Latvia as a "lower-middle-income" country and, in the 1990s, it faced many problems in turning its economy into a free-market system. Products include electronic goods, farm machinery, fertilizers, processed food, plastics, radios and vehicles. Latvia produces only about a tenth of the electricity it needs. It imports the rest from Belarus, Russia and Ukraine.

AREA 24,938 sq mi [64,589 sq km] **POPULATION** 2,367,000
CAPITAL (POPULATION) Riga (811,000)
GOVERNMENT Multiparty republic **ETHNIC GROUPS** Latvian 56%, Russian 30%, Belarussian 4%, Ukrainian 3%, Polish 2%, Lithuanian, Jewish **LANGUAGES** Latvian (official), Russian
RELIGIONS Lutheran, Russian Orthodox and Roman Catholic
CURRENCY Lats = 10 santimi

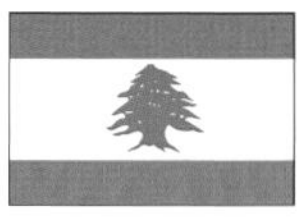
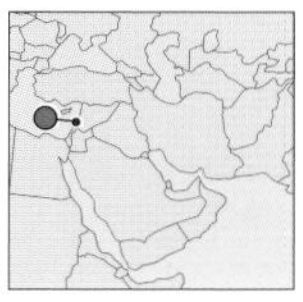

LEBANON

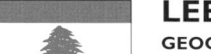

GEOGRAPHY The Republic of Lebanon is a country on the eastern shores of the Mediterranean Sea. Behind the coastal plain are the rugged Lebanon Mountains (Jabal Lubnan), which rise to 10,131 ft [3,088 m]. Another range, the Anti-Lebanon Mountains (Al Jabal Ash Sharqi), form the eastern border with Syria. Between the two ranges is the Bekaa (Beqaa) Valley, a fertile farming region.

The Lebanese coast has the hot, dry summers and mild, wet winters that are typical of many Mediterranean lands. Inland, onshore winds bring heavy rain to the western slopes of the mountains in the winter months, with snow at the higher altitudes.

POLITICS & ECONOMY Lebanon was ruled by Turkey from 1516 until World War I. France ruled the country from 1923, but Lebanon became independent in 1946. After independence, the Muslims and Christians agreed to share power, and Lebanon made rapid economic progress. But from the late 1950s, development was slowed by periodic conflict between Sunni and Shia Muslims, Druze and Christians. The situation was further complicated by the presence of Palestinian refugees who used bases in Lebanon to attack Israel.

In 1975, civil war broke out as private armies representing the many factions struggled for power. This led to intervention by Israel in the south and Syria in the north. UN peacekeeping forces arrived in 1978, but bombings, assassinations and kidnappings became almost everyday events in the 1980s. From 1991, Lebanon enjoyed an uneasy peace. But, Israel continued to occupy an area in the south. In the 1990s, Israel launched several attacks on pro-Iranian Hezbollah guerrillas in Lebanon, but all Israeli troops were withdrawn in May 2000.

Lebanon's civil war almost destroyed valuable trade and financial services that had been Lebanon's chief source of income, together with tourism. Manufacturing, formerly a major activity, was badly hit.

AREA 4,015 sq mi [10,400 sq km] **POPULATION** 3,678,000
CAPITAL (POPULATION) Beirut (1,500,000)
GOVERNMENT Multiparty republic
ETHNIC GROUPS Lebanese 80%, Palestinian 12%, Armenian 5%, Syrian, Kurdish **LANGUAGES** Arabic (official) **RELIGIONS** Islam 70%, Christianity 30% **CURRENCY** Lebanese pound = 100 piastres

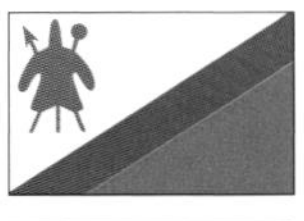
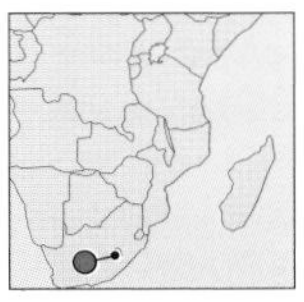

LESOTHO

GEOGRAPHY The Kingdom of Lesotho is a landlocked country, completely enclosed by South Africa. The land is mountainous, rising to 11,424 ft [3,482 m] on the northeastern border. The Drakensberg range covers most of the country.

The climate of Lesotho is greatly affected by the altitude, because most of the country lies above 4,921 ft [1,500 m]. Maseru has warm summers, but the temperatures fall below freezing in the winter. The mountains are colder. The rainfall varies, averaging around 28 inches [700 mm].

POLITICS & ECONOMY The Basotho nation was founded in the 1820s by King Moshoeshoe I, who united various groups fleeing from tribal wars in southern Africa. Britain made the area a protectorate in 1868 and, in 1971, placed it under the British Cape Colony in South Africa. But in 1884, Basutoland, as the area was called, was reconstituted as a British protectorate, where whites were not allowed to own land.

The country finally became independent in 1966 as the Kingdom of Lesotho, with Moshoeshoe II, great-grandson of Moshoeshoe I, as its king. Since independence, Lesotho has suffered instability. The military seized power in 1986 and stripped Moshoeshoe II of his powers in 1990, installing his son, Letsie III, as monarch. After elections in 1993, Moshoeshoe II was restored to office in 1995. But after his death in a car crash in 1996, Letsie III again became king. In 1998, an army revolt, following an election in which the ruling party won 79 out of the 80 seats, caused much damage to the economy, despite the intervention of a South African force intended to maintain order.

Lesotho is a "low-income" developing country. It lacks natural resources. Agriculture, mainly at subsistence level, light manufacturing and money sent home by Basotho working abroad are the main sources of income.

AREA 11,718 sq mi [30,350 sq km] **POPULATION** 2,208,000
CAPITAL (POPULATION) Maseru (130,000)
GOVERNMENT Constitutional monarchy
ETHNIC GROUPS Sotho 99% **LANGUAGES** Sesotho and English (both official) **RELIGIONS** Christianity 80%, traditional beliefs 20%
CURRENCY Loti = 100 lisente

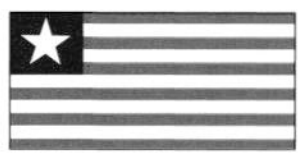
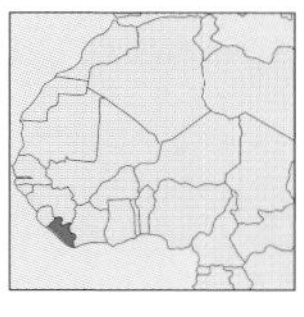

LIBERIA

GEOGRAPHY The Republic of Liberia is a country in West Africa. Behind the coastline, 311 mi [500 km] long, lies a narrow coastal plain. Beyond, the land rises to a plateau region, with the highest land along the border with Guinea. Liberia has a tropical climate with high temperatures and high humidity all through the year. The rainfall is abundant all year round, but there is a particularly wet period from June to November. The rainfall generally increases from east to west.

POLITICS & ECONOMY In the late 18th century, some white Americans in the United States wanted to help freed black slaves to return to Africa. In 1816, they set up the American Colonization Society, which bought land in what is now Liberia.

In 1822, the Society landed former slaves at a settlement on the coast which they named Monrovia. In 1847, Liberia became a fully independent republic with a constitution much like that of the United States. For many years, the Americo-Liberians controlled the country's government. US influence remained strong and the American Firestone Company, which ran Liberia's rubber plantations, was especially influential. Foreign companies were also involved in exploiting Liberia's mineral resources, including its huge iron-ore deposits.

In 1980, a military group composed of people from the local population killed the Americo-Liberian president, William R. Tolbert. An army sergeant, Samuel K. Doe, was made president of Liberia. Elections held in 1985 resulted in victory for Doe. From 1989, the country was plunged into civil war between various ethnic groups. Doe was assassinated in 1990 and the struggle with rebel groups continued. West African peacekeeping forces arrived in Liberia and, in 1995, a ceasefire was agreed. A council of state, composed of former warlords, was set up and, in 1997, one of the warlords, Charles Taylor, was elected president. A ceasefire in 1998 led to the withdrawal of the peacekeeping forces. But unrest continued and, in 2002, a state of emergency was declared.

Liberia's civil war devastated its economy. Three out of every four people depend on agriculture, though many of them grow little more than they need to feed their families. Major food crops include cassava, rice and sugarcane, while rubber, cocoa and coffee are exported. But the most valuable export is iron ore.

Liberia also obtains revenue from its "flag of convenience," which is used by about one-sixth of the world's commercial shipping, exploiting low taxes.

AREA 43,000 sq mi [111,370 sq km] **POPULATION** 3,288,000
CAPITAL (POPULATION) Monrovia (962,000)
GOVERNMENT Multiparty republic **ETHNIC GROUPS** Kpelle 19%, Bassa 14%, Grebo 9%, Gio 8%, Kru 7%, Mano 7%
LANGUAGES English (official), Mande, Mel, Kwa
RELIGIONS Christianity 40%, Islam 20%, traditional beliefs and others 40% **CURRENCY** Liberian dollar = 100 cents

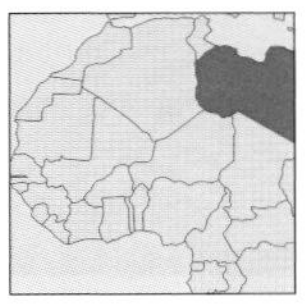

LIBYA

GEOGRAPHY The Socialist People's Libyan Arab Jamahiriya, as Libya is officially called, is a large country in North Africa. Most people live on the coastal plains in the northeast and northwest. The Sahara, the world's largest desert which occupies 95% of Libya, reaches the Mediterranean coast along the Gulf of Sidra (Khalij Surt).

The coastal plains in the northeast and northwest have Mediterranean climates, with hot, dry summers and mild, sometimes wet winters. Inland, the average yearly rainfall drops to 4 inches [100 mm] or less.

POLITICS & ECONOMY Italy took over Libya in 1911, but lost it during World War II. Britain and France then jointly ruled Libya until 1951, when the country became an independent kingdom.

In 1969, a military group headed by Colonel Muammar Gaddafi deposed the king and set up a military government. Under Gaddafi, the government took control of the economy and used money from oil exports to finance welfare services and development projects. Gaddafi was criticized for supporting terrorist groups around the world, and Libya became isolated from the mid-1980s. In 1998, he tried to restore Libya's reputation by surrendering for trial two Libyans suspected of planting a bomb on a PanAm plane which exploded over the Scottish town of Lockerbie in 1988. In 2001, one of the Libyans was found guilty and the other acquitted of the bombing. Gaddafi also compensated the family of a British policewoman killed in 1984 in London. However, in 2002, Libya remained on the US blacklist for its alleged support for international terrorism.

The discovery of oil and natural gas in 1959 led to the transformation of Libya's economy. Once one of the world's poorest countries, it has become Africa's richest in terms of its per capita income. It remains a developing country because of its dependence on oil, which accounts for nearly all of its export revenues.

Agriculture is important, although Libya has to import food. Crops include barley, citrus fruits, dates, olives, potatoes and wheat. Cattle, sheep and poultry are raised. Libya has oil refineries and petrochemical plants. Other manufactures include cement and steel.

AREA 679,358 sq mi [1,759,540 sq km] **POPULATION** 5,369,000
CAPITAL (POPULATION) Tripoli (960,000)
GOVERNMENT Single-party socialist state **ETHNIC GROUPS** Libyan Arab and Berber 97% **LANGUAGES** Arabic (official), Berber
RELIGIONS Islam (Sunni) **CURRENCY** Libyan dinar = 1,000 dirhams

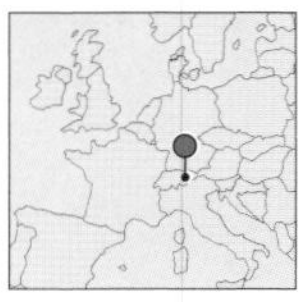

LIECHTENSTEIN

The tiny Principality of Liechtenstein is sandwiched between Switzerland and Austria. The River Rhine flows along its western border, while Alpine peaks rise in the east and south. The climate is relatively mild. Since 1924, Liechtenstein has been in a customs union with Switzerland. Taxation is low and the country is a haven for foreign companies. In 2003, the people voted to give their head of state, Prince Hans Adam II, sovereign powers.

AREA 61 sq mi [157 sq km] **POPULATION** 33,000 **CAPITAL** Vaduz

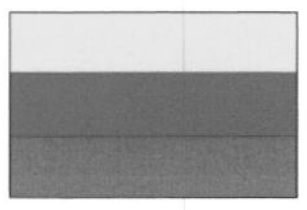

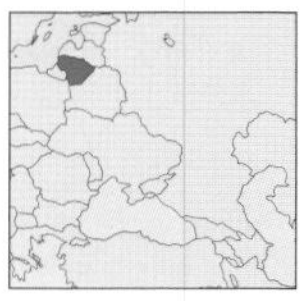

LITHUANIA

GEOGRAPHY The Republic of Lithuania is the southernmost of the three Baltic states which were ruled as part of the Soviet Union between 1940 and 1991. Much of the land is flat or gently rolling, with the highest land in the southeast.

Winters are cold. January's temperatures average 27°F [–3°C] in the west and 21°F [–6°C] in the east. Summers are warm, with average temperatures in July of 63°F [17°C]. The average rainfall in the west is about 25 inches [630 mm]. Inland areas are drier.

POLITICS & ECONOMY The Lithuanian people were united into a single nation in the 12th century, and later joined a union with Poland. In 1795, Lithuania came under Russian rule. After World War I (1914–18), Lithuania declared itself independent, and in 1920 it signed a peace treaty with the Russians, though Poland held Vilnius until 1939. In 1940, the Soviet Union occupied Lithuania, but the Germans invaded in 1941. Soviet forces returned in 1944, and Lithuania was integrated into the Soviet Union. In 1988, when the Soviet Union was introducing reforms, the Lithuanians demanded independence. Their language is one of the oldest in the world, and the country was always the most homogenous of the Baltic states, staunchly Catholic and resistant of attempts to suppress their culture. Pro-independence groups won the national elections in 1990 and, in 1991, the Soviet Union recognized Lithuania's independence.

Since 1991, Lithuania has sought to reform its economy and introduce a private enterprise system. Lithuania has also drawn closer to the West and, in 2002, the European Union invited it to become a member in 2004.

The World Bank classifies Lithuania as a "lower-middle-income" developing country. Lithuania lacks natural resources, but manufacturing, based on imported materials, is the most valuable activity.

AREA 25,200 sq mi [65,200 sq km] **POPULATION** 3,601,000
CAPITAL (POPULATION) Vilnius (580,000)
GOVERNMENT Multiparty republic
ETHNIC GROUPS Lithuanian 80%, Russian 9%, Polish 7%, Belarussian 2% **LANGUAGES** Lithuanian (official), Russian, Polish
RELIGIONS Mainly Roman Catholic **CURRENCY** Litas = 100 centai

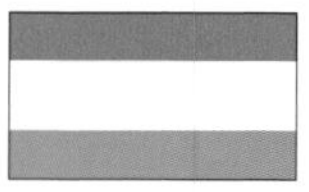

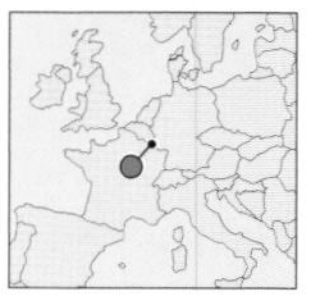

LUXEMBOURG

GEOGRAPHY The Grand Duchy of Luxembourg is one of the smallest and oldest countries in Europe. The north belongs to an upland region which includes the Ardenne in Belgium and Luxembourg, and the Eifel highlands in Germany.

Luxembourg has a temperate climate. The south has warm summers and falls, when grapes ripen in sheltered southeastern valleys. Winters are sometimes severe, especially in upland areas.

POLITICS & ECONOMY Germany occupied Luxembourg in World Wars I and II. In 1944–5, northern Luxembourg was the scene of the famous Battle of the Bulge. In 1948, Luxembourg joined Belgium and the Netherlands in a union called Benelux and, in the 1950s, it was one of the six founders of what is now the European Union. Luxembourg has played a major role in Europe. Its capital contains the headquarters of several international agencies, including the European Coal and Steel Community and the European Court of Justice. The city is also a major financial center.

Luxembourg has iron-ore reserves and is a major steel producer. It also has many high-technology industries, producing electronic goods and computers. Steel and other manufactures, including chemicals, rubber products, glass and aluminum, dominate the country's exports. Other major activities include tourism and financial services.

AREA 1,000 sq mi [2,590 sq km] **POPULATION** 449,000
CAPITAL (POPULATION) Luxembourg (76,000)
GOVERNMENT Constitutional monarchy (Grand Duchy)
ETHNIC GROUPS Luxembourger 71%, Portuguese 10%, Italian 5%, French 3%, Belgian 3% **LANGUAGES** Luxembourgish (official), French, German **RELIGIONS** Roman Catholic 95%
CURRENCY Euro = 100 cents

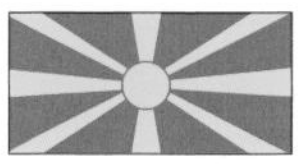

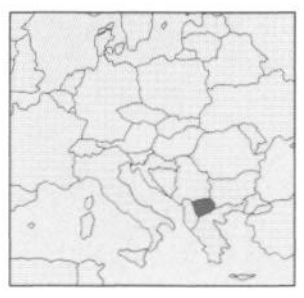

MACEDONIA (FYROM)

GEOGRAPHY The Republic of Macedonia is a country in southeastern Europe, which was once one of the six republics that made up the former Federal People's Republic of Yugoslavia. This landlocked country is largely mountainous or hilly. Macedonia has hot summers, though highland areas are cooler. Winters are cold and snowfalls are often heavy. The climate is fairly continental in character and rain occurs throughout the year.

POLITICS & ECONOMY Until the 20th century, Macedonia's history was closely tied to a larger area, also called Macedonia, which included parts of northern Greece and southwestern Bulgaria. This region reached its peak in power at the time of Philip II (382–336 BC) and his son Alexander the Great (336–323 BC). After Alexander's death, his empire was split up and it gradually declined. The area became a Roman province in the 140s BC and part of the Byzantine Empire from AD 395. In the 6th century, Slavs from eastern Europe settled in the area, followed by the Bulgars from central Asia in the 9th century. The Byzantine Empire regained control in 1018, but Serbia took Macedonia in the early 14th century. In 1371, the Ottoman Turks conquered the area and ruled it for more than 500 years. In 1913, at the end of the Balkan Wars, the area was divided between Serbia, Bulgaria and Greece. At the end of World War I, Serbian Macedonia became part of the Kingdom of the Serbs. Croats and Slovenes, which was renamed Yugoslavia in 1929. After World War II, Yugoslavia became a Communist country under ex-partisan leader Josip Broz Tito.

Tito died in 1980 and, in the early 1990s, the country broke up into five separate republics. Macedonia declared its independence in September 1991. Greece objected to this territory using the name Macedonia, which it considered to be a Greek name. It also objected to a symbol on Macedonia's flag and a reference in the constitution to the desire to reunite the three parts of the old Macedonia.

Macedonia adopted a new clause in its constitution rejecting any Macedonian claims on Greek territory and, in 1993, the United Nations accepted the new republic as a member under the name of The Former Yugoslav Republic of Macedonia (FYROM).

By the end of 1993, all the countries of the EU, except Greece, were establishing diplomatic relations with the FYROM. In 1995, Greece lifted its trade ban, when Macedonia agreed to redesign its flag and remove territorial claims from its constitution. In 2001, fighting along the Kosovo border spilled over into northwestern Macedonia. It was attributed to nationalists who want to create a Great Albania, including part of Macedonia. The uprising ended when the Macedonian government gave its Albanian-speakers increased rights.

The World Bank describes Macedonia as a "lower-middle-income" developing country. Manufactures dominate the country's exports. Macedonia mines coal, but imports all its oil and natural gas. The country is self-sufficient in its basic food needs.

AREA 9,927 sq mi [25,710 sq km] **POPULATION** 2,055,000
CAPITAL (POPULATION) Skopje (541,000) **GOVERNMENT** Multiparty republic **ETHNIC GROUPS** Macedonian 67%, Albanian 23%, Turkish 4%, Romanian 2%, Serb 2% **LANGUAGES** Macedonian and Albanian (both official) **RELIGIONS** Macedonian Orthodox, Islam
CURRENCY Dinar = 100 paras

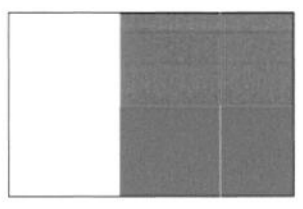

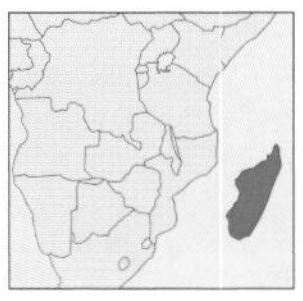

MADAGASCAR

GEOGRAPHY The Democratic Republic of Madagascar, in southeastern Africa, is an island nation, which has a larger area than France. Behind the narrow coastal plains in the east lies a highland zone, mostly between 2,000 ft and 4,000 ft [610 m to 1,220 m] above sea level. Broad plains border the Mozambique Channel in the west.

Temperatures in the highlands are moderated by the altitude. The winters (from April to September) are dry, but heavy rains occur in summer. The eastern coastlands are warm and humid. The west is drier and the south and southwest are hot and dry.

POLITICS & ECONOMY People from Southeast Asia began to settle on Madagascar around 2,000 years ago. Subsequent influxes from Africa and Arabia added to the island's diverse heritage, culture and language.

French troops defeated a Malagasy army in 1895 and Madagascar became a French colony. In 1960, it achieved full independence as the Malagasy Republic. In 1972, army officers seized control and, in 1975, under the leadership of Lt-Commander Didier Ratsiraka, the country was renamed Madagascar. Parliamentary elections were held in 1977, but Ratsiraka remained president of a one-party socialist state. In 2002, the country came close to civil war when Ratsiraka and his opponent, Marc Ravalomanana, both claimed victory in presidential elections. Ravalomanana was eventually recognized as president and Ratsiraka went into exile.

Madagascar is one of the world's poorest countries. The land has been badly eroded because of the cutting down of the forests and overgrazing of the grasslands. Farming, fishing and forestry employ about 80% of the people. The country's food crops include bananas, cassava, rice and sweet potatoes. Coffee is the leading export.

AREA 226,656 sq mi [587,040 sq km] **POPULATION** 16,473,000
CAPITAL (POPULATION) Antananarivo (1,053,000)
GOVERNMENT Republic **ETHNIC GROUPS** Merina 27%, Betsimisaraka 15%, Betsileo 11%, Tsimihety 7%, Sakalava 6%
LANGUAGES Malagasy and French (both official)
RELIGIONS Traditional beliefs 52%, Christianity 41%, Islam 7%
CURRENCY Malagasy franc = 100 centimes

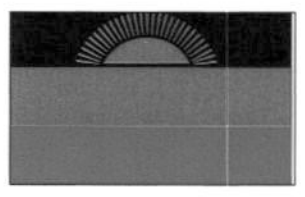

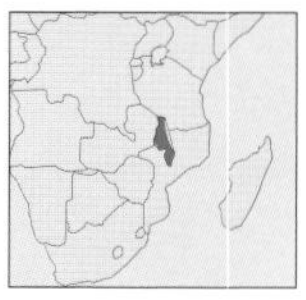

MALAWI

GEOGRAPHY The Republic of Malawi includes part of Lake Malawi, which is drained by the River Shire, a tributary of the River Zambezi. The land is mostly mountainous. The highest peak, Mulanje, reaches 9,843 ft [3,000 m] in the southeast.

While the low-lying areas of Malawi are hot and humid all year round, the uplands have a pleasant climate. Lilongwe, at about 3,609 ft [1,100 m] above sea level, has a warm and sunny climate. Frosts sometimes occur in July and August, in the middle of the long dry season.

POLITICS & ECONOMY Malawi, then called Nyasaland, became a British protectorate in 1891. In 1953, Britain established the Federation of Rhodesia and Nyasaland, which also included what are now Zambia and Zimbabwe. Black African opposition, led in Nyasaland by Dr Hastings Kamuzu Banda, led to the dissolution of the federation in 1963. In 1964, Nyasaland became independent as Malawi, with Banda as prime minister. Banda became president when the country became a republic in 1966 and, in 1971, he was made president for life. Banda ruled autocratically through the only party, the Malawi Congress Party. A multiparty system was restored in 1993. Banda and his party were defeated in elections in 1993. Bakili Muluzi became president and was re-elected in 1999. Banda died in 1997.

Malawi is one of the world's poorest countries. More than 80% of the people are farmers, but many grow little more than they need to feed their families.

AREA 45,745 sq mi [118,480 sq km] **POPULATION** 10,702,000
CAPITAL (POPULATION) Lilongwe (395,000)
GOVERNMENT Multiparty republic
ETHNIC GROUPS Maravi (Chewa, Nyanja, Tonga, Tumbuka) 58%, Lomwe 18%, Yao 13%, Ngoni 7%
LANGUAGES Chichewa and English (both official)
RELIGIONS Protestant 55%, Roman Catholic 20%, Islam 20%
CURRENCY Kwacha = 100 tambala

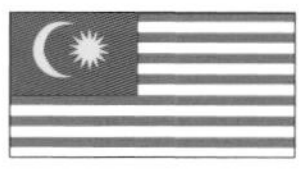
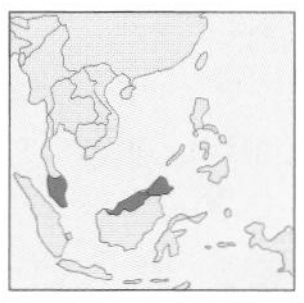

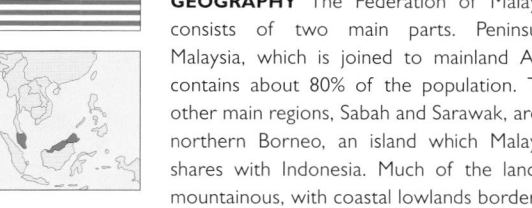

MALAYSIA

GEOGRAPHY The Federation of Malaysia consists of two main parts. Peninsular Malaysia, which is joined to mainland Asia, contains about 80% of the population. The other main regions, Sabah and Sarawak, are in northern Borneo, an island which Malaysia shares with Indonesia. Much of the land is mountainous, with coastal lowlands bordering the rugged interior. The highest peak, Kinabalu, reaches 13,455 ft [4,101 m] in Sabah.

Malaysia has a hot equatorial climate. The temperatures are high all through the year, though the mountains are much cooler than the lowland areas. The rainfall is heavy throughout the year.

POLITICS & ECONOMY Japan occupied what is now Malaysia during World War II, but British rule was re-established in 1945. In the 1940s and 1950s, British troops fought a war against Communist guerrillas, but Peninsular Malaysia (then called Malaya) became independent in 1957. Malaysia was created in 1963, when Malaya, Singapore, Sabah and Sarawak agreed to unite, but Singapore withdrew in 1965.

From the 1970s, Malaysia achieved rapid economic progress and, by the mid-1990s, it was playing a major part in regional affairs, especially through its membership of ASEAN (Association of Southeast Asian Nations). However, together with several other countries in eastern Asia, Malaysia was hit by economic recession in 1997, including a major fall in stock market values. In response to the crisis, the government ordered the repatriation of many temporary foreign workers and initiated a series of austerity measures aimed at restoring confidence and avoiding the chronic debt problems affecting some other Asian countries.

The World Bank classifies Malaysia as an "upper-middle-income" developing country. Malaysia is a leading producer of palm oil, rubber and tin. Manufacturing now plays a major part in the economy. Manufactures are diverse, including cars, chemicals, a wide range of electronic goods, plastics, textiles, rubber and wood products.

AREA 127,316 sq mi [329,750 sq km] **POPULATION** 22,662,000
CAPITAL (POPULATION) Kuala Lumpur (1,145,000)
GOVERNMENT Federal constitutional monarchy
ETHNIC GROUPS Malay and other indigenous groups 58%, Chinese 27%, Indian 8% **LANGUAGES** Malay (official), Chinese, English **RELIGIONS** Islam 53%, Buddhism 17%, Chinese folk religionist 12%, Hinduism 7%, Christianity 6%
CURRENCY Ringgit (Malaysian dollar) = 100 cents

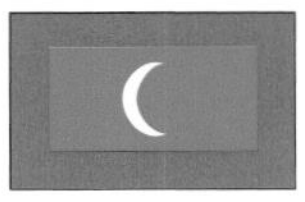
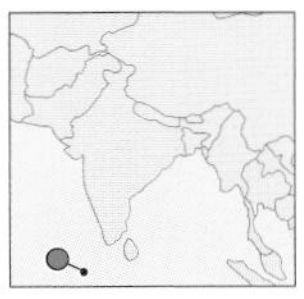

MALDIVES

The Republic of the Maldives consists of about 1,200 low-lying coral islands, south of India. The highest point is 79 ft [24 m], but most of the land is only 6 ft [1.8 m] above sea level. The islands became a British territory in 1887 and independence was achieved in 1965. Tourism and fishing are the main industries.

AREA 115 sq mi [298 sq km] **POPULATION** 320,000 **CAPITAL** Malé

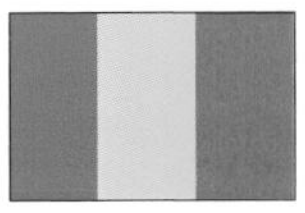
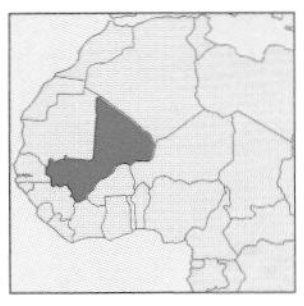

MALI

GEOGRAPHY The Republic of Mali is a landlocked country in northern Africa. The land is generally flat, with the highest land in the Adrar des Iforhas on the border with Algeria.

Northern Mali is part of the Sahara, with a hot, practically rainless climate. But the south has enough rain for farming.

POLITICS & ECONOMY France ruled the area, then known as French Sudan, from 1893 until the country became independent as Mali in 1960.

The first socialist government was overthrown in 1968 by an army group led by Moussa Traoré, but he was ousted in 1991. Multiparty democracy was restored in 1992 and Alpha Oumar Konaré was elected president. Konaré stood down in 2002 and Ahmadou Toure, who had restored democracy in 1992, was elected president.

Mali is one of the world's poorest countries and 70% of the land is desert or semidesert. Only about 2% of the land is used for growing crops, while 25% is used for grazing animals. Despite this, agriculture employs more than 80% of the people, many of whom still subsist by nomadic livestock rearing.

AREA 478,837 sq mi [1,240,190 sq km] **POPULATION** 11,340,000
CAPITAL (POPULATION) Bamako (810,000) **GOVERNMENT** Multiparty republic **ETHNIC GROUPS** Bambara 32%, Fulani (or Peul) 14%, Senufo 12%, Soninke 9%, Tuareg 7%, Songhai 7%, Malinke (Mandingo or Mandinke) 7% **LANGUAGES** French (official), Voltaic languages
RELIGIONS Islam 90%, traditional beliefs 9%, Christianity 1%
CURRENCY CFA franc = 100 centimes

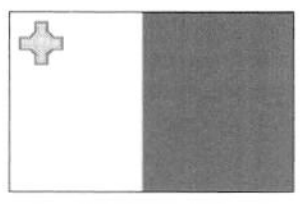
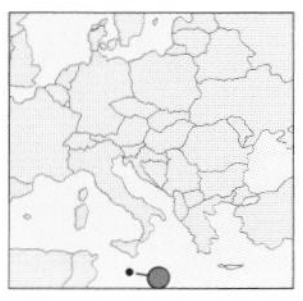

MALTA

GEOGRAPHY The Republic of Malta consists of two main islands, Malta and Gozo, a third, much smaller island called Comino lying between the two large islands, and two tiny islets.

Malta's climate is typically Mediterranean, with hot and dry summers and mild and wet winters. The sirocco, a hot wind that blows from North Africa, may raise temperatures considerably during the spring.

POLITICS & ECONOMY During World War I (1914–18) Malta was an important naval base. In World War II (1939–45), Italian and German aircraft bombed the islands. In recognition of the bravery of the Maltese, the British King George VI awarded the George Cross to Malta in 1942. In 1953, Malta became a base for NATO (North Atlantic Treaty Organization). Malta became independent in 1964, and in 1974 it became a republic. In 1979, Britain's military agreement with Malta expired, and Malta ceased to be a military base when all the British forces withdrew. In the 1980s, the people declared Malta a neutral country. In the 1990s, Malta applied to join the European Union. The application was scrapped when the Labor Party won the elections in 1996. However, after the Labor Party was defeated in 1998, the European Union in 2002 invited Malta to become a member in 2004. The Maltese people voted in favor of this move in 2003.

The World Bank classifies Malta as an "upper-middle-income" developing country. It lacks natural resources, and most people work in the former naval dockyards, which are now used for commercial shipbuilding and repair, in manufacturing industries and in the tourist industry.

Manufactures include chemicals, processed food and chemicals. Farming is difficult, because of the rocky soils. Crops include barley, fruits, potatoes and wheat. Malta also has a small fishing industry.

AREA 122 sq mi [316 sq km] **POPULATION** 397,000
CAPITAL (POPULATION) Valletta (102,000)
GOVERNMENT Multiparty republic **ETHNIC GROUPS** Maltese 96%, British 2% **LANGUAGES** Maltese and English (both official)
RELIGIONS Roman Catholic 91% **CURRENCY** Maltese lira = 100 cents

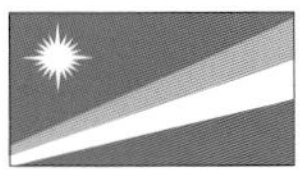
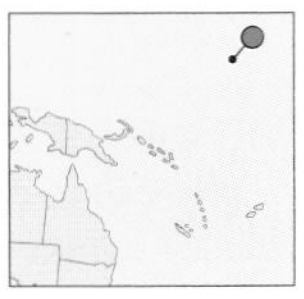

MARSHALL ISLANDS

The Republic of the Marshall Islands, a former US territory, became fully independent in 1991. This island nation, lying north of Kiribati in a region known as Micronesia, is heavily dependent on US aid. The main activities are agriculture and tourism.

AREA 70 sq mi [181 sq km] **POPULATION** 74,000
CAPITAL Dalap-Uliga-Darrit, on Majuro island

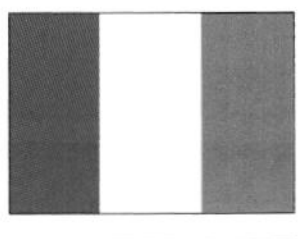
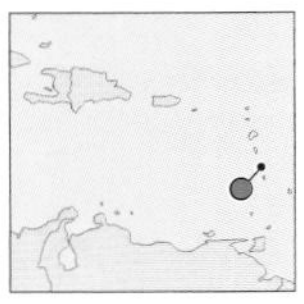

MARTINIQUE

Martinique, a volcanic island nation in the Caribbean, was colonized by France in 1635. It became a French overseas department in 1946. Tourism and agriculture are major activities. About 70% of Martinique's gross domestic product is provided by the French government, allowing for a good standard of living.

AREA 425 sq mi [1,100 sq km]
POPULATION 422,000 **CAPITAL** Fort-de-France

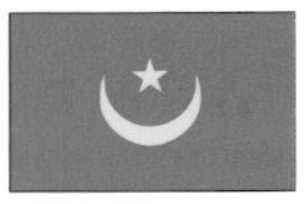
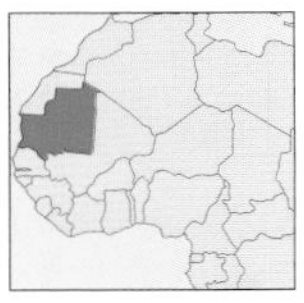

MAURITANIA

GEOGRAPHY The Islamic Republic of Mauritania in northwestern Africa is nearly twice the size of France. But France has more than 28 times as many people. Part of the world's largest desert, the Sahara, covers northern Mauritania and most Mauritanians live in the southwest.

The amount of rainfall and the length of the rainy season increase from north to south. Much of the land is desert, with dry northeast and easterly winds throughout the year. But southwesterly winds bring summer rain to the south.

POLITICS & ECONOMY Originally part of the great African empires of Ghana and Mali, France set up a protectorate in Mauritania in 1903, attempting to exploit the trade in gum arabic. The country became a territory of French West Africa and a French colony in 1920. French West Africa was a huge territory, which included present-day Benin, Burkina Faso, Guinea, Ivory Coast, Mali, Niger and Senegal, as well as Mauritania. In 1958, Mauritania became a self-governing territory in the French Union and it became fully independent in 1960.

In 1976, Spain withdrew from Spanish (now Western) Sahara, a territory bordering Mauritania to the north. Morocco occupied the northern two-thirds of this territory, while Mauritania took the rest. But Saharan guerrillas belonging to POLISARIO (the Popular Front for the Liberation of Saharan Territories) began an armed struggle for independence. In 1979, Mauritania withdrew from the southern part of Western Sahara, which was then occupied by Morocco. In 1991, the country adopted a new constitution when the people voted to create a multiparty government. Multiparty elections were held in 1992 and 1996–7.

The World Bank classifies Mauritania as a "low-income" developing country. Agriculture employs 40% of the people. Some are herders who move around with herds of cattle and sheep, though recent droughts forced many farmers to seek aid in the cities.

AREA 397,953 sq mi [1,030,700 sq km] **POPULATION** 2,829,000
CAPITAL (POPULATION) Nouakchott (735,000)
GOVERNMENT Multiparty Islamic republic
ETHNIC GROUPS Moor (Arab-Berber) 70%, Wolof 7%, Tukulor 5%, Soninke 3%, Fulani 1%
LANGUAGES Arabic and Wolof (both official), French
RELIGIONS Islam 99% **CURRENCY** Ouguiya = 5 khoums

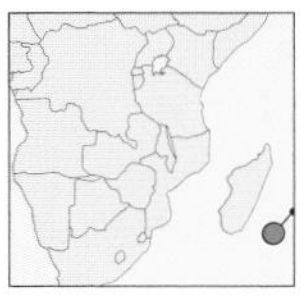

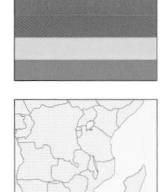

MAURITIUS

The Republic of Mauritius, an Indian Ocean nation lying east of Madagascar, was previously ruled by France and Britain until it achieved independence in 1968. It became a republic in 1992. Sugar production is in decline but tourism is vital to the economy.

AREA 718 sq mi [1,860 sq km]
POPULATION 1,200,000 **CAPITAL** Port Louis

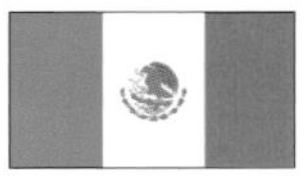
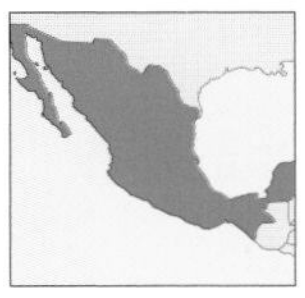

MEXICO

GEOGRAPHY The United Mexican States, as Mexico is officially named, is the world's most populous Spanish-speaking country. Much of the land is mountainous, although most people live on the central plateau. Mexico contains two large peninsulas, Lower (or Baja) California in the northwest and the flat Yucatán peninsula in the southeast.

The climate varies according to the altitude. The resort of Acapulco on the southwest coast has a dry and sunny climate. Mexico City, at about 7,546 ft [2,300 m] above sea level, is much cooler. Most rain occurs between June and September. The rainfall decreases north of Mexico City and northern Mexico is mainly arid.

POLITICS & ECONOMY In the mid-19th century, Mexico lost land to the United States, and between 1910 and 1921 violent revolutions created chaos.

Reforms were introduced in the 1920s and, in 1929, the Institutional Revolutionary Party (PRI) was formed. The PRI ruled Mexico effectively as a one-party state until it was finally defeated in 2001. The new president, Vicente Fox, faced many problems, including unemployment and rapid urbanization especially around Mexico City, demands for indigenous rights by Amerindian groups, and illegal emigration to the United States.

The World Bank classifies Mexico as an "upper-middle-income" developing country. Agriculture is important. Food crops include beans, maize, rice and wheat, while cash crops include coffee, cotton, fruits and vegetables. Beef cattle, dairy cattle and other livestock are raised and fishing is also important.

But oil and oil products are the chief exports, while manufacturing is the most valuable activity. Mexico is the world's leading silver producer, and it also mines copper, gold, lead, zinc and other minerals. Many factories near the northern border assemble goods, such as car parts and electrical products, for US companies. These factories are called *maquiladoras*. Hope for the future lies in increasing economic cooperation with the USA and Canada through NAFTA (North American Free Trade Association), which came into being on January 1, 1994.

AREA 756,061 SQ MI [1,958,200 SQ KM] **POPULATION** 103,400,000
CAPITAL (POPULATION) Mexico City (15,643,000)
GOVERNMENT Federal republic
ETHNIC GROUPS Mestizo 60%, Amerindian 30%, White 9%
LANGUAGES Spanish (official)
RELIGIONS Roman Catholic 90%, Protestant 5%
CURRENCY New peso = 100 centavos

MICRONESIA

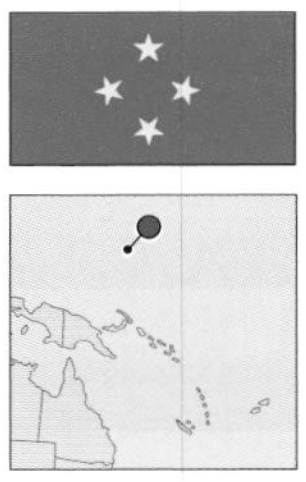

The Federated States of Micronesia, a former US territory covering a vast area in the western Pacific Ocean, became fully independent in 1991. The main export is copra. Fishing and tourism are also important.

AREA 272 SQ MI [705 SQ KM]
POPULATION 136,000 **CAPITAL** Palikir

MOLDOVA

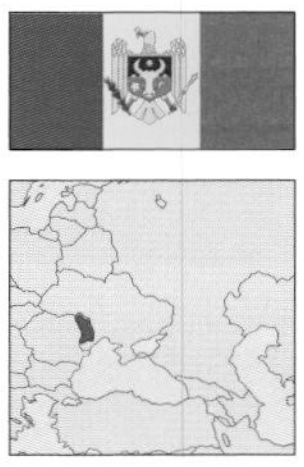

GEOGRAPHY The Republic of Moldova is a small country sandwiched between Ukraine and Romania. It was formerly one of the 15 republics that made up the Soviet Union. Much of the land is hilly and the highest areas are near the center of the country.

Moldova has a moderately continental climate, with warm summers and fairly cold winters when temperatures dip below freezing point. Most of the rain comes in the warmer months.

POLITICS & ECONOMY In the 14th century, the Moldavians formed a state called Moldavia. It included part of Romania and Bessarabia (now the modern country of Moldova). The Ottoman Turks took the area in the 16th century, but in 1812 Russia took over Bessarabia. In 1861, Moldavia and Walachia united to form Romania. Russia retook southern Bessarabia in 1878.

After World War I (1914–18), all of Bessarabia was returned to Romania, but the Soviet Union did not recognize this act. From 1944, the Moldovan Soviet Socialist Republic was part of the Soviet Union.

In 1989, the Moldovans asserted their independence and ethnicity by making Romanian the official language and, at the end of 1991, Moldova became an independent country. In 1992, fighting occurred between Moldovans and Russians in Trans-Dniester, a mainly Russian-speaking area east of the River Dniester. The first multiparty elections were held in 1994, when a proposal to unite with Romania was rejected. Economic problems made the government unpopular and, in 2001, Moldova became the first former Soviet state to return the Communist party to power in a general election.

In terms of its GNP per capita, Moldova is Europe's poorest country. Agriculture is the leading activity and products include fruits, maize, tobacco and wine. Moldova has few natural resources and it imports materials and fuels for its industries. Light industries, such as food processing and factories making household appliances, are increasing.

AREA 13,010 SQ MI [33,700 SQ KM] **POPULATION** 4,435,000
CAPITAL (POPULATION) Chişinău (658,000)
GOVERNMENT Multiparty republic
ETHNIC GROUPS Moldovan 65%, Ukrainian 14%, Russian 13%, Gagauz 4%, Jewish 2%, Bulgarian
LANGUAGES Moldovan/Romanian (official)
RELIGIONS Eastern Orthodox
CURRENCY Leu = 100 bani

MONACO

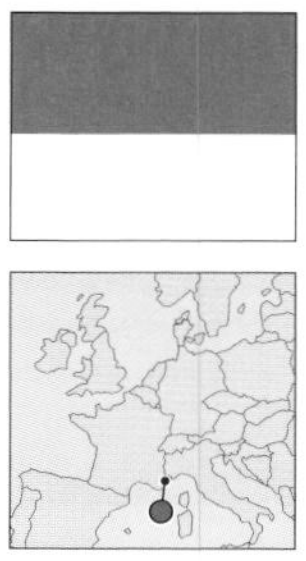

The tiny Principality of Monaco consists of a narrow strip of coastline and a rocky peninsula on the French Riviera. Its considerable wealth is derived largely from banking, finance, gambling and tourism. Monaco's citizens do not pay any state tax. Its attractions include the Monte Carlo casino and such sporting events as the Monte Carlo Rally and the Monaco Grand Prix.

AREA 0.6 SQ MI [1.5 SQ KM] **POPULATION** 32,000 **CAPITAL** Monaco

MONGOLIA

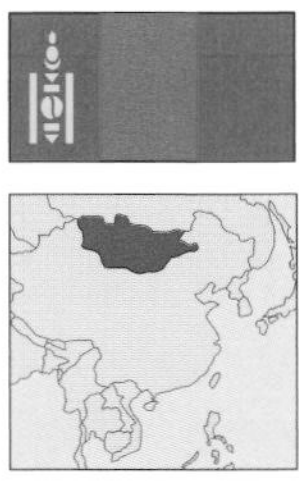

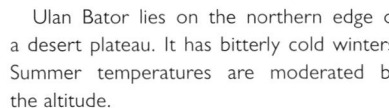

GEOGRAPHY The State of Mongolia is the world's largest landlocked country. It consists mainly of high plateaux, with the Gobi Desert in the southeast.

Ulan Bator lies on the northern edge of a desert plateau. It has bitterly cold winters. Summer temperatures are moderated by the altitude.

POLITICS & ECONOMY In the 13th century, Genghis Khan united the Mongolian peoples and built up a great empire. Under his grandson, Kublai Khan, the Mongol empire extended from Korea and China to eastern Europe and present-day Iraq.

The Mongol empire broke up in the late 14th century. In the early 17th century, Inner Mongolia came under Chinese control, and by the late 17th century Outer Mongolia had become a Chinese province. In 1911, the Mongolians drove the Chinese out of Outer Mongolia and made the area a Buddhist kingdom. But in 1924, under Russian influence, the Communist Mongolian People's Republic was set up. From the 1950s, Mongolia supported the Soviet Union in its disputes with China. In 1990, the people demonstrated for more freedom, and free elections in June 1990 resulted in victory for the Mongolian People's Revolutionary Party, which was composed of Communists. Communist rule ended in 1996, when the Democratic Union coalition won power. But the Communists regained power in 2000, though they were expected to continue free-market policies.

The World Bank classifies Mongolia as a "lower-middle-income" developing country. Most people were once nomads, who moved around with their herds of sheep, cattle, goats and horses. Under Communist rule, most people were moved into permanent homes on government-owned farms. But livestock and animal products remain leading exports. The Communists also developed industry, especially the mining of coal, copper, gold, molybdenum, tin and tungsten, and manufacturing. Minerals and fuels now account for around half of Mongolia's exports.

AREA 604,826 SQ MI [1,566,500 SQ KM] **POPULATION** 2,694,000
CAPITAL (POPULATION) Ulan Bator (673,000)
GOVERNMENT Multiparty republic **ETHNIC GROUPS** Khalkha Mongol 85%, Kazakh 6% **LANGUAGES** Khalkha Mongolian (official), Turkic, Russian **RELIGIONS** Tibetan Buddhist (Lamaist)
CURRENCY Tugrik = 100 möngös

MONTSERRAT

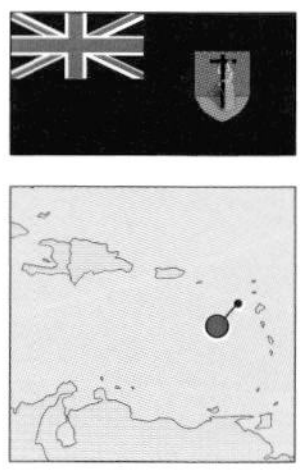

Monserrat is a British overseas territory in the Caribbean Sea. The climate is tropical and hurricanes often cause much damage. Intermittent eruptions of the Soufrière Hills volcano between 1995 and 1998 led to the emigration of many of the inhabitants and the virtual destruction of Plymouth, the capital, in the southern part of the island.

AREA 39 SQ MI [102 SQ KM] **POPULATION** 8,000 (prior to the volcanic activity) **CAPITAL** Plymouth

MOROCCO

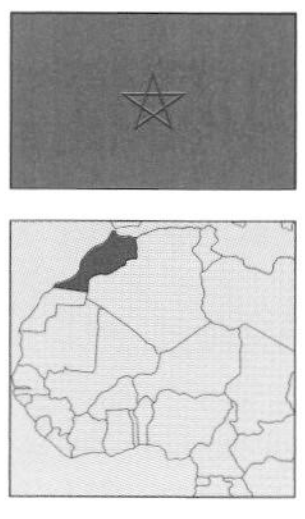

GEOGRAPHY The Kingdom of Morocco lies in northwestern Africa. Its name comes from the Arabic Maghreb-el-Aksa, meaning "the farthest west." Behind the western coastal plain the land rises to a broad plateau and ranges of the Atlas Mountains. The High (Haut) Atlas contains the highest peak, Djebel Toubkal, at 13,665 ft [4,165 m]. East of the mountains, the land descends to the arid Sahara.

The Atlantic coast of Morocco is cooled by the Canaries Current. Inland, summers are hot and dry. The winters are mild. In winter, between October and April, southwesterly winds from the Atlantic Ocean bring moderate rainfall, and snow often falls on the High Atlas Mountains.

POLITICS & ECONOMY The original people of Morocco were the Berbers. But in the 680s, Arab invaders introduced Islam and the Arabic language. By the early 20th century, France and Spain controlled Morocco, which became an independent kingdom in 1956. Although Morocco is a constitutional monarchy, King Hassan II ruled the country in a generally authoritarian way since his accession to the throne in 1961 to his death in 1999. His son and successor Mohamed VI faced several problems, including the future of Western Sahara which Hassan II had vigorously claimed for Morocco.

Morocco is classified as a "lower-middle-income" developing country. It is the world's third largest producer of phosphate rock, which is used to make fertilizer. One of the reasons why Morocco wants to keep Western Sahara is that it, too, has large phosphate reserves. Farming employs 34% of Moroccans. Chief crops include barley, beans, citrus fruits, maize, olives, sugar beet and wheat. Processed phosphates are exported, but most of Morocco's manufactures are for home consumption. Fishing and tourism are also important.

AREA 172,413 SQ MI [446,550 SQ KM] **POPULATION** 31,168,000
CAPITAL (POPULATION) Rabat (1,220,000)
GOVERNMENT Constitutional monarchy **ETHNIC GROUPS** Arab 70%, Berber 30% **LANGUAGES** Arabic (official), Berber, French
RELIGIONS Islam 99%, Christianity 1%
CURRENCY Moroccan dirham = 100 centimes

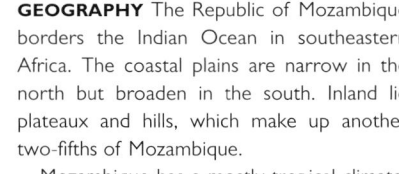

MOZAMBIQUE

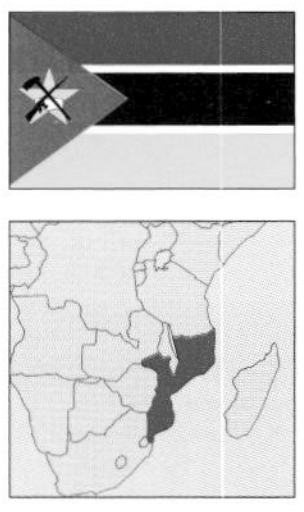

GEOGRAPHY The Republic of Mozambique borders the Indian Ocean in southeastern Africa. The coastal plains are narrow in the north but broaden in the south. Inland lie plateaux and hills, which make up another two-fifths of Mozambique.

Mozambique has a mostly tropical climate. The capital Maputo, which lies outside the tropics, has hot and humid summers, though the winters are mild and fairly dry.

POLITICS & ECONOMY In 1885, when the European powers divided Africa, Mozambique was recognized as a Portuguese colony. But black African opposition to European rule gradually increased. In 1961, the Front for the Liberation of Mozambique (FRELIMO) was founded to oppose Portuguese rule. In 1964, FRELIMO launched a guerrilla war, which continued for ten years. Mozambique became independent in 1975.

After independence, Mozambique became a one-party state. Its government aided African nationalists in Rhodesia (now Zimbabwe) and South Africa. But the white governments of these countries helped an opposition group, the Mozambique National Resistance Movement (RENAMO) to lead an armed struggle against Mozambique's government. Civil war, combined with droughts, caused much suffering in the 1980s. In 1989, FRELIMO declared that it had dropped its Communist policies and ended one-party rule. The war ended in 1992 and multiparty elections in 1994 heralded more stable conditions. In 1995 Mozambique became the 53rd member of the Commonwealth.

In the early 1990s, the UN rated Mozambique as one of the world's poorest countries. The second half of the 1990s saw a surge in economic growth, but huge floods in 2000 and 2001 proved to be a major setback. About 80% of the people are poor and agriculture is the main activity. Crops include cassava, cotton, maize, rice and tea.

AREA 309,494 SQ MI [801,590 SQ KM] **POPULATION** 19,608,000
CAPITAL (POPULATION) Maputo (2,000,000)
GOVERNMENT Multiparty republic **ETHNIC GROUPS** Indigenous tribal groups (Shangaan, Chokwe, Manyika, Sena, Makua, others) 99%
LANGUAGES Portuguese (official), many others
RELIGIONS Traditional beliefs 48%, Roman Catholic 31%, Islam 20%
CURRENCY Metical = 100 centavos

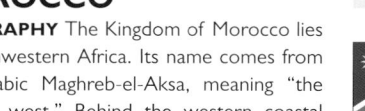

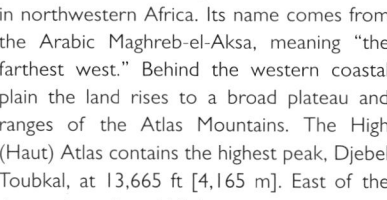

NAMIBIA

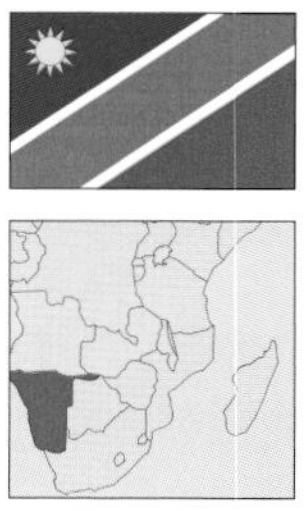

GEOGRAPHY The Republic of Namibia was formerly ruled by South Africa, which called it South West Africa. The country became independent in 1990. The coastal region contains the arid Namib Desert, which is virtually uninhabited. Inland is a central plateau, bordered by a rugged spine of mountains stretching north–south. Eastern Namibia contains part of the Kalahari Desert, a semidesert area which extends into Botswana.

Namibia is a warm and arid country. Lying at 5,500 ft [1,700 m] above sea level, Windhoek has an average annual rainfall of about 15 inches [370 mm], often occurring during thunderstorms in the hot summer months.

POLITICS & ECONOMY During World War I, South African troops defeated the Germans who ruled what is now Namibia. After World War II, many people challenged South Africa's right to govern the territory and a civil war began in the 1960s between African guerrillas and South African troops. A ceasefire was agreed in 1989 and Namibia became independent in 1990. In the 1990s, the government pursued a policy of "national reconciliation." An enclave on the coast, called Walvis Bay (Walvisbaai), remained part of South Africa until 1994, when it

was transferred to Namibia. In 1999, a secessionist group staged an unsuccessful uprising in the Caprivi Strip.

Namibia is rich in mineral reserves, including diamonds, uranium, zinc and copper. Minerals make up 90% of the exports. But farming employs about two out of every five Namibians. Sea fishing is also important, though overfishing has reduced the yields of the country's fishing fleet. The country has few industries, but tourism is increasing.

AREA 318,434 sq mi [825,414 sq km] **POPULATION** 1,821,000
CAPITAL (POPULATION) Windhoek (126,000)
GOVERNMENT Multiparty republic **ETHNIC GROUPS** Ovambo 50%, Kavango 9%, Herero 7%, Damara 7%, White 6%, Nama 5%
LANGUAGES English (official), Ovambo, Afrikaans, German
RELIGIONS Christianity 90% (Lutheran 51%)
CURRENCY Namibian dollar = 100 cents

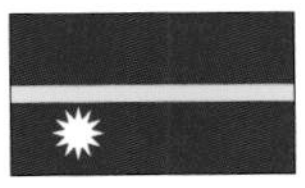
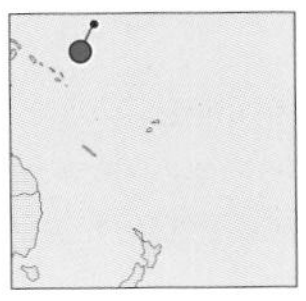

NAURU

Nauru is the world's smallest republic, located in the western Pacific Ocean, close to the equator. Independent since 1968, Nauru's prosperity is based on phosphate mining, but the reserves are running out.

AREA 8 sq mi [21 sq km] **POPULATION** 12,000
CAPITAL Yaren

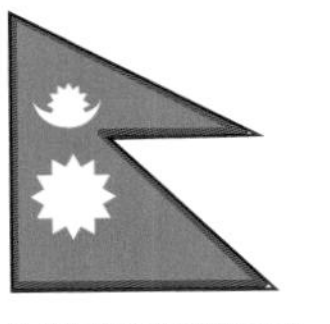
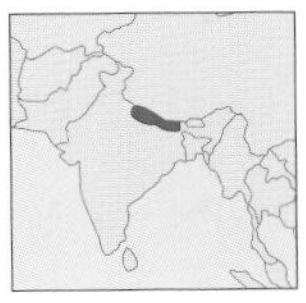

NEPAL

GEOGRAPHY Over three-quarters of Nepal lies in the Himalayan region, culminating in the world's highest peak (Mount Everest, or Chomolongma in Nepali) at 29,035 ft [8,850 m]. As a result, climatic conditions vary widely according to the altitude.

POLITICS & ECONOMY Nepal was united in the late 18th century, although its complex topography has ensured that it remains a diverse patchwork of peoples. From the mid-19th century to 1951, power was held by the royal Rana family. Attempts to introduce a democratic system in the 1950s failed. The first democratic elections in 32 years were held in 1991, but, by the early 21st century, Nepal faced many problems, including the activities of Maoist guerrillas. However, in 2003, a ceasefire was agreed with the Maoist rebels. In 2001, King Birendra and other members of the royal family were shot dead by Crown Prince Dipendra in a family dispute.

Agriculture remains the chief activity in this overwhelmingly rural country and the government is heavily dependent on aid. Tourism, centered around the high Himalaya, grows in importance each year, although Nepal was closed to foreigners until 1951. There are also ambitious plans to exploit the hydroelectric potential offered by the ferocious Himalayan rivers.

AREA 54,363 sq mi [140,800 sq km] **POPULATION** 25,874,000
CAPITAL (POPULATION) Katmandu (535,000)
GOVERNMENT Constitutional monarchy **ETHNIC GROUPS** Nepalese 53%, Bihari 18%, Tharu 5%, Tamang 5%, Newar 3%
LANGUAGES Nepali (official), local languages
RELIGIONS Hinduism 86%, Buddhism 8%, Islam 4%
CURRENCY Nepalese rupee = 100 paisa

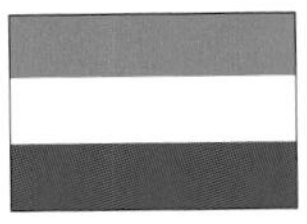
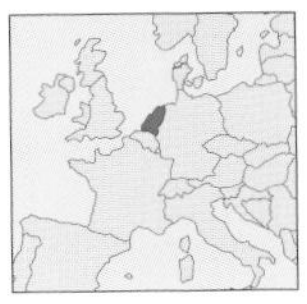

NETHERLANDS

GEOGRAPHY The Netherlands lies at the western end of the North European Plain, which extends to the Ural Mountains in Russia. Except for the far southeastern corner, the Netherlands is flat and about 40% lies below sea level at high tide. To prevent flooding, the Dutch have built dykes (sea walls) to hold back the waves. Large areas which were once under the sea, but which have been reclaimed, are called polders. Because of its position on the North Sea, the Netherlands has a temperate climate, with mild, rainy winters.

POLITICS & ECONOMY Before the 16th century, the area that is now the Netherlands was under a succession of foreign rulers, including the Romans, the Germanic Franks, the French and the Spanish. The Dutch declared their independence from Spain in 1581 and their status was finally recognized by Spain in 1648. In the 17th century, the Dutch built up a great overseas empire, especially in Southeast Asia. But in the early 18th century, the Dutch lost control of the seas to England.

France controlled the Netherlands from 1795 to 1813. In 1815, the Netherlands, then containing Belgium and Luxembourg, became an independent kingdom. Belgium broke away in 1830 and Luxembourg followed in 1890.

The Netherlands was neutral in World War I (1914–18), but was occupied by Germany in World War II (1939–45). After the war, the Netherlands Indies became independent as Indonesia. The Netherlands became active in West European affairs. With Belgium and Luxembourg, it formed a customs union called Benelux in 1948. In 1949, it joined NATO (the North Atlantic Treaty Organization), and the European Coal and Steel Community (ECSC) in 1953. In 1957, it became a founder member of the European Economic Community (now the European Union) and, in 2002, it adopted the euro as its sole unit of currency. In 2002, an anti-immigration group made sweeping gains in national elections. It joined a coalition government, which collapsed later that year. The group's vote collapsed in new elections in 2003.

The Netherlands is a highly industrialized country and industry and commerce are the most valuable activities. Its resources include natural gas, some oil, salt and china clay. But the Netherlands imports many of the materials needed by its industries and it is, therefore, a major trading country. Industrial products are wide-ranging, including aircraft, chemicals, electronic equipment, machinery, textiles and vehicles. Agriculture employs only 5% of the people, but scientific methods are used and yields are high. Dairy farming is the leading farming activity. Major products include barley, flowers and bulbs, potatoes, sugar beet and wheat.

AREA 16,033 sq mi [41,526 sq km] **POPULATION** 16,068,000
CAPITAL (POPULATION) Amsterdam (1,115,000); The Hague (seat of government, 700,000)
GOVERNMENT Constitutional monarchy
ETHNIC GROUPS Dutch 95%, Indonesian, Turkish, Moroccan
LANGUAGES Dutch (official), Frisian
RELIGIONS Roman Catholic 34%, Protestant 21%, Islam 4%
CURRENCY Euro = 100 cents

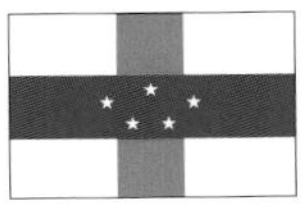
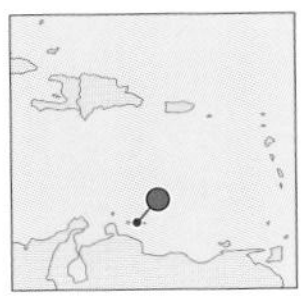

NETHERLANDS ANTILLES

The Netherlands Antilles consists of two different island groups; one off the coast of Venezuela, and the other at the northern end of the Leeward Islands, some 500 mi [800 km] away. They remain a self-governing Dutch territory. The island of Aruba was once part of the territory, but it broke away in 1986. Oil refining and tourism are important activities.

AREA 383 sq mi [993 sq km] **POPULATION** 214,000 **CAPITAL** Willemstad

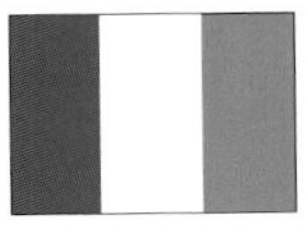
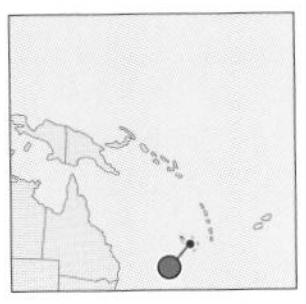

NEW CALEDONIA

New Caledonia is the most southerly of the Melanesian countries in the Pacific. A French possession since 1853 and an Overseas Territory since 1958. In 1998, France announced an agreement with local Melanesians that a vote on independence would be postponed until 2014. The country is rich in mineral resources, especially nickel.

AREA 7,174 sq mi [18,580 sq km] **POPULATION** 208,000 **CAPITAL** Nouméa

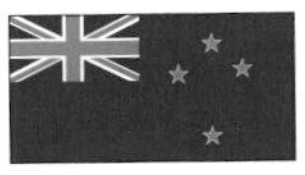
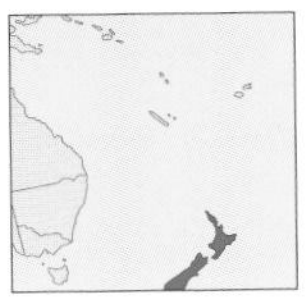

NEW ZEALAND

GEOGRAPHY New Zealand lies about 994 mi [1,600 km] southeast of Australia. It consists of two main islands and several other small ones. Much of North Island is volcanic. Active volcanoes include Ngauruhoe and Ruapehu. Hot springs and geysers are common, and steam from the ground is used to produce electricity. The Southern Alps, which contain the country's highest peak Mount Cook (Aoraki), at 12,313 ft [3,753 m] form the backbone of South Island. The island also has some large, fertile plains.

Auckland in the north has a warm, humid climate throughout the year. Wellington has cooler summers, while in Dunedin, in the southeast, temperatures sometimes dip below freezing in winter. The rainfall is heaviest on the western highlands.

POLITICS & ECONOMY Evidence suggests that early Maori settlers arrived in New Zealand more than 1,000 years ago. The Dutch navigator Abel Tasman reached New Zealand in 1642, but his discovery was not followed up. In 1769, the British Captain James Cook rediscovered the islands. In the early 19th century, British settlers arrived and, in 1840, under the Treaty of Waitangi, Britain took possession of the islands. Clashes occurred with the Maoris in the 1860s but, from the 1870s, the Maoris were gradually integrated into society.

In 1907, New Zealand became a self-governing dominion in the British Commonwealth. The country's economy developed quickly and the people became increasingly prosperous. However, after Britain joined the European Economic Community in 1973, New Zealand's exports to Britain shrank and the country had to reassess its economic and defense strategies and seek new markets. The world recession led the government to cut back on welfare spending in the 1990s. The preservation of Maori culture and Maori rights are other major issues.

New Zealand's economy has traditionally depended on agriculture, but manufacturing now employs twice as many people as agriculture. Meat and dairy products are the most valuable agricultural products. Sheep numbered less than 22 million in 2002. Their importance has greatly declined as the area under cattle, deer and vineyards has increased. Major crops include barley, fruits, potatoes and other vegetables, and wheat. Fishing is also important.

AREA 103,737 sq mi [268,680 sq km] **POPULATION** 3,908,000
CAPITAL (POPULATION) Wellington (329,000)
GOVERNMENT Constitutional monarchy
ETHNIC GROUPS New Zealand European 74%, New Zealand Maori 10%, Polynesian 4% **LANGUAGES** English and Maori (both official) **RELIGIONS** Anglican 24%, Presbyterian 18%, Roman Catholic 15%
CURRENCY New Zealand dollar = 100 cents

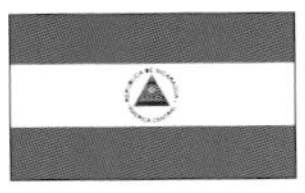
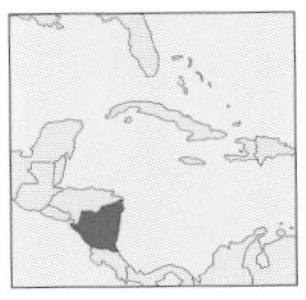

NICARAGUA

GEOGRAPHY The Republic of Nicaragua is a large country in Central America. In the east is a broad plain bordering the Caribbean Sea. The plain is drained by rivers that flow from the Central Highlands. The fertile western Pacific region contains about 40 volcanoes, many of which are active, and earthquakes are common.

Nicaragua has a tropical climate. Managua is hot throughout the year and there is a marked rainy season from May to October. In October 1998, Hurricane Mitch caused great devastation in Nicaragua. The Central Highlands and Caribbean region are cooler and wetter. The wettest region is the humid Caribbean plain.

POLITICS & ECONOMY In 1502, Christopher Columbus claimed the area for Spain, which ruled Nicaragua until 1821. By the early 20th century, the United States had considerable influence in the country and, in 1912, US forces entered Nicaragua to protect US interests. From 1927 to 1933, rebels under General Augusto César Sandino, tried to drive US forces out of the country. In 1933, US marines set up a Nicaraguan army, the National Guard, to help to defeat the rebels. Its leader, Anastasio Somoza Garcia, had Sandino murdered in 1934 and, from 1937, Somoza ruled as a dictator.

In the mid-1970s, many people began to protest against Somoza's rule. Many joined a guerrilla force, called the Sandinista National Liberation Front, named after General Sandino. The rebels defeated the Somoza regime in 1979. In the 1980s, the US-supported forces, called the "Contras," launched a campaign against the Sandinista government. The US government opposed the Sandinista regime, under Daniel José Ortega Saavedra, claiming that it was a Communist dictatorship. A coalition, the National Opposition Union, defeated the Sandinistas in elections in 1990. In 1996 and again in 2001, the Sandinista candidate Daniel Ortega was defeated in presidential elections.

In the early 1990s, Nicaragua faced many problems in rebuilding its shattered economy. Agriculture is the main activity, employing nearly half of the people. Coffee, cotton, sugar and bananas are grown for export, while rice is the main food crop.

AREA 50,193 sq mi [130,000 sq km] **POPULATION** 5,024,000
CAPITAL (POPULATION) Managua (864,000)
GOVERNMENT Multiparty republic
ETHNIC GROUPS Mestizo 69%, White 17%, Black 9%, Amerindian 5%
LANGUAGES Spanish (official), Misumalpan
RELIGIONS Roman Catholic 85%
CURRENCY Córdoba oro (gold córdoba) = 100 centavos

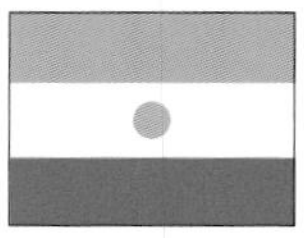

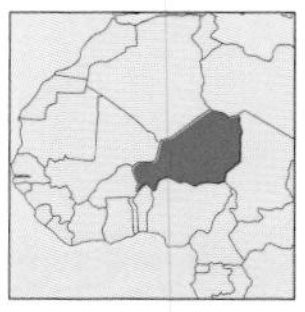

NIGER

GEOGRAPHY The Republic of Niger is a landlocked nation in north-central Africa. The northern plateaux lie in the Sahara Desert, while Central Niger contains the rugged Aïr Mountains. The most fertile, densely populated region is the Niger valley in the southwest.

Niger has a tropical climate and the south has a rainy season between June and September. The north is practically rainless.

POLITICS & ECONOMY Since independence in 1960, Niger, a French territory from 1900, has suffered severe droughts. Food shortages and the collapse of the traditional nomadic way of life of some of Niger's people have caused political instability. After a period of military rule, a multiparty constitution was adopted in 1992, but the military again seized power in 1996. Later that year, the coup leader, Col. Ibrahim Barre Mainassara, was elected president. He was assassinated in 1999, but parliamentary rule was rapidly restored and Tandja Mamadou was elected president in November.

Niger's chief resource is uranium and it is the fourth largest producer in the world. Some tin and tungsten are also mined, although other mineral resources are largely untouched.

Despite its resources, Niger is one of the world's poorest countries. Farming employs 76% of the population, but only 3% of the land can be used for crops and 8% for grazing.

AREA 489,189 sq mi [1,267,000 sq km] **POPULATION** 10,640,000
CAPITAL (POPULATION) Niamey (398,000)
GOVERNMENT Multiparty republic
ETHNIC GROUPS Hausa 56%, Djerma 22%, Tuareg 8%, Fula 8%
LANGUAGES French (official), Hausa, Djerma
RELIGIONS Islam 98% **CURRENCY** CFA franc = 100 centimes

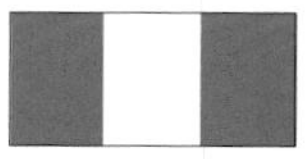

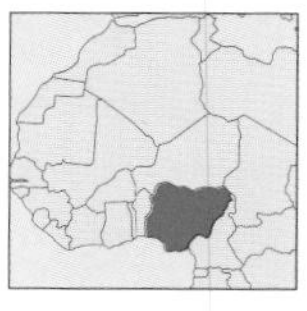

NIGERIA

GEOGRAPHY The Federal Republic of Nigeria is the most populous nation in Africa. The country's main rivers are the Niger and Benue, which meet in central Nigeria. North of the two river valleys are high plains and plateaus. The Lake Chad basin is in the northeast, with the Sokoto plains in the northwest. The south contains hilly uplands and coastal plains.

The south has high temperatures and rain throughout the year. The north is drier and often hotter than the south.

POLITICS & ECONOMY Nigeria has a long artistic tradition. Major cultures include the Nok (500 BC to AD 200), the Ife, a major Yoruba culture which developed about 1,000 years ago, and the Benin, which flourished between the 15th and 17th centuries. Britain gradually extended its influence over the area in the second half of the 19th century.

Nigeria became independent in 1960 and a federal republic in 1963. A federal constitution dividing the country into regions was necessary because Nigeria contains more than 250 ethnic and linguistic groups, as well as several religious ones. Local rivalries have long been a threat to national unity, and six new states were created in 1996 in an attempt to overcome this. Civil war occurred between 1967 and 1970, when the people of the southeast attempted unsuccessfully to secede during the Biafran War. Between 1960 and 1998, Nigeria had only nine years of civilian government. In 1998–9, civilian rule was restored. A former general, Olusegun Obasanjo, was elected president and he was re-elected in 2003. His government faced many problems, including religious clashes in the north, where several states adopted *sharia* (Islamic law).

Nigeria is a developing country with great potential. Its chief natural resource is oil, which accounts for most of its exports. Agriculture employs 43% of the people and the country is a major producer of cocoa, palm oil and palm kernels, groundnuts (peanuts) and rubber. Industry is increasing and manufactures include cement, chemicals, fertilizers, textiles and timber.

AREA 356,668 sq mi [923,770 sq km] **POPULATION** 129,935,000
CAPITAL (POPULATION) Abuja (339,000)
GOVERNMENT Federal multiparty republic
ETHNIC GROUPS Hausa and Fulani 29%, Yoruba 21%, Ibo (or Igbo) 18%, Ijaw 10%, Kanuri 4%
LANGUAGES English (official), Hausa, Yoruba, Ibo
RELIGIONS Islam 50%, Christianity 40%, traditional religions 10%
CURRENCY Naira = 100 kobo

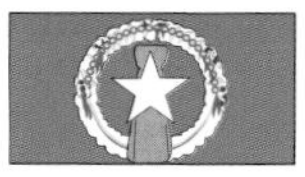

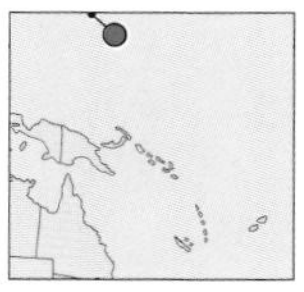

NORTHERN MARIANA ISLANDS

The Commonwealth of the Northern Mariana Islands contains 16 mountainous islands north of Guam in the western Pacific Ocean. In a 1975 plebiscite, the islanders voted for Commonwealth status in union with the USA and, in 1986, they were granted US citizenship.

AREA 184 sq mi [477 sq km] **POPULATION** 77,000 **CAPITAL** Saipan

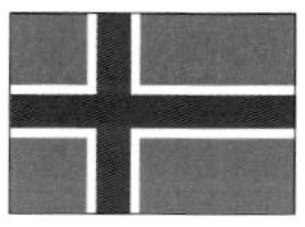

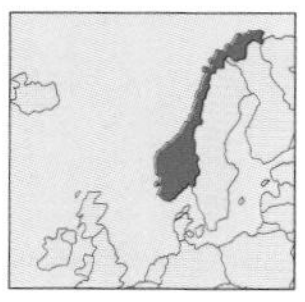

NORWAY

GEOGRAPHY The Kingdom of Norway forms the western part of the rugged Scandinavian peninsula. The deep inlets along the highly indented coastline were worn out by glaciers during the Ice Age.

The warm North Atlantic Drift off the coast of Norway moderates the climate, with mild winters and cool summers. Nearly all the ports are ice-free throughout the year. Inland, winters are colder and snow cover lasts for at least three months a year.

POLITICS & ECONOMY Under a treaty in 1814, Denmark handed Norway over to Sweden, but it kept Norway's colonies – Greenland, Iceland and the Faroe Islands. Norway briefly became independent, but Swedish forces defeated the Norwegians and Norway had to accept Sweden's king as its ruler.

The union between Norway and Sweden ended in 1903. During World War II (1939–45), Germany occupied Norway. Norway's economy developed quickly after the war and the country now enjoys one of the world's highest standards of living. In 1960, Norway, together with six other countries, formed the European Free Trade Association (EFTA). In 1994, the Norwegians voted against joining the EU.

Norway's chief resources and exports are oil and natural gas which come from wells under the North Sea. Farmland covers only 3% of the land. Dairy farming and meat production are important, but Norway has to import food. Norway has many industries powered by cheap hydroelectricity.

AREA 125,050 sq mi [323,900 sq km] **POPULATION** 4,525,000
CAPITAL (POPULATION) Oslo (502,000)
GOVERNMENT Constitutional monarchy
ETHNIC GROUPS Norwegian 97%
LANGUAGES Norwegian (official)
RELIGIONS Lutheran 88%
CURRENCY Krone = 100 ore

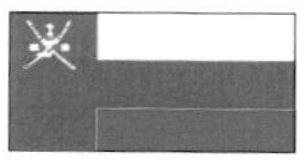

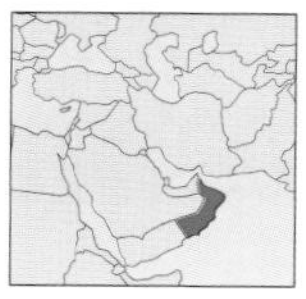

OMAN

GEOGRAPHY The Sultanate of Oman occupies the southeastern corner of the Arabian peninsula. It also includes the tip of the Musandam peninsula, overlooking the strategic Strait of Hormuz.

Oman has a hot tropical climate. In Muscat, temperatures may reach 117°F [47°C] in summer.

POLITICS & ECONOMY British influence in Oman dates back to the end of the 18th century, but the country became fully independent in 1971. Since then, using revenue from oil, which was discovered in 1964, the absolute ruler, Qaboos ibn Said, and his government have sought to modernize the country. In 2000, Oman held its first direct elections to its consultative parliament. Unusually for the Gulf region, two women were returned.

The World Bank classifies Oman as an "upper-middle-income" country. Oil accounts for the bulk of the exports, while huge natural gas deposits were discovered in 1991. However, agriculture remains important. Major crops include alfalfa, bananas, coconuts, dates, limes, tobacco, vegetables and wheat. Some cattle are raised and fishing, especially for sardines, is important. But Oman still has to import food.

AREA 82,031 sq mi [212,460 sq km] **POPULATION** 2,713,000
CAPITAL (POPULATION) Muscat (350,000)
GOVERNMENT Monarchy with consultative council
ETHNIC GROUPS Omani Arab 74%, Pakistani 21%
LANGUAGES Arabic (official), Baluchi, English
RELIGIONS Islam (Ibadiyah), Hinduism
CURRENCY Omani rial = 100 baizas

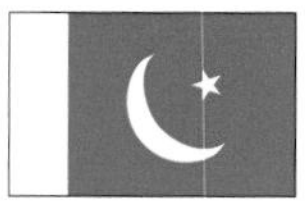

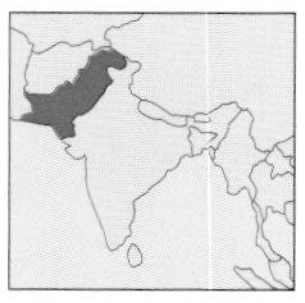

PAKISTAN

GEOGRAPHY The Islamic Republic of Pakistan contains high mountains, fertile plains and rocky deserts. The Karakoram range, which contains K2, the world's second highest peak, lies in the northern part of Jammu and Kashmir, which is occupied by Pakistan but claimed by India. Other mountains rise in the west. Plains, drained by the River Indus and its tributaries, occupy much of eastern Pakistan. Arid areas include the Thar Desert and the Baluchistan plateau. Most of Pakistan has hot summers and mild winters, though the mountains have cold winters. The rainfall is generally sparse.

POLITICS & ECONOMY Pakistan was the site of the Indus Valley civilization which developed about 4,500 years ago. But Pakistan's modern history dates from 1947, when British India was divided into India and Pakistan. Muslim Pakistan was divided into two parts: East and West Pakistan, but East Pakistan broke away in 1971 to become Bangladesh. In 1948–9, 1965 and 1971, Pakistan and India clashed over the disputed territory of Kashmir. In 1998, Pakistan responded in kind to a series of Indian nuclear weapon tests, provoking global controversy.

Pakistan has been subject to several periods of military rule, but elections in 1988 led to Benazir Bhutto becoming prime minister. She was removed from office in 1990, but she returned as prime minister between 1993 and 1996. In 1997, Narwaz Sharif was elected prime minister, but a military coup in 1999 brought General Pervez Musharraf to power. In 2001, Pakistan supported the Western assault on Taliban forces in Afghanistan. In 2002, voters agreed to extend Musharraf's term in office by five years. He made constitutional changes to increase his own powers, but he received a setback in national elections when Islamic parties received substantial support.

According to the World Bank, Pakistan is a "low-income" developing country. The economy is based on farming or rearing goats and sheep. Agriculture employs nearly half the people. Major crops include cotton, fruits, rice, sugarcane and wheat.

AREA 307,374 sq mi [796,100 sq km] **POPULATION** 147,663,000
CAPITAL (POPULATION) Islamabad (525,000)
GOVERNMENT Military regime **ETHNIC GROUPS** Punjabi 60%, Sindhi 12%, Pashtun 13%, Baluch, Muhajir
LANGUAGES Urdu (official), many others
RELIGIONS Islam 97%, Christianity, Hinduism
CURRENCY Pakistan rupee = 100 paisa

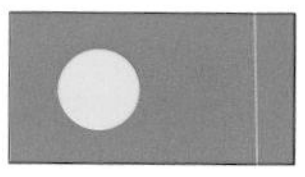

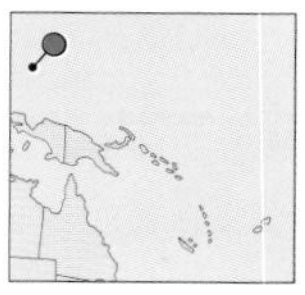

PALAU

The Republic of Palau became fully independent in 1994, after the USA refused to accede to a 1979 referendum that declared this island nation a nuclear-free zone. In December 1994 Palau joined the United Nations. The economy relies heavily on US aid, tourism, fishing and subsistence agriculture. The main crops include cassava, coconuts and copra.

AREA 177 sq mi [458 sq km] **POPULATION** 19,000 **CAPITAL** Koror

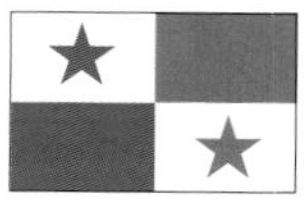

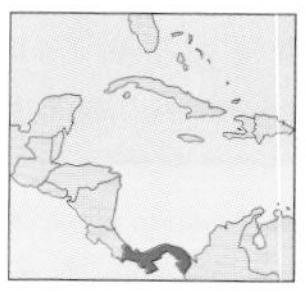

PANAMA

GEOGRAPHY The Republic of Panama forms an isthmus linking Central America to South America. The Panama Canal, which is 50.7 mi [81.6 km] long, cuts across the isthmus. It has made the country a major transport center.

Panama has a tropical climate. Temperatures are high, though the mountains are much cooler than the coastal plains. The main rainy season is between May and December.

POLITICS & ECONOMY Christopher Columbus landed in Panama in 1502 and Spain soon took control of the area. In 1821, Panama became independent from Spain and a province of Colombia.

In 1903, Colombia refused a request by the United States to build a canal. Panama then revolted against Colombia, and became independent. The United States then began to build the canal, which was opened in 1914. The United States administered the Panama Canal Zone, a strip of land along the canal. But many Panamanians resented US influence and, in 1979, the Canal Zone was returned to Panama. Control of the canal itself was handed over by the USA to Panama on December 31, 1999.

Panama's government has changed many times since independence, and there have been periods of military dictatorships. In 1983, General Manuel Antonio Noriega became

Panama's leader. In 1988, two US grand juries in Florida indicted Noriega on charges of drug trafficking. In 1989, Noriega was apparently defeated in a presidential election, but the government declared the election invalid. After the killing of a US marine, US troops entered Panama and arrested Noriega, who was convicted by a Miami court of drug offences in 1992. However, Panama held national elections in 1994. In 1999, Mireya Moscoso became Panama's first woman president.

The World Bank classifies Panama as a "lower-middle-income" developing country. The Panama Canal is an important source of revenue and it generates many jobs in commerce, trade, manufacturing and transport. Away from the Canal, the main activity is agriculture, which employs 16% of the people.

AREA 29,761 SQ MI [77,080 SQ KM] **POPULATION** 2,882,000
CAPITAL (POPULATION) PANAMA CITY (452,000)
GOVERNMENT MULTIPARTY REPUBLIC **ETHNIC GROUPS** MESTIZO 70%, BLACK AND MULATTO 14%, WHITE 10%, AMERINDIAN 6%
LANGUAGES SPANISH (OFFICIAL) **RELIGIONS** ROMAN CATHOLIC 84%, PROTESTANT 5% **CURRENCY** US DOLLAR; BALBOA = 100 CENTÉSIMOS

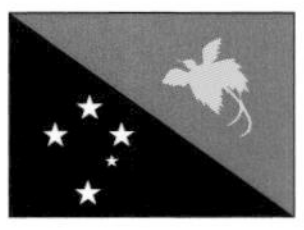
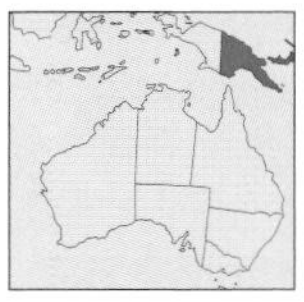

PAPUA NEW GUINEA

GEOGRAPHY Papua New Guinea is an independent country in the Pacific Ocean, north of Australia. It is part of a Pacific island region called Melanesia. Papua New Guinea includes the eastern part of New Guinea, the Bismarck Archipelago, the northern Solomon Islands, the D'Entrecasteaux Islands and the Louisiade Archipelago. The land is largely mountainous.

Papua New Guinea has a tropical climate, with high temperatures throughout the year. Most of the rain occurs during the monsoon season (from December to April), when the northwesterly winds blow. Winds blow from the southeast during the dry season.

POLITICS & ECONOMY The Dutch took western New Guinea (now part of Indonesia) in 1828, but it was not until 1884 that Germany took northeastern New Guinea and Britain took the southeast. In 1906, Britain handed the southeast over to Australia. It then became known as the Territory of Papua. When World War I broke out in 1914, Australia took German New Guinea and, in 1921, the League of Nations gave Australia a mandate to rule the area, which was named the Territory of New Guinea.

Japan invaded New Guinea in 1942, but the Allies reconquered the area in 1944. In 1949, Papua and New Guinea were combined into the Territory of Papua and New Guinea. Papua New Guinea became fully independent in 1975.

Since independence, the government has worked to develop its mineral reserves. One of the most valuable mines was on Bougainville, in the northern Solomon Islands. But the people of Bougainville demanded a larger share in the profits of the mine. Conflict broke out, the mine was closed and the Bougainville Revolutionary Army proclaimed the island independent. But their attempted secession was not recognized internationally. An agreement to end the conflict was signed in 1998 and the island was granted local autonomy in 2000.

The World Bank classifies Papua New Guinea as a "lower-middle-income" developing country. Agriculture employs three out of every four people, many of whom produce little more than they need to feed their families. Minerals, notably copper and gold, are the most valuable exports.

AREA 178,703 SQ MI [462,840 SQ KM] **POPULATION** 5,172,000
CAPITAL (POPULATION) PORT MORESBY (174,000)
GOVERNMENT CONSTITUTIONAL MONARCHY **ETHNIC GROUPS** PAPUAN, MELANESIAN **LANGUAGES** ENGLISH (OFFICIAL), PIDGIN ENGLISH, ABOUT 800 OTHERS **RELIGIONS** TRADITIONAL BELIEFS 34%, ROMAN CATHOLIC 22%, LUTHERAN 16% **CURRENCY** KINA = 100 TOEA

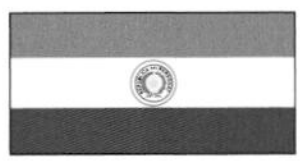
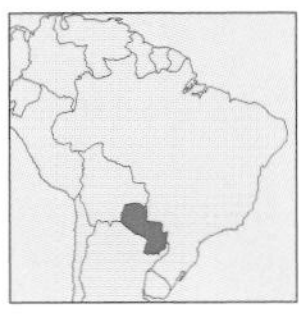

PARAGUAY

GEOGRAPHY The Republic of Paraguay is a landlocked country and rivers, notably the Paraná, Pilcomayo (Brazo Sur) and Paraguay, form most of its borders. A flat region called the Gran Chaco lies in the northwest, while the southeast contains plains, hills and plateaux. Northern Paraguay lies in the tropics, while the south is subtropical. Most of the country has a warm, humid climate.

POLITICS & ECONOMY In 1776, Paraguay became part of a large colony called the Vice-royalty of La Plata, with Buenos Aires as the capital. Paraguayans opposed this move and the country declared its independence in 1811.

For many years, Paraguay was torn by internal strife and conflict with its neighbors. A war against Brazil, Argentina and Uruguay (1865–70) led to the deaths of more than half of Paraguay's population, and a great loss of territory.

General Alfredo Stroessner took power in 1954 and ruled as a dictator. His government imprisoned many opponents. Stroessner was overthrown in 1989. Free multiparty elections were held in 1993 and 1998. However, the return of democracy often seemed precarious because of rivalries between politicians and army leaders, together with economic problems arising partly from those experienced in neighboring Argentina and Brazil. The World Bank classifies Paraguay as a "lower-middle-income" developing country. Farming and forestry are the most important activities. Paraguay produces hydroelectricity and exports power to its neighbors.

AREA 157,046 SQ MI [406,750 SQ KM] **POPULATION** 5,884,000
CAPITAL (POPULATION) ASUNCIÓN (945,000)
GOVERNMENT MULTIPARTY REPUBLIC **ETHNIC GROUPS** MESTIZO 90%, AMERINDIAN 3% **LANGUAGES** SPANISH AND GUARANÍ (BOTH OFFICIAL)
RELIGIONS ROMAN CATHOLIC 96%, PROTESTANT 2%
CURRENCY GUARANÍ = 100 CÉNTIMOS

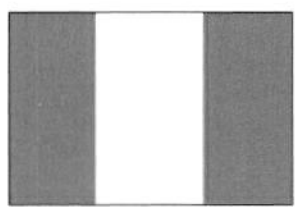
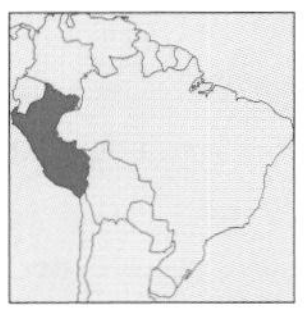

PERU

GEOGRAPHY The Republic of Peru lies in the tropics in western South America. A narrow coastal plain borders the Pacific Ocean in the west. Inland are ranges of the Andes Mountains, which rise to 22,205 ft [6,768 m] at Mount Huascarán, an extinct volcano. East of the Andes lies the Amazon basin.

Lima, on the coastal plain, has an arid climate. The coastal region is chilled by the cold, offshore Humboldt Current. The rainfall increases inland and many mountains in the high Andes are snow-capped.

POLITICS & ECONOMY Spanish conquistadors conquered Peru in the 1530s. In 1820, an Argentinian, José de San Martín, led an army into Peru and declared it independent. But Spain still held large areas. In 1823, the Venezuelan Simon Bolívar led another army into Peru and, in 1824, one of his generals defeated the Spaniards at Ayacucho. The Spaniards surrendered in 1826. Peru suffered much instability throughout the 19th century.

Instability continued in the 20th century. In 1980, when civilian rule was restored, a left-wing group called the Sendero Luminoso, or the "Shining Path," began guerrilla warfare against the government. In 1990, Alberto Fujimori, son of Japanese immigrants, became president. In 1992, he suspended the constitution and dismissed the legislature. The guerrilla leader, Abimael Guzmán, was arrested in 1992, but instability continued. Following his victory in disputed presidential elections in 2000, Fujimori resigned and sought sanctuary in Japan. In 2001, Alejandro Toledo became the first Peruvian of Amerindian descent to be elected president.

The World Bank classifies Peru as a "lower-middle-income" developing country. Agriculture employs 35% of the people and major food crops include beans, maize, potatoes and rice. Fish products are exported, but the most valuable export is copper. Peru also produces lead, silver, zinc and iron ore.

AREA 496,223 SQ MI [1,285,220 SQ KM] **POPULATION** 27,950,000
CAPITAL (POPULATION) LIMA (LIMA-CALLAO, 6,601,000)
GOVERNMENT TRANSITIONAL REPUBLIC **ETHNIC GROUPS** QUECHUA 45%, MESTIZO 37%, WHITE 15% **LANGUAGES** SPANISH AND QUECHUA (BOTH OFFICIAL), AYMARA **RELIGIONS** ROMAN CATHOLIC 90%
CURRENCY NEW SOL = 100 CENTAVOS

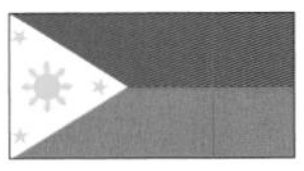
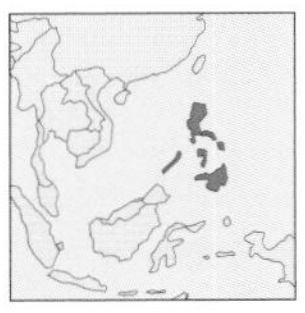

PHILIPPINES

GEOGRAPHY The Republic of the Philippines is an island country in southeastern Asia. It includes about 7,100 islands, of which 2,770 are named and about 1,000 are inhabited. Luzon and Mindanao, the two largest islands, make up more than two-thirds of the country. The land is mainly mountainous.

The country has a hot tropical climate. The dry season runs from December to April. The rest of the year is wet. Much of the rainfall comes from the typhoons which periodically strike the east coast.

POLITICS & ECONOMY The first European to reach the Philippines was the Portuguese navigator Ferdinand Magellan in 1521. Spanish explorers claimed the region in 1565 when they established a settlement on Cebu. The Spaniards ruled the country until 1898, when the United States took over at the end of the Spanish–American War. Japan invaded the Philippines in 1941, but US forces returned in 1944. The country became fully independent as the Republic of the Philippines in 1946.

Since independence, the country's problems have included armed uprisings by left-wing guerrillas demanding land reform, and Muslim separatist groups, crime, corruption and unemployment. The dominant figure in recent times was Ferdinand Marcos, who ruled in a dictatorial manner from 1965 to 1986. His successors were Corazon Aquino (1986–92), Fidel Ramos (1992–8), and Joseph Estrada, who resigned after massive public protests against his alleged corruption in 2001. He was succeeded by Vice-President Gloria Arroyo. She faced continuing problems in trying, with American help, to defeat the Muslim terrorist groups in the south.

The Philippines is a developing country which has a "lower-middle-income" economy. Agriculture employs 45% of the people. The main foods are rice and maize, while such crops as bananas, cocoa, coconuts, coffee, sugarcane and tobacco are all grown commercially. Manufacturing now plays an increasingly important role in the economy.

AREA 115,300 SQ MI [300,000 SQ KM] **POPULATION** 84,526,000
CAPITAL (POPULATION) MANILA (8,594,000)
GOVERNMENT MULTIPARTY REPUBLIC **ETHNIC GROUPS** TAGALOG 30%, CEBUANO 24%, ILOCANO 10%, HILIGAYNON ILONGO 9%, BICOL 6%
LANGUAGES PILIPINO (TAGALOG) AND ENGLISH (BOTH OFFICIAL), SPANISH, MANY OTHERS
RELIGIONS ROMAN CATHOLIC 83%, PROTESTANT 9%, ISLAM 5%
CURRENCY PHILIPPINE PESO = 100 CENTAVOS

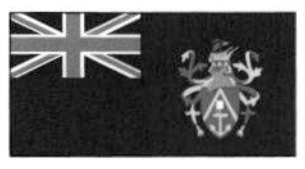
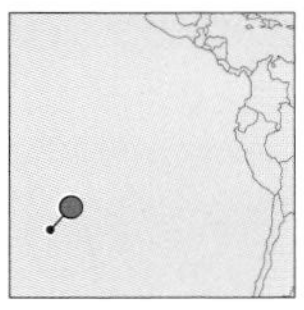

PITCAIRN

Pitcairn Island is a British overseas territory in the Pacific Ocean. Its inhabitants are descendants of the original settlers – nine mutineers from HMS *Bounty* and 18 Tahitians who arrived in 1790.

AREA 19 SQ MI [48 SQ KM] **POPULATION** 50
CAPITAL ADAMSTOWN

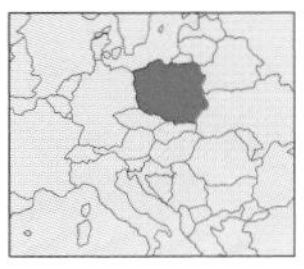

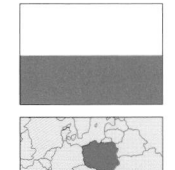

POLAND

GEOGRAPHY The Republic of Poland faces the Baltic Sea and, behind its lagoon-fringed coast, lies a broad plain. A plateau lies in the southeast, while the Sudeten Highlands straddle part of the border with the Czech Republic. Part of the Carpathian Range (the Tatra) lies in the southeast.

Poland's climate is influenced by its position in Europe. Warm, moist air masses come from the west, while cold air masses come from the north and east. Summers are warm, but winters are cold and snowy.

POLITICS & ECONOMY Poland's boundaries have changed several times in the last 200 years, partly as a result of its geographical location between the powers of Germany and Russia. It disappeared from the map in the late 18th century, when a Polish state called the Grand Duchy of Warsaw was set up. But in 1815, the country was partitioned, between Austria, Prussia and Russia. Poland became independent in 1918, but in 1939 it was divided between Germany and the Soviet Union. The country again became independent in 1945, when it lost land to Russia but gained some from Germany. Communists took power in 1948, but opposition mounted and eventually became focused through an organization called Solidarity.

Solidarity was led by a trade unionist, Lech Walesa. A coalition government was formed between Solidarity and the Communists in 1989. In 1990, the Communist party was dissolved and Walesa became president. But Walesa faced many problems in turning Poland toward a market economy. In presidential elections in 1995, Walesa was defeated by ex-Communist Aleksander Kwasniewski. However, Kwasniewski continued to follow westward-looking policies and he was re-elected president in 2000. Poland joined NATO in 1999 and, in 2002, it was invited to become a member of the European Union in May 2004.

Poland has large reserves of coal and deposits of various minerals which are used in its factories. Manufactures include chemicals, processed food, machinery, ships, steel and textiles.

AREA 120,726 SQ MI [312,680 SQ KM] **POPULATION** 38,625,000
CAPITAL (POPULATION) WARSAW (1,626,000)
GOVERNMENT MULTIPARTY REPUBLIC **ETHNIC GROUPS** POLISH 98%, UKRAINIAN 1%, GERMAN 1% **LANGUAGES** POLISH (OFFICIAL)
RELIGIONS ROMAN CATHOLIC 94%, ORTHODOX 2%
CURRENCY ZLOTY = 100 GROSZY

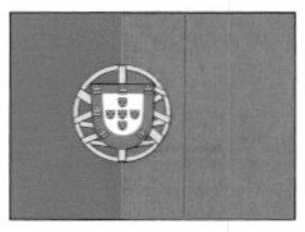
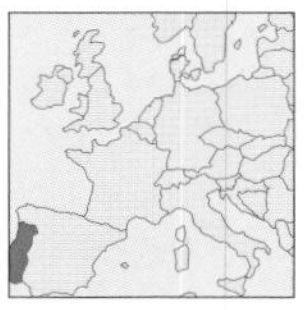

PORTUGAL

GEOGRAPHY The Republic of Portugal is the most westerly of Europe's mainland countries. The land rises from the coastal plains on the Atlantic Ocean to the western edge of the huge plateau, or Meseta, which occupies most of the Iberian peninsula. Portugal also contains two autonomous regions, the Azores and Madeira island groups.

The climate is moderated by winds blowing from the Atlantic Ocean. Summers are cooler and winters are milder than in other Mediterranean lands.

POLITICS & ECONOMY Portugal became a separate country, independent of Spain, in 1143. In the 15th century, Portugal led the "Age of European Exploration." This led to the growth of a large Portuguese empire, with colonies in Africa, Asia and, most valuable of all, Brazil in South America. Portuguese power began to decline in the 16th century and, between 1580 and 1640, Portugal was ruled by Spain. Portugal lost Brazil in 1822 and, in 1910, Portugal became a republic. Instability hampered progress and army officers seized power in 1926. In 1928, they chose Antonio de Salazar to be minister of finance. He became prime minister in 1932 and ruled as a dictator from 1933.

Salazar ruled until 1968, but his successor, Marcello Caetano, was overthrown in 1974 by a group of army officers. The new government made most of Portugal's remaining colonies independent. Free elections were held in 1978. Portugal joined the European Community (now the European Union) in 1986 and, on January 1, 2002, the euro replaced the escudo as Portugal's sole official unit of currency.

Agriculture and fishing were the mainstays of the economy until the mid-20th century. However, manufacturing is now the most valuable sector.

AREA 35,670 sq mi [92,390 sq km] **POPULATION** 9,609,000
CAPITAL (POPULATION) Lisbon (2,561,000)
GOVERNMENT Multiparty republic
ETHNIC GROUPS Portuguese 99%
LANGUAGES Portuguese (official)
RELIGIONS Roman Catholic 95%, other Christians 2%
CURRENCY Euro = 100 cents

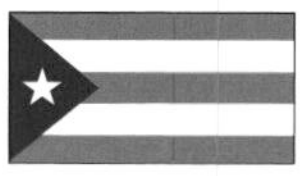
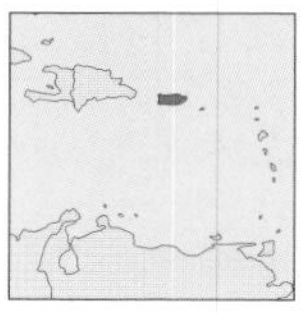

PUERTO RICO

The Commonwealth of Puerto Rico, a mainly mountainous island, is the easternmost of the Greater Antilles chain. The climate is hot and wet. Puerto Rico is a dependent territory of the USA and the people are US citizens. In 1998, 50.2% of the population voted in a referendum on possible statehood to maintain the status quo. Puerto Rico is the most industrialized country in the Caribbean. Tax exemptions attract US companies to the island and manufacturing is expanding. The chief exports are chemicals and chemical products, machinery and food.

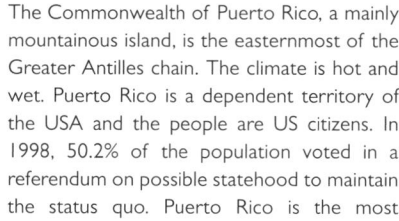

AREA 3,436 sq mi [8,900 sq km] **POPULATION** 3,958,000
CAPITAL San Juan

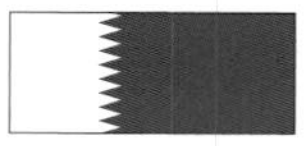
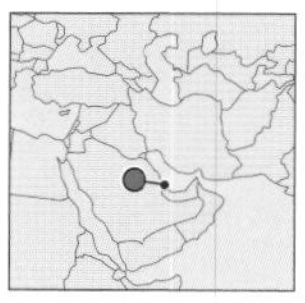

QATAR

The State of Qatar occupies a low, barren peninsula that extends northward from the Arabian peninsula into the Gulf. The climate is hot and dry. Qatar became a British protectorate in 1916, but it became fully independent in 1971. Oil, first discovered in 1939, is the mainstay of the economy of this prosperous nation.

AREA 4,247 sq mi [11,000 sq km] **POPULATION** 793,000 **CAPITAL** Doha

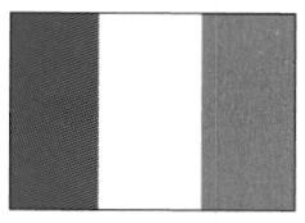
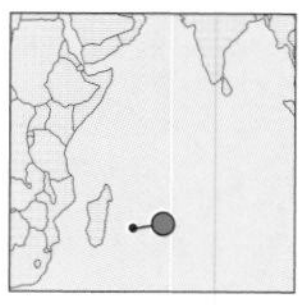

RÉUNION

Réunion is a French overseas department in the Indian Ocean. The land is mainly mountainous, though the lowlands are intensely cultivated. Sugar and sugar products are the main exports, but French aid, given to the island in return for its use as a military base, is important to the economy.

AREA 969 sq mi [2,510 sq km]
POPULATION 744,00 **CAPITAL** St-Denis

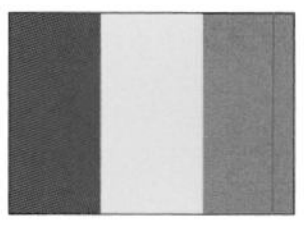
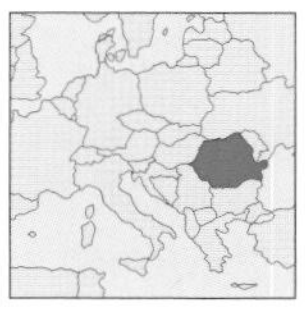

ROMANIA

GEOGRAPHY Romania is a country on the Black Sea in eastern Europe. Eastern and southern Romania form part of the Danube river basin. The delta region, near the mouths of the Danube, where the river flows into the Black Sea, is one of Europe's finest wetlands. The southern part of the coast contains several resorts. The heart of the country is called Transylvania. It is ringed in the east, south and west by scenic mountains which are part of the Carpathian mountain system.

Romania has hot summers and cold winters. The rainfall is heaviest in spring and early summer, when thundery showers are common.

POLITICS & ECONOMY From the late 18th century, the Turkish empire began to break up. The modern history of Romania began in 1861 when Walachia and Moldavia united. After World War I (1914–18), Romania, which had fought on the side of the victorious Allies, obtained large areas, including Transylvania, where most people were Romanians. This almost doubled the country's size and population. In 1939, Romania lost territory to Bulgaria, Hungary and the Soviet Union. Romania fought alongside Germany in World War II, and Soviet troops occupied the country in 1944. Hungary returned northern Transylvania to Romania in 1945, but Bulgaria and the Soviet Union kept former Romanian territory. In 1947, Romania officially became a Communist country.

In 1990, Romania held its first free elections since the end of World War II. The National Salvation Front, led by Ion Iliescu and containing many former Communist leaders, won a large majority. A new constitution, approved in 1991, made the country a democratic republic. Elections held under this constitution in 1992 again resulted in victory for Ion Iliescu, whose party was renamed the Party of Social Democracy (PDSR) in 1993. But the government faced many problems. In 1996, the center-right Democratic Convention defeated the PDSR, led by Emil Constantinescu, who became president. But Iliescu was re-elected president in 2000.

According to the World Bank, Romania is a "lower-middle-income" economy. Under Communist rule, industry, including mining and manufacturing, became more important than agriculture.

AREA 91,699 sq mi [237,500 sq km] **POPULATION** 22,318,000
CAPITAL (POPULATION) Bucharest (2,028,000)
GOVERNMENT Multiparty republic **ETHNIC GROUPS** Romanian 89%, Hungarian 7%, Roma 2% **LANGUAGES** Romanian (official), Hungarian, German **RELIGIONS** Romanian Orthodox 70%, Protestant 6%, Roman Catholic 3%
CURRENCY Romanian leu = 100 bani

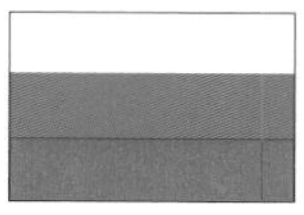
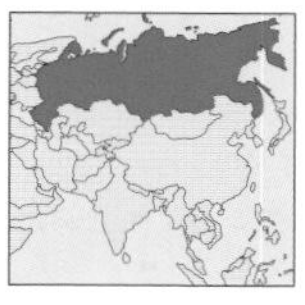

RUSSIA

GEOGRAPHY Russia is the world's largest country. About 25% lies west of the Ural Mountains in European Russia, where 80% of the population lives. It is mostly flat or undulating, but the land rises to the Caucasus Mountains in the south, where Russia's highest peak, Elbrus, at 18,481 ft [5,633 m], is found. Asian Russia, or Siberia, contains vast plains and plateaux, with mountains in the east and south. The Kamchatka peninsula in the far east has many active volcanoes. Russia contains many of the world's longest rivers, including the Yenisey-Angara and the Ob-Irtysh. It also includes part of the world's largest inland body of water, the Caspian Sea, and Lake Baikal, the world's deepest lake.

Moscow has a continental climate with cold and snowy winters and warm summers. Krasnoyarsk in south-central Siberia has a harsher, drier climate, but it is not as severe as parts of northern Siberia.

POLITICS & ECONOMY In the 9th century AD, a state called Kievan Rus was formed by a group of people called the East Slavs. Kiev, now capital of Ukraine, became a major trading center, but, in 1237, Mongol armies conquered Russia and destroyed Kiev. Russia was part of the Mongol empire until the late 15th century. Under Mongol rule, Moscow became the leading Russian city.

In the 16th century, Moscow's grand prince was retitled "tsar." The first tsar, Ivan the Terrible, expanded Russian territory. In 1613, after a period of civil war, Michael Romanov became tsar, founding a dynasty which ruled until 1917. In the early 18th century, Tsar Peter the Great began to westernize Russia and, by 1812, when Napoleon failed to conquer the country, Russia was a major European power. But during the 19th century, many Russians demanded reforms and discontent was widespread.

In World War I (1914–18), the Russian people suffered great hardships and, in 1917, Tsar Nicholas II was forced to abdicate. In November 1917, the Bolsheviks seized power under Vladimir Lenin. In 1922, the Bolsheviks set up a new nation, the Union of Soviet Socialist Republics (also called the USSR or the Soviet Union).

From 1924, Joseph Stalin introduced a socialist economic program, suppressing all opposition. In 1939, the Soviet Union and Germany signed a non-aggression pact, but Germany invaded the Soviet Union in 1941. Soviet forces pushed the Germans back, occupying eastern Europe. They reached Berlin in May 1945. From the late 1940s, tension between the Soviet Union and its allies and Western nations developed into a "Cold War." This continued until 1991, when the Soviet Union was dissolved.

The Soviet Union collapsed because of the failure of its economic policies. From 1991, President Boris Yeltsin introduced democratic and economic reforms. Yeltsin retired in 1999 and, in 2000, was succeeded by Vladimir Putin. Putin has sought to develop increasing contacts with the West, though Russia opposed the invasion of Iraq in 2003. However. the secessionist conflict in Chechenia, which claimed the lives of more than 4,500 Russian troops in 1999–2002, reveals that Russia's sheer size and ethnic diversity make national unity hard to achieve.

Russia's economy was thrown into disarray after the collapse of the Soviet Union, and in the early 1990s the World Bank described Russia as a "lower-middle-income" economy. Russia was admitted to the Council of Europe in 1997, essentially to discourage instability in the Caucasus. More significantly still, Boris Yeltsin was invited to attend the G7 summit in Denver in 1997. The summit became known as "the Summit of the Eight" and it appeared that Russia will now be included in future meetings of the world's most powerful economies. Industry is the most valuable activity, though, under Communist rule, manufacturing was less efficient than in the West, and the emphasis was on heavy industry. Today, light industries producing consumer goods are becoming important. Russia's adundant resources include oil and natural gas, coal, timber, metal ores and hydroelectric power.

Most farmland is still government-owned or run as collectives. Russia is a major producer of farm products, though it imports grains. Major crops include barley, flax, fruits, oats, rye, potatoes, sugar beet, sunflower seeds, vegetables and wheat.

AREA 6,592,800 sq mi [17,075,000 sq km] **POPULATION** 144,979,000
CAPITAL (POPULATION) Moscow (8,405,000) **GOVERNMENT** Federal multiparty republic **ETHNIC GROUPS** Russian 82%, Tatar 4%, Ukrainian 3%, Chuvash 1%, more than 100 others
LANGUAGES Russian (official), many others
RELIGIONS Mainly Russian Orthodox, Islam, Judaism
CURRENCY Russian rouble = 100 kopeks

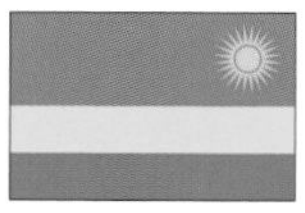
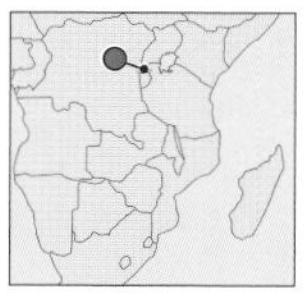

RWANDA

GEOGRAPHY The Republic of Rwanda is a small, landlocked country in east-central Africa. Lake Kivu and the River Ruzizi in the Great African Rift Valley form the country's western border.

Kigali stands on the central plateau of Rwanda. Here, temperatures are moderated by the altitude. The rainfall is abundant, but much heavier rain falls on the western mountains.

POLITICS & ECONOMY Germany conquered the area, called Ruanda-Urundi, in the 1890s. However, Belgium occupied the region during World War I (1914–18) and ruled it until 1961, when the people of Ruanda voted for their country to become a republic, called Rwanda. This decision followed a rebellion by the majority Hutu people against the Tutsi monarchy. About 150,000 deaths resulted from this conflict. Many Tutsis fled to Uganda, where they formed a rebel army. Burundi became independent as a monarchy, though it became a republic in 1966. Relations between Hutus and Tutsis continued to cause friction. Civil war broke out in 1994 and in 1996 the conflict spilled over into Congo (then Zaïre), where Zaïrean Tutsis staged a rebellion. This led to political instability.

According to the World Bank, Rwanda is a "low-income" developing country. Most people are poor farmers. Food crops include bananas, beans, cassava and sorghum. Some cattle are raised.

AREA 10,170 sq mi [26,340 sq km] **POPULATION** 7,398,000
CAPITAL (POPULATION) Kigali (235,000) **GOVERNMENT** Republic
ETHNIC GROUPS Hutu 84%, Tutsi 15%, Twa 1%
LANGUAGES French, English and Kinyarwanda (all official)
RELIGIONS Roman Catholic 53%, Protestant 24%, Adventist 10%
CURRENCY Rwanda franc = 100 centimes

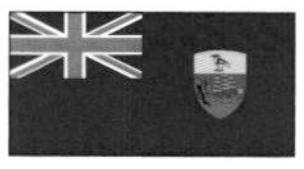
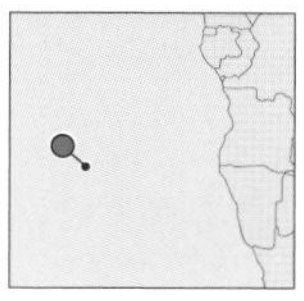

ST HELENA

St Helena, which became a British colony in 1834, is an isolated volcanic island in the south Atlantic Ocean. Now a British overseas territory, it is also the administrative center of Ascension and Tristan da Cunha.

AREA 47 SQ MI [122 SQ KM]
POPULATION 7,000 **CAPITAL** JAMESTOWN

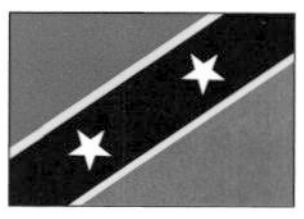
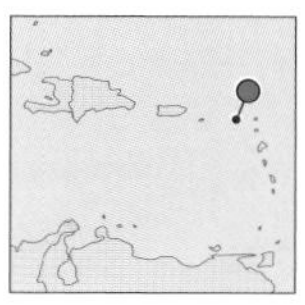

ST KITTS AND NEVIS

The Federation of St Kitts and Nevis comprises two well-watered volcanic islands, with mountains rising to around 3,300 ft [1,000 m]. The islands were the first in the Caribbean to be colonized by Britain (in 1623 and 1628), and they became an independent country in 1983. In 1998, a vote for the secession of Nevis fell short of the two-thirds majority required. Tourism has replaced sugar as the principal earner.

AREA 139 SQ MI [360 SQ KM] **POPULATION** 39,000
CAPITAL BASSETERRE

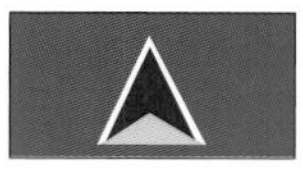
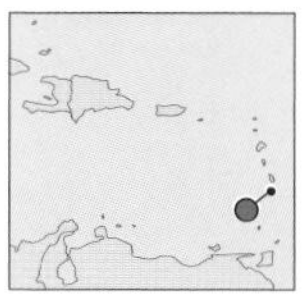

ST LUCIA

St Lucia, which became independent from Britain in 1979, is a mountainous, forested island of extinct volcanoes. It exports bananas and coconuts, and now attracts many tourists.

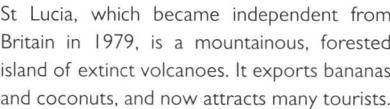

AREA 236 SQ MI [610 SQ KM]
POPULATION 160,000 **CAPITAL** CASTRIES

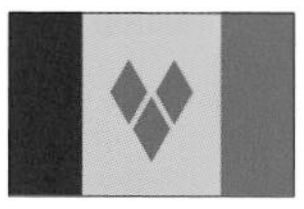
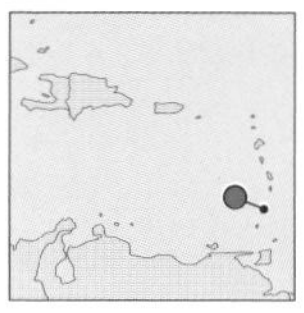

ST VINCENT AND THE GRENADINES

St Vincent and the Grenadines achieved its independence from Britain in 1979. Tourism is growing, but the territory is less prosperous than its neighbors.

AREA 150 SQ MI [388 SQ KM]
POPULATION 116,000 **CAPITAL** KINGSTOWN

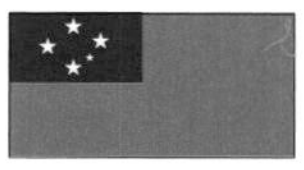
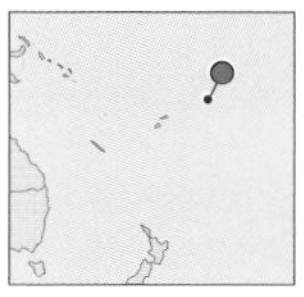

SAMOA

The Independent State of Samoa (formerly Western Samoa) comprises two islands in the South Pacific Ocean. Governed by New Zealand from 1920, the territory became independent in 1962. Exports include coconut cream and beer.

AREA 1,097 SQ MI [2,840 SQ KM]
POPULATION 179,000 **CAPITAL** APIA

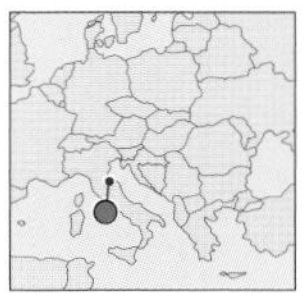

SAN MARINO

San Marino in northern Italy has been independent since 885 and a republic since the 14th century. It is the world's oldest republic. It has a friendship and cooperation treaty with Italy dating back to 1862. The state is governed by an elected council and has its own legal system. It has no armed forces and the police are "hired" from the Italian constabulary. The chief occupations are tourism, limestone quarrying, textiles and winemaking.

AREA 24 SQ MI [61 SQ KM] **POPULATION** 28,000 **CAPITAL** SAN MARINO

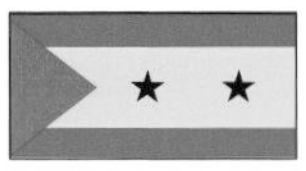
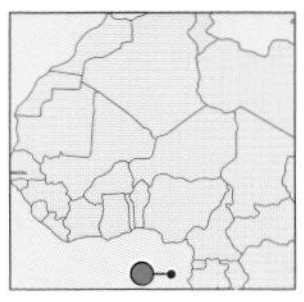

SÃO TOMÉ AND PRÍNCIPE

The Democratic Republic of São Tomé and Príncipe, a mountainous island territory west of Gabon, became a Portuguese colony in 1522. Following independence in 1975, the islands became a one-party Marxist state, but multiparty elections were held in 1991.

AREA 372 SQ MI [964 SQ KM] **POPULATION** 170,000 **CAPITAL** SÃO TOMÉ

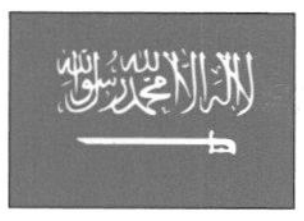
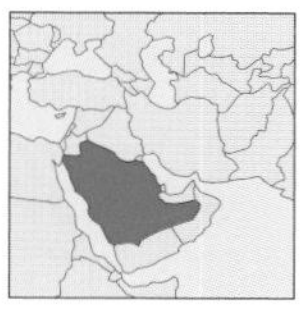

SAUDI ARABIA

GEOGRAPHY The Kingdom of Saudi Arabia occupies about three-quarters of the Arabian peninsula in southwest Asia. Deserts cover most of the land. Mountains border the Red Sea plains in the west. In the north is the sandy Nafud Desert (An Nafud). In the south is the Rub' al Khali (the "Empty Quarter"), one of the world's bleakest deserts.

Saudi Arabia has a hot, dry climate. In the summer months, the temperatures in Riyadh often exceed 104°F [40°C], though the nights are cool.

POLITICS & ECONOMY Saudi Arabia contains the two holiest places in Islam – Mecca (or Makka), the birthplace of the Prophet Muhammad in AD 570, and Medina (Al Madinah) where Muhammad went in 622. These places are visited by many pilgrims.

Saudi Arabia was poor until the oil industry began to operate on the eastern plains in 1933. Oil revenues have been used to develop the country and Saudi Arabia has given aid to poorer Arab nations. The monarch has supreme authority and Saudi Arabia has no formal constitution. In the first Gulf War (1980–8), Saudi Arabia supported Iraq against Iran. But when Iraq invaded Kuwait in 1990, it joined the international alliance to drive Iraq's forces out of Kuwait in 1991. In 2001, relations with the US became strained after the terrorist attacks on September 11, 2001, partly because many alleged terrorists were Saudi nationals. However, Saudi Arabia denounced the attacks.

Saudi Arabia has about 25% of the world's known oil reserves, and oil and oil products make up 85% of its exports. But agriculture still employs 48% of the people. Irrigation and desalination schemes have increased crop production, while the government continues to diversify the country's economy.

AREA 829,995 SQ MI [2,149,690 SQ KM]
POPULATION 23,513,000
CAPITAL (POPULATION) RIYADH (1,800,000)
GOVERNMENT ABSOLUTE MONARCHY WITH CONSULTATIVE ASSEMBLY
ETHNIC GROUPS ARAB 90%, AFRO-ASIAN 10%
LANGUAGES ARABIC (OFFICIAL) **RELIGIONS** ISLAM 100%
CURRENCY SAUDI RIYAL = 100 HALALAS

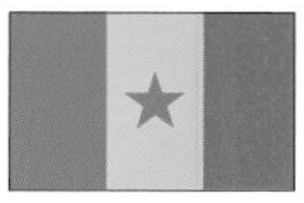
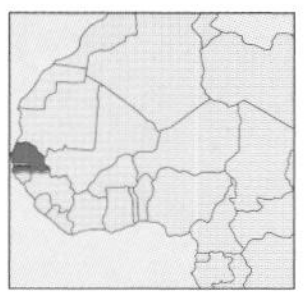

SENEGAL

GEOGRAPHY The Republic of Senegal is on the northwest coast of Africa. The volcanic Cape Verde (Cap Vert), on which Dakar stands, is the most westerly point in Africa. Plains cover most of Senegal, though the land rises gently in the southeast.

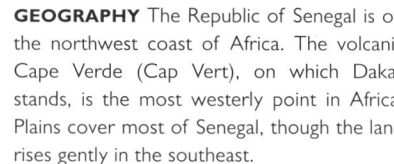

Dakar has a tropical climate, with a short rainy season between July and October.

POLITICS & ECONOMY In 1882, Senegal became a French colony, and from 1895 it was ruled as part of French West Africa, the capital of which, Dakar, developed as a major port and city.

In 1959, Senegal joined French Sudan (now Mali) to form the Federation of Mali. But Senegal withdrew in 1960 and became the separate Republic of Senegal. Its first president, Léopold Sédar Senghor, served until 1981, when he was succeeded by Abdou Diouf, who was later made "president for life." However, in 2000, Diouf was defeated in presidential elections by Abdoulaye Wade.

Senegal and The Gambia have always enjoyed close relations despite their differing French and British traditions. In 1981, Senegalese troops put down an attempted coup in The Gambia and, in 1982, the two countries set up a defense alliance, called the Confederation of Senegambia. But this confederation was dissolved in 1989.

According to the World Bank, Senegal is a "lower-middle-income" developing country. It was badly hit in the 1960s and 1970s by droughts, which caused starvation. Agriculture still employs 81% of the population though many farmers produce little more than they need to feed their families. Food crops include groundnuts, millet and rice. Phosphates are the country's chief resource, but Senegal also refines oil which it imports from Gabon and Nigeria. Dakar is a busy port and has many industries.

AREA 75,954 SQ MI [196,720 SQ KM] **POPULATION** 10,590,000
CAPITAL (POPULATION) DAKAR (1,905,000)
GOVERNMENT MULTIPARTY REPUBLIC
ETHNIC GROUPS WOLOF 44%, PULAR 24%, SERER 15%
LANGUAGES FRENCH (OFFICIAL), TRIBAL LANGUAGES
RELIGIONS ISLAM 92%, TRADITIONAL BELIEFS AND OTHERS 6%, CHRISTIANITY (MAINLY ROMAN CATHOLIC) 2%
CURRENCY CFA FRANC = 100 CENTIMES

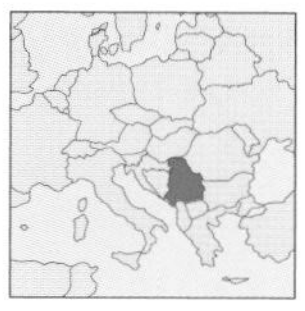

SERBIA AND MONTENEGRO

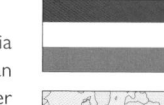

GEOGRAPHY Serbia and Montenegro are two of the six republics which made up the country of Yugoslavia until it broke up in the early 1990s. From the early 1990s, Serbia and Montenegro were known as the Federal Republic of Yugoslavia. But, in 2003, the two republics became semi-independent and adopted the name of the Union of Serbia and Montenegro.

Behind the coastline on the Adriatic Sea lies an upland region, including the Dinaric Alps and part of the Balkan Mountains. The Pannonian plains, which are drained by the River Danube, are in the north. The coast has a Mediterranean climate. The interior highlands have bitterly cold winters and cool summers. The wettest season is the summer, but there is also plenty of sunshine.

POLITICS & ECONOMY People who became known as the South Slavs began to move into the region around 1,500 years ago. Each group, including the Serbs and Croats, founded its own state. But, by the 15th century, foreign countries controlled the region. Serbia and Montenegro were under the Turkish Ottoman empire.

In the 19th century, many Slavs worked for independence and Slavic unity. In 1914, Austria-Hungary declared war on Serbia, blaming it for the assassination of Archduke Francis Ferdinand of Austria–Hungary. This led to World War I and the defeat of Austria–Hungary. In 1918, the South Slavs united in the Kingdom of the Serbs, Croats and Slovenes, which consisted of Bosnia-Herzegovina, Croatia, Dalmatia, Montenegro, Serbia and Slovenia. The country was renamed Yugoslavia in 1929. Germany occupied Yugoslavia during World War II, but partisans, including a Communist force led by Josip Broz Tito, fought the invaders.

From 1945, the Communists controlled the country, which was called the Federal People's Republic of Yugoslavia. But after Tito's death in 1980, the country faced many problems. In 1990, non-Communist parties were permitted and non-Communists won majorities in elections in all but Serbia and Montenegro, where Socialists (former Communists) won control. Yugoslavia split apart in 1991–2 with Bosnia-Herzegovina, Croatia, Macedonia and Slovenia proclaiming their independence. The two remaining republics of Serbia and Montenegro became the new Yugoslavia.

Fighting broke out in Croatia and Bosnia-Herzegovina as rival groups struggled for power. In 1992, the United Nations withdrew recognition of Yugoslavia because of its failure to halt atrocities committed by Serbs living in Croatia and Bosnia. In 1995, Yugoslavia was involved in the talks that led to the Dayton Peace Accord, which brought peace to Bosnia-Herzegovina. But the issue of Yugoslav repression of minorities flared up again in 1998 in Kosovo, a province where the majority are ethnic Albanians. In response to Serb ethnic cleansing, NATO forces began an offensive against Yugoslavia. A Serb withdrawal was agreed in June 1999. Many Montenegrins wanted to secede and set up their own nation separate from Serbia. In 2002, Serbia and Montenegro agreed to set up a loose union, giving both republics semi-independence. Montenegro agreed that they would not secede from this union, which came into being in 2003, for at least three years.

Under Communist rule, manufacturing became increasingly important in Yugoslavia. But in the early 1990s, the World Bank described what is now Serbia and Montenegro as a "lower-middle-income" economy. Resources include bauxite, coal, copper and other metals, oil and natural gas. Manufactures, which form the main exports, include aluminum, machinery, plastics, steel, textiles and vehicles. Farming remains important. Crops include fruits, maize, potatoes, tobacco and wheat. Cattle, pigs and sheep are raised.

AREA 39,449 SQ MI [102,170 SQ KM] **POPULATION** 10,657,000
CAPITAL (POPULATION) BELGRADE (1,598,000)
GOVERNMENT FEDERAL REPUBLIC
ETHNIC GROUPS SERB 62%, ALBANIAN 17%, MONTENEGRIN 5%, HUNGARIAN, MUSLIM, CROAT
LANGUAGES SERBO-CROAT (OFFICIAL), ALBANIAN
RELIGIONS CHRISTIANITY (MAINLY SERBIAN ORTHODOX), ISLAM
CURRENCY NEW DINAR = 100 PARAS

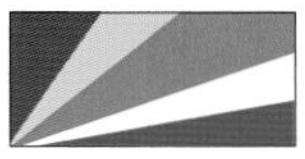
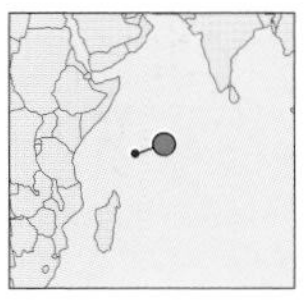

SEYCHELLES

The Republic of Seychelles in the western Indian Ocean achieved independence from Britain in 1976. Coconuts are the main cash crop and fishing and tourism are important.

AREA 176 SQ MI [455 SQ KM]
POPULATION 80,000 **CAPITAL** VICTORIA

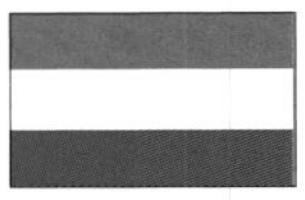

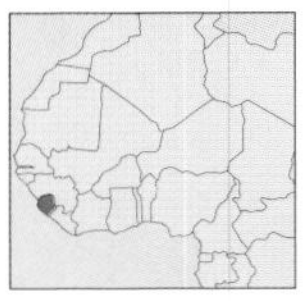

SIERRA LEONE

GEOGRAPHY The Republic of Sierra Leone in West Africa is about the same size as the Republic of Ireland. The coast contains several deep estuaries in the north, with lagoons in the south. The most prominent feature is the mountainous Freetown (or Sierra Leone) peninsula.

Sierra Leone has a tropical climate, with heavy rainfall between April and November.

POLITICS & ECONOMY A former British territory, Sierra Leone became independent in 1961 and a republic in 1971. It became a one-party state in 1978, but, in 1991, the people voted for the restoration of democracy. The military seized power in 1992 and a civil war caused much destruction in 1994–5. Elections in 1996 were followed by another military coup. In 1998, the West African Peace Force restored the deposed President Ahmed Tejan Kabbah. In 1999, a peace agreement followed further conflict. As part of this agreement, Foday Sankoh, one of the rebel leaders, became vice-president. However, he was arrested in 2000 and charged with war crimes. Conflict resumed, but another ceasefire was agreed. Disarmament continued through 2001 and, in 2002, the war seemed to be over.

The World Bank classifies Sierra Leone among the "low-income" economies. Agriculture provides a living for 70% of the people, though farming is mainly at subsistence level. The most valuable exports are minerals, including diamonds, bauxite and rutile (titanium ore). The country has few manufacturing industries.

AREA 27,699 sq mi [71,740 sq km] **POPULATION** 5,615,000
CAPITAL (POPULATION) Freetown (505,000)
GOVERNMENT Single-party republic **ETHNIC GROUPS** Mende 35%, Temne 30%, Creole **LANGUAGES** English (official), Mende, Temne, Krio **RELIGIONS** Islam 60%, traditional beliefs 30%, Christianity 10%
CURRENCY Leone = 100 cents

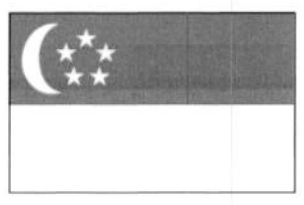

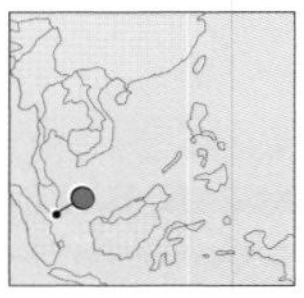

SINGAPORE

GEOGRAPHY The Republic of Singapore is an island country at the southern tip of the Malay peninsula. It consists of the large Singapore Island and 58 small islands, 20 of which are inhabited.

Singapore has a hot, humid climate. Temperatures are high and rainfall is heavy throughout the year.

POLITICS & ECONOMY In 1819, Sir Thomas Stamford Raffles (1781–1826), agent of the British East India Company, made a treaty with the Sultan of Johor allowing the British to build a settlement on Singapore Island. Singapore soon became the leading British trading center in South-east Asia and it later became a naval base. Japanese forces seized the island in 1942, but British rule was restored in 1945.

In 1963, Singapore became part of the Federation of Malaysia, which also included Malaya and the territories of Sabah and Sarawak on Borneo. In 1965, Singapore broke away and became independent.

The People's Action Party (PAP) has ruled Singapore since 1959. Its leader, Lee Kuan Yew, served as prime minister from 1959 until 1990, when he resigned and was succeeded by Goh Chok Tong. Under the PAP, the economy has expanded rapidly though some consider its rule rather dictatorial.

The World Bank classifies Singapore as a "high-income" economy. A skilled work force has created a fast-growing economy, but the recession in 1997–8 was a setback. Trade and finance are leading activities. Manufactures include electronic products, machinery, scientific instruments, textiles and ships. Singapore has a large oil refinery. Petroleum products and manufactures are the main exports.

AREA 239 sq mi [618 sq km] **POPULATION** 4,453,000
CAPITAL (POPULATION) Singapore City (3,866,000)
GOVERNMENT Multiparty republic
ETHNIC GROUPS Chinese 77%, Malay 14%, Indian 8%
LANGUAGES Chinese, Malay, Tamil and English (all official)
RELIGIONS Buddhism, Islam, Christianity, Hinduism
CURRENCY Singapore dollar = 100 cents

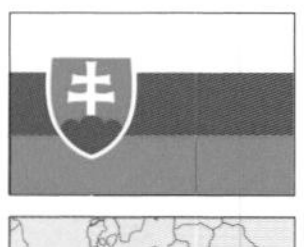

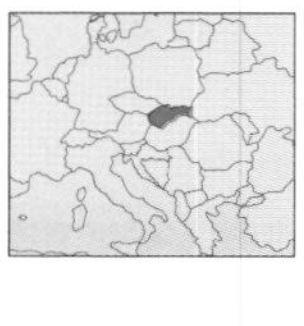

SLOVAK REPUBLIC

GEOGRAPHY The Slovak Republic is a predominantly mountainous country, consisting of part of the Carpathian range. The highest peak is Gerlachovka in the Tatra Mountains, which reaches 8,711 ft [2,655 m]. The south is a fertile lowland.

The Slovak Republic has cold winters and warm summers. Kosice, in the east, has average temperatures ranging from 27°F [–3°C] in January to 68°F [20°C] in July. The highland areas are much colder. Snow or rain falls throughout the year. Kosice has an average annual rainfall of 24 inches [600 mm], the wettest months being July and August.

POLITICS & ECONOMY Slavic peoples settled in the region in the 5th century AD. They were subsequently conquered by Hungary, beginning a millennium of Hungarian rule and suppression of Slovak culture.

In 1867, Hungary and Austria united to form Austria–Hungary, of which the present-day Slovak Republic was a part. Austria–Hungary collapsed at the end of World War I (1914–18). The Czech and Slovak people then united to form a new nation, Czechoslovakia. But Czech domination led to resentment by many Slovaks. In 1939, the Slovak Republic declared itself independent, but Germany occupied the country. At the end of World War II, the Slovak Republic again became part of Czechoslovakia.

The Communist party took control in 1948. In the 1960s, many people sought reform, but they were crushed by the Russians. In the late 1980s, demands for democracy mounted and a non-Communist government took office in 1990. Elections in 1992 led to victory for the Movement for a Democratic Slovakia headed by a former Communist and nationalist, Vladimir Meciar, and the independent Slovak Republic came into existence on January 1, 1993.

Independence raised national aspirations among Slovakia's Magyar-speaking community, but relations with Hungary deteriorated when the Magyars felt that administrative changes under-represented them politically. The government also made Slovak the only official language. The government's autocratic rule and human rights record provoked international criticism. In 1998, Meciar's party was defeated and Mikulas Dzurinda replaced Meciar as prime minister. In 2002, the European Union and the North Atlantic Treaty Organization invited the Slovak Republic to become a member of both organizations in 2004.

Before 1948, the Slovak Republic's economy was based on farming, but Communist governments developed manufacturing industries, producing such things as chemicals, machinery, steel and weapons. Since the late 1980s, many state-run businesses have been handed over to private owners.

AREA 18,932 sq mi [49,035 sq km] **POPULATION** 5,422,000
CAPITAL (POPULATION) Bratislava (451,000)
GOVERNMENT Multiparty republic
ETHNIC GROUPS Slovak 86%, Hungarian 11%, Roma 2%
LANGUAGES Slovak (official), Hungarian
RELIGIONS Roman Catholic 60%, Protestant 8%, Orthodox 4%
CURRENCY Koruna = 100 halierov

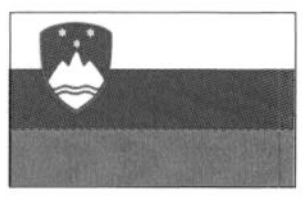

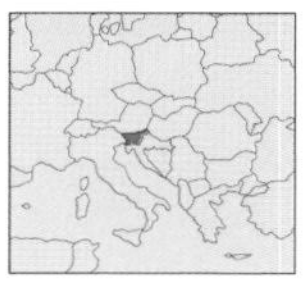

SLOVENIA

GEOGRAPHY The Republic of Slovenia was one of the six republics which made up the former Yugoslavia. Much of the land is mountainous, rising to 9,393 ft [2,863 m] at Mount Triglav in the Julian Alps (Julijske Alpe) in the northwest. Central Slovenia contains the limestone Karst region. The Postojna caves near Ljubljana are among the largest in Europe.

The coast has a mild Mediterranean climate, but inland the climate is more continental. The mountains are snow-capped in winter.

POLITICS & ECONOMY In the last 2,000 years, the Slovene people have been independent as a nation for less than 50 years. The Austrian Habsburgs ruled over the region from the 13th century until World War I. Slovenia became part of the Kingdom of the Serbs, Croats and Slovenes (later called Yugoslavia) in 1918. During World War II, Slovenia was invaded and partitioned between Italy, Germany and Hungary, but, after the war, Slovenia again became part of Yugoslavia.

From the late 1960s, some Slovenes demanded independence, but the central government opposed the breakup of the country. In 1990, when Communist governments had collapsed throughout Eastern Europe, elections were held and a non-Communist coalition government was set up. Slovenia then declared itself independent. This led to fighting between Slovenes and the federal army, but Slovenia did not become a battlefield like other parts of the former Yugoslavia. The European Community recognized Slovenia's independence in 1992. The electors returned a coalition led by the Liberal Democrats in 1992, 1996 and 2000. In 2002, the European Union and the North Atlantic Treaty Organization invited Slovenia to become a member of both organizations in 2004.

The reform of the formerly state-run economy caused problems for Slovenia. However, it has enjoyed considerable economic progress, with one of Europe's fastest growing economies. In 1992, the World Bank classified Slovenia's economy as "upper-middle-income."

Manufacturing is the leading activity and manufactures are the main exports. Manufactures include chemicals, machinery and transport equipment, metal goods and textiles. Slovenia mines some iron ore, lead, lignite and mercury. Agriculture and forestry employ 10% of the people. Fruits, maize, potatoes and wheat are major crops, and many farmers raise animals.

AREA 7,817 sq mi [20,251 sq km] **POPULATION** 1,933,000
CAPITAL (POPULATION) Ljubljana (280,000)
GOVERNMENT Multiparty republic
ETHNIC GROUPS Slovene 88%, Croat 3%, Serb 2%, Bosnian 1%
LANGUAGES Slovene (official), Serbo-Croat
RELIGIONS Mainly Roman Catholic
CURRENCY Tolar = 100 stotin

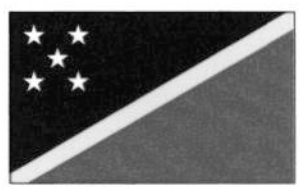

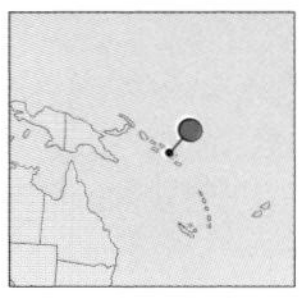

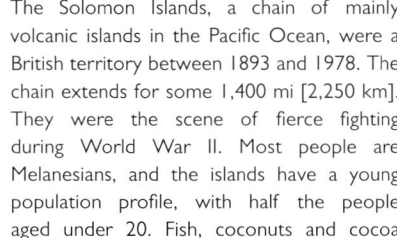

SOLOMON ISLANDS

The Solomon Islands, a chain of mainly volcanic islands in the Pacific Ocean, were a British territory between 1893 and 1978. The chain extends for some 1,400 mi [2,250 km]. They were the scene of fierce fighting during World War II. Most people are Melanesians, and the islands have a young population profile, with half the people aged under 20. Fish, coconuts and cocoa are leading products, though development is hampered by mountainous, forested terrain.

AREA 10,954 sq mi [28,370 sq km] **POPULATION** 495,000
CAPITAL Honiara

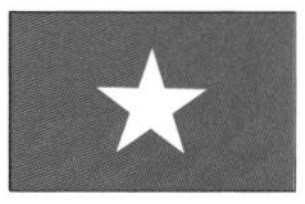

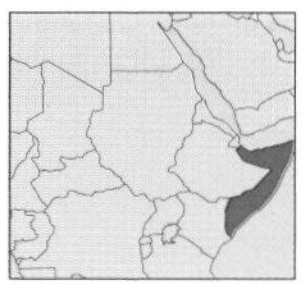

SOMALIA

GEOGRAPHY The Somali Democratic Republic, or Somalia, is in a region known as the "Horn of Africa." It is more than twice the size of Italy, the country which once ruled the southern part of Somalia. The most mountainous part of the country is in the north, behind the narrow coastal plains that border the Gulf of Aden.

Rainfall is light throughout Somalia. The wettest regions are the south and the northern mountains, but droughts often occur. Temperatures are high on the low plateaus and plains.

POLITICS & ECONOMY European powers became interested in the Horn of Africa in the 19th century. In 1884, Britain made the northern part of what is now Somalia a protectorate, while Italy took the south in 1905. The new boundaries divided the Somalis into five areas: the two Somalilands, Djibouti (which was taken by France in the 1880s), Ethiopia and Kenya. Since then, many Somalis have longed for reunification in a Greater Somalia.

Italy entered World War II in 1940 and invaded British Somaliland. But British forces conquered the region in 1941 and ruled both Somalilands until 1950, when the United Nations asked Italy to take over the former Italian Somaliland for ten years. In 1960, both Somalilands became independent and united to become Somalia.

Somalia has faced many problems since independence. Economic problems led a military group to seize power in 1969. In the 1970s, Somalia supported an uprising of Somali-speaking people in the Ogaden region of Ethiopia. But Ethiopian forces prevailed and, in 1988, Somalia signed a peace treaty with Ethiopia. The cost of the fighting weakened Somalia's economy. In the 1990s, Somalia gradually broke apart. In 1991, the people in what was formerly British Somaliland set up the "Somaliland Republic," although it never received international recognition. The northeast, which was called Puntland, also seceded from Somalia, while civil war, based on clan rivalry, raged in the south. US troops sent into the south by the UN in 1993 were forced to withdraw in 1994 and the clan warfare continued. However, hopes of reunification were raised in 2000, when a three-year transitional Assembly was set up in the south, following a peace conference held in Djibouti.

Somalia is a developing country, whose economy has been shattered by drought and war. Catastrophic flooding in late 1997 displaced tens of thousands of people, further damaging the country's infrastructure and destroying hopes of economic recovery.

Many Somalis are nomads who raise livestock. Live animals, meat and hides and skins are major exports, followed by bananas grown in the wetter south. Other crops include citrus fruits, cotton, maize and sugarcane. Mining and manufacturing remain relatively unimportant in the economy.

AREA 246,201 sq mi [637,660 sq km] **POPULATION** 7,753,000 **CAPITAL (POPULATION)** Mogadishu (997,000) **GOVERNMENT** Single-party republic, military dominated **ETHNIC GROUPS** Somali 85%, Arab 1% **LANGUAGES** Somali and Arabic (both official), English, Italian **RELIGIONS** Islam 99% **CURRENCY** Somali shilling = 100 cents

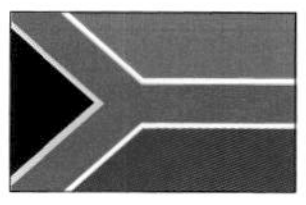

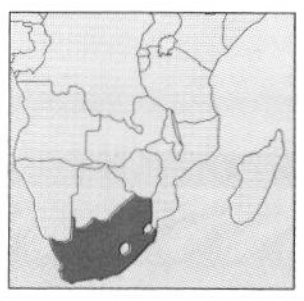

SOUTH AFRICA

GEOGRAPHY The Republic of South Africa is made up largely of the southern part of the huge plateau which makes up most of southern Africa. The highest peaks are in the Drakensberg range, which is formed by the uplifted rim of the plateau. The coastal plains include part of the Namib Desert in the northwest. Most of South Africa has a mild, sunny climate. Much of the coastal strip, including Cape Town, has warm, dry summers and mild, rainy winters. Inland, large areas are arid.

POLITICS & ECONOMY Early inhabitants in South Africa were the Khoisan. In the last 2,000 years, Bantu-speaking people moved into the area. Their descendants include the Zulu, Xhosa, Sotho and Tswana. The Dutch founded a settlement at the Cape in 1652, but Britain took over in the early 19th century, making the area a colony. The Dutch, called Boers or Afrikaners, resented British rule and moved inland. Rivalry between the groups led to Anglo-Boer Wars in 1880–1 and 1899–1902.

In 1910, the country was united as the Union of South Africa. In 1948, the National Party won power and introduced a policy known as apartheid, under which non-whites had no votes and their human rights were strictly limited. In 1990, Nelson Mandela, leader of the African National Congress (ANC), was released from prison. Multi-racial elections were held in 1994 and Mandela became president. After Mandela's retirement in 1999, his successor, Thabo Mbeki, led the ANC to victory in the elections. Mbeki faces many problems, including a health crisis arising from a government estimate in 2002 that 11.4% of the total population was infected with the HIV virus.

South Africa is Africa's most developed country. However, most of the black people are poor, with low standards of living. Natural resources include diamonds, gold and many other metals. Mining and manufacturing are the most valuable activities.

AREA 470,566 sq mi [1,219,916 sq km] **POPULATION** 43,648,000 **CAPITAL (POPULATION)** Cape Town (legislative, 2,350,000); Pretoria (administrative, 1,080,000); Bloemfontein (judiciary, 300,000) **GOVERNMENT** Multiparty republic **ETHNIC GROUPS** Black 76%, White 13%, Colored 9%, Asian 2% **LANGUAGES** Afrikaans, English, Ndebele, North Sotho, South Sotho, Swazi, Tsonga, Tswana, Venda, Xhosa and Zulu (all official) **RELIGIONS** Christianity 68%, Islam 2%, Hinduism 1% **CURRENCY** Rand = 100 cents

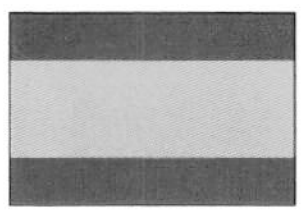

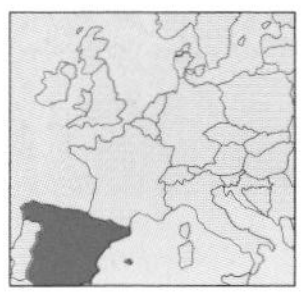

SPAIN

GEOGRAPHY The Kingdom of Spain is the second largest country in Western Europe after France. It shares the Iberian peninsula with Portugal. A large plateau, called the Meseta, covers most of Spain. Much of the Meseta is flat, but it is crossed by several mountain ranges, called sierras.

The northern highlands include the Cantabrian Mountains (Cordillera Cantabrica) and the high Pyrenees, which form Spain's border with France. But Mulhacén, the highest peak on the Spanish mainland, is in the Sierra Nevada in the southeast. Spain also contains fertile coastal plains. Other major lowlands are the Ebro river basin in the northeast and the Guadalquivir river basin in the southwest. Spain also includes the Balearic Islands in the Mediterranean Sea and the Canary Islands off the northwest coast of Africa.

The Meseta has a continental climate, with hot summers and cold winters, when temperatures often fall below freezing point. Snow frequently covers the mountain ranges on the Meseta. The Mediterranean coasts have hot, dry summers and mild winters.

POLITICS & ECONOMY In the 16th century, Spain became a world power. At its peak, it controlled much of Central and South America, parts of Africa and the Philippines in Asia. Spain began to decline in the late 16th century. Its sea power was destroyed by a British fleet in the Battle of Trafalgar (1805). By the 20th century, it was a poor country.

Spain became a republic in 1931, but the republicans were defeated in the Spanish Civil War (1936–9). General Francisco Franco (1892–1975) became the country's dictator, though, technically, it was a monarchy. When Franco died, the monarchy was restored. Prince Juan Carlos became king.

Spain has several groups with their own languages and cultures. Some of these people want to run their own regional affairs. In the northern Basque region, some nationalists have waged a terrorist campaign. A truce in 1998 was ended in 1999 when talks failed to produce results. In 2003, Spain's Supreme Court voted to ban Batasuna, the Basque separatist party.

Since the late 1970s, a regional parliament with a considerable degree of autonomy has been set up in the Basque Country (called Euskadi in the indigenous tongue and Pais Vasco in Spanish). Similar parliaments have been initiated in Catalonia in the northeast and Galicia in the northwest. All these regions have their own languages.

The revival of Spain's economy, which was shattered by the Civil War, began in the 1950s and 1960s, especially through the growth of tourism and manufacturing. Since the 1950s, Spain has changed from a poor country, dependent on agriculture, to a fairly prosperous industrial nation.

By the early 1990s, agriculture employed 10% of the people, as compared with industry 35% and services, including tourism, 55%. Farmland, including pasture, makes up about two-thirds of the land, with forest making up most of the rest. Major crops include barley, citrus fruits, grapes for winemaking, olives, potatoes and wheat.

Spain has some high-grade iron ore in the north, though otherwise it lacks natural resources. But it has many manufacturing industries. Manufactures include cars, chemicals, clothing, electronics, processed food, metal goods, steel and textiles. The leading manufacturing centers are Barcelona, Bilbao and Madrid.

AREA 194,896 sq mi [504,780 sq km] **POPULATION** 38,383,000
CAPITAL (POPULATION) Madrid (3,030,000)
GOVERNMENT Constitutional monarchy
ETHNIC GROUPS Castilian Spanish 72%, Catalan 16%, Galician 8%, Basque 2% **LANGUAGES** Castilian Spanish (official) 74%, Catalan 17%, Galician 7%, Basque 2%
RELIGIONS Roman Catholic 99%
CURRENCY Euro = 100 cents

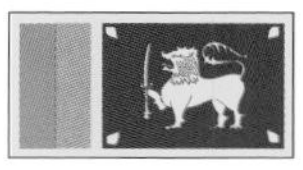

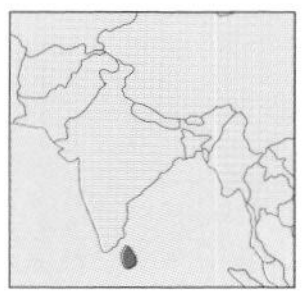

SRI LANKA

GEOGRAPHY The Democratic Socialist Republic of Sri Lanka is an island nation, separated from the southeast coast of India by the Palk Strait. The land is mostly low-lying, but a mountain region dominates the south-central part of the country.

The western part of Sri Lanka has a wet equatorial climate. Temperatures are high and the rainfall is heavy. Eastern Sri Lanka is drier than the west of the country.

POLITICS & ECONOMY From the early 16th century, Ceylon (as Sri Lanka was then known) was ruled successively by the Portuguese, Dutch and British. Independence was achieved in 1948 and the country was renamed Sri Lanka in 1972.

After independence, rivalries between the two main ethnic groups, the Sinhalese and Tamils, marred progress. In the 1950s, the government made Sinhala the official language. Following protests, the prime minister made provisions for Tamil to be used in some areas. In 1959, the prime minister was assassinated by a Sinhalese extremist and he was succeeded by Sirimavo Bandanaraike, who became the world's first woman prime minister.

Conflict between Tamils and Sinhalese continued in the 1970s and 1980s. In 1987, India helped to engineer a ceasefire. Indian troops arrived to enforce the agreement, but withdrew in 1990 after failing to subdue the main guerrilla group, the Tamil Tigers, who wanted to set up an independent Tamil homeland in northern Sri Lanka. In 1993, the country's president was assassinated by a suspected Tamil separatist. Offensives against the Tamil Tigers continued until hopes of peace were raised in 2002, with the signing of a long-term ceasefire.

The World Bank classifies Sri Lanka as a "low-income" developing country. Agriculture employs half of the work force, and coconuts, rubber and tea are exported. Rice is the chief food crop. Manufacturing is concerned mainly with processing agricultural products and producing textiles.

AREA 25,332 sq mi [65,610 sq km] **POPULATION** 19,577,000
CAPITAL (POPULATION) Colombo (1,863,000)
GOVERNMENT Multiparty republic
ETHNIC GROUPS Sinhalese 74%, Tamil 18%, Sri Lankan Moor 7% **LANGUAGES** Sinhala and Tamil (both official)
RELIGIONS Buddhism 69%, Hinduism 16%, Christianity 8%, Islam 7%
CURRENCY Sri Lankan rupee = 100 cents

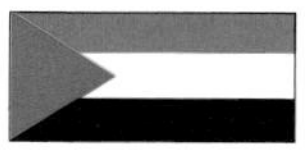

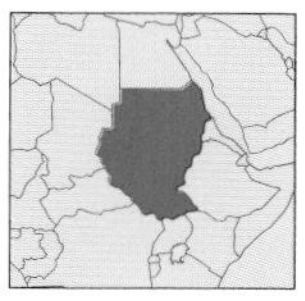

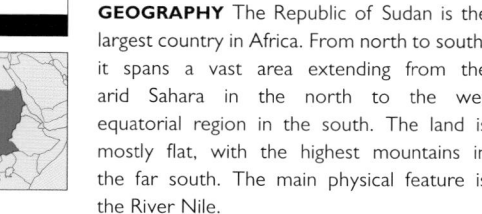

SUDAN

GEOGRAPHY The Republic of Sudan is the largest country in Africa. From north to south, it spans a vast area extending from the arid Sahara in the north to the wet equatorial region in the south. The land is mostly flat, with the highest mountains in the far south. The main physical feature is the River Nile.

The climate of Khartoum represents a transition between the virtually rainless northern deserts and the equatorial lands in the south. Some rain falls in Khartoum in summer.

POLITICS & ECONOMY In the 19th century, Egypt gradually took over Sudan. In 1881, a Muslim religious teacher, the Mahdi ("divinely appointed guide"), led an uprising. Britain and Egypt put the rebellion down in 1898. In 1899, they agreed to rule Sudan jointly as a condominium.

After independence in 1952, the black Africans in the south, who were either Christians or followers of traditional beliefs, feared domination by the Muslim northerners. For example, they objected to the government declaring that Arabic was the only official language. In 1964, civil war broke out and continued until 1972, when the south was given regional self-government, though executive power was still vested in the military government in Khartoum.

In 1983, the government established Islamic law throughout the country. This sparked off further conflict when the Sudan People's Liberation Army (SPLA) in the south launched attacks on government installations. The fighting continued into the 21st century. In 1998, the government announced that it accepted the idea of a referendum on the secession of the south, though definitions of the "south" varied. In 2002–3, the government signed memoranda of understanding with the SPLA, holding out hope of a total end to the hostilities.

AREA 967,493 sq mi [2,505,810 sq km] **POPULATION** 37,090,000 **CAPITAL (POPULATION)** Khartoum (925,000) **GOVERNMENT** Military regime **ETHNIC GROUPS** Sudanese Arab 49%, Dinka 12%, Nuba 8%, Beja 6%, Nuer 5%, Azande 3% **LANGUAGES** Arabic (official), Nubian, Dinka **RELIGIONS** Islam (mainly Sunni) 70%, traditional beliefs 25%, Christianity 5% **CURRENCY** Dinar = 10 Sudanese pounds

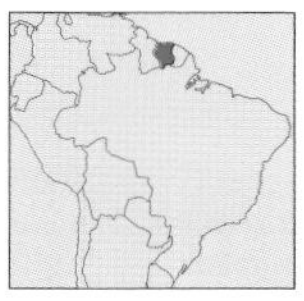

SURINAME

GEOGRAPHY The Republic of Suriname is sandwiched between French Guiana and Guyana in northeastern South America. The narrow coastal plain was once swampy, but it has been drained and now consists mainly of farmland. Inland lie hills and low mountains, which rise to 4,199 ft [1,280 m].

Suriname has a hot, wet and humid climate. Temperatures are high throughout the year.

POLITICS & ECONOMY In 1667, the British handed Suriname to the Dutch in return for New Amsterdam, an area that is now the state of New York. Slave revolts and Dutch neglect hampered development. In the early 19th century, Britain and the Netherlands disputed the ownership of the area. The British gave up their claims in 1813. Slavery was abolished in 1863 and, soon afterward, Indian and Indonesian laborers were introduced to work on the plantations. Suriname became fully independent in 1975, but the economy was weakened when thousands of skilled people emigrated from Suriname to the Netherlands. Following a coup in 1980, Suriname was ruled by a military dictator, Dési Bouterse. The adoption of a new constitution led to the restoration of democracy in 1988, though another military coup occurred in 1990. Elections were held in 1996, but instability, deteriorating relations with the Netherlands and economic problems continued. In 1999, Bouterse was convicted in absentia in the Netherlands of having led a cocaine-trafficking ring during and after his tenure in office.

The World Bank classifies Suriname as an "upper-middle-income" developing country. Its economy is based on mining and metal processing. Suriname is a leading producer of bauxite, from which the metal aluminum is made.

AREA 63,039 sq mi [163,270 sq km] **POPULATION** 436,000
CAPITAL (POPULATION) Paramaribo (201,000)
GOVERNMENT Multiparty republic **ETHNIC GROUPS** Asian Indian 37%, Creole (mixed White and Black) 31%, Indonesian 14%, Black 9%, Amerindian 3%, Chinese 3%, Dutch 1% **LANGUAGES** Dutch (official), Sranantonga **RELIGIONS** Hinduism 27%, Roman Catholic 23%, Islam 20%, Protestant 19%
CURRENCY Suriname guilder = 100 cents

SWAZILAND

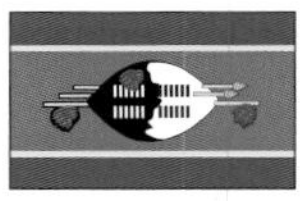

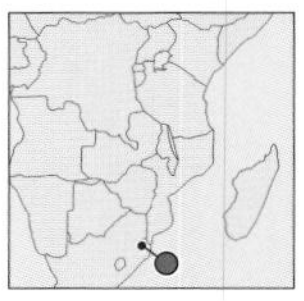

GEOGRAPHY The Kingdom of Swaziland is a small, landlocked country in southern Africa. The country has four regions which run north–south. In the west, the Highveld, with an average height of 3,950 ft [1,200 m], makes up 30% of Swaziland. The Middleveld, between 1,150 ft and 3,280 ft [350 m to 1,000 m], covers 28% of the country. The Lowveld, with an average height of 886 ft [270 m], covers another 33%. Finally, the Lebombo Mountains reach 2,600 ft [800 m] along the eastern border.

The Lowveld is almost tropical, with an average temperature of 72°F [22°C] and low rainfall. The altitude moderates the climate in the west.

POLITICS & ECONOMY In 1894, Britain and the Boers of South Africa agreed to put Swaziland under the control of the South African Republic (the Transvaal). But at the end of the Anglo–Boer War (1899–1902), Britain took control of the country. In 1968, when Swaziland became fully independent as a constitutional monarchy, the head of state was King Sobhuza II. Sobhuza died in 1982 and was succeeded by one of his sons, Prince Makhosetive, who, in 1986, was installed as King Mswati III. Elections in 1993 and 1998, in which political parties were banned, failed to satisfy protesters who opposed the absolute monarchy. But Mswati continued to rule by decree. In 2003, he announced that democracy was not suitable for the Swazi people.

The World Bank classifies Swaziland as a "lower-middle-income" developing country. Agriculture employs 74% of the people, and farm products and processed foods, including soft drink concentrates, sugar, wood pulp, citrus fruits and canned fruit, are the leading exports. Many farmers live at subsistence level, producing little more than they need to feed their own families. Swaziland is heavily dependent on South Africa and the two countries are linked through a customs union.

AREA 6,703 SQ MI [17,360 SQ KM] **POPULATION** 1,124,000
CAPITAL (POPULATION) MBABANE (42,000)
GOVERNMENT MONARCHY **ETHNIC GROUPS** SWAZI 84%, ZULU 10%, TSONGA **LANGUAGES** SISWATI AND ENGLISH (BOTH OFFICIAL)
RELIGIONS PROTESTANT 55%, ISLAM 10%, ROMAN CATHOLIC 5%
CURRENCY LILANGENI = 100 CENTS

SWEDEN

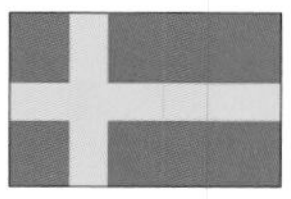

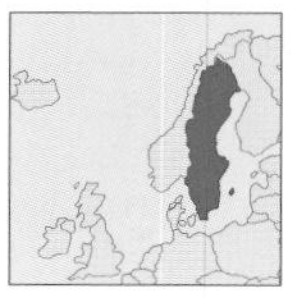

GEOGRAPHY The Kingdom of Sweden is the largest of the countries of Scandinavia in both area and population. It shares the Scandinavian peninsula with Norway. The western part of the country, along the border with Norway, is mountainous. The highest point is Kebnekaise, which reaches 6,946 ft [2,117 m] in the northwest.

The climate of Sweden becomes more severe from south to north. Stockholm has cold winters and cool summers. The far south is much milder.

POLITICS & ECONOMY Swedish Vikings plundered areas to the south and east between the 9th and 11th centuries. Sweden, Denmark and Norway were united in 1397, but Sweden regained its independence in 1523. In 1809, Sweden lost Finland to Russia, but, in 1814, it gained Norway from Denmark. The union between Sweden and Norway was dissolved in 1905. Sweden was neutral in World Wars I and II. Since 1945, Sweden has become a prosperous country. In 1995, it joined the European Union. However, many people were sceptical about the advantages of EU membership and Sweden did not adopt the euro, the single EU currency, in 1999.

Sweden has wide-ranging welfare services. But many people are concerned about the high cost of these services and the high taxes they must pay. In 1991, the Social Democrats, who had built up the welfare state, were defeated. They were re-elected in 1994, 1998 and 2002, but they tried to control public spending and expand the economy.

Sweden is a highly developed industrial country. Major products include steel and steel goods. Steel is used in the engineering industry to manufacture aircraft, cars, machinery and ships. Sweden has some of the world's richest iron ore deposits. They are located near Kiruna in the far north. But most of this ore is exported, and Sweden imports most of the materials needed by its industries. Sweden also has a major forestry industry.

Development of hydroelectricity has made up for the lack of oil and coal. In 1996, a decision was taken to decommission all of Sweden's nuclear power stations. This is said to be one of the boldest and most expensive environmental pledges ever made by a government.

AREA 173,730 SQ MI [449,960 SQ KM] **POPULATION** 8,877,000
CAPITAL (POPULATION) STOCKHOLM (727,000)
GOVERNMENT CONSTITUTIONAL MONARCHY
ETHNIC GROUPS SWEDISH 91%, FINNISH 3% **LANGUAGES** SWEDISH (OFFICIAL), FINNISH **RELIGIONS** LUTHERAN 89%, ROMAN CATHOLIC 2%
CURRENCY SWEDISH KRONA = 100 ÖRE

SWITZERLAND

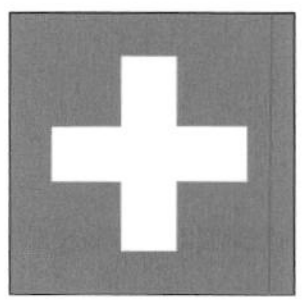

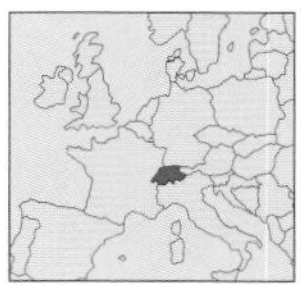

GEOGRAPHY The Swiss Confederation is a landlocked country in Western Europe. Much of the land is mountainous. The Jura Mountains lie along Switzerland's western border with France, while the Swiss Alps make up about 60% of the country in the south and east. Four-fifths of the people of Switzerland live on the fertile Swiss plateau, which contains most of Switzerland's large cities.

The climate of Switzerland varies greatly according to the height of the land. The plateau region has a central European climate with warm summers, but cold and snowy winters. Rain occurs all through the year. The rainiest months are in summer.

POLITICS & ECONOMY In 1291, three small cantons (states) united to defend their freedom against the Habsburg rulers of the Holy Roman Empire. They were Schwyz, Uri and Unterwalden, and they called the confederation they formed "Switzerland." Switzerland expanded and, in the 14th century, defeated Austria in three wars of independence. After a defeat by the French in 1515, the Swiss adopted a policy of neutrality, which they still follow. In 1815, the Congress of Vienna expanded Switzerland to 22 cantons and guaranteed its neutrality. Switzerland's 23rd canton, Jura, was created in 1979 from part of Bern. Neutrality combined with the vigor and independence of its people have made Switzerland prosperous. In 1993 and again in 2001, the Swiss people voted against starting negotiations to join the European Union. However, in 2002, the Swiss voted by a narrow majority to join the United Nations.

Although lacking in natural resources, Switzerland is a wealthy, industrialized country. Many workers are highly skilled. Major products include chemicals, electrical equipment, machinery and machine tools, precision instruments, processed food, watches and textiles. Farmers produce about three-fifths of the country's food – the rest is imported. Livestock raising, especially dairy farming, is the chief agricultural activity. Crops include fruits, potatoes and wheat. Tourism and banking are also important. Swiss banks attract investors from all over the world.

AREA 15,942 SQ MI [41,290 SQ KM] **POPULATION** 7,302,000
CAPITAL (POPULATION) BERN (942,000) **GOVERNMENT** FEDERAL REPUBLIC **ETHNIC GROUPS** GERMAN 65%, FRENCH 18%, ITALIAN 10%, ROMANSCH 1% **LANGUAGES** FRENCH, GERMAN, ITALIAN AND ROMANSCH (ALL OFFICIAL) **RELIGIONS** ROMAN CATHOLIC 46%, PROTESTANT 40%
CURRENCY SWISS FRANC = 100 CENTIMES

SYRIA

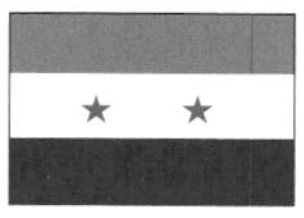

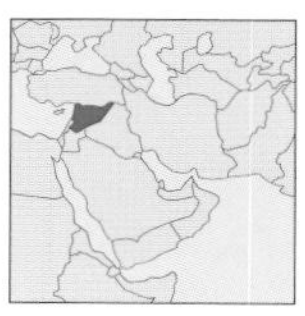

GEOGRAPHY The Syrian Arab Republic is a country in southwestern Asia. The narrow coastal plain is overlooked by a low mountain range which runs north–south. Another range, the Jabal ash Sharqi, runs along the border with Lebanon. South of this range is the Golan Heights, which Israel has occupied since 1967.

The coast has a Mediterranean climate, with dry, warm summers and wet, mild winters. The low mountains cut off Damascus from the sea. It has less rainfall than the coastal areas. To the east, the land becomes drier.

POLITICS & ECONOMY After the collapse of the Turkish Ottoman empire in World War I, Syria was ruled by France. Since independence in 1946, Syria has been involved in the Arab–Israeli wars and, in 1967, it lost a strategic border area, the Golan Heights, to Israel. In 1970, Lieutenant-General Hafez al-Assad took power, establishing a stable but repressive regime. In 1999, Syria had talks with Israel concerning the future of the Golan Heights. These talks formed part of an attempt to establish a peace settlement for the entire east Mediterranean region. Following the death of Assad in 2000, his son, Bashar Assad, succeeded him.

The World Bank classifies Syria as a "lower-middle-income" developing country. But it has great potential for development. Its main resources are oil, hydroelectricity from the dam at Lake Assad, and fertile land. Oil is the main export; farm products, textiles and phosphates are also important. Agriculture employs about 26% of the work force.

AREA 71,498 SQ MI [185,180 SQ KM] **POPULATION** 17,156,000
CAPITAL (POPULATION) DAMASCUS (1,394,000)
GOVERNMENT MULTIPARTY REPUBLIC
ETHNIC GROUPS ARAB 90%, KURDISH, ARMENIAN, OTHERS
LANGUAGES ARABIC (OFFICIAL) **RELIGIONS** ISLAM 90%, CHRISTIANITY 9% **CURRENCY** SYRIAN POUND = 100 PIASTRES

TAIWAN

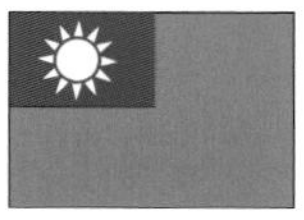

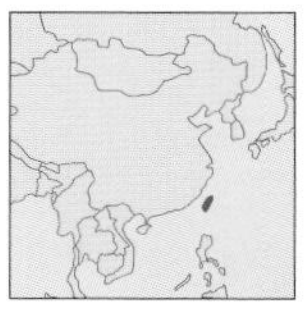

GEOGRAPHY High mountain ranges run down the length of the island, with dense forest in many areas. The climate is warm, moist and suitable for agriculture.

POLITICS & ECONOMY Chinese settlers occupied Taiwan from the 7th century. In 1895, Japan seized the territory from the Portuguese, who had named it Isla Formosa, or "beautiful island." China regained the island after World War II. In 1949, it became the refuge of the Nationalists who had been driven out of China by the Communists. They set up the Republic of China, which, with US help, launched an ambitious program of economic development. Today, it produces a wide range of manufactured goods. Mainland China regards Taiwan as one of its provinces, though reunification seems unlikely in the foreseeable future.

AREA 13,900 SQ MI [36,000 SQ KM] **POPULATION** 22,548,000
CAPITAL (POPULATION) TAIPEI (2,596,000)
GOVERNMENT UNITARY MULTIPARTY REPUBLIC
ETHNIC GROUPS TAIWANESE (HAN CHINESE) 84%, MAINLAND CHINESE 14%
LANGUAGES MANDARIN (OFFICIAL), MIN, HAKKA
RELIGIONS BUDDHISM 43%, TAOISM AND CONFUCIANISM 49%
CURRENCY NEW TAIWAN DOLLAR = 100 CENTS

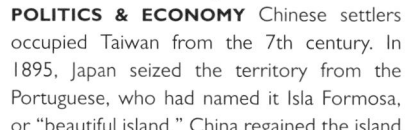

TAJIKISTAN

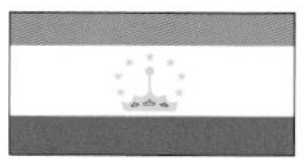

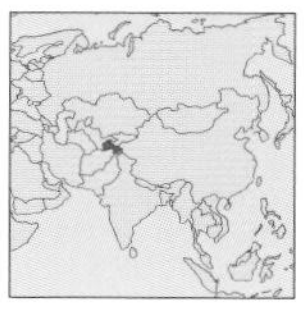

GEOGRAPHY The Republic of Tajikistan is one of the five central Asian republics that formed part of the former Soviet Union. Only 7% of the land is below 3,280 ft [1,000 m], while almost all of eastern Tajikistan is above 9,840 ft [3,000 m]. The highest point is Communism Peak (Pik Kommunizma), which reaches 24,590 ft [7,495 m]. The main ranges are the westward extension of the Tian Shan Range in the north and the snow-capped Pamirs in the southeast. Earthquakes are common throughout the country.

Tajikistan has a severe continental climate. Summers are hot and dry in the lower valleys, and winters are long and bitterly cold in the mountains.

POLITICS & ECONOMY Russia conquered parts of Tajikistan in the late 19th century and, by 1920, Russia took complete control. In 1924, Tajikistan became part of the Uzbek Soviet Socialist Republic, but, in 1929, it was expanded, taking in some areas populated by Uzbeks, becoming the Tajik Soviet Socialist Republic.

While the Soviet Union began to introduce reforms during the 1980s, many Tajiks demanded freedom. In 1989, the Tajik government made Tajik the official language instead of Russian and, in 1990, it stated that its local laws overruled Soviet laws. Tajikistan became fully independent in 1991, following the breakup of the Soviet Union. As the poorest of the ex-Soviet republics, Tajikistan faced many problems in trying to introduce a free-market system.

In 1992, civil war broke out between the government, which was run by former Communists, and an alliance of democrats and Islamic forces. A ceasefire was agreed in 1996, and in 1997 representatives of the opposition were brought into the government. Presidential elections were held in 1999, followed by parliamentary elections in 2000.

The World Bank classifies Tajikistan as a "low-income" developing country. Agriculture, mainly on irrigated land, is the main activity and cotton is the chief product. Other crops include fruits, grains and vegetables. The country has large hydroelectric power resources and it produces aluminum.

AREA 55,520 SQ MI [143,100 SQ KM] **POPULATION** 6,720,000
CAPITAL (POPULATION) DUSHANBE (524,000)
GOVERNMENT TRANSITIONAL DEMOCRACY
ETHNIC GROUPS TAJIK 65%, UZBEK 25%, RUSSIAN 3%, TATAR, KYRGYZ, UKRAINIAN, GERMAN **LANGUAGES** TAJIK (OFFICIAL), UZBEK, RUSSIAN
RELIGIONS ISLAM (MAINLY SUNNI) 80%
CURRENCY SOMONI = 100 DIRAMS

TANZANIA

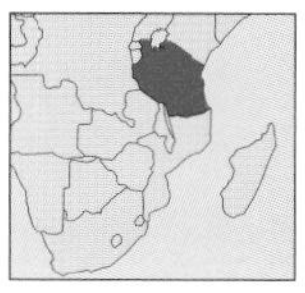

GEOGRAPHY The United Republic of Tanzania consists of the former mainland country of Tanganyika and the island nation of Zanzibar, which also includes the island of Pemba. Behind a narrow coastal plain, most of Tanzania is a plateau, which is broken by arms of the Great African Rift Valley. In the west, this valley contains lakes Nyasa and Tanganyika. The highest peak is Kilimanjaro, Africa's tallest mountain.

The coast has a hot and humid climate, with the greatest rainfall in April and May. The inland plateaus and mountains are cooler and less humid.

POLITICS & ECONOMY Mainland Tanganyika became a German territory in the 1880s, while Zanzibar and Pemba became a British protectorate in 1890. Following Germany's defeat in World War I, Britain took over Tanganyika, which remained a British territory until its independence in 1961. In 1964, Tanganyika and Zanzibar united to form the United Republic of Tanzania. The country's president, Julius Nyerere, pursued socialist policies of self-help (*ujamaa*) and egalitarianism. Many of its social reforms were successful, though the country failed to make economic progress. Nyerere resigned as president in 1985, although he retained much influence until his death in 1999. His successors, Ali Hassan Mwinyi and, from 1995, Benjamin Mkapa, introduced more liberal economic policies.

Tanzania is one of the world's poorest countries. Crops are grown on only 4.2% of the land, yet agriculture employs 80% of the people. Food crops include bananas, cassava, maize, millet and rice.

AREA 364,899 sq mi [945,090 sq km] **POPULATION** 37,188,000
CAPITAL (POPULATION) Dodoma (204,000)
GOVERNMENT Multiparty republic
ETHNIC GROUPS Nyamwezi and Sukuma 21%, Swahili 9%, Hehet and Bena 7%, Makonde 6%, Haya 6%
LANGUAGES Swahili and English (both official)
RELIGIONS Christianity (mostly Roman Catholic) 45%, Islam 35% (99% in Zanzibar), traditional beliefs and others 20%
CURRENCY Tanzanian shilling = 100 cents

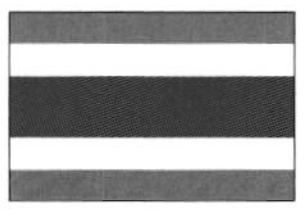

THAILAND

GEOGRAPHY The Kingdom of Thailand is one of the ten countries in Southeast Asia. The highest land is in the north, where Doi Inthanon, the highest peak, reaches 8,514 ft [2,595 m]. The Khorat plateau, in the northeast, makes up about 30% of the country and is the most heavily populated part of Thailand. In the south, Thailand shares the finger-like Malay peninsula with Burma and Malaysia.

Thailand has a tropical climate. Monsoon winds from the southwest bring heavy rains between the months of May and October. The rainfall in Bangkok is lower than in many other parts of Southeast Asia, because mountains shelter the central plains from the rain-bearing winds.

POLITICS & ECONOMY The first Thai state was set up in the 13th century. By 1350, it included most of what is now Thailand. European contact began in the early 16th century. But, in the late 17th century, the Thais, fearing interference in their affairs, forced all Europeans to leave. This policy continued for 150 years. In 1782, a Thai General, Chao Phraya Chakkri, became king, founding a dynasty which continues today. The country became known as Siam, and Bangkok became its capital. From the mid-19th century, contacts with the West were restored. In World War I, Siam supported the Allies against Germany and Austria-Hungary. But in 1941, the country was conquered by Japan and became its ally. However, after the end of World War II, it became an ally of the United States.

Since 1967, when Thailand became a member of ASEAN (the Association of Southeast Asian Nations), its economy has grown, especially its manufacturing and service industries. However, in 1997, it suffered recession along with other fast-developing countries in eastern Asia, and its economic policies had to be modified.

The economy still depends on agriculture, which employs more than two-fifths of the people. Rice is the chief crop. Cassava, cotton, maize, rubber, sugarcane and tobacco are also grown. Thailand also mines tin and other minerals. However, the chief exports are manufactures, including food products, machinery, timber products and textiles. Tourism is another major source of income.

AREA 198,116 sq mi [513,120 sq km] **POPULATION** 62,354,000
CAPITAL (POPULATION) Bangkok (7,507,000)
GOVERNMENT Constitutional monarchy
ETHNIC GROUPS Thai 75%, Chinese 14%, Malay 4%, Khmer 3%
LANGUAGES Thai (official), Chinese, Malay, English
RELIGIONS Buddhism 94%, Islam 4%, Christianity 1%
CURRENCY Thai baht = 100 satang

TOGO

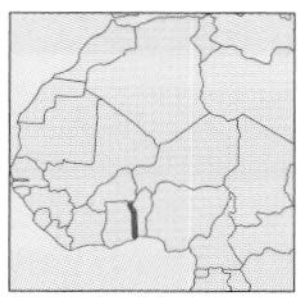

GEOGRAPHY The Republic of Togo is a long, narrow country in West Africa. From north to south, it extends about 311 mi [500 km]. Its coastline on the Gulf of Guinea is only 40 mi [64 km] long and it is only 90 mi [145 km] at its widest point.

Togo has high temperatures all through the year. The main wet season is from March to July, with a minor wet season in October and November.

POLITICS & ECONOMY Togo became a German protectorate in 1884 but, in 1919, Britain took over the western third of the territory, while France took over the eastern two-thirds. In 1956, the people of British Togoland voted to join Ghana, while French Togoland became an independent republic in 1960.

A military regime took power in 1963. In 1967, General Gnassingbe Eyadema became head of state and suspended the constitution. Under a new constitution adopted in 1992, multiparty elections were held in 1994. However, in 1998, paramilitary policies stopped the count in the presidential elections when it became clear that Eyadema had been defeated. As a result, the leading opposition parties boycotted the elections in 1999 and 2002.

Togo is a poor, developing country. Farming employs 67% of the people and major food crops include cassava, maize, millet and yams. The leading export is phosphate rock, which is used to make fertilizers.

AREA 21,927 sq mi [56,790 sq km] **POPULATION** 5,286,000
CAPITAL (POPULATION) Lomé (590,000)
GOVERNMENT Multiparty republic **ETHNIC GROUPS** Ewe-Adja 43%, Tem-Kabre 26%, Gurma 16% **LANGUAGES** French (official), Ewe, Kabiye
RELIGIONS Traditional beliefs 50%, Christianity 35%, Islam 15%
CURRENCY CFA franc = 100 centimes

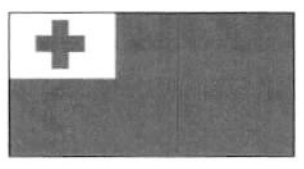

TONGA

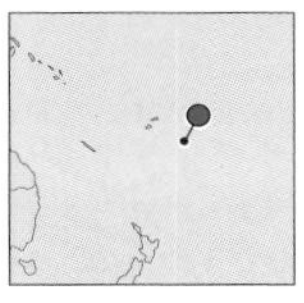

The Kingdom of Tonga, a former British protectorate, became independent in 1970. Situated in the South Pacific Ocean, it contains more than 170 islands, 36 of which are inhabited. Agriculture is the main activity; coconuts, copra, fruits and fish are leading products.

AREA 290 sq mi [750 sq km] **POPULATION** 106,000 **CAPITAL** Nuku'alofa

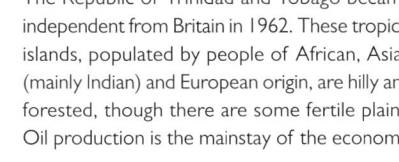

TRINIDAD AND TOBAGO

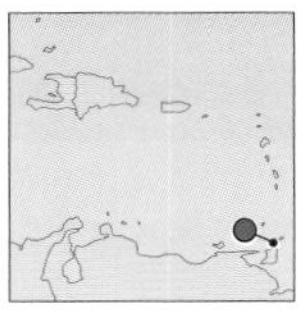

The Republic of Trinidad and Tobago became independent from Britain in 1962. These tropical islands, populated by people of African, Asian (mainly Indian) and European origin, are hilly and forested, though there are some fertile plains. Oil production is the mainstay of the economy.

AREA 1,981 sq mi [5,130 sq km]
POPULATION 1,164,000 **CAPITAL** Port-of-Spain

TUNISIA

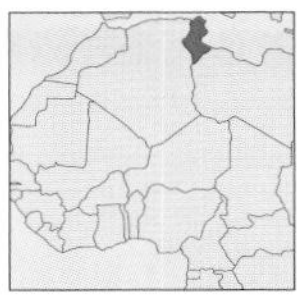

GEOGRAPHY The Republic of Tunisia is the smallest country in North Africa. The mountains in the north are an eastward and comparatively low extension of the Atlas Mountains. To the north and east of the mountains lie fertile plains, especially between Sfax, Tunis and Bizerte. In the south, low-lying regions contain a vast salt pan, called the Chott Djerid, and part of the Sahara Desert.

Northern Tunisia has a Mediterranean climate, with dry, sunny summers, and mild winters with a moderate rainfall. The average yearly rainfall decreases toward the south.

POLITICS & ECONOMY In 1881, France established a protectorate over Tunisia and ruled the country until 1956. The new parliament abolished the monarchy and declared Tunisia to be a republic in 1957, with the nationalist leader, Habib Bourguiba, as president. His government introduced many reforms, including votes for women, but various problems arose, including unemployment among the middle class and fears that Western values introduced by tourists might undermine Muslim values. In 1987, the prime minister Zine el Abidine Ben Ali removed Bourguiba from office and succeeded him as president. He was elected in 1989 and re-elected in 1994 and 1999.

The World Bank classifies Tunisia as a "middle-income" developing country. The main resources and chief exports are phosphates and oil. Most industries are concerned with food processing. Agriculture employs 22% of the people; major crops being barley, dates, grapes, olives and wheat. Fishing is important, as is tourism.

AREA 63,170 sq mi [163,610 sq km] **POPULATION** 9,816,000
CAPITAL (POPULATION) Tunis (1,827,000)
GOVERNMENT Multiparty republic **ETHNIC GROUPS** Arab 98%, Berber 1%, French **LANGUAGES** Arabic (official), French
RELIGIONS Islam 99% **CURRENCY** Dinar = 1,000 millimes

TURKEY

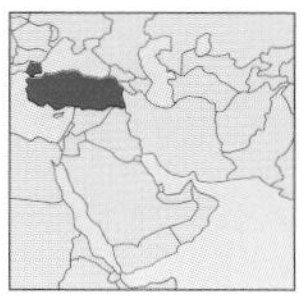

GEOGRAPHY The Republic of Turkey lies in two continents. European Turkey, also called Thrace, lies west of a waterway linking the Mediterranean and Black seas. Most of Asian Turkey consists of plateaux and mountains, which rise to 16,945 ft [5,165 m] at Mount Ararat (Agri Dagi) near the border with Armenia. Earthquakes are common.

Central Turkey has a dry climate, with hot, sunny summers and cold winters. The driest part of the central plateau lies south of the city of Ankara, around Lake Tuz. The west has a Mediterranean climate, but the Black Sea coast has cooler summers.

POLITICS & ECONOMY In AD 330, the Roman empire moved its capital to Byzantium, which it renamed Constantinople. Constantinople became capital of the East Roman (or Byzantine) empire in 395. Muslim Seljuk Turks from central Asia invaded Anatolia in the 11th century. In the 14th century, another group of Turks, the Ottomans, conquered the area. In 1453, the Ottoman Turks took Constantinople, which they called Istanbul.

The Ottoman Turks built up a large empire which finally collapsed during World War I (1914–18). In 1923, Turkey became a republic. Its leader Mustafa Kemal, or Atatürk ("father of the Turks"), launched policies to modernize and secularize the country.

Since the 1940s, Turkey has sought to strengthen its ties with Western powers. It joined NATO (North Atlantic Treaty Organization) in 1951 and it applied to join the European Economic Community in 1987. But Turkey's conflict with Greece, together with its invasion of northern Cyprus in 1974, have led many Europeans to treat Turkey's aspirations with caution. Political instability, military coups, conflict with Kurdish nationalists in eastern Turkey and concern about the country's record on human rights are other problems. Turkey has enjoyed democracy since 1983, though, in 1998, the government banned the Islamist Welfare Party, which it accused of violating secular principles. In 1999, the Muslim Virtue Party (successor to Islamist Welfare Party) lost ground. The largest numbers of parliamentary seats were won by the ruling Democratic Left Party and the far-right National Action Party. However, in the elections in 2002, the moderate Islamic Justice and Development Party (AKP) won 362 of the 500 seats in parliament, while none of the parties in the former ruling coalition won 10% of the vote. In 2003, Turkey opened its airspace to American aircraft during the Iraq war.

The World Bank classifies Turkey as a "lower-middle-income" developing country. Agriculture employs 37% of the people, and barley, cotton, fruits, maize, tobacco and wheat are major crops. Livestock farming is important and wool is a leading product. Turkey produces chromium, but manufacturing is the chief activity. Manufactures include processed farm products and textiles, cars, fertilizers, iron and steel, machinery, metal products and paper products.

AREA 300,946 sq mi [779,450 sq km] **POPULATION** 67,309,000
CAPITAL (POPULATION) Ankara (3,294,000)
GOVERNMENT Multiparty republic
ETHNIC GROUPS Turkish 80%, Kurdish 20%
LANGUAGES Turkish (official), Kurdish
RELIGIONS Islam 99% **CURRENCY** Turkish lira = 100 kurus

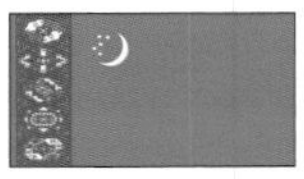

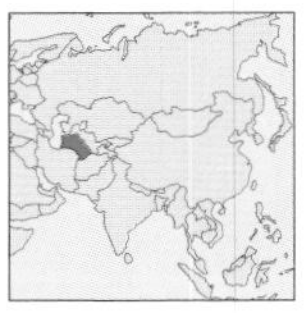

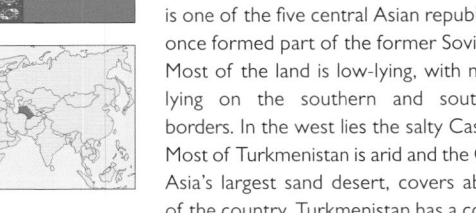

TURKMENISTAN

GEOGRAPHY The Republic of Turkmenistan is one of the five central Asian republics which once formed part of the former Soviet Union. Most of the land is low-lying, with mountains lying on the southern and southwestern borders. In the west lies the salty Caspian Sea. Most of Turkmenistan is arid and the Garagum, Asia's largest sand desert, covers about 80% of the country. Turkmenistan has a continental climate, with average annual rainfall varying from 3 inches [80 mm] in the desert to 12 inches [300 mm] in the mountains. Summer months are hot, but winter temperatures drop well below freezing point.

POLITICS & ECONOMY Just over 1,000 years ago, Turkic people settled in the lands east of the Caspian Sea and the name "Turkmen" comes from this time. Mongol armies conquered the area in the 13th century and Islam was introduced in the 14th century. Russia took over the area in the 1870s and 1880s. After the Russian Revolution of 1917, the area came under Communist rule and, in 1924, it became the Turkmen Soviet Socialist Republic. The Communists strictly controlled all aspects of life and discouraged religion. But they improved such services as education, health, housing and transport.

In the 1980s, when the Soviet Union began to introduce reforms, the Turkmen began to demand more freedom. In 1990, the Turkmen government stated that its laws overruled Soviet laws. In 1991, Turkmenistan became fully independent after the breakup of the Soviet Union. But the country kept ties with Russia through the Commonwealth of Independent States (CIS).

In 1992, Turkmenistan adopted a new constitution, allowing for the setting up of political parties, providing that they were not ethnic or religious in character. But, effectively, Turkmenistan remained a one-party state and, in 1992, Saparmurad Niyazov, the former Communist and now Democratic Party leader, was the only candidate. In 1994, a referendum prolonged Niyazov's term of office to 2002, while, in 1999, the parliament declared him president for life. In 2002, Niyazov survived an attempt on his life.

Faced with many economic problems, Turkmenistan began to look south rather than to the CIS for support. As part of this policy, it joined the Economic Cooperation Organization which had been set up in 1985 by Iran, Pakistan and Turkey. In 1996, the completion of a rail link from Turkmenistan to the Iranian coast was seen as a highly significant step for the future economic development of Central Asia.

Turkmenistan's chief resources are oil and natural gas, but the main activity is agriculture, with cotton, grown on irrigated land, as the main crop. Grain and vegetables are also important. Manufactures include cement, glass, petrochemicals and textiles.

AREA 188,450 SQ MI [488,100 SQ KM] **POPULATION** 4,689,000 **CAPITAL (POPULATION)** ASHKHABAD (536,000) **GOVERNMENT** SINGLE-PARTY REPUBLIC **ETHNIC GROUPS** TURKMEN 77%, RUSSIAN 17%, UZBEK 9%, KAZAKH 2%, TATAR **LANGUAGES** TURKMEN (OFFICIAL), RUSSIAN, UZBEK, KAZAKH **RELIGIONS** ISLAM **CURRENCY** MANAT = 100 TENESI

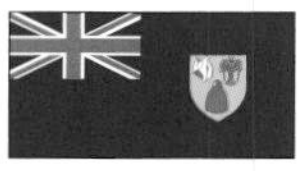

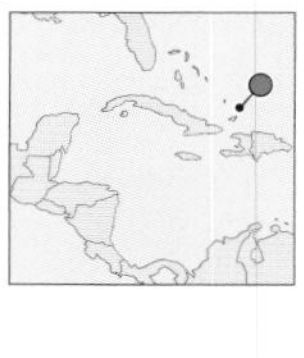

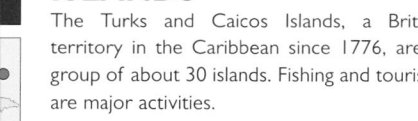

TURKS AND CAICOS ISLANDS

The Turks and Caicos Islands, a British territory in the Caribbean since 1776, are a group of about 30 islands. Fishing and tourism are major activities.

AREA 166 SQ MI [430 SQ KM]
POPULATION 19,000 **CAPITAL** COCKBURN TOWN

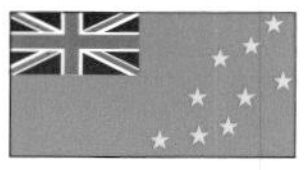

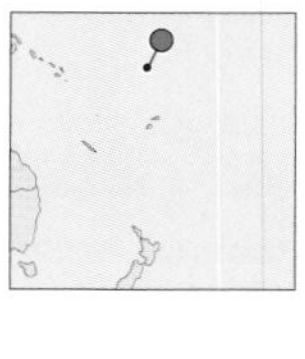

TUVALU

Tuvalu, formerly called the Ellice Islands, was a British territory from the 1890s until it became independent in 1978. It consists of nine low-lying coral atolls in the southern Pacific Ocean. Copra is the chief export.

AREA 9 SQ MI [24 SQ KM] **POPULATION** 11,000
CAPITAL FONGAFALE

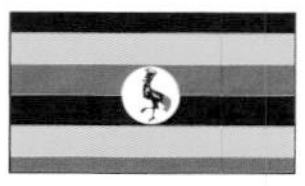

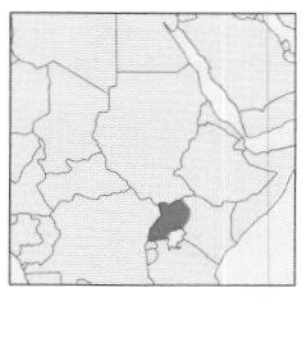

UGANDA

GEOGRAPHY The Republic of Uganda is a landlocked country on the East African plateau. It contains part of Lake Victoria, Africa's largest lake and a source of the River Nile, which occupies a shallow depression in the plateau.

The equator runs through Uganda and the country is warm throughout the year, though the high altitude moderates the temperature. The wettest regions are the lands to the north of Lake Victoria, where Kampala is situated, and the western mountains, especially the high Ruwenzori range.

POLITICS & ECONOMY Little is known of the early history of Uganda. When Europeans first reached the area in the 19th century, many of the people were organized in kingdoms, the most powerful of which was Buganda, the home of the Baganda people. Britain took over the country between 1894 and 1914, and ruled it until independence in 1962.

In 1967, Uganda became a republic and Buganda's Kabaka (king), Sir Edward Mutesa II, was made president. But tensions between the Kabaka and the prime minister, Apollo Milton Obote, led to the dismissal of the Kabaka in 1966. Obote also abolished the traditional kingdoms, including Buganda. Obote was overthrown in 1971 by an army group led by General Idi Amin Dada. Amin ruled as a dictator. He forced most of the Asians who lived in Uganda to leave the country and had many of his opponents killed.

In 1978, a border dispute between Uganda and Tanzania led Tanzanian troops to enter Uganda. With help from Ugandan opponents of Amin, they overthrew Amin's government. In 1980, Obote led his party to victory in national elections. But after charges of fraud, Obote's opponents began guerrilla warfare. A military group overthrew Obote in 1985, though strife continued until 1986, when Yoweri Museveni's National Resistance Movement seized power. In 1993, Museveni restored the traditional kingdoms, including Buganda where a new Kabaka was crowned. Museveni held elections in 1994 but political parties were not allowed. Museveni was elected president in 1996 and 2001. In 2003, the president announced that multiparty democracy would be restored, but he gave no date for the change.

The strife since the 1960s has greatly damaged the economy, but the economy grew during a period of stability in the 1990s. The situation worsened when Uganda intervened militarily in Congo (then Zaïre) in 1998. Agriculture dominates the economy, employing 80% of the people. The chief export is coffee.

AREA 91,073 SQ MI [235,880 SQ KM] **POPULATION** 24,699,000
CAPITAL (POPULATION) KAMPALA (954,000)
GOVERNMENT REPUBLIC IN TRANSITION
ETHNIC GROUPS BAGANDA 17%, KARAMOJONG 12%, BASOGO 8%, ITESO 8%, LANGI 6%, RWANDA 6%, BAGISU 5%, ACHOLI 4%, LUGBARA 4%
LANGUAGES ENGLISH AND SWAHILI (BOTH OFFICIAL), GANDA
RELIGIONS ROMAN CATHOLIC 33%, PROTESTANT 33%, TRADITIONAL BELIEFS 18%, ISLAM 16%
CURRENCY UGANDA SHILLING = 100 CENTS

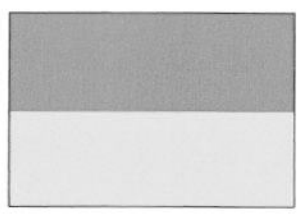

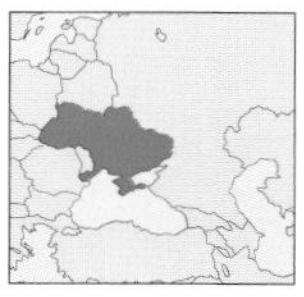

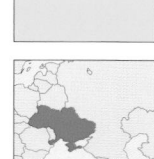

UKRAINE

GEOGRAPHY Ukraine is the second largest country in Europe after Russia. It was formerly part of the Soviet Union, which split apart in 1991. This mostly flat country faces the Black Sea in the south. The Crimean peninsula includes a highland region overlooking Yalta.

Ukraine has warm summers, but the winters are cold, becoming more severe from west to east. In the summer, the east of the country is often warmer than the west. The heaviest rainfall occurs in the summer.

POLITICS & ECONOMY Kiev was the original capital of the early Slavic civilization known as Kievan Rus. In the 17th and 18th centuries, parts of Ukraine came under Polish and Russian rule. But Russia gained most of Ukraine in the late 18th century. In 1918, Ukraine became independent, but in 1922 it became part of the Soviet Union. Millions of people died in the 1930s as a result of Soviet policies, while millions more died during the Nazi occupation (1941–4).

In the 1980s, Ukrainian people demanded more say over their affairs. The country became independent in 1991. Leonid Kuchma, who became president in 1994, came under fire in the early 2000s for maladministration and for his alleged involvement in the murder of a journalist. Conflict between the president and the parliament led to the sacking of prime minister Victor Yushchenko in 2001 and of his successor, Anatoly Kinakh, in 2002.

The World Bank classifies Ukraine as a "lower-middle-income" economy. Agriculture is important. Crops include wheat and sugar beet, which are the major exports, together with barley, maize, potatoes, sunflowers and tobacco. Livestock rearing and fishing are also important industries.

Manufacturing is the chief economic activity. Major manufactures include iron and steel, machinery and vehicles. Ukraine has large coalfields. The country imports oil and natural gas, but it has hydroelectric and nuclear power stations. In 1986, an accident at the Chernobyl (Chornobyl) nuclear power plant caused widespread nuclear radiation. The plant was finally closed in 2001.

AREA 233,100 SQ MI [603,700 SQ KM] **POPULATION** 48,396,000
CAPITAL (POPULATION) KIEV (2,621,000)
GOVERNMENT MULTIPARTY REPUBLIC
ETHNIC GROUPS UKRAINIAN 73%, RUSSIAN 22%, JEWISH 1%, BELARUSSIAN 1%, MOLDOVAN, BULGARIAN, POLISH
LANGUAGES UKRAINIAN (OFFICIAL), RUSSIAN
RELIGIONS MOSTLY UKRAINIAN ORTHODOX
CURRENCY HRYVNIA = 100 KOPIYKAS

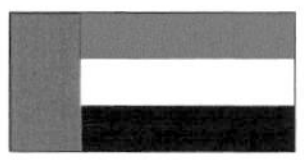

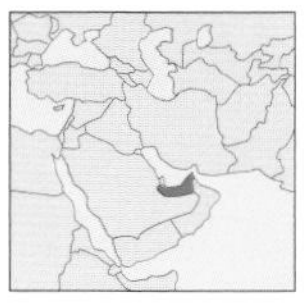

UNITED ARAB EMIRATES

The United Arab Emirates were formed in 1971 when the seven Trucial States of the Gulf (Abu Dhabi, Dubai, Sharjah, Ajman, Umm al Qawayn, Ra's al Khaymah and Al Fujayrah) opted to join together and form an independent country. The economy of this hot and dry country depends on oil production, and oil revenues give the United Arab Emirates one of the highest per capita GNPs in Asia.

AREA 32,278 SQ MI [83,600 SQ KM] **POPULATION** 2,446,000
CAPITAL ABU DHABI

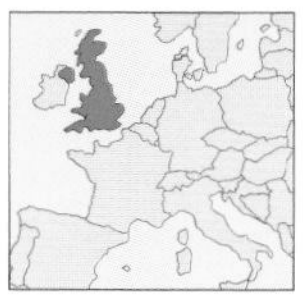

UNITED KINGDOM

GEOGRAPHY The United Kingdom (or UK) is a union of four countries. Three of them – England, Scotland and Wales – make up Great Britain. The fourth country is Northern Ireland. The Isle of Man and the Channel Islands, including Jersey and Guernsey, are not part of the UK. They are self-governing British dependencies.

The land is highly varied. Much of Scotland and Wales is mountainous, and the highest peak is Scotland's Ben Nevis at 4,406 ft [1,343 m]. England has some highland areas, including the Cumbrian Mountains (or Lake District) and the Pennine range in the north. But England also has large areas of fertile lowland. Northern Ireland is also a mixture of lowlands and uplands. It contains the UK's largest lake, Lough Neagh.

The UK has a mild climate, influenced by the warm Gulf Stream which flows across the Atlantic from the Gulf of Mexico, then past the British Isles. Moist winds from the southwest bring rain, but the rainfall decreases from west to east. Winds from the east and north bring cold weather in winter.

POLITICS & ECONOMY In ancient times, Britain was invaded by many peoples, including Iberians, Celts, Romans, Angles, Saxons, Jutes, Norsemen, Danes, and Normans, who arrived in 1066. The evolution of the United Kingdom spanned hundreds of years. The Normans finally overcame Welsh resistance in 1282, when King Edward I annexed Wales and united it with England. Union with Scotland was achieved by the Act of Union of 1707. This created a country known as the United Kingdom of Great Britain.

Ireland came under Norman rule in the 11th century, and much of its later history was concerned with a struggle against English domination. In 1801, Ireland became part of the United Kingdom of Great Britain and Ireland. But in 1921, southern Ireland broke away to become the Irish Free State. Most of the people in the Irish Free State were Roman Catholics. In Northern Ireland, where the majority of the people were Protestants, most people wanted to remain citizens of the United Kingdom. As a result, the country's official name changed to the United Kingdom of Great Britain and Northern Ireland.

The modern history of the UK began in the 18th century when the British empire began to develop, despite the loss in 1783 of its 13 North American colonies which became the core of the modern United States. The other major event occurred in the late 18th century, when the UK became the first country to industrialize its economy.

The British empire broke up after World War II (1939–45), though the UK still administers many small, mainly island, territories around the world. The empire was transformed into the Commonwealth of Nations, a free association of independent countries which numbered 54 in 2001.

The UK has retained an important world role. For example, in 2001, it played a prominent role in creating a broad alliance to counter international terrorism following the attacks on the United

States. It was also a prominent member of the coalition force which invaded Iraq in 2003. However, the UK has recognized that its economic future lies within Europe. It became a member of the European Economic Community (now the European Union) in 1973. In the early 21st century, most people accepted the importance of the EU to the UK's economic future. But some feared a loss of British identity should the EU ever evolve into a political federation.

The UK is a major industrial and trading nation. It lacks natural resources apart from coal, iron ore, oil and natural gas, and has to import most of the materials it needs for its industries. The UK also has to import food, because it produces only about two-thirds of the food it needs. In the first half of the 20th century, Britain was a major exporter of cars, ships, steel and textiles. But many industries have suffered from competition from other countries, with lower labor costs. Today, industries have to use high-technology in order to compete on the world market.

The UK is one of the world's most urbanized countries, and agriculture employs only 1% of the people. Production is high because of the use of scientific methods and modern machinery. However, in the early 21st century, especially following the outbreak of foot-and-mouth disease in 2001, questions were raised about the future of rural industries. Major crops include barley, potatoes, sugar beet and wheat. Sheep are the leading livestock, but beef and dairy cattle, pigs and poultry are also important. Fishing is another major activity and the UK is one of the largest fishing countries in the EU. Important catches include cod, haddock, plaice and mackerel.

Service industries play a major part in the UK's economy. Financial and insurance services bring in much-needed foreign exchange, while tourism has become a major earner.

AREA 94,202 SQ MI [243,368 SQ KM] **POPULATION** 59,778,000
CAPITAL (POPULATION) LONDON (8,089,000)
GOVERNMENT CONSTITUTIONAL MONARCHY
ETHNIC GROUPS WHITE 94%, ASIAN INDIAN 1%, PAKISTANI 1%, WEST INDIAN 1%
LANGUAGES ENGLISH (OFFICIAL), WELSH, GAELIC
RELIGIONS ANGLICAN 57%, ROMAN CATHOLIC 13%, PRESBYTERIAN 7%, METHODIST 4%, BAPTIST 1%, ISLAM 1%, JUDAISM, HINDUISM, SIKHISM
CURRENCY POUND STERLING = 100 PENCE

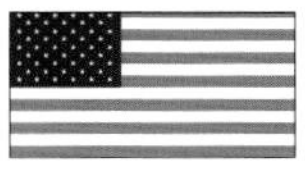
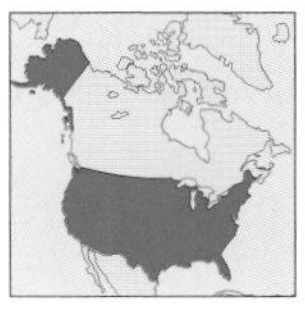

UNITED STATES OF AMERICA

GEOGRAPHY The United States of America is the world's fourth largest country in area and the third largest in population. It contains 50 states, 48 of which lie between Canada and Mexico, plus Alaska in northwestern North America, and Hawaii, a group of volcanic islands in the North Pacific Ocean. Densely populated coastal plains lie to the east and south of the Appalachian Mountains. The central lowlands drained by the Mississippi–Missouri rivers stretch from the Appalachians to the Rocky Mountains in the west. The Pacific region contains fertile valleys, separated by mountain ranges.

The climate varies greatly, ranging from the Arctic cold of Alaska to the intense heat of Death Valley, a bleak desert in California. Of the 48 states between Canada and Mexico, winters are cold and snowy in the north, but mild in the south, a region which is often called the "Sun Belt."

POLITICS & ECONOMY The first people in North America, the ancestors of the Native Americans (or American Indians) arrived perhaps 40,000 years ago from Asia. Although Vikings probably reached North America 1,000 years ago, European exploration proper did not begin until the late 15th century.

The first Europeans to settle in large numbers were the British, who founded settlements on the eastern coast in the early 17th century. British rule ended in the War of ndependence (1775–83). The country expanded in 1803 when a vast territory in the south and west was acquired through the Louisiana Purchase, while the border with Mexico was fixed in the mid-19th century. The Civil War (1861–5) ended slavery and the serious threat that the nation might split into two parts. In the late 19th century, the West was opened up, while immigrants flooded in from Europe and elsewhere.

During the late 19th and early 20th centuries, industrialization led to the United States becoming the world's leading economic superpower and a pioneer in science and technology. It took on the mantle of the champion of Western democracy and, following the breakup of the former Soviet Union, it became the world's only superpower. But the attacks on the country on September 11, 2001, revealed its vulnerability to terrorists and rogue states. The response was vigorous. In 2001, it attacked the Taliban government in Afghanistan, which was protecting al Qaida terrorists, and, in 2003, it led a coalition force to overthrow the regime in Iraq and remove its weapons of mass destruction.

The United States has the world's largest economy in terms of the total value of its production. Although agriculture employs only about 2% of the people, farming is highly mechanized and scientific, and the United States leads the world in farm production. Major products include beef and dairy cattle, together with such crops as cotton, fruits, groundnuts, maize, potatoes, soybeans, tobacco and wheat.

The country's natural resources include oil, natural gas and coal. There are also a wide range of metal ores which are used in manufacturing industries, together with timber, especially from the forests of the Pacific northwest. Manufacturing is the single most important activity, employing about 14% of the population. Major products include vehicles, food products, chemicals, machinery, printed goods, metal products and scientific instruments. California is now the leading manufacturing state. Many southern states, petroleum rich and climatically favored, have also become highly prosperous in recent years.

AREA 3,618,765 SQ MI [9,372,610 SQ KM] **POPULATION** 280,562,000
CAPITAL (POPULATION) WASHINGTON, D.C. (4,466,000)
GOVERNMENT FEDERAL REPUBLIC
ETHNIC GROUPS WHITE 70%, HISPANIC 13%, AFRICAN AMERICAN 12.7%, ASIAN 4%
LANGUAGES ENGLISH (OFFICIAL), SPANISH, MORE THAN 30 OTHERS
RELIGIONS PROTESTANT 56%, ROMAN CATHOLIC 28%, ISLAM 2%, JUDAISM 2% **CURRENCY** US DOLLAR = 100 CENTS

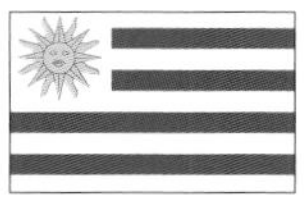
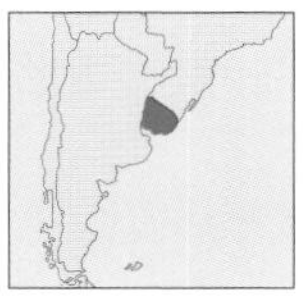

URUGUAY

GEOGRAPHY Uruguay is South America's second smallest independent country after Suriname. The land consists mainly of flat plains and hills. The River Uruguay, which forms the country's western border, flows into the Río de la Plata, a large estuary which leads into the South Atlantic Ocean.

Uruguay has a mild climate, with rain in every month, though droughts sometimes occur. Summers are pleasantly warm, especially near the coast. The weather remains relatively mild throughout the winter.

POLITICS & ECONOMY In 1726, Spanish settlers founded Montevideo in order to halt the Portuguese gaining influence in the area. By the late 18th century, Spaniards had settled in most of the country. Uruguay became part of a colony called the Viceroyalty of La Plata, which also included Argentina, Paraguay, and parts of Bolivia, Brazil and Chile. In 1820 Brazil annexed Uruguay, ending Spanish rule. In 1825, Uruguayans, supported by Argentina, began a struggle for independence. Finally, in 1828, Brazil and Argentina recognized Uruguay as an independent republic. Social and economic developments were slow in the 19th century, but, from 1903, Uruguay became stable and democratic.

From the 1950s, economic problems caused unrest. Terrorist groups, notably the Tupumaros, carried out murders and kidnappings. The army crushed the Tupumaros in 1972, but the army took over the government in 1973. Military rule continued until 1984 when elections were held. In the early 21st century, Uruguay faced many economic problems, many of which were the result of the economic crisis in its neighbor, Argentina, and its imposition of banking controls.

The World Bank classifies Uruguay as an "upper-middle-income" developing country. Agriculture employs only 4% of the people, but farm products, notably hides and leather goods, beef and wool, are the leading exports, while the leading manufacturing industries process farm products. The main crops include maize, potatoes, wheat and sugar beet. Uruguay depends largely on hydro-electric power for energy and exports electricity to Argentina.

AREA 68,498 SQ MI [177,410 SQ KM] **POPULATION** 3,387,000
CAPITAL (POPULATION) MONTEVIDEO (1,379,000)
GOVERNMENT MULTIPARTY REPUBLIC
ETHNIC GROUPS WHITE 88%, MESTIZO 8%, MULATTO OR BLACK 4%
LANGUAGES SPANISH (OFFICIAL)
RELIGIONS ROMAN CATHOLIC 66%, PROTESTANT 2%, JUDAISM 1%
CURRENCY URUGUAY PESO = 100 CENTÉSIMOS

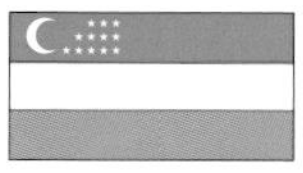
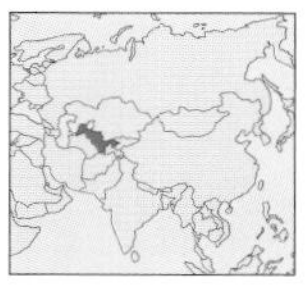

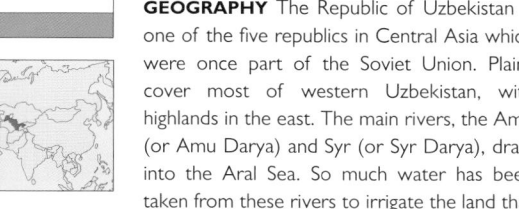

UZBEKISTAN

GEOGRAPHY The Republic of Uzbekistan is one of the five republics in Central Asia which were once part of the Soviet Union. Plains cover most of western Uzbekistan, with highlands in the east. The main rivers, the Amu (or Amu Darya) and Syr (or Syr Darya), drain into the Aral Sea. So much water has been taken from these rivers to irrigate the land that the Aral Sea shrank from 25,830 sq mi [66,900 sq km] in 1960 to 12,989 sq mi [33,642 sq km] in 1993. The dried-up lake area has become desert, like much of the rest of the country.

Uzbekistan has a continental climate. The winters are cold, but the temperatures soar in the summer months. The west is extremely arid, with an average annual rainfall of about 8 inches [200 mm].

POLITICS & ECONOMY Russia took the area in the 19th century. After the Russian Revolution of 1917, the Communists took over and, in 1924, they set up the Uzbek Soviet Socialist Republic. Under Communism, all aspects of Uzbek life were controlled and religious worship was discouraged. But education, health, housing and transport were improved. In the late 1980s, the people demanded more freedom and, in 1990, the government stated that its laws overruled those of the Soviet Union. Uzbekistan became independent in 1991 when the Soviet Union broke up, but it retained links with Russia through the Commonwealth of Independent States. Islam Karimov, leader of the People's Democratic Party (formerly the Communist Party), was elected president in December 1991. In 1992–3, many opposition leaders were arrested because the government said that they threatened national stability. In 1994–5, the PDP was victorious in national elections and, in 1995, a referendum extended Karimov's term in office until 2000, when he was again re-elected. In 2001, Karimov declared his support for the United States in its campaign against terrorist bases in Afghanistan.

The World Bank classifies Uzbekistan as a "lower-middle-income" developing country and the government still controls most economic activity. The country produces coal, copper, gold, oil and natural gas.

AREA 172,740 SQ MI [447,400 SQ KM] **POPULATION** 25,563,000
CAPITAL (POPULATION) TASHKENT (2,118,000)
GOVERNMENT SOCIALIST REPUBLIC **ETHNIC GROUPS** UZBEK 80%, RUSSIAN 5%, TAJIK 5%, KAZAKH 3%, TATAR 2%, KARA-KALPAK 2%
LANGUAGES UZBEK (OFFICIAL), RUSSIAN **RELIGIONS** ISLAM 88%, EASTERN ORTHODOX 9% **CURRENCY** SOM = 100 TYIYN

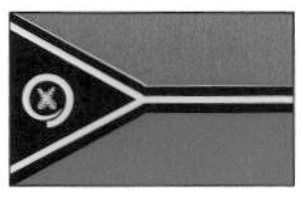
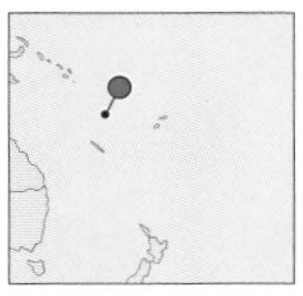

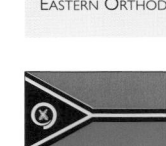

VANUATU

The Republic of Vanuatu, formerly the Anglo-French Condominium of the New Hebrides, became independent in 1980. It consists of a chain of 80 islands in the South Pacific Ocean. Its economy is based on agriculture and it exports copra, beef and veal, timber and cocoa.

AREA 4,707 SQ MI [12,190 SQ KM]
POPULATION 196,000 **CAPITAL** PORT-VILA

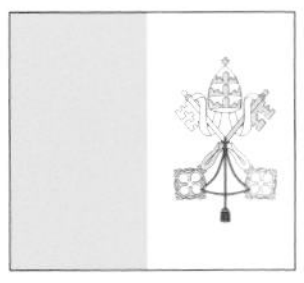
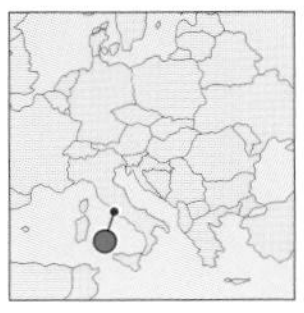

VATICAN CITY

Vatican City State, the world's smallest independent nation, is an enclave on the west bank of the River Tiber in Rome. It forms an independent base for the Holy See, the governing body of the Roman Catholic Church.

AREA 0.17 SQ MI [0.44 SQ KM]
POPULATION 1,000

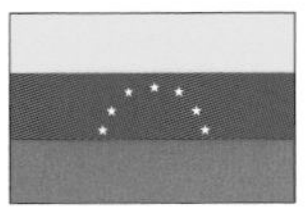
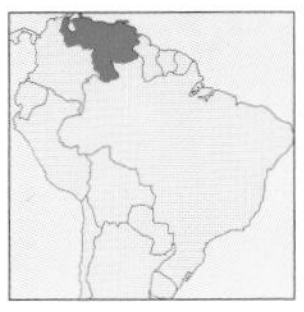

VENEZUELA

GEOGRAPHY The Bolivarian Republic of Venezuela, in northern South America, contains the Maracaibo lowlands around the oil-rich Lake Maracaibo in the west. Andean ranges enclose the lowlands and extend across most of northern Venezuela. The Orinoco river basin, containing tropical grasslands called *llanos*, lies between the northern highlands and the Guiana Highlands in the southeast. The Orinoco is Venezuela's longest river.

Venezuela has a tropical climate. Temperatures are high

throughout the year on the lowlands, though the mountains are much cooler. The rainfall is heaviest in the mountains. But much of the country has a marked dry season between December and April.

POLITICS & ECONOMY In the early 19th century, Venezuelans, such as Simón Bolívar and Francisco de Miranda, began a struggle against Spanish rule. Venezuela declared its independence in 1811. But it only became truly independent in 1821, when the Spanish were defeated in a battle near Valencia.

The development of Venezuela in the 19th and the first half of the 20th centuries was marred by instability, violence and periods of harsh dictatorial rule. But Venezuela has had elected governments since 1958. The country has greatly benefited from its oil resources which were first exploited in 1917. In 1960, Venezuela helped to form OPEC (the Organization of Petroleum Exporting Countries) and, in 1976, the government of Venezuela took control of the entire oil industry. In 1999, Hugo Chavez, who had staged an unsuccessful coup in 1992, was elected president. Chavez survived an attempted coup in April 2002 and a crippling general strike staged by his opponents between December 2002 and February 2003.

The World Bank classifies Venezuela as an "upper-middle-income" developing country. Oil accounts for 80% of the exports. Other exports include bauxite and aluminum, iron ore and farm products. Agriculture employs 8% of people and cattle ranching is important; dairy cattle and poultry are also raised. Major crops include bananas, cassava, citrus fruits, coffee and rice. The chief industry is petroleum refining. Other manufactures include aluminum, cement, processed food, steel and textiles.

AREA 352,143 sq mi [912,050 sq km] **POPULATION** 24,288,000
CAPITAL (POPULATION) Caracas (1,975,000)
GOVERNMENT Federal republic **ETHNIC GROUPS** Mestizo 67%, White 21%, Black 10%, Amerindian 2% **LANGUAGES** Spanish (official), Goajiro **RELIGIONS** Roman Catholic 96%
CURRENCY Bolívar = 100 céntimos

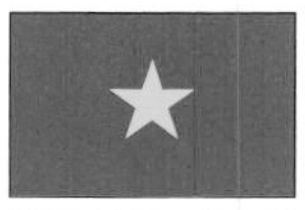
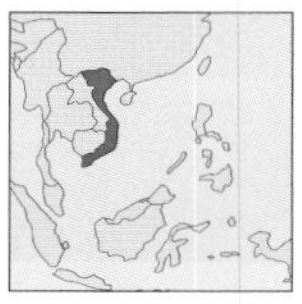

VIETNAM

GEOGRAPHY The Socialist Republic of Vietnam occupies an S-shaped strip of land facing the South China Sea in Southeast Asia. The coastal plains include two densely populated, fertile delta regions: the Red (Hong) delta facing the Gulf of Tonkin in the north, and the Mekong delta in the south.

Vietnam has a tropical climate, though the driest months of January to March are a little cooler than the wet, hot summer months, when monsoon winds blow from the south-west. Typhoons (cyclones) sometimes hit the coast, causing much damage.

POLITICS & ECONOMY China dominated Vietnam for a thousand years before AD 939, when a Vietnamese state was founded. The French took over the area between the 1850s and 1880s. They ruled Vietnam as part of French Indochina, which also included Cambodia and Laos.

Japan conquered Vietnam during World War II (1939–45). In 1946, war broke out between a nationalist group, called the Vietminh, and the French colonial government. France withdrew in 1954 and Vietnam was divided into a Communist North Vietnam, led by the Vietminh leader, Ho Chi Minh, and a non-Communist South.

A force called the Viet Cong rebelled against South Vietnam's government in 1957 and a war began, which gradually increased in intensity. The United States aided the South, but after it withdrew in 1975, South Vietnam surrendered. In 1976, the united Vietnam became a Socialist Republic.

Vietnamese troops intervened in Cambodia in 1978 to defeat the Communist Khmer Rouge government, but it withdrew its troops in 1989. In the 1990s, Vietnam began to introduce reforms. In 1995, the United States opened an embassy in Hanoi and, in 2000, a major trade pact was agreed by the countries.

The World Bank classifies Vietnam as a "low-income" developing country and agriculture employs 67% of the population. The main food crop is rice. The country also produces chromium, oil (which was discovered off the south coast in 1986), phosphates and tin.

AREA 128,065 sq mi [331,689 sq km] **POPULATION** 81,098,000
CAPITAL (POPULATION) Hanoi (3,056,000)
GOVERNMENT Socialist republic **ETHNIC GROUPS** Vietnamese 87%, Tho (Tay), Chinese (Hoa), Tai, Khmer, Muong, Nung
LANGUAGES Vietnamese (official), Chinese
RELIGIONS Buddhism 55%, Roman Catholic 7%
CURRENCY Dong = 10 hao = 100 xu

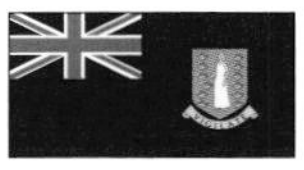
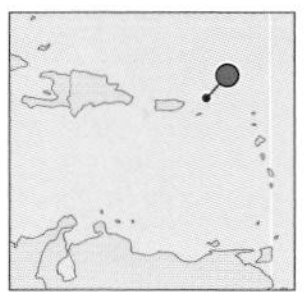

VIRGIN ISLANDS, BRITISH

The British Virgin Islands, the most northerly of the Lesser Antilles, are a British overseas territory, with a substantial measure of self-government.

AREA 59 sq mi [153 sq km]
POPULATION 21,000 **CAPITAL** Road Town

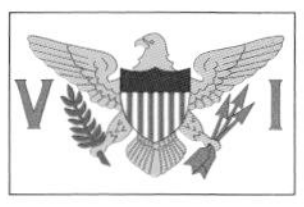

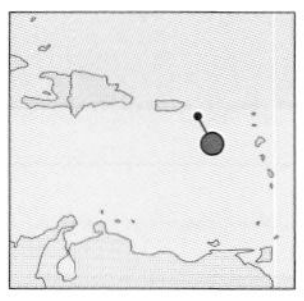

VIRGIN ISLANDS, US

The Virgin Islands of the United States, a group of three islands and 65 small islets, are a self-governing US territory. Purchased from Denmark in 1917, its residents are US citizens and they elect a non-voting delegate to the US House of Representatives.

AREA 130 sq mi [340 sq km]
POPULATION 123,000 **CAPITAL** Charlotte Amalie

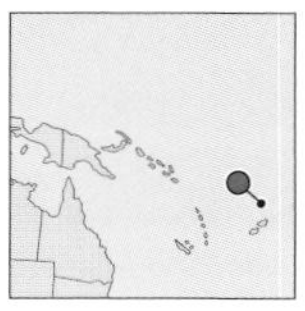

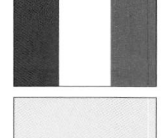

WALLIS AND FUTUNA

Wallis and Futuna, in the South Pacific Ocean, is the smallest and the poorest of France's overseas territories. French aid remains vital to an economy based on subsistence agriculture.

AREA 77 sq mi [200 sq km]
POPULATION 16,000 **CAPITAL** Mata-Utu

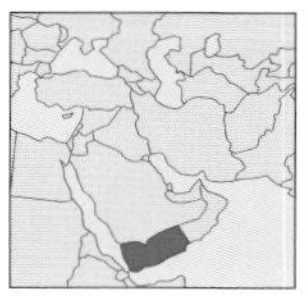

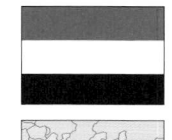

YEMEN

GEOGRAPHY The Republic of Yemen faces the Red Sea and the Gulf of Aden in the southwestern corner of the Arabian peninsula. Behind the narrow coastal plain along the Red Sea, the land rises to a mountain region called High Yemen. The climate ranges from hot and often humid conditions on the coast to the cooler highlands. Most of the country is arid. The south coasts are particularly hot and humid.

POLITICS & ECONOMY After World War I, northern Yemen, which had been ruled by Turkey, began to evolve into a separate state from the south, where Britain was in control. Britain withdrew in 1967 and a left-wing government took power in the south. In North Yemen, the monarchy was abolished in 1962 and the country became a republic.

Clashes occurred between the traditionalist Yemen Arab Republic in the north and the formerly British Marxist People's Democratic Republic of Yemen but, in 1990, the two Yemens merged to form a single country. Further conflict occurred in 1994, when southern secessionist forces were defeated. In 1998 and 1999, militants in the Aden-Abyan Islamic army sought to destabilize the country. In 2000, suicide bombers, thought to be part of the al Qaida network, steered a craft into a US destroyer in Aden harbor, killing 17 sailors, while, in 2002, three American missionaries were shot in a hospital in the south.

The World Bank classifies Yemen as a "low-income" developing country. Agriculture employs up to 63% of the people. Herders raise sheep and other animals, while farmers grow such crops as barley, fruits, wheat and vegetables in highland valleys and around oases. Cash crops include coffee and cotton.

Imported oil is refined at Aden and petroleum extraction began in the northwest in the 1980s. Handicrafts, leather goods and textiles are manufactured. Remittances from Yemenis abroad are a major source of revenue.

AREA 203,849 sq mi [527,970 sq km] **POPULATION** 18,701,000
CAPITAL (POPULATION) Sana' (972,000) **GOVERNMENT** Multiparty republic **ETHNIC GROUPS** Arab 96%, Somali 1% **LANGUAGES** Arabic (official) **RELIGIONS** Islam **CURRENCY** Rial = 100 fils

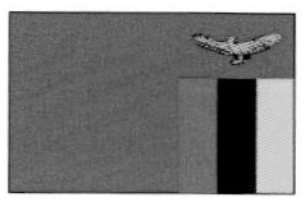
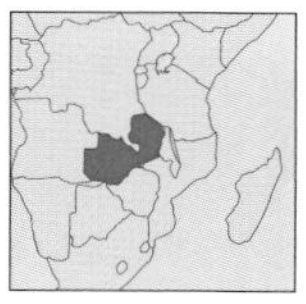

ZAMBIA

GEOGRAPHY The Republic of Zambia is a landlocked country in southern Africa. Zambia lies on the plateau that makes up most of southern Africa. Much of the land is between 2,950 ft and 4,920 ft [900 m to 1,500 m] above sea level. The Muchinga Mountains in the northeast rise above this flat land. Lakes include Bangweulu, which is entirely within Zambia, together with parts of lakes Mweru and Tanganyika in the north. Zambia lies in the tropics, but temperatures are moderated by the altitude.

POLITICS & ECONOMY European contact with Zambia began in the 19th century, when the explorer David Livingstone crossed the River Zambezi. In the 1890s, the British South Africa Company, set up by Cecil Rhodes (1853–1902), the British financier and statesman, made treaties with local chiefs and gradually took over the area. In 1911, the Company named the area Northern Rhodesia. In 1924, Britain took over the government of the country.

In 1953, Britain formed a federation of Northern Rhodesia, Southern Rhodesia (now Zimbabwe) and Nyasaland (now Malawi). Because of African opposition, the federation was dissolved in 1963 and Northern Rhodesia became independent as Zambia in 1964. Kenneth Kaunda became president and one-party rule was introduced in 1972. However, a new constitution was adopted in 1990 and, in 1991, Kaunda's party was defeated and Frederick Chiluba became president. Chiluba was re-elected in 1996. Chiluba stood down in 2001 and his party's candidate, Levy Mwanawasa, was elected president.

Copper is the main resource, accounting for 80% of Zambia's exports in 1997. Zambia also produces cobalt, lead, zinc and gemstones. Agriculture employs 69% of workers, as compared with 4% in industry and mining. Major food crops include cassava, fruits and vegetables, maize, millet and sorghum, while cash crops include coffee, sugarcane and tobacco. The production of copper products in the leading industrial activity.

AREA 290,586 sq mi [752,614 sq km] **POPULATION** 9,959,000
CAPITAL (POPULATION) Lusaka (982,000)
GOVERNMENT Multiparty republic **ETHNIC GROUPS** Bemba 36%, Maravi (Nyanja) 18%, Tonga 15% **LANGUAGES** English (official), Bemba, Nyanja, and about 70 others **RELIGIONS** Christianity 68%, Islam, Hinduism **CURRENCY** Kwacha = 100 ngwee

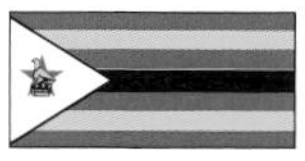
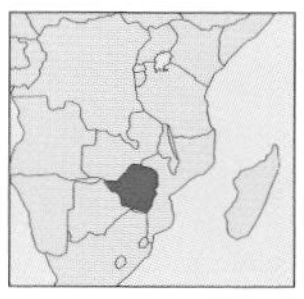

ZIMBABWE

GEOGRAPHY The Republic of Zimbabwe is a landlocked country in southern Africa. Most of the country lies on a high plateau between the Zambezi and Limpopo rivers between 2,950 ft and 4,920 ft [900 m to 1,500 m] above sea level. From October to March, the weather is hot and wet, but in the winter, daily temperatures can vary greatly.

POLITICS & ECONOMY The Shona people became dominant in the region about 1,000 years ago. The British South Africa Company, under the statesman Cecil Rhodes (1853–1902), occupied the area in the 1890s, after obtaining mineral rights from local chiefs. The area was named Rhodesia and later Southern Rhodesia. It became a self-governing British colony in 1923. Between 1953 and 1963, Southern and Northern Rhodesia (now Zambia) were joined to Nyasaland (Malawi) in the Central African Federation.

In 1965, the European government of Southern Rhodesia (then called Rhodesia) declared their country independent but Britain refused to accept this. Finally, after a civil war, the country became legally independent in 1980, though rivalries between the Shona and Ndebele people threatened stability. Order was restored when the Shona prime minister, Robert Mugabe, brought his Ndebele rivals into his government. In 1987, Mugabe became the country's executive president and, in 1991, the government renounced its Marxist ideology. Mugabe was re-elected president in 1990 and 1996. During the late 1990s, Mugabe threatened to seize white-owned farms without paying compensation to the owners. Despite international pressure, landless "war veterans" began to occupy white farms. The situation worsened in the early 2000s, resulting in violence and murder. In 2002, Mugabe was re-elected president amid accusations of electoral irregularities. The Commonwealth suspended Zimbabwe's membership for 12 months. However, in 2003, violence against Mugabe's opponents appeared to be increasing.

The World Bank classifies Zimbabwe as a "low-income" developing country. The country has valuable mineral resources and mining accounts for a fifth of the country's exports. Agriculture employs 27% of working people. Maize is the chief food crop, while cash crops include cotton, sugar and tobacco. Cattle ranching is another important activity.

AREA 150,873 sq mi [390,579 sq km] **POPULATION** 11,377,000
CAPITAL (POPULATION) Harare (1,189,000)
GOVERNMENT Multiparty republic **ETHNIC GROUPS** Shona 71%, Ndebele 16%, other Bantu-speaking Africans 11%, White 1%, Asian 1% **LANGUAGES** English (official), Shona, Ndebele
RELIGIONS Christianity 45%, traditional beliefs 40%
CURRENCY Zimbabwe dollar = 100 cents

INTRODUCTION TO WORLD GEOGRAPHY

The Universe

About 13.7 billion years ago, time and space began with the most colossal explosion in cosmic history: the so-called "Big Bang" that is believed to have initiated the universe. According to current theory, in the first millionth of a second of its existence it expanded from a dimensionless point of infinite mass and density into a fireball about 19 billion miles across; and it has been expanding ever since.

It took almost a million years for the primal fireball to cool enough for atoms to form. They were mostly hydrogen, still the most abundant material in the universe. But the new matter was not evenly distributed around the young universe, and a few billion years later atoms in relatively dense regions began to cling together under the influence of gravity, forming distinct masses of gas separated by vast expanses of empty space. To begin with, these first proto-galaxies were dark places: the universe had cooled. But gravitational attraction continued, condensing matter into coherent lumps inside the galactic gas clouds. About 3 billion years later, some of these masses had contracted so much that internal pressure produced the high temperatures necessary to bring about nuclear fusion: the first stars were born.

There were several generations of stars, each feeding on the wreckage of its extinct predecessors as well as the original galactic gas swirls. With each new generation, progressively larger atoms were forged in stellar furnaces and the galaxy's range of elements, once restricted to hydrogen, grew larger. About 9 billion years after the Big Bang, a star formed on the outskirts of our galaxy with enough matter left over to create a retinue of planets. Nearly 5 billion years after that human beings evolved.

The Sun is one of more than 100 billion stars in the home galaxy alone. Our galaxy, in turn, forms part of a local group of approximately 30 similar structures, some much larger than our own; there are at least 100 billion other galaxies in the universe as a whole. The most distant ever observed, a highly energetic galactic core known only as quasar PC 1247 +3406, lies about 12 billion light-years away.

Life of a Star

For most of its existence, a star produces energy by the nuclear fusion of hydrogen into helium at its core. The duration of this hydrogen-burning period – known as the main sequence – depends on the star's mass; the greater the mass, the higher the core temperatures and the sooner the star's supply of hydrogen is exhausted. Dim, dwarf stars consume their hydrogen slowly, eking it out over 1,000 billion years or more. The Sun, like other stars of its mass, should spend about 10 billion years on the main sequence; since it was formed less than 5 billion years ago, it still has half its life left.

Once all a star's core hydrogen has been fused into helium, nuclear activity moves outward into layers of unconsumed hydrogen. For a time, energy production sharply increases: the star grows hotter and expands enormously, turning into a so-called red giant. Its energy output will increase a thousandfold, and it will swell to a hundred times its present diameter.

After a few hundred million years, helium in the core will become sufficiently compressed to initiate a new cycle of nuclear fusion: from helium to carbon. The star will contract somewhat, before beginning its last expansion, in the Sun's case engulfing the Earth and perhaps Mars. In this bloated condition, the Sun's outer layers will break off into space, leaving a tiny inner core, mainly of carbon, that shrinks progressively under the force of its own gravity: dwarf stars can attain a density more than 10,000 times that of normal matter, with crushing surface gravities to match. Gradually, the nuclear fires will die down, and the Sun will reach its terminal stage: a black dwarf, emitting insignificant amounts of energy.

However, stars more massive than the Sun may undergo another transformation. The additional mass allows gravitational collapse to continue indefinitely: eventually, all the star's remaining matter shrinks to a point, and its density approaches infinity – a state that will not permit even subatomic structures to survive.

The star has become a black hole: an anomalous "singularity" in the fabric of space and time. Although vast coruscations of radiation will be emitted by any matter falling into its grasp, the singularity itself has an escape velocity that exceeds the speed of light, and nothing can ever be released from it. Within the boundaries of the black hole, the laws of physics are suspended, but no physicist can ever observe the extraordinary events that may occur.

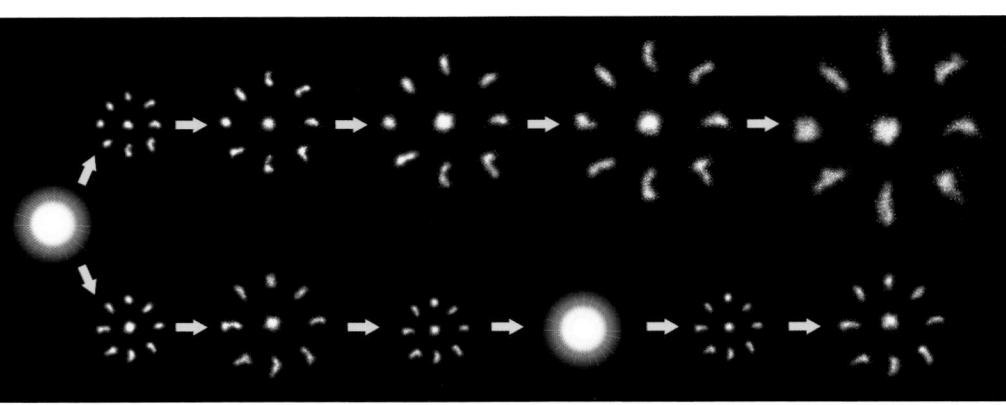

The End of the Universe

The likely fate of the universe is disputed. One theory (*top left*) dictates that the expansion begun at the time of the Big Bang will continue "indefinitely," with aging galaxies moving further and further apart in an immense, dark graveyard. Alternatively, gravity may overcome the expansion (*bottom left*). Galaxies will fall back together until everything is again concentrated at a single point, followed by a new Big Bang and a new expansion, in an endlessly repeated cycle.

The first theory is supported by the amount of visible matter in the universe; the second assumes there is enough dark material to bring about the gravitational collapse.

Galactic Structures

Many of the universe's 100 billion galaxies show clear structural patterns, originally classified by the American astronomer Edwin Hubble in 1925. Spiral galaxies like our own (*top row*) have a central, almost spherical bulge and a surrounding disk composed of spiral arms. Barred spirals (*bottom row*) have a central bar of stars across the nucleus, with spiral arms trailing from the ends of the bar. Elliptical galaxies (*far left*) have a uniform appearance, ranging from a flattened disk to a near sphere. So-called SO galaxies (*left row, right*) have a central bulge, but no spiral arms. Most galaxies, however, have no obvious structure at all.

Galaxies also vary enormously in size, from dwarfs only 2,000 light-years across to great assemblies of stars 80 or more times larger.

The Home Galaxy

The Sun and its planets are located in one of the spiral arms, a little less than 28,000 light-years from the galactic center and orbiting around it in a period of 200 million years. The center is invisible from the Earth, masked by vast, light-absorbing clouds of interstellar dust. The Galaxy is probably around 12 billion years old and, like other spiral galaxies, has three distinct regions. The central bulge is about 30,000 light-years in diameter. The disk in which the Sun is located is not much more than 1,000 light-years thick, but 100,000 light-years from end to end. Around the Galaxy is the halo, a spherical zone 300,000 light-years across, studded with globular star clusters and sprinkled with individual suns.

Globular clusters

Bulge

Disk

Solar System

Star Charts

Star charts are drawn as projections of a vast, hollow sphere with the observer in the middle. Each circle below represents slightly more than one hemisphere, centered on the north and south celestial poles respectively – projections of the Earth's poles in the heavens. At the present era, the north pole is marked by the star Polaris; the south pole has no such convenient reference point.

Astronomical coordinates are normally given in terms of "Right Ascension" for longitude and "Declination" for latitude or altitude. Since the stars appear to rotate around the Earth once every 24 hours, Right Ascension is measured eastward – counterclockwise – in hours and minutes and is marked around the edge of the map. One hour is equivalent to 15 angular degrees; zero on the scale is the point at which

the Sun crosses the celestial equator at the spring equinox, known to astronomers as the First Point in Aries. Unlike the Sun, stars always rise and set at the same point on the horizon. Declination measures (in degrees) a star's angular distance above or below the celestial equator and is marked on the vertical line.

To use the maps, first choose the one for your hemisphere and hold it with the month at the bottom. The stars in the lower part of the map are then due south (or north, in the southern hemisphere) at about 1 AM local time, not allowing for summer or daylight saving time. Their exact position above the horizon depends on your latitude. The closer to the Equator you live, the higher in the sky these stars will appear. Some additional stars from the map for the other hemisphere will be visible in the lower sky.

Stars near the top of the map will be below the opposite horizon at this date and time but will be visible at other times of the night and year. The sky appears to move counterclockwise around the celestial pole during the course of the day (clockwise in the southern hemisphere), so the same stars will be visible at 11 PM a month earlier.

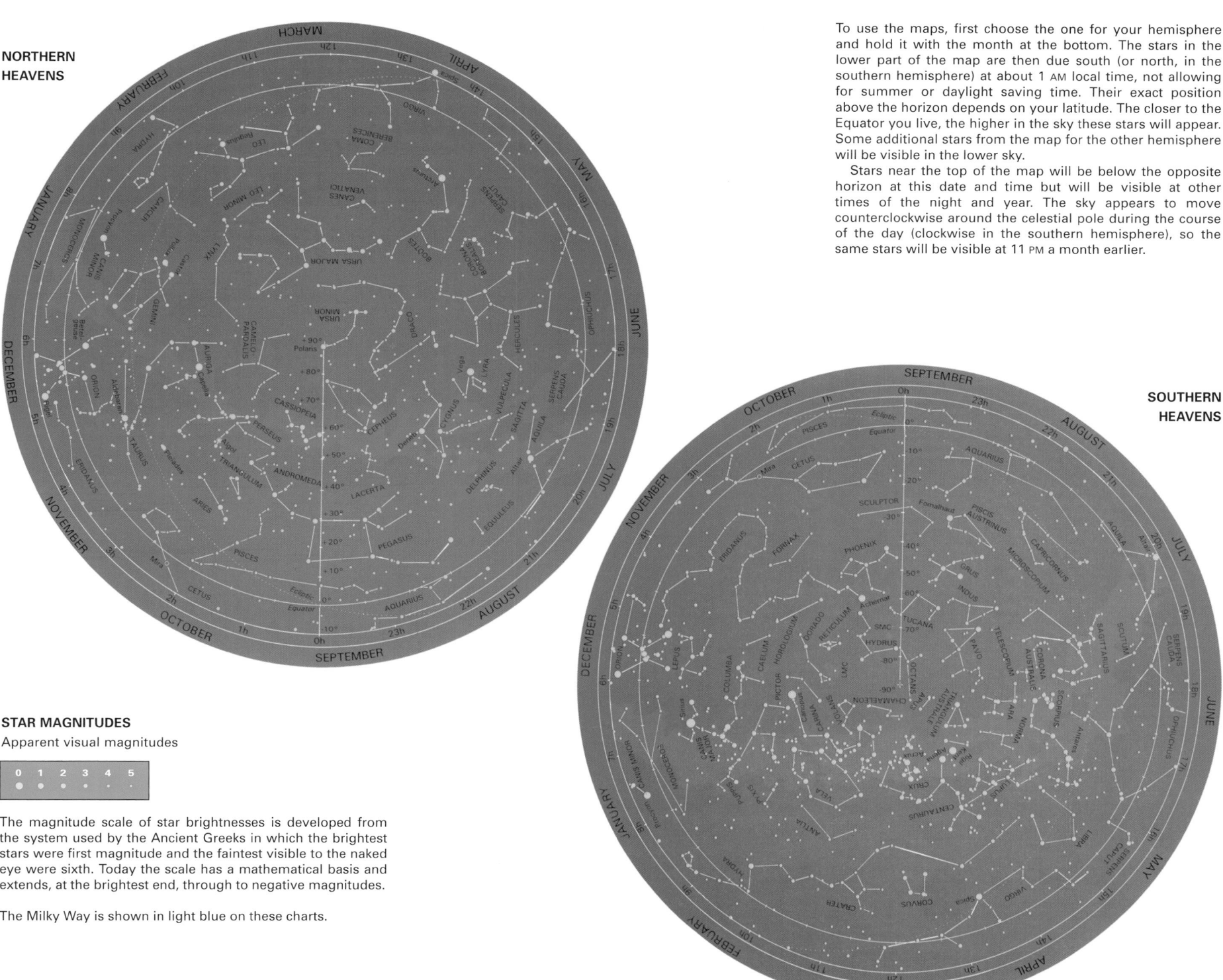

NORTHERN HEAVENS

SOUTHERN HEAVENS

STAR MAGNITUDES

Apparent visual magnitudes

The magnitude scale of star brightnesses is developed from the system used by the Ancient Greeks in which the brightest stars were first magnitude and the faintest visible to the naked eye were sixth. Today the scale has a mathematical basis and extends, at the brightest end, through to negative magnitudes.

The Milky Way is shown in light blue on these charts.

THE NEAREST STARS

The 20 nearest stars, excluding the Sun, with their distance from Earth in light-years*

Proxima Centauri	4.25	Many of the nearest stars, like
Alpha Centauri A	4.3	Alpha Centauri A and B, are
Alpha Centauri B	4.3	doubles, orbiting about the
Barnard's Star	6.0	common center of gravity
Wolf 359	7.8	and to all intents and
Lalande 21185	8.3	purposes equidistant from
Sirius A	8.7	Earth. Many of them are dim
Sirius B	8.7	objects, with no name other
UV Ceti A	8.7	than the designation given
UV Ceti B	8.7	by the astronomers who
Ross 154	9.4	investigated them. However,
Ross 248	10.3	they include Sirius, the
Epsilon Eridani	10.7	brightest star in the sky,
Ross 128	10.9	and Procyon, the seventh
61 Cygni A	11.1	brightest. Both are far larger
61 Cygni B	11.1	than the Sun; of the nearest
Epsilon Indi	11.2	stars, only Epsilon Eridani is
Groombridge 34A	11.2	similar in size and luminosity.
Groombridge 34B	11.2	
L789-6	11.2	* A light-year equals approx.
Procyon A	11.4	5,900 billion miles.
Procyon B	11.4	

THE CONSTELLATIONS

The constellations and their English names

Andromeda	Andromeda	Circinus	Compasses	Lacerta	Lizard	Piscis Austrinus	Southern Fish
Antlia	Air Pump	Columba	Dove	Leo	Lion	Puppis	Ship's Stern
Apus	Bird of Paradise	Coma Berenices	Berenice's Hair	Leo Minor	Little Lion	Pyxis	Mariner's Compass
Aquarius	Water Carrier	Corona Australis	Southern Crown	Lepus	Hare	Reticulum	Net
Aquila	Eagle	Corona Borealis	Northern Crown	Libra	Scales	Sagitta	Arrow
Ara	Altar	Corvus	Crow	Lupus	Wolf	Sagittarius	Archer
Aries	Ram	Crater	Cup	Lynx	Lynx	Scorpius	Scorpion
Auriga	Charioteer	Crux	Southern Cross	Lyra	Lyre	Sculptor	Sculptor
Boötes	Herdsman	Cygnus	Swan	Mensa	Table	Scutum	Shield
Caelum	Chisel	Delphinus	Dolphin	Microscopium	Microscope	Serpens	Serpent
Camelopardalis	Giraffe	Dorado	Swordfish	Monoceros	Unicorn	Sextans	Sextant
Cancer	Crab	Draco	Dragon	Musca	Fly	Taurus	Bull
Canes Venatici	Hunting Dogs	Equuleus	Little Horse	Norma	Level	Telescopium	Telescope
Canis Major	Great Dog	Eridanus	Eridanus	Octans	Octant	Triangulum	Triangle
Canis Minor	Little Dog	Fornax	Furnace	Ophiuchus	Serpent Bearer	Triangulum Australe	Southern Triangle
Capricornus	Goat	Gemini	Twins	Orion	Orion	Tucana	Toucan
Carina	Keel	Grus	Crane	Pavo	Peacock	Ursa Major	Great Bear
Cassiopeia	Cassiopeia	Hercules	Hercules	Pegasus	Winged Horse	Ursa Minor	Little Bear
Centaurus	Centaur	Horologium	Clock	Perseus	Perseus	Vela	Sails
Cepheus	Cepheus	Hydra	Water Snake	Phoenix	Phoenix	Virgo	Virgin
Cetus	Whale	Hydrus	Sea Serpent	Pictor	Easel	Volans	Flying Fish
Chamaeleon	Chameleon	Indus	Indian	Pisces	Fishes	Vulpecula	Fox

THE SOLAR SYSTEM

Lying 28,000 light-years from the center of one of billions of galaxies that comprise the observable universe, our Solar System contains nine planets and their moons, innumerable asteroids and comets, and a miscellany of dust and gas, all tethered by the immense gravitational field of the Sun, the middling-sized star whose thermonuclear furnaces provide them all with heat and light. The Solar System was formed about 4.6 billion years ago, when a spinning cloud of gas, mostly hydrogen but seeded with other, heavier elements, condensed enough to ignite a nuclear reaction and create a star. The Sun still accounts for almost 99.9% of the system's total mass; one planet, Jupiter, contains most of the remainder.

By composition as well as distance, the planetary array divides quite neatly in two: an inner system of four small, solid planets, including the Earth, and an outer system, from Jupiter to Neptune, of four much larger planets composed of lighter materials, such as gas, liquid and ice. Between the two groups lies a scattering of rocky asteroids, perhaps as many as 400,000. They may be debris left over from the inner Solar System's formation. The outermost planet, Pluto, may simply be the largest of a number of bodies composed of rock and ice orbiting beyond Neptune, similarly left over from the formation of the outer Solar System.

By the 1990s, however, the Solar System also included some newer anomalies: several thousand spacecraft. Most were in orbit around the Earth, but some had probed far and wide around the system. The valuable information beamed back by these robotic investigators has transformed our knowledge of our celestial environment.

Much of the early history of science is the story of people trying to make sense of the errant points of light that were all they knew of the planets. Now, men have themselves stood on the Earth's Moon; probes have landed on Mars and Venus, and orbiting radars have mapped far distant landscapes with astonishing accuracy. In the 1980s, the US Voyager probes skimmed all four major planets of the outer system, bringing new revelations with each close approach. Only Pluto, inscrutably distant in an orbit that takes it 50 times the Earth's distance from the Sun, remains unvisited by our messengers.

Orbits of the Planets

The planets of the Solar System and their orbits, showing the relative position of each planet at the vernal equinox of 1992.

Orbits are drawn to exact scale, but with the Sun and planets greatly enlarged for clarity. The Solar System is shown from the viewpoint of an observer a few light-hours distant in the direction of the constellation Hercules. Seen from such a position, above the plane of the ecliptic, all the planets revolve about the Sun in a counterclockwise direction. The perspective view exaggerates the elliptical form of all the planetary orbits: only Pluto and Mercury follow paths that deviate noticeably from circularity. Near perihelion – its closest approach to the Sun – Pluto actually passes inside the orbit of Neptune, an event that last occurred in 1983. Pluto did not regain its station as the Sun's outermost planet until February 1999.

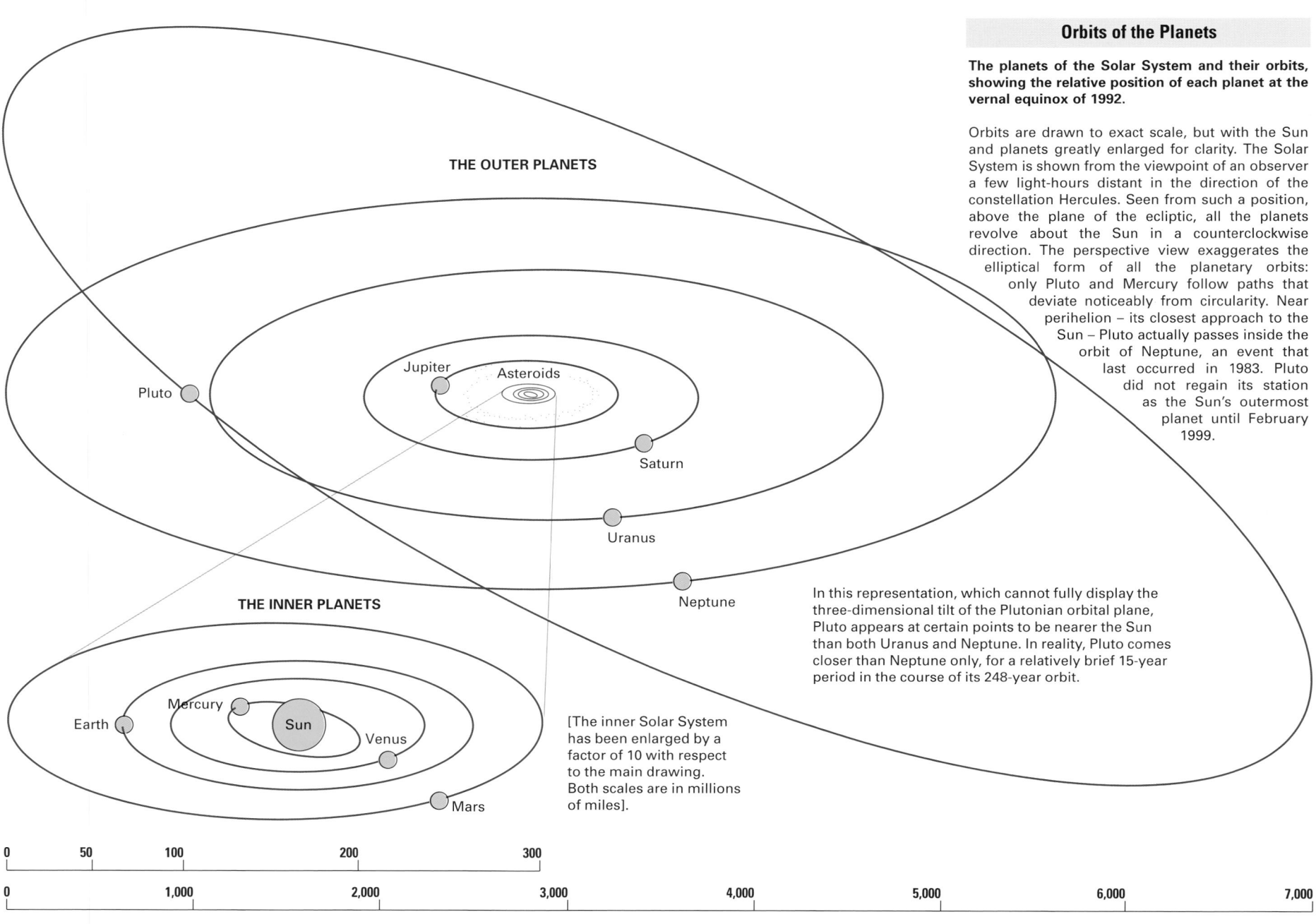

THE OUTER PLANETS

Pluto · Jupiter · Asteroids · Saturn · Uranus · Neptune

THE INNER PLANETS

Earth · Mercury · Sun · Venus · Mars

In this representation, which cannot fully display the three-dimensional tilt of the Plutonian orbital plane, Pluto appears at certain points to be nearer the Sun than both Uranus and Neptune. In reality, Pluto comes closer than Neptune only, for a relatively brief 15-year period in the course of its 248-year orbit.

[The inner Solar System has been enlarged by a factor of 10 with respect to the main drawing. Both scales are in millions of miles].

| 0 | 50 | 100 | 200 | 300 |
| 0 | 1,000 | 2,000 | 3,000 | 4,000 | 5,000 | 6,000 | 7,000 |

Planetary Data

	Mean distance from Sun (million miles)	Mass (Earth = 1)	Period of orbit (Earth days/years)	Period of rotation (Earth days)	Equatorial diameter (miles)	Average density (water = 1)	Surface gravity (Earth = 1)	Escape velocity (miles/sec)	Number of known satellites
Sun	–	332,946	–	25.4	865,000	1.41	27.9	383.7	–
Mercury	36.0	0.055	87.97d	58.67	3,031	5.44	0.38	2.64	0
Venus	67.2	0.815	224.7d	243.00	7,521	5.25	0.90	6.44	0
Earth	93.0	1.0	365.3d	1.00	7,926	5.52	1.00	6.95	1
Mars	141.6	0.11	687.0d	1.028	4,222	3.94	0.38	3.13	2
Jupiter	483.4	317.9	11.86y	0.411	89,405	1.33	2.64	37.03	60
Saturn	886.7	95.2	29.46y	0.427	74,898	0.71	1.16	22.12	31
Uranus	1,783.3	14.6	84.01y	0.748	31,763	1.27	0.79	13.11	21
Neptune	2,794.3	17.2	164.8y	0.710	31,403	1.77	0.98	15.29	11
Pluto	3,666.1	0.002	247.7y	6.39	1,444	2.02	0.06	0.75	1

Planetary days are given in sidereal time – that is, with respect to the stars rather than the Sun. Most of the information in the table was confirmed by spacecraft and often obtained from photographs and other data transmitted back to the Earth. In the case of Pluto, however, only Earthbound observations have been made, and no spacecraft will encounter it until well into the 21st century. Given the planet's small size and great distance, figures for its diameter and rotation period have only recently been confirmed.

Pluto is not massive enough to account for the perturbations in the orbits of Uranus and Neptune that led to its discovery in 1930, but it is now widely believed that these perturbations can be explained away as observational errors made by the earlier observers.

4

The Planets

Mercury is the closest planet to the Sun and hence the fastest-moving. It is very hot, with a cratered, wrinkled surface very similar to that of Earth's Moon. It is small and has no gravity, hence there is no significant atmosphere.

Venus has much the same physical dimensions as Earth. Its dense atmosphere is composed of 97% CO_2 resulting in a runaway greenhouse effect that makes the Venusian surface, at 890°F, the hottest of all the planets in the Solar System. Radar mapping shows the land to be relatively level, with volcanic regions whose sulfurous discharges explain the sulfuric-acid rains reported by soft-landing space probes before they succumbed to Venus' fierce climate.

Earth seen from space is easily the most beautiful of the inner planets; it is also, and more objectively, the largest, as well as the only home of known life. Living things are the main reason why the Earth is able to retain a substantial proportion of corrosive and highly reactive oxygen in its atmosphere, a state of affairs that contradicts the laws of chemical equilibrium; the oxygen in turn supports the life that constantly regenerates it.

Mars, smaller and cooler than the Earth, is nevertheless the most likely planet other than Earth where life may have formed. Vast water channels show that it was once warmer and wetter; there may still be traces of former simple life forms, though whether life could thrive in its current cold, dry and thin atmosphere is doubtful. The ice caps are mainly frozen carbon dioxide, though data from NASA's probe, Mars Odyssey, launched in 2001, suggests that vast reservoirs of water ice may lie a few centimeters beneath the surface over much of the planet. But the surface itself is a dustbowl, where occasional storms whirl dust high into the atmosphere.

Jupiter masses almost three times as much as all the other planets combined; had it scooped up rather more matter during its formation, it might have evolved into a small companion star for the Sun. The planet is mostly gas, under intense pressure in the lower atmosphere above a core of fiercely compressed hydrogen and helium. The upper layers form strikingly-colored rotating belts, the outward sign of the intense storms created by Jupiter's rapid diurnal rotation. Close approaches by spacecraft have shown an orbiting ring system and discovered several previously unknown moons: Jupiter has at least 60 moons, though many are extremely small.

Saturn is structurally similar to Jupiter, rotating fast enough to produce an obvious bulge at its equator. It is composed of 89% hydrogen and 11% helium, and has wind velocities in the outer atmosphere of 1,600 feet per second. Ever since the invention of the telescope, however, Saturn's rings have been the feature that has attracted most observers. Voyager probes in 1980 and 1981 sent back detailed pictures that showed them to be composed of thousands of separate ringlets, each in turn made up of tiny icy particles.

Uranus was unknown to the ancients. Although it is faintly visible to the naked eye, it was not discovered until 1781. Its interior is largely water, with an atmosphere of hydrogen, helium and some methane, which gives the planet its blue-green color. Observations in 1977 suggested the presence of a faint ring system, amply confirmed when Voyager 2 swung past the planet in 1986.

Neptune is always more than 2.5 billion miles from Earth, and despite its diameter of over 31,000 miles, it can only be seen by telescope. Its 1846 discovery was the result of mathematical predictions by astronomers seeking to explain irregularities in the orbit of Uranus, but until Voyager 2 closed with the planet in 1989, very little was known of it. Like Uranus, it has a ring system; recent observations have revealed a total of 11 moons.

Pluto is the most mysterious of the solar planets, if only because even the most powerful telescopes can scarcely resolve it from a point of light to a disk. It was discovered as recently as 1930, as the result (like Neptune) of perturbations in the orbits of the two then outermost planets. Its small size, as well as its eccentric and highly tilted orbit, has led to suggestions that it is a former satellite of Neptune, somehow liberated from its primary. In 1978 Pluto was found to have a moon of its own, Charon, apparently half the size of Pluto itself.

Mean distance from the Sun in million miles (not to scale)

Mercury	36.0
Venus	67.2
Earth	93.0
Mars	141.6
Jupiter	483.4
Saturn	886.7
Uranus	1,783.3
Neptune	2,794.3
Pluto	3,666.1

Diagram not drawn to scale

TIME AND MOTION

The basic unit of time measurement is the day, that is, one rotation of the Earth on its axis. Our present calendar is based on the solar year of 365.24 days, the time taken by the Earth to orbit the Sun.

Calendars based on the movements of the Sun and Moon have been used since ancient times. The average length of the year, according to the Julian Calendar introduced by Julius Caesar, was about 11 minutes too long. The cumulative error was rectified in 1582 by the Gregorian Calendar, when Pope Gregory XIII decreed that the day following October 4 was October 15, and in that century years did not count as leap years unless they were divisible by 400. England finally adopted the reformed calendar in 1752, when it was 11 days behind the European mainland.

The rotation of the Earth on its axis causes day and night. Because the Earth rotates through 360° every 24 hours, the world is divided into 24 time zones centered on lines of longitude at 15° longitude.

The tilt of the Earth's axis, also called the obliquity of the ecliptic, accounts for the seasons which are so familiar in the middle latitudes. But geological evidence shows that, over long periods of time, climates change, and the advances and retreats of the ice during the Pleistocene Ice Age may have been caused by regular variations in the Earth's tilt, its orbit around the Sun, and changes in the season when it is closest to the Sun (perihelion).

Earth Data

Aphelion (maximum distance from Sun):
94,452,780 miles

Perihelion (minimum distance from Sun):
91,342,080 miles

Angle of tilt (obliquity of the ecliptic): 23° 27' 08"

Length of year – solar tropical (equinox to equinox): 365.24 days

Length of year: 365 days, 5 hours, 48 minutes, 46 seconds of mean solar time

Superficial area:
197,000,000 sq miles

Land surface:
57,500,000 sq miles (29.2%)

Water surface:
139,500,000 sq miles (70.8%)

Equatorial circumference:
24,903 miles

Polar circumference:
24,860 miles

Equatorial diameter:
7,926 miles

Polar diameter: 7,900 miles

Equatorial radius:
3,963.4 miles

Polar radius: 3,950 miles

Volume of the Earth:
$260,000 \times 10^6$ cu miles

Mass of the Earth:
6.5×10^{21} tons

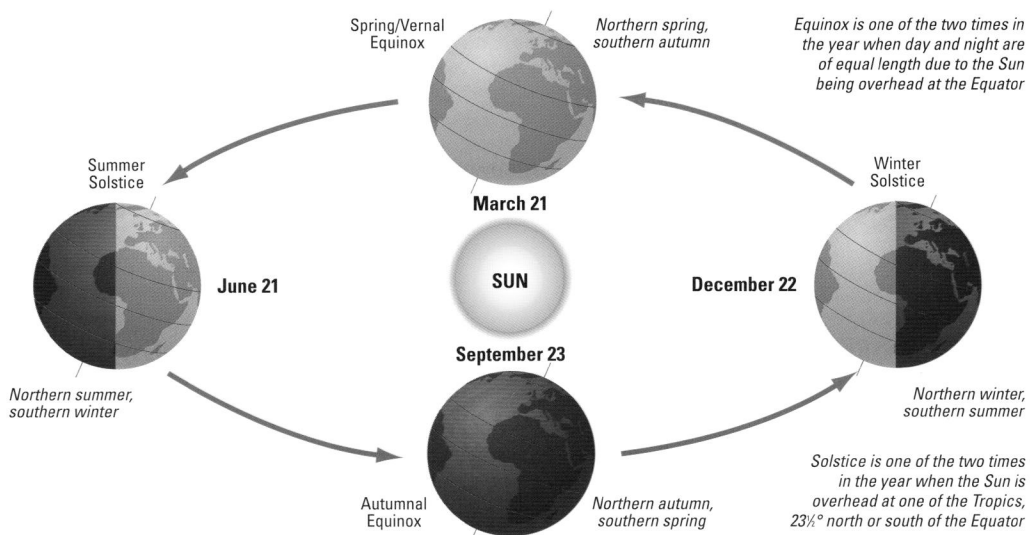

Equinox is one of the two times in the year when day and night are of equal length due to the Sun being overhead at the Equator

Solstice is one of the two times in the year when the Sun is overhead at one of the Tropics, 23½° north or south of the Equator

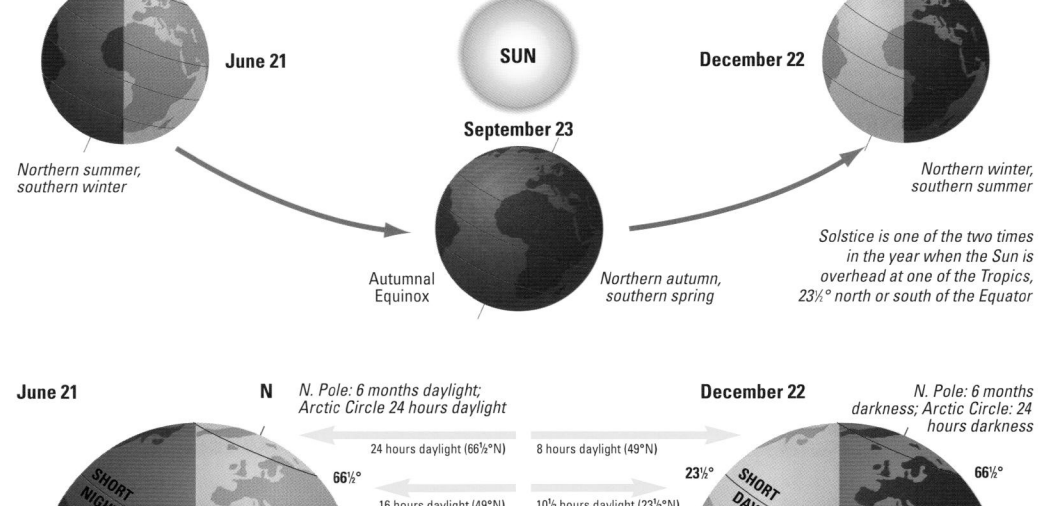

The Seasons

Seasons occur because the Earth's axis is tilted at an angle of approximately 23½°. When the northern hemisphere is tilted to a maximum extent toward the Sun, on June 21, the Sun is overhead at the Tropic of Cancer (latitude 23½° North). This is midsummer, or the summer solstice, in the northern hemisphere.

On September 22 or 23, the Sun is overhead at the Equator, and day and night are of equal length throughout the world. This is the autumnal equinox in the northern hemisphere. On December 21 or 22, the Sun is overhead at the Tropic of Capricorn (23½° South), the winter solstice in the northern hemisphere. The overhead Sun then tracks north until, on March 21, it is overhead at the Equator. This is the spring (vernal) equinox in the northern hemisphere.

In the southern hemisphere, the seasons are the reverse of those in the north.

Day and Night

The Sun appears to rise in the east, reach its highest point at noon, and then set in the west, to be followed by night. In reality, it is not the Sun that is moving but the Earth rotating from west to east. The moment when the Sun's upper limb first appears above the horizon is termed sunrise; the moment when the Sun's upper limb disappears below the horizon is sunset.

At the summer solstice in the northern hemisphere (June 21), the Arctic has total daylight and the Antarctic total darkness. The opposite occurs at the winter solstice (December 21 or 22). At the Equator, the length of day and night are almost equal all year.

The Sun's Path

The diagrams on the right illustrate the apparent path of the Sun at (A) the Equator, (B) in mid-latitude (45°), (C) at the Arctic Circle (66½°), and (D) at the North Pole, where there are six months of continuous daylight and six months of continuous night.

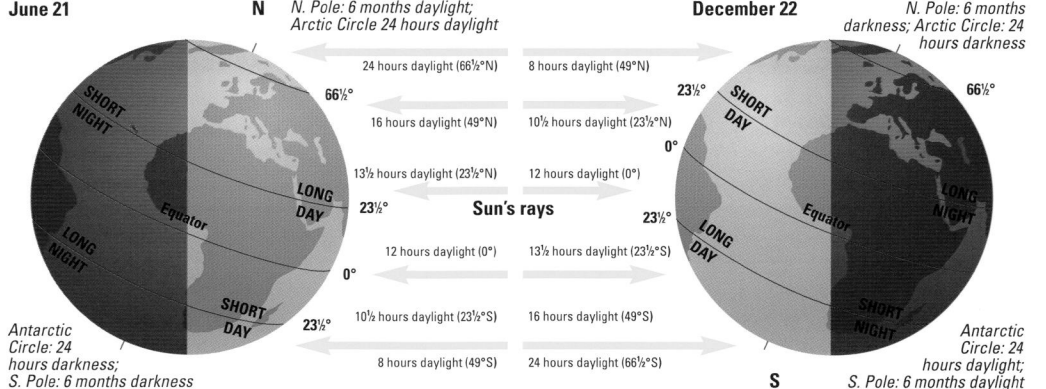

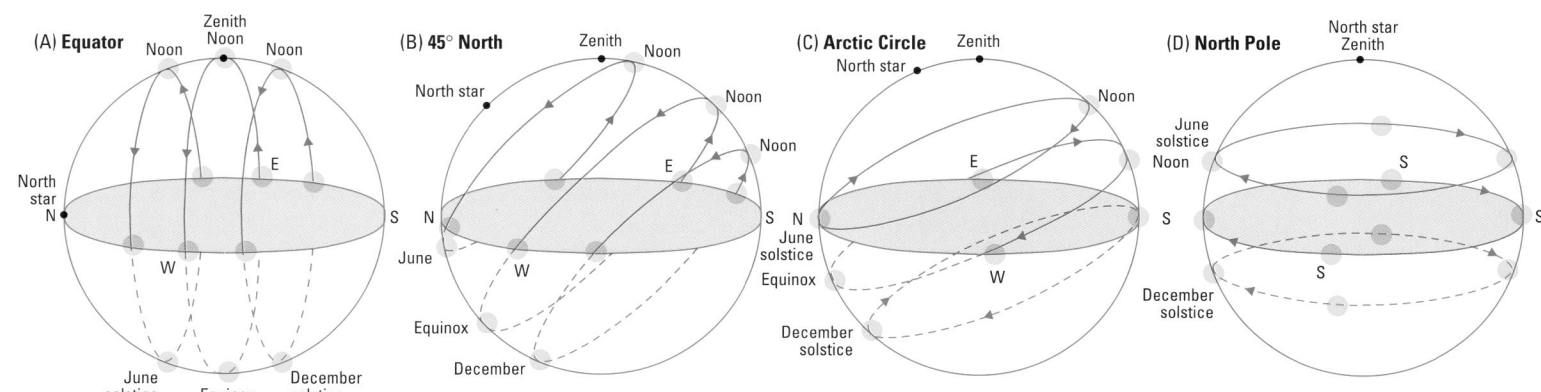

Sunrise and Sunset

The term equinox comes from two Latin words meaning "equal night." At the spring and autumnal equinoxes, the Sun is vertically overhead at the Equator and all places on Earth have 12 hours of darkness and 12 hours of daylight. The graphs showing sunrise and sunset show that these occasions on March 21 and on September 22 or 23. The graphs also show that, because the Sun remains high in the sky throughout the year, the length of the day and night at the Equator remain roughly the same throughout the year, with sunrise occurring around 6 AM and sunset at around 6 PM. The further north or south one travels, the greater the difference between the number of hours of daylight and darkness. For example, the graph (*right*) shows that at latitude 60°N sunrise varies from just after 9 AM in midwinter (on December 22 or 23) to about 2.30 AM in midsummer (around the summer solstice on June 21). By contrast, the second graph (*far right*) shows that sunset at latitude 60°N occurs at about 2.45 PM in midwinter and 9.20 PM in midsummer.

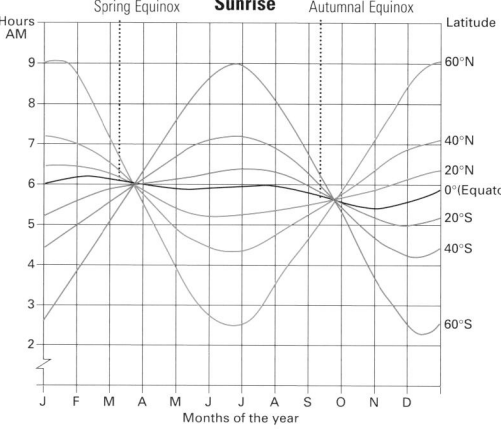

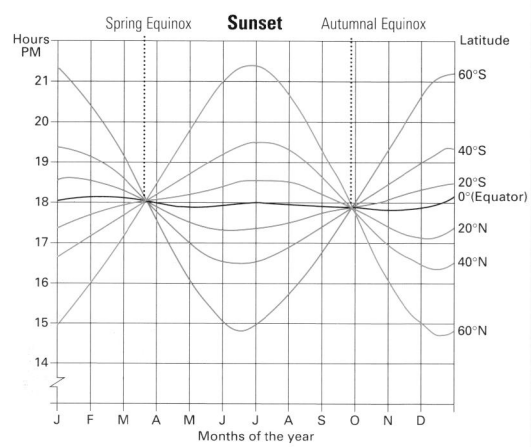

The Moon

The Moon rotates more slowly than the Earth, making one complete turn on its axis in just over 27 days. Since this corresponds to its period of revolution around the Earth, the Moon always presents the same hemisphere or face to us, and we never see "the dark side." The interval between one full Moon and the next (and between new Moons) is about 29½ days – a lunar month. The apparent changes in the shape of the Moon are caused by its changing position in relation to the Earth; like the planets, it produces no light of its own and shines only by reflecting the rays of the Sun.

Phases of the Moon

Distance from Earth: 221,463 miles – 252,710 miles; Mean diameter: 2,160 miles; Mass: approximately 1/81 that of Earth; Surface gravity: one-sixth of Earth's; Daily range of temperature at lunar equator: 350°F; Average orbital speed: 2,300 mph

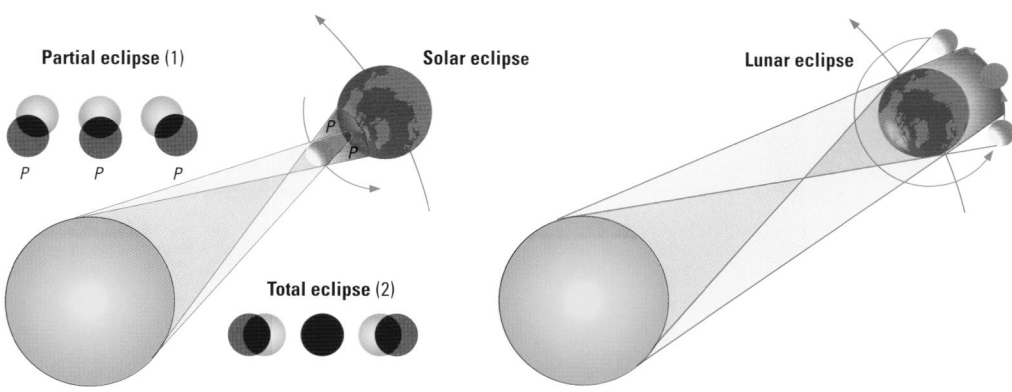

New Moon · Crescent · First quarter · Gibbous · Full Moon · Gibbous · Last quarter · Crescent · New Moon

Moon Data

Distance from Earth
The Moon orbits at a mean distance of 238,731 miles, at an average speed of 2,300 mph in relation to the Earth.

Size and mass
The average diameter of the Moon is 2,160 miles. It is 400 times smaller than the Sun but is about 400 times closer to the Earth, so we see them as the same size. The Moon has a mass of 7,975 × 10^19 tons, with a density 3.344 times that of water.

Visibility
Only 59% of the Moon's surface is directly visible from Earth. Reflected light takes 1.25 seconds to reach Earth – compared to 8 minutes 27.3 seconds for light to reach us from the Sun.

Temperature
With the Sun overhead, the temperature on the lunar equator can reach 243°F. At night it can sink to −261°F.

Eclipses

When the Moon passes between the Sun and the Earth it causes a partial eclipse of the Sun (1) if the Earth passes through the Moon's outer shadow (P), or a total eclipse (2) if the inner cone shadow crosses the Earth's surface. In a lunar eclipse, the Earth's shadow crosses the Moon and, again, provides either a partial or total eclipse.

Eclipses of the Sun and the Moon do not occur every month because of the 5° difference between the plane of the Moon's orbit and the plane in which the Earth moves. In the 1990s only 14 lunar eclipses were possible, for example, seven partial and seven total; each was visible only from certain, and variable, parts of the world. The same period witnessed 13 solar eclipses – six partial (or annular) and seven total.

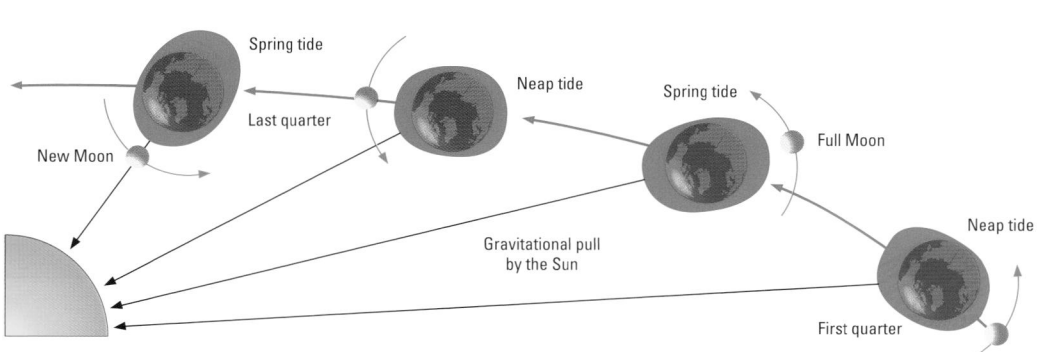

Partial eclipse (1) · Solar eclipse · Lunar eclipse · Total eclipse (2)

Tides

The daily rise and fall of the ocean's tides are the result of the gravitational pull of the Moon and that of the Sun, though the effect of the latter is only 46.6% as strong as that of the Moon. This effect is greatest on the hemisphere facing the Moon and causes a tidal "bulge." When the Sun, Earth and Moon are in line, tide-raising forces are at a maximum and Spring tides occur: high tide reaches the highest values, and low tide falls to low levels. When lunar and solar forces are least coincidental with the Sun and Moon at an angle (near the Moon's first and third quarters), Neap tides occur, which have a small tidal range.

Time Zones

The Earth rotates through 360° in 24 hours, and so moves 15° every hour. The world is divided into 24 standard time zones, each centered on lines of longitude at 15° intervals. At the center of the first zone is the Prime meridian or Greenwich meridian. All places to the west of Greenwich are one hour behind for every 15° of longitude; places to the east are ahead by one hour for every 15°. When it is 12 noon at the Greenwich meridian, 180° east it is midnight of the same day – while 180° west the day is just beginning. To overcome this, the International Date Line was established, approximately following the 180° meridian. Thus, if you traveled eastward from Japan (140°E) to Samoa (170°W), you would pass from Sunday night into Sunday morning.

10 — Hours slow or fast of UT or Coordinated Universal Time

— Zones using UT (GMT)

— Zones slow of UT (GMT)

- - - - International boundaries

— Zones fast of UT (GMT)

— Half-hour zones

— Time zone boundaries

— International Date Line

— Actual Solar Time when time at Greenwich is 12:00 (noon)

Note: Certain of the above time zones are affected by the incidence of "Summer Time" in countries where it is adopted.

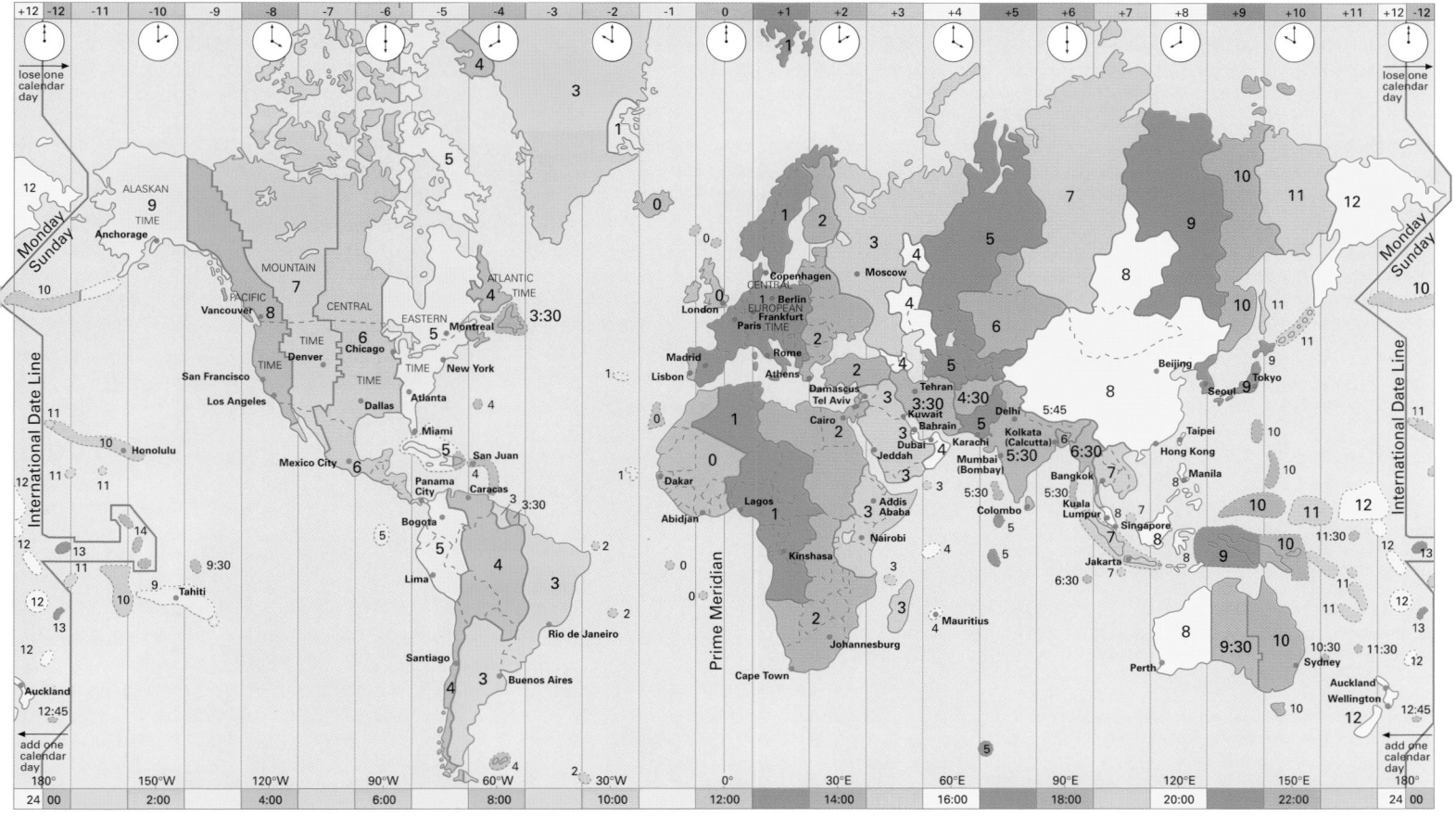

Projection: Mercator

OCEANS

Seawater

The chemical composition of the sea, by percentage, excluding the elements of water itself

Chloride (Cl)	55.04%
Sodium (Na)	30.61%
Sulfate (SO₄)	7.69%
Magnesium (Mg)	3.69%
Calcium (Ca)	1.16%
Potassium (K)	1.10%
Bicarbonate (HCO₃)	0.41%
Bromide (Br)	0.19%
Boric Acid (H₃BO₃)	0.07%
Strontium (Sr)	0.04%
Fluoride (Fl)	0.003%
Lithium (Li)	trace
Rubidium (Rb)	trace
Phosphorus (P)	trace
Iodine (I)	trace
Barium (Ba)	trace
Arsenic (As)	trace
Caesium (Cs)	trace

Eleven constituents account for over 99% of the salt content of seawater, but seawater also contains virtually every other element. In natural conditions, its composition is broadly consistent across the world's seas and oceans; but in coastal areas, especially, variations are sometimes substantial. The oceans are about 35 parts water to one part salt.

Atoll Building

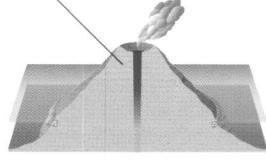

Volcano rises from ocean floor

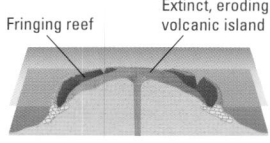

Fringing reef · Extinct, eroding volcanic island

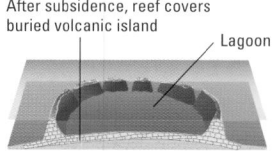

After subsidence, reef covers buried volcanic island · Lagoon

A coral atoll usually begins existence as a bare volcanic peak, thrusting above the surface of the ocean. A colony of coral – organisms with calcium carbonate skeletons – forms itself in the shallow water around the peak. The volcano is eroded and slowly sinks, leaving the coral forming a ring of hard limestone around its remnant. In time, the barrier reef of an atoll is all that remains.

The last 40 years have been described as the "Space Age," but another exciting and perhaps even more important area of discovery, proceeding at the same time, has been the exploration of "inner space," namely the oceans which cover more than 70% of our planet. The study of the ocean floor and oceanic islands has revealed features that help to explain how continents move, and how the movements are related to earthquakes and volcanic activity.

Manned submersibles have established that life exists even in the deepest trenches, where the pressure reaches 1,000 atmospheres, the equivalent of the force of six and a half tons bearing down on every square inch. Further exploration in the pitch-black environment of the ocean ridges has revealed strange forms of marine life around scalding hot vents. The creatures include giant tubeworms, blind shrimps, and bacteria, some of which are genetically very different from any other known life forms. In 1996, an analysis of one micro-organism revealed that at least half of its 1,700 or so genes were hitherto unknown. This environment, which is based on chemicals, not sunlight, may resemble the places where life on Earth first began.

Another vital area of contemporary research concerns the interactions between the oceans and the atmosphere, as exemplified in the El Niño–Southern Oscillation (ENSO), and the bearing that these have on climatic change.

Most geographers divide the world's ocean waters into four areas: the Pacific, Atlantic, Indian, and Arctic oceans. The most active zone in the oceans is the sunlit upper layer, where the water is moved around by wind-blown currents. It is the home of most sea life and acts as a membrane through which the ocean breathes,

The El Niño Phenomenon

The importance of the ocean–atmosphere interaction is nowhere more dramatically demonstrated than in the El Niño phenomenon of the southern Pacific Ocean.

Under normal conditions, called La Niña, surface water flows eastward from South America (*see diagram right, top*) under the influence of trade winds. Near the coast, cold, nutrient-rich water (dark blue) rises to the surface and spreads westward. In the western Pacific, sea surface temperatures reach 82°F or more and warm air rises, creating a low-pressure air system and causing heavy rains. The rising air spreads out and some of it descends over South America and the eastern Pacific, creating a high-pressure air system from which winds blow westward. This rotating system is called a Walker Circulation Cell.

An El Niño event, also called an El Niño–Southern Oscillation cycle, or ENSO cycle, is characterized by a reversal of currents, whereby the eastward-moving South Equatorial Current extends much further to the east and the trade winds weaken. The upwelling of cold water off South America is greatly reduced and surface water temperatures rise, causing a drastic reduction in fish life. The heaviest rainfall is over the eastern Pacific, while Southeast Asia is drier than usual. Warm air rises in the east, spreads out, and descends in the western Pacific, which becomes a high-pressure area, as shown on the second diagram (*right, below*).

During an intense El Niño, such as in 1982–3 when sea temperatures in the eastern Pacific rose by 11°F, the effects of the current and wind reversals affect the weather around the world. In Australia and Southeast Asia, the monsoon rainfall is reduced, while, in 1983–4, a severe drought occurred in the Sahel, south of the Sahara, and also in southern Africa. The southeast coast of the United States also suffered storms and heavy rainfall, and even Europe experienced changes in weather patterns, possibly as a result of consequent changes in the course of the jet stream.

Life in the Oceans

An imaginary profile of the typical coastal and oceanic zones is shown, with a selection of the life forms that might occur in the water off the Pacific Coast of Central America. The animals illustrated are not drawn to scale as the range of sizes is too great. Most marine life is confined to the first 650 feet, the upper sunlit (photic) zone, where sunlight can still penetrate. Plant and animal plankton, the basis of life in the ocean, occur in great quantities in all zones.

In the pelagic environment (open sea), vertical gradients, including those of light, temperature and salinity, determine the distribution of organisms. From the tidal zone at the coastline, the continental shelf, geologically still part of the continental landmass, drops gently to about 650 feet – the sunlit zone. At the end of the shelf, the seabed falls away in the steeper angle of the continental slope. The subsequent descent to the deep ocean floor, known as the continental rise, is more gentle, with gradients between 1 in 100 and 1 in 700 until the abyssal plains and hills between 8,000 and 19,500 feet below the surface.

The deep sea floor contains seamounts, some of which are capped by coral reefs, ocean ridges, the longest mountain chains on Earth, and deep ocean trenches, especially in the Pacific Ocean where six trenches reach depths of more than 33,000 feet, including the Mariana Trench at 36,161 feet deep.

Each of these zones contains a distinctive community of species adapted to the different conditions of salinity, temperature and light intensity. Indeed, a few organisms have been found even in the abyssal darkness of the great ocean trenches.

absorbing great quantities of carbon dioxide and partly exchanging it for oxygen.

As the depth increases, so light fades and temperatures fall until just before 3,000 feet where there is a marked temperature change at the thermocline, the boundary between the warm surface zone and the cold deep zone. Below the thermocline, slow currents are caused by density differences between bodies of water with varying temperatures and salinity.

Scientists have found evidence that the frequency of the El Niño event, which normally occurs every two to seven years, may have increased in recent years with warm conditions persisting in the eastern Pacific from 1990 until mid-1995, an unprecedented length of time during the 114 years for which data exist. Another intense El Niño occurred in 1997–8, with resultant freak weather conditions across the entire Pacific region. Scientists do not know the causes of the El Niño event, though some researchers are investigating possible connections between major volcanic eruptions in the tropical Pacific region, the ENSO cycle and atmospheric circulation.

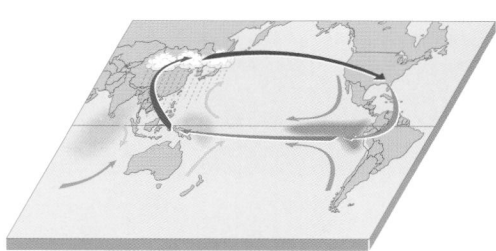

Normal year – Walker Circulation Cell

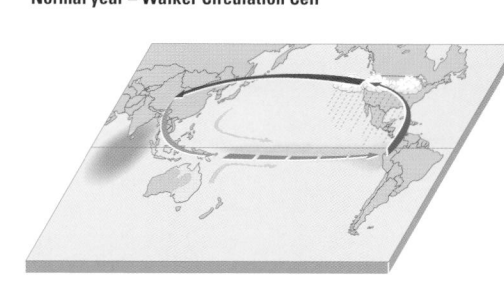

El Niño event

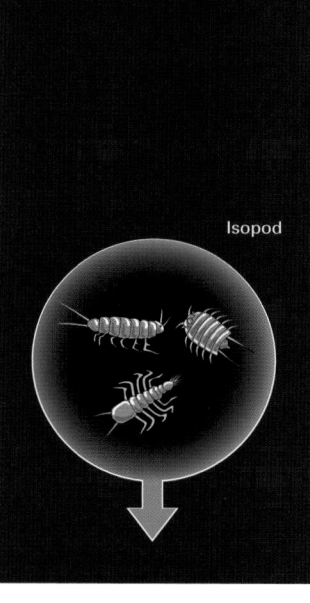

SEA LEVEL

Crab · Seaweed · Jellyfish · Anchovy · Green turtle · Dolphin

SUNLIT ZONE
650 feet

Marlin · Bonito · Snake eel · Blue Whale

TWILIGHT ZONE
3,000 feet

Phytoplankton and zooplankton · Lantern fish · Ray · Sperm whale · Deep-sea squid

DARK ZONE
19,500 feet

Anglerfish · Halosaur · Sea cucumber · Sponge

TRENCH ZONE
33,000 feet

Isopod

Ocean Currents

JANUARY CURRENTS AND TEMPERATURES
(Northern Hemisphere: winter)

ACTUAL SURFACE
TEMPERATURE

°F
- 86
- 68
- 50
- 32
- 14
- − 4
- − 22
- − 40

OCEAN CURRENTS

Cold	Warm	Speed (knots)
←	←	Less than 0.5
←	←	0.5 – 1.0
←	←	Over 1.0

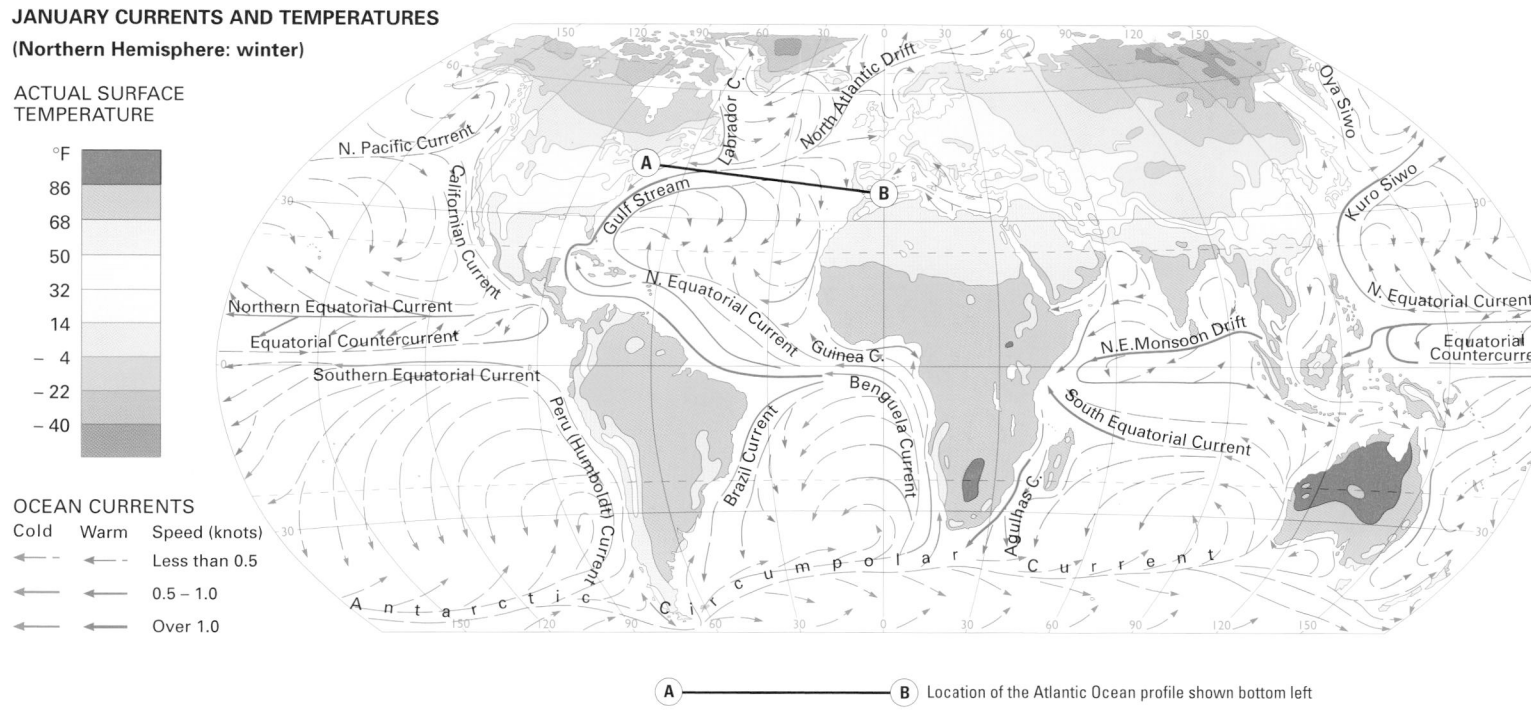

(A) ———————— (B) Location of the Atlantic Ocean profile shown bottom left

JULY CURRENTS AND TEMPERATURES
(Northern Hemisphere: summer)

ACTUAL SURFACE
TEMPERATURE

°F
- 86
- 68
- 50
- 32
- 14

OCEAN CURRENTS

Cold	Warm	Speed (knots)
←	←	Less than 0.5
←	←	0.5 – 1.0
←	←	Over 1.0

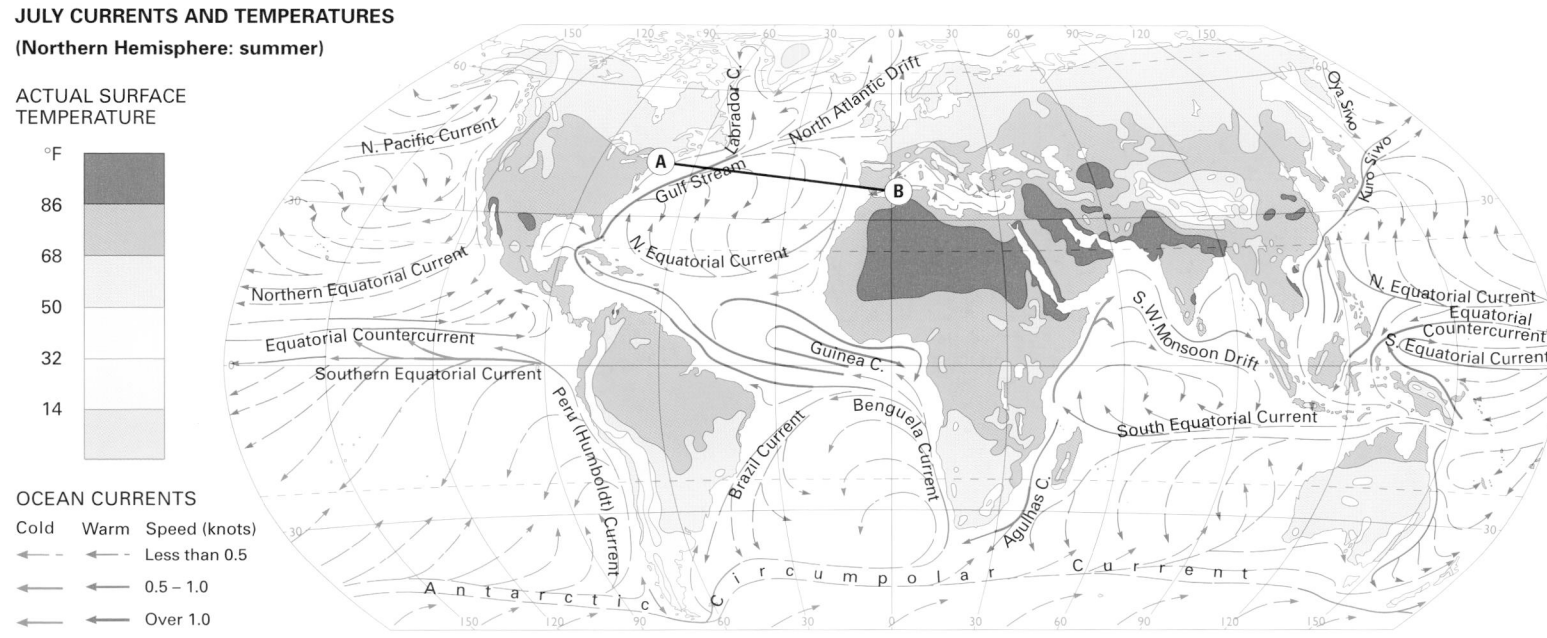

Moving immense quantities of energy as well as billions of tons of water every hour, the ocean currents are a vital part of the great heat engine that drives the Earth's climate. They themselves are produced by a twofold mechanism. At the surface, winds push huge masses of water before them; in the deep ocean, below an abrupt temperature gradient that separates the churning surface waters from the still depths, density variations cause slow vertical movements.

The pattern of circulation of the great surface currents is determined by the displacement known as the Coriolis effect. As the Earth turns beneath a moving object – whether it is a tennis ball or a vast mass of water – it appears to be deflected to one side. The deflection is most obvious near the Equator, where the Earth's surface is spinning eastward at 1,000 mph; currents moving poleward are curved clockwise in the northern hemisphere and counterclockwise in the southern.

The result is a system of spinning circles known as gyres. Warm currents move constantly from the Equator toward the poles, while cold water moves in the reverse direction. In this way, ocean currents act like a thermostat, helping to regulate temperatures around the world.

Depending on the annual movements of the prevailing wind belts, some currents on or near the Equator may reverse their direction in the course of the year, a variation on which Asia's monsoon rains depend and whose occasional failure has brought disaster to millions of people.

Topography of the Ocean Floor

Profile of the Atlantic Ocean

The deep ocean floor was once believed to be flat, but maps compiled from readings made by sonar equipment show that it is no more uniform than the surface of the continents. The profile (*below*) shows some of the features on the Atlantic Ocean floor between Massachusetts in North America and Gibraltar (*for location of profile, see maps above*). Around the continents are shallow continental shelves composed of rocks which are less dense than the underlying oceanic crust. The continents end at the top of the steep continental slope, which descends to the abyss via the continental rise, made up of sediments washed down from the continental shelves. The abyss contains large plains overlain by oozes, but the plains are broken by volcanic seamounts and guyots (flat-topped seamounts), a few of which reach the surface as islands. The other main feature is the Mid-Atlantic Ridge, through which runs a rift valley where new crustal rock is being formed as the plates on either side move apart.

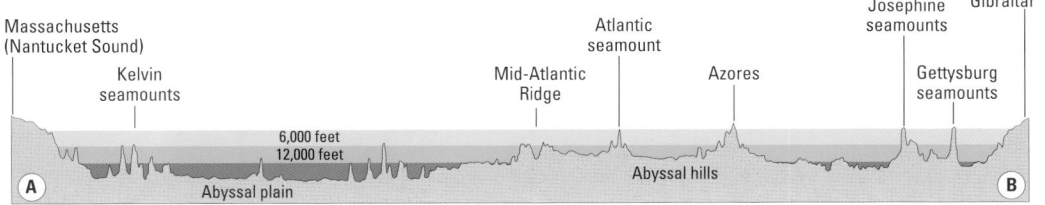

Topography of the ocean floor around Australia

In the image on the right, land areas are shown in gray, with shaded relief. The colors represent sea depth, with red representing the shallowest areas, through yellow and green to dark blue (the deepest). The data for the sea topography are from the Seasat radar satellite. The deep blue area in the upper left is the Java Trench which forms the boundary between the Indian-Australian plate and the Eurasian plate. In the top right, the New Guinea trench, which has a maximum depth of 29,865 feet, forms the border of the Indian-Australian and Pacific plates. Alongside the trenches are volcanic islands formed from magma, created as the edge of the Indian-Australian plate is subducted and melted.

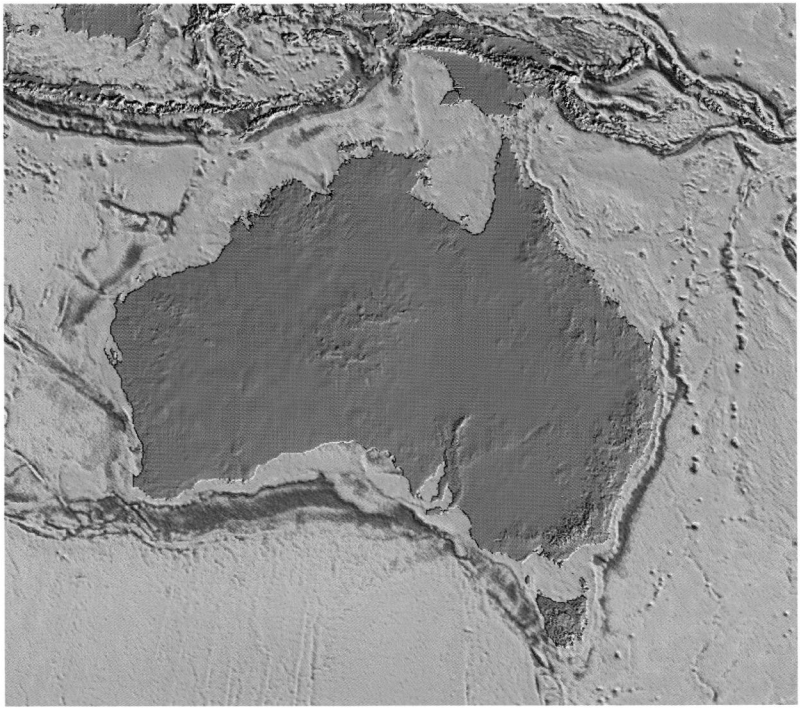

GEOLOGY OF THE EARTH

Every year, earthquakes and volcanic eruptions cause much destruction throughout the world. Such phenomena were once thought to be unconnected, but since the late 1960s, scientists have understood that these events are surface manifestations of the tremendous forces operating in the Earth's interior that are slowly but constantly changing the face of our planet.

The Earth is divided into three zones. The crust, a brittle, low-density zone, overlies the dense mantle. Separating the crust from the mantle is a distinct boundary called the Mohorovičić (or Moho) discontinuity. Enclosed by the mantle is the Earth's core, which consists mainly of iron and nickel.

Temperatures inside the Earth range from about 1,600°F in the upper mantle to perhaps 9,000°F in the core. Heat creates convection currents in a semimolten part of the mantle called the asthenosphere. Above the asthenosphere is the lithosphere, a solid layer about 40 miles thick, consisting of the crust and part of the mantle. The lithosphere is divided into rigid plates, moved around by the currents in the asthenosphere, a process named plate tectonics.

The Earth was formed around 4.6 billion years ago. Lighter elements floated toward the surface, where they formed crustal rocks. The oldest rocks so far discovered are about 4 billion years old, while the oldest fossils occur in rocks formed around 3.5 billion years ago. An explosion of life occurred at the start of the Cambrian period, 570 million years ago. The fossil record since the start of the Cambrian has enabled scientists to piece together the story of life on Earth.

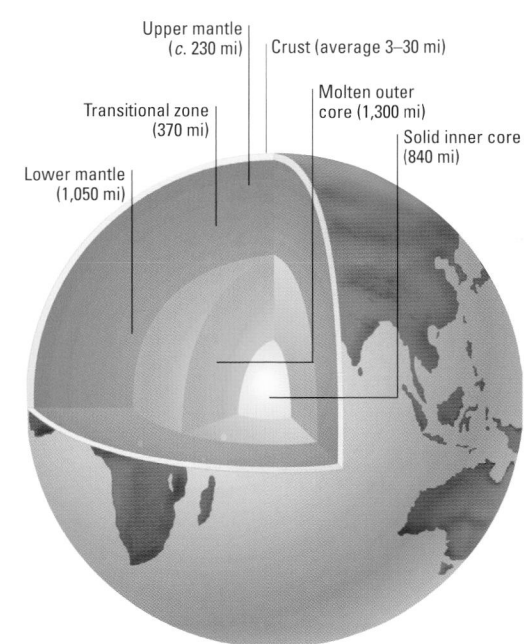

Upper mantle (c. 230 mi)
Crust (average 3–30 mi)
Transitional zone (370 mi)
Molten outer core (1,300 mi)
Lower mantle (1,050 mi)
Solid inner core (840 mi)

Plate Tectonics

In the early 20th century, the German scientist Alfred Wegener and others noticed similarities between the shapes of the continents. From a study of rocks and fossils in widely separated continents, they suggested that the continents had once been joined together and that somehow they had drifted apart. But no one knew of a mechanism that might cause continents to drift. However, in the 1950s and 1960s, evidence from studies of the ocean floor suggested that the low-density continents rest on huge slow-moving plates.

Seafloor spreading in the Indian Ocean and continental plate collision

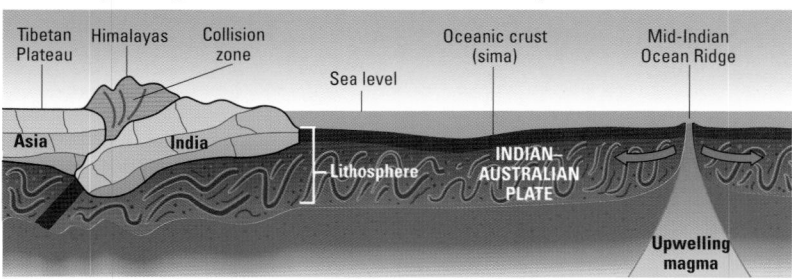

Tibetan Plateau | Himalayas | Collision zone | Oceanic crust (sima) | Mid-Indian Ocean Ridge
Sea level
Asia | India | Lithosphere | INDIAN–AUSTRALIAN PLATE | Upwelling magma

Seafloor spreading in the Atlantic Ocean and plate collision

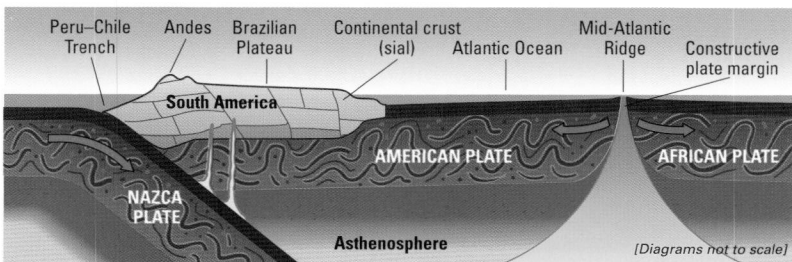

Peru-Chile Trench | Andes | Brazilian Plateau | Continental crust (sial) | Atlantic Ocean | Mid-Atlantic Ridge | Constructive plate margin
South America
AMERICAN PLATE | AFRICAN PLATE
NAZCA PLATE
Asthenosphere | [Diagrams not to scale]

The huge ridges that run through the oceans represent boundaries between plates. Here plates are diverging at rates of approximately 1–2 inches a year. Molten magma from the mantle rises along a central rift valley to form new crustal rock. These ocean ridges, which are active zones where earthquakes and volcanic eruptions are common, are called constructive plate margins. Destructive plate margins, which occur when two plates converge, are marked by deep ocean trenches as one plate is forced under the other. The descending plate is melted to produce the magma that fuels volcanoes alongside the trenches. Movements of descending plates are often sudden and violent, triggering earthquakes in overlying continental areas. Where two continents collide, their margins are buckled up to form fold mountain ranges. A third type of plate margin, the transform fault, is not illustrated above. Along these plate margins, such as California's San Andreas fault, plates are moving parallel to each other.

The debate about plate tectonics is not over. Questions still arise as to why some active volcanoes lie far from plate margins, and why major earthquakes occur in midplate areas.

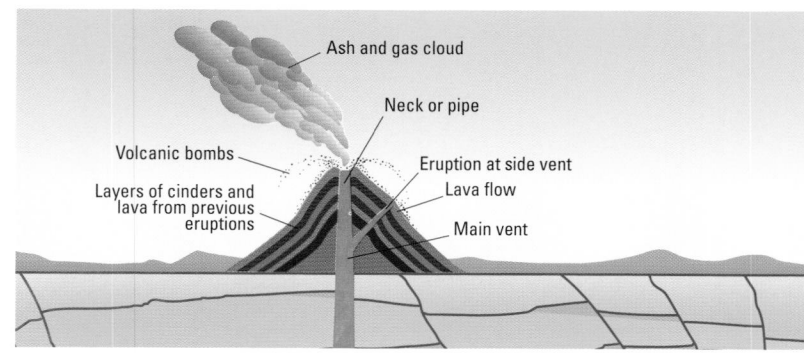

Ash and gas cloud
Neck or pipe
Volcanic bombs
Eruption at side vent
Layers of cinders and lava from previous eruptions
Lava flow
Main vent

Continental Drift

In 1915, Alfred Wegener produced a series of world maps proposing that, around 200 million years ago, the continents had been joined together in a supercontinent which he called Pangaea. This land mass started to break up about 180 million years ago and the parts drifted to their present positions. The arrows on the present-day world map (*below*) shows that the continents are still on the move.

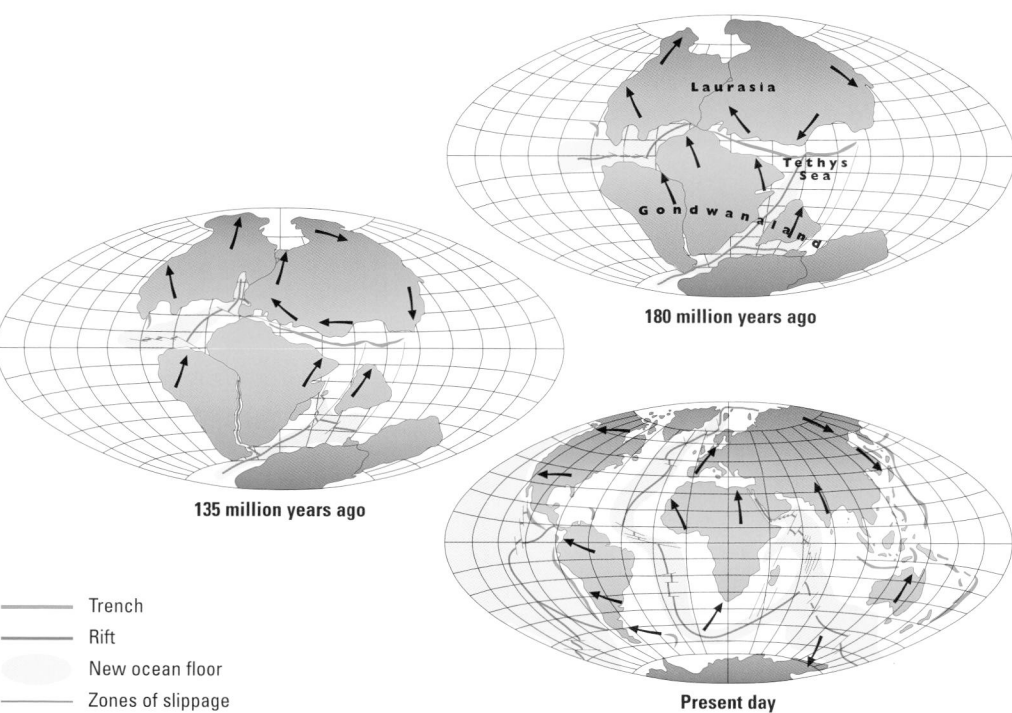

Laurasia
Tethys Sea
Gondwanaland
180 million years ago

135 million years ago

Present day

— Trench
— Rift
 New ocean floor
— Zones of slippage

Distribution of Volcanoes

Volcanoes occur when hot liquefied rock beneath the Earth's crust is pushed up by pressure to the surface as molten lava. There are some 550 known active volcanoes, around 20 of which are erupting at any one time.

• Submarine volcanoes
▲ Land volcanoes active since 1700
— Boundaries of tectonic plates

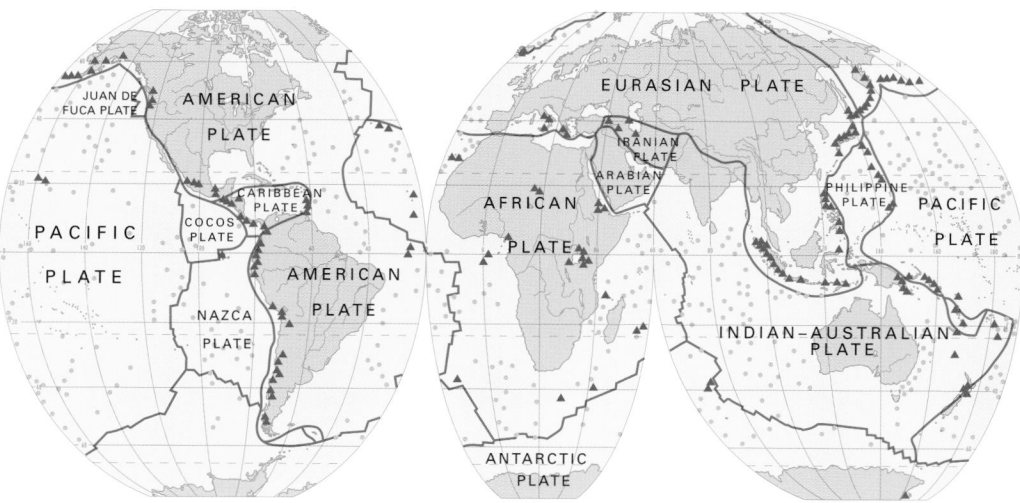

JUAN DE FUCA PLATE | AMERICAN PLATE
PACIFIC PLATE
CARIBBEAN PLATE
COCOS PLATE
NAZCA PLATE
AMERICAN PLATE
EURASIAN PLATE
IRANIAN PLATE
ARABIAN PLATE
AFRICAN PLATE
PHILIPPINE PLATE
PACIFIC PLATE
INDIAN–AUSTRALIAN PLATE
ANTARCTIC PLATE

Geological Time

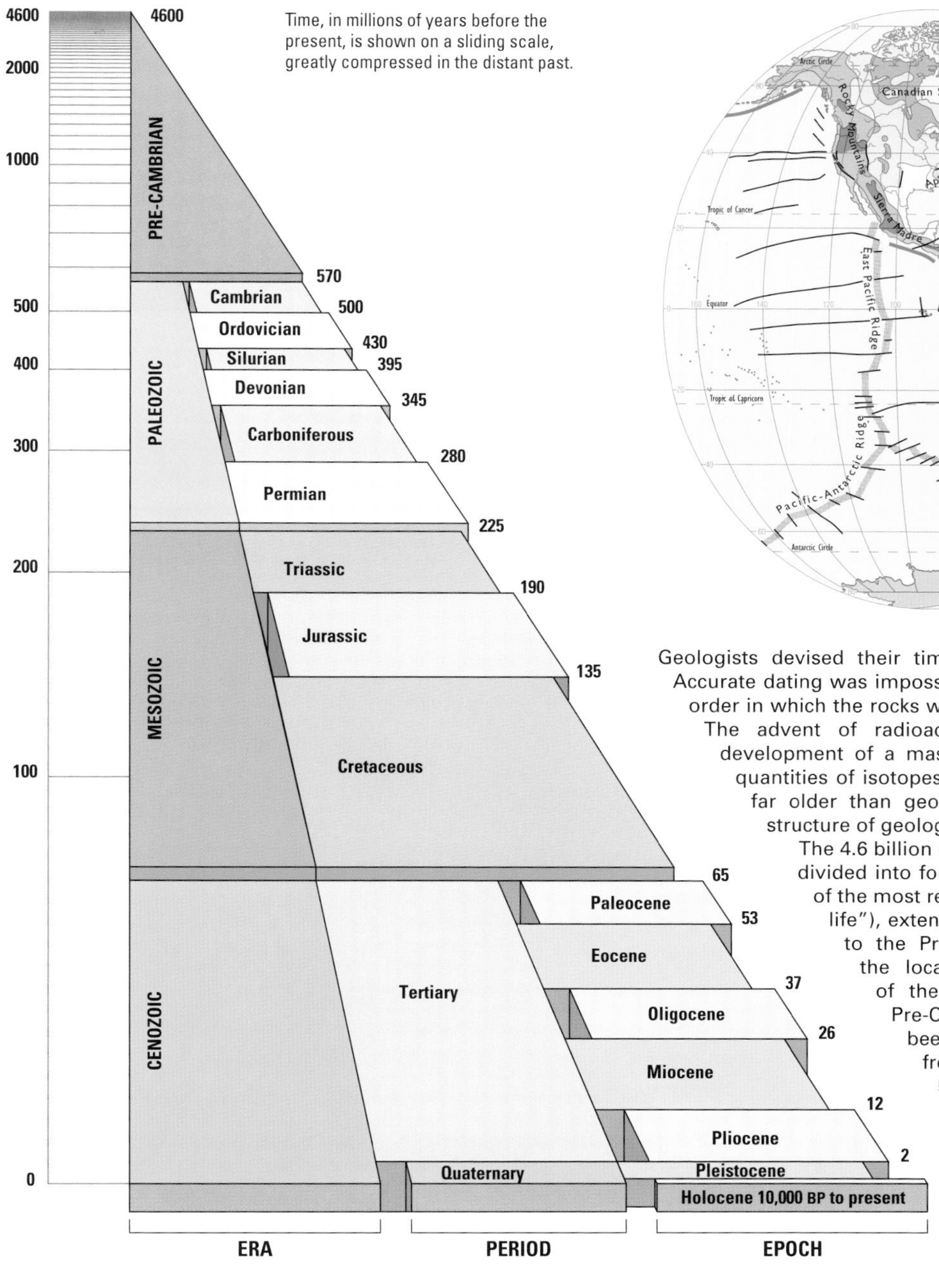

4600 Time, in millions of years before the present, is shown on a sliding scale, greatly compressed in the distant past.

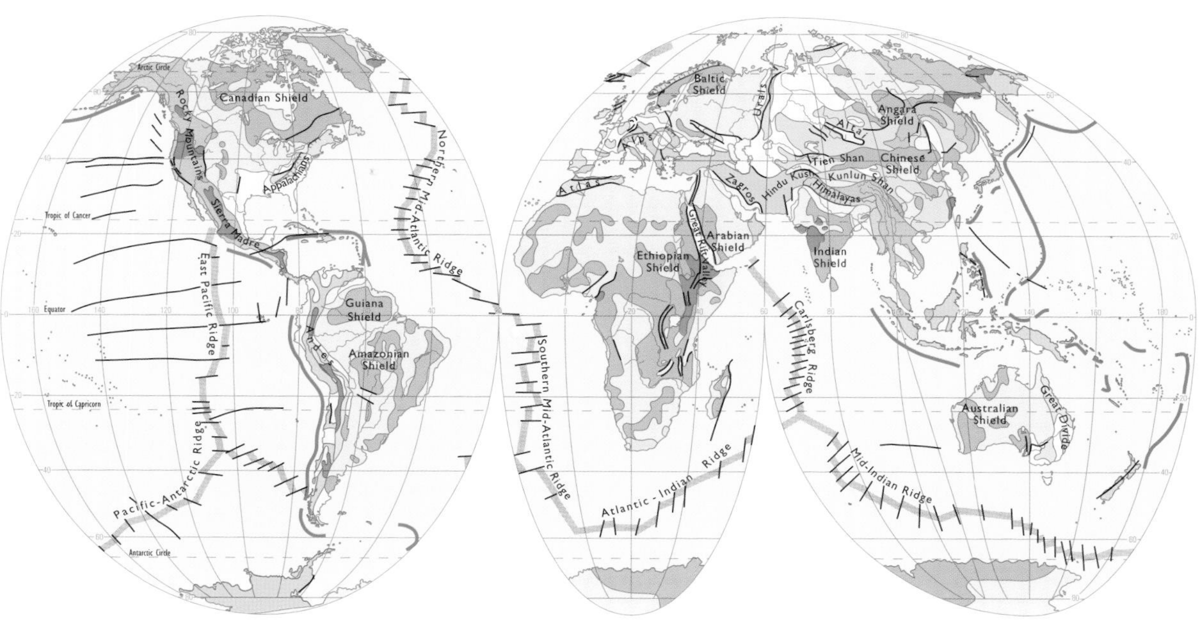

ERA	PERIOD	EPOCH
PRE-CAMBRIAN		
PALEOZOIC	Cambrian (570–500)	
	Ordovician (500–430)	
	Silurian (430–395)	
	Devonian (395–345)	
	Carboniferous (345–280)	
	Permian (280–225)	
MESOZOIC	Triassic (225–190)	
	Jurassic (190–135)	
	Cretaceous (135–65)	
CENOZOIC	Tertiary	Paleocene (65–53)
		Eocene (53–37)
		Oligocene (37–26)
		Miocene (26–12)
		Pliocene (12–2)
	Quaternary	Pleistocene (2–)
		Holocene 10,000 BP to present

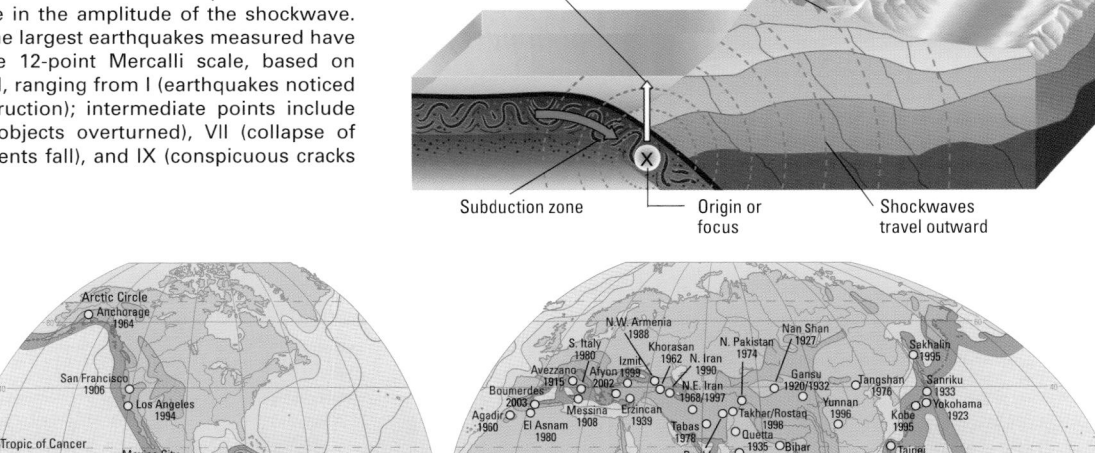

Geologists devised their timescale on the basis of relative, not calendar, ages. Accurate dating was impossible and estimates were often bitterly disputed, but the order in which the rocks were formed could be deduced from careful observation. The advent of radioactive dating – culminating in the 1950s with the development of a mass spectrometer capable of accurately measuring tiny quantities of isotopes – appears to have settled the arguments. The Earth is far older than geologists first imagined, but their painstakingly-created structure of geological time has withstood the advent of high technology.

The 4.6 billion (4,600 million) years since the formation of the Earth are divided into four great eras, further split into periods and, in the case of the most recent era, epochs. The present era is the Cenozoic ("new life"), extending backward through "middle life" and "ancient life" to the Pre-Cambrian, named after the Latin word for Wales, the location of some of the earliest known fossils. Most of the Earth's geological history is encompassed by the Pre-Cambrian: though traces of ancient life have since been found, it was largely the proliferation of fossils from the beginning of the Paleozoic era onward, some 570 million years ago, which first allowed precise subdivisions to be made.

Like the Cambrian, most are named after regions exemplifying a period's geology. Others – such as the Carboniferous ("coal-bearing") or the Cretaceous ("chalk-bearing") – are more directly descriptive.

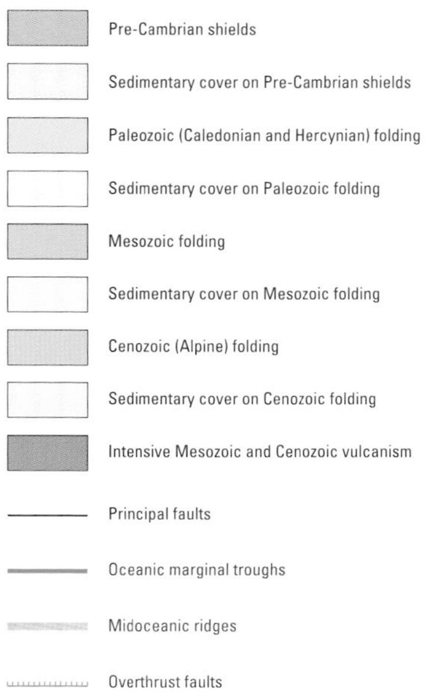

- Pre-Cambrian shields
- Sedimentary cover on Pre-Cambrian shields
- Paleozoic (Caledonian and Hercynian) folding
- Sedimentary cover on Paleozoic folding
- Mesozoic folding
- Sedimentary cover on Mesozoic folding
- Cenozoic (Alpine) folding
- Sedimentary cover on Cenozoic folding
- Intensive Mesozoic and Cenozoic vulcanism
- Principal faults
- Oceanic marginal troughs
- Midoceanic ridges
- Overthrust faults

Earthquakes

Earthquake magnitude is usually rated according to either the Richter or the Modified Mercalli scale, both devised by seismologists in the 1930s. The Richter scale measures absolute earthquake power with mathematical precision: each step upward represents a tenfold increase in the amplitude of the shockwave. Theoretically, there is no upper limit, but the largest earthquakes measured have been rated at between 8.8 and 8.9. The 12-point Mercalli scale, based on observed effects, is often more meaningful, ranging from I (earthquakes noticed only by seismographs) to XII (total destruction); intermediate points include V (people awakened at night; unstable objects overturned), VII (collapse of ordinary buildings; chimneys and monuments fall), and IX (conspicuous cracks in ground; serious damage to reservoirs).

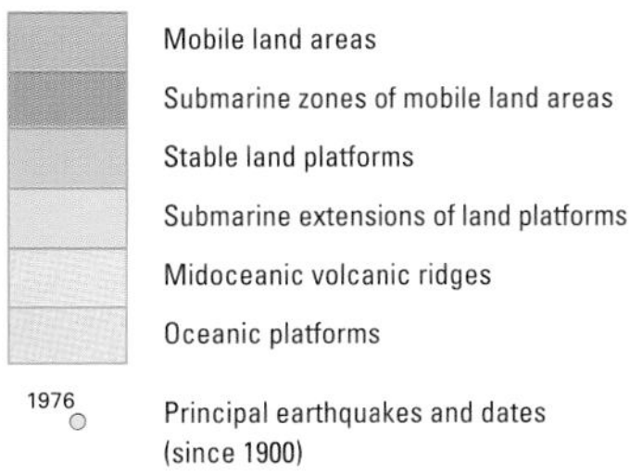

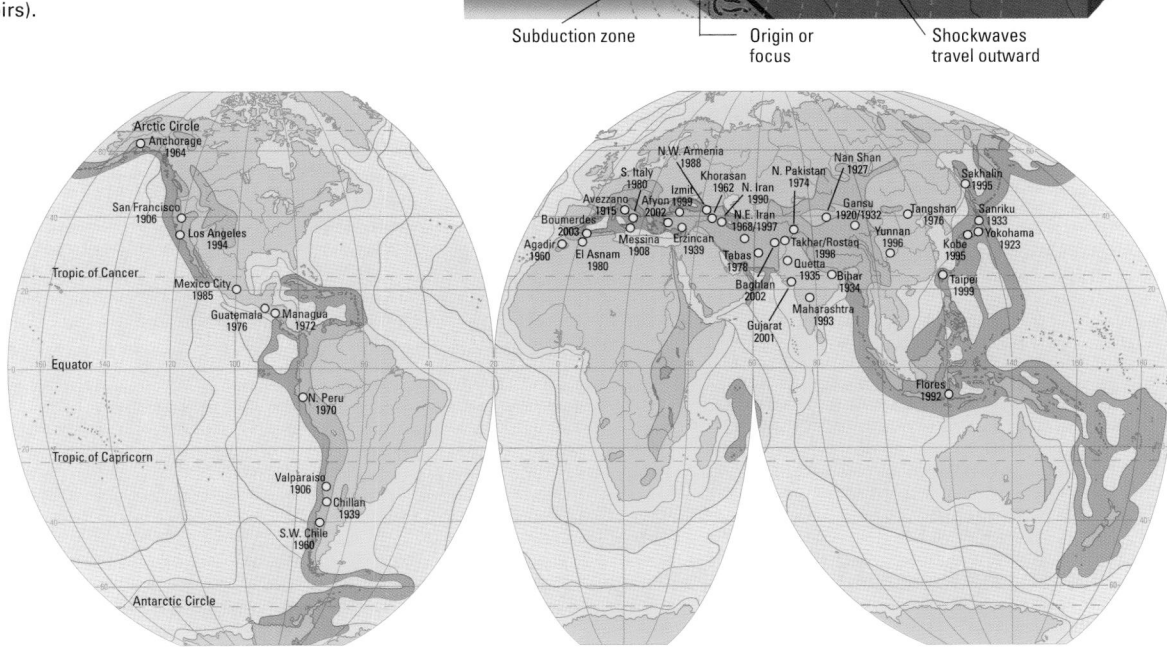

- Mobile land areas
- Submarine zones of mobile land areas
- Stable land platforms
- Submarine extensions of land platforms
- Midoceanic volcanic ridges
- Oceanic platforms

1976 ○ Principal earthquakes and dates (since 1900)

Earthquakes are a series of rapid vibrations originating from the slipping or faulting of parts of the Earth's crust when stresses within build up to breaking point. They usually happen at depths varying from 5–20 miles. Severe earthquakes cause extensive damage when they take place in populated areas, destroying structures and severing communications. Most initial loss of life occurs due to secondary causes such as falling masonry, fires and flooding.

Notable Earthquakes Since 1900

Year	Location	Mag.	Deaths
1906	San Francisco, USA	7.7	3,000
1906	Valparaiso, Chile	8.6	22,000
1908	Messina, Italy	7.5	83,000
1915	Avezzano, Italy	7.5	30,000
1920	Gansu (Kansu), China	8.6	180,000
1923	Yokohama, Japan	8.3	143,000
1927	Nan Shan, China	8.3	200,000
1932	Gansu (Kansu), China	7.6	70,000
1933	Sanriku, Japan	8.9	2,990
1934	Bihar, India/Nepal	8.4	10,700
1935	Quetta, India*	7.5	60,000
1939	Chillan, Chile	8.3	28,000
1939	Erzincan, Turkey	7.9	30,000
1960	S. W. Chile	9.5	2,200
1960	Agadir, Morocco	5.8	12,000
1962	Khorasan, Iran	7.1	12,230
1964	Anchorage, USA	9.2	125
1968	N. E. Iran	7.4	12,000
1970	N. Peru	7.7	66,794
1972	Managua, Nicaragua	6.2	5,000
1974	N. Pakistan	6.3	5,200
1976	Guatemala	7.5	22,778
1976	Tangshan, China	8.2	255,000
1978	Tabas, Iran	7.7	25,000
1980	El Asnam, Algeria	7.3	20,000
1980	S. Italy	7.2	4,800
1985	Mexico City, Mexico	8.1	4,200
1988	N.W. Armenia	6.8	55,000
1990	N. Iran	7.7	36,000
1992	Flores, Indonesia	6.8	1,895
1993	Maharashtra, India	6.4	30,000
1994	Los Angeles, USA	6.6	51
1995	Kobe, Japan	7.2	5,000
1995	Sakhalin Is., Russia	7.5	2,000
1996	Yunnan, China	7.0	240
1997	N. E. Iran	7.1	2,400
1998	Takhar, Afghanistan	6.1	4,200
1998	Rostaq, Afghanistan	7.0	5,000
1999	Izmit, Turkey	7.4	15,000
1999	Taipei, Taiwan	7.6	1,700
2001	Gujarat, India	7.7	14,000
2002	Afyon, Turkey	6.5	44
2002	Baghlan, Afghanistan	6.1	1,000
2003	Boumerdes, Algeria	6.8	2,200

The most devastating quake ever was at Shaanxi (Shenshi) province, central China, on January 3, 1556, when an estimated 830,000 people were killed.

* now Pakistan

LANDFORMS

The theory of plate tectonics has offered new insights as to how the Earth works, elucidating mysteries concerning continental drift, volcanic eruptions and earthquakes. It has also contributed to our understanding of how plate collisions can squeeze up layers of sediments on seabeds into fold mountain ranges, such as the Himalayas.

Yet even as mountains rise, natural forces are wearing them away. In hot, dry climates, mechanical weathering, a result of rapid temperature changes, causes the outer layers of rocks to peel away, while, in cold mountain regions, boulders are prised apart when water freezes in cracks in rocks. Chemical weathering is responsible for hollowing out limestone caves and decomposing granites.

Climatic conditions have a great bearing on the principal agent of erosion in any particular area. Running water is most important in moist temperate regions. In cold regions, ice is the major agent of erosion, and in many mountain ranges, U-shaped valleys are evidence of the erosive power of valley glaciers. Ice sheets molded much of the Earth's surface

during the Ice Ages, the most recent of which, in the northern hemisphere, ended only 10,000 years ago. Polar climates also shape the scenery of the periglacial areas that border bodies of ice. Such areas are subject to constant freeze-thaw action, which creates such features as pingos (domed mounds).

Climatic change has also affected many of the landforms in hot deserts, which were shaped by running water at a time when the deserts enjoyed much wetter climates. However, the major agent of erosion in deserts today is wind-blown sand, which erodes rock strata to form mushroom-shaped rocks and caves.

The surface of the Earth is under constant assault from tectonic processes and the agents of erosion. The products of erosion, fragments of rock such as sand, are deposited to form sedimentary rocks. Metamorphic rocks are created when igneous or sedimentary rocks are buried and metamorphosed by heat and pressure. Eventually the rocks are recycled to form magma, which rises upward to start the rock cycle all over again.

The Rock Cycle

James Hutton first proposed the rock cycle in the late 1700s after he observed the slow but steady effects of erosion.

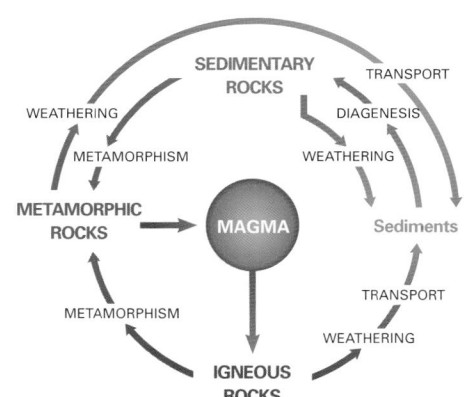

Rocks are divided into three types, according to the way in which they are formed:

Igneous rocks, including granite and basalt, are formed when magma cools inside the Earth's crust or on the surface.

Metamorphic rocks, such as slate, marble, and quartzite, are formed below the Earth's surface by the compression or baking of existing rocks.

Sedimentary rocks, like sandstone and limestone, are formed on the surface of the Earth from the remains of living organisms and eroded fragments of older rocks.

Mountain Building

Mountains are formed when pressures on the Earth's crust caused by continental drift become so intense that the surface buckles or cracks. This happens where oceanic crust is subducted by continental crust or, more dramatically, where two tectonic plates collide: the Rockies, Andes, Alps, Urals, and Himalayas resulted from such impacts. These are all known as fold mountains because they were formed by the compression of the rocks, forcing the surface to bend and fold like a crumpled rug. The Himalayas are formed from the folded former sediments of the Tethys Sea, which was trapped in the collision zone between the Indian–Australian and Eurasian plates.

The other main mountain-building process occurs when the crust fractures to create faults, allowing rock to be forced upward in large blocks; or when the pressure of magma within the crust forces the surface to bulge into a dome, or erupts to form a volcano. Large mountain ranges may reveal a combination of these features; the Alps, for example, have been compressed so violently that the folds are fragmented by numerous faults and intrusions of molten igneous rock.

Over millions of years, even the greatest mountain ranges can be reduced by the agents of erosion (especially rivers) to a low, rugged landscape known as a peneplain.

Types of faults: Faults occur where the crust is being stretched or compressed so violently that the rock strata break in a horizontal or vertical movement. They are classified by the direction in which the blocks of rock have moved. A normal fault results when a vertical movement causes the surface to break apart; compression causes a reverse fault. Horizontal movement causes shearing, known as a strike-slip fault. When the rock breaks in two places, the central block may be pushed up in a horst fault, or sink (creating a rift valley) in a graben fault.

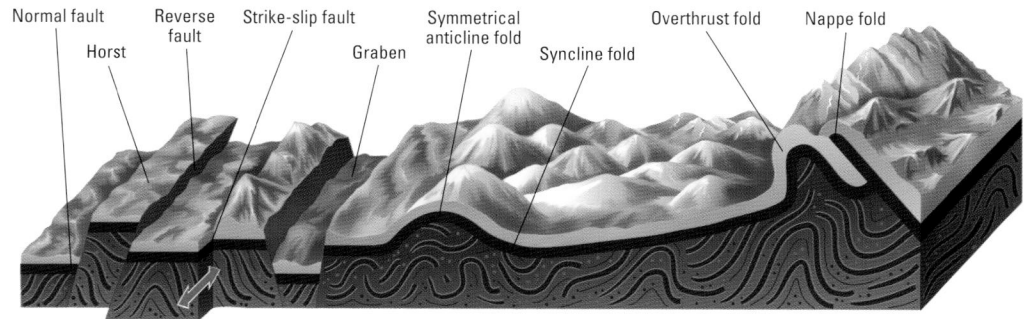

Types of fold: Folds occur when rock strata are squeezed and compressed. They are common, therefore, at destructive plate margins and where plates have collided, forcing the rocks to buckle into mountain ranges. Geographers give different names to the degrees of fold that result from continuing pressure on the rock. A simple fold may be symmetric, with even slopes on either side, but as the pressure builds up, one slope becomes steeper and the fold becomes asymmetric. Later, the ridge or "anticline" at the top of the fold may slide over the lower ground or "syncline" to form a recumbent fold. Eventually, the rock strata may break under the pressure to form an overthrust and finally a nappe fold.

Continental Glaciation

The mass balance is defined as the difference between glacier accumulation and ablation (melting), and is expressed as water equivalent in millimeters. A minus indicates a reduction in the depth or length of a glacier. As can be seen from this geographically diverse selection, glaciers are retreating in many areas worldwide. The most dramatic and serious example of this phenomenon is the continuing distintegration of several large Antarctic ice-shelves.

The extent to which glacial retreat is due to global warming, or to longer term climatic fluctuations, remains a matter for debate.

Many landforms in the northern hemisphere were shaped by ice sheets and meltwater during the Pleistocene Ice Age, which began about 2 million years ago. During the Ice Age, the ice sheets periodically advanced and retreated. The first map (*below left*) shows the ice cover at its greatest extent about 200,000 years BP (before the present), when it covered about 30% of the land surface, as compared with

10% today. About 18,000 years BP, the ice covered most of Canada and extended as far south as the Bristol Channel in England. Around the ice sheets, land areas experienced periglacial conditions.

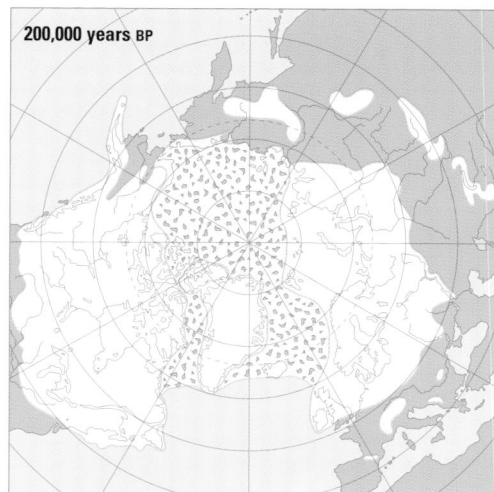

200,000 years BP

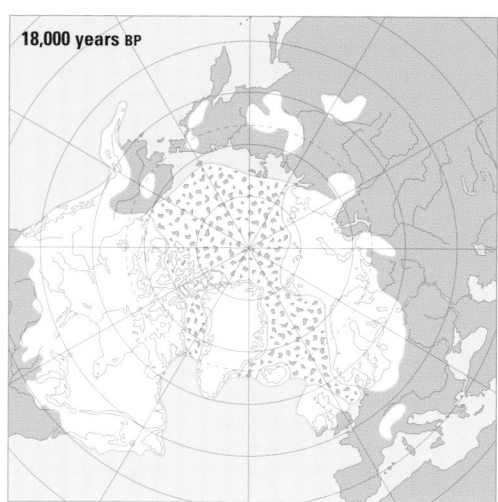

18,000 years BP

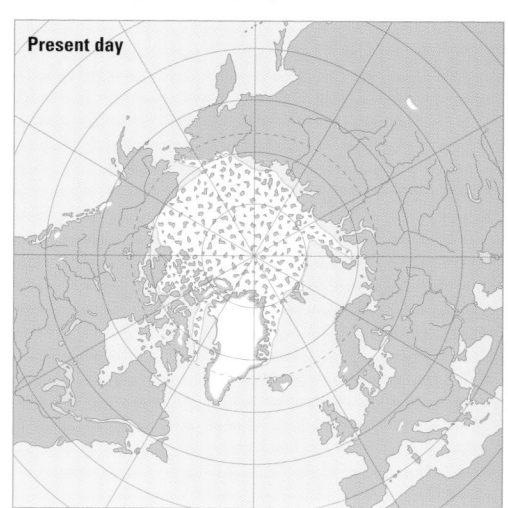

Present day

Natural Landforms

Natural landforms reflect the influence of plate tectonics through mountain-building and the generation of new rocks from the interior, together with the agents of erosion: running water, ice, winds, and coastal waves. Over millions of years, mountains are gradually eroded, producing landforms that reflect the major forces that have been at work, as well as the underlying geology, the climatic conditions, which often vary over time, and the vegetation cover. The stylized diagram (*below*) shows some major natural landforms found in the midlatitudes.

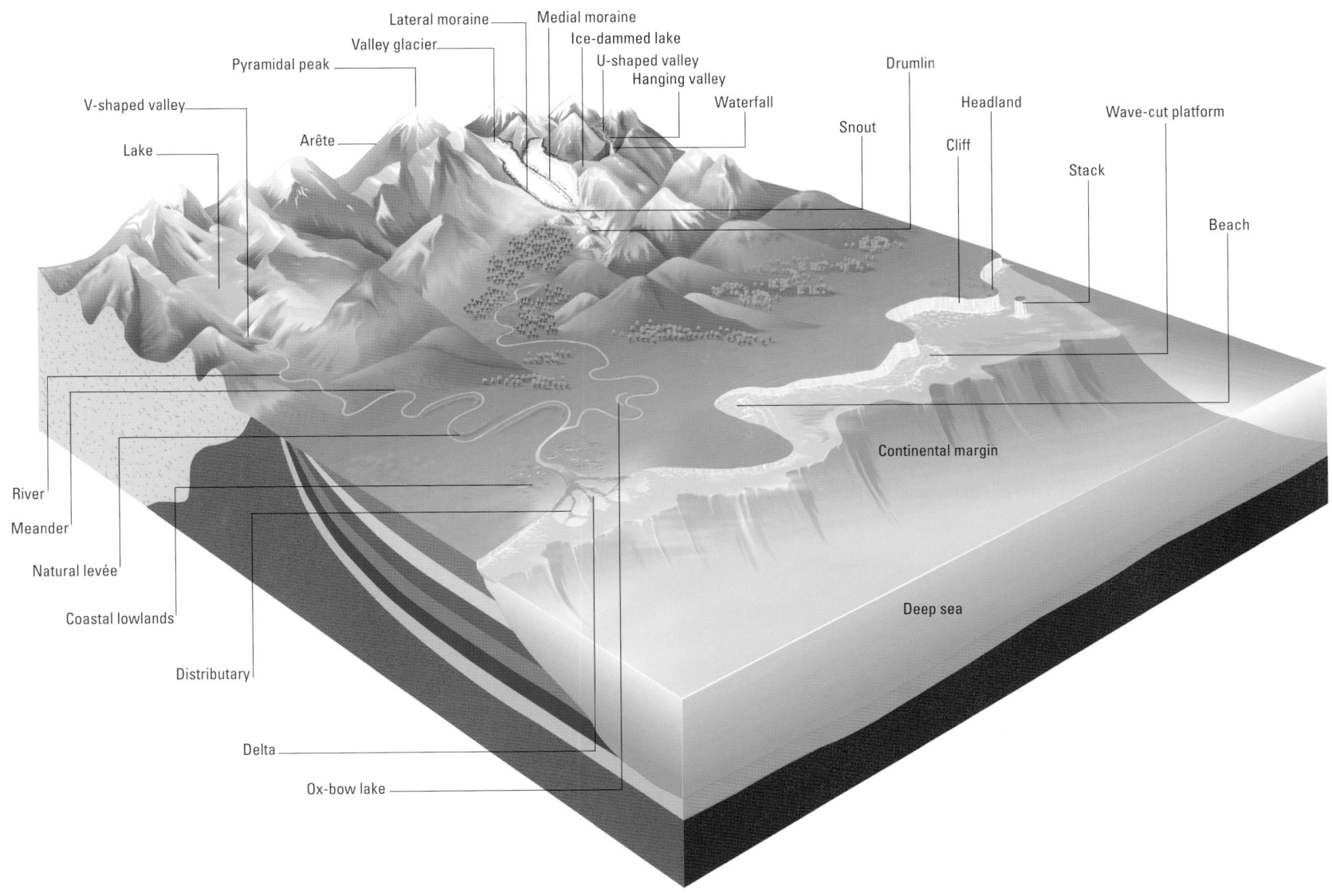

Desert Landforms

Deserts are defined as places with an average annual precipitation of 10 inches per year, though places with a higher rainfall and a high evaporation rate may also qualify as deserts. The three types of desert landforms are known by their Arabic names, a reflection of the fact that the Sahara in North Africa is the world's largest desert. Sand desert, called erg, covers about one-fifth of the world's deserts. The rest is divided between hammada (areas of bare rock) and reg (broad plains covered by loose gravel or pebbles).

The shapes of dunes in sand deserts reflect the character of local winds. Where winds are constant in direction, the sand often piles up in crescent-shaped dunes, called barchans. Barchans are constantly on the move and their forward march, unless halted by vegetation, may overwhelm settlements at oases. Seif dunes, named after the Arabic word for "sword," are long ridges of sand that lie parallel to the direction of the wind, but where winds are variable, the sand sheets are often featureless.

Erg

Wind-blown sand is an effective agent of erosion, but because of the weight of sand grains, this type of erosion is confined to within 7 feet of the land surface, creating caves and mushroom-shaped rocks.

In assessing desert landforms, it is important to remember that other processes were at work in the past when the climate was very different from today. For example, cave paintings suggest that the Sahara had a much wetter climate after the end of the Ice Age and only began to dry up after about 5000 BC. However, human action, including overgrazing and the cutting down of trees for firewood, can turn a grassland region into desert – a process known as desertification.

Hammada

Reg

Surface Processes

Catastrophic changes to landforms are periodically caused by such phenomena as avalanches, landslides, and volcanic eruptions, but most of the processes that shape the Earth's surface operate extremely slowly in human terms. One estimate, based on a study of landforms in the United States, suggests that, on average, just over 3 feet of land is removed from the entire surface of the country every 29,500 years. However, the terrain and the climate have a great effect on the erosion rate. For example, on cold plains, such as the Hudson Bay lowlands, the rate drops to around 3 feet for every 154,200 years, while in wet, tropical mountain areas, the rate may reach 3 feet for every 1,300 years.

Chemical weathering is at its greatest in warm, humid regions, while mechanical weathering, or the physical breakup of rocks, predominates in cold mountain or hot desert regions. The most familiar type of chemical weathering is caused by the reaction of rainwater containing dissolved carbon dioxide on limestone. This leads to the creation of labyrinthine cave networks dissolved by groundwater. Mechanical weathering includes frost action, while in hot deserts, rapid temperature changes cause the outer layers of rocks to expand and contract until they crack and peel away, a process called exfoliation.

The most important product of weathering is soil, which consists of rock fragments and humus, the decayed remains of plants and animals, together with living organisms, including vast numbers of micro-organisms. Soils vary in character according to the climate, ranging from the heavily leached, red laterite soils of wet tropical areas to the fertile, brown soils of dry grasslands. Soils are important because they support plants, which in turn anchor the soil and act as a protection against erosion. Soil erosion is greatest on sloping land because the steeper the slope, the greater the tendency for the soil to creep or flow downhill. The degree of movement of soil and rock downhill under the influence of gravity, called mass wasting, depends on a slope's stability. The stability may be disturbed by earthquakes or by heavy rain (water acts as a lubricant and increases the weight of the overlying material), which may trigger flows, slides or large falls of rock.

Running water is probably the world's leading agent of erosion and transportation. The energy of a river depends on several factors, including its velocity and volume, and its erosive power is at its peak when it is in full flood, sweeping soil, pebbles and even boulders along its course, cutting downward into the bedrock or widening its valley. Sea waves also exert tremendous erosive power during storms, when they hurl pebbles and large rocks against the shore, undercutting cliffs and hollowing out caves. Headlands are often attacked on both sides, forming caves, then a natural arch and eventually an isolated stack. Glacier ice forms in mountain hollows, called cirques, and spills out to form valley glaciers, which transport rocks shattered by frost action. As a glacier moves, rocks embedded in the base and sides scrape away bedrock, eroding steep-sided, flat-bottomed, U-shaped valleys. Evidence of past glaciation in mountain regions includes cirques, knife-edged ridges, or arêtes, and pyramidal peaks, or horns.

Geologists once considered that landforms evolved from "young," newly uplifted mountainous areas, through a "mature" hilly stage, to an "old age" stage when the land was reduced to an almost flat plain, or peneplain. This theory, called the "cycle of erosion," fell into disuse when it became evident that so many factors, including the effects of plate tectonics and climatic change, constantly interrupt the cycle, which takes no account of the highly complex interactions that shape the surface of our planet.

THE ATMOSPHERE

The atmosphere is a meteor shield, a radiation deflector, a thermal blanket, and a source of chemical energy for the Earth's diverse life forms. Five-sixths of its mass is in the lowest layer, the troposphere, which ranges in thickness from 11 to 6 miles between the Equator and the poles. Powered by the Sun, the air is always on the move, flowing generally from high- to low-pressure areas. The troposphere is the layer where virtually all weather phenomena, including clouds, precipitation and winds, occur. Above the troposphere is the stratosphere, which contains the important ozone layer and extends to about 30 miles above the Earth's surface. Beyond 60 miles, atmospheric density is lower than most laboratory vacuums.

Circulation of the Air

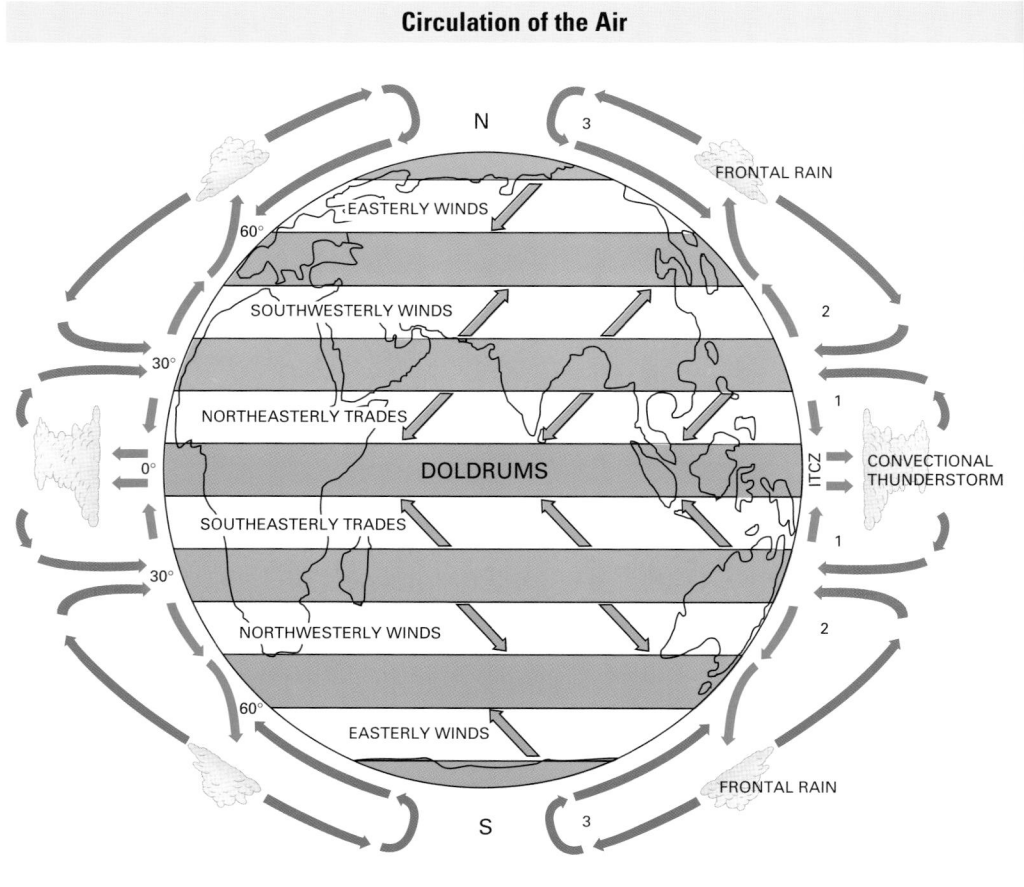

High pressure
Low pressure
Warm air
Cold air
Surface winds
Clouds

1 Hadley Cell
2 Ferrel Cell
3 Polar Cell

ITCZ Intertropical convergence zone

Structure of the Atmosphere

400 mi — Hubble Space Telescope — pressure 10^{-8}mb

exosphere

300 mi — 10^{-22}mb

International Space Station

250 mi

200 mi — 10^{-16}mb

Space Shuttle

thermosphere

150 mi

120 mi — 10^{-10}mb

aurorae

90 mi

mesosphere

60 mi — 10^{-3}mb

meteor trails

30 mi — ozone layer

stratosphere

6 mi — Concorde — 10^3mb

troposphere

Mount Everest 29,035 feet

Chemical Composition

Gaseous composition of the principal atmospheric layers

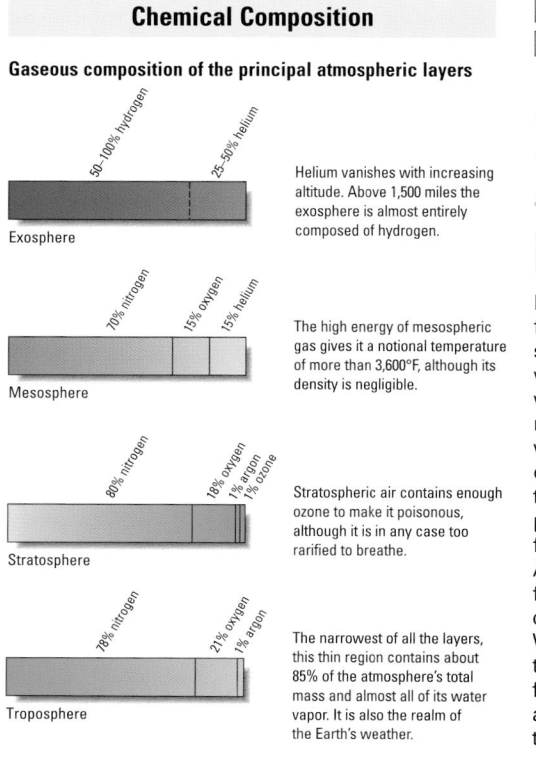

50–100% hydrogen | 25–50% helium
Exosphere

Helium vanishes with increasing altitude. Above 1,500 miles the exosphere is almost entirely composed of hydrogen.

70% nitrogen | 15% oxygen | 15% helium
Mesosphere

The high energy of mesospheric gas gives it a notional temperature of more than 3,600°F, although its density is negligible.

80% nitrogen | 18% oxygen | 1% argon | 1% ozone
Stratosphere

Stratospheric air contains enough ozone to make it poisonous, although it is in any case too rarified to breathe.

78% nitrogen | 21% oxygen | 1% argon
Troposphere

The narrowest of all the layers, this thin region contains about 85% of the atmosphere's total mass and almost all of its water vapor. It is also the realm of the Earth's weather.

Frontal Systems

Depressions, or cyclones, form along the polar front where dense polar easterlies meet warm subtropical westerlies. Depressions occur when warm air flows into waves in the polar front, while cold air flows in behind it, creating rotating air systems that bring changeable weather. Along the warm front (the boundary on the ground between the warm and cold air), the warm air flows upward over the cold air, producing a sequence of clouds which help forecasters to predict a depression's advance. Along the cold front, the advancing cold air forces warm air to rise steeply. Towering cumulonimbus clouds form in the rising air. When the cold front overtakes the warm front, the warm air is pushed above ground level to form an occluded front. Cloud and rain persist along occlusions until temperatures equalize, the air mixes, and the depression dies out.

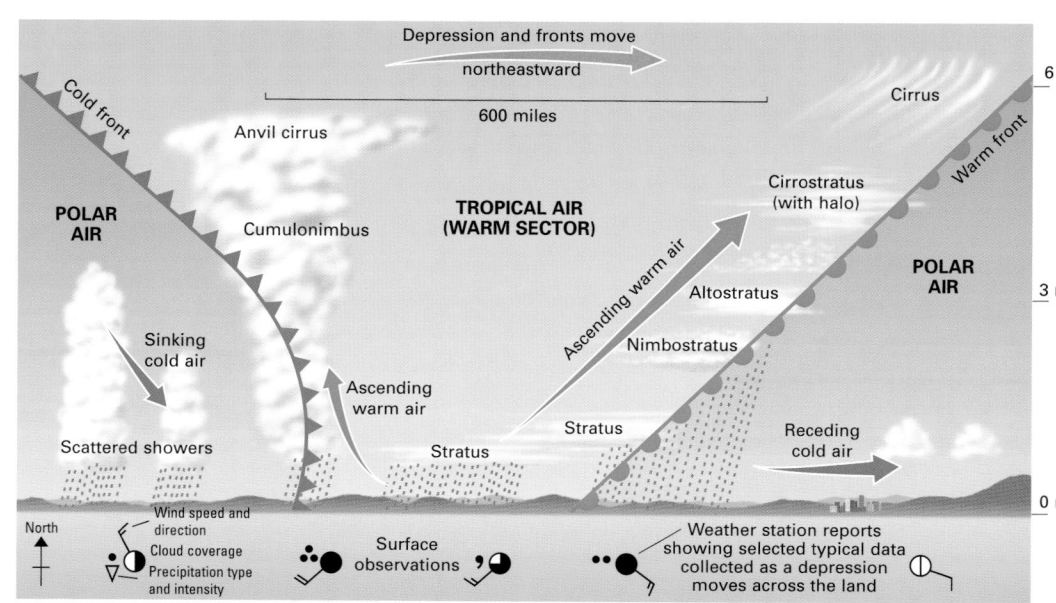

Air Masses

Air masses are bodies of air whose characteristics are broadly the same over a large area. Around the Equator, where the Sun's heat creates relatively high surface temperatures, warm air rises to create a zone of low pressure called the doldrums. The air cools and finally spreads out toward the poles. Around latitudes 30° north and south, the air sinks back to the surface, becoming warmer as it descends and creating zones of high pressure called the horse latitudes.

The high- and low-pressure zones are both areas of comparative calm, but between them lie the prevailing trade wind belts. Air also flows north and south from the high-pressure horse latitudes and these airflows meet up with cold, dense air flowing from the poles along the polar front. This basic circulatory system is complicated by the Coriolis effect, brought about by the spinning Earth. Because of the Coriolis effect, the prevailing winds do not flow directly north–south but are deflected to the right in the northern hemisphere and to the left in the southern. Along the polar front, depressions form where the polar easterlies meet the westerlies.

The first classification of clouds was developed by a London chemist, Luke Howard, in 1803, and it was later modified by the World Meteorological Organization. The main types are divided into three groups according to their altitude, and into subgroups according to their shape, which vary from hairlike filaments (cirrus), heaps or piles (cumulus), and layers (stratus). Each cloud carries some kind of message, though not always a clear one, to weather forecasters.

Classification of Clouds

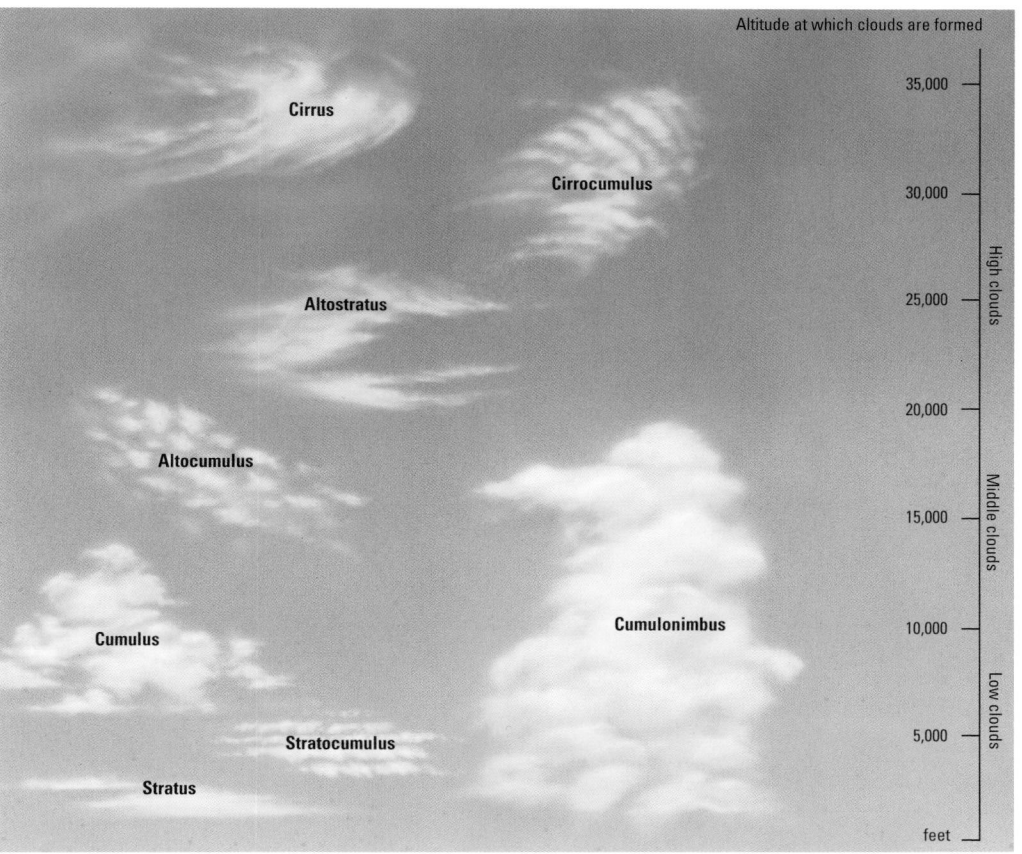

Clouds form when damp, usually rising, air is cooled. Thus they form when a wind rises to cross hills or mountains; when a mass of air rises over, or is pushed up by, another mass of denser air; or when local heating of the ground causes convection currents.

The types of clouds are classified according to altitude as high, middle, or low. The high ones, composed of ice crystals, are cirrus, cirrostratus, and cirrocumulus. The middle clouds are altostratus, a gray or bluish striated, fibrous or uniform sheet producing light drizzle, and altocumulus, a thicker and fluffier version of cirrocumulus.

Low clouds include nimbostratus, a dark gray layer that brings rain or snow; cumulus, a detached heap, dark at the base; stratus, which forms dull, overcast skies at low levels; and stratocumulus, which consists of fluffy grayish-white layers.

Cumulonimbus, associated with storms and rains, heavy and dense with a flat base and a high, fluffy outline, can be tall enough to occupy middle as well as low altitudes.

Pressure and Surface Winds

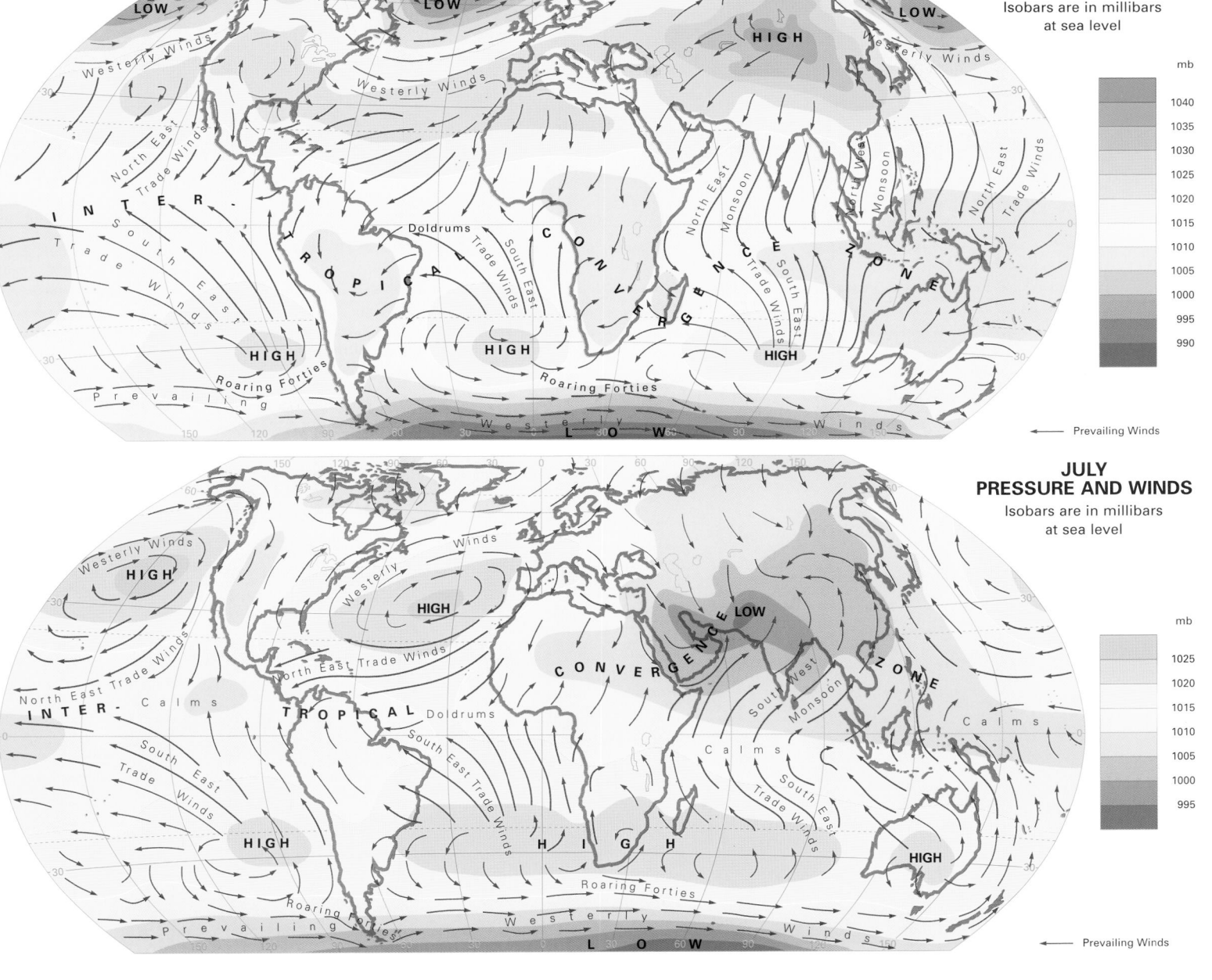

JANUARY PRESSURE AND WINDS
Isobars are in millibars at sea level

JULY PRESSURE AND WINDS
Isobars are in millibars at sea level

Climate Records

Pressure and winds

Highest barometric pressure: Agata, Siberia, 1,083.8 mb at altitude 862 ft [262 m], December 31, 1968.

Lowest barometric pressure: Typhoon Tip, 300 mi [480 km] west of Guam, Pacific Ocean, 870 mb, October 12, 1979.

Highest recorded wind speed: Mt Washington, New Hampshire, USA, 231 mph [371 km/h], April 12, 1934. This is three times as strong as hurricane force on the Beaufort Scale.

Windiest place: Commonwealth Bay, George V Coast, Antarctica, where gales frequently reach over 200 mph [320 km/h].

Worst recorded storm: Bangladesh (then East Pakistan) cyclone*, November 13, 1970 – over 300,000 dead or missing. The 1991 cyclone, Bangladesh's and the world's second worst in terms of loss of life, killed an estimated 138,000 people.

Worst recorded tornado: Missouri/Illinois/Indiana, USA, March 18, 1925 – 792 deaths. The tornado was only 300 yds [275 m] wide.

Tropical cyclones are known as hurricanes in Central and North America, as typhoons in the Far East, and as willy-willies in northern Australia.

Climate

For more information:

9 Ocean currents
14 Circulation of the air
15 Classification of clouds
Pressure and winds
18 Hydrological cycle
19 Natural vegetation
21 Greenhouse effect
22 Global warming

Weather is the day-to-day or hour-to-hour condition of the air, while climate is weather in the long term, the seasonal pattern of hot and cold, wet and dry, averaged over a long period. Most classifications of climate are based on a system developed by a Russian meteorologist, Vladimir Köppen, in the early 19th century. Using a code based on letters and a classification centered on two main features, temperature and precipitation, he identified five main climatic types: tropical (A), dry (B), warm temperate (C), cold temperate (D), and polar (E). A highland mountain climate (H) was added later to account for the variety of altitudinal climatic zones on high mountains. Each of these main regions was then further subdivided.

Latitude is a major factor in determining climate, but other factors add to the complexity. They include the differential heating of land and sea, the distance from the sea, the effect of mountains on winds, and the influence of ocean currents. For example, New York City, Naples, and the Gobi Desert share almost the same latitude, but their climates are very different.

Climates are not indefinitely stable. During the last Ice Age, the Earth underwent alternating cold periods, called glacials, separated by warm interglacials. The Milankovich theory suggests such cycles may be caused by variations in the Earth's path around the Sun, changing from almost circular to elliptical every 95,000 years, and variations in the Earth's tilt from 21.5° to 24.5° every 42,000 years. Another factor is that the Earth is now closest to the Sun in the middle of winter in the northern hemisphere and furthest away in summer. But 12,000 years ago, at the height of the last glacial period, the northern winter fell with the Sun at its most distant.

Studies of these cycles suggest that we are now in an interglacial with a new glacial period on the way. However, many scientists believe that global warming, largely a result of burning fossil fuels and deforestation, may be occurring much faster than the great, slow cycles of the Solar System.

Tropical rainy climates
All mean monthly temperatures above 64°F.
- Af Rain forest climate
- Am Monsoon climate
- Aw Savanna climate

Dry climates
Low rainfall combined with a wide range of temperatures
- BS Steppe climate
- BW Desert climate

Warm temperate rainy climates
The mean temperature is below 64°F but above 26°F and that of the warmest month is over 50°F.
- Cw Dry winter climate
- Cs Dry summer climate
- Cf Climate with no dry season

Cold temperate rainy climates
The mean temperature of the coldest month is below 26°F but that of the warmest month is still over 50°F.
- Dw Dry winter climate
- Df Climate with no dry season

Polar climates
The mean temperature of the warmest month is below 50°F, giving permanently frozen subsoil.
- ET Tundra climate

The mean temperature of the warmest month is below 32°F, giving permanent ice and snow.
- EF Polar climate

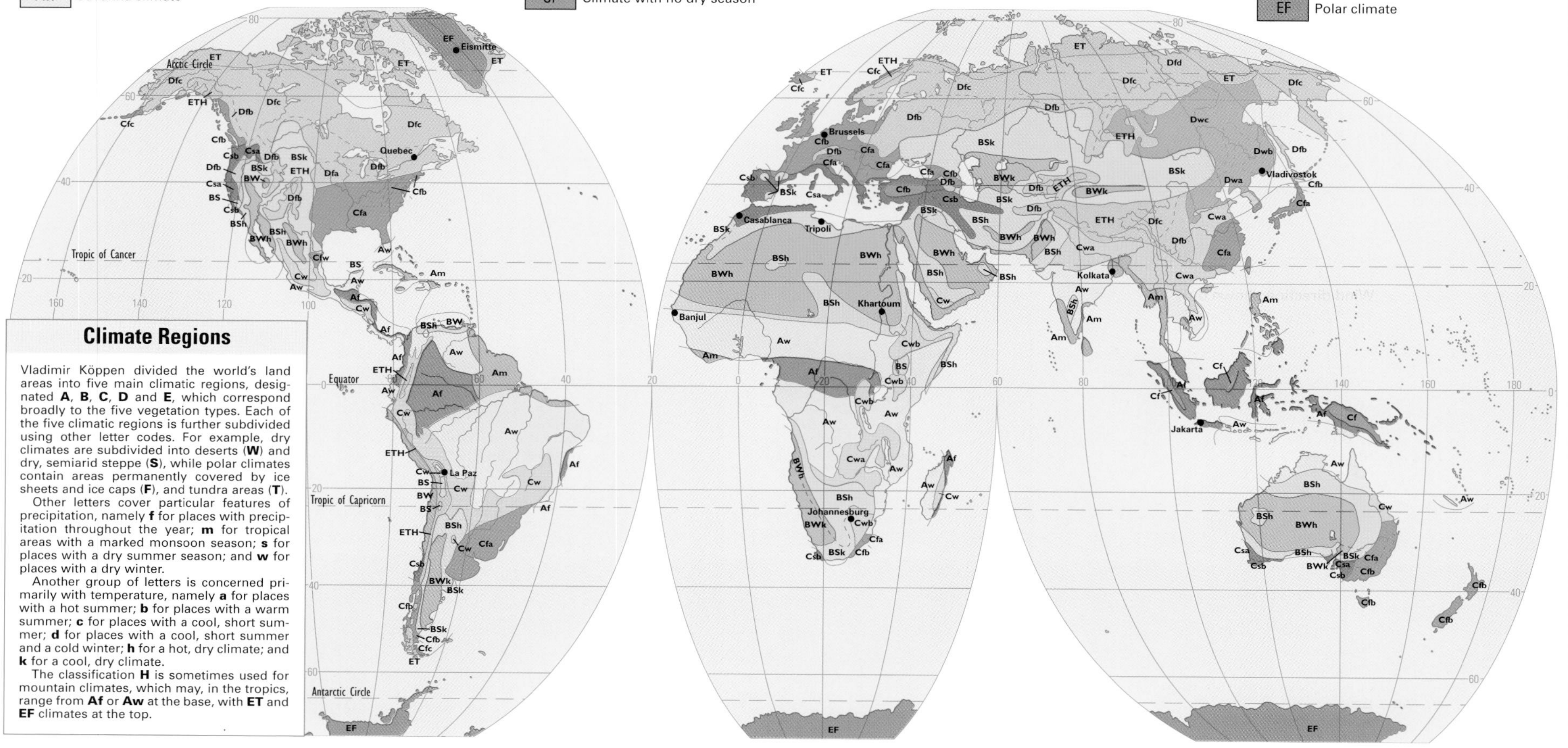

Climate Regions

Vladimir Köppen divided the world's land areas into five main climatic regions, designated **A**, **B**, **C**, **D** and **E**, which correspond broadly to the five vegetation types. Each of the five climatic regions is further subdivided using other letter codes. For example, dry climates are subdivided into deserts (**W**) and dry, semiarid steppe (**S**), while polar climates contain areas permanently covered by ice sheets and ice caps (**F**), and tundra areas (**T**).

Other letters cover particular features of precipitation, namely **f** for places with precipitation throughout the year; **m** for tropical areas with a marked monsoon season; **s** for places with a dry summer season; and **w** for places with a dry winter.

Another group of letters is concerned primarily with temperature, namely **a** for places with a hot summer; **b** for places with a warm summer; **c** for places with a cool, short summer; **d** for places with a cool, short summer and a cold winter; **h** for a hot, dry climate; and **k** for a cool, dry climate.

The classification **H** is sometimes used for mountain climates, which may, in the tropics, range from **Af** or **Aw** at the base, with **ET** and **EF** climates at the top.

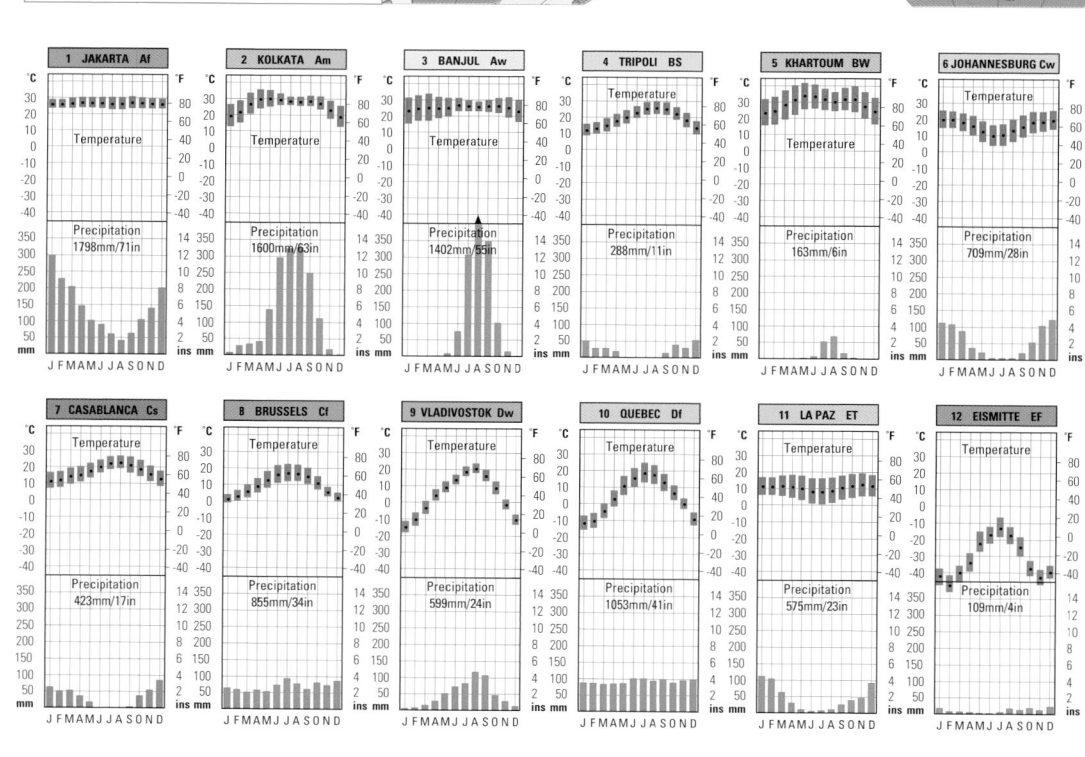

Climate and Weather Terms

Anticyclone: area of high pressure with light winds and generally quiet weather.
Absolute humidity: amount of water vapor contained in a given volume of air.
Cloud cover: amount of cloud in the sky; measured in oktas (from 1 – 8), with 0 clear, and 8 total cover.
Condensation: the conversion of water vapor, or moisture in the air, into liquid.
Cyclone: violent storm resulting from counterclockwise rotation of winds in the northern hemisphere and clockwise in the southern: called hurricane in N. America, typhoon in the Far East.
Depression: area of low pressure. The pressure gradient is toward the center.
Dew: water droplets condensed out of the air after the ground has cooled at night.
Dew point: temperature at which air becomes saturated (reaches a relative humidity of 100%) at a constant pressure.
Drizzle: precipitation where drops are less than 0.02 inches [0.5 mm] in diameter.
Evaporation: conversion of water from liquid into vapor, or moisture in the air.
Front: the dividing line between two air masses.
Frost: dew that has frozen when the air temperature falls below freezing point.
Hail: frozen rain; small balls of ice, often falling during thunderstorms.
Hoar frost: formed on objects when the dew point is below freezing point.
Humidity: amount of moisture in the air.
Isobar: cartographic line connecting places of equal atmospheric pressure.
Isotherm: cartographic line connecting places of equal temperature.
Lightning: massive electrical discharge released in thunderstorm from cloud to cloud or cloud to ground, the result of the top becoming positively charged and the bottom negatively charged.
Precipitation: measurable rain, snow, sleet, or hail.
Prevailing wind: most common direction of wind at a given location.
Rain: precipitation of liquid particles with diameter larger than 0.02 inches [0.5 mm].
Relative humidity: amount of water vapor contained in a given volume of air at a given temperature.
Snow: formed when water vapor condenses below freezing point.
Thunder: sound produced by the rapid expansion of air heated by lightning.
Tornado: severe funnel-shaped storm that twists as hot air spins vertically (waterspout at sea).
Whirlwind: rapidly rotating column of air, only a few feet across, made visible by dust.

Climate Change

Human factors, such as the emission of greenhouse gases through the burning of fossil fuels and deforestation, have contributed to global warming. The histogram (*below*) shows in blue the average global temperatures from 1860 (when sufficient observations became available for global averages to be calculated) to 1996. The red line is a 10-year running average. Overall, there is an upward trend, particularly so since the 1970s, when global warming became a matter of concern in scientific circles. The large year-to-year changes indicate the Earth's natural climatic variability and the influence of such factors as major volcanic eruptions.

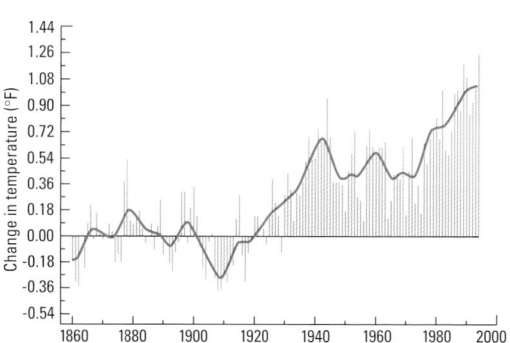

Data from the Hadley Center for Climate Research and Prediction

Beaufort Wind Scale

Named after the 19th-century British naval officer who devised it, Admiral Beaufort, the Beaufort Scale assesses wind speed according to its effects. It was originally designed as an aid for sailors, but has since been adapted for use on the land. It is used internationally.

Scale	Wind speed mph	km/h	Effect
0	0–1	0–1	**Calm** Smoke rises vertically
1	1–3	1–5	**Light air** Wind direction shown only by smoke drift
2	4–7	6–11	**Light breeze** Wind felt on face; leaves rustle; vanes moved by wind
3	8–12	12–19	**Gentle breeze** Leaves and small twigs in constant motion; wind extends small flag
4	13–18	20–28	**Moderate** Raises dust and loose paper; small branches move
5	19–24	29–38	**Fresh** Small trees in leaf sway; crested wavelets on inland waters
6	25–31	39–49	**Strong** Large branches move; difficult to use umbrellas; overhead wires whistle
7	32–38	50–61	**Near gale** Whole trees in motion; difficult to walk against wind
8	39–46	62–74	**Gale** Twigs break from trees; walking very difficult
9	47–54	75–88	**Strong gale** Slight structural damage
10	55–63	89–102	**Storm** Trees uprooted; serious structural damage
11	64–72	103–117	**Violent storm** Widespread damage
12	73+	118+	**Hurricane**

The Monsoon

Monsoon is the term given to the seasonal reversal of wind direction, most noticeably in Southeast Asia. It results from a combination of factors: the extreme heating and cooling of large land masses in relation to the less marked changes in temperature of the adjacent seas; the northward movement of the Intertropical Convergence Zone (ITCZ); and the effect of the Himalayas on the circulation of the air.

In early March, which normally marks the end of the subcontinent's cool season and the start of the hot season, winds blow outward from the mainland. But as the overhead Sun and the ITCZ move northward, the land is intensely heated, and a low-pressure system develops. The southeast trade winds, which are drawn across the Equator, change direction and are sucked into the interior to become southwesterly winds, bringing heavy rain. By November, the overhead Sun and the ITCZ have again moved southward and the wind directions are again reversed. Cool winds blow from the Asian interior to the sea, losing any moisture on the Himalayas before descending to the coast.

Temperature

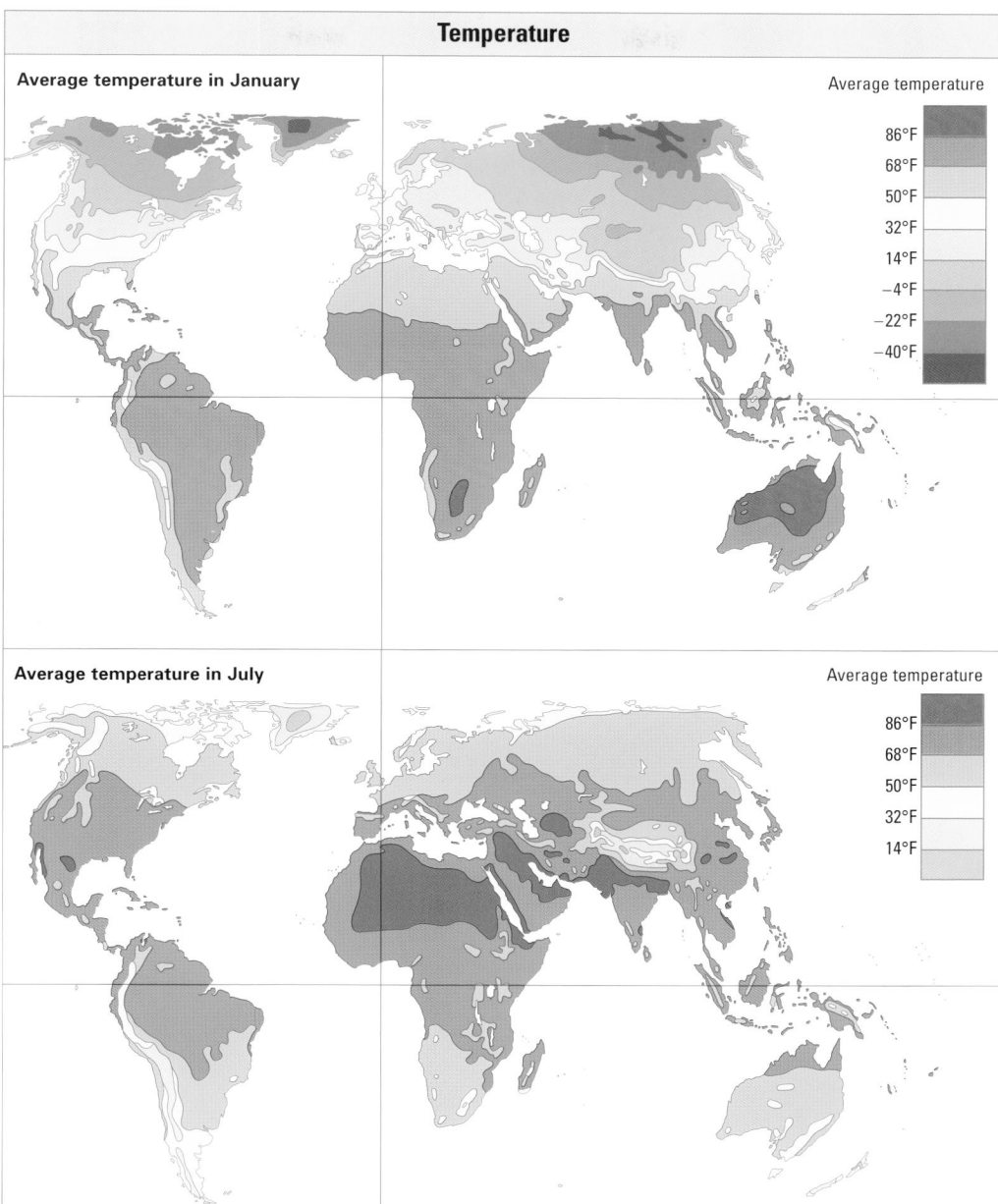

Average temperature in January

Average temperature

86°F
68°F
50°F
32°F
14°F
−4°F
−22°F
−40°F

Average temperature in July

Average temperature

86°F
68°F
50°F
32°F
14°F

Precipitation

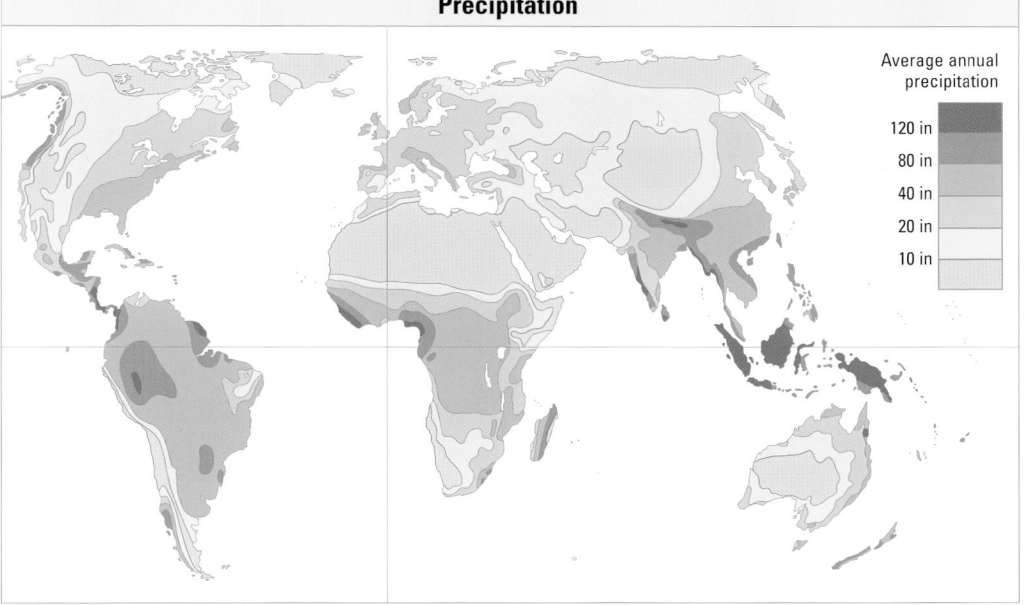

Average annual precipitation

120 in
80 in
40 in
20 in
10 in

March – Start of the hot, dry season. The ITCZ is over the southern Indian Ocean.

July – The rainy season. The ITCZ has migrated northward; winds blow onshore.

November – The ITCZ has returned south. The offshore winds are cool and dry.

Monthly rainfall (inches)

>16
8–16
4–8
2–4
1–2
<1

→ wind direction
— ITCZ

Climate Records

Temperature

Highest recorded temperature: Al Aziziyah, Libya, 136.4°F [58°C], September 13, 1922.

Highest mean annual temperature: Dallol, Ethiopia, 94°F [34.4°C], 1960–6.

Longest heatwave: Marble Bar, W. Australia, 162 days over 100°F [38°C], October 23, 1923, to April 7, 1924.

Lowest recorded temperature (outside poles): Verkhoyansk, Siberia, −90°F [−68°C], February 6, 1933. Verkhoyansk also registered the greatest annual range of temperature: −94°F to 98°F [−70°C to 37°C].

Lowest mean annual temperature: Polus Nedostupnosti, Pole of Cold, Antarctica, −72°F [−57.8°C].

Precipitation

Driest place: Calama, N. Chile: no recorded rainfall in 400 years to 1971.

Wettest place (average): Tututendo, Colombia: mean annual rainfall 463.4 in [11,770 mm].

Wettest place (12 months): Cherrapunji, Meghalaya, N.E. India, 1,040 in [26,470 mm], August 1860 to August 1861. Cherrapunji also holds the record for rainfall in one month: 115 in [2,930 mm], July 1861. (*See maps below*.)

Wettest place (24 hours): Cilaos, Réunion, Indian Ocean, 73.6 in [1,870 mm], March 15–16, 1952.

Heaviest hailstones: Gopalganj, Bangladesh, up to 2.25 lb [1.02 kg], April 14, 1986 (killed 92 people).

Heaviest snowfall (continuous): Bessans, Savoie, France, 68 in [1,730 mm] in 19 hours, April 5–6, 1969.

Heaviest snowfall (season/year): Paradise Ranger Station, Mt Rainier, Washington, USA, 1,224.5 in [31,102 mm], February 19, 1971, to February 18, 1972.

WATER AND VEGETATION

Without the hydrological cycle, whereby water is constantly recycled between the oceans, the atmosphere and the land, the continents would be barren. Precipitation enables plants to grow and soils to form, creating the world's natural vegetation regions and the ecosystems that support animal life. Running water also plays a major role in shaping landforms. Yet in many parts of the world, people do not have safe water to drink and suffer from diseases caused by water-borne organisms and pollution. In 2002, an estimated 1 billion people lacked access to safe water and 2.6 billion lacked basic sanitation.

UN experts argue that the world demand for water is increasing at about twice the rate of population growth. They have predicted that, by 2025, half of the world's population will face water shortages. This could lead to conflict and even boundary wars, especially because 300 major rivers cross national frontiers and access to their water is likely to be disputed.

The Hydrological Cycle

The world's water balance is regulated by the constant recycling of water between the oceans, atmosphere, and land. The movement of water between these three reservoirs is known as the hydrological cycle. The oceans play a vital role in the hydrological cycle: 74% of the total precipitation falls over the oceans and 84% of the total evaporation comes from the oceans. Water vapor in the atmosphere circulates around the planet, transporting energy as well as the water itself. When the vapor cools, it falls as rain or snow. The whole cycle is driven by the Sun.

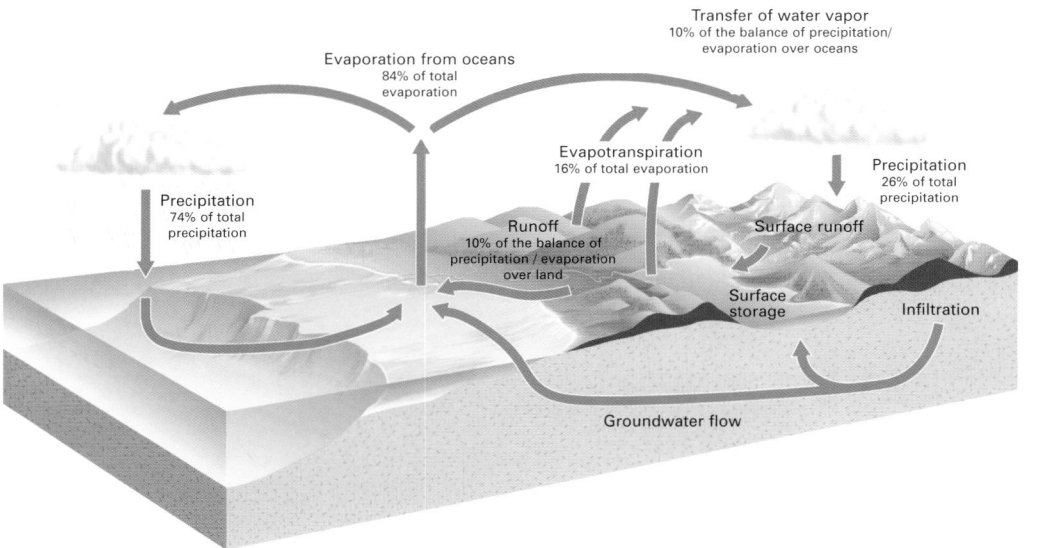

Water Distribution

The distribution of planetary water, by percentage. Oceans and ice caps together account for more than 99% of the total; the breakdown of the remainder is estimated.

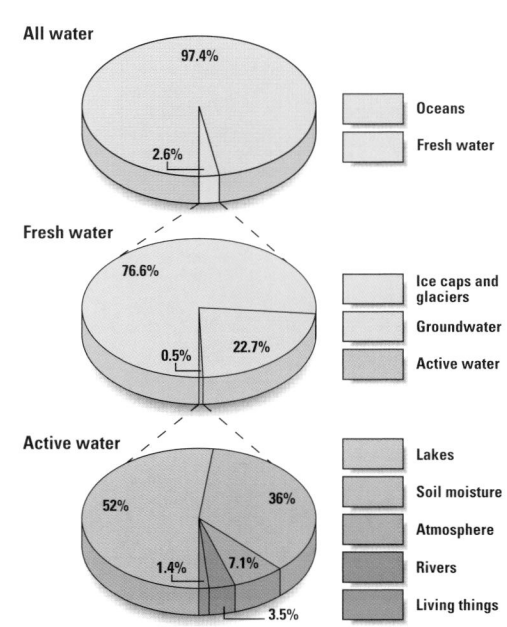

All water
- 97.4% Oceans
- 2.6% Fresh water

Fresh water
- 76.6% Ice caps and glaciers
- 0.5% Groundwater
- 22.7% Active water

Active water
- 52% Lakes
- 36% Soil moisture
- 1.4% Atmosphere
- 7.1% Rivers
- 3.5% Living things

Almost all the world's water is 3,000 million years old, and all of it cycles endlessly through the hydrosphere, though at different rates. Water vapor circulates over days, even hours; deep ocean water circulates over millennia; and ice-cap water remains solid for millions of years.

Water Utilization

The percentage breakdown of water usage by sector, selected countries (latest available year)

- Domestic
- Industrial
- Agriculture

Algeria
Australia
Egypt
France
Ghana
India
Mexico
Poland
Russian Fed.
Saudi Arabia
UK
USA

Water Runoff

Annual freshwater runoff by continent in cubic miles

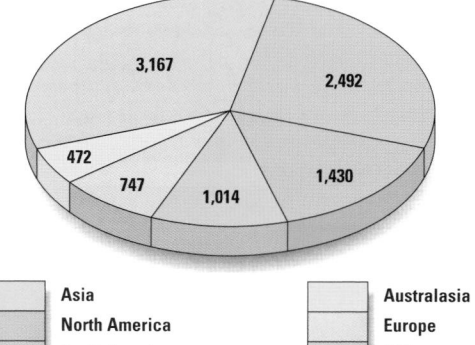

3,167
2,492
472
747
1,014
1,430

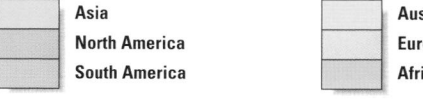

- Asia
- North America
- South America
- Australasia
- Europe
- Africa

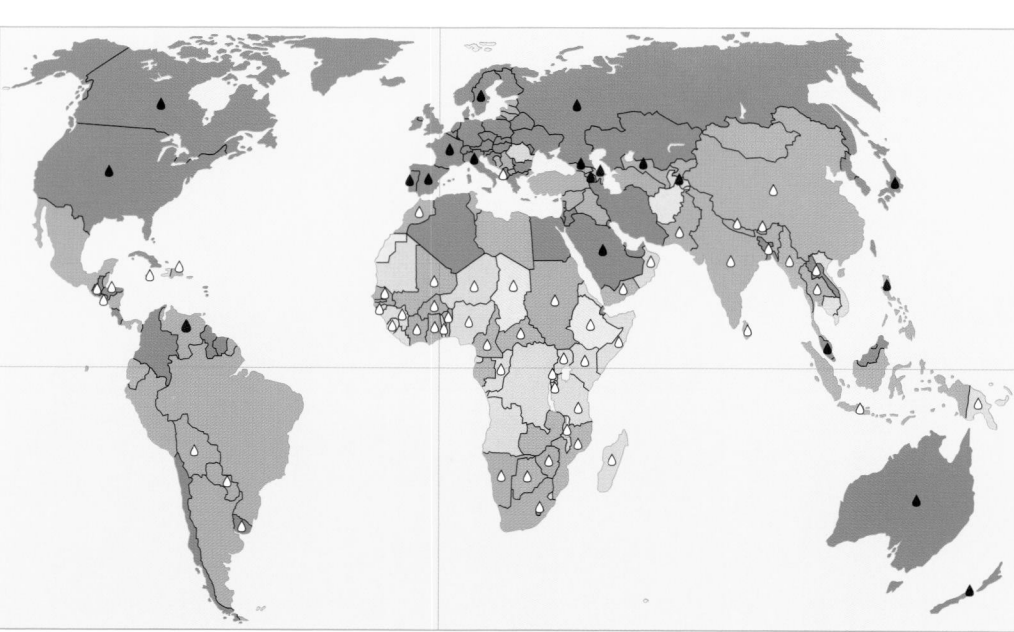

Water Supply

Percentage of total population with access to safe drinking water (2000)

- Over 90% with safe water
- 75 – 90% with safe water
- 60 – 75% with safe water
- 45 – 60% with safe water
- 30 – 45% with safe water
- Under 30% with safe water

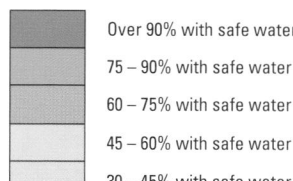

△ Under 80 liters average per capita daily water consumption

▲ Over 320 liters average per capita daily water consumption

80 liters of water a day is considered necessary for a reasonable quality of life

Least well-provided countries

Afghanistan	13%	Cambodia	30%
Ethiopia	24%	Mauritania	37%
Chad	27%	Angola	38%
Sierra Leone	28%	Oman	39%

Watersheds

The world's major rivers; the rank of the world's 20 longest is shown in square brackets, led by the Nile and the Amazon.

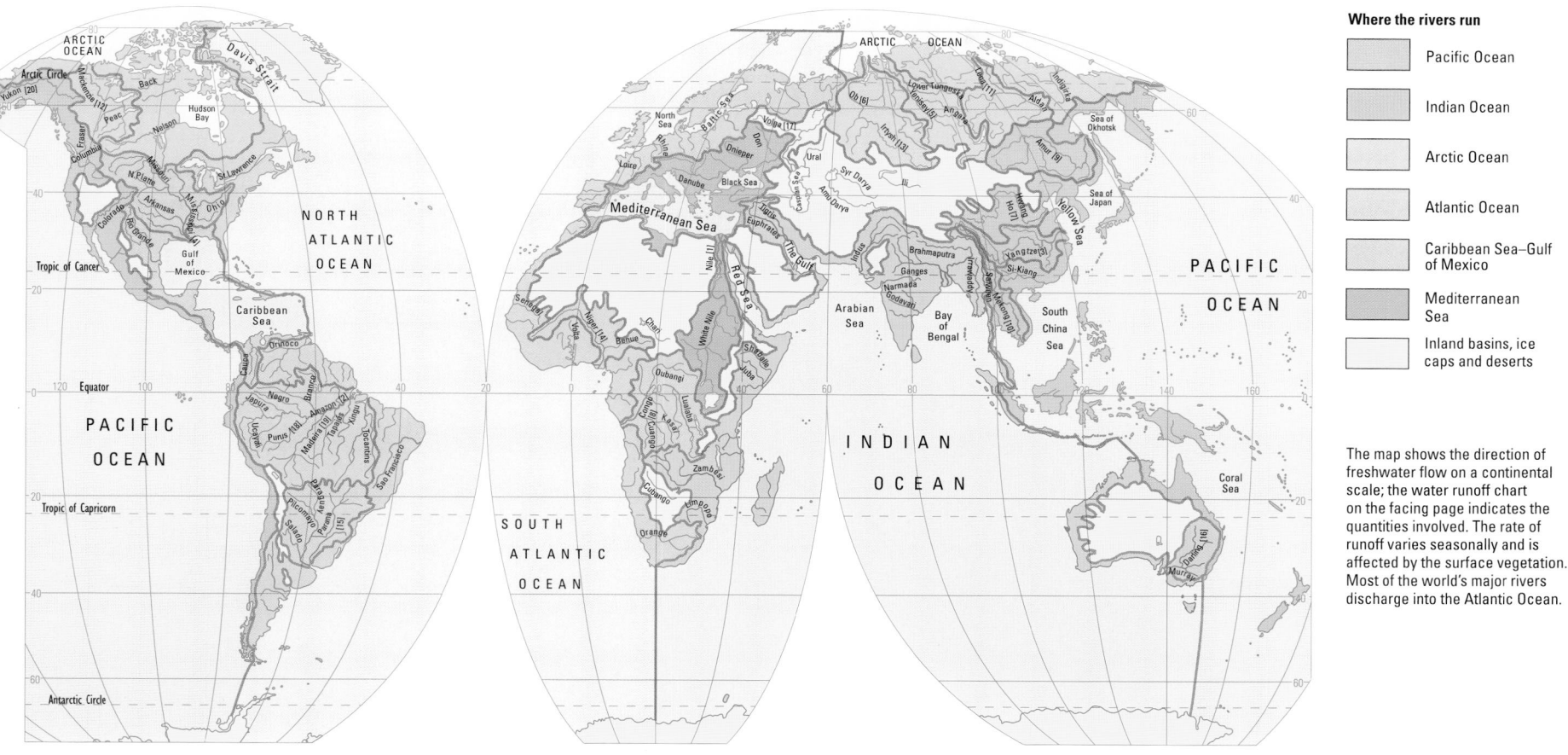

Where the rivers run

- Pacific Ocean
- Indian Ocean
- Arctic Ocean
- Atlantic Ocean
- Caribbean Sea–Gulf of Mexico
- Mediterranean Sea
- Inland basins, ice caps and deserts

The map shows the direction of freshwater flow on a continental scale; the water runoff chart on the facing page indicates the quantities involved. The rate of runoff varies seasonally and is affected by the surface vegetation. Most of the world's major rivers discharge into the Atlantic Ocean.

Annual Sediment Yield

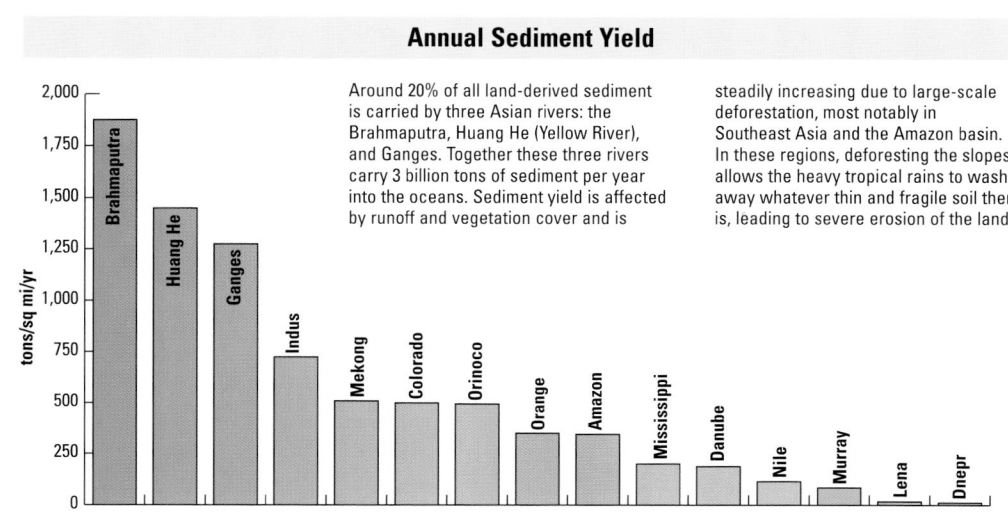

Around 20% of all land-derived sediment is carried by three Asian rivers: the Brahmaputra, Huang He (Yellow River), and Ganges. Together these three rivers carry 3 billion tons of sediment per year into the oceans. Sediment yield is affected by runoff and vegetation cover and is steadily increasing due to large-scale deforestation, most notably in Southeast Asia and the Amazon basin. In these regions, deforesting the slopes allows the heavy tropical rains to wash away whatever thin and fragile soil there is, leading to severe erosion of the land.

Land Use by Continent

The proportion of productive land has reached its upper limit in Europe, and in Asia more than 80% of potential cropland is already under cultivation.

- Forest
- Permanent pasture and rough grazing
- Permanent crops and plantations
- Arable
- Non-productive

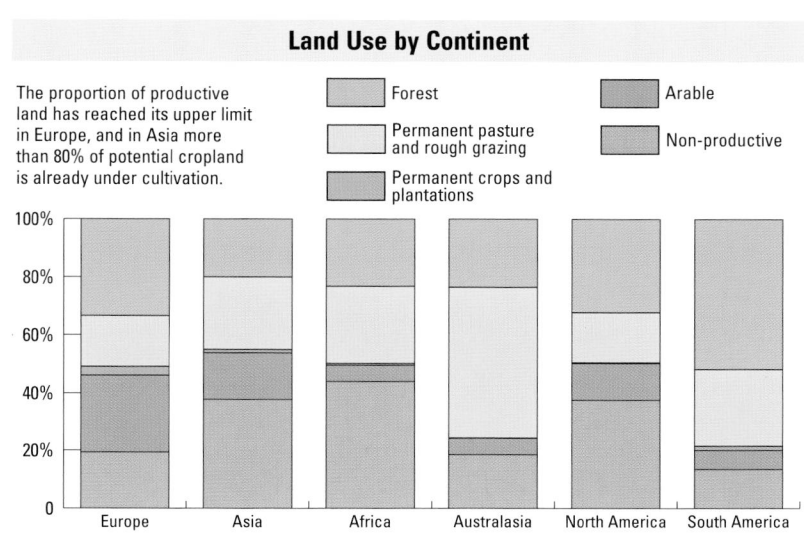

Natural Vegetation

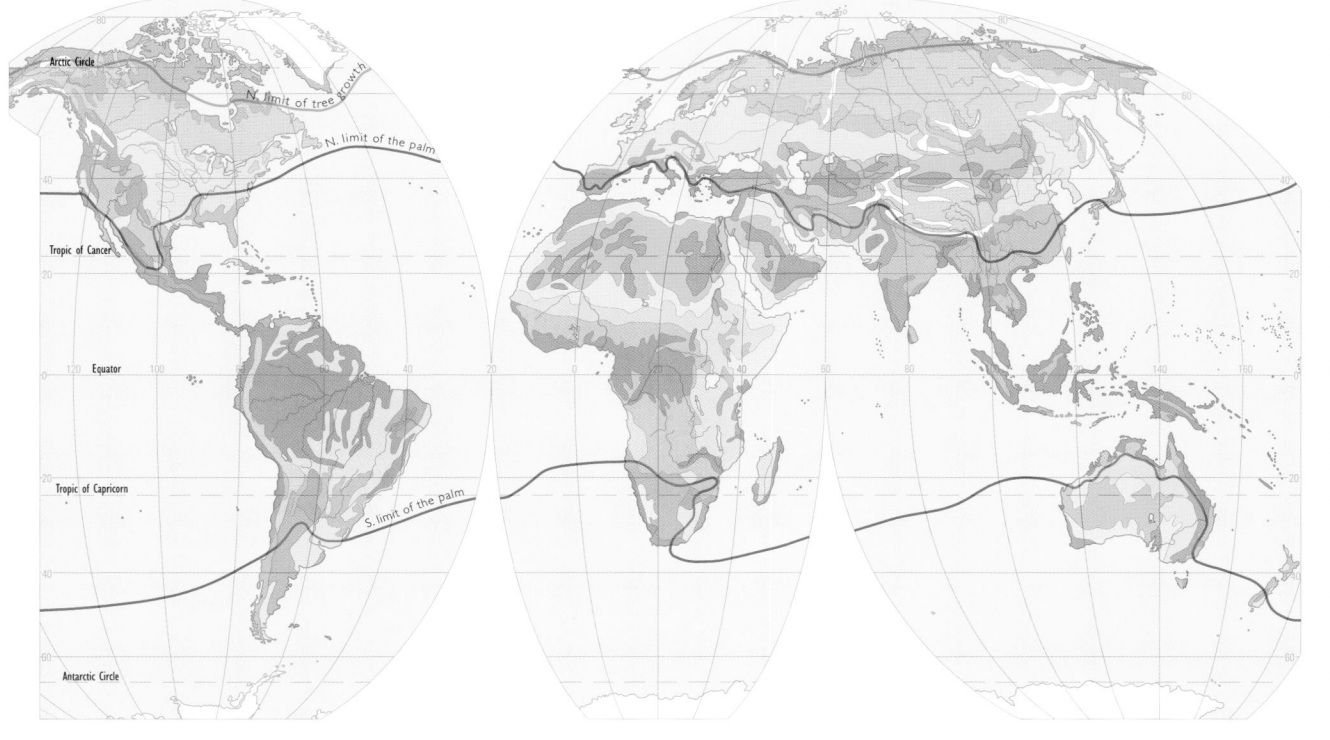

- Tropical rain forest
- Subtropical and temperate rain forest
- Monsoon woodland and open jungle
- Subtropical and temperate woodland, scrub and bush
- Tropical savanna, with low trees and bush
- Tropical savanna and grasslands
- Dry semidesert, with shrub and grass
- Desert shrub
- Desert
- Dry steppe and shrub
- Temperate grasslands, prairie and steppe
- Mediterranean hardwood forest and scrub
- Temperate deciduous forest and meadow
- Temperate deciduous and coniferous forest
- Northern coniferous forest (taiga)
- Mountainous forest, mainly coniferous
- High plateau steppe and tundra
- Arctic tundra
- Polar and mountainous ice desert

The map illustrates the natural "climax vegetation" of a region, as dictated by its climate and topography. In most cases, human agricultural activity has drastically altered the vegetation pattern. Western Europe, for example, lost most of its broadleaf forest many centuries ago, while elsewhere irrigation has turned some natural semidesert into productive land. The various vegetation regions support different kinds of animals and, in an undisturbed state, they are highly developed biological communities, or biomes.

The blue line on the map represents the northern limit of tree growth, and the red lines indicate the northern and southern limits of palm growth.

THE NATURAL ENVIRONMENT

Recent discoveries of life forms in some of the world's most hostile environments, such as around the black smokers along the ocean ridges, prepared the way for the announcement by NASA scientists in 1996 that they had found microfossils in a Martian meteorite. But other scientists were sceptical, believing them to be natural mineral structures and not evidence of extraterrestrial life.

Until further evidence is available, the Earth remains the only planet where we know for sure that life exists. According to the fossil record, life on Earth appeared at least 3.5 billion years ago. Since then, it has evolved from its primitive beginnings to its modern biodiversity, including millions of plants, animals and micro-organisms. Living organisms have not only adapted to the environ-ment but they have also changed their environment to suit themselves. For example, the Earth's early atmosphere contained little oxygen but the emergence of multicelled, oxygen-producing algae, around 2 billion years ago, led to the creation of an oxygen-rich atmosphere. This enabled land animals to populate the ancient continents.

The amount of the greenhouse gas carbon dioxide in the atmosphere would steadily increase from its present 0.03% were it not for plants. Without them, the Earth's atmos-phere would, in a few million years, be similar to that of Venus, where surface temperatures reach 890°F. The Earth has evolved into a complex control system, sensing and reacting to changes and tending always to maintain the balance it has achieved.

Much discussion has centered on how that balance changes. Only recently, scientists were suggesting that we may be living in an interglacial stage of the Pleistocene Ice Age. From the 1980s, however, predictions of future climates have concentrated more on global warming, caused by pollution which has led to an increase in greenhouse gases in the atmosphere. Interference in the natural cycles that control the environment may have consequences that are hard to predict.

Furthermore, we are currently experienc-ing a period of mass extinction of species, causing a rapid reduction in our planet's biodiversity. In 2002, a report by the Inter-national Union for the Conservation of Nature listed 11,167 organisms facing extinction. This was 121 more than in 2000.

Biodiversity in California

The photograph (*left*) is a false-color satellite image of central California in the southwestern United States. The large inlet of the Pacific Ocean is San Francisco Bay. San Francisco lies just below the entrance to the bay, with Oakland on the far side and San Jose to the southeast. California, nick-named the Golden State, is the third largest state in the United States and the most populous.

Because of its varied terrain and climate, California has a wide range of diverse habitats within a relatively small area. East of the forested Coast Ranges (the gray and red areas just inland from the bay) lies the fertile Central Valley, which appears as a red and blue checkerboard. The Sierra Nevada is the red area in the top right-hand corner. In the northwest and southwest of the state (*not shown here*) lie parts of the Basin and Range region, much of which is desert. It includes Death Valley, which contains the country's lowest point on land at 282 feet below sea level.

Forests cover about 40% of California and they include bristlecone pines, thought to be the oldest living things on Earth, together with coastal red-woods, the world's tallest trees. Wildlife is still abundant, though some species, such as the rare California condor, are on the endangered list.

The state has achieved much to protect its biodiversity. It contains eight of the 56 national parks in the United States. Two of them, Death Valley and Joshua Tree, were designated national parks as recently as 1994, as part of a conservation measure, including the protection of large areas of wilderness in the deserts.

California has vast resources and, were it a separate nation, it would rank among the world's ten most productive in terms of the total value of its goods and services. This means that, like the United States as a whole, it has resources, which many developing countries lack, to finance conservation measures. For example, the World Conservation Union reported in 1996 that 8% of mammals were threatened in the United States, as compared with 32% in the Philippines and 44% in Madagascar, two countries where habitat destruction has been on a large scale.

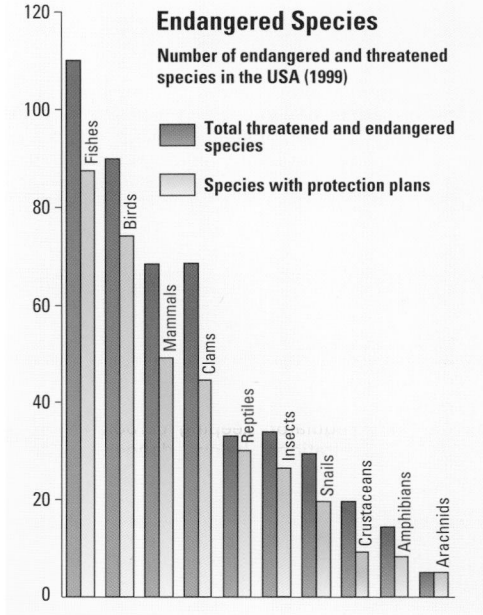

Endangered Species

Number of endangered and threatened species in the USA (1999)

■ Total threatened and endangered species
□ Species with protection plans

(Categories shown: Fishes, Birds, Mammals, Clams, Reptiles, Insects, Snails, Crustaceans, Amphibians, Arachnids)

Threatened Mammals

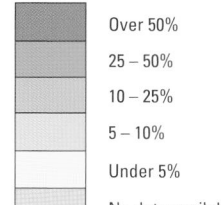

Percentage of mammal species classified as threatened (2002)
Many scientists believe we are currently experiencing a period of mass extinction of species rivaling five other periods in the past half a billion years. Among the most threatened mammals are elephants, primates, and rhinoceroses.

- Over 50%
- 25 – 50%
- 10 – 25%
- 5 – 10%
- Under 5%
- No data available

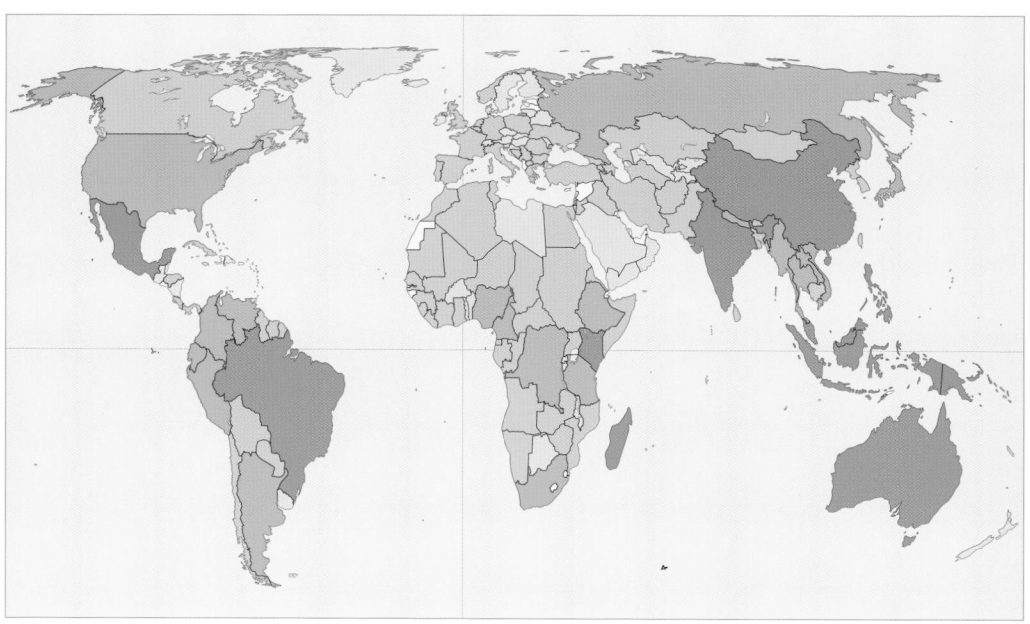

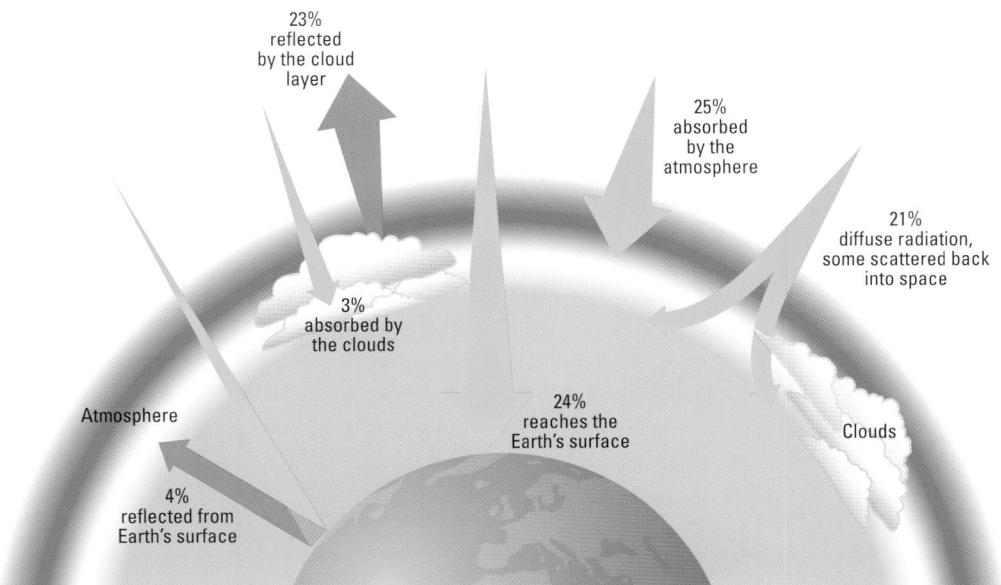

23% reflected by the cloud layer

25% absorbed by the atmosphere

21% diffuse radiation, some scattered back into space

3% absorbed by the clouds

Atmosphere

24% reaches the Earth's surface

Clouds

4% reflected from Earth's surface

The Earth's Energy Balance

Apart from a modest quantity of internal heat from its molten core, the Earth receives all of its energy from the Sun. If the planet is to remain at a constant temperature, it must reradiate exactly as much energy as it receives. Even a minute surplus would lead to a warmer Earth, a deficit to a cooler one. The temperature at which thermal equilibrium is reached depends on a multitude of interconnected factors. Two of the most important are the relative brightness of the Earth – its index of reflectivity, called the "albedo" – and the heat-trapping capacity of the atmosphere – the celebrated "greenhouse effect" (*see below*).

Because the Sun is very hot, most of its energy arrives in the form of relatively short-wave radiation: the shorter the waves, the more energy they carry. Some of the incoming energy is reflected straight back into space, exactly as it arrived; some is absorbed by the atmosphere on its way toward the surface; some is absorbed by the Earth itself. Absorbed energy heats the Earth and its atmosphere alike. But since its temperature is very much lower than that of the Sun, the outgoing energy is emitted at much longer infrared wavelengths. Some of the outgoing radiation escapes directly into outer space; some of it is reabsorbed by the atmosphere. Atmospheric energy eventually finds its way back into space, too, after a complex series of interactions. These include the air movements we call the weather and, almost incidentally, the maintenance of life on Earth.

This diagram (*left*) does not attempt to illustrate the actual mechanisms of heat exchange, but gives a reasonable account (in percentages) of what happens to 100 energy "units." Short-wave radiation is shown in yellow, long-wave in orange.

The Carbon Cycle

Most of the constituents of the atmosphere are kept in constant balance by complex cycles in which life plays an essential and indeed a dominant part. The control of carbon dioxide, which if left to its own devices would be the dominant atmospheric gas, is possibly the most important, although since all the Earth's biological and geophysical cycles interact and interlock, it is hard to separate them even in theory and quite impossible in practice.

The Earth has a huge supply of carbon, only a small quantity of which is in the form of carbon dioxide. Of that, around 98% is dissolved in the sea; the fraction circulating in the air amounts to only 340 parts per million of the atmosphere, where its capacity as a greenhouse gas is the key regulator of the planetary temperature. In turn, life regulates the regulator, keeping carbon dioxide concentrations below danger level.

If all life were to vanish from the Earth tomorrow, the atmosphere would begin the process of change immediately, although it might take several million years to achieve a new, inorganic stability. First, the oxygen content would begin to fall away; with no more assistance than a little solar radiation, a few electrical storms and its own high chemical potential, oxygen would steadily combine with atmospheric nitrogen and volcanic outgassing. In doing so, it would yield sufficient acid to react with carbonaceous rocks such as limestone, releasing carbon dioxide. Once carbon dioxide levels exceeded about 1%, its greenhouse power would increase disproportionately. Rising temperatures – well above the boiling point of water – would speed chemical reactions; in time, the Earth's atmosphere would consist of little more than carbon dioxide and superheated water vapour.

Living things, however, circulate carbon. They do so first by simply existing: after all, the carbon atom is the basic building block of living matter.

During life, plants absorb carbon dioxide from the atmosphere and, along with various chemicals, as soluble salts from the soil, incorporating the carbon into their structure – leaves and trunks in the case of land plants, shells in the case of plankton and the tiny creatures that feed on it. The oxygen thereby freed is added to the atmosphere, at least for a time. The carbon is returned to circulation when the plants die or is passed up the food chain to the herbivores, and then to the carnivores that feed on them. As organisms at each of these trophic levels die, they decay, releasing the carbon, which then combines once more with the oxygen released during life. However, a small proportion of carbon, about one part in 1,000, is removed almost permanently, buried beneath mud on land or at sea, sinking as dead matter to the ocean floor. In time, it is slowly compressed into sedimentary rocks such as limestone and chalk.

But in the evolution of the Earth, nothing is quite permanent. On an even longer timescale, the planet's crustal movements force new rock upward in midocean ridges. Limestone deposits are moved, and sea levels change; ancient carboniferous rocks are exposed to weathering, and a little of their carbon is released to be fixed in turn by the current generation of plants.

The carbon cycle has continued quietly for an immensely long time, and without gross disturbance there is no reason why it would not continue almost indefinitely in the future. However, human beings have found a way to release fixed carbon at a rate far faster than existing global systems can re-circulate it. The fossil fuels – coal, oil, gas, and peat deposits – represent the work of millions of years of carbon accumulation; but it has taken only a few human generations of high-energy scavenging to endanger the entire complex regulatory cycle.

pool of CO_2 in atmosphere

combustion photosynthesis

respiration respiration respiration

CO_2

CO_2

decay organisms

respiration

death

carbonification, gradual production of fossil fuels

death

decay organisms

peat

coal

oil and gas

N.B. The thickness of the Earth's atmosphere is proportionately much thinner than the peel of an apple.

The Greenhouse Effect

Constituting less than 1% of the atmosphere, the natural greenhouse gases (water vapor, carbon dioxide, methane, nitrous oxide, and ozone) have a hugely disproportionate effect on the Earth's climate, and even its habitability. Like the glass panes in a greenhouse, the gases are transparent to most incoming short-wave radiation, which passes freely to heat the planet beneath. But when the warmed Earth retransmits that energy, in the form of longer-wave infrared radiation, the gases function as an opaque shield preventing some of it from escaping, so that the planetary surface (like the interior of a greenhouse) stays relatively hot.

Over the last 150 years, there has been a gradual increase in the levels of greenhouse gases (with the exception of water vapor, which remains a constant in the system). These increases are causing alarm – global warming associated with a runaway greenhouse effect could bring disaster – and, what is more, predictions suggest that there could be a further rise of 2.5–8°F by the year 2100. A serious reduction in the greenhouse gases would be just as damaging; a total absence of CO_2, for example, would leave the planet with a temperature roughly 60°F colder than at present.

Sun

Less heat escapes into space

Outgoing long-wave radiation (infared) is radiated back into space

Increased greenhouse gases means that more long-wave radiation is reflected back to Earth

Atmosphere

The atmosphere of the Earth gets hotter as more heat is trapped

Increased greenhouse gases act as a shield to long-wave radiation

Incoming short-wave radiation (ultraviolet) reaches the surface of the Earth

PEOPLE AND THE ENVIRONMENT

In 1996, the Intergovernmental Panel on Climate Change issued a report stating that "The balance of evidence suggests a discernible human influence on global climate through emissions of carbon dioxide and other greenhouse gases." The report acknowledged that average global temperatures have risen by about 0.9°F since the mid-19th century, though there were still reasons for caution on attributing this entirely to actions taken by humans.

Human interference with nature is nothing new, at least since people turned from hunting and gathering to agriculture more than 10,000 years ago. At first, human actions seemed to have no ill effects because the systems that regulate the global environment were able to absorb damage. But from the late 18th century, the Industrial Revolution and the population explosion have caused massive pollution that threatens to overwhelm the Earth's ability to cope.

The 20th century experienced many disasters, including the dumping of industrial wastes in rivers and seas, accidents at nuclear power stations, and the creation of acid rain through the release of sulfur dioxides and nitrous oxides by the burning of fossil fuels. The release of greenhouse gases are held to be the main reason for global warming, while CFCs (chlorofluorocarbons) have damaged the ozone layer in the stratosphere, the planet's screen against ultraviolet radiation.

In December 1998, an international conference in Kyoto, Japan, reached an agreement to reduce the emission of greenhouse gases by 5.2% by 2012. But, in the early 21st century, the USA, which produces about a third of all emissions, opposed the Kyoto protocol.

Global warming will lead to melting ice sheets and the flooding of fertile coastal plains. Computer models suggest that it might affect ocean currents so that northwestern Europe, which owes its mild climate to the Gulf Stream, could expect bitterly cold winters. Some models have suggested that cloud cover could increase, reflecting more solar energy back into space and thus start a new Ice Age.

In many tropical areas, deforestation is making productive land barren, while in the dry grasslands bordering deserts, the removal of plant cover is causing desertification. But human ingenuity can respond to this crisis in planet management.

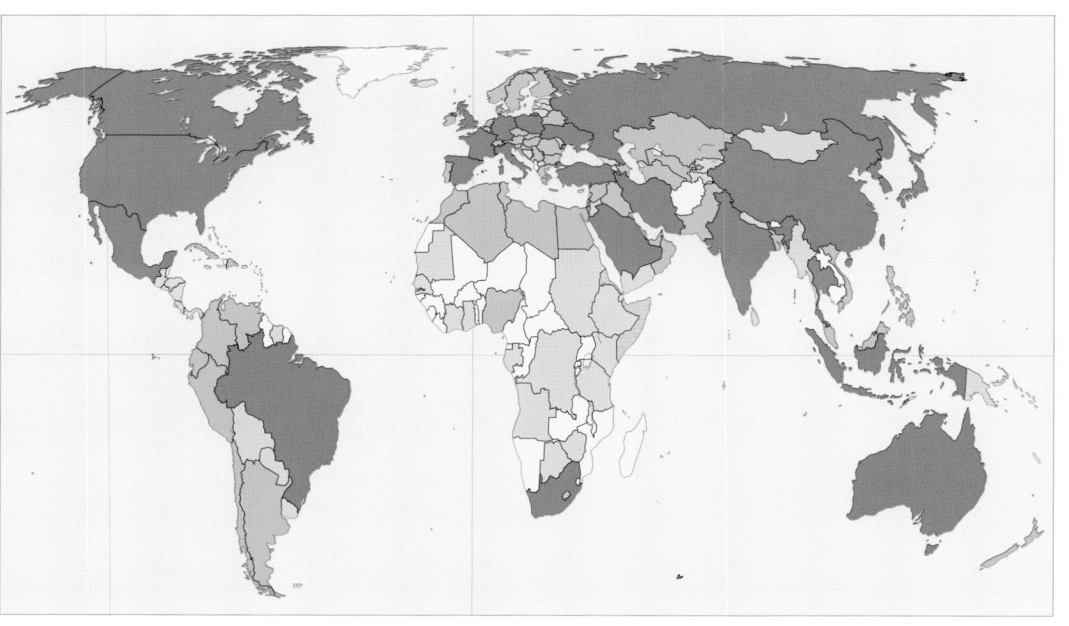

Global Warming

Carbon dioxide emissions in tons (1998)

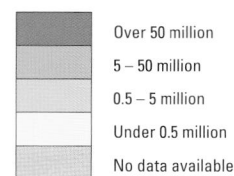

- Over 50 million
- 5 – 50 million
- 0.5 – 5 million
- Under 0.5 million
- No data available

High atmospheric concentrations of heat-absorbing gases appear to be causing a rise in average temperatures worldwide – up to 3°F [1.5°C] by the year 2020, according to some estimates. Global warming is likely to bring about a rise in sea levels that may flood some of the world's densely populated coastal areas.

Evidence of global warming is attributed mainly to the Greenhouse Effect, caused by the emission of certain gases, notably carbon dioxide (CO_2), into the atmosphere since the start of the Industrial Revolution. At first, much of the CO_2 was absorbed by the oceans. However, the vast increase in fuel combustion since 1950 has led CO_2 content in the atmosphere to increase gradually from 280 parts per million to more than 370 parts per million by 2002. Despite international action to control emissions of some greenhouse gases, CO_2 levels are still rising.

Greenhouse Power

Relative contributions to the Greenhouse Effect by the major heat-absorbing gases in the atmosphere

The chart combines greenhouse potency and volume. Carbon dioxide has a greenhouse potential of only 1, but its concentration of 350 parts per million makes it predominate. CFC 12, with 25,000 times the absorption capacity of CO_2, is present only as 0.00044 ppm.

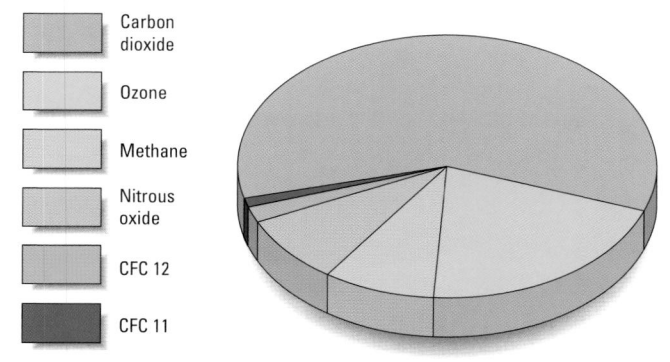

- Carbon dioxide
- Ozone
- Methane
- Nitrous oxide
- CFC 12
- CFC 11

Carbon Dioxide

Estimated percentage share of total world CO_2 emissions (2000)

USA, China, Russia, Japan, India, Germany, Canada, UK

Temperature Rise

The rise in average temperatures caused by carbon dioxide and other greenhouse gases, assuming present trends continue (1960–2020)

Recorded change — Projected changes

1960 1970 1980 1990 2000 2010 2020

°F +3 +2 +1 0 -1

The Thinning Ozone Layer

Total atmospheric ozone concentration in the southern and northern hemispheres (Dobson Units, 2000)

In 1985, scientists working in Antarctica discovered a thinning of the ozone layer, commonly known as an "ozone hole." This caused immediate alarm because the ozone layer absorbs most of the Sun's dangerous ultraviolet radiation, which is believed to cause an increase in skin cancer, cataracts, and damage to the immune system. Since 1985, ozone depletion has increased and, by 2002, the ozone hole over the South Pole was estimated to be three times as large as the USA. The false-color images (*right*) show the total atmospheric ozone concentration in the southern hemisphere (in September 2000) and the northern hemisphere (in March 2000) with the ozone hole clearly identifiable at the center. The data is from the Tiros Ozone Vertical Sounder, an instrument on the American TIROS weather satellite. The colors represent the ozone concentration in Dobson Units (DU). Scientists agree that ozone depletion is caused by CFCs, a group of manufactured chemicals used in air conditioning systems and refrigerators. In a 1987 treaty most industrial nations agreed to phase out CFCs and a complete ban on most CFCs was agreed after the end of 1995. However, scientists believe that the chemicals will remain in the atmosphere for 50 to 100 years. As a result, ozone depletion will continue for many years.

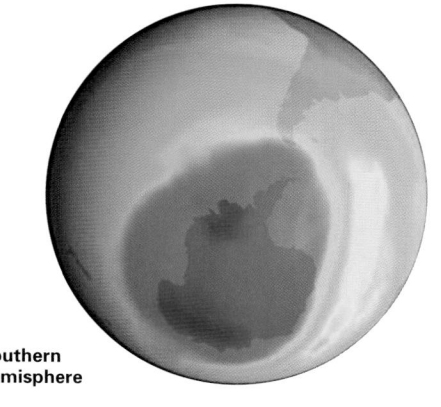

Southern hemisphere

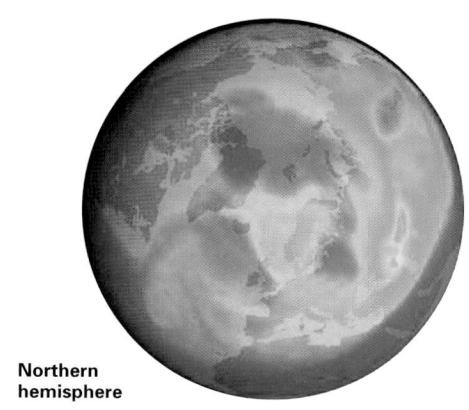

Northern hemisphere

World Pollution

Acid rain and sources of acidic emissions (latest available year)

Acid rain is caused by high levels of sulfur and nitrogen in the atmosphere. They combine with water vapor and oxygen to form acids (H_2SO_4 and HNO_3) which fall as precipitation.

- Regions where sulfur and nitrogen oxides are released in high concentrations, mainly from fossil fuel combustion

- Major cities with high levels of air pollution (including nitrogen and sulfur emissions)

Areas of heavy acid deposition

pH numbers indicate acidity, decreasing from a neutral 7. Normal rain, slightly acid from dissolved carbon dioxide, never exceeds a pH of 5.6.

- pH less than 4.0 (most acidic)
- pH 4.0 to 4.5
- pH 4.5 to 5.0
- Areas where acid rain is a potential problem

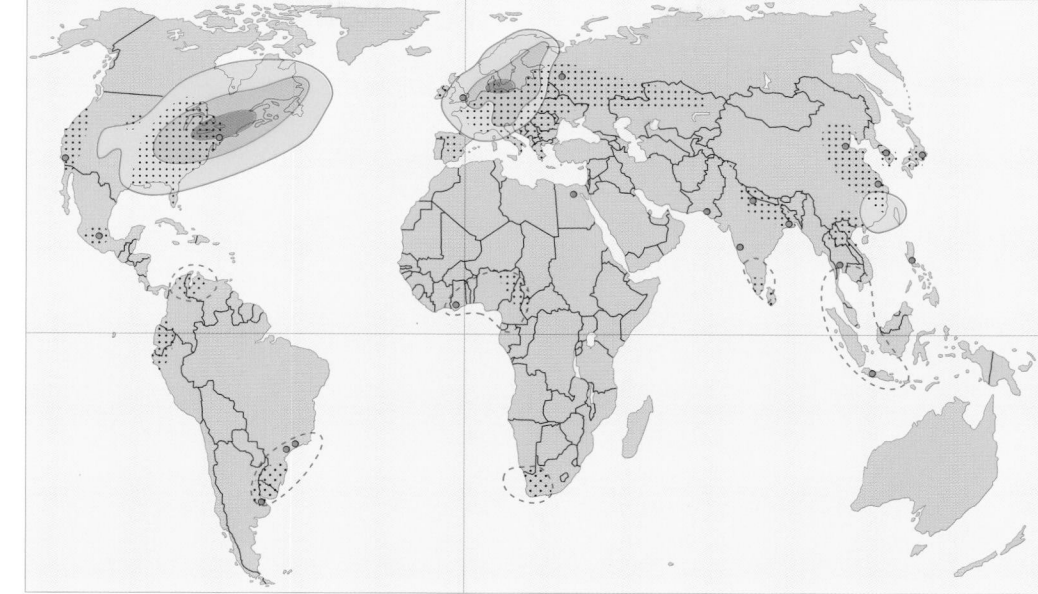

Desertification

- Existing deserts
- Areas with a high risk of desertification
- Areas with a moderate risk of desertification
- Former areas of rain forest
- Existing rain forest

Deforestation

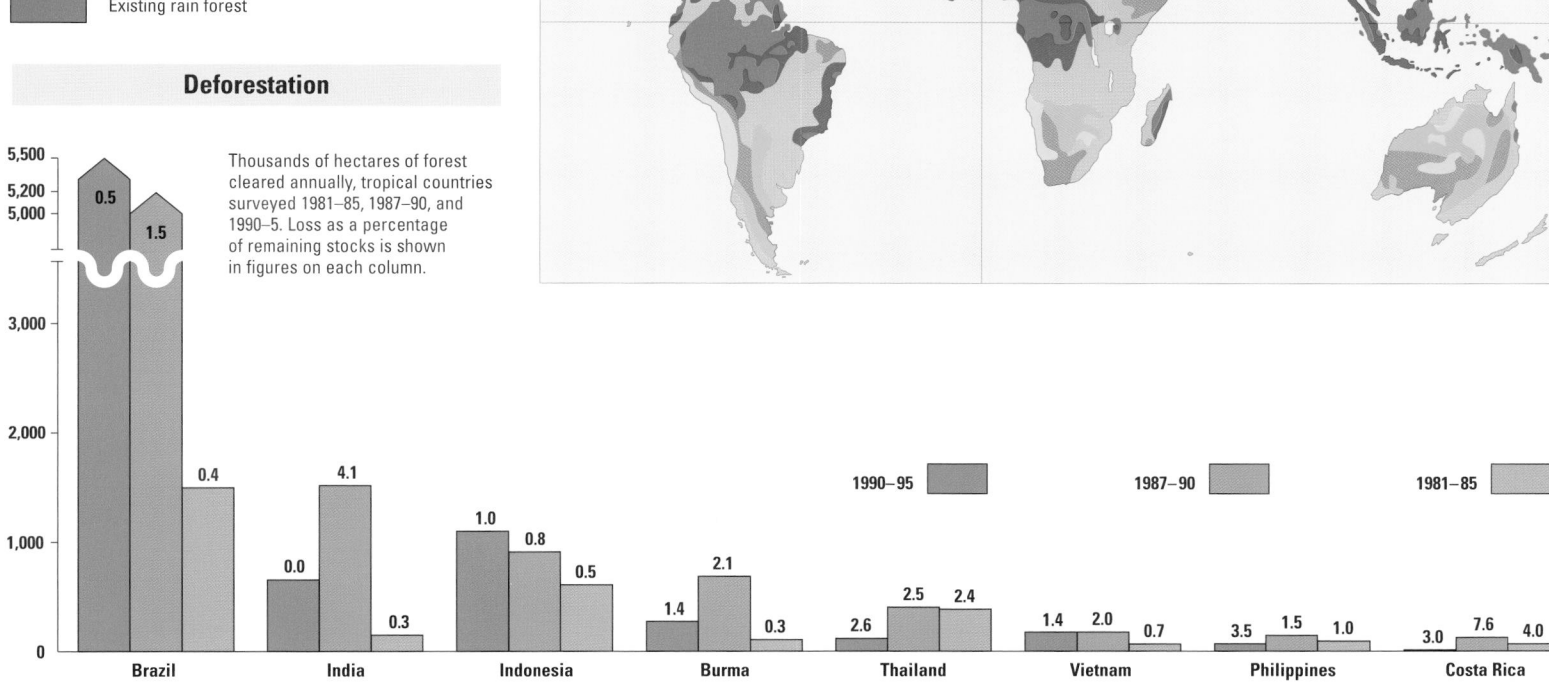

Thousands of hectares of forest cleared annually, tropical countries surveyed 1981–85, 1987–90, and 1990–5. Loss as a percentage of remaining stocks is shown in figures on each column.

1990–95   1987–90   1981–85

Water Pollution

- Severely polluted sea areas and lakes
- Polluted sea areas and lakes
- Areas of frequent oil pollution by shipping
- Major oil tanker spills
- Major oil rig blow outs
- Offshore dumpsites for industrial and municipal waste
- Severely polluted rivers and estuaries

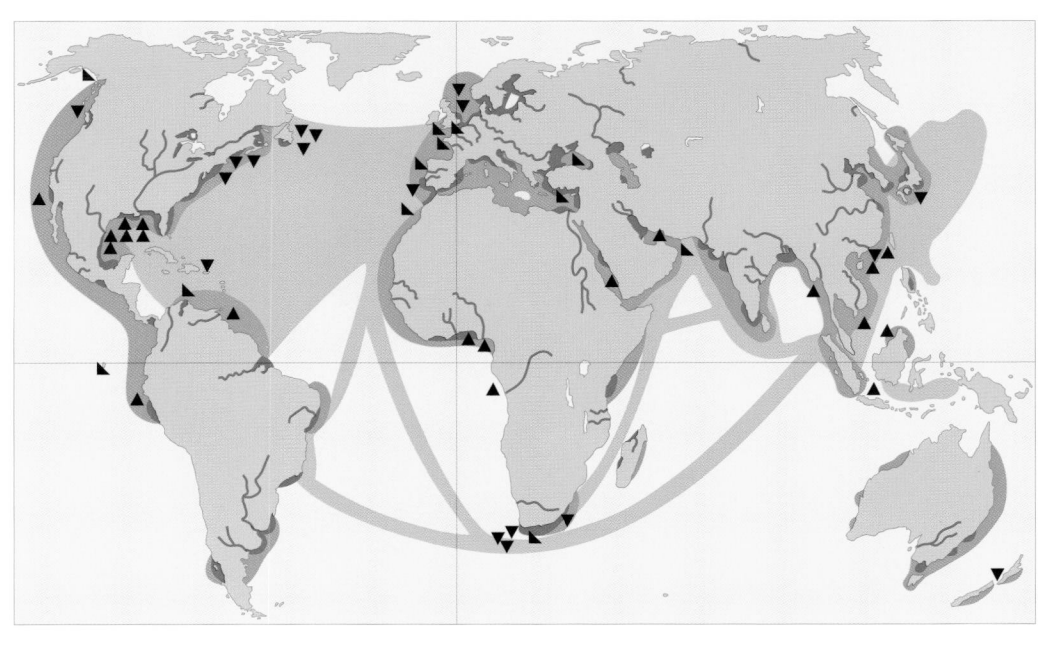

Antarctica

The vast Antarctic ice sheet, containing some 70% of the Earth's fresh water, plays a crucial role in the circulation of the atmosphere and oceans, and hence in determining the planetary climate. The frozen southern continent is also the last remaining wilderness – the largest area to remain free from human colonization.

Ever since Amundsen and Scott raced for the South Pole in 1911, various countries have pressed territorial claims over sections of Antarctica, spurred in recent years by its known and suspected mineral wealth: enough iron ore to supply the world at present levels for 200 years, large oil reserves and, probably, the biggest coal deposits on Earth.

However, the 1961 Antarctic Treaty set aside the area for peaceful uses only, guaranteeing freedom of scientific investigation, banning waste disposal and nuclear testing, and suspending the issue of territorial rights. By 1990, the original 12 signatories had grown to 25, with a further 15 nations granted observer status in subsequent deliberations. However, the Treaty itself was threatened by wrangles between different countries, government agencies and international pressure groups.

Finally, in July 1991, the belated agreement of the UK and the USA assured unanimity on a new accord to ban all mineral exploration for a further 50 years. The ban can only be rescinded if all the present signatories, plus a majority of any future adherents, agree. While the treaty has always lacked a formal mechanism for enforcement, it is firmly underwritten by public concern generated by the efforts of environmental pressure groups such as Greenpeace, which has been foremost in the campaign to have Antarctica declared a "World Park."

However, from the mid-1990s, the continent appeared to be under threat from global warming, which some scientists believe was the cause of the breakup of ice shelves along the Antarctic peninsula. Rising temperatures have also disturbed the breeding patterns of Adelie penguins.

In December 2002, oil slicks from the 77,000-ton *Prestige* tanker, which broke up off Spain, caused environmental damage to the north coast of Spain and, in 2003, to the southwest coast of France. This was a small incident by comparison with some earlier events, such as the collision between the *Atlantic Empress* and the *Aegean Captain* in July 1979. This was the worst tanker incident ever. It polluted the Caribbean with 1,890,000 barrels of crude oil. Oil spills, however, declined in the 1980s, from a peak of 750,000 tons in 1979 to less than 50,000 tons in 1990. The most notorious spill of that period – when the *Exxon Valdez* ran aground in Prince William Sound, Alaska, in March 1989 – released only 267,000 barrels, a relatively small amount when compared with the 2,500,000 barrels spilled during the Gulf War of 1991. Oil spillage, poisoned rivers, and domestic sewage have in recent years badly contaminated parts of the oceans.

POPULATION

In 8000 BC, following the development of agriculture, the world had an estimated population of 8 million and by AD 1000 it was about 300 million. The onset of the Industrial Revolution in the late 18th century led to a population explosion. The 1,000 million mark was passed by 1850, it doubled by the 1920s, and doubled again to 4,000 million by 1975.

In the 1990s, UN demographers estimated that the world's population, which passed the 6 billion mark in 1999, would reach 8.9 billion by 2050 and only level out in 2200, at a peak of around 11 billion. However, in the early 21st century, after the rate of population growth had shown signs of decline, the Institute for Applied Systems Analysis, suggested that the world's population might peak at about 9 billion in 2070. Whatever the global projections, everyone agreed that the greatest population growth will be in the developing countries.

The developing world includes what the World Bank (2001) describes as low-income economies (average per capita GNP of US $420), lower-middle-income economies (average per capita GNP of US $1,200), and upper-middle-income economies (average per capita GNP of US $4,870). Most developing countries are in Africa, Asia, and Latin America. The developed world, made up of high-income, industrialized economies (average per capita GNP of US $26,440), contains Australasia, most of Europe and North America, and Japan.

In developing countries, a high proportion of the population is young and so these countries face high expenditure on education and health. In developed countries, the population pyramids are becoming top-heavy, with increasingly aging populations.

Most Crowded Nations

Population per square mile (2002 est.)

1.	Monaco	32,000
2.	Singapore	18,554
3.	Vatican City	5,000
4.	Malta	3,308
5.	Maldives	2,667
6.	Bahrain	2,523
7.	Bangladesh	2,382
8.	Barbados	1,629
9.	Taiwan	1,622
10.	Nauru	1,500

Least Crowded Nations

Population per square mile (2002 est.)

1.	Mongolia	4.5
2.	Namibia	5.7
3.	Australia	6.6
4.	Suriname	6.9
5.	Iceland	7.0
6.	Botswana	7.1
7.	Mauritania	7.1
8.	Libya	7.9
9.	Canada	8.3
10.	Guyana	8.4

Largest Nations

The world's most populous nations, in millions (2002 est.)

1.	China	1,284
2.	India	1,046
3.	USA	281
4.	Indonesia	231
5.	Brazil	176
6.	Pakistan	148
7.	Russia	145
8.	Bangladesh	133
9.	Nigeria	130
10.	Japan	127
11.	Mexico	103
12.	Philippines	85
13.	Germany	83
14.	Vietnam	81
15.	Egypt	71
16.	Ethiopia	68
17.	Turkey	67
18.	Iran	67
19.	Thailand	62
20.	UK	60
21.	France	60
22.	Italy	58
23.	Congo (Dem.Rep.)	55
24.	Ukraine	48
25.	South Korea	48

Population Density

Inhabitants per square mile

- Over 500
- 250 – 500
- 125 – 250
- 65 – 125
- 15 – 65
- 8 – 15
- 3 – 8
- Under 3

Urban population

- ■ Over 10,000,000
- ● 5,000,000 – 10,000,000
- · 1,000,000 – 5,000,000

Places marked are conurbations, not city limits; San Francisco itself, for example, has an official population of less than a million.

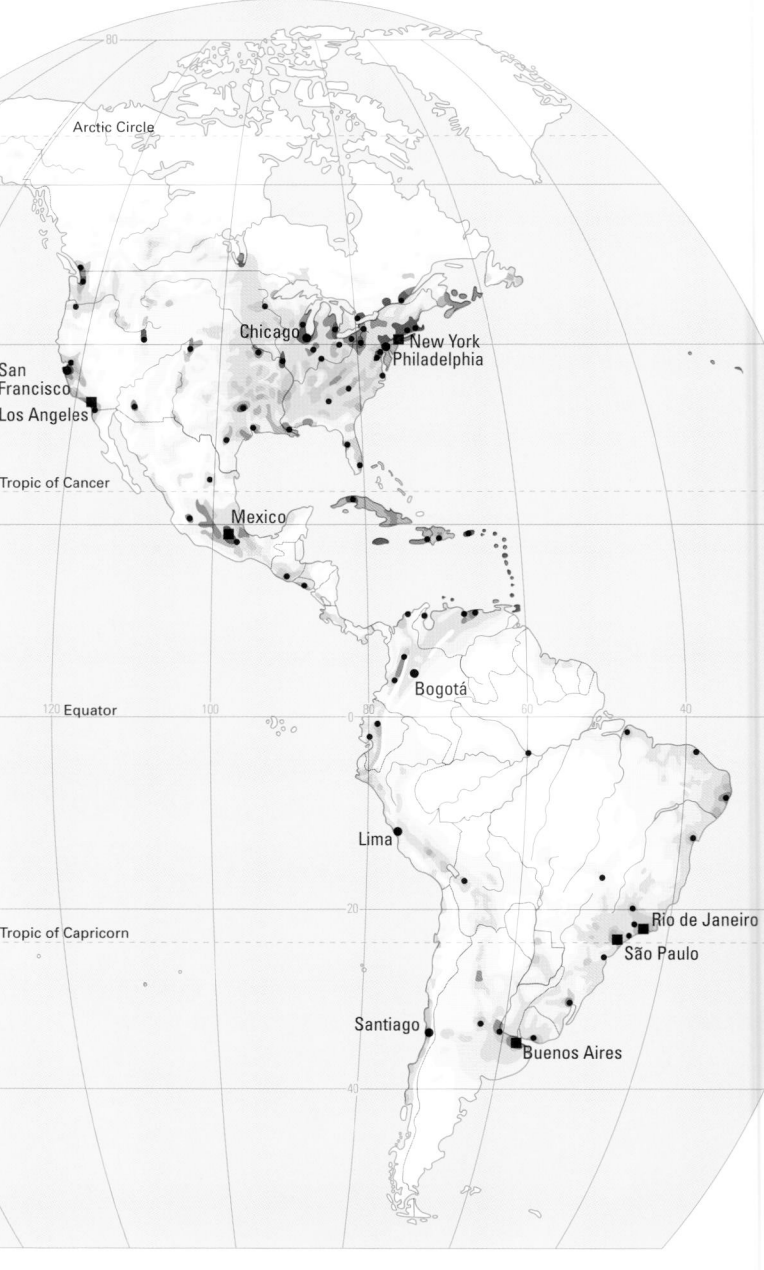

Rates of Growth

The world population doubled between 1950 and 1990. Small rates of population growth led to dramatic increases over two or three generations. The table below translates annual percentage growth into the number of years required to double a population.

% change	Doubling time
0.5	139.0
1.0	69.7
1.5	46.6
2.0	35.0
2.5	28.1
3.0	23.4
3.5	20.1
4.0	17.7

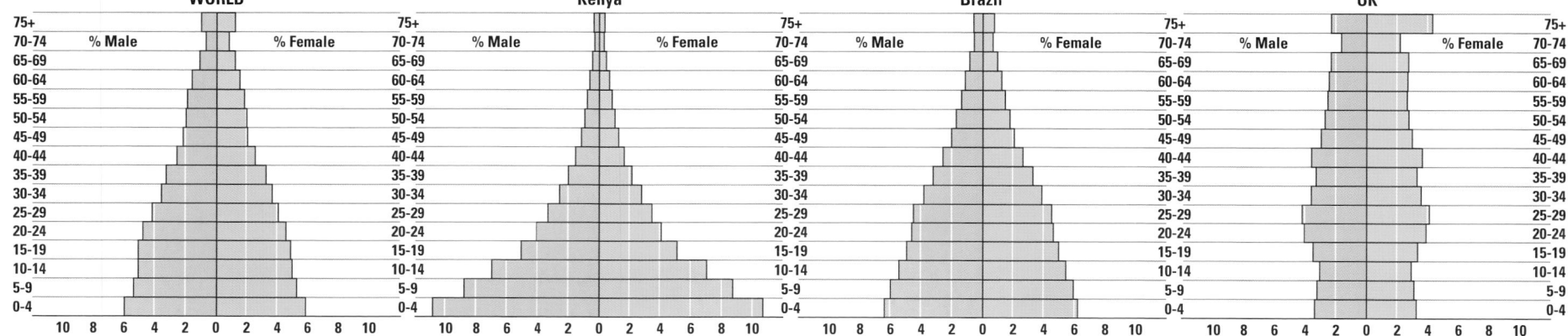

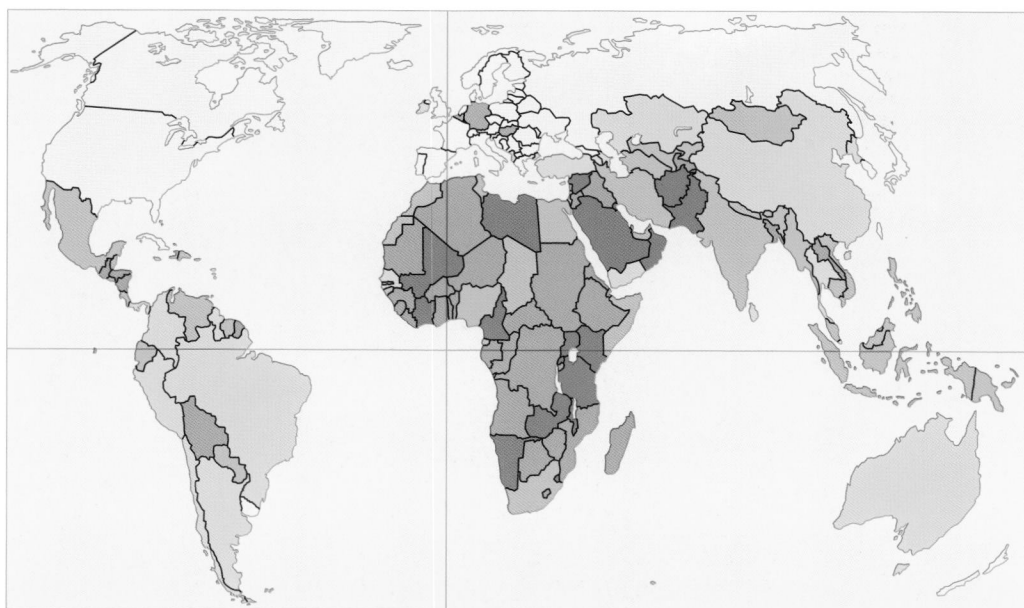

Population Change 1990–2000

The population change for the years 1990–2000

- Over 40% population gain
- 30 – 40% population gain
- 20 – 30% population gain
- 10 – 20% population gain
- 0 – 10% population gain
- No change or population loss

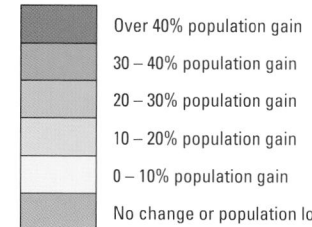

Top 5 countries		Bottom 5 countries	
Kuwait	+75.9%	Belgium	−0.1%
Namibia	+62.5%	Hungary	−0.2%
Afghanistan	+60.1%	Grenada	−2.4%
Mali	+55.5%	Germany	−3.2%
Tanzania	+54.6%	Tonga	−3.2%

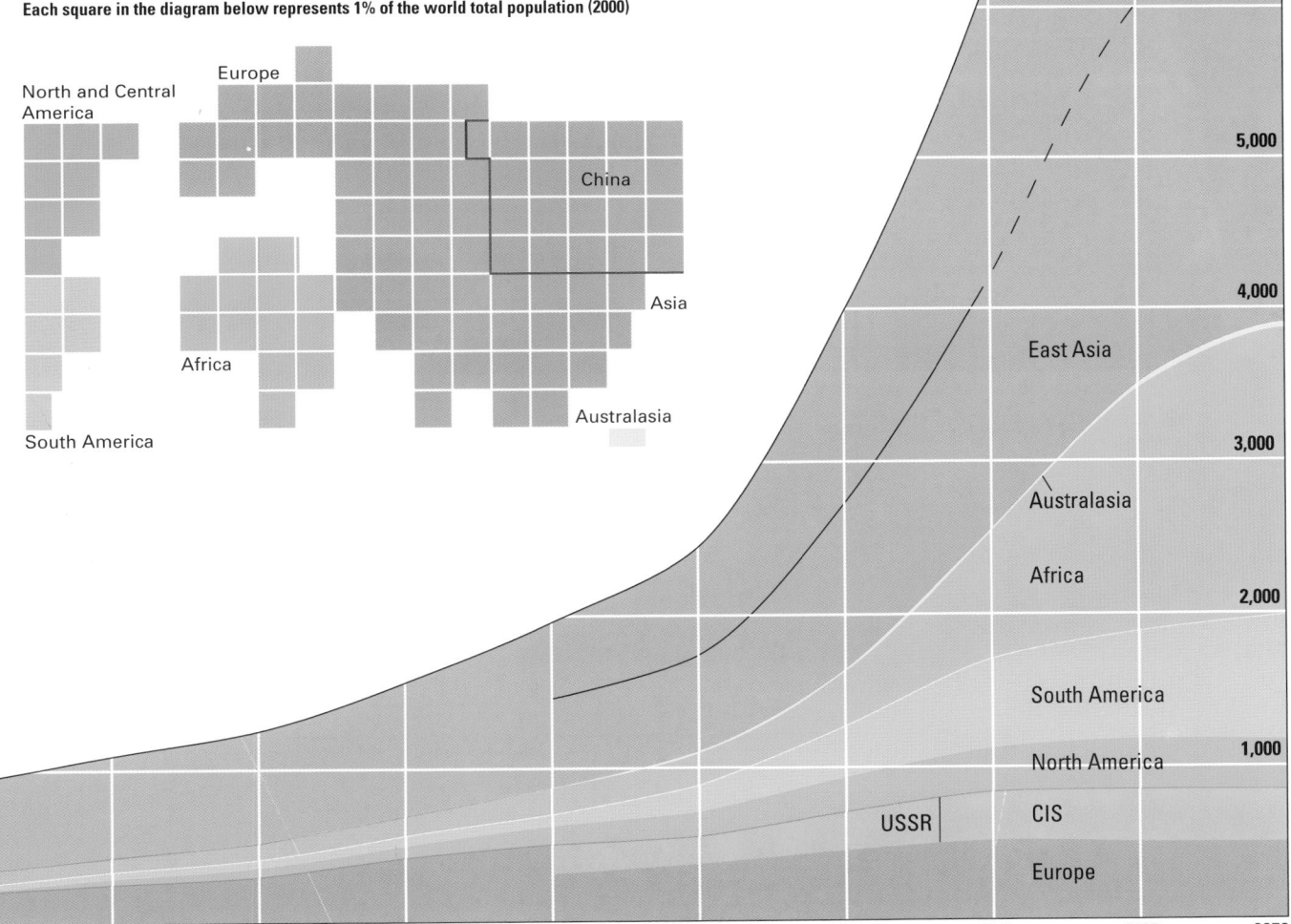

London
Paris
Moscow
Istanbul
Tehran
Cairo
Karachi
Delhi
Mumbai (Bombay)
Kolkata (Calcutta)
Dacca
Chennai (Madras)
Bangkok
Shenyang
Beijing
Tianjin
Seoul
Tokyo
Osaka
Shanghai
Hangzhou
Wenzhou
Chongqing
Guangzhou
Manila
Jakarta

Arctic Circle
Tropic of Cancer
Equator
Tropic of Capricorn

Demographic Extremes

Most men per 100 women (latest available year)		Fewest men per 100 women (latest available year)	
1. Qatar	193.3	1. Latvia	84.3
2. U. Arab Em.	176.4	2. Ukraine	86.8
3. Bahrain	133.7	3. Russia	88.0
4. Saudi Arabia	125.1	4. Estonia	88.7
5. Oman	113.4	5. Belarus	88.8
6. Trin. & Tob.	111.3	6. Lithuania	89.7
7. Brunei	110.3	7. Georgia	91.4
8. Tunisia	109.8	8. Hungary	91.6
9. Libya	108.2	= Moldova	91.6
10. Hong Kong	107.6	10. Swaziland	92.4

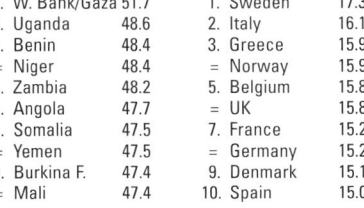

Percentage of people aged under 15 (latest available year)		Percentage of people aged over 65 (latest available year)	
1. W. Bank/Gaza	51.7	1. Sweden	17.3
2. Uganda	48.6	2. Italy	16.1
3. Benin	48.4	3. Greece	15.9
= Niger	48.4	= Norway	15.9
= Zambia	48.2	5. Belgium	15.8
6. Angola	47.7	= UK	15.8
7. Somalia	47.5	7. France	15.2
8. Yemen	47.5	= Germany	15.2
9. Burkina F.	47.4	9. Denmark	15.1
= Mali	47.4	10. Spain	15.0

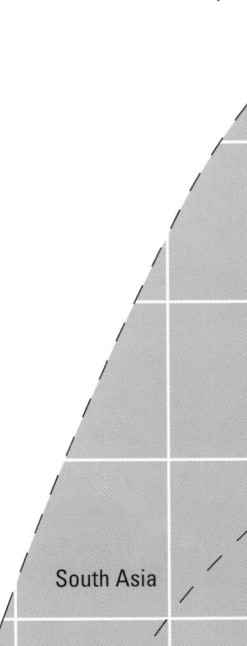

Growth by Continent

Predicting population trends can never be an exact science, since accurate census data are not always available and even contemporary figures are based partly on deduction. Numbers for years after 2000 are long-term extrapolations involving projections of current growth rates, and become increasingly speculative as they advance into the future.

Population by continent in millions, 1990–2025, with estimated annual growth rates.

	1990	2000	2025	% growth, 1990–2000	% growth, 2000–2025
Africa	641	860	1,589	2.97	2.50
South America	437	523	709	1.82	1.23
Asia	3,080	3,650	4,923	1.71	1.20
Australasia	24	28	34	1.44	0.64
North America	277	300	339	0.81	0.50
Europe	787	825	882	0.47	0.27
World	**5,246**	**6,185**	**8,476**	**1.66**	**1.27**

The graph (*below*) shows the extraordinary explosion of the world's population which has occurred in the last 250 years, with projections showing the predicted rate of growth in the 21st century. According to 1996 UN figures, the annual rate of world population growth between 1990 and 1995 fell to 1.48%, as compared with 1.57% predicted in a UN report in 1994. As a result of such data, future projections have to be constantly revised. In 1996, the most likely scenario was that population growth would continue until around 2080 and then start to decline. But very different predictions can be made. For example, high birth rates and fast declining death rates could give the world a population of 23,000 million by 2100. Another scenario, based on such assumptions as rampant disease and falling birth rates, would indicate a fall in world population of 4 million. Demographers give each of these predictions a probability of less than 1%.

Population by Continent

Each square in the diagram below represents 1% of the world total population (2000)

North and Central America
Europe
China
Asia
Africa
Australasia
South America

CITIES

Following the development of agriculture more than 10,000 years ago, people began to live in farming villages. Around 5,500 years ago, the world's first cities appeared in the lower Tigris and Euphrates valleys in Mesopotamia. Cities were founded in Ancient Egypt around 5,000 years ago and in China around 3,600 years ago. By contrast with the villages, most people in the early cities were not engaged in farming. Instead, they worked in craft industries, in government services, in religion and in trade. The cities became centers of early civilizations and, through trade, their influence spread far and wide. However, they were dependent on the surrounding farming communities for their food and other materials.

In 1750, prior to the start of the Industrial Revolution, barely 3% of the world's population lived in urban areas. By 1850, London and Paris had more than a million people, and, by 1900, 14% of the world's population lived in cities. By 1950, the world had 83 cities with more than a million people, and

by 1996, there were 280. By 2015, experts predict that there will be more than 500. New York City was the only city with a population in excess of 10 million in 1950; by 2015 the experts predict 27 such cities worldwide, the majority located in the developing world.

However, predictions have to be constantly revised in the light of new data. For example, in the late 1990s, UN demographers calculated that urban areas then accounted for 50% of the world's population. But after much lower census figures emerged for many cities in the early 21st century, the UN demographers had to push back the date when half of the world's population would be living in cities to 2007.

Urbanization is greatest in industrialized countries. For example, in 2000, 77.2% of the people in the United States lived in urban areas. However, in low-income countries, which contained nearly 60% of the world's population in the late 1990s, only 28% lived in urban areas.

The rapid rate of urbanization has created

many social problems, especially in cities which have been unable to provide enough jobs and services for the new arrivals. Many of the new city dwellers come from rural areas and take time to adjust to urban life and employment possibilities.

A typical city in a developing country contains millions of people living, often illegally, in shanty towns (or "informal settlements"), while thousands live on the streets. Yet many of these shanty towns are healthier than the industrial cities of 19th-century Europe and North America. Indeed, surveys have shown that the migrants to the cities in developing countries are less likely to face poverty than they are in rural areas, while benefiting from greater access to healthcare services and education.

Modern cities face many problems, including pollution, crime, and unemployment. Yet, given competent central and local government, they are capable of generating the wealth they need to solve them, as well as making a major contribution to the economy.

The Urbanization of the Earth

City-building, 1850–2000; each white spot represents a city of at least 1 million inhabitants.

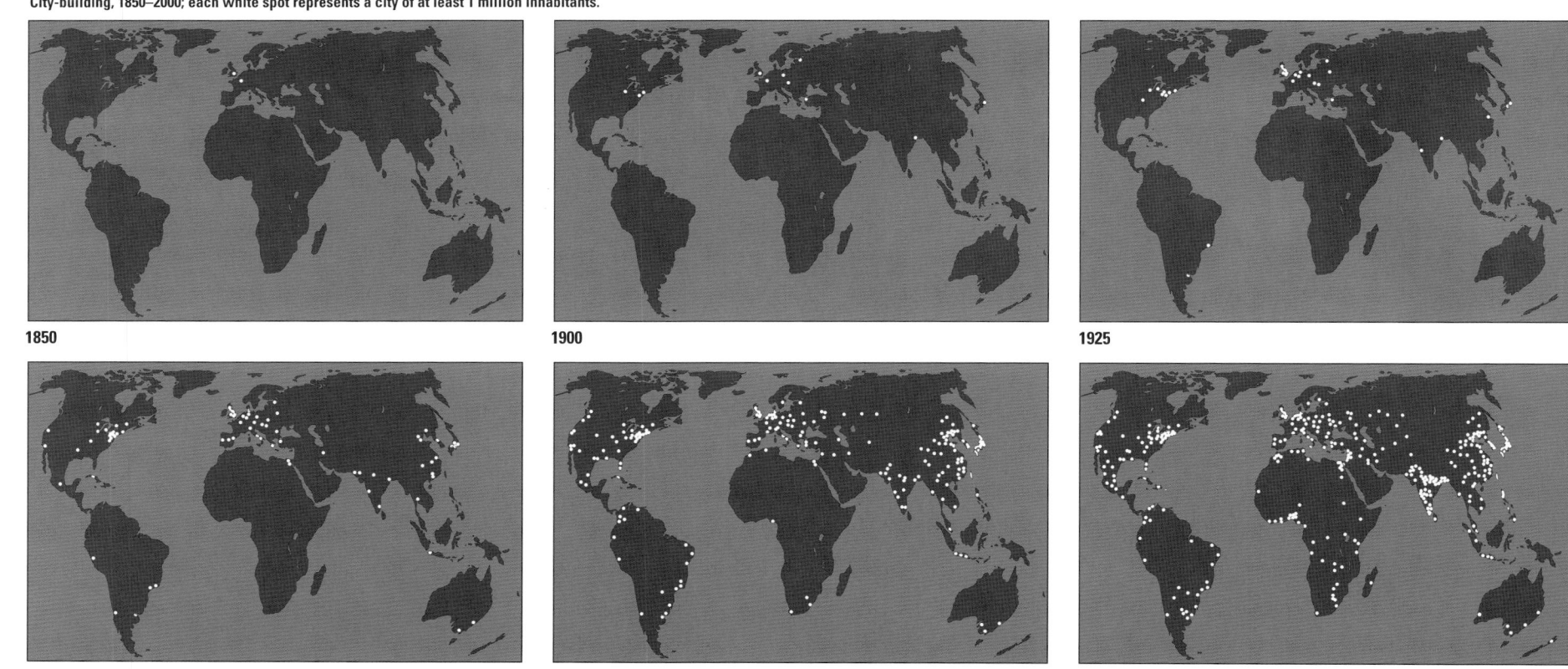

1850   1900   1925

1950   1975   2000

Urban Population

Percentage of total population living in towns and cities (2000)

Most urbanized

Belgium	97%
W. Sahara	96%
Singapore	93%
UAE	93%
Iceland	93%

Over 80%	
60 – 80%	
40 – 60%	
20 – 40%	
Under 20%	

Least urbanized

Rwanda	6%
Bhutan	7%
East Timor	7%
Burundi	9%
Nepal	11%

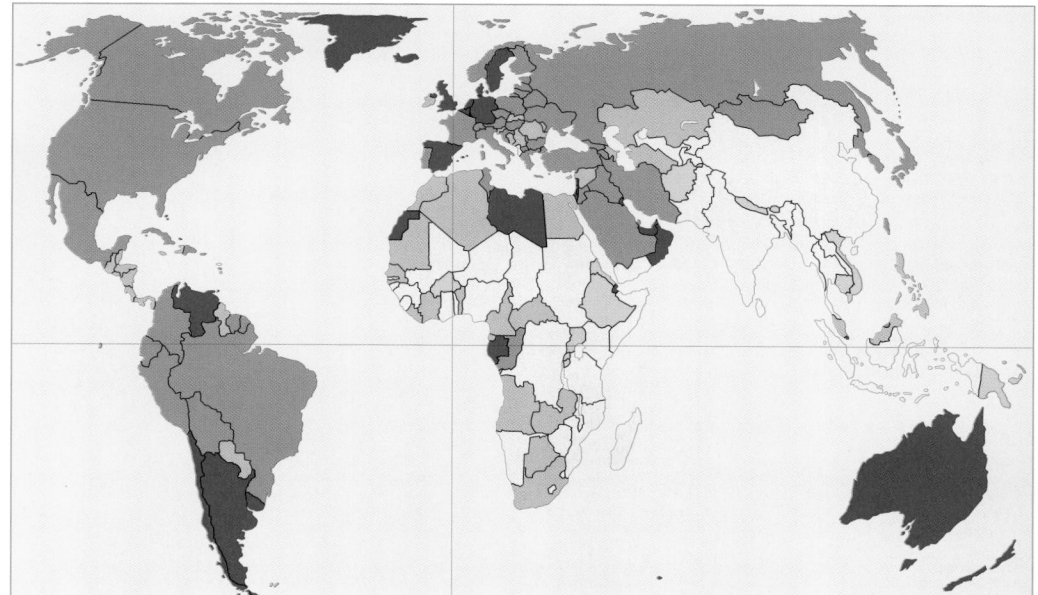

Expanding Cities

The growth of some of the world's largest cities in millions, 1950–2015.
Comparisons of city populations over time are problematic due to changes in the definition of the city limits.
These figures attempt to take such changes into consideration. The figure for London is the metropolitan region.

■ 1950   ■ 2015

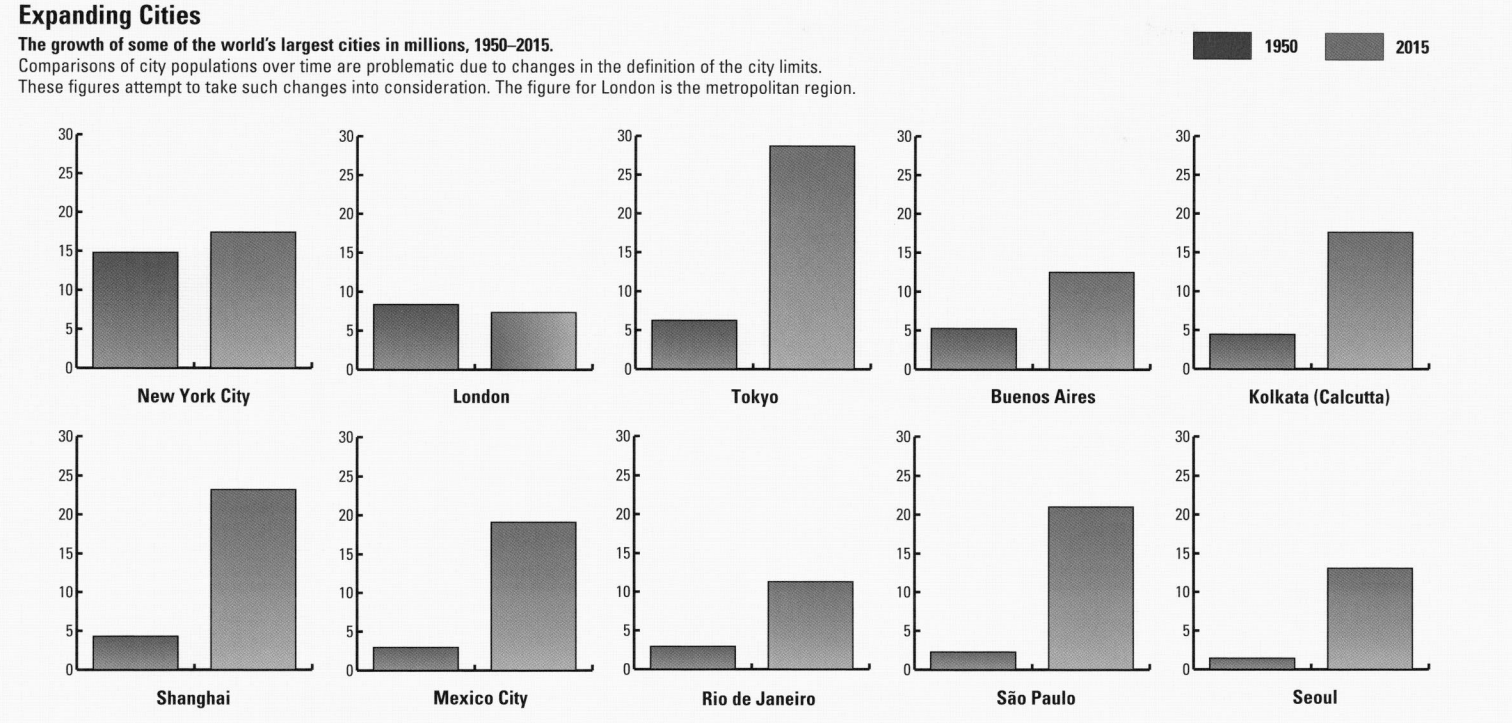

New York City | London | Tokyo | Buenos Aires | Kolkata (Calcutta)
Shanghai | Mexico City | Rio de Janeiro | São Paulo | Seoul

The graphs show the projected growth of megacities between 1950 and 2015. New York City, the world's largest city in 1950, reached a peak in 1970, but it has experienced periods of negative growth. London's population also declined between 1970 and 1985, before resuming a modest rate of increase. In both cases, the divergence from world trends is explained in part by counting methods. Each lies at the center of a great agglomeration, and definitions of the "city limits" may vary over time. Also, in developing countries, many areas around the megacities, which are counted as urban, are rural in character. The rates of city population growth in developing countries have also often been over-estimated. For example, it was once predicted that Kolkata (Calcutta) would have a population of 40 million by the late 1990s. The reason why many estimates have proven incorrect is partly explained by a new trend, namely that rapid urban growth is now greatest, in some regions, in the smaller cities. For example, the main expansion in West Bengal is no longer in Kolkata (Calcutta), but in a rash of small cities across the state.

Cities in Danger

In mid-2002, a "brown haze," 2 mi [3 km] high, covered much of southern Asia. Caused mainly by the burning of coal and biomass, it caused respiratory diseases and deaths. Alarm concerning urban air pollution had been expressed much earlier, but controls since the 1980s had proved difficult to enforce and expensive to install.

Those taking part in the United Nations' Global Environment Monitoring System (*see right*) frequently show dangerous levels of pollutants ranging from soot to sulfur dioxide and photo-chemical smog; air in the majority of cities without such sampling equipment is likely to be at least as bad. Traffic, a major source of air pollution worldwide, loses Thailand's work force 44 working days each year.

Urban Air Pollution

The world's most polluted cities: number of days each year when sulfur dioxide levels exceeded the WHO threshold of 150 micrograms per cubic meter (averaged over 4 to 15 years, 1970s – 1980s)

Sulfur dioxide is the main pollutant associated with industrial cities. According to the World Health Organization, more than seven days in a year above 150 µg per cubic meter bring a serious risk of respiratory disease: at least 600 million people live in urban areas where SO_2 concentrations regularly reach damaging levels.

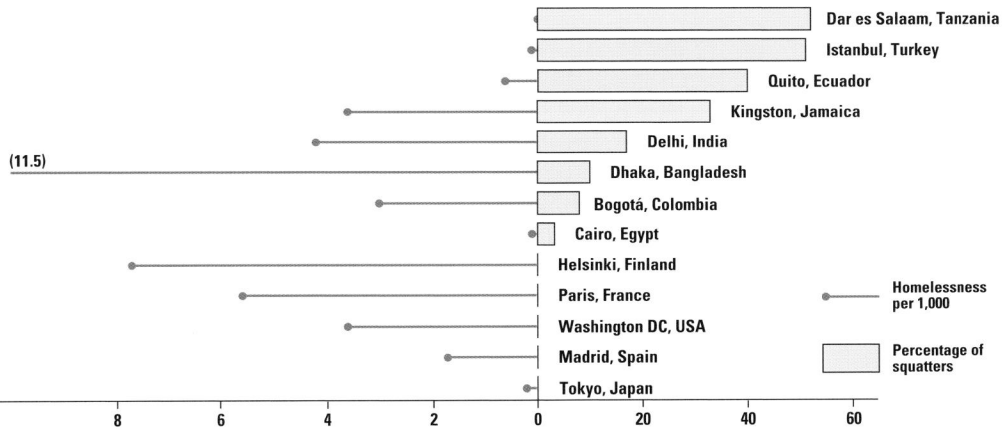

Manila, Philippines
Kolkata (Calcutta), India
Milan, Italy
Zagreb, Croatia
Guangzhou, China
Madrid, Spain
Beijing, China
Xian, China
Seoul, South Korea
Tehran, Iran
Shenyang, China

120   90   60   30

Urban Housing Needs

Proportion of the population living in squatter settlements and the number of homeless per thousand, for selected cities.

Urbanization in most developing countries has been proceeding so rapidly that local governments have been unable to provide the necessary services and housing. In some cities, many people find their homes in squatter settlements, frequently without power, water and sanitation. Yet these communities are often a dynamic part of the city's economy, while their inhabitants sometimes take all kinds of initiatives, including the setting up of their own local government and self-help associations. Some of the world's richest cities also have a homeless underclass, although calculating the numbers of people involved is problematic. Yet it is the case that homelessness and unemployment are currently affecting an increasing number of people in the developed world.

Dar es Salaam, Tanzania
Istanbul, Turkey
Quito, Ecuador
Kingston, Jamaica
Delhi, India
(11.5)   Dhaka, Bangladesh
Bogotá, Colombia
Cairo, Egypt
Helsinki, Finland
Paris, France — Homelessness per 1,000
Washington DC, USA
Madrid, Spain — Percentage of squatters
Tokyo, Japan

8   6   4   2   0   20   40   60

Largest Cities

Early in the 21st century for the first time in history, the majority of the world's population will live in cities. Below is a list of all the cities with more than 10 million inhabitants, based on estimates for the year 2015.

1.	Tokyo–Yokohama	28.7
2.	Mumbai (Bombay)	27.4
3.	Lagos	24.1
4.	Shanghai	23.2
5.	Jakarta	21.5
6.	São Paulo	21.0
7.	Karachi	20.6
8.	Beijing	19.6
9.	Dhaka	19.2
10.	Mexico City	19.1
11.	Kolkata (Calcutta)	17.6
12.	Delhi	17.5
13.	New York City	17.4
14.	Tianjin	17.1
15.	Manila	14.9
16.	Cairo	14.7
17.	Los Angeles	14.5
18.	Seoul	13.1
19.	Buenos Aires	12.5
20.	Istanbul	12.1
21.	Rio de Janeiro	11.3
22.	Lahore	10.9
23.	Hyderabad	10.6
24.	Bangkok	10.4
25.	Osaka	10.2
26.	Lima	10.1
27.	Tehran	10.0

City populations are based on urban agglomerations rather than legal city limits. In some cases where two adjacent cities have merged into one concentration, such as Tokyo–Yokohama, they have been regarded as a single unit.

Urban Advantages

Despite overcrowding and poor housing, living standards in the developing world's cities are almost invariably better than in the surrounding countryside. Resources – financial, material and administrative – are concentrated in the towns, which are usually also the centers of political activity and pressure. Governments – frequently unstable, and rarely established on a solid democratic base – are usually more responsive to urban discontent than rural misery.

In many countries, especially in Africa, food prices are kept artificially low, appeasing the underemployed urban masses at the expense of agricultural development. The imbalance encourages further cityward migration, helping to account for the astonishing rate of post-1950 urbanization and putting great strain on the ability of many nations to provide even modest improvements for their people.

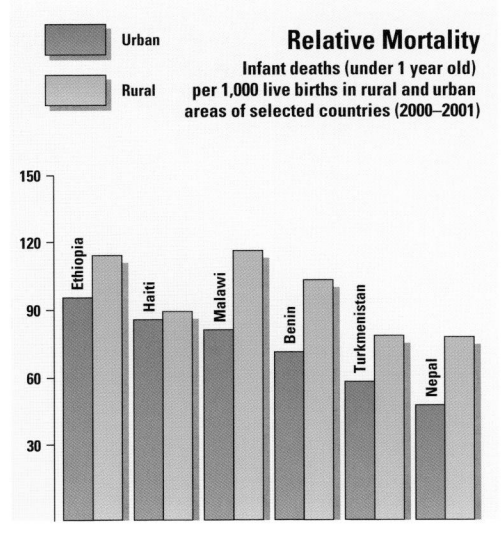

■ Urban ■ Rural
Relative Mortality
Infant deaths (under 1 year old) per 1,000 live births in rural and urban areas of selected countries (2000–2001)

Ethiopia | Haiti | Malawi | Benin | Turkmenistan | Nepal

150   120   90   60   30

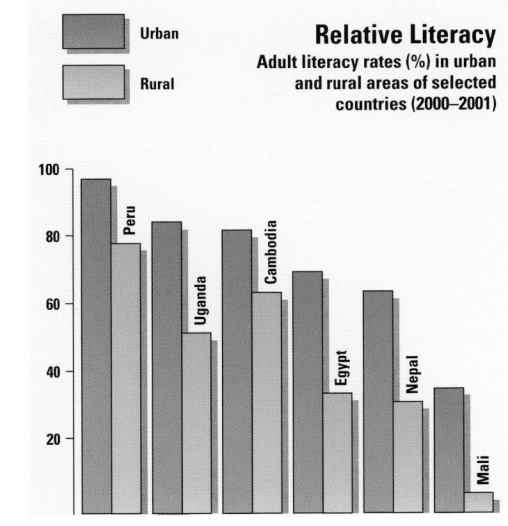

■ Urban ■ Rural
Relative Literacy
Adult literacy rates (%) in urban and rural areas of selected countries (2000–2001)

Peru | Uganda | Cambodia | Egypt | Nepal | Mali

100   80   60   40   20

CARTOGRAPHY BY PHILIP'S. COPYRIGHT PHILIP'S

27

THE HUMAN FAMILY

Racial, language and religious differences have led to appalling acts of inhumanity throughout history. Yet strictly speaking, all human beings belong to one species, *Homo sapiens*, which has no subspecies. The differences between the three racial types which most people identify – namely Caucasoid, Mongoloid, and Negroid – reflect not so much evolutionary differences as long periods of separation.

Migration has recently mingled the various groups to an unprecedented extent, and most nations now have some degree of racial mixing. For example, the United States has often been called a melting pot, because of the large numbers of people from various geographical locations which make up the population. The country has

no official language but, until recently, English was spoken by the vast majority of the people. But in recent years, some of the immigrants from Mexico, Cuba and other parts of Latin America have not learned English and speak only Spanish. This development disturbs those Americans who believe that the use of English binds the nation together, and several states have passed laws stating that English is their only official language.

Language is fundamental to human culture and any particular language is almost the definition of that particular culture. Because definitions of languages vary, estimates of the total number range from 3,000 to 6,000, although most are spoken by only a few people. The world's languages

are grouped into families, the largest of which are the Indo-European and Sino-Tibetan. Chinese, a Sino-Tibetan language, is spoken by more people as a first language than any other. English, an Indo-European tongue, ranks second, but it is the leading international language, because so many people speak it as their second tongue.

Like language, religion encourages cohesion in single human groups and it satisfies a deep human need by assigning people a place in a divinely ordered world. Religion is a way in which a culture can express its individuality. For example, the rise of Islamic fundamentalism in the late 20th century was partly an expression of resentment that secular Western values were being imposed on Muslims.

World Migration

The greatest voluntary migration was the colonization of North America by 30–35 million European settlers during the 19th century. The greatest forced migration involved 9–11 million Africans taken as slaves to America between 1550 and 1860. The migrations shown on the map below are mostly international, as population movements within borders are not usually recorded. Many of the statistics are necessarily estimates as so many refugees and migrant workers enter countries illegally and unrecorded. Emigrants may have a variety of motives for leaving, thus making it difficult to distinguish between voluntary and involuntary migrations.

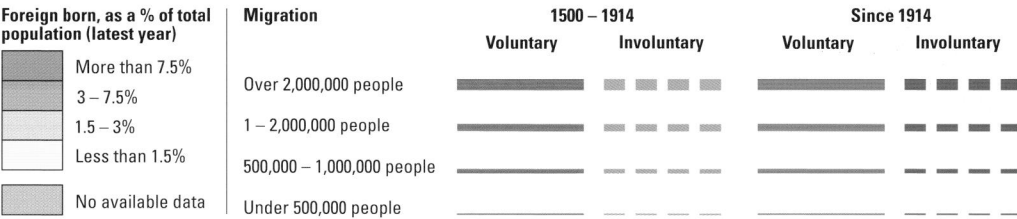

Foreign born, as a % of total population (latest year):
More than 7.5%
3 – 7.5%
1.5 – 3%
Less than 1.5%
No available data

Migration:
Over 2,000,000 people
1 – 2,000,000 people
500,000 – 1,000,000 people
Under 500,000 people

1500 – 1914: Voluntary / Involuntary
Since 1914: Voluntary / Involuntary

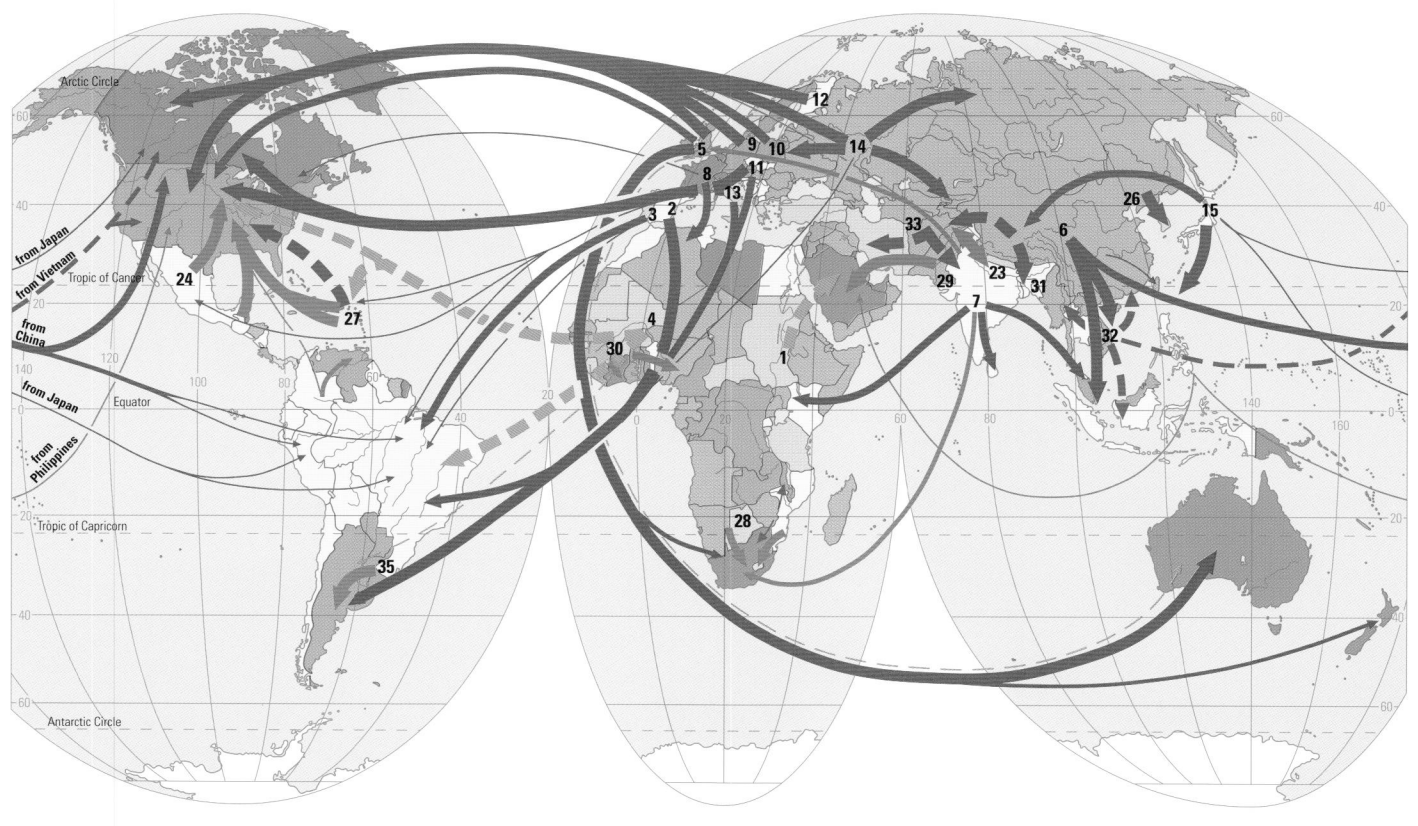

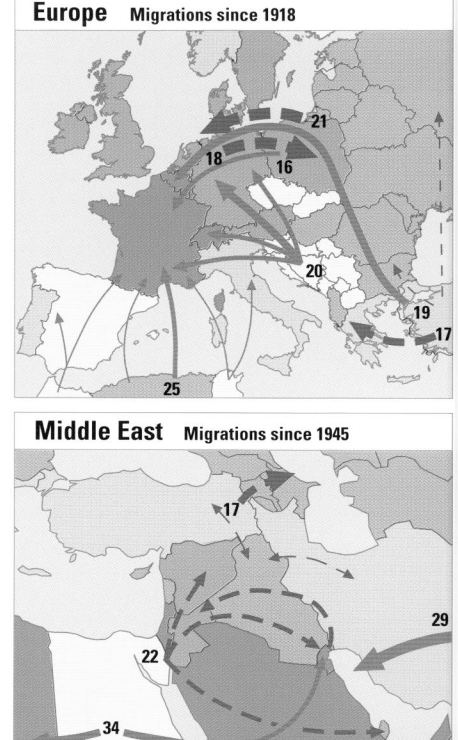

Europe Migrations since 1918

Middle East Migrations since 1945

Building the USA

US Immigration, 1920 and 2000

For decades the USA was the magnet that attracted millions of immigrants, notably from Central and Eastern Europe, the flow peaking in the early years of the 20th century. By the mid-1990s the proportion of immigrants had increased again to pre-World War II rates, reaching almost 10% by 2000. However, the balance of origin had swung from Europe to Latin America and Asia, as the graphs below indicate.

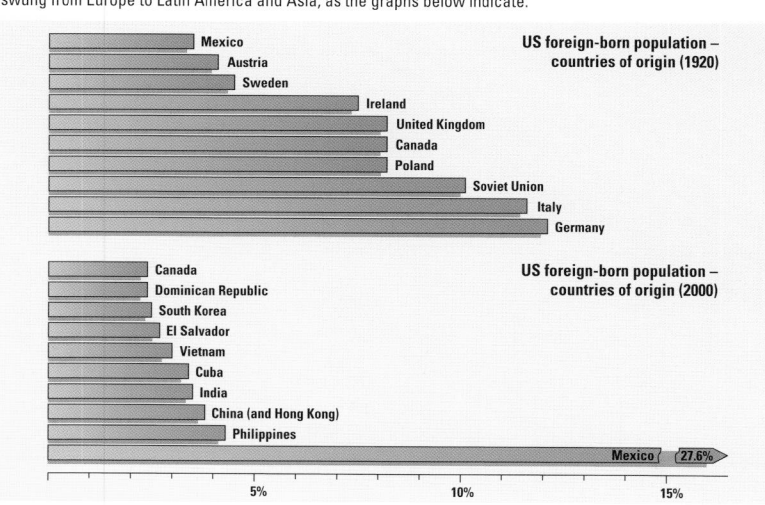

US foreign-born population – countries of origin (1920):
Mexico, Austria, Sweden, Ireland, United Kingdom, Canada, Poland, Soviet Union, Italy, Germany

US foreign-born population – countries of origin (2000):
Canada, Dominican Republic, South Korea, El Salvador, Vietnam, Cuba, India, China (and Hong Kong), Philippines, Mexico 27.6%

Major world migrations since 1500 (over 1 million people)

1. North and East African slaves to Arabia (4.3m)..........1500–1900
2. Spanish to South and Central America (2.3m) 1530–1914
3. Portuguese to Brazil (1.4m) 1530–1914
4. West African slaves to South America (4.6m)............1550–1860
   to Caribbean (4m).....................1580–1860
   to North/Central America (1m) ...1650–1820
5. British and Irish to North America (13.5m) 1620–1914
   to Australasia and
   South Africa (3m)...............................1790–1914
6. Chinese to Southeast Asia (22m) 1820–1914
   to North America (1m) 1880–1914
7. Indian migrant workers (3m)................................1850–1914
8. French to North Africa (1.5m) 1850–1914
9. Germans to North America (5m)...........................1850–1914
10. Poles to North America (3.6m)............................1850–1914
11. Austro-Hungarians to North America (3.2m) 1850–1914
    to Western Europe (3.4m)............1850–1914
    to South America (1.8m)............1850–1914
12. Scandinavians to North America (2.7m) 1850–1914
13. Italians to North America (5m) 1860–1914
    to South America (3.7m)............1860–1914
14. Russians to North America (2.2m) 1880–1914
    to Western Europe (2.2m)............1880–1914
    to Siberia (6m)............................1880–1914
    to Central Asia (4m)....................1880–1914

15. Japanese to Eastern Asia, Southeast Asia
    and America (8m)..................................1900–1914
16. Poles to Western Europe (1m) 1920–1940
17. Greeks and Armenians from Turkey (1.6m) 1922–1923
18. European Jews to extermination camps (5m)............1940–1944
19. Turks to Western Europe (1.9m) 1940–
20. Yugoslavs to Western Europe (2m) 1940–
21. Germans to Western Europe (9.8m) 1945–1947
22. Palestinian refugees (2m)....................................1947–
23. Indian and Pakistani refugees (15m) 1947
24. Mexicans to North America (9m)............................1950–
25. North Africans to Western Europe (1.1m) 1950–
26. Korean refugees (5m)......................................1950–1954
27. Latin Americans and West Indians to
    North America (4.7m)..............................1960–
28. Migrant workers to South Africa (1.5m) 1960–
29. Indians and Pakistanis to The Gulf (2.4m)..................1970–
30. Migrant workers to Nigeria and Ivory Coast (3m)......1970–
31. Bangladeshi and Pakistani refugees (2m)....................1972
32. Vietnamese and Cambodian refugees (1.5m) 1975–
33. Afghan refugees (6.1m)..1979–
34. Egyptians to The Gulf and Libya (2.9m) 1980–
35. Migrant workers to Argentina (2m) 1980–
36. Mozambique refugees (1.7m).................................1985–
37. Yugoslav/Balkan refugees (1.7m)..........................1992–
38. Rwanda/Burundi refugees (2.6m)...........................1994–

Predominant Languages

INDO-EUROPEAN FAMILY
1	Balto-Slavic group (incl. Russian, Ukrainian)
2	Germanic group (incl. English, German)
3	Celtic group
4	Greek
5	Albanian
6	Iranian group
7	Armenian
8	Romance group (incl. Spanish, Portuguese, French, Italian)
9	Indo-Aryan group (incl. Hindi, Bengali, Urdu, Punjabi, Marathi)
10	**CAUCASIAN FAMILY**

AFRO-ASIATIC FAMILY
11	Semitic group (incl. Arabic)
12	Kushitic group
13	Berber group

14	**KHOISAN FAMILY**
15	**NIGER-CONGO FAMILY**
16	**NILO-SAHARAN FAMILY**
17	**URALIC FAMILY**

ALTAIC FAMILY
18	Turkic group (incl. Turkish)
19	Mongolian group
20	Tungus-Manchu group
21	Japanese and Korean

SINO-TIBETAN FAMILY
22	Sinitic (Chinese) languages (incl. Mandarin, Wu, Yue)
23	Tibetic-Burmic languages
24	**TAI FAMILY**

AUSTRO-ASIATIC FAMILY
25	Mon-Khmer group
26	Munda group
27	Vietnamese

28	**DRAVIDIAN FAMILY** (incl. Telugu, Tamil)
29	**AUSTRONESIAN FAMILY** (incl. Malay-Indonesian, Javanese)
30	**OTHER LANGUAGES**

First-language speakers, in millions (1999)
Mandarin Chinese	885m
Spanish	332m
English	322m
Bengali	189m
Hindi	182m
Portuguese	170m
Russian	170m
Japanese	125m
German	98m
Wu Chinese	77m
Javanese	76m
Korean	75m
French	72m
Vietnamese	68m
Yue Chinese	66m
Marathi	65m
Tamil	63m
Turkish	59m
Urdu	58m

Languages form a kind of tree of development, splitting from a few ancient proto-tongues into branches that have grown apart and further divided with the passage of time. English and Hindi, for example, both belong to the great Indo-European family, although the relationship is only apparent after much analysis and comparison with non-Indo-European languages such as Chinese or Arabic; Hindi is part of the Indo-Aryan subgroup, whereas English is a member of Indo-European's Germanic branch; French, another Indo-European tongue, traces its descent through the Latin, or Romance, branch. A few languages – Basque is one example – have no apparent links with any other, living or dead. Most modern languages, of course, have acquired enormous quantities of vocabulary from each other.

Distribution of Living Languages

The figures refer to the number of languages currently in use in the regions shown.

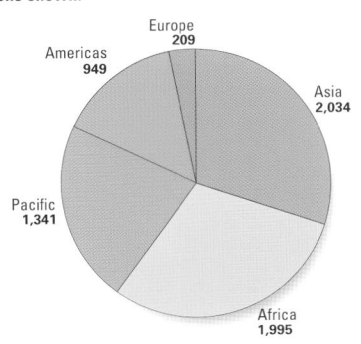

Europe 209
Americas 949
Asia 2,034
Pacific 1,341
Africa 1,995

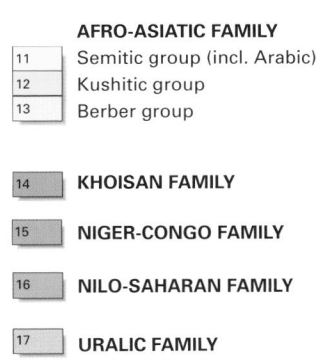

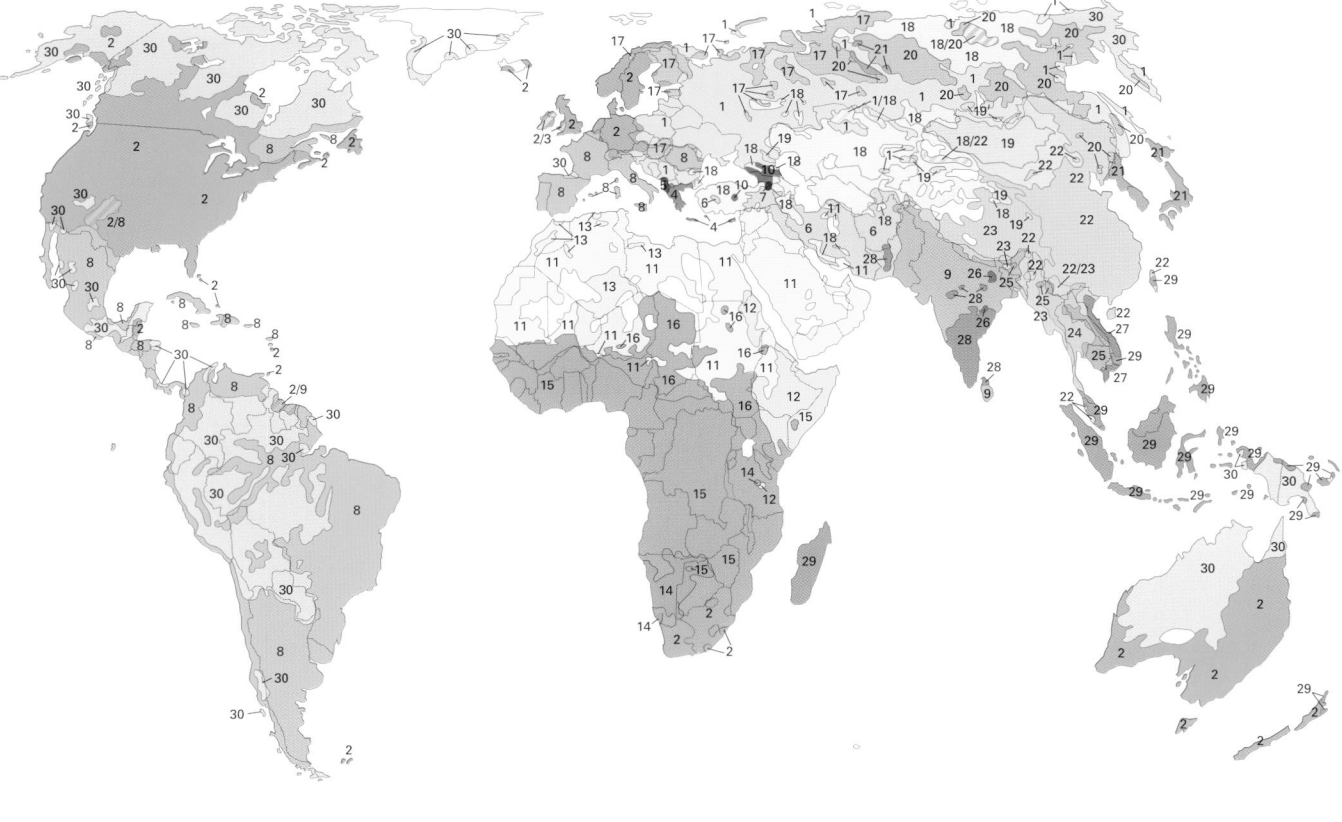

Predominant Religions

▲	Roman Catholicism
	Orthodox and other Eastern Churches
•	Protestantism
	Sunni Islam
	Shia Islam
	Buddhism
	Hinduism
	Confucianism
✦	Judaism
	Shintoism
	Tribal Religions

Religions are not as easily mapped as the physical contours of the land. Divisions are often blurred and frequently overlapping: most nations include people of many different faiths – or no faith at all. Some religions, like Islam and Christianity, have proselytes worldwide; others, like Hinduism and Confucianism, are restricted to a particular area, though modern migrations have taken some Indians and Chinese very far from their cultural origins. It is also difficult to show the degree to which religion controls daily life: Christian Western Europe, for example, is now far less dominated by its religion than are the Islamic nations of the Middle East. Similarly, figures for the major faiths' adherents make no distinction between nominal believers enrolled at birth and those for whom religion is a vital part of existence.

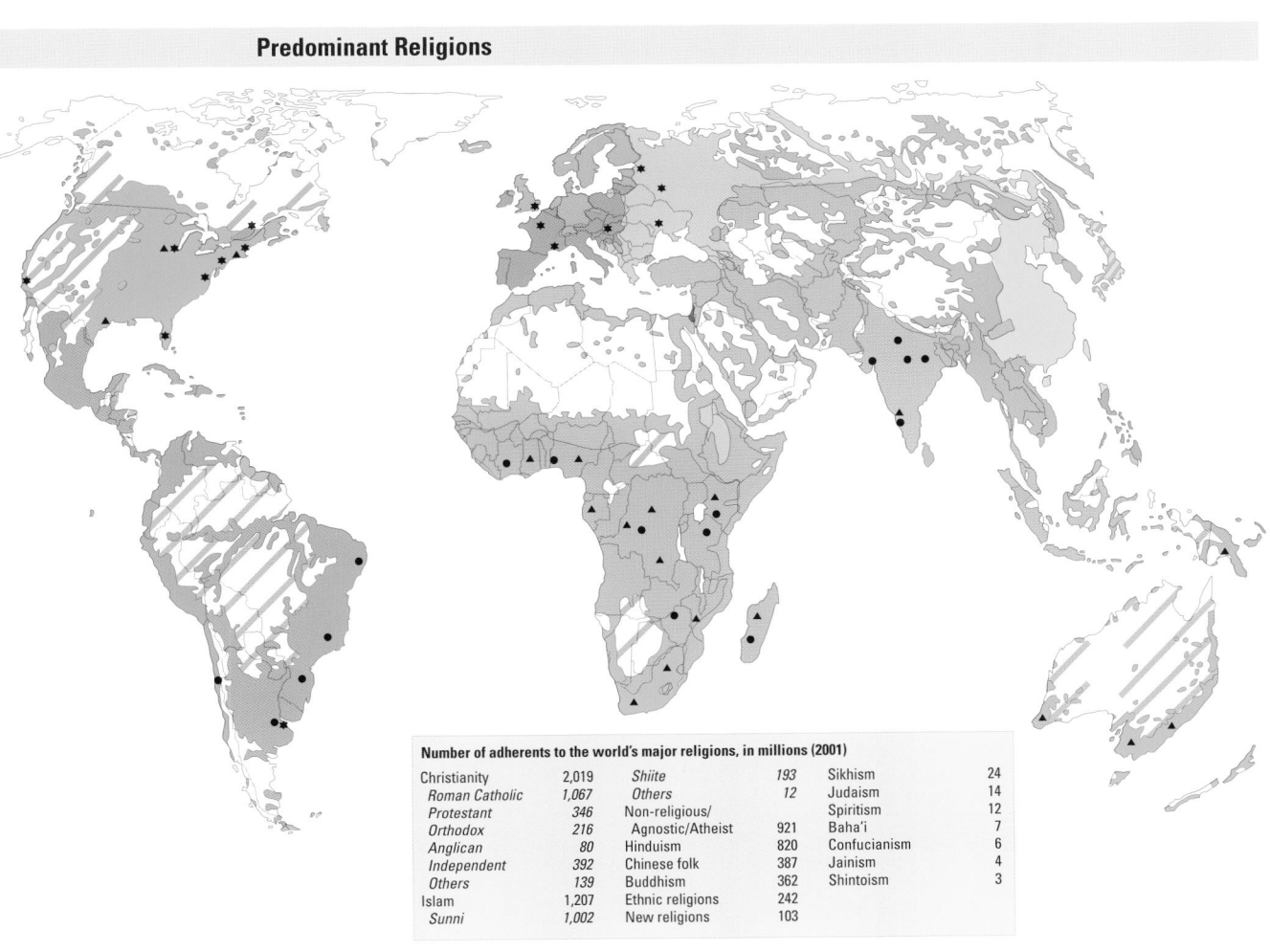

Number of adherents to the world's major religions, in millions (2001)
Christianity	2,019	*Shiite*	193	Sikhism	24
Roman Catholic	1,067	*Others*	12	Judaism	14
Protestant	346	Non-religious/		Spiritism	12
Orthodox	216	Agnostic/Atheist	921	Baha'i	7
Anglican	80	Hinduism	820	Confucianism	6
Independent	392	Chinese folk	387	Jainism	4
Others	139	Buddhism	362	Shintoism	3
Islam	1,207	Ethnic religions	242		
Sunni	1,002	New religions	103		

CONFLICT AND COOPERATION

For more information:
28 Migration
29 Religion

The 20th century witnessed two world wars, followed by a Cold War which several times threatened to erupt into a third world war, fought with nuclear weapons. The Cold War was marked by a great number of conflicts. Some were colonial wars, as the empires of the first half of the century fell apart, some were border wars, and some were civil wars. All the wars have caused great suffering among civilians, many of whom were forced to join the ranks of the world's refugees.

In the late 1980s, many people hoped that the end of the Cold War, following the collapse of Communist regimes in the former Soviet Union and Eastern Europe, would herald a new era of international stability. Instead, old ethnic and religious antagonisms surfaced in many areas, leading to civil war in such places as Chechenia, in Russia, and the former Yugoslavia. Nationalist rivalries, suppressed under Communist rule, replaced ideological factors as the major cause of conflict.

War is a very human activity, with no real equivalent in any other species. Yet humans also function well when they co-operate. Evolution has made this so. Hunter-gatherers in cooperative bands were far more effective than animals that prowled. Agriculture, urbanization and industrialization all depend on the ability of humans to cooperate.

The creation of the United Nations in 1945 held out hope that the world's nations, tired of war, would have the means to control humanity's aggressive instincts. Although the UN lacks the power to halt conflicts, it has often helped to achieve negotiation. Economic pressures have led to another kind of cooperation, the creation of common markets and economic unions, such as ASEAN in Southeast Asia, the European Union and NAFTA in North America.

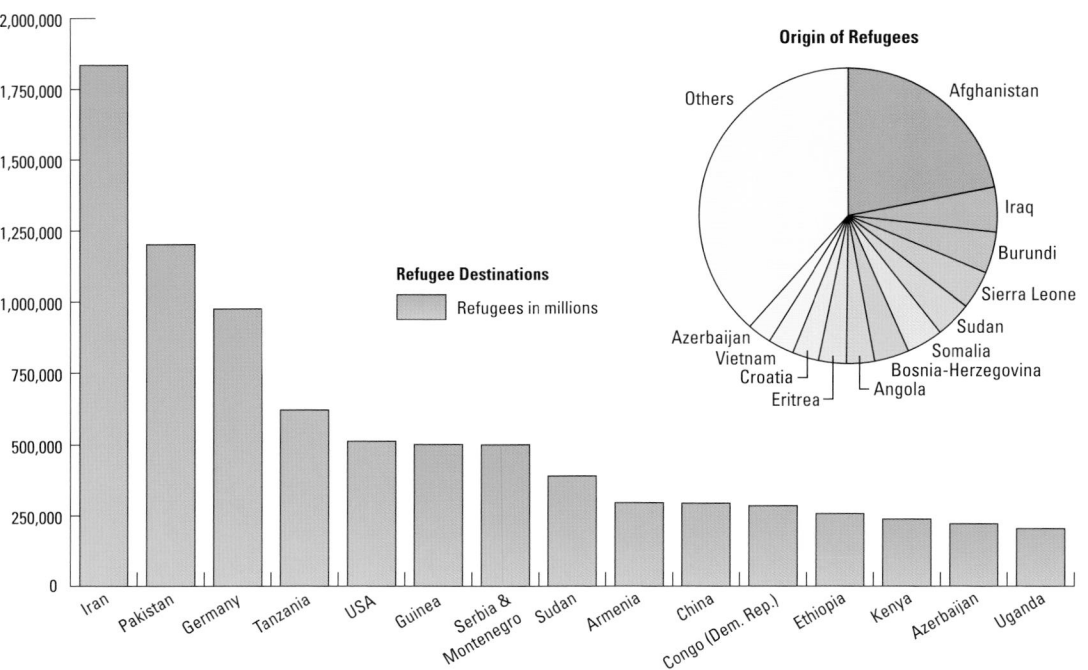

The World's Refugees

Refugees by host nation (bar chart, left) and by nation of origin (pie chart, left) (2000). The source is the United Nations High Commission for Refugees (UNHCR). The 3.2 million Palestinian refugees living in Jordan, Syria, Lebanon, Gaza and the West Bank fall under the mandate of United Nations Relief and Works Agency (UNRWA) and are not included on the graphs.

The pie chart shows the origins of the world's refugees, while the bar chart below shows their destinations. According to the United Nations High Commission for Refugees (UNHCR) in 2000 there were 12.1 million refugees. However, the UNHCR definition of a refugee, "a person who has left or remains outside their own country because they have a well-founded fear of persecution, or because their safety is threatened by events seriously disturbing public order," does not include people who are in a refugee-like situation but who have not been formally recognized. In 2000, there were a further 5.3 million people who were internally displaced, and a total "population of concern" 21.1 million people, worldwide.

All but a few who cross international boundaries seek asylum in neighboring countries, which are often the least equipped to deal with them. Lacking any rights or power, they frequently become an unwelcome burden to their hosts. Usually, the best any refugee can hope for is rudimentary food and shelter in temporary camps. Many Palestinians have been forced to live in camps since 1948.

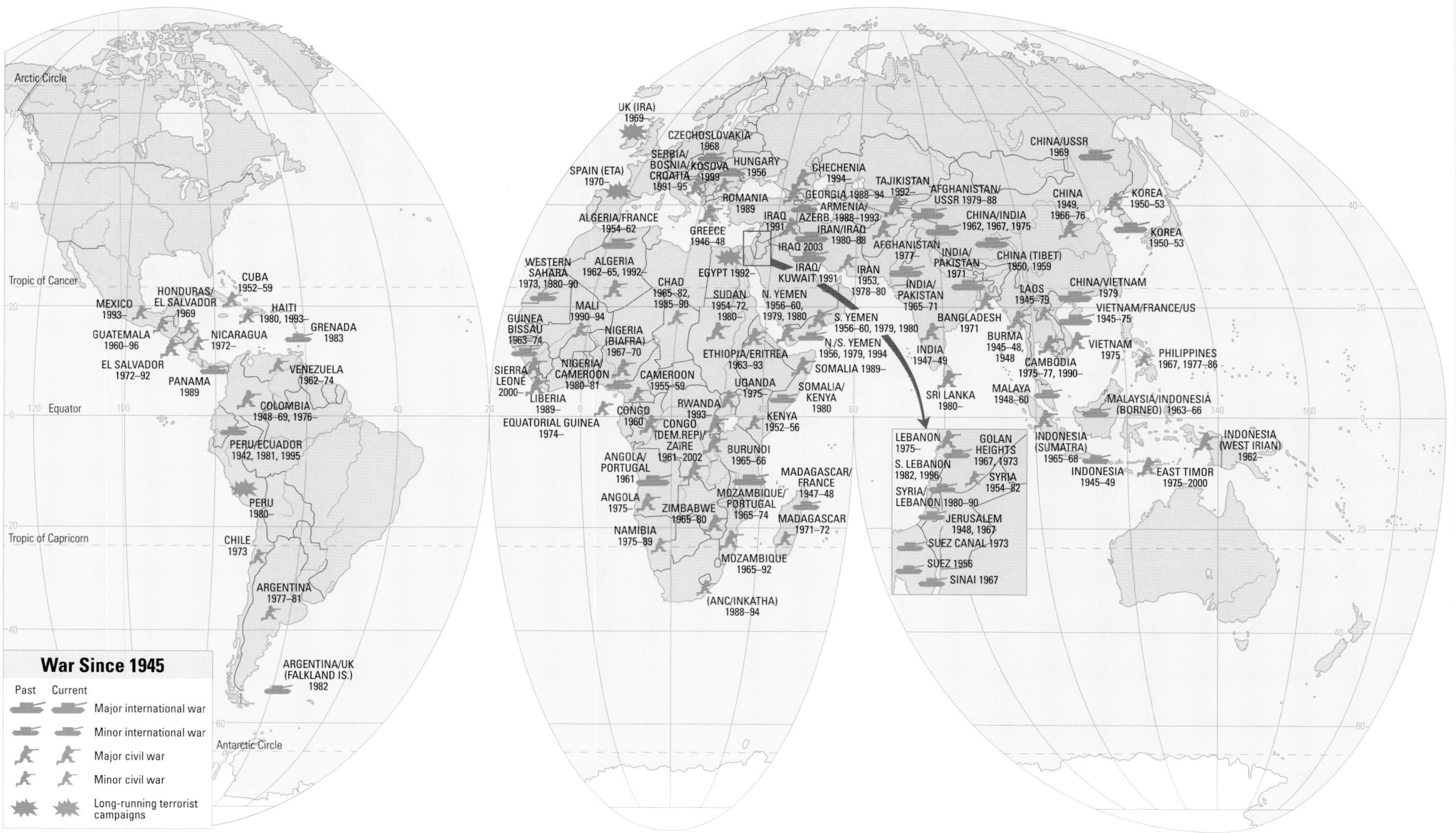

War Since 1945

Past	Current	
		Major international war
		Minor international war
		Major civil war
		Minor civil war
		Long-running terrorist campaigns

United Nations

The United Nations Organization was born as World War II drew to its conclusion. Six years of strife had strengthened the world's desire for peace, but an effective international organization was needed to help achieve it. That body would replace the League of Nations which, since its inception in 1920, had failed to curb the aggression of at least some of its member nations. At the United Nations Conference on International Organization held in San Francisco, the United Nations Charter was drawn up. Ratified by the Security Council and signed by the 51 original members, it came into effect on October 24, 1945.

The Charter set out the aims of the organization: to maintain peace and security, and develop friendly relations between nations; to achieve international cooperation in solving economic, social, cultural and humanitarian problems; to promote respect for human rights and fundamental freedoms; and to harmonize the activities of nations in order to achieve these common goals.

The United Nations has five principal organs :
The General Assembly
The forum at which member nations discuss moral and political issues affecting world development, peace and security meets annually in September, under a newly-elected President whose tenure lasts one year. Any member can bring business to the agenda, and each member nation has one vote.
The Security Council
A legislative and executive body, the Security Council is the primary instrument for establishing and maintaining international peace by attempting to settle disputes between nations. It has the power to dispatch UN forces, and member nations undertake to provide armed forces, assistance and facilities. The Security Council has ten temporary members elected by the General Assembly for two-year terms, and five permanent members – China, France, Russia, UK, and USA.
The Economic and Social Council
By far the largest United Nations executive, the Council operates as a conduit between the General Assembly and the many United Nations agencies it instructs to implement Assembly decisions, and whose work it coordinates. The Council also commissions studies on economic conditions, collects data and makes recommendations to the Assembly.
The Secretariat
This is the staff of the United Nations, and its task is to administer the policies and programs of the UN and its organs, and assist and advise the Head of the Secretariat, the Secretary-General – a full-time, non-political appointment made by the General Assembly.
The Trusteeship Council
This no longer administers any of the original 11 trust territories as they are all now independent.
The International Court of Justice (the World Court)
The World Court is the judicial organ of the United Nations. It deals only with United Nations disputes and all members are subject to its jurisdiction. There are 15 judges, elected for nine-year terms by the General Assembly and the Security Council.

The social and humanitarian operations of the UN include:
United Nations Development Program (UNDP) Plans and funds projects to help developing countries make better use of their resources.
United Nations International Childrens' Fund (UNICEF) Created at the General Assembly's first session in 1945 to help children in the aftermath of World War II, it now provides basic health care and aid worldwide.
Food and Agriculture Organization (FAO) Aims to raise living standards and nutrition levels in rural areas by improving food production and distribution.
United Nations Educational, Scientific and Cultural Organization (UNESCO) Promotes international cooperation through broader and better education.
World Health Organization (WHO) Promotes and provides for better health care, public and environmental health and medical research.

United Nations agencies are involved in many aspects of international trade, safety and security:
International Maritime Organization (IMO) Promotes unity amongst merchant shipping, especially in regard to safety, marine pollution and standardization.
International Labor Organization (ILO) Seeks to improve labor conditions and promote productive employment to raise living standards.
World Meteorological Organization (WMO) Promotes cooperation in weather observation, reporting and forecasting.
World Trade Organization (WTO) On January 1, 1995, the WTO replaced GATT. It advocates a common code of conduct and its aim is the liberalization of world trade.
Disarmament Commission Considers and makes recommendations to the General Assembly on disarmament issues.
International Atomic Energy Agency (IAEA) Fosters development of peaceful uses for nuclear energy and establishes safety standards.

The World Bank comprises three United Nations agencies:
International Monetary Fund (IMF) Cultivates international monetary cooperation and expansion of trade.
International Bank for Reconstruction and Development (IBRD) Provides funds and technical assistance to developing countries.
International Finance Corporation (IFC) Encourages the growth of productive private enterprise in less developed countries.

Membership There are two independent states which are not members of the UN – Taiwan and Vatican City. Official languages are Chinese, English, French, Russian, Spanish, and Arabic.
Funding The UN regular budget for 2002 was US $1.3 billion. Contributions are assessed by the members' ability to pay, with the maximum 22% of the total (USA's share), the minimum 0.01%. The 15-country EU pays over 37% of the budget.
Peacekeeping The UN has been involved in 54 peacekeeping operations worldwide since 1948.

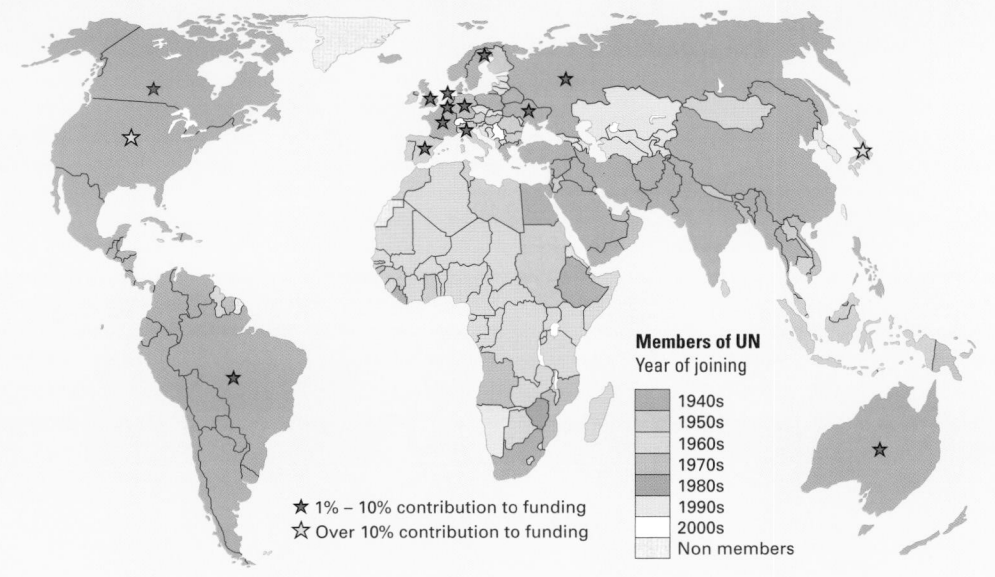

Members of UN
Year of joining

- 1940s
- 1950s
- 1960s
- 1970s
- 1980s
- 1990s
- 2000s
- Non members

★ 1% – 10% contribution to funding
☆ Over 10% contribution to funding

Military Spending

Military expenditure as a % of GDP (2000)

1. Eritrea	22.9%	14. Turkey	4.9%
2. Angola	21.2%	15. Singapore	4.8%
3. Saudi Arabia	11.6%	16. Zimbabwe	4.8%
4. Oman	9.7%	17. Sri Lanka	4.5%
5. Jordan	9.5%	18. Pakistan	4.5%
6. Ethiopia	9.4%	19. Djibouti	4.4%
7. Kuwait	8.2%	20. Armenia	4.4%
8. Israel	8.0%	21. Morocco	4.2%
9. Brunei	7.6%	22. Bahrain	4.0%
10. Syria	5.5%	23. Russia	4.0%
11. Burundi	5.4%	24. Turkmenistan	3.8%
12. Yemen	5.2%	25. Iran	3.8%
13. Greece	4.9%	26. Botswana	3.7%

It is worth noting that the total amount of expenditure varies considerably depending on the size of the economy, so that although the percentages show the importance given to military spending within each country, they give no idea as to the total expenditure. In 2001, for example, the USA spent a total of US $281 billion, Russia US $44 billion, France US $40 billion, Japan US $38.5 billion, and the UK US $37 billion. In 2001, the USA also provided the most military assistance worldwide, providing US $3.5 billion.

The period 1987–98 saw a decline in global military spending which generated what the United Nations Development Program termed a "peace dividend." Between 1998–2001, however, global expenditure increased by 7.4%. Unfortunately, there is no clear link between reduced military spending and enhanced expenditure on human development. Moreover, the poorest regions of the world (notably sub-Saharan Africa) failed to contain their military spending and, in some cases, it increased.

International Organizations

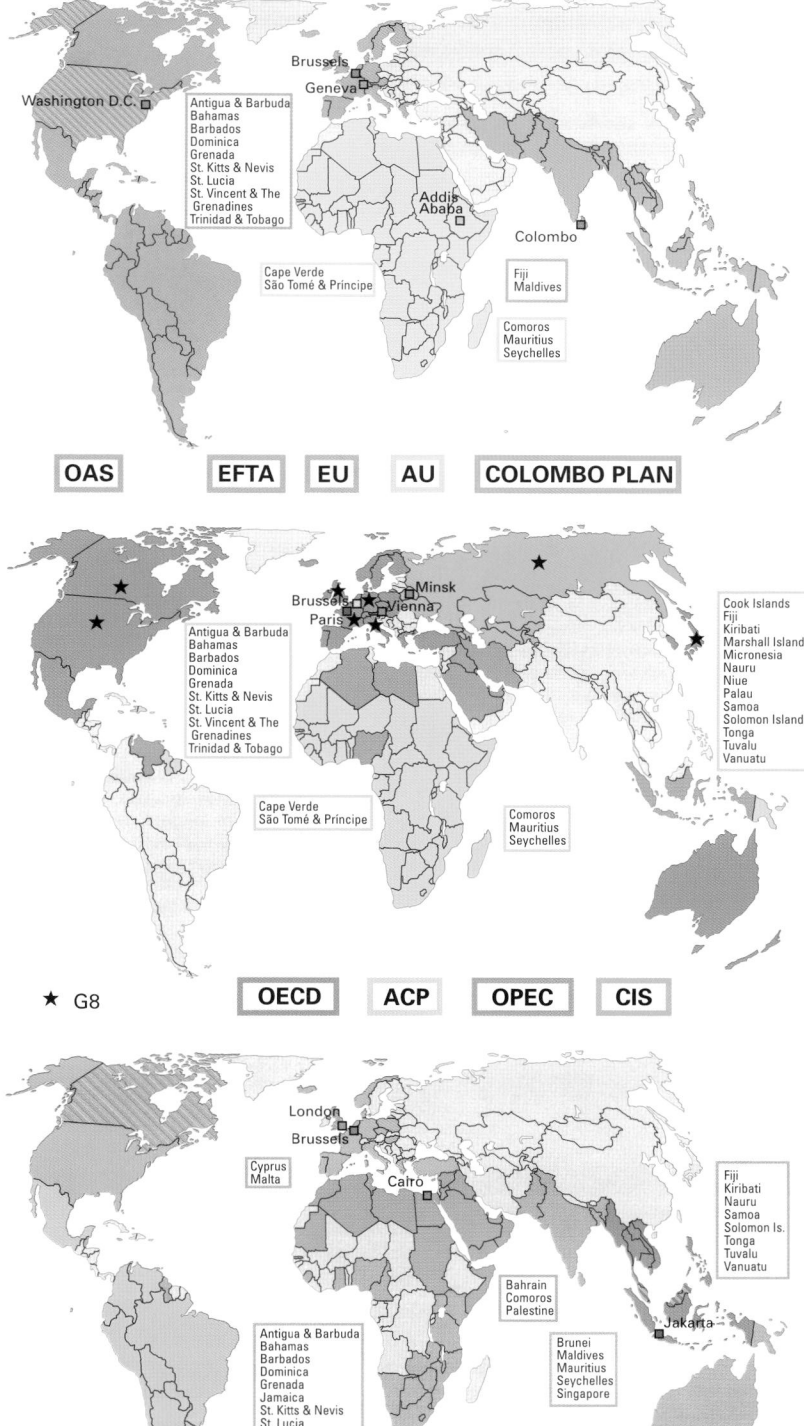

OAS   EFTA   EU   AU   COLOMBO PLAN

★ G8   OECD   ACP   OPEC   CIS

NATO   LAIA   ARAB LEAGUE   COMMONWEALTH   ASEAN

ACP African-Caribbean-Pacific (formed in 1963). Members enjoy economic ties with the EU.
ARAB LEAGUE (1945) Aims to promote economic, social, political and military cooperation.
ASEAN Association of Southeast Asian Nations (formed in 1967). Cambodia joined in 1999.
AU The African Union was set up in 2002, taking over from the Organization of African Unity (1963). It has 53 members. Working languages are Arabic, English, French, and Portuguese.
CIS The Commonwealth of Independent States (formed in 1991) comprises the countries of the former Soviet Union except for Estonia, Latvia and Lithuania.
COLOMBO PLAN (formed in 1951) Its 25 members aim to promote economic and social development in Asia and the Pacific.
COMMONWEALTH The Commonwealth of Nations evolved from the British Empire; it comprises 16 nations recognizing the British monarch as head of state, 32 republics and 5 indigenous monarchies, giving a total of 53. Nigeria was suspended in 1995, but reinstated in 1999.
EFTA European Free Trade Organization (founded 1960). Since Austria, Finland, Portugal, and Sweden left to join the EU, it has four members: Iceland, Liechtenstein, Norway, and Switzerland.
EU The European Union evolved from the European Community (EC) in 1993. The original body, the European Coal and Steel Community (ECSC), was created in 1951 following the signing of the Treaty of Paris. The 15 members of the EU – Austria, Belgium, Denmark, Finland, France, Germany, Greece, Ireland, Italy, Luxembourg, Netherlands, Portugal, Spain, Sweden, and the UK – aim to integrate economies and coordinate social development. In 2002, the EU invited ten countries – Cyprus, the Czech Republic, Estonia, Hungary, Latvia, Lithuania, Malta, Poland, the Slovak Republic, and Slovenia – to join the organization on May 1, 2004.
LAIA The Latin American Integration Association (formed in 1980) superceded the Latin American Free Trade Association formed in 1961. Its aim is to promote freer regional trade.
NATO North Atlantic Treaty Organization (formed in 1949). It continues despite the winding up of the Warsaw Pact in 1991. The Czech Rep., Hungary and Poland were the latest to join in 1999.
OAS Organization of American States (formed in 1948). It aims to promote social and economic co-operation between countries in the developed North America and developing Latin America.
OECD Organization for Economic Cooperation and Development (formed in 1961). It comprises 29 major free-market economies. The "G8" is its "inner group" of leading industrial nations, comprising Canada, France, Germany, Italy, Japan, Russia, UK, and the USA.
OPEC Organization of Petroleum Exporting Countries (formed in 1960). It controls about three-quarters of the world's oil supply. Gabon formally withdrew from OPEC in August 1996.

AGRICULTURE

When harvests are bad and world grain reserves fall, an old debate is revived, namely whether the population explosion will cause major food crises in the 21st century.

Experts estimate that 3 billion tons of cereals will be needed to feed the world's population in 25 years' time, as compared with 1.9 billion tons at present. To expand food production to this extent, some argue, will place great strain on the environment.

Other experts argue that there should be no food crises. World grain production tripled between 1950 and 1990, largely as a result of the Green Revolution, during which genetically improved, high-yield varieties of maize, rice and wheat, the world's three leading staple crops, were developed. These new varieties have helped many developing countries to achieve food surpluses and prevent widespread starvation. However, some people oppose the use of genetically modified crops. In 2002, with severe droughts causing starvation, Zambia and Zimbabwe refused large maize donations from the USA because they might be genetically modified.

The only region of the world which seems likely to suffer food shortages in the 21st century is sub-Saharan Africa, where in the late 1990s the average daily calorie intake was 6% less than what was needed and where the population is expected to double in 20 years. Improved land management and a huge increase in global trade, especially in food distribution, is necessary if sub-Saharan Africans are not to go hungry.

The development of agriculture more than 10,000 years ago transformed human existence more than any other major advance. By supporting larger populations, it led to the growth of early civilizations and later it sustained people in the industrial cities which sprang up in the 19th century.

Today, agricultural production varies a great deal between the developed world, where it is highly mechanized and employs few people, such as 2% of the work force in the United States, and the developing world, such as sub-Saharan Africa, where it employs 66% of the work force. Many Africans are engaged in subsistence farming, providing the basic needs of their families but not contributing to the national economy. Much of Africa also suffers from economic mismanagement, as well as civil war and corruption.

Political problems have also affected food production in other parts of the world. The former USSR had much excellent farmland, but the failure of the collectives and state farms to maintain sufficiently high levels of production helped to bring about the collapse of Communism.

Farmers are under great pressure not only to maintain high levels of production but to increase them. However, the cultivation of marginal areas is one of the prime causes of soil erosion and desertification.

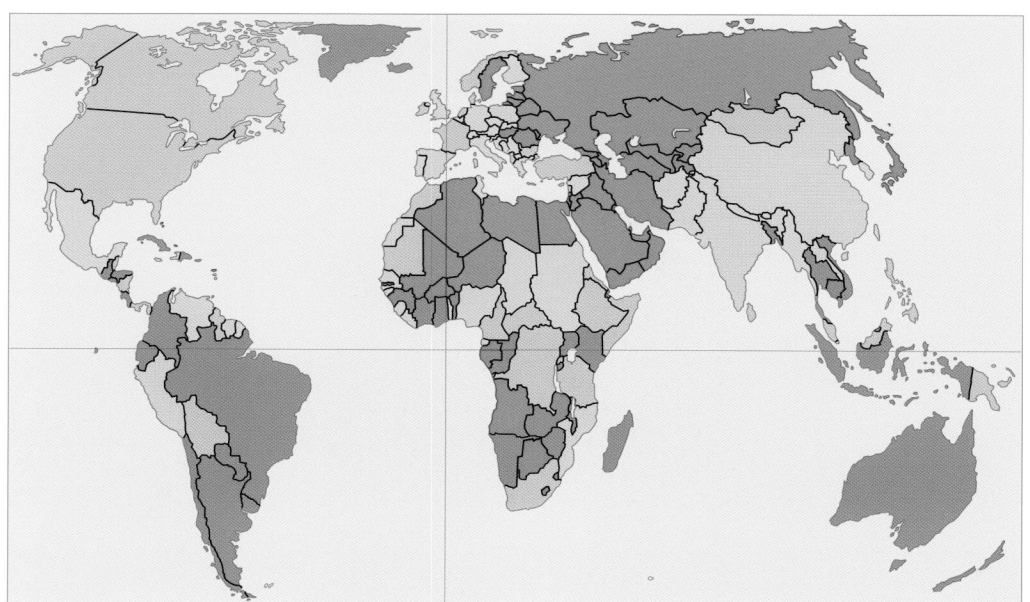

Self-sufficiency in Food

Balance of trade in food products as a percentage of total trade in food products – S.I.T.C. Classes 0, 1 and 4 (latest available year)

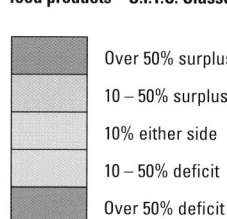

Over 50% surplus
10 – 50% surplus
10% either side
10 – 50% deficit
Over 50% deficit

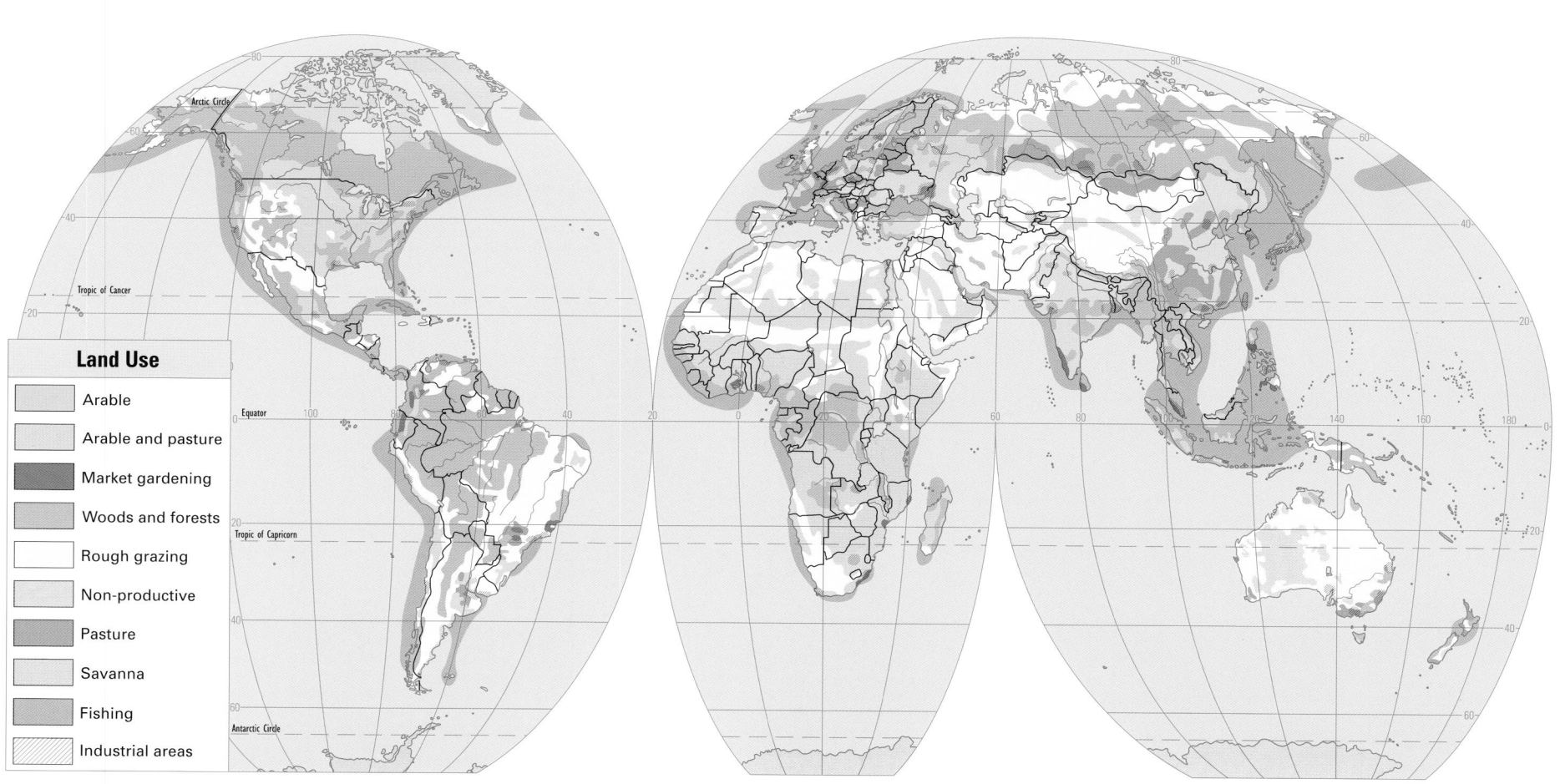

Land Use

Arable

Arable and pasture

Market gardening

Woods and forests

Rough grazing

Non-productive

Pasture

Savanna

Fishing

Industrial areas

Staple Crops

Wheat: Grown in a range of climates, with most varieties – including the highest-quality bread wheats – requiring temperate conditions. Mainly used in baking, it is also used for pasta and breakfast cereals.

China 18.9% India 12.2% USA 11.0% France 5.7% Russia 5.5% Canada 4.6%

World total (2000): 576,317,000 tons

Maize: Originating in the New World and still an important human food in Africa and Latin America, in the developed world it is processed into breakfast cereals, oil, starches and adhesives. It is also used for animal feed.

USA 36.4% China 21.8% Brazil 7.0%

World total (2000): 590,791,000 tons

Oats: Most widely used to feed livestock, but eaten by humans as oatmeal or porridge. Oats have a beneficial effect on the cardiovascular system, and human consumption is likely to increase.

Russia 29.7% Canada 9.9% USA 8.2% Australia 6.7% Germany 5.6%

World total (2000): 25,953,000 tons

Millet: The name covers a number of small-grained cereals, members of the grass family with a short growing season. Used to produce flour, meal and animal feed, and fermented to make beer, especially in Africa.

India 33.2% Nigeria 18.3% China 16.1% Niger 6.4%

World total (2000): 27,255,000 tons

Sugars

Sugarcane: Confined to tropical regions, cane sugar accounts for the bulk of international trade in sugar. Most is produced as a foodstuff, but some countries, notably Brazil and South Africa, distil sugar cane to make motor fuels.

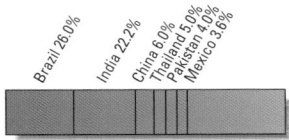

Brazil 26.0% India 22.2% China 6.0% Thailand 5.0% Pakistan 4.0% Mexico 3.6%

World total (2000): 1,278,093,000 tons

Cereals are grasses with starchy, edible seeds; every important civilization has depended on them as a source of food. The major cereal grains contain about 10% protein and 75% carbohydrate. Grain contributes more than any other group of foods to the energy and protein content of the human diet. Starchy tuber crops or root crops are second in importance after cereals as staple foods; easily cultivated, they provide high yields for little effort.

Rice: Thrives on the high humidity and temperatures of the Far East, where it is the traditional staple food of half the human race. Usually grown standing in water, rice responds well to continuous cultivation, with three or four crops annually.

China 34.0% India 21.7% Indonesia 9.0% Bangladesh 4.8% Vietnam 4.4% Thailand 3.6%

World total (2000): 598,852,000 tons

Potatoes: The most important of the edible tubers, potatoes grow in well-watered, temperate areas. Weight for weight less nutritious than grain, they are a human staple as well as an important animal feed.

China 16.0% Russia 14.0% Poland 6.7% India 6.3% Ukraine 5.2%

World total (2000): 311,288,000 tons

Soya: Beans from soya bushes (soybeans) are very high (30–40%) in protein. Most are processed into oil and proprietary protein foods. Consumption since 1950 has tripled, mainly due to the health-conscious developed world.

USA 47.1% Brazil 20.4% China 10.7% Argentina 9.6%

World total (2000): 161,993,000 tons

Cassava: A tropical shrub that needs high rainfall (over 125 inches annually) and a 10–30 month growing season to produce its large, edible tubers. Used as flour by humans, as cattle feed and in industrial starches.

Nigeria 19.2% Brazil 15.6% Thailand 11.1% Congo (D.R.) 10.7% Indonesia 9.4% Ghana 4.2%

World total (2000): 172,737,000 tons

Sugar beet: Closely related to the beetroot, sugar beet's yield after processing is indistinguishable from cane sugar. It is replacing sugarcane imports in Europe, to the detriment of the developing countries that rely on it as a major cash crop.

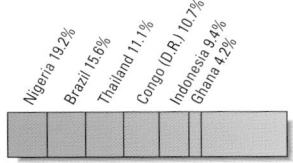

France 11.5% Ukraine 11.2% Germany 9.8% USA 9.6% Russia 7.2% Italy 5.0% Poland 5.0% Turkey 4.2%

World total (2000): 244,780,000 tons

Food and Population

Comparison of food production and population by continent

The left column indicates the % of world food production and the right shows population in proportion.

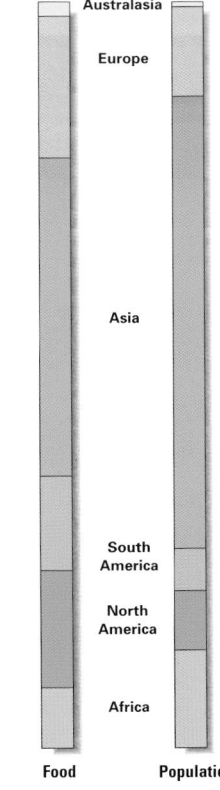

Australasia
Europe
Asia
South America
North America
Africa

Food   Population

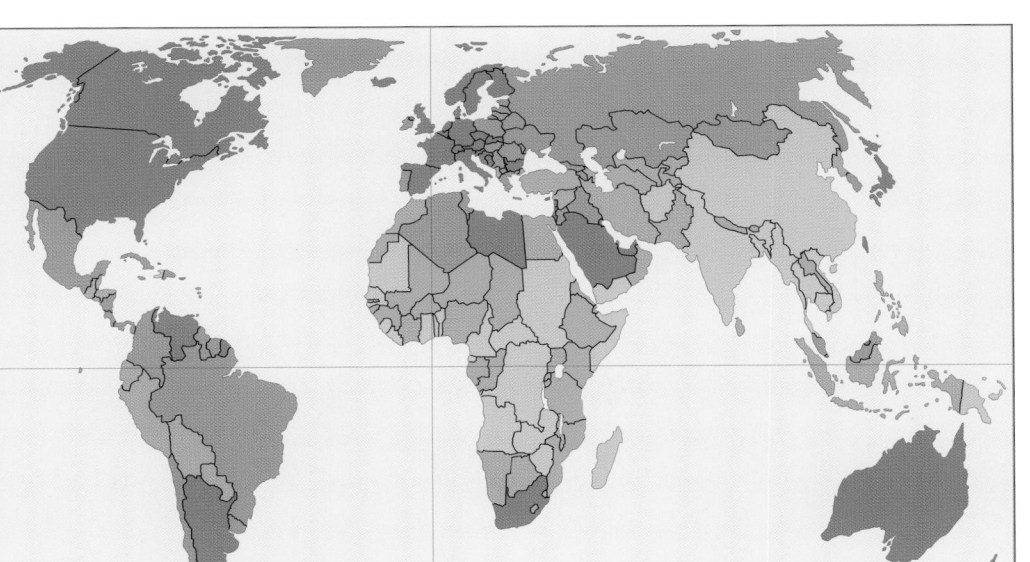

Agricultural Population

Percentage of the total population dependent on agriculture for their livelihood (2000)

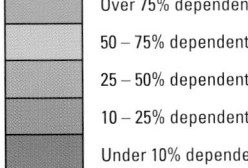

Over 75% dependent
50 – 75% dependent
25 – 50% dependent
10 – 25% dependent
Under 10% dependent

Top 5 countries		Bottom 5 countries	
Bhutan	93.7%	Singapore	0.1%
Nepal	93.0%	Brunei	0.7%
Burkina Faso	92.3%	Bahrain	1.0%
Burundi	90.4%	Kuwait	1.1%
Rwanda	90.3%	Qatar	1.3%

Animal Products

Traditionally, food animals subsisted on land unsuitable for cultivation, supporting agricultural production with their fertilizing dung. But free-ranging animals grow slowly and yield less meat than those more intensively reared; the demands of urban markets in the developed world have encouraged the growth of factory-like production methods. A large proportion of staple crops, especially cereals, are fed to animals, an inefficient way to produce protein but one likely to continue as long as people value meat and dairy products in their diet.

Cheese: Least perishable of all dairy products, cheese is milk fermented with selected bacterial strains to produce a foodstuff with a potentially immense range of flavors and textures. The vast majority of cheeses are made from cow's milk, although sheep and goat cheeses are highly prized.

USA 23.5% France 10.8% Germany 9.6% Italy 6.0% Netherlands 4.6%

World total (2000): 16,045,000 tons

Beef and Veal: Most beef and veal is reared for home markets, and the top five producers are also the biggest consumers. The USA produces nearly a quarter of the world's beef and eats even more.

USA 21.7% Brazil 8.6% China 6.5% Russia 5.5% Argentina 4.6% France 3.0%

World total (2000): 57,170,000 tons

Milk: Many human groups, including most Asians, find raw milk indigestible after infancy, and it is often only the starting point for other dairy products such as butter, cheese and yoghurt. Most world production comes from cows, but sheep's milk and goats' milk are also important.

USA 15.2% Russia 8.4% India 8.9% Germany 6.0% France 5.5% Brazil 3.7%

World total (2000): 2,504,000 tons

Butter: A traditional source of vitamin A as well as calories, butter has lost much popularity in the developed world for health reasons, although it remains a valuable food. Most butter from India, the world's largest producer, is clarified into ghee, which has religious as well as nutritional importance.

India 19.0% USA 8.9% Germany 7.2% France 6.7% Pakistan 6.2% New Zealand 4.6%

World total (2000): 7,049,000 tons

Pork: Although pork is forbidden to many millions, notably Muslims, on religious grounds, more is produced than any other meat in the world, mainly because it is the cheapest. It accounts for about 90% of China's meat output, although per capita meat consumption is relatively low.

China 45.1% USA 9.7% France 4.9% Germany 4.3% Russia 3.3%

World total (2000): 90,909,000 tons

Crisis in Africa

Each year 40 million people, almost half of whom are children, die from starvation and related diseases. In 2000, 600 million people worldwide were estimated to be suffering from malnutrition. Africa suffers from more natural disasters than any other continent; pests such as locusts destroy crops, and tropical storms and floods ruin harvests. Famines periodically affect parts of Africa causing widespread hardship, even though enough food is produced worldwide to feed everyone. One major phenomenon that affects the weather over tropical and subtropical regions areas around the world, is called El Niño. It occurs when there is unusual warming in the tropical eastern Pacific Ocean, causing changes in the wind and pressure systems. Normal years are called La Niña (*see page 8, The El Niño Phenomenon*). El Niño years included 1973–4, 1982–3, 1986–7, 1992, 1997–8, and 2002.

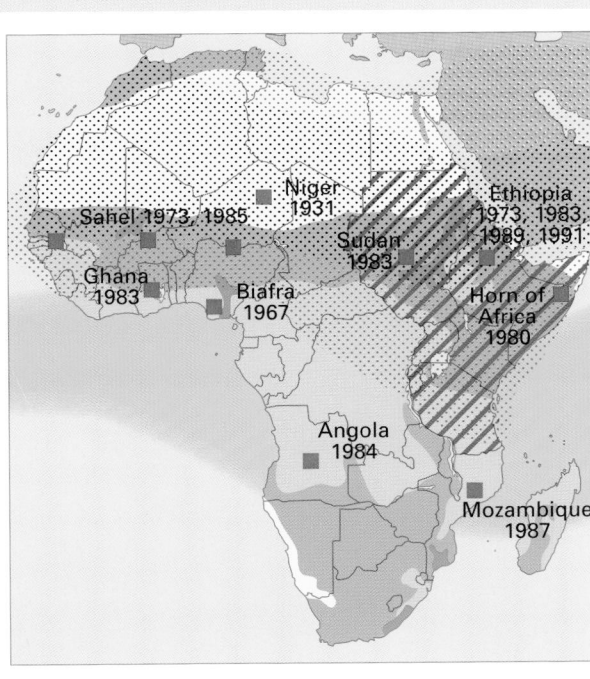

Niger 1931
Sahel 1973, 1985
Ethiopia 1973, 1983, 1989, 1991
Ghana 1983
Sudan 1983
Biafra 1967
Horn of Africa 1980
Angola 1984
Mozambique 1987

Ocean areas affected by El Niño and La Niña temperature fluctuations

Crop Failure

Areas liable to periodic crop failure

Areas where crop failures are rare

Desert

Desert Locusts

Areas liable to invasions by desert locusts

Areas affected by 1993 swarm of desert locusts

Countries affected by four years of continuous drought 1996–2000

Areas liable to flood

 Major famines since 1900 (with dates)

33

ENERGY

Every year, the world's energy consumption is about the equivalent of what would come from burning 9 billion tons of oil (9,000 MtOe) – a 20-fold increase since 1850. Two-fifths of this total actually comes from burning oil and most of the rest comes from coal and natural gas.

The oil crises in the 1970s precipitated concern over dependence on finite fossil fuels as the primary source of energy, and growing environmental awareness has added impetus to the search for alternative energy resources.

Fossil fuel combustion damages the environment through the release of gases and particulate matter, but two other major sources of energy, hydroelectricity and nuclear power, are also controversial. For example, hydroelectricity production involves flooding large areas to create reservoirs, while nuclear power stations generate dangerous radioactive wastes and can cause major disasters. Significantly, by 2002, five European countries – Belgium, Germany, the Netherlands, Spain, and Sweden – had plans to

phase out the use of nuclear energy.

Alternative energy resources may soon provide a much larger proportion of the world's energy consumption, especially in developing countries. Solar and wind energy may become important in such countries as China and India, while tidal, wave and geothermal energy all have potential in appropriate areas. Experts have calculated that solar power could, in theory, supply between five and ten times the present electricity supply of developing countries.

Conversions

For historical reasons, oil is still traded in barrels. The weight and volume equivalents shown below are all based on average density "Arabian light" crude oil, and should be considered approximate.

The energy equivalents given for a ton of oil are also somewhat imprecise: oil and coal of different qualities will have varying energy contents, a fact usually reflected in their price on world markets.

1 barrel:
0.15 tons
159 liters
35 Imperial gallons
42 US gallons

1 ton:
7.33 barrels
1,185 liters
256 Imperial gallons
261 US gallons

1 ton oil:
1.5 tons hard coal
3.0 tons lignite
12,000 kWh

1 gallon (Imperial):
227,42 cubic inches
1.201 US gallons
4,546 liters

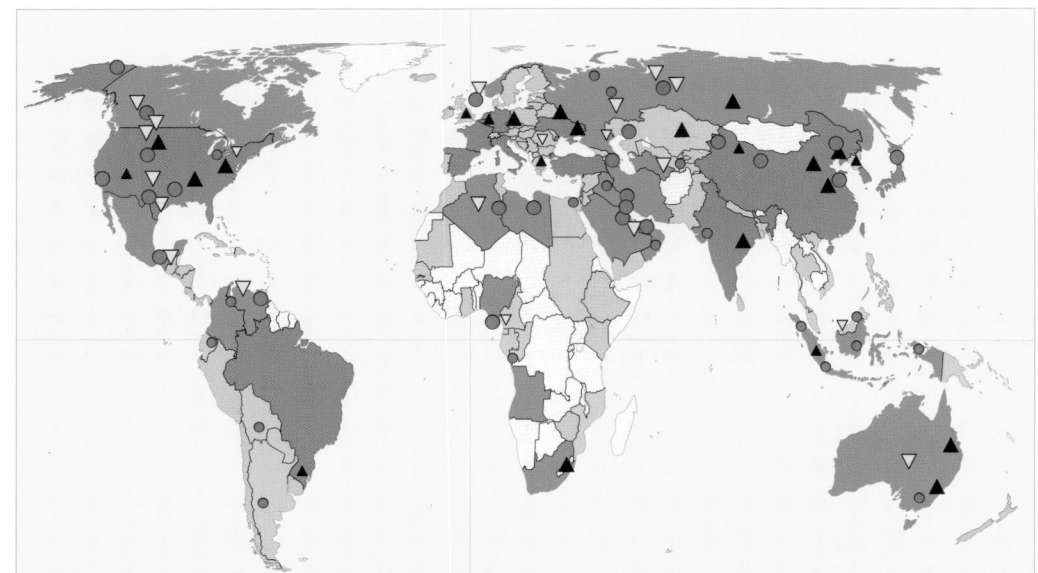

Energy Balance

Difference between energy production and consumption in millions of tons of oil equivalent (MtOe) (2000)

Energy surplus ↑

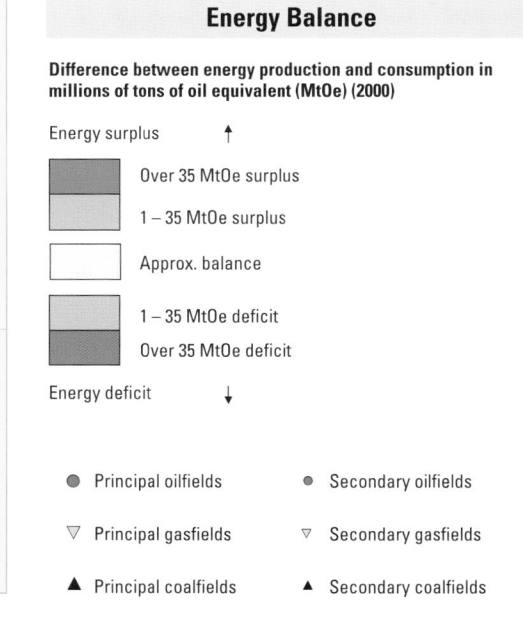

- Over 35 MtOe surplus
- 1 – 35 MtOe surplus
- Approx. balance
- 1 – 35 MtOe deficit
- Over 35 MtOe deficit

Energy deficit ↓

- ● Principal oilfields   ⬤ Secondary oilfields
- ▽ Principal gasfields   ▽ Secondary gasfields
- ▲ Principal coalfields   ▲ Secondary coalfields

World Energy Consumption

Energy consumed by world regions, measured in million tons of oil equivalent in 2001. Total world consumption was 9,125 MtOe. Only energy from oil, gas, coal, nuclear, and hydroelectric sources are included. Excluded are fuels such as wood, peat, animal waste, wind, solar, and geothermal which, though important in some countries, are unreliably documented in terms of consumption statistics.

Oil   Gas   Coal   Nuclear   Hydro

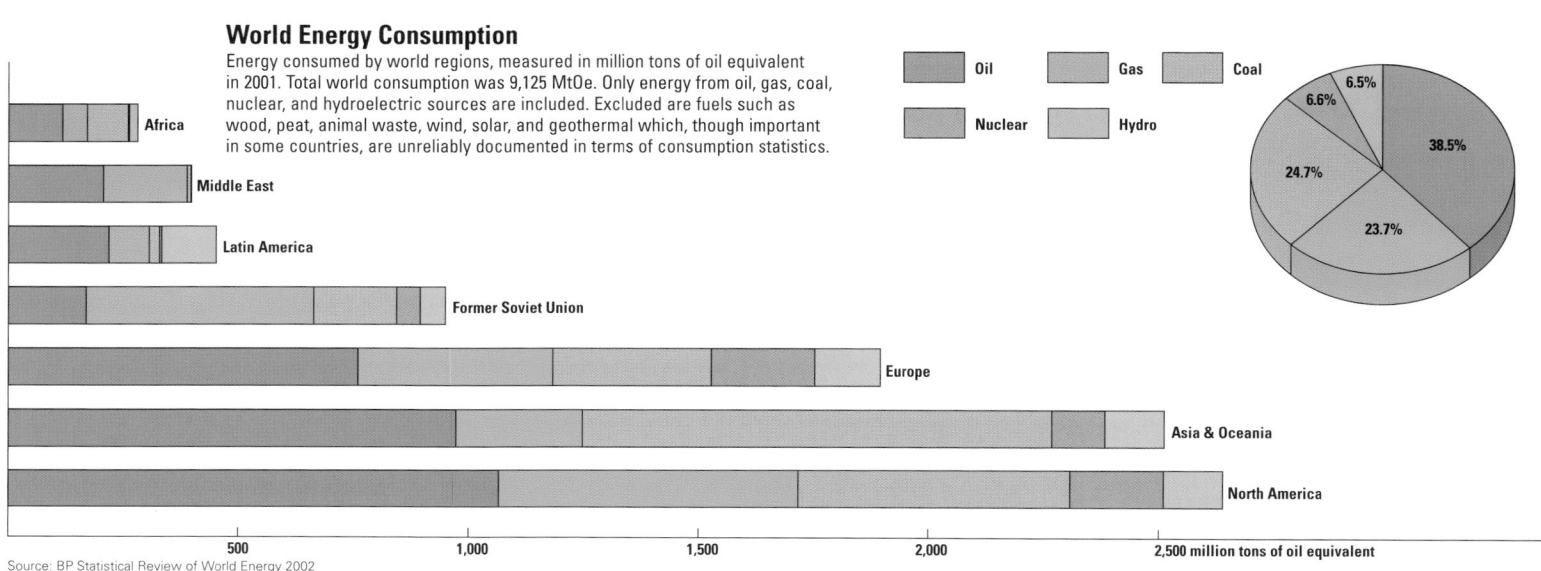

- Africa
- Middle East
- Latin America
- Former Soviet Union
- Europe
- Asia & Oceania
- North America

500   1,000   1,500   2,000   2,500 million tons of oil equivalent

Pie chart: 38.5%, 23.7%, 24.7%, 6.6%, 6.5%

Source: BP Statistical Review of World Energy 2002

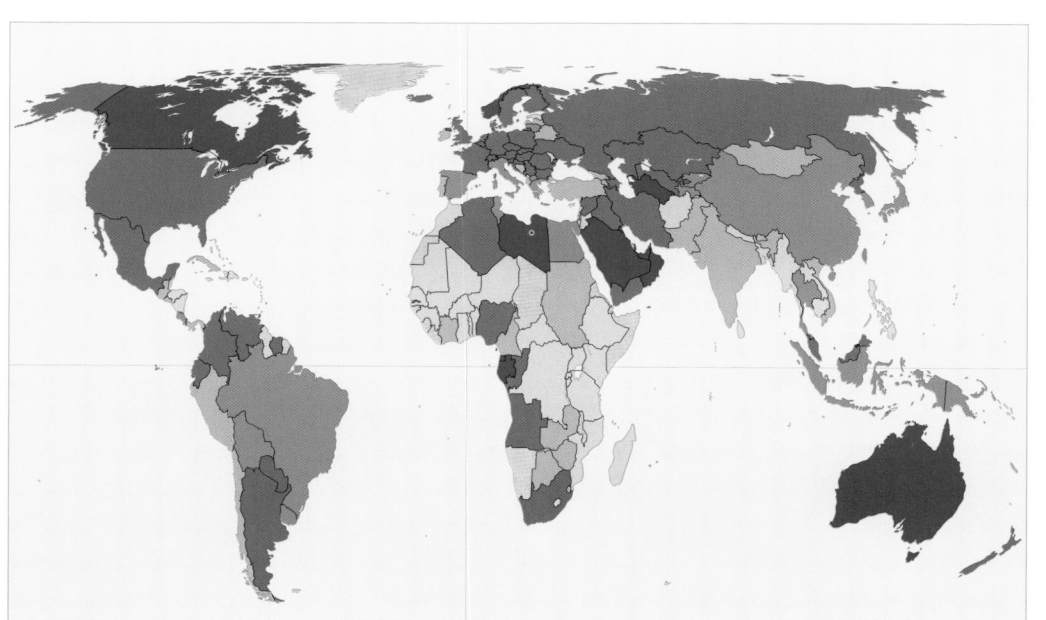

Energy Production

Energy production in tons of oil equivalent per capita (2000)

- Over 10
- 1 – 10
- 0.5 – 1
- 0.1 – 0.5
- Under 0.1
- No data available

In developing countries traditional fuels are still very important. These so-called biomass fuels include wood, charcoal and dried dung. The pie chart (right) highlights the importance of biomass in terms of energy consumption in Nigeria. Collecting fuelwood can be a time-consuming task, sometimes taking all day.

Nigeria

Biomass   Oil   Gas

Oil Movements

Major world movements of oil in millions of tons (2001)

1.	Middle East to Asia (not China or Japan)	316.7
2.	Middle East to Japan	208.8
3.	Former Soviet Union to Europe	181.2
4.	Middle East to Europe	176.2
5.	Middle East to USA	138.0
6.	South and Central America to USA	126.3
7.	North Africa to Europe	96.9
8.	Canada to USA	88.0
9.	Mexico to USA	70.8
10.	West Africa to USA	68.1
11.	Europe to USA	46.2
12.	Middle East to Africa	41.0
13.	West Africa to Asia (not China or Japan)	36.9
14.	West Africa to Europe	34.9
15.	Middle East to China	34.2
16.	Asia (not China) to Japan	34.2

Total world imports . . . . 2,159,300,000 tons

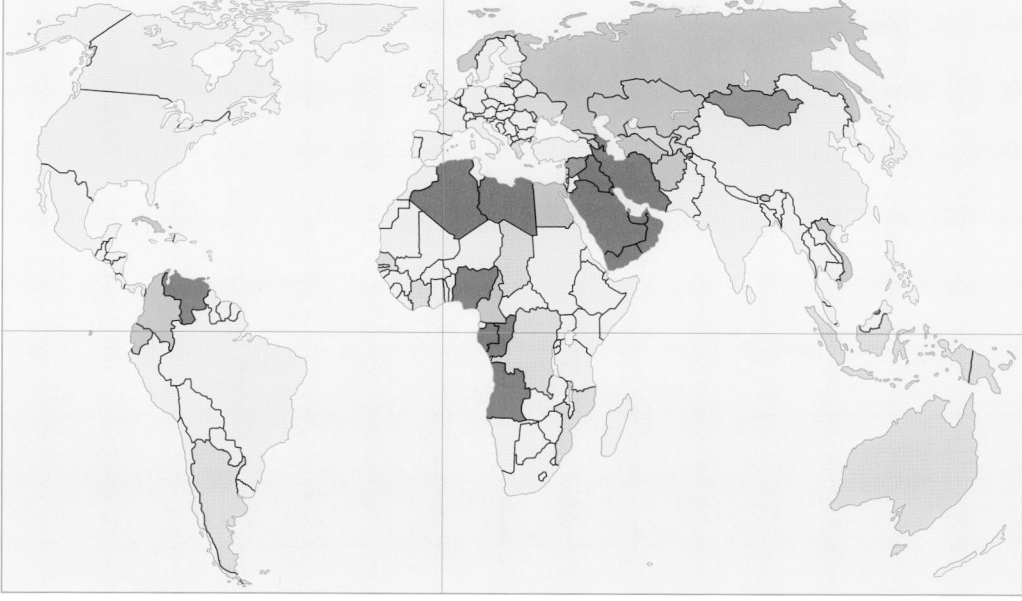

Fuel Exports

Fuels as a percentage of total value of exports (1999)

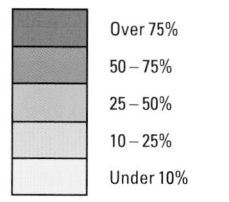

- Over 75%
- 50 – 75%
- 25 – 50%
- 10 – 25%
- Under 10%

In the 1970s, oil exports became a political issue when OPEC sought to increase the influence of developing countries in world affairs by raising oil prices and restricting production. But its power was short-lived, following a fall in demand for oil in the 1980s, due to an increase in energy efficiency and development of alternative resources.

World Coal Reserves

World coal reserves (including lignite) by region and country, thousand million tons (2001)

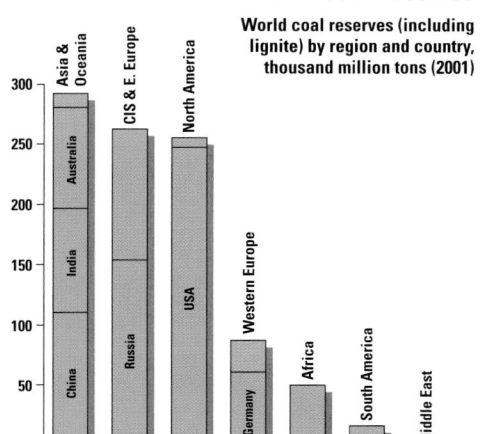

World Gas Reserves

World natural gas reserves by region and country, thousand million tons of oil equivalent (2001)

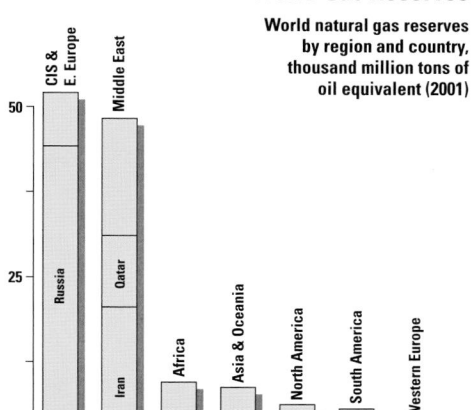

World Oil Reserves

World oil reserves by region and country, thousand million tons (2001)

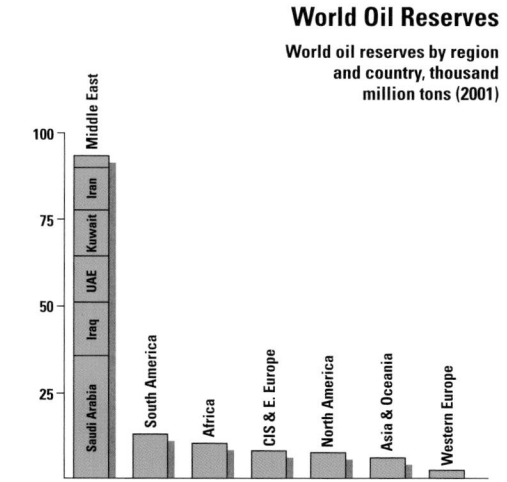

Nuclear Power

Major producers by percentage of world total (2000) and by percentage of domestic electricity generation (1999)

Country	% of world total production	Country	% of nuclear as proportion of domestic electricity
1. USA	30.5%	1. Lithuania	76.1%
2. France	15.7%	2. France	75.1%
3. Japan	12.6%	3. Belgium	58.2%
4. Germany	6.7%	4. Slovak Rep.	47.5%
5. Russia	4.6%	5. Sweden	44.2%
6. South Korea	4.1%	6. Ukraine	41.6%
7. UK	3.8%	7. Bulgaria	41.4%
8. Canada	2.9%	8. South Korea	39.1%
9. Ukraine	2.8%	9. Hungary	38.1%
= Sweden	2.8%	10. Slovenia	35.9%

Although the 1980s were a bad time for the nuclear power industry (major projects ran over budget and fears of long-term environmental damage were heavily reinforced by the 1986 disaster at Chernobyl), the industry picked up in the early 1990s. Whilst the number of reactors is still increasing, however, orders for new plants have shrunk. In 1997, the Swedish government began to decommission the country's 12 nuclear power plants.

Renewable Energy

Average annual solar irradiance in kWh/m^2, with selected major hydroelectric and geothermal power stations

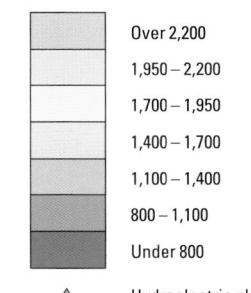

- Over 2,200
- 1,950 – 2,200
- 1,700 – 1,950
- 1,400 – 1,700
- 1,100 – 1,400
- 800 – 1,100
- Under 800

- △ Hydroelectric plants
- ● Geothermal plants

Hydroelectricity

Major producers by percentage of world total (2000) and by percentage of domestic electricity generation (1999)

Country	% of world total production	Country	% of hydroelectric as proportion of domestic electricity
1. Canada	13.1%	1. Bhutan	99.9%
2. USA	12.0%	2. Paraguay	99.8%
3. Brazil	11.1%	= Zambia	99.8%
4. China	8.5%	4. Norway	99.1%
5. Russia	6.1%	5. Ethiopia	98.1%
6. Norway	4.6%	6. Congo (Rep. Dem.)	97.9%
7. Japan	3.3%	7. Tajikistan	97.8%
8. India	3.1%	8. Cameroon	97.3%
9. France	2.8%	9. Albania	97.2%
10. Sweden	2.7%	= Laos	97.2%

Countries heavily reliant on hydroelectricity are usually small and non-industrial: a high proportion of hydroelectric power more often reflects a modest energy budget than vast hydroelectric resources. The USA, for instance, produces only 8.5% of its power requirements from hydroelectricity; yet that 8.5% amounts to more than three times the hydropower generated by most of Africa.

Alternative Energy Resources

Solar: Each year the Sun bestows upon the Earth almost a million times as much energy as is locked up in all the planet's oil reserves, but only an insignificant fraction is trapped and used commercially. In a few installations around the world, mirrors focus the Sun's rays on to boilers, whose steam generates electricity by spinning turbines.

Wind: Caused by uneven heating of the Earth, winds are themselves a form of solar energy. Windmills have been long used for wind power; recent models, often arranged in banks on wind-swept high ground or off coastlines, usually generate electricity. Wind-power figures are given in the table (*right*) – it is the world's fastest growing energy source. In 2002, Germany, the USA, Spain, and Denmark produced nearly 16,000 MW.

Tidal: The energy from tides is potentially enormous, although only a few installations have so far been built to exploit it. In theory at least, waves and currents could also provide almost unimaginable power, and the thermal differences in the ocean depths are another huge well of potential energy. But work on extracting it is still at the experimental stage.

Geothermal: The Earth's temperature rises by 1°F for every 50 feet descent, with much steeper temperature gradients in geologically active areas. El Salvador, for example, produces 39% of its electricity from geothermal power stations, whilst the USA is the world's leading producer. Some of the oldest and most successful applications are in Iceland, where 86% of all households are heated by geothermal energy.

Biomass: The oldest of human fuels ranges from animal dung, still burned in cooking fires in much of North Africa and elsewhere, to sugarcane plantations feeding high-technology distilleries to produce ethanol for motor-vehicle engines. In Brazil and South Africa, plant ethanol provides up to 25% of motor fuel. Throughout the developing world, most biomass energy comes from firewood: although accurate figures are impossible to obtain, it may yield as much as 10% of the world's total energy consumption.

Wind Power

World wind energy generating capacity, in megawatts

1980	10
1982	90
1984	600
1986	1,270
1988	1,580
1989	1,730
1990	1,930
1991	2,170
1992	2,510
1993	3,050
1994	3,710
1995	4,820
1996	6,115
1997	7,630
1998	9,600

Wind power is the fastest growing source of energy. Between 1998 and 2002, world production more than doubled.

MINERALS

The use of metals played a vital part in the evolving technologies of early peoples. Copper first came into use around 10,000 years ago, bronze about 5,000 years ago, and iron 3,300 years ago. In the early stages of the Industrial Revolution, the location of coal, iron ore and water power usually determined the location of new industries. But due to continuing improvements in transport, including oil pipelines, industries can now be located almost anywhere.

Minerals are distributed unevenly and some industrial countries, lacking their own mineral resources, import most of the raw materials they need. Some imports come from mineral-rich countries, such as Australia, but others come from developing countries, especially in Africa and South America.

Most of the developing countries export unprocessed ores, losing out on the much higher revenues gained from exporting metals.

Most minerals come from land deposits, because undersea deposits, with the exception of oil reserves under the continental shelves, have been regarded as inaccessible. But shortages of terrestrial minerals may one day encourage exploitation of the ocean floor.

Mineral Exports

Exports of mine and quarry products as a percentage of total value of exports (2000)

- Over 60%
- 30 – 60%
- 15 – 30%
- 1 – 15%
- Under 1%
- No data available

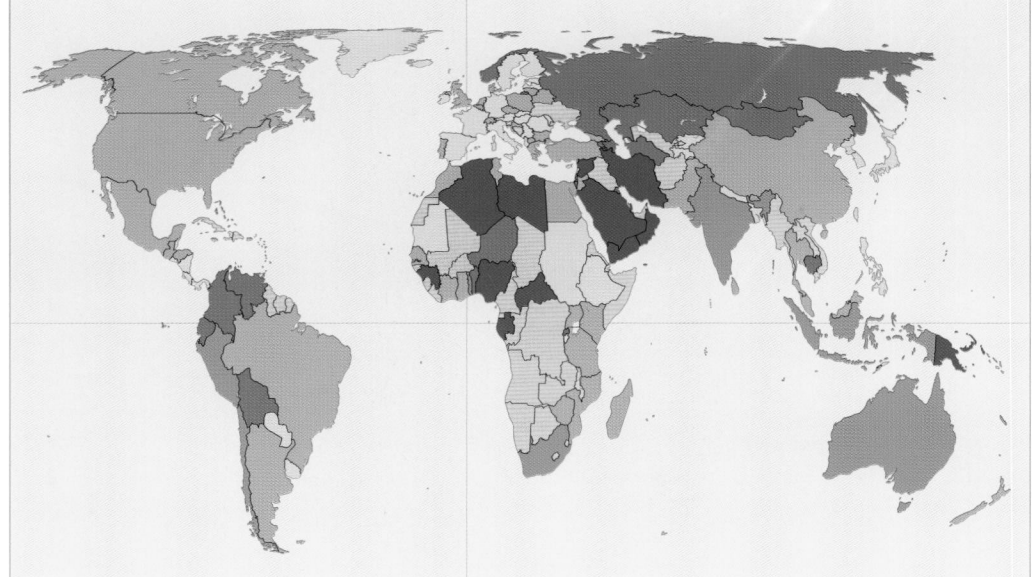

Uranium

In its pure state, uranium is an immensely heavy, white metal; but although spent uranium is employed as projectiles in anti-missile cannons, where its mass ensures a lethal punch, its main use is as a fuel in nuclear reactors, and in nuclear weaponry. Uranium is very scarce: the main source is the rare ore pitchblende, which itself contains only 0.2% uranium oxide. Only a minute fraction of that is the radioactive U^{235} isotope, though so-called breeder reactors can transmute the more common U^{238} into highly radioactive plutonium.

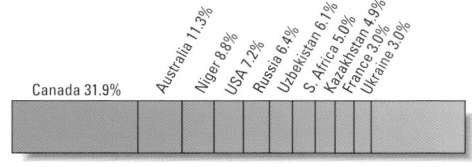

Canada 31.9% | Australia 11.3% | Niger 8.8% | USA 7.2% | Russia 6.4% | Uzbekistan 6.1% | S. Africa 5.0% | Kazakhstan 4.9% | France 3.0% | Ukraine 3.0%

World total (2000): 34,746 tons

Metals

* Figures for aluminum are for refined metal; all other figures refer to ore production.

The world's leading producers of aluminum ore (bauxite) in 2000 were as follows:

1. Australia 38.6%
2. Guinea 11.8%
3. Brazil 10.4%
4. Jamaica 8.8%
5. China 6.3%
6. India 4.9%
7. Venezuela 3.5%
8. Suriname 3.1%
9. Russia 3.1%
10. Guyana 2.6%

The figures shown above are in stark contrast to the figures showing aluminum production on the right. Australia, for example, produces 38.6% of the world's bauxite but only 5.9% of the aluminum metal. Guinea and Jamaica account for over 20% of the bauxite mined but have no smelters and export virtually all of it to countries like the USA and Canada.

Diamond

Most of the world's diamond is found in kimberlite, or "blue ground," a basic peridotite rock; erosion may wash the diamond from its kimberlite matrix and deposit it with sand or gravel on river beds. Only a small proportion of the world's diamond, the most flawless, is cut into gemstones – "diamonds"; most is used in industry, where the material's remarkable hardness and abrasion resistance finds a use in cutting tools, drills and dies. Australia produced 31.6% of the world's total in 2000. The other main producers are the Democratic Republic of the Congo (24.7%), Russia (20%), South Africa (10.5%), and Botswana (8.5%). Natural diamonds now account for less than 10% of all industrial diamond output. Synthetic diamond production in centers such as Ireland, Japan, Russia, and the USA far exceeds it.

Aluminum: Produced mainly from its oxide, bauxite, which yields 25% of its weight in aluminum. The cost of refining and production is often too high for producer-countries to bear, so bauxite is largely exported. Lightweight and corrosion resistant, aluminum alloys are widely used in aircraft, vehicles, cans, and packaging.

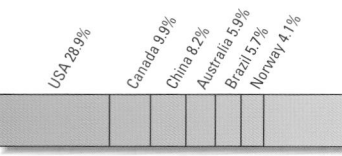

USA 28.9% | Canada 9.9% | China 8.2% | Australia 5.9% | Brazil 5.7% | Norway 4.1%

World total (2000): 23,900,000 tons *

Lead: A soft metal, obtained mainly from galena (lead sulfide), which occurs in veins associated with iron, zinc and silver sulfides. Its use in vehicle batteries accounts for the USA's prime consumer status; lead is also made into sheeting and piping. Its use as an additive to paints and petrol is decreasing.

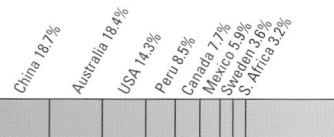

China 18.7% | Australia 18.4% | USA 14.3% | Peru 8.5% | Canada 7.7% | Sweden 3.6% | S. Africa 3.2%

World total (2000): 2,980,000 tons *

Tin: Soft, pliable and non-toxic, used to coat "tin" (tin-plated steel) cans, in the manufacture of foils and in alloys. The principal tin-bearing mineral is cassiterite (SnO_2), found in ore formed from molten rock. Producers and refiners were hit by a price collapse in 1991.

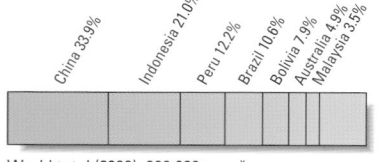

China 33.9% | Indonesia 21.0% | Peru 12.2% | Brazil 10.6% | Bolivia 7.9% | Australia 4.9% | Malaysia 3.5%

World total (2000): 200,000 tons *

Gold: Regarded for centuries as the most valuable metal in the world and used to make coins, gold is still recognized as the monetary standard. A soft metal, it is alloyed to make jewelry; the electronics industry values its corrosion resistance and conductivity.

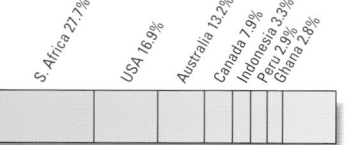

S. Africa 27.7% | USA 16.9% | Australia 13.2% | Canada 7.9% | Indonesia 3.3% | Peru 2.9% | Ghana 2.9%

World total (2000): 2,445 tons *

Copper: Derived from low-yielding sulfide ores, copper is an important export for several developing countries. An excellent conductor of heat and electricity, it forms part of most electrical items, and is used in the manufacture of brass and bronze. Major importers include Japan and Germany.

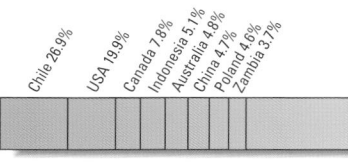

Chile 26.9% | USA 19.9% | Canada 7.6% | Indonesia 5.1% | Australia 4.8% | China 4.7% | Poland 4.6% | Zambia 3.7%

World total (2000): 12,900,000 tons *

Mercury: The only metal that is liquid at normal temperatures, most is derived from its sulfide, cinnabar, found only in small quantities in volcanic areas. Apart from its value in thermometers and other instruments, most mercury production is used in anti-fungal and anti-fouling preparations, and to make detonators.

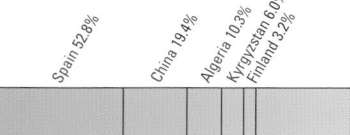

Spain 52.8% | China 19.4% | Algeria 10.3% | Kyrgyzstan 6.0% | Finland 3.2%

World total (2000): 1,800 tons *

Zinc: Often found in association with lead ores, zinc is highly resistant to corrosion, and about 40% of the refined metal is used to plate sheet steel, particularly vehicle bodies – a process known as galvanizing. Zinc is also used in dry batteries, paints, and dyes.

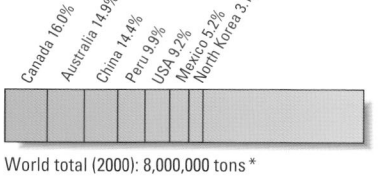

Canada 16.0% | Australia 14.9% | China 14.4% | Peru 9.9% | USA 9.2% | Mexico 5.2% | North Korea 3.1%

World total (2000): 8,000,000 tons *

Silver: Most silver comes from ores mined and processed for other metals (including lead and copper). Pure or alloyed with harder metals, it is used for jewelry and ornaments. Industrial use includes dentistry, electronics, photography, and as a chemical catalyst.

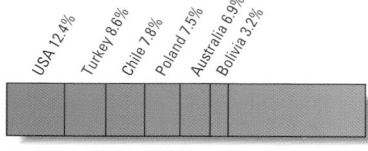

USA 12.4% | Turkey 8.6% | Chile 7.8% | Poland 7.5% | Australia 6.9% | Bolivia 3.2%

World total (2000): 17,900 tons *

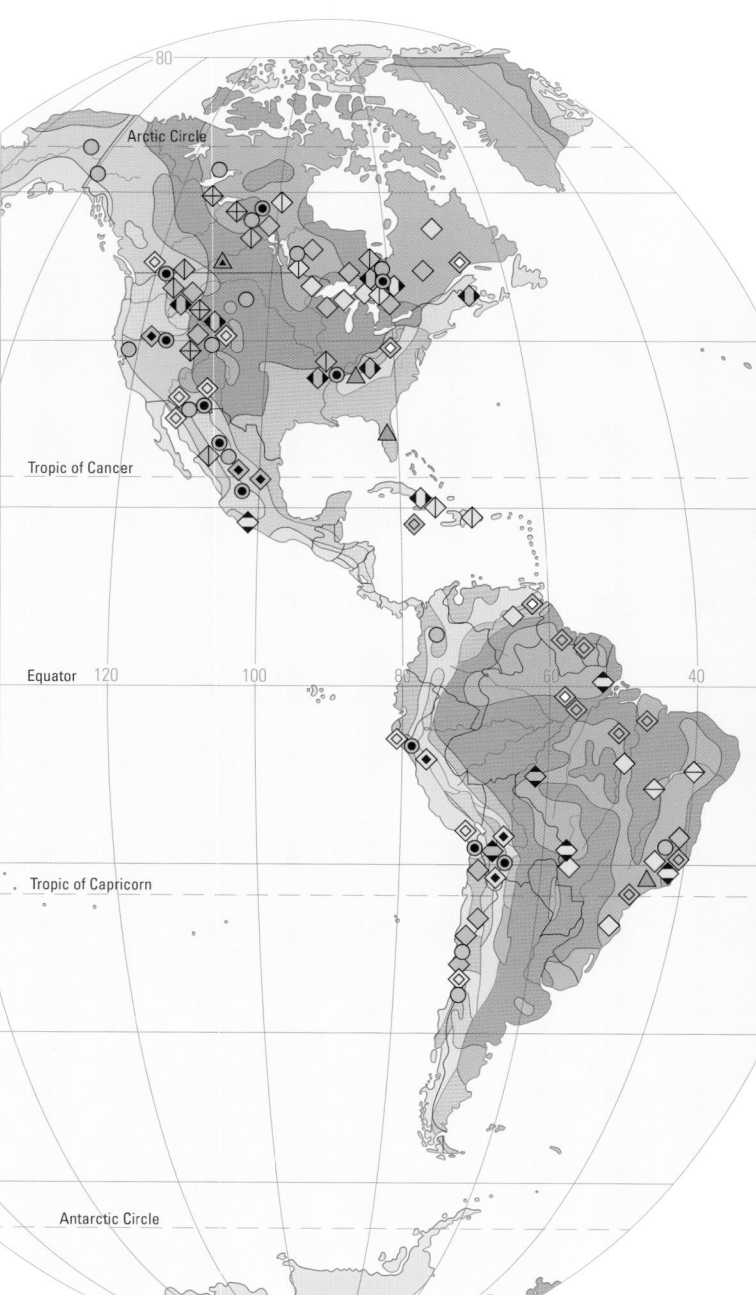

Strategic Minerals

Ever since the art of high-temperature smelting was discovered, some time in the second millennium BC, iron has been by far the most important metal known to man. The earliest iron plows transformed primitive agriculture and led to the first human population explosion, while iron weapons – or the lack of them – ensured the rise or fall of entire cultures.

Widely distributed around the world, iron ores usually contain 25–60% iron; blast furnaces process the raw product into pig iron, which is then alloyed with carbon and other minerals to produce steels of various qualities. From the time of the Industrial Revolution, steel has been almost literally the backbone of modern civilization, the prime structural material on which all else is built.

Iron smelting usually developed close to the sources of ore and, later, to the coalfields that fueled the furnaces. Today, most ore comes from a few richly-endowed locations where large-scale mining is possible. Iron and steel plants are generally built at coastal sites so that giant ore carriers, which account for a sizable proportion of the world's merchant fleet, can easily discharge their cargoes.

World total production of iron ore (2000): 1,010,000,000 tons

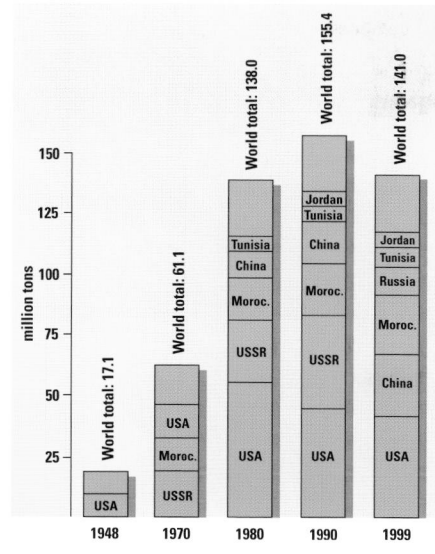

World production of phosphates in millions of tons (1999): Phosphate production is vital to the economies of several small countries. Nauru, for example, is heavily dependent on phosphate exports – the island has one of the world's richest deposits. In 1999, 500,000 tons were mined, employing 1,000 people. In Togo, earnings from phosphate exports have superseded all agricultural exports.

Percentage of total world phosphate production (1999)

1. USA	28.8%	7. Brazil	2.9%
2. China	17.8%	8. Israel	2.9%
3. Morocco	17.0%	9. South Africa	2.1%
4. Russia	7.9%	10. Syria	1.5%
5. Tunisia	5.7%	11. Senegal	1.3%
6. Jordan	4.3%	12. India	1.2%

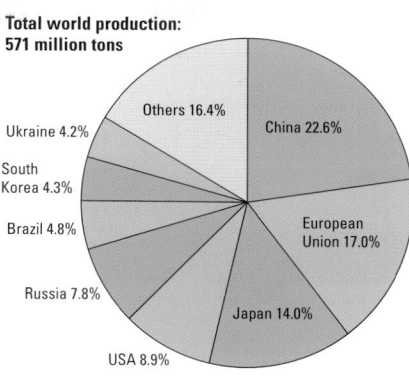

World production of pig iron (2000): All countries with an annual output of more than 1 million tons are shown

Total world production: 571 million tons

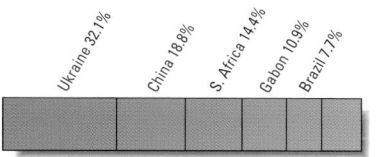

Manganese: In its pure state, manganese is a hard, brittle metal. Alloyed with chrome, iron and nickel, it produces abrasion-resistant steels; manganese-aluminum alloys are light but tough. Found in batteries and inks, manganese is also used in glass production. Manganese ores are frequently found in the same location as sedimentary iron ores. Pyrolusite (MnO_2) and psilomelane are the main economically-exploitable sources.

World total (2000): 7,450,000 tons (metal content)

Chromium: Most of the world's chromium production is alloyed with iron and other metals to produce steels with various different properties. Combined with iron, nickel, cobalt, and tungsten, chromium produces an exceptionally hard steel, resistant to heat; chrome steels are used for many household items where utility must be matched with appearance – cutlery, for example. Chromium is also used in the production of refractory bricks, and its salts for tanning and dyeing leather and cloth.

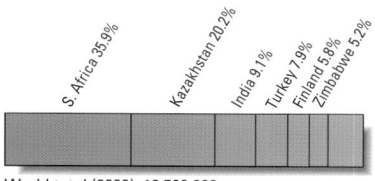

World total (2000): 13,700,000 tons

Nickel: Combined with chrome and iron, nickel produces stainless and high-strength steels; similar alloys go to make magnets and electrical heating elements. Nickel combined with copper is widely used to make coins; cupro-nickel alloy is very resistant to corrosion. Its ores yield only modest quantities of nickel – 0.5% to 3.0% – but also contain copper, iron and small amounts of precious metals. Japan, USA, UK, Germany, and France are the principal importers.

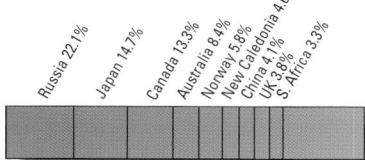

World total (2000): 1,230,000 tons

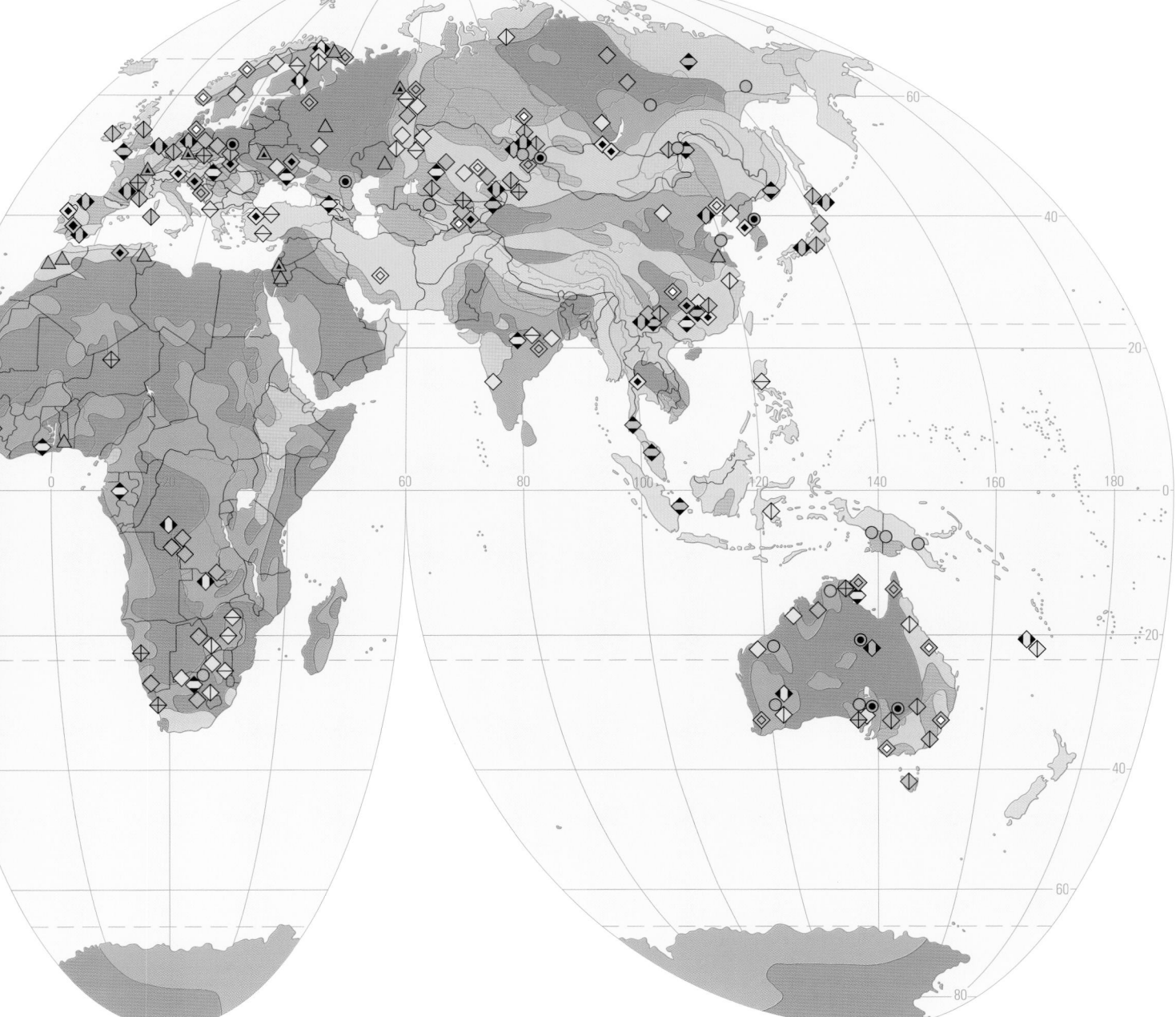

Distribution of Minerals

Structural Regions

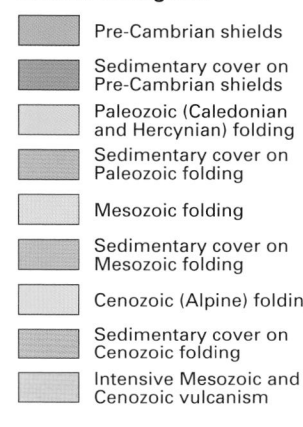

- Pre-Cambrian shields
- Sedimentary cover on Pre-Cambrian shields
- Paleozoic (Caledonian and Hercynian) folding
- Sedimentary cover on Paleozoic folding
- Mesozoic folding
- Sedimentary cover on Mesozoic folding
- Cenozoic (Alpine) folding
- Sedimentary cover on Cenozoic folding
- Intensive Mesozoic and Cenozoic vulcanism

Distribution

Iron and ferroalloys

- Chrome
- Cobalt
- Iron Ore
- Manganese
- Molybdenum
- Nickel Ore
- Tungsten

Non-ferrous metals

- Bauxite (Aluminum)
- Copper
- Lead
- Mercury
- Tin
- Zinc
- Uranium

Precious metals and stones

- Diamonds
- Gold
- Silver

Fertilizers

- Phosphates
- Potash

Manufacturing

The Industrial Revolution which began in Britain in the late 18th century, represented a major technological advance in the evolution of human society. It enabled a group of countries to become prosperous by replacing expensive human labor with increasingly sophisticated machinery. In economic terms, manufacturing is the transformation of raw materials, energy, labor and machines into finished goods, which have a higher value than the various elements used in production.

The economies of countries can be compared by reference to their per capita Gross National Products (or per capita GNPs), namely, the total value of goods and services produced in a country in a year, divided by the population.

The industrialized, or developed, countries accounted for 15% of the world's population in 2000 with an average per capita GNP of more than US $25,000. On the other hand, low-income developing countries, with small industrial sectors, accounted for 34% of the world's population. Their per capita GNPs are less than $755, with some as low as $200.

Kenya, with its low-income economy, had a per capita GNP in 2000 of US $350. Agriculture employs 19% of the people, industry 18%, and services 64%. The main industries are the processing of agricultural imports and import substitution (making such necessities as cement, footwear, and textiles). Heavy industry plays only a small part. By contrast, Germany had a per capita GNP in 2000 of $25,120. Agriculture employs only 2% of the population, with 30% in industry, and 68% in services. Germany's industrial sector differs greatly from Kenya's, with its emphasis on vehicles, machinery, chemicals, and electronics.

Since the 1970s, some former developing countries in eastern Asia achieved rapid economic growth through industrialization. Despite setbacks in the late 1990s, they demonstrated that a developing industrial sector can transform an economy, which starts off with certain advantages, such as low labor costs. But economic success also depends on such factors as education to provide skills, and regulations that attract foreign investors. China, whose economy grew by more than 9% per year between 1989 and 2002, satisfies many of these criteria, though its record on human rights leaves much to be desired.

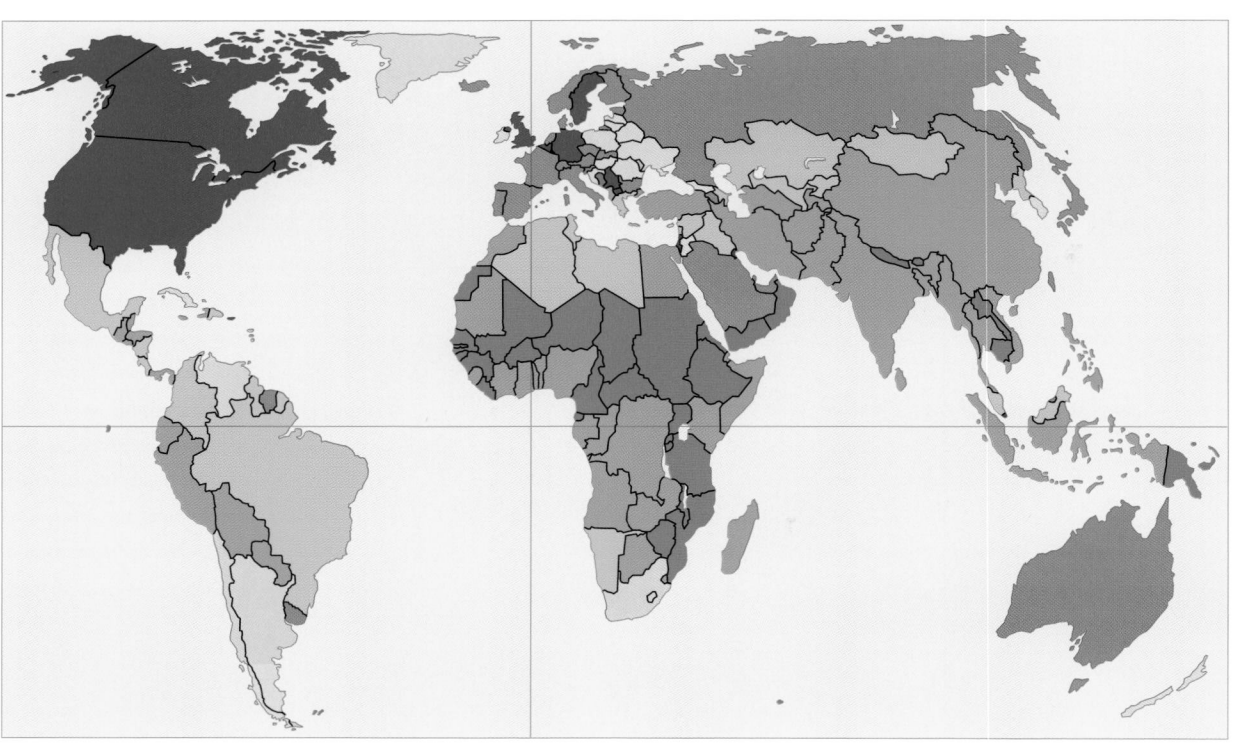

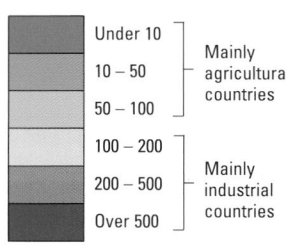

Employment

The number of workers employed in manufacturing for every 100 workers engaged in agriculture (latest available year)

Under 10	Mainly agricultural countries
10 – 50	
50 – 100	
100 – 200	Mainly industrial countries
200 – 500	
Over 500	

Selected countries (latest available year)

Singapore	8,860
UK	1,270
Belgium	820
Germany	800
Kuwait	767
Bahrain	660
USA	657
Israel	633

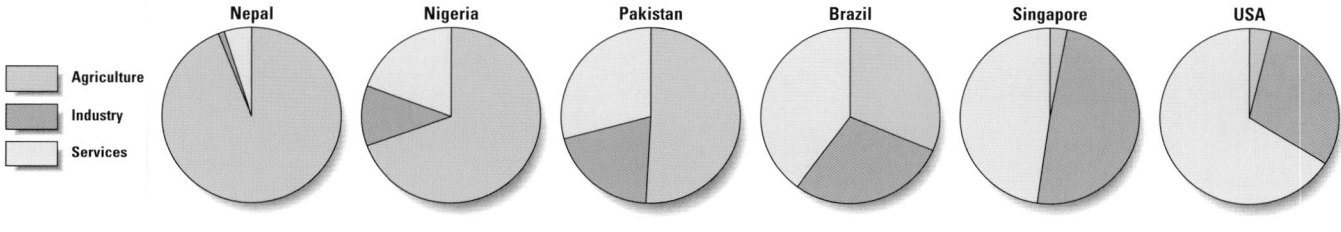

Nepal Nigeria Pakistan Brazil Singapore USA

Agriculture
Industry
Services

Division of Employment

Distribution of workers between agriculture, industry and services, selected countries (latest available year)

The six countries selected illustrate the usual stages of economic development, from dependence on agriculture through industrial growth to the expansion of the service sector.

The Work Force

Percentages of men and women between 15 and 64 in employment, selected countries (latest available year)

The figures include employees and the self-employed, who in developing countries are often subsistence farmers. People in full-time education are excluded. Because of the population age structure in developing countries, the employed population has to support a far larger number of non-workers than its industrial equivalent. For example, more than 52% of Kenya's people are under 15, an age group that makes up less than a tenth of the UK population.

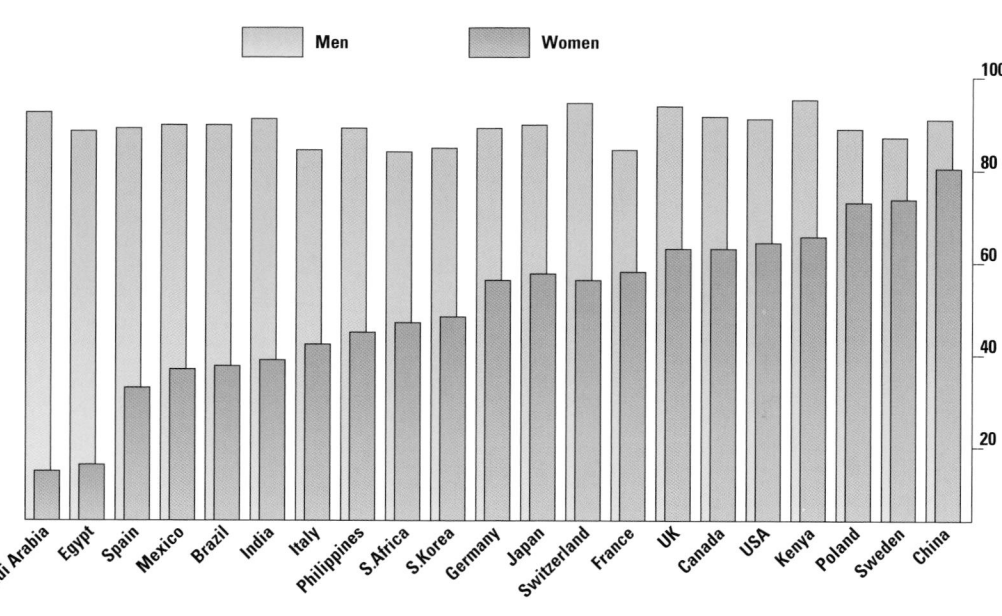

Men   Women

Saudi Arabia, Egypt, Spain, Mexico, Brazil, India, Italy, Philippines, S.Africa, S.Korea, Germany, Japan, Switzerland, France, UK, Canada, USA, Kenya, Poland, Sweden, China

Wealth Creation

The Gross National Income (GNI) of the world's largest economies, US $ million (2001)

1.	USA	9,900,724	21.	Austria	194,463
2.	Japan	4,574,164	22.	Hong Kong	176,157
3.	Germany	1,947,951	23.	Turkey	168,335
4.	UK	1,451,442	24.	Denmark	166,345
5.	France	1,377,389	25.	Poland	163,907
6.	China	1,130,984	26.	Norway	160,577
7.	Italy	1,123,478	27.	Saudi Arabia	149,932
8.	Canada	661,881	28.	Indonesia	144,731
9.	Spain	586,874	29.	South Africa	125,486
10.	Mexico	550,456	30.	Greece	124,553
11.	Brazil	528,503	31.	Finland	124,171
12.	India	474,323	32.	Thailand	120,871
13.	South Korea	447,698	33.	Venezuela	117,169
14.	Netherlands	385,401	34.	Iran	112,855
15.	Australia	383,291	35.	Portugal	109,156
16.	Switzerland	266,503	36.	Israel	104,128
17.	Argentina	260,994	37.	Egypt	99,406
18.	Russia	253,413	38.	Singapore	99,404
19.	Belgium	239,779	39.	Ireland	88,385
20.	Sweden	225,894	40.	Malaysia	86,510

Patterns of Production

Breakdown of industrial output by value, selected countries (latest available year)

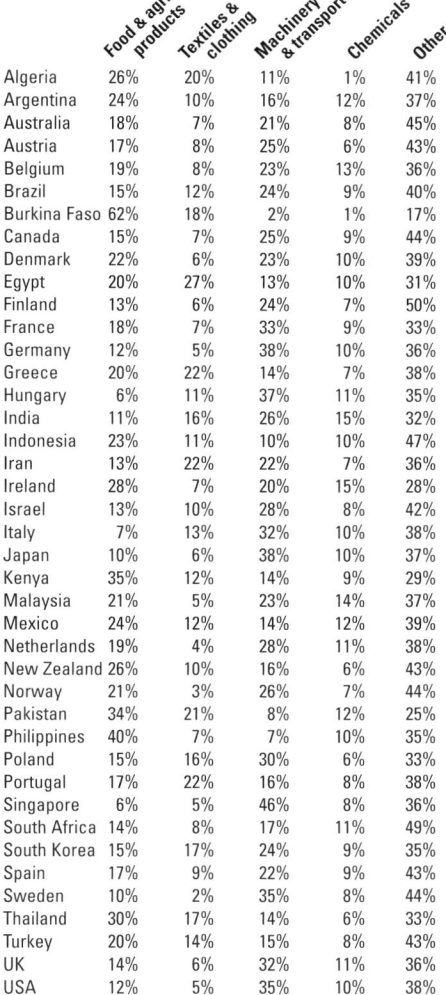

	Food & agric. products	Textiles & clothing	Machinery & transport	Chemicals	Other
Algeria	26%	20%	11%	1%	41%
Argentina	24%	10%	16%	12%	37%
Australia	18%	7%	21%	8%	45%
Austria	17%	8%	25%	6%	43%
Belgium	19%	8%	23%	13%	36%
Brazil	15%	12%	24%	9%	40%
Burkina Faso	62%	18%	2%	1%	17%
Canada	15%	7%	25%	9%	44%
Denmark	22%	6%	23%	10%	39%
Egypt	20%	27%	13%	10%	31%
Finland	13%	6%	24%	7%	50%
France	18%	7%	33%	9%	33%
Germany	12%	5%	38%	10%	36%
Greece	20%	22%	14%	7%	38%
Hungary	6%	11%	37%	11%	35%
India	11%	16%	26%	15%	32%
Indonesia	23%	11%	10%	10%	47%
Iran	13%	22%	22%	7%	36%
Ireland	28%	7%	20%	15%	28%
Israel	13%	10%	28%	8%	42%
Italy	7%	13%	32%	10%	38%
Japan	10%	6%	38%	10%	37%
Kenya	35%	12%	14%	9%	29%
Malaysia	21%	5%	23%	14%	37%
Mexico	24%	12%	14%	12%	39%
Netherlands	19%	4%	28%	11%	38%
New Zealand	26%	10%	16%	6%	43%
Norway	21%	3%	26%	7%	44%
Pakistan	34%	21%	8%	12%	25%
Philippines	40%	7%	7%	10%	35%
Poland	15%	16%	30%	6%	33%
Portugal	17%	22%	16%	8%	38%
Singapore	6%	5%	46%	8%	36%
South Africa	14%	8%	17%	11%	49%
South Korea	15%	17%	24%	9%	35%
Spain	17%	9%	22%	9%	43%
Sweden	10%	2%	35%	8%	44%
Thailand	30%	17%	14%	6%	33%
Turkey	20%	14%	15%	8%	43%
UK	14%	6%	32%	11%	36%
USA	12%	5%	35%	10%	38%
Venezuela	23%	8%	9%	11%	49%

Industry and Trade

Manufactured goods (including machinery and transport) as a percentage of total exports (1999)

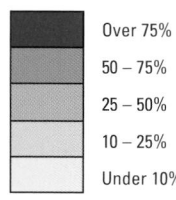

- Over 75%
- 50 – 75%
- 25 – 50%
- 10 – 25%
- Under 10%

Countries most dependent on the export of manufactured goods

Malta	91%
Bangladesh	90%
China	90%
Japan	88%
South Korea	83%
Luxembourg	83%
Pakistan	83%

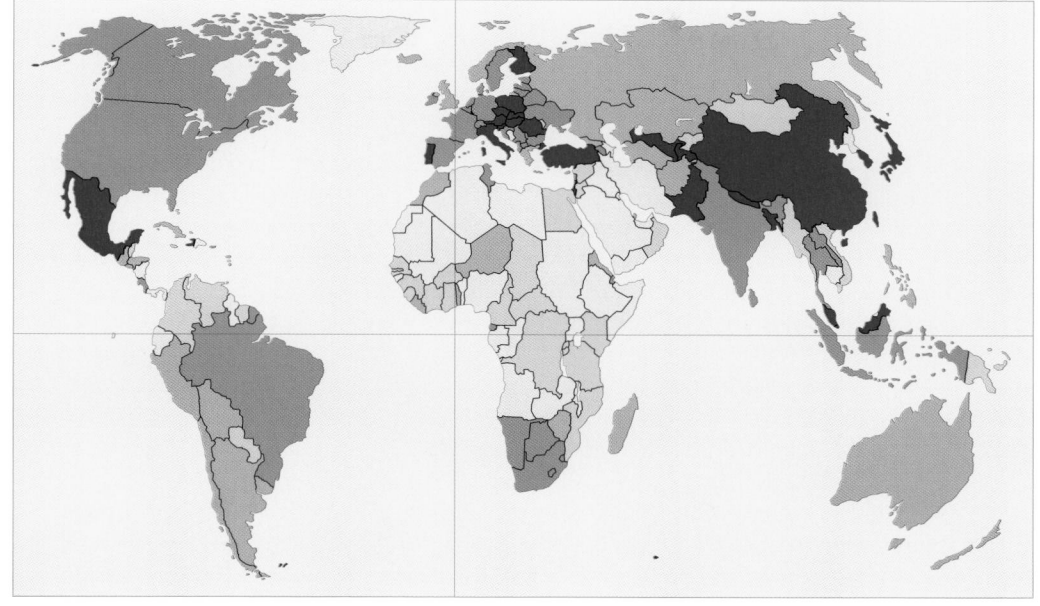

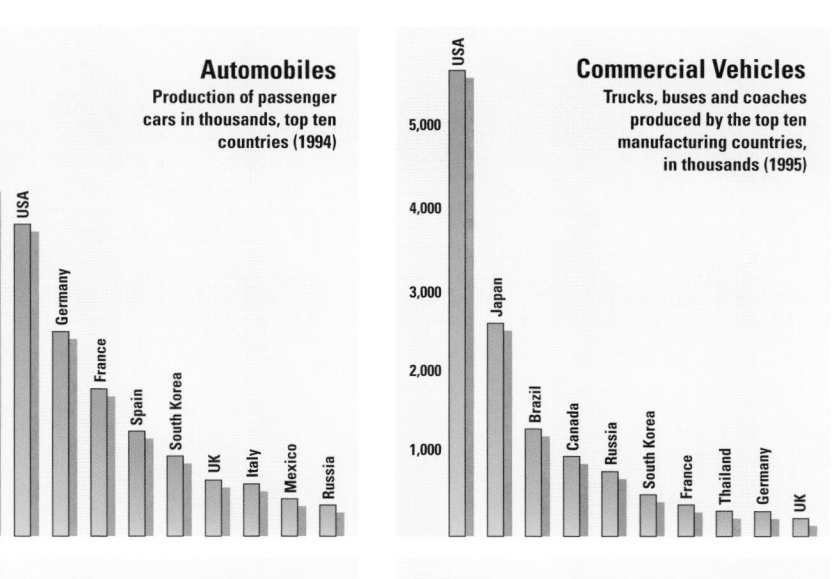

Automobiles
Production of passenger cars in thousands, top ten countries (1994)

Commercial Vehicles
Trucks, buses and coaches produced by the top ten manufacturing countries, in thousands (1995)

Television & Radio Receivers
Production of television and radio receivers in thousands, top ten countries (1998)

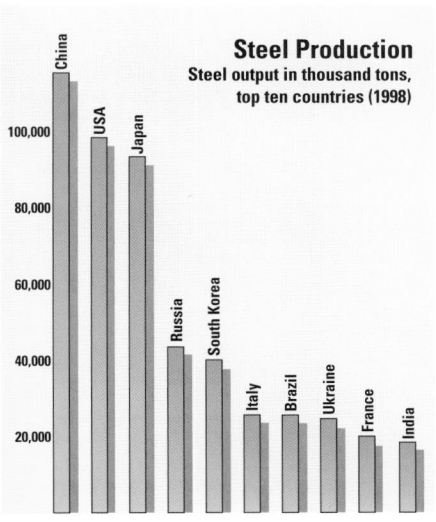

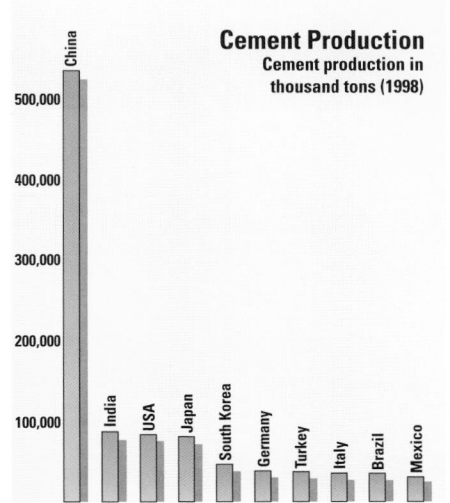

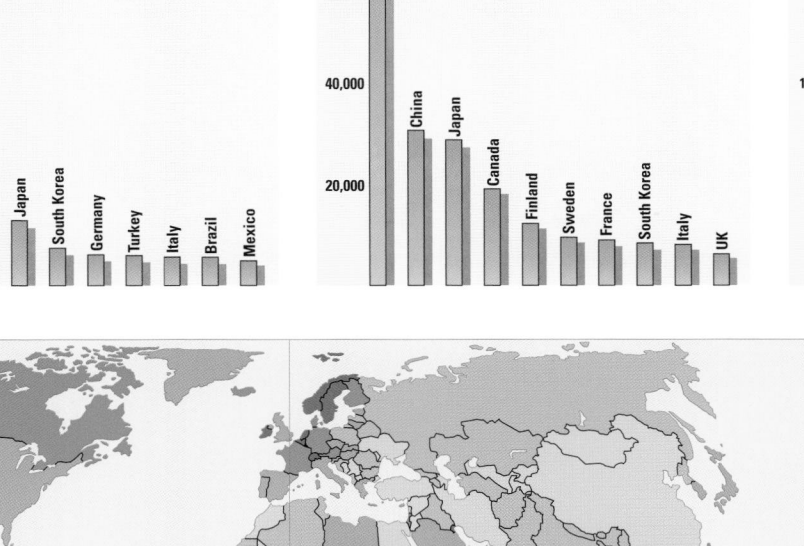

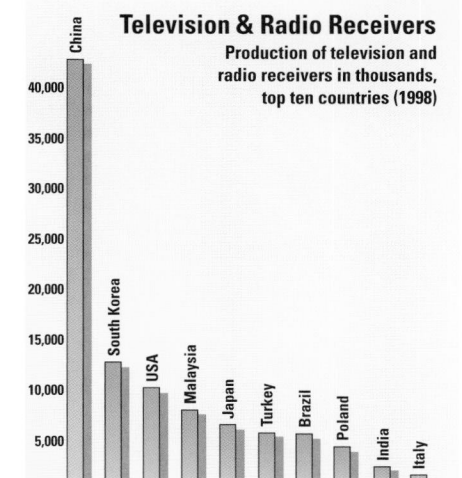

Steel Production
Steel output in thousand tons, top ten countries (1998)

Cement Production
Cement production in thousand tons (1998)

Paper & Cardboard
Paper and cardboard production in thousand tons (1999)

Sulfuric Acid
Production in thousand tons (1998)

Industrial Output

Industrial output (mining, manufacturing, construction, energy and water production), US $ billion (latest available year)

1.	Japan	1,941
2.	USA	1,808
3.	Germany	780
4.	France	415
5.	UK	354
6.	Italy	337
7.	China	335
8.	Brazil	255
9.	South Korea	196
10.	Spain	187
11.	Canada	174
12.	Russia	131
13.	Netherlands	107
14.	Australia	98
15.	Switzerland	96
16.	India	94
17.	Argentina	87
18.	Belgium	83
=	Indonesia	83
20.	Austria	79

21.	Sweden	73
22.	Saudi Arabia	67
=	Thailand	67
24.	Mexico	65
25.	Turkey	51
26.	Denmark	50
27.	Finland	46
=	Poland	46
29.	Norway	44
30.	Malaysia	37
=	Portugal	37
32.	Ukraine	34
33.	Greece	33
34.	Singapore	30
35.	Venezuela	29
=	Israel	29
37.	Chile	24
=	Colombia	24
=	Hong Kong	24
=	Philippines	24

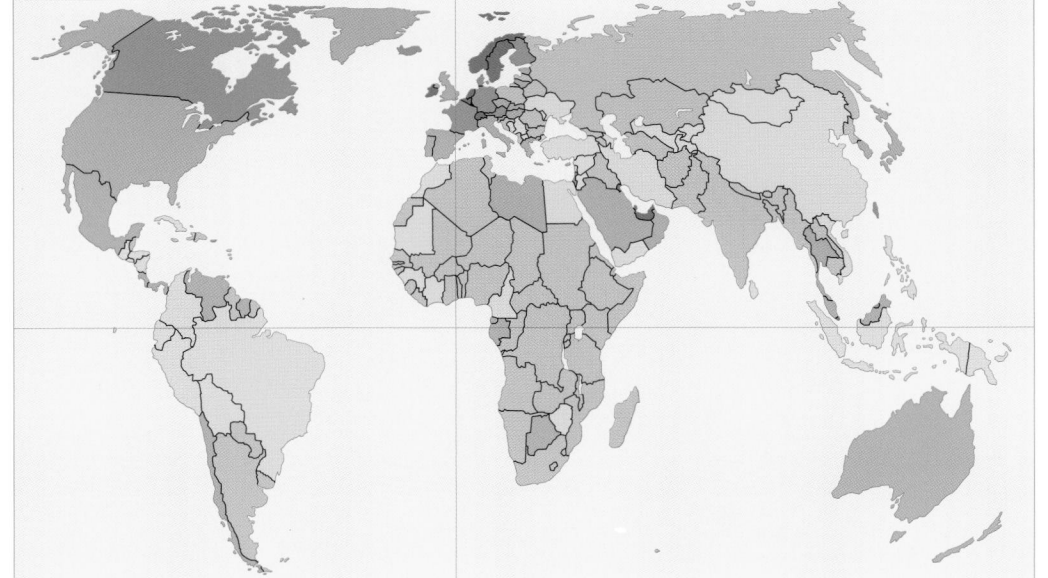

Exports Per Capita

Value of exports in US $, divided by total population (2000)

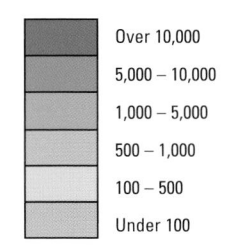

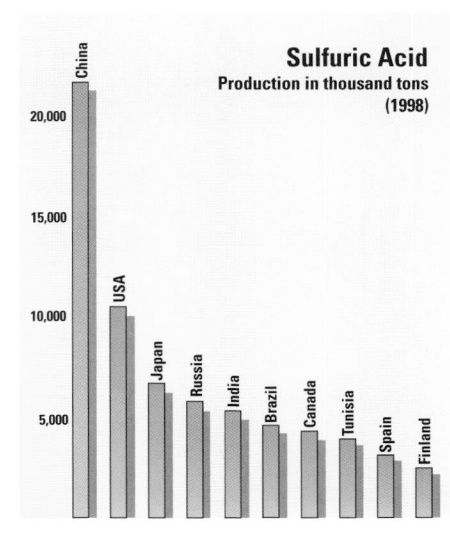

- Over 10,000
- 5,000 – 10,000
- 1,000 – 5,000
- 500 – 1,000
- 100 – 500
- Under 100

[UK 4,728] [USA 2,791]

Highest per capita

Kuwait	113,614
Liechtenstein	78,848
Singapore	31,860
Aruba (Neths)	31,429
Hong Kong (China)	28,290
Ireland	19,136

TRADE

Trade played a vital role in the growth of early civilizations and it was later a spur to European exploration and coloniz-ation. The colonial powers grew rich by exporting cheap manufactures, such as clothing and footwear, while obtaining primary products from their colonies.

From the late 19th century to the early 1950s, as transport technology improved, primary products, especially oil in the later stages of this period, dominated world trade. However, since that time, manufac-tures have become the chief commodities in world trade, which is dominated by the industrialized countries. Nearly half of all world trade flows between the developed market economies of the European Union, the United States and Japan, although a number of Asian economies, notably China, Malaysia, Singapore, South Korea, Taiwan, and Thailand, increased their share in the 1990s.

China's remarkable economic growth meant that, by 2002, it had overtaken Japan to become the fourth biggest exporter to the United States. China's low production costs, especially its cheap labor, was estimated to be one-twentieth of those of Japan, making its high-quality exports highly competitive in price. Growth in world trade is regarded as a sign of eco-nomic health, as is a favorable balance of trade (or trade surplus) in any country.

World Trade

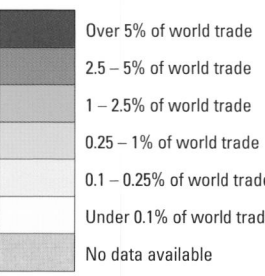

Percentage share of total world exports by value (2000)

- Over 5% of world trade
- 2.5 – 5% of world trade
- 1 – 2.5% of world trade
- 0.25 – 1% of world trade
- 0.1 – 0.25% of world trade
- Under 0.1% of world trade
- No data available

The Main Trading Nations

The imports and exports of the top ten trading nations as a percentage of world trade (2001). Each country's trade in manufactured goods is shown in dark blue.

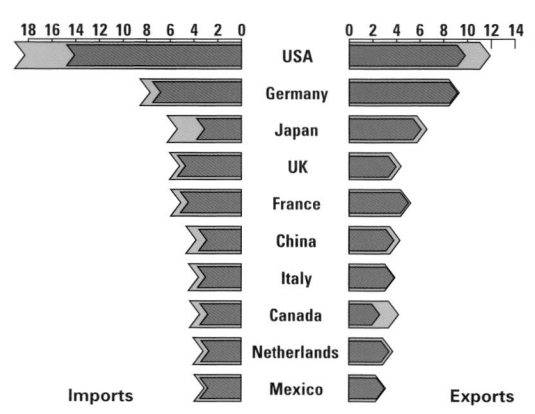

USA, Germany, Japan, UK, France, China, Italy, Canada, Netherlands, Mexico

Imports — Exports

Dependence on Trade

Exports as a percentage of GDP (2001)

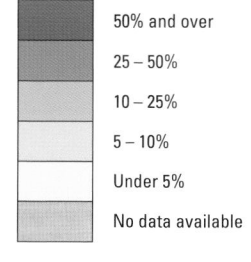

- 50% and over
- 25 – 50%
- 10 – 25%
- 5 – 10%
- Under 5%
- No data available

Major Exports

Leading manufactured items and their exporters (2000)

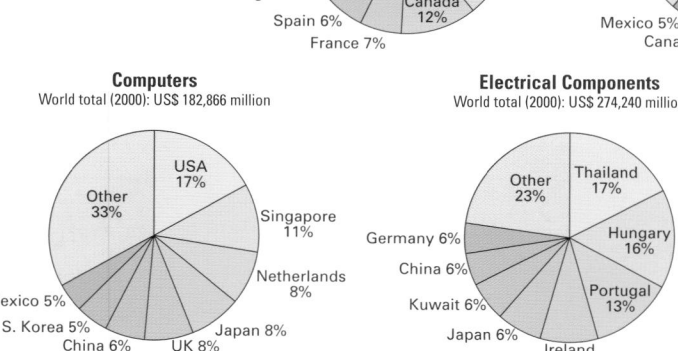

Motor Vehicles
World total (2000): US$ 299,334 million
Germany 20%, Japan 19%, Canada 12%, France 7%, Spain 6%, Belgium 6%, Mexico 5%, USA 5%, UK 5%, S. Korea 4%, Italy 2%, Other 10%

Telecommunications Gear
World total (2000): US$ 214,456 million
USA 12%, UK 8%, Japan 8%, Germany 7%, China 6%, France 6%, Sweden 6%, Canada 5%, Mexico 5%, Other 39%

Petrol Products
World total (2000): US$ 153,410 million
Singapore 8%, Netherlands 8%, Russia 7%, Saudi Arabia 6%, S. Korea 6%, USA 5%, Belgium 5%, UK 4%, Kuwait 3%, Germany 3%, Other 45%

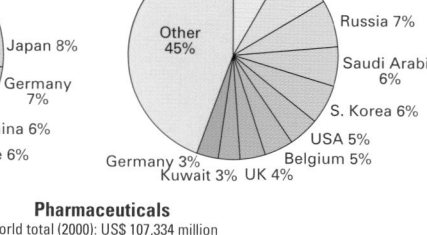

Computers
World total (2000): US$ 182,866 million
USA 17%, Singapore 11%, Netherlands 8%, Japan 8%, UK 8%, China 6%, S. Korea 5%, Mexico 5%, Other 33%

Electrical Components
World total (2000): US$ 274,240 million
Thailand 17%, Hungary 16%, Portugal 13%, Ireland 9%, Japan 6%, Kuwait 6%, China 6%, Germany 6%, Other 23%

Pharmaceuticals
World total (2000): US$ 107,334 million
USA 12%, Germany 12%, UK 10%, Switzerland 10%, France 10%, Italy 6%, Belgium 6%, Other 34%

Traded Products

Major manufactures traded by value, in millions of US $ (2000)

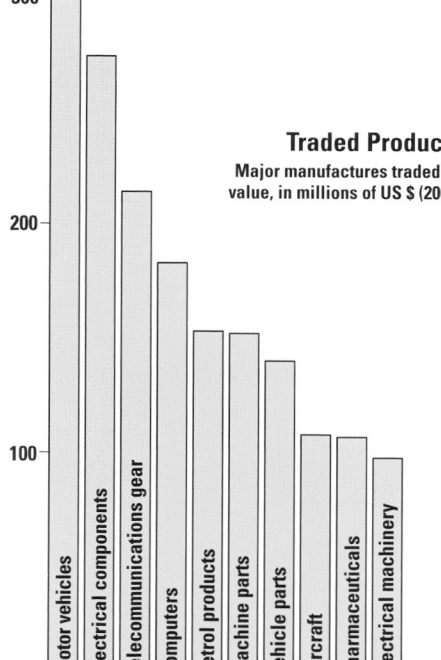

Motor vehicles, Electrical components, Telecommunications gear, Computers, Petrol products, Machine parts, Vehicle parts, Aircraft, Pharmaceuticals, Electrical machinery

World Shipping

While ocean passenger traffic is nowadays relatively modest, sea transport still carries most of the world's trade. Oil and bulk carriers make up the majority of the world fleet, although the general cargo category is the fastest growing. Two innovations have revolutionized sea transport. The first is the development of the roll-on/roll-off (Ro-Ro) method where lorries or even trains loaded with freight are driven straight on to the ship, thus saving time. The second is containerization in which goods are packed into containers (the dimensions of which are fixed) at the factory, driven to the port and loaded on board by specialist machinery.

Almost 30% of world shipping sails under a "flag of convenience," whereby owners take advantage of low taxes by registering their vessels in a foreign country the ships will never see, notably Panama and Liberia.

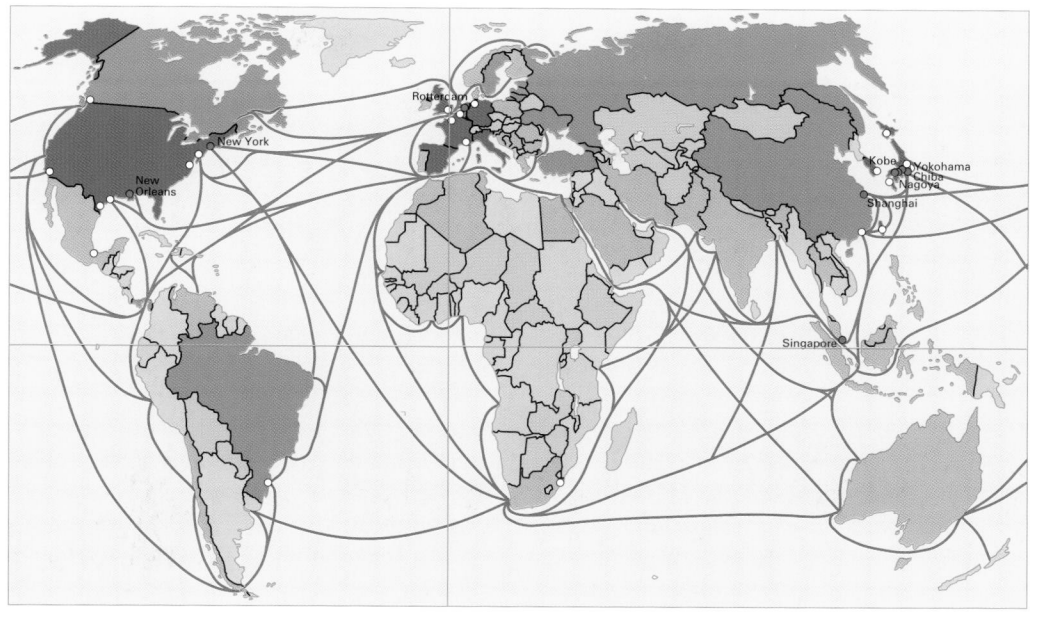

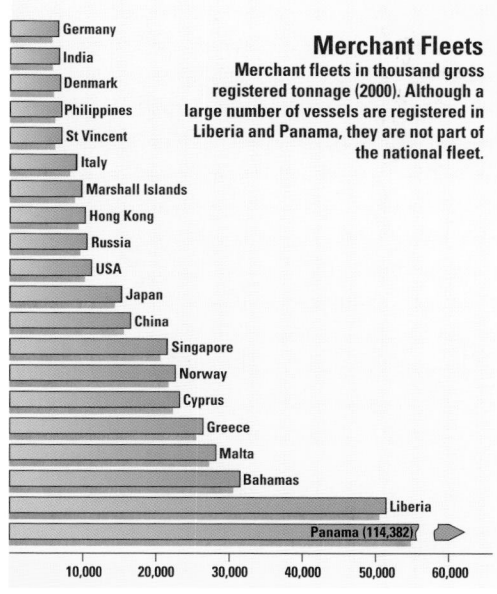

Merchant Fleets
Merchant fleets in thousand gross registered tonnage (2000). Although a large number of vessels are registered in Liberia and Panama, they are not part of the national fleet.

Germany, India, Denmark, Philippines, St Vincent, Italy, Marshall Islands, Hong Kong, Russia, USA, Japan, China, Singapore, Norway, Cyprus, Greece, Malta, Bahamas, Liberia, Panama (114,382)

10,000 20,000 30,000 40,000 50,000 60,000

Types of Vessels
World merchant fleet by type of vessel and deadweight tonnage (2000)

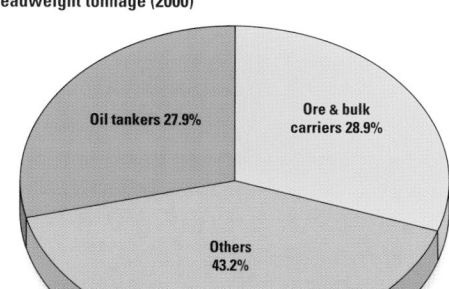

Oil tankers 27.9%
Ore & bulk carriers 28.9%
Others 43.2%

The Great Ports
Total cargo traffic, in million tons (2000)

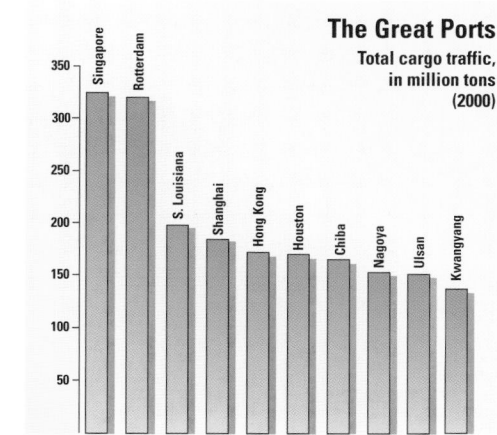

Singapore, Rotterdam, S. Louisiana, Shanghai, Hong Kong, Houston, Chiba, Nagoya, Ulsan, Kwangyang

Freight

Freight unloaded in millions of tons (latest available year)

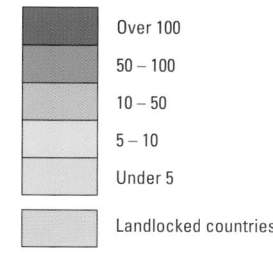

Over 100
50 – 100
10 – 50
5 – 10
Under 5
Landlocked countries

Major seaports

● Over 100 million tons per year
○ 50 – 100 million tons per year
— Major shipping routes

Trade in Primary Products

Primary products (excluding fuels, metals, and minerals) as a percentage of total export value (2000)

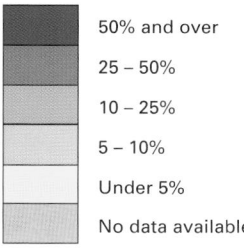

50% and over
25 – 50%
10 – 25%
5 – 10%
Under 5%
No data available

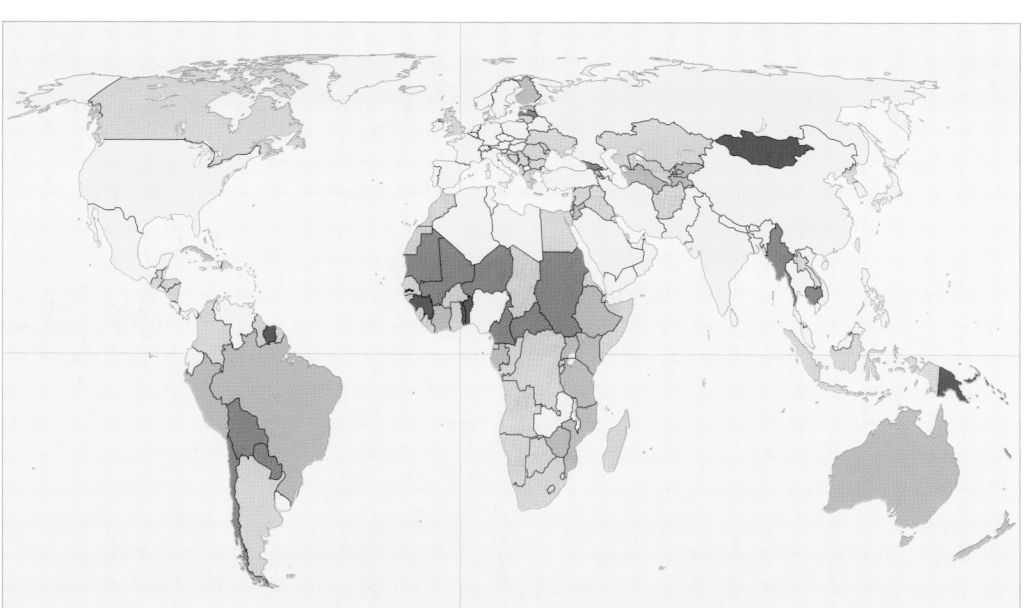

Primary products are raw materials or partly processed products which form the basis for manufacturing. They are the necessary requirements of industries and include agricultural products, minerals and timber, as well as many semi-manufactured goods such as cotton, which has been spun but not woven, wood pulp or flour. Many developed countries have few natural resources and rely on imports for the majority of their primary products. The countries of Southeast Asia export hardwoods to the rest of the world, whilst many South American countries are heavily dependent on coffee exports.

Balance of Trade

Value of exports in proportion to the value of imports (2000)

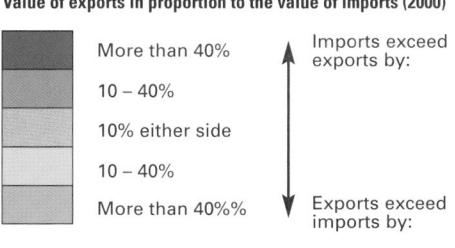

More than 40%   Imports exceed exports by:
10 – 40%
10% either side
10 – 40%
More than 40%%   Exports exceed imports by:
No data available

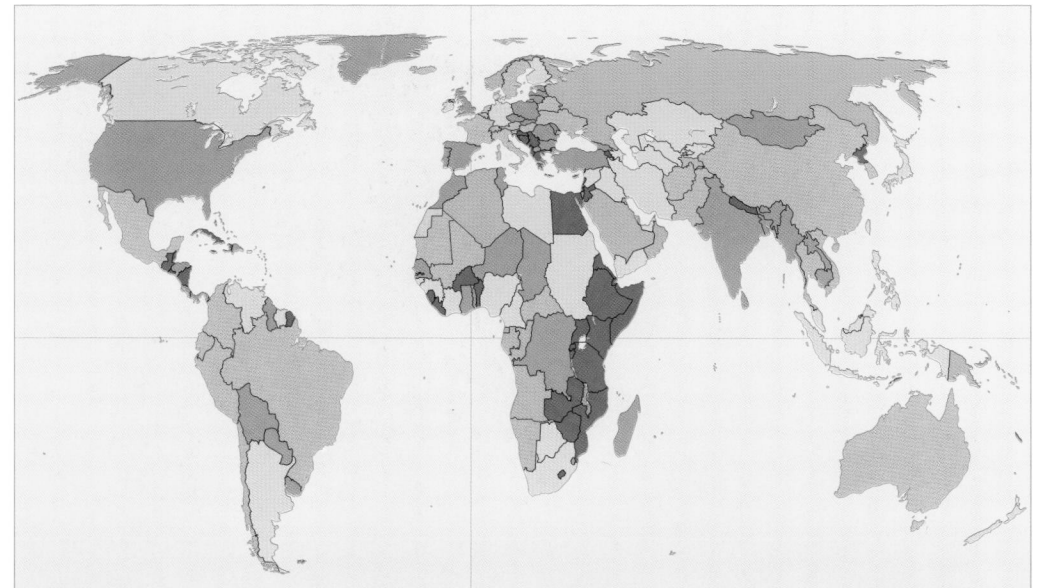

The total world trade balance should amount to zero, since exports must equal imports on a global scale. In practice, at least $100 billion in exports go unrecorded, leaving the world with an apparent deficit and many countries in a better position than public accounting reveals. However, a favorable trade balance is not necessarily a sign of prosperity: many poorer countries must maintain a high surplus in order to service debts, and do so by restricting imports below the levels needed to sustain successful economies.

Air Freight

Trends in air freight in million ton-km*, selected countries (1995–9)

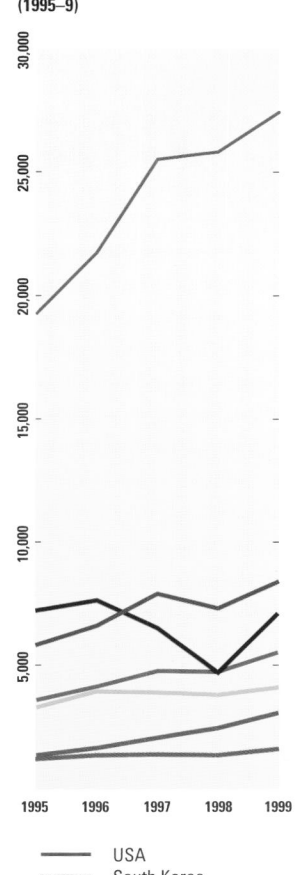

30,000
25,000
20,000
15,000
10,000
5,000

1995 1996 1997 1998 1999

USA
South Korea
UK
Singapore
Netherlands
China
Malaysia

* Equivalent to million tons of air freight flown over 1 million km [650,000 miles] per year.

Air transport is important to countries of considerable size; where ground terrain is difficult; when crossing short stretches of sea; and where goods are of high value, light in weight or perishable. The deregulation of airlines (in the USA since 1978 and the EU in 1993) has led to increased competition and lower fares.

HEALTH

Until the late 1990s, when the full extent of the AIDS crisis emerged, average life expectancies at birth were rising almost everywhere. By 2000, they ranged from 78 years in high income economies to 47 in sub-Saharan Africa. These figures represented an enormous advance on the situation in 1880, when citizens of Berlin had an estimated life expectancy of 30 years.

The ravages of AIDS have been greatest in southern Africa. One of the worst affected countries is Botswana, where nearly 40% of the adult population were thought to be infected by 2002. In Botswana, life expectancies were expected to fall to 27 years in 2010 instead of an original estimate of 74 years. However, in much of the world, average life expectancies are still increasing. The rises are attributed to improvements in agriculture and, hence, nutrition, as well as health education, an increase in sanitation and the quality of drinking water, together with advances in medicine.

Besides AIDS, the people of the developing world are subject to another affliction – malnutrition. Below, the map on this page shows that in most of Africa, Asia and Latin America, the average daily calorie supply per person is so low as to cause malnutrition. (The daily requirement rated adequate by the World Health Organization is between 2,300 and 2,500 calories per day.) Malnutrition is a serious condition. For example, among pregnant women it causes high rates of child mortality.

Deficiency diseases occur when people do not have a balanced diet. Protein deficiency causes stunting and kwashiorkor, which can be fatal, especially among young children, while vitamin deficiencies cause such illnesses as beri beri, pellagra, scurvy, and rickets. Iron deficiency causes anemia, while a lack of iodine causes mental retardation. A UN report in the early 1990s reported that iodine deficiency affected 458 million women world-wide, as compared with 238 million men. Women's nutritional problems are especially acute in southern Asia. For example, the UN report stated that 88% of pregnant women in India were anemic, as compared with 15% in developed countries.

Infectious diseases in association, directly or indirectly, with deficient diets, continue to affect people in developing countries, especially the countries in the low human development category, where only 32% of the people have access to sanitation and 68% to safe water supplies.

Around the turn of the century, a WHO report stated that infectious diseases cause over 16 million deaths a year. Most of the victims are young and otherwise fit people in developing countries. The major killers are AIDS, cholera, dysentery, malaria, measles, pneumonia, respiratory infections, tuber-culosis, and typhoid. Many of these diseases are preventable and, according to the United Nations Children's Fund, an investment of US $25,000 million per year, about half of the money spent annually on cigarettes in Europe alone, would have saved the lives of all the children who currently die from avoidable diseases.

Infectious diseases are much less important as causes of death in developed countries, where cancer and circulatory diseases, such as atherosclerosis and hypertension, which cause strokes and heart attacks, are the most common causes of fatality. Because these diseases tend to kill older people, they are relatively less important in developing countries where people have shorter lifespans.

Harmful habits are also generally practiced more by the rich than the poor. For example, smoking is an important cause of death in developed countries, though, curiously, the Japanese, with an average life expectancy of 81 years in 2000, are among the highest tobacco consumers. Similarly, high alcohol consumption, although it has bad effects on health, does not seem to affect longevity. The leading consumers, the French, had a life expectancy of 79 years in 2000.

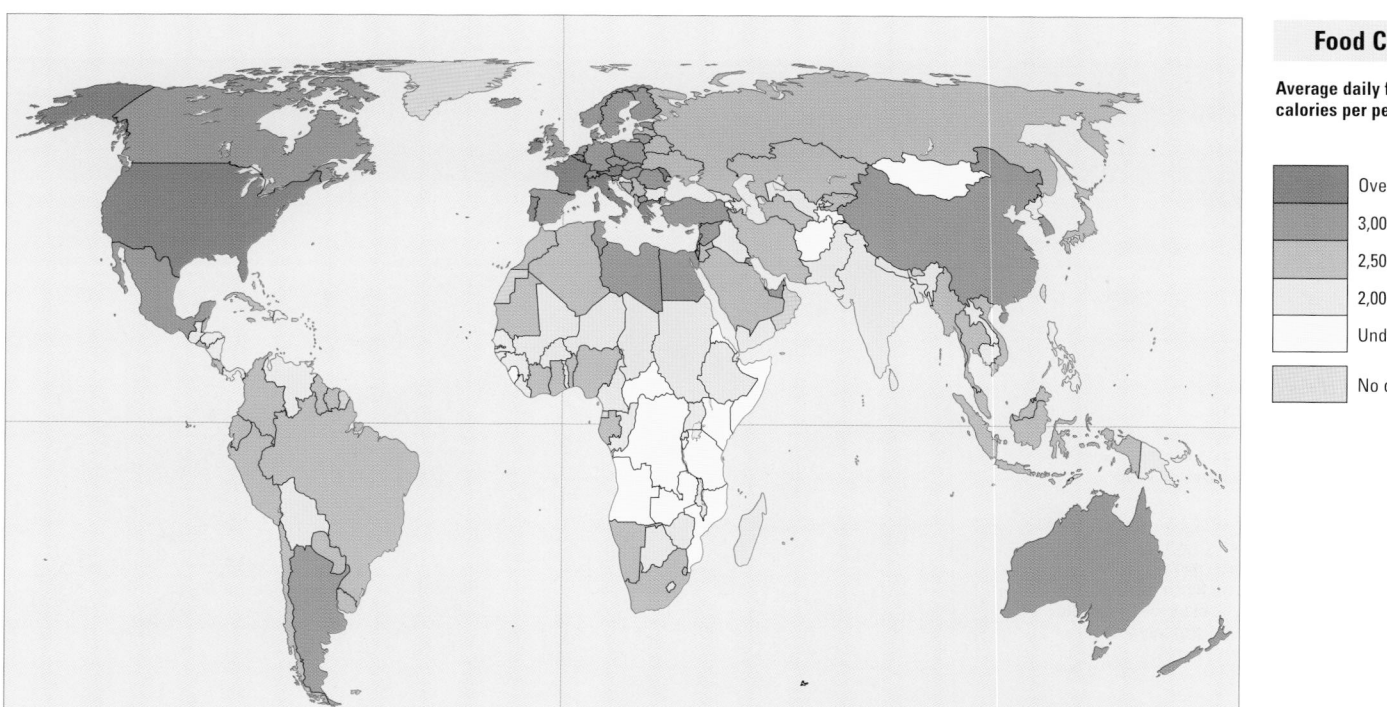

Food Consumption

Average daily food intake in calories per person (2000)

- Over 3,500 calories
- 3,000 – 3,500 calories
- 2,500 – 3,000 calories
- 2,000 – 2,500 calories
- Under 2,000 calories
- No data available

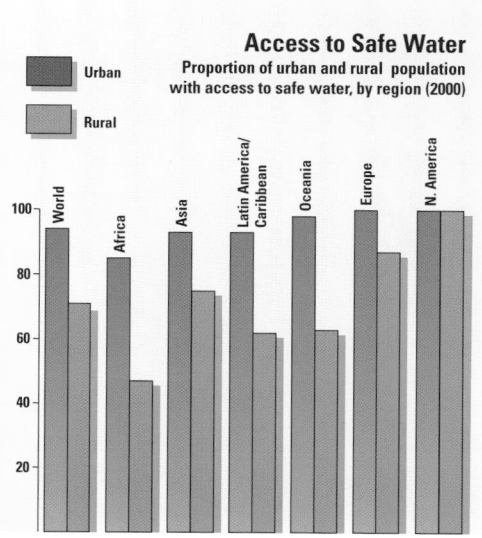

Access to Safe Water
Proportion of urban and rural population with access to safe water, by region (2000)

Urban
Rural

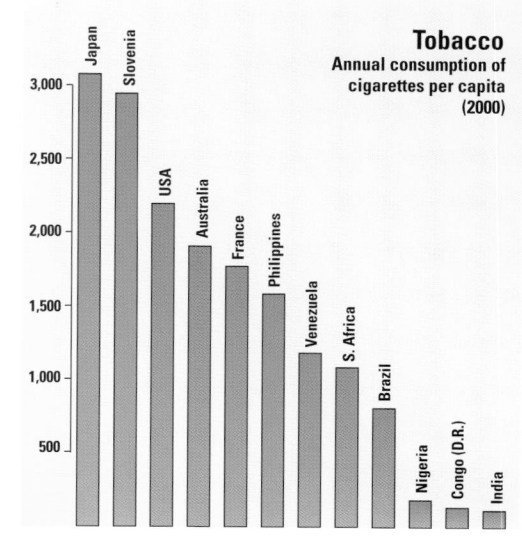

Tobacco
Annual consumption of cigarettes per capita (2000)

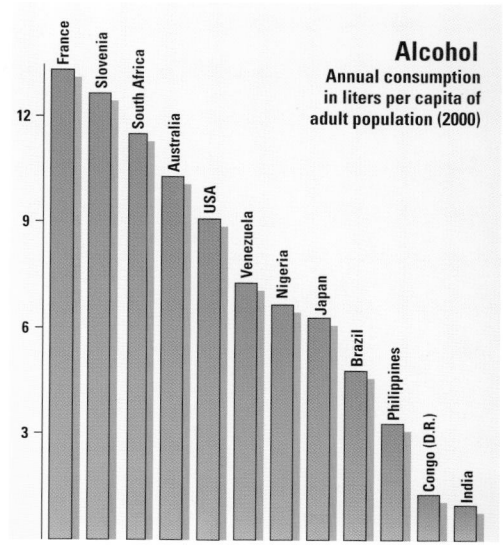

Alcohol
Annual consumption in liters per capita of adult population (2000)

Life Expectancy

Years of life expectancy at birth, selected countries (1997)

The chart shows combined data for both sexes. On average, women live longer than men worldwide, even in developing countries with high maternal mortality rates. Overall, life expectancy is steadily rising, though the difference between rich and poor nations remains dramatic.

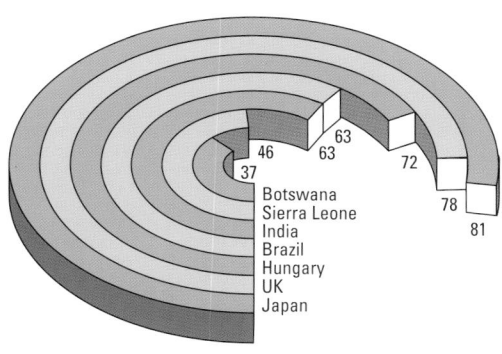

37 Botswana
46 Sierra Leone
63 India
63 Brazil
72 Hungary
78 UK
81 Japan

Infant Mortality

Number of babies who died under the age of one, per 1,000 births (2000)

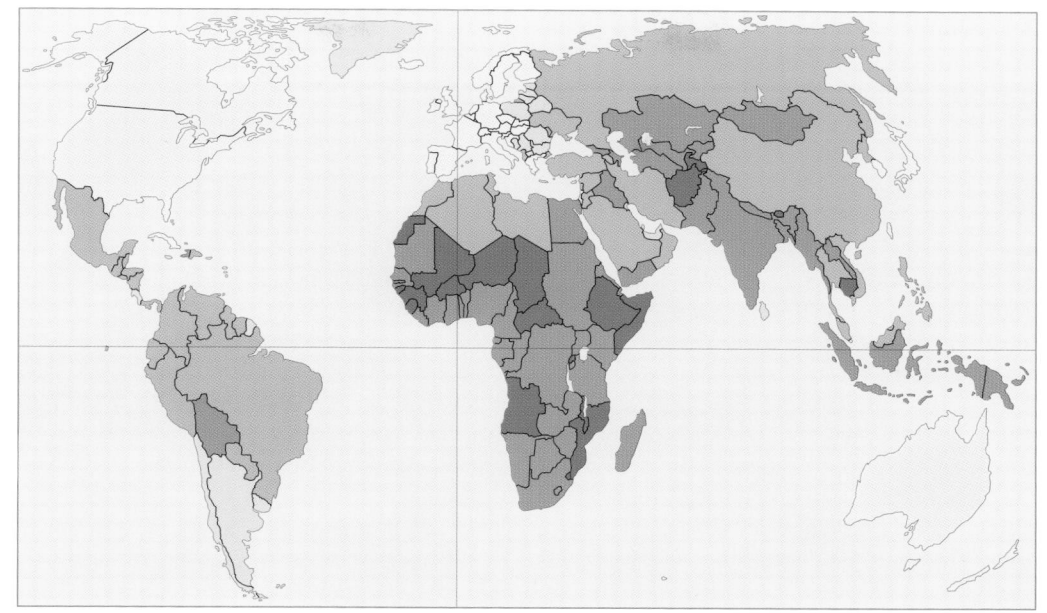

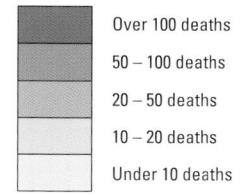

Over 100 deaths
50 – 100 deaths
20 – 50 deaths
10 – 20 deaths
Under 10 deaths

Highest infant mortality
Afghanistan .... 137 deaths
Western Sahara .... 134 deaths
Malawi .... 131 deaths

Lowest infant mortality
Iceland .... 5 deaths
Finland .... 4 deaths
Japan .... 4 deaths

Expenditure on Health

Public health expenditure per capita, in US $ (1998)

Countries with the highest spending		Countries with the lowest spending	
USA	.$4,271	Mozambique	.$8
Switzerland	.$3,857	Tanzania	.$8
Norway	.$3,182	Sierra Leone	.$8
Denmark	.$2,785	Indonesia	.$8
Luxembourg	.$2,731	Chad	.$7
Iceland	.$2,701	Laos	.$6
Germany	.$2,697	Niger	.$5
France	.$2,288	Madagascar	.$5
Japan	.$2,243	Burundi	.$5
Netherlands	.$2,173	Ethiopia	.$4

The allocation of limited funds for health care in developing countries is rarely evenly spread – the quality of treatment can vary enormously from place to place within the same country. Urban dwellers tend to have much better access to health provisions than those living in rural areas.

Medical Provision

Doctors per 100,000 population, selected countries (2000)

Although the ratio of people to doctors gives a good approximation of a country's health provision, it is not an absolute indicator. Raw numbers may mask inefficiency and other weaknesses: the high proportion of physicians in Hungary, for example, has not prevented infant mortality rates more than twice as high as in the United Kingdom.

The definition of a doctor also varies from nation to nation. As well as registered medical practitioners, it may include trained medical assistants – an especially important category in developing countries, where they provide many of the same services as fully qualified physicians, including simple operations.

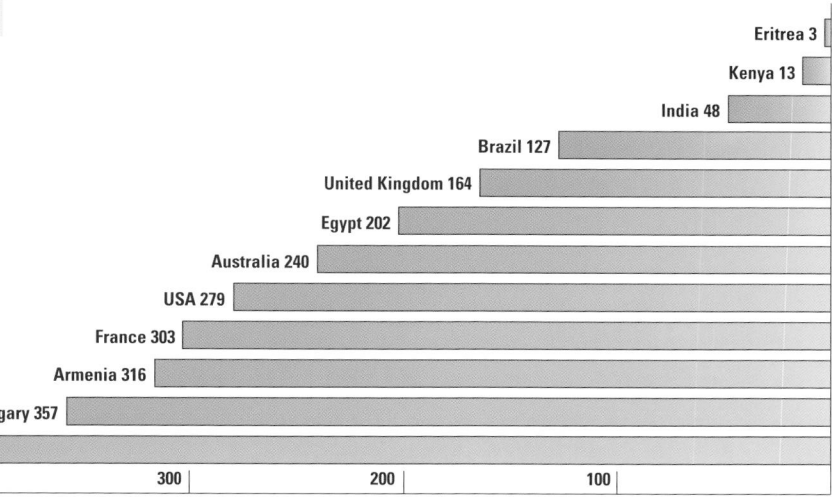

Eritrea 3
Kenya 13
India 48
Brazil 127
United Kingdom 164
Egypt 202
Australia 240
USA 279
France 303
Armenia 316
Hungary 357
Italy 554

600 | 500 | 400 | 300 | 200 | 100

The Aids Crisis

The Acquired Immune Deficiency Syndrome (AIDS) was first identified in 1981 when American doctors found otherwise healthy young men succumbing to rare infections. By 1984 the cause had been traced to the Human Immunodeficiency Virus (HIV) which can remain dormant for many years and perhaps indefinitely: only half of those known to carry the virus in 1981 had developed AIDS ten years later.

In Western countries in the 1990s, most AIDS deaths were among male homosexuals or needle-sharing drug-users. However, the disease is spreading fastest among heterosexual men and women, which is its usual vector in the developing world where most of its victims live.

In 2002, 25 million people had already died of AIDS and another 42 million were infected with the HIV virus. Around 30 million of them live in Africa. In some southern African countries, more than a third of the population carries the virus. In South Africa, which has the largest number of HIV infections, about 6 million people were expected to die of the disease between 2002 and 2012.

Most people who die of AIDS are young. AIDS also has other serious consequences. A report by UNAIDS and UNICEF stated that the number of children orphaned by AIDS rose threefold between 1996 and 2002, reaching an all-time high of 13.4 million.

Causes of Death

■ Accidents, poisoning and violence
■ Respiratory and digestive diseases
■ Nervous and circulatory diseases
■ Metabolic disorders
■ Cancers
■ Infectious and parasitic diseases

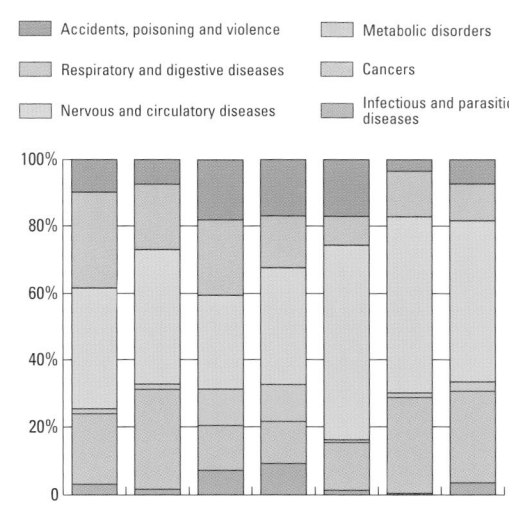

China | Japan | Mexico | Morocco | Russia | UK | USA

Circulatory Disease in Europe

Diseases of the circulatory system per 100,000 people (latest available year)

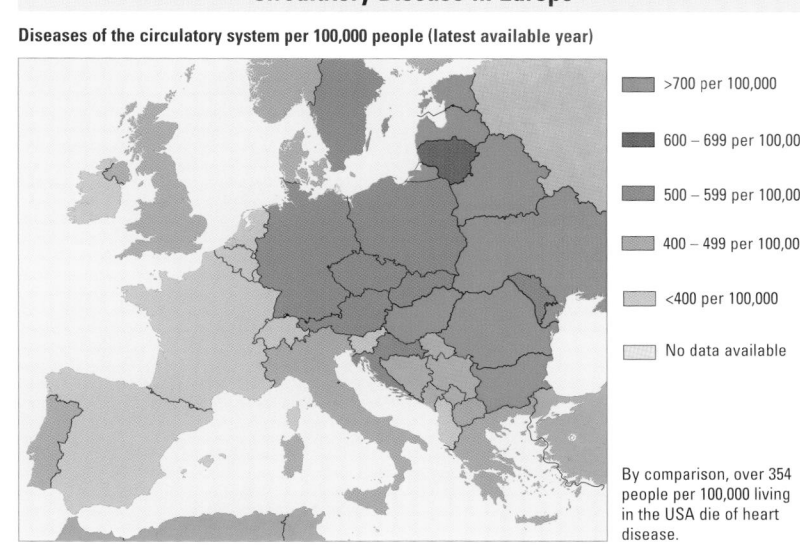

>700 per 100,000
600 – 699 per 100,000
500 – 599 per 100,000
400 – 499 per 100,000
<400 per 100,000
No data available

By comparison, over 354 people per 100,000 living in the USA die of heart disease.

AIDS

Cases reported in 1999

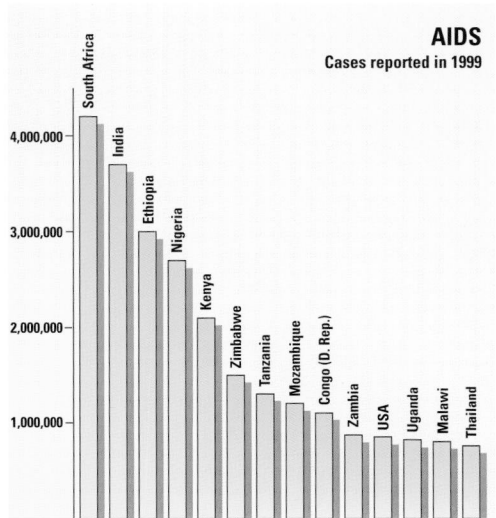

South Africa
India
Ethiopia
Nigeria
Kenya
Zimbabwe
Tanzania
Mozambique
Congo (D. Rep.)
Zambia
USA
Uganda
Malawi
Thailand

Sanitation

Percentage of the population with access to sanitation services, selected countries (latest available year)

■ Urban
■ Rural

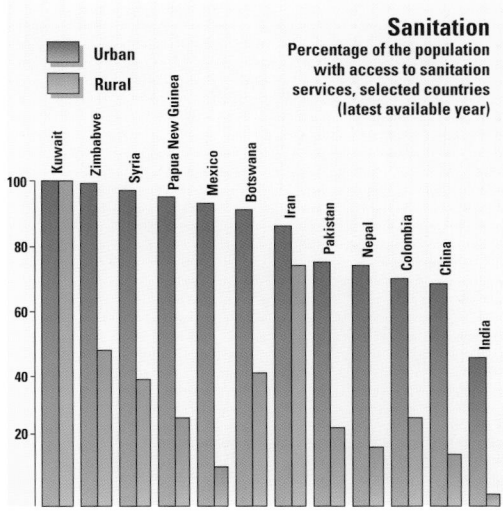

Kuwait
Zimbabwe
Syria
Papua New Guinea
Mexico
Botswana
Iran
Pakistan
Nepal
Colombia
China
India

Malaria

Cases of malaria per 100,000 people exposed to malaria-infected environments, selected countries* (latest available year)

* data are not available for Africa where 80% of malaria cases occur

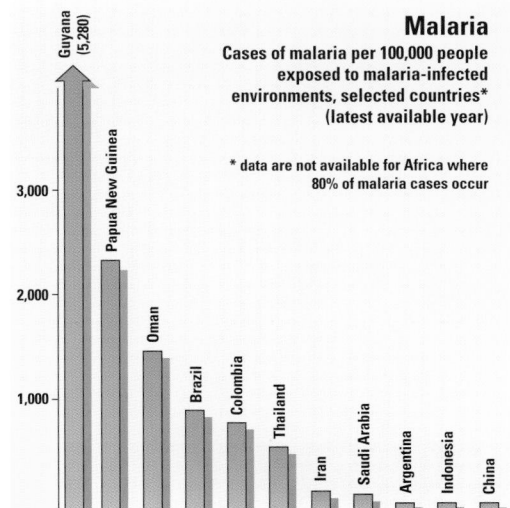

Guyana (5,280)
Papua New Guinea
Oman
Brazil
Colombia
Thailand
Iran
Saudi Arabia
Argentina
Indonesia
China

Infectious and parasitic diseases, such as malaria, which claimed 2.5 million lives in 2002, remain a scourge in the developing countries. Respiratory infections and injury also claim more lives in developing countries, which lack the drugs and the medical personnel to deal with them. Developing countries lack the basic services taken for granted in developed nations. For example, in rural Africa in 2000, only 49% of the population had access to sanitation and 44% to safe water, with the situation being worse in rural areas. By contrast, circulatory diseases and cancer are the main causes of death in the rich, industrialized countries. For example, in the UK in the 1990s, circulatory diseases, which cause heart attacks and strokes, accounted for nearly half the deaths, with cancer accounting for nearly a quarter.

WEALTH

Currencies

Currency units of the world's most powerful economies

1. USA: US dollar ($, US $) = 100 cents
2. Japan: Yen (Y, ¥) = 100 sen
3. EU: euro = 100 cents
4. UK: Pound sterling (£) = 100 pence
5. Canada: Canadian dollar (C$, Can$) = 100 cents
6. China: Renminbi yuan (RMBY, $, Y) = 10 jiao = 100 fen
7. Brazil: Cruzeiro real (BRC) = 100 centavos
8. India: Indian rupee (Re, Rs) = 100 paisa
9. Australia: Australian dollar ($A) = 100 cents
10. Switzerland: Swiss franc (SFr, SwF) = 100 centimes
11. South Korea: Won (W) = 100 chon
12. Sweden: Swedish krona (SKr) = 100 ore
13. Mexico: Mexican peso (Mex$) = 100 centavos
14. Denmark: Danish krone (DKr) = 100 øre
15. Norway: Norwegian krone (NKr) = 100 øre
16. Saudi Arabia: Riyal (SAR, SRIS$) = 100 halalah
17. Indonesia: Rupiah (Rp) = 100 sen
18. South Africa: Rand (R) = 100 cents

On January 1, 2002, three years after the launch of Europe's single currency, euro banknotes and coins were brought into circulation in the 12 member states of the European Union that had adopted the euro. Their former national currencies remained in dual circulation with the euro until the end of February 2002. The 12 countries in the euro area are: Austria, Belgium, Germany, Greece, Finland, France, Ireland, Italy, Luxembourg, the Netherlands, Portugal, and Spain.

Perhaps the most glaring differences in the world today are those between the rich and the poor. The World Bank divides countries into three main groups based on average economic production expressed in terms of per capita GNP (Gross National Product). They are the low-income economies, including most African countries and much of Asia; the middle-income economies, including most of Latin America and most of the former USSR; and the high-income economies of Canada, the United States, Western Europe, Japan, and Australia.

Per capita GNPs are a measure of the total goods and services produced by a country divided by the population, and then converted into US dollars at official exchange rates. They are useful indicators of a country's prosperity, though, like all statistics, they must be treated with care. For example, the prices for goods and services in China are far cheaper than they are in the United States. China's per capita GNP in 2000 was $840 (as compared with $34,100 in the USA), but the PPP (Purchasing Power Parity) estimate of China's per capita GNP was considerably higher at $3,920. Another problem with per capita GNPs is that they are averages, which often conceal wide internal variations.

The pattern of poverty varies from region to region. In Latin America, much progress has been made through industrialization, though startling inequalities still exist between rich and poor. China and other countries in eastern Asia, including South Korea and Taiwan, have followed Japan's example in pursuing export-led industrial policies. The success of China's Special Economic Zones, where foreign investment is encouraged, has led to a huge rise in China's per capita GNP.

Solutions to poverty in Africa are much harder to find because of its high population growth, civil wars, natural disasters, and high inflation rates. Although Africa receives more aid than any other continent, aid is only a partial solution. Much aid has been wasted on overambitious projects, in the servicing of huge national debts, or lost by inexperienced or corrupt governments. One initiative in some African countries has been to improve the infrastructure and develop tourism, creating employment and providing much-needed foreign currency. But tourism alone cannot solve the problems of under-development.

The International Monetary Fund and the World Bank argue that real economic progress in Africa will be achieved only when African countries create market-friendly economies that encourage trade through export-led manufacturing, while at the same time strictly controlling public spending on welfare, the civil service and other areas.

Continental Shares

Shares of population and of wealth (GNP) by continent

These generalized continental figures show the startling difference between rich and poor but mask the successes or failures of individual countries. Japan, for example, with less than 4% of Asia's population, produces almost 70% of the continent's output. Within countries, the difference between rich and poor can also be startling. In Brazil, for example, the richest 20% of the population own 60% of the wealth.

Population

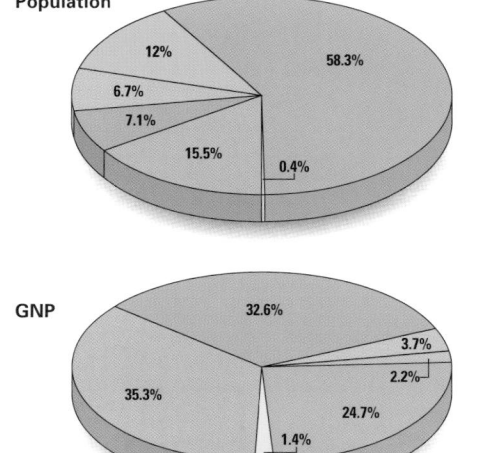

GNP

Europe   Asia   South America
Australia   Africa   North America

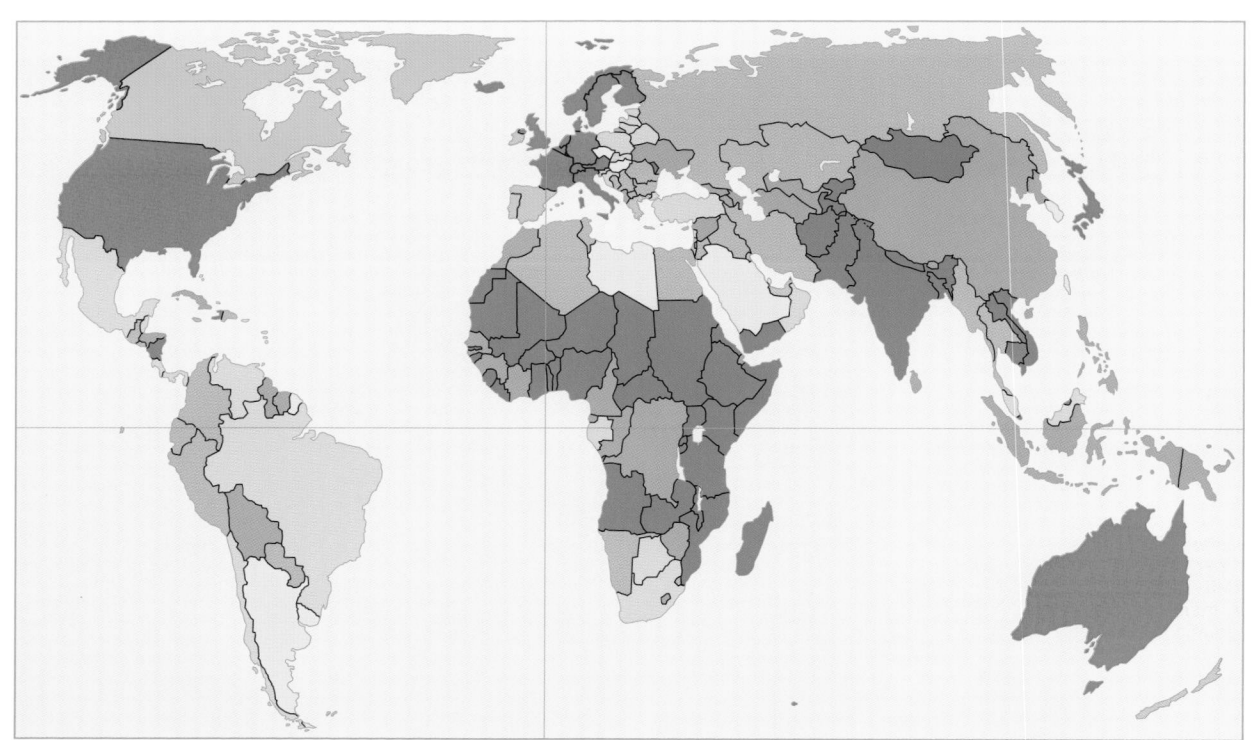

Levels of Income

Gross National Income per capita: the value of total production divided by the population (2000)

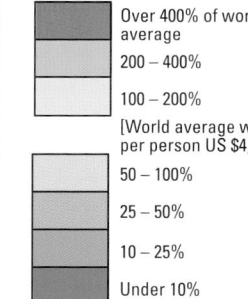

- Over 400% of world average
- 200 – 400%
- 100 – 200%
- [World average wealth per person US $4,890]
- 50 – 100%
- 25 – 50%
- 10 – 25%
- Under 10%

Top 5 countries

Luxembourg	$42,060
Switzerland	$38,140
Japan	$35,620
Norway	$34,530
Bermuda	$34,470

Bottom 5 countries

Ethiopia	$100
Burundi	$110
Sierra Leone	$130
Eritrea	$170
Malawi	$170

Indicators

The gap between the world's rich and poor is now so great that it is difficult to illustrate on a single graph. Within each income group (as defined by the World Bank), however, comparisons have some meaning. The wealth gap in many developing countries, though, is wide, with a small, rich class and a large, impoverished majority, while many high-income countries contain an underclass of unemployed and homeless people.

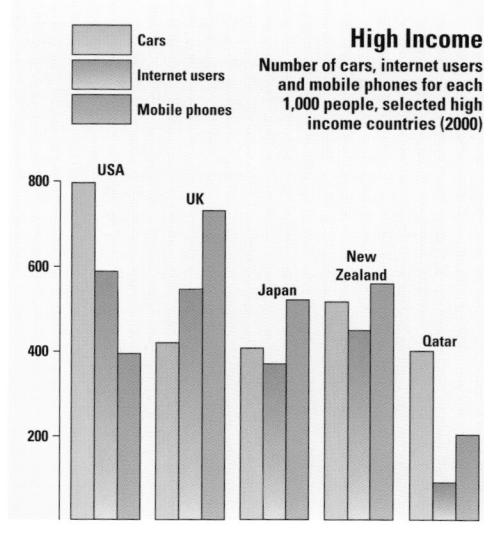

High Income

Number of cars, internet users and mobile phones for each 1,000 people, selected high income countries (2000)

Cars / Internet users / Mobile phones

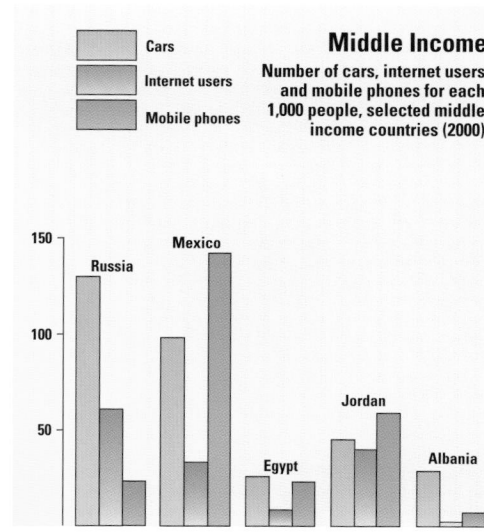

Middle Income

Number of cars, internet users and mobile phones for each 1,000 people, selected middle income countries (2000)

Cars / Internet users / Mobile phones

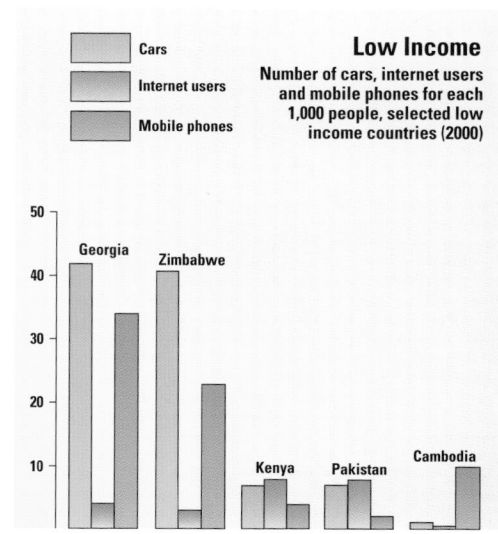

Low Income

Number of cars, internet users and mobile phones for each 1,000 people, selected low income countries (2000)

Cars / Internet users / Mobile phones

World Tourism

Passenger miles flown (the number of passengers multiplied by the distance flown from the airport of origin) (1999)

Over 60,000 million

30,000 – 60,000 million

6,000 – 30,000 million

600 – 6,000 million

Under 600 million

No data available

○ Major airports (handling over 25 million passengers in 2001)

Leisure and tourism is the world's second largest industry in terms of revenue generated. Small economies in attractive areas are often completely dominated by tourism: in some Caribbean islands, tourist spending provides over 90% of the total income and is the biggest foreign exchange earner. In cash terms the USA is the world leader: its 2000 earnings exceeded US $82 billion, though that sum amounted to approximately 0.9% of its total GDP. Of the 51 million visitors to the USA, 29% came from Canada and 20% from Mexico. Germany spends the most on overseas tourism; this amounts to over US $50,000 million. The next biggest spenders are the USA, Japan, and the UK.

The world's busiest airport in terms of total number of passengers is Atlanta (75.9 million passengers in 2000); the busiest international airport is London's Heathrow.

Aid Donors

Development aid by donor country, in millions of US $ and as a percentage of donor's GNI (2001)

Not all aid is given in cash grants: much is delivered in the form of cheap loans or technical assistance. Since the 1970s, OECD countries belonging to the Development Assistance Committee (DAC) have agreed in principle to give 0.7% of their GNI. Most have failed to meet their commitment. In 2001, four countries exceeded this level. They were Denmark (1.0%), Netherlands (0.8%), Norway (0.8%) and Sweden (0.8%).
The countries with the largest aid budgets were the United States (US $11,429 million) and Japan (US $9,847 million).

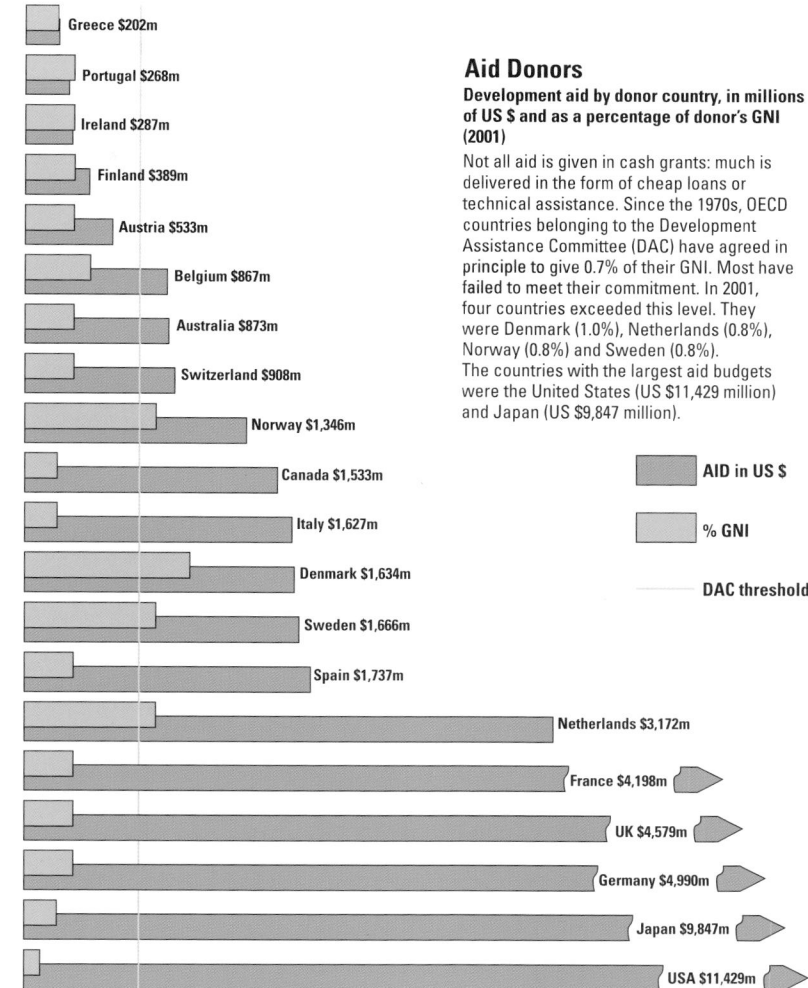

AID in US $

% GNI

DAC threshold

State Finance

Inflation rates, shown on the map (*right*) are an index of a country's financial stability and usually of its prosperity. Annual inflation rates above 20% are usually marked by slow or even negative growth of the GNP. Above 50%, it becomes hyperinflation and an economy is reeling. In the late 1980s and early 1990s, many high-income countries had to contend with annual inflation rates of 10% or more, while Japan, the growth leader, had an average inflation rate of 1.3% between 1985 and 1994.

The per capita GNI figures listed below are useful indicators of economic success or failure, but they do not account for living costs. Nor do they reveal the gaps between the rich and poor within countries.

Market-friendly policies, including low taxes and state spending, liberal trade policies and a welcome for foreign investors, are major factors in countries that have enjoyed rapid economic growth since 1980. For example, the setting up of Special Economic Zones in eastern China has led to a spectacular rise in the per capita GNP. Other successful countries included South Korea and Singapore, although an Asian market crash in 1997 temporarily halted the dramatic economic expansion of these countries.

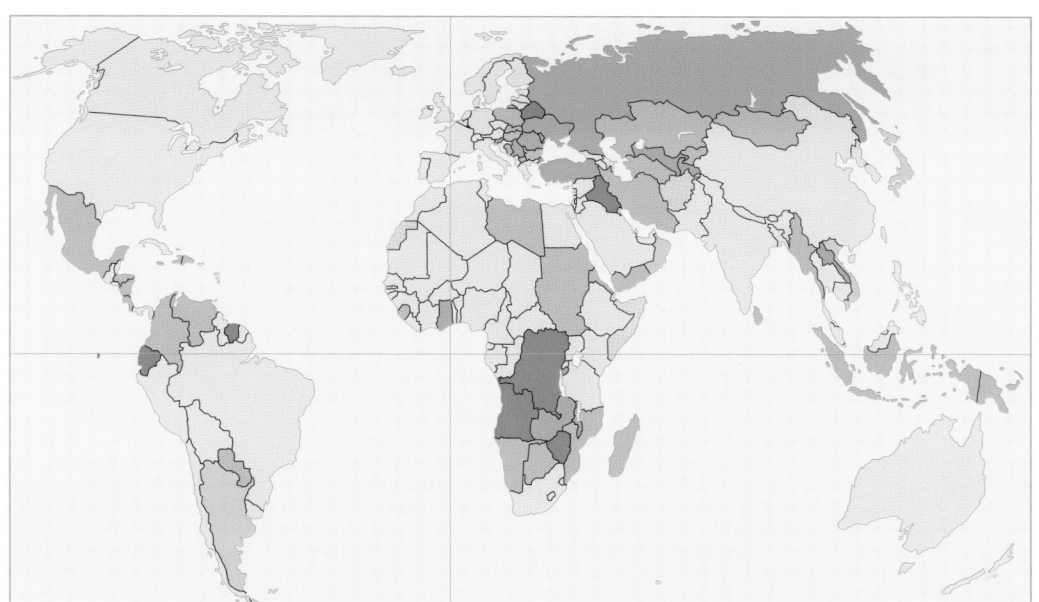

Inflation

Average annual rate of inflation (2000)

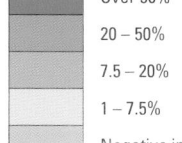

Over 50%

20 – 50%

7.5 – 20%

1 – 7.5%

Negative inflation

No data available

Highest average inflation
Congo (Dem. Rep.) 1,423%
Angola 740%
Turkmenistan............................ 407%

Lowest average inflation
Antigua and Barbuda .... –11.5%
Argentina* .... –3.1%
Bahrain .... –0.1%

* During 2002, Argentina experienced a sharp rise in inflation which is not reflected on this map.

The Wealth Gap

The world's richest and poorest countries, by Gross National Income per capita in US $ (2001)

1. Luxembourg	41,770	1. Ethiopia	100
2. Switzerland	36,970	2. Burundi	100
3. Japan	35,990	3. Sierra Leone	140
4. Norway	35,530	4. Guinea-Bissau	160
5. USA	34,870	5. Tajikistan	170
6. Denmark	31,090	6. Niger	170
7. Iceland	28,880	7. Malawi	170
8. Sweden	25,400	8. Eritrea	190
9. UK	24,230	9. Chad	200
10. Netherlands	24,040	10. Mozambique	210
11. Finland	23,940	11. Mali	210
12. Austria	23,940	12. Burkina Faso	210
13. Germany	23,700	13. Rwanda	220
14. Belgium	23,340	14. Nepal	250
15. Ireland	23,060	15. Madagascar	260
16. France	22,690	16. Togo	270
17. Canada	21,340	17. Tanzania	270
18. Australia	19,770	18. Central African Rep.	270
19. Italy	19,470	19. Cambodia	270
20. Spain	14,860	20. Uganda	280

GNI per capita is calculated by dividing a country's Gross National Income by its total population.

Growth in GNI

GNI per capita annual growth rate (1998–9)

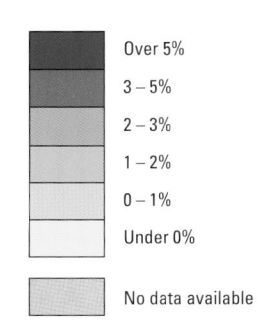

Over 5%

3 – 5%

2 – 3%

1 – 2%

0 – 1%

Under 0%

No data available

Countries with highest growth rates
Equatorial Guinea 15.0%
Mozambique 10.0%
Palau 10.0%
South Korea 10.0%
Guinea-Bissau 9.5%

STANDARDS OF LIVING

Wealth is a basic factor in determining standards of living. Everywhere, the rich have more of everything, including higher average life expectancies, while the poor have to spend most of their income on basic human needs, such as food and clothing. Yet poverty and wealth are relative terms. Slum dwellers living on social security in an industrial society feel their poverty acutely, but they have far more resources than an average African living in a rural area.

In 1990 the United Nations Development Program published its first Human Development Index (HDI), an attempt to construct a comparative scale by which a simplified form of well-being might be measured. The HDI, expressed as a value between 0 and 0.999, combines figures for life expectancy and literacy with a wealth scale, based on Purchasing Power Parity. The world's countries are divided into three groups, those with a high HDI (0.800 and above); those with a medium HDI (0.500 to 0.799); and those with a low HDI (below 0.500).

In 2002, Norway was top in the world rankings and Sierra Leone was bottom. In fact, of the 36 countries with a low HDI, 29 were from Africa, 6 from Asia, plus Haiti from the Caribbean. Besides having

low per capita GNPs, the average life expectancy in these countries was 59 years, while the adult literacy rate was 58%. By comparison, the average life expectancy at birth in countries in the high HDI group was 78 years, while the literacy rate was 98%.

Comparisons between countries with similar per capita GNPs reveal the effects of government actions. For example, the World Bank classifies both India and China as low-income economies, but India's HDI at 0.577 is much lower than that of China, at 0.726. This reflects not only China's economic progress in the 1980s and 1990s, but also differences in average life expectancies (63 years in India and 70 years in China), and adult literacy rates (52% in India and 82% in China).

Disparities in standards of living exist not only between countries but also between individuals, groups and regions within countries. For example, income distribution figures for 1995 show that, in the United States, the poorest 20% of households received less than 4% of the income.

Other contrasts exist in developing countries between rural communities, where incomes are low and basic services are often in short supply, and urban areas, where even those living in slums are

generally better off than their rural neighbours. Other striking differences exist between men and women. For example, while adult literacy rates for men and women living in developed countries are more or less the same, large differences exist in many developing countries. In 2001, in countries in the lowest HDI category, only 64% of women were literate, as compared with 73% of men.

Female education is a factor in population control, especially as women's fertility rates appear to fall in direct proportion to the amount of secondary education they receive. This point was acknowledged in 1994 by the UN Population Fund, which defined four main objectives relating to women and population control. They were: the reduction of maternal, infant and child mortality; better education, especially for girls; universal access to reproductive health services; and gender equality.

Statistical analysis presents many problems of interpretation, especially when trying to define such intangible factors as a sense of well-being. For example, education helps create wealth; but are rich countries wealthy because their people are well educated, or are they well educated because they are rich?

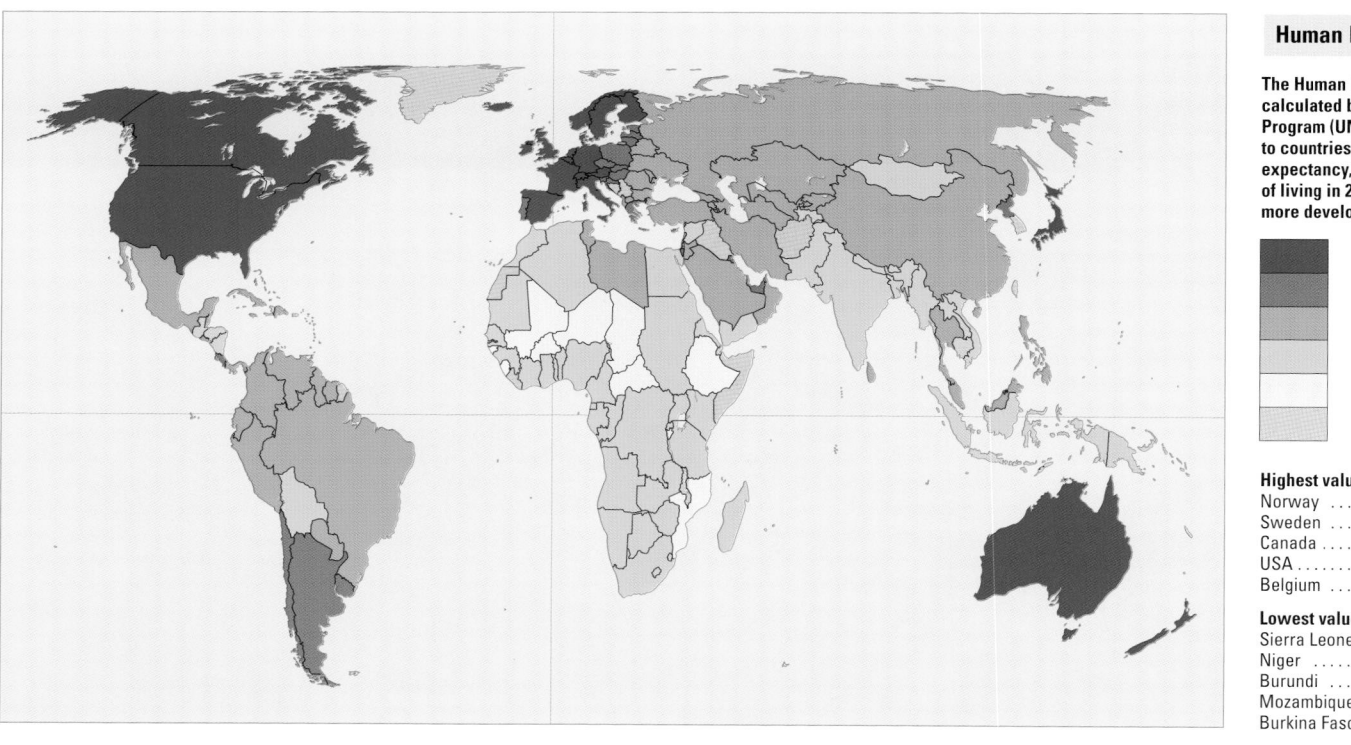

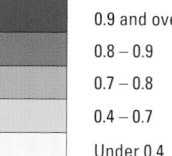

Human Development Index

The Human Development Index (HDI), calculated by the UN Development Program (UNDP), gives a value to countries using indicators of life expectancy, education and standards of living in 2000. Higher values show more developed countries.

- 0.9 and over
- 0.8 – 0.9
- 0.7 – 0.8
- 0.4 – 0.7
- Under 0.4
- No data available

Highest values
Norway 0.942
Sweden 0.941
Canada 0.940
USA 0.939
Belgium .0.939

Lowest values
Sierra Leone 0.275
Niger 0.277
Burundi .0.313
Mozambique 0.322
Burkina Faso 0.325

Education

The developing countries made great efforts in the 1970s and 1980s to bring at least a basic education to their people. Primary school enrolments rose above 60% in all but the poorest nations. Figures often include teenagers or young adults, however, and there are still an estimated 300 million children worldwide who receive no schooling at all. A lack of resources has restricted the development of secondary and higher education. Most primary school education is free in the poorer countries, but fees are often paid for secondary and higher education, thus heightening the differences between rich and poor.

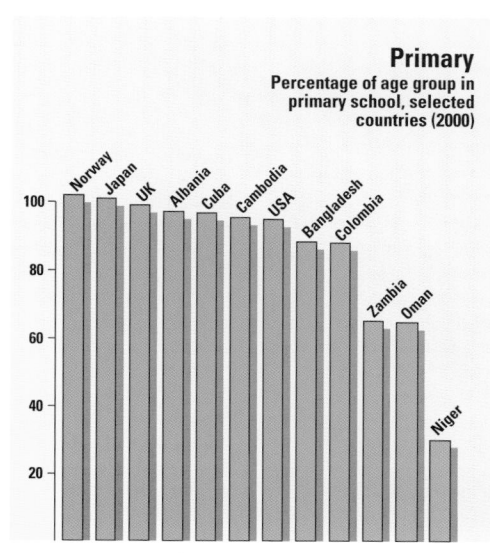

Primary
Percentage of age group in primary school, selected countries (2000)

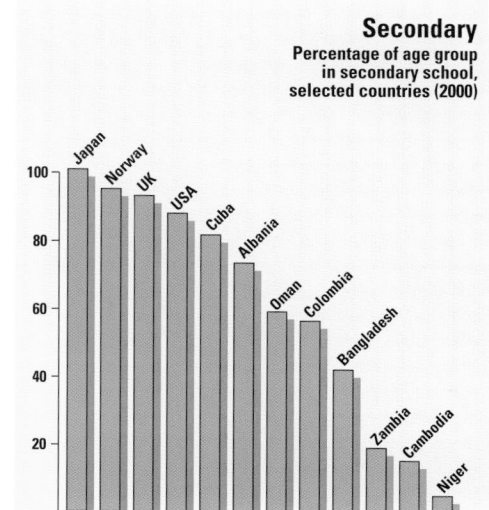

Secondary
Percentage of age group in secondary school, selected countries (2000)

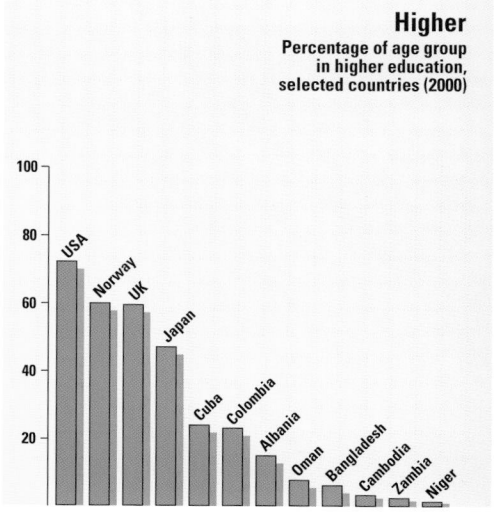

Higher
Percentage of age group in higher education, selected countries (2000)

Distribution of Spending

Percentage share of household spending (latest available year)

A high proportion of the average income of households in developing nations is spent on basic needs such as food and clothing. In most Western countries food and clothing account for less than 25% of expenditure.

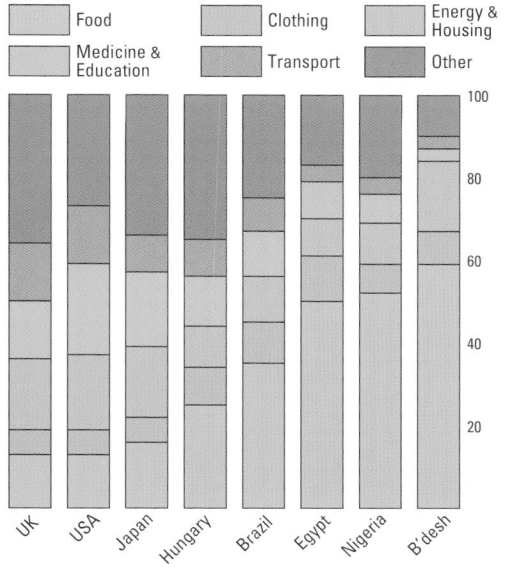

Food	Clothing	Energy & Housing
Medicine & Education	Transport	Other

Distribution of Income

Percentage share of household income from poorest fifth to richest fifth, selected countries (latest available year)

The graph (*below*) shows that wealth is not distributed evenly throughout the population of the six countries. In every country worldwide the richest 20% of the population have a disproportionately high percentage of the income. This disparity between rich and poor is nowhere more pronounced than in Brazil, where the richest 20% of the population have over 60% of the income. The poorest 20%, on the other hand, have less than 5%.

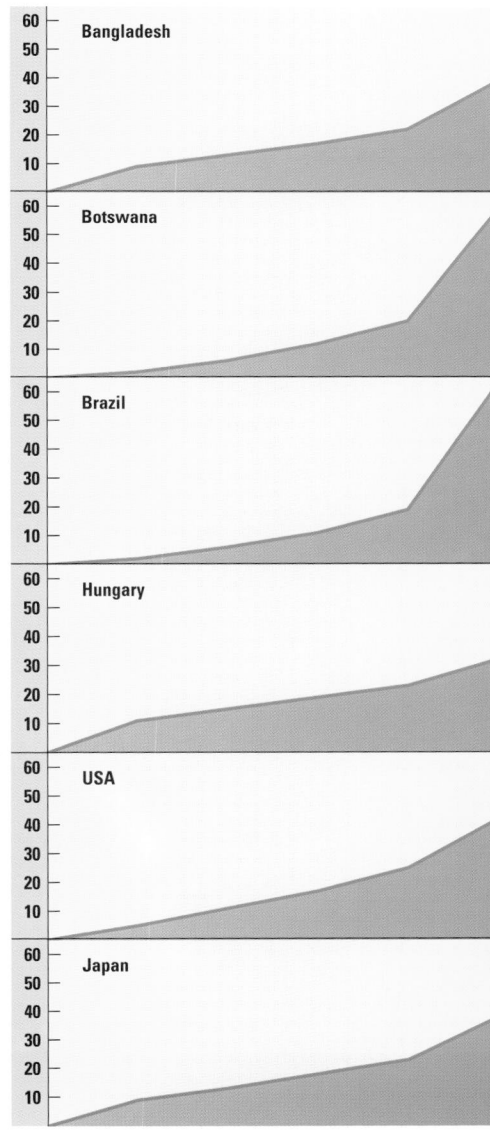

Fertility and Education

Fertility rates compared with female education, selected countries (1995–2000)

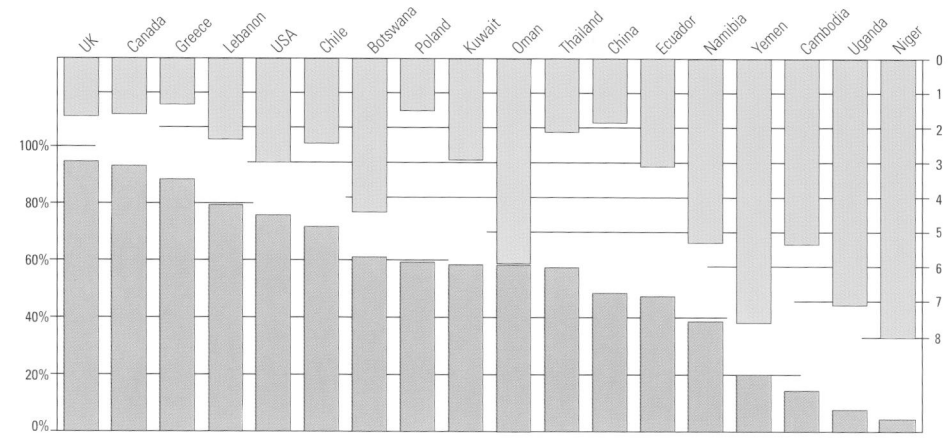

Fertility rate: average number of children borne per woman

Percentage of females aged 12–17 in secondary education

Access to secondary education is closely linked to low fertility rates in developed countries. By contrast, in many developing countries, women's lives are dominated by agriculture, or they lack access to secondary and higher education for cultural reasons, as in Muslim countries. Such disparities are reflected in women's parliamentary representation which is only one-seventh that of men, despite the emergence of such figures as Mrs Indira Gandhi, India's former prime minister. Female wages are also, on average, only two-thirds of those of men.

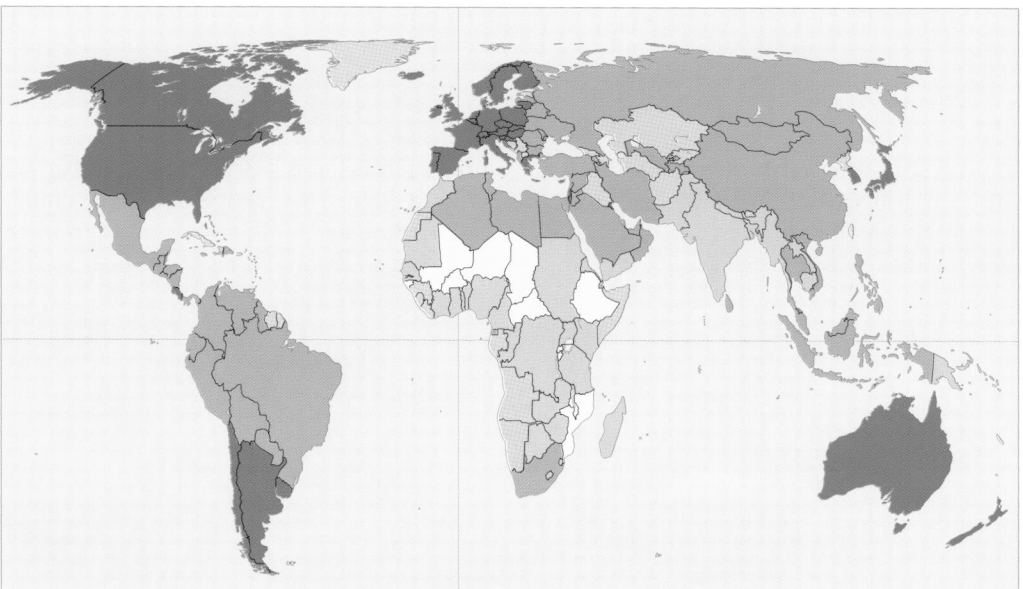

Gender Development Index

The Gender Development Index (GDI) shows economic and social differences between men and women by using various UNDP indicators (2002). Countries with higher values of GDI have more equality between men and women.

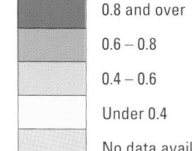

- 0.8 and over
- 0.6 – 0.8
- 0.4 – 0.6
- Under 0.4
- No data available

Highest values

Norway	.0.941
Australia	.0.938
Canada	.0.938
USA	.0.937

Lowest values

Niger	.0.263
Burundi	.0.306
Mozambique	.0.307
Burkina Faso	.0.312

Car Ownership

Proportion of the world's vehicles, by region

North America
Western Europe
Asia
E.Europe & CIS
Others

TOTAL = 312 million vehicles

Motor cars per 100 people

Lebanon	73.1
Brunei	57.5
Italy	56.8
Luxembourg	56.1
USA	51.8

Standards of Living in the USA by Race, Age and Region

A comparison of measures of income and education, by selected characteristics (2001–2)

Median income per household (US $), by age and region		Per capita income (US $), by race and Hispanic origin of householder		Percentage of persons aged 25 and over who have completed High School, by race or origin		
15–24 years	28,196	ALL RACES	22,851	ALL RACES	1975	62.5
25–34 years	45,086	White	24,127		2001	84.1
35–44 years	53,320	Black	14,953	White	1975	64.5
45–54 years	58,045	Asian and Pacific Is.	24,277		2001	84.4
55–64 years	45,864	Hispanic (any race)	13,003	Black	1975	42.5
65 years and over	23,118				2001	78.7
Northeast	45,716	The poorest 20% of households received just 3.6% of the income, whereas the richest 20% received 48.2%.		Hispanic	1975	37.9
Midwest	43,834				2001	57.0
South	38,904					
West	45,687					

Regional Inequality in Italy

Gross Domestic Product (GDP) per capita in Italy, by region (1999)

- Over US $20,000
- $16,000 – $19,999
- $12,000 – $15,999
- $8,000 – $11,999
- Under $8,000

The average GNI (Gross National Income) per capita for Italy was US $20,170. By comparison, the GNI for the UK was US $23,590; for the USA $31,910; and for the EU $22,250.

The number of inhabitants per doctor, another social indicator, varies from less than 500 in the north-west of Italy to over 800 in the far south (the *Mezzogiorno*), with a national average of 607.

The southern part of Italy, known as the *Mezzogiorno* (or "Land of the midday sun"), has been described as the poorest part of the European Union. It is identifiable on the map (*left*) as all the regions with a GDP per capita of less than US $12,000 (including the two islands of Sicily and Sardinia), plus Abruzzi whose capital is L'Aquila.

The *Mezzogiorno* region suffers from a lack of mineral and energy resources, industry, commerce, services, and skilled labor. As a result, standards of living in the region are well below the rest of Italy and Europe. Employment is predominantly agricultural and small-scale.

The north of Italy accounts for 60% of the population but 80% of the GDP, whereas the *Mezzogiorno* accounts for 40% of the population and only 20% of the GDP. Manpower surpluses in the south led to emigration to other parts of Europe and the Americas. It has also led, especially in the last 50 years, to inter-regional migration from the islands and the southern mainland to the north. The main regions attracting migrants were the northwest – the prosperous Liguria–Piedmont–Lombardy triangle with its great industrial cities of Genoa, Milan, and Turin – and the Venetia region in the northeast. As a result, the north has experienced much higher population growth rates than the rest of Italy.

In 1996 the Northern League, one of Italy's political parties, exploited the regional differences by declaring the north to be the independent "Republic of Padania." However, only a small minority of northerners supports secession.

— MT EVEREST, CHINA/NEPAL —

Part of the Himalaya range, Mt Everest – the highest
mountain in the world at 29,035 ft (8,850 m) – lies just
north of center in this image. The two arms of the Rongbuk
glacier flow away from the triangular shaded north wall, with
the Kangshung glacier due east. The international boundary
between China and Nepal bisects the peak, which was
first climbed on May 28, 1953.

CITY MAPS

CITY MAPS

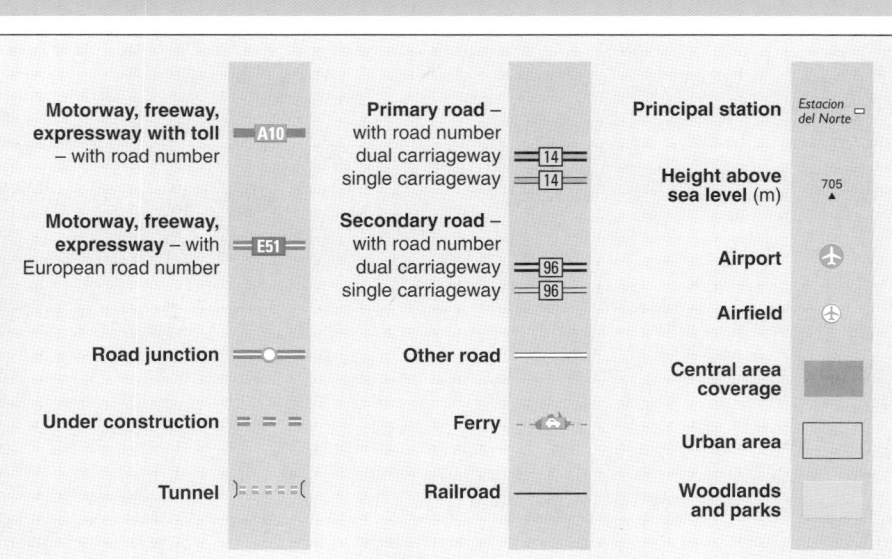

CENTRAL AREA MAPS

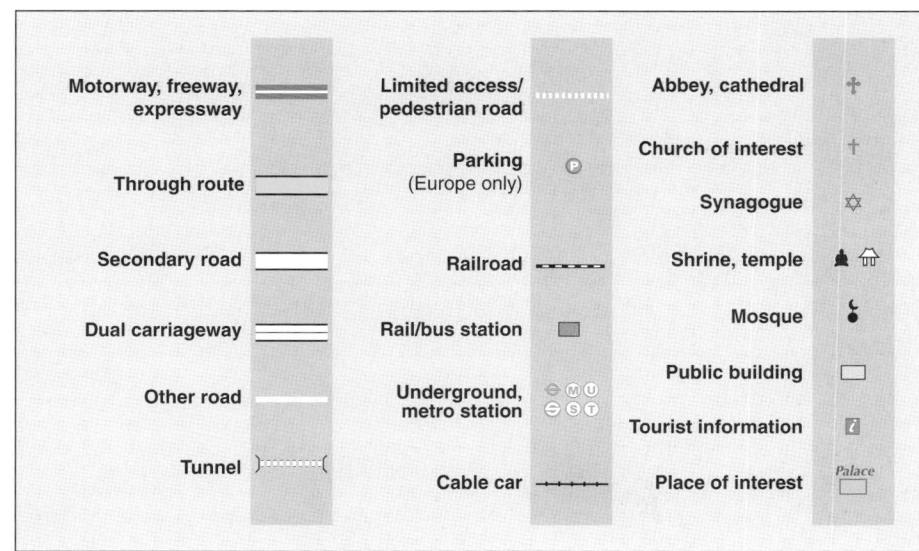

AMSTERDAM

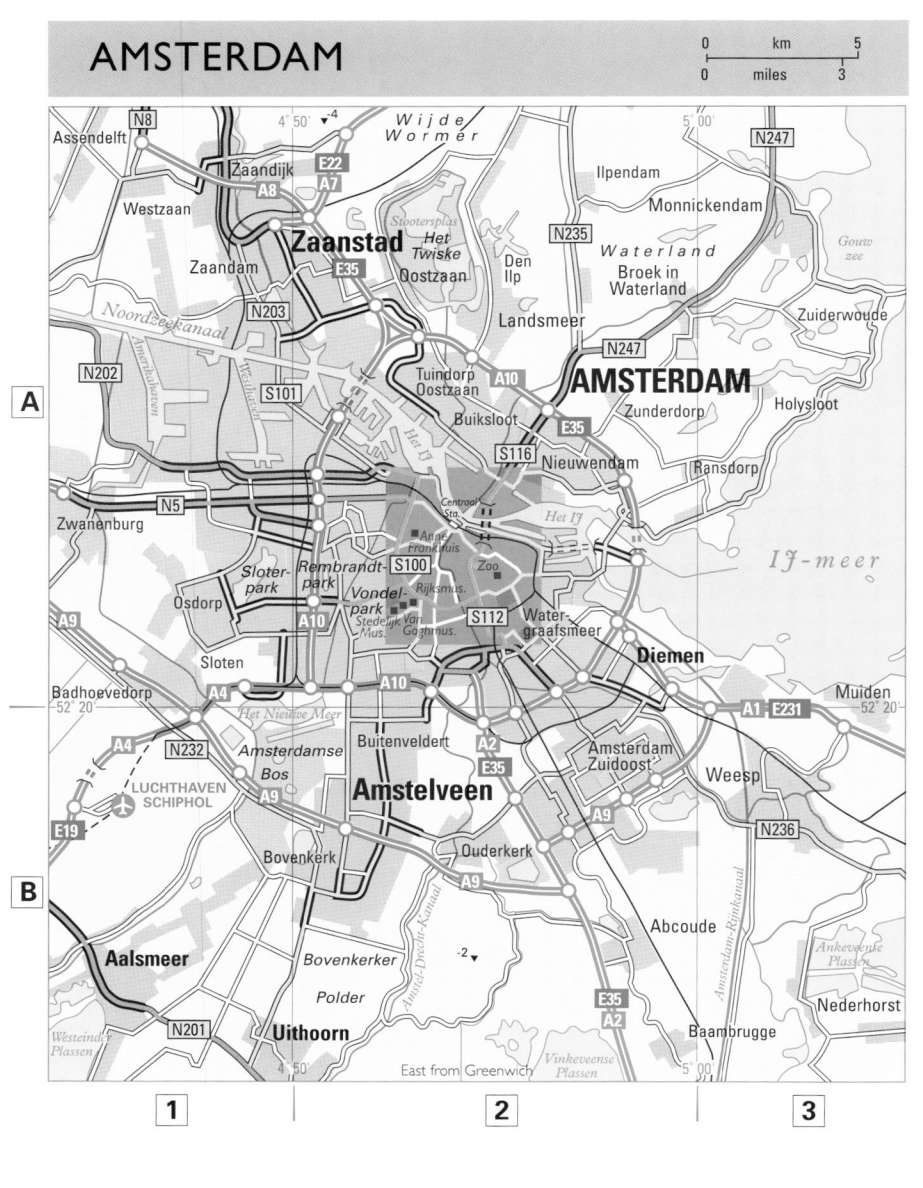

CENTRAL AMSTERDAM

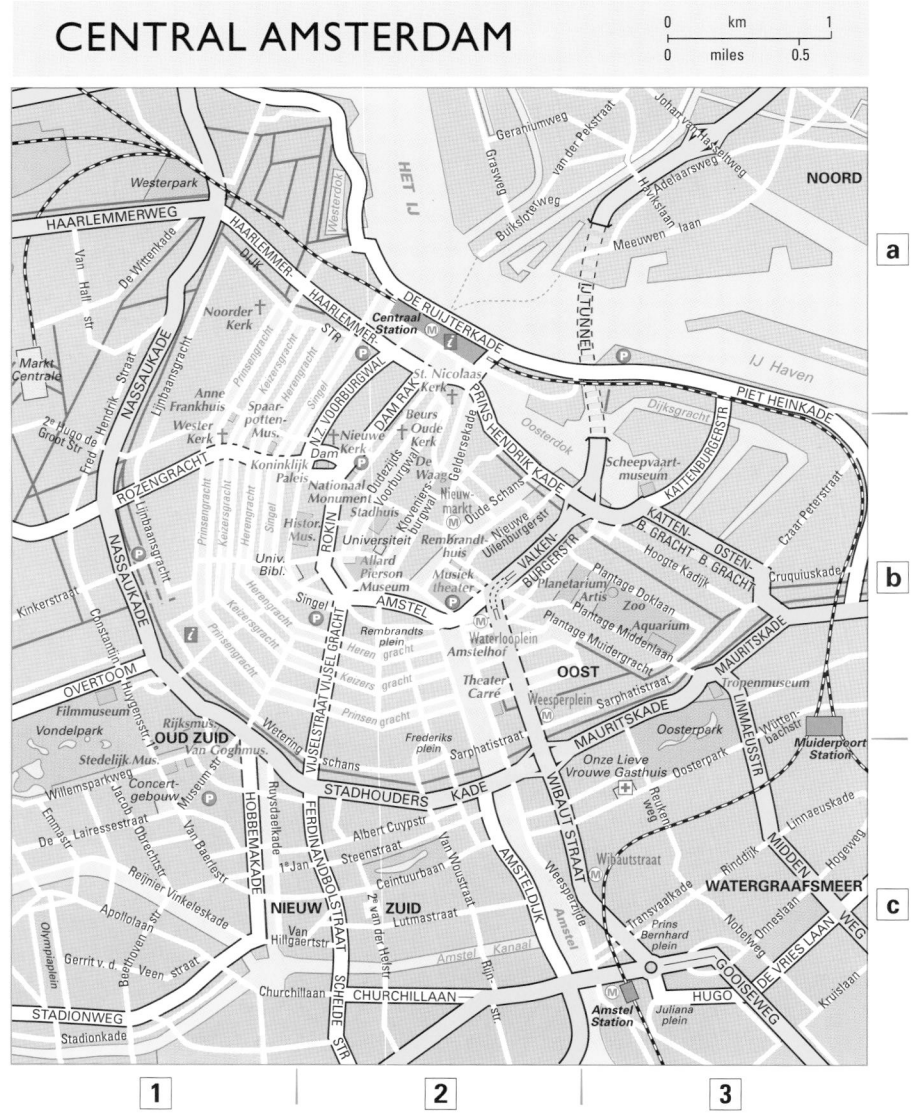

ATHENS

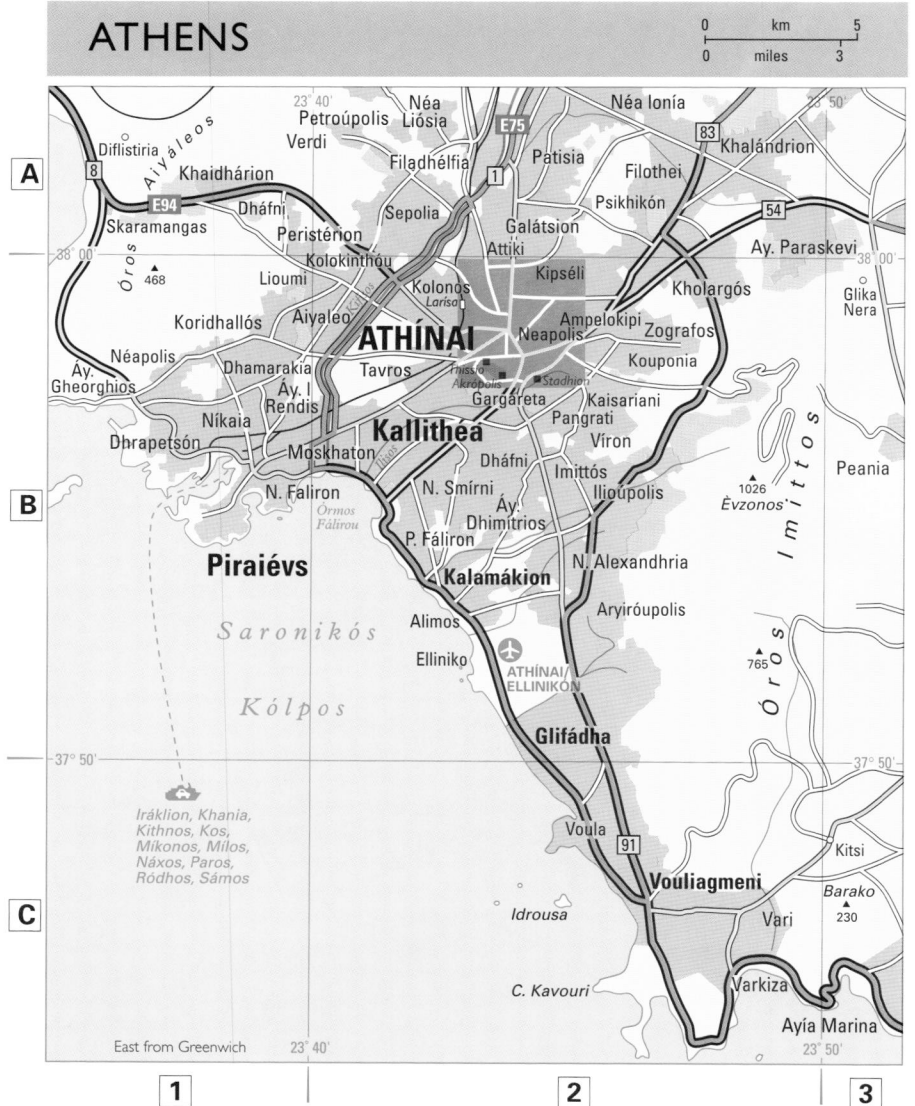

CENTRAL ATHENS

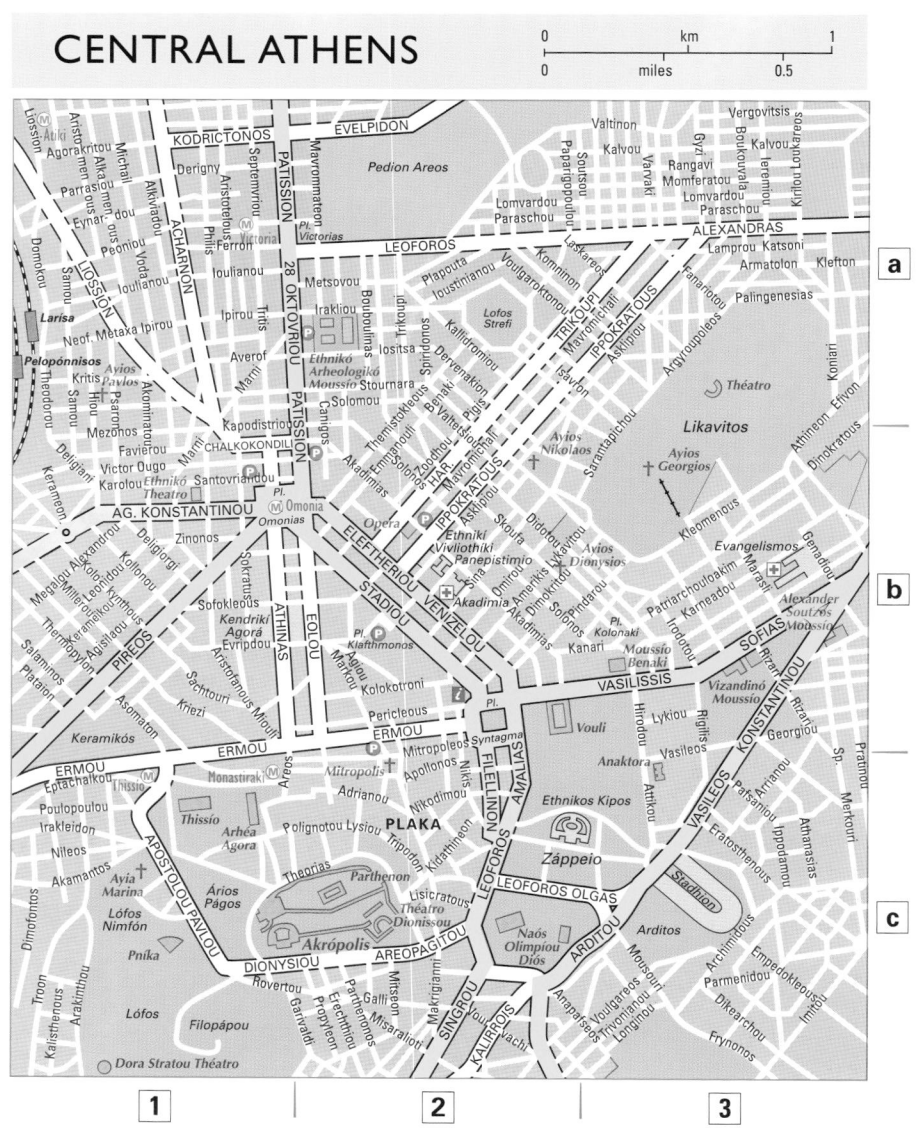

ATLANTA

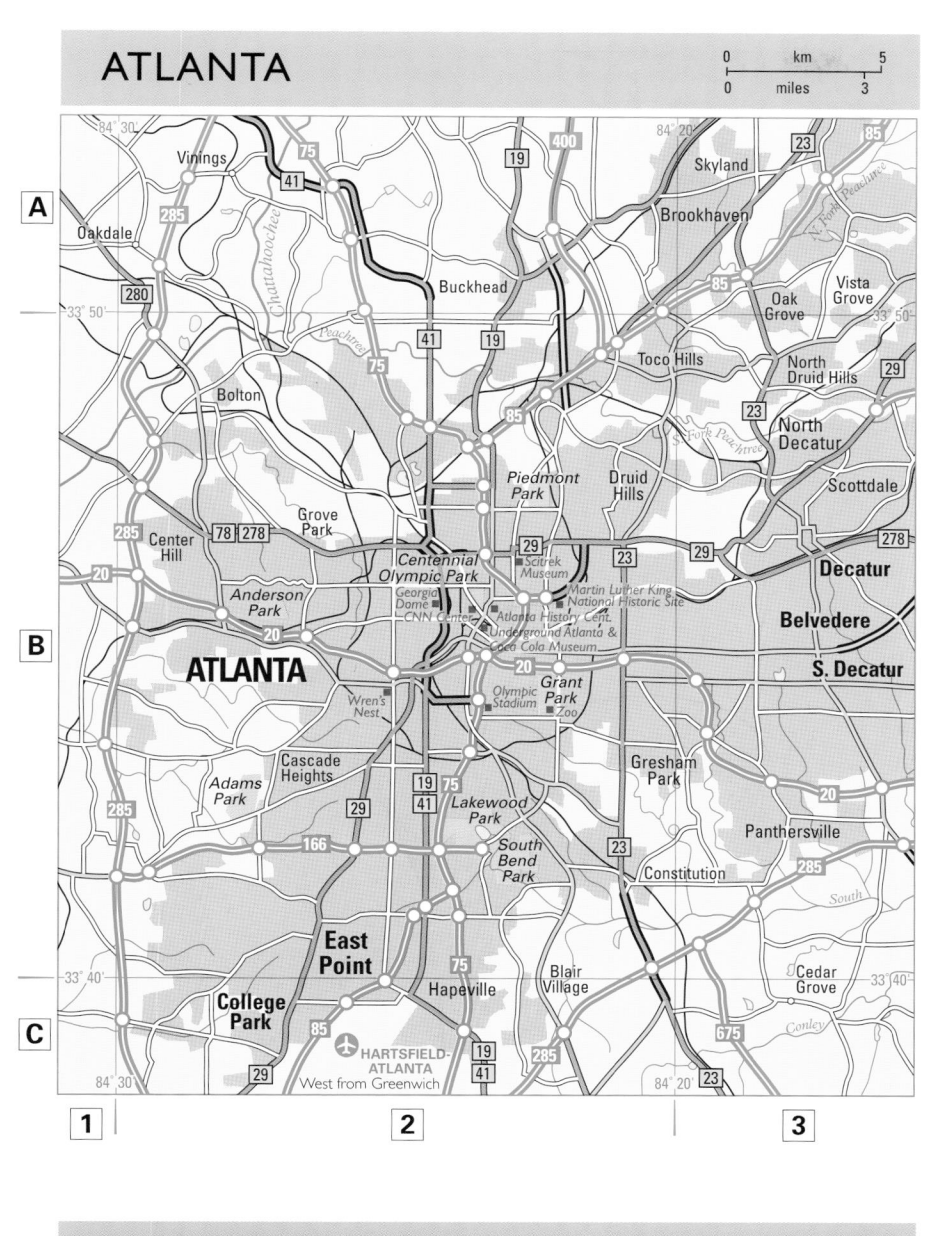

BAGHDAD

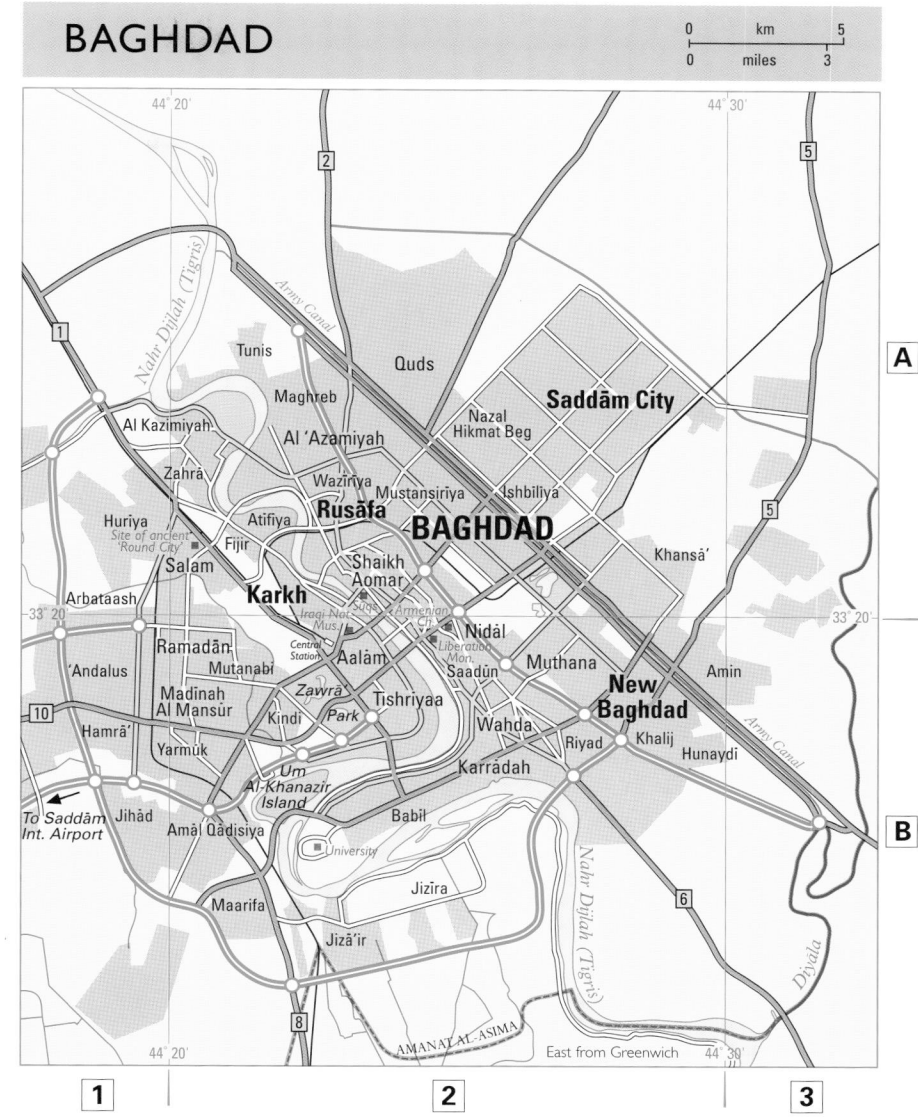

BANGKOK

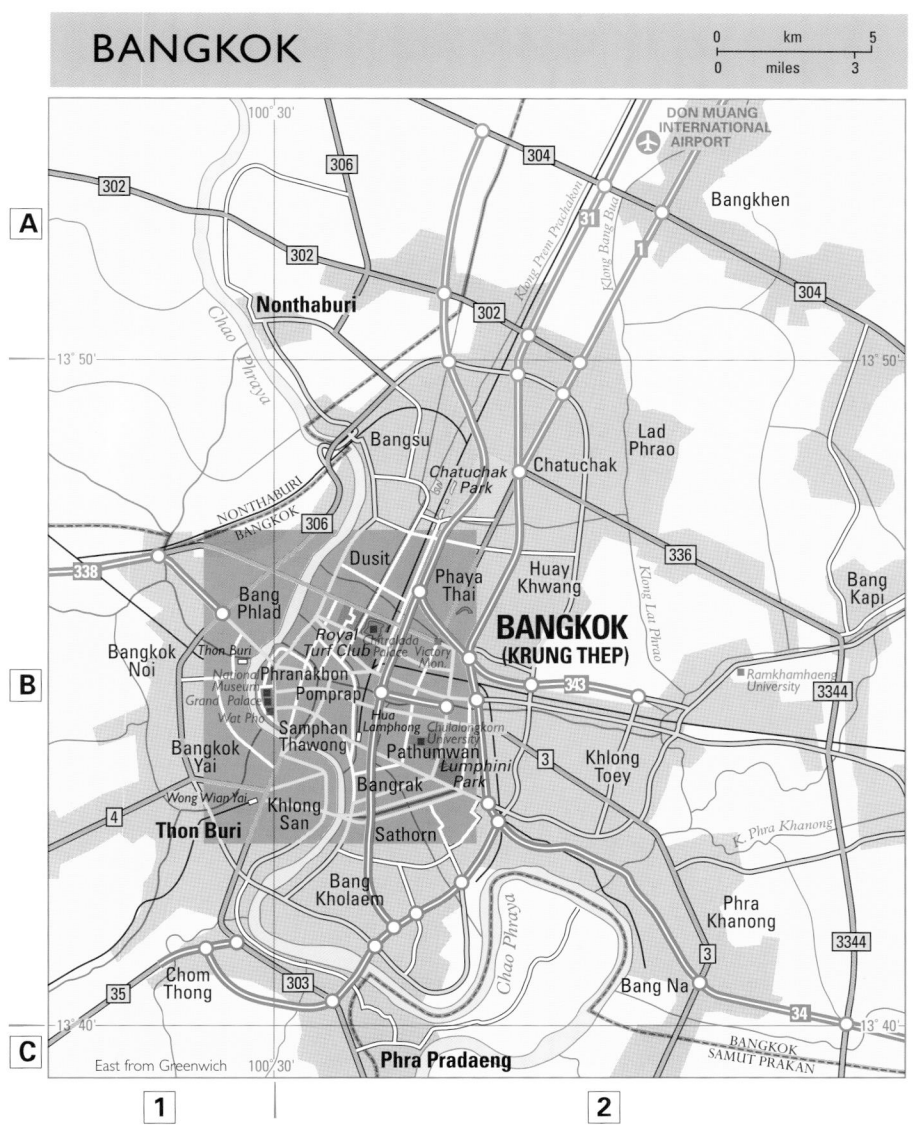

CENTRAL BANGKOK

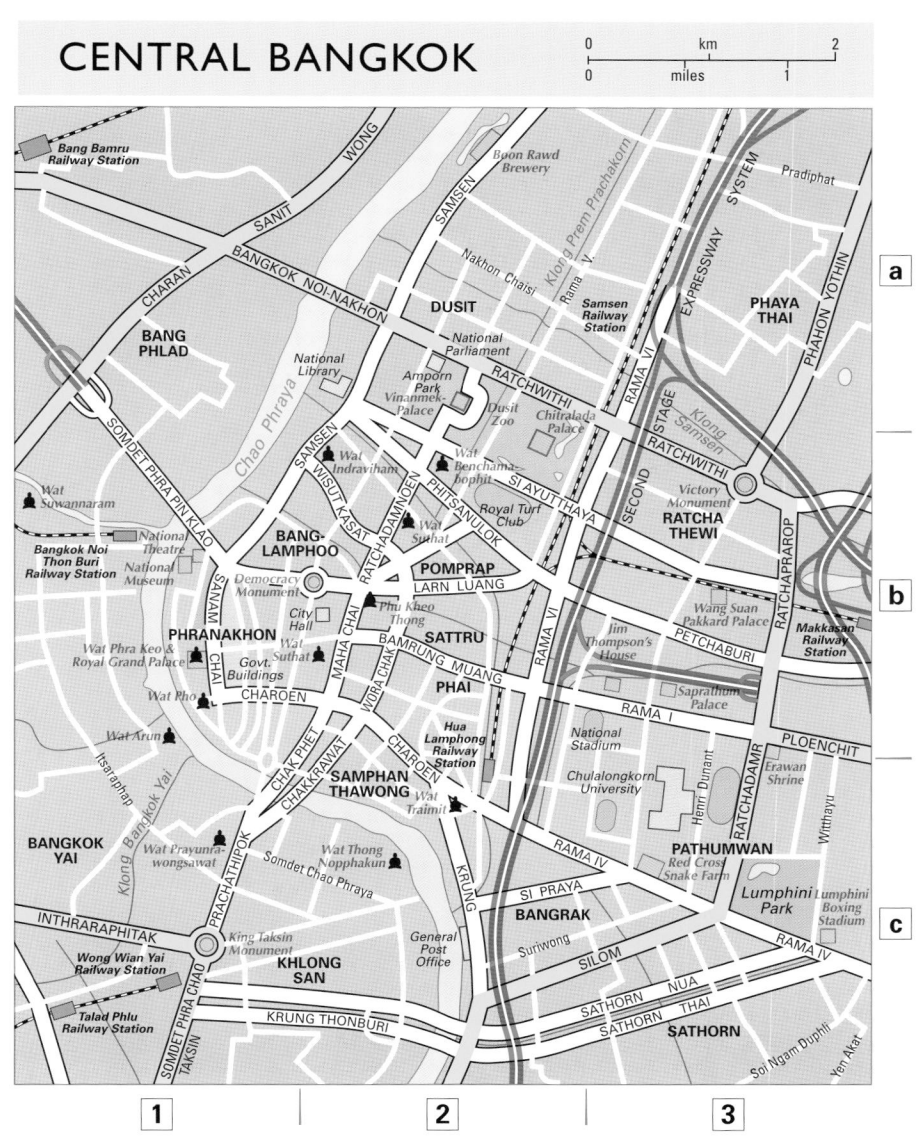

BARCELONA

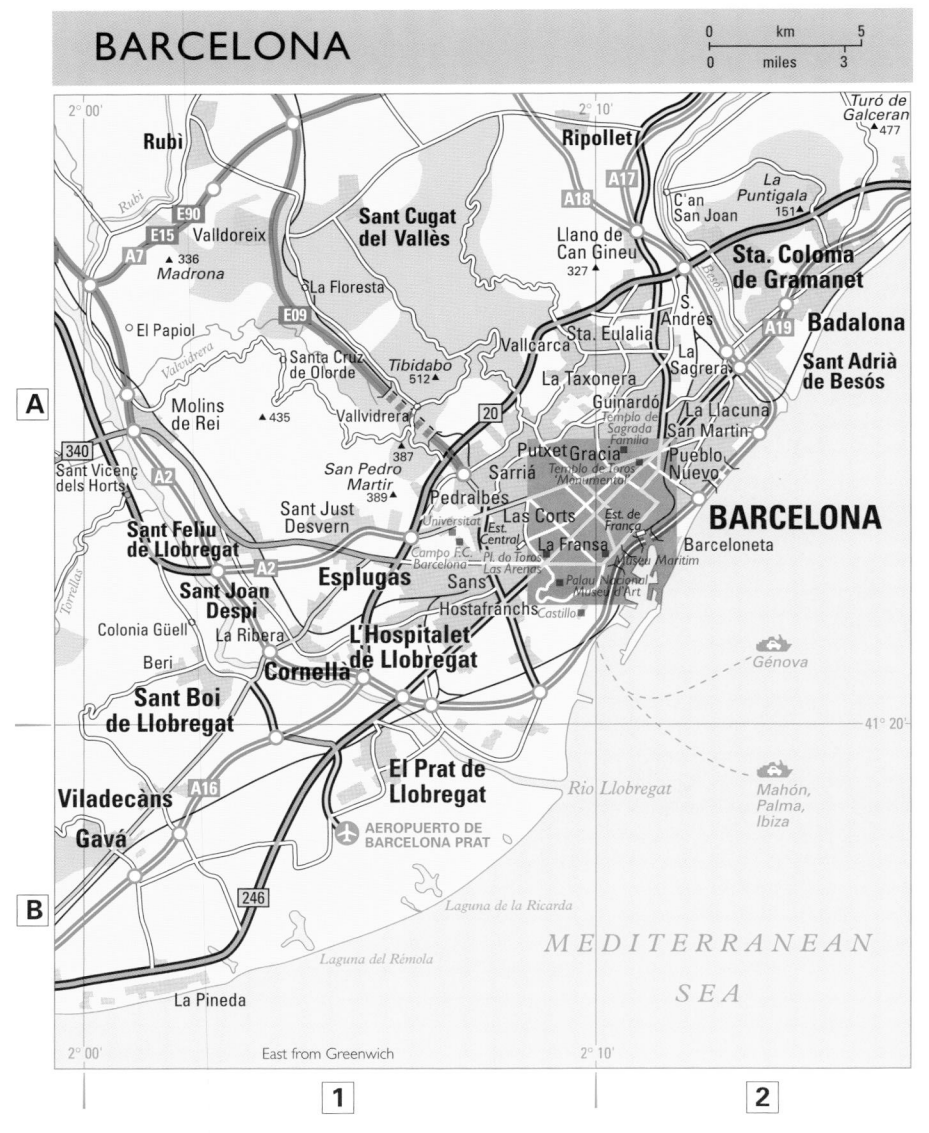

CENTRAL BARCELONA

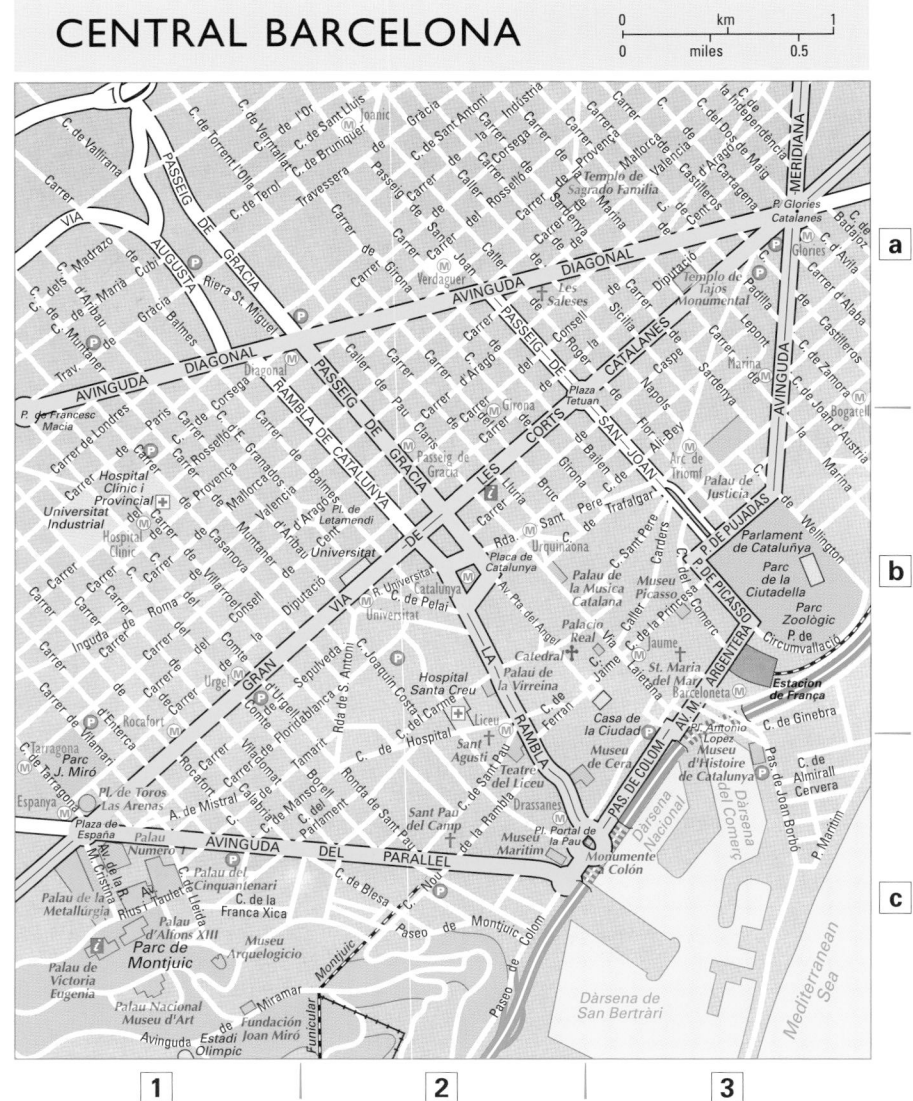

BEIJING

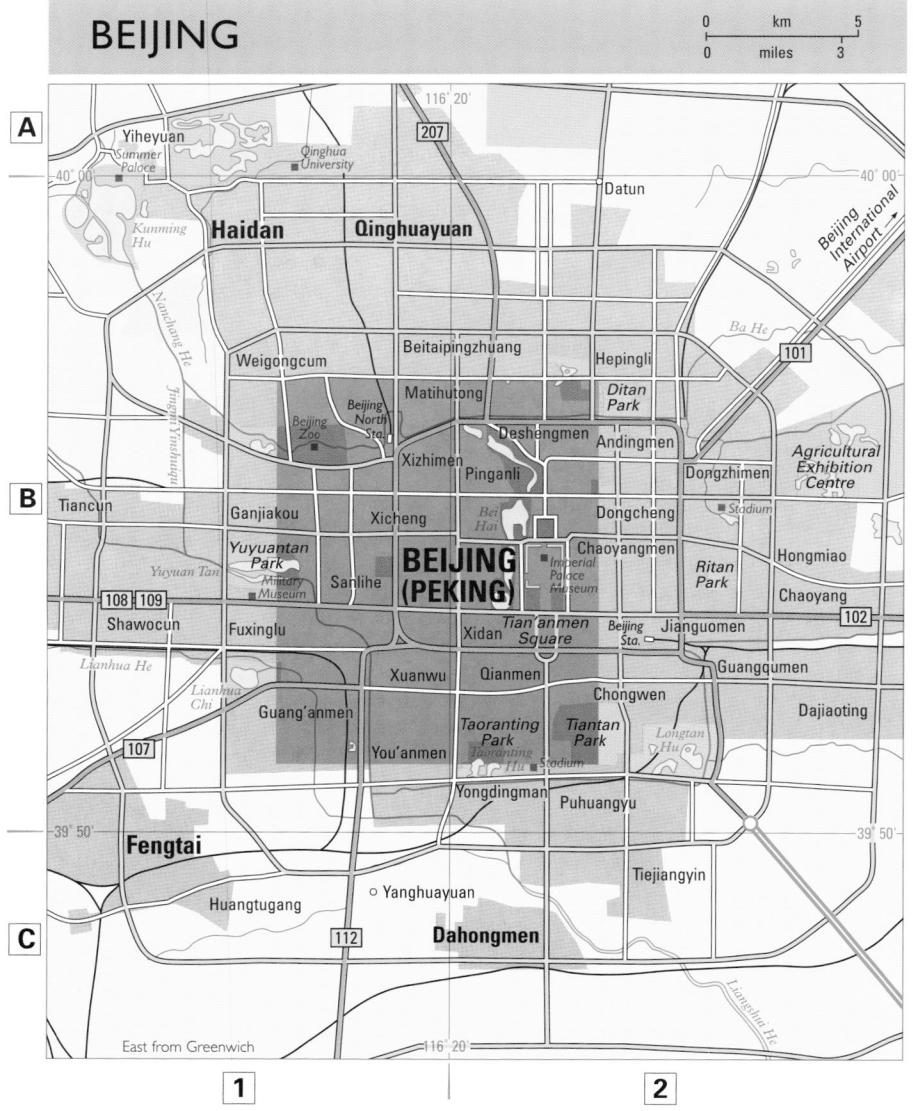

CENTRAL BEIJING

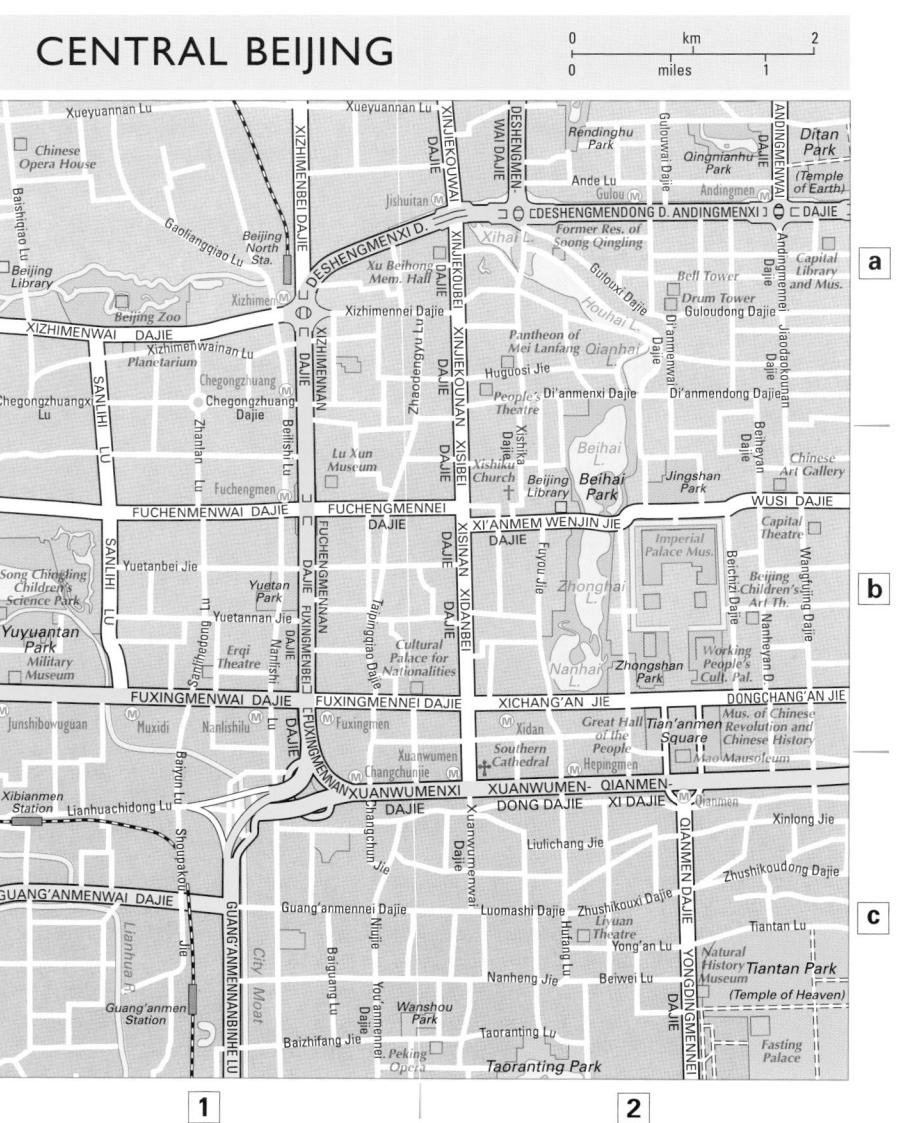

BERLIN

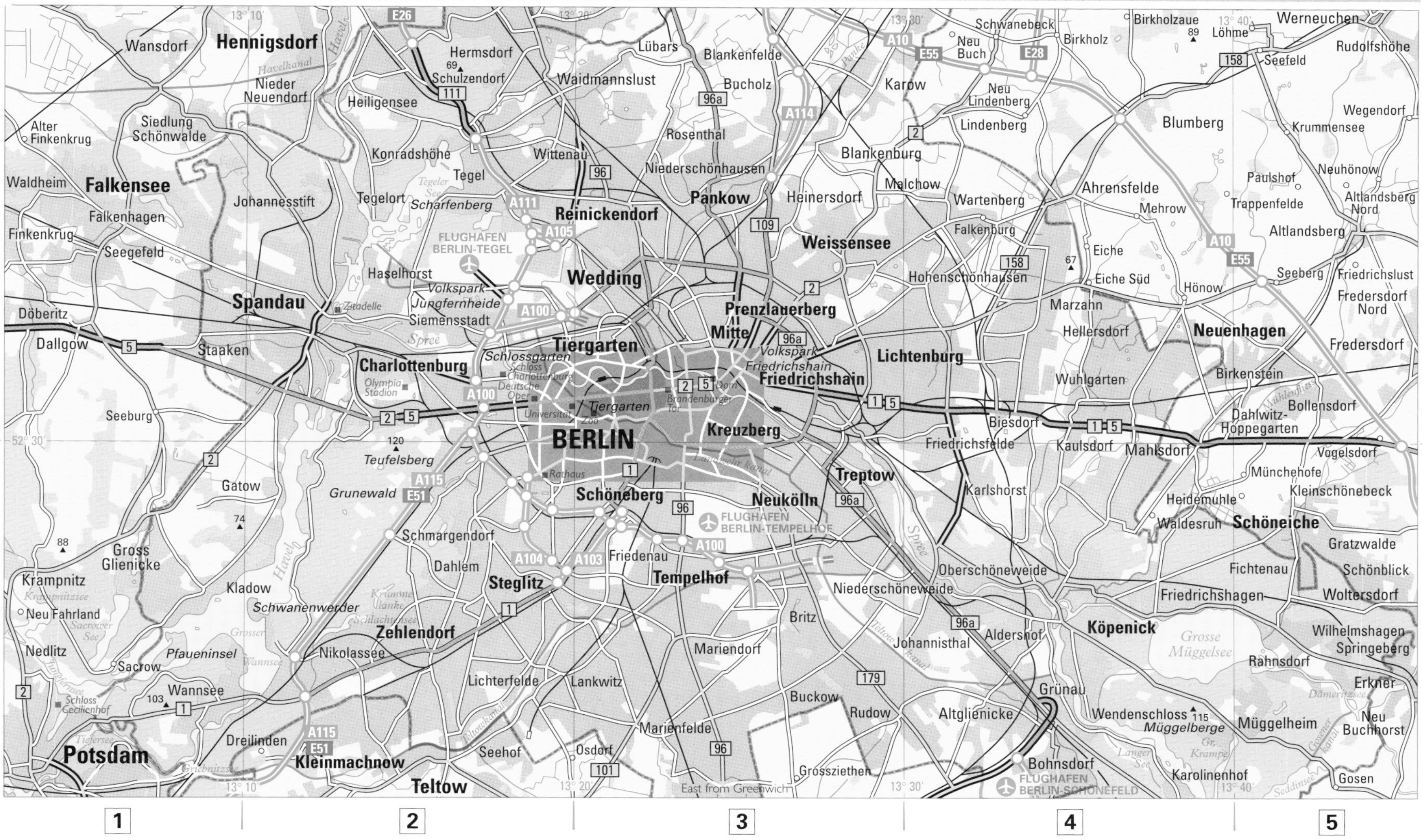

CENTRAL BERLIN

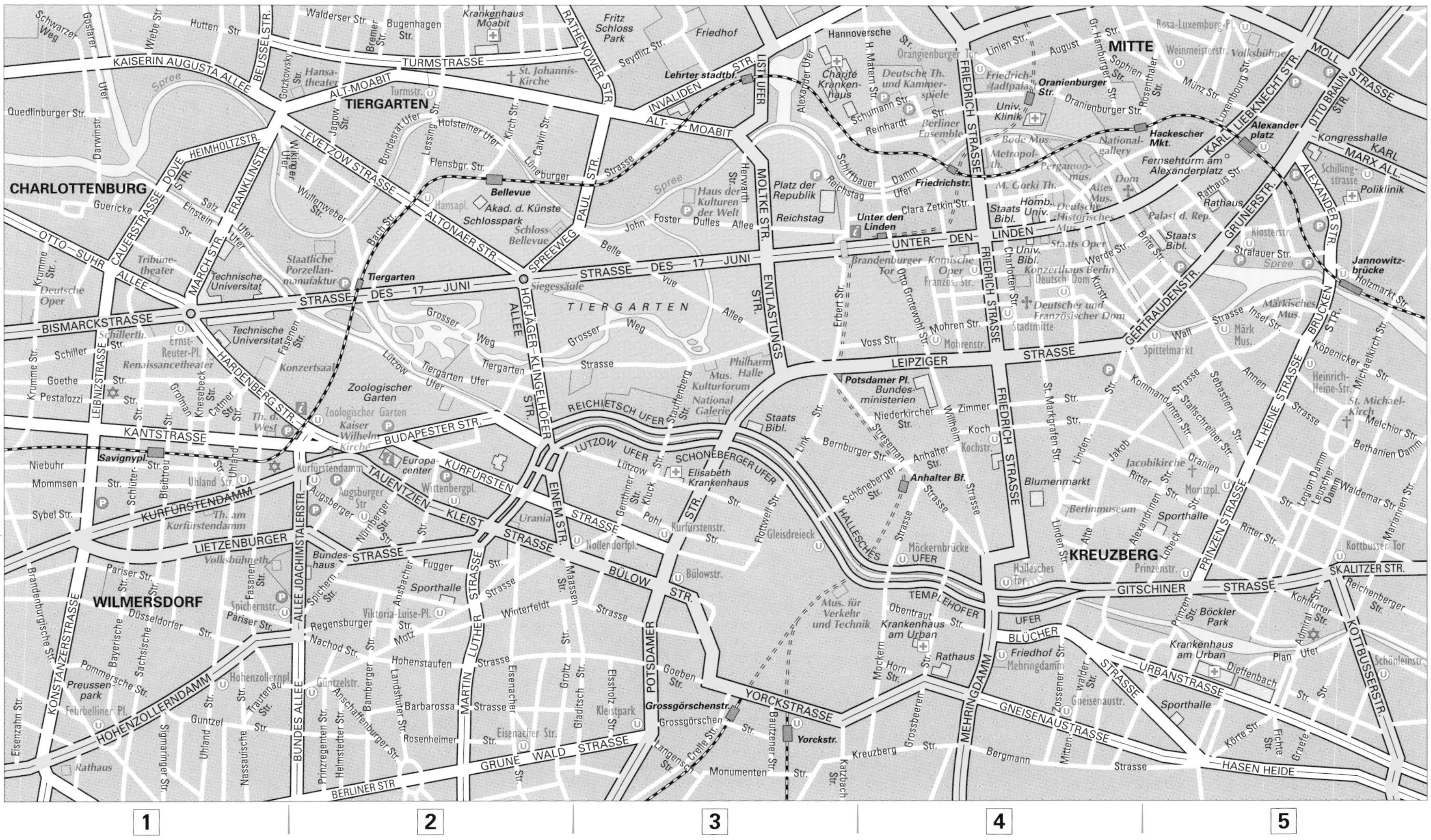

BOSTON

km 5
miles 3

Great Meadows 71° 20' Nat. Wildlife Refuge
Bedford
Burlington
HY.
71° 10'
Wakefield
North Saugus
Breakheart Reservation Greenwood
71° 00'
Spring Pond
Marblehead

East Acton
West Bedford
Woburn
Stoneham
North Res.
Lynn Woods Res.
Breeds Pond
Clifton

Yankee Division
Saugus
Lynn

2
Concord
North Lexington
Horn Pond
West Lynn
Swampscott

West Concord
LAURENCE G. HANSCOM FIELD
Minute Man Natural History Park
Cambridge St.
Winchester
Middlesex Fells Reservation
Walter D. Stone Mem. Zoo
Mt. Hood Mem. Park
Melrose
Nahant Bay

Fairhaven Hill
Lincoln
East Lexington
114
Arlington Heights
West Medford
Malden
ATLANTIC OCEAN

Fairhaven Bay
Sandy Pond
Lexington
Medford
Revere
Nahant

A
North Sudbury
South Lincoln
Concord Turnpike
Arlington
East Arlington
Tufts Univ.
Everett
Beachmont
East Point
A

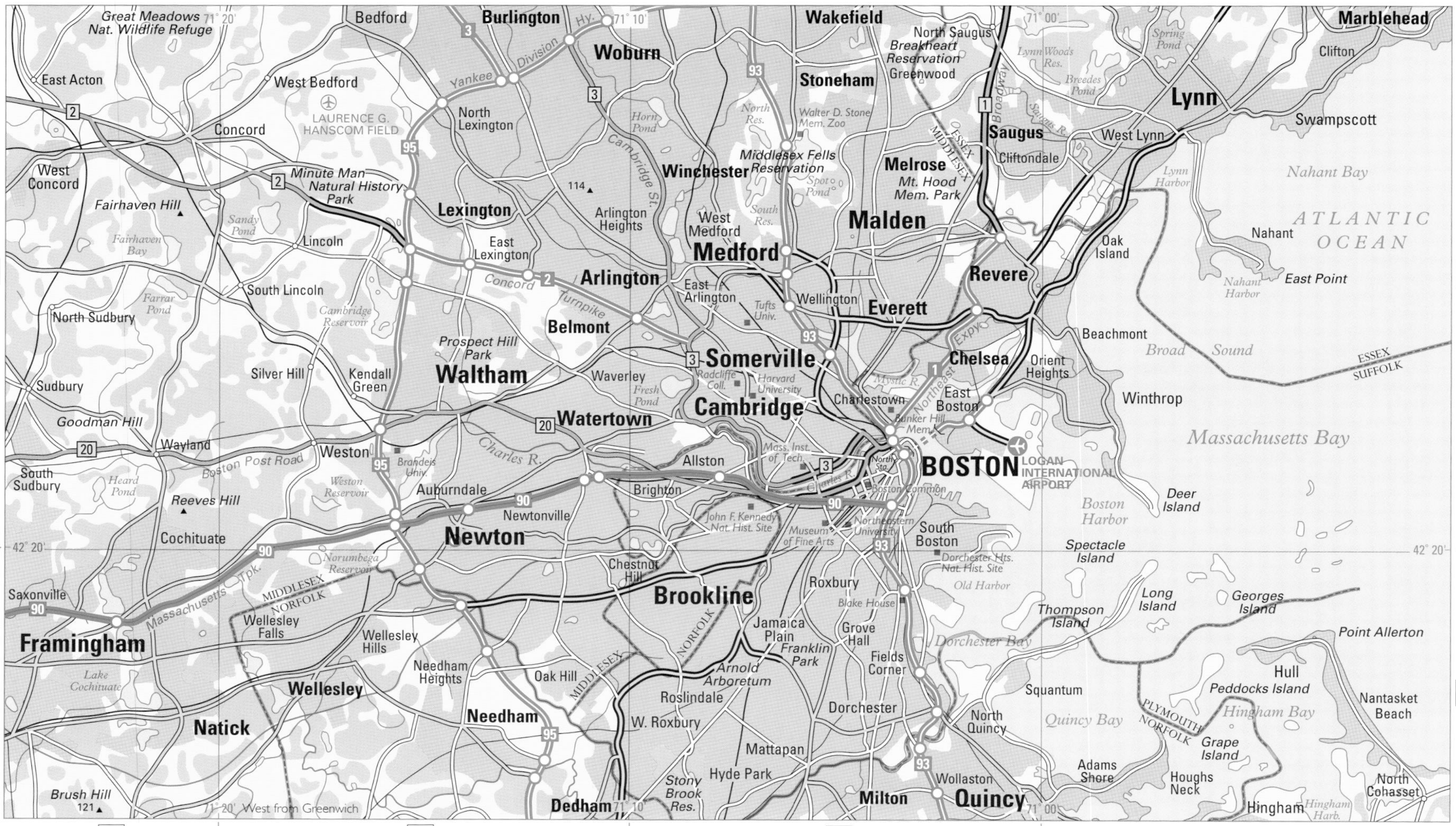

Sudbury
Farrar Pond
Belmont
Wellington
Chelsea
Orient Heights
ESSEX SUFFOLK

Goodman Hill
Prospect Hill Park
Waltham
Waverley
Fresh Pond
Radcliffe Coll.
Somerville
Harvard University
Charlestown
East Boston
Broad Sound
Winthrop

Silver Hill
Kendall Green
Watertown
Cambridge
Bunker Hill Mem.
Logan International Airport

Wayland
Weston
Auburndale
Allston
Mass. Inst. of Tech.
BOSTON
Massachusetts Bay

Heard Pond
Reeves Hill
Weston Reservoir
Newtonville
Brighton
John F. Kennedy Nat. Hist. Site
Museum of Fine Arts
South Boston
Deer Island
Boston Harbor

Cochituate
Norumbega Reservoir
Newton
Chestnut Hill
Northeastern University
Dorchester Hts. Nat. Hist. Site
Old Harbor
Spectacle Island

42° 20'
42° 20'

Saxonville
Wellesley Falls
Wellesley Hills
Brookline
Roxbury
Blake House
Grove Hall
Thompson Island
Long Island
Georges Island

B
Framingham
Needham Heights
Oak Hill
Jamaica Plain
Franklin Park
Fields Corner
Dorchester Bay
Point Allerton
B

Lake Cochituate
Wellesley
Arnold Arboretum
Roslindale
Grape Island
Hull
Peddocks Island
Nantasket Beach

Natick
Needham
W. Roxbury
Dorchester
North Quincy
Squantum
Quincy Bay
Hingham Bay

Brush Hill 121
Mattapan
Stony Brook Res.
Hyde Park
Wollaston
Adams Shore
Houghs Neck
North Cohasset

West from Greenwich
Dedham
Milton
Quincy
Hingham

1 **2** **3** **4**

BRUSSELS

km 5
miles 3

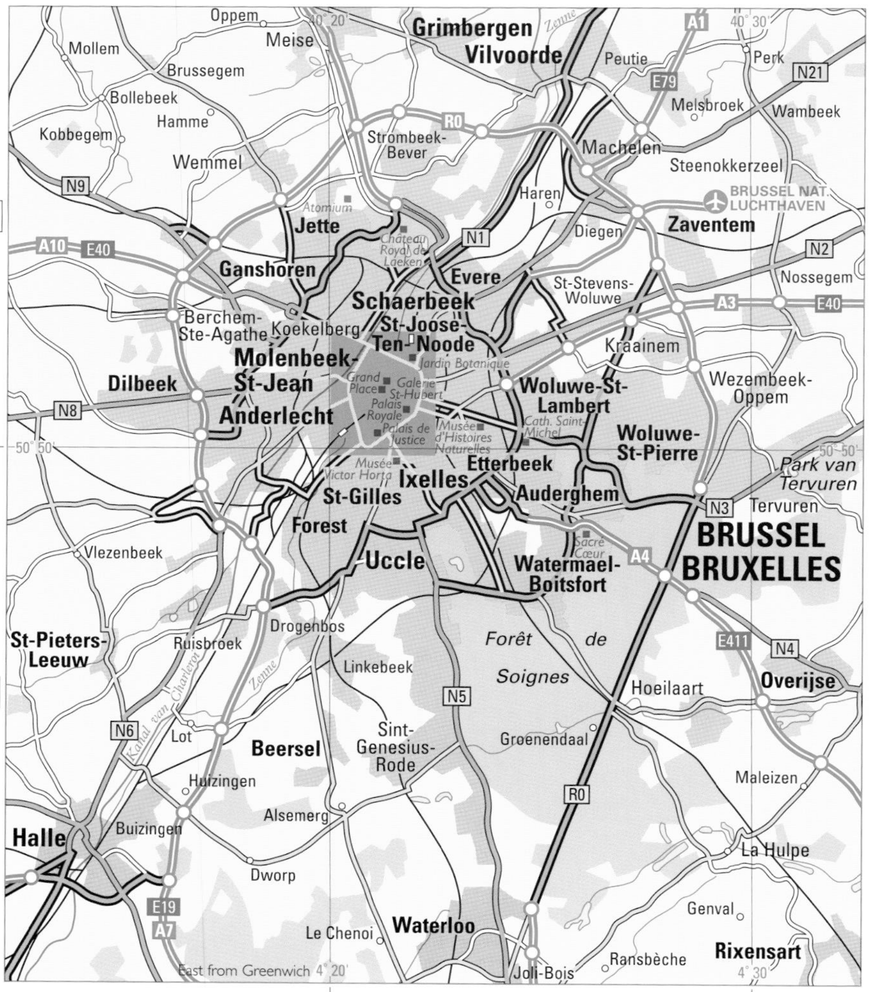

Oppem
Meise
Grimbergen
Vilvoorde
Peutie
Perk
N21
A1

Mollem
Brussegem
Bollebeek
Hamme
Wemmel
Strombeek-Bever
Melsbroek
Wambeek
E79

Kobbegem
N9
Machelen
Steenokkerzeel
BRUSSEL NAT. LUCHTHAVEN

A
Atomium
Jette
Evere
Haren
Diegen
Zaventem
N2
E40
A

Ganshoren
Berchem-Ste-Agathe
Koekelberg
Schaerbeek
St-Joose-Ten-Noode
St-Stevens-Woluwe
Nossegem

Dilbeek
Molenbeek-St-Jean
Anderlecht
Jardin Botanique
Grand Place
Palais Royale
Woluwe-St-Lambert
Coth. Saint Michel
Kraainem
Wezembeek-Oppem

N8
Ixelles
Etterbeek
Woluwe-St-Pierre
Park van Tervuren

Vlezenbeek
St-Gilles
Forest
Auderghem
BRUSSEL BRUXELLES
A4

50° 50'
St-Pieters-Leeuw
Uccle
Sacre
Watermael-Boitsfort
E411
N4

Ruisbroek
Drogenbos
Linkebeek
Forêt de Soignes
Overijse

Halle
N6
Beersel
Sint-Genesius-Rode
Groenendaal
R0

E19
A7
Buizingen
Huizingen
Alsemberg
La Hulpe

Dworp
Waterloo
Le Chenoi
Genval
Rixensart

East from Greenwich 4° 20'
Ransbèche
Joli-Bois
4° 30'

1 **2** **3**

CENTRAL BRUSSELS

km 1
miles 0.5

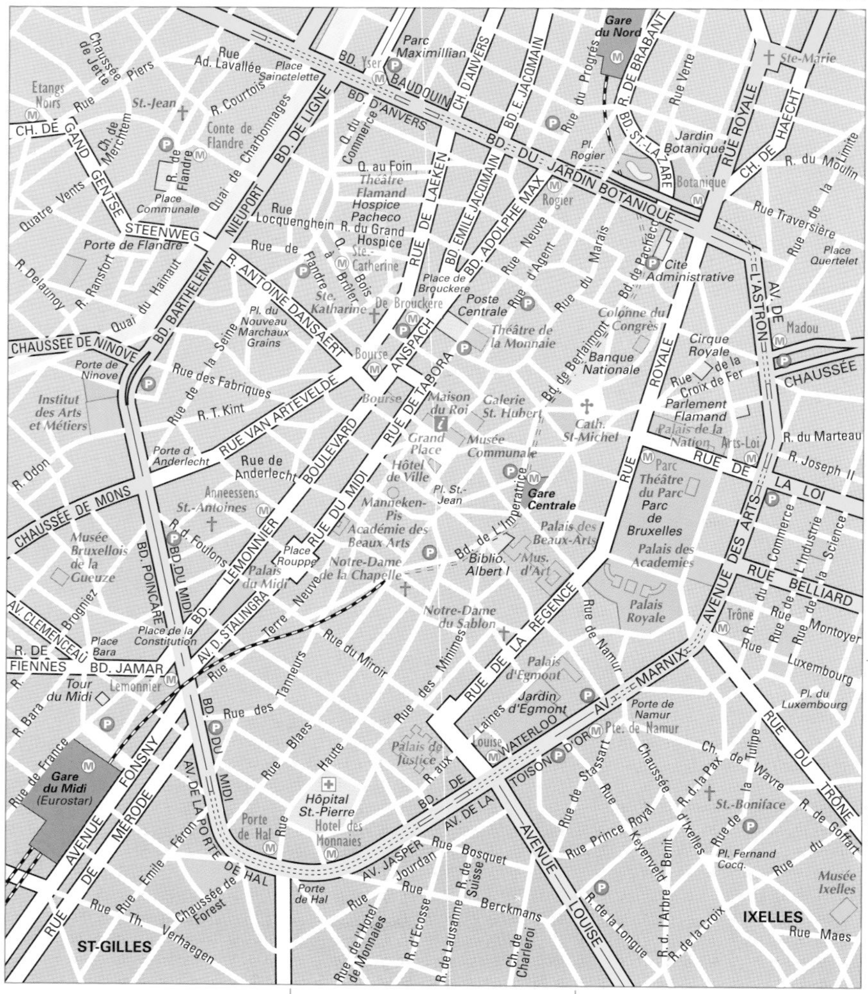

Gare du Nord
Parc Maximillien
Ste-Marie

a
Jardin Botanique
Botanique
Madou
a

Théâtre Flamand
Place de Brouckère
Colonne du Congrès
Cirque Royale
Place Quertelet

Bourse
Grand Place
Cath. St-Michel
b
Gare Centrale
Palais des Beaux-Arts
Parc de Bruxelles
Palais des Academies
R. de la Loi

Notre-Dame du Sablon
Palais Royale

Palais de Justice
Place du Grand Sablon
Jardin d'Egmont
Porte de Namur

Gare du Midi (Eurostar)
Hôpital St-Pierre
Palais de Justice
c
Louise
IXELLES
Musée Ixelles

ST-GILLES
Porte de Hal

1 **2** **3**

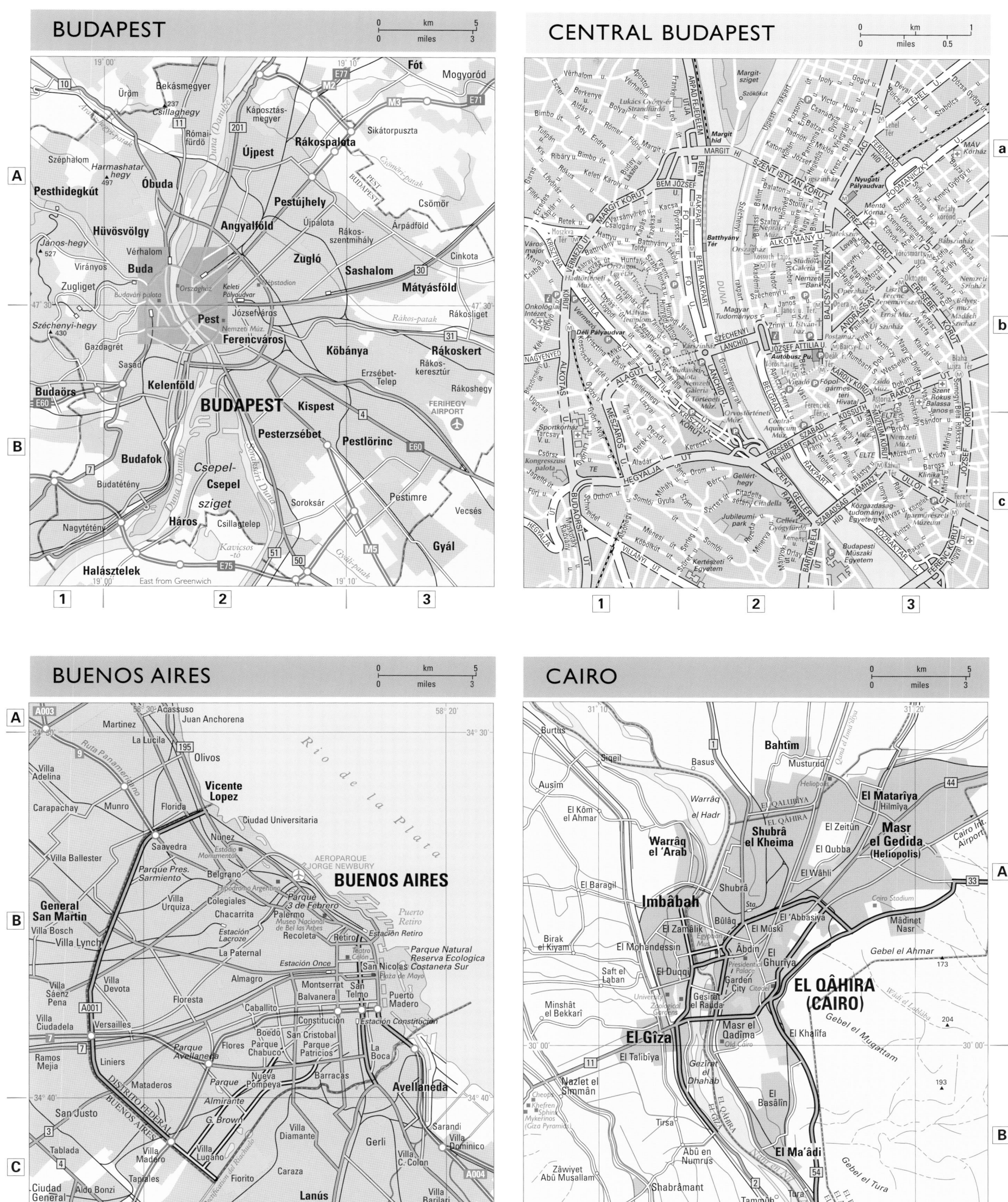

CALCUTTA (KOLKATA)

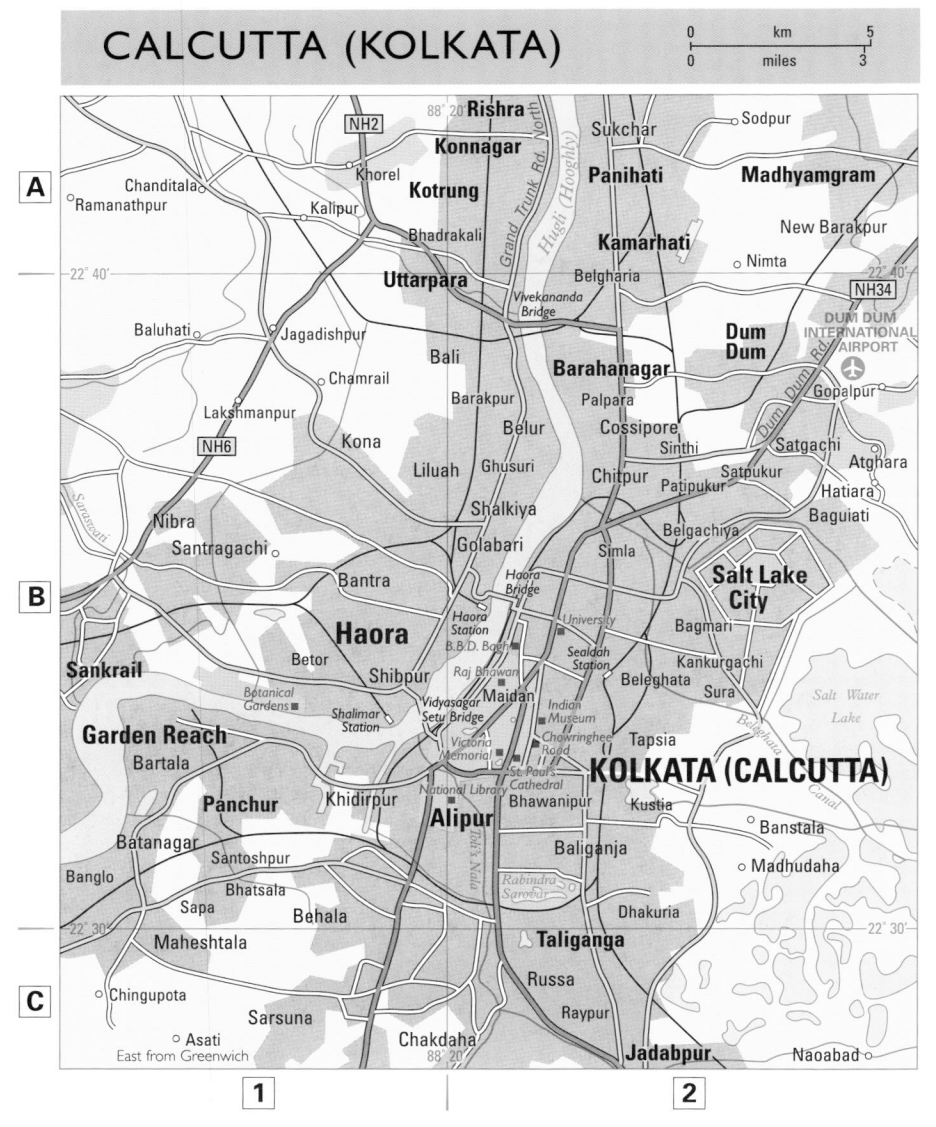

CANTON

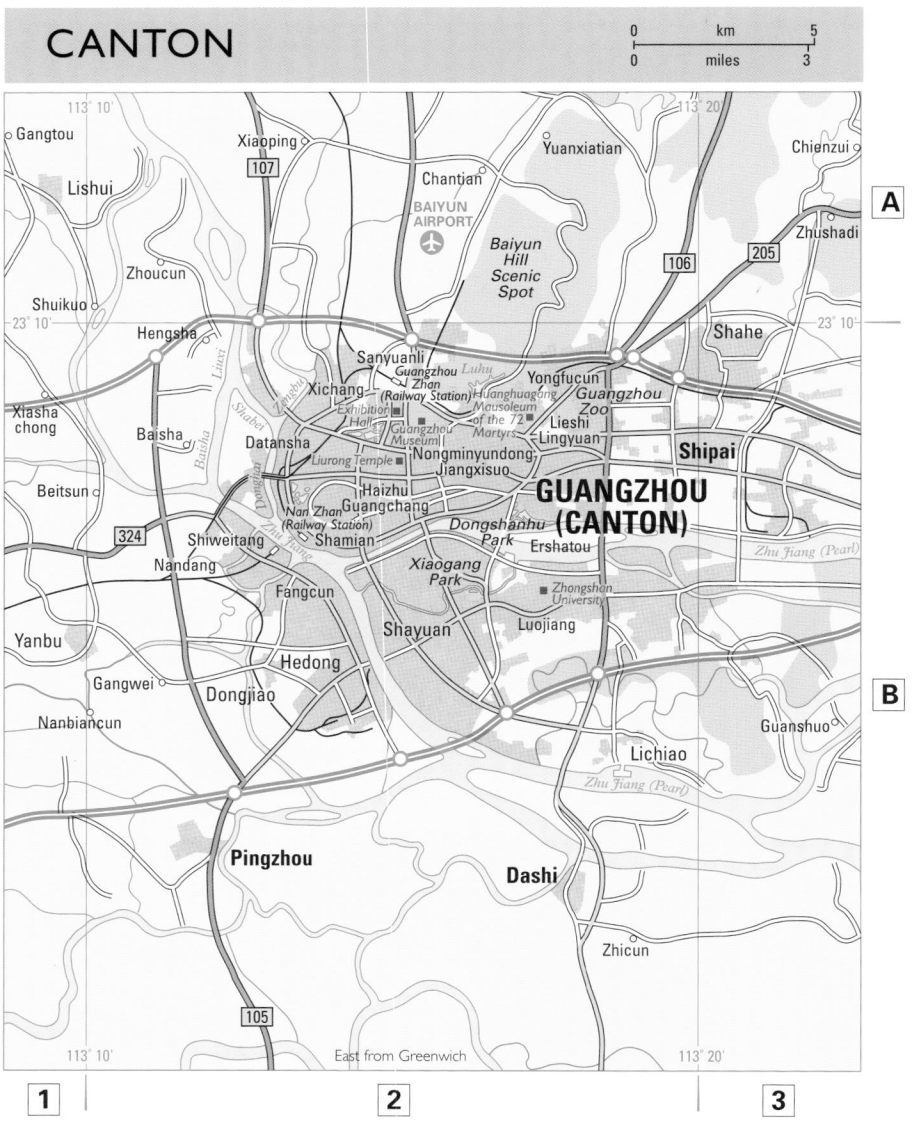

CAPE TOWN

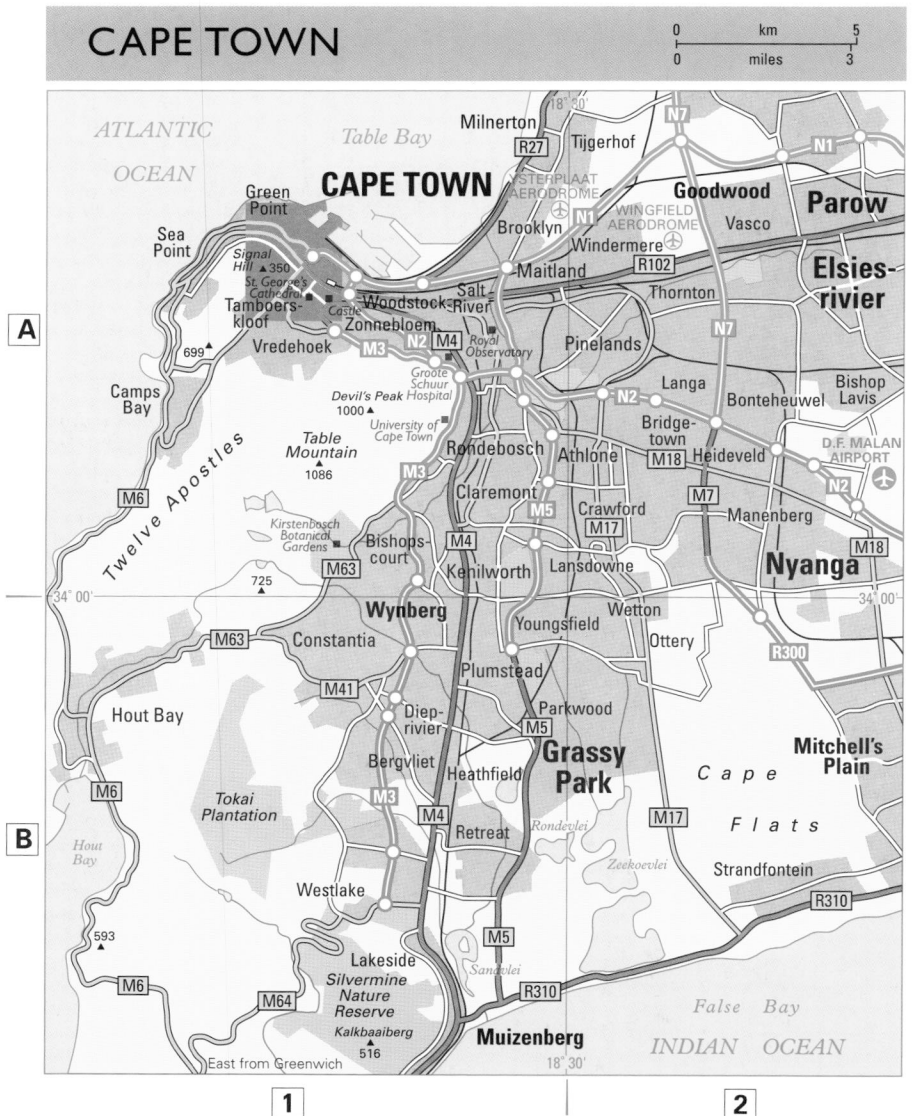

CENTRAL CAPE TOWN

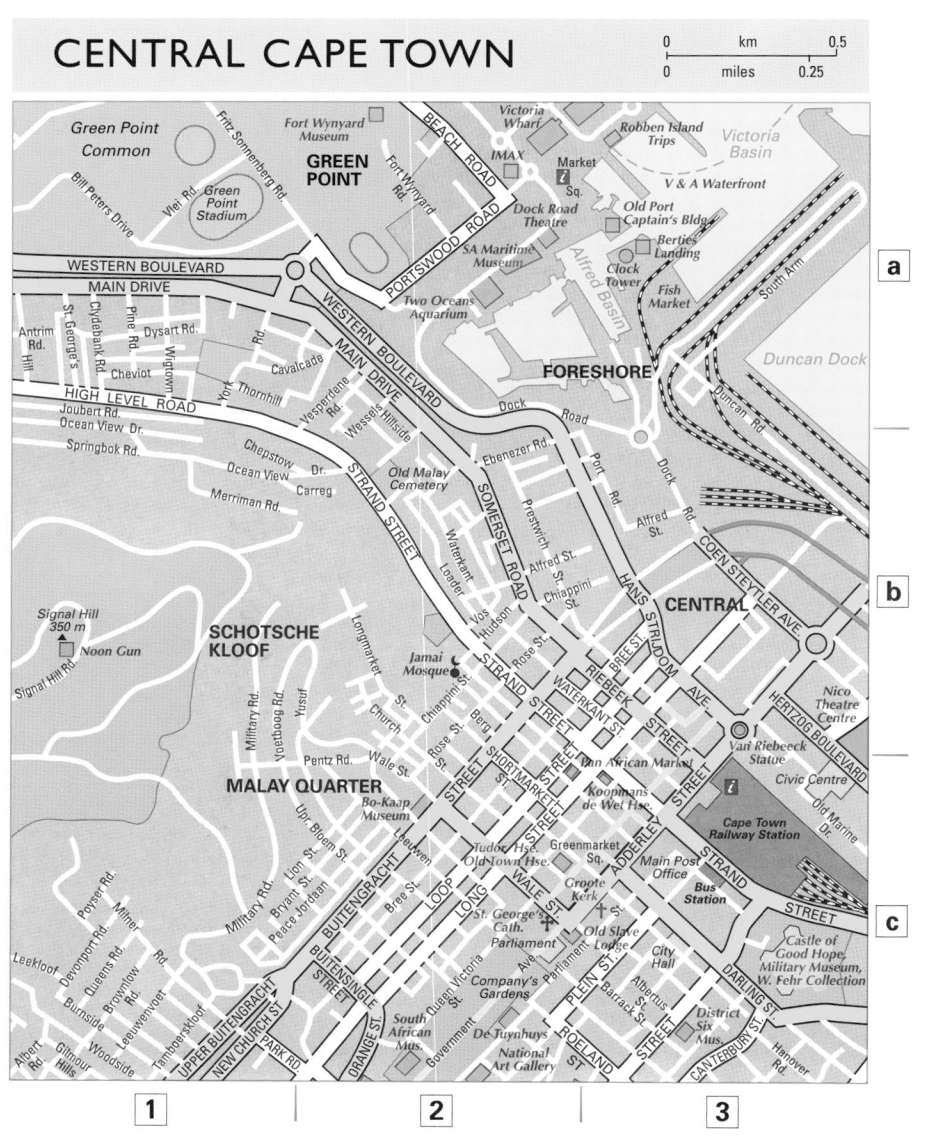

CHICAGO

km 0 — 5
miles 0 — 3

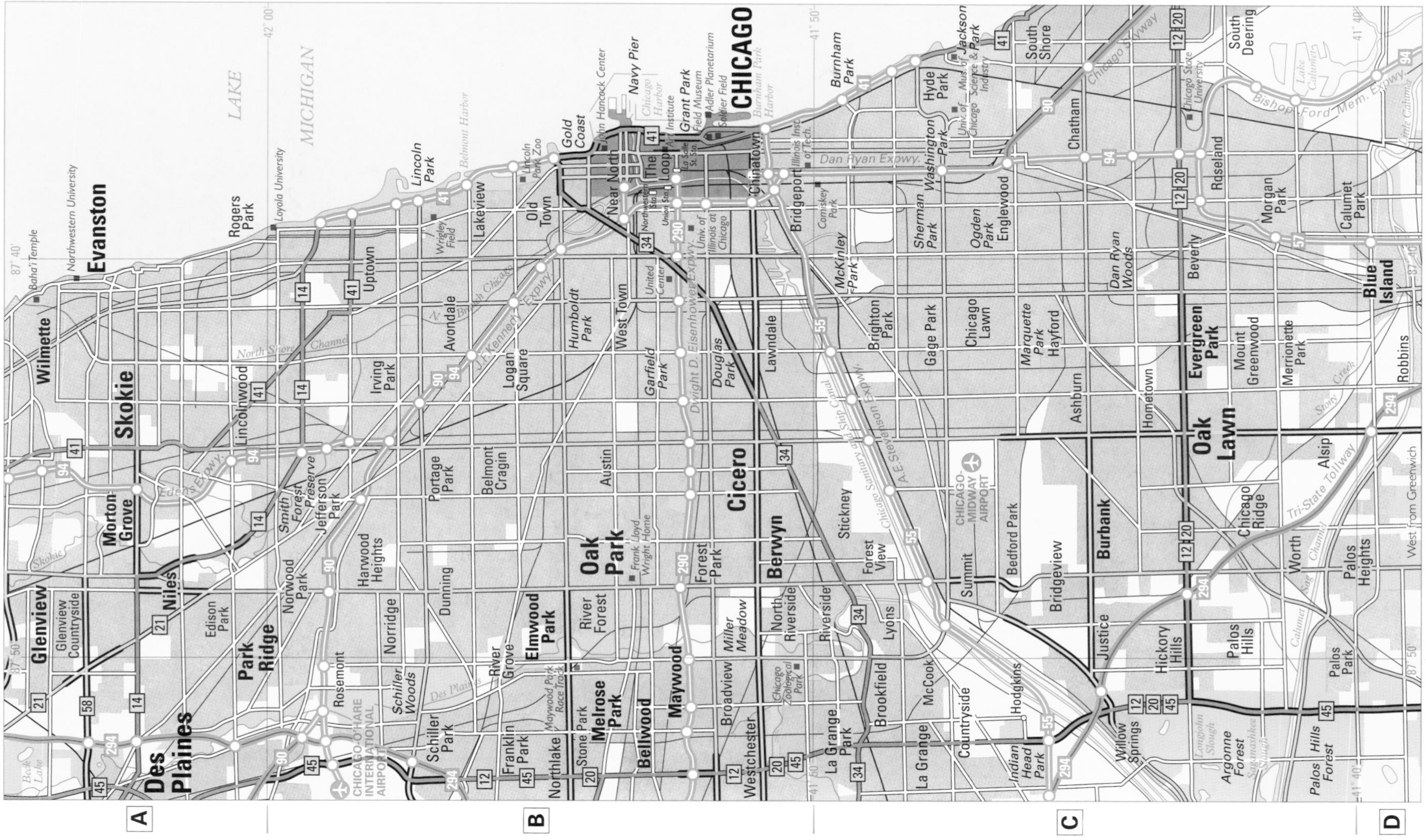

LAKE MICHIGAN

CHICAGO

Evanston
Wilmette
Skokie
Glenview
Morton Grove
Niles
Park Ridge
Des Plaines
Glenview Countryside
Edison Park
Norridge
Harwood Heights
Norwood Park
Schiller Park
Franklin Park
Melrose Park
Bellwood
Maywood
Broadview
Westchester
La Grange Park
La Grange
Countryside
Indian Head Park
Willow Springs
Hodgkins
McCook
Brookfield
Riverside
North Riverside
Forest View
Lyons
Stickney
Summit
Bedford Park
Bridgeview
Justice
Hickory Hills
Palos Hills
Palos Park
Palos Heights
Worth
Chicago Ridge
Alsip
Burbank
Oak Lawn
Hometown
Evergreen Park
Mount Greenwood
Merrionette Park
Robbins
Blue Island
Beverly
Morgan Park
Calumet Park
Roseland
Chatham
South Shore
South Deering
Hyde Park
Washington Park
Englewood
Ogden Park
Sherman Park
Gage Park
Chicago Lawn
Marquette Park
Ashburn
Brighton Park
McKinley Park
Bridgeport
Chinatown
Cicero
Berwyn
Oak Park
Elmwood Park
River Forest
River Grove
Stone Park
Northlake
Schiller Woods
Rosemont
Dunning
Portage Park
Belmont Cragin
Austin
Lawndale
Douglas Park
Garfield Park
Humboldt Park
West Town
Logan Square
Avondale
Irving Park
Uptown
Lakeview
Old Town
Gold Coast
Near North
The Loop
Grant Park
Lincoln Park
Lincolnwood
Rogers Park
Lincoln Park Zoo
Wrigley Field
Navy Pier
Burnham Park
Jackson Park
Chicago Science & Industry
Adler Planetarium
Soldier Field
Dan Ryan Woods

CHICAGO–O'HARE INTERNATIONAL AIRPORT
CHICAGO–MIDWAY AIRPORT

Northwestern University
Loyola University
Baha'i Temple
Univ. of Illinois at Chicago
Frank Lloyd Wright Home
Maywood Park Race Track
Argonne National Laboratory
Palos Hills Forest

Dan Ryan Expwy.
Kennedy Expwy.
Eisenhower Expwy.
Dwight D. Eisenhower Expwy.
A. E. Stevenson Expwy.
Bishop Ford Mem. Expwy.
Chicago Skyway
Tri-State Tollway
West Tom Greenwich

Des Plaines River
North Shore Channel
Chicago Sanitary & Ship Canal
Calumet River

CENTRAL CHICAGO

km 0 — 1
miles 0 — 0.5

LAKE MICHIGAN

Outer Harbor
Navy Pier
Olive Park
Lake Point Tower
Ohio St Beach
Streeter Dr
Oak St Beach
GOLD COAST
John Hancock Center
Water Tower Place
NEAR NORTH
Wrigley Bldg
Tribune Tower
Northwestern Memorial Hosp.
Merchandise Mart
RIVER NORTH
Chicago River
North Branch
South Branch
Chicago River
Northwestern Sta.
Union Sta.
Main Post Office
Opera House
City Hall & County Bldg
Marshall Field's
Prudential Building
Randolph St. Sta.
Van Buren St. Sta.
La Salle St. Sta.
THE LOOP
PRINTER'S ROW
SOUTH LOOP
CHINATOWN
Grant Park
Art Institute of Chicago
Buckingham Fountain
Roosevelt Road Sta.
Shedd Aquarium
Adler Planetarium
Field Museum of Nat. History
Soldier Field
Burnham Park
Burnham Park Harbor
Merrill C. Meigs Field
McCormack Place East
McCormack Place West
Chicago Harbor
Chicago Yacht Club

N LAKE SHORE DRIVE
S LAKE SHORE DRIVE
SOUTH LAKE SHORE DRIVE EAST
SOUTH LAKE SHORE DRIVE WEST
E SOLIDARITY DR
LAKE SHORE DR E

N Larrabee Street
N Hudson Avenue
N Kingsbury St
New Orleans St
N Clark St
N LaSalle St
N Dearborn St
N State Street
N Wabash
N Rush St
N Michigan Avenue
N Wells St
N Franklin St
E Division St
E Oak St
E Chestnut St
E Delaware Pl
E Chicago Avenue
E Superior St
E Huron St
E Erie St
E Ontario St
E Ohio St
E Grand Ave
E Illinois St
McClurg Court
Fairbanks Court
Columbus Drive
Michigan Avenue
N Wacker Dr
S Wacker Dr
W Wacker Dr
E Wacker Drive
Lake St
Randolph
Washington
Madison
Monroe Drive
Jackson Drive
Adams St
Congress Drive
Congress Pkwy
Van Buren St
Harrison St
W Polk St
Roosevelt Road
Cermak Road
S Michigan Avenue
S Wabash Ave
S State Street
S Clark Street
S Dearborn
S Wells Street
S Franklin
S Canal Street
S Clinton
Wentworth Ave
Archer Ave
S Prairie Ave
S Calumet Ave
Indiana Avenue
W 14th St
W 16th St
W 18th St
W 21st St

COPYRIGHT PHILIP'S

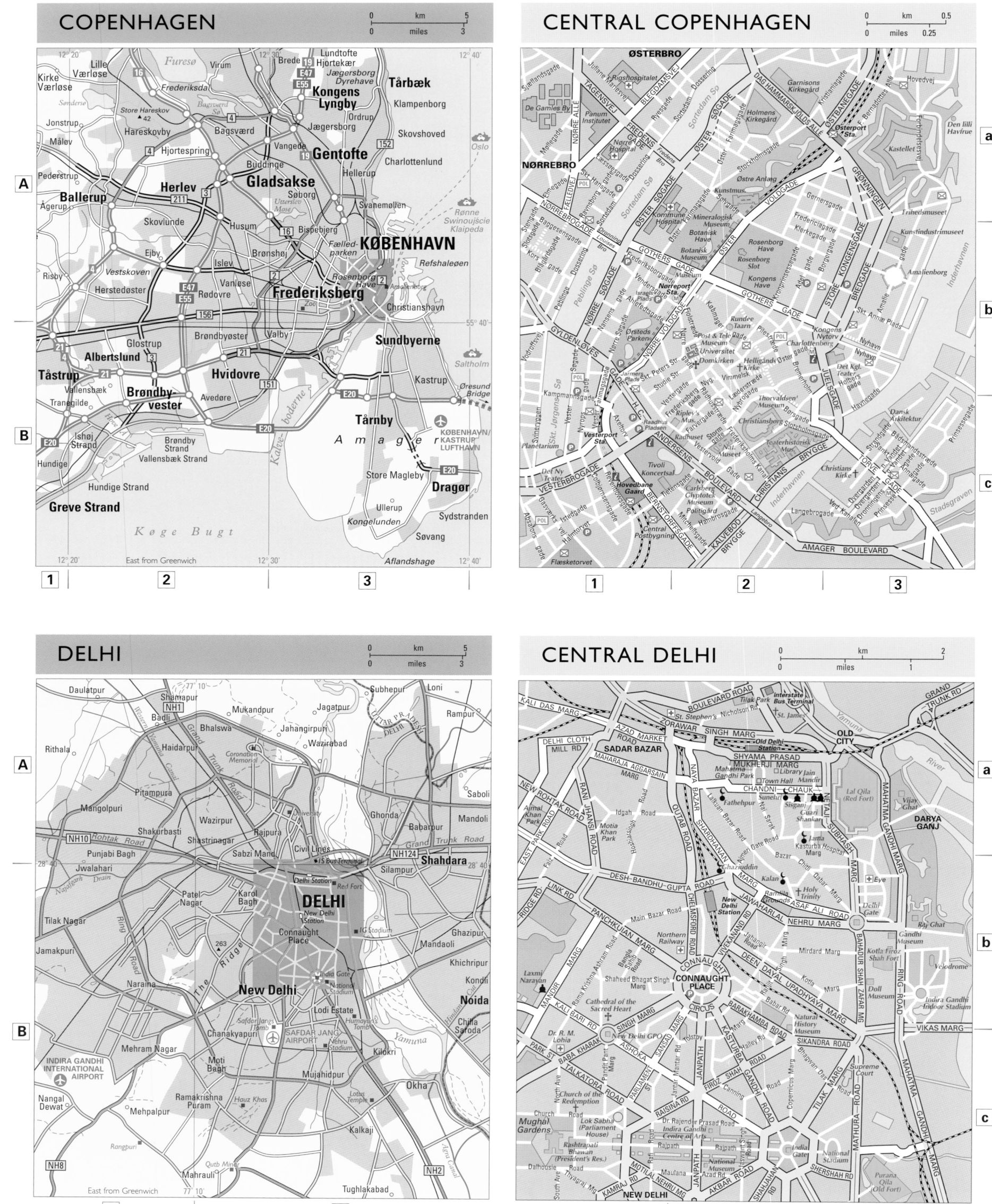

COPENHAGEN

km 5
miles 3

CENTRAL COPENHAGEN

km 0.5
miles 0.25

ØSTERBRO

a

NØRREBRO

b

c

1 2 3

DELHI

km 5
miles 3

CENTRAL DELHI

km 2
miles 1

OLD CITY

a

DARYA GANJ

b

CONNAUGHT PLACE

c

NEW DELHI

1 2 3

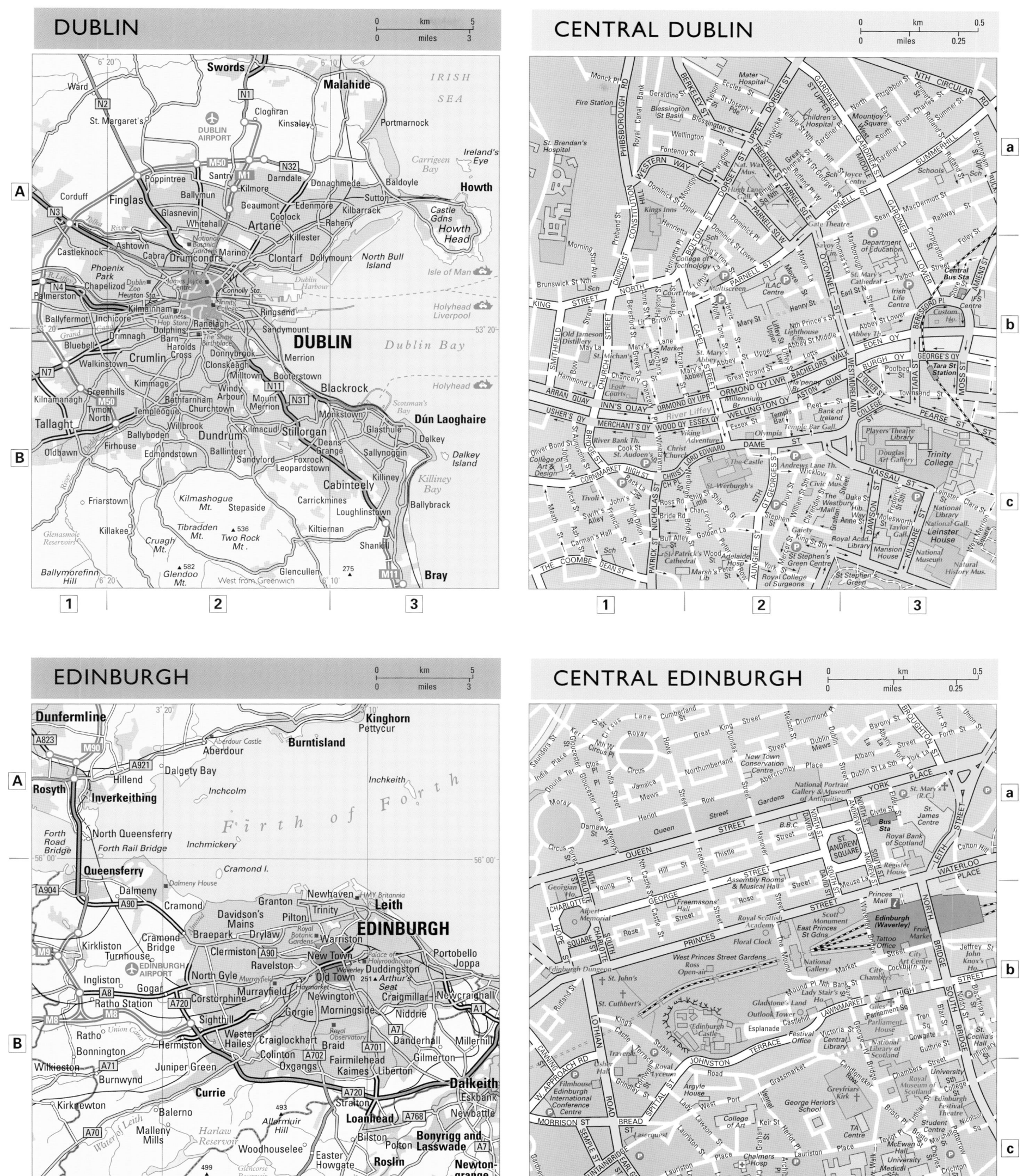

HELSINKI

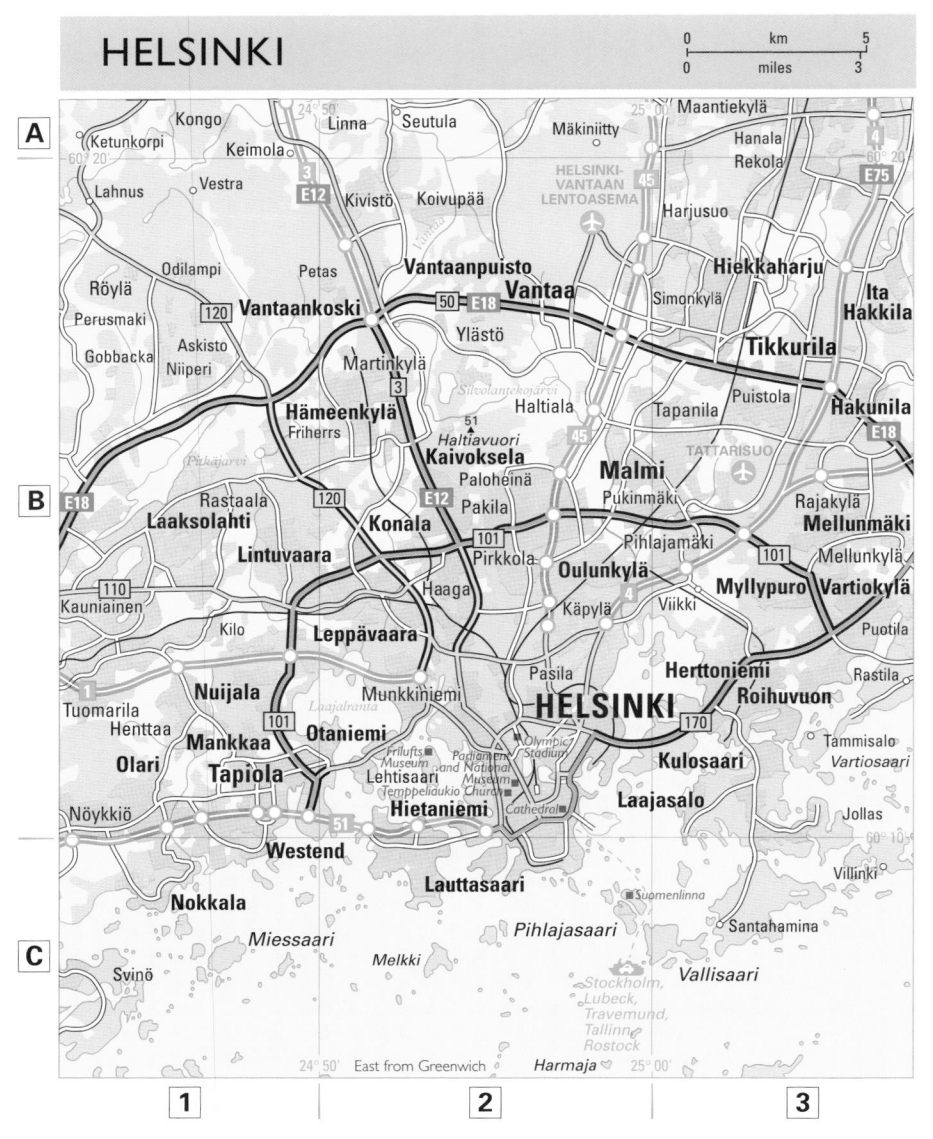

ISTANBUL

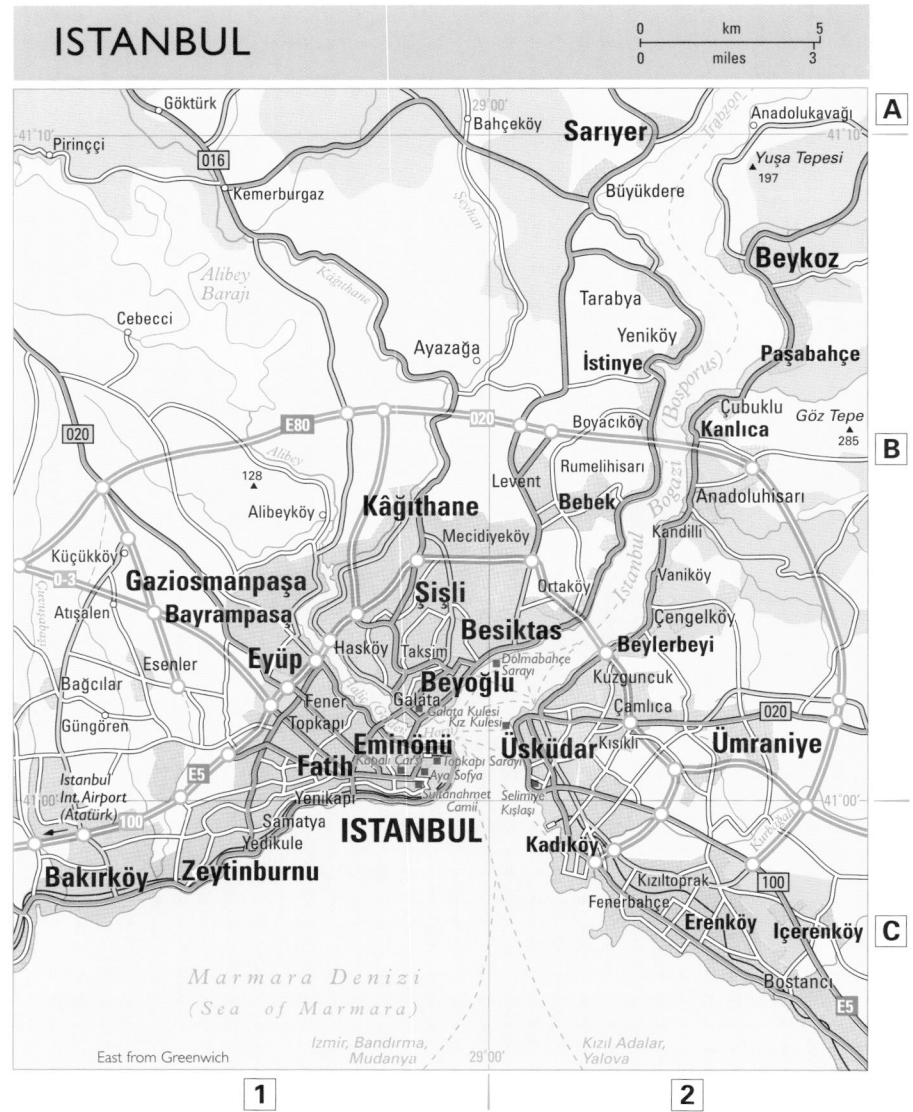

HONG KONG

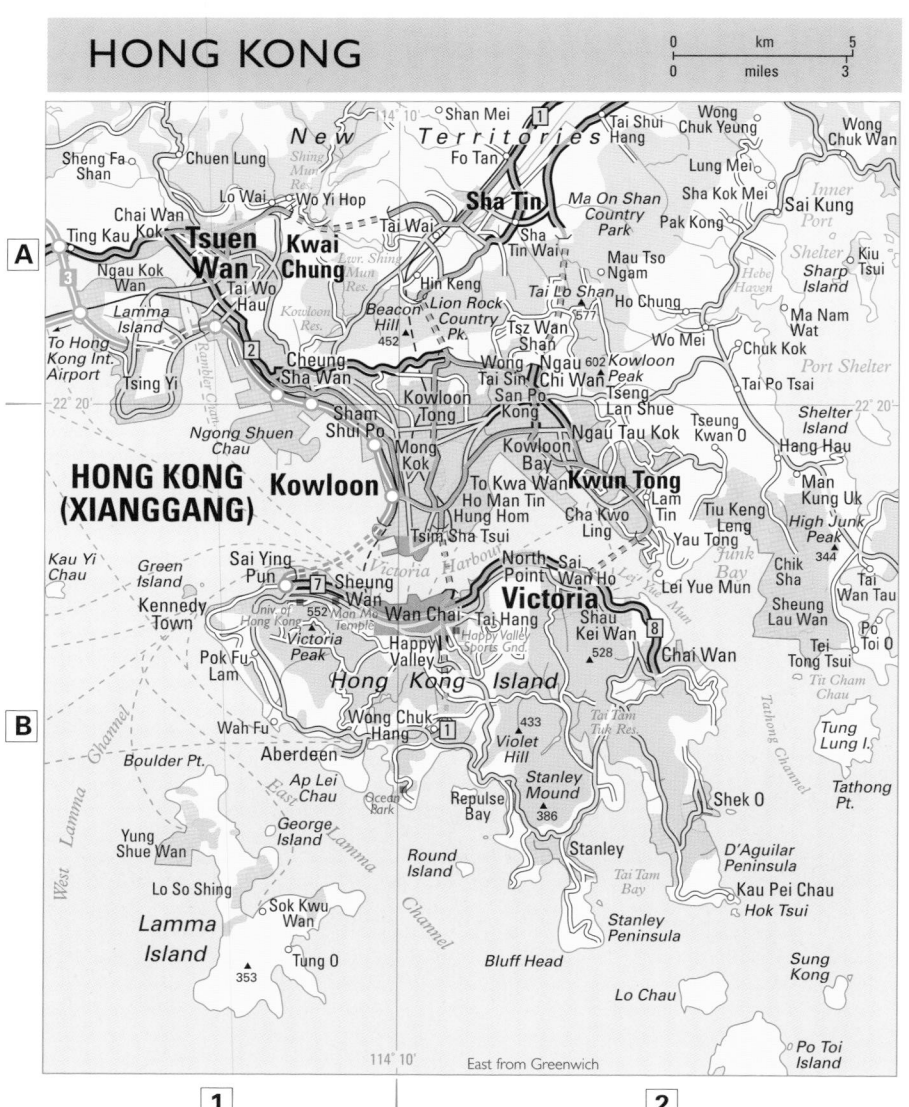

CENTRAL HONG KONG

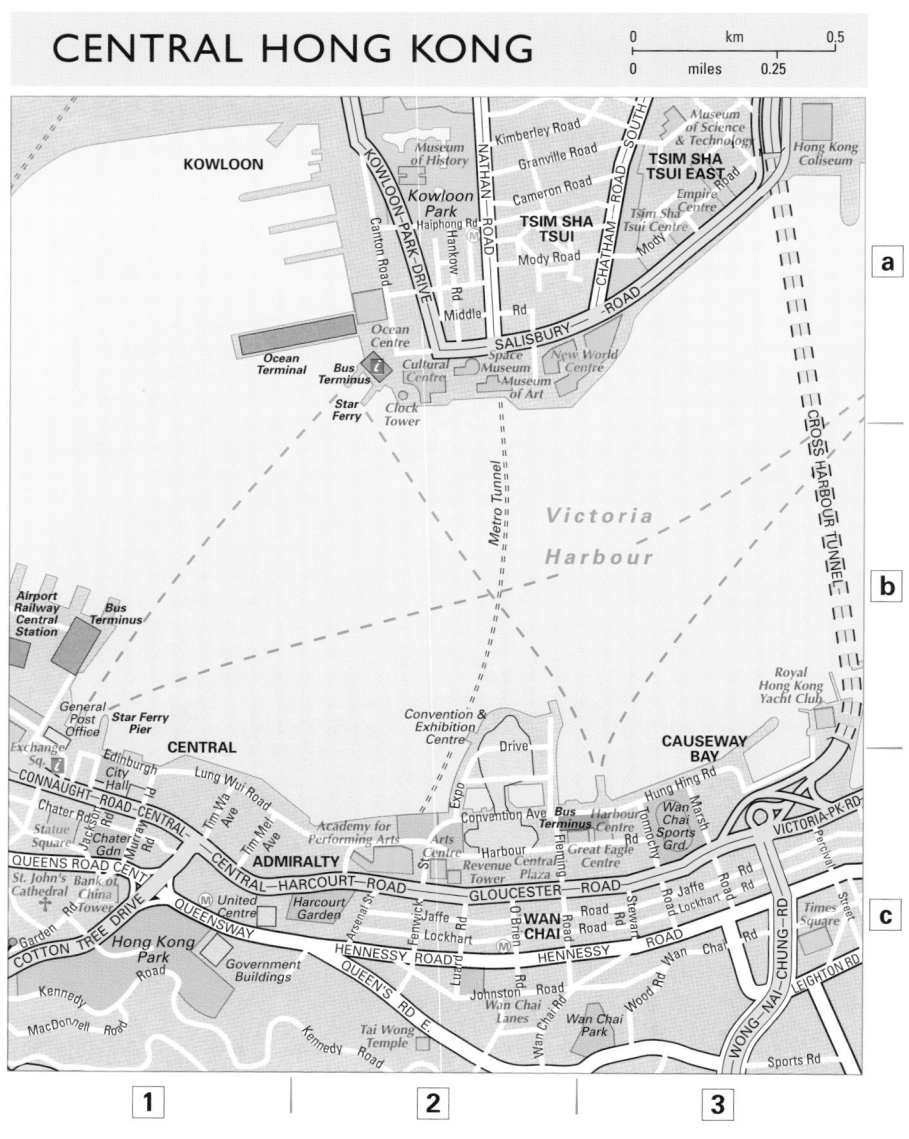

JERUSALEM

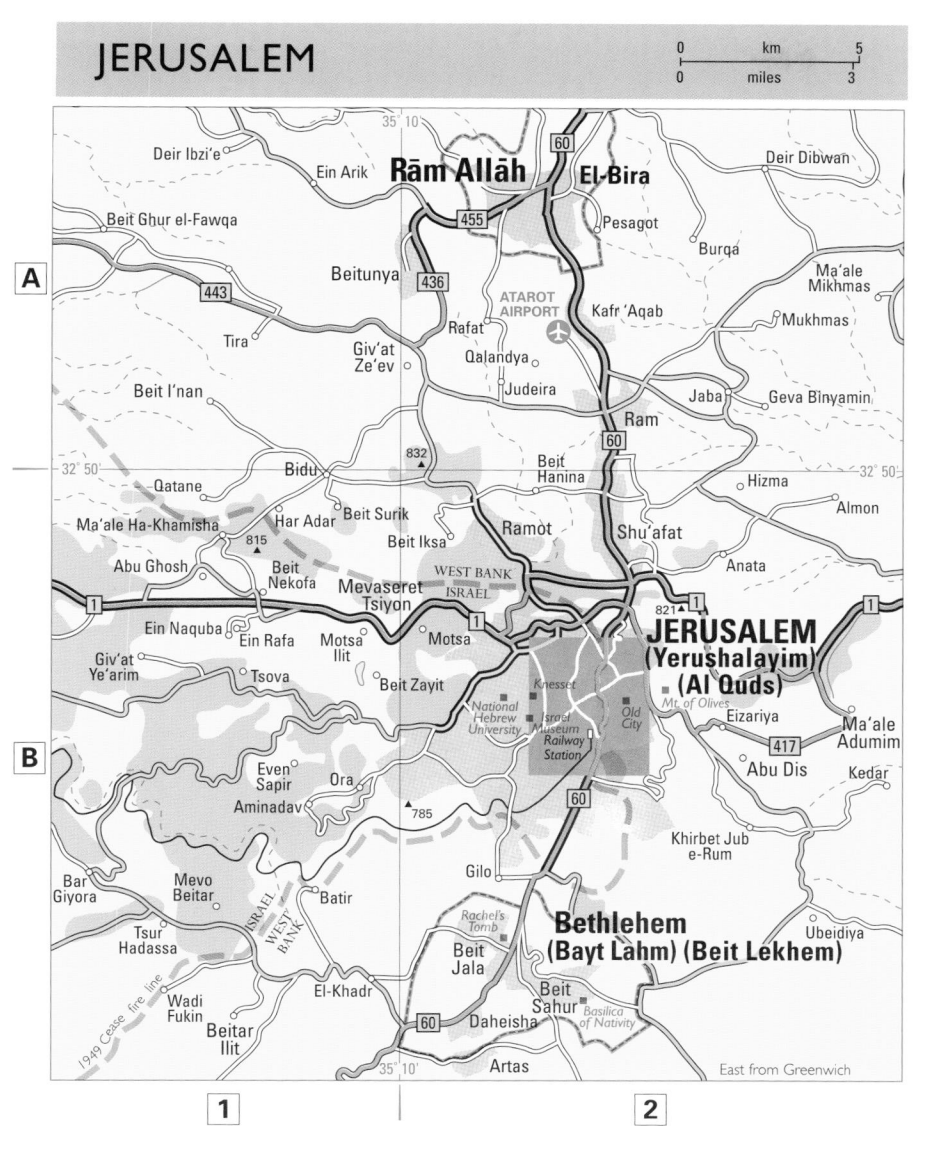

CENTRAL JERUSALEM

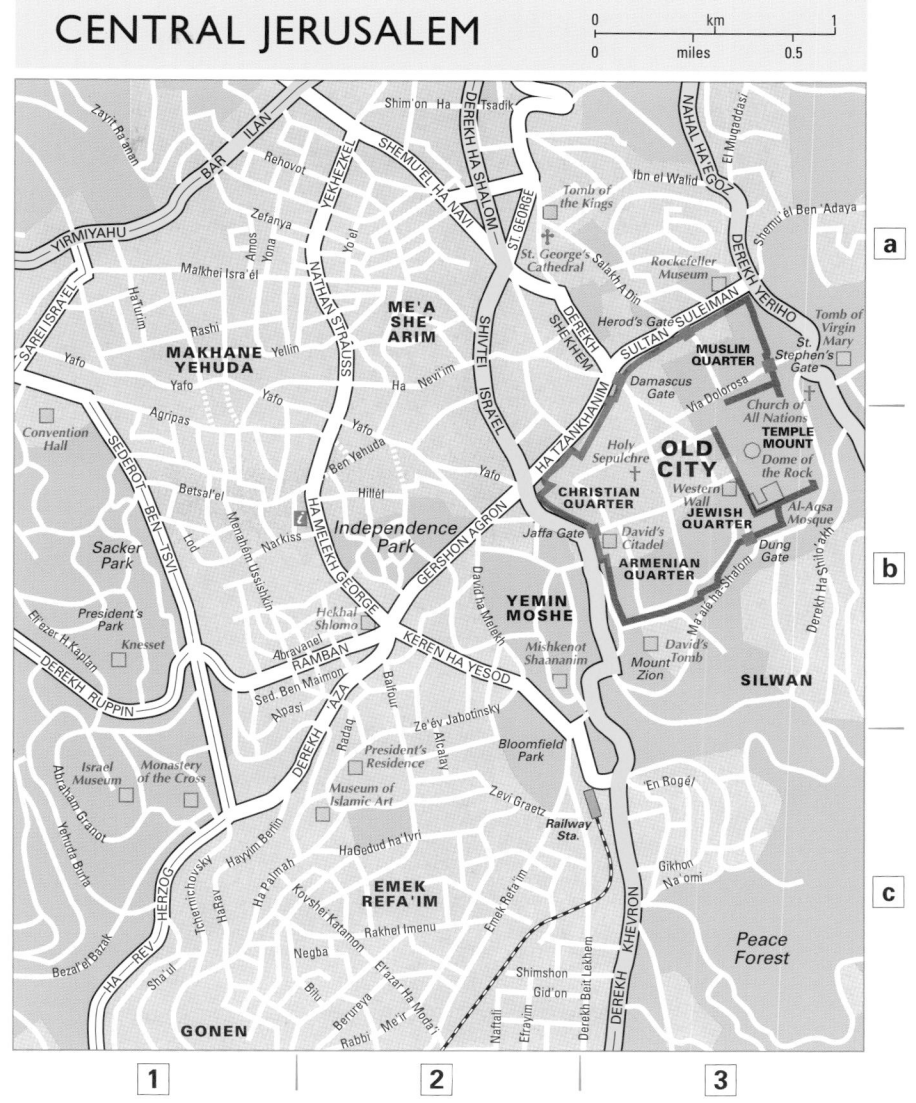

JAKARTA

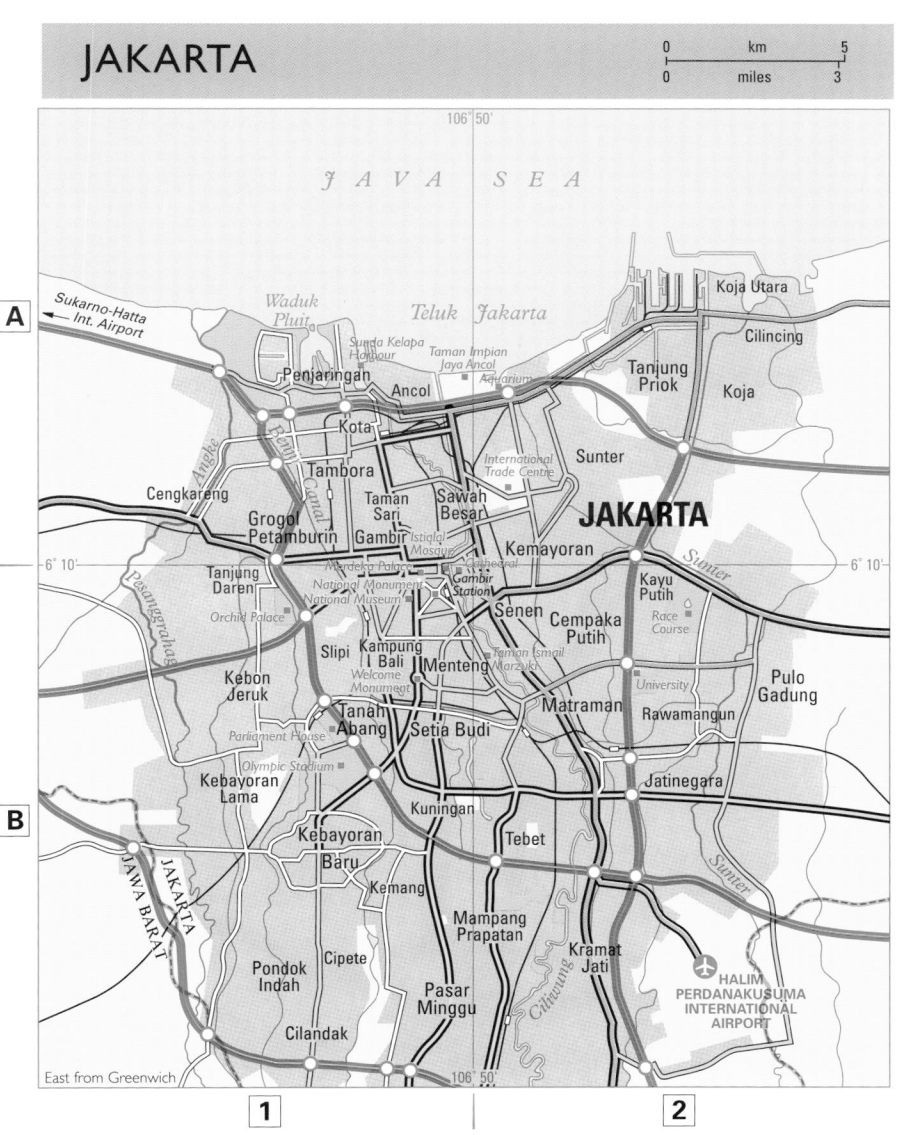

JOHANNESBURG

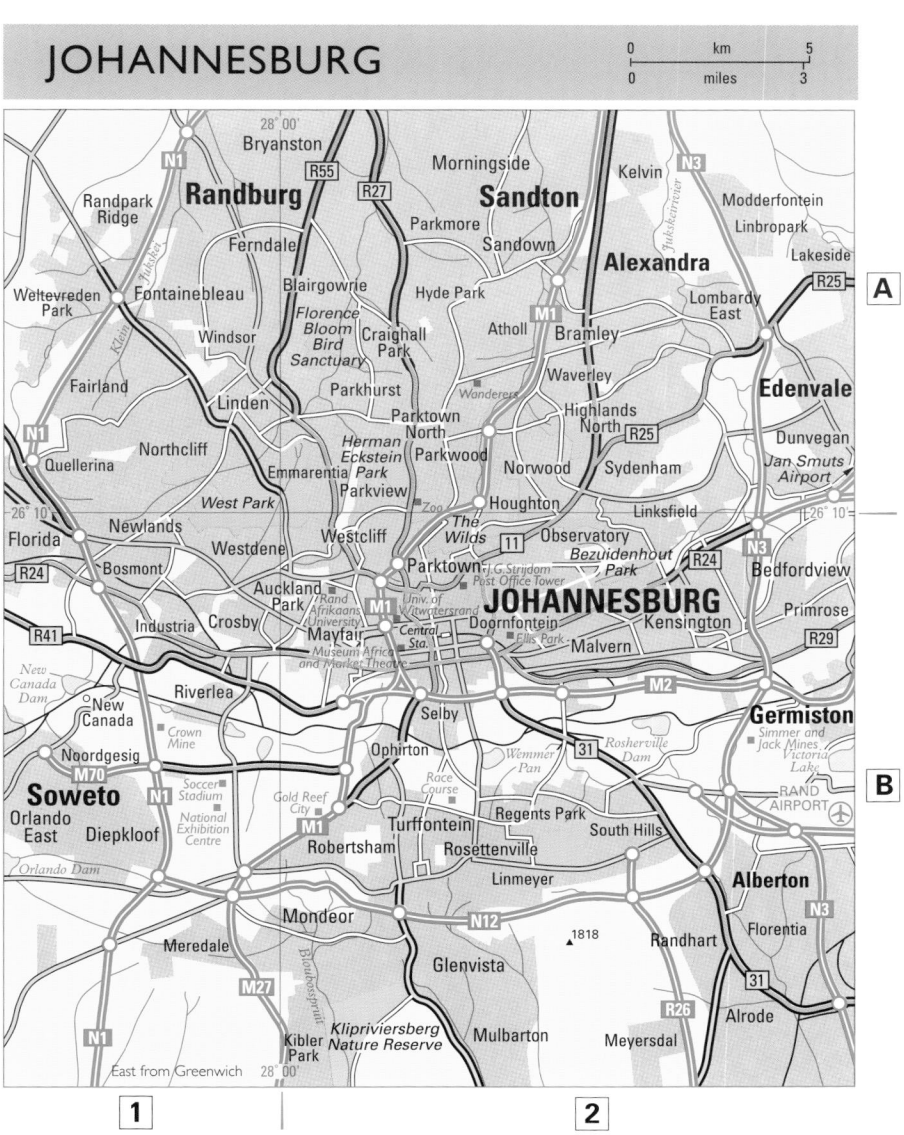

KARACHI

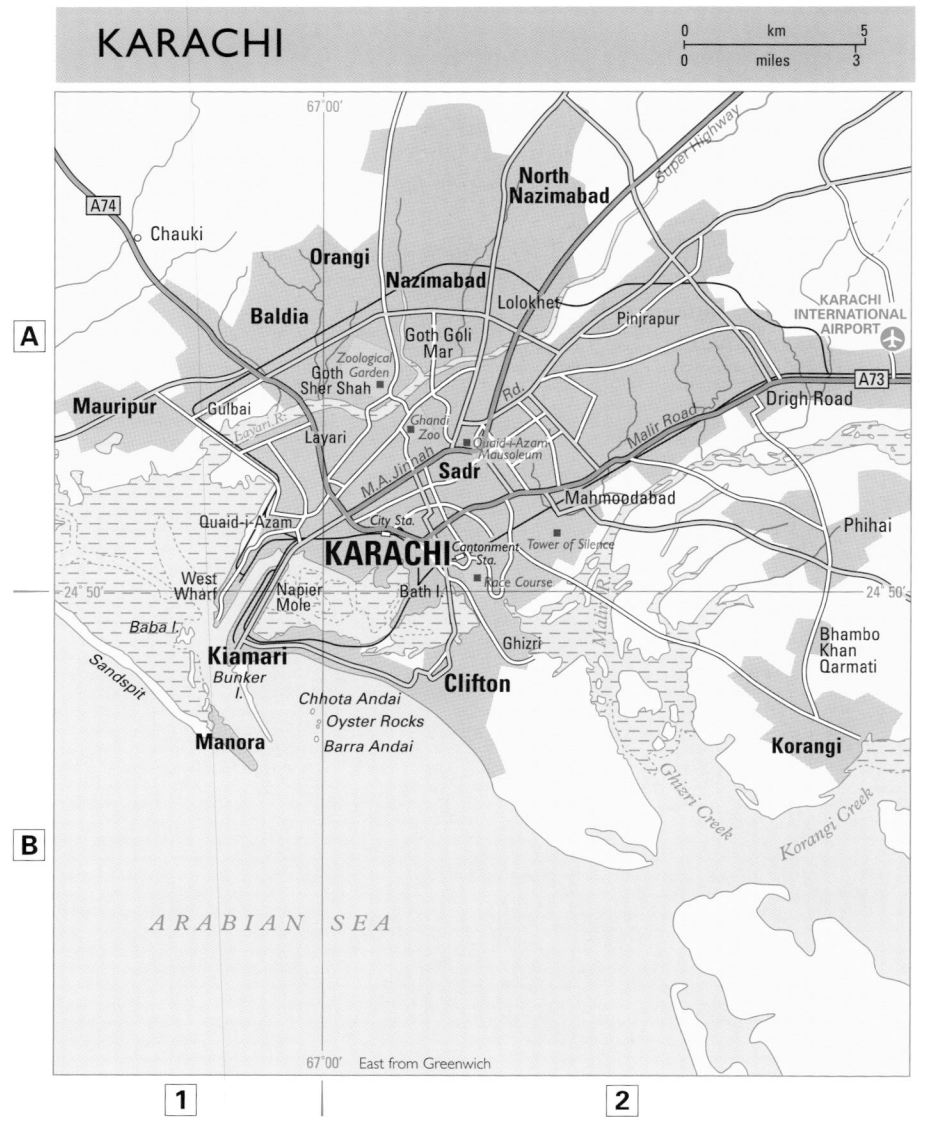

LAGOS

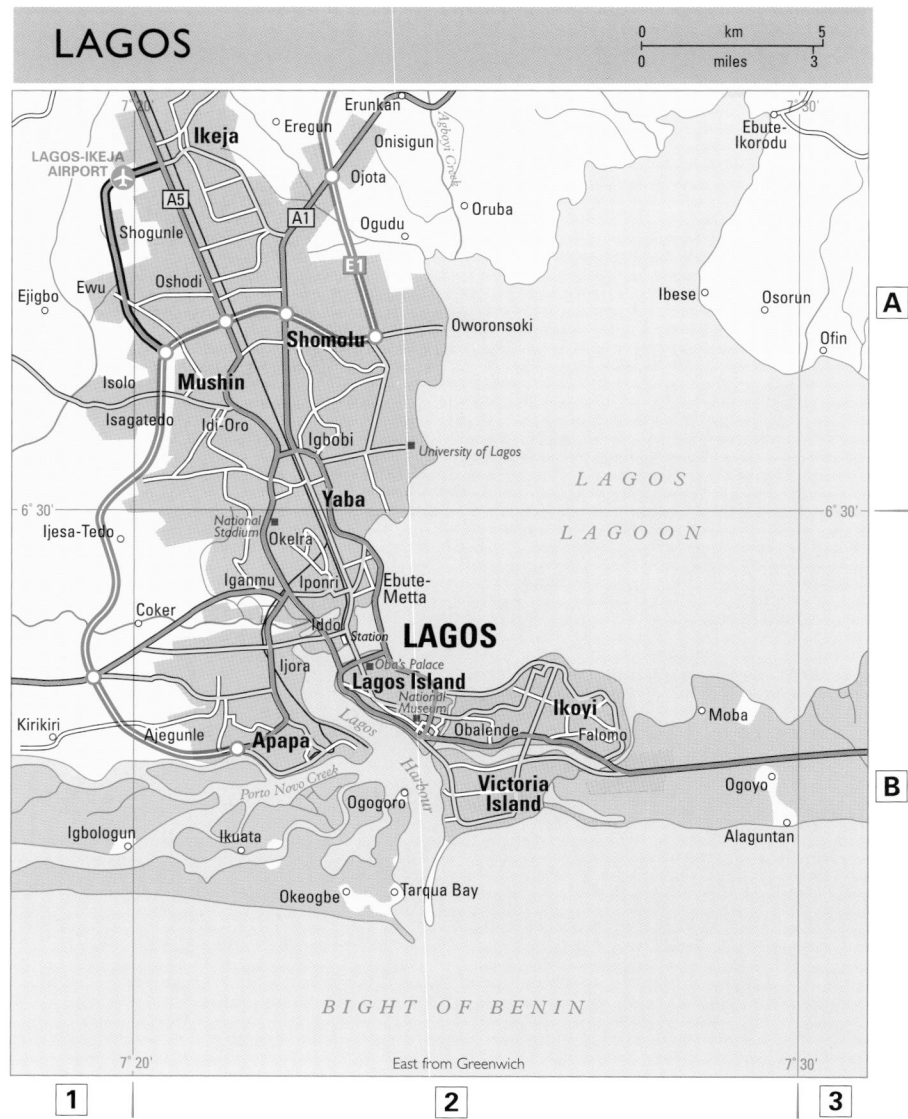

LISBON

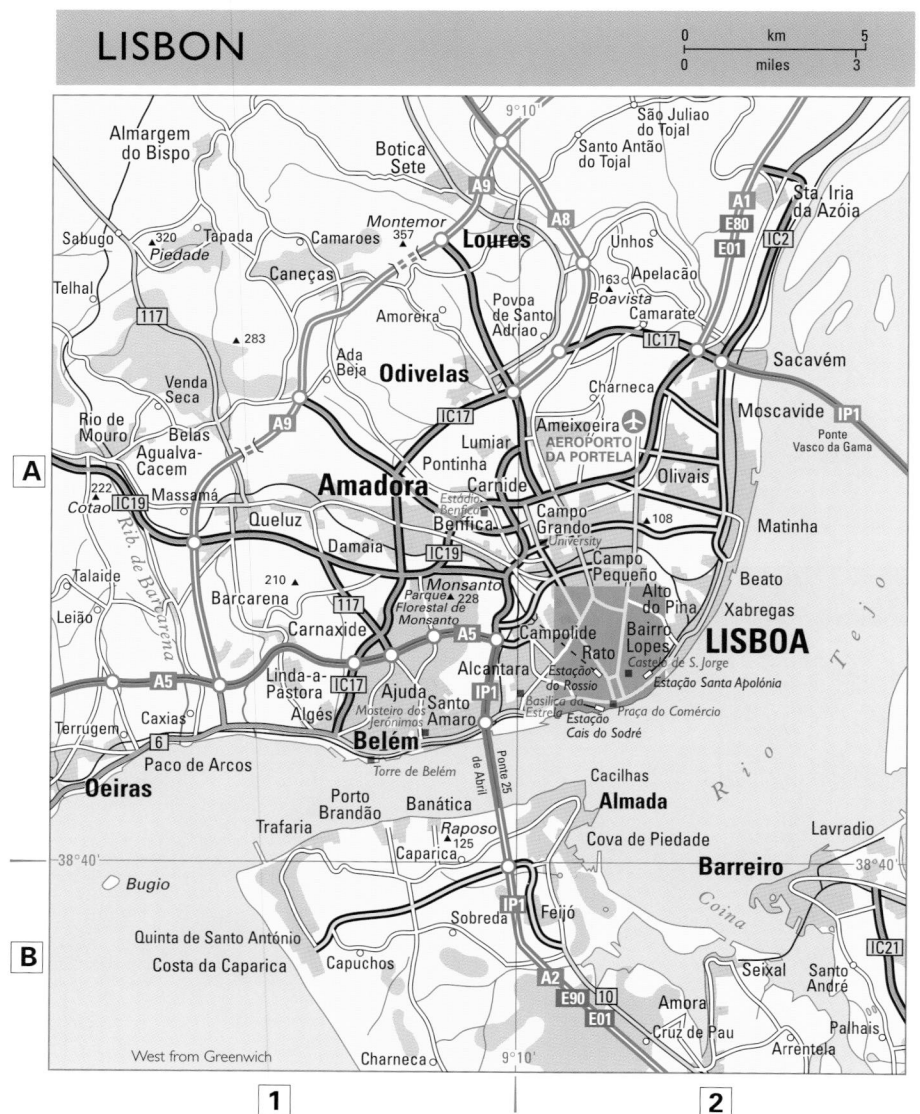

CENTRAL LISBON

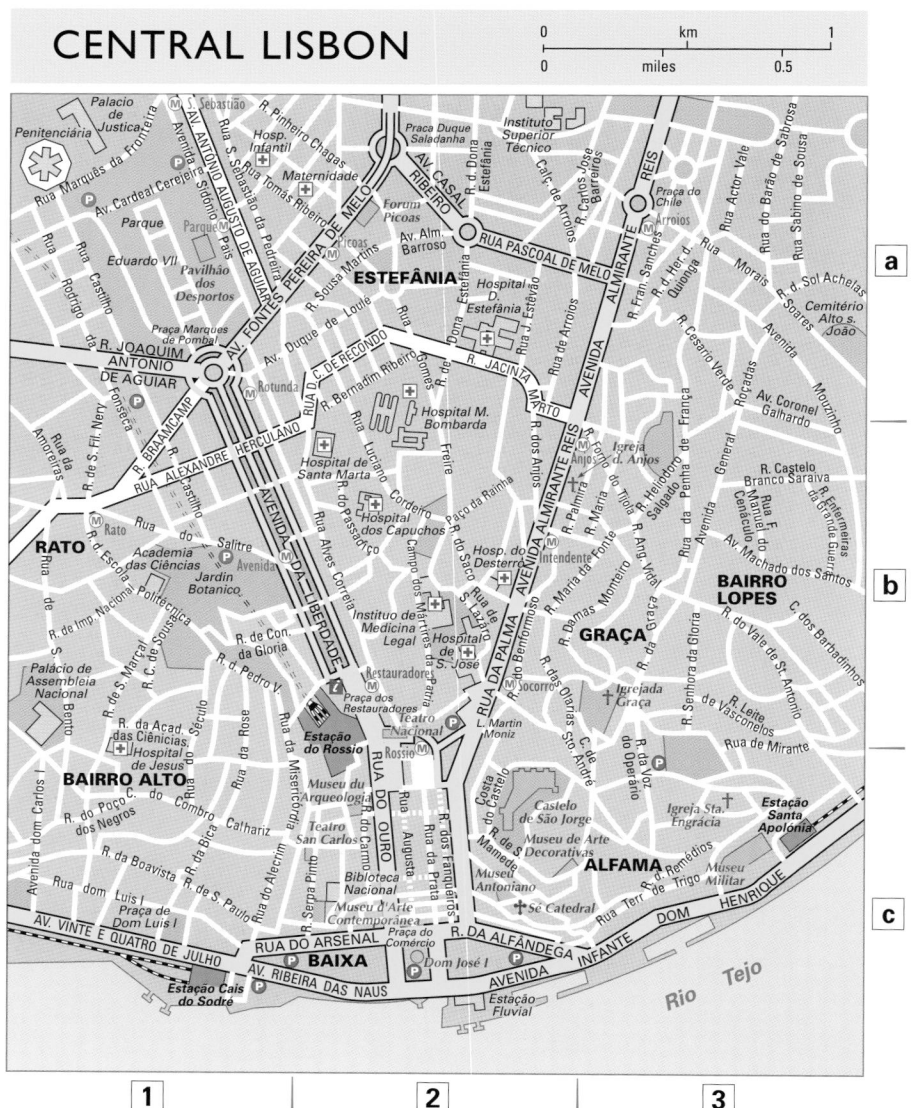

LONDON

km 0 — 5
miles 0 — 3

Northwood · Stanmore · Barnet · Finchley · Colney Hatch · Wood Green · Waltham Forest · Woodford · Stansted Airport · Havering-atte-Bower · Harold Hill

Hatch End · Harrow Weald · Belmont · Hendon · Mill Hill · Church End · Muswell Hill · Hornsey · Tottenham · Woodford · Hainault · Collier Row · Romford

Pinner Green · Queensbury · East Finchley · Crouch End · Haringey · Walthamstow · Redbridge · Gidea Park · Gallows Corner

Harrow · Greenhill · Kenton · Hampstead Garden Suburb · Golders Green · Highgate · Stamford Hill · Leyton · Leytonstone · Wanstead · Ilford · Seven Kings · Goodmayes · Becontree · Hornchurch · Havering

Hillingdon · Brent · Camden · Islington · Hackney · Stratford · Newham · Barking · Dagenham

Ealing · Acton · Paddington · Holborn · City · Tower Hamlets · Poplar · West Ham · East Ham · Canning Town · North Woolwich

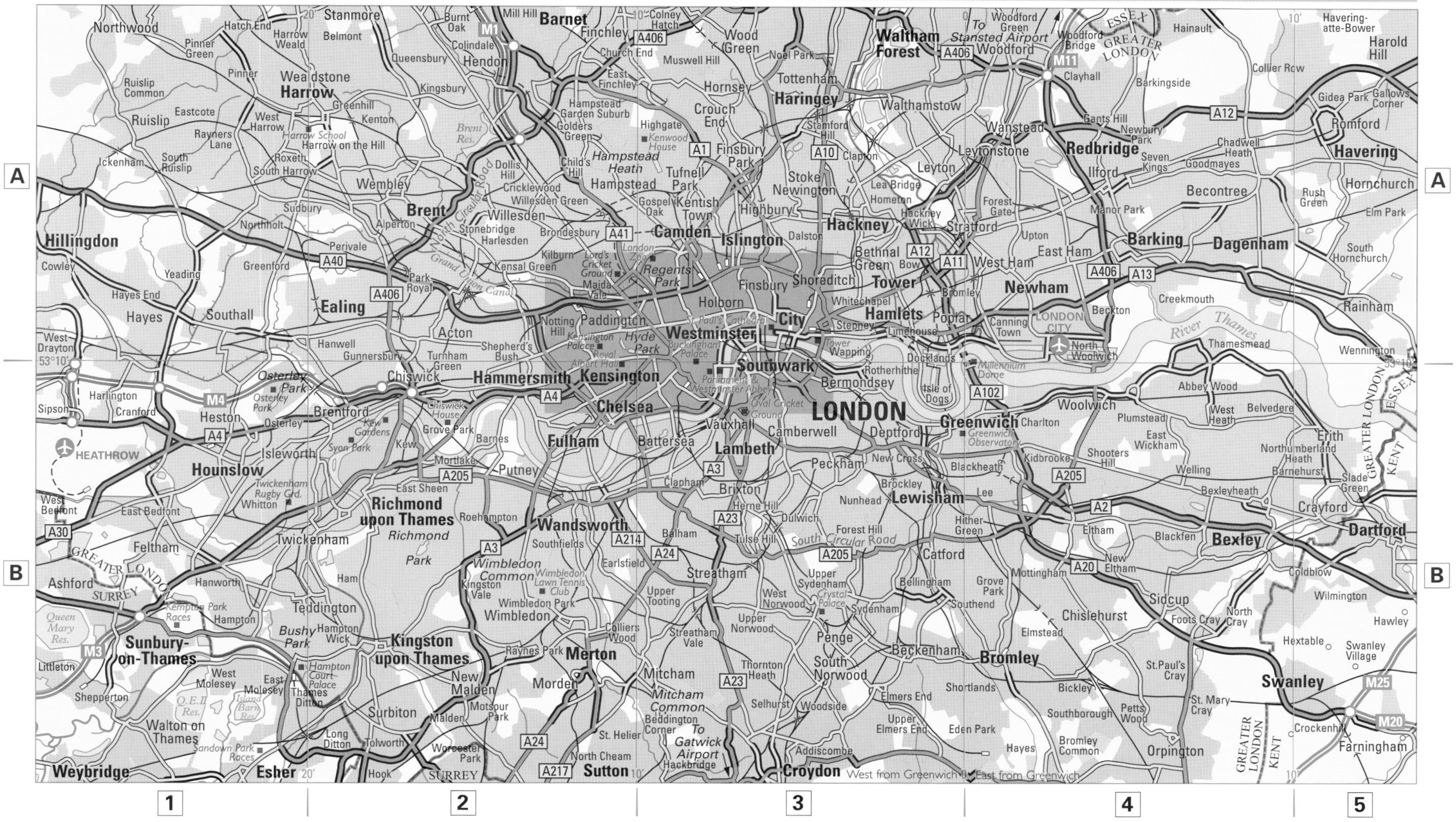

Heathrow · Hounslow · Isleworth · Chiswick · Hammersmith · Kensington · Westminster · Southwark · LONDON · Greenwich · Woolwich

Richmond upon Thames · Twickenham · Putney · Fulham · Chelsea · Battersea · Lambeth · Camberwell · Deptford · Charlton · Plumstead · Erith

Wimbledon Common · Wandsworth · Clapham · Brixton · Peckham · New Cross · Lewisham · Blackheath · Bexleyheath · Crayford · Dartford

Kingston upon Thames · Merton · Mitcham · Streatham · Dulwich · Catford · Eltham · Sidcup · Chislehurst · Bexley

Sunbury-on-Thames · New Malden · Morden · Sutton · Croydon · Penge · South Norwood · Beckenham · Bromley · Orpington · Swanley · Farningham

West from Greenwich | East from Greenwich

CENTRAL LONDON

km 0 — 2
miles 0 — 1

KENSAL RISE · WEST KILBURN · ST. JOHN'S WOOD · MAIDA VALE · WESTBOURNE GREEN · REGENT'S PARK · London Zoo · King's Cross · HOXTON · SHOREDITCH

PADDINGTON · BAYSWATER · Marylebone · BLOOMSBURY · Euston · St. Pancras · King's Cross Thameslink · CLERKENWELL · Farringdon · Barbican

NOTTING HILL · HYDE PARK · KENSINGTON GARDENS · MAYFAIR · SOHO · HOLBORN · Moorgate · Liverpool St · CITY · Whitechapel Art Gall.

Kensington Palace · Serpentine Gallery · Apsley House & Wellington Mus. · ST. JAMES'S · Trafalgar Square · St. Paul's · Bank · Leadenhall · Fenchurch St

KENSINGTON · KNIGHTSBRIDGE · BELGRAVIA · Buckingham Palace · Charing Cross · Waterloo East · SOUTHWARK · London Bridge · The Monument · HMS Belfast · Tower Gateway (DLR)

SOUTH KENSINGTON · BROMPTON · Victoria · Houses of Parliament · Westminster Abbey · Lambeth Pal. · BOROUGH · The Design Museum

CHELSEA · PIMLICO · Tate Britain · LAMBETH · Imperial War Mus. · Elephant & Castle · NEWINGTON · BERMONDSEY

KENNINGTON · The Oval Cricket Gd. · WALWORTH · Burgess Park · River Thames

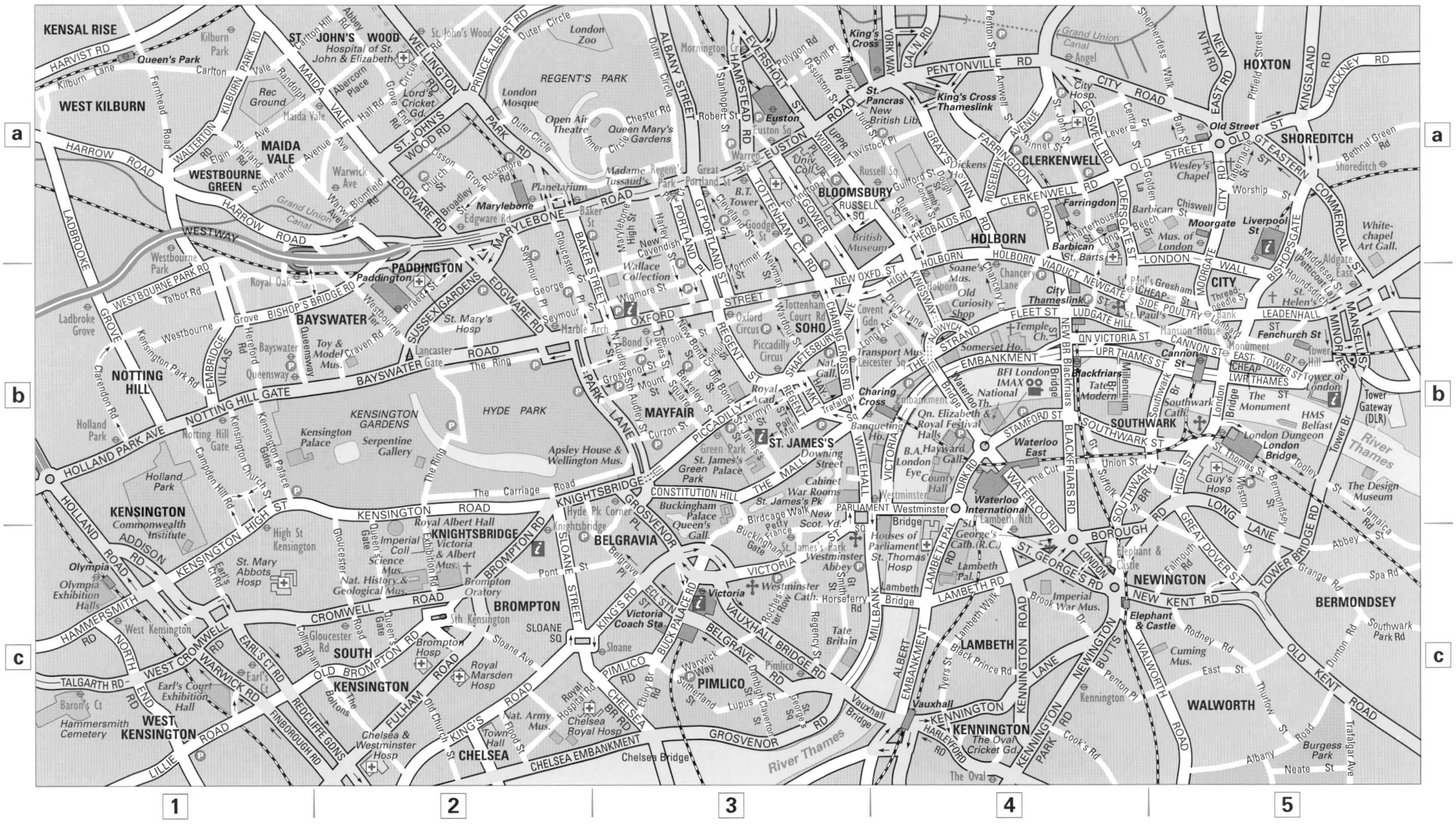

COPYRIGHT PHILIP'S

LOS ANGELES

0 km 5
0 miles 3

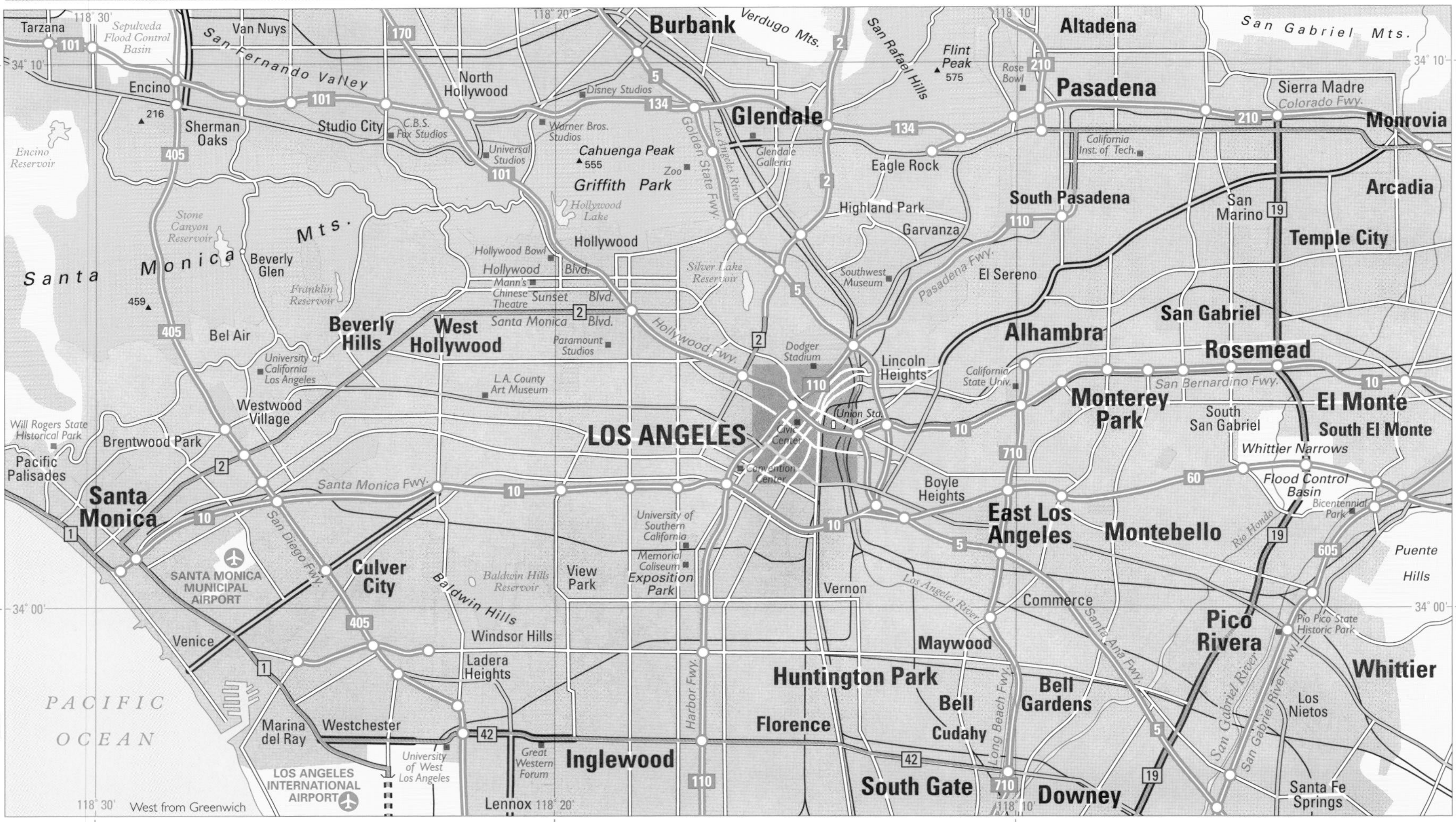

A Tarzana 101 Sepulveda Flood Control Basin Van Nuys 170 Burbank Verdugo Mts. Altadena San Gabriel Mts. A
34° 10' 118° 30' 118° 20' 118° 10' 34° 10'
Encino 101 North Hollywood Flint Peak 575 Rose Bowl 210 Pasadena
216 Sherman Oaks Studio City Disney Studios 134 Glendale California Inst. of Tech. Monrovia
C.B.S. Warner Bros. Studios 134 210
Encino Reservoir Cahuenga Peak 555 Universal Studios 101 Glendale Galleria Eagle Rock Sierra Madre Colorado Fwy.
Griffith Park Zoo South Pasadena Arcadia
459 Hollywood Lake Highland Park 110 San Marino 19
Santa Monica Mts. Hollywood Bowl Hollywood Bowl Garvanza El Sereno Temple City
405 Beverly Glen Hollywood Mann's Chinese Theatre Sunset Blvd. Southwest Museum Pasadena Fwy. San Gabriel
Bel Air Hollywood Blvd. 2 California State Univ. Alhambra Rosemead
Franklin Reservoir Santa Monica Blvd. Silver Lake Reservoir 2
Beverly Hills West Hollywood Paramount Studios Dodger Stadium 110 Lincoln Heights San Bernardino Fwy. El Monte B
B Westwood Village University of California Los Angeles L.A. County Art Museum 2 Union Sta. Monterey Park South San Gabriel South El Monte
Will Rogers State Historical Park Brentwood Park LOS ANGELES Civic Center Whittier Narrows
Pacific Palisades 2 Convention Center Boyle Heights 710 60 Flood Control Basin Bicentennial Park
Santa Monica Fwy. 10 East Los Angeles Montebello 19 Puente Hills
Santa Monica 10 University of Southern California 10 605
SANTA MONICA MUNICIPAL AIRPORT San Diego Fwy. Memorial Coliseum Exposition Park Vernon Commerce Santa Ana Fwy. Pio Pico State Historic Park Whittier
34° 00' Culver City Baldwin Hills Reservoir View Park 1 34° 00'
Venice 405 Baldwin Hills Windsor Hills Maywood Pico Rivera Los Nietos
1 Ladera Heights Harbor Fwy. Huntington Park Bell Gardens
Marina del Ray Westchester Great Western Forum 42 Florence Bell Cudahy Santa Fe Springs C
C PACIFIC OCEAN University of West Los Angeles 110 Inglewood South Gate 710 Downey 19
LOS ANGELES INTERNATIONAL AIRPORT Lennox 118° 20' 42
118° 30' West from Greenwich

1 2 3 4

LIMA

0 km 5
0 miles 3

A 77° 10' Bocanegra Los Olivos Independencia Huascar 77° A
12° LIMA CALLAO Avenida Panamericana Norte San Juan de Lurigancho 12°
Chavarria 755 Cerro San Jeronimo
Cerro La Milla Cerro Observatorio 465
AEROPUERTO INTERNACIONAL JORGE CHAVEZ San Martin de Porras 242 Rimac
Rimac Rimac El Agustino
Terminal Maritimo Carmen de La Legua Estacion Desamparados Palacio do Gobierno El Congreso Cerro El Agustino 482
Callao La Victoria LIMA B
B Fuerte Real Felipe Breña Campo de Marte Estadio Nacional San Luis
La Punta Bellavista Parque de las Leyendas Jesus Maria Parque de la Reserva Museo de la Nacion
La Perla Univ. Catolica Museo Nacional
San Miguel Pueblo Libre Lince Hipodromo de Monterrico San Borja
Isla Fronton Magdalena Huaca Juliana San Isidro
San Isidro Surquillo
Miraflores Avenida Panamericana Sur
PACIFIC OCEAN Vista Alegre
12° 10' Santiago de Surco 12° 10'
Barranco
Cerro Morro Solar 273 La Campiña C
C Chorrillos
Punta La Chira La Encantada
77° 10' West from Greenwich 77°

1 2 3

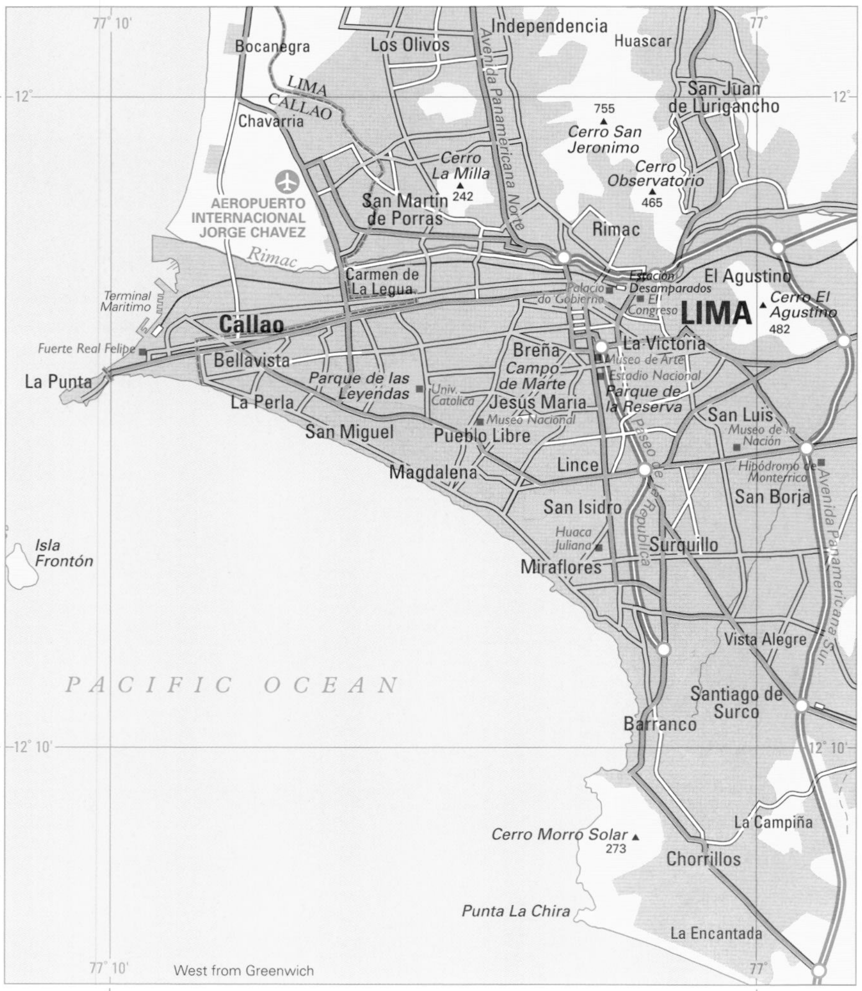

CENTRAL LOS ANGELES

0 km 1
0 miles 0.5

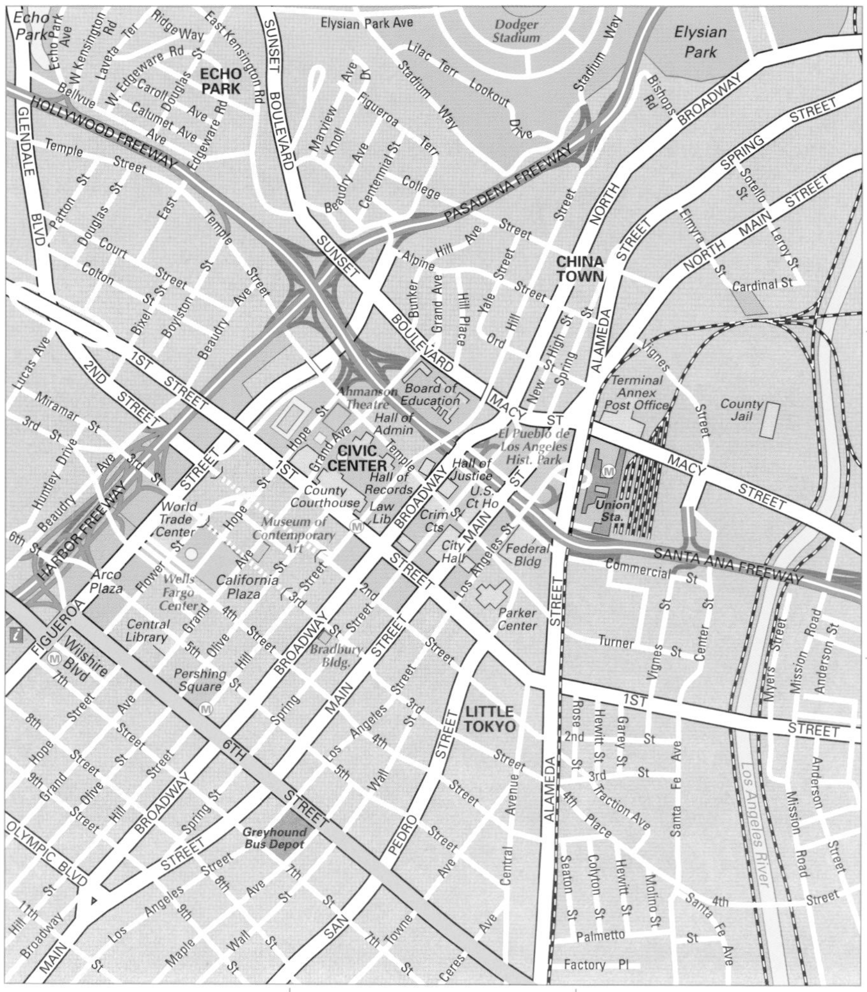

Echo Park Elysian Park Ave Dodger Stadium Elysian Park a
Hollywood Freeway ECHO PARK Sunset Boulevard Pasadena Freeway BROADWAY SPRING STREET NORTH MAIN STREET
GLENDALE BLVD CHINA TOWN ALAMEDA Cardinal St
Temple Street County Jail
HARBOR FREEWAY 1ST STREET Board of Education Hall of Admin CIVIC CENTER El Pueblo de Los Angeles Hist. Park MACY ST b
World Trade Center County Courthouse Hall of Records Union Sta. SANTA ANA FREEWAY
FIGUEROA Arco Plaza Wells Fargo Center California Plaza Museum of Contemporary Art Los Angeles St City Hall Federal Bldg
Central Library 2ND STREET BROADWAY MAIN STREET Parker Center LITTLE TOKYO ALAMEDA 1ST STREET c
Pershing Square BROADWAY SPRING MAIN SAN PEDRO ST
OLYMPIC BLVD Greyhound Bus Depot
BROADWAY 6TH STREET

1 2 3

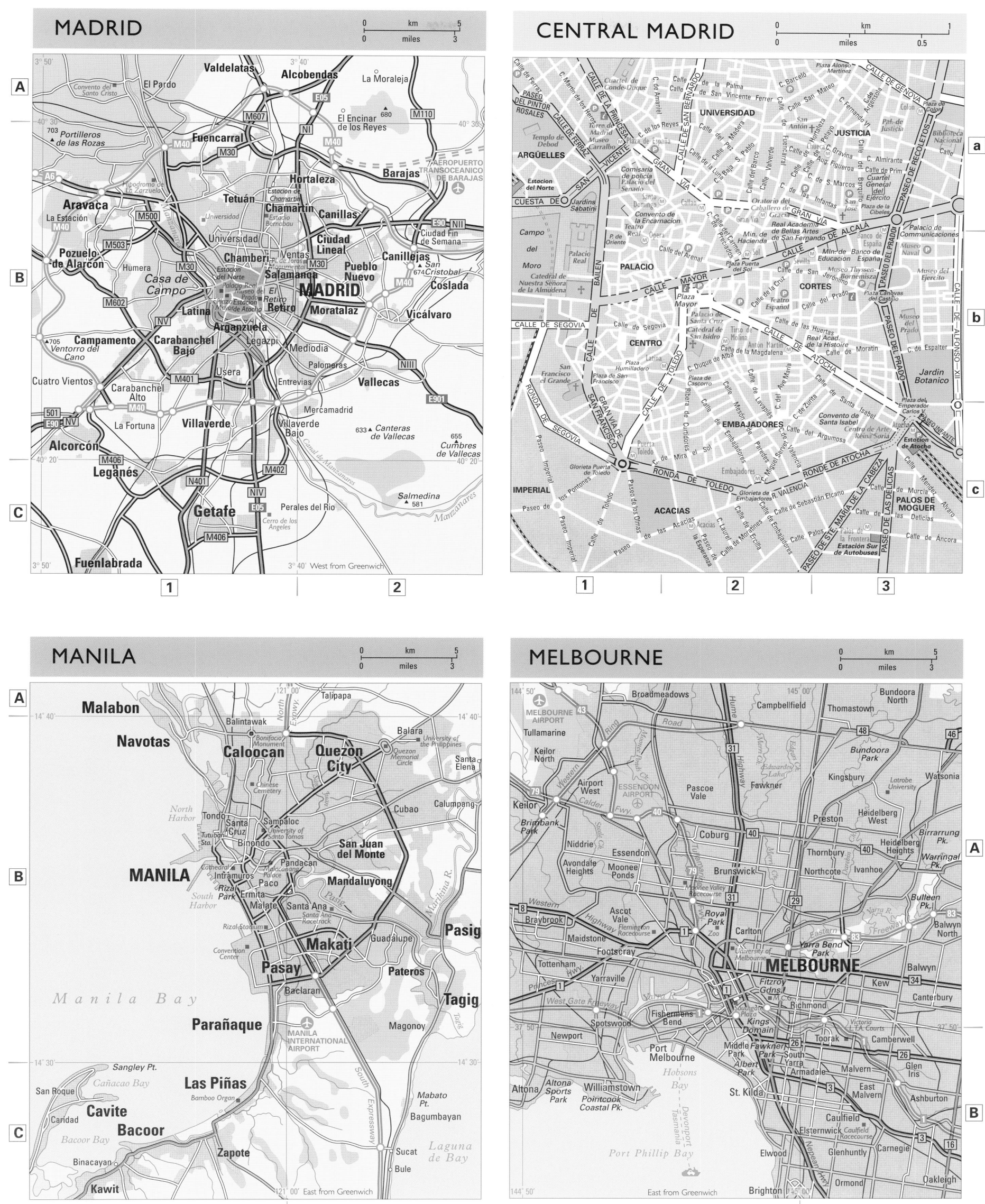

MADRID

km 5
miles 3

A
Convento del Santo Cristo
El Pardo
Valdelatas
Alcobendas
La Moraleja
E05
M607
Portilleros de las Rozas
703
Fuencarral
N1
El Encinar de los Reyes
680
M110
M40
M30
M40
Hortaleza
Barajas
A6
Aravaca
La Estación
Hipódromo de la Zarzuela
Tetuán
Estación de Chamartín
AEROPUERTO TRANSOCEANICO DE BARAJAS
M40
Pozuelo de Alarcón
M503
Humera
M30
Chamartín
Universidad
Canillas
E90
N II
B
Casa de Campo
M602
Salamanca
Ciudad Lineal
Canillejas
San Cristóbal
674
Coslada
Latina
Retiro
MADRID
Pueblo Nuevo
M40
Arganzuela
El Retiro
Moratalaz
Vicálvaro
Campamento
Carabanchel Bajo
Legazpi
Mediodia
Palomeras
N III
Ventorro del Cano
705
Cuatro Vientos
Carabanchel Alto
M401
Usera
Entrevias
Vallecas
E901
501
La Fortuna
Villaverde
Villaverde Bajo
Mercamadrid
Canteras de Vallecas
633
Alcorcón
40° 20'
M406
M402
Cumbres de Vallecas
655
40° 20'
Leganés
N401
NIV
Salmedina
581
C
Getafe
E05
Perales del Rio
Cerro de los Ángeles
M406
3° 40' West from Greenwich
Fuenlabrada

1   2

CENTRAL MADRID

km 1
miles 0.5

(Central Madrid street map with detailed labels)

1   2   3

MANILA

km 5
miles 3

A
Malabon
Talipapa
North Expwy.
Balintawak
Balara
University of the Philippines
14° 40'
Navotas
Bonifacio Monument
Quezon Memorial Circle
Santa Elena
Caloocan
Quezon City
Chinese Cemetery
Cubao
Calumpang
North Harbor
Tondo
Santa Cruz
Sampaloc
University of Santo Tomas
Santa Mesa
Binondo
San Juan del Monte
B
MANILA
Cathedral
Intramuros
Malacañang Palace
Pandacan
Mandaluyong
Rizal Park
Ermita
Paco
Marikina R.
Malate
Santa Ana
Pasig
Rizal Stadium
Santa Ana Racetrack
Convention Center
Makati
Guadalupe
Pateros
Pasay
Pasig
Tagig
Manila Bay
Baclaran
Parañaque
Magonoy
14° 30'
MANILA INTERNATIONAL AIRPORT
Sangley Pt.
Cañacao Bay
Las Piñas
Bamboo Organ
Mabato Pt.
Bagumbayan
San Roque
Caridad
C
Cavite
Bacoor
Zapote
Sucat
Bule
Laguna de Bay
Bacoor Bay
Binacayan
Kawit
121° 00' East from Greenwich

1   2

MELBOURNE

km 5
miles 3

A
144° 50'
145° 00'
MELBOURNE AIRPORT
43
Broadmeadows
Campbellfield
Thomastown
Bundoora North
Tullamarine
31
Hume
Keilor North
Edwardes Lake
48
46
Bundoora Park
Watsonia
79
Airport West
Essendon Airport
Pascoe Vale
Fawkner
Kingsbury
Latrobe University
Keilor
Calder Fwy
40
Coburg
Preston
Heidelberg West
Birrarrung Pk.
Brimbank Park
Niddrie
Essendon
40
Thornbury
Heidelberg Heights
40
Warringal Pk.
Avondale Heights
Moonee Ponds
Brunswick
Northcote
Ivanhoe
A
8
Western
Moonee Valley Racecourse
31
29
Bulleen Pk.
Braybrook
Ascot Vale
Royal Park
Carlton
Yarra Bend Park
83
Balwyn North
Maidstone
Flemington Racecourse
Zoo
University of Melbourne
Balwyn
Tottenham
Footscray
1
MELBOURNE
Kew
34
West Gate Freeway
Fitzroy Gdns.
Richmond
Canterbury
Yarraville
Eastern Freeway
Camberwell
37° 50'
Fishermens Bend
Kings Domain
26
37° 50'
Newport
Spotswood
Victoria T.A. Courts
Glen Iris
Port Melbourne
Middle Park
Toorak
26
Altona
Williamstown
Albert Park
South Yarra
Armadale
Malvern
3
Altona Sports Park
St. Kilda
East Malvern
Ashburton
B
Pointcook Coastal Pk.
Hobsons Bay
Caulfield
16
Elsternwick
Caulfield Racecourse
3
Port Phillip Bay
Devonport Tasmania
Elwood
Glenhuntly
Carnegie
Ormond
Oakleigh
Brighton
Nepean
144° 50'
East from Greenwich

1   2

MEXICO CITY

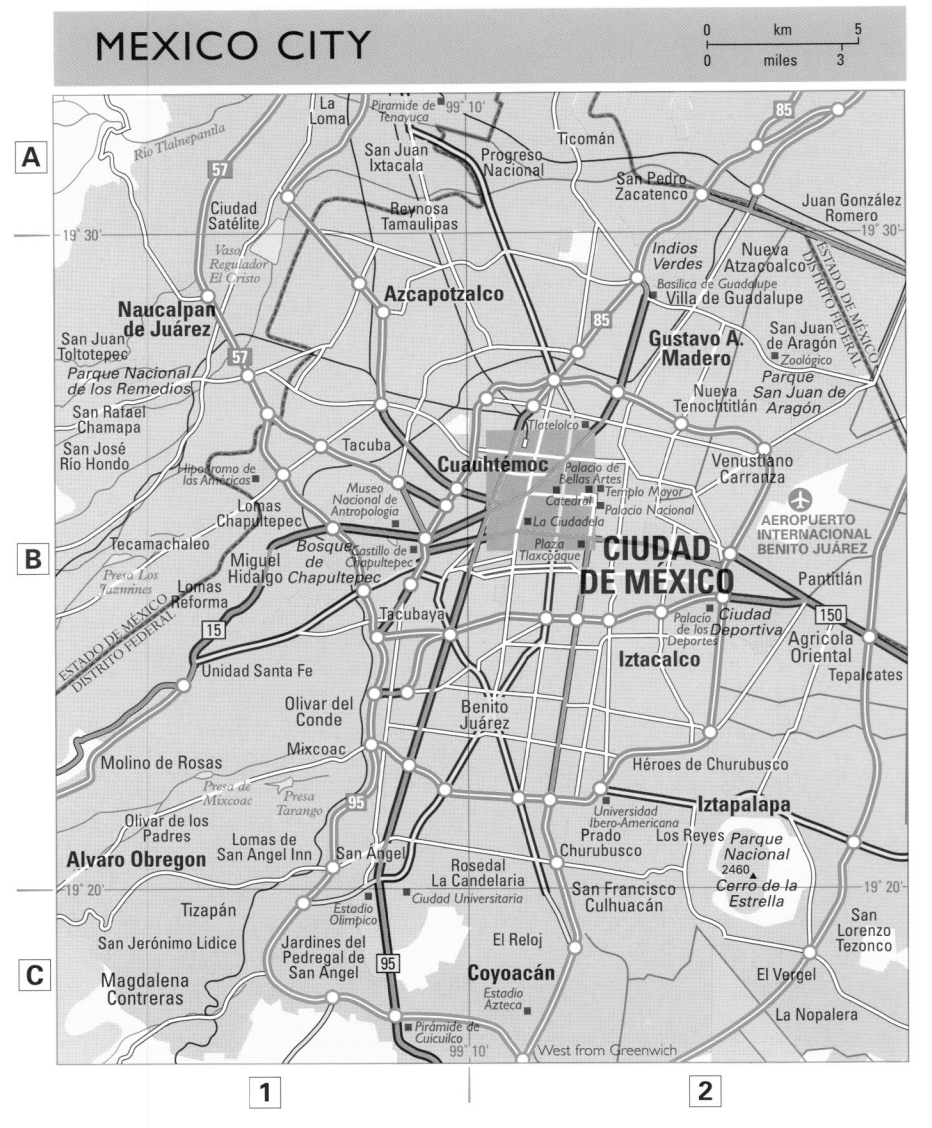

CENTRAL MEXICO CITY

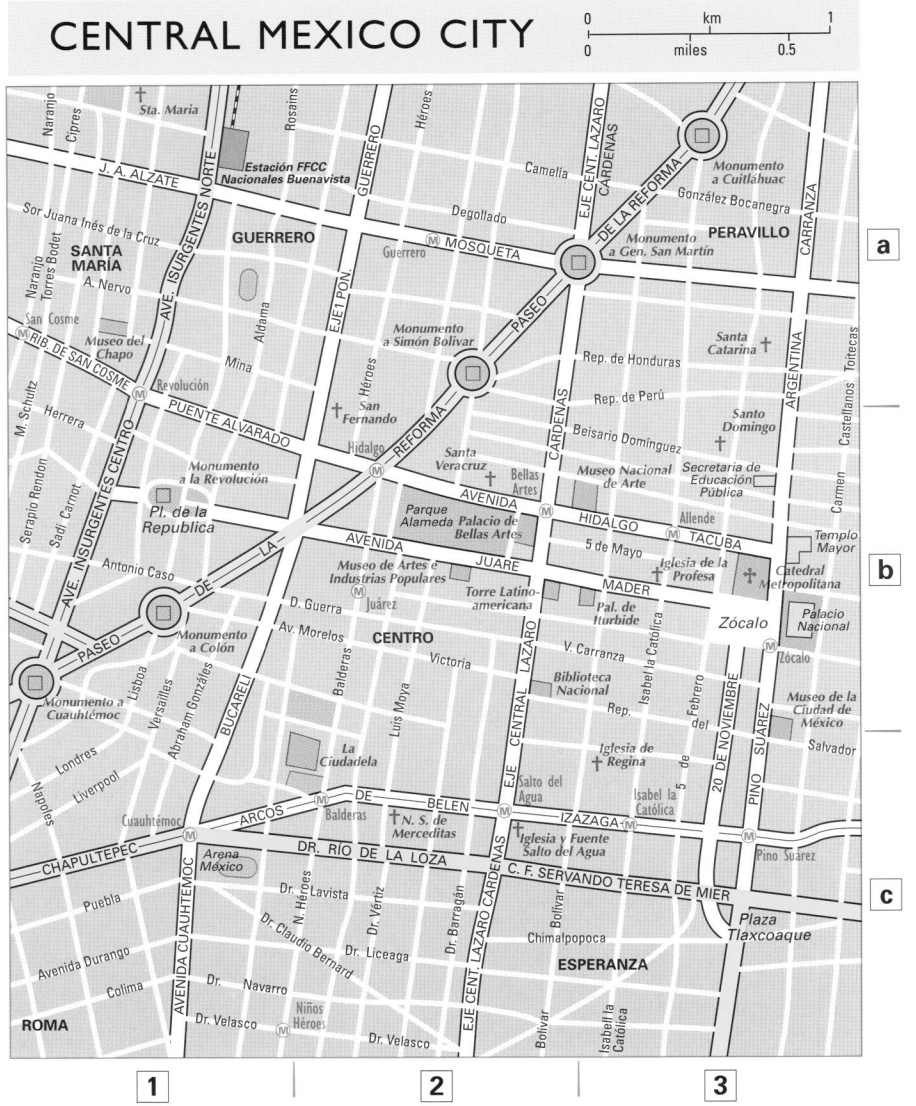

MIAMI

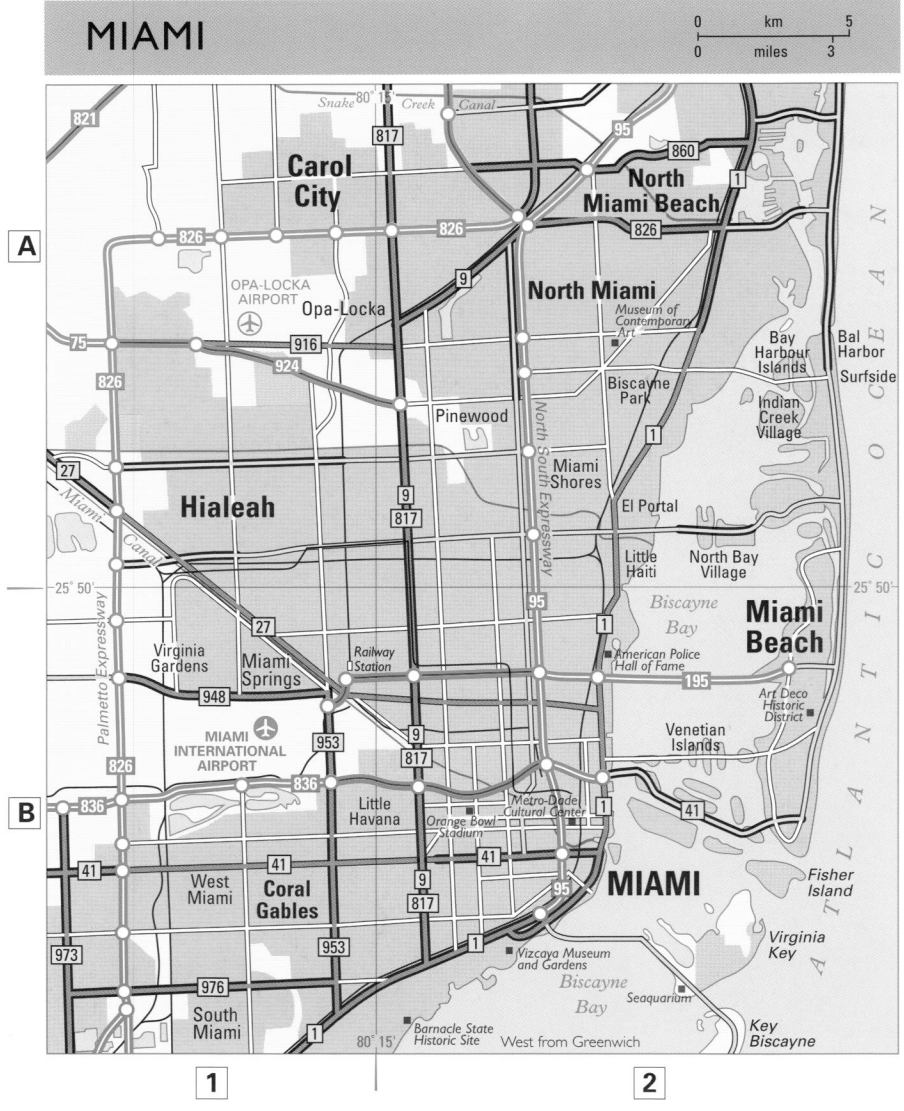

MILAN

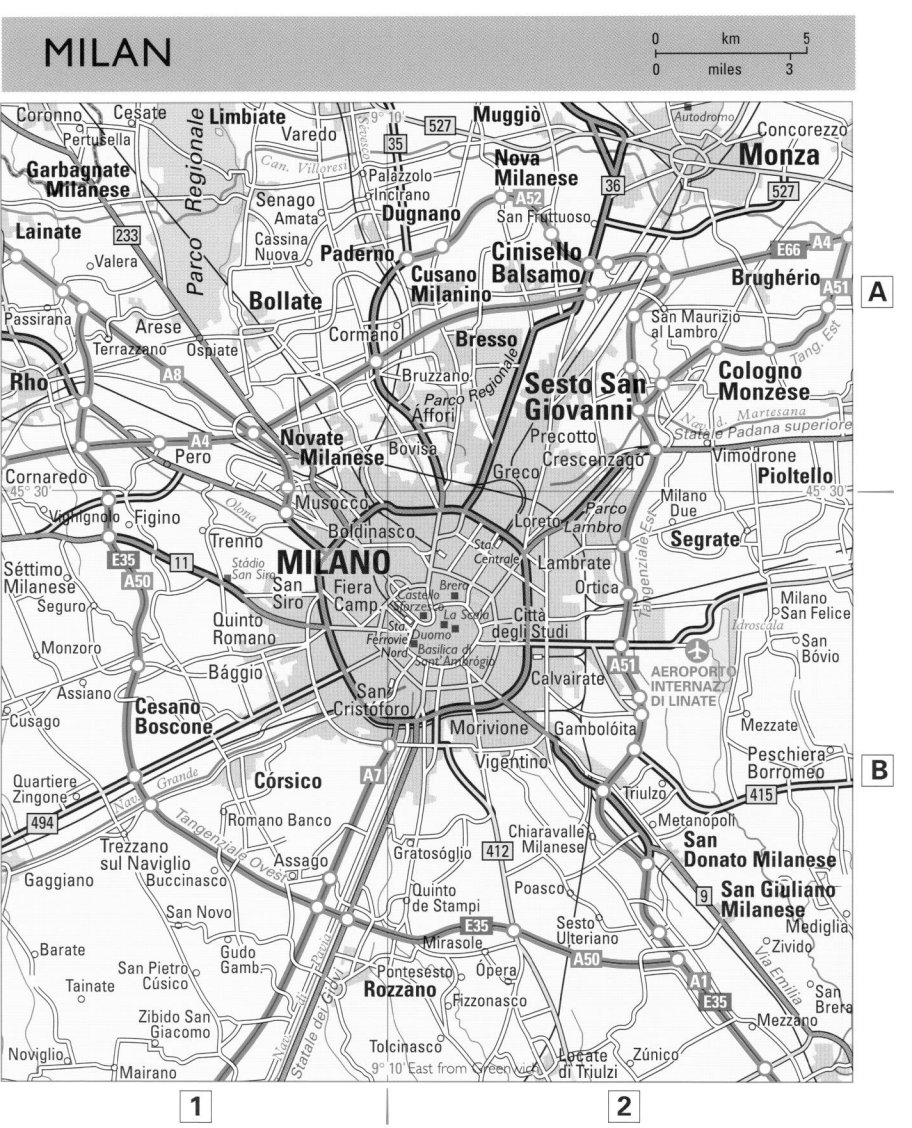

MOSCOW

km 0 — 5
miles 0 — 3

Novonikolyskoye
Putilkovo
Mitino
Sheremetyevo Airport
Bratsevo
Khimki-Khovrino
Degunino
Vladykino
Babushkin
157
Medvezhiy Ozyora
Medvezhiy Ozyora
Almazova
Chernyovo
Penyagino
Tushino
Nikolskiy
Petrovsko-Razumovskoye
Pekhra-Pokrovskoye
Krasnogorsk
Pavshino
Strogino
Timiryazev Park
Dzerzhinskiy Park
Ostankino
Bogorodskoye
Galyanovo
Vostochnyy
140
Balashikha
Novaya
Golyevo
Myakinino
Pokrovsko-Sresnevo
Petrovskiy Park
Sokolniki Park
Izmaylovo
Vishnyaki
Gorenki
Troitse-Lykovo
Khorosovo
Sokolniki
Izmayloskiy Park
Leportovo
Nikolyskoye
Arkhangelyskoye
Zakharkovo
Rublovo
Mnevniki
Frunze
Dzerzhinskiy
Sverdlov
MOSKVA
Yaroslavl Station
Kazan Station
Bauman Kursk Station
150
Novogireyevo
Perovo
Reutov
Saltykovka
Serebryanka
Zheleznodorozhnyy
Barvikha
Romashkovo
Cherepkovo
Krasno-Presnenskaya
Red Square St. Basil's Cath. Lenin Museum
Zhdanov
Kuskovo
Plyushchevo
Kutsino
Fenino
Poduskino
Nemchinovka
Krylatskoye
Kiev Station
Kremlin
Tretyakov Art Gallery
Pavelet Station
Veshnyaki
Kosino
Kozhukhovo
Temnikovo
Novoivanovskoye
Barvikha
Kuntsevo
Fili-Mazilovo
Davydkovo
Lenin
Gorky Park
Moskvoretskiy
Vykhino
Zhulebino
94
Mikhelysona
Chornaya
Lochino
Mamonovo
Bakovka
Zarechye
Luzhniki Sports Centre Lenin Stadium
Lomonosov University
Leninskiye Gory
Moscow Circus
Oktyabrskiy
Tekstilyshchik
Kuzyminki
Marusino
Odintsovo
Meshcherskiy
Ochakovo
Aminyevo
Ramenki
150
Cheryomushki
Nogatino
Lyublino
Nekrasovka
Ko'enevo
Nikulino
Yugo-Zarad
Dyakovo
Maryino
Lyubertsy
Kuryanovo
Kotelyniki
Tomilino
Kraskovo
Choboty
Solntsevo
Troparevo
Zyuzino
Volkhonka-Zil
Kapotnya
Chkalová
Malakhovka
Peredelkino
Orlovo
Belyayevo Bogorodskoye
250
Certanovo
Lenino
Brateyevo
Borisovo
Tokarevo
Vnukovo
Rasskazovka
Rümyantsevo
Dzerzhinskiy
East from Greenwich

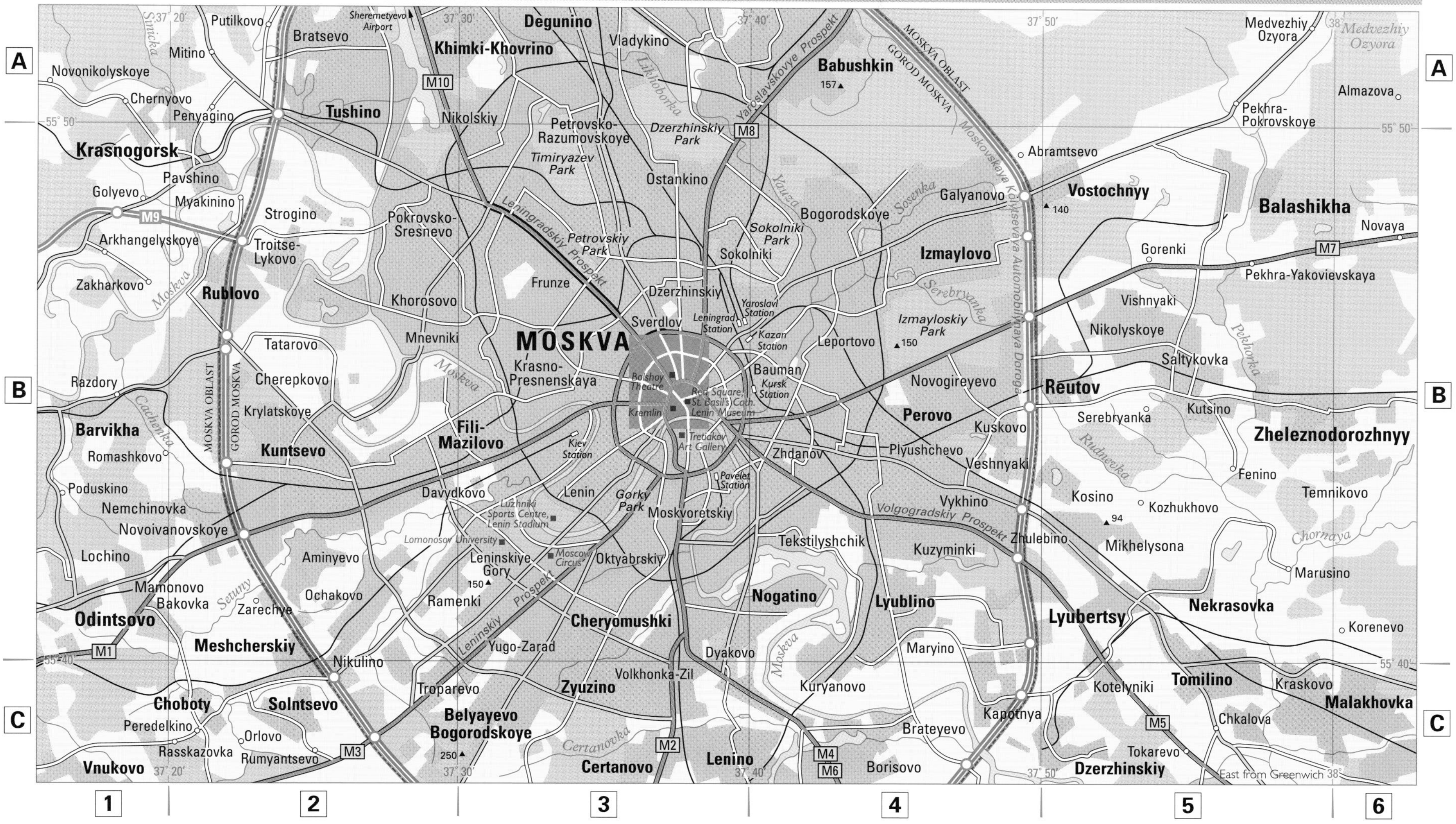

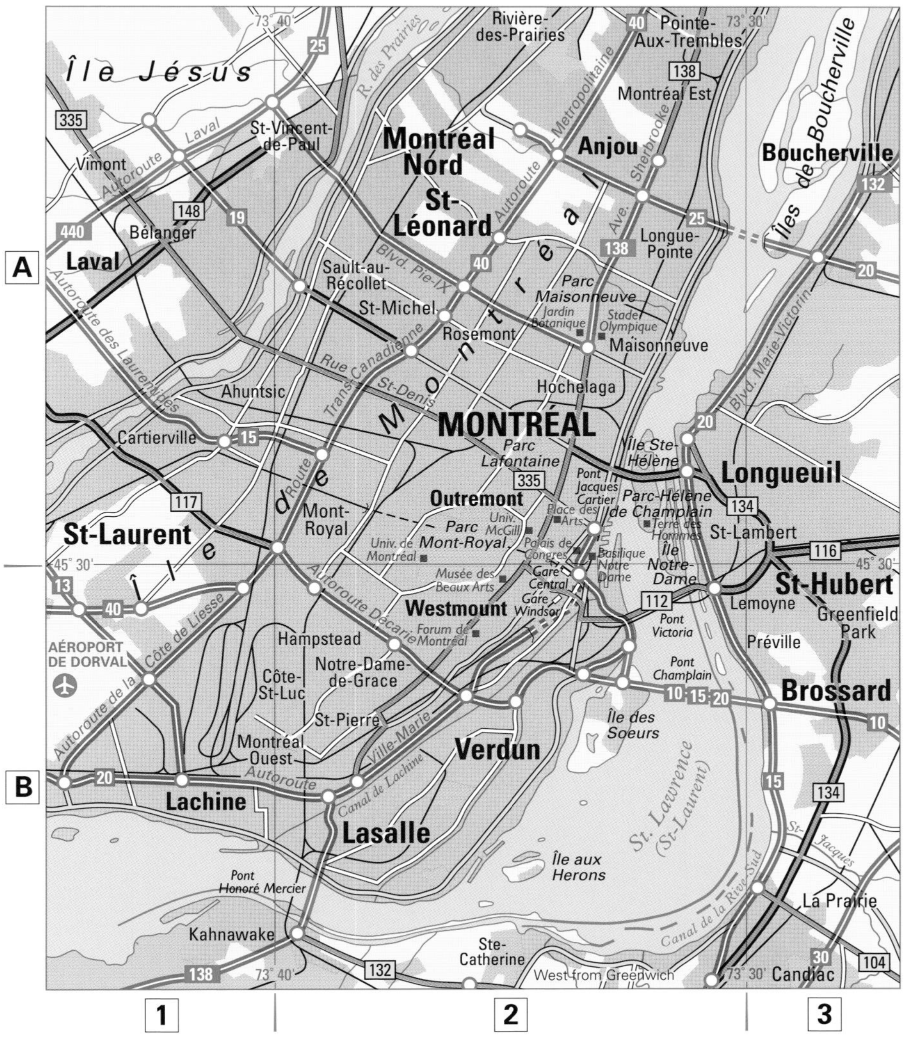

A B C
1 2 3 4 5 6

MONTRÉAL

km 0 — 5
miles 0 — 3

Île Jésus
Rivière-des-Prairies
Pointe-Aux-Trembles
Laval
St-Vincent-de-Paul
Montréal Nord St-Léonard
Anjou
Boucherville
Vimont
Bélanger
Longue-Pointe
Laval
Sault-au-Récollet
St-Michel
Parc Maisonneuve Jardin Botanique
Rosemont
Stade Olympique
Maisonneuve
Ahuntsic
Hochelaga
Cartierville
Parc Lafontaine
Île Ste-Hélène
Longueuil
St-Laurent
Outremont
Mont-Royal
Univ. McGill
Univ. de Montréal
Parc du Mont-Royal
Musée des Beaux Arts
Basilique Notre-Dame
Gare Central
Parc Hélène de Champlain Île Notre-Dame
St-Lambert
Westmount
Forum de Montréal
Gare Windsor
St-Hubert
Greenfield Park
Hampstead
Lemoyne
Préville
Côte-St-Luc
Notre-Dame-de-Grace
St-Pierre
Île des Soeurs
Montréal Ouest
Verdun
Brossard
Lachine
Lasalle
Île aux Herons
St. Lawrence (St-Laurent)
Kahnawake
Pont Honoré Mercier
Ste-Catherine
La Prairie
Candiac
West from Greenwich

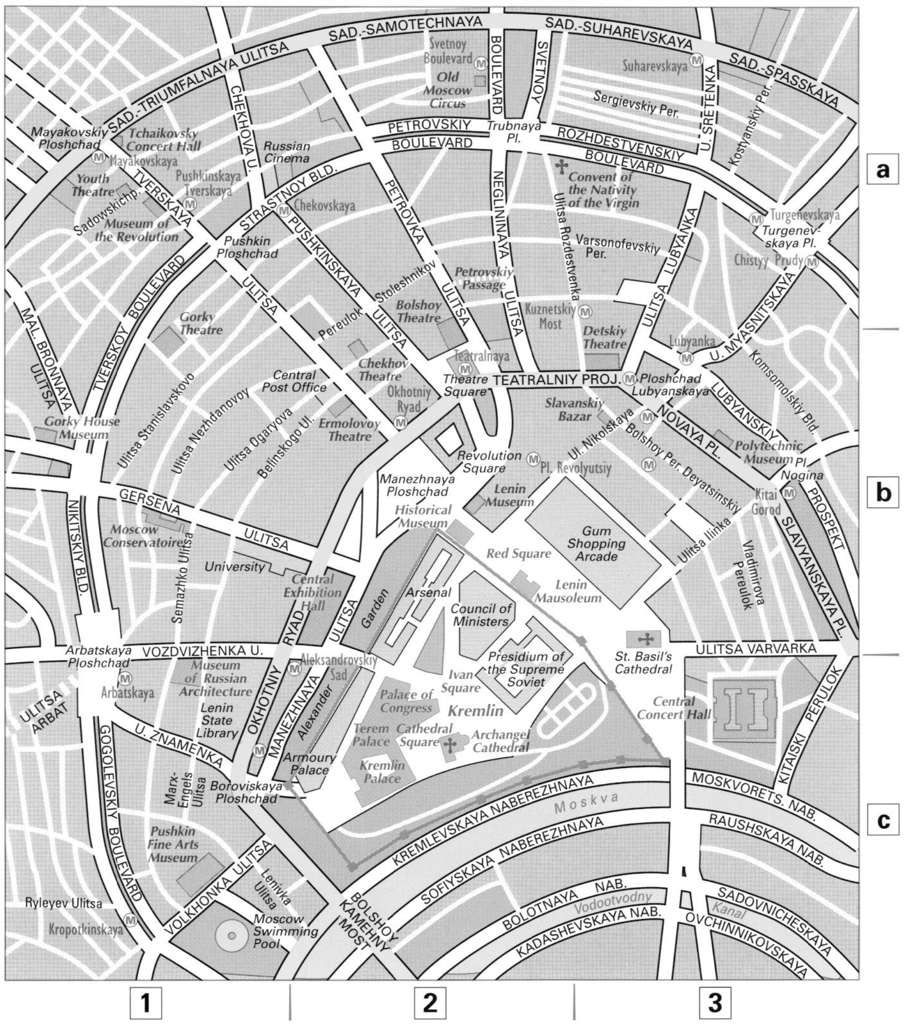

A B
1 2 3

CENTRAL MOSCOW

km 0 — 1
miles 0 — 0.5

a b c
1 2 3

MUMBAI

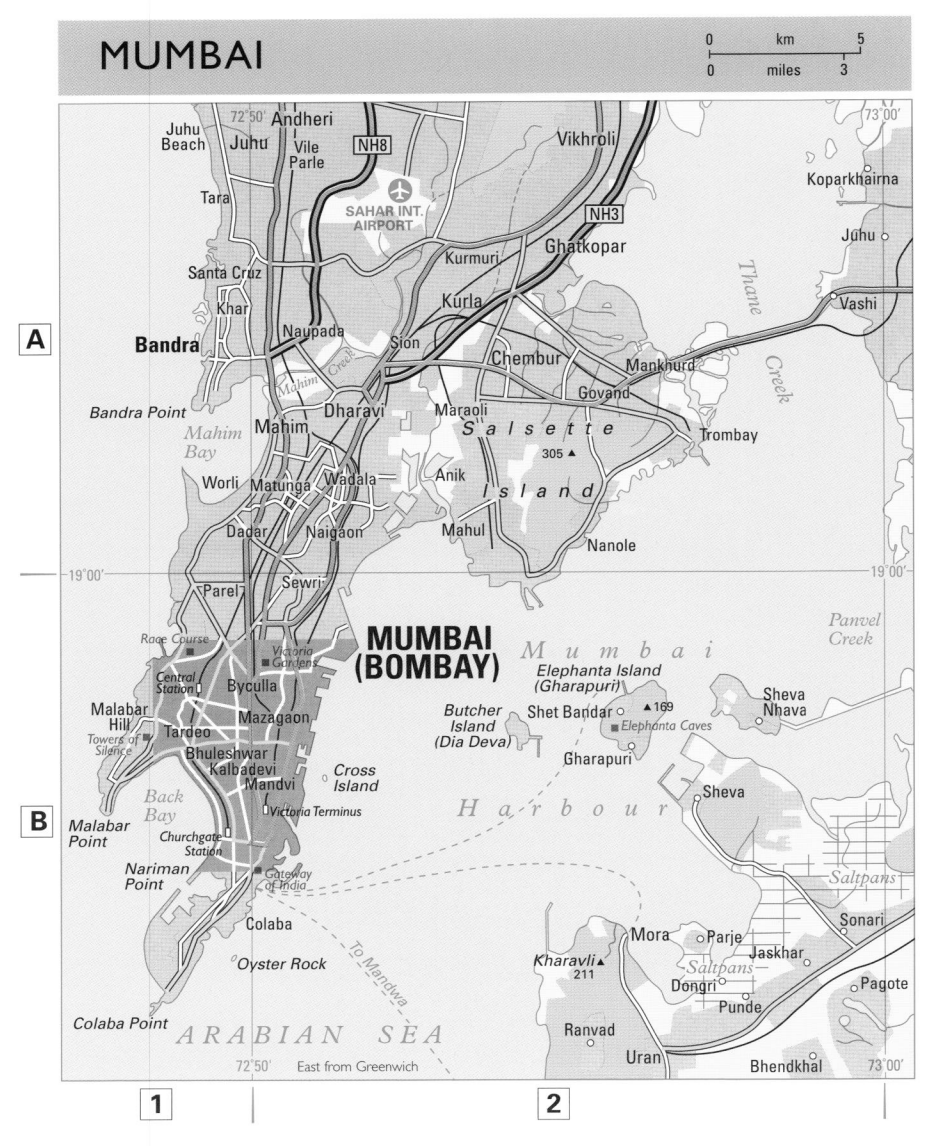

CENTRAL MUMBAI

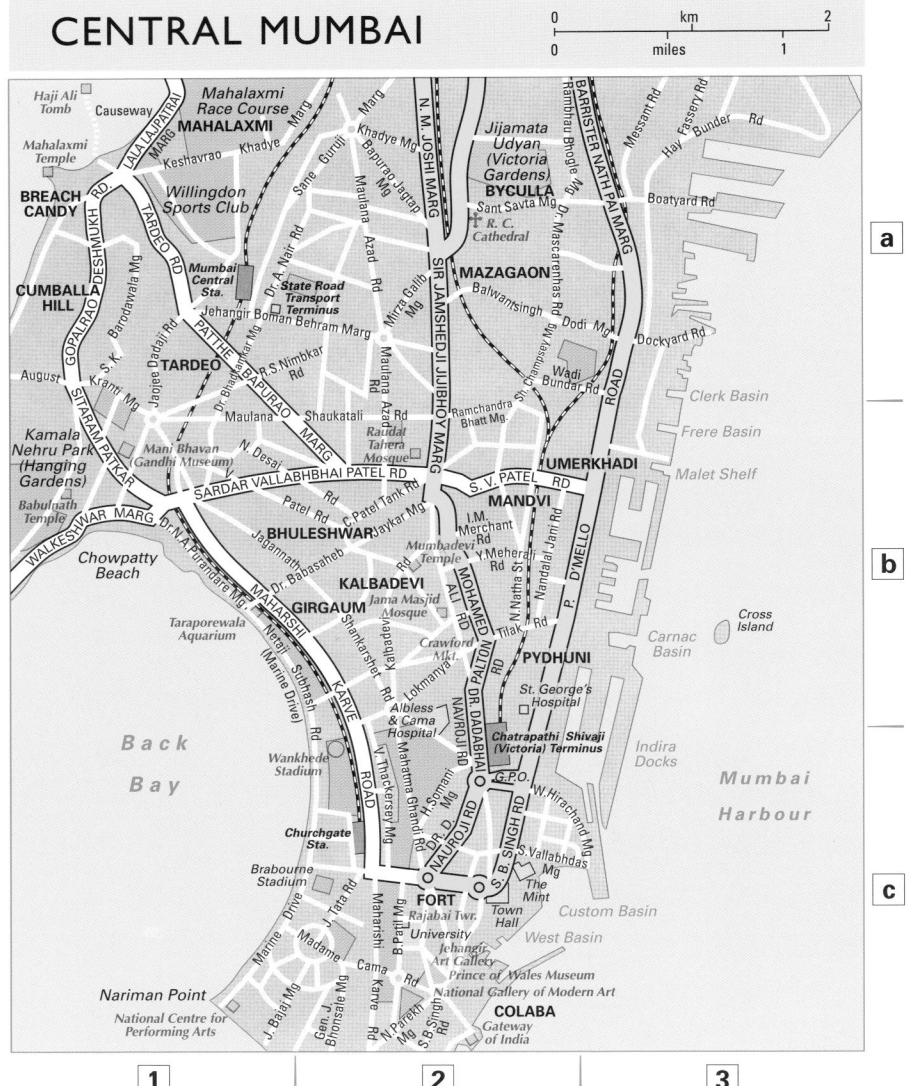

MUNICH

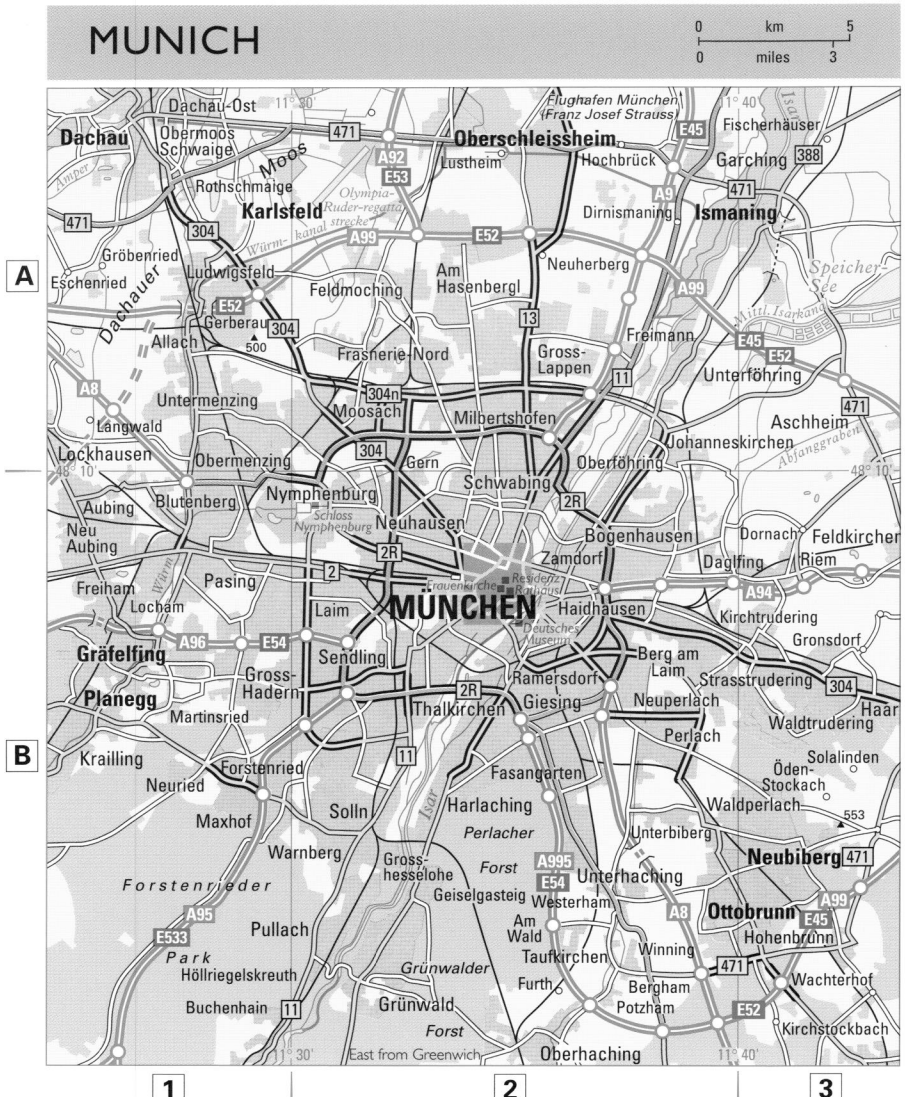

CENTRAL MUNICH

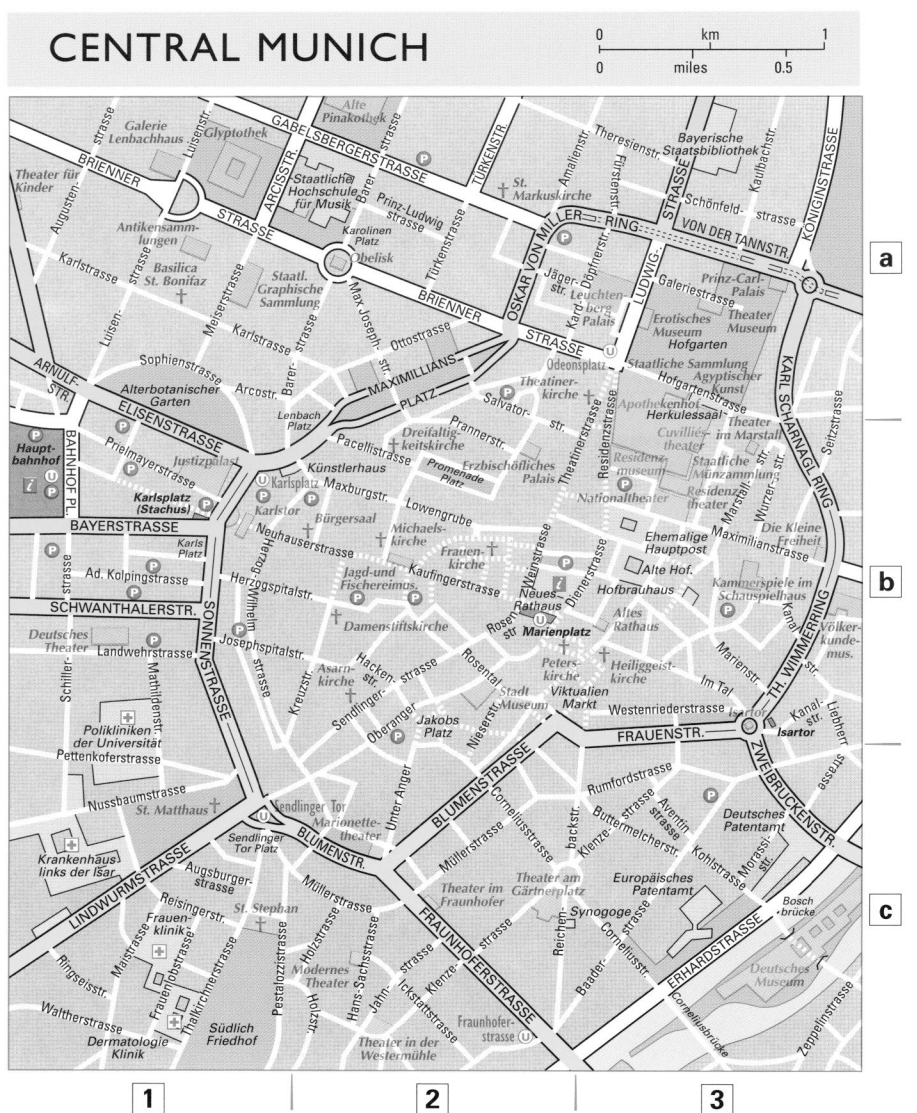

NEW YORK

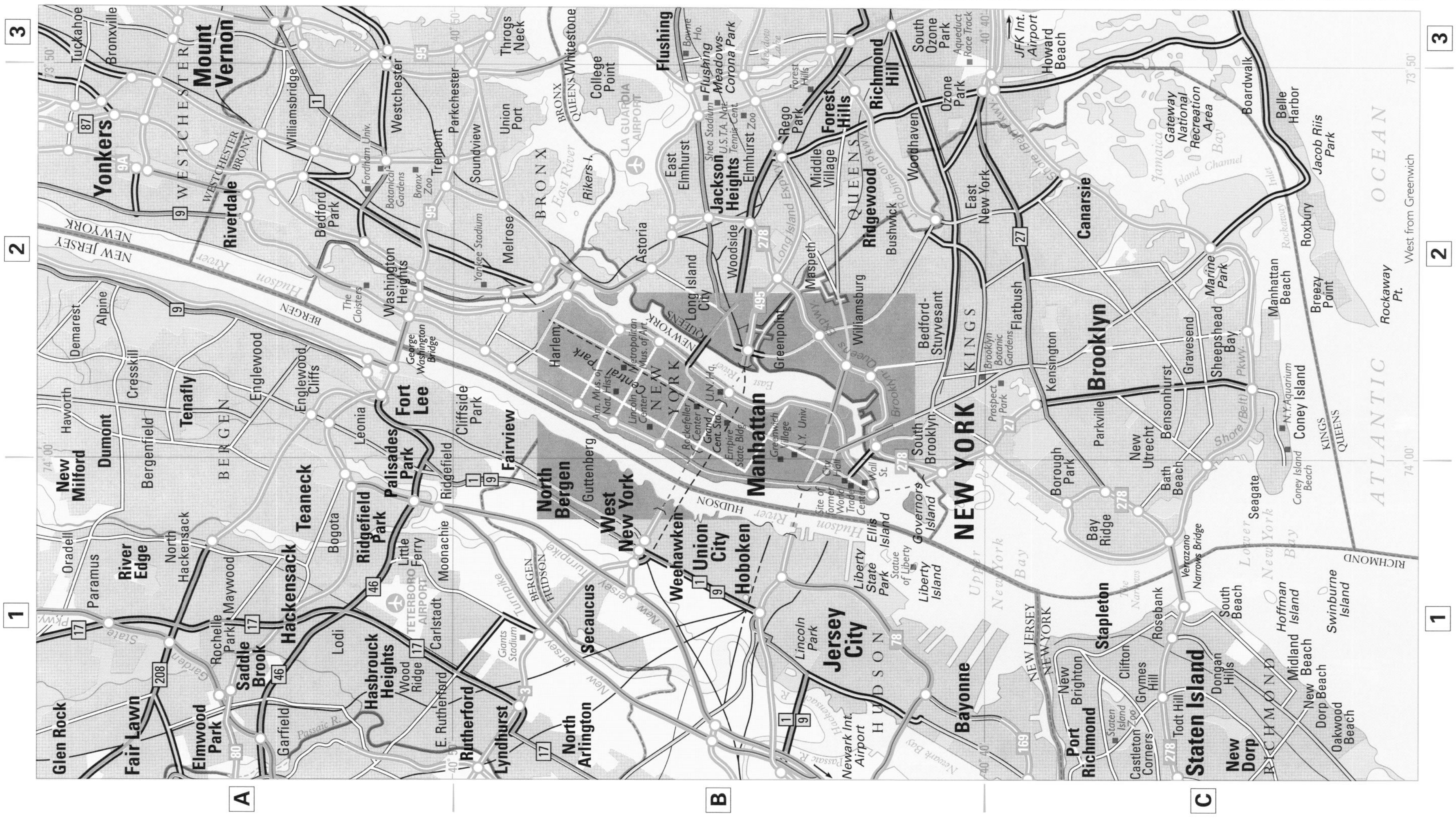

CENTRAL NEW YORK

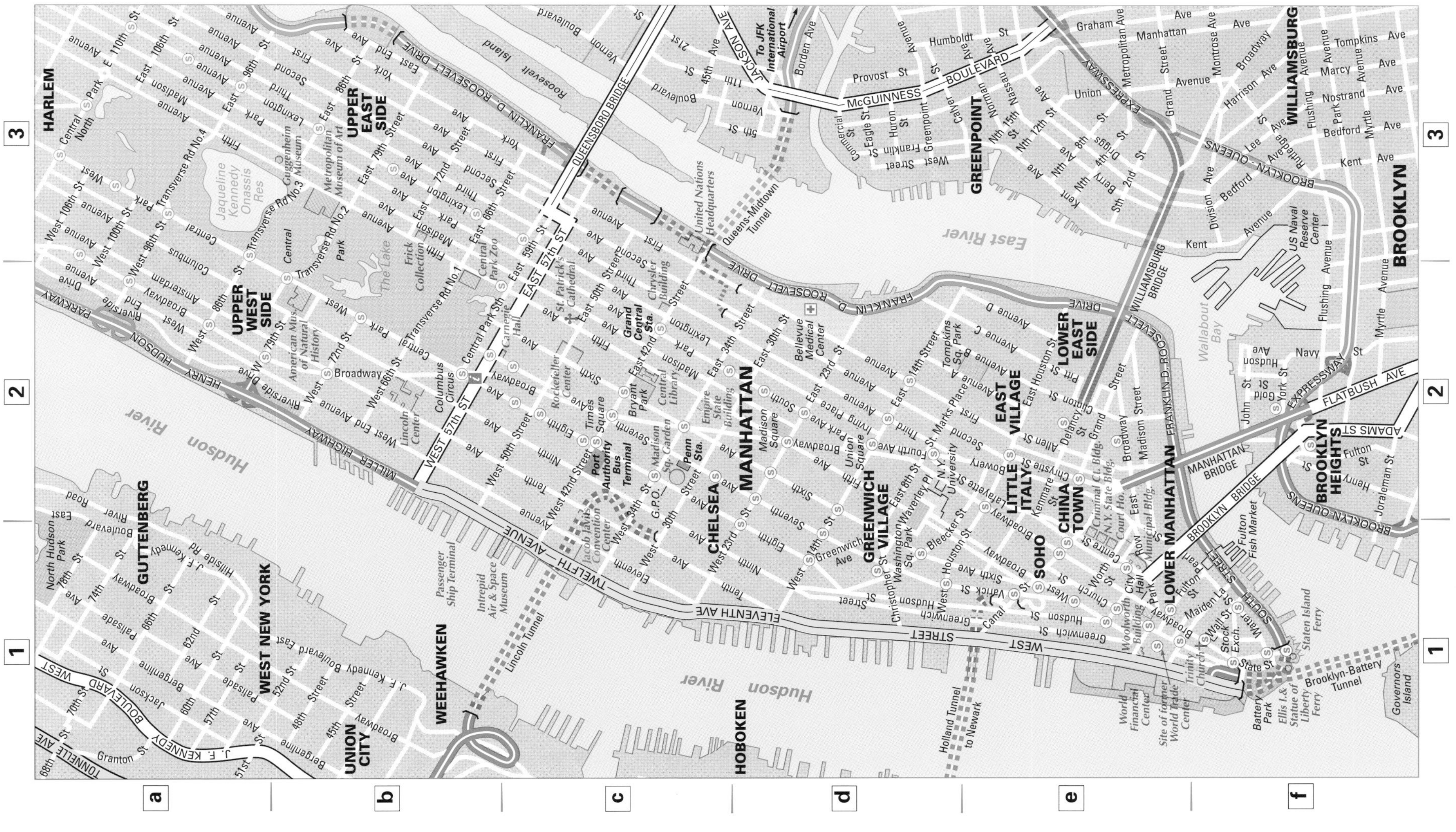

OSAKA

0 km 5
0 miles 3

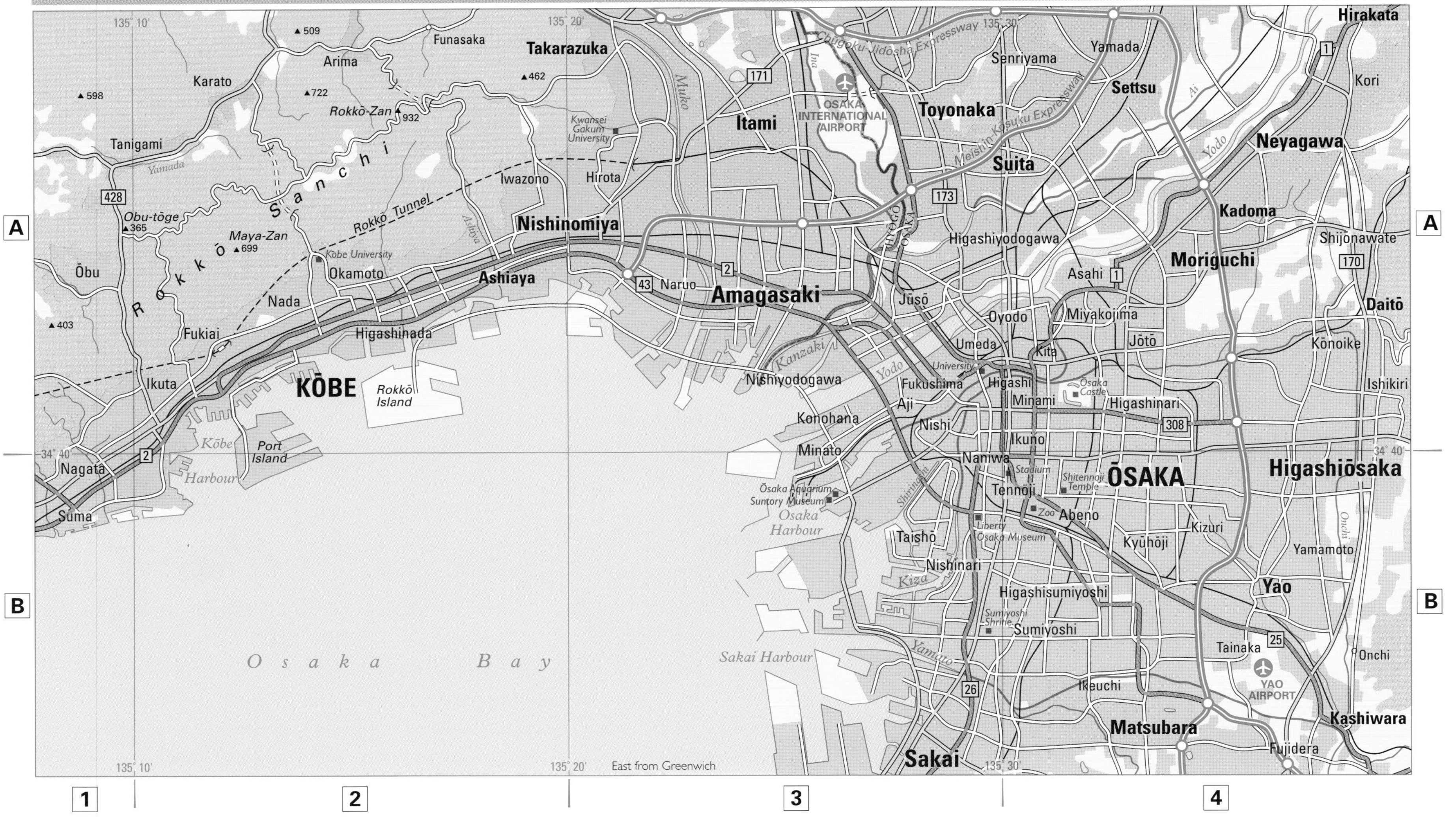

135° 10'
▲ 509
Funasaka
Takarazuka
135° 20'
Chugoku Jidoshado Expressway 135° 30'
Yamada
Senriyama
Hirakata
Karato
Arima
▲ 462
OSAKA INTERNATIONAL AIRPORT
Toyonaka
Settsu
Kori
▲ 598
▲ 722
Rokkō-Zan
932
Itami
171
Kwansei Gakuin University
Meishin Expressway
Suita
Neyagawa
11
Tanigami
Yamada
Iwazono
Hirota
Higashiyodogawa
173
Kadoma
Shijonawate
428
Rokkō Sanchi
Rokkō Tunnel
Asahi
1
Moriguchi
170
Obu-tōge
▲ 365
Maya-Zan
▲ 699
Kōbe University
Okamoto
Nishinomiya
43
Naruo
Amagasaki
Jūsō
Ōyodo
Miyakojima
Jōtō
308
Daitō
Ōbu
Nada
Ashiaya
Umeda
Kita
Kōnoike
▲ 403
Fukiai
Higashinada
Yodo
Fukushima
Higashi
Osaka Castle
Higashinari
Ishikiri
Ikuta
Nishiyodogawa
Aji
Nishi
Minami
34° 40'
Nagata
KŌBE
Rokkō Island
Konohana
Ikuno
Higashiōsaka
Suma
2
Kōbe Harbour
Port Island
Minato
Naniwa
ŌSAKA
Osaka Aquarium Suntory Museum
Tennōji
Shitennō Temple
Zoo
Abeno
Yamamoto
Osaka Harbour
Liberty Osaka Museum
Taishō
Kizuri
Yao
Nishinari
Kyūhōji
25
Higashisumiyoshi
Tainaka
Onchi
Sumiyoshi Shrine
Sumiyoshi
YAO AIRPORT
Osaka Bay
Kiga
Ikeuchi
Kashiwara
26
Matsubara
Fujidera
Sakai
135° 20'
East from Greenwich
135° 30'
Sakai Harbour

1 2 3 4
A A
B B

OSLO

0 km 5
0 miles 3

60° 00'
10° 30'
Tryvannshøgda
▲ 531
10° 40'
Maridalen
10° 50'
60° 00'
By
OSLO AKERSHUS
Bogstadvatn
Maridalsvatnet
▲ 418
Holmenkollen
Kjelsås
Gorud
Burudvatn
Alnsjøen
Rødtvet
Bærums Verk
Ila
Røa
Ris
RING 3
Ulleval
4
163
379
Lijordet
168
OSLO
Sinsen
Alna
E6
Kolsås
Haslum
Ullern
RING 2
Skøyen
Tøyen
E16
160
Stabekk
Lysaker
Universitet Vestbane
Domkirke
Bryn
Bryn
164
Hovik
166
Norsk Folke Museum
Sentralst.
Ryen
Tanum
Akershus Slott
Oppsal
Sandvika
Snarøya
Forebu
Hovedøya
Bøler
E18
E6
Slependen
Nesøya
Bekkelaget
Hvalstad
Nesbru
Ostøya
Frederikshavn Helsingborg København Hirtshals, Kiel
Nesoddtangen
Lambertseter
Østmark-kapellet
Brønnøya
Lindøya
Ormøya
Nordstrand
Asker
165
Holmenfjorden
Oksval
Malmøya
Ljabru
E18
Konglungen
Flaskebekk
Skoklefall
155
Hauketo
Blåstad
▲ 215
Torvik
Klemetsrud
167
Vollen
157
Ingierstrand
Kolbotn
Siemmestad
Nesodden
E6
Fjellstrand
Gjersjøen
Hasle
156
Svestad
Oppegård
Svaxad
Blylaget
152
Myrvoll
59° 50'
10° 30'
Nærsnes
Garder
East from Greenwich
▲ 134
Oppegård
10° 40'
10° 50'
E18

1 2 3 4
A A
B B

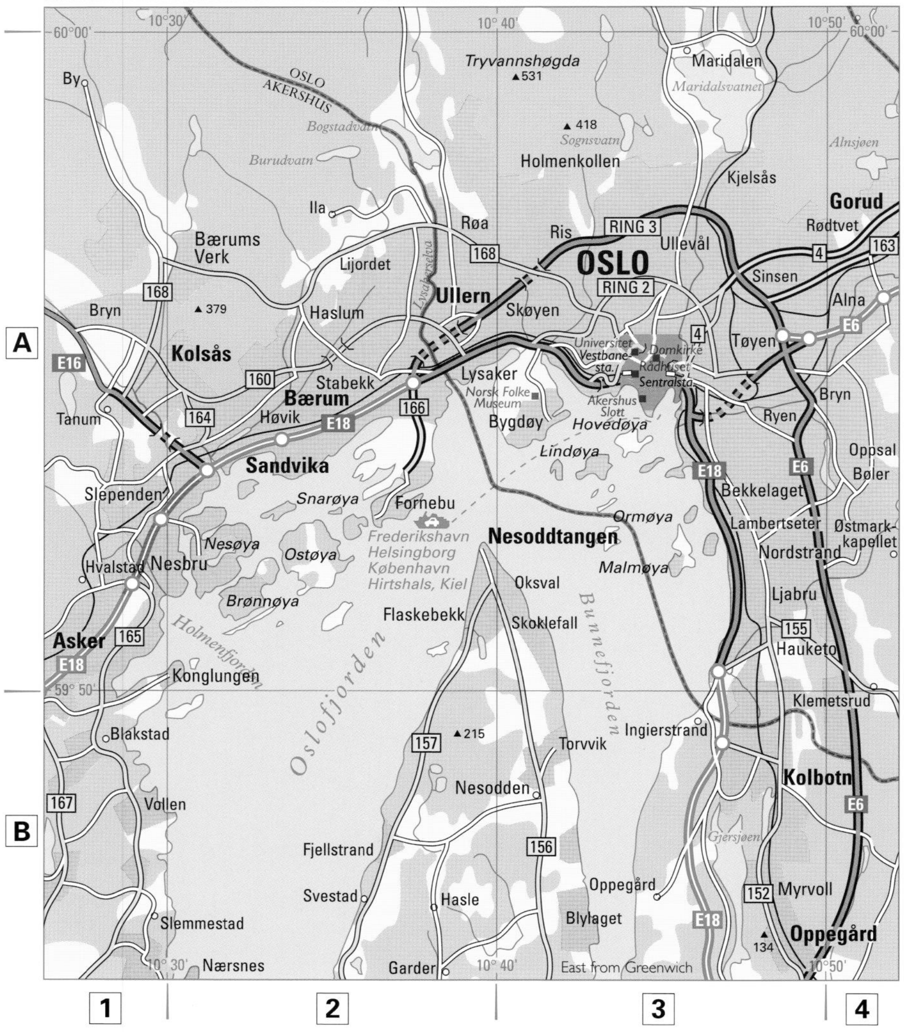

CENTRAL OSLO

0 km 0.5
0 miles 0.25

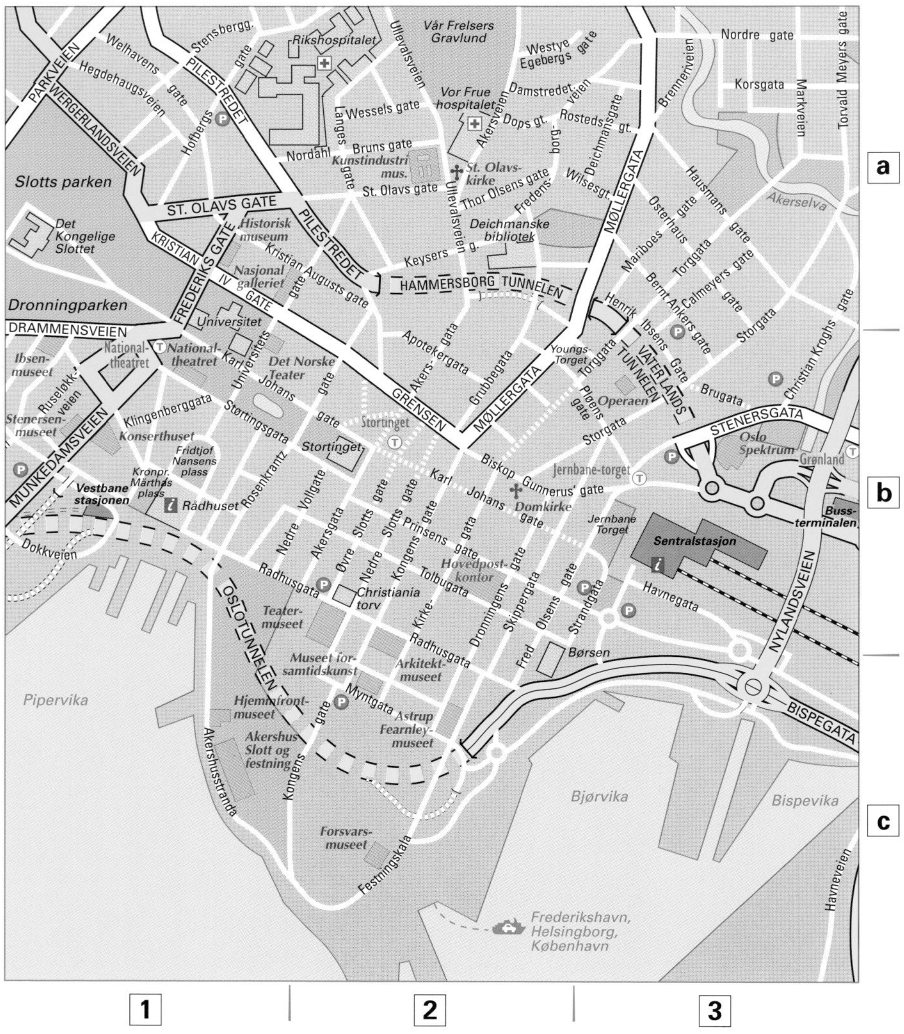

PARKVEIEN
Wethavens
Stensberg gt.
Vår Frelsers Gravlund
Westye Egebergs gate
Nordre gate
Korsgata
Torvald Meyers gate
Rikshospitalet
WERGELANDSVEIEN
Hegdehaugsveien
PILESTREDET
Ullevålsveien
Damstredet
Bremerveien
Markveien
Langes
Wessels gate
Rostedsgate
Akerselva
Slotts parken
Nordahl
Bruns gate
Vor Frue hospitalet
St. Olavs kirke
Deichmanske
Hausmanns gate
ST. OLAVS GATE
Thor Olsens gate
Storgata
a
Kunstindustri mus.
St. Olavs gate
KRISTIAN IV's GATE
Det Kongelige Slottet
Historisk museum
Kristian Augusts gate
Deichmanske bibliotek
HAMMERSBORG TUNNELEN
Henrik
Bernt Ankers gate
Dronningparken
FREDRIKS GATE
Nasjonal galleriet
Keysers
GRENSEN
MØLLERGATA
DRAMMENSVEIEN
Universitet
Pløens
Brugata
Ibsen-museet
Nationalt.theatret
Karl Johans
Youngs Torget
Christian Krohgs gate
STENERSGATA
Rosenkrantz'
Stortinget
Oslo Spektrum
Operaen
b
Stenersens museum
Konserthuset
Storingsgata
Biskop Gunnerus' gate
Granland
MUNKEDAMSVEIEN
Kronpr. Marthas plass
Fridtjof Nansens plass
Stortinget
Jernbane-torget
BUSS terminalen
Vestbane stasjonen
Rådhuset
Rådhusgata
Domkirke
Sentralstasjon
Nedre Slotts gate
Karl Johans gate
Hovedpost kontor
Teater-museet
Pipervika
Christiania torv
Prinsens gate
Børsen
Museet for samtidskunst
Myntgata
Arkitekt-museet
Fred. Olsens gate
Strandgata
NYLANDSVEIEN
Hjemmefront-museet
Åstrup Fearnley museet
OSLO TUNNELEN
Havnegata
c
Akershus Slott og festning
Forsvars-museet
Festningsbrygga
Bjørvika
Frederikshavn, Helsingborg, København
Bispevika
Havneveien
BISPEGATA

1 2 3
a
b
c

PARIS

0 km 5
0 miles 3

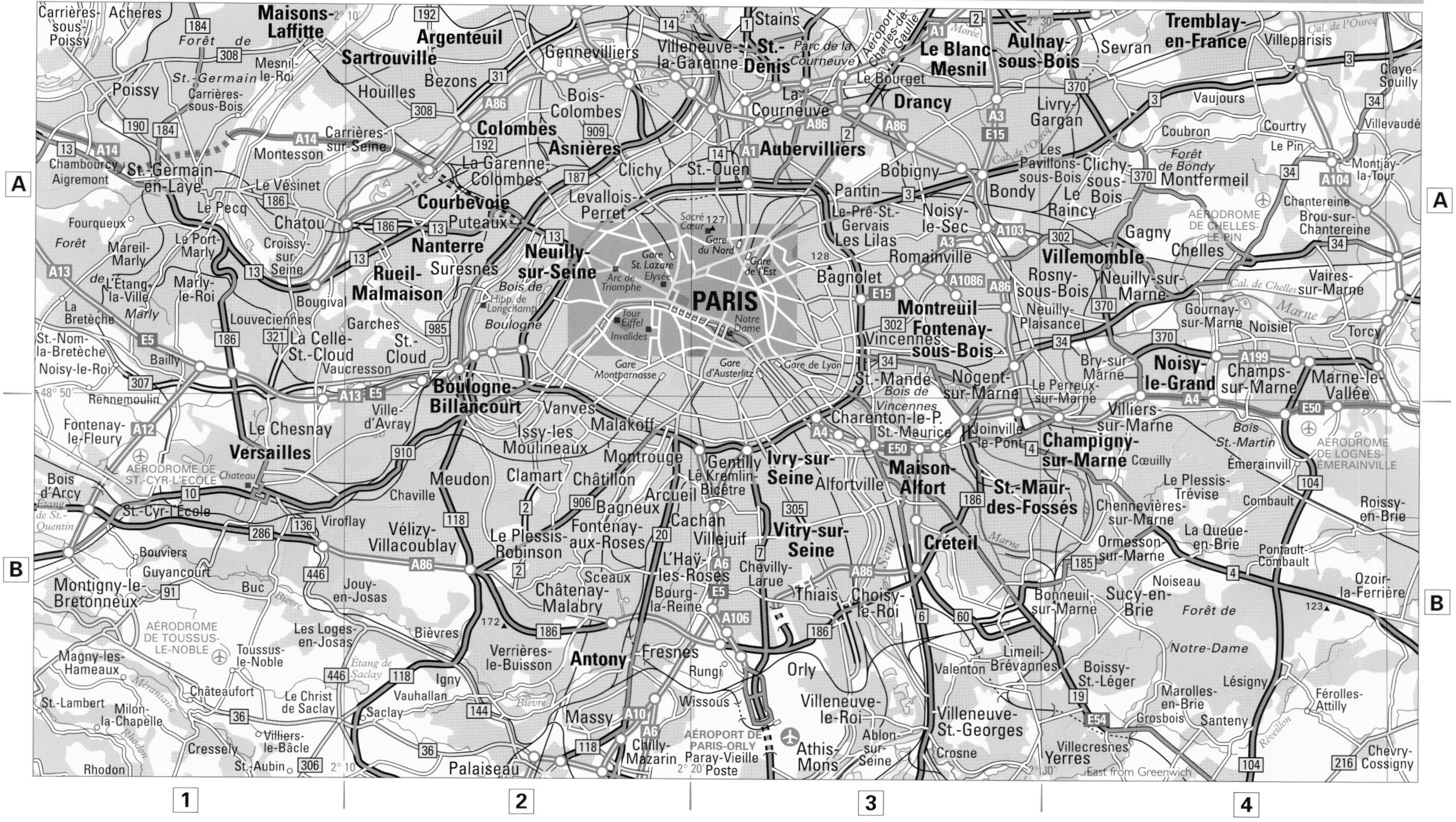
A
B
1
2
3
4
Maisons-Laffitte
Argenteuil
Sartrouville
St.-Denis
Le Blanc-Mesnil
Aulnay-sous-Bois
Tremblay-en-France
Colombes
Asnières
Aubervilliers
Drancy
St.-Germain-en-Laye
Courbevoie
Nanterre
Neuilly-sur-Seine
Rueil-Malmaison
PARIS
Montreuil
Fontenay-sous-Bois
Villemomble
Noisy-le-Grand
Boulogne-Billancourt
Versailles
Ivry-sur-Seine
Maison-Alfort
St.-Maur-des-Fossés
Champigny-sur-Marne
Vitry-sur-Seine
Créteil
Antony
AÉROPORT DE PARIS-ORLY
AÉRODROME DE TOUSSUS-LE-NOBLE
AÉRODROME DE ST.-CYR-L'ÉCOLE
AÉRODROME DE CHELLES-LE-PIN
AÉRODROME DE LOGNES-EMERAINVILLE
East from Greenwich

CENTRAL PARIS

0 km 1
0 miles 0.5

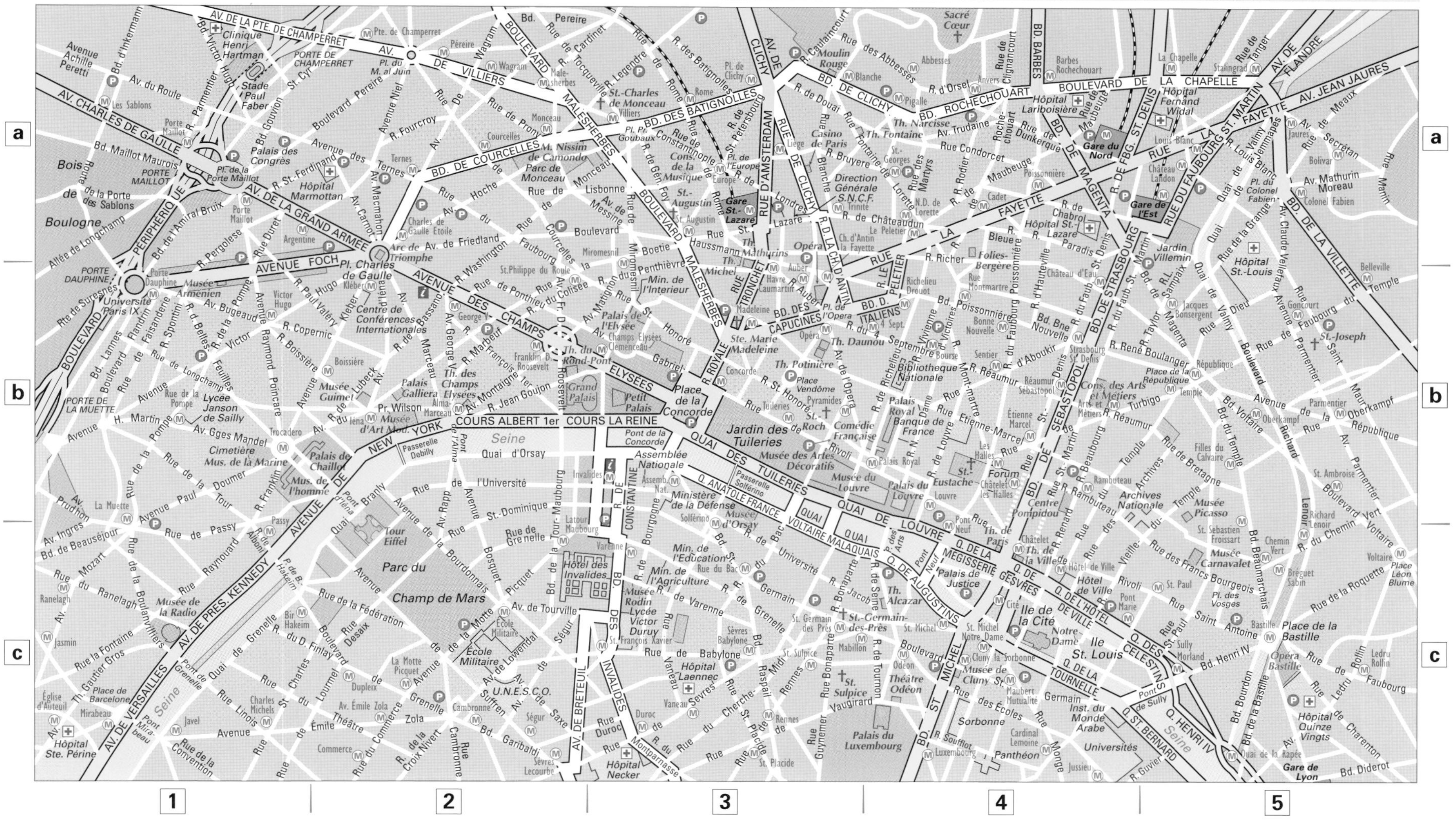
a
b
c
1
2
3
4
5
AV. CHARLES DE GAULLE
BD. DE COURCELLES
BD. DES BATIGNOLLES
BD. DE CLICHY
BD. ROCHECHOUART
BOULEVARD DE LA CHAPELLE
AV. DE LA GRANDE ARMÉE
AVENUE FOCH
AVENUE DES CHAMPS ELYSÉES
COURS ALBERT 1er
COURS LA REINE
QUAI DES TUILERIES
QUAI DE LOUVRE
Arc de Triomphe
Gare St.-Lazare
Gare du Nord
Gare de l'Est
Opéra
Jardin des Tuileries
Palais du Louvre
Tour Eiffel
Parc du Champ de Mars
Hôtel des Invalides
Centre Pompidou
Ile de la Cité
Ile St. Louis
Notre-Dame
Palais du Luxembourg
Place de la Bastille
Gare de Lyon
Seine
Bois de Boulogne

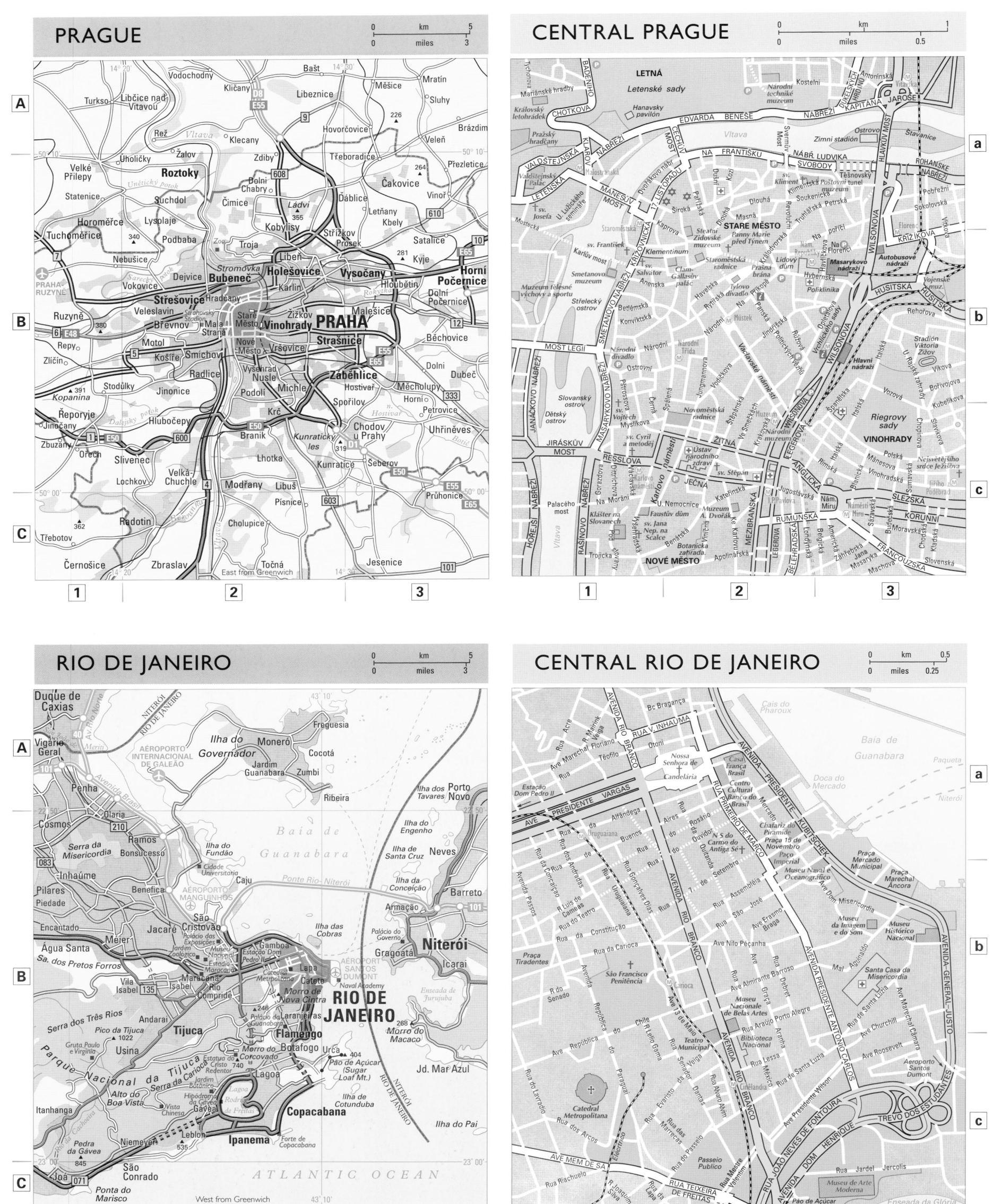

ROME

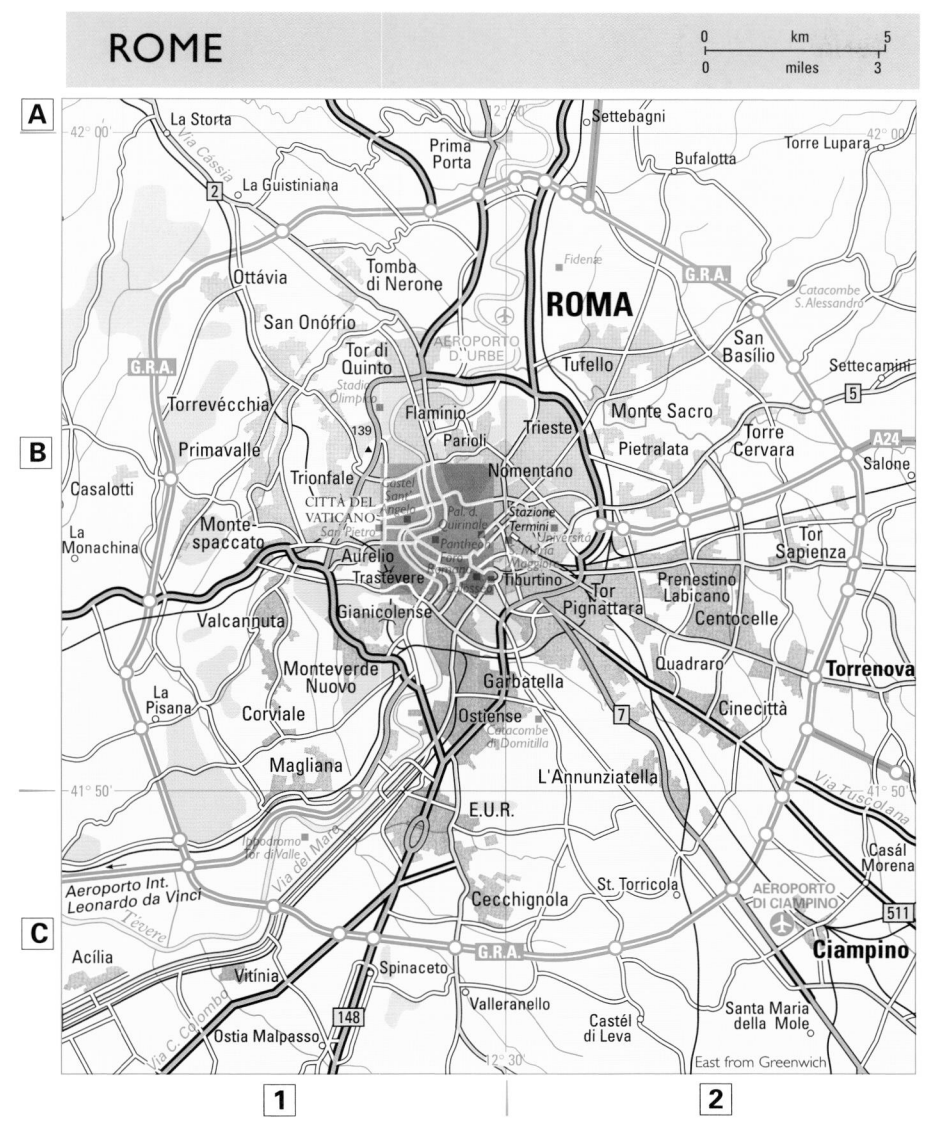

CENTRAL ROME

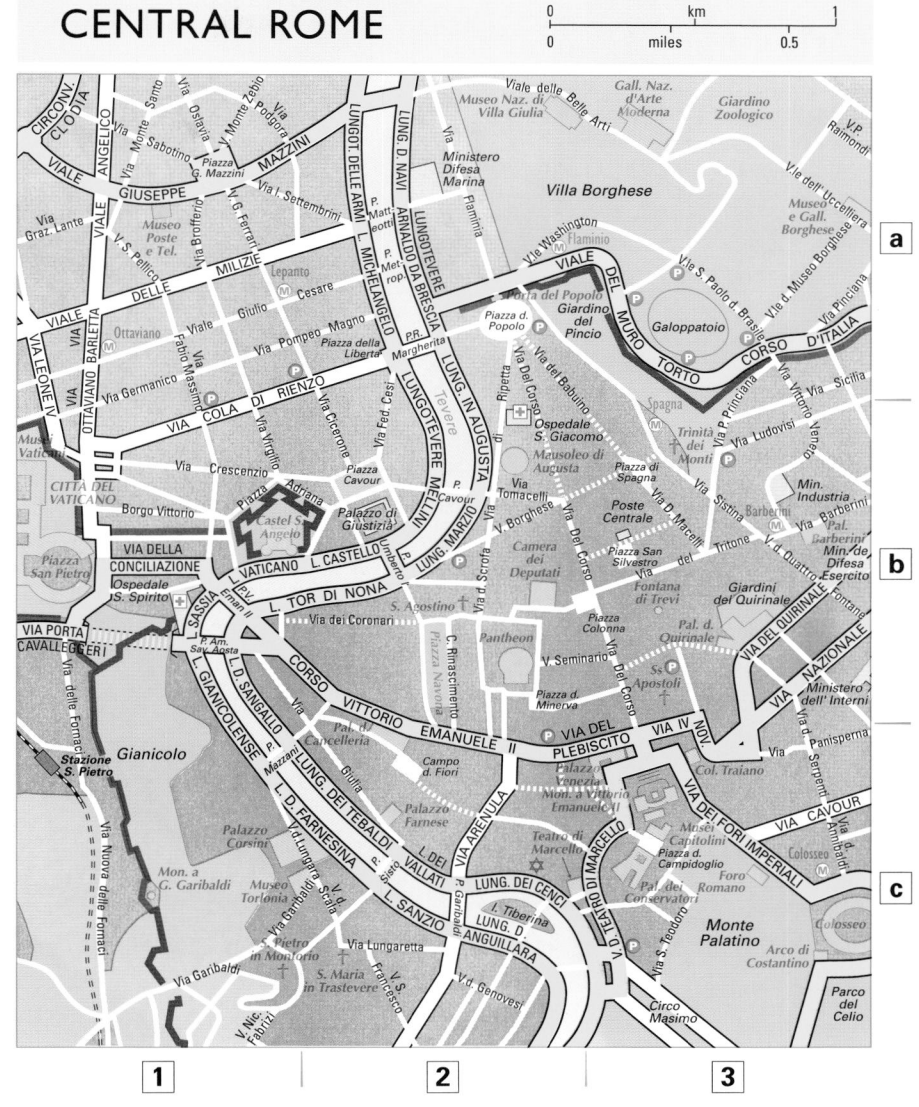

SAN FRANCISCO

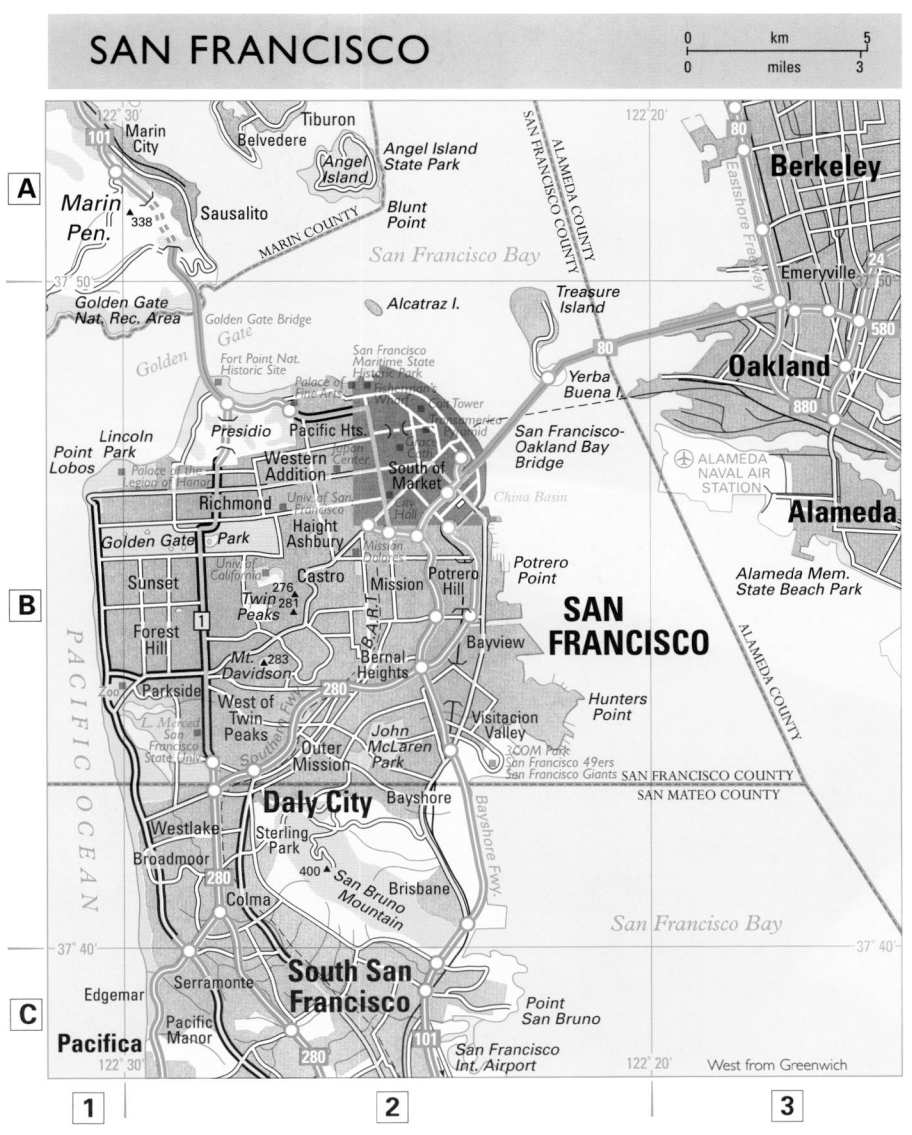

CENTRAL SAN FRANCISCO

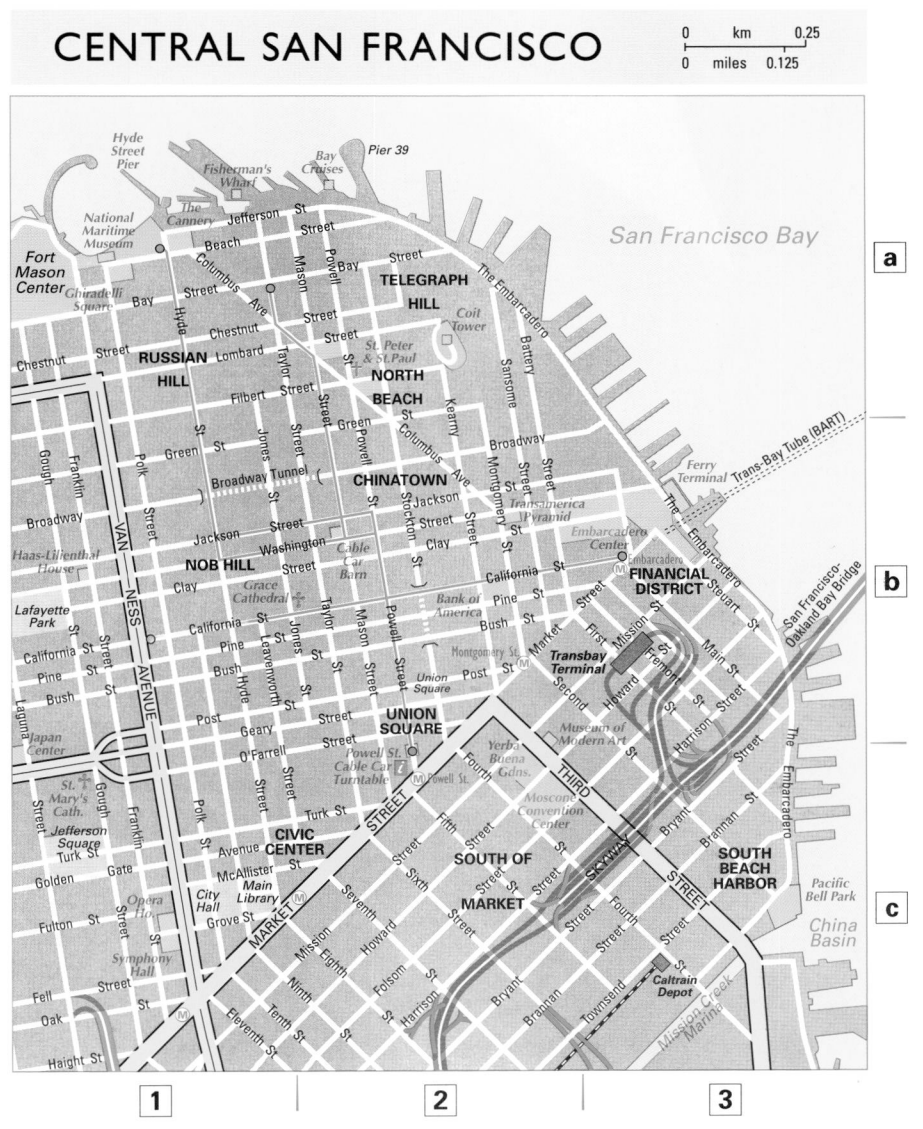

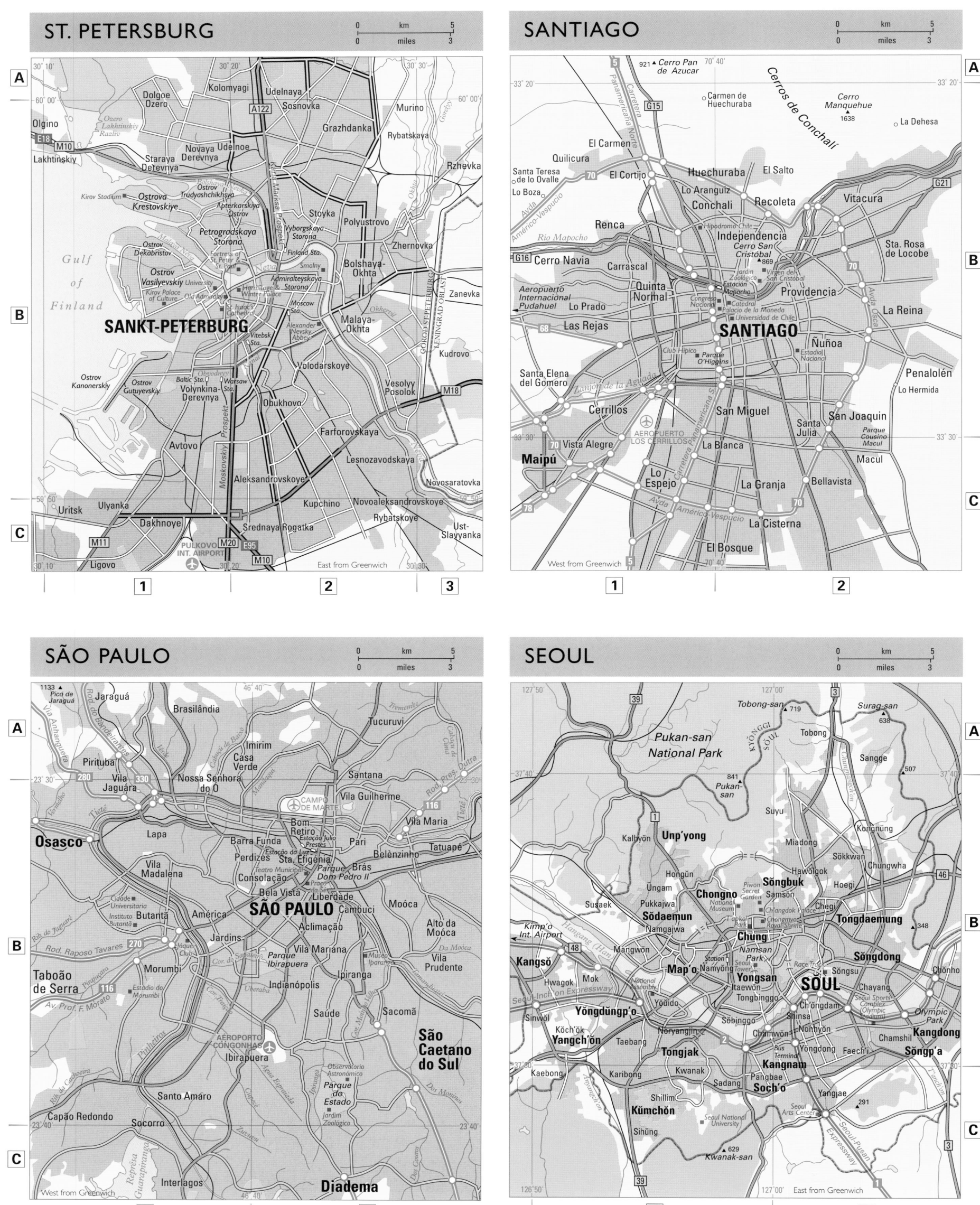

ST. PETERSBURG

km 0 — 5
miles 0 — 3

Olgino
Dolgoe Ozero
Kolomyagi
Udelnaya
Sosnovka
Murino
A122
Staraya Derevnya
Lakhtinskiy
Novaya Udelnoe Derevnya
Grazhdanka
Rybatskaya
Rzhevka
Kirov Stadium
Ostrova Krestovskiye
Ostrov Trudyashchikhsya
Apterkarskiy Ostrov
Stoyka
Polyustrovo
Zhernovka
Petrogradskaya Storona
Vyborgskaya Storona
Finland Sta.
Bolshaya-Okhta
Ostrov Dekabristov
Fortress of St. Peter & St. Paul
Admiralteyskaya Storona
Smolny
Ostrov Vasilyevskiy
University
Winter Palace
Moscow Sta.
Zanevka
Kirov Palace of Culture
Old Admiralty
St Isaac's Cathedral
Alexander-Nevsky Abbey
Malaya-Okhta
Okkervil
Kudrovo
Gulf of Finland
SANKT-PETERBURG
Vitebsk Sta.
Volodarskoye
Ostrov Kanonerskiy
Ostrov Gutuyevskiy
Baltic Sta.
Warsaw Sta.
Volynkina-Derevnya
Obukhovo
Vesolyy Posolok
M18
Avtovo
Farforovskaya
Lesnozavodskaya
Novosaratovka
Aleksandrovskoye
Ulyanka
Srednaya Rogatka
Kupchino
Novoaleksandrovskoye
Uritsk
Dakhnoye
Rybatskoye
Ust-Slavyanka
M11
PULKOVO INT. AIRPORT
M20
E95
M10
Ligovo
East from Greenwich

A B C
1 2 3

SANTIAGO

km 0 — 5
miles 0 — 3

921 Cerro Pan de Azucar
Cerro Manquehue 1638
La Dehesa
El Carmen
Carmen de Huechuraba
Cerros de Conchalí
Quilicura
Santa Teresa de lo Ovalle
Lo Boza
El Cortijo
Huechuraba
El Salto
Vitacura
Renca
Lo Aranguiz
Conchalí
Recoleta
Cerro Navia
Hippodromo Chile
Independencia
Sta. Rosa de Locobe
Carrascal
Cerro San Cristóbal 869
Jardín Zoológico San Cristóbal
Aeropuerto Internacional Pudahuel
Lo Prado
Quinta Normal
Estación Mapocho
Congreso Nacional
Providencia
La Reina
Las Rejas
Palacio de la Moneda
Catedral
Universidad de Chile
SANTIAGO
Ñuñoa
Santa Elena del Gomero
Club Hípico
Parque O'Higgins
Estadio Nacional
Penalolén
Lo Hermida
Cerrillos
AEROPUERTO LOS CERRILLOS
Vista Alegre
San Miguel
Santa Julia
San Joaquin
Parque Cousino Macul
Maipú
La Blanca
Macul
Lo Espejo
La Granja
Bellavista
La Cisterna
El Bosque
West from Greenwich

A B C
1 2

SÃO PAULO

km 0 — 5
miles 0 — 3

1133 Pica de Jaraguá
Jaraguá
Brasilândia
Tucuruvi
Imirim
Casa Verde
Pirituba
Santana
Vila Jaguára
Nossa Senhora do Ó
Vila Guilherme
CAMPO DE MARTE
Vila Maria
Osasco
Lapa
Bom Retiro
Estação Júlio Prestes
Pari
Belènzinho
Tatuapé
Vila Madalena
Barra Funda
Perdizes
Estação da Luz
Sta. Efigènia
Parque Dom Pedro II
Brás
Cidade Universitaria
Butantã
Consolação
Teatro Municipal
Bela Vista
Liberdade
Moóca
Instituto Butantã
América
SÃO PAULO
Cambuci
Alto da Moóca
Jardins
Aclimação
Da Moóca
Vila Prudente
Morumbi
Jóquei Club
Parque Ibirapuera
Vila Mariana
Museu Ipiranga
Taboão de Serra
116
Estadio do Morumbi
Indianópolis
Ipiranga
Saúde
Sacomã
AEROPORTO CONGONHAS
São Caetano do Sul
Ibirapuera
Observatorio Astronómico
Parque do Estado
Santo Amaro
Jardim Zoológico
Capão Redondo
Socorro
West from Greenwich
Interlagos
Diadema

A B C
1 2

SEOUL

km 0 — 5
miles 0 — 3

Tobong-san 719
Surag-san 638
Pukan-san National Park
Tobong
Sangge 507
Pukan-san 841
Suyu
Kongnung
Kalbyŏn
Unp'yong
Miadong
Sökkwan
Chungwha
Hongŭn
Piwon Secret Garden
Songbuk
Hoegi
Susaek
Ŭngam
Pukkajwa
Chongno
Samsön
Chegi
National Museum
Ch'angdok Palace
Tongdaemung 348
Söul Station
Södaemun
Chung
Namsan Park
Söngdong
Kangsö
Mangwŏn
Map'o
Yongsan
Itaewön
SÖUL
Chonho
Hwagok
Mok
National Assembly
Yŏido
Namyŏng
Söul Tower
Tongbinggo
Ch'ongdam
Chayang
Kimp'o Int. Airport
Olympic Park
Yŏngdŭngp'o
Sinsha
Olympic Stadium
Kangdong
Sinwŏl
Köch'ŏk
Noryangjin
Söbinggo
Chamwŏn
Söngp'a
Yangch'ön
Taebang
Yŏngdong
Faech'i
Chamshil
Tongjak
Kwanak
Bus Terminal
Kangnam
Kaebong
Karibong
Sadang
Pangbae
Soch'o
Yangjae 291
Shillim
Kümch'ön
Seoul National University
Seoul Arts Center
Kwanak-san 629
Sihüng
East from Greenwich

A B C
1 2

SHANGHAI

km 5
miles 3

A

Liuhang
Tangqiao
Yangjiazhuang
Wusong
Baoshan
Yinhangzhen
Gaoqiao
Chang J. (Yangtse)
31° 20'

Dachang
Airfield
Jiangwan
Wujiaochang
Donggou
Beijiao
Dachang
Heping Park
Yangpu Park
Fuxing Dao
Zhenru
Hongkou Park
Zhabei
Hongkou
Yangpu
Oingningsi
Yangpu Bridge
Zhoujiazhen
Zhenru
Putuo
Shanghai Zhan
Huangpu Park
Huangpu
Yangjing

B
312

Beixing Jing Park
Changfeng Park
Jingan
People's Park
People's
Huangpu
Pudong Dadao
Shanghai Zoo
Zhongshan Park
Changning
Xi Zhan
Fuxing Park
Old City
Puxi
Nanshi
Pudong New Area
318

Xujiahui
Xuhui
Nanpu Bridge
Beicai
Hongqiao
Hongqiao Airport
Longhua Park
Nanshi
Zhoujiadu
Chuanyang
31° 10'
Longhua Pagoda
Caoheijing
Sanlintang

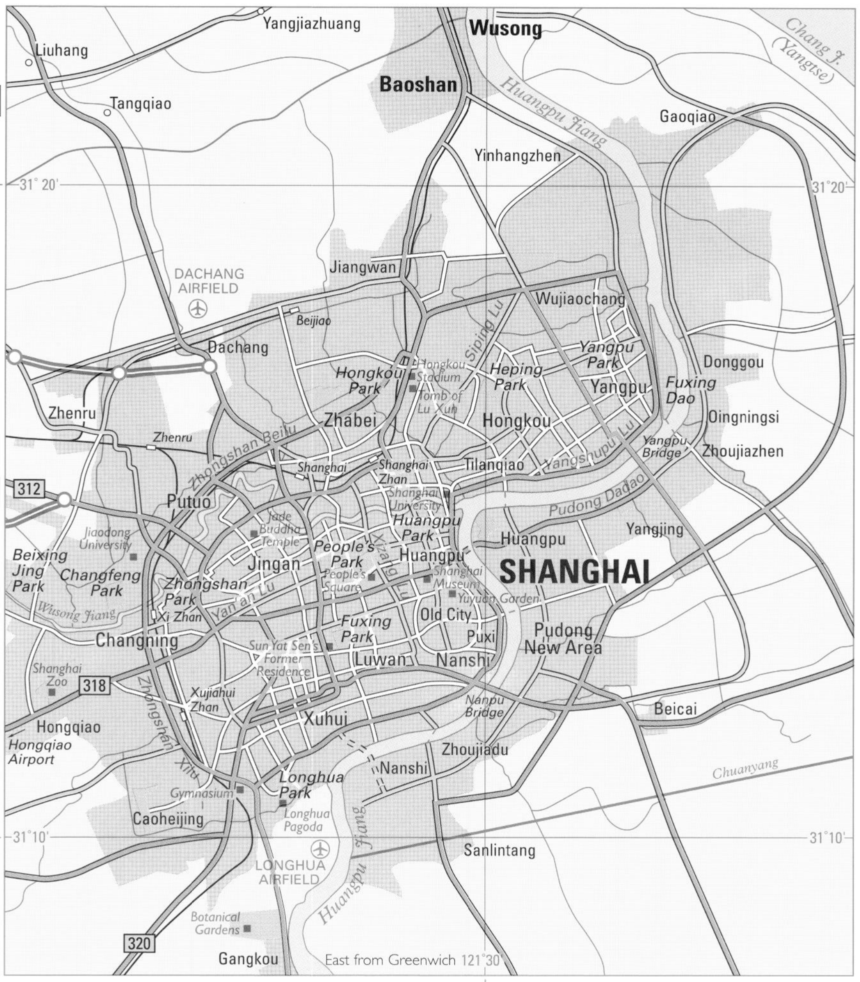

C
LONGHUA AIRFIELD
320
Botanical Gardens
Gangkou
East from Greenwich 121° 30'
Huangpu Jiang

1   2

CENTRAL SINGAPORE

km 1
miles 0.5

Istana (President's Residence)
Kandang Kerbau Hospital
BUKIT TIMAH ROAD
Cuff Rd
Central Park
ORCHARD ROAD
Sultan Mosque
a
Bus Station

Faber House
ORCHARD
Orchard Plaza
PENANG ROAD
Bencoolen
St. Joseph's Church
COLONIAL DISTRICT

KILLINEY
Dhoby Ghaut
BOULEVARD
Singapore Hist. Mus.
Singapore Art Museum
b
Sacred Heart Church
Fort Canning Park
CITY CENTRE
Fort Canning Reservoir
Van Kleef Aquarium
City Hall
St. Andrew's Cathedral
War Memorial Park

RIVER VALLEY ROAD
Hong San See Temple
Singapore Philatelic Mus
Supreme Court
Parliament Hse
Esplanade Park
Victoria Concert Hall & Theatre

HAVELOCK ROAD
MERCHANT ROAD
Melaka Mosque
Boat Quay
Raffles Landing Site
Empress Pl Museum
Merlion Park
c
Marina Bay
Pearl's Hill City Park
Pearl's Hill Reservoir
People's Park Complex
CHINATOWN
Sri Mariamman Temple
Clifford Pier
SENTOSA

1   2   3

SINGAPORE

km 10
miles 6

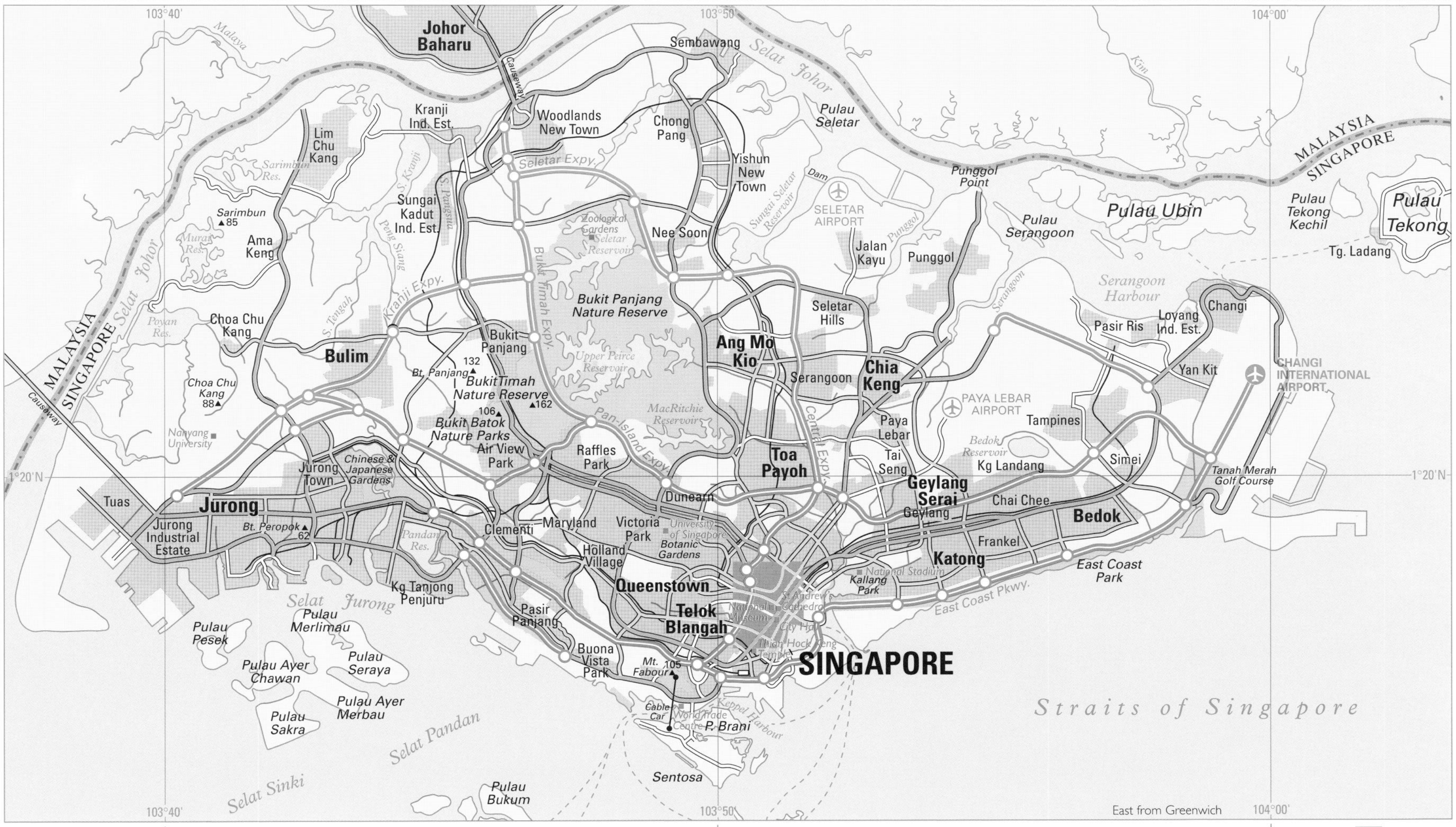

103° 40'
103° 50'
104° 00'
Johor Baharu
Sembawang
Selat Johor
Pulau Seletar
MALAYSIA
SINGAPORE

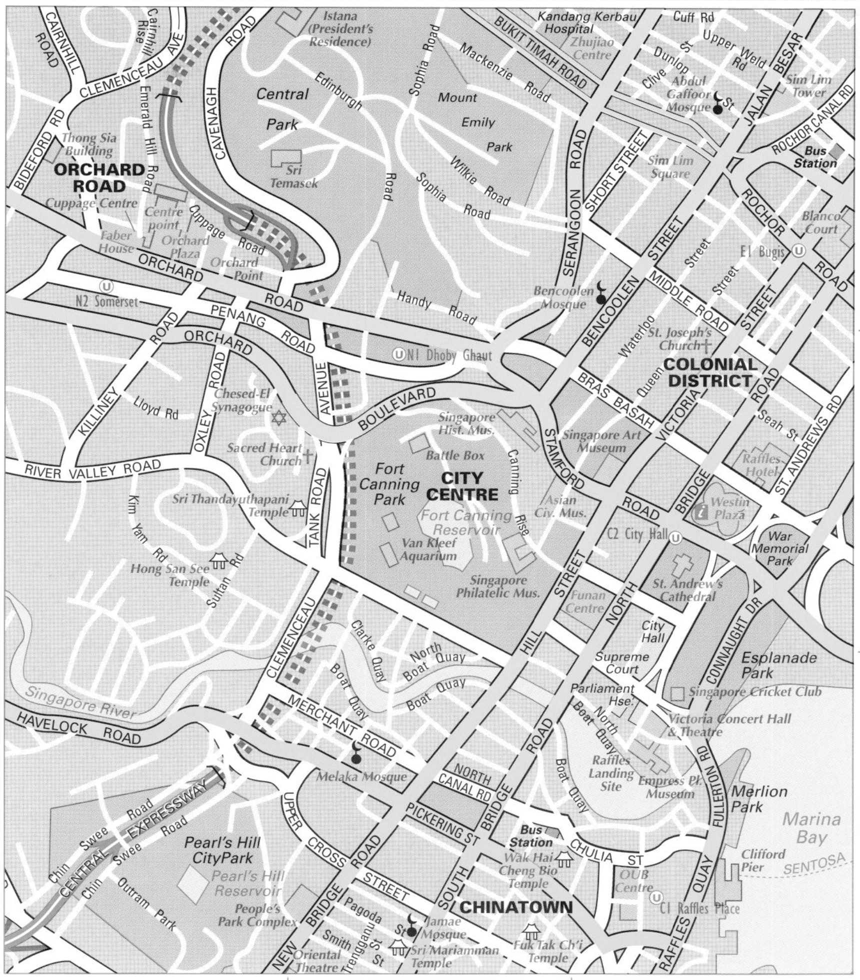

A
Kranji Ind. Est.
Woodlands New Town
Chong Pang
Yishun New Town
Punggol Point
Pulau Ubin
Pulau Tekong Kechil
Pulau Tekong
Lim Chu Kang
Sarimbun Res.
Sungai Kadut Ind. Est.
Zoological Gardens
Seletar Reservoir
SELETAR AIRPORT
Tg. Ladang
Ama Keng
Nee Soon
Jalan Kayu
Punggol
Pulau Serangoon
Serangoon Harbour
Choa Chu Kang
Bukit Panjang Nature Reserve
Seletar Hills
Pasir Ris
Loyang Ind. Est.
Changi
Bulim
Bukit Panjang
Ang Mo Kio
Chia Keng
Yan Kit
CHANGI INTERNATIONAL AIRPORT
Bukit Timah Nature Reserve
MacRitchie Reservoir
Serangoon
Paya Lebar
PAYA LEBAR AIRPORT
Tampines
Bukit Batok Nature Parks
Air View Park
Raffles Park
Toa Payoh
Tai Seng
Bedok Reservoir
Simei
Tanah Merah Golf Course
1° 20'N
Jurong Town
Chinese & Japanese Gardens
Clementi
Maryland
Victoria Park
Botanic Gardens
Geylang Serai
Geylang
Chai Chee
Bedok
Jurong
Jurong Industrial Estate
Kg Tanjong Penjuru
Holland Village
Queenstown
Telok Blangah
Katong
Frankel
East Coast Park
Pasir Panjang
Buona Vista Park
Mt Faburu
SINGAPORE
Tuas
Pulau Pesek
Pulau Merlimau
Pulau Ayer Chawan
Pulau Seraya
Pulau Ayer Merbau
Pulau Sakra
Selat Jurong
Selat Pandan
Cable Car
World Trade Centre
P. Brani
Sentosa
Pulau Bukum
Selat Sinki
Straits of Singapore
East from Greenwich 104° 00'

1   2   3   4

STOCKHOLM

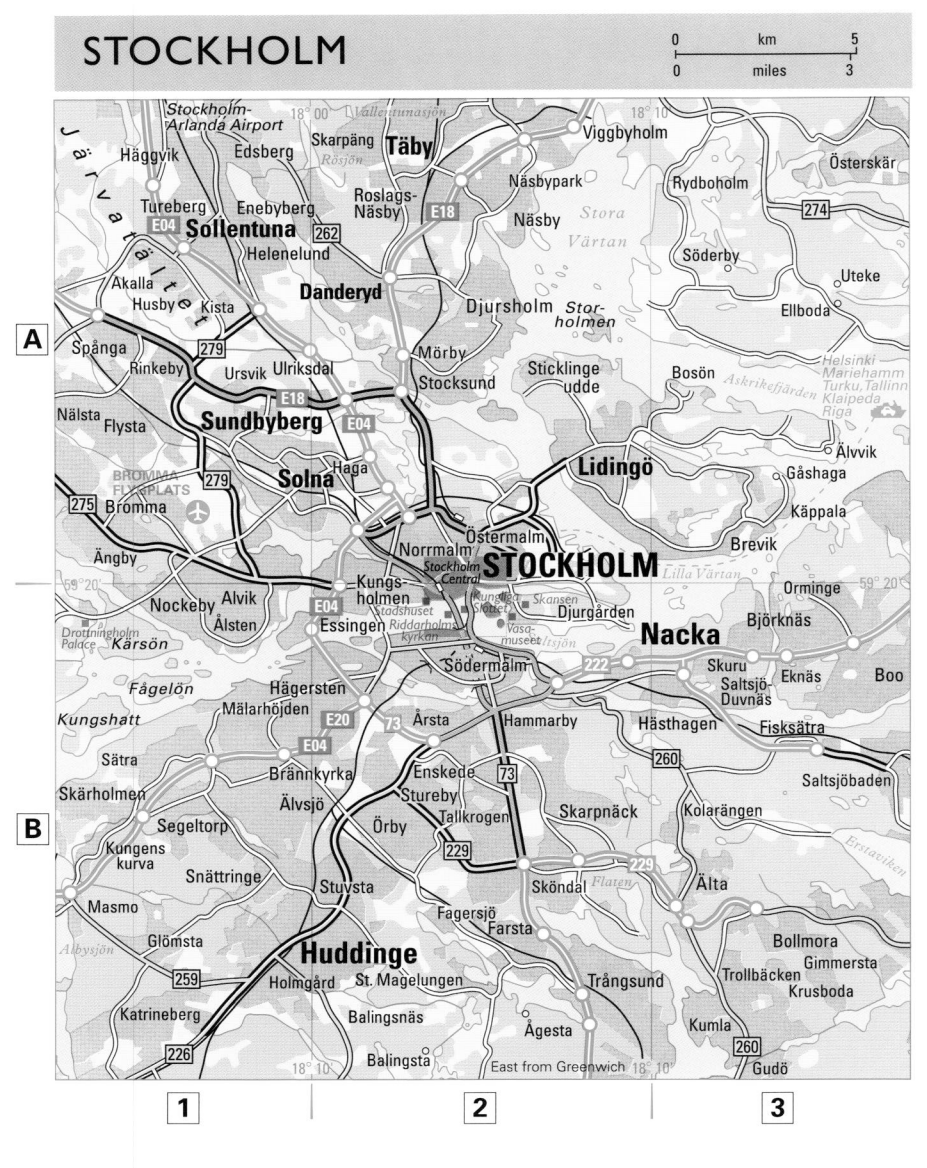

CENTRAL STOCKHOLM

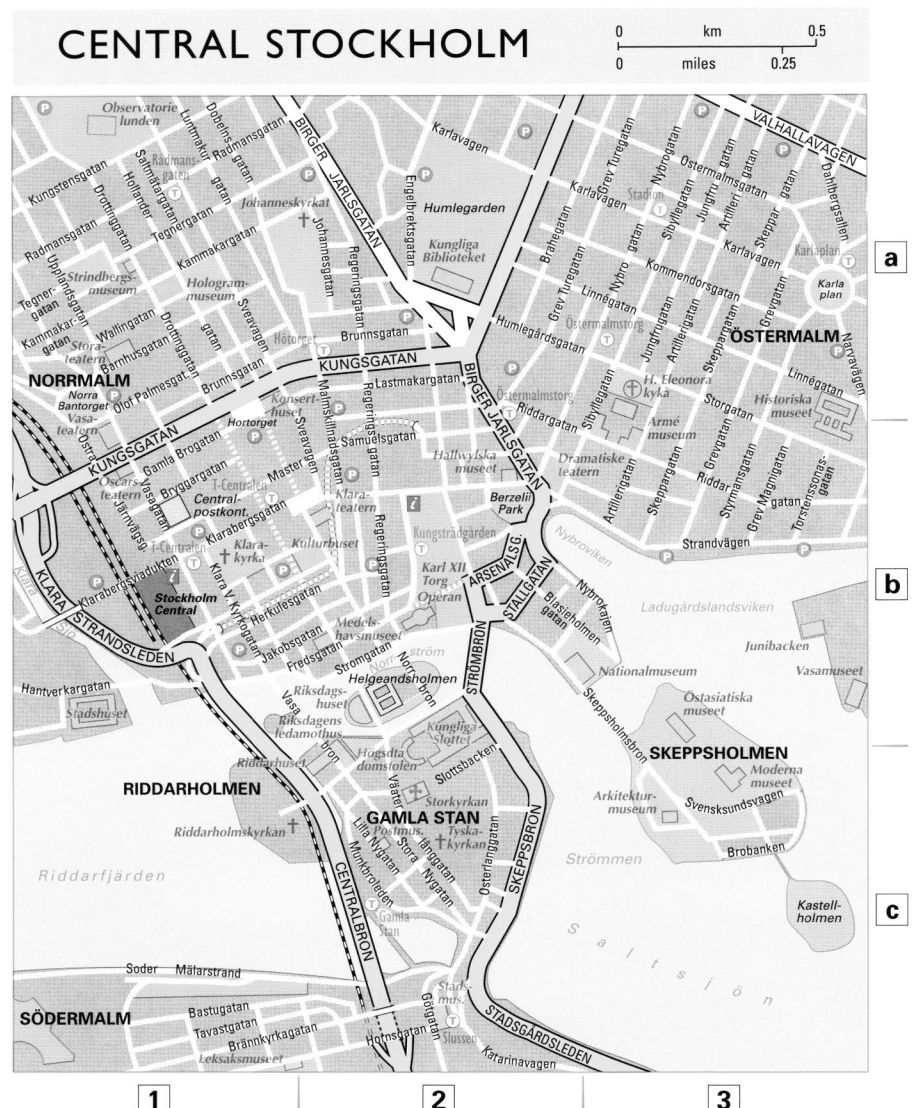

SYDNEY

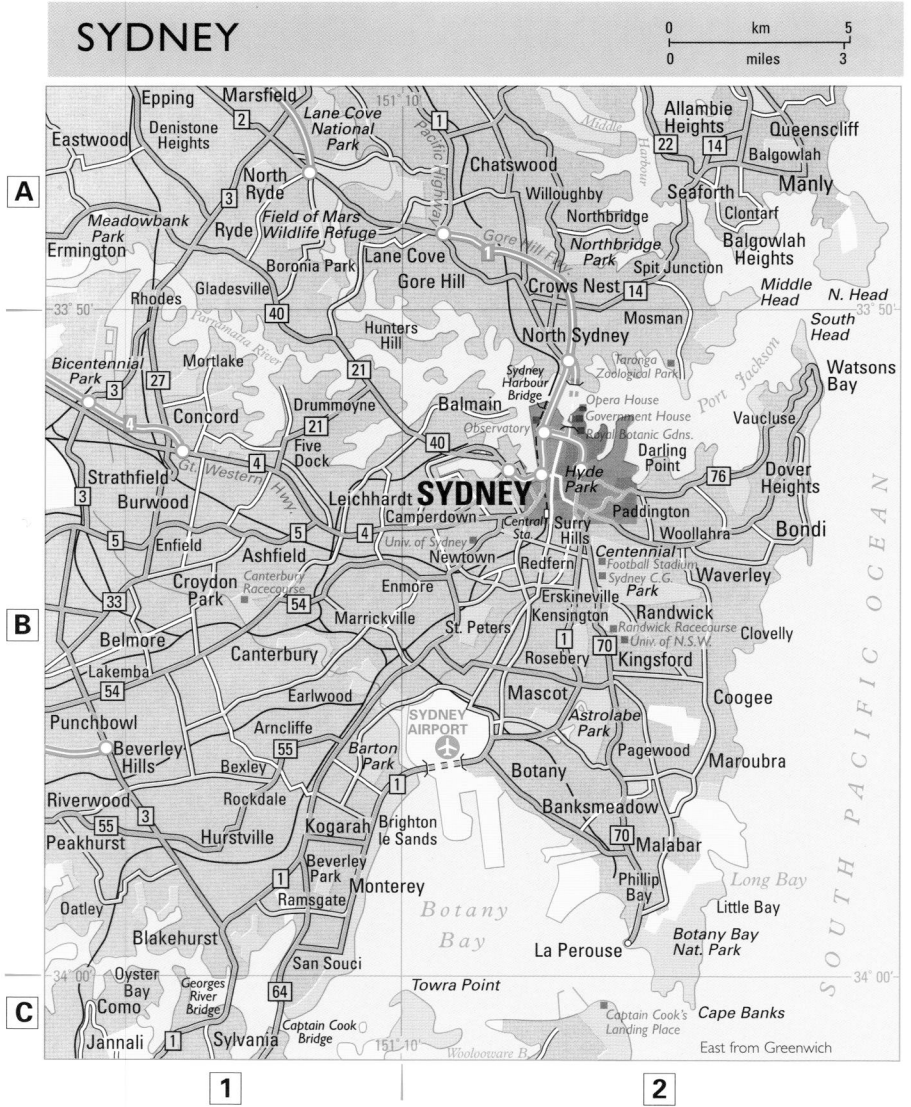

CENTRAL SYDNEY

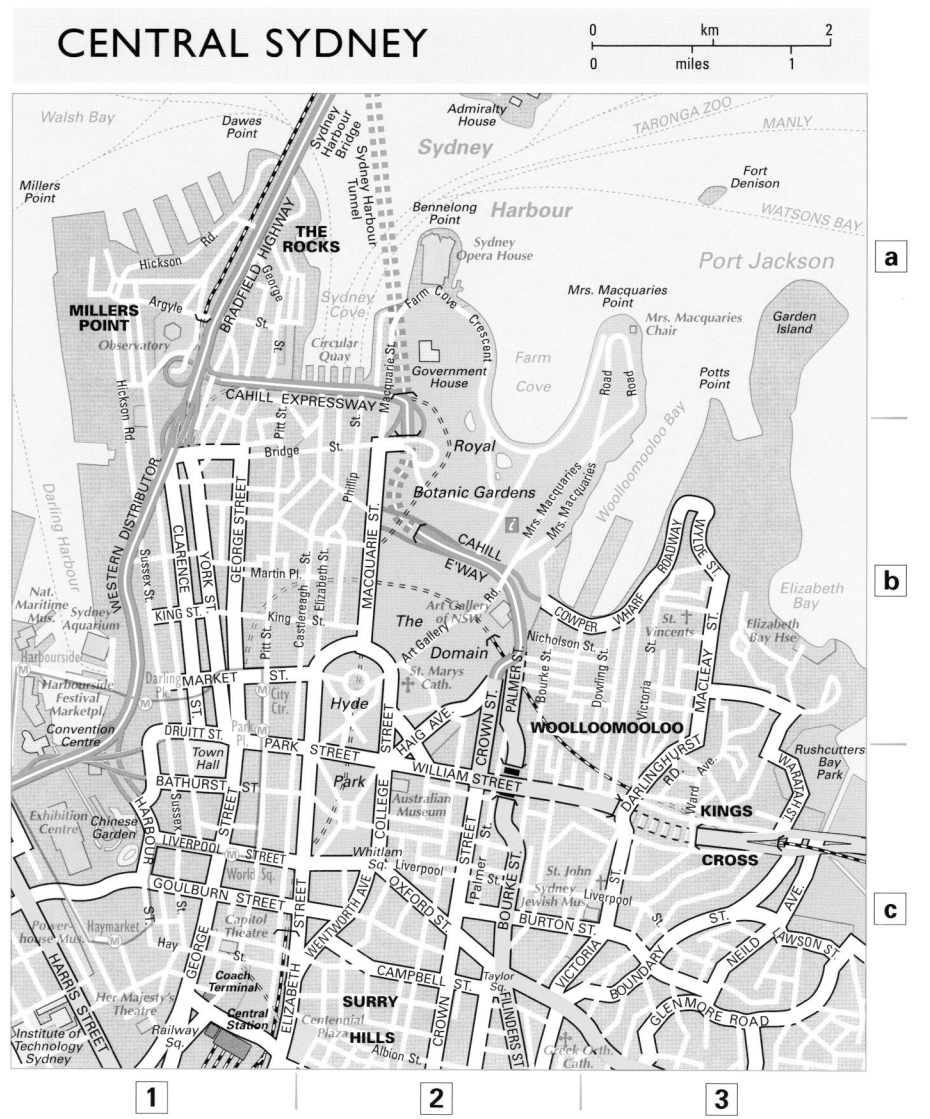

TOKYO

km 5
miles 3

A

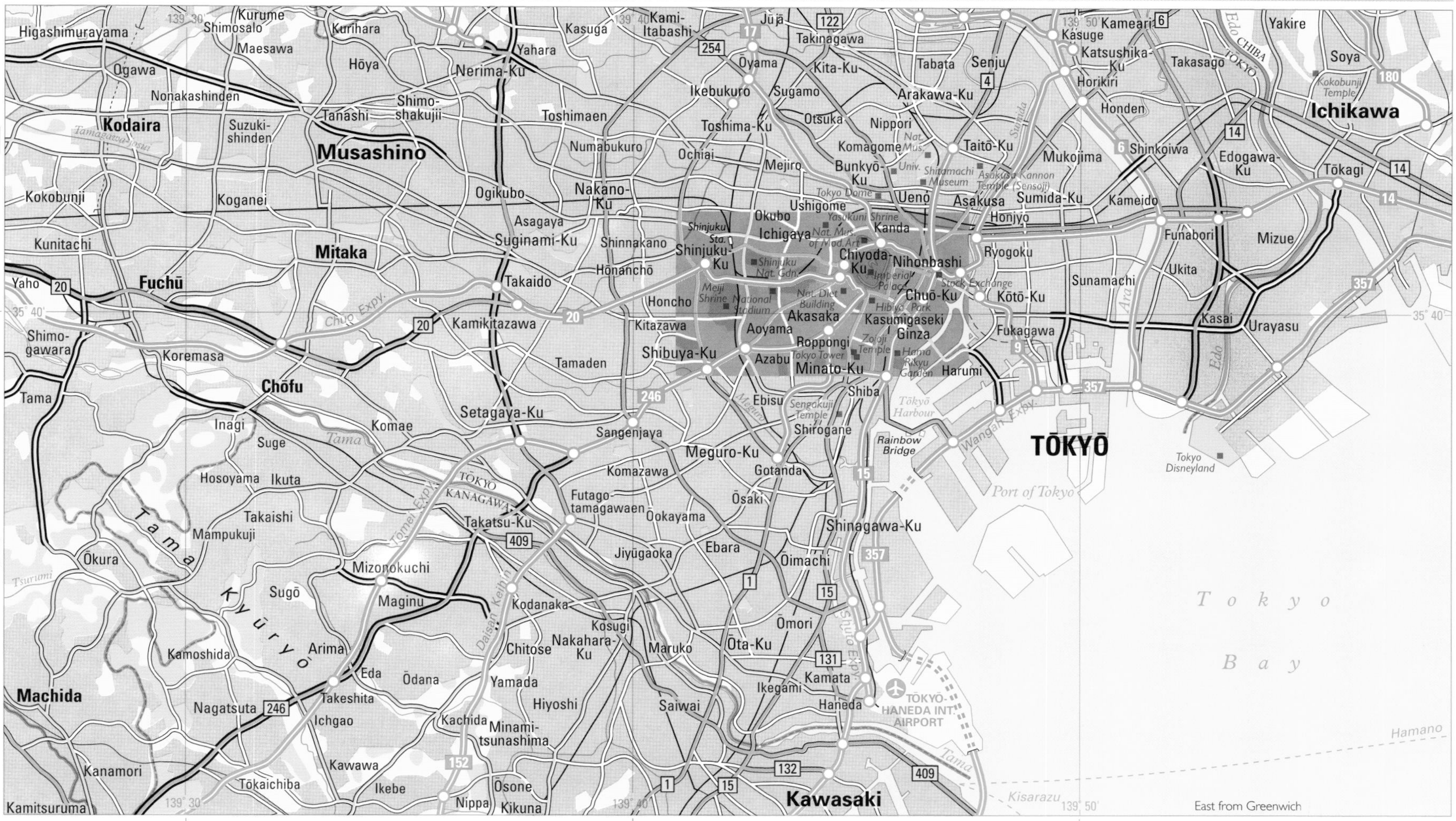

Higashimurayama Kurume Shimosalo Kami-Itabashi Jūjō Takinagawa Kameari Yakire Soya
Kodaira Ogawa Kurihara Kasuga Oyama Kita-Ku Tabata Senju Katsushika-Ku Takasago Kokubun Temple Ichikawa
Nonakashinden Maesawa Hōya Tanashi Ikebukuro Sugamo Ōtsuka Arakawa-Ku Horikiri Honden Shinkoiwa Edogawa-Ku
Kokobunji Suzuki-shinden Shimo-shakujii Toshimaen Nippori Taitō-Ku Mukojima Tōkagi
Koganei Nakano-Ku Toshima-Ku Okubo Asakusa Honjyo Sumida-Ku
Musashino Asagaya Suginami-Ku Mejiro Bunkyō-Ku Ueno Ryogoku Funabori Mizue
Mitaka Ogikubo Shinnakano Ichigaya Kanda Nihonbashi Ryogoku Kameido Ukita Kasai
Fuchū Yaho Takaido Honancho Shinjuku-Ku Chiyoda-Ku Chūō-Ku Kōtō-Ku Urayasu
Kokobunji Kamikitazawa Honcho Akasaka Kasumigaseki Ginza Fukagawa
Shimo-gawara Kitazawa Aoyama Roppongi Ginza Harumi
Chōfu Koremasa Tamaden Shibuya-Ku Azabu Minato-Ku Shiba Port of Tokyo
Inagi Suge Setagaya-Ku Sangenjaya Ebisu Shirogane Rainbow Bridge TŌKYŌ
Tama Komae Futago-tamagawaen Meguro-Ku Gotanda Tokyo Disneyland
Hosoyama Ikuta Takaishi Komazawa Ōsaki Tokyo Bay
Mampukuji Mizonokuchi Ookayama Shinagawa-Ku
Ōkura Sugō Jiyūgaoka Ebara Ōimachi
Machida Takatsu-Ku Kodanaka Yamada Maruko Ōmori Tokyo
Nagatsuta Takeshita Chitose Nakahara-Ku Hiyoshi Ōta-Ku Bay
Kamashida Arima Eda Ōdana Kosugi Kamata Haneda Hamano
Kanamori Ichgao Minami-tsunashima Saiwai TOKYO-HANEDA INT. AIRPORT
Kamitsuruma Tōkaichiba Ōsone Kawawa Kisarazu East from Greenwich
Nippa Kikuna Kawasaki

1 2 3 4

CENTRAL TOKYO

km 1
miles 0.5

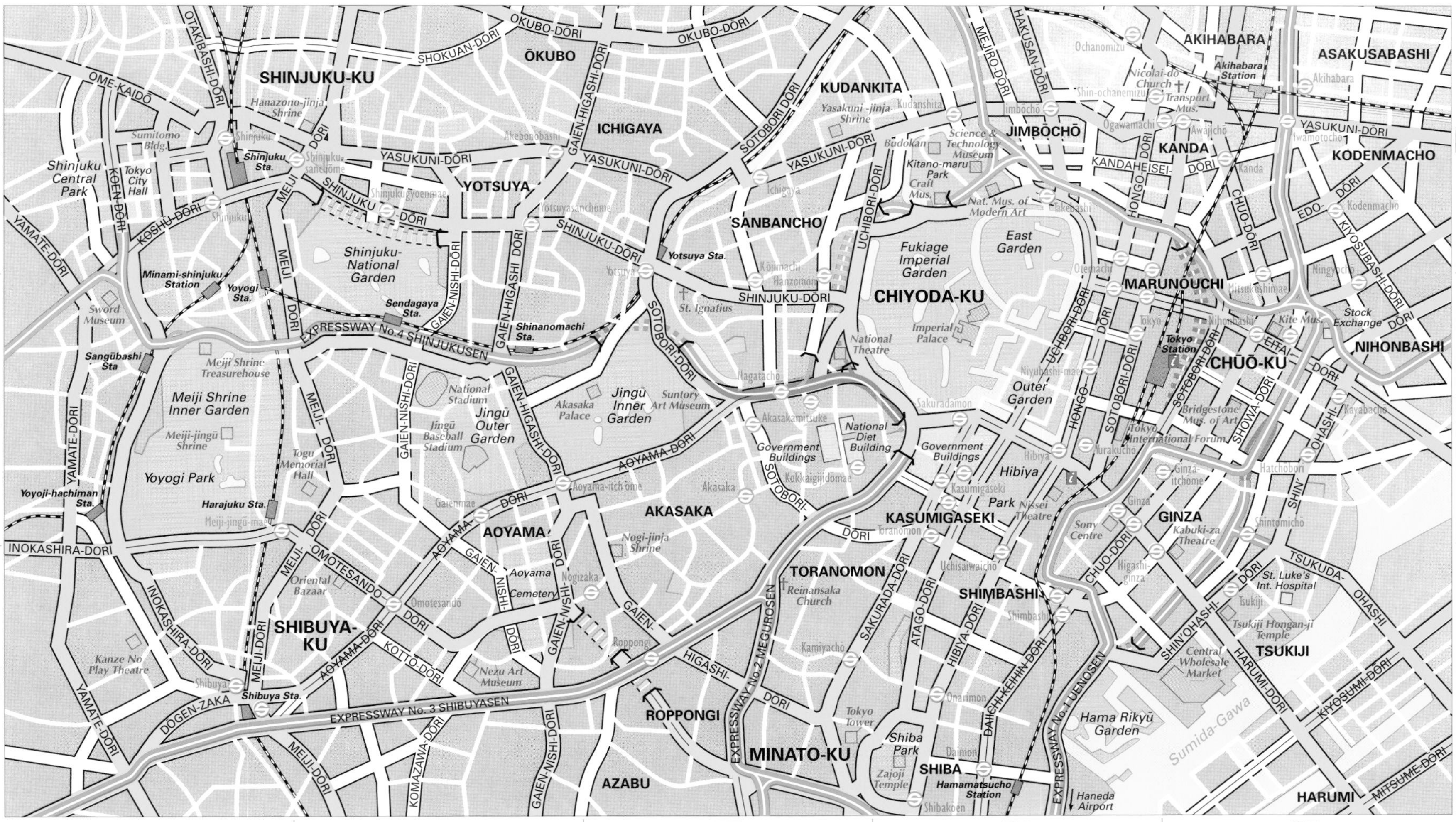

a

SHINJUKU-KU ŌKUBO OKUBO-DORI AKIHABARA ASAKUSABASHI
OME-KAIDO SHOKUAN-DORI KUDANKITA Akihabara Station KODENMACHO
Shinjuku Central Park Tokyo City Hall ICHIGAYA JIMBOCHO KANDA
Shinjuku Sta. YOTSUYA YASUKUNI-DORI SANBANCHO
Minami-shinjuku Station Yoyogi Sta. SHINJUKU-DORI Fukiage Imperial Garden MARUNOUCHI NIHONBASHI
Sword Museum Shinjuku National Garden Yotsuya Sta. CHIYODA-KU East Garden Stock Exchange
Sangūbashi Sta. Sendagaya Sta. Shinanomachi Sta. Tokyo Station CHŪŌ-KU

b

Meiji Shrine Treasurehouse National Stadium Jingū Outer Garden National Theatre Imperial Palace
Meiji Shrine Inner Garden Jingū Baseball Stadium Akasaka Palace Suntory Art Museum Outer Garden
Meiji-jingū Shrine Jingū Inner Garden National Diet Building Bridgestone Mus. of Art
Yoyogi Park Togu Memorial Hall Government Buildings Government Buildings Hibiya Park GINZA
Yoyoji-hachiman Sta. Harajuku Sta. AOYAMA-DORI KASUMIGASEKI Kabuki-za Theatre
INOKASHIRA-DORI AKASAKA Sony Centre SHIMBASHI St. Luke's Int. Hospital

c

Kanze No Play Theatre Oriental Bazaar Aoyama Cemetery Nogi-jinja Shrine TORANOMON Tsukiji Honganji Temple
SHIBUYA-KU OMOTESANDO Reinanzaka Church Central Wholesale Market TSUKIJI
Shibuya Sta. Nezu Art Museum ROPPONGI Tokyo Tower Hama Rikyū Garden
DOGEN-ZAKA EXPRESSWAY No. 3 SHIBUYASEN MINATO-KU Shiba Park Hamamatsucho Station
AZABU Zojoji Temple Haneda Airport HARUMI Sumida-Gawa

1 2 3 4 5

TEHRAN

km 0 5
miles 0 3

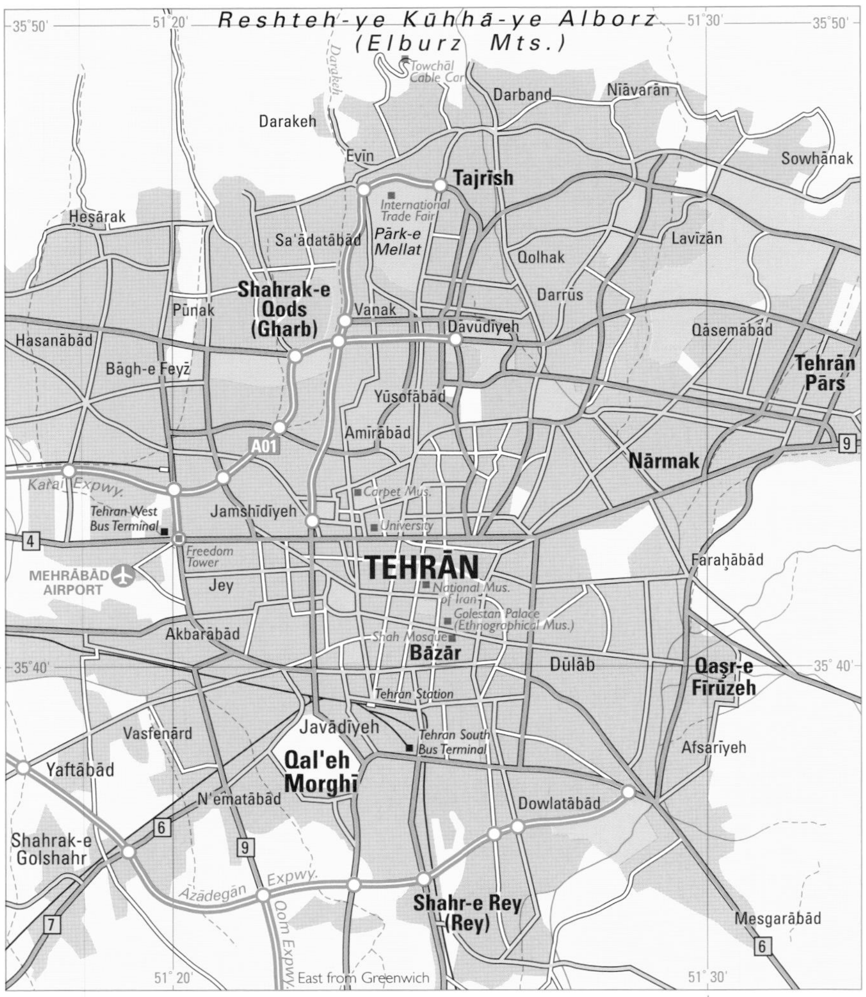

Reshteh-ye Kūhhā-ye Alborz
(Elburz Mts.)

Towchāl Cable Car
Darband
Niāvārān
Darakeh
Darakeh
Evin
Tajrīsh
Sowhānak
Sa'ādatābād
Pārk-e Mellat
International Trade Fair
Lavizān
Heşārak
Qolhak
Shahrak-e Qods (Gharb)
Pūnak
Vanak
Darrūs
Tehrān Pārs
Hasanābād
Bāgh-e Feyž
Dāvudiyeh
Qāsemābād
Yūsofābād
A01
Amirābād
Nārmak
Karaj Expwy.
Jamshīdiyeh
Corpet Mus.
University
Farahābād
Tehrān West Bus Terminal
Freedom Tower
Jey
TEHRĀN
National Mus.
of Iran
Golestan Palace
(Ethnographical Mus.)
MEHRĀBĀD AIRPORT
Akbarābād
Shah Mosque
Bāzār
Dūlāb
Qasr-e Firūzeh
Tehran Station
Vasfenārd
Javādiyeh
Tehran South Bus Terminal
Afsariyeh
Yaftābād
N'ematābād
Qal'eh Morghī
Dowlatābād
Shahrak-e Golshahr
6
9
Āzādegān Expwy.
Shahr-e Rey (Rey)
Mesgarābād
7
Qom Expwy.
East from Greenwich

A B

1 2 3

TIANJIN

km 0 5
miles 0 3

205
Xiaodian
Da Yunhe
Beicang
Xinkai He
A
Yixingbu
Dabizhuang
Hanjiashū
Zhangguizhuang
Nandian
Dingzigu
Xigu Park
Tianjin Xi Zhan (Railway Station)
Xigu
Hebei
Stadium
Ziya He
104
Hongqiao
The Grand Mosque
Hubei (Grand Mercy) Temple
Old Chinese District
Dongmenwài
Zhangguizhuang
Ximenwài
Hedong
Tianjin Zhan (Railway Station)
Dongjuzi
TIANJIN (TIENTSIN)
Nanmenwài
Heping
Dazhigu
Da Yunhe (Grand Canal)
Nankai
Antiques Market
Tianjin University
Nankai University
Renmin Park
Xinanlou
Tiaoyuan Pavilion
Balitai
Natural History Museum
Jianshan Park
Hexi
Shuishang Park
Aquatic Park
Hai He
Liqizhuang
Huidui
105
205
East from Greenwich 117°10'
39°00'

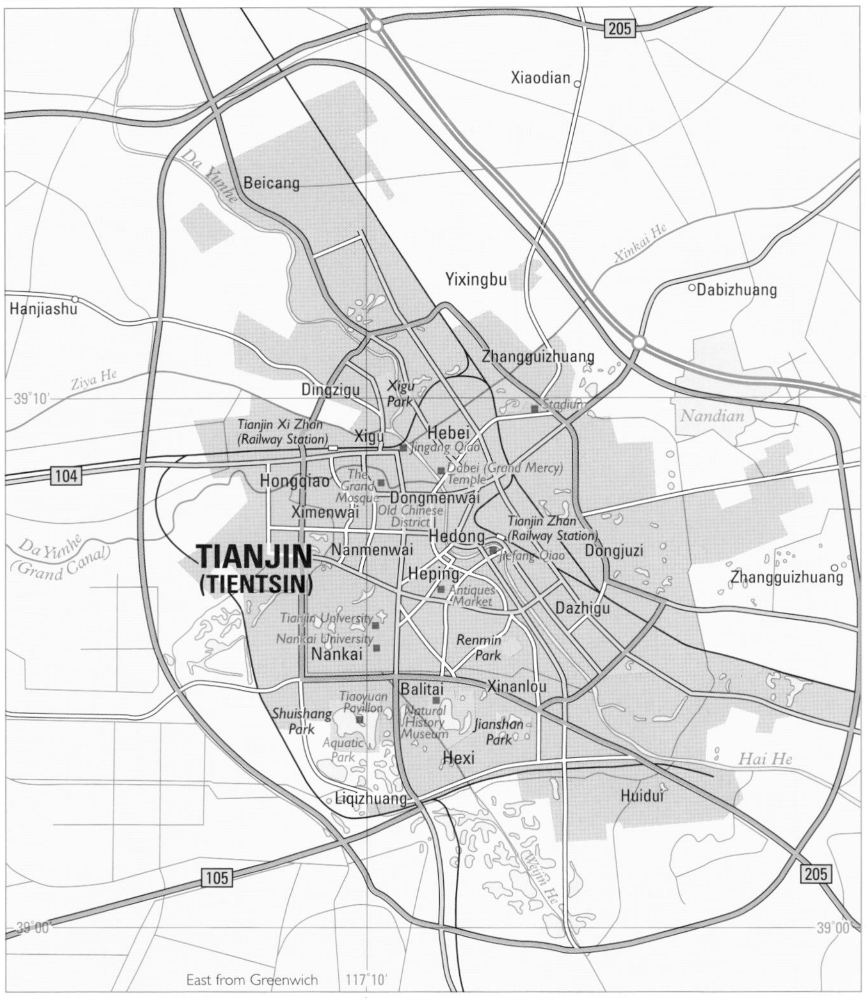

A B C

1 2

TORONTO

km 0 5
miles 0 3

79°40' 79°30' 79°20' 79°10' Fairport

407
Markham
Thornhill
Brown
West Rouge
Rouge Hill
27
Pine Grove
Concord
Edgeley
Newtonbrook
Agincourt
Malvern
Highland Creek
Port Union
Woodbridge
Fisherville
Willowdale
404
2A
Black Creek Pioneer Village
York University
11
Northmount
Woburn
West Hill
Humber Summit
North York
Lansing
401
Bendale
Beaumonte Heights
Armour Heights
York Mills
Wexford
Scarborough
Highland Creek
A
Thistletown
400
DOWNSVIEW AIRPORT
Don Mills
Cliffside
427
Kipling Heights
Downsview
Lawrence Heights
Wilket Creek Park
Danforth
2
Rexdale
Humberlea
401
Ontario Science Centre
Malton
Weston
Thorncliffe
Demonia Park
Woodbine Race Track
11
Leaside
Birch Cliff
27
Forest Hill
East York
5
409
Humber Valley Village
York
Casa Loma
Riverdale Park
Kew Gardens
401
TORONTO INTERNATIONAL AIRPORT (LESTER B. PEARSON)
Lambton Mills
Mount Dennis
5
University of Toronto
43°40'
Etobicoke
Islington
Kingsway
Swansea
Parliament Buildings
City Hall
Hanlon
Markland Wood
427
Humber Bay
High Park
CN Tower & SkyDome
Old Fort York
Union Stn.
TORONTO
Burnhamthorpe
Summerville
Parkdale
Gardiner Expwy.
B
New Toronto
Exhibition Place
TORONTO CITY CENTRE AIRPORT
Toronto Harbour
Mimico
Toronto Islands
Island Park
LAKE ONTARIO
Elizabeth Way
Queen
2
Gibraltar Point
Cooksville
Mississauga
Long Branch
79°40' 79°30' 79°20' West from Greenwich 79°10'

A B

1 2 3 4

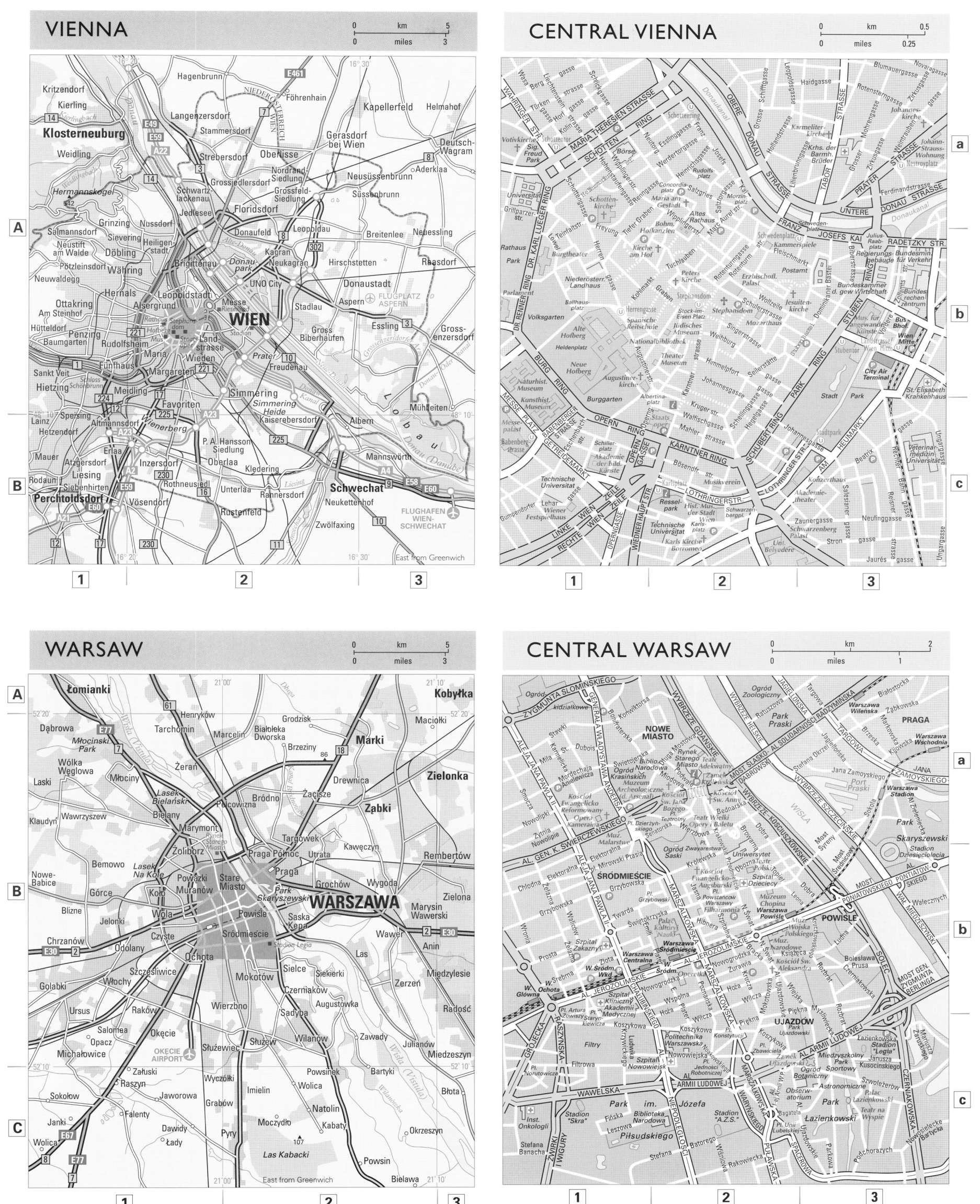

WASHINGTON

0 km 5
0 miles 3

A
B
C
1
2
3
4
5
77°20'
77°10'
77°00'
76°50'
39°00'
38°50'
Dranesville
Great Falls
Potomac
Cabin John Regional Park
Great Falls Park
99
Chevy Chase View
Silver Spring
Oak View
Greenbelt
Woodmont
Bethesda
Chevy Chase
Avenel
Adelphi
Langley Park
College Park
Univ. of Maryland
Berwyn Heights
Greenbelt Park
Lanham
Seabrook
Cabin John
Glen Echo
MARYLAND
VIRGINIA
Rock Creek Park
Lewisdale
Takoma Park
University Park
East Pines
New Carrollton
Glen Mar Park
Somerset
Chillum
Riverdale
Reston
Belle View
Westgate
Brookmont
Brightwood
Hyattsville
Edmondston
Dulles Int. Airport
Dulles Airport Access Rd.
Wolf Trap Farm Park
Langley
Univ. of the Dist. of Col.
The Catholic University of America
Mount Rainier
Landover Hills
Glenarden
McLean
Nat. Zoological Park
Washington Cath.
Trinity College
Bladensburg
Kent Village
American University
WASHINGTON
DISTRICT OF COLUMBIA
MARYLAND
Tysons Corner
Hunters Valley
Pimmit Hills
Franklin Park
Northern Va. Reg. Park
Marymount University
Georgetown
Trinidad
National Arboretum
Kenilworth Aquatic Gardens
Cheverly
Fairmount Heights
Palmer Park
Vale
Vienna
Dunn Loring
The White House
Union Station
Seat Pleasant
Oakton
Falls Church
Seven Corners
Arlington
Rosslyn
Vietnam Veterans Mem.
Lincoln Memorial
U.S. Capitol
Library of Congress
Kettering
Lee Hwy.
Hillwood
Arlington Nat. Cemetery
Jefferson Memorial
Mason Mem. Br.
Fort Dupont Park
Capitol Heights
Millwood
Ritchie
Arlington Blvd.
Broyhill Park
Pentagon
East Potomac Park
Oakland
East Arlington
Coral Hills
District Heights
Annalee Heights
Anacostia
Holmes Run Acres
Culmore
WASHINGTON NATIONAL AIRPORT
Forestville
Fairfax
Little River Tpk.
Baileys Crossroads
Suitland
Parklawn
PRINCE GEORGES
George Mason University
Hillcrest Heights
Morningside
Annandale
Alexandria
Silver Hill
Glassmanor
Potomac River
Forest Heights
Temple Hills
ANDREWS AIR FORCE BASE
Kings Park
Fairfax Station
Kings Park West
North Springfield
Oxon Hill
Camp Springs
L. Accotink
Capital Beltway
Huntington
West Springfield
Springfield
Franconia
Woodrow Wilson Memorial Bridge
South Lawn
Butts Corner
Rose Hill
Fort Foote Village
Groveton
Oaklawn
West from Greenwich
495
29
50
66
95/495
395
295
95

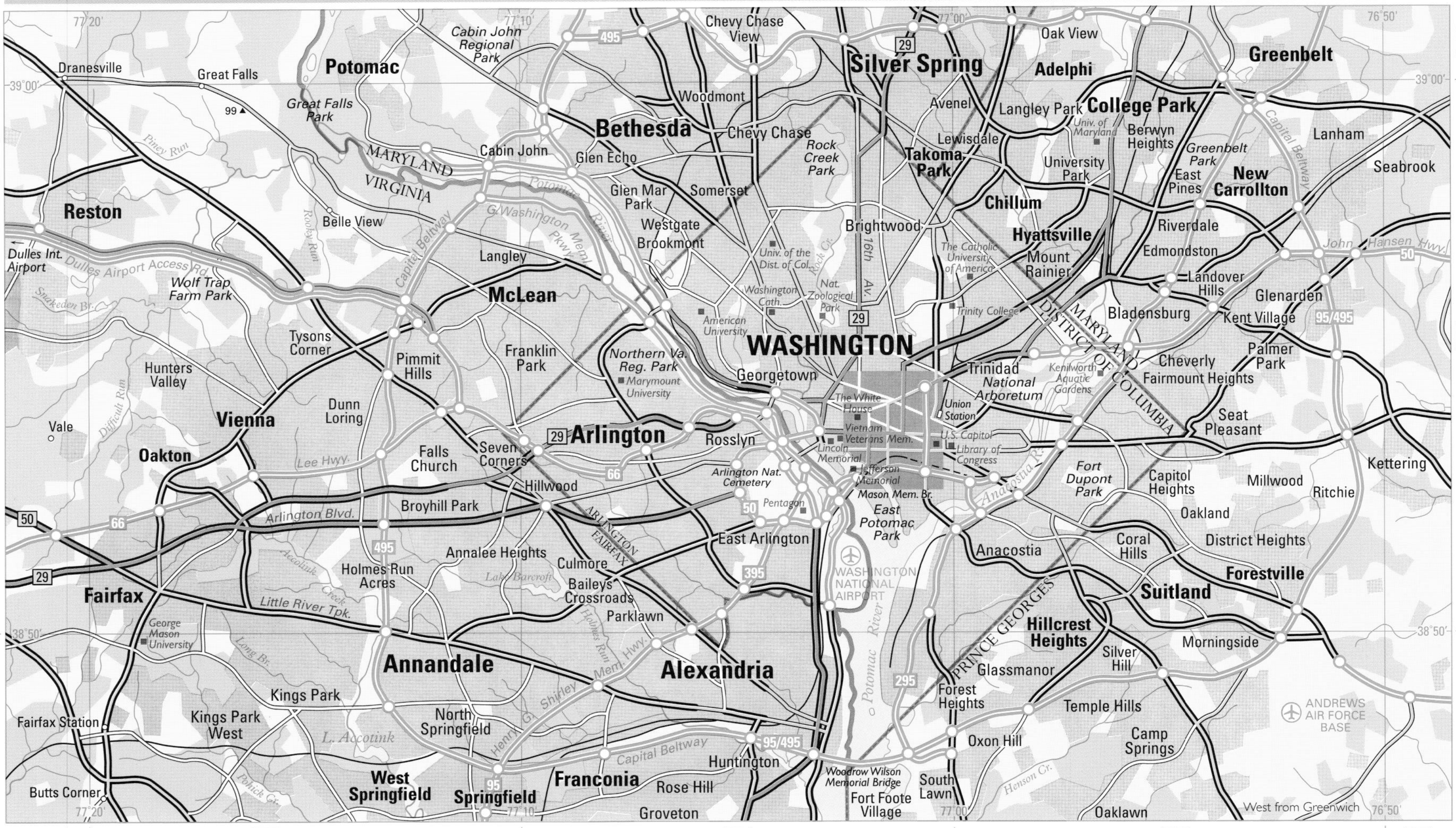

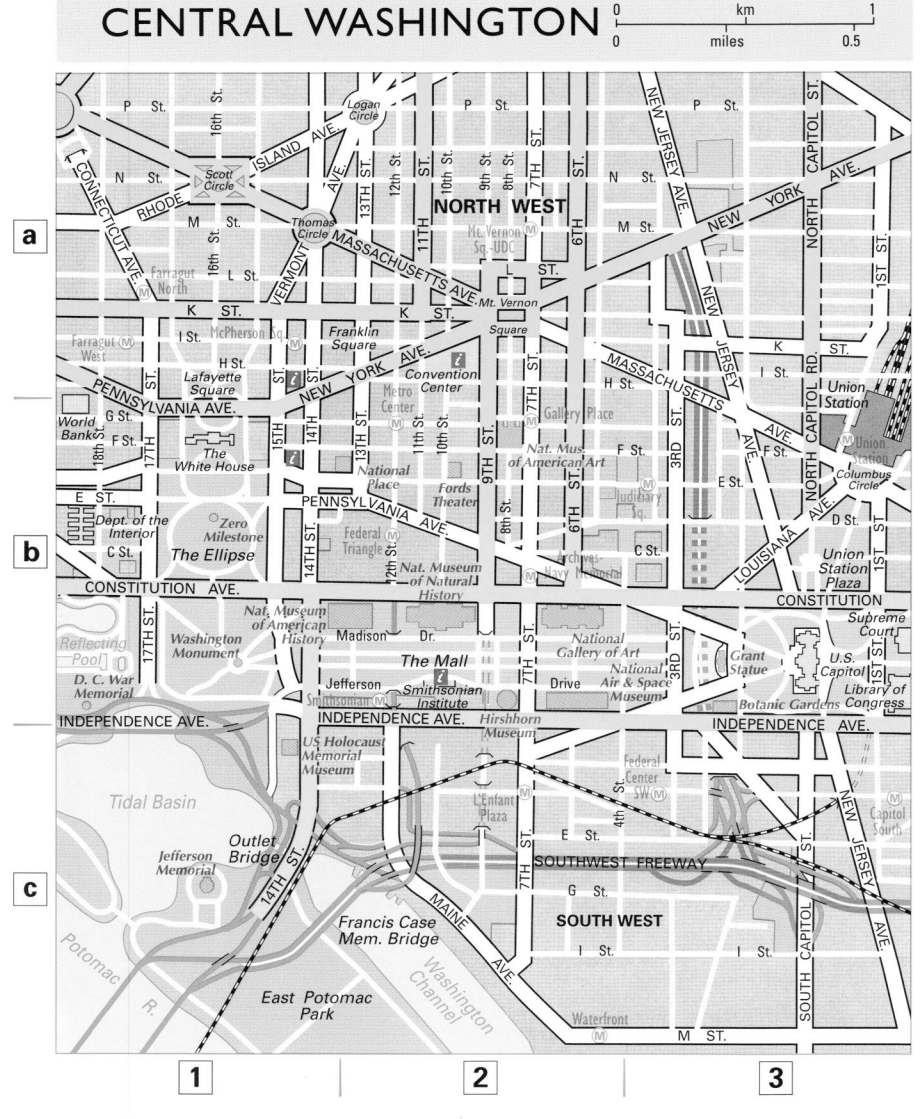

CENTRAL WASHINGTON

0 km 1
0 miles 0.5

a
b
c
1
2
3
P St.
Logan Circle
N St.
Scott Circle
RHODE ISLAND AVE.
CONNECTICUT AVE.
NORTH WEST
Thomas Circle
MASSACHUSETTS AVE.
Mt. Vernon Sq.-UDC
NEW YORK AVE.
NEW JERSEY AVE.
NORTH CAPITOL ST.
Farragut North
K ST.
McPherson Sq.
Franklin Square
Mt. Vernon Square
Farragut West
Lafayette Square
Convention Center
Metro Center
Union Station
PENNSYLVANIA AVE.
World Bank
Gallery Place
The White House
National Place
Judiciary Sq.
Columbus Circle
E ST.
Fords Theater
Dept. of the Interior
Zero Milestone
Federal Triangle
The Ellipse
Nat. Museum of Natural History
Union Station Plaza
CONSTITUTION AVE.
Nat. Museum of American History
Reflecting Pool
Washington Monument
Madison Dr.
National Gallery of Art
Supreme Court
D. C. War Memorial
The Mall
Grant Statue
U.S. Capitol
Jefferson Dr.
Smithsonian Institute
National Air & Space Museum
Library of Congress
Botanic Gardens
INDEPENDENCE AVE.
Hirshhorn Museum
US Holocaust Memorial Museum
Tidal Basin
Federal Center SW
L'Enfant Plaza
Capitol South
Jefferson Memorial
Outlet Bridge
14TH ST.
SOUTHWEST FREEWAY
SOUTH WEST
Francis Case Mem. Bridge
MAINE AVE.
SOUTH CAPITOL ST.
Potomac R.
East Potomac Park
Washington Channel
Waterfront
M ST.

WELLINGTON

0 km 5
0 miles 3

A
B
C
1
2
Rock Pt.
175°50'
Elsdon
Porirua East
58
Cook Strait
459 Colonial Knob
Porirua
Haywards
Linden
408
Pipinui Pt.
Tawa
Manor Park
41°10'
Western Hutt Road
Redwood
457 Belmont
Taita
Stokes Valley
Johnsonville-Porirua Mwy.
Avalon
Glenside
Normandale
Lower Hutt
Naenae
Korokoro
Paparangi
Waterloo
Johnsonville
Newlands
Petone
Gracefield
445
Khandallah
Hutt Road
Seaview
Ngaio
Ngauranga
Somes Island
Wainuiomata
Lowry Bay
Otari Open Air Museum
Port Nicholson
Wadestown
Old St. Paul's Church
Parliament and Beehive
Railway Station
WELLINGTON
Days Bay
Botanic Gardens
Maritime Museum
Pt. Halswell
Karori
Mount Victoria
196
Ward I.
Hataitai
Eastbourne
National Museum and Art Gallery
Brooklyn
Miramar
706 McKerrow
Evans Bay
Zoo
Kilbirnie
Seatoun
WELLINGTON INTERNATIONAL AIRPORT
248 Mount Cameron
570 Mount Grace
Island Bay
Lyall Bay
Owhiro Bay
41°20'
Picton
Pencarrow Head
East from Greenwich
175°50'

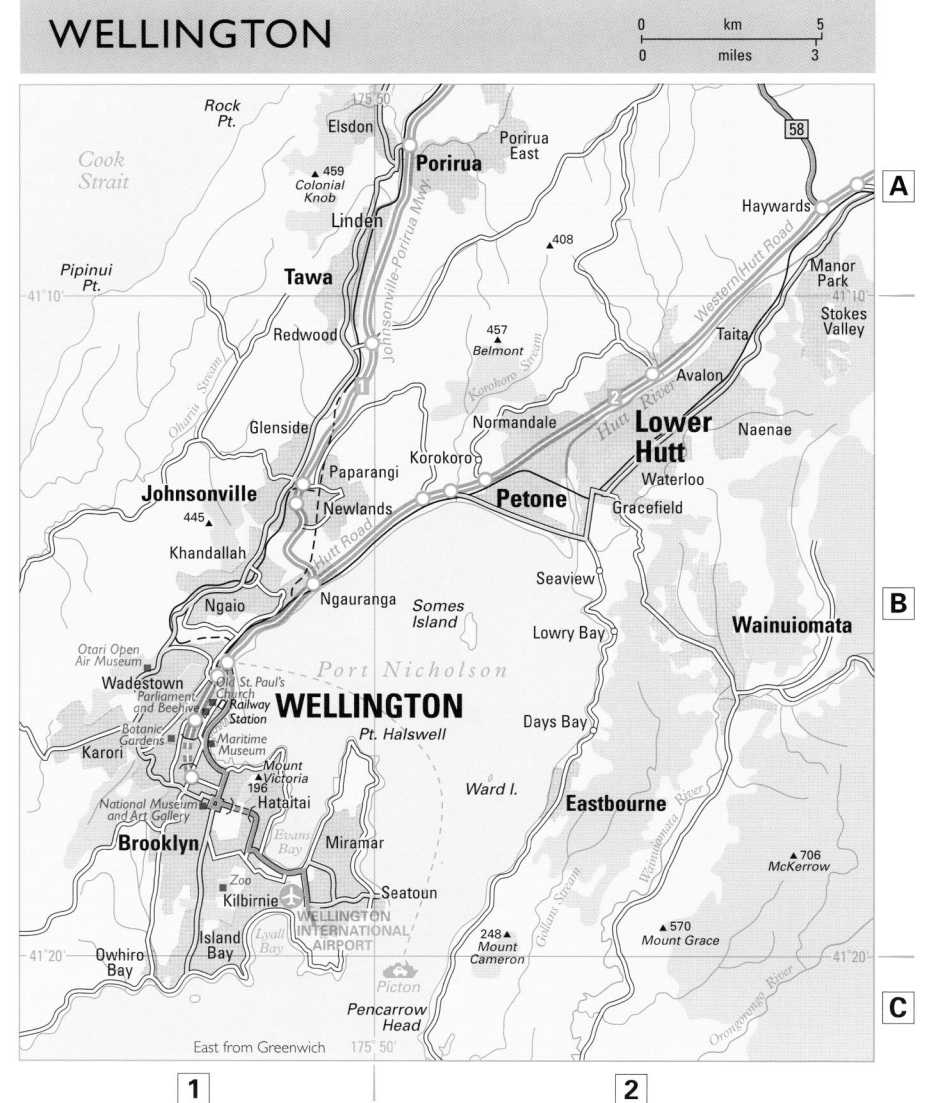

INDEX TO CITY MAPS

The index contains the names of all the principal places and features shown on the City Maps. Each name is followed by an additional entry in italics giving the name of the City Map within which it is located.

The number in bold type which follows each name refers to the number of the City Map page where that feature or place will be found.

The letter and figure which are immediately after the page number give the grid square on the map within which the feature or place is situated. The letter represents the latitude and the figure the longitude. Upper case letters refer to the City Maps, lower case letters to the Central Area Maps. The full geographic reference is provided in the border of the City Maps.

The location given is the centre of the city, suburb or feature and is not necessarily the name. Rivers, canals and roads are indexed to their name. Rivers carry the symbol → after their name.

An explanation of the alphabetical order rules and a list of the abbreviations used are to be found at the beginning of the World Map Index.

A

Aalām, *Baghdad* **3** B2
Aalsmeer, *Amsterdam* **2** B1
Abbey Wood, *London* **15** B4
Abcoude, *Amsterdam* **2** B2
Ābdin, *Cairo* **7** A2
Abeno, *Osaka* **22** B4
Aberdeen, *Hong Kong* **12** B2
Aberdour, *Edinburgh* **11** A2
Aberdour Castle, *Edinburgh* **11** A2
Abfanggraben →, *Munich* **20** A3
Ablon-sur-Seine, *Paris* **23** B3
Abramtsevo, *Moscow* **19** B4
Abu Dis, *Jerusalem* **13** B2
Abû en Numrus, *Cairo* **7** B2
Abu Ghosh, *Jerusalem* **13** B1
Acacias, *Madrid* **17** c2
Acassuso, *Buenos Aires* **7** A1
Accotink Cr. →, *Washington* **32** B2
Acheres, *Paris* **23** A1
Acilia, *Rome* **25** C1
Aclimação, *São Paulo* **26** B2
Acton, *London* **15** A2
Açúcar, Pão de, *Rio de Janeiro* **24** B2
Ada Beja, *Lisbon* **14** A1
Adams Park, *Atlanta* **3** B2
Adams Shore, *Boston* **6** B4
Addiscombe, *London* **15** B3
Adelphi, *Washington* **32** A4
Aderklaa, *Vienna* **31** A3
Admiralteyskaya Storona, *St. Petersburg* **26** B2
Āffori, *Milan* **18** A2
Aflandshage, *Copenhagen* **10** B3
Afsariyeh, *Tehran* **30** B2
Agboyi Cr. →, *Lagos* **14** A2
Ågerup, *Copenhagen* **10** A1
Ågesta, *Stockholm* **28** B2
Agincourt, *Toronto* **30** A3
Agora, Arhéa, *Athens* **2** c1
Agra Canal, *Delhi* **10** B2
Agricola Oriental, *Mexico City* **18** B2
Agua Espraiada →, *São Paulo* **26** B2
Agualva-Cacem, *Lisbon* **14** A1
Agustino, Cerro El, *Lima* **16** B2
Ahrensfelde, *Berlin* **5** A4
Ahuntsic, *Montreal* **19** A1
Ai →, *Osaka* **22** A4
Aigremont, *Paris* **23** A1
Air View Park, *Singapore* **27** A2
Airport West, *Melbourne* **17** A1
Aiyaleo, *Athens* **2** B2
Aiyáleos, Óros, *Athens* **2** B1
Ajegunle, *Lagos* **14** B2
Aji, *Osaka* **22** A3
Ajuda, *Lisbon* **14** A1
Akalla, *Stockholm* **28** A1
Akasaka, *Tokyo* **29** b3
Akbarābād, *Tehran* **30** A2
Akersus Slott, *Oslo* **22** A3
Akihabara, *Tokyo* **29** a5
Akrópolis, *Athens* **2** c2
Al 'Azamiyah, *Baghdad* **3** A2
Al Quds = Jerusalem, *Jerusalem* **13** B2
Alaguntan, *Lagos* **14** B2
Alameda, *San Francisco* **25** B3
Alameda, Parque, *Mexico City* **18** b2
Alameda Memorial State Beach Park, *San Francisco* **25** B3
Albern, *Vienna* **31** B2
Albert Park, *Melbourne* **17** B1
Alberton, *Johannesburg* **13** B2
Albertslund, *Copenhagen* **10** B2
Albysjön, *Stockholm* **28** B1
Alcantara, *Lisbon* **14** A1
Alcatraz I., *San Francisco* **25** B2
Alcobendas, *Madrid* **17** A2
Alcorcón, *Madrid* **17** B1
Aldershof, *Berlin* **5** B4
Aldo Bonzi, *Buenos Aires* **7** C1
Aleksandrovskoye, *St. Petersburg* **26** B2
Alexander Nevsky Abbey, *St. Petersburg* **26** B2
Alexander Soutzos Moussio, *Athens* **2** b3
Alexandra, *Johannesburg* **13** A2
Alexandra, *Singapore* **27** B2
Alexandria, *Washington* **32** C3
Alfama, *Lisbon* **14** c3
Alfortville, *Paris* **23** B3
Algés, *Lisbon* **14** A1
Alhambra, *Los Angeles* **16** B4
Alibey →, *Istanbul* **12** B1
Alibey Barajı, *Istanbul* **12** B1
Alibeyköy, *Istanbul* **12** B1
Alimos, *Athens* **2** B2
Alipur, *Calcutta* **8** B1
Allach, *Munich* **20** A1
Allambie Heights, *Sydney* **28** A2
Allard Pierson Museum, *Amsterdam* **2** b2
Allermuir Hill, *Edinburgh* **11** B2
Allerton, Pt., *Boston* **6** B4
Allston, *Boston* **6** A3
Almada, *Lisbon* **14** A2
Almagro, *Buenos Aires* **7** B2
Almargem do Bispo, *Lisbon* **14** A1
Almazovo, *Moscow* **19** A6
Almirante G. Brown, Parque, *Buenos Aires* **7** C2
Almon, *Jerusalem* **13** B2
Almond →, *Edinburgh* **11** B2
Alnabru, *Oslo* **22** A4
Alnsjøen, *Oslo* **22** A4
Alperton, *London* **15** A2
Alpine, *New York* **21** A2
Alrode, *Johannesburg* **13** B2
Alsemberg, *Brussels* **6** B1
Alsergrund, *Vienna* **31** A2
Alsip, *Chicago* **9** C2
Älsten, *Stockholm* **28** B1
Älta, *Stockholm* **28** B3
Altadena, *Los Angeles* **16** A4
Alte-Donau →, *Vienna* **31** A2
Alte Hofburg, *Vienna* **31** b1
Alter Finkenkrug, *Berlin* **5** A1
Altes Rathaus, *Munich* **20** b3
Altglienicke, *Berlin* **5** B4
Altlandsberg, *Berlin* **5** A5
Altlandsberg Nord, *Berlin* **5** A5
Altmannsdorf, *Vienna* **31** B1
Alto da Moóca, *São Paulo* **26** B2
Alto do Pina, *Lisbon* **14** A2
Altona, *Melbourne* **17** B1
Alvaro Obregon, *Mexico City* **18** B1
Alvik, *Stockholm* **28** B1
Älvsjo, *Stockholm* **28** B2
Älvvik, *Stockholm* **28** A3
Am Hasenbergl, *Munich* **20** A2
Am Steinhof, *Vienna* **31** A1
Am Wald, *Munich* **20** B2
Ama Keng, *Singapore* **27** A2
Amadora, *Lisbon* **14** A1
Amagasaki, *Osaka* **22** A3
Amager, *Copenhagen* **10** B3
Amāl Qādisiya, *Baghdad* **3** B2
Amalienborg, *Copenhagen* **10** b3
Amata, *Milan* **18** A1
Ameixoeira, *Lisbon* **14** A2
América, *São Paulo* **26** B1
Amin, *Baghdad* **3** B2
Aminadov, *Jerusalem* **13** B1
Aminyevo, *Moscow* **19** B2
Amīrābād, *Tehran* **30** A2
Amora, *Lisbon* **14** B2
Amoreira, *Lisbon* **14** A1
Ampelokipi, *Athens* **2** B2
Amper →, *Munich* **20** A1
Amstel, *Amsterdam* **2** b2
Amstel →, *Amsterdam* **2** c2
Amstel-Drecht-Kanaal, *Amsterdam* **2** B2
Amstel Station, *Amsterdam* **2** c3
Amstelhof, *Amsterdam* **2** b2
Amstelveen, *Amsterdam* **2** B2
Amsterdam, *Amsterdam* **2** A2
Amsterdam-Rijnkanaal, *Amsterdam* **2** B3
Amsterdam Zoo, *Amsterdam* **2** b3
Amsterdam Zuidoost, *Amsterdam* **2** B2
Amsterdamse Bos, *Amsterdam* **2** B1
Anacostia, *Washington* **32** B4
Anadoluhisarı, *Istanbul* **12** B2
Anadolukavağı, *Istanbul* **12** A2
Anata, *Jerusalem* **13** B2
Ancol, *Jakarta* **13** A1
'Andalus, *Baghdad* **3** B1
Andarai, *Rio de Janeiro* **24** B1
Anderlecht, *Brussels* **6** A1
Anderson Park, *Atlanta* **3** B2
Andingmen, *Beijing* **4** B2
Andrews Air Force Base, *Washington* **32** C4
Ang Mo Kio, *Singapore* **27** A3
Angby, *Stockholm* **28** A1
Angel I., *San Francisco* **25** A2
Angel Island State Park, *San Francisco* **25** A2
Angke, Kali →, *Jakarta* **13** A1
Angyalföld, *Budapest* **7** A2
Anik, *Mumbai* **20** A2
Anin, *Warsaw* **31** B2
Anjou, *Montreal* **19** A2
Annalee Heights, *Washington* **32** B2
Annandale, *Washington* **32** C2
Anne Frankhuis, *Amsterdam* **2** a1
Antony, *Paris* **23** B2
Anyangch'on, *Seoul* **26** C1
Aoyama, *Tokyo* **29** b2
Ap Lei Chau, *Hong Kong* **12** B1
Apapa, *Lagos* **14** B2
Apelação, *Lisbon* **14** A2
Apterkarskiy Ostrov, *St. Petersburg* **26** B2
Ar Kazimiyah, *Baghdad* **3** B1
Ara →, *Tokyo* **29** A4
Arakawa-Ku, *Tokyo* **29** A3
Arany-hegyi-patak →, *Budapest* **7** A2
Aravaca, *Madrid* **17** B1
Arbataash, *Baghdad* **3** A1
Arc de Triomphe, *Paris* **23** a2
Arcadia, *Los Angeles* **16** B4
Arceuil, *Paris* **23** B2
Arco Plaza, *Los Angeles* **16** b1
Arese, *Milan* **18** A1
Arganzuela, *Madrid* **17** B1
Argenteuil, *Paris* **23** A2
Argonne Forest, *Chicago* **9** C1
Argüelles, *Madrid* **17** a1
Arima, *Osaka* **22** A2
Arima, *Tokyo* **29** B2
Ários Págos, *Athens* **2** c1
Arkhangelskoye, *Moscow* **19** B1
Arlington, *Boston* **6** A2
Arlington, *Washington* **32** B3
Arlington Heights, *Boston* **6** A2
Arlington Nat. Cemetery, *Washington* **32** B3
Armação, *Rio de Janeiro* **24** B2
Armadale, *Melbourne* **17** B2
Armenian Quarter, *Jerusalem* **13** b3
Armour Heights, *Toronto* **30** A2
Arncliffe, *Sydney* **28** B1
Arnold Arboretum, *Boston* **6** B3
Árpádföld, *Budapest* **7** A3
Arrentela, *Lisbon* **14** B2
Ārsta, *Stockholm* **28** B2
Art Institute, *Chicago* **9** c2
Artane, *Dublin* **11** A2
Artas, *Jerusalem* **13** B2
Arthur's Seat, *Edinburgh* **11** B3
Aryiróupolis, *Athens* **2** B2
Asagaya, *Tokyo* **29** A2
Asahi, *Osaka* **22** A4
Asakusa, *Tokyo* **29** A3
Asakusabashi, *Tokyo* **29** a5
Asati, *Calcutta* **8** C1
Aschheim, *Munich* **20** A3
Ascot Vale, *Melbourne* **17** A1
Ashburn, *Chicago* **9** C2
Ashburton, *Melbourne* **17** B2
Ashfield, *Sydney* **28** B1
Ashford, *London* **15** B1
Ashiya, *Osaka* **22** A2
Ashiya →, *Osaka* **22** A2
Ashtown, *Dublin* **11** A2
Askisto, *Helsinki* **12** B1
Askrikefjärden, *Stockholm* **28** A3
Asnières, *Paris* **23** A2
Aspern, *Vienna* **31** A2
Aspern, Flugplatz, *Vienna* **31** A3
Assago, *Milan* **18** B1
Assemblée Nationale, *Paris* **23** b3
Assendelft, *Amsterdam* **2** A1
Assiano, *Milan* **18** B1
Astoria, *New York* **21** B2
Astrolabe Park, *Sydney* **28** B2
Atarot Airport, *Jerusalem* **13** A2
Atghara, *Calcutta* **8** B2
Athens = Athínai, *Athens* **2** B2
Athínai, *Athens* **2** B2
Athinai-Ellinikón Airport, *Athens* **2** B2
Athis-Mons, *Paris* **23** B3
Athlone, *Cape Town* **8** A2
Atholl, *Johannesburg* **13** A2
Atifiya, *Baghdad* **3** A2
Atişalen, *Istanbul* **12** B1
Atlanta, *Atlanta* **3** B2
Atlanta History Center, *Atlanta* **3** B2
Atomium, *Brussels* **6** A2
Attiki, *Athens* **2** A2
Atzgersdorf, *Vienna* **31** B1
Aubervilliers, *Paris* **23** A3
Aubing, *Munich* **20** B1
Auburndale, *Boston* **6** A2
Aucherdinny, *Edinburgh* **11** B2
Auckland Park, *Johannesburg* **13** B2
Auderghem, *Brussels* **6** B2
Augusta, Mausoleo di, *Rome* **25** b2
Augustówka, *Warsaw* **31** B2
Aulnay-sous-Bois, *Paris* **23** A3
Aurelio, *Rome* **25** B1
Ausim, *Cairo* **7** A1
Austerlitz, Gare d', *Paris* **23** A3
Austin, *Chicago* **9** B2
Avalon, *Wellington* **32** B2
Avedøre, *Copenhagen* **10** B2
Avellaneda, *Buenos Aires* **7** C2
Avenel, *Washington* **32** B4
Avondale, *Chicago* **9** B2
Avondale Heights, *Melbourne* **17** A1
Avtovo, *St. Petersburg* **26** B1
Ayazağa, *Istanbul* **12** B1
Ayer Chawan, P., *Singapore* **27** B2
Ayer Merbau, P., *Singapore* **27** B2
Ayía Marina, *Athens* **2** C3
Ayía Paraskevi, *Athens* **2** A2
Áyios Dhimitrios, *Athens* **2** B2
Áyios Ioánnis Rendis, *Athens* **2** B1
Azabu, *Tokyo* **29** c3
Azcapotzalco, *Mexico City* **18** B1
Azteca, Estadia, *Mexico City* **18** C2
Azucar, Cerro Pan de, *Santiago* **26** A1

B

Baambrugge, *Amsterdam* **2** B2
Baba I., *Karachi* **14** B1
Babarpur, *Delhi* **10** A2
Babushkin, *Moscow* **19** A4
Back B., *Mumbai* **20** B1
Baclaran, *Manila* **17** B2
Bacoor, *Manila* **17** C1
Bacoor B., *Manila* **17** C1
Badalona, *Barcelona* **4** A2
Badhoevedorp, *Amsterdam* **2** A1
Badli, *Delhi* **10** A1
Bærum, *Oslo* **22** A2
Bağcılar, *Istanbul* **12** B1
Bàggio, *Milan* **18** B1
Bāgh-e-Feyz, *Tehran* **30** A1
Baghdād, *Baghdad* **3** A2
Bagmari, *Calcutta* **8** B2
Bagneux, *Paris* **23** B2
Bagnolet, *Paris* **23** A3
Bagsværd, *Copenhagen* **10** A2
Bagsværd Sø, *Copenhagen* **10** A2
Baguiati, *Calcutta* **8** B2
Bagumbayan, *Manila* **17** C2
Bahçeköy, *Istanbul* **12** A1
Bahtim, *Cairo* **7** A2
Baileys Crossroads, *Washington* **32** B3
Bailly, *Paris* **23** A1
Bairro Alto, *Lisbon* **14** c1
Bairro Lopes, *Lisbon* **14** b3
Baisha, *Canton* **8** B2
Baisha →, *Canton* **8** B2
Baixa, *Lisbon* **14** c2
Baiyun Airport, *Canton* **8** B2
Baiyun Hill Scenic Spot, *Canton* **8** B2
Bakırköy, *Istanbul* **12** C1
Bakovka, *Moscow* **19** B2
Bal Harbor, *Miami* **18** A2
Balara, *Manila* **17** B2
Balashikha, *Moscow* **19** B5
Baldia, *Karachi* **14** A1
Baldoyle, *Dublin* **11** A3
Baldwin Hills, *Los Angeles* **16** B2
Baldwin Hills Res., *Los Angeles* **16** B2
Balgowlah, *Sydney* **28** B2
Balgowlah Heights, *Sydney* **28** A2
Balham, *London* **15** B3
Bali, *Calcutta* **8** B1
Baliganja, *Calcutta* **8** B2
Balingsnäs, *Stockholm* **28** B2
Balingsta, *Stockholm* **28** B2
Balintawak, *Manila* **17** B1
Balitai, *Tianjin* **30** B2
Ballerup, *Copenhagen* **10** A2
Ballinteer, *Dublin* **11** B2
Ballyboden, *Dublin* **11** B2
Ballybrack, *Dublin* **11** B3
Ballyfermot, *Dublin* **11** A1
Ballymorefinn Hill, *Dublin* **11** B1
Ballymun, *Dublin* **11** A2
Balmain, *Sydney* **28** B2
Baluhati, *Calcutta* **8** B1
Balvanera, *Buenos Aires* **7** B2
Balwyn, *Melbourne* **17** A2
Balwyn North, *Melbourne* **17** A2
Banática, *Lisbon* **14** A1
Banco do Brasil, Centro Cultural, *Rio de Janeiro* **24** a2
Bandra, *Mumbai* **20** A1
Bandra Pt., *Mumbai* **20** A1
Bang Kapi, *Bangkok* **3** B2
Bang Kholaem, *Bangkok* **3** A2
Bang Na, *Bangkok* **3** B2
Bang Phlad, *Bangkok* **3** a1
Bangkhen, *Bangkok* **3** A2
Bangkok = Krung Thep, *Bangkok* **3** B2
Bangkok Noi, *Bangkok* **3** B1
Bangkok Yai, *Bangkok* **3** B1
Banglamphoo, *Bangkok* **3** b2
Banglo, *Calcutta* **8** B1
Bangrak, *Bangkok* **3** B2
Bangsu, *Bangkok* **3** B2
Bank, *London* **15** b5
Bank of America, *San Francisco* **25** b2
Bank of China Tower, *Hong Kong* **12** c1
Banks, C., *Sydney* **28** C2
Banksmeadow, *Sydney* **28** B2
Banstala, *Calcutta* **8** B2
Bantra, *Calcutta* **8** B1
Baoshan, *Shanghai* **27** A1
Bar Giyora, *Jerusalem* **13** B1
Barahanagar, *Calcutta* **8** B2
Barajas, *Madrid* **17** B2
Barajas, Aeropuerto Transoceanico de, *Madrid* **17** B2
Barakpur, *Calcutta* **8** A2
Barberini, Palazzo, *Rome* **25** b3
Barbican, *London* **15** a4
Barcarena, *Lisbon* **14** A1
Barcarena, Rib. de →, *Lisbon* **14** A1
Barcelona, *Barcelona* **4** A2
Barcelona-Prat, Aeropuerta de, *Barcelona* **4** B1
Barceloneta, *Barcelona* **4** A2
Barking, *London* **15** A4
Barkingside, *London* **15** A4
Barnes, *London* **15** B2
Barnet, *London* **15** A2
Barra Andai, *Karachi* **14** B2
Barra Funda, *São Paulo* **26** B2
Barracas, *Buenos Aires* **7** B2
Barranco, *Lima* **16** B2
Barreiro, *Lisbon* **14** B2
Barreto, *Rio de Janeiro* **24** B2
Bartala, *Calcutta* **8** B1
Barton Park, *Sydney* **28** B1
Bartyki, *Warsaw* **31** C2
Barvikha, *Moscow* **19** B1
Bastille, Place de la, *Paris* **23** c5
Basus, *Cairo* **7** A2
Batanagar, *Calcutta* **8** B1
Bath Beach, *New York* **21** C1
Bath I., *Karachi* **14** B2
Batir, *Jerusalem* **13** B1
Batok, Bukit, *Singapore* **27** A2
Battersea, *London* **15** B3
Battery Park, *New York* **21** f1
Bauman, *Moscow* **19** B4
Baumgarten, *Vienna* **31** A1
Bay Harbour Islands, *Miami* **18** A2
Bay Ridge, *New York* **21** C1
Bayonne, *New York* **21** B1
Bayshore, *San Francisco* **25** B3
Bayswater, *London* **15** b2
Bayt Lahm = Bethlehem, *Jerusalem* **13** B2
Bayview, *San Francisco* **25** B2
Bāzār, *Tehran* **30** A2
Beachmont, *Boston* **6** A4
Beacon Hill, *Hong Kong* **12** A2
Beato, *Lisbon* **14** A2
Beaumont, *Dublin* **11** A2
Beaumonte Heights, *Toronto* **30** A1
Bebek, *Istanbul* **12** B2
Běchovice, *Prague* **24** B3
Beck L., *Chicago* **9** A1
Beckenham, *London* **15** B3
Beckton, *London* **15** A4
Becontree, *London* **15** A4
Beddington Corner, *London* **15** B3
Bedford, *Boston* **6** A2
Bedford Park, *Chicago* **9** C2
Bedford Park, *New York* **21** A2
Bedford Stuyvesant, *New York* **21** B2
Bedford View, *Johannesburg* **13** B2
Bedok, *Singapore* **27** B3
Bedok, Res., *Singapore* **27** A3
Beersel, *Brussels* **6** B1
Behala, *Calcutta* **8** B1
Bei Hai, *Beijing* **4** B2
Beicai, *Shanghai* **27** B2
Beicang, *Tianjin* **30** A1
Beihai Park, *Beijing* **4** b2
Beijing, *Beijing* **4** B1
Beit Ghur el-Fawqa, *Jerusalem* **13** A1
Beit Hanina, *Jerusalem* **13** B2
Beit Iksa, *Jerusalem* **13** B2
Beit I'nan, *Jerusalem* **13** A1
Beit Jala, *Jerusalem* **13** B2
Beit Lekhem = Bethlehem, *Jerusalem* **13** B2
Beit Nekofa, *Jerusalem* **13** B1
Beit Sahur, *Jerusalem* **13** B2
Beit Surik, *Jerusalem* **13** B1
Beit Zayit, *Jerusalem* **13** B1
Beitaipingzhuan, *Beijing* **4** B1
Beitar Illit, *Jerusalem* **13** B1
Beitsun, *Canton* **8** B2
Beitunya, *Jerusalem* **13** A2
Beixing Jing Park, *Shanghai* **27** B1
Békásmegyer, *Budapest* **7** A2
Bekkelaget, *Oslo* **22** A3
Bel Air, *Los Angeles* **16** B2
Bela Vista, *São Paulo* **26** B2
Bélanger, *Montreal* **19** A1
Belas, *Lisbon* **14** A1
Belas Artes, Museu Nacionale de, *Rio de Janeiro* **24** b2
Beleghata, *Calcutta* **8** B2
Belém, *Lisbon* **14** A1
Belém, Torre de, *Lisbon* **14** A1
Belènzinho, *São Paulo* **26** B2
Belgachiya, *Calcutta* **8** B2
Belgharia, *Calcutta* **8** B2
Belgrano, *Buenos Aires* **7** B2
Belgravia, *London* **15** c3
Bell, *Los Angeles* **16** C3
Bell Gardens, *Los Angeles* **16** C4
Bell Tower, *Beijing* **4** a2
Bellavista, *Lima* **16** B2
Bellavista, *Santiago* **26** C2
Belle Harbor, *New York* **21** C2
Belle View, *Washington* **32** B2
Bellevue, Schloss, *Berlin* **5** a2
Bellingham, *London* **15** B3
Bellwood, *Chicago* **9** B1
Belmont, *Boston* **6** A2
Belmont, *London* **15** A2
Belmont, *Wellington* **32** B2
Belmont Harbor, *Chicago* **9** B3
Belmore, *Sydney* **28** B1
Belur, *Calcutta* **8** B2
Belvedere, *Atlanta* **3** B3
Belvedere, *London* **15** B4
Belvedere, *San Francisco* **25** A2
Belyayevo Bogorodskoye, *Moscow* **19** C3
Bemowo, *Warsaw* **31** B1
Benaki, Moussío, *Athens* **2** b3
Bendale, *Toronto* **30** A3
Bendkhal, *Mumbai* **20** B2
Benefica, *Rio de Janeiro* **24** B1
Benfica, *Lisbon* **14** A1
Benito Juárez, *Mexico City* **18** B2
Benito Juárez, Aeropuerto Int., *Mexico City* **18** B2
Bensonhurst, *New York* **21** C2
Berchem-Sainte-Agathe, *Brussels* **6** A1
Berg am Laim, *Munich* **20** B2
Bergenfield, *New York* **21** A2
Bergham, *Munich* **20** B2
Bergvliet, *Cape Town* **8** B1
Beri, *Barcelona* **4** A1
Berkeley, *San Francisco* **25** A3
Berlin, *Berlin* **5** A3
Bermondsey, *London* **15** B3
Bernabeu, Estadio, *Madrid* **17** B1
Bernal Heights, *San Francisco* **25** B2
Berwyn, *Chicago* **9** B2
Berwyn Heights, *Washington* **32** B4
Besiktas, *Istanbul* **12** B2
Besós →, *Barcelona* **4** A2
Bethesda, *Washington* **32** B3
Bethlehem, *Jerusalem* **13** B2
Bethnal Green, *London* **15** A3
Betor, *Calcutta* **8** B1
Beurs, *Amsterdam* **2** b2
Beverley Hills, *Sydney* **28** B1
Beverley Park, *Sydney* **28** B1
Beverly, *Chicago* **9** C3
Beverly Glen, *Los Angeles* **16** B2
Beverly Hills, *Los Angeles* **16** B2
Bexley, *London* **15** B4
Bexley, *Sydney* **28** B1
Bexleyheath, *London* **15** B4
Beykoz, *Istanbul* **12** B2
Beylerbeyi, *Istanbul* **12** B2
Beyoğlu, *Istanbul* **12** B1
Bezons, *Paris* **23** A2
Bezuidenhout Park, *Johannesburg* **13** B2
Bhadrakali, *Calcutta* **8** A2
Bhalswa, *Delhi* **10** A2
Bhambo Khan Qarmati, *Karachi* **14** B2
Bhatsala, *Calcutta* **8** B1
Bhawanipur, *Calcutta* **8** B2
Bhuleshwar, *Mumbai* **20** b2
Białołeka Dworska, *Warsaw* **31** B2
Biblioteca Nacional, *Rio de Janeiro* **24** c2
Bicentennial Park, *Sydney* **28** B1
Bickley, *London* **15** B4
Bidu, *Jerusalem* **13** B1
Bielany, *Warsaw* **31** B1
Bielawa, *Warsaw* **31** C2
Biesdorf, *Berlin* **5** A4
Bièvre →, *Paris* **23** B1
Bièvres, *Paris* **23** B2
Bilston, *Edinburgh* **11** B2
Binacayan, *Manila* **17** C1
Binondo, *Manila* **17** B1
Birak el Kiyam, *Cairo* **7** A1
Birch Cliff, *Toronto* **30** A3
Birkenstein, *Berlin* **5** A5
Birkholz, *Berlin* **5** A4
Birkholzaue, *Berlin* **5** A4
Birrarung Park, *Melbourne* **17** A2
Biscayne Bay, *Miami* **18** B2
Biscayne Park, *Miami* **18** A2
Bishop Lavis, *Cape Town* **8** A2
Bishopscourt, *Cape Town* **8** A1
Bispebjerg, *Copenhagen* **10** A3
Biwon Secret Garden, *Seoul* **26** B1
Björknas, *Stockholm* **28** B3
Black Cr. →, *Toronto* **30** A2
Blackfen, *London* **15** B4
Blackheath, *London* **15** B4
Blackrock, *Dublin* **11** B2
Bladensburg, *Washington* **32** B4
Blair Village, *Atlanta* **3** C2
Blairgowrie, *Johannesburg* **13** A2
Blakehurst, *Sydney* **28** B1
Blakstad, *Oslo* **22** B1
Blankenburg, *Berlin* **5** A3
Blankenfelde, *Berlin* **5** A3
Blizne, *Warsaw* **31** B1
Bloomsbury, *London* **15** a3
Blota, *Warsaw* **31** C3
Blue Island, *Chicago* **9** C2
Bluebell, *Dublin* **11** B1
Bluff Hd., *Hong Kong* **12** B2
Blumberg, *Berlin* **5** A4
Blunt Pt., *San Francisco* **25** A2
Blutenburg, *Munich* **20** B1
Blylaget, *Oslo* **22** B3
Bo-Kaap Museum, *Cape Town* **8** c2
Boa Vista, Alto do, *Rio de Janeiro* **24** B1
Boardwalk, *New York* **21** C3
Boavista, *Lisbon* **14** A2
Bobigny, *Paris* **23** A3
Bocanegra, *Lima* **16** A2
Boedo, *Buenos Aires* **7** B2
Bogenhausen, *Munich* **20** B2
Bogorodskoye, *Moscow* **19** B4
Bogota, *New York* **21** A1
Bogstadvatnet, *Oslo* **22** A2
Bohnsdorf, *Berlin* **5** B4
Bois-Colombes, *Paris* **23** A2
Bois-d'Arcy, *Paris* **23** B1
Boissy-St.-Léger, *Paris* **23** B4
Boldinasco, *Milan* **18** B1
Bøler, *Oslo* **22** A4
Bollate, *Milan* **18** A1
Bollebeek, *Brussels* **6** A1
Bollensdorf, *Berlin* **5** A5
Bollmora, *Stockholm* **28** B3
Bolshaya-Okhta, *St. Petersburg* **26** B2
Bolton, *Atlanta* **3** B2
Bom Retiro, *São Paulo* **26** B2
Bombay = Mumbai, *Mumbai* **20** B2
Bondi, *Sydney* **28** B2
Bondy, *Paris* **23** A3
Bondy, Forêt de, *Paris* **23** A4
Bonifacio Monument, *Manila* **17** B1
Bonneuil-sur-Marne, *Paris* **23** B4
Bonnington, *Edinburgh* **11** B1
Bonnyrig and Lasswade, *Edinburgh* **11** B3
Bonsucesso, *Rio de Janeiro* **24** B1
Bonteheuwel, *Cape Town* **8** A2
Boo, *Stockholm* **28** A3
Booterstown, *Dublin* **11** B2
Borisovo, *Moscow* **19** C4
Borle, *Mumbai* **20** A2
Boronia Park, *Sydney* **28** A1
Borough Park, *New York* **21** C2
Bosmont, *Johannesburg* **13** B1
Bosön, *Stockholm* **28** A3
Bosporus = Istanbul Boğazi, *Istanbul* **12** B2
Bostancı, *Istanbul* **12** C2
Boston Harbor, *Boston* **6** A4
Botafogo, *Rio de Janeiro* **24** B1
Botanisk Have, *Copenhagen* **10** b2
Botany, *Sydney* **28** B2
Botany B., *Sydney* **28** B2
Botany Bay Nat. Park, *Sydney* **28** B2
Botič →, *Prague* **24** B3
Botica Sete, *Lisbon* **14** A1
Boucherville, *Montreal* **19** A3
Boucherville, Is. de, *Montreal* **19** A3
Bougival, *Paris* **23** A1
Boulder Pt., *Hong Kong* **12** B1
Boulogne, Bois de, *Paris* **23** A2
Boulogne-Billancourt, *Paris* **23** A2
Bourg-la-Reine, *Paris* **23** B2
Bouviers, *Paris* **23** B1
Bovenkerk, *Amsterdam* **2** B2
Bovenkerker Polder, *Amsterdam* **2** B2
Bovisa, *Milan* **18** A2
Bow, *London* **15** A3
Bowery, *New York* **21** e2
Boyacıköy, *Istanbul* **12** B2
Boyle Heights, *Los Angeles* **16** B3
Bradbury Building, *Los Angeles* **16** b2
Braepark, *Edinburgh* **11** B2
Braid, *Edinburgh* **11** B2
Bramley, *Johannesburg* **13** A2
Brandenburger Tor, *Berlin* **5** A3
Brani, P., *Singapore* **27** B3
Branik, *Prague* **24** B2
Brännkyrka, *Stockholm* **28** B2
Brás, *São Paulo* **26** B2
Brasilândia, *São Paulo* **26** A1
Brateyevo, *Moscow* **19** C4
Bratsevo, *Moscow* **19** A2
Bray, *Dublin* **11** B3
Braybrook, *Melbourne* **17** A1
Brázdim, *Prague* **24** A3
Breach Candy, *Mumbai* **20** a1
Breakheart Reservation, *Boston* **6** A3
Brede, *Copenhagen* **10** A3
Breeds Pond, *Boston* **6** A4
Breezy Point, *New York* **21** C2
Breitenlee, *Vienna* **31** A3
Breña, *Lima* **16** B2
Brent, *London* **15** A2
Brent Res., *London* **15** A2
Brentford, *London* **15** B2
Brentwood Park, *Los Angeles* **16** B2
Brera, *Milan* **18** B2
Bresso, *Milan* **18** A2
Brevik, *Stockholm* **28** A3
Břevnov, *Prague* **24** B2
Bridgeport, *Chicago* **9** B3
Bridgetown, *Cape Town* **8** A2
Bridgeview, *Chicago* **9** C2
Brighton, *Boston* **6** A3
Brighton, *Melbourne* **17** B1
Brighton le Sands, *Sydney* **28** B1
Brighton Park, *Chicago* **9** C2
Brightwood, *Washington* **32** B3
Brigittenau, *Vienna* **31** A2
Brimbank Park, *Melbourne* **17** A1
Brisbane, *San Francisco* **25** B2
British Museum, *London* **15** a3
Britz, *Berlin* **5** B3
Brixton, *London* **15** B3
Broad Sd., *Boston* **6** A4
Broadmeadows, *Melbourne* **17** A1
Broadmoor, *San Francisco* **25** B2
Broadview, *Chicago* **9** B1
Broadway, *New York* **21** e1
Brockley, *London* **15** B3
Brödno, *Warsaw* **31** B2
Brödnowski, Kanal, *Warsaw* **31** B2
Broek in Waterland, *Amsterdam* **2** A2
Bromley, *London* **15** B4
Bromley Common, *London* **15** B4
Bromma, *Stockholm* **28** A1
Bromma flygplats, *Stockholm* **28** A1
Brompton, *London* **15** c2
Brøndby Strand, *Copenhagen* **10** B2
Brøndbyøster, *Copenhagen* **10** B2
Brøndbyvester, *Copenhagen* **10** B2
Brondesbury, *London* **15** A2

WORLD MAPS

SETTLEMENTS

■ **PARIS**   ◉ Rotterdam   ◉ Livorno   ◉ Brugge   ⊚ Exeter   ○ *Torremolinos*   ○ *Oberammergau*   ○ *Thira*

Settlement symbols and type styles vary according to the scale of each map and indicate the importance of towns on the map rather than specific population figures

▫ *Vaduz*   Capital cities have red infills

⬠   Urban Agglomerations

∴   Ruins or Archaeological Sites

⌣   Wells in Desert

ADMINISTRATION

──────   International Boundaries

╌╌╌╌╌   Internal Boundaries

PERU   Country Names

╌╌╌╌╌   International Boundaries (Undefined or Disputed)

⬡   National Parks

KENT   Administrative Area Names

International boundaries show the *de facto* situation where there are rival claims to territory

COMMUNICATIONS

══════   Motorways, Freeways and Expressways

──────   Principal Railways

ᴸᴴᴿ ✈   Principal Airports

──────   Principal Roads

╌ ╌ ╌   Railways Under Construction

⊕   Other Airports

──────   Other Roads

──────   Other Railways

⋯⋯⋯⋯   Principal Canals

⊣···⊢   Road Tunnels

⊣···⊢   Railway Tunnels

⋈   Passes

PHYSICAL FEATURES

∿∿∿   Perennial Streams

⬭   Intermittent Lakes

▲ 8850   Elevations in metres

╌ ╌ ╌   Intermittent Streams

⬭   Swamps and Marshes

▼ 8500   Sea Depths in metres

⬭   Perennial Lakes

❄   Permanent Ice and Glaciers

1134   Height of Lake Surface Above Sea Level in metres

ELEVATION AND DEPTH TINTS

Height of Land above Sea Level

in metres

| 6000 | 4000 | 3000 | 2000 | 1500 | 1000 | 400 | 200 | 0 |

in feet

| 18 000 | 12 000 | 9000 | 6000 | 4500 | 3000 | 1200 | 600 |

Land Below Sea Level

| 6000 | 12 000 | 15 000 | 18 000 | 24 000 | in feet

| 0 | 200 | 2000 | 4000 | 5000 | 6000 | 8000 | in metres

Depth of Sea

Some of the maps have different contours to highlight and clarify the principal relief features

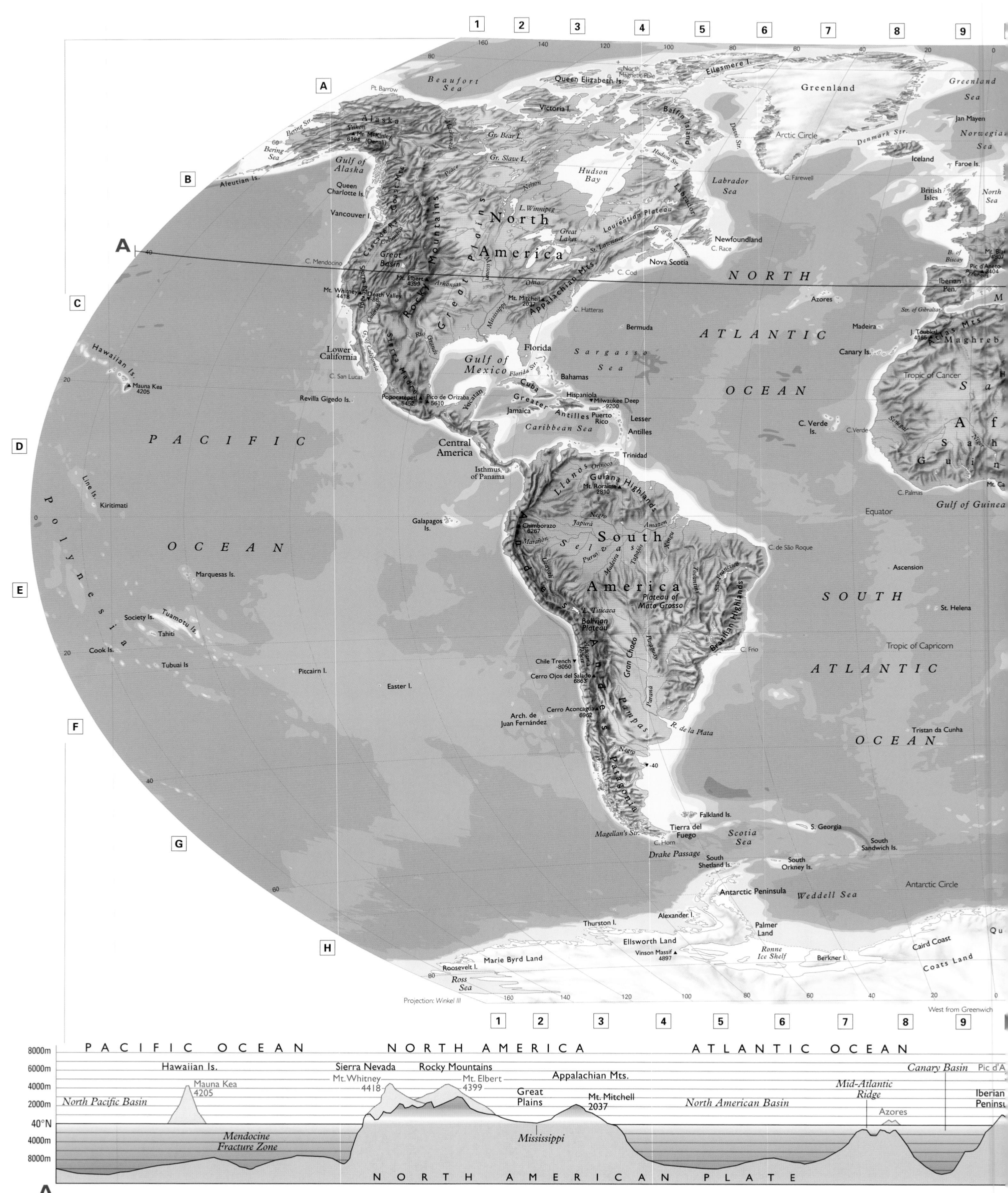

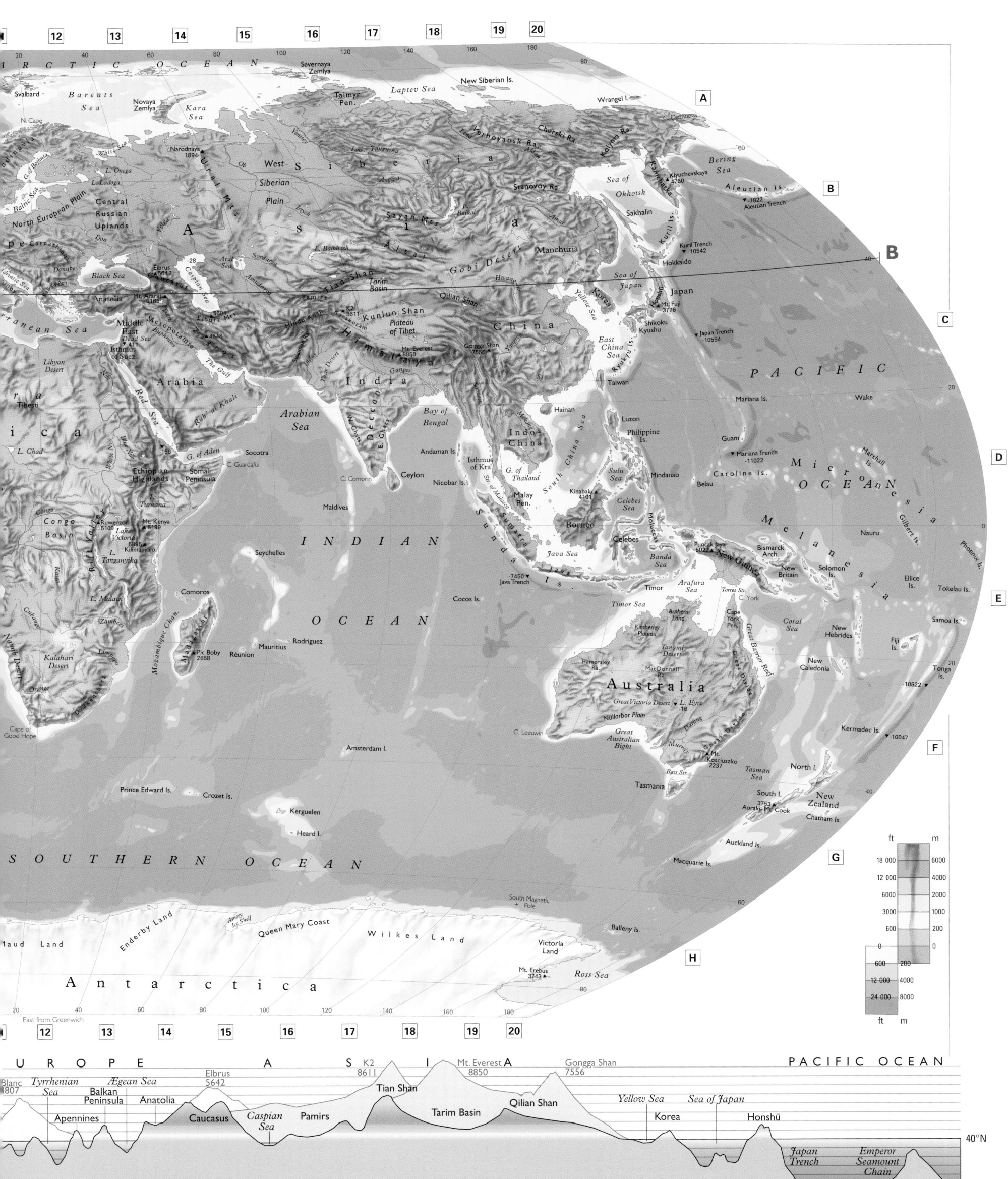

Hanoi ◉ Capital Cities

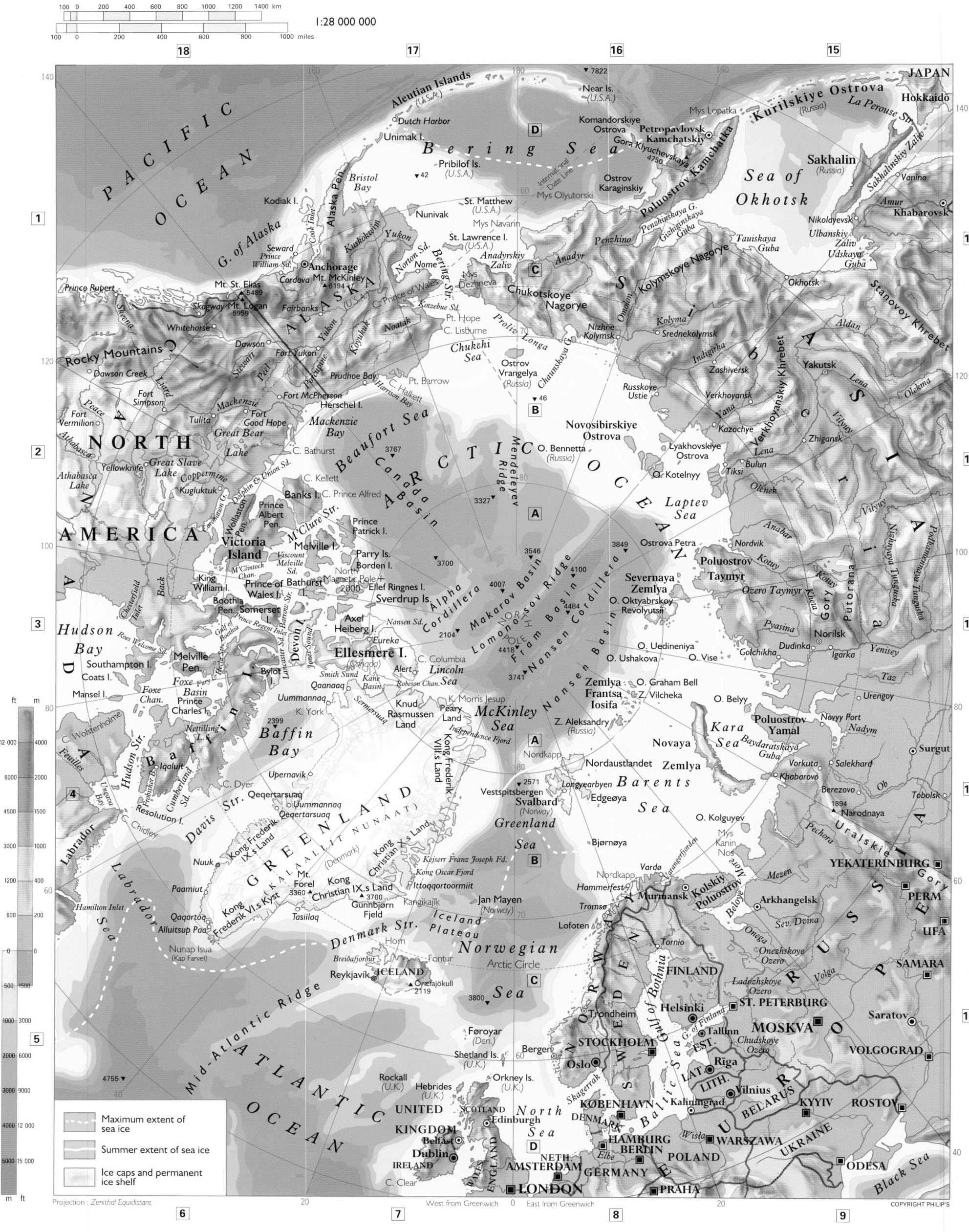

Maximum extent of sea ice

Summer extent of sea ice

Ice caps and permanent ice shelf

Projection : Zenithal Equidistant

West from Greenwich

East from Greenwich

COPYRIGHT PHILIP'S

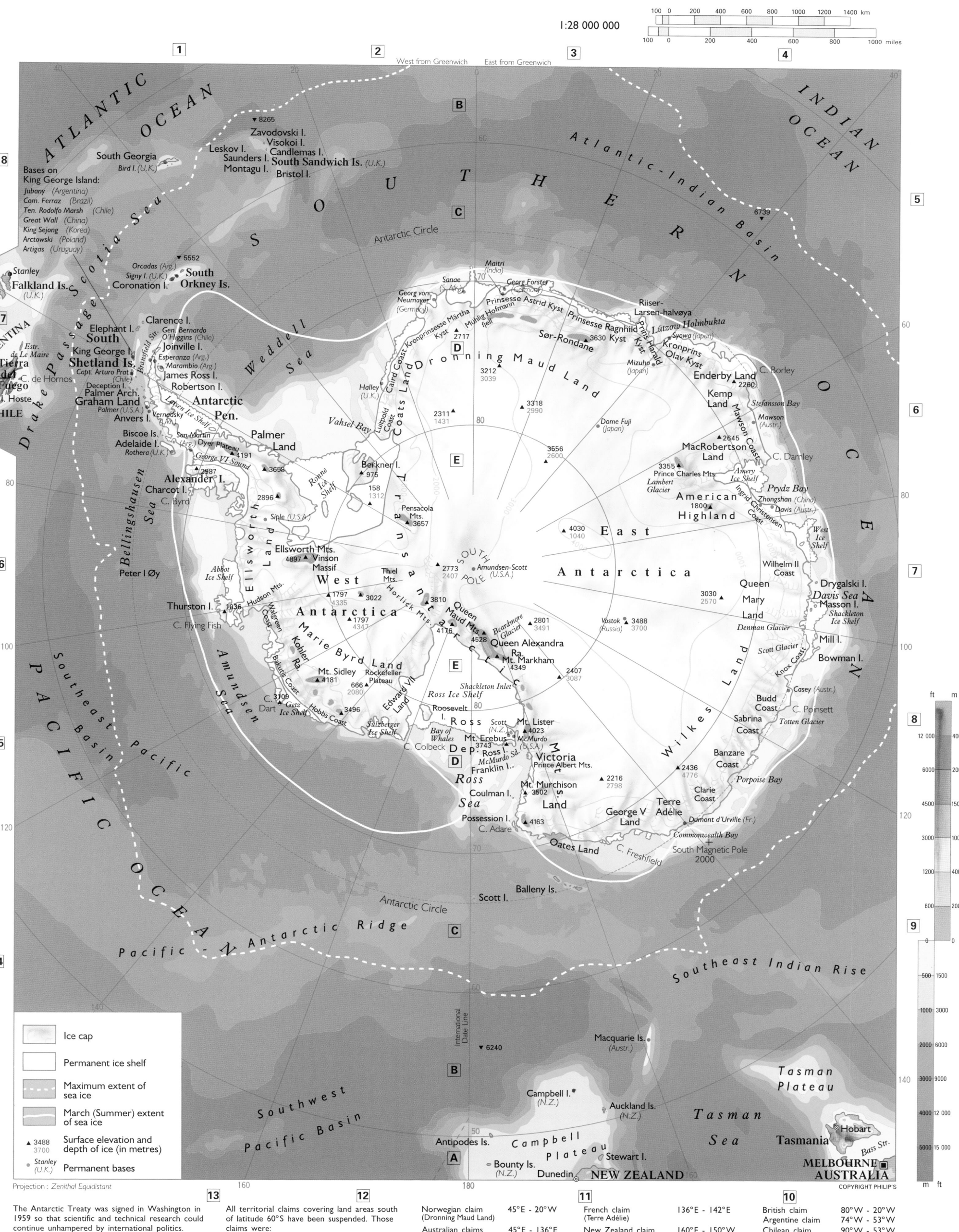

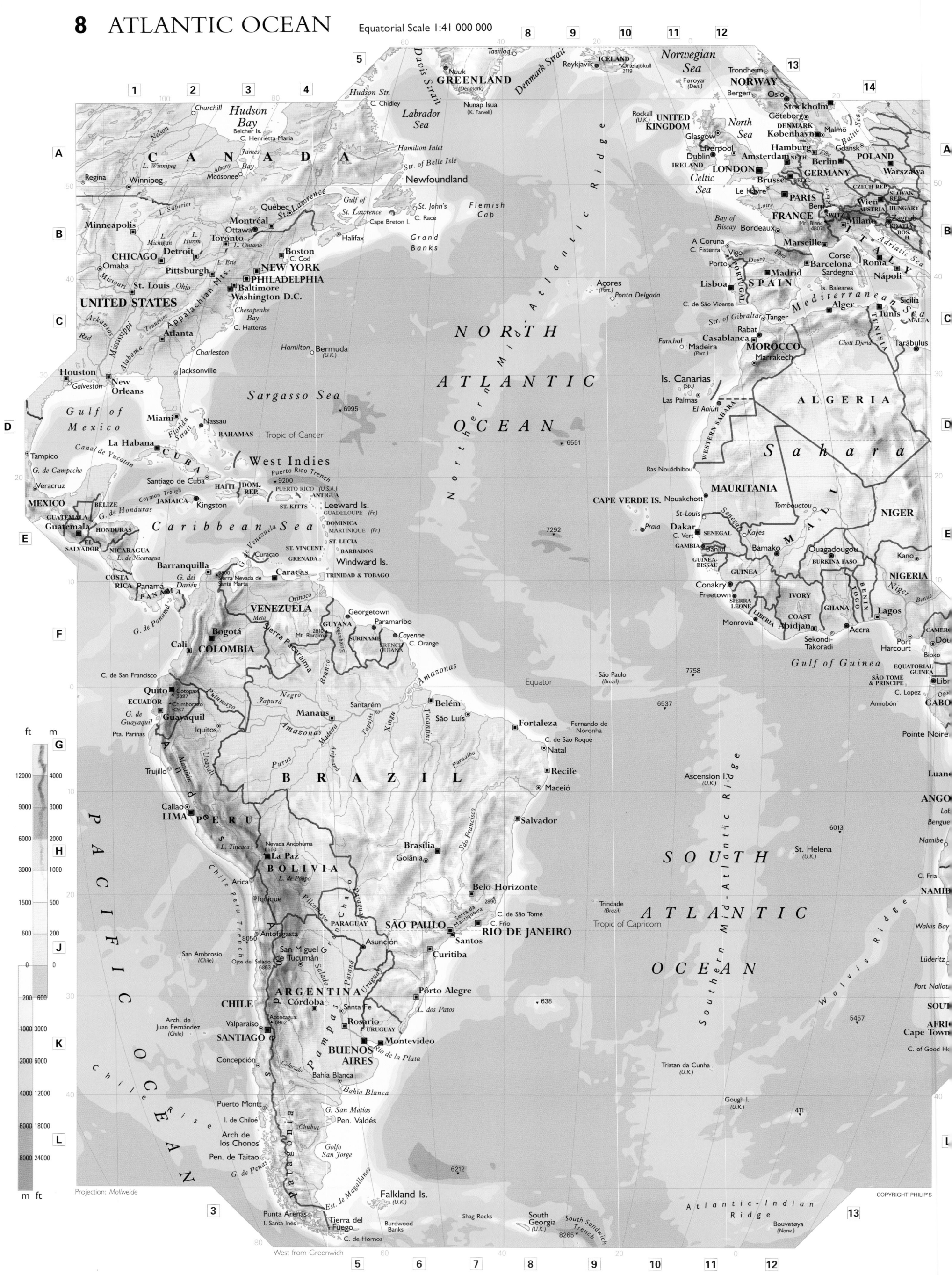

Projection: Mollweide

West from Greenwich

COPYRIGHT PHILIP'S

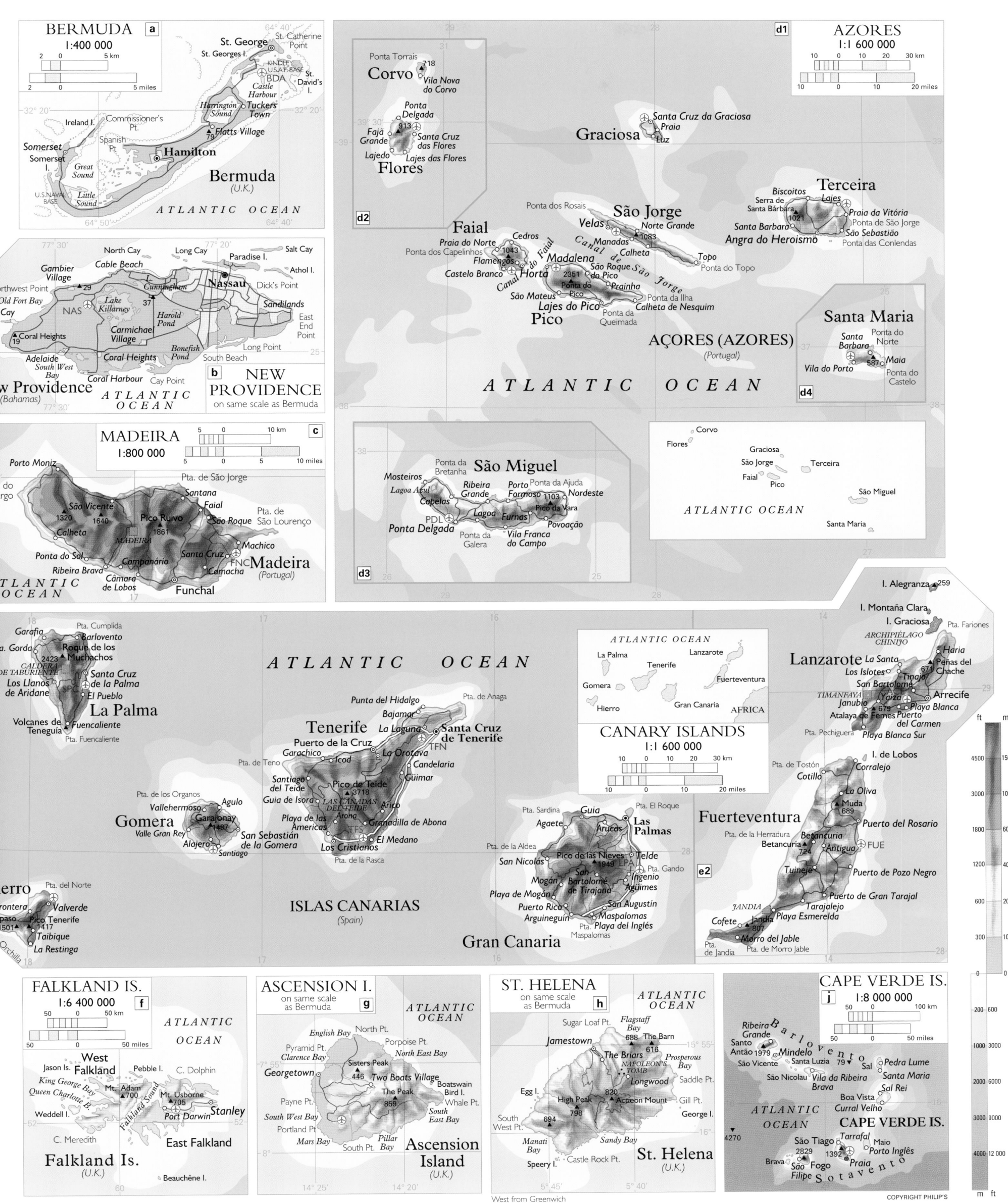

BERMUDA
1:400 000

St. George
St. Georges I.
St. Catherine Point
KINDLEY U.S.A.F. BASE
BDA
St. David's I.
Castle Harbour
Tuckers Town
Harrington Sound
Flatts Village
Ireland I.
Commissioner's Pt.
Somerset
Somerset I.
Spanish Pt.
Great Sound
Little Sound
U.S. NAVAL BASE
Hamilton
Bermuda
(U.K.)
ATLANTIC OCEAN

NEW PROVIDENCE
on same scale as Bermuda

North Cay
Cable Beach
Long Cay
Paradise I.
Salt Cay
Athol I.
Gambier Village
Cunningham
Nassau
Dick's Point
Northwest Point
Old Fort Bay
Cay
NAS
Lake Killarney
37
Harold Pond
Carmichae Village
Sandilands
East End Point
Coral Heights
19
Adelaide
South West Bay
Coral Heights
Bonefish Pond
South Beach
Long Point
Cay Point
Coral Harbour
w Providence
(Bahamas)
ATLANTIC OCEAN

MADEIRA
1:800 000

Porto Moniz
Pta. de São Jorge
. do argo
Santana
São Vicente
1320
1640
Faial
São Roque
Pta. de São Lourenço
Pico Ruivo
1861
MADEIRA
Machico
Calheta
Ponta do Sol
Campanário
Santa Cruz
Camacha
Ribeira Brava
Câmara de Lobos
FNC **Madeira**
(Portugal)
Funchal
TLANTIC OCEAN

AZORES
1:1 600 000

Ponta Torrais
718
Corvo
Vila Nova do Corvo
Ponta Delgada
913
Fajã Grande
Santa Cruz das Flores
Lajedo
Lajes das Flores
Flores
Santa Cruz da Graciosa
Praia
Graciosa
Luz
Ponta dos Rosais
Velas
São Jorge
Norte Grande
1083
Manadas
Calheta
Biscoitos
Serra de Santa Bárbara
Terceira
Lajes
1021
Praia da Vitória
Ponta de São Jorge
São Sebastião
Ponta das Conlendas
Faial
Praia do Norte
Cedros
1043
Ponta dos Capelinhos
Flamengos
Madalena
Canal do Faial
São Roque
do Pico
Canal de São Jorge
Topo
Ponta do Topo
Castelo Branco
Horta
2351
Prainha
São Mateus
Ponta do Pico
Ponta da Ilha
Lajes do Pico
Calheta de Nesquim
Pico
Ponta da Queimada
AÇORES (AZORES)
(Portugal)
Santa Barbara
Angra do Heroismo

Santa Maria
Santa Barbara
Ponta do Norte
Vila do Porto
587
Maia
Ponta do Castelo

ATLANTIC OCEAN

São Miguel

Ponta da Bretanha
Mosteiros
Lagoa Azul
Ribeira Grande
Porto Formoso
Ponta da Ajuda
Nordeste
Capelas
Lagoa
Furnas
1103
Pico da Vara
PDL
Ponta Delgada
Povoação
Ponta da Galera
Vila Franca do Campo

Corvo
Flores
Graciosa
São Jorge
Terceira
Faial
Pico
São Miguel
Santa Maria
ATLANTIC OCEAN

CANARY ISLANDS
1:1 600 000

ATLANTIC OCEAN
La Palma
Lanzarote
Tenerife
Gomera
Fuerteventura
Hierro
Gran Canaria
AFRICA

Pta. Cumplida
Garafia
ta. Gorda
Barlovento
Roque de los Muchachos
2423
CALDERA DE TABURIENTE
Santa Cruz de la Palma
SPC
Los Llanos de Aridane
El Pueblo
La Palma
Volcanes de Teneguía
Fuencaliente
Pta. Fuencaliente

ierro
Pta. del Norte
Frontera
Valverde
lpaso
Pico Tenerife
1501
1417
Taibique
705
La Restinga
Orchilla

Punta del Hidalgo
Pta. de Anaga
Bajamar
La Laguna
Santa Cruz de Tenerife
Tenerife
Puerto de la Cruz
TFN
Garachico
Icod
La Orotava
Candelaria
Pta. de Teno
Santiago del Teide
Pico de Teide
3718
Güimar
Guia de Isora
LAS CAÑADAS DEL TEIDE
Arico
Pta. de los Organos
Agulo
Playa de las Américas
Granadilla de Abona
Gomera
Garajonay
1487
TFS
El Medano
Valle Gran Rey
San Sebastián de la Gomera
Los Cristianos
Alojero
Santiago
Pta. de la Rasca

ISLAS CANARIAS
(Spain)

Pta. Sardina
Guia
Pta. El Roque
Agaete
Arucas
Las Palmas
San Nicolas
Pico de las Nieves
Telde
LPA
Pta. Gando
Mogán
San Bartolomé de Tirajana
1949
Ingenio
Agüimes
Playa de Mogán
Puerto Rico
San Augustín
Arguineguín
Maspalomas
Playa del Inglés
Pta. Playa Blanca
Maspalomas

Gran Canaria

I. Alegranza
259
I. Montaña Clara
I. Graciosa
Pta. Fariones
ARCHIPIÉLAGO CHINIJO
Haria
Lanzarote
La Santa
Peñas del Chache
Los Islotes
671
Tinajo
San Bartolomé
TIMANFAYA
Janubio
Yaiza
Arrecife
Atalaya de Femes
Playa Blanca
Puerto del Carmen
Pta. Pechiguera
Playa Blanca Sur

I. de Lobos
Pta. de Tostón
Corralejo
Cotillo
La Oliva
Muda
689
Puerto del Rosario
Fuerteventura
Pta. de la Herradura
Betancuria
FUE
Betancuria
724
Antigua
Tuineje
Puerto de Pozo Negro
JANDIA
Tarajalejo
Puerto de Gran Tarajal
Cofete
Jandia
Playa Esmerelda
Pta. de Jandia
Morro del Jable
Pta. de Morro Jable

FALKLAND IS.
1:6 400 000

ATLANTIC OCEAN
West Falkland
Jason Is.
Pebble I.
C. Dolphin
King George Bay
Queen Charlotte B.
Mt. Adam
700
Mt. Usborne
705
Port Darwin
Stanley
Weddell I.
Falkland Sound
East Falkland
C. Meredith
Falkland Is.
(U.K.)
Beauchêne I.

ASCENSION I.
on same scale as Bermuda

English Bay
North Pt.
Pyramid Pt.
Clarence Bay
Porpoise Pt.
North East Bay
Sisters Peak
Georgetown
Two Boats Village
446
Boatswain Bird I.
Payne Pt.
The Peak
859
South East Bay
South West Bay
Pillar Bay
Portland Pt.
Mars Bay
South Pt.
Ascension Island
(U.K.)

ST. HELENA
on same scale as Bermuda

ATLANTIC OCEAN
Sugar Loaf Pt.
Flagstaff Bay
688
The Barn
Jamestown
616
The Briars
NAPOLEON'S TOMB
Prosperous Bay
Longwood
Saddle Pt.
Egg I.
820
Gill Pt.
High Peak
Actaeon Mount
George I.
694
798
South West Pt.
Manati Bay
Sandy Bay
St. Helena
(U.K.)
Speery I.
Castle Rock Pt.

CAPE VERDE IS.
1:8 000 000

Ribeira Grande
Barlovento
Santo Antão
1979
Mindelo
São Vicente
Santa Luzia
79
Sal
Pedra Lume
São Nicolau
Vila da Ribeira Brava
Santa Maria
Sal Rei
Boa Vista
Curral Velho
ATLANTIC OCEAN
CAPE VERDE IS.
4270
Tarrafal
São Tiago
Maio
2829
Porto Inglês
1392
Praia
Brava
São Filipe
Fogo
Sotavento

West from Greenwich

COPYRIGHT PHILIP'S

ft m
4500 1500
3000 1000
1800 600
1200 400
600 200
300 100
0 0
200 600
600 1000
1000 3000
2000 6000
3000 9000
4000 12 000
m ft

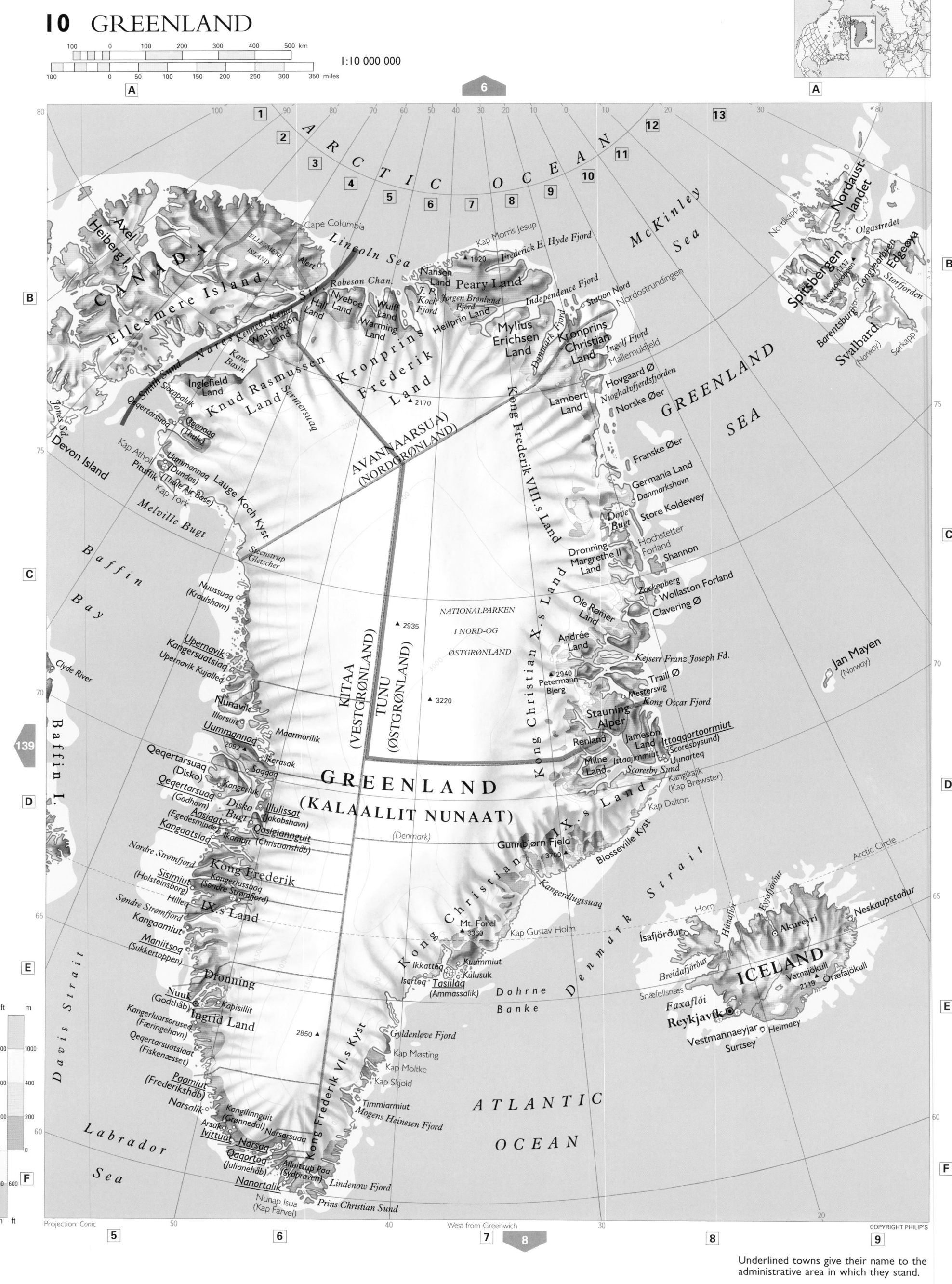

1:10 000 000

Projection: Conic

West from Greenwich

COPYRIGHT PHILIP'S

Underlined towns give their name to the administrative area in which they stand.

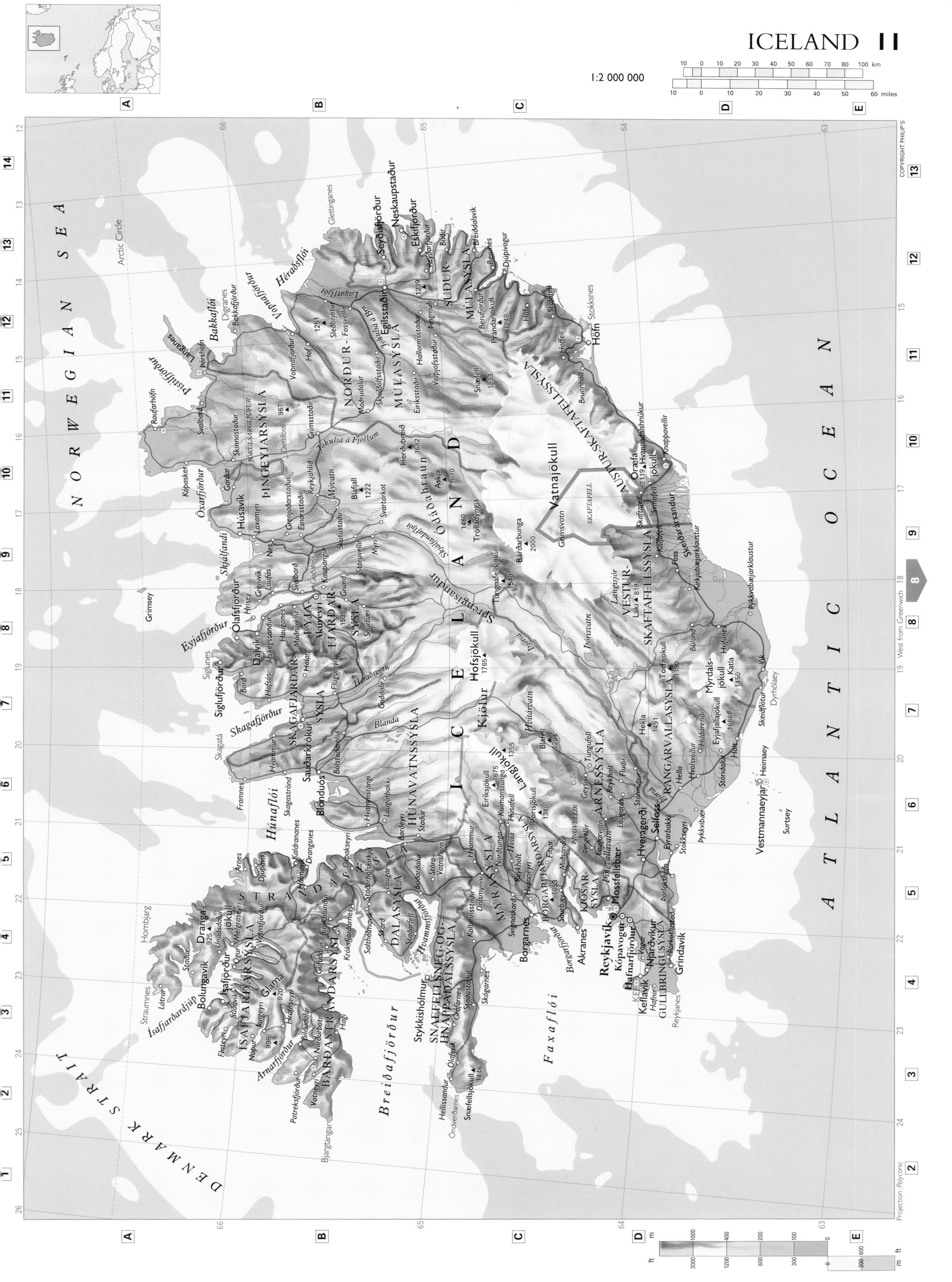

ICELAND 11

1:2 000 000

1:16 000 000

1:16 000 000

100 0 100 200 300 400 500 600 700 800 km
100 0 100 200 300 400 500 miles

COPYRIGHT PHILIP'S

■ LONDON Capital Cities

Projection: Bonne

West from Greenwich   East from Greenwich

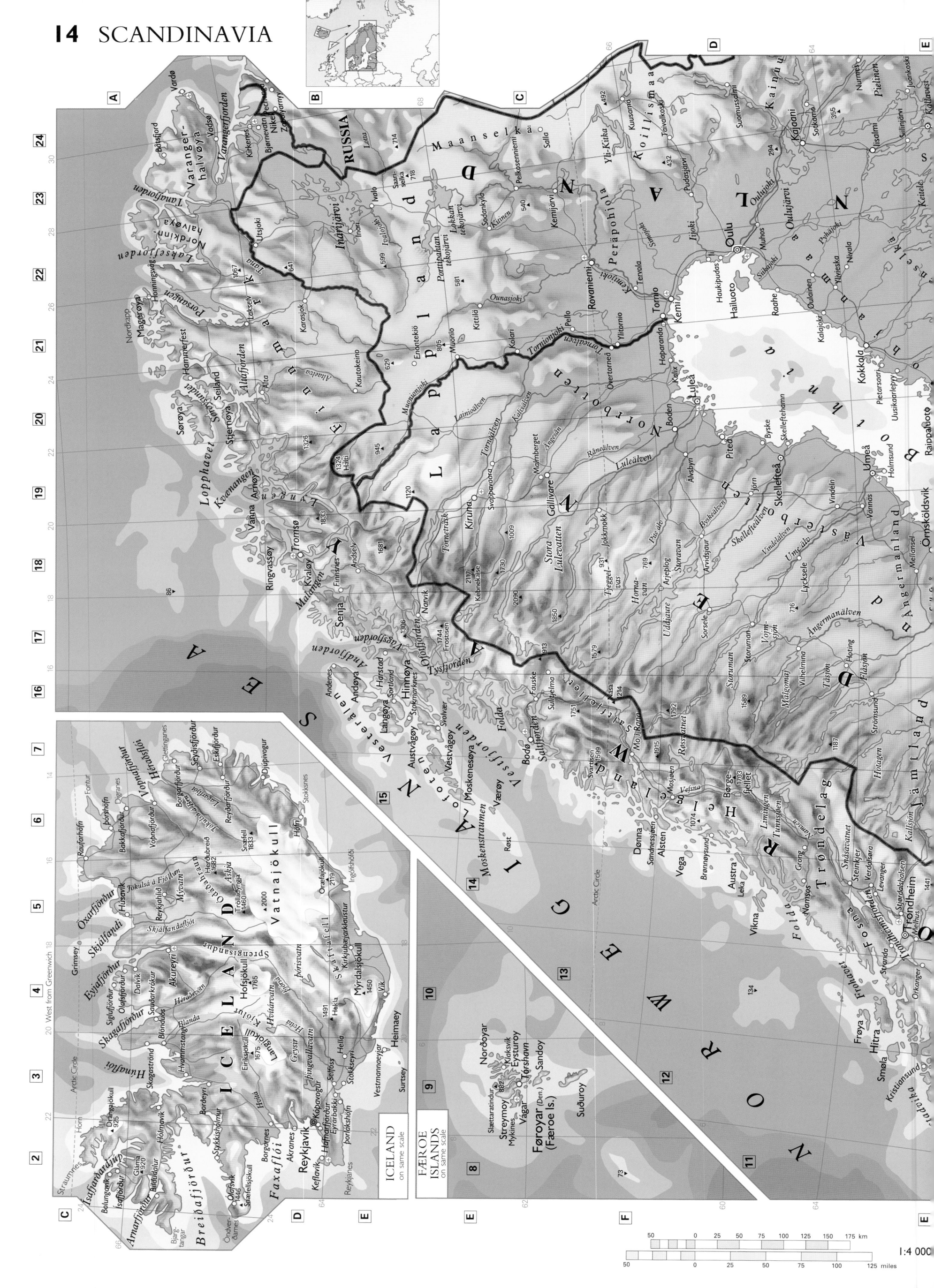

ICELAND
on same scale

FÆROE
ISLANDS
on same scale

50 25 0 25 50 75 100 125 150 175 km

50 0 25 50 75 100 125 miles

1:4 000

1:2 000 000

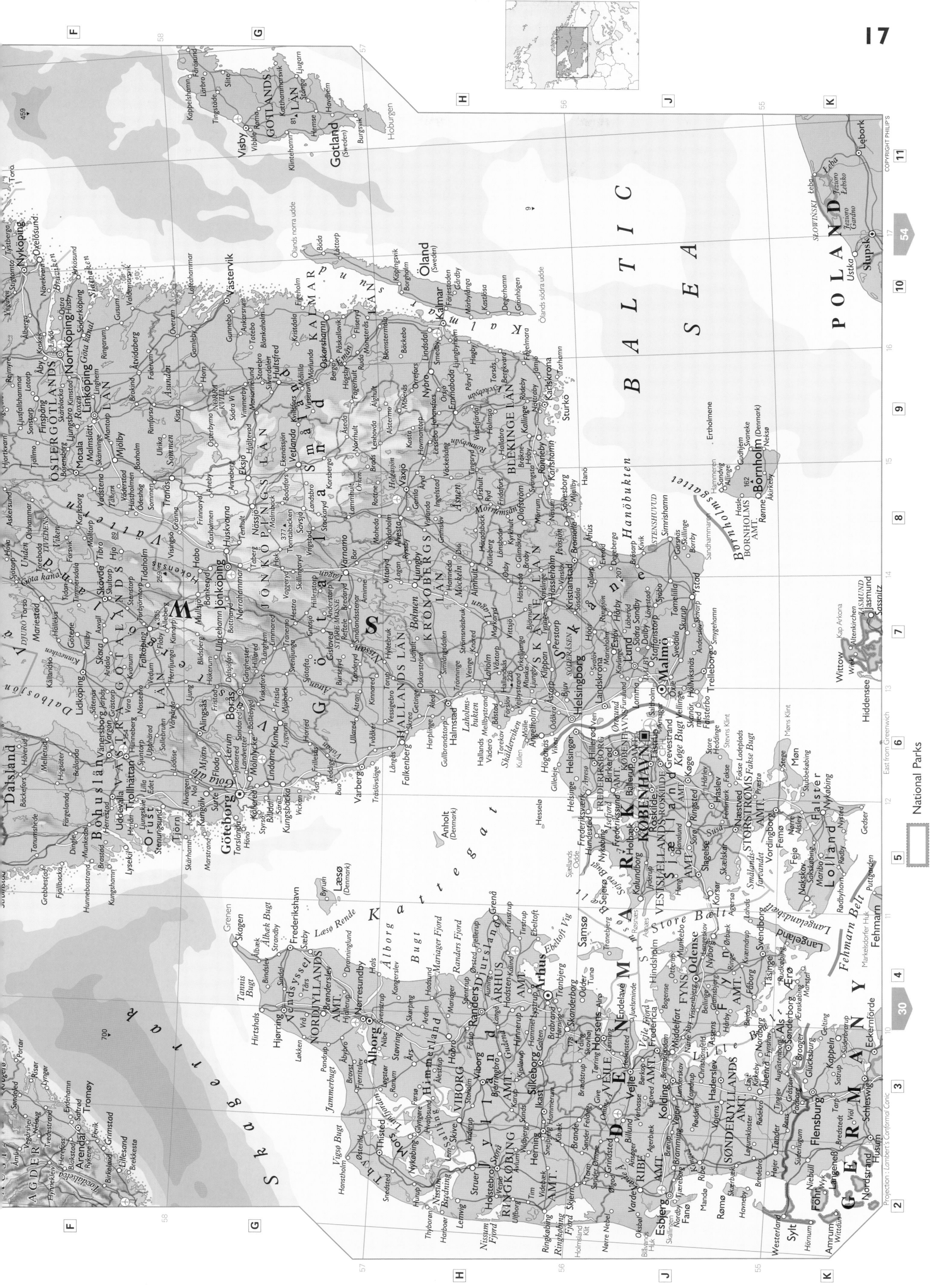

1:2 000 000

10 0 10 20 30 40 50 60 70 80 90 km
10 0 10 20 30 40 50 60 miles

NORWEGIAN SEA

Projection: Lambert's Conformal Conic

East from Greenwich

COPYRIGHT PHILIP'S

National Parks

1:1 600 000

Key to English unitary
authorities on map

25 HARTLEPOOL
26 DARLINGTON
27 STOCKTON-ON-TEES
28 MIDDLESBROUGH
29 REDCAR AND CLEVELAND
30 BLACKPOOL
31 BLACKBURN WITH DARWEN
32 HALTON
33 WARRINGTON
34 KINGSTON UPON HULL
35 NORTH EAST LINCOLNSHIRE
36 STOKE-ON-TRENT
37 TELFORD AND WREKIN
38 DERBY CITY
39 CITY OF NOTTINGHAM
40 LEICESTER CITY
41 RUTLAND
42 PETERBOROUGH
43 MILTON KEYNES
44 LUTON
45 NORTH SOMERSET
46 CITY OF BRISTOL
47 BATH AND NORTH EAST SOMERSET
48 SWINDON
49 READING
50 WOKINGHAM
51 WINDSOR AND MAIDENHEAD
52 SLOUGH
53 BRACKNELL FOREST
54 THURROCK
55 SOUTHEND-ON-SEA
56 MEDWAY
57 PLYMOUTH
58 TORBAY
59 POOLE
60 BOURNEMOUTH
61 SOUTHAMPTON
62 PORTSMOUTH
63 BRIGHTON AND HOVE

Key to Welsh unitary
authorities on map

15 SWANSEA
16 NEATH PORT TALBOT
17 BRIDGEND
18 RHONDDA CYNON TAFF
19 MERTHYR TYDFIL
20 CAERPHILLY
21 BLAENAU GWENT
22 TORFAEN
23 CARDIFF
24 NEWPORT

NORTH SEA

IRISH SEA

North Channel

SCOTLAND

NORTHERN IRELAND

ISLE OF MAN

ISLES OF SCILLY
on same scale

National Parks in England and Wales

Forest Parks in Scotland

1:1 600 000

Key to Scottish unitary authorities on map
1 CITY OF ABERDEEN
2 DUNDEE CITY
3 WEST DUNBARTONSHIRE
4 EAST DUNBARTONSHIRE
5 CITY OF GLASGOW
6 INVERCLYDE
7 RENFREWSHIRE
8 EAST RENFREWSHIRE
9 NORTH LANARKSHIRE
10 FALKIRK
11 CLACKMANNANSHIRE
12 WEST LOTHIAN
13 CITY OF EDINBURGH
14 MIDLOTHIAN

ORKNEY IS.
on same scale
ORKNEY
North Ronaldsay
Papa Westray
Westray
Sanday
Rousay
Eday
Stronsay
Brough Hd.
Stromness
Shapinsay
Mainland
Kirkwall
Hoy
Scapa Flow
St. Mary's
Burray
South Ronaldsay
Dunnet Hd.
Stroma
Duncansby Head
John o' Groats
Thurso
Sinclair's Bay

SHETLAND IS.
on same scale
Muckle Flugga
Unst
Haroldswick
Yell
Fetlar
Esha Ness
Ulsta
Out Skerries
Sullom Voe
Whalsay
St. Magnus Bay
Voe
Papa Stour
Walls
Lerwick
Bressay
Foula
Scalloway
West Burra
Boddam
Sumburgh Hd.

ATLANTIC OCEAN

SCOTLAND

NORTH SEA

WESTERN ISLES
Lewis
Stornoway
Broad Bay
Eye Peninsula
Harris
North Uist
Benbecula
South Uist
Barra

OUTER HEBRIDES
Sea of the Hebrides
Skye
Cuillin Hills
Rhum (Rùm)
Eigg
Muck
Coll
Tiree
Mull
Iona
Islay
Jura
Colonsay
Oronsay
Gigha
Arran
Goat Fell 874

C. Wrath
Durness
Cape Wrath
Sutherland
Reay Forest
Ben Hope 927
Ben More Assynt 998
Caithness
Thurso
Dunnet Hd.
John o' Groats
Wick
Lybster
Helmsdale
Ord of Caithness
Golspie
Brora
Lairg
Bonar Bridge
Dornoch
Tain
Moray Firth
Lossiemouth
Elgin
Buckie
Cullen
Banff
Macduff
Fraserburgh
Peterhead
MORAY
Forres
Nairn
Inverness
Keith
Huntly
BUCHAN
Ellon
Cruden Bay
ABERDEENSHIRE
Aberdeen
Inverurie
Stonehaven
Grampian Mountains
Cairngorm Mts.
Ben Macdhui 1309
Braemar
Ballater
Banchory
ANGUS
Montrose
Arbroath
Forfar
Brechin
Dundee
Perth
PERTH AND KINROSS
Ben Lawers 1214
Ben Nevis 1342
Fort William
LOCHABER
Glen Coe
Rannoch Moor
Pitlochry
Blairgowrie
St. Andrews
Fife Ness
FIFE
Glenrothes
Kirkcaldy
Stirling
STIRLING
Loch Lomond
ARGYLL AND BUTE
Oban
LORN
Inveraray
Dunoon
Greenock
Helensburgh
Dumbarton
Glasgow
Paisley
Hamilton
East Kilbride
Motherwell
Coatbridge
Airdrie
Cumbernauld
Falkirk
EDINBURGH
Livingston
Dalkeith
Musselburgh
Haddington
Dunbar
North Berwick
EAST LOTHIAN
PENTLAND HILLS
Peebles
Galashiels
Melrose
Kelso
SCOTTISH BORDERS
Hawick
Jedburgh
The Cheviot 816
CHEVIOT HILLS
Selkirk
Moffat
Lockerbie
Dumfries
DUMFRIES & GALLOWAY
Stranraer
Newton Stewart
Kirkcudbright
Wigtown
Whithorn
Mull of Galloway
Girvan
Ayr
Prestwick
Troon
Kilmarnock
SOUTH AYRSHIRE
NORTH AYRSHIRE
EAST AYRSHIRE
SOUTH LANARKSHIRE
Lanark
Biggar
Cumnock
Solway Firth

NORTHERN IRELAND
Larne
Belfast
Bangor
Newtownards
Carrickfergus
Donaghadee

NORTH CHANNEL

ENGLAND
Newcastle-upon-Tyne
Gateshead
Carlisle
Penrith
CUMBRIA
NORTHUMBERLAND
Berwick-upon-Tweed
Hadrian's Wall
Morpeth
Alnwick
DURHAM
Bishop Auckland
Barnard Castle

Forest Parks in Scotland

West from Greenwich

Projection : Lambert's Conformal Conic

COPYRIGHT PHILIP'S

1:1 600 000

10 0 10 20 30 40 50 60 70 80 km
10 0 10 20 30 40 50 miles

SCOTLAND
Mull of Oa · Kintyre · Brodick · Arran · Firth of Clyde · Campbeltown · Mull of Kintyre · Ailsa Craig · Cairnryan · Stranraer · Portpatrick · L. Ryan

ATLANTIC OCEAN

Inishtrahull · Malin Hd. · Tory I. · Horn Hd. · Sheep Haven · Mulroy B. · Lough Swilly · Fanad Hd. · Malin Pen. · Carndonagh · Moville · Buncrana · Inishowen Pen. · Giants Causeway · Fair Hd. · Rathlin I. · Ballycastle · Mts. of Antrim · North Channel

Bloody Foreland · Gweedore · Errigal 752 · Derryveagh Mts. · Rathmelton · L. Foyle · Portstewart · Portrush · Coleraine · Limavady · Ballymoney · Garron Pt. · GLENARIFF · Trostan 554 · Larne · Portpatrick

Inishfree B. · Aran I. · The Rosses · GLENVEAGH · Londonderry · LONDONDERRY · Roe · Ballymena · Randalstown Ballyclare · Larne · 269

Crohy Hd. · Gweebarra B. · Dawros Hd. · Letterkenny · DONEGAL · Lifford · Strabane · Sion Mills · Newtownstewart · Sawel Mt. 683 · Sperrin Mts. · Magherafelt · Moneymore · Antrim · Newtownabbey · Carrickfergus · Bangor · Donaghadee

Loughros More B. · Rossan Pt. · Slieve League 601 · Killybegs · Donegal · Derg · Castlederg · TYRONE · Omagh · Dungannon · Cookstown · Coalisland · L. Neagh · Belfast · Lisburn · Comber · Newtownards · Ards Pen. · Portaferry

St. John's Pt. · Donegal Bay · Ballyshannon · Bundoran · Erne · ULSTER · Dromore · Irvinestown · Enniskillen · FERMANAGH · Lower L. Erne · Upper L. Erne · Clones · Monaghan · Blackwater · Aughnacloy · Armagh · Craigavon · Lurgan · Portadown · Banbridge · Tandragee · Ballynahinch · Downpatrick · Ballyquintin Pt. · St. John's Pt. · Lagan · DOWN · Saintfield · Strangford L.

Broad Haven · Erris Hd. · Mullet Pen. · Belmullet · Downpatrick Hd. · Killala B. · 380 · Sligo Bay · Sligo · SLIGO · Collooney · L. Allen · LEITRIM · Belturbet · Annalee · Castleblaney · ARMAGH · Middletown · Keady · Newry · Mourne Mts. · Slieve Donard 852 · Newcastle · Dundrum B. · Carlingford L.

Inishkea North · Inishkea South · Blacksod Bay · Achill Hd. · 672 · Achill I. · Corraun Pen. · Nephin 806 · L. Conn · Ballina · Swinford · Charlestown · Boyle · Carrick-on-Shannon · Leitrim · L. Gowna · Cavan · Kingscourt · CAVAN · Carrickmacross · LOUTH · Dundalk · Dundalk Bay · Clogher Hd.

Clare I. · Clew Bay · Westport · Castlebar · MAYO · Knock · Ballyhaunis · Castlerea · ROSCOMMON · L. Sheelin · Oldcastle · Blackwater · Ceanannus Mor (Kells) · Ardee · Dunleer · Drogheda

Inishturk · Killary Harbour · Croagh Patrick 765 · Mweelrea 819 · CONNEMARA · Ballinrobe · Claremorris · Ballaghaderreen · Roscommon · LONGFORD · Granard · Castlepollard · MEATH · An Uaimh (Navan) · Balbriggan · Lambay I.

Inishbofin · Inishshark · Slyne Hd. · Clifden · Oughterard · Lough Mask · Lough Corrib · Tuam · GALWAY · Glennamaddy · Longford · Lough Ree · IRELAND · Leinster · Mullingar · WESTMEATH · Athboy · Trim · Royal Canal · Swords · Rush · Malahide · Howth Hd.

Bertraghboy B. · Kilkieran B. · Galway Bay · Galway · Athenry · Ballinasloe · Athlone · Moate · Brosna · Edenderry · Allen · Maynooth · DUBLIN · Dublin · Dun Laoghaire

Aran Is. · Inishmore · Inishmaan · Inisheer · Black Hd. · BURREN · Gort · Slieve Aughty 368 · Loughrea · Clara · Tullamore · OFFALY · Bog of Allen · KILDARE · Droichead Nua · Naas · Clondalkin · Bray · Greystones · 123

Cliffs of Moher · Hags Hd. · Liscannor Bay · Ennistimon · Slieve Bloom · Portumna · Shannon · Birr · Mountmellick · Portarlington · Kildare · Monasterevin · Poulaphouca Res. · Kippure 754 · WICKLOW · WICKLOW MTS.

Mal Bay · Mutton I. · Tulla · Lough Derg · Roscrea · Slieve Bloom · Arderin 528 · Port Laoise · Athy · Lugnaquillia 926 · Wicklow · Wicklow Hd.

Loop Hd. · Kilkee · Kilrush · Ennis · CLARE · Sixmilebridge · Killaloe · Nenagh · Templemore · LAOIS · Durrow · Carlow · Tullow · Rathdrum · Avoca · Arklow

Mouth of the Shannon · Ballybunion · Foynes · LIMERICK · Limerick · Keeper Hill 694 · Thurles · Kilkenny · KILKENNY · Callan · Shillelagh · Gorey · Mizen Hd.

Kerry Hd. · Listowel · Rathkeale · Newcastle West · Golden Vale · TIPPERARY · Tipperary · Cashel · Slievenamon 722 · Mt. Leinster 796 · Bunclody · Cahore Pt.

Brandon B. · Smerwick Harbour · Brandon Mt. 953 · Tralee B. · Tralee · Slieve Mish 853 · Newmarket · Kanturk · Mitchelstown · Kilfinnane · Galtymore 920 · Galty Mts. · Caher · Carrick-on-Suir · Clonmel · Suir · WEXFORD · Enniscorthy · New Ross · Wexford · Wexford Harbour · Rosslare · Rosslare Harbour · Greenore Pt. · Carnsore Pt.

Great Blasket I. · Dingle · KERRY · Maine · Buttevant · Fermoy · Blackwater · Knockmealdown Mts. 795 · Lismore · Comeragh Mts. 792 · Clonmel · Waterford · Tramore · Tramore B. · Hook Hd. · Saltee Is.

Inishvickillane · Dunmore Hd. · Killorglin · Killarney · L. Leane · Macroom · WATERFORD · Dungarvan · Dungarvan Harbour · St. George's Channel

Valencia I. · Puffin I. · Great Skellig · Cahirciveen · Carrauntoohill 1041 · Macgillycuddy's Reeks · KILLARNEY · Boggeragh Mts. 646 · Mallow · Blarney · CORK · Midleton · Youghal · Youghal B. · St. David's Hd. · St. David's · St. Brides Bay

Ballinskellig B. · Scariff I. · Kenmare River · Kenmare · Caha Mts. 707 · Glengarriff · Dunmanway · Macroom · Cork · Passage West · Cobh · Crosshaven · Cork Harbour · 115 · WALES

Dursey I. · Crow Hd. · Castletown Bearhaven · Bear I. · Bantry Bay · Bantry · Bandon · Bandon · Kinsale · Old Head of Kinsale

Dunmanus B. · Mizen Hd. · Skull · Long I. · Baltimore · Sherkin I. · Clear I. · C. Clear · Fastnet Rock · Skibbereen · Clonakilty · Clonakilty B. · Galley Hd.

CELTIC SEA

IRISH SEA

Projection: Lambert's Conformal Conic · West from Greenwich · COPYRIGHT PHILIP'S

National Parks

10 0 10 20 30 40 50 60 70 80 90 km
1:2 000 000
10 0 10 20 30 40 50 60 miles

NORTH SEA

UNITED KINGDOM

NETHERLANDS

Amsterdam

's-Gravenhage (Den Haag)

Rotterdam

BELGIUM

Brussel (Bruxelles)

Antwerpen

Gent (Gand)

Brugge

LUXEMBOURG

Luxembourg

GERMANY

NORDRHEIN WESTFALEN

Dortmund

Köln

Düsseldorf

Essen

RHEINLAND-PFALZ

SAARLAND

Saarbrücken

FRANCE

PARIS

Reims

Nancy

Strasbourg

National Parks

Underlined towns give their name to the
administrative area in which they stand.

COPYRIGHT PHILIP'S

1:4 000 000

50 0 25 50 75 100 125 150 175 km

50 0 25 50 75 100 125 miles

COPYRIGHT PHILIP'S

GERMANY

BELGIUM

LUXEMBOURG

SWITZERLAND

ITALY

AUSTRIA

LIECH.

UNITED KINGDOM

SPAIN

ANDORRA

F R A N C E

Corse (Corsica)

MEDITERRANEAN SEA

English Channel

Bay of Biscay

Golfe du Lion

Paris

Projection: Conical with two standard parallels

East from Greenwich

West from Greenwich

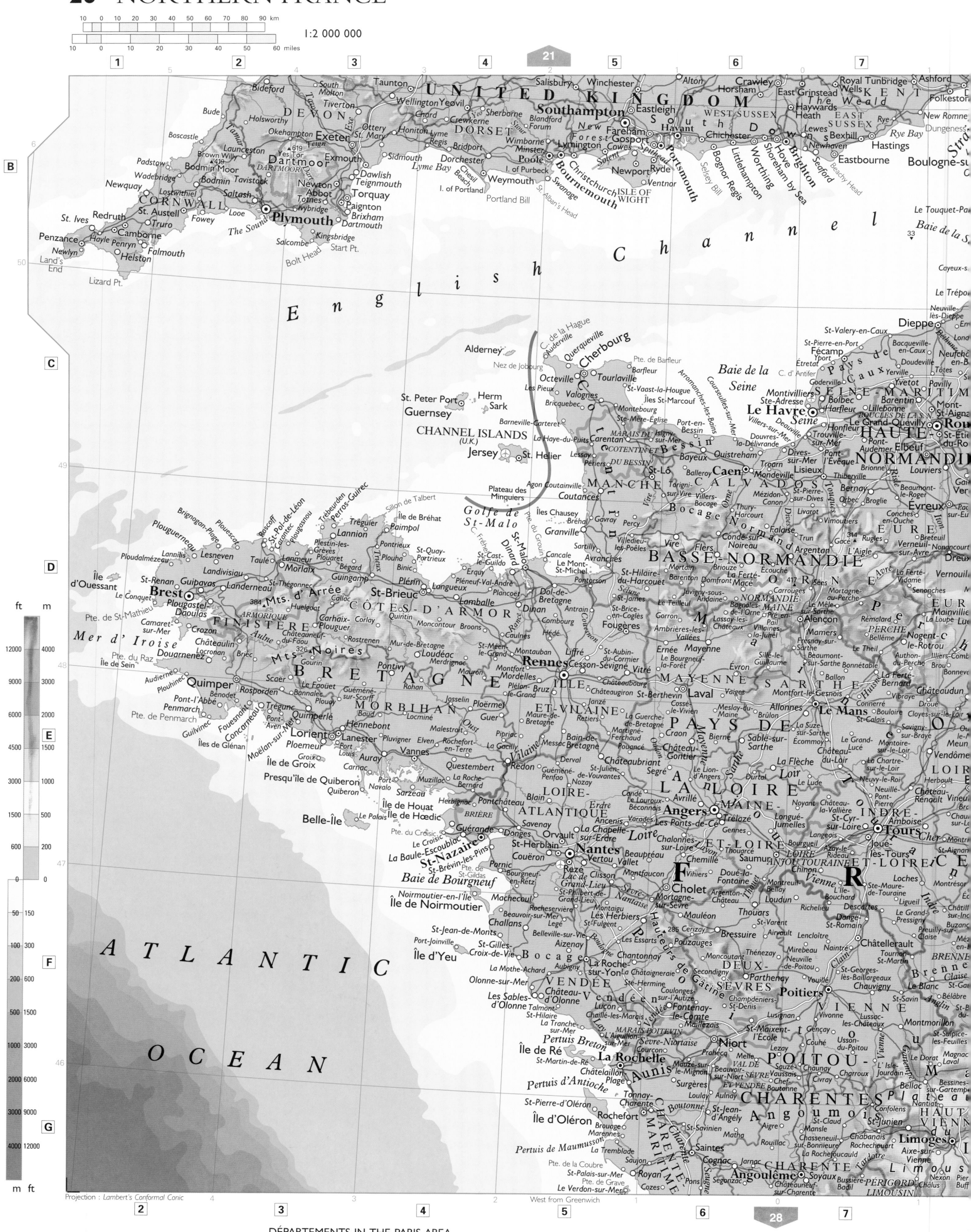

10   0 10 20 30 40 50 60 70 80 90 km
10   0   10   20   30   40   50   60 miles

1:2 000 000

DÉPARTEMENTS IN THE PARIS AREA
1 Ville de Paris   3 Val-de-Marne
2 Seine-St-Denis   4 Hauts-de-Seine

Projection : Lambert's Conformal Conic

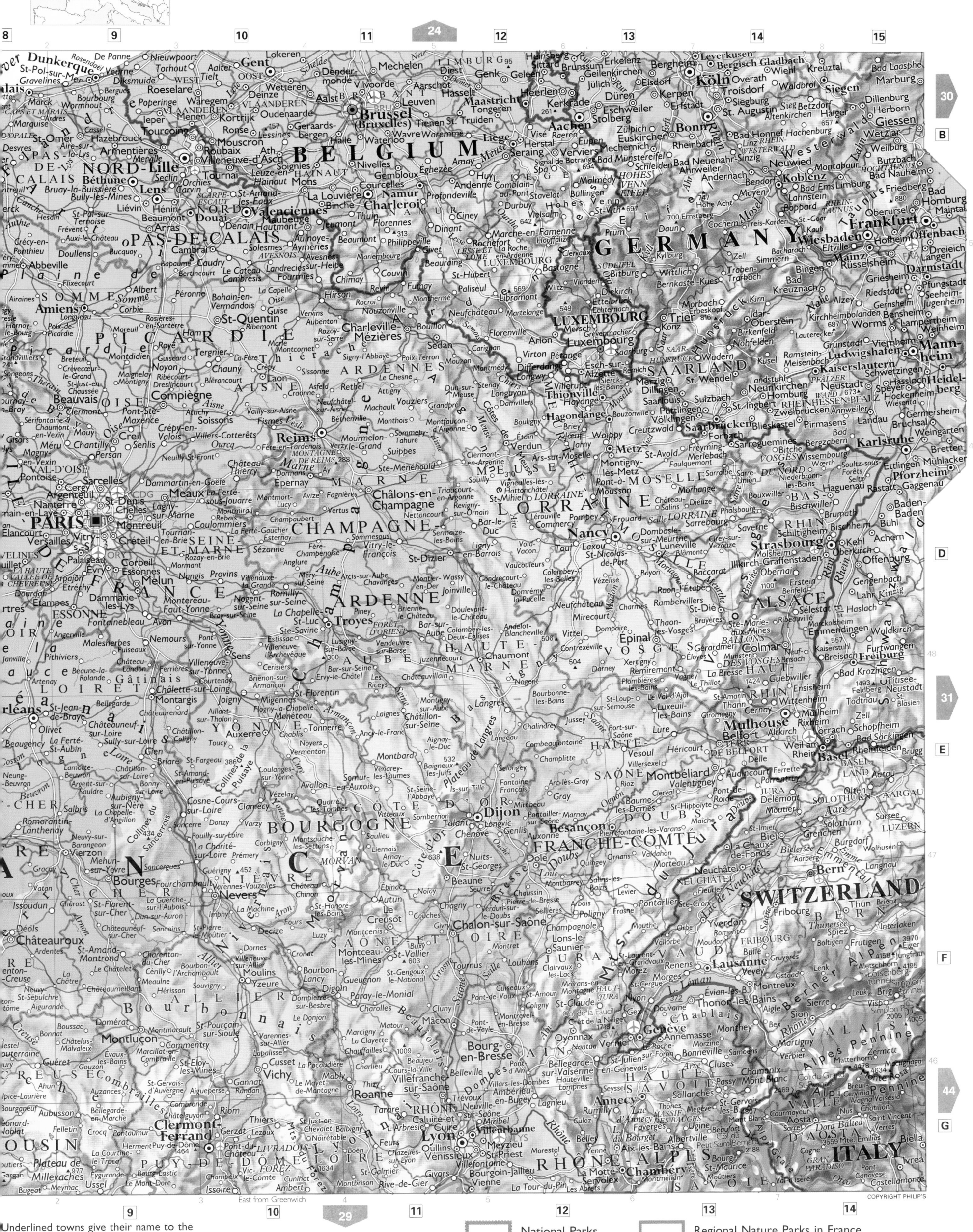

Underlined towns give their name to the
administrative area in which they stand.

National Parks

Regional Nature Parks in France

COPYRIGHT PHILIP'S

1:2 000 000

National Parks   Regional Nature Parks in France

COPYRIGHT PHILIP'S

1:2 000 000

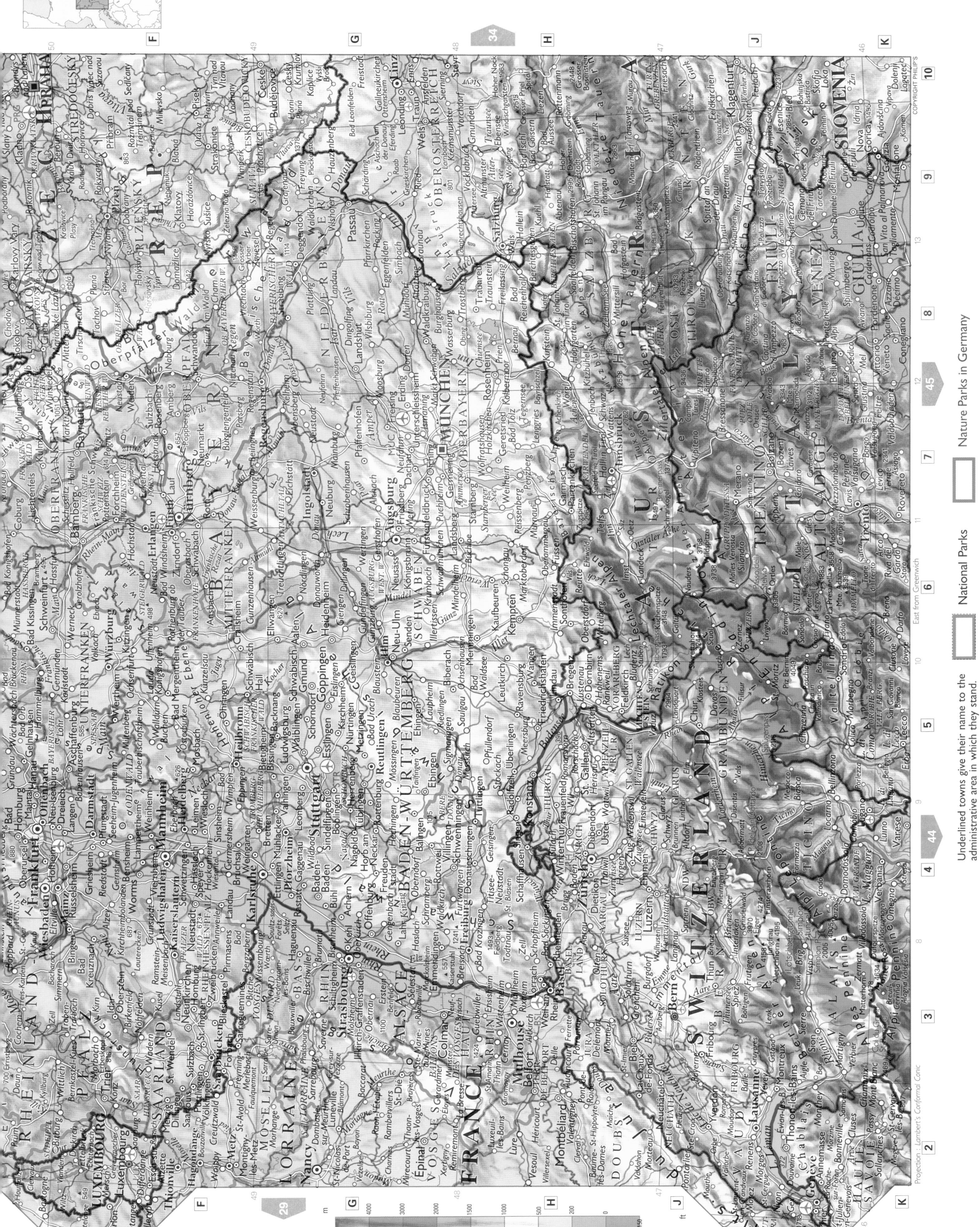

Underlined towns give their name to the
administrative area in which they stand.

Nature Parks in Germany

National Parks

East from Greenwich

COPYRIGHT PHILIP'S

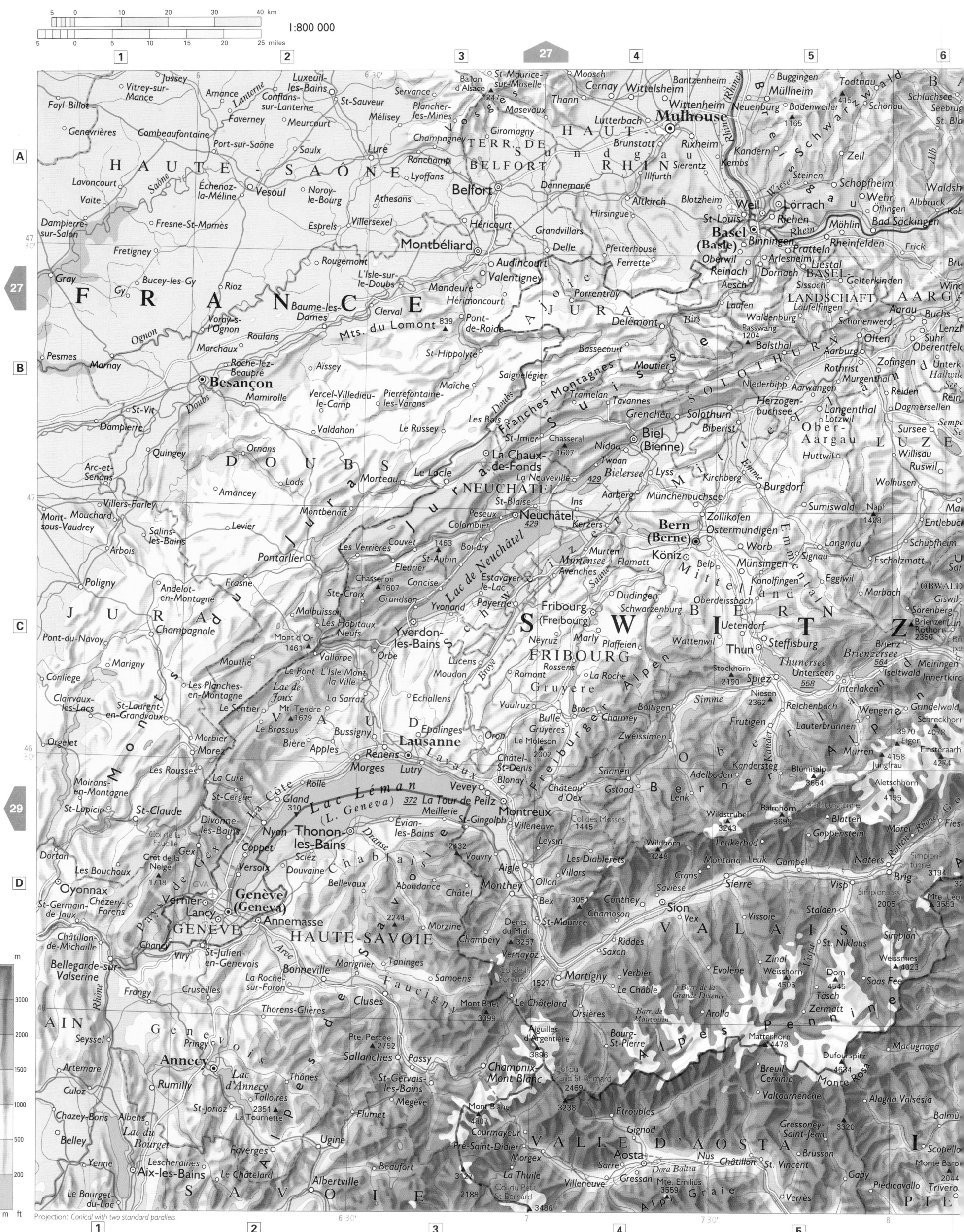

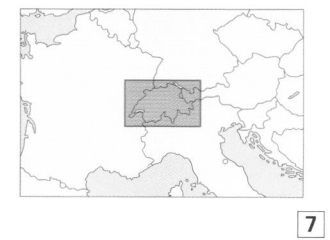

1:2 000 000

Projection : Lambert's Conformal Conic

National Parks

Underlined towns give their name to the administrative area in which they stand.

East from Greenwich

COPYRIGHT PHILIP'S

1:4 000 000

50 0 25 50 75 100 125 150 175 km
50 0 25 50 75 100 125 miles

Projection: Conical with two standard parallels

NORTH SEA

BALTIC SEA

DENMARK

UNITED KINGDOM

NETHERLANDS

BELGIUM

LUXEMBOURG

FRANCE

GERMANY

SWITZERLAND

AUSTRIA

CZECH

ITALY

SLOVENIA

ADRIATIC SEA

HAMBURG · BERLIN · BREMEN · Hannover · Hamburg · Kiel · Lübeck · Rostock · Schwerin · Magdeburg · Leipzig · Dresden · Erfurt · Frankfurt · Mainz · Wiesbaden · Stuttgart · München (Munich) · Nürnberg · Augsburg · Köln (Cologne) · Düsseldorf · Dortmund · Essen · Duisburg · Bonn

AMSTERDAM · ROTTERDAM · 's-Gravenhage (Den Haag) · Utrecht · Groningen

BRUSSEL (Bruxelles) · Antwerpen · Gent · Liège · Namur · Charleroi

PARIS · Lille · Reims · Metz · Nancy · Strasbourg · Dijon · Lyon · Marseille

BERN · Zürich · Genève · Basel · Lausanne

WIEN · Innsbruck · Salzburg · Graz · Klagenfurt

PRAHA (Prague) · Plzeň · České Budějovice · Liberec

MILANO (Turin) · TORINO · Torino · Genova · Bologna · Venezia (Venice) · Verona · Padova

LJUBLJANA · Trieste

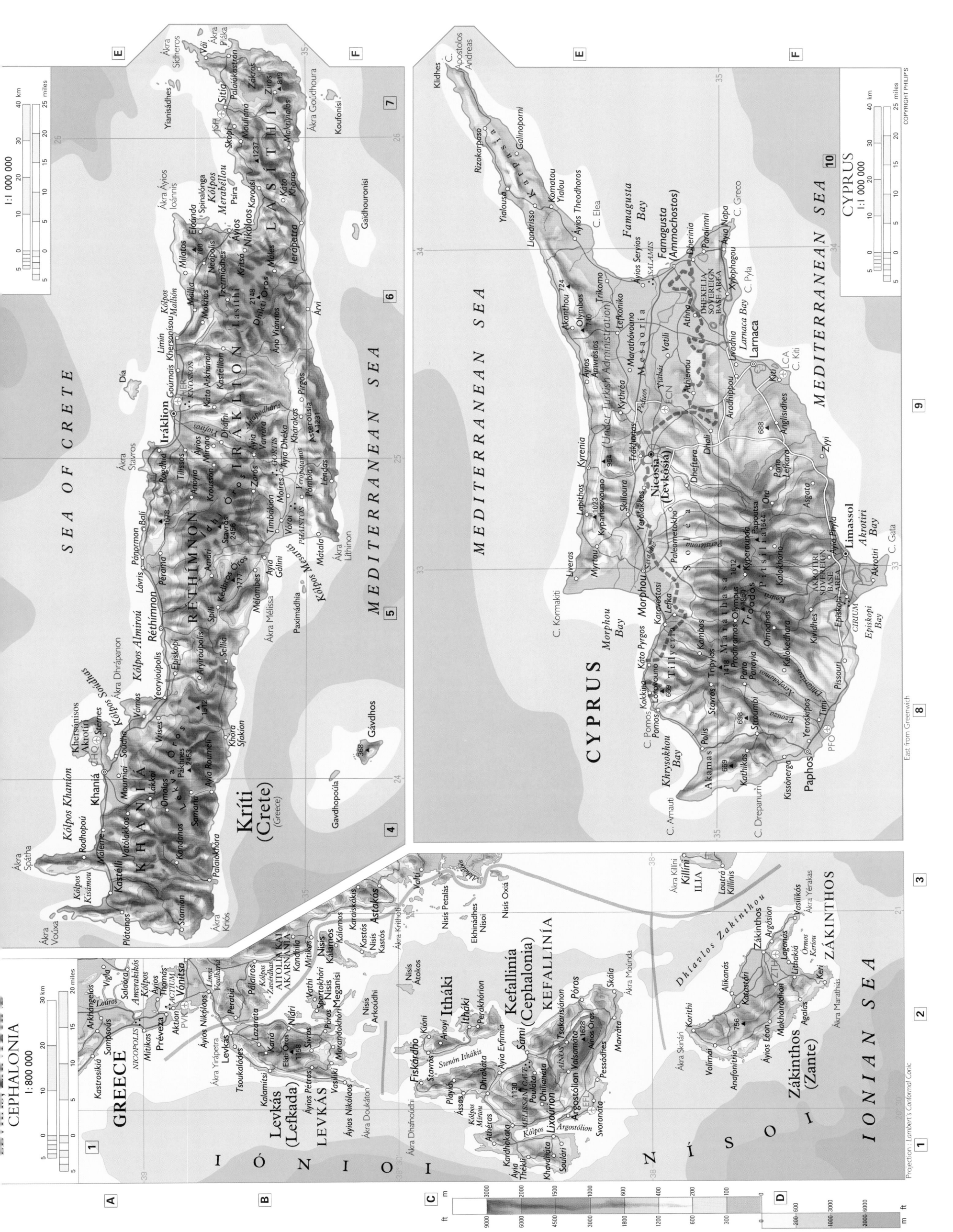

CEPHALONIA
1:800 000

GREECE

Levkás
(Lefkáda)

LEVKÁS

AITOLÍA KAI
AKARNANÍA

Kefallinía
(Cephalonia)

KEFALLINÍA

Zákinthos
(Zante)

ZÁKINTHOS

IÓNIOI NÍSOI

IONIAN SEA

SEA OF CRETE

KHANÍA

RÉTHÍMNON

IRÁKLION

LASÍTHI

Kríti
(Crete)
(Greece)

Gávdhos

MEDITERRANEAN SEA

1:1 000 000

CYPRUS

Kárpasos

Famagusta
Bay

(Under Turkish Administration)

Mesaoría

Nicosia
(Levkosía)

Tróodos

Maráthasa

Limassol

CYPRUS

MEDITERRANEAN SEA

MEDITERRANEAN SEA

1:1 000 000

East from Greenwich

Projection: Lambert's Conformal Conic

COPYRIGHT PHILIP'S

1:2 000 000

MEDITERRANEAN

SEA

ATLANTIC

OCEAN

National Parks

Nature Parks in Spain and Portugal

1:2 000 000

National Parks

Underlined towns give their name to
administrative area in which they sta

Projection : Lambert's Conformal Conic

East from Greenwich

odsko-Posavska   4 Medimurska   8 Virovitičko-Podravska
privničko-Križevačka 6 Požeško-Slavonska   10 Zagreba čka
apinsko-Zagorska   7 Varaždinska

Nature Parks in Italy

Inter-entity boundaries as agreed
at the 1995 Dayton Peace Agreement

COPYRIGHT PHILIP'S

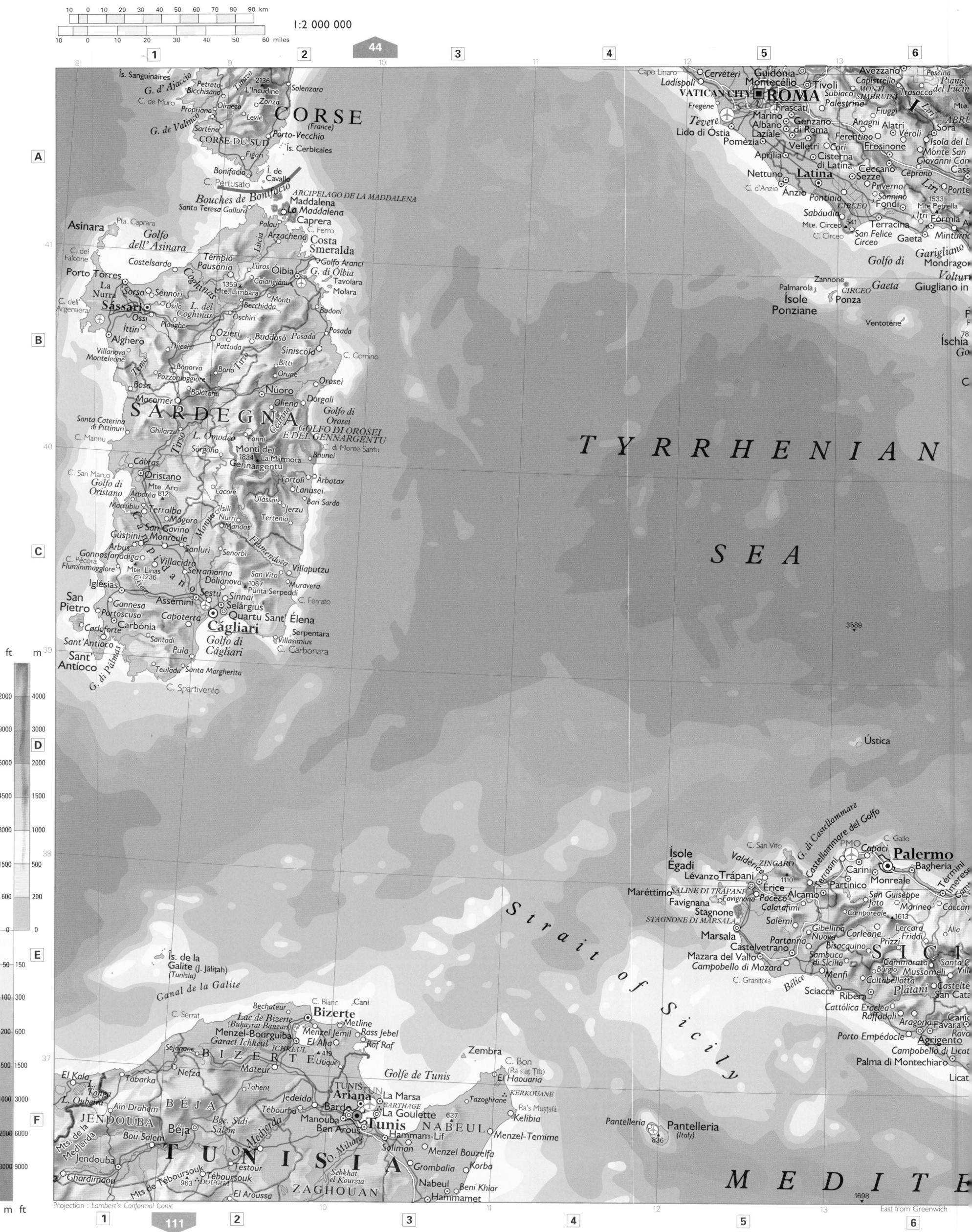

Nature Parks in Italy   National Parks

Underlined towns give their name to the
administrative area in which they stand.

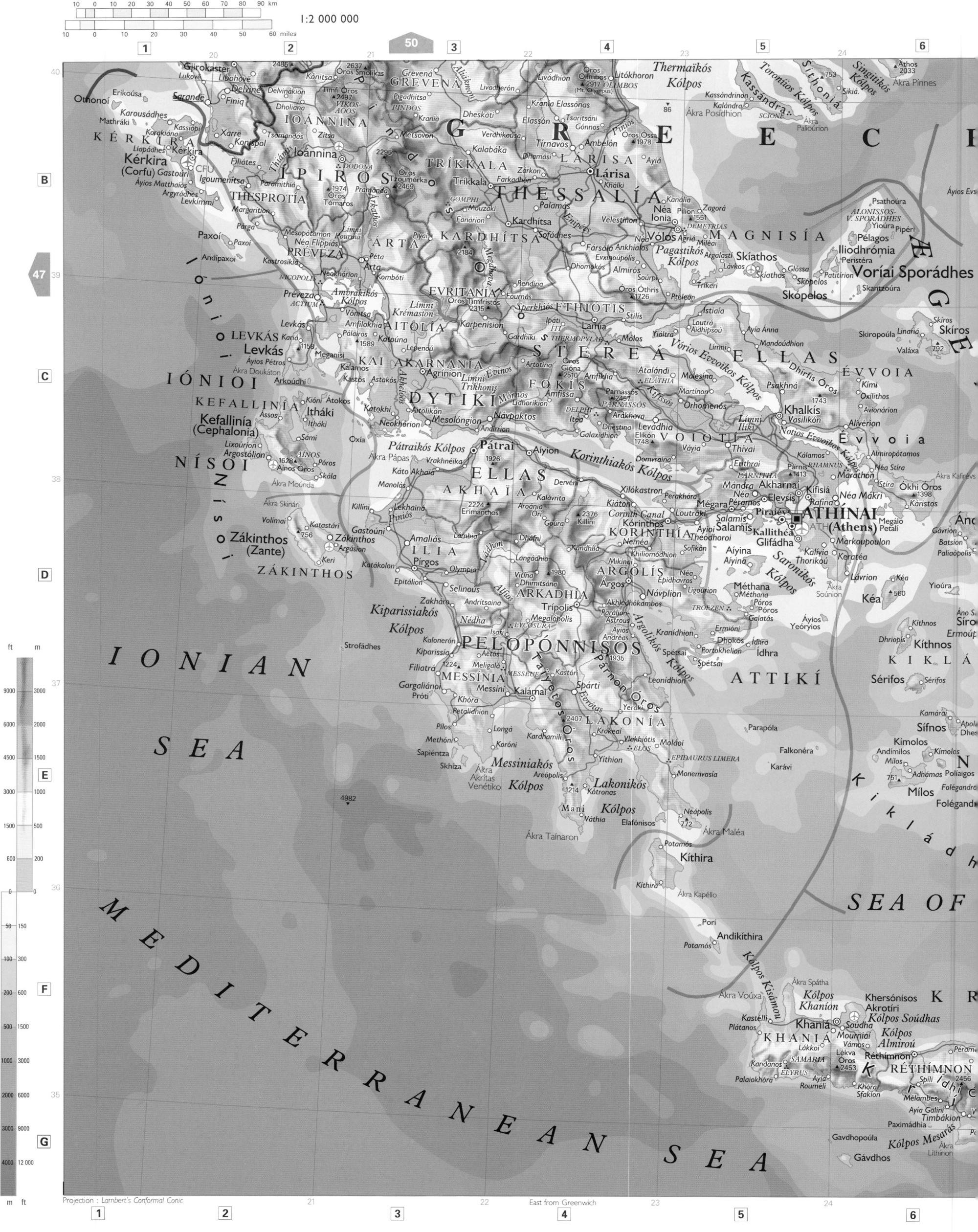

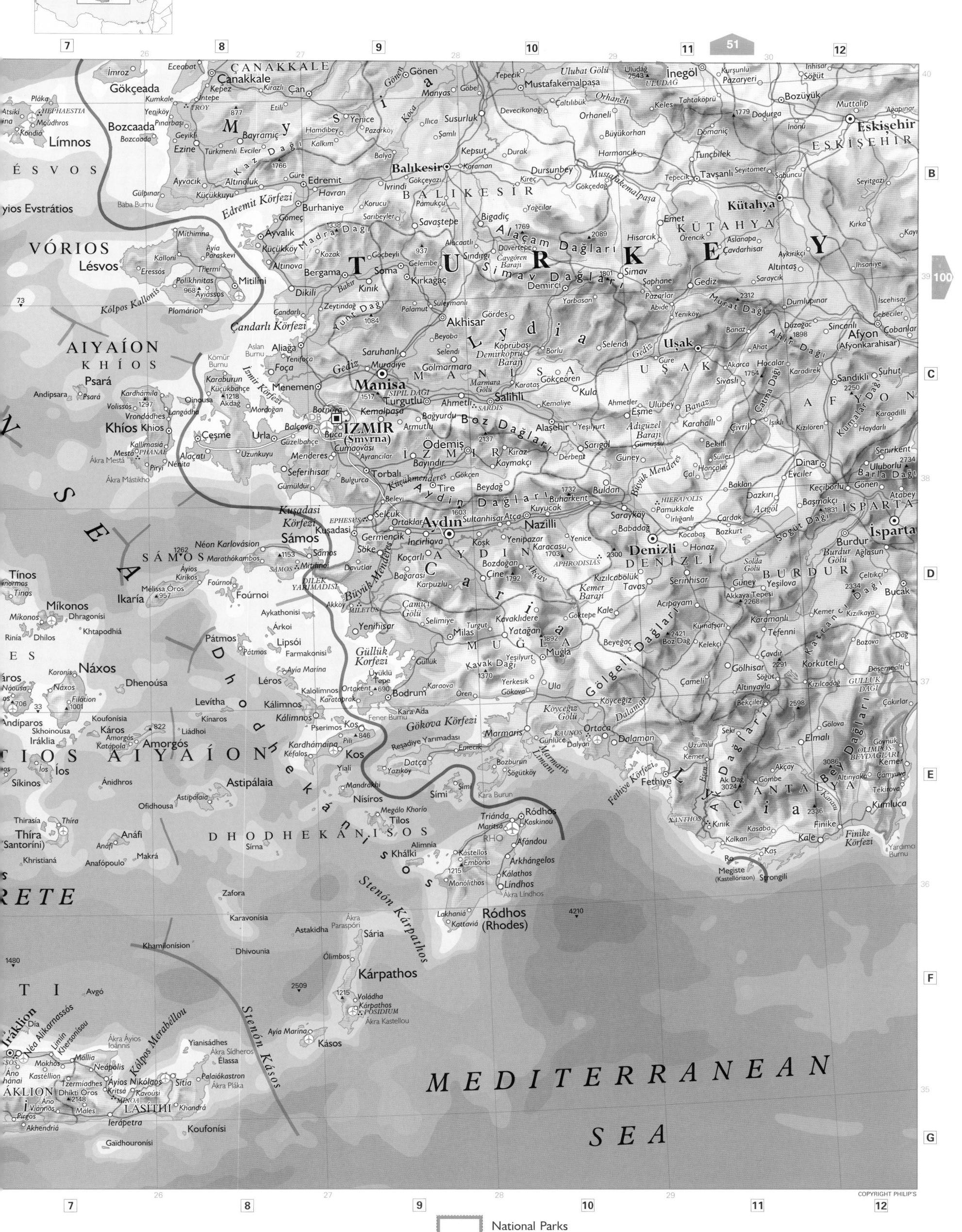

National Parks

Projection : Lambert's Conformal Conic

East from Greenwich

BLACK SEA

BULGARIA

ROMANIA

TURKEY

Marmara Denizi (Sea of Marmara)

Thrakikón Pélagos

Major towns and places:

BUCUREŞTI (Bucharest), Ploieşti, Piteşti, Târgovişte, Giurgiu, Alexandria, Caracal, Câmpulung, Sinaia, Buzău, Brăila, Galaţi, Tulcea, Constanţa, Mangalia, Medgidia, Cernavodă, Silistra, Ruse, Pleven, Svishtov, Gabrovo, Veliko Tūrnovo, Sliven, Yambol, Burgas, Varna, Dobrich, Balchik, Kavarna, Shumen, Razgrad, Tūrgovishte, Stara Zagora, Plovdiv, Pazardzhik, Dimitrovgrad, Khaskovo, Kūrdzhali, Smolyan, Edirne, Kırklareli, Lüleburgaz, Tekirdağ, İstanbul, Üsküdar, Kartal, Pendik, Gebze, Kocaeli (İzmit), Gölcük, Bandırma, Bursa, İnegöl, Gemlik, Yalova, Çanakkale, Gelibolu (Gallipoli), Keşan, Alexandroúpolis, Komotiní, Xánthi, Kavála, Thásos, Samothráki, Límnos

Dunărea (Danube), Delta Dunărea, Braţul Chilia, Braţul Sulina, Braţul Sfântu Gheorghe, Lacul Razim, Lacul Sinoie

Kamchiya, Burgaski Zaliv, Nos Emine, Maslen Nos, Nos Kaliakra

Saros Körfezi, Çanakkale Boğazı (Dardanelles), Gökçeada, Bozcaada, İmroz, Marmara, İstanbul Boğazı (Bosporus)

Stara Planina, Rodopi, Pirin, Botev 2376, Golyam Perelik 2191, Musala

National Parks

Underlined towns give their name to the administrative area in which they stand.

1:2 000 000

Projection : Lambert's Conformal Conic

Administrative divisions in Croatia:
1 Brodsko-Posavska   5 Osječko-Baranjska   9 Vukovarsko-Srijemska
2 Koprivničko-Križevačka 6 Požeško-Slavonska
4 Medimurska   8 Virovitičko-Podravska

East from Greenwich

Inter-entity boundaries as agreed
at the 1995 Dayton Peace Agreement

National Parks

Underlined towns give their name to the administrative area in which they stand.

1:2 000 000

10 0 10 20 30 40 50 60 70 80 90 km
10 0 10 20 30 40 50 60 miles

Gulf of Riga

Riga
Jūrmala
Salacgrīva
Ruhnu
Kolkasrags

LATVIA
Ventspils
Liepāja
Talsi
Tukums
Dobele
Jelgava
Bauska
Kuldīga
Saldus
Irbes saurums (Kura kurk)

LITHUANIA
Šiauliai
Mažeikiai
Telšiai
Klaipėda
Palanga
Šilutė
Tauragė
Kaunas
Marijampolė

KALININGRAD (Russia)
Kaliningrad
Sovetsk
Chernyakhovsk
Gusev
Baltiysk
Svetlogorsk

B A L T I C   S E A

SWEDEN
Jönköping
Nässjö
Västervik
Kalmar
Karlskrona
Karlshamn
SMÅLAND
KALMAR LÄN
BLEKINGE LÄN
JÖNKÖPINGS LÄN

Gotland (Sweden)
Visby
GOTLANDS LÄN

Öland (Sweden)

Bornholm (Denmark)
Rønne
BORNHOLMS AMT.
Hanöbukten

POLAND
Gdańsk
Gdynia
Sopot
Gulf of Gdańsk / Zatoka Gdańska
Elbląg
Słupsk
Koszalin
Kołobrzeg
Wejherowo
Lębork
Tczew
Olsztyn
Ostróda
Iława
Kwidzyn
POMORSKIE
WARMIŃSKO-MAZURSKIE
ZACHODNIO-POMORSKIE
Mazury

Hrodna

Underlined towns give their name to the
administrative area in which they stand.

National Parks

Projection: Lambert's Conformal Conic

East from Greenwich

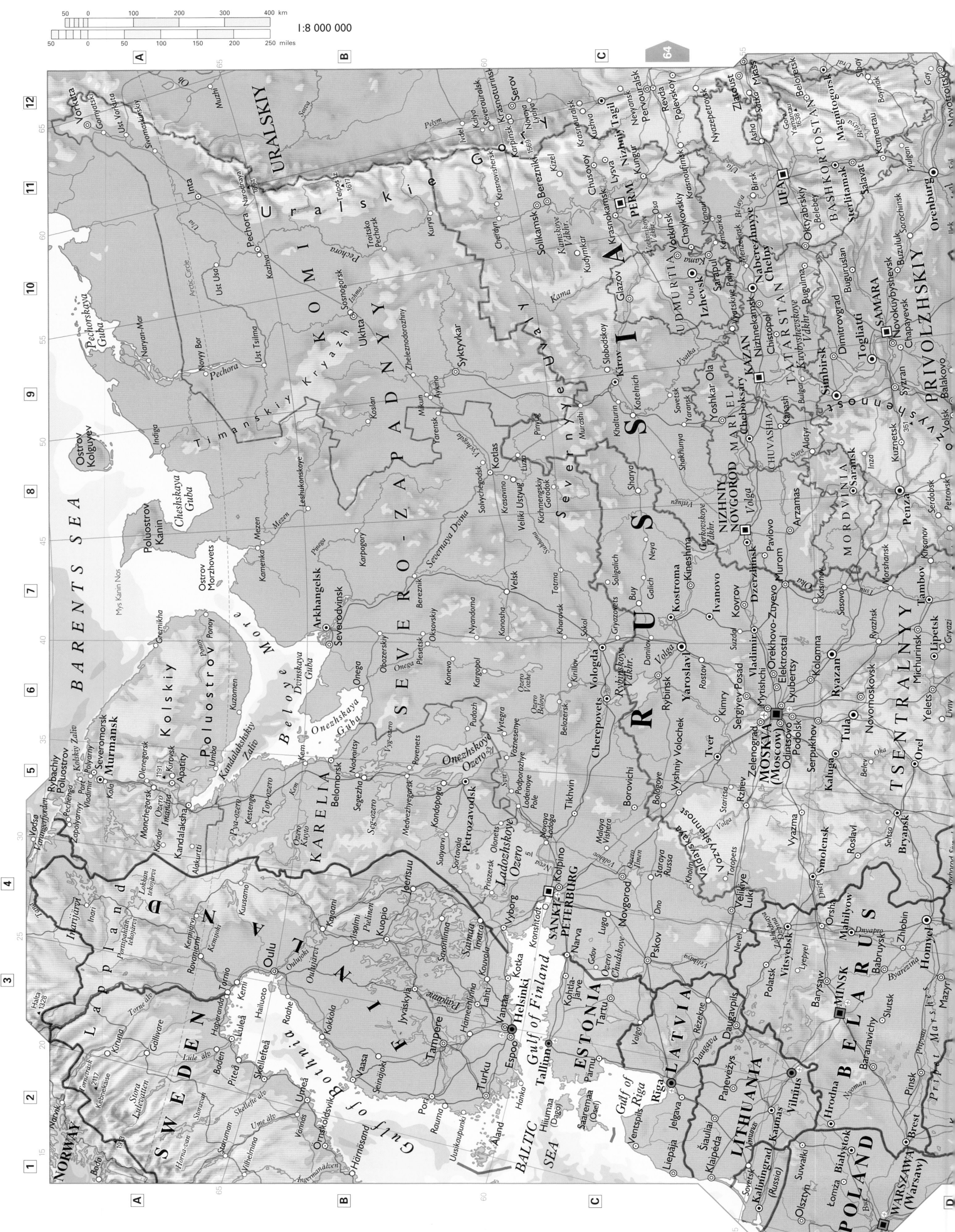

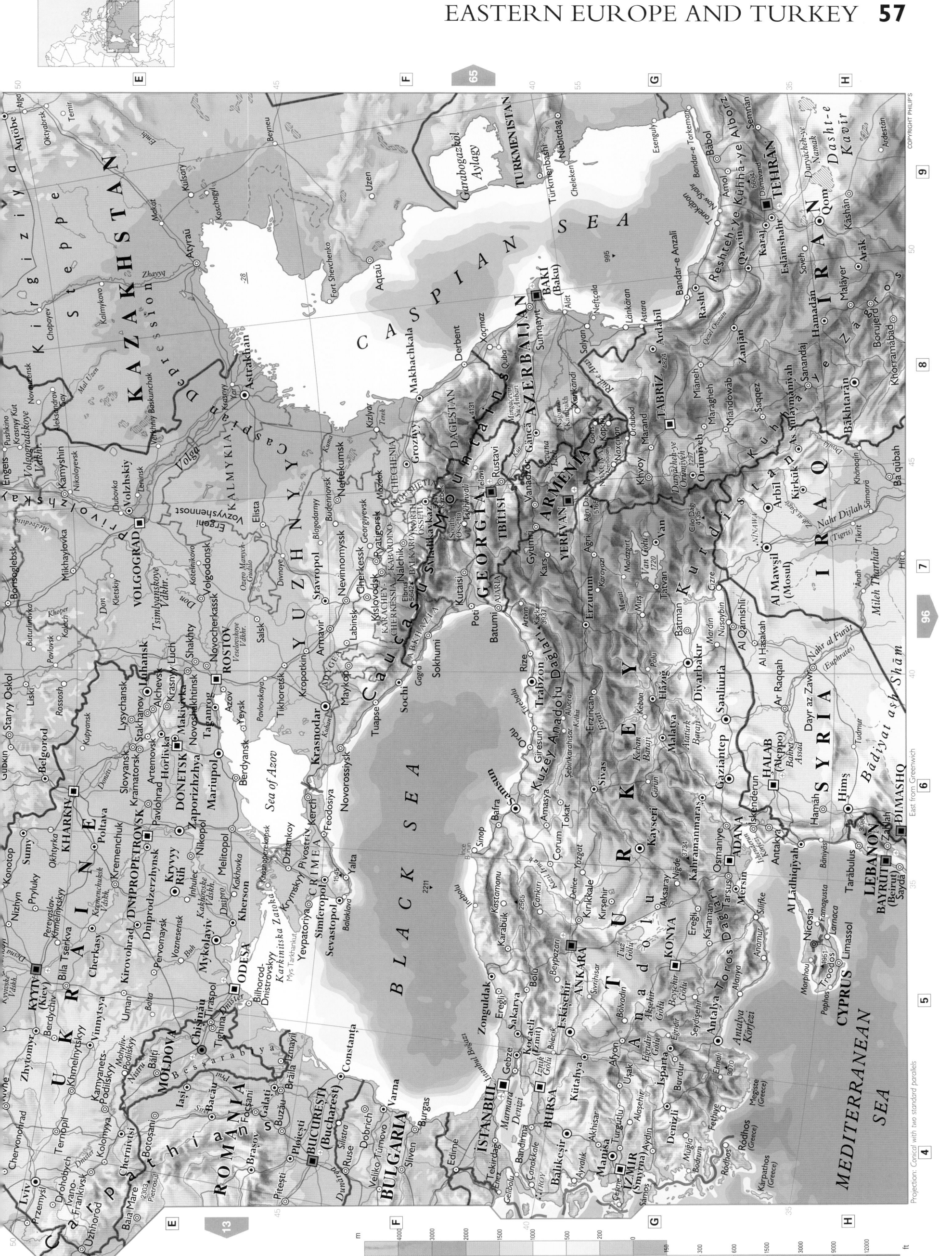

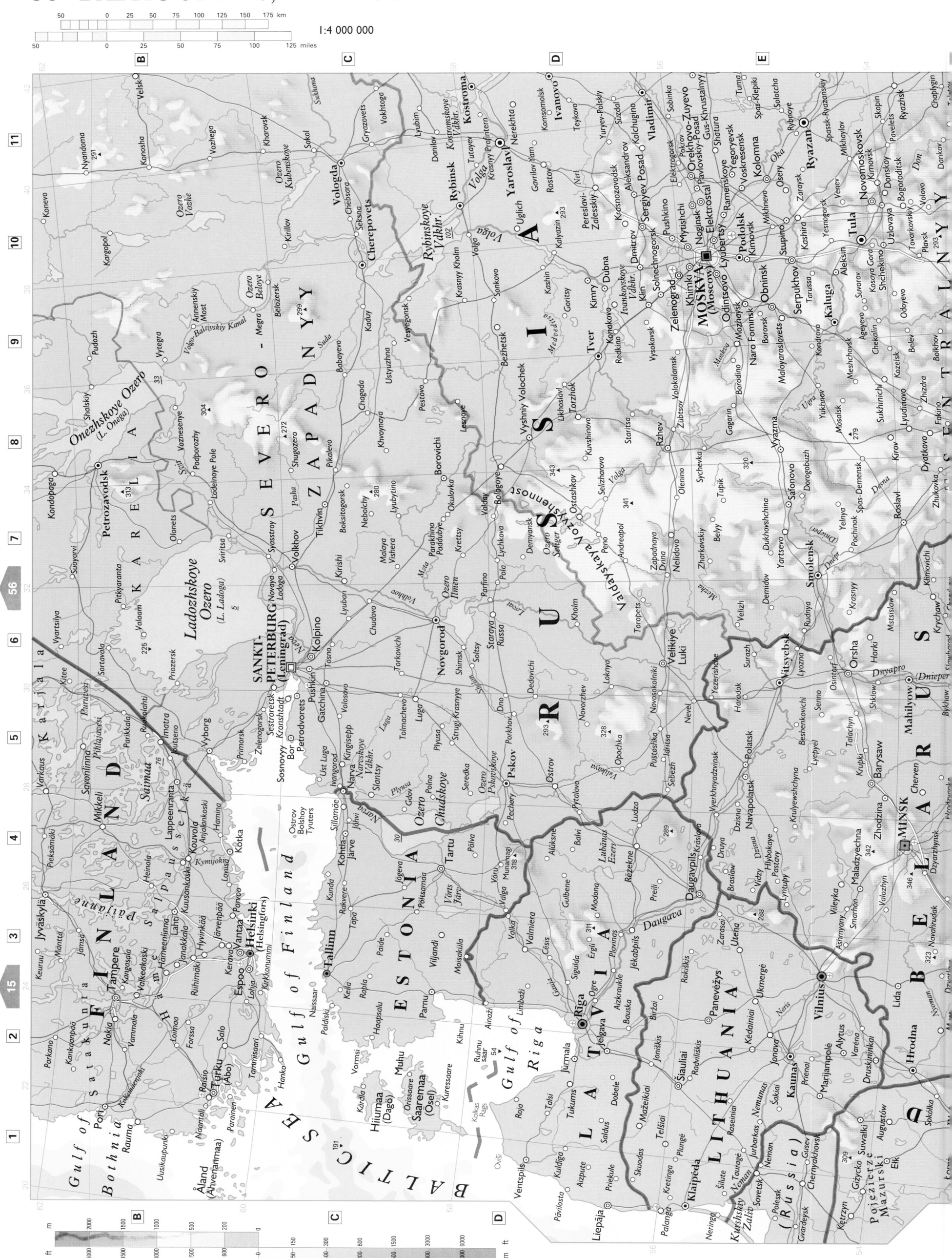

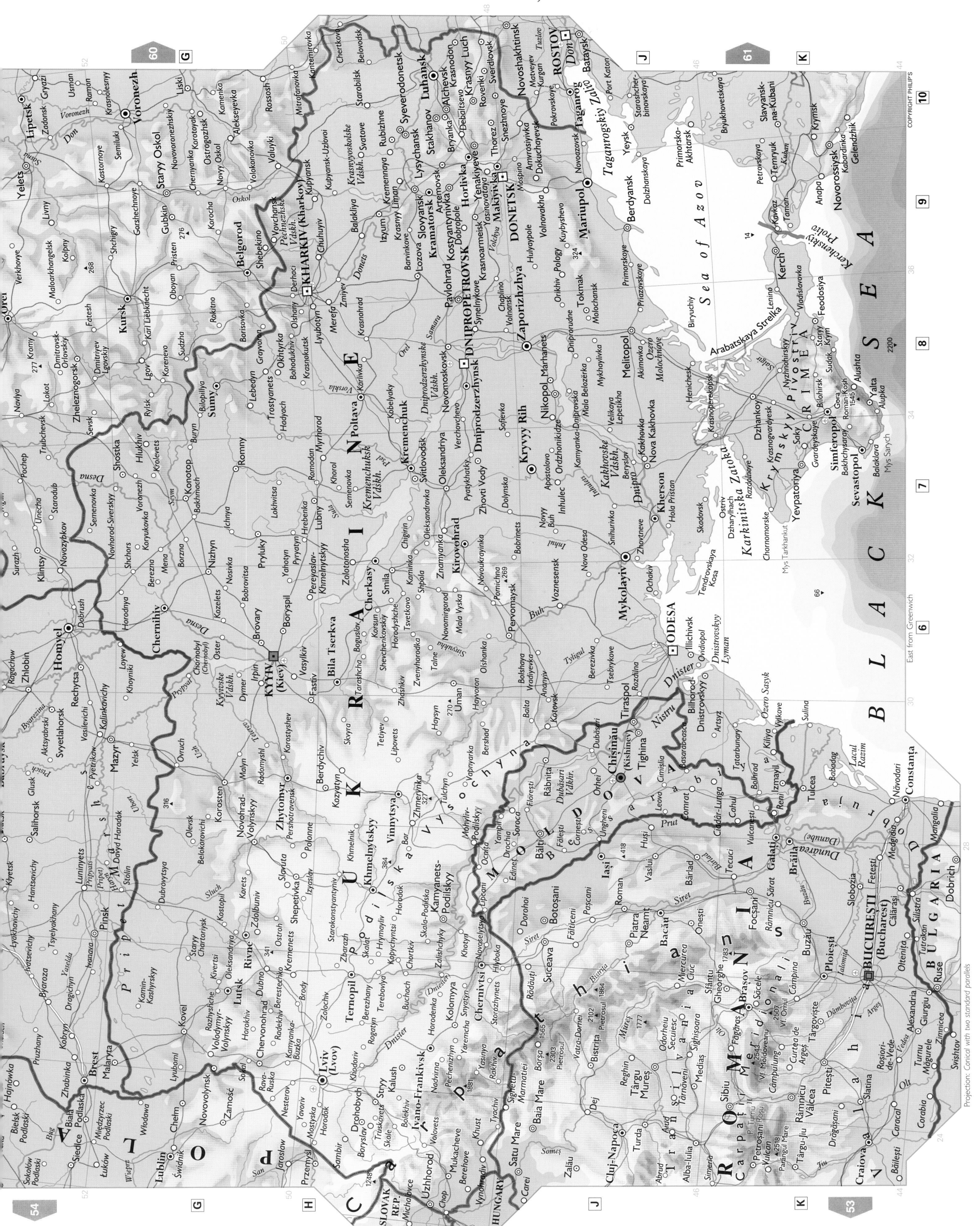

Projection: Conical with two standard parallels

East from Greenwich

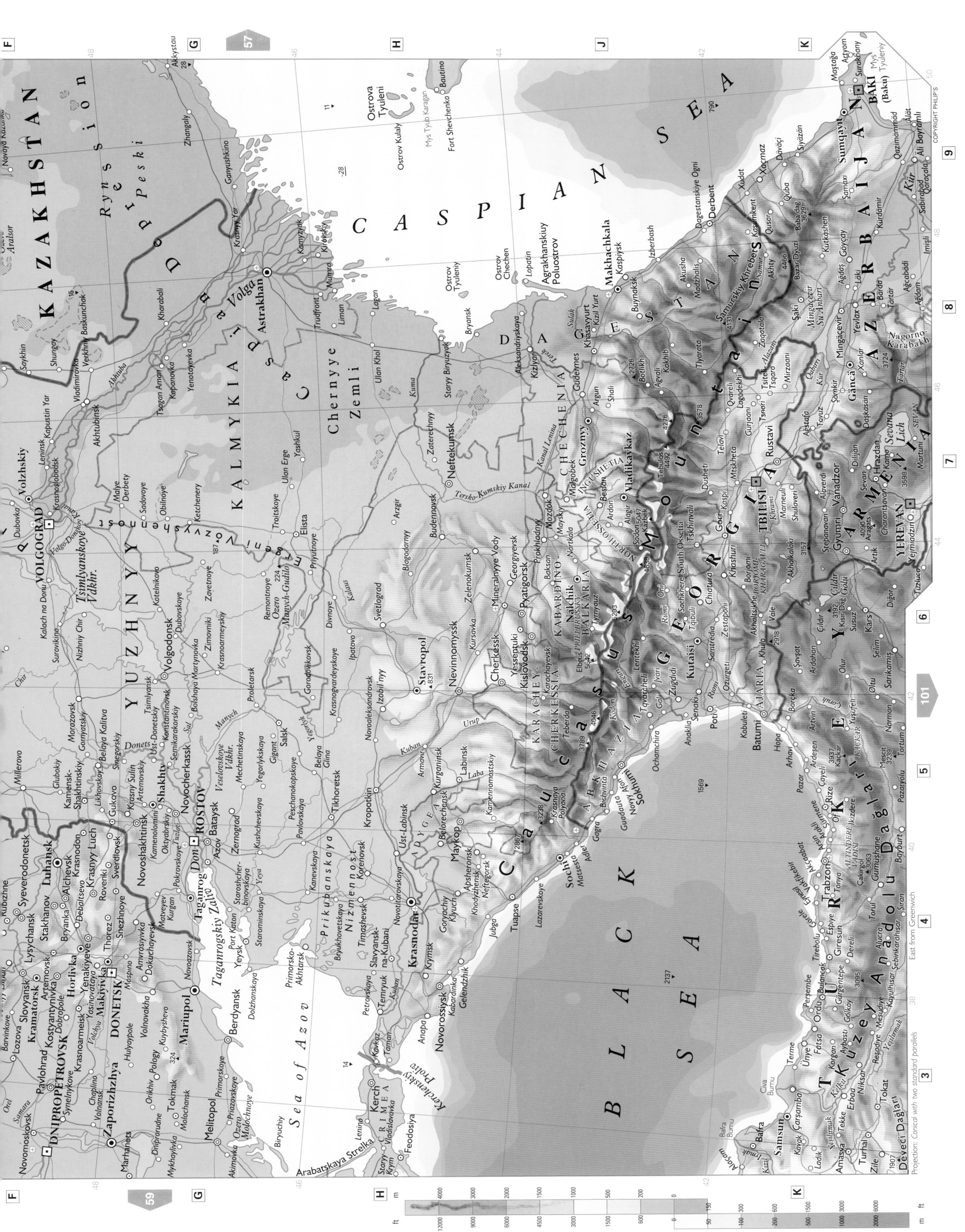

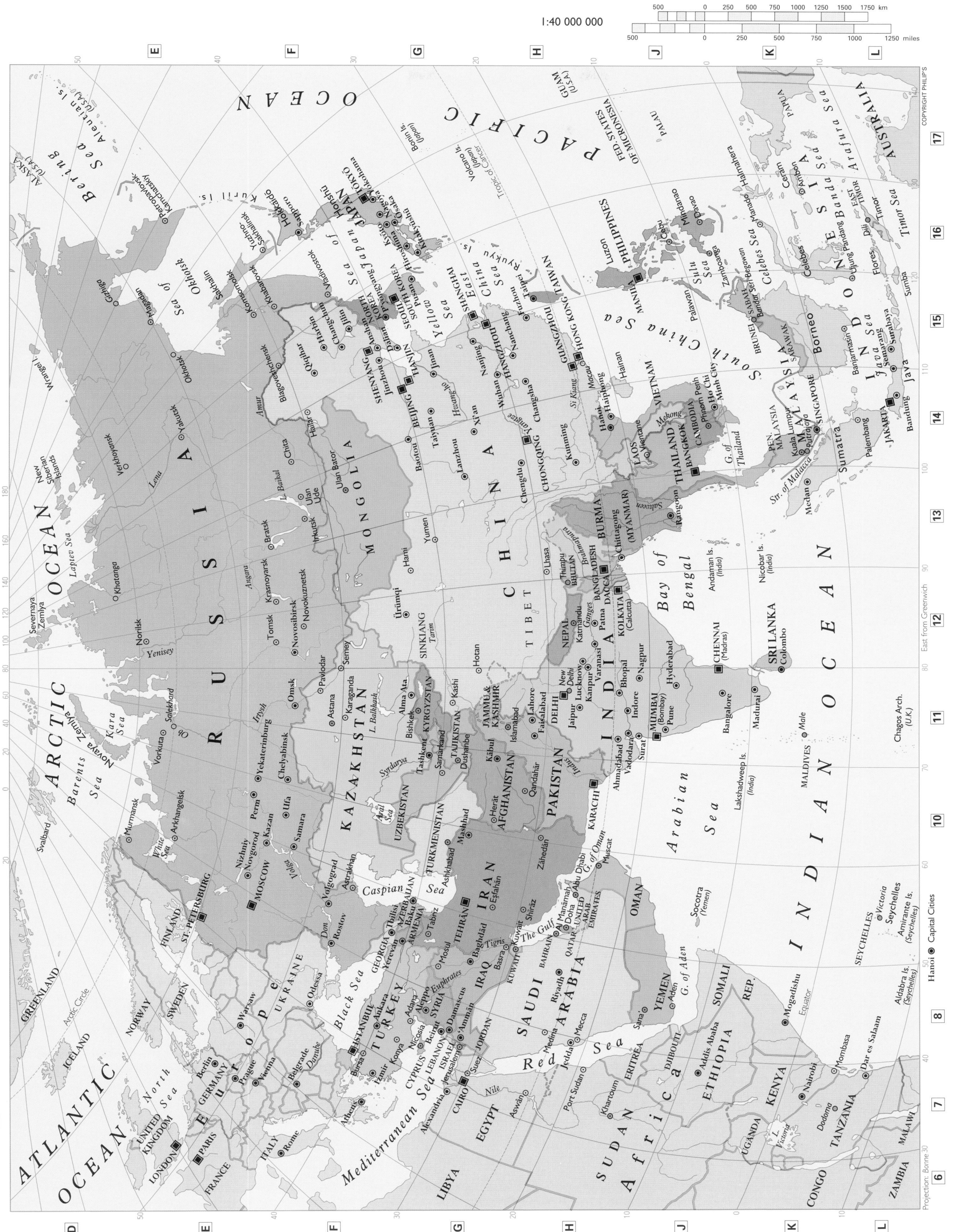

1:4 000 000

50 0 25 50 75 100 125 150 175 km
50 0 25 50 75 100 125 miles

KOMI

Severnyye Uvaly

RUSSIA

Pinyug
Kazhim
Gora Denezhkin Kamen 1493
Kalya
Lozva
Pelym

Krasnoye
Murashi
Nagorsk
Lesnoy
Kosa
Veslyana
Gayny
Kama
Cherdyn
Krasnovishersk
1065
Pokrovsk-Uralskiy
Severouralsk
Volchansk
Krasnoturinsk
Serov

Yurya
Belaya Kholunitsa
Chernaya Kholunitsa
Kirs
Peskovka
Yuria
Borovsk
Solikamsk
937
Gora Konzhakovskiy Kamen 1569
Kytlym
Karpinsk
Sosva
Sosva
Gari

Slobodskay
Khalturin
Kirov
Omutninsk
Zalazna
Kudymkar
Pozhva
Usolye
Berezniki
Kamskoye Vdkhr.
Aleksandrovsk
Kizel
Ugleuralskiy
Gubakha 993
Kachkanar
Lobva
Lyalya
Novaya Lyalya
Verkhoturye
Bolotovskoye

Novovyatsk
Kirovo-Chepetsk
Chapetsk
Zuyevka
Falenki
Yar
Glazov
337
Kama
Chermoz
Dobryanka
Usva
Gremyachinsk
Pashiya Verkhnyaya Tura
Kushva
Krasnouralsk
Nizhnyaya Salda
Turinsk

Kotelnich
Sovetsk
Sorvizhi
284
Nolinsk
Uni
Kez
Balezino
Nytva
Ocher
Krasnokamsk
PERM
Lysva
Chusovoy
Chusovaya
482
Nizhniy Tagil
746
Verkhnyaya Salda
Alapayevsk
Irbit
Nitsa

MARI EL
Yoshkar Ola
Medvedevo
Yaransk
Medvedok
Arkul
Kilmez
Izhevsk
Votkinsk
Kungur
452
Svetya
Verkhniy Tagil
Nevyansk
Rezh
Artemovskiy
Bulanash
Troitskiy

Yakshur Bodya
UDMURTIA
Uva
Votkinskoye Vdkhr.
Chaykovskiy
Osa
Achit
Kuzino
Revda
Pervouralsk
YEKATERINBURG
Verkhniy Ufaley
Asbest
Sukhoy Log
Talitsa
Pyshma

Mariinskiy Posad
Krasnogorskiy
Arsk
Kukmor
Malmyzh
Mozhga
Sosnovka
Sarapul
Kambarka
Yanaul
Krasnoufimsk
Chernushka
Oktyabrskiy
Mikhaylovski
678
Nizhniye Sergi
Polevskoy
Syseri
Beloyarskiy
Bogdanovich
Kamensk Uralskiy
Dalmatovo

Volzhsk
Zelenodolsk
Kozlovka
KAZAN
Mamadysh
Yelabuga
Menzelinsk
Nizhnekamskoye Vdkhr.
Neftekamsk
Belaya
Birsk
Ufa
Blagoveshchensk
517
Verkhniye Kigi
Nyazepetrovsk
Kasli
Techa
Shadrinsk

Kamskoye Ustye
Buinsk
Tetyushi
Bulgar
Bilyarsk
Chistopol
Naberezhnyye Chelny
Nizhnekamsk
Aktash
Zainsk
Almetyevsk
Dyurtyuli
Kushnarenkovo
Minyar
Yuryuzan
Asha
Katav Ivanovsk
Bakal
Satka
Berdyaush
Kusa
Zlatoust
Miass
Chebarkul
Karabash
Kyshtym
Argayash
Miass
CHELYABINSK
Kopeysk
Novosineglazovskiy
Korkino
Yemanzhelinsk

TATARSTAN
Kuybyshevskoye Vdkhr.
23
Cherdakly
Leninogorsk
Bugulma
Tuymazy
Oktyabrskiy
383
Chishmy
UFA
Iglino
Inzer
1406
Gora Iremel 1582
Verkhniye Avzyan
Uchaly
Plast
Yuzhnouralsk
Uvelskiy
Oktyabrskoye
Troitsk
Uy

Simbirsk
Novoulyanovsk
Sengiley
Dimitrovgrad
Isakly
Sernovodsk
Belebey
420
Rayevskiy
Davlekanovo
Krasnousolskiy
Gora Yamantau 1638
Tirlyanskiy
Beloretsk
Verkhneuralsk
Buskul
Komsomolets
Toguzak

Novodevichye
Nurlat
Bugulma
Priyutovo
Bugulma
PRIVOLZHSKIY
Zhigulevsk
375
Krasnyy Yar
Timashevo
Kinel
Pokhvistnevo
Abdulino
Buguruslan
Ponomarevka
Sterlitamak
Petrovskoye
481
Salavat
Ishimbay
1039
1118
Verkhniy Avzyan
Magnitogorsk
Varna
452
Kartaly
Rudnyy

Oktyabrsk
Syzran
Kashpirovka
Chapayevsk
Privolzhye
SAMARA
Novokuybyshevsk
Buzuluk
Otradnyy
Krotovka
Grachevka
Tok
Sorochinsk
Meleuz
Belaya
Kumertau
Sibay
859
Baymak
758
Kizilskoye
Ordzhonikidze
Lisakovsk

Pugachev
Pestravka
Bolshaya Glushitsa
Alekseyevka
Totskoye
Andreyevka
Bolshaya Chernigovka
Novo-Sergiyevskiy
405
Bulanovo
Tyulgan
Chernyy Otrog
Iriklinskoye Vdkhr.
414
Krasnoyarskiy
Yelizavetinka
Zhetiqara
Zhaltyr

Obshchi Syrt
Ozernoye
Perevolotskiy
Ilek
Orenburg
Saraktash
Ural
Kuvandyk
Iriklinskiy
Gay
Novoorsk
418
Ozërnyy
Turgayskaya Stolovaya Strana

Ozinki
Darinskoye
Zhayyq
Kamenka
Burli
Aksay
Ilek
Krasnyy Kholm
Pervomayskiy
Sol Iletsk
Akbulak
Mednogorsk
Novotroitsk
Orsk
Yasnyy
Dombarovskiy
Kumak
Svetlyy
Aktasty
Tolybay

Oral
Vladimorka
Ozero Shalkar
Shalkar
Chingirlau
Ural
Martuk
Leninskoye
509
Novoorsk
Khromtau
Zhabasak

KIRGIZIYA
Chapayev
Dzhambeyty
Shalkar
Karatobe
Novoalekseyevka
Aqtöbe
Alga
Novorossiyskoye
Qarabutaq
Igiz
Mugodzhary

KAZAKHSTAN
Steppe

Furmanovo
Karsha
Bolshoy Uzen
Bolshaya Klyohd
Oktyabrskiy

ft m
3000 1000
1500 500
600 200
50
0

1:4 000 000

50 25 0 25 50 75 100 125 150 175 km
50 0 25 50 75 100 125 miles

COPYRIGHT PHILIP'S

KAZAKHSTAN

UZBEKISTAN

KYRGYZSTAN

TAJIKISTAN

TURKMENISTAN

AFGHANISTAN

CHINA

XINJIANG UYGUR

Kyzyl Kum

Peski Taukum

Peski Moyynqum

Qaratau (Karatau)

Zailiyskiy Ala Too

Kirghiz Range

Talas Ala Too

Fergana Range

Turkestan Range

Zeravshan Range

Karakoram Range

Kunlun Shan

Tien Shan

Pamir

Gorno-Badakhshan

Hindu Kush

Northern Areas PAKISTAN

ALMATY (Alma Ata)

Bishkek (Frunze)

TOSHKENT (Tashkent)

Shymkent

Taraz (Dzhambul)

Namangan

Andizhon

Farghona

Qoʻqon (Kokand)

Osh

Khujand

Samarqand

Bukhoro

Qarshi

Navoiy

Jizzakh

Dushanbe

Qonduz

Mazar-e Sharif

Termiz

Kashi (Kashgar)

Shache (Yarkand)

Ysyk-Köl

Balqash Köl

Syrdarya

Amudarya

Qyzylorda

East from Greenwich

Projection: Conical with two standard parallels

1:16 000 000

	RUSSIA
1	Adygea
2	Karachey-Cherkessia
3	Kabardino-Balkaria
4	North Ossetia
5	Ingushetia
6	Chechenia
7	Dagestan
8	Mordvinia
9	Chuvashia
10	Mari El
11	Tatarstan
12	Udmurtia
13	Khakassia

AZERBAIJAN
14 Naxçıvan

GEORGIA   UKRAINE
15 Ajaria   17 Crimea
16 Abkhazia

Projection: Conical Orthomorphic with two standard parallels

East from Greenwich

1:12 000 000

Projection: Bonne

East from Greenwich

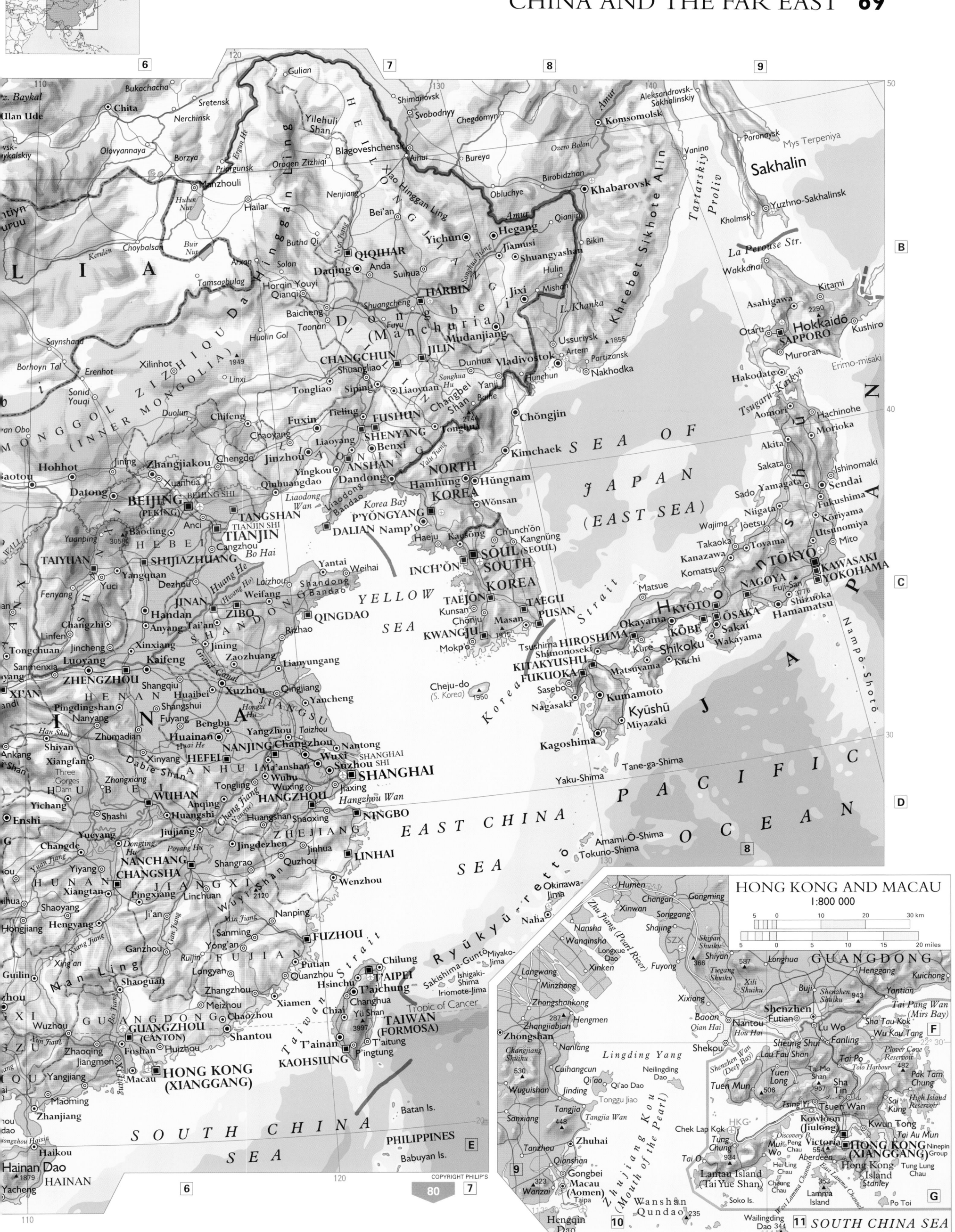

HONG KONG AND MACAU
1:800 000

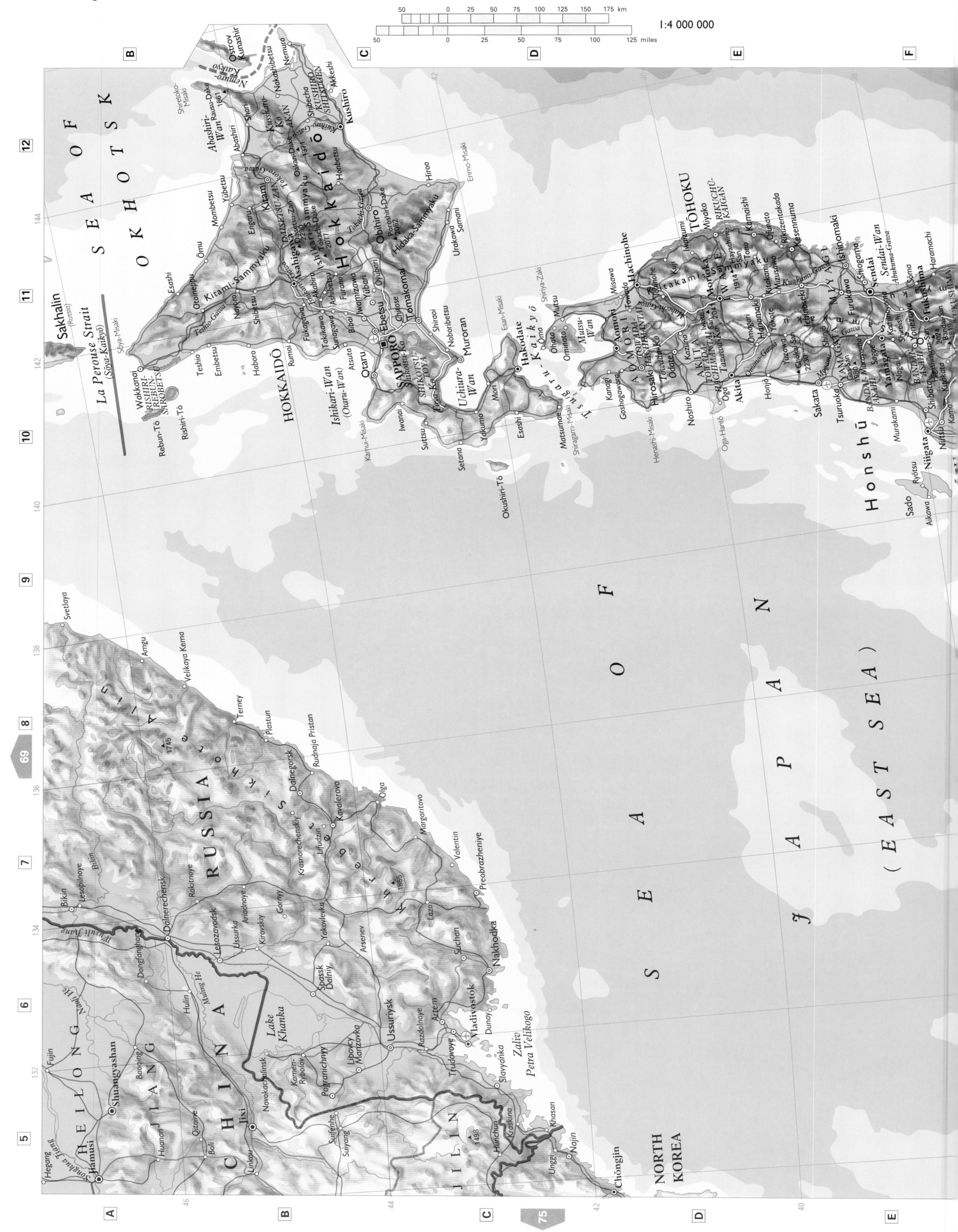

50   0   25   50   75   100   125   150   175 km

50   0   25   50   75   100   125 miles

1:4 000 000

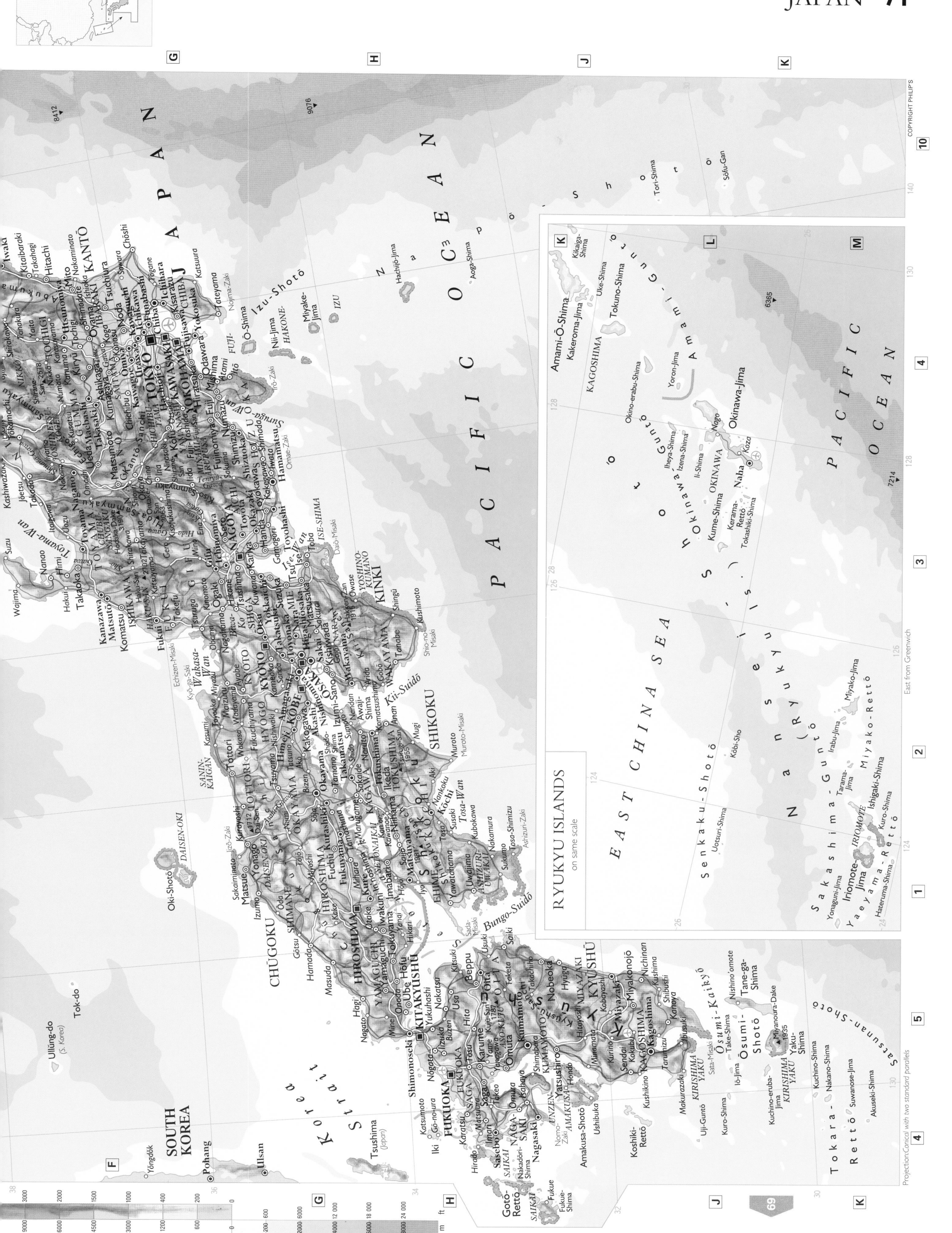

RYUKYU ISLANDS
on same scale

PROJECTION: Conical with two standard parallels

COPYRIGHT PHILIP'S

10 0 10 20 30 40 50 60 70 80 90 km
10 0 10 20 30 40 50 60 miles
1:2 000 000

1 **2** **3** **4** **5** **6**

SEA OF JAPAN
(EAST SEA)

A

Yŏngdŏk

Chŏngha

P'ohang

SOUTH KOREA

Oki-Shotō
Daimanji-San
Dōgo ▲608
Saigō
DAISEN-OKI

B

CHŪGOKU-DISTRICT

HONSHŪ

Korea Strait

DAISEN-OKI
Hi-no-Misaki
Hirata
Matsue
Shinji-Ko
Sakaiminato
Yonago
Kurayoshi
Tottori
SANIN-KAIGAN
Iwami
Toyooka
Hidaka
Kasumi

C

Tsushima
Kamiagata
Kamitsushima
Kara-Saki
Mitsushima
Izuhara
Kō-Saki
Higasi-Suidō

Taisha
Izumo
Yasugi
Dai-Sen
1729
Chizu
Wakasa
Suga-no-Mine
1510
Wadayama

Ōda
Sanbe-San
1126
Daito
Kisuki
Dōgo-San
1269
Katsuyama
Ochiai
Tsuyama
Yamasaki
HYŌGO

Yunotsu
Gōtsu
Miyoshi
Shōbara
Niimi
Tōjō
Yanahara
Sayō
Kasai

Hamada
SHIMANE
Masuda
HIROSHIMA
Fuchū
Ibara
Takahashi
Sōja
OKAYAMA
Bizen
Saidaiji
Okayama
Himeji
Takasago

Aono-Yama
908
Kanmuri-Yama
1339
Yoshida
Kake
Yakage
Kamo
Kurashiki
Tamano
Shōdo-Shima
Tonoshō
Akō
Kakogawa

D

FUKUOKA
KITAKYŪSHŪ
Shimonoseki
YAMAGUCHI
Higashi-Hiroshima
HIROSHIMA
Hatsukaichi
Kure
Takehara
Mihara
Onomichi
Fukuyama
Kasaoka
Ieshima-Shotō
SETO-NAIKAI
Harima-Nada
Awaji-Shima

E

Kyūshū
KYŪSHŪ-DISTRICT

NAGASAKI
Nagasaki
KUMAMOTO
Kumamoto
MIYAZAKI
OITA
Beppu
Ōita

Shikoku
SHIKOKU-DISTRICT
KOCHI
EHIME
TOKUSHIMA
KAGAWA

F

Kagoshima
KAGOSHIMA
Miyazaki
Nichinan

Shinkansen line   National Parks

Projection:
Lambert's Conformal Conic

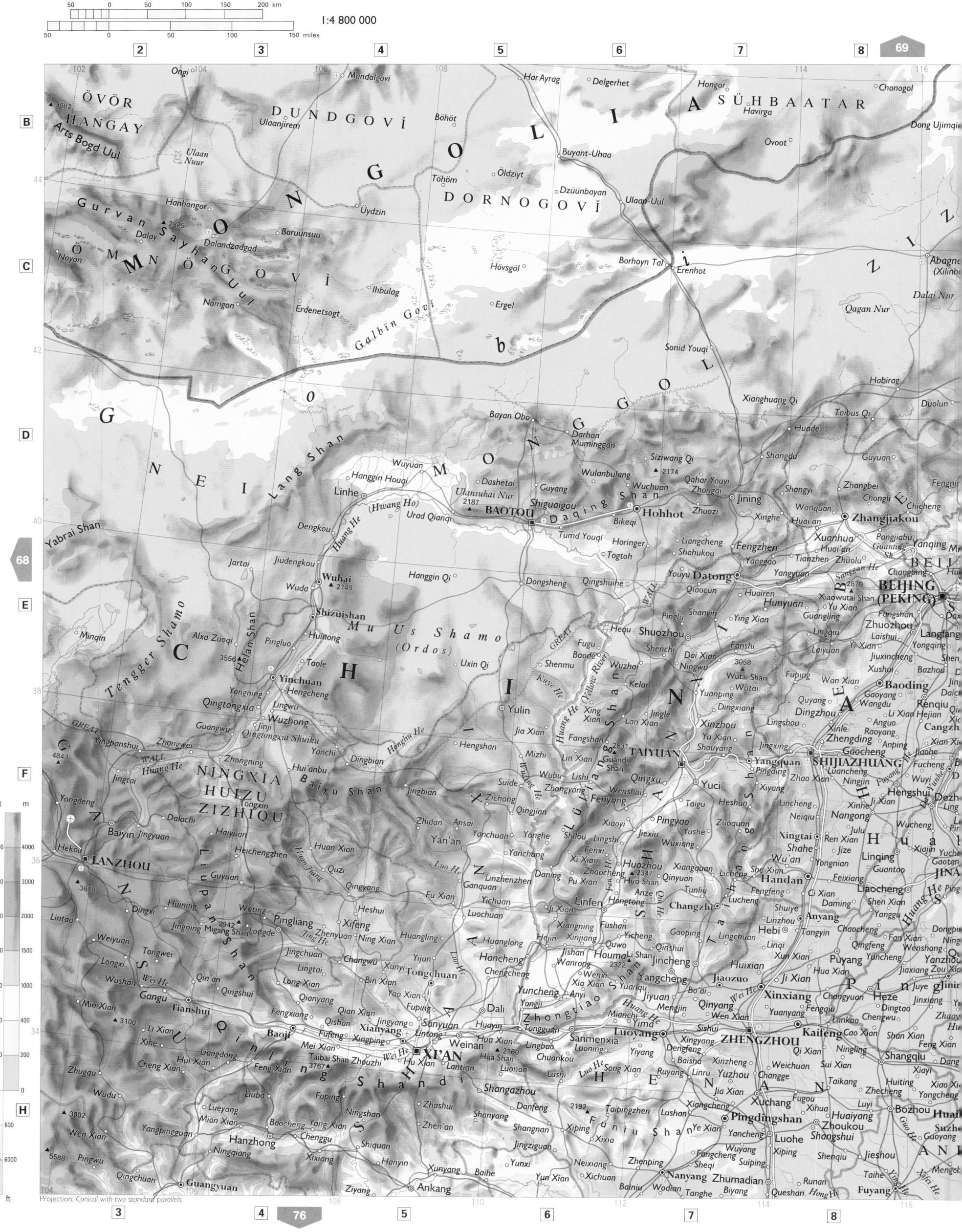

Projection: Conical with two standard parallels

Horqin Youyi Qianqi
(Ulanhot)
Zhenlai
HARBIN
Bin Xian
Linkou
Jixi
Turiy Rog
Lake Khanka

Baicheng
Da'an
Maoxing
Zhaoyuan
Shuangcheng
Acheng
Yanshou
HEILONGJIANG
Mudan Jiang
RUSSIA

Tuquan
Taonan
Anguang
Changchunling
Sanchahe
Lalin
Yimianpo
Yushu
Shanhetun
Wuchang
Shangzhi
Zhangguangcailing
Hengdaohezi
Maqiaohe
Xiachengzi
Pogranichnyy

Qagan
Nur Qian
Gorlos
Fuyu
Beitaolaizhao
Songhua
Lalin He
Mudanjiang
Hailin
Muling
Suiyang
Sufenhe

Tongyu
Shenjingzi
Nong'an
Dehui
Gangyao
Wulajie
Jiutai
Shulan
Ning'an
Dongjingcheng
Dongning
Golenki
Ussuriysk

JILIN
CHANGCHUN
JILIN
Jiaohe
Emu
Jingpo Hu
Chunyang
Dunhua
Daxinggou
Wangqing
Shixian
Luozigou
Razdolnoye
Artëm
Tavrichanka
Vladivostok

Tongliao
Kailu
Gongzhuling
Yitong
Panshi He
Huadian
Mingyuegue
Tumen
Longjing
Namyang
Hunchun
Slavyanka
Posyet

Siping
Liaoyuan
Dongfeng
Huinan
Baishan
Erdao Jiang
Antu
Helong
Hoeryong
Musan
Kraskino
Sōsura
Najin

SHENYANG
FUSHUN
Tieling
Qingyuan
Hunjiang
Tonghua
Linjiang
Changbai
Paektu-san
Hyesan
Chōngjin
Kyōngsōng
Chuuronjang
Ondaejin

YELLOW SEA
(Huang Hai)

PUSAN

JAPAN
Sasebo
Nagasaki

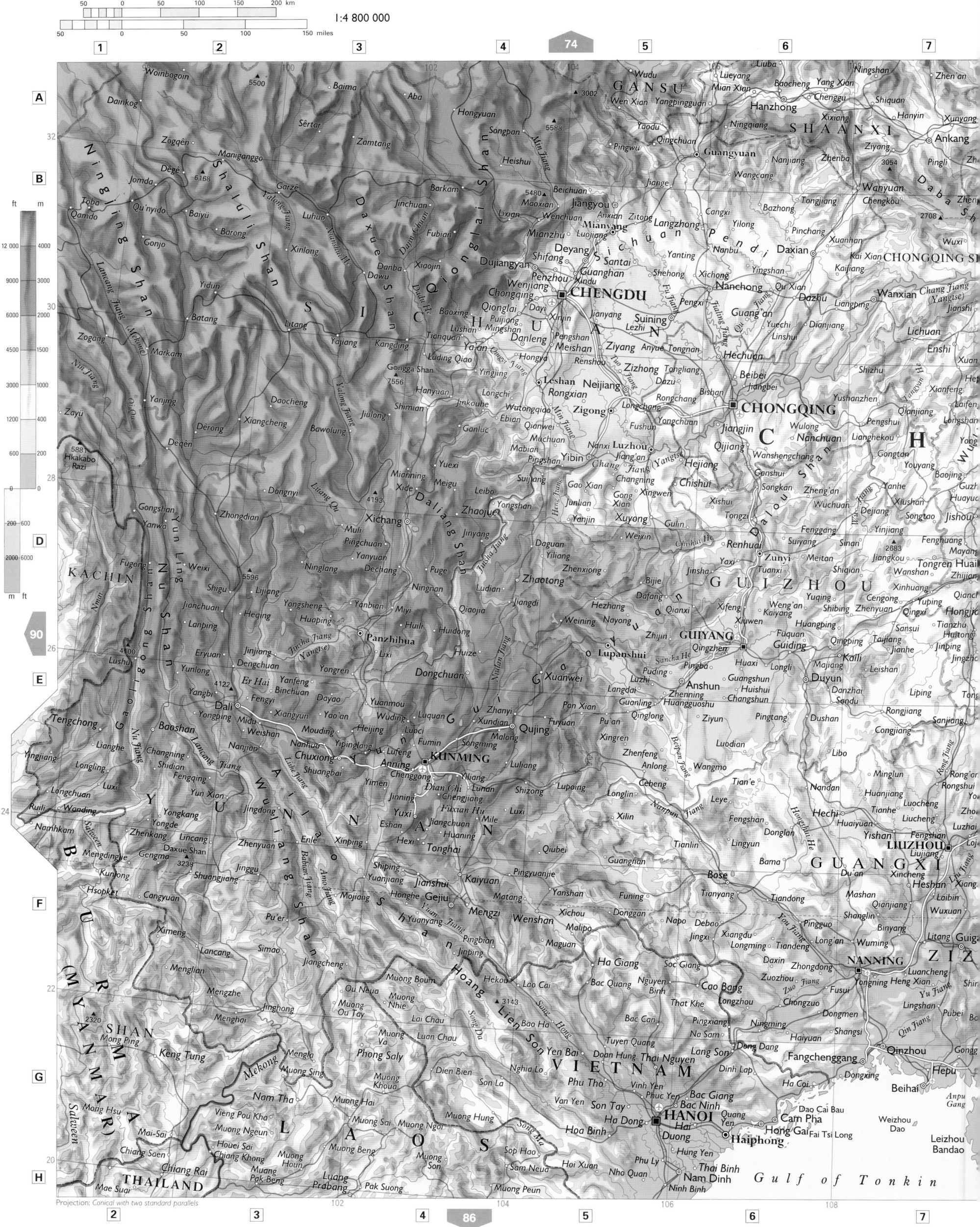

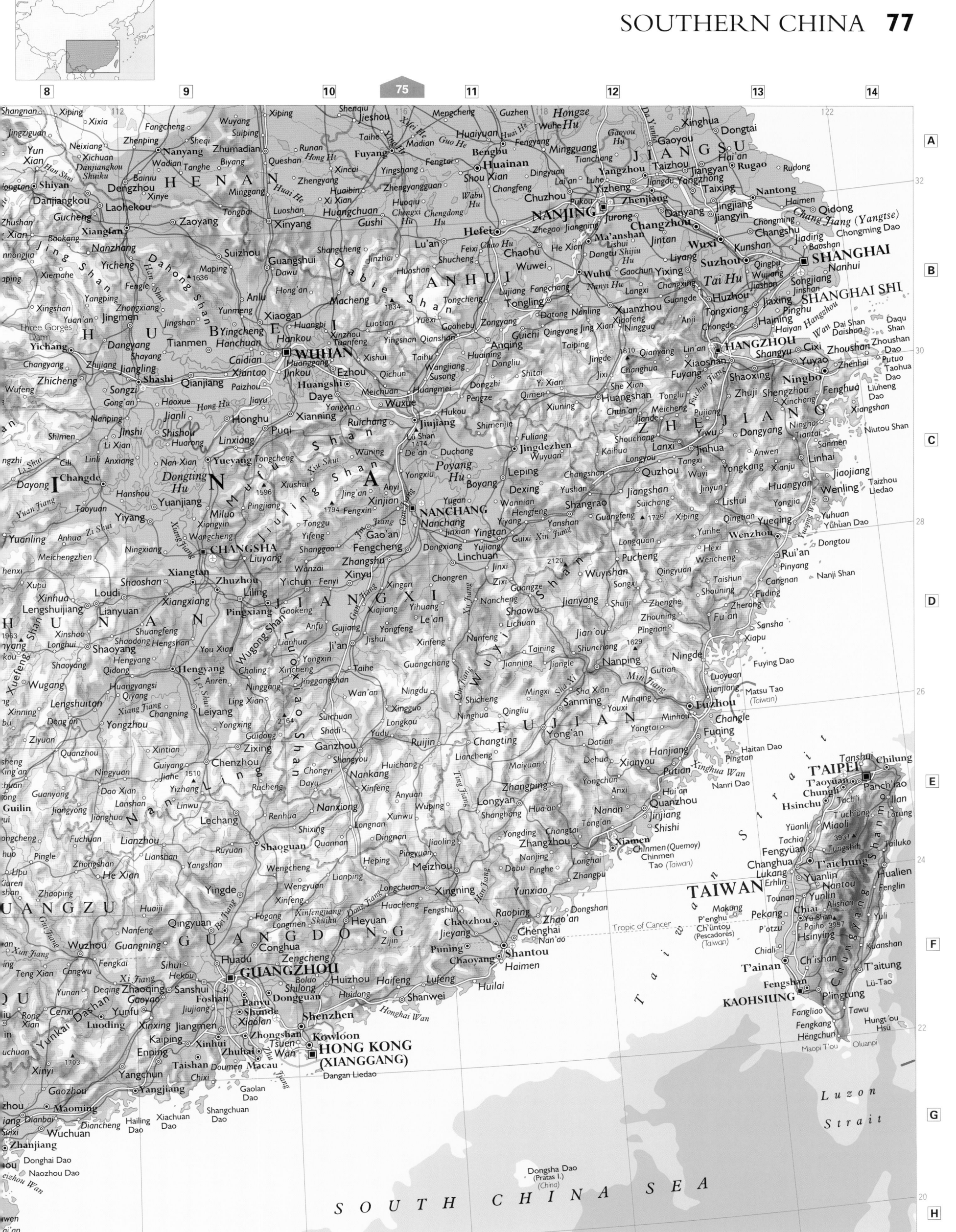

1:10 000 000

Projection: Mercator

East from Greenwich

JAVA AND MADURA
1:6 000 000

50 0 50 100 150 200 250 300 km
50 0 50 100 150 200 miles

BALI
1:1 600 000

10 0 10 20 30 km
10 0 10 20 miles

JAKARTA
Merak Serang Tangerang
Anyer-Kidul Pulau Rangkasbitung Karawang Pamanukan Kandanghaur Indramayu Kepulauan Karimunjawa Bawean Sangkapura
Selat Pandeglang Jatinegara Subang Jatibarang Cirebon Tg. Bugel
Sunda Panaitan Labuan BARAT Purwakarta Sumedang Majalengka Brebes Pemalang Pekalongan Rembang Kragan Tuban Madura
Tanjung Cianjur Kuningan Tegal Kendal Demak Kudus Muria Blora Tanjung Pangkah Bangkalan Sampang Pamekasan Sumenep
Guhakolak Bogor Bandung Garut Ciamis Slamet Wonosobo Purwodadi Cepu SEMARANG Gresik Tambuku
Pelabuhan Sukabumi Pengalengan Tasikmalaya Banyumas Magelang Salatige Boyolali SURABAYA Sidoarjo Selat Madura
Ratu Genteng Sindangbarang Cilacap Purwokerto Kebumen TENGAH Yogyakarta Surakarta Madiun Pare Arjuna Pasuruan Probolinggo Situbondo
Nusa Kambangan Karanganyar Bantul Wonogiri Ponorogo Kediri Ngawi Malang Bondowoso
Wates Wonosari Pacitan Trenggalek Tulungagung TIMUR Lumajang Banyuwangi
Nusa Barung Pasirian Jember Bali

BALI
Tanjung Batugondang Pulau Menjangan Kubutambahan
Gunung Ketapang Gilimanuk Singaraja Tejakula
Raung Banyuwangi Glagah Cekik Gerokgak Lovina Bayun Gunung Kintamani Batur Tianyar Kubu
Jambewangi Melaya Merbuk Seririt Songan
Kabat Rogojampi Negara Busungbiu Gunung Bedugul Batur Gunung Culik
Genteng Srono Mendoyo Pupuan Batukau Baturiti Agung Amed Tanjung
Tegalsari Beluki Muncar Perancak Yehbuah Belimbing Jatiluwih Tegallalang Rendang Karangasem Tirtagangga Pamenang
Tjluring Pasar Bojera Blahkiuh Bangli (Amlapura)
Pekutatan Bajatrejo Bali Tabanan Sibang Gianyar Klungkung Candi Dasa Lombok
Jawa Semenanjung Sembung Sukawati Kusamba Selat Lombok
Tanjung Purwo Blambangan Denpasar Danginpuri Sanur Selat Montongbuwoh Ampenan
Teluk Kuta DPS Toyapakeh Badung Suwana Tanjung Mataram Lembuak
Jimbaran Nusa Dua Nusa Bebera Teluk Terang
Uluwatu Tanjung Mebulu Bukit Penida Tanjung Gerung Lembar
Badung Abah Blongas

17 INDIAN OCEAN 18

Main map

Luzon
Claveria Babuyan Chan. C. Engaño
Bacarra Laoag Aparri Tuao Tuguegarao
Batac Ilagan
Bangued Bontoc Solano Palanan Pt.
Vigan Bayombong Palanan
San Fernando Baguio C. San Ildefonso
Bolinao Lingayen G. San Jose
Dagupan Tarlac Cabanatuan Casiguran
Iba Cabanatuan Polillo Is.
Mt. Pinatubo San Fernando
Olongapo Angeles Quezon City Lamon Bay
Manila B. Cavite MANILA Santa Cruz Daet
Bataan Lipa Lucena Calauag Catanduanes
Lubang Is. Batangas Calapan Naga Virac
Calavite Marinduque Tabaco Legazpi Mayon Volcano Sorsogon
Mamburao Mindoro Burias Bulan San Bernardino Str.
Sablayan Halcon Romblon Masbate Laoang Oras Samar
Semirara Panay Masbate Taft General MacArthur
Culion Kalibo Roxas Visayan Sea Catbalogan Borongan
Panay Iloilo Cadiz San Carlos Ormoc Leyte Baybay Guiuan
Bacolod Negros Mandaue Cebu Maasin Dinagat
Dumaguete Tanjay Siquijor Bohol Tagbilaran Surigao Siargao
Dipolog Oroquieta Iligan Cagayan de Oro Butuan Lianga
Sindangan Liloy Ozamiz Malaybalay Tandag
Kabasalan Sibuguey Pagadian Mindanao Bislig
Zamboanga Isabela Cotabato Talayan Tagum Davao Mati
Basilan Str. Parang Illana B. Datu Piang Digos
Jolo Kiamba General Santos Malita C. San Agustin
Balimbing Tawitawi Sarangani B. Sarangani

SULU SEA
CELEBES SEA
PACIFIC OCEAN

Kepulauan Nanusa
Karakelong
Kepulauan Talaud
Kepulauan Kawio Beo Salibabu
Pulau Sangihe Kaburuang
Karakitang Siau
Kepulauan Sangihe
Tahulandang

Merir (Palau)
Tobi (Palau) Helen Atoll (Palau)

Sopi Berebere Morotai
Doi Galela Tobelo
Bangka Ibu Akelamo Kepulauan Asia
Manado Kema Mayu Jailolo Kepulauan Mapia
Amurang Kotamobagu Ternate Halmahera Kepulauan Ayu
Tondano Gorontalo Tidore Teluk Buli Waigeo
Malino Tilamuta Makian Weda Patani Gebe Selpele Wakre Kepulauan Dampier
Tomini Moutong Kayoau Teluk Weda Selat Sorong Waibeem Biak
UTARA Kasiruta Gani Jazirah Doberai Klamono Kwoka Manokwari Supiori
TENGAH Kepulauan Bacan Mandioli Batanta Kofiau Sailolof Seget Numfoor Warsa Biak
Teluk Tomini Togian Poh Peleng Obilatu Kawasi Bisa Sesepe Lenmalu Misool Ransiki Padaido
SULAWESI Luwuk Banggai Mangole Adua Inanwatan Wasian Wariap Yapen
Toboli Parigi Tojo Tokala Taliabu Sanana Wahai Waru Nabire Bintuni Wendesi Serui
Poso Kolonodale Kepulauan Sula Piru Seram Bula Fakfak Waghete Teluk Cenderawasih
Sulawesi (Celebes) Mondeodo Namlea Amahai (Ceram) Weri Enaratoli Puncak Jaya PAPUA
SELATAN Malamala Manui Buru Kayeli Tehoru Kokas Babo Pegunungan Puncak Trikora
Palopo Danau Towuti Lima Namrole Ambon Geser Kaimana Uta Tembagapura Wamena
Rantemario Masamba Mekongga Kendari Saparua Kepulauan Manggawitu Pegunungan Maoke
Pinrang Singkang Kolaka Monse Wowoni Gorong Adi Amamapare Jayawijaya
Parepare Pampanua Buapinang Kepulauan Watubela Yapero Oksibil
Watampone Pising Buton Bandanaira Kai Besar Mandala
Sinjai Muna Raha Lawele Kepulauan Banda Tual Har Kola Gumzai Teluk Flamingo Agats
Bantaeng Kabaena Wangiwangi Tukangbesi Kai Kecil Banda Elat Dobo Wokam Mindiptana
Bulukumba Binongko Batauga Nila Molu Wangal Rebi Sewer Kepulauan Aru Tanahmerah
Benteng Serua Trangan Tafermaar Gomogomo Pirimapun
Kepulauan Bonerate Daya Gunungapi Wuliaru Larat Kepulauan Tanimbar Bade
Tanahjampea Kalao Damar Teun Alusi Saumlaki Pulau Dolak Muting
Bonerate Kalaotoa Wetar Wesiri Romang Barat Eliase Adaut Kimaam Okaba
Sunda Is. Sangeang Ilwaki Kisar Moa Lakor Babar Sermata Masela Selaru Pulau Komoran Merauke
Flores Ruteng Larantuka Adonara Pantar Atauro Baucau Leti Tutuala Leti Tanjung Vals

BANDA SEA
ARAFURA SEA
INDIAN OCEAN

NUSA TENGGARA TIMUR
Sumba Ende Maumere Solor Alor Selat Dili Viqueque EAST TIMOR
Waingapu Bima Sawu Sea Kefamenanu (E. Timor)
Sumba Kupang Nikiniki
Baing Sawu Raijua Dana Baa Roti

PAPUA NEW GUINEA

1:3 200 000

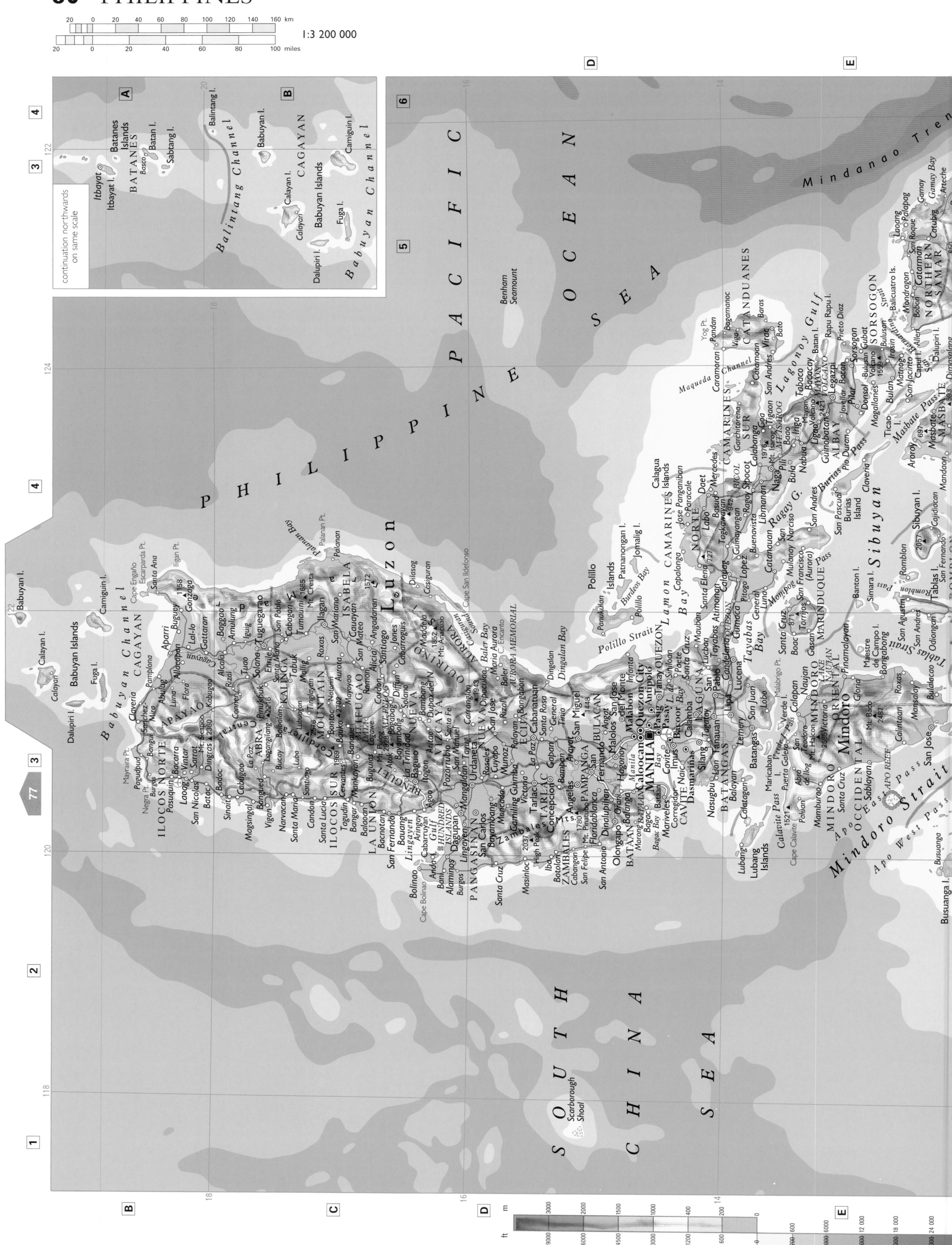

A

Batanes Islands
BATANES
Itbayat I.
Itbayat I.
Basco
Batan I.
Sabtang I.
Balintang I.

Balintang Channel

B

Balintang I.
Babuyan I.
CAGAYAN
Camiguin I.
Calayan
Calayan I.
Babuyan Islands
Fuga I.
Dalupiri I.

Babuyan Channel

continuation northwards on same scale

D

E

Mindanao Trench

P H I L I P P I N E   P A C I F I C   O C E A N   S E A

Benham Seamount

L u z o n

Palanan Bay
Palanan Pt.
Palanan
Cape San Ildefonso

Polillo
Polillo Islands
Burdeos Bay
Jomalig I.
Panananongan I.
Polillo I.
Patnanongan I.
Panukulan
Polillo Strait

Dingalan Bay
Dingalan

AURORA MEMORIAL

CAMARINES NORTE
Calagua Islands
Calagua
Labo
Daet
Paracale
Jose Panganiban

Maqueda Channel
Caramoran
San Andres
Pandan
Yog Pt.

CATANDUANES
Bagamanoc
Virac
Baras
Bato

Lagonoy Gulf
Rapu Rapu I.
Prieto Diaz

SORSOGON
Gubat
Bulusan
Volcano 1553
Irosin
San Jacinto
Matnog

Ticao Pass
Ticao I.
Masbate
MASBATE
Mandaon
Balud
Cataingan
Dimasalang

NORTHERN SAMAR
Catarman
Laoang
Palapag
Gamay Bay
Catubig
Arteche

Laoang
San Roque
Catubig
Allen

SOUTH
CHINA
SEA

Scarborough Shoal

Mindoro Strait
Apo West Pass
Apo East Pass
APO REEF

Busuanga I.
Busuanga

m
3000
2000
1500
1000
400
200
0

ft
9000
6000
4500
3000
1200
600
0
200-600
2000 6000
4000 12 000
6000 18 000
8000 24 000

COPYRIGHT PHILIP'S

Projection: Lambert Conformal Conic

East from Greenwich

CELEBES SEA

SULU SEA

S U L U   S E A

Visayan Sea

Bohol Sea

Camotes Sea

Mindanao

Negros

Leyte

Samar

Panay

Cebu

Bohol

Palawan

MALAYSIA

Borneo

SABAH

Moro Gulf

Davao Gulf

Illana Bay

Panay Gulf

Tañon Strait

Surigao Strait

Bassilan Strait

Sibutu Passage

Balabac Strait

Templar Bank

EASTERN SAMAR

SAMAR

BILIRAN

LEYTE

SOUTHERN LEYTE

SURIGAO DEL NORTE

SURIGAO DEL SUR

AGUSAN DEL NORTE

AGUSAN DEL SUR

DAVAO ORIENTAL

DAVAO

DAVAO DEL NORTE

DAVAO DEL SUR

BUKIDNON

MISAMIS ORIENTAL

MISAMIS OCCIDENTAL

LANAO DEL NORTE

LANAO DEL SUR

NORTH COTABATO

SOUTH COTABATO

SULTAN KUDARAT

MAGUINDANAO

ZAMBOANGA DEL NORTE

ZAMBOANGA DEL SUR

NEGROS OCCIDENTAL

NEGROS ORIENTAL

CEBU

BOHOL

SIQUIJOR

CAMIGUIN

AKLAN

CAPIZ

ILOILO

ANTIQUE

GUIMARAS

PALAWAN

SARANGANI

Zamboanga

Davao

Cagayan de Oro

Iligan

Cebu

Bacolod

Tacloban

Surigao

Butuan

General Santos

Koronadal

Cotabato

Marawi

Dumaguete

Tagbilaran

Puerto Princesa

Jolo

Bongao

Tawi-tawi Group

Sulu Archipelago

Cuyo Islands

Cagayan Islands

Mt. Apo 2954

Sandakan

Turtle Islands

1:5 600 000

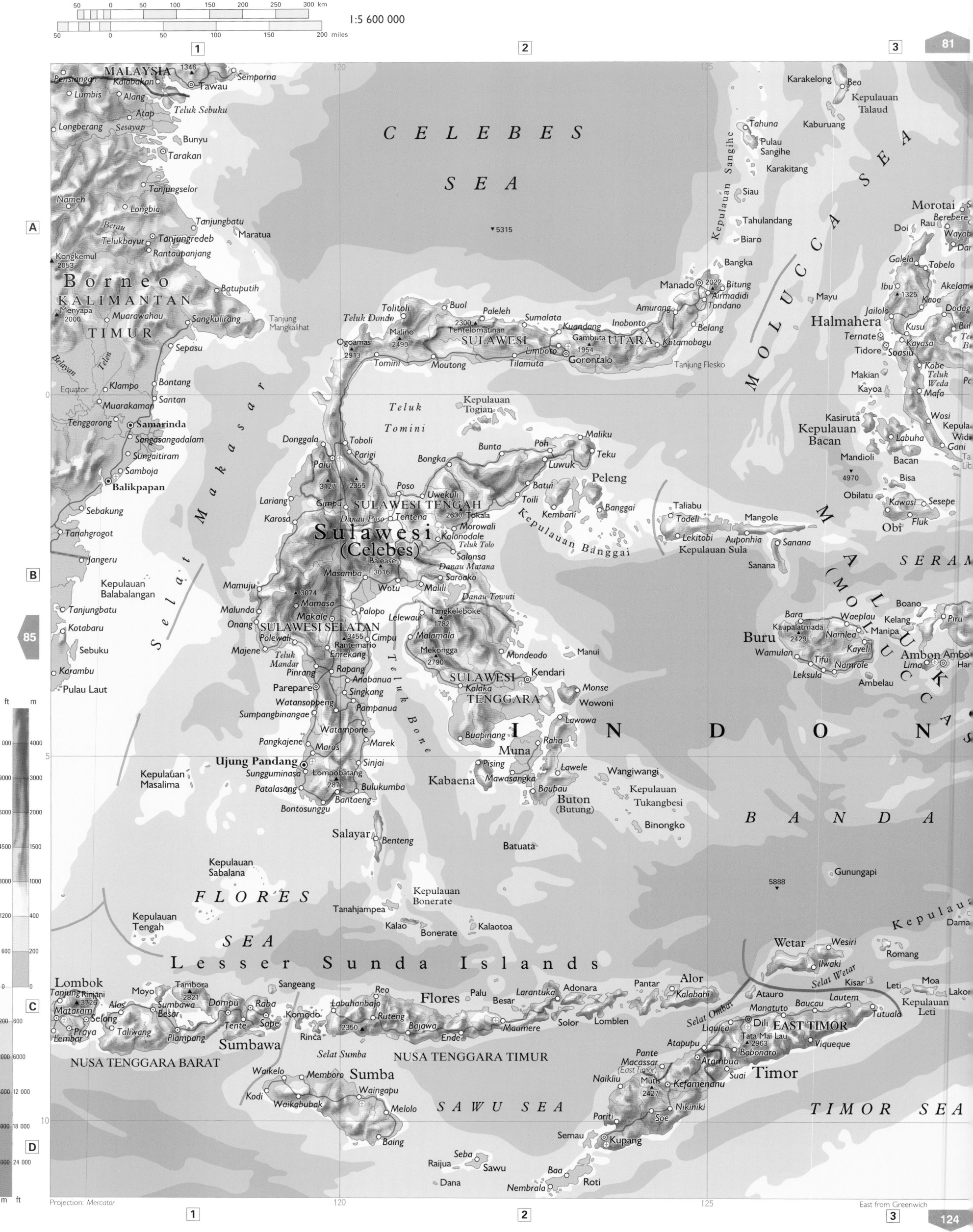

Projection: Mercator

East from Greenwich

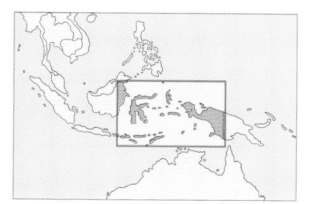

PACIFIC

OCEAN

Tobi
(Palau)   Helen
Atoll

Kepulauan
Asia

Kepulauan
Mapia

HALMAHERA

Kepulauan
Ayu

Selat Jailolo
Gebe
Kabarai
Umera   Selpele   Wakre   Waigeo
SEA   Gag   Saonek   Warmandi
Gam   Batanta   Susapor   Peg. Tamrau   Waibeem
Kepulauan Raja Ampat   Makbon   2452   Kwoka   Kaironi   Manokwari
Salawati   Samate   Sorong   Klamono   Jazirah Doberai   Warkopi   Number   Supiori   Sansundi
Kofiau   Sailolof   Seget   Konda   (Vogelkop)   3100   2926   Ransiki   Korim   Biak   Bosnik
Adua   Lenmalu   Teminabuan   Mogoi   Wasian   Wariap   Num   Wardo   Biak   Kepulauan
Misool   Inanwatan   Bintuni   Rumberpon   Ansus   Serui   Padaido
Kepulauan   Teluk Berau   Waar   Roon   Teluk   Yapen   Kepulauan
Segaf   Tanjung   Peg.   Saga   Babo   Wendesi   Cenderawasih   Waren   Ambai
Paa   Wahai   Hoti   Fatagar   Kokas   Fakfak   Semenanjung   Wosimi   Kepulauan   Nuboai   Barapasi
Sawai   Binaiya   Bula   Weri   Bomberai   Wenut   Bawe   Moor   Nabire   Napanwainami
Masohi   3019   Waru   Karas   Ibonma   Teluk   Kwatisore
Tehoru   Haya   Geser   Karufa   Arguni   Kaimana   Lobo
Seram   Kepulauan   Teluk   Aiduma   Modowi
(Ceram)   Gorong   Manggawitu   Kamrau   Wanapiri   Uta
Bandanaira   Kepulauan   Adi   Aiduna   Kokonau   Timika
Kepulauan   Watubela   Aidama   Amamapare   Yapero
Banda   I   A
Kur   Kepulauan
Kai   Har   Agats   Kaima
7440   Kepulauan   Tuaf   Kai Besar   Teluk Flamingo
Tayandu   Gumzai   Kola   Banda   Atsy   Pulau
Serua   Kai   Dobo   Wokam   Elat
Kecil   Sewer   Kobroor   Pirimapun   Kepi
Nila   Wangal   Penambulai   Tg. De Jongs   Kassue   Bade
Teun   Maikoor   Kobba   Kepulauan   Odammun
Molu   Rebi   Aru   Gomogomo
Trangan   Koba   Workai   Pulau   Kurik
Fordate   Tafermaar   Kepulauan   Dolak   Kimaam
Wuliaru   Larat   Tanjung   Jin   Okaba   Kumbe
Selu   Watmuri   Ngabordamlu   Pulau   Merauke
Sera   Yamdena   Komoran
Babar   Tepa   Bukrane   Alusi
Masela   Adaut   Saumlaki
Kepulauan   Eliase   Selaru   Kepulauan
Babar   Tanimbar

New
Guinea
PAPUA
Pegunungan Van Rees
Tariku
Tembagapura
Pegunungan Sudirman   Trikora
Enarotali   Puncak
Waghete   Puncak   5029   Jaya   4730
Peg. Tiyo   Pegunungan   Maoke   Pegunungan Jayawijaya
Baliem

Tanjung
D'Urville   Mataboor   Kepulauan
Bonoi   Apauwar   Kumamba
Danau   Sarmi
Rombebai   Saberania   Teluk
Mamberamo   Ansudu   Walckenaer   Demta
Genyem   Jayapura
Krau   Danau   Yos Sudarso
Sentani   Vahimo
Bewani

Mindiptana
Tanahmerah
Asike
Abemarre
Muting

PAPUA NEW GUINEA

E   S   I   A

ARAFURA   SEA

Tanjung Vals

4625

Equator

132

COPYRIGHT PHILIP'S

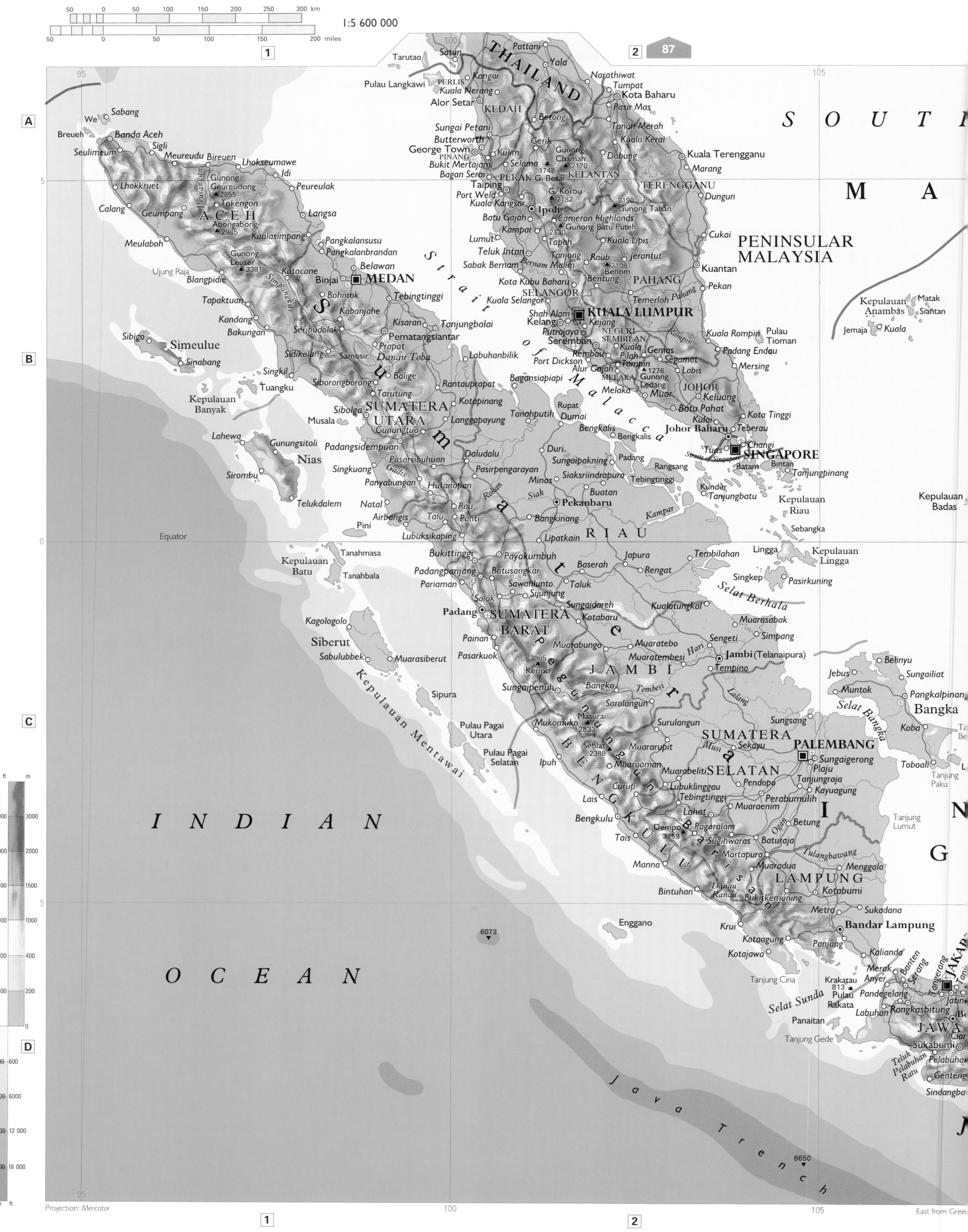

1:5 600 000

Projection: Mercator

East from Gree

3 4 81 115 5

A

CHINA SEA

SULU SEA

Balambangan — Banggi
Tg. Sempang — Kudat — Malawali
Mengayau — Senaja — Jambongan
Langkon — Datong
Kota Belud — Mt. Palin — 1216
Tuaran — 2579 — G. Tambuyukan
Kota Kinabalu — 4101 — Teluk — Sandakan
Penampang — Gunong Kinabalu — Labuk — Tanjong Pisau
Ranau — 2000 — Mt — Klagan
LABUAN — G. Trus Madi — Meutapok — Lamag — Batu
Beaufort — 2649 — Tambunan — Beluran — Puteh
Labuan — Sipitang — **SABAH** — G. Lumaku — Kuamut — Tungku — Litang
BRUNEI — Tenom — Banjaran Maitland — Lahad Datu — Labian
Bandar Seri Begawan — Lawas — Sapulut — Banjaran Brassey — Teluk Lahad
Kuala Belait — Limbang — Pensiongan — Kunak — 1346 — Datu — Sibutu
Lutong — Seria — Bangar — Kalabakan — Tawau — Semporna
Miri — Lumbis — Alang — Teluk — **PHILIPPINES**
Marudi — 2371 — Sebuku

MALAYSIA

Laut — Telukbutun
Kepulauan — Natuna — Besar
Natuna — Ranai — Binjai
Midai — Subi — Serasan
Kepulauan — Natuna Selatan
Kepulauan — Tambelan

Niah — Gunong Mulu — Long Akah — Longberang — Bunyu
Tanjong Kidurong — Tinjar — Pegunungan Kapuas — Nameh — Longbia — Tarakan
Bintulu — Baram — 1641 — Longjelai — Tanjungselor
Tubau — Bukit Kalulong — Gunong Iran — Longagung — Berau — Tanjungbatu
Oya — Mukah — Tatau — Bukit Batu Bora — 2988 — Telukbayur — Tanjungredeb — Maratua
Dalat — 1429 — Longnawan — **KALIMANTAN** — Rantaupanjang
Tanjong Sirik — Belaga — 2012 — Batubrok — **TIMUR** — Muarawahau — Sangkulirang — Tanjung Mangkalihat
Sibu — Bukit Batu — Kubumesaai — Menyapa — 2000 — Batuputih
Bintangor — Kanowit — Kapit — 2240 — Nahabuan — Longboh — Sangkulirang
Sarikei — Rajang — Hulu — Nangamentebah — 1730 — Tabang — Sepasu
Sematan — Tanjong Sipang — Boven Kapuas — Pegunungan Muller — 1744 — Murung — Tabang — Telen — Klampo
Paloh — Tanjong Po — Kuda — 1770 — Muarajuloi — Longiram — Bontang
Lundu — Bau — Saratok — Putussibau — Muarakaman — Santan
Sambas — Kuching — Debak — Sri Aman — Danau Luar — Tenggarong
Gunong Bungo — 996 — Simunjan — Engkilili — Danau Sentarum — Purukcahu — **Samarinda**
Singkawang — Serian — Bandar — Semitau — Songosangadalam
Bengkayang — 1701 — Balaikarangan — Balaisabut — Seipinang — Sungaitiram
Niut — Danau — Menate — Muaratewe — Samboja
Mempawah — Ngabang — Sintang — Jempang — **Balikpapan**
Jungkat — Sekadau — Nangamau — **KALIMANTAN** — Muarabenangin
Pontianak — Nangapinoh — 1758 — **TENGAH** — Teweh — Sebakung
Sungaidurian — Tayan — Gunung Saran — Pegunungan Schwaner — Rantaupanjang — Tanahgrogot
Kapuas — 2278 — Kotabaru — Seipinang — Buntok — Ampah — Tanjung
Padangtikar — Telukbatang — Rantauputut — Kasongan — Palangkaraya — Tamianglayang
Maya — Sukadana — Tumbangsamba — Bawan — Pujon — Amuntai — Jangeru
Sandai — Kotawaringin — Sampit — Kotabesi — Barabai — Besar
Nangatayap — Marau — Riam — Sampi — Pulangpisau — Kandangan — 1892
Kepulauan — Ketapang — Panopah — Kualakurun — Kualakapuas — Marabahan
Karimata — Kualapesaguan — Kotawaringin — Semuda — Pangkoh — Rantau — **KALIMANTAN**
Padang — Kendawangan — Sukaraja — Kuala Kuala — **Banjarmasin** — Banjarbaru — **SELATAN**
Tanjungpandan — Sukamara — Kumai — Martapura — Kotabaru
510 — Manggar — Kualajelai — Teluk Sampit — Pelaihari — Pegunungan — Tanjungbatu
Gantung — Belitung — Kualapembuang — Tanjung — Batakan — Satui — Pagatan — Sebuku
Dendang — Tanjung Sambar — Puting — Tanjung — Jorong — Kintap — Karambu — Pulau Laut
Selatan — Batakan

Selat Karimata

Borneo — *Kalimantan*

Equator 0

Sulawesi (Celebes) — Donggala — Palu — Lariang — Karosa — Mamuju — Mamasa — Malunda — Makale — Onang — Polewali — Majene — Enrekang — Pinrang — Rapang — Parepare — Watansoppeng — Sumpangbinangae — Pangkajene — Maros

B

C

82

INDONESIA

Greater Sunda Islands

Kepulauan Laut Kecil

Kepulauan Balabalangan

Ujung Pandang — Sungguminasa — 2871 — Bantaeng — Patalasang — Bontosunggu

JAVA SEA

Kepulauan Karimunjawa — Kepulauan Masalembo — Bawean — Sangkapura

Kepulauan Masalima

FLORES SEA

Kepulauan Kangean — Pabean — Puteran — Kepulauan Sabalana — Kepulauan Tengah
Sumenep — Sapudi — Sepanjang

BANDUNG — Indramayu — Jatibarang — Cirebon — Pamanukan — Subang — Majalengka — Kuningan — Ciremay — Brebes — Tegal — Pemalang — Pekalongan — Batang — Kendal — **SEMARANG** — Demak — Jepara — Muria — 1602 — Kudus — Rembang — Krogan — Tuban — Lamongan — **Madura** — Bangkalan — Sampang — Pamekasan — Sumenep
Garut — Tasikmalaya — 3078 — Banjar — Slamet — Wonosobo — 3265 — Purwodadi — Pati — Blora — Bojonegoro — Gresik — **SURABAYA** — Sidoarjo — Selat Madura
Ciamis — 3428 — **JAWA TENGAH** — Salatiga — Gundih — Ngawi — Cepu — Mojokerto — Pasuruan
Purwokerto — Banyumas — Magelang — 3317 — Surakarta — Sragen — Madiun — Jombang — Bangil — Probolinggo — Panarukan
Cilacap — Kebumen — Sleman — Klaten — Wilis — Kertosono — Arjuna — 3339 — Panarukan — Bondowoso
Nusa Kambangan — Karanganyar — **YOGYAKARTA** — Lawu — 2563 — Kediri — **Malang** — 3676 — Kraksaan — Jember — Rambipuji
Wates — Ponorogo — Blitar — Semeru — Lumajang — Pasirian
YOGYAKARTA — Trenggalek — Tulungagung — Wlingi — Pacitan — Nusa Barung

(Java)

BALI SEA

Lesser Sunda Islands

Bali — Singaraja — Moyo — Tambora — Sangeang
Banyuwangi — Agung — 3142 — Karangasem — 3726 — Alas — Sumbawa — Dompu — Raba — Labuhanbajo
Negara — Klungkung — Rinjani — Tanjung — Selong — Besar — Tente — Sape — Komodo
Tabanan — Mataram — Selong — Plampang — Rinca
Denpasar — Penida — Lembar — Praya — Taliwang — **Sumbawa** — Flores
BALI — Lombok — **NUSA TENGGARA BARAT**

D

3 4 110 115 5

COPYRIGHT PHILIP'S

1:4 800 000

Projection: Alber's Equal Area with two standard Parallels
East from Greenwich

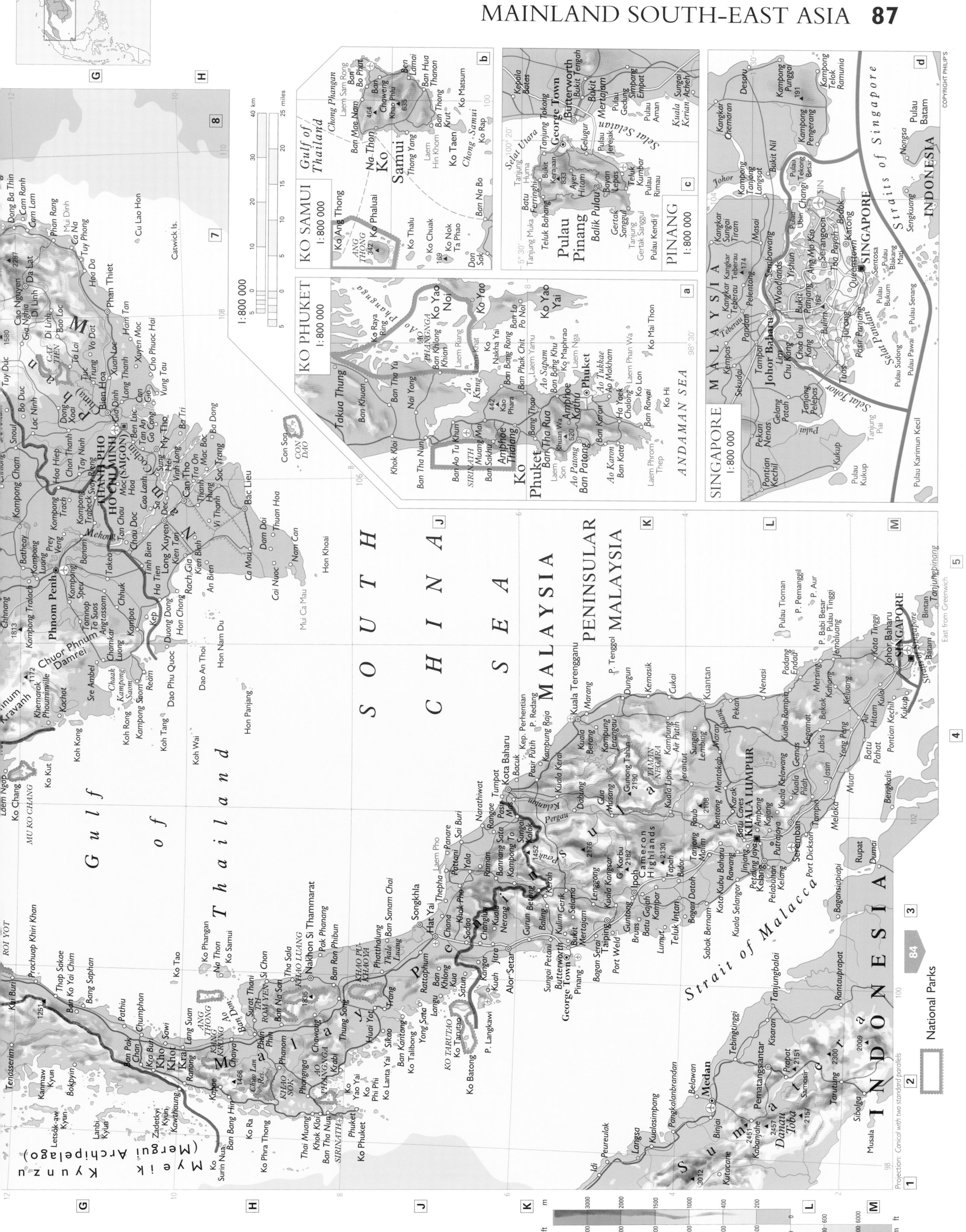

COPYRIGHT PHILIP'S

KO SAMUI 1:800 000

Gulf of Thailand

Ko Samui

KO PHUKET 1:800 000

Andaman Sea

Ko Phuket

PINANG 1:800 000

Pulau Pinang

George Town

SINGAPORE 1:800 000

SINGAPORE

Straits of Singapore

MALAYSIA

INDONESIA

South China Sea

PENINSULAR MALAYSIA

KUALA LUMPUR

Gulf of Thailand

Thailand

Phnom Penh

THÀNH PHO HO CHÍ MINH (SAIGON)

INDONESIA

Sumatra

Strait of Malacca

Myeik (Mergui Archipelago)

Kyunzu

National Parks

Projection: Conical with two standard parallels

East from Greenwich

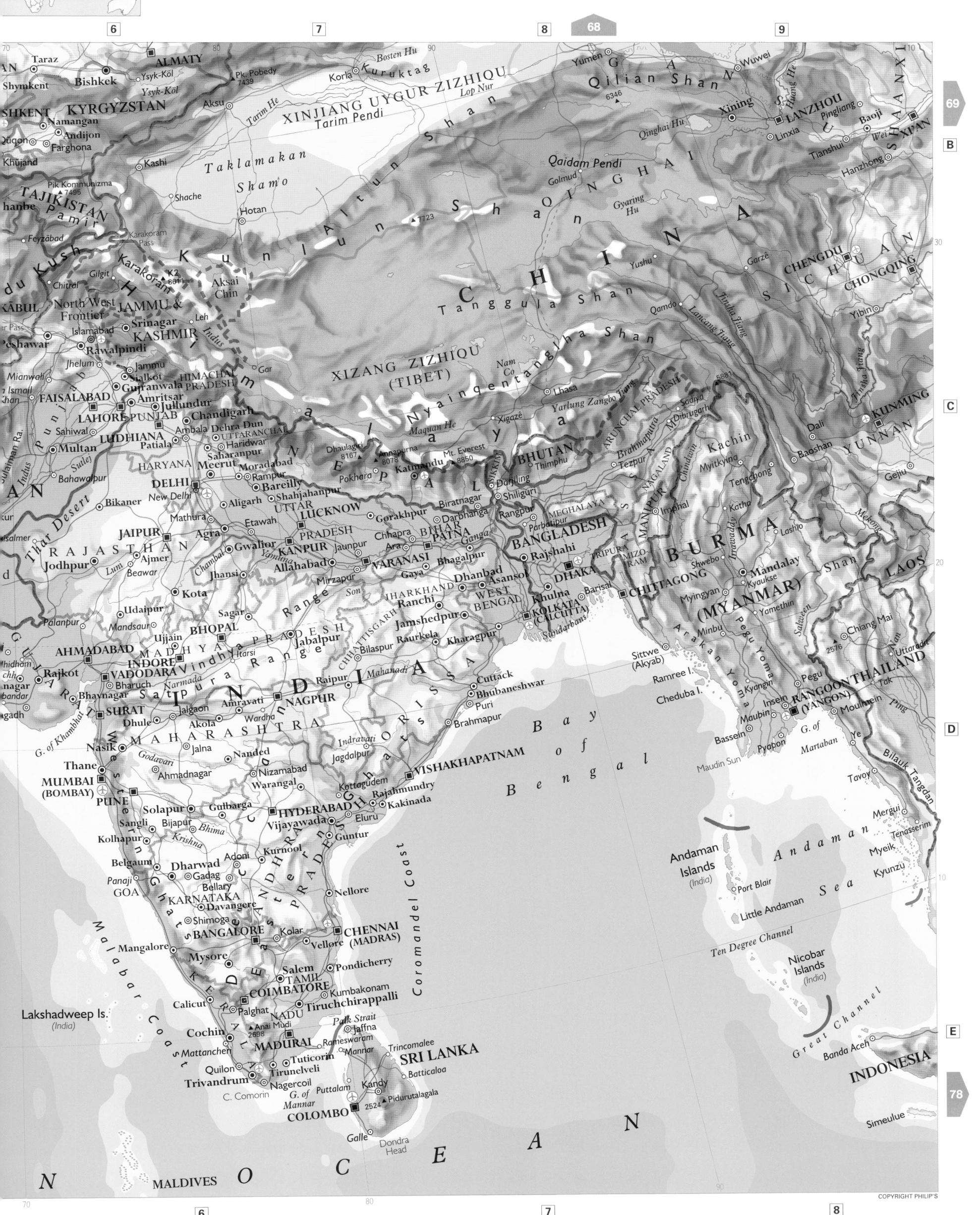

1:4 800 000

50 0 50 100 150 200 km
50 0 50 100 150 miles

1 2 3 4 68 5 6 7

ft m
18 000 6000
12 000 4000
9000 3000
6000 2000
4500 1500
3000 1000
1200 400
600 200
0 0
200 600
2000 6000
m ft

CHINA

XIZANG ZIZHIQU (TIBET)

NEPAL

SIKKIM

BHUTAN

ARUNACHAL PRADESH

INDIA

ASSAM

NAGALAND

MANIPUR

MEGHALAYA

BANGLADESH

DHAKA

TRIPURA

MIZORAM

WEST BENGAL

KOLKATA

CHITTAGONG

CHIN

SAGAING

KACHIN

YUNNAN

CHINA

SHAN

MANDALAY

BURMA (MYANMAR)

MAGWE

PEGU

KAYAH

ARAKAN

IRRAWADDY

RANGOON (YANGON)

THAILAND

MON

BAY OF BENGAL

INDIAN OCEAN

Mouths of the Ganges

Mouths of the Irrawaddy

G. of Martaban

The Sandheads

Sundarbans

Brahmaputra

Yarlung Zangbo Jiang (Brahmaputra)

Himalaya

Tropic of Cancer

Projection: Conical with two standard parallels

East from Greenwich

COPYRIGHT PHILIP'S

1:5 600 000

50 0 50 100 150 200 250 300 km
50 0 50 100 150 200 miles

65

TURKMENISTAN

UZBEKISTAN

TAJIKISTAN

Dushanbe

CHINA

Pik Kommunizma 7495

Gorno Badakhshan

Pamir

Karakoram Ra

IRAN

MASHHAD

Herāt

HERAT

BĀDGHĪS

FĀRYĀB

Safid Kuh

GHOWR

Mazar-e Sharīf

BALKH

SAMANGAN

BAGHLAN

Hindu Kush

QONDUZ

TAKHAR

BADAKHSHAN

NURISTĀN

JAMMU AND KASHMIR

Gilgit

Srinagar

Chitral

NORTH WEST FRONTIER

BĀMĪĀN

Koh-i-Baba

KĀBUL

KĀBUL

PARVAN

KAPISA

VARDAK

NANGARHAR

Jalālābād

Peshawar

Khyber Pass

Mardan

Islāmābād

RAWALPINDI

AFGHANISTAN

ORUZGAN

GHAZNI

PAKTIA

Gardēz

Ghazni

KHOWST

Tribal Areas

Kohat

Bannu

Jhelum

Gujrat

Siālkot

Amritsar

FARĀH

ZĀBOL

PAKTIKA

Sulaiman Range

Dera Ismail Khan

GUJRANWALA

FAISALABAD

LAHORE

NĪMRŪZ

HELMAND

Qandahār

QANDAHĀR

Rīgestān

Toba Kakar

Zhob

PUNJAB

Multan

Bhatinda

Zāhedān

Quetta

Chāh Gay Hills

BALUCHISTAN

Sibi

Bahawalpur

Thar Desert

INDIA

RAJASTHAN

Bīkaner

IRAN

Dasht-i

Ras Koh Range

Kalat

Khuzdar

SIND

Jacobābād

Sukkur

Khairpur

Jodhpur

Makran Coast Range

Gwādar

Pasni

Ormara

KARACHI

HYDERABAD

Mirpur Khas

Rann of Kachchh

ARABIAN SEA

Tropic of Cancer

Mouths of the Indus

GUJARAT

Little Rann

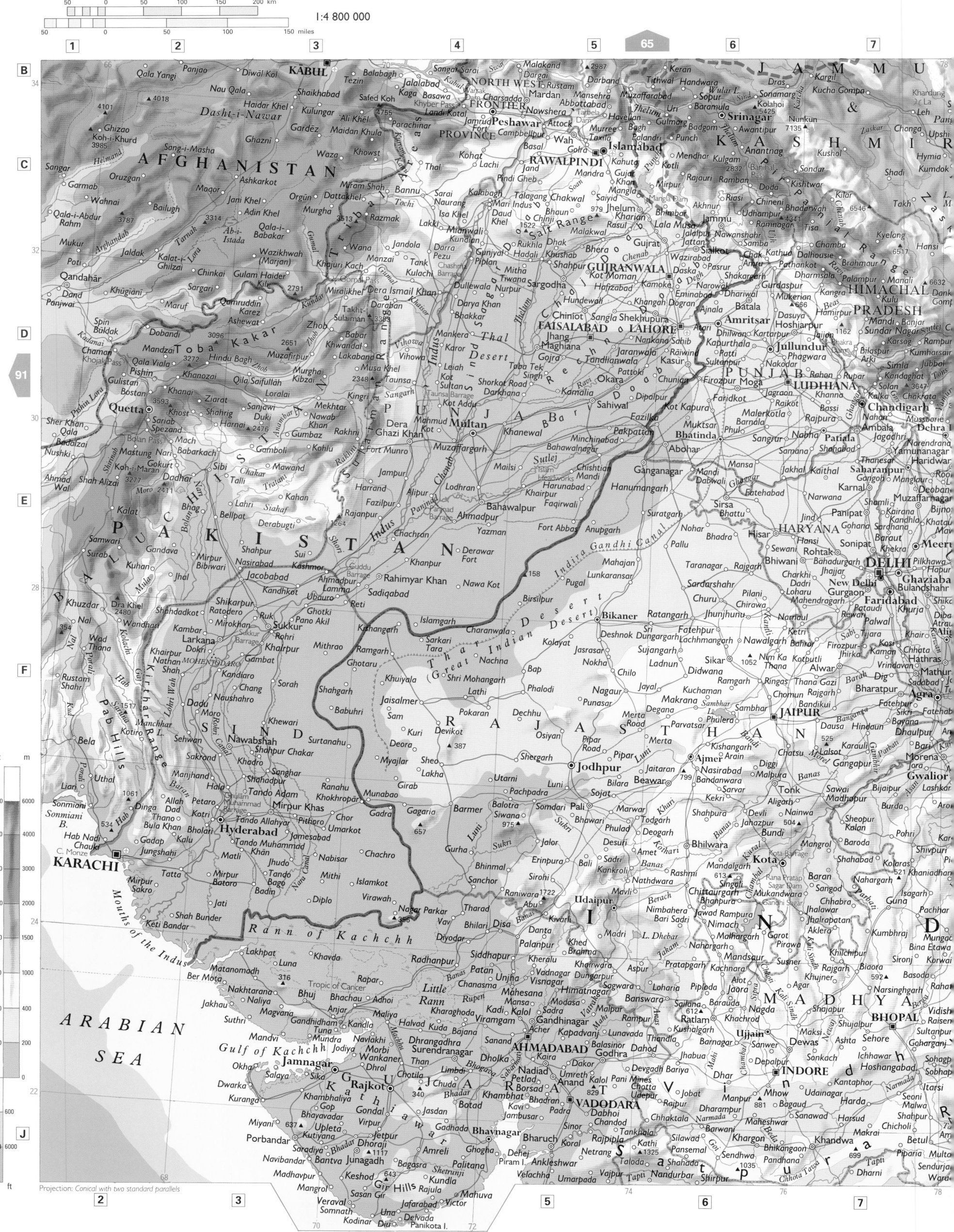

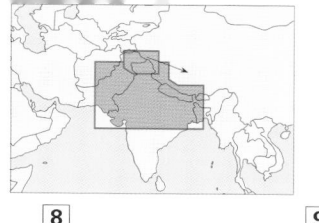

JAMMU AND KASHMIR
on same scale

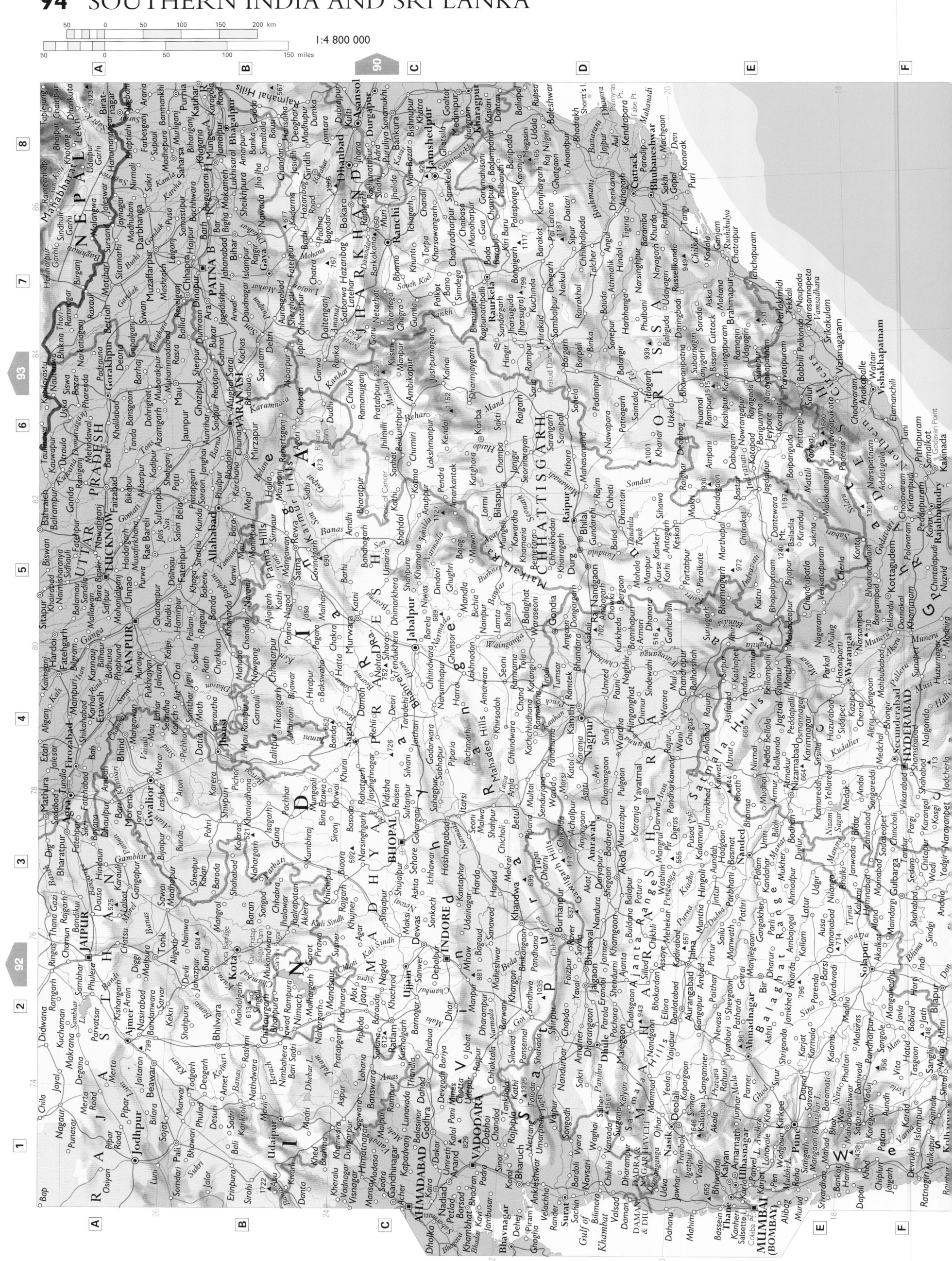

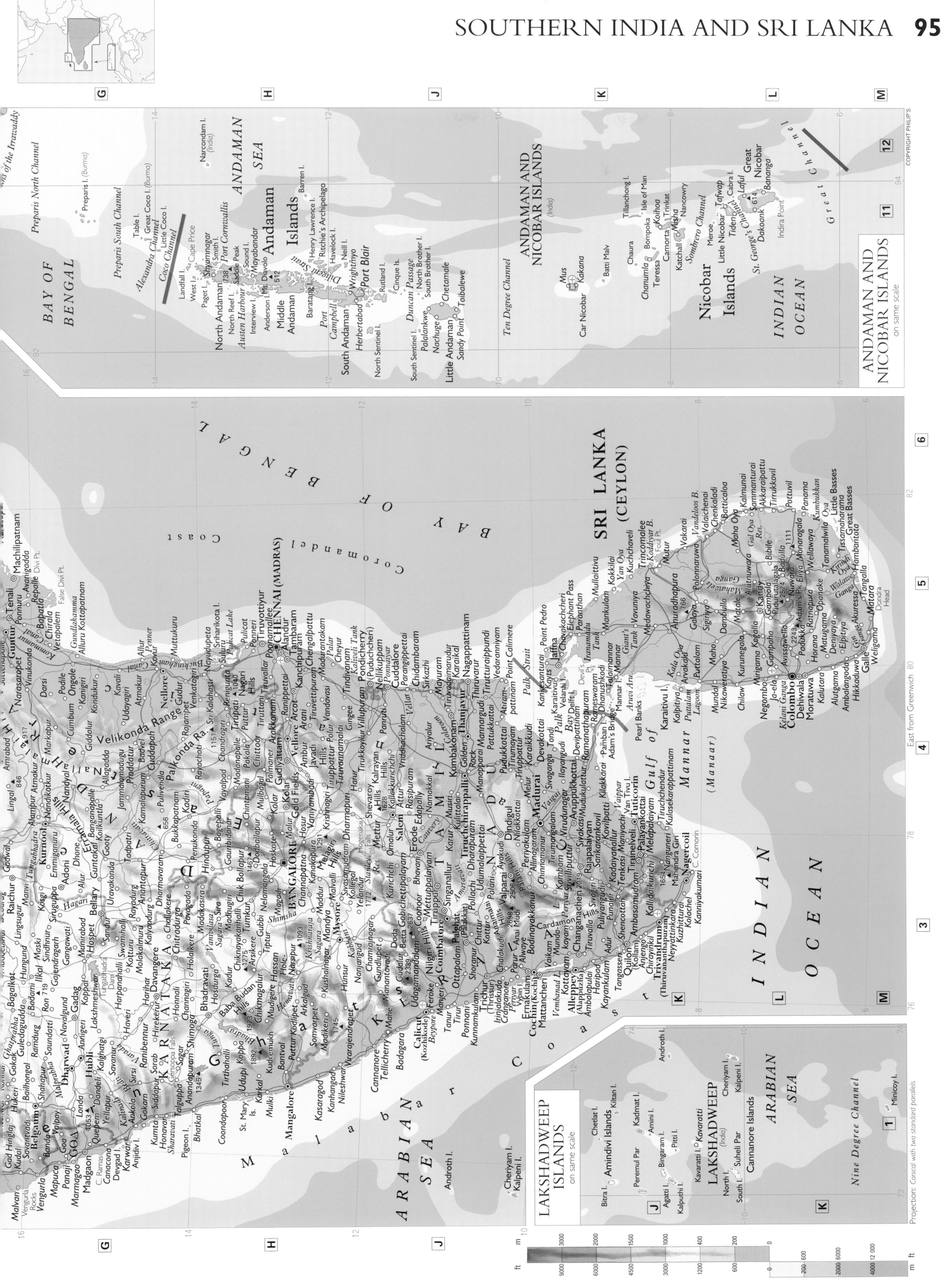

BAY OF BENGAL

ANDAMAN SEA

ANDAMAN AND NICOBAR ISLANDS (India)

ANDAMAN AND NICOBAR ISLANDS on same scale

Andaman Islands

Nicobar Islands

INDIAN OCEAN

SRI LANKA (CEYLON)

COROMANDEL COAST

CHENNAI (MADRAS)

BANGALORE

KARNATAKA

TAMIL NADU

Gulf of Mannar

ARABIAN SEA

Malabar Coast

GOA

LAKSHADWEEP ISLANDS on same scale

LAKSHADWEEP (India)

Minicoy I.

Nine Degree Channel

Projection: Conical with two standard parallels

COPYRIGHT PHILIP'S

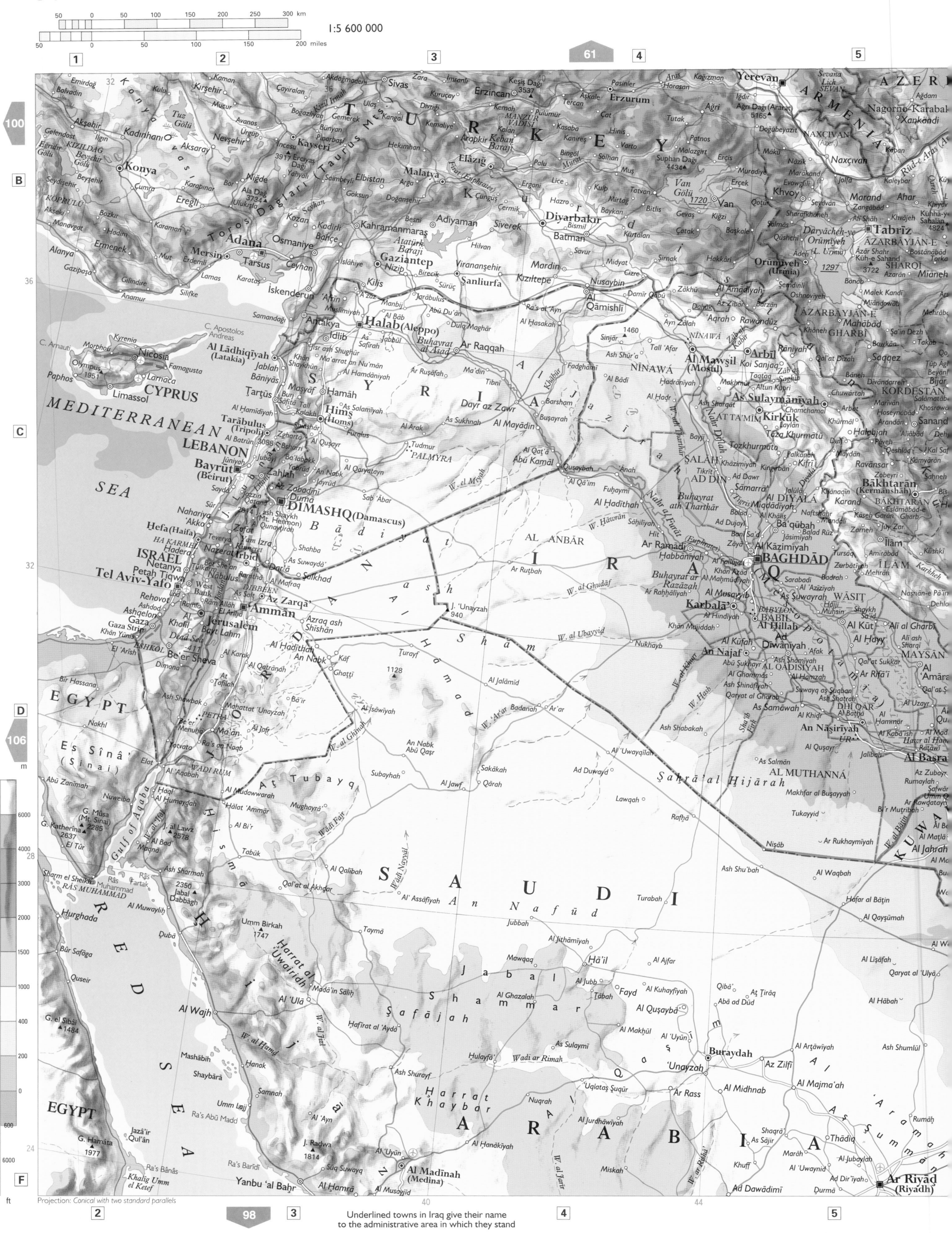

1:5 600 000

Projection: Conical with two standard parallels

Underlined towns in Iraq give their name
to the administrative area in which they stand

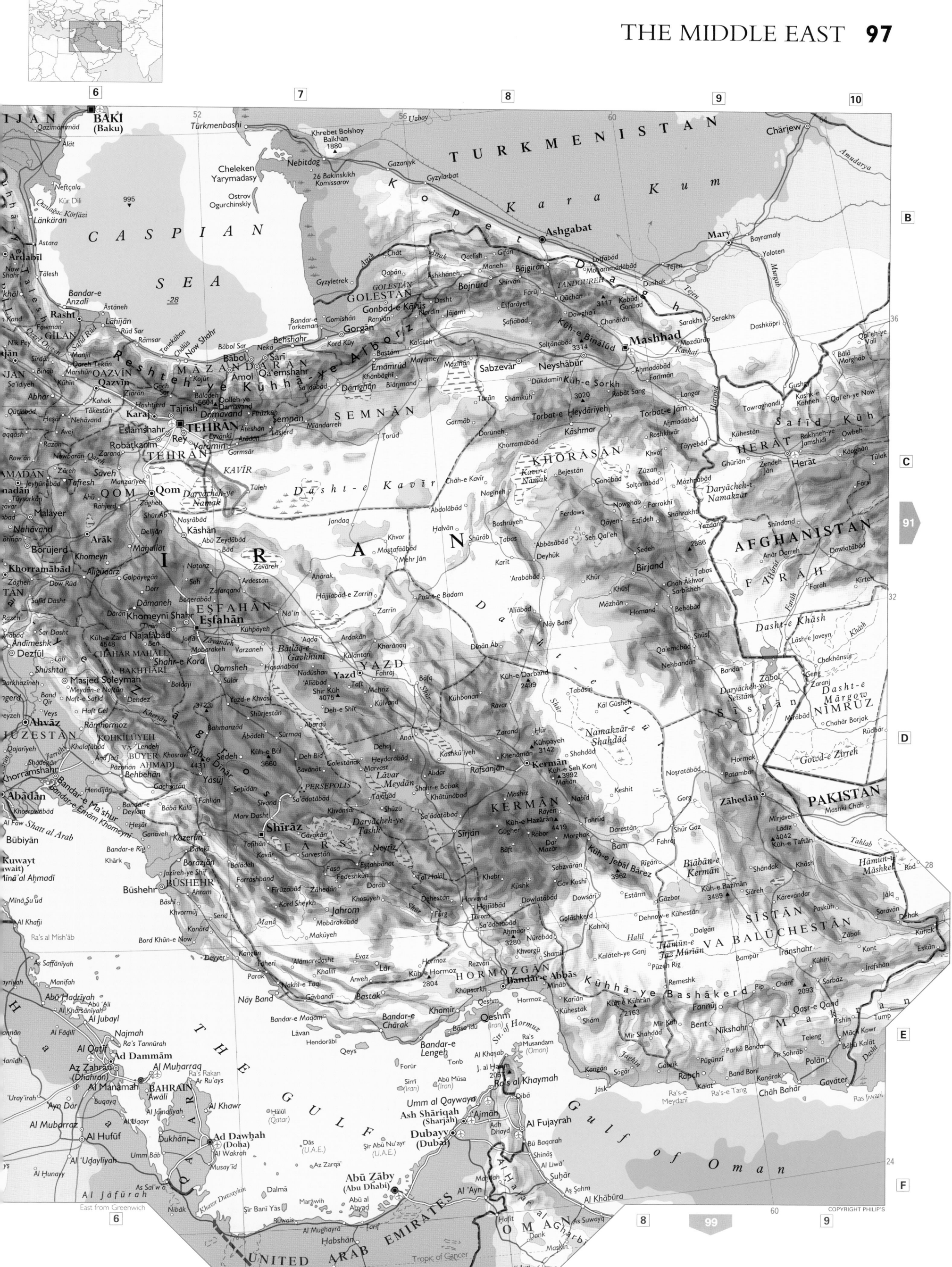

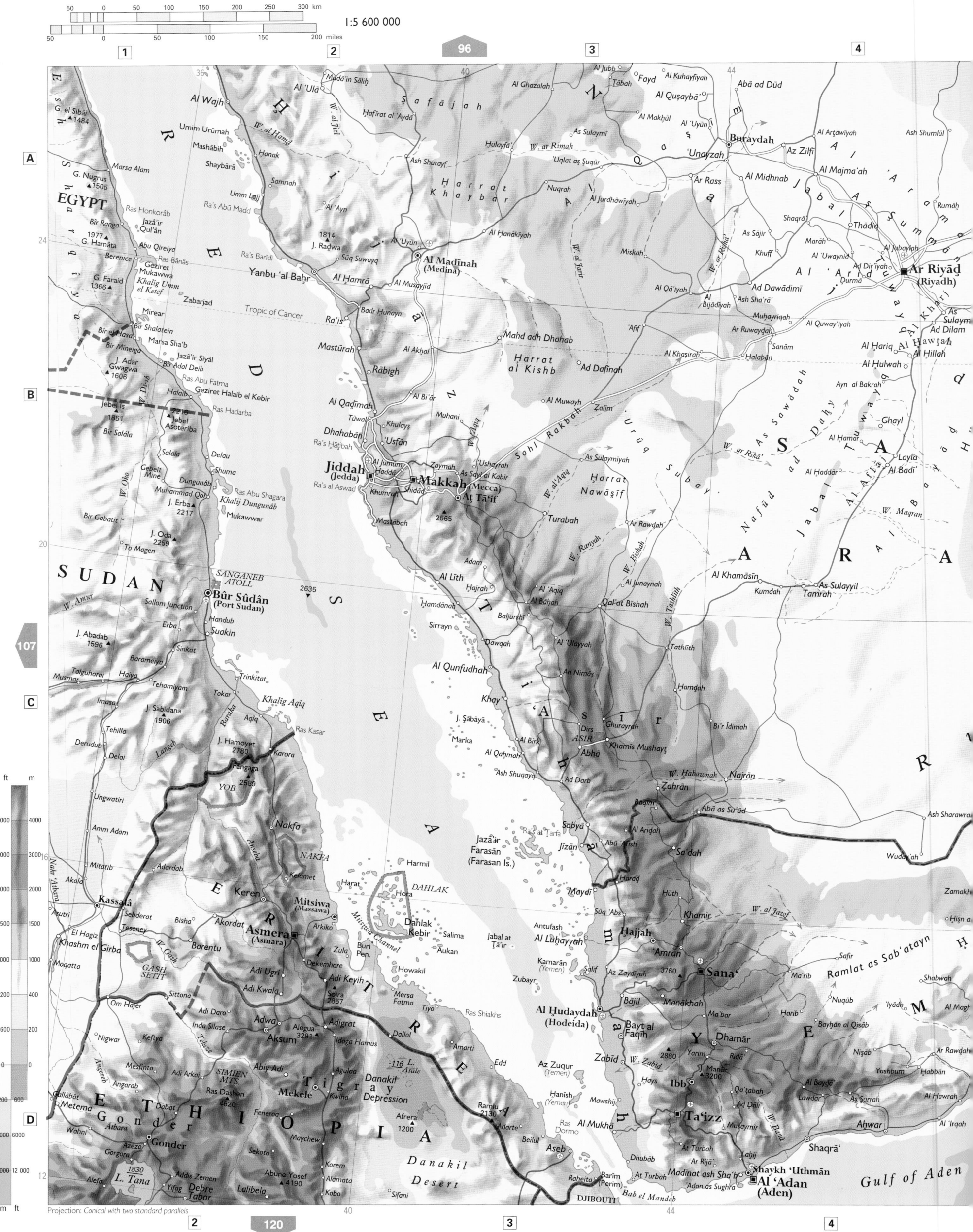

1:5 600 000

Projection: Conical with two standard parallels

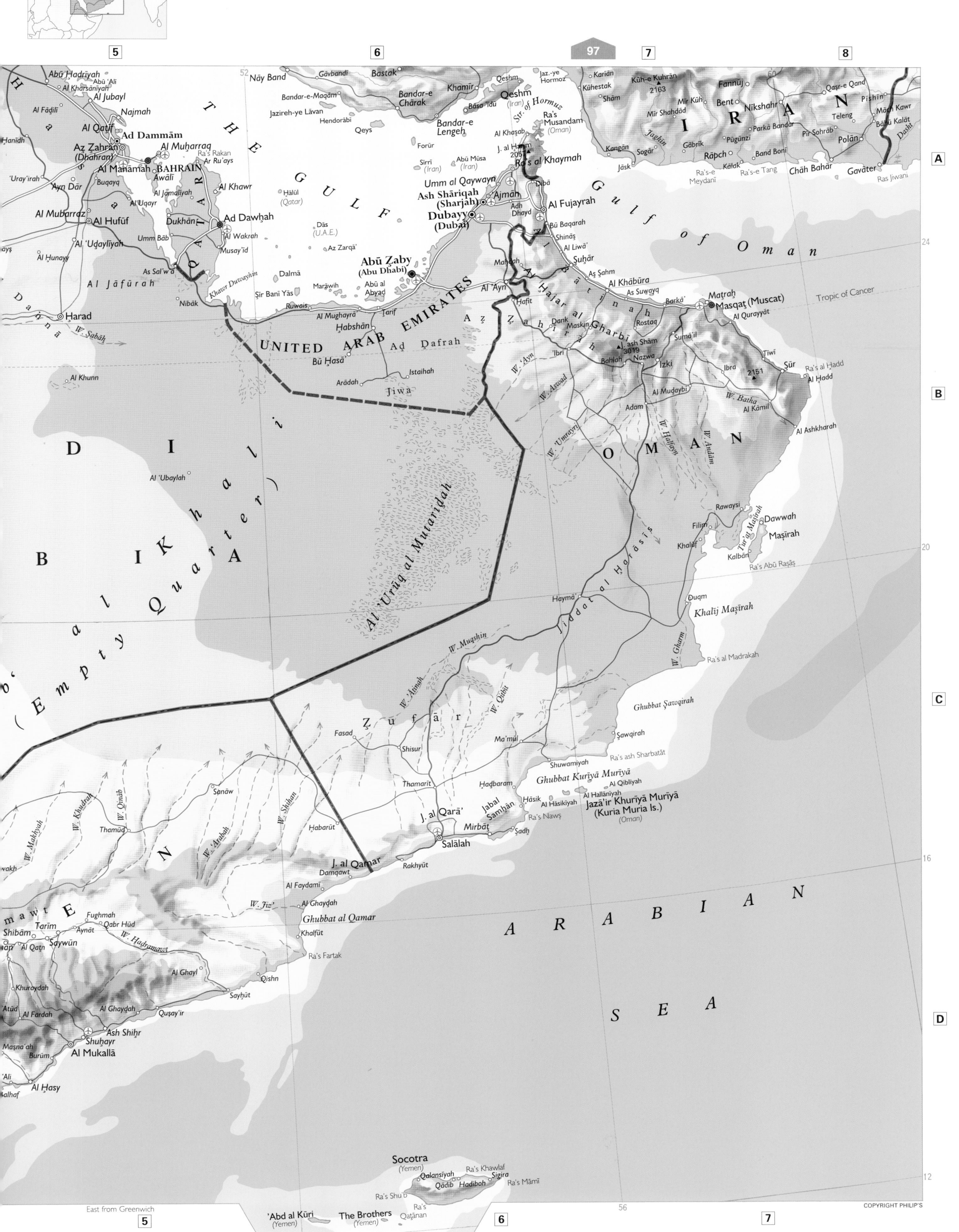

52   Nāy Band   Gāvbandi   Bastak   Khamir   Qeshm   Jaz-ye Hormoz   Kariān   Kūh-e Kuhrān 2163   Fannūj   Qaşr-e Qand

Abū Hadrīyah   Bandar-e Maqām   Bandar-e Chārak   Qeshm   Qeshm (Iran)   Bāsa Idū   Sham   Mīr Kūh   Bent   Nīkshahr   Teleng   Pīshīn   Mād Kawr

Al Kharsānīyah   Jazireh-ye Lāvan   Hendorābī   Bandar-e Lengeh   Ra's Musandam (Oman)   Al Khaşab   Mīr Shahdād   Gābrīk   Pūgūnzī   Parkā Bandar   Pīr Sohrāb   Bāhū Kalāt Dashtī

Al Jubayl   Forūr   J. al Hārīm 2052   Kangān   Şogār   Rāpch   Band Bonī   Polān

Al Fādilī   Qeys   Sirrī (Iran)   Abū Mūsā (Iran)   Ra's al Khaymah   Jāsk   Ra's-e Meydanī   Ra's-e Tang   Chāh Bahār   Gavāter   Ras Jiwani

Najmah   Hālūl (Qatar)   Umm al Qaywayn   Dibā

Ad Dammām   Ra's Rakan Ar Ru'ays   Ash Shāriqah (Sharjah)   Ajmān   Al Fujayrah   Bū Baqarah

Az Zahrān (Dhahran)   Al Muharraq   Dās (U.A.E.)   Dubayy (Dubai)   Adh Dhayd   Shināş   Aş Şahm

Al Manāmah BAHRAIN   Al Khawr   Abū Zaby (Abu Dhabi)   Al Liwā'   Şuḥār   As Suwayq   Barkā'   Maţraḥ

'Uray'irah   Ayn Dār   Buqayq   Al Jamalīyah   Musay'īd   Şīr Banī Yās   Marāwiḥ   Al 'Ayn   Hafīt   Al Khābūra   Masqaţ (Muscat)

Al Mubarraz   Al Hufūf   Dukhān   Umm Bāb   Dalmā   Abū al Abyad   Al Ayn   Danḳ   Maskin   Rostaq   Sumā'il   Al Qurayyāt   Tropic of Cancer

Al 'Udaylīyah   As Sal'wā   Khawr Duwayhin   Dabb'ah   Maḥdah   Gharbī   ash Shām 3019   Baḥlah   Nazwā   Izki   Tīwī

Harad   Nibāk   Al Mughayrā   Ţarif   Ad Dafrah   'Ibrī   Adam   Al Muḍaybi   Ibra   2151   Şūr   Ra's al Hadd

Al Jāfūrah   Bū Haşā   Istaihah   Arādah   Jiwa   W. Asyad   W. Batha Al Kāmil   Al Hadd

W. Sabāh   Al Khunn   W. 'Umrayri   Al Ashkharah

D I B A L   K H A L I   Al 'Ubaylah   Al 'Urūq al Mutaridah   O M A N   Raways

B   (E m p t y   Q u a r t e r)   Haymā   Filim   Dawwah   Maşīrah

Jiddat al Harāsīs   Khalaff   Kalbān   Ra's Abū Rasāş

W. Muqshin   Duqm   Khalīj Maşīrah

W. Annah   W. Ghazm   Ra's al Madrakah

Z u f ā r   W. Qitbīt   Ghubbat Şawqirah

Fasad   Ma'mul   Şawqirah

Shisur   Thamarit   Shuwamīyah   Ra's ash Sharbatāt

Şanāw   Haqbaram   Ghubbat Kurīyā Murīyā   Al Qibliyah

Thamūd   Thamarit   Hāsik   Al Hāsikīyah   Jazā'ir Khurīyā Murīyā (Kuria Muria Is.) (Oman)

W. 'Arnbah   Jabal Samḥān   Ra's Nawş   Şadḥ   Al Hallānīyah

J. al Qarā'   Mirbāţ

Habarūt   Salālah

J. al Qamar   Rakhyūt

Damqawt

Al Faydamī   A R A B I A N

W. Jīz'   Al Ghaydah   Qamar

Ghubbat al Qamar

Fughmah   Qabr Hūd   Khalfūt   S E A

Tarīm   Aynāt   W. Hadramawt   Ra's Fartak

Shibām   Saywūn   Al Qaţn

Al Ghayl

Khuraydah   Qishn   Sayhūt

Aţūd   Al Fardah   Al Ghaydah   Quşay'ir

Ash Shihr

Maşna'ah   Burūm   Al Mukallā

'Ali   Al Haşy

Socotra (Yemen)   Qalansīyah   Ra's Khawlaf   Sigira

Qādib   Hadiboh   Ra's Māmī

Ra's Shu'b

T H E   G U L F   Q A T A R   U N I T E D   A R A B   E M I R A T E S   A z   Z a h i r a   A l   H a j a r   a l   G h a r b ī   Al Bātinah   Gulf of Oman   I R A N   Str. of Hormuz

D A N N Ā   Dahnā   A l   J ā f ū r a h   R U B '   a l   K H A L I   Al 'Urūq al Mutaridah

Tropic of Cancer

50 25 0 25 50 75 100 125 150 175 km
50 0 25 50 75 100 125 miles

1 : 4 000 000

1 26 2 28 3 30 32 **59** 5 34 6 36 7

B L A C K S E A

A **BULGARIA**

Stara Zagora
Yambol
Aytos
Burgas
Nos Emine
1830
2206

51

Elkhovo
Michurin
Arda
Kırklareli
Yıldız Dağları
1018
Demirköy
İğneada Burnu
Kerempe Burnu
İnce Burun
Sinop

B Orestiás
Edirne
Pınarhisar
Saray
İstanbul Boğazı
(Bosporus)
Zonguldak
Kilimli
Amasra
Cide
İnebolu
Abana
Çatalzeytin
Ayancık
Gerze
Bafra Burnu
Civa Burnu

Hayrabolu
Uzunköprü
Muratlı
Çorlu
Çatalca
İSTANBUL
Kocaeli (İzmit)
Kandıra
Karasu
Kozlu
Ereğli
Devrek
Karabük
Araç
Safranbolu
Daday
Küre
Küre Dağları
Devrekâni
Gökırmak
Boyabat
Kastamonu
Durağan
Alaçam
1670
Bafra
Samsun
Terme
Ünye
Fatsa
Korgan
Kayabaşı

Évros
İpsala
Keşan
Malkara
Tekirdağ
Şarköy
Büyükçekmece
Gebze
1220
Kartal
Darıca
Şile
Sapanca
Hendek
Akyazı
Düzce
Bolu
Gerede
Çerkeş
Ilgaz
2565
Tosya
Osmancık
İskilip
Çankırı
Merzifon
Gümüşhacıköy
Suluova
Havza
Ladik
Tekke
Erbaa
Niksar
Reşadiye
B

1600
Samothráki
Gökçeada
Eceabat
Gelibolu
Biga
Gönen
Bandırma
Karacabey
Mudanya
Gemlik
Yalova
Golcük
Orhangazi
İznik
İznik Gölü
Geyve
Göynük
Mudurnu
Seben
2378
Kızılcahamam
Kızılırmak
Çubuk
Ayaş
Kalecik
Çankırı
Bozkazlar
Sungurlu
Çorum
Mecitözü
Amasya
Turhal
Zile
1907
Tokat
Yeşilırmak
Çırçır

C Lésvos
968
Mitilini
Ayvalık
Bergama
Soma
Balya
Burhaniye
Edremit
Susurluk
Bigadiç
Alaçam Dağları
2289
Dursunbey
Tavşanlı
Kütahya
Emet
Simav
Gediz
Altıntaş
Seyitgazi
Eskişehir
Alpu
Mihalıçcık
Sivrihisar
Haymana
Polatlı
Gölbaşı
Elmadağ
ANKARA
Kırıkkale
Keskin
Bâlâ
Koman
Kırşehir
Yerköy
Yozgat
Sorgun
Delice
Ortaköy
Akdağmadeni
Yıldızeli
2235
Sivas
Ulaş
Şarkışla
Gemerek
Kangal
Tohma
Tecer Da

Manisa
Menemen
1297
1153
İZMİR (Smyrna)

D **GREECE**
MEDITERRANEAN SEA
2775

E **CYPRUS**
Nicosia
Kyrenia
Morphou
Famagusta
Larnaca
Limassol
Olympus
1951
Troodos
Paphos
Episkopi

48

F

G **ISRAEL**
ISRAEL

Projection: Conical with two standard parallels

106 3 4 5 6 7

- - - Division between Greeks and Turks
in Cyprus; Turks to the North.

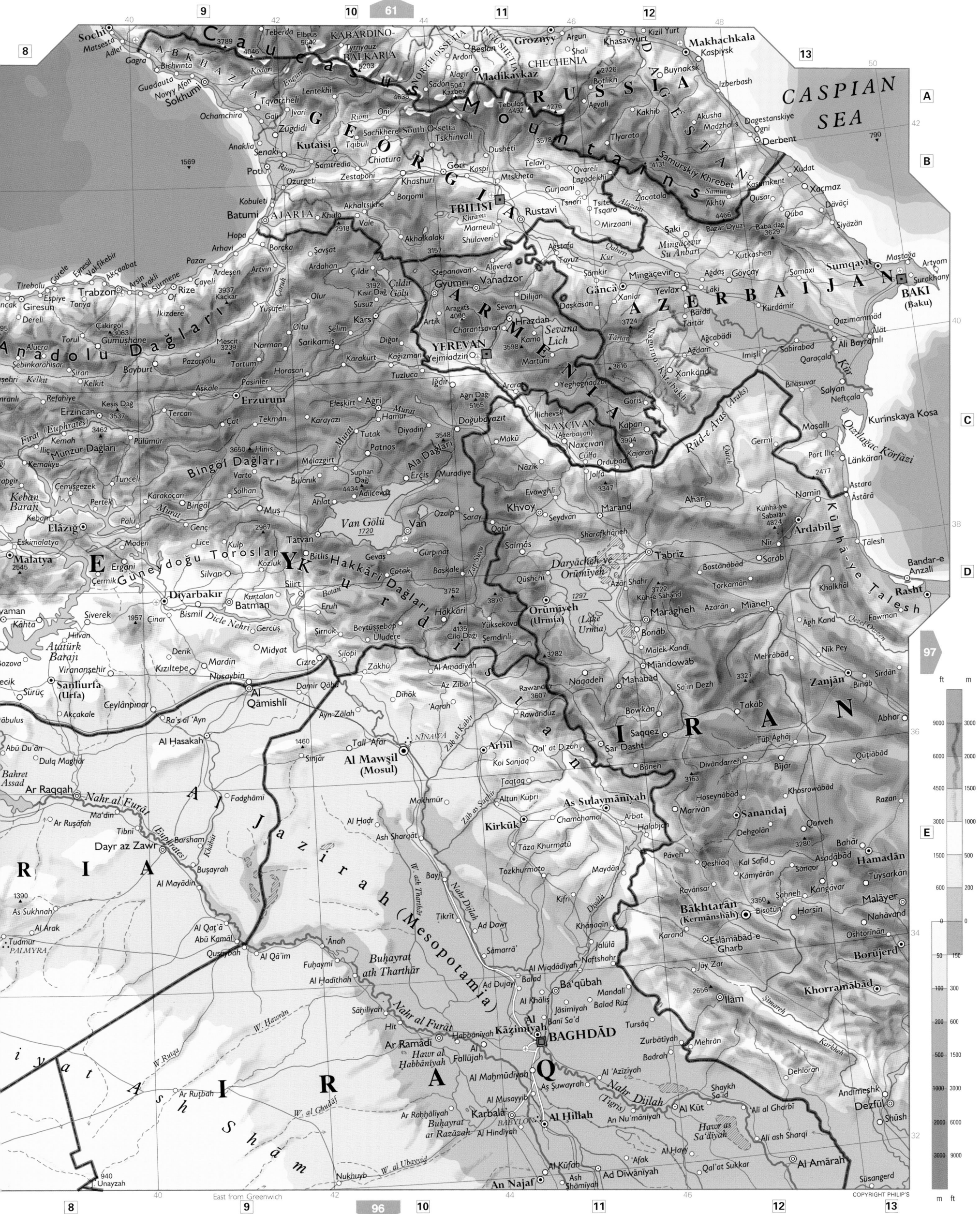

100 0 100 200 300 400 500 600 km
1:12 000 000
100 0 100 200 300 400 miles

1 **2** **3** 101 **4** **5** **6** **7**

LEBANON
BAYRŪT (BEIRUT)
DIMASHQ (DAMASCUS)
SYRIA
Jabal ad Durūz 1801
ISRAEL
Tel Aviv-Yafo
Ashdod
Hera
'AMMĀN
JORDAN
Jerusalem
Gaza
West Bank
Bûr Sa'îd (Port Said)
Qanâ es Suweis
Ismâ'ilîya
El Suweis (Suez)
Elat
Ma'ān
Al 'Aqabah
Khalîg el Suweis
Es Sinâ'
G. Mûsa 2637
Hurghada
Bûr Safâga
2187
Tabûk 2578
Al Muwayliḥ
Al Wajh
EGYPT
Qena
Quseir
El Uqsur
Idfû
Kôm Ombo
Aswân
Sadd el Aali
Buheirat en Naser
Wadi Halfa
Kosha
Delgo
3rd Cataract
Dongola
4th Cataract
Kareima
Ed Debba
Abu Hamed
Berber
Atbara
Ādarama
Wad Hamid
Shendî
6th Cataract
5th Cataract
Nahr en Nîl

IRAQ
Ar Ruṭbah
BAGHDĀD
Al Amarah
Karbalā
An Najaf
An Nāṣirīyah
Al Başrah
Ābādān
Khorrāmshahr
Hafar al Bāṭin
Rafḥā
Al Jawf
An Nafūd
Ḥā'il
Buraydah
'Unayzah
Al Madīnah
Yanbu' al Bahr
Rābigh
Al Līth
Makkah (Mecca)
2565
Aṭ Ṭā'if
Turabah
As Sulayyil
Laylā
JIDDAH (JEDDA)
SAUDI
ARABIA
Tropic of Cancer
AR RIYĀḌ (RIYADH)
Ḥaraḍ
Al 'Ubaylah
Rub' al Khālī (Empty Quarter)

Al Kuwayt
KUWAIT
Ḥasā
Al Qaṭīf
Ad Dammām
BAHRAIN
Al Manāmah
QATAR
Al Mubarraz
Al Hufūf
Ad Dawḥah (Doha)
Dubayy (Dubai)
Abū Ẓaby (Abu Dhabi)
Al 'Ayn
UNITED ARAB EMIRATES
Ra's al-Khaymah
Ra's Musandam (Oman)
Ash Shāriqah (Sharjah)
Gulf of Oman
Ṣuḥār
Maṭraḥ
Masqaṭ
Sūr
Ras al Hadd
Nazwā 3019
OMAN
Khalūf
Khalīj Maṣīrah
Maṣīrah
Ras al Madrakah
J. Khurīyā Murīyā
Salālah
Mirbāṭ
Rās Fartak
Sayḥūt
Ḥaḍramawt
Shibām 2469
Niṣāb
Al Mukallā
 Aḥwar
Shaqrā'
Al 'Adan (Aden)
Bāb el Mandeb
Gulf of Aden
Abd al Kūrī
Bereda
Ras Asir
Socotra (Yemen)
Hadiboh

IRAN
Khvor
Birjand
Farāh
AFGHANISTAN
ESFAHĀN 4548
Ahvāz
Yazd
Daryācheh-ye Seistan
Zābol
Kūhhā-ye Zagros
PERSEPOLIS
Shīrāz
Kāzerūn
Būshehr
Deyyer
Jahrom
Neyrīz
Kermān
Zāhedān
Bam
Dashi-e Lut
The Gulf
Khamīr
Qeshm
Bandar-e Abbas
Gābrīk
Bampūr
Str. of Hormuz

Bādiyat ash Shām
Dash
Al (Mesopotamia)
Nahr Dijlah
Nahr al Furāt
Būbiyān
J. Khārk

RED SEA
Ḥijāz
'Asīr
Najd
Ras Bānās
Bîr Shalatein
Halaib
Ras Hadarba
Muhammad Qol 2259
Bûr Sûdân
Suakin
Sinkat
Trinkitat
Haiya
Karora 2780
Nakfa
Akordat
ERITREA
Asmera
Massawa
Zula
Dahlak Kebir
Farasān
Jīzān
Najrān
Abhā
Khamir
Sana'
YEMEN
Al Ḥudaydah
Ḥanish
Kamaran
Al Luḥayyah
Djebel Manār 3350
Ta'izz
Al Mukhā
Aseb

Es Sahrâ en Nûbîya
Omdurmân
El Khartûm (Khartoum)
Kassalâ
Khashm el Girba
El Gedaref
SUDAN
Wad Medanî
Gezira
Singa
Ed Dueim
Kôstî
Umm Ruwaba
Ed Damazin
Nîl el Azraq
Sûdd
Bahr el-Jebel
Malakâl
Sobat
Bôr
Pibor Post
Tali Post
Juba
Mongalla
Kapoeta
Torit
Bahr el-Ghazal
Yei
Kajo Kaji 3187

ETHIOPIA
Aksum
Adigrat
-116
Adwa
Mekele
Ras Dashen 4620
Lalibela 4190
Gonder
1830
Danakil Desert
L. Tana
Bahir Dar
Debre Tabor
Debre Markos
Dese
Bure
Nekemte
ADDIS ABEBA
Debre Zeyit
Awash
Nazret
3202
Dembidolo
Metu
Gore
Jima 3686
Awasa
Yirga Alem
Omo
Shashemene
Asela
Ginir
Mt. Batu 4307
Goba
Dila
Kibre Mengist
Negele
L. Abaya
L. Shamo
Arba Minch
Chew Bahir
375
L. Turkana
Mega
Moyale
Dolo
Imi
Scebeli
Kebri Dehar
Ogaden
Las Anod
Harer
Jijiga
3381
Dire Dawa
Tadjoura
DJIBOUTI
Djibouti 156
Dikhil
Zeila
L. Abbé
Tendaho
Dese
Karin
Berbera
Hargeisa
Burao
Gardo
Bender Beila
Erigavo 2406
El Gal
Dante
Ras Hafun
Bosaso
Garoe
SOMALI REP.
Eil
Galcaio
Sinadogo
El Dere
Obbia
Belet Uen
Ferfer
Lugh Ganana
Wabi Scebeli
Bardera
Bur Acaba
Baidoa
Dolo
Dif
Wajir
El Wak
MUQDISHO (MOGADISHU)
Merca
Juba

UGANDA
Arua
Gulu 3084
Pakwach
Murchison Falls
Lira
Moroto
Soroti
L. Albert
L. Kyoga
Mbale
4321
Masindi
Kitale
Lodwar
South Horn
Marsabit
KENYA
2441
1919

Malakâl
Bahr el-Jebel

INDIAN OCEAN

East from Greenwich

Projection: Sanson-Flamsteed's Sinusoidal

COPYRIGHT PHILIP'S

ft m
12 000 4000
9000 3000
6000 2000
4500 1500
3000 1000
1200 400
600 200
0 0
200 600
1000 3000
2000 6000
4000 12 000
m ft

106
107

1:2 000 000

10 0 10 20 30 40 50 60 70 80 100 km
10 0 10 20 30 40 50 60 miles

CYPRUS

Paphos
Episkopi
Limassol
Akrotiri Bay
Episkopi Bay
C. Gata

MEDITERRANEAN SEA

Hims (Homs)
Al Hamidiyah
Tall Kalakh
Shinshar
Furqlus
Halba

ASH SHAMAL
Al Mina'
Tarabulus (Tripoli)
Al Hirmil
Al Qusayr
H I M S
Zgharta
Qurnat as Sawda 3088
Bsharri
Al Buray̆j 2464
Al Qaryatayn
Al Batrun
Qartaba
Ibrahim
Jubayl
An Nabk
Bi'r Ghadir
Juniyah
Bikfayya
2628 Sannin
Ba'labakk
2616
Yabrud

BAYRUT (Beirut)
Alayh
Ash Shuwayfat
Ad Damur
JABAL LUBNAN
Zahlah
Sirghaya
An Nabk
Khan Abu Shamat
SYRIA

LEBANON
Sayda (Sidon)
Jazzin
1942 J. al Barak
Az Zabadani
DIMASHQ
Dumayr

An Nabatiyah at Tahta
ash Shaykh (Mt. Hermon) 2814
Daraya
DIMASHQ (Damascus)
DAM
Qatana
Al Hajanah

Sur (Tyre)
AL JANUB
Qiryat Shemona
Golan Heights
O. Mas'ada
Al Kiswah
A'waj
Buraq
B A D I Y A T A S H S H A M

Nahariyya
Me'ona
Al Qunaytirah
As Sanamayn
Burag

'Akko (Acre)
Mifraz Hefa
Hagalil
Qiryat Yam HAZAFON
Zefat
Fiq
Shaykh Miskin
W. Al Harir
Shahba'
JABAL AD DURUZ

Hefa (Haifa)
Teverya (Tiberias)
Yam -210 Kinneret
Saham al Jawlan
Dar'a
As Suwayda 1800
AS SUWAYDA

Qiryat Ata
Daliyat el Karmel
HA KARMEL
Nazerat (Nazareth)
Yarmuk
Salah

Umm el Fahm
Tayiba
IRBID
Busra ash Sham
Salkhad
Malah

TEL MEGIDDO
Afula
Irbid
Ar Ramtha
AL MAFRAQ

CAESAREA
Jenin
Bet She'an
AJLUN 'Ajlun
J. Umm ad Dana
Al Mafraq
Umm al Qittayn

ISRAEL
Hadera
Hanna-Karkur
Pardes
SHOMRON
Tubas
Irbid
Jarash
Karak

Netanya
Tulkarm
SAMARIA
N. az Zarqa
JARASH

HAMERKAZ
Nabulus
DIBBEEN

Herzliyya
Kefar Sava
Petah Tiqwa
SHILO
AL BALQA'
Az Zarqa

Benē Beraq
Ramat Gan
As Salt
Wadi as Sir
AMMAN
Azraq ash Shishan

Tel Aviv-Yafo
Bat Yam
West Bank
-289 Karama
Na'ur
AZ ZARQA

Rishon le Ziyyon
Lod
Ramla
Ram Allah
El Ariha (Jericho)
AMM
At Tunayb

Yavne
Rehovot
Jerusalem (Yerushalayim) (Al Quds)
Ma'daba
'AMMAN

Ashdod
Qiryat Mal'akhi
Bet Shemesh
Bayt Lahm (Bethlehem)
MA'DABA
Dhiban
Al Hadltha

Ashqelon
Qiryat Gat
TEL LAKHISH
Al Khalil (Hebron)
W. al Huydan

Gaza
N. Shiqma
Az Zahiriya
W. al Mawjib

Gaza Strip
Sederot
ESHKOL
Har Yehuda
-411
Al Karak
AL KARAK

Khan Yunis
Rafah
Be'er Sheva (Beersheba)
Arad
Al Mazar
1305

Be'er Sheva
Sedom
Al Mazar

El 'Arish
Bir el Garârât
Bor Mashash
Dimona
W. al Hasa

Bur Sa'id (Port Said)
Bur Fu'ad
Ras Burun
Sabkhet el Bardawil
El Daheir
-333
At Tafilah
AT TAFILAH

Romani
Bir el 'Abd
Bir Kaseiba
Bir Lahfan
HADAROM
Sedom

El Qantara
Bir el Duweidar
Bir el Jafir
W. 'Arish
Qezi'ot
Sedé Boqer
JORDAN

Isma'iliya
Talata
Bir Madkur
SHAMAL SINI
Birein
-121
At Tafilah

ISMA'ILIYA
Khamsa
El Buheirat el Murrat el Kubra (Great Bitter L.)
Muweilih
Mizpe Ramon
1072
Jash Shawmari

Gineifa
Bir el Malhi
Bir Hasano
Bir Beiqa
Hanegev
Rujm Talat al Jama'a 1736
Al Jafr
Qa'el Jafr
MA'AN

Bir el Thamada
G. Yi'Allaq 1094
W. Qiraiya
El 'Agrud
N. Paran
PETRA
Wadi Musa
Ma'an

Mamarr Mitla
Bir Gebeil Hisn
W. el Bruk
W. Mahashim
N. Hiyyon
Bi'r al Mari

El Suweis (Suez)
Adabiya
Uyun Musa
948 G. el Kabrit
Nakhl
Ain Sudr
El Kuntilla
Yotvata
Ra's an Naqb
Mahattat ash Shidiyah

EGYPT
W. el Giddi
El Thamad
W. el 'Aqaba
Al Aqabah
Ra's an Naqb 1435
Batn al Ghul
SAUDI

Sina (Sinai)
1592 1754
Bi'r al Qattar
WADI RUM
ARABIA

Ghubbet el Bus
Ras Matarma
G. el Kabrit
El Wabeira
Bir Abu Muhammad
'En 'Avrona
Bir al Butayyihat
Elat
Al 'Aqabah
Rum
At Tubayq

1272
EL SUWEIS
Bir Abu Sanduq
JANUB SINI
Bir el Biarat
Al 'Aqabah
Gulf of Aqaba
Al Mudawwarah

W. Abu Ga'da
Bir el Heist
1165
W. an Nuqeib
Haql

Projection: Polyconic
East from Greenwich
COPYRIGHT PHILIP'S

=== 1974 Cease Fire Lines

National Parks

ft m
9000 3000
6000 2000
4500 1500
3000 1000
1200 400
600 200
0 0
200 600
2000 6000
m ft

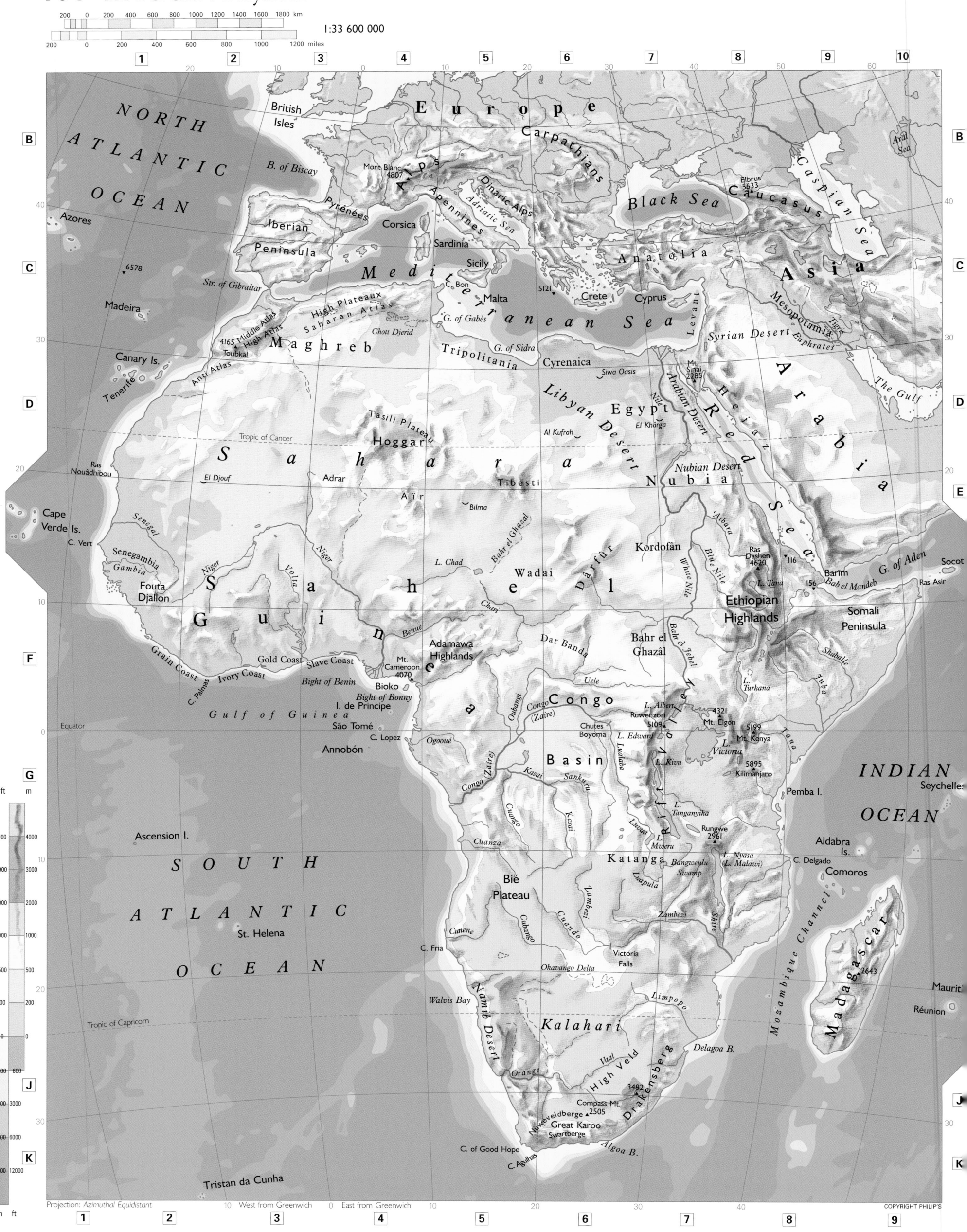

1:33 600 000

Projection: Azimuthal Equidistant

COPYRIGHT PHILIP'S

1:33 600 000

200 0 200 400 600 800 1000 1200 1400 1600 1800 km

200 0 200 400 600 800 1000 1200 miles

1:6 400 000

50 0 50 100 150 200 250 300 km
50 0 50 100 150 200 miles

THE NILE DELTA
1:3 200 000

MEDITERRANEAN SEA

Inset (The Nile Delta):
Bîr Sa'îd (Port Said), Dumyât (Damietta), El Mansûra, Ismâ'îlîya, Zagazig, El Suweis (Suez), Rashîd (Rosetta), EL ISKANDARÎYA (Alexandria), Damanhûr, El Mahalla el Kubra, Tanta, Shibîn el Kôm, Benha, Qalyûb, EL QÂHIRA (Cairo), El Gîza, Imbâba, Heliopolis, Helwân, Shubrâ el Kheima, El Faiyûm, Beni Suef, Baltim, Kafr el Sheikh, Mît Ghamr

Main map places:
Amman, Jerusalem (Al Quds), Tel Aviv–Yafo, Gaza, Be'er Sheva, ISRAEL, JORDAN, Ma'ân, Al 'Aqabah, Gulf of 'Aqaba, Es Sînâ' (Sinai), Suez, El Suweis, Khalîg el Suweis, EL QÂHIRA (Cairo), El Gîza, Heliopolis, Helwân, El Faiyûm, Beni Suef, El Minya, Mallawi, Asyût, Sohâg, Qena, El Uqsur (Luxor), Karnak, VALLEY OF THE KINGS, Esna, Idfu, Kôm Ombo, Aswân, El Sadd el 'Âli (High Dam), Buheirat en Nâser (Lake Nasser), Abu Simbel, Wadi Halfa

EL ISKANDARÎYA (Alexandria), Damanhûr, Tanta, El Mansûra, Dumyât, Bîr Sa'îd (Port Said), Rashîd (Rosetta), El Alamein

SAUDI ARABIA, Al Madînah (Medina), Makkah (Mecca), Jiddah (Jedda), Yanbu' al Bahr, Râbigh, Al Qunfudhah, Abha

Tropic of Cancer

Es Sahrâ' esh Sharqîya, Es Sahrâ el Gharbîya (Western Desert), El Wâhât el Khârga, El Wâhât ed Dâkhla, El Wâhât el Farâfra, El Wâhât el Baharîya, Siwa

Es Sahrâ en Nûbîya (Nubian Desert), AN NÎL EL AHMAR, BAHR EL AHMAR, Bîr Sûdân (Port Sudan), Suakin, Berber, Atbara, Dongola, Kerma, Merowe

ESH SHAMÂLÎYA, ESH SHAMÂL, Nukheila (Merga), Gebel Abyad, Gilf el Kebir, Hadabat el Gilf el Kebir

East from Greenwich

∴ UNESCO World Heritage Sites

National Parks

Nature Reserves and
Game Reserves

East from Greenwich

COPYRIGHT PHILIP'S

Projection: *Lambert's Equivalent Azimuthal*

YEMEN

ERITREA

DJIBOUTI

ETHIOPIA

SOMALI REP.

KENYA

UGANDA

CENTRAL AFRICAN REPUBLIC

CONGO

SUDAN

DARFUR

KORDOFAN

Asmera (Asmara)

ADDIS ABEBA (Addis Ababa)

El Khartûm (Khartoum)

Omdurmân

L. Tana

L. Turkana (L. Rudolf)

Blue Nile

White Nile

1:6 400 000

50 0 50 100 150 200 250 300 km
50 0 50 100 150 200 miles

MEDITERRANEAN SEA

GREECE
Dhodhekánisos
Kríti
Iráklion
Réthimnon
Khaniá
Neápolis
Ierápetra

Strait of Sicily

ITALY
CATANIA
Siracusa
Caltanissetta
Ragusa
Agrigento
Sicilia
MALTA
Valetta
Lampedusa
Pantelleria
Linosa

TUNISIA
TUNIS
Bizerte
CONSTANTINE
Sousse
Monastir
Mahdia
Sfax
Gabès
Djerba
Kairouan
Zarzis
Ben Gardane

EL OUED
El Oued
Tozeur
Nefta
Gafsa

ALGERIA
ILLIZI
In Amenas
Ghat

Tarābulus (Tripoli)
Al Khums
Misrātah
Zuwārah
Az Zāwiyah
Gharyān
LEPTIS MAGNA
SABRATHA
OEA
Zliten
Tarhūnah

GHUDĀMIS
Ghudāmis

Tripolitania
Al Hammādah al Hamrā

Surt
Khalij Surt (Gulf of Sidra)

Banghāzī (Benghazi)
Ajdābiyā
Al Marj
Darnah
Tūkrah
Zāwiyat al Baydā'
AL JABAL AL AKHDAR
DARNAH
AL FATIH
Tubruq
TUBRUQ

CYRENAICA
Ajdābiyā

LIBYA
SABHAH
Sabhah
MARZŪQ
Marzūq
AWBĀRĪ
Awbārī
Idehan Awbārī
Idehan Murzūq
Fezzān
Al Kufrah
AL KUFRAH

EGYPT
Sahra
Siwa
Al Jaghbūb

Tropic of Cancer

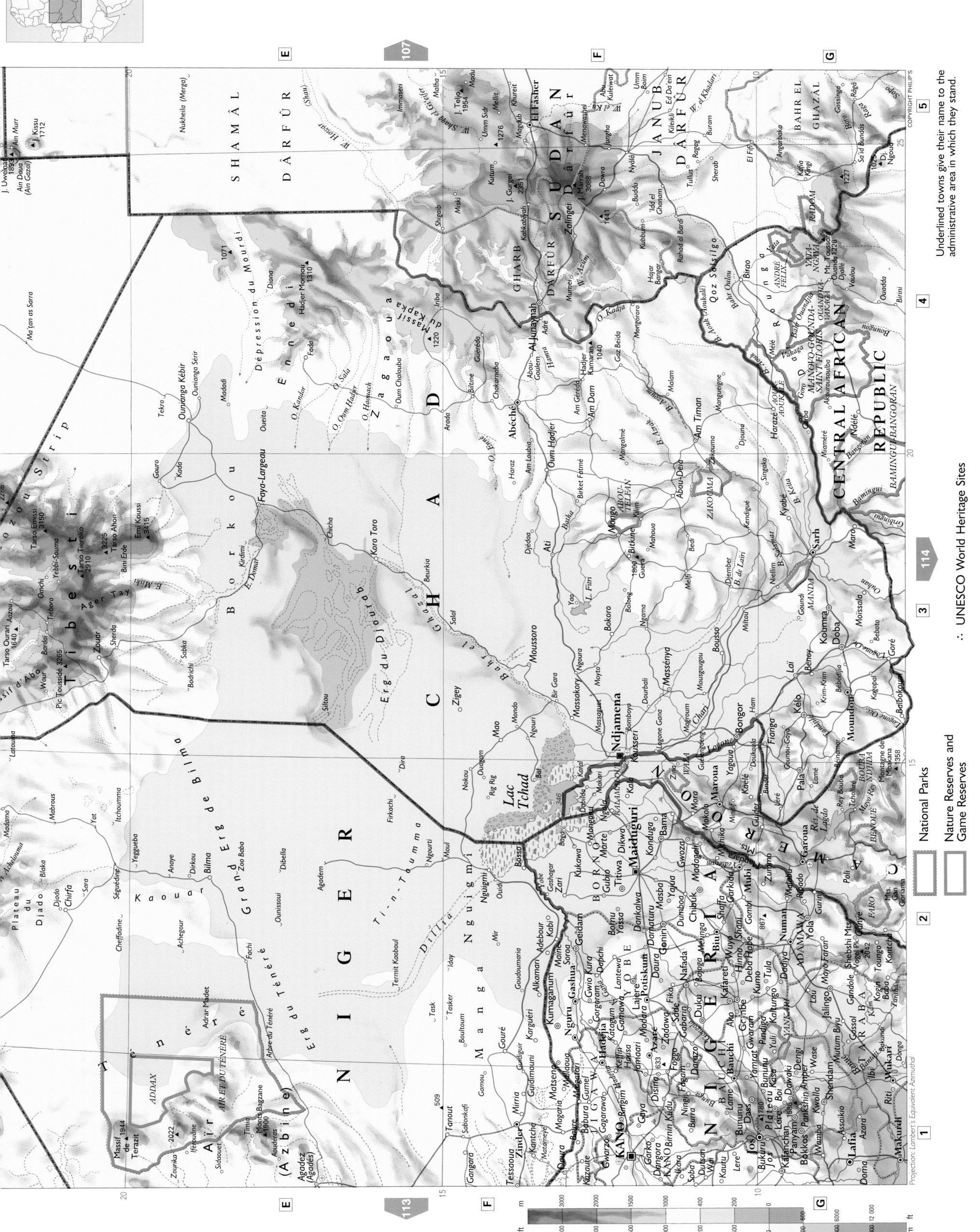

∴ UNESCO World Heritage Sites

Underlined towns give their name to the administrative area in which they stand.

National Parks

Nature Reserves and Game Reserves

COPYRIGHT PHILIP'S

Projection: Lambert's Equivalent Azimuthal

50   0   50   100   150   200   250   300 km
1:6 400 000

50   0   50   100   150   200 miles

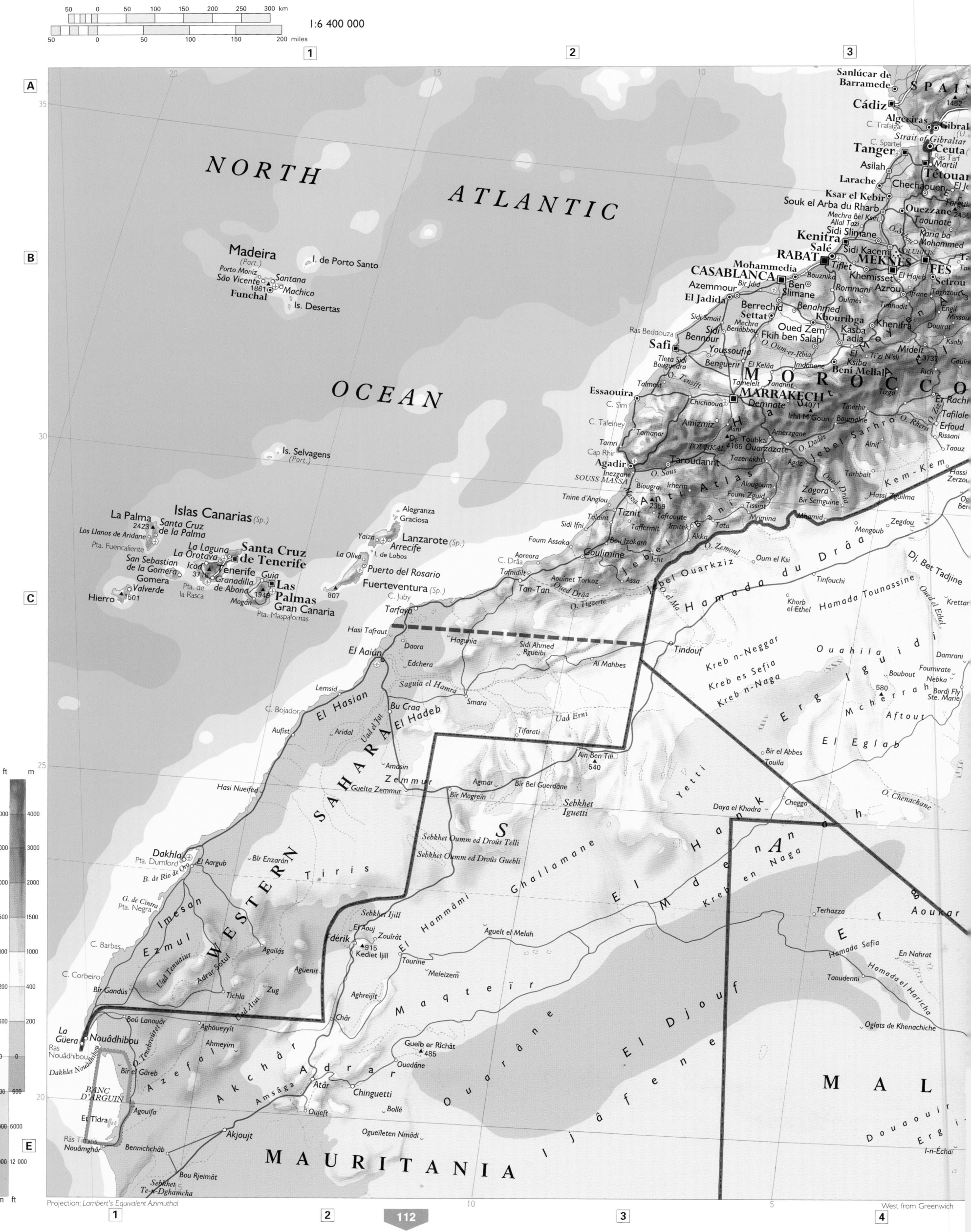

1   **2**   **3**

A

N O R T H   A T L A N T I C

Sanlúcar de
Barramede   **SPAIN**

Cádiz
Algeciras
C. Trafalgar   Gibral
Strait of Gibraltar
C. Spartel
Tanger   **Ceuta**
Ras Tarf
Asilah   Martil
Larache   Chechaouen   El Je
Taounate   Fergui

Ksar el Kebir
Souk el Arba du Rharb   Ouezzane
Mechra Bel Ksiri   Taounate
Sidi Slimane   Karia ba
Kenitra   Allal Tazi   OULUBIS
Salé   Sidi Kacem
RABAT   **MEKNÈS**

B   Mohammedia   **FES**
CASABLANCA   Tiflet   Sefrou
Azemmour   Bouznika   El Hajeb   Ifrane
Ben   Khemisset   Azrou   Taghzout
El Jadida   Slimane   Oulmès   Timhadit
Berrechid   Benahmed   Imouzzer
Safi   Settat   Khouribga   Kenifra   Douirat
Sidi Smail   Mechra   Kasba   Ksabi
Bennour   Benabbou   Fkih ben Salah   Tadla   El
Ras Beddouza   Youssoufia   O. Oumm-er-Rbia   Tizi N'sli
Benguerir   El Kelâa   Midelt
Essaouira   Talmest   Imdahne   Beni Mellal   Rich   3731

Madeira
(Port.)
Porto Moniz   Santana
São Vicente   Machico   Tamelelt   **MOROCCO**
1861   **Funchal**   Chichaoua   Tananni   4071
Is. Desertas   **MARRAKECH**   Tinerhir   El Rachi
C. Sim   Demnate   Boumalne   Tafilale
Amizmiz   Ihil M'Goun   Tizga   Erfoud
C. Tafelney   Asni   Amerzgane   Rissani
Tamri   Di. Toubkal   Ouarzazate   O. Rhers   Taouz
Agadir   TOUBKAL 4165   Tazenakht   Alnif
Cap Rhir   Inezgane   O. Sous   Agd   Kem-Kem
SOUSS MASSA   Biougra   Foum Zguid   Zagora   Hassi Zguilma
Tnine d'Anglou   Tissint   Bir Semguine
C   Tiznit   Talaint   Irherm   2359   Mhamid   Bir
I. de Porto Santo   Taffrout   Tofroute   Bou Izakarn   Zegdou
Sidi Ifni   Tata   Mrimina   Bera
Is. Selvagens   Foum Assaka   O. Zemoul   Oum el Ksi   Zerzou
(Port.)   Aoreora   Akka
C. Drâa   Di. Bet Tadjine
Tafnidilt   Aouinet Torkoz   Assa   Mengoub

Alegranza   Goulimine   Tinfouchi
Graciosa   Tan-Tan   Oued Drâa   Hamada   Hamada Tounassine
Islas Canarias *(Sp.)*   O. Tigzerte   du   Khorb   Ouled
Yaiza   **Lanzarote** *(Sp.)*   Drâa   el Ethel   Krettar
La Palma   Arrecife
2423   Santa Cruz   La Oliva   Kreb n-Neggar   Krettar
Los Llanos de Aridane   de la Palma   I. de Lobos   Hasi Tafraut   Kreb es Sefia   Ouahila
Pta. Fuencaliente   **Santa Cruz**   Daora   Sidi Ahmed   Kreb es Sefia   Damrani
La Laguna   **de Tenerife**   Hagunia   Rgueibi   Kreb-Naga   Fourate
La Orotava   Guia   Edchera   Tindouf   Boubout   Nebka
San Sebastian   Icod   **Tenerife**   **El Aaiún**   Al Mahbes   Bir el Abbes   580   Bordj Fly
de la Gomera   3718   Granadilla   Saguia el Hamra   Mcherrah   Ste. Marie
Gomera   de Abona   1949   Lemsid   Smara   Aftout
Valverde   Puerto del Rosario   Bu Craa   Uad Erni   Bir el Abbes
Hierro   1501   807   **Las Palmas**   El Hasian   El Hadeb   Aïn Ben Tili
Mogán   **Gran Canaria**   C. Bojador   Aufist   Tifarati   540   Touila
Pta. Maspalomas   C. Juby   Aridal   Amosin   O. Chenachane
Tarfaya   Zemmur   Agmar   Bîr Bel Guerdâne   El Eglab

Hasi Nueifed   Guelta Zemmur   Bîr Mogrein   Sebkhet
Iguetti   Daya el Khadra   Chegga

25   Sebkhet Oumm ed Droûs Telli   S   Terhazza
Sebkhet Oumm ed Droûs Guebli

Dakhla   El Aargub   Bîr Enzarân   Ghallamane
Pta. Durnford   El Hammâmi   Hamada Safia
B. de Río de Oro   Sebkhet Ijill   En Nahrat
G. de Cintra   Fdérik   Zouîrat   Aguelt el Melah   Hamada el Haricha
Pta. Negra   Agailás   915   Taoudenni
C. Barbas   Kediet Ijill   Tourine   Maqteïr
C. Corbeiro   Ag
Aguenit   Meleizem   Oglats de Khenachiche
La Güera   Bîr Gandús   Tichla   Zug   Aghreijît   Ouarâne
Nouâdhibou   Boû Lanoûar   Adrar Souf   Châr   Guelb er Rîchât   El Djouf
Ras   Aghoueyyit   Uad Atui   485
Nouâdhibou   Ahmeyim   Ouadâne
Dakhlet Nouâdhibou   Bîr el Gâreb   Chinguetti   **MAL**
Agouifa   Atâr
Et Tîdra   Oujeft   Bollé
BANC   Ogueileten Nmâdi   Douaouir
D'ARGUIN   Akjoujt   Ergi
Ràs Timiris   Bennichchâb
Nouâmghâr   Bou Rjeimât   I-n-Échaï
Sebkhet
Te-n-Dghamcha   **MAURITANIA**

Projection: Lambert's Equivalent Azimuthal

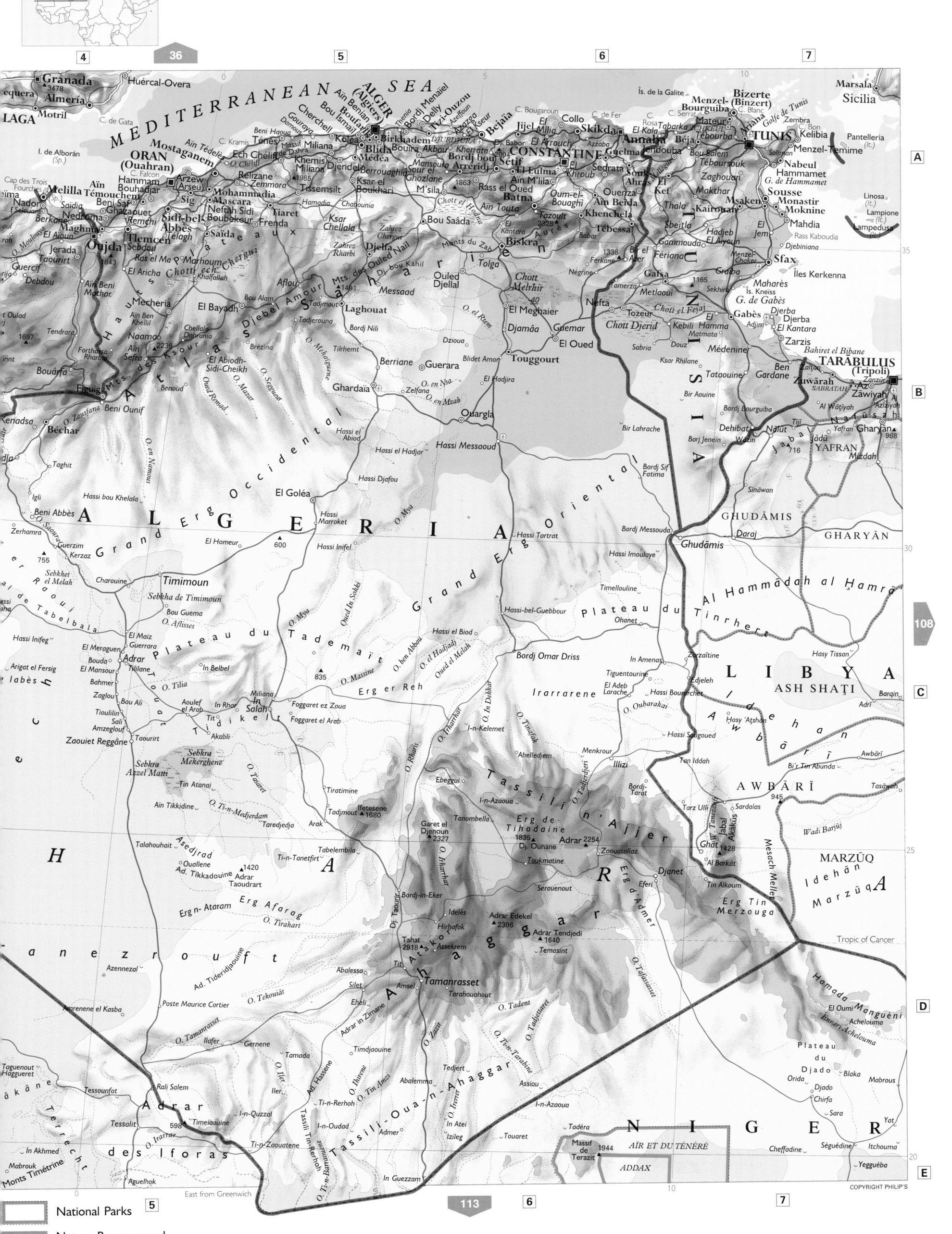

MEDITERRANEAN SEA

Granada
Almería
Motril
I. de Alborán (Sp.)
ORAN (Ouahran)
Mostaganem
Melilla
Nador
Oujda
Tlemcen
Béchar

ALGER (Algiers)
Blida
Médéa
Tissemsilt
Relizane
Mascara
Saïda
Laghouat
Ghardaïa
Ouargla
El Goléa
Timimoun

CONSTANTINE
Sétif
Batna
Biskra
Touggourt
El Oued
Hassi Messaoud

TUNIS
Bizerte (Binzert)
Sousse
Sfax
Gabès
Médenine
TARABULUS (Tripoli)
Zuwārah
Zāwiyah

Marsala
Sicilia
Pantelleria (It.)
Lampedusa

ALGERIA
LIBYA

Grand Erg Occidental
Grand Erg Oriental
Plateau du Tademaït
Plateau du Tinrhert
Al Hammādah al Ḥamrā
GHUDĀMIS
GHARYĀN

Ghudāmis
In Salah
Adrar
Reggane

Tamanrasset
Tahat 2918
Ahaggar
Tassili n'Ajjer
Djanet
Ghāt
MARZŪQ
AWBĀRĪ
ASH SHAŢI

Tropic of Cancer

Adrar des Iforas
Tessalit

NIGER
AĪR ET du TÉNÉRÉ
ADDAX
Plateau du Djado

East from Greenwich

COPYRIGHT PHILIP'S

National Parks

Nature Reserves and Game Reserves

∴ UNESCO World Heritage Sites

1:6 400 000

Projection : Lambert's Equivalent Azimuthal

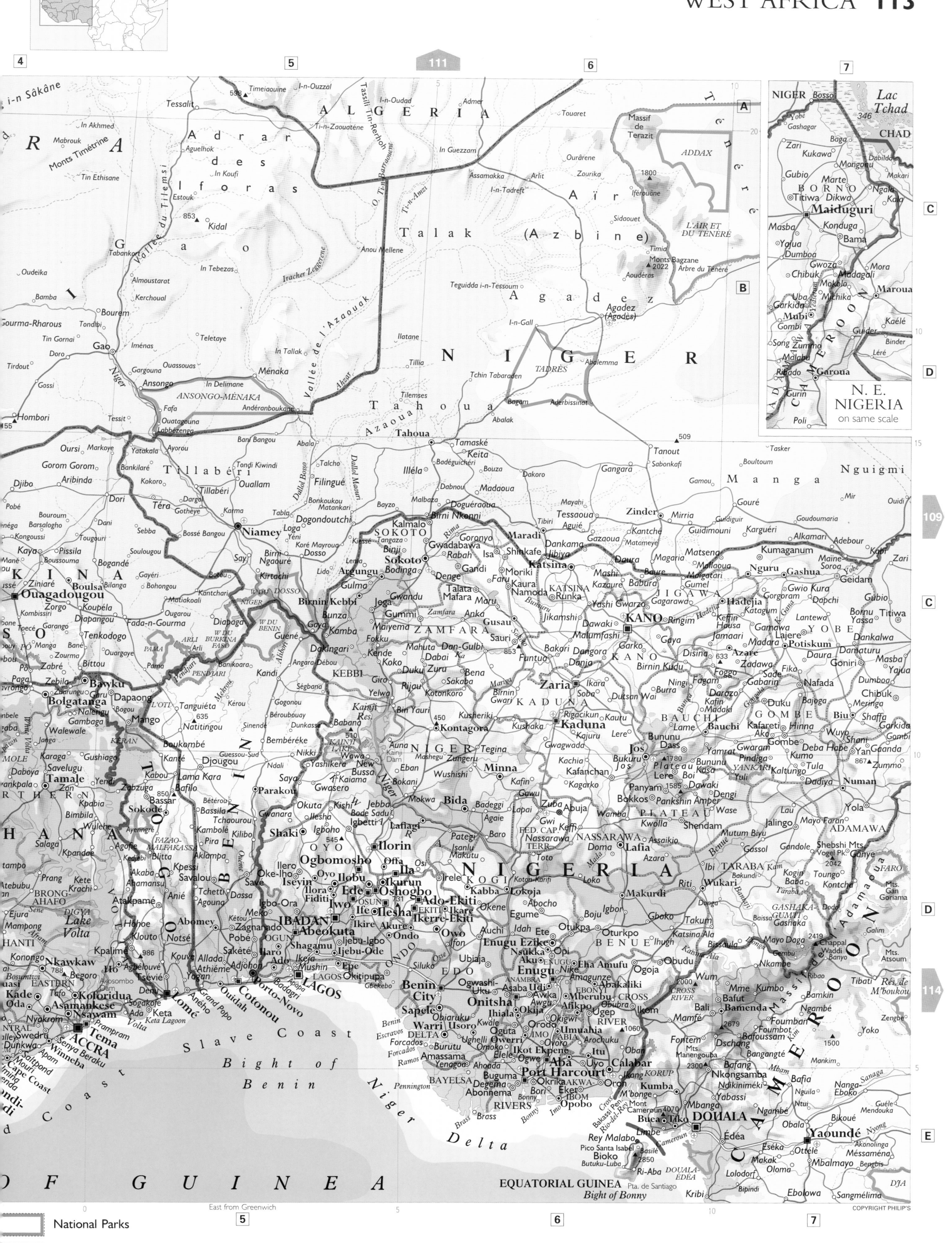

N. E.
NIGERIA
on same scale

National Parks

Nature Reserves and
Game Reserves

∴ UNESCO World Heritage Sites

East from Greenwich

COPYRIGHT PHILIP'S

1:6 400 000

50 0 50 100 150 200 250 300 km

50 0 50 100 150 200 miles

SUDAN

CHAD

CENTRAL AFRICAN REPUBLIC

NIGERIA

CAMEROON

EQUATORIAL GUINEA

GABON

CONGO

DEM. REP. OF THE CONGO

BANGUI

DOUALA

Yaoundé

Libreville

Port-Gentil

Kisangani

Bata

Malabo

Bioko

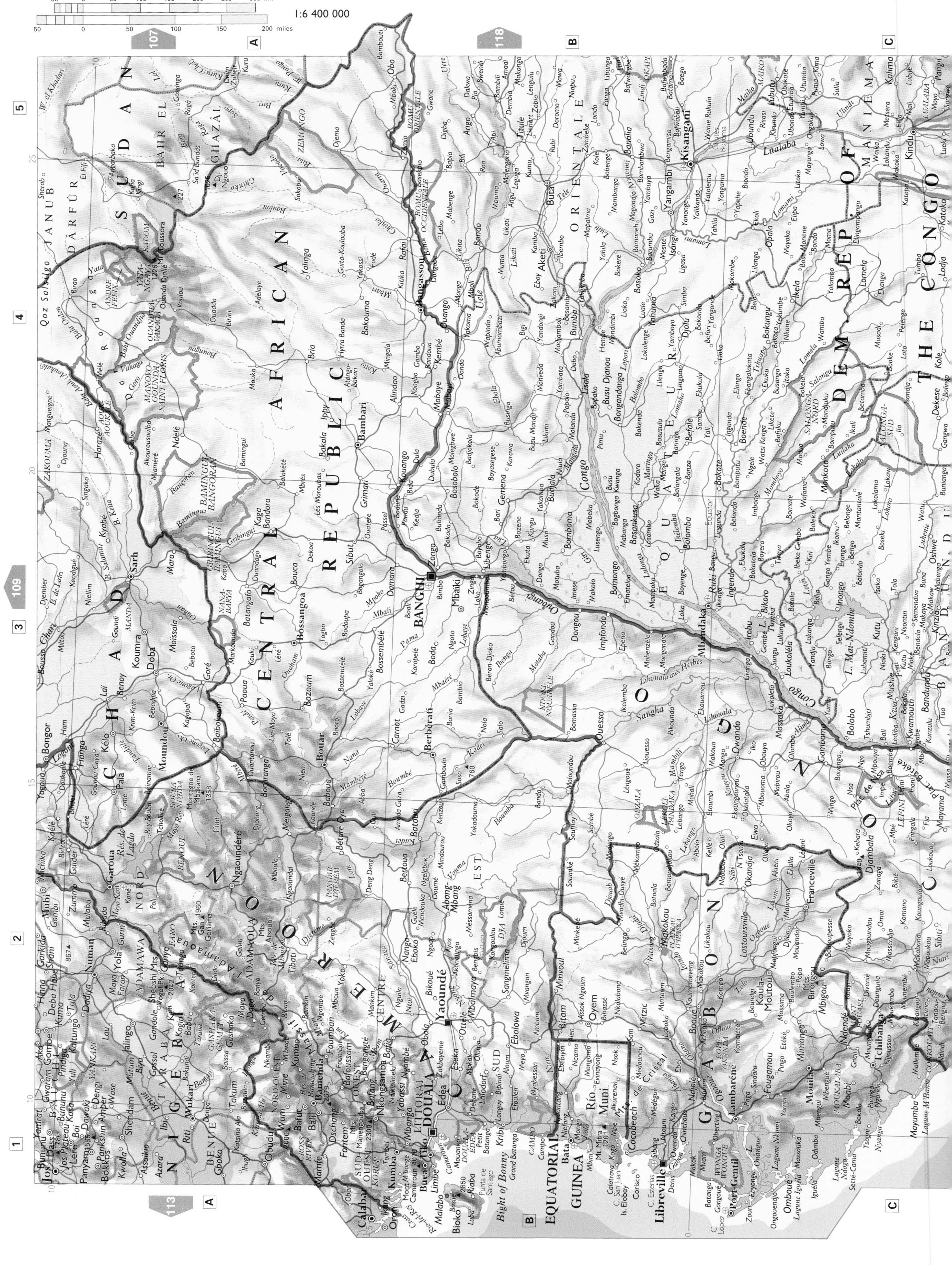

SÃO TOMÉ
AND PRÍNCIPE
on same scale

Príncipe
948 ▲ Caroço
Santo
António

I. Pedras Tinhosas

São Tomé

Pico de
São Tomé
2024 ▲
São Tomé

Gago Coutinho

Porto Alegre

National Parks

Nature Reserves and
Game Reserves

∴ UNESCO World Heritage Sites

COPYRIGHT PHILIP'S

Projection: Lambert's Equivalent Azimuthal

115

1　　**2**　　**3**

Ponta
Albina
Tombua　NAMIBE

Pta. da
Marca

NAMIBE
IONA

C U N E N E　　M U P A N E

C U A N D O   C U B A N G O

LONGA-MAVINGA
LUIANA

W E S T E R N

S O U T H
ZAMBIA

L U E N G U É

A N G O L A

CAPRIVI   Strip

Livingstone
Victoria Falls

Oshakati
Ondangwa
O v a m b o l a n d

CHOBE
Okavango
Delta

HWANGE

ETOSHA
Etosha Pan

KAUDOM

MOREMI
NXAI PAN

MAKGADIKGADI
Makgadikgadi
Salt Pans

B

Tsumeb
Grootfontein

SKELETON
COAST

Otjiwarongo

WATERBERG
PLATEAU

Kaukauveld
Sandveld

Maun
Ngami
Depression

N A M I B I A

Damaraland

C E N T R A L
K A L A H A R I

Serowe
Palapye

BRANDBERG

Omaruru

Windhoek

B O T S W A N A

Mahalapye

C

Swakopmund

Rehoboth

Mochudi

Walvis Bay

Tropic of Capricorn

Molepolole
Gaborone
Ramotswa

K a l a h a r i

Kanye
Lobatse

PILANESBERG

NAMIB-
NAUKLUFT

Mariental
N a m a l a n d

GEMSBOK
KGALAGADI
TRANSFRONTIER

MABUASEHUBE

N O R T H - W E S T

D

Keetmanshoop

KALAHARI
GEMSBOK

Lüderitz

A T L A N T I C

AI-AIS AND FISH
RIVER CANYON

AUGRABIES
FALLS

Kimberley

F R E E
S T A T E

Welkom

Oranjemund
Alexander Bay

RICHTERSVELD

Upington

Bloemfontein

Port Nolloth

O C E A N

S O U T H   A F R I C A

Springbok
Namaqualand

NORTHERN   CAPE

De Aar

E A S T E R N

E

Queenstown

Great
Karoo

C A P E

Vredenburg
Saldanha

Beaufort
West

Oudtshoorn

Port Alfred

George

Uitenhage

CAPE TOWN

W E S T E R N   C A P E

PORT ELIZABETH

CAPE PENINSULA
C. of Good Hope
C. Agulhas

1　　**2**　　**3**

National Parks

Nature Reserves and
Game Reserves   ∴ UNESCO World Heritage Sites

MADAGASCAR

on same scale

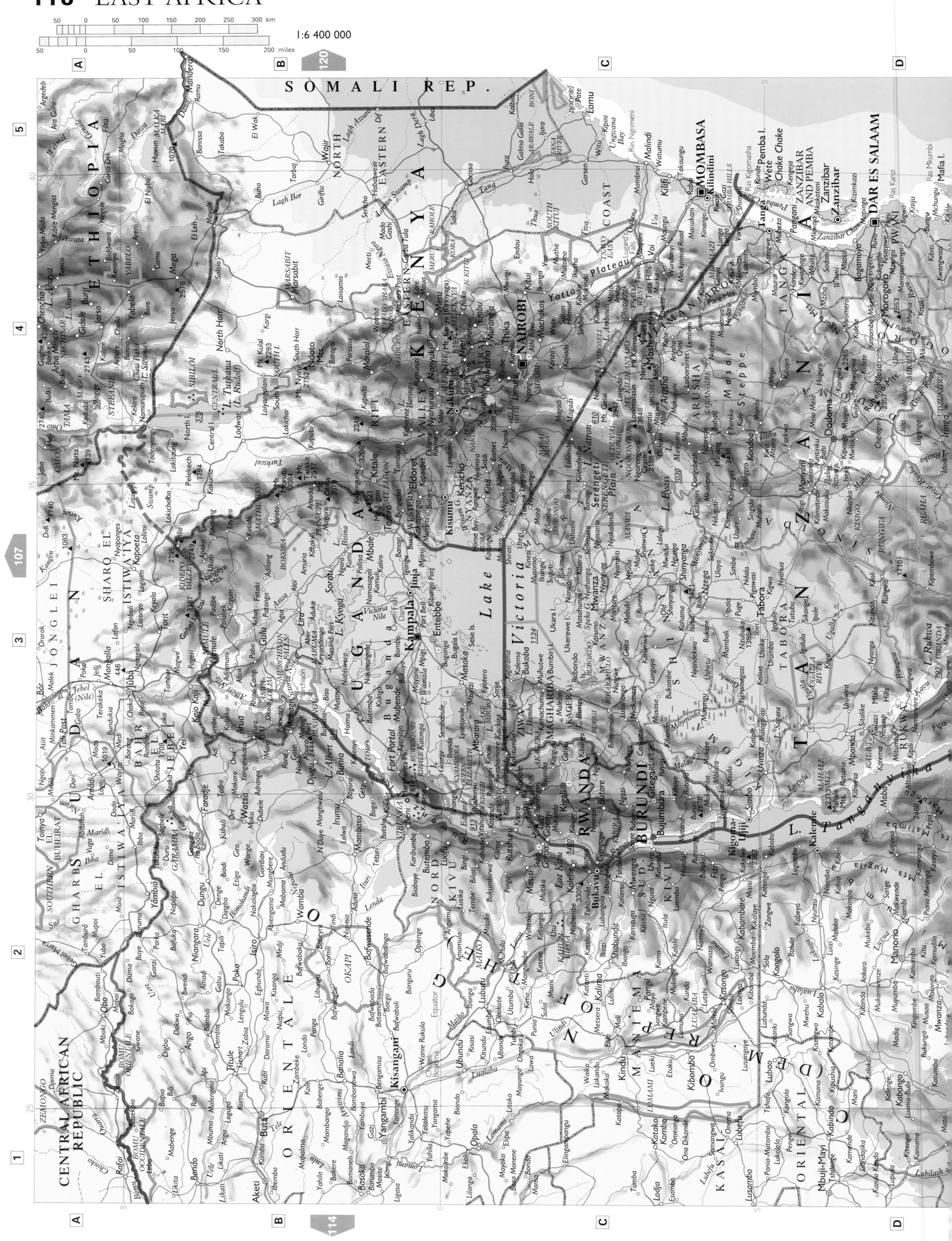

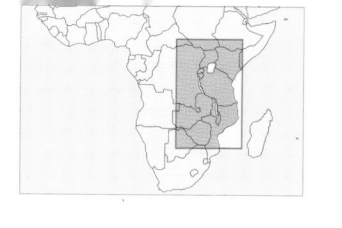

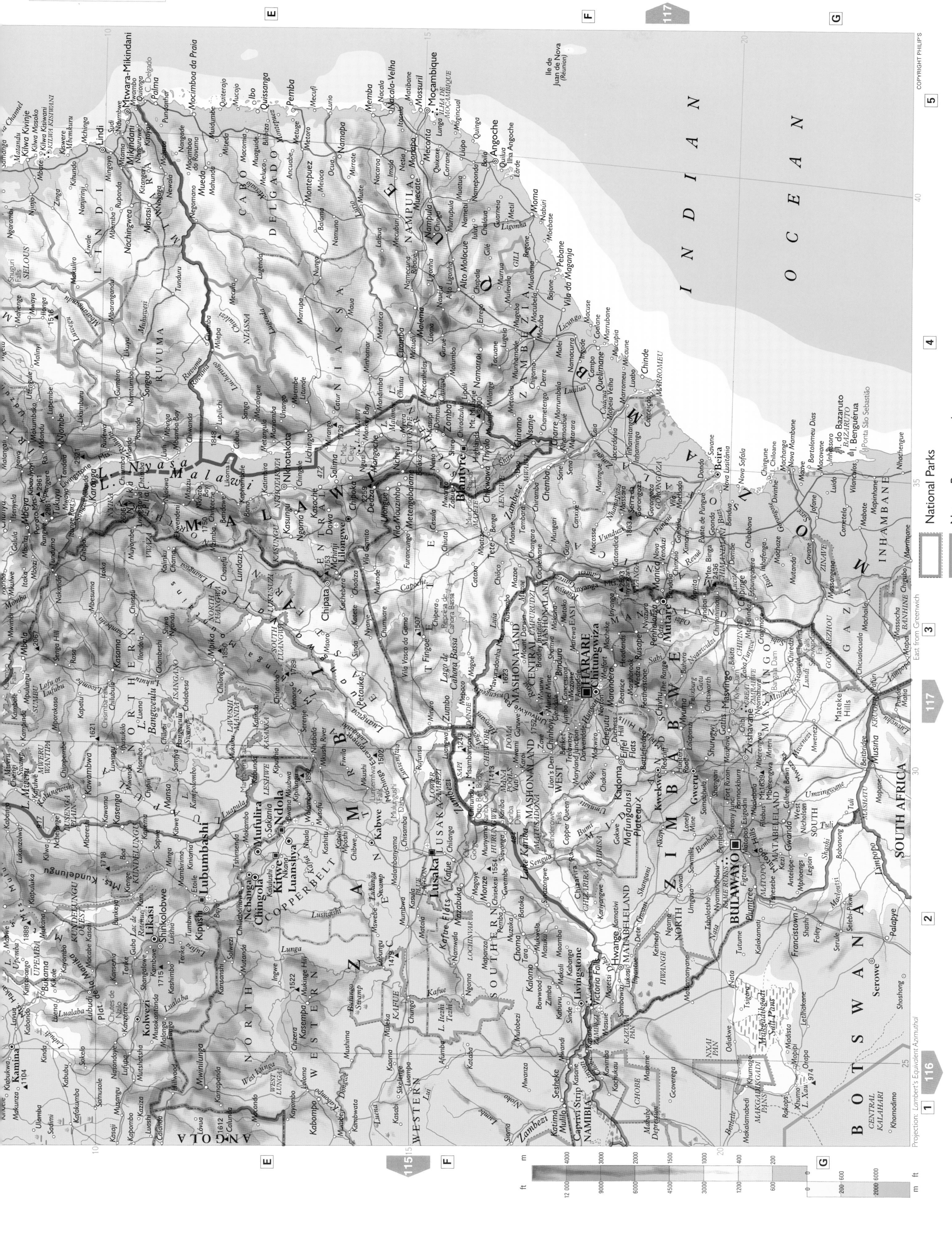

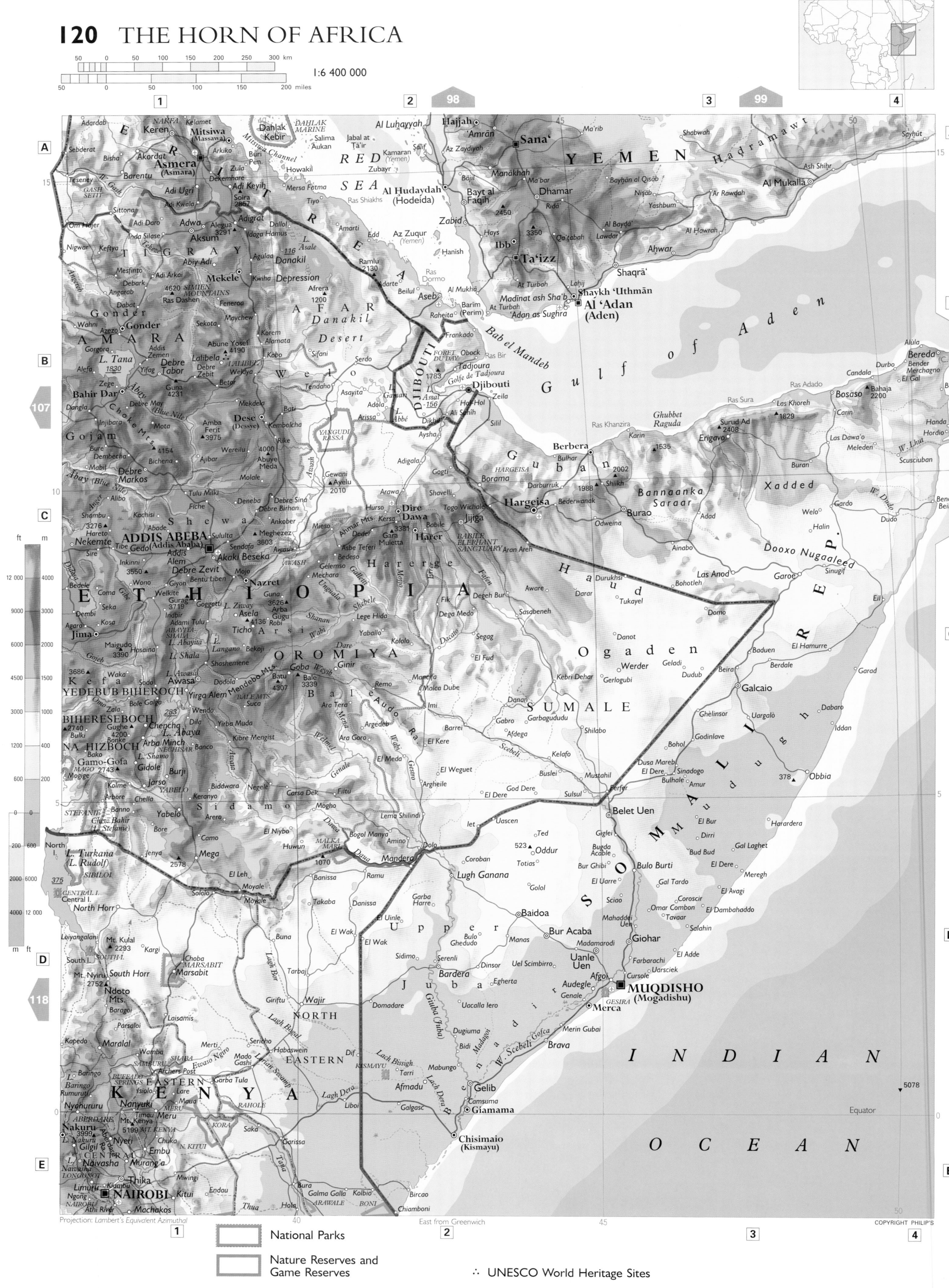

1:6 400 000

National Parks

Nature Reserves and
Game Reserves

◇ UNESCO World Heritage Sites

Projection: Lambert's Equivalent Azimuthal

East from Greenwich

COPYRIGHT PHILIP'S

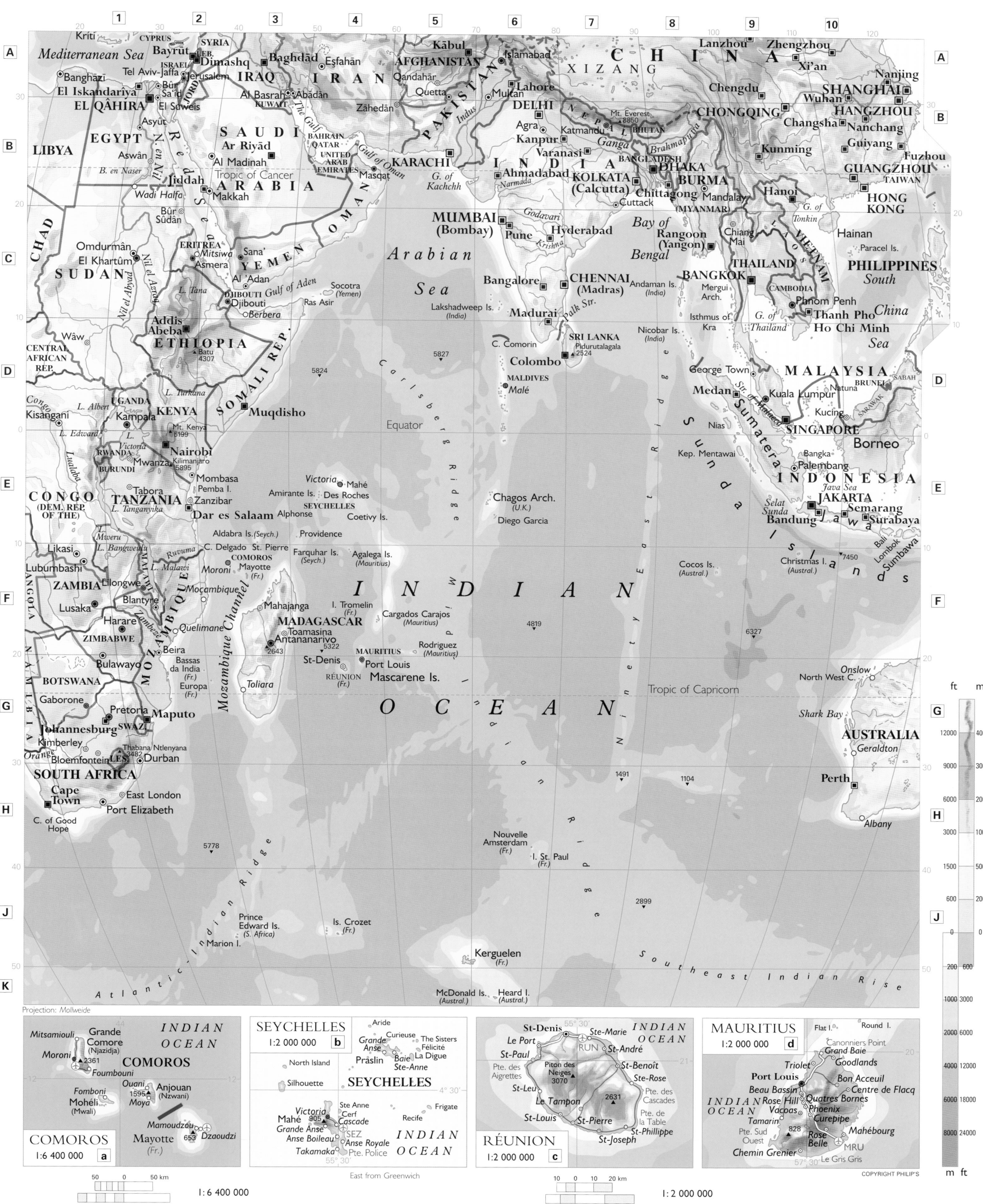

1:16 000 000

Projection: *Lambert's Equivalent Azimuthal*

East from Greenwich

1:6 400 000

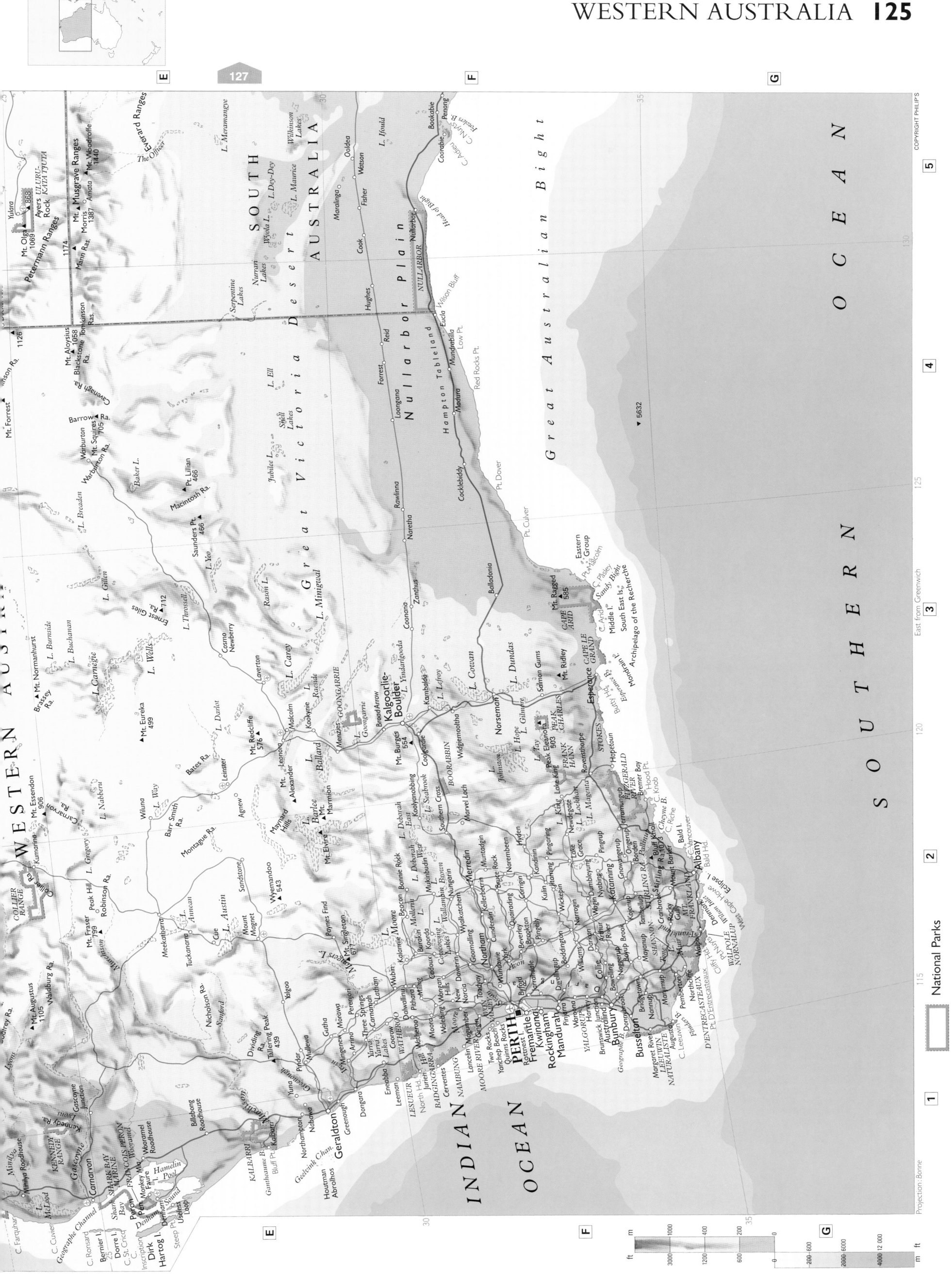

1:6 400 000

50 0 50 100 150 200 250 300 km
50 0 50 100 150 200 miles

WHITSUNDAY ISLANDS
1:2 000 000

10 0 10 20 30 40 50 60 km
10 0 10 20 30 40 miles

CORAL SEA

GLOUCESTER I.
Gloucester I.
Hayman I.
Hook I.
WHITSUNDAY
Whitsunday I.
ISLANDS
Long I.
Whitsunday Long Pass.
Lindeman I.
Hamilton I.
Shaw I.
Bowen
C. Conway
Connemara
Foxdale
Airlie Beach
CONWAY
Proserpine
Repulse Bay
Midge Point
Mt. McGuire
820
738▲ Mt. McGuire
Kelsey Creek
SOUTH CUMBERLAND Is.
Seaforth
Kuttabul
Farleigh
Mackay
Bloomsbury
Clarke
QUEENSLAND
Yalboroo
EUNGELLA
Kungurri
Mirani
Marian
Walkerston
Eton
Mt. Dalrymple
1259 ▲
Netherdale
Broken River Ra.
Gargett
Calen

CUMBERLAND
Carlisle I.
Brampton I.
St. Bees I.
Cumberland Islands
Hillsborough Channel
Bucasia
Slade Pt.

CORAL SEA

Magdelaine Cays
Coringa Is.
Lihou Reefs and Cays
Diamond Is.
Tregrosse Is.
Abington Reef
Herald Cays
Holmes Reefs
Flinders Reefs
Osprey Reef
Bougainville Reef

Great Barrier Reef

GREAT BARRIER REEF (FAR NORTH)
GREAT BARRIER REEF (CAIRNS)
GREAT BARRIER REEF (CENTRAL)
GREAT BARRIER REEF (CAPRICORN)

Capricorn Channel
Swain Reefs
Lady Elliott I.
Capricorn Group
Curtis I.
Gladstone
Port Curtis
Rockhampton
C. Clinton
C. Manifold
BYFIELD
Water Park Pt.
Townshend I.
Broad Sd.
Percy Is.
Northumberland Islands
Mt. Arthur Pt.
Mackay
Cumberland Islands
Seaforth
Whitsunday I.
Hook I.
Gloucester I.
Bowen
Bowling Green Bay
Townsville
Cleveland
Great Palm I.
Halifax Bay
Ingham
Hinchinbrook I.
HINCHINBROOK I.
Lucinda
Cardwell
Tully
Mission Beach
Dunk I.
Cairns
GREAT BARRIER REEF
C. Tribulation
Port Douglas
Mossman
Daintree
Cooktown
Cape Flattery
Lizard I.
Howick Group
Bedford
Cape Melville
Princess Charlotte Bay
C. Direction

CORAL SEA

Gulf of Carpentaria

York
Thursday I.
C. York
Prince of Wales I.
Horn I.
Turtle Head I.
Sharp Pt.
Shelburne Bay
Temple B.
Weymouth
Cullen Pt.
Port Musgrave
Mapoon
Weipa
Duifken Pt.
Albatross Bay
Aurukun
Archer River
Pera Hd.
C. Keer-Weer
Edward River

Cape York Peninsula
Great Dividing Range
IRON RANGE
MUNGKAN KANDJU

Mornington I.
C. Van Diemen
Wellesley Is.
Bentinck I.
Burketown
Karumba
Normanton
Croydon
Georgetown
Gilbert River
Chillagoe
Mareeba
Atherton
Ravenshoe
Herberton
Innisfail
Babinda
Gordonvale

Barkly Tableland

NORTHERN TERRITORY
QUEENSLAND

Arnhem Land
Goulburn Is.
Warruwi
C. Wessel
Wessel Is.
Elcho I.
Nhulunbuy
Yirrkala
C. Arnhem
Groote Eylandt
Umbakumba
Angurugu
C. Shield
Caledon Bay
Blue Mud Bay
C. Grey
Woodah I.
Bickerton I.
C. Beatrice
Maria I.
Sir Edward Pellew Group
Vanderlin I.
Port McArthur
Borroloola
Limmen Bight
Port Roper
McArthur River
Robinson
Calvert
Nicholson
Gregory Downs

Camooweal
Mount Isa
Cloncurry
Julia Creek
Richmond
Hughenden
Winton
Boulia
Bedourie
Birdsville

SIMPSON DESERT

Daly Waters
Newcastle Waters
Elliott
Dunmarra
Renner Springs
Tennant Creek
Barkly Roadhouse
Wauchope
Barrow Creek
Ti Tree
Alice Springs
MacDonnell Ranges
1128
Tropic of Capricorn
Finke
Santa Teresa
Erldunda

Diamantina
Windorah
Thomson
Longreach
Blackall
Barcaldine
Jericho
Emerald
Blackwater
Dawson Range
Biloela
Monto
Gympie
Dalby
Roma
Charleville
Quilpie
Thargomindah

TASMAN SEA

NEW SOUTH WALES

SOUTH AUSTRALIA

QUEENSLAND

VICTORIA

TASMANIA

BRISBANE
SYDNEY
CANBERRA
MELBOURNE
ADELAIDE
Newcastle
Wollongong
Gold Coast
Tweed Heads

Bass Strait
King Island
Flinders Island
Furneaux Group
Cape Barren I.
Bass Strait

National Parks

on same scale

LAKE EYRE
Lake Torrens
Lake Gairdner
Lake Frome

Darling Range
Grey Range
Barrier Range
Flinders Ranges

Broken Hill

Hobart
Launceston
Devonport

East from Greenwich

Projection: Bonne

COPYRIGHT PHILIP'S

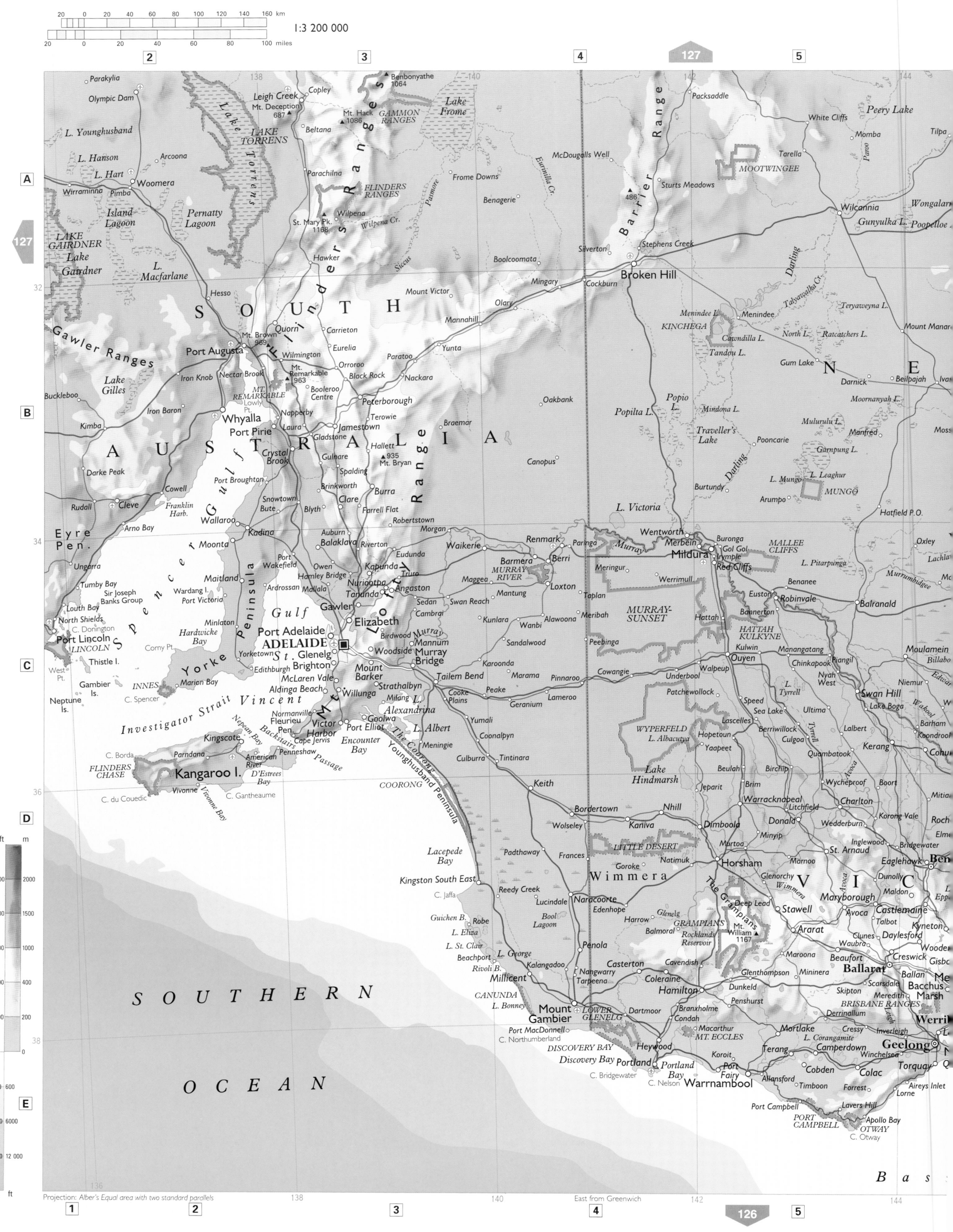

1:3 200 000

Projection: Alber's Equal area with two standard parallels

East from Greenwich

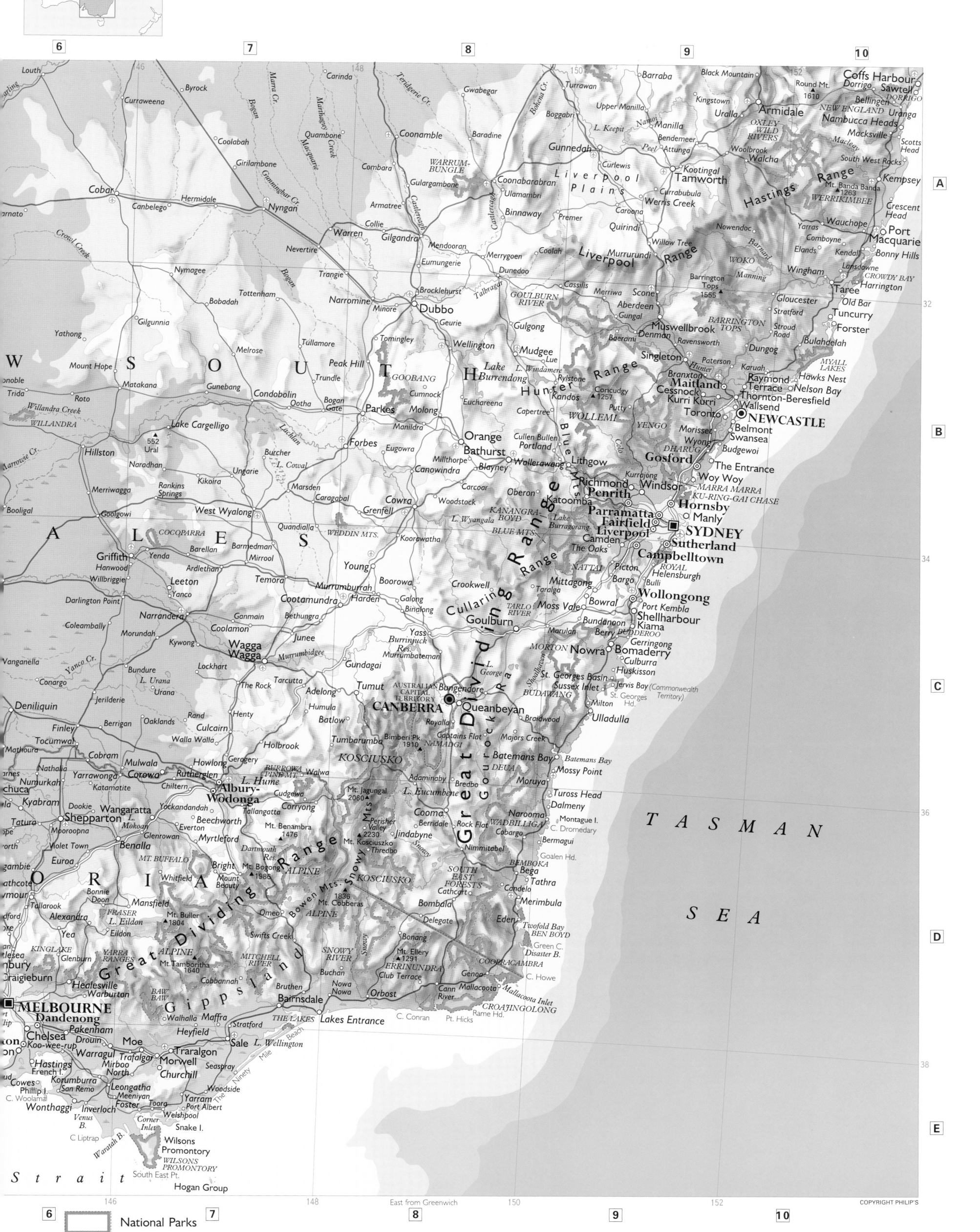

National Parks

1:2 800 000

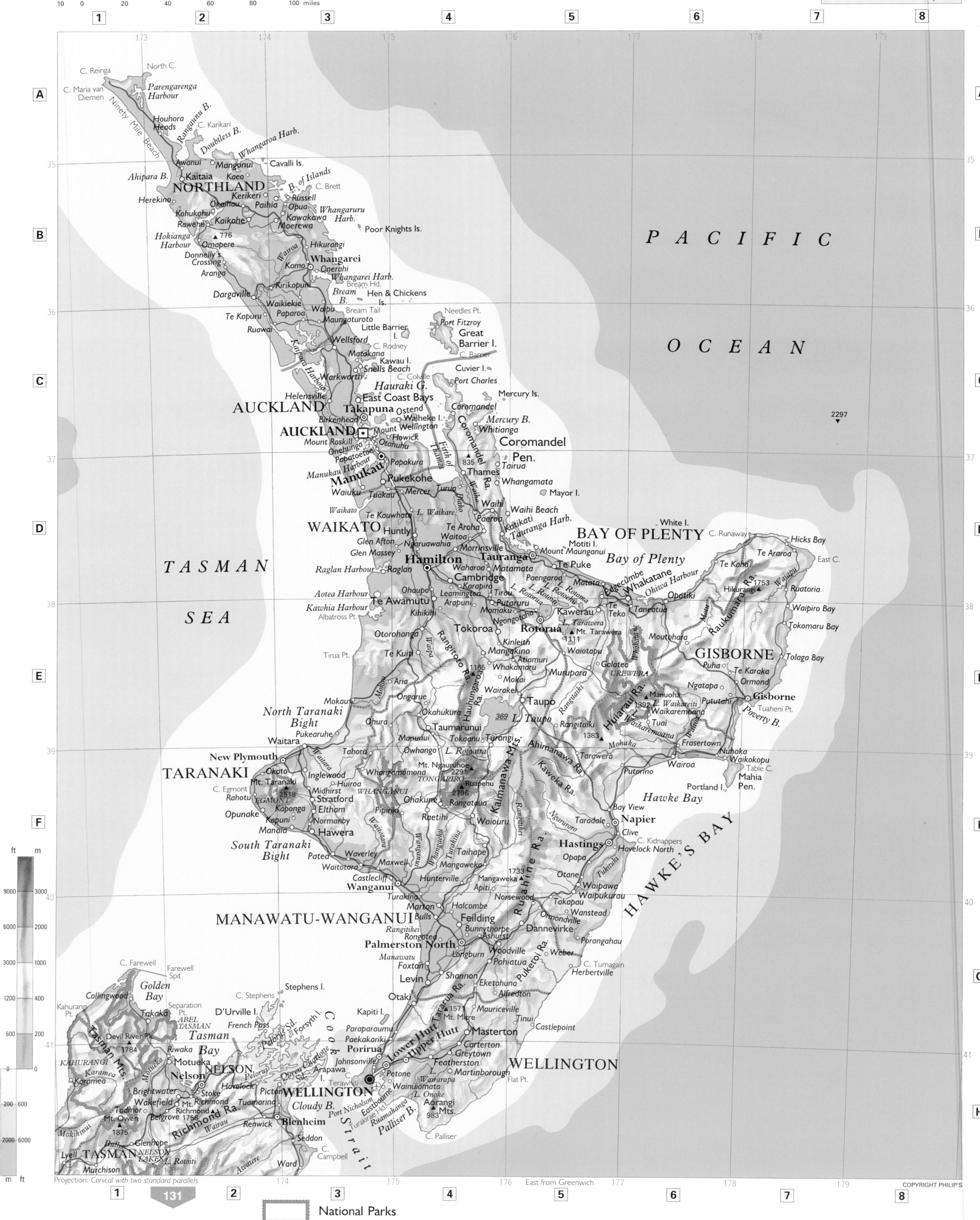

PACIFIC

OCEAN

TASMAN

SEA

NORTHLAND

C. Reinga
North C.
C. Maria van Diemen
Parengarenga Harbour
Houhora Heads
Rangaunu B.
Awanui
C. Karikari
Doubless B.
Mangonui
Kaeo
Cavalli Is.
Kaitaia
Whangaroa Harb.
Ahipara B.
Kerikeri
Paihia
B. of Islands
Herekino
Okaihau
Russell
C. Brett
Kohukohu
Opua
Rawene
Kawakawa
Whangaruru Harb.
Kaikohe
Moerewa
Hokianga Harbour
Omapere
776
Poor Knights Is.
Donnelly's Crossing
Kamo
Hikurangi
Aranga
Onerahi
Whangarei
Dargaville
Kirikopuni
Whangarei Harb.
Waikiekie
Bream Hd.
Hen & Chickens Is.
Te Kopuru
Wapu
Bream B.
Paparoa
Maungaturoto
Ruawai
Bream Tail
Needles Pt.
Wellsford
Little Barrier I.
Port Fitzroy
Great Barrier I.
Matakana
C. Rodney
Kawau I.
C. Barrier
Warkworth
Snells Beach
Cuvier I.
Helensville
Hauraki G.
C. Colville
Port Charles
AUCKLAND
East Coast Bays
Coromandel
Mercury Is.
Takapuna
Ostend
Waiheke I.
Mercury B.
Birkenhead
Mount Wellington
Whitianga
AUCKLAND
Howick
Coromandel Pen.
Coromandel
Mount Roskill
Otahuhu
835
Onehunga
Papatoetoe
Tairua
Manukau Harbour
Papakura
Thames
Manukau
Pukekohe
Whangamata
Waiuku
Tuakau
Mercer
Turua
Mayor I.
Waikato
Te Kauwhata
L. Waikare
Waihi
Waihi Beach

WAIKATO
Huntly
Te Aroha
Katikati
Tauranga Harb.
Glen Afton
Waitoa
Paeroa
BAY OF PLENTY
White I.
C. Runaway
Glen Massey
Ngaruawahia
Morrinsville
Motiti I.
Hicks Bay
Raglan Harbour
Hamilton
Matamata
Mount Maunganui
Te Araroa
Raglan
Tauranga
Te Kaha
East C.
Aotea Harbour
Cambridge
Te Puke
Bay of Plenty
Edgecumbe
1753
Kawhia Harbour
Ohaupo
Karapiro
Paengaroa
Matata
Whakatane
Hikurangi Ra.
Ruatoria
Albatross Pt.
Te Awamutu
Leamington
Tirau
Putaruru
Rotoehu
Ohiwa Harbour
Opotiki
Ngongotaha
Mamaku
Kawerau
Te Teko
Taneatua
Waipiro Bay
Kihikihi
Arapuni
L. Rotorua
Moutohora
Tokomaru Bay
Otorohanga
Rotorua
Te Kuiti
Tokoroa
Mt. Tarawera
L. Tarawera
GISBORNE
Puha
Tolaga Bay
Tirua Pt.
Kinleith
1111
Waiotapu
UREWERA
Te Karaka
Mangakino
Galatea
Atiamuri
Murupara
Ngatapa
Ormond
Mokau
Aria
Whakamaru
Waikaremoana
Pututahi
Gisborne
Ongarue
Mokai
1392
L. Waikaremoana
Waikaremoana
Mokau
Wairake
Rangitaiki
Mamuoha
Tuai
Tuaheni Pt.
Taupo
369
Poverty B.
North Taranaki Bight
Okahukura
Taumarunui
L. Taupo
1383
Waitara
Pukearuhe
Ohura
Manunui
Tokaanu
Turangi
Ahimanawa Ra.
New Plymouth
Okato
Tahora
Owhango
L. Rotoaira
Tarawera
Mohaka
Frasertown
Putorino
Wairoa
TARANAKI
Mt. Taranaki
Inglewood
Whangamomona
Mt. Ngauruhoe
Kaweka Ra.
Nuhaka
Waikokopu
C. Egmont
2518
Huiroa
2291
TONGARIRO
Table C.
Rahotu
Midhirst
Stratford
Ruapehu
Mahia Pen.
Kaponga
Eltham
2796
WHANGANUI
Rangataua
Kaimanawa Mts.
Portland I.
Opunake
Kapuni
Normanby
Ohakune
Bay View
Hawke Bay
Manaia
Hawera
Raetihi
Waiouru
Taradale
South Taranaki Bight
Patea
Waverley
Maxwell
Pipiriki
1733
Napier
Clive
C. Kidnappers
Waitotara
Mangaweka
Hastings
Havelock North
Castlecliff
Hunterville
Mangawera
Opapa
Wanganui
Turakina
Apiti
Otane
Norsewood
Waipawa
HAWKE'S BAY
Marton
Halcombe
Ormondville
Takapau
Waipukurau
Bulls
Feilding
Wanstead
MANAWATU-WANGANUI
Rangitikei
Bunnythorpe
Dannevirke
Porangahau
Rongotea
Ashurst
Palmerston North
Woodville
Weber
Foxton
Longburn
Pahiatua
C. Turnagain
Manawatu
Shannon
Herbertville
Levin
Eketahuna
Alfredton
Otaki
Mauriceville
C. Stephens
Stephens I.
Kapiti I.
1571
Tinui
Castlepoint
Paraparaumu
Mt. Mitre
Masterton
Paekakariki
Carterton
Porirua
Greytown
Lower Hutt
Upper Hutt
Featherston
Johnsonville
Martinborough
WELLINGTON
Petone
Wainuiomata
Flat Pt.
WELLINGTON
Eastbourne
L. Onoke
Wairarapa
Palliser B.
C. Palliser

TASMAN
C. Farewell
Farewell Spit
Golden Bay
Collingwood
Separation Pt.
D'Urville I.
French Pass
Kahurangi Pt.
Takaka
ABEL TASMAN
Tasman
Devil River Pk.
1784
Riwaka
Pelorus Sd.
Queen Charlotte Sd.
KAHURANGI Mts.
Motueka
Forsyth I.
Karamea
NELSON
Havelock
Picton
Cook Strait
Brightwater
Stoke
Terawhiti
Wakefield
Nelson
Richmond
Arapawa I.
Tadmor
Richmond
1756
Port Nicholson
Mt. Owen
Belgrove
Richmond Ra.
Cloudy B.
Aorangi Mts.
1875
Blenheim
983
Glenhope
Wairau
Renwick
Turakirae Hd.
Lyell
TASMAN
NELSON LAKES
Seddon
Murchison
L. Rotoiti
Awatere
Ward
C. Campbell

National Parks

Projection: Conical with two standard parallels

East from Greenwich

COPYRIGHT PHILIP'S

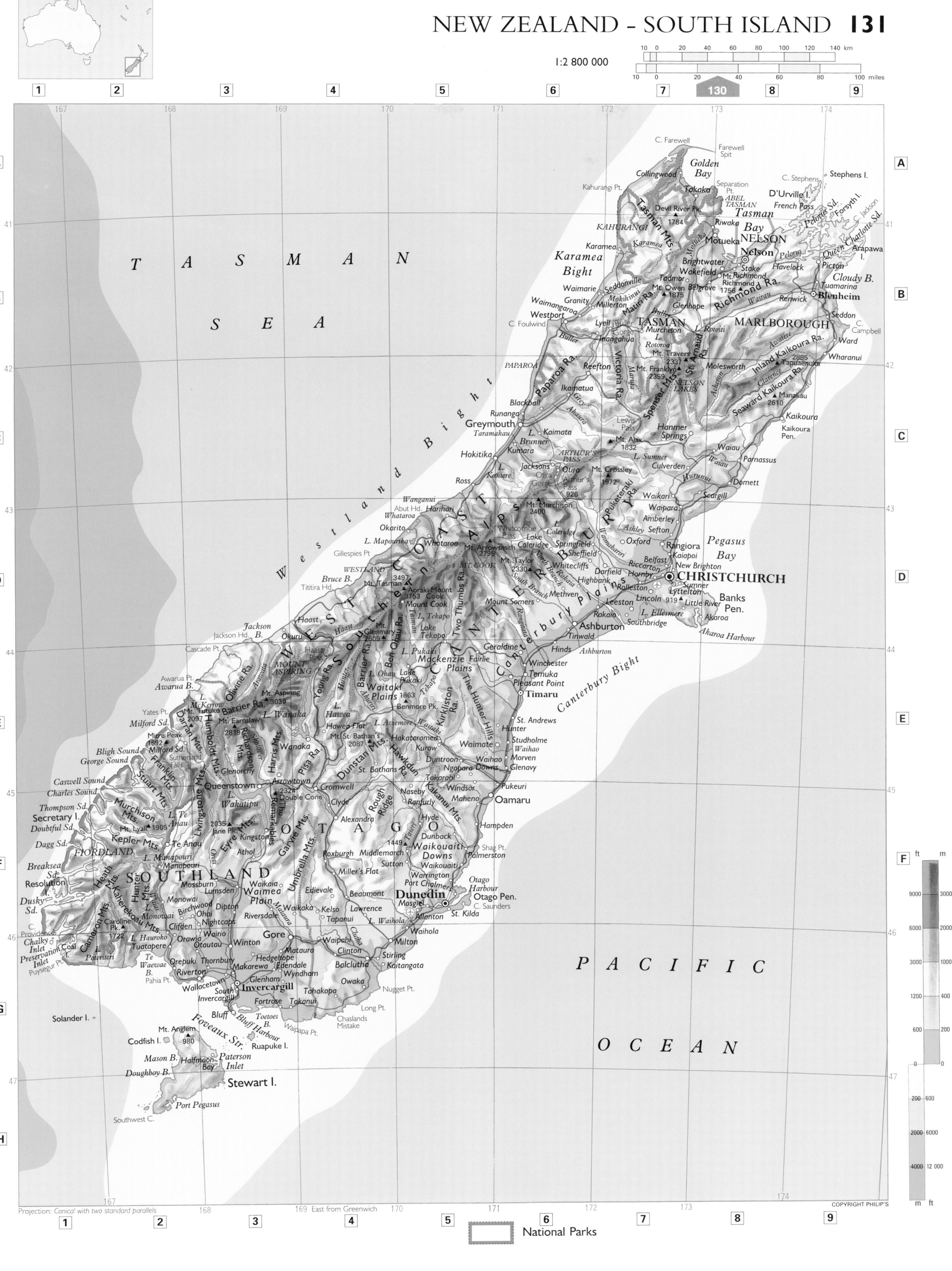

National Parks

Projection: Conical with two standard parallels   East from Greenwich   COPYRIGHT PHILIP'S

50 0 50 100 150 200 km

1:5 200 000

50 0 50 100 150 miles

COPYRIGHT PHILIP'S

PACIFIC OCEAN

NORTH SOLOMONS

Lyra Reef
Nuguria Is.
Sable I.
Green Is.

Kilinailau Is.
C. Hanpan
Buka I.
Hutjena
C. L'Averdy
Tinputz
Mt. Balbi 2715
Torokina
Kunua
Sohano
Lemankoa
Panguna
Mt. Takuam 2251
Arawa
Kieta
Toka
Boku

Bougainville I.
Moupena Pt.
Bougainville Trench 9140
Shortland I.
Treasury Is. (Solomon Is.)

Solomon Islands

NEW IRELAND

St. Matthias Group
Mussau I.
Tabalo
Eloaua I.
Emirau I.
Tench I.

New Hanover
Tingwon Group
Taskul
Noipuos
Ungat
Djaul I.
North C.
Kavieng

Schleinitz 1481
Tatau I.
Tabar Is.
Simberi I.
Lakuramau
Konos
Lihir Group
Lihir I.
Namatanai
Matomatanai

Hans Meyer Ra.
Verron Ra.
Lossu I.
Metlik
C. St. George

Tanga Is.
Boang I.
Malendok I.
Feni Is.
Babase I.
Ambitle I.

St. George's Channel

Bismarck Archipelago

Bismarck Sea

New Ireland

Watom I.
Rabaul
Kokopo
Gazelle Peninsula
Mt. Sinewit 2438
Sumpun
Wide Bay
Pomio
Jacquinot Bay
Crater Pt.
Matong

Kimbe Bay
Hoskins
Ewasse
Ubai
Kimbe
Talasea
Willaumez Pen.
Nakanai Mts.

NEW BRITAIN
New Britain 8320
Mt. Ulawun

Lolobau I.
Ulamona
Gasmata
C. Anukur
C. Kablungu
C. Dampier

2027
Whiteman Ra.
Nukulu
Waku
Kandrian
Arawe Is.

Garove I.
Witu Is.
Unea I.
Ottilien Reef
Whirlwind Reef

Sog Sog
C. Gloucester
Aumo

WEST NEW BRITAIN
WEST SOLOMON SEA

Solomon Sea

EAST NEW BRITAIN

NORTHERN

PACIFIC OCEAN

MANUS

Admiralty Islands
Hermit Is.
Ninigo Group
Aua I.
Wuvulu I.

Sori
Lorengau
Momote
Manus I.
Los Negros I.
Rambutyo I.
Baluan I.
South West Pt.
Kabuli

Tong I.
Circular Reef
Sherburne Reef

Madang

Long I.
Crown I.
Tolokiwa I.
Umboi I.
Sakar I.
Sialum
Siassi
Vitiaz Strait
Dampier Strait

Karkar I.
Bagabag I.
Manam I.
Bogia
Bibi
Matuka

Finisterre Ra.
Adelbert Range
Bismarck Range
Finschhafen
C. Cretin
Tami Is.

Wasu
Kabwum
Huon Peninsula
Saidor
Dumpu
Bena
Boana
Lae
Morobe
Lasanga I.

Huon Gulf

MOROBE

Wau
Bulolo
Mumeng
Wonenara
Menyamya
Aseki

Kaintantu
Goroka
Kundiawa
Mt. Wilhelm 4508
Mt. Michael 3647
Crater Mt. 3231

EASTERN HIGHLANDS
CHIMBU
WESTERN HIGHLANDS
ENGA
SOUTHERN HIGHLANDS

Mount Hagen
Mt. Giluwe 4368
Mt. Ialibu 3647
Mendi
Tari
Kandep
Wabag
Laiagam
Porgera
Koroba
Kopiago

Mt. Bosavi 2507
Muller
Nomad
Kikori
Baimuru
Erave
Kutubu

Mt. Capella 3993
Telefomin
Oksapmin
Mt. Ayang 3505
Mt. Fubilan
Ningerum

EAST SEPIK
WEST SEPIK

Wutung
Vanimo
Aitape
Wewak
Maprik
Angoram
Dreikikir
Lumi
Nuku

Sepik
April
Yuat
Keram
Karawari

NEW GUINEA

Central Range
Kagua
Ialibu

PAPUA

GULF

WESTERN

Kikori
Kerema
Baimuru
Ihu

Gulf of Papua

Deception Bay

Aramia
Bamu
Balimo
Wasua
Emeti
Boze

Fly
Lake Murray
Nomad
Kunga
Daru
Parama I.
Bristow I.
Kiwai I.
Purutu I.
Wabuda I.
Umuda I.

Bogui I. (Australia)
Sibidiri
Morehead
Tondo

Wegm
Mari

INDONESIA

Gulf of Papua

Port Moresby
Bereina
Iokea
Kairuku
Kupiano
Kwikila
Hula
Keppel Pt.
Hood Pt.
Abau
Amazon Bay
C. Rodney

Owen Stanley Range
Mt. Victoria 4035
Mt. Albert Edward 3990
Kokoda
Popondetta
Buna
Afore
Sirri
Tufi
Wanigela

CENTRAL

NORTHERN

Kumusi
C. Ward Hunt
C. Nelson
Dyke Ackland Bay
Mt. St. Mary
Mt. Suckling 3676
Mt. Simpson 2883
Sibium Mts.

WARIA

D'Entrecasteaux Islands
Goodenough I.
Fergusson I.
Normanby I.
Samarai
East Cape
Milne Bay
Dogura
Rabaraba

MILNE BAY

Trobriand Islands
Kiriwina
Kitava I.
Kaileuna I.
Losuia
Woodlark I.
Guasopa
Madau I.
Egum Atoll
Marshall Bennett Is.
Vakuta I.

Lusancay Is. and Reefs
Conflict Group
Deboyne
Dumoulin Is.

Louisiade Archipelago
Misima I.
Bwagaoia
Tagula I.
Sudest I.
The Calvados Chain
Tawa Tawa Mal Reef
Rossel I.

Pocklington Reef

Coral Sea

AUSTRALIA

Cape York
Peninsula
York
Shelburne Bay
C. Grenville
Temple Bay
Cullen Pt.

Great Barrier Reef

Torres Strait
Saibai I. (Australia)
Moa I.
Badu I.
Wednesday I.
Thursday I.
Prince of Wales I.
Horn I.
Turtle Head I.
Sharp Pt.
Endeavour Strait

Projection: Lambert Conformal Conic

East from Greenwich

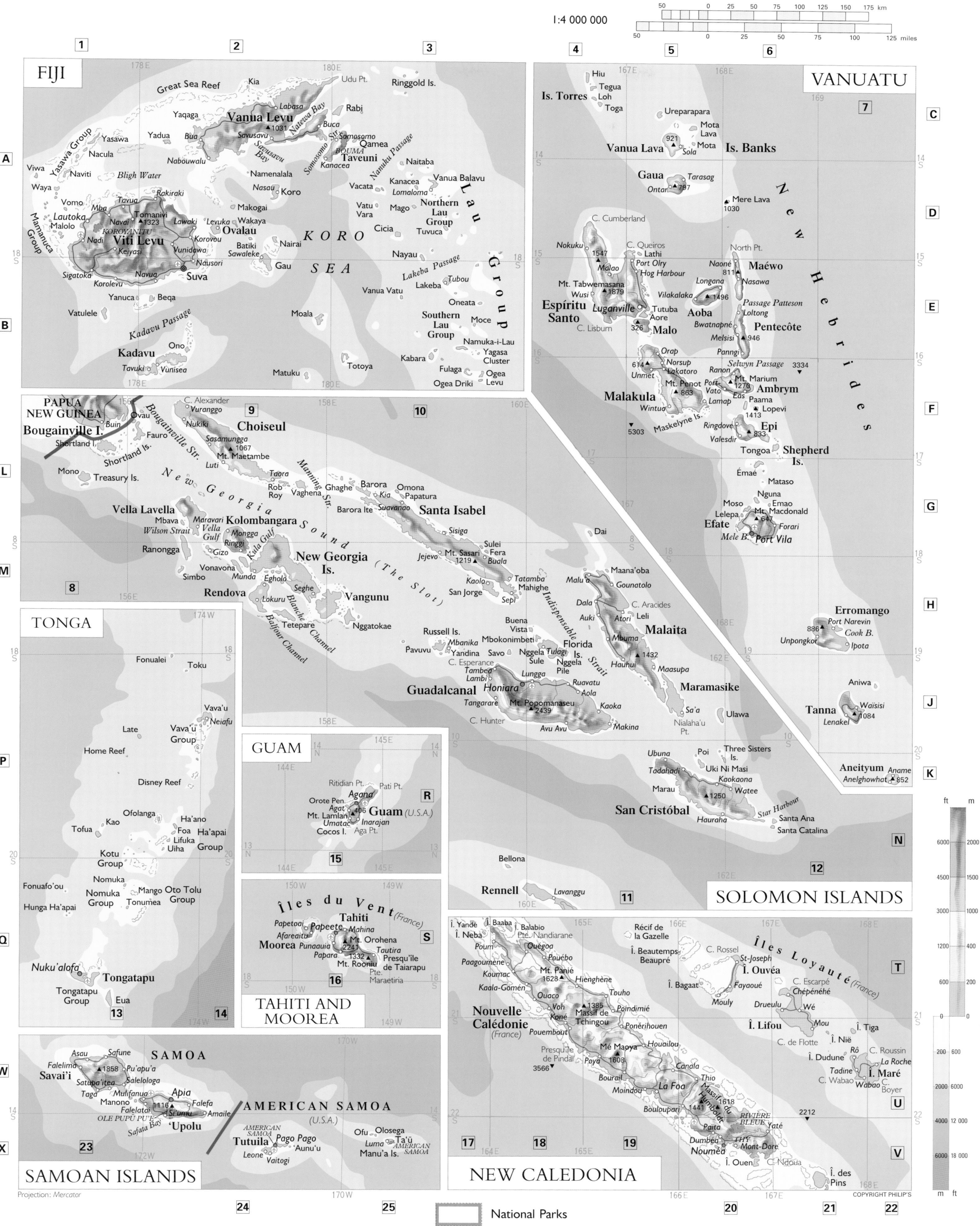

7 8 9 10
6

1 2 3 4 5

Bering Sea

Okhotsk
Sea of Okhotsk
Poluostrov Kamchatka
Komandorskiye Ostrova (Russia)
Near Is. (U.S.A.)
Andreanof
Petropavlovsk-Kamchatskiy
7822
Aleutian
Aleutian Trench

R U S S I A
Yekaterinburg
Tomsk
Lena
Ob
MOSKVA
Volga
Novosibirsk
Irkutsk
Oz. Baykal
Chita
Amur
Astana (Aqmola)
Semey
Blagoveshchensk
Khabarovsk
Sakhalin
La Perouse Str.
Kurilskiye Ostrova (Russia)
Kuril Trench
10,542
Emperor Seamount Chain

KAZAKHSTAN
Aral Sea
Balqash Köl
Altai
MONGOLIA
Ulaanbaatar
Changchun
Harbin
Sapporo
Vladivostok
Hakodate
Sea of Japan
How

Almaty
Ürümqi
SHENYANG
Sendai
Midway Is. (U.S.A.)
Toshkent
KYRGYZSTAN
BEIJING
TIANJIN
Dalian
SOUL
NORTH KOREA
SOUTH KOREA
Nagoya
Kyōto
TOKYO
Yokohama
JAPAN
Fuji-San 3776

TAJIKISTAN
C H I N A
Taiyuan
Huang He
Qingdao
Kitakyūshū
Osaka
Shikoku
10,554
Japan Trench
Lisianski I. (U.S.A.)

AFGHANISTAN
Kabul
Srinagar
Kunlun Shan
Lanzhou
Xi'an
Nanjing
SHANGHAI
Kyūshū
Ogasawara Gunto (Japan)
Minami-Tori-Shima (Japan)

PAKISTAN
Himalaya
XIZANG
CHONGQING
Wuhan
HANGZHOU
East China Sea
Kazan-Rettō (Japan)

Lahore
DELHI
NEPAL
Lhasa
Mt Everest 8850
Chang J.
Changsha
Fuzhou
Ryūkyū-rettō (Japan)

Kanpur
Ganga
Brahmaputra
Kunming
GUANGZHOU
Taipei
Marcus
Necker Ridge
Wake I. (U.S.A.)

INDIA
KOLKATA (Calcutta)
DHAKA
Mandalay
Macau
HONG KONG
TAIWAN
NORTHERN MARIANAS (U.S.A.)
Saipan
P A

Hyderabad
BANGLADESH
BURMA
Irrawaddy
Salween
LAOS
Hanoi
Hainan
Luzon
C. Engano
GUAM (U.S.A.)
11,022
Mariana Trench
MARSHALL IS.
Bikini Atoll
Enewetak Atoll

CHENNAI (Madras)
BANGKOK
THAILAND
CAMBODIA
Mekong
Paracel Is.
MANILA
PHILIPPINES
Yap
Caroline Is.
Micronesia
Dalap-Uliga-Darrit

SRI LANKA
Phnom Penh
Thanh Pho Ho Chi Minh
South China Sea
Mindoro
Samar
10,497
Truk
Jaluit I.

Colombo
Nicobar Is. (India)
G. of Thailand
Palawan
Sulu Sea
Mindanao
Koror
Pohnpei
Palikir
PALAU
FEDERATED STATES OF MICRONESIA
Butaritari

MALAYSIA
4101
BRUNEI
SABAH
Celebes Sea
Maluku
Melanesia
Tarawa
Gilbert Is.
Banaba
Abariringa
Endurbay

Kuala Lumpur
PEN. MALAYSIA
SINGAPORE
Borneo
SARAWAK
Sulawesi
Buru
Seram
Puncak Jaya 5029
PAPUA
PAPUA NEW GUINEA
Admiralty Is.
Bismarck Arch.
New Ireland
NAURU
Phoenix Is.
Howland I. (U.)
Baker I. (U.)

Sumatera
Palembang
Java Sea
Ujung Pandang
Banda Sea
7440
New Guinea
Rabaul
New Britain
Bougainville
SOLOMON IS.
KIRIBATI

I N D O N E S I A
JAKARTA
Jawa
Surabaya
Flores Sea
Flores
EAST TIMOR
Arafura Sea
Lae
Port Moresby
Honiara
Guadalcanal
TUVALU
Fongafale
Tokelau (N.Z.)

Selat Sunda
Bali
Sumbawa
Sumba
Timor
Torres Strait
C. York
Santa Cruz I.
9165
Rotuma
Is. Wallis & Futuna (Fr.)
SAMOA
Apia

Cocos Is. (Austral.)
Christmas I. (Austral.)
Java Trench
C. Arnhem
Darwin
Gulf of Carpentaria
Louisiade Arch.
Coral Sea
VANUATU
Espíritu Santo
Port Vila
Vanua Levu
Viti Levu
Suva

INDIAN
Broome
North West C.
Mount Isa
Cairns
Townsville
Great Barrier Reef
Is. Chesterfield
FIJI
Nuku'alofa
TONGA

OCEAN
AUSTRALIA
Alice Springs
Rockhampton
NEW CALEDONIA (Fr.)
Nouméa
Is. Loyauté
7570
10,822
Tonga Trench

Geraldton
L. Eyre
Brisbane
Great Dividing Ra.
Norfolk I. (Austral.)
Kermadec Is. (N.Z.)

Perth
Great Australian Bight
Darling
Sydney
Canberra
Mt. Kosciuszko 2237
Lord Howe I. (Austral.)
Kermadec Trench 10,047

Albany
Adelaide
Murray
Tasman Sea
Auckland
Cook Strait
NEW ZEALAND
Chatham Is. (N.Z.)

Melbourne
Bass Str.
Tasmania
Hobart
Aoraki Mt. Cook 3753
Christchurch
Wellington

Nouvelle Amsterdam (Fr.)
I. St. Paul (Fr.)
Mid-Indian Ridge
Dunedin
Invercargill
Bounty Is. (N.Z.)

Is. Crozet (Fr.)
Kerguelen (Fr.)
Auckland Is. (N.Z.)
Antipodes Is. (N.Z.)
Campbell I. (N.Z.)
Macquarie I. (Austral.)

Heard I. (Austral.)

ft m
12 000 4000
9000 3000
6000 2000
3000 1000
1500 500
600 200
0 0
200 600
1000 3000
2000 6000
4000 12 000
6000 18 000
8000 24 000
m ft

Projection: Mollweide's Homolographic
East from Greenwich
40 60 80 100 120 140 160 180

B C D E F G H L M N

1 2 3 4 5 6 7 8 9 10

11 **12** **13** **14** **15** **16** **17** **18** **19** **20**

Arctic Circle

ALASKA
(U.S.A.)
Anchorage

Bristol Bay

Gulf of Alaska

Juneau

Is. (U.S.A.)

Prince of Wales I.
(U.S.A.) Prince Rupert
Queen Charlotte Is.
(Canada)

C A N A D A

Edmonton

L. Winnipeg

Newfoundland

N O R T H

Vancouver
Vancouver I.
Victoria
Seattle

Calgary

Regina

Winnipeg

St. Lawrence

B

Portland

Boise

Snake

R O C K Y

L. Superior

Québec

St. John's

50

Minneapolis

Missouri

Montréal
L. Huron Ottawa
L. Michigan Toronto
Detroit

Boston

C

Salt Lake
City

Denver

CHICAGO

Buffalo
L. Ontario
Pittsburgh
L. Erie

NEW YORK
PHILADELPHIA
Baltimore
Washington D.C.

A T L A N T I C

Sacramento

4418

Kansas City

St. Louis
Cincinnati

40

C. Mendocino

6741

SAN FRANCISCO

Colorado

UNITED STATES

Oklahoma City
Memphis

Atlanta

Appalachian Mts.

C. Hatteras

Bermuda
(U.K.)

D

LOS ANGELES
San Diego

Phoenix

Dallas

Mississippi

Jacksonville

Sargasso Sea

30

Guadalupe
(Mex.)

Ciudad
Juárez

M E

Baja California

Houston

San Antonio

New
Orleans

Gulf of Mexico
Monterrey
Miami

La Habana

BAHAMAS

O C E A N

E

Tropic of Cancer

C. San Lucas

Gulf de California

X

CUBA

Florida Str.

West Indies

Honolulu
Oahu
4205
Hawaii

HAWAIIAN IS.
(U.S.A.)

Is. Revilla Gigedo
(Mex.)

Guadalajara

MEXICO
5610
Puebla
C

Mérida

Canal de Yucatan

JAMAICA

9200
HAITI
Kingston

7680

DOMINICAN REP.
PUERTO
RICO
(U.S.A.)

Leeward
Is.

20

F

C I F I C

Johnston I.
(U.S.A.)

Acapulco

O

I. Clipperton
(Fr.)

GUATEMALA
Guatemala
San Salvador
EL SALVADOR

BELIZE

HONDURAS
NICARAGUA
Managua

Caribbean Sea

Barranquilla

Maracaibo

BARBADOS

Windward Is.

Caracas

10

Orinoco

VENEZUELA

G

Palmyra Is.
(U.S.A.)
Teraina
Tabuaeran
Kiritimati

B

Jarvis I.
(U.S.A.)

North West Christmas Ridge

San José
COSTA
RICA
Colón
PANAMA
Panamá

I. del Coco
(Costa Rica)

Medellín

I. de Malpelo
(Colombia)

Cali

Bogotá

COLOMBIA

Quito
ECUADOR

Equator

Galápagos
(Ecuador)

0

E A N

Malden I.

Guayaquil

Amazonas

Iquitos

O

Starbuck I.

C. Palinas

BRAZIL

H

SAMOA
A.)

Tongareva

Pukapuka Manihiki

Vostok I.

Is. Marquises

Trujillo

Suwarrow Is.

Caroline I.
(Millennium I.)
Flint I.

Is. de la
Société

Is. Tuamotu

6369

PERU

10

J

Papeete Tahiti

Australis Seamount Chain

Mururoa

 Is. Tuamotu

Tuamotu Ridge

LIMA
Cuzco

L. Titicaca

Nevada Ancohuma
6550

Arequipa
6866
Peru-
Arica

La Paz
BOLIVIA

Cook Is.
(N.Z.)

FRENCH POLYNESIA

East Pacific Ridge

Tropic of Capricorn

Iquique
Chile

20

K

Rarotonga

Is. Tubuai

Ducie I.

Pitcairn I.
(U.K.)

Sala-y-Gómez
(Chile)

Antofagasta

PARAGUAY

Asunción

Rapa

San Felix
(Chile)

8050
Trench

San Ambrosio
(Chile)

San Miguel
de Tucumán

30

I. de Pascua
(Chile)

Córdoba

Pôrto
Alegre

L

Arch. de
Juan Fernández
(Chile)

Valparaíso

Aconcagua
6962

Rosario

URUGUAY

BUENOS
AIRES

Montevideo

40

Chile Rise

SANTIAGO

Rio de la Plata

Concepción

ARGENTINA

SOUTH

M

Pacific-Antarctic Ridge

ATLANTIC

6212

OCEAN

50

Punta Arenas

Est. de Magallanes
Tierra del Fuego

Falkland Is.
(U.K.)

South Georgia
(U.K.)

N

C. de Hornos

160 140 120 100 80 60 West from Greenwich 40 20

COPYRIGHT PHILIP'S

100 0   200 400   600   800 1000   1200   1400 km

1:28 000 000

100 0   200   400   600   800   1000 miles

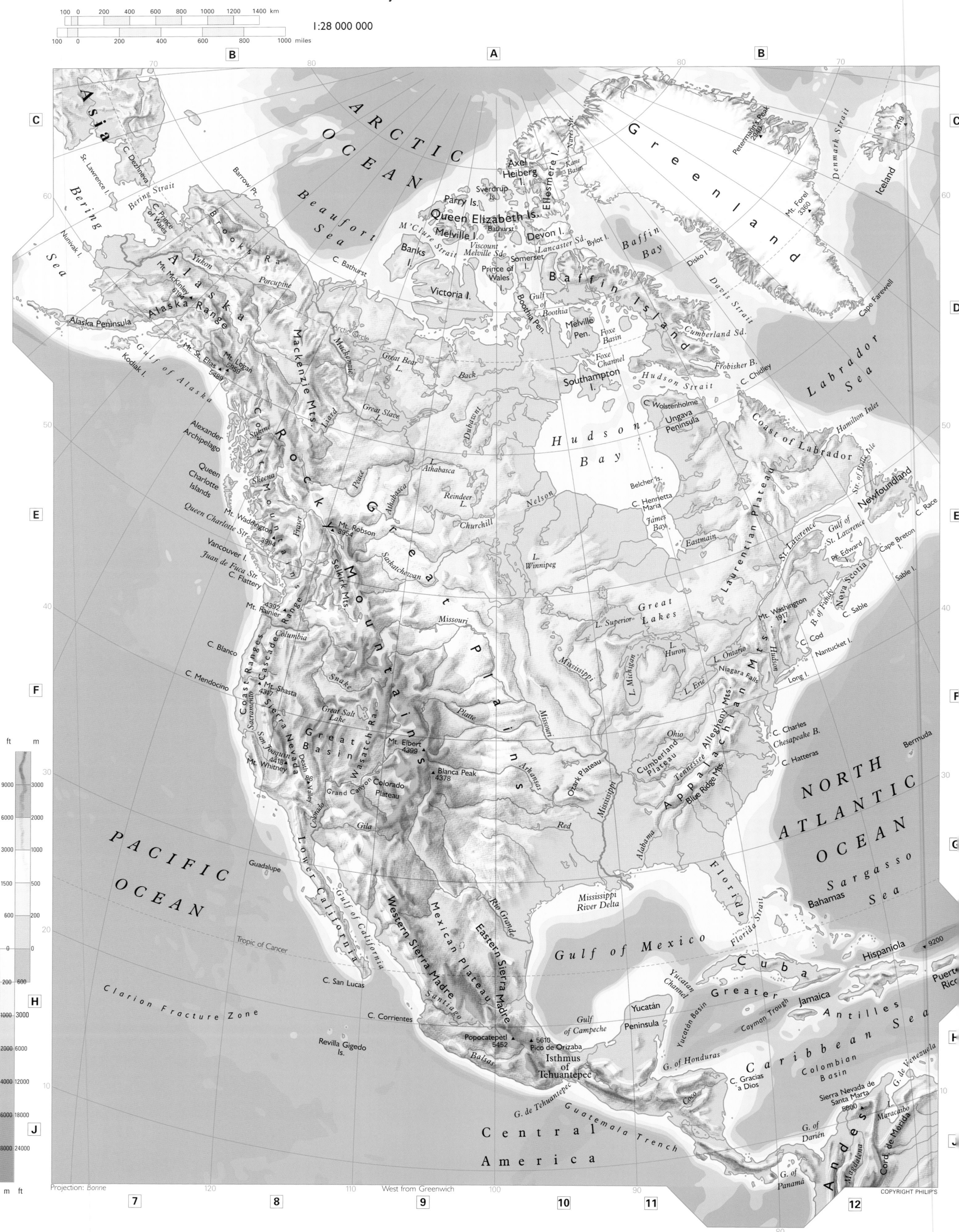

Projection: Bonne

West from Greenwich

COPYRIGHT PHILIPS

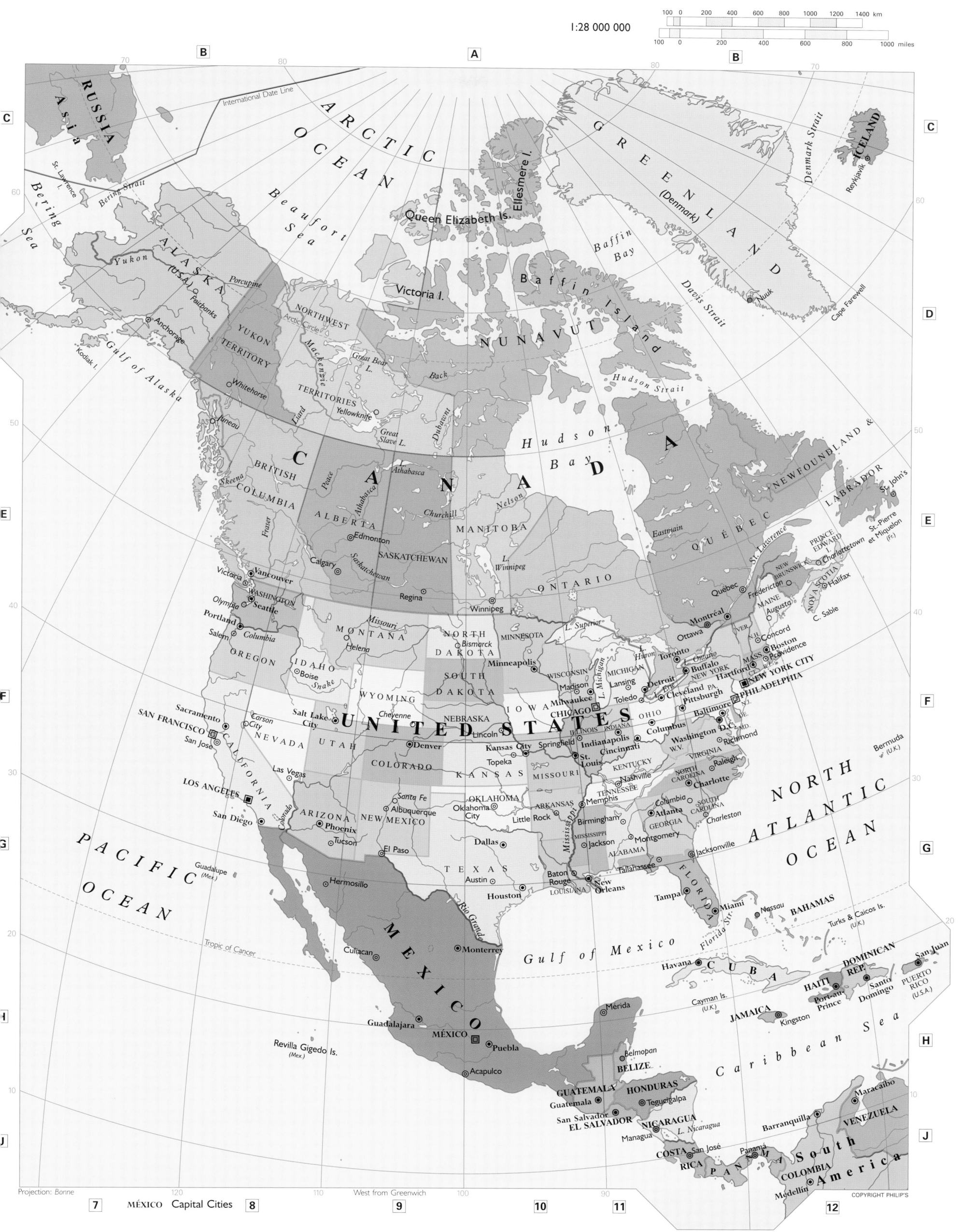

1:28 000 000

100 0   200   400   600   800   1000   1200   1400 km
100 0   200   400   600   800   1000 miles

Projection: Bonne

West from Greenwich

COPYRIGHT PHILIP'S

MÉXICO Capital Cities

100 0 100 200 300 400 500 600 km
100   0   100   200   300   400 miles

1:12 000 000

Projection : Bonne

ft	m
9000	3000
6000	2000
4500	1500
3000	1000
1200	400
600	200
0	0
200	600
2000	6000
4000	12 000
m	ft

ALASKA
1:24 000 000

100 0 100 200 300 400 500 600 km
100   0   100   200   300   400 miles

West from Greenwich

West from Greenwich

COPYRIGHT PHILIP'S

1:5 600 000

| 1 | 2 | 3 | 4 | 5 |

National Parks

Projection: Lambert's Equivalent Azimuthal

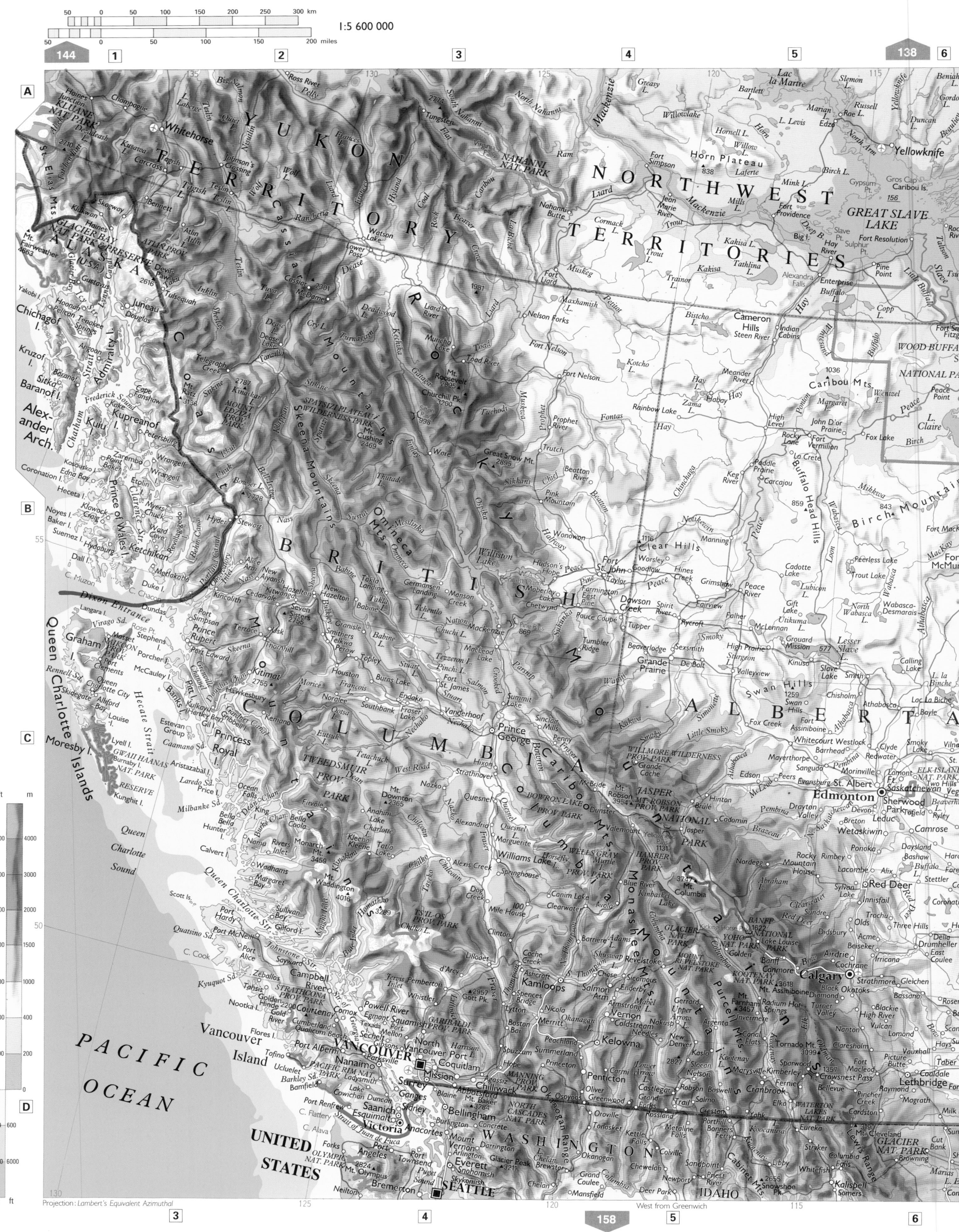

50 0 50 100 150 200 250 300 km

1:5 600 000

50 0 50 100 150 200 miles

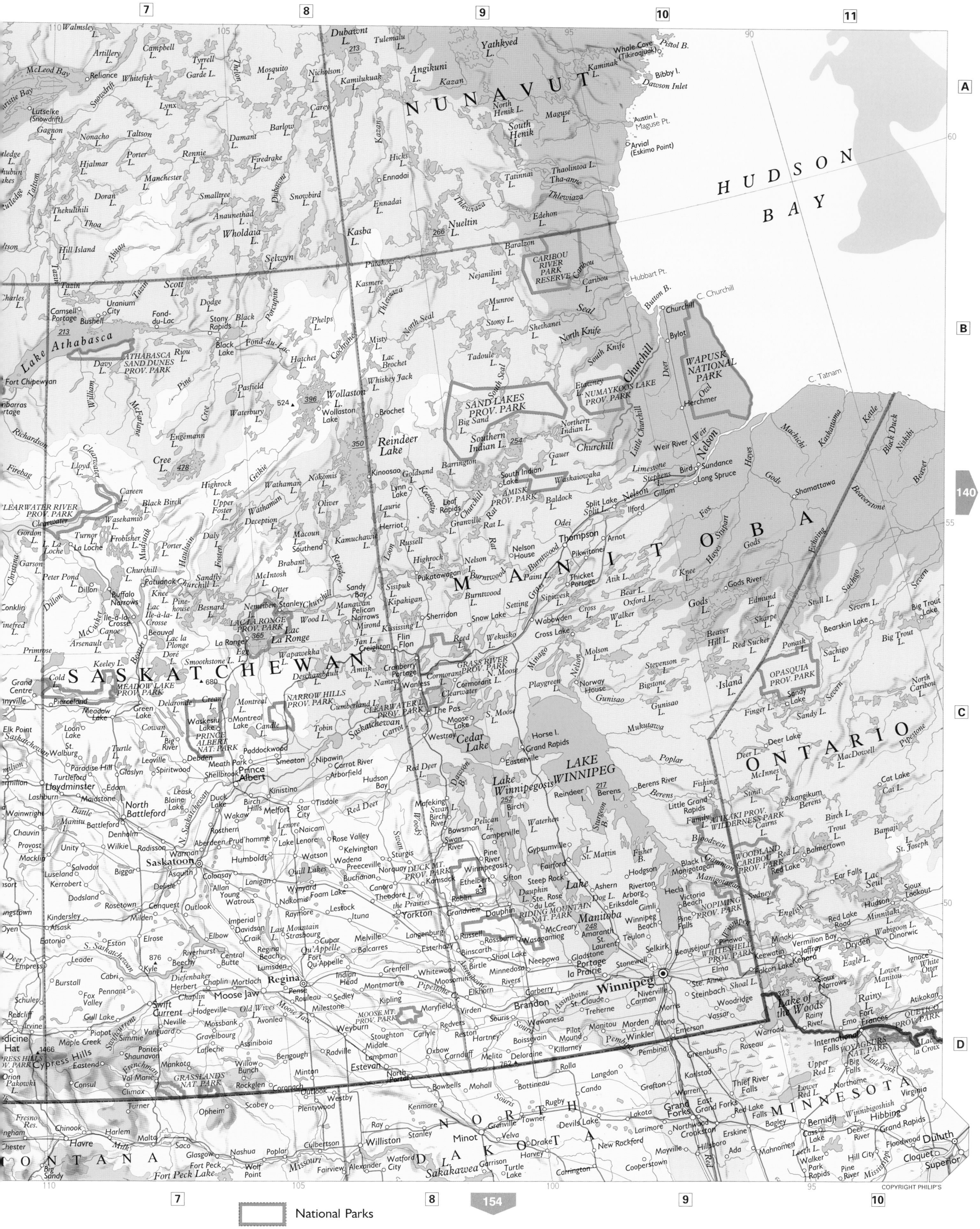

National Parks

1:8 000 000

ARCTIC OCEAN

BEAUFORT SEA

CHUKCHI SEA

RUSSIA

Chukotskiy Poluostrov

BERING SEA

PACIFIC OCEAN

Gulf of Alaska

Aleutian Islands

Andreanof Islands

Islands of Four Mountains

Rat Islands

Near Is.

Brooks Range

Alaska Range

Chugach Mts.

Kenai Peninsula

Kodiak I.

Alaska Peninsula

NORTH-WEST TERRITORIES

CANADA

YUKON TERRITORY

BRITISH COLUMBIA

Alexander Archipelago

Anchorage

Fairbanks

Barrow

Nome

Kotzebue

Juneau

Ketchikan

Projection: Bipolar oblique conic conformal

COPYRIGHT PHILIPS

1:2 000 000

10 0 10 20 30 40 50 60 70 80 90 km
10 0 10 20 30 40 50 60 miles

HAWAIIAN ISLANDS
1:20 000 000

Tropic of Cancer

Lehua I. Kauai Oahu Molokai
Niihau Kaula I. Lanai Maui
Kahoolawe Hawaii

H a w a i i a n   I s l a n d s

PACIFIC OCEAN

Kure I. Midway Is.

Pearl and Hermes Reef
Lisianski I.
Laysan I.
Maro Reef
Gardner Pinnacles
French Frigate Shoals
Necker I.
Nihoa

Projection: Albers Equal Area

COPYRIGHT PHILIP'S

National Parks

West from Greenwich

Hawaii

Kauhola Pt.
Upolu Pt. Hawi
Kohala Mts.
Kukuihaele
Malae Pt.
Kawaihae Bay
PUUKOHOLA HEIAU
NAT. HISTORICAL SITE
Kiholo Bay
KALOKO-HONOKOHAU
NAT. HISTORICAL PARK
Keahole Pt.
Kailua Kona
Keauhou
Kealakekua
Captain Cook
Keokea
Honaunau
PUUHONUA O HONAUNAU
NAT. HISTORICAL PARK
Kealia
Miloli
Papa
Ka Lae
Pohue Bay
Kauna Pt.

Kohala
1678▲
Waimea
(Kamuela)
Mauna Kea
▲4205
Hualalai
▲2521
Mauna Loa
▲4169
HAWAII
VOLCANOES
NATIONAL
PARK
Puu o 2096
Keokeo

Honokaa
Paauilo
Ookala
Laupahoehoe
Papaaloa
Honomu
Pepeekeo
Papaikou
Hilo
Hilo Bay
Keaau
Mountain View
Kurtistown
Glenwood
Volcano
Kilauea
Crater
Pahoa
Kalapana
Lelewi Pt.
Cape
Kumukahi
Opihikao

Pahala
Naalehu
Honuapo Bay
Kaalualu Bay

1340▲

PACIFIC OCEAN

Alenuihaha Channel

Maui

Puu Kukui Puuwela
Lahaina Honokowai Paia Hana
Lower Wailuku Kahului Makawao
Waikapu Puunene
Olowalu Pukalani HALEAKALA
Kihei NAT. PARK
Keawakapu 3055▲
Keokea Haleakala Kaupo
Crater
Makena Ulupalakua

Paawai
West
Maui Mts.

Lanai
Lanai City
Palaoa Pt.
Kaumalapau

Lua Makiki
450▲

Kahoolawe

Kealaikahiki Channel
Kalohi Channel
Kealaikahiki Pt.

Molokai
Kalaupapa
KALAUPAPA
NAT. HIST. PARK
Hoolehua 1515 Pukoo
Kaunakakai Kamalo
Kualapuu
Maunaloa
Laau Pt.
Kamakou 450

Pailolo Channel
Pukoo Channel
C. Halawa

Kaiwi Channel

Oahu
Kahuku Pt.
Laie
Kaaawa
Haleiwa
Waialua
Wahiawa
Kaneohe
Kailua
Kaala 1231
Waianae
Waimanalo
HONOLULU
Aiea
Ewa Beach
Nanakuli
Barbers Pt.
Kaena Pt.
Makapuu Pt.
446▲

PACIFIC OCEAN

Kauai Channel

3026▲

Kauai
Haena
Mokuaeae I.
Kilauea
Anahola
Hanalei
Kapaa
Waimea Wailua
Kawaikini Hanamaulu
1598▲ Lihue
Kekaha Koloa
Poipu
Nohili Pt. Hanapepe
Mana Makahuena Pt.
Puolo Pt.
1598▲

Puuwai Lehua I.
390▲
Paniau Pueo Pt.
Halalii
Kawaihoa Pt.
Niihau

PACIFIC OCEAN

Kaulakahi Channel

Kaieie Channel

OAHU
1:500 000

PACIFIC OCEAN

Kaena Pt.
Mokuauia I.
Kahuku
Laie
Kahana
Punaluu
Kaaawa
Hauula
Waialee
Sunset Beach
Waimea
Waimea Bay
Waialua
Haleiwa
Kawailoa Beach
Puaena Pt.
Waialua Bay
Mokuleia
Kawela
Kaneohe
Kaneohe Bay
Kailua
Kailua Bay
Mokapu Peninsula
Mokolea Rock
Mokulua Is.
Manana I.
Makapuu Pt.
Waimanalo
Waimanalo Bay
Waimanalo Beach
Koko Head
Hanauma Bay

Mokumanu I.

Whitmore Village
Wahiawa
Mililani Town
Wahiawa Res.
Waipio Acres
Waipio
Waipahu
Pearl City
Aiea
HONOLULU
Waikiki
Diamond Head
Kapahulu 232▲
Kaimuki
Kapalama
Halawa Heights
Pearl Harbor
USS ARIZONA
MEMORIAL
Ford I.
Waipio Pen.
Pearl Harbor
Ewa
Ewa Beach
Barbers Pt.

Waianae
Maili
Nanakuli
Makaha
Makakilo City
Kunia
Lualualei
Kaala 1231
Palikea Pk. 914▲
Kepuhi Bay
Lahilahi Pt.
Pokai Bay
Maili Pt.
Kaneilio Pt.

Koolau Range
Koolau Mts.
Waianae Range
Waianae Mts.

HONOLULU COUNTY

Mamala Bay

Kaiwi Channel

PACIFIC OCEAN

ft m
12 000 4000
9000 3000
6000 2000
4500 1500
3000 1000
1800 600
600 200
0 0

Projection: Lambert's Conformal Conic

1:9 600 000

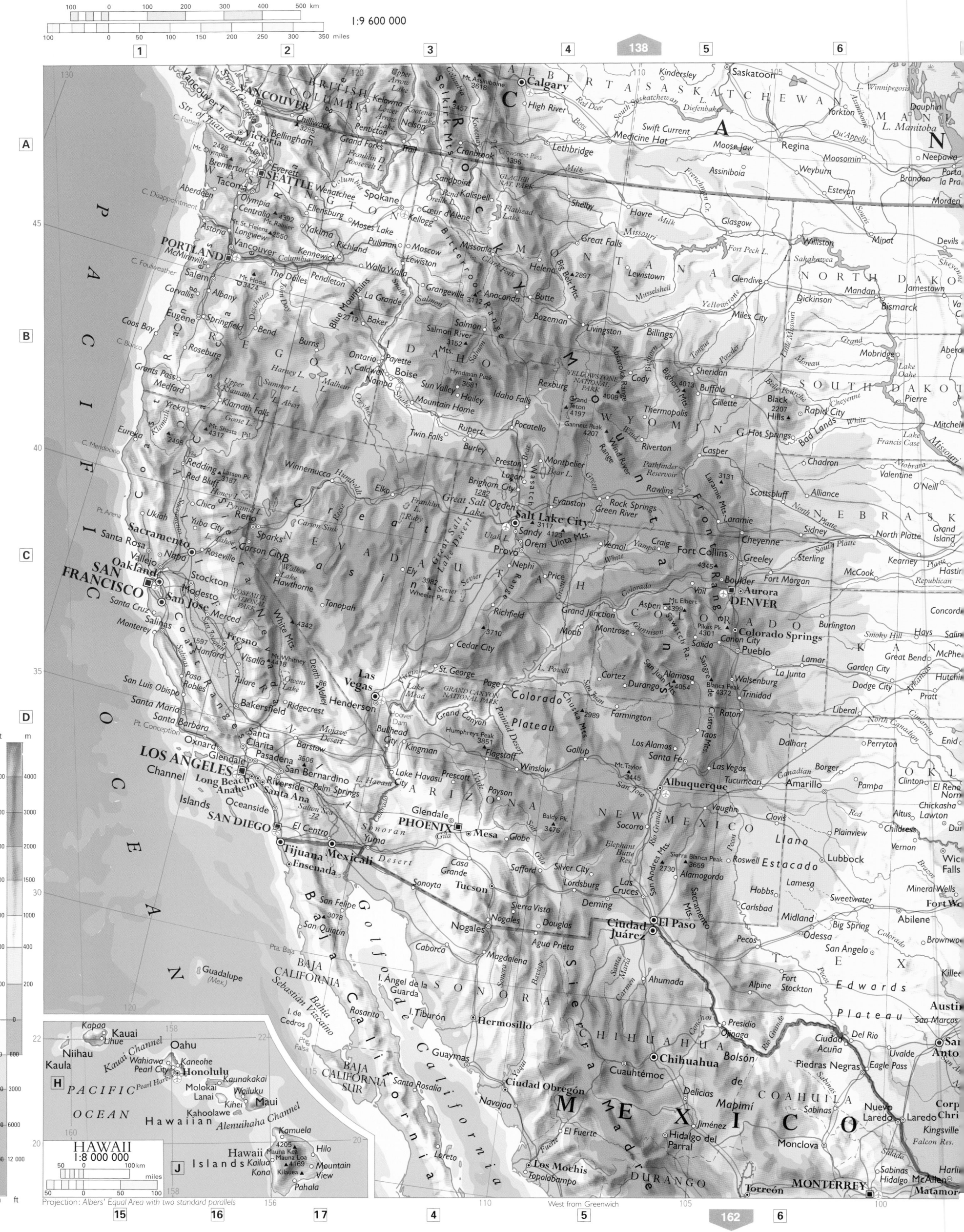

Projection: Albers' Equal Area with two standard parallels

HAWAII
1:8 000 000

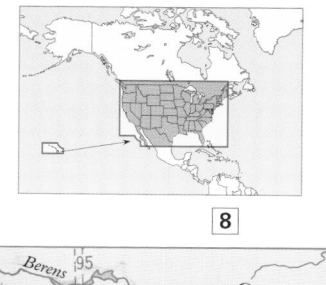

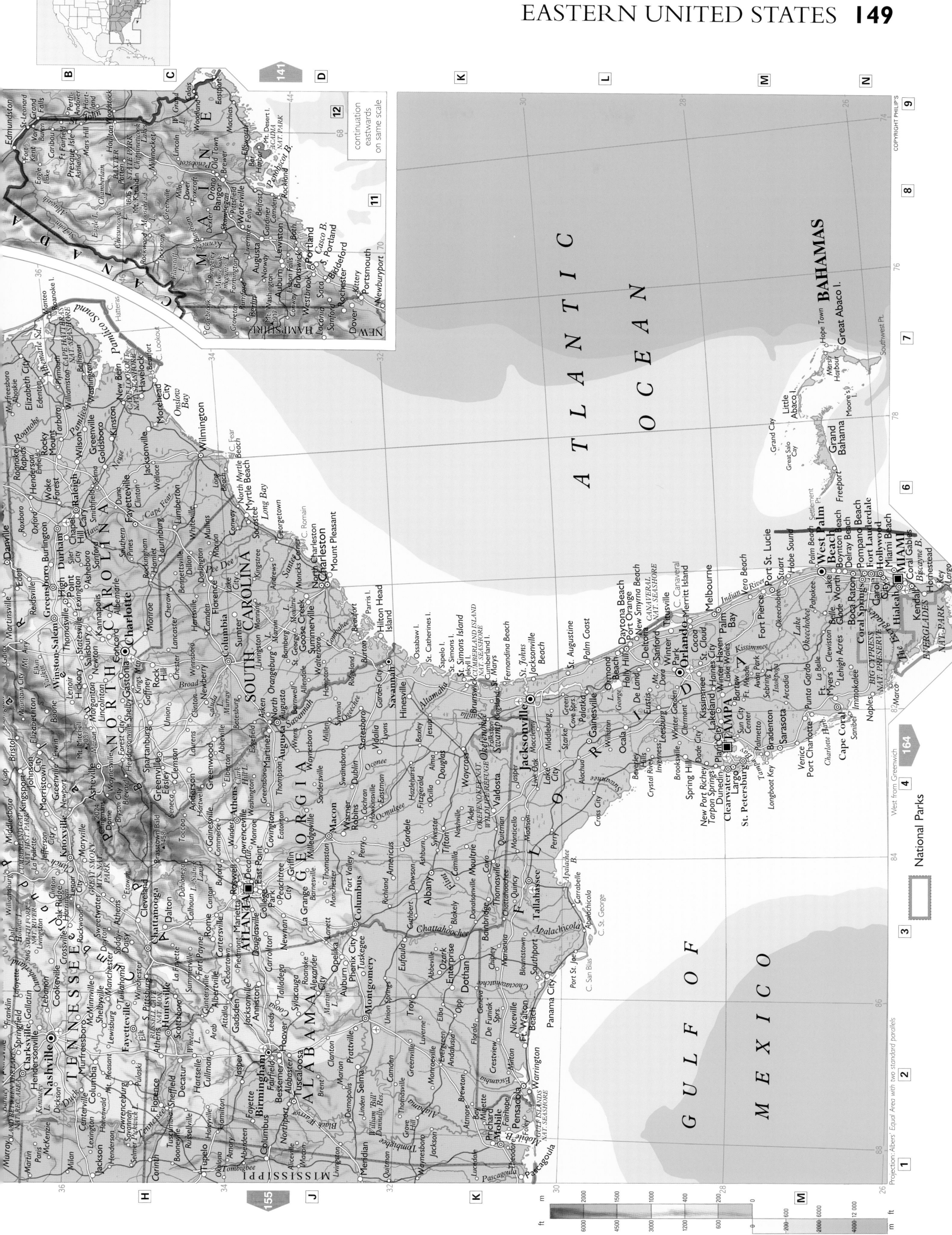

ATLANTIC OCEAN

GULF OF MEXICO

BAHAMAS

Great Abaco I.

Grand Bahama

MAINE

NEW HAMPSHIRE

National Parks

West of Greenwich

Projection: Albers' Equal Area with two standard parallels

COPYRIGHT PHILIP'S

continuation eastwards on same scale

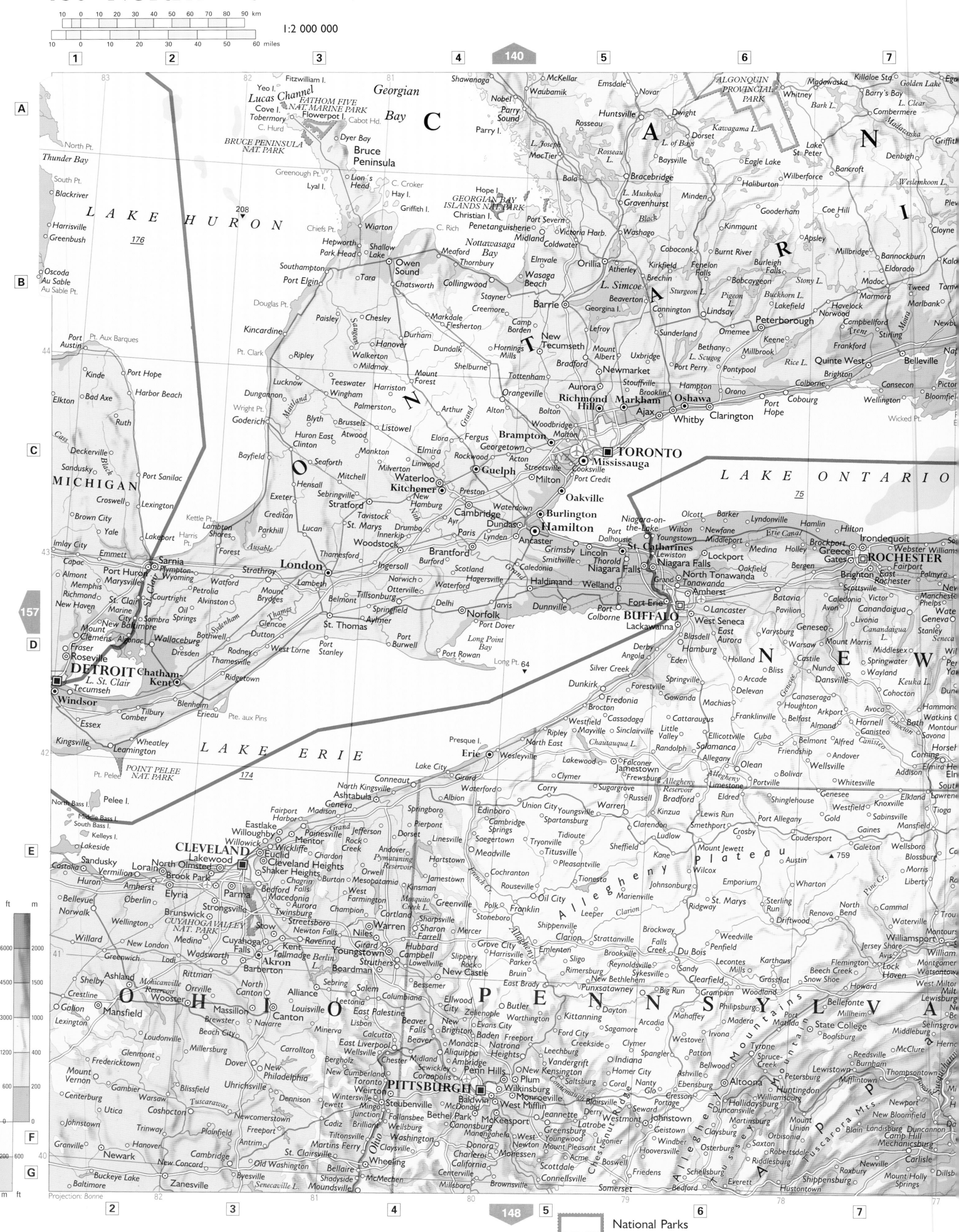

National Parks

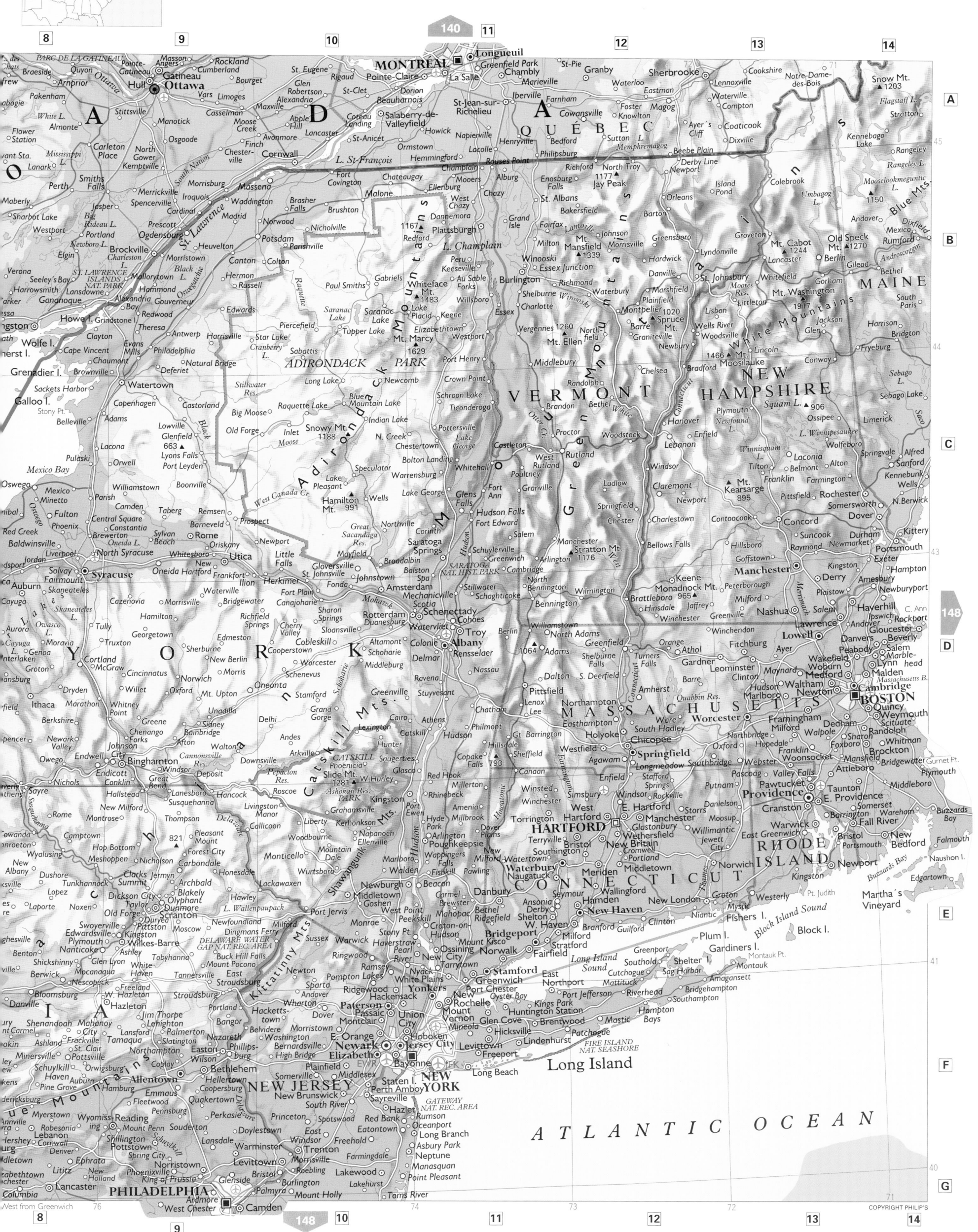

1:2 000 000

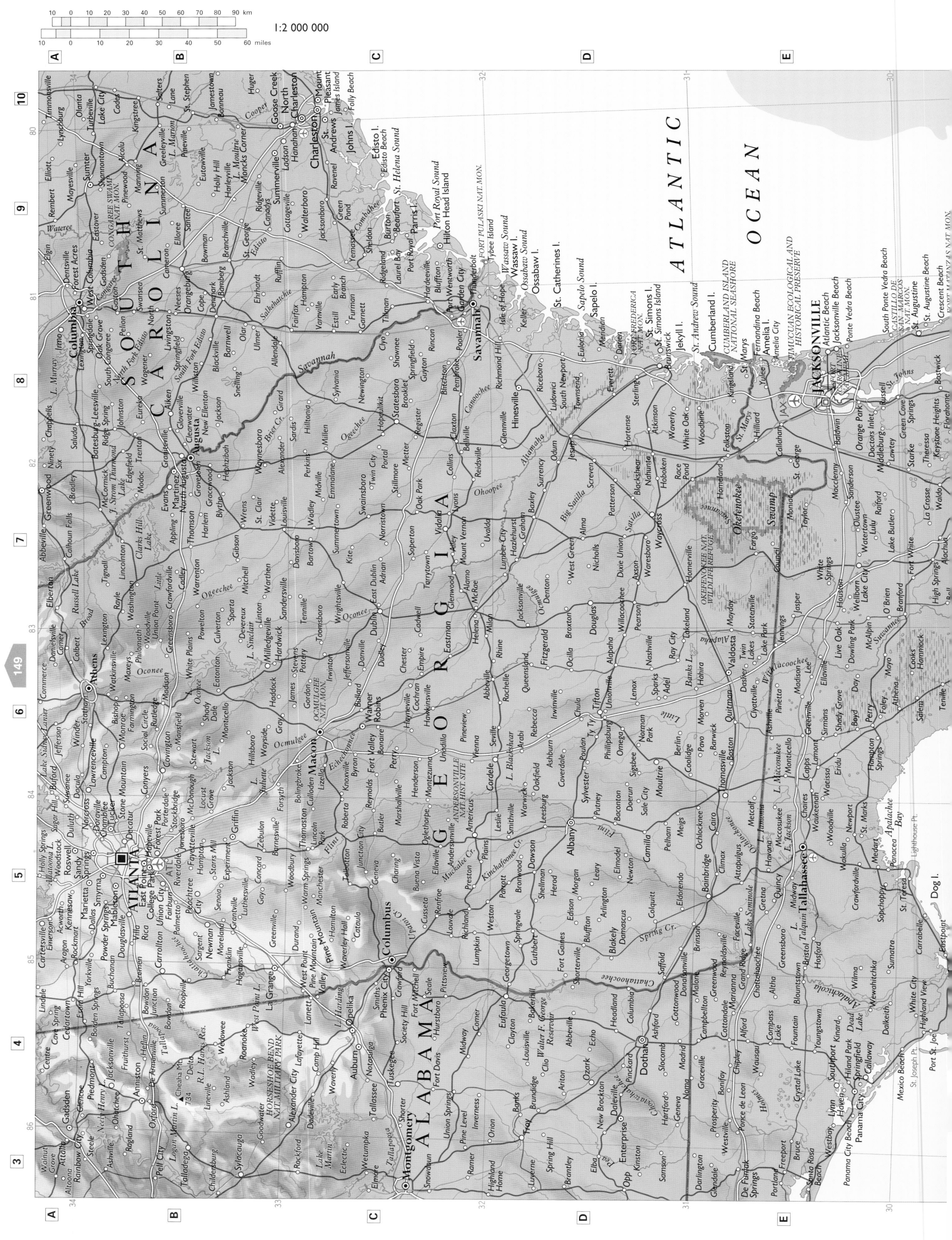

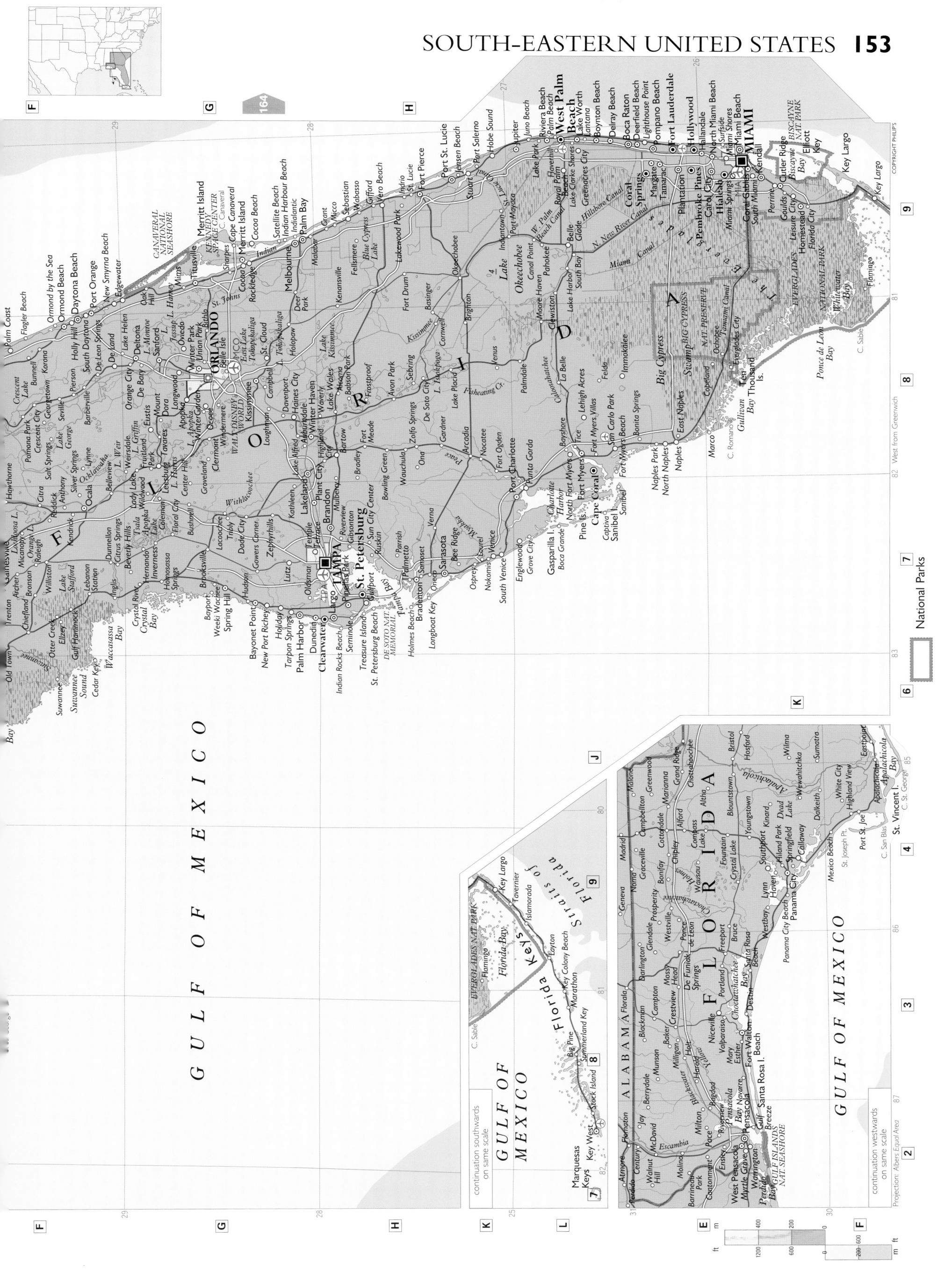

GULF OF MEXICO

GULF OF MEXICO

GULF OF MEXICO

National Parks

F L O R I D A

A L A B A M A

Florida Keys

Straits of Florida

EVERGLADES NAT. PARK

continuation southwards
on same scale

continuation westwards
on same scale

Projection: Albers Equal Area

1:4 800 000

50 0 50 100 150 200 km
50 0 50 100 150 miles

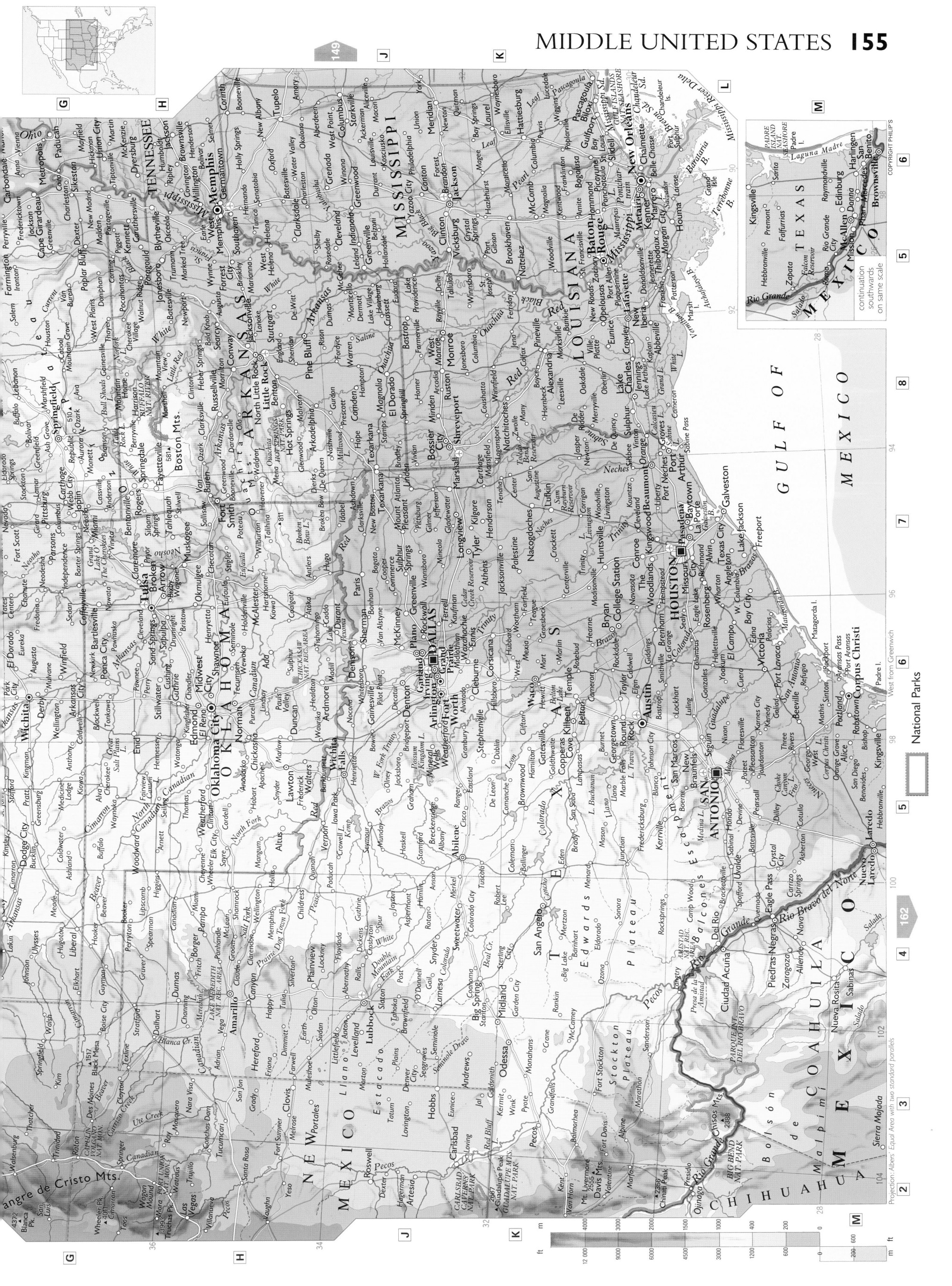

continuation
southwards
on same scale

National Parks

Projection: Albers' Equal Area with two standard parallels

West from Greenwich

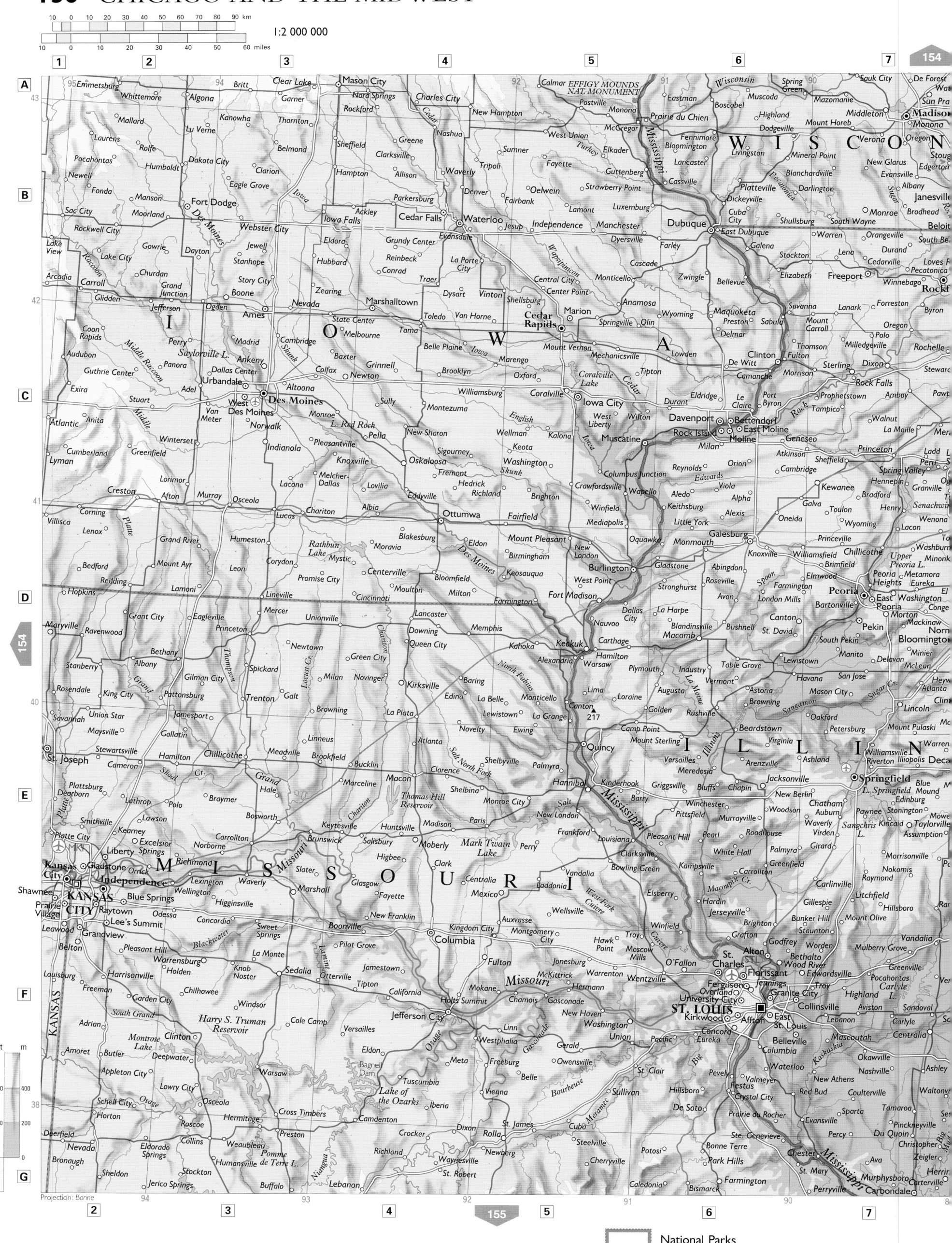

National Parks

Projection: Bonne

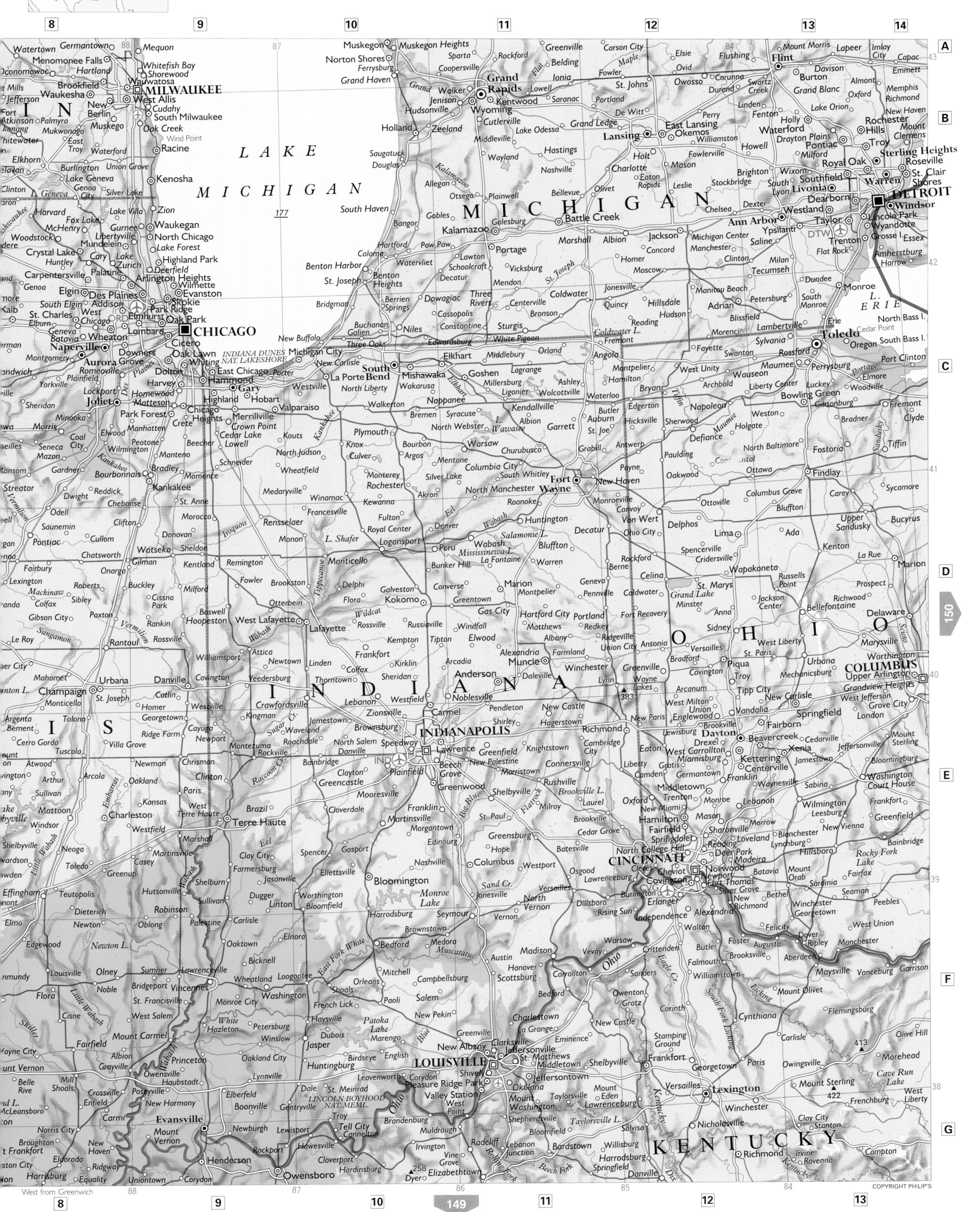

COPYRIGHT PHILIP'S

50 0 50 100 150 200 km

1:4 800 000

50 0 50 100 150 miles

154
142
SASKATCHEWAN
ALBERTA
BRITISH COLUMBIA
CANADA
MONTANA
WYOMING
IDAHO
WASHINGTON
OREGON
NEVADA
UTAH
Bighorn Mountains
Salmon River Mountains
Sawtooth Range
Bitterroot Range
Cascade Range
Blue Mountains
Columbia Basin
Great Salt Lake
Great Salt Lake Desert
Uinta Mountains
Wind River Range
Absaroka Range
Lewis Range
Swan Range
Cabinet Mountains
Clearwater Mountains
Wallowa Mts.
Harney Basin
Snake River Plain
Owyhee
Warner Mts.
Klamath Mts.
Coast Ranges
Sierra Nevada
Medicine Bow Mts.
Ruby Mts.
Shoshone Mountains
Toiyabe Ra.
Santa Rosa Range
Independence Mts.
Steens Mountain
Olympic Mts.
Strait of Juan de Fuca
Puget Sound
VANCOUVER
Victoria
SEATTLE
Tacoma
Olympia
Spokane
PORTLAND
Salem
Eugene
Medford
Boise
Idaho Falls
Pocatello
Salt Lake City
Ogden
Provo
Helena
Great Falls
Billings
Butte
Missoula
Bozeman
Casper
Laramie
Reno
Carson City
Sacramento
Lethbridge
Medicine Hat
Swift Current

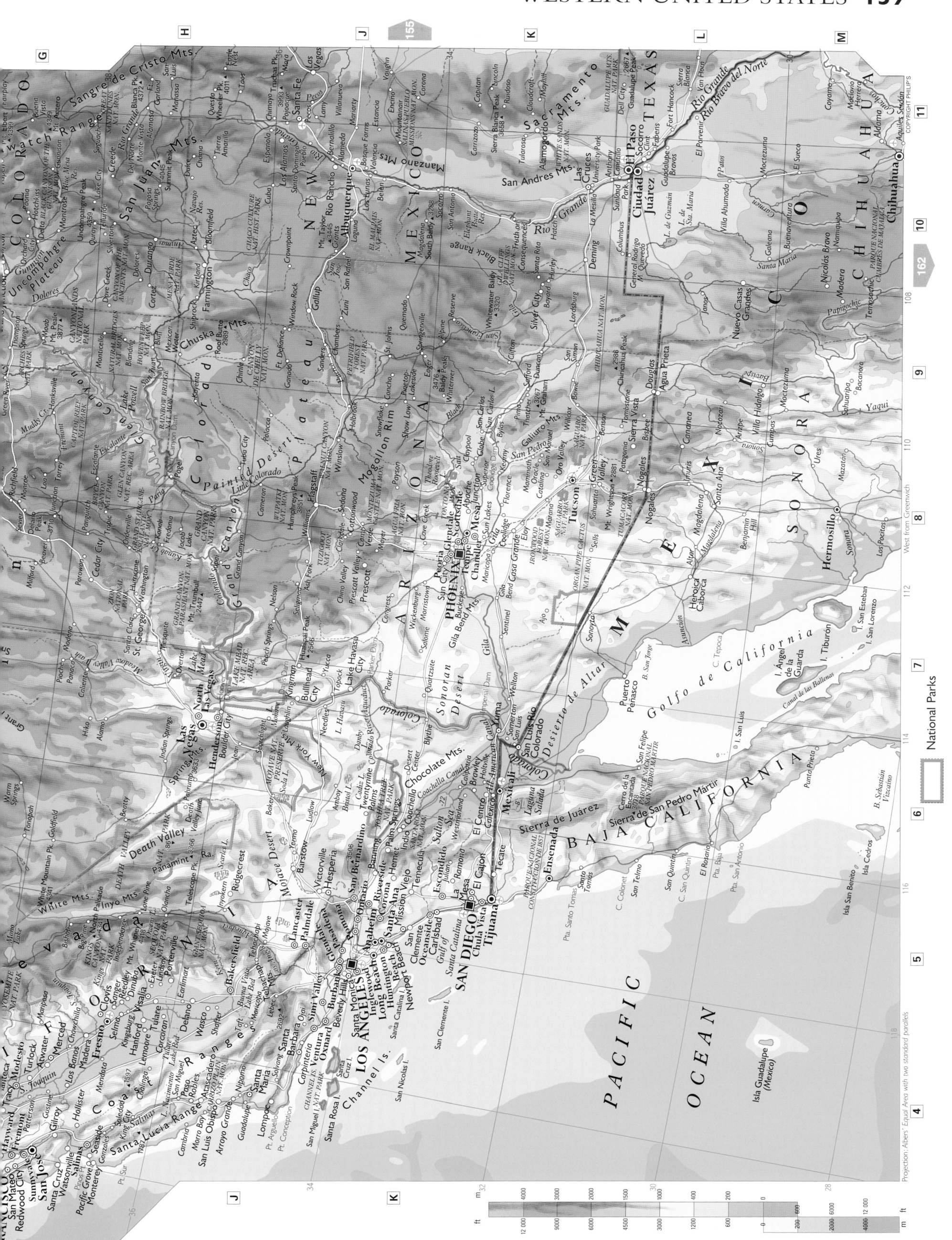

National Parks

Projection: Albers' Equal Area with two standard parallels

COPYRIGHT PHILIP'S

1:2 000 000

159

WESTERN WASHINGTON REGION
on same scale

PACIFIC OCEAN

1:6 400 000

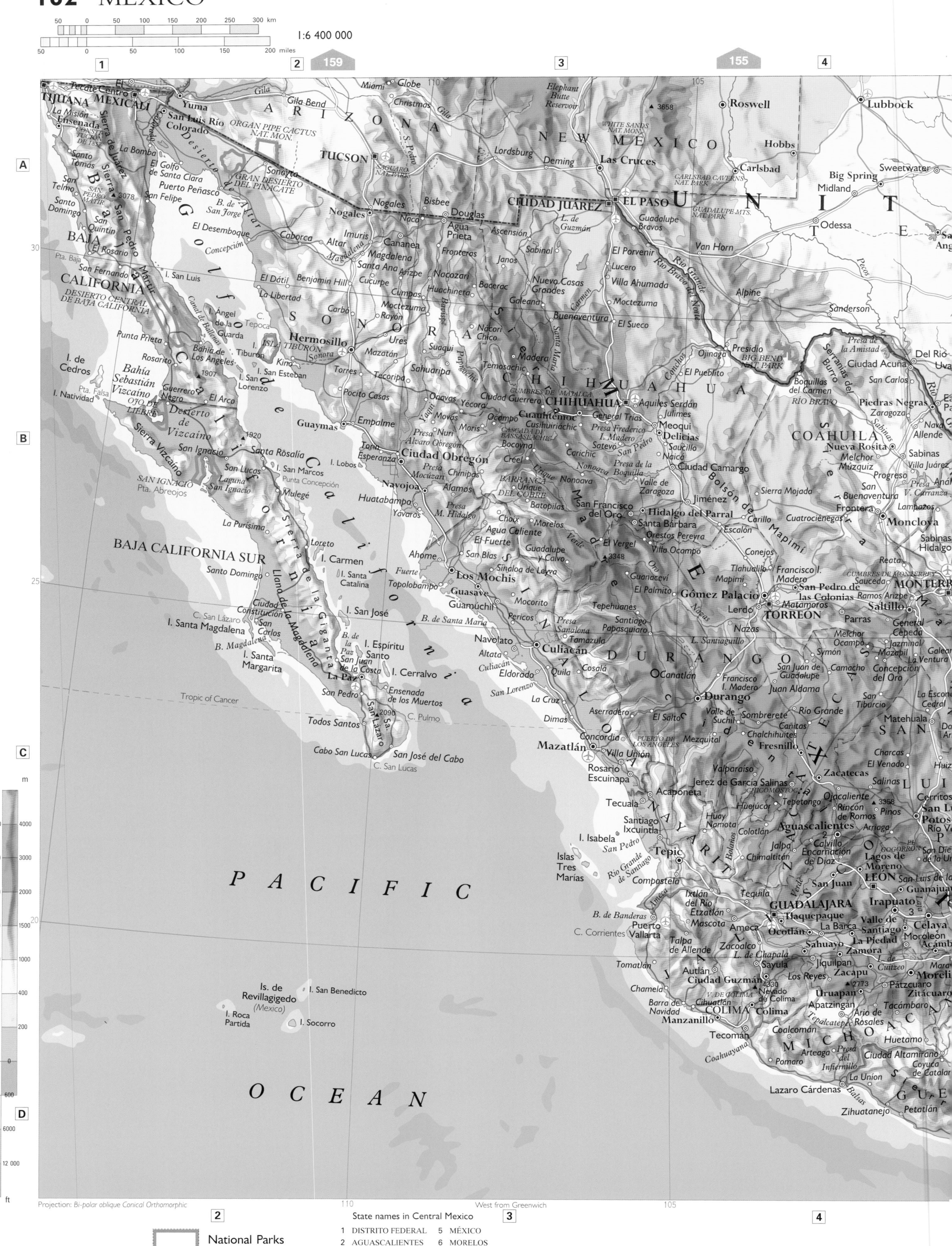

PACIFIC

OCEAN

Projection: Bi-polar oblique Conical Orthomorphic

National Parks

State names in Central Mexico

1	DISTRITO FEDERAL	5	MÉXICO
2	AGUASCALIENTES	6	MORELOS
3	GUANAJUATO	7	QUERÉTARO
4	HIDALGO	8	TLAXCALA

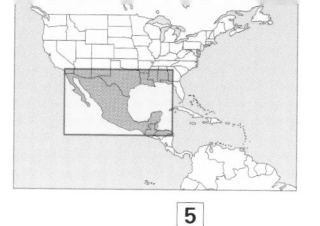

149

5 6 7 8

GULF OF MEXICO

GOLFO DE CAMPECHE

UNITED STATES

TEXAS · LOUISIANA · MISSISSIPPI · ALABAMA · GEORGIA · FLORIDA · ARKANSAS

Tropic of Cancer

CUBA

YUCATÁN · QUINTANA ROO · CAMPECHE · TABASCO · CHIAPAS · OAXACA · VERACRUZ · PUEBLA

GUATEMALA · BELIZE · HONDURAS

Golfo de Tehuantepec

164

COPYRIGHT PHILIP'S

50 0 50 100 150 200 250 300 km
50 0 50 100 150 200 miles

JAMAICA
1:2 400 000
10 0 10 20 30 40 50 km
10 0 10 20 30 miles

a

CARIBBEAN SEA

Montego Bay
Lucea
Falmouth
Runaway Bay
St. Ann's Bay
Galina Point
Port Maria
Annotto Bay
Negril
Cambridge
Wakefield
The Cockpit Country
Mount Denham 985
Ocho Rios
Dry Harbour Mountains
Moneague
Port Antonio
South Negril Pt.
Savanna-la-Mar
Maggotty
Don Figuero Mts.
Mandeville
Santa Cruz Mts.
Black River
May Pen
Linstead
Spanish Town
Portmore
The Blue Mountains
2256 Blue Mountain Peak
John Crow Mts.
Morant Point
Great Pedro Bluff
Alligator Pond
Portland Bight
KINGSTON
Morant Bay
Port Morant
Portland Point

A

1 I. Desterrada
I. Pérez (Mexico)

2 GULF OF MEXICO

3 L. Okeechobee
West Palm Beach
U.S.A.
Fort Myers
Naples
Everglades
C. Romano
Fort Lauderdale
Boca Raton
Freeport
Little Abaco I.
Hope Town
Grand Bahama
Northwest Providence Channel
Great Abaco I.

4

EVERGLADES NAT. PARK
Hialeah
MIAMI
C. Sable
Florida Bay
Bimini Is.
Berry Is.
Nicolls Town
Andros Town
Nassau
New Providence
Adelaide
Andros Island
BA
Eleuthera
Governor's
Portsm
Dunmore T

Dry Tortugas (U.S.A.)
Key West
Florida Keys
Straits of Florida
Santaren Channel
Cay Sal Bank
Canal Nicholás
Great Bahama Bank
Great Guana Cay
Great Exuma
Exuma Sound

LA HABANA (Havana)
Marianao
Guanabacoa
Santa Cruz del Norte
Matanzas
Cárdenas
Bahía Honda
Guanajay
San Antonio de los Baños
Güines
Jovellanos
Colón
Sagua la Grande
Caibarién
Jumento Cays
La Esperanza
Los Palacios
Pinar del Río
Guane
San Luis
Batabanó
Jagüey Grande
Santa Clara
Placetas
Morón
Cayo Romano
Duncan Town
La Fé
Nueva Gerona
I. de la Juventud
Cienfuegos
Trinidad
Sancti Spíritus
Júcaro
Ciego de Ávila
Nuevitas
Puerto Manatí
Corrientes
C. San Antonio
Arch. de los Canarreos
Arch. de Jardines de la Reina
Tunas de Zaza
Florida
Camagüey
Santa Cruz del Sur
Golfo de Guacanayabo
Victoria de las Tunas
Manzanillo
Gibara
HOLGUÍN
Sori
Bayamo
Sierra Maestra 1994
SANTIAGO DE CU

Cayman Islands (U.K.)
George Town
Grand Cayman
Cayman Brac
Little Cayman
C. Cruz

7680

Is. Santanilla (Swan Islands) (Honduras)

Montego Bay
Lucea
Falmouth
St. Ann's Bay
Port Maria
Negril
Cambridge
JAMAICA
Port Antonio
South Negril Pt.
Savanna-la-Mar
Black River
Mandeville
May Pen
Spanish Town
KINGSTON
Port
Pedro Cays (Jamaica)

B

Progreso
Dzilam de Bravo
Río Lagartos
El Cuyo
Punta Yalkubul
C. Catoche
Cancún
Mérida
Motul
Temax
Izamal
Espita
Tizimín
El Díaz
YUCATÁN
DZIBILCHALTÚN
Maxcanú
Sotuta
Valladolid
Puerto Morelos
Calkiní
Ticul
MAYAPÁN
CHICHÉN ITZÁ
Tenabo
UXMAL
Peto
Cozumel
Isla Cozumel
Campeche
Champotón
Hopelchén
Bolonchenticul
Felipe Carrillo Puerto
Vigia Chico
B. de la Ascensión
SIAN KA'AN
B. del Espíritu Santo
San José Carpizo
Chenkán
Edzná
QUINTANA ROO
MEXICO
Ciudad del Carmen
Términos
I. del Carmen
Pedro Antonio Santos
Bacalar
Chetumal
B. de Chetumal
Banco Chinchorro
PANTANOS DE CENTLA
Palizada
Balancán
CALAKMUL
Orange Walk
Corozal
Ambergris Cay
CAMPECHE
Tenosique
MIRADOR-RÍO AZUL
Uaxactún
San Pedro
Turneffe Is.
Palenque
SIERRA DE LACANDÓN
LAGUNA DEL TIGRE
San Ignacio
Belmopan
Belize City
Ocosingo
MONTES AZULES
L. Petén Itzá
Flores
JIKAL
BLUE HOLE
Middlesex
La Independencia
La Libertad
Benque Viejo
1120
BELIZE
Dangriga
Comitán
LAGUNAS DE MONTEBELLO
Sayaxché
CHIQUIBUL
Maya Mts.
Monkey River
Golfo de Honduras
Is. de la Bahía
San Luis
Punta Gorda
San Antonio
Roatán
Puerto Castilla
GUATEMALA
3993
Livingston
Puerto Barrios
Puerto Cortés
Tela
La Ceiba
Trujillo
Iriona
C. Camarón
Punta Patuca
Bajo Nuevo (Colombia)
Cuilco
Cuchumatanes
Cobán
L. de Izabal
RÍO DULCE
Motagua
San Pedro Sula
PICO BONITO
Balfate
Savá
Olanchito
Brus Laguna
Laguna Caratasca
San Marcos
Huehuetenango
Totonicapán
Sololá
Sierra de las Minas
El Progreso
Yoro
Arenal
RÍO PLÁTANO
Mosquitia
Ayutla
ATITLÁN
Antigua
Jalapa
Zacapa
Santa Bárbara
El Jaral
HONDURAS
Coco (Segovia)
C. Falso
Quetzaltenango
Chichicastenango
Chiquimula
Santa Rosa de Copán
L. de Yojoa
Comayagua
Juticalpa
Catacamas
Patuca
C. Gracias a Dios
Mazatenango
COPÁN
La Esperanza
Siguatepeque
PATUCA
Puerto Cabo Gracias á Dios
Retalhuleu
GUATEMALA
La Paz
Tegucigalpa
Danlí
Kisalaya
San José
Amatitlán
Escuintla
Suchitoto
Yuscarán
Coco
Cayos Miskitos (Nicaragua)
Ahuachapán
Santa Ana
Nueva San Salvador
Cojutepeque
Nacaome
Choluteca
Somoto
Bonanza
Siuna
Pta. Gorda
Acajutla
SAN SALVADOR
Zacatecoluca
La Unión
Jinotega
Saslaya
Puerto Cabezas
Sonsonate
San Miguel
G. de Fonseca
Estelí
Matagalpa
Tuma
Tungla
Usulután
Puerto Morazán
El Sauce
Muy Muy
Prinzapolca
EL SALVADOR
Chinandega
Cord. Isabelia
San Pedro del Norte
Río Grande
Corinto
León
Boaco
Siquia
Santo Domingo
Punta de Perlas
La Paz Centro
L. de Managua
Juigalpa
Rama
El Bluff
Is. del Maíz (Nicaragua)
NICARAGUA
MANAGUA
Masaya
Granada
Bluefields
Diriamba
Jinotepe
Lago de Nicaragua
Cord. de Yolaina
Cayos Roncador (Colombia)
Rivas
I. de Ometepe
I. de Providencia (Colombia)
San Juan del Sur
San Carlos
Cayos de Albuquerque (Colombia)
B. de Salinas
La Cruz
Los Chiles
San Juan del Norte
I. de San Andrés (Colombia)
GUANACASTE
C. Santa Elena
SANTA ROSA
G. de Papagayo
Liberia
Cord. de Guanacaste
B. de San Juan del Norte
PALO VERDE
TORTUGUERO
C. Velas
Santa Cruz
Nicoya
COSTA RICA
Cord. Central
Guápiles
Siquirres
Limón
Carmona
Pen. de Nicoya
Alajuela
San José
Puntarenas
Esparza
Cartago
Pta.
C. Blanco
Bribri
Bocas del Toro
Nombre de Dios
Archipiélago de San Blas
CARTA
RICA
Pandora
Panama Canal
Portobelo
Golfo del Darién
G. de Nicoya
Puerto Quepos
Chirripó
Cord. de Talamanca
AMISTAD
Almirante
Changuinola
Chiriquí
G. de los Mosquitos
Colón
L. Gatún
Balboa
Serranía de San Blas
I. de San Bernar
B. de Coronado
Puerto Cortés
San Vito
Volcán Barú 3374
Boquete
Concepción
PANAMÁ
Chepo
La Palma
Golfo de San Miguel
CORCOVADO
Buenos Aires
Chiriquí Grande
3837
David
Remedios
Río Hato
Penonomé
Chimán
Yaviza
Pen. de Osa
Golfito
Pta. Burica
Puerto Armuelles
Santiago
Sona
Aguadulce
Arch. de las Perlas
I. del Rey
DARIÉN
El Real
Golfo de Panamá
G. Dulce
Pta. Mariato
I. de Coiba
Chitré
Las Tablas
Garachiné
COIBA
G. de Chiriquí
Pen. de Azuero
Pocrí
Monte
I. de Cebaco
Tonosí
I. Jicarón
Punta Mala
CERRO HOYA

C

D

E

PACIFIC OCEAN

2

1

GUADELOUPE
1:1 600 000
Pointe de la Grande Vigie
61° 30'
16° 30'
Port-Louis
Grande-Terre
Pointe Allègre
Petit-Canal
Moule
La Désirade
Ste-Rose
Pointe-à-Pitre
Ste-Anne
Pointe Noire
Gosier
Pointe des Châteaux
Basse-Terre
GUADELOUPE (Fr.)
Îles de la Petite Terre
Bouillante
1467
Soufrière
Capesterre-Belle-Eau
Marie-Galante
16°
St-Louis
Basse-Terre
Trois-Rivières
204
Capesterre
Grand-Bourg
Pte. des Basses
61° 30'
Îles des Saintes

MARTINIQUE
Cap St-Martin
Basse-Pointe
1463
Le Prêcheur
Montagne Pelée
Ste-Marie
Presqu'île de la Caravelle
St-Pierre
La Trinité
Le Robert
St-Joseph
Le François
Fort-de-France
Le Lamentin
Le St-Esprit
Rivière-Salée
Rivière-Pilote
Le Marin
MARTINIQUE (Fr.)
14° 30'
Pte. d'Enfer

GUADELOUPE AND MARTINIQUE
1:1 600 000
10 0 10 20 30 40 50 60 km
10 0 10 20 30 40 miles

Projection: Bi-polar oblique Conical Orthomorphic

80

ATLANTIC OCEAN

PUERTO RICO d
1:2 400 000
10 0 10 20 30 40 50 km
10 0 10 20 30 miles

PUERTO RICO (U.S.A.)
Pta. Agujereada
Isabela
Aguadilla
Arecibo
Barceloneta
Manati
Vega Baja
San Juan
SJU
Rio Grande
Bayamón
Carolina
Fajardo
Mayagüez
San Sebastian
Utuado
Adjuntas
Cordillera Central
Cerro de Punta 1338
Sierra de Luquillo
Dewey
Culebra
San German
Uroyan Mts.
Yauco
Cayey
Humacao
Naguabo
Vieques
Esperanza
Pta. Aguila
Guanica
Ponce
Coamo
Guayama
Yabucoa
I. Caja de Muertos

VIRGIN ISLANDS e
1:1 600 000
10 0 10 20 30 km
10 0 10 20 miles

Virgin Islands (U.K.)
Rufling Pt.
The Settlement
Anegada
East Pt.
Great Camanoe
Virgin Is. (U.S.A.)
Jost Van Dyke I.
Hans Lollik I.
Guana I.
Virgin Gorda
Beef I.
Spanish Town
Tortola
Road Town
Peter I.
Charlotte Amalie
St. John I.
St. Thomas I.
VIRGIN IS.

ST. LUCIA f
1:800 000
5 0 10 km
5 0 5 10 miles

Cap Point
Pte. Hardy
Gros Islet
Esperance Bay
Castries
Marquis
Babonneau
L'Anse la Raye
Canaries
Millet
Dennery
Soufrière
Soufrière Bay
Mt. Gimie 950
750 Petit Piton
Micoud
Vierge Pt.
Gros Piton Pt. 796
Gros Piton
Choiseul
ST. LUCIA
Laborie
Vieux Fort
C. Moule à Chique

ATLANTIC OCEAN
Crabhill
North Point
Spring Hall
Fustic
Boscobelle
Portland
245 Bellepaine
BARBADOS
Speightstown
Bathsheba
Hillcrest
Westmoreland
Mt. Hillaby 340
Martin's Bay
Alleynes Bay
Bridgefield
Massiah Street
Holetown
Jackson
Ragged Pt.
Six Cross Roads
Black Rock
Ellerton
Edey
The Crane
Bridgetown
Ivy
Oistins
St. Martins
Carlisle Bay
Worthing
Oistins Bay
Chancery Lane
South Point
BGI

BARBADOS g
1:800 000
5 0 10 km
5 0 5 10 miles

ATLANTIC OCEAN
Tropic of Cancer

's Town
The Bight
Cat I.
Salvador I.
Conception I.
Rum Cay
Long I.
Clarence Town
Crooked I. Passage
Samana Cay
Albert Town
Snug Corner
Plana Cays
Mayaguana I.
Verde
Acklins I.
Mira por vos Cay
Crooked I.
Hogsty Reef
Caicos Passage
Turks & Caicos (U.K.)
Little Inagua I.
Caicos Is.
Cockburn Town
Turks Is.
Lake Rose
INAGUA
Turks Island Passage
Great Inagua I.
Matthew Town

Moa
Baracoa
Pta. de Maisi
Maisi
Guantánamo (U.S.A.)
Paso de los Vientos (Windward Passage)
Cap-Haïtien
Monte Cristi
LA ISABELA
Puerto Plata
Santiago de los Cabelleros
Milwaukee Deep 9200
Puerto Rico Trench
Jean Rabel
Port-de-Paix
Fort Liberté
Cord.
La Vega
San Francisco de Macoris
Nagua
Samana
Cap-à-Foux
G. de la Gonâve
Gonaïves
Central
Hinche
ARMANDO BERMUDEZ
Pico Duarte 3175
Sanchez
Sabana de la Mar
LOS HAITISES
Î. de la Tortue
St-Marc
Jérémie
Î. de la Gonâve
HAITI
DOMINICAN REP
San Pedro de Macoris
Higüey
La Romana
Dame
PORT-AU-PRINCE
San Juan
SANTO DOMINGO
Hato Mayor
C. Engaño
Marie
Massif de la Hotte
Petit
Goâve
2280
SIERRA DE BAHORUCO
Azua de Compostela
San Cristóbal
ESTE
B. de Yuma
Saona
Les Cayes
Aquin
Jacmel
L. Enriquillo
Barahona
Pedernales
Isla Mona (U.S.A.)
Pointe-à- Gravois
î. à Vache
I. Beata
C. Beata
Hispaniola
Mona Passage
Aguadilla
Arecibo
Bayamón
SAN JUAN
Carolina
Virgin Gorda
Tortola (U.K.)
Anegada
Sombrero (U.K.)
Anguilla (U.K.)
Ponce
Mayagüez
1338
Caguas
Fajardo
St. Thomas
Road Town
St.-Martin (Fr.)
PUERTO RICO (U.S.A.)
Charlotte Amalie
Virgin Is. (U.S.A.)
St. Maarten (Neth.)
St.-Barthélemy (Fr.)
Barbuda
Christiansted
Saba (Neth.)
Frederiksted
St. Croix
St. Eustatius (Neth.)
ST. KITTS & NEVIS
ANTIGUA & BARBUDA
St. John's
Basseterre
Nevis
Antigua
Redonda
Montserrat (U.K.)
Guadeloupe Passage
Ste-Rose
Moule
La Désirade
GUADELOUPE (Fr.) 1467
Pointe-à-Pitre
Basse-Terre
Marie-Galante (Fr.)
Grand-Bourg
I. des Saintes (Fr.)
Dominica Passage
Portsmouth
DOMINICA 1447
Roseau
MORNE TROIS PITONS
Martinique Passage
Mt. Pelée 1397
Ste-Marie
Fort-de-France
Le François
Rivière-Pilote
MARTINIQUE (Fr.)
St. Lucia Channel
Castries 950
ST. LUCIA
Soufrière
St. Vincent Passage
Soufrière 1234
St. Vincent
Kingstown
Speightstown
Bridgetown
BARBADOS
ST. VINCENT & THE GRENADINES
Hillsborough
Grenadines
St. George's
GRENADA

C A R I B B E A N   S E A

Antilles
Lesser Antilles
Leeward Islands
Windward Islands
Lesser Antilles

I. de Aves (Venezuela)

Aruba (Neth.)
Oranjestad
Curaçao
Bonaire
NETH. ANTILLES
Willemstad
ARC. LOS ROQUES
I. Orchila (Ven.)
I. Blanquilla (Ven.)
Is. Los Hermanos (Ven.)
Tobago
Scarborough
Pta. Gallinas
MACUIRA
Pen. de la Guajira
Is. Las Aves (Ven.)
Is. Los Roques (Ven.)
I. La Tortuga (Ven.)
Is. Los Testigos (Ven.)
Port of Spain
Galera Point
Trinidad
COLOMBIA
Riohacha
Uribia
C. San Román
Pen. de Paraguaná
Punta Cardón
MEDANOS DE CORO
Puerto Cumarebo
NUEVA ESPARTA
I. de Margarita
Porlamar
Pen. de Paria
Güiria
Arima
Rio Claro
Santa Marta
GUAJIRA
Punto Fijo
Coro
La Vela de Coro
CERRO EL COPEY
La Asunción
Dragon's Mouth
San Fernando
TRINIDAD & TOBAGO
TAYRONA
SA. DE SAN LUIS
Tucacas
LAGUNA LA RESTINGA
Caribe
TRUJILLO
S. NEVADA DE STA. MARTA
San Rafael
Altagracia
Puerto Cabello
Maiquetía
La Guaira
Carúpano
Cumaná
SUCRE
G. de Paria
Maturín
Santa Marta 5800
Cienaga
FALCÓN
Maracay
CARACAS
VARGAS
Higuerote
Puerto La Cruz
MOCHIMA
TURIMIQUIRE
CARIPE
Ciénaga Grande
Soledad
San Felipe
YARACUY
Los Teques
Rio Chico
Barcelona
Caicara
Caripito
Sabanalarga
Fundación
Villa del Rosario
Santa Rita
Cabimas
LARA
Carora
Valencia
Villa de Cura
San Juan de los Morros
Aragua de Barcelona
Anaco
MONAGAS
MARIUSA
Valledupar
Ciudad Ojeda
BARQUISIMETO
TEREBINA
MIRANDA
GUATOPO
Ocumare del Tuy
El Tigre
DELTA
Calamar
CESAR
Machiques
Mene Grande
Acarigua
COJEDES
Valle de la Pascua
El Sombrero
Cantaura
Tucupita
MAGDALENA
ZULIA
Lago de Maracaibo
Trujillo
PORTUGUESA
GUARICO
Calabozo
Santa Maria de Ipire
AMACURO
SERRANIA PERIJA
Betijoque
Valera
El Guache
Guanare
El Báúl
Pariaguan
Ciudad Guayana
MARACAIBO
Maracaibo
MÉRIDA
Trujillo
Guanare Portuguesa
Sierra Imataca
NORTE DE SANTANDER
La Concepción
San Carlos del Zulia
El Banco
CATATUMBO-BARI
Encontrados
BARINAS
Barinas
Libertad
GUARICO-GUARIQUITO
Soledad
El Pao
Ciudad Bolívar
Ocaña
Mompós
TACHIRA
CATATUMBO
SANTANDER
MÉRIDA
Ciudad Bolivia
San Fernando de Apure
Guri
BOLIVAR
Cúcuta
Santa Bárbara
San Antonio
PAPO-CAPARO
Bruzual
Achaguas
Apure
Caicara
Embalse de Guri
El Callao
Upata
Guasipati
Tumeremo

West from Greenwich

National Parks

COPYRIGHT PHILIP'S

4000 3000 2000 1500 1000 400 200 0
600 6000 12 000 18 000 24 000 ft
12 000 9000 6000 4500 3000 1200 600 0
200 2000 4000 6000 8000 m

100 0 200 400 600 800 1000 1200 1400 km

1:28 000 000

100   200   400   600   800   1000 miles

Projection: Lambert's Azimuthal Equal Area

COPYRIGHT PHILIP'S

1:28 000 000

100 0   200 400 600 800 1000 1200 1400 km

100 0   200   400   600   800   1000 miles

1   **2**   **3**   **4**   **5**   **6**   **7**

Tropic of Cancer

Havana   BAHAMAS   Turks & Caicos Is.
C U B A   (U.K.)

A

HAITI   DOMINICAN
Port-au-   REP.   San Juan   Virgin Is.
JAMAICA   Prince   (U.K.)
Kingston   PUERTO   ST. KITTS   ANTIGUA &
                RICO   & NEVIS   BARBUDA
MEXICO   (U.S.A.)   Basse-Terre   GUADELOUPE
BELIZE   DOMINICA   (Fr.)
                            Fort-de-France   MARTINIQUE
GUATEMALA   HONDURAS   (Fr.)
Guatemala   Tegucigalpa   Castries   ST. LUCIA
San Salvador   NICARAGUA   ST. VINCENT   BARBADOS
EL SALVADOR   Managua   C. de   Kingstown   Bridgetown
        COSTA   San José   la Aguja   GRENADA   St. George's
        RICA   Panamá   Barranquilla   Port of
            PANAMA   Cartagena   Maracaibo   Caracas   Spain   TRINIDAD &
                Barquisimeto   TOBAGO
                San Cristóbal   Valencia
        Medellín   Bucaramanga   Orinoco   Ciudad Guayana
            Bogotá   VENEZUELA   Georgetown
        Cali   RORAIMA   GUYANA   Paramaribo
                COLOMBIA   SURINAME   Cayenne
                                        FRENCH   C. Orange
                                        GUIANA

B

Caribbean Sea

Aruba   Curaçao

Cúcuta

Magdalena

Gulf of Panamá

Gulf of Darién

C

NORTH

ATLANTIC

OCEAN

AMAPÁ

Branco

Essequibo

Galapagos Is.   Quito   Equator
(Ecuador)   ECUADOR   Putumayo   Japurá   Amazon   Marajó   Belém
Guayaquil   Napo   Iquitos   I.
G. of Guayaquil   Marañón   AMAZONAS   Manaus   Santarém   São Luís
        Purus   Amazon   Fortaleza
    Chiclayo   Ucayali   Juruá   Madeira   PARÁ   MARANHÃO   C. de
    Trujillo   A C R E   Purus   Teresina   São Roque
    Chimbote   Pôrto Velho   Tapajós   CEARÁ   Natal
            RONDÔNIA   Tocantins   PIAUÍ   RIO G.
PERU   TOCANTINS   DO NORTE
Callao   LIMA   B R A Z I L   PARAÍBA
    Cuzco   Madre de Dios   Araguaia   PERNAMBUCO   Campina Grande
    L.   MATO GROSSO   GOIÁS   Recife
    Titicaca   Mamoré   DIS. FED.   São Francisco   ALAGOAS   Maceió
        BOLIVIA   Santa Cruz   Cuiabá   Goiânia   Brasília   SERGIPE   Aracaju
    Arequipa   La Paz   Cochabamba   BAHÍA   Salvador
        Sucre   MINAS GERAIS
PACIFIC   MATO GROSSO
                DO SUL   Belo   ESPÍRITO
Iquique   Paraguay   Paraná   Ribeirão   Horizonte   SANTO
                        Prêto   Juiz   Vitória
                PARAGUAY   SÃO PAULO   de Fora   Campos
Antofagasta   Pilcomayo   PARANÁ   Campinas   R. DE J.
    San Félix   Salta   Asunción   SÃO   Niterói
    (Chile)   PAULO   RIO DE
Tropic of Capricorn   San Ambrosio   Resistencia   Paraná   SANTA CATARINA   JANEIRO
        (Chile)   Corrientes   Uruguay
                San Miguel   RIO GRANDE
                de Tucumán   DO SUL   Pôrto Alegre

D

E

F

Arch. de Juan Fernández   Córdoba   Santa Fe   Pelotas
(Chile)   San Juan   A   Rosario   URUGUAY
    Viña del Mar   Mendoza   R   Paraná   Montevideo
    Valparaíso   G   BUENOS AIRES
    SANTIAGO   C   E   La Plata   Río de la Plata
    Talca   H   N   SOUTH
    Concepción   I   T   Bahía   Mar del Plata
        L   I   Blanca
    Valdivia   E   N   Colorado   ATLANTIC
            A   Negro   Viedma

G

OCEAN

PACIFIC

OCEAN

Puerto Montt

Comodoro Rivadavia
Gulf of San Jorge

Gulf of Penas   Chubut   OCEAN

H

West Falkland   FALKLAND IS.
            (U.K.)
Magellan's Str.   Stanley
Punta Arenas   East Falkland
    Tierra del Fuego   South Georgia
C. Horn   (U.K.)

Projection: Lambert's Azimuthal Equal Area

60 West from Greenwich 50

COPYRIGHT PHILIP'S

1   **2**   **3**   **4**   **5**   **6**   **7**

■ LIMA Capital Cities

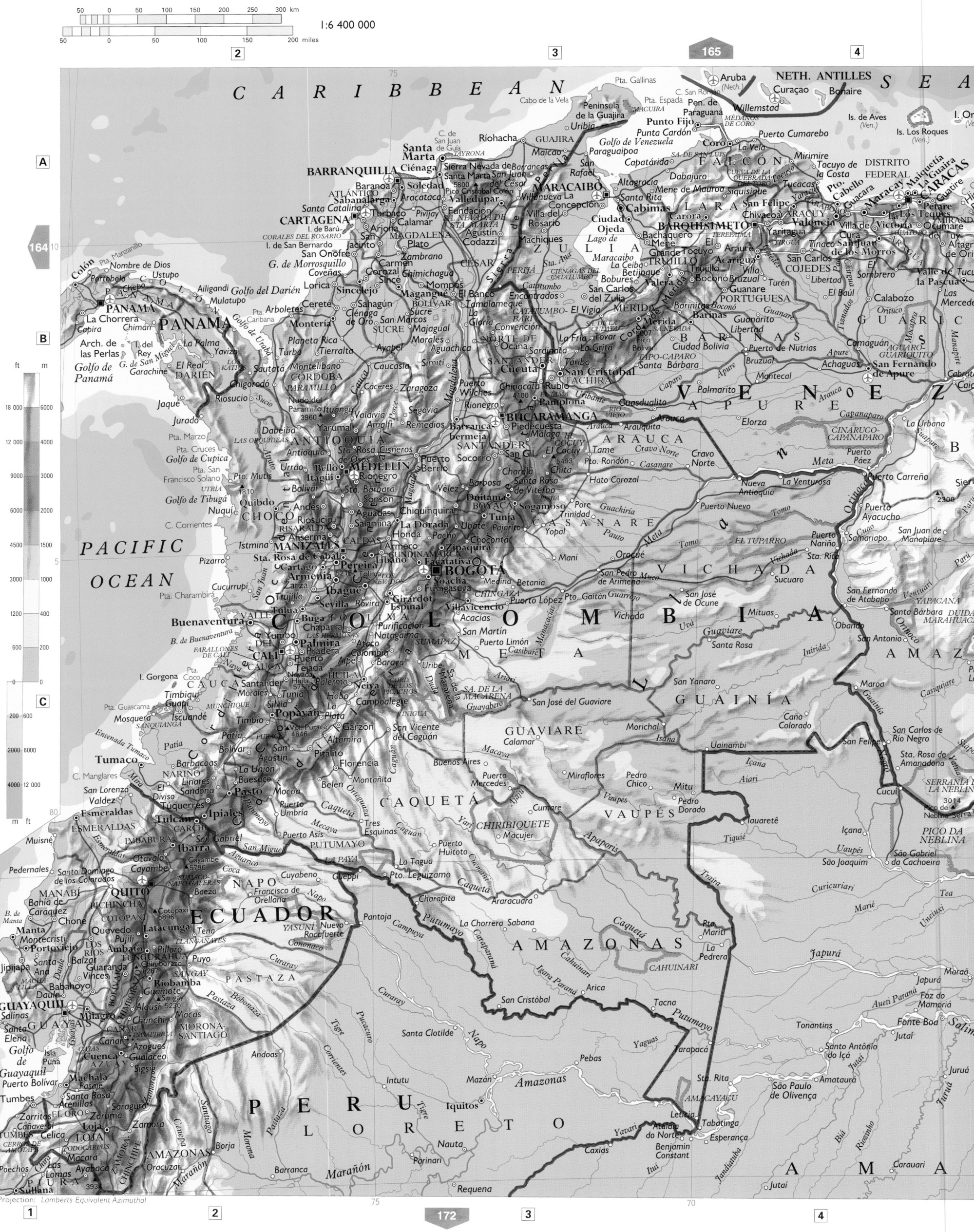

1:6 400 000

Projection: Lamberts Equivalent Azimuthal

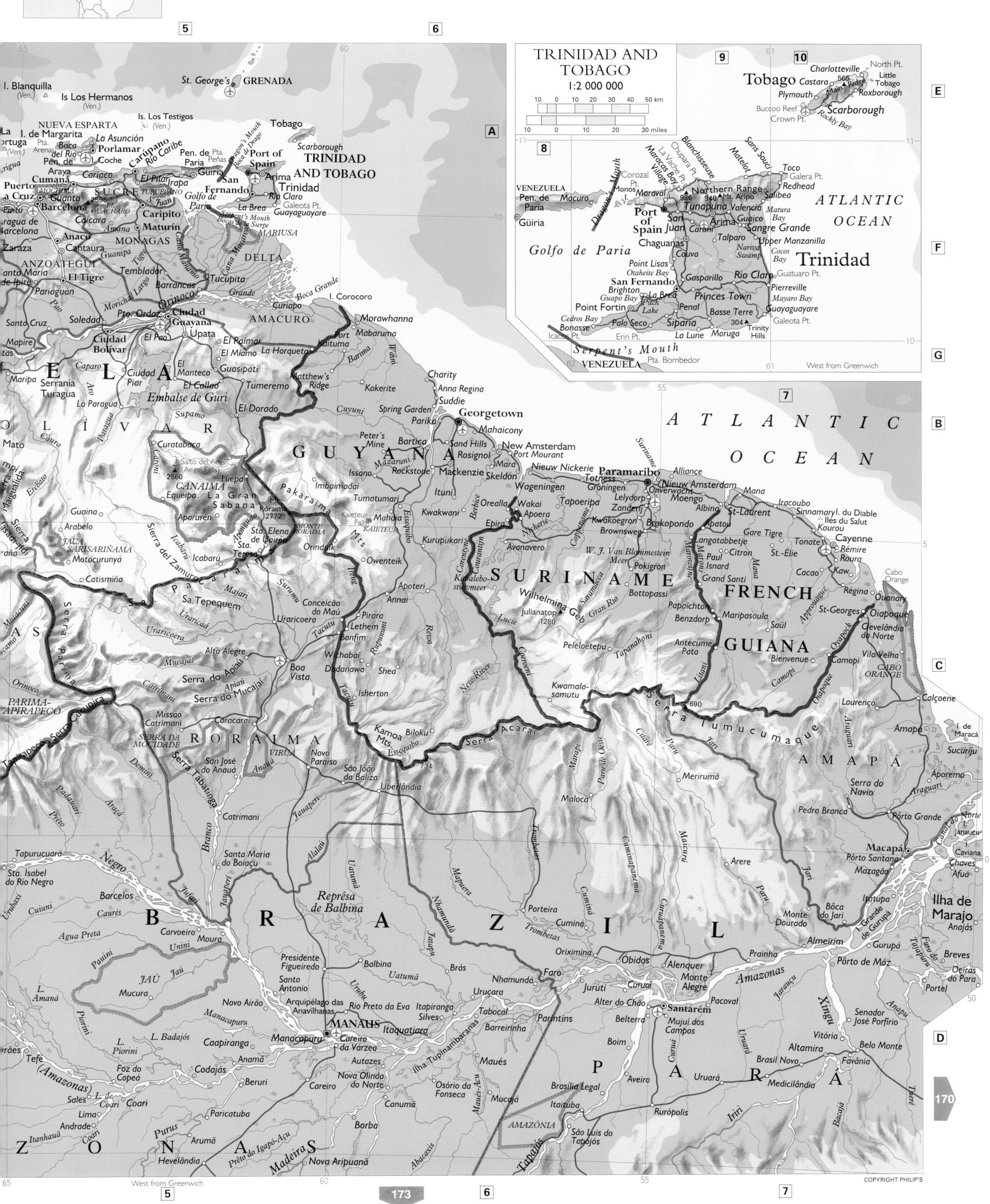

TRINIDAD AND TOBAGO
1:2 000 000

10 0 10 20 30 40 50 km
10 0 10 20 30 miles

9

10

Tobago
Charlotteville
North Pt.
Castara
565
Little
Tobago
Plymouth
Main Ridge
Roxborough
Scarborough
Buccoo Reef
Crown Pt.
Rockly Bay

E

-11-

8

VENEZUELA
Pen. de
Paria
Macuro

Güiria

Dragon's Mouth
Corozal
Pt.
Monos
Chupara Pt.
La Vacha Pt.
Maracas Bay
Maraval
Blanchisseuse
Sans Souci
Toco
Galera Pt.
Redhead
Salibea
Matelot
Northern Range
936
940 Mt. Aripo
Tunapuna
Valencia
Guaico
Matura
Bay
Sangre Grande
**Port of
Spain**
San
Juan
Arima
Carom
Chaguanas
Talparo
Upper Manzanilla
Couva
Narisa
Swamp
Cocos
Bay
Point Lisas
Otaheite Bay
Gasparillo
San Fernando
Brighton
La Brea
Guapo Bay
Pitch
Lake
Point Fortin
Penal
Cedros Bay
Bonasse
Palo Seco
Icacos Pt.
Erin Pt.
La Lune
Moruga

Golfo de Paria

Rio Claro
Pierreville
Mayaro Bay
Princes Town
Basse Terre
Guayaguayare
Siparia
304▲
Trinity
Hills
Galeota Pt.
Guatuaro Pt.

Trinidad

*ATLANTIC
OCEAN*

F

Serpent's Mouth
Pta. Bombedor
VENEZUELA
West from Greenwich
61
62

G

10

A

B

C

D

West from Greenwich

170

COPYRIGHT PHILIP'S

1:6 400 000

50 0 50 100 150 200 250 300 km
50 0 50 100 150 200 miles

A T L A N T I C   O C E A N

Equator

CABO ORANGE

AMAPÁ

Macapá

Ilha de Marajó

BELÉM (Pará)

PARÁ

Tocantins

MARANHÃO

SÃO LUÍS (Maranhão)

Bacabal

Teresina

PIAUÍ

CEARÁ

FORTALEZA (Ceará)

Parnaíba
Sobral
Crateús
Crato
Juàzeiro do Norte
Iguatu

Petrolina

RIO GRANDE DO NORTE

NATAL
Macau
Mossoró
Açu

PARAÍBA

JOÃO PESSOA (Paraíba)

Campina Grande
Patos
Sousa

PERNAMBUCO

RECIFE (Pernambuco)
Olinda
Jaboatão
Caruaru
Garanhuns
Palmares

ALAGOAS

MACEIÓ
Penedo
União dos Palmares

Chapada das Mangabeiras

Serra do Penitente

Imperatriz

Carolina

Balsas

TOCANTINS

Araguaína

Serra dos Carajás

Xingu

Tocantins

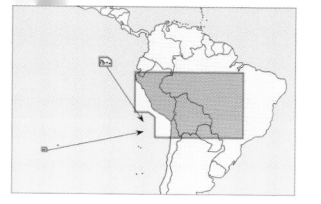

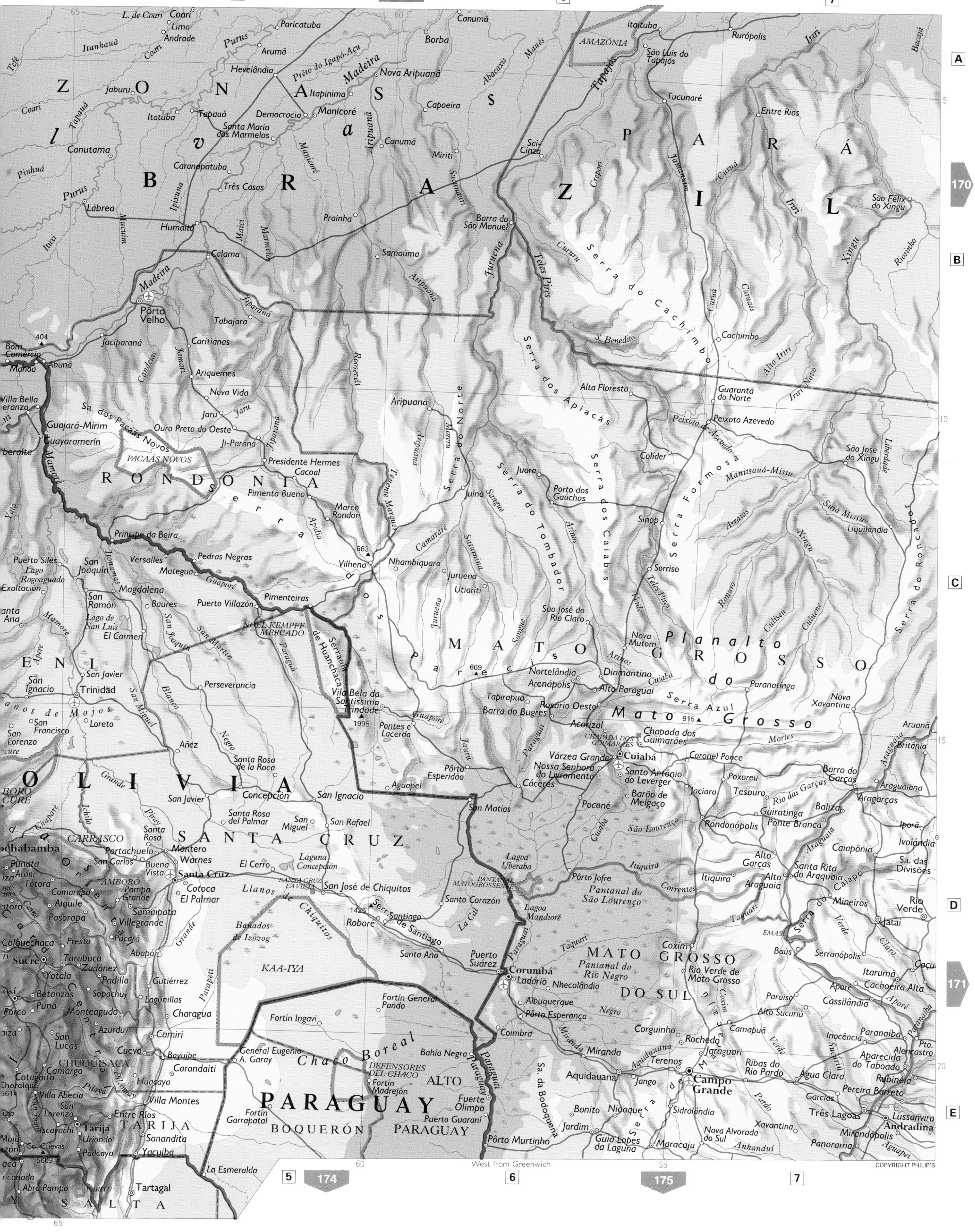

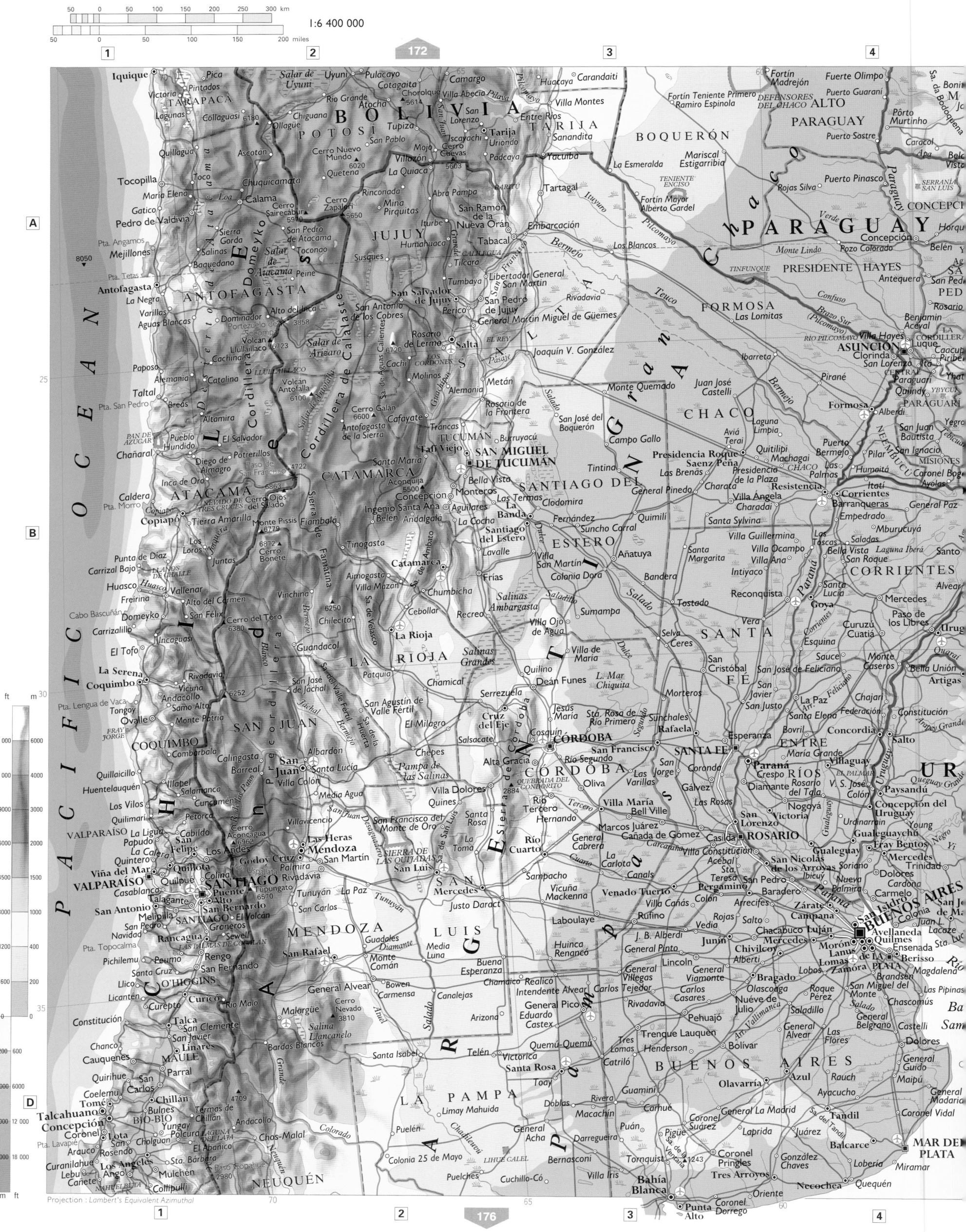

1:6 400 000

Projection : Lambert's Equivalent Azimuthal

National Parks

50 0 50 100 150 200 250 300 km
50 0 50 100 150 200 miles

1:6 400 000

174   175

Projection: Lambert's Equivalent Azimuthal

COPYRIGHT PHILIP'S

National Parks

West from Greenwich

PACIFIC OCEAN

SOUTH ATLANTIC OCEAN

FALKLAND ISLANDS (U.K.)
(ISLAS MALVINAS)

West Falkland   East Falkland   Stanley

GEOGRAPHICAL GLOSSARY

This is a list of the geographical terms from various foreign languages that are found in the place names on the maps and in the index. Each is followed by the language and its English meaning.

Afr. Afrikaans
Alb. Albanian
Amh. Amharic
Ar. Arabic
Belo. Belorussian
Berb. Berber
Bulg. Bulgarian
Burm. Burmese
Cat. Catalan
Chin. Chinese
Czec. Czech
Dan. Danish
Dut. Dutch
Est. Estonian
Fr. French
Gae. Gaelic
Ger. German
Gr. Greek
Heb. Hebrew
Hin. Hindi
Hung. Hungarian
I.-C. Indo-Chinese
Ice. Icelandic
It. Italian
Indo. Indonesian
Jap. Japanese
Kaz. Kazakh
Kor. Korean
Kyrg. Kyrgyz
Lapp. Lapp (Sami)
Lat. Latvian
Lith. Lithuanian
Malag. Malagasy
Mong. Mongolian
Nor. Norway
Pash. Pashto
Per. Persian
Pol. Polish
Port. Portuguese
Rom. Romanian
Russ. Russian
Sin. Sinhalese
Ser.-Cr. Serbo-Croat
Slov. Slovene
Som. Somali
Sp. Spanish
Swe. Swedish
Tib. Tibetan
Turk. Turkish
Ukr. Ukrainian
Viet. Vietnamese

-á *Ice.* river
-å *Dan., Nor., Swe.* stream
-abad *Farsi, Russ.* town
Abyad *Ar.* white mountain
Ada, Adasi *Turk.* island
Addis *Amh.* new
Adrar *Ar., Ber.* mountains
Aiguille *Fr.* peak
Aïn, Aïn (A.) *Ar.* spring
Ákra *Gr.* cape, point
Akrotíri *Gr.* cape, point
Alb *Ger.* mountains
Albufera *Span.* lagoon
-ålen *Nor.* islands
Alpen *Ger.* mountain ranges
Alpes *Fr.* mountains
Alpi *It.* mountains
Alt *Ger.* old
Alta, Alto *Port.* high, upper
Altos *Span.* mountains
-älv, -älven *Swe.* stream, river
Amtskommune (Amt.) *Dan.* first-order administrative division
-ån *Swe.* river
Anse *Fr.* bay
Ao *Thai* bay
Appennino *It.* mountain range
Archipel *Fr.* archipelago
Archipiélago (Arch.) *Span.* archipelago
Arcipélago *It.* archipelago
Arquipélago (Arq.) *Port.* archipelago
Arrecife *Span.* reef
Arroyo (Arr.) *Span.* stream
-ås, -åsen *Nor., Swe.* hill
Ayios *Gr.* island
Ayn *Ar.* well, waterhole

Baai, -baai *Afr., Dut.* bay
Bāb *Ar.* gate, strait
Bäck, -bäcken *Swe.* stream
Back, -backen, *Swe.* hill
Bad, -baden *Ger.* spa
Badia *Cat.* bay
Bādiyah, Bādiyat *Ar.* desert
Bæk *Dan.* stream
Bælt *Dan.* strait
Baharu *Malay* new
Bahía (B.) *Span.* bay
Bahiret *Ar.* lagoon
Bahr *Ar.* sea, lake, river
Bahra Bahrat *Ar.* lake
Baía (B.) *Port.* bay
Baie (B.) *Fr.* bay
Baixa, Baixo *Port.* lower
Baja, Bajo *Span.* lower
Bakke *Nor.* hill
Bala *Farsi* upper
Ballon *Fr.* dome
Baltă *Rom.* marsh, lake
Ban *Lao, Thai* village
-Bana *Jap.* cape
Banc *Fr.* bank
Banco *Span.* bank
Bandao *Chin.* peninsula
Bandar *Ar., Malay* port, harbour
Bandar *Farsi* bay
Banja *Ser.-Cr.* spa, resort
Banjaran *Malay* mountain range
Baraji *Turk.* dam
Barat *Indo., Malay* western
Barrage (Barr.) *Fr.* dam
Barragem (Barr.) *Port.* dam, reservoir
Bas, basse *Fr.* lower
Bassin *Fr.* basin
-batang *Indo.* river
Baṭlaq *Farsi* marsh
Batu *Malay* mountain
Bayt *Heb.* house, village
Bazar *Hin.* market, bazaar
-beek *Afr., Dut.* river
Be'er *Heb.* well
Bei *Chin.* north, northern
Beinn, Ben *Gae.* mountain
Beit *Heb.* village
Belaya, Belo, Beloye, Belyy *Russ.* white
Belogorye *Russ.* hills, mountain range
Bender *Som.* harbour
Berg(e), -berg(e) *Afr., Ger.* mountain(s)
-berg, -en, -et *Nor., Swe.* hill, mountain, rock
Besar *Indo., Malay* big
Bet *Heb.* house, village
Bir, Bîr, Bi'r *Ar.* well
Birkat, Birket *Ar.* lake, marsh, well
Bishti *Alb.* cape
-bjerg *Dan.* hill, point
Blaenau *Welsh* upland
-bo *Chin.* lake
Boca *Port., Span.* river mouth, inlet
Bodden *Ger.* bay, inlet
Bogaz, Boğazı *Turk.* channel, strait
Bogd *Mong.* mountain range
Bois *Fr.* woods
Boka *Ser.-Cr.* gulf, inlet
Bolshoi, Bolshaya, Bolshoye (Bol.) *Russ.* great, large
Bordj (Bj.) *Ar.* fort
-borg *Dan., Nor., Swe.* castle, fort
Bory *Pol.* woods
Bosque *Span.* woods
-botn *Nor.* valley floor
Bouche(s) *Fr.* mouth(s)
Braţul *Rom.* distributary stream, branch
-bre, -breen *Nor.* glacier
Bredning *Dan.* bay
Brücke *Ger.* bridge
-brug *Dut.* bridge
-brunn *Swe.* well, spring
Bucht *Ger.* bay
Bugt *Dan.* bay
-bugten *Dan.* bay
Buheirat *Ar.* lake, reservoir
Bukit *Malay* hill
-bukt, -a *Nor.* bay
-bukten *Swe.* bay
-bulag *Mong.* spring
Bulag *Chin.* lake
Bulu *Malay* mountain
Bum *Burm.* mountain
Būr *Ar.* port
Burg. *Ar.* fort
Burg, -burg *Ger.* castle
Burnu, Burun *Turk.* cape
Butt *Gae.* promontory
Büyük *Turk.* big
-by *Dan., Nor., Swe.* town
-byen *Nor., Swe.* town

Cabeza *Span.* peak, hill
Cabo (C.) *Port., Span.* headland, cape
Cachoeira *Port.* waterfall
Cala Cat. *It.* bay
Camp Port. *Span.* land, field
Câmpia *Rom.* plain
Campo *It., Port., Span.* plain
Campos *Span.* upland
Canal (Can.) *Fr., Port., Span.* canal, channel
Canale (Can.) *It.* channel
Canalul (Can.) *Ser.-Cr.* canal
Cao Nguyen *Thai* plateau, tableland
Cap (C.) *Cat., Fr.* cape
Capo (C) *It.* cape
Carn *Gae.* hill
Carse *Gae.* valley
Catarata *Port., Span.* cataract
Cauce *Span.* intermittent stream
Causse *Fr.* limestone plateau
Cay, Cayi, -cay, -cayi *Turk.* river
Cayo(s) *Span.* rock(s), islet(s)
Cefn *Welsh* hill
Cerro *Span.* hill, peak
Česká, Český, České *Czec.* Czech
Chaco *Span.* jungle
Chaîne(s) *Fr.* mountain range(s)
Chang *Chin.* mountain
Chapa *Span.* hills, upland
Chapada *Port.* hills, upland
Chaung *Burm.* stream, river
Chi *Chin.* small lake
-ch'ŏn *Kor.* river
-chŏsuji *Kor.* reservoir
Chott *Ar.* salt lake, depression
Chu *Tib.* river
Chute *Fr.* waterfall
Città *It.* city
Ciudad *Span.* city
Co *Tib.* lake
Cochilla (Coch.) *Port.* hills
Col *Fr., It.* pass
Colina(s) *Span.* hill(s)
Colle *It.* pass
Colline(s) *Fr.* hill(s)
Conca *It.* plain, basin
Cordillera (Cord.) *Span.* mountain range
Costa *It., Port., Span.* coast
Côte *Fr.* coast, slope, hill
Coteaux *Fr.* hills
Cuchilla *Span.* hills
Cuenca *Span.* river basin
Cu-Lao *Viet.* island

Da *Chin.* big
Da *Viet.* river
Daban *Mong.* pass
Dağ(ı) *Turk.* mountain(s)
Dāgh *Farsi* mountain
Dağları *Turk.* mountain range
-dai, -daichi *Jap.* plateau
-Dake *Jap.* mountain
-dal, -e *Dan., Swe.* valley
-dal, -en *Swe., Nor.* valley, stream
Dalay Mong. large lake
-ðalir, -ðalur *Ice.* valley
-damm, -en *Swe.* lake
Danau *Malay* lake
Dao *Chin., Viet.* island
Dar *Ar.* region
Darya *Russ.* river
Daryācheh *Farsi* marshy lake, lake
Dasht *Farsi* desert, steppe
Daung *Burm.* mountain, hill
Dayr *Ar.* monastery
Debre *Amh.* hill
Deli *Ser.-Cr.* mountain
Deniz, -i *Turk.* sea
Département (Dépt.) *Fr.* first-order administrative division
Dere *Turk.* stream
Desierto (Des.) *Span.* desert
Détroit *Fr.* strait
Dhar *Ar.* region, mountain range
Diep *Dut.* channel
Dijk *Dut.* dyke
Ding *Chin.* mountain
Dingzi *Chin.* hill, mountain
Djebel (Dj.) *Ar.* mountain
-djúp *Ice.* fjord
-djupet *Swe.* channel, sound
-Do *Jap., Kor.* island
Dolina *Russ.* valley
Dolna, Dolni *Bulg.* lower
Dolna, Dolne, Dolny *Russ.* lower
Dolni *Czec.* lower
Dolok (D.) *Malay* mountain
-dong *Kor.* village, town
Dong *Chin.* east, eastern
Donja, Donji *Ser.-Cr.* lower
-dorf *Ger.* village
-dorp *Afr.* village
-drif *Afr.* ford
-dybet *Dan.* marine channel
Dzong *Tib.* town, settlement
Dzüün *Mong.* east, eastern

-egga *Nor.* peak
-eiland, -en (eil.) *Afr., Dut.* island(s)
Eilean *Gae.* island
-elv, -a *Nor.* river
Embalse *Span.* reservoir
'Emeq *Heb.* plain, valley
Ensenada *Span.* bay
Erg *Ar.* sand desert
Estero *Span.* estuary
Estrada *Span.* bay
Estrecho *Span.* strait
Estuaire *Fr.* estuary
Estuario *Span.* estuary
Étang *Fr.* lagoon, lake
-ey, -jar *Ice.* island(s)
-ežeras *Lith.* lake
-ezers *Lat.* lake

Falaise *Fr.* cliff
-fallet *Swe.* waterfall
Farihy *Malag.* lake
Faro *Span.* lighthouse
-feld *Ger.* field
-fell *Ice.* mountain, hill
Feng *Chin.* mountain range
Fiume (F.) *It.* river
-fjäll, -en, -et *Swe.* hill(s), mountain(s), ridge
-fjärden *Swe.* fjord
Fjeld *Dan.* mountain
-fjell, -et *Nor.* mountain range
-fjord, -en *Dan., Nor., Swe.* fjord
-fjorður *Ice.* fjord, bay, inlet
Fleuve (Fl.) *Fr.* river
-flói *Ice.* bay, marshy country
Fluss (F.) *Ger.* river
Foce, Foci *It.* mouth(s)
Folyó (F.) *Hung.* river
-fonn *Nor.* glacier
-fontein *Afr.* fountain, spring
Forêt *Fr.* forest
-fors, -en *Swe.* waterfall, rapids
-foss, -en *Ice., Nor.* waterfall
Forst *Ger.* forest
Foum *Ar.* pass
Fuente *Span.* source
-furt *Ger.* ford
Fylke *Nor.* first-order administrative division

-gang *Chin.* bay, harbour
-gang *Kor.* river
Ganga *Hin., Sin.* river
Gangri *Tib.* mountain
Gaoyuan *Chin.* plateau
-gat *Dan.* sound
-Gata *Jap.* lake
-gau *Ger.* district
-Gawa *Jap.* river
Gebel (G.) *Ar.* mountain
Gebirge (Geb.) *Ger.* hills, mountains
Gezirat, Geziret *Ar.* island
Ghat *Hin.* range of hills
Ghiol *Rom.* lake
Ghubbat *Ar.* bay, inlet
Gjiri *Alb.* bay
Gjol *Alb.* lagoon, lake
Glava (Gl.) *Ser.-Cr.* mountain, peak
Glen *Gae.* valley
Gletscher (Gl.) *Ger.* glacier
Gobi *Mong.* desert
Gol *Mong.* river
Göl *Azeri, Turk.* lake
Golfe (G.) *Fr.* gulf
Golfo (G.) *It., Span.* gulf
Gölü *Turk.* lake
Gomba *Tib.* settlement
Gora, Góra *Bulg., Russ., Ser.-Cr., Pol.* mountain
Gorje *Ser.-Cr.* hills, mountains
Gorno *Russ.* mountainous
-gorod *Russ.* small town
Gory, Góry *Pol., Russ.* mountain
-grad *Bulg. Russ., Ser.-Cr.* town, city
-grada *Russ.* ridge
Gran *It., Span.* big, great
Grand, -e *Fr.* big, great
Groot (Gt.) *Afr., Dut.* big, great
Gross, -e, -en, -er *Ger.* big, great(er)
Grupo *Span.* group
Gruppo *It.* group
Guan *Chin.* pass
Guba (G.) *Russ.* bay
-Guntō *Jap.* island group
Gunong, Gunung (G.) *Indo., Malay* mountain
Gurā *Rom.* passage

Hadabat *Ar.* plateau
Hadjer *Ar.* mountain
-hafen *Ger.* harbour, port
Haff *Ger.* bay, lagoon
Hai *Chin.* lake, sea
Haixia *Chin.* channel, strait
Halbinsel *Ger.* peninsula
Halvø *Dan.* peninsula
Halvøya *Nor.* peninsula
Hāmad, Hamada, Hammādah, Hammādat *Ar.* stony desert, plateau
-hamn *Swe., Nor.* harbour, anchorage
Hāmūn *Farsi* marsh, lake
-Hantō *Jap.* peninsula
Har(e) *Heb.* hill(s), mountain(s)
Hassi (Hi.) *Ar.* well
-haug *Nor.* hill
Hav, Havet *Nor., Swe.* sea
-havn *Dan., Nor.* bay, harbour
Havre *Fr.* harbour
Hawd *Ar.* oasis
Hawr *Ar.* lake, marsh
He *Chin.* river
-hegység *Hung.* hills, forest
Heide *Ger.* heath, moor
Helodranon' *Malag.* bay
Higashi *Jap.* east, eastern
-ho *Kor.* lake
-hø *Nor.* peak
Hoch *Ger.* high
Hochland *Afr.* highland
Hoek, -hoek *Afr., Dut.* cape, point
-höfn *Ice.* harbour, port
-hög, -en, -högar, -högarna *Swe.* hill(s), peak, mountain
Höhe *Ger.* height
Hohen *Ger.* high, upper
-hoi *Chin.* bay
-høj, -e *Dan.* hills
-holm, -holme, -holmen *Dan., Nor., Swe.* island
Hon *Viet.* island
Hoog *Dut.* high
Hora *Czec., Ukr.* mountain
-horn *Ger.* peak
Hory *Czec.* mountains, hills
-hot *Mong.* town
-hoved *Dan.* point, headland, peninsula
-hrad *Czec.* town
Hráun *Ice.* lava
-hsi *Chin.* river
-hsia *Chin.* gorge, strait
-hsien *Chin.* district
Hu *Chin.* lake, reservoir
Huk *Dan., Ger.* cape
-huk *Swe.* cape
Huken *Nor.* cape

Idd *Ar.* well
Idehan *Ar., Ber.* sandy plain, dunes
-ike *Jap.* lake
Île(s) (I(s).) *Fr.* island(s)
Ilha(s) (I(s).) *Port.* island(s)
imeni *Russ.* 'in the name of'
Inish *Gae.* island
Insel(n) (I.) *Ger.* island(s)
Irmak *Turk.* river
'Irq *Ar.* dunes
Isla(s) (I(s).) *Span.* island(s)
Iso *Fin.* big, great
Isol, -a, -e (I.) *It.* island(s)
Isthme *Fr.* isthmus
Istmo *Span.* isthmus
-iwa *Jap.* island

Jabal *Ar.* mountain range
Järv *Est.* lake
järvi *Fin.* lake, bay, pond
-jaur, -javre *Lap.* lake
Jazā'ir *Ar.* islands
Jazīra, jazīrat *Ar.* island
Jazireh *Farsi* island
Jebel *Ar.* mountain
Jezero *Ser.-Cr.* lake
Jezioro *Pol.* lake
Jiang *Chin.* river
Jiao *Chin.* cape
-Jima *Jap.* island
Jøkulen *Nor.* glacier, ice cap
-joki *Fin.* river
-jökull *Ice.* glacier, ice cap
Jūras Līcis *Lat.* bay, gulf

Kaap (K.) *Afr.* cape
-kai *Jap.* bay, channel, sea
-kaikyō *Jap.* strait
-kaise *Lap.* mountain
kalnas *Lith.* hill
Kamennyy *Russ.* stony
Kampong *Cam.* village
Kampung *Malay* village
-kanaal *Dut.* canal
Kanal *Dan.* channel, gulf
Kanal *Ger., Swe.* canal
-kanal *Ser.-Cr.* channel, canal
Kanava *Fin.* canal
Kang *Kor.* river, bay
Kap (K.) *Dan., Ger.* cape, point
-kapp *Nor.* cape, point
-kaupstaður *Ice.* market town
-kaupunki *Fin.* town
Kavīr *Farsi* salt desert
Kébir *Ar.* great
Kecil *Malay* lesser, little
Kefar *Heb.* village, hamlet
-Ken *Jap.* first-order administrative division
Kep, -i (K.) *Alb.* cape
Kepulauan (Kep.) *Indo., Malay* archipelago
Keski- *Fin.* middle, central
Khalig, Khalīj *Ar.* gulf
-khamba *Tib.* source, spring
Khawr *Ar.* bay, channel, wadi
Khlong *Thai* river
Kho Khot *Thai* isthmus
Khōr *Farsi* bay, estuary
Khrebet *Russ.* mountain range
Kita- *Jap.* north
Klein,-e, -er *Ger.* small
-klint *Dan.* cliff
Klintar *Swe.* hills
-kloof *Afr.* gorge, pass
Knude *Dan.* point
-Ko *Jap.* lake
Ko *Thai* island
-kōchi *Jap.* mountainous region
-kōgen *Jap.* plateau
Kohi *Pash.* mountains
Kol *Kaz., Kyrg.* lake
Kólpos *Gr., Turk.* gulf, bay
Kolymskoye *Russ.* mountain range
Kompong *Malay* landing place
-kop *Afr.* hill
-kopf *Ger.* hill
-köping *Swe.* market town
Körfäzi *Azer.* gulf
Körfezi *Turk.* gulf
Kosa *Russ., Ukr.* spit
-koski *Fin.* rapids
-kraal *Afr.* native village
-kraj *Czec., Pol., Ser.-Cr.* region
Krasnyy *Russ.* red
Kryazh *Russ.* ridge, hills
Kuala *Malay* bay
-kuan *Chin.* pass
Kūh(ha) *Farsi* mountain(s)
Kul *Russ.* lake
-kulle *Swe.* hill
Kum *Russ.* sandy desert
Kumpu *Fin.* hill
Kwe *Burm.* bay, gulf
-kylä *Fin.* village
Kyst, -en *Dan., Nor.* coast
Kyun(zu) *Burm.* island(s)

La *Tib.* pass
-laagte *Afr.* watercourse

Lääni *Fin.* first-order administrative division
Lac (L.) *Fr.* lake
Lacul (L.) *Rom.* lake, lagoon
Lago (L.) *It., Port., Span.* lake, lagoon
Lagoa (L.) *Port.* lagoon
Lagos *Port., Span.* lakes
Laguna (L.) *It., Span.* lagoon, lake
Lagune (L.) *Fr.* lake
-laht *Est.* bay
Lahti *Fin.* bay, gulf, cove
Lakhti *Russ.* bay, gulf
Lam *Thai* river
Lampi *Fin.* lake
Län *Swe.* first-order administrative division
Land *Ger.* first-order administrative division
-land *Dan.* region
-land *Afr., Nor.* land, province
Lande *Fr.* heath
Laut *Indo.* sea
Law *Gae.* hill, mountain
Līcis *Lat.* gulf
Lido *It.* beach, shore
Liedao *Chin.* islands
Lilla *Swe.* small
Lille *Dan., Nor.* small
Liman *Russ.* bay, gulf
Límni (L.) *Gr.* lake
Ling *Chin.* mountain range
-linna *Fin.* fort
Llano *Span.* prairie, plain
Llyn *Welsh* lake
Loch (L.) *Gae.* lake, inlet
Lough (L.) *Gae.* lake, inlet
Lum *Alb.* river
Lund *Dan.* forest
-lund, -en *Swe.* wood(s)
-luoto *Fin.* island

-maa *Est.* island
Madīnat *Ar.* town, city
Madiq *Ar.* strait
Maja *Alb.* mountains
-mäki *Fin.* hill, hillside
Mal *Alb.* mountain
Maloye, Malyy, Malyya *Russ.* little, small
Mala, Mali, Malo *Ser.-Cr.* little, small
Malaya *Belo.* small
Malé *Czec., Slovak* small
Mali *Alb.* mountain
-man *Kor.* bay
Mar *Span.* lagoon, sea
Marais *Fr.* marsh
Mare *It.* sea
Mare *Rom.* great
Marisma *Span.* marsh
-mark *Dan., Nor.* land
Marsā *Ar.* anchorage, bay, inlet
Masabb *Ar.* river mouth, estuary
Massif *Fr.* upland, mountains
Mato *Port.* forest
Mazar *Farsi* shrine, tomb
Meer, -meer *Afr., Dut., Ger.* lake, sea
-men *Chin.* bay, gorge, channel
Mesto *Ser.-Cr., Czec.* town
Mezzo *It.* middle
Midbar *Heb.* wilderness
Mierzeja *Pol.* spit
Mifraz *Heb.* bay
Mina *Ar.* port
Minami *Jap.* south, southern
-misaki *Jap.* cape, point
Mittel *Ger.* central, middle
-mo *Nor., Swe.* heath, island
-mon *Swe.* heath
Mong *Burm.* town
Mont(s) (Mt(s).) *Fr.* hill(s), mountain(s)
Montagna (Mt.) *It.* mountain
Montagne(s) (Mt(s).) *Fr.* hill(s), mountain(s)
Montaña(s) (Mt(s).) *Span.* mountain(s)
Montanyes *Cat.* mountains
Monte(s) (Mte(s).) *It., Port., Span.* mountain(s)
Monti (Mti.) *It.* mountains
More *Russ.* sea
Mörön *Mong.* river
Moyen *Fr.* central, middle
Muang *Malay* town
Mui *Viet.* cape
Mull *Gae.* promontory
Mund, -mund *Afr.* mouth
Munkhafed *Ar.* depression
Munte (Mte.) *Rom.* mount
Munţi(i) (Mti.) *Rom.* mountain(s)
Muong *Malay* village
Myit *Burm.* river
Myitwanya *Burm.* mouths of river
Mynydd *Welsh* mountain
-myr *Nor., Swe.* swamp
-mýri *Ice.* swamp
Mys (M.) *Russ.* cape

-Nada *Jap.* bay, gulf
-næs *Dan.* point, cape
Nafūd *Ar.* sandy desert
Nagorye *Russ.* hills, mountains
Nagy *Hung.* big
Nahal (N.) *Heb.* river
Nahr (N.) *Ar.* river, stream
Najd *Ar.* plateau, pass
Nakhon *Thai* town
Nam *Kor., Viet.* river
-nam *Kor.* south
Namakzār *Per.* salt flat
Nan *Chin.* south, southern
-nao *Chin.* lake
-näs *Swe.* cape
Neder *Dut.* lower
Nedre *Nor.* lower
Nei *Chin.* inner
Nek *Afr.* pass
-nes *Ice., Nor.* cape
Ness, -ness *Gae.* promontory, cape
Nevada, Nevado *Span.* snow-capped mountain
Nez *Fr.* cape
Nieder *Ger.* lower
-niemi *Fin.* cape, point, peninsula, island
Nieuw, -e *Dut.* new
Nishi *Jap.* west, western
Nisos, Nisoi *Gr.* island(s)
Nizhneye, Nizhniy *Russ.* lower
Nizina *Belo., Pol.* lowland
Nizmennost *Russ.* plain, lowland
Nízni *Czec.* lower
Noord *Dut.* north, northern
Nord *Fr.* north, northern
Norra *Swe.* north, northern
Nørre *Dan.* north, northern
Norte *Port., Span.* north, northern
Nos *Bulg., Russ.* cape, point
Nosy *Malag.* island
Nouveau, Nouvelle *Fr.* new
Nova, Novi *Bulg., Port., Serb.-Cr.* new
Novaya, Novo, Novoye, Novyy *Russ.* new
Nové, Nový *Czec., Slovak* new
Novo *Port.* new
Nowa, Nowe, Nowy *Pol.* new
Nudo *Span.* mountain
Nueva, Nuevo *Span.* new
Nur *Chin.* lake
Nur *Tib.* peak
Nuruu *Mong.* mountain range
Nusa *Indo.* island
Nuur *Mong.* lake
Ny *Dan., Nor., Swe.* new

-ø *Dan., Nor.* island
-ö *Swe.* island,
-öar, -na *Swe.* islands
Ober *Ger., Ukr.* upper
Oblast *Russ.* administrative division
Öbor *Mong.* inner
Occidental *Fr., Span.* western
-odde *Dan., Nor.* point, peninsula, cape
Oeste *Span.* west, western
Oglat *Ar.* well
Oji *Alb.* bay
Ojo *Span.* spring
-Oki *Jap.* bay
-ön *Swe.* island
Ondör *Mong.* upper
Oost(er) *Dut.* east(ern)
Oraşu *Rom.* city
Ord *Gae.* point
Óri *Gr.* mountains
Oriental, -e *Fr., Span.* east, eastern
Órmos *Gr.* bay
Óros *Gr.* mountain(s)
Ort *Ger.* point, cape
Ost *Ger.* east
Øst(er) *Den., Nor.* east(ern)
Öst(ra) *Swe.* east(ern)
Ostriv *Ukr.* island
Ostrov(a) *Russ.* island(s)
Otok(i) *Ser.-Cr.* island(s)
Ouabi, Ouadi (O.) *Ar.* dry watercourse, wadi
Oud, -e *Dut.* old
Oued, -i (O.) *Ar.* watercourse
Ouest *Fr.* west, western
Ouzan *Farsi* river
Ova, -si *Turk.* plains, lowlands
Over- *Dan., Dut.* upper
Över-, Övre *Nor., Swe.* upper
-øy, -a *Nor.* island(s)
Oya *Hin.* point
Oya *Sin.* river
Ozero, Ozera (Oz.) *Russ., Ukr.* lake(s)

-pää *Fin.* hill(s), mountain
Pahta *Lapp.* hill
Pampa(s) *Span.* plain(s)
Pantanal *Port.* marsh
Pantano *Span.* reservoir
Pantao *Chin.* peninsula
Parbat *Urdu* mountain
Pas *Fr.* strait
Paso (P.) *Span.* pass
Passage *Fr.* channel
Passe *Fr.* channel
Passo (P.) *It.* pass
Pasul (P.) *Rom.* pass
Patam *Hin.* small village
Patna, -patnam *Hin.* small village
Pegunungan *Indo., Malay* mountain range
Pei, -pei *Chin.* north
Pélagos *Gr.* sea
Pen *Welsh* hill
Peña *Span.* rock, peak
Pendi *Chin.* basin, depression
Péninsule *Fr.* peninsula
Penisola (Pen.) *It.* peninsula
Pereval (Per.) *Russ.* pass
Pervo-, Pervyy- *Russ.* first
Pertuis *Fr.* channel, strait
Peski *Russ.* sand desert
Petit, -e *Fr.* small
Phanom *Thai* mountain
Phnum *Cam.* mountain
Phou *Lao.* mountain
Phu *Thai, Viet.* mountain
Piano *It.* plain
Pic *Cat., Fr.* peak
Pico(s) *Span.* peak(s)
-piggen *Dan.* peak
Pik *Russ.* peak
Pingyuan *Chin.* plain
Pique *Fr.* peak
Piton *Fr.* peak
Pivostriv *Ukr.* peninsula
Piz, Pizzo *It.* peak
Plage *Fr.* beach
Plaine *Fr.* plain
Planalto *Port.* plateau
Planina (Pl.) *Bulg., Ser.-Cr.* mountain range
Plato *Russ., Bulg.* plateau
Playa *Span.* beach
-po *Chin.* lake, wetland
Pointe (Pte.) *Fr.* point, cape
Pojezierze *Pol.* lakes
Polder *Dut.* reclaimed farmland
-pólis *Gr.* city, town
Poluostrov (Pov.) *Russ.* peninsula
Półwysep *Pol.* peninsula
Pont *Fr.* bridge
Ponta (Pta.) *Port.* point, cape
Ponte *Port.* bridge
Poort *Afr.* passage, gate
-poort *Dut.* port
Porta *Port.* pass
Porţile *Rom.* gate
Portillo *Span.* pass
Porto *It., Port., Span.* port
Potámi, Potamós *Gr.* river
Pradesh *Hin.* state
Praia *Port.* beach, shore
Presa *Span.* reservoir
Presqu'île *Fr.* peninsula
Prokhod *Bulg.* pass
Proliv *Russ.* strait
Promontorio *Span.* promontory
Průsmyk (Pr.) *Czec.* pass
Pueblo *Span.* village
Puerto (Pto.) *Span.* port
Puig *Cat.* peak
Pulau (P.) *Indo., Malay* island
Puna *Span.* desert plateau
Puncak *Indo.* peak
Punta (Pta.) *It., Span.* point, peak
Puy *Fr.* peak

Qal'at *Ar.* fort
Qanat *Ar.* canal
Qasr *Ar.* fort
Qiryat *Heb.* town
Qiuling *Chin.* plateau
Qolleh *Farsi* mountain
-qundao *Chin.* islands

Rach *Viet.* river
Rags *Lat.* cape
Rambla *Cat.* river
Ramlat *Ar.* sandy desert
Rão (R.) *Port.* river
Rann *Hin.* swampy region
Rao *I.-C.* river
Ras *Amh., Ar., Farsi* cape, point
Récif(s) *Fr.* reef(s)
Recife(s) *Port.* reef(s)
Reka *Bulg.* river
Repede *Rom.* rapids
Represa *Port.* reservoir
Reshteh *Farsi* mountain range
-rettō *Jap.* group of islands, chain
Ria *Port., Span.* estuary, bay
Ribeirão (R.) *Port.* river
Ribera (R.) *Span.* river bank
Rijeka *Ser.-Cr.* river
Rio (R.) *Port., Span.* river
Rivier (R.) *Afr., Dut.* river
Riviera *It.* coastal plain, coast
Rivière (R.) *Fr.* river
Roca *Span.* rock
Rocca *It.* rock, peak
Roche *Fr.* rock
Rt *Ser.-Cr.* cape, point
Rubh', Rubha *Gae.* cape, point
-rück *Ger.* ridge
Rūd *Farsi* stream, river
Rudohorie *Slovak* mountains
Rzeka (R.) *Pol.* river

-saar *Est.* island
-saari *Fin.* island
Sabkhat, Sabkhet *Ar.* salt flats
Sadd *Ar.* dam
Sagar,-a *Hin., Urdu* lake
Sahrā *Ar.* desert
-Saki *Jap.* cape, point
Salar *Span.* salt flat
Salina(s) *Span.* salt marsh(es)
-salmi *Fin.* strait, sound, lake, channel
Saltsjöbad *Swe.* resort
-Sammyaku *Jap.* mountain range
Samut *Thai* gulf
San (S.) *It., Port., Span.* saint
-San *Jap., Kor.* hill, mountain
-Sanchi *Jap.* mountain range
Sankt (St.) *Ger., Russ.* saint
-sanmaek *Kor.* mountain range
-sanmyaku *Jap.* mountain range
Santa (Sta.) *It., Port., Span.* saint
Santo (Sto.) *It. Port., Span.* saint
São (S.) *Port.* saint
Sarīr *Ar.* desert
Sasso *It.* mountain
Satu *Rom.* village
Saurums *Lat.* strait
Sebkha, Sebkhet *Ar.* salt flat
See, -see *Ger.* lake
-şehir *Turk.* town
Selat *Indo., Malay* strait
Selatan *Indo.* southern
-selkä *Fin.* bay, lake, ridge, hills
Selo *Ser.-Cr., Russ.* village
Selva *Port., Span.* forest, wood
Seno *Span.* bay, sound
Serir *Ar.* stony desert
Serra (Sa.) *Cat., Port.* range of hills
Serranía *Span.* mountain ridge
Severo, Severnaya, Severnoye, Severnyy (Sev.) *Russ.* north, northern
Sfântu *Rom.* saint
Shahr, -shahr *Farsi* city, town
Shamo *Chin.* desert
Shan *Chin.* hills, mountains
Shankou *Chin.* pass
Shanmo *Chin.* mountain range
Sharm *Ar.* bay
Shatt *Ar.* river mouth, estuary
-Shima *Jap.* island
Shimāli *Ar.* northern
-Shotō *Jap.* group of islands
-shui *Chin.* river
-shuiku *Chin.* reservoir
Sierra (Sa.) *Span.* mountain range
-sjö, -sjön, -sjø *Swe., Nor.* lake
-sjøen *Dan.* sea
-sjór *Ice.* lake
-sker *Ice.* island
-skär *Swe.* island, rock, cape
-skog, -skogen *Nor., Swe.* wood(s)
-skov *Dan.* forest
Slieve *Gae.* hill, mountain
Sø *Dan., Nor.* lake
Söder, Södra *Swe.* south, southern
Sør *Nor.* south, southern
Solonchak *Russ.* salt lake, marsh
Sønder, Søndra *Dan.* south, southern
Song *Viet.* river
Souk *Ar.* market
-spitze *Ger.* peak, mountain
-spruit *Afr.* stream
Sredna, Sredno *Bulg.* middle, central
Sredne, Sredneye *Russ.* middle, central
Srednja *Ser.-Cr.* middle, central
-stad *Afr., Nor., Swe.* town
-stadt *Ger.* town
-staður *Ice.* town
Stara, Stari *Ser.-Cr.* old
Stará, Staré, Stary *Czec.* old
Staraya, Staroye, Staryy *Russ.* old
Stare, Staro, Stary *Ukr.* old
Stausee *Ger.* reservoir
Stenón *Gr.* strait, pass
Step *Russ.* steppe
Stor, -a *Swe.* big
Store *Dan.* big
-strand *Dan., Ger., Nor., Swe.* beach
-strede *Nor.* straits
Strelka *Russ.* spit
-strete *Nor.* straits
Stretto (Str.) *It.* strait
Strædet (Str.) *Dan.* strait
-ström, -strömmen *Swe.* stream(s)
-stroom *Afr.* large river
Sud *Fr.* south, southern
Süd, -er *Ger.* south, southern
Suid *Afr.* south, southern
-Suidō *Jap.* strait, channel
Sul *Port.* south, southern
Sûn *Burm.* cape
-sund, -et *Swe., Nor.* sound, estuary, inlet
Sungai *Indo., Malay* river
Sur *Span.* south, southern
Sveti *Bulg.* saint
Syd *Dan., Swe.* south, southern
Sýsla *Ice.* first-order administrative division

-tag *Uighur* mountain
Tai -tai *Chin.* tower
-Take *Jap.* mountain
Tal *Mong.* plain, steppe
-tal *Ger.* valley
Tall *Ar.* hills
Tanjona *Malag.* cape, point
Tanjung, Tanjong (Tg.) *Indo., Malay.* cape, point
Tao *Chin.* island
Tasik *Malay* lake
Tassili *Ar.* rocky plateau
Tau *Russ.* mountain range
Taung *Burm.* mountain
Taungdan. *Burm.* mountain range
Taunggya *Burm.* pass
-tekojärvi *Fin.* reservoir
Teluk *Indo., Malay* bay, gulf
Ténéré *Berb.* desert
Tengah *Indo.* middle, central
-thal *Ger.* valley
Thok *Tib.* town
Tien *Chin.* lake, marsh
Tierra *Span.* land, country
Timur *Indo.* eastern
-tind *Nor.* peak
-ting *Chin.* mountain
Tjärn, -en, -et *Swe.* lake
-Tō *Jap.* island
Tong *Kor.* village, town
Tong *Burm., Thai, Kor.* mountain range
Tonlé *Cam.* lake
Top *Dut.* peak
-topp, -en *Nor.* peak
-träsk *Swe.* lake, swamp
Tsangpo *Tib.* large river
Tso *Tib.* lake
Tsu *Jap.* entrance, bay
Tsui *Chin.* cape, point
Tulur *Ar.* hill
-tunturi *Fin.* hill(s), mountain(s), ridge

Uad *Ar.* dry watercourse, wadi
Über *Ger.* upper
-udde, -udden *Swe.* point, cape
Uebi *Som.* river
Ujung *Indo., Malay* cape
Unter- *Ger.* lower
Us *Mong.* water
Ust, Ustye *Russ.* river mouth
Utara *Indo.* north, northern
Uttar *Hin.* north, northern
Uul *Mong., Russ.* mountain range

-vaara *Fin.* hill, mountain ridge, peak
Vaart *Dut.* canal
-våg *Nor.* bay
Val *Fr., Port., Span.* valley
Valea *Rom.* valley
-vall, -en *Swe.* mountain
Valle *It., Span.* valley
Vallée *Fr.* valley
Valli *It.* lake, lagoon
-város *Hung.* town
-varre *Nor.* mountain
Väst, Västra *Swe.* west, western
-vatn *Ice., Nor.* lake
-vatnet *Nor.* lake
-vatten, vattnet *Swe.* lake
-vecchio *It.* old
Vechi *Rom.* old
-ved, -veden *Swe.* hills
Veld, -veld *Afr.* field
Velha, Velho *Port.* old
Velika, Velike, Veliki, Veliko *Ser.-Cr., Slov.* big, large
Velikaya, Velikiy *Russ.* big, large
Velká, Velké, Velký *Czec.* big, large
Verkhne, Verkhniy *Russ.* upper
-vesi *Fin.* water, lake, bay, sound, strait
Vest, Vester, Vestre *Dan., Nor.* west, western
-vidda *Nor.* plateau
Vieille, Vieux *Fr.* old
Vieja, Viejo *Span.* old
Vig *Dan.* bay, inlet, cove, lagoon, lake
-vík *Ice.* bay
-vik, -a, -en *Nor., Swe.* bay, gulf, inlet, lake
Vila *Port.* small town
Villa *Span.* town
Ville *Fr.* town
Vinh *Viet.* bay
Vîrful (Vf.) *Rom.* peak, mountain
-viz *Hung.* river
-víztároló *Hung.* reservoir
-vlei *Afr.* lake, salt pan
-vliet *Dut.* canal
-vloer *Afr.* salt pan
Vodokhranilishche (Vdkhr.) *Russ.* reservoir
Vodoskovyshche (Vdskh.) *Ukr.* reservoir
Volcán (Vol.) *Span.* volcano, mountain
Vorota *Russ.* pass, channel, strait
Vostochno, Vostochnyy *Russ.* east, eastern
-vötn *Ice.* lakes
Vozvyshennost *Russ.* heights, uplands
Vozyera *Belo.* lake
Vrata *Bulg.* gate, pass
Vrchovina *Czec.* mountainous country
Vrch(y) *Czec.* mountain (range)
Vung *Viet.* bay, gulf
-vuori *Fin.* mountain, hill
Vychodné *Slovak* east, eastern
Vysochyna *Ukr.* upland

-waard *Dut.* polder
Wadi (W.) *Ar.* dry watercourse
Wāhāt *Ar.* oasis
Wald *Ger.* forest, mountains
-Wan *Chin., Jap.* bay, harbour
Wāw *Ar.* well
Webi *Amh.* river
Wes *Afr.* west, western
Wielka, Wielki, Wielko *Pol.* big, large
Woestyn *Afr.* desert
Wysoka, Wysoki *Pol.* upper
Wyżyna *Pol.* plateau

Xi *Chin.* river
Xia *Chin.* gorge, strait
Xiao *Chin.* small

Yam *Heb.* sea
-Yama *Jap.* mountain
-yan *Chin.* gorge, island
Yang *Chin.* bay, sea, sound
Yangi *Russ.* new
Yazovir *Bulg.* reservoir
Yeni *Turk.* new
Yli *Fin.* upper
Ynys *Welsh* island
Yoma *Burm.* mountain range
Ytre-, Ytter- *Nor., Swe.* outer
-yuan *Chin.* stream
Yugo- *Ser.-Cr.* south, southern
Yunhe *Chin.* canal
Yuzhni, Yuzhno *Russ.* south, southern

-Zaki *Jap.* point
Zalew *Pol.* lagoon, swamp
Zaliv *Russ.* bay, gulf
-Zan *Jap.* mountain
Zangbo *Tib.* stream, river
Zapadnaya, Zapadno, Zapadnyi (Zap.) *Russ.* west, western
Zatoka *Pol., Ukr.* bay, gulf
-zee *Dut.* lake, sea
Zemlya *Russ.* land, island(s)
Zhang *Chin.* mountain
-zhou *Chin.* island
Zhong *Chin.* middle, central
Zhou *Chin.* island
Zizhiqu *Chin.* autonomous region
Zuid, Zuider *Dut.* south, southern

INDEX TO WORLD MAPS

How to use the index

The index contains the names of all the principal places and features shown on the World Maps. Each name is followed by an additional entry in italics giving the country or region within which it is located. The alphabetical order of names composed of two or more words is governed primarily by the first word and then by the second. This is an example of the rule:

Mīr Kūh, *Iran*	97 **E8**	26 22N 58 55 E
Mīr Shahdād, *Iran*	97 **E8**	26 15N 58 29 E
Mira, *Italy*	45 **C9**	45 26N 12 8 E
Mira por vos Cay, *Bahamas*	165 **B5**	22 9N 74 30W
Miraj, *India*	94 **F2**	16 50N 74 45 E

Physical features composed of a proper name (Erie) and a description (Lake) are positioned alphabetically by the proper name. The description is positioned after the proper name and is usually abbreviated:

Erie, L., *N. Amer.* 150 **D4**   42 15N 81 0W

Where a description forms part of a settlement or administrative name however, it is always written in full and put in its true alphabetic position:

Mount Olive, *U.S.A.* 156 **E7**   39 4N 89 44W

Names beginning with M' and Mc are indexed as if they were spelled Mac. Names beginning St. are alphabetized under Saint, but Sankt, Sint, Sant', Santa and San are all spelt in full and are alphabetized accordingly. If the same place name occurs two or more times in the index and all are in the same country, each is followed by the name of the administrative subdivision in which it is located.

The number in bold type which follows each name in the index refers to the number of the map page where that feature or place will be found. This is usually the largest scale at which the place or feature appears.

The letter and figure which are in bold type immediately after the page number give the grid square on the map page, within which the feature is situated. The letter represents the latitude and the figure the longitude. A lower case letter immediately after the page number refers to an inset map on that page.

In some cases the feature itself may fall within the specified square, while the name is outside. This is usually the case only with features which are larger than a grid square.

The geographical co-ordinates which follow the letter-figure references give the latitude and longitude of each place. The first co-ordinate indicates latitude – the distance north or south of the Equator. The second co-ordinate indicates longitude – the distance east or west of the Greenwich Meridian. Both latitude and longitude are measured in degrees and minutes (there are 60 minutes in a degree).

The latitude is followed by N(orth) or S(outh) and the longitude by E(ast) or W(est).

Rivers are indexed to their mouths or confluences, and carry the symbol ➻ after their names. The following symbols are also used in the index: ■ country, ☑ overseas territory or dependency, ☐ first order administrative area, △ national park, ◠ other park (provincial park, nature reserve or game reserve), ✈ (LHR) principal airport (and location identifier).

How to pronounce place names

English-speaking people usually have no difficulty in reading and pronouncing correctly English place names. However, foreign place name pronunciations may present many problems. Such problems can be minimised by following some simple rules. However, these rules cannot be applied to all situations, and there will be many exceptions.

1. In general, stress each syllable equally, unless your experience suggests otherwise.
2. Pronounce the letter 'a' as a broad 'a' as in 'arm'.
3. Pronounce the letter 'e' as a short 'e' as in 'elm'.
4. Pronounce the letter 'i' as a cross between a short 'i' and long 'e', as the two 'i's in 'California'.
5. Pronounce the letter 'o' as an intermediate 'o' as in 'soft'.
6. Pronounce the letter 'u' as an intermediate 'u' as in 'sure'.
7. Pronounce consonants hard, except in the Romance-language areas where 'g's are likely to be pronounced softly like 'j' in 'jam'; 'j' itself may be pronounced as 'y'; and 'x's may be pronounced as 'h'.
8. For names in mainland China, pronounce 'q' like the 'ch' in 'chin', 'x' like the 'sh' in 'she', 'zh' like the 'j' in 'jam', and 'z' as if it were spelled 'dz'. In general pronounce 'a' as in 'father', 'e' as in 'but', 'i' as in 'keep', 'o' as in 'or', and 'u' as in 'rule'.

Moreover, English has no diacritical marks (accent and pronunciation signs), although some languages do. The following is a brief and general guide to the pronunciation of those most frequently used in the principal Western European languages.

		Pronunciation as in
French	é	day and shows that the e is to be pronounced; e.g. Orléans.
	è	mare
	î	used over any vowel and does not affect pronunciation; shows contraction of the name, usually omission of 's' following a vowel.
	ç	's' before 'a', 'o' and 'u'.
	ë, ï, ü	over 'e', 'i' and 'u' when they are used with another vowel and shows that each is to be pronounced.
German	ä	fate
	ö	fur
	ü	no English equivalent; like French 'tu'
Italian	à, é	over vowels and indicates stress.
Portuguese	ã, õ	vowels pronounced nasally.
	ç	boss
	á	shows stress
	ô	shows that a vowel has an 'i' or 'u' sound combined with it.
Spanish	ñ	canyon
	ü	pronounced as w and separately from adjoining vowels.
	á	usually indicates that this is a stressed vowel.

Abbreviations

A.C.T. – Australian Capital Territory
A.R. – Autonomous Region
Afghan. – Afghanistan
Afr. – Africa
Ala. – Alabama
Alta. – Alberta
Amer. – America(n)
Arch. – Archipelago
Ariz. – Arizona
Ark. – Arkansas
Atl. Oc. – Atlantic Ocean
B. – Baie, Bahía, Bay, Bucht, Bugt
B.C. – British Columbia
Bangla. – Bangladesh
Barr. – Barrage
Bos.-H. – Bosnia-Herzegovina
C. – Cabo, Cap, Cape, Coast
C.A.R. – Central African Republic
C. Prov. – Cape Province
Calif. – California
Cat. – Catarata
Cent. – Central
Chan. – Channel
Colo. – Colorado
Conn. – Connecticut
Cord. – Cordillera
Cr. – Creek
Czech. – Czech Republic
D.C. – District of Columbia
Del. – Delaware
Dem. – Democratic
Dep. – Dependency
Des. – Desert
Dét. – Détroit
Dist. – District
Dj. – Djebel
Domin. – Dominica
Dom. Rep. – Dominican Republic

E. – East
E. Salv. – El Salvador
Eq. Guin. – Equatorial Guinea
Est. – Estrecho
Falk. Is. – Falkland Is.
Fd. – Fjord
Fla. – Florida
Fr. – French
G. – Golfe, Golfo, Gulf, Guba, Gebel
Ga. – Georgia
Gt. – Great, Greater
Guinea-Biss. – Guinea-Bissau
H.K. – Hong Kong
H.P. – Himachal Pradesh
Hants. – Hampshire
Harb. – Harbor, Harbour
Hd. – Head
Hts. – Heights
I.(s). – Île, Ilha, Insel, Isla, Island, Isle
Ill. – Illinois
Ind. – Indiana
Ind. Oc. – Indian Ocean
Ivory C. – Ivory Coast
J. – Jabal, Jebel
Jaz. – Jazīrah
Junc. – Junction
K. – Kap, Kapp
Kans. – Kansas
Kep. – Kepulauan
Ky. – Kentucky
L. – Lac, Lacul, Lago, Lagoa, Lake, Limni, Loch, Lough
La. – Louisiana
Ld. – Land
Liech. – Liechtenstein
Lux. – Luxembourg
Mad. P. – Madhya Pradesh

Madag. – Madagascar
Man. – Manitoba
Mass. – Massachusetts
Md. – Maryland
Me. – Maine
Medit. S. – Mediterranean Sea
Mich. – Michigan
Minn. – Minnesota
Miss. – Mississippi
Mo. – Missouri
Mont. – Montana
Mozam. – Mozambique
Mt.(s) – Mont, Montaña, Mountain
Mte. – Monte
Mti. – Monti
N. – Nord, Norte, North, Northern, Nouveau
N.B. – New Brunswick
N.C. – North Carolina
N. Cal. – New Caledonia
N. Dak. – North Dakota
N.H. – New Hampshire
N.I. – North Island
N.J. – New Jersey
N. Mex. – New Mexico
N.S. – Nova Scotia
N.S.W. – New South Wales
N.W.T. – North West Territory
N.Y. – New York
N.Z. – New Zealand
Nac. – Nacional
Nat. – National
Nebr. – Nebraska
Neths. – Netherlands
Nev. – Nevada
Nfld. – Newfoundland
Nic. – Nicaragua
O. – Oued, Ouadi
Occ. – Occidentale

Okla. – Oklahoma
Ont. – Ontario
Or. – Orientale
Oreg. – Oregon
Os. – Ostrov
Oz. – Ozero
P. – Pass, Passo, Pasul, Pulau
P.E.I. – Prince Edward Island
Pa. – Pennsylvania
Pac. Oc. – Pacific Ocean
Papua N.G. – Papua New Guinea
Pass. – Passage
Peg. – Pegunungan
Pen. – Peninsula, Péninsule
Phil. – Philippines
Pk. – Peak
Plat. – Plateau
Prov. – Province, Provincial
Pt. – Point
Pta. – Ponta, Punta
Pte. – Pointe
Qué. – Québec
Queens. – Queensland
R. – Rio, River
R.I. – Rhode Island
Ra. – Range
Raj. – Rajasthan
Recr. – Recreational, Récréatif
Reg. – Region
Rep. – Republic
Res. – Reserve, Reservoir
Rhld.-Pfz. – Rheinland-Pfalz
S. – South, Southern, Sur
Si. Arabia – Saudi Arabia
S.C. – South Carolina
S. Dak. – South Dakota
S.I. – South Island
S. Leone – Sierra Leone
Sa. – Serra, Sierra

Sask. – Saskatchewan
Scot. – Scotland
Sd. – Sound
Serbia & M. – Serbia & Montenegro
Sev. – Severnaya
Sib. – Siberia
Sprs. – Springs
St. – Saint
Sta. – Santa
Ste. – Sainte
Sto. – Santo
Str. – Strait, Stretto
Switz. – Switzerland
Tas. – Tasmania
Tenn. – Tennessee
Terr. – Territory, Territoire
Tex. – Texas
Tg. – Tanjung
Trin. & Tob. – Trinidad & Tobago
U.A.E. – United Arab Emirates
U.K. – United Kingdom
U.S.A. – United States of America
Ut. P. – Uttar Pradesh
Va. – Virginia
Vdkhr. – Vodokhranilishche
Vdskh. – Vodoskhovyshche
Vf. – Vírful
Vic. – Victoria
Vol. – Volcano
Vt. – Vermont
W. – Wadi, West
W. Va. – West Virginia
Wall. & F. Is. – Wallis and Futuna Is.
Wash. – Washington
Wis. – Wisconsin
Wlkp. – Wielkopolski
Wyo. – Wyoming
Yorks. – Yorkshire

A

A 'Âli an Nîl □, Sudan 107 F3 9 30N 33 0 E
A Baña, Spain 42 C2 42 58N 8 46W
A Cañiza, Spain 42 C2 42 13N 8 16W
A Coruña, Spain 42 B2 43 20N 8 25W
A Estrada, Spain 42 C2 42 43N 8 27W
A Fonsagrada, Spain 42 B3 43 8N 7 4W
A Guarda, Spain 42 D2 41 56N 8 52W
A Gudiña, Spain 42 C3 42 4N 7 8W
A Rúa, Spain 42 C3 42 24N 7 6W
Aachen, Germany 30 E2 50 45N 6 6 E
Aadorf, Switz. 33 B7 47 30N 8 55 E
Aalborg = Ålborg, Denmark 17 G3 57 2N 9 54 E
Aalen, Germany 31 G6 48 51N 10 6 E
Aalst, Belgium 24 D4 50 56N 4 2 E
Aalten, Neths. 24 C6 51 56N 6 35 E
Aalter, Belgium 24 C3 51 5N 3 28 E
Äänekoski, Finland 15 E21 62 36N 25 44 E
Aarau, Switz. 32 B6 47 23N 8 4 E
Aarberg, Switz. 32 B4 47 2N 7 16 E
Aarburg, Switz. 32 B5 47 19N 7 54 E
Aare →, Switz. 32 A6 47 33N 8 14 E
Aargau □, Switz. 32 B6 47 26N 8 10 E
Aarhus = Århus, Denmark 17 H4 56 8N 10 11 E
Aarlen = Arlon, Belgium 24 E5 49 42N 5 49 E
Aarschot, Belgium 24 D4 50 59N 4 49 E
Aarwangen, Switz. 32 B5 47 15N 7 46 E
Aasiaat, Greenland 10 D5 68 43N 52 56W
Ab-i-Istada, Afghan. 91 B2 32 29N 67 55 E
Ab-i-Panja = Pyandzh →, Asia 65 E4 37 6N 68 20 E
Aba, China 76 A3 32 59N 101 42 E
Aba, Dem. Rep. of the Congo 118 B3 3 58N 30 17 E
Aba, Nigeria 113 D6 5 10N 7 19 E
Âbâ, Jazîrat, Sudan 107 E3 13 30N 32 31 E
Abacaxis →, Brazil 169 D6 3 54 S 58 47W
Abadab, J., Sudan 106 D4 18 54N 35 56 E
Ābādān, Iran 97 D6 30 22N 48 20 E
Abade, Ethiopia 107 F4 9 22N 38 3 E
Ābādeh, Iran 97 D7 31 8N 52 40 E
Abadin, Spain 42 B3 43 21N 7 29W
Abadla, Algeria 111 B4 31 2N 2 45W
Abaeté, Brazil 171 E2 19 9 S 45 27W
Abaeté →, Brazil 171 E2 18 2 S 45 12W
Abaetetuba, Brazil 170 B2 1 40 S 48 50W
Abagnar Qi, China 74 C9 43 52N 116 2 E
Abah, Tanjung, Indonesia 79 K18 8 46 S 115 38 E
Abai, Paraguay 175 B4 25 58 S 55 54W
Abak, Nigeria 113 E6 4 58N 7 50 E
Abakaliki, Nigeria 113 D6 6 22N 8 2 E
Abakan, Russia 67 D10 53 40N 91 10 E
Abala, Congo 114 C3 1 17 S 15 35 E
Abala, Niger 113 C5 14 56N 3 22 E
Abalak, Niger 113 B6 15 22N 6 21 E
Abalemma, Algeria 111 D6 20 51N 5 59 E
Abalemma, Niger 113 B6 16 12N 7 50 E
Abalessa, Algeria 111 D5 22 58N 4 47 E
Abana, Turkey 100 B6 41 59N 34 1 E
Abancay, Peru 172 C3 13 35 S 72 55W
Abanga →, Gabon 114 C2 0 20 S 10 30 E
Abano Terme, Italy 45 C8 45 22N 11 46 E
Abapó, Bolivia 173 D5 18 48 S 63 25W
Abarán, Spain 41 G3 38 12N 1 23W
Abariringa, Kiribati 134 H10 2 50 S 171 40W
Abarqū, Iran 97 D7 31 10N 53 20 E
Abashiri, Japan 70 B12 44 0N 144 15 E
Abashiri-Wan, Japan 70 C12 44 0N 144 30 E
Abau, Papua N. G. 132 F5 10 11 S 148 46 E
Abaújszántó, Hungary 52 B6 48 16N 21 12 E
Abava →, Latvia 54 A8 57 6N 21 54 E
Ābay = Nîl el Azraq →, Sudan 107 D3 15 38N 32 31 E
Abay, Kazakhstan 66 E8 49 38N 72 53 E
Abaya, L., Ethiopia 107 F4 6 30N 37 50 E
Abayita-Shala Lakes △, Ethiopia 107 F4 7 40N 38 37 E
Abaza, Russia 66 D9 52 39N 90 6 E
Abba, C.A.R. 114 A3 5 20N 15 11 E
Abbadia di Fiastra ⌓, Italy 45 E10 43 12N 13 24 E
Abbadia San Salvatore, Italy 45 F8 42 53N 11 41 E
'Abbāsābād, Iran 97 C8 33 34N 58 23 E
Abbay = Nîl el Azraq →, Sudan 107 D3 15 38N 32 31 E
Abbaye, Pt., U.S.A. 148 B1 46 58N 88 8W
Abbazia = Opatija, Croatia 45 C11 45 21N 14 17 E
Abbé, L., Ethiopia 107 E5 11 8N 41 47 E
Abbeville, France 27 B8 50 6N 1 49 E
Abbeville, Ala., U.S.A. 152 D4 31 34N 85 15W
Abbeville, Ga., U.S.A. 152 D6 31 59N 83 18W
Abbeville, La., U.S.A. 155 L8 29 58N 92 8W
Abbeville, S.C., U.S.A. 152 A7 34 11N 82 23W
Abbiategrasso, Italy 44 C5 45 24N 8 54 E
Abbot Ice Shelf, Antarctica 7 D16 73 0 S 92 0W
Abbottabad, Pakistan 92 B5 34 10N 73 15 E
Abbou, O. ben →, Algeria 111 C5 28 32N 5 14 E
Abd al Kūrī, Yemen 99 D6 12 5N 52 20 E
Ābdar, Iran 97 D7 30 16N 55 19 E
'Abdolābād, Iran 97 C8 34 12N 56 30 E
Abdulino, Russia 64 E4 53 42N 53 40 E
Abdulpur, Bangla. 90 C2 24 15N 88 59 E
Abéché, Chad 109 F4 13 50N 20 35 E
Abejar, Spain 40 D2 41 48N 2 47W
Abekr, Sudan 107 E2 12 45N 28 50 E
Abel Tasman △, N.Z. 131 A8 40 59 S 173 3 E
Abemarre, Indonesia 83 C6 7 1 S 140 9 E
Abengourou, Ivory C. 112 D4 6 42N 3 27W
Abenójar, Spain 43 G6 38 53N 4 21W
Åbenrå, Denmark 17 J3 55 3N 9 25 E
Abensberg, Germany 31 G7 48 48N 11 51 E
Abeokuta, Nigeria 113 D5 7 3N 3 19 E
Aber, Uganda 118 B3 2 12N 32 25 E
Aberaeron, U.K. 21 E3 52 15N 4 15W
Aberayron = Aberaeron, U.K. 21 E3 52 15N 4 15W
Aberchirder, U.K. 22 D6 57 34N 2 37W
Abercorn = Mbala, Zambia 119 D3 8 46 S 31 24 E
Abercorn, Australia 127 D5 25 12 S 151 5 E
Aberdare, U.K. 21 F4 51 43N 3 27W
Aberdare △, Kenya 118 C4 0 22 S 36 44 E
Aberdare Ra., Kenya 118 C4 0 15 S 36 50 E
Aberdeen, Australia 129 B9 32 9 S 150 56 E
Aberdeen, Canada 143 C7 52 20N 106 8W
Aberdeen, China 69 G11 22 15N 114 9 E
Aberdeen, S. Africa 116 E3 32 28 S 24 2 E
Aberdeen, U.K. 22 D6 57 9N 2 5W
Aberdeen, Ala., U.S.A. 149 J1 33 49N 88 33W
Aberdeen, Idaho, U.S.A. 158 E7 42 57N 112 50W
Aberdeen, Md., U.S.A. 148 F7 39 31N 76 10W
Aberdeen, Ohio, U.S.A. 157 F13 38 39N 83 46W
Aberdeen, S. Dak., U.S.A. 154 C5 45 28N 98 29W
Aberdeen, Wash., U.S.A. 160 D3 46 59N 123 50W
Aberdeen, City of □, U.K. 22 D6 57 10N 2 10W
Aberdeenshire □, U.K. 22 D6 57 17N 2 36W
Aberdovey = Aberdyfi, U.K. 21 E3 52 33N 4 3W
Aberdyfi, U.K. 21 E3 52 33N 4 3W
Aberfeldy, U.K. 22 E5 56 37N 3 51W
Aberfoyle, U.K. 22 E4 56 11N 4 23W
Abergavenny, U.K. 21 F4 51 49N 3 1W
Abergele, U.K. 20 D4 53 17N 3 35W
Abernathy, U.S.A. 155 J4 33 50N 101 51W
Abert, L., U.S.A. 158 E3 42 38N 120 14W
Aberystwyth, U.K. 21 E3 52 25N 4 5W
Abhā, Si. Arabia 98 C3 18 0N 42 34 E
Abhar, Iran 97 B6 36 9N 49 13 E
Abhayapuri, India 90 B3 26 24N 90 38 E
Abia □, Nigeria 113 D6 5 30N 7 35 E
Abide, Turkey 49 C11 38 55N 29 20 E
Abidiya, Sudan 106 D3 18 18N 34 3 E
Abidjan, Ivory C. 112 D4 5 26N 3 58W
Abilene, Kans., U.S.A. 154 F6 38 55N 97 13W
Abilene, Tex., U.S.A. 155 J5 32 28N 99 43W
Abingdon, U.K. 21 F6 51 40N 1 17W
Abingdon, Ill., U.S.A. 156 D6 40 48N 90 24W
Abingdon, Va., U.S.A. 149 G5 36 43N 81 59W
Abingdon, I. = Pinta, I., Ecuador 172 a 0 35N 90 44W
Abington Reef, Australia 126 B4 18 0 S 149 35 E
Abitau →, Canada 143 B7 59 53N 109 3W
Abitibi →, Canada 140 B3 51 3N 80 55W
Abitibi, L., Canada 140 C4 48 40N 79 40W
Abiy Adi, Ethiopia 107 E4 13 39N 39 3 E
Abkhaz Republic = Abkhazia □, Georgia 61 J5 43 12N 41 5 E
Abkhazia □, Georgia 61 J5 43 12N 41 5 E
Abminga, Australia 127 D1 26 8 S 134 51 E
Abnûb, Egypt 106 B3 27 18N 31 4 E
Åbo = Turku, Finland 15 F20 60 30N 22 19 E
Abo, Massif d', Chad 109 D3 21 41N 16 8 E
Abocho, Nigeria 113 D6 7 35N 6 56 E
Abohar, India 92 D6 30 10N 74 10 E
Aboisso, Ivory C. 112 D4 5 30N 3 5W
Abolo, Congo 114 B2 0 8N 14 16 E
Abomey, Benin 113 D5 7 10N 2 5 E
Abong-Mbang, Cameroon 114 B2 4 0N 13 8 E
Abongabong, Indonesia 84 B1 4 15N 96 48 E
Abonnema, Nigeria 113 E6 4 41N 6 49 E
Abony, Hungary 52 C5 47 12N 20 3 E
Abor Hills, India 90 A5 28 25N 94 46 E
Aborlan, Phil. 81 G2 9 26N 118 33 E
Aboso, Ghana 112 D4 5 23N 1 57W
Abou-Deïa, Chad 109 F3 11 20N 19 20 E
Abou-Goulem, Chad 109 F4 13 37N 21 38 E
Abou-Telfan ⌓, Chad 109 F3 12 2N 18 58 E
Aboyne, U.K. 22 D6 57 4N 2 47W
Abra □, Phil. 80 C3 17 35N 120 45 E
Abra de Ilog, Phil. 80 E3 13 27N 120 44 E
Abra Pampa, Argentina 174 A2 22 43 S 65 42W
Abraham L., Canada 142 C5 52 15N 116 35W
Abrantes, Portugal 43 F2 39 24N 8 7W
Abreojos, Pta., Mexico 162 B2 26 50N 113 40W
Abri, Esh Shamâliya, Sudan 106 C3 20 50N 30 27 E
Abri, Janub Kordofân, Sudan 107 E3 11 40N 30 21 E
Abrolhos, Banka, Brazil 171 E4 18 0 S 38 0W
Abrud, Romania 52 D8 46 19N 23 5 E
Abruzzo □, Italy 45 F10 42 15N 14 0 E
Absaroka Range, U.S.A. 158 D9 44 45N 109 50W
Abtenau, Austria 34 D6 47 33N 13 21 E
Abu, India 92 G5 24 41N 72 50 E
Abū al Abyad, U.A.E. 97 E7 24 11N 53 50 E
Abū al Khaşīb, Iraq 97 D6 30 25N 48 0 E
Abū 'Alī, Si. Arabia 97 E6 27 20N 49 27 E
Abū 'Alī →, Lebanon 103 A4 34 25N 35 50 E
Abū 'Arīsh, Si. Arabia 98 C3 16 53N 42 48 E
Abu Ballas, Egypt 106 C2 24 26N 27 36 E
Abu Deleiq, Sudan 107 D3 15 57N 33 48 E
Abu Dhabi = Abū Z̧āby, U.A.E. 97 E7 24 28N 54 22 E
Abu Dis, Sudan 106 D3 19 12N 33 38 E
Abu Dom, Sudan 107 D3 16 18N 32 25 E
Abū Du'ān, Syria 101 D8 36 25N 38 15 E
Abu el Gairi, W. →, Egypt 103 F2 29 35N 33 30 E
Abu Fatma, Ras, Sudan 106 C4 22 25N 36 25 E
Abu Gabra, Sudan 107 E2 11 2N 26 50 E
Abu Ga'da, W. →, Egypt 103 F1 29 15N 32 53 E
Abu Gelba, Sudan 107 E3 13 11N 31 52 E
Abu Gubeiha, Sudan 107 E3 11 30N 31 15 E
Abu Habl, Khawr →, Sudan 107 E3 12 37N 31 0 E
Abū Ḩadrīyah, Si. Arabia 97 E6 27 20N 48 58 E
Abu Hamed, Sudan 106 D3 19 32N 33 13 E
Abu Haraz, An Nîl el Azraq, Sudan 106 D3 18 1N 33 58 E
Abu Haraz, El Gezira, Sudan 107 E3 14 35N 33 30 E
Abu Haraz, Esh Shamâliya, Sudan 106 D3 19 8N 32 18 E
Abu Higar, Sudan 107 E3 12 50N 33 59 E
Abū Kamāl, Syria 101 E9 34 30N 41 0 E
Abu Kuleiwat, Sudan 107 E2 12 20N 26 0 E
Abū Madd, Ra's, Si. Arabia 96 E3 24 50N 37 7 E
Abu Matariq, Sudan 107 E2 10 59N 26 9 E
Abu Mendi, Ethiopia 107 E4 11 48N 35 42 E
Abū Mūsā, U.A.E. 97 E7 25 52N 55 3 E
Abū Qaşr, Si. Arabia 96 D3 30 21N 38 34 E
Abu Qir, Egypt 106 H7 31 18N 30 0 E
Abu Qireiya, Egypt 106 C4 24 5N 35 28 E
Abu Qurqâs, Egypt 106 B3 28 1N 30 44 E
Abū Rashāsh, Ra's, Oman 99 B7 20 10N 58 38 E
Abu Shagara, Ras, Sudan 106 C4 21 4N 37 19 E
Abu Shanab, Sudan 107 E2 13 58N 27 49 E
Abu Simbel, Egypt 106 C3 22 18N 31 40 E
Abū Şukhayr, Iraq 101 G11 31 54N 44 30 E
Abu Sultân, Egypt 106 H8 30 24N 32 21 E
Abu Tabari, Sudan 106 D2 17 32N 28 32 E
Abu Tig, Egypt 106 B3 27 4N 31 15 E
Abu Tiga, Sudan 107 E3 12 47N 34 12 E
Abu Tineitin, Sudan 107 E3 14 24N 31 1 E
Abu Uruq, Sudan 107 D3 15 52N 30 25 E
Abu Zabad, Sudan 107 E2 12 25N 29 10 E
Abū Z̧āby, U.A.E. 97 E7 24 28N 54 22 E
Abū Zeydābād, Iran 97 C6 33 54N 51 45 E
Abufari, Brazil 173 B5 5 25 S 62 59W
Abuja, Nigeria 113 D6 9 5N 7 32 E
Abukuma-Gawa →, Japan 70 E10 38 6N 140 52 E
Abukuma-Sammyaku, Japan 70 F10 37 30N 140 45 E
Abulug, Phil. 80 B3 18 27N 121 27 E
Abumombazi, Dem. Rep. of the Congo 114 B4 3 42N 22 10 E
Abunã, Brazil 173 B4 9 40 S 65 20W
Abunã →, Brazil 173 B4 9 41 S 65 20W
Abune Yosef, Ethiopia 107 E4 12 5N 39 12 E
Aburatsu, Japan 72 F3 31 34N 131 24 E
Aburo, Dem. Rep. of the Congo 118 B3 2 4N 30 53 E
Abut Hd., N.Z. 131 D5 43 7 S 170 15 E
Abuye Meda, Ethiopia 107 E4 10 30N 39 49 E
Abuyog, Phil. 81 F5 10 45N 125 0 E
Abwong, Sudan 107 F3 9 2N 32 14 E
Åby, Sweden 17 F10 58 40N 16 10 E
Aby, Lagune, Ivory C. 112 D4 5 15N 3 14W
Abyad, Sudan 107 E2 13 47N 26 24 E
Åbybro, Denmark 17 G3 57 10N 9 44 E
Acacías, Colombia 168 C3 3 59N 73 46W
Acadia △, U.S.A. 149 C11 44 20N 68 13W
Acajutla, El Salv. 164 D2 13 36N 89 50W
Açallândia, Brazil 170 C2 5 0 S 47 30W
Acámbaro, Mexico 162 D4 20 0N 100 40W
Acanthus, Greece 50 F7 40 27N 23 47 E
Acaponeta, Mexico 162 C3 22 30N 105 20W
Acapulco, Mexico 163 D5 16 51N 99 56W
Acará, Brazil 170 B2 1 57 S 48 11W
Acarai, Serra, Brazil 169 C6 1 50N 57 50W
Acaraú, Brazil 170 B3 2 53 S 40 7W
Acari, Brazil 170 C4 6 31 S 36 38W
Acarí, Peru 172 D3 15 25 S 74 36W
Acarigua, Venezuela 168 B4 9 33N 69 12W
Acatlán, Mexico 163 D5 18 10N 98 3W
Acayucan, Mexico 163 D6 17 59N 94 58W
Accéglio, Italy 44 D4 44 28N 7 0 E
Accomac, U.S.A. 148 G8 37 43N 75 40W
Accous, France 28 E3 43 0N 0 36W
Accra, Ghana 113 D4 5 35N 0 6W
Accrington, U.K. 20 D5 53 45N 2 22W
Acebal, Argentina 174 C3 33 20 S 60 50W
Aceh □, Indonesia 84 B1 4 15N 97 30 E
Acerra, Italy 47 B7 40 57N 14 22 E
Aceuchal, Spain 43 G4 38 39N 6 30W
Achacachi, Bolivia 172 D4 16 3 S 68 43W
Achaguas, Venezuela 168 B4 7 46N 68 14W
Achalpur, India 94 D3 21 22N 77 32 E
Achao, Chile 176 B2 42 28 S 73 30W
Acharnes = Akharnaí, Greece 48 C5 38 5N 23 44 E
Achegour, Niger 109 E2 19 10N 11 54 E
Acheloos = Akhelóös →, Greece 48 C3 38 19N 21 7 E
Achelouma, Niger 109 D2 22 12N 12 50 E
Achelouma, E. →, Niger 109 D2 21 55N 13 35 E
Acheng, China 75 B14 45 30N 126 58 E
Achenkirch, Austria 34 D4 47 32N 11 45 E
Achensee, Austria 34 D4 47 26N 11 45 E
Acher, India 92 H5 23 10N 72 32 E
Achern, Germany 31 G4 48 37N 8 4 E
Acheron →, N.Z. 131 C8 42 16 S 173 4 E
Achill Hd., Ireland 23 C1 53 58N 10 15W
Achill I., Ireland 23 C1 53 58N 10 1W
Achim, Germany 30 B5 53 1N 9 3 E
Achinsk, Russia 67 D10 56 20N 90 20 E
Achisay = Ashchysay, Kazakhstan 65 B4 43 35N 68 53 E
Achit, Russia 64 C6 56 48N 57 54 E
Achouka, Gabon 114 C2 0 52 S 9 45 E
Acıgöl, Turkey 49 D11 37 50N 29 50 E
Acıpayam, Turkey 49 D11 37 26N 29 22 E
Acireale, Italy 47 E8 37 37N 15 10 E
Ackerman, U.S.A. 155 J10 33 19N 89 11W
Ackley, U.S.A. 156 B3 42 33N 93 3W
Acklins I., Bahamas 165 B5 22 30N 74 0W
Acme, Canada 142 C6 51 33N 113 30W
Acme, U.S.A. 150 F5 40 8N 79 26W
Acobamba, Peru 172 C3 12 52 S 74 35W
Acomayo, Peru 172 C3 13 55 S 71 38W
Aconcagua, Cerro, Argentina 174 C2 32 39 S 70 0W
Aconquija, Mt., Argentina 174 B2 27 0 S 66 0W
Acopiara, Brazil 170 C4 6 6 S 39 27W
Açores, Is. dos, Atl. Oc. 8 C9 38 0N 27 0W
Acorizal, Brazil 173 D6 15 12 S 56 22W
Acornhoek, S. Africa 117 C5 24 37 S 31 2 E
Acquapendente, Italy 45 F8 42 44N 11 52 E
Acquasanta Terme, Italy 45 F10 42 46N 13 24 E
Acquasparta, Italy 45 F9 42 41N 12 33 E
Acquaviva delle Fonti, Italy 47 B9 40 54N 16 50 E
Ácqui Terme, Italy 44 D5 44 41N 8 28 E
Acraman, L., Australia 127 E2 32 2 S 135 23 E
Acre = 'Akko, Israel 103 C4 32 55N 35 4 E
Acre □, Brazil 172 B3 9 1 S 71 0W
Acre →, Brazil 172 B4 8 45 S 67 22W
Acri, Italy 47 C9 39 29N 16 23 E
Acs, Hungary 52 C3 47 42N 18 2 E
Actæon Mt., St. Helena 9 h 15 58 S 5 42W
Actium, Greece 39 B2 38 57N 20 45 E
Acton, Canada 150 C4 43 38N 80 3W
Açu, Brazil 170 C4 5 34 S 36 54W
Acul = Vidin, Bulgaria 50 C6 43 59N 22 50 E
Acuña, Mexico 162 B4 29 18N 100 55W
Acworth, U.S.A. 152 A5 34 4N 84 41W
Ad Dafinah, Si. Arabia 98 B3 23 18N 41 58 E
Aḑ Ḑafrah, U.A.E. 99 B6 23 30N 54 30 E
Ad Dahnā, Si. Arabia 99 A5 24 30N 48 10 E
Aḑ Ḑāli', Yemen 98 D4 13 42N 44 44 E
Ad Dammām, Si. Arabia 97 E6 26 20N 50 5 E
Ad Dāmūr, Lebanon 103 B4 33 44N 35 27 E
Ad Darb, Si. Arabia 98 C3 18 2N 43 7 E
Ad Dawādimī, Si. Arabia 96 E5 24 35N 44 15 E
Ad Dawḩah, Qatar 97 E6 25 15N 51 35 E
Ad Dawr, Iraq 101 E10 34 27N 43 47 E
Aḑ Ḑiffah, Libya 108 B4 30 30N 24 30 E
Ad Dilam, Si. Arabia 98 B4 23 55N 47 10 E
Ad Dir'īyah, Si. Arabia 96 E5 24 44N 46 35 E
Ad Dīwānīyah, Iraq 101 F11 32 0N 45 0 E
Ad Dujayl, Iraq 101 F11 33 51N 44 14 E
Ad Duwayd, Si. Arabia 96 D4 30 15N 42 17 E
Ada, Ghana 113 D5 5 44N 0 40 E
Ada, Serbia & M. 52 E5 45 49N 20 9 E
Ada, Minn., U.S.A. 154 B6 47 18N 96 31W
Ada, Ohio, U.S.A. 157 D13 40 46N 83 49W
Ada, Okla., U.S.A. 155 H6 34 46N 96 41W
Adabiya, Egypt 103 F1 29 53N 32 28 E
Adad, Somali Rep. 120 C3 9 27N 46 49 E
Adair, C., Canada 139 A12 71 30N 71 34W
Adaja →, Spain 42 D6 41 32N 4 52W
Adak, U.S.A. 144 L3 51 45N 176 45W
Adak I., U.S.A. 144 L3 51 45N 176 45W
Ådalsbruk, Norway 18 D8 60 43N 11 19 E
Adam, Oman 99 B7 22 15N 57 28 E
Adam, Mt., Falk. Is. 9 f 51 34 S 60 4W
Adamantina, Brazil 171 F1 21 42 S 51 4W
Adamaoua, Massif de l', Cameroon 113 D7 7 20N 12 20 E
Adamawa □, Nigeria 113 D7 9 20N 12 30 E
Adamawa Highlands = Adamaoua, Massif de l', Cameroon 113 D7 7 20N 12 20 E
Adamello ⌓, Italy 44 B7 46 4N 10 28 E
Adamello, Mte., Italy 44 B7 46 9N 10 30 E
Adami Tulu, Ethiopia 107 F4 7 53N 38 41 E
Adaminaby, Australia 129 D8 36 0 S 148 45 E
Adamovka, Russia 64 F7 51 32N 59 56 E
Adams, Mass., U.S.A. 151 D11 42 38N 73 7W
Adams, N.Y., U.S.A. 151 C8 43 49N 76 1W
Adams, Wis., U.S.A. 154 D10 43 57N 89 49W
Adams, Mt., U.S.A. 160 D5 46 12N 121 30W
Adam's Bridge, Sri Lanka 95 K4 9 15N 79 40 E
Adams L., Canada 142 C5 51 10N 119 40W
Adam's Peak, Sri Lanka 95 L5 6 48N 80 30 E
Adamuz, Spain 43 G6 38 2N 4 32W
Adana, Turkey 100 D6 37 0N 35 16 E
Adanero, Spain 42 E6 40 56N 4 36W
Adapazarı = Sakarya, Turkey 100 B4 40 48N 30 25 E
Adar Gwagwa, J., Sudan 106 C4 22 15N 35 20 E
Adarama, Sudan 107 D3 17 10N 34 52 E
Adare, C., Antarctica 7 D11 71 0 S 171 0 E
Adarte, Eritrea 107 E5 13 18N 42 8 E
Adaut, Indonesia 83 C4 8 8 S 131 7 E
Adavale, Australia 127 D3 25 52 S 144 32 E
Adda →, Italy 44 C6 45 8N 9 53 E
Addatigala, India 94 F6 17 31N 82 3 E
Addax ⌓, Niger 109 E1 19 17N 9 22 E
Addis Ababa = Addis Abeba, Ethiopia 107 F4 9 2N 38 42 E
Addis Abeba, Ethiopia 107 F4 9 2N 38 42 E
Addis Alem, Ethiopia 107 F4 9 0N 38 17 E
Addis Zemen, Ethiopia 107 E4 12 7N 37 47 E
Addison, Ill., U.S.A. 157 C8 41 55N 88 0W
Addison, N.Y., U.S.A. 150 D7 42 1N 77 14W
Addo, S. Africa 116 E4 33 32 S 25 45 E
Addo △, S. Africa 116 E4 33 30 S 25 50 E
Adebour, Niger 113 C7 13 17N 11 50 E
Ādeh, Iran 96 B5 37 42N 45 11 E
Adel, Ga., U.S.A. 152 D6 31 8N 83 25W
Adel, Iowa, U.S.A. 156 C2 41 37N 94 1W
Adelaide, Australia 128 C3 34 52 S 138 30 E
Adelaide, Bahamas 9 b 25 4N 77 31W
Adelaide, S. Africa 116 E4 32 42 S 26 20 E
Adelaide I., Antarctica 7 C17 67 15 S 68 30W
Adelaide Pen., Canada 138 B10 68 15N 97 30W
Adelaide River, Australia 124 B5 13 15 S 131 7 E
Adelanto, U.S.A. 161 L9 34 35N 117 22W
Adelaye, C.A.R. 114 A4 7 7N 22 49 E
Adelboden, Switz. 32 D5 46 29N 7 33 E
Adele I., Australia 124 C3 15 32 S 123 9 E
Adélie, Terre, Antarctica 7 C10 68 0 S 140 0 E
Adelie Land = Adélie, Terre, Antarctica 7 C10 68 0 S 140 0 E
Adelong, Australia 129 C8 35 16 S 148 4 E
Adelsk, Belarus 54 E10 53 24N 23 47 E
Ademuz, Spain 40 E3 40 5N 1 13W
Aden = Al 'Adan, Yemen 98 D4 12 45N 45 0 E
Aden, G. of, Asia 88 D3 12 30N 47 30 E
Adendorp, S. Africa 116 E3 32 15 S 24 30 E
Aderbissinat, Niger 113 B6 15 34N 7 54 E
Adh Dhayd, U.A.E. 97 E7 25 17N 55 53 E
Adhoi, India 92 H4 23 26N 70 32 E
Adi, Indonesia 83 B4 4 15 S 133 30 E
Adi Arkai, Ethiopia 107 E4 13 35N 37 57 E
Adi Daro, Ethiopia 107 E4 14 20N 38 14 E
Adi Keyih, Eritrea 107 E4 14 51N 39 22 E
Adi Kwala, Eritrea 107 E4 14 38N 38 48 E
Adi Ugri, Eritrea 107 E4 14 58N 38 48 E
Adieu, C., Australia 125 F5 32 0 S 132 10 E
Adieu Pt., Australia 124 C3 15 14 S 124 35 E
Adigala, Ethiopia 107 E5 10 24N 42 15 E
Adige →, Italy 45 C9 45 9N 12 20 E
Adigrat, Ethiopia 107 E4 14 20N 39 26 E
Adıgüzel Barajı, Turkey 49 C11 38 13N 29 14 E
Adilabad, India 94 E4 19 33N 78 20 E
Adilcevaz, Turkey 101 C10 38 47N 42 43 E
Adirondack ⌓, U.S.A. 151 C10 44 0N 74 20W
Adirondack Mts., U.S.A. 151 C10 44 0N 74 0W
Adis Abeba = Addis Abeba, Ethiopia 107 F4 9 2N 38 42 E
Adıyaman, Turkey 101 D8 37 45N 38 16 E
Adjim, Tunisia 108 B2 33 47N 10 50 E
Adjohon, Benin 113 D5 6 41N 2 32 E
Adjud, Romania 53 D12 46 7N 27 10 E
Adjumani, Uganda 118 B3 3 20N 31 50 E
Adjuntas, Puerto Rico 165 d 18 10N 66 43W
Adlavik Is., Canada 141 B8 55 0N 58 40W
Adler, Russia 61 J4 43 28N 39 52 E
Adliswil, Switz. 33 B7 47 19N 8 32 E
Admer, Algeria 111 D6 20 21N 5 27 E
Admer, Erg d', Algeria 111 D6 24 0N 9 5 E
Admiralty G., Australia 124 B4 14 20 S 125 55 E
Admiralty I., U.S.A. 142 B2 57 30N 134 30W
Admiralty Is., Papua N. G. 132 B4 2 0 S 147 0 E
Adnan Menderes, İzmir ✈ (ADB), Turkey 49 C9 38 23N 27 6 E
Ado, Nigeria 113 D5 6 36N 2 56 E
Ado-Ekiti, Nigeria 113 D6 7 38N 5 12 E
Adok, Sudan 107 F3 8 10N 30 20 E
Adola, Ethiopia 107 E5 11 14N 41 44 E
Adonara, Indonesia 82 C2 8 15 S 123 5 E
Adoni, India 95 G3 15 33N 77 18 E
Adony, Hungary 52 C3 47 6N 18 52 E
Adour →, France 28 E2 43 32N 1 32W
Adra, India 93 H12 23 30N 86 42 E
Adra, Spain 43 J7 36 43N 3 3W
Adrano, Italy 47 E7 37 40N 14 50 E
Adrar des Iforas, Algeria 111 C4 27 51N 0 11 E
Adrar Madet, Niger 109 E2 18 54N 10 35 E
Adrasman, Tajikistan 65 C4 40 38N 69 58 E
Adré, Chad 109 F4 13 40N 22 20 E
Adrī, Libya 108 C2 27 32N 13 2 E
Ádria, Italy 45 C9 45 3N 12 3 E
Adrian, Ga., U.S.A. 152 C7 32 33N 82 35W
Adrian, Mich., U.S.A. 157 C12 41 54N 84 2W
Adrian, Mo., U.S.A. 156 F2 38 24N 94 21W
Adrian, Tex., U.S.A. 155 H3 35 16N 102 40W
Adrianople = Edirne, Turkey 51 E10 41 40N 26 34 E
Adriatic Sea, Medit. S. 12 G9 43 0N 16 0 E
Adua, Indonesia 83 B3 1 45 S 129 50 E
Adula-Gruppe, Switz. 33 D8 46 30N 9 3 E
Adung Long, Burma 90 A6 28 7N 97 42 E
Adur, India 95 K3 9 8N 76 40 E
Adwa, Ethiopia 107 E4 14 15N 38 52 E
Adygea □, Russia 61 H5 45 0N 40 0 E
Adzhar Republic = Ajaria □, Georgia 61 K6 41 30N 42 0 E
Adzhibakul = Qazimämmäd, Azerbaijan 61 K9 40 3N 49 0 E
Adzopé, Ivory C. 112 D4 6 7N 3 49W
Ægean Sea, Medit. S. 49 C7 38 30N 25 0 E
Aerhtai Shan, Mongolia 68 B4 46 40N 92 45 E
Ærø, Denmark 17 K4 54 52N 10 25 E
Ærøskøbing, Denmark 17 K4 54 53N 10 24 E
Aesch, Switz. 32 B5 47 28N 7 36 E
Aëtós, Greece 48 D3 37 15N 21 50 E
Afafi, Massif d', Niger 109 D3 22 11N 15 10 E
'Afak, Iraq 101 F11 32 4N 45 15 E
Afándou, Greece 38 E12 36 18N 28 12 E
Afar □, Ethiopia 107 E5 12 0N 41 0 E
Afarag, Erg, Algeria 111 D5 23 50N 2 47 E
Afareaitu, Tahiti 133 S16 17 33 S 149 47W
Åfarnes, Norway 18 B4 62 40N 7 32 E
Afdega, Ethiopia 120 C2 6 4N 43 30 E
Affoltern, Switz. 33 B6 47 17N 8 27 E
Affreville = Khemis Miliana, Algeria 111 A5 36 11N 2 14 E
Affton, U.S.A. 156 F6 38 33N 90 20W
Afghanistan ■, Asia 91 B2 33 0N 65 0 E
Afgoi, Somali Rep. 120 D2 2 7N 44 59 E
'Afīf, Si. Arabia 98 B3 23 53N 42 56 E
Afikpo, Nigeria 113 D6 5 53N 7 54 E
Aflisses, O. →, Algeria 111 C5 28 40N 0 50 E
Aflou, Algeria 111 B5 34 7N 2 3 E
Afmadu, Somali Rep. 120 D2 0 31N 42 4 E
Afogados da Ingàzeira, Brazil 170 C4 7 45 S 37 39W
Afognak I., U.S.A. 144 G9 58 15N 152 30W
Afore, Papua N. G. 132 E5 9 9 S 148 23 E
Afragóla, Italy 47 B7 40 55N 14 18 E
Afram →, Ghana 113 D4 7 0N 0 52W
Afrera, Ethiopia 107 E5 13 16N 41 5 E
Africa 104 E6 10 0N 20 0 E
'Afrīn, Syria 100 D7 36 32N 36 50 E
Afşin, Turkey 100 C7 38 14N 36 55 E
Afton, Iowa, U.S.A. 156 C2 41 2N 94 12W
Afton, N.Y., U.S.A. 151 D9 42 14N 75 32W
Afton, Wyo., U.S.A. 158 E8 42 44N 110 56W
Aftout, Algeria 110 C4 26 50N 3 45W
Afuá, Brazil 169 D7 0 15 S 50 20W
'Afula, Israel 103 C4 32 37N 35 17 E
Afumba, Zambia 115 F4 15 38 S 24 56 E
Afyon, Turkey 49 C12 38 45N 30 33 E
Afyon □, Turkey 49 C12 38 25N 30 30 E
Afyonkarahisar = Afyon, Turkey 49 C12 38 45N 30 33 E
Aga, Egypt 106 H7 30 55N 31 10 E
Aga Pt., Guam 133 R15 13 15N 144 43 E
Agadem, Niger 109 E2 16 50N 13 11 E
Agadès = Agadez, Niger 113 B6 16 58N 7 59 E
Agadez, Niger 113 B6 16 58N 7 59 E
Agadir, Morocco 110 B3 30 28N 9 55W
Agaete, Canary Is. 9 e1 28 6N 15 43W
Agaie, Nigeria 113 D6 9 1N 6 18 E
Agailás, Mauritania 110 D2 22 37N 14 22W
Again, Sudan 107 F2 8 28N 29 55 E
Agalás, Greece 39 D2 37 43N 20 47 E
Agalega Is., Mauritius 121 F4 11 0 S 57 0 E
Agana, Guam 133 R15 13 28N 144 45 E
Ağapınar, Turkey 49 B12 39 48N 30 47 E
Agar, India 92 H7 23 40N 76 2 E
Agar →, India 94 D6 21 0N 82 57 E
Agaro, Ethiopia 107 F4 7 50N 36 38 E
Agartala, India 90 D3 23 50N 91 23 E
Agăş, Romania 53 D11 46 28N 26 15 E
Agassiz, Canada 142 D4 49 14N 121 46W
Agat, Guam 133 R15 13 25N 144 40 E
Agats, Indonesia 83 C5 5 33 S 138 0 E
Agatti I., India 95 J1 10 50N 72 12 E
Agattu I., U.S.A. 144 K4 52 25N 173 35 E
Agawam, U.S.A. 151 D12 42 5N 72 37W
Agbélouvé, Togo 113 D5 6 35N 1 14 E
Agboville, Ivory C. 112 D4 5 55N 4 15W
Ağcabädi, Azerbaijan 61 K8 40 5N 47 27 E
Ağdam, Azerbaijan 61 L8 40 0N 46 58 E
Ağdaş, Azerbaijan 61 K8 40 44N 47 22 E
Agde, France 28 E7 43 19N 3 28 E
Agde, C. d', France 28 E7 43 16N 3 28 E
Agdz, Morocco 110 B3 30 47N 6 30W
Agdzhabedi = Ağcabädi, Azerbaijan 61 K8 40 5N 47 27 E
Agen, France 28 D4 44 12N 0 38 E
Ageo, Japan 73 B11 35 58N 139 36 E
Ager Tay, Chad 109 E3 20 0N 17 41 E
Agerbæk, Denmark 17 J2 55 36N 8 48 E
Agersø, Denmark 17 J5 55 13N 11 12 E
Ageyevo, Russia 58 E9 54 10N 36 27 E
Aggteleki △, Hungary 52 B5 48 27N 20 36 E
Āgh Kand, Iran 97 B6 37 15N 48 4 E
Aghios Efstratios = Áyios Evstrátios, Greece 48 B6 39 34N 24 58 E
Aghios Oros = Áthos, Greece 51 F8 40 9N 24 22 E
Aghireşu, Romania 53 D8 46 53N 23 15 E
Aghoueyyît, Mauritania 110 D1 21 10N 15 6W
Aghreïjît, Mauritania 110 D2 21 58N 12 11W
Aginskoye, Russia 67 D12 51 6N 114 32 E
Ağlasun, Turkey 49 D12 37 39N 30 31 E
Agly →, France 28 F7 42 46N 3 3 E
Agmar, Mauritania 110 C2 25 18N 10 50W
Agnew, Australia 125 E3 28 1 S 120 31 E
Agnibilékrou, Ivory C. 112 D4 7 10N 3 11W
Agnita, Romania 53 E9 45 59N 24 40 E
Agno, Switz. 33 E7 45 59N 8 53 E
Agnone, Italy 45 G11 41 48N 14 22 E
Ago, Japan 73 C8 34 20N 136 51 E
Agofie, Ghana 113 D5 8 27N 0 15 E
Agogna →, Italy 44 C5 45 4N 8 54 E
Agogo, Sudan 107 F2 7 50N 28 45 E
Agön, Sweden 16 C11 61 34N 17 23 E
Agon Coutainville, France 26 C5 49 2N 1 34W
Agoo, Phil. 80 C3 16 20N 120 22 E
Ágordo, Italy 45 B9 46 18N 12 2 E
Agori, India 93 G10 24 33N 82 57 E
Agouna, Benin 113 D5 7 39N 1 47 E
Agout →, France 28 E5 43 47N 1 41 E
Agra, India 92 F7 27 17N 77 58 E
Agrakhanskiuy Poluostrov, Russia 61 J8 43 42N 47 36 E
Agram = Zagreb, Croatia 45 C12 45 50N 15 58 E
Agramunt, Spain 40 D6 41 48N 1 6 E
Agreda, Spain 40 D3 41 51N 1 55W
Ağri, Turkey 101 C10 39 44N 43 3 E
Agri →, Italy 47 B9 40 13N 16 44 E
Ağrı Dağı, Turkey 101 C11 39 50N 44 15 E
Ağri Karakose = Ağri, Turkey 101 C10 39 44N 43 3 E
Agriá, Greece 48 B5 39 20N 23 1 E
Agrigento, Italy 46 E6 37 19N 13 34 E
Agrinio = Agrínion, Greece 48 C3 38 37N 21 27 E
Agrínion, Greece 48 C3 38 37N 21 27 E
Agrópoli, Italy 47 B7 40 21N 14 59 E
Ağstafa, Azerbaijan 61 K7 41 7N 45 27 E
Água Branca, Brazil 170 C3 5 50 S 42 40W

‘Aqdā, *Iran* **97 C7** 32 26N 53 37 E
Aqîq, *Sudan* **106 D4** 18 14N 38 12 E
Aqîq, Khalîg, *Sudan* **106 D4** 18 20N 38 10 E
‘Aqīq, W. al →, *Si. Arabia* **98 B3** 20 16N 41 40 E
Aqköl, *Kazakhstan* **65 A7** 45 0N 75 39 E
Aqköl, *Kazakhstan* **65 B5** 43 36N 70 45 E
Aqmola = Astana, *Kazakhstan* **66 D8** 51 10N 71 30 E
Aqqum, *Kazakhstan* **65 A2** 44 50N 65 8 E
‘Aqrah, *Iraq* **101 D10** 36 46N 43 45 E
Aqshī, *Kazakhstan* **65 B8** 43 59N 76 19 E
Aqsū, *Kazakhstan* **65 B4** 42 25N 69 50 E
Aqsügek, *Kazakhstan* **65 A7** 44 37N 74 30 E
Aqsümbe, *Kazakhstan* **65 A3** 44 26N 67 33 E
Aqtaū, *Kazakhstan* **66 E6** 43 39N 51 12 E
Aqtöbe, *Kazakhstan* **57 D10** 50 17N 57 10 E
Aquidauana, *Brazil* **173 E6** 20 30 S 55 50W
Aquidauana →, *Brazil* **173 D6** 19 44 S 56 50W
Aquiles Serdán, *Mexico* **162 B3** 28 37N 105 54W
Aquin, *Haiti* **165 C5** 18 16N 73 24W
Aquitain, Bassin, *France* **25 D3** 44 0N 0 30W
Aquitaine □, *France* **28 D3** 44 25N 0 30W
Aqyrtöbe, *Kazakhstan* **65 B6** 42 59N 72 7 E
Aqzhar, *Kazakhstan* **65 B5** 43 8N 71 37 E
Ar Rachidiya = Er Rachidia, *Morocco* **110 B4** 31 58N 4 20W
Ar Rafīd, *Syria* **103 C4** 32 57N 35 52 E
Ar Raḩḩālīyah, *Iraq* **101 F10** 32 44N 43 23 E
Ar Ramādī, *Iraq* **101 F10** 33 25N 43 20 E
Ar Raml, *Libya* **108 C3** 26 45N 19 40 E
Ar Ramthā, *Jordan* **103 C5** 32 34N 36 0 E
Ar Raqqah, *Syria* **101 E8** 35 59N 39 8 E
Ar Rass, *Si. Arabia* **96 E4** 25 50N 43 40 E
Ar Rawḑah, *Si. Arabia* **98 B3** 21 16N 42 50 E
Ar Rawḑah, *Yemen* **98 D4** 14 28N 47 17 E
Ar Rawshān, *Si. Arabia* **106 C5** 20 2N 42 36 E
Ar Rifā‘ī, *Iraq* **96 D5** 31 50N 46 10 E
Ar Rijā‘, *Yemen* **98 D4** 13 1N 44 35 E
Ar Riyāḑ, *Si. Arabia* **96 E5** 24 41N 46 42 E
Ar Ru‘ays, *Qatar* **97 E6** 26 8N 51 12 E
Ar Rukhaymīyah, *Iraq* **96 D5** 29 22N 45 38 E
Ar Ruşāfah, *Syria* **101 E8** 35 45N 38 49 E
Ar Ruţbah, *Iraq* **101 F9** 33 0N 40 15 E
Ar Ruwayḑah, *Si. Arabia* **98 B4** 23 40N 44 40 E
Ara, *India* **93 G11** 25 35N 84 32 E
Ara Goro, *Ethiopia* **107 F5** 5 48N 41 18 E
Ara Tera, *Ethiopia* **107 F5** 6 38N 40 57 E
Arab, *U.S.A.* **149 H2** 34 19N 86 30W
‘Arab, Bahr el →, *Sudan* **107 F2** 9 0N 29 30 E
Arab, Khalîg el, *Egypt* **106 A2** 30 55N 29 0 E
Arab, Shatt al →, *Asia* **97 D6** 30 0N 48 31 E
‘Araba, W. →, *Egypt* **106 J8** 28 19N 33 31 E
‘Arabābād, *Iran* **97 C8** 33 2N 57 41 E
‘Arabah, W. →, *Yemen* **99 C5** 18 5N 51 26 E
Araban, *Turkey* **100 D7** 37 28N 37 44 E
Arabatskaya Strelka, *Ukraine* **59 K8** 45 40N 35 0 E
Arabba, *Italy* **45 B8** 46 30N 11 52 E
Arabelo, *Venezuela* **169 C5** 4 55N 64 13W
Arabi, *U.S.A.* **152 D6** 31 50N 83 44W
Arabia, *Asia* **62 G8** 25 0N 45 0 E
Arabian Desert = Es Sahrâ’ Esh Sharqîya, *Egypt* **106 B3** 27 30N 32 30 E
Arabian Gulf = Gulf, The, *Asia* **97 E6** 27 0N 50 0 E
Arabian Sea, *Ind. Oc.* **88 D5** 16 0N 65 0 E
Arabistan = Khūzestān □, *Iran* **97 D6** 31 0N 49 0 E
Araç, *Turkey* **100 B5** 41 15N 33 21 E
Aracaju, *Brazil* **170 D4** 10 55 S 37 4W
Aracataca, *Colombia* **168 A3** 10 38N 74 9W
Aracati, *Brazil* **170 B4** 4 30 S 37 44W
Araçatuba, *Brazil* **175 A5** 21 10 S 50 30W
Araceli, *Phil.* **81 F2** 10 33N 119 59 E
Aracena, *Spain* **43 H4** 37 53N 6 38W
Aracena, Sierra de, *Spain* **43 H4** 37 50N 6 50W
Aracides, C., *Solomon Is.* **133 M11** 8 21 S 161 0 E
Aračinovo, *Macedonia* **50 D5** 42 1N 21 34 E
Araçuaí, *Brazil* **171 E3** 16 52 S 42 4W
Araçuaí →, *Brazil* **171 E3** 16 46 S 42 2W
‘Arad, *Israel* **103 D4** 31 15N 35 12 E
Arad, *Romania* **52 D6** 46 10N 21 20 E
Arad □, *Romania* **52 D6** 46 20N 22 0 E
Arada, *Chad* **109 F4** 15 0N 20 20 E
Arādān, *Iran* **97 C7** 35 21N 52 30 E
Aradhippou, *Cyprus* **39 F9** 34 57N 33 36 E
Arafura Sea, *E. Indies* **83 C5** 9 0 S 135 0 E
Aragarças, *Brazil* **173 D7** 15 55 S 52 15W
Aragats, *Armenia* **61 K7** 40 30N 44 15 E
Aragon, *U.S.A.* **152 A4** 34 2N 85 3W
Aragón □, *Spain* **40 D4** 41 25N 0 40W
Aragón →, *Spain* **40 C3** 42 13N 1 44W
Aragona, *Italy* **46 E6** 37 24N 13 27 E
Aragua □, *Venezuela* **168 B4** 10 0N 67 10W
Aragua de Barcelona, *Venezuela* **169 B5** 9 28N 64 49W
Araguacema, *Brazil* **170 C2** 8 50 S 49 20W
Araguaçu = Paraguaçu Paulista, *Brazil* **175 A5** 22 22 S 50 35W
Araguaçu, *Brazil* **171 D2** 12 49 S 49 51W
Araguaia △, *Brazil* **170 D2** 10 30 S 50 0W
Araguaia →, *Brazil* **170 C2** 5 21 S 48 41W
Araguaiana, *Brazil* **173 D7** 15 43 S 51 51W
Araguaína, *Brazil* **170 C2** 7 12 S 48 12W
Araguari, *Brazil* **171 E2** 18 38 S 48 11W
Araguari →, *Brazil* **169 C8** 1 15N 49 55W
Araguatins, *Brazil* **170 C2** 5 38 S 48 7W
Arain, *India* **92 F6** 26 27N 75 2 E
Araioses, *Brazil* **170 B3** 2 53 S 41 55W
Arak, *Algeria* **111 C5** 25 20N 3 45 E
Arāk, *Iran* **97 C6** 34 0N 49 40 E
Araka, *Sudan* **107 G3** 4 20N 30 23 E
Arakan □, *Burma* **90 F5** 19 0N 94 15 E
Arakan Yoma, *Burma* **90 F5** 20 0N 94 40 E
Arákhova, *Greece* **48 C4** 38 28N 22 35 E
Arakkonam, *India* **95 H4** 13 7N 79 43 E
Arakli, *Turkey* **101 B8** 41 6N 40 2 E
Araks = Aras, Rūd-e →, *Asia* **61 K9** 40 5N 48 29 E
Aral, *Kazakhstan* **66 E7** 46 41N 61 45 E
Aral Sea, *Asia* **66 E7** 44 30N 60 0 E
Aral Tengizi = Aral Sea, *Asia* **66 E7** 44 30N 60 0 E
Aralsk = Aral, *Kazakhstan* **66 E7** 46 41N 61 45 E
Aralskoye More = Aral Sea, *Asia* **66 E7** 44 30N 60 0 E
Aralsor, Ozero, *Kazakhstan* **61 F9** 49 5N 48 12 E
Aramac, *Australia* **126 C4** 22 58 S 145 14 E
Aramia →, *Papua N. G.* **132 D2** 7 55 S 143 22 E
Aran →, *India* **94 E4** 19 55N 78 12 E
Aran Areh, *Ethiopia* **120 C2** 9 2N 43 54 E
Aran I., *Ireland* **23 A3** 55 0N 8 30W
Aran Is., *Ireland* **23 C2** 53 6N 9 38W
Aranda de Duero, *Spain* **42 D7** 41 39N 3 42W
Arandān, *Iran* **96 C5** 35 23N 46 55 E
Aranđelovac, *Serbia & M.* **50 B4** 44 18N 20 34 E
Aranga, *N.Z.* **130 B2** 35 44 S 173 40 E
Arani, *Bolivia* **173 D4** 17 34 S 65 46W
Arani, *India* **95 H4** 12 43N 79 19 E
Aranjuez, *Spain* **42 E7** 40 1N 3 40W
Aranos, *Namibia* **116 C2** 24 9 S 19 7 E
Aransas Pass, *U.S.A.* **155 M6** 27 55N 97 9W
Aranyaprathet, *Thailand* **86 F4** 13 41N 102 30 E
Arao, *Japan* **72 E2** 32 59N 130 25 E
Araouane, *Mali* **112 B4** 18 55N 3 30W
Arapahoe, *U.S.A.* **154 E5** 40 18N 99 54W
Arapari, *Brazil* **170 C2** 5 34 S 49 15W
Arapawa I., *N.Z.* **131 B9** 41 11 S 174 17 E
Arapey Grande →, *Uruguay* **174 C4** 30 55 S 57 49W
Arapgir, *Turkey* **101 C8** 39 5N 38 30 E
Arapiraca, *Brazil* **170 C4** 9 45 S 36 39W
Arapongas, *Brazil* **175 A5** 23 29 S 51 28W
Arapuni, *N.Z.* **130 E4** 38 4 S 175 39 E
Ar‘ar, *Si. Arabia* **96 D4** 30 59N 41 2 E
Araracuara, *Colombia* **168 D3** 0 24 S 72 17W
Araranguá, *Brazil* **175 B6** 29 0 S 49 30W
Araraquara, *Brazil* **171 F2** 21 50 S 48 0W
Araras, *Brazil* **171 F2** 22 22 S 47 23W
Ararás, Serra das, *Brazil* **175 B5** 25 0 S 53 10W
Ararat, *Armenia* **101 C11** 39 48N 44 50 E
Ararat, *Australia* **128 D5** 37 16 S 143 0 E
Ararat, Mt. = Ağrı Dağı, *Turkey* **101 C11** 39 50N 44 15 E
Arari, *Brazil* **170 B3** 3 28 S 44 47W
Araria, *India* **93 F12** 26 9N 87 33 E
Araripe, Chapada do, *Brazil* **170 C3** 7 20 S 40 0W
Araripina, *Brazil* **170 C3** 7 33 S 40 34W
Araruama, L. de, *Brazil* **171 F3** 22 53 S 42 12W
Araruna, *Brazil* **170 C4** 6 52 S 35 44W
Aras, Rūd-e →, *Asia* **61 K9** 40 5N 48 29 E
Aratāne, *Mauritania* **112 B3** 18 24N 8 32W
Araticu, *Brazil* **170 B2** 1 58 S 49 51W
Arauca, *Colombia* **168 B3** 7 0N 70 40W
Arauca □, *Colombia* **168 B3** 6 40N 71 0W
Arauca →, *Venezuela* **168 B4** 7 24N 66 35W
Arauco, *Chile* **174 D1** 37 16 S 73 25W
Araújos, *Brazil* **171 E2** 19 56 S 45 14W
Arauquita, *Colombia* **168 B3** 7 2N 71 25W
Araure, *Venezuela* **168 B4** 9 34N 69 13W
Arawa, *Ethiopia* **107 F5** 9 57N 41 58 E
Arawale ⌓, *Kenya* **118 C5** 1 24 S 40 9 E
Arawata →, *N.Z.* **131 E3** 44 0 S 168 40 E
Arawe Is., *Papua N. G.* **132 D5** 6 6 S 149 0 E
Araxá, *Brazil* **171 E2** 19 35 S 46 55W
Araya, Pen. de, *Venezuela* **169 A5** 10 40N 64 0W
Arayat, *Phil.* **80 D3** 15 10N 120 46 E
Arba Gugu, *Ethiopia* **107 F5** 8 40N 40 15 E
Arba Minch, *Ethiopia* **107 F4** 6 0N 37 30 E
Arbat, *Iraq* **101 E11** 35 25N 45 35 E
Árbatax, *Italy* **46 C2** 39 56N 9 42 E
Arbedo, *Switz.* **33 D8** 46 12N 9 3 E
Arbi, *Ethiopia* **107 F4** 9 4N 35 7 E
Arbīl, *Iraq* **101 D11** 36 15N 44 5 E
Arboga, *Sweden* **16 E9** 59 24N 15 52 E
Arbois, *France* **27 F12** 46 55N 5 46 E
Arboletes, *Colombia* **168 B2** 8 51N 76 26W
Arbon, *Switz.* **33 A8** 47 31N 9 26 E
Arbore, *Ethiopia* **107 F4** 5 3N 36 50 E
Arboréa, *Italy* **46 C1** 39 46N 8 35 E
Arborfield, *Canada* **143 C8** 53 6N 103 39W
Arborg, *Canada* **143 C9** 50 54N 97 13W
Arbre du Ténéré, *Niger* **113 B7** 17 50N 10 4 E
Arbroath, *U.K.* **22 E6** 56 34N 2 35W
Arbuckle, *U.S.A.* **160 F4** 39 1N 122 3W
Arbus, *Italy* **46 C1** 39 30N 8 33 E
Arc →, *France* **29 C10** 45 34N 6 12 E
Arc-lès-Gray, *France* **27 E12** 47 28N 5 34 E
Arcachon, *France* **28 D2** 44 40N 1 10W
Arcachon, Bassin d’, *France* **28 D2** 44 42N 1 10W
Arcade, *Calif., U.S.A.* **161 L8** 34 2N 118 15W
Arcade, *N.Y., U.S.A.* **150 D6** 42 32N 78 25W
Arcadia, *Fla., U.S.A.* **153 H8** 27 13N 81 52W
Arcadia, *Ind., U.S.A.* **157 D10** 40 11N 86 1W
Arcadia, *Iowa, U.S.A.* **156 B1** 42 5N 95 3W
Arcadia, *La., U.S.A.* **155 J8** 32 33N 92 55W
Arcadia, *Pa., U.S.A.* **150 F6** 40 47N 78 51W
Arcanum, *U.S.A.* **157 E12** 39 59N 84 33W
Arcata, *U.S.A.* **158 F1** 40 52N 124 5W
Arcévia, *Italy* **45 E9** 43 30N 12 56 E
Archangel = Arkhangelsk, *Russia* **56 B7** 64 38N 40 36 E
Archar, *Bulgaria* **50 C6** 43 50N 22 54 E
Archbald, *U.S.A.* **151 E9** 41 30N 75 32W
Archbold, *U.S.A.* **157 C12** 41 31N 84 18W
Archena, *Spain* **41 G3** 38 9N 1 16W
Archenu, J., *Chad* **109 D4** 22 15N 24 45 E
Archer, *U.S.A.* **153 F7** 29 32N 82 32W
Archer →, *Australia* **126 A3** 13 28 S 141 41 E
Archer B., *Australia* **126 A3** 13 20 S 141 30 E
Archer Bend = Mungkan Kandju △, *Australia* **126 A3** 13 35 S 142 52 E
Archers Post, *Kenya* **118 B4** 0 35N 37 35 E
Arches △, *U.S.A.* **159 G9** 38 45N 109 25W
Archidona, *Spain* **43 H6** 37 6N 4 22W
Archipel-de-Mingan △, *Canada* **141 B7** 50 13N 63 10W
Archipiélago Chinijo △, *Canary Is.* **9 e2** 29 20N 13 30W
Archipiélago Los Roques △, *Venezuela* **165 D6** 11 50N 66 44W
Arci, Mte., *Italy* **46 C1** 39 47N 8 45 E
Arcidosso, *Italy* **45 F8** 42 52N 11 33 E
Arcila = Asilah, *Morocco* **110 A3** 35 29N 6 0W
Arcipelago de la Maddalena △, *Italy* **46 A2** 41 14N 9 24 E
Arcipelago Toscano △, *Italy* **44 F7** 42 45N 10 15 E
Arcis-sur-Aube, *France* **27 D11** 48 32N 4 10 E
Arckaringa Cr. →, *Australia* **127 D2** 28 10 S 135 22 E
Arco, *Italy* **44 C7** 45 55N 10 53 E
Arco, *U.S.A.* **158 E7** 43 38N 113 18W
Arcola, *U.S.A.* **157 E8** 39 41N 88 19W
Arcoona, *Australia* **128 A2** 31 2 S 137 1 E
Arcos de Jalón, *Spain* **40 D2** 41 12N 2 16W
Arcos de la Frontera, *Spain* **43 J5** 36 45N 5 49W
Arcos de Valdevez, *Portugal* **42 D2** 41 55N 8 22W
Arcot, *India* **95 H4** 12 53N 79 20 E
Arcoverde, *Brazil* **170 C4** 8 25 S 37 4W
Arcozelo, *Portugal* **42 E3** 40 32N 7 47W
Arctic Bay, *Canada* **139 A11** 73 1N 85 7W
Arctic Ocean, *Arctic* **6 B18** 78 0N 160 0W
Arctic Red River = Tsiigehtchic, *Canada* **138 B6** 67 15N 134 0W
Arctic Village, *U.S.A.* **144 B11** 68 8N 145 32W
Arctowski, *Antarctica* **7 C18** 62 30 S 58 0W
Arda →, *Bulgaria* **51 E10** 41 40N 26 30 E
Arda →, *Italy* **44 C7** 45 2N 10 2 E
Ardabīl, *Iran* **97 B6** 38 15N 48 18 E
Ardabīl □, *Iran* **97 B6** 38 15N 48 20 E
Ardahan, *Turkey* **101 B10** 41 7N 42 41 E
Ardakān = Sepīdān, *Iran* **97 D7** 30 20N 52 5 E
Ardakān, *Iran* **97 C7** 32 19N 53 59 E
Ardala, *Sweden* **17 F7** 58 22N 13 19 E
Ardales, *Spain* **43 J6** 36 53N 4 51W
Årdalstangen, *Norway* **18 C4** 61 14N 7 43 E
Ardèche □, *France* **29 D8** 44 42N 4 16 E
Ardèche →, *France* **29 D8** 44 16N 4 39 E
Ardee, *Ireland* **23 C5** 53 52N 6 33W
Arden, *Canada* **150 B8** 44 43N 76 56W
Arden, *Denmark* **17 H3** 56 46N 9 52 E
Arden, *Calif., U.S.A.* **160 G5** 38 36N 121 33W
Arden, *Nev., U.S.A.* **161 J11** 36 1N 115 14W
Ardenne, *Belgium* **24 E5** 49 50N 5 5 E
Ardennes = Ardenne, *Belgium* **24 E5** 49 50N 5 5 E
Ardennes □, *France* **27 C11** 49 35N 4 40 E
Ardentes, *France* **27 F8** 46 45N 1 50 E
Arderin, *Ireland* **23 C4** 53 2N 7 39W
Ardeşen, *Turkey* **101 B9** 41 12N 41 2 E
Ardestān, *Iran* **97 C7** 33 20N 52 25 E
Ardez, *Switz.* **33 C10** 46 47N 10 12 E
Árdhas →, *Greece* **51 E10** 41 40N 26 30 E
Ardhéa, *Greece* **50 F6** 40 58N 22 3 E
Ardila →, *Portugal* **43 G3** 38 12N 7 28W
Ardino, *Bulgaria* **51 E9** 41 34N 25 9 E
Ardivachar Pt., *U.K.* **22 D1** 57 23N 7 26W
Ardlethan, *Australia* **129 C7** 34 22 S 146 53 E
Ardmore, *Okla., U.S.A.* **155 H6** 34 10N 97 8W
Ardmore, *Pa., U.S.A.* **151 G9** 39 58N 75 18W
Ardnamurchan, Pt. of, *U.K.* **22 E2** 56 43N 6 14W
Ardnave Pt., *U.K.* **22 F2** 55 53N 6 20W
Ardon, *Russia* **61 J7** 43 10N 44 18 E
Ardore, *Italy* **47 D9** 38 11N 16 10 E
Ardres, *France* **27 B8** 50 50N 1 59 E
Ardrossan, *Australia* **128 C2** 34 26 S 137 53 E
Ardrossan, *U.K.* **22 F4** 55 39N 4 49W
Ards Pen., *U.K.* **23 B6** 54 33N 5 34W
Arduan, *Sudan* **106 D3** 19 54N 30 20 E
Ardud, *Romania* **52 C7** 47 37N 22 52 E
Åre, *Sweden* **16 A7** 63 22N 13 15 E
Arecibo, *Puerto Rico* **165 d** 18 29N 66 43W
Areia Branca, *Brazil* **170 B4** 5 0 S 37 0W
Arena, Pt., *U.S.A.* **160 G3** 38 57N 123 44W
Arenal, *Honduras* **164 C2** 15 21N 86 50W
Arenales, Cerro, *Chile* **176 C2** 47 5 S 73 40W
Arenápolis, *Brazil* **173 C6** 14 26 S 56 49W
Arenas = Las Arenas, *Spain* **42 B6** 43 17N 4 50W
Arenas, Pta., *Venezuela* **169 A5** 10 31N 64 14W
Arenas de San Pedro, *Spain* **42 E5** 40 12N 5 5W
Arendal, *Norway* **18 F5** 58 28N 8 46 E
Arendsee, *Germany* **30 C7** 52 52N 11 27 E
Arenillas, *Ecuador* **168 D1** 3 33 S 80 10W
Arensburg = Kuressaare, *Estonia* **15 G20** 58 15N 22 30 E
Arenys de Mar, *Spain* **40 D7** 41 35N 2 33 E
Arenzano, *Italy* **44 D5** 44 24N 8 41 E
Arenzville, *U.S.A.* **156 E6** 39 53N 90 22W
Areópolis, *Greece* **48 E4** 36 40N 22 22 E
Arequipa, *Peru* **172 D3** 16 20 S 71 30W
Arequipa □, *Peru* **172 D3** 16 0 S 72 50W
Arere, *Brazil* **169 D7** 0 16 S 53 52W
Arero, *Ethiopia* **107 G4** 4 41N 38 50 E
Arès, *France* **28 D2** 44 47N 1 8W
Arévalo, *Spain* **42 D6** 41 3N 4 43W
Arezzo, *Italy* **45 E8** 43 25N 11 53 E
Arga, *Turkey* **96 B3** 38 21N 37 59 E
Arga →, *Spain* **40 C3** 42 18N 1 47W
Argalastí, *Greece* **48 B5** 39 13N 23 13 E
Argamakmur, *Indonesia* **84 C2** 3 35 S 102 0 E
Argamasilla de Alba, *Spain* **43 F7** 39 8N 3 5W
Argamasilla de Calatrava, *Spain* **43 G6** 38 44N 4 4W
Arganda, *Spain* **42 E7** 40 19N 3 26W
Arganil, *Portugal* **42 E2** 40 13N 8 3W
Argao, *Phil.* **81 G4** 9 52N 123 36 E
Argásion **39 D2** 37 45N 20 56 E
Argayash, *Russia* **64 D8** 55 29N 60 52 E
Argedeb, *Ethiopia* **107 F5** 6 11N 41 13 E
Argelès-Gazost, *France* **28 E3** 43 0N 0 6W
Argelès-sur-Mer, *France* **28 F7** 42 34N 3 1 E
Argens →, *France* **29 E10** 43 24N 6 44 E
Argent-sur-Sauldre, *France* **27 E9** 47 33N 2 25 E
Argenta = North Little Rock, *U.S.A.* **155 H8** 34 45N 92 16W
Argenta, *Canada* **142 C5** 50 11N 116 56W
Argenta, *Italy* **45 D8** 44 37N 11 50 E
Argenta, *U.S.A.* **157 E8** 39 59N 88 49W
Argentan, *France* **26 D6** 48 45N 0 1W
Argentário, Mte., *Italy* **45 F8** 42 24N 11 9 E
Argentat, *France* **28 C5** 45 6N 1 56 E
Argentera, *Italy* **44 D4** 44 12N 7 5 E
Argenteuil, *France* **27 D9** 48 57N 2 14 E
Argentia, *Canada* **141 C9** 47 18N 53 58W
Argentiera, C. dell’, *Italy* **46 B1** 40 44N 8 8 E
Argentière, Aiguilles d’, *Switz.* **32 E4** 45 58N 7 2 E
Argentina ■, *S. Amer.* **176 B3** 35 0 S 66 0W
Argentine Basin, *S. Amer.* **166 H5** 45 0 S 58 0W
Argentino, L., *Argentina* **176 D2** 50 10 S 73 0W
Argenton-Château, *France* **26 F6** 46 59N 0 27W
Argenton-sur-Creuse, *France* **27 F8** 46 36N 1 30 E
Argeş □, *Romania* **53 F9** 45 0N 24 45 E
Argeş →, *Romania* **53 F11** 44 5N 26 38 E
Arghandab →, *Afghan.* **91 C2** 31 30N 64 15 E
Argheile, *Ethiopia* **107 F5** 5 19N 42 4 E
Argo, *Sudan* **106 D3** 19 28N 30 30 E
Argolikós Kólpos, *Greece* **48 D4** 37 20N 22 52 E
Argolís □, *Greece* **48 D4** 37 38N 22 50 E
Argonne, *France* **27 C12** 49 10N 5 0 E
Árgos, *Greece* **48 D4** 37 40N 22 43 E
Argos, *U.S.A.* **157 C10** 41 14N 86 15W
Árgos Orestikón, *Greece* **50 F5** 40 27N 21 18 E
Argostoli = Argostólion, *Greece* **39 C2** 38 11N 20 29 E
Argostólion, *Greece* **39 C2** 38 11N 20 29 E
Argostólion, Kólpos, *Greece* **39 C1** 38 10N 20 27 E
Arguedas, *Spain* **40 C3** 42 11N 1 36W
Arguello, Pt., *U.S.A.* **161 L6** 34 35N 120 39W
Arguineguín, *Canary Is.* **9 e1** 27 46N 15 41W
Argun, *Russia* **61 J7** 43 18N 45 52 E
Argun →, *Russia* **67 D13** 53 20N 121 28 E
Argungu, *Nigeria* **113 C5** 12 40N 4 31 E
Arguni, T., *Indonesia* **83 B4** 3 6 S 133 42 E
Argus Pk., *U.S.A.* **161 K9** 35 52N 117 26W
Argyle, L., *Australia* **124 C4** 16 20 S 128 40 E
Argyll ⌓, *U.K.* **22 E4** 56 6N 5 0W
Argyll & Bute □, *U.K.* **22 E3** 56 13N 5 28W
Arhavi, *Turkey* **101 B9** 41 21N 41 18 E
Århus, *Denmark* **17 H4** 56 8N 10 11 E
Århus Amtskommune □, *Denmark* **17 H4** 56 15N 10 15 E
Aria, *N.Z.* **130 E4** 38 33 S 175 0 E
Ariadnoye, *Russia* **70 B7** 45 8N 134 25 E
Ariamsvlei, *Namibia* **116 D2** 28 9 S 19 51 E
Ariana, *Tunisia* **108 A2** 36 52N 10 12 E
Ariano Irpino, *Italy* **47 A8** 41 9N 15 5 E
Ariari →, *Colombia* **168 C3** 2 35N 72 47W
Aribinda, *Burkina Faso* **113 C4** 14 17N 0 52W
Arica, *Chile* **172 D3** 18 32 S 70 20W
Arica, *Colombia* **168 D3** 2 0 S 71 50W
Arico, *Canary Is.* **9 e1** 28 9N 16 29W
Arid, C., *Australia* **125 F3** 34 1 S 123 10 E
Arida, *Japan* **73 C7** 34 5N 135 8 E
Aridal, *W. Sahara* **110 C2** 25 59N 13 54W
Aride, *Seychelles* **121 b** 4 13 S 55 40 E
Ariège □, *France* **28 F5** 42 56N 1 30 E
Ariège →, *France* **28 E5** 43 30N 1 25 E
Arieş →, *Romania* **53 D8** 46 24N 23 20 E
Arigat el Fersig, *Algeria* **111 C4** 27 35N 2 7W
Arihā, *Israel* **106 A4** 31 51N 35 27 E
Arilje, *Serbia & M.* **50 C4** 43 44N 20 7 E
Arílla, Ákra, *Greece* **38 B9** 39 43N 19 39 E
Arima, *Trin. & Tob.* **169 F9** 10 38N 61 17W
Aringay, *Phil.* **80 C3** 16 26N 120 21 E
Arinos →, *Brazil* **173 C6** 10 25 S 58 20W
Ario de Rosales, *Mexico* **162 D4** 19 12N 102 0W
Ariogala, *Lithuania* **54 C10** 55 16N 23 28 E
Aripo, Mt., *Trin. & Tob.* **169 F9** 10 45N 61 15W
Aripuanã, *Brazil* **173 B5** 9 25 S 60 30W
Aripuanã →, *Brazil* **173 B5** 5 7 S 60 25W
Ariquemes, *Brazil* **173 B5** 9 55 S 63 6W
Arisaig, *U.K.* **22 E3** 56 55N 5 51W
Arîsh, W. el →, *Egypt* **106 A3** 31 9N 33 49 E
Arissa, *Ethiopia* **107 E5** 11 10N 41 35 E
Aristazabal I., *Canada* **142 C3** 52 40N 129 10W
Arita, *Japan* **72 D1** 33 11N 129 54 E
Aritao, *Phil.* **80 C3** 16 18N 121 2 E
Ariton, *U.S.A.* **152 D4** 31 36N 85 43W
Arivonimamo, *Madag.* **117 B8** 19 1 S 47 11 E
Ariyalur, *India* **95 J4** 11 8N 79 8 E
Ariza, *Spain* **40 D2** 41 19N 2 3W
Arizaro, Salar de, *Argentina* **174 A2** 24 40 S 67 50W
Arizona, *Argentina* **174 D2** 35 45 S 65 25W
Arizona □, *U.S.A.* **159 J8** 34 0N 112 0W
Arizpe, *Mexico* **162 A2** 30 20N 110 11W
Årjäng, *Sweden* **16 E6** 59 24N 12 8 E
Arjeplog, *Sweden* **14 D18** 66 3N 17 54 E
Arjepluovve = Arjeplog, *Sweden* **14 D18** 66 3N 17 54 E
Arjona, *Colombia* **168 A2** 10 14N 75 22W
Arjona, *Spain* **43 H6** 37 56N 4 4W
Arjuna, *Indonesia* **85 D4** 7 49 S 112 34 E
Arka, *Russia* **67 C15** 60 15N 142 0 E
Arkadak, *Russia* **60 E6** 51 58N 43 30 E
Arkadelphia, *U.S.A.* **155 H8** 34 7N 93 4W
Arkadhía □, *Greece* **48 D4** 37 30N 22 20 E
Arkaig, L., *U.K.* **22 E3** 56 59N 5 10W
Arkalgud, *India* **95 H3** 12 46N 76 3 E
Arkalyk = Arqalyk, *Kazakhstan* **66 D7** 50 13N 66 50 E
Arkansas □, *U.S.A.* **155 H8** 35 0N 92 30W
Arkansas →, *U.S.A.* **155 J9** 33 47N 91 4W
Arkansas City, *U.S.A.* **155 G6** 37 4N 97 2W
Arkaroola, *Australia* **127 E2** 30 20 S 139 22 E
Árkathos →, *Greece* **48 B3** 39 20N 21 4 E
Arkhangelo-Pashiskiy Zavod = Pashiya, *Russia* **64 B7** 58 33N 58 26 E
Arkhángelos, *Préveza, Greece* **39 A2** 39 6N 20 42 E
Arkhángelos, *Ródhos, Greece* **38 E12** 36 13N 28 7 E
Arkhangelsk, *Russia* **56 B7** 64 38N 40 36 E
Arkhangelskoye, *Russia* **60 E5** 51 32N 40 58 E
Arki, *India* **92 D7** 31 9N 76 58 E
Arkiko, *Eritrea* **107 D4** 15 33N 39 30 E
Arklow, *Ireland* **23 D5** 52 48N 6 10W
Árkoi, *Greece* **49 D8** 37 24N 26 44 E
Arkona, Kap, *Germany* **30 A9** 54 42N 13 26 E
Arkösund, *Sweden* **17 F10** 58 29N 16 56 E
Arkoúdhi Nisís, *Greece* **39 B2** 38 33N 20 43 E
Arkport, *U.S.A.* **150 D7** 42 24N 77 42W
Arkticheskiy, Mys, *Russia* **67 A10** 81 10N 95 0 E
Arkul, *Russia* **60 B10** 57 17N 50 3 E
Arkville, *U.S.A.* **151 D10** 42 9N 74 37W
Årla, *Sweden* **16 E10** 59 17N 16 40 E
Arlanda, Stockholm ✈ (ARN), *Sweden* **16 E11** 59 41N 17 56 E
Arlanza →, *Spain* **42 C6** 42 6N 4 9W
Arlanzón →, *Spain* **42 C6** 42 3N 4 17W
Arlbergpass, *Austria* **34 D3** 47 9N 10 12 E
Arles, *France* **29 E8** 43 41N 4 40 E
Arlesheim, *Switz.* **32 B5** 47 30N 7 37 E
Arli, *Burkina Faso* **113 C5** 11 35N 1 28 E
Arli △, *Burkina Faso* **113 C5** 11 35N 1 28 E
Arlington, *S. Africa* **117 D4** 28 1 S 27 53 E
Arlington, *Ga., U.S.A.* **152 D5** 31 26N 84 44W
Arlington, *N.Y., U.S.A.* **151 E11** 41 42N 73 54W
Arlington, *Oreg., U.S.A.* **158 D3** 45 43N 120 12W
Arlington, *S. Dak., U.S.A.* **154 C6** 44 22N 97 8W
Arlington, *Tex., U.S.A.* **155 J6** 32 44N 97 7W
Arlington, *Va., U.S.A.* **148 F7** 38 53N 77 7W
Arlington, *Vt., U.S.A.* **151 C11** 43 5N 73 9W
Arlington, *Wash., U.S.A.* **160 B4** 48 12N 122 8W
Arlington Heights, *U.S.A.* **157 B9** 42 5N 87 59W
Arlon, *Belgium* **24 E5** 49 42N 5 49 E
Arltunga, *Australia* **126 C1** 23 26 S 134 41 E
Armagh, *U.K.* **23 B5** 54 21N 6 39W
Armagh □, *U.K.* **23 B5** 54 18N 6 37W
Armagnac, *France* **28 E4** 43 50N 0 10 E
Armançon →, *France* **27 E10** 47 59N 3 30 E
Armando Bermudez △, *Dom. Rep.* **165 C5** 19 3N 71 0W
Armatree, *Australia* **129 A8** 31 26 S 148 28 E
Armavir, *Russia* **61 H5** 45 2N 41 7 E
Armenia, *Colombia* **168 C2** 4 35N 75 45W
Armenia ■, *Asia* **61 K7** 40 20N 45 0 E
Armeniş, *Romania* **52 E7** 45 13N 22 17 E
Armenistís, Ákra, *Greece* **38 E11** 36 8N 27 42 E
Armentières, *France* **27 B9** 50 40N 2 50 E
Armero, *Colombia* **168 C3** 4 58N 74 54W
Armidale, *Australia* **129 A9** 30 30 S 151 40 E
Armilla, *Spain* **43 H7** 37 9N 3 37W
Armori, *India* **94 D4** 20 28N 79 59 E
Armorique ⌓, *France* **26 D3** 48 22N 3 50W
Armour, *U.S.A.* **154 D5** 43 19N 98 21W
Armstrong, *B.C., Canada* **142 C5** 50 25N 119 10W
Armstrong, *Ont., Canada* **140 B2** 50 18N 89 4W
Armur, *India* **94 E4** 18 48N 78 16 E
Armutlu, *Bursa, Turkey* **51 F12** 40 31N 28 50 E
Armutlu, *İzmir, Turkey* **49 C9** 38 24N 27 34 E
Arnaía, *Greece* **50 F7** 40 30N 23 38 E
Arnarfjörður, *Iceland* **11 B3** 65 48N 23 40W
Arnaud →, *Canada* **139 B12** 59 59N 69 46W
Arnauti, C., *Cyprus* **39 E8** 35 6N 32 17 E
Arnay-le-Duc, *France* **27 E11** 47 10N 4 27 E
Arnedillo, *Spain* **40 C2** 42 13N 2 14W
Arnedo, *Spain* **40 C2** 42 12N 2 5W
Árnes, *Iceland* **11 A5** 66 1N 21 31W
Årnes, *Norway* **18 D8** 60 7N 11 28 E
Árnessýsla □, *Iceland* **11 C6** 64 15N 20 30W
Arnett, *U.S.A.* **155 G5** 36 8N 99 46W
Arnhem, *Neths.* **24 C5** 51 58N 5 55 E
Arnhem, C., *Australia* **126 A2** 12 20 S 137 30 E
Arnhem B., *Australia* **126 A2** 12 20 S 136 10 E
Arnhem Land, *Australia* **126 A1** 13 10 S 134 30 E
Árnissa, *Greece* **50 F5** 40 47N 21 49 E
Arno →, *Italy* **44 E7** 43 41N 10 17 E
Arno Bay, *Australia* **128 B2** 33 54 S 136 34 E
Arnold, *U.K.* **20 D6** 53 1N 1 7W
Arnold, *U.S.A.* **160 G6** 38 15N 120 20W
Arnoldstein, *Austria* **34 E6** 46 33N 13 43 E
Arnon →, *France* **27 E9** 47 13N 2 1 E
Arnot, *Canada* **143 B9** 55 56N 96 41W
Arnøy, *Norway* **14 A19** 70 9N 20 40 E
Arnprior, *Canada* **140 C4** 45 26N 76 21W
Arnsberg, *Germany* **30 D4** 51 24N 8 5 E
Arnsberger Wald ⌓, *Germany* **30 D4** 51 25N 8 20 E
Arnstadt, *Germany* **30 E6** 50 50N 10 56 E
Arnswalde = Choszczno, *Poland* **55 E2** 53 7N 15 25 E
Aro →, *Venezuela* **169 B5** 8 1N 64 11W
Aroab, *Namibia* **116 D2** 26 41 S 19 39 E
Aroánia Óri, *Greece* **48 D4** 37 56N 22 12 E
Aroche, *Spain* **43 H4** 37 56N 6 57W
Arochuku, *Nigeria* **113 D6** 5 21N 7 54 E
Aroeiras, *Brazil* **170 C4** 7 31 S 35 41W
Arolla, *Switz.* **32 D4** 46 2N 7 29 E
Arolsen, *Germany* **30 D5** 51 23N 9 2 E
Aron, *India* **92 G6** 25 57N 77 56 E
Aron →, *France* **27 F10** 46 50N 3 28 E
Arona, *Canary Is.* **9 e1** 28 6N 16 40W
Arona, *Italy* **44 C5** 45 46N 8 34 E
Aroroy, *Phil.* **80 E4** 12 31N 123 24 E
Arosa, *Switz.* **33 C9** 46 47N 9 41 E
Arosa, Ría de, *Spain* **42 C2** 42 28N 8 57W
Årøysund, *Norway* **18 E7** 59 10N 10 27 E
Arpajon, *France* **27 D9** 48 36N 2 15 E
Arpajon-sur-Cère, *France* **28 D6** 44 53N 2 28 E
Arpaşu de Jos, *Romania* **53 E9** 45 47N 24 37 E
Arqalyk, *Kazakhstan* **66 D7** 50 13N 66 50 E
Arque, *Bolivia* **172 D4** 17 48 S 66 23W
Arrah = Ara, *India* **93 G11** 25 35N 84 32 E
Arrah, *Ivory C.* **112 D4** 6 40N 3 58W
Arraias, *Brazil* **171 D2** 12 56 S 46 57W
Arraias →, *Mato Grosso, Brazil* **173 C7** 11 10 S 53 35W
Arraias →, *Pará, Brazil* **170 C2** 7 30 S 49 20W
Arraiolos, *Portugal* **43 G3** 38 44N 7 59W
Arran, *U.K.* **22 F3** 55 34N 5 12W
Arras, *France* **27 B9** 50 17N 2 46 E
Arrasate, *Spain* **40 B2** 43 4N 2 30W
Arrats →, *France* **28 D4** 44 6N 0 52 E
Arreau, *France* **28 F4** 42 54N 0 22 E
Arrecife, *Canary Is.* **9 e2** 28 57N 13 37W
Arrecifes, *Argentina* **174 C3** 34 6 S 60 9W
Arrée, Mts. d’, *France* **26 D3** 48 26N 3 55W
Arresø, *Denmark* **17 J6** 55 58N 12 6 E
Arriaga, *Chiapas, Mexico* **163 D6** 16 15N 93 52W
Arriaga, *San Luis Potosí, Mexico* **162 C4** 21 55N 101 23W
Arribes del Duero ⌓, *Spain* **42 D4** 41 11N 6 39W
Arrilalah, *Australia* **126 C3** 23 43 S 143 54 E
Arrino, *Australia* **125 E2** 29 30 S 115 40 E
Arriondas, *Spain* **42 B5** 43 23N 5 11W
Arrojado →, *Brazil* **171 D3** 13 24 S 44 20W
Arromanches-les-Bains, *France* **26 C6** 49 20N 0 38W
Arronches, *Portugal* **43 F3** 39 8N 7 16W
Arros →, *France* **28 E3** 43 40N 0 2W
Arrow, L., *Ireland* **23 B3** 54 3N 8 19W
Arrowhead, L., *U.S.A.* **161 L9** 34 16N 117 10W
Arrowsmith, Mt., *N.Z.* **131 D5** 43 20 S 170 55 E
Arrowtown, *N.Z.* **131 E3** 44 57 S 168 50 E
Arroyo de la Luz, *Spain* **43 F4** 39 30N 6 38W
Arroyo del Puerco = Arroyo de la Luz, *Spain* **43 F4** 39 30N 6 38W
Arroyo Grande, *U.S.A.* **161 K6** 35 7N 120 35W
Års, *Denmark* **17 H3** 56 48N 9 30 E
Ars, *Iran* **96 B5** 37 9N 47 46 E
Ars-sur-Moselle, *France* **27 C13** 49 5N 6 4 E
Arsenault L., *Canada* **143 B7** 55 6N 108 32W
Arsenev, *Russia* **70 B6** 44 10N 133 15 E
Arsi, *Ethiopia* **107 F4** 7 45N 39 0 E
Arsiero, *Italy* **45 C8** 45 48N 11 21 E
Arsikere, *India* **95 H3** 13 15N 76 15 E
Arsin, *Turkey* **101 B8** 41 8N 39 55 E
Arsk, *Russia* **60 B9** 56 10N 49 50 E
Árskógssandur, *Iceland* **11 B8** 65 56N 18 27W
Årsunda, *Sweden* **16 D10** 60 31N 16 45 E
Árta, *Greece* **48 B3** 39 8N 21 2 E
Artà, *Spain* **38 B4** 39 41N 3 21 E
Árta □, *Greece* **48 B3** 39 15N 21 5 E
Arteaga, *Mexico* **162 D4** 18 50N 102 20W
Arteche, *Phil.* **80 E5** 12 17N 125 22 E
Arteijo = Arteixo, *Spain* **42 B2** 43 19N 8 29W
Arteixo, *Spain* **42 B2** 43 19N 8 29W
Artem = Artyom, *Azerbaijan* **61 K10** 40 28N 50 20 E
Artem, *Russia* **70 C6** 43 22N 132 13 E
Artemovsk, *Russia* **67 D10** 54 45N 93 35 E
Artemovsk, *Ukraine* **59 H9** 48 35N 38 0 E
Artemovskiy, *Rostov, Russia* **61 G5** 47 45N 40 16 E
Artemovskiy, *Yekaterinburg, Russia* **64 C8** 57 21N 61 54 E
Artenay, *France* **27 D8** 48 5N 1 50 E
Artern, *Germany* **30 D7** 51 22N 11 18 E
Artesa de Segre, *Spain* **40 D6** 41 54N 1 3 E
Artesia = Mosomane, *Botswana* **116 C4** 24 2 S 26 19 E
Artesia, *U.S.A.* **155 J2** 32 51N 104 24W
Arth, *Switz.* **33 B7** 47 4N 8 31 E
Arthington, *Liberia* **112 D2** 6 35N 10 45W
Arthur, *Canada* **150 C4** 43 50N 80 32W

C

D

E

G

K

O

X

Z

KEY TO EUROPEAN MAP PAGES

 **Large scale maps**
(>1:3 900 000)

 Medium scale maps
(1:4 000 000 – 1:9 900 000)

 Small scale maps
(<1:10 000 000)

Arctic Circle

11

ICELAND

WORLD COUNTRY INDEX

14

19 · 22

22

23 · 20

IRELAND · UNITED KINGDOM · 24

26

28 · FRA

42 · 40

ANDORRA

PORTUGAL · SPAIN · 38

MOROCCO